REBELLION

Also by Peter Ackroyd

Fiction

The Canterbury Tales: A Retelling
The Trial of Elizabeth Cree
The Last Testament of Oscar Wilde
Chatterton
First Light
English Music
Dan Leno and the Limehouse Golem
Milton in America
The Plato Papers
The Clerkenwell Tales
The Lambs of London
The Fall of Troy
The Casebook of Victor Frankenstein
The Death of King Arthur

Nonfiction

The Collection: Journalism, Reviews, Essays, Short Stories, Lectures
(edited by Thomas Wright)
London Under: The Secret History Beneath the Streets
Dressing Up: Transvestism and Drag: The History of an Obsession
London: The Biography
Albion: The Origins of the English Imagination
Thames: Sacred River
Venice: Pure City
T. S. Eliot
Dickens
Blake
The Life of Thomas More
Shakespeare
Chaucer
J. M. W. Turner
Newton
Poe: A Life Cut Short
Foundation: The History of England from Its Earliest Beginnings to the Tudors
Tudors: The History of England from Henry VIII to Elizabeth I

Peter Ackroyd

REBELLION

THE HISTORY OF ENGLAND

FROM JAMES I TO THE GLORIOUS REVOLUTION

THOMAS DUNNE BOOKS

New York

THOMAS DUNNE BOOKS.
An imprint of St. Martin's Press.

 For information, address St. Martin's Publishing Group, 120 Broadway, New York, NY 10271.

www.thomasdunnebooks.com
www.stmartins.com

The Library of Congress has cataloged the hardcover edition as follows:

Ackroyd, Peter, 1949–
Rebellion : the history of England from James I to the Glorious Revolution / Peter Ackroyd. — First U.S. Edition.
p. cm.
First published in Great Britain by Macmillan as a set, complete in 6 volumes, under the common title: The history of England; Rebellion is volume 3 in that series.
Includes bibliographical references and index.
ISBN 978-1-250-00363-8 (hardcover)
ISBN 978-1-4668-5599-1 (e-book)
1. Great Britain—History—Stuarts, 1603–1714. 2. Stuart, House of. I. Ackroyd, Peter, 1949– History of England. II. Title.
DA375.A25 2014
941.06—dc23

2014026045

ISBN 978-1-250-07024-1 (trade paperback)

First published in Great Britain under the title *Civil War* by Macmillan, an imprint of Pan Macmillan, a division of Macmillan Publishers Limited

First Paperback Edition: September 2015

D 10 9

Contents

List of illustrations

1

A new Solomon

Sir Robert Carey rode furiously from London to Edinburgh along the Great North Road, spending one night in Yorkshire and another in Northumberland; he arrived at Holyrood Palace, 'be-bloodied with great falls and bruises' after a journey of more than 330 miles. It was late at night on Saturday 26 March 1603. He was ushered into the presence of King James VI of Scotland and, falling to his knees, proclaimed him to be 'King of England, France and Ireland'. He gave him as testimony a sapphire ring that his sister, Lady Scrope, had thrown to him from a window at Richmond Palace immediately after the death of Elizabeth I. 'I have', he told his new sovereign, 'a blue ring from a fair lady.'

'It is enough,' James said. 'I know by this you are a true messenger.' The king had previously entrusted this ring to Lady Scrope in the event of the queen's death.

A body of prelates and peers had already met Sir Robert Cecil, the principal councillor of the old queen, at Whitehall Gate before they proceeded with him to the cross at Cheapside where Cecil proclaimed James as king; bonfires and bells greeted the news of the swift and easy succession. Cecil himself declared that he had 'steered King James's ship into the right harbour, without cross of wave or tide that could have overturned a cock-boat'. The councillor had entered a secret correspondence with James before Elizabeth's death; he had urged the Scottish king to nourish 'a heart of adamant in a world of feathers'.

On 5 April James left Edinburgh to travel to his new realm. He had been the king of Scotland for thirty-six years, ever since he had assumed the throne at the age of thirteen months after the forced abdication of his mother Mary Queen of Scots. He had been a successful if not a glorious monarch, managing to curb the pretensions of an argumentative clergy and of a fractious nobility. From his earliest years the restive and combative spirit of the Scottish lords ensured that, in the words of the French ambassador, he had been nourished in fear. Yet he had by guile and compromise held on to his crown. Now, as he told his followers, he was about to enter the Land of Promise. He had already written to the council at Westminster, asking for money; he did not have the funds to finance his journey south.

The king did not perhaps expect so effusive and jubilant a welcome from his new subjects. He recalled later how 'the people of all sorts rid and ran, nay rather flew to meet me'. They came to gaze at him, since none of them had experienced the rule of a male monarch. He himself was impressed by the prosperity of the land and by the evident wealth of its rulers. He said later that the first three years of his reign were 'as a Christmas'. It took him a month to reach London, largely because he wished to avoid the funeral of his predecessor. He had no great fondness for Elizabeth; she had prevaricated over his right to the succession and, perhaps more significantly, had ordered the execution of his mother.

He reached York by the middle of April, where Cecil came to greet him. 'Though you be but a little man,' the king told him, 'we shall surely load your shoulders with business.' At Newark-on-Trent he gave orders that a cutpurse, preying upon his retinue, should summarily be hanged; he had not properly been informed on the provisions of English common law. It is an indication that he was still, in many important respects, a foreigner. At Burghley-by-Stamford he fell from his horse and broke his collar bone. Slowly he made his way to London. For three or four days he rested in Hertfordshire at Robert Cecil's country home, Theobalds House, at which seat he took pleasure in creating many knights.

He was so generous with titles that he was accused of improvidence. The reign of Elizabeth witnessed the creation of 878 knights; in the first four months of the king's rule, some 906 new men were awarded that honour. The queen had knighted those whom she considered to be of genuine merit or importance; James merely considered knighthood to be a mark of status. He was said to have knighted a piece of beef with the words 'Arise, Sir Loin'. On another occasion he did not catch the name of the recipient and said, 'Prithee, rise up, and call thyself Sir What Thou Wilt.' Other titles could be purchased with cash. The diminution in the importance of honour marks one of the first changes to the old Tudor system.

Those who were permitted into the king's presence may not have been entirely impressed. He was awkward and hesitant in manner; his legs were slightly bowed and his gait erratic, perhaps the consequence of rickets acquired in childhood. One admittedly hostile witness, Sir Anthony Weldon, also described him as forever 'fiddling about his codpiece'.

He was a robust and fluent conversationalist, who rather liked to hear the sound of his own voice, but the effect upon his English audience was perhaps impaired by the fact that he retained a broad Scots accent. If he was eager to talk, he was also quick to laugh. He could be witty, but delivered his droll remarks in a grave and serious voice. His manners were not impeccable, and he was said to have slobbered over his food and drink. He paid little attention to his dress, but favoured thickly padded doublets that might impede an assassin's dagger; ever since his childhood he had lived in fear of assault or murder. He was said to have a horror of naked steel. He had a restless, roving eye; he paid particular notice to those at court who were not known to him.

On 7 May he rode towards London, but was greeted 4 miles outside the city by the lord mayor and innumerable citizens. He lodged at the Charterhouse for four nights, and then made his way to the Tower, where he remained for a few days. While staying in the royal apartments he began an excited tour of his capital, 'secretly in his coach and by water', as one contemporary put it; he was particularly struck by the sight of the crown jewels, held at the palace in Whitehall. Here was the glittering and unmistakable evidence of his new-found wealth.

Yet London was not a pleasure-dome. Even as he approached it, the plague began its secret ministry in the streets and alleys; by the end of the summer it had claimed the lives of 30,000 citizens. A grand state entry had been planned for 25 July, the day of the coronation, but the fear of infected crowds curtailed the ceremony; there would be a crowning, but no state procession.

Even in these early months of the reign conspiracies began to mount against his throne. A group of gentlemen, among them Sir Walter Raleigh and Henry Brooke, Lord Cobham, were suspected of a scheme to depose James and to replace him with his cousin Arabella Stuart; like most conspiracies it was plagued by rumour, indecision and premature disclosure. Raleigh was arrested and consigned to the Tower, where two weeks later he attempted suicide; at his subsequent trial he was denounced by the attorney general, Sir Edward Coke, as 'a spider of hell'.

> *Raleigh:* You speak indiscreetly, barbarously and uncivilly.
> *Coke:* I want words sufficient to express thy viperous treasons.
> *Raleigh:* You want words, indeed, for you have spoken the one thing half a dozen times.

This was the end of what was called 'the Main Plot'. A 'Bye Plot' was also discovered, whereby the king was to be kidnapped by priests and forced to suspend the laws against Roman Catholics. It came to nothing, of course, except for the deaths of the principals engaged in it.

The time had come for the formal, if subdued, coronation of the king; the archbishop of Canterbury performed the ceremony expeditiously in the sight of an invited audience. James's consort, Anne of Denmark, agreed to receive her crown from the archbishop; as a Catholic, however, she refused to partake of Protestant communion. Being of a complaisant and gregarious disposition she caused very little trouble for the rest of her husband's reign. Her chaplain once remarked that 'the king himself was a very chaste man, and there was little in the queen to make him uxorious; yet they did love as well as man and wife could do, not conversing together'. After the ceremony the royal family left pestilential London for the healthier air of the country. James and Anne made their first 'progress' in the August of the year, making their way to Winchester and Southampton before turning north into Oxfordshire; in this, they were following the fashion of the king's illustrious predecessor.

James had already established, however, the foundations of his court and council. In particular he took care to reward his Scottish nobles with the most prominent positions in his personal retinue. The centre of his rule lay in the royal bedchamber, which was almost wholly staffed by the entourage that had followed him from his native land. This was a source of much discontent and disquiet among the English courtiers; it was said that the Scottish lords stood like mountains between the beams of the king's grace and themselves. Yet a new privy chamber was also established, half of Scots and half of English; the king revelled in his role as 'the pacifier', and this equal pairing evinced his moderation.

Among the English councillors the palm was awarded to Sir Robert Cecil and to the Howards. Henry Howard, earl of Northampton, was appointed as lord warden of the cinque ports at the beginning of 1604 and, a year later, lord privy seal; in the previous reign he had sent what James called 'Asiatic and endless volumes' of advice to Edinburgh. Thomas Howard, earl of Suffolk, was lord chamberlain. Cecil, soon to become Viscount Cranborne and then earl of Salisbury, was in fact pre-eminent; he was very small, with a hunched back, but he stood above the others. The king had told him that 'before God I count you the best servant that ever I had, albeit you be but a beagle'. He often addressed him as 'my little beagle'. Cecil managed parliament, and the revenues; he supervised Ireland and all foreign affairs. He was forever industrious, highly efficient and always courteous; he had borne with patience all the humiliating remarks about his appearance and physique. He was the ultimate civil servant and his cousin, Francis Bacon, once said of him that he might prevent public affairs getting worse but could not make them any better. That is perhaps too harsh; Cecil had so great a political intelligence that he may qualify as a statesman. Snapping at his heels, however, was Henry Howard.

Elizabeth's council had comprised some thirteen members; James soon doubled its size, but took great pleasure in avoiding its meetings. He favoured private deliberations, in the seclusion of his bedchamber, where he could then delegate responsibility. He preferred intimate meetings where his wit and common sense could compensate for his lack of dignity. He did not particularly like London in any case, and always preferred to go hunting in the countryside beyond; from this vantage James once wrote a complacent letter to his councillors, imagining them to be 'frying in the pains of purgatory' upon royal business. Yet he made quick and sudden visits to the capital, when his presence was deemed to be indispensable; he said that he came 'like a flash of lightning, both in going, staying there, and returning'.

The palace of Whitehall was a straggling complex of some 1,400 rooms, closets and galleries and chambers huddled together. It was a place of secrets and of clandestine meetings, of staged encounters and sudden quarrels. This is the proper setting for John Donne's satires as well as for Ben Jonson's two Roman plays on the nature of ambition and corruption. It is also the setting for the great age of the masque. A ball, or a comedy, was staged every other day.

Yet the court is also the most significant context for the collection of Thomas Howard, earl of Arundel, which came to include the architectural drawings of Palladio as well as the work of Holbein, Raphael and Dürer. The great lords and courtiers also built elaborate houses at Audley End, Hatfield and elsewhere. The earl of Northampton furnished his house in the Strand with Turkish carpets, Brussels tapestries and Chinese porcelain; he also owned globes, and maps of all the principal nations. This is the burgeoning world of Jacobeanism.

On his progress to London from Edinburgh, at the beginning of his reign, the king was given a petition; it was an appeal from his puritan subjects that became known as the 'millenary petition', bearing the signatures of 1,000 ministers of religion. In moderate terms it suggested to the king that the sign of the cross should be removed from the baptismal ceremony and that the marriage ring was unnecessary. The words 'priest' and 'absolution' should be 'corrected', and the rite of confirmation abolished. The cap and the surplice, the vestments of conformity, were not to be 'urged'.

The king himself liked nothing so much as doctrinal discussion, in which he could display his learning. The first important act of his reign, therefore, was to bring together a small number of clerics at his palace of Hampton Court where they might debate matters of religious policy and religious principle. Five distinguished and learned puritan ministers were matched against the leading ecclesiastics of the realm, among them the archbishop of Canterbury and eight bishops.

This was an age of religious polemic, perhaps prophesying the civil wars of the succeeding reign. On the side of the bishops were those generally satisfied with the doctrines and ceremonies of the established Church; they were moderate; they espoused the union of Church and state. They put more trust in communal worship than in private prayer; they acknowledged the role of custom, experience and reason in spiritual matters. It may not have been a fully formed faith, but it served to bind together those of unclear or flexible belief. It also suited those who simply wished to conform with their neighbours.

On the side of the puritans were those more concerned with the exigencies of the private conscience. They believed in the natural depravity of man, unless the sinner be redeemed by grace. They abhorred the practice of confession and encouraged intensive self-examination as well as self-discipline. They did not wish for a sacramental priesthood but a preaching ministry; they accepted the word of Scripture as the source of all divine truth. They took their compass from the stirrings of providence. Men and women of a puritan tradition were utterly obedient to God's absolute will from which no ritual or sacrament could avert them. This lent them zeal and energy in their attempt to purify the world or, as one puritan theologian put it, 'a holy violence in the performing of all duties'. Sometimes they spoke out as the spirit moved them. It was said, unfairly, that they loved God with all their soul and hated their neighbour with all their heart.

They were not at this stage, however, rival creeds; they are perhaps better regarded as opposing tendencies within the same Church, and their first formal confrontation took place at Hampton Court in the middle of winter. The proceedings of the first day, 14 January 1604, were confined to the king and his ecclesiastics. James debated with his bishops the changes suggested in the 'millenary petition'. On the second day the puritan divines were invited to attend. John Reynolds, the first to be called, argued that the English Church should embrace Calvinist doctrine. The bishop of London, Richard Bancroft, quickly intervened. He knelt down before the king and demanded that 'the ancient canon might be remembered', by which he meant that '*schismatici*' should not be permitted to speak against the bishops. James allowed the discussion on specific matters to continue.

In the subsequent debate the king seems to have been shrewd and judicious. He did not accede to the puritans' demand for Calvinism, but he did accept their proposal for an improved translation of the Bible. This request bore magnificent fruit in the King James translation published later in the reign. The delegates then discussed the problem of providing a learned ministry, and the difficulties of dealing with issues of private conscience. The king was willing to concede certain matters to the puritans, in the evident belief that a middle way would encourage unity within the Church. In the bitter weather the fires of Hampton Court roared, while the king sat in his furs; the bishops, and even the puritan delegates, were also clad in fur cloaks.

All seemed to be proceeding without much incident until Reynolds recommended that the bishops of the realm should consult with the 'presbyters'. At this, the king bridled. 'Presbyter', the term for the elder or minister of a Christian church, had for him unfortunate connotations. He had previously been outraged by the Presbyterian divines of Scotland, who did not always treat His Majesty with appropriate respect; they inclined towards republicanism and even egalitarianism. One of them, Andrew Melville, had called him to his face 'God's silly vassal'.

James now told Reynolds and his colleagues that they seemed to be aiming 'at a Scottish Presbytery which agreeth with monarchy as well as God and the devil'. He added that it would mean 'Jack and Tom, and Will and Dick, shall meet, and at their pleasure censure me and my council and all our proceedings'. He concluded with advice to Reynolds that 'until you find that I grow lazy, leave it alone'. His motto from this time forward would be 'no bishop, no king'. He observed, as the puritan delegates left his presence, that 'if this be all they have to say, I shall make them conform themselves, or I will harry them out of the land, or else do worse'.

Two days later the king summoned the bishops for a further conference. He then called back the puritans, and ordered them to conform to the whole of the orthodox Book of Common Prayer reissued forty-five years before. The conference was over. The impending translation was the greatest benefit of the proceedings but, altogether, the conference cannot be counted a great success. It had now emerged that there was perhaps not one national Church, after all, but at least two Churches with different meanings and purposes.

The king was, as ever, delighted with his performance at Hampton Court. 'I peppered them soundly,' he said. The bishops had told him that he had spoken with the power of inspiration. 'I know not what they mean,' Sir John Harington wrote to his wife, 'but the spirit was rather foul-mouthed.' The king had said, at one point, 'A turd for this argument. I would rather my child were baptized by an ape as by a woman.' He also chastised the puritans by remonstrating 'Away with your snivelling!'

He was, however, in many respects a learned man. All his life he had argued, and debated, with his Scottish clergy. He delighted in theological controversy, and according to an early observer 'he apprehends clearly, judges wisely and has a retentive memory'. The king also believed himself to be a master of the written word and composed volumes on demonology, monarchy, witchcraft and smoking. On his accession medal he is crowned with a laurel wreath, a sure sign of his literary pretensions. He even replied to 'rayling rhymes' published against him with his own doggerel verse. In 1616 he collected all of his prose writings into a folio volume, the first English monarch ever to do so. So he became known, sometimes sarcastically, as 'the British Solomon'.

John Whitgift, archbishop of Canterbury, now close to death, realized that the conclusion of the Hampton Court conference was by no means the end of religious controversy. He knew well enough that parliament, about to meet, contained many lords and gentlemen of a puritan persuasion. The king had decided to ride in state through the capital four days before the opening of parliament on 19 March 1604. Now that the threat of plague had lifted it was declared that people from every 'county, borough, precinct, city, hamlet' had flocked to give praise to the new monarch. Seven triumphal arches, in the style of imperial Rome, were erected along the processional route from the Tower to Whitehall. Yet magnificence did not necessarily command assent.

It was a large parliament, eager to take the measure of James I. In his opening speech the king made some remarks upon the state of religion and admonished the puritans for 'being ever discontented with the present government'. When it became clear that the Commons were more concerned with various matters of privilege and grievance, James rebuked them 'as a father to his children'. Further causes of contention soon emerged.

A dispute had arisen over the election of a member for Buckinghamshire and the ensuing argument pitched king against parliament. On 5 April the Speaker delivered a message from James that he desired 'as an absolute king' that there might be a conference between the Commons and the judges. No monarch had spoken to parliament in that manner for years. Silence and amazement followed this peremptory request, whereupon one member stood up and said that 'the prince's command is like a thunderbolt; his command upon our allegiance like the roaring of a lion; to his command there is no contradiction'.

That was not necessarily the case. In the middle of April it was proposed that James should assume the title of king of Great Britain, with the union of his kingdoms; it might have been deemed a mere formality under the circumstances. But the Commons were not so easily to be persuaded. What kind of union was being proposed? Economic? Constitutional? By what laws will this 'Britain' be governed? There might be a flood of Scots taking up all posts and honours. How could the common law of England be consistent with the legal traditions of Scotland or even with the customs of Ireland?

The king himself was adamant. 'I am the husband,' he said, 'and all the whole isle is my lawful wife; I am the head and it is my body.' Did they wish him to be a polygamist with two separate wives? The debate lingered into the succeeding year with what the king called 'many crossings, long disputations, strange questions, and nothing done'. He had a vision of a united kingdom with one law, one language and one faith; yet the practicalities of the period rendered the ambition useless. The English demanded, for example, that the Scots be taxed at the same rate as themselves; the Scots demurred, pleading poverty. The Commons had already agreed that since 'we cannot make any laws to bind *Britannia* . . . let us proceed with a leaden foot'. The king's enthusiasm for the project was as great as his anger against the opponents of union.

Parliament then turned its attention to matters of religion, and in particular to the work of the Hampton Court conference. It was here, as we have seen, that Archbishop Whitgift sensed trouble from the great puritan gentry who had already taken their seats. By the end of May the Commons had brought in two bills, one of which was directed against pluralists and non-residents; these men, who held more than one clerical living or were keen to relegate their duties, included some of the most prominent members of the established Church. The bias of the Commons was clear enough. The second bill expressed the desire for 'a learned and godly ministry', a request tantamount to a demand for puritanism.

The king was vexed, and by way of justification a parliamentary committee drew up a 'form of apology and satisfaction', read to the Commons on 20 June, in which were defended such rights as freedom of speech and freedom from arrest. It was declared that 'our privileges and liberties are our true right and due inheritance, no less than our lands and goods'. It was a parliamentary way, perhaps, of introducing a Scottish king to the peculiar constitution of England. Another section stated that 'your majesty should be misinformed if any man should deliver that the kings of England have any absolute power in themselves either to alter religion . . . or to make any laws covering the same'. The 'form of apology' was never presented to the king; it may have been rejected by a majority as too extreme.

Without doubt, however, James came to hear of it; he resented its implication and was angered at its impudence. He came down to prorogue parliament on 7 July, where in the course of his speech he berated some of its members for being 'idle heads, some rash, some busy informers'. He said that in Scotland he was heard with respect whereas here there was 'nothing but curiosity from morning to evening to find fault with my propositions'. In Scotland 'all things warranted that came from me. Here all things suspected.' He added that 'you have done many things rashly, I say not you meant disloyally'. Then, at the conclusion, he advised that 'only I wish you had kept a better form. I like form as much as matter.'

He was perhaps waiting for the assistance of Richard Bancroft, newly installed as archbishop of Canterbury, who was a firm upholder of the royal prerogative and no lover of puritans. Even then Bancroft was steering the convocation of senior clergy towards a statement of general religious conformity; the canons of 1604 gave nothing to the puritans but demanded that they submit to the Book of Common Prayer and to the Thirty-Nine Articles. The sectarian ministers must conform or be deprived. The more draconian penalties were in truth rarely applied, but the measures marked the first schism in the history of the reformed English Church.

So the king had prorogued parliament with a very bad grace, little or nothing having been achieved by it. He stated at a later date that it was a body without a head. 'At their meetings,' he is reported to have said, 'nothing is heard but cries, shouts and confusion. I am surprised that my ancestors should ever have allowed such an institution to come into existence.' His opinion may have been shared by others. In the winter of 1604 Thomas Percy subleased a house beside the Palace of Westminster and, with the assistance of Guy Fawkes and other conspirators, began to excavate a tunnel.

2

The plot

In these early years the king was proclaimed as a Caesar, a David, a Noah, a Joash and even a Homer. He was a second Augustus, a true Josiah, a wise and religious sovereign. It is difficult to know what this bewildering wealth of parallels might signify, but one virtue soon became predominant. He was *'rex pacificus'* or *'Jacobus pacificus'*. Blessed was the peacemaker. His was the reign of the fig tree and the vine.

Others were not so satisfied by the pleasures of peace. 'Na, na,' James is supposed to have said after his coronation, 'we'll not need papists now.' He had wooed them in case of trouble, but could now afford to discard them. In February 1604, the Jesuit priests who owed all their obedience to Rome were banished from the realm. It was a sensible precaution, perhaps, but for fervent Catholics it was an ominous sign.

Among these was Thomas Winter, or Wintour, who had unsuccessfully appealed to Philip III of Spain for aid on behalf of the faithful. In the same month of February 1604, he visited his cousin, Robert Catesby, at Lambeth. Catesby was possibly a convert from Protestantism and therefore one in whom the Roman fire burned ever more brightly. It was he, rather than Guy Fawkes, who led what became known as the 'powder plot'. Catesby informed his cousin of his grand plan to blow up parliament with gunpowder, but of course he needed allies in the work. In April Winter travelled to Flanders from which place he brought back Fawkes himself. We may now refer to them as conspirators. 'Shall we always, gentlemen, talk,' Thomas Percy said, 'and never do anything?' In the following month an oath of secrecy was sworn before they made their way to a house behind the church of St Clement Eastcheap, where they met a Jesuit by the name of Gerard who administered to them the Holy Sacrament.

It was now agreed that a dwelling conveniently close to parliament must be found, but it was not until the beginning of December that a suitable property became available. On the 11th of the month they entered the house, carrying with them a stock of hard-boiled eggs and baked meats. By Christmas Eve the conspirators had dug their way down and, in the words of Thomas Winter, 'wrought under a little entry to the wall of the parliament house and underpropped it as we went with wood'. They believed that the next session would begin in February 1605, but now they learned that it was prorogued until the following October. They had more time. The gunpowder was being stored at Catesby's lodgings in Lambeth but, under conditions of great secrecy and security, it was brought to the house at Westminster. They had already made some progress in penetrating the 9-foot wall, but their work was impeded by the influx of water.

One day, soon after the gunpowder had been acquired, they heard a rustling sound above their heads. Fawkes went out of doors and cautiously investigated. He was met by Ellen Bright, coal merchant, who informed him that she was leaving the premises; it so happened that her cellar or vault ran under the parliament house itself. The deal was quickly settled; Thomas Percy, another conspirator, secured the lease of the space. An iron gate between the basement of the conspirators' house and Mrs Bright's cellar was opened, and Fawkes was able to smuggle some thirty-six barrels of gunpowder into the neighbouring vault. There was enough powder to destroy many thousands of people.

By September fresh barrels of gunpowder were acquired in order to replace those affected by damp. Funds were running low, however, and it was deemed advisable to bring in three other conspirators with money or property. Thirteen men were by this time apprised of the secret, leaving thirteen ways for the secret to be betrayed.

One of the newly recruited conspirators, Francis Tresham, pleaded strongly that his brother-in-law, Lord Monteagle, should be spared the general conflagration. Monteagle was a staunch Catholic who had already defended his Church in the House of Lords. The others demurred at the exception, however well meant. Monteagle was sitting down for dinner on 26 October, at his house in Hoxton, when a letter was brought to him by a messenger. He glanced at it and then requested one of his gentlemen to read it aloud.

'My lord, out of the love I bear to some of your friends, I have a care of your preservation. Therefore I would advise you, as you tender your life, to devise some excuse to shift of your attendance at this parliament . . . ' So it began. The correspondent then went on to warn that 'they shall receive a terrible blow this Parliament, and yet they shall not see who hurts them'. Monteagle immediately set out for Whitehall with the letter in his hand. He came upon Robert Cecil, now the newly created earl of Salisbury, sitting down to supper with some other members of the privy council.

Monteagle took Salisbury into an adjoining room, and showed him the document. Salisbury was at first inclined to dismiss the matter as a false alarm but, on his consulting his colleagues, the possibility of gunpowder as a 'terrible blow' was discussed. The lord chamberlain, the earl of Suffolk, knew intimately the interior of parliament; in particular he was aware of the damp and capacious cellars beneath the building. He, and other privy councillors, agreed that they should be searched before the beginning of the session that had been further postponed to 5 November; but they did not wish to act too precipitately for fear of scaring away the plotters.

The king had been hunting at Royston and, on his return to London at the beginning of November, the letter was shown to him. Instantly he agreed that it suggested 'some stratagem of fire and powder'. On the afternoon of Monday 4 November, Suffolk and Monteagle began their search on the excuse that they were looking for some property belonging to the king. Guy Fawkes opened the door of the cellar.

Suffolk: To whom do these coals and faggots belong?
Fawkes: They belong to Mr Thomas Percy, one of his majesty's gentlemen pensioners.

Thomas Percy was of course a known Catholic, at a time when there was some fear of Catholic disaffection. The king now ordered a further and more thorough search. At eleven o'clock that night a Westminster magistrate, Sir Thomas Knyvett, went down to the cellar with certain soldiers. The door was once more opened by Guy Fawkes. Knyvett then began to brush aside the coals and the bundles of wood only to discover the barrels of gunpowder. Fawkes made no attempt at flight or combat. He admitted that he intended to blow up the king and the two houses of parliament on the following morning. It seems that he was prepared to light a slow match and then to make his way to Wapping where he would take boat to Gravelines in France. When he was asked later, in formal questioning by the council, the reason for procuring so much gunpowder he replied that he wanted 'to blow the Scottish beggars back to their native mountains'. The king was informed of Fawkes's capture, and gave thanks for his miraculous deliverance.

It was, perhaps, not a miracle at all. Francis Tresham and Lord Monteagle may have conspired in the production of the letter, as a device to gain the favour of the king. It has also been suggested that Salisbury himself was aware of the conspiracy but allowed it to proceed as a way of catching out the Catholics; this is highly unlikely, but not wholly impossible.

News of the arrest, and the intended treason, soon spread. Robert Catesby and the other conspirators fled from London, hoping to create the conditions for a Catholic rising; but the Catholic gentlemen were not about to commit suicide. The principal fugitives then took refuge in Holbeche House, on the borders of Staffordshire, where a lighted coal or stray spark ignited the gunpowder they were carrying with them. Two or three were injured, and were inclined to see in the accident a sign of divine displeasure. One of them cried out, 'Woe worth the time that we have seen this day!' They then knelt in prayer before a picture of the Virgin. The sheriff of Worcester was on their track; his men surrounded the house and fired on its occupants. Some were killed, while the wounded were taken back to London; Catesby was among those shot dead.

Other conspirators were found in hiding over the next few days. On 27 January 1606, Guy Fawkes and seven others were brought for trial to Westminster Hall where all but one of them pleaded innocence. They were executed a few days later. The Jesuits, who had condoned if not connived in the plot, were soon enough taken to the scaffold. So ended 'the powder plot'. Seven years later the study of Robert Cotton, librarian and antiquarian, was found to contain certain sainted relics of the plotters, including a finger, a toe and a piece of a rib.

The king himself, despite his miraculous survival, was not comforted. The Venetian ambassador reported that 'the king is in terror, he does not appear nor does he take his meals in public as usual. He lives in the innermost rooms with only Scotsmen about him.' James seemed subdued and melancholy, occasionally giving vent to his anger against the Catholics. 'I shall most certainly be obliged to stain my hands with their blood,' he said, 'though sorely against my will.' It did not come to that.

The members of the Commons had continued their ordinary business on the day they were meant to be destroyed; a committee on Spanish trade was established, and a petition was discussed from a member asking to be excused on account of gout. Yet by the end of May 1606, they had passed an Act 'for the better discovering and repressing of popish recusants'; one of its provisions was an oath of allegiance, drawn up by Archbishop Bancroft, which acknowledged James to be the lawful king beyond any power of the pope to depose him. Catholics were obliged to attend the services of the established Church and to receive holy communion at least once a year; the penalties included fines or the impropriation of property. No recusant was to come within 10 miles of London, and a statute of the previous reign was revived prohibiting any recusant from travelling further than 5 miles from his or her home. No recusant could practise as an attorney or as a doctor.

These measures did not bring about the demise of the old faith. The Catholics merely withdrew from political activity during the reign of James and largely remained quiet or quiescent. Most of them were willing to accept the oath of allegiance in order to secure both peace and property; only the Jesuitically inclined were still eager to support the pretensions of the pope. James himself said of the oath that he wished to make a distinction between the doctrinaire Catholics and those 'who although they were otherwise popishly affected, yet retained in their hearts the print of their natural duty to their sovereign'. The previous sanctions against the puritans had been only hesitantly or partially imposed; the same policy of caution was now pursued against the Catholics. James had no wish to make martyrs out of his subjects. It was in any case far easier, in the early seventeenth century, to make laws than to enforce them.

The court of James I, its excesses having already become public knowledge, was now notorious for its laxity; drunkenness and dissimulation, venality and promiscuity, were its most significant characteristics. Freedom of manners was the only rule. The earl of Pembroke was believed to have a horror of frogs, so the king put one down his neck. The king himself had an aversion to pigs, and so Pembroke led one into the royal bedchamber. One courtier took into the palace at Whitehall 'four brawny pigs, piping hot, bitted and harnessed with ropes of sausages, all tied to a monstrous pudding'. The sausages were hurled about the room while the fools and dwarves of the court began leaping on one another's shoulders.

In *Sejanus, His Fall*, a play performed in the first year of the king's reign, Ben Jonson alluded to courtiers when he wrote that:

> We have no shift of faces, no cleft tongues,
> No soft and glutinous bodies that can stick
> Like snails on painted walls . . .

'If I were to imitate the conduct of your republic,' the king told the Venetian ambassador, 'and begin to punish those who take bribes, I should soon not have a single subject left.'

When the king of Denmark arrived in the summer of 1606 the courtiers of Whitehall were said by Sir John Harington 'to wallow in beastly delights' while the ladies 'abandon their sobriety and are seen to roll about in intoxication'. A great feast was held for the two sovereigns, in the course of which was shown a representation of Solomon and the Queen of Sheba. The lady who played the queen carried various gifts to the two kings 'but forgetting the steps arising to the canopy overset her caskets into his Danish majesty's lap and fell at his feet . . . His Majesty then got up and would dance with the Queen of Sheba, but he fell down and humbled himself before her, and was carried to an inner chamber and laid on a bed of state.'

Other actors in the pageant, such as Hope and Faith, 'were both sick and spewing in the lower hall'. Harington concluded that 'the gunpowder fright is got out of all our heads' and 'I ne'er did see such lack of good order, discretion and sobriety, as I have now done'. He yearned for the days of his godmother, the Virgin Queen, when a certain stateliness and severity touched the atmosphere of the court.

There could be no doubt that the new court differed markedly from its predecessor. The king was known to be devoted to his pleasures rather than what were considered to be his duties. He attended the fights of the Cockpit in Whitehall Palace twice a week, and, like his predecessor, loved to ride or hunt every day. When James rode up to the dead hart he dismounted and cut its throat with dispatch; he then sated the dogs with its blood before wiping his bloodied hands across the faces of his fellow horsemen.

It soon became clear that he did not enjoy the company of spectators at his sports. Quite unlike his predecessor he disliked and even detested crowds. When the people flocked about him he would swear at them and cry out, 'What would they have?' On one occasion he was told that they had come in love and reverence. To which he replied, in a broad Scots accent, 'God's wounds, I will pull down my breeches and they shall also see my arse.' He would bid 'A pox on you!' or 'A plague on you!' As a result of outbursts of anger such as this he became, in the words of the Venetian ambassador, 'despised and almost hated'.

He justified his exertions at the hunt on the grounds that his vigour was 'the health and welfare of them all', no doubt meaning both the court and the nation. Let his officers waste away in closets or at the council table. He must be strong and virile. In any case, he said, he could do more business in an hour than his councillors could manage in a day; he spent less time in hunting than other monarchs did in whoring. One day a favourite dog, Jowler, disappeared from the pack. On the following morning it reappeared with a note tied around its neck. 'Good Mr Jowler we pray you speak to the king (for he hears you every day and so doth he not us) that it will please his majesty to go back to London, for else the country will be undone.' When eventually James did return to Whitehall he feasted and played cards, at which sport he lost large sums of money.

James was continually and heavily in debt. He had thought to come into a realm of gold, but soon found his purse to be bare. Or, rather, he emptied it too readily. He bought boots and silk stockings and beaver hats in profusion. Court ceremonial was more lavish with the arrival of ever more 'gentlemen extraordinary'. There was a vogue at court for 'golden play' or gambling. The king loved masques and feasts, which were for him a true sign of regality. He wished to have a masque on the night of Christmas, whereupon he was told that it was not the fashion. 'What do you tell me of the fashion?' he enquired. 'I will make it a fashion.'

The king also purchased plate and jewels, which he then proceeded to distribute among his followers. It was said that he had given to one or two men more than his predecessor had given to all of her courtiers during the whole of her reign. The earl of Shrewsbury remarked that Elizabeth 'valued every molehill that she gave . . . a mountain, which our sovereign now does not'. His generosity to favourites and to courtiers was by the standard of any age in English history exceptional.

One particular favourite emerged in the spring of 1607. Robert Carr, twenty-one, was a model of affability and deportment; he was also exceptionally handsome. He took part in a tournament in the king's presence, but he was thrown from his horse and broke his leg. The king was much affected and ordered his own doctor to take charge of the young man; Carr was carried to the hospital at Charing Cross, where the king visited him every day. The patient was placed on a choice diet and, at the insistence of James, was surrounded by surgeons. It was clear to the courtiers that here was a man worth flattering. 'Lord!' one contemporary, Sir Anthony Weldon, wrote, 'how the great men flocked to see him, and to offer to his shrine in such abundance . . .' James had become infatuated with him and, by the end of the year, Carr had been knighted and appointed as a gentleman of the bedchamber. The king decided to educate as well as to promote him. He himself gave Carr lessons in Latin grammar and in the politics of Europe. And of course he lavished gold and jewels upon him. It was observed that the king 'leaneth on his arm, pinches his cheek, smoothes his ruffled garments . . .'

Sir John Harington was still seeking preferment at court after a lifetime of service to Elizabeth. Thomas Howard, earl of Suffolk, took him aside and offered some advice. He was told that the king 'doth wonderfully covet learned discourse' and 'doth admire good fashion in cloaths'. He was instructed to 'get a new jerkin well bordered, and not too short; the king saith, he liketh a flowing garment; be sure it be not all of one sort, but diversely coloured, the collar falling somewhat down, and your ruff well stiffened and bushy'. Eighteen courtiers had already been dismissed for not conforming to the king's taste in male attire.

Suffolk suggested to Harington that in his conversation he should not dwell too long on any one subject, and touch only lightly on the topic of religion. Never say that 'this is good or bad' but modestly state that 'if it were your majesty's good opinion, I myself should think so and so'. Do not ask questions. Do not speak about the character or temperament of anyone else at court. Remember to praise the king's horse, a roan jennet. You must say that the stars are bright jewels fit for Robert Carr's ears, and that the roan jennet surpasses Bucephalus and is worthy to be ridden by Alexander.

Suffolk also advised Harington that 'silence and discretion should be linked together, like dog and bitch'. The previous sovereign had always spoken of her subjects' 'love and good affections', but James preferred to talk of their 'fear and subjection'. Why did Harington wish to come to court in the first place? 'You are not young, you are not handsome, you are not finely.' So he must rely upon his learning, which the king would admire.

Soon enough James took Harington aside, and questioned him in his private closet. He quizzed him on Aristotle and other philosophers; he asked him to read out a passage from Ariosto, and praised his elocution. He then posed a series of questions to him. What do you think pure wit is made of? Should a king not be the best clerk [the most learned] in his own country? Do you truly understand why the devil works more with ancient women than with others? He told Harington that the death of his mother, Mary Queen of Scots, had been foretold and that at the time of her execution a bloody head was seen dancing in the air; he dilated on the powers of prophecy and recommended several books on the matter. The king concluded by discussing 'the new weed', tobacco, and declared that 'it would, by its use, infuse ill qualities on the brain'. So ended the audience. Harington passed through the court 'amidst the many varlets and lordly servants who stood around'. Yet he had passed the test, and was appointed as tutor to the young Prince Henry.

Reasons other than favouritism can be adduced for the king's indebtedness. The steady rise in prices, and the reluctance of landowners to pay further taxation, all contributed to the rise in the expenditure of the court above its income. The cost of an extended royal household, complete with wife and three children, was also very high. Queen Anne was extravagant and devoted to the delights of fashionable London; her husband had proposed that she might confine herself to the 3,000 dresses in the previous queen's wardrobe, but she did not care for some of the old fashions. She would appear at court in the guise of a goddess or a nymph, an Eastern sultana or an Arab princess.

James was perpetually surprised by his debts, and continually promised to be more economical; yet it was not in his nature to be thrifty. 'My only hope that upholds me,' he told Salisbury, 'is my good servants, that will sweat and labour for my relief.' But where was the money to be found? Certain taxes had been levied 'time out of mind', or at least since the latter years of the fourteenth century. 'Tonnage' was the duty levied on each 'tun' or cask of wine; 'poundage' was the tax raised on every pound sterling of exported or imported goods. James decided to revise the book of rates, however, and to impose new levies that came to be known as 'impositions'.

A merchant by the name of John Bate refused to pay. He drove a cartload of currants from the waterside before the customs officials had the opportunity to tax them; he was brought before the council, where he declared that the 'imposition' was illegal. His became a test case before the court of the exchequer which ruled that the king had absolute power in the matter; in all aspects of foreign trade, his prerogative was assured.

Nevertheless opposition arose in parliament, where there was talk of money being poured into bottomless coffers. In October 1607 James addressed his council on the pressing problems concerning 'this eating canker of want'. He promised to abide by any 'cure' they prescribed and to accept 'such remedies and antidotes as you are to apply unto my disease'. The case was not an easy one. Salisbury tried various expedients for raising money, by fining for long-forgotten transgressions or by extorting as many feudal 'aids' to the king as he could find.

Yet the Commons were not impressed by the measures. It was an ancient principle that the sovereign of England should 'live of his own'; he should maintain his estate, and bear the cost of government, out of his own resources. It was also universally believed that taxation was an extraordinary measure only to be raised in time of war. The first parliament of James I was summoned for five sessions from March 1604 to February 1611, and in that long period it acquired the beginning of a corporate identity largely lacking during the reign of Elizabeth. More business was enacted, and parliament sat for longer. In 1607, for example, the Commons instituted a 'committee of the whole house'. This committee could elect its own chairman, as opposed to the Speaker chosen by the sovereign, and could debate freely for as long as it wished. It was at the time seen as a remarkable innovation, and might be considered the harbinger of strife between court and parliament.

A group of disparate and variously inclined parliamentarians was not necessarily on the king's side. Francis Bacon wrote to the king that 'that opposition which was, the last parliament, to your majesty's business, as much as was not *ex puris naturalibus* but out of party, I conceive to be now much weaker than it was'. This did not yet embody the partisanship of later struggles, or the creation of 'parties' in the modern sense, but it suggests a change in national affairs. Some of the disputatious details have been recorded. Sir Edward Herbert 'plops' with his mouth at Mr Speaker. John Tey complains that Mr Speaker is 'clipping him off' and proceeds to threaten him.

The king had another doughty opponent. A legal dispute had arisen. Was there a distinction between those Scots born before James's accession to the English throne and those born after it? The king argued that those born after his accession were naturalized by common law and, therefore, could hold office in England. James turned to the judges whom he assumed to take his part. One of them refused to do so. Sir Edward Coke had been chief justice of the common pleas since 1605, and was an impassioned exponent of English common law. James had no real conception of common law, having been educated in the very different jurisprudence of Scotland. Coke believed, for example, that both sovereign and subject were accountable to a body of ancient law that had been conceived in practice and clarified by usage; it represented immemorial general custom, but it was also a law of reason. This was not, however, the king's opinion. He had already firmly stated that 'the king is above the law, as both the author and the giver of strength thereto'. From this it could be construed that the king possessed an arbitrary authority. James alleged, for example, that he could decide cases in person. Coke demurred: a case could only be judged in a lawcourt. Coke's own report tells the story of bad blood.

> *James:* I thought the law was founded on reason. I and others have reason as well as the judges.
>
> *Coke:* Although, sir, you have great endowments of nature, yet you are not learned in the laws of England. Causes are not to be decided by natural reason but by the artificial reason and judgment of law.

More debate followed.

> *James:* So then I am under the law? It is treason to affirm that!
>
> *Coke:* Bracton has said that the king should not be under man but under God and the law.

An observer noted that 'his majesty fell in that high indignation as the like was never known in him, looking and speaking fiercely with bended fist, offering to strike him, which the Lord Coke perceiving fell flat on all fours . . .' Coke might yield and beg for mercy, but over succeeding years the debate between the Crown and the law continued with ever greater volume and seriousness.

The manoeuvres of the court were never still. The favourite, now Sir Robert Carr, needed land to complement his title. By Carr's great good fortune Sir Walter Raleigh, still incarcerated, had forfeited his interest in the manor of Sherborne; he thought that he had conveyed it to his son, but the king's council believed otherwise. It was given to the favourite. Lady Raleigh, accompanied by her two sons, was admitted into the king's presence where she threw herself at his feet. 'I maun have the land' was his only reply. 'I maun have it for Carr.' This is the true voice of the king.

3

The beacons

In 1605 one of the king's 'learned counsel' presented him with a treatise that summoned up the spirit of a new age. Francis Bacon's 'Of the Proficience and Advancement of Learning Divine and Human' is better known to posterity as *The Advancement of Learning*; it can justifiably be said to have changed the terms of human understanding and the nature of knowledge. Bacon had been a royal servant for some years under the patronage of his uncle, Lord Burghley, and had been first enlisted in the court of Elizabeth. But the advent of a new king promised more tangible rewards and, soon after the accession, Bacon provided James with texts of advice on such matters as the union of Scotland with England and ecclesiastical polity.

Yet *The Advancement of Learning* was a work in quite another key, and one that helped to create the climate of scientific rationalism that characterized the entire seventeenth century. Bacon had first to clear away the clutter of inherited knowledge. In the early pages of the treatise 'the first distemper of learning' is denounced as that by which 'men study words and not matter'. Yet words, and not matter, had been the foundation of traditional learning for innumerable centuries, whether in the rhetorical humanism of the Renaissance or in the scholastic theology of the Middle Ages. Bacon declared, however, that 'men have withdrawn themselves too much from the contemplation of nature, and the observations of experience, and have tumbled up and down in their own reasons and conceits'. It was time to look at the world.

He further observed that:

> this kind of degenerate learning did chiefly reign amongst the schoolmen, who having sharp and strong wits, and abundance of leisure, and small variety of reading, but their wits being shut up in the cells of a few authors (chiefly Aristotle their dictator) as their persons were shut up in the cells of monasteries and colleges, and knowing little history, either of nature or of time, did out of no great quantity of matter, and infinite agitation of wit, spin out unto us those laborious webs of learning which are extant in their books . . . cobwebs of learning admirable for the fineness of thread and work, but of no substance or profit.

The clarity and cogency of his prose are the perfect instruments for his attack upon the ornateness and excessive ingenuity of the old learning. That is why Shelley cited Plato and Bacon as the two most influential of all the poet-philosophers.

Bacon was assaulting the methods and principles of previous human learning in favour of experiment and observation, which he believed to be central to true natural science. He was suggesting that the scholars and experimenters of the time should confine themselves 'to use and not to ostentation' and to 'matters of common sense and experience'. He warned that 'the more you remove yourselves from particulars, the greater peril of error you do incur'. At a later date this would be described as the 'scientific' disposition.

The purpose of all learning was, for Bacon, to promote the benefit and prosperity of humankind. The material world is to be understood and mastered by means of 'the laborious and sober inquiry of truth' which can be pursued only by 'ascending from experiments to the invention of causes, and descending from causes to the invention of new experiments'. This was a revolutionary statement of intent that places Bacon, and the Jacobean period, at the opening of the modern age.

Bacon desired an institutional, as well as an epistemological, change; he suggested that universities, colleges and schools be directed 'by amplitude of reward, by soundness of direction, and by the conjunction of labours'. We may see here the origin of the attitude that was to guide the Royal Society and to inform the inventive energies that emerged in the first years of the Industrial Revolution. Bacon himself was of a puritan disposition. He believed in the power of individual agency above the manifold allures of tradition and authority; he believed in observation rather than contemplation as the true instrument of practical reason. The beacons of utility and progress were always before him.

Bacon hoped that by their bright light 'this third period of time will far surpass that of the Grecian and Roman learning'. It would be fair to say that he helped to change the pace and the direction of that new learning. He entitled a later work *Instauratio Magna*, 'the great innovation' or foundation; the frontispiece of that book shows a ship sailing through the two Pillars of Hercules that traditionally signified the limits of knowledge as well as of exploration. It is an emblem of a journey of discovery in defiance of the motto '*nec plus ultra*', nothing further beyond. The reign of James I, therefore, can be said to mark the beginning of a voyage through strange seas of thought.

4

The god of money

The treasury was bare; the officers of the Crown were demanding their salaries, but there was no money to be found. Parliament was reluctant to vote taxes, and local officials in the counties were not zealous in collecting the proper revenues from their neighbours; much of the money raised on custom duties was diverted into the pockets of those who collected it.

When parliament reassembled in February 1610, it was in a fractious mood. Salisbury outlined the financial woes of the nation, but the members were more concerned to arrest the prodigal spending of the court rather than to vote new taxes. One of them, Thomas Wentworth, argued that it would be worse than useless to grant new moneys to the king if he refused to reduce his expenditure. He asked, 'To what purpose is it to draw a silver stream into the royal cistern, if it shall daily run out thence by private cocks?' Salisbury was not impressed. It was his understanding that the Commons had a duty to supply the needs of the king, after which their grievances might be addressed. The members, on the other hand, demanded that their complaints be answered before turning to the demands of the king.

A conference was called in which Salisbury put forward a long-meditated plan that became known as the 'great contract'. The king would give up his feudal dues and tenures in exchange for a guaranteed annual sum; the Commons offered £100,000, only half of the amount James required. Parliament still seemed to believe that he should and could be as economical, or as parsimonious, as his predecessor. The negotiations were suspended.

On 21 May the king summoned both houses of parliament into his presence and upbraided them for sitting fourteen weeks without relieving his necessities. He would listen to what they had to say about increased taxation, but he would not be bound by their opinions. They must not question the royal prerogative in such matters. The members answered that, if this were the case, then the king might lawfully claim all that they owned. A deputation, armed with a petition of right, met James at his palace in Greenwich. Realizing that he had perhaps gone too far, he welcomed them and explained that he had been misunderstood. He always knew when to draw back from confrontation, a lesson never learned by his two more earnest sons.

The debate on the great contract resumed on 11 June, with the concomitant issues of supplies, revenues, grievances and impositions. When the grievances were presented to the king on a long roll of parchment, he remarked that it might make a pretty piece of tapestry. Concessions were yielded on both sides, but there was no end in sight. On 23 July James prorogued the parliament, and the members dispersed to their constituencies where the details of the great contract would further be discussed. Naturally enough the towns and counties were more concerned with their injuries than with the poverty of the king. The whole debate had served only to demonstrate the gulf between king and country, between court and realm.

The king was irate at the lack of progress. He resolved that he would never again endure 'such taunts and disgraces as have been uttered of him'. If they came back and offered him all he wished, he would not listen to them. James had in any case already made a speech which rendered the political situation infinitely worse. In March 1610 he had assembled at Whitehall the Lords and the Commons. 'The estate of monarchy', he proclaimed, 'is the supremest thing upon earth: for kings are not only God's lieutenants upon earth, and sit upon God's throne, but even by God himself they are called Gods.' He went on to claim that kings 'exercise a manner or resemblance of divine power on earth'. The sovereigns of the world can 'make and unmake their subjects; they have power of raising and casting down; of life and death; judges over all their subjects and in all causes, and yet accountable to none but God only'. He admonished them that 'you cannot so clip the wing of greatness. If a king be resolute to be a tyrant, all you can do will not hinder him.' Did they really want him to be a mere doge of Venice?

James's sentiments were not necessarily very welcome to the members of parliament. A contemporary news-writer, John Chamberlain, noted that they were 'so little to their satisfaction that I hear it bred generally much discomfort'. If the parliament acquiesced in this bravura statement of kingship, 'we are not like to leave to our successors the freedom we received from our forefathers'.

James did not understand common law, as his confrontations with Coke had suggested, and seemed to be unaware that the principle of absolute sovereignty was not one the English would even remotely entertain. It was noted that 'the king speaks of France and Spain what they may do'. He did not realize, or pretended not to realize, that the sovereigns of those two countries were in a position very different from his own. He maintained the theory of divine right without any clear understanding of how it would operate in the context of parliamentary authority and the common law.

He may have adopted his position for less theoretical reasons. His hatred of the Presbyterian elders of Scotland derived from the fact that they directly challenged his authority. The nobility of that country, also, had been inclined to treat him as if he were one among equals. So his statements about his own powers are likely to have been in part a response to his difficult and sometimes dangerous position as king of Scotland. He had once observed that 'the highest bench is the sliddriest to sit upon'.

He might also have been acutely aware that his temperament and behaviour were not always impeccably regal; he slobbered and walked at an odd angle; he kissed and slavered over his handsome favourites. In compensation for his apparent weaknesses, therefore, he may have been all the more eager to maintain the doctrine of divine right.

Yet in truth his theoretical understanding was very different from his practical grasp of political realities. He never did behave like an absolute prince, and with rare exceptions took care to remain within the fabric of the laws; he was neither arbitrary nor erratic in his exercise of power. In return no serious attempt was made by the parliament to undermine his authority or to question his sovereignty.

The fate of kings was also an immediate concern. On 14 May 1610, Henri IV of France was assassinated in Paris by a Catholic zealot who believed regicide to be his religious duty. Ever fearful for his own life, James responded with a kind of panic. On hearing the news, according to the French ambassador, James 'turned whiter than his shirt'.

In the following month Prince Henry, the king's oldest son, was formally invested as prince of Wales. He was of an heroic or militant character, and a fierce proponent of Protestantism. Francis Bacon remarked that his face was long 'and inclining to leanness . . . his look grave, and the motion of his eyes rather composed than spirited, in his countenance were some marks of severity'. Henry's court eschewed the prodigality and drunkenness condoned by his father; it was a model of formality and propriety, where the sentence for swearing was a fine. At a time when the morals and manners of the king's court were known to be in decline, many believed that he was a true Christian prince who might save the nation for righteousness.

Henry was surrounded by men of a military bent, men of action; he had a keen interest in maritime affairs, and in the progress of colonial exploration. He immensely admired Sir Walter Raleigh, still incarcerated in the Tower, and remarked aloud that 'none but my father would keep such a bird in a cage'. He had an equally keen dislike of his father's bosom companions. Of Carr himself he is supposed to have stated that 'if ever he were king, he would not leave one of that family to piss against the wall'. If ever he were king . . . that was the overwhelming question for the country. Henry IX would no doubt have followed the martial example of Henry V. James, noting the popularity of his son's court, is supposed to have asked, 'Will he bury me alive?' When the king's fool, Archie, remarked that James looked upon Henry as a terror rather than as a comfort the king burst into tears.

Another royal imbroglio, albeit of a minor kind, emerged in the weeks after Henry's investiture. Arabella Stuart was the cousin of the king, and for the first six years of his reign she had enjoyed all the comforts and considerations of the court. She had even been considered as a replacement for James himself, by Raleigh and others, but she had taken no part in the plot. It was still of the utmost importance that she married wisely and well. At the beginning of 1610, however, she came to a pre-contractual arrangement with William Seymour, who by indirect and circuitous route had some small claim to the throne. This always aroused the horror of princes.

The couple agreed to renounce their plans but, in June, they took part in a secret ceremony of marriage at Greenwich. On hearing the news, the king raged. Seymour was instantly confined to the Tower while Arabella was taken to Lambeth before it was decided to send her further north to Durham. En route, at Barnet, she planned her escape. She disguised herself, according to a contemporary chronicler, John More, 'by drawing a pair of great French-fashioned hose over her petticoats, putting on a man's doublet, a man-like peruke, with long locks over her hair, a black hat, black cloak, russet boots, with red tops, and a rapier by her side'. She took ship for France at Leigh, but was overtaken by a vessel sent from Dover to arrest her. She was escorted to the Tower, where her reason gave way under the oppression of her trials, and she died insane four years later. It is a sad story of the perils and perfidies that attended anyone of high estate.

When a new session of parliament opened in the autumn of the year it was clear to everyone that Salisbury's idea of a 'great contract' between the king's necessities and the country's generosity was not to be obtained by any means. The Commons abandoned discussions on the matter by 8 November, with repeated animadversions against 'favourites' and 'wanton courtiers'. The Scots were also attacked as men with open mouths. The king was in a fury, and told the privy council that 'no house save the house of hell' could match the House of Commons. He went on to say that 'our fame and actions have been daily tossed like tennis balls amongst them'. He was inclined to blame Salisbury for putting too much trust in a parliament which he dubbed 'this rotten reed of Egypt'; he continued in biblical mode when he told him that 'your greatest error hath been that you ever expected to draw honey out of gall'. He adjourned and then dissolved parliament within a matter of weeks.

The economic woes of the king were not all of his own making. The fiscal system of England had to a large extent been formulated in the fourteenth century, and it could not deal with the problems attendant upon the seventeenth century. It simply did not work, especially in times of warfare, and all manner of fiscal expedients had to be found. Thus in the spring of the following year James offered to sell hereditary titles to any knights or esquires who desired them. The title of baronet could be purchased for £1,080 in three annual payments, but the overall gain to the exchequer of approximately £90,000 was not enough to balance the profusion of the king's expenditure. Peerages were put on the market four years later. When in 1616 Sir John Roper made over the sum of £10,000 to become Lord Teynham, he was given the nickname of Lord 10m. A seventeenth-century historian, Arthur Wilson, remarked that the multiplicity of titles 'made them cheap and invalid in the vulgar opinion; for nothing is more destructive to monarchy than lessening the nobility; upon their decline the commons rise and anarchy increases'.

The king had another scheme to raise money. It was proposed to him that his oldest son might be pleased to accept the hand of the Infanta Maria Anna, daughter of Philip III of Spain; at once James sent one of his envoys to Madrid. Robin Goodfellow in Ben Jonson's *Love Restored*, performed at court on Twelfth Night 1612, complained ''tis that impostor, PLUTUS, the god of money, who has stolen love's ensigns; and in his belied figure, reigns in the world, making friendships, contracts, marriages and almost religion'.

In the spring of that year James joined the Protestant Union that had been established four years earlier with the coalition of German states such as Brandenburg, Ulm, Strasbourg and the Palatinate; in this matter he was following the sympathies of his people. At the same time he agreed formally that his daughter, Elizabeth, should be engaged to Frederick V of the Palatinate. This was a large territory in the valley of the Rhine, and included cities such as Heidelberg and Düsseldorf; it had been a centre of Protestantism since the middle of the sixteenth century, and Frederick himself was the leading Calvinist in all of Europe. It seemed, therefore, to be an expedient union for a king of England who believed that he himself might become the champion of Protestantism.

He had the appropriate credentials. The King James version of the Bible had emerged in the previous year; it was the fruit of the Hampton Court conference of 1604, and quickly supplanted the Geneva Bible and the Bishops' Bible. Indeed it still remains for many the key translation of the Scriptures and the model of seventeenth-century English prose. It also became a touchstone for English literary culture: in 'On Translating Homer', Matthew Arnold remarked that there is 'an English book, and one only, where, as in the *Iliad* itself, perfect plainness of speech is allied with perfect nobleness; and that book is the Bible'. Its influence can be traced in the work of Milton and Bunyan, of Tennyson and Byron, of Johnson and Gibbon and Thackeray; the power of its cadence is to be found everywhere. The King James Bible invigorated the consciousness of the nation and inspired some of its most eloquent manifestations.

It also prompted a great wave of religious publications in English and, as Robert Burton said in his preface to *The Anatomy of Melancholy*, of books of divinity there was no end. 'There be so many books in that kind, so many commentaries, treatises, pamphlets, expositions, sermons, that whole teams of oxen cannot draw them.' There was also a glut of cheap religious pamphlets that espoused the wonders of God's providence and the evil fate of His enemies.

James consolidated his Protestantism with another measure. In the spring of 1611 George Abbot had been appointed archbishop of Canterbury in succession to Richard Bancroft. His principal qualification for the post, after the assassination of Henri IV, was his persistent and rigorous opposition to Roman Catholicism; he had already taken a leading role in the prosecution of two priests who were subsequently executed at Tyburn.

So it was that in the early spring of 1612 the last two persons convicted for heresy were condemned to death. Edward Wightman published his belief that Christ was 'a mere creature, and not both God and man in one person', and that he himself was the Messiah of the Old Testament. Bartholomew Legate had preached against the rituals and beliefs of the established Church, and had admitted to the king that he had not prayed for seven years. The king kicked out at him. 'Away, base fellow! It shall never be said that one stayed in my presence that hath never prayed to our Saviour for seven whole years together.' Legate was taken to the stake in Smithfield in March 1612, while Wightman followed him to the fire at Lichfield one month later. Wightman had the distinction, if it can be so called, of being the last heretic burned in England.

Another enemy of the state, or at least of convention, may be mentioned here. John Chamberlain relates that in February 1612, Moll Cutpurse, 'a notorious baggage that used to go in man's apparel', was brought to Paul's Cross 'where she wept bitterly and seemed very penitent; but it is since doubted that she was maudlin drunk, being discovered to have tippled three quarts of sack before she came to her penance'. It is an apt vignette of Jacobean London.

5

The angel

In the summer of 1612 King James went on a 'progress' of a month's duration, taking in Leicester, Loughborough, Nottingham and Newark. All around him he could see evidence of a prosperous and tranquil nation. A peace with Spain, and a commercial treaty with France, had encouraged trade while a series of good harvests maintained that happy condition. Dairy produce flowed into London from Essex, Wiltshire and Yorkshire; wool for export arrived at the ports from Wiltshire and Northamptonshire; cattle from North Wales and Scotland, sheep from the Cotswolds, were herded to the great market of Smithfield.

Other trades were also rising. 'Correct your maps,' the poet John Cleveland wrote, 'Newcastle is Peru.' Coal, in other words, was as plentiful and valuable as silver; its production was rising rapidly each year, and the coal traders bargained noisily at the Exchange in Billingsgate. In the hundred years from 1540, the production of iron also increased fivefold. From the port at Bristol sailed cutlery from Sheffield and tin from Cornwall in exchange for sugar and cereals from America and the Indies. Norwich was a safe haven for exiled weavers from France or Germany, while Chester dominated trade with Ireland.

The struggle against monopolies, begun late in the reign of Elizabeth, played its part in the economy of the country. A declaration of the House of Commons, in 1604, stated that 'merchandise being the chief and richest of all others, and of greater extent and importance than all the rest, it is against the natural right and liberty of the subjects of England to restrain it into the hands of some few'. Yet patents were still given for such activities as the draining of the fens, the manufacture of paper, the making of salt from sea water, the production of sword blades, and the production of iron without charcoal. The wealth of the monopolies testifies, if nothing else, to the variety of new products and techniques.

The yeomen were constructing bigger and better dwellings, while the poor left their huts of reed or wood and built cottages of brick or stone. Kitchens and separate bedrooms were introduced, while stairs replaced ladders and chairs took the place of benches; the vogue for more comfortable living continued after the reign of Elizabeth with the taste for crockery rather than wooden platters, and eventually for knives and forks rather than daggers and spoons. It is unwise to exaggerate the general prosperity of the country; areas of the direst poverty still existed, especially among the class of landless agricultural labourers and the wandering workmen of the cities. But the conditions of social and commercial life continued to improve.

One minister had no part in the king's progress of 1612. Robert Cecil, earl of Salisbury, died towards the end of May from an illness of unknown cause; his infirmity might perhaps have been compounded with his knowledge of the king's displeasure at his failure to improve the royal finances. He had preserved among his papers a letter, written in Italian, which compared those who loved the great and the powerful to the heliotrope 'which while the sun shines looks towards it with flowers alive and open, but when the sun sets closes them and looks another way'. In the end he longed for his life, 'full of cares and miseries', to be dissolved. In any case he was not mourned for long. The London news was that, even if he had lived, he had already lost all authority and credit. He had no friends left. Ben Jonson dismissed Salisbury by saying that he 'never cared for any man longer than he could make use of him'.

With the death of any great administrator, there was always a scramble for place and office. Francis Bacon was one who hoped that the demise of Salisbury would prove a blessing. The king himself was not unhappy to have been freed from the yoke of his councillor; he could now, as it were, rule for himself. He could be his own principal secretary. In the following year he discovered, much to his disgust, that Salisbury had for a long time been in the paid employment of Spain. Whom could James ever trust?

Robert Carr, now created Viscount Rochester, was the king's confidant while Henry Howard, the earl of Northampton, had become the principal minister of the new administration. Howard gathered about him a group of peers and other noblemen, some of whom were secret Catholics and almost all of whom favoured the Spaniards. Against them, in the counsels of the king, was a Protestant and anti-Spanish party under the nominal leadership of Lord Chancellor Ellesmere. With the balance of these divided counsels James might be able to steer the nation forward. Different men were given different responsibilities. John Chamberlain wrote, in the summer of 1612, that the king 'hath found the art of frustrating men's expectations, and holding them in suspense'.

Another death occurred at court. All had seemed well with the heir to the throne. Prince Henry was an assertive and athletic young man who excelled in masques as well as martial sports. But at the end of October 1612, he fell sick. He was playing cards with his younger brother, Charles, and a bystander, Sir Charles Cornwallis, noticed that 'his highness for all this looked ill and pale, spake hollow, and somewhat strangely with dead sunk eyes'. A doctor was called but over the next eleven days could do nothing to curb the slow invasion of a disease that has since been tentatively diagnosed as porphyria or, perhaps, typhoid fever.

A dead pigeon was put on the prince's head, and a dead cock at his feet, both freshly killed and still warm, to draw out the noisome humours. He died raving, to the authentic dismay and dejection of the court. He had been the emblem of England's future destiny and had promised an age of heroic adventure in the Protestant cause. Queen Anne wept alone, and a year later it was still not safe to mention her son to her; James mourned aloud with 'Henry is dead! Henry is dead!' The crown was now destined for Charles, a silent, shy and reserved prince quite unlike his brother.

A strange incident occurred soon after when, in the words of John Chamberlain, 'a very handsome young fellow, much about his age, and not altogether unlike him, came stark naked to St James's, while they were at supper, saying he was the prince's ghost, come from heaven with a message to the king'. He was questioned, to no effect, and was deemed to be either mad or simple. After two or three lashes of the whip, he was dismissed.

The king was temperamentally averse to protracted mourning, and had a natural distaste for a gloomy court. In February 1613, he celebrated with great splendour and spectacle the marriage of his only surviving daughter, Elizabeth, to Frederick V of the Palatinate. No one beneath the rank of baron was admitted to the ceremony, and the members of the royal family were stiff with the jewels embroidered onto their clothing. Twenty-five diamonds glittered from the king's velvet hatband. The crown jewels were also on display, among them a pendant of rubies and pearls known as the 'Three Brothers' and a 'great and rich jewel of gold' called 'the Mirror of Great Britain'. The princess herself seemed to mar the solemnity of the occasion by indulging in a low titter that eventually became a loud laugh. She was, perhaps, overwhelmed. On the following day the king visited the newly wedded couple and asked them what had happened in their ornate bed. It is believed that Shakespeare introduced the masque into the fourth act of *The Tempest* in order to celebrate their union.

A more sinister marriage was about to take place. In the middle of April 1613, Sir Thomas Overbury was committed to the Tower of London. This was on the face of it surprising since Overbury had been the close companion and confidant of the king's favourite, Viscount Rochester. It was reported, however, that Overbury had been confined on the king's realization that it was 'a dishonour to him that the world should have an opinion that Rochester ruled him and Overbury ruled Rochester'.

Yet there was more to it than that. Rochester had become enamoured of the young countess of Essex, Frances Howard, but was thwarted by the inconvenient fact that the lady had been married for seven years to Robert Devereux, 3rd earl of Essex. She had been a child bride who now regretted her early union. They had in any case always been a reluctant and resentful pair; with the prospect of Rochester before her, she grasped at the chance of freedom. She asked that her marriage be declared null and void on the grounds that Essex was physically incapable of siring a son. Her father, Thomas Howard, 1st earl of Suffolk, enthusiastically took her part; his daughter's marriage to the king's favourite could only raise his already high standing at court.

Essex was naturally aggrieved that his manhood had been questioned, especially since it might affect his chances of finding another wife. So it was intimated that, although Essex had not been successful with his first partner, he suffered from no disability that might prevent him from marrying again. A solemn commission was established to test the case and, like most solemn commissions, it took the easiest way out.

The king was in favour of the divorce, not least because it would delight and satisfy Viscount Rochester. When Frances Howard declared that her husband's impotence might have been a bewitchment, James was altogether on her side; had he himself not written a tract on witchcraft? The archbishop of Canterbury objected. But James had packed the commission. One churchman asked Essex 'whether he had affection, erection, application, penetration, ejaculation' to prove the consummation of the marriage; the hearings were filled with what one contemporary called 'indecent words and deeds'. A jury of twelve matrons examined Lady Frances herself for evidence of her virginity; the lady wore a veil throughout the proceedings, and it was suspected that a true virgin had taken her place. The divorce was of course granted according to the wishes of the sovereign. It was considered to be a notable instance of court corruption, and one that was widely noted and condemned.

Sir Thomas Overbury now enters the plot. As Rochester's close companion he despised the idea of this marriage, no doubt in part because he might lose his friend to the Howard cause at court. When it was believed that Overbury might know some infamous secret about Frances Howard, the king intervened. He asked Overbury to become one of his envoys in Russia, effectively banishing him from England. Overbury refused to take up the appointment, and was committed to the Tower; although in poor health, he was to be kept in close confinement until the marriage itself had been celebrated. That, at least, seems to have been the plan.

Frances Howard was of a different mind, however, and had determined to murder Overbury even before he stepped out of the

Tower. She had an accomplice, Mrs Turner, who was skilled in the management of poisons; Mrs Turner had a servant, Richard Weston, who by means of influence or bribery was appointed to be the keeper of the prisoner. Rochester was in the habit of sending wine, tarts and jellies to Overbury; it has been suggested, but not proved, that a poison was included in the sweet provisions. It is more likely that, with the connivance of Weston, the unfortunate man was slowly fed quantities of sulphuric acid or 'oil of vitriol'. Whatever the method of dispatch Overbury died at the beginning of autumn 1613, and was buried in the Tower. John Chamberlain wrote that 'he was a very unfortunate man, for nobody almost pities him, and his own friends speak that indifferently of him'. It was reported that all was calm and quiet at court; the talk was of masques and feasts and coming noble marriages.

On 26 December Frances Howard and Robert Carr, created earl of Somerset in the previous month, were united in marriage. This was four months after the death of Overbury, and no suspicion of malfeasance had emerged to trouble their marital bliss. At the ceremony the new countess of Somerset appeared with her long hair flowing down her shoulders as a token of virginity; she was, in the phrase of the time, 'married in her hair'. The king and the archbishop of Canterbury were among the congregation in the Chapel Royal, and rich gifts were showered upon the newly married couple. Soon enough, however, the revelation of their conduct would excite the greatest scandal of the king's reign.

It was time to summon a new parliament. The parlous state of the king's finances demanded it. All the departments of government were in urgent need of money; the ambassadors had not been paid their salaries, and the sailors of the fleet pleaded in vain; even the fortifications of the nation were in a state of disrepair. The councillors were voluble with suggestions and recommendations, but they were irresolute and uncertain. The nobles and lords around the king determined to ensure that court candidates were returned to parliament; they became known as the 'undertakers' but suspicion about their activities meant that few constituencies were willing to take their advice. They sent missives to the various towns and regions, but the practice became known as 'packing'. The constituencies wanted new men, untainted by connection to the court, and in fact two-thirds of the Commons were elected for the first time. This did not bode well for the king.

James opened the proceedings on 5 April 1614, with a conciliatory speech that promised reform while requesting more revenue. The Commons chose to ignore the message and instead complained that the 'undertakers' had violated freedom of election and the privileges of parliament. They did not wish to vote supplies to the king but preferred instead to challenge the king's right to levy 'impositions' or special taxes on imports and exports. In a second speech three days later James asked for a parliament of love; he wished to demonstrate his affection for his subjects, while the Commons must manifest their devotion to their sovereign. Yet the Commons were in restless and unyielding mood, full of hissing and jeering. One member, Christopher Neville, declared that the courtiers were 'spaniels to the king and wolves to the people'. There had never been a more disorderly house. It was compared to a cockpit and a bear-garden; the members were called 'roaring boys', street hooligans.

When the members refused James's order to debate supplies alone, he quickly dissolved parliament and committed five members to the Tower of London. The session had lasted less than three months and not one bill had received the royal assent. Thus it became known as the Addle or Addled Parliament. No assembly met again for seven years.

Supplies had not been granted to the king and, in his need for revenue, he redoubled his matrimonial negotiations with both Spain and France; the prize on offer to both parties was Charles, prince of Wales. Yet business of that nature takes time and, in the interim, he approached the City for a large loan; the City refused, on the indisputable grounds that the Crown was not worthy of credit. Thomas Howard, earl of Suffolk, was now appointed lord treasurer and immediately began to raise money by whatever means available; he levied fines, for example, on any new buildings erected within 7 miles of London.

At the time of the dissolution of parliament some of the bishops and great lords brought to the Jewel House of the Tower their best pieces of plate, for the purposes of sale, and the king determined that their example should be followed by the whole nation. So he requested a 'benevolence' from every county and borough in the land. The results, however, were not encouraging. Oliver St John, a gentleman of Marlborough, refused to send the king money on the grounds that the 'benevolence' was contrary to Magna Carta. He was brought before the Star Chamber and committed to the Tower. Eventually he was sentenced to a fine of £5,000 and imprisonment at the king's pleasure.

In the absence of parliament all eyes turned towards the court as the proper centre of affairs. The earl of Somerset, the favourite, was still the cynosure. He had been appointed lord chamberlain in 1614 and was in constant attendance upon the king; correspondence with the ambassadors and other worthies passed through his hands, and he controlled the vast machinery of patronage that acted as the engine of the court. Yet his association with the Howards through his marriage earned him the enmity of many courtiers, and it was widely rumoured that the rule of one man over the king was improper and undesirable.

It was time to introduce to the king another fair-faced minion. In the summer of 1614 a young man of twenty-two was presented to James. George Villiers, the son of a knight, had already been trained as a courtier; he had become practised in the arts of dancing and of fencing. He had also spent three years in France, where he had acquired a good manner further to adorn what was called 'the handsomest-bodied man in all of England'. He also had powerful allies, among them Archbishop Abbot and the queen. Abbot supported him in the hope of diminishing the influence of Somerset and the Howards, who favoured Catholic Spain. The queen, influenced by Abbot, pressed her husband to show favour to the young man. Villiers was accordingly appointed to be the royal cup-bearer, in constant attendance upon his sovereign, and in the spring of 1615 was knighted as a gentleman of the bedchamber.

Somerset, sensing a rival, protested. He alienated the king still more by constant complaint and insolent argument, leading James to remonstrate with him. 'Let me never apprehend that you disdain my person', the king wrote, 'and undervalue my qualities (nor let it not appear that your former affection is cold towards me).' He rebuked him for his 'strange streams of unquietness, passion, fury and insolent pride' as well as his 'long creeping back and withdrawing yourself from lying in my chamber, notwithstanding my many hundred times earnestly soliciting you to the contrary'. It is a strange letter for a sovereign to write to a subject, reflecting as it does the once extraordinary intimacy between them.

Villiers may already have interposed himself between the two men. In the summer of 1615 James travelled to Farnham Castle, home of the bishop of Winchester, where he was joined by his new gentleman of the bedchamber. At a later date Villiers questioned the king 'whether you loved me now . . . better than at the time which I shall never forget at Farnham, where the bed's head could not be found between the master and his dog'. It is an ambiguous reference, but it is at least open to an interesting interpretation.

Sir Francis Bacon, observing the workings of the Jacobean court, once wrote that 'all rising to great place is by a winding stair: and if there be factions, it is good, to side a man's self, whilst he is in the rising'. Bacon therefore attached himself to Villiers. He told him that, as the king's favourite, he should 'remember well the great trust you have undertaken. You are as a continual sentinel, always to stand upon your watch to give him true intelligence.'

In the summer of this year Somerset, sensing numerous plots rising against him, drew up a general pardon for himself for offences which he may or may not have committed. It was said by his enemies, for example, that he had purloined some of the crown jewels. At a meeting of the council, held on 20 July, the king ordered the lord chancellor, Francis Bacon himself, to seal the pardon 'at once, for such is my pleasure'. Bacon fell to his knees and begged him to reconsider. 'I have ordered you to pass the pardon,' James said as he walked out of the council chamber, 'and pass it you shall.' But as always he was hesitant and irresolute; the queen and other councillors argued against the decision which would allow Somerset to keep any of the jewels or other goods he might have taken from the king. It would set an unfortunate precedent. Eventually James left Whitehall without forming any certain decision.

This was only the beginning of Somerset's woes. In the early autumn of 1615 reports began to emerge that Sir Thomas Overbury had been poisoned in the Tower. One of the minor accomplices, an apothecary's boy, had fallen gravely ill and confessed to his part in the affair. It did not take long before the secret plot began to unravel. The lieutenant of the Tower was questioned. It was discovered that Richard Weston had been procured as the keeper of the prisoner. It was then revealed that he had been a servant of Mrs Turner. The trail now led in turn to Frances Carr, countess of Somerset, and to her husband.

The king, now thoroughly alarmed at a turn of events that might even touch the throne, asked his lord chief justice, Edward Coke, to make out a warrant against Somerset. Somerset remonstrated with James about this insult to his name and family. 'Nay, man,' the king exclaimed, 'if Coke sends for *me*, I must go.' He was supposed to have added, as the quondam favourite left his presence, 'The devil take thee, I will never see thee mair.'

Coke conducted a thorough investigation, and eventually reported to the king that Frances Carr had in the past used sorcery both to estrange her previous husband, the earl of Essex, and to inveigle her new lover. He further revealed that she had procured three different types of poison to be administered to Overbury.

On 24 May 1616, the countess of Somerset stood in front of the grand jury at Westminster; she was dressed all in black, except for ruff and cuffs of white lawn. Some of her letters were read out in court, apparently of an obscene character; when the crowd of spectators pressed forward to gaze at the magic scrolls and images she had employed in the course of her secret work, a large 'crack' was heard from the wooden stage. The crowd now believed that the devil himself had come into the court and that the noise signalled his anger at the disclosure of his wiles. Panic and confusion followed that could not be quelled for a quarter of an hour. Witches and demons were still in the Jacobean air.

The countess pleaded guilty to the charge of murder, perhaps on the understanding that the king always favoured clemency to the members of the nobility. Her husband appeared on the following day and declared himself to be not guilty of the crime, but his judges did not believe him. Man and wife were sentenced to death. They were spared the final penalty on the orders of the king, and instead were taken to the Tower where they remained for almost six years. The exposure of their fraud and betrayal, their profligacy and hypocrisy, served only further to undermine the court and the status of the king whose intimate associates they once had been. Mrs Turner, condemned to death for her part in the poison plot, said of the king's courtiers that 'there is no religion in the most of them but malice, pride, whoredom, swearing and rejoicing in the fall of others. It is so wicked a place as I wonder the earth did not open and swallow it up.'

At the beginning of the spring of this year the heir apparent, Charles, in the garden of Greenwich Palace, turned a water-spout 'in jest' upon Villiers. The favourite was much offended. Whereupon in an unusual show of anger the king boxed his son's ears, exclaiming that he had 'a malicious and dogged disposition'. Villiers was now known to his sovereign as 'Steenie', a babyish rendition of St Stephen; the reference was to the fact that those who looked upon the face of the saint declared it to be the countenance of an angel. The angel would soon be in charge.

6

The vapours

The most colourful and compelling account of early Jacobean London can be found in *The Seven Deadly Sins of London*, published in 1607. It is a work, little more than a pamphlet, written by Thomas Dekker in a period of seven days with all the vivacity and immediacy of swift composition. Dekker himself was a playwright and pamphleteer of obscure life and uncertain reputation, but in these respects he does not differ from most writers of the time.

He announces, to the city, that 'from thy womb received I my being, from thy breasts my nourishment'; in which case London must be judged a harsh nurse or mother. He complains that of all cities it is 'the wealthiest, but the most wanton. Thou hast all things in thee to make thee fairest, and all things in thee to make thee foulest.' At the time of James's accession it had been the 'only gallant and minion of the world' but 'hadst in a short time more diseases (than a common harlot hath) hanging upon thee'.

He paints the scene of the capital at midday where

> in every street, carts and coaches make such a thundering as if the world ran on wheels: at every corner, men, women and children meet in such shoals, that posts are set up of purpose to strengthen the houses, lest with jostling one another they should shoulder them down. Besides, hammers are beating in

> one place, tubs hooping in another, pots clinking in a third, water tankards running at tilt in a fourth: here are porters sweating under burdens, there merchants' men bearing bags of money, chapmen (as if they were at leap-frog) skip out of one shop into another, tradesmen (as if they were dancing galliards) are lusty at legs and never stand still: all are as busy as country attorneys at an assizes.

Yet the city takes on a different aspect at night. Dekker has a vision of London by candlelight, the companion 'for drunkards, for lechers, and for prodigals'. This was the time when 'mercers rolled up their silks and velvets: the goldsmiths drew back their plate, and all the city looked like a private playhouse when the windows are clapped down, as if some nocturnal or dismal tragedy were presently to be acted before all the tradesmen'. The bankrupt and felon had kept indoors for fear of arrest but, at night, 'began now to creep out of their shells, and to stalk up and down the streets as uprightly, and with as proud a gait, as if they meant to knock against the stars with the crowns of their heads'.

The prosperous citizen who in the day 'looked more sourly on his poor neighbours than he had drunk a quart of vinegar at a draught' now sneaks out of doors and 'slips into a tavern where either alone, or with some other that battles their money together, they so ply themselves with penny pots [of ale] . . . that at length they have not an eye to see withall, not a good leg to stand upon'. They reel into the night, have an altercation with a post on the way and end up in the gutter. Their apprentices, despite the oath of their indentures, 'make their desperate sallies out and quick retires in' with their pints. The three nocturnal pursuits of the city are drinking, dancing and dicing.

The prose of Thomas Dekker is crisp, strenuous and elliptical. He observes the Londoners at a bookstall in St Paul's Churchyard 'looking scurvily (like mules chomping upon thistles) on the face of a new book, be it never so worthy: and go (as ill favouredly) mewing away'. He notices the fact that the brothels of London have painted posts before them, and that their keepers always serve stewed prunes to their customers. He reports that the lattices for the windows of the alehouses are painted red. He observes the hackney men of Coleman Street, the butchers of Aldgate and the brokers of Houndsditch.

The dress of the Londoner 'is like a traitor's body that hath been hanged, drawn and quartered, and is set up in several places: his codpiece is in Denmark, the colour of his doublet and the belly in France: the wing and narrow sleeve in Italy: the short waist hangs over a Dutch butcher's stall in Utrecht; his huge slops [hose for the legs] speaks Spanish: Polonia gives him the boots'. It is a typical complaint concerning London's variegated fashions.

Dekker observes the disagreeable habits of other citizens. He alludes to the various 'tobacconists, shuttle-cock makers, feather-makers, cobweb lawn weavers, perfumers' as manifesting the qualities of 'apishness'; each one is 'a fierce, dapper fellow, more light-headed than a musician: as fantastically attired as a court jester: wanton in discourse: lascivious in behaviour; jocund in good company: nice in his trencher, and yet he feeds very hungrily on scraps of songs'.

Dekker abhors the common practice of marrying a young bride to a rich old man, 'though his breath be ranker than a muck-hill, and his body more dry than a mummy, and his mind more lame than Ignorance itself'. He complains about London landlords 'who for the building up of a chimney, which stands them not above thirty shillings, and for whiting the walls of a tenement, which is scarce worth the daubing, raise the rent presently (as if it were new put into the subsidy books) assessing it at three pounds a year more than ever it went for before'. This has all the bitterness of personal experience. Welcome to the world of Jacobean London.

Greed and avarice were also much on the mind of another Londoner. Ben Jonson's *Bartholomew Fair* was first performed in the Hope Playhouse at the end of October 1614; it was a long play, of some three hours, and began at two in the afternoon. On that stage the essence of London was quiddified. The Hope was also used for bear-baiting, on which occasions the stage was removed, and in the induction Jonson compares the theatre to the venue of the fair itself, 'the place being as dirty as Smithfield and as stinking every whit'. The stench of the dead or dying animals still lingered. The hazel nutshells and apple-cores might not have been swept away. *Bartholomew Fair* has the soul and substance of the Jacobean city somewhere within it. Its characters are the flesh and bone of London, in which all the people are merely players.

Canvas booths have been erected on the stage to give a simulacrum of the fair. A character comes on, and is soon joined by another, and then another, until a concourse of citizens is visible. They jeer, they swear, they laugh. They fight. They are obscene. They piss. They vomit. They cheat one another. A couple of them burst into song. Various plots and stories emerge only to fall back into the swelling tumult of the fair. Prostitutes and cutpurses rub against ballad-singers and tapsters.

Some of the characters adopt disguise, but in the end their true identities are revealed and their pretensions crossed or crushed. All authority is reviled. That is the way of the city. There is no real power except that of money, and no real considerations other than those of aggression and appetite. 'Bless me!' someone calls out. 'Deliver me, help, hold me! The Fair!' Mousetraps and ginger bread, purses and pouches, dolls and puppies, all are for sale. 'What do you lack, gentlemen? What is't you buy?' All the world's a fair. 'Buy any new ballads? New ballads?' A puppet show brings a conclusion to the play that has revealed London to be a panoply and a pageant, a prison and a carnival.

One of the guardian spirits of the fair is Ursla, the fat seller of ale and roast pig who is also a part-time bawd.

> *Ursla:* I am all fire and fat, Nightingale, I shall e'en melt
> away to the first woman, a rib, again, I am afraid.
> I do water the ground in knots as I go, like a great
> garden-pot, you may follow me by the Ss I make.

She has also a firm line in abuse.

> *Ursla:* You look as you were begotten atop of a cart in
> harvest-time, when the whelp was hot and eager. Go
> snuff after your brother's bitch, Mistress Commodity.

In the words of the play, she has a hot coal in her mouth.

The other great character of the fair is Jonson's parody of the puritan, Zeal-of-the-Land-Busy.

> *Busy:* Look not towards them, hearken not. The place is
> Smithfield, or the field of smiths, the grove of hobby
> horses and trinkets . . . They are hooks and baits, very

> baits, that are hung out on every side to catch you, and to hold you, as it were, by the gills, and by the nostrils, as the fisher doth . . .

He turns out to be, of course, an arrant voluptuary and hypocrite, amply confirming the suspicions that some people conceived of the godly in this period.

Jonson had said that he wished to present 'deeds and language, such as men do use'. He knew of what he wrote. By his own report he was 'brought up poorly' in London and when his mother took a second husband, a master bricklayer, the small family moved to a house in a lane off the Strand. He attended an elementary school in the neighbourhood before Westminster School and may have been about to attend a college at Cambridge; shortage of funds, however, did not permit the move. Instead he took up his stepfather's business of bricklaying, in which trade he laboured intermittently for some years. He later saw service in the Low Countries and, on his return to London, entered the world of theatre. So he was a child of the city, and *Bartholomew Fair* is his tribute to its teeming life.

Here are your 'pretenders to wit! Your Three Cranes, Mitre and Mermaid men.' These three taverns were the haunt of poetasters and men of supposed good taste. 'Moorfields, Pimlico Path or the Exchange' are mentioned a few moments later as places of resort for tired Londoners. In the puppet play at the close of the proceedings, the myth of Hero and Leander is set in the city.

> *Littlewit:* As, for the Hellespont, I imagine our Thames here; and then Leander I make a dyer's son, about Puddle Wharf; and Hero a wench o' the Bankside, who going over one morning to Old Fish Street, Leander spies her land at Trig Stairs.

It is remarkable that ordinary Londoners were supposed to be wholly familiar with the old story, perhaps from Marlowe's poem published sixteen years earlier.

Many of the play's allusions are lost to us, and many of the words are now strange or unfamiliar. A 'hobby-horse' was a prostitute. An 'undermeal' was a light snack. To 'stale' was to urinate.

When one character discloses that 'we were all a little stained last night', he means that they were drunk. 'Whimsies' were the female genitalia. A 'diet-drink' was a medicine. A Catholic recusant was derided as 'a seminary'.

The visitors to the fair often refer to 'vapour' or 'vapours' that can mean anything or nothing. To vapour is to talk nonsense or to brag; a vapour is a frenzy or a passing mood or a mad conceit of the town. In the popular 'game of vapours' each participant had to deny that which the previous speaker had just said. London seethed with vapours.

> *Quarlous:* Faith, and to any man that vapours me the lie,
> I do vapour that. [*Strikes him*].

It is in a sense like watching a foreign world, except that there are still flashes of recognition and understanding. And then once more we are part of the Jacobean city.

7

What news?

The trial of Somerset and his wife marked the beginning of a deterioration at court, where it was believed that the king had become both more cunning and more cowardly; his learning had once been praised but now behind his back he was called a pedant. His new fancy for Villiers provoked scorn, jealousy and even disgust. His own health also showed signs of decline. His doctor wrote subsequently that 'in 1616 pain and weakness spread to knees, shoulders and hands, and for four months he had to stay in a bed or in a chair'. He became impatient and morose and bad-tempered. The doctor went on to say that 'he is extremely sensitive, most impatient of pain; and while it tortures him with violent movements, his mind is tossed as well, thus augmenting the evil'.

James drank frequently and immoderately. He perspired heavily, and caught frequent colds; he was always sneezing. His face had become red; he was growing fat, and his hair was turning white. At the age of fifty, he was rapidly ageing. He was still averse to business and preferred to hunt, but now he rode more slowly and allowed his horse to be guided by grooms.

So the eyes of aspirants turned more often to the heir. Charles, at the age of fifteen, had acquired many of the virtues of a prince. He was a champion at tennis and at tilting; he delighted in horses and in masques; he was already a connoisseur of art and music. Yet he was also pious and reserved; he was silent and even secretive; he blushed at an indelicate word. He was 5 feet 4 inches in height, and had a pronounced stutter.

The Venetian ambassador reported that his chief endeavour 'is to have no other aim than to second his father, to follow him and do his pleasure and not to move except as his father does. Before his father he always aims at suppressing his own feelings.' So Charles grew to be uncertain and hesitant, apt to cling to the few maxims that he had already imbibed. He was too modest for his own good, perhaps stunned by the loquacity of his father and the beauty of Villiers. When he did try to act forcefully, in later life, he often descended into rash action without any thought of the consequences. His piety, and sense of divine mission, also rendered him humourless and strict.

In the summer of the year the king turned upon his judges. Edward Coke, the chief justice of the king's bench, had often angered James by his continual assertion of common law over the claims of royal power. The king called the judges before him in June 1616, and accused them of insubordination; they fell on their knees, pledging their loyalty and obedience. The king then asked each of them in turn whether they would consult with him before pronouncing on matters of the prerogative. All assented, with the notable exception of Coke himself, who simply answered that he would behave in a manner fitting for a high judge. The king turned upon him, calling him a knave and a sophist. James proceeded to the Star Chamber a few days later, where he delivered a long speech on his zeal for justice. 'Kings are properly judges,' he told his councillors, 'and judgement properly belongs to them from God . . . I remember Christ's saying, "My sheep hear my voice", and so I assure myself, my people will most willingly hear the voice of me, their own shepherd and king.' It was not the most modest of his pronouncements.

Coke was not destined to remain in the king's service for much longer. He was removed from the privy council and ordered to desist from his summer circuit of the kingdom; he was told to revise his law reports 'wherein (as his Majesty was informed) there were many exorbitant and extravagant opinions'. Five months later, in November 1616, he was dismissed from office. He was, in a phrase of the time, 'quite off the books'. The king had rid himself of a turbulent judge but, in the process, he had turned Coke into a martyr for the rule of law and the liberties of the people.

The nature and the character of the 'people', however, could be understood in a multitude of ways. The population itself was growing rapidly until 1620, with the consequence that the number of the poor also began to rise. As late as 1688 it was reported that over half of the population, both rural and urban, were below the level of subsistence. The purchasing power of the wages of agricultural labourers or minor craftsmen was in relative terms at its lowest point for generations. In 1616 it was recorded that in Sheffield, out of a population of little over 2,000, 725 persons were 'not able to live without the charity of their neighbours'; they were all 'begging poor'. There were 160 others who 'are not able to abide the storm of one fortnight's sickness but would thereby be driven to beggary'. Their children 'are constrained to work sore to provide them necessaries'.

The inequalities of society were such that, in this same period of want, the prosperity of the rural gentry and the wealthier citizens increased dramatically; this in itself may help to account for the great period of building and rebuilding that culminated in the Jacobean country house with its elaborate ornamentation and astonishing skyline.

It also became plain that, as the gentry increased in wealth and status, so the members of the old aristocracy lost some of their authority. The rise of the country gentleman in turn materially affected the power and prestige of the Commons, of which they were the most considerable element; it was said that they could buy out the Lords three times over. In a later treatise, *Oceana*, James Harrington stated that the work of government was 'peculiar unto the genius of a gentleman'. The decline in the fortunes of the old lords, in favour of the rising gentry, has been variously explained. It had to do with the loss of wealth and territory; but it was also the natural consequence of diminished military power. The king in any case had been selling peerages and the new baronetcies for cash, thus diminishing the honourable worth of any title.

As the gentry rose in influence, so there was a corresponding increase in what might be called the professional classes. The number of lawyers rose by 40 per cent between 1590 and 1630, in a period when doctors and surgeons also multiplied. The merchant class, too, was now thriving and was no longer considered to be a demeaning connection; the younger sons of squires were happy to become apprentices with the hope of an eventual rise to partnership. The division between rich and poor had been sharpened while, at the same time, the wealthier elements of society were drawing together.

The gentry now also controlled the machinery of local government. The lords-lieutenant and deputies, the sheriffs and justices of the peace, were indispensable for the order and safety of the country; the king and his council wholly relied upon them for such matters as the collection of taxes, the regulation of trade and the raising of troops for any foreign war. In turn a form of local government grew up at the quarter sessions, where the most important men of the county or borough met to discuss the business of the community. They were collectively known as the commission of the peace, and their clerk was called the clerk of the peace. Their authority filtered down to the high constables in the hundred and to the petty constables, the churchwardens and overseers of the poor in the parish.

The country gentry had also in large part taken against the court. In a local election of 1614 both candidates claimed to represent 'the country' and denied charges of 'turning courtier'. Soon enough 'court' and 'country' factions would manifest themselves. The ways of Whitehall were already deeply suspect. The king's extravagance required higher taxation. The practice of purveyance, by which the court could effectively seize goods and services for royal use, had become iniquitous. Rumours of the king's homosexual passions also circulated through the nation. At the beginning of 1617 George Villiers, now Viscount Villiers, was created earl of Buckingham and appointed Master of the Horse. His lands were extensive, his income immense, but he had also acquired a monopoly of patronage. Any aspirant for office had to transact his business with the earl, and Buckingham insisted that all his clients acknowledged him as their only patron. Lucy Hutchinson, a memoirist of puritan persuasion, wrote that he had risen 'upon no merit but that of his beauty and prostitution'.

An office was considered to be a family property. The great officials were permitted, and expected, to appoint their successors;

of course they made their choice after an appropriate fee was exacted. Negotiations took place between the incumbent of the office, the favourite for the post and the various aspiring candidates. Some officials were the private employees of other officials. All that mattered was who you knew and how rich you were. When the chancellorship of the duchy of Lancaster fell vacant in 1618, forty-three competitors vied for the post which was being sold for approximately £8,000. The administrators of the navy were particularly corrupt, taking bribes, appointing private servants as public officials, diverting supplies, paying themselves double allowances, ordering inferior material and pocketing the difference in cost, employing ships for merchant journeys and charging accordingly.

All transactions under the aegis of the Crown – gratuities and perquisites, annuities and pensions – came at a price. Samuel Doves wrote that 'on the 2nd of February last past, I had a hearing in the Court of Chancery and for that hearing, there stood one in the crier's place; to whom being demanded, I gave him eight shillings . . . and two men more which kept the door would have eight shillings more, which I paid. And when I was without the door, two men stayed me and would have two shillings more, which I paid.' You paid to have a stall in the marketplace; you paid for the right to sell or manufacture cloth. When a group of monopolists was granted the maintenance of the lighthouse at Dungeness, being rewarded with the tolls on all shipping that passed by, they provided only a single candle.

What's the news abroad? *Quid novi*? 'It were a long story to tell all the passages of this business,' John Chamberlain wrote, 'which hath furnished Paul's and this town very plentifully the whole week.' 'Paul's' was the middle aisle of the cathedral where gossips and men known as 'newsmongers' met to discuss all the latest rumours. It was customary for the lords and the gentry, the courtiers and the merchants, as well as men of all professions, to meet in the abbey at eleven and walk in the middle aisle till twelve; they met again after dinner, from three to six, when they discoursed on politics and business or passed on in low voices all the rumours and secrets of the town. A purveyor of court secrets was called 'one of our new principal verbs in Paul's, and well acquainted with all occurrents'. So the busy aisle became known as the 'ears' brothel' and its interior was filled with what a contemporary observer, John Earle, called 'a strange humming or buzz mixed of walking, tongues and feet'.

It was said that one of the vices of England was the prattling of the 'busie-body', otherwise known as an 'intelligencer'. Joseph Hall, in *Characters of Virtues and Vices* (1608), describes one such creature. 'What every man ventures in Guiana voyage, and what they gained, he knows to a hair. Whether Holland will have peace he knows and on what conditions . . . If he see but two men talk and read a letter in the street he runs to them and asks if he may not be partner of that secret relation.'

So we might read that 'the world is full of casting and touching Fabritio's great affair' or 'at the worst, the world is of opinion, that if they should come to jostle, both of them are made of as brittle metal, the one as the other'. The world says this; the world thinks that. 'Now-a-days what seems most improbable mostly comes soonest to pass.' 'There is a speech, of the king's going to Royston.' 'It is current in every man's mouth.' 'We were never at so low an ebb for matter of news, especially public, so that we are fain to set ourselves at work with the poorest entertainment . . .' 'There is some muttering of the change of officers . . . by which you may smell who looks and hopes to be lord chancellor.' The watermen regaled their customers with the news; the humble citizen sitting in the barber's chair heard the news. Some men made their living by sending manuscript newsletters into the country. Rumour could travel at a speed of 50 miles per night.

And so what news of court? The king travelled north in March 1617. He told his privy council in Scotland that 'we have had these many years a great and natural longing to see our native soil and place of our birth and breeding'; he called it, charmingly, a 'salmon-like instinct'. On his slow journey he was attended by many hundreds of courtiers who ate their way through the land like locusts before their arrival at Edinburgh in the middle of May. No one was sure how the visit was to be financed, and those on his route feared the worst. No English king had come this way for hundreds of years. When James reached the border he dismounted and lay on the ground between the two countries, proclaiming that in his own person he symbolized the union between Scotland and England.

Many of his councillors and nobles had not wanted to accompany James to his erstwhile home. They took no interest in, and had no happy expectations of, Scotland. For them it was an uncouth and even savage land. The queen herself declined to go with her husband, pleading sickness. One English courtier, Sir Anthony Weldon, wrote that this foreign country 'is too good for those that possess it, and too bad for others . . . there is a great store of fowl – as foul houses . . . foul linen, foul dishes and pots . . . The country, although it be mountainous, affords no monsters but women.'

The king brought with him candles and choristers as well as a pair of organs; he was intent upon making the Scottish Kirk conform to the worship of the Church of England, but he had only limited success. The Scottish ministers were wary of these 'rags of popery'. 'The organs are come before,' said one Calvinist divine, 'and after comes the Mass.' James also alienated many members of the Scottish parliament. In his speech at the opening of the session James expatiated on the virtues of his English kingdom; he told his compatriots that he had nothing 'more at heart than to reduce your barbarity to the sweet civility of your neighbours'. The Scots had already learned from them how to drive in gay coaches, to drink healths and to take tobacco. This could not have been received warmly.

And what other news? In the summer of 1617 Sir Walter Raleigh, newly released from the Tower for the purpose, sailed to Guiana in search of gold. The king had expressly ordered him not to injure the Spanish in any way; he was still seeking the hand of the infanta for his son. When Raleigh eventually reached the mouth of the Orinoco he sent a lieutenant, Lawrence Keymis, up the river to determine the location of a fabled mine of gold. On his way, however, Keymis attacked the Spaniards who held San Thome and, after an inconsequential combat in which Raleigh's son was killed, he was eventually forced to return to the main fleet. There was now no possibility of reaching the mine and Raleigh made an ignominious return to England. Keymis killed himself on board ship. The wrath of the king was immense and, sometimes, the wrath of the king meant death. James believed that he had been deliberately deceived by Raleigh on the presence of gold and that the unlucky explorer had unjustifiably and unnecessarily earned for him the enmity of Spain.

The Spanish king of course made angry complaints, through the agency of his notorious ambassador, the count of Gondomar. As a measure of conciliation or recompense, James sent Raleigh to the scaffold in the Old Palace Yard at Westminster. It was commonly believed that he had sacrificed him for the honour of the king of Spain. 'Let us dispatch,' Raleigh told his executioner. 'At this hour my ague comes upon me. I would not have my enemies think I quaked from fear.' On viewing the axe that was about to destroy him he is supposed to have said that 'this is a sharp medicine, but it is a physician for all diseases and miseries'. As the executioner was poised to deliver the blow he called out, 'Strike, man, strike!' He never did have time to finish his *History of the World* which he had begun to compose in 1607 while held in the Tower. He had started at the Creation but at the time of his death had only reached the end of the second Macedonian War in 188 BC.

What is the new news, smoking hot from London? In November 1617, the king issued a declaration to the people of Lancashire on the matter of Sunday sports and recreations; in the following year the *Book of Sports* was directed to the whole country. Archery and dancing were to be permitted, together with 'leaping, vaulting or any other such harmless recreation'; the king also graciously allowed 'May-games, Whitsun-ales and Morris-dances, and the setting up of May-poles'. Bear-baiting, bull-baiting and bowls, however, were forbidden. Clergy of the stricter sort were not favourably impressed by the pronouncement, which soon became known as 'The Dancing Book'. It came close to ungodliness and idolatry. One clergyman, William Clough of Bramham, told his congregation that 'the king of heaven doth bid you to keep his Sabbath and reverence his sanctuary. Now the king of England is a mortal man and he bids you break it. Choose whether [which] of them you will follow.' Soon enough those of a puritan persuasion would become the principal opponents of royal policy.

Ben Jonson's masque *Pleasure Reconciled to Virtue* was performed before the court at the beginning of 1618. It did not please everyone, and it was suggested that the playwright might like to return to his old trade of bricklaying. At the close of the performance, in the scene of dancing, the players began to lag. 'Why don't they dance?' the king called out. 'What did they make me come here for? Devil take you all, dance!' Whereupon Buckingham sprang up and, in the words of the chaplain of the Venetian embassy, 'danced a number of high and very tiny capers with such grace and lightness that he made everyone love him'. James himself demonstrated 'extraordinary signs of affection, touching his face'.

Yet Buckingham's enemies, most notably the Howard family, were determined to supplant him. They introduced another handsome youth to court by the name of Monson. They groomed him for the role, dressed him up and washed his face every day with curdled milk to improve its smoothness. But the king did not take to this new suitor. The lord chamberlain took Monson to one side and informed him that James was not pleased with his importunacy and continual presence; he ordered him to stay away from the king and, if he knew what was best for him, to avoid the royal court.

Buckingham began to use one of the first sedan chairs ever to be seen in the country; the people were indignant, complaining that he was employing men to take the place of beasts. Yet he was still in the ascendant, at which high point he would remain for the rest of the reign.

8

A Bohemian tragedy

In April 1618 a little book, bearing the royal arms, was published. It was entitled *The Peacemaker*, and it extolled the virtues of James as a pacifier of all troubles and contentions. The 'happy sanctuary' of England had enjoyed fifteen years of peace since the time of the king's accession, and so now 'let it be celebrated with all joy and cheerfulness, and all sing – *Beati Pacifici*'.

Contention, however, was about to manifest itself in the distant land of Bohemia (now roughly equivalent to the Czech Republic) which was ruled by the Holy Roman Emperor Matthias. In the month after the book's publication certain Protestant nobles of Bohemia stormed the imperial palace in Prague and threw the emperor's deputies out of the windows; Matthias had tried to impose upon them the rule of Archduke Ferdinand, a fierce Catholic and a member of the Habsburg family. The Bohemian rebels were soon in charge of their country, posing a challenge to the Catholic dynasty of the Habsburgs, which included Philip III of Spain.

The German Calvinists of course took up their cause, thus posing a problem for the king of England. The head of the Calvinist interest was none other than James's son-in-law, Frederick of the Palatinate. Yet James was also seeking the daughter of Philip III for his son. What was to be done? Was James to side with the Spanish Habsburgs against the Protestant party? Or was he to encourage his son-in-law to maintain the Bohemian cause? He prevaricated by sending an arbiter, but none of the combatants was really willing to entertain his envoy. Gondomar, the Spanish ambassador, remarked that 'the vanity of the present king of England is so great that he will always think it of great importance that peace should be made by his means, so that his authority will be increased'. It did not quite work out like that.

In March 1619 Matthias died, and Archduke Ferdinand was elected as the new Holy Roman Emperor. The Bohemians took the opportunity of formally deposing him as their sovereign and invited Frederick to take his place. Frederick hesitated only for a moment. James complained that 'he wrote to me, to know my mind if he should take that crown; but within three days after, and before I could return answer, he put it on'.

After Frederick had accepted their offer, he travelled to Prague in October in order to assume the throne. The Protestants of England were delighted. Here at last was the European champion they had needed. A great comet passed across the skies of Europe in the late autumn of 1618; its reddish hue and long tail were visible for seven weeks, and it became known as 'the angry star'. It was of course considered to be providential, a token or warning of great change. Could it portend the final defeat of the Habsburgs and even the Antichrist of Rome?

James's opinion was not entirely in keeping with that of his Protestant subjects. He was angered by what he considered to be Frederick's rashness in accepting the crown of Bohemia; his son-in-law was in that sense an aggressor flouting the divine right of kings. 'You are come in good time to England,' he told Frederick's envoy, 'to spread these principles among my people, that my subjects may drive me away, and place another in my room.' More significantly, he did not wish to drop the Spanish connection he had so carefully fashioned. And yet his daughter was now queen of Bohemia. Surely there was glory in that? It was the greatest dilemma of his reign, combining in deadly fashion his amity with Spain and his relationship with his fellow Protestants in Europe; he had tried to conciliate both forces, but now they threatened to tear him apart. So he prevaricated. The French ambassador reported that 'his mind uses its powers only for a short time, but in the long run he is cowardly'.

Relations with the Spanish were in a difficult and delicate balance. The business of the marriage of Prince Charles to the infanta was infinitely protracted, and popular opinion in England was one of dismay at a possible liaison with a Catholic power. In the event of marriage, therefore, the king was likely to be estranged from his subjects; but James was too eager for a vast Spanish dowry to heed any warnings. The Spanish in turn required that English Catholics be allowed to practise their religion freely, but the change in law would need the consent of parliament. Parliament would never concede any such request. All was in suspense. When a gentleman from the Spanish embassy rode down a child in Chancery Lane, a crowd developed and tried to seize him; he spurred his horse but the crowd of citizens, now swelled to the number of 4,000 or 5,000, followed him to the ambassador's house. They besieged it, breaking the windows and threatening to force the doors, until the lord chief justice arrived and took away the offender.

It was possible, to put it no higher, that Spain was planning to invade the Palatinate. James was in an agony of indecision, at one moment promising to send a large army to help his son-in-law and at another claiming that he was in no position to aid anyone. He did not wish to meddle in the matter. He could not afford a war, and the country was not ready for military action. Was the election of Frederick, in any case, legally valid? If not, any war on Frederick's behalf might then be unjust as well as unnecessary.

Politics, and diplomacy, could not be separated from the issues of religion; all were intimately related in a continent where the division between Catholic and Protestant was the single most important fact of the age. There were of course divisions within the ranks of Protestants themselves. At the end of 1618 a national synod of the Dutch Reformed Church was held in the city of Dordrecht, known colloquially as Dort, to which came six representatives from England. The debate was of vital interest to the king. It was concerned with the Calvinist doctrine of predestination which was denied by a Dutch theologian, Jacobus Arminius, and his followers. Arminius also condemned religious zealotry of the kind practised by his opponents. He declared that religion was about to suffer the same fate as the young lady mentioned by Plutarch; she was pursued by several lovers who, unable to agree among themselves, became violent and cut the woman to pieces so that each could have a portion of her. The Calvinists, holding the dominant faith of Holland, called Arminius and his supporters to account. The arguments, impassioned and even bitter, lasted for seven months.

An English puritan, Thomas Goodwin, noted that the reports of the synod 'began to be every man's talk and enquiry' and another English theologian, Peter Heylyn, stated that the debates 'wakened Englishmen out of "a dead sleep"'. Theologians were then of the utmost consequence in political as well as spiritual affairs; religion was, in this century, the principal issue by which all other matters were judged and interpreted. At the conclusion of the synod the Calvinists emerged triumphant and their opponents were either imprisoned or deprived of their ministry; 700 families of Arminians were driven into exile. For James it seemed to be a victory for the purity of religion, and one English divine, Francis Rous, excoriated Arminianism as 'the spawn of the papists'. The battle lines of Protestantism were set ever more firmly in stone. Arminianism would emerge in England at a slightly later date, with fatal consequences for the next king.

James was growing sick with the strain and tensions induced by Spain and the Palatinate. He was suffering from an unhappy combination of arthritis and gout together with what was called 'a shrewd fit of the stone'. The death of his wife, Anne of Denmark, in the early spring of 1619 caused a further decline in his health. The king's doctor noted 'continued fever, bilious diarrhoea . . . ulceration of his lips and chin. Fainting, sighing, dread, incredible sadness, intermittent pulse.' The king voided three stones and the pain was so great that he vomited. He seemed likely to die. Charles, Buckingham and the leading councillors were summoned from London to Royston, where he was staying, and he delivered what was considered to be a deathbed speech. Yet this was premature. Within a few days he began to recover, although he was still too weak to attend his wife's funeral in the middle of May. He had been informed that the best remedy for weak legs was the blood of a newly slaughtered deer; so for some weeks he was to be found, after the hunt, with his feet buried in the body of an animal that had just been brought down.

He returned to London at the beginning of June, dressed so

luxuriously that he was said to resemble a suitor rather than a mourner. He had some cause for celebration. The new Banqueting House was about to be completed, one of the few physical memorials of his reign that survive intact. It had been designed by Inigo Jones in the novel and controversial neoclassical style, conceived in the spirit of Palladio and of the Italian Renaissance; it was devised to represent the twin concepts of 'magnificence' and 'decorum', with the king presiding in its ornate and mathematically correct interior as both judge and peacemaker. The Banqueting House was the seat of majesty. It was also considered to be a suitable setting for the eventual reception of Charles and the infanta. Sixteen years later Rubens completed the canvases for the great ceiling; James here is depicted as a British Solomon, uniting the kingdoms of England and Scotland, while on the oval canvas that acts as centrepiece he is raised into heaven by the figures of Justice, Faith and Religion.

The cost was very high, approximately £15,000, at a time when the royal treasury was almost bare. The country itself was also suffering a financial crisis. The growing preference on the continent for cheaper local cloth, as opposed to the more expensive English woollens, and the competitive power of Dutch traders meant that there was a significant fall in economic activity. 'All grievances in the kingdom are trifles,' Sir Edwin Sandys told the Commons, 'compared with the decay in trade.' Lionel Cranfield, who became lord high treasurer in 1621, explained that 'trade is as great as ever, but not so good. It increases inwards and decreases outwards.' The balance of trade, in other words, was not in England's favour. This was one of those spasms of economic distress that have always hit the English economy, but in the early seventeenth century no one really understood what was happening.

Cranfield added that 'the want of money is because trade is sick, and as long as trade is sick, we shall be in want of money'. Too many manufactured goods were entering the country, among them the import of what were widely regarded as vain and unnecessary items such as wine and tobacco. The luxurious world was one of velvets and satins, of pearls and cloth of gold. Yet elsewhere economic failure had become endemic. The export of London broadcloths, in 1622, had fallen by 40 per cent from the figures of 1618; the hardship was compounded by the failure of the harvest in 1623. 'There are many thousands in these parts,' one Lincolnshire gentleman, Sir William Pelham, wrote, 'who have sold all they have even to their bed-straw, and cannot get work to earn any money. Dog's flesh is a dainty dish, and found upon search in many houses.' This is the context for the unrest and disturbance of the last years of James's reign.

It is also one of the principal causes for the number of English colonists seeking a new life in America. In the autumn of 1620 the *Mayflower* set sail from Plymouth; some of its passengers were religious separatists who had come from Leiden, in Holland, but the majority were English families looking for land and for material improvement. It has been estimated that over the next two or three decades some 60,000 left English shores, one third of them bound for New England. When they cross the Atlantic, they are lost from the purview of this history.

It was becoming increasingly likely that the Spanish would invade the Palatinate in revenge for Frederick's assumption of the Bohemian throne. A successful attack would have serious consequences for Protestantism in Europe and might well lead once more to Habsburg domination; an ambassador was sent to England, therefore, from the princes and free cities of the Protestant Union in Germany. The envoy did not receive a warm welcome from the king. James, divided in his loyalties, decided to do nothing. The archbishop of Canterbury, horrified at this desertion of the Protestant cause, pleaded with him to allow voluntary contributions from the clergy for the sake of their co-religionists. To this the king reluctantly assented.

He was of course still pursuing Spain for the hand of the infanta. He called the Spanish ambassador, Gondomar, to him. 'I give you my word,' he said, 'as a king, as a gentleman, as a Christian, and as an honest man, I have no wish to marry my son to anyone except your master's daughter, and I desire no alliance but that of Spain.' He took off his hat and wiped the sweat from his forehead. He had made an implicit admission, to the effect that he desired no alliance with Frederick or the German princes. What did Bohemia mean to him? It was a distant land of which he knew nothing, remarkable only for the scene of shipwreck in Shakespeare's *The Winter's Tale*, performed nine years before, in which it was miraculously granted a sea coast.

Gondomar quickly sent a message to Philip III that he could invade Frederick's territories without risk of a war with England. Thus began the struggle which eventually became known as the Thirty Years War, one of the most destructive conflicts in early modern European history that ravaged much of the Holy Roman Empire and spread to Italy, France, the Netherlands and Spain.

At the end of July 1620, the king set out on a progress. The Venetian ambassador reported that he seemed glad to leave London behind. He added that 'the king seems utterly weary of the affairs that are taking place all over the world at this time, and he hates being obliged every day to spend time over unpleasant matters and listen to nothing but requests and incitements to move in every direction and to meddle with everything'. James had remarked, 'I am not God Almighty.'

A few days later news reached him that a Spanish army of 24,000 soldiers was moving against the Palatinate; at the same time the Holy Roman Emperor Ferdinand, whose throne had been usurped, was marching upon Prague. 'What do you know,' James asked an adviser who had questioned him on the perilous situation. 'You are ignorant. I know quite well what I am about. All these troubles will settle themselves, you will see that very soon. I know what I am talking about.'

Yet he was troubled by what he now realized was Spanish duplicity. Gondomar had talked of conciliation while all the time Philip III had been planning for war. James summoned the ambassador to Hampton Court, where he raved about his double-dealing. Gondomar politely replied that he had never said that Spain would *not* invade the Palatinate, whereupon the king burst into tears. Could he not be allowed to defend his own children? His policy of compromise, bred out of vacillation and indecision, was in ruins.

The Spanish were victorious in November 1620, at the battle of White Mountain just outside Prague. The Protestant army was devastated, and Frederick was removed from his temporary kingdom of Bohemia. On the following day he fled for his life into the neighbouring region of Silesia; he could not even return to his homeland, since in the following summer the Spanish occupied half of the Palatinate. He and his wife, Elizabeth, were effectively exiles. In turn the Bohemian leaders of the Protestant rebellion were led to the scaffold and a new imperial aristocracy rose in triumph. The news alarmed and enraged the English public in equal measure, and it was not long before all the blame was being laid upon James.

The Venetian ambassador reported that 'tears, sighs and loud expressions of wrath are seen and heard in every direction'. Letters against the king were scattered in the streets threatening that if he did not do what was expected of him, the people would soon display their anger. All sympathies lay with his daughter Elizabeth, who had been forced to flee without the assistance or protection of her father. Prince Charles, in agony over the unhappy situation of his sister, shut himself in his chambers for two days. The king himself was said to be in great distress but, having recovered from the initial shock, was heard to murmur that 'I have long expected this'.

He very soon took on his favourite role as arbitrator or peacemaker. He devised a plan that might prove acceptable to all sides. Frederick would submit to the emperor and renounce any claim to Bohemia on condition that his Palatinate was returned to him untouched. There ensued a process of elaborate diplomatic negotiations that achieved nothing. A parody of the time noted that James would present his son-in-law with an army of 100,000 ambassadors.

It was time to call a parliament; it assembled in the middle of January 1621. It did not augur well that the king had to be carried to its opening in a chair. His legs and his feet were so weak that it was believed he would soon lose the use of them. He did not in any case desire to consult with the Commons on matters of policy. He was there to deliver his demands. He ordered them not to 'meddle with complaints against the king, the church or state matters'. He himself would ensure that the proposed Spanish match between his son and the infanta did not endanger the Protestant religion of England; he also stated that he would not allow his son-in-law's Palatinate to be broken up. And for that he needed money. It was the only reason he had summoned them. He had once said that he was obliged 'to live like a shell-fish upon his own moisture, without any public supply'. It was one of James's arresting similes.

A committee of enquiry had already estimated that a force for the protection of the Palatinate would cost approximately £900,000 each year; James, sensing the outrage such a sum would cause, asked for £500,000; parliament granted him £160,000 before turning its attention to such domestic grievances as the abuse of patents and monopolies by unscrupulous agents. It was the first meeting of parliament for almost seven years and, as such, became a clearing house for all the complaints and problems that had accrued in the interim. In the course of this first session some fifty-two bills were given a second reading.

The weather outside the chamber was bitter. John Chamberlain wrote at the beginning of February that 'the Thames is now quite frozen over, so that people have passed over, to and fro, these four or five days . . . the winds and high tides have so driven the ice in heaps in some places, that it lies like rocks and mountains, and hath a strange and hideous aspect'.

The depression of trade was the single most important theme for the assembly beside the frozen river. The gathering of members of parliament at Westminster gave the opportunity for the exporters, landlords and graziers among them to vent their complaints about falling prices and unsold wool. It was declared that poverty and want were rife. One member told his colleagues that 'I had rather be a ploughman than a merchant'. Disorderly interventions did not quell the embittered speeches. No parties had as yet emerged, in the modern sense, only individuals expressing vested interests or local grievances. It was becoming clear, however, that the political initiative was being grasped by parliament rather than by the king and council.

In the same session parliament drew up a petition against 'Jesuits, papists and recusants'. It was the only way they knew of unravelling the Spanish connection that the king favoured. The member for Bath, Sir Robert Phelips, raised the temperature by saying that if the papists were not checked they would soon comprise half of the king's subjects. So parliament acted. All recusants to be banished from London. All recusants to be disarmed by the justices of the peace. No subject of the king should hear Mass. James was in a quandary, suspended between his parliament and the king of Spain; it was reported that he would accept the principal recommendations but would reserve the particulars for further consideration. This was widely believed to be an evasion.

The feeling of the people against the Spaniards was now palpable. A caricature had been circulated at the beginning of 1621 that depicted the king of Spain, the pope and the devil as conspirators in another 'powder-plot'. The Spanish ambassador, Gondomar, was proceeding down Fenchurch Street when an apprentice called out, 'There goes the devil in a dung-cart.'

One of Gondomar's servants responded. 'Sir, you shall see Bridewell ere long for your mirth.'

'What! Shall we go to Bridewell for such a dog as thou!'

Eventually the apprentice and his companions were whipped through the streets, much to the indignation of the citizens.

Parliament itself was enthusiastic for Frederick's cause. When one member made a speech advocating war against the imperial forces the Commons responded with a unanimous vote, lifting their hats high in acclamation, and vowed to recover the Palatinate. James seemed for the moment to share their enthusiasm, but he was too shrewd or too wary to commit himself to a European war against the Catholic powers. He had in any case grown impatient with parliament. It had sat for four months, and spent most of its time in delivering to him requests and grievances. It had not addressed the necessities of the king, or his request for a further grant of money. So at the beginning of June 1621, he adjourned it.

At a later date a notable parliamentarian, Sir John Eliot, reflected upon the failure of this assembly. The king believed that the liberties of parliament encroached upon his prerogative, while in turn parliament feared he 'sought to retrench and block up the ancient privileges and liberties of the house'. So both sides became more intransigent, the king maintaining his royal power and the parliament standing upon its privileges. Eliot believed that there was a middle ground, but at the time it was overlooked.

This was the rock upon which the constitution would founder. An eminent nineteenth-century jurist, John, Baron Campbell, wrote that 'the meeting of parliament on 30 January, 1621, may be considered the commencement of that great movement, which, exactly twenty eight years afterwards, led to the decapitation of an English sovereign, under a judicial sentence pronounced by his subjects'. A portrait of the king, completed in this year by Daniel Mytens, shows James in his robes of state; he has a preoccupied, or perhaps a perplexed, expression.

When parliament met once more on 20 November, it was clear that its zeal and anger had not noticeably diminished. Its members were in a sense liberated by the absence of the sovereign; James had decided to leave London and, with Buckingham, travelled to Royston and Newmarket. The chamber was united in its horror of recent policies. Sir Robert Phelips was once again on the attack. The Catholic states of Europe were England's enemies, while in England the Catholics had grown so bold that they dared to talk of the Protestants as a 'faction'. Let no supply be granted to the king until the dangers, home and abroad, had been resolved. Edward Coke, now a leader of the malcontents, then rose to remind his colleagues that Spain had sent the Armada, that the sheep scab which destroyed many flocks came from the same country, and that the most disgusting disease to strike humankind – namely, syphilis – had spread from Naples, a city controlled by Spain. That country was the source and spring of all foulness.

The Spaniards were also attacked in violent terms when John Pym, soon to become the fiercest opponent to the pretensions of the Crown, rose to speak against the Catholic threat in England itself, where 'the seeds of sedition' were buried beneath 'the pretences of religion'. The Venetian ambassador reported that the members 'have complained bitterly because his majesty shows them [the Catholics] so much indulgence'. The sovereign was indeed the problem; he had asked for a supply, but had not properly disclosed his policy. What could his supporters say on his behalf? The parliament had also raised the matter of the prince's marriage. If the infanta of Spain eventually became the queen of England, one of her offspring would at a future date assume the throne; this would mean the return to the rule of a Catholic king. The members of the Commons drew up a petition in which they asked James to declare war on the Catholic powers of Europe and to marry his son to a Protestant.

When the king received word of this petition he is supposed to have cried out, 'God give me patience!' He wrote to the Speaker of the Commons complaining that 'some fiery and popular spirits' were considering issues that were beyond their competence to resolve; he demanded that no member should in the future dare to touch upon issues 'concerning our government or matters of state'. The

Spanish match was not open for discussion. He then issued a threat that he felt himself 'very free and able to punish any man's misdemeanours in parliament as well during their sitting as after'. He had effectively denied them any rights at all. Phelips described it as 'a soul-killing letter'.

The Commons then drew up a petition in which they asked the king not to believe ill-founded reports on their conduct; they also requested him to guarantee their privileges. When they came with the document to Newmarket, he called out, 'Stools for the ambassadors!' He realized now that they did indeed represent a separate power in the land. In response to the petition, however, he warned them not to touch his sovereign power. One member, Sir Nathaniel Rich, objected to these commands. He took offence at such royal demands as 'Meddle not with this business' or 'Go to this business first'. 'When I speak of freedom of speech,' he declared, 'I mean not licentiousness and exorbitancy, but speech without servile fear or, as it were, under the rod.'

On 18 December 1621, by candlelight in the evening, the Commons issued a 'protestation' in which they asserted that their privileges, and indeed their lives, 'are the ancient and undoubted birthright and inheritance of the subjects of England'. They had every right to discuss foreign affairs. Any matter that concerned the defence of the realm, or the state of religion, came within the scope of their counsel and debate. They demanded freedom of speech and freedom from arrest. James, now thoroughly exasperated, adjourned and then dissolved parliament. He called for the journal of the Commons and with his own hand ripped out the 'protestation'; it now had no status. 'I will govern', he said, 'according to the commonweal, but not according to the common will.' The 'commonweal' was the term for the general interests of the nation. He then consigned Coke and Phelips to prison and confined Pym to his house. 'It is certain,' Gondomar wrote, 'that the king will never summon another parliament as long as he lives.'

The dissolution marked the beginning of the end of James's authority in England. His policy had been a dead failure, and he had alienated all the citizens and gentry who took the side of the Commons. He had no money to fight any war on behalf of the Palatinate, and he was obliged to continue negotiations with Spain. It was also widely believed that Buckingham's advice lay behind the king's intransigence; the favourite was even more distrusted than before. The times were dangerous and uncertain.

The reputation of the king was now constantly under attack. He was accused of being lazy and improvident; his will was weaker than water. He was no more than the king of Spain's viceroy. In January 1622, a man was put upon the rack 'for saying that there would be a rebellion'. A manuscript libel by 'Tom-Tell-Truth' passed among the people, saying that James may be 'defender of the faith', according to his title, but the faith was that of the Catholics; he was head of the Church dormant, not the Church militant or triumphant. 'Tom' added that Gondomar had the golden key to the king's cabinet of secrets and that James himself had committed the most hideous depravities of which a human being was capable. This was a reference to the king's relationship with Buckingham. A preacher at Oxford, a young man named Knight, declared that it was 'lawful for subjects when harassed on the score of religion to take arms against their Prince in their own defence'. Soon enough James issued 'directions concerning preaching' in which the clergy were forbidden to make 'bitter invectives and indecent railing speeches' against the Catholics and were told to avoid 'all matters of state'. 'No man can now mutter a word in the pulpit', Buckingham boasted to the Spanish ambassador, 'but he is presently catched and set in straight prison.'

With the same wish to silence dissent the king proclaimed that 'noblemen, knights and gentlemen of quality' should return to their rural estates. It was claimed that this was a measure to promote hospitality in the countryside but it was widely believed that it was aimed at the gentry who, while residing in London, compounded their discontent by sharing their grievances.

The lawyers of Gray's Inn had decided to take some small cannon from the Tower in order to celebrate Twelfth Night. They shot them off in the dead of night, but the report was so loud that it awoke the king at Whitehall. He started out of his bed crying, 'Treason! Treason!' The whole court was in alarm, and the earl of Arundel ran to the royal bedchamber with his drawn sword in his hand. The false alarm had arisen from the king's own fears. He seemed to lack both moral and physical courage. The Venetian ambassador reported that he was 'too agitated by constant mistrust of everyone, tyrannized over by perpetual fear for his life, tenacious of his authority as against the parliament and jealous of his son's obedience, all accidents and causes of his fatal and almost desperate infirmity of mind, so harmful to the general welfare'.

On the day on which the dissolution of parliament was announced James was riding in the park at his palace of Theobalds when his horse stumbled and threw him into the New River that flowed through the grounds; the ice of January broke beneath him and he sank into the water until only his boots could be seen. He was rescued, and was none the worse after the incident, but it is an apt image of a hapless sovereign.

9
The Spanish travellers

Prince Charles was becoming impatient with the slow progress of the negotiations concerning his betrothal to the Infanta Maria Anna of Spain. The marriage itself had been contemplated twelve years before. Yet there had been endless wrangles about the status of Catholics in England, a sensitive affair that became embroiled with the disputes over the Palatinate and the general state of religious warfare in Europe. There was still some doubt whether the Spanish were in earnest about the match, and disputes arose over the size of the dowry; these doubts were not assuaged by the accession of Philip IV in 1621. It was not at all clear, to put it no higher, that parliament or people would support their sovereign's wishes in the matter. When in 1622 the king ordered that Catholic recusants should be released from prison, after they had given security for any subsequent appearance in court, the fear and anger of the Protestant majority were evident.

It was proposed that Buckingham, now lord high admiral, would himself sail to Madrid; it was also whispered that 'he intended to take his friend with him in secret, to bring back that beautiful angel'. The friend in question was Charles himself. The plan was dropped only to be replaced by another.

In February 1623, Charles and Buckingham approached the king with a scheme of their own devising. It would take too long for a fleet to be prepared for the voyage to Madrid. The effort of obtaining travel warrants for France would be immense. Their plan was to travel to Spain in disguise, with the intention of wooing and winning the most eligible woman in the world. For them it was a great adventure, a grand European romance. The king, sick and weary, seems to have assented; he rarely withstood the blandishments of his favourite or the urgent entreaties of his son.

On the morning after this interview, however, the king was not so sure. Cautious and wary as he was, he anticipated the perils with which the two young men would be surrounded. The heir to the throne would be in foreign hands. Animated by Charles's presence among them, the Spanish ministers might make further demands. An attempt might even be made to convert him. So he remonstrated with them both, and outlined the dangers that they might incur. In response Buckingham merely said that, if he broke his promise of the day before, no one would ever believe him again.

Whereupon James called for one of his principal foreign advisers, Sir Francis Cottington, who was himself a supporter of Spain and the Spanish marriage. 'Here are Baby Charles and Steenie,' the king told him, 'who have a great mind to go by post into Spain to fetch home the Infanta, who will have but two more in their company, and have chosen you for one, what think you of the journey?' Cottington replied that such an expedition was dangerous and unwise; the Spanish were certain to impose new conditions upon the marriage. At this James threw himself upon the bed. 'I told you this before,' he shouted. 'I am undone. I shall lose Baby Charles!'

Buckingham remonstrated angrily with Cottington until he was interrupted by the king. 'Nay, by God, Steenie, you are much to blame to use him so. He answered me directly to the question I asked him, and very honestly and wisely: and yet he says no more than I told you before he was called in.' Reluctantly, however, he renewed his assent to the perilous journey. It was also agreed that the three travellers should be joined by Endymion Porter, a courtier who had been brought up in Spain and might act as translator.

On the morning of 18 February, Charles and Buckingham set off from Buckingham's mansion in Essex; they were wearing false beards and travelled under the names of Tom and John Smith. It was all wildly improbable. They gave a boatman at Gravesend a gold piece and rode away without asking for change; the man convinced himself that they were duellists about to fight each other on a foreign field, and advised the magistrates of the town. An officer was dispatched to intercept them, but he failed to find them. As suspected assassins they were stopped at Canterbury. Buckingham had to take off his false beard in order to assure the mayor that he was the lord high admiral going secretly to inspect the fleet. Eventually they reached Dover, where Porter and Cottington had secured a boat. Soon after their departure the sighing king wrote to them. 'My sweet boys and dear venturous knights, worthy to be put in a new romance, I thank you for your comfortable letters, but think it not possible that you can be many hours undiscovered, for your parting was so blown abroad.' In Buckingham's absence the king had made him a duke, so that he was now pre-eminent even among the eminent.

The two *incogniti* sailed from Dover to Boulogne and, after two days in the saddle, they reached Paris. Two weeks later, after hard and weary riding, they eventually arrived in Madrid and knocked on the door of the English ambassador to Spain. John Digby, newly created earl of Bristol, was described by Edward Hyde, earl of Clarendon, as a man 'of a grave aspect, of a presence which drew respect . . .' He kept his countenance at the unexpected arrival of these two great men, and treated them with all deference and courtesy. But the news of Charles's arrival soon reached the ears of Gondomar, the erstwhile Spanish ambassador who had returned home the year before. He went to the Spanish prime minister, Olivares, with a brilliant smile. Olivares told him that 'one might think you had the king of England in Madrid'.

'If I have not got the king, at least I have got the prince.'

Olivares and Gondomar now approached Philip IV with the astounding news that the prince of Wales had come in person to claim the hand of his sister. But what did Charles mean by travelling all this way to Spain? The grandees came to the conclusion that he was now ready to change his religion. Philip and Charles then agreed that they should meet in the open air, thus avoiding all the pomp and circumstance of a formal audience. The prince did not have a large enough retinue to appear with dignity. So he was invited into the king's carriage, and a few days later he was conducted to the apartments reserved for him in the royal palace.

It was now widely believed that Charles was ready to convert, and indeed he gave no sign to the contrary. He continued to temporize on the matter, eager at all costs not to offend the Spaniards before he had obtained his wife. 'We think it not amiss', he and Buckingham wrote to James, 'to assure you that, neither in spiritual nor in temporal things, there is anything pressed upon us more than is already agreed upon.' They could not have been more wrong. The infanta herself declared that she would never agree to marry a Protestant. She had been told that she would be sleeping with a heretic who would one day burn in the fires of hell.

The foreign policy of England was now also entangled with Dutch affairs. On 27 February 1623, the principal merchant of the East India Company was tortured and then beheaded in Amboyna, now the Maluku islands of Indonesia; he was executed by order of the local Dutch governor, on the grounds that he was planning to attack the Dutch garrison. Nine other English merchants suffered the same fate, and the report of the incident provoked outrage in the nation on an unprecedented scale. It was the subject of plays and ballads, chapbooks and woodcuts, inflaming public opinion against the country across the North Sea.

In the following month some Dutch men-of-war chased privateers into the harbour of Leith and began firing at the town itself; this was considered by James to be an unwarrantable infringement of sovereign territory. A second incident of a similar kind occurred at Cowes, on the Isle of Wight. For the king the actions of the Dutch were intolerable. In retaliation he sent a letter to his son in Madrid, asking him to open negotiations with the Spanish for a joint attack upon the Netherlands which the two countries would then partition. On few occasions has so small a pretext been used for so great a war. Yet it came to nothing. James's anger cooled, and a compromise with the Netherlands was reached. His initial proposals, however, demonstrate how implicitly he still relied upon Spanish support; the whole episode also displays his impulsiveness and unpredictability.

Charles had not yet been given any opportunity of greeting his proposed bride, and so at the beginning of April he was invited to an audience with the queen of Spain and the infanta. The conversation was supposed to be limited to a few formal words of address, but the prince went so far as to speak of his affection for her. This was a grave breach of protocol in a court that maintained the strictest rules of behaviour. Charles realized that he had offended, and fell silent. The infanta herself was not impressed. The prince, however, had been profoundly affected by the sight of her; he wrote to England that she was even more beautiful than he had expected.

It was urged by his hosts that Charles might at least receive some instruction in the precepts of Catholicism. So he agreed to participate in a religious discussion with four Carmelite friars. Their meeting began in silence and, when one of the friars asked if he had any matter to propose for debate, he replied, 'Nothing at all. I have no doubts whatsoever.' Charles even went so far as to ask that the reformed English service might be conducted for him in the palace, whereupon Olivares sent for Cottington and told him that the entry of English chaplains would be resisted by force. This did not bode well for any settlement.

By May it had become clear to Buckingham and the prince that they had made a grave error in travelling to Madrid. If they had remained in England, all the conditions and qualifications could have been discussed by experienced diplomats; they themselves were simply confused and angered by all the demands now being made upon them.

Towards the end of that month a Spanish 'junta of theologians' decreed that the infanta must remain in her native land for twelve months after the marriage had been solemnized. In that period the king of England must prove his good intentions by allowing his Catholic subjects the free exercise of their religion; all penal laws against them were to be suspended. It was further suggested that the prince might also prefer to spend the following year in Spain. He would then enjoy to the utmost the fruits of the marriage.

Sir Francis Cottington returned to England with the news. 'My sweet boys,' James wrote, 'your letter by Cottington hath stricken me dead. I fear it shall very much shorten my days; and I am the more perplexed that I know not how to satisfy the people's expectation here, neither know I what to say in the council . . . Alas I now repent me sore, that ever I suffered you to go away.' He was in fact more concerned about his son than the changes of policy that the 'junta' had demanded. One observer noted that 'the king is now quite stupefied'. 'Do you think', he asked a courtier, 'that I shall ever see the prince again?' He burst into tears.

The prince himself was mired in indecision. He was told that the delay between the marriage and the infanta's departure for England could be shortened by six months. In an audience with Philip IV on 7 July, Charles assented to the terms. 'I have resolved', he said, 'to accept with my whole heart what has been proposed to me, both as to the articles touching religion, and as to the security required.' A few days before, he had made statements of precisely the opposite intent.

James knew well enough that parliament would never allow English Catholics permanent immunity from prosecution; and yet he feared that, if he did not sign the agreement demanded by the 'junta', his son would never be permitted to leave Madrid. He summoned the members of his privy council and pleaded with them to take an oath to uphold the Spanish terms. Faced with the importance of maintaining the king's authority, and alarmed by the prospect of the heir apparent being detained in the Spanish capital, the council reluctantly agreed to take the oath.

The decision of the king, taken in confusion and anxiety, was perhaps not a wise one. It taught the English Catholics that they must rely for their safety on a foreign power, and it told the English people that James was willing to make a bargain with Spain against the obvious wishes of parliament. The Roman Catholic Church, for many years after, was identified with contempt for the rule of law. It was believed by many that, while the prince was detained in Spain, Philip could extort any terms he wished. John Chamberlain wrote that 'alas our hands are bound by the absence of our most precious jewel'. It was widely noted that the crucifix, once the symbol of papistry, had been reinstalled in the royal chapel. Another chapel was even then being erected in St James's Palace for the imminent coming of the infanta. Buckingham's mother converted to Rome. When the archbishop of Canterbury told the king that the toleration of Catholics could not be permitted 'by the laws and privileges of the kingdom', it was related that the king 'swore bitterly and asked how he should get his son home again'.

Two weeks after this reported conversation, on 25 July 1623, Charles and Philip signed the marriage contract. James dispatched jewels of great price to his son as gifts for the expected bride. When the prince asked for horses to be also sent to him, the king answered that his coffers were now empty.

Yet, after all this intrigue and resentment, the marriage never took place. The prince had changed his mind once more. His affection for the infanta had been gradually displaced by his resentment at his treatment in Spain; the king and his courtiers were endlessly prevaricating on the departure of Maria Anna. His companion, Buckingham, had been regarded with ill-concealed distaste. On 28 August he took an oath committing himself to the marriage, but he had already decided to leave Madrid without her. Three weeks later he and Buckingham set sail from Santander to England. The news of their landing at Portsmouth, on 5 October, was the cause of general rejoicing; the blessed prince had been rescued from the jaws of the dragon. He had escaped the wiles of the harlot of Rome. Spain would no longer be able to command the councils of the king. When Charles crossed the Thames he was greeted with carillons of bells; the wealthy laid out tables of food and wine in the streets; debtors were released from prison and felons rescued from death. It was a day of rain and storm yet one contemporary counted 335 bonfires between Whitehall and Temple Bar; 108 bonfires were lit between St Paul's and London Bridge alone. A contemporary ballad set the tone:

> The Catholic king hath a little young thing
> Called Donna Maria his sister,
> Our prince went to Spain her love to obtain,
> But yet by good luck he hath missed her.

A shorter rhyme was also carried from street to street:

> On the fifth day of October,
> It will be treason to be sober.

The two men rode straight from London to the royal hunting lodge at Royston where king, son and favourite all wept. Yet not all was well with the happy family. Buckingham, an erstwhile supporter of Spain, fell into a fury at all things Spanish; the contempt for him in Madrid was now common knowledge. One Spanish courtier, speaking of Buckingham, had said that 'we would rather put the infanta headlong into a well than into his hands'. Charles was equally dissatisfied with his treatment at the hands of the Spanish court; they had denied him his bride and treated him like a fool. 'I am ready', he told his father, 'to conquer Spain, if you will allow me to do it.' At a stroke James's well-considered, if not always well-executed, policy of twenty years would be destroyed.

Yet Charles had learned some useful lessons in Madrid. He had been impressed by Spanish formality and protocol that emphasized the divinity hedged about a king; he had also become an admirer of the art collected by the Spanish royal family and took back with him, to England, a Titian and a Correggio among other notable paintings. In his own reign the taste of the court would be generally elevated even if some of these 'gay gazings', as the paintings were called, smacked of the old religion.

The popular prejudice against the Catholic cause was strikingly demonstrated when a garret attached to the French embassy in Blackfriars collapsed on 26 October 1623. A Catholic priest was preaching to a congregation of some 400 people when the floor gave way, pitching the people into the 'confession room' beneath. Over ninety were killed, among them eight priests and fifteen 'of note and rank'. It was widely believed that the accident was the direct result of God's particular judgement against the papists, and the bishop of London refused to allow any of the dead to be buried in the city's churchyards. A mob had also gathered outside the residence of the French ambassador, shrieking execrations against the old faith. Some of the survivors were assailed with insults or assaulted with mud and stones.

The press for war against Spain was growing ever stronger. The situation of the Protestants in Europe was worse than it had been for many decades. The imperial troops were undertaking the forced conversion of the people of Bohemia, while Frederick's erstwhile subjects in the Palatinate were suffering from religious persecution. The defeat of the forces of Christian of Brunswick, one of the last Protestant leaders still standing, heralded the supremacy of the Holy

Roman Emperor, Ferdinand II, and his fellow Habsburg Philip IV of Spain. Thomas Gataker, an English Protestant theologian, declared that 'the last hour is now running. And we are those on whom the end of the world is fallen.'

The king himself was growing weaker. A memoir on the king's health drawn up at the end of 1623 reported that he was 'easily affected by cold and suffers in cold and damp weather'; he used to enjoy hunting but 'now he is quieter and lies or sits more, but that is due to the weakness of his knee-joints . . . His mind is easily moved suddenly. He is very wrathful, but the fit soon passes off.' He was now opposed by his son and by his favourite; Charles and Buckingham, as impetuous in their hatred of Spain as they had once been recklessly in favour of a Spanish match, were now directing the pressure for war.

For Buckingham the chance of fighting a pious crusade against the heretic promised great rewards for his domestic reputation as well as for his private fortune; his post as lord high admiral guaranteed him a tenth of all prizes won upon the seas. The policy of 'the sharp edge', as it became known, might also allow the young prince to acquire some sort of military glory without which, as the example of his father showed, kingship lost half of its lustre. It was Charles, therefore, who began to assume command of state affairs. He took the chair of the privy council while his father preferred to remain in the country, where Buckingham was able to insulate the king from any Spanish overtures. The Venetian ambassador told his doge and senate that 'the balance of affairs leans to the side of the prince, while Buckingham remains at Newmarket to prevent any harm . . .'

A parliament assembled in February 1624, when the king's opening speech was tentative and hesitant. He could neither disown his son-in-law and the freedom of the Palatinate nor press for war against Spain and the imperialists. He did not know where to turn. In private he had ranted and sworn, pretending illness to avoid difficult decisions, demanding repose and even death to end his sufferings. In his public speech to parliament, he asked for help. He said that as a result of his son's fruitless journey to Madrid 'I awaked as a man out of a dream . . . the business is nothing advanced neither of the match nor of the palatinate, for all the long treaties and great promises'. In the past James had earnestly upheld his sole responsibility for the conduct of foreign affairs as part of his royal prerogative. But now 'I shall entreat your good and sound advice for the glory of God, the peace of the kingdom, and weal of my children'. Five days later Buckingham met the Lords and Commons in the Banqueting House where he whipped up their anger against the duplicitous Spaniards.

A peace party still existed at the court and council. The lord treasurer, the earl of Middlesex, was adamantly opposed to any war with Spain. There was no money left. It would be folly to embark on a foreign enterprise when there was not coin enough to pay the servants of the Crown in England. Charles and Buckingham, therefore, found it necessary to destroy him. At the beginning of April the earl was charged with various counts of financial corruption; he had no chance. 'Remove this strange and prodigious comet,' Sir John Eliot declared of him, 'which so fatally hangs over us.' He was impeached by the Commons and judged to be guilty by the Lords. James himself was much more aware of the dangers of such a proceeding than his son. He declared that Charles had set a dangerous precedent that would in time weaken the power of the throne. The prince, in other words, had invited parliament to collaborate with him in the destruction of one of the king's own ministers. Would it not be tempted to exploit some of its newfound power? James's prophecy would soon enough have the ring of truth.

For the time being, however, Charles and Buckingham could effectively lead the common cause described by one of their supporters as that of the 'patriots'; it was defined by its anti-Catholic and anti-Spanish animus abroad, together with its supposed fight against court corruption at home. For the first, and perhaps the last, time in his life Charles was in broad agreement with the gentlemen of the Commons and the country. At the end of February 1624, the Lords asked that any negotiations with Spain should be broken off. A deputation to the king in the following month requested the fitting of a fleet and the repair of maritime fortifications; the occupation of the Palatinate by Spanish and Bavarian troops should be ended.

For these measures James needed money and, at his urgent request, he was granted £300,000. But how was any war to be fought, and against whom was it to be directed? Against the Holy Roman Emperor or against the king of Spain? Or against Maximilian I, duke of Bavaria, who now controlled the Palatinate? The king prevaricated in his usual manner. 'But whether I shall send twenty thousand or ten thousand, whether by sea or land, east or west, by diversion or otherwise, by invasion upon the Bavarian [Maximilian I] or the Emperor, you must leave that to the king.' The parliament might wish for war with Spain, but it might be in the interests of the English king only to threaten war; the Spaniards might then agree to restore Frederick to his throne. Many in the court and council were themselves wary of a direct war against the Spanish; battles on sea or on land cost money, and money could only be raised by imposing fresh taxes.

The Spanish envoys had meanwhile found their way to the king through the connivance of certain courtiers. It soon reached the king's ear that they accused Buckingham of 'affecting popularity', and charged him with drawing up a plan that would effectively imprison James in a convenient country house so that the prince might rule in his name. They suggested that the favourite believed the king to be a poor old man unfit to govern. There may or may not have been truth to these claims but the king took the unexpected step of interrogating his councillors on the matter. All of them swore that they had never heard a whisper of treason from Buckingham. The favourite was saved.

James had signalled his willingness to prepare himself for the possibility of war 'if he could be seconded'. The only possible ally was Louis XIII of France; the French king, at least, had the power to stand against the Spanish or the imperialists in Germany. Soon after parliament had assembled, two envoys were sent from London to Paris with the instruction to seek the hand of the French king's sister, Henrietta Maria, for Charles. Their proposals were indeed welcomed; it was in the interests of France permanently to separate England from Spain. Louis was a better Frenchman than he was a Catholic, and had no reason to shrink from conflict with his co-religionists. Yet the French court insisted, at the beginning of the negotiations, that English Catholics be given the same liberties as the Spanish had demanded for them in the previous marriage treaty.

This was of course a perilous matter. It would test once more the king's good faith. By marrying a Catholic princess, also, Charles might alienate the very 'patriots' whom he had previously courted. The king therefore decided to prorogue parliament before news of the French demands became known. It had not been an unproductive assembly; it had passed thirty-five public Acts and thirty-eight private. The private Acts alone are evidence that the members were representing local demands and grievances on a significantly increased scale. But parliament had achieved more than that. With its impeachment of the lord treasurer, and its active collaboration with Charles and Buckingham, it had proved itself to be an indispensable limb of the body politic.

Preparations for war with Spain were begun. The Spanish ambassador noted 'the great joy and exultation of all the cobblers and zealous bigots of the town'. Cobblers were well known for their radical Protestant sympathies. The English 'mice', as they were called, were ready to take on the Habsburg 'cats'. On the departure of the Spanish legation from London the citizens cried out: 'All the devils in hell go with you, and for those that stay behind let Tyburn take them!' London and the suburbs were now the venue for newly recruited soldiers, all of them waiting for the happy beat of the drums.

A defensive league was formed with the seven United Provinces; envoys were sent to the kings of Sweden and Denmark with proposals for a holy crusade against the Catholic powers. This served further to excite the martial enthusiasm of the populace. The more realistic of the king's councillors doubted that the Palatinate could be fully recovered, or Spain defeated, but they hoped at least to assert English power and subdue Spanish pretensions. In the summer of 1624 a play by Thomas Middleton, *A Game at Chess*, was staged at the Globe where its satire of Gondomar and the Spanish clique at the English court was an unprecedented success; crowds besieged the theatre for nine days, while the laughter and general hubbub could be heard on the other side of the Thames. 'Sir, your plot's discovered!' one of Gondomar's aides bursts in to tell him. The ambassador asks him which of the 20,958 plots he means. He explains his methods.

With pleasant subtlety and bewitching courtship . . .
To many a soul I have let in mortal poison
Whose cheeks have cracked with laughter to receive it;
I could so roll my pills in sugared syllables
And strew such kindly mirth o'er all my mischiefs,
They took their bane in way of recreation.

Thus spoke the erstwhile Spanish ambassador on the stage.

An Anglo-French league was now likely but by no means certain. The French still insisted in principle that penal measures against English Catholics be lifted, and that they should be allowed to practise their religion in peace. Both the king and his son, however, had promised the last parliament that no articles in favour of the Catholics would ever be entertained. It was considered that, in the last resort, it would be better to go to war without the aid of the French than to force a crisis between Crown and parliament.

All the flexible skills of diplomacy had now to be deployed. An English envoy at the court of Louis XIII suggested to James that the French demands were made for 'their own honour' only, and that 'it will always be in your majesty's power to put the same in execution according to your own pleasure'. It was a policy of hypocrisy and prevarication but none the worse for that. Buckingham was equally sanguine. He was so intent upon martial glory in any Protestant crusade that he urged the king to accept the French terms. James was not willing to concede so much, but he was prepared to write a private letter to Louis in which he promised that his Catholic subjects 'shall enjoy all the liberty and freedom which concerns the secret exercise of their religion which was granted by the treaty of marriage made with Spain'. It was not quite enough. The French insisted upon their original demands, with the enthusiastic support of Buckingham. The king finally yielded, with the proviso that he should sign a letter and not a contractual engagement. It was vital now that parliament should not intervene; a promised summons in the late autumn was therefore postponed until the following year.

On 12 December 1624, the marriage articles were signed; the king's hands were so crippled with gout that he was obliged to apply a stamp rather than a signature. To this document Charles appended a secret engagement to the effect that 'I will promise to all the Roman Catholic subjects of the Crown of Great Britain the utmost of liberty and franchise in everything regarding their religion . . .' Twelve days later the courts were forbidden to prosecute recusants under the penal laws; all Catholics in confinement for their faith were then released from the prisons of England.

In this month the king wrote a plaintive letter to Buckingham.

> I cannot content myself without sending you this billet, praying God that I may have a joyful and comfortable meeting with you, and that we may make at this Christmas a new marriage, ever to be kept hereafter; for, God so love me, as I desire only to live in this world for your sake, and that I had rather live banished in any part of the earth with you, than live a sorrowful widow life without you, and so God bless you, my sweet child and wife, and grant that you may ever be a comfort to your dad and husband
>
> James R.

It was the last letter that Buckingham would ever receive from the king.

The time of war was approaching. Ernest, count of Mansfeld, the principal German ally of Frederick, came to England in search of troops; the soldiers of the previous summer, in their gay feathers and buff jerkins, had been volunteers. Now the county officials had to conscript local men for service and, naturally enough, they preferred to choose those for whom they had the least use. Some of the conscripts preferred radical action to avoid being pressed for service. One hanged himself for fear, while another ran into the Thames and drowned; one cut off all the fingers of his right hand, while another put out one of his eyes with salt. An observer wrote that 'such a rabble of raw and poor rascals have not lightly been seen, and they go so unwillingly that they must rather be driven than led'.

It had been said that an Englishman could not fight without his 'three Bs', namely bed, beef and beer. All three were, on this occasion, in pitifully short supply. Dover had no such commodities in large quantity, and only a few vessels had arrived to transport the men. Their eventual destination was, in any event, not at all clear. James had wished the men to land in France, thus implicating Louis XIII in the war against Spain and the empire; Louis refused them the possibility. So Mansfeld, at the end of January, was obliged to sail for Flushing and begin a march through Holland; his men were to go to the aid of the Dutch fortress city of Breda, then under siege by the Spanish.

Yet the English troops were ill-trained and ill-equipped; they had few provisions, and soon enough a hard frost descended on them, provoking contagious sickness. 'All day long,' one of their commanders, Lord Cromwell, wrote, 'we go about for victuals and bury our dead.' By the end of March a force of 12,000 was reduced to 3,000 armed men. Yet the folly was not blamed so much upon Mansfeld as upon Buckingham, whose military enthusiasm did not include attention to the details of policy or planning. The disaster did not bode well for the conduct of a more general war that the king would not live to see.

James had recovered from the gout that had afflicted him at the beginning of the year. Yet on 5 March 1625 he was attacked by what was known as a tertian ague, of which the symptoms were chills, fever and profuse sweating. He feared the worst but refused to accept the advice of his physicians. Instead he relied upon a posset drink recommended by Buckingham's mother, which seemed to do no good. It was whispered that, at the urging of her son, she had in fact poisoned him; she fell on her knees at the king's bedside and asked for justice against these accusations. 'Poisoned me?' the king asked fearfully. At which point, he swooned.

The end was now very near. On 25 March he suffered a stroke that affected his face and jaw. It was reported that his tongue had become so enlarged that he could not make himself understood. He was also beset by bouts of dysentery that left him drenched in his own filth. Two days later he left this life. With the great lords and prelates of the realm about him, according to a later memorial, 'without pangs or convulsions at all, *dormivit Salomon*, Solomon slept'. Unlike his mother and his son, James I died lying in his bed rather than kneeling on the scaffold. The surgeons, on opening the body, found no evidence of poison. In a letter of the time, by the Reverend Joseph Meade, it was reported that all of his vital organs were sound 'as also his head which was very full of brains; but his blood was wonderfully tainted with melancholy'.

His death was not greeted with much dismay or sorrow among the people. His foreign policy had been an utter failure, and his relations with parliament were at best acrimonious. His finances were in disrepair, and the sexual scandals of his reign were common knowledge. The day of his funeral was marred by foul weather so that any bystanders were greeted with muffled coaches and flaming torches. His passing was greeted, perhaps, with relief. The new king might prosecute the Protestant cause with more vigour and determination. Sir John Eliot wrote that 'a new spirit of life possessed all men'.

There was an alternative vision of the late king's rule. At his funeral service in Westminster Abbey, on 7 May, the bishop of Lincoln, John Williams, preached a sermon in which he praised James's direction of religion. The King James Bible is lasting evidence of his achievement. The bishop also remarked upon the fact that 'manufactures at home are daily invented, trading abroad exceedingly multiplied, the borders of Scotland peaceably governed . . .' In the reign of James, too, the English people had reached out to Virginia and New England; the merchants had visited the ports of Africa, Asia and America. Certainly, the central achievement had been that of peace, the one condition that the king sedulously strove to maintain. A courtier, Sir Anthony Weldon, left a less than flattering account of the king as indecisive, hesitant and cowardly; it was he who reported the opinion that James was 'the wisest fool in Christendom'. Yet he appended to his description the more favourable comment that 'he lived in peace, died in peace, and left all his kingdoms in a peaceable condition'. This would not be the epitaph of his son.

10

An interlude

At the beginning of 1625, while his father was still incapacitated by gout, Charles had organized what the Venetian ambassador called 'a splendid masque, with much machinery, and most beautiful scenery'; the prince and his companions danced for four hours after midnight, perhaps in anticipation of the regal splendours to come.

The masque was the great ceremonial occasion of the court, performed once or twice each year, that came to define Stuart kingship. A group of the nobility advanced upon an especially designed stage, their ornate and artificial dress perfectly consonant with the elaborate scenery all around them. Gold was a token of perfection, white was the colour of faith and blue represented the infinite heavens; shame was crimson while lust was scarlet. The colours which took most wonderfully to candlelight were white, carnation and sea-water green. Oil lamps and candles of white wax were used to impart brilliance to the scene. The old Banqueting House had in fact been destroyed by fire in 1619 when 'oiled paper' and other combustibles used in the entertainment were ignited.

Inigo Jones was the sole deviser and designer of the court masques, and he brought to his practice all the refinements of his art. The discipline and formality of his architecture prevailed in his stagecraft; he was particularly adept at contriving the mechanical devices or 'machines' that were the wonder of the age.

'If mathematicians had lost proportion,' it was said of one of his productions, 'there they might have found it.' He wished to create harmonies in spectacle just as in his architecture he evoked the harmonies of stone.

The texts of the masques were generally composed by Ben Jonson who chose to deploy moral statements and sentiments within euphonious and carefully crafted verse. The two men were not natural collaborators, however, and Jonson soon wearied of a form in which visual display took precedence over sense. He wrote in one poem, 'An Expostulation with Inigo Jones':

> O shows! Shows! Mighty shows!
> The eloquence of masques! What need of prose
> Or verse, or sense t'express immortal you?
> You are the spectacles of State!

Inigo Jones himself admitted that the masques were 'nothing else but pictures with light and motion'.

The stage itself was designed to create the illusion of an infinite perspective, moving from the reality of the king and assembled court into an idealized world where everything had its place and proportion. These perspective stages were a wholly new thing in England, introducing novel principles of symmetry and order. The power of art represented the art of power. The masque was conducted in a formal space in which the laws of nature could be chastened and subdued by the king himself, who sat on the line of perspective from which everything could be perfectly seen. Only in his presence could the seasons miraculously change, or trees walk, or flowers be transformed into human beings.

It was the perfect complement to the doctrine of the divine right of kings that James had professed early in his reign. He sat in the centre of the especially constructed auditorium so that the eyes of the audience were as much upon his regality as upon the performance itself. James had already written in his instruction manual to his elder son, *Basilikon Doron*, that a king 'is as one set on a stage, whose smallest actions and gestures all the people do gazingly behold'. Inigo Jones himself wrote that 'in heroic virtue is figured the king's majesty, who therein transcends as far common men as they are above beasts'.

The stage had three habitations. At the highest level was a metaphysical world populated by divine or allegorical figures; below this was the world of the court, in which the monarch was the emblem of order and authority; beneath these two worlds lay ordinary reality which, with its emblems of Vice and Disorder as well as various 'low' figures, provided the material for the 'anti-masque'. The anti-masques represented mutability and inconstancy; they embodied the threat of chaos that was wonderfully removed from the world of the idealized court. The king defeated all those who threatened or abused him. As Sir William Davenant wrote in his masque *Salmacida Spolia*:

> All that are harsh, all that are rude,
> Are by your harmony subdu'd;
> Yet so into obedience wrought,
> As if not forc'd to it, but taught.

The scene might suddenly change. A palace might become a bower, where fairy spirits tread upon trolls and other wicked things; Oberon may appear in a chariot, drawn by two white bears, before ascending into the air; a statue might breathe and walk; a feather of silk may become a cloud of smoke, surrounded by several circles of light in continual motion. A scene might be set in a courtyard or in a dungeon, in a bedchamber or in a desert. All was framed by a proscenium arch, the direct forebear of the modern theatrical space. That is why the English drama favoured interiors.

A courtier and diplomat, Dudley Carleton, noted of an early production in 1605 that 'there was a great engine at the lower end of the room, which had motion, and in it were the images of sea-horses with other terrible fishes, which were ridden by Moors . . . at the further end was a great shell in the form of a scallop, wherein were four seats; on the lowest sat the queen with my lady Bedford; on the rest were placed the ladies . . . their apparel was rich, but too light and courtesan-like for such great ones'. James never took part in the masques, but his wife and children delighted in them; they rehearsed their parts for as long as two months, emphasizing the importance that they placed upon them.

The speaking roles were performed by professional players while the music and song were provided by court musicians; the dancers and masquers, among them members of the royal family itself, remained mute. At the end of the proceedings they advanced into the dancing space, before the king, and invited members of the especially invited audience to dance with them. The concord of music therefore concluded a display in which the virtues of reason, order and good governance are all conjoined.

The dancers of the masque thus celebrate the restoration of an ideal order, a magical ritual designed to emphasize the Stuart vision of kingship and continuity. The masques therefore became known as 'court hieroglyphics'. It is not unimportant that foreign ambassadors were an integral part of the audience, since the masque was also a form of mystical diplomacy. It was meant to convey, by the expense of the production, the wealth and liberality of the sovereign; the more money spent, the more the glory and the more the praise. In 1618 James spent the unparalleled sum of £4,000 on one production. The fourteen ladies of another masque needed, for their costumes, 780 yards of silk. Yet the masques appealed to appetites other than sight. A lavish banquet, complete with orchestra, often preceded or accompanied the performance.

It was an age of music. In the years between 1587 and 1630 over ninety collections of madrigals, airs and songs were published. Madrigals were compositions for several voices without music, and airs were solo songs accompanied by instruments; the madrigal was the most artificial, and therefore considered the most delightful. Catches were sung by gentlemen in their taverns, by weavers at their looms and by tinkers in their workshops. A man who could not take part in a madrigal, or play the lute, was considered to be unfinished. Lutes and citherns were available in barbers' shops for the diversion of waiting customers. Music books were customarily brought to the table after supper was ended.

No epoch in the history of English music can excel the diversity of genius that flourished in this period. It was the age of Dowland and of Morley, of Campion and of Byrd, of Bull and of Gibbons. It was also the age of songs such as 'Lady, Lie Near Me', 'If All The World Were Paper', 'New, New Nothing' and 'Punk's Delight'. In the time of James, the island was filled with sounds and sweet airs.

In the closing months of 1611, the private theatre at Blackfriars echoed to such harmonies. Shakespeare's *The Tempest* was a work of musical theatre with professional singers and a consort of instruments. The stage directions tell their own story, requesting 'solemn and strange music', 'soft music', 'a strange hollow and confused noise'. 'Enter Ferdinand, and Ariel, invisible, playing and singing.' Ferdinand asks, 'Where should this music be? I' th' air, or th' earth?' It was everywhere, being 'dispersed' music that came from various parts of the stage. In this play Stephano sings sea shanties, while Caliban croons drunken catches. Music was played in the intervals between the acts, and at the close a ritual dance was performed by all of the actors. Music was also played as an accompaniment to scenes of wonder and of pathos, on Prospero's grounds that 'a solemn air' is 'the best comforter to an unsettled fancy'.

The music of the instruments was diverse. The soft and mournful notes of the recorder were accompanied by a consort of strings including viols, lutes and citherns. An organ was suitable for the solemn music of supernatural change and awakening. Ariel often enters with pipe and tabor. Thus Caliban reveals that

> Sometimes a thousand twangling instruments
> Will hum about mine ears; and sometimes voices . . .

The last song of the play is sung by Ariel. The words are those of Shakespeare and at a slightly later date they were given a setting by Robert Johnson, a musician attached to the court of the king. It is clear, however, that the melodic inspiration came to Shakespeare from folk tunes or ballads that were in the air at the time.

> Where the bee sucks, there suck I,
> In a cowslip's bell I lie;
> There I couch when owls do cry.

This is a song of freedom, chanted just before Prospero releases Ariel from his service; perhaps the spirit danced at the close. The part was performed by a boy, or a light-voiced singer, and the role may have been taken by the seventeen-year-old 'Jackie Wilson' who later handed down the settings for the song. Blackfriars was known as a 'private' theatre because it was enclosed by roof and walls; in such a setting, the music would have a more powerful and intimate effect.

The Tempest was also performed before the king at Whitehall on 1 November 1611, and owes some of its ritual and sweet melody to the masques of the court; actors from Shakespeare's company also took part in those masques. There was a marked cultural or courtly style in the early years of the seventeenth century.

The great plays of Shakespeare's maturity were written during the reign of James, *Othello* and *King Lear*, *Measure for Measure*, *Antony and Cleopatra* and *The Winter's Tale* among them. The witches of *Macbeth* were in part inspired by James's own interest in the phenomenon. The king was a more enthusiastic patron of the drama than Elizabeth had ever been. Six days after his arrival in London, from Scotland, he called together Shakespeare and the other members of the Lord Chamberlain's Company and issued to them letters patent that allowed them to perform as the King's Men. The actors were appointed to be grooms of the chamber a few months later.

The era of James I also encouraged other forms of drama. A cardinal, dressed in crimson silk, with a tippet or shoulder cape of sable, comes upon the stage. He is meditating upon a book.

Cardinal: I am puzzled in a question about hell:
He says, in hell there's one material fire,
And yet it shall not burn all men alike.
Lay him by. How tedious is a guilty conscience!
When I look into the fish-ponds in my garden
Methinks I see a thing armed with a rake
That seems to strike at me.

It does not occur to the cardinal that it may be his own reflection.

The Duchess of Malfi, by John Webster, is a defining drama of the period, and is one of a number of plays that subsequently have been brought together under the collective title of 'Jacobean tragedy'. Since it is the only literary genre that carries the name of the age, it may be of some importance for any understanding of it. It signifies melancholy, morbidity, restlessness, brooding anger, impatience, disdain and resentment; it represents the horror of life. The exuberance and optimistic inventiveness of the Elizabethan years have disappeared. The joy has gone. The vitality has become extremity and the rhetoric has turned rancid.

The duchess herself asks, 'Who am I?' To which comes the reply: 'Thou art a box of worm-seed, at best but a salvatory of green mummy. What's this flesh? A little curded milk, fantastical puff paste: our bodies are weaker than those paper prisons boys use to keep flies in – more contemptible, since ours is to preserve earth worms. Didst thou ever see a lark in a cage?' This is perhaps the quintessence of Jacobean dramatic style and can be compared to John Donne's contemporaneous verse on:

> This curdled milk, this poor unlitter'd whelp,
> My body . . .

The Duchess of Malfi was written for Shakespeare's company and was first performed towards the close of 1614 at the theatre in Blackfriars before a fashionable audience that would catch most of the allusions to the plays and poems of the day. In a theatrical world of death and murder, of graves and shrines, music was once again an essential element for conveying suspense and intensity.

The plot itself is a poor thing. The duchess, a widow, wishes to marry the steward of her household in a union which might be perceived to dishonour her. Her two brothers – Ferdinand, duke of Calabria, and one known only as the cardinal – conspire to be revenged upon her. By means of a spy and secret agent, Bosola, the duchess is captured and subjected to a range of mental tortures designed to induce insanity; she is presented with the severed hand of her husband, and a gaggle of mad people is brought into her presence. A curtain is drawn to show a tableau comprising the dead bodies of her husband and children. It is revealed in an aside to the audience that they are waxworks, but not until the *frisson* of their discovery has subsided. The duchess is in the end strangled, but not before being shown the cord that will dispatch her.

> *Duchess*: What would it pleasure me to have my throat cut
> With diamonds, or to be smothered
> With cassia, or to be shot to death with pearls?

On sight of her body Ferdinand utters what are the most famous words of the play:

> Cover her face; mine eyes dazzle; she died young.

Out of guilt and despair he then descends into murderous madness.

> One met the Duke 'bout midnight in a lane
> Behind St Mark's church, with the leg of a man
> Upon his shoulder; and he howled fearfully;
> Said he was a wolf . . .

The final scene concludes with a bloody conflict in which both Bosola and the cardinal are killed, bringing the sum total of fatalities in the play to ten. Enough has been quoted, perhaps, to convey the sensibility of the time as well as the taste of the Jacobean audience.

It is a world of secrecy and madness, where characters hide and wait. The duchess sees a trespasser in the mirror and trembles. The broken phrases are forced out. 'What is it?' 'What's that?' 'Oh fearful!' 'Why do you do this?' 'What's he?' A common exclamation is 'Ha!' Some of Webster's favourite words are 'foul', 'mist' and 'dunghill'. The dialogue, when not fabulously ornamental, is direct and rapid, almost a whisper. 'Can you guess?' 'No.' 'Do not ask then.'

The play might be described as morbid or as grotesque, the English version of *Grand Guignol*, were it not for the fact that it is possessed by a wild and almost frantic energy. That energy is part of the characters' desperation, their vitality and misery mingling in frightful images of fever and of death. They seem to be possessed by will and desire rather than belief; they are united only in the quest for survival in an unstable world. They run towards darkness. This is in fact a most significant image of the age and one to which, as we shall see, Hobbes's *Leviathan* is addressed. Indeed, this is a world from which God seems to have departed, leaving it in 'a mist'. There seems to be no meaning in the abyss of darkness that opens beneath their feet. It was also a time when, in the work of Francis Bacon, the natural world was being stripped of its association with the divine presence.

Where some like Bacon were possessed by the possibilities of progress in the natural sciences, others believed that the world was in the process of fatal decline. When in 1612 Galileo discovered the presence of spots upon the face of the sun, it was considered to be proof that even the heavens were in a state of dissolution.

Yet proof of decay also lay closer to home, and much of the atmosphere of *The Duchess of Malfi* is conveyed by the image of a corrupt court.

A Prince's court
Is like a common fountain, whence should flow
Pure silver-drops in general. But if't chance
Some cursed example poison't near the head
Death and diseases through the whole land spread.

This is likely to be an indirect allusion to the court of James I, already rendered suspect by whispers of corruption and malfeasance. The loss or abdication of authority is a context for the disorientation and instability that afflict all of the characters. That is why it is a play of scepticism, disillusion and disgust united in an overwhelming pessimism.

Pleasure of life, what is't? Only the good hours
Of an ague . . .

The figure of melancholy, therefore, might be used as the frontispiece to the play. Melancholy was the time's delight, its presiding deity. It had its own dark dress and its own music in the compositions of John Dowland such as 'In darkness let me dwell' and 'Flow my tears'. That pensive, fearful and tearful mood also had its greatest celebration and exposition in the reign of James with the publication of Robert Burton's *The Anatomy of Melancholy*. Burton was the master of melancholy in all its moods and phases. His great volume – more than 1,200 pages in its modern form – was first published in 1621 and went through six editions in his own lifetime.

Burton professed that 'all the world is melancholy, or mad, dotes, and every member of it'. We sense here the curiosity of his prose, at once precise and unsettled; it is a characteristically Jacobean touch. Melancholy is a disease both grievous and common, which he describes as 'a kind of dotage without a fever, having for his ordinary companions, fear and sadness, without any apparent occasion'.

So Burton follows it through all its declensions and divisions, its intervals and digressions; he creates three 'partitions' with a variety of sections and subsections into which the various types and forms of melancholy are arranged. There are sections entitled

'Miseries of Scholars', 'The Force of Imagination', 'Poverty and Want', 'Unfortunate Marriage' and 'Old Age'. He devotes a passage to 'Symptoms of Maids', Nuns' and Widows' Melancholy'. Hundreds of pages are consumed by 'Love Melancholy' and 'Religious Melancholy'. The madness, if such it is, can be caused by stars or spirits, by the quality of meat or wine, by catarrh or constipation, by bad air or immoderate exercise, by idleness or solitariness, by anger or discontent, by poverty or servitude or shame.

All was grist to his capacious mill, and he striates his narrative with stories, anecdotes, digressions, quotations, aphorisms and the most colourful detail. 'A young merchant going to Nordeling Fair in Germany, for ten days' space never went to stool; at his return he was grievously melancholy, thinking that he was robbed, and would not be persuaded but that all his money was gone . . . a Jew in France (saith Lodovicus Vives) came by chance over a dangerous passage or plank that lay over a brook, in the dark, without harm; the next day, perceiving what danger he was in, he fell down dead.'

He describes the inner working of obsessive temperaments who are 'to your thinking very intent and busy, still that toy runs in their minds, that fear, that suspicion, that abuse, that jealousy, that agony, that vexation, that cross, that castle in the air, that crotchet, that whimsy, that fiction, that pleasant waking dream, whatsoever it is'. He piles up heaps of words and throws himself into them; he has different voices, and different tones; he elaborates, and then qualifies his elaborations; he can be inconsistent and even contradictory. No opinion is stable, no judgement is certain. On eventually finishing the volume, you may feel that you know everything or that you know nothing.

He anatomized himself. He professed that 'I write of melancholy, by being busy to avoid melancholy'. He was a student of Christ Church, Oxford, until the time of his death, and he confessed that 'I have lived a silent, sedentary, solitary, private life, *mihi et musis* [for myself and the muses] in the university, as long almost as Xenocrates in Athens . . .' He was a cormorant of books whose library of 1,700 volumes of forgotten lore was both his refuge and his inspiration. Burton was the magpie scholar, curator of the world's learning, a lord of books who hoped that by quilting together references and allusions and quotations he could stitch so strong a cloth that he would be able to cover himself with it. He makes reference to more than 1,250 authors. His is a book in praise of books and a literary fancy in praise of reading. He wished to fashion an incantation to exorcize melancholy. The book concludes with an aphorism, 'Be not solitary, be not idle', and an epigraph:

SPERATE MISERI
CAVETE FELICES

You that are unhappy, hope. You that are happy, fear.

We are close, perhaps, to the religious spirit of the age. Lancelot Andrewes, bishop of Winchester, had on many occasions preached before James in the royal chapel and was well known to the court as he mounted the pulpit at Whitehall. He was tall and slim, with a long narrow face and expressive hands; he had a neatly trimmed beard and high forehead. In the winter of 1622 he had preached from the words of the text taken from St Matthew, '*vidimus enim stellam Ejus*', 'For we have seen his star':

> *Vidimus stellam*. We can well conceive that: any that will but look up, may see a star. But how could they see the *Ejus* of it, that it was His? Either that it belonged to any, or that He it was it belonged to. This passeth all perspective: no astronomy could show them this. What by course of nature the stars can produce, that they by course of art or observation may discover. But this birth was above nature. No trigon, triplicity, exaltation could bring it forth. They are but idle that set figures for it. The star should not have been His, but He the star's, if it had gone that way. Some other light, then, they saw this *Ejus* by.

The style is hard and elliptical, almost tortuous in its slow unwinding of the sense. It relies upon repetition and alliteration, parallel and antithesis. It is knotty and difficult, almost impossible for the hearers fully to understand. Yet it is the devotional style of the Jacobean period, fully mastered by a king who prided himself on his scholarship and erudition. Andrewes hovers over a word, even a syllable, eliciting its meaning by minute degrees; he is constantly questioning, refining and rephrasing. He does not express a thought but, rather, the process of thought itself; he dramatizes the act, or art, of creative reasoning. This is the luxuriant etymology of Jacobean scholarship, similar in its strenuous tone to the prose of Francis Bacon.

'Last we consider the time of their coming, the season of the year. It was no summer progress. A cold coming they had of it at this time of the year, just the worst time of the year to take a journey, and especially a long journey. The ways deep, the weather sharp, the days short, the sun farthest off, in *solsitio brumali*, O the very dead of winter.' The prose is disciplined and pure, evincing clarity of thought and expression as well as a great power of ordered analysis. It may not possess the inspired eloquence or impassioned fervour of the great Elizabethan preachers, but it is marked by what T. S. Eliot described as 'ordonnance, precision, and relevant intensity'. Andrewes moves forward in pulses of light; he stops and repeats a phrase for more lucidity; he is always reaching out for the full revelation of the interior sense. An association of words can lead him further forward, caressing or coaxing their intention; he professed that such meanings can 'strike any man into an ecstacy'.

The soaring cadence and expressive emotionalism evident in the sermons of John Donne may seem a world away from the concerted pressure of Andrewes's words; the articulations of any one culture, however, will not be very far apart. On 13 November 1622, the month before the bishop of Winchester gave his sermon to the king on the journey of the Magi, John Donne, the dean of St Paul's, entered the pulpit of the cathedral.

> The first word of the text is the cardinal word, the word, the hinge, upon which the whole text turns. The first word, *But*, is the *But*, that all the rest shoots at. First it is an exclusive word: something the Apostles had required, which might not be had; not that; and it is an inclusive word; something Christ was pleased to afford to the apostles, which they thought not of; not that, not that which you beat upon, *But*, but yet, something else, something better than that, you shall have.

The rapid associations are like a sudden peal of bells.

For Donne the sermon was a species of erudite oratory, a performance that like the plays of the Jacobean tragic stage would surprise and delight the audience. He must remind his auditors of the damnation of being 'secluded eternally, eternally, eternally, from the sight of God'. He must move and direct their emotions or else he had failed. That is why he exerts all the power of the macabre that John Webster had employed. So in one sermon Donne reminds his hearers that 'between that excremental jelly that thy body is made of at first, and that jelly which thy body dissolves to at last; there is not so noisome, so putrid a thing in nature'.

The settled truths of the old medieval faith had utterly gone. It was now necessary to argue and to convince. In this endeavour Lancelot Andrewes and John Donne were united. Yet this meant that they were sometimes engaged in tortuous and self-involved trials of the spirit; this was in many respects a sceptical, ambiguous and ambivalent age, at least in direct comparison with its predecessors, and against that unstable background both preachers protested and declaimed.

The syntactic parallels and paradoxes of both churchmen are attempts to riddle out individual truths and certainties from ambiguous matter. They needed to convince as much as to inspire their hearers. Yet the sermons are characterized by the caustic rhetoric that is so much part of the period. Donne preached that 'sects are not bodies, they are but rotten boughs, gangrened limbs, fragmentary chips, blown off by their own spirit of turbulency, fallen off by the weight of their own pride . . .' The immediacy and urgency of the language, with its rough cadence, are also part of Donne's secular poetry. We may note the pessimism and melancholy, anatomized in an earlier part of this chapter, that also underlie his being in the world. In one of his meditations he enquires about the source of his disease. 'They tell me that it is my melancholy. Did I infuse, did I drink in melancholy into my self? It is my thoughtfulness; was I not made to think? It is my study; doth not my calling call for that?' This is the true music of the Jacobean period, now come to a close.

11

Vivat rex

Charles Stuart had become king of England at the age of twenty-four. He was proclaimed on the same day as his father's death, 27 March 1625, and a contemporary at Cambridge wrote that 'we had thunder the same day, presently on the proclamation, and 'twas a cold season, but all fears and sorrows are swallowed up in joy of so hopeful a successor'. Had the new king not put himself at the head of the anti-Spanish alliance in England?

He was more severe and reserved than his father, with a strong sense of formality and order, and the change of tone at court was soon evident. Charles announced that during the reign of his 'most dear and royal father' idle and unnecessary people had thronged the court, bringing 'much dishonour to our house'. There were to be no more bawds or catamites. The new king had been impressed by the decorum of the Spanish court, where he had spent many months; he appreciated the privacy by which the royal family was protected, and the gravitas with which courtly affairs were conducted. The moral tone appealed to a young man who had become dismayed by the laxness and libertinism of his father's court. He began to dress in black. In the preface to his orders for the royal household he remarked that his purpose was 'to establish government and order in our court which from thence may spread with more order through all parts of our kingdom'. This art of control, however, might be more congenial in theory than in practice.

The Venetian ambassador noted that within days of his accession 'the king observes a rule of great decorum. The nobles do not enter his apartments in confusion as heretofore, but each rank has its appointed place.' The ambassador also reported that the king had drawn up rules and regulations that divided his day, from first rising, into separate compartments; there was a time for praying and a time for exercising, a time for business and a time for audiences, a time for eating and a time for sleeping. He did not wish his subjects to be introduced to him without warning; they were only to be sent for. Servants proffered meals to him on their bended knees, and such was the protocol around royal dining that he seldom if ever ate a hot meal; food took too long to serve. Whenever he washed his hands, those parts of the towel he touched were raised above the head of the gentleman usher who removed it from the royal presence.

Charles set to work in earnest at the beginning of April when he asked Buckingham and other grandees to review all aspects of foreign policy; the fraught relationship with Spain, and a possible alliance with France, were to be considered in the light of Charles's desire to recover the Palatinate for his brother-in-law. A committee was established, a few days later, in order to supervise the nation's defences in case of war. The new king then set up two further commissions to investigate financial fraud by the collectors of the customs and to examine the trade of the East India Company with Russia. It was a business-like start but, as is generally the case with the work of committees and commissions, it achieved very little.

Buckingham was still the principal councillor, as he had been in the reign of James; he stayed in the company of the king all day, and slept in a room next to the royal bedchamber. He possessed the golden key that allowed him entrance to all the apartments of the palace. It seemed that nothing could be done without him. He had an almost vice-regal status and was in part able to compensate for the king's unskilfulness in persuasion and management.

Charles had a stutter which, together with his want of natural fluency in conversation, led him to confess once that 'I know I am not good to speak much'. When he was a child his doctors had tried to cure the problem by putting small stones in his mouth, but this had provided no benefit. He tried to form complete sentences in his mind before uttering them, but the impediment remained. He was always shy and hesitant in speech. So he communicated with his household servants by means of gestures as much as words.

One of his principal advisers at a later date, the earl of Clarendon, noted that his insecurity led him to adopt the suggestions, or yield to the influence, of men who were in fact less capable than himself. He never really discerned the true merits or vices of those around him; he tended to confide in those who were merely boasters and adventurers while ignoring those of real, if silent, merit. The council about him consisted of professional courtiers, many of whom had been close to his father, while the others were friends or trusted servants. The principal decisions, however, were diverted from the full council to selective small groups or committees; suspicion and jealousy were therefore rife.

His first public appearance, in April, was at the port of Blackwall, on the north bank of the Thames, where he visited the royal fleet. He was small, just a little over 5 feet in height, and might be described as rather delicate than otherwise. Yet he had disciplined and trained himself in healthy exercise, so that his slight exterior was deceptive. He was of a pale complexion, set off in his youth by curly chestnut hair; he had a long face with grey eyes and full lips. He was of temperate habits, preferring plain beer to spiced wines, and of an apparently cool and dispassionate nature. He always blushed if he overheard indecent talk. If he could command his own passions, however, he might be able to control those of his kingdom. He collected aphorisms from the Stoics and neo-Stoics on the importance of cultivating detachment from the pressing issues of the moment. 'We have learnt to own ourself by retiring into ourself,' he once said. Yet acute observers, among them portrait painters, were able to sense that he concealed secret or hidden tension. His pace was rapid and hurried.

The potentially dangerous matter of his marriage to the French Catholic princess, Henrietta Maria, soon became the principal topic of London gossip. Many in the court, and in the country, deplored the alliance with a devotee of Rome and conjured up old fears of papal domination. Yet Charles was not inclined to heed any warnings. He had a Scottish father, a Danish mother, and a half-French grandmother in the person of Mary Queen of Scots; he was the perfect representative of the fact that the royal families of Europe were not necessarily nationalist or religious partisans.

The marriage was celebrated by proxy, on 1 May 1625, in front of the west door of Notre Dame; on the same day the king issued a declaration that 'all manner of prosecution' against Roman Catholics should 'be stayed and forborne, provided always that they behave themselves modestly therein'. This had been one of the stumbling blocks in the Spanish negotiations of previous years and a contemporary, John Chamberlain, now complained that 'we are out of the frying-pan into the fire'. In the middle of the month Buckingham himself travelled to Paris in order to accompany Henrietta Maria across the Channel and to expedite the proposed alliance between England and France; he hoped to persuade the French king to treat his Protestant subjects, the Huguenots, with the same tact as Charles was now displaying to the Catholics. He also wished to draw the French into open warfare against the Spanish. In both respects he was unsuccessful, and in any case his flair or arrogance was not to the taste of Louis XIII. He is reported to have worn a white satin suit sewn all over with diamonds, and to have flirted with the wife of the French king; he also danced a saraband in front of her dressed as a Pantaloon.

Henrietta Maria eventually arrived at Dover on 12 June and was taken to the castle where Charles rode to meet her. She seemed to be taller than he anticipated, and she noticed him glancing at her feet in case she were wearing shoes like stepladders. 'Sir,' she said, 'I stand upon mine own feet; I have no helps by art. Thus high I am, and am neither higher nor lower.' She had spirit, therefore, and was described by an English observer, Joseph Mead, as 'nimble and quick . . . in a word, a brave lady'. She was fifteen years old. Soon after her arrival she was discomfited by too much company in an overheated room. Mead reported that 'with one frown . . . she drove us all out of the chamber. I suppose none but a queen could have cast such a scowl.'

A new parliament for the new reign was of paramount importance. Charles would have been happy to recall the old one, since it had favoured his anti-Spanish cause, but he was informed that the death of James had brought it to an end. He should have known this element of constitutional practice. A parliament had been called for May, but the onset of the plague in thirteen parishes of the city led to its postponement for a month. Charles opened the assembly with a speech in which he pressed for money to finance the recovery of the Palatinate. It is not at all clear, however, that the members wished to be drawn into a continental war and instead they seemed intent on domestic matters. After they had observed a day of fasting, they delivered to the king a 'pious petition' in which was demanded the immediate execution of 'all the existing laws against Catholic recusants and missionaries'. The king had married a Catholic princess and, against the opinion of the country, had granted toleration to her co-religionists. The wrath of the Commons was then turned against one of the king's chaplains, Richard Montagu, who in a theological tract effectively denied the Calvinist notion of predestination; the book was declared to be in contempt of the house, and the unfortunate divine was taken into custody.

Only now were the king's finances given consideration. His plea for wartime expenditure was not taken very seriously, on the good grounds that no proper plans or policies had been brought forward. The incompetence of Buckingham, in the ill-timed and ill-executed march towards Breda at the end of the previous reign, was also borne in mind; why give money to inept commanders? 'We know yet of no war,' Sir Robert Phelips said, 'nor of any enemy.' Parliament proposed to give to the king only one tenth of the sum which he had anticipated and, to compound the offence, the customs duties of tonnage and poundage were granted for only one year. All of his predecessors, ever since the time of Henry VI (1421–71), had been awarded them for the duration of their reigns. It is likely that the duties of one year were in fact only a temporary measure, until parliament had the opportunity to debate a permanent settlement. Yet this session had set a precedent. The resistance to increased taxation, and opposition to the king's religious policy, would be the prime movers of later discontent.

Charles was indignant at his lack of success, but he had no

strategy to deal with any parliamentary opposition; he had simply expected that his orders would be followed. Before any remonstrance could be entertained, in any case, the plague intervened. One courtier told his son that 'I . . . in earnest do marvel that anyone who may be called reasonable would be now in London'. The tolling of the neighbourhood bells could clearly be heard in the chamber of the Commons. Joseph Mead wrote, on 2 July, to one of his correspondents that 'my Lord Russell being to go to parliament, had his shoemaker to pull on his boots, who fell down dead of the plague in his presence'. On 11 July parliament was adjourned, to be convened once more in Oxford at the beginning of August.

The change of location did nothing to curb the rising hostility of the members to king and court. On a motion of Sir Edward Coke at the beginning of the session, the subsidies to the king were set to be thoroughly investigated, thus implying that parliament had the power to regulate the king's income at will. Another member rose brandishing a pardon the king had issued to a Jesuit, just the day after he had promised to uphold the 'pious petition' against Roman Catholics. A general silence followed. This affected the integrity and honour of the sovereign. It was agreed that they should wait to hear Charles's response. Charles had made contradictory promises to the French king and to parliament. Which would be the first to be broken?

Charles arrived from Woodstock three days later, and summoned the members to meet him in the hall of Christ Church. His mind was on matters of finance rather than of religion. He needed money for the fleet that Buckingham had collected, but the exchequer was bare. He found that his 'credit' was as yet too slim 'to set forth that navy now preparing'. He was, as usual, spare of words. He said that he would answer the religious petitions in two days' time.

It was still not at all clear how much money was required and to what purpose it would be put. Was a naval war against Spain contemplated? Or would an army be transported to aid the Palatinate? No one in the administration spoke with a certain voice. Why should the members of the Commons support a policy that they did not understand and upon which they had not been consulted? One declared that it would be better if parliament concentrated upon domestic and financial affairs, of which it did have cognizance, rather than concern itself with foreign imbroglios.

Buckingham now came under attack. It could be inferred from the speeches against him that he was incapable of controlling the government or of organizing any credible war effort. So now he bent with the wind. The information was conveyed that he and his master had never really believed in religious toleration for its own sake; it was merely a device to woo the Spanish and then the French. Buckingham was supposed to believe that the religious treaty drawn up with Louis XIII was merely for the sake of form, a piece of paper to appease the pope. The king, with his connivance, was ready to cultivate the Commons by turning on the Catholics.

'If you mean to put the laws into execution,' an envoy from the French court, Father Berulle, told him, 'I neither can nor will endure it, whatever sauce you may be pleased to add.'

'Begone,' Buckingham is supposed to have replied. 'I know that you are only at home in your breviary and your Mass.'

But the duke's evident lack of principle or consistency did not necessarily endear him to parliament. He had gathered together a fleet to boost his standing in the popular cause of war against Spain, but there was no money fully to prepare it. He was deemed to be too young, too rash and too inexperienced. In the ensuing debate, Sir Francis Seymour called out, 'Let us lay the fault where it is.' He then named the duke of Buckingham. Sir Edward Coke, sensing misgovernment and self-serving administrators, declared that 'the ship hath a great leak'. This was coming too close to the king. On 11 August he and his council decided that it was not fit for this parliament to continue. The excuse of the plague, steadily encroaching upon Oxford, was used to save Buckingham from possible impeachment. Where Charles believed that he was defending an honest and faithful minister, the parliamentarians were of the opinion that they were protecting the nation against a selfish and incapable favourite. The Oxford parliament had lasted eleven days. Charles blamed a few troublemakers and 'seditious men' for the turmoil, a miscalculation he would also make in later years.

It is already possible to gauge something of the king's character. He truly believed that his regal authority was paramount and that parliament was merely a compliant instrument to finance his requirements in war and peace. The simple declaration of his wishes was sufficient to command obedience. On state papers he would scrawl, 'Let it be done. C.R.' He had certain firm convictions that could not be altered by arguments or by events; if you agreed with him, you were a friend, but any who questioned his judgement were enemies from that moment forward. Once he had formulated a policy, he maintained it to the end. He could never see the point of view of anyone but himself, and this lack of imagination would one day cost him the throne.

He was so convinced of the rightness of his cause that he never acquired the easiness and bonhomie of either his father or his son. He remained to most of his subjects cold and reserved. The Venetian ambassador wrote that 'this king is so constituted by nature that he never obliges anyone, either by word or deed'. In succeeding years he would become enmeshed in the problems caused by his inability to use tact or craft in the affairs of the world. He once told a churchman that he could never have become a lawyer because 'I cannot defend a bad, nor yield in a good, cause'. He was in other words too righteous for his own good, or for the good of his kingdom.

The official war against Spain was declared in the early autumn of 1625, and in the same period a treaty was established between England and the Dutch republic. Yet the perennial problem of finance had not been solved and, as a desperate remedy, it was proposed that the crown jewels should be sold. The soldiers had been pressed into service but they remained unpaid; they roamed about Plymouth, where the people of south Devon would not or could not supply them with food. So the hungry men killed the available sheep and oxen in front of them. Three of their captains were named Bag, Cook and Love; the joke soon spread that they were Bag without money, Cook without Meat and Love without charity. This was a period when rumours spread throughout the country that the king had been touched by the plague; the report was untrue, but it represented the uncertain atmosphere of the time.

The English fleet under the command of Sir Edward Cecil, who had first seen service in the reign of Elizabeth, finally left harbour on 8 October after much abortive sailing through wind and rain. Its principal purpose was as yet undecided, except that it should in some way strike a blow against the Spanish coast. A council of war was called while the ships were at sea, when it was decided that an assault should be attempted upon Cadiz. The spirits of the men were raised when, at the advance of the English, the Spanish vessels fled the scene. The fort of Puntal, guarding the entrance to Cadiz harbour, was taken; but the attack had alerted the Spanish authorities to the dangers faced by the town.

While a blockade of Cadiz was attempted, news reached Cecil and his commanders that a large Spanish force was on its way to save the town; the English soldiers were disembarked and hurried to meet the threat, but the report was false. No enemy was in sight. Their forced march under a hot Spanish sun, however, had left them without provisions. Casks of wine were taken from neighbouring villages and dwellings; the men gorged themselves on the drink until they were senseless. It was said that every man became his own vintner. The Spanish defenders of Cadiz fell upon them and engaged in a general frenzy of slaughter. The siege of Cadiz, and the occupation of Puntal, were therefore abandoned in embarrassing failure.

The English vessels had also been charged to intercept the Spanish silver sailing from Mexico, but they were in no condition to confront anything. Their hulks were rotten, and their tackle frail. Whether through corruption or neglect, their supplies had been insufficient from the beginning. The drink, possibly a medley of wine and water, was foul; the food was evil-smelling 'so as no dog in Paris Garden would eat it'. Paris Garden was part of the noisome suburb of Southwark. In the middle of November Cecil ordered his ships to return to England. It was a complete, and humiliating, fiasco. An enquiry was held, but such was the conflicting evidence and prejudiced testimony that it was considered best to bury the matter in a public silence.

An attempt was then made to avert the wrath of the country. At the beginning of November the execution of the penal laws against the Catholics was instituted once more; the fines and confiscations were to be used for the defence of the realm. It was reported that at Whitehall 'they look strange on a papist'. Yet there was no stronger papist than the queen. Charles's disillusion with Louis XIII for failing to assist him now seems to have extended to his sister, and especially to her entourage of Capuchin friars. Their rituals and orisons were not welcome at the English court, in which Buckingham was still hoping to lead a Protestant league against Spanish and imperial pretensions.

The king and queen were dining together when her Catholic confessor tried to anticipate the grace being said by a Protestant cleric. He began praying in Latin, in a loud voice, according to Joseph Mead, 'with such a confusion, that the king, in a great passion, instantly rose from the table, and, taking the queen by the hand, retired into the bedchamber. Was this not a priestly discretion?' Charles was heard to state that a man must be master in his own house. But he had also to prove himself master of his own kingdom.

12

A fall from grace

The day of Charles's formal coronation came on Candlemas, 2 February 1626, a little under a year since his accession to the throne. Henrietta Maria refused to accompany her husband to what she considered to be an heretical service, and so he proceeded alone; the queen watched some of the events from an apartment in the gatehouse of the palace yard. Charles did not go on the customary procession through the streets of London, however, and there was neither banquet nor masque after the ceremony; the plague was still leaving its mark. There was little rejoicing at the service itself. When the newly crowned king was presented to the people, they remained largely silent. The earl of Arundel, the lord marshal, then ordered them to cry out 'God save King Charles' at which juncture a few shouts of homage were heard.

Charles wore a cloak of white rather than a robe of regal scarlet; this was considered by many to be an unfortunate innovation in an ancient ceremony. The coronation oath was also carefully changed by William Laud, the bishop of St David's, with a prayer that the king might have 'Peter's key of discipline, Paul's doctrine'. This was not at the time considered to be ominous but, at a later date, Laud was accused of conferring absolute power upon the king to the injury of the people. Any ill will or resentment was at this time, however, largely directed against Buckingham rather than his sovereign.

Parliament met four days later in a state of seething discontent at Buckingham's mismanagement of the expedition to Cadiz. He may have tried to waive blame by pleading that he had been conducting diplomatic negotiations at the time in The Hague, but this did not satisfy the angry members. Sir John Eliot, member for St Germans in Cornwall, had witnessed the return of the fleet to Plymouth after the debacle; he had seen the men, diseased and half-starved, staggering off their ships. He had also seen some of them die in the streets, mortally infecting the people of the town. He did not forget these scenes of suffering, and he placed all the blame for them on the folly and pride of the king's favourite.

The king opened proceedings with a customary short and blunt speech. 'I mean to show what I should speak', he said, 'in actions.' He offered no apologies or explanations for what had transpired; he simply asked for more money. When Eliot rose to speak he demanded that no further supply should be granted until an account had been given of previous sums. He called for the inspection of the admiralty ledgers which, as vice-admiral of Devon, he was uniquely well placed to examine.

But he made a wider plea to the king. 'Sir, I beseech you cast your eyes about! View the state we are in! Consider the loss we have received! Weigh the wrecked and ruined honour of our nation!' Eliot might be described as one of the first great parliamentarians in English history, ready to curb the abuses of the royal prerogative. He went on to say that 'our honour is ruined, our ships are sunk, our men perished; not by the sword, not by the enemy, not by chance, but, as the strongest predictions had discerned and made it apparent beforehand, by those we trust'. The aspects of international affairs were not promising. The Catholic forces of the Holy Roman Emperor were advancing through Bohemia and Germany; the Protestants of France were being threatened, and even destroyed, by the French king.

A committee was established in order to enquire into the problems of the state finances, but it came to no settled conclusions. On 10 March, therefore, Charles let it be known that he wished for an immediate supply for the necessities of the state without any further questions of his past or future conduct being raised. The statement raised the temperature of the debates. The member for Boroughbridge,

Sir Ferdinando Fairfax, wrote to his father that 'if we give nothing, we not only incense the king, who is in his own nature extremely stiff, but endanger a ruin of the commonweal, as things now stand; and if we do give, it may perhaps not be employed in the right way, and the more we part with, the more we shall want another time to bestow'.

It was now generally believed that the cause of all grievances was the duke of Buckingham. He had appointed incompetent officers and was responsible for the calamity at Cadiz. He had taken Crown lands for his friends and family. He had sold many of the offices of state and acquired others for his own aggrandizement. His mother and his father-in-law were both recusants, and might be considered enemies of the state. He was the man to be named.

The king replied to the parliamentarians at Whitehall five days later in a speech in which he declared that 'I would not have the House to question my servants, much less one that is so near me'. He added that 'I would you would hasten for my supply, or else it will be worse for yourselves, for if any ill happen, I think I shall be the last that shall feel it'. Sir John Eliot, addressing his colleagues two days later, counselled steadfastness. 'We have had a representation of great fear,' he said, 'but I hope that shall not darken our understandings.' The king once more ordered them to desist. 'Remember', Charles told them, 'that parliaments are altogether in my power for their calling, sitting, and dissolution; therefore, as I find their fruits good or evil, they are to continue, or not to be.'

The Commons, in no mood now for retreat, still pursued the duke; they were hounds slipped off the leash, all the more confident because they knew that the Lords were supporting them; the nobility, too, had had enough of the overweening favourite. The old peerage were incensed by his control of patronage and by his domination of the king. The earl of Bristol, who as ambassador at the court of Spain had witnessed the conduct of Buckingham in Madrid, brought his own testimony against the favourite. He charged him with the attempt to change the prince's religion; he accused him of kneeling to the sacrament 'to give the Spaniards a hope of the prince's conversion'. He was in effect denouncing Buckingham for treason.

The king was irate at what he considered to be the vainglory of the houses. Yet they were not to be diverted. On 10 May a deputation was drawn up to prepare the articles of impeachment against Buckingham; one of its members, Sir Dudley Digges, stated in perhaps unprecedented terms that 'the laws of England have taught us that kings cannot command ill or unlawful things. And whatsoever ill events succeed, the executioners of such designs must answer for them.' Digges also compared Buckingham to a comet, exhaled 'out of base and putrid matter'. When the members of the deputation presented themselves to Buckingham, however, it was reported that he laughed in their faces. The duke knew the loyalty, or rigidity, of the king. Charles would never abandon him.

The day of the impeachment debate was an occasion for passion and theatrical confrontation. When one member, John Glanville, delivered an exordium in favour of parliament Buckingham 'jeered and fleered' him. 'My lord,' Glanville replied, 'do you jeer me? Are these things to be jeered at? My lord, I can show you a man of greater blood than your lordship, as high in place and power, and as deep in the favour of the king as you, who hath been hanged for as small a crime as the least of these articles contain.'

Sir John Eliot rose to launch a general invective against the favourite. 'What vast treasures he has gotten! What infinite sums of money, and what a mass of lands!' The banquets, the buildings, the costumes, the gold and the silver were the visible tokens of his greed; his wealth was keeping the sovereign, and the nation, poor. Eliot then hinted at the prevailing rumour that Buckingham and his mother had poisoned James I. He compared the duke to a legendary beast, known to the ancients as Stellionatus, that was 'so blurred, so spotted' that it was filled with foulness. By this extraordinary speech, the king was of course much offended.

On the following day, 11 May, the king visited the Lords where he tried to exonerate Buckingham from all the charges attached to him by the Commons. 'I can bear witness,' he said, 'to clear him in every one of them.' On the same day the lower house broke up in turmoil when it was discovered that Sir John Eliot and Sir Dudley Digges had been taken to the Tower. When the Speaker rose on 12 May to commence business he was told to 'sit down'. There was to be 'no business until we are righted in our liberties'. The French ambassador warned the king that if his power did not prevail, he would be as impotent as the doge of Venice, who could do nothing without the approval of his senate.

Parliament stood firm and finally prevailed. Within a week both Digges and Eliot were set at liberty. It was not a good precedent for the king, who appeared to be resolute but in truth prevaricated. He then compounded the offence by appointing Buckingham to be chancellor of the university at Cambridge; such was the displeasure of the Commons that they drew up a general remonstrance for Buckingham's dismissal from public life.

The war of words now intensified. Charles responded with the demand that parliament should proceed immediately to pass a Subsidy Bill, furnishing him with more funds, or he would be obliged 'to use other resolutions'. The Commons debated the matter and decided that the remonstrance should come before any bill for subsidies. They had not in fact proved the charges of venality and corruption laid against Buckingham, but they now pressed for his forced resignation on the sole grounds that the Commons did not trust him. If they succeeded in their purpose, their authority would then outweigh that of the sovereign himself.

If parliament on the other hand were forced to yield, and to grant Charles supply without the redress of grievances, it would set an unfortunate precedent in which the king might be the permanent victor; the members did not, in a current phrase, wish to give posterity a cause to curse them. Court and parliament, at cross-purposes one with another, had reached an impasse. A conversation between the king and Buckingham was overheard and widely reported. 'I have in a manner lost the love of my subjects,' Charles is supposed to have told him. 'What wouldst thou have me do?' On 14 June the king determined to dissolve parliament. The Lords begged for two days more to resolve the situation. The king replied quickly enough. 'Not a minute.'

The day before the dissolution of what was called 'this great, warm, ruffling parliament' a storm of thunder, lightning and hail fell upon the Thames at Westminster and created the phenomenon of a 'whirlwater' or 'water-pillar'. The water was dissolved into a mist and formed a great revolving funnel some 30 yards across and 10 feet in height; the interior was hollow and white with froth. This prodigy of nature crossed the Thames and then began to beat against the walls of the garden of York House, the residence of the duke of Buckingham; as it struck against the bricks it broke into a thick smoke, as if it came from a chimney, and rose high into the air. It then vanished out of sight with two or three peals of thunder. It was considered to be an omen, and perhaps a warning to the duke himself.

Handbills were printed on clandestine presses and distributed through the streets of London.

> Who rules the kingdom? *The king.*
> Who rules the king? *The duke.*
> Who rules the duke? *The devil.*

Three days after the dissolution the king ordered that all copies of the parliamentary remonstrance against Buckingham should be destroyed. By continuing to favour the duke, Charles had provoked a determined and vocal opposition in parliament; the antagonism did not as yet directly touch the person of the king himself, but there were some who looked ahead to possible changes in public affairs. A great constitutional historian, Leopold von Ranke, once suggested that the coming conflict between king and parliament was the product of 'historical necessity'; whether we accept the phrase or not, it is at least evident that there were forces at work that could not easily be contained or averted.

In the course of this parliament, amid the turmoil of domestic affairs, the bishops had also been considering the issues of religion. In particular they had debated the controversy between the puritan members of the Church and those who were already known as 'Arminians'. These latter were the clergy who believed in the primacy of order and ritual in the customary ceremonies; they preached against predestination and in favour of the sacraments, and had already earned the condemnation of the Calvinists at the Synod of Dort seven years earlier. Some of them were dismissed as mere papists under another name, but in fact they were as much estranged from the Catholic communion as they were from the puritan congregation; they wished for a purified national Church, and their most significant supporter was already William Laud, a prominent bishop now in royal favour. The English Arminians in turn became known as 'Laudians', with one of their central precepts concerning 'the beauty of holiness' by which they meant genuflections and bowings as well as painted images. There was even room to be made for an incense pot.

The Arminians had been in an equivocal position during the previous reign because of James's residual Calvinist sympathies and his unwillingness to countenance doctrinal controversy. His son was made of sterner, or more unbending, material. In the weeks after James's death, Bishop Laud prepared for the new king a list of senior churchmen, with the letters 'O' or 'P' appended to their names; 'O' meant orthodox and 'P' signalled a puritan. So the lines were drawn.

The powerful bias towards 'adoration', with all the ritual and formality it implied, was deeply congenial to the young king who had already brought order and ceremony to his court; just as he delighted in masques, so he wished for a religion of splendour and mystery. Charles had in any case a deep aversion to puritanism in all of its forms, which he associated with disobedience and the dreadful notion of 'popularity'; he thought of cobblers and tailors and sharp-tongued dogmatists. Above all else he wanted a well-ordered and disciplined Church, maintaining undeviating policies as well as uniform customs, with the bishops as its principal representatives. It was to be a bulwark in his defence of national stability. Laud himself used to quote the phrase '*stare super antiquas vias*' – it was important to stand upon ancient roads.

With a sermon delivered in the summer of 1626, Laud aimed a direct hit against the puritans by claiming that the Calvinists were essentially anti-authoritarian and therefore anti-monarchical. In the following year George Abbot was deprived of his powers as archbishop of Canterbury and replaced by a commission of anti-Calvinist bishops. When one Calvinist bishop, Davenant of Salisbury, delivered a sermon in which he defended the doctrine of predestination, he was summoned before the privy council; after the prelate had kissed the king's hand, Charles informed him that 'he would not have this high point meddled withal or debated, either the one way or the other, because it was too high for the people's understanding'. After 1628 no Calvinist preachers were allowed to stand at Paul's

Cross, the centre for London sermons. A joke soon followed, asking a question about the Arminians' beliefs.

'What do the Arminians hold?'
'All the best livings in England.'

Yet the Calvinists, and the puritans, did not go gently into the dark. The victory of the Laudian cause in the king's counsels, more than anything else, stirred the enmity between opposing religious camps that defined the last years of his reign. It should be added, however, that these doctrinal discontents wafted over the heads of most parish clergy and their congregations who attended church as a matter of habit and took a simple attitude towards the gospels and the commandments.

Within a few weeks of the dissolution of parliament Charles finally determined to banish his wife's priests and ladies-in-waiting from his court. While parliament had still been in session the queen's religious counsellors advised her to go on a pilgrimage to Tyburn, in bare feet, in order to pray for the souls of those Catholics who had been executed there. It was soon murmured she had offered up her prayers for the cause of dead traitors rather than of martyrs.

Resentment, and even anger, had already risen between husband and wife. She was merry enough with her French followers but in the presence of the king she was sullen and morose; she apparently took no delight in his company. They quarrelled over her wish to distribute some of her lands and houses among her entourage. 'Take your lands to yourself,' Charles himself reports her as saying. 'If I have no power to put whom I will into these places, I will have neither lands nor houses of you. Give me what you think fit by way of pension.'

'Remember to whom you speak,' the king replied. 'You ought not to use me so.'

They continued to argue and, in the king's own recollection of the scene, 'then I made her both hear me and end that discourse'. The court, too, had ears.

At the beginning of August, after a meeting of the privy council, Charles called for the queen. She declined the invitation on the grounds that she had a toothache. So with his council in attendance he proceeded to the queen's private chambers where he found her

French attendants, according to a contemporary letter-writer, Mr Pory, 'unreverently dancing and curvetting in her presence'. He summarily brought the party to a close, and took Henrietta Maria to his own chambers where he told her that he was sending the French attendants back to Paris 'for the good of herself and the nation'. The queen was momentarily bewildered but then, in a fit of temper or frustration, broke the windows in the chamber with her bare hands in order to speak to her people in the courtyard below. Whereupon the women 'howled and lamented as if they were going to an execution'.

The loudest protests could not prevail against the king's angry will. For some days the French refused to leave the queen's court. At that point Charles lost all patience. He commanded Buckingham 'to send all the French away tomorrow out of the town; if you can, by fair means – but stick not long in disputing – otherwise force them away, driving them away like so many wild beasts until you have shipped them, and so the devil go with them! Let me hear of no answer but the performance of my command.' He could use a peremptory tone even with his favourite.

Eventually, under the escort of the Yeomen of the Guard, the French boarded the vessels for their return. As they went down to the Thames by the river stairs of Denmark House, a crowd of Londoners hooted and jeered at them; one of them threw a stone that knocked off the hat of Mme de Saint-Georges. The whole episode incensed the French king, who told the English envoy that his sister had been cruelly treated. It was not a propitious moment to alienate Louis XIII.

The dissolution of the parliament, for example, led ineluctably to urgent attempts to raise money for the king's war against Spain. A loan of £100,000 was requested from the merchants of London, with the crown jewels as security. The appeal was denied. In the following month it was proposed that the freeholders of the various counties would provide a 'free gift' to the Crown; the clergy were ordered 'to stir up all sorts of people to express their zeal to God and their duty to the king'. Charles also decided that he must continue to levy the customs revenues of 'tonnage and poundage' even though parliament had not given its consent. When contributions to the 'free gift' were about to be collected in Westminster

Hall, the cry was raised of 'A parliament! A parliament!' Throughout August and September the refusal to contribute to the king's coffers became widespread. It was then decreed that the king's plate should be sold.

In the middle of August 200 pressed soldiers and sailors made their weary way from Portsmouth to London in order to demand the money still owed to them. By chance or design they came upon the duke of Buckingham's coach; they stopped it and pleaded for redress. Buckingham promised to deal with their demands later in the day, but he escaped by way of the Thames and returned to the security of York House. This was in any case a time of deep distress among the general populace. The great nineteenth-century historian of prices, Thorold Rogers, stated that 'I am convinced, from the comparison I have been able to make between wages, rents and prices, that it was a period of excessive misery among the mass of the people and the tenants, a time in which a few might have become rich, while the many were crushed down into hopeless and almost permanent indigence'. The condition of England now looked to some to be beyond repair. One contemporary asked, 'Is it not time to pray?'

13

Take that slime away

The king's war against Spain and the imperial forces was not going well. Christian of Denmark had depended upon subsidies from his nephew, Charles, but of course no money was forthcoming; on 27 August 1626, his demoralized forces were defeated by the armies of the Catholic League at Lutter in Lower Saxony. As a result the Protestants of north-west Europe could become the prey of the imperialist armies. On hearing the news of the battle Charles abandoned his summer progress and returned to London where he told the Danish ambassador that he would defend King Christian 'even at the risk of his own crown and hazarding his life'. The king's council wished to send four regiments, each comprising 1,000 men, to Denmark, but how were they to be paid?

After the failure of the 'free gift' proposed for the king, and the small sums of money raised by the sale of his plate, the time had come for more severe and aggressive measures. In the autumn of 1626 the king imposed what was essentially a forced loan, and demanded from the counties the equivalent of five parliamentary subsidies. His decision was in part prompted by his deep reluctance to call another parliament. He would manage his finances without the meddling of certain malicious members. He wrote to the various lords-lieutenant of the counties ordering them to put forward the names of their local dignitaries, with details of the amounts they could afford; he also wrote to the peers, asking them to be generous in their financial support. He condemned those who cried out against the loans as 'certain evil-disposed persons'; he declared that he must have the money to subsidize himself and his armed forces and that the duty of all true subjects, in the absence of parliamentary agreement, was 'to be a law unto themselves'. He might have added, in a phrase of the period, that 'need knows no law'.

The general response of the country seems for once to have been favourable. The exigencies of the country, and the possible defeat of the Protestant cause, prompted most communities into payment. It was granted that, in an emergency, the king had the right to call upon special aid. The people of Thetford in Norfolk, for example, 'were all very willing to yield'. By November the forced tax had raised something close to £250,000, sufficient for the king's immediate requirements. Charles himself admitted that the money had been 'more readily furnished than I could have expected in these needy times'.

The judiciary was uncertain about the legality of any forced loan, however, and refused to sign a paper of consent to its imposition. The king called in the chief justice and dismissed him from his office as a warning and encouragement to others. He threatened to sweep all recalcitrant magistrates from their benches, but in so doing he damaged the authority of the judges as well as his own. It was reported that from this time forward they were no longer considered to be impartial or disinterested, and it was long remembered that the king had demanded the resignations of those who refused to accede to his requests. If they possessed opinions of their own, they were to be treated with contempt.

Some were still unwilling to pay the forced loan. The wealthier of these recalcitrants were summoned before the privy council, where they were either dispatched to prison or confined in private houses away from their homes and families; the poorer of them were pressed into the army or navy, where their bodies might serve instead of their money. Among those who refused payment were five knights, who decided to challenge the legality of the loan in the courts and were subsequently placed in their county prisons. They would become the cause of much discontent against the king.

Another opponent acquired great popularity in later years. John

Hampden, a Buckinghamshire squire and former member of parliament, was summoned at the end of January 1627 to explain his refusal to pay the forced loan. 'I could be content to lend,' he replied, 'but fear to draw on myself that curse in Magna Carta which should be read twice a year against those who infringe it.' He was claiming, in other words, that the king had challenged the fundamental rights and liberties of the people. He was consigned to the Gatehouse prison at Westminster for a year and was so strictly held that, according to a contemporary account, 'he never did afterwards look like the same man he was before'. Fifteen years later, in the same prison, Richard Lovelace wrote that:

> Stone walls do not a prison make,
> Nor iron bars a cage . . .

Hampden's mind remained at liberty. He became a celebrated parliamentary commander in the eventual civil war.

Charles's angry will may have begun to cloud his judgement. On the urgent submissions of the duke of Buckingham, it was now proposed to send a naval expedition against France in order to help the rebellion of the Huguenots against Louis XIII. For some months an unofficial maritime war had been taking place between the two countries, leading to the seizure of goods and ships in mutually escalating fashion. At the beginning of December 1626, an order was issued for the capture of all French vessels found in English waters. Three weeks later it was discovered that six or eight ships purchased by Louis from the Low Countries were now at Le Havre ready to sail against England; they had to be either taken or destroyed.

The king was at this time contemplating a war against both France and Spain. To fight against one power was serious enough, but to fight against two at the same time might have been considered akin to folly. In the spring of 1627 new levies of men were dispatched to Portsmouth. It was the old story. Many of them were described as 'base rogues'; there was no clothing for them, and the surgeons had not been paid. Their lordships in the council were happy to issue general orders without caring to follow them up; they were incapable of estimating military costs, and were often ignorant of local geography. They sent regiments to be billeted without informing the relevant county authorities. They were preparing to send wheat to the proposed army in France, but provided no means to grind it. The absence of any working bureaucracy proved fatal. The confusion could have been prevented only if local self-government had been somehow rendered compatible with national conscription. How could a war in Europe be maintained by the men and administrative machinery of the parishes and counties? A national army raised to fight overseas could be managed only by some form of central administration. The conditions of Stuart England made that impossible. So chaos ensued. The pressed men appeared at Portsmouth:

> With an old motley coat and a malmsey nose,
> With an old jerkin that's out at the elbows,
> And with an old pair of boots drawn on without hose,
> Stuffed with rags instead of toes.

The talk of a further expedition against France meant that London, according to Edward Hyde, earl of Clarendon, 'was full of soldiers, and of young gentlemen who intended to be soldiers, or as like them as they could; great licence used of all kinds, in clothes, in diet, in gaming'. It was a city of dice and whores.

On 11 June the king himself reviewed the fleet at Portsmouth and dined aboard the admiral's vessel, where all were merry. The jokes and antics of the king's fool, Archie, were said to have been memorable. The notion of English superiority at sea, despite the failure at Cadiz, persisted. The fleet sailed on 27 June 1627, with two principal purposes. The first was to contest the ambition of Richelieu, the pre-eminent minister of Louis XIII, to make his sovereign the master of the sea. That role was reserved for England. The second aim of the enterprise was to transport certain regiments to the port of La Rochelle, on the Atlantic coast of France; the Huguenots of that town had taken over its administration and were engaged in a struggle for their religious liberty with the French king. The neighbouring island of Rhé was already under royal control. Buckingham's strategy was to occupy that part of it which managed the approaches to La Rochelle.

So on the afternoon of 12 July the men leapt into the landing craft, covered by the fire from their ships. Buckingham was everywhere among them, encouraging them and urging them on. Yet his bravado was not enough. The men themselves were ill-disciplined, and not all of them were inclined to fight; some lingered on board and others did not take up the positions assigned to them. Those who reached the shore were in no hurry to move against the enemy. Buckingham went among them with his cudgel to drive them forward. All this was to no avail.

The French seized the opportunity and rode down upon the English bands, threatening to drive them into the sea. Yet somehow a line of defence was established and the French forces, in difficult and swampy terrain, decided to retreat to the safe fortifications of the citadel of St Martin. Buckingham then ordered that the fort should be placed under siege.

The siege turned into a blockade, but the suffering multiplied on both sides. The women and children within the fort cried out for mercy and for pity, where none were available, while Buckingham's men were worn down by disease and lack of rations. He sent urgent messages to London for more troops and more supplies but the exchequer was, as always, empty. As winter came closer, the English forces grew weaker; they were now practically without food, money, or ammunition. It was reported in the middle of October that the English officers on Rhé were 'looking themselves blind' by scanning the seas with their telescopes for the sight of English ships.

A last desperate assault was made upon the fort, but it was discovered that the scaling ladders were too short. There was nothing for it but to retreat. Yet even this was bungled. On 30 October the English were about to cross by wooden bridge to a smaller island from which they hoped to embark upon their ships; but it was not properly defended. Under prolonged fire the infantry and cavalry were lost in confusion. Many of them were shot down, while others drowned. It was estimated that 4,000 Englishmen had been killed, while the rest eventually made their weary way back to Portsmouth or to Plymouth. La Rochelle had not been relieved. A contemporary, Denzil Holles, observed that 'every man knows that, since England was England, it received not so dishonourable a blow'. It was written of Buckingham himself:

> And now, just God, I humbly pray
> That thou wilt take that slime away.

It was the second signal disaster, in the space of two years, under the duke's command. His flags were now hanging in the cathedral of Notre Dame as a token of the nation's shame. The people were soon calling him 'the duke of Fuckingham'. Yet the king greeted his favourite with a cheerful face and effectively placed all the blame upon his own shoulders. 'In this action you have had honour,' Charles told him, 'all the shame must light upon us here remaining at home.' In truth Buckingham was not entirely culpable. He was a brave man but he was no strategist, a failure compounded by his scant attention to detail. Much of the fault, however, must lie with the administration at home that signally failed to provide the requisite money and supplies to its army overseas.

The king called a council of war in which he pressed for money to finance another expedition to La Rochelle which he had bound himself in honour to defend. His advisers counselled him once more to call parliament. It was the only way to raise money without a thousand complaints and legal challenges. Despite the fact that he expected only remonstrance and debate and petition from its members, he suffered himself to be persuaded.

The atmosphere of parliament in 1628 was not promising. At the beginning of February, a month before the members met, letters had been sent out by the king explaining the necessity for 'ship-money' to furnish another fleet. 'Ship-money' had been a medieval device by which at times of crisis the navy was supplied with boats from the maritime towns; Charles now wished to extend ship-money over the entire country, and to raise it in terms of coin rather than craft. He ordered that the relevant county officials should 'proceed according to the true worth of men's lands and estates'. The fresh attempt to levy taxes, on a dubious legal principle, provoked furious discontent. Many of the towns and counties refused to pay. Lincolnshire rejected 'the unusual and unexpected charge'; Somerset excused itself on the grounds that it 'will be a precedent of a charge which neither they nor their predecessors did ever bear'. Charles, realizing that his will would be openly flouted and his orders disobeyed, conceded the matter a few days later. He had decided 'wholly to rely on the love of our people in parliament'.

He was deluding himself. Love was in short supply at Westminster. The king and favourite had not prepared the ground adequately for further demands upon the nation's resources, and the court had made little effort to pack the Commons with its natural supporters at a time of crisis. A large number of those who met on 17 March 1628 were local men with local grievances; those who had refused to support the forced loan, for example, were almost sure of seats. A dependant of the duke of Buckingham, Sir Robert Pye, was named for one of the constituencies. The rallying cry went up for 'A Pye! A Pye! A Pye!' To which his adversaries called out 'A pudding! A pudding! A pudding!' and others joined in with 'A lie! A lie! A lie!' It was believed that the 'patriots' might trump the 'court party', and that parliament would not last eight days. It was even suspected by some that Charles and Buckingham had engineered such a result. If the parliament did not vote funds to the king, he would dismiss it and blame it for weakness and incapacity at a time of national danger.

When the king opened proceedings he declared that 'these are times for action'; he wanted money, and was not interested in 'tedious consultations'. He then piled insult upon insult by claiming that he did not intend to threaten them 'for I scorn to threaten any but my equals'. It was becoming clear that the major confrontation would not be with Buckingham, the object of the previous parliament, but with the king himself.

The mood of the Commons was not helped by the captivity of the five knights who, in the previous year, had been imprisoned for declining to pay the forced loan to the king. It was pleaded on their behalf that to refuse an illegal loan was no crime; if there was no crime, they could not remain in prison. The knights brought forward writs of habeas corpus to free themselves from illegal detention and declared that, according to Magna Carta, 'no man should be imprisoned except by the legal judgement of his peers or by the law of the land'.

The king's defenders stated in return that the knights were imprisoned at the especial command of their sovereign, and that no other cause was necessary. There followed suitable obfuscation from the judges of the case. They decreed that they would not give the prisoners bail, but that the crown prosecution should at some stage show cause for their further detention. It was an ambiguous judgment but contemporary observers interpreted it as a victory for the king. He would now be able to commit his subjects to prison without due cause. No redress against his sovereign will was permitted.

Sir Edward Coke therefore brought in a bill that prohibited anyone from being detained in prison without trial for more than two months; but this was not enough to avert the growing anger of the Commons. If the king could imprison his subjects for not providing him with money, as he had done in the case of the dissenting knights, where would his dominion end? 'Upon this dispute,' Eliot declared, 'not alone our lands and goods are engaged, but all that we call ours. These rights, these privileges, which made our fathers free men, are in question.' Thomas Wentworth, soon to become one of the most prominent men of the age, stood up to argue that there should be no more illegal imprisonment, no more pressing of men for foreign service, no forced loans and no billeting of soldiers on unwilling households.

At the beginning of April a committee of the Commons agreed three resolutions to be put to the king. No free man might be consigned to prison without cause; everyone had the right to a writ of habeas corpus; every prisoner was to be freed or bailed if no cause could be shown for his detention. The king was growing impatient. He wished the members to vote him financial supply without any delay. He did not understand why they were so insistent upon their so-called liberties. 'For God's sake,' he said, 'why should any hinder them of their liberties?' Parliament was not to be moved. The members decided to draw up a bill on the liberty of persons and property before even considering any matters of money.

Charles seemed to believe that this was no longer a simple matter of grievances to be redressed in the ancient fashion, but an attempt to limit royal sovereignty. A message came to the Commons that the king had taken note that 'this House pressed not upon the abuses of power but upon power itself'. 'Power' was a grand word, but what was its meaning? The debate continued, with the king suggesting that all would be well if only the monetary supply was granted. It was a question of relying upon 'his royal word and promise'. On 5 May a parliamentary remonstrance was presented to him on the matters under dispute. The king, in reply, was willing to pledge that he would not act in the manner he had done in the past; but he refused to allow that any of his future actions could be determined by parliament. The uses of 'power' could be curtailed, in other words, but 'power' itself remained his to wield as he saw fit.

This was not a satisfactory conclusion. The royal promises were too vague. No fundamental principles had been agreed. It was still not clear whether the king was above the law or the law above the king. A committee was drawn up to prepare a 'petition of right' which itself became an important statement of constitutional principle; the notable historian, Thomas Babington Macaulay described it as 'the second great charter of the liberties of England'. It cited the statutes passed in the reigns of Edward I and Edward III; it deplored the fact that 'your people have been in diverse places assembled and required to lend certain sums of money unto your majesty', and demanded that 'no freeman be taken or imprisoned' without due process of law. It also complained that 'great companies of soldiers and mariners have been dispersed into diverse counties of the realm'. The petition really contained nothing novel or radical, despite the king's autocratic sensitivities, and can most profitably be interpreted as a conservative document essentially restating what many considered to be the ancient constitution of the country. It can be concluded, however, that the king was not trusted in the same way as some of his predecessors.

By the end of May, after much debate, the petition had been adopted by both the Commons and the Lords; to sweeten what might be for Charles a bitter pill it was also agreed to offer the king five subsidies. In other circumstances he would no doubt have rejected the petition as a sheer abrogation of his rights and duties, but his foreign policy was in disarray. La Rochelle had still received no aid from England, despite the promises the king had made, and the fall of key German towns to the imperialist forces meant that English intervention in north-western Europe had for all practical purposes come to an inglorious end.

So the king was in urgent need of the money from parliament if he was to retain any shred of honour in foreign policy. Yet he prevaricated. He asked the judges certain leading questions concerning the petition, to which they gave cautious replies. 'Gentlemen,' he told the assembled parliamentarians before granting them his answer, 'I am come here to perform my duty. I think no man can think it long, since I have not taken so many days in answering the petition as you spent weeks in framing it . . .' His impatience was clear. With his finances in parlous state, and his foreign devices wrecked, all these men could do was debate and debate about the 'rights' of the people. The king then announced his reply to the petition. He declared merely that 'right should be done according to the laws and customs of the realm'. His words gave no comfort at all, since it was still the privilege of the king to judge what those 'laws' and 'customs' actually were.

The men of parliament were neither impressed nor reassured. When they met to consider their answer they remained seated for a while in a profound and melancholy silence; when certain members did eventually rise to their feet, their speeches were often interrupted by their tears. Sir John Eliot summoned up their spirits with the stern declaration that at home and abroad all was confused and uncertain. Our friends overseas had been defeated, and our enemies had prospered. The cause of Protestantism in Germany, and the recapture of the Palatinate, had been sacrificed as a result of the king's obsessions with a war against the French king. One member, Humphrey May, was about to interrupt him; but the rest of the house called out to Eliot, 'Go on! Go on!'

'If he goes on,' May said, 'I hope that I may myself go out.'

'Begone! Begone!'

But May stayed to listen to Eliot's oratory. 'Witness [the journey] to Cadiz! Witness the next! Witness that to Rhé! Witness the last! And I pray to God we shall never have more such witnesses! . . . Witness all! What losses we have sustained! How we are impaired in munition, in ships, in men!' At the close of his impassioned peroration he demanded a statement of grievances, or 'remonstrance', to be addressed to the king.

It seems that he was about to name Buckingham as the source of all regal problems, but he was stopped from doing so by the Speaker. The king then sent a message, absolutely forbidding the members further to discuss matters of state on pain of instant dismissal. In the face of this command, touching the liberties of parliament, one member after another rose to speak; others sat on the benches and wept. Joseph Mead, the contemporary writer of newsletters, reported that 'there appeared such a spectacle of passions as the like had seldom been seen in such an assembly, some weeping, some expostulating, some prophesying of the fatal ruin of our kingdom . . . I have been told by a Parliament man that there were above an hundred weeping eyes; many who offered to speak being interrupted and silenced by their own passions.' It was a sensitive and tearful age, in which political and religious controversy were not to be distinguished from personal passion. Eventually Sir Edward Coke rose to ask, 'Why may we not name those that are the cause of all our evils? The duke of Buckingham – that *man* is *the grievance of grievances*.' At that remark the Commons erupted in acclamations. It was said that, when one good hound recovers the scent, the rest come in with a full cry.

On 7 June Charles, now aware of the danger to his favourite and acutely conscious that his financial needs must be satisfied, took his seat upon the throne in the Lords. In front of the peers, and the members of the Commons who crowded to the bar, he ordered that his previous inconclusive answer to the 'petition of right' should be removed and that new words take its place. '*Soit droit fait comme il est désiré*.' This was the usual formula of assent that conferred legality on parliamentary measures: 'Let right be done as is desired.' He then added that 'now I have performed my part. If this parliament have not a happy conclusion, the sin is yours. I am free from it.' The result was delight in parliament itself, and celebration in the streets beyond; the bells were rung and the bonfires were kindled.

Yet the general satisfaction did not prevent parliament from pressing still further against the king. The remonstrance against Buckingham was presented to Charles on 17 June, to which he responded with a few words. He would consider their grievances 'as they should deserve'. Buckingham himself was not disturbed by the charges against him and is reported to have said that 'it makes no matter what the Commons or parliament do, for without my leave and authority they shall not be able to touch the hair of a dog'.

The Commons, not happy with the royal reception of their remonstrance, then went into committee on the question of the king's finances. The king ordained that the parliament should end in the next week. Whereupon a second remonstrance was prepared declaring that the king's collection of customs duties and other taxes without parliamentary assent was 'a breach of the fundamental liberties of this kingdom'. Before the debate could commence the king prorogued the assembly.

So ended the parliamentary session. It has sometimes been seen as one of the most significant in the history of that institution. The members had reminded the king that he was not permitted to violate the liberties of his subjects, and they had obtained from him the recognition of those rights they believed to be most important. Yet the celebrations on the street were perhaps premature. Three days after the conclusion of the proceedings, the king ordered a recall of the second answer he had given 'to be made waste paper'. He also ordered the reprinting of his first unsatisfactory answer, together with a series of qualifications to his second answer. In his closing speech to parliament, he had said that 'my meaning . . . was not to grant any new privileges but to re-edify your old', which could mean anything or nothing.

He prevaricated in his usual fashion, therefore, and as a result diminished the respect in which he was held. It was difficult to believe now in his good faith. One contemporary diarist, John Rous, noted that 'our king's proceedings have caused men's minds to be incensed, to rave and project [scheme]'. It could of course be claimed, on his behalf, that he was merely protecting the power and authority of the sovereign. It is worth noting that the young Oliver Cromwell, member for the town of Huntingdon, was also part of this parliament.

On the evening of 13 June, thirteen days before the prorogation, Buckingham's physician and astrologer was noticed leaving the Fortune Theatre in the northern suburbs of the city; his name was Doctor Lambe. A crowd of apprentices recognized him and began to cry out, 'The duke's devil! The duke's devil!'; they pursued him towards a cookhouse in Moorgate Street where he paid a group of sailors to guard him. By the time he left the cookhouse the mob had grown in size; he told them that he 'would make them dance naked', no doubt at the end of a rope. Still the people followed him, but at Old Jewry his guard beat them off. The crowd was now intent upon violence and, forcing him towards the Windmill Tavern in Lothbury, they beat him senseless with sticks and stones. One of his eyes was kicked out as he lay upon the cobbles. He was taken to a compter or small prison in Poultry where he died on the following morning.

A couplet was soon being repeated everywhere:

> Let Charles and George [Buckingham] do what they can
> Yet George shall die like Dr Lambe.

When the rhyme was discovered among a scrivener's papers he confessed that he had heard it from one Daniel Watkins, who had in turn heard it recited by an illiterate baker's boy. A Suffolk cleric recalled that 'about September 3 I had related to me this foolish and dangerous rhyme, fruit of an after-wit'. So poems and ballads, commonly known as 'libels', circulated throughout the kingdom; they were often left on stairs or nailed to doors or pinned to gates. Some were even put in the open hands of conveniently placed statues. When the attorney general prosecuted a group of minstrels for singing scurrilous ballads about Buckingham, he referred to these 'libels' as 'the epidemical disease of these days'. They are evidence of the political consciousness of the nation and of the 'lower sort', otherwise largely unheard. Even the baker's boy had opinions about the king and 'George'.

The temperature of the nation was also being raised by the publication of printed 'courants' or 'corantos' in ever-increasing quantity; these were regular newsletters or news pamphlets that were circulated in taverns and in marketplaces together with the 'libels' that accompanied any great movement in the affairs of state. While many were printed, others were written by hand. The written varieties were considered more reliable, perhaps because they seemed to be more immediate or perhaps because of the authority of the correspondent. One of the writers of these papers called himself 'your faithful Novellante' or newsmonger; this is of course the derivation of the 'novel'.

In a similar movement of information any great stir in the county towns also reached the capital. The newsletters often deliberately helped to provoke controversy or division, so that, for example, the growing polarization between 'court' and 'country' – between 'courtiers' and 'patriots' – can only have been assisted by their partisan accounts. Ben Jonson's masque, *News from the New World*, portrayed a writer of newsletters declaring that 'I have friends of all ranks and of all religions, for which I keep an answering catalogue of dispatch wherein I have my Puritan news, my Protestant news and my Pontifical news'.

Manuscript copies of the proceedings and debates of parliament of 1628, known as 'separates', were also issued at this time in perhaps the first example of parliamentary reporting. The great speeches of Sir John Eliot and others were thus available to the public, reinforcing the conclusion that parliament had indeed come to represent the will and voice of the people. It is perhaps significant that these papers were often to be found in the libraries of the gentry.

After parliament had been prorogued, the king gave orders that all the gunpowder in London should be taken under royal control. The impression of overweening authority, close to arbitrariness, was further strengthened by the investiture of William Laud as the bishop of London in the following month. His exaltation of the king's authority, and his demand for exact conformity, did not endear him to the 'patriots' of the kingdom who were eager to curb the royal prerogative.

The king also elevated Sir Thomas Wentworth to the peerage. Wentworth had previously taken the part of parliament but, after the publication of the 'petition of right', he came to accept the king's position on matters of sovereign control; he had arrived at the conclusion that the Commons were not fit to manage the affairs of the nation. He was condemned for abandoning his principles but he believed that parliament, not he himself, had changed. He was soon to say in a speech that 'the authority of a king is the keystone which closes up the arch of order and government'. With men such as Laud and Wentworth around him, what might the sovereign not dare to undertake? The atmosphere of the city was uneasy. It was reported that the citizens were filled with alarm, and were taking up arms for their own defence. It was rumoured that the duke and the king were ready to confront their enemies. No one knew what might happen next.

14

I am the man

The plight of La Rochelle, still besieged by the forces of Louis XIII after the forced withdrawal of the English army, was extreme. Its inhabitants were reduced to eating grass and boiled cow-hides. It was reported that they cut off the buttocks of the dead, lying in the churchyard, for sustenance. The honour of the king, and of Buckingham, determined that they must once more come to the aid of the city. So in the spring and summer of 1628 a fleet was fitted out at Plymouth. The normal delays ensued. 'I find nothing', Buckingham wrote, 'of more difficulty and uncertainty than the preparations here for this service of Rochelle.' He was so despised at home that he had been asked to wear protection in order to ward off any attempt at assassination. He replied that 'a shirt of mail would be but a silly defence against any popular fury. As for a single man's assault, I take myself to be in no danger. There are no Roman spirits left.'

On the morning of 23 August, the duke was staying at the house of Captain Mason on Portsmouth High Street; Mason was a naval administrator as well as an officer. Buckingham was at breakfast with his colleagues and some representatives from La Rochelle; after the meal was over, he came down into the hall of the house. He stopped to converse with one of his officers when a man, who had been standing in the passage, stepped forward and plunged a knife into his chest with the words 'God have mercy upon thy soul!' Buckingham staggered back but, crying out 'Villain!' managed to draw the knife from the wound. He tried to pursue his assailant but fell against a table before dropping to the floor.

A great outcry went up among those assembled. The foreigners were suspected, and men cried out, 'A Frenchman! A Frenchman!' Others shouted, 'Where is the villain? Where is the butcher?'

'I am the man. Here I am.' John Felton, with his sword in his hand, came forward. He might have been killed where he stood, but some of Buckingham's officers surrounded him. The wife and sister-in-law of the dead man rushed to the corpse. 'Ah, poor ladies,' Dudley Carleton informed the queen, 'such was their screechings, tears and distractions that I never in my life heard the like before, and hope never to hear the like again.'

The news reached the king while he was at prayer in the royal chapel. When it was whispered in his ear his face betrayed little emotion and he stayed in his place until the service was over. Then he hurried to his private apartments, closed the doors and wept. It was reported that the king used to refer to him as 'my martyr'. Charles believed, in other words, that his favourite had been murdered for carrying out his orders.

Under examination it was revealed that John Felton had served in the disastrous expedition to Rhé, and that Buckingham had denied him promotion. The insult was compounded by the fact that Felton's wages had not arrived. When he asked the duke how he was supposed to live, Buckingham is supposed to have replied that he could hang himself if he had not the means to survive. Felton returned to London, where he brooded on his misfortunes; he read the latest pamphlets, which accused Buckingham of poisoning the former king and of being the source of all the grievances of the realm. Four days before the assassination he purchased a tenpenny knife at a cutler's shop on Tower Hill; he then visited a church in Fleet Street and asked the cleric for prayers as 'a man much discontented in mind'. He made his way to Portsmouth, largely on foot, where he performed the deed. He had sewn certain messages in the crown of his hat, among them one in which he announced himself to be an executioner rather than an assassin: 'He is unworthy of the name of a gentleman or a soldier, in my opinion, that is afraid to sacrifice his life for the honour of God, his king, and country.' He had been the righteous killer of a reprobate who had brought Charles and England into jeopardy.

In that opinion, he was almost universally sustained by the response of the people. The joy at Buckingham's death was widespread and prolonged. Celebratory healths to Felton were drunk in the taverns of London, and congratulatory verses passed from hand to hand. When he was taken through Kingston on his way to the Tower, an old woman cried out, 'God bless thee, little David.' When he arrived at the Tower itself, a large crowd had gathered to greet him, calling, 'The Lord comfort thee! The Lord be merciful to thee!' Charles was much offended by these manifestations of popular sentiment, and he wrapped himself more deeply in the mantle of cold authority.

The day before Felton's arrival at the Tower, Buckingham's funeral had taken place at Westminster Abbey in a hurried and apparently graceless manner with approximately one hundred mourners. But even this ceremony was mere theatre. The body had been privately interred the night before, to avoid any demonstrations against it by the London crowds. The poet and dramatist James Shirley wrote an appropriate epitaph:

> Here lies the best and worst of fate,
> Two kings' delight, the people's hate.

Felton himself, after due trial, was executed at Tyburn; his body was then displayed in chains at Portsmouth dressed in the same clothes he wore when he killed the duke.

The king now took sole charge of the administration. It was reported by his secretaries that he dispatched more business in two weeks than Buckingham had managed in three months. He told his privy council that he would postpone the opening of parliament until the following year. He retained the same ministers as before, but of course he did not trust them as much as he had trusted the duke. There would be no more royal favourites except, perhaps, for Henrietta Maria, who, after the death of Buckingham entered a much more intimate relationship with her husband; it soon became apparent that, after the initial discord, the royal family was at last a happy one. The poet and courtier Thomas Carew claimed that

Charles had 'so wholly made over all his affections to his wife that he dare say that they are out of danger of any other favourite'. Carew's friend, William Davenant, composed some dialogue at the time for a play entitled *The Tragedy of Albovine, King of Lombardy*:

'The king is now in love.'
'With whom?'
'With the queen.'
'In love with his own wife! That's held incest in court.'

Six children followed this reconciliation.

Buckingham had not sailed for La Rochelle, after all. Yet in the early autumn of the year a third expedition was sent to the besieged town; it was no more successful than its predecessors. The fleet dared not take the initiative, and its fire-ships were sunk by French ordnance. When the English did eventually land, they were repelled with firmness by the French besiegers. The king's promises of assistance had come to nothing. So in October 1628, the authorities of the town signed a treaty of surrender to the French king; their great walls were demolished. Whereupon Louis XIII announced a policy of toleration to his Protestant subjects, who were to enjoy freedom of worship throughout his kingdom. The fears of the Protestants had been based upon the mistaken belief that their religion was in danger of being extirpated, and it could be said that the foreign policy of Charles I represented a thorough misunderstanding of the policy of Louis XIII.

In the absence of Buckingham the king was more uncertain and irresolute than ever. Should he make a treaty with France against Spain, or a treaty with Spain against France? There was no question of waging outright war against either nation. The king did not have the resources to do so, or any realistic prospect of raising money by other means. In any case the zeal for war was rapidly ebbing in the country. There might be some delay in signing the relevant treaties, but a period of peace had become inevitable.

A day after the assassination of Buckingham a prominent courtier, Sir Francis Nethersole, remarked that 'the stone of offence being removed by the hand of God, it is to be hoped that the king and people will now come to a perfect unity'. Yet the opening of the parliament in January 1629 did not bode well for national harmony. The abiding issue was still that of religion. A royal declaration had been issued in the parliamentary recess that 'the Church has the right to decree ceremonies, and authority to decide controversies of religion'. But what Church? William Laud, now bishop of London, had helped to draw up the proclamation and in the same period a number of his supporters had been promoted to vacant sees. These were the Arminians or 'high churchmen' who rejected the precepts and practices of Calvinism.

For parliament this was a direct challenge to the old and familiar creed of the Church. Sir John Eliot told his parliamentary colleagues that the prelates, with the king's authority, might 'order it which way they please and so, for aught I know, to bring in Popery and Arminianism, to which we are told we must submit'. Another member, Christopher Sherland, said of the Arminians that 'they creep into the ears of his Majesty, and suggest, that those that oppose them, do oppose his Majesty . . .'

It had become a confrontation, therefore, between the Calvinists of the old Church and the Arminian bishops of the new. The recently appointed prelates declared that theirs was the true creed of the Church of England and condemned their opponents as puritan, synonymous with zealotry and nonconformity. It was claimed, for example, that the Calvinists were ready to take up the cause of individual conscience against the precepts of the established faith and the prerogative of the sovereign. The Arminian bishops were in turn accused by their opponents of preaching passive obedience and the divine right of kings. The Calvinists believed in predestination, grace and the gospel; the Arminians put their faith in free will, the sacraments and deference to ceremonial order. It was not conceived by any contemporary that these were controversies that could stir a civil war, but this was the moment when members of parliament and members of the court party began to take sides.

The Commons, animated by the speeches of Eliot and others, affirmed that they alone had the right to determine the religion of the country. John Pym, who had already earned the king's wrath, stated that 'it belongs to the duty of parliament to establish true religion and to punish false'. The members resolved that the faith they espoused was that agreed in the reign of Elizabeth 'and we do reject the sense of the Jesuits and Arminians'. The king, perhaps justifiably, considered this to be a breach of his prerogative in spiritual matters; he was, after all, 'supreme governor' of the Church of England. The Commons had also laid aside matters of 'tonnage and poundage', the customs duties destined for the king's purse, thus depriving him of his traditional revenue. Charles adjourned parliament on 25 February for a week. Both sides were in fact vying for mastery.

This was the point when Eliot decided to appeal to the country in the face of an obvious threat. If the king took the further step of dissolving parliament, its future would be uncertain. If he could obtain his revenues elsewhere, there was no reason at all why he should ever summon it again. He had had, in any case, enough of parliament; he called it 'that noise'. The Arminians were eager to avoid parliaments, also, for the simple reason that they believed they would be persecuted by them; they were of course wholly justified in their suspicion. Eliot had already said of them that 'they go about to break parliaments, lest parliaments should break them'.

So all things were leading to a final quarrel. On 2 March the Speaker, Sir John Finch, announced to the Commons that it was the king's wish that they should adjourn for a further eight days. Such a request had in the past always been accepted. Now the members stood up shouting, 'No! No!' Finch moved to rise from his chair, thus abruptly ending the session, but some of the members barred his way and thrust him back to his seat. 'God's wounds,' Denzil Holles told him, 'you shall sit till we please to rise.' Eliot then announced that the members would have the privilege of adjourning themselves after he had read out a declaration of their intentions.

'What would any of you do,' Finch asked, 'if you were in my place? Let not my desire to serve you faithfully lead to my ruin.' He was in an impossible situation, with incompatible loyalties to parliament and to the king. Some members, realizing the gravity of the approaching confrontation, rose to leave. But the serjeant-at-arms was ordered to close the doors; when he hesitated, another member locked the doors and put away the key.

Eliot once more demanded that the declaration he had prepared should be read. 'I am not less the king's servant for being yours,' the Speaker replied. 'I will not say that I will not put the reading of the paper to the question, but I must say, I dare not.' Eliot then spoke out in a ferocious attack upon the evil councillors that surrounded the king; he also assaulted Arminianism as an open door to popery.

Knocks were heard on the outer door. The king had ordered the serjeant-at-arms to bring away the mace, thus depriving the proceedings of any authority. Sir Peter Heyman then turned upon the Speaker. 'I am sorry', he told him, 'that you must be made an instrument to cut up the liberties of the subject by the roots . . . The Speaker of the House of Commons is our mouth, and if our mouth will be sullen and will not speak when we have it, it should be bitten by the teeth and ought to be made an example; and for my part I think it not fit you should escape without some mark of punishment to be set upon you by the House.' This was one of the first indications of the arbitrary and authoritarian impulses of some parliamentarians.

Talk of punishment was vain, however. It was whispered that the king had sent a guard to force its way into the chamber and end the proceedings. So Denzil Holles swiftly proposed three resolutions. Anyone who tried to introduce popery or Arminianism into the kingdom would be considered a capital enemy. Anyone who should advise the levying of customs duties, without the authority of parliament, would similarly be considered as an enemy. If any merchant should voluntarily agree to pay the duties of 'tonnage and poundage', he would be 'reputed a betrayer of the liberty of England and an enemy to the same'. The resolutions were thereupon adopted. Having delivered his message to the nation, Holles asked that the house now adjourn itself, to which there were immediate calls of 'Ay! Ay!' The doors were thrown open and the triumphant parliamentarians streamed out to announce the news. They would not meet again for another eleven years.

Two days later the king announced the dissolution of parliament, and at the same time nine of its members were arrested. Sir John Eliot was the particular object of the king's wrath; Charles blamed his angry tirades against Buckingham for the favourite's death. In his speech to the Lords Charles did not censure the majority of the Commons, but reserved his anger for 'some few vipers amongst them that did cast this mist of undutifulness over most of their eyes'. It was reported that he was afterwards in very good spirits.

A few days later was published *His majesties declaration of the causes which moved him to dissolve the last parliament*, in which he declared that the men whom he imprisoned had 'more secret designs which were only to cast our affairs into a desperate condition, to abate the powers of our crown and to bring our government into obloquy that in the end all things may be overwhelmed with anarchy and confusion'. He was not alone in this belief. Many considered that the members had gone too far in their opposition to the king. Even a fervently Protestant MP, Simonds D'Ewes, considered that the events of 2 March represented 'the most gloomy, sad and most dismal day for England that happened in five hundred years last past'; he also blamed the turmoil on 'diverse fiery spirits in the House of Commons'.

The immediate aftermath of the dissolution was one of dismay and bewilderment. The majority of the merchants refused to pay the customs duties demanded of them, on the grounds that a future parliament would condemn them as betrayers of the kingdom; so they simply declined to trade. Their recalcitrance lasted for two months until the prospect of financial ruin weakened their resolution.

The nine members of parliament arrested after the scenes in the chamber remained in prison. They could no longer appeal to the Lords or the Commons but they could take their case to the courts; they could appeal to the rule of law in a fundamental attempt to question the powers of the king. They claimed parliamentary privilege, and in particular 'freedom of speech in debate' that had been asserted by the Speaker since the late sixteenth century; four of them, including Eliot, refused to answer questions on anything pertaining to parliamentary business. The king wished them to be tried for conspiracy and treason, but the judges were reluctant to do so. The question of privilege was vexatious, and Charles eventually asked them to cease speaking in riddles.

At the beginning of May the imprisoned men sought to obtain their release on the grounds of habeas corpus, according to the precepts of the 'petition of right'. After much argument and debate the judges decided that the prisoners had indeed the right to bail;

the king then demanded that they reach no verdict until they had consulted their colleagues on the judiciary. This was essentially an appeal for delay, so that the long legal vacation could intervene; the men would therefore languish in gaol for the duration of the summer. At the beginning of October the prisoners were taken from the Tower to Serjeants' Inn, where they were promised their release as long as they signed a bond of good behaviour; most of them refused to do so, on the grounds that this would implicitly justify their arbitrary imprisonment for the last eight months. They were intent upon inflicting the maximum embarrassment on the king and his officers.

The Venetian ambassador wrote that 'affairs grow more bitter every day, and by these disputes the king has made his people see that he can do much more than they may have imagined'. The imprisoned members were testing, piece by piece, the lengths to which Charles would go. When the chief judge of the exchequer made it clear that he was inclined to support parliamentary privilege, the king suspended him from office. It was clear that the guilt of the prisoners was simply to be assumed. The king's action seems to have clarified the opinion of the remaining judges, who declared that the defendants were indeed punishable by law.

The members of parliament had reached the end of the legal process. Three of them, including Eliot, were once more imprisoned at the king's pleasure; the others were detained for shorter periods before being released. It had been a victory for the king, in theory, but it had gravely impaired his authority and reputation. He had revealed himself to be inclined to arbitrary and perhaps illegal measures in order to sustain his sovereignty; he saw treachery and conspiracy in what others considered to be justifiable dissent; he was wilful, and even implacable. Yet those who supported him put a different interpretation upon his actions. Charles had conducted himself in the manner of a true sovereign; he was determined to rule the country without the intervention of enemies or malcontents. He was guided by God. This may be considered to be the tone or principle of the next period of his reign.

15

The crack of doom

After the dissolution of parliament in March 1629, the king entered upon a period of personal government that lasted for eleven years. To all intents and purposes he had begun an experiment in absolute monarchy, with the prospect of an acquiescent nation obeying his commands. He was not ill-equipped for that role. One prominent lawyer, Sir Robert Holborne, observed that 'the king could drive a matter into a head with more sharpness than any of his privy council'. Yet in practice he delegated much of his work to various officials, preferring the pleasures of the hunt to the world of practical affairs.

It was in certain respects a time of silence. There were no debates in parliament, and no elaborate declarations or proclamations from the throne. As in a masque, the king had no need to speak; his presence itself ensured majesty and harmony. As in a masque, also, he could command the workings of the great stage of the world. Charles had a high enough opinion of his supreme office, not unmixed with moral self-righteousness, to believe this.

In the absence of parliament, and with a relatively tame judiciary, the freedoms of the subject were to a certain extent reliant upon the judgement and goodwill of the sovereign. The people of England were simply asked to trust his benevolent intentions. It is true that in many respects he was a gentle monarch, in the course of whose reign no political executions took place. Yet some still considered him to be a tyrant riding over the liberties of the nation and parliament. The continued detention of Sir John Eliot and two colleagues was cited as an example.

Unparliamentary government was not in itself fruitless. It was a time of improvements in transport, with roads repaired and new canals dug; the national postal service was improved, with a regular post on the principal roads taking the place of an irregular system of carriers; in the absence of any national emergency, the administration of local government was strengthened and extended. That domestic peace, however, depended upon external tranquillity. The king could not afford war. And, as long as he could raise sufficient money for his own government by fines and taxation, there was no need to call parliament.

The foreign policy of the nation therefore, in a sense, made itself. Peace was concluded with France in the spring of 1629 and, nineteen months later, a truce was arranged with Spain. By the treaty with France Charles was obliged to abandon the cause of the Protestant Huguenots on the understanding that the principles of his marriage treaty with Louis XIII need not be strictly applied; he need not, for example, grant freedom of worship to Roman Catholics.

The peace with Spain made no mention of the restoration of the Palatinate to Charles's sister and brother-in-law; the fate of the region was now the subject of promises and expressions of goodwill. In another clause of the treaty it was agreed that Spanish silver could be minted in England before being shipped to Antwerp, where the Spanish were engaged in fighting the Protestant Dutch. It was an open question whether these alliances with the Catholic powers would become a cause of dissent in England. Some believed the people to be cheerful and acquiescent; others suggested that the anger or antagonism against the king had simply been driven below the surface.

The public reaction to both pacts, however, was subdued. Little interest was taken in the matter. Charles had no European policy as such, except for the wish that his sister might be returned to the Palatinate with her husband; but with no army or money to enforce his desires he was reduced to inaction. Money was the key. It was said that Henrietta Maria herself had been obliged to close the shutters of her private apartments in case visitors saw the ragged coverlets of her bed. There were times when, roused by Protestant appeals in Europe for assistance, the king asked his council what he might do. He was told that a new parliament would need to be called to raise the money. This was unthinkable. So nothing was done. The French ambassador remarked that lack of revenue made the English government one 'from which its friends can hope for no assistance, and its enemies need fear no harm'.

The king's discomfort was compounded when a new Protestant champion arose in Europe to counter the imperialist triumphs in Poland and Bohemia, Austria and Bavaria, Flanders and the Rhineland. In 1629 the king of Sweden, Gustavus Adolphus, marched into Germany and embarked upon a military conquest as unexpected as it was unprecedented. His chancellor wrote that 'all the harbours of the Baltic, from Kalmar to Danzig, throughout Livonia and Prussia, are in his majesty's hands'. Gustavus Adolphus had created a new Swedish empire and thereby took on the mantle of a Protestant Messiah, the Lion of the North.

How was the English king to treat with such a man? Gustavus Adolphus demanded men and materials from a fellow Protestant king. But if Charles entered into an alliance with the Swedish king, his important friendship with Spain would come to an end; and the trade with Spain was very important. If he refused an alliance with Gustavus Adolphus, he would lose honour and influence if the Swede was eventually victorious.

So Charles prevaricated and tried half-measures to maintain his credit on both sides. He agreed that a private force of 6,000 Scottish soldiers, under the command of the marquis of Hamilton, could join the Swedish army; but the expedition was a disaster, made worse by epidemic disease and insubordination. The king then sent a delegation to the Swedish king 'to enter into a league . . . upon emergent occasions'. This could mean anything or nothing. In practice it meant nothing. At one point Charles banned the news gazettes from reporting on the Swedish victories because they cast such an unhappy light on his own ineffectiveness.

The fortunes of the Swedish king came to an end in a battle outside Leipzig, where his body was found among a heap of naked corpses. The king of England had done nothing to counsel or to assist him. English inaction, or inertia, had created what one anonymous pamphleteer, in 'The Practice of Princes', described as 'a Hispanolized, Frenchified, Romanized or Neutralized' policy. Yet there may have been virtue in that. One week of war can undo a decade of peace. England escaped the devastation that was inflicted upon central Europe.

Funds still had to be raised by one means or another. The fines against the illegal enclosure of common land were more strenuously exacted. The king also raised much money from a great scheme to drain the fens of eastern England. Many articles of ordinary consumption were granted for a fee to monopolists, who could then set their own prices; the articles included iron and salt, pens and playing cards, starch and tobacco, seaweed and spectacles, combs and gunpowder, hats and hops. Patents could also be purchased for such projects as the manufacture of turf or the weighing of hay and straw, for 'the gauging of red herring' and the gathering of rags. In a contemporary anti-masque an actor came on stage with a bunch of carrots on his head, representing a 'projector' or speculator 'who begged a patent of monopoly as the first inventor of the art to feed capons fat with carrots'. The king demanded from the Vintners' Company a payment of £4 on every tun of wine; when they refused to pay the new tax, the Star Chamber forbade them to cook and serve meat for their customers. The loss of trade meant that they came to an 'understanding' with the court, amounting to £30,000 a year.

There was also the curious case of soap. The Company of Soapmakers was in 1631 granted a monopoly to manufacture soap made out of domestic ingredients, such as vegetable oil, rather than out of imported whale oil or fish oil. The company agreed in turn to pay the king an annual tax of £20,000.

The previous soap manufacturers were prosecuted in the Star Chamber for selling the old product; many of them were fined and some of them were imprisoned, while their pans and vats were destroyed. They were of course incensed at their loss of livelihood, but many housewives also complained that the new soap did not wash as well as the old. In seventeenth-century England even the most domestic disputes had a religious dimension. It was believed that the Company of Soapmakers was in fact controlled by the Catholic friends of Henrietta Maria; some of the new monopolists were rumoured to be financed by the Jesuits. Many Protestant households, therefore, objected to the new soap on theological grounds. It became known as the Popish Soap.

So the authorities put on a public demonstration of the efficacy of the new soap. In the Guildhall, under the gaze of the lord mayor, the aldermen and the lieutenant of the Tower, two washerwomen used the rival products in tubs placed beside each other. It was meant to prove that the new soap cleaned and lathered better, but the demonstration does not seem to have persuaded the London public. Eighty great ladies signed a testimonial to the effect that their maids preferred the new soap. This also had no noticeable effect. The old soap was still being sold under the counter. Another demonstration by washerwomen in Bristol was meant to prove that the new product washed 'as white . . . and as sweet, or rather sweeter' than the old. This may be considered a harbinger of modern advertising campaigns. It also made little impression. The old soap was still being manufactured and, as a result of its scarcity, sold at a much higher price.

More personal exactions were made by the king. Individuals were summoned for taxes they had not thought to pay. In 1630, for example, a royal commission was set up to fine those gentlemen who had not taken up knighthoods at the time of the king's coronation. It was a legal requirement that had faded out of memory through disuse. Those who were summoned were aggrieved at this unexpected imposition, and most tried to excuse themselves. Yet they were not successful. By these means the king raised the money he wished for, but at the expense of the affection and loyalty of some of his subjects.

Other expedients were also practised. Royal rights over forest lands were resurrected; those who had encroached upon forest boundaries were charged large sums. Those who had built houses in London 'upon new foundations' were also fined. Mr Moor had erected forty-two new houses in the neighbourhood of St Martin-in-the-Fields, for example, and was fined £1,000 and ordered to demolish the houses; when he refused, the sheriffs took them down and sold the materials to pay the fine.

What, then, was the king's general attitude to the property of his subjects? Could he take it away at will? If he could impose new taxes on his people without recourse to the courts or to parliament, might he not be able to emancipate the Crown from its traditional obligations? Many suggested that the king could indeed tax without consent, and that public good took precedence over private right. Others in turn argued that the Englishman's right to the property of his goods and estates was absolute, and could not be removed from him by any court or sovereign. Domestic peace was also unsettled by the disastrous harvest of 1630, which pushed up the price of grain from 4 shillings to 14 shillings a bushel; the prospect of starvation alarmed many communities, and food riots occurred in Kent, Hampshire and elsewhere.

The fractious atmosphere of the time was also evident in the court's actions against the notable antiquary Robert Cotton. His library had been sealed up, in the belief that it contained ancient tracts and pamphlets that took the side of parliament against the king. History had to be cleansed. One tract was found, according to the archbishop of York, 'containing a project how a prince may make himself an absolute tyrant'. Cotton was taken into custody, and interrogated by the Star Chamber before being released. Yet his life of study was effectively over. He was no longer allowed to enter his library and learned men were advised to cease their visits to him. He told one friend that 'my heart is broken'. He was so worn by anguish and grief that, according to Simonds D'Ewes, 'his face, which had been formerly ruddy and well-coloured, such as the picture I have of him shows, was wholly changed into a grim, blackish paleness near to the resemblance and hue of a dead visage'. He expired soon after, the victim of a nervous and turbulent time.

At the end of 1629 William Laud had, with the assent of the king, composed a 'Declaration on the Articles of Religion'. It was designed to impose order and uniformity upon the English Church by prescribing the forms of worship, the words of the prayers and even the gestures of the clergy. It was ordained that all clerics must accept to the letter the Thirty-Nine Articles, a demand which would in effect prohibit any discussion by Calvinists on such matters as predestination; these were condemned by the bishop of Chichester as 'deep and dark points which of late have so distracted and engarboyled the world'. The declaration was conceived thoroughly in the spirit of the monarch, who believed in order above all things.

Certain observers thereby concluded that Church and nation were to be reduced to uniformity.

Laud was, in the capital, considered to be little more than a papist in love with ritual and with ceremony. A paper was scattered about the streets of London declaring 'Laud, look to thyself, be assured thy life is sought. As thou art the fountain of all wickedness, repent thee of thy monstrous sins, before thou be taken out of the earth.' Laud was not discomfited. 'Lord,' he wrote in his diary, 'I am a grievous sinner; but I beseech thee, deliver my soul from them that hate me without cause.' An opponent of Laud by the name of Alexander Leighton, having written an appeal to parliament entitled 'Sion's Plea against the Prelacy', was condemned to the Fleet Prison for life; he was also to be taken to the pillory at Westminster and whipped before one of his ears was cut off, one side of his nose slit, and his face branded with the mark of 'S.S.' for 'Sower of Sedition'. He was then to be returned to prison for a period of recuperation before being whipped again and his other ear removed. He was afterwards 'to be shut up in close prison, for the remainder of his life'. Part of this sentence was remitted, for the sake of decency, but he was not released from prison until 1641 by which time he could not see, hear, or walk.

His wife was also briefly committed 'for her disordered tongue', according to a news-writer of March 1630, 'and a button maker for putting his mouth to the keyhole of the prison door where he lay, and crying aloud "Stand to it, doctor, and shrink not" and such like words'. In the following month an oatmeal-maker was brought before a religious commission for his unorthodox opinions. He was condemned by the bishop of Winchester, another ally of Laud, as a 'frantic, foolish fellow'. The maker of oatmeal replied, 'Hold thy peace, thou tail of the beast that sittest at the lower end of the table.'

The king expressed his appreciation of Laud's work, however, by appointing him as chancellor of Oxford University in the spring of 1630. Laud worked at once to re-establish order and decorum in the ancient university. The students had previously venerated Bacchus and Venus who were, as Laud wrote, 'the cause of all our ills in church and state'. Discipline was to be restored, thus promoting order and harmony; extravagant dress and long hair were not to be permitted, and alehouses were to be regulated. In the course of Laud's chancellorship, new buildings were erected and new studies were placed upon the curriculum with learned clerics to expound them. The city was refurbished, as it were, in glowing vestments.

The glory of Charles I was also celebrated. In 1630 the lord treasurer, Richard Weston, commissioned a statue of the king on horseback; it was a noble decoration for the garden of his country house in Roehampton. It soon became the abiding image of Charles's rule. In 1633 Van Dyck portrayed the king riding through a triumphal arch in the classical style; the king becomes a Roman conqueror. Two years later the same artist composed *Charles I on Horseback*, in which the king calmly and effortlessly directs the steed on which he rides. Images of chivalry, and of the Christian knight, are conflated with the representation of order.

It is also an image of the sovereign controlling animal nature, bringing the strength and energy of the horse into harness with his own will and desire. The Spanish ambassador, in the same spirit, had once flattered Charles by noting that the horses upon which he was mounted 'laid down all their natural and brutish fierceness in his presence'. The equestrian portraits are thereby a depiction of the manner in which reason must be able to control passion. This is of a piece with Charles's own conception of his rule and of his evident belief that he must control his own nature, by restraint and formality, before he could properly govern the entire kingdom. Art was for the king one of the great emblems of power. Yet it was more than that.

Lucy Hutchinson observed that 'men of learning and ingenuity in all the arts were in esteem and received encouragement from the king, who was a most excellent judge and great lover of paintings, carvings, gravings and many other ingenuities . . .' Charles had seen the artistic wealth of the royal court in Madrid and wished to cultivate a similar state of magnificence. He was in addition an adept and instinctive judge of painting and sculpture; if he had not been a king, he would have been a connoisseur. He was able to recognize the identity of an artist at first glance; this was known as a 'knowledge of hands'. He knew where '*gusto*', passion or taste, was to be found. He commissioned Rubens, Mytens, Inigo Jones and Van Dyck; by the end of his reign he had collected some 500 paintings and tapestries, among them nine Correggios, thirteen Raphaels and forty-five Titians. The Dutch once sent him five paintings to persuade him to resolve a dispute about herring fisheries; the city of Nuremberg gave him two Dürers. He also collected coins and medals; he enjoyed composing music. His love of order was everywhere apparent. When a collection of the busts of senators and emperors of ancient Rome reached Whitehall, he himself took pains to arrange them in chronological order.

A papal emissary to England recalled the occasion when the king, in the company of Inigo Jones, was informed that a consignment of paintings had arrived from the Vatican; he 'rushed to see them, calling to him Jones . . . the very moment Jones saw the pictures he greatly approved of them, and in order to study them better threw off his coat, put on his eyeglasses, took a candle, and together with the king, began to examine them very closely, admiring them very much . . .' The gift included works by Leonardo and Andrea del Sarto. This excitement reveals a sovereign very different from the conventional image of his coldness and reserve. Rubens was to say of Charles's court that it was remarkable 'not only for the splendour of the outward culture' but for 'the incredible quality of excellent pictures, statues and ancient inscriptions which are to be found in this court . . . I confess I have never seen anything in the world more rare.'

The authority of the king's image was amplified by the evidence of his fertility. In the spring of 1630 Henrietta Maria presented him with a son and heir, also to be named Charles. She wrote to a friend in France that her child was 'so serious in all that he does that I cannot help deeming him far wiser than myself'. The baby never clenched his fists, and so it was predicted that he would be a king of great liberality. He was also healthy and strong, looking at four months as if he were already a year old. So the birth augured well. The infant Charles was also the first in English history to be born as heir to the three kingdoms.

Thomas Carew, gentleman of the bedchamber, told the earl of Carlisle that the king and queen were 'at such a degree of kindness as he would imagine him a wooer again and her gladder to receive his caresses than he to make them'. Charles wrote to his mother-in-law, Marie de' Medici, that 'the only dispute that now exists between us is that of conquering each other by affection'. More importantly, perhaps, the birth of a son seemed to indicate that the Stuart dynasty might continue until the crack of doom.

16

The shrimp

All seemed quiet. The appearance of calm may have been deceptive, but it was peaceful enough in comparison with the violent years yet to come. Edward Hyde, 1st earl of Clarendon, claimed in his *History of the Rebellion and Civil Wars in England* that during the personal rule of Charles 'the like peace and plenty and universal tranquillity for ten years was never enjoyed by any nation'. Another historian, Sir Philip Warwick, in his *Memoirs of the Reign of Charles I*, wrote that 'from the year 1628 unto the year 1638, I believe England was never master of a profounder peace, nor enjoyed more wealth, or had the power and form of godliness more visible in it'.

On 9 January 1631, *Love's Triumph*, a masque devised by Inigo Jones and Ben Jonson, introduced Henrietta Maria as the Queen of Love in Callipolis or 'the city of beauty and goodness'. When the scene dissolved the 'prospect of the sea' appeared, into which setting the king himself walked in the guise of Neptune with a train of sea-gods and Cupids. He was then apostrophized as 'the centre of proportion, sweetness, grace!' At the end of the performance 'the throne disappears, in place of which there shooteth up a palm tree with an imperial crown on the top'.

In that same month, by royal command, a 'book of orders' was published. It decreed that two justices of the peace should meet each month in petty sessions to maintain the operations of local government. The overseers of the poor were to ensure that poor children were placed in apprenticeships; the constables and churchwardens of the parish were ordered to discipline offenders and to chase away vagrants. It was also the responsibility of the two justices to make certain that the roads were in a good state of repair and that, in general, law and order were imposed. They were also obliged to submit reports to London concerning 'how they found the counties governed'.

Although the king himself may not have drawn up these provisions, they bear all the marks of his paternal authority and of his predilection for good order. Charles was also determined that the local gentry and nobility should play an active part in the government of their neighbourhoods; a proclamation was issued ordering any of them still dwelling in London to return to the countryside where they belonged. At a later date another royal declaration ordered that urban vintners should stop selling tobacco and that innkeepers should not dress or serve game birds; this was believed to be a device to make the city less attractive to the country gentry.

The servants of the Crown were going about their duties. At the beginning of March William Laud preached at Paul's Cross in celebration of the sixth anniversary of the king's accession. He remarked that 'some are so waspishly set to sting that nothing can please their ears unless it sharpen their edge against authority'; he added, in sententious fashion, that 'I hope I shall offend none by praying for the king'.

The king's other great councillor, Sir Thomas Wentworth, had been dispatched to York as lord president of the north in order to curb disorder. At the beginning of 1632 he was further promoted to become lord deputy of Ireland, where his cause of promoting 'good and quiet government' could be tested. He was a man of strong will and of commanding temper. He believed implicitly in royal authority and in public duty. He told one of his relatives that 'a life of toil and labour' was his effective destiny. The portraits of him by Van Dyck show him to be profoundly animated by zeal or, perhaps, by vision.

Laud and Wentworth shared similar precepts and preoccupations that were embraced by them under the name of 'Thorough', by which they meant a disciplined and energetic response to the problems of the realm. They would not be diverted from their self-imposed task, and held nothing but contempt for those ministers of the state whom they regarded as lax, cowardly, or concerned only with enrichment. The administration of the king and his councillors – parliament was put to one side – should be enabled to push through those policies that were in the public interest. The vital alliance was that between Church and Crown in the cleansing of the kingdom.

The lord treasurer, the earl of Portland, was described by them as 'Lady Mora' or 'Lady Delay'; Laud also described the chancellor of the exchequer, Lord Cottington, as 'Lady Mora's waiting maid' who 'would pace a little faster than her mistress did, but the steps would be as foul'. This represented the difference between complaisant councillors and committed reformers.

Wentworth, like Laud, believed that only royal sovereignty could bring order out of disorder and discipline out of anarchy. As lord deputy of Ireland, therefore, he was inclined to drive himself over any opposition, to consolidate the authority of the king, to lead the people – and in particular the recent English settlers – into the pastures of obedience and docility. He was intent upon recovering the powers of the king, as he said, by 'a little violence and extraordinary means'. By his own light he succeeded, but only at the cost of arousing hostility and even hatred. He brought to his task a less than attractive combination of austerity and obstinacy. It was said, in *A Collection of Anecdotes and Remarkable Characters*, that 'his sour and haughty temper' meant that he expected 'to have more observance paid to him than he was willing to pay to others'.

Laud was more practical than the inspired Wentworth. The bishop wrote to the lord deputy that 'for the State, indeed my Lord, I am for thorough . . . and it is impossible for me to go thorough alone'. 'Thorough' and 'through', spelt in an identical way in the seventeenth century, were for all intents and purposes the same word. Laud added that 'besides, private ends are such blocks in the public way, and lie so thick, that you may promise what you will, and I must perform what I can and no more'. Nevertheless Wentworth was relentless, describing himself at his subsequent trial as 'ever desiring the best things, and never satisfied I had done enough, but did always desire to do better'.

In this period, too, the proclamations of the privy council were given legislative authority; the privy councillors could make laws on those matters which the actual courts of law neglected or avoided. The other governors of the realm maintained the emphasis upon law and order. It was reported in London by a news-writer, John Pory, that 'on Sunday, in the afternoon and after supper, till midnight, my lord mayor visited as many taverns as he could, and gave warning to the vintners not to suffer any drinking in their houses, either that day or night; and the same afternoon also he passed Moorfields and put down the wrestling of the western with the northern men, which was there usual on that afternoon'. The Star Chamber also enjoyed new authority with its enforcement of the proclamations from the council and its pursuit of transgressors.

One of the most prominent of these public offenders, William Prynne, had already aroused controversy with his strongly puritan opinions. He wrote tracts and pamphlets endlessly, his servant bringing him a bread roll and pot of ale every three hours; he was known as a 'paper-worm'. John Aubrey wrote that he 'was of a strange saturnine complexion', and Christopher Wren said that he had the countenance of a witch.

In the late autumn of 1632 Prynne's *Histriomastix: A Scourge of Stage Players* launched a general assault upon the plays and players of London, with a particular attack upon the practice of boys playing female roles and of women themselves appearing on the stage. He wrote that the actresses were 'notorious whores' and asked if 'any Christian woman be so more than whorishly impudent as to act, to speak publicly on a stage (perchance in man's apparel and cut hair), in the presence of sundry men and women'.

Unfortunately for Prynne the queen, Henrietta Maria, took part in a theatrical pastoral entitled *The Shepherds' Paradise* just a few weeks after the publication of his tract. The play itself was in the best possible taste. It was recorded of its audience that 'my lord chamberlain saith that no chambermaid shall enter, unless she will sit cross-legged on the top of a bulk'. It was a serious affair, and was of such complexity that the production lasted for seven or eight hours.

Nevertheless Prynne's attack upon female players was interpreted as an attack upon the queen herself; he had also denounced public dancing as a cause of shame and wickedness, and it was well known that the queen was fond of dancing. Prynne was sent to the Tower, where he faced prosecution by the Star Chamber and by the high commission on religious affairs. He was sentenced to imprisonment for life, fined £5,000 and expelled from Lincoln's Inn where he had practised law. The severity of the judgment was enhanced by the brutal order that both of his ears should be cut off as he stood in a public pillory. The sentence was duly carried out. One of his ears was cut away at Westminster, and the other in Cheapside.

Another opponent of the court, Sir John Eliot, died in confinement at the end of 1632. The king's enmity against him was such that, despite pleas for his health, he had never been allowed to leave the Tower in the course of his imprisonment. He had sent a petition to the king in which he declared that 'by reason of the quality of the air I am fallen into a dangerous disease'; he also stated that 'I am heartily sorry I have displeased your majesty'. The king replied that the petition was not humble enough. Eliot's humiliation was continued after his death. His son petitioned the king to allow his father's body to be carried into Cornwall for burial. Charles scrawled at the bottom of the petition, 'Let Sir John Eliot's body be buried in the church of that parish where he died.' He was in other words to be interred in the Tower.

A sequence of letters between the members of the Barrington family, in the early months of 1632, gives the flavour of the time. Thomas Barrington, writing from Holborn, informs his mother that 'women are cruel this year, Saturn reigns with strong influence: another wife has given her husband a potion of melted lead, but it was because he came home drunk'. His wife, Judith Barrington, wrote to her mother-in-law that 'I find all my friends sick or dying, the air is so bad . . . Here is little news stirring, much expected at the latter end of this week . . . This day was the poor woman burned in Smithfield that poisoned her husband, which is wondered at the cruelty, since there was so much cause of mercy to her.' A week or so later she reported that 'the smallpox is so much here that we wish ourselves with you'. In May Thomas Barrington wrote that 'the current of London runs so contrary and diverse courses as that we know not which way to fasten on certain truths'. London was the city of disease, of cruelty and of false reports.

In the spring of 1633 the king returned to his homeland. He made a leisurely journey northwards, and reached Edinburgh by the middle of June. His relations with Scotland in the past had not been entirely happy; at the beginning of his reign he had asked for the restitution of Church lands in Scotland to the Crown. The measure was not in the end advanced, but it stirred bad blood. When some Scottish lords came to defend the existing landowners, the king made a characteristic remark. 'My lord,' he said to the leader of the deputation, 'it is better the subject suffer a little than all lie out of order.' Charles himself did not seem especially to like the Scots and, in particular, the Highlanders, whom he described as 'that race of people which in former times hath bred so many troubles'. Yet his principal feeling was one of indifference rather than hostility.

He was crowned as king of Scotland in Holyrood Abbey on 18 June, and it was remarked that he had been happy to wait eight years for the privilege. The delay showed no overriding desire to endear himself to his people. The coronation itself was marked of course by ritual and formal ceremony that did not impress the natives; for most Scots, brought up in the Presbyterian faith, it smacked of prelacy and popery.

One of the complaints advanced by the Scots concerned the introduction of English ritual into the service. Yet the chief proponent of that ritual was about to be raised to the highest see. When Bishop Laud came into the king's presence for the first time after the journey to Scotland he was greeted with unfamiliar words. 'My Lord's Grace of Canterbury, you are very welcome.' Charles had just heard of the death of George Abbot, the previous archbishop.

As bishop of London Laud had been the king's principal religious adviser, but his authority had been ill-defined. Now as archbishop he became the source and spring of English religion, with an energy and purpose that the king himself lacked. Yet, at the beginning of his ministry, he was beset by anxiety. He wrote to Thomas Wentworth that 'there is more expected from me than the craziness [infirmity] of these times will give me leave to do'. Nevertheless like Sisyphus he was ready to put his shoulder to the stone.

He was a man of quick temper, small in stature, inclined to

irritability and impatient of contradiction. His harshness and rigour quickly made him enemies, particularly among the puritans whom he excoriated. He was known as 'the shrimp', 'the little urchin' and 'the little meddling hocus-pocus'. The king's fool, Archie, made a pun before a royal dinner. 'Give great praise to God, and little laud to the Devil.' Yet no one could question the new archbishop's sincerity or personal honesty. One English diplomat, Sir Thomas Roe, told the queen of Bohemia that Laud was 'very just, incorrupt . . . a rare counsellor for integrity'.

Thomas Carlyle described him as 'a vehement, shrill voiced character confident in its own rectitude, as the narrowest character may the soonest be. A man not without affections, though bred as a college monk, with little room to develop them: of shrill, tremulous, partly feminine nature, capable of spasms, of most hysterical obstinacy, as female natures are.' He was something between an Oxford don and a bureaucrat. A portrait of him by Van Dyck represents him as austere and quizzical. Not that he would have put much faith in the artist. He described his paintings as 'vanity shadows'.

He was highly superstitious and kept a record of his uneasy dreams. He dreamed that he gave the king a drink in a silver cup; but Charles refused it, and called for a glass. He dreamed that the bishop of Lincoln jumped on a horse and rode away. On one night 'I dreamed that I had the scurvy; and that forthwith all my teeth became loose. There was one in especial in my lower jaw, which I could scarcely keep in with my finger till I had called for help.'

Soon enough his influence was being felt. In October 1633 he and the king caused to be republished King James's *Declaration of Sports*, which had granted a degree of entertainment and recreation on the Sabbath. The king's 'good people' were not to be discouraged from dancing or archery, while the sports of leaping and vaulting were also permitted; 'may-games, whit ale and morris dances, and the setting up of maypoles' were perfectly acceptable to the authorities. It was almost like a return to the more picturesque religion of earlier centuries. For the Calvinists and the stricter sorts of Protestant, the *Declaration of Sports* was a poisoned document set to destroy true religion. Certainly it had unforeseen consequences. A seventeenth-century historian, Thomas Fuller, wrote that many of his contemporaries were 'of opinion that this abuse of the Lord's Day was a principal procurer of God's anger, since poured out on this land, in a long and bloody civil war'. The vicar of Enmore in Somerset declared from the pulpit that 'whatsoever the king is pleased to have done, the king of heaven commands us to keep the Sabbath'.

In the same period it was determined that the plain communion table should be moved from the middle of the church to the eastern end where it was to be railed off; it then more closely resembled the altars of the old faith. The priests now bowed towards it, and some of them employed the sign of the cross to bless it. William Prynne had already satirized the Eucharistic rite when the celebrant . . .

> came near the bread, which was cut and laid in a fine napkin, and then he gently lifted up one of the corners of the said napkin, and peeping into it till he saw the bread (like a boy that peeped after a bird-nest in a bush), and presently clapped it down again, and flew back a step or two, and bowed very low three times towards it . . . then he laid his hand upon the gilt cup . . . so soon as he pulled the cup a little nearer to him he let it go, flew back and bowed again three times towards it.

This was a keen burlesque of the services imposed by Laud.

The archbishop was concerned to augment the beauty and holiness of the rites of the Church, thus inducing respect if not awe. He had previously complained that ''tis superstition nowadays for any man to come with more reverence into a church, than a tinker and his bitch into an alehouse'. It soon became a serious offence for a minister not to bow his head at the name of Jesus. Choirboys came in two by two, and were instructed never to turn their backs upon the altar. Music returned to the cathedrals.

Laudianism, however, was not popery. The archbishop had a distaste for Roman Catholicism that was quite genuine. He was hoping to create a truly national Church devoid of the zealotry and intolerance of the puritans as well as the Mariolatry and superstitions of the papists. He had no appetite or aptitude for theological argument and, on the everlasting debate between free will and predestination, he said only that 'something about these controversies is unmasterable in this life'. He was indifferent towards Geneva and Rome, and looked only towards the king.

Laud was also attempting to fashion religious developments of a structural kind; he appointed only bishops who were of firmly anti-Calvinist persuasion. Charles himself believed that the episcopacy was the fundamental buttress of his sovereignty; no bishop, as his father had said, implied no king. It was believed essential to augment clerical power. The corporations of cathedral towns were called upon to appoint more clerics as justices of the peace, and were further obliged to attend Sunday service in their ceremonial robes. Within a short time Laud was joined by two bishops in the king's council; Bishop Juxon of London, who had been only the king's chaplain two years before, was appointed as lord treasurer of the kingdom. The last cleric to fill the post had been promoted in the reign of Henry VII (1485–1509). England might be considered to have re-entered the world of medieval polity.

A series of 'visitations' to the various parishes followed in order to investigate cases of clerical disobedience and nonconformity. In Manchester, for example, twenty-seven clerics were charged with failing to kneel at the time of communion. Richard Mather of Toxteth, near Liverpool, admitted that he had never worn the surplice. 'What!' exclaimed the Visitor, 'Preach fifteen years and never wear a surplice? It had been better for him that he had gotten seven bastards!'

The old processions and festivals also returned. With the re-publication of *Declaration of Sports* came a general relaxation of social custom. The ritual of 'beating the bounds' was soon followed by the parishes of London; such holy days as All Saints were celebrated once more. The custom of the Lord of Misrule returned with its attendant atmosphere of party games, dancing and drinking of spiced ale. These feasts had never completely died away but, in the new atmosphere of anti-puritanism, they flourished.

The king was further to test the loyalty of the nation. In the autumn of 1634 writs of ship-money were issued once again, for the first time in a period of peace. They had previously been sent out in 1626 and 1627, in the face of a threat of war against both France and Spain; payments had been grudging, but they had been made, and so it was deemed plausible to repeat the exercise. The proximate cause for the reintroduction of the tax was the prospect of new combinations in Europe. The French and Dutch had entered an unlikely alliance to dominate the continent, and a secret treaty between England and Spain was believed to be necessary.

There was no hope, however, that the members of the king's own council would countenance the fact of an English force taking the part of Spain against the Dutch; how could the king ally himself with the pre-eminent Catholic power attacking a Protestant republic? Once again Charles relied upon intrigue with any or every party that seemed likely to favour him. He had to conceal his alliance with Spain and pretend that the ships were being prepared as a defence against attacks from all quarters. It was said that English trade had to be protected from Tunis and Turkey as much as from France or Spain. So the king claimed the right of sovereignty in all of his seas, including the English Channel and the North Sea.

The first writs of ship-money were dispatched only to the ports and to the towns along the coasts; they were ordered to provide a sum sufficient to fit out a certain number of ships as well as to maintain them and their crews for six months. The money was to be given to a collector appointed by the Crown. London alone attempted to oppose the tax, having been required to raise one fifth of the total, but was quickly subdued by threats and talk of treason. The Venetian ambassador commented of ship-money that 'if it does not altogether violate the laws of the realm, as some think it does, it is certainly repugnant to usage and to the forms hitherto observed'.

Yet for what purpose was the fleet being prepared? What was the king to do with his newly fitted ships? Was it enough that they should enforce his sovereignty of the seas by making sure that passing vessels struck their flags and lowered their topsails? In the spring of 1635 the first fleet raised by ship-money finally took sail. The forty-two vessels, nineteen of them over 50 tons, set forth with orders to curb piracy, protect English traders, prevent the Dutch from fishing in English waters and, according to one news-writer, Edward Rossingham, 'to preserve the sovereignty of the narrow seas from the French king who hath a design long to take it from us and therefore he hath provided a very great navy'. They were meant, in other words, to do everything and nothing.

So ship-money had indeed been raised, out of fear or loyalty, and the success of the tax ensured its survival; in the following year it was enlarged to take in the whole country. It was argued that, since the counties and urban corporations were interested in their 'honour, safety and profit', it was appropriate that 'they should all put to their helping hands'. The appeal worked, and the tax of 1635 became the model for the next five years in which 80 per cent of the money demanded was actually paid.

In 1634 the first hackney carriages were allowed to stand for hire in the streets of London, a novelty that generated the usual amount of horror and indignation. It was proposed that no hackney could be hired for a journey of less than 3 miles. The suggestion was accepted on the grounds that too many coaches going on brief expeditions would create a 'lock' or traffic-jam in the streets, damage the pavements and increase the price of hay. Other contemporaries suggested that no unmarried gentleman should be allowed to ride in a hackney carriage without being accompanied by his parents.

17

Sudden flashings

In the summer of 1636 Charles and Henrietta Maria paid a visit to Oxford; it was now, in essence, Laud's university. Yet only the academic officials paid homage to the royal couple. As they rode through the streets there were no calls of 'God save the king'. The scholars and the citizens alike were silent. This did not bode well, and was a salutary reminder that Charles was steadily building up grievances among his people.

Among the aristocracy and the greater gentry, for example, much anger had been aroused by the exactions of the various courts Charles had established to extort money – the court of wards and the court of forest law principal among them. Of the former it was said that even those devoted to the Crown saw that they might be destroyed, rather than protected, by the law. Of the latter, the fines for encroachment upon the royal forests had, according to Clarendon, 'brought more prejudice upon the court, and more discontent upon the king, from the most considerable part of the nobility and gentry in England, than any one action that had its rise from the king's will and pleasure'.

Charles was also in the process of alienating his subjects elsewhere. He had unilaterally published a body of 'canons' to be adopted by the Scottish Church; the people themselves interpreted these requirements as nothing more than new laws imposed upon them by strangers. No one could receive the sacrament except upon his or her knees. No man should cover his head during the divine service. No person should engage in spontaneous prayer. The clergy should not allow private meetings for the expounding of Scripture. These were all novel commandments, and caused much disquiet that soon enough would break out in riot.

The puritan reaction in England to the Laudian orthodoxy was no less strong if, perhaps, more carefully concealed. In London, for example, a secret network of conventicles and discussion groups had been established; they communicated with each other by means of manuscript tracts and sermon notes as well as by conferences and 'conversations' behind closed doors. This was a world of fasts, of prayer meetings and of scriptural discussions in such centres of sectarianism as Coleman Street and Friday Street in the capital.

Lady Eleanor Davies, who had the reputation among the godly of Lichfield as a prophetess, entered Lichfield Cathedral on one communion day at the end of 1636 with a brush and kettle. She announced that she had come to sprinkle her 'holy water' on the hangings and newly decorated communion table; the holy water itself was composed of tar, pitch and puddle-water which she then liberally distributed with her brush. She was deemed to be out of her wits and sent to Bethlehem Hospital. By curious chance Charles and Henrietta Maria had visited that institution just a few months before, according to Edward Rossingham, 'to see the mad folks where they were madly entertained. There was every one in his humour. Two mad women had almost frighted the king and queen, and all their attendants, out of the house, by their foul talk.'

Lady Eleanor Davies was not alone in her disgust at the Laudian innovations. One puritan writer, John Bastwick, complained that 'the Church is now as full of ceremonies as a dog is full of fleas'. Oliver Cromwell, looking back at the end of his life, remarked in a speech to parliament that Laud and his allies had wished 'to innovate upon us in matters of religion, and so to innovate as to eat out the core and power and heart and life of all religion, by bringing on us a company of poisonous popish ceremonies . . .' The conditions were, in a phrase of the day, 'too hot to last'.

In the summer of 1637 three sectarians were led before the Star Chamber on the charge of maligning the bishops of England.

William Prynne was well known to the judges, and four years earlier had lost his ears before being consigned to the Tower; yet somehow he had managed to write pamphlets in his prison cell which were then smuggled away by friendly visitors.

He was joined now in court by Henry Burton and John Bastwick. In *The Litany of John Bastwick* the latter had written, 'From plague, pestilence and famine, from bishops, priests and deacons, good Lord, deliver us!' When the chief justice saw Prynne he asked the officers of the court to hold back his hair so that he might see the scars of the mutilated ears. 'I had thought Mr Prynne had no ears,' he said, 'but methinks he hath ears.' The executioner had not been as savage in his punishment as he might have been, which left open the possibility that a further assault might finally sever them altogether. The sentences were as brutal as they were predictable. Loss of ears, and life imprisonment, were the verdicts upon the three men.

Many contemporaries were still unsympathetic to the condemned. News-writer John Burgh remarked that 'they are desperate mad factious fellows, and covet a kind of puritanical martyrdom or at least a fame of punishment for religion'. In that expectation they were successful. The previous sentence upon Prynne had been carried out with no obvious signs of public displeasure. Now the three men were cheered to the foot of the pillory, their path strewn with herbs and flowers. They stood in the pillory for two hours. They were not attacked with dirt or stones. They talked freely and cheerfully to the crowd around them, and their words were greeted by some with applause and shouts of approval. Burton's wife sent him a message that 'she was more cheerful of that day than of her wedding day'.

After two hours it was time for the more severe punishment. The hangman began to cut away at the ears of Burton, and as each ear was severed there came a roar of pain from the members of the crowd, so deep was their sympathy with the victims. When the blood came streaming down upon the scaffold, some of the crowd dipped their handkerchiefs in it. The stumps of Prynne's ears were further mutilated in a very contemptuous and brutal fashion. Bastwick was similarly treated. The fortitude of the men, in not flinching during their ordeal, aroused much admiration.

The prisoners were then taken out of London to their respective dungeons in the castles of Carnarvon, Launceston and Lancaster.

When Prynne travelled with his gaolers along the Great Northern Road, he was greeted with shouts of sympathy. When Burton left London by the Western Road, calls of 'God bless you!' echoed around him. Bastwick was followed by what seemed very like a triumphal procession. It was not a victory for Archbishop Laud. The rigour of the punishment had not overawed the crowd and Wentworth told the archbishop that 'a prince that loseth the force and example of his punishments loseth withal the greatest part of his domain'. The fate of the three men only served to alienate still further those who believed that Laud and the king were becoming a weight upon the body politic. The archbishop's own chaplain, Peter Heylyn, later wrote that the whole occasion 'was a very great trouble to the spirits of many very moderate and well-meaning men'. A proverb was current: 'To break an egg with an axe'.

The news from Edinburgh was even more disturbing. In the spring of 1637 a new Service Book for Scotland was published by the king. It applied much of the English Book of Common Prayer and abolished most of John Knox's Book of Common Order. It was in effect another English imposition, bearing all the marks of the intervention of Archbishop Laud. It was first read in public at St Giles, recently become the cathedral church of Edinburgh. The dean ascended the pulpit, but when he began to recite the words of the new book, shouts of abuse came from the women of the congregation. 'The Mass is entered among us!' 'Baal is in the church!' The bishop of Edinburgh then stepped forward to calm the angry women and begged them to desist from profaning 'holy ground'. This was not a phrase to be used in front of a puritan assembly, and further abuse was screamed against him; he was denounced as 'fox, wolf, belly god'. One of the women hurled her stool at him which, missing its target, sailed perilously close to the head of the dean.

The magistrates were then called to clear the church but the women, once ejected, surrounded the building; its great doors were pummelled and stones were flung at its windows as the unhappy ceremony proceeded to its end. Cries could be heard of 'a pape, a pape, anti-Christ, stone him, pull him down!' When the bishop came out, the women shouted 'get the thrapple out of him' or cut his windpipe; he barely escaped with his life. This was not a spontaneous combination of irate worshippers, however, but a carefully organized assault on the Service Book; certain nonconformist gentry and clergy had been planning the event for approximately three months, even though the scale of the riot was not perhaps anticipated. The incident became known as 'Stony Sunday'.

On hearing the news of the riots in Edinburgh the king ordered the immediate suppression of the malcontents. In a city where the majority of the populace was on their side, this was not a plausible command. Laud asked the Scottish bishops if they were ready to 'cast down the milk they have given because a few milkmaids have scolded at them. I hope they will be better advised.' Yet the archbishop was the one in need of counsel. The Edinburgh magistrates stated that no member of the clergy would be able to read the new service. Most of the ministers abhorred its contents, and all of them feared further riot.

Petitions were now arriving from all parts of Scotland deploring the papistical intentions of the new prayer book, so far from the old form and worship of the Kirk. The Scottish council wrote to the king that 'the murmur and grudge' at the innovations were unprecedented. Their remonstrances became all the more urgent after a second riot broke out in Edinburgh; the news had spread that the lord provost had tried to prevent a petition against the Service Book from reaching London. The petitioners, as they became known, were now by far the largest element in the city.

A moderate Presbyterian minister, Robert Baillie, confided to his journal that 'what shall be the event, God knows . . . the whole people thinks popery at the doors; the scandalous pamphlets which come daily new from England add oil to this flame; no man may speak anything in public for the king's part, except he would have himself marked for a sacrifice to be killed one day'.

Charles did not know what to do. He had not anticipated such an unwelcome act of defiance and disobedience. It is reported that his first words were 'I mean to be obeyed'. Yet how was he to enforce his will? He had no army, and only unwilling support from his representatives in Scotland. A solution to the immediate impasse was then suggested by members of the Scottish privy council. The petitioners would leave Edinburgh and return to their homes, leaving a group of commissioners to speak and act in their name. It was clear that, in effect, these commissioners would become the voice of Scotland.

It is possible to see the incidents in Edinburgh as a prelude to the more fatal antagonisms that led to civil war in England; yet no one at the time could have conceived such an outcome. One event just followed another in apparently random or at least unconnected fashion, and only at a later date could a pattern be discerned. Some time afterwards, for example, Henrietta Maria called the new order of service for Scotland 'that fatal book'. But who would have believed that a woman throwing a stool would mark the beginning of a great war?

Scotland had set an example of defiance that was regarded with admiration by some in England. Charles ruled over three kingdoms that were as vitally connected as filaments in a web; a disturbance in one part affected the equilibrium of the whole. Another great controversy concerning the king's authority now emerged in London. In the summer of 1637 the king decided to call John Hampden before the court of the exchequer for refusing to pay his portion of ship-money. Hampden had been imprisoned ten years earlier for declining the king's forced loan, but the experience does not seem to have curbed his independence.

At the beginning of the year twelve senior judges had declared that, in the face of danger to the nation, the king had a perfect right to order his subjects to finance the preparation of a fleet; in addition they declared that, in the event of refusal, the king was entitled to use compulsion. Leopold von Ranke believed that 'the judges could not have delivered a more important decision; it is one of the great events of English history'. The royal prerogative had become the foundation and cornerstone of government. Simonds D'Ewes wrote that if indeed it could be exacted lawfully, 'the king, upon the like pretence, might gather the same sum ten, twelve, or a hundred times redoubled, and so to infinite proportions to any one shire, when and as often as he pleased; and so no man was, in conclusion, worth anything'. It was a powerful argument, to be tested in the trial of John Hampden.

The court case lasted from November 1637 until the following summer and was watched with extreme interest by the political nation. It was a test of power between sovereign and subject, and was considered to be one of the most significant cases ever put to judgement. The prosecution essentially rested upon two points. The

Crown contended that all precedents, from the time of the Anglo-Saxons, allowed the king to gather money for his navy; Hampden in turn maintained that previous methods of taxation had in no way resembled the recent writs for ship-money sent to the inland counties. The Crown also defended the reasonableness of its claim for financial assistance in the face of foreign danger; by the time any parliament could be assembled to debate the matter, the country might have been attacked or even invaded. Hampden argued that the writs had been sent out six months before any ships were fitted, and there had been ample time for an assembly at Westminster; the writs were in any case contrary to statutes forbidding any tax without the consent of parliament.

The court was packed with spectators. A squire from Norfolk had come to London simply to attend the trial but when he arrived 'at peep of day', the crowd was already so great that he could get only 2 or 3 yards from the door of the court. Those who did obtain entrance seem largely to have taken Hampden's part. When one of his counsels, Oliver St John, opened the defence he was according to a puritan observer, Robert Woodford, 'much applauded and hummed by the bystanders, though my lord Finch [the chief justice] signified his displeasure for it'; at the close of St John's argument, 'they adventured to hum him again'. The argument continued beyond the walls of the court, where debates between the opposing sides could become very fierce. The vicar of Kilsby, in Northamptonshire, had exhorted his congregation 'to pay his majesty's dues'; whereupon the parish constable told him that the king's taxes were worse than the pharaoh's impositions upon the Israelites. Conversations of a similar kind took place all over the realm.

The judges deliberated and eventually gave a decision in favour of the court, seven against five. It was the smallest of all possible majorities for the king. Nevertheless the words of the chief justice in his support were repeated throughout the country. Finch declared that 'acts of parliament to take away his royal power in the defence of the kingdom are void'. Or, as another judge had put it, '*rex est lex*' – the king *is* the law. The ancient rights of Englishmen were of no importance, and the declarations of Magna Carta or the 'petition of right' were inconsequential. Neither law nor the parliament could bind the king's power. Clarendon, in his *History of the Rebellion*, states that 'undoubtedly my Lord Finch's speech made ship-money much more abhorred and formidable than all the commandments by the council table and all the distresses taken by the sheriffs of England'.

When a judge at the Maidstone assizes read out the judgment of the court in London the people, according to a contemporary, Sir Roger Twysden, 'did listen with great diligence and after the declaration made I did, in my conceit, see a kind of dejection in their very looks . . .' A justice of the peace in Kent wrote in a memorandum that 'this was the greatest cause according to the general opinion of the world was ever heard out of parliament in England. And the common sort of people are sensible of no loss of liberty so much as that hath joined with it a parting from money.' The opposition to ship-money became much more fierce than before; some refusing to pay now cited the arguments made by those judges who had favoured John Hampden.

In the middle of the trial, on 9 February 1638, the king issued a proclamation to Scotland in which he stated that 'we find our royal authority much impaired' and declared that all protests against the new prayer book would be deemed treasonable. The king's response was characteristic. Any attempt to curb his power was of course treachery and he believed that, if he made any compromise or accommodation, he would be fatally weakened; he did not want to become as powerless as the doge of Venice and he informed his representative in Scotland, the marquis of Hamilton, that he was 'resolved to hazard my life rather than suffer authority to be condemned'. He was not simply referring to his authority but to the concept of 'authority' itself. Yet he could be wily and secretive at the same time, and told Hamilton that 'I give you leave to flatter them with what hopes you please'. Since the leaders of the prayer book rebellion were essentially traitors, they could be deceived and betrayed with impunity.

In response the commissioners in Edinburgh, representing the petitioners, drew up a national covenant in which the precepts of the Kirk were re-established. Among its declarations was one that the innovations of the new prayer book 'do sensibly tend to the re-establishing of the popish religion and tyranny, and to the subversion and ruin of the true reformed religion and of our liberties, laws and estates'. The people were in truth not rebelling against their king per se, but at the alliance of secular and religious authority that he had come to represent. The elect were now bound to God in solemn contract, as the Israelites once had been, with a clear moral obligation to fulfil His commands. 'If thou walk before me, and serve me, and be perfect . . . I am willing to enter into covenant with thee' (Genesis, 17: 1–2). The national covenant was carried in triumph through the streets, accompanied by crowds of women and children who alternately cheered and wept.

The people of Scotland took their lead from the inhabitants of Edinburgh and signed the covenant in their hundreds of thousands, declaring that they would rather die than accept the new liturgy. They raised their right hands to heaven before they took up the pen. Many of the orthodox Scottish bishops fled to England, with the archbishop of St Andrews, John Spottiswoode, lamenting that 'all we have been doing these thirty years past is now thrown down at once'. This came from the king's attempt to master his subjects in the same way as he mastered his horse.

The responses of others were mixed. The great minister of France, Richelieu, was inclined to support and even to aid the Scottish rebels on the grounds that trouble for the English king was always welcome. In turn Charles did not wish the world to believe that his authority had been spurned by some of his subjects; all his life he feared to appear weak. The English dissenters, already excited and agitated by the trial of John Hampden, welcomed the defiant actions of the Scots; many of them hoped that the Scottish example might be followed closer to home. The most impassioned denunciations of the king's policy could be read in the verses and broadsides distributed in the streets of London.

Laud wrote to Wentworth that 'my misgiving soul is deeply apprehensive of no small evils coming on'. Wentworth himself was urging the king to stricter measures. He believed that, if the arrogance and bravado of the Scots were not 'thoroughly corrected', it would be impossible to know how far the evil of dissension might spread. Some people were already wary of the coming conflict. When in 1638 one of the godly in the Wiltshire village of Holt found a beggar at his door he refused to give him alms on the grounds that 'shortly you will be pressed for war, and then you will fight against us'.

When the general assembly of the Church of Scotland met in Glasgow Cathedral towards the end of November, the bishops were charged with violating the boundaries of their proper authority. The marquis of Hamilton attended in the name of the king, and he reported to his master that 'my soul was never sadder than to see such a sight; not one gown amongst the whole company, many swords but many more daggers – most of them having left their guns and pistols in their lodgings'. The voting of course went against the orders and wishes of the king. Hamilton thereupon declared the assembly dissolved but, after he had left the church, the delegates voted to continue their debate. They also passed a resolution declaring that the Kirk was independent of the civil power, in effect stripping Charles of any religious supremacy he had previously claimed.

For the next three weeks the delegates revised the whole form of the Scottish faith that had recently been imposed upon them. The new liturgy was abolished. The bishops were excommunicated. The king's writ no longer ran in Scotland.

The preparations for war were now intensified. The king ordered a convoy of military supplies to be sent from the Tower to Hull while the marquis of Hamilton advised him to take in hand the further fortification of Berwick, Carlisle and Newcastle. The lords-lieutenant of the counties were ordered to organize and exercise their local militias for readiness in combat. The leaders of the Scots, in turn, divided their country into seven military regions from which recruits would be taken; the commissioners also requested that the Scots mercenaries, fighting for the cause of Protestantism in Germany, should come home for a more significant war. Their lord general, Alexander Leslie, knew that they would bring with them new forms of military training and expertise taught by Dutch and Swedish commanders. It was believed that they would be a far more professional force than their English adversaries.

Omens were noticed and reported. A Yorkshire gentleman, Sir Henry Slingsby, confided to his diary an old prophecy that, after the victories of the Saxons and Normans, England would next be mastered by the Scots. Freak winds and lightning were seen. Henry Hastings reported to his father that, at eight o'clock one evening, the clouds dispersed to reveal apparitions 'like men with pikes and muskets, but suddenly the scene being changed they appeared in two bodies of armed men set in battalion, and then a noise was heard and sudden flashings of light seen and streaks like smoke issuing out of these clouds'. The forces of war were gathering.

18

Venture all

At the beginning of 1639 Charles sent out a summons for the soldiers of his kingdom to meet him at York. The peers of the realm were ordered to appear in person, together with the retinues that befitted their status. The trained bands – the local militia made up of citizens – of the north were required to attend under the command of the lords-lieutenant of their counties. The rest of the men were conscripted, mainly from the midlands; they were formerly ploughmen or carters or thatchers, and had no stomach for a fight. Neither trained nor organized, they were being sent to unknown regions of the country for a cause about which they knew very little or nothing.

The men raised from Herefordshire attacked and wounded their officers before returning to their towns and villages. Other conscripts proceeded to pillage the hamlets through which they passed. They tore down the hated enclosures that parcelled up previously common land; they fired the gaols and freed the prisoners, many of whom had been detained for refusing to pay royal taxes; they attacked the undergraduates of Oxford; the more precise of them attacked the altars and communion rails of the churches. They were, as one royalist commander, Lord Conway, put it, 'more fit for Bedlam or Bridewell' than the king's service.

The peers and nobles, gathered about the king by old feudal bonds, were equally reluctant to risk their lives in the royal cause. Many of them pleaded sickness, and the majority of them travelled to York against their will. If the king lost, their lands and even their lives might not be spared by the Scottish covenanters; if he won, and became supreme, their liberties would be further at risk. The prospect of another parliament, for example, would recede even further into the distance. The puritan party, in particular, had no reason or desire to fight against their co-religionists in Scotland. It would be an act of faithlessness on an unparalleled scale. Many of them believed that the war was being fought on behalf of the episcopate, and that its principal aim was to restore the bishops to their authority in Scotland. So the war became known as *bellum episcopale* or the Bishops' War. It was all the more hated by some because of it.

Yet it was abhorred principally because it was an unfamiliar and unwelcome intrusion into the affairs of the nation. England had avoided foreign wars, and enjoyed domestic peace, for many years; no shots had been fired, and no drums heard, in the land. Yet that quiet was about to be shattered. Sir Henry Slingsby wrote that it was 'a thing most horrible that we should engage ourself in a war one with another, and with our own venom gnaw and consume ourself'. The long period of peace also meant that the instruments of war had been degraded; the swords and muskets and pikes, laid aside, were now tarnished or broken. Horses were in short supply.

At the end of March 1639, the king rode into York to meet his army. Charles and his principal officers were lodged at the King's House, the residence of the lord president of the north, while other officers and gentry found room in the various inns of the city such as the Talbot and the Dragon. The king was also graciously pleased to watch his 'cavaliers' exercising on their horses in the meadows known as the 'ings'. The 'cavaliers' were now a recognizable body of officers attached to the king's cause; some of them were already professional soldiers who had seen service in the European wars, while others were the sons of gentlemen in search of martial glory. Many of them, however, earned a reputation as braggarts and as anti-puritan bullies given to drink and gaming. According to a pamphlet of the time, 'Old News Newly Revived', anyone with 'a tilting feather, a flaunting periwig, buff doublet, scarlet hose, and a sword as big as a lath' could be mistaken for one. They were now ready to fight what one of the king's men, Sir Francis Windebank, in turn castigated as 'those scurvy, filthy, dirty, nasty, lousy, itchy, scabby, shitten, stinking, slovenly, snotty-nosed, logger-headed, foolish, insolent, proud, beggarly, impertinent, absurd, grout-headed, villainous, barbarous, bestial, false, lying, roguish, devilish . . . damnable, atheistical, puritanical crew of the Scottish Covenant'.

The king seems to have presumed, as Clarendon put it in his *History of the Rebellion*, that his calling together the peers of the realm with their retinues meant that 'the glory of such a visible appearance of the whole nobility would at once terrify and reduce the Scots'. In that presumption he was quite wrong. He could not even rely upon the nobility itself. Alarmed by talk of collusion with the covenanters, the king demanded that the lords and gentry at York should take an oath of allegiance. Two of them declined, Lord Brooke and Viscount Saye refusing to do so on the grounds that it was unconstitutional to demand any such oath that had not been approved by parliament. Saye added that, since the crowns of England and of Scotland were now unified, he could not take it upon himself to kill a Scot. Charles remonstrated with him angrily: 'My lord, there be as good men as you that will not refuse to take it, but I find you averse to all my proceedings.' He ordered that both men be arrested.

It was the talk of the city, and it seems to have been generally agreed that the peers had become martyrs to the king's will. Charles was soon advised that they had done nothing illegal in refusing the oath; much to his chagrin he was obliged to release them. His authority had suffered another grave blow. It transpired soon enough that Viscount Saye had indeed been in secret discussion with the leaders of the covenant cause. They held the puritan creed in common, and their clandestine collaboration would be significant in the events of later months.

On 1 May Charles advanced to Durham. His envoy to Scotland and now commander of his ships, the marquis of Hamilton, wrote to him that 'your majesty's affairs are in desperate condition. The enraged people here run to the height of rebellion, and walk with a blind obedience as by their traitorous leaders they are commanded . . . You will find it a work of great difficulty and of vast expense to curb them by force, their power being greater, their combination stronger than can be imagined.' Hamilton, himself a Scot, declared that 'next to hell I hate this land'. His discomfort was also heightened by his mother's threat that, if he returned in arms to his native country, she would shoot him.

Charles could not afford 'expense' of any kind. By the best estimate he had enough money to support his army to the end of the summer, but no longer. By the end of May, however, the lord treasurer announced that the revenue was exhausted. The knight marshal, Sir Edmund Verney, wrote to his son that 'our men are very raw, our arms of all sorts naught, our victual scarce, and provision for horses worse'.

The Scots were soon on the move. The drums were beaten, morning and evening, to summon the soldiers for divine service; they listened to two sermons each day in support of their cause. When the men were not engaged in martial exercise, they studied the Scriptures or sang hymns or prayed aloud. It was a formidable force. At the beginning of June they set up an armed camp at Kelso on the Scottish borders. The king ordered the earl of Holland to march 3,000 men to the north and drive them out. So the earl led his cavalry forward to test the purposes of the Scots. The English forces climbed an incline from which they could see the enemy below them. Holland was about to order a charge when a cloud of dust could be seen approaching very quickly; this was taken to be the token of a larger Scottish army. The English retreated in order but in haste; discretion, as on many other occasions, surmounted valour. It was said that they were spared a slaughter by the elders of the covenant who only wished for the strangers to leave their country.

The fiasco was a double blow to the English forces. They had not only been humiliated by the Scots but the Scottish lord general, Alexander Leslie, seemed to know in advance the movement of Holland's men. It looked very much as if there was a spy or traitor in the camp. Sir Edmund Verney wrote once more to his son that 'I think the king dares not stir out of his trenches. What counsels he will take, or what he will do, I cannot divine.' It had become clear to everyone that the enterprise was a huge mistake.

On 5 June Alexander Leslie arrived with an army of 12,000 men, and encamped on a hill about 11 miles from the king's position. Charles was devoid of fear, or indeed of any other emotion except perhaps curiosity; he took a view of the Scottish forces through his telescope. 'Come let us go to supper,' he said, 'the number is not considerable.' Yet he could not afford to fight them. The Scots were well-disciplined and ready to fight for 'Christ's Crown and Covenant'; he had only an ill-organized and largely apathetic army already painfully aware of its lack of provisions.

The king had to gain time to prepare himself more fully for armed warfare. The Scots, in turn, were reluctant to invade England; the temper of an aroused nation would then be such that victory was by no means certain. Parliament might be called, and all the material wants of the king resolved. It could become a hard fight. So the conditions were right to obtain a truce and agree to a treaty. On 11 June six commissioners from the Scots and six commissioners from the king sat down together at Berwick in the tent of the earl of Arundel; Charles himself then joined them.

The covenanters were described by one Scottish historian as 'men a little too low for heaven, and much too high for earth'. But on this occasion they were willing at least to treat with the king. In the event the negotiations at Berwick meant nothing. Ambiguities, confusions and caveats were the sum of all talk so that in the end, according to Clarendon, 'there were not two present who did agree in the same relation of what was said and done . . .' Nobody meant what he said, or said what he meant. The treaty was merely a paper peace and within six months the antagonists were preparing for a later and greater conflict. The first Bishops' War, a war without a set battle, had come to an end.

Charles I had hoped to lead a glittering army to victory but had instead been forced to come to terms with a people that had, to all intents and purposes, become a separate nation beyond his power to command. The Scots gained the reputation that he himself had forfeited. It was more painful for him to lose authority than to part with his lifeblood. He had come to realize the reluctance of many of the peers and gentry to join him in his quarrel. So he disbanded the army without thanking any of its commanders, who had undergone the sacrifice of bringing up their men, and without giving honours to his faithful followers. The earl of Essex, one of the great nobles whom the king distrusted, was dismissed without a word. Soon enough he would become a principal opponent of the king.

Charles was anxious and dissatisfied. When the Scots published a document that purported to contain the matter of the treaty it was burned in London by the common hangman. The covenanters proclaimed, however, that in maintaining their own rights they were also fighting for English liberties; they insinuated that the proscription or exclusion of their religion would infallibly lead to the destruction of the cause of puritanism in England.

There were many of that nation who agreed with them, Pym and Hampden among them; for these Englishmen, the Scottish defiance of a stubborn and authoritarian king was an inspiration. Letters passed between the 'malcontents' or 'malignants' of both nations, as the king called them, in the hope of planning a common strategy to preserve their religion. The earl of Northumberland wrote that 'the north is now the scene of all our news'; the theatre of the three kingdoms was now situated in Edinburgh. English politics now became thoroughly mingled with Scottish affairs.

The king had also lost authority on the high seas. In the autumn of 1639 a Spanish fleet had been discovered in the Channel by a Dutch squadron and, after a hot pursuit, took refuge in the Downs off the coast of east Kent; Charles offered, for a large sum, to take the Spaniards under his protection and convey them to the coast of Flanders. Yet the Dutch were unwilling to lose their prey and, with reinforcements, they attacked the Spanish vessels and sank many of them. The English fleet, under the command of Vice-Admiral Pennington, merely looked on as the security of their home waters was violated. The sea road to Dover was known as 'the king of England's imperial chamber', but that king had failed in his first duty of protecting it.

The paralysis of Charles was part of a much wider problem of foreign policy where, in want of money and preoccupied by the problem of Scotland, he was obliged to play off one party against another in the hope of something 'turning up'. France, Holland and Spain had to be appeased equally.

On 27 July, just before he left Berwick, Charles had summoned an emissary sent by Thomas Wentworth from Ireland; they held a long and secret conversation on matters that the king would not confide to paper. Wentworth had already told the king that he should conclude an armistice, and postpone any attack upon the Scots until he was quite certain that he could defeat them. Charles now merely sent a message to the lord deputy, saying, 'Come when you will, you shall be welcome.' The king was already scheming.

Wentworth returned from Dublin in the autumn of the year, and at once became the king's most trusted councillor. He possessed all the self-confidence and energy that the king himself lacked. One courtier, Sir Philip Warwick, recorded that 'his countenance was cloudy, while he moved or sat thinking; but when he spoke, either seriously or facetiously, he had a lightsome and very pleasant air'.

Wentworth urged Charles to take the affairs of Scotland into his own hands, and in addition to call parliament in order to be supplied with funds. The king of course distrusted and even despised the members at Westminster, but Wentworth believed that he could organize a court party which would be able to outmanoeuvre any opposition from such familiar suspected persons as Pym and Hampden. The king would also be absolved of the charge of absolutism, of wishing to rule without parliament, and might once again earn the approval of the nation. If the members of the Commons did not cheerfully grant his demands, in the face of evident danger from the Scots, then the world would know who to blame. Within a few months Wentworth received the earldom of Strafford.

At the end of 1639, therefore, parliament was summoned. The news was greeted with relief by those who had feared the complete abandonment of conventional government. Others were not so sanguine, however, and the Venetian ambassador reported that 'the long rusted gates of parliament cannot be opened without difficulty'. The king's councillors professed to believe that the newly elected parliament, shocked by the insolence of the Scots, would rally around the king.

The general election proceeded apace, with all sides and factions trying to organize support in an informal way. Only sixty-two of the elections were contested, with the other candidates selected by the principal landowners in the country and by the municipal corporations of the towns and cities. Other members of parliament were chosen by individual patrons who owned the right of nomination. A contested election was considered to be a mark of failure by the local elite to resolve matters satisfactorily.

The contested seats were indeed scenes of great division; there had been no such competition for eleven years. The court sent out lists of its favoured candidates as soon as the writs were issued. The local ministers preached to their congregations largely in favour of puritan candidates, while the peers supporting the court often tried to bribe or intimidate the electors of their regions. Newsletters and speeches abounded, as did the more nebulous reports of rumour and gossip. Violence, and threats of violence, were commonplace. A verse was circulated in opposition to the court party:

> Choose no ship sheriff, nor court atheist,
> No fen drainer, nor church papist.

There were no 'parties' in the modern sense, of course, merely individuals with various interests or principles who might or might not form an association with those who largely agreed with them. Some of them described themselves as 'good commonwealthmen' or 'patriots' who played upon the people's fears of taxation and popery. Other candidates tried to rally the electors to the cause of king and country. The tide was against them. It was said by a Kentish gentleman, Sir Roger Twysden, that 'the common people had been so bitten with ship-money that they were very averse from a courtier'; in Leicestershire the freeholders, who made up the constituency, were opposed to one candidate because 'he is a courtier and has been sheriff and collected the ship-money'.

It has been estimated that, of the sixty or so candidates nominated or supported by the court, only fourteen were successful. It would be fair to say, however, that the majority of those elected were not partisan in any obvious sense; they were individuals who came to Westminster with a lively sense of local complaints and who, when congregated together, might find that they had grievances in common.

Preparations for another war against Scotland were even then being made. It was intended to press into service 30,000 foot-soldiers from the counties south of the Humber, the northern counties having given service in the last war. The covenanters were equally active in Scotland, where a call to arms was about to be issued. It did not seem possible that war could be avoided. A group of covenanters came to London, where it was reported that they held secret consultations with their English allies.

The newly elected parliament opened on 13 April 1640, in great excitement. The wife of the earl of Bridgewater was advised to procure a place at a window by six o'clock in the morning, in order to watch the passing scenes at Westminster; after that time the press of the people in the street would make it impossible for her to reach the house. John Finch, newly appointed as lord keeper of the great seal, made an opening speech on behalf of the king in which he dilated upon the threat that the Scots posed to the country; the king had been obliged to raise an army in its defence and, for the payment of that army, he needed funds. Finch revealed that a bill had already been prepared with all the relevant measures in place; it was only necessary for parliament to pass it. Then, and only then, would the grievances of individual members be discussed. He stated that 'the king did not require their advice but an immediate vote of supplies'. It was noted that Finch had at no stage mentioned the primary source of discontent, the ship-money which was once again being exacted.

The members soon made their reply to the lord keeper's speech. On the first day of the session the earl of Northumberland wrote that 'their jealousies and suspicions appear upon every occasion and I fear they will not readily be persuaded to believe the fair and gracious promises that are made to them by the king'. In this opinion he was correct. The member for Colchester, Harbottle Grimstone, delivered a speech in which he stated that the invasion of individual liberties at home was more threatening than the ambitions of any enemy abroad. On the following day petitions from the various counties, complaining about unjust exactions, were presented to the Commons.

On 17 April John Pym rose to speak on the nature of parliamentary authority. He declared that 'the powers of parliament are to the body politic as the rational faculties of the soul to man'. He was asserting more than the usual claims of parliamentary privilege; he was outlining what amounted to a new theory of government without any mention of the divine right of kings. He then turned to the matter of religion, and condemned the innovations introduced by Laud and others; they had managed only to raise 'new occasions of further division' and to dismay 'the faithful professors of the truth'. The grievances of his eleven years' silence now poured forth in an attack upon ship-money, monopolies, forest law and the other measures that the king had imposed. When he sat down he was greeted with cries of 'A good oration!'

There was one group or faction in this parliament that helped to shape the session. The Providence Island Company had first been established to assist the emigration of 'godly' settlers to an island off the coast of what is now Nicaragua; it was hoped that a little republican commonwealth would then emerge that would finance itself with tobacco and cotton. Among the begetters of this scheme were the most prominent puritans in the country, among them Oliver St John, John Pym, John Hampden, Viscount Saye and Lord Brooke; the most eminent of them, however, was the earl of Warwick. All of these men now took their seats in parliament, both in the Commons and in the Lords, where they could plan their strategy in concert. They had familial as well as religious connections, lending them a unity and strength of purpose that were almost without precedent. The court party, in contrast, was riven with conflicts over personality and policy.

On 21 April the king summoned both houses to Whitehall, and demanded that the financial subsidies be granted to him. Two days later the Commons went into committee and requested a conference with the Lords on the grounds that 'until the liberties of the House and kingdom were cleared, they knew not whether they had anything to give or no'. At this act of defiance Charles was extremely angry. On 1 May the Commons decided by a large majority to call before them a cleric who had stated that the king had the authority to make laws without parliament; this was considered by the court to be another act of insubordination. On the following day the king demanded an immediate answer to his request for money; he was met with prevarication. On 4 May Charles sent another message in which he agreed to give up the collection of ship-money in return for twelve subsidies amounting to approximately £850,000. The committee of the Commons again broke up without reaching any definite conclusions. One of the royal councillors, Sir Henry Vane, told the king that there was now no hope that they 'would give one penny'.

It had become apparent, at least to the court party, that the Commons had no real desire to support the king's war against Scotland; it might even be supposed that they were leaning towards the Scottish covenanters. The king had asked for supplies five times, and five times he had been rebuffed. He had twice appeared in person, to no palpable effect. He had tried to negotiate but his offers had been rejected with silence. He had pressed for speed in their decisions, with the possibility of an imminent invasion from the north, but parliament had been dilatory and evasive.

Rumours now reached the king that, under the influence of Pym, a petition was even then being drawn up asking him to come to terms with the Scots. He summoned the Speaker and forbade him take his place on the following day, thus avoiding the possibility of any debate. He then hurried to the Lords and on 5 May summarily dissolved the parliament. Since it had endured for only three weeks, it became commonly known as the 'stillborn parliament'; posterity christened it the 'Short Parliament'. It had achieved nothing, but it had changed everything. It had given voice to the frustration and anger of the country at the behaviour of the king; it had become a national forum where none had existed before.

One newly elected MP, Edward Hyde, who would later become better known as Lord Clarendon, was disconsolate. He supported the king but did not know what the future might hold for him. He wrote later that one of the leaders of the parliamentary revolt, Oliver St John, 'observing a cloudiness in me, bade me "be of good comfort; all would go well; for things must be worse before they could be better"'. St John added that 'we must not only sweep the house clean below, but must pull down all the cobwebs which hang in the top and corners'. He was hoping for a crisis or disaster, in other words, that would overturn the familiar order.

Another member may be introduced here. Sir Philip Warwick came into the house later in the same year,

> and perceived a gentleman whom I knew not, very ordinarily apparelled; for it was a plain cloth suit that seemed to have been made by an ill country tailor; his linen was plain and not very clean and I remember a speck or two of blood upon his

> little band which was not much larger than his collar; his hat was without a hatband; his stature was of a good size; his sword stuck close to his side; his countenance swollen and reddish; his voice sharp and untunable and his eloquence full of fervour.

Such was the young Oliver Cromwell, who had sat unnoticed in the parliamentary sessions of 1628 and 1629. Now he had found his voice.

On the afternoon of the dissolution the king's council met in which the newly ennobled earl of Strafford, according to notes taken at the time, advised the king to 'go on with a vigorous war as you first designed, loosed and absolved from all rules of government, being reduced to extreme necessities. Everything is to be done that power must admit.' He added that 'you have an army in Ireland you may employ here to reduce this kingdom'. It was, perhaps, not clear which 'kingdom' needed to be reduced; this was an ambiguity that would cost him dear.

The dissolution aroused much discontent. The calling of the first parliament for eleven years had been hailed as a victory and as a deliverance from bondage; yet it had ended in defeat. Clarendon recalled that 'there could not a greater damp have seized upon the spirits of the whole nation'. The king blamed 'the cunning of some few seditiously affected men'; he genuinely believed, for example, that the members of the Providence Island Company were in direct contact with his Scottish enemies in an effort to defeat him.

Many in London and elsewhere, however, were ready to condemn the king and his councillors, principal among them the earl of Strafford and Archbishop Laud. Strafford now became known as 'black Tom Tyrant', the hatred for him compounded by the suspicion that he was indeed planning to bring over an Irish army to subdue English dissent. Yet William Laud was still the principal target. He was, in the judgement of many, the secret power behind the throne.

On 7 May, two days after the dissolution, the lord mayor and his aldermen were summoned before the council and ordered to provide the king with a loan of £200,000. If they refused they were to return three days later with a list of the wealthiest Londoners who could furnish the necessary funds. On 10 May they returned, bearing no list. 'Sir,' Strafford said to the king, 'you will never do good to these citizens of London till you have made examples of some of these aldermen. Unless you hang up some of them, you will do no good upon them.' The king did not execute them, but he did commit four of them to prison. This added more fuel to the fire that was about to break out in the streets.

Placards had been posted at the Royal Exchange, and elsewhere, calling upon the apprentices to meet at St George's Fields in Southwark and 'hunt William the fox, the breaker of the parliament'. A force of 500 attempted, on the night of 11 May, to storm the archbishop's palace at Lambeth; the protestors were driven off by gunfire from the trained bands. Three days later the prisons that held some of the rioters were broken open, and the men released. The trained bands of Essex, Kent and Hertfordshire were summoned to the capital where they successfully restored a semblance of peace. Yet there were still victims. One captured apprentice was, on the orders of the king, tortured on the rack in the vain hope that he would name his accomplices; his crime had been to beat the drum in the vanguard of the rioters. It was the last example of judicial torture in English history. A sailor was convicted of high treason for attempting to open the gates of Lambeth Palace with a crowbar; he was hanged, drawn and quartered as punishment for his mighty offence.

The anger against the archbishop was augmented by the deliberations of the convocation. This body of the higher clergy always met at the time of parliament but, on this occasion, it was not dissolved after the abrupt conclusion of the recent short session. It continued to meet, granted a subsidy to the king, and announced seventeen new canons that exalted the sovereign's power. It was ordered that, four times in each year, the clergy should preach to their congregations on the theme of divine right. It was further decreed that all of the clergy must take an oath to maintain both the doctrine and the discipline of the Church and not to allow any alteration in its government by 'archbishops, bishops, deans and archdeacons etc.'. This became known derisively as 'the etcetera oath'. How could clerics obey a ruling of which the contents were so uncertain? Without the assent of parliament, in any case, the decree was illegal. When the chancellor of the bishop of London entered one church to exact the oath, with a great mace carried before him, the verger stopped him with the words: 'I care nothing for you, nor for your artichoke.' The new canons were similarly derided. A drawing by Wenceslaus Hollar depicted some clergymen standing about a faulty cannon as Laud lights it. A verse beneath it read:

> This cannon's sealed, well forg'd, not made of lead
> Give fire. Oh no, 'twill break and strike us dead.

The Scots were greatly heartened by events in England. A parliament met in Edinburgh at the beginning of June, despite an effort by Charles to prorogue it. Its members now believed that the people of England were no longer inclined to support their king; they passed into law, without royal assent, various Acts that removed the bishops from the Kirk and materially diminished the king's authority. It was a tacit declaration of war.

Yet what could the king do? He had formed no fresh army, and the troops still quartered at Newcastle after the last conflict were untrained and impoverished. Once more the king demanded ship-money from London. The sheriffs went from house to house to exact the tax but only one man, in the entire City of London, agreed to pay it. Schemes for loans from France, and from Genoa, came to nothing.

The labourers and craftsmen of England were again pressed into service, in the king's army, for a cause about which they knew or cared little. News of disorder came from most of the southern counties, and one of the first open mutinies broke out in Warwickshire. Some men of Devon, stopping at Wellington in Somerset, murdered a Roman Catholic lieutenant who refused to accompany them to church. When all of these unlikely and unwilling recruits arrived at Selby, in North Yorkshire, their commander described them as 'the arch-knaves of the country'. Thus began the Second Bishops' War.

19

A great and dangerous treason

In July 1640, the lord general of the Scottish forces, Alexander Leslie, began to create the nucleus of an army to take the fight once more into England. His intention was first to seize Newcastle; with its mineral wealth in his hands, he knew that he could exert pressure upon London that depended upon 'sea-coal' for its fuel. He believed that he would meet no resistance from the northern counties; the dissolution of parliament, and the general belief in a 'popish plot' led by Laud, had put an end to any appetite for a struggle against Scotland. Leslie's contacts in England had in fact assured him that the next parliament, when summoned, would demand peace; otherwise, it would give no financial assistance to the king. There may have been a closer connection. It seems probable that the leaders of the 'godly' cause in England had effectively invited the Scots to invade as a way of curbing or destroying the power of an authoritarian king. Leslie's march would be welcomed by some, therefore, and treated with indifference by the rest.

On the morning of 20 August the king set out from London to meet his forces in the north. On that night a Scottish army of 25,000 men crossed the Tweed. As soon as they entered English territory, their ministers formed the vanguard with Bibles in their hands. A declaration was issued to the effect that they were not marching against the English but against the papists, the Arminians and the prelates. They would remain in England until their grievances were heard by a new parliament.

They informed the people of Northumberland, too, that they would not take any food or drink without paying for it; they were well disciplined and respectful. Thomas Wentworth, the earl of Strafford, had hoped that the mere sight of an invading army would enrage all good Englishmen, but that proved not to be the case. The English commander in the north, Viscount Conway, noted that 'the country doth give them all the assistance they can. Many of the country gentlemen do come to them, entertain and feast them.' In London, after the king's departure, all was in confusion. A courtier, Sir Nicholas Byron, wrote that 'we are here, and in every place, in such distraction as if the day of judgment were hourly expected'. The constable of the Tower was ordered to prepare his fortress for a possible siege. Meanwhile the Scots were still marching southward.

Viscount Conway had been ordered to fortify the banks of the Tyne, and to defend Newcastle; he left two-thirds of his troops to protect the city, and took the remainder some 4 miles above Newcastle to a ford in the river at Newburn. The Scots took up a commanding position on the north bank, from where they fired on the enemy; the English soldiers, unaccustomed to gunshot, fled after some of their number were killed. The cavalry also retired in disarray. It was the first major victory of the Scots over the English for 300 years. Charles I had failed in battle, the single most important disgrace that stained the honour of a king. The battle of Newburn might also be considered the first of the civil war, since two rival parties had fought on English soil.

After their egregious defeat the English army retired to the borders of Yorkshire, leaving Durham and Northumberland in the hands of the enemy. The vital city of Newcastle had already surrendered. The earl of Strafford wrote to his friend, Sir George Radcliffe, from Northallerton in North Yorkshire where he had gone to meet the fleeing army:

> Pity me, for never came any man to so lost a business. The army altogether necessitous and unprovided of all necessaries . . . Our horse all cowardly; the country from Berwick to York in the power of the Scots; an universal affright in all;

> a general disaffection to the king's service, none sensible of his dishonor. In one word, here alone to fight with all these evils, without anyone to help. God of his goodness deliver me out of this, the greatest evil of my life.

The news of the royal defeat at Newburn was greeted with celebrations in London. Twelve peers of puritan persuasion, among them the earls of Warwick and Bedford, now issued in the traditional manner a 'petition' to the monarch in which they called for a parliament to resolve the grievances and evils of the nation; they stated that 'your whole kingdom [has] become full of fears and discontents'. They were following a carefully prepared strategy. If the king declined to act on their advice, they themselves were prepared to summon parliament, just as the barons of Henry III had threatened almost 400 years before.

The king reacted in a thoroughly medieval way. He received the petition while at York, and summoned a great council of the peers. He may have hoped that they might raise large sums of money, without the assistance of parliament, but in this hope he was destined to be disappointed. Archbishop Laud was more realistic, and believed that the great council would lead inevitably to the calling of another parliament that might bode no good.

So the peers of England met in the hall of the deanery at York on 24 September. They represented a vast social power; they exercised local authority over tenants and dependants but they also wielded political power by means of their influence in county and borough elections. In his opening speech to them the king announced that he would indeed summon parliament to meet at the beginning of November; it was hoped that, on the basis of this undertaking, the City would be ready to lend him money. He said further that an 'army of rebels' was lodged within the kingdom and he wished for the peers' advice so that 'we might justly proceed to the chastisement of these insolencies'.

In the debate that followed it was eventually decided that commissioners should be sent to negotiate with the invaders. The Scots had already demanded money from the northern counties where they were lodged; they now insisted that the payments be maintained by the leading gentry, and that Charles should call parliament, where a peace treaty could be agreed. They trusted parliament, in other words, rather than the king. On these conditions they would remain where they were, and not proceed any further into an unhappy and divided kingdom.

Negotiators from both sides met at Ripon, where it was concluded that the king would pay the Scots £25,000 a month until a peace treaty had been reached. It seemed likely that only parliament could supply such a sum. The peers at York were asked to advise the acceptance or rejection of the agreement. It was of course no contest. The king had no choice but to submit to the claims of the invaders and to call parliament. The experiment of absolute monarchy had come to an end.

In his diary entry for 30 October John Evelyn noted that 'I saw his majesty (coming from his northern expedition) ride in pomp and a kind of ovation, with all the marks of a happy peace, restored to the affections of his people, being conducted through London with a most splendid cavalcade'. Edward Rossingham wrote to Viscount Conway that 'we are all mad with joy here that his majesty does call his parliament, and that he puts his Scotch business into the hands of his peers who, the hope is here, will make peace upon any conditions'. The earl of Northampton considered 'one word of four syllables', namely parliament, was 'like the dew of heaven'.

Others were not so sanguine. A few days before the king's arrival into the city Archbishop Laud had entered his study, in search of certain manuscripts, only to find his portrait by Van Dyck lying face down upon the floor. He was a superstitious man. 'I am almost every day threated with my ruin in Parliament,' he confided to his diary. 'God grant this be no omen.'

The 'godly' parliamentarians were well prepared. They met at the house of John Pym, close to Gray's Inn, where their plans were discussed in detail. They became known as 'the Junto', with Pym their leader in the Commons and the earl of Bedford their representative in the Lords. They knew the disposition of the Scots and in turn the covenanters relied upon the help of their English friends in parliament to engineer the necessary changes in religion. This was the 'Protestant Cause'.

The voting in the parliamentary elections was unusually combative, with eighty-six contests outside the charmed circle of seats where only one uncontested member stood. The king's party was again at a disadvantage, with local as well as religious interests matched against the courtiers and their acolytes. Of twelve lawyers chosen by the king to be selected, for example, only three were appointed. On 3 November the king travelled to the new parliament by water in order to avoid the public gaze. The Venetian ambassador noted that the lack of ceremony 'shows more clearly than ever to his people that he consents to the summons merely from compulsion . . . and not of his own free will to please the people'. Who could have guessed that this parliament would last, with intervals, for almost twenty years?

As soon as they were assembled in debate, the members of the Commons issued a catalogue of grievances against the conduct of the king's councillors, Strafford and Laud chief among them. The dissolution of the 'Short Parliament', before any measures of reform could be agreed, had not improved the temper of the members; 60 per cent of them had sat in the previous assembly and they were now more belligerent than ever. Yet the largest group in the Commons was still that of the landed gentry, who were essentially conservative and not inclined to innovation. They did not want to destroy the king or the orthodox constitution. They wanted government to be restored upon the old model. Yet they, too, had been grievously disappointed. They had watched the king lose a war. They had seen him alienate his natural supporters. They had observed him in the company of the popish courtiers around his wife. They had witnessed the disruption of law and order in their regions.

All of the parliamentarians now understood their strength. They knew that the king relied upon them to salvage him from his distress; if parliament did not supply him with funds, he would not be able to pay the Scottish army as he had agreed to do. Alexander Leslie might then order a march upon Whitehall, with no English army to prevent his progress. As long as the Scots remained in England, therefore, parliament was supreme.

In the debate that followed the opening, one member remarked that it was common knowledge that the judges had overthrown the law and that the bishops had overthrown the gospel. Another intimated that a popish plot was being hatched by some about the king. Yet another rose to complain that the government was the weakest for generations and had produced nothing but national disgrace; it was surmised that those who had most loudly proclaimed the king's authority had also been those who had wasted the king's money.

When John Pym rose to speak the members were already much agitated. Pym began by saying that 'the distempers of the time are well known'. Much of his bitterness was reserved for Strafford himself, whom he believed to be the author of 'a design to alter law and religion'. Many contemporaries and colleagues were taking Pym's side. The Scots believed that Strafford was the cause of the war between the two nations. The puritans hated him. The City, now more powerful than ever, remembered how he had threatened its aldermen with hanging. He had created an absolute rule during his period of government in Ireland, and it was believed that he wished to repeat the experiment in England.

Strafford was aware of the perils of his position. He could have stayed in York, safe from the depredations of parliament, but the king urged him to join him in Whitehall; he assured him that 'he should not suffer in his person, honour or fortune'. The king's promises were, in the event, worth nothing at all. Strafford wrote that 'I am tomorrow in London with more dangers beset, I believe, than ever any man went with out of Yorkshire . . .'.

John Pym in turn had some reason to fear Strafford. When the earl arrived in London on 9 November he advised the king to provide the evidence that would implicate Pym and his colleagues in a treasonable association with the Scots. That evidence, perhaps of intercepted letters, has never since emerged. News reached Westminster that Strafford was ready to 'prefer an accusation of high treason against diverse members of both houses of parliament'; they would no doubt include Warwick, Saye and Brooke from the Lords with Pym, Hampden and others from the Commons.

It was agreed by the king and his councillors that the defences of the Tower should immediately be strengthened; the fortification was meant as a warning to the City. The Tower was also the likely destination for those about to be arrested. Strafford was quoted as saying that 'he hoped the City would be subdued in a short time'.

On 11 November the king was expected to travel to the Tower and inspect its garrison.

On that day rumours of an attempted coup reached Westminster. The Commons ordered that all strangers should be cleared from the lobby. Strafford took his seat in the House of Lords, but said nothing; he was biding his time. Yet Pym knew of the accusations against himself and his colleagues. He had to remove Strafford before Strafford could destroy him. In a phrase of the time, 'my head or thy head'.

In a speech delivered to the Commons Pym attacked one of Strafford's most notable allies, Sir Francis Windebank, for concealing a popish plot. It might or might not be interpreted as an attack upon Strafford himself, but it was a method by which Pym could test the readiness of his colleagues to take action against his enemies. Another member, John Clotworthy, now suggested or insinuated that Strafford planned to use the Irish army 'ready to march where I know not' in order to curb dissent in England.

It was moved that a committee be established to consult with the Lords on the accusations; this committee was packed with Strafford's enemies, and a 'charge' against the earl was swiftly prepared and presented to the Commons. Some members urged caution and delay in the assault upon Strafford, but Pym replied that any procrastination 'might probably blast all their hopes'.

With a throng of members around him Pym then went to the Lords in order to accuse Strafford of high treason, and to recommend that he be 'sequestered from Parliament'. If the Lords wished to know the grounds of this serious charge, 'particular articles and accusations' against him would be delivered to them shortly. Strafford had been told of the events then unfolding. 'I will go,' he said, 'and look my accusers in the face.' It must be said that the Lords themselves had many grievances against the king's arrogant and difficult adviser and, on his entry, he was commanded by them to withdraw. An order was then passed committing Strafford to the custody of the gentleman usher. He was directed to enter the chamber and to kneel while the order was read to him. He asked permission to speak, but was refused; his sword was taken from him before he was led away.

In his *History of the Rebellion* Clarendon wrote that the crowd looked upon the earl without pity, 'no man capping to him, before whom that morning the greatest in England would have stood discovered'. No man had taken off his hat in respect.

'What is the matter?' someone asked him.

'A small matter, I warrant you,' he replied.

Another called out, 'Yes indeed, high treason is a small matter.'

Strafford was effectively removed from public life. Charles had lost his principal councillor. It was widely assumed that a great work had been accomplished. The king was obliged to disperse the garrison he had established within the Tower and to dismantle the guns that had recently been mounted. His attempt to coerce or overawe his opponents had failed, in another of those humiliating reversals that had become associated with his rule.

With the threat of dissolution or a coup now removed, parliament could begin its work on what it believed to be wholesale renovation. A public fast was observed on 17 November as a way of enlisting divine assistance in this task. Some sixty-five committees were established to investigate all cases of abuse and corruption. One of them was devoted to seeking out and removing 'persecuting, innovating or scandalous' ministers, justices of the peace and other royal officers; when its members requested 'informations from all parties' to assist them, hundreds of individuals descended upon Westminster with their own particular grievances.

A committee for petitions was then established to deal with their complaints. Warwick, Brooke, Essex, Bedford and Saye and their colleagues were in command of its actions. It sat in the Painted Chamber at Westminster and became an alternative court of law, investigating all aspects of the government's work. Parliament had in the past been summoned simply to transact the king's business; now it busied itself about national affairs without any reference to the king.

The evidence against Strafford was presented on 24 November 1640, and was formulated in the first article of the indictment against him. The Commons was asked to declare that 'Thomas, earl of Strafford hath traitorously endeavoured to subvert the fundamental laws and government of the realms of England and Ireland, and instead thereof to introduce an arbitrary and tyrannical government against law'. In his speech to the Commons Pym argued that the accusations amounted to a great and dangerous treason, animated by malice and guided by evil mischief. He accused the earl of attempting to spread discord between the king and the people. It had become clear that Strafford could not be allowed to survive; if he evaded the charge of treason he might become the focus of royalist hopes, and might even herald the resumption of non-parliamentary government.

At the end of November the three dissenters who had been mutilated and imprisoned at the behest of Archbishop Laud – Prynne, Burton and Bastwick – returned in triumph to the capital; they wore rosemary and bay in their hats, and flowers were strewn before them. Rosemary was the herb of remembrance and bay of victory. It was for Henry Burton, a puritan divine, 'a sweet and glorious day, or time, which the sun of righteousness, arising over *England*, was now about to procure for us'. That bright dawn still depended on the presence of the covenanters in the north, and in the early days of December parliament voted subsidies for the Scottish army.

Arguments over religion were the soul of this first session of what became known as the 'Long Parliament', outweighing any concerns over secular misgovernment. Already the devout were in full pursuit of the Arminians. A London crowd had burst into St Paul's Cathedral where it destroyed the altar and tore up the book of the new liturgy. At Stourbridge Fair a preacher stirred up a crowd by calling out 'Pardon! Pardon! Pardon!' for the superstition and idolatry imposed by those in authority. In Brislington, Somerset, a dissenting minister who had been suspended from office preached to his flock beneath the shade of a tree in the street, whereupon the congregation led him back to the church and gave him the key.

On 11 December the citizens of London presented a petition to parliament for 'reformation in church government'. It declared that 'the government of archbishops and lord bishops, deacons and archdeacons etc. . . . has proved prejudicial and very dangerous both to the church and commonwealth'; it urged that this ecclesiastical government should be destroyed 'with all its dependencies, roots and branches'. Fifteen hundred supporters gathered in Westminster Yard, well-dressed, well-organized and good-tempered, and after delivering their petition they returned quietly to their homes. The 'root and branch' petition, as it came to be known, was passed by Pym to a committee where it remained for some months.

More immediate remedies were at hand. On 16 December the canons passed by convocation in the spring of the year, among them 'the etcetera oath', were voted by parliament to be illegal. It was now time to attack the archbishop himself. On 18 December Laud was impeached and taken into custody. He was accused of fostering doctrines that lent support to the king's arbitrary measures, and of using the courts both to impose innovations in worship and to silence the true professors of religion. One member of parliament, Harbottle Grimstone, described him as 'the root and ground of all our miseries and calamities'. Other bishops soon joined him in the Tower. The bishop of Ely, Matthew Wren, was to spend seventeen years in confinement. Parliament could be as vindictive and as authoritarian as the king, perhaps because both parties believed that they were fulfilling the divine will.

Someone had scribbled, on the door of St Stephen's Chapel at Westminster, an appeal to 'remember the judges'. Their time was not long in coming. All those who had supported the king in their judgments were questioned or arrested. Many of the king's courtiers now fled the approaching storm. Sir Francis Windebank, whom Pym had accused of concealing a Catholic conspiracy, was rowed at night across the Channel. Lord Keeper Finch fled the country for Holland on the day he was impeached.

The members of parliament now determined to consolidate their strength. On 24 December it was recommended that 'the English lord commissioners', which in effect meant the puritan lords who had launched the petition for parliament in the summer, should be responsible for the disbursement of money to the Scots. Five days later Pym advised that the customs officials, who were the king's principal financial agents, should 'forbear to pay anything' to the exchequer until authorization was 'settled by Parliament'; his proposal was carried without any division. The king now lacked the resources even to pay his own household expenses.

In this last week of December it was further agreed that parliament should meet at fixed times with or without the co-operation of the king. The 'Triennial Act' was passed to compel parliaments to meet every three years. The Venetian ambassador reported that 'if this innovation is introduced, it will hand over the reins of government completely to Parliament, and nothing will be left to the king but mere show and a simulacrum of reality, stripped of credit and destitute of all authority'. It remained to be seen whether Charles would willingly relinquish his powers. The contest had only just begun.

20

Madness and fury

The new year, 1641, was for the godly a time of jubilation. It was the year in which, according to cant phrases of the time, a period of 'great affliction' was succeeded by an age of 'seasonable mercies'. Some writers were dating their letters '*annus mirabilis*' or '*anno renovationis*'. It was a golden year in which God's goodness and mercy to the nation were vouchsafed. A pamphleteer, John Bond, exulted in 'England's Rejoicing for the Parliament's Return' that 'papists tremble . . . Arminians tumble . . . the priests of Baal lament their fortunes'. For those of a royalist persuasion, however, the year marked the culmination of all their woes that had begun at the battle of Newburn.

The king was in desperate straits with his authority and revenue threatened, and with his principal counsellors languishing in the Tower. Henrietta Maria was enraged at the situation of the royal household, and continued to argue for more determined measures against her husband's opponents. She even wrote to the Vatican asking for a large loan, perhaps with the intention of raising troops.

Charles himself did not surrender to the calamity that faced him. His health was good, and he was not inclined to anxiety; he maintained a daily regimen of prayer and exercise; he enjoyed an excellent appetite. He believed implicitly that the enemies of the Lord's anointed would of necessity fail, and that all traitors would eventually be brought to the bar of justice.

On 23 January Charles summoned both houses of parliament to the Banqueting House at Whitehall, and delivered a speech in which he complained about the obstructions placed in his path by men who 'put no difference betwixt reformation and alteration of government'. Yet he seemed willing to compromise, and promised to return the laws of religious polity to the 'purest times of Queen Elizabeth's days'. He stated further that 'whatsoever part of my revenue shall be found illegal, or heavy to my subjects, I shall be willing to lay it down'. He had in effect cancelled the exaction of ship-money, and curbed all other questionable ways of raising revenue.

The status of his most faithful servant was still in doubt. It was already whispered at court that Strafford must rely upon his own protestations of innocence and, if they should fail, upon the mercy of parliament. Charles was unwilling to fight for his quondam counsellor; he seems to have realized that only Strafford's death could preface the reconciliation he desired with his people. At the end of the month the charges were drawn up against the earl; twenty-eight separate articles, covering the last fourteen years of his career, were outlined over two hundred sheets of paper.

At the beginning of February the Commons voted £300,000 to the Scots under the name of 'brotherly assistance'; the two nations were not to be divided. They needed one another, for the moment, in their confrontation with the king. They also needed the 'Triennial Bill' that guaranteed the meeting of parliament on a regular basis. The bill was a grievous blow to the royal prerogative, and Charles had been most reluctant to give his assent; his power would be limited, and his authority compromised. Yet on 16 February he was persuaded to concede the issue, partly from advice that he would receive no money after any refusal. So he declared in the old Norman fashion that '*le roi le veut*', 'the king wishes it'. In private the king raged. In effect the Act made him reliant upon parliament and gave that assembly the permanent existence that it had never known before. The bells of London rang out. The earl of Leicester wrote in his commonplace book that now 'the parliament which is a corporation never dies, nor ceases at the death of the king, that is, the death of the king is no determination of it, and it is not likely that they will be weary of their immortality'.

It had already been rumoured that a new privy council was about to emerge that would reflect the wishes of the Commons as well as of the king. The earl of Bedford was to become lord treasurer while his lieutenant in the Commons, John Pym, would be chancellor of the exchequer; the earl of Bristol would be made lord privy seal. On 19 February seven other members of the puritan Junto were nominated to be privy councillors, among them Viscount Saye and the earls of Essex and Bedford. Clarendon wrote in his *History* that they were 'all persons at that time very gracious to the people or the Scots . . . had all been in some umbrage at court and most in visible disfavour'.

The king had declared himself indirectly to be a moderate, therefore, equally ready to forgive his erstwhile enemies and to trim or turn his policies in the light of complaints directed against them. Yet at the same time he had also managed to divide the opposition against him. Many in parliament did not share the religious enthusiasm of the Scottish covenanters and had no wish to see the English Church remodelled to satisfy their demands; others were already beginning to resent the amount of money being spent for the maintenance of the Scottish army in the north. If Charles could gain the support of such men, parliamentary assistance would be at hand in his fight against the Junto.

The compromise with the puritans of parliament did not in the end succeed. The king had insisted that, in order to take up the offices of state he had promised to them, they must agree to retain the bishops in the Lords and to save Strafford's life. They in turn demanded to be granted the offices before doing anything at all. No grand reconciliation was possible.

On 24 February Strafford was brought from the Tower to the chamber of the House of Lords in order to answer the charges laid against him. It was noticed with surprise that the king had taken his place upon the throne, by which he indicated his support for the earl. When the king eventually departed, however, it was resolved that the proceedings would have to begin all over again. Strafford defended himself with eloquence and wit, throwing into serious doubt the result of any trial. Within days it was reported that the parliamentary leaders were unsure how to proceed with their case. It was easy to proclaim Strafford to be a traitor, but a more difficult matter to prove it in open court.

His trial opened on 22 March, when he was taken by barge from the Tower to Westminster Hall. He was dressed entirely in black, as a dramatic token of sorrow, and the hall itself became known to the participants as 'the theatre'. This was the spectacle that might determine the fate of the nation, as the prisoner fought for his life and for the cause of the king. Negotiations of course continued behind the scene. The puritan grandees were ready to spare Strafford's life, for example, if the king agreed to grant them the great offices of state.

On the first day the peers of the realm filed into their places on both sides of the hall; tiers of seats had been placed, on either side of the peers, for the Commons. A committee of the Lords had already decided that it was not proper for the king himself to be present; so an empty throne stood at the northern end of the improvised courtroom while the king and queen were in fact sitting in seats behind, like a box in a theatre. Strafford himself was to stand on a dais at the southern end, facing both houses of parliament. The visual impression, in fact devised by Inigo Jones, was of one man against all the representatives of the nation. The hall was packed with spectators who made much clamour and 'clattering'; it was remarked by one observer, Robert Baillie, that there was 'much public eating, not only of confections but of flesh and bread, bottles of beer and wine going thick from mouth to mouth without cups'.

When the twenty-eight articles of impeachment were read out to him, Strafford was seen to smile; he could already see the legal difficulties that beset his accusers. They were attempting to prove treason on the basis of an accumulation of several separate charges. A remark passed around at the time was: you know at first sight whether a man is short or tall, you do not need to measure the inches. With Strafford's supposed treachery, you would need to count the inches carefully. At one point Strafford said that 'opinions may make a heretic, but that they make a traitor I never heard till now'. The days passed, with witnesses and questions and arguments, in the course of which Strafford seemed to delight in outwitting the counsels for the prosecution; they in turn were considered to be bombastic and hectoring.

It soon became clear to the members of the Junto that their cause could be lost, and they began to suspect that a majority of the peers was in fact secretly or openly supporting the cause of Strafford. When on 10 April the Lords allowed an adjournment for the prisoner to consult his notes before making a closing speech, the Commons protested in fury. They rose in consternation. Some of them, according to the parliamentary notes of Simonds D'Ewes, called out, 'Withdraw! Withdraw!', which was misheard by others as 'Draw! Draw!'; their hands went to the hilts of their swords in anticipation of battle. The confusion delighted Strafford to the extent that 'he could not hide his joy'; the king, in his box behind the throne, was seen to laugh. The two houses of parliament were in dispute.

The members of the Commons returned to their chamber in the afternoon, and at this opportune moment certain notes taken at a previous meeting of the privy council were conveniently revealed. This was the council during which Strafford had told the king that 'you have an army in Ireland you may employ here to reduce this kingdom'. The earl's accusers interpreted this 'kingdom' to be England rather than Scotland. This of course was treason. The Commons readily agreed. A Bill of Attainder was drawn up, a medieval device whereby both houses of parliament could try and condemn an enemy of the kingdom without the formality of a trial. It was also a way of persuading the Lords to vote for Strafford's death without the burden of legal proof.

On 19 April the king ordered all military officers immediately to return to their regiments. When a negotiator from Scotland had an audience with the king two days later, he reported that 'his mind seems to be on some project here shortly to break out'. It was also rumoured that the French, exhorted by the queen, were about to invade. What the leaders of the Junto most feared was a dissolution of parliament, a device that would result in the immediate cancellation of both the trial and the proposed attainder. They called out their supporters, and a crowd of many thousands gathered at Westminster in the belief that dangerous measures were about to be introduced. On 19 April, too, the Commons passed the Bill of Attainder against the earl of Strafford. Those of the Commons who had not supported the decision were derided as 'Straffordians or enemies to their country'; their names were listed and placed on posts and other visible locations in the city. The members of the godly party were not above intimidation and violation of parliamentary privilege.

When the Commons passed the attainder the king wrote to Strafford to reassure him once again he had his word that his life, honour, or fortune would not be touched. On the last day of the proceedings in Westminster Hall, 29 April, Strafford seemed merry. Oliver St John then rose to deliver a three-hour tirade against the prisoner which was of such eloquence that it profoundly influenced the intentions of the peers; when he finished, the spectators in the hall broke into applause. Two days later the king addressed both houses of parliament from the throne. In his speech he emphasized that he would never act against his conscience; this was taken to mean that he would veto any attainder against his counsellor. Let them find Strafford guilty only of a misdemeanour, and he would act. The king also refused to disband his Irish army, which in turn raised fears of military action.

He stayed for a while after his oration, looking for supporters, but Simonds D'Ewes reported 'there was not one man gave him the least hum or colour of plaudit to his speech, which made him, after some time of expectation, depart suddenly'. It was widely believed that he had intruded in a matter still under parliamentary debate, which was considered by the Commons to be 'the most unparalleled breach of privilege that had ever happened'. It seemed that a confrontation between king and parliament was inevitable.

Rumours of plots and counter-plots were soon everywhere. For some weeks a vessel, chartered by Strafford's secretary, had been moored in the Thames. The boat could easily take an escaped prisoner to France. Some of the reports proved to be true. On Sunday 2 May, Sir John Suckling, courtier and army commander, poet and gambler, called sixty men to the White Horse Tavern in Bread Street; they wore battledress of buff cloth and carried swords as well as pistols. They were supposed to gain entrance to the Tower of London, in the guise of reinforcements, where they would at once overwhelm the guard and secure Strafford's liberty. It was a wild scheme, made all the more improbable by the sight of sixty armed men milling about in the middle of London. Their presence was quickly known and interpreted, the news passed immediately to the leaders of parliament. A tumultuous crowd of Londoners gathered about the Tower to defend it against any invasion.

The rumours of a military rebellion, and plans for the flight of

Strafford, had thoroughly alarmed the people of London. A fresh crowd gathered on Monday outside the doors of the Lords, bellowing for the execution of Strafford; some of them cried that if they could not have his life, they would take that of the king. The parliamentary journal for that day wrote of the members of the Junto that 'they caused a multitude of tumultuous persons to come down to Westminster armed with swords and staves, to fill both the palace-yards and all the approaches to both houses with fury and clamour and to require justice, speedy justice, against the earl'. It was clear that Strafford would die. Oliver St John, one of the parliamentary leaders, had said that it was right and proper to knock wolves and foxes on the head. It was also remarked that 'stone dead hath no fellow'.

When the Commons assembled, Sir John Pennington spoke of Suckling's unsuccessful gathering. Thomas Tomkins added that 'many Papists were newly come to London'. The king had been misled by false counsellors and, as John Pym put it, 'he that hath been most abused doth not yet perceive it'. The parliament must open the eyes of the king.

It was now proposed that a religious manifesto should be published. The 'Grand Remonstrance' devised by the Commons was in a sense an English version of the Scottish covenant, binding those who signed it to an oath that they would remain loyal to 'the true reformed Protestant religion' against 'popery and popish innovation'. The remonstrance claimed that during the present session of the parliament its members had 'wrestled with great dangers and fears, the pressing miseries and calamities, the various distempers and disorders which had not only assaulted, but even overwhelmed and extinguished the liberty, peace and prosperity of this kingdom'. It was printed and circulated throughout the country, addressing and inspiring what might now be called a parliamentary party.

On 5 May the Commons, fearful of a papist uprising, ordered the towns, cities and counties of England to ensure that their arms and ammunition were well prepared. A papist plot amounted, in this context, to a royal plot. On that day a new bill was passed allowing parliament to remain in session until it voted for its own dissolution. It has been said that this was the moment that reform turned into revolution; it deprived the monarch of his right to govern.

The Lords themselves had directed that an armed force should take command of the Tower, thus divesting the king of responsibility for military affairs. It was another blow to his authority. The earl of Stamford proposed a motion 'to give God thanks for our great deliverance, which is greater than that from the Gunpowder Treason [of 5 November 1605]. For by this time, had not this plot been discovered, the powder had been about our ears here in the parliament house, and we had all been made slaves.' The threat of military force had alarmed the Lords as much as the Commons; on 8 May, the Bill of Attainder against Strafford was passed by the upper house.

A delegation from both houses of parliament now carried the document of attainder to the Banqueting House for the king's signature; the members were accompanied by a crowd of approximately 12,000 calling out, 'Justice! Justice!' The king, understandably cast down and demoralized, said that he would give his response on Monday morning; this delay did not please the crowd, who had promptly gathered again outside Palace Gate. If the king refused to sign the attainder it was predicted that the palace would be attacked, and that the king and queen would be captured.

Charles conferred with his bishops and his privy councillors, most of whom urged him to sign the bill condemning Strafford to death. The archbishop of York told him that 'there was a private and a public conscience; that his public conscience as a king might not only dispense with, but oblige him to do, that which was against his private conscience as a man'. Slowly and reluctantly he assented; he had promised to protect the earl's life and fortune, but now for reasons of state he was obliged to break his word. In the process he had been humiliated and weakened almost beyond repair. Pym, on hearing the news of the king's capitulation, raised his hands in exaltation and declared, 'Has he given us the head of Strafford? Then he will refuse us nothing!'

On 12 May Strafford went to his death on Tower Hill in front of what was said to be the largest multitude ever gathered in England. Crowds of 200,000 people watched his progress in an atmosphere of carnival and rejoicing. The lieutenant of the Tower asked him to make the short journey from the prison to the scaffold by coach, thus avoiding public fury; Strafford is supposed to have replied that

'I dare look death in the face and, I hope, the people too. Have you a care that I do not escape, and I care not how I die, whether by the hand of the executioner or the madness and fury of the people.' As he walked to his death he looked up at the window of the chamber in which Laud was confined, and saw the archbishop waiting for him there. He asked for 'your prayers and your blessings', but the cleric fell into a dead faint.

In his speech from the scaffold the earl declared that 'I wish that every man would lay his hand on his heart, and consider seriously whether the beginning of the people's happiness should be written in letters of blood'. He knelt in prayer for half an hour, and then laid himself down on the block. It took one stroke. The spectators rushed through the streets of London waving their hats and shouting, 'His head is off! His head is off!' In his prison Archbishop Laud observed, a few days later, that Strafford had served 'a mild and gracious prince who knew not how to be, or to be made, great'.

1. James I of England and James VI of Scotland, in the characteristically regal pose of hand on hip.

2. Anne of Denmark, James's spouse, who became a key artistic patron in the 'Jacobean' age.

3. James in front of his lords, temporal and spiritual.

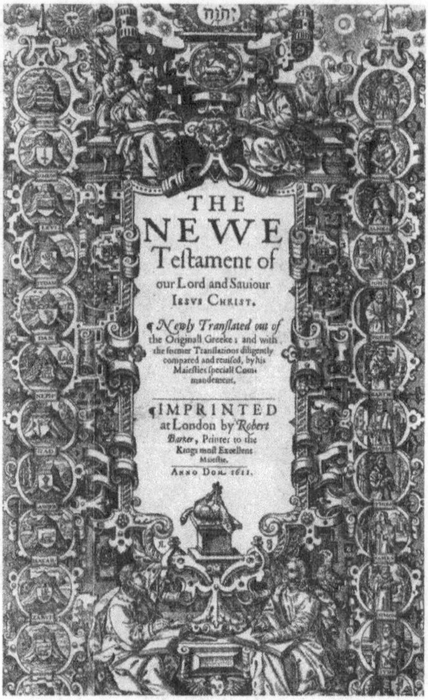

THE NEWE Testament of our Lord and Sauiour Iesvs Christ.

Newly Translated out of the Originall Greeke: and with the former Translations diligently compared and reuised, by his Maiesties speciall Commandement.

IMPRINTED at London by Robert Barker, Printer to the Kings most Excellent Maiestie.

Anno Dom. 1611.

4. The title page of the King James Bible, one of the lasting memorials of his reign.

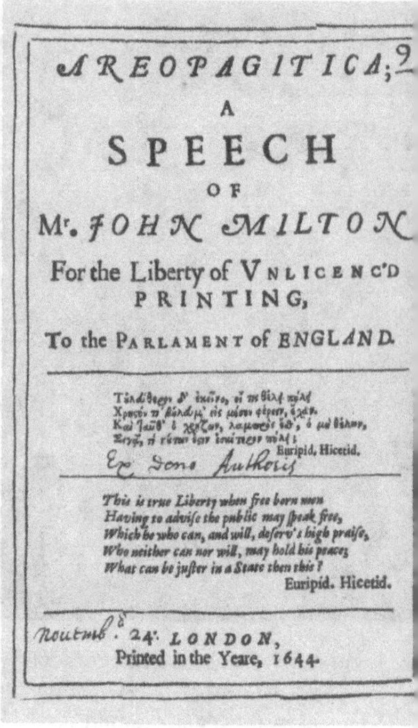

AREOPAGITICA;

A SPEECH OF Mr. JOHN MILTON For the Liberty of VNLICENC'D PRINTING, To the PARLAMENT of ENGLAND.

Euripid. Hicetid.

Ex Dono Authoris

This is true Liberty when free born men
Having to advise the public may speak free,
Which he who can, and will, deserv's high praise,
Who neither can nor will, may hold his peace;
What can be juster in a State then this?

Euripid. Hicetid.

Novemb. 24. LONDON, Printed in the Yeare, 1644.

5. The title page of John Milton's *Areopagit* an eloquent plea against censorship.

6. George Villiers, 1st duke of Buckingham, loved by two sovereig and hated by the people.

7. Henry, prince of Wales, the supposed saviour of Protestant Europe, who did not live long enough to fulfil his destiny.

8. Charles, the future Charles I, as the prince of Wales in armour.

9. Elizabeth, daughter of James I, who was briefly queen of Bohemia, otherwise known as the Winter Queen.

10. A double portrait of the unhappy Charles I and his wife, Henrietta Maria.

11. Three out of seven of Charles I's children, painted by Anthony Van Dyck.

12. A disapproving illustration of the Rump Parliament, after the purge of the Long Parliament in December 1648.

The Rump and dreggs of the hous of Com: remaining after the good members were purged out.

13. What the Cavaliers are supposed to have done with the Puritans.

CRUELTIES OF THE CAVALIERS, 1644.

14. Thomas Wentworth, 1st earl of Strafford, the dour supporter of absolute monarchy.

15. A plan of the Battle of Naseby, the outcome of which wrecked the king's chances in the summer of 1645.

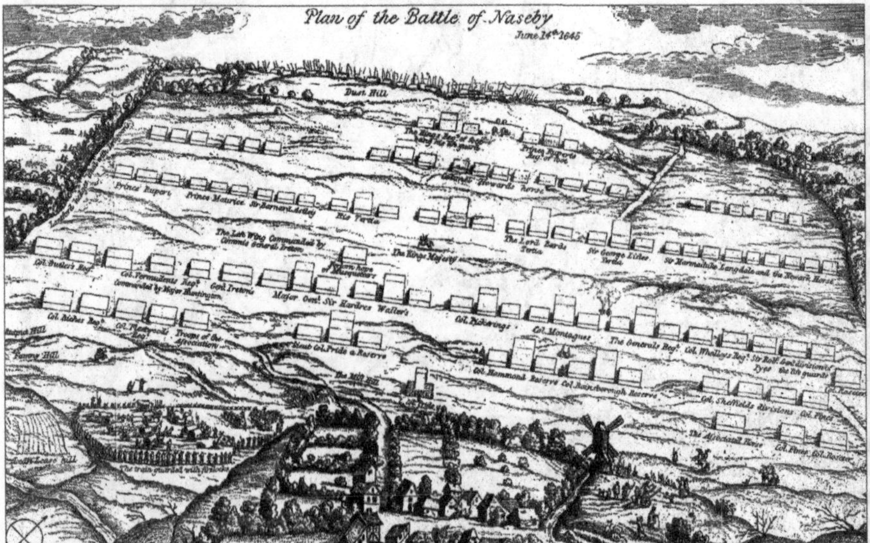

16. Prince Rupert of the Rhine, Charles I's senior commander, brave, but also foolhardy.

17. The trial of Charles I in Westminster Hall.

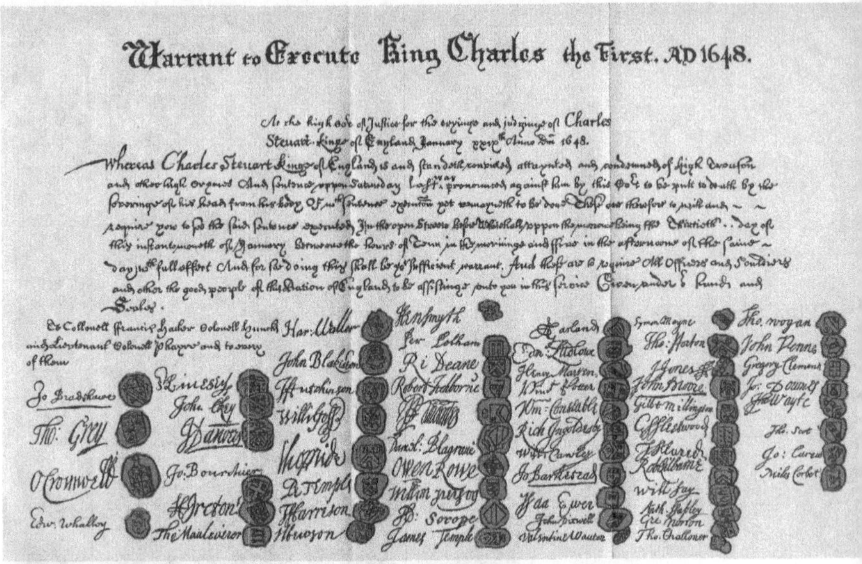

Warrant to Execute King Charles the First. AD 1648.

At the high Court of Justice for the tryinge and judginge of Charles Steuart Kinge of England January xxix^th Anno Dni 1648.

Whereas Charles Steuart Kinge of England is and standeth convicted attaynted and condemned of High Treason and other high Crymes And sentence uppon Saturday last was pronounced against him by this Court to be putt to death by the severinge of his head from his body Of wch sentence execucon yet remayneth to be done These are therefore to will and require you to see the said sentence executed In the open Streete before Whitehall uppon the morrowe being the Thirtieth day of this instante moneth of January betweene the houres of Tenn in the morninge and Five in the afternoone of the same day wth full effect And for soe doing this shall be yor sufficient warrant And these are to require All Officers and Souldiers and other the good people of this Nation of England to be assistinge unto you in this service Given under our hands and Seales.

To Collonell Francis Hacker Colonell Huncks and Lieutenant Colonell Phayre and to every of them

Jo. Bradshawe, Tho. Grey, O. Cromwell, Edw. Whalley, M. Livesey, John Okey, J. Danvers, Jo. Bourchier, H. Ireton, Tho. Mauleverer, Har. Waller, John Blakiston, J. Hutchinson, Willi. Goffe, Tho. Pride, Pe. Temple, T. Harrison, J. Hewson, Hen. Smyth, Per. Pelham, Ri. Deane, Robert Tichborne, H. Edwardes, Daniel Blagrave, Owen Rowe, William Purefoy, Ad. Scroope, James Temple, A. Garland, Edm. Ludlowe, Henry Marten, Vinct. Potter, Wm. Constable, Rich. Ingoldesby, Willi. Cawley, Jo. Barkstead, Isaa. Ewer, John Dixwell, Valentine Wauton, Symon Mayne, Tho. Horton, J. Jones, John Moore, Gilbt. Millington, G. Fleetwood, J. Alured, Robt. Lilburne, Will. Say, Anth. Stapley, Gre. Norton, Tho. Challoner, Tho. Wogan, John Venn, Gregory Clement, Jo. Downes, Tho. Wayte, Tho. Scot, Jo. Carew, Miles Corbet

18. The result of the trial: a death warrant.

19. Cromwell, the chief of men until his death in 1658.

21

A world of change

While the trial of Strafford continued, the Commons seemed uncertain about the direction of other public business. Parliament did nothing but, in the phrase of the time, beat the air. On one occasion, after prayers had been said, the members of the Commons lapsed into silence and simply looked at one other; they did not know where to begin. On another occasion, according to a contemporary account, the Speaker stood up and asked what question he should put to them; answer came there none. A loss of initiative in the cause of reform was one of the reasons for a public fast in April.

Yet the death of the earl seems finally to have lent stimulus to the proceedings. The sight of blood quickened the appetite, and in July a series of fresh initiatives was debated and agreed. It seemed that the king himself had become almost an irrelevance in the business of renovating the kingdom. The familiar grant of tonnage and poundage was made to him but on the understanding that his previous exactions had been illegal; no new money was to be given to the royal household without permission of parliament. Of course parliament itself needed revenues both for work at home and for payment to the Scots. A new subsidy was imposed upon the counties and a poll tax introduced to raise additional income. This did not endear parliament to many of the people.

The old centres of royal authority were abolished. The council of the north, the religious court of high commission and the Star Chamber were all swept away. Ship-money was condemned as contrary to the law. The limits of the royal forests were declared to be those that had obtained in the twentieth year of James I. The dissolution of the Star Chamber, in particular, lifted the final impediment to public expression. That body had decreed, four years before, that no book could be published without a licence; the order was now dead. Even before the chamber had been dissolved the appetite for news was fed by pamphlets and tracts eagerly passed from hand to hand, most of them predicting great innovations in Church and state. There were 900 of these publications issued in 1640, 2,000 in 1641 and 4,000 in 1642.

The number of print shops doubled in this decade, but they were joined by what were described in one satirical pamphlet as 'upstart booksellers, trotting mercuries and bawling hawkers'. Wandering stationers and balladmongers would call out, 'Come buy a new book, a new book, newly come forth'. Pamphlets with titles such as 'Appeal to Parliament', 'A Dream, or News from Hell' and 'Downfall of Temporising Poets' abounded. It was no longer necessary to go to the bookstalls about St Paul's or the Exchange to find newssheets. They were sold on the streets of London. Broadsheets cost a penny, eight-page pamphlets a penny or twopence. One commentator derided Pym's 'twopenny speeches'. A member of the congregation in Radwinter, Essex, threw a religious pamphlet to his curate, saying, 'There is reading work for you, read that.' The mixture of information and opinion was compounded by plays, processions, ballads, playing cards, graffiti, petitions and prints.

The leading members of the Commons published their speeches which, according to the puritan Richard Baxter in his autobiography, were 'greedily brought up throughout the land, which greatly increased the people's apprehension of their danger'. The king himself was moved to write against these 'poisoners of the minds of his weak subjects; amazed by what eyes these things are seen, and by what ears they are heard'. Yet pamphleteering was not confined to the godly men of the parliament. The sermons of the principal preachers were also distributed. From the pulpit came a multitude of declarations and denunciations; but the pulpit also acted as a distributor of news. The cleric might explain the events of the day, or the week, and comment upon them to his excited congregation. The Presbyterian minister Robert Baillie said that 'many a sore thrust got both men and women thronging into our sermons'. The words from the church were then taken up in discussions at the taverns and the shops, the streets and the markets.

Yet the pamphlets were not simply directed against one or other of the factions then gaining ground. They were part of a vigorous debate on the ideas and ideals of political and religious life. What were the grounds of a just monarchy? Was there in truth an ancient constitution? Were king, parliament and people uniquely joined? The publication and dissemination of these concepts materially helped to extend and to inform the political nation. The radicals used the printing presses to disseminate their own opinions of Church and state, leading John Milton to proclaim that London had become 'the mansion house of liberty' with its citizens 'sitting by their studious lamps, musing, searching, revolving new notions and ideas wherewith to present, as with their homage and their fealty the approaching reformation'.

Yet the royalists fought back with their own pamphlets. Richard Carter, in 'The Schismatic Stigmatised', attacked the dissenting preachers who were even then crowding Westminster and its environs. 'And instead of orthodox divines, they set up all kinds of mechanics, as shoe-makers, cobblers, tailors and glovers . . . these predicant mechanics and lawless lads do affect an odd kind of gesture in their pulpits, vapouring and throwing heads, hands and shoulders this way, and that way, puffing and blowing, grinning and gurning.' A doggerel verse circulated through the streets:

When women preach, and cobblers pray,
The fiends in hell make holiday.

The parishes of London were indeed filled with dissenters of any and every kind. A separatist congregation met at a house in Goat Alley, off Whitecross Street; they arrived in twos or threes, and one man stood at the door to warn of any approaching strangers. The man appointed to preach stood in the middle of the room while the others gathered in a circle about him. Among these lay preachers were, according to a political satire sold in the streets, 'Greene the feltmaker, Spencer the horse-rubber, Quartermine the brewer's clerk, with some few others, that are mighty sticklers in this new kind of talking trade, which many ignorant coxcombs call preaching'.

The conventional clergy of the Church were derided in the streets and sometimes their surplices were stripped from their backs. The cry went up, 'There goes a Jesuit, a Baal-priest, an Abbey-lubber, one of Canterbury's whelps . . .' When a bishop went up to the pulpit in St Olave's, in Old Jewry, some hundred 'rude rascals' called out, 'A Pope! A Pope! A Pope!'

In this fevered atmosphere rumours of every kind circulated like hurricanes. It was said that a papist cavalry was concealed in caves in Surrey; it was reported that a plot had been hatched to blow up the Thames with gunpowder and thus drown the city. One of Pym's colleagues, Sir Walter Earle, told the Commons that a conspiracy had been discovered to demolish parliament; in their excitement the members leaned forward in their seats better to hear him, and part of the floor of the gallery gave way. One member exclaimed that he smelled gunpowder and another, leaving his seat, shouted that 'there was hot work and a great fire within'. The news soon spread, and a mob flew to Westminster. It was of course a false alarm, but the sudden panic testifies to the agitated state of the capital.

It was a world of change; as the king had said to parliament earlier in the year, 'You have taken the government all in pieces.' 'The Brothers of the Blade', a dialogue issued in 1641, considered 'the vicissitudes and revolutions of the states and conditions of men in these last days of the world'. 'Revolution' meant in conventional terms recurrence or periodic return; in these years it became associated with more earthly disorder. It was widely believed that the times were awry; anxiety and even despair were experienced by many. Brilliana Harley, a royalist letter-writer, expressed her belief that 'things are now in such a condition that if the Lord does not put forth his helping hand his poor children will be brought low'.

In the weeks after Strafford's death the king seems to have become resigned to his loss of power. He signed the bill for abolishing tonnage and poundage, telling both houses of parliament that 'I never had other design but to win the affections of my people'. He made a leading puritan, the earl of Essex, his lord chamberlain. Yet he was in fact playing for time.

There were already the makings of a king's party from those outraged at the pretensions of parliament in assuming executive powers; others were displeased at the idea of a puritan state Church controlled by parliamentary lay commissioners in place of bishops. The 'root and branch' party, which favoured such a change, was still in a minority. In this year many petitions reached Westminster from those who wished to preserve the Church and protect the Book of Common Prayer from more change. Some supported the maintenance of the episcopacy on the basis that the office was good even if the man was indifferent. From Oliver Cromwell's own county of Huntingdon, for example, it was pleaded that 'the form of divine service expressed and contained in the book of common prayer' was the best. These petitioners wished to extirpate those immoderate and bitter reformers who fomented nothing but trouble and disorder in the churches of the country.

It is hardly surprising, therefore, that those who were moderate or orthodox in their religion were beginning to take the side of the king and to believe that the political settlement imposed by parliament had gone far enough. Instead of relief and liberty, it had brought anxiety and division. The imposition of taxes had not improved the temper of the nation. One gentlewoman from Yorkshire, Margaret Eure, wrote: 'I am in such a great rage with parliament as nothing will pacify me, for they promised us all should be well, if my lord Strafford's head were off, and since then there is nothing better, but I think we shall be undone with taxes.' It was agreed by many that the king should take wise counsel but few accepted that parliament had the power to choose who those counsellors should be. It was also possible that the king could still divide the Lords from the Commons; in June 1641, the peers threw out a bill excluding the bishops from their number. They were not prepared to consider any 'further reformation'.

In the same month of June John Pym introduced what were known as the 'ten propositions', measures that were designed to increase parliamentary control of the king's court and council. All priests and Jesuits were to be banished from the court and, in particular, from the queen's entourage. Henrietta was defiant; she would obey her husband, she said, but not 400 of his subjects. Another proposition demanded that the king remove his 'evil' counsellors, and insisted that none in future were to be appointed unless they were such 'as his people and Parliament may have just cause to confide in'. The armies of Scotland and of England were to be disbanded as quickly as possible. There was no reference to the king. This might be seen as a step towards a republican government, however carefully obscured by the rhetoric of loyalty.

The 'ten propositions' had been in part prompted by the king's recent and carefully resolved decision to travel to Scotland. It was feared that in fact his destination would be York, rather than Edinburgh, where he might take control of his English army garrisoned there; hence the call that the English and Scottish armies should stand down. But if he did indeed journey to Edinburgh, what then? He might, for example, enlist his native subjects in some attack upon Westminster. If he agreed to grant the Scots the 'pure' religion they demanded, and allowed them to resume their just liberties, they might return to their old allegiance to the Stuarts; Charles had already written to the earl of Argyll, chief of Clan Campbell, with the pledge to 'establish the affections of my people fully to me'. If the Scottish and English armies were joined together, under the command of the king, they would represent an almost irresistible force.

John Pym and his supporters were now seized with anxiety and alarm. They even convened parliament on Sunday morning, at the beginning of August, to debate the nature of the threat. They begged for a delay to the king's journey, and he consented to a pause of one day. He had in the interim been engaged in talks with the Scottish commissioners and, according to the Venetian ambassador, the Scots were boasting that 'they would do all in their power to place the king in his authority once again. When he appeared in Scotland, all political differences would be at an end, and they would serve their natural prince as one man in such a cause.'

As the king prepared to go on his journey a crowd gathered in Westminster entreating him not to leave. It may be that his presence in London acted as a form of reassurance, at a time of great disorder, or it may be that some in the crowd suspected his intentions. He went to parliament on the morning of his departure in a mood of ill-concealed hostility and impatience. He named a commission of twenty-two men who would administer affairs in his absence; among them was the earl of Newcastle, a notable enemy to the parliamentary cause.

The Commons immediately retired to their chamber and debated the means 'of putting the kingdom into a posture of defence'. An 'ordinance' was passed, the first of its kind, appointing several key parliamentarians to attend the king in Scotland; they were of course to be spies rather than companions, hoping to supervise his actions. An ordinance had in the medieval period been a device by means of which the king could make a declaration without the consent of parliament; now the two houses were issuing ordinances without the consent of the king. Another confrontation seemed to be inevitable.

Charles was greeted in Edinburgh with every sign of acclamation. He at once proceeded to gain the approval of the Scots. He attended the services of the Scottish Church with an outward display of piety, and agreed to the demand of the covenanters that bishops be excluded from the reformed Church. He attended the sessions of the Scottish parliament, and agreed to the terms of an Anglo-Scottish union whereby his powers over parliament and the army were severely circumscribed. Some at Westminster believed that they might obtain similar benefits, but it occurred to others that Charles had simply managed to neutralize the Scots in any future conflict.

In these months parliament had begun to govern; it paid the army, and it issued orders to royal officials such as the lieutenant of the Tower. It had made decrees about the liturgy and the forms of religious worship. Laud had been impeached and imprisoned, while Strafford had been executed; various of the supposed 'evil counsellors', among them Lord Keeper Finch, had fled. The judges and sheriffs who had supported the king's exactions had been summoned to parliament and asked to explain their conduct. The Star Chamber, the northern council and the high commission, the seats of Charles's rule, had been abolished. Laud's judicial victims, such as Prynne and Bastwick, had been liberated and brought back to London in triumph. Most importantly, perhaps, it had been decreed that the present parliament could not be prorogued without its own consent.

It is possible, however, to see these developments in another light. Parliament had acted in an arbitrary and imperious manner.

It had misinterpreted the polity or unwritten constitution of the country, and arrogated powers to itself that it had never before possessed. It had illegally hounded Strafford to death. It had colluded with the king's enemies and an alien army. It had organized mobs to intimidate its opponents. It had proposed a new system of religion to be enforced upon an unwilling people. It had passed a bill ensuring its permanence. In the process the king had been stripped of his royal prerogative and had suffered a severe defeat in all the matters that touched him most closely. He had always said that his enemies wished to relegate him to the status of the doge of Venice. He was not mistaken.

22

Worse and worse news

Parliament reassembled on 20 October 1641, determined to wring from the king the same concessions that the Scottish parliament had already obtained from him. This was the period when the title of 'King Pym' came into general use. John Pym had started his career, perhaps surprisingly, as a receiver of Crown lands, and he was in general a good man of business. He was the great orchestrator of parliamentary affairs and had the ability to direct various men and factions towards one end; he was an effective, if not eloquent, debater but his real energy and power lay in his handling of parliamentary committees. By his use of such committees, in fact, he proved that parliament could govern as ably as the king. He sat close to the Speaker in the Commons, together with the other parliamentary leaders, and it was reported that 'the Speaker diligently watches the Eye of Pym'.

He was shrewd, and tireless, with a fierce hatred of popery and a genuine commitment to what he considered to be the true religion; his maiden speech was an attack upon one of his colleagues who had branded a Sabbath bill as a 'puritan' bill, and in another speech he declared that 'no impositions are so grievous as those that are laid upon the soul'. He possessed a round face, full lips and heavy jowls; he also sported a curling moustache and short pointed beard.

Yet he was not necessarily of a severe disposition; he was known for his cheerfulness and conviviality.

At the beginning of this session a letter was delivered to him as he sat in his place in the Commons. A gentleman had hired a messenger on Fish Street Hill, and given him a shilling to deliver the missive. When Pym opened it a rag dropped out that was, in the words of Clarendon, 'foul with the foulness of a plague sore'; it was a rag that had covered a plague wound. It was accompanied by a letter that denounced Pym for treason and threatened that, if the plague did not kill him, a dagger surely would. It ended with 'repent, traitor'.

Pym and his colleagues were now intent upon stripping Charles of his prerogative power, namely his ability to appoint his officers and councillors without reference to parliament. Yet they had first to deprive the upper house of its majority in favour of the king, and so they moved to expel the thirteen bishops who sat there. A bill was passed by the Commons to disqualify any cleric from accepting secular office, but naturally enough it was delayed by the Lords themselves.

Pym tried to raise the temperature of the debate with news of fresh army plots and of a furore in Edinburgh, where three covenanter lords had fled the king's court in fear of their lives; this became known as 'the incident'. The king then fervently declared before the Scottish parliament that he had played no part in any such plot to assassinate them and asked for 'fair play'. The fact that the principal conspirator had been Will Murray, the groom of the king's bedchamber, served to throw doubt upon the king's protestations of innocence. Whether true or not, the rumours only deepened parliamentary alarm about the king's intentions; it simply confirmed the fact, known by all, that he could not be trusted. Yet, in turn, why should he trust those who conspired against his throne? It still seemed very likely, in the early days of the parliament, that any attempt at more radical reform would come to nothing. Many members were now of the opinion that the changes in religion, in particular, were coming on too fast. Here were the makings of the king's party.

Just at that moment, at the very beginning of November, news reached parliament that a rebellion had broken out in Ireland. The information was brought to the Commons by seventeen privy councillors, and Clarendon reported that 'there was a deep silence . . . and a kind of consternation'. It aroused all the fears of the Protestants of England, and one courtier who had been asked to remain at Westminster and report on parliament, Edward Nicholas, wrote to the king in Edinburgh that 'the alarm of popish plots amaze and fright the people here more than anything'. It was reported that papists were storing weapons and stocking gunpowder. A pamphlet circulated with the question 'Oh ye blood-thirsty papists, what are your intents?' The rebellion came as a cataclysmic shock, but the conditions for it had been slowly gathering.

There were three defined elements in Irish society. The New English were the Protestant settlers who had established themselves after the Reformation; they controlled the Dublin parliament and were intent upon imposing English 'standards' upon the natives. The Old English had arrived before the Reformation, some as early as the twelfth century, and had become so acclimatized that they identified themselves with Ireland rather than with England; many of them were Catholic while some merely conformed in public to the Protestant Church of Ireland. They owned about one third of the best land. The third group, known by their masters as the 'mere Irish' or 'natives', made up the largest part of the population but, like most of the downtrodden of the earth, have left little record of their loyalties or beliefs.

But the Irish and the Old English had much cause for grievance. The Crown had in previous years confiscated one quarter of the land that had been held by the Anglo-Irish gentry and by the native Irish; it had already been decided, in the reign of James I, that no landowner could have the title to his land unless he could prove that he held proper feudal tenure. If he could not provide these credentials, his lands might be confiscated and planted with new English or Scottish settlers. Thus James had presented the citizens of London with 40,000 acres in County Derry, the territory therefore becoming known as Londonderry. The six counties of Ulster had also largely fallen into the hands of Scottish Presbyterians. The dismal state of the Church of Ireland, and the zealous work of Jesuit missionaries, had in any case emboldened the Catholic cause. The Catholics had good reason for resentment; they were unable to educate their children, and their priests, given no benefices, were forced to rely upon the charity of their parishioners. Fines could also be imposed upon those who did not attend Protestant services.

Many forces were therefore at work in the revolt. The Irish Catholic leaders, who included the Old English, drew up a remonstrance in which they claimed to be rising up for the safety of their religion and for the defence of their lives and estates. They were aware of the proceedings of the English parliament, and of the concessions made by the king to the Scottish Presbyterians, and so felt all the more keenly the injustice to their native religion; they feared also that the reformers or 'puritan faction of England' had so deep a detestation of Catholicism that they would impose more restraints upon, and exact new duties from, them. They might even go further and in a statement of Irish grievances it was suggested that the Scots and English, combined, might 'come into Ireland, with the Bible in one hand and the sword in the other, for to plant their puritan, anarchical religion among us, otherwise utterly to destroy us'. Why should Irishmen not rise up in their own defence before it was too late? This was a grand irony of the period. The negotiations between England and Scotland had the result of forcing Ireland into revolt. Charles had found it impossible in practice to administer three kingdoms, when each one had pledged its loyalty to a separate religion.

On 23 October 1641, they rose up against their English masters. A rebellion in Dublin on the previous day had been partly discovered and quelled, but insurrection spread through the land. Parties of armed men would ravage an English-owned plantation, and then retire to their own territory; others would actively supplant the English owners and replace them with the former proprietors. The English fugitives sought refuge in the nearest army garrison, where they remained in fear and consternation.

The more radical members of the Commons were already preparing a remonstrance to the king with the purpose of appealing for renewed public support, when news of what was called an Irish 'massacre' invested their efforts with fresh urgency. The most frightful reports had reached them. It was stated that many thousands of Protestants had been killed, that women had been raped and mutilated, that babies had been burned. A pamphlet, 'Worse and Worse News from Ireland', revealed the list of war crimes. A letter read out to the House of Commons alleged that the Irish rebels in Munster were engaged in

> exercising all manner of cruelties, and striving who can be most barbarously exquisite in tormenting the poor Protestants, wheresoever they come, cutting off the privy members, ears, fingers and hands, plucking out their eyes, boiling the heads of little children before their mothers' faces, and then ripping out their mothers' bowels, stripping women naked, and standing by them being naked, whilst they are in travail [labour], killing the children as soon as they are born, ripping up their mothers' bellies as they are delivered . . .

The more sober truth was that approximately 5,000 English Protestants had been killed, and that an equal number of Irish Catholics had fallen in the course of the English counter-attack.

On 5 November Pym rose from his seat to pledge his life and estate to the cause of suppressing the rebellion but added that 'unless the king would remove his evil counsellors, and take such counsellors as might be approved by Parliament, we should account ourselves absolved from this engagement'. A bill was then passed that 'supplicated' the king to employ only men acceptable to parliament. On 8 November Pym told the Lords that, if the king rejected their supplication, he and his fellows would have to 'resolve some such way of defending Ireland from the rebels as may concur to the securing of ourselves'. Parliament, in other words, would be in charge of organizing and directing its own Protestant army that might in turn be employed to defend its own cause. The king would become merely a figurehead or talisman.

This was the occasion for the debate on a document that later became known as the 'Grand Remonstrance', a lengthy tract of some 204 clauses that anatomized the history of abuses perpetrated by the 'malignant party' close to the king. These evil counsellors had set out 'a malignant and pernicious design of subverting the fundamental laws and principles of government, upon which the religion and justice of this kingdom are firmly established'. It was a catalogue of errors and abuses that was designed to inflame the temper of the nation, and thus to check the resurgence of loyalty towards the king.

Violent objections were raised to what amounted to a manifesto; some believed that it was an act of treachery against the king, while others believed that the Commons had no right to produce such a remonstrance without the agreement of the Lords. Sir Edward Dering, the royalist member for Kent, said that 'when I first heard of a remonstrance I presently imagine that like faithful councillors we should hold up a glass to his majesty . . . I did not dream that we should remonstrate downward, tell stories to the people and talk of the king as a third person'.

Pym sensed that a royalist party was acquiring more support. He agreed that certain clauses of the remonstrance might be amended or deleted but 'it is time to speak plain English, lest posterity shall say that England was lost and no man durst speak the truth'. The final debate took place on 22 November and went on through that winter afternoon; it continued in candlelight until one o'clock in the morning. When the house finally divided Pym had gained the victory by eleven votes. It was said that the decision was like that of a 'starved jury', alluding to the custom of depriving jurors of meat and drink until they had reached a verdict. But the narrowness of the result meant that the king had created a sizeable party.

As soon as the division was announced some of the royalists entered their protestations. One member, Sir Geoffrey Palmer, accused the majority of being 'a rabble of inconsiderable persons, set on by a juggling Junto'. When a motion was introduced that the remonstrance should be published at once, the tempers of the opposing sides erupted. Some waved their hats in the air while others, according to Simonds D'Ewes, 'took their swords in their scabbards out of their belts and held them by their pommels in their hands, setting the lower part on the ground'. Sir Philip Warwick wrote that 'I thought we had all sat in the valley of the shadow of death; for we, like Joab's and Abner's young men, had catched at each other's locks and sheathed our swords in each other's bowels'. The significance of the occasion is marked by Oliver Cromwell, who said on leaving the chamber that 'if the remonstrance had been rejected, I would have sold all I had the next morning, and never have seen England more'.

*

Edward Nicholas wrote to the king on the first day of the debate on 8 November, that 'it relates all the misgovernment and unpleasing things that have been done by ill counsels (as they call it) . . . if your majesty come not instantly away [from Edinburgh to London] I trouble to think what will be the issue of it'. So Charles returned to London from Edinburgh seventeen days later and, on his entrance into the City, he was met by a cavalcade. He told those assembled to greet him that he would maintain the good old laws and the Protestant religion. He would do this 'if need be, to the hazard of my life and all that is dear unto me'.

It is likely that the welcome from the City was a genuine one. The 'former tumults and disorders', as Charles called them, were no better for commerce than the new taxes that were being imposed by parliament upon the merchants and men of business. A fund of loyalty for the king also existed among the prosperous sort who were averse to the radicalism of his opponents; they disliked the spectacle of apprentices and minor tradesmen quoting Scripture at them, and they feared any uprising of the multitude. The Venetian ambassador had already reported that anonymous placards had been posted in the streets of the city, naming the lords of the puritan Junto as traitors and the authors of sedition.

Charles knighted the lord mayor amid cries of 'God bless and long live King Charles and Queen Mary', the name by which Henrietta Maria was often known, after which he rode in procession, accompanied by 1,000 armed men, to the Guildhall for a great banquet. The conduits at Cornhill and Cheapside ran with claret as the bells rang and the bonfires blazed. It was a ceremony of ancient provenance and it emphasized the virtues of the traditional order. No guests from the Commons were invited to the feast at the Guildhall.

The king was encouraged, however, by his greeting in the City and by the fact that the remonstrance had been strongly resisted by so many members of the Commons. Determined to surrender nothing more, the king was resolved to extirpate his enemies under the forms of law. The parliament had destroyed Strafford by ingenious means of attainder, and it was open to him to use the same or similar methods.

Just before the king had left Scotland he, too, had received the news that his Irish subjects had erupted in rebellion. He had appeased one of his kingdoms only to find another in arms. His first reaction was simply the hope that the revolt 'may hinder some of these follies in England', by which he may have meant that the desperate news might bring parliament to its senses. Yet it could be lent a more sinister meaning. Could the Irish not be treated as a threat to the puritans?

Pym and his colleagues were inclined to blame Charles for the rebellion in a more direct sense. Some of the Irish rebels claimed that they had a commission from the king under the great seal 'to arrest and seize the goods, estates and persons of all the English Protestants'. It was a false claim, but at the time it persuaded Pym that the king had deliberately fomented the revolt in order to raise a force against the parliament; that Charles was willing to tolerate Catholicism in Ireland in return for the support of the 'Old English' in his fight against parliament. It was said of the Irish rebels that England 'is that fine sweet bit which they so long for and their cruel teeth so much water at'.

There was bitter controversy over the size and direction of the military campaign in Ireland. The king said that one man, rather than 400 men, was best able to direct a campaign; the Junto naturally disagreed, claiming that Charles could not raise an army without the express approval of parliament. In the last two months of the year the earl of Warwick set about creating what was essentially a parliamentary force. Charles wanted a wholly volunteer force composed of his supporters, while the Junto insisted upon pressing men into service. At every stage in the process the Commons, with a small majority against the king, was opposed by the Lords.

In the event only one regiment was sent to Ireland, at the end of the year, and a further force of 5,000 men arrived five months later. The English garrisons in Ireland were essentially left to fight their own battles. It might be fair to assume that Pym and his fellows wished to muster their resources for a conflict closer to home.

23

A world of mischief

At the end of 1641 a royalist member of parliament, Sir Henry Slingsby, wrote that 'I cannot say we have had a merry Christmas, but the maddest one that ever I saw'. He added that 'I never saw the court so full of gentlemen, every one comes thither with his sword . . . Both factions talk very big and it is a wonder there is no more blood yet spilt, seeing how earnest both sides are.' The citizens had come to Westminster, their swords by their sides, ready to protect the puritan members. John Venn, one of the London members of parliament, said in a shop off Cheapside that 'you must go to the parliament with your swords, for that party which is best for the commonwealth is like to be over-voted'. The parliament itself had been warned many times of threats against its activities and even its life.

On 21 December elections were held in London for the common council and the results favoured the puritan cause. On that day the king dismissed the lieutenant of the Tower, Sir William Balfour, and appointed Thomas Lunsford in his place; Lunsford was known to be a zealous and sometimes violent partisan of the king, and was therefore deeply distrusted. If any of the parliamentary or civic leaders were arrested, he would be sure to hold them fast. Simonds D'Ewes wrote that 'all things hastened apace to confusion and calamity, from which I scarce saw any possibility in human reason for this poor Church and kingdom to be delivered'.

The lightning flash was reserved for the thirteen bishops who sat in the Lords; they provided the majority for the king which was able to override all the bills and declarations of the Commons. When the Lords gathered in Westminster at the end of December a crowd of apprentices and others began to call out, 'No bishops! No popish lords!' The archbishop of York lunged at one of the noisiest of the participants, but he himself was hustled and his gown torn. The Lords then asked the Commons to join with them in a declaration against riotous assemblies, to which Pym answered, 'God forbid the House of Commons should proceed in any way to dishearten people to obtain their just desires in such a way.' He was on the side of the mob who had threatened the bishops.

An opposing force, made up of military volunteers and soldiers of fortune, had also gathered in the city; they had come to serve the king in Ireland and elsewhere, but they could also be guaranteed to turn upon the crowds who supported parliament. They might prove useful if the king should ever attempt to mount a *coup d'état*. One London news-writer, John Dillingham, reported that these soldiers 'offered their majesties to untie the knot' before adding 'what was meant you may judge'.

This was the period in which the terms of 'roundhead' and 'cavalier' became common currency, deriving from the short hair of the citizens and the long locks of the royalist soldiers. The latter term, deriving from *caballeros* or Spanish troops, was meant to be one of abuse but it soon became associated with honour and gallantry. It should be remembered that the leaders of the parliamentary cause, in the Commons and in the Lords, also wore their hair long as befitted the members of their social rank.

With the steady formation of two antagonistic powers, there was already talk of a civil war. Argument and dissension sprang up everywhere. Two days after Christmas the crowds once more gathered around Westminster to demand a response from the Lords to another petition against the bishops; a group of soldiers fell upon them but the citizens fought back with ferocity inspired by fear. They attacked the troops with sticks and stones and cudgels; some sailors joined them with truncheons until the soldiers were beaten down or had run away. A number of apprentices had been arrested and detained in the Mermaid Tavern; a group of their fellows stormed the tavern and released them. On the following morning soldiers charged out of Westminster Abbey and fell upon the citizens with their swords and pistols; that afternoon, they hacked at a group of apprentices. In retaliation the citizens threatened to shut up their shops and refrain from trade.

In the Lords the bishops sat huddled in the torchlight, listening to the rage and menace of the crowds. They were forced to leave the chamber by means of subterfuge, some of them under the protection of the great lords and others directed to secret passages out of the building. The earl of Huntingdon reported that 'ten thousand prentices were betwixt York House and Charing Cross with halberds, staves and some with swords. They stood so thick that we had much ado to pass with our coaches, and though it were a dark night their innumerable number of links [lights] made it as light as day. They cried "no bishops, no papist lords", looked in our coaches whether there were any bishops therein, that we went in great danger.'

On the following morning the citizens and apprentices returned to Westminster with the stated intention of murdering any bishops who dared to venture forth. Whenever they spied a bishop's boat coming across the Thames they called out, 'A bishop! A bishop!' and prevented him from landing. It is likely, but not proven, that these angry assemblies were in fact planned and organized by the parliamentary party to bring additional pressure upon the king.

On 29 December a group of twelve bishops laid the complaint that they had been 'violently menaced, affronted, and assaulted, by multitudes of people' and that in their enforced absence the proceedings of the Lords were void. This was tantamount to asserting that, without the bishops, any parliament was illegal. The members of the Commons were incensed at what they considered to be the arrogance of the claim, and on the following day the bishops were impeached for high treason and sent to the Tower on a bitter night of snow and frost. The senior dignitaries of the Church, including both archbishops, were now behind locked doors. It was possible that, in their absence, the puritan Junto would at last be able to pass its radical measures through the Lords. The king was by no means alone in his policy of coercion and conspiracy.

On the following day a large number of the king's old military officers, described by Simonds D'Ewes as 'desperate and loose persons', were seen milling about the court and the environs of Westminster. John Pym ordered that the doors of the chamber be locked. He then declared that he had discovered a plot to destroy the Commons before nightfall. It was yet another rumour thrown upon the fire.

On the first day of the new year, 1642, matters came to a head. Committees from the Commons and the remaining Lords met at the Guildhall to consider their strategy. It was agreed that the trained bands should be summoned on the authority of parliament; at this meeting plans may also have been drawn up to impeach the queen for communing with the Catholic rebels in Ireland. The threat was, perhaps, designed to provoke the king into violent action. The trained bands were indeed raised for the cause of parliament, effectively placing London under its control; to summon armed troops without the king's permission was an act of treason, but nobody seemed to care any more.

Charles was in any case already drawing up plans to impeach certain members of parliament; he had said previously that their correspondence with the Scots, at time of war, 'shall not be forgotten'. On 3 January the charges against Lord Mandeville, John Pym, John Hampden, Arthur Haselrig, Denzil Holles and William Strode were read to the Lords. On the following day Pym sent a delegation to the common council of London, newly elected in the puritan interest, to plead for help; on that day the council elected a 'committee of safety' for the city.

It was not a moment too soon, since the king was ready to strike later that day. Pym had been alerted to the assault, perhaps by spies at the court, and prepared for a notable act of theatre. The accused men took their seats in the Commons early in the afternoon, knowing full well that the king would be informed of their presence. At three o'clock Charles left Whitehall with an armed guard of 300 men and made his way to Westminster. The news reached the Commons and the indicted members slipped from their seats and hid in the court of the king's bench before being rowed into the City; even as they made their departure the king's party could be heard clattering on the stairs into the lobby. The king entered the chamber of the Commons alone but the doors were left open so that the members could see the armed force waiting outside.

'Gentlemen,' Charles said, 'I am sorry to have this occasion of coming unto you.' He asked for the accused members to be surrendered to him. He then realized that his bluff had been called. He looked about him, and saw that they were gone. 'I do not see any of them,' he muttered, 'I think I should know them.' He added that 'I am come to tell you that I must have them, wheresoever I find them. Is Mr Pym here?' There came no answer. 'Well, well! 'Tis no matter. I think my eyes are as good as another's.' He then asked the Speaker to help him find the offending members.

'May it please your majesty,' Speaker Lenthall replied, 'I have neither eyes to see nor tongue to speak in this place, but as this House is pleased to direct me, whose servant I am here; and I humbly beg your majesty's pardon that I cannot give any other answer than this to what your majesty is pleased to demand of me.'

There followed what contemporaries described as a 'long pause' or a 'dreadful silence'. 'Well,' the king eventually said, 'since I see all the birds are flown, I do expect from you that you will send them unto me as soon as they return hither. If not, I will seek them myself, for their treason is foul, and such a one as you will thank me to discover. But I assure you, on the word of a king, I never did intend any force, but shall proceed against them in a legal and fair way, for I never meant any other.' He left much discomfited as the cries of 'Privilege! Privilege' were raised all around him.

The members of the king's party in the Commons realized at once that he had committed a major, and perhaps fatal, blunder; his authority was for the moment lost, and in a mood of understandable dismay they meekly submitted to the decision of parliament to adjourn itself to the hall of one of the London guilds as a place of greater safety. On the evening of the failed attempt the city had all the air of an armed camp. Barricades were set up and chains drawn across the principal thoroughfares; the people of the suburbs, as well as the city itself, offered their support to parliament in case Charles's army should march against them. The women boiled water ready to throw upon any encroaching cavaliers. The members who had absconded were now safely concealed in a house on Coleman Street, a notable centre for radical sectarians. The call went up among some that the king was unworthy to live. Charles had effectively lost the capital.

Yet London was not the only place of disaffection. In the days immediately following, thousands of men from Kent and Buckinghamshire, Northamptonshire and Leicestershire, Essex and Sussex, rode or marched to Westminster with petitions for parliament. They complained in general about the decay of trade provoked by the divisions and distempers in the state. The country was, as a result of the crisis, confronted by sudden economic decline; the loss of confidence restricted trade, and the tradesmen and merchants of London hoarded their money in the hope of better times. The majority of the people yearned for peace. It is important to note, however, that the petitioners from Kent and elsewhere had addressed parliament as the centre of authority in the nation.

On 10 January the king left London for Hampton Court, arriving so quickly and unexpectedly that the beds had not been prepared for him and his family. He told the Dutch ambassador that he had feared for the safety of his wife in the capital; he would not see London again until he returned nine years later as a prisoner. On the following day the members of parliament who had been charged by Charles with high treason came back by water to Westminster where they were greeted by triumphant crowds.

The military arsenal of the nation was placed at Hull, where 20,000 weapons and 7,000 barrels of gunpowder were secured. The king appointed the earl of Newcastle to be the governor of the port and arsenal but he was circumvented by the swift action of a young parliamentarian, John Hotham, who persuaded the mayor of Hull to admit his men. His father, Sir John Hotham, was then appointed as the town's governor.

The Commons drew up a declaration to the officials of all the counties urging them 'to put themselves in a position of defence', and a day or two later asked them to nominate their own lieutenant-generals in the place of those loyal only to the king. The king then sent a letter to Westminster in which he proposed that he would preserve the privileges of its members and protect the interests of true religion in exchange for a commitment to preserve his authority and his revenues. The Lords wished to send a simple reply of thanks but the Commons responded with the demand that the fortresses and militia of the country should be placed in the hands of their supporters.

At the end of January Charles summoned all of his faithful lords to Windsor, to which castle he had now retired; fourteen of the peers joined him there, thus tipping the majority of those remaining in Westminster to the side of the puritan Junto. The lords of the puritan coalition could now rely on a majority in their own house to pass all the necessary legislation. Thus on 5 February the Commons sent up to the Lords a bill concerning the exclusion of the bishops from parliament. The pace quickened. By the middle of that month Charles and Henrietta Maria were at Canterbury, on their way to Dover where the queen would embark for Holland. She was travelling ostensibly to escort her daughter to an arranged marriage with the prince of Orange, but she also had more covert aims; she was attempting to buy men and *matériel* since, as she told the Venetian ambassador, 'to settle affairs it was necessary to unsettle them first'.

The bill for the exclusion of the bishops now reached the king. He was advised that, if he did not give royal assent to the document, the queen's journey might be prevented by parliamentary supporters; the queen herself then added her voice urging him to assent. As far as she was concerned, the bishops were dispensable. So Charles consented, even though he had promised in his coronation oath to maintain the ecclesiastics in all their privileges. He may have calculated, however, that he could rescind his decision at a later time and in more favourable circumstances.

When Charles travelled back to his palace at Greenwich, he sent for his eldest son. He was determined to keep the prince of Wales with him as a guarantee for the preservation of the royal family; father and son would remain together for the next three years through all the vicissitudes of warfare. The members of parliament now asked him to stay in the vicinity of Westminster; his presence elsewhere might provoke conflict and danger. He replied that 'for my residence near you, I wish it might be so safe and honourable that I had no cause to absent myself from Whitehall; ask yourself whether I have not'. He did not, in other words, feel safe in proximity to parliament and the citizens of London.

On the following day he set out for royalist York rather than the capital. While en route, at Newmarket a parliamentary delegation came to him in order to present their case; they read out a declaration in which all the king's actions, including his recent attempt to arrest the five members of the Commons, were detailed. The king was very uneasy. 'That's false,' he said at one point. 'That's a lie!' He gave his answer to them the next day. 'What would you have? Have I violated your laws? Have I denied to pass any bill for the ease and security of my subjects?' He then added, 'I do not ask what you have done for me.'

The earl of Pembroke, a member of the puritan Junto, urged the king to return and set out his demands or wishes. 'I would whip a boy in Westminster School', Charles replied, 'that could not tell that by my answer.' Pembroke then asked him to grant power over the army to parliament. 'By God,' the king said, 'not for an hour!' He added that 'you have asked that of me in this, which was never asked of a king'. A king would not surrender his troops to what was effectively the enemy.

On 16 March the members of the Commons issued a proclamation claiming supreme power for parliament within the nation. When Lords and Commons 'shall declare what the law of the land is, to have this not only questioned and controverted, but contradicted, and a command that it should not be obeyed, is a high breach of the privilege of Parliament'. At the same time the members issued an ordinance requiring the leaders of the local militias to be appointed by them; these men would in turn raise forces on behalf of parliament. An Act was then passed to levy new taxes for that cause, much to the horror of the regional communities.

The members of parliament were becoming unpopular. Clarendon wrote that 'their carriage was so notorious and terrible that spies were set upon, and inquiries were made upon, all private, light, casual discourses which fell from those that were not gracious to them'. It seemed to many that they had become despots rather than representatives, inquisitors rather than champions. As a supporter of the Crown Clarendon may have been a biased witness, but he mentioned the case of one member of the Commons who was expelled from the house and sent to prison for having said that parliament could not provide a guard for itself without the king's consent.

There was as yet no necessity for war. The local communities of the realm were at peace; the borough sessions, the leet courts and the quarter sessions still met. Bread was weighed and the quality of ale was measured. In the wider world it still seemed possible that a political solution could be reached. Neither side appeared to have the power, or resources, to raise and command an army. No one wanted to be found guilty of having started a civil war. Nobles on both sides were eager for some form of compromise.

The king, in the company of his son, made a slow journey to York. Charles heard an oration at Cambridge as the cry of '*Vivat rex!*' came from the scholars; the sheriff, however, did not appear to greet him. The prince of Wales reported to his sister that their father was 'disconsolate and troubled'. The king's reception in Yorkshire was not designed to reassure him. He had arrived at York with only thirty-nine gentlemen and seventeen guards, but the gentry did not flock to his side; the recorder of York, in his address of welcome, urged him 'to hearken unto and condescend unto' his parliamentary opponents. Margaret Eure, the Yorkshire gentlewoman mentioned before, expressed the wish: 'Oh that the sweet parliament would come with the olive branch in its mouth. We are so many frighted people; for my part if I hear but a door creak I take it to be a drum. Things stand in so ill a condition here as we can make no money of our coal-pits.' This may be said to summarize the mood of the nation, a compound of fear and dismay. No one could quite believe what was happening. Surely a solution could be found? The participants seemed to be sleep-walking towards disaster.

The king himself still professed a measure of optimism, saying that he could easily assemble an army of 16,000 men. He declared that he would raise a force in Cheshire and descend upon the rebels in Ireland. He wrote to parliament explaining that he had 'firmly resolved to go with all convenient speed into Ireland, to chastise those wicked and detestable rebels'; he added that, for this purpose, he intended to raise a force of 2,000 foot and 200 horse which should be armed 'from my magazine at Hull'. He may of course have had a different enemy in mind.

Here lay the problem. Hull was in the hands of parliament represented by its governor, Sir John Hotham. Hotham knew, as well as anyone, that the king may have required arms for 'wicked and detestable rebels' closer to home than Ireland. He also knew that the king would soon ride out and demand obedience. The members of parliament had already anticipated this action, and had told him not to open the town gates except by their authority. The members stated later that 'the king's supreme and royal pleasure is exercised and declared in this high court of law and counsel [themselves], after a more eminent and obligatory manner than it can be by personal act or resolution of his own'. They could not have declared in a clearer or more unambiguous manner that they were the masters now.

In the last week of April Charles approached Hull with a company of 300 horsemen, preceded by a message that he had come to dine with the governor. Sir John Hotham resolved with the municipal leaders to curtail any triumphant entry; when the king arrived he found the gates shut and the drawbridge raised with a guard upon the ramparts. He demanded entrance as their lawful sovereign, but was told by Hotham that 'I dare not open the gates, being intrusted by the Parliament with the safety of the town'. Charles replied that 'I believe you have no order from the Parliament to shut the gates against me or to keep me out of the town'. To which Hotham answered that the king's force was so great that 'if it were admitted I should not be able to give a good account of the town'. It seems that Hotham then told him that he might enter with a company of twelve men. He refused the condition as an affront to his person and, to the sound of a trumpet, proclaimed Hotham to be a traitor. His dignity, and his self-respect, had been deeply injured.

When he returned to York he sent a message to parliament acquainting the members with the insult given to him by Hotham 'who had the impudence to aver that Parliament had directed him to deny His Majesty entrance'. The two houses stated in reply that 'Sir John Hotham had done nothing but in obedience to the commands of both Houses of Parliament' and that 'the declaring of him a traitor, being a member of the House of Commons, was a high breach of the privilege of Parliament'. They also ordered the sheriff of Yorkshire to 'suppress' any further forces raised by the king. All parties prophesied a world of woe.

24

Neither hot nor cold

In the spring of 1642 the two houses resolved that 'the king, seduced by wicked counsels, intends to make a war against the Parliament'. So they began to prepare men and arms. In May a levy of 16,000 soldiers was ordered. The trained bands of London were secured for service, and were mustered in Finsbury Fields; the weapons at Hull were transferred to the Tower. A forced loan, to be repaid at an interest of 8 per cent, helped to fill the coffers of the parliamentary treasury with coin or with plate. In the course of this spring parliament nominated the earl of Warwick to be lord high admiral of the English fleet. He worked quickly to gain the loyalty of his men, and ships that supported the cause of the king were promptly boarded and overpowered. Clarendon later observed that 'this loss of the whole navy was of unspeakable ill consequence to the king's affairs'. A king of England without sovereignty of the sea could scarcely be considered a king at all.

Men and money were also arriving for the king at York. Members of the nobility and the clergy, together with the gentry and the scholars of both universities, sent him jewellery and plate as well as ready money. Some ventures were less successful. The queen dispatched a vessel from Holland containing ammunition and sixteen pieces of cannon, but it was captured off Yarmouth. Just as parliament had sent out a 'militia ordinance' to recruit troops, so the king now sent out 'commissions of array' to raise a volunteer army. These commissions were formal documents, written in Latin and impressed with the great seal, sent to every city and county in the nation; they named certain leading men who would secure their territory for the king and at the same time gather men and money for the royal cause. Yet the soldiers on either side had not yet necessarily been raised to fight; they might be used to deter the other side from violence or to provide support in any subsequent negotiations.

The contradictory commands of the militia ordinance and the commissions of array caused much disquiet. While walking in Westminster on a May morning a notable moderate and former soldier, Sir Thomas Knyvett, was approached by two men of parliament who brought with them an order 'to take upon me, by virtue of ordinance of Parliament, my company and command again'. He told his wife that 'I was surprised what to do, whether to take or refuse'; he accepted it, however, since this 'was no place to dispute'. Then a few hours later 'I met with a declaration point blank against it by the king'. He consulted with others in the same predicament, and they agreed that they would be obliged to follow their consciences in the matter. Meanwhile, Knyvett wrote, 'I hold it good wisdom and security to keep my company as close to me as I can in these dangerous times, and stay out of the way of my new masters till these first musterings be over.' These are the words of a modest and relatively impartial man caught between the two factions. His voice, like that of many others, would soon be muffled by the increasingly rebarbative tones of those urging stronger and stronger action against their opponents. One Londoner who refused to follow the lead of parliament was advised 'to leave the town lest his brains were beaten out by the boys in the streets'.

Events now had a momentum of their own, each move prompting a counter-move and each rumour producing a further reaction. Bulstrode Whitelocke, a parliamentary supporter, remarked later that 'it is strange to note how we have insensibly slid into this beginning of a civil war, by one unexpected accident after another, as waves of the sea, which have brought us thus far'. Many volumes have been written on the social or religious 'cause' or 'causes' of the civil war, but one principal motive may simply have been that of fear. Pym and his colleagues knew that, if the king were to prevail, they could all suffer a traitor's death.

One parliamentarian, Lord Wharton, wrote in June 1642 to the chief justice who was with the king at York. He asked him how it was that the kingdom did not contain one person of prudence and skill 'to prevent the ruin coming upon us'? His colleagues at Westminster were not disloyal, and he knew that those about the king 'wish and drive at an accommodation'. So why could not an agreement be reached by both sides? Thomas Knyvett believed, two years later, that 'the best excuse that can be made for us, must be a fit of lunacy'.

At the beginning of June parliament, guided by Pym's opportune and careful management, delivered 'nineteen propositions' to the king; among them was the wish, or command, that the king dismiss his forces and accept the validity of the militia ordinance. He was to accept the religious reforms outlined by the members of parliament and to exclude popish peers from the Lords. His principal officers should be appointed only with the approval of parliament, and all important matters of state must be debated there. The document became in the words of one parliamentarian, Edmund Ludlow, 'the principal foundation of the ensuing war'. Ludlow said that the question came to this: 'whether the king should govern as a god by his will and the nation be governed by force like beasts; or whether the people should be governed by laws made by themselves, and live under a government derived from their own consent'.

The king of course rejected the demands out of hand with the words '*nolumus leges Angliae mutari*' – we do not wish the laws of England to be changed. He said that acceptance of parliamentary demands would ensure that he became 'but the outside, but the picture, but the sign, of a king'. The propositions were 'a mockery' and 'a scorn'. Yet some still held back from confrontation. A parliamentarian, Sir Gilbert Pickering, wrote to a friend that 'there are now some overtures of accommodation . . . and most men think they smell the air of peace. Yet provide for war.' Seventeen counties sent forth petitions for such an 'accommodation' between the two sides.

At the beginning of July it was reported that the royalists had mustered in Herefordshire, Worcestershire and Warwickshire; it was soon known that the king had placed himself at the head of a force of cavalry. On 11 July parliament declared that the king had already begun the war, thus diverting any blame for beginning the conflict. On the following day the earl of Essex was placed in charge of a parliamentary army, and the king promptly declared him to be a traitor. The first blood was shed three days later, when a townsman of Manchester died from wounds inflicted by a group of royalist troopers. The two sides now competed to seize control of the munitions of the local militias.

A 'committee of safety' was set up by parliament which, through the summer and autumn, began to organize soldiers, weaponry and supplies; it was a high command in another sense, since it oversaw military strategy and communicated between parliament and the commanders in the fields.

The two sides were now beginning to acquire a definite shape. The early supporters of the king were prompted by loyalty and by the doctrine of obedience. Sir Edmund Verney expressed it best by saying of the king that 'I have eaten his bread and served him near thirty years, and will not do so base a thing as to forsake him'. Verney lost his life, shortly after writing this, in the first great battle of the conflict. His sense of honour overrode all other considerations. It was a question of what was known as 'the old service' or 'the good old cause'.

A majority of the peers and the greater landowners supported the king, since his privileges guaranteed their own. Twice as many families of the gentry also took the king's part. The puritan gentry, of course, were parliamentarians. A puritan divine, Richard Baxter, anatomized the situation very well. He claimed that 'on the parliament's side were the smaller part, as some thought, of the gentry in most of the counties, and the greatest part of the tradesmen and freeholders, and the middle sort of men, especially in those corporations [towns] and counties which depend on clothing and such manufactures'. An element of popular or lower-class royalism, still to be recognized today, was evident in the zeal of porters and watermen, butchers and labourers, for the king's cause in the larger towns and cities; the language of the street often condemned 'parliament dogs' and 'parliament whores'. They wore red ribbons in their hats as a sign of their allegiance.

Religious dissenters overwhelmingly took the side of parliament, of course, while the Roman Catholics and those of orthodox faith supported the king or, for fear of reprisals, remained neutral. The universities and cathedral cities were largely for the king, although the clergy were often opposed by the aldermen, while the dockyards and chief ports were for parliament. A great number of towns, however, wished to stay out of the conflict altogether.

In the most general terms the north and west were sympathetic towards the king while the south-east, and London in particular, supported the parliamentary cause. Yet all of the counties were divided. The north of Lincolnshire was largely royalist, for example, while the south remained generally for parliament. It has been recorded of Derbyshire that the belt of iron and coal in the eastern stretch of the county was royalist while the lead areas of the north supported parliament. This may be an aspect of human society rather than of geology; the lead areas contained many independent small masters, while the areas of coal and iron depended upon larger enterprises controlled by a single master or landlord. In other counties the wooded areas containing isolated and self-sufficient parishes harboured the puritan cause, while the communal villages exploiting 'mixed' farming took the royalist side.

More subtle calculations have also been made. It has been estimated that the royalists were slightly younger than the parliamentarians, this statistic boosted by the fact that many young men joined the king in a spirit of bravado as well as patriotism; in parliament itself the royalist members had been on average eleven years younger than their puritan colleagues. It is clear that the judges of the land were divided in their allegiance, some of them worried by the constitutional pretensions of the king, while the staff of the various offices of the state were more likely to be active parliamentarians. The lawyers, too, had a long history of hostility towards the courtiers.

The majority of the population were neither hot nor cold; they may have been indifferent to the opinions of either side, but they were alarmed and intimidated by the change that had come over the kingdom. The partisans on both sides had provoked the conflict, and it was they who would end it. The rest stood by and waited. They did not care about the form of government, according to one member of parliament, Arthur Haselrig, as long 'as they may plough and go to market'. Some said that the affair should be decided by a throw of the dice.

Sir William Waller, the parliamentary general in the west, wrote to his royalist counterpart, Sir Ralph Hopton, that 'my affections to you are so unchangeable that hostility itself cannot violate my friendship to your person; but I must be true to the cause wherein I serve'. He declared that he hated a war without a true enemy but 'I look upon it as *opus domini* [the work of the Lord] . . . We are both on the stage and we must act those parts that are assigned to us in this tragedy. Let us do it in a way of honour, and without personal animosities.' This is one of the noblest sentiments uttered in the period.

There was not a town or county that remained undivided by opinion and argument; factional conflict was everywhere apparent from the largest town to the humblest parish. Some sportsmen named their packs of hunting dogs 'roundheads' or 'cavaliers', and the children in the streets would engage in mock battles under those names.

Many families were also split in their allegiances, although it was sometimes believed that this was a convenient ploy to save family property if one or the other party finally prevailed. First sons were likely to be royalist, while younger sons remained 'neutral' or 'doubtful'. Yet not all family differences were settled amicably. Sir John Oglander, who took no part in the conflict, wrote in his commonplace book that 'thou wouldest think it strange if I should tell thee there was a time in England when brothers killed brothers, cousins cousins, and friends their friends'.

On the afternoon of 22 August Charles rode into Nottingham, where the royal standard was taken from the castle and fixed in the ground beside him. It was a silk flag with the royal arms and a motto, 'Give Caesar his due'; it was suspended from a long pole that was dyed red at the upper part, and was said to resemble a maypole. The king quickly scanned the proclamation of war, and corrected certain words. The declaration was then read in an uncertain voice by the herald, after the trumpets had sounded, but all threw their hats into the air and called out: 'God save King Charles and hang up the roundheads.' The standard was blown down that night in the middle of a storm. Clarendon reported that 'a general sadness covered the whole town, and the king himself appeared more melancholic than he used to be'. The civil war had begun.

25

The gates of hell

By the late summer of 1642 the king had managed to gather an army, partly comprised of the trained bands of the counties who remained loyal to him and partly of the ready supply of volunteers animated by loyalty or by the desire for pay and plunder. By the time he left Nottingham he was leading seven or eight regiments of infantry, and on his subsequent march he was joined by several regiments of cavalry; altogether he had the command of some 14,000 men.

Others might soon be inclined to join them since, at the beginning of September, parliament declared that those who opposed its intentions were 'delinquents' or 'malignant and disaffected persons' whose property could be confiscated. Those who had favoured the king without taking any action for him, or those who had remained neutral, now believed themselves to be threatened. The declaration further divided the nation into two parties. Many landowners and grandees who had taken no part in the struggle now decided to raise forces for their king so that their own lives and estates might be defended. Simonds D'Ewes, the parliamentarian diarist, confessed that the declaration 'made not only particular persons of the nobility and others but some whole counties quite desperate'. The king was greatly hearted by his opponents' error, and confidently expected many more recruits to his cause. In that hope, he was not mistaken.

On 9 September the earl of Essex rode out to his army at

Northampton. He took with him a coffin and a winding sheet as a token of his fidelity to the end. He commanded an army of 20,000 men and it was widely believed that he would defeat the king with ease. Clarendon wrote of him that 'his pride supplied his want of ambition, and he was angry to see any other man respected more than himself, because he thought he deserved it more, and did better requite it'. He was a man of great wealth and power. He liked to be known as 'his excellence', and was considered to have no equal but the king. He had the habits, and the manners, of a great lord like those of the Wars of the Roses. But it was not yet clear that he was a great commander. His reserve and his aloof manner were perhaps mistaken for wisdom. He was not a natural rebel, in any case, and his position at the head of the parliamentary forces rendered him deeply uneasy. It seems that his ultimate purpose was to detach the king from his 'evil councillors' and bring him back to London in the role of a constitutional monarch working alongside parliament. That is not what his parliamentary allies required.

In the course of this autumn some 40,000 men were gathered, and by the summer of 1643 the number had risen to 100,000. The armies were in many respects equally matched. They contained many men who believed that the war would be a short one, and that they would return to their fields in time for the next harvest; it was widely considered that one great battle would decide the issue. Many of them were poor and had been pressed into service by their landlords or employers.

From one Shropshire village, in the army of the king, were a farmer in debt, the son of a man who had been hanged for horse-stealing, a decayed weaver, a vagrant tailor and a family of father and three sons who lived in a cave. The soldiers on both sides were sometimes scorned as 'the off-scourings of the nation'. Men were released from prison and pressed into service. It was said that some of the best trainees were butchers, because they were used to the sight of blood. For some the war came as a welcome relief from more mundane suffering, and such men eagerly sought the opportunity to seize money or goods. One veteran, Colonel Birch, recalled that 'when I was in the army some said, "Let us not go this way, lest the war be ended too soon"'. They were also given provisions that were more plentiful than their food at home; the normal ration was supposed to be 2 pounds of bread or biscuit and 1 pound of meat or cheese each day. They were allowed one bottle of wine or two bottles of beer.

The royalist troops in particular were accused of drunkenness and lechery, and in the early months of the war it was reported that a group of them had murdered an eight-months pregnant woman in Leicestershire. Nehemiah Wallington, a puritan artisan from Eastcheap, wrote that 'they swagger, roar, swear, and domineer, plundering, pillaging or doing any other kind of wrong'.

Yet the abuses were not reserved to one side. The royalists may have wrecked the taverns, but the parliamentarians desecrated the churches. The climate of war turns men into animals. It was said that, when troops were quartered in a church or hall, the smell they left behind was frightful. They pissed and defecated in corners. They often brought with them contagious diseases that became known as 'camp fever'.

Many of the soldiers had of course volunteered out of genuine conviction. The parliamentary soldiers often chanted psalms as they marched, and the ministers preached to them upon such texts as the sixty-eighth psalm, 'Let God arise, let his enemies be scattered . . .' More secular rivalries also animated them; it was reported that the men of Herefordshire fought against the men of Gloucestershire, the Lancastrians against the Northumbrians.

The men carried pikes or muskets, but some were still armed with bows and arrows in the old fashion. The pike itself was supposed to be 18 feet long, with a steel head, but many of the soldiers cut it down as too cumbersome; the pikemen were also armed with a short sword. The muskets were charged with weak gunpowder and the men were advised to shoot only when the weapon was close up against the body of the enemy; since there were no cartridges, the musketeer held two or three bullets in his mouth or in his belt. They had to load and then fire with a lighted cord known as a 'match'. Others preferred to shoot arrows from their guns. They wore leather doublets and helmets that looked like iron pots.

Not all of the troops, however, were untrained or ill-prepared. There were professional soldiers among them who had fought in France, Spain and the Low Countries. Mercenaries were also used on both sides. Many of the commanders had seen service on the

European mainland. These were men who had perused such manuals as *Warlike Directions* or *Instructions for Musters and Arms*; they were the leaders who would have to give basic training to their troops. 'Turn the butt ends of your muskets to the right . . . Lay your muskets properly on your shoulders . . . Take forth your match. Blow off your coal. Cock your match . . . Present. Give fire.'

A first skirmish or encounter took place near Worcester. Essex had moved his army towards the town and, on hearing the news, the king sent Prince Rupert to support the royalist stronghold. Rupert of the Rhine was the king's nephew and, at the age of twenty-three, had already enjoyed great success as a military commander. His expertise, and his experience, were considered to be invaluable. He was high-spirited and fearless; he was also rash and impatient. Yet on this occasion, in a limited engagement, he routed the parliamentary cavalry and killed most of its officers.

Clarendon wrote that the incident 'gave his troops great courage and rendered the name of Prince Rupert very terrible, and exceedingly appalled the adversary'; he added that 'from this time the Parliament began to be apprehensive that the business would not be as easily ended as it was begun'. Oliver Cromwell himself had grave reservations about the conduct of the parliamentary army. He told his cousin, John Hampden, that 'your troopers are most of them decayed serving men and tapsters, and such kind of fellows, and their [royalist] troopers are gentlemen's sons, younger sons, and persons of quality'. Cromwell believed that if parliament were to prevail, a new and more glorious force should be formed.

There was perhaps still one way to avert the conflict. The parliamentarian grandee of Worcestershire, Lord Brooke, declared that he wished 'to avoid the profusion of blood'. So he offered his royalist counterpart in the county, the earl of Northampton, to 'try the quarrel by sword in single combat'. A duel might therefore have decided the course of the civil war. It was a medieval expedient but it emphasizes the extent to which this war was essentially still seen as a baronial combat. Yet the political and social world had changed since the fifteenth century.

The king moved with his army to Shrewsbury, only 50 miles away from the parliamentary forces. For three weeks both sides remained close to one another, but neither made any move. No one was eager for battle. Charles decided to press the issue and advance towards London. Essex was obliged to prevent him. The earl also wished to present a petition to the king, but Charles refused to see him. Why should he parley with a traitor?

The king moved forward slowly towards London, but Essex remained on his trail. The first battle of the civil war took place at Edgehill, in southern Warwickshire, where the royalist forces had rested on the evening of 22 October; the parliamentary army was only a short distance away and Charles had decided to attack from the summit of a range of hills that gave him the advantage. It was an uncertain struggle, with Rupert's cavalry for a while in the ascendant but the parliamentary infantry holding its own. Both sides claimed the victory, when in truth neither prevailed. The number of the dead amounted to a little over 1,000. A trooper wrote to his mother that 'there was a great deal of fear and misery about that field that night'.

It was the first experience of battle for most of the participants, and it came as a salutary shock. The soldiers had been badly organized and Rupert's cavalry, in particular, had run out of control. Many of the men and some of the commanders, weary and disgusted at the slaughter, fled for their homes. The king, never before in a war, was himself horrified by the death of some of his most loyal commanders. He seems also to have been alarmed by the extent of the enemy, and murmured before the battle that he did not expect to see so many arrayed against him. The earl of Essex was equally dismayed. He had hoped that one great battle would resolve the issue, but the result had been bloody and uncertain. Might this be a harbinger of the whole war? He had raised his standard against his sovereign, however, and there was no easy way forward.

The king was urged by Rupert immediately to march upon London, but instead Charles rode with his men 20 miles south to Oxford, where he had determined to establish his headquarters. It was from here, at the beginning of November, that he once more set out for the capital. On the news of his approach the terrified citizens took up whatever weapons they possessed; parliament sent a delegation to the royal camp to open negotiations but the king, while giving gracious words, still pressed forward. Prince Rupert attacked a parliamentary force at Brentford, 8 miles out of London, and then proceeded to fire some of the houses in the town; the word 'plunder' now entered the English vocabulary. It was to be the prince's method throughout the war.

The citizens of London decided, under the direction of their parliamentary masters, to make a stand. The apprentices and trained bands, to the number of 6,000, were assembled in Chelsea Field near the village of Turnham Green in Chiswick. The earl of Essex went into the city and pleaded for more men, until eventually a ragged army of 24,000 Londoners advanced to Turnham Green close to the royalist army. On Sunday 13 November, the two forces stood face to face without giving way. The king, fearing any grievous loss of life, withdrew to Hounslow. Even his most ardent supporters would have hesitated before launching a general assault upon the city itself. Yet he had lost his best, and last, chance to defeat his enemies. He was not given the credit for his mercy, however, and his withdrawal at the last minute was considered to be a public humiliation. Thus it was presented, at least, in the printing presses controlled by parliament.

A pause in hostilities prompted calls from some quarters for peace and accommodation. Parliament raised four proposals for the attention of the king; it already knew that he would reject them. A crowd of Londoners approached the common council calling for 'Peace and truth!' whereupon someone shouted out, 'Hang truth! We want peace at any price!' Demands for an end to hostilities were frequent throughout the course of the war but, at each stage of the process, the activists won their cause over their more diffident colleagues. The more combative members of parliament, for example, believed that a peace with the king would amount to capitulation. Instead they began to make approaches to Scotland in an attempt to gain military aid.

It was also important that more money should be raised. On 25 November it was agreed that an assessment should be levied upon London, but that was only the beginning. In the next few weeks and months John Pym worked to pass legislation concerning land taxes, general assessments, confiscations, property taxes and rises in excise duty. All men of property were obliged to make contributions to the public funds, on the understanding that the money would eventually be repaid by 'public faith', an obscure and possibly meaningless phrase. The levies were excused on the familiar grounds of necessity and imminent danger. In the following year an order went out that those who had not voluntarily contributed would be fined one fifth of their income from land and one twentieth of the value of their personal property.

The king now established his household and himself in Christ Church, Oxford, while Prince Rupert moved into St John's College. All Souls became an arsenal while the king's council assembled at Oriel. A strange change came over the face of the university. The main quadrangle of Christ Church was turned into a cattle-pen. It became a substitute court, also, with satires and love poems circulating from hand to hand.

Both sides now considered their strategies for the conflict to come. The royalist plan was slowly to descend on London from the north and the west, with Prince Rupert and his cavalry offering assistance from Oxford. The ports of Plymouth and Bristol in the west, and Hull in the north-east, were to be seized from parliament so that they could not become a menace to the flanks of any advancing armies. Parliament in turn already held London as well as the counties of the south-east and the midlands; it had determined to form them into 'associations' so that they could more easily combine and co-operate in the face of the enemy.

Oliver Cromwell held true to his intention, expressed to his cousin, John Hampden, of creating a regiment that would be a match for 'the gentlemen' of the other side; he picked industrious and active men from a range of occupations whom Richard Baxter, a leader of the puritans, considered to be 'of greater understanding than common soldiers'. If any of them swore he was fined a shilling; if he became drunk, he was set in the stocks. They became known, sometimes in praise and sometimes in irony, as 'godly' or 'precious' men.

The first news was kind to Charles and his forces. One of his commanders, the earl of Newcastle, took York and seemed firmly in command of the northern counties. The king himself stormed Marlborough and seized it from a parliamentary force; he was, according to the French ambassador, 'prodigal of his exertions . . . more frequently on his horse than in his coach, from morning till night marching with his infantry'. Parliamentary prisoners were often sent to Coventry under armed guard; hence the familiar expression.

Many still held to the belief that it would soon be over, their confidence strengthened by the opening of negotiations at Oxford between the two sides at the beginning of February 1643. Parliament had drafted some propositions for peace; in particular the king would be obliged to honour the bills already approved by parliament and allow the trial of certain 'delinquents'. Although these terms were not to the king's liking he maintained that 'I shall do my part and take as much honey out of the gall as I can'. In a private communication, however, he wrote that God himself could not 'draw peace out of these articles'. He replied with a list of conditions, the first of which was the return to him of his forts, revenues and ships. A few days later parliament voted that his answer was no answer at all. The hopes for peace were short-lived.

The pace of the war was quickened with the return of the queen, Henrietta Maria, together with money and fresh arms from her brief exile. A severe and prolonged tempest kept her at sea. 'Comfort yourselves, my dears,' she told her attendants, 'queens of England are never drowned.' After she had landed at Bridlington in Yorkshire some ships in the service of parliament bombarded with cannon fire the house in which she lodged, forcing her to take refuge under a bank in a field. Parliament then destroyed her chapel in Somerset House, and a painting by Rubens that had been placed over the high altar was thrown into the Thames. Yet 'Her She Majesty Generalissima', as she styled herself, was not cowed. She travelled from York to her husband in Oxford with 3,000 infantry, thirty companies of horse and six cannon. In the early spring of 1643 John Evelyn recorded in his diary that the whole of southern England saw an apparition in the air; it was a shining cloud, in the shape of a sword with its point reaching towards the north 'as bright as the moon'.

The balance of the fighting in subsequent months seemed to be tilting towards the side of the royalists, but nothing was decided. The battles were small and often indecisive, but local victories were won on both sides. The best troops were those who fought for their own territories, naturally enough, but no large-scale engagement changed the fortunes of war.

It was fought, piece by piece, across the nation without much central planning or control. Leeds had to be taken by the royalists, for example, to relieve the earl of Newcastle who might then go on to assist the earl of Derby who was hard-pressed in Lancashire. The king's forces were besieging Gloucester but an army of Londoners under the command of Essex relieved it. The royalists were making gains in the north, but they lost the key town of Reading. Taunton fell to them, but Plymouth was saved by the parliamentary fleet. Small wars erupted in almost all of the counties. The citizens of one town might furnish a force for parliament while the adjacent manor houses collected troops for the king. Very little of the action was co-ordinated properly. Opposing armies would come upon one another by chance. No one knew what was really happening.

London was harassed by fears and rumours, its population swollen by refugees from the fighting elsewhere. In the spring of 1643 a great defensive earthwork began to rise around the city, and many houses in the suburbs were demolished to provide clean lines of fire from twenty-eight 'works' or forts that were ranged along it. Ramparts were constructed behind a ditch 3 yards wide, and the total height of the fortifications in some places reached 18 feet; the 'wall' surrounded the city in a circuit of 11 miles. Much of it was built within three months by the citizens themselves. The Venetian ambassador estimated that 20,000 men, women and children were engaged in the work; the 'furious and zealous people', as John Evelyn described them, were so enthusiastic that they even worked on Sundays. No trace of this great wall of London survives.

The city also had to be defended from the enemy within. It was believed that one third of the population still supported the king, and that many royalists had infiltrated the trained bands. At the beginning of June a royalist plot was discovered to take over the city and to arrest the leading parliamentarians; loose talk by some of the conspirators led to their arrest and interrogation. There was another enemy inside the city. It was ordered that the Cheapside Cross should be removed from the site where it had stood for 350 years; all other 'popish monuments' were also to be destroyed.

In May 1643 a small skirmish acquired, in retrospect, much significance. Oliver Cromwell was 2 miles outside Grantham with a small force of horsemen when he came across a division of royalists; they were twice the size of his company but at once he gave the signal to charge. Speed and surprise were always his favourite methods of warfare. The royalists broke ranks and fled from the scene or, as Cromwell himself put it, 'with this handful it pleased God to cast the scale'. A number of 'godly' men, inspired by their commander, had defeated an apparently stronger enemy.

At the beginning of July the spiritual world was to be set in order. An assembly of divines met at Westminster to administer a thorough purging of faith and worship, religious discipline and religious government. They were to draw up a 'directory' to take the place of the Book of Common Prayer, and to compile a 'confession of faith' to which all men must subscribe. This was the true heart and inspiration for the civil struggle that had so lately begun. The commissioners first met in Henry VII's chapel but, as the weather grew bleaker, they withdrew into the relative comfort of the Jerusalem Chamber. They sat for five years, and engaged in more than 1,000 meetings from nine in the morning until one or two in the afternoon.

They wept, and fasted, and prayed. Robert Baillie, one of the new Scottish commissioners, described that

> after Dr Twisse had begun with a brief prayer, Mr Marshal prayed large two hours most divinely. After, Mr Arrowsmith preached one hour, then a psalm, thereafter Mr Vines prayed near two hours, and Mr Palmer preached one hour, and Mr Seaman prayed near two hours, then a psalm. After Mr Henderson brought them to a short, sweet conference of the heart confessed in the assembly, and other seen faults to be remedied, and the convenience to preach against all sects, especially Baptists and antinomians.

The syntax might be faulty, but the fervour is evident.

When they were not at prayer they debated predestination, election, justification and reprobation. They also discussed more political affairs. Ought the state to impose one form of religion, or should the free will of the individual decide the matter? Ought the state to punish those of a faith different from that of the majority? For a month they considered the role of individual congregations within the broad unity of a Presbyterian regime. What did it say in Scripture about these topics? How had the Church of Antioch been related to the Church of Jerusalem? Thus solemnly they debated with one another. The Scottish Presbyterian divines argued with their English puritan counterparts; the English were all in favour of a 'civil league' that would keep 'a door open in England to independency' while the Scots favoured a 'religious covenant'. It was never likely, however, that the English would accept the full rigour of the Scottish religion or that parliament would concede predominance to any national Church. Oliver Cromwell himself was a notable Independent who favoured toleration and plurality; many of the leaders of the parliamentary army shared his convictions.

A few days after the formal opening of the Westminster assembly Essex made a startling proposal. He suggested that the terms of truce given to Charles at Oxford should be offered to him again. If the king refused them once more, he should withdraw from the field so that the two armies could settle the matter in one pitched battle. It was a form of duel. This proposition could not be construed as a serious one, but it does emphasize the attachment of Essex to an old chivalric code. This was not, however, an age of chivalry. Pym declared the notion to be 'full of hazard and full of danger'. It was the first serious indication from Essex of weakness or doubt about the progress of the war, and it was the cause of much apprehension. He was now, according to a newsletter, the *Parliament Scout*, 'abused in pictures, censored in pulpits, dishonoured in the table talk of the common people'.

A number of reversals dismayed the parliament. At Roundway Down, in Wiltshire, a parliamentary army was vanquished and those who survived were taken prisoner; among them were the members of a regiment completely clad in armour, known as 'the Lobsters'. At Chalgrove, in Oxfordshire, the royalists were the victors again and John Hampden died of his wounds. Prince Rupert stormed and overcame Bristol, the second city of the kingdom; this victory was followed by the surrender of Poole and Dorchester, Portland and Weymouth. Gainsborough and Lincoln would soon be lost.

A 'peace party' had now grown up in the Lords, thoroughly shaken by news of the defeats, but Pym and his cohorts faced them down with the help of intimidation by the London mobs. But the *mobile vulgus* could be fickle. In the second week of August 2,000 or 3,000 women descended on Westminster with white ribbons in their hats. Simonds D'Ewes recorded that they 'came down in great confusion and came to the very door of the House of Commons, and there cried as in diverse other places, Peace, Peace'. He added that they 'fell upon all that have short hair' and cried out, 'A roundhead! A roundhead!'

Parliament was rendered even more unpopular by the imposition of a new tax called 'excise', a flat rate charged upon commodities such as meat, salt and beer. The king in turn raised money through voluntary donations and a tax raised on the royalist counties known as 'the contribution'; nevertheless his funds were very much lower than those of parliament.

Charles had again taken the offensive and was marching towards Gloucester. Cromwell wrote to parliament that 'you must act lively! Do it without distraction! Neglect no means!' On 10 August the royalist army had reached the city; Charles invited the officers of Gloucester to submit and, on their refusal, he encircled it and laid siege for three weeks without gaining entry. On 5 September a parliamentary force under the command of the earl of Essex arrived on the scene and, in the face of failure and exhaustion, Charles's forces withdrew.

It was the first major success of parliament for many months, and was greeted by jubilation in London and Westminster. In his history of the war Clarendon wrote that 'the Parliament had time to recover their broken forces and more broken spirits, and may acknowledge to this rise the greatness to which they afterwards aspired'. He also wrote that on the royalist side there was 'nothing but dejection of mind, discontent and secret mutiny'. On the withdrawal from Gloucester the prince of Wales asked his father if they were going home. Charles replied that 'we have no home'.

The forces of the earl of Essex could not remain in Gloucester indefinitely, since they were needed elsewhere. The royalist army waited in the neighbourhood for their eventual withdrawal, with the purpose of cutting them off from London. For a few days the troops turned and manoeuvred, marched and counter-marched, both sides making for London. The king's men spent one unhappy night of wind and rain before pursuing the enemy as far as the town of Newbury in west Berkshire. On 20 September a battle ensued that lasted all day with the parliamentary forces pushing slowly against the royalists through winding lanes and hedges; the soldiers of the king held on to their position, keeping the enemy from the road to London, but they eventually withdrew that night. They were thoroughly exhausted, and it seems likely that they had run out of ammunition. It had not been a battle notable for tactics or for strategy but rather a grim and bloodstained stalemate; all had depended, in the phrase of the period, on 'push of pike'. Both sides of course claimed the victory.

It is easy to recite the names and dates of battles but less simple to describe their nature. In truth they were composed of a hundred desperate struggles between individuals who had no notion of what was going on around them; there would have been waves of panic fear when a group of men was consumed with the horror of dying and fled; it would have been impossible for the commanders to direct the action except by impetuous chance and sudden instinct. It was a flailing, wavering, shuddering mass of men and horses. Victory, or defeat, was largely a matter of chance.

The terror and confusion were such that both sides believed that they had advanced upon the burning gates of hell. A royalist captain, Richard Atkyns, recalled of one conflict that

> the air was so darkened by the smoke of the powder that for a quarter of an hour together (I dare say), there was no light seen, but what the fire of volleys shot gave: and 'twas the greatest storm that I ever saw, in which thought I knew not whither to go, nor what to do, my horse had two or three musket bullets in him immediately which made him tremble under me at a rate, and I could hardly with spurs keep him from lying down, but he did me the service to carry me off to a led horse, and then died.

A more prominent royalist commander, William Cavendish, described how 'the two main bodies joining made such a noise with shot and clamour of shouting, that we lost our ears, and the smoke of powder was so thick that we saw no light, but what proceeded from the mouth of guns'. Chaos descended. The savage shouts, and the screams of the wounded or the dying, resounded through the darkened air.

26

The women of war

The reader may grow tired of the deeds of arms and men. If women were not exactly invisible in the period of civil war, they were still at a notable disadvantage in the affairs of the world. Yet exceptions can be found. In the summer of 1638 Lucy Apsley married John Hutchinson, who at the opening of the war enlisted in the parliamentary army. He was an Independent, like Cromwell, and was therefore acceptable to the army command; in 1643 he was appointed to be governor of Nottingham Castle. He was one of those who eventually signed the king's death warrant. Some years after the war was over Lucy Hutchinson wrote for her eldest son an account of this unhappy time. It was eventually published under the title of *Memoirs of the Life of Colonel Hutchinson.*

The book is not a history of the war in the style of Clarendon, but rather a vivid and intimate account of its proceedings from the point of view of a committed participant. Although Lucy Hutchinson is ostensibly writing an encomium on the life and career of her husband, her own character and beliefs continually break through. She even provides a brief sketch of her early years that emphasizes how unusual she was among her contemporaries. She disliked plying the obligatory needle and thread, and had a horror of playing with other children. When she was forced to mingle with her young contemporaries she delivered lectures to them and made it quite plain that she detested their company. She abhorred their 'babies', better known now as dolls. She infinitely preferred the 'serious discourses' of the adults which she memorized and repeated. In the time allowed for play she preferred to apply herself to her books.

So the account of the war itself springs from the pen of a spirited and remarkable character. It is not a record of battles and sieges, but in large part a collection of character portraits and of first-hand accounts of life in the field of conflict. She describes these portraits as 'digressions' but in fact they convey the human face of the war, with all its threats and suspicions, hypocrisies and lies. She rejects the name of 'roundhead' for her husband, for example, on the grounds that he had a full head of hair. Since it was not cropped short, however, his puritan comrades distrusted him.

Lucy Hutchinson's memoir is in fact most revealing for its account of the internecine suspicion and conflict between the members of the puritan party; John Hutchinson was at odds with his army council in Nottingham, for example, while the members of parliament and the army were always in conflict. Even the leaders of the various parliamentary contingents were themselves 'so emulous of one another, and so refractory to commands, and so peeking in all punctilios of superiority' that it was surprising they could ride together on the same field.

A command came from Westminster for John Hutchinson to gather together all the horse he could spare for the relief of Montgomery Castle; as a consequence, he proceeded to consult with the political committee of the local members of parliament that had oversight of Nottingham. Lucy Hutchinson reports that her husband asked that a number of soldiers be requisitioned, to which request they replied '*None*'. Hutchinson, falling into a rage, reminded the committee that a direct order from parliament had to be obeyed. She describes the members as 'factious little people' who fomented squabbles, divisions, delays and scandals. Their behaviour only added to the chaos of war.

She herself was courageous at times of crisis. A few months before her husband took charge of Nottingham he was run to ground in Leicester, where a royal warrant was issued for his arrest. A sudden trumpet alerted her family to the presence of the king's troops but Hutchinson 'stayed not to see them, but went out at the other end as they came in'; he may have escaped through one of the city gates, or perhaps through a 'geat' or opening. Lucy Hutchinson, then heavily pregnant, remained to confront the officers.

> *Captain*: 'It is a pity you should have a husband so unworthy of you that he has entered some faction and dare not be seen with you.'
>
> *Lucy Hutchinson*: 'You are mistaken sir. My husband would not hide himself from you, or not dare to show his face.'

Then Lucy told a lie. She called down her brother-in-law, George Hutchinson, and announced to the captain that this man was in truth her husband. The subterfuge worked; John Hutchinson got clean away while George eventually obtained his liberty. It was a close-run thing, however, and is testimony to the dreadful risks that Lucy Hutchinson was willing to run.

She recounts in some detail the siege of Nottingham by the king's army, marked by no great strategic initiative but by endless bickering and argument among those who were besieged. 'What is the cause to me,' one doctor asked John Hutchinson, 'if my goods be lost?'

'You might prevent that hazard by securing them in the castle.'

'It pities me to spoil them. I had rather have the enemy have them than that they should be spoiled in the removal.' The doctor then rebuked Hutchinson 'for countenancing the godly townsmen' to whom he referred as 'puritanical prick-eared rascals'. He infinitely preferred the 'malignants' or royalists.

When John Hutchinson was eventually charged with colluding in the execution of the king, after the war was over, Lucy Hutchinson forged a letter in his name to the Speaker of the House of Commons with the request that he should not be taken into custody but called to account when he was needed. Her forgery was accepted. She was a formidable woman. Her husband, however, eventually died in prison for complicity in another plot. He gives the impression of being an impulsive and contentious man who was supported by a strong-minded and strong-principled woman; it is impossible to estimate how many other such relationships flourished in the Civil War. The evidence suggests, however, from the exploits of Lucy Hutchinson to the female crowds who often assembled at

Westminster, that there was a tradition of adventurous women who helped to fuel the conflict. In the ballad literature of the time it is suggested that some women dressed as men in order to join the armies of either side.

It should be noted of course that Lucy Hutchinson came from a relatively privileged family and was not in that sense necessarily representative of her sex; but older and deeper traditions of female liberty persisted still. Puritanism itself was uniquely susceptible to the authority of women, and actively promoted a partnership of the sexes in religious duties and devotions; many puritan women became part of an informal network of communication, for example, exchanging manuscripts and treatises between neighbouring families. Some of them also took part in forming congregations and nominating ministers. Letters, manuscripts and commonplace books testify to a distinct religious and intellectual female community.

The wives of certain Baptist, and 'leveller', leaders shared their husbands' faith to the extent that they inhabited the same prison cells. Other women were intent upon defending their homes when they were placed under siege. Lady Elizabeth Dowdall defended Kilfenny Castle, in Limerick, on her own initiative even though her husband was himself on the premises. She wrote that on 'the ninth of January, the High Sheriff of the county, and all the power of the county, came with three thousand men to besiege me. They brought two sows [cannon] and thirty scaling-ladders against me. They wrote many attempting letters to me to yield to them which I answered with contempt and scorn.'

Other royalist women played their own part in the civil struggle. Ann, Lady Fanshawe, was the daughter of Sir John Harrison, a child of superior birth who was educated in the usual fashion with needle, thread, virginals and lute; but above all else she enjoyed riding and 'was I wild to that degree . . . I was that which we graver people call a hoyting girl'. All the clichés and stereotypes of childhood tend to fall apart in the face of direct testimony. Were girls and women really as servile or as domesticated as the courtesy books suggest? Could all the domestic novels, the family portraits and the sentimental poetry have got it wrong? Perhaps only the plays, with their rampant and mischievous women, got it right.

Fanshawe came from a fiercely royalist family and, at the opening of hostilities, her brother joined the king at Nottingham; her father was threatened with transportation to 'the plantations' while all of his goods were sequestrated by parliament. He was put under house arrest, but managed to escape and to join the king at Oxford. She fled with him, as she put it, 'from as good houses as any gentlemen of England . . . to a baker's house in an obscure street'. But she coped with the overcrowding, the sickness, the plague, the lack of supplies and the general fear of catastrophe. This was wartime Oxford.

In 1644 she married her second cousin, Sir Richard Fanshawe, who was even then a member of the council attached to the prince of Wales with the title of secretary of war. As such he and his family moved in tandem with the prince's court. Ann Fanshawe rarely writes of the war itself but reserves her comments for the peripatetic life she was obliged to endure. She was not without resource. She procured a pass for her husband through the good offices of 'a great Parliament man whose wife had formerly been obliged to our family'. She carried £300 of money from London to Paris without being searched. The household travelled to Cork, perhaps to gain money or support, but at the beginning of October 1649, 'by a fall of a stumbling horse (being with child), broke my left wrist'.

While she lay in bed that night, her wrist bound, she was roused by the news that the Irish were firing the town after it had been taken by Cromwell. Her husband had gone to Kinsale on business; pregnant and in pain she gathered together her husband's manuscripts for fear of seizure and managed to pack in wooden crates all of their portable belongings, including clothes and linen; she also managed to conceal £1,000 in gold or silver which, to their puritan assailants, would have been a treasure worth killing for. At three o'clock in the morning, attended only by a man and a maid, she walked by the light of a taper into the crowded marketplace where she was confronted by 'an unruly tumult with their swords in their hands'.

Bravely enough, she demanded to see the commander-in-chief of the Protestant forces. By great good fortune he had once served with Sir Richard Fanshawe, in different circumstances, and under the weight of her entreaties and in light of her evident plight he granted her a safe conduct. Bearing the pass she walked unmolested 'through thousands of naked swords' until she reached Red Abbey, a fourteenth-century Augustinian establishment that acted as a meeting place. Here she took out some loose coin and hired a neighbour's cart, into which she piled all of her belongings, before making her way to her husband in Kinsale. It is a story of bravery to match any told by the soldiers of either side.

On another stage of her adventure she was aboard a Dutch ship with her husband when a Turkish galley, well manned, advanced towards them. She was ordered by the captain to go below, on the grounds that if the Turks saw a woman they would know the ship to be part of a merchant fleet and therefore attack it. If they spied only men, they might believe it to be a man-of-war. Once she had gone below she called for the cabin boy and, giving him half a crown, purchased his cap and coat. Suitably concealed she returned to her husband's side on deck.

She seems to have been an expert at disguise. On another occasion she dressed herself as a 'plain' or 'lowly' woman in order to obtain a pass for a journey to Paris. She made her way to the parliamentary military headquarters at Wallingford House in Whitehall.

> 'Woman, what is your husband and your name?'
>
> 'Sir, he is a young merchant, and my name is Anne Harrison.'
>
> 'Well, it will cost you a crown.'
>
> 'That is a great sum for me but, pray, put in a man, my maid, and three children.'
>
> 'A malignant would give me five pounds for such a pass.'

Once she had received it she managed by careful penwork to change the name from 'Harrison' to 'Fanshawe'; there was no need for further concealment because she was already known to the 'searchers' at Dover, having passed that way before.

'Madame,' one of the 'searchers' told her, 'I little thought that they would give pass to so great a malignant, especially in such a troublesome time as this.'

Even in times of war certain known opponents could still come and go as they pleased.

Ann Fanshawe wrote her memoirs in the 1670s, after the death of her husband, for the benefit and education of her family. They are a notable addition to the literature of the civil conflict, but they also throw an indirect but welcome light upon the otherwise generally hidden women of the war.

27

The face of God

In the middle of November 1643, parliament announced itself to be the supreme power in the land by authorizing the use of a 'great seal' to replace that of the king; on one side were the arms of England and Ireland while on the other was engraved an image of the Commons sitting in their chamber. One of their most important members, however, was no longer present. John Pym had been the key strategist of the parliamentary cause; he had been the quiet revolutionary, playing his cards largely behind the scenes, exploiting temporary setbacks or victories, and in some part controlling the mobs of London. Cautiously and slowly he had maintained the direction and impetus of the movement against the king.

His death from cancer of the lower bowel only reinforced the divisions and factions at Westminster, where some wished for an honourable settlement with the king and others demanded total victory. Disagreements were also evident in the royal court at Oxford, where questions of immediate tactics and general strategy were furiously debated; some wanted an attack upon London, for example, while others favoured the capture of the south-west. One of the king's courtiers, Endymion Porter, remarked that God would have to intervene in order to cure all the divisions between the royal supporters; as is so often the case, the most bitter fights were between those on the same side.

At the end of January 1644, Charles summoned a parliament of his supporters at Oxford to which came the great majority of the Lords and approximately one third of the Commons. There were now two parliaments in the country striving for mastery. The ceremony for the opening of the Oxford parliament took place in Christ Church Hall, and in his customary address the king said that 'he desired to receive any advice from them which they thought would be suitable to the miserable and distracted condition of the kingdom'. He had also taken the precaution of bringing over from Ireland some of the regiments of the army he had dispatched to extirpate the rebels.

In the following month the Westminster parliament established a 'committee of both kingdoms'. In one of the most important circumstances of the war 20,000 Scots had already, in the middle of January, crossed the border to support the parliamentary cause; after prolonged negotiations with their English allies, they had come to defend the common Protestant faith in the form of a 'solemn league and covenant' between the two nations. It had been voted by parliament at the beginning of February that this covenant should be taken and sworn by every Englishman over the age of eighteen; the names of those who refused to take the oath would be sent to Westminster. A new committee, composed of English and Scottish representatives, would manage the direction of the war; among its members were the earl of Essex and Oliver Cromwell.

The advantage lay now for the first time with parliament. In a battle at Cheriton in Hampshire, the royalist forces were overwhelmingly defeated; the parliamentary cavalry was now more than a match for its royalist counterpart. Oliver Cromwell himself had been promoted to become lieutenant-general of the 'eastern association', where he began to form the cavalries of seven counties into a coherent fighting force. With its command of London and many of the significant ports, in any case, the financial resources of parliament were far greater than those of the king. Charles had armies of approximately half the size of those commanded by his enemy. Many people, on both sides, recognized that his cause would suffer the more the war was prolonged.

In the early summer of the year two parliamentary armies, under the command of the earl of Essex and Sir William Waller respectively, advanced upon Oxford in order to hold the king in a vice of their making. The king managed to make his escape with 7,000 men and, on 6 June, fled to Worcester. He had also received news that his forces in York were besieged, and wrote from Worcester to Prince Rupert 'in extreme necessity'. Charles urged his nephew to ride to the relief of York in order to save the cause.

Prince Rupert arrived outside York, in the last days of June, only to find that the forces of the parliamentary besiegers had made a tactical retreat. Animated by bravado or by faith in his strategy he pursued his enemy to Marston Moor, in the north of the country, for what might have been a final confrontation. The parliamentary soldiers, wearing white handkerchiefs or white pieces of paper in their caps, were the stronger force; they were the first to charge, from the advantage of higher ground, and their sudden onslaught scattered the royalists. An eyewitness, Arthur Trevor, wrote that 'the runaways on both sides were so many, so breathless, so speechless, so full of fears, that I should not have taken them for men'.

In what was the largest battle ever fought on English soil, 4,000 of the king's troops had been killed, and his army had disintegrated. In a letter to his brother-in-law, Valentine Walton, Cromwell said of the enemy that 'God made them as stubble to our swords'. Prince Rupert, in a spirit of mockery rather than admiration, dubbed the victorious commanders as 'Ironsides'. The cities of York and Newcastle surrendered. It was a notable victory for parliament and, at least in retrospect, it marked a turning point of the civil war.

The victory of Cromwell at Marston Moor lifted him to eminence in parliament no less than on the field of battle. One of his most notable opponents, the earl of Clarendon, admitted that he possessed 'a great spirit, an admirable circumspection and sagacity, and a most magnanimous resolution'. He was resolute and fearless, and thus a fitting adversary for a king.

He had not distinguished himself in early life and seems happy to have farmed the flat land of the south-east midlands. He once declared that 'I was by birth a gentleman living neither in any considerable height nor yet in obscurity'. He was one of what were called the 'middling sort'. Yet even in that enviable condition he was not free from superstitious terror, and in his first years of married life he consulted a London physician who recorded in his case-book that Cromwell was '*valde melancholicus*'; by this he meant that his patient was nervous or depressed to an abnormal degree. Another doctor had suggested that he suffered from hypochondria and indeed, under stress or nervous excitement, he would sometimes fall ill.

His religion was the most important aspect of his character. His depression of spirits may have been the context or the catalyst for the sudden revelation – we do not know when it was vouchsafed – that he was one of 'the elect'. The blinding light of God's grace surrounded him, and he was transformed. He wrote to his cousin, Elizabeth St John, that 'I live (you know where) in Mesheck, which they say signifies Prolonging; in Kedar, which signifies blackness; yet the Lord forsaketh me not'. The reference is to the 120th psalm: 'Woe is me, that I sojourn in Mesech, that I dwell in the tents of Kedar!' This scriptural allusiveness and simple piety are at the heart of Cromwell's faith.

He knew that he had been saved by the grace of God, and the certainty of redemption lay behind all of his judgements; he believed implicitly in the power of divine will to guide the actions of men. He waited on providence. He prayed for a sign. He wrote that 'we follow the Lord that goeth before'. He sought for the divine meaning of the events occurring around him and saw all things in the context of the eternity of God. Since he had a private sense of what he called 'true knowledge' or 'life eternal', he was impatient of religious debate and doctrinal niceties. What did they matter before the overwhelming power of God? He once said that 'I had rather that Mahometanism were permitted among us than that one of God's children should be persecuted'.

His first years in parliament were not particularly auspicious; he was regarded as a forceful and impetuous, rather than elegant, speaker whose manner was sometimes clumsy or unprepossessing. But together with his family connections at Westminster – the puritan party was in some sense a wide circle of relatives – he fought steadily and assiduously for the parliamentary cause. He was adept at committee work, and was blessed with an acute understanding of human character. Yet he professed not to have been ambitious on his own behalf but rather for the cause he had chosen.

Cromwell was of singular appearance. The London doctor whom he had consulted noted that he had pimples upon his face. These seem to have been supplanted by warts on his chin and forehead. His thick brown hair was always worn long over the collar, and he had a slim moustache; a tuft of hair lay just below his lower lip. He had a prominent nose and one of his officers, Arthur Haselrig, once said to him that 'if you prove false, I will never trust a fellow with a big nose again'; his eyes, in colour somewhere between green and grey, were described by Andrew Marvell as being of 'piercing sweetness'. He was about 5 feet 10 inches in height and, according to his steward, John Maidstone, 'his body was well compact and strong'; he had a 'fiery' temperament but was very quickly settled, and was 'compassionate . . . even to an effeminate measure'. He was often boisterous in company, with a taste for rough country humour; there were times indeed when, according to Richard Baxter, he displayed too much 'vivacity, hilarity, and alacrity, as another man hath when he hath drunken a cup too much'.

Like his opponents he thoroughly enjoyed hawking and the pursuits of the field; he also liked to play bowls. He had a great love of music and one of his colleagues, Bulstrode Whitelocke, recalled that 'he would sometimes be very cheerful with us, and laying aside his greatness he would be exceeding familiar with us, and by way of diversion would make verses with us and everyone must try his fancy. He commonly called for tobacco, pipes and a candle, and would now and then take tobacco himself; then he would fall again to his serious and great business.'

That great business was, at the latter end of 1644, to drive the war forward until the king surrendered; in this purpose, however, he was not supported by other parliamentary commanders. The earl of Essex and the earl of Manchester, in particular, were in favour of some accommodation with Charles; it was suspected by some, therefore, that they were less than zealous in their military offensives. Manchester used to say that it was easy to begin a war, but no one could tell where it would end. He was in command of the eastern association, with Cromwell as his lieutenant-general, and the earl's desire for peace led to a complete breakdown in trust between the two men. Manchester in particular had an impatient dislike of sectarians and what he called 'fanatics', among whom he placed Cromwell himself.

At a council of war the following exchange took place.

Manchester: If we beat the king ninety and nine times yet he is king still and so will his posterity be after him; but if the king beat us once we shall all be hanged and our posterity made slaves.

Cromwell: My lord, if this be so why did we take up arms at first? This is against fighting ever hereafter. If so, let us make peace, be it ever so base.

Cromwell had already written to his brother-in-law that 'we have some among us much slow in action'.

The argument between the two military commanders came to a head after an inconclusive battle with the king at Newbury, where it seemed that Manchester had deliberately held back his army. He is supposed to have said to one of his colleagues, who urged instant action, that 'thou art a bloody fellow. God send us peace, for God does never prosper us in our victories to make them clear victories.' It was now believed, by Cromwell and others, that Manchester had become a traitor to the cause.

Towards the end of November Cromwell came into the Commons in order to denounce Manchester; the earl's 'backwardness of all action' and his 'averseness to engagement' sprang from his unwillingness to prosecute the war 'to a full victory'. He was therefore questioning his loyalty. Three days later Manchester returned fire, in the Lords, and charged his opponent with insubordination and slander. Cromwell was accused of saying that he hoped for a day when there would be no peers left in England. The 'peace party' on the parliamentary side now considered a move to impeach Cromwell for treason, but was persuaded that it was not wise to do so. A single sheet of print was found in the streets of the city attacking Essex and Manchester with the words 'Alas poor parliament, how art thou betrayed!'

On 9 December Cromwell pressed home his advantage. He told the Commons that 'it is now a time to speak, or forever hold the tongue. The important occasion now is no less than to save a nation out of a bleeding, nay almost dying, condition which the long continuance of war hath already brought it into, so that without a more speedy, effectual and vigorous prosecution of the war . . . we shall make the kingdom weary of us and hate the name of

Parliament'. He realized that only a clear victory over the king would decide the issue.

The eastern association had already informed the 'committee of both kingdoms' that local contributions were not enough to maintain an army, and the committee therefore decided 'to consider of a frame or model of the whole militia'. This was Cromwell's opportunity. It had become time to reorganize the various armies on a different basis, and for Cromwell the most obvious model was that of his own regiment of 'godly' men. He had said that 'I had rather have a plain russet-coated captain that knows what he fights for, and loves what he knows, than that which you call a gentleman and is nothing else'.

Immediately after Cromwell's speech another member of the Commons, Zouch Tate, rose to suggest a thorough reorganization of the army. It was first necessary to dismiss such fractious and incompetent commanders as Essex and Manchester. So Tate, no doubt in collaboration with Cromwell, proposed what was called 'a self-denying ordinance' by means of which no member of either house could take on a military command or an official place in the state. This removed at a stroke the noble earls. In theory it also removed Cromwell but it was widely and correctly believed that an exception would be made for such a successful military leader. The whole business might therefore be seen as an enterprising bid by Cromwell for sole command.

It may be worth remarking that this session of parliament was the one that abolished Christmas. The traditional festival was deemed by the Commons to encourage 'liberty to carnal and sensual delights' and instead the day was to become one of fast and penance.

Cromwell had told his colleagues that until 'the whole army were new modelled and governed under a stricter discipline' there would be no certain or ultimate victory. So the force became known as the New Model Army, known to its enemies as the 'New Noddle'. It was effectively a standing army from which all aristocratic commanders had been displaced; no English army had ever before been so constituted. It was to be organized on a national basis, and financed by a new national tax; the morale of the soldiers would therefore be maintained by consistent payment. It was to be professional, disciplined and purposeful. Its commander, known as 'Black

Tom' for his muddy complexion, was Sir Thomas Fairfax, who had previously been in charge of parliament's northern army.

It was an amalgamation of older regiments rather than a new army, but it was designed to be a more stable and coherent force drawn up with the sole purpose of defeating the king in battle. That is why Essex and Manchester had been removed from any military command. The commission given to Fairfax made no mention of the old provision that he was bound to preserve the king's safety on the field of battle. New muskets, swords and pistols were manufactured; the coats of the infantry were of red cloth, becoming the standard uniform for the next 200 years.

Some of its officers believed in a religious mission for themselves and their soldiers; Cromwell's regiment, for example, considered itself to be a 'gathered Church'. 'Go now,' one preacher declared, 'and fight the battles of the Lord!' It is unlikely that the rest of the army shared that godly purpose, but they may have been animated by the zeal of their more pious fellows.

But what was now meant by the godly? Cromwell and his colleagues favoured the Independent cause in religion, effectively espousing toleration in England; the earl of Manchester and his supporters had adopted the Presbyterian cause with no room for other sects or groups. In this endeavour they were supported by their Scottish allies. Even while parliament was debating the arrangements of the new army, the Book of Common Prayer was abolished and a puritan Directory of Worship took its place; this new text was to be delivered to the people by means of a national Presbyterian system. That system was not destined to last for very long.

One of the great expositors of the Book of Common Prayer was now led to the scaffold. On 10 January 1645, Archbishop Laud was taken from the Tower to the place of death on Tower Hill. He told the people assembled there that 'this is a very uncomfortable place'. As he knelt for the executioner, he prayed aloud for 'grace of repentance to all bloodthirsty people, but if they will not repent, O Lord, confound all their devices'. Essex lamented the old man's death. 'Is this', he asked, 'the liberty which we promised to maintain with our blood?' The political philosopher Thomas Hobbes wrote that 'it was done for the entertainment of the Scots'. It had been a year of much blood.

There was now very little intention of compromise on either side, but some brief negotiations took place at Uxbridge in February 1645. The two parties divided the town, with the parliamentary team in one inn and the royalist delegation in the other. Nothing was achieved, of course, but the king was still sanguine about his chances. Despite the disaster at Marston Moor he had not yet been decisively defeated, and he believed that the divisions in the opposite party between Independents and Presbyterians would work to his advantage. He was calm and indomitable, sustained by his belief that no one could touch the Lord's anointed. His commanders, and his forces, were still a match for those of parliament.

He had also received welcome news from Scotland where his principal supporter, the earl of Montrose, had already won notable victories over the Scottish covenanters. 'Give me leave', Montrose wrote to him, 'with all humility to assure your majesty that through God's blessing I am in the fairest hopes of reducing this kingdom to your majesty's obedience.' This in turn rendered the covenanting army in the north uneasy, distracted by the argument that they should withdraw from England and return to fight for their home territory. Charles was firmly persuaded that the fortunes of battle might still be with him.

The new campaign opened in the spring of 1645. At the beginning of May the New Model Army, under the command of Sir Thomas Fairfax, was about to begin the siege of Oxford. In the course of this action he received another message from Westminster. Charles had summarily taken his army into the east midlands, where he stormed and sacked the parliamentary town of Leicester. Fairfax now decided to follow him, with Oliver Cromwell as his second-in-command.

The great confrontation could no longer be delayed. On 14 June the two armies were in the fields outside the village of Naseby, in Leicestershire, where the parliamentary army had a large advantage in numbers. When the parliamentary forces made a tactical withdrawal to reach higher ground, Prince Rupert mistook the movement for a retreat; so with his cavalry he made for the enemy. Cromwell managed to beat them back, and then charged the royalist infantry. The king's soldiers resisted for a while but, under the combined assault of Fairfax and Cromwell, they fell apart and fled. They were pursued by the parliamentary troopers for 14 miles before they reached the safety of Leicester.

Naseby was a devastating defeat for the king. His infantry had been destroyed and 5,000 of his men, together with 500 officers, had been captured; his arms and artillery had been taken. The women of the royalist camp were treated with great ferocity; those from Ireland were 'knocked on the head' – killed is another word – while those from England had their faces slashed with daggers. Oliver Cromwell, after the battle, declared that 'this is none other than the hand of God, and to Him alone belongs the glory'. Clarendon concluded that at Naseby 'the king and the kingdom were lost'.

For the king, indignity was heaped upon dismay. Among the wagons captured after the battle was one that contained all of his private correspondence. When the king's cabinet was opened, it revealed the extent of his dealings with the Irish Catholics in search of troops; it also disclosed his plans to use French, or Swedish, soldiers for the sake of his cause. It could now be asserted that the New Model Army was truly a national army ready to defend England, and at Naseby it had decisively proved its worth. It had also demonstrated that the Independent cause was now the strongest. Cromwell himself was the man singled out for future glory and, according to Bulstrode Whitelocke, he began 'to grow great even to the envy of many'. Yet many also believed that God was with him.

Most of the king's supporters and councillors believed that his case was desperate, and that he must yield to necessity by negotiating with parliament. The king himself on occasions feared the worst and, in a secret letter to his son, wrote that 'if I should at any time be taken prisoner by the rebels, I command you . . . never to yield to any conditions that are dishonourable, unsafe to your person, or derogatory to royal authority'. Yet he refused to have 'melancholy men' about him; he chose to entertain himself with sports and pastimes. He wandered about the country between Hereford, Oxford and Newark; these were three of his last remaining fortresses in his kingdom.

Prince Rupert, whose rashness may have cost Charles the battle of Naseby, now hurried on to Bristol; he needed to make that city safe against an enemy army that might descend upon it at any moment. From there he wrote to a colleague that 'his majesty hath now no way left to preserve his posterity, kingdom and nobility, but by a treaty'. When he was shown the letter the king was incensed. In his reply he wrote that in his role as a soldier or statesman 'I must say there is no probability but of my ruin'; yet as a king and a Christian he knew that 'God will not suffer rebels and traitors to prosper'.

This was not necessarily so. At Langport to the south of Bristol, on 10 July 1645, the New Model Army, fresh from its victory at Naseby, decisively defeated the royalist army of the south-west; the cavalry of the king had been destroyed, and his last hope of winning the contest seemed to be over. Cromwell exulted. 'To see this,' he said, 'is it not to see the face of God?'

28

The mansion house of liberty

One parliamentary occasion has gone unnoticed in this account of victories and defeats on the field. An ordinance of 14 June 1643 had been passed 'to prevent and suppress the licence of printing'. It was declared necessary to suppress the 'great late abuses and frequent disorders in printing many false, forged, scandalous, seditious, libellous, and unlicensed papers, pamphlets, and books to the great defamation of religion and government'; a committee of censors, therefore, was appointed to license new publications and to seize any that were unlicensed.

One republican deplored what he considered to be this reversion to the evil practices of the past that had no place in the new world for which he so devoutly wished. The Presbyterian members of parliament, who were largely behind the measure, might as well 'kill a man as kill a good book; who kills a man kills a reasonable creature, God's image: but he who destroys a good book, kills reason itself, kills the image of God, as it were, in the eye. Many a man lives a burden to the earth: but a good book is the precious life blood of a master spirit, imbalmed and treasured up on purpose to a life beyond life.' This is the unmistakable prose of John Milton.

Milton was a Londoner animated by a spirit of enquiry and an awareness of his own genius. From an early age he pored over his books by candlelight in Bread Street, brooding over fables and histories until he had knowledge and time enough to compose the fables and history of his own country. He was a born republican, averse to authority and discipline in any of its forms. There would come a time when he would denounce Charles I in Latin, so that the world might hear. He declared that England was 'the elect nation', a prophecy endorsed by other clerics and divines of the period, thus emphasizing the millennial aspirations of the seventeenth century.

In 1637, in his twenty-ninth year, Milton wrote in a letter that 'my genius is such that no delay, no rest, no care or thought almost of anything, holds me aside until I reach the end I am making for, and round off, as it were, some great period in my studies'. He read as if for life; for him, it *was* life. Yet the storms of the world would soon surround him, obscuring for a time that bright particular star by which he set his course.

He had studied at Cambridge and followed his period at that university with an intensive course of private scholarship that continued for some eight years. Blessed with a fair face, and an even fairer mind, he began a tour among the devoted scholars and learned poets of Europe; his voyage of sweet discovery was curtailed, however, when he was obliged to return to London in 1639 at the time of the Bishops' War.

He had studied with the overriding ambition to become a poet that the world would not willingly ignore. But the desperation of the age turned him from poetry to prose, to the language of men in debate and conflict. He began writing his pamphlets against the bishops in 1641 and indulged his taste for polemic at a time of delusion and disagreement. In *The Reason of Church Government* he denounced those prelates who 'have glutted their ingrateful bodies' with 'corrupt and servile doctrines'; they were fed 'scraggy and thorny lectures . . . a hackney course of literature' and were filled with 'strumpet flatteries . . . corrupt and putrid ointment'. They were scum and harlots and open sepulchres. The language of the streets, which he heard all around him, came naturally to a Cockney visionary.

Milton wrote his treatise *Areopagitica* in Aldersgate Street; but the little pamphlet in due course made its way around the world as the most eloquent and inspiring defence of the freedom of expression. For this founding statement upon the liberty of speech he modelled himself upon the Attic orators who had once spoken to the Athenian people; the Areopagus was the rock upon which the final court of appeal held its sessions. Milton was clearly adverting to the republican and even democratic status of the English parliament which he described as 'that supreme and majestic tribunal'. He wrote copiously and elegantly, constructing sentences that have been described as baroque palaces, but all the time his style was tempered by the urgency and seriousness of the puritan cause.

Areopagitica was ready for the press by the autumn of 1644, two or three months after Cromwell's victory at Marston Moor; hopes for the Independent cause were high, and Milton himself was touched by the optimism of the moment. All was still possible. On the title page was printed:

AREOPAGITICA

A SPEECH OF MR JOHN MILTON

For the Liberty of UNLICENC'D PRINTING,

To the PARLIAMENT OF ENGLAND.

Milton's passion for free speech, for liberty of thought and conscience in the making of a new world, was a powerful corrective to all the obfuscators and doctrinaires of parliament who had partly triumphed with the signing of the solemn league and covenant with the Scots in the previous year. He railed against those with closed minds, of which the Presbyterians were the largest number. Censorship and licensing would be 'the stop of truth'. The people of England would suffer from the change, when 'dull ease and cessation of our knowledge' would inevitably lead to 'obedient uniformity' or to 'rigid external formality'.

He insisted that 'we must not think to make a staple commodity of all the knowledge in the land, to mark and license it like our broad-cloth and wool packs'. He recalled his travels into Italy where he visited Galileo 'grown old, a prisoner to the Inquisition'. If the silence of conformity were to be imposed upon England, too, it would 'soon put it out of controversy that bishops and presbyters are the same to us both name and thing'. What if the Presbyterians were no better than the Laudian Church writ in sterner letters?

What did the censors and opponents of freedom have to fear? 'He that can apprehend and consider vice with all her baits and seeming pleasures, and yet abstain, and yet distinguish, and yet prefer that which is truly better, he is the true warfaring Christian. I cannot praise a fugitive and cloistered virtue, unexercised and unbreathed, that never sallies out and sees her adversary, but slinks out of the race, where that immortal garland is to be run for, not without dust and heat.' Milton's phrases rise like waves before they fall upon the shore, the poetry of his being flooding beneath them. His sentences are grave, sonorous and magniloquent but not untouched by the occasional asperity of irony or wit.

In *Areopagitica* he addresses the political nation with an encomium that proclaims the fervent seriousness of the time. 'Lords and Commons of England, consider what Nation it is whereof ye are, and whereof ye are the governors: a Nation not slow and dull, but of a quick, ingenious and piercing spirit, acute to invent, subtle and sinewy to discourse, not beneath the reach of any point the highest that human capacity can soar to.' It is an excellent tribute to the intellectual resources of the country in this period of conflict and argument. Milton considered England to be particularly blessed by what he called 'the favour and love of heaven'. It was this faith that gave strength and optimism to the puritan cause.

He writes, too, of London as a beacon of that cause. 'Behold now this vast City; a City of refuge, the mansion house of liberty, encompassed and surrounded by His protection . . . Under these fantastic terrors of sect and schism we wrong the earnest and zealous thirst after knowledge and understanding which God hath stirred up in this City.' He is suggesting that there is nothing to fear in the proliferation of sectarians and schismatics; they are all part of the glory of God.

Of all the writers of the period Milton is the one most able to embody the seriousness and the determination of the religious cause. In the loftiness of his mind, in the dignity and grandeur of his most stately utterances, we may glimpse the essential nobility of the age. 'Methinks I see in my mind a noble and puissant Nation rousing herself like a strong man after sleep, and shaking her invincible locks. Methinks I see her as an eagle muing [renewing] her mighty youth, and kindling her undazzled eyes at the full midday beam; purging and unscaling her long abused sight at the fountain itself of heavenly radiance . . .'

In later years Milton served as Latin secretary for Cromwell and the protectorate, in which capacity he served the puritan cause as faithfully as before. Yet disillusion would set in soon enough, followed by bitterness and despair. Like many of his generation he was, by the end of Cromwell's rule and the return of the king, beset by misery and isolation, bewilderment and grief.

29

A game to play

The last twelve months of war were confused and uncertain. No one knew when, or how, it would end. The king no longer had the resources to fight any more major battles; he held on to a few cities such as Bristol and Worcester, but his strength was essentially limited to individual fortresses or garrisons. A campaign of siege warfare had begun, with parliamentary forces coming upon one royalist stronghold after another. The rules of siege were well known to all the participants. After the defence had put up as good a fight as they could, they could then demand a 'parley' and bargain upon the terms of surrender; if they capitulated, they were spared. If they refused to surrender, they were likely to be stormed and massacred.

In this weary and bloody period groups of men and women emerged ready to defy and fight both parties in order to save their neighbourhoods. The 'clubmen' were called after the primitive weapons they often carried. The farmers and yeomen of Wiltshire and Dorset, for example, had already established bands of watchmen to seize any soldiers caught in the act of plunder and to march them back to their respective camps for punishment. They did not know which side was winning or losing. They did not know of Naseby or of Langport. They wished only to preserve their lives and property.

Now some countrymen, armed with sickles or scythes as well

as clubs, took the offensive. They gathered to protect their harvests and their granaries with the message that:

> If you offer to plunder and take our cattle
> You may be sure we'll give you battle.

If the clubmen had any other message, it was simply that the two sides should come together and that the war should be ended. Clubmen risings took place in several counties, from Sussex to South Wales, but particularly in those regions that, as one of their leaders put it, had 'more deeply . . . tasted the misery of this unnatural internecine war'. Money and supplies had been extorted from them; soldiers had been quartered upon them against their will; local authority had often broken down. They wanted a return to order and to the 'known laws'.

The unsettled mood of the localities may perhaps be traced in the large number of witch trials in the period. Three days after the battle of Naseby thirty-six supposed witches were put on trial at the Essex assizes, and all but one of them were executed on the charge of black art and of conjuring up the devil. It has been estimated that, in this summer, one hundred old and young women were executed. This was a world of anxiety.

The king was now reduced to limited forays to lift a siege here or support a town there, but he lived in fear of any parliamentary army bearing down upon him; he was concerned that, if he were captured, he would suffer at the hands of the puritan troops. He received some comfort from the fact that the Scots seemed prepared to negotiate with him. They were ready to break with parliament, now that it was beginning to incline towards Cromwell and the Independent cause. They had been accused of doing little since their first arrival in England, and their payments were in arrears.

Yet this small hope for the royalist cause was almost overwhelmed by the news that Bristol had fallen; Prince Rupert had signed a treaty of surrender. Sir Thomas Fairfax had surrounded the city towards the end of August and laid siege. By the beginning of September Rupert realized that he could hold out no longer. He did not have enough troops to defend the walls of the city, and the citizens were increasingly desperate. Fairfax was growing impatient and directed an assault against some royalist defenders; when they had been cut down he sent the terms of surrender to his combatant. The prince accepted and, on 11 September, evacuated the town.

The loss of the second city of the kingdom was a grievous blow to the king, who at once suspected a plot to suborn him. He even considered the possibility that Rupert was about to launch a military coup and remove him from the throne before negotiating a truce with parliament. 'Nephew!' he wrote in anger, 'though the loss of Bristol be a great blow to me, yet your surrendering it as you did is of so much affliction to me, that it makes me not only forget the consideration of that place, but is likewise the greatest trial of my constancy that hath yet befallen me; for what is to be done, after one that is so near to me as you are, both in blood and friendship, submits himself to so mean an action?' He dismissed him from his service, and advised him to return home. The prince had not been a popular figure and, as he marched out of Bristol, the citizens cried out, 'Give him no quarter! Give him no quarter!'

Two or three days later the cause of the king was shaken further with the news that the forces of Montrose in Scotland had been defeated, and that the earl had fled back to the Highlands. The king's best hope had gone. In this period it was ordered by parliament that 'the boarded masque house at Whitehall' should be pulled down and its materials sold. The days of the cavalier were coming to an end.

In October Prince Rupert made his way to Newark Castle, where the king was lodged. He strode up to his uncle and told him that he had come to give him an account of his conduct at Bristol; the king would not speak to him and sat down to supper, during which he ignored him. Eventually he allowed his nephew to give evidence before a council of war, the members of which decided that the prince had not been guilty of any want of courage or fidelity. He could have done no other but surrender or face the entire destruction of his troops and of the town. The king reluctantly accepted the verdict, with the proviso that he believed his nephew could have held out longer. Charles left Newark a few days later, and quickly made what had now become a dangerous journey back to Oxford.

In his extremity the king began negotiating with various parties in order to preserve himself. He had already told his son to sail for France and remain under the protection of his mother who had sailed from Falmouth in the summer. Now he sought to divide the two principal groups in parliament by dealing separately with the Independents and the Presbyterians; he seemed willing to grant liberty of conscience to the former while inclining towards the latter on the grounds that the army was too democratic. He told his wife that 'I had great reason to hope that one of the factions would so address themselves to me that I might without difficulty obtain my so just ends'. He had opened provisional negotiations with the Scots, also, and was still attempting to treat with the Irish.

The fighting in the last few months of the war became sporadic and desultory. Prince Rupert set out from Oxford on cavalry raids, but achieved little. The royalist troops on the border of Wales and England tried desperately to hold on to Chester and its related ports in the hope of welcoming an Irish army. That army never arrived and, in any case, Chester eventually fell. Sir Thomas Fairfax conducted the parliamentary campaign in the west against a divided and demoralized enemy. A royalist army was raised to confront him but, at Torrington, it fell to pieces.

In the last battle of the great civil war, near Stow-on-the-Wold in Gloucestershire, the royalist forces were soon overpowered and surrendered en masse. The royalist commander, Sir Jacob Astley, told his captors that 'you have now done your work and may go play, unless you fall out among yourselves'. And that is what they proceeded to do.

The king, now facing ruin, tried to buy time with various proposals, secret or otherwise. He offered to come to Westminster, but his overture was rejected; it was considered likely that he would try to detach one faction and place himself at its head. Charles himself wrote that 'nothing will satisfy them but the ruin, not only of us, our posterity and friends, but even monarchy itself'. Eventually he decided that he would go over to the Scots; he was their native king, after all, and they did not share the levelling principles of his principal parliamentary opponents. He would be secure both in conscience and in honour; he would also be under the protection of a large army.

The Scots themselves had to act warily, since they did not wish to antagonize their paymasters at Westminster. They would be obliged to come upon the king, as it were, by accident. On 27 April

1646, the king left Oxford in disguise as a servant, and by a circuitous route made his way to the Scottish army at Newark. The Scottish commanders told their English allies that this was a 'matter of much astonishment' to them.

Soon enough Charles realized that he was as much a prisoner as a guest. When he tried to give the word of command to his guard he was interrupted by the lord general, Alexander Leslie, who told him that 'I am the older soldier, sir; your majesty had better leave that office to me'. It seems likely that the Scots wished to keep their king as a hostage until parliament paid them the money they were owed. They took him to Newcastle, where almost at once he became subject to their demands. He must sign the covenant. He must impose Presbyterianism on all of his people. He must abandon the Book of Common Prayer. When one minister told him that his father, James VI, would welcome such a settlement the king replied that 'I had the happiness to know him much better than you'. 'I never knew', he wrote to his wife, 'what it was to be barbarously treated before.' Yet he pretended to compromise while playing for time; he hoped that his opponents would become further divided, and he believed that fresh aid would come from France or Ireland or the Highlands or anywhere.

At the end of July, parliament sent the king a number of propositions to which he should accede if he wished to retain the throne. He should embrace Presbyterianism and extirpate the bishops; he should persecute Independents or Catholics, and give up his army for twenty years. Privately he swore that he would not surrender 'one jot' but in his public response he agreed to consider the demands in a mild and obliging spirit. He wrote privately to his wife that he had to deliver 'a handsome denying answer', an unenthusiastic response that would not alienate his captors. All of these secret letters were written in code and smuggled out of his quarters.

The flight of the king to the Scottish army had precipitated the final split between the forces of his enemies. The Scottish army and parliament now deeply distrusted one another, and their differences were reflected in the open divisions between the Presbyterians and Independents at Westminster. It is of no importance whether we choose to call them religious sects or political parties; now they were both. They were known as 'factions' or 'juntoes' or 'cabals'.

The Presbyterian cause, in its ideal state, proposed that its Church should rule by inherent right as the one divinely ordained form of religious government, and that no other churches or sects should be permitted. The Independent cause rested on the belief that a true Church was a voluntary association of believers and that each congregation had the right to self-government; it was Calvinist in tendency but it favoured toleration. Cromwell had said that 'he that ventures his life for the liberty of his country, I wish he trust God for the liberty of his conscience'. A Presbyterian divine stated, however, that 'to let men serve God according to the persuasion of their own consciences, was to cast out one devil that seven worse might enter'. Another Presbyterian divine, Thomas Edwards, published a book entitled *Gangraena* in which he listed the heresies of the radical sectarians, each one to be crushed in its egg 'before it comes to be a flying serpent'. Here, then, was the great divide. In the broadest secular terms the Presbyterians supported parliament, while the Independents favoured the army.

Conflicts and divisions arose frequently in parliamentary debate. On one occasion the Commons spent the day discussing matters of religion until darkness fell upon the assembly; a motion was advanced to bring in candles, but this was disputed. When a division was called it was already too dark to count the members on either side, and it was suggested that candles be introduced to resolve the issue. But could candles be brought in before the house had formally requested them? So the affairs of the nation were determined. This was a new age of political life.

The eventual refusal of the king to take the covenant undermined his value to the Scottish Presbyterians, who now thought it best to make a bargain with parliament. On receipt of the moneys owing to them, they would hand back the sovereign; under these circumstances, perhaps, Charles might negotiate a treaty with their allies at Westminster. So for the sum of £400,000 he was surrendered. The haggling over money damaged their credibility, however, and the earl of Lauderdale predicted that it 'would make them to be hissed at by all nations; yeah, the dogs in the street would piss upon them'. As the army marched out of Newcastle, leaving the king behind, the fishwives of the city cried out, 'Judas! Judas!' The king himself said that they had sold him at too cheap a rate.

Charles set out for parliamentary custody at the beginning of February 1647 almost as a conquering hero, and cheering crowds lined his route. At Ripon he touched for the king's evil, thus asserting his divine power over the disease of scrofula. At Nottingham the lord general of the New Model Army, Sir Thomas Fairfax, dismounted and kissed his hand. The king arrived at Holmby House, in Northamptonshire, in the middle of February. He remained for five months; he spent much time in his private quarters or 'closet', played at bowls or rode in the neighbourhood.

The Presbyterians and their supporters at Westminster now began to plan for the disbandment of the New Model Army and for its replacement by a less sectarian and more reliable force. They also ignored the English army's demands for payment of arrears in wages, and for an indemnity against prosecution for any actions committed in the late war. It was now becoming a dangerous dispute between army and parliament. In this period Oliver Cromwell collapsed, and almost died, from something known as an 'impostume in the head'; it was some kind of swelling or abscess, perhaps in part induced by nervous strain.

The sectarians and supporters of the army, or as they called themselves 'well-affected persons', sent a 'Large Petition' to parliament in which they asserted the supreme authority of the people; they also demanded that the Lords and Commons exempt 'matters of religion and God's worship from the compulsive and restrictive power of any authority upon earth'. Among these passionate sectarians emerged a group that were known as 'the levellers'. Royalist newsletters had given them the name, since 'they intend to set all straight, and raise a parity and community in the kingdom'. We might perhaps describe them as spiritual egalitarians.

They were essentially a London group who issued several hundred tracts, and could muster perhaps a few hundred sympathizers; their colour was sea-green and they wore sea-green scarves or ribbons. One of their unofficial leaders, John Lilburne, wrote to Cromwell in this year that he and his co-religionists 'have looked upon you as the most absolute single-hearted great man in England, untainted or unbiased with ends of your own'.

The army itself was in a state of agitation close to mutiny, and sent a petition of complaint to Sir Thomas Fairfax. In turn parliament passed a declaration denouncing 'enemies of the state and disturbers of the peace'. The army that had saved parliament was therefore branded as an enemy, which in turn was considered to be in effect a declaration of war. 'The Apology of the Soldiers to their Officers', published at the beginning of May, complained that their intentions were 'grossly and foully misconstrued' and asked 'Was there ever such things done by a parliament . . . is it not better to die like men than to be enslaved and hanged like dogs?'

Against this background the people of England suffered. This year, 1646, marked the beginning of six terrible harvests in a period when the price of bread doubled and the cost of meat rose by more than a half. The agriculture of England was its life and staple; its partial collapse therefore shook the already troubled kingdom.

The members of the New Model Army were quartered at Saffron Walden, where some parliamentary commissioners came to recruit soldiers for service in Ireland; they were greeted with complaints and questions. The troops wanted to know when, in particular, their arrears of payment would be met; they received no coherent response. Eight of the ten cavalry regiments then chose representatives who would in time become known as 'adjutators' (or, as their opponents called them, 'agitators') for the army's cause. Cromwell pleaded for a compromise, arguing that if parliamentary authority 'falls to nothing, nothing can follow but confusion'. Yet parliament was in turn determined to crush the army, on the principle that 'they must sink us, or we sink them'. It was now being whispered that the army sought an accommodation with the king, whereby it might contrive to destroy the Presbyterian cause. Fairfax explained that Charles had become 'the golden ball cast between the two parties'. Which way would he roll, or be rolled?

The army leaders believed that parliament was about to establish a new army with the king at its head, so they moved to act first. At six in the morning of 4 June 1647, the king emerged from Holmby House to be confronted by a party of 500 horse, drawn up in neat ranks, under the command of Cornet Joyce. Joyce asked permission to escort Charles to some other place. The king demanded to see his commission, but Joyce prevaricated. 'I pray you, Mr Joyce, deal with me ingenuously and tell me what commission you have.'

'Here is my commission.'

'Where?'

Joyce turned around and gestured towards the assembled horsemen. 'It is behind me.'

'It is as fair a commission,' the king replied, 'and as well written as I have seen a commission written in my life: a company of as handsome, proper gentlemen, as I have seen a great while.'

The New Model Army took him to the village of Childerley outside Cambridge. Charles did not particularly care in whose camp he rested; it was enough for him, as he put it, to set his opponents by the ears. Yet, with the king in its hands, the army had now become a political as well as a military force. The role of Cromwell in the Holmby House plot has never been clear; Joyce visited him five days before the action, however, and it is not likely that they discussed horsemanship. When Cromwell told the king that Joyce had acted entirely on his own initiative Charles retorted that 'I'll not believe you unless you hang him'. In fact Joyce received promotion and a generous pension.

On the day after Charles had been taken to Childerley Hall the regiments met near Newmarket in order to draw up a 'solemn engagement' in which they pledged to stay together until their legitimate demands were met. 'Is that the opinion of you all?' 'It is, of all, of all.' There were also cries of 'Justice, justice, we demand justice!' A new 'general council of the army' was established, with Cromwell among its members. He had ridden to the army headquarters at Newmarket from London, having heard rumours that the Presbyterians were about to consign him to the Tower. He had endeavoured to hold the peace between the opposing factions, but now he formally took the army's part as its chief representative.

On hearing the news of the king's seizure, parliament convened and hastily granted all arrears of pay to the New Model Army; the city fathers now demanded that a force of cavalry be raised for the defence of the capital. The army itself was on the move and marched to Triploe Heath, 7 miles nearer London, and began to advance ever closer to the city. Cromwell wrote a letter to the civic authorities, asking for a just settlement of the liberties of the people under the aegis of parliament; he warned, however, that if the army met concerted opposition it would be freed from the blame for 'all that ruin which may befall that great and populous city'.

When the army reached St Albans, a little over 20 miles from London, *The Declaration of the Army* was published in which were proposed shorter and more representative parliaments beyond the reach of oligarchy or regal authority; no force in the nation should have 'unlimited power'. Its author was Sir Henry Ireton, Cromwell's new son-in-law. The *Declaration* was accompanied by charges against eleven named Presbyterian members of parliament; they were accused of treasonable dealings with royalists at home and abroad. Parliament seemed willing and able to defend them but, on 26 June 1647, the eleven men thought it prudent to withdraw from Westminster and eventually to flee abroad. This was the period in which 'purge' entered the English political vocabulary. The great constitutional historian Henry Hallam wrote that on this day 'may be said to have fallen the legislative power and civil government of England'.

Throughout the month of June the leaders of the army were in constant and courteous contact with the king. It is clear enough that they still wished to reach a settlement which would allow him to retain his throne with altered powers; he was the only power that might conceivably unite the nation now dangerously divided between army and parliament. Yet he was still beset by accusations of hypocrisy and double-dealing. At one point the king told Henry Ireton that 'I shall play my game as well as I can'; to which Ireton replied that 'if your majesty have a game to play, you must give us also liberty to play ours'.

The New Model Army had by now worked its way around to Reading, which provided a more convenient route to London. The more radical of the 'agitators' now pressed for a final march upon the city, but Cromwell favoured delay and negotiation. Ireton had drafted a policy document, *Heads of the Proposals*, that effectively repeated the propositions set out in *The Declaration of the Army* including a biennial parliament and a new council of state.

Parliament, noticeably more moderate or more fearful after the expulsion of the eleven members, voted to accept the proposals. They agreed in particular that control of the city militia should be returned to the old committee of militia, which meant effectively that the city force would be under the command of the now dominant army. The Lords and Commons, however, had not calculated the ferocious response of the Presbyterians in London itself who feared for their lives and property if the army came to rule. A crowd of citizens and apprentices accompanied a deputation of Londoners and besieged the Lords, shouting that 'they would never come out' unless they reversed their decision. Another crowd, or mob, burst into the Commons and demanded that they repeal their earlier judgement. 'Vote! Vote!' The members were too terrified to do anything other than comply. Parliament had proved itself to be at the mercy of any powerful group, and was thus unable to legislate for anything; sixty of the Independent members, together with the Speaker, now fled to the army at Reading for safety. They lent added legitimacy to the soldiers' cause.

The *Heads of the Proposals* had been submitted for the king's consideration. Some of the terms were mild enough. The bishops would not be abolished but deprived of the power of coercion; the old liturgy and the new covenant would have equal force in a broad context of religious liberty and toleration. The army and navy would be returned to the king after ten years. Only five royalists would be excluded from pardon. If Charles had accepted these terms, he could have returned to the throne with his honour intact. The king, however, rejected the document without giving it any serious consideration. His stated response was that 'you cannot be without me. You will fall to ruin if I do not sustain you.' One of his advisers, Sir John Berkley, whispered to him, 'Sir, your majesty speaks as if you had some secret strength and power that I do not know of.' The moderates on both sides now began to lose all hope.

The intimidation of parliament by the London mob, and the failure of negotiations with the king, prompted the New Model Army finally to march upon London. A brigade of horse took Southwark on the night of 3 August, and the civic leaders of the city woke up to find their principal avenue across London Bridge in the hands of what must now be called the enemy. The sudden occupation 'struck them dead', according to Clarendon, and 'put an end to all their consultation for defence'. Their only object now was to conciliate those whom they had previously offended and to prevent the army from firing and plundering their mansions.

The whole army of 18,000 men, under the command of Sir Thomas Fairfax, now entered the city; Cromwell rode at the head of the cavalry, while Fairfax sat in a carriage beside Cromwell's wife. Fairfax was met at Hyde Park by the mayor and aldermen, who proffered a formal apology and offered him a gold cup; he refused to accept the gift, and sent them on their way. With the Speaker and the members of the Commons with him, he seemed now to represent the legitimate authority of the nation. One puritan Londoner, Thomas Juxon, wrote after watching the soldiers marching through the streets of London, that ''tis remarkable that it never was in the minds of the army to carry it so far; but were brought to it, one thing after another, and that by the designs of their enemies'. The army also made sure that the great defensive wall, erected by Londoners at the beginning of the war, was pulled down. Fairfax did not intend a military occupation of the city, however, and established the army headquarters some 6 miles away at Putney.

Charles, now residing at Hampton Court, was willing graciously to listen to the proposals put forward by Cromwell and the other leaders of the army; but he was resolute in defence of his interests, and refused to compromise. Many Independent members were willing, and indeed eager, to dispense altogether with the king. They even accused Cromwell of pursuing his own self-interest in continuing to negotiate with him; it was whispered that he was about to be honoured as the new earl of Essex.

Yet Cromwell was in truth becoming angry and frustrated at the king's constant prevarications and refusals; he began seriously to doubt his sincerity. At some point, towards the end of October, he refused to travel any more to Hampton Court. Those who attended the monarch now began to notice an alteration in the manners and civility of the soldiers who were stationed about him; the king's guard was doubled.

30

To kill a king

The army now began to take stock of its power and its situation. The levellers made an early contribution to the debate when in October they published a pamphlet, 'The Case of the Armie Truly Stated', in which they demanded a more representative parliament; they maintained the then revolutionary doctrine that all power was 'originally and essentially in the whole body of the people of this nation'. No mention, therefore, was made of king or lords. They had support among the more radicalized soldiers who agreed with their call for national renovation. 'The Case of the Armie' was swiftly followed by the 'Agreement of the People' that argued for a new political order based upon a written constitution. Both sets of proposals seemed to be guiding the army towards the establishment of a republic.

Some of the principal officers, Cromwell among them, did not support the more extreme measures being canvassed; it was proposed, therefore, that the arguments be tested in open debate. The deliberations were held at St Mary's Church, on the southern side of Putney Bridge, at the end of October and lasted for three weeks; gathered here were the several generals, together with four representatives from each of the thirty-two regiments. The importance of the proceedings was not lost upon any of the participants, and indeed the 'Putney debates' of 1647 remain one of the most significant expressions of English political thought.

On the first day Edward Sexby, one of the representatives of the soldiers, complained that 'we have laboured to please a king, and, I think, except we go about to cut all our throats, we shall not please him'. Cromwell then remarked that the radical 'Agreement of the People' was naively formulated in the belief that a new constitution could be created without any consideration of English tradition or precedent. He had been told that faith would make a way through all difficulties but 'we are very apt all of us to call that faith, that perhaps may be but carnal imagination, and carnal reasonings'. He was suggesting that expediency and self-deception may be at the heart of political revolution. He also made more practical criticisms. All of this change was to be achieved in the name of the people but he questioned, 'Were the spirits and temper of the people of this nation prepared to receive and to go along with it?'

A defining moment of the debate arrived when Thomas Rainsborough, one of the representatives of the levelling movement, declared that 'I think that the poorest he that is in England has a life to live as the greatest he' and should therefore be allowed the vote. It was a call that was not to be answered until 1918. Henry Ireton rejected the idea of manhood suffrage, however, and argued that the vote should be given to 'persons in whom all land lies, and those in corporations in whom all trading lies'. Only those with a financial stake in the country, in other words, should be allowed to determine its direction.

At one point in the proceedings Cromwell was moved to declare that 'the foundation and the supremacy is in the people, radically in them', but he also argued that the sovereign authority must be that of a parliament however constituted. In this uncertain time the force of power was absolutely required. He compared himself to a drowning man. 'If it have but the face of authority, if it be but a hare swimming over the Thames, I will take hold of it rather than let it go.' A more ominous note, for the king, emerged when Captain Bishop claimed that the woes of the nation came from 'a compliance to preserve that man of blood' by which he meant Charles. The captain was alluding to a passage from the second Book of Samuel: 'Thou art taken in thy mischief because thou art a bloody man.' The phrase soon became commonplace.

The final set of proposals that emerged from Putney did not

reflect the demands of the levellers or the debate about the future of the king; it was designed only to preserve the unity of the army. It recommended an extended franchise but maintained the ancient framework of king, Commons and Lords with the Commons in effective control. The commanders of the army then brought the debates to a summary close by ordering all of the participants to return to their regiments. A partial mutiny by some of the more radical troops was quickly put down. A restructuring of the army, in the following year, allowed its leaders to remove those soldiers of suspect sympathies.

The king now confounded everyone by escaping from Hampton Court. He had gone down some private stairs and, meeting with two associates, fled south. He seemed to have had no certain destination but eventually decided to make for the Isle of Wight where he had the sea at his back. He left behind some papers, one of which was an anonymous letter warning him of the danger of assassination. He also left a letter to parliament in which he asked to 'be heard with freedom, honour and safety, and I shall instantly break through this cloud of retirement and show myself ready to be *pater patriae*'.

The governor of the Isle of Wight, Robert Hammond, received this father of the nation with no little apprehension; he was under the command of the army, and had no wish to disobey his superiors. But he was violently opposed to the levellers in the ranks and could guarantee the king's safety from their attentions. It may also have suited Cromwell to leave the king on the island; he was far from the reach both of the more sanguinary levellers and of the Scots who might wish to negotiate with him. In the best possible circumstances the king might even take to the sea and journey to exile in France.

The king was now in Carisbrooke Castle under guard. He could set himself up as an object for auction, as it were, with many prospective bidders. Cromwell might still wish to come to an accommodation with him. Despite Robert Hammond's best endeavours, the Scots might somehow be able to find a way of communicating with him. Almost as soon as he was ensconced in the castle he began to practise his subterfuges; he concealed messages in the lining of gloves, he engaged in secret conversations with his servants, he drew up elaborate plans for sending and receiving clandestine letters.

This was the period in which Cromwell openly broke with the king and spoke bitterly against him in the army council. There is a story, never fully substantiated, that Cromwell intercepted a secret letter to the queen in which Charles announced that he would make an arrangement with the Scots rather than with the army. It was soon remarked at Westminster that, in Carisbrooke, Charles had thrown a bone between two spaniels and laughed at their enmity. That alone would have been enough to turn Cromwell against him. He now began to sympathize with the position of the more radical soldiers as resolute anti-monarchists. He observed that 'if we cannot bring the army to our sense, we must go to theirs'.

Cromwell's suspicions were soon confirmed. Towards the end of December the king, after secret negotiations with the Scottish commissioners, signed an agreement known as 'the Engagement'. He promised to introduce Presbyterianism as the state religion for an initial three years; he would confirm the 'solemn league and covenant' in the English parliament, but would not oblige his subjects to take its oath. In return the Scots would support Charles's demand for a personal treaty and the disbandment of all English armies; a Scottish army would then be dispatched to London to expedite 'a full and fair parliament'. The document was sealed in lead and buried in the garden of the castle. He then refused to deal with a parliamentary deputation, at which point Colonel Hammond dismissed the king's servants and doubled his guard.

Charles: Shall I have liberty to go about to take the air?
Hammond: No. I cannot grant it.

On 3 January 1648, the Commons passed the 'Vote of No Addresses' by a majority of fifty. No more communications, or proposals, would be put to the king. Cromwell fully supported the decision on the grounds that the people should not 'any longer expect safety and government from an obstinate man whose heart God has hardened'. The council of the army also pronounced that it would stand by the kingdom and parliament 'without the king and against him'.

Yet at a subsequent dinner the army was still manifestly divided.

The commanders argued amongst themselves about the relative merits of 'monarchical, aristocratical or democratical government', but could come to no conclusion. At the end of the discussion Cromwell, in one of those fits of boisterousness or hysteria that punctuated his career, threw a cushion at one of the protagonists, Edmund Ludlow, before running downstairs; Ludlow pursued him, and in turn pummelled him with a cushion.

Colonel Hammond was soon informed that a treaty with the Scots had been signed while the king was in his safe-keeping, and he determined to find it. He entered the king's chamber without warning; the king rose from his bed in alarm and put on his gown; Hammond proceeded to search its pockets, at which point Charles struck him. It was reported that, against all precedent, the colonel returned the blow.

The king's incarceration incensed those who supported the royalist cause. Riots occurred in Ipswich and in Canterbury. A news-writer in London reported that 'the counties are full of discontent, many insurrections having been lately made, even near this city'. The majority of the newspapers and pamphlets were strongly royalist and on the anniversary of the king's accession, 27 March, celebratory bonfires blazed in the capital. Coach travellers, driven through the streets, were compelled to drink the king's health. The butchers of the city declared that if they could catch Colonel Hammond 'they would chop him as small as ever they chopped any of their meat'.

At the beginning of April the lord mayor sent some trained bands to disperse a crowd of apprentices in Moorfields; the crowd turned on the bands, captured their weapons and marched off shouting on behalf of 'King Charles!' Petitioners, seeking the rule of a king again, flocked to London from Kent, Essex and Surrey. The cavaliers were jubilant, and the Presbyterians once more gained a hold over parliament. In April the Commons passed a motion calling for a treaty with the king.

The signs of civil war were once more apparent. The first acts came from Wales where, in April, a royalist commander occupied Tenby Castle; soon enough the whole of South Wales had declared in the sovereign's favour. The leaders of the army spent a day in tears and prayers. How could it be that blood and battle had returned to the nation? Had the previous war been fought for no purpose? At a meeting of the New Model Army in Windsor it was concluded that 'it was our duty, if ever the Lord brought us back again in peace, to call Charles Stuart, that man of blood, to an account for the blood he had shed'.

The army council then ordered Cromwell to enter South Wales with two regiments of horse and three of foot; it took him six weeks to defeat the rebels. Other anti-parliamentary forces had emerged throughout the country, guided not so much by zeal for the king as dismay at the taxes and county committees imposed by parliament. Berwick and Carlisle were taken by the disaffected; Pontefract was also seized in a surprise attack, and Scarborough declared for the king. The men of Essex marched under a banner raised by a royalist commander, General Goring. A section of the fleet off the Downs also declared themselves for the king, and joined with the men of Kent in their revolt. It had also become clear that the Scottish army was being assembled on the border in order to fight for the king.

This represented a serious challenge to the authority of parliament but this second civil war, as it became known, ended once more in victory for the New Model Army. The Scottish army did not cross the border until July, by which time most of the risings in England and Wales had been put down by the army's superior military force; Cromwell dealt with the north, and Fairfax with the south. It had not been a war, but a series of scattered risings and outbreaks of fighting with no serious attempt to co-ordinate what might have been a successful rebellion. Without a coherent strategy the rebels were no match for the New Model. They had waited vainly for the Scots until it became too late to fashion serious resistance.

The second civil war had a bloody ending on its two principal fronts. The Scottish army, under the command of the duke of Hamilton, had made a slow progress southward through the rain and wind of an unseasonably cold summer; ill-trained, and much smaller than expected, it was sustained by no great cause, and as a consequence its morale was low. The New Model was at least bolstered by the knowledge that it was fighting an invasion force.

The two sides encountered each other at a pitched battle near the walls of Preston, on 17 August, in which the infantry of both armies pressed hard upon each other. The Scots were eventually pushed back, with the loss of 1,000 men. Cromwell pursued the remainder of the Scottish army which, battered and broken, laid down its arms. It was the first battle in which he enjoyed overall command, and it was his most signal victory.

All the remaining royalists from the south-east had fled behind the walls of Colchester where, in the middle of June, Sir Thomas Fairfax prepared for a long siege against them. It was the most distasteful and inglorious event of the entire civil war. Fairfax had decided to starve the city into submission until there came a time when the inhabitants, having exhausted the provisions of cats and dogs, were forced to devour soap and candles; it was reported that the royalist soldiers had told the inhabitants to eat their children. The royalist commander, the earl of Norwich, then sent 500 women and children out of the town; Fairfax refused to receive them and with threats they were driven back behind the walls. By the end of August, reduced, as it was said, 'by Captain *Storm* without and by Captain *Hunger* within', the royalists surrendered; two of their commanders were then put in front of a firing squad. This second phase of the civil war was more harsh and intense than the first; there was no longer time for mercy.

After his victory at Preston Cromwell believed that he had seen once more the hand of God. He trusted that he was doing the work of the Lord; that is why he waited upon divine providence to guide his actions and to direct his way forward. He was a blind mole in search of grace, sometimes surrounded by darkness, yet his faith in providence was his rock and his refuge. He wrote to a friend and colleague, Philip Wharton: 'I can laugh and sing in my heart when I speak of these things.'

The battle at Preston effectively marked the end of the second civil war, and of the turmoil that had mangled the kingdom since the king had first raised his banner six years before. It has been calculated that 100,000 soldiers and civilians died in the course of the conflict, and that a larger portion of the population perished than in the Great War of 1914–18. It has therefore justly been described as the bloodiest war in English history. One hundred and fifty towns, and fifty villages, suffered significant damage; 10,000 houses were destroyed.

In the course of the second civil war Charles made several attempts to escape from Carisbrooke Castle. He had never ceased to conspire, and to devise stratagems against his captors and his enemies; he would, for example, conceal coded messages in the heels of his servants' boots. Some supporters managed to smuggle to him a cutting tool and a supply of nitric acid, then known as *aqua fortis*, to dismantle the iron bars of his window; but the design was forestalled and came to nothing. On another occasion he tried to squeeze through the bars but became trapped, stuck between his chest and shoulders, and could only extricate himself with difficulty.

Yet after the final victory parliament still wished to treat with him, against the wishes of the army whose leaders had denounced him as 'a man of blood' who had effectively instigated the second civil war. The majority of the members of the Lords and Commons, together with the large part of the population, now wished for peace at any price. The king was therefore taken out of confinement in the castle and lodged with his friends and servants in Newport, to which town the parliamentary commissioners came. He sat under a canopy of state with his advisers behind him; the parliamentary delegation sat before him.

He was in a more tractable mood, no doubt because the victory of the New Model Army brought an effective end to his resistance. He wished to come to an agreement with parliament on the very good grounds that he feared the army much more. So within a few days he had conceded thirty-eight of their propositions and in return was granted four of his own. He submitted in large part to the religious demands of the commissioners, and agreed to give up control of the militia for a period of twenty years. The parliamentary negotiators were no doubt aware that he might renege on these promises if ever he returned to full power.

The king himself wrote to an adviser, Sir William Hopkins, that 'the great concession I made this day – the Church, militia and Ireland – was made merely in order to my escape . . . my only hope is that now they believe I dare deny them nothing, and so be less careful of their guards'. Yet at the same time he was ever mindful that a different fate might await him. He might be a king who had emasculated his sovereignty. He might be condemned to perpetual imprisonment. He might die upon the scaffold. He also feared assassination by friends of the army, and while at the castle had lived in terror of being poisoned by Hammond or one of his gaoler's associates.

One of the king's secretaries, Sir Philip Warwick, saw his master standing at a window with the parliamentary legation behind him and noticed that he was crying 'the biggest drops that ever I saw fall from an eye'. From the moment his servants had been withdrawn by order, he had neglected his personal appearance; his beard remained untrimmed while his clothes were worn and faded. His once luxurious hair had turned almost entirely grey, thus imparting a new shade of melancholy to his face.

The army was growing increasingly impatient with the negotiations at Newport and, in November, drew up a 'remonstrance' calling for 'exemplary justice' for the notorious man of blood. The leaders of the army were calling for his death. They had also begun the march back to London after completing their business against the Scots in the north.

On the first day of December the king was removed from the Isle of Wight and taken to Hurst Castle on the coast of Hampshire. Cromwell and his colleagues feared, rightly, that parliament had drawn up plans to invite him back to Westminster. They were also apprehensive of any kind of formal agreement between the two parties. Cromwell declared that any Newport treaty would be only a 'little bit of paper'. He wrote to Hammond that the king was 'an accursed thing' with whom there could be no agreement.

On 5 December parliament resolved to settle with the king on the basis of the terms concluded at Newport. On the following day Colonel Thomas Pride stood outside the chamber of the Commons with a list of names; he checked them off, one by one, as each member tried to enter. Some were allowed to go forward while others were detained or arrested by soldiers who stood behind him. The Presbyterian members, who favoured the Newport treaty, and other of the king's supporters, were summarily removed. It was the first, and last, military *coup d'état* in English history. It seems to have been engineered by Henry Ireton rather than by Oliver Cromwell, but when Cromwell returned to London that night from Yorkshire he declared that 'I was not acquainted with this design, yet, since it is done, I am glad of it'. As far as he was concerned, all the providences of God were coming together without his claiming responsibility for them.

In a dreary castle, on the edge of a stretch of shingle spit, the king was immured for two weeks; it was a place of mist and fog where the air was damp and heavy from the marshes that lay all around it. His room was small and dark, lit with candles even at noon, and from the slit of a window he could look out across the Solent. The soldiers brought in his meals 'uncovered', not wearing their hats. 'Is there anything more contemptible', he is supposed to have asked, 'than a despised prince?'

He must have known, or guessed, that all hope was at an end; the army was the master of the kingdom, and must now surely seek his death. Yet, like Cromwell, he was seized with a sense of destiny and of religious purpose; he believed that he might enjoy the fate of a martyr to a holy cause. He had meditated on all the sufferings and ignominies that were likely to befall him, and had hardened his resolve against the rebuffs of the world. Like Cromwell, too, he valued his own life less than the principles for which he fought. So even in this extremity he remained apparently calm and even cheerful.

After 'Pride's Purge', as it became known, approximately 200 members were left of the previous assembly; yet they now constituted the House of Commons and eventually became known as 'the Rump Parliament' or, as Clarendon interpreted it, 'the fag-end of a carcass long since expired'. Some of them had not stayed necessarily to support the army but to avert the prospect of direct military rule without any parliament at all.

On 19 December the king began the journey from Hurst Castle to Windsor where, by the order of the army officers, he was to be 'secured in order to the bringing of him speedily to justice'. Yet the nature of that 'justice' was unclear. Many in the army did not wish for a sentence of death. Despite his fierce words about the man of blood, Cromwell seems to have been among those who did not favour condign punishment. Charles might now be so chastened and so desperate that he would yield. The army, and perhaps a newly elected parliament, would thereby acquire legitimacy and authority if they held power with the assent of the king. In the event that he was tried and found guilty, he might be deposed rather than executed. Charles's death was as yet by no means a necessity.

Another consideration moved Cromwell. An envoy had been sent to Ireland by the king intent upon raising an army; if Charles could be dissuaded from following the project, another great threat would be lifted. The prospect of a royalist Ireland was enough to persuade Cromwell to make one last attempt at a settlement.

The army leaders then sent an envoy to Windsor in order to discuss the terms of a possible agreement, but the king refused to see him on the grounds that he had already 'conceded too much, and even so had failed to give satisfaction, and he was resolved to die rather than lay any further burden on his conscience'. So the prospect of death came ever nearer. The refusal of the king to make any further compromise seems to have persuaded Cromwell that he must indeed be tried and executed. He told the Commons that 'since the providence of God hath cast this upon us, I cannot but submit to providence'.

On New Year's Day 1649, the Rump Parliament passed without any opposition an ordinance for the king's trial on the grounds that he had contrived 'a wicked design totally to subvert the ancient and fundamental laws and liberties of this nation'; he had wished to make himself a tyrant and had prosecuted a cruel and bloody war for that purpose. The Lords rejected the ordinance, whereupon the Commons passed a resolution that 'the people are, under God, the original of all just power' and that they themselves represented the people. The Commons therefore declared themselves to be the supreme power in the state. They also passed an ordinance to establish a new high court of justice with 135 commissioners. In the event only 52 arrived on the appointed day of the king's trial. The army council was also divided. One of its members asserted that the king of England could be tried by no English court. Cromwell responded: 'I tell you, we will cut off his head with the crown upon it!'

Charles was to be brought from Windsor to St James's Palace on 19 January. When the king was told of the coming journey, he replied that 'God is everywhere'. The trial began on the following day. The soldiers brought him from the palace to Whitehall in a closed sedan chair, and then to Westminster in a curtained barge. The roll of judges was called and, when the name of Sir Thomas Fairfax was announced, a woman cried out that 'he has more wit than to be here'; it was the voice of his wife.

The king was conducted into Westminster Hall and sat down in the place provided without the least sign of unease; all the judges, according to Clarendon, were 'fixing their eyes upon him, without the least show of respect'. The solicitor general, John Cook, then read out the charges against him. 'Hold a little,' the king said. He tapped Cook on the shoulder with a silver-tipped cane but the official paid no attention. He tapped him twice more, when the silver tip came off and rolled across the floor. No one picked it up for him. A few days later he confessed that 'it really made a great impression on me'. It might also be seen as an omen of his beheading. When Cook called him 'a tyrant and a traitor', he laughed aloud. How could a sovereign be accused of treason when the meaning of treason was a crime against the sovereign? He did not understand that the word now denoted a trespass against the sovereign power of people and parliament. The king's state, formerly preserved in all honour and authority, had been turned into 'the state'.

After the recital the president of the court, John Bradshaw, asked him for an answer to the impeachment against him. Bradshaw sat in a crimson velvet chair before the king, with the judges arrayed behind him; the guard was ranged to the left and right of the prisoner as well as behind him. The spectators sat in galleries on either side, or stood at the lower end of the hall.

'I would know', the king asked, 'by what power I am called hither?' This was the supreme question. He added that 'there are many unlawful authorities in the world, there are robbers and highwaymen'. He had managed to overcome his habitual stammer.

He was informed that he had been brought to trial 'in the name of the people of England, of which you are elected king, to answer them'.

'England was never an elective kingdom, but a hereditary kingdom for near these thousand years.'

The dialogue continued a little longer until Bradshaw adjourned the proceedings. As the king passed the great sword of justice on the clerk's table he was heard to say, 'I have no fear of that.'

On the second day of the trial the king once more refused to plead. He did not recognize the authority of the court. Bradshaw ordered him to be taken away.

'I do require that I give in my reasons—'

'Sir, 'tis not for prisoners to require.'

'*Prisoners! Sir, I am not an ordinary prisoner.*'

On the third day he again refused to plead, declaring that 'it is the liberty of the people of England that I stand for'. He was asked to plead forty-three times, altogether, but he would not accept the authority of parliament over him. On 27 January the judges, sitting in the Painted Chamber at Westminster, declared the king to be 'a tyrant, traitor, murderer and a public enemy' who deserved death 'by the severing his head from his body'. Before sentence was passed upon him in the court Charles argued that the case was so serious that it should be put before a joint session of parliament. Some of the judges, anxious to be relieved of the responsibility of regicide, favoured the idea. 'Art thou mad?' Cromwell hissed at one of them. 'Canst thou not sit still and be quiet?' The king's proposal was not accepted.

After Bradshaw had read out the sentence of death Charles asked permission to speak.

'No, sir, by your favour, sir. Guard, withdraw your prisoner.'

'I may speak after the sentence. By your favour, sir, I may speak after the sentence ever.' He was roughly led away by his guard as he continued to cry out. 'By your favour, hold! The sentence, sir – I say, sir, I do – I am not suffered for to speak. Expect what justice other people will have.' All around him the soldiers and the spectators screamed, 'Justice! Justice! Justice!'

In truth the trial and death of the king were contrived by a small, if committed, minority who in no way represented the wishes of the nation. Two Dutch ambassadors pleaded for his life. Sir Thomas Fairfax made a similar supplication to the council of the army. The prince of Wales sent a blank sheet of paper, signed and sealed, so that parliament might write down any conditions it wished. These pleas were not enough. Cromwell and Ireton, in particular, were obdurate. The king must die. Otherwise there would be no safety for themselves or for the new commonwealth.

The last days of the king were for those around him a sorrowful mystery. On 29 January he burnt his papers and his ciphered correspondence. Two of his young children, Elizabeth and Henry, still in the hands of his enemies, were permitted to visit him. When they caught sight of their father, they both burst into tears. He told his thirteen-year-old daughter that he was about to die a glorious death for the liberty of the land and for the maintenance of the true religion. He told his ten-year-old son that the boy must not permit the army to place a crown on his head while his older brothers were still alive. The boy replied: 'I will sooner be torn in pieces first!' The king's guards wept. This was an age of tears.

On the last night of his life, 29 January 1649, the king slept soundly for approximately four hours. When he awoke he told his personal servant that 'this is my second marriage day'. He asked for two shirts since 'were I to shake through cold, my enemies would attribute it to fear'. When he left St James's Palace several companies of infantry were waiting to escort him to Whitehall Palace; the noise of their drums was so loud that the king could not be heard. He was taken to his bedchamber where he waited until parliament had passed a resolution prohibiting the announcement of any successor to the throne. He refused dinner but instead took a piece of bread and a glass of wine. At the appointed time he was escorted to the great Banqueting House.

It was so cold that the Thames had frozen. When he stepped out, from a window on the first floor, the low scaffold was before him; it was draped in black, and the two executioners were heavily disguised. Their identities have never been discovered. The cavalry were at either end of the street and armed guards kept back the people; spectators were on the rooftops, in the houses and in the street itself. The king tried to speak to them but they were too far off. So he dictated his last words to a shorthand writer and two attendants, among which was his declaration that 'a subject and sovereign are clear different things'. He then claimed that 'I die a martyr to the people' before lying down with his head upon the scaffold. The bishop of London was with him.

Bishop: There is but one stage more; it is turbulent and troublesome, but a short one. It will carry you from earth to heaven, and there you will find joy and comfort.
King: I go from a corruptible to an incorruptible crown.
Bishop: You exchange an earthly for an eternal crown – a good exchange.

One blow dispatched him. The principal executioner then took up the head and announced, in traditional fashion, 'Behold the head of a traitor!' At that moment, according to an eyewitness, Philip Henry, 'there was such a groan by the thousands then present, as I never heard before and desire I may never hear again'.

20. A contemporary tapestry celebrating the restoration of Charles II.

21. Charles II, the supposedly 'merry monarch'.

22. Catherine of Braganza, the wife of Charles II, who was reputed to have introduced tea-drinking to England.

23. Barbara Villiers, duchess of Cleveland, one of Charles II's many mistresses, who was described by John Evelyn as 'the curse of the nation'.

24. Nell Gwynne,
the orange-seller who
became a royal courtesan.

25. Louise de Kérouaille,
Charles's French mistress
who became duchess of
Portsmouth and who was
known by Nell Gwynne
as 'Squintabella'.

26. The earl of Rochester, rake and poet who did not mince his words.

27. Samuel Pepys, who turned the diary into an art form.

28. Sir Christopher Wren, the polymath who transformed London.

29. Sir Isaac Newton, arguably the greatest experimenter in English history.

30. Charles II in his role as patron of the Royal Society.

31. The members of the 'Cabal', a group of five self-interested councillors who ran a corrupt coalition around Charles II.

32. The duke of Monmouth, the illegitimate son who yearned to be king.

33. The duke of York, soon to become James II, with his wife and daughters.

34. A confused scene supposedly depicting the covert arrival of an infant, 'the warming-pan baby', to be passed off as James II's son.

35. The baby grows into James Francis Edward Stuart, better known to posterity as the 'Old Pretender' or the 'King Over the Water'.

36. James II throwing the great seal into the Thames as he escapes from England into France.

31

This house to be let

The death of the king had delivered a mortal shock to the body politic but as a pamphleteer, Marchamont Nedham, put it, 'the old allegiance is cancelled and we are bound to admit a new'. There was work to be done. The Rump Parliament passed an Act for the 'sale of the goods and personal estates of the late king'. The image of Charles was removed from all public buildings, and his statue at the Exchange was smashed into pieces; on its now empty pedestal were inscribed the words '*exit tyrannus, regum ultimus*' (the tyrant is gone, the last of the kings).

At the beginning of February the House of Lords, and the office of king, were formally abolished; kingship was declared to be 'unnecessary, burdensome and dangerous to the liberty and safety and public interest of the nation'. In theory the Rump Parliament now had unlimited authority, yet it was hardly representative of the people. It contained approximately ninety members, since the rest of them had been purged or had voluntarily withdrawn. Other members returned to parliament later, when they could not be charged with collaboration in the king's death, but of course all of them were divided in their principles and their allegiances. Under the pressure of immediate events, however, they remained a relatively coherent body; only later would it become clear that no consistent ideology could be expected from them. They were reformers rather than revolutionaries, driven by the force of events and circumstances. The Rump was essentially improvised rather than organized; it was born out of necessity and expediency.

Yet the army was also an indispensable power in the new state; Cromwell was a member of parliament as well as a leading army officer. Where did supremacy really lie? If the sword truly ruled, then the answer was obvious. But the main participants professed to believe that they had engineered a constitutional settlement under the aegis of parliament. The politics of ambiguity prevailed, in a situation where no single or fundamental authority was ever named.

A council of state, comprising some forty-one members with thirty-one of them coming from parliament itself, was established to determine policy. Cromwell was the presiding officer. Standing committees were set up for the army, for the navy, for Ireland and for foreign affairs in general. The most pressing concern was that of money; with an army of 70,000 soldiers to maintain and pay, funds were desperately needed. The councillors resorted to fresh taxation, pleas of loans from the City, and the confiscation of royalist estates. It did not help that this was a year of disastrous harvest, in which many inhabitants of Lancashire and Westmorland perished through starvation. Bulstrode Whitelocke reported that the magistrates of Cumberland certified that 30,000 people 'had neither bread nor seed corn, nor the means of procuring either'. Yet the council had other great tasks; it was expected to unify the three kingdoms, to assert the nation's ascendancy at sea and to protect commerce.

The councillors, faced with these burdens and charges, seem to have been largely enthusiastic and efficient. A French envoy, sent by Cardinal Mazarin to spy out the land, wrote that 'not only are they powerful by sea and land, but they live without ostentation, without pomp and without mutual rivalry. They are economical in their private affairs, and prodigal in their devotion to public affairs, for which each man toils as if for his private interest. They handle large sums of money, which they administer honestly, observing a strict discipline. They reward well and punish severely.' It was reported that in this period Oliver Cromwell and Henry Ireton were 'extremely well pleased' at the pace of affairs. Every revolution has its early heroic days.

In the middle of March Cromwell was chosen by the council

to become commander-in-chief of the army with the central purpose of subduing royalist Ireland. Scotland also posed a problem. Its government, on hearing of the king's execution, immediately proclaimed his eighteen-year-old son Charles II as king. The most serious threat came from Ireland, however, where the royalist lieutenant-general, the duke of Ormonde, was dominant. He had aligned himself with the confederate Catholics, rulers of two-thirds of the country after the rebellion of 1641, in support of the new king. Cromwell would soon go back to war.

In May the Rump passed a final Act that proclaimed England to be a free commonwealth; a kingdom had become a republic. All things must now be directed towards what was called the public good; and of course all things might be justified by invoking it. As Milton put it, 'more just is it, if it come to force, that a less number compel a greater to retain their liberty' than that a greater number compel the rest to be their fellow slaves. From this time, for example, we may date the emergence of the fiscal state with national taxation and public spending as its principal activities.

Yet this was also, according to the inscription on the new great seal, 'the first year of freedom, by God's blessing restored'. The revolution in public affairs now lent additional energy and purpose to religious enthusiasts and radicals of every kind. It was time for a new heaven and a new earth. A woman rose up among the congregation in Whitehall Chapel and stripped naked with the cry 'Welcome the Resurrection!'

The Ranters believed that to the pure all things were pure; Laurence Clarkson, 'the captain of the Rant', professed that 'sin had its conception only in imagination'. They might swear, drink, smoke and have sex with impunity. No earthly magistrate could touch them.

The Fifth Monarchy men and women were actively preparing for the reign of Christ and His saints that was destined to supersede the four monarchies of the ancient world; the reign of Jesus would begin in 1694. They would clap hands and jump around, calling out, 'Appear! Appear! Appear!'; they would be joined by travelling fiddlers and ballad-singers until they were in an emotional heat.

The Muggletonians also had apocalyptic and millenarian tendencies. They believed that the soul died with the body and would be raised with it at the time of judgment, and that God paid no attention to any earthly activities. They also asserted that heaven was 6 miles above the earth and that God was between 5 and 6 feet in height.

On 16 April some Diggers came to St George's Hill, near Weybridge in Surrey, where they proceeded to dig and sow seed in the common land. One of them, William Everard, proclaimed that he had been commanded in a vision to dig and plough the land. They believed in a form of agrarian communism by which the English were exhorted finally to free themselves from 'the Norman yoke' of landlords and owners of estates before 'making the earth a common treasury for all'.

The Quakers believed that no visible Church was necessary and that divine revelation was permitted to every human being; Christ might enter the soul and kindle an inner light. They also called for the abolition of lawyers and universities; they refused to pay tithes or to take off their hats in the presence of their 'superiors'. They were also known to disrupt the orthodox church services. They called each other 'saints' or 'friends of the truth' but, because of their tremblings and quiverings in worship, they became popularly known by the name now attached to them.

At the beginning of May a translation of the Koran was issued from the press. Religious liberty was contagious. Two months before, John Evelyn had attended an Anglican service in Lincoln's Inn Chapel.

Political, as well as religious, radicals were in the ascendant. John Lilburne, one of the levellers who had helped to promote agitation in the New Model Army, had turned against the new administration. In 'England's New Chains Discovered' he lambasted Cromwell and the army grandees for dishonesty and hypocrisy; he accused them of being 'mere politicians' who wished to aggrandize themselves while they pretended 'a waiting upon providence, that under the colour of religion they might deceive the more securely'. A pamphlet, 'The Hunting of the Foxes', complained that 'you shall scarce speak to Cromwell but he will lay his hand on his breast, elevate his eyes, and call God to record. He will weep, howl and repent, even while he does smite you under the fifth rib.'

Cromwell was incensed at the pamphlet and was overheard

saying at a meeting of the council of state, 'I tell you, sir, you have no other way to deal with these men but to break them in pieces . . . if you do not break them, they will break you.' By the end of March Lilburne and his senior colleagues had been placed in the Tower on the charge of treason. The levellers, however, were popular among Londoners for speaking home truths about the condition of the country. When thousands of women flocked to Westminster Hall to protest against Lilburne's imprisonment the soldiers told them to 'go home and wash your dishes'; whereupon they replied that 'we have neither dishes nor meat left'. When in May a group of soldiers rose in mutiny for the cause of Lilburne, Cromwell and Fairfax suppressed them; three of their officers were shot. As Cromwell said on another occasion, 'Be not offended at the manner of God's working; perhaps no other way was left.'

Assaults also came from the opposite side with royalist pamphlets and newsletters mourning 'the bloody murder and heavy loss of our gracious king' and proclaiming that 'the king-choppers are as active in mischief as such thieves and murderers need to be'. The authorities were now awake to the mischief of free speech, and in the summer of the year the Rump Parliament passed a Treason Act that declared it high treason to state that the 'government is tyrannical, usurped or unlawful, or that the Commons in parliament assembled are not the supreme authority of this nation'. There was to be no egalitarian or libertarian revolution. At the same time the council of state prepared 'An Act against Unlicensed and Scandalous Books and Pamphlets' that was designed to prohibit any pamphlets, papers or books issued by 'the malignant party'. A resolution was also passed by the Rump that any preacher who mentioned Charles Stuart or his son would be deemed a 'delinquent'.

On Tuesday 10 July, Cromwell left London and travelled west in a coach drawn by six horses. He was on his way to Ireland. He had hesitated at first, not wishing to leave the country in turmoil and confusion. But once he reached his decision, or professed to believe that providence had directed him, he was very firm. 'It matters not who is our commander-in-chief,' he once said, 'if God be so.' The army leaders had feared a royalist invasion from Ireland, although in truth there was very little chance of one. Nevertheless they could not endure an enemy close to England's shores; it presented a clear and dangerous menace to the new republic.

Cromwell arrived, in the middle of August, at a favourable moment; the royalist navy had been swept from the seas by the ships of the commonwealth, and the duke of Ormonde's army had been all but annihilated outside Dublin after a surprise attack by parliamentary forces. Cromwell wrote from his ship that 'this is an astonishing mercy'. He believed that he was indeed the Lord's chosen servant and, when he landed at the port of Dublin after a stormy crossing, he promised a crusade against 'the barbarous and bloodthirsty Irish'. They were for Cromwell vastly inferior both in race and in religion; he treated them as if they were less than human.

Cromwell wished to do his work rapidly and effectively but, despite his command of 20,000 men, no set battles were fought. Instead he proceeded to conquer the enemy in a series of sieges. He went first to the city of Drogheda, a little over 30 miles north of Dublin, where he summoned the royalist governor to surrender. On the following day, 11 September, having received no formal submission, he attacked; in a series of bloody battles and skirmishes the defenders were overwhelmed. According to Cromwell's express orders all those who were carrying weapons were put to the sword. That was the rule of war: 3,000 of the garrison, as well as all priests and friars, were killed. 'I am persuaded', Cromwell wrote, 'that this is a righteous judgement of God upon these barbarous wretches.' The slaughter has remained in the folk memory of Ireland to this day.

From Drogheda Cromwell and his men marched down to Wexford, a little over 70 miles south of Dublin, where there was yet more killing in the name of God. The city did not need to be stormed since the gate had been opened in the face of imminent attack; yet when the soldiers entered the town they began a fierce onslaught upon the inhabitants, many of whom begged for mercy in vain. It is reported that 200 women were killed beside what is now the Bull Ring; a memorial plaque is on the site of the massacre.

Cromwell stayed in Ireland for another nine months. Any hope that the Irish would capitulate after the spectacle of bloodshed in Drogheda and Wexford was soon dispelled, and he found himself engaged in a series of struggles against stubborn resistance. At the beginning of December he abandoned the siege of Waterford under a storm of rain, 'it being as terrible a day as ever I marched in all my life'. As soon as the army moved inland, away from the coast, the climate and geography of the country reduced them more quickly than did the enemy; fog and rain and mist descended upon them, while dysentery and malarial fever also did their work. Problems of supply were added to those of morale.

The war itself continued for another two years; it had acquired the character of what might be termed guerrilla warfare with the native forces attacking the invading army in a series of raids and skirmishes. Yet by his swift and punitive response Cromwell had achieved the task of destroying any potential for a royalist attack upon England.

The remaining enemy now lay in the north. The Scots had already invited King Charles II to travel to his kingdom, and negotiations between the two sides began in March at Breda, a city in the south of the Netherlands where the young king and his court resided. Parliament and the council of state were thoroughly alarmed at the conjunction, and Cromwell was soon made aware that his presence was needed at home. At the end of May 1650, he sailed for England, leaving behind him Henry Ireton as lord deputy of Ireland; when he landed at Bristol, he was given the welcome for a returning hero.

Charles II needed to find support wherever he could, and the chance of a Scottish army was not one to be missed. So aboard ship on 23 June, just before landing in Scotland, he signed a solemn oath to uphold the national covenant and to ensure that Presbyterianism became the official religion of England as well as of Scotland. He swore this in bad faith, having no regard for the Presbyterian cause or its proponents, but his immediate interests were of more importance. One Scottish negotiator, Alexander Jaffray, later concluded that 'he sinfully complied with what we most sinfully pressed upon him'. The king had learned, like his father, the arts of disguise and dissimulation. Yet his signature meant that war was now certain.

Sir Thomas Fairfax refused to lead the English army into Scotland on the grounds that the invasion would violate the 'solemn league and covenant' that had been signed between the two nations seven years before and never repealed. Cromwell countered with the question 'whether it is better to have this war in the bowels of another country or of our own'; his argument was persuasive and it was he who led the army once more. Fairfax, uncertain about the direction of the commonwealth and unwilling wholly to depose the king, now resigned as lord general. Cromwell was appointed to be his successor.

Cromwell crossed the border on 23 July with 11,000 horse and foot, but the enemy was not to be seen. The commander of the Scottish forces, David Leslie, had determined upon a strategy of harassment rather than open battle in order to cut off Cromwell's communication with England; he was successful in that regard, and Cromwell was forced to draw back to the coastal town of Dunbar 30 miles to the east of Edinburgh. Leslie then swept forward to ensure that Cromwell could have no contact with England. The commanders of both armies believed in divine providence and the sacredness of their cause; both sides fasted and prayed, their respective ministers exhorting them in long sermons. In the phrase of the time, only the harder nail would be able to drive out the other.

At Dunbar Leslie believed that the English were trapped between his army and the sea; he waited on high ground but the Scottish ministers in the camp persuaded him to move down towards the enemy. Cromwell saw the manoeuvre and exclaimed that 'God is delivering them into our hands; they are coming down to us'. And so it proved. The English called out, 'The Lord of Hosts!' while the battle cry of the Scots was 'The Covenant!' The Scots were routed after a brief resistance; 3,000 were killed and 10,000 captured. Very few English casualties were reported. A witness informed John Aubrey that, after the battle, Cromwell 'did laugh so excessively as if he had been drunk; his eyes sparkled with spirits'. The whole of southern Scotland now fell to the English. Other consequences followed. With the apparent judgement of God against them, the Presbyterian ministers lost much prestige and authority; never again would the covenanting movement maintain its previous power over Scotland.

The young king was now in desperate circumstances. After his submission to the presbyters in the early summer of 1650 he was now at Perth in the power of the 'committee of estates', who governed Scotland when parliament was not in session. He hated Scotland and despised the Presbyterian ministers who exhorted him and preached at him; he detested their hypocrisy, as he saw it, and was nostalgic for the simple pieties of the Church of England. After he heard of Leslie's defeat he tried to escape from his oppressors, but some troops from the 'committee of estates' managed to intercept him and to persuade him to return on the promise that he would be granted more powers. On the first day of 1651 Charles was crowned king of Scotland in Scone; the medieval village was the traditional and hallowed site of kingship.

Cromwell remained in Edinburgh for almost a year after his victory at Dunbar, while Leslie strengthened the remains of his army less than 40 miles north-west at Stirling. But there was no possibility of the two armies clashing in the vicinity; the nature of the terrain, and the wild weather of winter, made any campaign unlikely. In any case Cromwell fell dangerously sick in February 1651. He suffered from a 'feverish ague', perhaps contracted in Ireland and exacerbated by the campaign in Scotland; he had told his wife, the day after Dunbar, 'I grow an old man, and feel the infirmities of age marvellously stealing upon me.' He was on the brink of death on three separate occasions and, in alarm, parliament dispatched two physicians to his bedside. He himself was convinced that God had sent him sickness in order to test his faith.

By the early summer, however, he was fully recovered; he believed that he had been saved for a purpose, and almost at once took advantage of the more favourable weather to renew his campaign. In a series of manoeuvres he so arranged matters that the roads south to England remained open to the royalist forces. It might have seemed like an unpardonable blunder, but in fact Cromwell had wanted to remove the Scottish troops from Scotland where they could not otherwise be dislodged. He had set a trap that Charles now entered. Cromwell warned the Speaker of the Rump Parliament that 'I do apprehend that if the enemy goes for England, being some few days march before us, it will trouble some men's thoughts and may occasion some inconveniences'. Yet he believed that all would be well, and all manner of things would be well.

The king, hopeful that the royalists of England would flock to his banner, came across the border by way of Carlisle. Certain 'scares' and conspiracies had been reported in these early days; disaffected royalists met at racecourses or in taverns to plot their schemes but, without any organized direction, they remained inchoate. The government also sent agents provocateurs among them, known as 'decoy ducks'. In the spring of this year a royalist conspiracy was discovered in the City of London that involved several Presbyterian ministers; one of their number, Christopher Love, died on the scaffold. This was considered by some to be an affront to religion while others, such as John Milton, celebrated it as a blow against disobedience and treason.

Yet few supporters joined the king on his journey south, principally because the Scots were not popular among the English people; they could not support an ancient enemy, even if a lawful monarch led them forward. David Leslie himself was doleful and, when the king asked why he was so sad in the presence of such a spirited army, he replied quietly that 'he was melancholic indeed, for he knew that army, how well soever it looked, would not fight'. Nevertheless the king made his way down the north-western counties, through Cumberland and Cheshire and Staffordshire; he could not think of changing course towards London, since the regiments of the enemy were now pursing him. Cromwell's strategy had been entirely successful.

Charles took refuge at last in the perennially royal city of Worcester. 'For me,' the king said, 'it is a crown or a coffin.' Cromwell had not the patience to try a siege on this occasion but decided instead upon an immediate attack, on both sides of the town, by means of the Severn. With the royalist army at half the strength of its antagonist, the result was not really in doubt. Charles, watching the action from the tower of the cathedral, made one last effort to consolidate his forces in a battle that lasted for three hours. When he rallied some of his men for another fresh sally, they threw down their arms. 'Then shoot me dead,' he said, 'rather than let me live to see the sad consequences of this day.' Brave words were not enough, however, and by the early afternoon of 3 September 1651, the royalist army had been scattered to the winds. The young king disappeared into the greenwood, among the birds and foxes, where he could not be found. It was Oliver Cromwell's last battle and it was for him, as he wrote, 'a crowning mercy'.

The wanderings of the young king have become the stuff of legend; he made his secret way through England for forty-two days, and was concealed in eighty-two different hiding places; forty-five people, by the smallest count, knew who he was and where he was. Yet not one of them betrayed him. The image of the king still burned brightly in some loyal hearts. It was noted that many of those who preserved him were Roman Catholic.

In the course of his peregrinations he was disguised as a labourer; he hid in a barn, in a wood and on a farm. He adopted the disguise of the son of a tenant farmer, and was recognized in silence by the butler of the manor where he rested. He stayed in a 'priest hole', devised to protect visiting Jesuits, and lay concealed among the boughs of an oak tree in the grounds of Boscobel House. He dressed as a country man, in a worn leather doublet, and as a servant in a grey cloak. Posters were pasted in villages and market towns asking for the capture of 'a tall, black man, over two yards high'; the 'black' referred to his somewhat swarthy complexion. On one occasion he was surprised by the sound of bells and sight of bonfires, arranged after a false report of his death.

In Bromsgrove, Worcestershire, a blacksmith told him that the king should be hanged for bringing in the Scots. At Bridport, disguised as a servant, he entered a street that was filled with troops searching for him; he dismounted and led his horse as if he were taking it to a stable. At Brighton an innkeeper knelt down and kissed his hand, saying 'that he would not ask him who he was, but bid God bless him whither he was going'. One attempt at escape by sea was abandoned, but on 14 October he sailed from Shoreham to the relative safety of Normandy. On his return to France the young king was asked if he would ever return to Scotland, to which he replied that he would rather be hanged first. When he arrived at the French court he was still ragged and dirty after his adventures.

Cromwell returned in triumph to London bearing with him, like a Roman emperor, the prisoners whom he had taken. He was granted an income of £4,000 per year, and the palace at Hampton Court was bestowed upon him. There could be no doubt that he was the first man of the state.

Yet he came back to a city very different from that which he had left at the beginning of the Irish campaign. The first 'year of freedom', after the heady days of the council of state, had been less than glorious. The Rump Parliament had been almost overwhelmed with the pressure of business; it set up committees for legal or ecclesiastical reform, but then did nothing to carry their conclusions into effect. Accusations of favouritism, and even of corruption, were often heard. It was widely believed that its principal concern was for its own survival.

Parliament did pass a few bills, however, designed for the supposed good of the commonwealth; one of them was an Act making adultery a capital offence. It was not a great success. Four women, and no men, were executed. In many other respects the members of parliament seemed to have lapsed into a state close to inertia. It was reported that the present government was reduced to a 'languishing condition' in the provinces.

Yet Cromwell's triumphs were evident. Scotland was seized and strengthened by one of Cromwell's key generals, George Monck, and was governed by a military regime for the next eleven years; Cromwell remarked that 'I do think truly they are a very ruined nation'. No king of England had ever conquered Scotland. Ireland was in no better case; after Cromwell's withdrawal another general, Edmund Ludlow, practically completed the conquest of that country. The Act of Settlement, passed in the summer of 1652, condemned Catholic landowners to the wholesale or partial forfeiture of their estates while those who had actively supported the Irish rebellion were in theory condemned to death. Cromwell had achieved the unparalleled feat of ascendancy over the three kingdoms.

When he returned from his victory at Worcester he was told that great things were expected of him in peace no less than in war; it was his task, according to a letter sent to him, to 'ease the oppressed of their burdens, to release the prisoners out of bonds, and to relieve poor families with bread'. Yet he could only achieve these laudable aims through the agency of the Rump Parliament that seemed in no way inclined to obey his orders with the same promptness as the soldiers of the New Model Army. Those parliamentarians who were members of the council of state were in most respects still conscientious and diligent, yet others were not so easily inspired by Cromwell's zeal or vision.

Cromwell had argued for an immediate dissolution of parliament, making way for a fresh legislature that might deal with the problems attendant upon victory. Yet the members prevaricated and debated, finally agreeing to dissolve their assembly at a date not later than November 1654. They gave themselves another three years of procrastination. The army was by now thoroughly disillusioned with those members who seemed intent upon thwarting or delaying necessary legislation. The more committed soldiers believed them to be time-servers or worse, uninterested in the cause of 'the people of God'.

In truth the Rump was essentially a conservative body, while the army inherently favoured radical solutions; there was bound to be conflict between them. Yet Cromwell himself was not so certain of his course; he wished for godly reformation of the commonwealth but he also felt obliged, at this stage, to proceed by constitutional methods. He did not want to impose what was known as a 'sword government'. Another possibility was also full of peril. In the current state of opinion it was possible that, unless fresh elections were carefully managed, a royalist majority might be returned; this could not be permitted.

The condition of England was enough to cause dismay. The late wars had badly injured trade, with a consequent steep increase in unemployment; bands of beggars roamed the land in numbers not seen since the last century. The country gentry and other landlords were devastated by the various taxes imposed upon them; those who favoured the royalist cause found their lands in danger of confiscation or sale. The prisons were filled with debtors. The Church was in confusion, with radical sectaries and orthodox believers still engaged in recrimination and complaint. Episcopacy had been abolished but no other form of national Church government had taken its place; it was said that the mass of the people could not find ministers to serve them. Many called, without success, for legislation to abolish burdensome taxes, to simplify and improve the judicial process, to ease the public debt and to lower the cost of living.

One evening in the autumn of 1652, Cromwell was walking in St James's Park with a member of the council of state, Bulstrode Whitelocke. Cromwell asked his companion for his counsel on the present condition of affairs, remarking of the Rump Parliament that 'there is little hope of a good settlement to be made by them, really there is not'. Whitelocke then replied that 'we ourselves have acknowledged them the supreme power'.

Cromwell: What if a man should take upon him to be king?
Whitelocke: I think that remedy would be worse than the disease.
Cromwell: Why do you think so?
Whitelocke: As to your own person the title of king would be of no advantage, because you have the full kingly power in you already, concerning the militia, and you are general.

Cromwell went on to reflect, at least according to Whitelocke's diary, that 'the power of a king is so great and so high', that 'the title of it might indemnify in a great measure those that act under it'; it would in particular be useful in curbing 'the insolences and extravagances of those whom the present powers cannot control'. It is possible that the conversation sprang from hindsight on the part of Whitelocke but its purport is confirmed by Cromwell's remark in an earlier meeting of officers and parliamentarians that 'somewhat of a monarchical government would be most effectual, if it could be established with safety to the liberties of the people'. Certainly he believed that his military victories had been delivered to him by God. Why should his destiny now be in the hands of a Rump? He could have waited patiently for a sign but ambition and a sense of mission (they are not to be distinguished) soon drove him forward.

The army had already presented a petition of complaint to parliament in which it was recommended that miscreants in positions of authority should be replaced by 'men of truth, fearing God and hating covetousness'. This was a standard preamble based on Exodus 18:21. They listed many necessary reforms that needed 'speedy and effectual' redress. The members of the Rump promised to take such matters 'under consideration'.

Cromwell attempted to mediate between the officers and parliamentarians, although he believed that the Rump was in general guided by pride and self-seeking. He told a colleague that he was being pushed to action, the consideration of which 'makes my hair stand on end'. His practice was always to withdraw into himself, in a process of self-communing, before taking swift and decisive action.

The officers of the New Model Army had devoted the first week of 1653 to prayer and fasting, seeking for God's counsel. From this time forward the members of the Rump feared some form of military intervention. It was rumoured that parliament was preparing a bill for new elections, vetted by its own members, that would destroy the army's expectations of godly reformation; it was also claimed that parliament was about to remove Cromwell from the leadership of the army.

On 20 April Cromwell came into the chamber of the House of Commons, dressed in plain black, and took his seat; he had left a file of musketeers at the door of the chamber and in the lobby. He took off his hat and rose to his feet. He first commended the Commons for their early efforts at reform but then reproached them for their subsequent delays and obfuscations; he roamed down the middle of the chamber and signalled various individual members as 'whoremaster' and 'drunkard' and 'juggler'. He declared more than once that 'it is you that have forced me to do this, for I have sought the Lord night and day that he would rather slay me than put me upon the doing of this work'. He spoke, according to one observer, 'with so much passion and discomposure of mind as if he had been distracted'; he shouted, and kicked the floor with his foot.

In conclusion he called out, 'You are no parliament. I will put an end to your sitting.' He then called for the musketeers and pointed to the parliamentary mace lying on the table. 'What shall be done with this bauble? Here. Take it away.' He said later that he had not planned or premeditated his intervention and that 'the spirit was so upon him, that he was overruled by it; and he consulted not with flesh and blood at all'. This is perhaps too convenient an explanation to be altogether true. He had dissolved a parliament that, in one form or another, had endured for almost thirteen years. The Long Parliament, of which the Rump was the final appendage, had witnessed Charles I's attempt to seize five of its members and then the whole course of the civil wars; it had seen some of its members purged and driven away. It was not a ruin, but a ruin of that ruin. It ended in ignominy, unwanted and unlamented.

Cromwell remarked later that, at its dissolution, not even a dog barked. On the following day a large placard was placed upon the door of the chamber. 'This House to be let, unfurnished.'

32

Fear and trembling

The most powerful image of the age, after the demise of the Tudor line, was that of a society without divine sanction. In the early decades of the seventeenth century Jacobean tragedy, as we have seen, assumed a world without God where men and women struggle for survival. The civic broils of the 1640s had rendered the prospect of chaos only more acute. Out of that fear and insecurity came a book that has been described as the only masterpiece of political philosophy in the English language.

Thomas Hobbes had shown no signs of greatness. After a conventional humanist education at Oxford he became tutor and companion to William Cavendish, second son of the 1st earl of Devonshire; with that gentleman he undertook the almost obligatory European tour. On a subsequent journey, to Geneva, he experienced his moment of awakening. He happened to open a copy of Euclid's *Elements of Geometry* and was immediately impressed by the Greek mathematician's reliance on deduction through definitions and axioms; it was the method, not the matter, that inspired him. In that spirit he began to brood on the nature of human society.

He began work on *Leviathan, or the Matter, Form and Power of a Common Wealth Ecclesiastical and Civil* in the late 1640s, the volume eventually being published in 1651. It was begun at a time, therefore, of chaotic civil war; its writing continued through the trial and execution of a king; it was completed in a period when the political experiment of the Rump Parliament was being challenged by various sects and interests. Where was certainty, or safety, to be found? Hobbes was in any case of a timorous and fearful nature. He wrote, at the age of eighty-four, that 'fear and I were born twins'.

So *Leviathan* emerged from the very conditions of the time, or what he called 'the seditious roaring of a troubled nation'. He did not read other political or philosophical accounts; he believed 'that there can be nothing so absurd, but may be found in the books of philosophers'. He followed his own bright line of thought through all of its logical consequences. He would ponder and ruminate, then jot down the phrases and conclusions that came to him. One axiom would lead to another, and then to the next, so that he was inexorably guided towards his own vision of the world.

His clarity of purpose, and his rigorous method, allowed him to cut through all the political cant of the period; his was a thorough scepticism that pierced the pious platitudes and false generalizations, the truisms and solecisms, that always attend political discourse. He would proceed only upon first principles maintained by firm definition and vigorous argument. He stated that 'words are wise men's counters, they do but reckon by them; but they are the money of fools'.

So his argument opened. Stripped of order and security, men are at enmity one with another in 'a perpetual contention for honour, riches and authority'. The goad for action and conflict is preeminently 'a perpetual and restless desire for power'. The strength of one man is more or less equal to that of another, leading to an eternal war of all against all. Once the dire predicament is understood, a solution may be found amid the discord. The fear of death encourages prudence and the desire for self-preservation; the principles of reason might therefore be applied to the quest for peace, and for life rather than death. A form of contract might be agreed whereby each man is 'contented with so much liberty against other men as he would allow other men against himself'. Each man agrees that he will not do to another what he would not have done to himself.

This instinct for self-preservation then becomes the key element in what might be described as Hobbes's metaphysic whereby 'man which looks too far before him, in the care of future time, has his heart all the day long gnawed on by fear of death, poverty, or other calamity, and has no repose, nor pause of his anxiety, but in sleep'. This is the foundation of his theory of the state.

The contract between men is the beginning of wisdom. How is it to be maintained? It cannot be entrusted to the individuals themselves. It must be transferred to 'a common power set over them both, with right and force sufficient to compel performance'. There must be an authority that can enforce the contract in perpetuity; supreme authority demands supreme power and, as Hobbes puts it, 'covenants, without the sword, are but words'. To escape from fear and trembling, therefore, men must agree among themselves to create a system of such powerful control that no deviation or dissension, no unrest or cause of unrest, will be tolerated. They transfer their own prudence and reason to this other thing, this living absolutism that he names as 'great Leviathan'. This act of authorization is the mutual surrender of the natural rights of each man in order to create the sovereign power which will guide and protect them.

Leviathan will impose the religion of the state, thus avoiding the divisions that Hobbes saw all around. There will be no such thing as liberty of conscience, which simply created confusion and, in the case of England, bloodshed. Justice and truth are to be determined by civil authority rather than individual choice. Justice is simply what the law demands.

It did not matter whether this omnipotent authority was king, or conquering invader, or magistrate; it was only important that it existed, and that it was authorized to act and to will in place of individual action and private will. Only thus could true order be maintained. That is why some critics accused him of complying with the doctrine of the divine right of kings, while others attacked him for compounding with Cromwell's commonwealth.

In his preface to the Latin translation of his treatise he wrote that 'this great Leviathan, which is called the State, is a work of art; it is an artificial man made for the protection and salvation of the natural man, to whom it is superior in grandeur and power'. By the rigorous argument from first principles, Hobbes believed that he had uncovered the true imperatives of civil society. He was also convinced that he had written for the benefit of mankind, and in the last sentence of the work he concludes ironically that 'such truth, as opposeth no man's profit, nor pleasure, is to all men welcome'.

Leviathan created a sensation at the time, and it has been said that it inspired universal horror. The Commons proposed to burn the book, and one bishop suggested that Hobbes himself should be tied to the stake. It was so exact, so convincing in its logic, so simple in its argument, that it was difficult to repudiate without relying upon the political pieties and the cant that Hobbes had already attacked.

Nevertheless he was denounced as an atheist and as a materialist. Clearly he had no very great confidence in human nature, and described the character of any man's heart as 'blotted and confounded . . . with dissembling, lying, counterfeiting and erroneous doctrines'. He stated that 'the value, or WORTH of a man, is as of all other things, his price; that is to say, so much as would be given for the use of his power'. He added that 'to obey, is to honour, because no man obeys them whom they think have no power to help or hurt them'. His clarity of judgement is sometimes terrible; he has the savagery of the true moral philosopher, and *Leviathan* must rank as one of the central statements of the seventeenth century.

33

Healing and settling

Cromwell had engineered what was in effect a second revolution. He was now, by virtue of the sword, the indisputable head of state and sole source of power. The officers of the army concluded a dispatch with the encomium that 'we humbly lay ourselves with these thoughts, in this emergency, at your excellency's feet'. The ministers of Newcastle upon Tyne made 'their humble addresses to his godly wisdom'. Yet Cromwell did not intend or wish to be a dictator; he was still concerned with the constitutional niceties of his unique position.

He appointed a reformed council of state, with himself a prominent participant, but its thirteen members were in something of a quandary. They were in a situation without precedent, faced with the obligation of creating a constitution out of nothing. Some in the army wished for government by the council itself, perhaps with the assistance of a carefully selected parliament; others pressed for near universal male suffrage; yet others demanded a council of godly men on the model of the Jewish Sanhedrin.

Cromwell spent eight days locked in conversation with his councillors, and from their deliberations emerged a wholly original form of parliament. It was eventually agreed that members of the new assembly should be either nominated by the various Independent congregations or favoured by the army and by prominent individuals; those chosen were to be 'known persons, men fearing God, and of approved integrity'. One of the godly men chosen to serve was Isaac Praise-God Barebone, a leather merchant and preacher from London who, at his warehouse in Fleet Street, proclaimed the imminent coming of Jesus Christ. His colourful name and nature led to this nominated parliament becoming known as 'Barebone's Parliament'. There were 144 men who were nominees, and thus it was also called the 'Little Parliament'; it was indeed the smallest parliament to date ever to sit at Westminster.

It would be wrong, however, to conclude that all of its members were zealots; the preponderance of them held the rank of gentleman, and their number included a viscount and a baron as well as several baronets and knights. The provost of Eton and the high master of St Paul's School were among them. Yet, unsurprisingly, the radical element prevailed in their deliberations; those who burn hottest inflame the rest. No one wishes to be known as tepid or lukewarm. In his opening address to them, Cromwell remarked that 'we are at the threshold' and that 'you are at the edge of promises and prophecies'. It was supposed to mark the beginning of a new era.

The members of the new assembly were zealous and busy, but they were perhaps not worldly enough to judge the consequences of their decisions. They determined to abolish the court of chancery, for example, and drastically to simplify the law; some in fact demanded the abolition of the common law, to be substituted by the code of Moses. They voted to abolish tithes, a proposal that might have eventually led to the disestablishment of the Church and the violation of all rights of property.

The alarm and horror of the nation soon became manifest, and Cromwell realized that it was time to end an experiment that had lasted for just five months. He is reported to have said that he was more troubled now by fools than by knaves. A parliament of saints had gone to excess. He had learned that it was not possible to create instruments of power in an arbitrary manner; they had no stable foundation, and therefore veered wildly from side to side. In December the more conservative or moderate of the members were persuaded to launch a pre-emptive coup by voting in an early morning session that they should abdicate their powers; the radicals were in a prayer meeting at the time. The Speaker then took up the mace and led them in procession to Whitehall Palace where Cromwell was waiting to greet them. He professed later to being surprised by their arrival, but this is hard to credit.

A few of the godly remained in the chamber. An army officer entered and asked them, 'What do you here?'

'We are seeking the Lord.'

'Then you may go elsewhere for, to my certain knowledge, he has not been here these twelve years.'

The abrogation of this 'Little Parliament' was greeted with considerable relief by those whose livings had been threatened by it. The lawyers celebrated and, according to an Independent lay preacher, 'most men upon this dissolution take occasion to cry Aha, Aha'.

And then there was one. It was said that, in bringing an end to 'Barebone's Parliament', Cromwell took the crown from Christ and put it on his own head. One of his military associates, General John Lambert, had drawn up what was called an 'Instrument of Government' in which Cromwell would be granted power as Lord Protector of the British Republic. This 'Instrument' has the distinction of being the first, and the last, written constitution of England. Yet its system of checks and balances, including a council, did not dispel the impression that Cromwell was now an autocrat in all but name. Clarendon noted that 'this extraordinary man, without any other reason than because he had a mind to it . . . mounted himself into the throne of three kingdoms, without the name of king, but with a greater power and authority than had ever been exercised or claimed by any king'.

On 16 December 1653, Oliver Cromwell stood before a chair of state in Westminster Hall. He was dressed in a suit and cloak of black velvet, with long boots; a band of gold ran around his hat. He looked up and raised his right hand to heaven as he swore to observe all the articles of the new constitution; John Lambert then knelt and offered him a civic sword sheathed in its scabbard as a token of peaceful rule. In the proclamation of public acts he was now styled 'Olivarius Protector' in the same manner as 'Carolus Rex'. His passage through the streets was guarded by soldiers. He insisted that the series of nine paintings by Andrea Mantegna, *The Triumphs of Caesar*, should not be sold off but remain at his apartments in Hampton Court Palace. The proceedings of his court, in such matters as the reception of ambassadors, resembled those of Charles I. His son, Henry Cromwell, was greeted in the entertainment grounds of Spring Gardens with cries of 'Room for the prince'. Lucy Hutchinson wrote that for Cromwell's family to emulate regal state was as ridiculous as to dress apes in scarlet.

Many of his former supporters now railed at him for betraying the cause of godly reformation. He was accused of sacrificing the public good to ambition and was denounced as a 'dissembling perjured villain'. Biblical insults were hurled at him as the 'Old Dragon', the 'Little Horn', the 'Man of Sin' , and the 'Vile Person' of Daniel 11: 21. At the pulpit set up by Blackfriars one preacher, Christopher Feake, proclaimed that 'he has deceived the Lord's people'; he added that 'he will not reign long, he will end worse than the last Protector did, that crooked tyrant Richard. Tell him I said it.' Feake was brought before the council and placed in custody. The governor of Chester Castle, Colonel Robert Duckenfield, put it a little more delicately when he wrote to Cromwell that 'I believe the root and tree of piety is alive in your lordship, though the leaves thereof, through abundance of temptations and flatteries, seem to me to be withered much of late'.

In a sense the revolution was now over, with all attempts at radical reform at an end. Cromwell instituted a reign of quiet in which men of property might feel safe; in effect he inaugurated a gentry republic. It cannot be said that the new dispensation was received with any great enthusiasm, yet for many it must have been a relief after the disordered governance of recent years. For others, of course, it made no difference at all.

In the first eight months of their power the Lord Protector and the council, in the absence of parliament, passed more than eighty ordinances. Scotland and Ireland were to be incorporated within the commonwealth. The court of chancery was to be reformed. Duels were forbidden, and cock-fighting suppressed; horse racing was suspended for a period. Public drunkenness, and profanity, were punished with a fine or with a whipping. No more than 200 hackney carriages were allowed in London. The postal service was reformed, while the prisons and the public highways were improved. The treasury was reorganized. This was a practical administration.

Cromwell and the council were no less pragmatic in foreign affairs. The European powers were docile, perhaps in fear of a resurgent English navy that had recently challenged and defeated the Dutch. Peace was made with the Protestant nations, among them Sweden and Denmark. France and Spain vied with each other for the favour of the protectorate, in which equation Cromwell tended to incline towards the French side; he wanted to remove the influence of Charles II on the French court.

He also favoured balance in religious matters. An ordinance in the spring of 1654 established a commission of 'triers' who would check the qualities and qualifications of proposed clergymen. In the summer of the year commissioners were appointed to every county as 'ejectors' who would remove ministers guilty of ignorance, insufficiency, or scandalous behaviour. Cromwell supported religious liberty except for those who espoused pope or bishops. Anglicans were in theory no more tolerated than Roman Catholics, but in practice they were given tacit acceptance.

From a policy of benign neglect, Cromwell created a variegated Church made up of Presbyterians, Independents and Baptists. Doctrine was less important to him than spirit; dogma did not concern him as long as he could create a community that had what he called 'the root of the matter' within it. It has been described as not so much a national Church as a confederation of Christian sects. Some of the more committed Anglicans went into exile 'waiting for a day', as they put it, when Charles II might claim his throne. Yet many were not exercised by religion at all. In his diary entry for 11 May 1654, Evelyn noted that 'I now observed how the women began to paint themselves, formerly a most ignominious thing, and used only by prostitutes'.

Small groups of royalists frequented certain taverns of London, and of the provincial towns, where they engaged in plots against the protectorate. Where there are conspiracies, however, there are apt to be informers and suborners. In February 1654, eleven men were arrested at the Ship Tavern by the Old Bailey. It became clear, in the course of investigations, that a powerful group of royalists had been formed to incite a popular rebellion; it was known as the Sealed Knot. The exiled king was in constant and secret correspondence with his supporters, and seemed particularly interested in a scheme to assassinate Cromwell himself. He was to be shot after he had left Whitehall for Hampton Court on a Saturday morning.

Yet Cromwell had created a very efficient secret service under the command of John Thurloe, secretary to the council of state, and the details of the plot were known almost as soon as they were formulated. Alerted by his spy-master Cromwell took to the water on that morning and avoided an attack. Soon after the failure of the conspiracy the authorities mounted raids in London taverns and houses, in the course of which 500 people were arrested. Two of the leaders were executed, while others were transported to Barbados. An old Catholic priest was also seized and executed.

Yet the punishments did not deter other plotters, who would soon attempt to rise again. Cromwell was given a copy of a letter written by the new king in which Charles advised his supporters to 'consult with those you dare trust, and, if you are ready, agree upon a time . . .' Cromwell now always carried a gun. In a riding accident, later in the year, the pistol fired in his pocket and the wound kept him in bed for three weeks.

The occasion for a parliament, according to the 'Instrument of Government', had now come. On 4 September 1654, Cromwell addressed the new assembly in the Painted Chamber of Westminster Palace; he sat in the chair of state while the members were seated on benches ranged against the walls. 'Gentlemen,' he told them, 'you are met here on the greatest occasion that, I believe, England ever saw.' He then proceeded to speak for three hours on the various manifestations of God's providence in an oration that veered from messianic enthusiasm to scriptural exposition. He had called parliament, but 'my calling be from God'. He was thus reiterating, in his own fashion, the divine right of kings. He was above parliament. Yet he came to them not as a master but as a fellow servant. Now was a time for 'healing and settling'.

Yet the new parliament was by no means a compliant body. For some days its members had debated, without reaching any conclusion, whether they should give the protectorate their support. On 12 September they found the doors of their chamber closed against them, and they were asked once more to assemble in the Painted Chamber where the Protector wished to address them. He chided them for neglecting the interest of the state, 'so little valued and so much slighted', and he would not allow them to proceed any further unless and until they had signed an oath to agree to 'the form of government now settled'. All members had to accept the condition that 'the persons elected shall not have power to alter the government as it is hereby settled in one single person and a Parliament'. 'I am sorry,' he said, 'I am sorry, and I could be sorry to the death that there is cause for this. But there is cause . . .'

Some members protested and refused to sign, but the majority of them either agreed or at least submitted. Cromwell still did not attempt to guide the debates, but he became increasingly alarmed at their nature. He is reported to have said in this period that he 'would rather keep sheep under a hedge than have to do with the government of men'. Sheep were at least obedient. The members voted to restrict the power of the Protector to veto legislation; they also decided that their decisions were more authoritative than those of the council of state. They believed, in other words, that parliament should still be paramount in the nation. That was not necessarily Cromwell's view. From day to day they debated every clause of the 'Instrument of Government', with the evident wish to replace it with a constitution of their own. On 3 January 1655 they voted to reaffirm the limits to religious toleration; two days later they decided to reduce army pay, thus striking at Cromwell's natural constituency. On 20 January they began to discuss the formation of a militia under parliamentary control.

Two days later, Cromwell called a halt. He lambasted them for wasting time in frivolous and unnecessary discourse when they should have been considering practical measures for the general reformation of the nation. He told them that 'I do not know what you have been doing. I do not know whether you have been alive or dead.' He considered that it was not fit for the common welfare and the public good to allow them to continue; and so, farewell. The first protectorate parliament was dissolved. The larger problem, however, was not addressed. Could a representative parliament ever co-exist with what was essentially a military dictatorship?

Cromwell and the council once more reigned without challenge, but the price of power was eternal vigilance. In his speech of dissolution Cromwell had warned that 'the cavalier party have been designing and preparing to put this nation in blood again' together with 'that party of men called levellers'. The royalist supporters of the Sealed Knot had indeed survived, despite deportations and executions, and seem to have entered an unlikely association with the radical republicans who shared an interest in removing Cromwell from power. For those of a levelling tendency Cromwell was infinitely worse than Charles; he had used them, betrayed them and set himself up as a despot. Yet the royalists could not even agree among themselves. They had planned six different regional conspiracies in 1654, but the only rebellion was a short and ill-organized affair in the West Country. The spy-master, Thurloe, had done his work.

Cromwell had been considering a possible friendship or alliance with Spain, despite the fact that as a Catholic state it was one of the horns of the beast. He had said to a Spanish envoy that an alliance was possible on the conditions that the English were granted liberty of conscience within the Spanish dominions and that free trade be allowed between England and the West Indies. The envoy replied that this was 'to ask my master's two eyes'.

Without any agreement, therefore, Cromwell felt emboldened to test Spanish power in the sensitive area of the West Indies. He convinced himself that the action was part of a religious crusade against popery, and he trusted that the warfare would not spread to Europe; he was mistaken, or misguided, in both aspirations. At the end of 1654 Admiral William Penn and General Robert Venables set sail for Barbados with the order 'to gain an interest in that part of the West Indies in possession of the Spaniards'. They arrived safely enough, in the spring of the following year, but their expedition thereafter was not a success.

The English forces sailed to the island of Hispaniola with the purpose of subduing the city of Santo Domingo and taking its treasure. The men marched for four days through rough country in the burning sun with little fresh water; they were apparently untested soldiers who had no idea of the conditions they would confront. Exhausted and demoralized, they were an easy prey for a group of horsemen and cattle-herders who surprised them in ambush. The remaining members of the expedition, still under the command of Venables, managed to sail on to Jamaica where they were able to take and occupy the island. But at the time it seemed like a poor reward, with the additional risk that Spain might now declare a general war against the old enemy.

The news of the failure to rout Santo Domingo reached Cromwell towards the end of July. He locked himself in his room for an entire day. He had hoped to control the trade and treasure routes of the Spaniards, but he had been thwarted. The new republic had never suffered a military defeat before. He had seen himself as the protector and champion of Protestant interests, but the hand of God seems to have been against him. Cromwell had said, in reply to those who had originally questioned the wisdom of the expedition, that 'God had not brought us hither where we are but to consider the work that we may do in the world as well as at home'. Yet the Lord had not blessed this work in the world. This caused Cromwell the most painful reflections of his rule, and presaged the fears and doubts that would attend the last years of his protectorate. Wherein had he offended? Or was it the nation itself that had provoked God's anger?

It may not be coincidental, therefore, that soon after the disaster in the Indies a network of godly rule was established in England. The country was divided into eleven districts, or groups of counties; at the head of each was imposed a major-general of decidedly puritan inclinations. These army commanders were instructed to raise taxes and revive the local militia, to enquire into the conduct of clergy and teachers, to arrest any suspect persons and to prevent further royalist uprisings. Their costs were met by charges imposed on royalists alone. This became known as the 'decimation tax', taking one tenth of the 'malignants'' profits from the land, an injustice to which they were forced to submit without complaint. The newspapers and periodicals were suppressed, and no item of news could be printed without the permission of John Thurloe.

Cromwell was attempting that reformation of manners which the last parliament had signally failed to achieve. The major-generals were instructed 'to encourage and promote godliness and virtue' and, as a result, the pastimes of the people were largely suppressed. Colonel Pride, who had led the purge of parliament seven years before, raided the bear-garden at Bankside; he himself killed the bears, and then ordered his troops to wring the necks of the game-cocks in other parts of London. Alehouses were shut all over the country; stage plays as well as 'mirths and jollities' were forbidden.

One major-general, William Boteler, informed Thurloe that he had imprisoned 'drunken fellows' and others 'suspected to live only on the highway'; those accused of illegal brewing or of keeping a 'lewd house' were also arrested. Those who travelled on the Lord's day could be set in the stocks or placed in a cage; unmarried men and women who had 'carnal knowledge' of each other could be sent to a house of correction; those who swore or uttered profanities were heavily fined.

Public morals may have been improved by these measures, but public sympathy for Cromwell's regime was lost. The people did not wish to be governed, or corrected, by military officials with an attendant crew of spies and informers. Some of the major-generals were considered by the gentry to be low-born interlopers, and the natural leaders of the counties did not relish their loss of authority. A nation cannot be made virtuous by diktat or by government inspectors. The experience of the major-generals, with their troops of horse behind them, also helped to augment the national hatred for standing armies.

The experiment did not last for very long; the major-generals were sent to their counties in the autumn of 1655 and were summoned back to Westminster in the spring of the following year for consultation. With a great war against Spain growing ever more likely, fresh revenues were urgently needed; the major-generals seem to have persuaded a reluctant Cromwell to call another parliament rather than impose further taxation by decree. Thus they contrived their own fall. It was not likely that the representatives of the nation, however they were chosen, would tolerate a continuation of godly rule.

After the attack by Penn and Venables on the Spanish colonies in the Caribbean, Spain declared war on England as a natural and almost inevitable consequence. The West Indian adventure had become a European imbroglio with infinitely more dangerous possibilities. Spain and France were old enemies, however, and Cromwell now inclined towards the court of the young Louis XIV.

A commercial treaty was signed in the autumn of 1655, containing certain secret clauses about the expulsion of Charles II from French territory; the English king had in fact already left for Spa and Aachen. Charles then promptly fashioned an agreement with Spain that would allow him to live in the Spanish Netherlands (what is now Belgium and part of northern France); he promised that, on his accession, he would return Jamaica to the Spanish. He was disheartened, always in need of money; he was surrounded by squabbling courtiers. With no realistic prospect of regaining his throne, nothing could ease his distress of mind.

Cromwell was himself in no easy condition. The failure of the expedition to the West Indies, and the onset of war with Spain, had precipitated a sickness described by the French ambassador as 'a bilious colic, which occasionally flies to the brain'. He added that 'grief often persecutes him more than either of these, as his mind is not yet accustomed to endure disgrace'. Cromwell survived, but became even more aware of the extent to which the commonwealth relied upon his presence. Who else could preserve the unity and constancy of the state? He was showing signs of his age and of his cares; his hand trembled when he held his hat. 'Study still to be innocent,' he told his son, Henry. 'Cry to the Lord to give you a plain single heart.'

With the plans for a new parliament, and with the preparations for war, Cromwell and his councillors were hard pressed. The Venetian envoy observed that 'they are so fully occupied that they do not know which way to turn, and the Protector has not a moment to call his own'. Cromwell had no very sanguine expectations about parliament. He may have realized that, far from 'healing and settling', the rule of the major-generals had provoked fresh dissension; he must have feared in any case that the combined opposition of republicans and silent royalist supporters might produce a majority against him. He explained later, 'that it was against my judgement but I could have no quietness till it was done.'

The course of the election campaign was strenuous, and Thurloe wrote to Henry Cromwell that 'here is the greatest striving to get into Parliament that ever was known'. The call went out against the representatives of the military regime. 'No swordsmen! No decimators!' It was a further sign that the country was restless and discomposed. The council of state took measures of its own, however, and excluded approximately one hundred of the elected members for 'immorality' or 'delinquency'; it was another example of brute military power, and provoked much outrage in the country. How could this be called a free parliament?

Cromwell opened its proceedings on 17 September 1656, with a warning of the forces ranged against the country. England was at war with Spain, and the Spanish king was even then preparing to assist Charles Stuart in an invasion launched from Flanders. 'Why, truly,' he said employing his usual nervous syntax, 'your great enemy is the Spaniard. He is. He is a natural enemy, he is naturally so.' As for the enemy within, the levellers and the cavaliers were plotting to seize a seaport to welcome the king's forces.

In the course of a long and rambling speech Cromwell defended the major-generals for suppressing vice and for espousing the cause of true religion. And what of the forced taxation to pay for them? 'If nothing should be done but what is according to law, the throat of the nation may be cut while we send for some to make a law.' The tenor of this comment is similar to one he had made before, that government should be judged by what is good for the people and not by what pleases them. He was by instinct an authoritarian.

On the day of his speech, three conspirators met to take his life as he entered parliament; they hired a house that stood beside the east door of Westminster Abbey, and planned to shoot him as he left there on his way to the Painted Chamber. They were levellers who wished to return to the old form of a puritan republic. Yet, in the face of a crowd, they lost their nerve and dispersed; it was only the first attempt that the leader of the group, Miles Sindercombe, would undertake. Cromwell, meanwhile, dismissed all such threats as 'little fiddling things'. News soon came that might yet please the parliament and the nation. At the beginning of October Thurloe announced to parliament that Admiral Blake had seized several Spanish treasure ships on their way back to Cadiz; it was perhaps a sign that God was still with them. Parliament set aside a day for national thanksgiving.

A new Venetian ambassador, Giovanni Sagredo, came to England at this time and wrote that he found 'not elegant cavaliers but cavalry and infantry; instead of music and ballets they have trumpets and drums; they do not speak of love but of Mars . . . no patches on their faces but muskets on their shoulders; they do not neglect sleep for the sake of amusements, but severe ministers keep their adversaries in incessant wakefulness. In a word, everything here is full of disdain, suspicion and rough menacing faces . . .'

Parliament was variously and continually employed with private petitions and private bills as well as matters of state. A member complained that 'one business jostled out another'. It seemed likely that, just as its predecessor, it would achieve nothing of any consequence. Yet the religious zeal of its members was not in doubt when the case of James Naylor was put before them. He was a Quaker whose preachings aroused apocalyptic yearnings among his disciples; he was 'the hope of Israel' and 'the Lamb of God'. In the summer of the year he had entered Bristol as Christ had once gone into Jerusalem; two women led his horse while others cried out 'Holy, holy, holy, Lord God of Israel'. He was arrested and brought before the bar of parliament where he was questioned. 'I was set up,' he said, 'as a sign to summon this nation.'

A debate of nine days followed his appearance in which it was agreed that this horrid blasphemy was more dangerous to the nation than any Spanish warship; it struck at the heart of its relationship with God, than which nothing was more precious. 'Let us all stop our ears,' one member said, 'and stone him.' It was not clear whether parliament had the judicial power to punish him, yet the members voted that Naylor should be placed in the pillory and whipped through the streets; his tongue was to be bored through with a hot iron and the letter 'B' for blasphemer branded on his forehead. He would then be sentenced to an indefinite imprisonment.

The ordeal of the tongue and forehead took place at the end of the year. A diarist, Thomas Burton, noted that 'Rich, the mad merchant, sat bare-headed at Naylor's feet all the time. Sometimes he sang, and cried, and stroked his hair and face, and kissed his hand, and sucked the fire out of his forehead.' Naylor was patient, and the spectators were sympathetic to the plight of one who had endured the wrath of this parliament. Cromwell himself wished to know 'the grounds and reason' for its assumption of judicial power, but no response was ever made for the very good reason that the sentence was both arbitrary and unjustified. Some contemporaries warned that, if parliament felt itself able to condemn and punish one misguided man, who could feel safe?

At the beginning of 1657 a debate was held on a bill for maintaining the 'decimation tax' to subsidize the major-generals. To the surprise of many Cromwell's son-in-law, John Claypole, opposed the measure; this was generally believed to mean that the Protector had withdrawn his support from the godly commanders in the field. Parliament itself was in large measure composed of people from the communities who had been subject to the strict measures of the major-generals, and the bill was rejected by thirty-six votes. The pietistic experiment was ended.

Another question of governance was raised. Should not Cromwell now become king and the House of Stuart be replaced by the House of Cromwell? This would satisfy the yearning of many people for a return to a traditional form of government. If Cromwell were sovereign, he might be able to curb the pretensions of parliament that had already gone beyond its powers. The newsletters anticipated a sudden 'alteration of government'. On 19 January 1657, one member, John Ashe of Freshford, moved that Cromwell 'take upon him the government according to the ancient constitution'.

On 23 February Sir Christopher Packe brought forward a remonstrance, under the title of the 'humble petition and advice', to the effect that Cromwell should assume 'the name, style, title and dignity of king' and that the House of Lords should be restored. The fury of the opponents of monarchy, most particularly the military element, was unrestrained. General John Lambert declared that any such reversal would be contrary to the principles for which he and his fellow soldiers had fought. Kingship had been so bathed in blood that it could not be restored. This was not a theoretical point. Cromwell was informed that a group of soldiers had bound themselves on oath to kill him as soon as he accepted the title.

Four days after the 'humble petition' had been advanced, one hundred representatives of the army visited Cromwell at Whitehall where they pleaded with him to resist the offer of advancement. He told them that he liked the title of king as little as they did; it was nothing but a bauble or a feather in the hat. He then reviewed the history of the last few years, in which he stated that he had faithfully followed the advice of the army; he said that 'they had made him their drudge upon all occasions', yet they had not met with success. None of the parliaments, none of the constitutional proposals, had worked. He told them that 'it is time to come to a settlement'. A House of Lords, for example, was needed to check the pretensions of the Commons; they left him with their fury 'much abated', and a few days later another army delegation assured him that they would acquiesce in whatever he decided 'for the good of these nations'.

The debate in parliament lasted for more than a month and occupied twenty-four sittings, some of them lasting all day. Eventually, at the end of March, Cromwell was formally requested to assume the crown. He replied that he had lived for the last part of his life 'in the fire, in the midst of trouble', and he requested more time for reflection. It was thought that he would accept the role of king, if only to unite a predominantly conservative nation, but in truth he was in conflict with himself. He knew that his senior military colleagues were passionately opposed to the change, but he knew also that this might prove his last and best chance to return the country to its traditional ways. It was in his means to provide the conditions for a regular and stable government.

It was not a question of private ambition; as he had said many times, the crown and sceptre meant very little to him. He already had more power than any English king. So he struggled. Thurloe said that Cromwell had 'great difficulties in his own mind' and that 'he keeps himself reserved from everybody that I know of'; when a parliamentary delegation came to him, in the middle of April, 'he came out of his chamber half unready in his gown, with a black scarf around his neck'. No doubt he prayed incessantly for divine guidance, hoping that as in the past a resolve or a decision would be presented to him as if by an act of grace.

He heard vital news of God's providence in England's affairs when he was told that Admiral Blake had successfully maintained a siege of the Spanish coast and had destroyed another treasure fleet, thus disabling Spain as a maritime power. England now effectively controlled the high seas, an ascendancy that was unprecedented in its history. With colonies in Jamaica and Barbados, as well as those such as Virginia on the American mainland, Cromwell was the first statesman since the days of Walsingham to contemplate a global empire. As Edmund Waller put it,

Others may use the ocean as their road
Only the English make it their abode.

Pepys noted, in the pusillanimous years of Charles II, that 'it is strange how everybody do nowadays reflect upon Oliver and commend him, what brave things he did, and made all the neighbour princes fear him'.

Yet on the most pressing matter of monarchy he could not, or dare not, come to a decision. On 3 April he declared to a parliamentary delegation that he could not discharge his duties 'under that title'; five days later parliament urged him to reconsider, on which occasion it is reported that he delivered 'a speech so dark, that none knows whether he will accept it or not'. He may still have been waiting for divine guidance. He knew that it was proper and expedient that he should take the crown but, as he said, 'I would not seek to set up that which providence hath destroyed and laid in the dust, and I would not build Jericho again.' In the first week of May it is reported that he told a group of members of parliament that he had decided to accept the title; yet once more he changed his mind.

On 8 May he told parliament that he could not and would not become King Oliver I. 'At the best,' he said, 'I should do it doubtingly. And certainly what is so [done] is not of faith.' The protests of the army officers had in the end proved to be persuasive; two of them, Fleetwood and Desborough, had in fact married into Cromwell's family. They had told him that, if he accepted the crown, they would resign from all their offices and retire into private life. Other officers, who had been with him from the beginning and had fought with him through fire, also registered their strong disapproval. This was decisive. He could not at this late stage abandon his comrades and colleagues; he could not betray their trust or spoil their hopes. So his final answer to parliament was that 'I cannot undertake this government with the title of king'.

The only way forward was by means of compromise. Even if Cromwell would not be king, he could accept the other constitutional measures recommended by parliament; in particular it seemed just, and necessary, to re-establish the House of Lords as a check upon the legislature. On 25 May the 'humble petition' was presented again with Cromwell named as chief magistrate and Lord Protector, an appointment which he accepted as 'one of the greatest tasks that ever was laid upon the back of a human creature'. On 26 June 1657, Oliver Cromwell was draped in purple and in ermine for the ceremony of installation in Westminster Hall; upon the table before his throne rested the sword of state and a sceptre of solid gold. The blast of trumpets announced his reign. His office was not declared to be hereditary but he had been given the power to name his successor; it was generally believed that this would be one of his sons. So began the second protectorate, which was now a restored monarchy in all but name.

34

Is it possible?

There was a time for celebration. At the end of 1657 one of Cromwell's daughters, Frances, married Robert Rich, the grandson of the earl of Warwick, and the ceremonial matched the status of the pair. Music and song echoed through the corridors of Whitehall in honour of the occasion; the orchestra comprised forty-eight violins and fifty trumpets. Guns were fired from the Tower in the manner of previous royal weddings. There was even 'mixt dancing', men and women together, that continued until five o'clock the following morning. In the spirit of the festivity Cromwell was moved to spill sack-posset, a rich and creamy drink, over the dresses of the women and to daub the stools where they were to sit with sugar and spice. He had an almost rustic sense of fun. At the subsequent wedding of another daughter, Mary, the ceremony at Hampton Court included a masque in which Cromwell played the non-speaking role of Jove. It was an astonishing return to the customs of the Stuart kings.

The French envoy reported that 'another spirit' was abroad and that 'the preachers of old time are retiring because they are found too melancholic'. When Cromwell gave banquets for foreign envoys 'rare music' was always part of the occasion and, in the great hall of Hampton Court, two organs were placed for the use of a resident organist. It is to the credit of Cromwell, too, that under his rule the opera was introduced into England. The Protector was known to be a great lover of harmony, both of instruments and of voices.

Immediately after his installation Cromwell had adjourned parliament until the new year; when it reappeared, it would be in its old constitutional form of two houses. He had named his new council; it was the same as its predecessor, with the solitary exception of John Lambert who had resigned all of his offices and retired with a large pension. He had once believed that he would be the Protector's successor but he now realized that he would be pre-empted by another, and younger, Cromwell.

One of the principal tasks of the re-established council was to decide upon the nature of the new upper chamber, but some of their proceedings took place in the absence of the Protector. Cromwell was now being called, even by his intimates, 'the old man'; his signature was no longer bold and striking but tremulous. He spent much of the summer in the healthful air of Hampton Court, but he was suffering from painful catarrh.

The second session of the second protectorate parliament re-assembled on 20 January 1658, but immediately it began to confront the military regime. The members of the new House of Lords were largely chosen from Cromwell's most loyal supporters and, as a result, the Commons became antagonistic; some of the most inveterate of Cromwell's opponents, who had been excluded from the previous session on the grounds of 'immorality' or 'delinquency', were returned to Westminster where at once they began to question the authority of the 'other house'.

Cromwell summoned both houses to the Banqueting House, five days after they had first met, and urged them to be faithful to the cause. But his intervention had no material effect, and the Commons remained as hostile as before. One of its most formidable members, Sir Arthur Haselrig, made a speech in which he scorned the actions of the House of Lords in the past. 'And shall we now rake them up,' he asked, 'after they have so long laid in the grave?' An observer at Cromwell's court noted that the assertions of the Commons, and the divisions between the two houses, threw the Protector 'into a rage and passion like unto madness'. His anger was augmented by the fact that elements of the army in fact supported the Commons in its affirmation of supremacy.

On a cold morning, 4 February, Cromwell rose early and announced his determination to go to Westminster. He could not journey down the frozen Thames, and so impulsively he took the first coach for hire he could find. When he arrived in the retiring room of the Lords, his son-in-law and close military colleague, Charles Fleetwood, remonstrated with him on learning his intention. 'You are a milksop,' Cromwell said to him, 'by the living God I will dissolve the house.' And that was what he proceeded to do.

He told the Commons that 'you have not only disquieted yourselves, but the whole nation is disquieted'. With the prospect of invasion from abroad, and rebellion from within, they had done nothing. 'And I do declare to you here that I do dissolve this parliament. And let God be judge between you and me.' To which pious aspiration some of the members cried out, 'Amen!' Cromwell's latest, and last, constitutional experiment had come to an end. It was a sign of the radical anomaly of military rule that none of his parliaments had succeeded. He was now being openly criticized. The envoy from Venice reported that the people were 'nauseated' by the present government; the Dutch ambassador similarly noted that Cromwell's affairs were 'in troubled and dangerous condition' while a visitor from Massachusetts remarked that many men 'exclaim against him with open mouths'.

A royalist agent in London, Allan Broderick, reported to Edward Hyde that the army 'is infected with sedition' and that the treasury was exhausted; he added that the countries of Europe were 'cold friends or close enemies' and that the people of England were labouring under 'an unwearied restless spirit of innovation'. Yet Broderick said of Cromwell himself that 'the man is seemingly desperate, any other in his condition would be deemed irrecoverable, but as the dice of the gods never throw out, so is there something in the fortune of this villain that often renders ten to one no odds'.

This message was designed to encourage Charles Stuart. It was reported that the exiled king was waiting in Flanders with an army of 8,000 men, ready to strike at the first favourable opportunity. Another royalist insurrection was planned for the spring, but once more the plotters were betrayed and taken; four of them were found by Colonel Barkstead, the lieutenant of the Tower, in what he called 'a desperate malignant alehouse'. Other royalists were beheaded or hanged, drawn and quartered, but the majority were consigned to gaol.

Another fortunate throw of the dice also favoured Cromwell. In the early summer of the year the forces of the French and English scattered the Spanish just outside Dunkirk in the 'battle of the dunes'; Dunkirk, hitherto held by Spain, was then surrendered to England. It was the first piece of continental territory to fall into English hands since the time of Calais. Since there was a royalist contingent in the Spanish army, victory for Cromwell was all the sweeter. The French king now hailed him as 'the most invincible of sovereigns'. Yet this praise concealed the truth that the Protector's expenditure far outran his income; the exchequer was often bare and the pay of his soldiers was in arrears. It was said that his ministers had to go 'a-begging' to the merchants of the City.

Sickness was also in the air. A malignant fever, called 'the new disease', had arisen. In the spring of 1658 the new epidemic spread, in the words of a contemporary, Dr Willis, 'as if sent by some blast of the stars'. Cromwell himself laboured under the burden of personal rule to the extent that, as one of his servants, John Maidstone, said, 'it drank up his spirits'. His private suffering was then increased by the death of his most loved daughter, Elizabeth Claypole, at the beginning of August from an obscure or undiagnosed disease; the event, though long expected, had a violent effect upon him. Thurloe reported that 'he lay very ill of the gout and other distempers, contracted by the long sickness of my lady Elizabeth, which made great impressions on him'; he became dangerously ill, but then recovered sufficiently to ride in Hampton Court Park.

When one of the leaders of the Quakers, George Fox, visited Cromwell, however, he reported that 'I saw and felt a waft of death go forth against him, and when I came to him he looked like a dying man'. In the last week of August Cromwell fell sick again with a condition then known as 'tertian ague', a form of malaria with fits every three days. It began with chills and sensations of coldness which were followed by a stage of dry heat that ended in a drenching sweat.

He was taken back to Whitehall where, as Thurloe put it, 'our fears are more than our hopes'. Prayer meetings assembled throughout the capital. His condition varied from rally to relapse, as all the time he grew weaker, but he was said to have prayed for 'God's cause' and 'God's people'. He asked one of his doctors why he looked so sad.

'How can I look otherwise, when I have the responsibility of your life upon me?'

'You doctors think I shall die.' His wife was sitting by his bedside and he took her hand. 'I tell thee I shall not die of this bout; I am sure I shall not. Do not think I am mad. I tell you the truth.' He then told the astonished doctor that this was the answer God had given to his prayers. He also questioned one of his chaplains.

'Tell me. Is it possible to fall from grace?'

'It is not possible.'

'Then I am safe; for I know that I was once in grace.'

He had always been sustained by the notion that he was one of the elect; his pride and his piety were thereby combined, giving him that irresistible power to remove all obstacles in his path. Yet there were many times when he did not know what to do, when he waited for a sign. He once said that no man rises so high as one that does not know where he is going. He had reached the height of his command through a mixture of guile, zeal and adventitious circumstance; no one could have predicted the series of measures and counter-measures that had led to his ascendancy. It did not matter that he was inconsistent, in turns pragmatic and authoritarian, as long as the force of righteousness was with him. That is why he believed above all else in 'providence' as both the cause and justification of his actions.

On Thursday 2 September it became clear that he was dying. One of his physicians offered him a sleeping draught but he replied that 'it is not my design to drink or to sleep, but my design is to make what haste I can to be gone'. Five officers, called to the deathbed, testified that he had declared that his son, Richard Cromwell, should succeed him. He died on the afternoon of 3 September which had been called by him his 'fortunate day' as the anniversary of his victories at Dunbar and at Worcester. His battles were all now over.

When in 1650 Oliver Cromwell came back to England, after his successful campaign in Ireland, he was greeted by '*An* Horatian *Ode upon* Cromwel's *Return from* Ireland'. It has been described as the greatest political poem in the English language, but it is not the most transparent. Andrew Marvell was at this time a poet of no great account. He had been educated well, and had made the obligatory tour of Europe. He might have become a clergyman or secretary to some great man; instead he lived off the sale of some lands in the north, and revolved in the circles of London literature.

He seems to have first been attached to some royalist poets or poetasters but the crucial victories of Cromwell, and the execution of the king, gave him pause. It might be time to find patronage among the new rulers of the land, and it may be that he composed his 'Ode' with some such purpose in sight. Yet his words, distilled as if in an alembic, testify to his creative ambiguity and equivocation. His mind is so finely tempered that he can become both royalist and republican at the same time; he is open to all possible opinions, and thus finds it impossible to choose between them. He is in the position of one who, on coming to a judgement, realizes at the same time that the opposite is also true. We may therefore discuss Marvell here as representative of the confusion that must have been experienced by many others in this period of change and conflict. The poem itself was composed in the interval between Cromwell's return from Ireland and his subsequent campaign in Scotland.

In the opening lines of the 'Ode' Cromwell is one who finds fulfilment not in 'the inglorious Arts of Peace' but in 'advent'rous War' through which he takes his 'fiery way'. This might not necessarily be construed as a compliment but Marvell is withholding judgement as well as praise. He goes on to declare that:

> 'Tis Madness to resist or blame
> The force of angry Heavens flame:
> And, if we would speak true,
> Much to the Man is due.

This is as much as to say that Cromwell cannot be resisted and should not in any case be censored or condemned. He may have emerged into the light as part of the inexorable movement of time, or of historical necessity, but in that respect his personal failings are of no consequence. It was his destiny (providential or otherwise) to

> . . . cast the Kingdom old
> Into another Mold.
> Though Justice against Fate complain,
> And plead the antient Rights in vain:
> But those do hold or break
> As Men are strong or weak.

Cromwell is in other words a strong man whose strength is its own reward. If justice has been sacrificed in the process, it is a necessary and inevitable consequence of change. Cromwell is in any case a creature of 'Fate' rather than of 'Justice', decisive and undeflectable. A leader may be both redeemer and despot. It had often happened in the history of the world, and Marvell's contemporaries were thoroughly acquainted with the career of Julius Caesar.

So this is a poetry of doubt and ambiguity rather than of praise and affirmation, which may thus reflect a more general distrust and uncertainty concerning Cromwell's motives in these crucial years. It can only be confirmed that he has:

> Nor yet grown stiffer with Command,
> But still in the *Republick's* hand:
> How fit he is to sway
> That can so well obey.

It can at least be said that Cromwell has not become a tyrant. Marvell does not take sides because there are no sides to take, and we may recall T. S. Eliot's remark upon Henry James that 'he had a mind so fine that no idea could violate it'. Marvell's almost impenetrable reserve and self-effacement are also evident. He utters no real opinion of his own, and seems ready to retreat at almost any moment into silence. This, too, may have been the stance of many contemporaries in the face of Cromwell's supremacy.

Four years later Marvell applied himself once more to the phenomenon of Oliver Cromwell with 'THE FIRST ANNIVERSARY of the Government under O.C.'. This is a much more positive account of Cromwell's rule, but it would be fair to say that it is a panegyric on the nature of protectorate government rather than on the Protector himself. Cromwell is compared to Amphion who with his brother raised the city of Thebes by means of music. So:

No Note he struck, but a new Story lay'd
And the great Work ascended while he play'd.

Cromwell is here praised for creating a structure of government that will, like Thebes, endure. He has also been able to create a unique form of leadership that was an appropriate substitute for royal government:

For to be *Cromwell* was a greater thing,
Then ought below, or yet above a King:
Therefore thou rather didst thy Self depress,
Yielding to Rule, because it made thee Less.

This polity has created a system of government that avoids the extremes of liberty or oppression:

'Tis not a Freedome, that where All command;
Nor Tyranny, where One does them withstand:
But who of both the Bounders knows to lay
Him as their Father must the State obey.

As a result England was respected and feared by all of its neighbouring nations:

He seems a King by long Succession born,
And yet the same to be a King does scorn.
Abroad a King he seems, and something more,
At Home a Subject on the equal Floor.

This might be described as the 'party line' for Cromwell's adherents, and may or may not reflect Marvell's private thoughts on the matter. The difficulties of Cromwell's position as Protector, and the emergence of many agents of opposition to his rule, are not mentioned. Marvell is giving expression to the opinions of many people, however, who seem to have believed that the government of a Protector was more effective than the government of parliament. The poetry here is of great fluency and sophistication; it is precise but not pointed, hard but not wooden, eloquent but not facile.

The last poem by Marvell on Cromwell is also the most intimate. He had become by this time well known to the Protector's household; he had been asked to compose songs for the marriage of Mary Cromwell to Lord Fauconberg, and had been commissioned by Cromwell to write poems for Christina of Sweden. In 1657 he had been given employment as assistant to John Milton in Milton's position as Secretary of Foreign and Latin Tongues. So 'A Poem upon the Death of O.C.', written in 1658, was his last gift to an employer whom he may have come to love as well as admire. It seems more than likely that he was allowed to enter the death chamber and to view Cromwell's corpse:

> I saw him dead, a leaden slumber lyes,
> And mortal sleep over those wakefull eyes:
> Those gentle Rays under the lids were fled,
> Which through his looks that piercing sweetnesse shed;
> That port which so Majestique was and strong,
> Loose and depriv'd of vigour, stretch'd along:
> All wither'd, all discolour'd, pale and wan,
> How much another thing, no more that man?

35

The young gentleman

It was believed by some that after the death of Oliver Cromwell the fabric of the commonwealth would be torn apart; the centre would not hold. Yet the succession of his oldest son, Richard Cromwell, passed off without any commotion. No great public mourning was aroused by his father's death, and very little debate was instituted about his role or his legacy. John Evelyn witnessed the Protector's funeral where 'there were none that cried but dogs, which the soldiers hooted away with a barbarous noise, drinking and taking tobacco in the streets as they went'.

Richard Cromwell was a modest and self-effacing man with none of the natural authority or commanding presence of his father. He was, according to an appendix to James Mackintosh's *Eminent British Statesmen*, 'a person well skilled in hawking, hunting, horse-racing, with other sports and pastimes'. Allusions were made to 'Queen Dick'. He admitted soon after his accession that 'it might have pleased God, and the nation too, to have chosen out a person more fit and able for this work than I am'.

Yet almost at once he was engaged in the defining question of the moment. Should the army, or parliament, control this new gentry republic? Some of the army officers had already been demanding that they should have a commander-in-chief separate from the Protector, which meant in practice that they rejected the authority of the civil state. These officers were accustomed to meet at Wallingford House, the residence of Major-General Charles Fleetwood, who was their natural leader. Richard Cromwell, or 'the young gentleman' as he was known to some of them, did not concede their demand.

His position was strengthened in the election of a new parliament at the beginning of 1659, when a majority of the members seem to have been moderate or conservative men who supported the government of the protectorate and disliked the pretensions of the army; some of them were secret royalists, sustained by the impression or belief that the nation was with them. They demanded that all political activity in the army should come to an end, which at once aroused Fleetwood and his supporters. The soldiers refused to obey the order, and the few colonels who supported it found themselves abandoned by their men. Fleetwood, the regiments of the army with him at St James's, demanded that parliament be dismissed forthwith.

The impasse might have signalled the beginning of another war, but Richard Cromwell took fright at the prospect. He is reported to have said that 'for the preservation of my greatness (which is a burthen to me) I will not have one drop of blood spilt'. So he dissolved parliament and then, towards the end of May, abdicated his post as Protector. John Evelyn wrote in his diary that 'several pretenders and parties strive for the government: all anarchy and confusion; Lord have mercy on us!'

The leaders of the army decided against all precedent to revive the Rump Parliament that had been dissolved by Oliver Cromwell in the spring of 1653. In the beginning it had comprised some 200 members but the number had now fallen to 50. On their reappearance, however, they refused to be cowed by the authorities of the army and set about to reassert their power by granting the commission of officers to their Speaker rather than to Fleetwood. An open division between the two competing powers could not long be delayed.

A rebellion against the army, organized by a coalition of royalists and disaffected Presbyterians, was effectively put down in the summer by General John Lambert, who had returned from his retirement to play once more a leading role in military affairs, yet within two months he and eight other officers were dismissed by parliament for promoting a petition deemed to be seditious. Lambert then in turn expelled the Rump and instituted a very short reign of the army. A 'committee of safety' was formed consisting of twenty-three officers and committed to govern without the rule of 'a single person' and without a House of Lords.

The army itself was divided. One of its most senior officers, General George Monck, had been given the task by Oliver Cromwell of governing Scotland; from this vantage he looked upon the bewildering events in England with a wary and suspicious eye. He had thought of supporting Richard Cromwell but had then drawn back. He was considered by some to be a secret royalist. Now he refused to support Lambert and Fleetwood, but instead demanded the recall of the parliament so recently expelled.

It might seem that anarchy had been loosed upon the world, but the world went its own way. A contemporary, quoted in the Clarendon State Papers, observed that in London 'in all the hurly burly the streets were full, every one going about their business as if not at all concerned, and when the parliament sent unto the city to relieve them, they answered that they would not meddle with the dispute'. John Milton was not so sanguine and wrote that it was 'most illegal and scandalous, I fear me barbarous, or rather scarce to be exampled among any barbarians, that a paid army should . . . thus subdue the supreme power that set them up'.

Lambert was also forced to confront divisions among his own soldiers; they declared that they themselves would not fight Monck or anyone else, but would form a ring in which their officers could contest one against another in some form of prize fight; the troops stationed at Plymouth, and the entire fleet, then declared the Rump as the least worst alternative to unconstitutional military rule. They desired a justly established government as well as freedom of worship. On 24 December Fleetwood, declaring that 'God had spit in his face', delivered the keys of parliament to its Speaker, William Lenthall.

On that day the troopers now loyal to parliament marched to Lenthall's house in Chancery Lane, where they pledged to live and die with the assembly at Westminster. Lenthall, thus encouraged, decided to reconvene parliament on 26 December; the leading officers no longer had the will, or the support, to discourage him. On 4 January 1660, Lambert, who had made an unsuccessful attempt to march north and confront Monck, was now obliged to submit himself to the restored parliament; the members ordered him 'to one of his dwelling houses most remote from the City of London, in order to the quiet and peace of this commonwealth'. The confusion and uncertainty were the direct effect of Oliver Cromwell's inability to create a stable governance. Hartgill Baron, a royalist supporter, wrote that 'all things here at present are in so great a cloud that the most quick-sighted or wisest man living is not able to make a judgment of what may be the issue'. There were many, like him, who now looked to the king beyond the sea for deliverance from the chaos around them.

General Monck, at the end of 1659, began marching south from Edinburgh with 8,000 men. His intentions were not clear, perhaps not even to himself; he said only that he had come into England in order to maintain the commonwealth. He may have believed that the army's seizure of power had been misguided, but he was so taciturn and secretive that it is hard to be sure even of this. Pepys described him as 'a dull heavy man'.

When he arrived in London at the beginning of February many citizens called for 'a free parliament'; that meant the removal of the Rump and a return to the duly elected authority that had been purged by Colonel Pride eleven years before. Parliament responded by ordering Monck to enter the city in order to restore public order and to arrest its leading opponents. On 9 February Monck obeyed by removing all the gates, portcullises, posts and chains that were the symbols of the city's strength. The citizens believed that they had been betrayed and seem to have been beset with fear and dismay. It may have been that Monck deliberately set out to demonstrate the lengths to which parliament would go to protect its authority, and thus bring the people over to his side. No certainty is possible in the matter.

Two days later, however, the unfathomable Monck wrote a letter to the Rump with the order to dissolve itself and to call for fresh elections. The effect was immediate and profound; according to one pamphleteer, Roger L'Estrange, the people 'made bonfires very thick in every street and bells ringing in every church and the greatest acclamations of joy that could possibly be expressed'. Rumps of beef were roasted on every street-corner; rumps were tied on sticks and carried about; a great rump was turned on a spit on Ludgate Hill. Pepys reported that boys 'do now cry "kiss my parliament" instead of "kiss my arse", so great and general a contempt is the Rump come to . . .' Ten days later Monck made a short cut by readmitting all the members of the Long Parliament who had before been excluded. These had been largely Presbyterian in temper and had been removed precisely because of their willingness to negotiate a settlement with Charles I.

The newly restored parliament promptly decided to erase all the proceedings in the aftermath of Pride's Purge, which meant that it now resumed supreme authority in obtaining a settlement with the king. Lambert was sent to the Tower along with other members of the previous regime. On 6 March Pepys noted that 'everybody now drinks the king's health without fear, whereas before it was very private that a man dare do it'.

Charles II was still uncertain. He was not sure what Monck intended, and feared that the general might still set himself up as Lord Protector; there was even talk that Richard Cromwell might be asked to return to the post. Other supporters of the king did not trust Monck but believed that he would, in the old phrase, 'play fast and loose'. The king had experienced so many false hopes that now he could do nothing but wait. If he took any premature action, it might ruin everything. Monck himself was obliged to proceed very carefully. He may have surmised that the restoration of the king would be the best possible outcome for the nation but he could not yet fully support the popular mood; he had to maintain the unity of his army, and could not afford to alienate those who were still called 'commonwealth men'. He did not want to be suspected at this stage, as it was said, of 'carrying the king in his belly'. A month or two later it was reported that Monck was determined either to restore the king by his own actions, and thus reap the subsequent rewards, or to prevent Charles's return.

In the middle of March 1660, parliament dissolved itself and prepared the nation for a new assembly in the following month. The Long Parliament had finally come to an end, after a haphazard and interrupted rule of a little over nineteen years. In this month a known royalist supporter, Sir John Grenville, was smuggled into St James's Palace for a clandestine interview with Monck; Monck did not wish to write anything down but he intimated to Grenville, through an intermediary, that it might be fit and proper for the king to send him a letter setting out the intentions of the royal party. The general would then keep the letter in trust and reveal its contents at an appropriate time. By this happy subterfuge he might be able to ease the king's path to England. In another account of this secret affair Grenville had brought a letter from Charles to the general, offering Monck high office in a royal administration; the general replied that he had always intended to restore Charles. Whatever the exact circumstances it is clear that the king and the general were coming to an understanding.

At the beginning of April the king issued a 'declaration' from his temporary home at Breda in the Protestant Netherlands; no doubt he had consulted Monck's wishes or suggestions in their clandestine consultations. The king offered a free pardon and amnesty to anyone who swore allegiance to the Crown, with the exception of those who had voted for the late king's death; this was the only way of closing the chapter on the legacy of the civil war. Among other provisions was the promise of religious toleration to all peaceful Christians. Only thus could the struggles between Anglicans, Presbyterians and sectarians be resolved. Yet the king left all these measures to the final decision of parliament; this was seen by many to be a conciliatory gesture, but it also meant that parliament rather than king now incurred the responsibility of what might befall.

So all was set fair for the first elected parliament in almost two decades. It was known as the Convention Parliament since, in theory, no parliament could be called without a writ from the king to that effect. It soon became clear that many of a royalist persuasion had been elected; the king's friends had returned to Westminster. Charles's declaration was read to both Houses of Parliament and was received with enthusiasm. On the morning of 1 May the Lords, now with many royalist peers readmitted on the orders of General Monck, declared that 'according to the ancient and fundamental laws of this kingdom, the government is, and ought to be, by King, Lords and Commons'; the Commons assented that afternoon. It was now generally believed that a stable parliamentary government could only be established upon royal power. The republic had come to an end, and the aspirations of the army had been defeated.

On May Day, the once prohibited maypoles were set up all over the country. When the vice-chancellor and beadles of Oxford university tried to saw down a pole set up outside the Bear Inn, they were attacked by a crowd and beaten off. Pepys reported 'great joy all yesterday at London, and at night more bonfires than ever, and ringing of bells, and drinking of the king's health upon their knees in the streets, which methinks is a little too much'.

Charles II had removed to The Hague, where six members of the Lords and twelve members of the Commons were ushered into his presence; they presented the humble invitation and supplication of the parliament that his majesty should return and take the government of the kingdom into his hands. They also presented him with the sum of £50,000 to expedite his journey. Fourteen London citizens then came forward and offered the king a further £10,000. The city had not in previous years been wholly favourable to the royalist cause, and so its penitence was doubly appreciated. The king told them that he entertained a particular affection for London, as it was his place of birth, and knighted all of the citizens.

He set sail for England on 24 May, having embarked on a vessel newly christened *The Prince*; early on the morning of 26 May he arrived at Dover, where he knelt on the shore to give thanks. Monck was waiting for him, kneeling on the pier. The mayor of Dover presented him with a Bible; the king accepted it, saying 'it was the thing that he loved above all things in the world'. We may excuse him on this occasion of any attempt at irony.

Monck and the king travelled together to Canterbury where Charles listened to the Anglican service, according to the Book of Common Prayer, in the cathedral. Wherever he went he was surrounded by crowds. He had time to write to his youngest sister, Henrietta Anne, that 'my head is so dreadfully stunned with the acclamations of the people that I know not whether I am writing sense or nonsense'. From here the king progressed towards London to confirm and celebrate the fact of the Restoration.

36

Oh, prodigious change!

The return of Charles II was greeted with jubilation that was for the most part sincere. At Blackheath, just before entering the capital, he was met by what one newsletter described as 'a kind of rural triumph, expressed by the country swains, in a morris dance with the old music of the tabor and pipe'. It was believed that the restoration of the king would be accompanied by the revival of the old customs and traditions of the nation.

He rode in a dark suit through all the pomp of the procession, from the Strand to Westminster, raising his hat with its crimson plume time and time again. The streets were covered in flowers, and the houses hung with ornate tapestries; the sound of bells and trumpets mingled with the greetings of the crowd. John Evelyn noted in his entry for 29 May 1660, that 'I stood in the Strand and beheld it, and blessed God. And all this was done without one drop of blood shed, and by that very army which rebelled against him; but it was the Lord's doing, for such a restoration was never mentioned in any history, ancient or modern, since the return of the Jews from the Babylonish captivity; nor so joyful a day and so bright ever seen in this nation, this happening when to expect or effect it was past all human policy.'

As he passed under the gateway of the Banqueting House he glanced upwards to the site of his father's execution and at this point he came close to tears. When he was placed beneath the canopy of state such was the disorder and confusion that the king himself seemed to be in a daze. Yet he soon recovered himself. He had been greeted with such delight and enthusiasm that he remarked, with a smile, that he should have come back sooner. It was the wit of a man who had no illusions about human nature.

It was the king's thirtieth birthday, but he seemed older. His hair was already streaked with grey; men did not yet, in this period, wear wigs. The years of exile had made him lean, accentuating his height of 6 feet 2 inches. One contemporary, Sir Samuel Tuke, observed that 'his face is rather grave than severe, which is very much softened whensoever he speaks; his complexion is somewhat dark but much enlightened by his eyes, which are quick and sparkling'. With his large nose and heavy jaw, he was not handsome. He looked sad, and rather lugubrious, with a hint of dissipation and a trace of cruelty. 'Oddsfish,' he used to say, 'I am ugly.' 'Oddsfish' was a corruption of 'God's flesh'.

In this heady period he was affable to all he met, even to those whom he suspected of being his secret enemies. Yet behind this assumption of good humour he was calculating and even cunning. He had been brought up in the hard school of exile and, as he used to say, at all costs he wished to avoid 'going on my travels' once again. So his first decisions were made out of policy towards his erstwhile opponents rather than of gratitude to his friends. He believed that all men were governed by self-interest and therefore was not reluctant to consult his own.

When the king returned to his palace at Whitehall, it was much as he had remembered it from his childhood; it survived as a maze of a place with closets, cubby-holes, back staircases, corridors, corners and courtyards; it had grown piece by piece out of a variety of different dwellings and encompassed chapels, tennis courts and bowling greens. It covered 23 acres and contained approximately 2,000 rooms, some of which flooded when the Thames rose too high. The king loved the place, however, and rarely left it during the first full year of his reign. The great court as well as some of the terraces and galleries were in effect open to the public, and these areas were thronged with suitors hoping to gain the king's favour; others came simply to watch the splendour of majesty.

The king dined in public at midday, but he managed his business in the privacy of his bedchamber. There was also a secret closet beyond the chamber, to which few were ever admitted; soon enough this would testify to the king's penchant for secrecy and intrigue. The marquis of Halifax noted that 'he had backstairs to convey informations to him, as well as for other uses'; we may surmise what those other 'uses' were.

There was space enough at the palace for all of the king's principal councillors. Chief among them was a man who had been at his side for the years of exile. Edward Hyde, later to become the 1st earl of Clarendon and author of the monumental *History of the Rebellion*, was austere and assiduous even if, as he wrote himself, he was 'in his nature inclined to pride and passion'; he had a high opinion of his own judgement and rectitude, even to the point of lecturing his master on his shortcomings. His status was soon enhanced when his daughter, Mary Hyde, was married to the king's brother James, duke of York. It had been discovered that she was pregnant by him, prompting Samuel Pepys to recall how a wit once observed that 'he that doth get a wench with child and marries her afterward it is as if a man should shit in his hat and then clap it upon his head'.

Hyde, as lord chancellor, was one of a group of six confidants who formed what was called a 'secret committee' that, in the words of Hyde himself, was appointed by the king 'to consult all his affairs before they came to the public debate'. They were assisted by a privy council of some thirty to forty members, twelve of whom had carried arms against the king's father. Charles had decided to accommodate the recent past.

The king was at first diligent in his duties but he soon tired of the details of his administration. He grew easily bored at the meetings of his council and disliked the paperwork of office; it was reported by the marquis of Halifax that his ministers 'had to administer business to him as doctors do physic, wrap it up in something to make it less unpleasant'. It was also a convenient way for him to disown responsibility for certain policies. As he once said, 'My words are my own but my acts are my ministers'.

The sale and ownership of land were pressing issues. Many of the royalists had been forced to sell their estates in order to pay fines or to meet the 'decimation tax'. They now petitioned for their lands to be returned to them, but parliament decided that it was not in its power to reverse what had been in theory voluntary sales. The decision caused much resentment, and contributed to the feeling that the king had turned his back on his former supporters.

That feeling was compounded by one of the measures of the Convention Parliament in this year. An Act of Indemnity and Oblivion was passed, by means of which any crime or treason committed 'by virtue or colour' of parliamentary or regal authority over the last twenty-two years was to be 'pardoned . . . and put in utter oblivion'. All the rage of the past was therefore to be redeemed or, at least, forgotten. The measure incensed those royalists who believed themselves to have been injured by the actions of the military regime, and it was remarked that the king was consenting to an indemnity for his enemies and to oblivion for his friends.

The regicides, those who had signed the death warrant of the late king, were excepted from the indemnity. In the autumn of the year, in one of the few acts of vengeance perpetrated by the new administration, ten of these malefactors were hanged, drawn and quartered; they met their deaths with defiance and one of them had the strength, as his naked body was sliced open before disembowelling, to strike the executioner. Richard Cromwell had already fled from England to lead a life of decent obscurity in Europe. Charles was inclined to clemency, however, and when nineteen other regicides were about to be brought to trial for their lives he wrote to Clarendon that 'I must confess that I am weary of hanging except upon new offenses; let it sleep'.

It was a nice matter also to deal with the army. Under the command of Monck it had helped to place the king on his throne, but it might equally well be used to eject him from it. A poll tax was reintroduced to fund the payments of the soldiers' arrears and, by the autumn, they were retired; they returned, where possible, to their old homes and occupations. They were allowed to keep their swords, however, and the more radical of them still maintained 'the good old cause' of the republic. At the end of the year a declaration banned them from assembling in London, but in truth they posed no serious threat. Most of them melted away causing the preacher,

Richard Baxter, to observe that 'thus did God do a more wonderful work in the dissolving of this army than any of their greatest victories'.

Yet as always the cause of religion was pre-eminent, with a division of the clergy between those who avowed the Anglican persuasion and those who adopted the puritan or Presbyterian case. There was no particular example from the 'defender of the faith'. It is still difficult to write with any clarity of the king's religion. He died after being received into the Catholic Church, and it is possible that he had become a secret member of that faith even while in exile. Yet perhaps he did not have the conviction to espouse any particular creed; it was not his business to be pious but to be politic. The various forms of religion held no real interest for him and he used to tease his rigidly Catholic brother, James, about the scandalous lives of the popes. He was apt to say, of his own sexual escapades, that God would not damn a man for seeking a little pleasure. He had a light heart and an easy conscience.

Within a month of his return to England, however, Charles was busily engaged in the ceremony of 'the king's touch' whereby through the agency of God he could heal those afflicted with scrofula or 'the king's evil'. It was a signal instance of the divine dispensation that had made him the Lord's anointed and, as a spectacle of majesty, he deployed it frequently. Once a month, until the end of his reign, hundreds of scrofulous people flocked to the Banqueting House where with patience and dignity he laid his hands upon them.

The old order had been reasserted, but it had been subtly changed by the recent broils. The French ambassador, for example, wrote to Louis XIV that 'this government has a monarchical appearance because there is a king, but at bottom it is very far from being a monarchy'. The power of parliament had increased immeasurably after its success in the civil war; it was impossible for the king to raise money from his subjects, or to arrest any person, without its consent. Charles also now depended for his finances on the annual sum assigned to him by the members at Westminster.

The king's power had also diminished in other ways. The Star Chamber would not be revived. Any attempt at a large standing army would be treated with grave suspicion. The influence of the

City had also grown, and from the events of these years we may date the true beginning of a commercial and mercantile state.

The rule that had once radiated from one person, whether Stuart or Cromwell, had become more balanced and diffused. The departments of the two secretaries of state, devoted to the administration of domestic as well as foreign affairs, were established; permanent boards were also created for such business as the assignment and collection of taxation. The treasury broke away from royal control and became responsible for approving all payments. Thirty committees were soon in session and, later in 1660, a council of trade and a council of foreign plantations were at work.

Yet this was not a bureaucracy in the modern sense, since it was based upon patronage and the lavish giving or taking of 'fees' for services rendered. Many of the officials were not technically the servants of the state but were paid by more senior officials. The more important posts were considered to be private property, to be kept for life and subsequently sold to a close relative or to the highest bidder. It was not necessarily a corrupt system, since it represented the only way in which government could be made to work.

The central differences between the two epochs of republic and restored monarchy were less palpable. The people put no faith in paper constitutions, such as Cromwell had imposed; the religious dimension of public affairs was no longer as relevant as once it was, and piety eventually became a matter of private conscience. There would be no more zealotry at Westminster. Political theory more frequently became the preserve of philosophers, such as Locke and Hobbes, rather than of theologians. This may be the reason for the suggestion of many contemporaries that religious belief itself was in decline. Thomas Sprat, the chronicler of the Royal Society, noted that 'the influence which Christianity once obtained on men's minds is now prodigiously decayed'.

The certainties of the religious wars, if we may call them that, had begun to dissolve within a new public discourse that favoured reason and civility. A man might now gather his opinions from the coffee-house rather than from the church or conventicle (in the year of the king's restoration the drinks of tea, coffee and chocolate are first mentioned). The king was obliged by parliament to impose

Anglicanism upon the nation, as we shall see, but the puritans and dissenters could not in the end be silenced. Compulsion was eventually to be replaced by persuasion.

The formal coronation of Charles II was delayed until St George's Day, 23 April 1661, just two weeks before the opening of his first parliament. Charles II was the last monarch ever to ride in state through the streets of London on the day preceding the event, since he knew well enough that ceremony was at the centre of kingship. He ordered that all the ancient records should be studied so that the traditional solemnity of the occasion should be maintained; the crown jewels had been broken up and sold after his father's execution, but he ordered that a new set should replicate the old in every minute particular. He wore robes of gold and silver, together with a crimson cap of velvet lined with ermine. The first coronation mugs, sold as souvenirs, are a measure of the popularity of the occasion. The day itself was serene and fair but Pepys observed in his diary that, immediately after the ceremony, 'it fell a-raining and thundering and lightning as I have not seen it do for some years'. Some obvious prognostications were made.

Parliament met on 8 May; the proximity of the two occasions was a tribute to the notion of 'the crown in parliament', the title of supreme power in England. Since half of the new members came from families that had suffered in the royalist cause, it became known as 'the Cavalier Parliament'. They were for the most part young men but the king remarked that 'he would keep them till they got beards'; he fulfilled the promise by maintaining this parliament for a further eighteen years.

They of course supported his cause, and that of the bishops, but they were most intent on maintaining the privileges of the gentry from which they had largely come. The Presbyterians were in a small minority, and were in no position to check or obstruct what might be described as the conservative tide. In a series of Acts, over a period of five years, parliament enforced Anglican supremacy upon the nation. Two weeks after it met the 'solemn league and covenant', which had pledged the nation to a Presbyterian settlement with Scotland, was summarily burned by the common hangman at Westminster and other places in the city. John Evelyn remarked, 'Oh, prodigious change!'

By the Corporation Act of 1661, the municipal leaders of town or city were confined to those who received communion by the rites of the Church of England; the mayors and aldermen were also obliged to take an oath of allegiance and affirm that it was not lawful to take up arms against the king. The Act was designed to remove those of a nonconformist persuasion whose loyalty might be suspect.

An Act of Uniformity was passed in the following year which restricted the ministry to those who had been ordained by a bishop and who accepted the provisions of the Book of Common Prayer. These conditions effectively disqualified 1,700 puritan clergy, who were therefore ejected from their livings. It was the most sudden alteration in the religious history of the nation. Some said that it was an act of revenge by the Anglicans after their persecution during the days of the commonwealth, but it may also have been a means whereby the royalist gentry regained control of their parishes.

Some of the ejected clergy were reduced to poverty and the utmost distress. One of their number, Richard Baxter, recalled that 'their congregations had enough to do . . . to help them out of prisons, or to maintain them there'. John Bunyan, for example, was imprisoned in Bedford Prison for nonconformist preaching. He wrote that 'the parting with my wife and poor children hath often been to me in this place as the pulling of the flesh from the bones'; yet in his prison cell he dreamed of eternity.

Much popular derision was directed at the godly ministers. The dissenting preachers were mocked and hooted at in the street. Ben Jonson's *Bartholomew Fair*, in which puritans were roundly scorned, was revived with great popular success. The Quakers in particular were badly treated and, during the reign of Charles, 4,000 were consigned to prison; Clarendon had said that they were 'a sort of people upon whom tenderness and lenity do not at all prevail'.

Yet the rigour of the new law was averted in some areas. Many Presbyterians or 'church puritans' were more flexible in obeying the law; the clergy of these congregations might well retain their livings in acts of subtle compromise. Some authorities were in any case reluctant to enforce the law, and the ecclesiastical courts were not always efficient.

In two further Acts of subsequent years the attendance at religious assemblies, other than those of the official Church, was punished by imprisonment; no puritan clergyman or schoolmaster could come within 5 miles of a town or city. These measures did not reflect the king's promise of toleration for all honest Christians, as he had announced in the 'declaration' of Breda before sailing to England, but it is likely that he was being pressed by the young men of parliament; he acceded to their demands because he did not wish to lose their support in the funding of his revenues.

It would in the end prove impossible to subdue the whole body of nonconformist worshippers, now bound together by the pressure of shared persecution; but, by attempting to impose Anglican worship, the members of the 'Cavalier Parliament' opened up the great fissure between Anglicanism and dissenting faiths that would never be resolved. An informal network of meetings brought together Independents, Baptists and Presbyterians in sharp distinction to the established Church. No national religious settlement had been achieved. The days of the disputes between church and chapel would soon come.

Other measures followed in what was a series of busy parliamentary sessions. A new 'hearth tax' was passed in the spring of 1662, with a charge of 1 shilling for each hearth to be paid twice a year; the response was clamant and immediate. A saying passed through the streets of London to the effect that 'the bishops get all, the courtiers spend all, the citizens pay for all, the king neglects all and the devil takes all'. A Licensing Act was approved, by which it was ordered that no book might be published without the approval of an official censor; this was largely directed against nonconformist writings that would now come under the gaze of the bishop of London and the archbishop of Canterbury. The atmosphere of free debate that had pertained for much of Cromwell's rule came to an end.

These measures against 'toleration' came at a price. Pepys reported that all of the 'fanatics' were discontented and 'that the king do take away their liberty of conscience'; he deplored 'the height of the bishops who I fear will ruin all again'. The puritan clergy were ordered to abandon their livings on 24 August 1662, St Bartholomew's Day, and in many places the congregations came in great numbers to hear and lament their 'farewell sermons'. More spirited protest was also expected. Ever since the king's arrival in England minor uprisings by 'fanatics' had disturbed the peace, and through the spring and summer of 1662 fears rose of some concerted puritan resistance. A general rising was supposed to be planned for August, and from all over the country came reports of seditious meetings and treasonable speeches. Lord Fauconberg, lord-lieutenant of the North Riding of Yorkshire, claimed that in Lancashire 'not one man in the whole county intends to conform'; reports of the same nature came from his own county of Yorkshire and the West Country, while London was known to be the spiritual home of zealotry and sectarianism. The lords-lieutenant of the various counties were told to watch 'all those known to be of the Republic party'.

Yet these apprehensions were generally without foundation. The Anglican Church was now supreme under the leadership of the cleric who in 1663 was consecrated as archbishop of Canterbury; Gilbert Burnet wrote of Archbishop Sheldon that 'he seemed not to have a deep sense of religion, if any at all, and spoke of it most commonly as of an engine of government and a matter of policy'. The bishops, for example, had been returned to their seats in the House of Lords where they could exert a strong influence upon national legislation; yet it was also true that parliament, and not the Church, had taken control of the nature and direction of the national religion.

The actual faith of the people was no doubt as inchoate and confused as ever. One Lancastrian apprentice, Roger Lowe, recorded in 1663 that 'I was pensive and sad and went into the town field and prayed to the Lord, and I hope the Lord heard'.

At a meeting of the council, just after parliament had been summoned, Charles told his advisers that he had decided to marry the infanta of Portugal, Catherine of Braganza; he had already announced his preferences when he said that 'I hate Germans, or princesses of cold countries'. The mother of the intended bride, the queen regent of Portugal, had also offered £800,000 together with her colonial territories of Bombay and Tangier in order to sweeten the arrangement. English merchants were also to be permitted to trade freely throughout the Portuguese Empire, thus assisting England in its rivalry with the Dutch. In return Portugal wished to recruit English soldiers in its war with the neighbouring power of Spain, which was eager to take back its rebellious province. A marriage could accomplish a great deal.

Another matrimonial alliance completed what may be called the 'foreign policy' of Charles. His sister Henrietta was married off to the homosexual brother of Louis XIV and helped to inaugurate closer relations between France and England that came in the end to be too close. Louis XIV was feared and distrusted for his attempt to raise himself up as 'universal monarch' in the face of Spanish decline; nevertheless Charles admired his absolutist and centralized rule that he had some obscure hope of emulating.

The king travelled down to Portsmouth to meet his bride, and reported to Clarendon that 'her face is not so exact as to be called a beauty though her eyes are excellent good, and not anything in her face that in the least degree can shock one'. This may not amount to a ringing endorsement but, for a royal union, it was fairly satisfactory. Her teeth stuck out a little, and her hair was swept to the side in the Portuguese fashion. The king is said privately to have remarked, 'Gentlemen, you have brought me a bat.' One of Catherine's first requests was for a cup of tea, then a novelty. Instead she was offered a glass of ale.

She had arrived with what one contemporary, the comte de Gramont, described as 'six frights, who called themselves maids-of-honour and a duenna, another monster, who took the title of governess to those extraordinary beauties'. Much fun was also made of their great fardingales, or hooped skirts of whalebone beneath their dresses.

Catherine had some formidable competition. The king was known to be an insatiable and compulsive philanderer, and Pepys calculated that he had had seventeen mistresses even before the Restoration. John Dryden, in *Absalom and Achitophel*, characterized him thus:

> Then, Israel's monarch, after Heaven's own heart,
> His vigorous warmth did variously impart

To wives and slaves: and, wide as his command,
Scatter'd his Maker's image through the land.

Or, as the earl of Rochester put it more bluntly,

Restless he rolls from whore to whore,
A merry monarch, scandalous and poor.

By a previous lover, Lucy Walter, he had a son who would in 1663 become duke of Monmouth. His present mistress was Barbara Palmer, whose husband had been ennobled as the earl of Castlemaine; Lady Castlemaine soon became indispensable to his pleasure, and it was reported by Pepys that she ruled the king by employing 'all the tricks of Aretino [a poet of obscenity] . . . in which he is too able having a large—' The rest is silence. The lady was already heavily pregnant by the time that Catherine arrived in England.

The king's appetite for Lady Castlemaine was such that he appointed her to be his wife's lady-of-the-bedchamber. Catherine objected to the convenient arrangement, and her anger led to an estrangement between the royal couple. The new queen of England was receiving company at Hampton Court when her husband led Lady Castlemaine into the room; she may not have correctly heard her name since she received her calmly enough but, on being made aware of the lady's identity, she burst into tears before fainting. Clarendon was used by the king as a mediator and, in the end, the queen gave way and welcomed her rival.

In truth she had become devoted to her husband, and in no way wished to alienate his affections. She could do nothing, however, to fulfil her primary role; she seemed to be incapable of bearing children. It was not for want of trying. An Italian visitor at the court, Lorenzo Magalotti, heard that the queen was 'unusually sensitive to pleasure' and that after intercourse 'blood comes from her genital parts in such great abundance that it does not stop for several days'.

In time the king would become enamoured of another mistress, Frances Stewart, of whom the comte de Gramont said that it would be difficult to imagine less brain combined with more beauty. She was the model, complete with helmet and trident, for the figure of Britannia on British coins. Charles was always in love with someone or other. By seventeen of his known mistresses he had thirteen illegitimate children, some of whom became dukes or earls. The story of Nell Gwynn has often been told.

The royal court itself had become the object of much scandal and remark. Macaulay, in an essay for the *Edinburgh Review*, remarked of a no doubt exaggerated example that 'a dead child is found in the palace, the offspring of some maid of honour by some courtier, or perhaps by Charles himself. The whole flight of pandars and buffoons pounces upon it and carries it to the royal laboratory, where his majesty, after a brutal jest, dissects it for the amusement of the assembly, and probably of its father among the rest.'

The rule of the saints had been replaced by the rule of the sinners who seemed to compete with each other in drunkenness and debauchery. When a bishop preached in the royal chapel against 'mistaken jollity' the congregation laughed at him. When the court visited Oxford a scholar, Anthony Wood, observed that 'they were nasty and beastly, leaving at their departure their excrements in every corner, in chimneys, studies, coalhouses, cellars. Rude, rough, whoremongers; vain, empty, careless.' And of course they took their morals and manners from their royal leader. Other royal courts were no doubt characterized by profligacy and sexual licence – the court of William II comes to mind – but never had they been so widely observed and criticized.

A circle of 'wits' emerged around the king; among them were George Villiers, duke of Buckingham, and Charles, Sir Sedley. They were accustomed to meet in the apartments of the king's latest lover or in the lodgings of the notorious William Chiffinch who became 'keeper of the king's private closet', where their most notable contribution to court life was a number of highly obscene poems and stories. Their wit was manifested in verbal extravagance and dexterity, in puns and allusions, or, as Robert Boyle put it, 'a subtlety in conceiving things . . . a quickness and neatness in expressing them'.

There was much to ridicule. In the summer of 1663 Lord Sedley appeared naked on the balcony of the Cock Inn in Bow Street where, according to Samuel Pepys, he proceeded to enact 'all the postures of lust and buggery that could be imagined, and abusing of scripture'. He delivered a mock sermon in which he declared that 'he hath to sell such a powder as should make all the cunts in town run after him'. After the recital 'he took a glass of wine and washed his prick in it and then drank it off; and then took another, and drank the king's health'. He then took down his breeches and proceeded to 'excrementize'.

On the following day he was brought before the chief justice, who asked him if he had ever read Henry Peacham's *The Complete Gentleman*. He was then bound over to keep the king's peace on a bond of £500, whereupon he said that 'he thought he was the first man that paid for shitting'. The bond was paid with money borrowed from the king himself.

37

On the road

On the course of their journey Faithful and Christian came upon Talkative, a gentleman who 'was something more comely at a distance than at hand'. Then he conversed with his fellow travellers.

> *Talkative:* I will talk of things heavenly, or things earthly; things moral, or things evangelical; things sacred, or things profane; things past, or things to come; things foreign, or things at home; things more essential, or things circumstantial; provided that all be done to our profit.

He walked out of their way for a little, whereupon Christian and Faithful began to discuss their new companion.

Faithful: Do you know him, then?
Christian: Know him! Yes, better than he knows himself.
Faithful: Pray what is he?
Christian: His name is *Talkative*; he dwelleth in our town. I wonder that you should be a stranger to him, only I consider that our town is large.
Faithful: Whose son is he? And whereabout doth he dwell?
Christian: He is the son of one *Say-well*; he dwelt in *Prating*

Row; and is known of all that are acquainted with him, by the name of *Talkative* in *Prating Row*; and notwithstanding his fine tongue, he is but a sorry fellow.

Faithful: Well, he seems to be a very pretty man.

Christian: That is, to them who have not thorough acquaintance with him, for he is best abroad, near home he is ugly enough.

John Bunyan's *The Pilgrim's Progress* has often been characterized as the first English novel; it is as if he had the actual characters before him, in imagination, and simply wrote down what he heard; he also employed the plain speech of the time, to the extent that we can hear the ordinary people of the late seventeenth century talking to one another. Yet *The Pilgrim's Progress* is more than a novel.

John Bunyan, born in Bedfordshire in 1628, gathered the rudiments of learning while young but may have been largely self-educated; he was thoroughly acquainted with the vernacular Bible and with Foxe's *Acts and Monuments*, but in his youth he read the ballads and romances of the time. He joined the New Model Army at the age of fifteen, but it is not clear whether he saw any active service before his disbandment three years later.

After his marriage to a poor woman he entered a period of spiritual struggle, documented by *Grace Abounding*, in which he fell into despair and fearfulness before being tempted by false hope. He was still afflicted by anxiety and depression when in 1655 he joined a separatist church in Bedford; he began his preaching before that congregation where slowly he found strength and confidence. His ministry widened, therefore, and he came into conflict with the authorities. In 1661 he was consigned to Bedford Prison where, refusing to renounce his right to preach, he remained for the next eleven years. He wrote many books and treatises during this period, but none more popular and significant than *The Pilgrim's Progress*.

In part it might be read as an account of any seventeenth-century journey, over rough roads, encumbered by mud and puddles, endangered by mires and ditches, pits and deep holes. The travellers must sometimes reconnoitre steep hills where they may catch 'a slip or two'. Sometimes they go 'out of the way' and among 'turnings' and 'windings' lose themselves; 'wherefore, at last, lighting under a little shelter, they sat down there till the day brake; but being weary they fell asleep'. We hear the dogs barking at their presence. If they are unfortunate they may be taken for vagrants, and placed in the stocks or in the 'cage'. If they are fortunate they will find lodgings on the course of their journey, where they will be asked, 'What will you have?'

They must also face the dangers of robbers waiting for them along the road.

> So they came up all to him, and with threatening language bid him stand. At this *Little-Faith* looked as white as a clout, and had neither power to fight nor fly. Then said *Faint-Heart*, Deliver thy purse . . . Then he cried out, Thieves, thieves!

In the face of such dangers some travellers formed a company for the sake of friendship and security.

'Then I hope we may have your good company.'

'With a very good will, will I be your companion.'

'Come on, then, let us go together . . .'

Such snatches of conversation are often heard on the road. They are eager to meet one another and, leaning upon their staves, they talk. 'Is this the way?' 'You are just in your way.' 'How far is it thither?' 'Whence came you?' 'Have you got into the way?' One will greet another with 'What have you met with?' or 'What have you seen?' 'Whither are you going?' 'Back, back.' Some travellers want 'to make a short cut of it, and to climb over the wall'. What does it matter how they reach their destination? 'If we are in, we are in.'

The vividness of the prose is derived from its immediacy and contemporaneity. 'I met him once in the streets,' Faithful says of Pliable, 'but he leered away on the other side, as one ashamed of what he had done; so I spake not to him.' Christian says to a man, 'What art thou?' and is told, 'I am what I was not once.' He tells Hope, 'I would, as the saying is, have given my life for a penny . . . this man was one of the weak, and therefore he went to the wall . . . And when a man is down, you know, what can he do?' The simplicity and vigour have been tested on the anvil of suffering experience but they also derive from Bunyan's reading of the vernacular Bible. The words seem to come to him instinctively but they have absorbed the cadence and imagery of the Scriptures.

They come also from Bunyan's identity as a Calvinist. To read *The Pilgrim's Progress* is to return to that world of fierce struggle and debate in which deeply held religious faith was the only stay against the dark. Bunyan is nothing like the caricatures of Tribulation Wholesome, Snarl, or Zeal-of-the-Land-Busy, in seventeenth-century drama. He is too desperate and determined to be that. Christian decides to embark upon his journey alone 'because none of my neighbours saw their danger as I saw mine'. This is the heart of it, this awareness of imminent destruction. It is the source of what he calls his 'dumps' that might also be expressed as despair and distraction, of melancholy close to madness, afflicting those who believed themselves to be in danger of spiritual destruction. This fear animates the life of the seventeenth century. It is the fear of what Bunyan calls 'the bottomless pit . . . out of the mouth of which there came in an abundant manner smoke, and coals of fire, with hideous noises'. To be saved by the infinite and unlooked-for grace of God, unworthy though you be, is to experience the transformation of the spirit. It is a glimpse into the heart of the fervent spirituality of the seventeenth-century world.

38

To rise and piss

The prosperous citizen of London would wear a cloth doublet, open at the front to display his shirt and lawn scarf; breeches, stockings and buckled shoes completed the ensemble. For the outdoors he donned his wig and sugarloaf hat, together with a short cloak, and a sword at his side. His wife would naturally wear a brocaded silk dress, looped to display her quilted petticoat; her neck and shoulders were covered with a kerchief and she wore the fashionable French hood of the day.

The house in which they lived, in the period of Charles I and Cromwell, would have been perhaps too dull and plain for modern taste; the floors were of polished wood, some of the walls wainscoted and the ceilings panelled with oak. The rooms were solid and well-proportioned, but a little gloomy and confined; the floors creaked under foot. Only towards the end of the seventeenth century was there a general movement towards lighter and more gracious interiors.

The houses of those who were known as 'the middle rank' contained between three and seven rooms; the household would characteristically contain between four and seven people, including servants. In the more prosperous of these dwellings the hall, parlour and kitchen took up the ground floor while above them were one or two bedrooms. Of ornament there was very little. The windows rarely boasted curtains; carpets and armchairs were not widely used. Clocks, looking glasses and pictures were still relatively scarce but they were more in evidence towards the close of the period; this was also the time when the cabinet-maker, working in walnut and mahogany, became more popular. The richer households, however, might place hangings against some of the walls.

Their furniture was not comfortable, being comprised of high-backed chairs, stools, chests and benches with perhaps a few cushions to soften the hard wood. The dining table would have no ornament, and cutlery of the modern type was not in use; the crockery was of pewter rather than of earthenware. A display of plate might be set on the sideboard, but otherwise ostentation was still slight. The rooms were heated with coals. Sanitation was of the most rudimentary, with only the occasional mention of a pewter chamber pot or a 'close-stool'. There is no evidence of any utensils for washing.

The good citizen might engage in trade as a merchant or in commerce as a shopkeeper, but there was no firm distinction between the various avocations of the city. In the reign of Charles II 3,000 merchants could be found in the Royal Exchange, and in this period foreign trade, domestic industry and shipping all enjoyed rapid growth in advance of that period that became known to twentieth-century historians as the 'commercial revolution'. In *A Discourse of Trade*, published in 1670, Roger Coke stated that 'trade is now become the lady which in this present age is more courted and celebrated than in any former by all princes and potentates of the world'. The list of imported commodities included tobacco, sugar, indigo and ginger from the colonies as well as Indian calicoes and chintzes; a large proportion of these goods was then re-exported in English ships to continental Europe.

The gentry and the local administrators of the counties must not be forgotten since in this period they exercised full control of their neighbourhoods. It was a time when the old principles of the social hierarchy were reinforced. The 'Cavalier Parliament' had extended the authority of the local aristocracy in such matters as the control of the militia and the administration of the Poor Law. The justices of the peace had almost complete possession of local affairs, from imprisoning vagabonds to fining parish officials for breach of their duties.

The gentry had resumed their role as the leaders of local society, after the unfortunate experiment of republicanism, but they seemed not to have returned to their old complacency. Many of them, for example, paid very close attention to the new methods of agricultural practice. The farmers themselves were engaged in what were known as 'improvements' that increased the profitability of the land; in this period the country was able to export grain to mainland Europe.

A large class of 'professional men' had also emerged in this period; the lawyers and the doctors were principal among them, but accountants and professional administrators of estates were also to be found. Samuel Pepys has become for posterity the master of this world, and his diary does in some degree provide a mirror for his age. He is twenty-six at the time of his first entry; living with his wife in Axe Yard, near Downing Street, he is about to be appointed as secretary to Edward Mountagu, the lord admiral. This was the period when the Rump Parliament had reassembled and General Monck was beginning his march from Scotland.

And so we read that on 3 January 1660, 'Mr Sheply, Hawley and Moore dined with me on a piece of beef and cabbage, and a collar of brawn'. Meat was the principal item in the diets of the period, and it is characteristic that Pepys should have two types; dinner was eaten at noon. On another occasion Pepys sat down to a dish of marrow bones and a leg of mutton, a loin of veal and a dish of fowl together with two dozen larks. He also had dinners of fish but, on being offered a dish of sturgeon, 'I saw very many little worms creeping, which I suppose was through the staleness of the pickle'.

He drank ale and 'strong water' that was most probably gin. After dinner there was often a 'mad stir' with games and forfeits. Sports were of all kinds including one that Pepys called 'the flinging at cocks', in which sticks were hurled at a bird that was tethered by its leg or held down by some other means; whoever rendered it unconscious was allowed to cook and eat it. He also visited a cock-fight in a new pit by Shoe Lane. Other vignettes of the period emerge from his notations. A new disease sprang up in the autumn of 1661, consisting of 'an ague and fever'.

The cleanliness of the age is perhaps in doubt. He had 'like to have shit in a skimmer that lay over the house of office'. He made a cloth suit out of a cloak 'that had like to have been beshit behind a year ago'. 'This night I had a strange dream of bepissing myself, which I really did.' He was en route to the Guildhall, 'by the way calling to shit at Mr Rawlinson's'. He had forgotten his chamber pot one night, 'so was forced to rise and piss in the chimney'. In the theatre, 'a lady spat backward upon me by a mistake, not seeing me'. He sometimes washed himself with warm water, and sometimes washed his feet, but the occurrences were rare enough to merit mention. His wife, Elizabeth, visited a 'hot-house' and 'pretends to a resolution of hereafter being very clean – how long it will hold, I can guess'. Sure enough, on a later occasion, 'she spent the whole day making herself clean, after four or five weeks being in continued dirt'. Two months later, however, 'she finds that I am lousy, having found in my head and body above twenty lice, little and great'.

He was particular about his clothes. He ordered a coat of velvet, what he called a 'close-kneed coloured suit' with stockings of the same colour together with belt and a new gilt-handled sword, as well as a black cloth suit with white lining. In the autumn of 1663 he bought a new shag-gown, trimmed with gold buttons, and two periwigs. He then decided that the wig-maker should cut off his hair and make another periwig with it, and 'after I had caused all my maids to look upon it and they conclude it to become me'. Soon after he also purchased a black cloth suit trimmed with scarlet ribbon as well as a cloak lined with velvet. 'Clothes', he wrote, 'is a great matter.' He went into the street 'a little to show forsooth my new suit'. A poor fellow was one 'that goes without gloves for his hands'.

It was a society of spectacle and display, in which all the leading characters were also actors. In his bright costume and new wig he might promenade with his wife in certain select neighbourhoods, such as Gray's Inn, followed by 'a woman carrying our things'. It was quite usual to stop and enquire of a 'common' person if he or she were ready to fetch this or to deliver that for a small fee. Servants could be severely treated, even in the relatively peaceful household of the Pepyses; Pepys sometimes beat his boy until his wrist hurt and Elizabeth was obliged 'to beat our little girl; and then we shut her down into the cellar, and there she lay all night'.

His adventures with women are well enough known. When he

was observed kissing a woman in the window of a winehouse, someone in the street called out, 'Sir, why do you kiss the gentlewoman so?' and threw a stone towards the window. He decided to join the congregation of St Dionis Backchurch after he had noticed that a 'very great store of fine women there is in this church'. He was always ogling and touching. One young lady, in the congregation of another church, took some pins out of her pocket to prick him if he molested her. He wrote in code about his sexual encounters; 'mi cosa naked', for example, was 'my bare penis'. He 'had his way' and 'got it', as he said, on many occasions. Yet he could be less demanding. 'I got into the coach where Mrs Knipp was, and got her upon my knee (the coach being full) and played with her breasts and sung.'

Violence in the streets was not uncommon. During one altercation 'I did give him a good cuff or two on the chops; and seeing him not oppose me, I did give him another'. The constable and his watch were there to prevent mischief or riot; they once found Pepys's backyard door open 'and so came in to see what the matter was'.

Pepys often 'fell to cards'. Cards, and gaming in general, were the delight of the age; gambling was endemic in all classes of the society, and lotteries were used as a method of public finance. On one afternoon he paid 18 pence to join a 'coffee club' of the Rota that met in the Turk's Head Tavern in Gerrard Street; coffee-houses had come to London eight years before, and had immediately become a success among the merchants and lawyers of London. Yet the merchants and lawyers were not alone. Roger L'Estrange complained that 'every carman and porter is now a statesman, and indeed the coffee-houses are good for nothing else'. No regard was given to 'degrees or order' but in the coffee-house, according to Samuel Butler, the author of *Hudibras*, 'gentleman, mechanic, lord and scoundrel mix'.

In a city dominated by conversation and speculation, by news and gossip, they were the single most important venue of public recreation and of public information. London was characterized by its coffee-houses, and it became common to address letters to a citizen 'at the Grecian' or 'at the Rainbow'. Macaulay said that they almost became a political institution. Yet they were not wholly concerned with 'news piping hot'. On one visit Pepys 'sat long in good discourse with some gentlemen concerning the Roman empire'. At the end of 1664 he stepped into a coffee-house to taste the new drink of 'Jocolatte', 'very good'.

And then 'after dinner we had a pretty good singing and one, Hazard, sung alone after the old fashion'; music and song were everywhere. There were 'song rounds'. While he waited for a lawyer, 'I sat in his study singing'. Before he retired to his bed, he often played the lute. In one of the rooms of a coffee-house he heard a variety of Italian and Spanish songs as well as a canon for two voices on the words '*domine salvum fac regem*'. When he came for recreation to Epsom Wells he observed some townsmen, met by chance, singing together in company. Pepys and his young male servant were accustomed to sing psalms and motets together. During the time of the plague he hired a boat that already had a passenger, so that 'he and I sung together the way down'.

Like many of his contemporaries he seemed to have an open mind about the vagaries of faith and devotion. On one Sunday, 'I went out and looked into several churches'; if he liked the sermon he might stay until the end, but there were times when he slept through the oration. When the inventor Sir Samuel Morland and his wife entered a church with two footmen in livery the congregation took 'much notice of them', especially on 'going into their coach after sermon with great gazeing'. He observed also 'that I see religion, be it what it will, is but a humour . . . and so the esteem of it passeth as other things do'. There was always room for superstition, however. He carried a hare's foot as a charm against illness, but a companion noticed that it did not have the proper 'join' in it. No sooner did he touch his friend's charm than 'my belly begin to be loose and to break wind'.

In pursuit of his duties at the Navy Office it was a matter of routine to accept gifts from various claimants to office or privileges. On one occasion he was offered in turn a rapier, a vessel of wine, a gown, and a silver hatband, in return for 'a courtesy'. His master, Mountagu, told him that 'in the meantime I will do you all the good jobs I can' for making money. He was eager to make a profit from the hiring of some ships for service in Tangiers; he received a share of the proceeds 'which I did not demand but did silently consent to it'. When he was handed a packet containing money, he emptied out a piece of gold and some pieces of silver, all the time averting his eyes so 'that I might say I saw no money in the paper if ever I should be questioned about it'. Commerce of every kind was the essence of the state, and Pepys was keen to acquire a good wife for his brother 'worth two hundred pounds in ready money'. He noted that at court all was 'lust and gain'.

He had some interesting encounters. He recorded how one gentleman had served eight different governments in one year, 1659, 'and he did name them all, and then failed unhappily in the ninth, viz that of the king's coming in'. He was beside the king when a Quaker woman delivered a petition to him; Charles argued with her, 'she replying still with these words, "O King!" and "thou'd" him all along'. He conversed with an experimenter, John Spong, who told him 'that by his microscope of his own making he doth discover that the wings of a moth is made just as the feathers of the wing of a bird'. While he and Spong were talking, several sectarians were arrested for attending a service at a conventicle. Pepys added that 'they go like lambs, without any resistance'. It was common for men and women to weep in this period, whether out of joy or sorrow.

This was an age of much observation and experiment. An acquaintance brought to his house one evening a 12-foot glass, through which they endeavoured to see the moon, Saturn and Jupiter. He met Robert Hooke in the street by chance, and the experimenter told him that he could estimate the number of strokes a fly made with its wings 'by the note that it answers to in music during their flying'. Pepys had previously attended a lecture by Hooke on the art of felt-making. While travelling by boat from Rotherhithe to Gravesend, he read Robert Boyle's *Hydrostatical Paradoxes*.

He noticed 'a fine rarity: of fishes kept in a glass of water'. When he purchased a watch he found it so marvellous that he kept it in his hand 'seeing what a-clock it is 100 times'. He visited the country house of a goldsmith, Sir Robert Viner, where 'he showed me a black boy that he had that died of a consumption; and being dead, he caused him to be dried in an oven, and lies there entire in a box'. Black servants, slaves brought back from West Africa, had become very fashionable.

On Thanksgiving Day, 14 August 1666, in celebration of a recent sea victory over the Dutch, family and friends were very merry 'flinging our fireworks and burning one another and the people over the way'. They then began 'smutting one another with candle-grease and soot, till most of us were like devils'. They drank, and danced, and dressed up. One man put on the clothes of the serving boy and danced a jig; Elizabeth Pepys and her female friends put on periwigs. Pepys sometimes observed that, where there was no company, there was little pleasure.

Some phrases are redolent of the period. 'He talked hog-high.' 'I am with child that . . .' or 'I am in pain for . . .' meant I am anxious and impatient to be told something or for an imminent event. Someone's antics 'would make a dog laugh'. 'I did laugh till I was ready to burst.' 'As she brews, let her bake.'

As he was writing, one winter night, a watchman came by with his bell under the window and cried out, 'Past one of the clock, and a cold, frosty, windy morning.' And so to bed.

39

And not dead yet?

The early hopes for Charles's reign had now faded. It had become clear enough that he was a very poor match for Oliver Cromwell, and the erstwhile cavaliers were bitterly hostile to a corrupt court and a mismanaged government; the revenues were misused while the king himself was at the gambling table with what John Evelyn described as 'vast heaps of gold squandered away in a vain and profuse manner'. The great questions of state and of religion were left unsettled in an atmosphere of squabbling, cynicism, corruption and faction-fighting; the only thing that the king's ministers shared was mutual hatred. The king did not have the patience or the intellect to formulate clear lines of policy or enunciate the ideas that might sustain them. He was reticent and secretive, ever intent upon concealing his opinions on men or on measures. Clarendon wrote to the duke of Ormonde in 1662 that 'the worst is, the king is as discomposed as ever, and looks as little after his business, which breaks my heart, and makes me and other of your friends weary of our lives'.

Yet Clarendon himself, the most loyal and substantial figure of the regime, was also under attack. In the autumn of 1662 it emerged that he had been the prime agent in the sale of Dunkirk to the French; it had been captured by Cromwell's men from the Spanish, but the one continental possession in English hands was now to be delivered to the nation's old enemy. There were good reasons for the sale; the port was costly to maintain and was in no way essential to the national interest, but its surrender (so it was called) was considered to be an act of betrayal. Clarendon was accused of accepting French bribes, and the great mansion he was then building in London was dubbed 'Dunkirk House'. The merchants in particular feared that Dunkirk would be used as a base for privateers intent upon seizing their ships; when the mobs of London grew restless at the news of the sale, the gates of the city were shut and double guards posted in various sensitive locations.

At the close of the year the king attempted to heal the religious divisions of the nation by making a 'declaration of indulgence' in which he expressed his regret at his failure to introduce 'a liberty for tender consciences'; he proposed to ask parliament to give him the power to dispense some of his subjects from the Act of Uniformity and to begin removing penal legislation directed at those Roman Catholics 'as shall live peaceably, modestly and without scandal'. It is the clearest possible evidence that he believed parliament had gone too far in imposing Anglican orthodoxy upon the realm. For this, he may also have blamed Clarendon. The lord chancellor was at the time crippled with gout and forced to keep to his house; he was in no position to object.

Yet the king's appeal was ignored. When the fourth session of the 'Cavalier Parliament' assembled in February 1663, the Commons refused to ratify the declaration. The king therefore was obliged to drop the matter and retire from a possible confrontation. It was in truth a significant failure, since he had proved himself unable to sustain the power of his royal prerogative in religious issues. In the spring of 1663 a new Militia Act was passed that reformed the local militia and placed them under the control of the lords-lieutenant of each county; they were given adequate funds, and were thus able to recruit more men for their service. It was reported that the measure was necessary to combat the continual threat of conspiracy and sedition, but it was feared by some that the king might use the troops for other purposes.

The navy rather than the army, however, was the priority. When parliament resumed once more in the spring of 1664 one of its first measures was a declaration or 'trade resolution' against the Dutch, complaining that 'the subjects of the United Provinces' had invaded the king's rights in India, Africa and elsewhere by attacking English merchants and had committed 'damages, affronts and injuries' closer to home. It was believed that the Dutch wished to establish a trade monopoly throughout the known world, which was as dangerous as the 'universal monarchy' sought by Louis XIV.

The republic was therefore seen as a threat to English ships and to English commerce, but of course its very existence as a republic could be interpreted as an essential menace to the kingdom of England. The religion of the enemy was Calvinist in temper, and it was feared that the Dutch would support the cause of their co-religionists in England; they could thereby sow dissension against the king and the national faith. The 'trade resolution' was an aspect of the Anglican royalism asserted both by Lords and Commons. The fervour of the Commons, in particular, was matched by their actions. They agreed to raise the unprecedented sum of £2.5 million to assist the king in his prosecution of hostilities.

The formal declaration of war came, in February 1665, after months of preparation. The cause seems to have been largely popular, as far as such matters can be ascertained, particular among those merchants and speculators who would benefit from the embarrassment of Dutch trade; one of these was the king's brother, James, duke of York. He led the Royal Africa Company that specialized in the business of slavery, and he invested in other commercial ventures. The conflict has therefore been described as the first purely commercial war in English history. As one hemp merchant, Captain Cocke, put it, 'the trade of the world is too little for us two, therefore one must go down'.

A great victory was won at Lowestoft in the beginning of June under the leadership of the duke of York, when twenty-six Dutch vessels were seized or sunk. Each fleet would sail past the other firing its guns into the enemy's hull and rigging until one or more ships 'broke the line', in which case the disabled vessels would be boarded or sunk with fire-ships. The two sides 'knocked it out', in the phrase of the time, for several hours.

The sound of the guns was heard even in London, and in an essay John Dryden recalled that 'the noise of the cannon from both navies reached our ears about the city, so that all men being alarmed with it, and in a dreadful suspense about the event which we knew was then deciding, everyone went following the sound as his fancy led him . . .' The success would have been even greater if a courtier, while the duke of York was asleep in his cabin, had not called off the pursuit of the remaining ships, whether for fear of waking him, or of engaging once more with the enemy, is not known. In any case the momentum of the victory was not maintained in the wider war.

In August a squadron of English ships attacked a merchant convoy, but was beaten back. In the same month the fleet under the command of the earl of Sandwich was held off the Suffolk coast as a result of poor victualling, and then spent the next few weeks chasing Dutch ships through storm and rain. Some were captured but, when the prizes were dispersed among the flag officers, charges of fraud and theft were made against Sandwich; he never really managed to refute them, and the navy itself seemed complicit in corruption. The earl was deprived of his command and sent as an ambassador to Spain. Later in the year, when the English ships were laid up for repair, some Dutch vessels appeared at the mouth of the Thames and commenced a blockade; it was dispersed only when disease, and lack of supplies, forced them to return home. The blockade, however, had compounded the problems of high taxes and uncertain business that already beset the merchants. Overseas trade had been seriously set back by the war on the high seas, and the Baltic trade shrank away almost to nothing; woollen manufacture, the staple of England's exports, was similarly depressed. A war fought for trade had become a war fatal to trade.

Yet already a greater threat had emerged in the streets of London. In his diary entry for 7 June 1665, 'the hottest day that ever I felt in my life', Samuel Pepys noted that

> This day, much against my will, I did in Drury Lane see two or three houses marked with a red cross upon the doors, and 'Lord have mercy upon us' writ there – which was a sad sight to me, being the first of the kind that to my remembrance I ever saw. It put me into an ill conception of myself and my smell, so that I was forced to buy some roll tobacco to smell to and chew – which took away the apprehension.

The plague had come back to London; houses infected with the distemper were shut up, the victims still often within, and a red cross 1 foot in height was painted on the doors. Pepys had purchased tobacco as a medical precaution.

So began a time of peril and great fear. The first signs of the disease were 'tokens' of discoloured skin; after three or four days 'buboes' or carbuncles erupted over the body and, if they did not suppurate, death was certain. Many victims were tied to the bed in the event of frenzy.

The 'dead carts' or 'pest carts' trundled through the lanes and alleys with their burden of corpses to be discharged in one of the many pits dug for the purpose; it is reported that in their misery some of the living flung themselves among the piles of the dead. Some lay dead, or dying, in the streets. Others fled wailing to the fields around London. Some people locked themselves away, and those that ventured outside looked on one another fearfully. 'And not dead yet?' 'And still alive?' Some, desperate beyond fear, sang and danced and drank in promiscuous gatherings. Others fell into a stupor of despair. It was whispered that demons in human shape wandered abroad; they were known as 'hollow men', and those that they struck soon died.

Prophets and fanatics roamed the streets bawling out threats and warnings. One of them, walking naked with a pan of burning coals on his head, invoked the judgement of God on the sinful city. Through the searingly hot months of July and August the fury of the plague rose ever higher. The principal thoroughfares were all but overgrown with grass. In September fires of sea-coal, one fire for every twelve houses, were kept burning in the streets for three days and nights. Yet they had no effect. As many as 10,000 fatalities were listed each week in the bills of mortality. It seemed that soon enough the city would be empty. But by the beginning of December the sickness abated, and the new year witnessed a return of many London families who had fled in panic. It was estimated that 100,000 had died.

The new year, 1666, was one of ill omen. The number had long been considered significant, heralding perhaps the coming of the Antichrist; for some it signified fire and apocalypse. In its Latin form, 'MDCLXVI', it is unique for including every Roman numeral once and in reverse sequence. The solar eclipse at the beginning of July, in this year, convinced many that the end of days was coming.

The prognostications elsewhere were not good. The king of France had signed a defensive treaty with the Dutch and, at the beginning of the year, he declared war upon England. In truth he did not do much for the benefit of his new ally, but his intervention increased public anxiety about the conduct of hostilities. There was no money and the lord high treasurer, the 4th earl of Southampton, asked Samuel Pepys, clerk of the naval board, 'What would you have me do? I have given all I can for my life. Why will people not lend their money? Why will they not trust the king as well as Oliver?' The reference to Cromwell's success is interesting. The nation had received no benefit, and acquired no material gains, from these inconclusive and inglorious battles against the Dutch.

They were in any case still a formidable enemy. A battle at the beginning of June off the Flemish and English coasts lasted for four days, and at the end of it the English had lost twice as many ships and men as their rivals; the two sides had fought each other to exhaustion and, as one English commander put it, 'they were as glad to be quit of us as we of them'. It was a desperate and bloody fight, leaving 6,000 Englishmen dead. Many of them were found floating in the seas wearing their dark 'Sunday clothes'; they had previously been taken by the press-gangs on leaving church.

News then came, a week later, that the French had taken over the colonial possession of St Kitts. Louis XIV had decided to take a more active part in the maritime struggle and ordered his fleet to sea. The melancholy aspect of affairs convinced many that the government and the king were about to fall. A battle in late July was the occasion for some celebration, however, after the English fleet had pursued the fleeing Dutch over the North Sea for some thirty-six hours. The cry that had gone up before the engagement was: 'If we do not beat them now, we shall never do it!' But all of the participants were growing weary of a war that would last for another year.

London was not spared further horror. After the disaster of the plague, a small chimney fire at a bakery in Pudding Lane began a conflagration that would envelop most of the city. It was the very beginning of September 1666, after an unusually hot August had left the thatch and timber of the city bone dry; the fire was carried by strong south-east winds towards London Bridge and Fish Street.

It burned steadily towards the west, and John Evelyn noted that 'the noise and cracking and thunder of the impetuous flames, the shrieking of women and children, the hurry of people, the fall of towers, houses and churches, was like an hideous storm, and the air all about so hot and inflamed that at the last one was not able to approach it'. The molten lead from the roof of St Paul's ran through the streets, according to John Evelyn, 'glowing with fiery redness'. The Guildhall stood immured in flame like a burning coal. The people took to the water or fled to the fields in the north of the city, seeking safety from the burning drops that rained down upon them. The smoke now stretched for 50 miles. Yet not everyone ran in terror. The royal brothers, Charles and James, took an active part in exhorting, and even joining, those who were trying to contain the engulfing fires.

The fire abated after three days, having consumed five-sixths of the city and leaving a trail of destruction and desolation a mile and a half in length and half a mile in breadth. When John Evelyn clambered among the ruins, the ground still hot beneath his feet, he often did not know where he was. Yet the vitality of the city was not seriously harmed. The usual round of trade and commerce was established again within a year, and the work of rebuilding in brick and stone began; within two years of the Great Fire 1,200 houses had been constructed, and in the following year another 1,600. By 1677 most of the city was once again in place. It was said that it rose almost as quickly as it fell.

The year of ill omen, however, seemed to have fulfilled its destiny. In the month after the fire parliament reassembled in a state of gloom and anxiety. Rumours of conspiracy, by the French and Dutch, were everywhere. The Catholics, and the Quakers, were also blamed. One of those returned to parliament, Roger Pepys, cousin to Samuel, predicted that 'we shall all be ruined very speedily'. A general fast was imposed upon the nation as a penance for what John Evelyn described as 'our prodigious ingratitude, burning lusts, dissolute court, profane and abominable lives'. In the same period the king ordained that all French fashions should be banished from the court and that in their place a simple 'Persian' coat and tunic were to be worn; it was supposed to be a gesture towards thrift but it was essentially a token of his flippancy. The style was in any case soon abandoned.

After much debate, and intense scrutiny of the accounts provided by the Navy Board, the king was voted sufficient funds to fight another year of war; yet there was intense wrangling about the means of furnishing them. Should it be a hearth tax or a poll tax? Nobody seemed to know. As they talked and debated it was rumoured that the French were preparing an invasion, but this was discounted as a government ploy to hasten a decision.

The assessment was finally passed in the middle of January 1667, but of course the revenues were not collected. In the following month the Navy Board declared to the duke of York that 'we are conscious of an utter incapacity to perform what his majesty and your royal highness seem to look for from us'. The shipyards were laid up without supplies or repairs. The seamen, deprived of pay and even of the necessities of life, were provoked to riot on several occasions. The City refused to lend money, and the treasury was exhausted.

It was time for peace. The king and his council had tentatively begun the process of negotiation with the Dutch, and Charles himself was at the same time engaged in private negotiations with the French king; they had no reason to fight against each other, and it was eventually agreed that they should abstain from mutual hostilities. Charles also trusted that his fellow sovereign would be able to persuade or bully his Dutch allies into signing a similar agreement. Charles and Louis had sent their letters through Henrietta Maria, respectively mother and paternal aunt of the two men; the English king kept the matter secret from even his most intimate councillors, thus emphasizing his propensity for clandestine dealings.

In the meantime, to save expenditure, the privy council had no choice but to reduce the scale of naval operations; only a 'summer guard' of ships would be sent to sea in order to protect the merchant vessels. It was also believed that, given the increasingly futile nature of the war, hostilities were about to be suspended. This incapacity led directly to one of the most humiliating episodes in English naval history.

At the beginning of May 1667, a great conference between the warring parties was called at Breda; it soon became clear to the Dutch, however, that the English were not prepared to be over-generous in the negotiations. So they decided to try force for the final time to extort concessions and to hasten the progress of the discussions. In the following month, therefore, they launched a raid into the Thames estuary; they broke the defences of the harbour at Chatham and proceeded to burn four ships before towing away the largest ship of the fleet, the *Royal Charles*, and returning with it undamaged.

Panic ran through the streets of London. It was said that the Dutch were coming, and the trained bands were called out for the city's defence. In truth the enemy fleet could have found its way to London Bridge without much difficulty. It was reported that Harwich, Colchester and Dover were already burned. The reports were false but the events at Chatham were a symbolic, as well as a naval, disaster. One parliamentarian, John Rushworth, wrote that 'the people are ready to tear their hairs off their heads'. Sir William Batten, surveyor of the navy, exclaimed, 'By God! I think the devil shits Dutchmen!'

The Dutch now pressed their advantage and the king, humiliated at home and abroad, conceded some of their demands. The principle of negotiation was that of '*uti possidetis*', by means of which the parties retained possession of that which they had taken by force in the course of conflict. As a result, England lost much of the West Indies to France and the invaluable island of nutmeg, Run, part of Indonesia, to the Dutch. In return, however, it retained New Netherland; this was the colonial province of the Netherlands that included the future states of New York, New Jersey, Delaware and Connecticut. Yet at the time the gains did not match the loss of national prestige.

After the disaster at Chatham talk of corruption and conspiracy was once more in the air; some blamed the papists, and others even blamed the bishops. It was said that, at the time of the Dutch raid, the king was chasing a moth in the apartments of Lady Castlemaine. It was supposed by many that the nation was so mismanaged by the king that it would once more turn against the Stuarts and become a republic. Charles was the subject of distrust as well as dislike, and it was feared that he was colluding with Louis XIV in some popish plot to impose absolute rule. At times of peril and disaster, fear is contagious.

Yet opinion turned in particular against Clarendon who was,

quite unfairly, accused of mismanaging the war; he had in fact opposed it from the start, but he was a convenient scapegoat. He had always been disliked by the men and women about the king – whom John Evelyn described as 'the buffoons and the *misses*' – while an attempt to impeach him had already been made by the earl of Bristol in the Lords. But the chancellor was now in infinitely greater danger. It was being said that the king had turned against him. Charles disliked being lectured or patronized; serious men in any case made him feel uncomfortable. It was not that Clarendon annoyed the king; he bored him. He was disliked by parliament for his fervent support of the prerogative power of the king, and by dissenters for his equally vehement espousal of the established Church. Gilbert Burnet, the historian of his own time, wrote that 'he took too much upon him and meddled in everything, which was his greatest error'.

The enemies of Clarendon now gathered for the kill. His wife had died early in August, and his obvious grief incapacitated him from robustly defending himself. His absence from the privy council encouraged other councillors to speak against him; the king was told that Clarendon prevented the advice of others from reaching him and that he had denied any freedom of debate within the council chamber itself. Thus all the ills of the kingdom could, in one form or another, be blamed upon him. If he was removed, the hostility towards the administration might abate. Certainly his departure would gratify the Commons that had long despised him; it might help to lighten the mood of the next session.

In the middle of August the king sent the duke of York to the lord chancellor with the request that he resign his office. Clarendon unwisely refused and a week later, on 25 August, a more peremptory demand came that he should surrender the seals of office forthwith. Again, Clarendon refused. The affair was the sole news of the court, and it had become necessary for Charles to assert his authority against this overweening councillor. The king demanded the seals, in redoubled fury, and they were at last returned.

The king told one of Clarendon's allies, the duke of Ormonde, that 'his behaviour and humour was grown so unsupportable to myself, and to all the world else, that I could no longer endure it, and it was impossible for me to live with it, and do those things with the parliament that must be done or the government will be lost'. Yet the affair may not be as straightforward as that. Pepys was told that there were many explanations 'not fit to mention'. The king may genuinely have believed that the lord chancellor was no longer capable of service, but there are suggestions that in some way Clarendon had interfered with his love-life; he seems to have been instrumental, for example, in the sudden marriage of one of the king's mistresses. It is impossible now to untangle the myriad webs of court intrigue.

The pack was in full pursuit of Clarendon, now that royal favour had fallen away, and it was believed that the king had become very interested in his former confidant's prosecution. The charges brought against Clarendon by the Commons included illegal imprisonment of various suspects, the intention of imposing military rule, and the sale of Dunkirk to the French. Since the lord chancellor had always been an advocate of arbitrary government, the charges may have been in large measure true. The Lords, however, resolved that Clarendon could not be committed; they seem to have concluded that one of their own members should not be impeached on a whim of the lower house. The king wondered aloud why his once chief minister was still in the country, and by the end of November it was rumoured that he would pick a tribunal of peers prepared to try Clarendon and execute him. The earl now heeded the advice of those closest to him and secretly took ship for France where he began an exile in the course of which he would write perhaps the most interesting history of his times.

It is now pertinent to note that after the forced abdication of the lord chancellor the administration of the king's affairs became ever more murky and corrupt. In the absence of Clarendon the senior councillors were now Clifford, Arlington, Buckingham, Ashley Cooper and Lauderdale, whose initials spelled out 'cabal'; for ever afterwards, the word was employed to designate secretive and self-interested administration. They were an alphabetical coalition, and in truth they can now be seen as mere ciphers in the game of politics; their policies brought nothing about, and their principal object was to make as much money as they could from their period of office before the wheel turned. Clifford, in particular, was known as 'the Bribe Master General'.

They suited the king, however, because he could manipulate them. George Savile, the 1st marquess of Halifax, wrote that 'he lived with his ministers as he did with his mistresses; he used them, but he was not in love with them'. The king was now in charge of all affairs and, without the interference of Clarendon, he could bend and twist in whichever way he wished. So arose one of the most devious and inconsistent periods of English history.

In the beginning the acknowledged first minister was George Villiers, 2nd duke of Buckingham, described by Gilbert Burnet as one who was 'never true either to things or persons, but forsakes every man and departs from every maxim, sometimes out of levity and unsettledness of fancy and sometimes out of downright falsehood'. This was a fit companion for a king. He had already emerged as one of the circle of wits at court, but now he had ambitions to be a statesman as well as a satirist.

He was the son of the ill-fated 1st duke, assassinated by John Felton at the beginning of the reign of Charles I. He was thereafter brought up in the royal household in the company of Charles II, and had shared many exploits with the young king; he had fought beside him at Worcester. His rise after the fall of Clarendon was still remarkable, however, he having previously only obtained the rank of Master of the Horse. The king consulted him on all matters of importance, and the foreign ambassadors generally applied to him for advice before being admitted to the king's presence.

If Buckingham had one abiding principle, it was that of religious toleration; he had so many religious whims and fancies of his own that he was happy to allow freedom of thought to others. The nonconformists were in any case now in a more secure position than before. Fears of a papist court and of a papist queen, and a prevailing belief that the 'Great Fire of London' had been concocted by Roman Catholics in the service of France, gave sectarians and dissenters a novel air of loyalty and trustworthiness.

Quakers began to meet in London, and soon enough monthly assemblies were in place all over the country; they were safer now than at any previous time. The Baptists of Bristol regathered. The Conventicle Act of 1664 was effectively dead, and was formally abolished in 1668. Certain Presbyterian ministers prepared the ground for a separate Church if they could not be assimilated within the established one. At the sessions and assizes of the realm Catholic recusants, rather than nonconformists, were presented for judgement.

The bishop of Norwich preached a sermon in 1666 in which he declared that 'it is an honour which learned men owe to one another to allow liberty of dissent in matters of mere opinion'. That liberty was already apparent in the survival of Brownists, Fifth Monarchy men, Sabbatarians, Muggletonians, Ranters, Anabaptists, General Baptists, Particular Baptists and Familists. We may invoke the words of John Bunyan, 'I preached what I felt, what I smartingly did feel.' They were perhaps not a force to challenge the popular Anglicanism of the high-church party, but the once stringent laws against them were now unenforced or only hesitantly invoked. A contemporary tract, *Discourse of the Religion of England, 1667*, observed that nonconformists were 'spread through city and country; they make no small part of all ranks and all sorts of men. They are not excluded from the nobility, among the gentry they are not a few; but none are more important than they in the trading part of the people.' That is why London was a city of dissent.

From this period, then, we can trace the emergence of the doctrine known as Latitudinarianism that propounded comprehension and tolerance in all matters of doctrine and practice. The 'Latitude men', as they were known, emphasized the power of reason as 'the candle of the Lord' and believed that such matters as liturgy and ritual were 'things indifferent'. This might be said to be the unwritten principle of eighteenth-century Anglicanism. God, and Christianity, were no longer mysterious.

40

The true force

In the early autumn of 1664 a young scholar visited Stourbridge Fair, just outside Cambridge, where he purchased a prism; he took the instrument back to his lodging at Trinity College where 'having darkened my chamber, and made a small hole in my window-shuts, to let in a convenient quantity of the sun's light, I placed my prism at his entrance, that it might be thereby refracted to the opposite wall'. By these means did Isaac Newton experiment with 'the celebrated phenomena of colours'.

In this year, too, he also experimented upon himself. He inserted a bodkin or large needle 'betwixt my eye and the bone as near to the backside of my eye as I could'; at the risk of blinding himself, he wished to alter the curve of his retina and observe the results. These were the preliminary steps to his theory of colour that would revolutionize the discipline of optics; it was he who made the discovery that white light was not some primary or basic hue but a mixture of all the other colours in the spectrum. The conclusion was so contrary to the principles of common sense that no one had ever considered it before.

So began the career of the most remarkable mathematicians of the seventeenth century and one who, more than anyone else, has shaped the perceptions of the modern world. The scientists of NASA, in the United States, still use the calculations of Isaac

Newton. The two years after he purchased the prism at Stourbridge Fair were his years of glory, during which he penetrated the mysteries of light and gravitation. The story of the falling apple may or may not be accurate but it is true enough that, at the age of twenty-three, he began his exploration of the enigma of that force which held the world and universe together. John Maynard Keynes was to call him 'the last of the magicians'.

The time came when he was obliged to enter the public world of seventeenth-century science and, at the end of 1671, he allowed his 6-inch reflecting telescope to be displayed to the Fellows of the Royal Society. Newton had made the instrument himself, fashioning his own tools for the purpose, and it was taken in triumph to Charles II, who marvelled at it. Newton was duly elected a Fellow of the Royal Society, to which institution he was attached for the rest of his life.

The Royal Society may be deemed to be the jewel of Charles II's reign. At the end of November 1660, a group of physicians and natural scientists announced the formation of a 'college for the promoting of physic-mathematical experimental learning'; they were in part inspired by Francis Bacon's vision of 'Solomon's House' in *The New Atlantis*, and they shared Bacon's passion for experimental and inductive science. They were men of a practical and pragmatic temper, with a concomitant interest in agriculture as well as navigation, manufactures as well as medicine. All questions of politics or religion were excluded from the deliberations of the Fellows, and indeed their pursuit of practical enquiry was in part designed to quell the 'enthusiasm' and to quieten the spiritual debates that had helped to foment the late civil wars. They met each week, at Gresham College in Bishopsgate, where papers were read on the latest invention or experiment. It was in their company that Sir Isaac Newton first propounded his revolutionary theories of light.

The last four decades of the seventeenth century in fact witnessed an extraordinary growth in scientific experiment to the extent that, in 1667, the historian of the Royal Society, Thomas Sprat, could already celebrate the fact that 'an universal zeal towards the advancements of such designs has not only overspread our court and universities, but the shops of our mechanicks, the fields of our gentlemen, the cottages of our farmers, and the ships of our merchants'.

An enquiring and inventive temper was now more widely shared, whereby the whole field of human knowledge became the subject of speculation. The Fellows of the Royal Society debated a method of producing wind by means of falling water; they explored the sting of a bee and the feet of flies; they were shown a baroscope that measured changes in the pressure of the air and a hygroscope for detecting water in the atmosphere; they set up an enquiry into the state of English agriculture and surveyed the methods of tin-mining in Cornwall. They conducted experiments on steam, on ventilation, on gases and on magnetism; thermometers, pumps and perpetual motion machines were brought before them. The origins of the industrial and agricultural 'revolutions', conventionally located in the eighteenth century, are to be found in the previous age. In the seventeenth century, providentially blessed by the genius of Francis Bacon at its beginning, we find a general desire for what Sprat described as 'the true knowledge of things'.

At a meeting of the society in the early months of 1684 Edmund Halley, Christopher Wren and Robert Hooke were discussing the dynamics of planetary motion. Halley put a question to them. Could the force that keeps the planets moving around the sun decrease as an inverse square of its distance? Wren and Hooke agreed that this was very likely, but no one had as yet been able to prove the point. So Halley travelled to Cambridge, where he consulted Newton on the problem of the sun and the revolving planets. Newton readily concurred in Halley's hypothesis.

'How do you know this?'

'Why, I have calculated it.'

This was a reply that, as in Halley's words, struck him 'with joy and amazement'. No one had ever done it before. By the end of the year Newton had revisited his calculations and had produced a short treatise, *De motu corporum in gyrum*, that deciphered and proved mathematically the motion of bodies in orbit. He pressed on with his deliberations and, within the space of eighteen months, had completed the treatise that would confer upon him the acclamation of the world. He formulated the three laws of motion that are the foundation of his theory of universal gravitation, a revolutionary principle that proclaims the universe to be bound together by one force that can be mathematically promulgated and understood. It was the great revelation of the seventeenth century. Newton had understood the cosmos, and made it amenable to human laws. There was indeed a force that bound the sun and all the stars. 'It is now established', he wrote, 'that this force is gravity, and therefore we shall call it gravity from now on.'

Newton was eventually chosen to become president of the Royal Society and for the last twenty years of his life governed its meetings with a somewhat forbidding dignity. He ruled that there should be no 'whispering, talking nor loud laughters. If dissensions rose in any sort . . . they tended to find out truth, but ought not to arise to any personality.' These were to be the new truths of science, objective and impersonal, as adumbrated in seventeenth-century London. One Fellow, William Stukeley, recalled that 'everything was transacted with great attention and solemnity and decency' for in truth this was the century in which science became a new form of religion with its laws and principles treated as matters of unassailable dogma. Newton himself declared that natural philosophy now 'consists in discovering the frame and operations of Nature and reducing them, as far as may be, to general rules or laws, establishing these rules by observations and experiments, and thence deducing the causes and effects of things'. This is our inheritance from the seventeenth century.

41

Hot news

The casual deviousness of the king soon became apparent when at the beginning of 1668 he negotiated a 'Triple Alliance' with the Dutch republic and Sweden to oppose the French armies that had already occupied part of the Spanish Netherlands; it was a general defensive league against the encroaching power of the French and, at the time, it was regarded as a great stroke of policy. It was considered to be better to be allied with two Protestant powers against a common Catholic enemy. It was, more pertinently, meant to prove to Louis XIV that England still possessed significant influence in the game between the states.

Yet the king wrote to his sister residing at the French court, Henrietta, duchess of Orléans, that 'I have done nothing to prejudice France in the agreement'. Even as he allied himself with the Dutch, in fact, he was preparing to move ever closer to France in a secret plan to destroy their republic. He had the ability to pursue two different, and indeed opposing, policies at the same time. Feeling great admiration for his cousin, Louis XIV, he also needed the French king's money and perhaps, in some future contingency, his men. Louis ruled the most powerful state in Europe, and it was much better to be his ally than his enemy; he was also part of the family and, in dynastic terms, family was more important than country.

Suspicion was in the air. Pepys reported that in London 'people do cry out in the streets . . . that we are betrayed by people about the king and shall be delivered up to the French'. In the 'bawdy-house riots' of the spring, the apprentices of London revised the ancient custom of attacking brothels on Shrove Tuesday. But this was no ritual performance; fifteen of their leaders would be tried for high treason, and four of them were hanged. The demonstrations involved thousands of people, and lasted for five days.

The riots began on Easter Monday when some brothels in Poplar were attacked and demolished; the insurrection spread on the following day to Moorfields, East Smithfield and Holborn. On Wednesday the apprentices, swelled by an appreciable force from Southwark, attacked the bawdy-houses of Moorfields. They did not form an inchoate crowd: they were mustered into regiments and marched behind flags; they carried iron bars and axes. Some of the more notorious prisons were also besieged.

The king himself professed not to understand the motive of the apprentices in attacking the brothels. 'Why, why, do they go to them, then?' he is reported to have asked. But in fact the brothels were a sign, or token, of what was for many a larger problem. In attacking the brothels the Londoners were attacking the perceived morals of the court and, in opposing its morals, they were disowning its principles. One of their cries was that 'ere long they would come and pull Whitehall down'.

The king's favourite mistress, Lady Castlemaine, had converted to Roman Catholicism at the end of 1663. She was a sign, therefore, of the court's leaning towards papistry and was a target of much virulent comment as a 'whore' and worse. That is another reason why the brothels were attacked. The bishops were also condemned for keeping mistresses, and the archbishop of Canterbury was rumoured to retain a prostitute; other prelates were 'given to boys'. When the apprentices called out for 'reformation' they were giving voice to the pleas of the dissenters who distrusted or hated the established Church.

So sexual laxity was associated with papistry, and papistry with treason, and treason with the king of France. It was an unstable compound of rumour and fear, but all the more potent for that. The rioters could not have discerned the king's secret purposes but, in their distrust, they were in fact close to the truth. Soon after the formation of the 'Triple Alliance' Buckingham entered negotiations with the duchess of Orléans in France. Charles meanwhile apologized to the French envoy for having entered the treaty with Holland and Sweden insinuating that he would like to establish a much closer union with Louis. In the spring of 1668 the king decided to prorogue parliament for what turned out to be the unprecedented period of seventeen months; in its absence he might more easily plot and plan.

At the beginning of 1669 he sprang a surprise. He called his brother, James, and three of his most important councillors to his private chamber where with tears in his eyes he announced his desire for conversion to the Catholic faith. His brother was soon to be received into that communion, and would remain a staunch and indeed almost hysterical Catholic for the rest of his life. The honesty and fidelity of the king are more doubtful. If Charles was preparing himself for negotiations with the devout French king, what could be better than to declare his espousal of the same religion?

A secret emissary was sent to the French court in March with the offer of an offensive and defensive alliance together with a request for men, money and ships in the event of a war with the Dutch. Charles also promised to declare himself a Catholic if, in return, Louis XIV would give him the sum of £200,000 to secure himself against public wrath. He never did make any such announcement, and it seems that he was converted only on his deathbed; he was adept at the arts of dissimulation and hypocrisy even in the great affairs of state.

Throughout this year, and the first half of the next, negotiations between the two kings continued in absolute secrecy. The English ambassador in Paris, and the French ambassador in London, were not informed. Charles's anti-Catholic ministers were not told. The king continued negotiations with the Dutch as if nothing in the world had changed. By late summer or early autumn 1669, Charles and Louis reached agreement. Louis would come to Charles's aid whenever the English king announced his Catholicism, and the two would join together in an assault upon the Dutch.

Henrietta, duchess of Orléans, arrived at Dover in the middle of May 1670, with diverse documents from the French court that she gave to her brother. Among these was a secret paragraph which read that 'the king of England, being convinced of the truth of the Roman Catholic religion, is resolved to declare it, and to reconcile himself with the Church of Rome as soon as the state of his country's affairs permit'. Charles hoped and believed that the majority of his subjects had such affection for him that they would not protest 'but as there are unquiet spirits who mask their designs under the guise of religion, the king of England, for the peace of his kingdom, will avail himself of the assistance of the king of France'. The king was still engaged in subterfuge against his most intimate councillors. He allowed Buckingham, for example, to negotiate a version of the treaty that did not contain this important paragraph concerning the king's conversion to Roman Catholicism. Instead he was asked to press on with a treaty of alliance that made no mention of the secret. He was not aware of the collusion. It is unlikely that Charles ever had any intention of announcing his conversion, however, and the commitment was in large part a ploy to bind the French king more tightly to him.

The financial reward granted to the king was not large. He was to be paid £140,000 – half in advance – as a token of the French king's favour. He was also to be paid approximately £210,000 during each year of the proposed war with the Dutch, with the first instalment to be sent to him three months before the actual declaration of hostilities. The king of England had become a pensionary of the king of France, and had in effect sold his sovereignty. Another difficulty was apparent. If the French king should ever release into the world the secret paragraph, Charles's hold over his subjects might be destroyed; so Louis had a potent weapon in any confrontation with his fellow sovereign.

The counterfeit treaty was signed towards the close of the year, while the secret agreement reached earlier in the spring was not revealed even to the king's confidants. The alliance with Louis against the Dutch, however, could not be concealed for ever. The popular sentiment against France was already very strong, and the Venetian ambassador commented that 'although the king may join France, his subjects will not follow him'. A rumour was spread that French agents were kidnapping English children to take their blood as a cure for Louis's supposed leprosy. It was clear to the king's men that, if there was to be a war with the Dutch, it would have to be very short and very successful before public anger turned against them.

Yet how was any proposed war to be financed? In the intervals between various recesses and prorogations, parliament voted only modest supplies. The French pension itself was not over-generous. The king's own hereditary revenues were all pledged to repay old debts but, as a sign of boldness or desperation, it was determined to postpone the repayment of all those loans. This became known as 'the stop', imposed on 2 January 1672. All payments due from the exchequer were cancelled, so that incoming revenues could be spent upon the preparations for war.

The principal victims were the goldsmiths operating as bankers, who in turn passed on the loss and refused to discharge to their clients the cash they held on deposit. It seemed that 'the stop' might also soon be put to trade itself. Yet another casualty, however, was the king, who at a stroke lost credibility; the financial probity of the government was severely undermined and it was not at all clear that anyone would lend to it again. One contemporary confided to his diary that the decision 'will amaze all men and ruin thousands'.

In the spring of 1672, the French declared war on the Dutch; Charles immediately followed their example, and justified hostilities by citing the attempts of the republic to supplant English trade and to harass English traders. He also mentioned the fact that he was personally insulted by Dutch caricatures and publications. Two days before the call to war, Charles had honoured another undertaking to Louis by issuing a 'declaration of indulgence' that included his Catholic subjects. The nonconformists were granted complete freedom of worship while the Roman Catholic 'recusants' were permitted to worship in their private houses. It was a signal use of the royal prerogative at a time when parliament was not in session. Licences to hold public meetings were now generously and variously distributed to the nonconformists. John Bunyan was one of those released from prison. It may also have occurred to dissenters and Catholics that their new religious liberties now depended upon royal favour.

The measure could also have been designed to assist the king's brother, who had recently been received into the Catholic communion.

James, duke of York, by his own account, had been converted after reading certain tracts for and against the Roman faith; he also perused church histories and came to the conclusion that none of the English reformers 'had power to do what they did'. His faith was a matter of conviction and principle; for his brother it was a question of expediency.

It was said by the earl of Arlington that the 'declaration of indulgence' was so intended 'that we might keep all quiet at home while we are busy abroad'. Yet hostilities had already begun. In the middle of March an English squadron attempted to detain and board a rich Dutch fleet of merchant vessels on its way home from Smyrna and Malaga. Its commander had been warned in advance, however, and was accompanied by a convoy that allowed him to elude the English enemy. It was a humiliation for Charles, who had also been deprived of the treasure he had hoped to capture. The affair did not bode well for the greater war.

The duke of York had been appointed as lord high admiral, but Charles played a large part in preparing and arming the fleet. In the early summer of 1672 an inconclusive battle took place near Sole Bay, off the coast of Suffolk, in which both sides claimed success. Since the original plan of the English was to sail across the North Sea and blockade the Dutch in their home ports, they could hardly be described as the victors. It was clear enough that this would be no easy fight for the seas. The French fleet, ostensibly present to aid their allies, had played no part in the battle and thus earned the angry rebukes of the English; soon enough, in popular opinion, the French would be far more hated than the Dutch. John Evelyn observed in his diary entry for 27 June that the inconclusive battle 'showed the folly of hazarding so brave a fleet, and losing so many good men, for no provocation but that the Hollanders exceeded us in industry, and in all things but envy'.

The armies of Louis XIV had more success. They poured across the Rhine in the first two weeks of June and attacked the territories of the United Provinces; there seemed no possibility of withstanding their advance, and some of the principal cities were obliged to open their gates to the invaders. The fires from the French camps could be seen from Amsterdam. Of the seven republics of the United Provinces, only Holland and Zealand remained unconquered. At this perilous juncture the Dutch opened their dykes and flooded the country to prevent any further French advance. The land war came to a peremptory halt.

Charles had asked for a further £1 million from the French king, for the maintenance of the war, but Louis had refused. So Charles had no choice but to recall parliament in the hope of obtaining funds. Parliament returned in February 1673. In its absence a war had been declared and a declaration of religious indulgence had been issued. It might have seemed superfluous to requirements, except that it knew its power over the raising of money. The king had hoped to meet its members after a successful campaign against the Dutch, but that possibility had been removed.

A new lord chancellor had become the king's official spokesman in the lords. The earl of Shaftesbury would soon become the most controversial man in the kingdom but, in these years, he was one of the most vigorous supporters of the royal prerogative; Charles would eventually describe him as 'the weakest and wickedest man of the age' but at this time he relied upon his judgement as an administrator and adviser. Shaftesbury had been an enthusiastic supporter of Oliver Cromwell, and even a member of the Barebone's Parliament, but by dint of eloquence and industry he had managed to exorcize his interesting past. He would in turn inspire one of the most powerful pieces of satirical verse when he was denounced by John Dryden in *Absalom and Achitophel*:

> For close designs, and crooked counsels fit;
> Sagacious, bold and turbulent of wit:
> Restless, unfixt in principles and place;
> In pow'r unpleas'd, impatient of disgrace.
> A fiery soul which, working out its way,
> Fretted the pigmy-body to decay.

Parliament met in an unsettled and fractious mood. It was angry in particular that the king had seen fit to issue a declaration of religious indulgence without obtaining its consent; his action was deemed to be unconstitutional. Parliament was not necessarily opposed to the Dutch war but, if it was to vote supplies for the continuation of hostilities, its authority must be reasserted. The Commons then passed a resolution that parliamentary statutes concerning religion could not be suspended or cancelled except by Act of Parliament, thus denying the king's power in matters of 'indulgence'.

Charles tried to resist with the help of the Lords but, in desperate need of money, eventually he submitted. After a number of rancorous exchanges he cancelled the declaration of indulgence and said that 'what had been done with respect to the suspension of the penal laws should never be drawn into consequence'. The king broke the seal of the original declaration with his own hands. Bonfires were lit in the streets of London and, by the end of the month, Charles had received the supply of funds he so badly needed.

Parliament had taken aim at papists rather than dissenters, since the Catholic recusants were still believed to pose a threat to the state. Abednego Seller, in *The History of Passive Obedience*, suggested that 'treason in papists is like original sin to mankind; they all have it in their natures, though many of them may deny it, or not know it'. Some members believed that the 'declaration' had in fact been part of a papist plot concocted by Charles and Louis to impose that religion upon England.

So in March 1673, the Commons passed a measure that became known as the Test Act. All aspirants to office or to a place of trust were to swear the oath of royal supremacy as well as the oath of allegiance, thus placing king before pope; they were also obliged to take the sacrament according to the rite of the Church of England and to swear that 'I declare that I believe there is not any transubstantiation in the sacrament of the Lord's Supper, or in the elements of bread and wine, at or after the consecration thereof by any person whatsoever'. This struck at the heart of Catholic belief. When the king gave his assent to the Test Act a 'great hum' of approval arose in parliament. Charles was heard to say that he would now purge his court of all Catholics except his barber, 'whom he mean[s] to keep in despite of all their bills, for he was so well accustomed to his hand'. The remark had a point; the king trusted the Catholic who put a razor to his throat.

The first casualty was James, duke of York, who was obliged to retire from public life. He resigned as lord high admiral and command of the fleet was entrusted to Prince Rupert, who last appeared in these pages as the leader of the royalist cavalry during the Civil War. It was therefore advertised to the world that the king's brother and heir apparent was a Roman Catholic; immediately rumour and innuendo began to surround him. It was widely believed, for example, that the lord chancellor himself, the earl of Shaftesbury, was plotting against him in an effort to exclude him from the throne. When James did not receive communion with his brother in the royal chapel John Evelyn wrote in his diary that it 'gave exceeding grief and scandal to the whole nation, that the heir of it, and the son of a martyr for the Protestant religion, should apostatize. What the consequence of this will be, God only knows, and wise men dread.'

One of the king's principal councillors and one of the original 'cabal', Thomas Clifford, also resigned all of his posts. He was a secret Catholic, and it had been suggested that the Test Act was in part formulated by his rivals precisely in order to remove him from office. He died soon after. Confidence now flowed to yet another of Charles's ministers. Thomas Osborne, soon to become the earl of Danby, was a staunch Anglican who had opposed the Dutch war; he had also been a signal success as an administrator and, on Clifford's resignation, he was appointed to be lord treasurer.

The preparation for another year of hostilities with the Dutch was not undertaken with any great enthusiasm; the discovery of James's Catholicism called into further question the alliance with papist France and the attack upon a fellow Protestant state. The king himself is reported to have been vacillating and inconsistent, ready to prosecute war on one day and ready to retire from conflict on the next. Shaftesbury said of his master that 'there is not a person in the world, man or woman, that dares rely upon him or put any confidence in his word or friendship'.

In July Charles ordered Rupert to avoid any naval confrontation unless he could be sure to win it decisively. He had already returned to negotiations with the Dutch, and simply wished to apply pressure upon them. No such clear outcome emerged from the last sea battle of the war, the battle of the Texel, when the Dutch and English vessels fought a long and inconclusive struggle that left the waters filled with wreckage and floating bodies. It was notable, also, for the inactivity of the French fleet that simply stood apart and watched. Prince Rupert wrote later of the French admiral's reluctance to become involved that 'it wanted neither signal nor instruction to tell him what he should then have done; the case was so plain to every man's eye in the whole fleet'. It was now believed by many that Louis XIV was happy to watch the two maritime nations destroy one another's navies, thus adding more fire to the anger of the English against their nominal allies.

James increased the anti-Catholic bias of the nation by taking advantage of the parliamentary recess to betroth himself to a papist princess. His previous wife, Anne Hyde, had died two years earlier, leaving him with two Protestant daughters, Mary and Anne. The new bride was of quite another nature. Mary of Modena was fifteen but already a devout Catholic, and it was reported that the French king highly approved of the match and might even provide a dowry for the occasion. The imminent prospect of a royal Catholic dynasty was not one that the English favoured. When Mary eventually arrived in England she was generally greeted with sullen silence by the populace. When she was allowed to sit in the queen's presence, the English ladies 'humped' and walked out.

When parliament reconvened towards the end of October 1673, the outcry against the marriage was immediate. Sir William Temple declared that the effort to defeat papistry with the Test Act would come to nothing 'if it got footing so near the throne' and he begged the king to forbid the proposed match. A resolution to that effect was almost unanimously approved.

A broader assault upon the administration now began. Some of the members had already stated that they would not vote a penny more for the war unless and until they had a voice in its management. A resolution to that effect was amended with the proviso that no money should be granted until the previous supply of war funds had been collected. It was also found necessary to give room for a debate on 'grievances', principal among them the French alliance and the war against the Dutch. At the beginning of November it was declared that the standing army was also a 'grievance', perhaps not the most appropriate note to be struck during a war. On 5 November the old sport of pope-burning returned to the streets, when the effigy of Pope Clement X was set on fire by the London apprentices. A figure of a Frenchman was also used for target practice.

Charles was aware that his lord chancellor, the earl of Shaftesbury, had helped to foment opposition against his brother and that he was steadily becoming the leading spokesman for the Protestant interest. So he dismissed him from his councils, and appointed Heneage Finch as lord chancellor; it was reported that the king changed his mind six times, in as many hours, over the appointment. The Venetian envoy reported to the doge and senate that 'the king calls a cabinet council for the purpose of not listening to it, and the ministers hold forth in it so as not to be understood'.

Shaftesbury did not go quietly, however, and against the king's direct order remained in London to recruit allies for his anti-Catholic cause; for the rest of his political life he would organize the opposition to the king. When parliament met again at the beginning of 1674, after a brief prorogation, the attack moved on to the king's principal ministers who were 'popishly affected, or otherwise obnoxious and dangerous'. Lauderdale had ruled on the king's behalf in Scotland, and was accused of favouring absolutism; it was resolved therefore that the king should remove him from 'all his employments and from the royal presence and councils for ever'.

The duke of Buckingham was next to be arraigned and agreed to speak before the Commons; he tried to excuse himself by shifting the blame onto the ineptitude of others, and declared that 'I can hunt the hare with a pack of hounds but not with a pack of lobsters'. It was widely believed that the lobsters in question were the king and his brother. His wit did not impress the Commons, however, and it was determined that he should also be removed from all of his employments. Buckingham later complained that 'men ruined by their princes and in disgrace are like places struck with thunder; it is accounted unlawful to approach them'.

Arlington was then in turn impeached for treason and crimes of high misdemeanour, but his case was ceded to a special committee. The 'cabal' had in any case now been dissolved. It was obvious to everyone that the king was ready to sacrifice ministers when he had no further use for them.

He was also engaged in extreme and unwise deception. Shaftesbury had opposed the king's measures in part because he had become acquainted, by one means or another, with the secret treaty whereby Charles became the pensionary of the king of France in exchange for his conversion to Catholicism. At the opening of parliament in January 1674, however, Charles stated that rumours of 'secret articles of dangerous consequence' were completely untrue and he declared, 'I assure you, there is no other treaty with France, either before or since, not already printed, which shall not be made known.' He was perceived to fumble with his notes at this point.

It had now become clear that the war against the Dutch could not be continued; the Spanish had now entered an alliance with the enemy and it was unthinkable that England would also declare war against Spain. Too much trade was at stake. So the Dutch now appointed the Spanish envoy in London as an arbitrator for peace. It could not come soon enough for all the participants. The Dutch agreed to pay an indemnity and consented to salute the English flag at sea; this was really a question of saving face, on the English side, and the outcome was hardly enough to justify a costly and bloody war of two years' duration. The king announced the peace to parliament on 24 February, and then unexpectedly prorogued the session until November. The members of the Commons looked upon one another in amazement in light of the fact that, in the words of Lord Conway, 'they had sat so long upon eggs and could hatch nothing'. Conway also observed that 'now there will be a new game played at court, and the designs and interests of all men will be different from what they were'.

Thomas Osborne, who had emerged as the king's principal minister, was created earl of Danby in the summer of the year. He was a determined and pugnacious Yorkshireman who firmly believed that the Anglican faith was of paramount importance in unifying the nation and who had as a result favoured alliances with the Protestant states of Europe. He was determined to reform royal finances, and to maintain control over parliament by any and every means possible; those methods included clandestine payments to members from secret service funds and the select distribution of various titles or offices. Danby did his best to demonstrate that the king was wholly in favour of the Anglican cause, and that Charles was determined to maintain an anti-French and an anti-Catholic stance.

As a pronounced royalist and courtier he was of course opposed by the earl of Shaftesbury and by the duke of Buckingham who, abandoned by the king, now joined together in the campaign against the court. It has been often observed that in the creation of these factions and interests we may see the modest beginnings of 'party' in the contemporary sense. From 1674 forward an 'opposition' to the royal cause began to emerge in the Commons, with the aim of imposing restrictions upon the king's power and of upholding the supremacy of parliament.

Its members did not consider or call themselves a party, because the term implied disruption or disloyalty, yet in 1673 a member of parliament, Sir Thomas Meres, could speak of 'this side of the house and that side'. The term was considered to be unparliamentary but it was observed, for example, that a cluster of members sat together in the 'south-east corner' of the chamber. The 'court' and 'country' parties were also distinguished. The former were intent upon maintaining all the rights and privileges of the throne while the latter wished, according to the parliamentarian Sir John Reresby, 'to protect the country from being overburdened in their estates, in their privileges and liberties'.

In the spring of 1675 parliament reassembled. Here was another opportunity for Danby to reassert the primacy of orthodox Anglicanism at the court of Charles II. He had recently engaged in what Andrew Marvell called 'window-dressing' by taking in hand the rebuilding of St Paul's Cathedral after the Great Fire; the first stone of Christopher Wren's design was laid in the early summer. A brass statue of Charles I was also raised on its pedestal at Charing Cross.

Now in parliament, Danby wished to reintroduce a bill that compelled members of parliament and holders of public office to declare that resistance to the king was unlawful; they were also to be obliged to disown any alteration in Church or government. It was a measure designed to please what was still a 'Cavalier Parliament' in its fourteenth year. In a 'Letter from a Person of Quality' Shaftesbury denounced the proposal as a plot by 'high episcopal men and cavaliers' to establish an absolute government. In a speech to the Lords he had questioned that 'if a king would make us a province, and tributary to France, and subdue the nation by a French army, or to the papal authority, must we be bound in that case tamely to submit'? The question was never answered. A formal battle between the Lords and the Commons, over the extent of their respective rights, meant that no business could be introduced. Danby's measure failed, therefore, and the king prorogued parliament until October.

The summer of 1675 was spent in preparation and calculation. Some of the votes in the last session of parliament had been very close; there were occasions when frustration and anger erupted in mild violence as periwigs were pulled off and swords were drawn. On one occasion the Speaker had to bring the mace crashing down upon the table in order to restore order. Danby himself had been obliged to fight off charges of impeachment made against him by some of the Commons. So he was determined to create a majority for the court by what was called 'high bribing'. Some thirty members were given pensions on the excise while others were granted minor offices.

In this same summer Charles also received another subsidy from the French king on condition that he further prorogued parliament or, in the event of a difficult session in October, dissolved the assembly altogether. Louis did not wish his cousin to be forced into measures against the French, while at the same time envoys from Spain, the United Provinces and elsewhere were busily bribing individual members of the parliament. Everyone was bribing everyone else.

The parliament of the autumn was not a success; the Commons voted £300,000 for the navy, but then vetoed the introduction of any new money bills. In the Lords the supporters of Shaftesbury and Buckingham argued for a dissolution, on the grounds that the 'Cavalier Parliament' was now old and corrupt. So on 22 November the king, without attempting to make a speech, prorogued parliament once more for a further fourteen months.

A report compiled for Danby, after the session was over, reveals the calculations of one of his managers.

> *Sir Nicholas Slanning*. He was absent most part if not all last session. Lord Arundel should be sure to take care of him. *Mr Josiah Child*. I am loath to speak plain English, but if he were

> well observed he might be proved to be a capital offender. *Mr Joseph Maynard.* He seldom or never goes right. *Mr John Grubham Howe.* Your lordship knows who can influence him . . . *Sir Thomas Bide* is past cure. *Sir John Cotton.* He is a very good man, and rarely misses his vote, and then by mistake only. Some person (trusty) should always sit near him. *Sir John Newton.* I suspect he has been corrupted by Sir Robert Carr . . . *Mr Henry Monson.* Mr Cheney must take care of this gentleman, and that most particularly, for he is very uncertain unless one be at his elbow.

In the parliamentary recess Charles was angered into taking a clumsy and ill-considered measure to silence idle tongues. It was a winter of discontent at the failure of parliament and the maladministration of the king. So he agreed to issue a proclamation that closed all the coffee-houses of the city, in the knowledge that these were the places where his opponents gathered to plot and to plan. Those who followed Shaftesbury, for example, were accustomed to meet at Kid's Coffee House otherwise known as the Amsterdam. The government employed at least one 'coffee-house spy' to keep an account of their proceedings.

Some observers blamed the appetite for news and scandal on the consumption of coffee. In the days of the tavern, sack and claret created an atmosphere of gaiety; but the city chamberlain, Sir Thomas Player, complained that 'these sober clubs produce nothing but scandalous and censorious discourses, and at these nobody is spared'.

The king might also have taken the opportunity to close down the bookshops attended by the opposition which, in a memorandum, Danby described as devoted to spreading false news through city and country. The temperature of public debate and interest in the politics of the day was such that young law students flocked to the shops and stalls every afternoon, together with those citizens and gentry who were eager for the latest reports. The agents of every faction circulated among them, ready to lend their interpretation to any turn of events. The bookshops remained open, however, and such was the outcry over the closing of the coffee-houses that the proclamation was withdrawn. They had been shut down in January 1676, but were reopened ten days later. The volte-face was characteristic of the hesitation and confusion that beset all aspects of public policy.

At a later date, however, an attempt was made to exclude satires and newsletters that were composed, according to the king, by 'sordid mechanic wretches who, to gain a little money, had the impudence and folly to prostitute affairs of state'. Yet the appetite for news could not be curbed or diminished. There was only one newspaper that was granted official authorization, the *London Gazette*, but this consisted mainly of proclamations, official pronouncements and advertisements.

Everybody needed news. Everybody wanted news. News was known as 'hot'. It was a society of conversation so that rumour and gossip passed quickly through the streets. At times of more than usual excitement papers and pamphlets were dropped in the street and were eagerly snatched up and passed from hand to hand. Anonymous publications, without a printer's imprint, were also widely circulated. One owner of a coffee-house trained his parrot to squawk 'What's the news?' at his customers.

42

New infirmities

And what was the news? After the Commons had declined to pass any new money bills, Charles was once more compelled to turn to his French cousin for financial aid. It was agreed in the early months of 1676 that Louis would pay him a yearly pension, and that both kings would refrain from agreements with other powers without mutual consent. Charles told his brother about the arrangement and was congratulated for his fidelity to the Catholic sovereign. He also informed Danby, who was wholly opposed to any transactions with the French; he disapproved, and asked his master to take the advice of the privy council. Charles was in no mood to consult anyone, however; he wrote out the secret treaty in his own hand, and delivered it to the French ambassador. The king then retired to Windsor, where he supervised certain 'improvements' to the castle and went fishing.

When parliament reassembled in February 1677, after a prorogation of fifteen months, it was claimed by Shaftesbury and others that such a long suspension of proceedings was illegal; Buckingham proposed a motion to that effect and cited two statutes of Edward III, which ordained that parliament should meet 'once a year, or oftener, if need be'. This was considered to be an affront to the royal prerogative. Shaftesbury and Buckingham were ordered to retract their 'ill-advised' action and to ask pardon of king and

Lords. Both men refused and were promptly dispatched to the Tower for an indefinite period together with two other dissenting lords. Buckingham confessed his fault soon afterwards, and was released, while Shaftesbury preferred to remain in prison. 'What, my lord,' he called down to Buckingham as he departed the Tower, 'are you leaving us so soon?'

'Ay, my lord, you know that we giddy-pated fellows never stay long in one place at a time.'

France was still continuing its land war against the United Provinces, despite English withdrawal from the conflict, and in the spring of this year the French enjoyed a series of victories. The Commons reacted by reaffirming its animus against the French. The king was in any case suspect. He had in recent years acquired a French mistress, Louise de Kérouaille, made duchess of Portsmouth, thus binding his ties to the French court of which she was a prominent member as duchess of Aubigny. There is a famous story of the crowd threatening the coach of Nell Gwynn under the misapprehension that it contained the duchess; she called out, 'Be silent, good people! I am the *Protestant* whore!'

Charles was in every sense a Frenchified king. An address was issued by both Houses of Parliament calling upon him to allay the anxieties of the nation by entering appropriate alliances with the opponents of Louis. At an audience with one of the ambassadors from the United Provinces, he threw his handkerchief into the air with the exclamation, 'I care just that for parliament.'

On 23 May, however, the king invited the Commons to the Banqueting House in which he declared that 'I do assure you on the word of a king that you shall not repent any trust you repose in me'; he then proceeded to ask for a further supply of money, 'both to defend my subjects and offend my enemies'. They did not place very much faith in the king's word, however, and two days later they found themselves 'obliged (at present) to decline the granting your majesty the supply your majesty is pleased to demand'. They also called for the king to unite himself with the Dutch against the power of France.

An angry king then adjourned parliament on 28 May with a speech in which he said that 'could I have been silent, I would rather have chosen to be so, than to call to mind things so unfit for you to meddle with'. He had told the French ambassador, the month before, that 'I put myself in trouble with my subjects for love of the French king'. Soon enough he was negotiating for further supplies from his much loved cousin that would more than match the money withheld from him by parliament. He had adjourned that assembly to the summer, but in fact it did not meet again until the beginning of the following year.

In the meantime the earl of Danby endeavoured to burnish the Protestant credentials of the regime by furthering the scheme of marrying Mary, elder daughter of the duke of York and therefore niece of the king, to William of Orange. William was the leader of the United Provinces even then threatened by the French; since he was a Protestant champion, the union might have seemed unwise to a king who relied upon French money. Yet Charles assented to the match in part to placate the public clamouring for an alliance with the United Provinces, and in part with the hope that he might be able to negotiate some treaty of peace between William and Louis. He could then emerge as the saviour of Europe. He was, in short, looking both ways at once. The belief of Louis XIV that the English king was quite unreliable was amply confirmed. He suspended his financial subsidy, and rejected Charles's proposal for an extended truce between France and the United Provinces. The marriage between William and Mary was solemnized at the beginning of November, to much public rejoicing. The Protestant powers were matched.

Parliament met finally in the last week of January 1678, in a more amenable atmosphere. In his opening speech the king confirmed that he 'had made such alliances with Holland as are for the preservation of Flanders', and that he now required 'a plentiful supply'. The Commons resolved that all trade between England and France should be curtailed and that no peace could be made until France had withdrawn to its previous frontiers. In February the members proceeded to vote him £1 million for prosecuting the war against France. The money would not in fact be enough to wage a successful campaign, but Charles had in any case no intention of declaring war on Louis.

He was in a trap or, rather, by his double-dealing he had trapped himself. A period followed in which parliament was adjourned or reconvened on almost a monthly basis; the shortest session was 6 days and the longest 172 days while the recesses lasted from 10 days to 15 months. This aberrant pattern is a measure of the confusion into which public policy had fallen. Charles did not know where to turn. He wanted the French subsidy from Louis but he had also been promised by parliament £1 million to furnish the means to attack him. He was making active preparations for war against France, while at the same time assuring the French ambassador of his devotion to Louis.

Parliament was also thrown into doubt. It had voted funds to raise an army of 30,000 men, but what if the king should use that army for his own ends? Charles and Danby were consequently feared and distrusted. The French king was liberally distributing bribes to various parties, and all men complained that darkness and deep mist covered the affairs of state. Sir William Temple explained in his *Memoirs* that 'from these humours arose those uncertainties in our counsels that no man, who was not behind the curtain, could tell what to make of' the confused rumours and reports.

Towards the end of March 1678 the king instructed Danby to write to the English ambassador in Paris, Ralph Montagu, with an outline of possible peace proposals; Charles then demanded the payment of 6 million *livres* a year (more than £4,000 of gold) for three years, in return for using his influence with the Dutch to negotiate a treaty. The whole arrangement was to be hidden in the most complete secrecy and Montagu 'must not mention a syllable of the money'. In his own hand the king added that 'I approve of this letter'. It was perhaps the only way that he could have persuaded Danby to write it. Louis promptly refused the request, but Charles had left another hostage to fortune that would in time severely damage Danby himself.

Then Louis caught Charles unawares by making a separate peace with the United Provinces, leaving no room for the English king to manoeuvre himself into the good graces of one party or the other. He had in a sense been abandoned by his French cousin. This gave him pause for thought. He was walking through St James's Park on a summer morning, in the middle of August, when he was approached by a chemist who worked in the royal laboratory. Charles, ever affable and courteous, greeted Christopher Kirkby with a salutation.

Kirkby then informed him that a Jesuit plot had been detected against his life; the sovereign was to be stabbed or poisoned so that the Catholic James, duke of York, could be raised to the throne. Charles, always inclined to dismiss such conspiracies as little more than hot air, advised Kirkby to consult his confidential secretary. Some desultory enquiries followed, in the course of which a long indictment against certain Jesuits was discovered. The supposed author of this indictment, Titus Oates, was then brought before a committee of the privy council to justify his accusations. Thus began the episode that became known as the 'Popish Plot'.

Roger North described Oates as 'a low man, of an ill cut, very short neck; and his visage and features were most particular. His mouth was the centre of his face . . .' He had a low forehead, long nose, and huge chin; his voice was high, and his manner dramatic. Yet he was very plausible. He outlined the meetings and consultations of the Jesuits in confident detail, and went on to name two prominent men as the authors of the plot. He accused Sir George Wakeman, physician to the queen, of planning to poison Charles; he also cited Edward Coleman, her secretary and previously secretary to the duke of York. The Catholic heir apparent was therefore touched. One of the councillors who listened to this damning testimony, Sir Henry Coventry, observed that 'if he be a liar, he is the greatest and adroitest I ever saw'.

Then a sudden death seemed to confirm Oates's testimony. He had previously sworn an affidavit to the truth of these matters before a London magistrate, Sir Edmund Berry Godfrey; he had told Godfrey that he had attended a clandestine meeting of Jesuits at the White Horse Tavern in the Strand, where the various methods of assassinating the king were discussed. It seems that Godfrey was alarmed to see the name of an acquaintance, Edward Coleman, on the list of suspects. On 12 October Godfrey did not return to his home. Five days later his body was found in a ditch on Primrose Hill, run through with his own sword. A coroner's inquest then concluded that the body had been taken to Primrose Hill on the day it was discovered, and that multiple bruising about the upper part of it and, in particular, the neck was indication that he had been strangled. Had he been murdered by the Catholics in fear of their discovery? Had he been killed by the supporters of Oates, who feared that his lying would be proven? Had he committed suicide? The truth of the matter will never be known.

Alarms and prophecies were already circulating. In the previous year a blazing comet had hurtled through the sky, and in 1678 occurred three eclipses of the sun and two of the moon. William Dade's *Prognostication* divined 'frenzies, inflammations and new infirmities proceeding from cholerick humours' while John Partridge's *Calendarium Judaicum* predicted 'troubles from great men and nobles'. In this atmosphere of anxiety, the discovery of Godfrey's body prompted mass panic and hysteria about a possible Catholic rising. The lords-lieutenant of the counties were ordered to search the homes of Catholics for hidden weapons, and of course the more general fear of a French invasion in favour of an uprising was never far from the surface. It was also widely believed that many thousands of apparently orthodox Protestants were in fact Catholics in disguise, waiting for a sign. One contemporary observer, Sir John Reresby, wrote that 'it seemed as if the very cabinet of hell had been laid open'.

When the papers of Edward Coleman were taken it was revealed that he had written certain suspect letters to Jesuit priests, close to Louis XIV, asking for money on the grounds that he and his colleagues 'had a mighty work on their hands, no less than the conversion of three kingdoms'. It may have been a piece of bravura, and seemed to have no connection with the plot outlined by Oates, but in the present circumstances it was explosive.

The publication of this plot, together with the possible collusion of James, admirably suited the intentions of Shaftesbury who could come forward as the champion of Protestantism. He had left the Tower for his Dorset estates a few months before, after making a formal apology to the king, but he could now take up the cause of 'No Popery!' with fresh justification and enthusiasm. It had become his abiding purpose to exclude James from the throne of England. He commented later that 'I will not say who started the game, but I am sure I had the full hunting of it'.

When parliament reassembled on 21 October 1678, he and his supporters were in charge of the pack. Committees were established to secure the king's safety and to investigate the plot. Both Houses of Parliament unanimously carried a resolution that 'there has been, and still is, a damnable and hellish plot contrived and carried on by popish recusants, for the assassinating and murdering the king, and for subverting the government and rooting out and destroying the Protestant religion'. Oates appeared before the Commons on three consecutive days and, as a result of his testimony, five Catholic peers were arrested. A bill was passed that excluded Catholics from both houses. Shaftesbury proposed that the king should be asked to dismiss James, duke of York, from his council.

At the end of November Titus Oates further raised the temperature when he appeared at the bar of the House of Commons. 'I, Titus Oates, accuse Catherine, queen of England, of high treason.' This alarmed the members who voted that the queen and her household should be removed from Whitehall. The Lords were not so hasty, however, and examined the witnesses who had testified against her; they were not convinced of their veracity and suppressed the charges brought by Oates. The king had previously held a private interview with Oates during which the informer had laid the charges against his wife; he kept his temper but ordered that all of Oates's papers should be seized and that his consultations with other people should be supervised.

The king does not seem to have believed a word that Oates uttered, but he could not openly withstand the full force of Protestant rage. As one of his ministers, the marquis of Halifax, put it, 'it must be handled as if it were true, whether it were so or no'. Measures against papists were made more severe, therefore, and the five Catholic lords held in the Tower were impeached of high treason. A second Test Act was passed obliging all Catholics in the Lords or Commons to repeat the oaths of allegiance and supremacy. In the course of the debate one peer declared that 'I would not have so much as a popish man or a popish woman to remain here; not so much as a popish dog or a popish bitch; not so much as a popish cat to purr or mew about the king'. At the beginning of December Edward Coleman was dragged to Tyburn where he was hanged, drawn and quartered; in 1929 he was beatified as a Catholic martyr.

Another act of this political drama now opened with the decision of Ralph Montagu to attack the earl of Danby. It was he who, as ambassador in Paris, had received the earl's letter concerning a secret subsidy from the French king to Charles. He had lost his office in the summer of this year, for the crime of corrupting the daughter of the king's former mistress, Lady Castlemaine, and now sought revenge. Another party may also have been involved. Louis XIV, knowing of Danby's antipathy to the French cause, had reasons enough to want him removed.

On being elected to the Commons for the borough of Northampton, Montagu arranged that his 'secret letters' from Danby should be disclosed to parliament. It became apparent that Danby, with the approval of the king, had asked for a bribe from Louis at the same time as he had solicited funds from the Commons to raise an army against France. As Lord Cavendish put it, 'it will appear by those papers that the war with France was pretended, for the sake of an army, and that a great man carried on the interest of an army and popery'. In the Commons the member for Shaftesbury, Thomas Bennet, said that 'I wonder the House sits so silent when they see themselves sold for six million *livres* to the French'. The situation was rendered infinitely worse for Danby by the fact that the army itself was still in existence; the king had no money either to deploy it or disband it.

The earl could not survive. Seven articles of impeachment were passed against him, amongst them the charge of keeping up an army to subvert the government and of being 'popishly affected'. In the Lords Danby defended himself with vigour. He poured scorn upon his accuser, Montagu, for perfidy and duplicity against his royal master; he denied the charges and demanded a speedy trial.

Charles then decided to suspend the proceedings against his chief minister by proroguing parliament. At a meeting of the privy council in the first weeks of 1679 the king told his councillors that he would not seek their advice because they were more afraid of parliament than they were of him. He dissolved the assembly on 24 January. So ended the 'Cavalier Parliament' that had first met in 1661, just after the restoration of the king; it had lasted seventeen years and in that period had turned from an assembly of the king's supporters into a fractious and suspicious body ready to turn upon the king's ministers and even upon the king himself.

Yet Charles and his ministers influenced the country in ways of which they were wholly unaware. The ending of the naval war with the Dutch in 1674, for example, materially increased the volume of the country's export trade. The excise returns after that year rose markedly in such staple items as beer, ale, tea and coffee, which in turn indicates a sharp rise in consumption. The increase in revenue had a significant effect upon royal income, too, which began to rise. Contemporary reports also suggest that the 'middling classes' were now indulging their taste for imported 'luxuries' and that the labouring poor were purchasing such items as knitted stockings, earthenware dishes and brass pots. The 'commercial revolution' of the eighteenth century had its origins three or four decades earlier. The successful colonization of portions of North America and of the West Indies, undertaken in the realms of the early Stuart kings and under the protectorate of Oliver Cromwell, now found its fruit in the ever-increasing rate of trade. By 1685 the English had the largest merchant fleet in the world, and their vessels were filled with the merchandise of sugar, tobacco and cotton on their way to the great emporium of London.

Other evidence supports this picture of material advantage. By 1672, for example, stagecoaches ran between London and all the principal towns of the kingdom; it was reported that 'every little town within twenty miles of London swarms with them'. The ubiquity of the stagecoach is the harbinger of the reforms of transport in the next century, with the further development of turnpike roads and canals; the country was slowly quickening its pace while at the same time finding its unity.

It is now a commonplace of economic history that the 'agricultural revolution' of the eighteenth century in fact began in the middle of the seventeenth century. The introduction of new crops, and the steady spread of 'enclosures' designed to achieve cohesion and efficiency of farming land, were already changing the landscape of England. The abundance of grain, for example, was such that in 1670 cereal farmers were allowed to export their crop without any regard to its price in the domestic market.

John Houghton, in *Collection of Letters for the Improvement of Husbandry and Trade*, wrote in 1682 that 'since his majesty's most happy restoration the whole land hath been fermented and stirred up by the profitable hints it hath received from the Royal Society by which means parks have been disparked, commons enclosed, woods turned into arable, and pasture land improved by clover, St. Foine [a grass], turnips, coleseed [rape], parsley, and many other good husbandries, so that the food of the cattle is increased as fast, if not faster, than the consumption . . .' It is a sign that practical experiment and innovation were already proving fruitful.

Another revolution began during the reigns of the later Stuarts. The exact conditions for the whirlwind of invention, commerce and trade that comprised the industrial revolution may not yet have been present; but the atmosphere was changing. English shipbuilding reached an unprecedented and unrepeated 'peak' in the seventeenth century. From the mines of England issued more coal, tin and iron ore than ever before; the coal production of the north-east of England, for example, more than doubled between 1600 and 1685. The old trade of heavy cloths was now being replaced by that of lighter cloths made in what were known as 'woollen manufactories'. Sugar refineries, iron foundries and glass works were ubiquitous by the close of the seventeenth century. The industries of brewing and soap-boiling had already been created. The rapid growth of towns such as Manchester and Birmingham, Halifax and Sheffield, testified to the interdependence between industrialization and urbanization. Birmingham had under the Tudors been little more than a village but, by the turn of the century, it would have at least 8,000 inhabitants. The population of the whole country may have stabilized, but a larger proportion of it was now migrating from the country to the town.

The election in the early weeks of 1679, after the dissolution of the 'Cavalier Parliament', was necessarily fought on the choice between king and parliament. Since the mood of the country had turned against the king, after the revelation of the 'Popish Plot' and the disgrace of Danby, the new parliament was even more hostile to the court than its predecessor. The king himself remarked that a dog would be elected if it stood against a figure from court. Shaftesbury, the principal benefactor of this change of mood, calculated that 158 'courtiers' had been elected against 302 of the 'opposition'.

The king had to deal with two pressing matters in advance of negotiating with the new parliament. He met the earl of Danby and requested him to resign his office; in exchange he would be granted the title of marquis, and receive a large annual pension. Since most of his dependants had been voted out of parliament, his ministry was effectively already at an end. A new politics, of agitation and campaign, had emerged.

The archbishop of Canterbury had been asked to discuss with James, duke of York, the prospect of his returning to the Anglican communion; the duke refused. The king then summoned his brother and ordered him to retire beyond the seas as the only way of averting the displeasure of parliament. James fought hard against this sentence of exile but, at the beginning of March, made a lachrymose departure for the Spanish Netherlands on the pretext that he was visiting his daughter and new son-in-law, William of Orange.

Yet the new parliament would not be diverted from its pursuit of the 'Popish Plot' or the impeachment of Danby, especially after it was revealed that the earl had received a pardon from the king. A week after its assembly he resigned and in the following month he was sent to the Tower by the Lords. When Lord Halifax condemned the decision to confer a marquisate upon 'a traitor to his country' he fixed his eyes upon the king who was watching the proceedings. 'My God!' the king was said later to have exclaimed, 'how I am ill-treated; and I must bear it, and keep silence!'

In the spring of the year, just after the parliament had met, the king announced a change in the administration. He dissolved the privy council and established in its place a smaller council of thirty-three members comprising office-holders and independents. In what at the time seemed a surprising and even shocking move he appointed Shaftesbury as its lord president together with four members of parliament who had always been resolute in opposing him. His purpose may have been to tame or to corrupt these men, but the nominations may simply have afforded a screen to conceal his real intentions. Some of the new counsellors lost their former influence, in any case, and were widely regarded as having sold themselves to the king. The members of the council were soon divided among themselves, and proved to be singularly ineffective. That may also have been the king's intention. Charles distrusted all of them and confided to the earl of Aylesbury that 'they shall know nothing'. He was isolated, after

Danby had been removed from office, and he told Sir William Temple that 'he had none left with whom he could so much as speak of them in confidence'. In his fight against vigorous and well-organized parliamentary opponents, he was on his own.

Towards the end of April 1679, an address was introduced that was designed to exclude the duke of York from the crown of England; it was said that the 'Popish Plot' had been encouraged by his likely succession to the throne. It marked the formal beginning of what became known as the 'exclusion crisis', and was the cause of much partisan rancour. Pamphlets and verse satires came from the presses; the votes of parliament were published and widely disseminated. The 'exclusionists' in large part controlled the Commons, but legislation could not pass without the consent of the king and the Lords.

Nevertheless an Exclusion Bill quickly received its first and second readings; it pronounced that the duke of York had been seduced by papal agents into entering the Roman communion, and that it was the duty of parliament to exclude him from the throne. One member, Sir John Trevor, stated that 'the king's eyes are closed; he knows nothing of the danger that we are in . . .' The mood of hysteria was translated beyond the walls of parliament. It was said that the citizens slept with pistols beside them, and that their wives carried knives into the street. At the beginning of July Charles, exasperated by the proceedings, prorogued parliament. The unpopularity of his decision was such that he doubled the guards at Whitehall. Shaftesbury declared that the royal advisers should pay for the decision with their heads.

The session left only one permanent memorial in the form of a Habeas Corpus Act which decreed that no person could be unlawfully detained and that all those charged with felony or treason should be granted a speedy trial or discharge from prison. This was designed as a means of public safety in the event of James's ascending the throne. In his *Commentaries on the Laws of England* Sir William Blackstone wrote that 'the point of time at which I would choose to fix this *theoretical* perfection of our public law is the year 1679; after the habeas corpus act was passed, and that for licensing the press had expired . . .' The sudden prorogation had indeed meant that the laws inhibiting the press had not been renewed, so that the rage of party could now be fully conveyed in the public prints.

In the latter half of 1679, the terms of 'Whig' and 'Tory' became common currency. The Presbyterian rebels of Scotland, ever zealous for a stricter covenant, had been given the name of Whiggamores after the Scottish word for corrupt or sour whey; the Irish royalist Catholics, who had been reduced to banditry, had the Gaelic name of *toraihde*. Soon enough Shaftesbury's Whigs, who supported the Protestant Church and favoured the exclusion of James, would oppose Danby's Tories, who were prepared to countenance a Catholic king as part of the divine order of natural succession. The Whigs were the enemies of popery and arbitrary government, and thus wished to limit royal power; the Tories were determined to defend the monarch and the constitution against the onslaught of those whom they considered to be republicans or rebels. Various factions could of course be observed on both sides and a third group of 'trimmers', who pursued a middle course, was also evident. A sympathetic witness, the duke of Ormonde, described the 'trimmers' as using the language of 'moderation, unity and peace' combining the Whig concern for the maintenance of property and the true religion with the Tory desire for a secure monarchy and an untouched royal prerogative.

Moderation and unity were not readily apparent in a political nation violently divided. The Green Ribbon Club, perhaps the first ever political club, consisted of a variety of groups of Whigs including dissenters, lawyers and merchants; it met at the King's Head Tavern on the corner of Fleet Street and Chancery Lane, where it was accustomed to plan its strategy and to co-ordinate its tactics. As avowed supporters of Shaftesbury, its members wore green ribbons and thus identified themselves as a 'party'. They paid customary obeisance to the royal prerogative but more often than not they talked of their responsibilities to 'the people'; one phrase, '*salus populi suprema lex*', was often repeated: 'the safety of the people is the supreme law'. This would in effect have created a political revolution, albeit without the bloodshed of another civil war.

Charles believed that if his opponents managed to get rid of James he himself would surely follow. He was engaged in a battle for his survival. His opponents believed that, under increasing pressure, he would eventually submit and bar his brother from the throne; many now looked to the king's illegitimate son, the duke of Monmouth, a Protestant, as the next heir. Shaftesbury even argued that the king was pretending to oppose exclusion while all the time hoping to be 'forced' to agree to his natural son's accession. It is true that he had a low opinion of his brother. When James cautioned him from walking in St James's Park without a guard he replied, 'I am sure no man in England will take away my life to make you king.' It was unlikely, however, that Charles would deny James his lawful right to succeed.

The French ambassador observed that the king's 'conduct is so secret and impenetrable that even the most skilful observers are misled. The king has secret dealings and contacts with all the factions and those who are most opposed to his interests flatter themselves that they will win him over to their side.' The ambassador may have credited the king with too much cunning; it is possible that Charles simply moved from one expedient to the next.

The duke of Monmouth, the Protestant candidate for the succession, now covered himself with glory or at least with blood. A band of covenanters dragged the primate of Scotland, Archbishop Sharp, from his coach outside the town of St Andrews and stabbed him to death in front of his daughter; they then went on to defeat a royalist squadron sent after them. Monmouth was now dispatched to the north with a large army where, at Bothwell Bridge, he routed the covenanters. The subsequent repression of these enthusiasts became known as 'the killing time'. Monmouth became the hero of the hour, his ambitions for the throne significantly increased; as a Protestant he was Shaftesbury's preferred candidate, and James looked on in alarm from his exile in Brussels as the king's favour towards his natural son increased.

Charles had, a few months earlier, signed a document in which he explained that 'for the voiding of any dispute which may happen in time concerning the succession of the Crown, I do hereby declare in the presence of Almighty God that I never gave nor made any contract of marriage, nor was married to any woman whatsoever, but to my present wife Queen Catharine now living'. He had declared to the world that Monmouth was illegitimate, therefore, but the king was not inexpert at lying.

When Monmouth returned to London, the people assembled in the streets where bonfires were lit and toasts were drunk. He was considered by many to be the champion of the Protestant faith and, as the first illegitimate son of Charles II, the true heir to the throne. Despite the king's denial it was claimed that a 'black box', carefully concealed, contained a contract of marriage between Charles and Lucy Walters; Lucy Walters had been one of his first mistresses, while in continental exile, and had borne this particular son. Monmouth was handsome and affable, in every respect a royal boy, and on his journeys through the kingdom he was treated with as much ceremony as his father. Wherever he went he was escorted by columns of gentlemen and admirers. He was, in the words of Macaulay, 'the most popular man in the kingdom'. It is perhaps no wonder that his thoughts turned towards the crown. The shield that bore his coat of arms quartered the lions of England and the lilies of France as a symbol of his aspirations. He had even begun to 'touch' for the king's evil.

In July 1679, the king decided to turn the prorogation of parliament into a dissolution, pending a new general election; he was gambling that public sentiment had turned towards him. And indeed there were many now who questioned the wisdom and loyalty of Shaftesbury in his relentless pursuit of the duke of York. Yet at the hustings in the summer of the year the Whig Party, as we may now term it, was in full cry against the Catholic heir. When the clergy of Essex were believed to incline to the court interest, they were called 'dumb dogs . . . Jesuitical dogs . . . dark lanterns . . . Baal's priests . . . jacks and villains . . . the black guard . . . the black regiment of hell!' The Whigs were in turn dismissed by the Tories as a 'rabble' of disloyal and rebellious traitors. Lists were drawn up by both sides, noting down the names of 'the vile' and 'the worthy'. Sir Ralph Verney, soon to become a member of parliament, remarked that 'there are vast feuds in our Chilterns as well as in our Vale, occasioned by elections, and so 'tis, I suppose, all over England'.

But then all the problems of succession became more acute. Towards the end of August the king fell seriously ill, and was for two or three days in danger of death. James was summoned from Brussels to be by his brother's side, and perhaps to take the crown; he came to England disguised in a black wig. Meanwhile Monmouth's supporters began to intrigue on his behalf. The political nation was in confusion.

43

Or at the Cock?

On 12 January 1675, a conversation took place in London. It was ostensibly about china, that commodity then being the rage of the town. Lady Fidget desires some from a dear male acquaintance 'for he knows china very well, and has himself very good, but will not let me see it lest I should beg some'. The gentleman's name is Horner, whose welcome for Lady Fidget alarms her husband.

Sir Jaspar: Wife! My Lady Fidget! He is coming into you the back way!

Lady Fidget: Let him come, and welcome, which way he will.

Sir Jaspar: He'll catch you, and use you roughly, and be too strong for you.

Lady Fidget: Don't you trouble yourself, let him if he can.

Horner, having been detained in his chamber with Lady Fidget, is asked a few minutes later if he has any china left.

Horner: Upon my honour I have none left now.

Mrs Squeamish: Nay, nay, I have known you deny your china before now, but you shan't put me off so. Come.

Horner: This lady had the last there.

Lady Fidget: Yes indeed, madam, to my certain knowledge he has no more left.

Mrs Squeamish: Oh, but it may be he may have some you could not find.

Lady Fidget: What, d'ye think if he had any left, I would not have had it too? For we women of quality never think we have china enough.

The conversation took place on the stage of the Theatre Royal in Drury Lane. 'China' is course a euphemism for male sperm, as all the members of the audience knew, and *The Country Wife* by William Wycherley soon gained a reputation for indecency. Yet, in the 1670s, this was not considered to be a great offence. It was, perhaps, a quality to be praised.

Two companies of players were re-established immediately after the restoration of the king, the King's Players under the management of Thomas Killigrew and the Duke of York's Servants under Sir William Davenant. They played at first in makeshift venues until such time as suitable playhouses were erected. They did in any case cater for a considerably diminished audience since the great days of the Globe and the Fortune; the new theatrical public was largely made up of 'the quality' or 'the fashion' as well as those members of the middling classes who wished to emulate them.

The 'sparks' and 'wits' of the court were also in attendance and would, in the words of Etherege from *She Wou'd if She Cou'd*, roam 'from one play-house to the other play-house, and if they like neither the play nor the women, they seldom stay any longer than the combing of their periwigs, or a whisper or two with a friend; and then they cock their caps, and out they strut again'. The play began at half past three in the afternoon, and lasted for approximately two hours. The gentlemen brought their own wine with them and often made more noise than the players on the stage, hectoring or exchanging badinage with the actors.

In *The Country Wife* Horner feigns impotence in order to deceive husbands and enter into clandestine amours with their wives; among these is Margery Pinchwife, an innocent young bride from the country who is fiercely guarded by her husband. The usual complications of sexual farce ensue amid innuendo and double meaning, with the principal women desperate to enjoy Horner's favours by clandestine means. Lady Fidget herself does not deplore the hypocrisy of seeming virtuous. 'Our reputation! Lord, why should you not think that we women make use of our reputation, as you men of yours, only to deceive the world with less suspicion?' As Leigh Hunt once remarked of these seventeenth-century dramas, 'we see nothing but a set of heartless fine ladies and gentlemen, coming in and going out, saying witty things at each other, and buzzing in some maze of intrigue'.

But this is the heart of the comedies of the Restoration period. They reflect a hard, if brittle, society where the prize goes to the most devious or hypocritical; they represent a world in which all moral values are provisional or uncertain; they convey a general sense of instability in which no one knows quite what to believe or how to behave. It is the perfect complement to Restoration tragedy in which fantastic notions of love or valour are pitched past the reality of life or true feeling; they are contrived and sentimental vehicles for rant and rhetoric.

The comedies, unlike the tragedies, of the period are at least set in real time and real place. The time is always the present moment, and the place is always London.

Sparkish: Come, but where do we dine?
Horner: Even where you will.
Sparkish: At Chateline's?
Dorilant: Yes, if you will.
Sparkish: Or at the Cock?
Dorilant: Yes, if you please.
Sparkish: Or at the Dog and Partridge?

This was a world in which the participants must 'stay, until the chairs come', in which the prostitutes always wore vizards, and in which the women 'all fell a-laughing, till they bepissed themselves'. The protagonists are always those of the gentry or nobility, or at least those who aspire to be such; the playwrights were of the same mould, as were the members of the audience. Everyone knew everyone else but, in this multiple game of mirrors, we may glimpse the shape of the age.

The characters of course express themselves in prose; good conversation was considered be the medium of truth as well as of manners. Nothing was so delightfully true as that which was perfectly expressed. The notion of 'wit' is crucial here since, as Horner expresses it, 'methinks wit is more necessary than beauty, and I think no young woman ugly that has it, and no handsome woman agreeable without it'. Wit was not simply the effect of an epigram but, rather, the product of a fertile mind and keen observation. Wit was the currency of the court of Charles II.

The obscenity was also as much part of the court as of the stage. Horner apologizes to Lady Horner for bringing to her from France 'not so much as a bawdy picture, new postures, nor the second part of the *École des Filles*'. Pepys described the latter publication as 'the most bawdy, lewd book that ever I saw . . . so that I was shamed of reading it'. So the comic stage was used to strong meat. Yet not, perhaps, as strong as this:

> In liquid raptures I dissolve all o'er,
> Melt into sperm, and spend at every pore.
> A touch from any part of her had done 't:
> Her hand, her foot, her very look's a cunt.

The author, John Wilmot, earl of Rochester, was an indispensable element of the court of Charles II. At the age of seventeen, on Christmas Day 1664, he arrived at Whitehall bearing a letter to the king from the duchess of Orléans in France. Soon enough he was enrolled in the circle of wits that surrounded the king and by the spring of 1666 he had been appointed as one of the gentlemen of the bedchamber. He had all the qualities that the king admired. He was witty and he was fluent; he had a lightness of manner, and indeed of conscience, that were of paramount importance in such surroundings:

> That pattern of virtue, Her Grace of Cleveland,
> Has swallowed more pricks than the ocean has sand;
> But by rubbing and scrubbing so large it does grow,
> It is fit for just nothing but Signior Dildo.

He was sent to the Tower after attempting to abduct a lady; on his release, at the king's orders, he played a valiant or perhaps foolhardy role in one of the conflicts with the Dutch. His subsequent life at court principally consisted of liberal doses of drink and sex, interlarded with fashionable atheism or, as it was sometimes known, 'Hobbeism'. He recalled that at an atheistical meeting at the house of a 'man of quality' 'I undertook to manage the cause, and was the principal disputant against God and piety, and . . . received the applause of the whole company'. This conveys sufficiently the presiding atmosphere of Whitehall.

For five years he was, by his own account, continually drunk and was so little master of himself that he forgot many of his 'wild and unaccountable' actions. Like most of his contemporaries at court he was deeply engaged in the theatre of the time; in fact the drama can perhaps best be seen as an extension of the court itself. Rochester patronized playwrights such as Dryden and Otway; he wrote a comedy and a tragedy as well as various prologues. Yet he is still remembered principally for his satirical invectives and for his mastery of obscenity:

> Much wine had passed, with grave discourse,
> Of who fucks who, and who does worse . . .

A character in *The Country Wife* asks, 'Is it not a frank age? And I am a frank person.' The 'frankness' might have consisted principally of blasphemy and obscenity, but it was also part of a novel dispensation represented by the cogent social analysis of Thomas Hobbes and the decision of the experimenters of the Royal Society to deal in things and not in words. It was an attempt to see the world anew, after the realization that religious obscurantism and doctrinaire prejudices had previously brought England into confusion. Horace Walpole wrote that 'because the presbyterians and religionists had affected to call every thing by a scripture-name, the new court affected to call every thing by its own name'. It was time to clear away the rubble of untested assumptions, false rhetoric and standard appeals to authority or to tradition. This was the context for the ironical, cynical and materialist atmosphere of the Restoration court.

44

Noise rhymes to noise

When James arrived at his brother's sickroom in Windsor Castle he fell to his knees, and it is reported that the two men burst into tears. The king had recovered some of his strength and was already out of danger. Yet the two claimants to the throne, the dukes of York and Monmouth, were now in confrontation; each had his own band of supporters, but James for the moment had the upper hand. His sudden return to England had not caused an insurrection, as some had feared, and he had indeed been received with deference; the lord mayor and the aldermen of London, for example, had come to kiss his hand. He did not wish to return to exile in Brussels, and seems to have made it clear that he would leave England only if the duke of Monmouth also made his exit. It was agreed therefore that Monmouth would retire into Holland, out of harm's way, while James would be dispatched to Edinburgh as a kind of viceroy. He remained there for almost three years.

It had already become clear that, in the election of the summer, the Whigs had won the majority and that those who had voted against the 'exclusion' of James were generally turned out of office. Charles refused to allow this parliament to sit, however, and prorogued it to the beginning of the following year, 1680. He told his nephew, William of Orange, that he had no choice in the matter and that otherwise 'they would have his crown'; he also feared that the Commons would proceed to the impeachment of his brother and his wife for their Catholic beliefs. Few expected parliament to meet again.

Shaftesbury was discharged from his office as lord president of the new council, and at once entered his true role as leader of the opposition to the court and Crown. Yet he knew well enough that he had no real power unless or until parliament was assembled. The Commons was his praetorian guard. Almost at once, therefore, he planned to launch petitions from all parts of the country for its return. His organization was such that his agents, together with notable local men, went from parish to parish collecting marks and signatures. No one, not even the poorest, was overlooked.

On 17 November the Green Ribbon Club, opposed to Catholics and to the court, organized a great pageant in London in which it was claimed that 200,000 people took part. A variety of Catholic personages were in representation dragged through the streets, and the procession eventually halted in Fleet Street just by the King's Arms, the headquarters of the club; here effigies of the pope and of the devil, as well as sundry monks, nuns and Jesuits, were hurled into the flames of a fire accompanied by a great shout that, according to a pamphlet, 'London's Defiance to Rome', reached France and Rome 'damping them all with a dreadful astonishment'. Macaulay remarks in his *History of England* that two words became current at this time, 'mob' and 'sham'.

When the duke of Monmouth arrived in London unexpectedly from exile, he was greeted with bonfires and jubilant crowds as the natural Protestant successor to the throne; he was not so warmly received by his father, however, who told him to be gone from court. His son disobeyed on the grounds that he must stay in order to preserve the life of his father from the designs of the papists.

At the beginning of December 1679, with a party of fifteen other peers, Shaftesbury stopped Charles on his way to the royal chapel and presented him with a petition for the sitting of parliament. The king was so irate that he prorogued the assembly for a further eleven months and issued a proclamation against petitioning itself. His supporters were said to 'abhor' the conduct of those who were trying to force the king's hand; for a while grew up the factions of 'the Abhorrers' and 'the Petitioners'.

After some months of impasse Shaftesbury once more raised the temperature when in the early summer of 1680 he tried to present, to a Middlesex grand jury, the duke of York as a papist and the duchess of Portsmouth, Charles's mistress, as a prostitute. The latter had already attracted the dislike and suspicion of many, and it had often been suggested that she should be sent packing to France as soon as possible. Shaftesbury's action was of course an open affront to the king, and an obvious attempt to inflame public opinion. The king hastened to London from Windsor where he instructed the chief justice, William Scroggs, to dismiss the grand jury before it heard any evidence for the charges. The damage had been done, however, compounded by the fact that Shaftesbury received no rebuke.

When parliament finally met, towards the end of October, the Commons was full from the very first session. The king's ministers, known as 'the chits' because of their relative youth, had formulated what they hoped was a consistent policy; they intended to defuse the threat of exclusion by imposing limitations on the power of a future King James, and to seek an alliance with the United Provinces against the French. It was still important to signal hostility to Louis XIV, even though Charles had been engaged in constant negotiations to obtain money from him.

The Whigs were not to be averted from their purpose, however, and at the beginning of November a second Exclusion Bill against the duke of York was introduced. It received its third reading within nine days and was then sent up to the Lords. The duke of Monmouth came back to London from a triumphal tour of the West Country in order to participate in the discussions.

The king also attended this long session of the peers, from eleven in the morning to nine at night, and listened to them with eager attention. It had been believed that he would abandon his brother, however reluctantly, for the sake of public peace; he was known to fear, more than anything else, the outbreak of another civil war. But in fact he remained firm and made his feelings known during the course of the Lords' debate. When Monmouth expressed his concern for his father, Charles called out, 'It is a Judas kiss that he gives me!' The sentiments of the king may have helped to concentrate the minds of the Lords. They voted, sixty-three to thirty, against the Exclusion Bill. Shaftesbury's measure had failed.

It was hoped that the Commons might now suggest a compromise upon which both sides might agree, but no possibility of a middle way existed. The Commons passed a series of resolutions aimed at the exclusion of the duke of York; they stated that no supply of money could be voted under the circumstances, that the councillors of the king should be removed from public employment, and that any man who lent money to the king should be called to the bar of parliament. The king was advised to prorogue parliament once again and the Commons, speedily warned of this threat, met early on the morning of 10 January 1681, to vote that anyone who offered such advice was a traitor to the king and to the realm. The king therefore issued a proclamation dissolving parliament, and ordering that a new assembly should meet in Oxford within two months.

This aroused anger, resentment and no little anxiety among Shaftesbury and his followers. Oxford was known to be the most royalist of all English cities. They would have been even more concerned if they had learned that Louis XIV had proffered another bribe to the king. Louis offered to grant him an annual pension, larger than anything parliament would provide, as long as he refrained from joining in any attack upon France by Spain or others. A ban on French imports was also allowed to expire. Nothing was put in writing, and no signatures were required; it was simply a verbal agreement, mediated by envoys, between the two kings.

The new parliament, meeting on 21 March 1681, was no more willing than its predecessor to come to any agreement. Charles appeared before the two houses with a compromise. If James ever became king, his powers would be transferred to a regent. In the first instance that regent would be James's older daughter, Mary, princess of Orange, a Protestant; and, in the event of her decease, the regency would devolve upon his other Protestant daughter, Anne. This seemed on the face of it an eminently sensible arrangement, but the Commons refused to accept it. Instead it debated a third Exclusion Bill. Charles in fact seems genuinely to have wished for an agreement in the calmer atmosphere of Oxford, no less for the fact that he feared another civil war. That was another reason for his secret alliance with the French king; he might need men as well as money.

On 28 March, Charles, with his full regalia concealed in a covered sedan chair, proceeded to the Lords, who were sitting in the Geometry School of Oxford. He was about to spring a surprise. He appeared before the Lords in his ordinary clothes, but then he ordered his attendants to dress him in robe and crown. Thus attired he summoned the Commons. 'My lords and gentlemen,' he said to the two houses, 'all the world may see to what a point we are come, that we are not like to have a good end, when the divisions at the beginning are such: therefore, my lord chancellor, do as I have commanded you.' He now told his opponents, to their faces, that they had been dissolved and must disperse. He left Oxford immediately, and they had no choice but to follow. It was reported that 'the king's breath scattered them like leaves in autumn'.

Charles now believed that he could survive without any parliamentary funds. His pension from France, and the raising of customs revenue from luxury French imports now freely admitted, would grant him room to manoeuvre; his household expenditure had in any case been considerably reduced. He had decided to embark upon a period of personal rule without an opposition to divert or trouble him. In this respect the king was greatly assisted by what seemed to be a resurgence of loyalty towards the Stuart monarchy. The intransigence of Shaftesbury and his followers, in rejecting what seemed to be a just and sensible offer on the matter of the regency, could be contrasted with the moderation of the king. They had wanted to bully him into submission, but he had remained firm. He had resisted any attempt to alter the natural succession because it was repugnant to his conscience and to the laws of England. That is how the abortive Oxford parliament could be represented.

In his declaration 'to all his loving subjects, touching the causes and reasons that moved him to dissolve the last two parliaments' he stated that 'we assure ourself that we shall be assisted by the loyalty' of those 'who consider the rise and progress of the late troubles'. The 'late troubles' were the divisions that had led to the civil wars. 'And we cannot but remember that religion, liberty and property were all lost and gone when monarchy was shaken off, and could never be revived till that was restored.' He appealed, therefore, to the instincts of loyalty and stability that maintained the traditions of the nation.

He now turned his fury upon Shaftesbury and his allies who, with no likelihood of a parliament, began to lose strength as well as purpose. Charles was determined to exclude them from all public offices; he decided to remove them from the judicial bench and from the administration of the towns. Sixty members of parliament who had voted for exclusion were removed from nomination as justices of the peace. Some of the lords-lieutenant of the counties were dismissed, together with the lowlier recorders and town clerks. Since the nonconformists had played a large role in the opposition, the laws against dissenters were executed with more rigour; they, rather than Roman Catholics, were increasingly consigned to prison. One contemporary said that it was a form of civil war, with the law replacing the sword.

At the beginning of July 1681 Shaftesbury was taken into custody and brought before the king and council where he was accused of treason; the earl denied the charge but was in any case committed to the Tower. Yet there was a flaw in the royal project. Shaftesbury had a residence at Aldersgate, and so his case came within the jurisdiction of the City. London was still in the hands of those who opposed the court; it was still, for the king, enemy territory.

When the earl's case was heard in the Old Bailey, therefore, the grand jury was packed with prominent Whigs; the foreman had in fact been an exclusionist member of parliament. It was perhaps inevitable that a verdict of *ignoramus* – 'we do not know' – was given and Shaftesbury acquitted. Four days later he applied for bail and the king's son, the duke of Monmouth, offered to act as his surety. He was released and, that night, the streets rang out with the cries 'A Monmouth! A Shaftesbury!' In many places, however, a Whig demonstration was countermanded by a Tory manifestation; or, as Sir Roger L'Estrange put it in his *Observator*, 'Noise rhymes to Noise, and Noise must be opposed to Noise'.

Two days after the verdict had been given the king launched an investigation into London's charter, asking '*quo warranto*' or by what warrant did the City enjoy the corporate privileges that it claimed; it was a protracted and expensive procedure, replete with formal and legal niceties, which could easily be turned against the City corporation. Any pretext could be found or concocted by the court lawyers to justify a forfeiture. It was easier and less expensive to ask for a new charter, but this in turn might give the king power to remove 'disaffected' members of the corporation. It was a device that Charles had already been using to great effect.

Even before the *quo warranto* proceedings had ended, the court party was exercising all its influence to elect Tory sheriffs and a Tory mayor. Various subterfuges were employed. The keepers of the alehouses and coffee-houses were told that their licences would be revoked if they did not vote for the Tory candidates; most of the Whig candidates were removed from the poll on the grounds that they were Quakers, or were non-residents, or had refused to take the oaths, or were in some other way ineligible. The campaign of trickery and intimidation was successful, and the Tory candidates were elected. On the following day Shaftesbury left his house in Aldersgate and went into hiding before taking ship to Holland. He knew now that, in any new trial for high treason, his opponents would be able to control the juries. The king would finally claim his head. He died in Amsterdam at the beginning of the next year. It was his belief that the souls of men and women entered the stars at the moment of death; the spirit of Shaftesbury would kindle, perhaps, a very fiery comet.

Some London radicals were now convinced that Charles intended to create an absolute monarchy, and began to plot among themselves to resist any such attempt. It was reported by government informers that preparations had been made for an uprising by city dissenters, who were apparently resolved to capture the king and force him to act against his brother. In November 1682, hundreds of 'brisk boys' in the East End rioted with the call 'A Monmouth! A Monmouth!' Before he left for the continent Shaftesbury had joined with the duke in discussing an armed uprising in the event of the king's death.

All this plotting and planning concluded in what became known as the 'Rye House Plot'. Certain discontented Whigs – among them William, Lord Russell, Algernon Sidney and the earl of Essex – seem to have laid plans to ambush and kill the king and his brother on their way back from the races at Newmarket. The assassins would assemble at a lonely farmstead known as Rye House in Hertfordshire, for the purpose of 'lopping the two sparks'. The plot was betrayed by one of the minor conspirators, and in the early summer of 1683 the principal agents were arrested. Even as the trial of Russell proceeded, the news came that Essex had been found dead in the Tower with wounds about his throat. It was supposed that he had committed suicide, thus presuming guilt, but it is possible that he had been murdered to prove the reality of the plot against the royal brothers. It would provide a convenient opportunity for the king to destroy all of the prominent Whigs.

When Lord Russell's family pleaded for him the king replied that 'if I do not take his life he will soon have mine'. His beheading, in Lincoln's Inn Fields, was badly managed by the public hangman, Jack Ketch, who later issued an apology. When Algernon Sidney was also sentenced to death by the axe, he made a passionate statement of his innocence. The chief justice, Judge Jeffreys, rose and rebuked him. 'I pray God work in you a temper fit to go into the other world, for I see you are not fit for this.'

'My lord, feel my pulse and see if I am disordered. I bless God, I never was in better temper than I am now.'

Russell, Essex and Sidney became known as the first Whig martyrs.

The duke of Monmouth had also been implicated in the plot, and an indictment been drawn up against him. Yet he submitted to his father and signed a confession that 'he owned the late conspiracy' but was innocent of any design against the life of his father. On the following day he withdrew the statement, for fear that he had betrayed his erstwhile associates; whereupon he was banished from the court. John Evelyn reported in his diary, the entry of 15 July 1683, that 'the public was now in great consternation on the late plot and conspiracy; his Majesty very melancholy, and not stirring without double guards; all the avenues and private doors about Whitehall and the Park shut up, few admitted to walk in it'.

The news of the conspiracy helped to rouse further anger against Whigs and dissenters, and the king published a declaration against 'the factious party' that was read out from every pulpit. This provoked the publication of innumerable 'loyal addresses' that underlined the supremacy of the king. Charles had in effect won his battle against parliament. He was also about to conquer London. The *quo warranto* proceedings had come to a conclusion, and in the summer of 1683 the king's bench decided that the liberties of the city had been rendered forfeit and returned into the hands of the king.

Charles could now govern in any manner that he pleased. The earl of Danby, once pursued by the Commons, was promptly released from the Tower. The duke of York was granted extensive powers, and it seemed to many that he was already ruling in place of the king who more and more consulted only his pleasures. In the spring of 1684, in fact, the duke was reappointed to the privy council after an absence of eleven years. In this period Titus Oates, the instigator of the 'Popish Plot', was arrested for calling James a traitor; he was convicted and fined £100,000. This ensured that he remained in confinement for the foreseeable future.

An entry from Evelyn's diaries conveys the mood and atmosphere of the triumphant court with its 'inexpressable luxury, and prophanesse, gaming and all dissolution, and as if it were total forgetfulness of God'. The king was 'sitting and toying with his concubines', among them the duchess of Portsmouth, with a 'French boy singing love-songs, in that glorious gallery, whilst about twenty of the great courtiers and other dissolute persons were at basset round a large table, a bank of at least two thousand in gold before them'.

Yet the games of Charles II were about to end. In the early weeks of 1685 he suffered from prolonged attacks of gout which left him debilitated. On the morning of Monday 2 February, he arose early after a restless and fevered night; to his attendants he seemed lethargic and almost torpid. He was also confused in speech and action. Then he fell into convulsions, or as one of his doctors put it '*convulsivi motus*', that left him speechless for two hours; cantharides, or Spanish fly, was applied to his skin to promote blisters. The letting of his blood lent him some relief, and the king recovered his power of speech. The duke of York had been summoned, and arrived so rapidly that he was wearing one shoe and one slipper. The doctors now prepared powders to promote sneezing so that the pressure of 'the humours' upon the king's brain might be relieved; he was also given a solution of cowslip flowers and spirit of sal ammoniac.

The king gradually seemed to grow better but by Wednesday afternoon he was covered in a profuse cold sweat that was a stage in the progress of dissolution. A preparation known as 'spirit of human skull' was then applied. By noon on Thursday there was little hope; he suffered several fits but was conscious in the intervals between them.

On that Thursday evening he ended the vacillations of a lifetime and formally entered the Roman Catholic communion by the ministrations of a Benedictine monk, John Hudleston. When the bishops and other attendants had withdrawn, the monk was conducted to the death chamber by the duke of York through a secret door. There seems little reason to doubt this account. James wrote, and spoke, of it. Hudleston himself left a brief description of the event. The observers had indeed been excluded from the chamber for a period, and afterwards the king refused to receive Anglican communion.

After that rite his mind was clear and his speech composed. On the following morning he asked to be taken to a window where he might see the rising sun. By ten o'clock he was unconscious. He died, quietly and without pain, shortly before noon.

45

The Protestant wind

So on 6 February 1685, the new king, James II, ascended the throne in the face of sustained and organized opposition from Shaftesbury and the Whigs. He was fifty-two years of age, and in vigorous heath. He had already proved himself to be determined and decisive; he had remained faithful to his Catholic beliefs despite every attempt to persuade him otherwise. He was more resolute and more trustworthy than his brother, but he lacked Charles's geniality and perceptiveness. He seemed to have no great capacity for compromise and viewed the world about him in the simple terms of light and darkness; there was the monarchy and authority on one side, with republicanism and disorder on the other. His manner was stiff and restrained, his temper short.

The prospect of such a monarch, however, was not necessarily disagreeable. He was known to be more diligent and more scrupulous than his late brother, with a greater concern for economy in financial matters. He was the very model of a retired naval officer of moderate abilities. The court itself acquired quite a different tone. Where before there had been music and mirth and gambling there was now, according to Sir John Lauder, 'little to be but seriousness and business'.

James's first statement maintained his support for the Church of England as the truest friend to the monarchy. Yet a little more than a week after the old king's death, according to John Evelyn, James 'to the great grief of his subjects, did now, for the first time, go to mass publicly in the little Oratory at the duke's lodgings, the doors being wide set open'. When the host was elevated, the Catholics fell upon their knees while the Protestants hurried out of the chapel. The new king was proclaiming his faith to the nation. He built his church upon the rock of Peter, but on that rock he would eventually founder.

Louis XIV had already sent a large sum of money to James as a reserve fund, held by the French ambassador, in case any insurrection or opposition should rise against him; Louis knew well enough that the English king would now favour Catholicism as far as lay in his power. James's councillors were also aware, however, that parliament would have to pass any order for new taxation. James called in the French ambassador to explain the position. 'Assure your master', he told him according to the ambassador's own account, 'of my gratitude and attachment. I know that without his protection I can do nothing . . . I will take good care not to let the Houses meddle with foreign affairs. If I see in them any disposition to make mischief, I will send them about their business.'

He need not have concerned himself. Parliament met in the spring of 1685 and was overwhelmingly Tory or royalist in composition; in his speech he gave 'assurance, concerning the care I will have of your religion and property' and in return requested revenues for life. The members proceeded to vote him the funds; given the extraordinary increase in his excise revenue as a result of growing trade, they furnished him with more money than he actually required. They may have been given pause, however, by the king's reference to 'your religion'.

The only possible threat came from his late brother's illegitimate son, the duke of Monmouth, who still harboured ambitions for the throne. Sure enough the duke left his exile in Amsterdam and, on 11 June, appeared with a small force off the coast at Lyme; he had believed that after his landing a multitude of supporters would flock to his flag, and so arrived with no more than 150 followers. Monmouth planted his blue standard on the soil of England and pronounced James to be a usurper; he also declared that the traitorous king had poisoned his brother, set light to London in the

Great Fire, and encouraged the 'Popish Plot' as part of 'one continued conspiracy against the reformed religion and the rights of the nation'. He then took upon himself the title of King James II.

Some of the natives of Dorset and Somerset joined his small army as he marched towards Taunton and Bridgwater, but there were far fewer recruits than he had originally expected. He had no coherent strategy of campaign, and he was quickly overwhelmed by James's better-trained and better-armed soldiers. The battle of Sedgemoor was the last one to be fought upon English soil. Monmouth escaped from the field and was found lying under a bush, half-asleep from exhaustion, and covered with fern and nettles for camouflage.

No mercy was shown to the defeated. Monmouth himself was taken before the king; he knelt down and pleaded for his life. 'Is there no hope?' he finally asked. The king turned away in silence. The duke was beheaded upon Tower Hill, and became the victim of another botched execution by Jack Ketch.

The consequences for the people of the West Country were severe. Judge Jeffreys was sent among them to deal out punishment. The 'Bloody Assizes' became part of the folklore of the region. Many died in prison, 800 were transported to be slaves, while some 250 were sentenced to death. Twenty-nine were sentenced to die at Dorchester but the two executioners protested that they could not hang, draw and quarter so many men on a single day. A woman was beheaded for offering food and water to an escaping 'rebel'. 'Gentlemen,' Jeffreys said to the jury, 'in your place I would find her guilty, were she my own mother.' Jeffreys laughed aloud, joked and exulted at the plight of the prisoners who came before him. He used to say that he gave the defendants 'a lick with the rough side of my tongue'. 'I see thee, villain, I see thee with the halter already around thy neck.' When he was told that one prisoner relied upon parish alms he replied, 'I will ease the parish of the burden.'

The defeat of the rebellion confirmed the king's authority; he had triumphed over his enemies, and now set about the process of building a new state based upon his absolute power. He determined to abolish the Test Act, thereby allowing Catholics to assume control of various offices; he wished to repeal the Habeas Corpus Act, thereby granting him more control over his opponents, and to maintain his standing army of approximately 20,000 men. He needed an army to safeguard himself from any 'disturbances', without or within.

In the summer of the year, after the defeat of Monmouth, some 15,000 men were encamped on Hounslow Heath; a lawyer of the time, Sir John Lowther, recollected that the standing army came 'to the astonishment of the people of England' who had never heard of such a force in times of peace. The troops were soon billeted throughout the country where, under the guise of pursuing 'rebels', they might act as James's security force. Some of their time was spent in disrupting the gatherings of Baptists and Presbyterians who, in this period, were once again some of the most persecuted of the dissenting sects. With the close assistance of Samuel Pepys, also, the king was intent upon establishing a formidable navy; this was part of his determination to consolidate and exploit the colonial territories within India, North America and the West Indies. He can be considered, therefore, as one of the founders of the commercial and imperial state that emerged in the eighteenth century.

The twin bonds of royal autocracy and the Catholic religion ensured the amity of James II and Louis XIV, and there was naturally much alarm in England when, in the autumn of 1685, the French king cancelled the Edict of Nantes that guaranteed freedom of worship to his Protestant subjects. Could James follow the same path? It was of course unlikely that James would dare to take measures against the English national Church but he might attempt to check its powers. His attitude towards the Protestant Huguenots who fled to England was not encouraging; he believed them to be anti-monarchical and was not anxious that they remain in his kingdom. They stayed, however, settling in Spitalfields and elsewhere, and were essentially to create the silk industry of the country.

When parliament reassembled on the appointed day, 9 November, much apprehension was naturally felt by the king's supporters, the Tories, who also upheld the Anglican faith. 'Never was there a more devoted Parliament,' one contemporary observed, 'but you know the point of religion is a tender point.' The members of both houses were most alarmed by the fact that, in defiance of the Test Act, the king had already appointed Roman Catholic officers to the army and navy. The king declared, in his speech from the throne, that 'having had the benefit of their services in such a time of need and danger

[Monmouth's invasion], I will neither expose them to disgrace, nor myself to the want of them, if there should be a second rebellion to make them necessary to me'. It was soon made clear to him that the members of both houses, but particularly those of the Lords, were dismayed by his illegal and unparliamentary appointments. One brave peer, Viscount Mordaunt, stated that 'the evil which we are considering is neither future nor uncertain. A standing army exists. It is officered by papists. We have no foreign enemy. There is no rebellion in the land. For what, then, is this force maintained, except for the purpose of subverting our laws, and establishing that arbitrary power which is so justly abhorred by Englishmen?'

Eleven days after parliament had been summoned, James prorogued it until the following year; it was characteristic of his rule that he suppressed the assembly before it had the chance formally to challenge his authority. It was the first sign of the growing tension between the king and the political nation. Parliament never met again in the course of his short reign.

On the strength of his prerogative alone he now began to assist his co-religionists. He issued orders forbidding the celebration of 'gunpowder treason day', in which it was customary to burn an effigy of the pope; the edict was only partly successful. Various of the religious orders were once again settled in London; the Benedictines were ensconced at St James's, the Carmelite friars in the City, the Franciscans in Lincoln's Inn Fields and the Jesuits in the Savoy. A Catholic school was established by the Jesuits in that neighbourhood. One of James's most intimate advisers was a Jesuit priest, Edward Petre, who was placed in charge of the royal chapel and who lodged in the king's old apartments in Whitehall. By the end of the year five Roman Catholics were part of the privy council.

The king's morals, however, were not governed by strictly Catholic standards. His principal mistress, Catherine Sedley, was given a large mansion in St James's Square and soon acquired the title of countess of Dorchester. She seemed not to know the reason for his affection. 'It cannot be my beauty,' she said, 'for he must see that I have none; and it cannot be my wit, for he has not enough to know that I have any.'

The king often said that his purpose was to 'establish' or 're-establish' Roman Catholicism. He may have realized that he would not be able to impose his faith upon the nation and he knew well enough that his likely successor, Mary, was a fervent Protestant; he hoped only to put Catholicism on terms of equality with Anglicanism in the belief that the virtues of his religion would in time elicit many converts. He had hoped to persuade his Anglican and Tory supporters to accede to his wishes but instead he only managed further to antagonize them. When a Catholic chapel was established in Lime Street, a crowd of Londoners gathered to attack 'the mass house'; the trained bands were called out to disperse the crowd but demurred on the grounds that 'we cannot in conscience fight for popery'. The king's own stubborn and imperious temper did not help his cause. 'I will make no concession', he was accustomed to say. 'My father made concessions, and he was beheaded.'

His purpose was to purge the judicial bench of all those who might be disaffected from his policies or his powers. It has been estimated that in the course of his reign he replaced up to nine-tenths of the serving justices of the peace in each county; the replacements were Roman Catholics who, in the absence of a police force, became the principal agents of law and royal authority. The corporations of the towns and the lords-lieutenant of the counties were also purged. When the king subsequently relieved the archbishop of Canterbury of his duties at the privy council, the French ambassador observed that James had resolved to favour only those who supported his interests.

The case of *Gooden* v. *Hales* was brought forward, in the summer of 1686, as a test of power. At issue was the right of the king to dispense with the penalties of the law and to suspend their execution, with particular reference to the Test Act against Catholics. When four judges declared that any such decision would 'overturn the English constitution', he simply dismissed them from the bench. Even those once most loyal to the king were now dismayed. 'Everyone was astonished', John Evelyn wrote in his diary entry for 27 June. 'Great jealousies as to what would be the end of these proceedings.'

In this summer, too, the king established a commission for ecclesiastical causes for 'the prevention of indiscreet preaching'; it was in effect an institution designed to assert the rights of Roman Catholics. The commissioners had the power to deprive any cleric of his living or to excommunicate any layman, and, perhaps more importantly, they were given the authority to regulate the schools and universities of the kingdom.

It is not at all clear that the Catholics of England, who made up some 2 to 3 per cent of the population, welcomed the efforts of their Catholic king. He was stirring up resentment, and worse, against them. Riots against 'papists' had broken out in certain parts of the country. They were too few, in any case, to fill up all the offices that were becoming vacant. How could they become judges when they had previously been denied entrance to the Inns of Court?

James also began the scrutiny of all those in power. In the royal closet he interviewed those who held public office as well as the members of both houses of parliament; these individual encounters became known as 'closetings' whereby he demanded the acquiescence of each man in his religious policies. Those who demurred were dismissed. Lord Chesterfield reported that 'we do hear every post of so many persons being out of their employments that it seems like the account one has after a battle of those who miscarried in the engagement'. The king's proceedings created much anger and disaffection among those who, in other circumstances, would have been faithful to him.

At the same time James also decided to gain the loyalty, or at least the acquiescence, of the nation by granting religious liberty to all of his subjects. In a declaration of indulgence, issued in the spring of 1687, he suspended 'the execution of all penal laws for religious offences' and lifted 'the imposition of religious oaths or tests as qualifications for office'. Thus he materially assisted the case of his co-religionists while at the same time hoping to gain the gratitude of nonconformists. He may have believed that he could still rely upon the tacit support of the royalists and the Anglicans, even though they had been sorely stretched. In this judgement he may have been unwise. From this time forward, however, the dissenters flocked to their chapels and assemblies without the least hindrance; Macaulay observed that 'an observant traveller will still remark the date of 1687 on some of the oldest meeting houses'.

One sign of Anglican unease emerged in the king's decision to impose his will upon Oxford University. When the president of Magdalen College died, letters mandatory were sent by the king to the Fellows of that college for the election of Anthony Farmer; Farmer was in fact ineligible for the office, and was notable only for his Catholic sympathies. The Fellows proceeded to elect a Doctor Hough, in defiance of royal instructions. When the king visited Oxford in the course of his summer progress, he berated the recalcitrant Fellows and ordered them to leave his presence. 'Go home,' he said, 'and show yourselves good members of the Church of England. Get you gone, know I am your king. I will be obeyed and I command you to be gone.'

The recently appointed ecclesiastical commission then annulled the election of Hough, whereupon twenty-five of the Fellows of Magdalen resigned or were dismissed. The college now became essentially a Catholic stronghold, and Mass was performed daily in its chapel. It was a hollow victory for the king, however, who thereby managed to alienate a great number of the clergy and to lose any reputation he hoped to gain for religious tolerance. The Magdalen affair was widely reported, adding to the anger and dismay at the king's indifference to Anglican sensibilities.

It was widely reported, also, that in the course of the summer he made a pilgrimage to the 'holy well' in North Wales dedicated to St Winifred where he prayed for an heir. It was also noted that the king had knelt to the papal nuncio, Archbishop Adda, and implored his blessing. No English king had ever knelt before another man since the time of King John, and the posture was treated with embarrassment and even disgust. This was Catholicism with a vengeance. The envoy from Modena reported that 'such of the nobility as have any credit, standing, or power in the kingdom are rarely to be seen at court'. William of Orange, staunch defender of the Protestant cause, had sent an ambassador to London who held meetings with disaffected noblemen; the prince of Orange watched and waited.

William had been appointed captain general for life of the forces of the Dutch republic and, by right of his territory of Orange, he was also a sovereign prince. His mother was Mary, eldest daughter of Charles I, and his wife, Mary, was the daughter of the present king; no doubt he considered himself to be a rightful heir to the throne, on the supposition that James had no legitimate son. He was a staunch Calvinist, like the rest of his family, and the doctrine of predestination weighed heavily upon him. If he had one duty beyond all others it was to curb the power of France; he had seen Louis XIV invade his adopted country, only to be halted by the opening of the dykes. The imperial pretensions of the House of Bourbon had not been tamed, however, and William dedicated himself to the defence of the Protestant states of Europe from the forces of the French king.

By the end of 1687 James had decided to call parliament in order formally to repeal the Test Act and the other penal laws against the exercise of religious liberty. For that purpose he decided to renew the 'closeting' on a local and regional level by asking all office-holders and justices of the peace whether, if elected, they would vote for repeal; if they were not standing as members of the Commons, would they at least vote for candidates who were committed to doing so? If they answered in the negative, or were equivocal, they were to be dismissed from their posts. Over 1,000 men, for example, were expelled from the borough corporations. This was another action designed to infuriate the local gentry, as well as the corporations of the towns and cities; it also served further to alienate the Anglican Church, now confirmed in its belief that Catholicism served only to reinforce arbitrary government.

At the beginning of April 1688, government agents set out with 20 shillings a day in expenses in order to prepare the ground for the coming general election; they were to liaise with the leader of the 'court party' in each locality, arrange for the proper distribution of court literature and counter the work of the opposition. The king's aim was, in other words, to 'pack' his new parliament with his own supporters and thus clear the way for complete and uninterrupted rule. Subsequent events, however, ensured that no such parliament would ever meet.

It had already become clear that the queen, Mary of Modena, was with child. The prospect of a Catholic heir then became palpable, with all the anguish and anxiety that ensued among the Anglican and dissenting populations. The Stuart imperium might stretch on perpetually. On 7 May 1688, James reissued his declaration of indulgence, together with a promise to call parliament by the end of the year. An order followed that the declaration was to be read from the pulpits of every church on two successive Sundays. His

Jesuit adviser, Father Petre, had told him that the Anglican clergy 'should be made to eat their own dung'.

The order incited only rage and disobedience from the clergy. The archbishop of Canterbury and six other bishops printed a petition for its withdrawal, on the grounds that the dispensing power assumed by the king was in fact illegal. When the petition was presented to him the king was irate. 'This is a great surprise to me,' he told the bishops. 'I did not expect this from your Church, especially from some of you. This is a standard of rebellion!' The declaration of indulgence was in fact largely ignored. Of the 9,000 churches of England, it is estimated that it was read in 200. It was read in only seven, out of one hundred, in London. When its first words were pronounced in the church of St Gregory's by St Paul's, the whole congregation rose and withdrew. The angry will of the king now superseded any kind of caution or circumspection. He demanded that the seven bishops be consigned to the Tower and prosecuted for publishing a seditious libel.

William was watching events as they unfolded. A swift sailing boat was continually passing over the North Sea from London to The Hague, with messages and reports designed for the sole attention of the prince of Orange.

On 10 June 1688, a son was born to James and Mary of Modena. Many disbelieved the report. It was just too convenient that a Stuart heir should emerge at this particular moment. It was rumoured that a warming pan had been used to smuggle a newborn infant into the royal chamber. Five days after the birth of the prince of Wales the seven offending bishops were brought by barge from the Tower to Westminster Hall, where they were greeted with repeated cries of 'God bless the bishops!' The jury, after a night's deliberation, acquitted the bishops of publishing a seditious libel; on publication of the verdict, Westminster Hall rang with cheers and acclamations for half an hour. The news spread rapidly throughout the city, where bonfires were lit and church bells rang. Effigies of the pope were burned in the streets; in Somerset an effigy of the newborn prince was also set on fire. Most ominously for the king, perhaps, his soldiers encamped on Hounslow Heath cheered on receiving the news. When the king heard that the bishops had been acquitted, he said merely, 'So much the worse for them.'

Yet the decision had shaken the earth beneath his feet. On the day of the acquittal seven prominent men of state – among them the earls of Devonshire, Danby and Shrewsbury – sent a secret letter to William of Orange and informed him that the vast majority of the people were 'dissatisfied with the present conduct of the government' and were eager for a change. If William were to invade England, he would find the nation behind him. They told him that 'much the greatest part of the nobility and gentry' was opposed to the king and to his policies, and that on his landing they would 'draw great numbers' to his side.

Even in this extremity it is unlikely that they wished to remove James from the throne. They wanted William to act in the role of a Protestant saviour who would force the king to call a free parliament, which would then settle the religious affairs of the nation and extirpate all bias towards popery. Speed, and decision, were of the essence before the king could call a 'packed' parliament. William was in fact already making active preparations to assemble a field army and a fleet.

By the beginning of August the news of his intentions reached England. In his diary entry for 10 August 1688, John Evelyn noted that 'Dr Tenison now told me there would suddenly be some great thing discovered. This was the Prince of Orange intending to come over.' An envoy from the court of Louis XIV reached James a few days later, warning him of an imminent invasion and offering him French assistance. James refused to believe the message. Could his daughter Mary conspire with her husband to depose her father? It was not possible. Would William lead his forces on a perilous expedition abroad at a moment when his country was threatened by French power? No. It was more likely that the French were trying to frighten him into an alliance with Louis XIV, an alliance that would not be to the liking of the coming parliament.

The decision was not long delayed. On 28 September William of Orange announced the forthcoming invasion of England to the States General. On the same day James proclaimed to the nation that its object was 'an absolute conquest of these our kingdoms and the utter subduing and subjecting us and all our people to a foreign power' and that it had been promoted 'by certain wicked subjects for their own selfish ends'; the king also declared that he had 'declined any foreign succours'. He was on his own.

William then issued his own declaration in which he stated that he had been invited to come over the water by 'a great many lords both spiritual and temporal' and that he would come simply 'to have a free and lawful Parliament assembled as soon as is possible'. He did not mention any pretensions to the throne but stated only that 'we for our part will concur in everything that may procure the peace and happiness of the nation'. James wished to know who these 'many lords', inviting William to England, might be. He questioned the bishops and asked them to sign a paper declaring their 'abhorrence' of the invasion but, to his surprise and dismay, they refused to do so.

He now realized the full gravity of his position, and began to make desperate efforts to reverse the policies that had alienated his kingdom. He dismissed Father Petre from his councils. He issued a declaration promising that he would 'inviolably . . . preserve the Church of England' and bar Catholics from parliament. He pledged to restore to office those justices of the peace and other local leaders whom he had summarily dismissed in the spring of the year. He stated that he would readmit the Fellows of Magdalen College whom he had banished for disobedience, and agreed that he would terminate the ecclesiastical commission that had been responsible for their punishment. The charter of the City of London, rendered forfeit six years before, was now returned to the mayor and aldermen. Yet all these palliative measures came too late, and he was now despised for weakness and vacillation.

He was resolute enough, however, in organizing his defences. He fitted out more ships to join the squadrons already at sea; they now consisted of thirty-three large ships and sixteen fire-ships. Royal commissions were sent out for the creation of new regiments and additional men were appointed to existing ones; the militia of London and the counties were called up, and ordered to stand in readiness for the defence of their country. Battalions of infantry, and regiments of cavalry, were brought back from Ireland and Scotland to serve closer to home. Sir John Lowther, a baronet who supported the cause of William, recalled that 'nothing was left undone that might put the king in a posture to defend himself'. It was clearly within James's power to confront and defeat the invader.

William, prince of Orange, set sail in the middle of October; it was dangerously late in the season, and a gale drove his ships back. Now that he had made his decision, however, he was determined to go on. At the beginning of November he embarked for England once more with an east wind filling his sails; it became known as 'the Protestant wind'.

He did not come to 'save' Protestantism, however, except in a particular sense. His principal purpose was to find the means to contain and, if possible, curtail French power that was directed towards the United Provinces and elsewhere. He needed an English army, and English ships, for that endeavour. He could by no means be certain of the outcome. While preparing for the invasion he wrote to his principal councillor, Willem Bentinck, that 'my sufferings, my disquiet, are dreadful. I hardly see my way. Never in my life did I so much feel the need of God's guidance.' Yet he was a firm believer in predestination, and now chanced all. He could not be certain that he would be welcomed; he had been advised that the majority of the English would come to his side once he arrived, but he could not be sure of this.

It was believed that he would land in the north or in the east, and James's defences were accordingly clustered there; William himself was apprised of the decision, and determined that he would go to the relatively unprepared south-west. By the time he reached the coast of Devon, strong winds hampered the English fleet in pursuit and, at a subsequent council of war, it was determined that no attack should be made against what was considered to be a far stronger Dutch fleet. James subsequently averred that a conspiracy had been hatched among the captains, but it is far more likely that they were influenced by caution rather than treason.

The prince of Orange set foot on English soil at Brixham, at the southern end of Tor Bay, on 5 November. It was an auspicious day, the anniversary of the overthrow of the gunpowder plot and the dissolution of a papist conspiracy. The movements of William's troops, once they had disembarked, were hampered by rain and foul roads. By 9 November William had reached Exeter, where his men were able to rest, but he was not met with any enthusiasm; the citizens treated him coldly, and at a service of thanksgiving in the cathedral the canons and most of the congregation fled. William remained in the city for nine days but no one of renown or distinction came to him; he began to believe that he had been deceived about the situation in England and seemed willing to re-embark with his men. When some local gentry did enrol under his standard he declared that 'we expected you that dwelled so near the place of our landing would have joined us sooner'. The simple answer to his bafflement may have been that he had landed in a region where no one expected him. Supporters did now begin to march towards him.

Yet James II had not been able to take advantage of this interval in the conflict. He called back his troops who had been originally sent to the north but, when he joined them at their camp in Salisbury, he found both the officers and the men demoralized and divided. A strong king would have immediately launched an attack upon his enemy but James hesitated. Some of his commanders wished to press forward quickly, while others advised a retreat to London.

In this crisis the king himself broke down; he suffered from a catastrophic series of nosebleeds, tokens of his rising panic, that deprived him of rest. Some of his officers began to desert him and make their way to the prince of Orange, among them Lord Colchester, Lord Abingdon and Lord Cornbury; they trusted William's declaration that he had come to save the Protestant religion and to install a free parliament. A series of local risings, in favour of parliament and Protestantism, now increased the king's isolation; Nottingham and York, Leicester and Carlisle and Gloucester were some of the towns that declared for 'the Protestant religion and liberty'.

In an atmosphere of confusion and intense distrust the king, seized with apprehension at the news of the desertions, decided to retreat to London. He had in effect capitulated to William without a fight. Other senior officers, among them John Churchill and the earl of Berkeley, now decided to leave him and go over to William. When the king arrived at Whitehall, and an almost empty court, he was greeted with the news that his younger daughter, Anne, had also defected to the enemy. She was a staunch Anglican who had been horrified by her father's open espousal and encouragement of Catholicism. Under the protection of the bishop of London, she had escaped by hackney carriage to Nottingham.

The king did not know whom to trust or whom to believe any more. A courtier reported that 'the king is much out of order, looks yellow, and takes no natural rest'. He could sleep only with the assistance of opiates. He summoned to a council all the nobles and bishops who remained in the city; they advised him that he had no recourse except to call a free parliament. On 30 November he issued a proclamation to that effect, and combined with it a pardon to all those who had risen against him. But it was too late. He had already forfeited the trust and loyalty of many of those who had been closest to him.

William was on a slow march towards London, and the king had the choice of flight or resistance. Yet where would he find the arms and the men to withstand the invader? He sent some commissioners to treat with William at Hungerford, but this was a feint to disguise his true purpose. He had already provided for the safety of his wife and son; on the night of 9 December Mary of Modena, disguised as a laundress, escaped with her child to Calais. On 11 December the king himself fled and, with two Roman Catholic companions, he crossed the Thames to Vauxhall and there took horse. It is assumed that he threw the great seal of England into the waters, so that public order could not legally be maintained by his successor. He did not think of himself as abandoning his kingdom but, rather, finding temporary security before regaining his throne. Yet he had effectively surrendered the initiative to William, who could already regard himself as the next king of England.

On the news that the king had fled, the lords spiritual and temporal formed a temporary administration in order to negotiate with the prince of Orange for the return of a free parliament designed to restore 'our laws, our liberties and properties'. James's departure also provoked open fury against the papist enemy; the Catholic chapels of London were fired, while the residences of the Catholic ambassadors of Spain and Florence were ransacked.

Wild rumours now spread through the country that Irish troops under the command of the king had massacred the people of London and were marching to the north. It was reported that Birmingham had been fired by the papists; Nottingham and Stafford were then said to have been sacked, with Doncaster and Huddersfield following in the line of fire. When the rumours reached Leeds that the child-eating Irish were in the suburbs, Ralph Thoresby wrote in his diary that 'the drums beat, the bells rang backwards, the women shrieked and such dreadful consternation seized upon all persons'. The false alarm is a token of the hysterical anxiety into which the people had sunk. A doggerel song against the Irish came out of the consternation. 'Lillibulero' is a parody of papist sentiment and it became so popular that its composer, Thomas Wharton, declared that it had whistled a king out of three kingdoms:

> Now the heretics all go down
> Lillibulero bullen a la
> By Christ and St Patrick's the nation's our own
> Lillibulero bullen a la.

The music is still used as a signature tune by BBC Radio.

The king's departure from England was now interrupted when he was discovered on a customs boat about to sail from the Isle of Sheppey; he was disguised in a short black wig and was at first mistaken for a Jesuit. When he was brought to the port of Faversham he was soon recognized and taken to the mayor's house where he was guarded by the seamen who had found him; they wanted to claim their prize. He was by now thoroughly frightened and bewildered, at one moment pleading for a boat and at the next weeping over his misfortunes. An eyewitness, John Knatchbull, 'observed a smile in his face of an extraordinary size and sort; so forced, awkward and unpleasant to look upon that I can truly say I never saw anything like it'.

When informed of James's enforced sojourn in Faversham, no one in authority really knew what to do with him. He could not stay where he was. James himself then seems to have determined to return to London, where he might hold an interview with William; his messenger, bearing this news to the invader, was promptly arrested and consigned to the Tower. Who was the master now?

James, unaware of his envoy's fate, proceeded towards the capital; as he approached Blackheath on 16 December he was greeted by cheering crowds who were no doubt hoping for an accommodation between the two parties. They were largely comprised of the 'king and country' stalwarts among the people, but they represented a more general sense of relief. A royalist supporter noted after the event that in the streets between Southwark and Whitehall 'there was scarce room for coaches to pass through, and the balconies and windows besides were thronged'. The king himself was to write that it was 'liker a day of triumph than humiliation'.

A less enthusiastic welcome also awaited him. While resting at Whitehall that evening, he was advised that all the posts were to be taken up by the Dutch guards of the prince of Orange; he would in effect be a prisoner in his own palace. In the early hours of the next day he was woken by an order from the prince commanding him to leave London by nine in the morning and travel on to Ham House. He was to depart at that time because William himself was to enter London at midday and did not wish the people to be diverted by the sight of their king. The king obeyed the order, with the exception that he wished to remove to Rochester rather than to Ham. The wish was granted but it was still clear that the monarch was a helpless captive in his own kingdom.

William himself entered the capital on 18 December to be in turn greeted by cheering crowds, bells and bonfires. He was heralded as one who had come to redeem 'our religion, laws, liberties and lives', but a large element of the jubilation must have come from the fact that the Protestant religion had been restored without war or revolution. They had cheered the king two days before as one who had abandoned his Catholic policies; they could equally well cheer their Protestant saviour.

The king stayed at the house of a local baronet in Rochester for a few days, but every moment he was looking for a means of escape. He feared assassination or, at best, straight imprisonment. Yet he noted that the guards about him were not strict in the performance of their duties. In truth William wanted his rival to escape as the least worst outcome of their conflict. James's presence in the country caused difficulties of its own but, if it could be said that he had departed by his own wish, then he might be considered to have abdicated. On the night of 22 December he rose from his bed and departed through a conveniently opened back door; he walked through the garden to the shore of the Medway where a skiff was waiting for him.

Thus was accomplished what was variously called the great or prodigious 'Revolution' and what was eventually known as the 'Glorious Revolution'. A supporter of William, Bishop Burnet, wrote of the king that 'his whole strength, like a spider's web, was so irrevocably broken with a touch, that he was never able to retrieve what for want of judgement and heart, he threw up in a day'.

It was not a matter of a day, however, but of years. In his obstinacy and fervent piety he had miscalculated the nature of the country; he had advanced where he should have called a halt. He had pitted the power of central government against local government to the ultimate disservice of the nation. By assaulting the sensibilities of both Anglicans and Tories he had alienated his natural supporters, and by advancing the claims of Catholics he had touched upon a very sensitive prejudice. He may not have wanted to become an absolute king, but he acted as if that were his intention. The birth of an heir stretched that prospect indefinitely.

James II spent the rest of his life in France. It was said, in his court at the Château de Saint-Germain-en-Laye, that 'when you listen to him, you realize why he is here'. Thus ended the public life of the last Stuart king of England. We may leave the scene with the words of John Dryden from *The Secular Masque*:

> Thy wars brought nothing about;
> Thy lovers were all untrue.
> 'Tis well an old age is out,
> And time to begin a new.

Further reading

This is by no means an exhaustive list, but it represents a selection of those books the author found most useful in the preparation of this third volume.

General Studies

G. E. Aylmer: *The Struggle for the Constitution* (London, 1963).
J. C. D. Clark: *Revolution and Rebellion* (Cambridge, 1986).
Thomas Cogswell, Richard Cust and Peter Lake (eds): *Politics, Religion and Popularity* (Cambridge, 2002).
Richard Cust and Ann Hughes (eds): *Conflict in Early Stuart England* (London, 1989).
Godfrey Davies: *The Early Stuarts* (Oxford, 1959).
Kenneth Fincham (ed.): *The Early Stuart Church* (London, 1993).
S. R. Gardiner: *History of England, 1603–1642*. In ten volumes (London, 1899).
William Haller: *The Rise of Puritanism* (New York, 1938).
Christopher Hill: *Puritanism and Revolution* (London, 1958).
Derek Hirst: *Authority and Conflict* (London, 1986).
Ronald Hutton: *Debates in Stuart History* (London, 2004).
J. P. Kenyon: *The Stuart Constitution* (Cambridge, 1966).
Peter Lake: *Anglicans and Puritans?* (London, 1988).
Peter Lake and Steven Pincus (eds): *The Politics of the Public Sphere in Early Modern England* (Manchester, 2007).
John Lingard and Hilaire Belloc: *The History of England*. Volumes seven to ten (New York, 1912).
Judith Maltby: *Prayer Book and People in Elizabethan and Early Stuart England* (Cambridge, 1998).

Brian Manning: *The English People and the English Revolution* (London, 1976).
John Morgan: *Godly Learning* (Cambridge, 1986).
John Morrill, Paul Slack and Daniel Woolf (eds): *Public Duty and Private Conscience in Seventeenth Century England* (Oxford, 1993).
J. F. H. New: *Anglican and Puritan* (London, 1964).
Linda Levy Peck: *Court Patronage and Corruption in Early Stuart England* (London, 1990).
H. S. Reinmuth Jnr. (ed.): *Early Stuart Studies* (Minneapolis, 1970).
Conrad Russell: *Parliament and English Politics, 1621–1629* (Oxford, 1979).
——— *Unrevolutionary England* (London, 1990).
Kevin Sharpe, *Politics and Ideas in Early Stuart England* (London, 1989).
——— *Image Wars* (New Haven, 2010).
——— (ed.): *Faction and Parliament* (London, 1978).
Kevin Sharpe and Peter Lake: *Culture and Politics in Early Stuart England* (London, 1994).
Alan Smith: *The Emergence of a Nation State* (London, 1984).
J. P. Sommerville: *Politics and Ideology in England, 1603–1640* (London, 1986).
David Starkey (ed.): *The English Court* (London, 1987).
Margot Todd (ed.): *Reformation to Revolution* (London, 1995).
Howard Tomlinson (ed.): *Before the English Civil War* (London, 1983).
Hugh Trevor-Roper: *Historical Essays* (London, 1957).
——— *Catholics, Anglicans and Puritans* (London, 1987).
Nicholas Tyacke: *Anti-Calvinists* (Oxford, 1987).
——— (ed.) *The English Revolution* (Manchester, 2007).
David Underdown: *Revel, Riot and Rebellion* (Oxford, 1985).
J. Dover Wilson (ed.): *Seventeenth Century Studies* (Oxford, 1938).
Andy Wood: *Riot, Rebellion and Popular Politics in Early Modern England* (London, 2002).

James VI and I

Robert Ashton: *James by his Contemporaries* (London, 1969).
Bryan Bevan: *King James* (London, 1990).
Caroline Bingham: *James of England* (London, 1981).
Thomas Birch: *The Court and Times of James*. In two volumes (London, 1848).
Glenn Burgess: *Absolute Monarchy* (London, 1996).
Irene Carrier: *James* (Cambridge, 1998).
Thomas Cogswell: *The Blessed Revolution* (Cambridge, 1989).
James Doelman: *King James and the Religious Culture of England* (Cambridge, 2000).
Kenneth Fincham: *Prelate as Pastor* (Oxford, 1990).
Antonia Fraser: *King James* (London, 1974).
S. J. Houston: *James* (London, 1972).
Robert Lockyer: *James* (London, 1998).
David Matthew: *The Jacobean Age* (London, 1938).
——— *James* (London, 1967).
W. M. Mitchell: *The Rise of the Revolutionary Party* (New York, 1957).
W. B. Patterson: *King James and the Reunion of Christendom* (Cambridge, 1997).
Linda Levy Peck (ed.): *The Mental World of the Jacobean Court* (Cambridge, 1991).
Menna Prestwich: *Cranfield* (Oxford, 1966).
Walter Scott: *Secret History of the Court of James*. In two volumes (London, 1811).
Alan G. R. Smith (ed.): *The Reign of James* (London, 1973).
Alan Stewart: *The Cradle King* (London, 2003).
Roy Strong: *Henry, Prince of Wales* (London, 2000).
Roland Usher: *The Reconstruction of the English Church*. In two volumes (New York, 1910).
D. H. Willson: *King James* (London, 1956).

Charles I

G. E. Aylmer: *The King's Servants* (London, 1961).
Thomas Birch and Cyprien de Gamache: *The Court and Times of Charles I.* In two volumes (London, 1848).
Charles Carlton: *Charles I: The Personal Monarch* (London, 1983).
Hester Chapman: *Great Villiers* (London, 1949).
H. P. Cooke: *Charles I and his Earlier Parliaments* (London, 1939).
E. S. Cope: *Politics without Parliaments* (London, 1987).
Richard Cust: *Charles I: A Political Life* (London, 2005).
C. W. Daniels and John Morrill: *Charles I* (Cambridge, 1988).
Isaac Disraeli: *Commentaries on the Life and Reign of Charles I.* In five volumes (London, 1828–1831).
Christopher Durston: *Charles I* (London, 1998).
J. H. Hexter: *The Reign of King Pym* (Cambridge, Mass., 1961).
Christopher Hibbert: *Charles I* (London, 2007).
F. M. G. Higham: *Charles I* (London,1932).
Clive Holmes: *Why Was Charles I Executed?* (London, 2006).
David Matthew: *The Social Structure in Caroline England* (Oxford, 1948).
——— *The Age of Charles I* (London, 1951).
Brian Quintrell: *Charles I* (London, 1993).
L. J. Reeve: *Charles I and the Road to Personal Rule* (Cambridge, 1989).
Conrad Russell: *The Fall of the British Monarchies* (Oxford, 1991).
Kevin Sharpe: *The Personal Rule of Charles I* (New Haven, 1992).
Hugh Trevor-Roper: *Archbishop Laud* (London, 1940).
C. V. Wedgwood: *The King's Peace* (London, 1955).
——— *Thomas Wentworth* (New York, 1962).
G. M. Young: *Charles I and Cromwell* (London, 1935).

Oliver Cromwell

Maurice Ashley: *The Greatness of Oliver Cromwell* (London, 1957).
Hilaire Belloc: *Cromwell* (London, 1934).
John Buchan: *Cromwell* (London, 1934).
Barry Coward: *Oliver Cromwell* (London, 1991).

J. C. Davis: *Oliver Cromwell* (London, 2001).
C. H. Firth: *Cromwell* (London, 1901).
Antonia Fraser: *Cromwell* (London, 1973).
S. R. Gardiner: *Oliver Cromwell* (London, 1901).
Peter Gaunt: *Oliver Cromwell* (Oxford, 1996).
François Guizot: *Oliver Cromwell* (London, 1879).
Christopher Hill: *God's Englishman* (London, 1971).
Roger Howell: *Cromwell* (London, 1977).
Frank Kitson: *Old Ironsides* (London, 2004).
John Morley: *Oliver Cromwell* (London, 1904).
John Morrill (ed.): *Oliver Cromwell* (Oxford, 2007).
Micheál Ó Siochrú: *God's Executioner* (London, 2008).
C. V. Wedgwood: *Oliver Cromwell* (London, 1973).

Civil War

John Adamson: *The Noble Revolt* (London, 2007).
Michael Braddick: *God's Fury, England's Fire* (London, 2008).
Charles Carlton: *Going to the Wars* (London, 1992).
Edward, earl of Clarendon: *The History of the Rebellion and Civil Wars in England*. In six volumes (Oxford, 1888).
David Cressy: *England on Edge* (Oxford, 2007).
Richard Cust and Ann Hughes (eds): *The English Civil War* (London, 1997).
Barbara Donagan: *War in England, 1642–1649* (Oxford, 2008).
Anthony Fletcher: *The Outbreak of the English Civil War* (London, 1981).
S. R. Gardiner: *History of the Great Civil War*. In four volumes (London, 1888).
Peter Gaunt (ed.): *The English Civil War* (Oxford, 2000).
Ian Gentles: *The English Revolution* (London, 2007).
Christopher Hill: *The English Revolution* (London, 1940).
Ann Hughes: *The Causes of the English Civil War* (London, 1991).
Ronald Hutton: *The Royalist War Effort* (London, 1982).
D. E. Kennedy: *The English Revolution* (London, 2000).
John Kenyon: *The Civil Wars of England* (London, 1988).
Mark Kishlansky: *The Rise of the New Model Army* (Cambridge, 1979).

Jason McElligott and David Smith (eds): *Royalists and Royalism during the English Civil Wars* (Cambridge, 2007).
Allan Macinnes: *The British Revolution* (London, 2005).
Brian Manning (ed.): *Politics, Religion and the English Civil War* (London, 1973).
Michael Mendle (ed.): *The Putney Debates* (Cambridge, 2001).
John Morrill: *The Revolt of the Provinces* (London, 1976).
——— *The Nature of the English Revolution* (London, 1993).
——— (ed.) *Reactions to the English Civil War* (London, 1982).
Jason Peacey (ed.): *The Regicides and the Execution of Charles I* (London, 2001).
R. C. Richardson: *The Debate on the English Revolution* (London, 1977).
Ivan Roots: *The Great Rebellion* (London, 1966).
Conrad Russell (ed.): *The Origins of the English Civil War* (London, 1973).
David Scott: *Politics and War in the Three Stuart Kingdoms* (London, 2004).
Lawrence Stone: *The Causes of the English Revolution* (London, 1972).
John Stubbs: *Reprobates* (London, 2011).
David Underdown: *Pride's Purge* (Oxford, 1971).
Malcolm Wanklyn: *The Warrior Generals* (London, 2010).
C. V. Wedgwood: *The King's War* (London, 1958).
Austin Woolrych: *Britain in Revolution* (Oxford, 2002).
Blair Worden: *The Rump Parliament* (Cambridge, 1974).
——— *The English Civil Wars* (London, 2009).

Commonwealth and Protectorate

G. E. Aylmer (ed.): *The Interregnum* (London, 1972).
Toby Barnard: *The English Republic* (London, 1982).
Jakob Bowman: *The Protestant Interest in Cromwell's Foreign Relations* (Heidelberg, 1900).
Barry Coward: *The Cromwellian Protectorate* (Manchester, 2002).
C. H. Firth: *The Last Years of the Protectorate*. In two volumes (London, 1909).

S. R. Gardiner: *History of the Commonwealth and Protectorate*. In four volumes (London, 1903).
William Haller: *Liberty and Information in the Puritan Revolution* (New York, 1955).
Ronald Hutton: *The British Republic* (London, 1990).
William Lamont: *Godly Rule* (London, 1969).
Jason McElligott: *Royalism, Print and Censorship in Revolutionary England* (Woodbridge, 2007).
John Morrill (ed.): *Revolution and Restoration* (London, 1992).
Robert Paul: *The Lord Protector* (London, 1955).
David Smith (ed.): *Cromwell and the Interregnum* (Oxford, 2003).
Michael Walzer: *The Revolution of the Saints* (New York, 1974).
Austin Woolrych: *Commonwealth to Protectorate* (London, 1980).
——— *England without a King* (London, 1983).

Charles II

Maurice Ashley: *Charles II* (London, 1973).
Robert Bosher: *The Making of the Restoration Settlement* (London, 1951).
Hester Chapman: *The Tragedy of Charles II* (London, 1964).
Raymond Crawfurd: *The Last Days of Charles II* (Oxford, 1909).
Godfrey Davies: *The Restoration of Charles II* (London, 1955).
Antonia Fraser: *King Charles II* (London, 1979).
Tim Harris: *Restoration* (London, 2005).
Tim Harris, Paul Seaward and Mark Goldie (eds): *The Politics of Religion in Restoration England* (Oxford, 1990).
Cyril Hartmann: *Clifford of the Cabal* (London, 1937).
Ronald Hutton: *The Restoration* (Oxford, 1985).
———: *Charles II* (Oxford, 1989).
Matthew Jenkinson: *Culture and Politics at the Court of Charles II* (Woodbridge, 2010).
J. R. Jones: *The First Whigs* (Oxford, 1961).
——— *Charles II* (London, 1987).
——— (ed.) *The Restored Monarchy* (London, 1979).
J. P. Kenyon: *Robert Spencer, Earl of Sunderland, 1641–1702* (London, 1958).

Anna Keay: *The Magnificent Monarch* (London, 2008).
Maurice Lee Jnr: *The Cabal* (Urbana, 1965).
John Miller: *Charles II* (London, 1991).
——— *After the Civil Wars* (London, 2000).
Annabel Patterson: *The Long Parliament of Charles II* (New Haven, 2008).
Stephen Pincus: *Protestantism and Patriotism* (Cambridge, 1996).
Paul Seaward: *The Cavalier Parliament and the Reconstruction of the Old Regime* (Cambridge, 1988).
Thomas Slaughter: *Newcastle's Advice to Charles II* (Philadelphia, 1984).
Jenny Uglow: *A Gambling Man* (London, 2009).
Brian Weiser: *Charles II and the Politics of Access* (Woodbridge, 2003).

James II

John Callow: *The Making of King James II* (Stroud, 2000).
Eveline Cruickshanks (ed.): *By Force or By Default?* (Edinburgh, 1989).
Lionel Glassey (ed.): *The Reigns of Charles II and James II* (London, 1997).
Tim Harris: *Revolution* (London, 2006).
J. R. Jones: *The Revolution of 1688 in England* (London, 1972).
T. B. Macaulay: *The History of England from the Accession of James II* (London, 1848).
John Miller: *Popery and Politics in England* (Cambridge, 1973).
——— *James II* (London, 1978).
W. A. Speck: *Reluctant Revolutionaries* (Oxford, 1988).
——— *James II* (London, 2002).

Culture and Society

I have not included studies of individual authors mentioned in the text.

Maurice Ashley: *Life in Stuart England* (London, 1964).
David Cressy: *Bonfires and Bells* (London, 1989).

Eveline Cruickshanks (ed.): *The Stuart Courts* (Stroud, 2000).
Anthony Fletcher and Peter Roberts (eds): *Religion, Culture and Society in Early Modern Britain* (Cambridge, 1994).
Ian Gentles, John Morrill and Blair Worden (eds): *Soldiers, Writers and Statesmen of the English Revolution* (Cambridge, 1998).
Johanna Harris and Elizabeth Scott-Baumann: *The Intellectual Culture of Puritan Woman* (London, 2011).
Alan Houston and Steve Pincus (eds): *A Nation Transformed* (Cambridge, 2001).
Ronald Hutton: *The Rise and Fall of Merry England* (Oxford, 1994).
N. H. Keeble: *The Restoration. England in the 1660s* (Oxford, 2002).
W. K. Jordan: *The Development of Religious Toleration in England* (London, 1936).
Gerald MacLean: *Culture and Society in the Stuart Restoration* (Cambridge 1995).
Allardyce Nicoll: *Stuart Masques* (New York, 1968).
Rosemary O'Day: *The English Clergy* (Leicester, 1979).
David Ogg: *England in the Reign of Charles II*. In two volumes (Oxford, 1934).
Stephen Orgel: *The Jonsonian Masque* (Cambridge, Mass., 1965).
Stephen Orgel and Roy Strong: *Inigo Jones. The Theatre of the Stuart Court*. In two volumes (London, 1973).
Graham Parry: *The Golden Age Restor'd* (Manchester, 1981).
R. Malcolm Smuts: *Court Culture and the Origins of a Royalist Tradition in Early Stuart England* (Philadelphia, 1987).
——— (ed.) *The Stuart Court and Europe* (Cambridge 1996).
John Spurr: *England in the 1670s* (Oxford, 2000).
Roy Strong: *Art and Power* (Woodbridge, 1984).
Blair Worden: *Literature and Politics in Cromwellian England* (Oxford, 2007).

Index

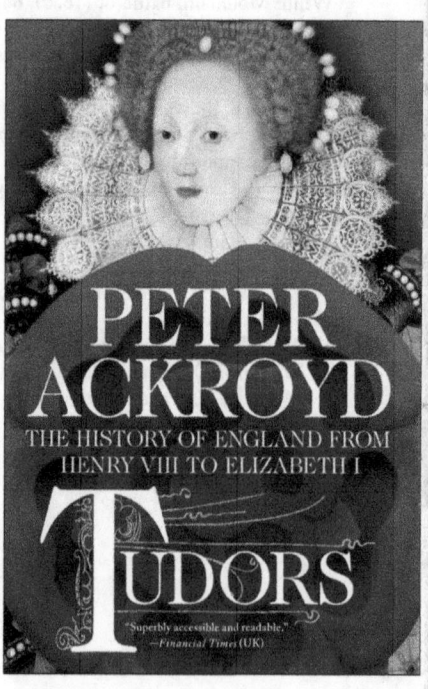

ALEXIS LICHINE

Encyclopédie des vins et des alcools

DE TOUS LES PAYS

Avec la collaboration de W. Fifield
et l'assistance de J. Bartlett,
J. Stockwood, K. Philson
et A. Gay

ROBERT LAFFONT

Première édition 1980
Première réimpression édition révisée 1981
Deuxième réimpression édition révisée 1982
Troisième réimpression édition révisée 1983
Quatrième réimpression 1984
Cinquième réimpression édition révisée 1985
Sixième réimpression 1986
Septième réimpression 1987
Huitième réimpression édition actualisée 1988
Neuvième réimpression 1991

Cet ouvrage a été publié aux États-Unis
par Alfred A. Knopf à New York sous le titre
Alexis Lichine's Encyclopedia
of Wines and Spirits

ISBN : 2-221-05668-X

A Sacha et Sandra,
qui furent élevés dans le Médoc,
avec l'espoir que ce livre
les aidera à former leur goût.

Préface

Ce livre est destiné aux consommateurs et à ceux qui, par profession, sont amenés à parler du goût, des traditions, des qualités du vin, des différences subtiles entre un cru et un autre et des inévitables limitations des vins fins produits sur une superficie restreinte. De telles connaissances augmentent, dans des proportions qu'on ne saurait mesurer, la joie que procure une bonne bouteille. Elles aident aussi à dissiper les nuées d'ignorance et de préjugés qui prévalent dans un domaine qui est encore enveloppé de mystère. Quelques-uns de ceux qui s'y engagent avec crainte ne sont pas encore certains que le vin est fait avec du raisin. C'est pourquoi nous accordons une telle place dans cet ouvrage aux sciences de la viticulture et de la vinification. On trouvera des renseignements détaillés sur ces sujets — ainsi que sur l'histoire, la valeur et la manière de servir le vin — dans les chapitres qui précèdent les données classées par ordre alphabétique de notre encyclopédie.

Étant donné que nous ne disposons pas d'un espace illimité, il nous a été impossible d'accorder un article à chaque élément et à chaque mot ; le lecteur en trouvera donc quelques-uns dans des rubriques de plus grande importance. Cependant nous n'avons pas appliqué des règles étroites et inflexibles. Le vin est un sujet d'une souplesse infinie et nous avons traité chacun de ses aspects selon son importance propre sous la rubrique qui nous a paru le mieux appropriée. Nous invitons donc avec insistance le lecteur à se servir de l'index qui, en cas de doute, lui signalera toutes les références à chaque aspect particulier d'un sujet, quel qu'il soit. Les appendices offrent une documentation complète sur des matières telles que la tonnellerie, la capacité des bouteilles, d'utiles tables de conversion et des listes de châteaux du Bordelais qui ne sont pas classés malgré leurs mérites, ainsi que des listes complètes du registre des vignobles allemands.

Les données quantitatives de production citées dans le texte sont des chiffres basés sur une moyenne, sauf lorsqu'il est indiqué avec précision qu'il s'agit de la production d'une année type. Ces quantités varient naturellement d'une année à l'autre. Les lois et règlements cités dans l'encyclopédie étaient en vigueur au moment où l'ouvrage fut mis sous presse, mais certains sont sujets à de amendements annuels.

Afin d'indiquer clairement au lecteur si nous traitons d'un vin authentiq d'une imitation, nous avons écrit les noms de vins tels que Xérès,

Bourgogne, etc., avec une majuscule lorsqu'il s'agit réellement du vin authentique ayant légalement droit à cette appellation en Espagne, au Portugal ou en France.

Mon premier livre, *Vins de France,* fut si bien accueilli et a atteint de tels tirages, qu'il m'a décidé d'écrire un ouvrage sur les vins et spiritueux du monde entier (1967), suivi ensuite du *Guide des vins et vignobles de France* (1979). Néanmoins, je n'aurais pu accomplir cette tâche sans la collaboration des personnes suivantes :

Pierre Perromat, propriétaire viticulteur et ex-président national de l'Institut national des appellations d'origine (I.N.A.O.), première personnalité des vins de France, qui a pu consacrer quelques instants de son temps, ô combien précieux, pour nous livrer ses appréciations sur certaines pages de cet ouvrage.

Feu Herr Karl Ress, non seulement dégustateur émérite mais aussi personnage dont le dévouement sincère à son bien-aimé Rheingau en fait une source inestimable de renseignements sur cette région et sur d'autres régions vinicoles d'Allemagne. Le fils, Joachim, a suivi les traces de son père défunt de façon remarquable, et a apporté sa généreuse contribution à chaque édition révisée.

Le docteur Franz Werner Michel du Stabilisierungsfonds für Wein de Mayence s'est rendu particulièrement utile en vérifiant la mise à jour de la rubrique allemande, mise à jour que les lois allemandes de 1971 sur les vins avaient rendu nécessaire.

M. Peter M.F. Sichel de New York, dernier membre de ce fidèle trio qui s'est tant dévoué pour assurer la rubrique allemande.

Le docteur Maynard Amerine, œnologue américain des plus éminents, dont la collaboration technique a été sollicitée par des gouvernements du monde entier. Ses œuvres, reflétant sa connaissance scientifique sur la vinification contemporaine, sont respectées par des savants français tels que les docteurs Peynaud et Ribéreau-Gayon. Amateur de vin, il met en évidence qu'il ne s'agit pas seulement d'une science mais aussi d'une des grâces de la civilisation.

M. Patrick Léon, autrefois chez Alexis Lichine et C°, et aujourd'hui chez le baron Philippe de Rothschild, qui passa de longues heures, parfois fort avant dans la nuit, à étudier les petits vignobles de France et leur production, de telle sorte qu'aucun autre ouvrage, même en France, ne fournit une masse aussi complète de statistiques.

M. Claude Taittinger, qui nous a prodigué son temps et ses connaissances afin que l'article sur la Champagne soit aussi complet que possible et qu'il fasse indiscutablement autorité.

Feu François Hine, négociant en Cognac à Jarnac, dont le caractère jovial est aussi estimé que ses marchandises sur le plan international.

MM. Protin et Friedas de l'Office international du vin de Paris, qui eurent l'amabilité de nous fournir d'importants renseignements statistiques sur tous les pays producteurs de vin du monde, ainsi que quelques-unes des cartes dont nous avions pensé nous servir pour la publication d'un atlas des vins.

M. Pierre Bréjoux, ancien inspecteur général, membre de l'I.N.A.O., qui vérifia personnellement l'article consacré à son cher Anjou et nous concéda gracieusement son temps pour la préparation d'une rubrique consacrée aux récentes Appellations Contrôlées.

Docteur Philippe Dufaye, qui abandonna la médecine pour se consacrer à la viticulture à Châteauneuf-du-Pape, estimant qu'il mènerait une vie plus pleine et plus heureuse en traitant la nature du sol plutôt que celle de l'homme.

Feu professeur Georges Portman, qui par son action inlassable en faveur du vin a apporté la preuve à l'affirmation de son illustre prédécesseur, Louis Pasteur, à savoir que le vin était la plus saine et la plus hygiénique des boissons. Je lui suis particulièrement reconnaissant de sa contribution au chapitre « Le vin et la santé ».

M. Georges Dubœuf qui est devenu, grâce à sa compétence pour le choix des vins et à ses efforts en faveur des exploitants du Beaujolais, une des personnalités les plus en vue de cette région viticole ; sans oublier son collaborateur M. Michel Brun.

L'Office international du vin, et son éminent secrétaire, qui m'ont permis de consulter librement la masse des documents qu'ils avaient réunis pour leur Atlas viticole du monde, ce qui m'a aidé dans l'établissement d'une partie des cartes contenues dans ce livre.

Pour rassembler tous les renseignements de ce livre commencé en 1955 qui vit finalement le jour en 1967, il a fallu partager des milliers de repas avec des amis versés dans le vin et venus chez moi du monde entier. Marie Lasserre, Carmen Arcennathury, Marie-José et Bernard Taveira, grâce à leur cuisine et leurs services, ont su inspirer ces amis qui ont tant contribué à ce livre.

Les cinquante et quelques courtiers, distributeurs, propriétaires et amis informés qui contribuèrent à la révision de la classification des vins de Bordeaux se trouvant p. 225. Une fois que les pressions politiques et les préjugés ont été écartés, les personnes objectives, dotées d'un esprit constructif, peuvent alors classer les vins rouges de la Gironde. Les opinions de ces conseillers, opinions données en toute franchise, seront gardées anonymes comme convenu, ceci afin de ne pas nuire à leur activité professionnelle quotidienne dans la région bordelaise.

Le docteur Bruno Roncarati de Londres, qui est à l'origine de la vaste gamme des vins italiens d'appellation contrôlée (vins D.O.C.).

Mlle Jane Stockwood, qui travaille diligemment avec moi depuis vingt ans et qui partagea mon dépit lorsqu'une dactylographe détruisit par inadvertance un cinquième du manuscrit et me prêta une main secourable pour reconstituer les textes disparus. Sans elle, le manuscrit n'aurait jamais atteint la table de l'éditeur.

M. John Laird, amoureux du vin, qui fournit une aide précieuse pendant la longue année que dura la révision de ce livre en 1974. S. Perkins et Martin Sinkoff, qui collaborèrent à sa mise à jour en 1978 et en 1979. K. Philson qui poursuivit leur travail en 1980, 1981 et 1988. Anne Gay qui travailla plus d'une année avec acharnement pour aider à réactualiser cette cinquième édition en 1988. Françoise Rosenthal et Pascale Carissimo Bodemer des Éditions Robert Laffont. Il faut aussi remercier Kerry Stewart qui, pour l'édition de 1988, a remis complètement à jour la rubrique allemande.

Tous ceux qui me furent proches durant onze années, depuis 1956, alors que je croyais avec optimisme que la 1re édition de ce livre serait terminée en 1959 et non pas en 1967. Et les nombreux amis qui, armés de patience, travaillèrent aux révisions de 1974 et 1987 qui ne devaient être qu'une mise à jour, mais qui devinrent vite des expansions de l'encyclopédie.

Bien d'autres, trop nombreux pour que je puisse les citer tous ici, m'ont fourni une aide considérable. J'en donne la liste en fin de volume.

ALEXIS LICHINE

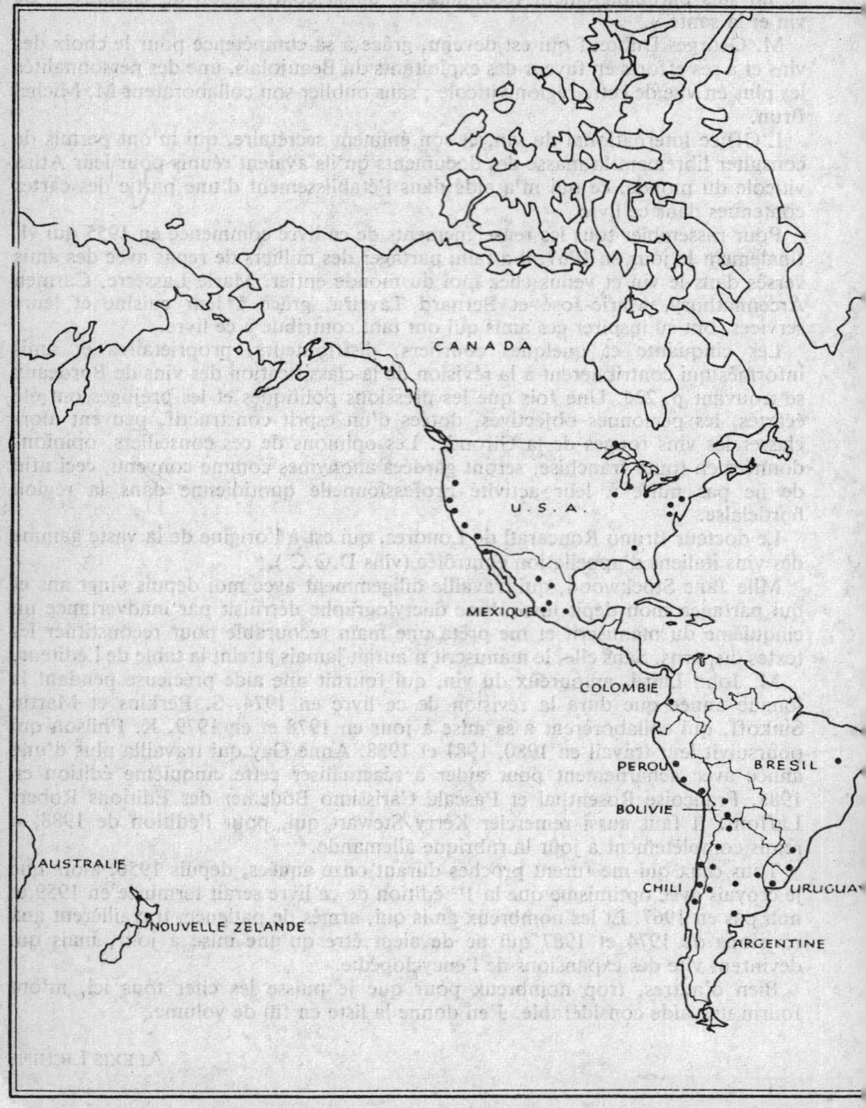
CANADA
U.S.A.
MEXIQUE
COLOMBIE
PEROU
BRESIL
BOLIVIE
CHILI
URUGUAY
ARGENTINE
AUSTRALIE
NOUVELLE ZELANDE

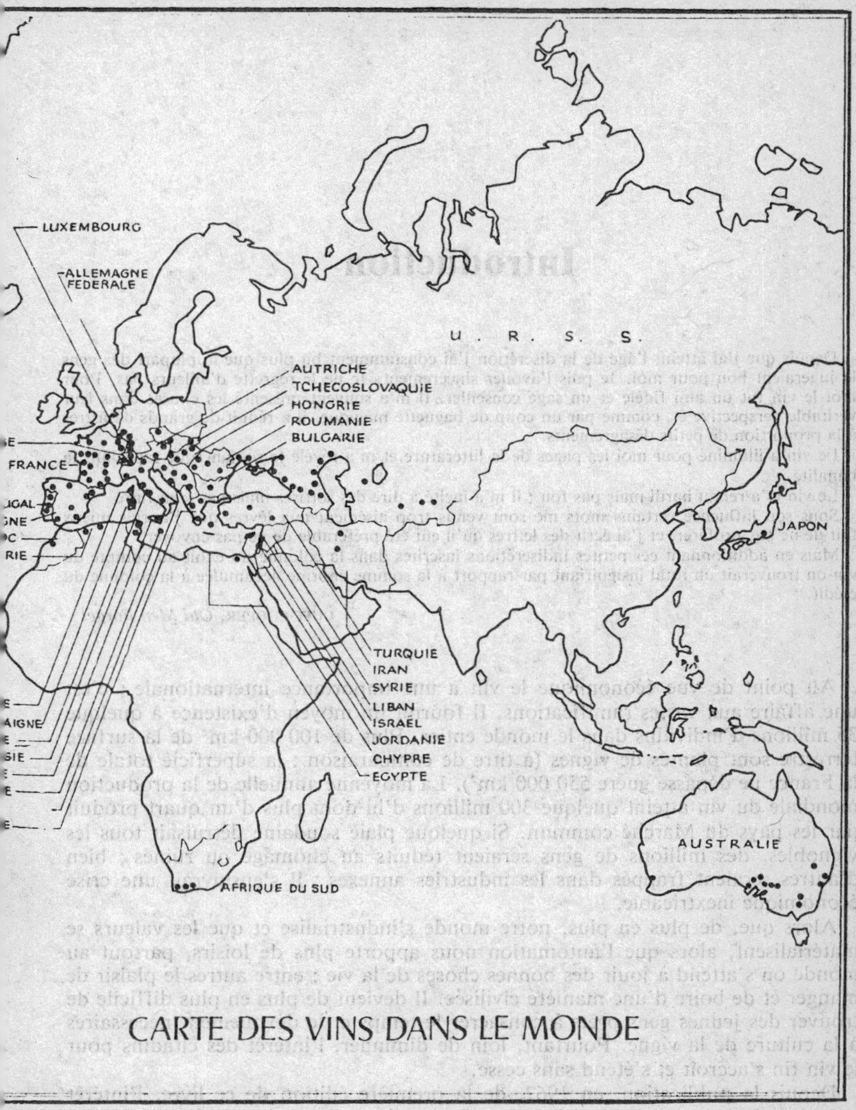

CARTE DES VINS DANS LE MONDE

Introduction

Depuis que j'ai atteint l'âge de la discrétion j'ai constamment bu plus que la plupart des gens le jugeraient bon pour moi. Je puis l'avouer sincèrement. Je ne le regrette d'ailleurs pas. Pour moi le vin fut un ami fidèle et un sage conseiller. Il m'a souvent présenté les choses dans leur véritable perspective et, comme par un coup de baguette magique, il a réduit de grands désastres à la proportion de petits désagréments.

Le vin a illuminé pour moi les pages de la littérature et m'a révélé le romanesque tapi dans la banalité.

Le vin m'a rendu hardi mais pas fou ; il m'a incité à dire des sottises mais pas à en faire.

Sous son influence certains mots me sont venus trop aisément aux lèvres que j'aurais mieux fait de ne pas proférer, et j'ai écrit des lettres qu'il eût été préférable de ne pas envoyer.

Mais en additionnant ces petites indiscrétions inscrites dans la colonne du débit au compte du vin on trouverait un total insignifiant par rapport à la somme énorme accumulée à la colonne du crédit.

DUFF COOPER, *Old Men Forget*

Au point de vue économique le vin a une importance internationale ; c'est une affaire aux vastes ramifications. Il fournit un moyen d'existence à quelque 35 millions d'individus dans le monde entier. Plus de 100 000 km² de la surface terrestre sont plantés de vignes (à titre de comparaison : la superficie totale de la France ne dépasse guère 550 000 km²). La moyenne annuelle de la production mondiale du vin atteint quelque 300 millions d'hl dont plus d'un quart produit par les pays du Marché commun. Si quelque plaie soudaine détruisait tous les vignobles, des millions de gens seraient réduits au chômage ou ruinés ; bien d'autres seraient frappés dans les industries annexes ; il s'ensuivrait une crise économique inextricable.

Alors que, de plus en plus, notre monde s'industrialise et que les valeurs se matérialisent, alors que l'automation nous apporte plus de loisirs, partout au monde on s'attend à jouir des bonnes choses de la vie : entre autres le plaisir de manger et de boire d'une manière civilisée. Il devient de plus en plus difficile de trouver des jeunes gens prêts à consacrer le temps et le dévouement nécessaires à la culture de la vigne. Pourtant, loin de diminuer, l'intérêt des citadins pour le vin fin s'accroît et s'étend sans cesse.

Depuis la publication, en 1967, de la première édition de ce livre, l'intérêt pour les vins n'a cessé de croître dans le monde entier, et particulièrement aux États-Unis. Il existe encore des gens convaincus que seuls, les Premiers Crus classés du Médoc sont de bons vins ; ce sont maintenant les vins rouges les plus chers du monde ; mais le néophyte d'esprit plus ouvert, dont le portefeuille ne sera pas nécessairement bien garni, appréciera cette nouvelle édition pour l'attention particulière qu'elle porte aux crus illustres de presque tous les pays producteurs de vin du globe. Bien qu'en 1973, les vins de Bordeaux et quelques Bourgognes aient vu leur prix fluctuer considérablement, l'importance des nombreux autres vins ne peut que continuer à augmenter. La formidable expansion de la viticulture en Californie (et la hausse de prix des vins californiens de première catégorie) est un exemple parmi d'autres de cet intérêt toujours croissant. Les nouvelles lois allemandes, italiennes, espagnoles, sud-africaines, américaines et australiennes réglementant la production des vins en sont une autre conséquence. Après avoir subi les prix records des premières années de l'explosion mondiale du vin, le consommateur peut enfin se tourner vers les vins bonifiés (au prix plus modique) de nombreux pays.

Ainsi, le vin, un des premiers objets d'intérêt de l'homme civilisé, est à la fois un secteur économique capital et un des plaisirs capitaux de la vie. L'écart considérable qui sépare les chiffres de consommation annuelle de vin par individu dans les différents pays sont intéressants à lire. La France qui, depuis des siècles, est le premier pays du monde pour la qualité et la diversité de ses vins, a incontestablement joué un rôle prépondérant et a donné au monde entier le goût du bien manger et du bien boire. Elle arrivait largement en tête avec l'Italie avec une consommation d'environ 82 l ; toutes deux sont aujourd'hui devancées par le Portugal qui est en première place avec une consommation de 84 l par tête ; puis vient l'Argentine avec 66 l. Les Espagnols se contentent modestement de 57 l de leur propre production. En un an, l'Américain moyen boira quelque 9 l ; un peu plus que l'Anglais, mais 1/5 de la consommation d'un Grec, d'un Suisse, d'un Chilien, d'un Autrichien ou encore d'un Luxembourgeois. Le Russe, qui buvait très peu de vin, a vu récemment le vignoble de son pays s'étendre de 50 % et il boit désormais sensiblement plus que l'Américain, mais son vin sera probablement d'une qualité inférieure au vin que consomment les Américains et les Australiens.

Les pays dont les habitants boivent le plus en quantité ne sont pas toujours ceux qui s'attachent le plus à la qualité. L'Angleterre, la Belgique et les États-Unis importent certaines des plus fines bouteilles de France et, malgré la consommation relativement faible *per capita* de ces pays, on y disposera de plus de grands vins français chaque année que n'en auront les Français eux-mêmes qui, depuis quelques années, découvrent de plus en plus la hiérarchie de leurs propres vins.

Les gens, voyageant de plus en plus, acquièrent le goût du bon vin ; l'usage civilisé de poser une bonne bouteille sur la table gagne du terrain. Alors on se demande parfois : la demande dépassera-t-elle l'offre ? Ces six dernières années, cela s'est vu pour quelques vins de qualité supérieure de par le monde, d'où une hausse importante des prix au début des années 80. Le vignoble de certaines régions peut encore s'accroître. La Bourgogne a atteint son maximum et certaines zones d'appellation contrôlée célèbres sont extraordinairement petites : 19 km² pour tout le Chablis ; comparez ce chiffre aux milliers de bouteilles portant l'étiquette Chablis qu'on trouve sur les tables de restaurant du monde entier et tirez-en vos conclusions.

De nos jours, on réclame sans cesse plus de toute chose produite plus vite et à meilleur marché. S'il en est une qui ne saurait répondre à cette exigence, c'est bien le Grand Vin. On peut le produire d'une façon très onéreuse sans pour autant en augmenter la quantité. Produit en masse, il cessera d'être un vin fin. Les meilleurs vins ont toujours été produits par des vignes à très faible rendement qu'on taille court afin d'orienter toute l'énergie de la plante vers l'élaboration de fruits de qualité supérieure, ce qui réduit aussi la quantité de ces fruits. Étant donné que le viticulteur ne peut pas obtenir à la fois quantité et qualité, on a édicté des lois sages pour limiter la production, en France particulièrement. Voilà pourquoi les statistiques figurant dans ce livre indiquent les quantités que peut produire chaque cru, mais ne donnent pas la moindre idée de celles qu'un négociant sans scrupule peut livrer sur le marché en étirant sa marchandise comme un accordéon et en collant à ses bouteilles des étiquettes qui indiquent des appellations, des crus et même des régions auxquelles sa marchandise n'a pas droit. Ces pratiques malhonnêtes ont eu cours dans bien des pays.

Il y a actuellement surabondance de vins en vrac provenant de nombreux pays, et en particulier d'Espagne, d'Australie et de certaines régions de la France méridionale. On observe depuis 1980 une augmentation de 20 % de la production mondiale, ce qui donne, au total, plus de 400 millions d'hl par an ; ceci s'explique par la surproduction de vins ordinaires. Cette tendance ne peut être enrayée qu'en assortissant plus judicieusement au sol les meilleures variétés et en étant plus rigoureux dans le choix de microclimats appropriés. Jusqu'en 1977, la moitié de la production de la Californie était du raisin de table et des raisins secs. Aujourd'hui l'État se consacre davantage aux meilleures variétés de *Vinifera.*

En outre, le B.A.T.F. ou *the Bureau of Alcohol, Tobacco and Firearms* (Bureau pour l'alcool, le tabac et les armes) du gouvernement américain ainsi que l'État de Californie auraient intérêt à s'inspirer des lois concernant les Appellations d'Origine Contrôlée promulguées en France et dans d'autres pays membres du Marché commun. Un nombre d'appellations renommées ou de noms de lieux ont été promulgués aux États-Unis. Cependant, un contrôle plus rigoureux portant sur les aires de production devrait être effectué en Californie, où nombreux sont les vins médiocres qui s'abritent sous l'étiquette de vins de qualité produits par les meilleures entreprises vinicoles des comtés du nord.

Récemment de nombreux changements sont intervenus dans la vente et la distribution mondiale du vin en vrac, ainsi les énormes importations de vin algérien de la part de l'Union Soviétique. Avant l'indépendance algérienne, la majeure partie de la production du pays était utilisée pour le coupage du vin du Midi ou « vin ordinaire » français, et pour relever certains Bourgognes. Actuellement, l'Union Soviétique tente de lutter contre la surconsommation de Vodka par la promotion de vins algériens, et les Français importent des vins italiens — qui ont un taux d'alcool élevé — pour remplacer le vin algérien. Cette opération s'est révélée avantageuse depuis la dévaluation de la lire et depuis que le Marché commun permet l'importation de ces vins sans frais de douane.

Dans cet ouvrage, je me suis efforcé de présenter le vin tel qu'on le trouve aujourd'hui. En insistant sur la faible production des grands vignobles, j'espère guider le consommateur dans les méandres des nomenclatures et des coupages interdits — par opposition à ceux qui sont honnêtes et licites. La tendance contemporaine vers un produit standard (c'est-à-dire d'une qualité constante et d'une quantité correspondant à la demande) est en vogue partout. Or elle suscite des difficultés pour les viticulteurs. La vendange d'une année n'est pas la même que celle de l'année précédente. Le producteur peut donc honnêtement mélanger l'une à l'autre pour obtenir une marchandise uniforme. Mais il n'est pas au monde une seule cuve de coupage capable de donner un vin à la fois standard et de la plus haute qualité. Voilà un des sujets auxquels le présent ouvrage est consacré. Le consommateur moyen de vin ne peut espérer jouir chaque jour d'un des plus grands vins. C'est évident. Même s'il lui était possible d'en faire la dépense, il n'y aurait bientôt plus assez de vin pour tout le monde. Mais les quantités de vins sains et honnêtes sont heureusement assez grandes. Le Bordelais, par exemple, est une des régions où la surface des vignobles classés pourrait s'accroître de 30 %. Le consommateur qui pensait autrefois que le summum de la qualité était le Château-Lafite s'est instruit et ses connaissances s'étendent désormais jusqu'aux Quatrièmes et Cinquièmes Crus. Il serait comblé si certains négociants s'habituaient à un étiquetage honnête, mais il ne devrait pas espérer acheter un véritable Pommard au prix d'un bourgogne rouge ordinaire. L'expérience lui enseignera que pour le prix d'un Liebfraumilch (nom dénué de sens s'il en fut jamais, malgré la loi allemande de 1971 sur les vins et les règlements du Marché commun de 1982) du commerce, il peut se procurer un vin de bon cru du Rhin ou de la Moselle et doubler ainsi son plaisir.

Comme l'écrivit Ernest Hemingway dans *Mort dans l'après-midi :* « Celui dont la connaissance et l'éducation sensorielle augmentent peut tirer du vin un plaisir infini ».

Dans ce livre je me suis efforcé d'aider le lecteur à faire la distinction entre les petits et les grands vins, à les comparer les uns aux autres et à éduquer ainsi son palais, à développer son goût et augmenter son plaisir. Je citerai à nouveau Hemingway : « Le vin est une des matières les plus civilisées du monde, une des choses matérielles qui ont été poussées au plus haut degré de perfection, qui offre un plus large choix de jouissance et de satisfaction qu'aucune autre chose que l'on peut acheter à des fins purement sensorielles ».

CHAPITRE PREMIER

Histoire du vin

L'histoire du vin s'enchevêtre inextricablement à celle de l'homme. Nous savons que la civilisation naquit de l'agriculture : quand les premiers nomades semèrent des graines et attendirent la récolte, leurs errances cessèrent. On pourrait dire avec plus d'exactitude que la civilisation commença avec le vin car la vigne prend plus de temps à produire que n'importe quelle autre plante et ne donne de raisins pour la vignification qu'au bout de quatre ans. Après avoir passé quatre ans en un endroit quelconque, la tribu nomade s'était bien stabilisée et pratiquait déjà quelques arts domestiques.

Nous ne savons pas quand l'homme commença à boire du vin, mais il l'accepta comme un don des dieux : les Égyptiens l'attribuaient à Osiris, les Grecs à Dionysos, les Arméniens soutiennent que Noé planta le premier vignoble près d'Erivan. Étant donné qu'on a trouvé des pépins de raisin dans les cavernes préhistoriques on pourrait admettre que le vin est plus ancien que l'histoire ; il n'est pourtant guère vraisemblable que l'homme des cavernes ait su faire fermenter ses raisins. Quand il fit cette découverte ce fut sans doute fortuitement. Selon une légende, un roi de Perse qui raffolait des raisins, en conserva dans une grande jarre marquée *poison*. Quelque temps plus tard, une des beautés de son harem qu'il négligeait, lasse de la vie, but le breuvage contenu dans cette jarre... Le poison était devenu si délicieux que, rassérénée, elle en porta un gobelet au roi ; il but, accorda de nouveau ses faveurs à la dame et décréta que dorénavant il fallait laisser fermenter les raisins. Quelle que soit la manière dont les Perses le découvrirent, ils aimèrent certainement le vin ; selon Hérodote, ils discutaient en conseil de l'État toutes les questions importantes deux fois de suite : la première fois en buvant et la fois suivante à jeun.

La Mésopotamie et les flancs du Caucase comptèrent à coup sûr parmi les première régions vinicoles ; la Scène de Libation du panneau « Standard » d'Our, qui se trouve actuellement au British Museum, date de la première moitié du troisième millénaire avant l'ère chrétienne. En Égypte on plantait des vignes pour faire des vins funéraires peu après 3 000 av. J.-C. ; les premières légendes au sujet de la consommation du vin en Chine datent sensiblement de la même période. En tout cas, on estime que la Grèce — premier pays d'Europe où l'on fit du vin — apprit cet art de l'Orient et aussi, très certainement de l'Égypte.

Les plus anciennes traces écrites du vin en Égypte sont les sceaux sur les bouchons des amphores trouvées dans les tombeaux de la période prédynastique.

Aux premiers temps, le roi possédait sa propre vigne d'où provenaient les vins funéraires et (selon H.F. Lutz) un lopin planté de vigne à usage domestique lui fournissait son vin de table. Les vignobles appartenant à des personnages importants portaient déjà des noms : Ramsès III (1198-1166 av. J.-C.) planta les célèbres vignes de Kan-Komet de même que de nouveaux vignobles dans les oasis. Une vigne de Zoser porte un nom d'une longueur remarquable : « Loué soit Horus qui est au seuil des cieux ». Les Égyptiens désignaient parfois plus succinctement le vin de ce cru en ces termes : « breuvage d'Horus ». D'autre part, certains sceaux peuvent être considérés comme des modèles de clarté, notamment celui-ci : « En l'année XXX bon vin du vaste terrain irrigué du Temple de Ramsès II à Per-Amon. Le chef des vinificateurs, Toutmès ». Il serait à souhaiter que toutes les étiquettes soient aussi honnêtes, explicites et rédigées aussi simplement.

Étant donné l'uniformité de la température en Afrique, la récolte ne différait guère en qualité d'une année à l'autre. Le sol est d'une importance vitale pour la vigne, partout où elle pousse ; les Égyptiens se souciaient du site de leurs vignobles car ils savaient déjà que les vignes poussaient mieux à proximité du Delta où elles étaient irriguées tous les ans par la crue du Nil ; mais les terrains marécageux ne leur convenant pas, on les plantait sur des levées artificielles entourées de murs.

Les reliefs et peintures des tombeaux nous offrent aujourd'hui de clairs tableaux de la vie en Égypte antique. On y voit les ouvriers vendanger avec des couteaux à lame incurvée ressemblant à la faucille dont on se sert encore à l'occasion. Les femmes cueillaient les grappes et les jetaient dans des hottes d'osier portées par les hommes ou bien dans des paniers accrochés à un balancier posé sur les épaules. C'est ainsi que le raisin allait aux presses. Les Égyptiens faisaient fermenter leur vendange dans des cuves en bois d'acacia. Ils le foulaient au rythme d'une chanson entraînante, accompagnée de claquements de mains. Ce spectacle est encore familier à tous ceux qui ont assisté aux vendanges sur les bords du Douro ou en Espagne.

Le parallèle avec les temps modernes ne s'arrête pas là. Un certain Bilgaï, « surveillant de la Forteresse de la mer », nota sans vergogne sur une stèle qu'il avait imposé à la population une redevance de 23 568 mesures de vin en plus de ce qui était dû au percepteur des taxes. En outre, le code d'Hammourabi (Babylone, 2000 av. J.-C.) précise les conditions dans lesquelles il est permis d'acheter du vin : le marchand qui ne donnait pas la mesure devait être jeté à l'eau. En ce temps, comme aujourd'hui, la fraude sévissait dans les affaires de vin [1].

LES PLUS CÉLÈBRES TYPES DE VINS

Nous savons peu de chose quant au vin des gens du commun car ils n'avaient pas les moyens de se faire enterrer dans de grands tombeaux ni de faire graver leur histoire et leurs méditations sur la pierre. Probablement buvaient-ils du vin de palme et de dattes ainsi que de la bière d'orge. Le vin royal et celui des riches était surtout blanc.

Le *Maréotique*. Produit par des vignes proches du site sur lequel Alexandrie

1. Pour plus de détails sur l'histoire du vin, se reporter à la rubrique des vins de l'Antiquité (p. 155 et suiv.). Pour l'histoire locale, voir les régions et pays vinicoles : Bordeaux, Bourgogne, États-Unis, etc.

fut bâtie par la suite. C'était un blanc doux, léger, apte à être conservé et doué d'un bouquet odorant. Il fut connu des siècles plus tard à Rome. Selon Horace ce serait le Maréotique qui aurait embrasé le cœur de Cléopâtre.

Le *Taniotique.* Athénée (env. 200 de notre ère) le considère comme meilleur que le Maréotique. Vin blanc, verdâtre, doux, onctueux, aromatique, légèrement astringent. (Athénée disait que les amateurs de vin égyptien mangeaient volontiers du chou bouilli avant les banquets et buvaient ensuite l'eau de cuisson de ces choux pour guérir leur gueule de bois).

Le *Sebennyticum.* D'après Pline, ce vin était fait avec trois éléments différents : du raisin de Thasos, un raisin dit de suie, et de la résine de pin.

Les Égyptiens conservaient leur vin dans des amphores scellées du même type que celles des Grecs et, comme ils ne produisaient pas assez, ils importaient du vin de Grèce, de Phénicie et de Syrie.

Le vin est cité 155 fois dans l'Ancien Testament et 10 fois dans le Nouveau. Dans le Livre des Nombres on apprend qu'au moment de l'Exode, les Hébreux regrettaient de laisser derrière eux les vins d'Égypte ; mais ils auraient eu tort de s'inquiéter car la vigne verdoyait au pays des Philistins et sur la plaine de Sharon, et la Palestine se couvrit de riches vignobles. La vigne prolifère abondamment dans les pays situés à l'est de la Méditerranée ainsi qu'autour de la Caspienne et de la mer Noire. Au chapitre XXVII d'Ézéchiel, nous lisons que Damas était un grand centre commercial de vin : « ton marchand... de vin de Helbon ».

On célébrait aussi le vin de Byblos. Syriens et Phéniciens expédiaient leur vin par les vieilles pistes de caravanes vers l'Arabie, l'Égypte, l'Inde et même la Chine. Les rois de Perse achetaient leur célèbre Chalybon. On plantait aussi des vignes en Arabie qui produisaient de grandes quantités de vin, surtout du rouge.

On trouve de nombreuses références au vin de Babylone, dans les inscriptions et les œuvres d'art ainsi que dans le Talmud. Le sud du pays ne convenait pas à la vigne comme le delta du Nil ; il fallait donc planter sur des levées construites à main d'homme. Mais dans le nord, sol et climat étaient favorables et, à une certaine époque, les vins de Babylone furent très estimés ; on les expédiait jusqu'en Arabie. Le roi Melchisédech offrit du vin bénit à Abraham (Genèse, XIV). A la Fête des tabernacles on brûlait du vin en guise de sacrifice. Cette coutume établit un lien avec le roi d'Assyrie Nabuchodonosor qui consacrait au dieu païen Mardouk des vins aux noms étranges, ainsi qu'avec Assurbanipal de Ninive qui se livrait à de généreuses libations de vin sur les pierres angulaires, les objets sacrés, les lions tués à la chasse et les ennemis décapités. A Haïti, au cours des cérémonies vaudou, on fait encore des libations aux dieux. Comment s'étonner de cette coutume puisque les dieux primitifs sont anthropomorphes ? Et que peut-on offrir de meilleur à celui que l'on veut honorer ?

Les Grecs anciens offraient aussi des libations à leurs dieux. Dès avant les temps homériques, ils buvaient du vin. Le bouclier d'Achille était décoré de pampres ; la coupe d'or de Nestor est encore célèbre ; Ulysse et ses compagnons faisaient bonne chère, s'abreuvant de vin doux. Les Grecs aimaient consommer leur vin vieux coupé d'eau. Ces vins doux, foulés dans des cuves de pierre et mûris dans des poteries, devaient ressembler au Malvoisie d'aujourd'hui. Hésiode, le poète et paysan de Béotie, qui écrivit *Les Travaux et les Jours* vers l'an 700 av. J.-C., plantait et taillait ses vignes selon des méthodes qui furent appliquées depuis lors par d'innombrables générations (*voir* ANTIQUITÉ, VINS DE L').

On discute encore le *Pramnien* et le pur *Maronéen* que décrivit Homère et on les regrette. Selon certains auteurs, les crus de la Grèce antique, lorsqu'ils arrivaient à maturité, offraient la quintessence du vin fin. Aucun de nos contemporains ne saurait contredire cette opinion. Pourtant les poteries enduites de poix dans lesquelles les Grecs conservaient une bonne part de leur vin, parfois coupé d'eau de mer et additionné d'aromates, ne devaient pas contenir des breuvages conformes à nos goûts actuels.

Les Grecs transplantèrent très certainement quelques-unes de leurs vignes à vin en Grande-Grèce : leurs colonies de Sicile et d'Italie méridionale. Ils devaient y faire leur vin de la même façon que dans leur pays d'origine. Cependant, à mi-hauteur de la Botte, les Étrusques (venus d'Asie Mineure, dit-on) buvaient déjà du vin. Épris de luxe, ils donnaient des banquets somptueux présidés par leurs femmes. Leur dieu du vin s'appelait Foufluns. C'est leur pays (actuellement la province de Toscane) qui produit certains des meilleurs vins italiens.

Les Romains ont donc dû hériter naturellement de la viticulture. Comme les Grecs, ils faisaient des vins rouge, blanc et ambré ; eux aussi le buvaient volontiers « bitumé et à la saumure », parfois mélangé à de l'eau de mer et exposé dans des fumoirs. Comme le dit Tovey, en vieillissant ces vins devaient être « réduits à l'état de sirop, rendus bourbeux et épais au point qu'il fallait les filtrer à travers un tissu et les dissoudre à l'eau chaude ». En réalité, le *fumarium* servait à donner du moelleux au vin par la chaleur plutôt que par la fumée ; ce procédé n'est pas sans analogie avec la maturation des vins de Madère à proximité de fours ; les jarres des Romains étaient protégées par une épaisse couche de plâtre ou de poix. Les Grecs de Phocée s'établirent à Marseille quelque six cents ans avant notre ère. Elle fut certainement la première ville de Gaule où l'on produisit un vin véritable. Lorsque les vins provenaient de Marseille, les Romains se plaignaient de « vins enfumés » car ils appréciaient particulièrement les vins doux, voire sirupeux, qui n'ont pas besoin d'être additionnés de matières âcres pour être conservés. Sans doute ressemblaient-ils au *Lágrima* que l'on fait aujourd'hui à Málaga (*voir* LÁGRIMA et ANTIQUITÉ, VINS DE L').

Les Romains répandirent la culture de la vigne dans les pays qu'ils conquirent et colonisèrent. En l'an 92 de notre ère l'empereur Domitien ordonna d'arracher la moitié de toutes les vignes de l'Empire afin de développer les cultures vivrières et de parer à la surproduction du vin. On n'est pas obligé de croire que cet ordre fut exécuté. La Gaule produisait déjà une bonne quantité de vin et le caractère de ses habitants étant déjà sans doute analogue à celui des Français d'aujourd'hui, ils n'exécutèrent probablement pas cet ordre de bon gré, voire pas du tout. Qu'ils aient obéi ou non, leurs descendants furent sans doute soulagés quand l'empereur Probus abrogea cet édit en 280.

Quand on recommença à planter des vignes ouvertement, elles se répandirent au-delà des anciennes régions viticoles de Marseille, Bordeaux, la vallée du Rhône et la péninsule Ibérique ; elles gagnèrent les régions les plus septentrionales de la France ainsi que l'Allemagne et même la Grande-Bretagne. Lorsqu'Ausone, professeur bordelais, poète et consul, accompagna l'empereur Valentinien en Moselle, il établit une comparaison entre les vignes soignées et les larges fleuves de France et d'Allemagne, et tous deux le charmèrent. En Allemagne comme en France, Charlemagne encouragea la culture de la vigne. En un temps où le vin n'était bon que bu jeune, les Allemands se mirent à le conserver dans leurs énormes foudres. Ils ne tardèrent pas à promouvoir ainsi le goût du « vieux

Rhénan ». On cultiva le raisin en Alsace et des tonneaux de vin partirent pour Colmar et Strasbourg pour être ensuite expédiés en Allemagne. Le vin arriva jusqu'en Angleterre, où il était connu — et hautement apprécié — sous le nom de *Osey* ou *Aussey*. On le mentionne dans le *Piers Plowman* de Langland, écrit vers la moitié du XIVe siècle. Le christianisme aussi se répandait. On construisait partout des monastères et des protecteurs, nobles et royaux, les dotaient de vignobles, particulièrement en Bourgogne, où plusieurs vins, notamment les vins de Beaune, étaient connus à Rome. Charlemagne lui-même (vers l'an 800) avait ses propres vignes à Corton (d'où le nom du grand vignoble Corton-Charlemagne). Vers l'an 1100, les cisterciens établirent le Clos de Vougeot et produisirent aussi du vin à Chablis. Par leurs connaissances et leur esprit industrieux, les moines devinrent les maîtres de la viticulture : on avait besoin du vin pur de la vigne pour le sacrement et pour subsister. Cluny, en Bourgogne, fut un grand centre monastique. Quand sa règle se relâcha, les sévères cisterciens rompirent avec l'ordre et propagèrent l'Évangile ainsi que la vigne partout où ils s'établirent, en France et au-delà de ses frontières.

Au début du Moyen Age, les moines surtout cultivaient la vigne dans les comtés méridionaux d'Angleterre. Mais les habitants de Grande-Bretagne importaient aussi du vin du Rhin et du nord de la France. En dépit du mariage d'Henri II avec Éléonore d'Aquitaine (*Voir* BORDEAUX) c'est seulement au début du XIIIe siècle que les vins de Bordeaux (vins gascons) commencèrent à être importés en quantité notable en Angleterre, en Flandre et dans les ports de la Hanse. Une liste des vins établie à l'attention du roi Jean ne mentionne que les endroits situés à l'extrême nord — Gaillac, Auxerre et la région du Rhin. Aucune mention n'est faite de vins de Gascogne. Pourtant, quelques années plus tard, le roi dégustait ces vins et octroyait des faveurs et des réductions d'impôts aux bourgeois de Bordeaux. Des marchands anglais firent le voyage à la saison des vendanges, et s'y établirent quelques semaines pour négocier avec les Bordelais.

On ne tarda pas à raffoler du vin gascon en Angleterre où on l'appelait *claret* (Clairet). Au début du XIVe siècle, les Anglais purent se procurer des vins de table venant d'Espagne, du Portugal, ainsi que des vins doux crétois et cypriotes. Le Malvoisie vint d'abord de Grèce ; mais quand les Turcs occupèrent la Grèce continentale on exporta le vin de Candie (en Crète) et des autres îles. Les transports étaient souvent effectués par les Vénitiens qui, sous le règne de Richard III, apportaient déjà en Europe occidentale le légendaire Helbon de Damas. En Angleterre, ils devaient livrer avec chaque tonneau dix ifs du Levant propres à la fabrication des arcs. L'État exerçait une surveillance stricte à l'intérieur du pays aussi. Des fonctionnaires montaient à bord des navires marchands pour inventorier la cargaison et vérifier la qualité du vin. Le roi prélevait une *prise* sur chaque chargement. Quoique le vin fût bon marché, le menu peuple n'en buvait pas librement. Chaque ville n'avait droit qu'à un nombre déterminé de tavernes ; seuls les pairs et les gens à revenus considérables étaient autorisés à détenir chez eux plus d'un demi-hectolitre. Pourtant, lorsqu'il monta sur le siège archiépiscopal d'York, certain prélat en acheta et en distribua cent tonneaux. Le vin n'était d'ailleurs pas aussi fort que de nos jours.

Au moment même où le Proche-Orient exportait du vin vers l'Europe, ce breuvage était interdit aux musulmans. Cette prohibition n'était peut-être pas observée scrupuleusement. On sait notamment que certains Turcs consommaient volontiers le jus de la treille. Néanmoins les accroissements territoriaux de l'Islam accrurent parallèlement le nombre des populations abstèmes. Pour vendre leur vin aux Turcs, les moines astucieux de Carbonnieux, dans la région de Bordeaux, le baptisèrent : « Eau minérale de Carbonnieux ». Néanmoins les croisés auraient trouvé de nouvelles variétés de cépages au pays des Sarrasins. Ils en auraient rapporté les raisins sucrés de muscat. Plantés en ce temps-là au pied des Pyrénées, ce sont ces ceps qui produisent de nos jours les Muscats de Frontignan, de Lunel et de Rivesaltes. Remarquons aussi que les Sarrasins abstinents enseignèrent l'art de la distillation aux Européens.

Étant donné qu'au Moyen Age tous les vins étaient consommés jeunes, certains devaient être très acides et corsés. Surtout pour les banquets, on les rendait plus agréables en y ajoutant du miel, des épices et notamment du piment. On obtenait ainsi « la force du vin, la douceur du miel et le parfum des aromates ». De ces breuvages ressemblant plus aux liqueurs qu'aux vins de table, le plus célèbre était l'Hippocras, tant chanté par les poètes. Un autre, le Clarry, devait, selon toute évidence, être élaboré à partir du vin Clairet. Mais la situation géographique de la Bourgogne et ses mauvaises routes la rendant difficile d'accès, ses vins étaient peu connus en Angleterre et dans les capitales du nord. Leur célébrité commença à s'établir dans leur propre région, où ducs et princes venaient souvent en guerre contre les rois français. En 1395, Philippe le Téméraire de Bourgogne édicta des lois visant à conserver intacte la qualité des vins, bannissant ainsi le raisin de qualité inférieure — le Gamay — et essayant d'évincer les vins d'autres régions, susceptibles d'être utilisés pour allonger le Bourgogne. Il transféra sa cour — et une partie de son vin — dans ses terres de Belgique, à Bruxelles. La Bourgogne fut aussi dûment appréciée par les papes pendant leur exil à Avignon. En 1443, Nicolas Rolin, chancelier de Philippe le Bon, fonda l'Hôtel-Dieu, ou Hospice, à Beaune.

Les vignobles de Champagne, plantés par les Romains, produisirent, durant le Moyen Age et pendant deux cents ans, des vins rouges plats qui furent d'abord bonifiés avec les vins de l'Ile-de-France et vendus à l'étranger bien avant les productions gasconnes. Saint Rémi, qui baptisa Clovis à Reims en 496, possédait des vignobles dans cette région, où on le considérait comme le protecteur des vins. Henri VIII d'Angleterre et le cardinal Wolsey achetèrent de ce vin, qui fut très apprécié par les rois du Valois ; l'un d'eux, Henri IV, fut le premier à donner le nom de *Champagne* aux productions de Reims et d'Épernay.

Au temps d'Elisabeth Ire, l'aristocratie anglaise buvait encore abondamment du vin mais le prix du vin français s'était élevé et le menu peuple en buvait donc moins ; il consommait plus de bière. D'autre part, le Xérès et les « sacks » étaient déjà en vogue. (Le nom de *sacks* s'appliquait aux vins des environs de Jerez et des Canaries — *voir le mot* SACKS). Cependant Jacques Ier resta fidèle au Clairet ; l'autère Cromwell qui haïssait le rire et détruisait le beau était pourtant assez humain pour apprécier le bon vin. L'*Osey* garda sa célébrité, mais en 1618 la guerre de Trente ans éclata et les vignobles furent en grande partie détruits ; le commerce ne redevint florissant que deux siècles plus tard.

Charles II ramena de France la mode du Champagne qu'encouragea aussi le philosophe et homme d'esprit français Saint-Évremont, à cette époque exilé en Angleterre. Les vins de Reims et d'Épernay étaient déjà alors des vins blancs ou *vins gris,* avec une mince écume évanescente. Ce ne fut que dans les dernières années du siècle que l'on reconnut au frère cellérier Dom Pérignon l'exclusivité de la découverte du Champagne à peu près tel que nous le connaissons aujourd'hui. On savait que le roi Louis XIV prisait le Bourgogne rouge, et il s'ensuivit une concurrence acharnée entre les vignerons de cette région et ceux de Champagne : on appela des experts pour débattre sur les qualités respectives des produits rivaux. Sous la Régence et pendant le règne de Louis XV, le Champagne fut à l'honneur à la Cour, et certains gros négociants virent leur renommée s'établir à commencer par Ruinart en 1729. Environ un siècle plus tard, ce vin pétillant fut amélioré par l'addition d'une liqueur de tirage au goût sucré, et par les progrès apportés au dégorgement, ce qui permet de débarrasser les bouteilles de leur dépôt (*voir* CHAMPAGNE).

Guillaume d'Orange et ses successeurs allemands imposèrent lourdement les vins français et, en 1703, le traité de Methuen accorda un traitement extraordinairement préférentiel au Porto. Ce n'était pas encore le breuvage fortifié que nous connaissons de nos jours mais simplement un vin de table portugais. Les Anglais qui le jugeaient très inférieur au Bordeaux s'en plaignaient. Bon nombre s'abstinrent d'en boire et lui préférèrent le « vin de Florence ». Les moines riches se tournèrent, hélas ! vers le gin qu'ils burent sans mesure. On consomma aussi en Angleterre du vin du Rhin et du vin de table espagnol, notamment du Xérès ; au début du XVIIIe siècle on n'entendait plus guère parler du sack. Le Clairet arrivait, évidemment, en contrebande ; mais petit à petit le goût de Porto se répandit, peut-être parce qu'on commençait à le « fortifier ». (Cet usage date probablement de 1715, ou à peu près). Avec le temps les expéditeurs de Porto apprirent à fortifier eux-mêmes leur vin et à le porter à maturation comme ils le font actuellement ; vers la fin du XVIIIe siècle c'était devenu le plus populaire quoique l'Hermitage, le Champagne et le Madère fussent encore assez en faveur.

Jusqu'alors on achetait le vin en barriques de toutes dimensions et pour le consommer on le tirait directement dans des cruches. Mais au cours du XVIIIe siècle la bouteille prit à peu près la forme que nous lui connaissons de nos jours. C'est en 1781 que le premier Clairet fut versé dans une bouteille bien ronde pour être conservé dans les caves de Château-Lafite.

Quand éclata la Révolution française, les vignobles des nobles et de l'Église passèrent aux mains du peuple. Quelques années plus tard, Napoléon sécularisa les vignobles d'Allemagne, ce qui fut une révolution presque aussi importante aux yeux des vignerons allemands. En France, depuis lors, les domaines ont été divisés, de génération en génération, en petites parcelles, mais dans le Bordelais on reconstitua les grandes propriétés. Talleyrand devint notamment propriétaire du Château-Haut-Brion. Quelques esprits subtils attribuent aux talents de son cuisinier les succès diplomatiques qu'il remporta au Congrès de Vienne. Au cours des repas exquis qu'il offrait, il travaillait ses invités aux vins fins et les opposait les uns aux autres. Son principal adversaire, Metternich, s'enorgueillit plus tard de l'acquisition d'un des plus grands domaines viticoles allemands : Schloss Johannisberger. Vers le milieu du XIXe siècle on planta la vigne dans de nouveaux pays : Afrique du Sud, Australie et surtout Amérique.

Quand Leif Ericson traversa l'Atlantique aux environs de l'an 1000, il découvrit un pays couvert de vignes sauvages et le baptisa « Vineland ». Plus tard les immigrants européens se livrèrent à de nombreuses expériences avec des vignes importées d'Europe ; finalement ils découvrirent que, si la *Vitis vinifera* s'acclimatait fort bien en Californie, il valait mieux, à l'origine, s'en tenir aux variétés indigènes dans les États de l'est (*voir* ÉTATS-UNIS).

On n'aurait jamais imaginé que la vigne américaine lorsqu'elle proliférait dans l'isolement était en train d'acquérir une immunité vis-à-vis de certaines maladies et de certains parasites qui, eux-mêmes, ne cessaient de se fortifier par sélection naturelle. Mais lorsqu'on importa en Europe des vignes américaines il y a à peu près un siècle, les parasites se répandirent sur des vignes qui, elles, n'étaient pas immunisées. C'est ainsi qu'au cours de la seconde moitié du XIXe siècle presque tous les vignobles d'Europe furent ravagés par le pou térébrant nommé phylloxéra. En vérité cette plaie s'étendit au monde entier et le vin, tel que nous le connaissons, aurait fort bien pu disparaître de notre planète. Par bonheur, les plants qui avaient provoqué le désastre offraient en même temps le remède : on découvrit que les variétés européennes de vigne pouvaient être greffées sur des souches américaines immunisées contre le phylloxéra. Que résulta-t-il finalement de ce greffage, en ce qui concerne la qualité ? Il est impossible de se prononcer avec certitude à ce sujet. D'après certains, les vins sont meilleurs qu'« avant le phylloxéra » ; d'autres le nient. La lente adaptation de la vigne au sol et au climat doit avoir le temps de s'effectuer. C'est un processus graduel, comme nous l'a appris toute l'histoire du vin.

Mais l'histoire de la vigne américaine en Europe ne résout pas celle du vin au Nouveau Monde. En ce qui concerne les États-Unis, au temps de la domination britannique on ne buvait que des vins européens. D'après des documents de l'époque on peut se faire une idée des goûts et des exigences des Américains de ce temps-là. L'écrivain Washington Irving était un célèbre amateur de vin et nous possédons bon nombre de ses lettres et reçus au sujet des commandes de barriques qu'il passait en France et en Espagne. Il y en avait bien d'autres mais nous ne citerons que des passages de deux lettres écrites de France — bien avant qu'il devint président des États-Unis — par Thomas Jefferson, un véritable expert : la première, en 1792, à Henry Sheaff négociant de Philadelphie et la seconde, en 1817, au président James Monroe, à la Maison-Blanche :

Bourgogne, les meilleurs vins de Bourgogne sont Montrachet, un vin blanc. Il est fait par deux personnes, à savoir, Monsr de Clermont, et Monsieur de Sassnet, ce dernier loue à Monsr de La Tour. nouveau il coûte 48 sous la bouteille, et 3 livres quand il est bon à boire.

Meursault, un vin blanc, la meilleure qualité s'appelle Goûte d'Or, il coûte six sous la bouteille nouveau, je ne crois pas qu'il supportera le transport, mais le Montrachet le supportera à la bonne saison.

Chambertin, Vougeau, Beaune, sont des vins rouges, de la première qualité, et sont les seuls vins rouges de Bourgogne qui supporteront le transport et même ceux-là exigent d'être déplacés à la meilleure saison, et de n'être exposés ni à la grande chaleur ni au grand froid. nouveaux ils coûtent 48 sous la bouteille et 3 livres, vieux. Je crois presque impossible d'amener ici en bon état n'importe quel vin de Bourgogne.

Champagne, le Champagne Mousseux ou pétillant n'est jamais servi sur une bonne table en France. Les connaisseurs ne boivent que le plat ou non mousseux.

Vins rouges de Bordeaux. Quatre crus sont plus célèbres que tous les autres. Ce sont Château-Margau, Tour de Ségur, Hautbrion et De La Fite. vieux, ils coûtent 3 livres la bouteille : mais ils sont tellement négociés à l'avance qu'il est impossible d'en obtenir, si vous le souhaitez, les commerçants vous enverront un vin portant n'importe lequel de ces noms, et vous feront payer 3 livres la bouteille : mais je me permettrai d'affirmer qu'il n'a jamais été envoyé en Amérique une bouteille d'un de ces vins par un commerçant, et qu'il est donc vain d'en rechercher ; car je défie n'importe qui de les distinguer des vins de la plus proche qualité à savoir.

Rohan-Margau, qui est fait par Madame de Rohan, c'est ce que j'importe pour moi-même et j'estime qu'il vaut n'importe lequel des quatre crus. Il y a aussi les vins de Dabadie, la Rose Quirouen et Durfort qui sont considérés comme aussi bons que celui de Madame Rohan. pourtant je préfère le sien. ces vins coûtent 40 sous la bouteille quand ils ont atteint l'âge d'être bus.

Vins blancs de Bordeaux.

Grave. le meilleur s'appelle Pontac, et il est fait par Mons' de Lamont, il coûte 18 sous la bouteille.

Sauterne, c'est le meilleur vin blanc de France (sauf Champagne et Hermitage) le meilleur est fait par Mons' de Lur-Salur et coûte, à l'âge de 4 ans (quand il est bon à boire) entre 20 et 24 sous la bouteille, on fait deux autres vins blancs dans les mêmes parages qui s'appellent Prignac et Barsac, certains les estiment, mais à Paris on préfère le Sauterne qui est bien meilleur selon mon jugement. ils coûtent le même prix, un grand avantage du Sauterne c'est que son bouquet se développe le jour où l'on ouvre la bouteille et qu'il est meilleur après avoir été débouché quelque temps.

M. Fenwick, consul des États-Unis à Bordeaux, est bien informé au sujet de ces vins et il en a fourni au Président et à moi-même d'authentiques et bons. Il serait le mieux à même pour s'efforcer de vous procurer des vins du sud de la France qui sont très excellents et très bon marché, disons 10 ou 12 sous la bouteille, ceux du Roussillon sont les meilleurs...

Je vous ai promis que, lorsque j'aurais reçu et goûté les vins que j'ai commandés en France et en Italie, je vous donnerais une note sur ceux que j'estimerais dignes de vos achats. Ce sont les suivants :

Vin blanc liquoreux d'Hermitage de M. Jourdan à Tains. Il coûte à peu près 0,82 la bouteille livré à bord... Il y a encore un autre vin à vous citer, c'est un vin de Florence nommé Montepulciano, qu'Appleton est le mieux à même de vous fournir. Il connaît en particulier le cru qui est tout à fait meilleur et qu'il m'a envoyé d'habitude. Il sait aussi par expérience comment le faire mettre en bouteille et emballer pour qu'il supporte la traversée, ce qu'il ne fait pas sans précautions exceptionnelles. J'en ai importé tous les ans depuis dix ou douze ans et je ne crois pas avoir perdu 1 bouteille sur 100.

Vers le milieu du XIXe siècle, les tarifs douaniers entre l'Angleterre et la France avaient tellement baissé que la bourgeoisie anglaise se mit à boire du Clairet. Toutefois Cyrus Redding écrivit quelques années plus tôt que, endurcis par un long régime de vins fortifiés, les palais anglais n'étaient plus capables d'apprécier un grand cru de Bordeaux à l'état pur et naturel et que, particulièrement pour le marché anglais, on « sophistiquait » les Clairet fins avec du Cahors, de l'Hermitage, du Benicarlos et même de l'eau-de-vie de vin. Les Premiers Crus, y compris ceux de l'« année de la Comète » (1811), subissaient ce traitement ; et lorsque Nathaniel Johnston — qui s'était établi, avec un certain nombre d'étrangers, dans le commerce des vins de Bordeaux — exprima le désir de boire un verre de l'excellent 1798 non coupé, il exigea que plusieurs bouteilles de « Lafite pur » soient mises de côté spécialement pour lui.

Redding pensait qu'on ne pouvait adultérer le Bourgogne, parce que sa délicatesse et son bouquet exquis sont inimitables. (Il nous semble étrange aujourd'hui que cet auteur ait cru impossibles des imitations acceptables obtenues par coupage ou chaptalisation excessive.) Barry, écrivain du XVIIIe siècle, jugeait aussi le Bourgogne trop délicat pour voyager et il n'était en effet guère connu en Angleterre en ce temps-là.

Ajoutons que, même si les réserves de M. Redding sur le Clairet préparé à l'usage des Anglais étaient justifiées, une race de fins connaisseurs apparut dans la seconde moitié du XIXe siècle ; on cite encore aujourd'hui les louanges qu'ils décernèrent aux grands millésimes de l'ère préphylloxérienne des années 1860 à 1880. A leur époque, les Anglais devaient avoir le droit d'acheter leur Clairet dans l'état pur. C'est aussi au milieu de ce siècle qu'apparurent deux maladies désastreuses de la vigne : l'oïdium, considéré comme la pire plaie jusqu'à ce qu'apparût le phylloxéra.

Autre événement capital : la classification officielle des vins de Bordeaux (fondée sur des valeurs antérieures mais qui n'étaient pas officielles). Cette classification porta évidemment sur les grands crus du Médoc en 1855. Le commerce du vin entrait dans l'ère de l'organisation grâce à la jurisprudence. La nécessité d'exercer un contrôle sur les appellations d'origine, afin de rendre difficile, sinon impossible, de faire passer un vin inférieur pour un grand vin, apparaissait clairement. La campagne commença au bord du Douro pour protéger la bonne réputation du Porto. Elle se poursuivit en France, au début de notre siècle, et les lois sur les appellations contrôlées furent votées en 1936. Elles pourraient utilement servir de modèle pour tous les autres pays viticoles du monde (*voir* APPELLATION D'ORIGINE CONTRÔLÉE).

Le vin devient de plus en plus cher, mais la demande n'a jamais été aussi grande et la production s'épanouit. L'Office international du vin — groupe de travail comprenant viticulteurs et législateurs — a évalué la production des 40 pays participants : en 1949, elle dépassait sensiblement 150 millions d'hl, elle s'élève maintenant à plus de 300 millions d'hl (46 pays participants).

En notre temps de mécanisation, l'homme revient au vin de la terre : breuvage de la civilisation.

CHAPITRE II

Histoire des alcools et de la distillation

Au Moyen Age, l'alcool de vin portait un nom latin : *aqua vitae ;* ce mot survit de nos jours dans le suédois et le norvégien « aquavit » et le danois « akvavit ». Il a une valeur symptomatique puisqu'il signifie tout simplement : eau-de-vie.

Dès l'Antiquité grecque, Aristote écrivait : « On peut rendre l'eau de mer potable par distillation. Après avoir été convertie en vapeurs humides elle redevient liquide ». On dit qu'un Grec avait découvert ce phénomène rien qu'en observant comment la vapeur se condense à la surface inférieure d'un couvercle de marmite.

En fait de médicaments les Anciens ne connaissaient guère, nous le savons, que le vin et les simples. Dès l'époque des Égyptiens on utilisait en abondance fleurs, plantes et épices qu'on faisait cuire, macérer ou infuser à des fins pharmaceutiques ou culinaires. Le liquide aromatisé et salutaire était conservé dans du vin ou de l'eau, à l'abri de l'air, dans des jarres bien closes. Si on ne le pratiqua pas constamment, l'art de la distillation reparut épisodiquement au cours de l'histoire. Pour autant que nous le sachions, on distilla d'abord l'eau et les parfums. Ce sont les Arabes qui distillèrent l'alcool au début de Moyen Age. Au Xe siècle, le philosophe Avicenne donna une description complète de l'alambic mais il ne cite pas le mot alcool qui devait pourtant être employé dès cette époque. Alcool dérive de l'arabe, comme alchimie. Son étymologie présente une particularité curieuse : les Arabes liquéfiaient une certaine poudre noire, faisaient bouillir le liquide ainsi obtenu et laissaient ensuite la vapeur se condenser puis se solidifier ; c'est ainsi qu'ils obtenaient le khôl avec lequel les beautés des harems se fardaient les paupières. Quand les Arabes commencèrent à distiller le vin, ils donnèrent au produit obtenu le même nom qu'à ce fard : *al khôl,* parce qu'on le fabriquait par le même procédé.

En réalité les Arabes révélèrent aux Européens la science de la distillation comme bien d'autres procédés divers de l'alchimie qui tint une grande place dans les sciences du Moyen Age. Les deux premiers noms qui aient une réelle importance en ce qui concerne la distillation sont ceux d'Arnaud de Villeneuve (mort en 1313) — un Catalan qui enseignait à l'université de Montpellier et fut peut-être le premier à traiter de l'alcool par écrit — et son élève Raymond Lulle, philosophe et chimiste qui poursuivit les expériences de Villeneuve. Lulle était né en 1235 à Majorque. En son temps le traité de Villeneuve sur les vins et spiritueux faisait autorité.

« L'eau-de-vie, écrivit Lulle, est une émanation de la Divinité, un élément récemment révélé aux hommes et qui leur fut caché durant l'Antiquité parce que la race humaine était alors trop jeune pour avoir besoin de ce breuvage destiné à raviver les énergies en notre temps de décrépitude ». Villeneuve était encore plus enthousiaste. Pour lui, l'alcool était la panacée cherchée depuis longtemps, l'élixir de vie, vieux rêve des alchimistes. Les alchimistes ne découvrirent jamais ce qu'ils cherchaient — le secret de la transmutation des métaux vils en or et l'élixir de la vie éternelle — mais au cours de leurs recherches ils trouvèrent bien des choses. C'est eux qui jetèrent les bases de la chimie scientifique et s'ils ne parvinrent jamais à mettre au point le véritable *aqua vitae,* ils se servirent abondamment de l'eau-de-vie et nous en léguèrent l'usage.

Pour le public en général, l'*aqua vitae* était un médicamment et en avait le goût. On l'appelait aussi *aqua ardens :* eau de feu. Les fruits et les herbes qu'on y ajoutait dissimulaient son goût et contribuaient à guérir les malades. Puis vint le temps où le public se mit à boire alcool de vin et liqueurs à des fins autres que médicinales. On expérimenta diverses plantes pour en améliorer la saveur. Sauf dans des régions favorisées, comme celle de Cognac, les Français s'ingéniaient encore à résoudre ce problème à la fin du XVIIIe siècle. C'est alors qu'en 1800 Adam inventa la rectification de l'alcool, c'est-à-dire une redistillation qui supprime le *mauvais goût.* Malheureusement elle supprime tous les goût de l'alcool, bons et mauvais. Les Français, qui avaient élaboré des concoctions d'herbes et de fruits pour masquer le mauvais goût de l'alcool y revinrent pour lui donner une saveur.

On vendait l'*aqua vitae* en Italie dès le Moyen Age ; elle apparut à peu près à la même époque en Irlande sous un nom gaélique : *uisge beatha,* obtenue par distillation de la bière d'orge. Au cours des siècles « l'eau-de-vie » porta divers noms dans ce pays et finit par s'implanter sous celui de whisky.

Le whisky écossais naquit dans les Highlands. Au XVe siècle on en buvait couramment dans ce pays : c'était du pur whisky de malt. Il se répandit petit à petit jusqu'aux Lowlands et à la cour d'Écosse. D'abord les Anglais préférèrent la bonne eau-de-vie française de Cognac, miraculeux distillat des vins secs et acides de la Charente. Depuis longtemps les navires des pays du nord mouillaient à La Rochelle, surtout pour y charger du sel. Puis les habitants de la région se mirent à vendre aussi leur vin. Plus tard, pour occuper moins de place dans les bateaux — et peut-être aussi pour échapper aux taxes — ils se mirent à bouillir leur vin qui voyagea mieux après cette métamorphose. A l'origine ils pensaient ramener le vin à son état originel en lui ajoutant de l'eau après son débarquement ; mais on ne tarda pas à découvrir qu'il avait meilleur goût tel quel. Un certain Croix-Marron, qui aurait joué un grand rôle dans cette affaire, aurait déclaré : « En faisant cuire mes vins j'ai découvert leur âme ».

Selon un rapport datant de 1688, on ne pouvait guère vendre à l'étranger le vin de la Charente mais « ...quand les vins blancs sont convertis en eau-de-vie, ce qui est l'usage, les flottes anglaises et danoises abordent aux ports de la Charente pour en embarquer ». On peut donc estimer que le Cognac a établi sa réputation dès cette époque. On l'appelait « brandy », nom qui pourrait fort bien venir de l'allemand « Branntwein » (vin brûlé) et les Français l'appelaient couramment « brandevin ». En 1622 et 1650 on écrivit parfois en Angleterre « brand wine », ce qui signifierait vin de marque.

On apprendra avec intérêt qu'au début on distillait l'alcool surtout à la maison et que les dames les plus distinguées étaient expertes en cet art domestique, aussi banal que celui de la cuisine. De même le whisky écossais était élaboré presque entièrement au foyer ; on réservait le meilleur aux chefs locaux dans les Highlands. Les métayers brassaient leurs surplus de grain pour en faire du whisky. Les rois de la dynastie de Hanovre interdirent l'usage des alambics individuels et imposèrent de lourdes taxes sur la distillation collective ; mais dans les régions montagneuses presque inaccessibles, les distillateurs indépendants prirent le maquis.

On estime qu'en 1800 les Écossais distillaient clandestinement quelque 23 000 hl par an et la quantité produite de manière licite était à peu près nulle. D'année en année, la quantité de whisky qui passait dans les Lowlands et franchissait même la frontière anglaise aurait atteint jusqu'à 14 000 hl par an. A une certaine époque on compta jusqu'à 200 points de distillation illicite dans la vallée étroite mais célèbre de Glenlivet ; c'est de là que vient peut-être de nos jours le meilleur whisky exempt de coupages.

Les distillateurs écossais étaient assez audacieux pour élaborer leur potion illicite tout à fait ouvertement. Il leur suffisait de choisir un vallon facile à défendre et de s'y rendre armés jusqu'aux dents. En 1823, le gouvernement anglais réduisit les droits sur le whisky afin d'encourager la distillation licite de bons alcools. Mais les alambics interdits étaient si bien entrés dans les mœurs que lorsqu'un casse-cou nommé George Smith vint établir une distillerie opérant conformément à la loi dans la vallée même de Glenlivet, on estima qu'il faisait preuve d'une extrême effronterie. Ses *Mémoires* ne nous indiquent pas comment il faisait son whisky mais il nous révèle le secret de sa réussite. Il embaucha les plus hardis lascars qu'il put trouver et, en montant la garde avec eux par équipes pendant vingt-quatre heures par jour, il évita qu'on incendiât son installation, comme on le fit à quelques autres aussi audacieux que lui mais moins malins. En prenant pied à Glenlivet, Smith sonna le glas d'une ère. Le triste déclin de la distillation illicite apparaît dans les statistiques d'alambics repérés en Écosse : en 1834, 692 ; en 1835, 177 ; en 1854, 73 ; en 1864, 19 ; en 1874, 6. La race des contrebandiers de l'alcool se mourait comme celle des romanesques brigands de grands chemins du siècle précédent.

C'est au XVIIIe siècle qu'on commença à produire du whiskey aux États-Unis. (L'orthographe whisky prévaut au Canada, en Angleterre et en Écosse ; celle de whiskey aux États-Unis et en Irlande). La distillation du seigle et de l'orge était devenue une habitude tellement invétérée en 1794 que l'imposition de taxes et de contrôles provoquèrent une rébellion armée en Pennsylvanie. Vaincus, les distillateurs partirent vers l'Ouest en grand nombre ; ils préféraient les Peaux-Rouges aux agents du fisc. Quelques années plus tôt on avait commencé à faire du whiskey de maïs dans le canton de Bourbon, au Kentucky ; quand les réfugiés arrivèrent de l'Est, le commerce prospéra. A l'origine on produisit du whiskey de maïs pour simplifier les expéditions ; sur les pistes montagneuses du Kentucky un cheval de somme ne pouvait guère porter que quatre boisseaux de maïs, mais il portait l'équivalent de 24 boisseaux si le grain était transformé en alcool. Ce whiskey de maïs prit le nom de Bourbon : celui du canton où il était né.

Un autre élément incita les cultivateurs à distiller leur maïs : les prix du whiskey au Kentucky. En 1782 — à peu près à l'époque où s'établirent les premières distilleries de Bourbon — un tribunal du canton de Jefferson fixa à quinze dollars la demi-pinte (guère plus de 23 cl) le prix du whiskey au Kentucky.

Les Indiens avaient déjà donné l'exemple en fabriquant leur propre alcool de maïs appelé nohelick. (Plus à l'ouest, sur les terres encore inconnues des émigrants, les Apaches distillaient le même breuvage sous le nom de tiesouine). Le premier qui imita les Peaux-Rouges au Kentucky pourrait être Elijah Craig. En tout cas cet intrépide prêcheur baptiste « considérait cette activité comme aussi honorable que n'importe quelle autre. Les prêtres eux-mêmes estiment qu'accorder leur approbation à cette manufacture n'est pas faillir à leur haute mission et qu'ils peuvent même s'y livrer personnellement ou en boire un peu pour le bien de leur estomac ».

La rectification ou redistillation, inventée par Adam et dont nous avons déjà parlé, déclencha un bouleversement complet dans la production des spiritueux. Même dans la région de Cognac (où aujourd'hui encore on ne rectifie jamais l'eau-de-vie qui continue à être distillée en alambic selon les méthodes traditionnelles) on adopta de nouvelles méthodes d'exportation il y a quelque trois quarts de siècle pour faire face à la concurrence des alcools rectifiés. Longtemps expédié en barils, le Cognac fut exporté en bouteilles pour que distillateurs et expéditeurs assurent la qualité de leur marchandise. S'ils avaient continué à l'envoyer dans des futailles leur alcool risquait d'être « allongé » et adultéré pendant le voyage ou à l'arrivée. Autre conséquence de cette révolution : l'eau-de-vie des Charentes prit le nom de la petite agglomération d'où elle était expédiée et c'est alors qu'on commença à l'appeler Cognac.

Le rhum — alcool de canne à sucre des Antilles — eut des débuts agités aux Iles. C'était le breuvage traditionnel des hommes qui combattaient sur les routes maritimes des bâtisseurs d'empires ; quand les marins n'en touchaient pas leur juste ration, la mutinerie était à craindre. Les habitants des colonies anglaises d'Amérique consommaient aussi ce jus ardent de la canne. Il est permis de dire que, dans une certaine mesure, le rhum les excita à la rébellion et les amena ainsi à constituer un pays indépendant : les États-Unis. Quand elle taxa le rhum, l'Angleterre provoqua en effet autant de colère qu'en imposant le thé. Les rapports entre l'histoire du rhum et celle de la flibuste, qui ravageait les routes maritimes des Espagnols, sont encore plus romanesques. Les pirates mouillaient à l'abri de petites anses, aux Barbades, à la Jamaïque et sur les côtes d'autres îles pour embarquer leurs cargaisons de rhum frais. De nos jours, nous buvons en général un rhum plus apprivoisé. C'est encore la rectification qui a provoqué ce bouleversement. A force de redistillations répétées on élimine tous les sous-produits de n'importe quel liquide. Dans bien des rhums rectifiés il ne reste plus grand-chose de la vigueur ni du bouquet de la canne à sucre, notamment dans les rhums légers de Porto Rico et de Cuba ; alors que le Demarara de l'ancienne Guyane britannique et le rhum de la Jamaïque et de la Martinique sont plus forts, plus savoureux, plus sucrés.

Les véritables effets de la rectification apparaissent surtout dans la grande popularité du gin et de la vodka. Foncièrement l'un et l'autre sont des spiritueux rendus insipides par la redistillation ; dans le cas du gin on le traite pour lui rendre un goût. La faveur dont le gin jouit aux États-Unis est due à la popularité du cocktail nommé Martini. C'est au temps de la prohibition que des mixtures complexes d'alcool apparurent partout aux États-Unis et se répandirent dans le monde entier sous le nom de cocktail. Dérivant probablement des anciens punchs froids et du « mint julep », ils se développèrent et se multiplièrent certainement parce qu'il fallait donner une saveur moins écœurante aux gins illicites et synthétiques fabriqués par des moyens artisanaux et qu'on appelait alors « gin de baignoire ». De nos jours le cocktail — autrefois si complexe — devient de plus en plus simple. Le Martini emporte la préférence générale, c'est simplement du gin additionné d'un soupçon de vermouth, concoction tolérable quand ces ingrédients sont de bonne qualité.

La vodka est le dernier spiritueux en vogue. A l'origine on la distillait en Russie, en Pologne, dans les Balkans et aux pays baltes. Elle est désormais faite avec du grain, aux États-Unis, en France et dans d'autres pays à travers le monde. La marque Smirnoff fut achetée par une firme américaine à un réfugié russe blanc en 1939. Tel fut le point de départ de la mode qui se répandit après la Seconde Guerre mondiale.

CHAPITRE III

Le vin et la santé

Le vin peut être considéré à juste titre comme le plus sain et le plus hygiénique de tous les breuvages.
LOUIS PASTEUR

Le vin est le plus noble des cordiaux que nous offre la nature.
JOHN WESLEY
(fondateur du méthodisme)

Le vin est un aliment.
OLIVER WENDELL HOLMES

La magie du vin lui est intrinsèque, elle est aussi complète. Elle suscite la confiance, une sensation de bien-être, l'euphorie, et prédispose ainsi l'homme qui boit modérément du vin à être heureux et dispos — car le vin est un tonique pour le convalescent. Le vin incline à la détente, il stimule l'appétit — processus bien compris en notre temps d'études psychologiques mais qui échappe encore en partie à la démonstration scientifique. Le comportement d'un rat de laboratoire ne nous indiquera pas grand-chose sur la manière dont le vin influence un homme fatigué ou débilité ; cet homme n'éprouvera pas la même chose après une injection hypodermique de vin que lorsqu'il élève un verre de vin pétillant vers la lumière, hume son bouquet et fait rouler la première gorgée autour de sa langue. Le secret du vin ne réside pas seulement dans son composant alcoolique car le vin possède des vertus que ne partagent pas les autres breuvages alcooliques. Parmi les substances chimiques qui composent le vin — qui n'a pas encore été analysé complètement — il y a des quantités infinitésimales d'esters qui contribuent dans une large mesure à lui donner son arôme, son goût et l'ensemble de ses caractéristiques, mais qui sont trop subtils pour avoir été isolés jusqu'à présent par les chimistes. Chose étonnante : la recherche scientifique contemporaine nous prouve que l'art traditionnel de la vinification, datant des premiers âges de l'humanité, est parfaitement logique et sain selon les conceptions d'aujourd'hui. Sous la froide lumière de la science, des pratiques qui, à première vue, sembleraient dictées par la superstition ont acquis une nouvelle autorité.

L'étude du vin porte nécessairement à la fois sur les effets spécifiques de chacun de ses composants et sur l'effet général du composé. On estime en France que les buveurs de vin sont joyeux, que les buveurs de bière sont lourds et ont l'esprit lent, que les buveurs de spiritueux sont nerveux, emportés et ont souvent mauvais caractère. Voici ce que dit le professeur Arnozan :

« La consommation quotidienne du vin, en quantité modérée, excite légèrement les facultés intellectuelles et finit par donner des caractéristiques particulières : le vin aiguise l'esprit, anime, rend plus aimable, confère une grande facilité d'assimilation, suscite une sorte d'assurance. Tels sont les traits de l'homme qui use chaque jour du vin ».

N'oublions pas que Grecs et Romains ne furent pas les seuls à boire du vin dans l'Antiquité et que si Français, Espagnols, Italiens en boivent de nos jours, les Anglais ne s'en privaient pas durant la période la plus aventureuse et la plus vivante de leur histoire.

LE VIN EN TANT QU'ALIMENT

Selon sa richesse en sucre et en alcool un litre de vin équivaut à quelque 600 à 1 000 calories. L'analyse du vin a déjà permis d'isoler plus de cent composants. D'après les travaux de E.J. Underwood, publiés en 1940, il contient des vitamines A, B, et C, ainsi que les treize minéraux nécessaires à la vie humaine, à savoir : calcium, phosphore, magnésium, sodium, potassium, chlore, soufre, fer, cuivre, manganèse, zinc, iode et cobalt.

La vitamine B est présente dans le vin en quantité notable. Les vins rouges sont plus riches que les blancs en ce qui concerne maints éléments comestibles, parce que la peau des raisins participe à leur fermentation : tel n'est pas le cas des vins blancs. Pourtant des recherches faites au Collège d'agriculture de Californie ont établi que vins rouges et vins blancs contiennent autant de vitamines B, de même que les vins secs et les vins de liqueur. Les vins blancs auraient une plus forte teneur en riboflavine ; certains en contiendraient une proportion égale aux 2/3 de celle qu'on trouve dans le lait frais. Le complexe de la vitamine B reste stable dans le vin et n'est pas détérioré par le vieillissement. Mais le jus de raisin, pasteurisé ou frigorifié pour l'empêcher de fermenter, perd sa vitamine B, y compris la riboflavine dont la proportion peut atteindre 120 microgrammes pour cent grammes, avec 50 microgrammes de thiamine et autres éléments.

Outre ces vitamines et minéraux, qui contribuent au bon fonctionnement de l'organisme et à son métabolisme, le vin contient des éléments nutritifs dans les sucres du raisin (la dextrose, notamment, mérite d'être signalée), des matières polyphénoliques, des protéines et de l'alcool. (« On a démontré que les sucres naturels du raisin dans le vin sont volontiers absorbés par l'organisme humain et sont même un aliment souhaitable, que l'alcool de vin fournit rapidement de l'énergie calorique et que le vin contient du fer, certainement utile à l'élaboration du sang. » — *Encyclopaedia Britannica*.) 95 % de l'énergie contenue dans l'alcool sont convertis à fin d'utilisation immédiate ainsi que l'a dit Neumann, en Allemagne, au début de notre siècle et que l'ont confirmé Atwater et Benedict. « L'alcool éthylique est absorbé directement et progressivement pourvu que l'estomac ne soit pas vide » (Starling). « Apporté par le sang en tous les points de l'organisme, l'alcool est brûlé dans les tissus » (Duroy, Perrin et Lallemand).

On reconnaît la valeur nutritive du vin en Espagne où il est soumis au même contrôle de prix que le pain. En raison des qualités nutritives des autres ingrédients du vin, son contenu alcoolique est assimilé plus lentement par le corps et utilisé plus efficacement que s'il était absorbé dans des breuvages d'un plus fort degré. Les recherches du professeur Georges Portmann, de Bordeaux — président du Comité international pour l'étude scientifique du vin — et de Max Eylaud ont révélé que si une petite quantité d'alcool est capable d'accroître la vigueur de la machine humaine dans la proportion de 15 %, une double ou triple dose n'a pas un effet proportionnel ; on a découvert d'autre part que l'absorption d'une grande quantité d'alcool suscite un effet d'inhibition qui en diminue l'utilité.

Les vins naturels contiennent environ 11 % d'alcool (11°) ce qui représente la proportion la plus efficace, croit-on. Plus surprenant encore : en tant que désinfectant interne l'alcool agit plus puissamment en solution dans le vin et même dans un mélange de vin et d'eau. L'accroissement de l'effet prophylactique avec la diminution de la teneur en alcool resta complètement incompréhensible jusqu'à ces tout derniers temps, lorsqu'on découvrit que certains éléments composant le vin, autres que l'alcool, empêchent ou ralentissent la prolifération de certains micro-organismes fauteurs de maladies qui affligent le corps humain.

Le vin et la perte de poids

Diverses enquêtes et expériences ont établi des coefficients et graphiques qui permettent de prévoir mathématiquement les effets du vin sur le système humain. Pris en dilution d'environ 10 à 11 % — la saturation du vin naturel — l'alcool est oxydé par l'organisme dans la proportion suivante : 1 g d'alcool par kilo de poids en 24 heures, à condition que l'absorption ait lieu par petites doses espacées qui disparaissent dans le métabolisme sans laisser de résidus dans le sang, l'urine ou autres excrétions analysables. C'est l'excès d'alcool et non la quantité assimilable qui cause l'ébriété. Il est donc facile de calculer ainsi la quantité idéale d'alcool à absorber pour reconstituer et stimuler l'énergie sans laisser de déchets : 1 g d'alcool par kilo de poids du consommateur et par jour.

Sachant que ce gramme d'alcool fournit 7 calories, un individu de corpulence moyenne pourra dissiper 500 calories par jour ou à peu près (75 kg autorisent l'absorption de 75 g d'alcool et 75 fois 7 calories = 525 cal). La consommation calorique de l'homme dans les conditions normales s'élève en moyenne à 3 000 calories. Le vin peut donc lui fournir 17 % de ses besoins dans ce domaine. Eh bien ! il se trouve que, dans une grande partie du monde, le vin joue exactement ce rôle. Voilà une expérience de laboratoire vérifiée à une échelle gigantesque en bien des pays où le vin fait partie du régime alimentaire habituel depuis des milliers d'années.

Cette formidable expérience humaine a été confirmée sous une surveillance bien plus étroite par W.O. Atwater et d'autres membres de l'Académie des sciences des États-Unis. Ils observèrent dans une chambre calorimétrique trois hommes âgés de 25 à 33 ans, conditionnés par des genres de vie différents, un Suédois, un Américain et un Canadien, l'un d'eux habitué à boire du vin et les deux autres abstèmes. Le régime alimentaire comportait 72 g d'alcool par jour. On nota la chaleur qu'ils dissipaient et on analysa les sous-produits de leur métabolisme. L'alcool fournissait 20 % des calories qu'ils dissipaient au repos et 14 % de la même dissipation en période de travail. On constata que l'alcool remplace protéines, hydrates de carbone et matières grasses, et protège les protéines et les autres matières organiques provenant d'autres sources. Le poids des trois hommes demeura constant pendant toute la durée de l'expérience.

L'importance du vin dans le régime alimentaire a été résumée comme suit par Georges Portmann, professeur de médecine à l'université de Bordeaux et l'une des plus hautes autorités européennes en fait de vin et d'hygiène : « Le vin peut être utilisé pour remplacer 500 calories de matières grasses ou de sucre dans le régime alimentaire quotidien. Ces calories seront complètement consumées et n'ajouteront pas un gramme au poids du corps. Consommé de cette manière, le vin peut être très utile à ceux qui souhaitent perdre du poids, mais à condition de supprimer dans les autres aliments les 500 calories fournies par le vin ».

Des expériences poursuivies aux États-Unis et en Italie ont montré que non seulement le vin remplace les calories fournies d'ordinaire par les hydrates de carbone mais qu'en même temps il diminue le besoin d'hydrates de carbone et permet de vivre sans absorber les aliments sucrés qui augmentent le poids. Quoiqu'on ne soit pas tout à fait d'accord sur ce sujet, il semble avoir été démontré qu'en diminuant la masse des aliments absorbés, l'alcool allège dans la même proportion la tâche des glandes digestives.

La bouteille de vin courante (75 cl) fournit 525 calories alcooliques si le vin titre 10°. Si on le considère seulement comme un aliment, une bouteille de vin naturel par jour représente la consommation souhaitable d'un individu pesant 75 kg à condition qu'il se livre à un travail manuel. S'il ne fait pas d'effort physique, la dose doit être réduite : un demi-litre de vin à 10° suffira. Quoique cette partie du régime alimentaire fournisse à l'homme 1/6 de la nourriture qui lui est nécessaire, elle ne peut pas augmenter son poids.

LE VIN ET LE MANQUE D'APPÉTIT

Alors que le vin diminue le besoin en hydrates de carbone, les vins blancs secs et encore plus le vin rouge stimulent les nerfs olfactifs et les papilles gustatives. Ils excitent donc les appétits paresseux. Par contre, l'alcool contenu dans les cocktails et les apéritifs *paralyse* l'appétit.

Dilué comme il l'est dans le vin et associé avec des sucres, des acides et la vitamine B^2, l'alcool stimule le flux de la salive, de l'acide chlorhydrique et les sécrétions gastriques — comme le font, dans une certaine mesure, les jus de fruit. Autrement dit, le vin déclenche la faim et active l'appétit. S.P. Lucia, professeur à l'École de médecine de l'université de Californie, décrit ainsi ce qui se passe quand on absorbe une dose trop brutale d'alcool : « Néanmoins, si la concentration d'alcool dépasse le degré optimal, son effet coagulant sur l'albumine, des variations de la pression osmotique et d'autres altérations physico-chimiques provoqueront un arrêt de sécrétions [1] ».

Les acides tartique et acétique ainsi que les tanins des vins secs, blancs ou rouges stimulent l'appétit sans que l'alcool y soit pour quoi que ce soit. Afin d'étudier ce phénomène, ces acides furent absorbés dans des solutions non alcooliques par 21 sujets, hommes et femmes, âgés de 22 à 53 ans, au cours d'une expérience à l'Institut de recherche médicale d'Oakland (Californie), en 1953. Ces personnages poursuivaient leurs activités habituelles (travail de bureau)

---

1. *Wine as Food and Medecine* (Le vin en tant qu'aliment et médicament), Blakiston C° Ltd., New York et Toronto, 1954.

et certains jours prenaient les acides dérivés du vin avec leur repas et même, dans certains cas, à la place des repas.

Après avoir vérifié le bon état des fosses nasales du sujet, en le faisant expirer sur une surface de métal poli (qui devait présenter des taches nuageuses de dimensions et de consistance égales), on lui introduisit dans la narine un tube de gomme pure. Ce tube aboutissait à un ballon d'où l'on pouvait injecter de l'air dans les narines dans des conditions permettant un contrôle absolu. Grâce à cette méthode on dosait la quantité exacte de n'importe quel parfum insufflé dans les narines. L'arôme choisi pour toute l'expérience était celui d'un café de marque banale.

On constata que la sensibilité olfactive diminue toujours après un repas normal. Ce phénomène fut mesuré et inscrit sur un graphique. Quand les acides accompagnaient le repas, la sensibilité olfactive ne variait pas. Dans ce cas, la ligne figurant ce phénomène sur le graphique coupait en droite ligne à travers les zigzags enregistrés après les autres repas. Cette expérience démontrait qu'après un repas ordinaire l'individu perd normalement l'aptitude à être stimulé par l'odeur d'une substance apéritive. Au contraire, les acides dérivés du vin maintiennent cette aptitude et suppriment l'impression de satiété qui suit d'ordinaire un repas plantureux.

D'autre part, on a isolé récemment dans le vin rouge un ingrédient autre que les acides et qui stimule l'appétit d'une manière encore incomplètement connue.

Le vin en tant que médicament

Le vin est utilisé comme médicament, soit comme tonique à toutes fins, soit pour le traitement spécifique d'un grand nombre de maladies. Son plus grand intérêt, c'est probablement qu'il peut stimuler l'énergie et soutenir le moral, préparant ainsi le terrain pour la guérison. C'est aussi un agent alcalin.

Les propriétés thérapeutiques et antiseptiques du vin étaient connues et appréciées dès les temps les plus anciens. Un papyrus de l'ancienne Égypte nous transmet une ordonnance médicale dans laquelle le vin jouait un rôle essentiel. Dans son *Anabase,* Xénophon signale l'ordre par lequel Cyrus enjoint à ses troupes d'emporter du vin afin de le mélanger, tant qu'il y en aura, à l'eau des pays étrangers. Au XIXe siècle on recommandait encore de mélanger du vin aux eaux polluées qui répandaient le choléra. Depuis le temps d'Homère jusqu'à une époque assez proche de la nôtre, on se servait du vin pour laver et panser les blessures. Hippocrate l'ordonnait comme diurétique et pour apaiser les fièvres. Galien dressa une liste des vins et de leurs diverses vertus curatives. Au Moyen Age et encore plus tard, on mélangeait au vin diverses thériaques, des composés pharmaceutiques d'herbes, épices, sécrétions d'animaux fabuleux. Jusqu'au siècle dernier on employait encore de grandes quantités de vin dans les hôpitaux et dans la pratique de la médecine privée : les blancs comme diurétiques, le Bourgogne rouge contre la dyspepsie, les Bordeaux rouges pour les désordres de l'estomac et la diarrhée, les vins allemands pour les nerfs, le Champagne contre la nausée et le catarrhe, le Porto et le Xérès pendant la convalescence. De nos jours encore, le vin sert de base à divers médicaments. S'il est moins en faveur auprès du corps médical, c'est en raison du mouvement général contre les breuvages alcoolisés et de la découverte de nouveaux remèdes.

Le vin pur, exempt de toute adultération, n'en a pas moins des effets curatifs spécifiques en cardiologie, neurologie et gériatrie, notamment les suivantes :

1. En France, on estime en général qu'en raison de leur richesse en tartre certains vins augmentent les sécrétions intestinales quoique des vins rouges à teneur élevée en tanin les diminuent. On sait depuis longtemps que ces vins rouges apaisent la diarrhée, notamment par l'influence du tanin sur le gros intestin. (Ces vertus sont celles des bons vins, surtout des Bordeaux ; des vins adultérés par le coupage avec des crus de qualité inférieure n'auront pas le même effet bénéfique). Le vin a aussi un effet curatif sur la colite et les hémorroïdes.

2. Le vin est indispensable dans les régimes pauvres en sodium. Un verre de vin contient de 1,3 à 9,9 mg de sodium alors qu'un œuf en contient 40 mg ; un verre de lait, 120 mg ; 100 g de certains fromages, 800 mg, et une tranche de pain blanc, 215 mg.

3. Les personnes qui boivent régulièrement du vin risquent moins les calculs de la vessie.

4. « C'est le plus sûr de tous les sédatifs », selon Haggard et Jellinek.

5. Les vins riches en fer agissent sur l'anémie provoquée par la carence de ce métal.

Un désinfectant

On a toujours su que le vin et l'alcool tuent les microbes tant à l'intérieur qu'à l'extérieur du corps.

Dès le temps de la Rome antique on s'interrogeait sur l'efficacité prophylactique du vin, ce qui incita un élève du Collège de pharmacie de l'université de Californie, John Gardner, à tenter d'isoler un ingrédient du vin rouge — autre que l'alcool — capable de tuer le staphylocoque doré et d'autres bactéries. Nombre de micro-organismes, y compris le microbe du typhus, sont anéantis par l'alcool et par certains acides du vin. Le vin ordinaire est aussi capable de tuer le bacille de la dysenterie. Même très dilué, le vin rouge peut purifier des eaux polluées. L'usage universel du vin rouge mêlé à l'eau autrefois, dans bien des pays du monde, a contribué dans une mesure inestimable à préserver la vie humaine sur terre. Même dans les pays où l'eau pure est abondante, son action bactéricide est utile. Le vin absorbé avec le repas agit dans le tube digestif contre les micro-organismes absorbés avec les légumes, les fruits ou des tissus infectés parfois présents dans les fruits de mer et autres aliments consommés crus.

Un vin titrant 9° ou plus retarde ou interdit la libération pendant la digestion des nématodes qui provoquent la trichine, comme l'indiquent J.B. McNaught et G.N. Perce dans *The Protective Action of Alcohol in Experimental Trichinosis* (L'action protectrice de l'alcool dans la trichine expérimentale) [*American Journal of Clinical Pathology,* 1931]. « Je regretterais d'abandonner l'usage du vin contre les formes graves de fièvre entérique et pulmonaire », dit Sir William Osler, éminent médecin canadien. Le vin est aussi bien connu dans le traitement de la bronchite et de la grippe.

Le vin n'est pas composé que d'alcool et la consommation de l'alcool ne conduit pas obligatoirement a l'alcoolisme

Nous sommes désormais certains de ceci : une petite quantité de vin stimule, une grande quantité de vin assomme. Les cocktails (et bien des apéritifs) sont des déprimants ; s'ils semblent avoir un effet inverse c'est parce qu'ils libèrent le buveur de ses inhibitions. Mais le vin naturel ne contient en général que 10 % d'alcool et le cocktail, 40 % ou plus. Autre différence : le vin contient d'autres éléments que l'alcool et qui agissent sur l'organisme. Une forte dose d'alcool coupe le flux de la bile. Celle que contient le vin naturel (10 %) stimulera au contraire ce flux. Le professeur Georges Portmann a dit jadis : « Le vin est un complexe équilibré et vivant comme on n'en trouve nulle par ailleurs. Savez-vous quelque chose au sujet des aliments et de la vie et croyez-vous que l'équilibre et la vitalité ne comptent pour rien ? C'est la seule chose que l'homme consomme et qui vient directement de la terre à l'état vivant. »

C'est l'excès et non l'habitude du vin qui peut faire du mal — il en va de même pour les alcools. Toutefois, le vin contenant moins d'alcool présente moins de danger. Les anciennes théories concernant les maladies provoquées par l'alcool ont été démenties pour la plupart car ces maladies étaient souvent provoquées par des carences alimentaires, notamment en vitamines. En 1827, Bright suggérait que l'inflammation des reins qui porte son nom — maladie de Bright — était parfois provoquée par l'alcool. Or il a été démontré depuis qu'elle n'a aucun rapport avec l'alcool qui, au contraire, aide les reins à fonctionner.

Si le buveur s'alimente convenablement, même une forte consommation d'alcool provoquera difficilement la cirrhose du foie ; pris en quantité modérée, l'alcool a même un effet stimulant sur le foie. On ne connaît actuellement aucun mal provoqué par le vin naturel, sauf s'il est consommé en quantité très excessive.

CHAPITRE IV

La vigne

Selon les botanistes, la vigne à vin appartient à la famille des Ampélidacées qui comprend aussi diverses plantes grimpantes et rampantes *(Ampelopsis et Parthenocissus quinquefolia,* baie et qu'il ne faut pas confondre avec le lierre, *Hedera helix).* Des dix genres que comprend cette famille — appelée aussi Vitacées — un seul — le genre *Vitis* — importe aux vignerons, quoique certains autres soient aussi capables de produire des raisins. (On a essayé de faire du vin avec des raisins du genre *Ampelocissus*, mais il était trop léger et trop aigre et l'expérience ne mérite pas d'être répétée). Le genre *Vitis* suffit d'ailleurs car ses plants prospèrent sous tous les climats tempérés. Dans l'hémisphère Nord ils poussent à l'état sauvage entre le 35e degré de latitude au sud, et le 50e degré au nord ; on le cultive entre le 38e et le 53e. Ce genre se divise en deux sous-genres : *Euvites* et *Muscadiniae*, eux-mêmes subdivisés en plusieurs espèces. Les variétés de chaque espèce prolifèrent énormément.

L'espèce *Vinifera*, du sous-genre *Euvites*, du genre *Vitis*, nous fournit tous les grands vins du monde. On a tout lieu de croire qu'elle est originaire de Transcaucasie et c'est dans les pays chauds du bassin méditerranéen qu'elle s'est le mieux développée ; c'est là aussi qu'elle a été domestiquée par les premières civilisations à leur début. De la côte orientale de la Méditerranée elle a été transplantée en Grèce, puis en Italie, enfin en Gaule, jusqu'à la côte atlantique et sur les rives du Rhin.

Beaucoup plus tard, on planta des vignes d'Europe aux États-Unis (surtout en Californie), en Australie, Afrique du Sud et du Nord, Amérique du Sud. *Vitis vinifera* a quelques rivales en ce qui concerne la production du vin, mais qui lui sont bien inférieures ; ce sont des espèces indigènes d'Asie occidentale et d'Amérique. Aucune de ces espèces ne compte réellement en fait de viticulture : pourtant on en cultive quelques-unes au Japon et, au plus profond de la crise provoquée par le phylloxéra, le Japon exporta vers la France du vin de *Vitis coignetiae*. (Lorsqu'on greffe *Vitis vinifera* sur des souches de ces autres espèces, le fruit a un goût attrayant mais sa fermentation donne quelque chose ressemblant plus à la liqueur douce qu'à notre jus de la treille). En Amérique du Nord, ces espèces de vigne sont cultivées largement à l'est des États-Unis et au Canada. En France, et dans d'autres pays, on les utilise comme porte-greffes résistant au phylloxéra. C'est évidemment des variétés de *Vitis vinifera* qui sont greffées dessus.

I. Sous-genre euvites

A. Espèces américaines

1) Régions tempérées
(zone orientale)

Vitis labrusca	*Vitis aestivalis*
Vitis lincecunici	*Vitis bicolor*

(zone centrale)

Vitis riparia	*Vitis rupestris*
Vitis rubra	*Vitis monticola*
Vitis berlandieri	*Vitis cordifolia*
Vitis candicans	*Vitis cinerea*

(zone occidentale)

Vitis californica	*Vitis arizonica*

2) Régions torrides
(Floride et les Bahamas)

Vitis coriacea	*Vitis gigas*

(zones tropicale et équatoriale)

Vitis bourgaeana	*Vitis caribaea*

B. Espèces de l'Asie orientale (liste incomplète)

1) Régions tempérées

Vitis amurensis	(Japon, Mongolie, île Sakhaline)
Vitis coignetiae	(Japon, île Sakhaline, Corée)
Vitis thunbergii	(Japon, Corée, Formose, sud-ouest de la Chine)
Vitis flexuosa	(Corée, Japon, Inde, Népal)
Vitis romaneti	(Chine)
Vitis piasezkii	(Chine)
Vitis armata	(Chine)
Vitis wilsonae	(Chine)
Vitis rutilans	(Chine)
Vitis pagnucii	(Chine)
Vitis pentagona	(Chine)
Vitis romanetia	(Chine)
Vitis davidii	(Chine)

2) Régions subtropicales

Vitis retordi	(Tonkin)
Vitis balansaeana	(Tonkin)
Vitis lanata	(Inde, Népal, Dekkan, Chine méridionale, Birmanie)
Vitis pedicellata	(Himalaya)

C. Espèce européenne (ainsi que d'Asie occidentale et centrale)
Vitis vinifera

II. Sous-genre muscadiniae

Espèces (nord-américaines)

Vitis rotundifolia	*Vitis munsoniana*	*Vitis popenaei*

La classification des espèces du genre *Vitis* donne lieu à discussion ; les classifications botaniques sont toujours plus ou moins arbitraires et, dans les meilleurs des cas, les savants ne sont pas tous d'accord. Néanmoins, la classification la plus largement acceptée, particulièrement en Europe et chez les spécialistes des États-Unis, est celle qu'utilisait le professeur Branas (peut-être celui qui fut le plus éminent ampélographe du monde) dans ses cours à l'École nationale d'agriculture de Montpellier, France (*voir* tableau p. 33).

Du côté américain de l'Atlantique, la plupart des vignerons ont adopté la classification du savant américain Bailey. Les Européens la considèrent comme moins exacte au point de vue académique, mais elle n'en est pas moins extrêmement efficace au point de vue pratique. La classification de Bailey comporte quelques différences de nomenclature et répartit autrement les subdivisions. Voici les plus notables différences de nomenclature : *Vitis riparia* devient *Vitis vulpina ; Vitis bicolor* devient *Vitis argentifolia*. Bailey divise aussi *Vitis caribaea* en deux espèces distinctes : *Vitis tiliaefolia* et *Vitis sola ;* les Européens considèrent ces deux variétés comme des mutations de la même.

L'HYBRIDATION

La classification des vignes est d'autant plus difficile qu'on peut pratiquer des croisements d'où résultent des hybrides possédant certaines caractéristiques de l'un ou de l'autre. Ces « mulets » semblent appartenir à une espèce originale. On pratique l'hybridation artificielle à une grande échelle aux États-Unis et bon nombre des meilleurs vins de l'est du pays sont faits avec ces vignes hybrides résultant d'efforts poursuivis pendant le dernier siècle et demi — cela s'explique du fait que, pour diverses raisons, *Vitis vinifera* ne s'y acclimate pas.

Mais les Américains ne sont pas les seuls à s'intéresser aux hybrides. On trouve des laboratoires de viticulture dans à peu près tous les pays viticoles du monde et en France, notamment, on y procède constamment à des expériences. Les hybrides français — croisement de *Vitis vinifera* avec des espèces américaines ou de la même *Vinifera* avec des hybrides — portent le nom de celui qui les a réalisés ; c'est ainsi qu'on connaît Baco, Seibel et Couderc, dans les vignobles du monde entier. Divers hybrides couvrent de vastes surfaces viticoles à l'est des États-Unis, au Canada, dans le sud de la France, en Italie et en Espagne. Quoiqu'ils aient un rendement supérieur à celui de *Vitis vinifera* et qu'ils résistent mieux aux maladies, ils ne donnent qu'un vin honnête, de prix accessible, mais rien de plus. Néanmoins, dans le monde entier, les chercheurs s'ingénient à pratiquer des croisements pour obtenir l'hybride idéal à grand rendement, résistant aux maladies et offrant quand même des fruits d'une qualité équivalente à celle de *Vitis vinifera*. Cependant, les grands vins continuent à être produits exclusivement par cette seule *Vitis vinifera*. Mieux encore, comme durant les derniers siècles, ils sont produits par les mêmes vignobles, très peu nombreux.

LE SOL

Les œnologues — savants qui étudient le vin et la vigne — affirment que quatre facteurs déterminent la qualité de n'importe quel vin : le sol, le climat, la variété de vigne et l'homme. Des facteurs moindres entrent dans l'équation — tels que la levure — mais à titre accessoire. Les quatre que nous avons énoncés sont essentiels. Pour obtenir un grand vin, il faut que tous quatre soient liés l'un à l'autre, qu'ils se soutiennent et se complètent mutuellement, chacun ajoutant des qualités indispensables. Dans cette combinaison, la vigne l'emporte et aussitôt après vient le sol sur lequel elle pousse.

Le sol qui convient à la vigne doit être « noble » ; les éléments qui lui confèrent cette noblesse sont difficiles à analyser. Son attribut le plus remarquable, c'est une pauvreté évidente car souvent la vigne prospère mieux sur une terre où rien d'autre ne pousse.

Les vestiges fossilisés trouvés dans les calcaires oolithiques de Bourgogne ont donné naissance à ce paradoxe bourguignon : « Si notre sol n'était pas le plus riche du monde, il serait le plus pauvre ». De même, la craie à peine fertile de Champagne, les graviers sablonneux du Bordelais, les terres schisteuses de la vallée de la Moselle, en Allemagne, nourrissent des plants dont les raisins donnent les plus grands vins du monde. En vertu de la même règle, des terres riches et fécondes sur la côte française de la Méditerranée et dans la vallée du Pô, en Italie, ne produisent guère plus que de *bons vins ordinaires*.

Ces terres pauvres doivent contenir un certain genre de richesse : de faibles traces de nombreux éléments. Une des plus grandes gloires du vin réside dans les nuances de son goût et de son bouquet, dues, au moins en partie, à l'action et l'interaction des éléments qui nourrissent la vigne.

Sans entrer dans les détails, disons que ces oligo-éléments sont présents dans le roc et la terre en quantités relativement faibles. Il s'agit notamment de minéraux : bore, cobalt, cuivre, iode, manganèse, molybdène,nickel, sélénium, vanadium, zinc, etc. Si leur teneur est trop élevée, ils peuvent être nocifs pour la plante ; ils n'en sont pas moins indispensables en petite quantité.

Quoiqu'on n'ait pas poussé les recherches à ce sujet sur les vignes, les effets de ces oligo-éléments sur les plants ont été démontrés de manière spectaculaire dans les vergers et les vignes des États-Unis où un accroissement minime de la teneur en bore du sol a éliminé un défaut de la pulpe des pommes. Des résultats semblables ont été obtenus en ce qui concerne d'autres éléments dans divers pays tels que l'Allemagne et l'Australie. On pense que ces traces d'éléments agissent sur la vigne en contrôlant le rythme de croissance, en modifiant son complexe enzymatique. Les éléments du sol qui nourrissent la vigne confèrent au raisin saveur et arôme distincts. Le type et le nombre des levures qui provoquent la fermentation peuvent avoir une influence considérable sur le vin (*voir* CHAPITRE V : COMMENT FAIT-ON LE VIN ?).

De très faibles modifications du sol affectent le vin fait avec les raisins des vignes poussant sur ce sol. Mais il faut évidemment que les bases essentielles soient présentes pour que ces oligo-éléments jouent un rôle de quelque importance. Les vignes produisent leurs meilleurs fruits sur des terrains quartzeux, calcaires, schisteux, dont la composition granuleuse favorise le drainage. C'est ainsi que l'on obtient les raisins les plus mûrs. L'azote et l'humus donnent à la vigne de quoi produire son feuillage luxuriant. Mais la qualité du fruit en souffre. On trouve une faible quantité de fer dans le terrain des meilleures vignes, mais s'il y en a trop, le vin sera difficile à clarifier et à stabiliser (certains experts, pourtant, affirment que le fer du matériel de vinification, plutôt que celui du sol, provoque ce désordre). Quand ces éléments sont tous présents en quantité diverse, leur interaction dictera la qualité du fruit.

Il en résulte que celui qui se propose d'acheter un vignoble peut prédire sans grandes difficultés où la vigne poussera le mieux ; quant à préciser sur quel point du sol son produit atteindra à la grandeur, c'est une affaire de temps, d'expériences et, dans une large mesure, de chance.

LE CLIMAT

La chaleur et la pluie exercent une influence directe sur la vigne. Des hivers froids — mais pas trop — assez pluvieux, des étés longs et chauds sans être torrides, avec un peu de pluie — mais modérée — voilà le temps le plus souhaitable. Les premiers froids, à la fin de l'automne et au début de l'hiver, endorment la vigne ; pendant ce sommeil, le bois durcit et mûrit ; mais un hiver trop froid tuera les ceps. L'été doit être assez chaud pour que le fruit mûrisse. Un bon ensoleillement en fin d'été hâtera la maturation intérieure du raisin. C'est pour cela que, dans les régions tempérées et fraîches, les vignerons doivent vendanger aussi tard que possible pour profiter des derniers rayons de soleil que le sort leur accordera. La dernière semaine d'été, ou à peu près, on se décidera à vendanger si le temps est clément. Un fort ensoleillement tardif donnera un vin très agréable ; mais il sera médiocre, sinon pire, en cas de pluie. La pluie n'est la bienvenue que pendant l'hiver et au début du printemps car les maladies de la vigne se développent surtout par temps chaud et humide ; au cours des arrière-saisons pluvieuses le fruit risque de pourrir sur la plante. Le manque de soleil ne permettra pas au raisin de mûrir aussi complètement que pendant les étés bien ensoleillés.

Parmi les influences climatiques indirectes il faut citer la fréquence et la gravité des gelées, de la grêle et du vent. Les gelées tardives, au mois de mai, peuvent détruire toute la récolte de l'année. La grêle ou de très forts vents en fin d'été détruiront ou arracheront les raisins avant la vendange.

D'autres facteurs sont également importants comme la proximité de l'eau, car les lacs et les fleuves atténuent les variations extrêmes de température ou la situation de la vigne sur un flanc de coteau qui donnera des résultats différents selon son orientation. La plupart des grands vignobles sont plantés sur des terrains inclinés, ce qui les expose mieux au soleil et permet un bon drainage du sol. On le constate aussi bien dans le Bordelais où les vignes sont plantées sur des croupes à peine inclinées que dans les vallées du Rhin et de la Moselle où les pentes sont abruptes.

Il faut évidemment trouver exactement la variété de vigne qui convient à chaque sol, sous chaque climat. La Bourgogne nous en donne une preuve frappante : les nobles vins rouges de la Côte-d'Or sont faits avec du Pinot Noir et dans le Beaujolais — à moins de cinquante kilomètres de là — on cultive le Gamay. Même une si faible distance détermine des différences capitales : dans la Côte-d'Or, le Gamay donne un vin ordinaire ; dans le Beaujolais le Pinot Noir produit des vins plats et insipides. Cependant, chaque variété plantée à sa place donne les meilleurs résultats, qui peuvent être sublimes.

Le dernier facteur capital, c'est l'homme. Dans toute entreprise humaine il faut admettre la possibilité de l'erreur humaine. C'est seulement quand l'homme est le plus habile et la nature la plus généreuse que l'on fera de grands vins. Certes l'homme déploiera son habileté après la vendange. Mais s'il n'a pas contribué à amener le raisin à la maturité qui convient, la récolte méritera à peine ses efforts. Soigner ses raisins est une tâche ardue et accablante. Le vigneron consciencieux n'a guère de loisirs et ne peut espérer se livrer à d'autres activités.

LA PRÉPARATION DU SOL

Préparer le sol pour y planter de la vigne exige les plus grands soins ; c'est une tâche épuisante. Dans certaines régions vinicoles — les coteaux abrupts de la vallée du Rhin, en Allemagne, et de la vallée du Douro, au Portugal, notamment — le vigneron sera peut-être obligé de détruire des rochers à la dynamite, d'aménager des terrasses et même de porter de la terre à l'endroit voulu afin d'en avoir assez pour nourrir sa vigne. Ailleurs en Europe il faut défoncer le sol, c'est-à-dire labourer en profondeur. Parfois l'opération est plus poussée : le labourage assure aération et ensoleillement du fond autant que de la surface, sans les mêler, ou bien on mélange la terre de surface avec celle du fond, où encore on travaille le fond en agitant le moins possible la surface. Cette tâche peut être d'une complication désespérante parce que nombre de vignes européennes sont plantées sur des terrains inclinés où le vigneron ne peut pas se servir du tracteur et parfois pas même du cheval ; sur certains, il doit utiliser des outils à main. Après ce labourage on pratique habituellement une culture de couverture qui enrichira la terre pendant un ou deux ans. Alors seulement le sol sera prêt pour la plantation de la vigne. On utilisera des ceps d'un an parfois et plus souvent de deux ans.

En Californie et dans les autres régions où l'on plante de nouvelles vignes, il est souvent facile d'aplanir le sol, au moins en bas des coteaux, et l'on peut alors se servir de tracteurs. D'ordinaire, dans ce cas-là on défriche, laboure et plante en quelques jours. Les sols sont vierges et très fertiles. Une culture de couverture destinée à enrichir le sol n'est pas nécessaire. La mécanisation permet à une équipe peu nombreuse de planter bien des hectares. En Californie à l'origine, puis aujourd'hui dans le monde entier, on détruit les champignons ou les autres maladies du sol par la fumigation.

La reproduction de la vigne

La vigne peut se reproduire de bien des manières qui ne sont pas toutes pratiquées par le viticulteur. La botanique nous enseigne que le raisin est destiné par la nature à protéger et nourrir le pépin et que la vigne se reproduirait normalement par semis. Pour le vigneron, ce serait certainement la méthode la moins pratique. Pour qu'elle se reproduise de cette manière, la fleur de la vigne doit être pollinisée ; or le pollen peut provenir d'une fleur de la même variété ou non. Si c'est celui d'une autre variété qui féconde la fleur, on obtiendra un hybride. Étant donné que le vigneron souhaite une réplique exacte de la vigne qu'il cultive, que le semis exige un équipement coûteux de serres, de pots et d'abris pour le protéger, le vigneron abandonne cette tâche aux laboratoires agricoles ou aux spécialistes d'hybridation, bref, aux pépiniéristes de la vigne.

Bouturage, ou plutôt marcottage, telle fut la manière traditionnelle de propager la vigne, mais depuis l'épidémie phylloxérienne, au siècle dernier, on y recourt plus rarement. Le marcottage consistait en ceci : laisser se développer et s'allonger une pousse, l'incliner vers le sol, en couvrir une partie de terre ; il s'y formait des racines ; lorsque celles-ci étaient suffisamment développées on séparait la marcotte de la plante mère pour la transplanter ailleurs. Les vignerons procédaient plus souvent par provignage, opération dérivée de la précédente : ils plantaient une vieille souche en n'y laissant qu'une seule pousse ; cette pousse alimentait des racines neuves, tout en se nourrissant elle-même aux vieilles racines tant qu'elles survivaient. On conçoit qu'ainsi le plant nouveau avait exactement les caractéristiques de l'ancien.

Ces méthodes ne sont plus guère utilisées de nos jours à cause du phylloxéra. La plupart des vignes à vin contemporaines sont des *Vitis vinifera* greffées sur des souches de variétés américaines ou d'hybrides. Marcottage ou provignage produirait un plant à racines de *Vitis vinifera* vulnérable au phylloxéra. Pourtant, on reproduit la vigne par marcottage en certaines parties de Château-Prieuré-Lichine, depuis 1958, sans constater aucun inconvénient. En Californie, où le sol et le climat semblent immuniser contre le phylloxéra, 65 % des vignes sont plantées sur leurs propres racines, de même qu'à Chypre, en Turquie, dans toute l'Asie Mineure et dans certaines régions d'Allemagne.

La seule manière pratique de propager la vigne de nos jours, c'est le bouturage. De jeunes branches, coupées en automne ou en hiver pendant le sommeil de la vigne, sont conservées jusqu'au printemps dans du sable ou de la sciure de bois ; puis on les plante dans un sol fertile où leurs racines se développent. Au bout d'un an, ou à peu près, ces jeunes plants sont assez vigoureux pour supporter la transplantation. Les sarments ainsi enracinés appartiennent évidemment aux espèces américaines ou hybrides qui servent de porte-greffes à la *Vitis vinifera*. Les viticulteurs procédent soient au greffage sur table, soit au greffage sur place. La première méthode consiste à greffer une pousse de *Vitis vinifera* (scion) sur une souche (sujet), dans un pot, à l'abri. Ce n'est qu'après cicatrisation de la blessure que la nouvelle vigne sera transplantée et pourra développer ses racines dans la terre. La seconde consiste à greffer le scion sur une souche déjà plantée à l'endroit où elle se développera.

En Californie, la rapide expansion des vignobles a entraîné un essor considérable de la demande en souches de vignes. Une méthode de reproduction accélérée a été conçue et est aujourd'hui couramment utilisée : des tiges mûres sont taillées en segments portant chacun un bourgeon ; ceux-ci sont cultivés en chambre à une température de 30°C et reçoivent de fines vaporisations d'eau intermittentes. Lorsque des feuilles apparaissent sur les nouvelles pousses, celles-ci sont à leur tour taillées en segments portant un bourgeon-plus-une-feuille. Ces segments sont trempés dans une hormone de culture, puis plantés dans la chambre à vaporisation. Grâce à cette méthode, appelée reproduction par vaporisation, une vigne de cinq ans d'âge peut produire des milliers de nouvelles souches par an.

Quelle que soit la méthode utilisée, le résultat est le même : une nouvelle vigne à vin est née. Mais il faudra attendre quatre ans pour qu'elle produise des raisins dignes d'être transformés en vin. Cependant, il existe maintes variétés qui produisent au bout de trois ans.

LA CULTURE DE LA VIGNE

En simplifiant à l'excès, on peut dire que durant la première année d'existence de la vigne les vignerons se soucient surtout du développement des racines ; durant la seconde année, de celui de branches fortes et bien placées ; enfin, à partir de la troisième année, ils veillent à ce qu'elle donne des fruits de la meilleure qualité possible. En réalité ils se soucieront de ces trois éléments pendant toute l'existence du cep. Mais pendant la jeunesse de celui-ci, ils ont une importance encore plus grande.

Voici quelles sont les parties de la vigne au-dessus du sol :

— LE TRONC, corps de la vigne ;

— LES BRAS, autrement dit les branches qui aboutissent aux pousses, aux sarments et aux bourgeons.

1. LES POUSSES de chaque saison comprennent :

a) un nouveau feuillage ;

b) les vrilles (pousses minces, parfois fourchues, qui s'entortillent autour des supports destinés à soutenir les branches) ;

c) les sarments qui s'articulent sur le bois de l'année précédente ou plus ;

d) les gourmands : pousses nées de la souche au-dessous de la greffe.

2. LES SARMENTS, pousses de plus d'un an et arrivées à maturité ; les plus importantes sont les pousses à fruit : celles qui porteront les raisins de l'année.

3. LES BOURGEONS, courtes et minces tiges qui se divisent en trois catégories :

a) le prompt bourgeon, qui donnera les fruits au printemps suivant ;

b) les bourgeons de renouvellement, qui donneront les sarments de l'année suivante ;

c) les bourgeons de remplacement qui serviront à remplacer les branches existantes.

Par la taille et le palissage — opérations différentes mais étroitement interdépendantes — le vigneron ne conserve que les portions de sa vigne nécessaires à assurer une bonne qualité constante de bons fruits. La taille consiste donc à supprimer les pousses en surnombre en conservant celles qui, par leur forme et leur orientation, rendront le travail plus facile.

LA TAILLE

Le but de la taille est d'obtenir un équilibre optimal entre la croissance de la vigne et la quantité de la récolte. Si l'on cultive la vigne sans la soumettre à la taille, elle produira plus de raisin qu'elle ne peut en mûrir. Par contre, une taille trop sévère limiterait de façon excessive la croissance générale de la vigne. L'idéal est d'obtenir une zone feuillue la plus étendue possible, afin qu'elle puisse mûrir la plus grande quantité de fruits possible à des conditions optimales. L'importance de la taille à pratiquer dépendra de la fertilité du sol, de la vigueur de la vigne, de la chaleur du climat et de la quantité d'eau disponible. Lorsque le temps est chaud, le sol fertile et la vigne vigoureuse, une taille longue — qui consiste à laisser au moins quatre bourgeons ou « yeux » sur chaque tige — peut être pratiquée, car la vigne a l'énergie nécessaire pour supporter une récolte et un feuillage abondants. De même, on peut utiliser un plus grand nombre de tuteurs de taille normale, qui supporteront une croissance plus importante. Le nombre, la longueur et le positionnement des tuteurs dépendront du système de palissage utilisé. En Californie, on utilise de plus en plus le système à espaliers pour les raisins destinés à produire des vins de première catégorie. Ceci nécessite un treillis coûteux, mais ainsi plusieurs tiges, chacune avec quinze ou vingt yeux, peuvent être laissées sur chaque vigne. Dans les régions au climat plutôt froid, comme l'Allemagne et le Nord de la France, la vigne sera plus faible. C'est pourquoi on adopte fréquemment le palissage en gobelet avec une taille à petit tuteur *(voir ci-dessous).*

Dès que la vigne est mûre et que la forme désirée a été établie, on décide de la quantité à tailler en fonction des performances de la vigne lors de la saison antérieure. Si la récolte était équilibrée à ce moment, on laisse alors à la vigne le même nombre d'yeux qu'il y avait de tiges l'année précédente, alors que si la vigne avait surproduit, le nombre de tiges (et par conséquent la quantité de la récolte) doit être réduit.

Le palissage

Le genre de taille et les facteurs qui décideront de son choix détermineront aussi la manière dont la vigne sera liée en cordon, en gobelet ou en espalier.

1. Le tronc de la vigne taillée et liée en cordon est orienté dans une seule direction, verticale, horizontale ou oblique.

La taille du cordon donne lieu à un grand nombre de variantes. La plus utilisée est celle où le tronc est incliné sur le côté pour pousser parallèlement au sol. Il est généralement soutenu par des fils de fer attachés à des piquets. La quantité de pousses qui divergent vers le haut ou vers le bas sera déterminée au gré du vigneron, de même que le nombre de bourgeons, ou d'yeux, sur chaque pousse. Cette méthode, qui exige de l'habileté, récompense le vigneron adroit par une vendange abondante. Elle ne peut être appliquée à toutes les variétés de vignes et on ne l'utilise pas normalement pour les plus fines qui produisent le moins de fruits.

La taille la plus répandue, celle qu'on utilise partout au monde pour les vins fins dérive du cordon, c'est le guyot. Cette taille conserve une branche en plus du tronc. Les tiges qui poussent sur cette branche sont liées à des fils. Elle est particulièrement efficace pour les vignes dont les nœuds basilaires sont stériles et celles dont les grappes sont petites et compactes. En Californie, le type de cordon le plus courant a la forme d'un T, avec le tronc se ramifiant en deux branches horizontales.

2. La taille en gobelet ne conserve qu'un seul tronc vertical d'où divergent plusieurs branches obliques qui donnent à la plante la forme d'un gobelet. Son avantage c'est que la vigne n'a pas besoin de support, que le travail et l'entretien du plant sont faciles. Néanmoins, si les bourgeons basilaires sont stériles, on ne peut pas l'utiliser et, dans certains cas, les vignes vigoureuses ont des grappes mal placées.

3. Dans le cas de la taille en espalier, le tronc se termine par une ou deux branches et plusieurs sarments qui sont en général tous liés sur un même plan. On les palisse sur des fils de fer et plus généralement sur un treillage qui les soutient. La taille en espalier donne lieu à des variantes innombrables, y compris les treilles, aussi ornementales qu'utiles, des jardins bien tenus.

Le cycle de la vigne

Le cycle végétatif annuel de la vigne commence au printemps : le sommeil hivernal se termine et la sève commence à couler dans la plante. Au bout de cinq à six semaines, les feuilles apparaissent, les bourgeons gonflent le long des sarments en déchirant la mince pellicule ligneuse qui les protégeait durant l'hiver. Les bourgeons sont alors petits et ont un aspect laineux. De même, les feuilles à leur naissance sont ténues. C'est la phase du *débourrement* à partir de laquelle commence la *croissance*. Remarquons que les feuilles apparaissent nettement avant les fruits, contrairement à ce qui se passe chez bien d'autres plantes. L'époque du débourrement dépend surtout de la chaleur du sol et aussi, dans une certaine mesure, du moment auquel on a taillé la vigne.

Si la taille a eu lieu pendant l'hiver, ce qui est le cas général, l'apparition des bourgeons a lieu à la date normale. Mais si le vigneron a taillé sa vigne lorsque la sève coulait déjà, le débourrement sera retardé dans des proportions variables allant jusqu'à une quinzaine de jours. La taille tardive implique la perte d'une grande quantité de sève. Bien qu'elle n'ait pratiquement aucune valeur nutritive, les vignerons estiment qu'une telle perte ne peut que nuire à la vigne, aussi préfèrent-ils éviter la taille tardive. Pourtant, dans les régions où les gelées tardives sont à craindre, cette pratique peut être utile en retardant le débourrement jusqu'à ce que le danger de gel soit passé. La taille tardive, dite aussi taille verte, oblige à supprimer des pousses fraîches.

En Californie, on procède à une double taille. Entre la fin de l'automne et le milieu de l'hiver, on laisse aux longues tiges quatre à huit yeux, au lieu de deux à quatre. Ceux qui sont à l'extrémité de la tige ont le temps de continuer à croître, mais les pousses sont coupées immédiatement à leurs dimensions normales pour qu'elles n'épuisent pas leurs réserves d'amidon. Grâce à cette méthode, une seconde taille pourra être faite sans hâte car il n'y a pas à craindre que la croissance commence trop tôt. Cependant le débourrement est retardé de cinq à quatorze jours.

Les jeunes pousses font leurs feuilles et ensuite des grappes de fleurs. Chacune de ces grappes est constituée par d'infimes boutons et l'ensemble offre déjà l'aspect d'une grappe de raisin miniature. Au début, chacune de ces petites fleurs est recouverte par une capsule qui disparaît à l'anthèse en révélant les organes de la reproduction.

La fleur de la plupart des vignes comprend le pistil femelle en forme de cône et cinq étamines mâles, également vigoureux. Le pistil est constitué par l'ovaire, le style et le stigmate ; les étamines par des filaments portant des petits sacs de pollen appelés anthères. Quand ces sacs s'ouvrent, le pollen se disperse, ses grains sont englués par le stigmate où ils germent. Son calice s'allonge le long du style jusqu'à pénétrer dans l'ovaire où la fécondation a lieu.

La plupart des *Vitis vinifera* sont hermaphrodites : les organes mâles et femelles sont aussi développés les uns que les autres sur tous les plants. Mais d'autres vignes ont des fleurs dont les organes, soit mâles soit femelles, sont atrophiés. Le vigneron devra veiller à disperser à bon escient vignes mâles et vignes femelles. Le pollen des premières fécondera l'ovaire des secondes qui porteront des fruits. Les vignes hermaphrodites se fécondent elles-mêmes : le pollen des étamines tombe sur le style de la même fleur. Dans le cas des vignes unisexuées, il faut que le pollen d'une vigne atteigne le pistil d'une autre vigne. Si la rencontre n'a pas lieu, il n'y aura pas du tout de fruits. Le raisin sera toujours le rejeton de la vigne qui le porte. En cas de croisement, les transformations n'auront lieu que dans le pépin qui n'intéresse pas le viticulteur.

La fleur de vigne dure à peu près quinze jours pendant lesquels le temps a une importance capitale car le rendement en dépendra entièrement. Si le plant ne fleurit pas correctement ni complètement, on assistera alors à la *coulure (voir* PATHOLOGIE DE LA VIGNE, *ci-après)*. Si la coulure est grave, la vigne ne produira pas de raisin. Dans des circonstances normales, quand la fleur disparaît, elle fait place à de très petites baies vertes qui grossiront et mûriront groupées en grappes.

La floraison est suivie par la lente croissance du fruit. Les grains sont alors tout verts, riches en chlorophylle et ils assimilent le carbone, exactement comme les feuilles. Ils se développent en volume ; au point de vue chimique ils ne changent guère ; c'est à peine si leur acidité augmente légèrement.

La phase suivante commence généralement en août. C'est la *véraison :* le raisin change de couleur ; va du vert à l'or, ou bien il devient d'un rouge violacé ou encore d'une blancheur verdâtre translucide. C'est alors seulement qu'a lieu la maturation proprement dite.

Voici à peu près la durée de ces phases successives :

Débourrement	72 à 75 jours
Floraison	10 à 20 jours
Développement initial du raisin	40 à 45 jours
Maturation proprement dite	48 à 50 jours
Total	170 à 190 jours

Ce tableau ne correspond qu'aux *cépages de première époque* car les différentes variétés de vigne ont des fruits qui mûrissent en un temps plus ou moins long. A ce point de vue, la classification la plus couramment admise est celle du Français Pulliat. En prenant comme élément de base le Chasselas doré, Pulliat dressa le tableau suivant, à la fin du siècle dernier :

Catégorie		*Époque de maturation avant ou après chasselas doré*
Précoces	très tôt	10 jours avant
1re époque	tôt	à peu près en même temps
2e époque	début mi-saison	12 jours après
3e époque	mi-saison	24 jours après
4e époque	tard	36 jours après

Le système de Pulliat n'est pas le meilleur pour prédire la date de maturité, car il ne tient pas compte des circonstances locales et des influences climatiques. Il ne donne qu'un schéma de comparaison entre les différentes variétés de raisin.

La méthode de Winkler et Amerine permet de déterminer plus exactement le temps de maturation. Elle est fondée sur la quantité totale de chaleur exigée par chaque catégorie pour mûrir. Lorsqu'on connaît les caractéristiques de la variété à ce point de vue, les variantes météorologiques permettent de prédire la date à laquelle le raisin sera mûr.

Après la véraison, il se transforme tout en continuant à grossir. Il a alors atteint son maximum d'acidité qui diminuera cependant que sa teneur en sucre augmentera. Ces phénomènes s'accélèrent au fur et à mesure de la maturation. Le raisin est *mûr* quand sa teneur en sucre atteint le maximum et n'augmentera plus. Il sera alors prêt à être vendangé ou bien pour une dernière phase, celle de la *pourriture noble*. Dans certains cas on assiste à un accroissement *apparent* de la teneur en sucre après la fin de la maturation ; il s'agit en réalité de l'évaporation de l'eau contenue dans le fruit.

Dans certaines régions vinicoles, notamment dans le Barsac et le Sauternes du Bordelais et, dans une moindre mesure, dans certains vignobles de la Moselle et du Rhin, un champignon microscopique provoque une moisissure cendrée du raisin appelée la pourriture noble. Elle hâte le processus et donne ainsi des vins extrêmement doux (*voir* BOTRYTIS CINEREA, POURRITURE NOBLE et *ci-après* POURRITURE GRISE).

Pendant la période de maturation, une sorte de « fleur » cireuse, la pruine, couvre le raisin et le protège de l'excès de soleil, en même temps qu'elle capture les levures qui provoqueront la fermentation.

Pendant que la vigne se prépare à livrer ses fruits, nombre de maladies la guettent. Elles sont d'autant plus redoutables que le temps est plus humide : parce qu'elles s'aggravent plus rapidement sur des raisins mouillés et aussi parce que la pluie élimine par lavage les produits chimiques utilisés par les vignerons pour les prévenir, les freiner ou les guérir.

Nous trouverons ci-après la liste des plus importantes de ces maladies ainsi que leurs antidotes.

La pathologie de la vigne

Les maux qui peuvent frapper la vigne se divisent en deux grandes catégories : les accidents et maladies non parasitaires et les maladies d'origine parasitaire. Le premier groupe comprend les calamités provoquées par le climat, le sol, et l'homme ; le second, les maladies provoquées par virus, bactéries, cryptogames et insectes.

LES ACCIDENTS ET LES MALADIES NON PARASITAIRES

1°) Le climat

La *gelée* est le pire danger climatique. Quoique la plupart des vignes soient plantées en des lieux où les gelées auront l'effet le plus faible possible, celles qui se produisent peuvent avoir des conséquences dévastatrices. Le dur hiver de 1956 diminua la production de 90 % pour certains crus de la région de Bordeaux. En partie parce que de tels hivers sont rares (depuis 1709, le Bordelais n'avait pas connu d'hiver aussi froid que celui de 1956 !) les vignerons ne savent pas quelles mesures prendre pour défendre leurs vignes. En général la vigne est en danger si la température tombe au-dessous de moins 15 °C pendant l'hiver et de moins 4 °C au printemps, quand la vigne commence à porter ses premières feuilles. Bien des variétés américaines de vigne résistent beaucoup mieux au froid que *Vitis vinifera*. Le cépage Bêta — hybride de *Vitis labrusca* et de *Vitis riparia* —, répandu au nord des États-Unis et au Canada, supporte des températures inférieures à moins 20 °C et *Vitis amurensis* prospère sous le climat prodigieusement rigoureux de l'île Sakhaline (malheureusement elle n'a pas encore donné de raisin, ni pour la table ni pour le vin). Dans les régions viticoles exceptionnellement froides, il arrive qu'on couvre la vigne de terre pendant l'hiver. C'est ce qui se passe épisodiquement en Russie, Hongrie, Bulgarie, Asie Mineure et Canada. Les gelées tardives de printemps sont aussi des périls, mais nous avons vu que la taille tardive peut retarder la floraison jusqu'à ce que le danger soit passé.

Dans de nombreuses régions de la Californie, les gelées de début printemps sont courantes et peuvent détruire la majorité d'une récolte en tuant les jeunes pousses. Autrefois, les viticulteurs employaient des appareils de chauffage à mazout ou à butane qu'ils plaçaient dans les vignobles pour les empêcher de geler, ou bien ils installaient des propulseurs à moteur appelés machines à vent qui diffusaient l'air plus chaud du dessus. Aujourd'hui la méthode la plus efficace pour combattre les gelées de printemps consiste à installer des tourniquets aériens à proximité de sources d'eau. Pendant les grands froids, les tourniquets diffusent constamment une couche d'eau sur les vignes, les protégeant du gel par la chaleur délivrée lorsque l'eau gèle. Cette méthode, bien que coûteuse, est si efficace qu'elle permet à des vignobles d'être plantés et cultivés avec succès dans des zones auparavant inexploitables à cause des gelées de printemps ou d'automne.

La *chaleur* peut aussi endommager la vigne, mais à condition de dépasser

43 °C, limite critique. Des étés aussi torrides n'affligent normalement que les seuls vignobles d'Afrique du Nord où le sirocco — vent chaud, sec et déshydratant — provoque des dégâts énormes surtout quand il souffle de manière prolongée.

La *grêle* lèse feuilles et branches, parfois les déchire, ce qui affaiblit la vigne. Les orages de grêles tardifs peuvent détruire totalement la récolte. Pour se défendre contre ce fléau, on lançait naguère encore des fusées dans les nuages de grêle pour hâter la précipitation : faire crever le nuage avant qu'il arrive au-dessus de la vigne ou provoquer une réaction qui transforme la glace en eau. Mais le procédé laisse à désirer en raison de l'altitude des nuages de grêle et de la vitesse à laquelle ils se forment.

Le *vent* de tempête casse les pousses, arrache feuilles et fruits. Certains vents salés venant de l'océan brûlent les vignes du Médoc jusqu'à 80 km à l'intérieur des terres.

2°) Le sol

La *sécheresse* jaunit les feuilles et si on ne trouve pas une manière quelconque d'arroser la vigne, elle dégénère ou meurt.

L'*inondation* peut noyer la vigne, mais il lui faut un certain temps. Si la vigne est inondée pendant moins de dix semaines, elle peut survivre. Cette particularité incita les vignerons à inonder leurs vignes pour combattre le phylloxéra : l'eau noyait le parasite avant que la vigne en soit affectée.

La *chlorose* est un jaunissement des feuilles dû à une carence en chlorophylle. En Europe, ce phénomène est souvent dû à un excès de calcium dans le sol, d'où résulte une déficience en fer. Selon leurs variétés, les vignes résistent plus ou moins à ce mal qui n'affecte pratiquement pas *Vitis vinifera*. Le traitement consiste en addition de sulfate ferreux au sol, en raison d'une théorie selon laquelle un excès de calcium empêcherait la vigne d'assimiler le fer. Étant donné que *Vitis berlandieri* résiste assez bien à la chlorose, on l'utilise comme porte-greffes.

Les *déficiences du sol* sont dues surtout à la carence en bore, potassium ou zinc. Le manque de zinc est assez courant en Californie et en Australie où l'on ajoute du zinc au sol. Le manque de bore est plus répandu ; on le traite soit en augmentant la teneur en bore de la terre, soit en injectant directement cet élément dans la vigne.

La *toxicité du sol* est due le plus souvent à un excès de sel. Le choix des porte-greffes peut en venir à bout (des hybrides, surtout ceux d'un croisement avec *Vitis candicans*, originaire des marais du Mississipi, résistent très bien au sel). On peut aussi laver la terre en l'inondant pendant un temps assez court à l'eau douce. Un excès de bore peut aussi avoir des effets toxiques.

3°) La vigne

La *coulure* : on dit que la fleur a *coulé* quand elle s'est désséchée sans être fécondée. Le mal peut aussi affecter le raisin lui-même quand il n'est encore qu'une toute petite baie verte et dure, au premier stade de son développement. Le mauvais temps est la cause principale de la coulure car la fleur ne peut s'épanouir et être fécondée que par temps chaud et ensoleillé. Une croissance trop rapide peut aussi provoquer la coulure. Ce phénomène est généralement dû à un mauvais équilibre entre la greffe et le porte-greffes et le remède consiste à greffer sur une souche appropriée au raisin que l'on souhaite produire.

On donne le nom de *millerandage* à une disparité entre la dimension des divers grains de la même grappe. Si la floraison et la fécondation n'ont pas été complètes, certains raisins restent à l'état initial — verts, durs, gros comme des chevrotines — alors que les autres se développent et mûrissent normalement. Pour les vignes à vin, c'est une maladie, mais c'est l'état normal de certaines espèces, comme celles de Corinthe, qui produisent des raisins à consommer secs.

Le *rougeau* — rougissement des feuilles — n'est pas dû à un virus ni à un autre parasite quelconque, mais à une blessure qui interrompt le flux de la sève. Si la lésion se trouve au-dessus du sol, on éliminera la partie blessée si possible. Si elle se trouve sous le sol, c'est-à-dire aux racines, un engrais au potassium aura parfois un effet salutaire, surtout si les racines ne sont pas trop développées.

4°) L'homme

La *brunissure* est due à une surproduction de raisin par une vigne insuffisamment taillée. Des taches brunes apparaissent alors sur les feuilles, qui tombent. La qualité du fruit en souffre et, finalement, le cep perdra ses réserves d'énergie et périra. Pris à son début, le mal peut être curable : il suffit de ne laisser la vigne porter qu'une quantité réduite de grappes. Mais si le plant est déjà épuisé, il est perdu.

La vigne peut aussi être atteinte — *brûlée* — par des insecticides, des fongicides, des engrais chimiques et parfois aussi par les fumées d'usines avoisinantes. La cause est alors une erreur humaine, tant dans les soins que dans l'implantation de la vigne, et les plants en souffrent.

LES MALADIES D'ORIGINE PARASITAIRE

1°) Les virus

La *dégénérescence infectieuse* ou *court noué* est une maladie virale qui semble n'être apparue qu'à la suite du phylloxéra. La vigne contracte ce mal par le sol infecté d'un virus : *Xiphema index*. La feuille jaunit le long de ses nervures entre lesquelles apparaissent des mouchetures ; elle prend des formes anormales, les sarments bifurquent et se multiplient latéralement ; les fleurs se présentent en grappes doubles, parfois multiples. Cette maladie apparaît par taches, de-ci, de-là sur le vignoble et se répand lentement. Telles sont ses trois caractéristiques : elle raccourcit progressivement la vie de la vigne ; elle réside dans le sol ; on ne lui connaît jusqu'à présent aucun traitement. Le labourage contribue à aggraver et répandre cette maladie. Jusqu'à présent, la seule solution consiste à arracher les vignes atteintes par le mal et à ne labourer que légèrement ou pas du tout. Cette dégénérescence a les conséquences suivantes : si la vigne vivait jusqu'à une centaine d'années avant le phylloxéra, sa longévité est réduite à quarante ans pour la première génération et à quinze pour la seconde. Si la *court noué* ne lui laisse plus que quatre ans d'existence, la vigne ne produira plus de vin. On peut nettoyer le sol en arrachant tous les pieds atteints et ceux qui les entourent, en laissant la terre en friche jusqu'à ce que toutes les vieilles racines pourrissent et en procédant à des fumigations de D.D. (dichloropropane dichloropropylène).

La *maladie de Pierce* sévit en Californie. Les feuilles jaunissent le long des nervures, leur bord brûle ; les sarments sont trop petits, le fruit se colore et fane prématurément. La vigne ne dure plus que d'un à cinq ans. Le mal est dû au même virus que celui du nanisme de l'alfa transporté par des insectes. Traitement : arracher les vignes atteintes est inutile ; c'est l'insecte vecteur qui doit être attaqué avec un pesticide puissant.

D'autres maladies à virus provoquent des dégâts considérables : l'une donne à l'écorce l'aspect du bouchon, l'autre jaunit les nervures des feuilles, avec une autre les feuilles s'enroulent. Il y a aussi la mosaïque.

2°) Les bactéries

La *maladie d'Oléron* se manifeste par des taches sur les feuilles et les grappes de fleurs ; elle détruit les parois intérieures des cellules. Née en Europe, elle ne sévit plus guère que dans le vignoble de l'Afrique du Sud. On estime que des vaporisations au cuivre et la stérilisation des instruments de taille l'ont fait disparaître en Europe.

3°) Les cryptogames ou champignons

L'*anthracnose* est la seule maladie importante de la vigne d'origine européenne. Des petites taches en forme de polygone apparaissent sur les feuilles, les fruits et les pousses. Le cryptogame qui le provoque vit en liberté, c'est pourquoi on a gardé les *Vitis vinifera* hors de l'est des États-Unis, malgré le froid hivernal de cette région ; le *black rot* (pourriture noire), s'il n'est pas contrôlé, est aussi une menace. On traite l'anthracnose au sulfate de cuivre (CuSo4) ; on en utilise 7 000 t chaque année en France pour combattre le mildiou. On l'applique généralement sous forme de *bouillie bordelaise*, contenant des proportions variées de sulfate de cuivre, de chaux, et d'eau.

L'*apoplexie*, plus exactement dénommée *esca*, doit son appellation familière à la mort foudroyante de la vigne en temps de canicule. Cette maladie sévit sur toutes les plantes, partout au monde. Elle est due à un champignon microscopique qui pénètre dans le bois, y libère un enzyme. Emporté par la sève, cet enzyme tue la plante au-delà du point de pénétration. Il semble que l'arséniate de soude combatte efficacement ce mal, mais on ne sait pas encore pour quelle raison.

Le *black rot*, autrement dit pourriture noire, est une infection d'origine américaine. Elle se manifeste par l'apparition de taches grises mouchetées de noir sur les organes verts de la plante. Le fruit se ride, fane et brunit. On applique le même traitement au sulfate de cuivre que pour l'anthracnose. La pourriture noire est particulièrement redoutée dans les États de l'est des États-Unis parce que le traitement par la bouillie bordelaise y est inefficace.

Extrêmement rare, l'*excoriose* attaque surtout les branches. On le traite à la bouillie bordelaise.

Le *mildiou*, ainsi nommé en Europe, est en réalité un faux mildiou en Amérique d'où il est originaire. Son agent, le *Plasmopora viticola*, s'attaque aux portions vertes de la vigne, mais seulement avant la véraison. Des taches huileuses, qui deviennent blanches par la suite, se forment sous les feuilles et s'étalent. Il en apparaît aussi sur les pousses juste au-dessus des bourgeons et elles peuvent attaquer fleurs et fruits. Le mildiou ne se manifeste que par forte chaleur très humide. Étant donné qu'il est propagé par le vent, il peut avoir des effets dévastateurs partout où il a frappé. (La plupart des espèces américaines résistent au mildiou et on ne les traite pas contre cette maladie aux États-Unis). Le cryptogame qui le provoque vit donc en liberté dans les vignes des États de l'est des États-Unis. C'est pourquoi il se manifesta en Europe dès qu'on y importa des plants américains.

L'*oïdium* (ainsi appelé en Europe) est le véritable mildiou en Amérique. C'est la première plaie des vignes importées des États-Unis. Elle causa des ravages importants aux vignobles français dès 1854, année au cours de laquelle elle détruisit 20 % des vignes. L'oïdium freine la croissance de la vigne, attaque les feuilles, fait éclater les raisins avant leur développement. Si on ne le traite pas, la vigne — surtout la vulnérable *Vinifera* — mourra en quelques années. Les vins faits avec des raisins affectés par cette maladie ont mauvais goût, mauvaise odeur, vilaine couleur et un faible degré d'alcool. Même si les feuilles d'un seul cep ont été attaquées par l'oïdium, les conséquences se feront sentir sur tout le vin. On combat cette maladie par des pulvérisations de soufre dont les vignerons français consomment 10 000 tonnes par an.

Le *pourridié* se développe sur les parties ligneuses, racines, troncs, branches. Les racines supérieures se développent au détriment des plus profondes qui sont les plus utiles et qui s'affaiblissent. Le pourridié est plus particulièrement virulent dans les sols sablonneux et se manifeste souvent près des cours d'eau. Le seul traitement consiste à arracher la vigne, désinfecter le sol et le laisser en friche jusqu'à ce que le champignon responsable du mal ait disparu. Il s'agit, soit de l'*Armillaria mellea*, soit de *Rosellina necatrix* ou *Dematophora necatrix*.

La *pourriture grise* est due au même champignon microscopique qui provoque la pourriture noble à laquelle on doit les vins doux de Sauternes, d'Allemagne, et de Hongrie. A une température de 25 °C, par temps humide et surtout après qu'une autre maladie a affaibli la vigne, on voit apparaître une pourriture grise qui tache les feuilles et altère les fruits. En général, cette pourriture est une maladie. C'est seulement dans certaines conditions — forte humidité suivie de temps chaud — qu'elle peut devenir la pourriture noble recherchée par certains vignerons (*voir* BOTRYTIS CINEREA).

Le *rot blanc* apparaît sur les raisins au moment de leur maturation et les fait éclater. Un traitement immédiat au cuivre ou au bisulfite de sodium s'impose.

Le *rot brun* se manifeste, comme son nom l'indique, par apparition de taches brunes entre les nervures, sur les feuilles basilaires. Cette maladie, d'origine cryptogamique, se manifeste seulement dans les vignobles de régions où les hivers sont froids et secs, condition nécessaire à la vie du champignon qui en est la cause. Il faut traiter la maladie, dès le début de son apparition, au sulfate. Elle sévit particulièrement en Allemagne.

4°) Les animaux parasites

Les animaux parasites de la vigne ne sont pas les mêmes partout. Ceux qui sévissent en France n'existent pas forcément en Afrique du Sud, en Californie, ni même en Espagne. Néanmoins, voici une liste des plus virulents.

L'*acariose* est due à un acarien (araignée) infime, aussi petit que le sarcopte de la gale. Cet animal se nourrit de la jeune feuille et du fruit. On le détruit par pulvérisation de cuivre.

L'*érinose (Phytoptus vitis* ou *Eriophyes vitis)* est une mite de taille microscopique qui provoque des cloques sur les feuilles, les fleurs, et les raisins. La plupart des vignes lui résistent, et celles qui en sont atteintes sont traitées avec la solution généralement utilisée pour combattre l'oïdium.

L'*altise* est un insecte — coléoptère sauteur qui se nourrit de feuilles auxquelles son passage donne l'aspect d'une très fine dentelle. On la détruit avec des insecticides.

L'*anguillule* est un nématode — ver mince comme un fil — qui perce les racines et y forme des nœuds ressemblant à ceux du phylloxéra. *Vitis vinifera* est particulièrement vulnérable à ce nématode. Étant donné que le mal porte sur les racines, le choix d'un porte-greffes résistant écarte le danger. Toutefois, si les anguillules prolifèrent en quantité excessive dans le sol, il faudra désinfecter celui-ci au D.D. Ce ver est le plus grand ennemi de la vigne après le phylloxéra.

Divers papillons *(Eudemis, Cochylis* et *Polychronis viteana)* sont aussi des parasites de la vigne : leurs larves se repaissent des grappes de raisin sans les détruire complètement d'ailleurs, mais en les rendant vulnérables à d'autres maux. On les détruit à l'arsenic et au DDT.

Enfin le *phylloxéra* sévit dans le monde entier sauf au Chili ainsi que sur quelques point isolés, de-ci, de-là. Ce pou térébrant de la vigne est originaire d'Amérique. Il se manifesta en Europe en 1868, après l'épidémie d'oïdium et provoqua le plus grand désastre viticole depuis le Déluge. Ses ravages ont bouleversé la viticulture européenne et provoqué le « grand débat » qui dure depuis cent ans parmi les connaisseurs : le vin postphylloxérien vaut-il celui d'autrefois ? (*Voir* cette question et les problèmes soulevés par le phylloxéra parmi les articles classés par ordre alphabétique).

La *pyrale* se nourrit du feuillage et du fruit de la vigne. On la détruit, comme les papillons, avec l'arsenic et au DDT.

Enfin, une nouvelle menace pèse sur les vignes de l'est des États-Unis : la *Popillia japonica*, minuscule coléoptère qui s'attaque aux feuilles et aux fruits. On la détruit au DDT et avec des insecticides à base d'arsenic. Le mal ne s'est pas encore répandu en Californie ni en Europe.

Un calendrier de vignobles

La liste des calamités qui guettent la vigne nous donne une idée des soins que le vigneron doit lui apporter. Ses tâches ne se limitent pas à cela. Le détail des travaux et l'époque choisie pour les accomplir varient suivant la région et les traditions. Le calendrier ci-dessous présente la succession des travaux effectués au château Prieuré-Lichine, appartenant à l'auteur de cette encyclopédie, et situé dans la commune de Margaux dans la région bordelaise. Ailleurs, les tâches seront assez semblables. Pourtant même dans les vignobles voisins on constate de légères variantes.

Automne. Fin septembre ou octobre, la vendange dure plus de quinze jours. Elle est suivie par un nettoyage général des sillons jusqu'à leur extrémité, où vignerons et instruments agricoles font demi-tour pour reprendre un autre sillon. Un labourage d'automne aère le sol. Il est procédé de telle sorte que la terre couvre et protège le point de greffage sensible au froid.

Hiver. La taille dure tout l'hiver. C'est à cette même saison qu'on remplace les piquets et les fils de fer qui les relient l'un à l'autre, afin de supporter les branches et troncs de la vigne.

Printemps. Un second labourage aère de nouveau le sol. Des femmes suivent la charrue, armées de râteaux spéciaux pour tirer la terre entre les plants où le soc ne passe pas. Ce travail s'appelle déchausser la vigne. Quand les bourgeons apparaissent, on supprime ceux qui sont en trop. On élimine aussi les *repousses :* rameaux poussant sur le porte-greffes. En avril ou mai : troisième labourage.

C'est aussi à cette saison qu'on plante de nouvelles vignes, pour remplacer celles qui sont épuisées.

Été. On arrache les mauvaises herbes. En juin on attache les sarments aux fils de fer. On les écime ou on les pince pour éviter un développement excessif. C'est surtout en cette saison qu'on pulvérise et arrose la vigne avec les produits nécessaires pour lutter contre la maladie. Selon la saison et la vigne, le vigneron traitera jusqu'à huit fois sa vigne au cours d'un seul été. Un quatrième labourage supprime les mauvaises herbes. Le raisin mûrit.

Automne. Les raisins sont mûrs, on vendange et le cycle recommence par le nettoyage, la taille et la récolte des sarments : sarmentage.

CHAPITRE V

Comment fait-on le vin ?

Le vin est le jus fermenté du raisin : la fermentation transforme le sucre du raisin en alcool. On peut faire toutes sortes d'espèces de breuvage dénommés à tort vin avec nombre de fruits et de baies. Mais le vin proprement dit n'est fait qu'avec du raisin et rien d'autre. C'est un dérivé naturel du raisin après la vendange, le transport au pressoir (pour les blancs) et la vinification dans des vastes cuves où a lieu la fermentation. Les réactions biochimiques de la fermentation sont provoquées par des levures. Ces végétaux microscopiques prolifèrent d'eux-mêmes dans le milieu naturellement riche que constitue le jus frais de raisin. Ils produisent des enzymes qui convertissent le sucre en alcool par toute une succession de réactions chimiques donnant divers autres produits que l'alcool, notamment du gaz carbonique.

Si un processus aussi naturel que la fermentation était livré au hasard, il en résulterait tout simplement un mauvais vinaigre. Pourtant le premier vin goûté par l'homme ne devait pas être autre chose que le produit d'un hasard heureux. Quoique l'événement ne fût pas consigné dans l'histoire, il eut des conséquences historiques. Désormais et depuis des siècles, le bon vin provient d'une bonne vinification plutôt que de la chance. D'abord, à force d'essais et d'erreurs, plus tard grâce à l'expérimentation scientifique, les hommes ont appris à améliorer leurs techniques de vinification.

Les découvertes de Louis Pasteur (1822-1895) ont répandu une nouvelle lumière sur les idées scientifiques des premiers producteurs de vin. Elles ont fourni une explication logique à des pratiques ancestrales dont certaines remontaient à la Grèce et à la Rome antiques. En réalité les savants n'ont pas tellement modifié l'art de la divination, mais ils ont montré pourquoi certaines choses doivent être faites comme on les fait et ils ont encouragé la pratique des méthodes les plus sages. Leur action contribua aussi à éliminer les mauvais vins et à apprendre aux vignerons à sauver une vendange qui, auparavant, eût été désastreusement inutilisable.

Le raisin

L'ingrédient fondamental du vin n'est autre que le raisin. Arrivé à sa maturité parfaite, il possède certaines caractéristiques spécifiques qui diffèrent d'ailleurs considérablement d'une variété de vigne à l'autre. Sa pulpe, sa peau et — à quelques exceptions près — son pépin contribuent à certaines qualités du vin.

La peau du raisin donne surtout du tanin et des matières colorantes. Pigments et tanin se trouvent dans les vacuoles des cellules de la peau. Tant que ces cellules sont vivantes il est très difficile d'en extraire les colorants. On dispose de plusieurs méthodes pour provoquer la mort de ces cellules et l'effondrement de leurs parois internes : chaleur, alcool, désintégration physique. C'est au second élément qu'on recourt d'ordinaire de la manière suivante : on laisse jus et peau fermenter ensemble jusqu'à ce que la quantité d'alcool suffise pour rendre les parois perméables, ce qui libère les pigments. La libération des matières colorantes s'accroît et atteint son maximum au bout de quelques jours puis diminue. Le temps durant lequel on laisse les peaux et le jus fermenter ensemble est le facteur le plus important dont dépend la couleur du vin. Pour avoir des vins rosés on ne laisse les peaux dans le jus que pendant un temps limité ; pour des vins blancs on enlève la peau dès le début ; enfin, pour le vin rouge, la peau reste présente dans le jus jusqu'à ce que la fermentation soit terminée. Quelques rares variétés de raisins (raisins teinturiers) présentent cette particularité : les matières colorantes sont situées dans les couches intérieures de la pulpe ; le jus de fruit est donc coloré d'un rouge foncé, tendant sur le violet, alors que tous les autres raisins, quelle que soit leur couleur apparente, ont un jus aussi incolore que l'eau. Les tanins passent aussi de la peau et de la pulpe dans le jus pendant le cuvage.

La différence essentielle entre les vins blancs et les vins rouges réside plus dans leur teneur en tanin que dans leur couleur.

Dans certains cas, la peau fournit aussi une odeur qui peut être agréable ou désagréable. Maintes variétés de *Vitis vinifera* ont un arôme frais et léger : l'haleine du raisin. Ce parfum est plus perceptible quand le vin est jeune mais disparaît avec l'âge qui développe le bouquet (cette remarque nous amène à préciser qu'il ne faut pas confondre arôme et bouquet). Certaines vignes de l'est des États-Unis, particulièrement *Vitis labrusca*, ont un mauvais arôme caractéristique *(fox)* qu'on appelle en français le *foxé*. Odeur étrange et parfois désagréable à ceux qui sont habitués aux vins européens. Cette variété n'est pas autorisée en France. Bon nombre de viticulteurs américains de l'est et canadiens ne laissent leur vin cuver que pendant un temps aussi court que possible, pour empêcher cette caractéristique de se développer.

La pulpe représente 80 à 90 % du poids du raisin. En ce qui concerne la composition du raisin mûr, elle dépend de la variété et des circonstances. Néanmoins, le savant français Jules Ventre l'a déterminée dans son *Traité de vinification pratique et rationnelle* (*voir* tableau p. 52). La pulpe et la peau constituent donc les éléments essentiels dans la fabrication du vin. Le pépin va aussi dans la cuve mais il contient du tanin et surtout une substance huileuse et résineuse qui rendrait le vin imbuvable si elle se mélangeait au moût. Il faut donc prendre garde à ne pas briser les pépins dans le pressoir. Un autre élément peut entrer dans la composition du vin : le jus de la rafle (ensemble des pédoncules et pédicelles auxquels sont accrochés les grains de raisin). Riche en tanin, la rafle passera dans la cuve pour la fabrication de certains vins peu charpentés. Mais dans la plupart des cas, on élimine cet élément avant de mettre le jus dans la cuve de fermentation.

Dans quelques très petites exploitations vinicoles d'Europe, c'est à la main qu'on arrache les grains de la grappe, mais en général on se sert d'un instrument appelé égrappoir et l'opération s'appelle : éraflage ou égrappage. En ce qui concerne les vins blancs, le pépin doit absolument être éliminé en raison des tanins qu'il contient. Sa présence donnerait au jus ou au moût, et plus tard au vin, un coloris brun pareil à celui d'une pomme talée (meurtrie ou mordue, puis exposée à l'air). Cette coloration brune se développerait alors très rapidement, à peu près en une heure, au contact de l'air.

La vendange

Le moment choisi pour la vendange a des conséquences importantes sur la qualité du vin. Quand il s'agit de faire des vins fins, on suit la maturation du raisin avec le plus grand soin et on ne les récolte qu'au tout dernier moment possible, surtout dans les régions froides où il est extrêmement difficile d'arriver à une maturité parfaite.

Dans les régions plus chaudes on vendange quand sucre et acides ont atteint l'état d'équilibre convenant à l'élaboration du vin désiré.

Aussitôt cueillies les grappes de raisin rouge sont égrappées ou éraflées et versées dans la cuve de fermentation. Un retard — même de quelque douze heures seulement — pourrait provoquer de graves difficultés :

1. les éléments destinés naturellement à donner le bouquet s'oxyderaient en présence de trop d'air, ce qui donnerait au vin un arôme désagréable ;
2. des bactéries ou des moisissures, aussi indésirables les unes que les autres, se mettraient à attaquer le sucre et gâteraient le vin.

Composition du raisin mûr

Composants	*Proportions en %*	*Remarques*
Eau	70 à 80	
Matière sèche	15 à 30	
Hydrates de carbone		
Sucres	12 à 27	Hexoses : dextrose et lévulose
Pectines	0,1 à 1	Y compris des gommes
Pentosanes	0,1 à 0,5	Aussi petite quantité de pentoses
Inositol	0,05	
Acidité totale		
Acide malique	0,1 à 0,5	Selon région, variété, saison
Acide tartrique	0,2 à 0,8	Surtout du bitartrate de potassium (crème de tartre)
Acide citrique	0,02	
Tanin	0,0 à 0,2	
Azote	0,01 à 0,2	Surtout protéines, acides aminés, ammoniac
Matières minérales	0,2 à 0,6	

La fermentation

Yves Renouil et Paul de Traversay ont donné cette définition de la fermentation alcoolique : un phénomène biochimique qui transforme le sucre en alcool éthylique et gaz carbonique.

Avant les expériences de Pasteur (environ 1857) la fermentation restait un mystère. C'est seulement à une époque relativement récente que l'on a étudié systématiquement ce phénomène. La liste suivante nous donne les éléments présents dans le moût puis dans le vin.

ÉLÉMENTS PRÉSENTS			
MOÛT		VIN	
Eau		*Eau*	
Sucres :		*Sucres :*	
Glucose	Pentoses	Glucose	Pentoses
Fructose	Sucrose	Fructose	
		Alcools :	
		Éthanol	Isoamyle
		Glycérol	Amyle actif
		2,3-Butanédiol	Isobutyle
		Acétoïne	*n*-propyle
		(Butylène-glycol 2-3)	
Esters		*Esters :*	
		Acétate d'éthyle	Lactate —
		Succinate —	autres esters
Acides :		*Acides :*	
Tartrique	Citrique	Tartrique	Succinique
Malique	Ascorbique	Malique	Lactique
		Citrique	Acétique
Minéraux :		*Minéraux :*	
Sodium	Magnésium	Sodium	Fer
Potassium	Fer	Potassium	Phosphore
Calcium	Phosphore	Calcium	Cuivre
		Magnésium	Soufre
Substances azotées :		*Substances azotées :*	
Ammoniac		Ammoniac	
Acides aminés		Acides aminés	
Protéines		Protéines	
Substances phénoliques		*Acétaldéhyde*	
Pigments		*Substances phénoliques*	
Vitamines		*Pigments*	
		Vitamines	

On trouvera dans le *Traité d'œnologie* de Ribéreau-Gayon et Peynaud la quantité approximative de chacune de ces matières présentes dans le vin, selon les dernières expériences connues.

La plupart des composants du moût se retrouvent à un certain degré dans le vin. La quantité de sucre diminue beaucoup pendant la fermentation, surtout dans les vins secs. Mais des matières nouvelles apparaissent au cours du même phénomène. Ce sont elles qui font du vin autre chose qu'un simple mélange d'eau, d'acide et d'alcool.

Pour simplifier, disons donc que la fermentation consiste essentiellement en transformation des sucres hexoses — dextrose et lévulose — en alcool et gaz carbonique par l'action des levures. La formule n'a pas changé depuis Gay-Lussac (1778-1850) :

$$\underset{\text{(Sucres hexoses)}}{C_6H_{12}O_6} \rightarrow \underset{\text{(Alcool éthylique)}}{2C_2H_6O} + \underset{\text{(Gaz carbonique)}}{2CO_2}$$

Quoique cette formule exprime le début et la fin de la fermentation — c'est-à-dire les matières présentes avant et après le phénomène — elle n'est exacte qu'à 90 %. En effet, au cours de la fermentation, 10 % des sucres se transforment en produits tels que : glycérine, butylène-glycol, aldéhydes, etc. La formule de Gay-Lussac simplifie donc une succession complexe de réactions chimiques. Selon Amerine et Joslyn (*Table Wines* (« Vins de table ») University of California Press, 1951), la molécule de dextrose passe par douze états intermédiaires stables avant de constituer l'alcool. La décarboxylation a lieu pendant tout le phénomène au cours duquel le gaz carbonique (CO_2) apparaît à plusieurs reprises. En outre, une trentaine de substances organiques et non organiques doivent être présentes pour que le processus donne un résultat satisfaisant.

Voici donc la définition qu'Amerine et Joslyn donnent de la fermentation : « Essentiellement, une succession d'oxydoréductions réversibles, tant intermoléculaires qu'intramoléculaires, et de phosphorylations ainsi qu'une décarboxylation irréversible. »

Les levures

Agents indispensables de la fermentation, les levures n'agissent qu'indirectement ; en réalité elles excrètent certains enzymes qui rendent cette réaction possible. Nombre de micro-organismes sont capables de déterminer la fermentation, mais tous ne sont pas utiles à l'élaboration du vin. Les levures diffèrent quant au genre, à l'espèce et à la variété ; la combinaison de variétés trouvées en un endroit ne sera jamais exactement la même qu'ailleurs.

La famille de levures *Saccharomyces cerevisiae*, variété *ellipsoideus* (vulgairement : levure de bière de forme ellipsoïde), fournit les ouvrières de la transformation des sucres de vinificateurs.

Il convient de remarquer que toutes les levures sont classées selon leurs caractéristiques morphologiques et physiologiques. On peut dresser leur nomenclature parce qu'une vingtaine d'entre elles existent sous une forme invariable dans le monde entier.

Les levures *Saccharomyces* se présentent sous un très grand nombre de variétés d'hybrides et de mutants. Cette famille n'en a pas moins un intérêt capital : les enzymes qu'elle excrète font fermenter le sucre plus complètement que n'importe quels autres. Mais ce n'est pas la seule levure qui contribue à la fermentation ; on doit à d'autres le bouquet et le goût ; on estime que le nombre et le type de levures ont un effet considérable sur la qualité du vin. Cependant, les meilleures levures ne donneront pas un bon vin à partir d'un raisin médiocre. En apportant la dernière touche à la qualité, les levures accessoires jouent un rôle important.

Comme nous l'avons vu précédemment les levures se collent à la pruine, à l'extérieur du raisin. Elles existent donc dans l'atmosphère ambiante du vignoble. C'est très précisément de celles-là qu'on se sert pour la vinification dans les régions qui produisent des vins fins.

Les siècles de viticulture en Europe occidentale ont permis de découvrir quantité d'excellentes levures de vin et le danger d'une « mauvaise » fermentation due à de mauvaises levures a été considérablement réduit. Dans les pays de viticulture récente, comme la Californie et l'Australie, il existe pourtant un tel risque d'endommagement causé par des levures sauvages impures qui prolifèrent que l'on ajoute immédiatement du bioxyde de soufre pour empêcher leur croissance. On inocule ensuite au moût une levure pure de culture, souvent importée de régions vinicoles européennes. Les différences entre les levures utilisées expliquent les nuances de goût et de bouquet. Mais le climat et le choix des variétés importent beaucoup plus. Il se pourrait que la touche finale, qui fait la gloire des vins les plus prestigieux, soit une teneur légèrement supérieure en esters due à quelque levure sauvage. Néanmoins, le même vin pourrait être gâché par les mêmes esters, si leur teneur était trop élevée.

Le bon sens et la science exigent que, pour obtenir des résultats heureux et constants, on utilise des levures de race pure d'une qualité connue et cultivées à cet effet. On ne connaît pas encore assez bien ces micro-organismes et les mélanges offerts par les laboratoires ne peuvent pas toujours être utilisés avec une certitude totale.

Pour le profane, la cuve dans laquelle le vin fermente rapidement suggère l'idée d'un chaudron de sorcière. Et le bruit qu'il entend lui rappelle une ruche d'abeilles en fureur. Mais on recourt de moins en moins à ce système de fermentation. L'amélioration du matériel, des connaissances et des techniques amène à faire fermenter le moût sous des températures moins élevées, parfois dans des réservoirs clos. Ce phénomène qui durait autrefois quelques jours peut actuellement se prolonger durant plusieurs semaines.

Les levures prolifèrent rapidement dans le moût frais ; après leur multiplication initiale, on en trouve plus de cent millions de cellules dans un seul millilitre de moût. Cette proportion variera selon la température et les aliments que les levures trouvent dans chaque moût.

Sans ajout de levure de culture, il ne faudra qu'incorporer des quantités minimes de bioxyde de soufre car il détruit facilement la levure naturelle. Si par contre on utilise des levures de culture, on pourra alors ajouter un peu de bioxyde de soufre pour empêcher la croissance de la levure sauvage. La culture pure peut être acclimatée au bioxyde de soufre et s'épanouira rapidement sans en être incommodée.

Les levures du vin fermentent efficacement entre 10 et 32 °C. En général les vins blancs sont meilleurs s'ils fermentent aux environs de 18 à 20 °C. Quant aux vins rouges, pour lesquels on fait aussi fermenter la peau, ils atteignent leur maximum de qualité en fermentant à des températures plus élevées.

Tous les producteurs de vin connaissent le danger d'un blocage de fermentation provoqué par l'apparition de matières toxiques qui paralysent les levures. Ces matières sont produites par les levures elles-mêmes si la température de fermentation s'élève jusqu'à 34 ou 38 °C. Il s'agit donc de prendre toutes les mesures pour éviter ce phénomène.

Dans certaines régions, une fermentation incomplète est un grave souci. On ignore pour quelle cause il peut en être ainsi. Peut-être est-ce dû à l'utilisation de levures qui tolèrent mal l'alcool, à la faible valeur nutritive des raisins ou à une fermentation à trop haute ou trop basse température.

Les vins rouges

On obtient du vin rouge en faisant fermenter du raisin avec sa peau pendant un temps plus ou moins long selon le genre de vin, les caractéristiques particulières de chaque vendange et aussi les traditions régionales. Dans le Bordelais, on laissait le vin quatre à six semaines dans la cuve de fermentation. Cette vieille mode n'est plus en faveur que dans quelques rares propriétés. Selon la méthode moderne, le vin ne cuve que de 9 à 20 jours ; les vins sont plus légers, plus souples et consommables plus tôt puisqu'ils contiennent moins de tanin fourni par la peau. Remarquons toutefois que certains des plus jeunes vignerons du Bordelais reviennent actuellement à un cuvage prolongé de trois semaines. En réalité la durée de cuvaison doit être adaptée à la qualité du raisin et au type de vin à réaliser. En Bourgogne on procède d'une manière totalement différente. Depuis la fin de la Première Guerre mondiale, la durée de cuvage est aussi réduite que possible : optimum, 5 à 7 jours ; maximum, 8 à 9 jours. Elle vient récemment d'être prolongée à 15 jours.

Pendant la fermentation, la pulpe et la masse de peau, qui donnent couleur et tanin, flottent sur le jus où elles forment le *chapeau.* Dans les grandes cuves, ce chapeau atteint l'épaisseur de 60 cm à 1 m. Divers procédés permettent de mêler les éléments du chapeau au jus :

1. on crève le chapeau deux ou trois fois par jour ;
2. on installe une espèce de cheminée dans la cuve, le liquide en fermentation s'y élève et retombe sur le chapeau comme l'eau dans la lessiveuse ;
3. on pose une espèce de couvercle trop étroit mais lourd sur le chapeau, pour le faire tomber dans le jus en ébullition.

Cependant, la méthode la plus courante en France est la suivante : on pompe le jus par une ouverture inférieure de la cuve et on le répand sur le chapeau.

Quand la fermentation est terminée, on soutire le liquide et le chapeau tombe au fond de la cuve. On presse ce résidu pour en extraire le vin qu'il peut contenir encore. Le premier résultat de ce pressurage peut être conservé à part ou ajouté à la masse ; les produits des pressurages suivants seront vinifiés séparément pour faire un vin ordinaire à l'usage des ouvriers de la propriété. Le vin soutiré est mis en tonneaux de chêne où il mûrit. Le vin vieillit dans du bois pour s'y clarifier et se débarrasser de la lie. D'autres réactions physico- et biochimiques s'y produisent ; les fermentations alcooliques puis malolactiques s'y terminent. Divers composants en suspension dans le vin tombent au fond par *précipitation* (lire ce mot dans le même sens que pour la pluie considérée comme précipitation atmosphérique). Or ces opérations ne peuvent avoir lieu qu'en présence d'oxygène qui pénètre dans le tonneau à travers le bois dont la porosité correspond exactement à celle qui est nécessaire. Si toutefois elle est insuffisante, on ne fermera pas hermétiquement la bonde. C'est seulement après toutes ces transformations que le vin pourra être soutiré une dernière fois pour mise en bouteille.

Dans ses *Études sur le vin,* Pasteur remarqua que, sans oxygène, le vin ne mûrissait pas et ne survivait même pas à son amertume première. Dans une barrique de bois, en vieillissant, il n'aura plus la même teneur en alcool. Si le contenant est placé en un lieu sec, l'eau du vin s'évaporera plus rapidement que l'alcool ; dans un lieu humide, au contraire, l'alcool diminuera plus vite dans le vin. L'évaporation augmentera légèrement la concentration des composants non volatils, mais dans une mesure à peine perceptible pour la plupart des vins secs. D'autre part, l'oxydation du gaz sulfureux ($SO_2 + O_4 \rightarrow SO_4$) augmentera l'acidité du vin ; la concentration du liquide (10 à 15 %) aura le même effet. Ajoutons à cela l'action des bactéries.

Le vieillissement initial et le soutirage

Durant la première année de vieillissement, on conserve le vin rouge dans une barrique dont la bonde joue librement. Dans la plupart des chais ou caves un ouvrier veille à ce que la barrique reste constamment pleine en y ajoutant du vin : une fois par semaine l'hiver et deux fois par semaine l'été. Cette opération vise à compenser l'évaporation. Elle s'appelle *ouillage* (*voir* ce mot). Si le niveau du vin baissait dans le contenant, des bactéries indésirables se développeraient à la surface au contact de l'air et leur activité provoquerait une acidité volatile excessive. Au cours des mois, le vin perd en partie l'âpreté de son tanin, ce qui le rend moins dur au goût. La fermentation malolactique (*voir* ci-après le paragraphe sur la fermentation secondaire) atténue l'amertume. La couleur devient moins vive et, au bout d'un an, le vin sera d'un rouge foncé. Toutefois la teinte peut être affectée par la teneur en acide sulfureux.

Pendant la première phase, le vin se repose et toutes les particules en suspension tombent lentement dans le fond. Ensuite, on soutire le vin pour le transférer dans une barrique propre et stérile. Lie et autres sédiments restent dans le premier. Selon la tradition, le moment idéal pour le soutirage est celui où se trouvent réunies les trois conditions suivantes : pleine lune, vent du nord, temps clair. Or, la science confirme ce qui semble inspiré par la superstition. Ces conditions, en effet, impliquent une forte pression atmosphérique et c'est en de telles circonstances que le vin travaille moins activement. (Quand la pression atmosphérique est basse, les gaz qui émanent du liquide sont capables d'agiter les lies les plus légères ; elles passeront avec le vin du premier dans le second tonneau). Mais rares sont les vinificateurs de quelque importance qui peuvent s'offrir le luxe d'attendre longtemps les caprices favorables de la nature. En fin de compte, l'effet de la pression atmosphérique est tellement faible qu'on peut le négliger sans dommage. Étant donné que la plupart des bactéries nocives se rassemblent dans la lie, le soutirage libère le vin du danger d'infection. Les lies sont rassemblées et, en se posant, elles donnent encore une petite quantité de vin de qualité inférieure, généralement réservé au personnel. Durant la première année on soutire le vin quatre fois. S'il ne s'agit que d'un petit vin, il est mis en bouteille à la fin de cette même année ou bien vendu en baril pour être consommé en carafes remplies au fausset. Quant au vin fin, il exige plus de soin.

Les vins de qualité vieillissent donc un an de plus en tonneau, mais généralement pas plus longtemps. Durant cette seconde année, la bonde est enfoncée et on tourne le baril afin qu'elle soit à la partie inférieure. Elle reste ainsi humide, et l'on obtient une fermeture hermétique. L'oxydation se poursuit pourtant parce que le bois, grâce à sa porosité, permet à une certaine quantité d'air d'atteindre le vin. Pendant cette seconde année on le soutirera encore deux ou trois fois. En le retirant de la barrique, en général, on le filtre et même on le stabilise par certains traitements variant selon la région. L'oxydation fait alors place à la réduction et le bouquet commence à se développer. Pendant cette seconde année, le vin se transforme de manière moins notable. La couleur devient plus foncée et son goût se précise. Le contact du bois révèle son caractère et lui donne du moelleux. Les précipitations se poursuivent encore.

Le vin se repose ainsi encore une année et parfois plus longtemps. Les soutirages continuent. Juste avant de le mettre en bouteille ou de l'expédier, le vinificateur procède à la clarification.

La clarification

La clarification, ou collage, assure un vin parfaitement clair, débarrassé de toutes les particules en suspension et contribue aussi à le stabiliser en interdisant la précipitation de certaines protéines, pigments, matières polyphénoliques, selon le genre de collage auquel on recourt. Une matière colloïdale introduite dans le tonneau coagule en les attirant toutes les infimes particules qui peuvent flotter dans le vin. Puis elles tombent vers le fond. Les matières recommandées pour le vin rouge sont la gélatine, le blanc d'œuf, le sang, etc. Ces agents organiques ont une action chimique ou qui peut être considérée à la fois comme chimique et physique. Surtout en Californie, mais ailleurs aussi, on utilise d'autres agents de clarification : des matières non organiques telles que l'argile espagnole [1], dont le composant actif est le kaolin, et une glaise du Wyoming, dénommée bentonite, diluée à l'eau chaude avant d'être mise au contact du vin. Quand la sédimentation est faite, on soutire le vin une dernière fois pour le mettre en bouteille ou l'expédier en baril.

Pour donner des résultats satisfaisants, la clarification doit avoir lieu au moins six mois après les vendanges, c'est-à-dire quand la fermentation initiale et la fermentation malolactique (*voir ci-après* LA FERMENTATION SECONDAIRE DES VINS ROUGES ET BLANCS) sont terminées. Le vin doit être inerte pour que le dépôt ne soit pas agité. On en conclut évidemment qu'elle doit être précédée par un soutirage correct. L'opération sera plus facile par température stable.

Si le vin doit être sulfité, le traitement doit lui être administré la veille de la clarification. Les petites additions d'anhydride sulfureux paralysent temporairement les micro-organismes. Chez certains vinificateurs français, sauf dans les régions de vins fins, la clarification est désormais presque considérée comme une pratique désuète. On la remplace par un filtrage. Les filtres utilisés à cet effet sont de types divers mais servent tous à atteindre le même but : rendre le vin clair en l'exposant à l'air le moins possible. Dans les centres plus importants de vinification, on clarifie par centrifugation les vins qui doivent être vendus aussitôt que possible (quelques mois après la fermentation). On y procède par plusieurs soutirages successifs, chacun suivi de centrifugation ; après conservation au froid (— 4 °C) pendant 8 ou 15 jours, on procède à une dernière centrifugation et à un filtrage avant la mise en bouteille.

Le filtrage ne nuit pas au vin s'il est fait par quelqu'un de compétent et en utilisant des filtres appropriés. Dans la plupart des centres de vinification modernes on filtre une fois après soutirage ou clarification et toujours avant la mise en bouteille. Pourvu que l'élément filtrant soit constitué par une matière adéquate et que les pompes utilisées maintiennent le vin à l'abri de l'air, le vin s'en porte bien. En réalité, ce filtrage ne saurait remplacer complètement le collage. Cette dernière opération, en effet, fait plus que clarifier le vin. Elle

1. Terre du nord de l'Espagne. Elle a la particularité de gonfler énormément au contact de l'eau.

améliore son goût, lui assure un meilleur équilibre et il restera clair dans la bouteille pendant plus longtemps.

LES VINS BLANCS

Précisons avant tout que la vinification n'est pas la même pour les vins blancs secs et les vins blancs doux. D'autre part, des vins spéciaux tels que le Xérès, autrement dit les vins vinés, sont traités à part dans cet ouvrage (*voir* XÉRÈS).

Les vins blancs sont doux ou secs — plus ou moins doux ou plus ou moins secs — selon que la conversion du sucre en alcool est plus ou moins complète. Les vins doux sont sucrés parce que le sucre ne fermente plus à partir de 15 ou 16° d'alcool. La fermentation qui produit de l'alcool se freine d'elle-même quand elle a achevé sa tâche. Dans la pratique, les vins secs fermentent jusqu'à ce que tout le sucre ait été converti.

Les vins blancs doux

On obtient des vins doux par quatre méthodes différentes : 1. en utilisant du raisin si riche en sucre qu'il ne se convertira pas totalement en alcool ; 2. en arrêtant la fermentation artificiellement, généralement par un agent chimique ; 3. en soutirant à plusieurs reprises pendant la fermentation ; 4. en ajoutant de l'alcool soit au moût avant la fermentation, soit dans la cuve pendant le processus — il doit s'agir, évidemment, d'alcool de vin. (Une variante de la quatrième méthode consiste à ajouter du sucre au vin, mais les résultats sont mauvais et cette pratique est généralement réprouvée).

1. Les raisins assez riches en sucre pour arrêter eux-mêmes leur propre fermentation sont rares. On en trouve surtout dans la région de Sauternes, les vallées du Rhin et de la Moselle et certaine partie de la Hongrie. Dans tous les cas, le vigneron laisse les raisins sur la vigne jusqu'à ce que la pourriture noble se soit formée et ait provoqué certaines transformations chimiques. En réalité la pourriture noble n'augmente pas la teneur en sucre mais élimine de l'eau. On peut obtenir le même résultat en séchant les raisins. Ce qui se fait dans certaines contrées de France, d'Italie et d'Espagne. Mais ce procédé ne diminue pas l'acidité en même temps que la proportion d'eau.

2. La manière la plus courante d'arrêter artificiellement la fermentation consiste à ajouter de l'anhydride sulfureux. Ce remarquable agent chimique tue levures et micro-organismes mais a moins d'effet sur ceux qui sont utiles que sur les indésirables. Si on en met de trop, tous seront exterminés et la fermentation cessera complètement ; dans ce cas une partie du sucre ne sera pas convertie en alcool. Si trop d'anhydride sulfureux reste dans le vin il lui donnera le goût et l'odeur désagréables du soufre : défaut de bien des vins blancs doux et demi-doux de qualité médiocre. Une autre méthode consiste à pasteuriser et à filtrer jusqu'à stérilisation. On peut aussi utiliser l'éthylpyrocarbonate (fongicide extrêmement efficace). Dans tous ces cas les ferments seront tués ou éliminés avant la conversion de tout le sucre.

3. Quelle que soit la méthode utilisée, il faut que le vin soit à une température proche de 0 °C au maximum. Sinon, le traitement n'est pas efficace.

4. L'addition d'alcool, avant ou pendant la fermentation, l'empêche ou l'arrête ; le sucre reste donc en l'état au moins pour une partie. Bien des vins vinés sont fabriqués ainsi. Les vinificateurs usent aussi d'une variante, aussi

bien pour les vins rouges que blancs. Ils ajoutent à la fois du sucre et de l'alcool à du jus de raisin : mélange auquel certains refusent le nom de vin.

Les vins demi-doux

Les vins blancs de table contenant seulement de 1 à 3 % de sucre résiduel obtiennent un succès croissant, particulièrement en Californie et en Allemagne. Ces vins faibles en alcool sont très courants en Californie, où on les obtient en fermentant le jus sec, puis en l'adoucissant avec un concentré de jus de raisin non fermenté. On stabilise ensuite le tout par procédé chimique ou bien par un filtrage stérile.

Le pressurage des raisins

Nous avons vu que pour faire du vin blanc il importe de retirer dès que possible les peaux du jus de raisin. Les raisins sont donc écrasés et pressés aussitôt arrivés à l'entrepôt de vinification. Le jus est soutiré immédiatement pour fermenter seul. Les vins blancs de haute qualité ne sont faits qu'avec le *vin de goutte,* c'est-à-dire celui qui s'écoule au début du pressurage. En effet, plus le pressurage est énergique, plus la qualité décroît.

La clarification du moût

En Californie pour obtenir un vin blanc de la meilleure qualité, il est fondamental que le jus soit aussi libre que possible de solides en suspension avant la fermentation. (En France, c'est le débourbage). Le procédé traditionnel consiste à laisser les solides se déposer pendant une nuit, puis à soutirer le jus clair du dépôt. Depuis quelques années, on utilise de plus en plus fréquemment des centrifugeuses, qui permettent une clarification optimale du moût blanc.

La fermentation et le soutirage

Les vins blancs sont mis à fermenter soit dans de vastes cuves soit dans des barriques de quelque 300 l maximum comme dans le cas des vins français de qualité. L'Allemagne à ce point de vue fait exception. Les grands vins y fermentent dans d'énormes foudres. Le secret des vins blancs fins réside dans une fermentation contrôlée, lente et à basse température. En ce qui concerne la maturation en fût, l'oxygène joue un rôle moins important pour les vins blancs que pour les rouges et ne contribue guère à leur amélioration.

On ne remplit que partiellement les cuves parce que le moût se dilate et une écume et des particules de pulpe montent vers le sommet ; si le contenant était plein, il déborderait et ce serait une perte.

Néanmoins, la fermentation des vins blancs en barrique est probablement de moins bonne qualité que dans une cuve de 4 000 ou 5 000 l, à condition, évidemment qu'il s'agisse dans les deux cas du même jus de raisin. La *seule* raison pour laquelle les Français s'en tiennent aux barriques de bois c'est parce qu'autrefois ils n'avaient rien d'autre. C'est devenu une tradition qui malheureusement ne permet pas d'agir sur la température autant qu'il serait souhaitable. Pour atteindre leur meilleure qualité, les vins blancs doivent être à l'abri de l'oxygène et une barrique de 300 l à moitié pleine est une mauvaise protection.

Dès que le tumulte de la première fermentation a cessé, la lie commence à se déposer. On procède alors à un soutirage léger ; si cette opération éliminait les levures actives avec celles qui sont épuisées, la fermentation s'arrêterait. Dans certaines régions vinicoles ce premier soutirage est extrêmement léger parce qu'en supprimant toutes les particules on empêcherait de s'accomplir la fermentation secondaire ou malolactique (*voir ci-après* LA FERMENTATION SECONDAIRE DES VINS ROUGES ET BLANCS) qui diminue l'acidité. A l'inverse, dans les pays chauds comme la Californie, on prend grand soin d'empêcher cette fermentation malolactique car on y traite des moûts peu acides.

Outre les légers soutirages périodiques, on contrôle la température. La plupart des vignerons estiment que la température optimale de fermentation se situe entre 16 et 21 °C ; certains préfèrent même une température plus basse. Une fermentation lente et fraîche conserve le goût fruité du raisin et donne un vin d'une plus grande finesse qu'une fermentation rapide.

Dans les pays plus chauds où il est permis d'ajouter de l'acide, on encourage parfois la fermentation malolactique puis on ajuste l'acidité du vin en y ajoutant ensuite une quantité appropriée d'acide tartrique ou citrique. Encore faut-il surveiller le vin car les réactions malolactiques peuvent se produire à plusieurs reprises, soit pendant la fermentation alcoolique initiale, soit dans les mois qui suivent. Le plus sûr moyen d'y parer est l'utilisation judicieuse de l'anhydride sulfureux ; de même des soutirages complets et une clarification précoce y contribuent. La fermentation à basse température diminuera aussi la possibilité de fermentation malolactique.

En général, on maintient aussi basse que possible la température de fermentation. C'est surtout une affaire d'équilibre. Les centres de vinification de Californie, bien équipés, ne laissent pas la température de leurs vins blancs atteindre 16 °C. Et la température moyenne ne dépasse guère 10 °C. Le soutirage sert aussi à réduire la vitesse de la fermentation mais il peut l'arrêter complètement, ce qui n'est pas sans danger pour le vin.

Le vieillissement initial des vins blancs

On conserve les vins blancs à une température inférieure à celle des vins rouges. Les tartrates et autres substances en dissolution — plus remarquables dans les vins blancs que dans les vins rouges — se précipitent mieux à basse température et, de nos jours, la plupart des gens préfèrent des vins parfaitement clairs. Malgré toutes les précautions, il arrive que des particules de bitartrate de potassium apparaissent en suspension dans le vin, sous la forme de petits flocons blancs comme neige. Quoique généralement insipides, ils nuisent à l'aspect du breuvage. Si le vin est conservé à la basse température appropriée et s'il n'est pas mis en bouteille trop tôt — avant que les particules n'aient eu le temps de précipiter — ces flocons n'apparaissent généralement pas

La clarification et la mise en bouteille

Les vins blancs secs sont mis en bouteille jeunes, plus jeunes que les vins blancs doux. Souvent un an ou dix-huit mois en barrique suffisent à les clarifier ; on soutire et on « colle » le vin, soit pour être mis en bouteille, soit pour le vendre en barrique. La clarification des vins blancs est un processus semblable à celui du vin rouge, sauf en ce qui concerne le choix de l'agent : ichtyocolle (colle de poisson), surtout ou bien sang et caséine. En réalité la plupart des vins blancs atteignent la qualité la meilleure si le collage a lieu à la bentonite.

Sauf si on les a conservés dans du bois très neuf dont ils auraient recueilli une grande quantité de tanin, l'utilisation d'agents organiques pour le collage est sujet à controverses. On se sert aussi de nouvelles substances : poudre de nylon et très rarement P.V.P. (polyvinylpyrrolidone). Ces substances contribuent à stabiliser les vins et a les empêcher de prendre une couleur marron. Les vins blancs doux sont souvent collés à la bentonite qui en élimine les protéines, ce qui facilite leur stabilisation. Le vieillissement en bouteille a lieu selon les mêmes principes pour les vins blancs et les vins rouges ; il demande moins de temps pour les secs et plus pour les doux. En général l'amateur de vin blanc sec apprécie l'arôme frais du raisin ; il consomme donc son vin jeune. Quant aux vins blancs doux leur bouquet ne se développe qu'au bout de plusieurs années de conservation en bouteille et dure beaucoup plus longtemps ; les plus prestigieux ont conservé leur excellence pendant un demi-siècle et même plus.

La fermentation secondaire des vins rouges et blancs

Bien des vins subissent une fermentation secondaire parfois concurremment à la principale et plus souvent après. Il ne s'agit pas d'une transformation de sucre en alcool, mais d'une conversion de l'acide malique en acide lactique et gaz carbonique, sous l'effet d'une bactérie. Précisons que ce phénomène *n'est pas* celui qui rend mousseux les vins de Champagne et autres. Le gaz contenu par ces vins est dû à une seconde fermentation alcoolique, généralement provoquée artificiellement, soit dans la bouteille (méthode champenoise), soit dans des cuves ou réservoirs clos (procédé Charmat) [*voir* CHAMPAGNE et CHARMAT].

Si la fermentation secondaire a lieu avant la mise en bouteille, le gaz se dissipera et il en résultera simplement un vin moins acide. Un soutirage supplémentaire sera souvent bénéfique.

La fermentation malolactique présente une importance énorme en ce qui concerne les vins très acides de Suisse et les œnologues bordelais lui attribuent, pour une bonne part, l'excellence des vins rouges de leur région. Il est bon que la fermentation secondaire s'achève peu après la première. S'il n'en est pas ainsi elle pourra avoir lieu six ou neuf mois plus tard, voire un an.

On ne connaissait jusqu'à ces dernières années aucun moyen de provoquer à volonté et au moment choisi cette désacidification biologique. Mais dès qu'elle a commencé on peut l'activer en utilisant un grand contenant parce qu'un important volume de liquide conserve la chaleur de la fermentation plus longtemps qu'une petite quantité. Si la fermentation secondaire commence ou continue en bouteille, le gaz y est confiné et le vin devient mousseux et prend souvent un mauvais goût. Si la quantité de gaz qu'il contient n'est pas trop forte, on peut éliminer ce défaut en l'aérant, soit en le faisant tourner dans son verre ou en le faisant passer d'un verrre dans un autre. Mais si on vous sert au restaurant un vin présentant ce défaut, le plus simple est de le refuser.

Grâce aux progrès de la science œnologique on est arrivé récemment à un point où il devient possible de cultiver en laboratoire des bactéries qui provoquent la réaction malolactique. Il suffit donc désormais au vigneron d'en ajouter à son vin après la fermentation pour que les deux phénomènes se produisent successivement. Naguère il arrivait parfois qu'une mauvaise variété de bactéries malolactiques détermine goût et arôme désagréables et gâche le vin.

On peut désormais éviter cet accident en utilisant des bactéries de type connu. Ce procédé permet aussi d'échapper aux inconvénients de la fermentation secondaire en bouteille et de faire mûrir le vin plus rapidement.

Le vieillissement des vins

Tous les vins ne s'améliorent pas avec l'âge. Certains — notamment les blancs secs — sont meilleurs dans leur jeunesse. Les autres, et surtout la plupart des vins fins, s'améliorent, tant en barrique qu'en bouteille, mais finissent par dépasser leur point d'excellence, se dégrader et perdre complètement leurs qualités. Que se produit-il dans le vin lorsqu'il vieillit ? L'acidité diminue ; l'alcool, les acides et autres composants se transforment et s'associent de manières innombrables et complexes pour former de nouveaux composés : esters, aldéhydes, acétals et ainsi de suite — il se produit aussi une précipitation des sels.

Le professeur E. Peynaud, président honoraire de la station œnologique de Bordeaux, divise les vins en deux catégories nettement tranchées : — 1. Les vins vinés tels que le Porto et le Xérès, dont l'excellence est due à un processus d'oxydation et de formation d'aldéhydes, notamment l'acétaldéhyde. (D'autres oxydations se produisent parallèlement et le vin prélève aussi une partie de ses composants dans le bois de la barrique.) — 2. Les vins qui atteignent leur point culminant à l'abri de l'air, c'est-à-dire sans phénomènes d'oxydation. Les vins de cette seconde catégorie doivent l'essentiel de leurs caractéristiques au raisin : le Bordeaux, par exemple, est surtout fait avec du Cabernet et le Bourgogne avec du Pinot Noir. Là, c'est l'âge qui détermine le développement du bouquet ; ce phénomène ne se produit que dans les vins de la seconde catégorie auxquels le raisin fournit le bouquet à condition qu'ils vieillissent à l'abri de l'air et lorsque de bonnes conditions de réduction leur sont assurées.

Le vieillissement en fût est important en ce sens qu'il hâte la stabilisation et la clarification du vin et lui fournit certaines caractéristiques provenant du bois. Mais la quantité d'oxygène qui entre en contact avec le vin en fût et l'importance de son rôle sont encore controversées et peut-être surestimées. En tout cas, à partir du moment où le vin est en bouteille, on ne peut plus le soigner ni le traiter.

Le vieillissement en bouteille des vins fins n'est pas encore complètement compris. Les savants ne sont, en général, pas d'accord avec les vinificateurs ; selon les premiers, il n'entre que très peu d'air à travers le bouchon et cet air n'aurait guère d'influence, peut-être pas du tout. Le professeur J. Ribéreau-Gayon, de l'université de Bordeaux, indique dans son impressionnant traité d'œnologie : « La quantité d'oxygène qui pénètre normalement dans la bouteille est infinitésimale, sinon nulle ; on ne saurait vraisemblablement lui attribuer un rôle important ». Il en donne comme preuve le fait que le vin vieillit aussi bien dans des éprouvettes hermétiquement closes que dans des bouteilles dont le goulot est obturé par un bouchon. Étant donné que ces questions sont encore mal comprises, il ne semble pas que l'on puisse espérer provoquer dans un proche avenir un vieillissement artificiel. Or, voilà longtemps que les chercheurs se préoccupent de ce problème.

En général, ceux qui ne sont pas habitués à la prudence des savants, ne tiennent pas compte de l'air enfermé dans la bouteille avec le vin. Peut-être est-ce cette faible quantité qui joue un rôle dans les transformations qui caractérisent le vieillissement. En moyenne, toute bouteille de vin contient un minimum de 8 à 10 mm^3 d'air dans le goulot. Si le bouchon reste humide pendant le vieillissement, il ne pénétrera vraisemblablement plus d'air dans la bouteille et c'est celui qui s'y trouve déjà qui provoquera certaines réactions. On doit donc prendre un soin extrême pour réduire autant que possible la quantité d'air renfermée dans la bouteille ; les oxydations seront réduites au minimum et les réductions auront lieu quand même. Des traitements artificiels peuvent conférer au vin un bouquet généralement dû à l'âge. Ces procédés semblent déjà prometteurs au moins pour certains vins ordinaires.

Les pratiques exceptionnelles

Le vigneron doit toujours envisager la possibilité d'une température défavorable pendant la maturation du raisin et, par conséquent, prévoir la possibilité d'une vendange insuffisamment ou mal mûrie. Autrefois, c'était un désastre. De nos jours, certains moyens permettent d'obtenir quand même un vin de qualité courante. Voici certaines de ces méthodes :

La *chaptalisation* — ainsi nommée car ce fut Jean-Antoine Chaptal (1756-1832) qui proposa, au début du XVIIIe siècle, d'ajouter du sucre aux moûts insuffisamment sucrés. Sa méthode fut adoptée en Allemagne où on l'appela *gallisation* (en hommage au docteur Jean-François Gall et plus couramment : *Anreicherung,* enrichissement). Il n'est pas inutile d'insister sur ce point : le sucre doit être ajouté au moût, mais jamais au vin.

La chaptalisation permet au raisin insuffisamment sucré de donner un vin dont la teneur en alcool s'harmonise avec ses autres qualités. L'hydrolyse du sucre ordinaire (saccharose) produit des sucres hexoses (dextrose et lévulose) lorsqu'on l'ajoute au moût, et la fermentation a lieu normalement. Si l'on n'en abuse pas, la chaptalisation donne une teneur en alcool qui s'équilibre mieux avec les autres composants du vin. Mais on en abuse malheureusement dans certaines régions et elle donne alors un semblant de vin fabriqué avec des peaux de raisin, du sucre et des acides. Ce procédé est répandu en Allemagne et en Bourgogne et on y recourt même jusque dans le Bordelais. Il doit être autorisé par l'administration dans chaque cas particulier. En Bourgogne, où l'on y procède malheureusement tous les ans, on permet à certains grands vins d'être trop abondamment sucrés. Dans les régions où le soleil est assez chaud pour donner aux raisins une teneur suffisante en sucre, la chaptalisation est inutile. Le *Dictionnaire du vin* de MM. Renouil et de Traversay estime que la chaptalisation a un rôle avantageux plus complexe et qu'elle ne se limite pas à augmenter le degré d'alcool étant donné que la fermentation du sucre donne aussi des sous-produits tels que glycérol, acide succinique, etc., qui exercent une influence considérable sur le goût du vin. Cette opération diminue aussi l'âpreté excessive de certains vins en précipitant la crème de tartre.

La chaptalisation est interdite en Californie.

La *désacidification* : quand le temps est vraiment mauvais, le raisin peut non seulement manquer de sucre, mais être trop acide. Pour venir à bout de ce défaut, il suffit de mélanger le vin trop acide avec un vin peu acide. Ce coupage est parfaitement légitime à condition que le breuvage ne soit pas vendu sous une *appellation* à laquelle il n'a pas droit. Moins souvent on y ajoute du carbonate de calcium qui agit sur les acides et les précipite. Mais cette méthode exige une extrême prudence sinon elle donne des résultats médiocres.

L'*acidification* : après un été exceptionnellement chaud, les raisins peuvent ne pas être suffisamment acides et fournir un vin plat, peu savoureux, voire insipide. On peut corriger légitimement ce défaut en ajoutant au moût une petite quantité d'acide tartrique (qui n'améliore pas la qualité des vins fins) ou bien des raisins moins mûrs — donc plus acides — provenant d'une floraison tardive de la vigne. Enfin, on peut aussi procéder par coupage avec des vins présentant une forte teneur en acide.

La *décoloration* : quand le vin blanc est teinté de rouge, un traitement au charbon de bois effacera cette coloration dans la mesure désirée. Malheureusement toutes les autres caractéristiques du vin disparaissent en même temps.

La *concentration* : la déficience en sucre peut être corrigée en ajoutant du moût concentré : bouilli, pour le débarrasser d'une partie de son eau. La déficience en alcool peut être traitée d'une manière analogue par coupage avec un vin dont la teneur en eau a été diminuée par congélation. Dans les deux cas, on provoque une augmentation de l'élément qui manquait au vin, soit sucre, soit alcool. Dans certains pays ces pratiques sont interdites. Lorsqu'elles augmentent la teneur en sucre et en alcool, elles augmentent aussi l'acidité, parfois au détriment du vin.

La *pasteurisation* : la stérilisation du vin par la chaleur est encore controversée. Bien des experts estiment que la chaleur tue le vin. Pourtant l'œnologue bordelais Ribéreau-Gayon assure que c'est une affaire de conditions sous lesquelles la stérilisation a lieu. La pasteurisation consiste à porter rapidement le vin à une température de 54 °C ; elle stérilise efficacement le vin en fût parce qu'elle détruit toutes les bactéries, mais elle est évidemment peu pratique et même impossible quand le vin est déjà en bouteille. C'est aussi un procédé compliqué et hasardeux, mais surtout parce que le matériel nécessaire à cette opération n'a pas été suffisamment mis au point. Dans certaines circonstances, la pasteurisation peut être très utile. Mais dans les régions de vins fins il vaux mieux l'éviter parce que le vin pasteurisé devient inerte. Néanmoins, dans bien des pays, la pasteurisation des vins de table doux et demi-doux, avant ou pendant la mise en bouteille, est devenue monnaie courante. Les vins ordinaires sont portés à 82 °C pendant une minute ou mis en bouteille entre 54 et 60 °C, puis rafraîchis lentement. Dans certains grands centres de vinification la concurrence a incité à un tel perfectionnement du système que pas une seule bouteille, sur les milliers qui sont remplies à l'heure, n'est gâchée par des levures ou bactéries, sauf en cas de bouchage défectueux ou de quelque accident imprévisible. Les conditions mécaniques pour la pasteurisation du vin sont maintenant assimilées. Des études récentes ont montré que plus le vin est chauffé et refroidi rapidement, moins il perd en qualité. On développe actuellement des méthodes de pasteurisation ultra-rapide, ce qui est coûteux et ne résout pas encore le problème de la recontamination du vin pendant sa mise en bouteille.

La composition du vin

Le vin est le composé de différents ingrédients qui s'associent de manière extrêmement complexe et inconstante. Étant donné son aptitude à se transformer de bien des manières entre la vendange et le moment où on le sert, on dit que le vin *vit*. Et en effet, il vit.

L'alcool

Le composant le mieux connu, mais pas le plus important, est l'alcool produit par la fermentation du jus de raisin, non alcoolisé à l'origine. L'alcool représente de 7 à 24 % du volume. Il s'agit surtout d'alcool éthylique. Mais une partie — moins de 0,15 % — est de l'alcool méthylique. Il est présent dans le vin en quantité variant de 36 à 350 mg/l. En outre, le vin contient des quantités

RÈGLES ÉLÉMENTAIRES DE LA VINIFICATION

Recommandations		*Défauts à éviter*
La propreté est indispensable. Veiller à ce que tout le matériel entrant en contact avec le vin soit propre. Éviter les ustensiles de fer ou d'alliages contenant du cuivre. Utiliser de préférence certains plastiques, le verre, l'acier inoxydable ou le bois aussi bien pour les outils que les cuves, les fûts et les conduits des pompes.	1	Goût et odeur désagréables Casse métallique ; détérioration, trouble microbien.
Vendanger dans les meilleures conditions permises par la température de l'année, alors que le raisin est suffisamment mûr. Apporter la vendange au pressoir en évitant de la souiller sur le sol.	2	Goût désagréable de moisi. Vin amer (amertume due à l'oïdium). Acidité excessive ou insuffisante. Trouble microbien, casse métallique
Presser rapidement pour les vins blancs, mais ne pas presser excessivement. Éviter l'oxydation du moût par la macération à l'air libre des raisins écrasés.	3	Manque de fraîcheur et de fruité. Excès de tanin. Trouble colloïdal. Casse oxydasique, moisissure.
Nettoyer le moût — et par conséquent le vin — par l'addition d'une dose d'anhydride sulfureux, petite mais suffisante.	4	Excès de protéines. Détérioration et trouble microbien. Casse oxydasique.
Contrôler la température de la fermentation pour la maintenir aussi bas que possible en évitant toutefois le froid qui l'arrêterait. Limiter attentivement le temps de fermentation des vins rouges. Se méfier de la détérioration qui peut être due à l'exposition du chapeau à l'air libre.	5	Excès de sucre en voie de réduction, moisissure. Excès d'acidité volatile et viscosité si la température est trop élevée.
Ouiller dès que la fermentation est terminée. Ne jamais laisser un vin soutiré en contact avec l'air.	6	Pullulation de levures mycodermiques, détériorations et nuages microbiens.
Sauf le blanc doux, le vin ne doit pas conserver la moindre trace de sucre en voie de réduction. (Pourtant dans bien des régions on tolère et même encourage une certaine teneur en sucres résiduels pour les vins blancs secs et rosés d'un degré d'alcool non excessif. Il est tout à fait possible de préserver heureusement de tels vins en utilisant l'acide sorbique et l'anhydride sulfureux. Bien des vins allemands contiennent du sucre résiduel considéré comme nécessaire pour certaines qualités.)	7	Piqûre lactique. Fermentation mannitique.
La forte teneur en alcool des grands vins blancs doux et moelleux permet de les préserver sans abuser de l'anhydride sulfureux. A l'inverse, les vins blancs mineurs, doux et moelleux, sont difficiles à conserver.		Fermentation secondaire.

RÈGLES ÉLÉMENTAIRES DE LA VINIFICATION

Recommandations		*Défauts à éviter*
Pour éviter de donner au vin une forte dose d'anhydride sulfureux, on peut le stériliser avant la mise en bouteille.		Prolifération et dépôt de levure.
Procéder aux soutirages aux moments appropriés et assez souvent, soit avec aération, soit à l'abri de l'air, selon les cas. Ne pas oublier que, dans une certaine mesure, la fermentation malolactique doit avoir lieu ou être évitée selon l'acidité que doit garder le vin. Cette opération exige néanmoins un soin constant, surtout en ce qui concerne les vins blancs. D'autres facteurs que l'acidité déterminent s'il doit y avoir ou non fermentation malolactique. Fronachon fait remarquer qu'elle dépend des substances nutritives, de l'aération, du pH et de l'acide sulfureux. C'est un système très complexe d'interactions qui empêche de prédire à coup sûr si tel vin subira naturellement la fermentation malolactique.	8	Excès ou insuffisance d'acidité. Viscosité.
Le vin atteindra sa maturité physique durant le premier hiver par précipitation des divers tartres. Les vins ordinaires, bus quelques mois après les vendanges, peuvent être traités à l'acide métatartrique ou, mieux, par réfrigération. Le filtrage aidera tous les vins à mûrir. La clarification sans recours excessif aux agents de collage contribuera à la maturation du vin.	9	Précipitations cristallines. Trouble colloïdal. Vins minces manquant de caractère, dus à un collage excessif. Coagulation des protéines.
Les coupages ne peuvent être recommandés que lorsqu'il est possible de marier des qualités qui se complètent mutuellement. Mieux vaut abaisser la classification d'un vin inférieur si ses qualités ne peuvent qu'être diluées, plutôt que de l'améliorer en le mélangeant à un meilleur vin de classification supérieure qui prête à confusion.	10	Absence de caractère.
Afin de garantir son produit, le producteur doit livrer au consommateur du vin en bouteille dont l'étiquette porte la garantie de celui qui a mis en bouteille, comme pour les eaux minérales, les breuvages non alcoolisés et les bières.	11	Détérioration et nuages microbiens. Qualités de conservation médiocres. Perte d'authenticité.
Étiqueter et mettre en vente les bouteilles de telle sorte qu'elles n'induisent pas le consommateur en erreur.	12	Étiquetage frauduleux susceptible de provoquer une intervention des autorités.

variables d'autres alcools : amylique, isoamylique, *n*-propylique, *n*-butylique, *sec*-butylique, iso-butylique, *a*-terpinolique et, peut-être, *n*-hexylique, *n*-heptylique et *sec*-nonyliuqe.

Alcool éthylique (éthanol). La teneur du moût en sucre détermine celle du vin en alcool éthylique. Elle varie, suivant la maturité du raisin, entre 7 et 16 % du volume (plus, si on a ajouté de l'alcool). Pour les vins fins, le degré d'alcool influence qualité et longévité ; il présente donc une importance capitale. Les acides du vin se combinent lentement avec l'alcool pour produire des esters. Les propriétés antiseptiques de l'alcool éthylique contribuent à paralyser la prolifération des bactéries et les désordres des levures — maux auxquels le vin est accessible.

Les acides

Les acides donnent au vin sa fraîcheur et sa vivacité. Le manque d'acides rend le vin plat et trop d'acides, imbuvable. Les acides organiques (tartrique, malique, etc.) sont ceux qui confèrent au vin les caractéristiques gustatives perçues par la pointe de la langue : sensation due à la présence d'ions d'hydrogène. Le breuvage vinifié à partir de raisins verts aura toujours une forte acidité totale et un faible pH. En ce qui concerne les alcools de vins, trop d'acidité est un défaut, mais une acidité modérée donne du corps.

En empêchant ou en ralentissant la pullulation des bactéries aussi nuisibles que celles de la fermentation mannitique (qui transforme le vin en mauvais vinaigre) l'acidité contribue à la conservation du vin. L'acidité agit aussi sur la stabilité et la couleur : plus la teneur en acide est élevée, plus la teinte est brillante. L'acidité totale d'un vin rouge jeune et sain s'élève en moyenne à 3 ou 4 g/l exprimés en acide sulfurique. Cette teneur est inférieure d'environ 25 % à celle du moût dont le vin est issu.

Les trois principaux acides du vin sont également présents dans le raisin. Ce sont les acides tartrique, malique et citrique. Le raisin est le seul fruit des pays tempérés qui recèle de l'acide tartrique. A part ces trois-là, le vin en contient d'autres qui résultent de la fermentation.

L'acide tartrique représente toujours plus de la moitié de l'acidité totale du vin ; l'acide malique 10 à 40 %, quant à l'acide citrique, on ne le trouve qu'en très faible quantité, de même que ceux qui sont produits par la fermentation, à savoir : acides succinique, lactique et acétique ; le vin contient aussi des traces infimes d'acides butyrique, caprique, caproïque, caprylique, formique, laurique, propionique ; et aussi de l'acide carbonique dans les vins mousseux. Les acides acétique, butyrique, carbonique, formique, propionique, sont des acides dits volatils. Les chimistes établissent un parallèle entre l'acidité volatile des vins et la température de l'homme, témoins de leur état de santé : l'une et l'autre existent à l'état permanent, mais on ne constate leur existence que lorsque quelque chose tourne mal, donc qu'elles croissent ou décroissent. Les autres sont appelés acides organiques « fixes ». La somme des acidités fixes et volatiles constitue l'acidité « totale » du vin, c'est-à-dire l'acidité tirable qu'on exprime habituellement en grammes d'acide tartrique ou d'acide sulfurique.

L'*acide tartrique* : c'est le plus important des acides fixes du vin et celui qui est le plus particulièrement associé au raisin ; on ne le trouve guère ailleurs dans la nature. La quantité d'acide présente dans le raisin diminue en raison de la combustion respiratoire pendant les périodes de température élevée. Si le moût n'est pas assez acide, il est permis de lui ajouter de l'acide tartrique. Toutefois, une trop forte concentration de cet acide donnera au vin une certaine astringence et même de la dureté.

L'*acide malique* : cet acide se trouve dans bien des fruits et légumes. La teneur du raisin en acide malique au moment de la vendange présente une importance considérable pour la vinification. La respiration cellulaire pendant la maturation du fruit abaisse la concentration de l'acide malique. Sous l'influence de certaines bactéries, cet acide subit une fermentation lactique. L'âpreté des vins cuvés après un été froid et la raideur des vins jeunes sont dus à l'acide malique qui détermine presque à lui tout seul le degré de maturité du raisin.

L'*acide citrique* est présent dans les raisins de toutes variétés aussi bien mûrs que verts. *Botrytis cinerea* en augmente la quantité. Les vins faits avec des raisins en état de pourriture noble contiennent en effet jusqu'à 1 g d'acide citrique/l. La quantité normale varie de 1 à 10 g/hl, étant moins élevée dans les vins rouges que dans les blancs. La bactérie qui provoque la fermentation malolactique peut agir aussi sur l'acide citrique qui produit alors une acidité volatile. La teneur en acide citrique varie d'un vin à l'autre et peut provoquer la casse. La quantité d'acide citrique qu'il est permis d'ajouter au vin varie d'un pays à l'autre.

L'*acide carbonique* se forme par réaction d'anhydride carbonique et d'eau ($CO_2 + H_2O = H_2CO_3$). La quantité d'acide carbonique présente dans le vin dépend de la quantité d'anhydride carbonique dissous. Dans les vins plats, on en trouve généralement 0,5 g/l. L'anhydride carbonique apparaît pendant la décomposition du sucre en fermentation alcoolique, par la décomposition de l'acide malique en fermentation malolactique, et pendant la respiration de toute levure ou bactérie dans le vin. C'est la production continuelle d'anhydride carbonique pendant la fermentation qui limite la quantité d'oxygène existante dans le vin, détruisant les bactéries acétiques qui provoquent l'acidité et permettant à la levure de produire de l'éthanol plutôt que de réduire le sucre à de l'anhydride carbonique et de l'eau. Pour le Champagne, l'anhydride carbonique est délibérément emprisonné dans la bouteille, ceci en ajoutant une dose supérieure de sucre fermentable à un vin sec et en cachetant la bouteille.

L'*anhydride sulfureux* : ajouté au vin, le bioxyde de soufre (SO_2) réagit avec l'eau en formant l'anhydride sulfureux (H_2SO_3). Un équilibre chimique s'établit entre le bioxyde de soufre et ses formes hydratées :

$$SO_2 + H_2O — H_2SO_3 — H^+ + HSO_3 — 2H^+ — SO_3$$

Le bioxyde de soufre est un antiseptique utilisé pour la protection des barriques de bois. On l'ajoute soigneusement au vin, qu'il protège contre la détérioration. L'anhydride sulfureux et l'acide sorbique sont actuellement les deux seuls antiseptiques autorisés par la loi en France. L'acide sulfureux est un antioxydant et un agent réducteur.

Parmi les vertus utiles de cet acide, il faut insister sur ses qualités antiseptiques qui agissent efficacement contre les maladies microbiennes provoquées par les levures indésirables et les bactéries. Le traitement au sulfite permet d'atténuer une fermentation trop violente, mais il n'est pas sans défauts : parce qu'il s'agit d'un solvant en contact avec différents métaux et minéraux, il peut causer du casse ferrique bleu et blanc et, dans les vins blancs, du casse cuivreux (*voir* LES DÉSORDRES DU VIN, *ci-après*). On sait aussi fort bien que les vins trop soufrés conservent une odeur et un goût désagréables.

Table des acides du vin (Selon J. Ribéreau-Gayon et E. Peynaud)
Acides organiques fixes Acides provenant du raisin : tartrique, malique, citrique. Produits par la fermentation : succinique, lactique, citramalique. Présents dans les raisins atteints par l'eudémis : gluconique, glycuronique. Provenant de l'oxydation de l'acide tartrique : bioxymalique, bioxytartrique. Encore insuffisamment étudiés dans le vin : glycolique, glyoxylique, glycérique, saccharique, acides gras à longue chaînes [1]. *Acides organiques volatils* Formique, acétique — ce dernier seulement est toujours présent dans le vin. *Acides minéraux* Chlorhydrique, sulfurique, sulfureux, orthophosphorique. Produit par la fermentation : carbonique.
Nota. — 1. Les études récentes du professeur Ribéreau-Gayon nous fournissent des lumières sur les deux premiers (glycolique et glyoxylique).

En France, quand un vin doit être sulfité, le traitement peut être appliqué au moût ou bien au produit de la fermentation. Il suffit à cet effet de verser l'un ou l'autre dans une barrique où l'on a fait brûler une mèche de soufre. Cette méthode désuète manque de précision. Des déchets de soufre non consumé peuvent rester au fond du baril et le bioxyde de soufre peut aussi s'évaporer par la bonde. La théorie selon laquelle 10 g de soufre donneront à la combustion 20 g de bioxyde de soufre est inexacte : dans des conditions favorables, on n'obtiendra que 15 g d'anhydride sulfureux qui ne seront tout à fait efficaces que si on injecte le gaz par la bonde. Dans une barrique de 225 l (capacité normale de la barrique bordelaise) on ne peut faire brûler qu'une demi-mèche de soufre. On peut donc en conclure que le soufre brûlé introduira dans le vin l'équivalent de son propre volume en bioxyde de soufre.

Une solution aqueuse banale d'anhydride sulfureux arrive à saturation aux environs de 5 à 6 % et ne peut pas être plus concentrée. Évidemment une solution de sulfite de potassium, bisulfite de potassium ou métabisulfite, peut être plus concentrée. A 5 ou 6 % la solution est très corrosive pour les métaux.

Bisulfites et métabisulfites devraient être utilisés sous forme de pilules ou de cristaux. Dans tous les pays vinicoles le traitement au sulfite fait l'objet de restrictions réglementaires limitant la teneur totale en acide sulfureux. Le bioxyde de soufre total est la somme du bioxyde de soufre libre et du bioxyde de soufre composé. La quantité de bioxyde de soufre libre diminue lentement jusqu'à un niveau d'équilibre parce qu'il se combine partiellement avec des aldéhydes, des pigments et des sucres. Une part du bioxyde de soufre s'oxyde en sulfate par contact avec l'oxygène en solution. La quantité de soufre libre est proportionnelle à la quantité totale lorsqu'on arrive à l'équilibre avec les matières qui entrent en combinaison (généralement au bout d'environ quinze jours). Ensuite, on constate une diminution lente par transformation chimique, mais le rapport entre bioxydes total et libre reste constant.

Habituellement on ajoute le bioxyde de soufre au moment de la mise en bouteille pour protéger le vin contre l'oxydation et pour combiner un acétaldéhyde inactivé. A longueur d'année, le bioxyde de soufre total diminuera considérablement. Néanmoins, si le vin est bien fait et dans la bouteille, cette perte n'aura pas de grandes conséquences.

LES MÉTHODES D'ACIDIFICATION AUTORISÉES DANS DIVERS PAYS PRODUCTEURS DE VIN

Algérie : Moûts : acide tartrique sans restriction pendant la fermentation ; acide citrique, 50 g au maximum par hectolitre après la fermentation. Vin : acide tartrique, interdit ; acide citrique, maximum 50 g/hl, à condition que le moût n'ait pas déjà été acidifié à cette dose.

Allemagne : Interdiction d'augmenter la teneur en acide.

Autriche : En principe, interdiction d'augmenter la teneur en acide.

Bulgarie : Acides tartrique et citrique, seulement pour les vins mousseux.

Espagne : Acide citrique pur, maximum 1 g/l. Acide tartrique, seulement dans les moûts ou vins de faible acidité, mais pas pour d'autres usages.

États-Unis : Acides tartrique, malique et citrique, dans des limites précises.

France : Moûts : acide tartrique ; vins : acide citrique, 0,5 g/l.

Acidité volatile

La principale source de l'acidité volatile de la plupart des vins est l'acide acétique. Néanmoins, d'autres acides — formique ou sulfureux, notamment, ou n'importe quel autre acide distillable à la vapeur — y concourent. L'odeur acétique du vin peut être attribuée dans bien des cas à l'acétate d'éthyle. La présence de ces matières chimiques est normale, elle n'est contestable qu'en cas de teneur excessive. En France on exprime l'acidité volatile en équivalence d'acide sulfurique ; elle se situe entre 0,3 et 0,7 g/l, au-delà de ce dernier chiffre, le vin en est affecté. De temps à autre en France on réglemente strictement le degré d'acidité tolérable du vin livré au commerce. D'après la législation actuelle, un vin est impropre à la vente en gros à partir de 0,9 g/l, et de 1,20 g pour la vente au détail. En Californie, les limites légales en ce qui concerne l'acidité volatile sont de 1,10 g/l pour les vins blancs et de 1,20 g/l pour les vins rouges, exprimés en acide acétique.

Sucre et glycérine

Le plus important sous-produit de la fermentation qui transforme le sucre en alcool est la glycérine (ou glycérol). Elle donne de la douceur et de l'onctuosité au vin et on lui a jadis attribué à tort les « jambes » : traces verticales à l'intérieur du verre dans lequel on fait tourner du vin. On sait désormais que ces jambes sont dues à l'alcool éthylique. On trouve dans le vin des composés apparentés à la glycérine, mais en très petite quantité ; ce sont : butylène-2,3, glycol, acétylméthylcarbinol et diacétyle. Il y reste du sucre, même dans un vin complètement « sec ». (Moins de 0,2 % est à peu près la norme pour les vins secs ; aussi dilué, ce sucre n'a plus aucun goût et ne fermentera pas non plus.) Une part de ce sucre est hexose — dextrose et lévulose, ce dernier étant le plus doux — et d'autres pentoses, surtout arabinose et xylose. Il y a aussi des composés apparentés tels que rhamnose, pentosanes et des pectines.

Aldéhydes et esters

Les aldéhydes sont des substances intermédiaires entre les alcools et les acides ; ils sont formés par l'oxydation de l'alcool. Quant aux esters, ils résultent de la combinaison de l'acide et de l'alcool. Les uns et les autres jouent un rôle important dans le vin, surtout en ce qui concerne le bouquet. L'aldéhyde qui importe le plus dans le vin est l'acétaldéhyde. On y trouve en outre des traces de formaldéhyde, propionaldéhyde, cinnamaldéhyde, œnanthaldéhyde, vanilline, éthylcétone, benzaldéhydes et, probablement, furfurol et acroléine, quoique les chimistes ne soient pas parfaitement catégoriques en ce qui concerne les deux derniers. Dans certains vins doux qui ont été chauffés — tels que le Madère et des imitations de Xérès — il y a aussi une trace d'hydroxyméthylfurfurol.

On divise les esters en deux groupes : (1) les esters volatils odorigènes, habituellement dérivés de l'acide acétique ; (2) les esters neutres et acides, des acides fixes, principalement tartrique et malique. L'acétate d'éthyle est de loin l'ester qui prévaut dans le vin. Mais d'autres sont présents à un degré plus ou moins élevé ; ils dérivent chacun des acides énumérés ci-dessus, plus des acides valérique, caproïque et pélargonique.

Extrait sec et cendre

Quand on chauffe avec précaution du vin dans une éprouvette, il se dissipe par ébullition en laissant un extrait. Si on porte ce dernier à des températures élevées, on n'obtient que de la cendre qui sert au chimiste à déterminer quels étaient ces sels et en quelle quantité ils se trouvaient dans le vin. Ce sont des chlorates, phosphates, silicates et sulfates ; parmi les minéraux on compte : potassium, calcium, magnésium, sodium, fer, cuivre et, en faible quantité : bore, iode, manganèse, molybdène, vanadium, titane, zinc, entre autres. Le type et la proportion de minéraux présents dans le vin dépend largement du sol sur lequel les raisins ont mûri et des minéraux qui ont nourri la vigne, ainsi que des éléments qui sont entrés en contact avec le vin.

Azote et vitamine

Les plus importants des sous-produits azotés sont les acides aminés dont quelques-uns disparaissent pendant la fermentation ou sont utilisés par les levures pour composer des alcools supérieurs. La levure elle-même produit d'autres acides aminés. Les amino-acides courants sont : alanine, arginine, acide aspartique, cystine, acide glutamique, glycine, histidine, isoleucine, leucine, lysine, méthionine, proline, sérine, thréonine, tryptophane, tyrosine, valine et phénylalanine. Parmi les vitamines on compte l'acide ascorbique, l'amide nicotinique, les acides pantothénique, *p*-aminobenzoïque ainsi que les autres vitamines suivantes : thiamine, riboflavine, pyridoxine, biotine et inositol.

Substances phénoliques et tanin

Les constituants phénoliques du vin sont un groupe complexe comprenant tanins, anthocyanes, catéchines et autres flavonoïdes, acides cinnamiques, etc. Les tanins sont surtout prédominants dans les pépins et les pétioles, et donnent un goût astringent au vin. Ils ont des qualités antiseptiques, contribuent à détruire les bactéries nocives, et font fonction d'anti-oxydants en protégeant le vin pendant son vieillissement. Plus un vin rouge fermente sur les peaux, plus la teneur en tanin est importante et, par conséquent, plus le vin s'améliorera avec l'âge. Pendant le vieillissement, les tanins sont soumis à des réactions oxydatives complexes et à des polymérisations avec des aldéhydes, pigments et autres constituants. Ainsi l'âpreté du vin jeune s'atténue peu à peu lorsque les tanins se combinent et précipitent. Toutes ces modifications contribuent largement à forger l'aspect et le caractère d'un bon vin bien vieilli.

Les anthocyanes sont les pigments rouges de base des raisins. Ils sont situés dans les cellules de la peau. Ils se libèrent pendant la fermentation, lorsque les peaux sont détruites par l'alcool. La quantité et le type d'anthocyane diffèrent suivant chaque variété de raisin. Par conséquent, la stabilité du pigment présent dans le vin fini sera aussi variable. Pendant le vieillissement, les anthocyanes s'assemblent et se libèrent en précipitant, de sorte qu'une très vieille bouteille peut avoir un dépôt de pigment et une couleur marron orangée, dus principalement à la présence des tanins. Les vins blancs contiennent généralement moins de 350 mg/l de phénols exprimés en acide gallique, alors que les vins rouges peuvent en contenir jusqu'à 3/l.

Les désordres du vin

Le vin jeune est vivant, en ce sens qu'il s'y produit constamment des actions et réactions biochimiques. Il est sujet à des maladies et à des désordres divers. On peut les diviser en maladies causées par des désordres biologiques et maladies provoquées par l'environnement physique.

Les désordres biologiques

L'action néfaste des bactéries et des levures indésirables peut avoir lieu soit à l'abri, soit au contact de l'air. Dans bien des cas il est extrêmement difficile de désigner avec certitude le micro-organisme fauteur du désordre ; la même bactérie peut causer, semble-t-il, des maladies différentes dans des circonstances différentes. La nomenclature des maladies change aussi au cours des années. La bactérie la plus commune est le lactobacille qui fera fermenter les acides malique et citrique sous certaines conditions. Ces bacilles ne sont dangereux que s'ils appartiennent à la variété qui métabolise d'autres substances que celles sur lesquelles elles ont un effet bénéfique ; ou s'ils dégagent odeur et goût ; ou encore si le vin est d'une si faible teneur en acidité qu'il deviendra plat et se déséquilibrera à la seconde fermentation. Voici quelques-unes des maladies les plus répandues.

La *maladie de l'aigre* est un désordre assez grave qui se manifeste par la formation d'une pellicule à la surface des vins jeunes exposés à l'air. On l'appelle encore *acescence,* piqûre, ou acétification. Provoquée par la bactérie du vinaigre décrite par Pasteur sous le nom de *Mycoderma aceti,* actuellement appelée *Acetobacter*, cette maladie provoque la formation abondante d'acide acétique et d'acétate d'éthyle aux dépens de l'alcool et donne au vin un goût désagréable qui le rend impropre à la consommation. On peut aisément prévenir ce mal, comme le précédent, en évitant d'aérer excessivement le vin, surtout par un ouillage et par une surveillance attentive du chai.

Les *fleurs du vin* : cette maladie, comme la précédente, se manifeste par l'apparition d'une pellicule de levure à la surface des vins jeunes exposés à l'air. Même remède que pour les précédentes : ouillage pour éviter l'aération du vin. Cependant, on encourage ce phénomène pour le *vin jaune* du Jura français et pour donner sa caractéristique particulière au Xérès.

La *fleur* est un microbe assez bénin qui se développe rapidement sur la surface du vin jeune en formant une mince pellicule. On confond souvent ce microbe avec les *fleurs du vin,* mais étudié au microscope, on s'aperçoit immédiatement de la différence. On peut aussi prévenir ce mal en limitant l'exposition du vin à l'air.

La *tourne* : le vin devient gazeux ; odeur et goût deviennent tout à fait désagréables comme dans le cas d'une acescence prononcée. Il se trouble et perd sa couleur. Cette maladie est due à une bactérie qui attaque l'acide tartrique. On constate à l'analyse chimique une perte de tartrate, une diminution de l'acidité fixe et une augmentation de l'acidité volatile. Ces phénomènes peuvent être vérifiés par une augmentation du pH.

La *graisse* : la présence de gaz carbonique produit une légère effervescence ; le vin devient visqueux et file comme de l'huile. La teneur en sucre diminue ; les acidités totale et volatile augmentent ; il se forme un dépôt gommeux. Cette maladie se manifeste surtout dans le Champagne et particulièrement chez le *rebêche* (Champagne de basse qualité provenant du dernier pressurage et qui n'est généralement pas livré au commerce).

L'*amertume* : un dépôt se forme, le vin devient amer et très acide. Cette maladie est provoquée par une bactérie qui attaque la glycérine. L'analyse chimique révèle une diminution de la glycérine et une augmentation des acidités totale et volatile.

On estime en général que ces trois dernières maladies sont provoquées par le lactobacille ou ferment lactique.

La *fermentation mannitique* se produit quand la température de fermentation s'élève à l'excès. Alors les levures utiles meurent et sont remplacées par des bactéries qui attaquent le sucre sans le convertir en alcool éthylique. Il en résulte un vin trouble, doux-amer, parfois au goût de moisi. Au lieu de convertir le sucre du raisin en alcool éthylique et gaz carbonique, la bactérie responsable de cette maladie, appartenant généralement à la famille des *Lactobacillus,* le décompose en acides acétique et lactique, gaz carbonique et mannite ; substance sucrée, non fermentescible. Cette maladie sévit particulièrement dans les pays chauds.

Les désordres chimiques (casses)

Il y a quatre types de casse : oxydasique, protéinique, ferrique et cuivrique.

La *casse oxydasique* est due à un enzyme (polyphénoloxydase) qui rend le vin trouble et change sa couleur au contact de l'air ; les vins rouges deviennent marrons et les blancs, jaunes ; un dépôt se forme au bout de quelque temps. Cette casse se produit souvent chez les vins faits avec des raisins un peu trop mûrs ou moisis. Les vins contenant une forte proportion d'alcool ou d'acide, ou encore plus particulièrement de tanin, sont ceux qui résistent le mieux à cette dissociation. Traitement préventif : usage judicieux de l'anhydride sulfureux ; addition d'acide ascorbique en son état naturel, 0,1 à 0,2 g/l ; chauffage 70-75 °C dans une cuve à pasteurisation ; addition de bentonite et de levure.

La *casse protéinique* : les vins blancs contiennent toujours une certaine quantité de substances protéiniques. S'il y en a trop, elles réagissent avec le tanin et se coagulent. Le vin se trouble ; puis il se forme un précipité. Autrefois cette casse donnait de grands tracas aux producteurs de vin blanc doux, mais la pratique du collage à la bentonite en vient à bout : cette matière élimine les substances protéiniques de telle sorte que le vin n'a plus besoin de vieillir pour que la disparition d'une quantité suffisante de tanin obtienne le même résultat.

La *casse ferrique* : au temps jadis, la vendange n'était en contact qu'avec le bois et les pieds nus. Puis on utilisa outils et procédés qui mettent le vin en contact avec du fer et du cuivre. Ces métaux agissent sur le vin, le troublent et altèrent son goût. La casse ferrique est due à une teneur excessive en fer qui réagit avec les phosphates en présence de l'air, en déterminant l'apparition d'un nuage bleu ou noir, suivi de précipitation dans les vins qui sont aussi riches en tanin mais peu acides. Parfois on laisse cette casse suivre son cours et le vin retrouve sa clarté de lui-même. Bien des vins rouges, jeunes et plus vieux, se troubleront par dissolution de l'oxygène et exposition à l'air. Les vins blancs aussi sont sujets à une forme de la casse phosphatoferrique s'ils sont riches en fer ou en acide phosphorique et exposés à l'air au cours du soutirage, de la mise en bouteille et plus particulièrement du filtrage. Un dépôt grisâtre apparaît alors ; l'aspect trouble disparaîtra si on conserve le vin à l'abri de l'air et de la lumière. Dans ce cas aussi la meilleure mesure préventive consiste à ne pas mettre le vin en contact avec des ustensiles de métal. Comme la casse cuivrique, la casse ferrique peut être évitée par *collage bleu* consistant à précipiter le métal par l'addition d'une dose infime de ferrocyanure de potassium (bleu de Prusse). Officiellement interdit dans bien des pays ce traitement est autorisé en d'autres, tels que l'Allemagne, et récemment en France, mais sous un sévère contrôle de l'administration.

Deux composés contenant du fer peuvent former des précipitations dans le vin. L'une, casse blanche, est due au phosphate ferrique et l'autre, casse bleue, au tanate ferrique. La première apparaît si le pH du vin est inférieur à 3,6 et la teneur en fer supérieure à 10 mg/l. Dans ces conditions, le fer s'associera au phosphate qui, normalement, est présent en quantité suffisante. Le fer doit être oxydé pour arriver à l'état ferrique. La meilleure mesure préventive consiste à éviter tout contact du vin avec du fer. Mais ce n'est pas toujours une solution pratique. On peut, soit aérer le vin et laisser la casse se développer et disparaître, ou bien éliminer le métal par traitement au ferrocyanure, dans les pays où il est autorisé. Ailleurs on se servira d'agents moins dangereux (tels que le *cufex* aux États-Unis, par exemple). En outre, l'addition d'acide citrique peut agir contre cette casse en complexant le fer, ce qui clarifie le vin.

La *casse cuivrique* est généralement due au sulfure de cuivre. Elle ne se formera pas en l'absence de protéines, mais floculera rapidement en leur présence. Le gaz sulfureux et le sulfure d'hydrogène doivent être présents ; alors, un précipité cuproprotéinique se forme rapidement. L'aération et l'addition d'une faible quantité de gomme arabique empêcheront cette précipitation. Le traitement par le froid, l'élimination du métal, le filtrage et autres procédés sauveront le vin.

La casse cuivrique peut se manifester dans les vins blancs ne contenant que quelques dixièmes de milligrammes de cuivre par litre si ces vins ont été conservés pendant un certain temps à l'abri de l'air, dans un lieu chaud et éclairé. On peut y remédier par collage à la bentonite qui élimine la substance protéinique. Étant donné que la casse cuivrique ne se développe qu'à la lumière, les vins vulnérables sont souvent mis en bouteille d'un vert foncé. Comme la casse ferrique, cette dissociation relève du collage bleu dans les rares pays où il n'est pas interdit.

Exposé simultanément à l'air et à la lumière, le cuivre s'oxyde, comme le vin. On peut donc prendre des mesures préventives avant de faire passer le vin dans des récipients ou conduits de cuivre, en les lavant avec une solution d'acide tartrique à la dose de 5 g/l puis en les rinçant à l'eau pure. Mieux vaut encore éviter tout contact entre le moût ou le vin et un objet quelconque en cuivre.

Les accidents

Quand le vin a mauvait goût pour une raison accidentelle, le vinificateur est généralement en cause. Des odeurs extrinsèques affectent le vin dans une bien plus grande mesure qu'on ne le réalise en général. Des vins peuvent être gâchés si on les conserve en des endroits où ils côtoient des matières aussi fortement odorigènes que pétrole, insecticides, tabac ou même parfums.

L'odeur des tonneaux moisis, des tuyaux et outils malpropres est dangereuse, car elle peut donner mauvait goût au vin. Caves et celliers anciens dans le genre « romantique », dont les Européens sont si fiers, soulèvent de véritables problèmes à ce sujet.

Odeurs et goûts indésirables peuvent aussi être dus à l'usage en quantité excessive de certaines matières utiles au traitement du vin, telles qu'acide sorbique, anhydride sulfureux, diéthylpyrocarbonate, etc.

Les mesures a prendre contre les désordres du vin

La *propreté des chais :* les toiles d'araignées sur les murs des chais, caves et celliers abritent des bactéries nocives. Il faut les éliminer et blanchir les murs sales avec une solution de chaux additionnée de 1 % de sulfate de cuivre. Les murs moisis ou salpêtrés doivent être frottés au carbonate de soude (1 kg/10 l d'eau bouillante). Après rinçage à l'eau claire, ces murs peuvent être enduits d'une solution tiède de permanganate de potassium à la dose de 1 %. Après balayage et grattage, les sols peuvent être traités au chlorure de calcium à 1 %, puis rincés à l'eau claire.

De temps en temps, il faut curer les caves de fermentation. Pressoirs et tonneaux, qui doivent toujours être bien frottés et rincés, devraient aussi être lavés avec une solution à 10 % de carbonate de soude puis à l'eau claire quand ils présentent une moisissure grise.

Le vin : une somme totale

Si le vin relevait de la géométrie, science où le tout est constitué par la somme des parties, on pourrait, au moins théoriquement, le reproduire en laboratoire. La complication accablante d'une pareille tâche apparaît dès qu'on pense à la liste des ingrédients qui composent le vin. Actuellement, selon les professeurs Ribéreau-Gayon et Peynaud de Bordeaux, les savants ont isolé, étudié et évalué quelque 200 substances différentes composant de 97 à 98 % du vin. Quant aux autres 2 à 3 %, tout aussi importants, nous n'en n'avons aucune idée ou presque. Nous ne savons même pas combien de matières différentes ils représentent. Mieux encore, si nous mélangeons tous les ingrédients connus dans la proportion adéquate, nous n'obtenons rien qui ressemble à du vin. On conçoit donc que, selon les plus éminents œnologues, le vin doit être jugé dans le verre à boire et non dans l'éprouvette.

CHAPITRE VI

La production des alcools

Les spiritueux consommables sont des breuvages d'une forte teneur en alcool obtenus par distillation, c'est-à-dire séparation par la chaleur de l'alcool éthylique et du vin ou autres liquides contenant de l'alcool. L'alcool s'évapore à une température plus basse que l'eau. La distillation consiste à tirer parti de cette différence de volatilité. Sous une pression atmosphérique normale, l'eau bout à 100 °C et l'alcool à 78,4 °C. Quand on porte n'importe quel mélange contenant de l'alcool à une température intermédiaire entre 78,4 et 100 °C, l'alcool se convertit en vapeur. Il s'agit alors de le récupérer par des tubulures et de le condenser en le rafraîchissant. On l'aura ainsi séparé du liquide original qui peut être du vin ou bien le liquide produit par la macération dans l'eau de grains ou de fruits écrasés. Si on est parti du vin, on aura de l'alcool de vin : Armagnac, Cognac. Dans le second cas on aura une liqueur de fruits ou bien du whisky, une quelconque vodka, voire du rhum en partant de la mélasse. Certaines vodkas sont faites avec de l'orge, d'autres avec de la pomme de terre. La diversité des spiritueux est quasi illimitée : eaux-de-vie de prune, de poire, eau-de-vie de cidre, etc. Tous ces breuvages sont des produits de la distillation. L'alcool s'évapore à des températures différant selon la quantité qui en est contenue dans le liquide initial. Plus la teneur du mélange en alcool est faible, plus elle sera forte, au contraire, dans le produit de la distillation.

L'ALAMBIC

L'appareil qui sert à la distillation s'appelle alambic. Il dérive du vieil alambic des alchimistes composé des trois parties suivantes : cucurbite, chapiteau, serpentin. Actuellement, si la cucurbite, verre à panse renflée, est remplacée par un récipient de métal, les trois parties jouent toujours le même rôle. Les vapeurs d'alcool s'élèvent du récipient jusqu'au chapiteau et passent dans un conduit pour aboutir à un serpentin où elles se condensent. Le récipient est chauffé soit au-dessus d'un feu, soit par de la vapeur introduite dans une jaquette qui l'entoure ou passant dans un serpentin qui fait le tour de la partie inférieure. Pour obtenir un distillat plus pur, on procède à une deuxième ou à une troisième distillation. A sa première distillation le vin, ou la bouillie de malt qui sert à faire du whisky, donne un alcool à 25°. A la seconde, les premières et dernières vapeurs sont éliminées et on ne conserve que celles qui sont émises lorsque l'ébullition va déjà bon train. On obtient alors un alcool titrant 60 à 70°.

L'alambic, utilisé selon les usages locaux, sert à la distillation du Cognac, ainsi qu'à celle des whiskys de malt, faits en Écosse et en Irlande. Mais la plupart des spiritueux sont désormais produits par des appareils à distillation dérivant de celui que Coffey inventa en 1830. Il consiste essentiellement en deux colonnes, longues et droites, nommées rectificateur et analyseur. Chacune comporte plusieurs compartiments divisés horizontalement par des plaques en cuivre perforées et qui communiquent les unes avec les autres par des tubulures. Les colonnes sont reliées l'une à l'autre par deux tuyaux ; l'un permet à la vapeur de passer du sommet de l'analyseur au fond du rectificateur et l'autre va du fond du rectificateur au sommet de l'analyseur. La vapeur entre dans cet appareil par le fond de l'analyseur. Le distillat rafraîchi monte vers le sommet du rectificateur, passe par un serpentin, tombe au bas de la colonne et remonte dans le tuyau relié au sommet de l'analyseur. Quand elle pénètre dans la colonne de l'analyseur, la vapeur chaude rencontre des vapeurs ascendantes. Elle est alors en voie de condensation, se liquéfie et tombe de compartiment en compartiment, d'un plateau à l'autre où les vapeurs ascendantes la réchauffent et emportent son composant alcoolique. C'est ainsi qu'à la fin de l'opération l'eau restant dans l'alcool tombe au fond de l'analyseur, alors que l'alcool volatilisé s'élève jusqu'au sommet de la colonne puis passe par le conduit qui le ramène au fond du rectificateur. L'opération se répète de la même manière : la vapeur s'élève vers le sommet de la colonne en réchauffant pendant son ascension le serpentin qui introduit dans l'appareil une nouvelle quantité de mixture. Parallèlement cette vapeur se refoidit en montant. Près du sommet du rectificateur, elle atteint un plateau où elle se condense. Ce plateau est muni d'un tuyau qui emporte l'alcool vers un autre serpentin où il refroidit pour être recueilli dans un autre récipient. Ces divers serpentins situés à des emplacements déterminés séparent l'alcool de certains aldéhydes et de substance volatiles, notamment l'alcool amylique.

Dans le cas de la distillation continue, l'appareil se recharge constamment. Le système est plus économique et surtout il permet à l'opérateur de prélever l'alcool au degré qui lui convient.

Les matières premières

Pour produire des spiritueux on se sert surtout du vin qui est lui-même un liquide contenant de l'alcool. Mais d'autres substances sucrées produisent de l'alcool par fermentation. Pour les distiller il faut les diluer dans l'eau. L'amidon des céréales se convertit en sucre fermentescible qui donne de l'alcool à la fermentation.

Pour une description complète de la fermentation et de la distillation des différents spiritueux, *voir* ci-après : GIN, RHUM, COGNAC, WHISKY-SCOTCH, etc.

Les sous-produits

Les spiritueux sont composés essentiellement d'alcool éthylique dilué dans l'eau. Il s'y trouve aussi divers ingrédients secondaires et tertiaires qui donnent à chaque breuvage ses caractéristiques essentielles. La matière première contient une quantité de substances qui survivent ou se tranforment à la fermentation et à la distillation et jouent leur rôle dans le processus de vieillissement. Ces diverses réactions influent sur l'état et la proportion des ingrédients secondaires qu'on retrouve dans le spiritueux à maturité. Les alcools de vin tels que Armagnac et Cognac contiennent après fermentation des substances présentes dans le vin : sels minéraux, acides fixes, substances taniques et organiques qui ne sont pas désirables dans le processus de distillation. Le distillateur d'eau-de-vie se soucie d'éléments volatils : alcools butylique, amylique, propylique, caproïque, etc. ; aldéhydes, esters (pour le bouquet du produit fini) et acides. Ces matières volatiles passent de la fermentation à la distillation et confèrent ses caractéristiques au produit fini. Extrêmement volatils, les aldéhydes passent dans le distillat et une certaine proportion d'entre eux se combine avec l'alcool pour former des acétals. L'acétification et l'estérification, qui se produiront plus tard, apportent leur contribution à l'arôme et au goût de l'eau-de-vie. Les aldéhydes sont d'une telle complexité qu'ils peuvent provoquer une certaine amertume. Une teneur excessive n'est donc pas souhaitable. C'est un des dangers auxquels le distillateur doit veiller.

On peut classer comme suit les substances secondaires des spiritueux.

1. *Alcools gras à longue chaîne*. On les appelle aussi alcools supérieurs en ce sens qu'ils sont supérieurs à l'éthanol ou alcool éthylique. Leur présence dans les spiritueux est déterminée par la matière première. Les whiskys distillés à l'alambic contiennent un mélange d'alcools supérieurs composés d'alcools iso-amylique, iso-butylique et propylique. Les whiskys d'un degré plus élevé produits par distillation continue (autrement dit rectification) contiennent moins de ces alcools supérieurs. On y trouve l'alcool propylique et iso-butylique en plus forte proportion que l'alcool iso-amylique. L'alcool neutre de grain servant à faire le gin ne contient guère d'alcools supérieurs. La distillation de la pomme de terre produit un spiritueux qui contient de l'alcool iso-butylique.

2. *Esters*. Ces substances sont formées pendant la fermentation et résultent d'une interaction de l'alcool et des acides. Les esters dérivés des acides gras se combinent avec de petites quantités d'alcool éthylique ou amylique ; le principal ester est l'acétate d'éthyle appelé aussi ester acétique ; notons également le valérate d'éthyle et le butyrate d'éthyle, etc.

3. *Acides*. Parmi les acides, celui qui atteint la teneur le plus élevée est l'acide acétique. Cette acidité varie avec le spiritueux qui contient aussi d'autres acides parmi lesquels les plus connus sont les acides butyrique, tartrique et succinique.

4. *Aldéhydes*. Ces substances résultent de l'oxydation de l'alcool éthylique. Le furfurol, ou aldéhyde pyromucique, apparaît au début de la distillation et diminue pendant le vieillissement en baril.

5. Les spiritueux contiennent aussi des *ingrédients tertiaires* tels que huiles essentielles, terpènes et substances volatiles. Ces composants tertiaires ajoutent aux caractéristiques particulières du breuvage.

Le vieillissement

Le temps pendant lequel le spiritueux vieillit en barrique, c'est-à-dire au contact du bois, déterminera aussi en partie ses caractéristiques. L'eau-de-vie de vin arrive à son plein épanouissement au bout de 10 à 20 ans. Quant au gin, spiritueux d'un haut degré d'alcool, il n'a guère besoin de vieillir et au bout d'un an il cesse de s'améliorer. En général les ingrédients secondaires énumérés ci-dessus augmentent avec l'âge. Le furfurol présente la particularité d'augmenter dans le whisky et de diminuer dans les autres spiritueux.

On n'insistera jamais assez sur l'importance de la futaille dans le vieillissement des alcools, sans négliger non plus les autres conditions de conservation. Le Cognac vieillit dans des fûts en chêne du Limousin qui améliorent sa qualité. Le chêne blanc, roussi par le feu, confère un goût particulier et des substances taniques aux whiskys, surtout à ceux d'Amérique. En général, l'eau s'évapore peu à peu à travers le bois. Il en résulte qu'au bout d'un certain temps la teneur en alcool augmente en proportion de la baisse de quantité de liquide. Un baril de whisky américain, titrant à l'origine 58,2°, titrera, au bout de six ans, 61,4° et 62,5° à huit ans. L'évaporation du liquide à travers le fût sera plus rapide si la cave est sèche que si elle est humide. Encore faut-il que la température reste constante.

Voir aussi à ce sujet : EAU-DE-VIE, COGNAC, GIN, RHUM, VODKA, WHISKY.

CHAPITRE VII

Le vin et les mets

Accoupler, occupation toujours divertissante, devient un véritable plaisir quand il s'agit de marier les aliments et le vin : lorsqu'on assemble ainsi des saveurs complémentaires, la combinaison offre un délice gastronomique infiniment supérieur à celui que procurent séparément l'une et l'autre. Un bon repas, bien cuisiné, servi de telle sorte qu'il séduise autant l'œil que l'appétit, est à lui seul un ravissement ; ajoutons-y un verre de vin — d'un rouge chaleureux ou d'un or translucide à peine teinté de vert — et la délectation est double. Le goût et l'arôme du vin renforcent énormément la saveur des aliments. En outre, ce breuvage provoque une sensation de bien-être — euphorie — et stimule l'imagination. C'est pour cela que depuis le temps de Socrate la table du repas est le siège traditionnel des propos de bon aloi.

L'habitude contemporaine de s'asseoir d'abord devant un cocktail puis de manger à la hâte pour s'éclipser au plus vite de la salle à manger afin de regarder la télévision avait brisé cette tradition. Par bonheur nous assistons dans le monde entier à une résurrection de l'intérêt suscité par le vin. Les gens qui préparent avec soin leurs réceptions et servent au cours du repas quelques bonnes bouteilles veillent d'ordinaire à ce que l'apéritif soit du Xérès, du Champagne sec ou un vermouth sec bien glacé. Essayer d'harmoniser le vin et les aliments n'est qu'une perte de temps si les breuvages ne s'accordent pas les uns aux autres ; le vin doit donc être précédé — ou suivi — par un dérivé du raisin et non du grain. Même le meilleur vin et le meilleur alcool de grain s'accordent mal.

Nos plus anciens ancêtres savaient déjà que les vins et les mets s'accordent à merveille. Au temps jadis on faisait d'abondants repas arrosés de vins nouveaux servis en carafes remplies directement au fausset du tonneau. Au XVIIIe siècle le vin commença à mûrir en bouteilles de verre et à partir de 1800, ce ne fut plus une boisson désaltérante que l'on buvait à grands traits. Les gens aisés de la campagne continuaient à faire des repas pantagruéliques et vidaient parfois leurs trois bouteilles par jour. Mais avec la renaissance de la bonne cuisine française — au temps de Carême et des autres grands cuisiniers — on commença à préparer les menus des dîners avec finesse et à choisir attentivement les vins appropriés à chaque plat. Les convives humèrent et dégustèrent ces breuvages. Même en ce temps-là et très avant dans le cours du XIXe siècle, les repas étaient encore plantureux et duraient à n'en pas finir. On trouvait devant chaque assiette une rangée formidable de verres.

Par comparaison avec nos vigoureux aïeux de l'époque victorienne nous mangeons et recevons très parcimonieusement. Pourtant, lors d'un dîner exceptionnel, au cours duquel on sert trois vins ou plus, on peut encore créer une symphonie classique des vins. A cette fin il faut veiller à ce que la succession des plats permette de servir des vins en ordre de qualité croissante. En outre, au lieu de vider son verre, chacun doit laisser un peu de vin dans le fond du premier afin de le comparer avec le contenu du second verre, et ainsi de suite jusqu'à ce qu'arrive la meilleure bouteille avec le fromage.

Le repas peut commencer avec un vin blanc sec, continuer avec un rouge, puis avec un rouge plus vieux ou plus fin, par exemple dans l'ordre suivant : un Chablis puis un Bordeaux rouge suivi d'un Bordeaux rouge plus vieux ou de plus grand cru. Selon les mets qui sont servis on peut boire successivement trois vins rouges en commençant toujours par le plus jeune pour monter vers le plus fin et souvent le plus vieux. En France, le fromage précède toujours le dessert et c'est avec le fromage que cesse le vin rouge. Alors, si l'amphitryon dispose d'un vin de dessert sucré, ce dernier apportera un contre-point à la douceur du dessert. Le Champagne (demi-sec) et le Vouvray conviennent bien aux fruits ; le Sauternes ou le Barsac s'accordent avec les gâteaux et les fruits les plus sucrés.

Offrir du vin est le geste d'hospitalité le plus charmant ; l'hôte tire de sa réserve le meilleur qu'il possède. Qu'il serve quatre vins ou un seul, le geste est le même. Un vin unique choisi pour se marier avec le plat de résistance obtiendra le plus de succès s'il convient aussi à l'entrée. Par exemple, s'il s'agit d'un Bordeaux, le repas pourrait commencer avec un soufflé au fromage. Considérons toutefois qu'il est tout aussi facile d'offrir une bouteille de vin blanc et une de rouge que d'en offrir deux de rouge. En France, où presque tout le monde boit quotidiennement du vin, la plupart des ménages se contentent d'une seule boisson ordinaire pour les repas courants. Mais le dimanche, les jours de fête, les baptêmes, communions et autres grandes occasions, se manifestent toujours sur la table du Français... parce qu'il y apparaît alors une bouteille exceptionnelle de bon vin. On mangera de la volaille, du poisson ou une viande qui seront propres à mettre en valeur les qualités particulières de ce vin.

Les combinaisons de vins et de mets

Selon la tradition certains vins accompagnent certains plats — le Chablis et l'huître s'accordent comme le pain et le beurre — et les pédants (qui sont hélas nombreux ! car il n'est guère de sujet sur lequel ceux qui en savent le moins soient aussi fastidieux) ont tendance à être extrêmement tyranniques à ce sujet. La plupart des règles sont pourtant bonnes parce qu'elles dérivent de plusieurs siècles d'expérience. Voici les principales : les vins blancs secs sont plus agréables avant les rouges ; les vins les plus fins ont meilleur goût quand ils sont servis après des vins moins fins de même type ; les vins doux ne sont pas bons du tout avec la viande — voilà longtemps qu'on sait tout cela. En outre, on constate que de nombreux vins sont étroitement apparentés à certains mets : avec les fameux saucissons de Lyon, rien ne vaut un jeune Beaujolais fruité produit dans la région ; dans la vallée de la Loire on arrose les rillettes de Tours avec les vins du pays : Sancerre, Vouvray ou Pouilly-Fumé.

Celui qui aime en faire à sa tête agira sagement en observant ces règles même si elles lui sont présentées par des gens pour qui le vin est un snobisme. Il aura grand avantage à les comparer avec les expériences qu'il pourrait être amené à faire en suivant ses propres caprices.

Quand on choisit ses vins pour soi-même, la considération la plus évidente est la suivante : la combinaison doit plaire à celui qui mange et boit ; un rosé léger qui s'accorde tellement bien avec le sandwich de midi sera une hérésie avec un plat fin du dîner. L'auteur de ce livre se rappelle avoir bu par une nuit torride aux Antilles un fin Bordeaux suivi par un grand Bourgogne rouge ; quoique les mets leur convinssent, la température ambiante ne leur valait rien. (Les règles ne sont utiles qu'à ceux qui savent les enfreindre et, sous les tropiques, un vin rosé ou blanc servi frappé est le plus agréable quel que soit le menu.) A l'inverse, un rosé frais, très plaisant par une chaude journée dans le sud de la France, ne conviendra pas du tout à un solide bifteck par une froide soirée d'hiver.

Certains mets détonnent de manière catastrophique avec certains vins, par exemple un curry chaud tuera un Bordeaux ; mais un vin blanc au goût nettement prononcé (un Gewürztraminer, notamment) supportera fort bien n'importe quel plat épicé. Quant aux anchois, aux kippers, aux sauces vinaigrées, ils sont mortels pour tous les vins et ne devraient jamais être servis dans un repas savamment arrosé.

TYPES DE VINS

Il est des vins qui peuvent se boire sans manger ou rien qu'avec un biscuit ; ce sont des vins très doux : Sauternes, Barsac ; en Allemagne, Beerenauslesen, Trockenbeerenauslesen Auslesen, vins Santo, Moscato et les vins de la dernière vendange, ainsi que les vins de liqueur : Xérès, Porto, Madère. Pourtant les vins naturels ne peuvent vraiment être appréciés qu'en harmonie avec un aliment. Un bon plat a besoin du vin pour le révéler et on gâche une bouteille si elle accompagne une succession discordante de saveurs.

VINS DE TABLE

Ce sont les vins que nous buvons aux repas. Ils titrent entre 9 et 14° et peuvent être rouges, rosés ou blancs, secs ou doux, légers ou corsés.

Les *vins blancs secs* s'associent traditionnellement avec les poissons et les fruits de mer. Le Chablis, comme nous l'avons déjà dit, se marie parfaitement avec l'huître, mais il n'y a pas que lui : Champagne, Muscadet, Graves, et autres vins blancs secs conviennent également. Le Bourgogne blanc aussi est excellent avec les crevettes, homards, langoustes et il s'harmonise en outre avec le jambon, le veau ou le poulet préparés avec une sauce au vin blanc. Le Montrachet est magnifique avec la sole au court-bouillon. Un Hermitage blanc sec est doté d'un goût si caractéristique qu'il peut s'équilibrer avec le curry et n'importe quel plat très épicé. En règle générale, rappelons-nous que les vins blancs secs sont légers et de goût délicat ; ils ne s'assortissent qu'aux mets présentant les mêmes qualités. Les plats lourds et riches dominent, voire écrasent, ces vins.

Les vins blancs doux sont délicieux avec les fruits sucrés et les gâteaux, nous le savons. Mais, pris au début du repas, leur goût sucré paralyse les papilles gustatives et coupe l'appétit. A la fin du repas, au contraire, cette même qualité est précisément très agréable et celle qu'il faut pour susciter une impression de bien-être et de satisfaction. Néanmoins, on servait couramment des Sauternes avec le poisson au début de notre siècle. De nos jours encore, certains Bordelais considèrent que ces vins conviennent aux poissons à goût prononcé comme le saumon, et le Sauternes peut aussi admirablement agrémenter un bon foie gras.

Les vins rouges sont presque exclusivement secs. (Il existe quelques vins rouges doux, mais ils sont à peu près dans la même catégorie que les vins rouges mousseux ; quoiqu'ils plaisent à certains, ils manquent généralement de distinction ; leur goût sucré les rend incompatibles avec les aliments). Partout au monde on consomme plus de vin rouge que de blanc. En Europe occidentale, îles Britanniques exceptées, le *vin ordinaire* est la boisson quotidienne du travailleur, et c'est un rouge.

Ce qu'il y a de plus marquant dans les vins rouges, c'est leur extrême variété : les vins blancs sont secs ou doux, pétillants ou non ; quant aux vins rouges, ils vont du vin léger au robuste vin très corsé ; chacun possède un goût caractéristique et des complexités résultant des qualités du sol et de la variété du raisin. Une règle s'impose à l'évidence : plus le mets est lourd, plus le vin doit être fort. Volailles, veau et autres viandes légères sont parfaitement arrosés par des vins rouges — et aussi par des vins blancs secs. Mais une viande plus riche, surtout saignante, exige un compagnon plus cordial ; les pâtés, les viandes en sauce et le gibier veulent des vins qui ont le plus de corps.

Le mets qui s'harmonise le mieux avec le vin, c'est le fromage ; mais il ne doit pas être trop fort, surtout avec un vin vieux et délicat. En raison de cette affinité on sert le vin le plus fin à la fin du repas avec le dernier plat qui précède le dessert : le fromage qui doit toujours être d'un goût discret.

Les vins mousseux

La plupart des vins mousseux sont blancs, très rarement rouges ; ils vont du sec au doux et sont parfois trop doux. Les amateurs de vin expérimentés dédaignent les vins rouges mousseux et doux parce qu'ils sont médiocres pour la plupart et même les meilleurs n'ont pas la distinction des vins blancs mousseux et doux. En outre, ils ne conviennent à aucun plat. D'autre part, dans certains pays, surtout en Italie, on en produit depuis des siècles et les Italiens semblent en être satisfaits.

Le Champagne est évidemment de loin et de beaucoup le meilleur vin blanc mousseux.

Bien des vins blancs mousseux portent ce nom ; mais seul le vin français, fait selon la véritable méthode champenoise, en Champagne, a droit à ce titre.

Il n'est d'ailleurs guère besoin d'être expert pour distinguer l'authentique de l'imitation dès la première gorgée. Pourtant bien des vins blancs mousseux sont très agréables ; comme le Champagne, ils peuvent être secs, demi-secs ou doux. Certains considèrent le Champagne comme le seul vin digne d'être bu ; il est certes délicieux en fin de soirée ; avant le repas s'il est sec ; avec le dessert (fruit ou pâtisserie), s'il est assez doux. Ses partisans les plus enthousiastes ne boivent rien d'autre pendant tout le repas ; ce n'est pas à recommander. Pourtant il n'y a guère de raisons valables pour ne pas le faire à condition toutefois de ne pas boire du *brut* avec les desserts sucrés, ni du doux avec des plats corsés ; ceux qui ont goûté d'autres vins à table et qui, par comparaison, préfèrent le Champagne n'ont aucune raison de s'en priver. En général on estime pourtant que le Champagne n'a pas assez de corps et trop de mousse pour s'harmoniser avec les aliments.

Mais ne doutons pas que lorsqu'il s'agit de baptiser un navire ou de trinquer au Nouvel An ou encore à la mariée, le Champagne, avec sa mousse, atteint au superlatif.

Vins de liqueur

Ces vins peuvent être blancs ou rouges, secs ou doux. Le Xérès sec (Fino ou Manzanilla) est considéré en général comme un apéritif parfait, surtout avant un repas au cours duquel on servira des vins fins. Bien des gens jugent le Porto incomparable après dîner. Pourtant certains préfèrent le Xérès ou le Madère doux.

Il existe aussi divers vins de liqueur qui ont moins de prestige mais sont fort appréciés dans leur propre pays : le Moscato italien, par exemple, et le *vin doux naturel* de Banyuls.

Autant savoir, cependant, que dans certaines parties du monde, hors d'Europe, on élabore des vins de liqueur à la fois trop sucrés et trop forts ; en réalité ce ne sont que des succédanés à bon marché de spiritueux. Personne ne pensera évidemment à boire ces vins de table — sauf, peut-être, un Xérès sec avec le potage.

Quelques règles élémentaires

Il est permis d'expérimenter à l'infini combinaisons et permutations de mets et de vins — et chacun peut faire une découverte pour son propre compte dans ce domaine. Néanmoins, pour éviter de gâcher un bon vin par erreur, mieux vaut observer les règles élémentaires que voici :

Les vins blancs secs ont meilleur goût avant les rouges ; les vins rouges sont d'autant meilleurs qu'ils sont servis après d'autres du même type mais de qualité moindre. Dans le second cas il est élégant — et très agréable — de servir plus d'un vin rouge avec un bon repas. En l'occurrence il est préférable de s'en tenir à une seule région : de servir par exemple un Bordeaux après un autre Bordeaux ou un Bourgogne après un autre Bourgogne. Nous conseillons aussi de servir les vins à l'inverse de leur âge : le plus jeune le premier. Quand les vins ont le même âge, le plus fin viendra en dernier.

Certains mets, certaines saveurs ne se marient avec aucun vin. Nous avons déjà cité le vinaigre et les hors-d'œuvres de poisson (anchois, kippers, etc.) au vinaigre. Nous y ajouterons l'oignon et l'ail qui rendent le palais réfractaire au vin. Les épices, le curry, la moutarde ont aussi des effets regrettables sauf si le vin a un goût assez prononcé pour dominer celui des mets.

Si l'on évite ces faux pas, mieux vaut ne pas se faire trop de souci au sujet de ce que l'on peut boire avec ceci ou cela (à moins, évidemment, que l'on soit en train de préparer une réception). Il existe des affinités naturelles entre les vins et les aliments et, bien plus souvent qu'on ne le croirait aussi, leur mariage donne d'heureux résultats.

CHAPITRE VIII

Servir le vin

Les vins blancs sont servis frais et les rouges à la température de la pièce dans laquelle ils sont bus. Encore faut-il les traiter avec le plus grand soin avant de les poser sur la table.

Dans la cave. Tout d'abord, si vous avez acheté un vin rouge vieux, un dépôt sera probablement formé. Alors posez la bouteille verticalement et laissez-la ainsi pendant un jour ou deux avant de la coucher dans le casier. De cette manière, le dépôt qui a été agité pendant le déplacement n'atteindra pas le goulot. Ensuite, couchez la bouteille à plat dans le casier, l'étiquette au-dessus pour pouvoir la lire d'un coup d'œil sans remuer la bouteille. Inutile de préciser, évidemment, que ces règles s'appliquent à tous les vins, rouges et blancs. Avant de transférer un vin rouge vieux de la cave à la table, il faut d'abord laisser la bouteille quelques heures dans la position verticale pour que le dépôt tombe au fond.

Demi-bouteilles et magnums. Acheter le vin par demi-bouteilles est une bonne affaire quand on veut y goûter ou lorsque, par habitude, on n'en consomme qu'une petite quantité à chaque fois ; mais les demi-bouteilles ne conviennent qu'aux vins jeunes et moyens, car les grands vins vieillissent prématurément dans les petits flacons et s'épanouissent avec plus de bonheur dans les magnums. La maturation s'effectue en effet plus lentement dans les très grosses bouteilles ; elles garantissent donc aux grands vins une maturation complète qui les poussera jusqu'au maximum de leur qualité — un vin vieilli trop vite n'arrive jamais aux plus hauts sommets.

Age et température. Les vins blancs doivent généralement être bus jeunes ; au bout de cinq ans ils perdront probablement leur fraîcheur et commenceront à s'oxyder. Pourtant un bon Bourgogne blanc peut vivre quelques années de plus. (Qu'est-ce qu'un vin jeune ? Un Bordeaux de bon cru et de bonne année ne dépasse pas quatre ans. Un Bourgogne rouge, moins de deux ans et demi).

Les vins blancs doivent être rafraîchis ; plus ils sont doux, plus ils doivent être servis frais. Ainsi, les grands Sauternes sont délicieux absolument glacés. Mais c'est une exception ; en général glacer est une erreur car le froid excessif oblitère goût et caractéristiques. Mieux vaut par exemple boire un Bourgogne blanc de qualité pas assez frais que trop froid. La plupart des gens mettent désormais leur vin dans le réfrigérateur. Dans ce cas une ou deux heures suffisent car la température idéale de consommation se situe entre cinq et dix degrés pour les vins blancs secs. Cependant l'usage du sceau à glace serait un meilleur moyen de rafraîchir car l'opération est plus rapide : vingt minutes suffisent. Le temps nécessaire pour frapper ainsi le vin dépend évidemment de la température à laquelle se trouvait la bouteille auparavant. Si vous n'avez pas de sceau à glace, mettez la bouteille en position inclinée dans un grand saladier plein de glace, pilée ou en cubes, baignant dans un peu d'eau. Ne débouchez la bouteille qu'au moment de servir.

Les vins rosés doivent être frappés comme les blancs.

Les vins rouges qui sont jeunes et corsés (les grands Médoc jeunes, par exemple) peuvent être débouchés quelques heures avant le repas. Les très jeunes gagneront à être débouchés la veille. Ce temps supplémentaire de respiration les aidera à acquérir maturité et mœlleux. En ce qui concerne le Beaujolais l'extrême jeunesse est un avantage : son cycle s'étend entre six mois et trois ans. Comme le vin blanc, on doit le déboucher au moment de le servir. Quoiqu'il ne doive pas être frappé dans les pays froids, mieux vaut le servir frais que chaud dans les pays tropicaux ou équatoriaux. Entre cinq et quinze ans d'âge le Bordeaux doit être débouché environ deux heures avant d'être bu ; mais un vin très vieux n'a pas besoin d'être aéré aussi longtemps ; s'il est vraiment très vieux et délicat (millésime antérieur à 1970), décantez-le à table ; même dans ce cas il peut faner et mourir un peu entre le premier et le second verre — alors que le vin rouge jeune s'améliorera et s'épanouira dans le verre.

Le décantage. La bouteille qui contient un dépôt de moins d'un quart de centimètre doit être manipulée avec le plus grand soin. Il faut d'abord la maintenir fermement dans la position où on l'a prise et en verser le contenu d'un mouvement continu dans une carafe propre en cristal, jusqu'au moment où le dépôt commence à monter au goulot ; alors, on cesse immédiatement. Afin de surveiller le dépôt, opérez en tenant la bouteille entre une source de lumière et vos yeux. Étant donné que le processus de décantage permet au vin de respirer, il est inutile de laisser la carafe débouchée. Cela dit, tous les vins rouges doivent être apportés à la salle à manger quelques heures avant le repas afin qu'il en prennent la température. Ils sont servis *chambrés*. Les réchauffer brusquement en les plaçant devant un feu ou en plongeant la bouteille dans l'eau chaude leur fait du mal. Le panier dans lequel on couche la bouteille évite d'agiter le dépôt chaque fois que l'on sert ; dans les restaurants, bien des garçons servent le vin par saccades et agitent ces paniers inconsidérément ; alors ce ne sont plus que des objets ajoutés sans raison au rituel souvent inintelligible du vin. Les vins rouges devraient être bus à 17 ou 18°.

Déboucher la bouteille

Avant de déboucher une bouteille de vin, coupez la capsule ou la cire avec la pointe d'un couteau, enlevez ensuite avec un linge propre la moisissure qui se forme habituellement sur le bouchon. Alors seulement, débouchez. Puis essuyez soigneusement la lèvre du goulot à l'intérieur.

Le tire-bouchon. Ne vous encombrez pas d'un engin compliqué avec roulette, levier et Dieu sait quoi ! Il ne ferait aucun mal aux vins jeunes mais il présente un danger pour les vins vieux dont le bouchon fragile risque de se pulvériser. Le meilleur, c'est le tire-bouchon en T ; choisissez-le avec une longue spirale car on utilise des bouchons longs pour les grands vins. La partie métallique qui pénètre dans le liège ne doit pas avoir la forme d'une lame mais celle d'une pointe parce que la lame découpe trop le bouchon. Toutefois s'il arrive que le bouchon se brise ou qu'avec l'âge, il soit devenu poudreux, on peut encore l'extraire par un mouvement de levier. Dans ce cas, couchez la bouteille pour que le vin presse sur le bouchon, et introduisez le tire-bouchon obliquement et tournez lentement ; ensuite vous exercez un mouvement de levier pour soulever l'extrémité la plus éloignée du bouchon vers le haut de la bouteille. On trouve parfois des bouchons défectueux. Il arrive qu'une veine, invisible à l'état neuf, se détériore et moisisse avec l'âge. Le vigneron ou le négociant n'y sont pour rien, cet accident peut arriver avec les meilleurs vins. Dans ce cas le vin aura un goût et une odeur désagréables : il sentira le bouchon. Au restaurant, le sommelier doit sentir le bouchon et vous l'apporter. Si le bon usage exige qu'on verse d'abord un peu de vin dans le verre du maître de maison, c'est pour qu'il s'assure avant de l'offrir à ses invités que son vin n'a pas le goût du bouchon. Parfois le mal est si léger que seul le premier verre s'en ressent ; quand vous débouchez le vin chez vous et qu'il présente un défaut, il vaut mieux mettre la bouteille de côté et voir plus tard si vous pourrez l'utiliser. Mais, au restaurant, on doit évidemment la renvoyer sur-le-champ.

VERSER LE VIN

Lors d'une réception intime, pour quatre ou cinq personnes, chez soi, on pose la bouteille sur la table devant le maître de maison et c'est lui qui verse à boire. S'il y a plus de monde autour de la table, on place une seconde bouteille à portée de la maîtresse de maison qui servira ceux qui sont assis le plus près d'elle. Quand c'est un domestique qui fait le service, il sert les dames d'abord en commençant par celle qui est assise à la droite du maître de maison ; il tourne ensuite autour de la table dans le sens des aiguilles d'une montre ; puis il sert les hommes en commençant par celui qui est à droite de la maîtresse de maison. A sa propre table, le maître de maison ne goûte pas le vin d'abord ; puisqu'il a ouvert la bouteille lui-même, il sait que ce vin ne sent pas le bouchon. En ce qui concerne l'ordre dans lequel les vins doivent être servis, voir chapitre VII.

Les verres. Choisissez des verres de cristal uni pour faire ressortir la couleur chaleureuse du vin. Des verres trop petits nuisent aux grands vins auxquels il faut assez de place pour qu'on les fasse tourner dedans et pour qu'ils « respirent » en exhalant leur bouquet. Les meilleurs verres sont grands, en forme de tulipes, clairs et minces ; la coupe proprement dite doit avoir la taille d'une pomme ou d'une orange. Il en existe de différentes formes pour différents vins. Mais la tulipe sied à tous, y compris au Champagne — dans la « coupe à Champagne » pas assez profonde, les bulles qui résultent de grands soins se dissiperont trop vite et le vin perdra une partie de son goût. (Cela nous amène à dire que le fouet à Champagne est un instrument malfaisant qui sert tout simplement à détruire une des caractéristiques distinctives du Champagne, résultant d'années de travail. Ceux auxquels les bulles sont désagréables feraient mieux d'acheter un Champagne de vieux millésime ou du Blanc de Blancs non mousseux.)

L'eau-de-vie, servie avec le café, ne doit pas être versée dans un petit verre à liqueur mais dans un ballon. Cela permet de réchauffer le verre dans la paume de la main et de faire tourner l'eau-de-vie à l'intérieur. Servez de préférence de bons Cognac, Armagnac, voire des marcs. En ce qui concerne les alcools blancs (eaux-de-vie de fruits telles que framboise, mirabelle, quetsch, kirsch), rafraîchissez d'abord le verre en y faisant tourbillonner un morceau de glace ; la fraîcheur donne du moelleux aux breuvages fortement alcoolisés.

Le Porto. En France, où le goût pour le Porto augmente chaque année, il se sert comme apéritif. Tandis qu'en Angleterre on le sert habituellement à la fin du repas, avant ou avec le café. Souvent les dames quittent la salle à manger à ce moment-là et les hommes jouissent entre eux de leur vin. Ils se passent la carafe dans le sens des aiguilles d'une montre.

Le tabac. En Angleterre, il est de mauvais ton de fumer quand on boit du bon vin. Les Français sont moins stricts et bien des vignerons fument en buvant du vin entre les repas, mais, heureusement, ils n'ont jamais adopté l'habitude américaine de fumer entre les plats.

CHAPITRE IX

Comment se constituer une cave

L'expression cave à vin évoque le temps où les hommes avaient de la place pour conserver leur Porto bouché et leur Bordeaux de l'ère préphylloxérienne ou bien l'époque où leurs pères vidaient trois bouteilles par jour et souffraient de la goutte. Une maison de campagne aux vastes caves est indiscutablement une bonne part de patrimoine ; mais même le propriétaire d'un deux-pièces-cuisine peut imiter le professeur Saintsbury et « s'accommoder d'un confort très inférieur », pourvu qu'il fasse preuve d'ingéniosité.

La cave à vin idéale devrait être spacieuse, aérée, sèche, à l'abri de la lumière et des vibrations ; sa température constante ne devrait pas dépasser 13°C. Cet idéal n'est évidemment pas souvent réalisable et, même en France, quelques caves seulement s'en approchent. Alors, faute de mieux, il faut ménager une resserre répondant au plus grand nombre possible de ces conditions. Il sera très utile de comprendre pourquoi elles sont idéales et dans quelle mesure elles ont de l'influence sur le vin.

« Un endroit spacieux, aéré, sec et d'une fraîcheur constante. » Le manque de place signifie évidemment que vous serez réduit à ne conserver qu'une quantité limitée de vin. Une bonne ventilation vous épargnera une atmosphère « renfermée » qui au bout de plusieurs années pénétrerait dans la bouteille à travers le bouchon, ce qui donnerait au vin goût et odeur de moisi. Une certaine humidité est même nécessaire ; elle empêche les bouchons de se dessécher prématurément. Il faut aussi un bon sol ; on l'obtient en couvrant parquet ou carrelage avec du gravillon : couche épaisse de deux à trois centimètres ; il faudra l'arroser légèrement de manière régulière ; ce gravier conservera l'humidité. Un excès d'humidité nuit à l'étiquette mais rarement au vin. Les gens assez fortunés pour disposer d'une vaste cave seraient avisés de faire changer les bouchons de leurs bouteilles tous les vingt-cinq à cinquante ans. On ne peut espérer une longévité plus élevée même du meilleur bouchon.

« A l'abri de la lumière et des vibrations. » Certaines maladies dont souffre le vin — telles que la casse protéique : précipité provoqué par un excès de protéine — ne se manifestent qu'à la lumière. Une forte luminosité peut aussi « rôtir » le vin, autrement dit le madériser ou l'oxyder, ce qui le rend prématurément plat, trouble et brunâtre comme le vin de Madère. Les vibrations qui agitent le vin le vieillissent aussi prématurément. Une maison située près d'une ligne de chemin de fer est donc mal appropriée à la constitution d'une cave. Pourtant, si les vibrations ne sont pas trop fréquentes ni trop violentes, le vin, conservé aussi près que possible du niveau de la terre, n'en souffrira pas excessivement.

« Une température constante de 13 °C » voilà le pire Croquemitaine de l'encaveur présomptif. Cependant le vin ne sera pas perdu même si la température s'élève jusqu'à 24 °C, à condition que l'élévation soit progressive ; il vieillira plus vite, c'est tout. Les vins vieux en particulier sont fragiles et ne se conserveront pas longtemps au-dessus de 16 °C. Entre 10 et 14 °C, les vins vieillissent normalement. S'ils peuvent en général s'adapter à des élévations presque imperceptibles de température, des variations brusques ne tarderont pas à les abîmer. Les conserver près d'une conduite d'eau chaude est une hérésie. Les logements où la température est élevée durant la journée et s'abaisse brusquement pendant la nuit font de mauvais celliers. En général, les vins rouges sont moins affectés que les blancs par la chaleur. Il faudra donc poser les blancs le plus près possible du sol dans la partie la plus fraîche de la resserre.

Il tombe sous le sens qu'une « cave à vin » ne doit pas forcément être en sous-sol. Avec un rien d'ingéniosité il est souvent possible d'aménager un débarras ou un placard pour conserver du vin à consommer assez rapidement. Dans ce cas-là on ne pourra pas acheter des grands vins dès leur enfance — époque où les prix sont plus avantageux — et les conserver jusqu'à ce qu'ils aient atteint l'âge de la pleine maturité ; pourtant divers bons vins peuvent être gardés à portée de la main à tout instant. Un buffet de vestibule, par exemple, ou un espace réduit sous un escalier, font aussi l'affaire. Vous pouvez alors commencer à tirer des plans sur ce que vous allez y mettre.

Sachons d'abord que tous les vins naturels — c'est-à-dire tous ceux qui ne sont pas additionnés d'alcool — doivent être conservés bouteille couchée pour que le vin mouille le bouchon et l'empêche de se ratatiner, ce qui permettrait à l'air d'entrer et détruirait le vin. Xérès, Porto, spiritueux et liqueurs peuvent être conservés bouteille debout car leur forte teneur en alcool les préservera. Cependant, étant donné que ces breuvages ne s'améliorent pas en bouteille, il est inutile d'en conserver une grande quantité, sauf en ce qui concerne le Porto et le Madère de grande année. Puisque vous voudrez probablement mettre vins et spiritueux dans le même cellier, il vous faudra des étagères pour poser les alcools debout et des casiers pour coucher vos bouteilles de vin.

On trouve des casiers de métal ou de bois à des prix raisonnables et qui conviennent parfaitement. Faute de mieux de petites caisses ou des cartons d'épicerie, couchés sur le côté, permettent des agencements satisfaisants. On peut aussi se faire faire des casiers sur mesure. Ils doivent être solides et avoir des formes appropriées en losanges pour qu'en retirant une bouteille on ne fasse pas tomber les autres. On peut aussi se servir de buses en terre cuite d'un diamètre convenable. Elles présenteront l'avantage de protéger les bouteilles contre les brusques variations de température. Inutile de choisir un casier trop grand. S'il offre une façade de 50 cm sur 50 cm il contiendra presque une caisse de vin. Sauf si vous tenez à stocker de grandes quantités de vin, ne couchez pas vos bouteilles les unes sur les autres. Le vin se conserve mieux quand il n'est pas remué. Chercher une bouteille sous ou derrière les autres agace le caviste et exaspère le vin.

Une fois que vous avez installé vos casiers, il ne vous manque pas grand-chose. Le thermomètre est le plus utile. Il vous faudra aussi des étiquettes et un livre de cave.

L'intérêt du thermomètre saute aux yeux. Il indique au premier coup d'œil si la température de votre cellier est propice à la conservation du vin. Les étiquettes doivent être en papier fort, évidemment, et attachées au goulot de la bouteille ; elles permettront de choisir sans remuer toutes les bouteilles. Enfin le livre de cave. Si vous ne conservez que six bouteilles, voire au maximum une caisse, cet accessoire peut paraître prétentieux. Mais il sera utile et, plus tard, en le feuilletant, il éveillera des souvenirs agréables. Quel que soit l'aspect de votre livre de cave, vous devrez y noter : le nom et le millésime du vin, la quantité achetée, la date de l'achat, le nom du fournisseur, celui du négociant qui le mit en bouteille et le prix que vous l'avez payé. Sur l'autre côté de la page vous ménagerez un espace pour inscrire la date de consommation et vos commentaires. Il est bon de consacrer une page entière à chaque vin, surtout quand on en achète plusieurs bouteilles.

La constitution de la cave donne du plaisir si on veut choisir une diversité bien équilibrée permettant de servir un vin approprié aux circonstances et aux mets. Cette variété implique des vins de catégorie, qualité et prix divers.

Dans les éditions antérieures à cette encyclopédie, j'avais établi une liste arbitraire pour constituer un fond de cave de trente-six bouteilles. Les consommateurs devenant plus sophistiqués de par le monde, les vins meilleurs qu'autrefois dans la plupart des pays et les goûts différents selon le marché et les pays, le consommateur doit se fier davantage au conseil de son négociant en vins et au plaisir de son palais.

CHAPITRE X

La valeur du vin

Acheter du vin est une bonne affaire à condition de trouver à son juste prix la bouteille qui convient à un but précis. A 25 francs, un faux Bourgogne est une mauvaise affaire ; mais 60 francs n'est pas un prix déraisonnable pour un authentique Richebourg. Un vin dont l'appellation d'origine désigne une vaste région — elle-même subdivisée en plusieurs appellations plus limitées et plus prisées — et portant l'étiquette d'un négociant qui procède à des coupages pour fournir une qualité et un goût constants d'année en année pourra être offert au même prix qu'un Bordeaux de cru classé. Même si ce négociant est digne de confiance, acheter un tel vin à ce prix-là est une mauvaise affaire ; il n'en irait pas de même s'il était vendu quelques dizaines de francs moins cher. Dans tous les cas, le facteur le plus important à considérer est le goût de l'acheteur : quelles que soient ses qualités et sa valeur, aucun vin n'est une bonne affaire s'il ne plaît pas et s'il ne se marie pas avec le plat qu'on entend déguster.

Pour l'amateur, la meilleure manière de sélectionner le vin qu'il préfère et d'apprendre lequel accompagne le mieux tel ou tel plat consiste à consulter un fournisseur honnête, qui connaît son affaire et qui est doué des qualités qui font le dégustateur. En Angleterre, plus que partout ailleurs, ainsi qu'en Amérique, il existe de vieilles maisons dans la grande tradition du commerce des vins, et ne serait-ce qu'une seule de celles-ci c'est déjà une mine d'informations et de conseils.

En France on achète directement chez le vigneron... et souvent chez l'épicier du coin. Même dans ce pays il n'est pas toujours facile, quand on habite une province vinicole, de se procurer du vin d'une autre région. Le négociant ou l'épicier d'un village de Bourgogne ne stocke guère que les produits locaux et ne fournira vraisemblablement pas du Bordeaux. Néanmoins, l'usage du vin —quel que soit le chauvinisme dont il s'assortit — fait partie de l'existence quotidienne. Le client est maintenant servi comme il le mérite, et le nombre de négociants en vins au fait de leur métier est en constante augmentation.

LE VIN DU FOYER

On achète du vin pour le boire un ou deux mois plus tard, ou bien pour le conserver en vue d'un usage ultérieur. Autrefois, quand on menait une vie stable et que l'on vivait dans des maisons bâties sur de vastes caves, la coutume voulait que l'on achetât un vin de bonne année aussitôt que possible et à un bon prix.

On le conservait en cave jusqu'à sa maturation. Lorsqu'il arrivait à son point de perfection le prix s'était élevé dans des proportions considérables. L'acheteur — ou le fils qui lui succédait — se félicitait de sa prévoyance. De nos jours on tend à vivre l'instant présent plutôt qu'à faire des projets d'avenir. On vit aussi dans des appartements où la place manque. On ne conserve donc plus guère de vin. La petite quantité qui peut être stockée dans un buffet moderne doit donc être choisie avec encore plus de soin. Le lecteur trouvera néanmoins au chapitre suivant des conseils sur la manière de se constituer une cave.

LES VINS A BAS PRIX

Bien des vins achetés pour la consommation courante appartiendront au type régional et seront probablement dénués de prétention. Mais il y a toute raison de croire qu'ils seront sains, d'un goût agréable et qu'ils ne démentiront pas ce que promet l'étiquette. Certaines étiquettes offrent de meilleures garanties que d'autres. Sur les vins français, cherchez les mots : *appellation contrôlée,* sur les vins espagnols : *denominación de origen ;* sur les vins italiens : *denominazione di origine controllata.* Les meilleures bouteilles des vignobles d'Afrique du Sud, d'Australie et de Californie seront de bonnes valeurs à des prix modérés ; mais elles n'en seront que meilleures si vous savez éviter les bouteilles qui s'octroient des appellations aussi vagues et infondées que « bordeaux sud-africain » ou encore « bourgogne californien » (car ne sont des Bordeaux, des Bourgognes que les vins nés dans les régions de Bordeaux et de Bourgogne). Cherchez plutôt les « vins de cépage » — c'est-à-dire des vins portant le nom de la variété de raisins dominante, tels le Riesling, Cabernet Sauvignon et Pinot Noir. S'il est aussi fait mention de l'endroit d'origine, le vin sera probablement de qualité supérieure à la moyenne.

Certains vins d'Amérique du Sud, notamment ceux du Chili, offrent de bonnes affaires et sont agréables à boire de même que certains vins italiens, espagnols ou portugais. Des vins plaisants viennent aussi de Yougoslavie ou de Hongrie : les meilleurs sont ceux qui portent un sceau de l'État. Vérifiez le millésime sur l'étiquette, il vous indiquera la durée de vieillissement de la bouteille si la couleur rouge est passée ; si possible, choisissez des vins âgés de trois à cinq ans.

En France et en Allemagne le choix est beaucoup plus vaste et l'éventail des prix plus ouvert ; la première question à vous poser à vous-même n'est autre que : « Ce vin est-il bien ce que prétend l'étiquette ? Est-il authentique ? »

LES VINS FRANÇAIS

La plupart des vins français vendus à l'étranger portent sur leur étiquette : « Appellation Contrôlée » ainsi que la mention « Produce of France ». Cette mention signifie qu'ils proviennent de l'aire de production figurant sur l'étiquette, qu'ils ont été faits en observant strictement des règles viticoles et vinicoles précises et qu'ils sont conformes à certaines règles minimales de qualité (*voir* APPELLATIONS D'ORIGINE CONTRÔLÉE).

Étant donné que la France produit annuellement une moyenne de quelques dix millions d'hectolitres de vin ayant droit à l'Appellation Contrôlée, les bouteilles qui portent cette inscription contiennent des vins de qualités extrêmement diverses. Quand on achète de ces vins il faut appliquer cette règle : plus le lieu d'origine est précisé, plus le vin sera bon ; un Médoc, par exemple, vaudra mieux qu'un simple Bordeaux ; un Margaux l'emportera sur un Médoc. Les vins d'Alsace font exception car la variété du raisin prévaut sur le lieu d'origine. Les meilleures bouteilles d'Alsace se vendent sous l'appellation de Riesling d'Alsace, Gewürztraminer et ainsi de suite. Dans quelques cas exceptionnels le nom du vignoble est aussi indiqué sur l'étiquette. Pour le plus grand nombre des vins français il faut posséder un minimum de connaissance concernant la géographie du pays. Il est impossible de choisir la bouteille dont les indications sont les plus précises quand on ne sait pas si Saint-Julien est dans le Haut-Médoc (ce qui est le cas) ou si le Haut-Médoc est à Saint-Julien (ce qui ne l'est pas).

Les vins fins français

Hormis le Champagne, les grands vins de France sont ceux de Bordeaux et de Bourgogne et les meilleurs échantillons portent le nom du vignoble où les raisins ont mûri. Si vous êtes prêt à dépenser le prix, nullement déraisonnable, auquel se vendent ces grands vins, la meilleure garantie d'en avoir pour votre argent, s'il s'agit d'un Bordeaux, c'est l'indication du château où il a été fait, avec la formule suivante : *Mis en bouteille au château.* En Bourgogne les vignobles sont tellement parcellaires que les vignerons mettaient rarement leur vin en bouteille eux-mêmes ; néanmoins aujourd'hui avec une demande grandissante pour des vins vendus directement de la propriété, la mise en bouteille par les viticulteurs est plus répandue que jamais. Ces vins portent l'indication *Mis au domaine,* ou quelque chose de semblable. A défaut d'une de ces deux formules, contentez-vous de l'étiquette d'un négociant digne de confiance. Parmi ceux-ci on peut citer : Bouchard Père et Fils, Louis Jadot, Louis Latour et Joseph Drouhin.

Le système d'étiquetage des vins est à peu près le même dans les autres régions, à ceci près que le nom du vignoble y est moins souvent indiqué. Le Champagne fait habituellement l'objet de coupage de vins appartenant à cette région, effectués par de grosses maisons dont les noms sont célèbres. Les meilleurs portent l'indication du millésime. (Les autres vins mousseux n'ont guère de valeur par comparaison avec le Champagne ; peu d'entre eux le valent, pourtant les taxes sur les mousseux à l'étranger situent le prix à peu près au même niveau). Les vins des autres régions font souvent l'objet de coupages eux aussi, quoique certains proviennent de vignobles déterminés, notamment le Châteauneuf-du-Pape, l'Hermitage, les Côtes du Rhône et le Tavel dans la vallée du Rhône, de même que l'Anjou, le Vouvray, le Pouilly-sur-Loire dans la vallée de la Loire. Ces vins peuvent être non seulement agréables mais admirables.

Les vins allemands

On ne fabrique pas un bon vin de manière économique, en particulier en Allemagne où il est si difficile de faire pousser la vigne et où les coûts de production sont si élevés. Il est physiquement et économiquement impossible à l'Allemagne de rivaliser avec ses voisins de l'ouest et du sud pour produire de grandes quantités de vin de table agréable à bas prix. Au mieux, 5 à 10 % d'une vendange annuelle moyenne (soit environ 10 millions d'hl pour 70 millions d'hl en France) permettent de fabriquer un vin de table appelé Deutscher Tafelwein ou Deutscher Landwein (vin de pays). On le consomme généralement durant les repas ou en ballons dans les cafés locaux, à proximité du lieu de production. Cela ne veut pas dire qu'il est rare ou cher de trouver des vins allemands, de consommation courante, d'une qualité décente. Au contraire, l'Allemagne produit de nombreux Qualitätsweine valables à des prix modérés. Ils revêtent un caractère régional et portent souvent les noms des villages les plus populaires (exemples : Bern, Piesporter Michelsberg, Niersteiner Gutes Domtal...) ou de districts, appelés Bereich en allemand, qui sont eux-mêmes habituellement nommés d'après les villages les plus connus de la région (exemples : Bereich Bernkastel, Bereich Johannisberg...) Liebfraumilch (célèbre depuis des siècles) et Moseltaler (créé en 1986) sont des vins de consommation courante, populaires et régionaux, sans nomenclature compliquée sur leur étiquette (aucun village, aucun vignoble, aucune variété de raisin). Leur production est définie par la loi (c.a.d. en type de variétés pouvant être utilisées pour la cuvée, ou de taux de sucres résiduels acceptés...). Pour faire le bon choix parmi ces vins régionaux, il faut regarder le nom du producteur ou de l'expéditeur imprimé sur les étiquettes. La cuvée finale ne peut être de qualité (et donc un bon choix) que si ses composants ont été sélectionnés pour des critères de qualité plutôt que des critères de bas prix. De nombreuses coopératives (Winzergenossenschaft ou Zentralkellerei) offrent un très bon choix. Il en est de même pour les expéditeurs fiables tels Sichel, Deinhard, Valckenberg ou St-Ursula pour n'en citer que quelques-uns.

Dans le bon secteur viticole, beaucoup considèrent que les vins blancs allemands sont de premier rang. Les Qualitätsweine mit Prädikat (vins de qualité avec une mention spéciale indiquant le degré de maturité des raisins à la vendange) s'échelonnent entre les vins Kabinett qui sont légers, délicats et élégants (généralement les plus secs des Prädikats), les vins Spaetlese plus mûrs et plus tardifs (fantastiques pour les repas lorsqu'ils sont secs — trocken, ou demi-secs — halbtrocken) et enfin les vins de type Auslese, riches et liquoreux, fabriqués à partir de raisins mûrs ou très mûrs, avec souvent une haute concentration en arôme ou en parfum. Les meilleurs de ces vins porteront généralement le nom d'un village suivi de celui d'un vignoble ainsi que de la variété de raisin. Le nom du producteur ou de l'expéditeur doit aussi être indiqué sur l'étiquette. Si le vin est mis en bouteilles au domaine (Erzeugerabfüllung : mis en bouteilles au château), il faut aussi le mentionner. Au XIXe siècle, il était courant de trouver de grands vins allemands ne comportant que le nom de leur village d'origine sur l'étiquette (Hochheimer, Bernkasteler, Oppenheimer) et il était admis qu'un vin blanc était un Riesling, un vin rouge un Spätburgunder (Pinot Noir). Prendre le temps de découvrir les nuances subtiles qui distinguent les villages, les vignobles et les variétés des meilleurs vins blancs allemands est une expérience très enrichissante.

LES PLUS GRANDS VINS

Tôt ou tard, tout amateur de vin sera tenté de goûter un des plus grands crus du monde. Qu'il prenne donc d'abord le temps d'éduquer son palais en commençant par des vins de moindre qualité, en apprenant à reconnaître une bonne bouteille quand il en passe une sur sa table. Ensuite seulement il pourra savourer le meilleur. Pour apprécier l'excellence d'un grand vin il faut le boire assez vieux ; il ne sera donc pas bon marché, c'est une vérité évidente, surtout si on l'achète lorsqu'il a achevé sa maturation chez un négociant, ce qui est actuellement le cas le plus courant. Que vous l'achetiez jeune pour le conserver ou plus tard pour consommation immédiate, vous serez bien avisé en refusant des risques inutiles lorsque vous projetez de telles agapes ; fiez-vous par conséquent à un nom illustre que l'élite des experts ne discute jamais (Château-Margaux, Chambertin, Château-d'Yquem, Montrachet) et choisissez une grande année. Les tables de millésimes, comme nous le disons ailleurs, ne sont pas aussi infaillibles qu'elles le paraissent : un grand vignoble ne produira vraisemblablement jamais un pauvre vin, même après le pire des étés ; un Chambertin ou un Château-Prieuré-Lichine de petite année pourra être très bon et moins cher que d'habitude ; mais arrivé à pleine maturité, le vin fin d'une grande année donnera des sensations incomparables. Recherchez des noms prestigieux parmi les Premiers, Seconds, Troisièmes, Quatrièmes et Cinquièmes Crus de Bordeaux (*voir* MÉDOC et BORDEAUX au chapitre *classification,* ainsi que parmi les *grands vins* de Bourgogne (*voir* BOURGOGNE) ou les vins fins allemands (*voir* ALLEMAGNE). Les meilleurs vins californiens proviennent des vallées du Napa et de Sonoma et d'autres localités viticoles de la côte septentrionale (*voir* ÉTATS-UNIS : Californie, pour le nom de quelques bonnes caves).

Le vin au restaurant

Celui qui veut en avoir pour son argent ne s'y prendra pas de la même manière au restaurant que chez le marchand de vin. En France le client de restaurant dédaigne volontiers la carte des vins à prix excessifs et commande une carafe de Beaujolais ou de rosé ; il se trouve que ce sont très souvent de bons vins. Voilà une méthode facile, mais elle ne résout pas le problème. La critique constructive serait plus efficace. Plaignez-vous, réclamez, n'hésitez pas, mais soyez raisonnables : le restaurateur doit couvrir ses frais généraux et faire un honnête bénéfice sur chaque bouteille. Il ne manque pas de restaurants qui ont une bonne cave et offrent une excellente carte des vins ; généralement leur réputation est faite et ils sont donc faciles à repérer. Par contre trop de restaurateurs poussent le chauvinisme jusqu'à l'esprit de clocher. Être fier des vins de sa région voilà qui est tout à fait normal. Mais une gamme où figurent toutes les régions productrices des vins de qualité semble nécessaire dans les restaurants qui prétendent avoir une carte des vins respectable. D'autres restaurateurs ne savent pas grand-chose en fait de vin ; si vous les traitez avec tact, ils se montreront peut-être prêts à apprendre et changeront de fournisseur pour adopter un négociant plus digne de confiance. Nous ne répéterons jamais assez qu'au restaurant le client « habitué » boit le vin qu'il mérite.

Les tables de millésimes

Pour connaître les grandes années, lisez les tables de millésimes, mais qu'elles ne vous hypnotisent pas : ces listes imprimées sont trop succinctes pour offrir plus que de très larges généralités. Les notes sur les millésimes que l'on trouve dans les catalogues des marchands de vin de première classe fournissent des renseignements plus complets, donc plus dignes de foi, mais elles ne peuvent évidemment pas indiquer les nombreuses exceptions à chaque règle.

Ceux qui consacrent leur existence à faire du vin sont d'accord sur un point : le vin est un complexe vivant, en évolution constante. En n'importe quelle année il commence par être « vert » généralement fruité, souvent dur ; il vieillira dans la barrique puis en bouteille pour acquérir du moelleux. Alors (ce sera peut-être des années après la mise en bouteille) il arrivera à son point culminant : un état d'excellence qui dure un temps variable. Les vins qui, selon les experts, vieilliront lentement jusqu'à la perfection et la conserveront sont mis en vedette sur les tables de millésimes. Ceux qui portent une mauvaise note sur ces tables peuvent quand même être agréables si on les boit jeunes. Ces notes accordées au vin ne peuvent pas tenir compte du fait que chaque vin réserve des surprises. Ceux de vignobles contigus, soignés par les vignerons expérimentés et amoureux de leur métier, peuvent quand même différer énormément l'un de l'autre. En Bourgogne, 1953 fut une bonne année ; pourtant bien des vignerons produisirent des vins blancs médiocres parce que leurs raisins contenaient trop de sucre et ont souffert par un excès d'acidité volatile. 1945 fut un bon millésime mais pas pour le Chablis dont les vignes furent massacrées par la grêle.

Quand on a bien saisi l'importance de ces réserves, une table des millésimes est néanmoins utile. Et voici des notes sur les dernières années.

Les derniers millésimes

Les facteurs qui déterminent la qualité du vin sont le terroir, le climat, le cépage et l'homme qui cultive la vigne, fait le vin et le soigne en cave ou en chai, si l'on admet qu'en principe la variété du raisin convient à la terre sur laquelle il est cultivé. Quand tous ces éléments se marient en une parfaite harmonie, l'acheteur peut espérer une bonne bouteille. Les tables de millésimes sont importantes certes, mais exagérer leur importance ne résoudra pas tous les problèmes de l'acheteur.

En admettant par hypothèse l'élimination de toute possibilité de fraude, l'expert est à même de choisir pour n'importe quelle année les meilleurs vins de Bordeaux mis en bouteille au château et de Bourgogne mis en bouteille au domaine. Encore faudra-t-il éliminer aussi les erreurs de la nature et de l'homme ; certaines grandes années produiront des vins décevants en raison d'une vendange prématurée ou à cause d'une erreur au cours de la vinification. La nature n'accorde pas à toute la superficie d'une région vinicole le même équilibre entre la pluie et le soleil au moment voulu.

Les tables de millésimes peuvent donc, au mieux, généraliser. Au cours des moins bonnes années, souvent condamnées catégoriquement comme « mauvaises années », on produit des vins fort agréables et parfois même de véritables délices ; l'acheteur pourra à l'occasion en découvrir un. C'est particulièrement vrai pour le vin rouge. Les vins blancs exigent un minimum d'ensoleillement ; sinon, une acidité excessive détruira leur équilibre. Au cours des années parfaites, le vin rouge aura un plus fort degré d'alcool, plus une abondance de tanin. Il en résultera un vin qui mettra longtemps à s'épanouir et décevra celui qui le boira trop tôt. C'est seulement avec les années qu'il atteindra sa qualité maximale et que le velours de l'âge remplacera la dure amertume du tanin.

Pour le Bordeaux rouge, la grande année est celle qui, grâce à un long ensoleillement, donnera aux raisins une forte teneur en sucre que la fermentation transformera en un fort degré d'alcool. Quelques grandes années, comme 1961, 1970, 1978, 1982, 1985 et 1986 auront probablement une place d'honneur sur la carte des crus, mais cette note ne leur sera décernée qu'en prévision de la « cote » qu'ils pourront espérer atteindre à leur pleine maturité. Parfois ces vendanges mémorables donnent une surabondance de tanin qui agit comme un corset pour maintenir la cohésion des différents éléments du vin pendant plusieurs années, jusqu'à ce que la maturation arrive à son point culminant. Cela ne se produira qu'au bout de 15 à 20 ans. Boire du 1961 en 1965 peut avoir déçu bien des amateurs. Le même 1961 aurait offert en 1976 une des jouissances esthétiques les plus mémorables qui soient accessibles à un être humain, pourvu que ce vin fût de grand cru.

Pour énoncer des règles générales, disons que les tables de millésimes importent plus en ce qui concerne les vins blancs que les rouges, étant donné qu'au cours des années pauvres l'excès d'acidité se manifeste par une certaine verdeur et que les défauts du vin sont donc plus apparents. Quant aux vins rouges, il faut tenir compte du cru où le raisin peut, en général, mûrir plus ou moins rapidement. Ces généralités peuvent d'ailleurs être contredites par les conditions dans lesquelles le vin est conservé et le climat sous lequel il sera consommé. La conservation à une température élevée fait mûrir prématurément alors que le vin mûrit plus lentement dans une cave parfaitement fraîche et qu'ainsi toutes les qualités qu'il recèle s'épanouiront pleinement. Compte tenu de toutes ces réserves, voici une liste de généralités au sujet des plus grandes régions vinicoles.

Bordeaux

1952. Très bonne année pour les vins rouges. Les plus grands crus, un peu durs, ne mûrirent que lentement. Les Saint-Émilion et Pomerol de 1952 surclassèrent ceux de 1953, mais il n'en alla pas ainsi pour les Médoc. D'une manière générale les 1952 ont duré plus longtemps que les 1953.

1953. Très grande année pour les vins rouges. Les 1953 ont vieilli plus rapidement que les 1952. Ils ont été dotés de gras, rondeur et équilibre parfaits. Peut-être ne durèrent-ils pas aussi longtemps que les 1952, mais arrivés à maturité, ils atteignirent le plus haut degré de perfection. Les conserver au-delà de 1980 serait tenter le diable.

1954. Les pessimistes condamnèrent cette vendange mais ils durent se rendre à la raison. Les vins rouges à bas prix offrirent d'excellentes occasions ; même si leur charme dura peu, il confondit les Cassandre.

1955. Très grande année pour les vins rouges, indiscutablement meilleure que 1952 et même que 1953 pour certains crus. Vins magnifiquement équilibrés.

En ce qui concerne les vins blancs, cette année-là fut parfaite pour ceux qui trouvent généralement le Sauternes trop doux.

1956. Vins rouges allant du médiocre au passable avec tendance à la dureté. On espérait que le cépage Merlot les attendrirait mais on fut déçu en raison de gelées du mois de février et ensuite d'une maturation excessive du raisin avant les vendanges.

Les Bordeaux blancs furent décevants.

1957. Bon millésime pour les vins rouges, mais en petite quantité. Jointe à l'inflation, cette production réduite fit monter les prix. Les vignerons qui vendangèrent tard bénéficièrent d'un mois d'octobre exceptionnel. Aujourd'hui encore une certaine dureté diminue leur agrément et les prive de rondeur.

1958. Vin très léger à maturation rapide, manquant de caractère pour justifier une conservation un tant soit peu prolongée. Aujourd'hui c'est probablement un vin buvable.

1959. On claironna que cette année serait la plus grande du siècle. La presse du monde entier en fit des manchettes. Ce ne fut pourtant pas un millésime exceptionnel. Dans l'ensemble les vins rouges se montrèrent corsés et harmonieux.

Ceux qui aiment les Barsac et les Sauternes parce qu'ils sont « les vins doux les plus riches et les plus racés du monde » n'oublieront pas 1959. Parfaitement équilibrés, les vins de ce millésime auraient dû restaurer une coutume qui se perd : servir du Sauternes avec le dessert.

1960. Quantité abondante de vin rouge.

1961. Une des plus petites années dont on se rappelle dans le Médoc. Le froid et la pluie au mois de mai gênèrent la floraison ; il en résultat une production ne s'élevant qu'à 40 ou 50 % des années précédentes. Puis un été chaud, suivi par un mois de septembre superbe, donna (en qualité sinon en quantité) une des meilleures récoltes depuis 1945. Compte tenu des nouvelles méthodes de vinification, les vins ont eu plus de rondeur que ceux de 1945, mais ne sont parvenus à leur plénitude qu'en 1975. Année à grand succès aussi pour les Saint-Émilion et Pomerol.

Grande année pour les vins doux de Sauternes et de Barsac. Certaines bouteilles de Sauternes dureront une trentaine d'années. Certains vins doux pourtant réussirent moins bien à cause des pluies d'octobre.

1962. Les très bons vins rouges furent consommables avant ceux de 1961.

1963. Quelques vins légers et buvables dans le Médoc ; un désastre pour le Saint-Émilion et le Pomerol. Après un été pluvieux, la vendange eut lieu dans de mauvaises conditions : pluie et froid. Une année à oublier, à quelques exceptions près.

1964. Année de grande abondance pour les vins rouges. Été magnifique suivi d'un excellent septembre, et les raisins mûrirent dans de bonnes conditions. On attendit tard pour vendanger dans certains châteaux du Médoc ; malheureusement il ne cessa plus de pleuvoir à partir du 8 octobre. Ce millésime, qui avait si bien commencé, provoqua des déceptions en ce qui concerne les raisins vendangés tardivement. Néanmoins l'année 1964 fut en général bonne dans le Médoc. Grand succès dans le Saint-Émilion et le Pomerol où les vendanges étaient terminées avant les pluies.

Les vignerons de Sauternes qui attendirent jusqu'à la fin octobre subirent un désastre.

1965. Été pluvieux. Bons vins.

1966. Grande année pour tout le Bordelais. Vins de coloration foncée et profonde, parfaitement équilibrés et d'une rondeur exceptionnelle. Les meilleurs depuis 1961, mais de caractère différent car ils s'apparentent légèrement à ceux de 1953. Maturation rapide.

Graves blancs : très bons. Barsac et Sauternes : 1/3 seulement très bons. Le reste, décevant.

1967. Plus léger que 1966. A donc vieilli plus rapidement. Bonne année pour la quantité. Cependant il ne faut acheter qu'à bon escient. Sauternes excellents.

1968. Vins légers en raison de l'été pluvieux. On put toutefois trouver des bouteilles agréables mais de valeur moyenne.

1969. Bon en Médoc ; décevant en Saint-Émilion et en Pomerol. Le temps froid et pluvieux pendant la floraison en juin réduisit la quantité de quelque 40 %. Ensoleillement très satisfaisant en juillet et août, suivi de pluies intermittentes en septembre. Trois semaines de chaleur exceptionnelle juste avant et pendant les vendanges sauvèrent la récolte. Vins blancs secs : bons. Sauternes et Barsac (doux) : tout juste passables.

1970. Très bonne année ; parmi les meilleures depuis 1961, caractérisée également par une abondance jamais atteinte depuis le début du siècle, qui malheureusement ne fit pas descendre les prix. De nombreux vins se sont affinés à des âges différents, et il ne serait pas négligeable d'effectuer une sélection dans cette optique, entre les vins à boire tôt, et ceux à garder pour la fin des années 80 ou même 90.

Les blancs, quant à eux, sont bons.

1971. L'inflation, la bonne qualité et la faible quantité furent les trois facteurs qui conduisirent à des prix qui semblaient astronomiques. Les rouges sont légers mais ne manquent pas de rondeur. Certains viticulteurs préfèrent les vins de 1971 à ceux de 1970, pour l'élégance, la race et le parfait équilibre des premiers — qualités qui ne se manifestèrent que vers la fin de 1976.

Dans l'ensemble, les vins blancs sont bons, avec quelques sommets exceptionnels en Sauternes, productions qui seront exquises jusqu'en l'an 2000.

1972. Après un été désespérément pluvieux, l'année fut plus ou moins sauvée par un début d'automne miraculeusement ensoleillé, qui dura de fin septembre jusqu'aux vendanges d'octobre. Les rouges, jeunes, montrèrent trop d'acidité, ils ne devinrent pas remarquables en vieillissant.

Les Barsac et Sauternes sont loin d'avoir la qualité des vins de 1971.

1973. Une récolte considérable, plus abondante encore que l'année-record 1970. Mais comme il fallait s'y attendre, l'énorme quantité impliquait une qualité moindre. La couleur est bonne, mais les rouges manquent de cette acidité qui leur aurait permis une grande longévité, et sont en outre plutôt légers. Les vins du Médoc ont eu plus de chance que ceux des Graves, de Saint-Émilion et Pomerol. Les meilleurs vins rouges ressemblent à ceux de 1967. Heureusement, en 1976, les prix ont baissé de 40 à 50 %, rehaussant ainsi à nouveau la valeur des grands Bordeaux.

Les blancs secs furent très acceptables si ce n'est bons ; les blancs doux, par contre, ne furent que très moyens. Les vignobles du Sauternes furent à plusieurs reprises détruits par la grêle.

1974. Une année plus que satisfaisante pour les vins rouges. L'abondance de la récolte et le fait que ces vins finirent par surplanter ceux de 1973 font de cette année une valeur sûre.

Les blancs secs sont bons, fruités et équilibrés sans excès d'acidité. Malheureusement la récolte en Sauternes fut désastreuse.

1975. Une année exceptionnellement brillante pour les vins rouges, donnant des vins riches, harmonieux, à maturation lente. Jamais une telle qualité n'avait été atteinte depuis 1970, et peut-être lui sera-t-elle même supérieure ; mais la quantité produite fut faible (50 % de moins qu'en 1974).

Des blancs secs excellents, un Barsac doux et un Sauternes superbe, que l'on doit au temps des derniers jours d'octobre et du début novembre.

1976. Toutes les bouteilles de 1976 peuvent être appréciées avant les grands crus de 1975 à maturation lente. Ainsi, les vins de 1976 étaient comparables à ceux de 1975, un peu dans la même mesure où les vins de 1971 l'étaient à ceux, très brillants, de 1970. Certains viticulteurs ont comparé la teneur des vins de 1976 à celle des vins de 1975, se prononçant en faveur des premiers. Malheureusement beaucoup de 1976 ont une tenue désappointante.

Les blancs secs qui ont été vendangés suffisamment tôt ont donné d'excellents résultats. Les Sauternes et Barsac ont beaucoup souffert des pluies d'octobre. Les raisins furent endommagés avant que le *Botrytis cinerea* puisse effectuer son processus de « pourriture noble ». Heureusement à cette époque, les vins rouges avaient déjà été récoltés.

1977. Après un été pluvieux et un mois d'août plutôt frais, il y eut une période de chaleur qui dura jusqu'à la fin des vendanges ; celles-ci, tardives, eurent lieu dans de très bonnes conditions pendant tout le mois d'octobre. Cette chaleur inespérée donna des vins riches en couleur, fruités quoiqu'un peu durs, mais leur maturation sera assez rapide. Il faudra opérer une certaine sélection. Quoique différents des vins de 1974, les vins de 1977 rentrent dans la même classe et sont indubitablement supérieurs à l'année 1972.

Les blancs secs sont de bons vins fruités ; leur acidité leur confère une fraîcheur agréable et en fait des vins qui vieillissent avec profit. Quant aux vins doux de Barsac et Sauternes, ils furent produits en quantités insignifiantes, mais certains sont acceptables.

1978. C'est un grand millésime. Les rouges ont une robe de couleur profonde et les vins ont tendance à être corsés. Après un mauvais été, un temps exceptionnellement chaud, avant et pendant les vendanges, a miraculeusement transformé un millésime qui aurait manqué de maturité en une année qu'on appréciera pendant quelques décennies. Bien que la qualité de ces vins soit égale, il est conseillé d'être très sélectif, surtout dans les Saint-Émilion et les Pomerol.

Les Bordeaux blancs secs — Graves et autres — étaient très bons. Barsac et Sauternes sont des vins doux, succulents.

1979. Une récolte particulièrement abondante pour les rouges. La qualité, très inégale d'une région à l'autre, reste cependant d'un très grand niveau. Les vins très colorés, ronds, souples se sont faits assez rapidement ; si l'on devait les comparer ce serait avec les vins de 1962. Ces caractéristiques sont celles du cépage Merlot et elles dominent cette année car il a mieux mûri que les Cabernet.

Comme pour les rouges, la récolte des blancs secs fut très abondante. La qualité est très satisfaisante. La pourriture noble s'est développée normalement et les vins sont plaisants, bien typés, assez pleins mais sans atteindre le point culminant de l'année 1971 ou de 1967.

1980. Bonne récolte. Les vins sont ronds, plaisants et à maturation rapide. C'est la quatrième récolte consécutive qui a bénéficié d'un temps favorable entre fin septembre et mi-octobre. En dépit des pluies tombées pendant les vendanges d'octobre, l'arôme et le tanin de quelques vins sont fort bons. Résultats assez décevants en Saint-Émilion et en Pomerol où la récolte fut moins importante (Merlot) que dans le Médoc. Les vins blancs secs sont fruités. Octobre et novembre furent spécialement favorables aux vins doux de Sauternes et Barsac, qui promettent d'être très bons. A Château-Yquem par exemple, 80 % de la récolte furent vendus sous son étiquette, en 1979 il n'y en eut que 40 %.

1981. Une très bonne année. Les vins sont plus souples que ceux de 1978 et peut-être plus durs que ceux de 1979. Ils sont taniques et de belle couleur. Quelques pluies intermittentes à la fin des vendanges (vers la mi-octobre) contribuèrent à enlever la dureté qu'ils auraient pu avoir.

Les producteurs de Barsac et Sauternes doux (vendangés après les vins rouges) ont produit de très bons vins.

1982. Des vins rouges superbes, mûrs, parfumés, longs en bouche et d'un grand avenir, feront ressortir 1982 comme une très grande année.

Les blancs secs sont excellents. Les Barsac et Sauternes qui ont fait l'objet de nombreuses cueillettes ont réussi une bonne année.

1983. La chaleur bénéfique, sans une goutte de pluie, qui a duré jusqu'à la fin des vendanges, a donné un très grand millésime. Certains grands propriétaires considèrent qu'il sera supérieur, en vieillissant, au déjà superbe millésime 82. La commune de Margaux fut particulièrement favorisée ainsi que certains crus de Saint-Émilion et Pomerol. En Sauternes, la qualité fut excellente.

1984. A la grande surprise et après bien des médisances, c'est un bon millésime qui ressemble beaucoup au 1981. La plupart des Merlots ont été atteints par la coulure, mais la partie vendangée était de bonne qualité et on a confondu à tort quantité et qualité.

A Saint-Émilion et à Pomerol les quantités sont très réduites mais la qualité, surtout dans le Médoc, est bonne.

Les Sauternes et les Barsac ont bénéficié d'une excellente arrière-saison et ont été très « botrytisés », ce qui prédit un très bon millésime, riche en sève.

1985. Grand millésime. Après une longue sécheresse on s'attendait à une petite vendange aux vins plutôt durs. Au contraire on obtint une récolte très importante. La quantité a permis de diluer la dureté. Ces vins pourraient ressembler à un croisement entre 1982 et 1983. Bien que la récolte fût un succès avec les Merlots du Médoc, ce fut moins vrai à Saint-Émilion et Pomerol.

A Sauternes, bonne maturité. Finalement en novembre l'humidité permit le développement du *botrytis*. Les vendanges se prolongèrent jusqu'en décembre. Sauternes connaît un assez grand millésime qui pourrait ressembler aux excellents 1983.

1986. Excellent millésime pour les Médoc. Un peu plus dur qu'en 1985. Semblable d'après certains à celui de 1961. Quoique riches en tanin, les vins sont en général meilleurs qu'en 1975 et 1970 car ils ne sont pas aussi âpres. 1986 est une année à Cabernet Sauvignon. Saint-Émilion et Pomerol ont produit de très bons vins mais n'égaleront pas la qualité exceptionnelle des Médoc.

Bonne année pour les Sauternes. Semblable à 1975, mais les vins murissent relativement vite.

BOURGOGNE

1959. Très abondante. Les vins rouges étaient fondus et ont eu assez de corps pour être classés dans les vins de grande garde : ils récompensèrent les gens patients, qui les conservèrent jusqu'à ce qu'ils eussent atteint une maturité glorieuse.

Les Bourgogne blancs atteignirent de hauts sommets. Cependant avec le recul du temps on constate que, faute d'acidité fixe pour conserver leur fraîcheur, il s'oxydèrent prématurément.

1960. Rouges légers et décevants, aussi bien dans la Côte-d'Or que dans le Beaujolais.

1961. Grande année pour les Bourgogne rouges, riches avec forte teneur en tanin, bien équilibrés et de belle couleur. Un fort degré d'alcool compensa la forte acidité des vins blancs qui furent excellents et méritèrent bien leur réputation.

1962. Rouges très fins, légers et bien équilibrés avec tendance à vieillissement rapide. Ils purent être consommés avant les vins de 1961.

1963. Désastre pour les Bourgogne rouges. Certains Bourgogne blancs furent buvables, mais rien de mieux.

1964. Certains Bourgogne rouges furent meilleurs que les Bordeaux. Ces vins d'une belle rondeur purent être bus assez tôt, comme le furent ceux de 1962. Ils étaient riches en bouquet. Quoique bien équilibrés, les blancs manquèrent plutôt d'acidité. Grande année pour le Beaujolais.

1965. Un désastre pour les vins rouges, dû aux innondations qui détruisirent de nombreux vignobles, et au manque de maturité.

1966. Les Bourgogne de la Côte-d'Or eurent bien des caractéristiques de ceux de 1964 : plénitude, rondeur, maturité rapide.

1967. Millésime satisfaisant, mais qui n'a pas le corps des 1966.

1968. Vins légers et décevants.

1969. Très grand millésime pour la Côte-d'Or. Ses vins ronds et pleins, d'une belle robe foncée, sont doués d'un caractère qui dure. En fait de qualité, cette région fut la plus comblée de France pour cette récolte.

Les vins blancs manquèrent d'acidité et sont aujourd'hui fanés.

1970. Les vins de la Côte-d'Or furent bons, sans plus. Alors que les 1969 de Bourgogne sont supérieurs aux Bordeaux, le contraire est vrai en 1970 où les Bordeaux ont produit une très grande année.

1971. La récolte fut peu importante, à cause du mauvais temps qui sévit pendant la floraison, suivi d'orages et de grêles. Les vins rouges se montrèrent pleins de corps, avec une bonne couleur, en dépit toutefois d'un certain manque de finesse pour certains, ce qui ne leur permit pas d'être comparés aux millésimes de 1969. 1971 est la meilleure année entre 1969 et 1976.

Des vins blancs pleins de corps ; un bon millésime, quoiqu'en faible quantité.

1972. Malgré le temps heureux pendant la récolte tardive d'octobre, le Pinot Noir et d'autres raisins à vin rouge manquaient de maturité. Certains rouges sont colorés et harmonieux, mais dans l'ensemble, ils ne s'éloignent pas de la moyenne. Une grande déception pour ce qui concerne les vins blancs.

1973. La quantité ne fut pas celle qu'on aurait pu espérer. Ces vins ne mériteront bientôt plus notre attention. Les blancs, meilleurs que les rouges, se sont éventés avec l'âge.

1974. Une année plutôt bonne, à égalité avec 1971. Des vins fruités avec un fort caractère de Pinot Noir. Une production surabondante, due aux incessantes pluies de septembre, en appauvrit la qualité.

De bons vins blancs qui étaient à consommer rapidement. Grande quantité.

1975. Une année très décevante. Les vins furent trop clairs, à cause des pluies.

Certains vins blancs furent bons, mais ils n'ont pas eu une grande longévité.

1976. Grand millésime. Une année exceptionnelle pour la Bourgogne, qui souffrait d'une pénurie de bons millésimes. Des vins pleins, ronds, riches en couleur et en caractère.

Des vins blancs pleins de corps, en dépit d'un manque d'acidité indispensable pour donner au vin sa fraîcheur.

Le Beaujolais produisit son meilleur cru depuis 1961.

1977. Produits en grande quantité, les vins perdirent en qualité et se montrèrent trop légers et sans corps. Il y a bien quelques exceptions.

1978. Est un très bon millésime, et les rouges, bons, veloutés, n'ont pas trop de tanin. On peut les comparer à ceux de 1962.

Les blancs se sont révélés bons sans avoir la mollesse de ceux de 1976. Les Chablis sont excellents.

1979. Une récolte importante de vins rouges dont la qualité irrégulière mais bonne reste inférieure à celle de 1978. Les vins fruités, d'assez belle couleur, manquent d'amplitude et de gras.

Pour les Beaujolais : une très importante quantité et une qualité très irrégulière (20 % ont produit une bonne qualité, 20 % une qualité acceptable ; malheureusement, 60 % peuvent être oubliés). La moitié de la production fut qualitativement inférieure à celle de 1977. Cette situation resta identique pour les Crus.

Les vins blancs, de constitution assez légère, étaient bien équilibrés et fruités, ils ne furent pas des vins de garde. Les vins blancs étaient meilleurs que les vins rouges. Les vins blancs de Chassagne ont été plus réussis que ceux de Puligny.

1980. Assez bonne année pour les vins rouges qui ont une maturation rapide et une qualité supérieure à celle des dernières années (à l'exception de 1976) mais en faible quantité. Les Meursault, Puligny et Chassagne ont donné des vins bien équilibrés et fruités ; un bon cru sans plus. Bonne récolte typique et légère dans le Beaujolais. Les petits vins eurent tendance à être acides, légers et ont dû être consommés rapidement.

1981. Les vins rouges sont de bonne couleur flatteuse en dépit d'un certain manque de caractère. La quantité fut exceptionnellement petite. Quelques pluies éparses durant les vendanges ont affaibli la très bonne qualité que l'on espérait. Les vins sont néanmoins plaisants. Dans le Beaujolais, bonne qualité assez homogène, les vins ont eu tendance à être assez charpentés.

Les blancs, meilleurs que les rouges, étaient fruités, élégants et ont bien vieilli.

1982. Bonne année pour les rouges. Vins tendres. La qualité fut homogène de belle couleur. Une production énorme pour les Beaujolais, mais une qualité inégale qui a demandé beaucoup de sélection.

Les blancs fruités, souples, élégants, avec une acidité assez basse, étaient supérieurs à ceux de 1981.

1983. Les rouges, vendangés dans d'excellentes conditons, ont produit un bon millésime, un peu tanique et dur ; la grêle détruisit malheureusement les grands vignobles de Vosne Romanée dans le cœur de la Côte de Nuits.

Les blancs ont été trop riches en alcool et s'avérèrent moins intéressants que ceux de 1982, qui étaient plats.

Les Beaujolais furent les meilleurs depuis 1976 ; vins fermes, moins fruités.

1984. Les vins rouges ont une belle couleur avec un goût un peu vert et acide ; millésime de qualité moyenne.

Les blancs, bien que fruités, manquent un peu de fond.

1985. Un bon millésime. Belle couleur. Les rouges sont meilleurs qu'en 1982 et 1984. Certains ressemblent à ceux de 1978 et 1979. Avec un peu de subtilité, ils auraient eu plus de caractère. Pour les blancs, la quantité fut abondante quoique diluée pour certains Puligny et Chassagne. On trouve quelques très bonnes exceptions.

1986. Année moyenne. Les Côtes de Beaune rouges sont légers. Les blancs sont meilleurs que les rouges.

Vins du Rhône

1959. Chaleur excessive qui brûla les vignes dans la vallée bien ensoleillée du Rhône. Les raisins arrivèrent à une très saine maturité et firent un très bon millésime. En ce qui concerne les autres crus de la vallée du Rhône, le raisin arriva à une aussi bonne maturité que dans les autres régions de la France.

1960. Très bon millésime. Seule la vallée du Rhône, favorisée par un temps remarquablement bon depuis la fructification jusqu'à la vendange, produisit des vins de très grande qualité cette année-là. Une des meilleures parmi les quinze dernières années.

1961. Comme les autres régions de France, la vallée du Rhône produisit des vins d'une qualité exceptionnelle.

1962. Année moyenne qui donna des vins plats manquant de caractère. Il y eut néanmoins quelques réussites de-ci, de-là.

1963. Année à oublier. Vins complètement dénués de couleur. Très nettement inférieurs à ceux de 1962.

1964. Année satisfaisante.

1965. Assez bonne année. La région des Côtes du Rhône, contrairement au reste de la France, ne manqua pas de soleil. Aux vendanges le temps fut idéal.

1966. En général un millésime d'une bonne qualité dans la vallée du Rhône. Quelques grands sommets. Certains vignerons ont fait des vins remarquables.

1967. La température assure à la vallée du Rhône plus de bons millésimes qu'à toutes les autres régions de France. Et cette région a produit en 1967, des vins supérieurs à ceux de 1966.

1968. Quelques vins agréables.

1969. Quantité faible. Très bonne qualité. Belle couleur. Principales réussites dans la Côte Rôtie, où l'on produisit d'excellents vins.

1970. Bonne année, en quantité comme en qualité.

1971. De passable à très bon.

1972. Bonne année pour la plupart des vins du Rhône, avec quelques exceptions.

1973. La qualité fut satisfaisante malgré un manque d'acidité et de fruité. Dans l'ensemble, des vins moyens.

1974. Qualité tout au plus moyenne avec quelques hauts et bas et une tendance décisive vers le bas plutôt que vers le haut.

1975. Bonne année dans l'ensemble avec, malheureusement, de nombreuses exceptions. De la couleur, du fruité, du caractère et dans certains cas, un excellent potentiel de longévité. Malheureusement quelques déceptions en ce qui concerne le Châteauneuf-du-Pape.

1976. La région des Côtes du Rhône fut parmi les plus favorisées. Un temps chaud et ensoleillé permit une récolte abondante de vins pleins, ronds et harmonieux, qui durent sur le palais comme en cave. On trouve donc un grand nombre de vins agréables. Les Châteauneuf-du-Pape et Tavel furent excellents.

1977. Passable. 30 % des vins, généralement de Condrieu, Côte Rôtie et Hermitage, furent de bonne qualité. Ceux de Châteauneuf-du-Pape et du sud des Côtes du Rhône furent médiocres. Les pluies de fin d'été se prolongèrent jusqu'aux vendanges dans le midi, gonflant les raisins et donnant des vins faibles et maigres.

1978. Excellent millésime.

1979. La quantité fut importante et la qualité très bonne. Néanmoins dans l'ensemble, les vins étaient bien constitués et bien colorés.

1980. Année satisfaisante, assez semblable à 1974.

1981. Qualité passable. Les vins manquent de corps. A Châteauneuf, les vins furent moyens. Dans les Côtes du Rhône, la qualité était satisfaisante sans haut de gamme.

1982. Très bonne qualité dans l'ensemble. Une sélection est à faire, allant du moyen jusqu'à de très bons vins. Les vins des Côtes Rôtie et de l'Hermitage sont d'un bon niveau de qualité, avec rondeur et souplesse, tandis que les Côtes du Rhône et les Châteauneuf-du-Pape ont un bon caractère, assez corsé. La qualité est bonne, et souvent supérieure.

1983. Très belle qualité. Très prometteuse. Les crus méridionaux, c'est-à-dire les Châteauneuf-du-Pape, ont produit un excellent ensemble aromatique et un millésime supérieur au déjà très bon 1982.

1984. L'optimisme, à la naissance de ce millésime, a été déçu dans la partie septentrionale tandis que les crus méridionaux ont produit un bon ensemble aromatique et un bon millésime.

1985. Un très grand millésime selon les autorités émérites du Rhône. La mention « exceptionnel » définit la meilleure qualité.

1986. De très bon vins. Néanmoins, dans les basses Côtes du Rhône, les grandes quantités produites ont affecté la qualité.

Vins de la Loire

1969. Bon millésime pour tous les vins de la Loire depuis le Pouilly jusqu'au Muscadet. Ce dernier fut excellent. Généralement fruité, le vin blanc fut tout à fait remarquable. A l'exception des vins doux, la qualité n'est plus qu'un lointain souvenir.

1970. L'abondante quantité produite nuisit à la qualité. Dans l'ensemble une bonne année pour la Loire. Excellente année pour le Pouilly-Fumé, mais ces vins sont maintenant oxydés.

1971. Bonne année, avec de l'excellent Muscadet maintenant oublié.

1972. Année plutôt mauvaise. Des blancs légers et sans caractère. A oublier.

1973. Année très abondante. La qualité fut passable, mais sans plus pour la plupart des vins. Un Muscadet honorable, bien que loin d'être parfait.

1974. Une production de vins fruités et équilibrés, peut-être un peu plats et manquant de caractère et d'acidité.

1975. Année un peu au-dessus de la moyenne mais de bons Muscadet.

Très bonne année en Anjou. Des vins assez bons dans le Vouvray, le Pouilly-Fumé et le Sancerre.

1976. Très bonne année dans le Muscadet. Mais la sécheresse qui s'abattit sur la France provoqua un mûrissement prématuré, qui pour ces vins signifia un grand manque d'acidité.

Dans d'autres régions de la Loire — Vouvray, Sancerre et Pouilly-Fumé — la quantité et la qualité furent dans l'ensemble très bonnes, en particulier pour le Vouvray.

1977. Bonne année. Quelques vins agréables furent produits.

1978. Bon millésime pour le Muscadet mais malheureusement produit en faible quantité. Le reste de la Loire a produit des vins de bonne qualité sauf à Pouilly-sur-Loire où les vignobles furent atteints par la grêle.

1979. Qualité satisfaisante. Les vins sont très nets, sans trop d'acidité mais bien équilibrés et fruités.

Quantités très importantes des vins décevants en Anjou à l'exception du cépage Cabernet, qualitativement le meilleur vin.

La production des vins du Vouvray, du double de celle de 1978, a été très abondante mais la qualité reste assez faible. La majeure partie de la récolte de 1979 fut utilisée pour l'élaboration des vins mousseux.

Comme pour l'ensemble du Val-de-Loire, la récolte des Pouilly-Fumé et des Sancerre était à peu près le double de celle de 1978. Cependant, les vins d'assez bonne qualité se montrent bien équilibrés quoiqu'un peu légers mais assez fruités et un peu flatteurs. Ils se boivent assez rapidement.

1980. Les Muscadet, un peu acides, manquent de maturité et sont de moins bonne qualité qu'en 1979. En Anjou les vins sont supérieurs à ceux de 1979.

1981. Bonne année pour les Muscadet (nettement supérieure à celles de 1979 et 1980). Les vins sont plus légers, parfumés, fruités et moins acides que les autres années. Contrairement aux années 1979 et 1980, les vins de 1981 sont de bonne qualité et bien équilibrés. Faible quantité également de Vouvray doux due aux pluies tardives qui empêchèrent le développement du *Botrytis* ou « pourriture noble ». A la différence de 1979, le Vouvray mousseux fut produit en quantité limitée, puisque la majeure partie de la récolte fut consacrée à de bons vins secs. Bonne année également pour le Pouilly-Fumé et le Sancerre ; les viticulteurs furent satisfaits en Anjou et en Saumur.

1982. L'abondante récolte de Muscadet a produit de bons vins fins, gouleyants, bien équilibrés et harmonieux, manquant un peu d'acidité mais ayant un bon arôme grâce à la richesse naturelle des moûts.

En Anjou et Saumur, récolte abondante, mais la qualité a des hauts et des bas, comme en Touraine. Les moelleux sont peut-être déficients à cause des pluies survenues pendant les vendanges. Les vins rouges feront une bonne année, fruités et élégants. Les Vouvray sont bien. Par contre, la pluie a empêché le *Botrytis,* donc c'est une année qui n'aura pas de vins liquoreux de grande classe.

Sancerre et Pouilly ont produit des vins fins et équilibrés ayant un riche bouquet, bien supérieurs à ceux des années précédentes.

1983. Bonne année le long de la Loire. Les Vouvray n'ont pas produit de vin doux.

1984. Généralement une passable année, surtout en Anjou. Comparativement, bonne réussite dans les Muscadet.

1985. D'un bout à l'autre de la Loire, les viticulteurs étaient joyeux. Le Muscadet était rond, agréable et a du corps. Le *Botrytis* a fait de merveilleux vins doux dans les Côteaux de Layon qui n'avaient rien produit depuis des années.

1986. Bon Muscadet fruité et léger à l'acidité satisfaisante. Le climat de la Loire fut agréable dans l'ensemble quoique frais. Des pluies ont empêché le développement du *Botrytis,* nécessaire à la fabrication de vins doux, sauf en Anjou.

ALSACE

1969. Bon millésime. Caractère satisfaisant.

1970. Bonne qualité, étant donné l'énorme récolte — une des plus importantes du siècle.

1971. Une gamme allant du bon au très bon, commençant avec des vins d'une teneur en alcool très élevée, ce qui détruit les caractéristiques habituelles des bons vins alsaciens : la légèreté, le brio, la facilité à se laisser boire.

1972. Quelques vins agréables qui ont manqué de profondeur tout en étant légèrement acides.

1973. Année la plus abondante en Alsace depuis la guerre à l'exception de 1970. Les vins manquèrent d'acidité, par conséquent, ils n'ont pas duré longtemps en bouteille et ont dû être bus jeunes.

1974. Très équilibrés, frais malgré les pluies incessantes pendant les vendanges, les vins ont dû être bus très jeunes.

1975. Une bonne année.

1976. Comme en Champagne, une production exceptionnelle. Grande qualité et grande quantité.

1977. Vins honnêtes au goût fruité, quoiqu'un peu durs.

1978. Ce bon millésime a une production inférieure à la normale. Les Riesling sont très réussis.

1979. Bon millésime, en quantités abondantes. Les vins étaient très bien équilibrés.

1980. Année passable dans l'ensemble, faible quantité notamment pour les Gewürztraminer.

1981. Qualité excellente (supérieure à celle de 1979). La récolte fut normale en quantité. Les Riesling, qui n'avaient pas été vendangés trop tôt furent excellents.

1982. Bonne année en qualité et quantité. Les vins sont charpentés avec un bouquet très prononcé.

1983. Très grande année, ayant produit de grands vins secs, ainsi que des grands vins doux connus sous le libellé de « vendange tardive ».

1984. Année moyenne avec certains vins très décevants.

Pour apprécier pleinement les vins alsaciens, il faut les boire jeunes, c'est-à-dire lorsqu'ils ont moins de cinq ans et gardent encore leurs qualités primordiales : la fraîcheur et le fruité, qu'ils ont tendance à perdre avec l'âge. Comme la plupart des vins blancs secs, les vins l'Alsace tendent à madériser.

1985. Un grand millésime. Certains propriétaires assurent qu'il était meilleur que le 1983. Le Gewürztraminer a plus de caractère que les millésimes précédents. Bon équilibre d'acidité.

1986. Une bonne année qui prouve que l'Alsace peut produire des vins de haute qualité. En outre, les bons producteurs ont appris à sélectionner leurs cuvées.

Champagne

Comme tous les vins blancs — mousseux ou non — le Champagne doit être bu assez jeune, soit dix ou quinze ans au plus après sa mise en bouteille. Ceci, bien que quelques connaisseurs s'acharnent à priser des bouteilles vieilles de plusieurs dizaines d'années. Comme tous les vins blancs, le Champagne a tendance à madériser avec l'âge, ce qui lui donne une couleur brunâtre et un goût de feuilles mortes. Une exception, toutefois, en ce qui concerne le Champagne non dégorgé qui vieillira bien en bouteille ; néanmoins, pour être bu, il devra être dégorgé et toutes les précautions dues à son âge et aux vins blancs en général devront être prises. On n'indique le millésime sur les bouteilles de Champagne que lorsqu'elles sont d'une qualité exceptionnelle, l'expression « millésime » peut être une garantie de qualité.

1961. Très bonne année.

1962. Quelques maisons ont fait un millésime.

1963. Faute de soleil, le vin fut plutôt acide, ce qui l'a rendu fort utile pour des coupages avec ceux d'autres années.

1964. Bon millésime et grande abondance. 93 millions de bouteilles d'un vin rond et charnu.

1965. Petite année qui ne peut pas être considérée comme un millésime.

1966. Vins magnifiques. Bouquet excellent et grande finesse.

1967. Des pluies du 5 au 21 septembre, une semaine juste avant les vendanges, ont altéré la qualité. Ce ne fut pas un millésime.

1968. Année désastreuse. Cette année ne fut pas millésimée.

1969. Bon millésime, bien équilibré et fortement charpenté. Quantité nettement faible.

1970. Récolte considérable, la plus abondante jamais enregistrée. La qualité fut satisfaisante.

1971. Très bonne année, mais la faible quantité produite entraîna des prix élevés.

1972. Cette année ne fut pas un millésime.

1973. Année pleinement satisfaisante.

1974. Un certain manque de caractère.

1975. Des vins de qualité satisfaisante, quoique ayant tendance à manquer d'acidité et à être un peu lourds.

1976. Millésime. Une production riche en quantité et en qualité.

1977. Cette année ne fut pas un millésime, mais les producteurs s'estimèrent satisfaits des vins obtenus.

1978. Récolte de qualité, bien que le mauvais temps en début de saison ait limité la production à 70 millions de bouteilles de moins que ce qu'il aurait fallu pour satisfaire la demande. Certaines maisons décidèrent de millésimer cette année.

1979. Récolte abondante et de bonne qualité. Certaines maisons ont fait des vins millésimés.

1980. Récolte catastrophiquement réduite, vins d'assez bonne qualité mais qui ont atteint des prix exorbitants.

1981. Assez bonne qualité, mais la quantité fut très insuffisante. Récolte désastreuse en raison de gelées tardives : seulement 350 000 pièces en 1981 comparées aux 420 000 en 1980 et aux 800 000 en 1979.

1982. La Champagne fut une des régions favorisées. La qualité fut bonne. La quantité énorme (1 300 000 pièces représentant 300 millions de bouteilles) compensa la pénurie causée par les vendanges désastreuses de 1980 et 1981.

1983. Comme en 1982, une très grande quantité avec plus de 300 millions de bouteilles. La qualité ne fut pas celle de 1982, donc l'année ne fut pas millésimée.

1984. Qualité moyenne qui n'a pas fait une année millésimée.

1985. « Extraordinaire ». Voici le mot employé pour qualifier ce millésime harmonieux, bien équilibré et d'une grande qualité. La quantité, cependant, était faible. On a produit 120 millions de bouteilles contre 190 millions vendues en 1985. La baisse de la quantité fut due aux gelées de janvier qui ont durement frappé la Champagne. Ainsi s'explique la perte de 30 à 40 millions de pieds de vigne.

1986. Bons vins, mais sans plus. La quantité est cependant satisfaisante et peut assurer les ventes annuelles.

RHIN ET MOSELLE

1959. Très grande année, comparable à 1949 et 1953. Vins riches en alcool et en sucre. Les vins les plus doux furent rares mais figurent dans l'histoire.

1960. Récolte très abondante mais de qualité inférieure à la moyenne.

1961. Bonne année sur la Moselle. Des déceptions sur le Rhin.

1962. A l'inverse de l'année précédente, le Rheingau fut favorisé, mais pas la Moselle.

1963. Grande quantité dans toutes les régions. Petite qualité.

1964. Bonne année avec de nombreux très hauts sommets.

1965. Sans intérêt.

1966. Bonne année, surtout pour les grands domaines où l'on commença à vendanger le 28 octobre.

1967. Qualités diverses : pour 1/3 : bon millésime avec quelques cas de réelle grandeur, qu'on ne trouva pas dans le 1966. Ces différences de qualité furent dues au mauvais temps pendant les vendanges.

1968. Vins légers et médiocres.

1969. Meilleur que 1966 et 1967. Un fort bouquet caractéristique, tel était le trait saillant de ce millésime élégant mais sans grandeur.

1970. Grands espoirs, malheureusement démentis par le temps froid et pluvieux des premiers jours d'octobre qui empêcha les raisins de mûrir convenablement. Les plus grands vignobles furent vendangés tardivement, et dans certains cas, la récolte n'eut lieu qu'à Noël. Ce délai eut d'heureuses conséquences sur la qualité des vins. Mais dans d'autres vignobles, l'énorme quantité vendangée entraîna un nivellement de qualité, bien que dans l'ensemble, l'année ait été de grand succès.

1971. Une des plus grandes années du siècle, et de loin. Les vins avaient ce merveilleux équilibre en sucre et en acidité qui classe les bons vins blancs allemands parmi les meilleurs du monde. Ils ont longue vie. Dans le Rheingau, 95 % de la récolte reçut le label de Qualitätswein mit Prädikat, appellation appliquée depuis cette année aux Kabinett, Spätlese, Auslese, etc.

1972. Après un été plutôt froid, les vins furent médiocres car les raisins n'étaient pas complètement mûrs. Des vins agréables et légers, mais sans plus.

1973. La plus grande récolte jamais enregistrée en Allemagne. Un été chaud et ensoleillé avait permis d'espérer un vin de bonne qualité. Pourtant, ils ne furent pas des meilleurs, à cause du manque de neige et de pluies en hiver qui endommagea les vignes dans quelques zones. Au moment des vendanges d'octobre 1973, la pluie fut incessante pendant plusieurs jours. Quelques journées particulièrement froides en décembre gelèrent de nombreux raisins dans certains grands vignobles du Rheingau. Seuls quelques vignerons purent produire du Eiswein.

1974. Une qualité médiocre due à un été perturbé par d'abondantes pluies qui se prolongèrent pendant les vendanges. Il y eut bien quelques vins agréables, à boire très jeunes, mais on ne produisit pas de Spätlese ni de Auslese.

1975. Grande année, certainement pas comparable à 1971, mais enfin avec une bonne quantité de vins de toute première qualité. Le Rheingau produisit 50 % de Qualitätswein. Le Mosel-Saar-Ruwer fut très honorable avec 45 % de Spätlese et 15 % de Auslese. Le Palatinat et le Rheinhessen produisirent 50 % de Qualitätswein et 15 % de Spätlese.

1976. Très grande année. Le temps exceptionnellement chaud qui favorisa l'Europe entière eut des conséquences particulièrement heureuses sur la production du Rheingau et de la Moselle. La teneur en sucre des raisins était si élevée au moment des vendanges — surtout dans le Rheingau — que les Riesling ne donnèrent qu'une quantité minime de vins au-dessous du niveau de Spätlese. On produisit en effet une énorme quantité de Auslese, ainsi que de Beerenauslese et de Trockenbeerenauslese (deux variétés généralement rares), plus peut-être que le marché ne pouvait en absorber. Les Müller-Thurgau et les Sylvaner furent plus ou moins décevants, ayant souffert de l'extrême chaleur. En Moselle, seule la moitié de la récolte normale put être vendangée, mais la qualité des vins doux fut aussi brillante que dans le Rheingau. Des vins doux et parfaitement équilibrés caractérisent cette année, où l'on trouva difficilement de bons vins bien secs.

1977. Année de qualité médiocre. Il lui aurait fallu beaucoup plus de soleil pour être classée parmi les grands millésimes. Les amateurs de vins secs allemands ont pu trouver un grand choix de bouteilles agréables.

1978. Année moyenne. Un début d'été froid et pluvieux a réduit la quantité et la qualité de la récolte. Les vins ressemblaient au 1977. Ils furent très buvables mais n'ont pas été des vins de garde.

1979. Bon millésime sans éclat. Les vins furent de bonne qualité sans être exceptionnels. Le gel de l'hiver 1978-1979 détruisit une bonne partie de certains vignobles, et les raisins récoltés furent soit en très faible, soit en trop grande quantité. En général, les Riesling donnèrent mieux que les Müller-Thurgau, à l'exception de la Saar et la Ruwer, où la récolte fut faible.

Dans le Rheinhessen et le Palatinat, les jeunes vignes furent presque entièrement détruites par les gels et la production fut réduite ; les Riesling, pourtant, étaient de bonne qualité. Dans le Rheingau, les vins furent de bonne qualité, mais sans plus ; la récolte fut abondante. Dans la Moselle, la Saar et la Ruwer, la récolte des Riesling fut abondante et de bonne qualité. Les autres cépages souffrirent du gel.

1980. Dans le Rheingau comme partout en Allemagne, le beau temps durant les vendanges ne fut pas suffisant pour effacer un été humide et froid. Production inférieure de 50 % à la normale et qualité médiocre. En Moselle, la récolte fut également réduite de 50 % et la qualité décevante. Dans la Saar et la Ruwer, les viticulteurs ne firent que 10 % de leur récolte habituelle et la qualité fut médiocre. Dans le Rheinhessen et le Palatinat la récolte fut réduite de moitié, mais la qualité fut assez bonne grâce aux nombreuses variétés de raisins *vinifera* qui résistèrent au froid de l'été.

1981. L'année débuta bien, jusqu'à la mi-septembre où quantité et qualité furent endommagées par des pluies continuelles qui se prolongèrent jusqu'à la fin du mois d'octobre. D'une manière générale, la récolte produisit des vins blancs secs. Il n'y eut pas de Spätlese ni d'Auslese. Dans la Saar-Ruwer et en Franconie, les gelées réduisirent la récolte de plus de 50 %.

1982. La qualité de la récolte fut dans l'ensemble moyenne et produisit fort peu de vin de qualité supérieure en raison des pluies abondantes et prolongées qui tombèrent au début des vendanges. Les nouvelles variétés de cépages produisirent des vins parfois très décevants, à faible acidité à cause de la sécheresse de l'été. Les vins de Kabinett et les Riesling traditionnels furent meilleurs, fruités et élégants. Une année moyenne pour les vins du Rhin, un peu meilleure en Moselle.

1983. Récolte très importante. Raisins parfaitement mûrs après un long été chaud. Kabinett, Spätlese et Auslese d'excellente qualité. L'automne chaud et sec ne permit toutefois pas à la pourriture noble de se développer. Ce grand millésime n'a donc compté que de rares sommets en Beerenauslese et Trockenbeerenauslese. Sans doute la plus belle récolte en Eiswein.

1984. Après un été froid et pluvieux suivi d'une période de sécheresse durant les vendanges, les vins produits allaient du médiocre au convenable. On a trouvé néanmoins beaucoup de bouteilles tout à fait buvables.

1985. Après trois mois chauds et secs, à partir de la fin août, le Rhin atteignit son niveau le plus bas jamais enregistré. Les régions traditionnelles de Riesling bénéficièrent de ce climat, mais de nouvelles variétés de raisin dans le Rheinhessen et le Palatinat, entre autres, souffrirent beaucoup de la sécheresse. La récolte fut d'assez bonne qualité donnant des vins clairs et typiques. En Moselle, on produisit un peu de Beerenauslese. L'arrivée de gelées importantes vers la mi-novembre permit la fabrication d'Eiswein dans toutes les régions. Bonne année pour de bons vins comme le Kabinett et le Spätlese, mais cependant aucun vin de niveau supérieur.

1986. L'année qui promettait d'être exceptionnelle en qualité ne fut que bonne en raison de quatre semaines de pluies froides tombées juste avant la récolte. Grande quantité de vins Prädikat dans les variétés tardives telles que le Riesling. Grosse production d'Eiswein.

CHAPITRE XI

Répertoire des vins et alcools

A

Abbocato

Nom donné en Italie au vin demi-doux, demi-sec.

Abocado

Nom donné en Espagne au vin mi-doux, de bouquet délicat.

Abricotine

Nom français d'une liqueur obtenue en faisant macérer des abricots dans de l'eau-de-vie de vin. D'une couleur ambre foncé, l'abricotine a le goût d'abricot avec une légère saveur d'amande due au noyau.

Abrogation

Le 5 décembre 1933, un 21ᵉ amendement à la Constitution des États-Unis abrogeait le 18ᵉ amendement qui interdisait vente, détention et transport de tout breuvage alcoolique sur toute l'étendue du pays. Cette abrogation rendait de nouveau légitime la fabrication, le commerce et la consommation de tous breuvages alcooliques. Néanmoins, en dépit de ce *repeal*, chaque État, chaque canton, chaque municipalité est à même d'imposer des restrictions de toute nature à ce sujet.

Abruzzi (Abruzzes)

Vins rouges et blancs. Centre-Est de l'Italie. Sur l'Adriatique.

Cette région montagneuse d'Italie produit quelques vins agréables mais de peu d'importance. Montepulciano et Cerasuolo d'Abruzzo sont rouges, légers et robustes. Le Montepulciano, produit en grande quantité (2 millions de caisses), doit son nom à la variété de raisin, mais il est parfois vinifié avec un peu de Sangiovese. Ce vin robuste, légèrement mousseux, a une couleur rubis et parfois, un arrière-goût douceâtre. Il est cultivé aux alentours de Canosa, Sannita, Casoli et d'autres villages et a sa propre D.O.C. (Denominazione di Origine Controllata). Le Cerasuolo est un vin d'un rose framboise D.O.C. ; comme le Montepulciano, il titre environ 12° d'alcool. Trebbiano d'Abruzzo, d'une couleur de paille, est neutre et sec, son nom provient aussi de la variété de raisin utilisée, Trebbiano d'Abruzzo ou Trebbiano Toscano. D'où qu'il provienne dans la région, il porte tout de même le label D.O.C. Ces vins sont peu exportés et on n'en trouve guère en Italie hors de leur région.

Voir ITALIE

Absinthe

Apéritif d'un vert clair, extrêmement fort, obtenu par infusion d'herbes — surtout anis et absinthe — dans de l'alcool. Considérée comme nocive pour les nerfs, l'absinthe a été bannie de la plupart des pays occidentaux, mais pas en Espagne où l'on voit souvent aux terrasses de cafés des buveurs d'absinthe discuter furieusement les dangers du breuvage qu'ils consomment.

L'absinthe fut inventée par le médecin français Ordinaire à Couvet (Suisse). Ordinaire vendit sa recette à un certain monsieur

Pernod, en 1797. On en consomma abondamment en Europe jusqu'à ce qu'elle fût interdite. Depuis, on fabrique nombre de succédanés tous anisés, mais ne contenant pas d'essence d'absinthe. Ces anis et pastis sont très populaires surtout dans le Sud de la France. Les deux marques commerciales les plus connues sont Pernod et Ricard.

Abzug

Littéralement : ce qui est tiré hors de quelques chose, donc tirage ou soutirage, ainsi que le produit du soutirage. L'expression allemande *Schloss Abzug* équivaut à mise en bouteille (tirage) au château.

Acariose

Maladie de la vigne qui étiole les jeunes pousses, et dont les causes varient d'un pays à l'autre. La croissance peut être ralentie ou même enrayée par les acariens *Calepitrimerus vitis* et *Phyllocoptes vitis,* ou par une variante de l'*Ériophyes vitis.*

Acescence

Formation d'une quantité excessive d'acide acétique et d'acétate d'éthyle dans le vin, souvent provoquée par trop de contact avec l'air. Une pellicule d'un gris translucide apparaît alors à la surface, elle est due à l'*Acetobacter.* Le vin est alors *piqué ;* il prend l'odeur d'acescence et un goût de vinaigre.

Voir CHAPITRE V

Acétification

Voir ACESCENCE

Acétique (acide)

Cet acide volatil est toujours présent dans le vin en très faible quantité. Si on laisse se développer librement les bactéries acétiques ou lactiques, il acétifiera le vin qui sera piqué, et tournera au vinaigre. Formule : CH_3COOH.

Voir CHAPITRE V

Achaïe

Province grecque du Péloponnèse longeant la côte méridionale du Golfe de Corinthe. La région produit une quantité non négligeable de rouges et de blancs, particulièrement autour de la ville de Patras.

Voir GRÈCE

Acide

Nom donné aux substances qui peuvent échanger un ou plusieurs atomes d'hydrogène avec un atome de métal ou son radical. Les acides sont des composants essentiels du vin auquel ils donnent fraîcheur et caractéristiques. L'acide est monoacide, biacide ou triacide, selon qu'il comporte 1, 2 ou 3 atomes échangeables d'hydrogène.

Les hydracides sont des combinaisons d'hydrogène avec un métalloïde ou un métal et un métalloïde. Ils portent un nom en « hydrique », par exemple : acides chlorhydrique, sulfhydrique. Les oxacides dérivent de l'action d'un anhydride sur l'eau ; en général leur nom se termine en « ique » (acide sulfurique, nitrique, par exemple) ; mais certains corps simples constituent différents oxacides de diverses valences. On les classe alors comme suit :

per......ique	acide persulfurique	$H_2S_2O_8$
..........ique	acide sulfurique	H_2SO_4
..........eux	acide sulfureux	H_2SO_3
hypo ...eux	acide hyposulfureux	$H_2S_2O_4$

(Source : Yves Renouil et Paul de Traversay, *Dictionnaire du vin*).

Voir ACIDE ; ACÉTIQUE

Acidité

Les acides, qui donnent au vin de la fraîcheur et du goût, en sont les constituants essentiels. Sans acidité le breuvage serait insipide. Trop acide, il devient âpre ou aigre. Mais quand l'équilibre est atteint, le vin a du goût et de la fraîcheur. Certains acides existent à l'état naturel dans le raisin, d'autres résultent de la fermentation. Les types d'acide et la quantité de chacun que l'on trouve dans chaque vin dépendent de la variété de raisin, du sol sur lequel pousse la vigne, du climat pendant l'été au cours duquel mûrit le raisin, des levures et autres micro-organismes ainsi que des substances ajoutées au vin pendant la vinification.

Les acides tartrique et malique sont les plus désirables dans le vin. L'acétique est au contraire le plus indésirable. L'acide citrique est un de ceux que l'on trouve en quantités infimes. Les vins mousseux contiennent aussi de l'acide carbonique.

Les experts reconnaissent trois types d'acidité : volatile, fixe, et totale qui est la somme des deux précédentes. L'acide acétique est l'acide volatil dominant, mais il y en a d'autres quantités infimes, notamment les acides butyrique, formique, propionique. L'acidité volatile est indispensable à la stabilité et au bouquet du vin, mais si elle est excessive, elle donne un goût désagréable du genre vinaigre. Parmi les acides fixes, ou stables, les plus importants sont les acides tartrique, malique et citrique. Les deux types forment l'ensemble de l'acidité totale.

Voir CHAPITRE V

Aconcagua (Vallée de l')

Vins rouges. Centre du Chili.

Une des meilleures régions vinicoles du Chili. On y cultive particulièrement le Cabernet et le Malbec. Production de vins forts, doués de finesse, bien équilibrés et de longue durée.

Voir CHILI

Acquavite

Ortographe italienne d'*aqua vitae* autrement dit : eau-de-vie.

Toutefois les Italiens prétendent volontiers qu'à l'origine l'orthographe n'était pas *aqua vitae* en latin, mais *aqua* ou *aqua di vite,* autrement dit, en italien : eau de vigne, désignant le liquide incolore obtenu par la distillation du vin. Selon les partisans de cette étymologie, l'orthographe se transforma plus tard, soit en raison de la vertu stimulatrice et vivifiante de l'eau-de-vie, soit par simple erreur et ce serait ainsi que l'orthographe la plus courante l'aurait emporté.

Acquit

Ou plus exactement : *acquit à caution :* document officiel qui accompagne en France toutes les expéditions de vins ou de spiritueux dont les taxes intérieures n'ont pas été payées. (Pour les expéditions dont la taxe a été payée le document s'appelle *congé.)* L'acquit est employé pour les exportations exemptes de taxe. La couleur du papier change selon le type de vin ou spiritueux et facilite l'identification. Le papier bulle désigne les vins ordinaires ; le vert désigne les vins d'appellation d'origine contrôlée ; le jaune d'or, l'Armagnac et le Cognac ; l'orange, les vins de liqueur d'appellation d'origine contrôlée. En général ce document reste en France. S'il accompagnait l'expédition jusqu'au destinataire et s'il était soumis à un contrôle strict, il y aurait moins d'exportations frauduleuses.

En 1959, les autorités douanières des États-Unis ont décidé que l'acquit serait légalement nécessaire pour toute importation commerciale de vins français.

Acre

Mesure de surface anglaise et américaine équivalant à 4 047 m², autrement dit, 0,405 ha.

Adega

Nom portugais de la *bodega.*

Voir BODEGA

Adige

Voir TRENTIN

Adom Atic

Un des principaux vins rouges d'Israël.

Voir ISRAËL

Advocaat

Breuvage ressemblant au lait de poule, généralement fait avec de l'eau-de-vie de vin et du jaune d'œuf, puis mis en bouteille. Aux Pays-Bas, l'advocaat titre entre 15 et

18° d'alcool. Il est si épais qu'on le consomme à la cuillère.

Afrique du Sud

Avec son climat sec et chaud et ses traditions viticoles remontant à trois siècles, l'Union sud-africaine est un pays producteur de vin mais malheureusement n'en consomme pas beaucoup. Bien que, Dieu merci ! on y ait tendance à adopter l'usage civilisé de prendre un verre de vin aux repas. La consommation excessive des liqueurs fortes — whisky, eau-de-vie (la plus forte par tête pour le monde entier) et gin — pose un problème que les autorités s'efforcent de résoudre. La grande amélioration de qualité des vins de table et des vins du type Xérès contribue sans doute à transformer les usages en fait de boisson. Il n'y a que quelques années, les faux Xérès étaient extrêmement durs et les vins de table rudes et sans aucune saveur qui permît de les distinguer les uns des autres. Mais il n'en est plus ainsi. On constate en outre une amélioration prodigieuse de la présentation, c'est-à-dire de l'étiquetage, des meilleurs vins de table au cours des dernières années.

Combien faudra-t-il de temps pour que les Africains du Sud consomment couramment du vin, actuellement réservé aux occasions exceptionnelles ? C'est difficile à dire, mais les perspectives semblent favorables. Depuis que les gros vins ordinaires à bon marché disparaissent, les vignerons font des vins de table qui, dans certains cas, atteignent une qualité moyenne supérieure à celle de leurs homologues européens. Ce n'est pas sans raison que leur consommation a triplé depuis 1945, selon des évaluations dignes de foi. Elle s'élève aujourd'hui à 11 l par tête et par an.

La région qui s'étend au sud-ouest de Cape Town est une de celles qui conviennent le mieux à la viticulture. Tempéré, le climat ne varie que très exceptionnellement dans de grandes proportions et les pluies abondantes sont rares avant la saison des vendanges. Les années mauvaises ne sont donc pas trop à craindre. Comme nous sommes dans l'hémisphère sud, la saison des vendanges commence en février ou mars et, dans les vignobles où l'on cultive plusieurs variétés de raisin, elles peuvent se prolonger pendant cinq à six semaines.

HISTOIRE DU VIN EN AFRIQUE DU SUD

En 1955, l'industrie sud-africaine du vin célébra son tricentenaire. C'est en effet à la fin de l'année 1654 que les premières boutures de vigne arrivèrent de Hollande au Cap. Sans doute s'agissait-il de petites pousses de 10 cm, provenant de jeunes vignes du Rhin. L'année suivante il en arriva de nouvelles, toujours de Hollande. C'étaient alors probablement des vignes Muscat, Green Grape (Groendruif), Muscatel et Steen, connue sous le nom de Steendruif en Afrikaans.

Le 2 février 1659, on pressura des raisins pour la première fois au Cap dans le but de faire du vin. Johan van Riebeeck écrivit dans son journal : « Aujourd'hui, loué soit le Seigneur ! on a fait du vin pour la première fois avec des raisins du Cap ».

Signalons le mérite de l'Association coopérative des vignerons d'Afrique du Sud à laquelle nous devons une chronologie des événements. En 1679, Simon Van der Stel devint gouverneur du cap de Bonne-Espérance, installa son domaine agricole à Groot Constantia et donna l'exemple aux colons en faisant des vins fins. Voici d'autres dates mémorables : 1688, des huguenots français arrivent et s'installent à Franschœk, Paarl, Drakenstein et Stellenbosch ; ils augmentent les plantations de vigne et améliorent la qualité des vins du Cap. 1711, les vins sud-africains commencent à être connus et un voyageur écrit cette phrase : « ...les vins de Constantia, célèbres dans le monde entier... ». On faisait ces vins à Wynberg. Ils étaient doux. 1805, les Anglais prennent possession du Cap et, en raison de leur guerre contre Napoléon, encouragent l'exportation des vins sud-africains vers la Grande-Bretagne. 1811, Sir John Cradock nomme le premier dégustateur officiel et le charge de veiller à la qualité des vins exportés. 1826, les exportations vers la Grande-Bretagne prospèrent ; vignerons et négociants investissent de grosses sommes. 1861, le gouvernement Gladstone baissa considérablement les tarifs pour l'importation des vins, ce dont l'Afrique du Sud profita. 1885, le phylloxéra ravage les vignes du Cap et les vignerons sont menacés de ruine totale. Pour venir à bout de ce fléau, ils greffent leurs vignes sur des souches américaines qui résistent au phylloxéra. Les vignes reprennent leur vigueur. Mais les vignerons sont menacés d'un désastre encore pire : la surproduction. 1917, les prix tombent si bas que les vignerons décident de s'organiser pour défendre leurs intérêts. 1918, fondation de l'Association coopérative des vignerons de l'Afrique du Sud, sous forme de société anonyme. On la connaît mieux de nos jours sous ses initiales K.W.V. En 1924, le parlement adopte la loi numéro 5 sur le contrôle des vins et spiritueux. La K.W.V. selon ses statuts détermine chaque année le prix minimal des vins destinés à la distillation. La nouvelle loi impose les mêmes règles à ceux qui ne sont pas membres de l'association, ce qui bouleverse l'industrie vinicole de l'Afrique du Sud. 1926, les exportations reprennent vers la Grande-Bretagne et la Hollande. 1931, l'Association des fermiers viticulteurs de l'Afrique du Sud (Londres) est fondée au Royaume-Uni sous forme de société anonyme dont la K.W.V. détient la moitié du capital. Cette association a pour but de veiller à la distribution, assurer la continuité des fournitures, uniformiser la quantité et stabiliser les prix. 1940, adoption d'un amendement n° 23 à la loi sur le contrôle des vins et des spiritueux, qui fixe le prix du bon vin vendu par le producteur ; elle autorise aussi la K.W.V. à limiter la production de l'alcool de vin. 1950, la K.W.V. devient seule propriétaire de l'Association des fermiers viticulteurs d'Afrique du Sud (Londres) Ltd.

Les régions vinicoles

En tant qu'activité agricole importante, la viticulture est limitée à une zone qui s'étend à l'ouest du Cap, entre 33° et 34° de latitude sud. Les régions où les pluies sont abondantes en été ne conviennent pas à la vigne ; mais il en pousse en altitude au Transvaal. Le nord du pays produit raisins de table et raisins secs. De bons raisins du Sauternais (Sémillon et Sauvignon blanc) sont cultivés avec autant de succès au Cap que près de Bordeaux. Mais la loi autorise à viner le vin au-delà de 16° ; cela indique qu'on n'a pas encore obtenu en Afrique du Sud un vin doux, pur, sucré naturellement, comme dans le Sauternais.

La zone viticole peut être divisée en deux régions distinctes : le secteur côtier et celui de Little Karoo. Le premier s'étend de la côte jusqu'à la première chaîne de montagnes et englobe les agglomérations de Stellenbosch, Paarl, Malmesbury, Ceres Tulbagh, ainsi que la vallée de Constantia. La seconde est située au-delà de la chaîne de Drakenstein et va jusqu'au mont Swartberg. Elle comprend les secteurs de Worcester, Robertson, Montagu, Oudtshoorn et Ladismith.

Le secteur des vignobles du Cap s'étend au sud-est du mont de la Table et couvre la péninsule du Cap. Situé à l'extrémité sud de la zone côtière, c'est le plus ancien pays viticole d'Afrique du Sud. Dans toute la région côtière, on cultive la vigne surtout à flanc de colline. Le rendement varie entre 7,5 et 15 hl/ha. On y fait des vins secs, rouges et blancs, et des imitations de Xérès et de Porto. Étant donné que les conditions climatiques varient peu, la qualité de ces vins reste constante d'une année à l'autre. On y cultive des raisins des variétés Hermitage, Steendruif (qui ressemble beaucoup au Sauvignon blanc), Grœndruif, Riesling, Cabernet Sauvignon, Clairette Blanche et les raisins qui donnent le Porto.

Dans la région de Little Karoo où il pleut moitié moins que dans la précédente et où les vignobles sont irrigués, le rendement s'élève à 15 et même 25 hl/ha. On y cultive des raisins Hermitage, Steendruif, Hanepoot, Muscatel et Sultana, qui donnent des vins doux, des vins du type Xérès et également des eaux-de-vie.

Dans la région côtière, le sol varie du sablonneux à un mélange lourd d'argile, sable et sédiments organiques, alors qu'au Little Karoo on trouve une couche épaisse de riches alluvions. Certains vignerons affirment que leur propriété comporte des sols d'origine diverse.

Les saisons de l'Afrique du Sud sont inversées par rapport à celles de l'Europe. Le printemps dure de septembre à novembre, l'été de décembre à février, l'automne de mars à mai, et l'hiver de juin à août. Les raisins achèvent de mûrir entre février et avril, et les vendanges commencent avant l'arrivée de l'automne.

Les types de vins

Les vins de Constantia étaient réputés dans les pays importateurs dès la fin du XVIIIe siècle et au début du XIXe. C'étaient déjà des vins de dessert. Ils sont encore de bonne qualité. Certains sont du type Porto et Muscat. Ceux du premier groupe sont faits avec des raisins Hermitage ou des variétés portugaises cultivées à Paarl, Stellenbosch et dans les régions avoisinantes. Les Porto sont produits suivant des normes portugaises. Aussi trouve-t-on du Porto blanc, du Ruby Port, du Tawny Port et même du Vintage Port. Quant au Muscat, il provient de raisins du même nom cultivés à Robertson, Montagu, Bonnievale et dans le secteur Nuy de Worcester.

La production de vin de type Xérès ne commença en Afrique du Sud qu'il y a environ 30 ans et c'est seulement en 1942 qu'on le fit selon le système de la *solera* (méthode traditionnelle de production du Xérès en Espagne). Il est intéressant de noter les ressemblances climatiques et géographiques qui existent entre Paarl, centre de la production vinicole sud-africaine, et les régions d'Andalousie d'où provient le Xérès.

Jerez de la Frontera est situé à 34°41' de latitude nord et Paarl à 33°45' de latitude sud.

Le Cap produit des vins légers et des vins corsés naturels. Les légers avec des raisins Cabernet, Hermitage et Shiraz, cultivés dans la vallée de Constantia, ainsi que dans celles de Stellenbosch et de Somerset West, plus proche de la côte ; les corsés avec des raisins Hermitage, Shiraz, Pontac et Gamay, cultivés à Paarl, Stellenbosch et Durbanville. Voilà déjà quelques années qu'on fait aussi des rosés dont la popularité augmente.

Paarl, Stellenbosch et Tulbagh produisent aussi des vins de table blancs, secs et demi-doux, dont la teneur en sucre doit être inférieure à 3 %. Ils sont faits avec des raisins Riesling du Cape, Gewurztraminer, Colombard, et Clairette Blanche. Les vins blancs représentent 85 % de la production.

Avec les raisins Riesling, Sauvignon blanc et un peu de Chenin Blanc, on fait aussi des vins mousseux, soit par fermentation naturelle, soit par insufflation de gaz carbonique.

Il est difficile de donner des statistiques exactes sur le produit des vendanges sud-africaines. Il faut se reporter à des rapports fournis par les vignerons. Y figurent non seulement les produits alcooliques, mais aussi les raisins de table et ceux qui sont destinés à être séchés. En outre, ils ne comportent aucune indication en ce qui concerne les principales régions de production de raisins secs. Toutefois, d'après les informations fournies par l'Association coopérative de producteurs de vins, voici quelle fut la production des différentes régions en 1983 :

Secteur	*Milliers d'hectolitres*
Olifants River	1 000 000
Malmesbury	750 000
Montagu	400 000
Orange River	700 000
Paarl	1 400 000
Robertson	1 400 000
Stellenbosch	1 300 000
Worcester	2 000 000
Total	8 950 000

Les alcools

Des breuvages alcooliques, titrant entre 60 et 78° ou 30 % à 39 % par volume, sont de plus en plus nombreux. On les fait selon les mêmes méthodes qu'en Europe. Mais la liqueur légendaire que les premiers colons du Cap appelaient Van der Hum est un produit typiquement sud-africain. Jadis, chacun l'élaborait chez soi, avec des écorces de mandarine *(naartjie)*. De nos jours, on emploie un produit synthétique pour lui donner du goût.

On distilla de l'eau-de-vie de vin, pour la première fois au Cap en l'an 1672. Actuellement, production et maturation de l'alcool de vin sont soumises à un strict contrôle d'État. Il titre 75° ou 43 % par volume. Les vins employés à la distillation sont faits avec du raisin cultivé autour de Worcester, Montagu et Robertson. Seuls les vins de chaudière de première qualité sont autorisés à la distillation et les produits doivent avoir l'approbation du Government Brandy Board. Tous les types d'eaux-de-vie de vin sud-africaines doivent contenir un minimum de 30 % d'eau-de-vie de vin distillée en alambic et mûrie pendant au mois trois ans en fûts de chêne importés avec l'approbation d'un commissaire du gouvernement. Si le bureau des eaux-de-vie certifie que l'alcool est un pur dérivé du vin, on lui applique une exonération fiscale. On a mis au point une échelle de réduction d'impôts plus élevée pour les eaux-de-vie vieillies. Les marques les plus connues sont Klipdriff, Oude Meester, Viceroy, Limousin, Richelieu, Martell et Bols.

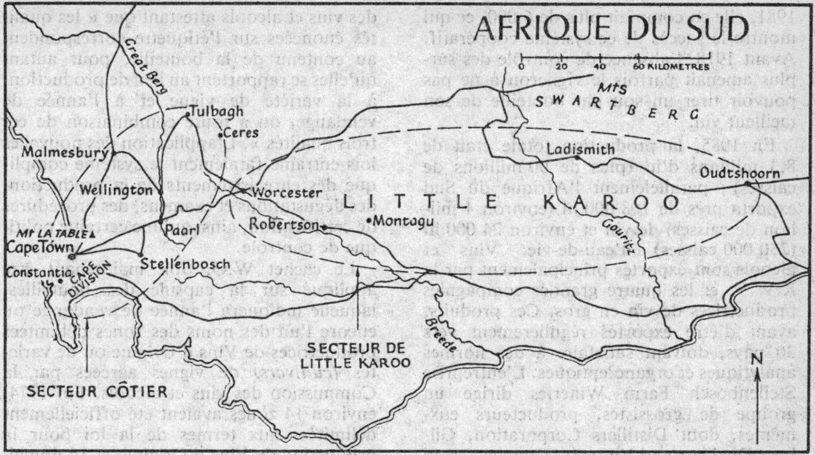

L'ORGANISATION DES INDUSTRIES DES VINS ET DES ALCOOLS

Au niveau de la production, l'industrie du vin est solidement organisée et cela, dans une large mesure, en raison de l'espèce de monopole dont jouit la K.W.V. dont nous avons parlé ci-avant. Fondée en 1918, cette association avait pour but : « de diriger, contrôler et réglementer la vente ainsi que les autres procédés par lesquels ses membres disposaient de leur produit, celui-ci étant le raisin, dans le but de leur assurer ou de chercher à leur assurer un revenu constamment valable ».

Au début, certains vignerons préférèrent se passer de l'appui que leur aurait fourni cette association coopérative. La loi de 1924 mit un terme à leur opposition, car l'acte de contrôle des vins et spiritueux imposait les mêmes conditions et obligations aux non-membres qu'aux membres de la K.W.V. Depuis lors, nul ne peut vendre, acheter ou distiller, ou convertir en spiritueux d'une manière quelconque, du vin sans le consentement de la K.W.V. ou sans passer par son intermédiaire. De même, aucun vigneron n'a le droit de vendre, distiller ou disposer autrement du vin, d'eau-de-vie, de spiritueux, provenant de son propre vin, que par l'intermédiaire ou avec le consentement de la K.W.V.

En vertu de ces statuts, l'association fixe chaque année le prix minimal du vin destiné à la distillation, évalue le surplus (c'est-à-dire la portion de la récolte que le marché local ne peut absorber) et indique quelle proportion de sa récolte chaque membre doit conserver, d'une part, et livrer gratuitement comme surplus à l'association, d'autre part. Le membre qui ne peut livrer le surplus indiqué parce qu'il a vendu toute sa récolte doit en verser l'équivalent en espèces. Les décisions de la coopérative ont force de loi. La K.W.V. n'a pas le droit de vendre ses produits pour utilisation en Afrique, au sud de l'équateur, sauf à des sociétés coopératives à fin de distillation et de vente en gros. En Afrique du Sud, on fait une distinction claire et nette entre ce qu'on appelle le « bon vin » et le « vin à distiller ». Le premier est destiné à être consommé en tant que vin et le second à être distillé pour obtenir de l'eau-de-vie ou d'autres spiritueux à base de vin.

En 1986, l'association fixa à 40 % le surplus de la récolte. Pour en disposer, elle trouva son meilleur débouché sur le marché traditionnel du Cap : la Grande-Bretagne. La K.W.V. possède cinq entreprises vinicoles en Afrique du Sud. Elles sont situées à Paarl, Stellenbosch, Robertson, Montagu et Worcester. La capacité totale de leurs entrepôts dépasse 2 000 000 hl. En 1959, la K.W.V. groupait 4 444 membres et, en

1981, elle en comptait plus de 6 000, ce qui montre le succès de ce système coopératif. Avant 1918, l'absence de contrôle des surplus amenait parfois le vigneron à ne pas pouvoir tirer un sou par bouteille de son meilleur vin.

En 1985, la production totale était de 8,3 millions d'hl (plus de 90 millions de caisses) ; parallèlement l'Afrique du Sud exporta près de 108 000 hl (environ 1 million de caisses) de vin et environ 24 000 hl (250 000 caisses) d'eau-de-vie. Vins et alcools sont exportés principalement par la K.W.V. et les quatre grandes compagnies productrices de vin en gros. Ces produits, avant d'être exportés régulièrement vers 30 pays, doivent satisfaire à des normes analytiques et organoleptiques. L'entreprise Stellenbosch Farm Wineries dirige un groupe de grossistes, producteurs eux-mêmes, dont Distillers Corporation, Gilbeys Distillers and Vintners, Douglas Green et Union Wine. Ces compagnies achètent ou fabriquent leur propre vin en grande quantité pour le mélanger ensuite, le faire vieillir, le mettre en bouteilles, le conserver ou le distribuer afin qu'il soit vendu au détail. Grâce à leurs installations de recherche, elles jouent un rôle important dans le développement des techniques viticoles et œnologiques récentes. Désormais, le commerce des vins sud-africains ne dépend plus des tarifs douaniers préférentiels, mais de leur qualité. La qualité de tous les vins du Cap est vérifiée par les commissaires du gouvernement avant exportation et le contrôle de l'alcool de vin, au point de vue fiscal, est un des plus stricts du monde. Toutes les eaux-de-vie expédiées par ce pays sont accompagnées d'un certificat indiquant leur âge, leurs méthodes de distillation et de vieillissement.

Alors que les pays vinicoles d'Europe ont reconnu depuis longtemps l'importance du lieu d'origine quant à l'identification et au « pedigree » des vins, l'Afrique du Sud resta dépourvue jusqu'en septembre 1973 de tout système approchant l'Appellation d'Origine Contrôlée française. Un tel système a enfin été adopté — après enquête menée par une commission gouvernementale placée sous la direction du Dr J.A. van Zyl — et mis en vigueur avec l'introduction du cachet W.O. (Wines of Origin, soit Vins d'Origine), qui est une véritable garantie de l'étiquette d'un vin. Le cachet est délivré par la Commission Sud-africaine des vins et alcools attestant que « les qualités énoncées sur l'étiquette correspondent au contenu de la bouteille, pour autant qu'elles se rapportent au lieu de production, à la variété de vigne et à l'année de vendange, ou à toute combinaison de ces trois qualités ». L'application des nouvelles lois entraîne fatalement le système compliqué des enregistrements de la production, des dégustations et examens, des procédures de certification, ainsi qu'une certaine politique de contrôle.

Le cachet W.O. doit maintenant être appliqué sur la capsule des bouteilles, laquelle indiquera l'année de vendange ou encore l'un des noms des zones délimitées productrices de Vins d'Origine ou de variétés *(cultivars)* de vignes agréées par la Commission des vins et alcools. Fin 1974, environ 14 zones avaient été officiellement délimitées aux termes de la loi pour la production de Vins d'Origine, et 14 domaines étaient agréés pour celle de « Vins de Domaine d'Origine ».

Les zones en question comprenaient Paarl, Piketberg, Robertson, Stellenbosch (y compris Caledon et Le Cap), Tulbagh, Worcester, Swartland, Swellendam, Constantia, Durbanville, Olifants River, Little Karoo, ainsi qu'un secteur appelé Boberg (zones de Conseil Divisionnaire de Paarl et Tulbagh). L'appellation Boberg est limitée aux vins de liqueur tels que les « Xérès » et « Portos ». Les meilleurs vins viennent de Malmesbury, Paarl, Stellenbosch, Tulbagh, Worcester, Constantia et Durbanville, ce dernier secteur étant connu pour ses vins rouges.

Des vins fins de qualité très améliorée sont à l'heure actuelle produits par un grand nombre de domaines, y compris Backsberg, Boschendal, Welgemeend, Fairview, Landskroon et Nederburg à Paarl ; Groot Constantia dans la zone de Cape Town ; Kanonkop, Vergenoegd, Simonsig, Spier, Uiterwyk, Meerlust, Le Bonheur et Vergenoegd situés à Stellenboosch ; enfin Alto, Theuniskraal et Twee Jongegezellen situé à Tulbagh. D'autres domaines particulièrement bons sont De Westhof, L'Ormarins et Hamilton Russell Vineyards.

Pour être qualifié Vin d'Origine, un vin doit être fait avec des raisins provenant uniquement de l'origine indiquée (et 80 % pour les vins vinés).

Un vin de domaine doit satisfaire à certaines normes de qualité définies par la

Commission et doit être entièrement produit ou fabriqué au domaine avec des raisins cultivés dans ce même domaine. On distingue entre les vins produits, fabriqués et mis en bouteille dans le même domaine, et les vins produits ou fabriqués au domaine, mais mis en bouteille autre part.

Pour être vendu ou exporté sous le nom d'une des variétés *(cultivar)* de vigne autorisées, un vin doit être fait avec au moins 75 % de la variété en question et être caractéristique de cette variété. Les vins dits « de qualité supérieure » doivent être faits avec 100 % du cépage en question.

Des dispositions sont actuellement prises pour les « Vins Supérieurs d'Origine » (ou W.O.S.), label de haute distinction octroyé aux vins de qualité supérieure.

Depuis l'introduction du Certificat d'Origine, le consommateur est davantage conscient des variations qui existent entre des vins de vignobles, de variétés et de cépages différents, ce qui se traduit par une plus grande gamme de prix. Tout ceci a poussé les producteurs à planter des cépages capables de produire des vins de meilleure qualité tels les Weisser Riesling, Sauvignon Blanc, Chardonnay, Gewürztraminer, Pinot Noir et Cabernet Sauvignon.

On devrait louer le Stellenbosch Research Institute pour son influence dans le développement de règles intelligentes de contrôle de qualité.

Agave.

Plante de la famille des amaryllidacées qui pousse en Amérique tropicale et surtout au Mexique. Dénommée aussi plante séculaire, l'agave a une sève abondante, dont les Mexicains tirent trois boissons : pulque, tequila et mescal.

Voir PULQUE, TEQUILA et MESCAL

Aglianico del Vulture (D.O.C.)

Vin d'un rouge profond chaleureux et durable, fait des raisins Aglianico dans les vignobles de Monte Vulture en Italie méridionale.

Voir BASILICATE

Agrafe

Lamelle de métal recourbée servant à retenir le premier bouchon de la bouteille de Champagne avant le *dégorgement* et le bouchage final.

Aguardiente

Nom général des spiritueux dans les pays de langue espagnole et plus précisément de l'eau-de-vie de vin dans les pays vinicoles et du rhum dans les pays de canne à sucre.

Ahr

État allemand : Rhénanie-Palatinat. Superficie : 430 ha environ. 70 % de vins rouges, 30 % de vins blancs.

Situé à l'extrême nord-ouest du pays, l'Ahr est l'un des plus petits des 11 vignobles allemands. Il tire son nom du fleuve Ahr qui se jette dans le Rhin juste au-dessous de Bonn. Bad Neuenahr est la capitale locale et une ville d'eaux. Tous les vignobles de la région sont regroupés dans un district, celui de Walporzheim-Ahrtal, qui consiste en un site vinicole collectif (Grosslage), Klosterberg.

Variétés de raisin : Spätburgunder ou Pinot Noir (37 %), Portugieser, variété rouge (26 %), Riesling (15 %) et Müller-Thurgau (12 %).

Vins : Le Spätburgunder épicé et velouté, le Portugieser léger, souple et fruité au caractère neutre et des vins blancs alertes et aciéreux.

Les vignobles nécessitent un travail intensif. Ils sont plantés sur des coteaux abrupts et des falaises d'ardoise et de sol volcanique, taillées en terrasses. C'est grâce au sol qui se réchauffe rapidement en conservant la chaleur et au micro-climat bénéfique dû au fleuve que les vignes peuvent survivre dans la région. La vallée de l'Ahr est abritée par le massif de l'Eiffel.

La majorité des 740 viticulteurs sont des vignerons à mi-temps, dont les exploitations mesurent en moyenne 0,64 ha. 90 % d'entre eux livrent leurs raisins et leur moût au négoce ou à l'une des 5 coopératives de la région. La première coopérative vinicole d'Allemagne fut fondée à Mayschoss, en 1868. La plupart du vin est consommée sur place ou achetée par les touristes.

La viticulture dans l'Ahr remonte à l'époque romaine et ici, comme partout ailleurs, c'est l'Église qui a entretenu les vignes au cours du Moyen Age. Kloster Marienthal, couvent augustin (du XIIe au XIXe siècle) et aujourd'hui propriété de l'État, est l'un des domaines les plus prestigieux de la région (Staatliche Weinbaudomäne Marienthal, dont l'étiquette porte l'aigle noir stylisé). Bien que les variétés rouges ne furent pas plantées avant 1680, le vin devint si populaire que, pendant les deux siècles et demi qui suivirent, les vins de l'Ahr furent exclusivement rouges.

Aiguebelle

Liqueur faite en France près de Valence. La formule aurait été découverte dans un monastère de la Trappe. Quelque cinquante herbes lui donnent son goût. Elle se présente en deux variétés — verte et jaune —, la verte est la plus forte.

Aiven

Alcool tatare obtenu en faisant fermenter du lait.

Aix-en-Provence

Vins rouges, blancs et rosés. Sud-Est de la France.

Les vignobles situés aux environs de la capitale de la Provence s'étendent sur des terrains rocheux jusqu'aux limites de la Côte d'Azur. Les vins sont agréables, généralement entêtants et tenaces. Ils sont parfaits quand on les consomme dans la région, légèrement rafraîchis, en été. Rouges et blancs ne sont pas négligeables, mais les rosés sont généralement les meilleurs.

Voir PROVENCE, COTEAUX D'AIX, COTEAUX DES BAUX

Akvavit

Orthographe danoise d'aquavit.

Alambic

Appareil servant à la distillation, particulièrement celle des spiritueux. Dans la région de Cognac, on distille encore le vin avec l'alambic le plus simple, dérivé de celui des alchimistes. Ailleurs, surtout par la distillation des alcools de grain (whisky, vodka, etc.) on se sert d'un appareil à distillation continue dérivé de celui qu'inventa Coffey.

Voir CHAPITRE VI et DISTILLATION

Alasch

Voir ALLASCH

Alavesa

Un des meilleurs vins de Rioja, en Espagne. (Le mot Alavesa figure fréquemment sur l'étiquette). Il ressemble à celui du Rhône.

Voir RIOJA

Alba Flora

Un vin blanc de Majorque (Baléares, Espagne).

Albana di Romagna

Principal vin de Romagne, région vinicole de la province italienne d'Émilie. Ce vin D.O.C. peut être sec, doux ou mousseurx, les bonnes années, il est doué d'un velouté remarquable.

Voir ITALIE

Albariza

Sol blanc calcaire typique de la région de Jerez, pays du Xérès espagnol, où l'on produit les meilleurs Finos et Manzanillas.

Alcamo (D.O.C.)

Vin rouge ou blanc de Sicile.

Voir SICILE

Alcool

Le principal, mais non le seul, composant du vin. Pendant la fermentation, les enzymes créés par les cellules de levure convertissent le sucre du jus de raisin en alcool et gaz carbonique. Dans le jus de raisin fermenté, les alcools se combinent avec les acides pour produire des esters. D'après Yves Renouil et Paul de Traversay, l'alcool est « le dérivé résultant de la substitution d'un radical hydroxyle à un atome d'hydrogène dans un hydrate de carbone ». L'alcool pur est un liquide incolore qui s'enflamme à des températures variant entre — 12°C pour l'alcool absolu (100°) et + 11°C pour l'alcool à 95°. Ses vertus antiseptiques jouent un rôle admirable dans le vin. L'alcool rectifié est obtenu par distillation continue.

Voir CHAPITRES V et VI, *voir* aussi DEGRÉ D'ALCOOL ; DISTILLATION ; RECTIFICATION

Alcool (Teneur en)

La proportion d'alcool contenue dans un vin, ou la force alcoolométrique de ce vin, est toujours exprimée, en France, en termes de volume à 15°C, déterminé selon le principe de Gay-Lussac : l'alcool pur a une force égale à 100 degrés, et la teneur en alcool est égale au nombre de litres d'alcool éthylique contenu dans 100 l de vin, ces deux volumes étant mesurés à une température de 15°C. Ainsi, un degré d'alcool correspond à 1 c.c. d'alcool pur contenu dans 100 c.c. de vin. La quantité d'alcool peut être exprimée en g/l à 20°C. (Renouil et de Traversay : *Dictionnaire du vin).*

L'évaluation britannique est effectuée sur la base du « Proof Gallon » et du « Proof Spirit ».

Le « Proof Spirit » est un alcool étalon pesant exactement — à une température de 11° — douze treizièmes d'une quantité égale en volume d'eau distillée. Il s'agit en effet d'un mélange d'eau et d'alcool contenant 49,28 % en poids et 57,1 % en volume d'alcool à 15,6°. Le « Proof Gallon » est une unité de volume et de teneur alcoolique égale à 4,5459631 litres de l'étalon « proof spirit ».

Pour calculer le contenu alcoolique, on utilise les degrés Sikes. Puisque, selon Gay-Lussac, l'« étalon » correspond à 57,1° un contenu alcoolique plus élevé est exprimé en degrés Sikes O.P. (Over Proof, c'est-à-dire au-dessus du niveau étalon), et 100 degrés Gay-Lussac correspondent à 75,9° Sikes O.P. Vice-versa, un contenu alcoolique plus faible est exprimé en degrés Sikes U.P. (Under Proof, c'est-à-dire au-dessous du niveau étalon) et dans ce cas, 100° Sikes U.P. correspondent à 0° Gay-Lussac. Aux États-Unis, la teneur en alcool d'un vin est exprimée en pourcentage de volume à 15°.

Voir APPENDICE

Aldéhyde

Liquide volatil obtenu par l'oxydation de l'alcool ; nombreux composés intermédiaires entre l'alcool et les acides. Ces aldéhydes jouent un rôle important dans le vin, surtout en ce qui concerne le bouquet.

Voir CHAPITRE IX

Ale

Bière blonde à partir du malt.

Voir BIÈRE

Aleatico

Raisin de la variété du Muscat, cultivé dans diverses régions d'Italie pour faire un vin rouge, doux et odorant.

Aleatico di Protoferraio

Vin de dessert de couleur rouge, doux, produit à l'île d'Elbe (15-16° d'alcool).

Voir TOSCANE

Aleatico di Puglia

Vin rouge D.O.C., foncé, doux, fort, consommé au dessert, produit dans la province de Pouille, en Italie.

Voir POUILLE

Alella

Vin blanc sec produit dans le village portant ce nom, en Catalogne espagnole, au nord de Barcelone. On y fait aussi du vin rouge.

Voir ESPAGNE

Aleyor

Vin rouge de Majorque, Espagne.
Voir ESPAGNE

Algérie

Jadis l'un des premiers pays producteurs de vin d'Europe, l'Algérie a réduit sa production et entrepris une réorganisation générale de ses industries du vin et du raisin. En 1961 — alors qu'elle était encore un département français — l'Algérie produisait près de 16 millions d'hl de vin et exploitait environ 360 000 ha de vignobles. L'Algérie se place maintenant en dix-neuvième position parmi les nations productrices de vin, après avoir été sixième en volume total pendant de longues années. La quasi-totalité de sa production est faite de vin rouge.

L'économie du vin en Algérie pose un problème exceptionnel. D'une part, en 1964, 35 à 40 % de la population active travaillait à la culture de la vigne, la vinification, le transport et le commerce du vin. Mais la plupart des Algériens sont musulmans et leur religion leur interdit formellement de boire du vin et n'importe quel breuvage alcoolique. Les vins algériens, de couleur foncée et entêtants, devaient donc trouver des débouchés à l'extérieur. Sur environ 10,5 millions d'hl produits, guère moins de 9,14 millions furent exportés.

Une bonne part de ce vin passa en France pour servir à des coupages avec des vins du Midi. Le reste entra aussi en France et dans d'autres pays, sous ses propres étiquettes, pour être vendu comme vin ordinaire d'usage quotidien. Quoique la France importât moins de vin, les viticulteurs du Midi et des autres régions de production massive protestèrent contre ces importations et firent pression sur le gouvernement pour en diminuer la quantité. Or, le traité d'Évian imposa à la France un *quota* déterminé d'importation et le gouvernement algérien insiste pour faire valoir ses droits à ce sujet. Problème économique en Algérie, le vin devient un problème de politique étrangère. Mais depuis l'indépendance de l'Algérie en 1962, la qualité s'est mise à baisser, les ouvriers musulmans ayant toujours travaillé jusqu'alors sous la direction de vignerons français. Il y eut également une importante baisse des exportations vers la France et les autres pays du Marché Commun. Les

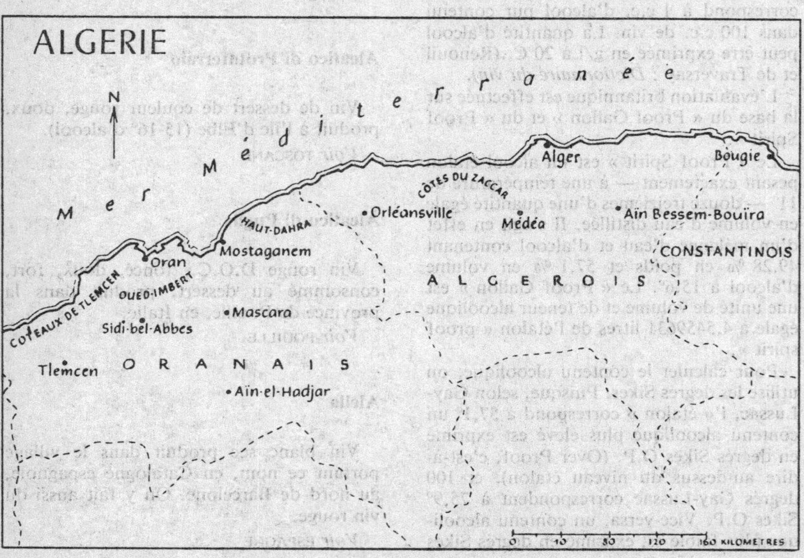

vignerons du Midi et d'autres régions productrices de vin en vrac protestèrent contre l'indépendance de l'Algérie en faisant pression sur le gouvernement pour que la quantité soit réduite.

Étant donné l'insignifiance des exportations vers la France et les autres pays du Marché commun, suite aux accords d'Évian le gouvernement algérien redirigea l'industrie vinicole. Le million d'hl de vin algérien autrefois vendu à la France est maintenant expédié en partie en Union Soviétique, Scandinavie et en Europe Orientale. Ce changement a amené les associés à remplacer les anciens pieds de vigne par de jeunes plants de raisins de table. Le programme vise à orienter l'agriculture algérienne vers une culture céréalière, à améliorer les terres exploitées, et simplement à planter des vignes saines à la place des vignes moins prospères. La surface consacrée au raisin à vin est réduite à 85 000 ha et la production est stabilisée autour du niveau actuel de 2,1 millions d'hl par an (23 millions de caisses).

L'Algérie avait autrefois tendance à produire de grosses quantités de vins. Ceux-ci étaient utilisés comme vins médecins dans le Midi, en Bourgogne et dans d'autres régions qui avaient besoin d'augmenter le taux d'alcool de leurs vins. Aujourd'hui, en dépit de l'interdiction du Coran pour toutes les boissons alcooliques, le gouvernement algérien s'est détourné des vins ordinaires pour produire 7 vins d'appellation d'origine garantie. La plupart sont des vins de qualité, et n'existaient pas avant 1970, date à laquelle tous les districts furent créés. La production, qui se décompose en 60 % de vins rouges, 30 % de blancs et 10 % de rosés, se répartit entre : des rouges et des rosés ordinaires, à forte teneur en alcool, exportés pour la plupart par bateaux-citernes ; des vins fins, rouges et rosés, dont on compte dix marques commerciales et des vins d'appellation d'origine garantie (V.A.O.G.), dont la liste figure un peu plus loin. L'Algérie n'exporte pas de vin blanc car sa couleur laisse à penser qu'il est oxydé. Jusqu'à ce que l'on ait trouvé le moyen de remédier à cette imperfection, on ne verra jamais de vin blanc algérien en dehors du pays. Les domaines sont immenses, travaillés avec des machines modernes. A la vendange on apporte le raisin dans des chais gigantesques où ils sont traités presque à la chaîne dans d'énormes cuves de fermentation en ciment. Pour libérer les cuves avant l'arrivée d'un autre apport de raisin, on ajoute au moût des levures sélectionnées pour assurer une fermentation rapide et saine. Dès que la fermentation est terminée, on soutire le vin dans d'autres énormes cuves. Il est ensuite vendu en barriques, par camions entiers ou en camions-citernes ou wagons-citernes. Le prix dépend du degré d'alcool. Pour les vins rouges, ce sont : Carignan, Cinsault (ou Cinsaut), Grenache, Alicante-Bouschet, Aramon, Morrastel ou Mourvèdre ; pour les blancs, Clairette, Listan, Ugni blanc, Faranah, Maccabéo et Merseguéra.

En général les vins rouges algériens qui constituent 60 % de la production du pays sont très caractérisés au point de vue goût et sont de couleur foncée. Leur teneur en alcool est supérieure à 11°. Ils atteignent couramment 15° à l'état naturel, avec une très faible acidité. Une telle teneur en alcool est extrêmement rare dans les pays plus frais où les étés ne sont pas assez chauds pour donner suffisamment de sucre au raisin. Étant donné que les vins du Midi de la France peuvent avoir une acidité élevée et être faibles en alcool (souvent pas plus de 9°), les vins algériens étaient souvent utilisés pour les « corriger » en leur donnant couleur, corps et degré d'alcool. Les vins de Mascara étaient vendus presque ouvertement par bien des négociants sous le nom de bourgogne.

Histoire du vin en Algérie

La culture de la vigne en Algérie date de l'Antiquité. Du vin de cette province de l'Empire était envoyé à Rome pour les délices des maîtres du monde méditerranéen. L'invasion musulmane ne sonna pas le glas de tous les vignobles malgré l'interdiction de l'alcool sous n'importe quelle forme car raisins de table et raisins secs y ont toujours été appréciés. Selon une hypothèse vraisemblable, le Muscat y prospéra comme fruit de table et on fit des recherches pour acclimater d'autres raisins de dessert. Cette consommation ne pouvait suffire à faire prospérer tous les vignobles et leur nombre de même que leur superficie diminuèrent.

Il fallut attendre plus de mille ans pour assister à la résurrection de la vigne en Algérie, sous le régime français. Quoique conquise à partir de 1830, l'Algérie ne fut plantée de nouveau en vignobles qu'à partir de 1865. Quand le phylloxéra dévasta les vignobles français, nombre de vignerons abandonnèrent leurs terres ruinées pour aller s'installer en Algérie. Dans bien des cas, ils plantèrent les vignes auxquelles ils étaient accoutumés dans la mère patrie : les Lyonnais firent venir du Gamay et du Pinot ; les Bourguignons, de même ; les Bordelais plantèrent du Cabernet ; les gens du Midi de l'Aramon ; Alsaciens et Lorrains qui fuyaient l'occupation allemande de leur province autant que le phylloxéra cultivèrent Chasselas et Pinot Gris. Partout on cultiva aussi Mourvèdre, Morrastel et Grenache. Mais le phylloxéra atteignit l'Algérie à son tour. Les plants de qualité furent abandonnés et on les remplaça par Carignan, Cinsault et Alicante-Bouschet, tous greffés sur des souches américaines. En ce qui concerne les vins blancs, les vignes utilisées sont principalement les Clairette, Merseguéra, Maccabéo et Ugni Blanc.

Aujourd'hui, tout le savoir-faire vient de travailleurs employés par des viticulteurs français avant l'indépendance, d'étudiants ayant appris l'œnologie en France, dans le Bordelais et en Bourgogne, ou de quelques ingénieurs agricoles ayant fait leur apprentissage dans des écoles techniques de viticulture algériennes.

RÉGIONS VITICOLES ALGÉRIENNES

Quelque 60 000 ha couvrent les coteaux des anciens départements d'Alger et d'Oran et ce sont ceux-là qui donnent les vins auxquels les autorités algériennes ont reconnu le statut de A.O.G., soit Appellation d'Origine Garantie. Les vins algériens les meilleurs sont souvent très agréables, plus souples et plus corsés que ceux du Midi.

Les meilleurs vins sont faits avec des vignes de variété Cinsault, Carignan, Grenache et Morrastel, quoique, dans certains cas particuliers, d'autres variétés soient autorisées. Les blancs sont faits avec des raisins des variétés Clairette et Muscat. Sur les coteaux on cultive aussi Cabernet, Grenache, Mourvèdre, Pinot et Syrah. Voici la liste des vins reconnus par les autorités algériennes en 1970. [Ils proviennent de sept zones d'Appellation d'Origine Garantie (V.A.O.G.).]

District d'Alger

Aïn-Bessem-Bouïra : vins rouges et rosés. C'est une petite région viticole située au sud d'Alger. Les vignobles sont plantés de 500 m à 700 m d'altitude.

Coteaux du Zaccar : vins rouges et blancs. Les versants des collines de Zaccar, autour de la ville de Miliala, produisent des vins rouges intéressants à partir du Pinot Noir et de Syrah.

Médéa : vins rouges, rosés et blancs. Cette région est située à l'ouest de Aïn-Bessem, au sud d'Alger. Plantée à une altitude de 1 300 m, ses hivers sont frais et ses étés chauds et secs. Elle produit de bons vins rouges vigoureux fabriqués à partir de Cabernet et de Pinot Noir.

District d'Oran

Coteaux de Mascara : vins rouges et rosés, peut-être les meilleurs vins d'Algérie faits à partir des raisins cultivés sur les coteaux environnant Mascara, sur le plateau de Ghriss. Ils sont très colorés et étaient connus autrefois sous le nom de vin teinturier. La région est capable de fabriquer des vins surprenants à partir de Cabernet Sauvignon, de Syrah et d'autres variétés cultivées en Algérie.

Coteaux de Tlemcem : rouges, rosés et blancs. Ce coteau est situé au sud-ouest d'Oran. Les vins que l'on y produit sont très robustes.

Dahra : vins rouges et rosés. La région de Dahra, au sud de la ville d'Oran, est constituée des zones suivantes : Taoughrite (ex-Paul Robert), Aïn Merane (ex-Rabelais), Mazouna (ex-Renault) et Khadra Achaacha (ex-Picard). Elle produisent des vins robustes à forte teneur en alcool, ainsi qu'un peu de vin connu autrefois sous le nom de Mostaganem.

Monts du Tessalah : rouges et rosés. Les vins rouges sont d'une couleur profonde. On les produit à partir des vignobles de ces coteaux, et plus spécialement autour de Sidi-bel-Abbès (quartier général de la Légion Étrangère française avant l'indépendance de l'Algérie).

Alicante

Vin rouge espagnol déjà connu au temps de Shakespeare sous le nom de « Tent ».

Voir ESPAGNE

Alicante-Bouschet

Raisin à vin rouge, de haut rendement, résultant des travaux poursuivis par les œnologues français L. et M. Bouschet au siècle dernier. Ces vignes, cultivées dans tout le Midi français, en Algérie et en Californie, donnent partout du vin de qualité inférieure, dénué de caractère, d'une faible acidité. D'abord d'une vive couleur, il fane ensuite rapidement.

Aligoté

Raisin blanc de Bourgogne qui donne un vin plaisant mais sans qualités exceptionnelles. Mieux vaut le consommer jeune car il a tendance à s'oxyder dans les trois ans.

Alkermès

Liqueur agréable mais excitante faite avec les larves d'un insecte du genre de la cochenille qu'on prit longtemps pour les baies du chêne kermès poussant sur les côtes de la Méditerranée. Ces chenilles, en effet, vivent sur cet arbre.

Allasch ou Alasch

Genre de kummel apprécié en Angleterre, Pologne et Russie. Cette liqueur porte le nom de la localité d'Allasch, proche de Riga (Lettonie, U.R.S.S.) célèbre pour ses graines de cumin, élément essentiel du kummel auquel il donne son goût.

Allemagne

« La noblesse des vins fins allemands est le fruit du combat pour la vie sous le climat le plus septentrional que puisse supporter la vigne. Les prix de revient sont plus élevés ; la culture plus intensive, la lutte contre les insectes et les maladies plus critique, l'amendement des terres plus indispensable que partout ailleurs ».

Ces propos du professeur Steinberg, directeur de la plus importante école de viticulture d'Allemagne, à Geisenheim, sur le Rhin, résume l'histoire des vins allemands. Quoique diverses régions vinicoles d'Allemagne se prétendent à tort les plus septentrionales du monde, il est exact que les vignes allemandes sont cultivées dans des zones les plus froides et celles dont le climat est le moins favorable à la vigne. Or la vigne accepte le défi. Les cépages, le Riesling notamment, produisent un vin d'or pur mais ils exigent en échange autant de ménagements qu'une *prima donna*.

La culture de la vigne y fait l'objet d'un contrôle sévère. Pour pouvoir planter un vignoble, il faut obtenir un permis des autorités régionales après avoir fait évaluer le sol, le climat, etc., et que le site ait été jugé apte à la viticulture, c'est-à-dire capable de produire des raisins assez mûrs pour fabriquer des vins de qualité. Les vignobles sont situés au sud-ouest du pays, le long du Rhin, de la Moselle et de leurs affluents. 100 000 ha environ sont plantés de vignes, soit moins de 1 % de la surface agricole allemande. 87 % des raisins sont utilisés à la fabrication du vin blanc. La production annuelle a été d'environ 8,8 millions (pratiquement 100 millions de caisses) d'hectolitres pour les dix dernières années. La majorité des 90 000 viticulteurs sont vignerons à mi-temps (ou durant leurs loisirs) et leur exploitation s'étend sur 1 ha ou moins. Les 2/3 livrent leurs raisins ou leur moût à des coopératives ou au négoce. Directement ou indirectement, on estime qu'environ 1 million d'individus vivent de l'industrie du vin. Le vin allemand est toujours consommé essentiellement en Allemagne, bien que la consommation par tête stagne à 25 l (dont une part croissante est importée). Les exportations s'élèvent à 1/3 des ventes totales. Les marchés principaux sont le Royaume Uni et les États-Unis, puis d'autres pays européens voisins non producteurs et le Japon.

Histoire du vin en Allemagne

La longue histoire du vin en Allemagne s'enchevêtre à celle des habitants de la vallée du Rhin, comme les entrelacs d'une tapisserie gothique. Il est toutefois possible d'en esquisser les grandes lignes.

On faisait sans doute déjà du vin en Allemagne dès le début de l'ère chrétienne. Les Romains occupèrent le pays, ils laissèrent leur empreinte sur la population, les agglomérations, les vins, les mœurs et les coutumes dans les vallées de la Moselle et du Rhin.

Après l'effondrement de l'Empire romain et dans la confusion qui s'ensuivit, les guerres féodales ravagèrent les vignobles. Puis le vignoble passa sous la protection de l'Église. Les monastères furent les grands promoteurs de la culture de la vigne.

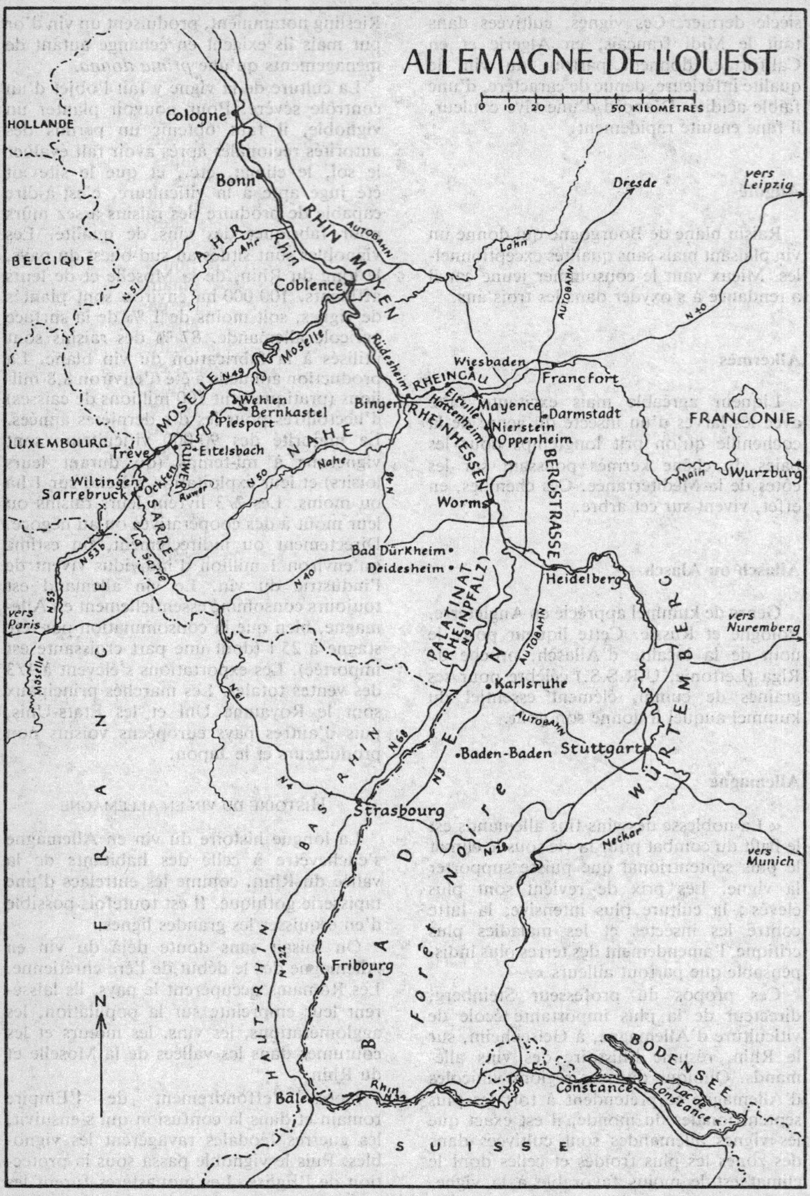
ALLEMAGNE DE L'OUEST
0 10 20 50 KILOMETRES
HOLLANDE
Cologne
Bonn
BELGIQUE
AHR
Ahr
Rhin
RHIN MOYEN
AUTOBAHN
Coblence
Lahn
Dresde
vers Leipzig
N 40
Wiesbaden
Francfort
RHEINGAU
Rüdesheim
Eltville
Hattenheim
Mayence
Darmstadt
Nierstein
Oppenheim
FRANCONIE
Main
Wurzburg
Bingen
RHEINHESSEN
BERGSTRASSE
Wehlen
Bernkastel
Piesport
MOSELLE
Moselle
N 49
N 51
LUXEMBOURG
Trève
Eitelsbach
RUWER
Ruwer
NAHE
Nahe
N 50
N 48
Wiltingen
Ockfen
Sarrebruck
SARRE
Sarre
N 53b
N 53
vers Paris
Worms
Bad Dürkheim
Deidesheim
N 40
Heidelberg
PALATINAT (RHEINPFALZ)
N 3
Karlsruhe
Baden-Baden
Stuttgart
vers Nuremberg
WURTEMBERG
N 61
N 68
N 4
BAS RHIN
Strasbourg
FRANCE
Neckar
N 28
vers Munich
Forêt Noire
BADE
Fribourg
N 422
HAUT RHIN
Bâle
Rhin
Constance
BODENSEE
Lac de Constance
SUISSE

Les moines étaient aussi des commerçants avisés et leurs affaires furent une source de revenus importants pour l'Église. Certains des anciens monastères peuvent encore être visités aujourd'hui. Leurs pressoirs gigantesques sont encore là, comme au temps des moines encapuchonnés. Une petite anecdote racontée à Kloster Eberbach résume l'esprit du temps. Le maître de chai de ce cloître surplombant le Rhin, goûtant le contenu d'un fût, y décela un goût de fer. Il courut, en grand désarroi, confier sa découverte au cuisinier qui goûta à son tour et découvrit quant à lui, non pas un goût de fer, mais de cuir. Tous deux s'empressèrent d'aller soumettre l'affaire au prieur qui goûta à son tour pour les départager. Il déclara que tous deux avaient tort car à son avis le vin avait un léger goût de bois. On vida le tonneau tout en goûtant et discutant. Enfin on y trouva, au fond, une clé attachée à un morceau de bois par une courroie de cuir.

Au cours du XVIIIe siècle, on peut noter, sous l'influence de l'Église et l'aristocratie, un plus grand goût pour la qualité. Dans certaines régions, notamment sur la Moselle et dans le Rheingau, des vignes de moindre importance furent arrachées et remplacées par du Riesling de haute qualité. Les vins supérieurs et les meilleurs crus furent conservés à dessein et stockés séparément dans une petite cave — Cabinet Keller — d'où le Prädikat Kabinett allemand tire son origine. Les mentions les plus anciennes d'un Cabinet Keller (dans ce contexte) remontent à 1728 (Schloss Vollrads) et 1730 (Kloster Eberbach). En dépit de la perte de quantité, la valeur qualitative des récoltes tardives fut reconnue par les meilleurs vignobles. Après la première vendange tardive « accidentelle », (Spätlese) en 1775, Schloss Johannisberg obtint des résultats exceptionnels et chercha à modifier la règle en vigueur en stipulant que la vendange devait être terminée au plus tard le 15 octobre, ce qui certainement est souhaitable pour les Riesling tardifs. Dès 1750, puis régulièrement après 1775, Schloss Johannisberg mit ses meilleurs vins en bouteilles. Avec l'avènement de la mise en bouteilles au domaine, apparut toute une série de capsules colorées pour distinguer les vins vendangés à divers stades de maturité. A la fin du siècle, grâce au développement de la lithographie par Senefelder, les étiquettes firent leur apparition.

En 1803, Napoléon sécularisa les vignobles allemands. Quelques grandes propriétés restèrent intactes comme, par exemple, celles qui étaient entretenues par l'État ou des institutions charitables (Bischöfliches Priesterseminar ou Friedrich Wilhelm Gymnasium, toutes deux à Trèves). Néanmoins, la plupart de ces domaines furent vendus aux enchères. Pour les viticulteurs qui purent racheter, ce fut l'occasion unique d'acquérir d'excellents sites, n'ayant, jusqu'à présent, appartenus qu'à l'Église. L'impact le plus important du Code Napoléon, basé sur la loi romaine, fut la fragmentation des vignobles par héritage. Le domaine ne pouvait être cédé dans son intégralité à un seul héritier mais devait être divisé à parts égales entre les descendants. Un vignoble avait donc plusieurs propriétaires. En conséquence, il fallut rebaptiser toutes les sections pour pouvoir identifier la parcelle de chaque fermier. On arriva à plus de 30 000 noms de crus qui furent regroupés en 2 600 sous la loi allemande sur les vins, de 1971.

A la fin du XIXe siècle, les progrès de la science et de la technologie améliorèrent les méthodes de culture de la vigne et la vinification. L'État créa des instituts de recherche et d'enseignement pour rendre la qualité meilleure, et, par conséquent, l'économie viticole. Le développement de coopératives fut aussi une mesure importante pour les vignerons à plein temps ou à temps partiel. Ce fut également à cette époque que des domaines (Rheingau, Pfalz, Moselle-Sarre-Ruwer), en quête de qualité, se regroupèrent par région pour commercialiser leurs vins « naturels » (non chaptalisés). Ils décidèrent de les vendre aux enchères afin que chaque producteur puisse obtenir un prix sur la base d'un marché plus large et puisse se faire connaître (car le résultat des ventes était toujours publié). En 1910, sous les auspices du Maire de Trèves, les groupes régionaux se rassemblèrent en une association, connue aujourd'hui sous le nom de Verband Deutscher Prädikats-und Qualitätsweingüter, ou VDP. La mention « naturel » obligatoire pour les vins vendus aux enchères par l'association, devint synonyme de haute qualité. La loi allemande sur les vins, de 1971, en interdit l'emploi pour la remplacer par le système des Prädikats. Tout comme leurs prédécesseurs, ils interdirent la chaptalisation. Aujourd'hui les 171 membres de l'Association des Domaines de Prädikat Allemand et Vin de Qualité sont basés dans presque toutes les régions. Ils organisent des foires, des ventes aux enchères et périodiquement des dégustations où leurs pairs s'assurent que la VDP ne regroupe que des domaines produisant régulièrement des vins de qualité supérieure à celle requise, au minimum, dans leur région. Les hauts standards de la VDP ont largement contribué à la réputation internationale des vins allemands. S'ils n'avaient pas recouru à la chaptalisation (en Allemagne « gallisation », ou procédé Gall), les petits vignerons auraient disparu. Cette addition de sucre au moût est désormais définie par la loi en ces termes : « Du sucre, ou du sucre dissous dans de l'eau pure, peut être ajouté au moût... à condition que ce soit dans le but de remédier à une carence en sucre ou en alcool ou de contrecarrer un excès naturel d'acidité, dans une mesure suffisante pour produire un vin de composition équivalente à celle des vins produits durant les bonnes années par un raisin de même espèce et origine... et à condition que le sucre soit ajouté avant fermentation ». Ce traitement permit aux viticulteurs d'étaler les mauvaises années auxquelles ils n'auraient pas survécu autrement. Il importe cependant de noter qu'aucun vin mis en bouteille au domaine (en allemand : *Originalabfüllung)* ne peut être *angereichert* (enrichi, autement dit chaptalisé) sauf si cela est fait conformément aux limites des nouvelles lois. *Voir ci-après au paragraphe* EXPORTATION ET LÉGISLATION DU VIN.

Durant les premières années d'après guerre, on remarqua une tendance prononcée vers la production de vins doux qui semble être la conséquence de la pénurie de sucre en Allemagne durant la guerre ; cette tendance s'est perpétuée. La vendange tardive de raisin moisi sauva les vignerons allemands à la fin du XVIIIe siècle. On ne sait pas exactement qui est à l'origine de cette pratique, mais on l'attribue en général à un évêque de Fulda. Par négligence, ce prélat aurait oublié de donner l'ordre de vendanger en temps voulu. Quand il se rappela ses vignes, les raisins étaient presque complètement pourris et il les abandonna aux paysans qui en tirèrent le glorieux élixir que nous connaissons. Cette méthode consistant à laisser le raisin dépasser la maturité jusqu'à la pourriture noble, à la fin de l'automne, produit en France les grands Sauternes et en Allemagne les Beerenauslesen et Trockenbeerenauslesen. Mais, surtout en Allemagne, la vendange tardive livre le raisin aux risques de gelées précoces. En outre ces raisins sont cueillis grain à grain, ce qui implique l'utilisation d'une main-d'œuvre plus nombreuse qui rend les prix trop élevés pour le marché contemporain du Rhin et de la Moselle.

Variétés de raisins

Le cépage utilisé présente une importance capitale dans tous les vignobles du monde ainsi qu'en Allemagne.

En Allemagne, 87 % de tous les vins sont blancs. Les rouges sont une spécialité très populaire dans le pays, mais mal connus ni appréciés à l'étranger. Ils se distinguent par leur acidité fruitée plus que tannique et sont souvent, selon leur variété et le fabricant, de couleur plus claire, d'une intensité et d'un corps plus légers que les autres vins rouges. Si l'on compare aux vins rouges du reste du monde, et tout chauvinisme mis à part, les vins rouges allemands ne sont pas de niveau international. Les variétés de raisins blancs les plus importantes sont les suivantes :

Riesling

Ce raisin fait les meilleurs vins blancs allemands. Une aristocratie d'acier, telle est la caractéristique principale du vin fait avec des Riesling, surtout quand la vigne a poussé sur le sol schisteux de la Moselle. Le fruit est petit, son rendement peu élevé, mais son caractère, sa durée, l'incomparable bouquet qui semble composé d'un mélange de fruits compensent, et au-delà, le manque de quantité. Il mûrit tard et résiste au froid. Mais si on l'éloigne de son habitat — Rhin, Moselle et Alsace — il lui arrive malheur et le vin qu'il produit n'est plus du Riesling que de nom. 20 % des vignobles allemands sont plantés de Riesling.

Silvaner

Plus douce que le Riesling, cette variété produit un vin plein et neutre à l'image du sol sur lequel elle est cultivée. C'était autrefois la vigne la plus plantée d'Allemagne. On l'épelle généralement « Sylvaner » en dehors de l'Allemagne. 8 % des vignobles allemands sont plantés de Silvaner.

Müller-Thurgau

Le croisement de Riesling et de Silvaner (hybridation des vignes et non mélange des vins) donne un produit au goût moins prononcé que celui du Riesling et qui rappelle le Muscat. Il produit des vins de consommation courante, plaisants et meilleurs lorsqu'ils sont consommés jeunes et frais. 1/4 des vignobles allemands sont plantés de Müller-Thurgau.

Kerner

Nouveau croisement obtenu à partir de Trollinger (variété rouge) et de Riesling (variété blanche). Les vins ressemblent moins aux Riesling, à cause de leur acidité vive et racée. Producteur abondant donnant un vin manquant de finesse (7 %).

Scheurebe

Croisement très réussi de Silvaner et de Riesling, dont le nom provient de son créateur, Georg Scheu. Vin à l'acidité alerte dont le bouquet et le goût rappellent celui du cassis, mais commun néanmoins (4,5 %).

Bacchus

Croisement de (Silvaner x Riesling) x Müller-Thurgau. Bouquet léger, fleurant le Muscat, acidité douce, bon corps (3,5 %).

Variétés de Burgunder (Bourgogne)

Grauburgunder ou Rulander (Pinot Gris) et Weissburgunder (Pinot Blanc), tous deux cultivés essentiellement à Bade. Spätburgunder (Pinot Noir), cultivé dans l'Ahr, à Bade et dans le Rheingau. Müllerrebe ou Schwarzriesling (Pinot Meunier), cultivé à Bade et dans le Wurtemberg. Autres variétés de rouge : Portugieser, Trollinger, Limberger.

Si un vin contient au moins 85 % d'une variété de raisin, celle-ci doit être mentionnée sur l'étiquette. Jusqu'en 1950, cet usage n'était pas courant car l'on pensait que les vins blancs n'étaient fabriqués qu'à partir de Riesling, et les rouges de Spätburgunder. Aujourd'hui, si la variété n'est pas mentionnée, il faut s'attendre à un vin typique de la région et probablement à une cuvée produite à partir de plusieurs variétés.

RÉGIONS VITICOLES ALLEMANDES

En Allemagne, les 100 000 ha de vignobles sont situés au sud-ouest du pays, entre le Lac de Constance (Bodensee) et Bonn. Les micro-climats jouent un rôle important dans la partie septentrionale de ces vignobles (qui s'étend sur le 50° de latitude, parallèle du Labrador ou de la Mongolie du nord), car les raisins ont besoin de tout ce que la nature peut leur donner pour mûrir. C'est pour cette raison que les régions viticoles allemandes se regroupent toutes le long du Rhin et de ses affluents. Les fleuves tempèrent le climat : en captant la chaleur à la manière de réflecteurs, ils maintiennent jour et nuit une température suffisante pour créer les brumes et brouillards qui protègent les vignobles des gelées précoces. Les vignobles se situent généralement sur les coteaux, orientés au sud, des vallées fluviales, entre la rivière et le sommet des collines coiffé d'une forêt protectrice — frontière naturelle et obstacle à leur expansion.

Cette zone est divisée en onze régions viticoles (bestimmte Anbaugebiete) ; chacune produit un vin typique (semblable en goût et en caractère), différent de celui des autres régions. Celles-ci sont décrites de façon détaillée sous leur rubrique ; voici cependant une liste sommaire où elles sont classées d'après leur taille et non pas leur qualité.

Rheinhessen

25 000 ha. 94 % de vins blancs, 6 % de vins rouges. Variétés de raisins : Müller Thurgau, Silvaner et Scheurebe.

Rhénanie-Palatinat

23 000 ha. 89 % de vins blancs, 11 % de vins rouges. Variétés de raisins : Müller Thurgau, Riesling et Kerner.

Bade

15 000 ha. 77 % de vins blancs, 23 % de vins rouges. Variétés de raisins : Müller Thurgau, Spätburgunder et Ruländer.

Moselle-Sarre-Ruwer

12 800 ha. 100 % de vins blancs. Variétés de raisins : Riesling, Müller Thurgau et Elbling.

Würtemberg

9 600 ha. 51 % de vins rouges, 49 % de vins blancs. Variétés de raisins : Riesling, Trollinger et Müllerrebe.

Franconie

5 200 ha. 97 % de vins blancs, 3 % de vins rouges. Variété de raisins : Müller Thurgau, Silvaner et Bacchus.

Nahe

4 600 ha. 98 % de vins blancs et 2 % de vins rouges. Variétés de raisins : Müller Thurgau, Riesling et Silvaner.

Rheingau

3 000 ha. 94 % de vins blancs, 6 % de vins rouges. Variétés de raisins : Riesling, Müller-Thurgau et Spätburgunder.

Rhin moyen

800 ha. 98 % de vins blancs, 2 % de vins rouges. Variétés de raisins : Riesling, Müller Thurgau et Kerner.

Ahr

426 ha. 70 % de vins blancs, 30 % de vins rouges. Variétés de raisins : Spätburgunder, Portugieser et Riesling.

Bergstrasse (Hessische Bergstrasse)

390 ha. 98 % de vins blancs, 2 % de vins rouges. Variétés de raisins : Riesling, Müller Thurgau et Ruländer.

Appellation d'origine

Il est obligatoire d'indiquer le nom de la région viticole sur l'étiquette d'un vin allemand de qualité. (Qualitätswein.) Il y a souvent plus de détails concernant l'origine du vin, tel que le nom du district ou du village joint au nom du site viticole collectif ou individuel. Plus l'appellation d'origine est spécifique, plus le goût et le caractère du vin sont particuliers — ceci à cause des différences de sols et de conditions de culture.

Chaque région est composée d'une ou de plusieurs sous-régions appelées *Bereiche*. Pour le Mosel-Saar-Ruwer, ces districts sont Bernkastel, Obermosel, Saar-Ruwer Zell et Moseltor. On entrevoit immédiatement l'origine des noms : dans certains cas (Saar-Ruwer) le nom géographique a été gardé pour la sous-région ; dans d'autres cas (Bernkastel) le nom d'une agglomération célèbre a été donné à une sous-région entière pour rendre plus attrayant un vin qui est en fait simplement régional. Ainsi un vin étiqueté *Bereich Bernkastel* peut être originaire de n'importe quel endroit de cette vaste région, mais un vin appelé *Berkasteler* ne peut être produit que dans les vignobles associés à la ville célèbre en question. Quoique les noms changent, la situation est sensiblement la même dans les autres régions d'Allemagne par exemple, Bereich Nierstein, Niersteiner.

Chaque *Bereich* est divisé en un ou plusieurs *Grosslagen*. Ce mot signifie littéralement « grande étendue », mais le *Grosslage* est plus spécifiquement une collection de vignobles semblables. Le principe selon lequel les noms des *Grosslagen* ont été choisis est quelque peu semblable à celui des *Bereiche*. Par exemple, dans le *Bereich* Bernkastel, un des *Grosslagen* porte le nom de Badstube, qui était aussi celui de l'un des meilleurs vignobles de la ville. Un vin portant l'étiquette Bernkasteler Badstube (depuis 1971) est un coupage régional, quoique provenant d'un bon secteur du *Bereich*. Les vins portant le nom d'un *Grosslage* devraient être de meilleure qualité que les simples vins de *Bereich*. Ils auront idéalement le goût et certaines caractéristiques des vins produits dans les vignobles du *Grosslage (voir ci-dessous)*, mais seront moins chers.

Chaque *Grosslage* est composé de vignobles individuels appelés *Einzellagen*. Leur nombre (environ 30 000) était si imposant qu'il prêtait à confusion et ce fut une des causes principales du vote de la loi vinicole de 1971. Pour qu'un vignoble puisse garder son nom, il doit avoir une superficie minimum de 5 à 10 ha selon le terrain. Les parcelles plus petites que le minimum légal furent absorbées ou regroupées en étendues suffisamment grandes pour porter un nom individuel. Ce regroupement eut pour résultat de réduire le nombre des vignobles à environ 42 600, mais aussi d'abolir plusieurs appellations respectables. Il est possible que la qualité de la production s'en soit également ressentie. Les vins d'un grand vignoble risquent d'être moins bons si ses vignes voisinent avec des cépages inférieurs. Les *Einzellagen* sont toujours associées aux villages. Le nom du village

SOMMAIRE DES APPELLATIONS D'ORIGINE	
Pour les vins allemands de qualité *(Qualitätswein b.A.)*	Exemple
11 régions viticoles *(bestimmtes Anbaugebiet = b.A.)* divisées en	Moselle-Sarre-Ruwer
34 districts *(Bereich)* divisés en	Bereich Bernkastel
152 sites viticoles collectifs *(Grosslage)* divisés en	Bernkasteler Badstube
2 600 sites viticoles individuels *(Einzellage)*	Bernkasteler Doktor

(+er) précède le nom du site individuel. Une agglomération et les vignobles qui l'entourent peuvent couvrir plus d'un *Grosslage*. Ainsi Bernkastel Kardinalsberg fait partie du *Grosslage* Kurfürstlay, alors que Bernkastel Doctor se trouve dans le *Grosslage* Badstube. Le nom de l'agglomération figurera toujours sur l'étiquette de vins de qualité qui sont produits dans un seul vignoble.

CLASSES DE QUALITÉ OU DEGRÉ DE MATURITÉ A LA VENDANGE

D'après la loi de la Communauté économique européenne relative au vin, il y a deux classes de qualité :

1º Vin de table *(Deutscher Tafelwein)*. Il s'agit de vins simples et agréables ne pouvant être faits qu'avec certaines variétés de raisin qui sont autorisées dans un des quatre secteurs suivants : Rhin-Moselle, Bayern, Neckar ou Oberrhein. Les noms de la région et de la personne qui a mis le vin en bouteille *(Abfüller)* figurent sur l'étiquette et les noms de marque sont maintenant autorisés. Le nom d'une variété de raisin peut être indiqué si le vin a été fait avec au moins 85 % de la variété en question.

Vin régional *(Deutscher Landwein)*. *Landwein* est une qualité supérieure de *Tafelwein*. Il doit être sec ou demi-sec. Comme *Tafelwein* peut n'indiquer que la région d'origine, par exemple Rhin ou Moselle, *Landwein* doit, en plus de la mention *Deutscher Landwein,* spécifier le nom de l'un des quinze villages particuliers et peut également porter le nom du *Bereich*.

2º Vin de qualité *(Qualitätswein Bestimmter Anbaugebiete)*. Plus fins et plus pleins que les premiers, ces vins doivent révéler le caractère typique de la région et de la variété de raisin. A cet effet, ils subissent le contrôle du gouvernement et d'un jury local. Ils doivent en outre avoir une teneur en alcool minimum (qui varie d'une région à l'autre) et ne peuvent être faits que dans l'une des onze régions vinicoles productrices de Vins de Qualités *(Bestimmter Anbaugebiete) :* Bade, Palatinat, Würtemberg, Franconie, Rheinhessen, Hessische Bergstrasse, Rheingau, Nahe, Mittelrhein, Mosel-Saar-Ruwer ou Ahr. (Voir plus haut pour la confrontation de ces régions aux secteurs de *Tafelwein)*. Si le vin réunit toutes les qualités requises, les autorités compétentes le reconnaissent et lui attribuent un numéro de contrôle *(amtliche Prüfungsnummer)* qui figurera sur l'étiquette avec les noms de la région et, si possible, des informations plus spécifiques sur l'origine — dans ce dernier cas, il faut toutefois qu'au moins 85 % de vin provienne de l'endroit. Les derniers 15 % peuvent provenir de n'importe quelle partie de cette même région. Le nom du vigneron sera également inscrit sur l'étiquette. Comme pour les *Tafelweine,* le nom de la variété de raisin pourra être ajouté si 85 % au moins du vin a été fait avec ladite variété.

Vin de Qualité avec Attributs spéciaux *(Qualitätswein mit Prädikat).* Ce sont les vins allemands de grande classe, faits exclusivement avec certaines variétés de raisins mûris à point, et produits dans un *Bereich* déterminé. Ils doivent titrer un minimum de 9° sans addition de sucre. Des fonctionnaires de l'État ont pour tâche de contrôler les raisins dans le vignoble et le moût dans la cave même. La date des vendanges est fixée et enregistrée par le village. Comme les vins de qualité simple, les vins de cette catégorie seront examinés et testés par différents jurys. S'ils se montrent pleinement satisfaisants, ceux-ci recevront enfin un numéro de contrôle. Les *Prädikat* sont les vins suivants : Kabinett, Spätlese, Auslese, Beerenauslese, Eiswein, Trockenbeerenauslese (voir pages suivantes la définition de ces vins). Les vins mis en bouteilles au domaine, jadis appelés *Original abfüllung,* portent maintenant la mention *Erzengerabfullung* (mis en bouteille par le producteur) ou *aus eigenem Lesegut* (mise personnelle du producteur). Aucun vin, même provenant d'un vignoble célèbre, ne se verra décerner un *Prädikat* s'il ne réunit pas les grandes qualités associées à son nom. Le classement d'un vin qui ne s'effectue plus en fonction du vignoble mais de sa qualité réelle, est un des grands triomphes de la nouvelle législation.

Voici une description des attributs spéciaux, ou Prädikate, par ordre de maturité croissante lors de la vendange. Il est important de se rappeler que les raisins les plus mûrs ont eu plus de temps pour développer des sucres naturels et pour absorber les minéraux contenus dans le sol. Les vins produits à partir de raisins mûrs sont plus charnus et d'une couleur plus profonde (plus dorée). Ceux produits à partir de raisins très mûrs sont plus riches (ce qui ne signifie pas nécessairement plus sucré), leur bouquet et leur arôme plus concentrés. Spätlese, par exemple, indique que DANS LE VIGNOBLE, les vins ont acquis au moins le minimum de sucre naturel (prescrit par la loi), nécessaire à la qualification pour cet attribut. Le jus de raisin naturellement sucré est fermenté pour donner un vin sec et c'est à ce point que, DANS LA CAVE, le fabricant décidera du style définitif de son vin. Il peut laisser son Spätlese comme il est, c'est-à-dire sec, ou il peut y ajouter un peu de jus de raisin non fermenté (et par conséquent toujours naturellement sucré) qu'il avait conservé (c'est la réserve sucrée) au Spätlese sec, et obtenir ainsi différents types de vin : demi-sec ou légèrement sucré. Un Spätlese qu'il soit sec, demi-sec ou doux, sera plus riche, plus intense qu'un Kabinett. La richesse est déterminée par la nature, le style ou le degré de douceur est, quant à lui, déterminé par le fabricant.

Kabinett. A l'origine, ce terme indiquait dans la nomenclature du Rheingau un vin de réserve spéciale, conservé dans un cellier « Cabinet » fermé à clé. Mais le sens de ce mot a pris une telle extension qu'il s'applique désormais à n'importe quelle bonne production à laquelle le propriétaire du domaine entend donner son nom. Pourtant il conserve un sens plus précis en ce qui concerne certains vignobles du Rheingau. Au terme de la loi de 1971, un *Kabinett* (l'orthographe *k* étant maintenant la seule reconnue) doit être fait avec des raisins mûris à point et ne doit pas avoir été sucré.

Spätlese. Signifie littéralement vendanges tardives. Les raisins doivent être récoltés 7 jours au moins après que les vendanges normales n'aient commencé. Les raisins sont plus mûrs que ceux utilisés pour la fabrication d'un Kabinett.

Auslese. Réfère à la vendange sélective. Les grappes trop mûres sont mises de côté, ce qui requiert un gros travail de la part de la main d'œuvre.

Beerenauslese. Autre forme de vendange sélective. Dans ce cas, chaque grain trop mûr est sélectionné et détaché de la grappe. Requiert beaucoup de main d'œuvre.

Eiswein. Signifie vin glacé. Il est fait à partir de raisins vendangés et pressurés alors qu'ils sont encore gelés. Ces raisins doivent être au moins aussi mûrs que ceux sélectionnés pour le Beerenauslese. Travail très coûteux en main-d'œuvre.

Trockenbeerenauslese. Réfère à la sélection individuelle de grains sur les grappes. Les grains ont été laissés dans la vigne pour se désécher et ressembler à des raisins secs. (Séché se dit Trocken). Travail très coûteux en main d'œuvre.

Les *Qualitätsweine b.A., Kabinett* et *Spätlese* (particulièrement secs ou demi-secs) sont excellents au cours d'un repas. L'*Auslese* est un vin riche à la douceur noble et fruitée ; il convient parfaitement en apéritif (à la place d'un Sherry par exemple), pour accompagner un pâté riche ou au dessert. *Berren- et Trockenbeerenauslese* et *Eiswein* sont extrêmement riches, délicieusement sucrés, doux et assez rares. Il est donc préférable de les boire seuls.

Futailles et unités de vente

Les meilleurs viticulteurs allemands vendent leurs vins aux enchères ou bien à la cave du producteur, au négociant par l'intermédiaire d'un courtier. Ce dernier type de vente s'appelle *Freihand* (vente à *main libre).* Les dimensions des fûts ne sont pas uniformes quoique on tende à généraliser l'usage de barriques contenant un certain nombre d'hl.

Dans le Rheingau, l'unité théorique est la pièce *(Stück) :* gros fût ovale de 1 200 l, qui sert généralement à la conservation en cave. Vendu aux enchères ou à *main libre,* le vin se traite par *Halbstück* (demi-pièce) qui contient 600 l. Il est plus généralement expédié en *Viertelstück* (quart de pièce) : baril rond de 300 l. Les vins les plus fins sont aussi négociés en bouteilles ou bien en caisses de bouteilles.

Dans la Moselle, les vins sont vendus dans de grands barils longs appelés *Fuder* (foudre) qui contenaient autrefois théoriquement 960 l. Mais durant les vingt-cinq dernières années, on tend à une normalisation fixant le contenu du *Fuder* à 1 000 l, ou 1 370 bouteilles. Les vins les plus fins sont aussi vendus en bouteille.

Les vins de Rheinhessen sont généralement vendus en *Stück* de 1 200 l et parfois en *Halbstück* de 600 l, ce qui est généralement le cas des plus fins. Dans cette région aussi, les vins supérieurs sont vendus en bouteille.

L'État est le plus grand propriétaire de vignobles de toute l'Allemagne. Ses domaines viticoles sont constitués en grande partie des anciennes propriétés de l'Église qui furent sécularisées en 1803 par Napoléon. Ils se situent pratiquement dans chaque région et comptent parmi les exploitations les plus belles et les plus prestigieuses du pays. Le Verwaltung des Staatsweingüter (Eltville), avec ses 190,5 ha, en est le plus grand. Il regroupe six propriétés dans le Rheingau et l'Hessische Bergstrasse, possède trois centres vinicoles et dirige l'ancien monastère cistercien de Kloster Eberbach (c'est aussi ici que sont stockés et vieillissent les vins de tous les domaines). Sur la base des prix d'enchères, voici le classement de quelques-uns des meilleurs crus du Rheingau : 1. Steinberger, 2. Rauenthaler Baiken, 3. Erbacher Marcobrunn, 4. Rüdesheimer Schlossberg, 5. Hochheimer Domdechaney.

Les coopératives vinicoles

Voilà 120 ans que le mouvement coopérateur est parti du Wurtemberg avec cette devise : « Nous avons beaucoup de vin, mais ni pain ni argent ». On comptait, au tout début du siècle, 113 coopératives. La première fédération nationale de coopératives fut constituée en 1930 et était à l'origine de l'actuel Deutscher Raiffeisenverband, organisation centrale administrative (et groupe de pression des 329 coopératives) allemandes, dont les six grandes caves régionales (Zentralkellereien) de Breisach à Bade, Gau-Bickelheim dans le Rheinhessen, Bernkastel dans la Moselle-Sarre-Ruwer, Bretzenheim dans le Nahe, Möglingen dans le Wurtemberg et Kitzingen-Repperndorf en Franconie. Dès leur création, les coopératives ont cherché à accroître le revenu peu élevé des vignerons. C'est aussi sous leur gouverne que fut améliorée la qualité des vins de petits producteurs ou producteurs à temps partiel, en accordant des primes à la qualité plutôt qu'à la quantité. Leur aptitude à traiter les raisins de leurs sociétaires et à les stocker sur de longues périodes a contribué à stabiliser les prix du marché. En terme de vinification, ces caves de coopératives figurent parmi les plus modernes et les plus efficaces du monde. Si l'on tient compte de leurs standards de haute qualité, on comprendra pourquoi 40 % des prix, attribués par la DLG (société allemande d'agriculture) aux meilleurs crus allemands lors de concours, sont décernés à des coopératives. Leurs ventes se répartissent en deux catégories : les petites coopératives locales qui fournissent habituellement des consommateurs régionaux, souvent par des ventes en direct ; les caves régionales et centrales capables de fournir régulièrement de grandes quantités de vins d'appellation à la distribution (qui commercialise 40 % des vins allemands), et de figurer avec succès sur les marchés d'exportation. Aujourd'hui les coopératives représentent entre 30 à 40 % des ventes annuelles de vins allemands. En 1985, elles regroupaient 68 000 membres. Le pourcentage d'adhérents aux coopératives, par région, est de : Bade et Wurtemberg, 85 % chacune, Hessische Bergstrasse et Ahr, 75 % chacune, Mittelrhein (Rhin moyen) 50-60 %,

Moselle-Saar-Ruwer (Moselle-Sarre-Ruwer) et Rheinpfalz (Palatinat) 30 % chacune, Nahe et Rheingau, 20 % chacune, Rheinhessen 12 %.

Aloxe-Corton (Appellation Contrôlée)

Bourgogne rouge et blanc. Côte de Beaune.

La commune d'Aloxe-Corton se trouve à l'extrémité nord de la Côte de Beaune, mais ses meilleurs vins blancs valent ceux qui portent la dénomination officielle de « Côte de Meursault » — dont l'extrémité sud produit les plus grands vins blancs — et ses vins rouges, les plus fins de la Côte de Beaune, comptent parmi les meilleurs de toute la Bourgogne. Mais afin d'obtenir ce que vous désirez, vous devez savoir ce qu'il faut demander.

Certains de ces vins portent simplement le nom d'Aloxe-Corton. Ce sont des vins agréables et parfois distingués, mais rarement grands. D'autres portent, outre le nom d'Aloxe-Corton, une dénomination particulière telle que Les Maréchaudes, ce qui signifie qu'ils proviennent d'un excellent vignoble sélectionné et qu'ils atteignent des sommets bien supérieurs aux normes minimales. Les plus grands de ces vins *ne* portent *pas* le nom d'Aloxe ; ils sont soit Corton tout seul, soit Corton suivi d'une autre dénomination plus spécifique. Les deux plus grands sont les suivants.

Corton

Du rouge, portant parfois la désignation exacte du vignoble qui les a produits : Corton-Bressandes, Corton-Renardes, par exemple.

Corton-Charlemagne

Le superbe vin blanc d'Aloxe, magnifiquement corsé. L'un des meilleurs vins blancs de la Bourgogne, donc l'un des plus grands vins blancs secs du monde.

Voir chacun de ces crus à sa place dans l'ordre alphabétique.

Les vignes poussent sur une colline isolée, à proximité de la grande route et dénommée La Montagne. Ses coteaux à pente douce sont couronnés par le paisible bois de Corton. Les sillons du vignoble qui font face à ce bois sont ceux de Corton. Mais plus bas se trouvent d'autres portions du même cru qui portent le nom de Bressandes, Renardes et Clos du Roi. Au même niveau que Corton se trouve Charlemagne qui est planté de Chardonnay, de même que la partie supérieur de Corton. Les vignerons du pays disent que le sommet des coteaux est meilleur pour les vins blancs et que ceux du milieu et du bas conviennent mieux aux rouges. Le sol explique cette particularité. Au sommet, il est léger et sec, teinté de blanchâtre par son sous-sol crayeux ; plus bas il devient ferrugineux et rougeâtre.

Aloxe est une des plus vieilles communes viticoles de la vénérable Côte de Beaune. Charlemagne, Henri II et Charles le Téméraire l'auraient possédée tour à tour et y auraient encouragé la culture de la vigne. Voltaire fut l'un des plus célèbres admirateurs de ces vins. Dans une lettre à M. Le Bault — qui construisit le château de Corton-Grancey — il écrit : « Votre vin est devenu une nécessité pour moi. Je donne un très bon Beaujolais à mes amis de Genève mais, en secret, je bois votre Corton ». Le Bault ne répondit pas mais écrivit en marge : « Cet homme est un vilain ». Le château de M. Le Bault a été rénové à maintes reprises depuis sa construction en 1749. De nos jours, complètement modernisé, il est entre les mains d'une bonne firme de négociants en vins, celle de Louis Latour.

Lequel est le meilleur de l'Aloxe rouge ou de l'Aloxe blanc ? Affaire de goût. Mais la plupart des vrais amateurs de vin sont prêts à se prononcer pour les deux. Les rouges sont puissants, corsés, capiteux, avec une tendance à la dureté dans leur jeunesse. Mais ils mûrissent magnifiquement et prennent alors un bel équilibre. Leur arôme superbe évoque celui de la violette. De tous les vins de la Côte de Beaune, Corton mérite particulièrement d'être conservé, car il se développe lentement et conserve ensuite sa majesté pendant des années. Les meilleurs Corton blancs sont parfois de la même classe que le Montrachet : le vin que bien des experts considèrent comme le plus grand blanc du monde entier. Ces vins ont une fermeté qui frise celle de l'acier et leur arôme est incomparable, surtout dans leur jeunesse. Des connaisseurs assurent qu'ils détectent aussi un parfum de cannelle dans son bouquet. Ce sont des vins d'une race exceptionnelle. Leur dégustation donne une énorme variété de sensations et laisse un arrière-goût durable.

La zone sur laquelle poussent les vignes d'Aloxe-Corton n'est guère considérable : quelque 240 ha pour toute la commune. Les meilleurs vignobles couvrent une superficie beaucoup moins élevée. Remarquons d'ailleurs que certains des vins qui ont droit à l'appellation contrôlée d'Aloxe-Corton proviennent de vignes débordant sur les communes voisines de Pernand-Vergelesses et Ladoix-Serrigny. La production d'une année moyenne peut atteindre 5 250 hl (58 000 caisses) de vin rouge. Ces statistiques ne comprennent pas les vignobles de Corton et Corton-Charlemagne qui produisent respectivement 2 000 hl (22 000 caisses) et 1 300 hl (14 000 caisses).

GRANDS CRUS

Vignobles		*Superficie approximative*
Corton	*Rouge*	100 ha
Corton-Charlemagne	*Blanc*	40 ha

ALOXE-CORTON

Les Meix	Les Genevrières
Les Petits-Vercots	Les Combes
Boulmeau	La Boulotte
Clos Boulmeau	Les Fournières
Les Chaillots	Les Planchets
Les Guérets	Les Vercots
Les Brunettes	Les Paulands
Les Sallières	Suchot
	Les Valozières

CORTON - PREMIERS CRUS

Clos du Roi	Les Grèves
Bressandes	Les Perrières
Renardes	Les Pougets
Chaumes	Les Maréchaudes
Fiètres	Les Vergennes
La Vigne au Saint	Le Rognet-Corton
Les Languettes	Le Clos du Corton

Alsace

Vin du Rhin français. Est de la France.

La route du vin part de Thann, près de la frontière suisse, et se dirige vers le nord en direction de Marlenheim, près de Strasbourg, en bordant le flanc Est des Vosges, barrière de sapins noirs entre la France et l'Allemagne.

La région des vins, officiellement divisée en Haut-Rhin et Bas-Rhin, est l'une des plus attirantes de France. Dans la partie inférieure, on trouve autant de vergers que de vigne, vergers qui produisent une partie des fruits destinés à la fabrication des merveilleuses eaux-de-vie : kirsch, fraise, framboise, poire. Bien que les pressoirs et les méthodes de vinification soient extrêmement modernes, il règne une atmosphère paisiblement rurale dans cette campagne, où les tracteurs s'ébranlent lentement vers les lieux de vendange, et où certains villages, avec leurs maisons décorées de bois, leurs nids de cigognes et leurs balcons fleuris, semblent sortir tout droit d'un conte de fées allemand.

Les vignes s'étendent entre le Rhin et les montagnes pendant plus de 120 km, de Thann au sud (Haut-Rhin) à Marlenheim au nord (Bas-Rhin), couvrant plus de 12 000 ha que se partagent de nombreux domaines de proportions souvent réduites, cultivés par 10 000 vignerons et leurs familles. Les vins tiennent leur nom de la variété de raisin : il n'y a qu'en Alsace où l'Appellation d'Origine est donnée suivant le cépage et non pas suivant le lieu d'origine. Les vins ayant droit à l'appellation de Vins d'Alsace sont faits avec des raisins classés de la façon suivante : *Variété Courante* — Chasselas ; *Variété de Qualité* — Sylvaner et Pinot Blanc (ou Clevner) ; *Variété Noble* — Riesling, Gewürztraminer, Muscat et Tokay-Pinot Gris. Les noms des vignobles n'ont pas ici grande importance, sauf quelques exceptions comme Rangen à Thann, Sonnenglanz à Beblenheim, Les Sorcières à Riquewihr, et d'autres vignobles rattachés aux villes classées à la rubrique *Célèbres Agglomérations Vinicoles d'Alsace,* p. 145.

HISTOIRE DU VIN EN ALSACE

On cultivait la vigne et on faisait du vin en Alsace avant la conquête romaine. Le Rhin est une voie d'eau navigable ; au

Moyen Age, les Alsaciens envoyaient leur vin à Cologne, d'où il partait pour la Scandinavie et l'Angleterre. L'Alsace s'appelait alors Aussay — mot dont l'orthographe n'était nullement fixée — et Shakespeare parle des vins d'Osoy.

La guerre de Trente Ans mit fin à la culture et au négoce. Elle marque l'un des premiers reculs de l'industrie du vin en Rhénanie, mais ce ne fut pas le dernier. La France participa à la troisième phase de la guerre contre l'empereur d'Allemagne et les principautés du sud de l'Empire. Elle y gagna par le traité de Westphalie (1648) la souveraineté sur les landgraviats de Haute et Basse Alsace, ainsi que le gouvernement de dix villes impériales de cette province.

Au XVIIIe siècle, les vins d'Alsace étaient en vogue en Autriche et en Suisse. Le contrôle de la qualité — fort ressemblant à celui de la législation française, quoique sous une forme primitive — était déjà en vigueur et *les magistrats de la vigne* — précurseurs des inspecteurs de l'I.N.A.O. actuel et de nos courtiers en vins, appelés en Alsace gourmets — surveillaient rigoureusement toutes les expéditions. Lieu d'origine du vin, conditions de production etc., tout était consigné sur un document qui accompagnait la marchandise. Les règlements interdisaient aussi de planter une proportion plus élevée de vignes à grand rendement de moindre qualité que de vignes nobles.

La Révolution française bouleversa le système de propriété et provoqua le morcellement des vignobles en parcelles. Pourtant, en 1870, les vignes d'Alsace prospéraient et les vins connus sous le nom de vins d'Alsace ou du Rhin français étaient appréciés. Mais la guerre éclata cette année-là entre la France et l'Allemagne et, en 1871, l'Alsace devint allemande. Pour protéger leur propre vin du Rhin, les Allemands interdirent aux Alsaciens de donner cette appellation aux leurs qui prirent alors le nom de vins d'Alsace. Pour des raisons économiques, l'Allemagne encouragea les vignerons à produire des vins à bon marché. La qualité baissa donc et se trouva au plus bas en 1918, quand les Français libérèrent l'Alsace.

Le retour de l'Alsace à la France provoqua une catastrophe sur le marché du vin alsacien, comme si la libération était un cadeau empoisonné pour les vignerons de cette province. En Allemagne, où les vins de la Moselle sont bons mais en faible quantité, les vins alsaciens à bon marché étaient très demandés. Mais la France étant alors le plus gros producteur mondial de vins de toutes qualités, du plus grand au plus ordinaire, les vins d'Alsace n'avaient pas de place sur le marché.

Les vignerons de la province réagirent avec courage et en furent récompensés. Ils s'ingénièrent à faire de nouveau des vins de la meilleure qualité possible et c'est ce qu'ils font encore de nos jours. Or, malgré l'extrême diversité et l'abondance de ses vins, la France n'en produisait nulle part ailleurs qui fussent dotés des qualités naturelles de ceux du Rhin. Légers et agréables, destinés à être bus plutôt que dégustés, les vins d'Alsace retrouvèrent bientôt une place sur le marché français.

L'Alsace vécut une nouvelle tragédie en 1944-1945 : les dernières batailles de la guerre semèrent la dévastation. Pourtant, le voyageur qui arrive actuellement de Lorraine et traverse les hauteurs paisibles entre les deux provinces n'imaginerait pas combien de vignes furent rasées et de vignobles détruits. Il s'en douterait encore moins en arrivant à Obey, dans la vallée où on l'accueillera avec un repas des plus succulents composé de foie gras, truites, saucisses, jambon et crème fouettée. Quelques dernières collines le séparent encore des vignobles. C'est alors seulement qu'il constatera à quel point l'Alsace a souffert. Mais la population a reconstruit énergiquement ses maisons et ses celliers, elle a aussi replanté ses vignes. De nos jours le négoce du vin, plus actif et plus important que jamais, fait face à une demande mondiale croissante des vins d'Alsace.

Chaque année, quelque 300 000 hl sont exportés vers l'étranger, les principaux acheteurs étant, par ordre décroissant, l'Allemagne, le Benelux, le Royaume-Uni, la Suisse, les États-Unis, le Canada, l'Italie, la Scandinavie, le Mexique et l'Afrique. Le Marché Commun s'attribue les trois quarts du vin destiné à l'exportation.

Si les vignobles alsaciens ont une histoire quelque peu mouvementée, il y a une grande continuité dans celle des vignerons : certaines firmes les plus connues aujourd'hui sont les mêmes familles qui, il y a déjà quatre cents ans, faisaient leur vin dans ces mêmes villages d'Alsace. Aujourd'hui, elles ne se contentent probablement plus de commercialiser leurs propres vins, mais aussi ceux des petits viticulteurs de leur région. Le vignoble alsacien produit des vins de caractère et de qualité différents — du Zwicker, vraisemblablement, ainsi qu'un ou plusieurs Riesling, Gewürztraminer, Pinot ou Muscat. Aussi les gros producteurs-distributeurs — qui ne produisent pas seulement les grands vins, mais mettent aussi en réserve différentes variétés qu'ils assemblent afin d'obtenir des vins caractéristiques — jouent-ils un rôle important dans le commerce des vins alsaciens. Depuis la dernière guerre mondiale, une nouvelle branche de ce commerce est née : celle des coopératives. Après la dernière guerre, quelques petits propriétaires décidèrent qu'en mettant leurs ressources en commun, ils pourraient plus facilement réhabiliter leur vignoble et retrouver leur prospérité. Maintenant réunies sous le sigle Union vinicole pour la diffusion des vins d'Alsace, ces coopératives contrôlent 15 % du marché. Traitant à égalité avec de vieilles maisons telles que Hugel, Dopff et Irion, Lorentz et

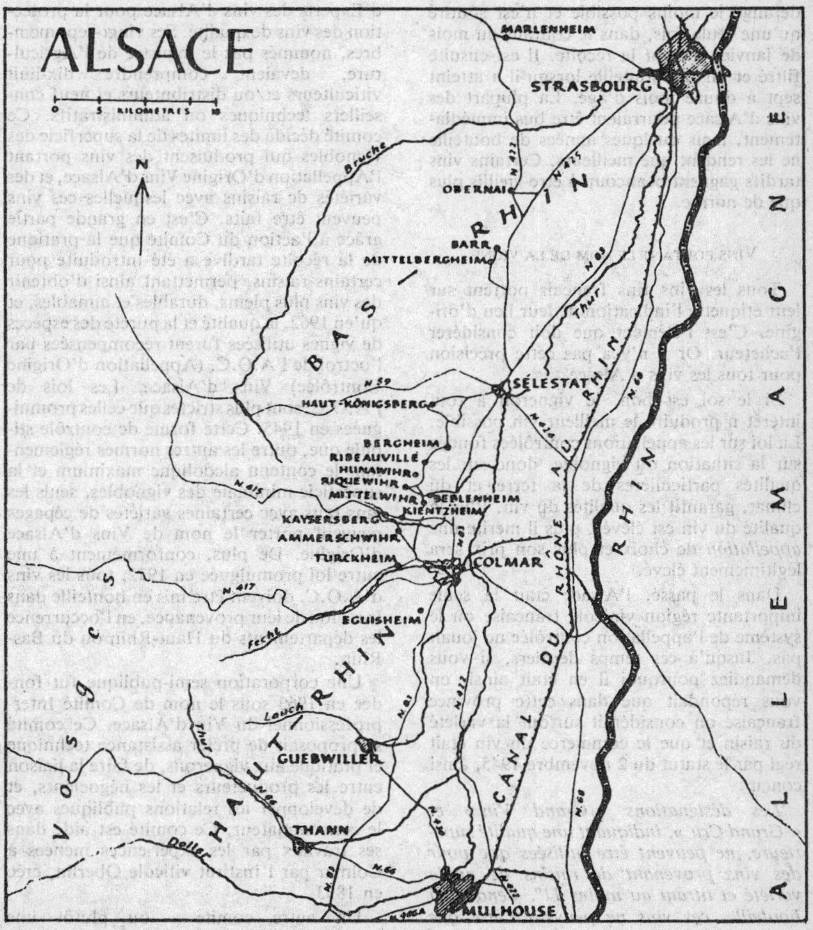

Willm, dont elles ne mettent pas en doute la prééminence, ces coopératives contribuent à la stabilisation des prix et au développement du commerce à grande échelle.

Dans les caves de ces grandes maisons de tradition familiale, on peut voir d'énormes cuves sur lesquelles des écussons, sculptés à même le bois, illustrent des sirènes et des dauphins. Ces grandes cuves sont toujours en usage, bien qu'une partie du vin soit maintenant encuvée dans de grands conteneurs en béton doublés de verre. Pour conserver toute sa fraîcheur, le vin est dérangé le moins possible et n'est soutiré qu'une seule fois, dans le courant du mois de janvier suivant la récolte. Il est ensuite filtré et mis en bouteille lorsqu'il a atteint sept à douze mois d'âge. La plupart des vins d'Alsace pourraient être bus immédiatement, mais quelques années de bouteille ne les rendent que meilleurs. Certains vins tardifs gagnent beaucoup à être vieillis plus que de norme.

Vins portant le nom de la vigne

Tous les vins fins français portent sur leur étiquette l'indication de leur lieu d'origine. C'est l'élément que doit considérer l'acheteur. Or il n'y a pas cette précision pour tous les vins d'Alsace.

Si le sol est bon, le vigneron a tout intérêt à produire le meilleur vin possible. La loi sur les appellations contrôlées fondée sur la situation du vignoble, donc sur les qualités particulières de la terre et du climat, garantit les qualités du vin. Plus la qualité du vin est élevée, plus il mérite une *appellation* de choix et plus son prix sera légitimement élevé.

Dans le passé, l'Alsace était la seule importante région vinicole française où le système de l'appellation contrôlée ne jouait pas. Jusqu'à ces temps derniers, si vous demandiez pourquoi il en était ainsi, on vous répondait que dans cette province française on considérait surtout la variété du raisin et que le commerce du vin était régi par le statut du 2 novembre 1945, ainsi conçu :

Les désignations « Grand Vin » et « Grand Cru », indiquant une qualité supérieure, ne peuvent être utilisées que pour des vins provenant de raisins de noble variété et titrant au moins 11°. Vendus en bouteille, ces vins ne peuvent l'être que dans les contenants connus sous le nom de bouteille de vin alsacienne.

Les viticulteurs alsaciens considérèrent ce règlement comme injuste car s'il les obligeait à n'utiliser que ce type de bouteilles, il n'interdisait nullement à leurs concurrents des autres régions de vendre leur vin dans des flacons de même forme. A force de réclamations, ils obtinrent un décret en 1955 qui mit fin à cette injustice. Ce décret accorde un quasi-monopole aux vins d'Alsace sur leurs bouteilles hautes et sveltes.

En 1945, on institua un comité régional d'Experts des vins d'Alsace pour la protection des vins de qualité. Ses vingt-sept membres, nommés par le ministre de l'Agriculture, devaient comprendre dix-huit viticulteurs et/ou distributeurs et neuf conseillers techniques ou administratifs. Ce comité décida des limites de la superficie des vignobles qui produisent des vins portant l'Appellation d'Origine Vins d'Alsace, et des variétés de raisins avec lesquelles ces vins peuvent être faits. C'est en grande partie grâce à l'action du Comité que la pratique de la récolte tardive a été introduite pour certains raisins, permettant ainsi d'obtenir des vins plus pleins, durables et aimables, et qu'en 1962, la qualité et la pureté des espèces de vignes utilisées furent récompensées par l'octroi de l'A.O.C. (Appellation d'Origine Contrôlée) Vins d'Alsace. Les lois de l'A.O.C. sont plus strictes que celles promulguées en 1945. Cette forme de contrôle stipule que, outre les autres normes réglementant le contenu alcoolique maximum et la superficie minimale des vignobles, seuls les vins faits avec certaines variétés de cépages peuvent porter le nom de Vins d'Alsace d'Origine. De plus, conformément à une autre loi promulguée en 1972, tous les vins d'A.O.C. doivent être mis en bouteille dans la région de leur provenance, en l'occurrence les départements du Haut-Rhin ou du Bas-Rhin.

Une corporation semi-publique fut fondée en 1963 sous le nom de Comité Interprofessionnel du Vin d'Alsace. Ce comité se proposait de prêter assistance technique et pratique aux vignerons, de faire la liaison entre les producteurs et les négociants, et de développer les relations publiques avec le consommateur. Ce comité est aidé dans ses travaux par les expériences menées à Colmar par l'Institut viticole Oberlin, crée en 1893.

Un autre comité — ou plutôt une

ancienne confrérie arborant capes écarlates et tricornes noirs — exerce par l'intermédiaire de ses règles volontairement rituelles une surveillance bénéfique sur les plus grands vins d'Alsace. Fondée au XIVe siècle à Ammerschwihr, la Confrérie Saint-Étienne était à l'origine connue sous le nom de *Herrenstubengesellschaft* (Guilde des conseillers municipaux). Les membres-fondateurs étaient des magistrats locaux et leurs amis, ils élisaient chaque année un grand-maître parmi tous les membres. C'était au grand-maître d'organiser les séances de dégustation durant lesquelles on jugerait des vins nouveaux, ainsi que le banquet annuel de la Saint-Etienne (bien que le saint patron de la Société soit en fait saint Diacre). La Confrérie disparut pendant la période de crise de la viticulture alsacienne. On la retrouve en 1947 en qualité de grand concile pour la région des vins d'Alsace. Son rôle consiste essentiellement à organiser des séances de dégustation au cours desquelles les meilleurs vins de la dernière récolte sont jugés et notés. Une douzaine de bouteilles des meilleurs grands crus sont mises de côtés comme pièces de collection et servent d'étalon aux membres viticulteurs. Les bouteilles les plus hautement appréciées porteront le sceau de la Confrérie, attaché avec un ruban doré. Chaque année, à l'occasion de la Foire aux vins de Colmar, la société sélectionne (sur examen et dégustation à yeux bandés) de nouveaux candidats susceptibles d'entrer dans ses rangs. Les membres de longue date reçoivent des visiteurs étrangers à l'occasion de la Foire pour déguster les vins proposés dans les différentes loges.

Célèbres agglomérations vinicoles d'Alsace

Les vignobles s'étendent en une longue bande se déroulant du nord au sud, le long de l'est des Vosges, là où la chaîne de montagnes touche la plaine du Rhin. Les zones les plus importantes se trouvent entre Riquewihr et Ribeauvillé, ainsi qu'autour des villages de Bard au nord, et de Guebwiller au sud. La plupart des gens qui se rendent en Alsace prennent la splendide Route du Vin. En partant de Strasbourg, ils pourront voir près de 50 des 100 communes détenant l'appellation Vins d'Alsace. Le visiteur pourra faire une première étape à Colmar, ville qui garde encore ses vieilles ruelles, quelques magnifiques maisons, ainsi que l'extraordinaire rétable d'Isenheim peint par Matthias Grüenewald au début du XVIe siècle. Le musée qui l'abrite est un ancien couvent. C'est aussi à Colmar qu'a lieu tous les ans la grande Foire aux Vins. Un lien particulier unit la ville de Colmar aux Ètats-Unis : il se trouve que Bartholdi, le sculpteur du Lion de Belfort de Colmar, est aussi l'auteur de la Statue de la Liberté. En outre, la partie plate de la région est le centre agricole du chou avec lequel on fait la choucroute, le plat alsacien le plus célèbre. Il se marie d'ailleurs beaucoup mieux avec les bières locales qu'avec le vin.

Obernai

Abritée par le mont Saint-Odile, cette commune du Bas-Rhin — avec ses fontaines, ses statues de la sainte, et sa charmante place du marché — n'est qu'un avant-goût des merveilles que le visiteur pourra découvrir sur la Route du Vin.

Barr

Située dans le Bas-Rhin aux pieds d'une vallée qui descend des plus hauts sommets vosgiens de la région, Barr est un petit bourg animé avec une bien jolie mairie. On y fait surtout du Sylvaner, mais aussi du bon Riesling.

Bergheim

La réputation des Traminer — plus particulièrement celui du vignoble de kanzlerberg de Bergheim — est des plus élevées. C'est un charmant village entouré de murs sous lesquels on passe par une voûte sculptée en l'an 1300. Dans certaines vieilles rues, les caniveaux sont si larges qu'il faut les traverser sur des petits ponts et leur eau est si claire que des femmes pendant longtemps y lavèrent leur linge.

Le centre de la ville est une place ombragée avec une belle mairie d'un côté et, de l'autre l'église paroissiale. Une tour de ce monument s'appelle la *Tour des Sorcières,* parce que de prétendues sorcières y furent jugées et condamnées au XVIe siècle.

Ribeauvillé

Ribeauvillé est un peu moins important. Dominée par trois châteaux perchés sur les collines, cette ville conservait la charmante tradition des cornemuseux. Chaque année, autrefois, le tintamarre de leur festival retentissait dans les vieilles rues tortueuses de Ribeauvillé. Précisons toutefois que, s'il n'y a plus de cornemuseux, il y a toujours les vins d'Alsace.

Riquewihr

Entourée de murs, épargnée par les guerres, Riquewihr est la plus ravissante agglomération vinicole de France, exception faite de Saint-Émilion et peut-être de Sancerre. Les rues pavées de pierres arrondies sont bordées de maisons des XVIe et XVIIe siècles, avec leurs enseignes hautes en couleur et leurs fenêtres fleuries. Elles sont rafraîchies par des fontaines. La cour d'une des vieilles auberges, entourée d'une treille, voilà un des meilleurs endroits du monde pour déguster un vin d'Alsace frais, d'or vert, dans un verre au long pied d'émeraude. L'endroit est riche en Riesling, Gewürztraminer, Muscat et Pinot. La nature calcaire du sol convient parfaitement au Riesling, qui prend un très bon bouquet. Les coteaux les plus prospères sont ceux de Sporen et Schœnenberg.

Kaysersberg

Déguster le vin dans une cave comme celle de feu Salzmann à Kaysersberg est une des expériences les plus romantiques que puisse s'offrir un amateur de vin.

La cour du domaine conserve intact son caractère gothique. C'est une relique du Moyen Age, dominée par les ruines d'un vieux château, dressées sur une éminence, au-delà du cours d'eau qui traverse la ville. Il se trouve que le docteur Schweitzer naquit dans ce village.

Ammerschwihr

Les vignes qui entourent ce bourg s'étendent en diretion des Vosges. Tours, murailles, fossés d'anciens châteaux y apparaissent de-ci, de-là. L'agglomération proprement dite est absolument nette, moderne, tout à fait neuve, car l'ancien Ammerschwihr fut rasé jusqu'au sol sans qu'en subsistât une seule pierre par les bombardements de décembre 1944 et janvier 1945. Le nouvel Ammerschwihr est aussi fonctionnel qu'une belle machine. Le restaurant de M. Gaertner, « Aux Armes de France » — un des meilleurs restaurants régionaux de France — offre fièrement foie gras et choucroute arrosés du vin des vignobles ressuscités d'Ammerschwihr, dont le Kaefferkopf est probablement le plus célèbre. A la fin de la guerre, la Herrenstubengesellschaft devint la Confrérie de Saint-Étienne.

Turckheim

Située au nord de Colmar, Turckheim est une commune pittoresque, avec ses vieux remparts percés de trois grandes portes. Son grand vignoble porte le nom de Brand.

Eguisheim

Ancien village bâti en cercle. Les Beyer — une vieille maison qui transmet sa science des vins de père en fils depuis le XVIe siècle, ce qui n'est pas exceptionnel en Alsace — vous offriront du Kougelhoff, le gâteau alsacien traditionnel, accompagné d'un Gewürztraminer parfumé et d'un doigt de Pinot Noir aux reflets rosés, vin local mineur mais agréable lorsque bu dans son cadre.

Guebwiller

Les habitants de ce pays produisent de très bons vins — surtout du Riesling — avec les raisins de leurs vignes plantées en terrasses au nord et au sud de l'agglomération. Les vignes sont haut perchées sur des coteaux si escarpés que des tracteurs s'y acharnent toute l'année à tasser le sol qui a tendance à glisser. Le meilleur vignoble est incontestablement Wannen.

Les variétés de raisins

Riesling et Gewürztraminer (ou Traminer-Gewürztraminer) sont les plus fins et la palme revient sans doute au Riesling. Les amateurs non alsaciens de vin d'Alsace ne sont pas d'accord à ce sujet, mais aucun dégustateur éclairé ne refuserait la première place au Riesling. Quant aux Alsaciens eux-mêmes ils affirment que le Riesling est le roi des vins.

En ce qui concerne les vins de qualité courante produits en grosse quantité, les meilleurs sont les Chasselas et Knipperlé.

Traminer — Gewürztraminer

Il règne une certaine confusion au sujet de ces deux noms et certains se demandent s'il existe réellement une différence entre les deux vins. En réalité le Gewürztraminer, vin de saveur épicée, n'est qu'une variante du Traminer qui ne se distingue guère de l'autre, mais qu'on préfère en général. En fait il a été décidé que seul le terme Gewürztraminer peut être utilisé, et que la vigne est une variante sélectionnée des anciennes espèces, les Traminer. Ce vin (fait avec un petit raisin rougeâtre au goût musqué) peut être légèrement douceâtre les meilleures années, mais il est en général passablement sec. Il reste une part de sucre résiduel dans le vin qui diffère du Riesling en ce sens que ce dernier, quand le raisin est bien mûr, éveille un souvenir incertain de muscat, alors qu'à même degré de maturité le Traminer-Gewürztraminer a un léger arôme de violette ou de rose. Il lui manque la race, la distinction et la rigidité d'acier propre aux très fins Riesling. Son goût et son bouquet prononcés manquent peut-être de subtilité pour le palais de certains. Le Traminer-Gewürztraminer est le vin blanc français le plus nettement caractérisé. Délicieusement fruité quand il est de première qualité, il accompagne à merveille les plats au goût très prononcé et fortement épicés, tels que le curry, on le sert aussi avec la viande et les fromages locaux.

Riesling

C'est le raisin qui donne les grands vins allemands du Rhin et de la Moselle. Le Riesling d'Alsace se marie magnifiquement avec les huîtres, le poisson et tous les fruits de mer ainsi qu'avec le fromage. Moins corsé que le Tokay d'Alsace et moins caractérisé que le Traminer, il a indiscutablement plus de classe que l'un et l'autre. Sec, fruité et frais, le Riesling peut atteindre à la plus grande élégance. La vigne s'épanouit sur un sol en grande partie calcaire. Les grands coteaux de Riesling se trouvent autour de Riquewihr, Kellenberg, Ribeauvillé et Dambach.

Tokay d'Alsace ou Pinot Gris

Bien des gens considèrent ce vin comme immédiatement inférieur au Riesling et au Traminer. Très corsé, il s'améliore en bouteille, qu'il soit sec ou légèrement doux. Selon une hypothèse, on le nommerait Tokay parce que les vignes de cette variété auraient été importées voici trois cents ans de la région de Tokaj en Hongrie. Ce vin n'a pas d'autre rapport avec le véritable Tokay de Hongrie, fait avec du raisin de la variété Furmint. Certains critiquent donc cette appellation qui induit en erreur. Le *Dictionnaire du vin* indique seulement que le nom de Tokay désigne en langage courant les vins alsaciens faits avec du Pinot gris. On le sert généralement avec du foie gras et des viandes.

Muscat d'Alsace

Muscat très sec, fruité, qui offre souvent un fin bouquet. C'est une autre vieille espèce, et un apéritif populaire en Alsace.

Sylvaner

Intermédiaire en fait de qualité entre les raisins courants tels que le Chasselas et les variétés plus fines. Agréable, léger, le vin qu'il donne convient pour les déjeuners rapides. Il présente parfois un piquant qui rafraîchit la bouche ou une « pointe de fraîcheur » comparable à celle des Sylvaner de même classe produits en Palatinat, de l'autre côté du Rhin. Il mérite d'être bu jeune. Sous certaines conditions, il a droit au titre de Grand Vin.

Pinot Blanc

Plus corsé en général que le Sylvaner auquel il ressemble un peu, il ne mérite quand même pas d'être classé parmi les vins distingués — quoique dans les meilleurs cas, il soit équilibré et de bouquet délicat. Parfois il est légèrement piquant. C'est un vin à servir avec du foie gras ou des viandes.

Chasselas

Ses vignes fournissent la plus grande part du vin de carafe. Léger, agréable, il titre, comme la moyenne des vins d'Alsace, entre 9 et 10°. Rarement vendu en bouteille, il est peu exporté. Pourtant une grande quantité de Chasselas sert de base aux vins de nombreux distributeurs.

Müller-Turgau

Ce croisement de Riesling et Sylvaner, qui gagne beaucoup de terrain en Allemagne, est très rare en Alsace où il produisait un vin semblable au Chasselas, mais pas aussi bon.

Knipperlé

Autre vin courant d'Alsace, pas tout à fait aussi bon que le Chasselas.

Zwicker

Ce nom n'est pas celui d'une variété de raisin. Lorsqu'il figure sur une étiquette, il désigne le coupage entre une variété noble et une courante. La plupart des vins alsaciens portant une marque quelconque inventée par un négociant ou un vigneron sont des Zwicker.

Edelzwicker

Coupage de variétés exclusivement nobles (*edel* signifie noble en Allemand et en alsacien).

Vin gris

Célèbre, sauf en Alsace, le vin rosé de cette province est plus souvent un mélange de rouge et de blanc qu'un véritable rosé, produit par la fermentation légère de raisin rouge. Les experts qui font autorité en vins d'Alsace tels que feu René Kuehn d'Ammerschwihr (ancien membre de la Chambre des députés et ancien délégué de la France aux Nations Unies) affirment que le meilleur vin rosé de leur province est l'authentique Rosé d'Alsace qui doit provenir du Pinot Noir et être fait avec des raisins de deux ou trois vignobles seulement dans chacune des trois ou quatre communes d'Alsace qui produisent du véritable rosé. On fait des quantités considérables de vins gris en Lorraine.

LES EAUX-DE-VIE D'ALSACE

Faites avec divers fruits, les eaux-de-vie d'Alsace sont célèbres sous le nom d'*alcools blancs* parce qu'elles ne vieillissent pas en fût, mais dans des poteries. En Alsace, vignes et vergers alternent entre Vosges et Rhin. Les quetschiers notamment abondent sur les plaines. Fraisiers, framboisiers et houx prospèrent à merveille dans les forêts à plus haute altitude.

Kirsch

C'est le plus important des alcools blancs. Comme l'indique son nom allemand, il est produit par la distillation de la cerise. Le noyau aussi est distillé. Il faut près de 30 kg de fruit pour obtenir environ onze bouteilles d'alcool à 50°. C'est à mi-hauteur entre la plaine et le sommet des Vosges que prospère le cerisier sauvage dont les fruits donnent le meilleur kirsch. Ceux de la région de Trois-Épis, immédiatement au-dessus d'Ammerschwihr, de Haut-Kœnigsbourg et de Sainte-Odile, sont les plus réputés.

Fraise

L'eau-de-vie de fraise provient de la distillation de fraises sauvages et cultivées. Quand elle est authentique elle est très bonne, mais aussi très chère.

Framboise

L'eau-de-vie de framboise ne s'obtient pas par les mêmes procédés que ceux utilisés pour la fabrication des autres eaux-de-vie de fruit. En effet, une eau-de-vie distillée directement et exclusivement à partir de framboises aurait un goût si concentré qu'elle serait pratiquement imbuvable. De plus, étant donné qu'il faut près de 30 kg de fruit pour obtenir un litre d'eau-de-vie de framboise ayant un pourcentage d'alcool suffisant, sa fabrication serait d'un coût prohibitif et son prix, tout aussi élevé. On obtient donc l'eau-de-vie de framboise par macération des fruits dans de l'alcool neutre sans l'exposer à l'oxygène. Le liquide obtenu est alors distillé pour devenir de l'eau-de-vie proprement dite. Ce procédé permet d'obtenir un litre d'eau-de-vie ayant le taux d'alcool désiré avec seulement 4 ou 5 kg de fruits.

Mirabelle

Faite avec de grosses prunes jaunes, cette eau-de-vie vient en général de Lorraine.
Voir MIRABELLE DE LORRAINE

Quetsche

Alcool fait avec les grosses prunes bleues dénommées quetsches. Cette eau-de-vie est courante et les arbres qui produisent le fruit prospèrent sur la plaine alsacienne.

Houx

Ce breuvage extraordinaire est distillé sur les hauteurs dominant Ammerschwihr. C'est un des plus rares et aussi un des plus chers au monde. L'Alsace en produit moins de 500 bouteilles par an. A cet effet on met à fermenter ensemble du sucre et des baies de houx, puis on distille le produit de cette macération.

Enzian

Alcool blanc obtenu en distillant les racines étonnamment longues de la gentiane jaune.

Reine-Claude

Cette variété de prunes, baptisée ainsi en l'honneur de la fille de Louis XII, n'est guère distillée. L'alcool qu'elle produit alors a un bouquet presque trop capiteux.

L'Alsace produit encore d'autres variétés d'alcools blancs faits à partir de l'abricot, la pêche, le fruit du sorbier et de l'alisier blanc, la myrtille et la mûre.

Altise

Insecte qui se nourrit des feuilles de la vigne.

Voir CHAPITRE IV

Amarone

Vin rouge italien de la Vénétie, semblable — en plus sec — au Recioto de la Valpolicella, fait avec des raisins séchés et spécialement sélectionnés. C'est un vin riche, concentré et fortement alcoolisé. Fort apprécié par les connaisseurs, ce D.O.C. demande à vieillir en bouteille.

Amber Dry

Nom sous lequel on vend souvent en Grande-Bretagne la Clairette du Languedoc *(voir ce mot).*

Ambonnay

Agglomération des environs de Reims, qui produit un des Premiers Crus de Champagne.

Amélioration

N'importe quel traitement du vin ou addition au vin ou au jus de raisin dans le but d'en améliorer la qualité.

Américain (Goût)

Nom donné au Champagne doux, surtout avant 1914, d'ailleurs tout à fait à tort car, en réalité, on n'exporte pas le Champagne doux vers les États-Unis.

Amer Picon

Marque d'un bitter français consommé en apéritif, fait de vin et d'alcool de vin, auxquels on ajoute de la quinine (pour lui donner son amertume), de l'écorce d'orange et d'innombrables herbes. Se consomme avec de la glace, dilué dans de l'eau et généralement adouci avec de la grenadine ou du cassis.

Amertume

Une des maladies du vin étudiée au CHAPITRE V. Elle se manifeste d'abord par l'apparition d'un dépôt et le vin tourne en vinaigre.

Aminaeen

Un des plus durables et des plus célèbres vins, au temps d'Auguste, auquel « même le royal Phanéen » rendait hommage (Virgile, *Les Géorgiques, II*).

Voir ANTIQUITÉ (VINS DE L')

Ammerschwihr

Agglomération vinicole d'Alsace *(voir* ALSACE).

Amontillado

Variété de Xérès de couleur moins pâle que le Fino, mais plus riche en bouquet. A l'état naturel il est sec. Pour exportation vers les pays anglo-saxons on lui ajoute du vin plus doux provenant du raisin Pedro Ximénez.

Voir XÉRÈS

Ampélidacées ou Ampélidés

Famille à laquelle appartient la vigne à vin. Des 10 genres que comporte cette famille, un seul, le genre *Vitis,* importe en vinification, quoique nombre d'autres soient capables de produire des raisins. *Vitis* se divise en deux sous-genres : *Euvites* et *Muscadinae,* chacun subdivisé en nombreuses espèces, notamment le premier. L'espèce *Vitis vinifera* est la plus cultivée car c'est elle qui donne les plus grands vins du monde. Née en Europe, elle a été transplantée sur les autres continents.

Voir CHAPITRE IV

Ampélographie

1. Étude descriptive, identification et classification des vignes.
2. Livre ou document décrivant les caractéristiques structurelles d'une vigne. Les commentaires écrits sont souvent accompagnés d'un dessin détaillé ou d'une photographie d'une feuille de chaque plante étudiée dans le livre.

Ampélothérapie

Traitement de maladies humaines ou animales par des raisins possédant des vertus thérapeutiques.

Amphore

Grand récipient de terre cuite et parfois de pierre, à deux petites anses, et qui servait aux temps anciens à conserver le vin ou l'huile.

Voir ANTIQUITÉ (VINS DE L')

Ancenis (Coteaux d')

Le Coteaux d'Ancenis est un V.D.Q.S. rouge, rosé ou blanc, titrant dans les trois cas au minimum 10°. Il s'agit d'un Cabernet ou de Gamay pour le rouge et le rosé ; de Chenin blanc ou de Pinot Beurot, pour le blanc.

Anglais (Goût)

Nom donné au Champagne très sec destiné au marché anglais.

Angleterre

Voir ROYAUME-UNI

Angelus (Château l')

Bordeaux rouge.
Commune de Saint-Émilion.

Un des nombreux Grands Crus, d'après la Classification des Saint-Émilion de 1955 et de 1986. Depuis 1924, le domaine appartient à la famille des Boüard. La vinification est faite selon des procédés très actuels, dans un chai moderne.

Superficie : 25 ha.
Production moyenne : 150 tonneaux, 13 000 caisses.

Angludet (Château -)

Bordeaux rouge. Commune de Cantenac-Margaux, en Haut-Médoc.

Dans la classification de 1855, Château-Angludet figure parmi les Crus Exceptionnels, juste au-dessous des Cinquièmes Crus. En cette année-là, ce vignoble traversait une mauvaise passe. Ce château appartient à la famille Sichel. Angludet mérite d'être promu à un rang plus élevé. Peter Sichel est aussi un des propriétaires de Château-Palmer.

Superficie plantée en vignes : 30 ha.
Production annuelle moyenne : 120 tonneaux, 12 000 caisses environ.

Angola (Vin d')

Breuvage obtenu par fermentation de la sève de palmier en Afrique Occidentale.

Angostura

Bitter à base de rhum fait à La Trinité (Trinidad), d'après la recette encore secrète de la famille Siegert, héritière de l'inventeur. Le docteur Siegert devint chirurgien général dans l'armée de Simon Bolivar pendant les guerres d'indépendance de l'Amérique du Sud. Il mit au point ce bitter à partir de diverses herbes et plantes afin de combattre les conséquences déprimantes du climat tropical. Le produit devint immédiatement si populaire que Siegert fonda, dès le début du XIXe siècle, la firme qui le commercialise encore.

Anguillule

Ver minuscule qui s'attaque aux racines de la vigne et provoque l'anguillulose *(voir* CHAPITRE IV).

Anhydride sulfureux

L'usage du soufre pour stériliser le vin est presque aussi ancien que le vin luimême : Dans l'*Iliade,* Achille soufre sa coupe avant de faire une libation en hommage à Zeus. Dans la vinification moderne, on diffuse de l'anhydride sulfureux (SO_2) sur les raisins à peine vendangés afin d'enrayer une fermentation précoce ; on en ajoute au vin en cours de fermentation, puis dans les tonneaux dans lesquels il séjournera. Injecté à petites doses, il garantira un vin sain sans altérer le goût ou l'arôme. Mais utilisé à trop fortes doses, il ne passera pas inaperçu (ce qui se produit assez fréquemment pour les blancs doux et demi-doux, de qualité médiocre, auxquels on injecte des doses massives d'anhydride sulfureux pour que le sucre non fermenté ne soit pas attaqué par les levures après la mise en bouteille).

Le soufre a pour acti n de détruire les levures indésirables. Par ce procédé, on élimine facilement microbes et bactéries, mais une quantité considérable de soufre sera nécessaire pour attaquer les levures *Saccharomyces.* C'est généralement en brûlant des mèches soufrées que l'on obtient l'anhydride sulfureux, qui est un gaz ; mais il existe également du SO_2 liquide comprimé ainsi que des tablettes de métabisulfite de potassium ($K_2S_2O_5$) qui lorsqu'on les dissout dans le vin donnent de l'anhydride sulfureux, de l'eau et une petite quantité de crème de tartre, qui est l'une des composantes normales du vin.

Voir SULFURISATION

Anis

Nom générique donné à divers apéritifs et liqueurs en France et en Espagne. Le goût qui domine est celui de l'anis étoilé. Cet anis était autrefois un des principaux composants de l'absinthe. On fabriqua ensuite des anis sans absinthe *(voir ce mot)* quand cette dernière fut interdite par la loi. Les apéritifs à l'anis sont consommés après dilution dans l'eau. Verts à l'état pur, ils prennent une teinte d'un gris trouble, à

ACTION PURIFICATRICE DE L'ANHYDRIDE SULFUREUX

Proportion d'acide sulfureux à ajouter (g/l)	*Acidité volatile exprimée en (g/l) acide sulfurique*	*Goût*	*Examen au microscope*	
			Liquide	*Dépôt*
trace	16,10	Sur et cassé	Bactéries de la tourne et de l'aigre	Levure et bactéries
0,050	0,76	Jaune, marron assez clair, léger goût de moisissure	Des bactéries	Levure assez pure
0,100	0,52	Légèrement rosâtre, mousseux, droit de goût	Absence de bactéries	Levure pure
0,150 0,200 0,250	0,47 0,45 0,36	Rose brillant, mousseux, droit de goût		

peine verdâtre, à l'addition de l'eau. Les pastis *(voir ce mot)* sont des boissons similaires, mais faits avec de la réglisse au lieu d'anis étoilé. Les marques Pernod, Ricard et Berger sont les plus connues parmi celles qui produisent des apéritifs et liqueurs à base d'anis. Quant à la liqueur d'anis, c'est l'une des liqueurs les plus populaires d'Espagne.

Anisette

Liqueur au goût de grain d'anis. Au retour des Indes occidentales, un voyageur en aurait confié la recette à une Bordelaise nommée Marie Brizard.

Anjou-Saumur

Blanc, rouge et rosé. Vallée de la Loire.

L'ancienne province de l'Anjou (dont les limites coïncidaient à peu près avec celles du département de Maine-et-Loire) compte plus de 13 000 viticulteurs. Ses vignobles s'étendent sur les coteaux dominant la rive gauche de la Loire, à l'ouest de la Touraine. L'Anjou et la Touraine se ressemblent de bien des manières. Les collines entourant Saumur sont faites des mêmes dépôts calcaires que ceux de Vouvray et, dans les deux régions, le vin vieillit dans des caves profondes creusées à flanc de colline. Dans l'Anjou, au sud et à l'ouest d'Angers, le sol arable, peu profond, couvre un lit de roc dur qui ressemble à celui de la Bretagne. Le pays des châteaux proprement dit se trouve en Touraine, mais en Anjou la Loire traverse un pays paisible, verdoyant, semé de vieux manoirs et châteaux, reliques du temps où les rois Plantagenêt d'Angleterre étaient aussi comtes d'Anjou. Au XIIIe siècle, les vins d'Anjou étaient très populaires en Angleterre. Plus tard, quand les Anglais importèrent surtout du Bordeaux, les Hollandais devinrent les meilleurs clients de l'Anjou. Leurs bateaux remontaient la Loire jusqu'à Rochefort-sur-Layon et même Saumur, pour embarquer les barriques. En ce temps-là, déjà, on exportait les meilleurs vins vers l'étranger par voie fluviale puis maritime et c'est seulement ceux de moins bonne qualité qui s'en allaient vers Paris par voie de terre.

Comme tous ceux de la vallée de la Loire, les vins d'Anjou sont frais et légers. Même les crus les moins cotés sont souvent charmants, mais on les trouve rarement hors de leur région d'origine. Les plus connus à l'étranger sont les rosés d'Anjou.

La production annuelle s'élève à 1 000 000 hl, dont 1/3 en vins blancs et presque tout le reste en rouges et rosés. L'Anjou produit aussi une faible quantité de vins rouges d'un intérêt relativement moindre. Les meilleurs Anjou blancs sont doux, comme ils l'étaient autrefois à peu près tous. L'évolution des goûts incita bien des viniculteurs à traiter leur vin en sec. Cette tendance est saine pour l'Anjou. Les vignobles capables de produire des vins naturellement doux continuent à le faire ; les autres — au raisin desquels il fallait ajouter du sucre — sont revenus à un produit naturellement sec. L'Anjou produit aussi du vin mousseux, surtout à Saumur et dans les environs, mais ce n'est pas le meilleur.

LE SOL ET LES VIGNES

Nous avons déjà indiqué que le sol de la région présente deux types différents : calcaire autour de Saumur et sur les coteaux bordant la Loire, d'une part ; dur et schisteux recouvert d'une mince couche d'argile siliceuse partout ailleurs. Ce sol est si mince que les vignerons doivent parfois pulvériser le roc à la dynamite pour planter leurs vignes. Faute de recourir à l'explosif, ils passeraient d'innombrables heures à travailler leur terre à la pioche.

Le seul cépage autorisé pour le vin blanc d'appellation contrôlée est le Chenin Blanc, courant en Anjou depuis le IXe siècle. Les vins rouges — faits surtout à Saumur et dans les communes de Souzay-Champigny, Chacé, Dampierre, Varrains, Saint-Cyr-en-Bourg, Brézé et Brain-sur-Allonnes — viennent du Cabernet Franc et accessoirement du Cabernet Sauvignon. Le Pineau d'Aunis, autrefois courant, cède maintenant du terrain au Cabernet. On fait en Anjou deux espèces de rosé : le Rosé d'Anjou avec des raisins Groslot, Gamay, Got, Noble et Pineau d'Aunis ; le Rosé de Cabernet, uniquement avec des raisins Cabernet. Ce dernier est le meilleur : plus fruité, plus frais, d'un goût plus net et d'une couleur plus engageante. Certains rosés d'Anjou sont secs, d'autres doux. En général le consommateur de la région demande de plus en plus des rosés doux.

Un tiers seulement du vin est vendu sous l'étiquette Anjou. Le reste, y compris les meilleurs, porte les noms des subdivisions d'appellation contrôlée. Ce sont ces noms que l'on trouve le plus souvent sur les bouteilles envoyées à l'étranger.

Les subdivisions vinicoles de l'Anjou-Saumur

Coteaux de la Loire (Appellation Contrôlée)

Cette zone s'étend sur les deux rives du fleuve. C'est une des meilleures et des plus connues de l'Anjou. Son sol de compositions et qualités diverses est favorable au Chenin Blanc qui fait place au Muscadet dans la région vinicole voisine, située à l'ouest de Montjean. Les vins varient en fonction du sol. Doux, quoique en général plus secs que ceux des Coteaux du Layon, ils sont légers et bien faits. Quelques-uns, un peu âpres dans leur jeunesse, prennent de la rondeur avec le temps. D'autres vins achèverons de s'épanouir après quelques années de bouteille.

Savennières, village attrayant, a droit à sa propre appellation contrôlée. Ses vins ont tendance à être secs ; faits avec du Chenin Blanc ils mûrissent lentement. Ses vignobles les plus appréciés sont : La Coulée-de-Serrant, la Roche-aux-Moines, qui donnent tous deux des vins fins et très élégants ; Château de Savennières, Château d'Epiré, Château de la Bizolière, Clos du Papillon et Clos de la Bergerie.

D'autres communes méritent d'être citées, notamment : Bouchemaine, La Possonnière, Saint-Georges-sur-Loire, Champtocé et Ingrandes, Montjean, La Pommeraye et une partie de Chalonnes.

Coteaux du Layon (Appellation Contrôlée)

Les quelque 50 km de vignobles de cette zone sont éparpillés au long du petit affluent de la Loire nommé Layon qui descend des collines près des Verchers et sinue ensuite d'un village vinicole à l'autre jusqu'à se jeter dans la Loire juste en amont de Chalonnes. Les vins des coteaux du Layon sont riches en alcool et ceux des meilleures vignes sont parfois vendangés après que la pourriture noble s'est développée. On obtient alors des vins doux qui sont probablement les plus fins de cette catégorie en Anjou. Mais on y fait aussi des vins secs. Les blancs doux sont plus corsés et durent plus longtemps que tous ceux des coteaux de la Loire. Au XVIIe siècle, ils eurent beaucoup de succès auprès des Hollandais ; maintenant, on les boit surtout dans le nord de la France et en Belgique.

Bonnezeaux. Ce grand cru de la région a droit à sa propre appellation contrôlée et compte presque pour une subdivision à lui tout seul. Les vignobles, dans la commune de Thouarcé, s'étendent à flanc de coteau en direction du cours d'eau. Un moulin à vent solitaire monte la garde audessus d'eux. Jadis il y en avait trois. Ces vignes produisent une quantité limitée de vin blanc doux, mœlleux et fruité.

Quarts de Chaume. A aussi sa propre appellation. Presque aussi distingué que le précédent (certains même disent que c'est le meilleur des coteaux du Layon), le vin blanc doux de ce vignoble situé près du village de Chaume, dans la commune de Rochefort, ressemble au Vouvray doux. Il est plus fruité qu'un Sauternes. Comme finesse, légèreté et bouquet, il est unique, pourtant il titre généralement entre 12 et 13°. Pendant un certain temps, le vignoble de Chaume appartenait à un seul propriétaire qui le louait en échange d'un quart de produit. Il se réservait le droit de choisir le secteur de la vigne d'où devait provenir sa part de vin. C'est ainsi que cette partie fut appelée Quarts de Chaume.

Six autres communes de cette zone ajoutent leur nom à l'appellation contrôlée Coteaux du Layon. Ce sont : Beaulieu-sur-Layon, Faye-d'Anjou, Rablay-sur-Layon, Rochefort-sur-Loire, Saint-Aubin de Luigné et Saint-Lambert-du-Lattay. A mi-cours du Layon on produit une quantité importante de vin blanc ; il n'a droit qu'à l'appellation la plus générale d'Anjou. Mais dans cette même zone le vin rosé domine.

Coteaux de l'Aubance (Appellation Contrôlée)

Les vins de cette petite zone des coteaux du Layon sont mieux connus dans leur région qu'ailleurs. Agréables, ils ont les qualités typiques de l'Anjou. Ce sont surtout des blancs mais n'ont pas tout le moelleux de ceux des coteaux de la Loire. Ils n'ent sont pas moins remarquables, surtout les demi-secs dont le caractère et le bouquet sont charmants. Les principales communes sont : Brissac ; Vauchrétien, d'où proviennent de bons vins blancs ;

Saint-Jean-des-Mauvrets, Juigné-sur-Loire, Saint-Melaine, Saint-Saturnin, Soulaines, Mozé, Mûrs, Denée qui est proche de Rochefort. Toutes ces communes font des vins assez semblables.

Coteaux du Loir

Cette ancienne subdivision d'Anjou, devenue A.O.C. dans les départements d'Indre-et-Loire et de la Sarthe, produit les vins des vignes cultivées dans la vallée du petit affluent de la Loire nommé le Loir. Ce sont des blancs agréables, des rouges sans intérêt et des rosés charmants.

Saumur-Champigny
et Coteaux de Saumur-Champigny
(A.O.C.)

La vieille ville de Saumur est dominée par un château sans grand intérêt architectural qui abrite un musée de l'art équestre. L'école de cavalerie de l'armée française se trouve à Saumur. Les rives du fleuve sont escarpées. Dans les falaises abruptes les vignerons ont creusé de vastes caves qui conviennent parfaitement au vieillissement du vin. Les crus les plus doux sont champagnisés. Mais le gros de la récolte consiste en vins secs ou demi-secs titrant entre 10 et 13° et parfois légèrement crémants.

Les mousseux de la Loire ont un goût qui leur est propre, nettement différent de celui du Champagne. Au même prix que le Champagne, le Saumur est surpayé. Ses producteurs sont pourtant imposés par certaines douanes étrangères à des taux aussi élevés que ceux de Champagne. Fait pour 2/3 avec du Chenin Blanc et 1/3 avec du Cabernet, le mousseux de la Loire est plus corsé et plus lourd que le Vouvray mousseux. Neuf communes du département de la Vienne partagent l'appellation de Saumur, notamment Pouançay, Berrie, Saint-Léger-de-Montbrillais, Ternay et Ranton.

L'appellation Coteaux de Saumur est actuellement délimitée par l'I.N.A.O. En principe, ses vignobles s'étendent sur les coteaux qui bordent la Loire. Dampierre joue un peu le rôle de capitale. Cette commune produit 2/3 de blancs et 1/3 de rouges et de rosés. Souzay-Champigny, Parnay et Turquant font des vins frais et fruités. Le vin blanc de Montsoreau est aisément reconnaissable à ses caractéristiques nettement tranchées. Situés sur le fleuve Thouet, Varrains et Chacé sont mieux connus pour leur rosé et leur rouge que pour leur petite production de blanc. Brezé, Epieds et Saix réussissent fort bien leur vin rouge, mais leur blanc est plus réputé. Saumur-Champigny, bon vin rouge de Champigny, agglomération située au sud de Saumur, provient également des nombreux villages environnants qui font eux aussi partie des Coteaux de Saumur. Parmi les vins rouges faits avec une grande partie de Cabernet Franc, Saumur-Champigny est, avec le Bourgueil et le Chinon, le meilleur vin rouge de la Loire.

Voir chacune des appellations traitées cidessus à sa place dans l'ordre alphabétique.

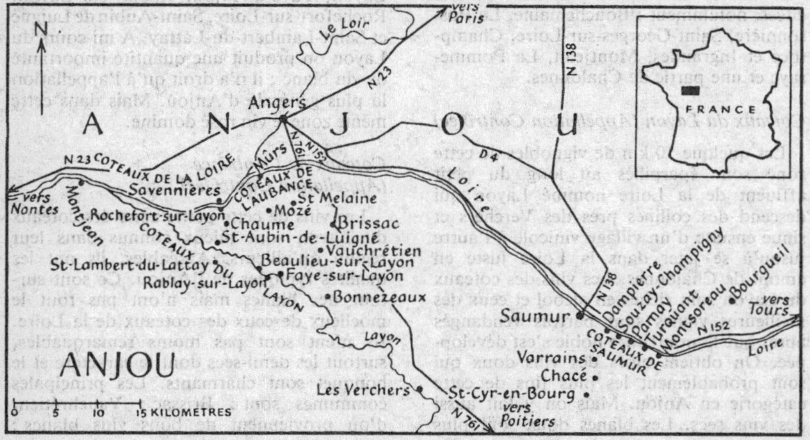

Anthracnose

Maladie de la vigne ; originaire d'Europe. *Voir* CHAPITRE IV et AUSTRALIE

Antilles

Le rhum — produit par la distillation de la canne à sucre — est né aux Antilles. On fait encore du rhum sur à peu près toutes les îles de cette mer, notamment les départements français et les anciennes Antilles britanniques.

Voir RHUM.

Antiquité (Vins de l')

Nous sommes fort bien renseignés au sujet du vin et de la vigne dans la Grèce et la Rome antiques. En fait de viticulture, notamment, les pratiques n'ont guère changé depuis environ 700 av. J.-C., quand Hésiode décrivit la plantation et la taille des vignes dans son domaine de Béotie. Mais les textes ne sauraient nous révéler quel était exactement le goût du vin que buvaient nos ancêtres. Malgré toute leur science, les spécialistes, tant historiens qu'œnologues, se laissent aller à des fantaisies personnelles qu'il leur serait difficile de prouver. L'un prétend que ces breuvages, bouillis jusqu'à ce qu'il n'en reste plus qu'une pâte bourbeuse, fumés, sucrés au miel, gâtés par la résine ou l'eau salée, nous auraient écœurés. D'autres au contraire soutiennent que les vins grecs conservés jusqu'à bonne maturation étaient exactement ce que prônaient les héros de l'Antiquité : les breuvages les plus divins dont l'homme ait jamais joui. On a recueilli au fond de la Méditerranée des amphores provenant de naufrages. Elles sont encore bouchées. Le nom de l'expéditeur ou du vigneron est déchiffrable. Mais si on ouvrait ces jarres, le liquide tentateur, à demi évaporé, serait insipide, saumâtre, et n'aurait pas le goût de vin.

Au XIXe siècle, l'historien Cyrus Redding croyait que les meilleurs crus antiques avaient probablement le goût de la Malvoisie ou des vins doux de Chypre qui étaient faits à cette époque selon la manière traditionnelle et qui le sont encore parfois de nos jours.

GRÈCE

La vigne poussa dès les temps les plus reculés en Grèce, sur la terre ferme et sur les îles, et les Grecs buvaient du vin. Le vin joue un rôle important dans les aventures d'Ulysse. Quand Nausicaa le trouva évanoui près d'un ruisseau, elle le ranima en lui donnant à manger et aussi en lui versant du vin qu'elle avait apporté dans une gourde en peau de chèvre. Plus tard, quand Ulysse arriva dans le palais royal, il banqueta avec Alcinoos et les prétendants, puis déclara : « Mélangez le breuvage et servez le vin à tous ceux qui sont dans la salle et offrons une libation à Zeus ». Et Pontonius mélangea le miel au vin, en versa dans la coupe de chacun pour la libation, puis il servit à la ronde.

Cette coutume pourrait rappeler les toasts de nos jours.

Vins doux

En général, il semble que les vins étaient doux. Celui avec lequel Ulysse enivra Polyphème lui avait été donné par Maron et c'était « un vin doux, sans mélange, un breuvage pour les dieux ». Maron cachait à ses serviteurs le tonneau contenant ce vin de réserve. Après avoir soutiré « ce vin rouge d'une douceur de miel » il le mélangeait dans un cratère d'argent avec de l'eau, à raison de 20 parts de vin pour 1 part d'eau. « Alors, une odeur merveilleusement douce s'élevait du mélange ». Le vin d'Hésiode devait aussi être doux, car il étalait les grappes au soleil et les y laissait pendant 10 jours après la vendange. Magon de Carthage procédait exactement de la même manière vers 550 av. J.-C.

Six cents ans plus tard, Columelle, donnant ses ordres pour faire du *passum optimum* (le meilleur vin sucré), disait que les raisins séchés au soleil devaient être étalés sur des cadres surélevés, couverts d'herbe, et y rester jusqu'à ce qu'ils soient assez flétris ; ensuite, ils seraient conservés pendant 6 jours dans une jarre avant le pressurage. Ce système ressemble d'assez près à la méthode de vinification des vins de paille contemporains.

Les vins doux n'ont jamais perdu leur attrait sur les habitants de l'Italie méridionale, de Chypre et les riverains de la mer Égée. On ne s'étonnera donc pas que les Grecs anciens les aient aimés et qu'ils aient préféré les vins vieux aux vins jeunes. De nos jours encore, le riche Commandaria de Chypre est doué d'une grande longévité.

On dit que les meilleurs vins grecs de l'Antiquité étaient faits avec un mélange de raisins noirs et blancs. Le célèbre Pramnien devait être un breuvage semblable au Tokay d'aujourd'hui.

Mélange des vins

Les vins grecs n'étaient pas tous purs et exempts de mélange. Souvent on mettait du miel dans les jarres. Plus tard Pline nous dit que les Grecs avaient l'habitude de donner de la vigueur à leur vin en l'additionnant de terre glaise, marbre pulvérisé et eau salée. Quoique certains affirment que les Grecs ne mêlaient pas de résine à leur vin, c'est fort probable, car la résine du pitchpin, très utilisée dans la viniculture romaine, survit encore dans celle de l'Italie actuelle, et il est probable que les Grecs l'utilisaient aussi. Mélanger de l'eau de mer au moût n'était pas tout à fait aussi grossier que cela nous semble aujourd'hui. Puisée en mer alors qu'elle était calme, cette eau était bouillie jusqu'à ce que les 2/3 s'évaporent. On y mêlait des épices, puis on la filtrait et on la conservait pendant plusieurs années avant de s'en servir.

Les Grecs mélangeaient aussi les vins entre eux pour les améliorer. Les meilleurs crus, devenus pâteux et épaissis par le miel au cours de leur vieillissement, ne pouvaient guère être consommés sans l'addition d'un breuvage plus léger. Les vins doux, en pleine maturité, devaient être filtrés avant consommation. On les coupait toujours à l'eau et les Grecs ne buvaient pas leur vin pur. Parfois, par raffinement, on y ajoutait quelques aromates.

Contenants : jarres, cratères, amphores.

A Athènes, lors des banquets, les convives (tous des hommes en règle générale) étaient allongés sur des sophas. Les esclaves mélangeaient le vin et l'eau dans des cratères et le servaient à la ronde avec des cruches. D'abord on offrait une libation, puis l'amphitryon, ou le chef du banquet, décrétait combien on boirait de vin et de quelle vigueur il serait.

Les *pithoi* (en latin : *dolia*) étaient les jarres dans lesquelles le vin fermentait. Pour assurer la conservation des vins les plus légers, on enduisait ces récipients de poix et on les enterrait.

Les amphores étaient de grandes jarres à deux anses dans lesquelles le vin vieillissait et que l'on apportaient dans la salle du banquet. L'*hydria* était un pot à couvercle qui servait à soutirer le vin des amphores pour l'apporter à table ou bien à apporter l'eau de la fontaine. Bol large, le *cratère* servait au mélange de l'eau et du vin. Enfin, chaque convive buvait soit dans un *kantharos* (tasse à deux anses), soit dans un *kylix* (gobelet étroit ressemblant à la flûte à champagne). Après avoir bu du vin, le Grec trouvait au fond du *kantharos* ou du *kylix* des dessins parfois étonnants. Faute de papier, et le papyrus étant rare, des artistes de talent ou de simples caricaturistes amateurs, ornaient de leurs œuvres le fond des tasses. Certains de ces dessins subsistent. Ils nous montrent les Grecs en train de banqueter, des joueuses de flûte, des danseuses qui les distrayaient pendant le repas ou des jeunes gens s'efforçant d'atteindre du pied des assiettes brandies au-dessus des têtes. C'était le jeu de *kottabos,* qui aurait été inventé en Sicile (alors Grande Grèce). En jetant la lie de sa coupe, le jeune homme invoquait souvent le nom d'une jeune femme.

Les femmes et le vin

Hormis des hétaïres, joueuses de flûte et danseuses, les femmes ne figuraient que rarement aux repas des hommes, mais quelques courtisanes avaient la tête solide et, à partir de Nausicaa, les femmes grecques burent en général du vin. Rien d'étonnant à cela, puisque c'était le breuvage courant.

Les anciens auteurs ont beaucoup écrit au sujet de la Grèce légendaire et de l'austérité qui régnait à Rome au début de son histoire ; en ces temps-là, les femmes ne buvaient que l'innocente *sapa* (jus de raisin non fermenté). Mais plus tard les femmes, dans une Rome plus sophistiquée, burent avec les hommes et quelques-unes s'enivrèrent. Elles participaient en grand nombre aux fêtes dionysiaques (originaires de Thrace) et c'était aussi elles qui s'exaltaient le plus au cours de ces cérémonies. Même quand l'adoration du dieu du Vin se réduisit à un rituel banal, sans danses de ménades, ni destructions, les femmes continuaient à célébrer le culte de Bacchus, tout particulièrement lors du pèlerinage à Delphes, comme le remarque Charles Seltman.

Rome

Les vignes sauvages prospèrent sur les côtes tempérées de la Méditerranée et tout permet de supposer que les habitants les plus primitifs de ces régions ont toujours fait des petits vins légers. Mais les Grecs, les Phéniciens et plus tard les Romains leur enseignèrent à tailler leur vigne et à faire du vin propre à la conservation. Les Grecs furent des navigateurs aventureux. On suppose que leur première colonie italique fut celle de Cumes, en Campanie, fondée par les Eubéens, probablement au VIIIe av. J.-C. A la fin du VIIe siècle av. J.-C. il y avait des villes grecques sur la côte orientale de Sicile, dans le golfe de Tarente et plus au nord. Il n'est pas prouvé que les Étrusques aient déjà fait de bons vins avec des raisins de vignes cultivées avant l'arrivée des Grecs, mais on considère en général comme certain qu'ils aimaient le luxe et les banquets auxquels les femmes participaient et buvaient leur part de vin. En général on croit que les Romains apprirent des Grecs viticulture et viniculture et qu'ils les enseignèrent ensuite aux habitants des pays qu'ils conquirent. Les premiers vins authentiques étaient des breuvages précieux et on ne les consommait qu'avec parcimonie. Ainsi, un général victorieux n'en offrait qu'une seule coupe à Jupiter. En un temps où l'on enseignait à faire prendre la viticulture au sérieux par les petits cultivateurs, Numa Pompilius (715-673 av. J.-C.) aurait interdit d'offrir des libations avec du vin de vignes non taillées.

La viticulture romaine

Le premier texte en latin qui nous indique comment les Romains traitaient leurs vignes et faisaient du vin est l'œuvre de Caton le Censeur (234-149 av. J.-C.) Grâce à son *De agri cultura,* dont Pline le Jeune parla avec admiration 200 ans plus tard, grâce à Pline l'Ancien lui-même et à Columelle (à peu près son contemporain), nous savons comment les Romains cultivaient la vigne, la plantaient, la greffaient, la taillaient, et nous sommes aussi au courant de la viniculture au premier siècle de notre ère et même avant.

Pline nous indique que de son temps encore on laissait, surtout en Campanie, les vignes devenir aussi hautes que des maisons et grimper le long des troncs jusqu'au sommet des arbres. Les travailleurs embauchés pour les tailler réclamaient un supplément de salaire en raison du risque d'accident. Il ajoute : « Ici, nous empêchons nos vignes de grandir en les taillant afin que leur vigueur se concentre dans les jeunes pousses ». D'après lui, le nombre des variétés de vigne en Grèce était incalculable. Il connaissait 80 bons vins italiens dont les meilleurs étaient faits avec des raisins aminéens (qu'il divisait en cinq variétés). En Toscane, les vignes nomantines, aux tiges rougeâtres, et les muscats prospéraient abondamment de son temps. Toutes ces variétés étaient indigènes. Parmi les vignes importées de Grèce, il citait le græcula (digne de rivaliser avec l'aminéen) et l'eugenia, d'abord transplantée à Taormina, puis dans la région d'Albe. Quant aux vignes de Rhétie et celles du pays des Allobroges, en Gaule, qui donnaient au vin un goût de résine, elles ne produisaient pas en Italie des boissons de qualité, mais ce désavantage était compensé par la quantité.

La viniculture romaine

Ce n'est pas le goût de pin des raisins allobroges qui déplaisait aux Romains. Ils le trouvaient même désirable puisqu'ils enduisaient leurs jarres à vin aussi bien à l'intérieur qu'à l'extérieur avec de la poix. Dans le XIIe livre de *Res rustica,* décrivant les innombrables tâches des domestiques, Columelle donne des indications précises à ce sujet. Puis il décrit diverses manières de conserver le moût : avec de la résine liquide, mélangée à de la cendre de vigne ; avec de l'eau salée et des herbes douces, ainsi que des épices. Afin que le vin vieillisse plus vite, les jarres devaient être conservées dans un grenier, au-dessus du *fumarium* où l'on brûlait du bois et des aromates. En ville, les vins qu'il fallait fumer pouvaient être conservés dans des celliers publics ou privés et on les traitait à peu près comme ceux d'aujourd'hui. La superstition selon laquelle il ne fallait soutirer le vin que lorsque le vent soufflait du nord paraît raisonnable quand on pense qu'en Italie le vent du sud est le sirocco qui rend fous bêtes et gens et fait cailler le lait. Pline considérait à juste titre que le fumage améliorait le goût du vin. Mais il s'élevait vigoureusement contre le vieillissement artificiel en fumoir des vins importés de Narbonne qu'il accusait aussi de contenir des herbes nocives et des drogues. Seul parmi les vins gaulois, celui de Marseille lui semblait acceptable. Il préférait les crus espagnols et considérait ceux de la Tarraconaise et des Baléares comme aussi estimables que les meilleurs vins italiens.

Les vins les plus estimés par les Romains

Les vins importés de Grèce étaient tenus en haute estime. Mais du vivant de Pline ils n'étaient plus aussi rares ni aussi riches que deux générations plus tôt lorsque, à un banquet, on n'en buvait jamais plus d'un seul verre. Au premier siècle de notre ère le Falerne rivalisait avec des vins grecs. Les Grecs des îles de Lesbos, Chio, Thassos, qui exportaient leurs meilleurs vins, connaissaient déjà la valeur de la publicité : des grappes de raisin ou la tête de Bacchus figuraient sur leurs pièces de monnaie. Mais les crus coûteux, aussi bien grecs qu'italiens, n'ont certainement jamais été goûtés par le menu peuple qui arrosait ses repas avec des breuvages aussi banals que notre vin ordinaire.

Les Romains faisaient du vin noir (rouge très foncé), du rouge clair, de l'ambré, et du blanc. Ceux qu'ils laissaient vieillir devaient être aussi forts que les vieux crus de Grèce. Dans son *Satiricon,* Pétrone nous montre le nouveau riche Trimalchion en train d'offrir, à son célèbre banquet, un petit verre tiré d'une amphore marquée : « Opimien muscadin, d'un siècle ». Et l'amphitryon s'exclame : « Hélas ! ce vin peut donc vivre plus longtemps qu'un homme ! Eh bien, goûtez-y et voyez s'il est resté bon depuis le consulat de Lucius Opimius ». Le millésime de 121 av. J.-C., aussi célèbre que celui de 1811, année de la comète, est un de ceux qui durèrent le plus longtemps de toute l'histoire du vin. Quand Pline y goûta, il était si épais et sec qu'il fallait gratter le fond de l'amphore pour l'en tirer et qu'on devait le mélanger à un vin plus jeune. Trimalchion offrit aussi à ses hôtes un *vino cotto* (vin cuit) « bouilli jusqu'à évaporation d'un tiers et conservé sous terre pour que survive sa vigueur ». Avant le repas on avait servi un *antepasti :* apéritif d'une douceur de miel ; ainsi que des olives, des saucisses chaudes, bref, des amuse-gueule qui figureraient à un cocktail d'aujourd'hui.

Quelques sources littéraires au sujet des vins de l'Antiquité

En grec

Homère. L'Iliade et l'Odyssée dont nous avons déjà cité plusieurs passages nous indiquent que les héros d'épopée buvaient couramment du vin et leurs femmes faisaient de même. Nous savons qu'ils l'aimaient doux et dilué avec de l'eau, nous savons aussi comment ils le servaient et offraient des libations au cours des festins princiers, entre le XIe et le VIIIe siècle avant notre ère.

Hésiode. Dans *Les Travaux et les Jours,* Hésiode nous donne le plus ancien compte rendu, simple mais trop succinct, de la viticulture européenne en son temps. Écrivant aux environs de l'an 700 av. J.-C., ce poète et paysan de Boétie réglait son calendrier sur les étoiles ; il plantait et taillait ses vignes à peu près de la même manière qu'un petit vigneron d'aujourd'hui. Son œuvre montre clairement qu'il devait travailler dur sur sa terre. Il se plaignait des princes du voisinage qui l'opprimaient.

Alkaeus, poète lyrique, qui vécut à Mytilène une centaine d'années après Hésiode, faisait partie de l'aristocratie de Lesbos. Les tyrans se succédaient sur l'île en ce temps-là. Il chanta l'amour, le vin et la patrie. Son « Buvons et dansons puisque Myrsilus est mort ! » servit de modèle à Horace pour son ode sur la mort de Cléopâtre qui commence par : « Nunc est bibendum ». Alkaeus fut banni pour raisons politiques et il se pourrait que Sappho ait été exilée au même moment.

Anacréon. Une génération plus tard, ou à peu près, Anacréon de Téos alla à Athènes. Poète lyrique lui aussi et bon compère, il chantait le vin et les guirlandes. Il dit du jeu de *Kottabos :* « Coups de talon s'envolant d'une coupe de Téos ».

Platon, Xénophon, Aristophane. Tous trois décrivent la manière de boire en leur temps, celui de l'Athènes classique : Aristophane, par des allusions dans ses comédies ; Platon et Xénophon qui écrivirent l'un et l'autre un *Banquet* dans lequel on se fait une idée de la manière dont les Grecs se comportaient à table.

Dioscoride. Depuis le 1er siècle de notre ère jusqu'au XVIIe son *Traité sur la matière médicale* fit autorité au sujet de toutes les substances utilisées en médecine ainsi que sur les vins naturels, médicinaux et aromatisés, tant grecs que romains.

Galien. Ce grand médecin de la cour de Marc Aurèle, né en Asie Mineure, était aussi un connaisseur en vins. En cherchant le meilleur Falerne dans les caves palatines à l'intention de son maître, il dédaignait tous ceux qui n'avaient pas encore atteint

20 ans d'âge. En rappelant la masse étonnante de ses écrits philosophiques et médicaux, Athénée signale son *Traité sur les vins.* Mais cet ouvrage a disparu.

Athénée. Cet écrivain, auteur d'un *Banquet des sophistes* (convives érudits, certes, mais pédants), nous laisse une source sans pareille de cancanages et d'informations exactes ou non. Au cours de longs propos et discussions sur le poisson, sur des devinettes, la manière de faire du vin et des soufflés au fromage, et d'utiliser correctement les mots, il insère des citations d'à peu près tous les auteurs de son temps (vers 230) et d'avant. Ce qu'il dit des différents genres de vin n'est pas sans intérêt, mais les fragments d'œuvres littéraires perdues qu'il a conservés à notre usage sont encore plus précieux. Il naquit à Naucratis, en Égypte. Son œuvre nous prouve qu'il fut grand lecteur et amassa des connaissances encyclopédiques. Dans son *Banquet des sophistes* il décrit un dîner chez Laurentinus, noble romain. Galien est l'un des hôtes.

En latin

Caton. Le premier rapport en latin sur la manière dont les Romains faisaient le vin nous apparaît dans *De agri cultura* de Caton le Censeur, un homme d'état entêté, né à la campagne en 234 av. J.-C. Deux cents ans plus tard, Pline cita quelques-uns de ses préceptes en les approuvant.

Marcus Varro (Varron). Cet « érudit historien » qui vécut au temps de César et d'Auguste écrivit un manuel d'agriculture intitulé *Rerum Rusticarum* toujours considéré comme le meilleur en son genre et auquel il ne s'attela qu'en sa 80e année. Il donne des instructions claires sur la manière de soigner la vigne et de faire du vin et cite les maximes des écrivains grecs qui le précédèrent ainsi que de Magon de Carthage.

Virgile. En raison de sa célébrité comme poète, la *Seconde Géorgique* est un des ouvrages les mieux connus sur la vigne (sinon le mieux connu). Pourtant Virgile manquait d'expérience agricole bien que son père fut cultivateur. On dit que Varron fut son maître. Pline remarque que Virgile, malgré tout son talent, ne parle que de 15 variétés de raisin.

Pline l'Ancien (23-79). Le livre XIV de sa *Naturalis Historia* est consacré à la vigne et à différents genres de vin dont il donne la recette. Dans cette œuvre il se réfère aux écrits les plus importants existant de son temps. Toujours curieux et dans le but d'augmenter ses connaissances scientifiques, il périt en s'approchant trop près du Vésuve en éruption.

Horace. Il connaissait le vin et cultivait la vigne. Dans ses *Odes* et ses *Satires,* il cite les célèbres crus de Chio, de Lesbos, le Caecubien et le Falerne. Selon lui, le vin de Lesbos était inoffensif et ne donnait pas mal à la tête. Il aimait le Calenien, provenant de vignes proches de celles de Falerne ; faute de pouvoir offrir de ce dernier, c'est du Calenien qu'il servait à Mécène.

Juvénal et *Martial.* Ces deux écrivains satiriques vécurent aux environs de l'an 100 de notre ère. Tous deux parlent du vin et des modes et coutumes de leur époque. Martial en particulier avait beaucoup à raconter : surtout des histoires fantaisistes au sujet des vins frelatés de Marseille.

Pétrone. On sait peu de chose à son sujet. Ce fut peut-être le Titus Petronius renommé pour sa paresse et sa dissipation, qui réussit quand même à devenir consul. Nous avons déjà parlé ci-avant du banquet de Trimalchion dans son *Satiricon.*

Columelle. On ne sait pas grand chose de lui non plus. Il semble qu'il soit né à Cadix, au début du 1er siècle de notre ère. Un de ses oncles — Columelle, lui aussi — cultivateur en Espagne, est parfois cité dans son œuvre. Il écrivit un livre d'arboriculture et un traité complet, remarquablement clair, sur l'agriculture et la viticulture romaines : *Res rustica* en douze livres. Dans les livres III et IV, il donne des indications détaillées sur la manière de préparer le sol et de planter la vigne ; dans le livre XII (Les responsabilités de la femme de l'intendant), il explique la manière de préparer la vendange, de faire du vin, de corriger les défauts éventuels du moût, etc.

Ausone. Cet érudit bordelais fut précepteur du futur empereur Gratien (fils de Valentinien), puis devint gouverneur d'une province de Gaule et enfin consul. En sa vieillesse il se retira dans sa villa parmi ses vignobles. Il posséda un vignoble à Pauillac, dans une petite propriété sur la Dordogne et, plus tard, un autre sur la Charente. Il n'est nullement certain qu'Ausone vécut sur l'emplacement actuel du château qui porte son nom. Au cours de ses voyages avec l'empereur, il visita la vallée de la Moselle qui l'enchanta parce qu'elle lui rappelait les vignobles du Bordelais. Dans ses œuvres pourtant, il parle plus de nourriture que de vin.

Quelques vins de l'Antiquité

La description que nous donnons des vins dont les noms ne sont pas oubliés dérive de ce qu'en disaient les écrivains énumérés ci-avant. Quelques-uns de ces auteurs se laissent emporter par leur lyrisme lorsqu'ils parlent de parfum de rose et de violette perceptibles dans le bouquet du vin... tout comme ceux d'aujourd'hui, d'ailleurs.

Grèce

Maronéen. Nous avons déjà indiqué que Ulysse enivra Polyphème avec ce vin. Selon Pline, ce serait le plus ancien de tous. Il aurait été fait avec des raisins de vignes cultivées près de la côte de Thrace. D'une couleur foncée, on le consommait généralement très dilué dans l'eau. Selon Pline, le Maronéen conservait de son temps toute sa vigueur.

Pramnien. C'est le vin le plus glorieux de l'Antiquité et la boisson favorite de Nestor. Selon Homère, Nestor aurait donné de ce breuvage « très fort et nourrissant » à Machaon, blessé, avec une collation d'oignon cru et de fromage de chèvre. C'est avec du Pramnien que Circé préparait sa potion magique. Ce vin était encore connu à Athènes au temps d'Aristophane... il ne l'aimait d'ailleurs pas. Selon Dioscoride, les raisins éjectaient leur jus d'eux-mêmes tant ils étaient lourds et produisaient ainsi un moût riche. Mais Athénée nous dit que le Pramnien n'était ni doux ni épais, mais sec, dur et extraordinairement fort.

Chian (de l'île de Chio). Selon plus d'un auteur, c'était le meilleur des vins grecs : « irréprochable et qui ne donne jamais mal à la tête ». Les deux meilleurs crus de l'île semblent avoir été le Phanéen et le vin d'Arisium. Horace se procura une barrique de Chian pour un festin et ordonna d'en couper la moitié avec deux parts d'eau pour une de vin, à l'usage des convives tempérants, et l'autre moitié à raison de deux parts de vin pour une d'eau pour ceux qui ne craignaient pas l'ivresse. Les habitants de l'île, grands dégustateurs, disaient que le fils de Dionysos lui-même leur avait appris à faire leur vin rouge foncé. C'était évidemment un breuvage doux et plutôt épais.

Lesbien. C'était aussi un vin doux « Comme il est doux le Pramnien de Lesbos », dit un des personnages cités par Athénée. Force nous est de conclure que Pramnien n'était pas une appellation d'origine, mais plutôt un type de vin. Quelques auteurs disent que le Lesbien était le meilleur de tous mais, selon Athénée, il aurait été moins astringent, plus diurétique et moins agréable que le Chian. On n'y mêlait pas d'eau de mer, dit-il.

Thasien. Ce « noble cru, riche et rosé » aurait pris du moelleux avec l'âge. Théophraste nous dit qu'il était « merveilleusement délicieux et savoureux ; ils brassent de la pâte avec du miel et la mettent dans les jarres, afin que le vin soit sucré par le miel et se parfume de lui-même ». Il fallait le filtrer pour le boire.

Cos. Le vin de cette île sur laquelle Hippocrate écrivit son fameux traité de médecine était blanc et fortement mélangé d'eau de mer. Caton donne une recette pour l'imiter avec du vin italien et du sel. D'après les auteurs anciens, le Cos donnait mal à la tête.

Byblos. A l'origine c'était le vin célèbre de Byblos, au nord de la Syrie. Probablement transplanta-t-on par la suite des vignes de Byblos en Thrace. Ce vin devait être doux et parfumé. Hésiode écrivit : « Quand l'été me lasse, quand les chèvres sont grasses et que le vin s'est épanoui, donnez-moi l'ombre d'un rocher et du vin de Byblos ».

Helbon ou *Chalybon.* Célèbre vin doux de Syrie, fait près de Damas et cité dans la Bible. C'était le préféré des rois de Perse.

Rome

Falerne. C'est le plus célèbre de tous les vins romains. Horace en chanta souvent les louanges. Pourtant Pline ne le classe que dans les seconds crus, tout en admettant qu'à son époque il était fort prisé. Il ajoute que seul le Falerne s'enflammait quand on l'allumait et qu'il y en avait de trois genres : léger et sec, jaune, doux et foncé. L'Opimien de Trimalchion était du Falerne. Selon Galien, ce vin n'était pas bon à boire avant sa 10e année. (Sans doute ne parlait-il pas de l'Opimien). Et il le disait encore meilleur à 15 et 20 ans, quoique fort capable de donner mal à la tête. En décrivant le Falerne fait avec les raisins de vignes cultivées sur les sols volcaniques de Campanie, près de Naples (où l'on produisait aussi du Massique). Redding nous dit qu'il était rêche, foncé et fort jusqu'à un âge avancé où il devenait moelleux, et il supposait que le Falerne de jadis ressemblait au Lacrima Christi d'aujourd'hui.

Setin. Pline classe ce vin dans les premiers crus, sans doute par diplomatie car c'était le préféré d'Auguste. Athénée aussi nous le dit de première qualité « comme le Falerne », mais plus léger et moins enivrant. On le faisait à Setia sur la voie Appienne.

Caecubien. Encore un premier cru, selon Pline. Athénée nous le dit racé, généreux et capiteux, mais n'atteignant son apogée qu'au bout de nombreuses années. Horace le connaissait. Le vignoble disparut quand Néron fit creuser un canal.

Albin. Divers auteurs citent le vin d'Albe qui semble avoir été de deux qualités : doux ou sec. Pline le range en troisième catégorie. On le disait bon pour l'estomac.

Sorrentin. Les opinions diffèrent au sujet de ce vin. Galien estimait qu'il n'était bon qu'à 25 ans. Les médecins le recommandaient pour la santé, mais Tibère y voyait un « vinaigre généreux ». Selon Pline il était fait avec des raisins aminéens de vignes taillées court et soutenues par des tuteurs.

Mamertin. Vin produit près de Messine en Sicile. Galien le trouvait léger, bien équilibré et agréable. César le mit à la mode quand, pour fêter son troisième consulat, en 46 av. J.-C., il fit distribuer quatre vins au lieu de deux : du Falerne, du Chian, du Lesbien et du Mamertin. On fait encore dans la même région un vin pale, de forte teneur alcoolique et qui porte pratiquement le même nom.

Apéritif

Terme très vague désignant pratiquement tous les alcools pris avant le déjeuner pour chatouiller le palais et ouvrir l'appétit. Différents vins fortifiés au goût prononcé — généralement vendus sous une étiquette exclusive telle que Byrrh, Lillet et Dubonnet — sont très répandus, ainsi que des alcools plus forts et les bitters, que l'on sert généralement avec de l'eau plate ou gazeuse : ce sont les Campari, Amer Picon et Pastis. Mais le meilleur apéritif est probablement le Champagne sec ou le Xérès.

Apoplexie

Maladie spectaculaire de la vigne.

Voir CHAPITRE IV

Appellation d'origine contrôlée (ou A.O.C.)

Lieu d'origine d'un vin français. L'appellation d'origine contrôlée n'indique pas seulement le lieu d'où provient le vin, mais aussi une certaine qualité dérivant des méthodes de culture et de vinification en honneur en ce lieu d'origine. La loi sur les appellations d'origine contrôlée est la plus souple, la plus claire et la plus efficace qui existe actuellement pour la protection des vins de qualité.

COMMENT S'APPLIQUE CETTE LOI

Les vins fins portent toujours l'indication du lieu où furent cultivés les raisins avec lesquels ils ont été faits. Étant donné les règles imposées à la production de ces vins de qualité, plus la superficie du lieu d'origine est restreinte, meilleur sera le vin. En partant de ce fait, les Français ont mis au point leur législation en établissant dans chaque région vinicole une série de cercles concentriques de plus en plus petits. Les plus exigus de ces cercles limitent les sols d'élite ; les procédés de vinification, les normes minimales y sont de plus en plus sévères au fur et à mesure que le cercle se rétrécit. Il en résulte que, plus l'appellation est précise, plus elle garantit un vin de haute qualité.

Voici un exemple typique : la vaste région vinicole de Bordeaux, dans le Sud-Ouest de la France. Imaginez un grand cercle dont Bordeaux serait le centre. Quiconque possède ou loue une terre à l'intérieur de ce cercle (excepté les terrains impropres à la viticulture) a le droit de cultiver des cépages pour faire du vin de Bordeaux. Tout près de la ville, à l'intérieur du grand cercle, en direction du nord-ouest se trouve la subdivision régionale du Haut-Médoc ; à l'est, celles de Saint-Émilion et de Pomerol. Chacune de ces subdivisions représente un plus petit cercle dans le grand cercle du

Bordelais. Tous les vins qui y sont faits ont droit à l'appellation de Bordeaux, mais ils en adopteront une autre, plus restrictive, s'ils correspondent à des normes minimales plus élevées : celles de leur subdivision. Dans chacun de ces plus petits cercles le terrain, en effet, est plus propice à la vigne, les normes plus sévères et les vins meilleurs.

La contraction des cercles ne s'arrête pas là. Dans le Haut-Médoc, par exemple, des cercles plus étroits délimitent des territoires communaux dont les meilleurs sont Margaux, Saint-Julien, Pauillac et Saint-Estèphe. Les vins de ces communes ont droit à l'appellation Haut-Médoc, mais les vignerons choisissent toujours une appellation plus restrictive si leur vin correspond aux normes de qualité plus sévères de leur subdivision.

Le rétrécissement des cercles continue presque à l'infini. Poussé jusqu'à l'extrême, il arrive à des conséquences étonnantes mais parfaitement logiques. En Bourgogne, notamment, un superbe vignoble a droit à une appellation contrôlée propre alors que sa superficie ne dépasse guère 3 ha. Mais pour être vendu sous l'appellation La Romanée, le vin de cette vigne doit être conforme à des normes extrêmement sévères... et c'est un nectar merveilleux.

Vignerons, négociants et consommateurs ont confiance en ce système. Plus l'appellation d'un vin est précise, plus son prix est élevé. Ainsi un Haut-Médoc coûte plus cher qu'un Bordeaux et un Saint-Estèphe plus cher qu'un Haut-Médoc et ainsi de suite. On peut accorder aux législateurs français le mérite d'avoir mis au point une législation telle que, grâce à elle, les prix sont presque toujours justifiés.

Ce que la loi contrôle

La législation sur les appellations d'origine contrôle tous les facteurs qui concourent à la qualité du vin, à tous les stades et dans tous les détails, à partir de la plantation de la vigne jusqu'à la bouteille dans laquelle le vin est livré au commerce ou expédié hors de France. Ce système paraît, à première vue, accablant et presque impraticable. Or il fonctionne fort bien, grâce aux relations faciles et harmonieuses entre les experts techniques et administratifs de l'Institut national des appellations d'origine, à Paris, et ceux qui opèrent dans chaque région vinicole. Cet Institut, couramment appelé l'I.N.A.O., donne des directives générales au sujet des contrôles. Les fonctionnaires appliquent ses directives en les adaptant à leur région ; le ministère de l'Agriculture élabore lois et règlements sur proposition de l'I.N.A.O., et les inspecteurs des fraudes veillent à leur application. Il existe des lois et règlements généraux s'appliquant à toute viticulture et viniculture françaises et d'autres portant sur une région d'ensemble ou une quelconque subdivision. L'ensemble de la législation implique toujours les précisions suivantes :

1. *Zone de production*. La composition géologique du sol jugée propice à la production du vin qui aura droit à l'appellation de la région est définie par la loi. Les experts procèdent alors à des études sur place et désignent les terrains correspondants à ces qualités. Seules les vignes plantées sur ces terrains-là, dans la zone délimitée, ont droit à l'appellation.

2. *Cépages autorisés*. Sur des sols différents et sous des cieux différents, la vigne de même variété produira des raisins de caractéristiques diverses. La loi précise donc les variétés de vigne qui, dans chaque circonscription vinicole, donneront droit à l'appellation d'origine. La sélection de ces variétés suit les meilleures pratiques traditionnelles locales.

3. *Teneur minimale en alcool*. L'alcool permet au vin de se conserver, par conséquent de vieillir jusqu'au point où il atteint son maximum de perfection. Si l'on permettait aux vignes de produire trop, les raisins ne contiendraient pas assez de sucre. Le vin perdrait son équilibre car sa teneur en alcool ne s'harmoniserait pas avec ses autres caractéristiques. La loi précise donc la teneur minimale en alcool du vin, en dehors de toute addition de sucre et donne ainsi une assurance de qualité.

4. *Les pratiques viticoles*. Amendement du sol, taille de la vigne et tous les soins qui lui sont donnés en général influent sur la qualité du vin. Toutes les pratiques viticoles sont donc étroitement réglementées. Pour chaque appellation d'origine, la loi précise le genre de taille. Elle tend toujours à éliminer les méthodes qui favorisent la quantité au détriment de la qualité.

5. *Limitation de la quantité*. Étant donné que la qualité est inversement proportionnelle à la quantité, la loi limite la production autorisée pour chaque vin d'appellation d'origine. Cette norme s'exprime en

hectolitres par hectare (hl/ha). Le rendement autorisé est d'autant plus faible que l'appellation est réservée à un secteur moins étendu.

6. *Les pratiques vinicoles.* Les pratiques traditionnelles de vinification propres à chaque région contribuent largement à la réputation des grands vins et leur confèrent une bonne part de leurs caractéristiques distinctives. Ces pratiques sont donc codifiées par la loi. Les contrôles de dégustation sont devenus de plus en plus fréquents.

7. *Distillation.* L'I.N.A.O. exerce aussi son contrôle sur les eaux-de-vie produites en France. Les procédés traditionnels de distillation qui firent la réputation de ces remarquables alcools sont aussi réglementés par la loi.

L'ÉVOLUTION DES LOIS

Au seuil du XXe siècle, l'avenir des vins de France était sinistre et ne promettait rien de bon. Plusieurs épidémies (ou, plus exactement, épiphyties) successives de la vigne, particulièrement celle du phylloxéra, sévissaient depuis plus de cinquante ans. Elles avaient réduit de vastes vignobles à des espèces de cimetières sur lesquels ne subsistaient plus, comme des stèles, que les piquets des vignes mortes. Les vignerons replantèrent dans la région méridionale des cépages productifs en terrains de plaine jadis réservés à la culture des céréales. En même temps, on en arrivait trop souvent, en dépit de la loi, à ajouter du sucre ou de l'eau aux résidus du pressurage, à laisser fermenter ce mélange et à le vendre ensuite sous le nom de vin. Les législateurs français intervinrent dans ce chaos en votant la loi du 1er août 1905 organisant la répression des fraudes. Elle sauva les vins ordinaires d'une grande crise. En outre, elle établissait le canevas d'après lequel on put organiser le contrôle des lieux d'origine pour tous les produits agricoles. Quoique encore insuffisante, elle fut imitée en bien des pays, mais jusqu'ici nulle part égalée. En ce qui concerne les vins fins, la loi fut complétée en 1908 afin de prévoir des délimitations par décrets du gouvernement. C'est ce que l'on appela la phase administrative de la législation sur les appellations d'origine. La législation n'avait pas tenu compte que les vins fins ne sont pas seulement le produit d'un lieu géographique, mais aussi d'un sol délimité, d'un raisin déterminé et de certains procédés de culture et de vinification. En contrôlant seulement le lieu géographique d'origine, sans imposer le respect de certaines pratiques traditionnelles de culture, et sans dégustations ou analyses, ces lois ouvraient la voie à deux abus : 1) les vins portant des grands noms pouvaient être faits sans les soins auxquels ils doivent leurs qualités inégalables ; 2) certains viticulteurs pouvaient profiter de la seule situation géographique de leurs vignes quel qu'en fût le cépage ; et en appliquant la loi à la lettre, rien ne les empêchait de vendre des vins médiocres sous une étiquette prestigieuse.

En réalité, la loi de 1908 ne faisait que codifier pour les vins la loi de 1905 portant sur l'ensemble des produits agricoles. C'est ainsi que furent fixées les zones géographiques de Bordeaux, de Banyuls, de la Clairette de Die, de Cognac et d'Armagnac. Mais le gouvernement fut incapable de prendre une décision satisfaisante pour la Champagne.

La région de Champagne s'étend sur plusieurs départements ; autrefois, les viticulteurs de la Marne contestaient à ceux de l'Aube le droit de conférer le nom de Champagne à leurs produits. La délimitation adoptée par le gouvernement était un compromis destiné à satisfaire les deux parties. Comme bien des décisions de ce genre, elle déplut aux deux camps. La contestation resta modérée jusqu'en 1910. Cette année-là, de terribles gelées donnèrent une des vendanges les plus désastreuses de l'histoire de la Champagne et les vignerons s'indignèrent. Selon eux, si la région avait été plus étroitement délimitée et si les négociants en avaient respecté les limites, les raisins se seraient vendus plus cher et les vignerons auraient pu économiser de quoi étaler une année défavorable. Remarquons qu'à cette époque la Champagne pouvait préparer des vins mousseux sans appellation, portant mention de l'adresse champenoise ; les raisins étaient souvent récoltés au-delà des limites de la Champagne. L'affaire alla si loin que des émeutes éclatèrent en janvier 1911 et l'armée fut envoyée pour rétablir l'ordre. En juin, on rectifia les limites de la région, ce qui provoqua de nouvelles émeutes. Plus tard au cours de la même année le parlement décida que la loi était inapplicable et la mit sous le boisseau sans rien offrir pour la remplacer.

Cette même année, la Chambre fut appelée à se prononcer sur une modification raisonnable de la loi antérieure. Les adversaires de cette législation avançaient l'argument suivant : « Pouvez-vous contester le droit d'un cultivateur à faire l'usage qui lui plaît du nom de sa propriété et des fruits de son sol ? » La réforme ne fut pas adoptée. Le député Jenouvrier fit une nouvelle tentative en 1914 et souligna le caractère collectif de cette législation. « La réputation dont jouissent ces produits résulte des efforts soutenus de maintes générations successives ; le fruit de leur labeur est devenu célèbre et le droit de propriété s'étend désormais sur l'ensemble de la commune et de la région. »

Après la Première Guerre mondiale, en 1919 une nouvelle loi fut votée. Jenouvrier y fit inclure son projet de réforme. Mais aucune clause ne restreignait les variétés de raisin, ne prévoyait une délimitation des sols ni des méthodes de culture et les autres éléments qui garantissent la qualité. La nouvelle loi eut des résultats aussi désastreux que la précédente, et même pires.

Appelée à se prononcer sur l'application de la loi, la Cour de Cassation interpréta la loi du point du vue strictement géographique en considérant que c'était là l'intention du législateur. C'était précipiter ainsi un mouvement désastreux : la plantation de vignes à gros rendement et à faible qualité dans les secteurs ayant droit à appellation d'origine. En rappelant le long combat qu'il mena pour en arriver à la loi telle que nous la connaissons maintenant, le député Capus indiqua les effets que celle de 1919 eut sur son pays d'origine : Barsac, dans le Bordelais. Les célèbres vins de Barsac — doux et riches — proviennent traditionnellement de raisins de Sauvignon et de Sémillon, cultivés sur les hauteurs de la commune. Dans les vallons et le *palus* — les terres basses et humides qui bordent la Garonne — on n'avait fait que du vin rouge ordinaire qui ne portait pas le nom de Barsac. Or, au cours des procès déclenchés par la loi de 1919, les tribunaux autorisèrent les producteurs qui cultivaient de la vigne dans les palus de Barsac à conférer l'appellation de Barsac à leurs vins médiocres quoique le sol ne pût leur donner les qualités de ce cru célèbre. Quelques vignerons regimbèrent parce que la loi de 1919 ne précisait rien au sujet des vignes, mais la plupart acceptèrent cette loi et firent ce qui était légal mais désastreux. Comme le dit Capus : « Les mauvaises lois font les mauvais citoyens ». On arracha les vignes de palus pour leur substituer des plants de raisin blanc ou bien on y greffa des hybrides à gros rendement et on fit du Barsac avec le raisin des palus. Il y eut pire ; les nobles vignes à faible rendement cultivées sur les coteaux ne pouvaient pas résister à la concurrence des nouvelles. Là aussi on arracha les plants de qualité pour leur substituer des hybrides à fort rendement. Des raz de marée vineux allant du médiocre à l'épouvantable déferlèrent sur le marché, dans des bouteilles portant le célèbre nom de Barsac. Les prix, évidemment, tombèrent. La réputation de Barsac aussi. Étant donné que le même phénomène pouvait se produire ailleurs, la réputation des vins français en souffrit dans le monde entier.

Cet état de choses nuisait aux viticulteurs autant qu'aux consommateurs. L'honnête vigneron qui dépensait argent et peine pour produire une petite quantité de grand vin était surclassé par ses concurrents sans scrupule qui produisaient beaucoup plus de vin sans aucune qualité mais vendu sous la même appellation d'origine. Bientôt des négociants étrangers se plaignirent parce que leurs clients ne voulaient plus payer les prix exigés pour une marchandise médiocre. Lorsque des gens avisés réclamèrent de nouveau, à cor et à cri, une législation plus stricte, il apparut que l'opinion publique avait tourné. Chéron, ministre de l'Agriculture, fut choqué, lors d'un voyage en Gironde, de voir arracher les vignes des grands crus pour planter des hybrides à plus fort rendement. On nomma une commission d'enquête.

Pendant toutes ces années, l'agitation régnait en Champagne. Les deux parties concurrentes — Marne et Aube — en appelèrent à l'arbitrage d'Édouard Barthe, président du groupe viticole de la Chambre. Ce dernier dressa un plan qui réglait de manière satisfaisante aussi bien les limites de la région que les conditions nécessaires pour produire du bon Champagne. Approuvé par toutes les associations de viticulteurs intéressés, ce plan fut incorporé sans modifications dans la nouvelle loi votée en 1927 qui amendait celle de 1919 sur les points suivants : elle limitait le lieu d'origine aux « surfaces comprenant des communes ou des fractions de communes aptes à produire le vin portant l'appellation » ; elle interdisait l'appellation aux vins provenant d'hybrides et de vignes autres que celles qui, selon la tradition, donnaient de grands vins. La loi de 1927 porta le nom de « Loi de l'appellation simple ». Quoique encore imparfaite, elle eut des conséquences heureuses. Dans le Barsac notamment, le palus retomba à son statut inférieur et on vit ressusciter les vignes nobles dans les régions qui observaient la loi. Mais cette réglementation était facultative. On l'observa dans certaines régions. Dans celle de Châteauneuf-du-Pape, le baron Le Roy, propriétaire lui-même, persuada les autres vignerons d'adopter librement une réglementation conforme à la qualité. Il la fit consacrer par voie judiciaire. D'autres appellations suivirent cet exemple, et une centaine furent ainsi délimitées.

La loi de 1927 ne se souciait encore que du lieu d'origine et des cépages. Elle dédaignait les autres facteurs qui concourent à la qualité du vin, notamment : limite quantitative de la récolte, teneur minimale en alcool, normes des soins à apporter à la vigne, notamment la taille, et à la vinification. Malgré ces imperfections, la loi de 1927 introduisait une nouveauté importante : le législateur français admettait que le nom du vin ne dépende pas uniquement de la situation géographique, mais aussi de la qualité de certains sols et de certains cépages. En vertu de cette nouveauté, elle ouvrait la voie à des mesures de contrôle plus strictes. En 1935, de nouvelles restrictions entrèrent en vigueur et les vins de France furent enfin régis par une commission qui est devenue depuis l'Institut national des appellations d'origine des vins et des eaux-de-vie (I.N.A.O.) dont les experts protègent la réputation des vins français, tant sur le marché national qu'à l'exportation.

Les effets des lois

Dès qu'une commune, une fraction de commune ou un groupe de communes acquièrent le droit à l'appellation contrôlée, la qualité de leurs produits s'élève. Conscient du fait que ses efforts seront désormais récompensés, le vigneron peine pour obtenir un produit de haute qualité. La seule existence de l'appellation contrôlée suffit par elle-même à prouver que le vin est bon. Il en résulte un double bénéfice : le vigneron vend son vin plus cher et le consommateur en a pour son argent. Il est regrettable que les autres pays vinicoles n'aient pas suivi plus tôt et plus étroitement l'exemple de la France. Mais rappelons-nous que le contrôle continue à porter principalement sur le lieu d'origine plus que sur le vin. En voici un exemple : l'appellation contrôlée Pommard signifie que la région du Pommard a été délimitée et que ses vins doivent présenter des normes minimales de qualité. Quant à contrôler le contenu des bouteilles, c'est beaucoup plus difficile, étant donné les effectifs limités dont disposent les services d'inspection. Il y a donc des failles dans cette loi et elle ne garantit pas toujours, dans tous les cas, l'authenticité des étiquettes.

Appellation simple

Avant l'institution des appellations contrôlées en 1935, les appellations d'origine étaient dites « simples ». Nous venons de voir qu'elles passèrent par une phase administrative puis par une phase judiciaire. Ces lois de 1905, 1908, 1919 et 1927 étaient insuffisantes. Elles furent abrogées.

Voir APPELLATION D'ORIGINE CONTRÔLÉE

Apple brandy

Nom anglais de l'eau-de-vie de pomme obtenue par distillation du cidre. La meilleure eau-de-vie de cidre française est le Calvados ; la variété américaine s'appelle applejack.

Voir CALVADOS et APPLEJACK

Applejack

Dans son acception la plus étroite, *applejack* ne désigne que l'eau-de-vie de pomme faite en Amérique. Mais les Américains eux-mêmes lui donnent un sens plus étendu car il s'applique aussi bien à la véritable eau-de-vie de pomme obtenue par la distillation du cidre qu'à un spiritueux plus grossier fait par des procédés primitifs. Ce second procédé, limité de nos jours aux régions écartées des grandes voies de communications, consiste à laisser le cidre fermenter au maximum, puis à le congeler.

Étant donné que l'eau gèle à une température plus élevée que l'alcool, la glace qui apparaît la première dans le mélange est de l'eau à l'état solide. Il suffit d'*écumer* la cuve pour en extraire l'eau. Le liquide qui reste est presque de l'alcool pur. Il s'agit au fond d'une distillation par le froid, procédé inverse de la distillation par la chaleur. L'applejack obtenu par ce procédé est un spiritueux très fort et légèrement huileux.

Autrefois les deux méthodes étaient utilisées à peu près partout aux États-Unis et l'applejack fut longtemps un des alcools les plus populaires du pays. Sans doute était-ce dû au fait qu'en ce temps-là la boisson la plus courante était un cidre d'une teneur en alcool assez faible : environ 6°. S'il faut en croire les écrits de l'époque, les premiers Américains aimaient boire sec et abondamment, d'où la popularité de l'applejack.

En réalité, les tout premiers colons des États-Unis ne buvaient ni cidre ni eau-de-vie de pomme pour la bonne raison qu'il n'y avait pas de pommiers en Amérique. Anglais et Danois importaient leur bière, puis les Britanniques plantèrent et semèrent houblon et orge en Nouvelle-Angleterre où ces deux plantes ne s'acclimatèrent pas. On planta alors des arbres fruitiers qui, au contraire, prospérèrent énormément et auraient même, dit-on, donné des fruits beaucoup plus tôt qu'ils ne le faisaient en Angleterre. Quand il y eut des pommiers, on fit du cidre, boisson consommée couramment en Angleterre depuis le XVIe siècle — et même plus tôt, sans doute. On écrivait alors ce mot « sider », qui dérive probablement du mot hébreu « shekar ». A l'origine, ce terme s'appliquait peut-être à n'importe quelle boisson forte et ce serait seulement à partir du XVIe siècle qu'il désigna particulièrement un breuvage fort fait avec du jus de pomme.

Étant donné que la Nouvelle-Angleterre n'était pas propice à la culture du houblon, ses habitants oublièrent la bière et se mirent à aimer le cidre, le rhum importé des Antilles, et fait plus tard sur place avec de la mélasse de même origine, et l'applejack. Bientôt Blancs et Peaux-Rouges qui s'éloignaient vers l'Ouest y implantèrent la culture du pommier, ainsi que l'art de fabriquer cidre et eau-de-vie de cidre. Plus tard, Hollandais et Allemands qui s'installèrent en Pennsylvanie brassèrent la bière avec grand succès ; d'autre part, Écossais et Irlandais qui arrivèrent en Amérique au début du XVIIIe siècle y lancèrent l'industrie du whisky. Cependant cidre et applejack restèrent les breuvages les plus consommés dans les zones rurales.

Les facteurs économiques qui encouragèrent les producteurs de céréales de Pennsylvanie à fabriquer du whisky en quantité, eurent les mêmes résultats sur les producteurs de pommes de la Nouvelle-Angleterre. En ce temps-là, les routes étaient mauvaises et il était risqué de transporter des cargaisons importantes ; on préférait donc fermenter ou distiller les fruits et céréales. De plus, les chargements d'alcool, plus légers et donc plus transportables, ouvraient des marchés plus intéressants. La Nouvelle-Angleterre — en particulier le Connecticut — était le premier producteur de cidre. Les ingénieux Yankees du Connecticut prouvèrent leur capacité d'adaptation au monde des alcools. En colorant le cidre avec du maïs indien, et en le laissant vieillir trois mois, ils obtenaient un alcool assez fort, de la couleur du Madère. C'est d'ailleurs sous ce nom qu'ils le vendaient aux naïfs Européens. On ne sait combien dura cette pratique, mais probablement pas très longtemps car le cidre était bien trop apprécié aux États-Unis pour être gaspillé à l'étranger.

Au temps de la Révolution, l'Américain était profondément convaincu que plus l'alcool était fort, plus il était bénéfique. Ainsi, il se mit allégrement à prendre grand soin de sa santé, commençant souvent sa journée avec du cidre ou de l'applejack au petit déjeuner. Il emportait même sa carafe aux champs. Toutes les manifestations de la vie sociale — mariages, enterrements, collations religieuses ou réunions politiques — étaient copieusement arrosées de rhum, de cidre (ou applejack) ou d'une sorte de punch très fort, ou bien des trois boissons à la fois. Lors d'un office religieux dans une église de la Nouvelle-Angleterre, quatre-vingt dix fidèles engloutirent trente bolées de punch avant la réunion matinale ; le soir, ils firent une consommation encore plus étonnante d'un mélange de toutes les boissons imaginables. Les alambics étaient de plus en plus abordables et de nombreux fermiers en achetèrent, élevant ainsi l'applejack au niveau d'un alcool distillé. Pourtant, on faisait encore beaucoup d'applejack de type congelé primitif. Il n'y a aucun doute sur le caractère détonnant du produit, si l'on en croit les habitués des tavernes locales qui l'appelaient « coup de hameçon au bleu », « essence décroche-gueule » ou, après que le centre de ce commerce se soit transféré dans le New-Jersey, « foudre du Jersey ».

Pour faire un bon applejack, il ne faut utiliser que le cidre sain, de bonne qualité, produit par des pommes bien mûres et c'est ce cidre que l'on distille. Autrefois on ne se servait à cet effet que de l'alambic et on en trouve encore quelques-uns de nos jours. Actuellement on procède par deux distillations successives. Le premier liquide recueilli titre environ 30° ; après seconde distillation, il titre entre 55 et 65°. On le coupe ensuite à l'eau ou à l'eau-de-vie de grain neutre pour ramener sa teneur à 42 ou 50°, selon les désirs du distillateur. Étant donné que la pomme est plus chère que le grain, un applejack pur coûterait trop cher. Au temps des hommes robustes qui firent la conquête du continent, on buvait l'applejack tout chaud tiré au robinet de l'alambic. Aujourd'hui l'applejack mûrit d'un à cinq ans dans des tonneaux de chêne conservés dans des entrepôts soumis à contrôle officiel.

Autrefois, on obtenait un alcool plus grossier et bien inférieur par une méthode pour le moins hasardeuse : on distillait le marc sans le presser auparavant. De même, on trempait quelquefois dans l'eau le marc duquel le jus avait été exprimé, puis on fermentait l'eau, ce qui donnait un alcool faible connu sous le nom de ciderkin. Aux temps coloniaux, on le faisait boire aux enfants.

Aux États-Unis, on nomme l'applejack : cider brandy, cider spirits, cider whisky et, parfois, tout simplement apple. Quoique ces noms soient strictement américains, on fait de l'eau-de-vie de pomme presque partout dans le monde et le plus célèbre de ces alcools est le Calvados de Normandie en France.

Voir CALVADOS

Apricot brandy

Alcool sec, non additionné de sucre, obtenu en distillant le jus d'abricot. Le produit original le plus célèbre était le Barack Pálinka, fait en Hongrie.

Voir HONGRIE et EAU-DE-VIE

Apricot liqueur

Nom d'un breuvage qu'il ne faut pas confondre avec l'eau-de-vie d'abricot. Il consiste en un mélange d'eau-de-vie de vin sucrée et d'abricots.

Apry

Liqueur d'une teinte brun roux, faite avec des abricots macérés dans de l'eau-de-vie de vin sucrée. C'est une production de la firme Marie-Brizard et Roger, Bordeaux, France.

Apulie

Ancien nom de la Pouille : province située dans le talon de la botte italienne.

Voir POUILLE

Aqua vitae

Tel est le premier nom donné à l'alcool, surtout à l'alcool de vin. Il signifie en latin : eau-de-vie. Toutefois les Italiens affirment que le nom d'origine n'était pas *aqua vitae,* mais *aqua vite* ou *acqua di vite* — soit « eau de vigne » en italien — par allusion au liquide translucide distillé du vin. Toujours d'après les Italiens, le nom actuel serait dû au pouvoir stimulant et revigorant de l'alcool, ou bien simplement à une déformation de l'orthographe.

Voir aussi AQUAVIT

Aquavit, Akvavit, Akevit

Alcool consommé dans les pays scandinaves et consistant soit en distillat de céréales, soit en alcool rectifié de pommes de terre. Dans les deux cas, il est parfumé avec certaines graines aromatiques — notamment le cumin et des épices. Les Scandinaves le boivent frappé et, selon la tradition, il arrose leur *smörgasbord.* Ce nom est évidemment une contraction du latin *aqua vitae,* signifiant eau-de-vie et désignant en Italie, depuis le XIIIe siècle, le produit obtenu en distillant du vin. La Suède est considérée en général comme le principal producteur d'aquavit, souvent appelé *snaps* dans le pays. La première licence de vente d'aquavit à Stockholm fut accordée en 1498. Durant le siècle suivant, on fabriqua ce breuvage en distillant du vin. Mais comme la vigne à vin ne pousse pas en Suède, il fallait importer le vin. L'aquavit était alors si cher qu'il servait surtout à des fins médicinales. Quand les soldats suédois apprirent à l'étranger comment on distille le grain, l'alcool devint moins cher dans leur pays. Si la récolte de céréales était mauvaise, les autorités interdisaient la distillation. On chercha des succédanés. Les expériences se portèrent d'abord sur des racines et des baies, puis, au XVIIIe siècle, on constata que la pomme de terre convenait parfaitement et, depuis lors, elle reste la principale source d'aquavit.

La plupart des distilleries suédoises de pomme de terre sont situées dans la province méridionale de Skane. Les pommes de terre épluchées sont d'abord bouillies à la vapeur sous pression. La masse d'amidon qui en résulte est mélangée à du malt écrasé (malt d'orge ou d'un mélange de plusieurs grains) pour convertir l'amidon en sucre. On ajoute alors à cette pâte des levures cultivées. La fermentation qui s'ensuit transforme le sucre en alcool. On élimine le goût de pomme de terre par rectification et il suffit dès lors d'y ajouter épices ou graines qui lui donnent son arôme.

On n'obtiendrait pas un aquavit de bonne qualité uniquement en diluant de l'alcool dans l'eau car il n'aurait aucun goût. On met donc l'alcool dilué en contact avec du charbon de bois de bouleau activé par l'effet de la vapeur à haute température. Ce procédé accroît la teneur de l'alcool en aldéhyde et détermine la formation d'une petite quantité d'esters qui donnent de la saveur. Quant aux épices choisies pour améliorer le goût de l'aquavit, ce sont surtout les graines de cumin, d'anis, de fenouil et des oranges amères.

Croire que l'aquavit doit être exempt de tout sucrage est une erreur très répandue. En réalité, le mot aquavit désigne en général n'importe quel alcool sec, épicé ou sucré, ainsi que l'eau-de-vie de vin (brännvin) qui, en Suède, est généralement, mais pas toujours, épicée mais non sucrée.

Actuellement on compte une vingtaine de marques d'aquavit en Suède. Celle d'O.P. Anderson l'emporte sur les autres sur le marché de l'exportation ; elle est parfumée aux graines de cumin, d'anis et de fenouil. Une autre marque bien connue est l'Odakra Taffel Aquavit qui apparut sur le marché en 1899 ; elle est légèrement épicée et généralement sèche. Overste Brännvin a un arôme plus épicé que celle de la marque O.P. Anderson et contient un peu plus de sucre. La Skáne Aquavit ressemble beaucoup à celle d'Anderson, mais elle est moins épicée.

Le Danemark vient immédiatement après la Suède pour la production de l'aquavit. Considérée comme la boisson nationale danoise et appelée couramment *schnapps,* elle couvre environ 70 % de la consommation de spiritueux du pays. C'est généralement un breuvage incolore et non sucré.

Les distilleries danoises furent fondées en 1881 et, jusqu'en 1914, la bouteille d'aquavit se vendait couramment l'équivalent de 75 centimes de l'époque. De nos jours, cette firme ne possède plus qu'une seule distillerie qui depuis 1923 jouit au Danemark du monopole exclusif de la fabrication de l'alcool et des levures. Parfois les Danois utilisent la pomme de terre et le grain. Ce dernier sert toujours pour l'exportation.

Aalborg Taffel Akvavit, qui apparut sur le marché en 1846, reste la plus connue des marques au Danemark et à l'étranger. Épicée au cumin, elle titre 43°. D'autres marques méritent d'être citées : Brødûm Kumenaquavit, au cumin et à la cannelle ; Aalborg Export Akvavit, qui a un léger goût de madère ; Harald Jensen Taffel Akvavit ; Perikum-Snaps.

La Norvège produit moins de spiritueux que la Suède et le Danemark. Voici ses marques les plus connues : Lysholm Aquavit, légère, élégante, plutôt délicate et mûrie dans des fûts de Xérès récemment vidés : Løiten Aquavit, type plus robuste et corsé. Linie Aquavit, alcool assez intéressant dont le nom fait allusion à la « traversée de la ligne » (l'équateur). Ce détail rappelle la vieille tradition selon laquelle les liqueurs sont améliorées par les voyages maritimes. De nos jours encore l'alcool de cette marque fait l'aller et retour Norvège-Australie-Norvège sur les cargos Wilhelmsen.

Aramon

Variété de raisin au rendement énorme qui donne des vins ordinaires. On le cultive surtout dans le Midi de la France et en Californie.

Arbois (Appellation Contrôlée)

Blanc, rouge et rosé. Est de la France.

Subdivision vinicole la plus connue du Jura. On y fait des vins blancs et rouges et des rosés qui comptent parmi les bons vins de France. *Voir* JURA.

Arche (Château d')

Bordeaux blanc. Commune de Sauternes.

Situés sur une colline près du village de Sauternes, ces vignobles classés Second Cru dans la Classification de 1855 font un vin bien équilibré. La propriété, une des plus anciennes de la région, appartient à M. Bastit-St-Martin. M. Pierre Perromat, ancien président de l'I.N.A.O. et propriétaire dans l'Entre-Deux-Mers, a actuellement pris Château d'Arche en exploitation.

Superficie : 42 ha.

Production moyenne : 50 tonneaux.

Ardine

Eau-de-vie d'abricot faite par la firme bordelaise Bardinet.

Aréomètre

Instrument servant de densimètre, autrement dit à mesurer le poids spécifique d'un mélange. La graduation de cet instrument est arbitraire. Elle diffère selon qu'il s'agit d'un aréomètre Œchslé ou d'un aréomètre Baumé, modèle qui nous intéresse particulièrement.

Cet instrument de mesure, qu'on appelle aussi mustimètre, est en usage depuis Chaptal (*voir ce nom et* CHAPITRE V) pour mesurer la densité du moût. Il se trouve gradué de telle sorte qu'il donne approximativement la teneur en alcool du vin obtenu par fermentation à partir du moût dans lequel on le plonge. Le degré Baumé correspond assez exactement à la densité d'un litre d'eau contenant 17,18 g de sucre.

Le mustimètre Baumé indique zéro dans l'eau distillée et 15° dans un mélange composé de 15 parts de sel marin et 85 parts d'eau pure. (Proportions en poids, non en volume).

Voir TABLES D'ÉQUIVALENCE DES DEGRÉS BAUMÉ, p. 170

TABLE D'ÉQUIVALENCE DE LA DENSITÉ D'UN VIN ET DU POIDS DE SUCRE QU'IL CONTIENT

Poids spécifique d'un vin sans sucre	*Quantité de sucre à ajouter pour obtenir le poids spécifique de 1 000 (en grammes par litre)*	*Poids spécifique du même vin après addition de sucre (en grammes par litre)*					
		9 g	*18 g*	*27 g*	*36 g*	*45 g*	*54 g*
990	25	994	998	0,1°	0,6°	1,1°	1,6°
991	22	995	998	0,3°	0,8°	1,3°	1,8°
992	20	996	1 000	0,4°	0,9°	1,4°	1,9°
993	17	997	0,2°	0,6°	1,1°	1,6°	2,1°
994	15	998	0,2°	0,7°	1,2°	1,7°	2,2°
995	12	999	0,4°	0,9°	1,4°	1,9°	2,4°
996	10	1 000	0,5°	1°	1,5°	2°	2,5°
997	7	0,1°	0,6°	1,1°	1,6°	2,1°	2,6°
998	5	0,2°	0,8°	1,3°	1,8°	2,3°	2,8°
999	2	0,4°	0,9°	1,4°	1,9°	2,4°	2,9°

Aréomètre

Table d'équivalence des degrés Baumé, des degrés d'alcool et de la gravité spécifique (à la température de 15 °C).

Degrés Baumé	*Teneur en alcool coef. pot. 17*	*Gravité spécifique*
6	5	1 043
7	6,2	1 051
8	7,4	1 058
9	8,6	1 066
10	9,9	1 074
11	11,1	1 082
12	12,4	1 090
13	13,7	1 099
14	15	1 107
15	16,4	1 116
16	17,7	1 124
17	19,1	1 133
18	20,5	1 142
19	22	1 151
20	23,4	1 160
21	24,9	1 170
22	26,4	1 179
23	27,9	1 189
24	29,5	1 199
25	31	1 209
26	32,6	1 219
27	34,3	1 230
28	35,9	1 240
29	37,6	1 251
30	39,3	1 262
31	41,1	1 273
32	42,9	1 284
33	44,7	1 296
34	46,5	1 308
35	48,5	1 320
36	50,3	1 332
37	52,3	1 344
38	54,2	1 357
39	56,3	1 370
40	58,5	1 383

Table d'équivalence des degrés Baumé, des degrés Œchslé et de la gravité spécifique (à la température de 15 °C).

Degrés Baumé	*Degrés Œchslé*	*Gravité spécifique correspondante*
0	0	1 000
0,1	0,7	1 000,7
0,2	1,4	1 001,4
0,3	2,1	1 002,1
0,4	2,8	1 002,8
0,5	3,5	1 003,5
0,6	4,2	1 004,2
0,7	4,9	1 004,9
0,8	5,6	1 005,6
0,9	6,3	1 006,3
1	7	1 007
1,1	7,7	1 007,7
1,2	8,4	1 008,4
1,3	9,1	1 009,1
1,4	9,8	1 009,8
1,5	10,5	1 010,5
1,6	11,2	1 011,2
1,7	11,9	1 011,9
1,8	12,6	1 012,6
1,9	13,3	1 013,3
2	14	1 014
2,1	14,7	1 014,7
2,2	15,4	1 015,4
2,3	16,1	1 016,1
2,4	16,8	1 016,8
2,5	17,5	1 017,5
3	21,2	1 021,2
4	28,5	1 028,5
5	35,9	1 035,9
6	43,4	1 043,5
7	51	1 051
8	58,7	1 058,7
9	66,5	1 066,5
10	74,5	1 074,5
11	82,5	1 082,5
12	90,7	1 090,7
13	99	1 099
14	107,4	1 107,4
15	116	1 116
16	124,7	1 124,7
17	133,5	1 133,5
18	142,4	1 142,5

Argentine

Avec un encépagement couvrant une superficie de plus de 300 km² (300 000 ha), 60 000 vignobles et environ 2 000 *bodegas*, l'Argentine est le plus gros producteur de vin de l'hémisphère sud et le cinquième du monde entier, après l'Italie, la France, l'Espagne et l'U.R.S.S. Sa production moyenne annuelle de 20 millions d'hl la place juste avant les États-Unis. Une faible partie (5 %) seulement de cette énorme quantité passe sur le marché mondial. Les exportations atteignirent leur maximum à la fin de la dernière guerre ; elles s'élevèrent alors à environ 113 650 hl, dont la plus grosse partie fut importée par l'Angleterre.

La baisse des exportations argentines est due, en partie, à l'augmentation de la consommation nationale ; en effet, pour une population de 30 millions d'habitants, la consommation moyenne annuelle est de 66 litres de vin par personne, soit la quatrième place mondiale. De plus, les méthodes de vinification traditionnelles (bien que convenant au goût national) produisaient un vin peu attrayant pour les marchés étrangers avisés. Cependant, depuis les dix dernières années, les importantes améliorations techniques, la modernisation des méthodes et l'importation d'équipement européen et de cultures de levures ont permis aux principaux producteurs d'être plus compétitifs sur le marché mondial sophistiqué. Environ 70 % de la production est du vin ordinaire, mais quelques *bodegas* se spécialisent dans les vins de qualité.

L'histoire du vin en Argentine

En 1566, le père jésuite Cedron planta la première vigne dans la région de Cuyo. Les tout premiers ceps des jésuites survivent dans la variété de raisins dénommés Criollas. Quoique descendante de vigne importée en Argentine il y a quatre cents ans, la Criolla Grande produit encore une grande quantité de vins quelconques, rouges légers, rosés et blancs. Depuis un siècle seulement les possibilités vinicoles de la région furent reconnues et exploitées par des immigrants français et italiens, qui entreprirent d'irriguer le désert de Mendoza en canalisant l'eau provenant de la fonte des neiges. Cette province est située à la frontière du Chili, au pied des Andes.

Régions vinicoles

La province de Mendoza située à environ 1 000 km à l'ouest de Buenos Aires, produit aujourd'hui près de 70 % du vin argentin et 40 % de ses terres cultivables sont consacrés à la vigne. La viticulture est la plus importante activité de cette province. On y compte environ 40 000 viticulteurs et plus de 1 000 *bodegas*, mais 20 % de la production sont assurés par neuf grandes sociétés propriétaires de vignobles, de chais, usines de mise en bouteille et circuits de vente s'étendant à toute l'Argentine. La production du rouge (provenant principalement des cépages Malbec, Bonarda, Tempranilla, Cabernet, Sauvignon, Merlot et Barbera) représente 30 % du total, les blancs 20 % (à partir des cépages Pedro Gimenez, Chenin, Sémillon, Tokay Friulano et Ugni Blanc), les rosés (des Criolla Grande, Cereza et Moscatel Rosado) et les raisins de tables 50 %.

Comme on peut s'y attendre dans un pays neuf et sous l'influence italienne, les procédés sont surtout ceux de la production quantitative. (Ce sont des viniculteurs français et non italiens qui, de génération en génération, se sont efforcés de perfectionner leur art.) Mendoza et la province voisine de San Juan offrant l'aspect d'immenses océans verdoyants couverts de pampres. C'est là qu'on trouve les plus grandes cuves à fermentation du monde entier. Les qualités positives mais dénuées de toute subtilité des vins argentins leur sont conférées par des méthodes de vinification massives. On fait parfois fermenter et vieillir ensemble jusqu'à 10 000 hl de vin. Inutile de dire qu'en de telles circonstances, les soins particuliers sont inconcevables. Une seule entreprise de viniculture de la ville de Mendoza traite à elle toute seule jusqu'à 900 000 hl de vin par an. On compte plus de 200 *bodegas* de ce genre dans cette même ville. La province totalise plus de 200 000 ha de vignobles.

Plus de la moitié de cette superficie totale est concentrée dans le nord de Mendoza, les variétés Criollas, Malbec et Pedro Ximenez — le nom de ce dernier étant d'ailleurs donné à tort — sont irriguées par des eaux des fleuves Tunuyán et Mendoza ainsi que par l'eau des sources. Dans les terres salines du nord-ouest de la province, les mêmes variétés sont prédominantes. Mais c'est dans la partie sud-ouest du nord de Mendoza que l'on produit les meilleurs vins d'Argentine. On y trouve du Malbec en quantité, et le vin est meilleur que son frère pourtant plus célèbre, le Cabernet Sauvignon. Tout en n'ayant rien de fabuleux, ce vin est certainement l'un des meilleurs que l'Argentine puisse offrir.

La vallée du fleuve Uco est la région vinicole centrale de Mendoza. Les Malbec, Tempranilla et Sémillon y sont les variétés les plus importantes. Dans le sud de la

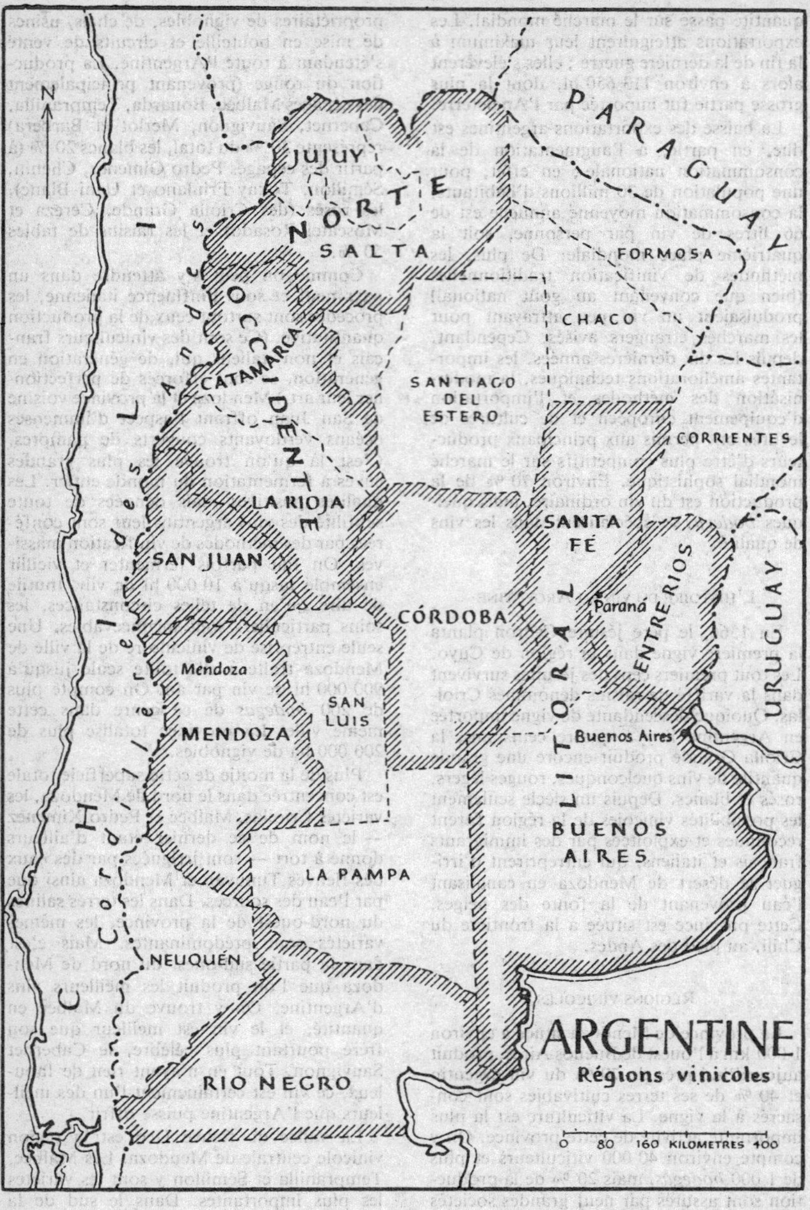
N
JUJUY
NORTE
SALTA
PARAGUAY
FORMOSA
CHACO
OCCIDENTE
CATAMARCA
SANTIAGO
DEL
ESTERO
CORRIENTES
LA RIOJA
SANTA
FÉ
SAN JUAN
ENTRE RIOS
Paraná
CÓRDOBA
LITORAL
URUGUAY
Mendoza
SAN
LUIS
MENDOZA
Buenos Aires
BUENOS
AIRES
LA PAMPA
NEUQUÉN
RIO NEGRO
CHILI
Cordillère des Andes
ARGENTINE
Régions vinicoles
0 80 160 KILOMETRES 400

province, on trouve plusieurs variétés qui produisent d'assez bons vins, notamment les Criollas, Malbec, Muscatel Rosé et Chenin. Les terres sont irriguées par les fleuves Atuel et Diamante.

Immédiatement au nord de Mendoza se trouve San Juan, province qui est, elle aussi, adossée à la chaîne des Andes et qui produit un vin plus lourd et plus riche. Les vignobles s'étendent sur environ 60 000 ha où se trouvent environ 400 *bodegas*. San Juan se trouve aussi plus près de l'équateur ; son climat est plus chaud et par conséquent ses vins plus forts : 20 % des vins argentins sont fait à San Juan, particulièrement dans les vallées de Zonda, Ullun et Tulun. Les moûts sont d'une haute teneur en sucre et d'une faible acidité ce qui les rend très appropriés pour leur concentration. Les variétés de raisin sont Moscatel de Alejandria, Pedro Gimenez et Ugni Blanc pour les blancs (40 %) ; Barbera, Nebbiolo, Berguignot, Bonarda, Malbec et Lambrusco pour les rouges (10 %) ; Cereza, Criolla Grande et Moscatel Rosado pour les rosés (50 % avec les raisins de tables). Étant donné que l'irrigation est aussi indispensable dans une province que dans l'autre, on n'y voit pas des coteaux couverts de vigne, comme en Europe. L'eau coulant dans les veines d'un réseau d'irrigation d'un vignoble plat a apporté aussi bien la mort que la vie aux vignes à vin de ce pays. Alors que dans la plupart des pays le phylloxéra a voyagé par la voie des airs pour passer d'une vigne à l'autre, en Argentine il pourrait fort bien passer par les conduits d'irrigation. Par contre, les Argentins se servaient de leurs aqueducs pour combattre cette maladie : les régions infestées étaient inondées pendant le temps nécessaire pour noyer le pou dévastateur et en libérer la vigne.

Les provinces de Rio Negro et Neuquén, au sud de celle de Mendoza, produisent, avec une centaines de *bodegas*, environ 5 % des vins argentins sur plus de 9 000 hectares. Étant donné que l'Argentine se trouve dans l'hémiphère sud, les vins les plus légers et les plus secs sont produits dans les régions les plus froides au climat le plus rigoureux, c'est-à-dire au sud. On les considère en général comme les meilleurs vins d'Argentine, quoique leur réelle qualité reste encore à prouver. Les variétés de raisin sont dans l'ensemble les mêmes que celles cultivées à San Juan (40 % pour les rouges, 50 % pour les blancs et 10 % pour les rosés et les raisins de table).

Outre les provinces de Mendoza, San Juan, Rio Negro et Neuquén, les autres régions vinicoles les plus importantes de la République d'Argentine sont plus au nord : La Rioja (environ 9 000 hectares), Salta, Jujuy et Catamarca (à peu près 5 000 hectares en tout).

Bien que la plupart des variétés européennes de *Vinifera* existent actuellement en Argentine, le nom du cépage paraissait rarement sur les étiquettes, les Argentins préférant voir leurs vins fins porter le nom de la propriété dont ils proviennent. Le Malbec donne environ les deux tiers du vin rouge argentin recherché — souvent mélangé —. Le Syrah est originaire du Rhône et les viticulteurs argentins en font un bon vin.

La confusion règne sur les noms et origines des vins et des raisins, et les appellations sont sujettes à des libertés : ainsi, le soi-disant Riesling argentin, tout en étant l'un des meilleurs vins blancs, peut, en fait, provenir de Sylvaner. Comme le Chardonnay, il a tendance à avoir un taux en alcool peu élevé (11 à 12°) et à se rapprocher plutôt des Mâcons français. Le Chenin Blanc est parfois désigné sous le nom de Pinot Blanc. Il faut également noter que deux variétés distinctes de Cabernet Sauvignon portent le même nom : l'un rappelle le Médoc, l'autre, beaucoup plus grossier est semblable à un vin du Midi. Les vins blancs, peu vinifiés dans les fûts de bois, attendaient trop longtemps avant d'être bus, ce qui donnait un vin manquant de fraîcheur et ayant un goût de barrique. Les vins rouges, eux aussi, vieillissaient souvent plus longtemps qu'ils n'auraient dû. Avec l'introduction de méthodes modernes de vinification, les viticulteurs désireux d'améliorer leurs chances de succès à l'exportation acquièrent des techniques de plus en plus perfectionnées et produisent de meilleurs vins, répondant davantage aux goûts étrangers. Il faut remarquer que les Argentins font preuve de beaucoup d'imagination lorsqu'il s'agit de créer des mélanges et des coupages, un exemple courant : celui des « soi-disant » Riesling et Chardonnay donnant un vin parfois déséquilibré, n'ayant ni début, ni milieu et finissant sur une note plate et oxydée. L'un des vins rouges les plus populaires du pays est fait de Barbera, de Syrah et de Malbec. Du moût condensé est exporté.

Les principaux exportateurs de vins de qualité sont : Penaflor S.A. à Mendoza (dont la production est vendue, en partie aux États-Unis, sous les marques « Andean Vineyards » et « Bodegas Trapiche »), Giol EEIC, Lopez et Toso. La maison Giol est connue pour ses Riesling, Cabernet et Pinot Gris ; Lopez pour ses Cabernet, Malbec, et Merlot ; Toso est réputé pour le Cabernet Sauvignon. Il y a aussi Eledar S.A., Estornell S.A. et El Trébol S.A.. Castel Chandon (Moët et Chandon de France), Crillon (Seagram) et Edmundo Navarro Correas (en collaboration avec Deutz de la Champagne) produisent des mousseux.

Argile d'Espagne

Silicate d'aluminium utilisé pour le collage ou la clarification des vins.

Arjan

Un des nombreux noms du koumiss, alcool obtenu par la fermentation du lait aigre de jument. C'est une boisson des Tartares.

Arkansas

Petite région vinicole des États-Unis. Les vignobles sont situés dans les montagnes de l'Ozark, au nord.

Voir ÉTATS-UNIS : ARKANSAS

Armagnac

Eau-de-vie de vin. Sud-Ouest de la France.

L'Armagnac est l'eau-de-vie du pays de d'Artagnan. Subdivision provinciale de l'ancienne Gascogne, l'Armagnac est aussi connu pour ses oies et ses chevaux. Ses habitants, au teint bronzé, au caractère vif, parlent encore volontiers de sorcières bonnes pour leurs amis et qui jettent de mauvais sort sur leur ennemis. Les Armagnacs descendent des Gaulois, des Romains, des Basques, des Wisigoths qui peuplèrent la Gascogne. On y trouve encore un certain nombre de protestants. Selon la tradition leurs propriétés sont signalées par des cyprès qui proclameraient leur foi. Le paysage vallonné est souvent noirci par des petits chênes noueux et des pins. En hiver, un vent froid y dévale des Pyrénées. En été, collines et vallons cuisent sous un soleil ardent. L'eau-de-vie d'Armagnac rappelle ce climat extrême ainsi que le caractère résolu de ceux qui le font. C'est un alcool corsé, au goût nettement caractérisé et fort. Il est souvent vendu en flacons plats, arrondis, au long cou, connus sous le nom de bouteilles basques ou « basquaises ». L'étiquette indique soit Armagnac, soit Bas-Armagnac. Ténarèze et Haut-Armagnac sont aussi des noms d'origine autorisés mais on les voit rarement, parce qu'ils désignent des régions de moindre qualité. Les termes *haut* et *bas* ont un sens purement géographique et ne qualifient en aucun cas la qualité du produit.

DÉLIMITATION

Afin de préciser son nom et de conquérir un marché à l'exemple de Cognac, l'eau-de-vie d'Armagnac fit l'objet d'une réglementation en 1909. Les limites de l'appellation d'origine englobent une bonne partie du département du Gers, plusieurs cantons du Lot-et-Garonne et un tout petit secteur des Landes. Les principaux centres de la région sont Condom pour le Ténarèze, Auch pour le Haut-Armagnac, Eauze pour le Bas-Armagnac. On traitait les affaires d'Armagnac à Eauze au marché du jeudi. Acheteurs et vendeurs discutent dans les petites rues étroites, goûtent et souvent se contentent de frotter une goutte d'eau-de-vie entre les mains et de la humer. Le Bas-Armagnac est la partie la plus occidentale. Le sol s'y abaisse vers la forêt des Landes. Son caractère sablonneux et argileux donne une grande finesse à l'eau-de-vie. 11 000 hectares de vignes sont cultivés pour être distillés en Armagnac. Pour porter le nom réservé de Bas-Armagnac, Ténarèze ou Haut-Armagnac, l'eau-de-vie doit être à 100 % originaire de ces terres et doit avoir été élaborée, mélangée et conservée dans des entrepôts distincts où elle n'a voisiné avec aucun alcool d'une autre catégorie traité par le même expéditeur. Au sud du Ténarèze où le sol est argileux et calcaire, l'Armagnac est plus léger et vieillit plus rapidement. A l'est, le Haut-Armagnac est surtout crayeux ; quoique le calcaire soit l'élément déterminant des meilleurs

Cognac, il n'a pas le même effet sur l'Armagnac qui, sur ce sol, est d'un type plus grossier et n'est guère vendu à l'état naturel. On s'en sert pour la fabrication des liqueurs dont le commerce joue un rôle important dans l'économie de l'Armagnac.

Millésimes

Bien qu'elle soit officiellement réglementée, la question de l'âge et des millésimes est encore discutée en Armagnac. Pour dater leurs eaux-de-vie, les producteurs et le Bureau national de l'Armagnac utilisent le même système que celui des Cognac. L'Armagnac est vinifié entre fin septembre et fin octobre, puis distillé presque immédiatement ; il est alors appelé *compte 00.* Le 30 avril de l'année suivante, les distillations doivent être terminées et la totalité de l'eau-de-vie distillée devient *compte 0.* Le 1er avril de chaque année, les eaux-de-vie gagnent officiellement une année de plus.

L'âge minimum à partir duquel l'Armagnac peut effectivement être vendu sous le nom d'Armagnac est le *compte 1* pour les Trois-Étoiles ou *compte 2* pour ses équivalents ; le V.S.O.P. doit être au moins *compte 4* et les *Extra* ou *Hors d'Age, compte 5.* Contrairement aux Cognac, les Armagnac peuvent encore porter un millésime ou une appellation spécifiques (sauf les bouteilles exportées aux États-Unis). Lorsqu'une étiquette d'Armagnac indique un alcool « de dix ans d'âge », il peut s'agir d'un coupage d'Armagnac d'années différentes, mais un Armagnac ne peut en aucun cas avoir moins de dix ans d'âge.

Certains vignerons préfèrent l'eau-de-vie millésimée qu'ils jugent supérieure aux coupages (encore s'agit-il seulement de certaines années particulièrement favorables). Quelques firmes livrent aussi au marché certains Armagnac millésimés et ne mélangent que ceux des autres années. On trouve de rares producteurs qui ne traitent que l'Armagnac millésimé. Dans leurs chais, les barils d'Armagnac sont alignés sur leurs supports en deux rangées ; chacun porte inscrit à la craie l'année de vendange. Le vigneron vous racontera volontiers que les clients viennent en grand nombre, de toutes les régions de France et de l'étranger, pour goûter les eaux-de-vie des différentes années et choisir celle qui leur convient. A quelques kilomètres de là, un viticulteur-expéditeur n'a plus de barils dans sa cave. Certains éleveurs conservent leurs très vieilles eaux-de-vie dans des bonbonnes en verre contenant généralement 30 l. Ne serait-ce pas le début d'un triste abandon des traditions ? Non, rassurons-nous car il ne s'agit que de vénérables millésimes. Nous avons découvert chez l'un d'eux des 1900, 1904, 1891, 1888 logés ainsi. L'éleveur en tire un échantillon, le flaire et nous le fait goûter.

Au bout de cinquante ans, l'Armagnac ne s'améliore plus dans les fûts de bois et même, se dégrade. Dans le verre, il ne changera ni en bien ni en mal, comme tous les autres alcools. Voilà pourquoi le viticulteur-expéditeur du Bas-Armagnac met ses vieux alcools dans le verre, les protège de tout changement, dès qu'ils ont atteint leur plein épanouissement.

Presque noircis par le chêne, les très vieux Armagnac ont un tel arôme qu'il subsiste parfois plus d'une semaine dans le verre vidé. Ces Armagnac millésimés sont en vérité des breuvages divins.

Pour pouvoir porter le millésime sur l'étiquette, l'Armagnac doit être celui d'une seule année. L'eau-de-vie coupée d'une année sur l'autre ne peut pas porter une date, la loi l'interdisant. Il est toutefois possible de mentionner un âge (10, 15, 20 ans, etc.), à condition que ce dernier soit celui de l'Armagnac le plus jeune entrant dans l'assemblage.

Les vignes autorisées en Armagnac

L'Armagnac est fait avec les vins blancs du Gers provenant des raisins suivants : Picpoul, Saint-Émilion, Colombard, Jurançon et Plant de Grèce (appelé Baco). Quoique autorisés, Blanquette, Mauzac, Clairette et Meslier sont moins utilisés. Le Folle Blanche était autrefois le plus répandu. Il cède constamment du terrain au Saint-Émilion et à d'autres ceps plus robustes.

Au cours des dernières années, le Baco 22 A a été inclus parmi les raisins autorisés, mais seulement dans les terrains sablonneux du Bas-Armagnac. C'est un hybride du Folle Blanche et du Noah américain. On discute encore passionnément ses mérites en Armagnac. Selon une règle élémentaire de la viticulture française, les vignes hybrides donnent des raisins de qualité inférieure et elle devraient être arrachées dans tous les vignobles ayant droit à une appellation contrôlée pour le vin. Sur le sol sablonneux du Bas-Armagnac pourtant, le Baco semble jusqu'à présent produire un vin dont la distillation donne une eau-de-vie d'aussi bonne qualité que le Picpoul ou le Folle Blanche. Peut-être est-il trop tôt cependant pour juger un produit qui doit mûrir pendant quelque quarante ans pour arriver au maximum de sa qualité.

COMPARAISON AVEC LE COGNAC

Il existe plusieurs différences foncières entre le Cognac et l'Armagnac. Le meilleur Armagnac est le produit d'un sol sablonneux, alors que les meilleures régions du Cognac sont les plus riches en craie. Le climat du Cognac est nettement maritime, doux et brumeux ; celui de l'Armagnac, plus rigoureux. L'Armagnac est plus proche de ses origines que le Cognac ; il n'est pas adouci par coupages ; c'est un produit naturel auquel il est inutile d'ajouter du sucre.

Bien des gens, et pas seulement des Gascons, préfèrent l'Armagnac de très bonne qualité au Cognac. Malheureusement il n'est pas toujours de très bonne qualité. On trouve trop d'Armagnac à bon marché et bien des gens qui ont l'habitude de cette eau-de-vie n'en connaissent même pas les meilleurs types. Les exportateurs d'Armagnac se sont fait le plus grand tort en faisant passer leur marchandise pour beaucoup plus vieille qu'elle ne l'était en réalité ! 99 ans d'âge ! telle était une gasconnade courante jusqu'à ce que la loi interdise cette pratique en 1951.

Les méthodes de distillation et de maturation sont différentes en ce qui concerne l'Armagnac et le Cognac. On insiste même délibérément sur ces différences.

On a procédé à une expérience intéressante à la coopérative d'eau-de-vie de Réans, près d'Eauze. Le produit de la distillation de vins de Bas-Armagnac de

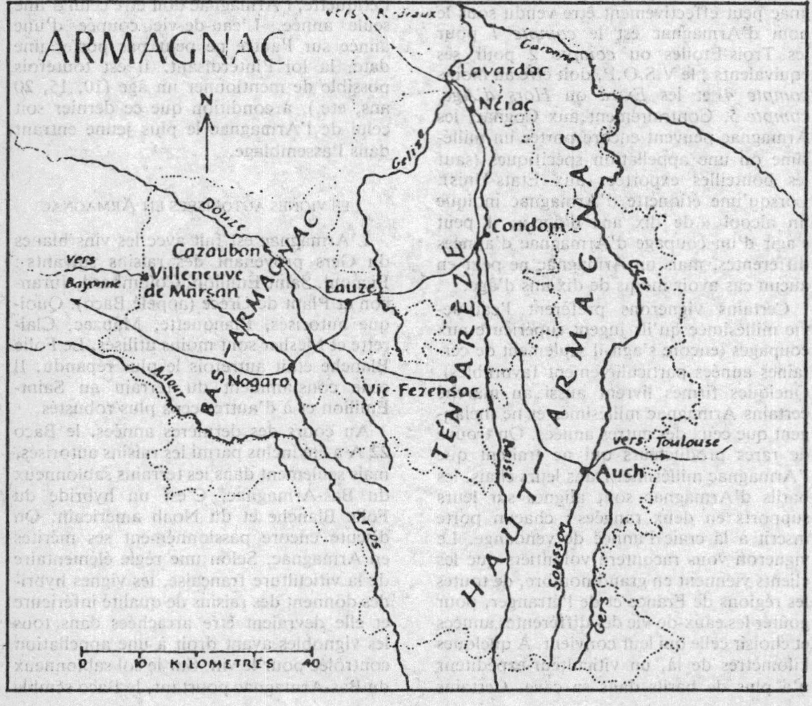

1952, provenant d'un seul alambic, fut versé dans des barils dont la moitié était en chêne du Limousin, identiques à ceux qui servent au vieillissement du Cognac. On scella à la cire toutes les bondes et on y apposa un sceau officiel. Quatre ans plus tard, en 1956, on goûta aux eau-de-vie. L'Armagnac conservé dans des barils du pays était bon. Quant aux fûts en chêne de Limousin, ils contenaient quelque chose qui n'était ni de l'Armagnac ni du Cognac. Cette expérience n'était d'ailleurs pas une fantaisie car le chêne se raréfie en Armagnac et son prix augmente. Pourtant il est désormais prouvé que l'Armagnac doit mûrir dans des fûts en chêne de son pays et rien d'autre.

On a aussi essayé de distiller de l'Armagnac avec les mêmes alambics qu'à Cognac. Le résultat a été consigné par la loi de 1936 qui exige la fabrication de l'Armagnac avec les appareils à distillation continue du pays. Le Cognac fait l'objet d'une double distillation dont le résultat final titre 70°. L'Armagnac ne peut dépasser 63° et en titre généralement 10 % de moins. Cela implique que l'alcool contient plus d'autres composants du raisin et qu'il a donc un goût plus particulier. A l'origine, les alambics de l'Armagnac ressemblaient à ceux de Cognac. C'est au XIXe siècle qu'on se mit à utiliser couramment l'appareil à distillation continue qui sert aujourd'hui. C'est essentiellement un alambic où les vapeurs sont raffinées par le vin lui-même *(Voir* CHAPITRE VI). Il est destiné à la distillation de vins titrant 9 à 10°. Une teneur plus élevée n'est pas souhaitable puisqu'il s'agit de conserver dans l'eau-de-vie le plus possible de substances non alcooliques qui lui donnent goût et arôme. Il en résulte que l'Armagnac conserve bien des éléments du goût et de l'odeur du vin. Il possède déjà un parfum étonnant, même quand il n'a pas atteint un an d'âge et qu'il est trop ardent pour la consommation. Cette jeune eau-de-vie est souvent consommée dans le café ; elle est dotée d'une fragrance capiteuse. L'Armagnac lance aujourd'hui un nouvel apéritif appelé Floc. C'est un vin doux, non fermenté, à base d'Armagnac. Environ 150 petits vignerons se partagent les vingt alambics itinérants. Le passage de cet alambic dans la campagne est un spectacle folklorique. Il ressemble à une vieille locomotive toute noire traversant le décor accidenté de l'Armagnac. Il s'arrête le soir. Sa gueule crache du feu nourri de branches de chêne. Il va d'une ferme à l'autre et c'est ainsi que ceux qui ne possèdent pas d'alambic distillent quand même le produit de leur vigne. Les principaux négociants en Armagnac étudient un nouveau type d'alambic qui produira une eau-de-vie tout aussi pure en éliminant certains éthers. Le temps de vieillissement en sera raccourci.

Si on a exporté du mauvais Armagnac c'est parce que les expéditeurs manquaient d'esprit de tradition. Si l'on en exporte encore moins que du Cognac, c'est parce que les producteurs ne savent pas faire connaître leur eau-de-vie par la publicité. Quelques-uns des meilleurs négociants et des plus importants viticulteurs ont désormais pris l'affaire en main. A leur tête se trouva feu le marquis de Montesquiou, duc de Fezensac, député au parlement français, qui géra son domaine — le château de Marsan — dont il fit une ferme modèle et un centre d'expérimentation. Il s'ingénia à maintenir les normes les plus élevées d'Armagnac et à protéger les petits viticulteurs contre certains négociants qui n'hésitaient pas à acheter l'alcool au plus bas prix pour le revendre le plus cher possible. Celui qui visite le château Marsan goûtera peut-être au plat gascon que préférait Henri IV : la poule au pot ; à la fin du repas, il dégustera un bon vieil Armagnac. Il en trouvera aussi une petite carafe dans sa chambre à coucher : une tradition que respecte l'amphitryon.

Parce que nous sommes dans le pays des Trois Mousquetaires, la plupart des firmes ont leur « réserve d'Artagnan ». Mais le seul homme vivant qui pourrait revendiquer ce nom prestigieux, n'est autre que le marquis de Montesquiou lui-même. Il descend en effet du maréchal d'Artagnan qui devint plus tard le héros d'Alexandre Dumas. D'Artagnan vivait en réalité au château de Castelmore, près de Lupiac, et ne s'appelait pas d'Artagnan. On peut voir au dessus du portail de cette demeure du XVIIe siècle, d'ailleurs mal entretenue, l'inscription suivante : « Ici naquit, vers 1615, d'Artagnan, de son vrai nom Charles de Batz ».

Depuis 1951, il existe en Armagnac une association comparable à celle de la Confrérie des chevaliers du Tastevin en Bourgogne et à la Commanderie du Bontemps dans le Médoc. Ces sociétés donnent à leurs membres de nombreuses occasions de se travestir, de prêter serment et de s'amuser de diverses manières. C'est aussi un excellent moyen d'attirer l'attention sur l'eau-de-vie de la région. En Gascogne, les membres de la Compagnie des Mousquetaires portent de hautes bottes, des chapeaux emplumés et de magnifiques moustaches. Le cardinal de Richelieu et le roi de France sont représentés à leurs réunions. Les Mousquetaires, de nos jours, se réunissent volontiers à Auch, ville bâtie au sommet d'une hauteur et couronnée par une cathédrale dont la construction commença au XIVᵉ siècle et fut terminée sous Louis XIV. Des centaines de personnages, merveilleusement sculptés dans le bois par un élève de Michel-Ange, décorent les bancs d'œuvre. On accède au parvis par un escalier abrupt partant du Gers. La statue de d'Artagnan se trouve à mi-chemin et c'est là que se réunissent les Mousquetaires de nos jours. Quant à d'Artagnan lui-même, sa statue le représente étonnamment jeune.

Armillaria root rot

Nom du pourridié en anglais. Il s'agit d'une maladie cryptogamique de la vigne.
Voir CHAPITRE IV

Arôme

L'opinion que l'on se fait d'un vin jeune en le jugeant du nez ; à ne pas confondre avec le bouquet. L'arôme du vin jeune provient directement de l'odeur des fruits frais avec lesquels il a été conçu, et non pas des esters qui se développent éventuellement dans un vin plus âgé. C'est surtout dans les vins qui, n'étant pas extrêmement secs, ont gardé un peu du sucre du raisin, que l'on trouve l'arôme le plus prononcé. Tel est le cas des Gewürztraminer, si aisément reconnaissables.

Arrack, arraki, arack, arak, raki, etc.

Ces noms dérivent du mot arabe signifiant : « jus » ou « sueur ». Ils désignent en général l'« alcool indigène ». Il y a probablement autant de genres d'arrack qu'il y a d'alcools locaux en Orient et en Europe orientale. Aux Indes orientales on fait de l'arrack en distillant la sève fermentée de palmier ou le suc du riz ; en Grèce, l'arrack est un alcool de grain ; au Moyen-Orient et en Égypte, un alcool de dattes ou de raisins. À Batavia, l'arrack est un rhum fortement aromatique, distillé sur l'île de Java. Le nombre et les espèces d'herbes et d'épices qui ont servi à parfumer cet alcool sont aussi vastes que l'imagination humaine. L'arrack est un alcool dur, fait pour les palais aguerris. « Celui qui a goûté l'arrack n'en oublie jamais le goût », dit un proverbe français.

Arroba

Mesure de vin, en Espagne, équivalant à 11,5 kg, soit à peu près le poids d'un panier de raisins. Théoriquement, 60 arrobas donnent un fût de 516 l de vin. Comme mesure de capacité, l'arroba équivaut à 16 ou 16,5 l.

Artichoke brandy

Voir EAU-DE-VIE D'ARTICHAUT

Asali

Miel fermenté consommé en Afrique orientale.

Asciutto

Mot italien désignant le vin sec.

Assemblage

Opération qui consiste à mélanger les vins provenant de différents vignobles en Champagne. Dans le Bordelais, on emploie le même terme pour le mélange des cuves ou des barriques contenant des vins issus de cépages différents.

Assmannshausen

Village du Rheingau, produisant de bons vins rouges, et spécialement réputé pour ses Spätburgunder (Pinot Noir) élégants et finement fruités. Les vignes s'épanouissent sur des pentes de quartzite et d'ardoise orientées au sud et extrêmement abruptes. *Meilleur cru :* Hoellenberg.

Voir RHEINGAU

Asti

Ville d'Italie célèbre pour son vin blanc mousseux : l'Asti Spumante ou Asti (D.O.C.), qui est un vin sec et surtout doux. Asti est aussi connu, quoique dans une moindre mesure, pour son Moscato d'Asti (D.O.C.).

Voir PIÉMONT

Astringence

En ce qui concerne le vin, ce mot désigne une âpreté due aux acides et au tanin. Elle indique parfois que le vin vieillira bien.

Asztali Bor

Nom hongrois du vin ordinaire (*Bor* signifie vin).

Athol Brose

Breuvage écossais à base de whisky auquel on ajoute soit du miel, soit de la bouillie d'avoine, soit encore les deux.

Attempérateurs

Tubes métalliques en forme de spirale que l'on immerge dans les cuves de fermentation et à travers lesquels on insuffle de l'eau chaude ou froide pour régler la température du moût en fermentation ou du jus de raisin.

Aubance

Voir COTEAUX DE L'AUBANCE, ANJOU

Aube

Département français situé dans la partie sud — moins importante — de la Champagne, avec environ 4 000 ha de vignes.

Voir CHAMPAGNE

Aude

Surtout rouge, mais aussi du blanc. Sud de la France.

Un des trois départements français qui produisent les plus grandes quantités de vin, les deux autres étant l'Hérault et le Gard. A eux trois, ils fournissent la masse des vins du Midi.

Les vignobles de l'Aude, proches du Roussillon, donc pas très éloignés de la frontière espagnole, produisent de très grandes quantités de vin dénué de distinction. Ce sont surtout des rouges avec une petite quantité de blancs et de rosés, plus particulièrement ceux de Limoux, de Corbières et du Minervois.

Aume

Tonneau utilisé surtout pour l'expédition des vins d'Alsace. Sa contenance de 114 l est égale à celle de la feuillette bourguignonne.

Aurum

Marque d'une liqueur italienne d'une couleur d'or pâle, à goût d'orange amère.

Auslese

Mot allemand désignant le vin fait seulement avec certaines grappes très mûres choisies sur la vigne. *Beerenauslese* est la sélection de certains grains choisis sur chaque grappe. *Trockenbeerenauslese :* opération consistant à ne choisir un par un que les grains de raisin trop mûrs.

Voir ALLEMAGNE

Ausone (Château-)

Bordeaux rouge. Commune et cru de Saint-Émilion.

Quoique la tradition lui accorde la première place parmi les vins de Saint-Émilion, Ausone est quelquefois considéré comme inférieur à Cheval-Blanc. Certains vont même jusqu'à lui préférer le Figeac. Pourtant le Château-Ausone se vend encore à des prix fabuleux.

Néanmoins, quand les vins de Saint-Émilion furent classés officiellement une première fois en 1955 puis en 1986, on plaça Ausone et Cheval-Blanc, selon la tradition, en tête des premiers grands crus, et les autres ensuite, par ordre alphabétique ; mais ils ne furent pas rangés dans une catégorie particulière.

D'après certains, Ausone serait bâti sur l'emplacement où se trouvait, au IVe siècle, la villa du poète romain Ausone. A en croire ce qu'écrivit Ausone, le vin de cette même villa était déjà le préféré de Jules César quelques siècles plus tôt. En tout cas, le vignoble est magnifiquement placé à l'extrémité ouest du village de Saint-Émilion, construit au XIe siècle, sur une éminence. Le château proprement dit domine le vignoble bien incliné vers le sud-est et, par endroits, planté en terrasses ; une route d'accès débouche sur un panorama inoubliable. En raison de sa situation privilégiée, Ausone échappa aux terribles gelées de février 1956. Les caves d'Ausone sont profondément enfoncées dans la pierre douce creusée il y a des siècles, et avec laquelle Saint-Émilion fut bâti.

Les vins de Château-Bel-Air, dont le vignoble est contigu, jadis vieillissaient aussi dans les caves d'Ausone. Les deux châteaux appartenaient à feu M. Dubois-Challon, une des principales personnalités de la Jurade de Saint-Émilion ; depuis sa mort en 1974, le Château-Ausone appartient en indivision à sa veuve et aux héritiers de Mme Cécile Vauthier, sa sœur.

Caractéristiques ; Moins robuste que bien des Saint-Émilion, le Château-Ausone n'en a pas moins une très belle plénitude et une distinction remarquable. La qualité superbe en 1976 justifia la validité de la classification d'Ausone.

Superficie : 7 ha.

Production moyenne : 30 tonneaux (2 500 caisses).

Australie

La production vinicole australienne fut bicentenaire en 1988. A l'exception des États-Unis, l'Australie est le pays qui a connu les plus grands développements et les transformations les plus importantes. Le vin y est produit dans tous les États, y compris dans les Territoires du Nord. En 1987, plus de la moitié de la production australienne (soit 350 millions de litres ou encore 39 millions de caisses de douze bouteilles chacune) provenait du sud du pays, considéré comme la région viticole par excellence. Le vin est très populaire en Australie où la consommation annuelle est de 21 litres par individu. Le pays totalise environ 65 000 ha de vignobles ; les régions viticoles se sont mutipliées. Bien que la culture de la vigne soit restreinte par les conditions climatiques généralement trop chaudes, trop arides ou trop humides, elle s'est néanmoins développée dans le quart sud du pays relativement plus frais.

L'Australie compte, dans un arc de 6 500 km, environ 600 entreprises vinicoles et 7 000 vignobles dans trente-trois régions distinctes, couvrant plus de quatre-vingts sous-districts et échantillonnant divers micro-climats et types de sols, tous favorables à la vigne. De nouvelles régions se développent lentement.

On prétend en Australie, dans les milieux viticoles, que « chaque année est une bonne année pour le vin » et qu'un climat régulier donne une qualité toujours égale.

Dans les régions qui produisent de bons vins, la variété de la qualité est fonction de la variété du sol : terre alluvionnaire riche et noire, terrains argileux, sablonneux, de graviers et basalte. Une petite région peut regrouper différents types de sols et être soumise à différents modes d'irrigation. Les dégâts provoqués par divers insectes, champignons et maladies varient suivant les méthodes de drainage et de surveillance. L'Australie est un vaste continent où de nouvelles régions sont sans cesse exploitées. Avec l'une des économies les plus stables du monde, elle offre à son industrie viticole un environnement économiquement sain. La demande pour un vin de table de très bonne qualité était si grande que seules d'infimes quantités de ses meilleurs vins étaient exportées. La production s'est aujourd'hui accrue.

Histoire du vin en Australie

Les premières vignes semblent être arrivées en Australie avec les premiers colons. Quand le capitaine Arthur Phillip quitta la Tamise à la tête d'une flotte de onze navires, sa cargaison comprenait « des plantes pour la colonie », parmi lesquelles se trouvaient les premières vignes qui furent plantées en Australie. Il débarqua à Sydney le 26 janvier 1788 et planta ses ceps à l'endroit où se trouve aujourd'hui le jardin botanique de la ville. On ne tarda pas à constater que le site était mal choisi pour la culture de la vigne car la proximité de l'océan créait une humidité ambiante favorable à une maladie cryptogamique qu'on identifia plus tard sous le nom d'anthracnose et plus couramment appelée « taches noires ».

Le premier qui fit une tentative sérieuse pour produire du vin à une échelle commerciale fut le capitaine John McArthur auquel une concession de terre fut accordée à environ 50 km de Sydney. Il baptisa son domaine Camden Park. Les autorités lui fournirent des souches de toutes les variétés qu'elles possédaient et il cultiva ensuite, avec un honnête succès, des ceps issus de semis. Plus tard, ses deux fils s'associèrent avec lui : James, né en 1798, et William, né en 1800. Les démêlés entre McArthur et le gouvernement Bligh sont bien connus en Australie. Ils portèrent même sur les pratiques courantes de la vinification. En 1807, McArthur importa deux alambics pour faire de l'eau-de-vie avec une partie de son vin. Bligh les fit saisir et réexpédier en Angleterre. Mieux encore, il fit comparaître McArthur en justice, l'accusant d'avoir importé illégalement ces appareils pour faire du rhum en dépit du monopole de fabrication de cet alcool en Nouvelle-Galles du Sud. Néanmoins la famille McArthur poursuivit ses efforts et joua un rôle important, non seulement dans la viticulture, mais aussi dans les affaires publiques.

Gregory Blaxland mérite aussi le titre de pionnier de la viticulture australienne car c'est le premier vigneron qui expédia son vin à Londres. La quantité n'était pas élevée : une centaine de litres de rouge, mais cette opération servit d'avant-coureur à un trafic très intense de bourgogne australien acheté par l'Angleterre. L'année suivante, Blaxland envoya 600 l du vin de son vignoble de Parramatta. Il se rendit encore célèbre quand il traversa la chaîne des Montagnes Bleues en compagnie de Wentworth et de Lawson. Cet exploit leur donna accès à des plaines fertiles situées au-delà des montagnes : découverte capitale pour le développement agricole de la Nouvelle-Galles du Sud.

En 1824, James Busby arriva à Sydney à l'âge de 24 ans. Ce remarquable jeune homme originaire d'Écosse n'avait passé que quelques mois dans les régions vinicoles françaises mais, depuis, il était obsédé par l'idée que la vigne avait un avenir illimité en Australie. Peu après son arrivée, il écrivit son premier livre : un traité sur la culture de la vigne et l'art de faire du vin. Le 8 mai 1824, on lui accorda une concession de quelque 800 ha dans la Hunter Valley. Il la baptisa Kirkton, nom auquel son vin donna par la suite de la notoriété. A cette époque, Busby s'entendit avec McArthur, Blaxland et d'autres vignerons déjà établis pour distribuer leurs ceps disponibles à quiconque voulait les planter.

Le génie de Busby s'illustra surtout lors de son voyage d'études viticoles dans les régions vinicoles d'Europe, et lorsqu'il introduisit sa grande collection de vignes en Australie. Celle-ci comptait presque toutes les meilleures variétés cultivées à l'époque en France et dans le sud de l'Espagne. Les vignes parvinrent sans dommages jusqu'à Sydney. Busby les offrit alors au gouvernement pour la formation d'un jardin expérimental qui se proposerait de « prouver leurs différentes qualités et propager de façon générale les variétés qui se montreraient les plus appropriées au climat ».

Jusqu'en 1925, l'Australie exporta presque exclusivement du faux bourgogne. En 1854, ce commerce n'avait qu'une valeur symbolique. C'est seulement en 1872 que la firme P. B. Burgoyne and Company commença ses opérations et que l'exportation prit de l'ampleur. Elle s'accrut et se maintint longtemps à quelque 34 000 hl par an. On vendit dans tout le Royaume-Uni le Harvest et le Tintara de Burgoyne ; le Rubicond de Gilbey ; le Keystone de Stephan Smith et l'Emeu de Pownall.

A la fin de la Première Guerre mondiale, le gouvernement Bruce-Page fut chargé de ramener à de saines occupations les soldats démobilisés. A cette époque, les vignerons établis au bord du Murray vendangeaient le raisin de Gordon Blanco à raison de 25 tonnes par hectare. Étant donné qu'il valait 12 livres australiennes la tonne, la viticulture semblait l'occupation idéale pour les anciens combattants.

Les gens du métier mirent le gouvernement en garde contre les plantations excessives. Il n'en tint pas compte. Quand les vignes portèrent leurs fruits, il y eut surabondance de raisin, ce qui provoqua une crise économique de la pire espèce. Incapable de résoudre ce problème, le gouvernement en confia la responsabilité aux viticulteurs. Le Conseil fédéral de viticulture déclara que le seul remède possible consistait à conquérir de nouveaux marchés en accordant des primes à l'exportation ; il en résulterait une nouvelle demande d'alcool sur ce même marché et on résorberait ainsi le surplus de Doradillo, variété de raisin propre à la distillation. Faute d'autres projets, le gouvernement accorda une prime substantielle aux exportateurs de vin, et une réduction de taxe sur l'eau-de-vie employée pour transformer les vins courants en vins de liqueur. Au total, les exportateurs touchaient près d'un shilling par litre de vin doux expédié à l'étranger. En quelques années ces mesures sauvèrent la situation.

L'exportation du vin de liqueur se développa et en 1927 elle atteignit plus de 171 000 hl. L'année 1936/37 fut la grande année des exportations. Environ 180 000 hl de vin furent exportés en Angleterre, tandis que 160 000 hl seulement étaient consommés en Australie. L'Australie, qui aime fabriquer de nouveaux vins, doit consommer toute sa production sur place. Seuls 5 % des vins sont exportés. Les principales sociétés d'exportation sont : Thomas Hardy and Sons/Emu, Lindemans, Orlando, Penfolds/Kaiser, Stuhl/Wynns, des coopératives vinicoles bien implantées

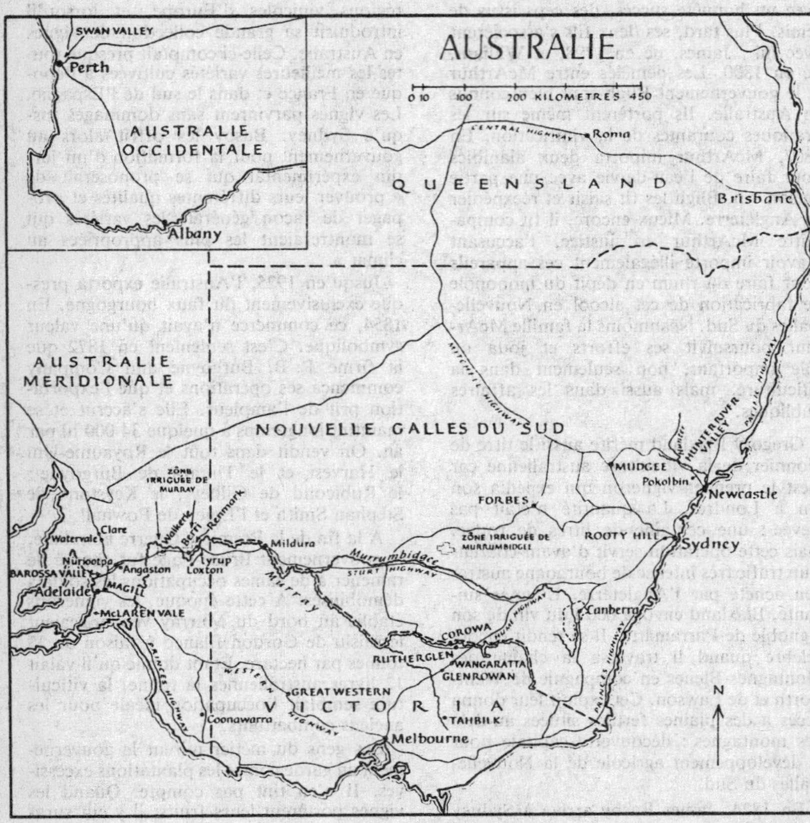

(Berri/Renmano), Mildara/Hamilton, McWilliams, Seppelts et Smith and Son (Yalumba/Hill Smith Estate). Les améliorations sont visibles dans les vignobles et dans les vins. La production est 9 fois plus importante qu'en 1936. L'Australie, aujourd'hui l'un des plus grands producteurs de vins de table, ne limite plus sa production aux grosses quantités de vins corsés et de rouges destinés au commerce britannique. Malgré ces récents développements, il est peu probable que la quantité de vin exportée revienne concurrencer en volume la consommation locale. Jusque dans les années 60, la population consommait peu de vin de table, puis dans les années 70, les vins rouges secs et les vins blancs secs devinrent populaires. A cette époque, la consommation augmenta sérieusement lorsque le vin fut vendu dans divers conditionnements (c'est-à-dire : bonbonnes, cubitainers, vrac, etc.). Vers 1985, plus de 60 % des ventes se firent sous des formes autres que les bouteilles, dont plus de 50 % furent vendus en cubitainers. Ces vins sont, dans l'ensemble, de bonne qualité et constituent de très bons vins ordinaires à consommer sur place.

Nouvelle-Galles du Sud

Plus vieil État du Commonwealth, la Nouvelle-Galles du Sud était aussi le plus ancien producteur de vin. Les plus importantes régions vinicoles sont : la Hunter Valley (au nord de Sydney), la zone d'irrigation Murrumbidgee (M.I.A.) située autour des districts de Griffith-Leeton (deuxième région viticole du pays qui produit 18 % des vins d'Australie), Mudgee et Forbes, et Cowra. La Hunter Valley demeure l'une des régions les plus renommées. La plupart des bons vins blancs, produits par les 40 centres viticoles, est coupée de sémillon. Les plus grands et plus anciens producteurs sont : Tyrrell's, Lindeman, McWilliams, Tulloch, Drayton et Wyndham Estate. Ce fut Tyrrell's qui implanta le Chardonnay dans la région. Toutes sortes de vins nouveaux furent produits à partir de cette variété. Les Chardonnay sont souvent portés à maturation dans des fûts neufs venant de France et des États-Unis car les bois locaux ne conviennent pas. Les Chardonnay et Sémillon, des vins de cépage, rivalisent avec les meilleurs du monde. De bonnes entreprises vinicoles, généralement récentes et petites, se sont créées. Parmi les nouveaux centres de qualité il convient de citer : Allandale, Lake's Folly, Robson, Brokenwood, Peterson's, Terrace Yale, Rothbury Estate, Sutherlands, Rosemount, Hunter Estate, Saxonvale, Hungerford Hill et Arrowfield, les cinq dernières étant des entreprises de taille non négligeable.

Le Shiraz, également connu sous le nom d'Hermitage, le Cabernet Sauvignon et plus tard le Pinot Noir ont été cultivés avec succès.

Les vastes vignobles irrigués de Griffith-Leeton, au centre du M.I.A., produisent de grosses quantités de vins (dont certains sont des mousseux) vendus pour la plupart en outre, ainsi que des porto, sherry, muscat et vermouth. On compte 21 centres vinicoles dont les plus importants sont : McWilliam's, Orlando, De Bortoli, San Bernardino pour les plus grands et Lillypilly Estate, Scenic Hill, et The College pour les plus petits.

La région de Mudgee est toujours une zone nouvelle en pleine expansion. Située en altitude, elle jouit d'un climat frais qui a attiré 16 centres intéressants. Le plus important, « Montrose Company », appartient à des Italiens. Quelques-uns des meilleurs vins proviennent de Huntington Estate, Botobolar et Miramar.

État de Victoria

Le plus ancien vignoble connu du Victoria fut planté en 1838 à Yering, dans la localité de Lilydale. Quoique la culture de la vigne eût commencé plus tard au Victoria qu'en Nouvelle-Galles du Sud et en Australie méridionale, les conditions favorables à cette culture y amenèrent un grand nombre de colons, si bien qu'en 1900 il y avait déjà 1 200 vignobles distincts répartis à peu près partout dans l'État de Victoria qui était déjà de beaucoup le plus gros producteur de vin australien. Voici les chiffres de production pour la saison 1899-1900 :

Australie méridionale	23 215 hl
Nouvelle-Galles du Sud	31 308 hl
Victoria	71 767 hl

Par malheur, le phylloxéra apparut à Geelong, puis à Bendigo, puis dans les vignes du nord-est et les régions viticoles furent dévastées. Nombre de vignerons reculèrent devant la dépense que représentait la reconstitution de leur vignoble avec des plants américains immunisés contre le phylloxéra. Dans les années 55, la production fut limitée aux zones irriguées de Mildura et Swan Hill, ainsi qu'à quelques petits vignobles producteurs de bons vins : Great Western près d'Ararat, Château Tahbilk dans le Victoria central, et les contrées du Nord-Est (Rutherglen, Wangaratta, Glenrowan et Milawa). Ces régions sont justement célèbres pour les muscat et tokay qu'on laisse vieillir en fûts pendant 30 à 50 ans. On y fait aussi quelques vins rouges secs et robustes. A Milawa, où le microclimat est plus frais, les Brown Brothers produisent un éventail étonnant de blancs et de rouges secs ainsi que quelques vins doux intéressants, vendangés tardivement.

Depuis la renaissance de son industrie du vin dans les années 60, le Victoria, pratiquement oublié pendant plus de 100 ans, est aujourd'hui en toute première place. Il compte 120 entreprises vinicoles regroupées dans les régions suivantes : Mildura-Robinvale (Sunraysia), troisième d'Australie par sa taille et qui produit environ 10 % de la production nationale, Rutherglen, Milawa-Glenrowan-King Valley, Great Western, Murray Valley, Goulburn Valley, Bendigo-Central Highlands, the Victorian Pyrenees, Yarra Valley, Geelong et Mornington Peninsula.

Parmi les nouvelles entreprises, les plus importantes sont : la firme franco-américaine Taltarni, Tisdall, Yellowglen et Balgownie (qui font partie de l'empire Mildara), Idyll, Le Amon, Redbank, Château Yarrinya, Lilydale et St Huberts. Pour les plus anciennes et les plus grosses, il faut citer : Brown Brothers, Château Tahbilk, Morris of Rutherglen, Baileys of Glenrowan, Bullers, Best's, Stanton et Killeen, Campbells, All Saints, Mildara, Mitchelton et Château Remy dirigé par la société française Remy. Une autre compagnie française, Moët, a investi dans un nouveau vignoble situé au centre du Victoria. Tous ont produit de merveilleux vins, essentiellement du Cabernet Sauvignon, du Pinot Noir, du Chardonnay, du Sauvignon Blanc et du Riesling, mais aussi du Marsanne et du Shiraz. Tous ces vins sont vendus sur place et ne sont que très rarement exportés vers les autres États australiens. Pourtant, certains comptent parmi les meilleurs jeunes vins du pays. La prospérité des années 65 a attiré toutes sortes d'amateurs : docteurs, dentistes, pharmaciens et avocats. La plupart d'entre eux ont disparu, laissant quelques bons vins : Cabernet Sauvignon, Pinot Noir, Chardonnay, Sauvignon Blanc et Riesling.

Le futur du Victoria est prometteur. Il y aura toujours une demande enthousiaste, en dépit des prix, pour ses bons vins produits en quantité limitée et ses vins supérieurs.

L'Australie Méridionale

La région Riverland, baignée par la Murray, est de loin la plus importante d'Australie. Elle produit 40 % des vins du pays. Ils proviennent, pour la plupart, de grosses coopératives appartenant aux viticulteurs des comtés de Renmark, Berri, Loxton et Waikerie. Les plus importantes sont : l'affaire familiale Angove's, l'association gigantesque Berri-Renmano, connue sous le nom de « Consolidated Cooperative Wineries Ltd » et Loxton Cooperative Ltd.

Aujourd'hui, la majorité des vins consommés par de nombreux Australiens est produite à partir des régions irriguées. La plupart des vins de table, très recherchés et appréciés, sont vendus par des producteurs nationaux et proviennent essentiellement de vignobles ensoleillés et irrigués. Quelques Chardonnay remarquables y ont été fabriqués récemment. Les 15 entreprises du Riverland, assez grandes à l'échelle australienne, peuvent offrir à présent une plus vaste gamme de vins à des prix extrêmement compétitifs.

Les zones de vignobles « secs », qui produisent pourtant la majeure partie des vins fins de table, s'étendent de Clare, située à plus de 100 km au nord d'Adélaïde, à Coonawarra, à 400 km au sud. La Barossa Valley, colonisée par les Allemands au milieu du siècle dernier, est la plus renommée. L'influence allemande y est toujours vive : les personnes âgées parlent le dialecte local (le Barossa Valley Deutsch) et on trouve encore des enseignes gothiques. Barossa, au nord-est d'Adélaïde, est la région d'Australie la plus riche en vignobles. On y compte 35 centres viticoles. Grandes et petites entreprises, certaines très pittoresques (comme par exemple Yalumba et Seppeltsfield, siège de plusieurs générations de Hill Smith et Seppelt) sont les curiosités de ce qui est devenu l'un des principaux comtés touristiques d'Australie.

Citons les noms de Wolf Blass, Penfold, Kaiser Stuhl, Orlando, Henschke, Krondorf, Masterson Barossa et Tollana qui obtiennent de bons résultats avec le Cabernet Sauvignon, le Shiraz ou leurs mélanges.

Les meilleurs vins blancs sont vinifiés à partir du Riesling et plus particulièrement du raisin venant des coteaux où prédominent les vignobles de Burings, Orlando et Yalumba.

La zone urbaine d'Adélaïde était, il y a peu de temps encore, très fière de ses vignobles réputés, tout proches du quartier des affaires, et qui produisaient beaucoup de vin. Mais l'expansion de la ville les a repoussés dans les plaines et les collines d'Adélaïde. Les conditions climatiques plus fraîches de ces dernières ont permis à quelques entreprises vinicoles dignes d'intérêt (comme Petaluma dont Bollinger, France, possède 20 % des parts) de produire des vins de grande qualité. Quant aux plaines d'Adélaïde, elles sont chaudes et sèches, mais les viticulteurs ont fait appel à des techniques avancées pour résoudre la plupart des problèmes. Le plus célèbre d'entre eux, Joe Grilli de Primo Estate, a su en peu de temps révéler des vins de caractère et d'une qualité exceptionnelle (en particulier un vin de style beerenauslese fabriqué à partir des raisins Riesling, botrytisés juste après les vendanges).

A seulement 45 mn d'Adélaïde commence une autre zone de production, celle de McLaren Vale au superbe complexe vinicole de Old Reynella, restauré juste après que Thomas Hardy and Sons l'ait racheté en 1982 et y ait installé son centre administratif. (Cette opération de 9 millions de dollars australiens a permis à la société familiale de retourner sur le lieu où elle fut fondée aux alentours de 1840). Les 50 centres vinicoles de McLaren Vale sont en général petits et situés sur les pentes de jolies collines où les vignes sont entourées de bosquets d'amandiers en fleurs. Les brises du Golf Saint-Vincent rafraîchissent le climat et permettent d'atteindre de hauts rendements ainsi qu'une bonne qualité. Autrefois connue pour ses Porto et ses vins rouges vigoureux destinés au commerce britannique et aux mélanges, la région s'illustre maintenant dans la production de rouges et de blancs parfumés. Les producteurs les plus célèbres sont : Hardy's, Reynella et Tintara y compris, Seaview, Pirramimma, Wirra Wirra, Woodstock, Hazelmere, Kay Brothers, d'Arenberg et Coriole. Malheureusement l'expansion d'Adélaïde menace les vignobles. Des mesures doivent être prises sans délai pour préserver leur futur.

Coonawarra, zone viticole du sud la plus fameuse du district (aux dires de certains la plus célébrée du pays), a le privilège incontesté d'être la seule région viticole d'Australie que l'on puisse délimiter géographiquement. Elle serpente et couvre toute une ceinture de « terra rossa », riche, rouge et grasse, bien définie : 14,4 km de long sur 200 m à 1,5 km de large. Une vaste nappe d'eau, sous-jacente à cette couche de calcaire, favorise l'irrigation naturelle et le drainage. Coonawarra n'a aucunement vu sa réputation faiblir lorsqu'elle a perdu ses vins les plus frais et les plus tardifs d'Australie au profit de vignobles plus récents comme Victoria's Geelong, Western Australia's Mount Barker-Frankland et l'île de Tasmanie.

Plus tard, après une nouvelle période de développement dans les années 70, au cours desquelles Coonawarra était décevante pour la qualité de ses raisins blancs, la région s'est rachetée en produisant d'excellents vins blancs et plus particulièrement un Riesling et un Sauvignon blanc. Les nouveaux plants de Chardonnay, qui produisent déjà, sont très prometteurs. Les vins sont faits, pour la plupart, à partir de Cabernet Sauvignon et ressemblent beaucoup aux Bordeaux. La plupart des gros producteurs australiens possèdent des vignobles à Coonawarra ou font appel aux raisins de cette région. De grosses sociétés comme Lindemans, Wynns, Mildara et Penfolds y sont établies. Les petits producteurs locaux tels Redman, Leconfield, Kidman, Brand's Laira et Hollick ont aussi de bons résultats à leur actif et un nombre non négligeable d'admirateurs. Les compagnies qui ne possèdent pas de vignobles à Coonawarra ou qui n'ont pu en acquérir davantage, développent les régions voisines et prometteuses de Keppoch et Padthaway qui jouissent d'un climat plus frais l'été, d'une bonne humidité et d'un drainage satisfaisant. La firme Thomas Hardy and Sons figure parmi les producteurs de bons vins à partir de ces vignobles.

Le district de Clare Valley/Watervale est peut-être le plus typique et pittoresque d'Australie. Chaud et sec, il y circule en permanence un souffle d'air. Cette région surprend par ses vins et ses créations séduisantes. Elle regroupe quelques-uns des vignobles australiens les plus anciens tels le Sevenhill Estate, exploité depuis 1848 par les Frères du Collège Jésuite de Saint-Aloysius. Ce Collège est le principal fournisseur de vins de messe aux pays du bassin Pacifique. Situés sur de petites collines calcaires, les vignobles ne sont généralement pas irrigués et produisent pour cette raison des vins épais et durables. La plupart des 16 exploitations sont petites, sauf la Stanley Wine Company, Quelltaler et Château Clare de Taylor qui produisent des vins blancs secs, aromatiques et fleuris, faits à partir de Riesling communément répandu.

L'Australie Occidentale

La région viticole se regroupe autour de Swan Valley (Vallée du Cygne) tout près de Perth. Les principaux producteurs sont le groupe Hardy et Sandalford. Bien que ces exploitations soient toujours florissantes, on pense que les vins de qualité proviendront, à l'avenir, des régions plus fraîches de l'État. La Swan Valley produit des vins rouges corsés, puissants et suaves et des blancs élégants et savoureux. On s'intéresse de plus en plus aux vins des régions de Margaret, de Frankland River dans le sud-ouest et de Mount Barker plus au sud. De petites entreprises viticoles, appartenant à des propriétaires qui ne font pas partie du monde du vin, continuent à se multiplier ; les vins, provenant de Evans and Tate, Leeuwin, Cape Mentelle (Cabernet, Hermitage, Zinfandel), Moss Wood (excellent Pinot Noir), Vasse Felix, Redmont, Forest Hill, Milyabrup, Plantagnet et beaucoup d'autres, méritent que l'on s'y attarde. Cette région pourrait devenir l'une des « nouvelles » régions viticoles du monde.

Tasmanie

L'île de Tasmanie et certaines de ses régions fraîches ont attiré des producteurs de qualité : Mo Estate, Heemskerk, Marion's et la nouvelle entreprise de Louis Roederer (France) et Piper Brook.

Queensland

La ceinture granitique de la région de Stanthorpe, plus fraîche que le reste des États viticoles, permet d'espérer la production d'un vin de qualité, et quelques Queenslanders consacrent tous leurs efforts pour y parvenir.

PRODUCTION D'UNE ANNÉE TYPE

État	*Production en hl*
Australie méridionale	2 000 000
Nouvelle-Galles du Sud	700 000
Victoria	500 000
Australie occidentale	50 000
Queensland	1 500
Total	3 251 500

Autriche

Les provinces occidentales comme Vorarlberg produisent peu de vin et en consomment la totalité. En Basse-Autriche, Burgenland, Styrie et autour de Vienne, la vigne couvre environ 58 000 ha. Les vignobles, où plus de 42 000 viticulteurs ont fait du vin pendant des générations, sont divisés en parcelles dont la plupart ne dépassent pas 20 ha. La production annuelle est d'environ 3 000 000 hl (soit 33 millions de caisses), dont 83 % de blanc et 17 % de rouge. Nombre de vignerons conservent le gros de la récolte dans leurs propres caves mais, lorsque les vendanges sont abondantes, coopératives et négociants en prennent une partie en charge. Les vignerons autrichiens s'associent aussi volontiers en coopératives auxquelles ils confient leur raisin pour vinification, conservation et vente. Leurs vins ont une bonne réputation de qualité. Les Autrichiens consomment entre 35 et 37 l par tête et par an : c'est déjà plus que l'Autriche ne produit. Ainsi, une bonne partie du vin (surtout rouge) est importée d'Espagne, d'Italie, de France, et de plus en plus de Hongrie, de Yougoslavie et des États balkaniques. Le taux d'importation annuel est actuellement d'environ 250 000 hl (près de 3 millions de caisses).

Il y a quelques années, la demande était telle que la quasi-totalité de la récolte du pays était consommée dans ses frontières. Mais la situation a changé et l'on voit maintenant des vins autrichiens à l'étranger — du Schluck, probablement fait avec du Gruener Veltliner, au liquoreux Spaetlesen et aux Auslese mis en bouteille au domaine. Le total annuel se chiffre à environ 420 000 hl (4,5 millions de caisses). Traditionnellement, le client principal est l'Allemagne, mais les ventes sur d'autres marchés — la Grande-Bretagne en particulier — sont en constante augmentation. Un institut œnologique créé en 1968 commence à réglementer les exportations tout en résolvant les anomalies et en remettant les choses en bon ordre.

En 1985, des lois très strictes, concernant les vins, furent votées pour remédier aux fraudes préalablement constatées. Sur les étiquettes figure le nom du village ou de la région d'origine et, moins souvent, celui d'un vignoble particulier. On n'y voit parfois que le seul nom de la variété de raisin, comme en Alsace. Quelquefois aussi les deux indications.

A titre d'exemple : Wachauer 1984 signifie vin des vendanges 1984 dans l'importante région vinicole de Wachau, en Basse-Autriche : Grüner Veltliner 1984, vin de l'année 1984 fait avec du raisin de la variété Grüner Veltliner ; enfin, Steiner Veltliner 1984 indique un vin de 1984 provenant de Stein, dans la région de Wachau et fait avec du raisin Grüner Veltliner.

Les meilleures bouteilles sont faites avec le Riesling et le Traminer. On trouve aussi des Spätlese (provenant des raisins cueillis tardivement). Parmi les noms qu'il est intéressant de trouver sur les étiquettes, citons : Krems, Klosterneuburg, Gumpoldskirchen, Retz, Vöslau, Nussdorf, Grinzing, Oggau et Rust. Ils figureront généralement avec la terminaison *er* du possessif.

Histoire du vin en Autriche

En l'an du Seigneur 955, Othon Ier ordonna de replanter en Autriche les vignobles abandonnés depuis l'effondrement de l'Empire romain. Ce furent les moines qui cultivèrent la vigne en Autriche, de même qu'en Bavière.

Tous les producteurs avaient le droit de vendre leurs produits *(Eigenbauwein)* hors taxes. Cette loi donne encore des soucis aujourd'hui en ce qui concerne les *Heurigen* (vins de l'année).

Quand un vigneron voulait mettre en vente son vin nouveau, il accrochait des branches devant sa maison. Le verbe allemand *aushängen* (accrocher dehors) servit à composer le nom de ces vins qui devinrent des *Hengelweine.*

Aucun ouvrage portant sur la viticulture autrichienne ne serait complet s'il ne mentionnait le docteur Lenz-Moser. L'importance de ses travaux sur les hybrides *vinifera* et surtout la méthode révolutionnaire de « haute culture » des vignes portant son nom sont maintenant reconnues dans tous les pays producteurs de vin. En Autriche, plus de 90 % des vignes sont cultivées d'après le système Lenz-Moser.

Régions vinicoles d'Autriche

Basse-Autriche

Environ 34 000 ha sont plantés en vigne dans cette province arrosée par le Danube ; c'est d'ailleurs le grenier de l'Autriche : on y cultive aussi céréales et primeurs. C'est également le pays des églises, des monastères baroques et des châteaux romantiques. C'est la seule région d'Europe où l'on voit des puits de pétrole parmi les vignobles. Les grandes régions vinicoles sont : Wachau, Kamptal-Donauland, Donauland-Carnuntum, Weinviertel et, au sud de Vienne, la région de Thermen. Les principales variétés de vins blancs sont les suivantes : Grüner Veltliner (vin local qui représente 44 % de toute la production autrichienne), Rheinriesling, Neuberger, Riesling-Sylvaner, Welsch-Riesling, Müller-Thurgau, Zierfandler (« Spätrot » rouge tardif), Muscat-Ottonel, Traminer, pour les vins rouges Blaufrankisch, Blauer Portugieser.

Le secteur *Danube (Donau)* commence à l'ouest de Willendorf avec la région de Wachau. C'est un pays ravissant qui s'étend entre Willendorf d'une part et Krems et Stein de l'autre. Les vignes en terrasses escaladent les hauteurs de gneiss et de micaschiste. Le district de Krems commence à Stein. Il appartient à la région de Wachau dont le sol de lœss (limon calcaire) est propice à la vigne. La forte déclivité des terrains exige la culture en terrasses. A Krems, ville célèbre dans l'hitoire du vin autrichien, on trouve de grandes caves pour la conservation d'importantes quantités de vin, une école de viniculture et un magnifique musée du vin. En 1964, on acheva la vendange le 10 décembre à Strass bei Krems. Outre les localités déjà mentionnées plus haut, Spitz, Dürnstein (site pittoresque au pied d'un château en ruine), Weissenkirchen et Loiben méritent aussi d'être citées. Dans les régions de Kamptal-Donauland et de Wachau, le Riesling donne un vin au beau bouquet qui est de plus en plus apprécié.

Les vignes s'étendent le long de la rive droite du Danube, depuis Oberansdorf jusqu'à Traismauer. La vallée de Kamp, sur la rive gauche du fleuve, est une importante région vinicole dont Langenlois est le centre principal. A l'est de cette vallée s'étend le district dénommé Am Wagram. Ses vignes en terrasses sur des hauteurs agrestes ressemblent beaucoup à celles de Krems. En aval, sur la rive droite, la vallée s'élargit dans le fertile Tullnerfeld, jusqu'à ce que la montagne se rapproche du fleuve à Greifenstein. Toute proche de Vienne se situe Klosterneuburg, ville d'ailleurs célèbre pour ses bons vins. On y trouve une école expérimentale de viticulture et d'immenses caves qui s'enfoncent sur trois étages successifs ; ce sont celles du Chorherrenstift.

Outre les noms déjà cités, ceux des localités suivantes méritent aussi de l'être : Zöbing, qui se distingue par son excellent Riesling, Strass et Schönberg ; dans la région de Klosterneuburg : Kahlenberg.

Au nord, sur la rive gauche du Danube, on produit du bon vin sur les coteaux de Bisamberg. En aval de Vienne, sur la rive droite, se trouve la région de Hainburg et Bruck.

Le *Weinviertel* s'étend au nord du Danube, autour de Retz et au sud des régions de Eggenburg, Hollabrunn et Ravelsbach. Il englobe aussi le secteur de Brünnerstrasse, à cheval sur la vieille route qui relie Vienne à Brünn et qui est l'un des plus productifs du pays. Dans l'ensemble, cette contrée fertile produit des vins légers et agréables ; au sud-ouest, le Veltliner donne des crus épicés et fruités et Matzen produit de bons vins rouges.

Citons parmi les principaux lieux d'origine du Weinviertel : Retz, Pulkau, Haugsdorf et Mailberg ; Eggenburg, Hollabrunn et Ravelsbach ; Poysdorf, Zistersdorf (« Steinberg »), Matzen, Wolkersdorf et Falkenstein.

La *région de Thermen*. Quelques excellents vignobles sont plantés sur les coteaux de la forêt viennoise. Gumpoldskirchen, au pied des hauteurs de Anninger, produit dans les bonnes années un vin très doux à partir de raisin cueilli tard et c'est le centre vinicole le plus connu. Baden et Traiskirchen produisent des vins ardents et épicés. Le vin rouge de Vöslau *(Vöslauer Rotwein)* est fait en partie avec du Blauer Portugieser.

Burgenland

Jusqu'en 1919, cette province du sud-est de l'Autriche appartenait à la Hongrie. De nos jours encore, bien des villages du Burgenland sont entièrement peuplés de Hongrois et de Croates. Le paysage n'est pas le même que dans les autres parties de l'Autriche. On pénètre déjà dans la *puszta* (la steppe hongroise) au milieu de laquelle se trouve le lac de Neusiedl dont les rives marécageuses sont plantées de roseaux où nichent des oiseaux qu'on ne trouve nulle part ailleurs en Europe. Riche en vergers et potagers, cette province est aussi favorable à la vigne qui couvre quelque 21 000 ha. Elle est répartie en quatre zones différentes : Neusiedlersee, Neusiedlersee-Hügelland, Mattersburg et Burgenland méridional.

Ici les variétés principales sont : Muscat-Ottonel, Pinot Blanc, Waelschriesling, Neuberger, Gruener Veltliner, Traminer, Bouvier (une vigne « indigène ») et Riesling et Muller-Thurgau — pour les vins blancs. Pour les rouges, on trouve les Blaufraenkisch (Gamay), Blauburgunder (Pinot Noir).

Le *district du Lac* est le plus important au point de vue vinicole. Ses vignobles entourent le lac de Neusiedl sur trois côtés. Ils sont protégés des vents froids du nord par les Karpathes et de ceux de l'est par les montagnes de Styrie. La surface lisse de l'immense lac retient et reflète la chaleur du soleil. On y fait d'excellents vins blancs à partir du Welschriesling et du Muscat-Ottonel ainsi que des rouges agréables avec le Blaufränkisch. A la fin des beaux étés on fera aussi du Ruster-Ausburch avec les raisins tard cueillis, notamment le Furmint. Sur le sol sablonneux du Seewinkel, les vignes ont échappé au phylloxéra. C'est une des rares régions d'Europe où l'on fait encore du vin provenant de vignes non greffées. Voici les principaux lieux d'origine du vin de cette contrée : Oggau, Mörbich, Sankt Margarethen et Rust.

Eisenstadt. Son principal centre est Gols où la vigne couvre une superficie de 900 ha. Proches du lac, les vignes plantées sur un sol sablonneux sont immunisées contre le phylloxéra et produisent les Sandweine

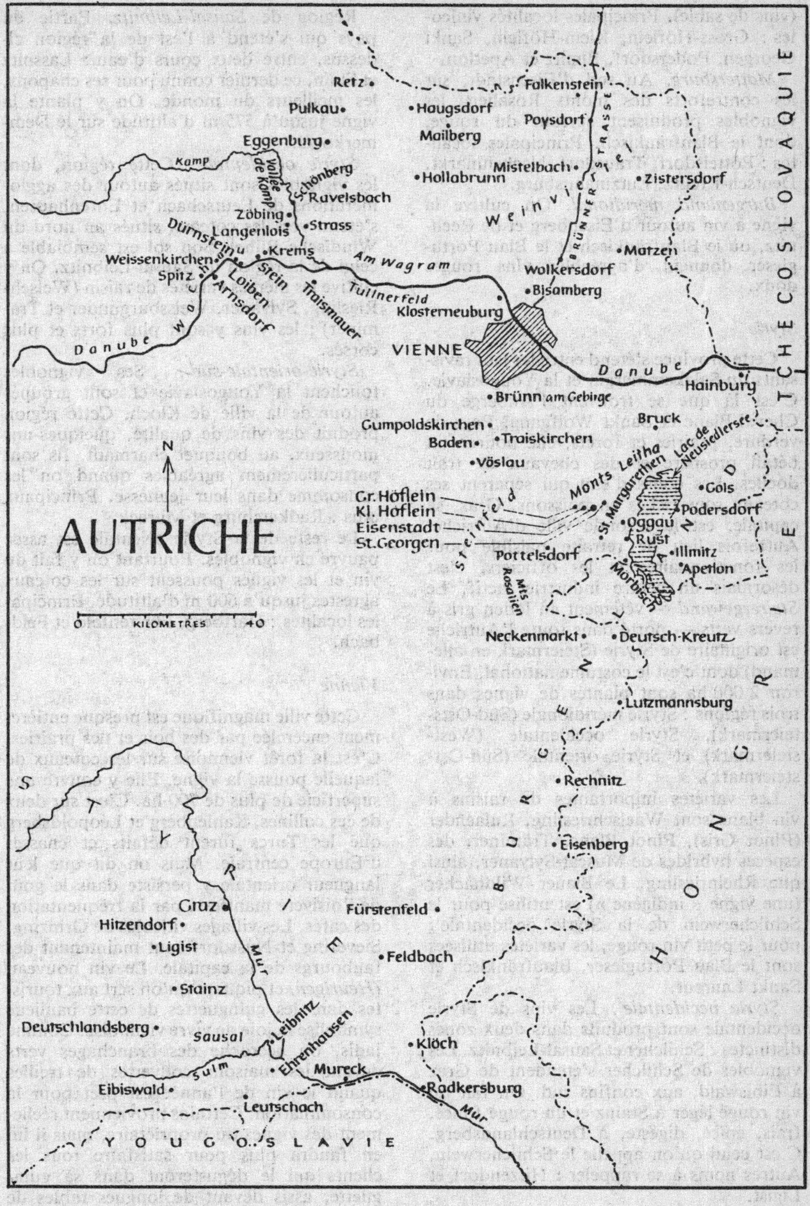
AUTRICHE
N
0 KILOMETRES 40
TCHECOSLOVAQUIE
HONGRIE
YOUGOSLAVIE
STYRIE
BURGENLAND
Retz
Pulkau
Eggenburg
Kamp
Vallée de Kamp
Schönberg
Ravelsbach
Zöbing
Strass
Langenlois
Dürnstein
Weissenkirchen
Krems
Spitz
Wachau
Loiben
Stein
Arnsdorf
Traismauer
Am Wagram
Tullnerfeld
Danube
Haugsdorf
Mailberg
Hollabrunn
Falkenstein
Poysdorf
Mistelbach
Zistersdorf
Weinviertel
Brünnerstrasse
Matzen
Wolkersdorf
Bisamberg
Klosterneuburg
VIENNE
Hainburg
Brünn am Gebirge
Gumpoldskirchen
Baden
Traiskirchen
Vöslau
Bruck
Monts Leitha
Lac de Neusiedlersee
Gols
Gr. Höflein
Kl. Höflein
Eisenstadt
St. Georgen
Steinfeld
St. Margarethen
Podersdorf
Oggau
Rust
Illmitz
Apetlon
Pottelsdorf
Mts Rosalien
Mörbisch
Neckenmarkt
Deutsch-Kreutz
Lutzmannsburg
Rechnitz
Eisenberg
Graz
Fürstenfeld
Hitzendorf
Ligist
Mur
Feldbach
Stainz
Deutschlandsberg
Sausal
Leibnitz
Ehrenhausen
Sulm
Klöch
Mureck
Eibiswald
Radkersburg
Leutschach

(vins de sable). Principales localités vinicoles : Gross-Höflein, Klein-Höflein, Sankt Georgen, Podersdorf, Illmitz et Apetlon.

Mattersburg. Au sud d'Eisenstadt, sur les contreforts des monts Rosalien, les vignobles produisent surtout du rouge, dont le Blaufränkisch. Principales localités : Pöttelsdorf, Trausdorf, Neckenmarkt, Deutsch-Kreutz, Lutzmannsburg.

Burgenland méridional. On cultive la vigne à vin autour d'Eisenberg et de Rechnitz, où le Blaufränkisch et le Blau Portugieser donnent d'agréables vins rouges doux.

Styrie

Cette province s'étend entre les lacs ravissants du Salzkammergut et la Yougoslavie. C'est là que se trouvent l'Auberge du Cheval-Blanc et Sankt Wolfgang. Pays de verdure, prairies et forêts, elle nourrit un bétail prospère et des chevaux de trait dociles. Les cours d'eau qui séparent ses coteaux sont riches en poissons. Graz, sa capitale, est la seconde ville d'Autriche. Autrefois lieu de retraite paisible pour les fonctionnaires et les officiers, c'est désormais un centre industriel actif. Le *Steirergewand* — vêtement en loden gris à revers verts — porté dans toute l'Autriche est originaire de Styrie (Steiermark en allemand) dont c'est le costume national. Environ 2 000 ha sont plantés de vignes dans trois régions : Styrie méridionale (Süd-Oststeiermark), Styrie occidentale (Weststeiermark) et Styrie orientale (Süd-Oststeiermark).

Les variétés importantes de raisins à vin blanc sont Waelschriesling, Rulaender (Pinot Gris), Pinot Blanc, Traminer, des espèces hybrides de Muscat-Sylvaner, ainsi que Rheinriesling. Le Blauer Wildbacher (une vigne « indigène ») est utilisé pour le Schilcherwein de la Styrie occidentale ; pour le petit vin rouge, les variétés utilisées sont le Blau Portugieser, Blaufränkisch et Sankt Laurent.

Styrie occidentale : Les vins de Styrie occidentale sont produits dans deux zones distinctes : Schilcher et Sausal-Leibnitz. Les vignobles de Schilcher s'étendent de Graz à Eibiswald, aux confins sud. On fait un vin rouge léger à Stainz et un rouge foncé, frais, épicé, digeste, à Deutschlandsberg. C'est celui qu'on appelle le Schilcherwein. Autres noms à se rappeler : Hitzendorf et Ligist.

Région de *Sausal-Leibnitz.* Partie du pays qui s'étend à l'est de la région ci-dessus, entre deux cours d'eau : Lassnitz et Sulm, ce dernier connu pour ses chapons, les meilleurs du monde. On y plante la vigne jusqu'à 575 m d'altitude sur le Demmerkogel.

Styrie occidentale : Cette région, dont les vignobles sont situés autour des agglomérations de Leutschach et Ehrenhausen, s'étend vers les coteaux situés au nord du Windische Bühel. Son sol est semblable à celui de la région de Sausal-Leibnitz. On y cultive les mêmes variétés de raisin (Welsch-Riesling, Sylvaner, Weissburgunder et Traminer) ; les vins y sont plus forts et plus corsés.

Styrie-orientale-sud : Ses vignobles touchent la Yougoslavie et sont groupés autour de la ville de Kloch. Cette région produit des vins de qualité, quelques-uns mousseux, au bouquet charmant. Ils sont particulièrement agréables quand on les consomme dans leur jeunesse. Principaux crus : Radkersburg et Mureck.

Le reste de la Styrie orientale est assez pauvre en vignobles. Pourtant on y fait du vin et les vignes poussent sur les coteaux agrestes jusqu'à 600 m d'altitude. Principales localités : Hartberg, Fürstenfeld et Feldbach.

Vienne

Cette ville magnifique est presque entièrement encerclée par des bois et des prairies. C'est la forêt viennoise sur les coteaux de laquelle pousse la vigne. Elle y couvre une superficie de plus de 700 ha. C'est sur deux de ces collines, Kahlenberg et Léopoldsberg que les Turcs furent défaits et chassés d'Europe centrale. Mais on dit que leur langueur orientale y persiste dans le goût de l'oisiveté manifesté par la fréquentation des cafés. Les villages viticoles de Grinzing, Sievering et Nussdorf sont maintenant des faubourgs de la capitale. Le vin nouveau *(Heurigen)* et piquant qu'on sert aux touristes dans les guinguettes de cette banlieue symbolise la joie de vivre viennoise. Comme jadis, on accroche des branchages verts devant les maisons couvertes de treilles quand le vin de l'année est prêt pour la consommation. Certains proviennent réellement des vignes du propriétaire, mais il lui en faudra plus pour satisfaire tous les clients qui le dégusteront dans sa guinguette, assis devant de longues tables de bois où ils chantent en s'accompagnant de guitares et cithares. Une nouvelle loi ne permet aux cafetiers que de vendre le vin provenant de leurs propres vignobles et il leur faut une dispense pour en acheter d'autre.

Principales variétés de raisin : Gruener Veltliner, Neuburger, et quelques vignes indigènes.

Auxey-Duresses
et Auxey-Duresses-Côte de Beaune
(Appellation Contrôlée)

Bourgogne rouge et blanc. Côte de Beaune.

Parmi les Côte de Beaune, l'Auxey fait figure de parent pauvre. Ses vins sont considérés comme agréables, sains de corps, parfum et couleur, mais peu distingués en général. Étant donné pourtant la différence de prix entre l'Auxey et les autres Côte de Beaune, en acheter est souvent un bon placement.

Quoique la liste des Premiers Crus n'ait pas encore été arrêtée, voici ceux qui sont considérés comme les meilleurs.

PREMIERS CRUS	*Superficie (ha)*
Les Duresses	10,6
Les Bas-de-Duresses	2,39
Reugne	3,16
Les Grands-Champs	4,86
Climat-du-Val (ou Clos-du-Val)	9,31
Les Écusseaux	6,43
Les Bretterins	2,02

Les vignes sont plantées à l'écart de l'agglomération, sur les collines, à une altitude un peu trop élevée pour donner des vins de première classe. Elles couvrent environ 170 ha dont une centaine a droit à l'appellation de Côte de Beaune en plus du nom de la commune et sont parfois un peu supérieurs aux autres. Auxey produit annuellement une moyenne de 1 100 hl de blanc et 3 200 hl de rouge. Les vins des meilleurs vignobles peuvent en ajouter le nom à celui de la commune.

N.B. Les vins vendus sous le nom de La Chapelle sont faits avec des raisins provenant d'une vigne autrefois distincte, désormais partagée entre Reugne et Les Bretterins.

Ava-Ava

Autre nom du Kava *(voir ce mot)*.

Avelsbach

Commune d'Allemagne située dans l'angle formé par la Moselle et la Ruhr. Ses vins sont classés tantôt dans un groupe. tantôt dans l'autre. Les crus les plus connus sont : Altenberg, Dom Avelsbach et Dom Herrenberg.

Voir RUHR ; MOSELLE

Avize

Village de Champagne, qui produit un des meilleurs Côte des Blancs.

Voir CHAMPAGNE

Ay

Agglomération proche d'Épernay, dans la vallée de la Marne. Ses caves s'étendent sous les vignobles des vignes à bon vin rouge de la région.

Voir CHAMPAGNE

B

Bacardi

1. Marque bien connue de rhum (maintenant d'origine cubaine) fait à Cuba, Porto-Rico, aux Bahamas, au Brésil et au Mexique.

2. Cocktail fait à partir du rhum.

Voir RHUM ; PORTO-RICO

Bacchus

1. Nom donné au dieu grec de la Vigne et du Vin, Dionysos, que les Romains assimilèrent à Liber, vieille divinité de l'Italie centrale qui présidait à la culture de la vigne.

2. Vigne hybride américaine. Ses raisins sont petits et noirs. Dans les meilleures conditions il produit un vin corsé et de qualité passable.

Voir DIONYSOS ; ANTIQUITÉ (VINS DE L')

Baco

Maurice Baco, botaniste français, dont les hybrides sont cultivés en France et en Amérique. Le Baco 1 est très répandu mais produit un meilleur vin dans l'État de New York qu'en France. Le Baco 22A est autorisé dans les sols sablonneux du Bas-Armagnac (France) pour faire la célèbre eau-de-vie de la région. Ses mérites sont encore discutés.

Bactérie

Organisme unicellulaire de taille microscopique sans parois cellulaires rigides ni noyau bien défini.

Bad Dürkheim

Voir DURKHEIM ; PALATINAT

Bad Kreuznach

Agglomération et région vinicole de la vallée de la Nahe *(voir ce mot).*

Badacsonyi Keknyelü

Le plus connu des vins de Badacsonyi (Hongrie). On fait dans cette région des rouges et des blancs ; le Kehnyelü est un blanc sec, légèrement teinté de vert, à boire au dessert.

Au sujet de ce type de vin et des autres Badacsonyi.

Voir HONGRIE

Bade

État allemand : Bade-Wurtemberg. Superficie : 15 000 ha environ, 77 % de vins blancs, 23 % de vins rouges.

Situation : les vignobles du pays de Bade forment une sorte de haie verte à la frontière sud-ouest de l'Allemagne. Ils commencent au bord du lac de Constance (en Allemagne : Bodensee), longent les coteaux de la Forêt-Noire, aux confins de la Suisse et de la France, puis suivent le cours du Rhin, parallèlement aux vignobles d'Alsace, jusqu'au Neckar aux alentours d'Heidelberg.

Ses vins sont les plus consommés en

Allemagne. Troisième plus grande région viticole, Bade est redevenue, de façon spectaculaire, une zone très importante ces trente dernières années et la qualité du vin s'est considérablement améliorée. Dans les années 1860, le grand-duché de Bade était le plus gros producteur de vin allemand, mais il souffrit particulièrement du phylloxéra et les superficies cultivées en vignes y diminuèrent de près de la moitié. La production locale subit ensuite une seconde catastrophe mais qui eut pour avantage une loi, celle-ci imposant l'arrachage des vignes hybrides. Et la superficie du vignoble diminua encore de 20 %. Mais la plantation de variétés telles que le Pinot Noir (Spätburgunder), le Pinot Gris (Ruländer), le Pinot Blanc (Weissburgunder), ainsi que du Müller-Thurgau, du Silvaner, du Traminer et un peu de Riesling permet d'espérer une amélioration générale des vins avec le vieillissement des ceps. Le Müller-Thurgau (un croisement de Riesling et de Silvaner) gagne rapidement du terrain dans cette région comme ailleurs.

Le pays de Bade, maintenant plus étendu que la région de la Moselle, a beaucoup profité de l'avènement des grandes coopératives. Ces organismes géants, qui contrôlent 90 % de la superficie des vignobles du pays de Bade, ont créé de nouveaux vignobles adaptés à la viticulture moderne. L'image de Bade s'est améliorée sous l'impulsion du mouvement coopératif et par l'introduction de toute une série de standards de qualité et de contrôles. L'application stricte de ces règles a permis à Bade d'obtenir la reconnaissance de son niveau de qualité exceptionnelle lors de concours nationaux. En conséquence, les prix atteignirent des niveaux comparables à ceux des vins de régions plus connues. Les caves centrales des coopératives de Bade, Zentralkellerei Badischer Winzergenossenschaften (ZBW), sont considérées comme étant les plus grandes et les plus modernes d'Europe. Cette organisation produit des vins de plus de 400 appellations chaque année. Les vins sont bien faits et typiques de leur origine et de leur variété.

Variétés de raisin : une bonne part du vin ordinaire est faite avec du raisin Müller-Thurgau et les rouges de meilleure qualité avec du Spätburgunder. Importée à l'origine de Bourgogne où on l'appelle Pinot Noir, cette variété est la plus cultivée en Allemagne pour le peu de vins rouges qu'on y peut trouver. Dans le pays de Bade, le Spätburgunder est aussi utilisé pour produire un vin rosé, le Weissherbst. Un autre vin rosé, également une spécialité locale, le Badisch, est fabriqué à partir d'un mélange de deux variétés de Bourgogne, le Spätburgunder et le Grauburgunder (Ruländer). De couleur claire, c'est malgré tout un vin au corps plein et d'une robustesse surprenante.

Le Gutedel, variété importée de Vevey, sur le lac de Genève, en 1780, donne le Mardgräfler, produit au-dessous de Fribourg, à l'angle sud-ouest de l'Allemagne. On le trouve aussi en quantité considérable en Suisse où il est connu sous le nom de Fendant et en France sous le nom de Chasselas.

Le Ruländer n'est rien d'autre que le Pinot Gris. Il doit son nom allemand au fait qu'un nommé Ruland l'importa de France. Il donne un vin doré qui peut être très riche et fruité, et dans les bonnes années assez corsé.

Le Riesling est assez important dans le pays de Bade. On en trouve sur le flanc sud du Kaiserstuhl et dans l'Ortenau, crus qui produisent les meilleurs vins de Bade.

Statistiques : Müller-Thurgau : 37 %, Spätburgunder : 22 %, Ruländer (a.k.a. Grauburgunder ou Pinot Gris) : 12 %, Gutedel (a.k.a. Fendant ou Chasselas) : 8 % et Riesling : 7 %.

Production annuelle basée sur une moyenne de dix ans : 1 200 000 hl (plus de 13 millions de caisses).

Les districts (Bereiche)

Le long vignoble en forme d'hameçon qui suit le Rhin depuis le lac de Constance jusqu'à Heidelberg comprend plusieurs subdivisions régionales ayant chacune ses propres caractéristiques de sol, de climat, et par conséquent de vins. Pour une liste complète des districts (Bereiche), sites viticoles collectifs (Grosslagen) et sites viticoles individuels (Einzellagen) (*voir* APPENDICE B).

Bereich Bodensee

Les vins de ce cru sont connus sous le nom de Seeweine, autrement dit : vins du lac. Ce nom rappelle l'influence sur les vignes du grand lac oblong. Le föhn — vent tiède qui souffle sur les régions alpestres d'Allemagne, d'Autriche et de Suisse —

doit avoir un effet encore plus marqué sur le vin de la région, en faisant mûrir rapidement les raisins. Le souffle chaud du föhn agit en effet sur les plantes, les animaux et les hommes ; on l'accuse de faire tourner le lait car il provoque la prolifération des insectes ; le Code pénal autrichien en tient compte comme circonstance atténuante dans les cas de violences.

Les meilleurs vins de Bodensee sont les Spätburgunder, Ruländer et Gewürztraminer. Chaque petit port lacustre est entouré de vignes mais presque tout le vin intéressant provient de Meersburg : le domaine — Domäne Meersburg — appartient à l'État de Bade-Wurtemberg. Aucun des vins du Bodensee n'échappe aux touristes. Les petits vapeurs du lac voguent d'un port à l'autre, tantôt un suisse, tantôt un allemand ; derrière se dressent des pics neigeux. Meersburg est un joyau médiéval serti dans la vigne ; son château, encore bien entretenu, a bon aspect malgré son âge : treize cents ans. Dans un restaurant en plein air, à la lumière des lanternes vénitiennes, au bord du lac, les vins qui arrosent la truite au bleu du lac paraissent meilleurs qu'ils ne le sont en réalité.

Bereich Markgräflerland

Ce nom dérive de *Markgraf* (margrave), titre de noblesse allemand équivalant à peu près à marquis et qui fut à l'origine celui des seigneurs gouvernant une marche (région frontalière). Le margrave Charles-Frédéric replanta des vignes en cette extrémité sud-ouest de l'Allemagne, à la fin du XVIIIe siècle, époque où prédominait le Gutedel importé de Vevey en Suisse. Il faut aussi mentionner le Müller-Thurgau et le Gewürztraminer.

Bereich Kaiserstuhl-Tuniberg

En arrivant d'Alsace, si vous traversez le Rhin sur le petit pont proche de Colmar et vous dirigez sur Fribourg-en-Brisgau, vous voyez à main gauche une éminence en forme de cône, couverte de vigne : le Kaiserstuhl. Ce plissement d'origine volcanique est composé d'un sol où l'argile se mêle à la lave. Ce terrain convient au vin rouge et donne aussi un vin blanc d'une teinte ambrée assez foncée. L'un comme l'autre sont assez corsés mûrs et vineux. Un tiers du Kaiserstuhl est planté de Müller-Thurgau, 25 % de Spätburgunder et Ruländer. Les meilleurs Ruländer prospèrent sur les coteaux sud et sud-ouest. Ils servent à fabriquer des vins au parfum concentré, relativement ardents et profonds. Il en est de même des Spätburgunder et Traminer. Les Riesling sont cultivés dans quelques crus isolés au nord et au sud du Kaiserstuhl. Parmi les villages les plus remarquables figurent Ihringen, Achkarren, Bickensohl, Oberrotweil, Schelingen, Leiselheim, Merdingen et Bahlingen.

Bereich Breisgau

Cette petite région, située juste au nord de Kaiserstuhl et de Markgräflerland, produit des vins qui sont plus légers, moins complexes mais assez plaisants. La ville de Fribourg, avec sa magnifique cathédrale (la tour est une des plus hautes constructions d'Europe) est située à l'extrême sud de la région ; au nord se trouve Lahr. Le *Weissherbst,* produit dans la vallée du Glotter près de Fribourg, est un des meilleurs vins du pays de Bade.

Bereich Ortenau

En fait de qualité, outre la région très restreinte de Kaiserstuhl, les meilleurs vins de Bade viennent de celle d'Ortenau, appelée aussi Bühler Gegend *(Bühl* désigne une localité et *Gegend* signifie région). Elle s'étend sur l'étroite zone de terre arable qui sépare le Rhin du massif montagneux et forestier, entre Offenburg, au sud, et Baden-Baden, au nord. Le sol est surtout composé de granit écrasé. Riesling et Traminer sont les blancs les meilleurs ; le Spätburgunder est le meilleur rouge. Citons parmi les villages de pointe (qui cultivent, en général, à la fois les variétés rouges et blanches) : Durbach, Ortenburg et Neuweier. Ici aussi, il est autorisé de mettre le vin en Bocksbeutel (bouteille en forme de flacon que l'on trouve traditionnellement en Franconie). Les villages suivants ont leur spécialité de vin rouge : Durbach, Sasbachwalden (Alde Gott), Kappelrodeck (Hex von Dasenstein) et Waldulm (Pfarrberg). L'Affenthaler est un vin populaire léger dont la bouteille a une forme très particulière où un singe est accroché à son côté.

Bereich Bergstrasse-Kraichgau

Cette région s'étend entre celles d'Ortenau et de Bergstrasse, juste au sud d'Heidelberg. Aujourd'hui, les vignobles sont plantés de Müller-Thurgau (50 %), Riesling, Weissburgunder et Ruländer.

Bereich Badisches Frankenland

Le plus au nord des *Bereiche* du pays de Bade, un peu isolé des principales sections viticoles. La plupart de ses vignes sont cultivées autour de Tauberbischofsheim et dans la vallée du fleuve Jagst, un affluent du Neckar.

Bagaceira

Spiritueux portugais fait à partir de peaux de raisin.

Balaton (lac)

Centre d'une des principales régions vinicoles de Hongrie.

Voir HONGRIE

Balestard-la-Tonnelle (Château)

Bordeaux rouge. Commune de Saint-Émilion.

L'un des plus vieux crus de la région, ce vignoble a été rendu célèbre par un poème de François Villon (1431-1463) qui en fait mention : *ce vin nectar/Qui porte le nom de Balestard.* La dynamique famille Capdemourlin — promotrice des plus dévouées des vins de Saint-Émilion — possède ce Grand Cru des classifications de 1955 et 1986.

Superficie : 8 ha.

Production moyenne : 40 tonneaux ; 4 000 caisses.

Balling ou Brix

Échelle hydrométrique servant à mesurer approximativement la teneur en sucre du jus de raisin, des vins doux et des solutions sucrées. L'échelle est calibrée de façon à indiquer en pourcentage le poids du sucrose lorsqu'immergée dans de telles solutions. L'hydromètre Brix est généralement calibré à 17,5 °C ou 20 °C, et le Balling à 60 °F.

Balthazar

Bouteille employée surtout en Champagne et qui convenait mieux à la présentation qu'à l'utilisation pratique. Sa contenance était équivalente à celle de 16 bouteilles normales de Champagne (12,8 l). N'est plus utilisée.

Banadry

Liqueur de banane faite par la firme Bardinet de Bordeaux.

Bandol

Appellation d'origine contrôlée de certains vins de Provence.

Voir PROVENCE

Banyuls (Appellation Contrôlée)

Vin de liqueur. Sud de la France.

Petite région vinicole avoisinant la localité de Banyuls, près de la frontière espagnole. Son vin de liqueur présente moins d'intérêt dans les pays où l'on peut acheter Xérès et Porto. Le Banyuls est un « vin doux naturel » (additionné d'alcool). On le consomme généralement en apéritif. Certains le prennent aussi avec le dessert.

Voir VINS DOUX NATURELS

Barbados Rhum

Rhum des Barbades.

Voir RHUM ; INDES OCCIDENTALES

Barbados Water

Un des premiers noms donnés au rhum. La Barbade est une île indépendante des Petites-Antilles, autrefois colonnie britannique, où l'on fit les premiers rhums.

Barbaresco

Vin rouge du Piémont. C'est l'un des meilleurs d'Italie. Solide, fort, il vieillit lentement et prend alors une saveur et une profondeur remarquables. Depuis 1981, il est autorisé à porter l'appellation *Denominazione di Origine Controllata e Garantita* (D.O.C.G.).

Voir PIÉMONT

Barbera

Raisin italien à vin rouge, cultivé surtout au Piémont *(voir ce mot).*

Barbera Amabile

Vin rouge italien doux, légèrement mousseux, fait avec du raisin Barbera très cultivé en Italie du Nord.

Bardolino (D.O.C.)

Vin rouge provenant des vignobles qui s'étendent entre Vérone et le lac de Garde, en Italie.

Voir VÉNÉTIE

Bärentrank

Littéralement : boisson d'ours. Ce breuvage est fait en Prusse orientale avec de l'alcool de pomme de terre et du miel.

Baril

Petit tonneau de capacité indéterminée.

Barolo

Vin rouge du Piémont. C'est un des meilleurs d'Italie. Robuste, lourd, à maturation lente. Son goût prononcé reste dans la bouche. Depuis 1980, il porte l'appellation *Denominazione di Origine Controllata e Garantita* (D.O.C.G).

Voir PIÉMONT

Barossa

Région vinicole proche d'Adélaïde en Australie méridionale.

Barrel

Mesure de capacité anglaise équivalant à 36 gallons britanniques (imperial gallons) soit 163,65 litres (sauf pour les vins et spiritueux). *Voir* tableau des mesures de capacité à l'APPENDICE B.

Barrica

Nom espagnol de la barrique de Bordeaux et aussi d'une certaine barrique espagnole.

Voir BARRIQUE

Barrique

Futaille spécifiquement bordelaise dont la capacité varie selon la région. La barrique contient 225 l, ce qui devrait équivaloir à 300 bouteilles de 75 cl, mais par tolérance on compte généralement 288 bouteilles ou 24 caisses de 12 bouteilles chacune. Dans le Bordelais, quatre barriques font un tonneau.

Voir TONNEAU ; APPENDICE B : tableaux.

Barriquot

Petit tonnelet sans capacité définie.

Barsac (Appellation Contrôlée)

Vin blanc doux. Région de Bordeaux.

Même dans l'esprit des connaisseurs, il règne parfois une certaine confusion entre Barsac et Sauternes : le Barsac est-il un Sauternes ou un autre cru ? En réalité on peut répondre aussi bien oui que non.

L'appellation d'origine contrôlée Barsac désigne des vins naturels, doux, blancs, produits autour de Barsac, c'est-à-dire au nord de la région délimitée des Sauternes, à quelque 40 km au sud-est de Bordeaux. Le Sauternes englobe cinq communes dont Barsac et Sauternes *(Voir à ce nom* la carte du SAUTERNAIS). Autrefois, chacune de ces localités avait sa propre appellation. Mais les communes autres que Sauternes produisaient peu. Voilà longtemps, on décida donc de les inclure sous l'appellation de Sauternes afin de disposer d'une production suffisante pour faire connaître ces vins doux sur le marché mondial. Barsac fut englobé, comme les trois autres communes, dans l'appellation Sauternes. Mais ses vins étaient déjà trop célèbres pour abandonner leur propre nom. Les autorités décidèrent par conséquent que les vins de Barsac, faits avec des raisins mûris dans la région délimitée de Sauternes et possédant toutes les caractéristiques de ce cru, auraient le droit de conserver leur nom traditionnel ou d'adopter celui de Sauternes. Dans la pratique, certains s'appellent Sauternes, d'autres Barsac, et d'autres encore portent les deux appellations qui sont aussi légitimes l'une que l'autre. La plus grande partie est livrée au commerce sous le nom de Barsac.

Sur les 13 Seconds Crus classés de Sauternes, 8 sont des Barsac. Mais on ne compte que 2 Barsac parmi les 11 Premiers Crus. Le Château-d'Yquem, unique Premier Grand Cru, classé au-dessus de tous les autres, se trouve au sud de Sauternes, c'est-à-dire à l'opposé de Barsac. Cependant Barsac peut s'enorgueillir de Château-Coutet et de Château-Climens : les deux Premiers Crus qui méritent d'être classés immédiatement après Château-d'Yquem. La plus aristocratique des cinq communes du Sauternes est Bommes, dont un tiers des vignobles sont des Premiers Crus. En général la qualité des vins est assez uniforme à Sauternes, Barsac et Preignac, dont le sol est intermédiaire entre celui des deux autres communes. Les vins du secteur sud, dont le terrain est plus pierreux et accidenté, sont un peu plus onctueux et riches en sucre. Les Barsaç tendent à être plus légers, plus fruités et à se développer plus rapidement. Les différences sont néanmoins très subtiles. Variété de raisins, méthodes de production et caractéristiques générales sont identiques. Contrairement au reste du Sauternais au sol vallonné, Barsac est en pays plat. Ses limites sont à peu près parallèles au cours du Ciron, ruisseau qui coupe le Sauternais en diagonale et se jette dans la Garonne.

Parcourir, par sécheresse, le circuit du Sauternais — succession de petites routes sinuant entre les vignobles et marquées de flèches dorées — inspire un sentiment de désolation. On ne voit que des sarments sans feuilles, pareils à des bras décharnés. Les gelées de février, certaines années, peuvent avoir à Barsac les effets les plus dévastateurs. Les pertes sont souvent moins graves pour les vignes de Sauternes plantées à flanc de coteau. Le sol de Barsac est moins pierreux, plus crayeux que celui de Sauternes, d'où la différence — d'ailleurs infime — entre les deux crus.

Crus classés de Sauternes situés en Barsac (*Classification de 1855*)	
Premiers Crus	
Château-Coutet	Château-Climens
Second Crus	
Château-Myrat	Château-Broustet
Château-Doisy-Dubroca	Château-Nairac
Château-Doisy-Daëne	Château-Caillou
Château-Doisy-Védrines	Château-Suau

Voir CHÂTEAU-CLIMENS ; CHÂTEAU-COUTET ; CHÂTEAU-CAILLOU ; SAUTERNES

Bartzch

Spiritueux produit par la fermentation d'herbes dans le nord de l'Asie. Il s'agit d'herbes n'ayant aucune autre utilité connue, de végétaux grossiers, dont les noms dans la langue du pays signifieraient : chardon à truie et fenouil à chien.

Basi

Spiritueux fait aux Phillipines à partir de canne à sucre fermentée.

Basilicate

Rouges et blancs. Sud de l'Italie. Sud de la Campanie, Nord de la Calabre.

Cette province est l'ancienne Lucanie. Le vin le plus connu de la région est l'Aglianico del Vulture (D.O.C.), d'un rouge profond, peu éclatant, tenace, chaleureux, produit par les vignes de Monte Vulture. Il est souvent très agréable. C'est sans aucun doute l'un des meilleurs vins d'Italie du Sud qui peut encore s'améliorer une fois mis en bouteille. Après avoir vieilli trois ans, dont deux en fûts, il devient *vecchio* (vieux) ; après cinq ans, *riserva* (réserve spéciale). Les vins de l'Italie méridionale ont tendance à prendre la saveur du sol volcanique, goût étrange et assez désagréable au premier contact. Le terrain du Monte Vulture n'exerce pas trop vigoureusement cette influence, c'est pourquoi son Aglianico est plus apprécié par les étrangers.

Muscat et Malvoisie abondent dans cette région vinicole comme partout en Italie. Tous deux se plaisent sous les climats chauds et se prêtent au traitement, dénommé en Italien *passito,* qui consiste à laisser les raisins sécher avant de les vinifier afin d'obtenir un vin plus fort et plus doux. Fait de manière normale ou par *passito*, le Basilicate peut être aussi bien rouge que blanc. Le premier titre jusqu'à 12°, le second jusqu'à 15°, mais aucun n'a la classe de l'Aglianico.

Basler Kirschwasser

Kirsch bâlois. Eau-de-vie de cerises suisse.
Voir KIRSCH

Bastardo

Raisin qui joue un rôle important dans la fabrication du Porto *(voir ce mot).*

Batailley (Château-)

Bordeaux rouge. Commune de Pauillac, en Haut-Médoc.

Situé à 1 500 m de la Gironde, sur une élévation de terrain, immédiatement au sud de Pauillac, ce vignoble est situé au-dessus des , Château-Pichon-Longueville et Château-Latour. Appartenant depuis 1942 à M. Marcel Borie et à son gendre, M. Casteja, — qui est aussi propriétaire du Château-Trottevieille, un des meilleurs vignobles de Saint-Émilion —, ce domaine est un des Cinquièmes Crus du Médoc d'après la classification de 1855. Le Château-Grand-Saint-Julien est un vignoble accessoire de la même propriété. Le vin jouit d'une bonne réputation.

Caractéristiques : Assez robuste, mais pas l'un des meilleurs.

Superficie : 55 ha.

Production moyenne : 270 tonneaux, 20 000 caisses.

Bâtard-Montrachet (Appellation Contrôlée)

Bourgogne blanc. Côte de Beaune. Commune : Puligny-Montrachet et une partie de Chassagne-Montrachet. Classification officielle : Grand Cru.

Voilà un des magnifiques Montrachet qui sont les plus grands blancs de Bourgogne et, par conséquent, comptent parmi les vins les plus grands du monde. Le Bâtard a presque la valeur du Chevalier-Montrachet, et n'est dépassé que par le seul grand Montrachet. La superficie plantée en vignes n'atteint pas 14,5 ha, un mur le sépare de la route derrière le village de Puligny. De Puligny, il se trouve sur la gauche, avec Bienvenue-Bâtard-Montrachet. Sur la droite de la route, que l'on atteint en passant sous une voûte de pierre, sont groupés : le Montrachet, Chevalier et Le Cailleret, autrefois nommé Les Demoiselles. Autre membre du trio Bâtard, Criots-Bâtard-Montrachet est situé à proximité ; c'est une petite vigne d'environ 1,6 ha, en totalité sur la commune de Chassagne-Montrachet. Bienvenue-Bâtard, guère plus vaste avec ses 3,6 ha, est partagé entre Puligny et Chassagne, comme Montrachet lui-même. Le rendement annuel de Bâtard-Montrachet s'élève à quelque 325 hl, bien peu de chose pour un vin aussi demandé dans le monde entier. Ne nous étonnons donc pas que ce Bâtard ait beaucoup de bâtards. Voilà pourquoi il importe tant de se renseigner sur les noms des négociants exportateurs et des vignerons qui mettent leur propre bon vin en bouteille au domaine.

Bâtard présente les mêmes caractéristiques que le grand Montrachet ; il est sec quoique rond, de grande élégance, avec un bouquet séduisant. Parfois ce vin est mieux réussi que le Montrachet lui-même.

Voir MONTRACHET ; PULIGNY-MONTRACHET

Batavia-Arrack

Arrack de Batavia (Java).
Voir ARRACK

Batzi

Eau-de-vie de pomme suisse, équivalent du Calvados français et de l'applejack américain.

Baumé

Échelle hydrométrique couramment utilisée pour mesurer la densité des moûts et des vins doux. Un degré Baumé est à peu près égal à 1,8 degré Brix.

Voir AÉROMÈTRE ; BALLING

Baux (Coteaux des)

Voir COTEAUX D'AIX, COTEAUX DES BAUX-DE-PROVENCE

Béarn (Appellation Contrôlée)

Vieille province française qui de nos jours représente la quasi-totalité du département des Basses-Pyrénées. Le vin le plus renommé de cette région est le Jurançon *(voir ce mot)*, un vin blanc doux. Ici, néanmoins, les vins ne viennent qu'en second lieu après la grande spécialité gastronomique régionale : la *sauce béarnaise* aux échalottes, au vinaigre et à l'estragon.

Beaujolais

Vin rouge. Sud de la Bourgogne.

Le Beaujolais est devenu l'un des vins rouges les plus consommés au monde. Comme une fille de la campagne à la fleur de l'âge, la fraîcheur fait son charme. C'est ainsi que le Beaujolais a séduit les capitales de tous les pays. Reste à savoir si la vertú de la belle survivra aux sollicitations d'aussi nombreux soupirants.

Avant tout le Beaujolais doit être consommé jeune. Ce n'est pas un vin à déguster mais à boire. Étant donné la manière dont on fait le Beaujolais maintenant, la fermentation varie de quatre à dix jours et les qualités du vin dépendent de la maturité atteinte par les raisins en fonction du temps durant l'été. C'est pourquoi il est léger, fruité et fleuri. Un Fleurie — quintessence du Beaujolais — est plus caractérisé qu'un cru plus réputé tel que Morgon et Moulin-à-Vent. Certains dégustateurs disent qu'ils décèlent un goût ou un arôme de pêche, d'abricot ou de rose, dans ce vin. Quoi que chacun puisse y trouver, ce seront toujours la fleur, le fruit et la fraîcheur qui lui donneront sa distinction et sa grâce. C'est la raison pour laquelle on doit le boire jeune — même si, dans une certaine mesure, on peut faire exception pour le Morgon et le Moulin-à-Vent.

Selon toute évidence un tel vin court le danger d'être ruiné par le succès. Tant le *vin bourru* qu'on vend en carafe dans les cafés de Paris que les Beaujolais de classe qui vont à l'étranger, tous risquent d'être allongés avec des vins provenant de régions à plus haut rendement.

Situé sur la rive occidentale de la Saône, le pays de Beaujolais a toujours été une étape pour ceux qui traversaient l'Est de la France sur son axe nord-sud. On y trouve en abondance des reliques de l'âge de pierre. César vainquit les tribus gauloises du Beaujolais. Son nom y subsiste ainsi que des vestiges de la civilisation gallo-romaine : murs en ruine, chapelles, surtout au nord, à proximité du Mâconnais et dans le nom de certaines localités comme Juliénas et Romanèche-Thorins. Au temps des croisades, la Saône marquait déjà la frontière orientale de la France. De cette époque date une coutume alors en usage chez ceux qui naviguaient sur la rivière. Ils ordonnaient cap au royaume quand ils voulaient que le pilote incline vers la rive du Beaujolais et cap à l'empire pour l'orienter vers l'autre rive.

Pourtant la vogue du Beaujolais est relativement récente. C'est au XVIIIe siècle qu'on commença à le charroyer jusqu'à la Loire, d'où il gagnait Paris par voie d'eau [1]. Jusqu'à ces derniers temps, le Beaujolais n'était guère consommé qu'à Lyon où on l'envoyait par la Saône. On connaît le dicton : « Lyon est arrosé par le Rhône, la Saône et le Beaujolais ». De nos jours encore, le Lyonnais commande son Beaujo-

1. Quoique connu depuis cette époque à Paris, le Beaujolais n'y est devenu vraiment très populaire que depuis une quarantaine d'années. Un correspondant parisien me suggèra une hypothèse à ce sujet : durant l'entre-deux-guerres, un journal, *Le Canard enchaîné*, exerça une forte influence sur la fraction libérale de la jeunesse française, celle qui subit les bouleversements de la Seconde Guerre mondiale, de l'Occupation et de la Libération. Or, plusieurs rédacteurs de cet hebdomadaire satirique étaient de fervents amateurs des vins du Beaujolais, particulièrement du Juliénas. En toute occasion ils en vantaient incidemment les mérites. Leurs lecteurs d'autrefois ayant atteint l'âge où l'on choisit son vin et où l'on peut le payer, il est vraisemblable que *Le Canard enchaîné* contribua à la promotion du Beaujolais.

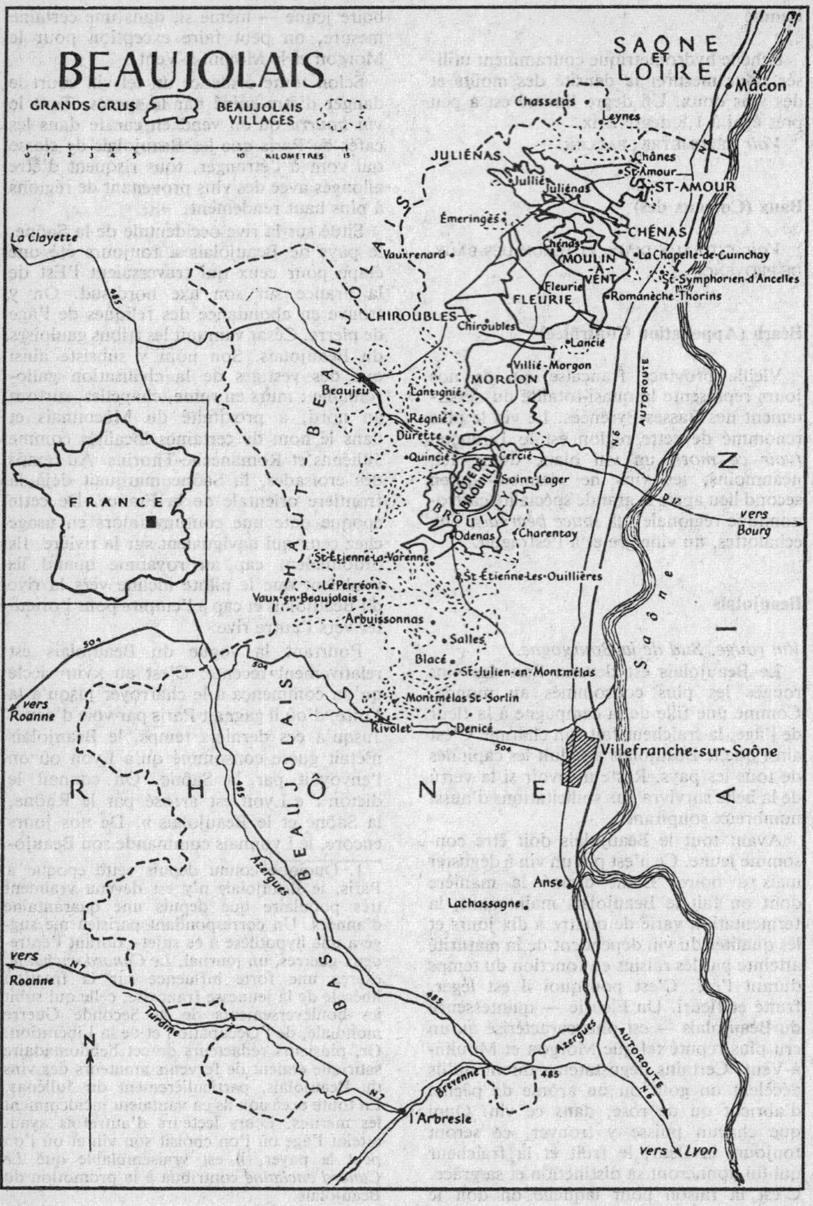
BEAUJOLAIS
GRANDS CRUS
BEAUJOLAIS VILLAGES
KILOMETRES
SAONE ET LOIRE
Mâcon
Chasselas
Leynes
JULIÉNAS
Chânes
St-Amour
Jullié
Juliénas
ST-AMOUR
Émeringes
CHÉNAS
Chénas
La Chapelle-de-Guinchay
Vauxrenard
MOULIN A VENT
St-Symphorien-d'Ancelles
Fleurie
FLEURIE
Romanèche-Thorins
La Clayette
CHIROUBLES
Chiroubles
Lancié
Villié-Morgon
MORGON
Beaujeu
Lantignié
Régnié
Durette
Quincié
Cercié
CÔTE DE BROUILLY
Saint-Lager
BROUILLY
FRANCE
Odenas
Charentay
vers Bourg
St-Étienne-la-Varenne
St-Étienne-Les-Ouillières
Le Perréon
Vaux-en-Beaujolais
Arbuissonnas
Salles
Blacé
St-Julien-en-Montmélas
Montmélas St-Sorlin
vers Roanne
Rivolet
Denicé
Villefranche-sur-Saône
R H Ô N E
HAUT BEAUJOLAIS
BAS-BEAUJOLAIS
AUTOROUTE
N6
Saône
Anse
Lachassagne
Azergues
vers Roanne
N7
Turdine
N
485
504
Brevenne
l'Arbresle
vers Lyon

lais en *pot*, pas en bouteille. Le pot contient 46 cl. On trouve encore de tels pots de grès gris ornés de dessins bleus. Ils étaient autrefois alignés sur les comptoirs et les tables des cafés de Lyon et les Lyonnais avalaient une bonne partie de la production du Beaujolais.

Le Beaujolais se trouve sur le parallèle qui sépare la France du Nord et celle du Sud. Au-dessus de cette ligne, les toits sont pointus ; au-dessous, ils sont de plus en plus plats. L'accent change et le jeu de boules devient un besoin impérieux. Tout le Beaujolais le prend au sérieux. On se groupe en clubs affiliés à des ligues et des journaux entiers ne sont consacrés qu'à ce seul sport. Il y a un terrain de boules dans le jardin de chaque café et on y trouve en général « Fanny », statuette de fille impudique que doit embrasser le perdant.

Jusqu'à ces derniers temps, le pays du Beaujolais vivait à l'écart des tourbillons de la vie moderne et, tout à coup, son vin l'a révélé au monde. Les gens du pays se transforment. Autrefois ils avaient les mœurs et les attitudes rurales communes à tous les habitants des autres régions vinicoles de France, mais voilà que le succès les rend difficiles, parce qu'on les sollicite. Le vin aussi a changé. Ce n'est plus du Bourgogne : appellation à laquelle il a droit s'il est conforme à certaines normes, notamment s'il est fait avec du Pinot ou s'il provient des neufs crus suivants du Beaujolais : Saint-Amour, Juliénas, Chénas, Moulin-à-vent, Fleurie, Chiroubles, Morgon, Brouilly et Côte de Brouilly. Mais maintenant le Beaujolais est planté de Gamay. « *Beaujolais suis* », disent volontiers les gens du pays avec autant d'orgueil que jadis les Rohan.

Un vin qui doit être bu très jeune et qui est parfois d'une faible teneur en alcool ne voyage pas bien. Ainsi, un Chiroubles ne devrait même pas se mettre en bouteille. Il faudrait le boire frais tiré du tonneau. Pourtant, on exporte ce vin vers les quatre coins du monde. Pis encore, trop de gens croient que la valeur du vin dépend de son degré. Les gens du pays en sont très affectés et ils s'indignent en entendant dire que le produit de leurs vignes est un « bon petit vin ». Alors certains essaient de le « grandir », c'est-à-dire en augmentent la teneur en alcool par un cuvage plus long qui lui fera perdre vraisemblablement sa fraîcheur. D'autres commencent à parler du « goût parisien ». Ils craignent que trop de Beaujolais se conforment à la manie des Parisiens qui préfèrent le degré d'alcool à la fraîcheur.

Depuis quelques années, la mode du Beaujolais nouveau fait fureur à l'étranger et à Paris. La préparation de la mise en bouteilles — car ce vin est expédié en bouteilles et non en tonneaux — nécessite des soutirages et des ultra-filtrages pour supprimer les dépôts et une nouvelle fermentation en bouteilles. Par ces préparatifs prématurés, c'est le cœur même du vin qui est sacrifié.

Restrictions, production, délimitation

Presque tout le Beaujolais est rouge, mais tout le vin produit par la région du Beaujolais ne l'est pas. Le Pinot-Chardonnay cultivé au nord du Beaujolais, à la limite du Mâconnais, porte l'appellation Mâcon, sauf une petite quantité dénommée Beaujolais blanc. Supérieur au Mâcon, il ressemble en moindre qualité au Pouilly-Fuissé, et provient principalement de la commune de Chaintres, haut-lieu du Pouilly-Fuissé, qui est la plus importante productrice de Beaujolais blanc avec environ 2 500 hl (plus de 25 000 caisses).

Les vins rouges des localités les plus importantes peuvent porter l'étiquette des Bourgogne car ce sont, en effet, des Bourgogne. Aujourd'hui, on a plutôt tendance à les nommer Beaujolais parce que le nom est plus populaire. Il est fait avec du Gamay qui donne un breuvage délicieux sur le sol du Beaujolais et un vin banal à quelque cinquante kilomètres au nord, dans la Côte-d'Or.

La région est divisée en deux secteurs viticoles : haut Beaujolais et bas Beaujolais (parfois appelé aussi « le Beaujolais du pays des Pierres dorées »). Le Nizerand, petit cours d'eau qui se jette dans la Saône, un peu en amont de Villefranche, sert de frontière entre ces deux secteurs ; Beaujolais au nord, jusqu'au Mâconnais, et bas Beaujolais au sud. Cette différenciation s'explique par une différence de sol. Avec le raisin Gamay, le climat équilibré entre la rigueur du nord et la douceur du sud, et la fermentation courte, les caractéristiques du sol ont une tendance marquée sur la nature du vin. Les meilleurs viennent du haut Beaujolais à sol granitique, avec forte teneur de manganèse dans le sous-sol (près de Romanèche-Thorins et de Fleurie, on trouve une ancienne mine de manganèse exploitée de la Révolution à la Première Guerre mondiale). Dans le bas Beaujolais, le sol est plus crayeux.

Le vignoble du Beaujolais commence à quelque 8 km au sud de Mâcon. Sa largeur ne dépasse guère une quinzaine de kilomètres et s'étend sur une longueur d'environ 90 km jusqu'à la banlieue lyonnaise. Les autorités l'ont soigneusement délimité. Au sud, il s'arrête à la Turdine ; à l'ouest, à une altitude d'environ 450 m, sur les pentes des monts du Lyonnais ; à l'est, à la route nationale n° 6 et à la Saône ; enfin, au nord, à la ligne de démarcation entre le Mâconnais et le Beaujolais, juste au-dessus d'un cours d'eau nommé Arlais. Hormis ce qui concerne une petite poche à Saint-Symphorien-d'Ancelles, en face de Romanèche-Thorins, le vignoble ne dépasse jamais la route nationale n° 6, pour la bonne raison qu'entre cette route et la Saône le terrain plat ne pourrait produire un vin digne du nom de Beaujolais.

Sur l'étendue ainsi circonscrite, on produit quatre catégories de vin : Beaujolais, Beaujolais-Supérieur, Beaujolais-Villages et neuf crus : Saint-Amour, Juliénas, Chénas, Moulin-à-Vent, Fleurie, Chiroubles, Morgon, Brouilly et Côte de Brouilly.

Beaujolais. Ce vin, qui peut titrer moins de 10° (9° pour le rouge et le rosé ; 9,5° pour le blanc), est produit dans les 59 communes qui n'ont pas droit à une appellation supérieure. Hormis deux bandes étroites dans le haut Beaujolais, tant du côté de la montagne que de la rivière, les vignes qui produisent ce vin sont presque toutes dans le bas Beaujolais. Presque toute la production est achetée en vrac Le rendement maximum autorisé est de 55 hl/ha avec une possibilité de 20 % de plus. Ces chiffres peuvent être modifiés chaque année selon la qualité de la récolte.

Déclassement : Les excédents vont à la distillerie.

Beaujolais-Supérieur. Les vins des mêmes communes, qui dépassent 10°, ont droit à cette appellation. Comme pour le Beaujolais simple, la production est limitée à 55 hl/ha avec des dépassements de 20 % autorisés.

Les 21 600 ha de vignobles du Beaujolais produisent environ 1 200 000 hl (13 millions de caisses) de vin par an, dont un peu plus de la moitié de Beaujolais. Les neufs crus représentent environ les deux tiers du reste, avec quelques 300 000 hl (plus de 3 millions de caisses) par an. Viennent ensuite plus de 350 000 hl (près de 4 millions de caisses) de Beaujolais-Villages et de Beaujolais-Supérieur.

On pratique deux méthodes de taille en Beaujolais : le guyot pour les vins des deux premières catégories *(voir* CHAPITRE IV) ; le gobelet, qui implique une taille courte où les sarments ne sont pas liés à des fils de fer et la vigne ne dépasse alors guère 30 cm de haut, est obligatoire pour les vins qui ont droit à l'appellation Beaujolais-Villages ou à celle des neuf crus.

Haut Beaujolais

Pour les neuf crus, le rendement ne doit pas dépasser 48 hl/ha (plus de 20 % de dépassement autorisé), sinon le vin tombe sous l'appellation simple de Beaujolais. Mais, en année exceptionnelle, les autorités permettent un certain dépassement, pourvu que la qualité soit satisfaisante. Les neuf crus forment un bloc entouré comme une île par Beaujolais-Villages. Ce secteur est le cœur du Beaujolais et c'est lui qui produit la plus grande partie du vin. Les vins qui n'appartiennent pas aux neuf crus et n'ont droit qu'à l'appellation officielle Beaujolais-Villages peuvent aussi porter sur l'étiquette le nom de leur commune avec la mention Beaujolais.

Bas Beaujolais

Les vignes qui ne bénéficient pas d'un sol granitique donnent des vins qui manquent de distinction et sont généralement plus légers, moins complets que ceux du haut Beaujolais.

Cependant, ils ressemblent un peu à ceux du Mâconnais, comme si les mêmes caractéristiques générales se retrouvaient aux deux extrémités du vrai pays de Beaujolais.

Au point de vue topographique, la région se présente comme un vaste sol, moucheté de fermes. A certains points, l'on est environné de clochers paroissiaux. Les coteaux ont une certaine déclivité, et les gens du pays aiment à la considérer comme une terre escarpée. Sans doute étaient-ils eux-mêmes plus farouches que leur décor, si nous en croyons les histoires racontées à Anse. Quand une fille tient tête aux hommes et semble difficile à amadouer, on dit qu'elle « est passée devant le four à Anse ». Toujours selon les on-dit, au temps de Napoléon, les femmes d'Anse traitaient les hommes comme des bêtes de somme et les torturaient devant le four s'ils regimbaient. Pis encore, elles auraient jeté au feu le prêtre du village qui essayait de mettre fin à ces pratiques barbares.

Beaujolais-Villages

Les communes suivantes ont droit à l'appellation contrôlée Beaujolais-Villages ou peuvent joindre leur nom à celui de Beaujolais :

1° Leynes, Pruzilly, Chânes et Saint-Vérand qui produisent du Beaujolais-Villages, bien sûr, mais aussi le célèbre Saint-Véran.

2° les communes suivantes, qui produisent surtout du rouge :
Communes du département de Saône-et-Loire : Leynes, Saint-Amour-Bellevue, Pruzilly, La Chapelle-de-Guinchay, Romanèche, Thorins, Chânes, Saint-Vérand, Saint-Symphorien-d'Ancelles.
Communes du département du Rhône : Juliénas, Jullié, Émeringes, Chénas, Fleurie, Chiroubles, Lancié, Villié-Morgon, Lantigné, Beaujeu, Cercié, Régnié-Durette, Quincié, Saint-Lager, Odenas, Charentay, Saint-Étienne-la-Varenne, Vaux, Le Perréon, Saint-Étienne-des-Ouillères, Blacé, Salles-Arbuissonas, Saint-Julien, Montmelas, Rivolé, Denicé, Les Ardillats, Marchampt, Vauxrenard.

Avant la fusion de Régnié avec Durette et de Salles avec Arbuissonas, ils étaient 31.

Crus

(classés en allant du plus corsé au plus léger)

Moulin-à-Vent (Appellation Contrôlée)

Réputé roi du Beaujolais, ce vin est considéré comme le premier parmi les crus nobles, à l'exception peut-être du Fleurie. Il doit son caractère à sa puissance et sa rondeur. Ce monarque du Beaujolais peut vieillir jusqu'à cinq ou sept ans en conservant une partie de son charme. Certaines années il est recommandé de ne pas le déguster avant deux ans.

Le moulin qui a donné son nom au vignoble et au vin est un cône de pierre qui se dresse, isolé comme un phare, depuis trois cents ans sur une mer de vignes. La route Paris-Côte d'Azur qui passe à 1 500 m de là, en direction de la Saône, a un aspect beaucoup plus moderne. Les enseignes au néon s'allument et s'éteignent en bordure de la chaussée et quelques-unes proclament : Moulin-à-Vent. Pourtant nulle part ailleurs on ne peut mieux apprécier le vrai Moulin-à-Vent.

Chénas est une appellation contrôlée, mais la plus grande partie du territoire de cette commune (environ 240 ha de vigne) est englobée dans le secteur qui a droit à l'appellation Moulin-à-Vent. Les vins de Chénas sont donc vendus sous le nom le plus célèbre des deux. De même, les 3/4 de la commune de Romanèche-Thorins (environ 650 ha) produisent du Moulin-à-Vent. Les vins de Thorins et de Moulin-à-Vent, fameux depuis longtemps, ont souvent été assimilés en raison de leurs qualités similaires et sont désormais tous étiquetés Moulin-à-Vent. Les vignes poussent sur un sol peu profond de granit en décomposition. Les racines des vignes plongent dans le rocher et continuent à le disloquer. La forte teneur en manganèse du sous-sol contribue certainement à donner de la race au vin.

A partir des 650 ha de l'Appellation Moulin-à-Vent, plus de 30 000 hl sont produits (300 000 caisses).

Juliénas (Appellation Contrôlée)

Ce vin conserve parfois assez longtemps l'agréable fruité de sa jeunesse. Avec le Morgon, c'est le plus durable du Beaujolais.

La production des 570 ha s'élève à quelque 30 000 hl (plus de 300 000 caisses). Château-Juliénas est le meilleur cru. Bessay et Château-Les-Capitans sont aussi des noms bien connus.

Morgon (Appellation Contrôlée)

C'est le plus dur des Beaujolais. Plus corsé aussi, il diffère des autres en ce sens qu'il n'est pas aussi délicieux en sa jeunesse mais s'améliore avec un peu d'âge. Un « vrai Morgon » n'est pas mis en bouteille moins de sept ou neuf mois après les vendanges et doit y rester au moins un an. Les Morgon les plus lourds ont des caractéristiques à cheval sur celles des Beaujolais les plus typiques et des Bourgogne. La zone ayant droit au nom de Morgon couvre environ 1 000 ha et c'est la plus vaste des neuf crus et produit quelque 55 000 hl (620 000 caisses) annuellement. Mais il n'existe pas vraiment de Morgon typique parce que le sol varie énormément sur cette surface. Le secteur nommé « vrai Morgon » et celui de Villié-Morgon produisent un vin généralement plus léger. Tout le Villié-Morgon ne s'appelle pas Morgon ; une certaine partie n'est que du Beaujolais-Villages. La meilleure de toutes les parcelles se trouve à flanc d'une colline nommée Côte de Py, au sol brunâtre de schiste décomposé. C'est ce « sol pourri », comme l'appellent les vignerons, qui donne le goût de terroir souvent présent dans le Morgon. Robuste, généralement gras, ces vins sont les seuls Beaujolais qui récompensent ceux qui les conservent. Toutefois la tendance actuelle dans le Morgon est aux vins légers. Leur « légèreté » ou leur « lourdeur » varieront d'année en année : en 1985 par exemple, les vins furent plus durs et plus vivaces que de coutume ; ils font pourtant exception à la nouvelle tendance.

Chénas (Appellation Contrôlée)

La plus grande partie de Chénas est englobée dans l'appellation Moulin-à-Vent. Une petite tranche de la commune dépasse pourtant cette localité en direction du nord et son vin est vendu sous le nom de Chénas. La production est minime [12 000 hl (130 000 caisses)] et les vins ne sont pas tout à fait aussi bons que le Moulin-à-Vent. Cependant, par leurs caractéristiques, ils s'en rapprochent souvent et ils pourraient vraisemblablement être un excellent placement.

Fleurie (Appellation Contrôlée)

Si Moulin-à-Vent est le roi du Beaujolais, Fleurie en est la reine. Si l'on adopte comme critère les caractéristiques typiques du Beaujolais, Fleurie est le plus fin. Avant qu'on n'eût strictement délimité les appellations d'origine — entre les deux guerres — presque tout le vin de Fleurie était vendu comme Moulin-à-Vent, dont le territoire est d'ailleurs contigu. Il en résulte que le nom de Fleurie n'était pas, jusqu'à récemment, aussi connu que celui de Moulin-à-Vent. Ce cru est le seul des grands Beaujolais qui se trouve entièrement dans une commune, celle de Fleurie, dont tous les vins n'ont d'ailleurs pas droit à cette appellation d'origine. Quelques vignes de l'ouest et du sud de la commune produisent du vin vendu comme Beaujolais, sans plus.

La caractéristique de ce vin, c'est son extrême fruité. Quoique ce soit un des Beaujolais les plus charpentés, il l'est moins que le Moulin-à-Vent et, de manière différente, que Morgon et Chénas.

Les quelque 830 ha de vignes produisent environ 40 000 hl (plus de 50 000 caisses) par an, dont 1/4 est vinifié à la cave coopérative dirigée à merveille par le successeur de Mme Chabert. Les meilleurs vignobles sont : Clos de la Roilette ; Grand Cour ; La Madone ; Les Moriers ; Augarant. On compte quelques 400 propriétaires de vignes à Fleurie.

Saint-Amour (Appellation Contrôlée)

Ce cru, le plus septentrional du Beaujolais, est presque contigu à celui de Pouilly-Fuissé, dans le Mâconnais. Sur près de 300 ha, il s'y produit du vin blanc vendu comme Mâcon blanc ou Beaujolais blanc, et assez similaire au Pouilly-Fuissé, et du vin rouge vendu comme Saint-Amour : l'un des plus fermement corsés du Beaujolais.

Blanc et rouge sont également fruités, et il faut les boire jeunes.

Les vignes poussent sur un sol de granit et d'ardoise couvert de cailloux dont certains sont aussi gros que des œufs. La plupart des coteaux sont orientés à l'est et au sud-est sur la hauteur de Bessay qui borde Juliénas et sur une plus petite colline nommée l'Église.

La production annuelle est de 13 000 hl (145 000 caisses).

Côte de Brouilly (Appellation Contrôlée)

Le territoire de ce cru est au milieu de celui de Brouilly. Ses quelque 300 ha de vigne donnent un vin plus caractéristique et plus corsé que celui de Brouilly. Il dure aussi plus longtemps. La production annuelle est de 17 000 hl (190 000 caisses).

Le mont de Brouilly se trouve exactement au milieu et à mi-hauteur d'une éminence au sommet de laquelle se dresse Notre-Dame-du-Raisin, entourée de broussailles. Ce monument date d'une centaine d'années. Des pénitents le construisirent dans l'espoir d'exorciser les vignes ravagées par l'oïdium. Le 8 septembre de chaque année, avant les vendanges, on s'y rendait en pèlerinage. Les amis du vin gravissaient la hauteur par un chemin sinueux, ce qui leur donnait soif. Au sommet on demandait, au cours d'une cérémonie religieuse, la protection du Seigneur pour la vendange à venir. Puis le Beaujolais de Côte de Brouilly était le bienvenu pour désaltérer les assoiffés sous le soleil de septembre.

Aujourd'hui, une association « Les Amis de Brouilly » organise une fête champêtre avec casse-croûte et Beaujolais. Les vignerons de Brouilly offrent, ce jour-là, le pain, le vin et le sel. C'est devenu une fête païenne !

Brouilly (Appellation Contrôlée)

C'est le cru le plus méridional. Il donne un vin fin. Ses vignes couvrent quelque 1 250 ha sur les communes de Saint-Léger, Cercié, Audenas, Charentay, Quincié et produisent près de 70 000 hl de vin par an (près de 800 000 caisses). Le centre, qui est la meilleure partie de Brouilly, a droit à une appellation distincte : Côte de Brouilly.

On fait du Brouilly dans les vastes caves du château de La Chaize construit par un neveu du père La Chaize, confesseur de Louis XIV. Le joli château Thiven se trouve exclusivement consacré au vin.

Chiroubles (Appellation Contrôlée)

Le vin de ce cru est habituellement aussi élégant que le Fleurie et moins dur que le Morgon, dont les vignobles sont contigus à celui de Chiroubles sur ses limites ouest.

Voilà un vin qui doit être consommé très jeune et l'idéal serait de ne pas le mettre en bouteille mais de le boire frais tiré du tonneau. Jusqu'à ces derniers temps, c'était le moins connu, mais il est en train de devenir le préféré des Français parmi les Beaujolais légers à maturation rapide.

En réalité, il titre un degré assez élevé d'alcool, mais on ne le sent pas au goût car il est velouté, léger, extrêmement fruité. Bu jeune, sa fraîcheur en fait un Beaujolais typique. On peut le consommer deux mois après la vendange et, en général, c'est précisément ce qu'il faudrait faire. La production du Chiroubles sur quelque 350 ha s'élève à environ 18 000 hl (200 000 caisses).

La statue qui convient le mieux à une ville vinicole de France se dresse au milieu de la place du village de Chiroubles, en face de l'église. Ce n'est pas celle de Napoléon, ni de Jeanne d'Arc, mais celle de l'estimable M. Pulliat, celui qui planta la première vigne greffée dans le Beaujolais, pendant la crise du phylloxéra. Les meilleurs vins de cette région proviennent du Domaine de Raousset et du vigneron Marcel Dufoux.

Beaujolais-Villages (Appellation Contrôlée)

Nom donné aux vins de 36 communes ou agglomérations du pays de Beaujolais. Après les neuf grands crus tels que Fleurie, Moulin-à-Vent, Morgon, etc., les Beaujolais-Villages sont les meilleurs des vins rouges agréables et frais qui connaissent actuellement une vogue furieuse en France et qui, partout ailleurs, deviennent populaires.

Voir BEAUJOLAIS

Beaulieu-sur-Layon

Commune de France dont le vin a droit à une appellation contrôlée. Elle est située dans les coteaux du Layon, en Anjou.

Voir ANJOU ; COTEAUX DU LAYON

Beaumes-de-Venise

On produit ce vin doux naturel et du vin de liqueur fait à partir de raisin de Muscat dans la commune de Beaumes, au sud de Gigondas et à l'est de Châteauneuf-du-Pape (Vaucluse). La bonne vinification de ce vin laisse penser qu'il sera très populaire aux États-Unis et plus tard dans d'autres pays. On y fabrique aussi des vins rouges et rosés.

Voir VINS VINÉS DE FRANCE

Beaune (Appellation Contrôlée)

Bourgogne rouge et blanc. Secteur : Côte de Beaune

La vieille ville qui porte ce nom est la plus importante de la région qui a droit à l'appellation Côte de Beaune. Ce n'est pas sans raison qu'on l'appelle la capitale des vins de Bourgogne. La longue histoire de cette ville est émaillée d'orages et de terreurs car bien des seigneurs, poussés par l'ambition, s'y disputèrent la suprématie. Ses murs ont été bâtis, rasés, puis rebâtis. Ses châteaux forts connurent le même sort. On trouve plus d'histoires, d'intrigues et de violence dans ses archives que dans celles des producteurs de films à Hollywood. Les malheurs de Beaune s'expliquent par sa position stratégique entre les deux anciennes places fortes d'Autun et de Besançon. Ses vignes aussi en faisaient un objet de convoitise. Signe des temps, les bureaux et les caves de la Maison Bouchard Père et Fils se trouvent dans le seul château fort médiéval qui subsiste à Beaune. Ce sont les dernières tours des remparts de Beaune qui servent au stockage du vin.

La vie changea au XVIIe siècle quand les citoyens de Beaune reforgèrent leurs sabres pour en faire des couteaux à tailler la vigne et tournèrent leur attention vers le vin. C'est depuis cette époque que Beaune est indiscutablement le centre des vins de Bourgogne et qu'elle jouit d'une réputation de prospérité et d'activité. Son énergie, son esprit d'entreprise assurent la prospérité non seulement du secteur Côte de Beaune, mais de tout le département de la Côte-d'Or. Les caves s'étendent sous les rues tortueuses et sous les maisons ornées d'enseignes ou de panneaux publicitaires. Restaurateurs et négociants en vins appâtent le touriste et l'acheteur éventuel pour l'attirer dans leurs entrepôts. Peu de temps après la dernière guerre mondiale l'étranger qui arrivait à Beaune trouvait facilement l'adresse de ces firmes, encore risquait-t-il fort de se tromper car les raisons sociales prêtaient à confusion. L'annuaire du téléphone indiquait une vingtaine de noms pour un seul numéro. Des négociants d'occasion, prompts à disparaître le cas échéant, adoptaient des raisons sociales ressemblant tellement à celles des négociants les plus réputés qu'ils étaient à deux doigts des poursuites judiciaires. Il ne manquait pas à Beaune de commerçants prêts à vous vendre n'importe quel vin, en n'importe quelle quantité, même supérieure à celle de la production. Pourtant, malgré tout cela, il régnait et il règne toujours à Beaune un amour sincère du vin de Bourgogne, la conviction qu'aucun autre au monde ne pourrait rivaliser avec lui, et un enthousiasme qu'on ne trouve nulle part ailleurs.

Rues étroites et tortueuses, tapage des gros camions qui transportent du vin, bourdonnement des conversations au sujet des millésimes, dégustation et prix, ce n'est pas tout ce qu'on trouve à Beaune. Hors de la ville, mais encore dans les limites de la commune, la superficie plantée en belles vignes est plus étendue que dans n'importe quelle autre agglomération de Côte-d'Or, quoique Pommard et Meursault produisent en général plus de vin par an. Les vins de ces vignes — rouges et blancs — sont vendus sous le nom de Beaune, parfois suivi de celui d'un certain vignoble. Parfois aussi leur étiquette ne porte que l'indication Côte de Beaune, ce qui signifie simplement qu'ils proviennent d'une vigne quelconque autorisée à utiliser le nom de Beaune (et de quelques autres aussi). Quand on les mélange avec du vin de certaines communes définies du coteau, ils peuvent aussi être vendus sous l'appellation Côte de Beaune-Villages.

Les plus remarquables vignobles de Beaune aujourd'hui sont pratiquement les mêmes que ceux qui furent classés au premier rang lors de la classification officielle des vins de Côte-d'Or, en 1860. En ce temps-là, on comptait huit Têtes de Cuvée et sept d'entre elles continuent à être considérées comme exceptionnelles. En 1936, les autorités firent figurer les huit anciennes Têtes de Cuvée dans la liste des 34 Premiers Crus : vignes de qualité supérieure dont les vins ont droit de porter à la fois le nom de la commune et celui du vignoble. Le meilleur cru est en général considéré comme celui des Grèves et particulièrement la fraction de cette vigne nommée l'Enfant-Jésus. Ce nom lui aurait été conféré jadis par des moines et dérive de l'expression suivante : « Ça vous glisse dans la gorge aussi facilement que le petit Jésus en culotte de velours ». Étant donné que les moines n'avaient pas l'impression de manquer de révérence, nul ne s'en offusque non plus en Bourgogne. Grèves est un des vins les plus épanouis et les plus suaves de Bourgogne. Le Clos des Mouches mérite d'être noté pour son caractère corsé (considérable pour un Beaune) et pour son élégance. Les Fèves vient légèrement après ; c'est une des plus petites vignes ; sa production est donc bien moindre ; ses vins sont remarquables par leur finesse et leur délicatesse ainsi que pour leur arôme prononcé. Beaune-Bressandes — à ne pas confondre avec Corton-Bressandes dans la commune voisine d'Aloxe-Corton — Les Marconnets, Champimonts, Les Cras, jouissent aussi d'une haute réputation ; leurs vins sont légers mais fermes, avec un bouquet caractérisé. Finesse, délicatesse, bouquet expressif et souvent remarquable, tels sont les caractéristiques dans lesquelles excellent les vins de Beaune.

Jadis on considérait que les Beaune atteignaient leur plénitude immédiatement après la vendange. Au XVIIe siècle, on buvait généralement le vin frais tiré du tonneau au lieu de le mettre en bouteille et on le vinifiait de manière à obtenir un breuvage très léger à maturation rapide et à consommer immédiatement. Ils sont encore assez légers, et assez prompts à vieillir, mais on les consomme beaucoup moins rapidement qu'autrefois. Deux années au moins de bouteille ne leur font aucun mal, bien au contraire. Quelques-uns des meilleurs se conserveront plus longtemps, mais ce sont des exceptions à la règle ; cinq années dans du verre leur suffiront généralement. Au-delà, ils sont tendance à faner.

La vente du vin aux enchères aux Hospices de Beaune est un grand événement annuel. Cet établissement charitable fonctionne depuis le XVe siècle et tire une part de ses revenus de la vente des vins provenant de vignes données à l'hospice par des Bourguignons philanthropes. La vente a toujours lieu le troisième dimanche de novembre. Elle attire des nuées d'acheteurs, surtout de France et de Belgique. Les prix atteints par les vins des Hospices de Beaune donnent la tendance des cours pour tous ceux de la Côte-d'Or dans le même millésime. Les Hospices possèdent des vignes sur tout le territoire de la Côte de Beaune ; ils vinifient leur propre vin et distillent aussi un marc de Bourgogne vendu en même temps que le vin *(voir* aussi HOSPICES DE BEAUNE).

Sur le territoire de la commune, 537 ha sont plantés en vignes dont le vin est du Beaune et 8,9 ha qui donnent du vin étiqueté Côte de Beaune (appellation plus générale à laquelle ont d'ailleurs droit les précédents). En années moyennes, Beaune produit quelque 8 700 hl de rouges et 200 hl de blancs. Les blancs sont rarement de la même classe que les rouges, mais il en est de délicats, parfumés, et souvent excellents. Le Beaune est surtout vendu en France mais les Pays-Bas en importent de grandes quantités, tant en raison de la proximité géographique que des liens historiques datant du temps de la Grande Bourgogne et aussi de la présence en Hollande de descendants des huguenots qui s'y réfugièrent au XVIIe siècle. L'Angleterre, la Suisse et les États-Unis en achètent également.

PREMIERS CRUS	*Superficie (ha)*
Les Marconnets	8,81
Les Fèves	4,29
Les Bressandes	21,80
Les Grèves	31,77
Les Clos des Mouches	24,85
Clos du Roi (en partie)	8,44
Sur-les-Grèves	4,57
Aux ou Les Cras	4,88
Le Clos de la Mousse	3,40
Les Teurons	21,52
Champimonts (ou Champ-Pimont)	16,59
Aux Coucherias (en partie)	9,27
En l'Orme	2,06
En Genêt	4,88
Les Perrières	3,24
A l'Écu	5,00
Les Cent-Vignes	23,31
Les Toussaints	6,88
Les Chouacheux	4,88
Les Boucherottes	8,66
Les Vignes Franches	10,15
Les Aigrots	22,00
Pertuisots	5,53
Tiélandry	1,78
Les Sizies	8,24
Les Avaux	13,75
Les Reversées	5,20
Le Bas des Teurons	7,24
Les Seurey	1,25
La Mignotte	2,35
Les Montrevenots (en partie)	9,07
Les Blanches Fleurs (en partie)	1,16
Les Épenottes (en partie)	13,63

Voir CÔTE DE BEAUNE

Beauregard (Château-)

Bordeaux rouge. Commune de Pomerol.

La propriété des Clauzel est exposée au sud du plateau de Pomerol et fait l'un des vins les plus sains de la région.

Superficie : 13 ha.

Production moyenne : 50 tonneaux.

Beau-Séjour-Bécot (Château-)

Bordeaux rouge. Commune et secteur de Saint-Émilion.

Ex-propriété du docteur Jean Fagouët, le Château appartient maintenant à M. Bécot avec le château La Carte. Le vignoble fut légitimement classé Premier Grand Cru dans le classement de Saint-Émilion jusqu'en 1986, année où il fut malheureusement déclassé en Grand Cru pour des raisons mal perçues. Ce vin mérite son classement antérieur.

Caractéristiques : Bon vin au fin bouquet.

Superficie : 16 ha.

Production moyenne : 85 tonneaux, 6 500 caisses.

Beauséjour-Duffau-Lagarosse (Château-)

Bordeaux rouge. Commune et secteur de Saint-Émilion.

Situés sur une petite colline, hors des murs de Saint-Émilion, d'où la vue s'étend sur les sinuosités paresseuses de la Dordogne, les deux Beauséjour ne formaient qu'un seul domaine jusqu'en 1869. Cette année-là, ce domaine fut divisé entre deux branches de la famille Ducarpe. Par son mariage, Mlle Ducarpe était devenue Mme Duffau-Lagarrosse. C'est elle et sa descendance qui héritèrent du château originel et de la partie du vignoble qui l'entoure immédiatement. Beauséjour-Duffau-Lagarrosse et Beau-Séjour-Bécot qui sont contigus furent tous deux classés parmi les Premiers Grands Crus de Saint-Émilion lors de la classification officielle de 1955. Il faut veiller à ne pas les confondre car sur leurs caisses les mots : Château-Beau-Séjour étaient souvent imprimés en plus gros caractères que le nom du propriétaire.

Caractéristique : Les vignes sont bien placées, entre Canon et Fourtet. Elles produisent de bons Saint-Émilion.

Superficie : 6 ha.

Production moyenne : 25 tonneaux, 2 000 caisses.

Beerenauslese

Mot allemand désignant la sélection des grains un à un sur la grappe et aussi les vins faits avec ces raisins.

Voir ALLEMAGNE

Beeswing

Nom que l'on donne en anglais à la croûte légère et mince qui se forme à la surface d'un vieux Porto en bouteille. Cette pellicule évoque l'aile *(wing)* transparente d'une abeille *(bee)*.

Bélair (Château-)

Bordeaux rouge. Commune et secteur de Saint-Émilion.

Le vignoble, orienté plein sud, appartient depuis 1974, à Mme Jean Dubois-Challon, veuve de feu M. Dubois-Challon, et copropriétaire du Château-Ausone avoisinant.

Jadis (jusqu'en 1974) les vins de Château-Bélair vieillissaient dans les caves de Château-Ausone. Bien des gens estiment qu'il n'y a pas lieu de faire de distinction entre les deux crus. D'autres, au contraire, conviennent que Bélair ressemble à Ausone, bien que moins fin et moins généreux la plupart des années.

Les origines romaines du vignoble ne sont pas absolument certaines ; mais, à coup sûr, il existait au XIVe siècle et appartenait même au gouverneur anglais de la Guyenne : Robert Knolles. Jusqu'en 1916, le domaine appartint à la famille des Cannolle — descendant vraisemblablement des Knolles. Lors des classifications de 1955 et 1986 des vins de Saint-Émilion, Bélair fut classé parmi les Premiers Grands Crus.

Caractéristiques : Un vin subtil et très agréable.

Superficie : 13 ha.

Production moyenne : 50 tonneaux, 4 000 caisses.

Belair-Marquis d'Aligre (Château-)

Bordeaux rouge. Commune de Soussans-Margaux, en Haut-Médoc.

Un des meilleurs vins de la petite commune de Soussans, dont la production a droit à l'appellation Margaux. C'est un Cru Exceptionnel d'après la classification de 1855. Nombre de ses vignes touchent celles du Château-Margaux. Le sol du vignoble est graveleux et le sous-sol caillouteux.

Superficie : 17 ha.

Production moyenne : 40 tonneaux.

Belgrave (Château-)

Bordeaux rouge. Commune de Saint-Laurent, en Haut-Médoc (Saint-Laurent n'est pas une appellation contrôlée et le vin de ce château est du Haut-Médoc).

Classé Cinquième Cru en 1855 et contigu au territoire de Saint-Julien, le domaine a changé plusieurs fois de nom dans le passé. Celui d'aujourd'hui, Belgrave, qu'il partage avec quelques autres vignobles du Bordelais, aurait été inspiré par le nom de Belgrave Square, à Londres. Il ne faut pas confondre son vin avec celui qui porte le nom de « Château-Bellegrave », de moindre qualité.

Caractéristiques : Depuis le fermage de Dourthe-Kresmann la qualité s'est considérablement améliorée.

Superficie : 55 ha.

Production moyenne : 260 tonneaux, 26 000 caisses.

Bellegarde

Commune de la grande plaine du Languedoc, où sont plantées des vignes de la variété Clairette, qui donne un petit vin blanc.

Voir CLAIRETTE DE BELLEGARDE

Bellet

Localité proche de Nice et appellation d'origine contrôlée. C'est un des meilleurs secteurs viticoles du Sud-Est.

Voir PROVENCE

Bench Grafting

Expression anglaise désignant le greffage sur table.

Voir CHAPITRE IV

Bénédictine D.O.M.

Liqueur célèbre et très populaire qui aurait été élaborée pour la première fois en 1510 au monastère des bénédictins de Fécamp par Dom Bernardo Vincelli, pour fortifier et rendre vigueur aux moines fatigués. On dit qu'elle aurait plu à François Ier lorsqu'en 1534 il passa dans la région et y goûta. Au cours de la Révolution française, le monastère fut détruit, l'ordre des bénédictins dispersé et la fabrication de la Bénédictine interrompue. Quelque 70 ans plus tard ou à peu près, la recette tomba entre les mains de M. Alexandre Legrand qui fonda l'entreprise séculière à laquelle on doit la liqueur actuelle. Cette firme n'a plus aucun rapport avec les bénédictins ni avec aucun ordre religieux quelconque, quoique chaque bouteille porte encore la formule ecclésiastique D.O.M. qui signifie *Deo optimo maximo.* Les tentatives de contrefaçon furent nombreuses et toutes échouèrent.

Cette liqueur d'un jaune verdâtre est faite d'eau-de-vie et de nombreuses herbes, plantes, racines, zestes, pelures, écorces. On dit qu'à n'importe quel moment trois personnes seulement et jamais plus en connaissent la recette exacte. Ces temps derniers, les directeurs de la firme constatèrent que de nombreux consommateurs commandaient leur Bénédictine panachée d'une quantité égale d'eau-de-vie de vin, afin de la boire moins douce. Ils ont donc lancé sur le marché une Bénédictine à leur marque portant la mention « B et B » (Bénédictine et Brandy).

Benicarlo

Vin rouge musclé produit dans la région de Castellon de la Plana, province de Valence, Espagne.

Bénin (Vin du)

Vin de palme ou sève de palme fermentée, fait et consommé au Niger.

Bentonite

Espèce d'argile du Wyoming découverte à Fort Benton, dans cet État. C'est un excellent agent de collage pour les vins blancs. Il leur permet de résister à la précipitation des protéides et au trouble dû à la présence accidentelle de cuivre. Son usage est autorisé par la loi.

Ce silicate hydraté d'aluminium, composé surtout de montmorillonite, gonfle dans l'eau et forme une pâte gélatineuse. Après cette dilution, on verse cette pâte dans le vin qu'il faut alors agiter vivement. La dose la plus satisfaisante s'élève ordinairement à environ 100 g de bentonite délayés dans deux litres d'eau au moins, par hectolitre de vin.

Voir CHAPITRE V : CLARIFICATION

Bercy

Quartier de Paris longeant la Seine, connu sous le nom de Quai de Bercy. C'est le centre de distribution de la plupart des vins de table de la capitale.

Bereich

Mot allemand signifiant « secteur ». Se réfère particulièrement à l'une des subdivisions des onze principales régions vinicoles allemandes.

Bergerac (Appellation Contrôlée)

Rouges et blancs. Sud-Ouest de la France.

Bergerac est situé à quelque 100 km de Bordeaux, les vins des deux régions se ressemblent. On y cultive les mêmes vignes et les méthodes viticoles sont les mêmes. On est donc tenté d'établir une comparaison entre les produits de ces deux régions, ce qui est flatteur pour Bergerac. Quelques vins de Bergerac, comme le Domaine de la Jaubertie, se sont considérablement améliorés.

Par elle-même, la ville est paisible, banale et même maussade. Elle ne vaudrait pas la peine d'être visitée si l'on ne tenait pas compte des châteaux forts qui protégeaient jadis la large et belle vallée de la Dordogne, en amont de Bergerac. Pendant la guerre de Cent Ans, on livra maintes batailles sur ces collines. Ceux qui y passent actuellement imaginent aisément les chevaliers jaillissant des fortifications en grand arroi de guerre.

Les vignes sont plantées au flanc des collines qui entourent la ville. Leur sol va du gravier sablonneux à l'argile quartzeux pour finir en argile crayeuse contenant des traces de fer. Les raisins appartiennent aux mêmes variétés que ceux de Bordeaux : Cabernet Sauvignon et, en moindre quantité, Cabernet Franc, et surtout le Merlot pour les rouges ; Sémillon, Sauvignon, Muscadelle, Ondenc et Chenin Blanc pour les blancs.

Pour les vins rouges n'ayant droit qu'à l'appellation d'origine la plus générale — Bergerac — les vignes Fer et Périgord sont autorisées. La région vinicole de Bergerac comporte d'autres appellations d'origine, à savoir :

Monbazillac (Appellation Contrôlée). Le plus important de la région. Appelé parfois « Sauternes du pauvre », il aura, en bonnes années, la plénitude et la richesse sucrée du Sauternes, mais il lui manque en général la finesse. Depuis quelques années, le Monbazillac accuse une baisse de qualité, car les vignerons ont abandonné les méthodes traditionnelles de récolte sélective. Il provient des vignes cultivées dans les communes de Monbazillac, Pomport, Rouffignac, Colombier et une partie de Saint-Laurent-des-Vignes.

Les vignobles s'étendent sur la rive sud de la Dordogne, face au nord. Voilà une exception à la règle générale selon laquelle l'orientation sud est la meilleure pour les vignes. Sol d'argile crayeuse avec de-ci, de-là, des veines de roches friables également calcaires. On laisse les raisins sur les vignes jusqu'à la fin de l'automne, comme dans le Sauternais, afin que la pourriture noble les attaque et élimine une bonne partie de leur eau. Les vignobles couvrent une superficie de quelque 2 500 ha qui produisent un peu plus de 40 000 hl (440 000 caisses).

Pécharmant (Appellation Contrôlée). C'est le meilleur des Bergerac rouges. Léger, il ressemble quelque peu aux Saint-Émilion mineurs (la subdivision vinicole du Bordelais la plus proche de Bergerac). On fait ce vin dans quatre communes qui sont situées au nord et à l'est de Bergerac. Les coteaux les plus proches de la ville sont considérés comme les meilleurs. Les 220 ha produisent rarement plus de 10 000 hl (environ 110 000 caisses).

Rosette (Appellation Contrôlée). Nom donné à des vins blancs demi-doux et rarement distingués, provenant de six communes dont trois ont droit au nom de Pécharmant pour le vin rouge. La production est de 800 hl (9 000 caisses) pour les très bonnes années.

Montravel (Appellation Contrôlée). Comprend Haut-Montravel et Côtes de Montravel. 15 communes situées en aval de Bergerac le produisent.

Les vignes sont plantées sur la rive nord du fleuve. Comme le Rosette, ces vins sont demi-doux. Montravel produit environ 18 000 hl (200 000 caisses) par an, pendant que Haut-Montravel et Côtes de Montravel produisent l'un et l'autre, à peu près, 6 000 hl (65 000 caisses) dans l'année.

Bergerac et Côtes de Bergerac (Appellation Contrôlée). Production : environ 250 000 hl (2,5 millions de caisses) par an, dont 2/3 de blanc. Ces appellations sont les plus générales de la région et les vins qui les portent seront moins bons que ceux qui ont droit à un nom plus précis.

Bergheim

Magnifique et très vieux village vinicole d'Alsace.

Voir ALSACE

Bergstrasse (Hessische Bergstrasse)

État allemand de Hesse. Superficie : 390 ha environ. 98 % de vins blancs, 2 % de vins rouges.

Cette région viticole, la plus petite d'Allemagne, est située le long de l'ancienne « Strata montana » (route de montagne) entre Darmstadt et Heidelberg. Elle est bordée par le Rhin à l'ouest et la forêt d'Oden à l'est. La Bergstrasse s'étend au sud de Heidelberg, mais cette section viticole appartient à l'État allemand de Bade-Wurtemberg (Bereich Badische Bergstrasse de Bade). Le district nord, près de Darmstadt, est celui de Umstadt, petite région plantée principalement en Müller-Thurgau. Le Bereich Starkenburg est le cœur de la région et regroupe les villes de Bensheim et Heppenheim. Le Riesling y est prédominant.

Variétés de raisin : Riesling (53 %), Müller-Thurgau (19 %), Ruländer ou Pinot Gris (8 %), Silvaner (8 %).

Vins : Ils sont vigoureux, riches et rafraîchissants grâce à un goût acide prononcé. On les a souvent comparés aux petits vins du Rheingau bien qu'ils aient plus de corps.

La majorité des vignobles sont plantés sur des coteaux abrupts (d'où un travail intensif) exposés au sud ou au sud-ouest. Le sol est composé de limons, de granite et de grès coloré décomposé autour de Heppenheim. Le climat est doux, en fait les arbres fruitiers fleurissent plus tôt que dans les autres districts d'Allemagne.

Les 740 producteurs de la région sont pour la plupart des viticulteurs à mi-temps ou des amateurs (et membres de coopératives) possédant moins de 50 ares de vignobles. En moyenne 75 % des vins produits dans le district de Starkenburg sont fabriqués par les coopératives régionales de Bergstrasse à Heppenheim. L'autre grande coopérative de la région est à Gross-Umstadt. Bensheim est réputé pour son vignoble, ainsi son prestigieux Domaine Viticole d'État. Les autres producteurs sont : Josef Mohr et Tobias Georg Seitz à Bensheim et Heinrich Freiberger et Hans Strauch à Heppenheim.

Hessisiche Bergstrasse est une petite région très agréable et hospitalière. La majorité du vin est consommée sur place — bonne raison pour assister à l'un des festivals du vin dans la ville de Heppenheim (en juin) et à Bensheim (en septembre).

Voir APPENDICE B

Bernkasteler Doctor (ou Doktor)

Parmi les grands vignobles les plus réputés de Moselle, le site de Doktor est celui qui produit le meilleur Riesling. Cette variété est cultivée sur un sol schisteux et jouit d'un micro-climat très favorable. En vieillissant, l'équilibre entre une maturité riche et une acidité fruitée des vins de Doctor assure à ses très bons blancs allemands leur haute réputation.

Les vins de Doktor sont cependant controversés. Leur qualité est-elle égale à leur réputation (et aux prix très élevés) ? Se mettra-t-on enfin d'accord sur la taille et la propriété de ce vignoble ?

Voir MOSELLE-SARRE-RUWER

Beychevelle (Château-)

Bordeaux rouges. Commune de Saint-Julien, en Médoc.

Le château, long, bas, avec une grande aile, est peut-être le plus important et le plus beau du Médoc. Il fut construit en 1757 dans le style où nous le trouvons actuellement, sur le site d'une ancienne forteresse féodale. Un énorme belvédère, d'au moins 50 mètres de long, domine des pelouses de gazon descendant vers la Gironde, sur quelque 800 mètres : perspective qui rappelle Versailles à plus petite échelle.

En 1984, les deux tiers des actions de ce Quatrième Cru (classification de 1855) détenues par la famille Achille-Fould furent vendues à une caisse de retraite. En 1986, après la mort brutale de son mari Aymar, député du Médoc et ancien secrétaire d'État, Mme Achille-Fould en prit la présidence, assistée de M. Foureau, le régisseur. En 1987, elle vendit ses parts, laissant la caisse de retraite seule propriétaire.

M. Achille-Fould raconta comment Beychevelle était entré dans le patrimoine de sa famille : son grand-père alla aux États-Unis et y épousa une Américaine. Plus tard, alors qu'ils parcouraient la France en touristes, ils passèrent par Beychevelle et il fut heureux d'entendre sa femme lui confier : « Voilà où je voudrais vivre ». Après quoi, il acheta le château.

Le nom de Beychevelle date du temps où le duc d'Epernon, grand amiral du royaume de France, était le seigneur du lieu. Pour lui rendre hommage, les navigateurs abaissaient leurs voiles en passant devant son château : *beyche velle* signifie en gascon baisse voile. Un autre souvenir du grand amiral subsiste : le deuxième vin est livré au commerce sous l'étiquette : Clos de l'Amiral.

Beychevelle est très connu en Angleterre et aux États-Unis.

Caractéristiques : Grande finesse : certains millésimes ont été des plus réussis.

Superficie : 70 ha.

Production moyenne : 280 tonneaux, 26 000 caisses.

Bhang (Bang)

Un « vin » fait en Inde par infusion dans l'eau de feuilles et pousses de chanvre (chanvre indien, évidemment).

Bianchello del Metauro (D.O.C.)

Vin blanc italien des Marches *(voir ce nom).*

Bianco

En italien : blanc. Ce mot désigne les vins blancs.

Bienvenue-Bâtard-Montrachet (A.O.C.)

Bourgogne blanc. Secteur : Côte de Beaune. Commune : Puligny-Montrachet et une partie de Chassagne-Montrachet. Classement officiel : Grand Cru.

Un des mémorables Montrachet qui sont les plus grands Bourgogne blancs. Le vignoble ne couvrant qu'environ 3,64 ha est contigu à celui de Bâtard-Montrachet. Les deux vins sont analogues par le caractère et la qualité. C'est seulement depuis les années cinquante qu'on distingue les Bienvenue des Criots et Bâtard. Autrefois, les vins de ces trois vignes étaient vendus sous le nom de Bâtard. Production moyenne : 125 hl.

Voir BÂTARD-MONTRACHET, et également PULIGNY-MONTRACHET

Bière

Les origines de la bière sont presque aussi lointaines que celles du vin ; tous les peuples en ont fait à toutes les phases de leur civilisation. Les tribus africaines en font avec du millet ; les Japonais avec du riz ; les habitants des Amériques, les Européens, les Australiens et bien d'autres font leur bière avec de l'orge. On en boit dans le monde entier, surtout en Belgique où la consommation annuelle s'élève à 135 l par tête et par an.

Bière est le nom général de toutes les espèces de bières blondes ou brunes, légères ou fortes, vendues à la pression, en bouteille ou en boîte de métal, faites avec du malt, du sucre, du houblon, de l'eau et du levain qui fait fermenter ces ingrédients. La qualité du breuvage dépend largement de ces matières premières et de leur aptitude à donner la bière souhaitée.

Le malt commence sa vie sous le nom d'orge. Des variétés spéciales de cette céréale sont cultivées soigneusement jusqu'à maturité. Ensuite on imbibe l'orge d'eau et on la laisse germer dans des conditions déterminées et surveillées afin que l'amidon se transforme en sucre soluble. Cela fait, on la sèche et on la fait griller ; légèrement pour obtenir une bière blonde, et plus intensément pour une bière brune.

Les sucres utilisés pour le brassage sont des sucres de canne, traités de diverses manières pour donner des goûts divers et une bière plus ou moins douce.

On cultive des variétés spéciales de houblon pour la brasserie qui n'utilise que la fleur : un cône de pétales d'or contenant résine et huiles. C'est le houblon qui donne à la bière sa pointe d'amertume.

L'eau de brasserie est en général traitée avec des sels minéraux convenant au type particulier de bière à fabriquer. Au temps où l'on n'analysait pas encore l'eau, les grands centres de brasserie apparurent là où une source ou un ruisseau convenaient particulièrement à certains types de bière. La bière de Pilsen, en Tchécoslovaquie, notamment, est brassée à l'eau naturelle et on la reconnaît comme l'une des meilleures du monde.

La levure, qui est composée d'organismes vivants, est l'agent qui fait fermenter la bière.

Le brassage n'est pas une opération très compliquée. Le malt est écrasé dans un moulin et versé dans l'eau à une température surveillée attentivement. La solution de sucre est soutirée. Des tambours rotatifs agitent le mélange pour que chaque grain baigne dans l'eau et que tout le malt soit utilisé. Il ne reste plus que les pellicules qui sont vendues, comprimées, pour l'alimentation du bétail. Le malt non encore fermenté qui s'appelle alors *wort (voir ce mot et* WHISKY) est pompé dans des bouilloires de cuivre où on lui ajoute houblon et sucre. On fait bouillir le wort pendant une heure ou deux. C'est à ce moment que le parfum et l'amertume du houblon se combinent à la douceur et au goût du malt et du sucre. Après ébullition, le houblon est retiré par filtrage. On rafraîchit le mélange, on le transfère dans un autre récipient et on y verse le levain qui agit sur le sucre, comme dans la fermentation du vin : transformation en alcool d'une part et gaz carbonique de l'autre. On conserve le gaz et l'on s'en sert pour rendre plus gazeuses les bières vendues en bouteille ou en boîte.

La fermentation prend plusieurs jours au bout desquels la masse de levure tombe au fond de la cuve de fermentation et s'y stabilise s'il s'agit de bière dite « lager ». S'il s'agit de blonde claire, nommée « ale », le levain, au contraire, s'accumule à la surface du liquide. Dans les deux cas, on le recueille. Il y en a alors beaucoup plus qu'à l'origine ; pendant la fermentation, en effet, les levures prolifèrent. La masse recueillie à la fin servira à provoquer d'autres fermentations et pourra être vendue aussi pour le traitement des humains et des animaux, car c'est un dépuratif et une source de vitamines.

Dans la plupart des pays où l'on consomme de la bière, le breuvage est conservé dans de grands réservoirs à une température proche de zéro degré, pour le stabiliser et lui assurer des qualités satisfaisantes et durables. Après filtrage, on le gazéifie au gaz carbonique et on l'expédie en barils, bouteilles ou boîtes. Désormais la plupart des bières sont pasteurisées (chauffées à 60 °C) pour détruire les plus infimes vestiges de levure qui pourraient subsister après filtrage. Ils pourraient, en effet, fermenter, se multiplier et troubler la couleur de la bière.

La bière vendue à la pression est désormais presque toujours livrée en barils de métal. C'est le mode de distribution le plus populaire dans les pays où l'on boit de la bière. Tous les récipients sont lavés et stérilisés avant d'être emplis. Les bouteilles et boîtes de métal sont remplies, étiquetées marquées, puis rassemblées en caisses par des machines capables de traiter plus de 600 bouteilles à la minute.

La qualité de la bière varie considérablement selon la brasserie qui la produit, l'habileté et le savoir-faire du brasseur. Une des plus fameuses est la Tuborg, produite à Copenhague et connue dans le monde entier. D'autres localités sont devenues célèbres grâce à leur bière : Pilsen en Tchécoslovaquie, Carlsberg au Danemark, Heineken en Hollande. Enfin, la Münchener vient de Munich. L'Angleterre et l'Irlande sont renommées pour leurs bières fortes, blondes ou brunes. Japon, Mexique, États-Unis, Australie, Cuba et Canada en produisent aussi d'excellentes.

Voici les principaux types de bière :

Lager

Bière fortement chargée de gaz carbonique. Son nom vient du verbe allemand *lagern :* emmagasiner. La Lager est une bière laissée au repos jusqu'à ce que tous les vestiges de fermentation soient éliminés. Ensuite on la gazéfie et on la met en bouteille. Sauf si l'étiquette indique le contraire, les bières américaines sont des Lager (mais ce terme est rarement utilisé aux États-Unis).

Ale

Espèce de bière qui, autrefois, était faite sans houblon et bue fraîche. Désormais il n'y a plus guère de différence, en Grande-Bretagne, entre l'Ale et les autres bières. Aux États-Unis, on la fait généralement fermenter à une température plus élevée que les autres et on utilise d'autres espèces de levure.

Stout

Bière brune et lourde, souvent un peu sucrée, avec un goût prononcé de malt, en général issue d'un mélange à forte proportion de houblon. Les Stout de Grande-Bretagne et d'Irlande sont célèbres, particulièrement les marques Guinness et Oyster Stout.

Porter

Semblable au Stout, mais moins forte, avec, en général, une lourde mousse crémeuse. Elle devrait son nom au fait que ce fut jadis le breuvage préféré des porteurs londoniens.

Bock

1. Bière lourde faite au printemps aux États-Unis avec, dit-on, les sédiments prélevés dans les cuves de fermentation, lors de leur rinçage annuel. La saison de la bière Bock ne dure en général qu'environ six semaines.

2. En France, le mot « bock » désigne un verre contenant 12,5 cl de bière vendue à la pression.

Bin

Mot anglais désignant l'endroit où l'on conserve les bouteilles de vin : une cave, une pièce quelconque d'appartement ou bien un buffet. Quand le commerçant vend le vin « in bin » (ou « ex bin ») cela signifie que le client doit payer l'emballage et la livraison.

Binger Rochusberg

Remarquable vin allemand du Rhin, originaire de Bingen. Le sol qui est composé de quartz et d'ardoise contribue à lui donner son caractère.

Voir RHEINHESSEN

Bitter

Breuvage spiritueux de degré alcoolique variable, parfumé avec des racines, des écorces et des herbes. La seule caractéristique commune de tous les Bitters est l'amertume et leurs prétentions thérapeutiques. A l'origine, c'étaient des élixirs et quelques-uns conservent ce nom. On les prend en apéritif ou en digestif ou bien on s'en sert pour préparer des cocktails. Voici quelques-uns des plus connus : Amer Picon (France), Angostura (Trinidad, mer des Caraïbes), Boonekamp's (Hollande), Campari (Italie), Fernet Branca (Italie) *(Voir chacun de ces noms),* Abbot's Aged Bitters (É.-U.), Law's Peach Bitters (Angleterre), Orange Bitters (Angleterre), Pommeranzen (Hollande et Allemagne), Secrestat (France), Unicum (Hongrie).

Black rot

Pourriture noire. Maladie de la vigne, originaire d'Amérique.

Voir CHAPITRE IV

Black Velvet

Velours noir. Mélange de Stout et de Champagne apprécié en Angleterre à l'époque édouardienne et encore consommé de nos jours, d'habitude pour arroser des huîtres.

Blagny (Appellation Contrôlée)

Seule appellation d'origine contrôlée de Bourgogne qui ne soit pas un nom de commune. Blagny n'est qu'un hameau à cheval sur les territoires de Meursault et de Puligny-Montrachet, en Côte de Beaune. A tout point de vue, son vin est semblable au Meursault. L'appellation Meursault-Blagny désigne les vins des meilleures vignes de Blagny contiguës à celles d'appellation Meursault. Les autres sont étiquetés Blagny ou Blagny-Côte de Beaune.

Voir MEURSAULT

Blanc de Blancs

Champagne fait uniquement avec du Chardonnay Blanc. Sa couleur claire permet de le distinguer aisément des Champagne dorés faits avec des raisins rouges. L'appellation Blanc de Blancs se répand un peu partout en France pour désigner les vins blancs faits avec des raisins blancs dans des régions autres que la Champagne.

Voir CHAMPAGNE

Blanc Fumé de Pouilly (Appellation Contrôlée)

Vin blanc sec de la vallée de la Loire, généralement appelé Pouilly-Fumé.

Voir POUILLY-SUR-LOIRE

Blanc de Noirs

Vin blanc fait avec des raisins rouges.

Voir CHAMPAGNE

Blanco

Chez les Espagnols, ce mot désigne aussi le vin blanc.

Blanquette de Limoux et Vin de Blanquette (Appellation Contrôlée)

Vin mousseux ou non. Sud-Ouest de la France.

La petite agglomération de Limoux, proche de Carcassonne, produit deux types de vin à partir des mêmes raisins. Le mousseux s'appelle Blanquette de Limoux ou Limoux Nature, et l'autre Vin de Blanquette. Tous deux doivent être faits avec au moins 70 % de Mauzac, 20 % de Chardonnay et pas plus de 10 % de Clairette Blanche, dans une région délimitée englobant 42 communes dont Blanquette est le centre.

Le mousseux, Blanquette de Limoux, s'est acquis une renommée. Il titre au moins 10° et il est traité comme le Champagne, par fermentation secondaire en bouteille. Récemment, grâce aux soins d'œnologues avertis, ce mousseux s'est beaucoup amélioré.

La petite quantité de vin qui n'est pas champagnisée doit aussi titrer 10° et il est en général légèrement pétillant. La région de Limoux produit en moyenne près de 50 000 hl de ces deux vins par an sur plus de 2 000 ha de vigne.

Voir LANGUEDOC

Blauer Portugieser

Vigne à vin rouge cultivée surtout dans la région de Vöslau, en Autriche et dans plusieurs régions d'Allemagne.

Blaufränkisch

Vigne à vin rouge, cultivée en Autriche, en Hongrie et ailleurs.

Blaye, Côtes de Blaye, Premières Côtes de Blaye (Appellation Contrôlée)

Rouges et blancs. Bordeaux.

Vins blancs et rouges, sans grande distinction produits dans la vieille et vaste région vinicole de la Gironde. Ces trois appellations contrôlées s'appliquent aux vins de la même origine : les environs de Blaye. Elles indiquent une gradation de qualité. Le Blaye et le Côtes de Blaye sont des vins blancs sans grande distinction ; pour avoir droit à cette dernière appellation, il doit correspondre à des normes légèrement plus sévères. Parmi les Premières Côtes de Blaye on compte 15 % de blanc et 85 % de rouge ; seules certaines bouteilles ayant droit à cette appellation méritent considération ; selon la norme, ces vins doivent être faits avec des variétés nobles, quoique pour les rouges on autorise jusqu'à 10 % de Prolongeau, Cahors et Béquignol.

Les vins blancs sont secs. S'ils sont étiquetés doux, ils seront demi-doux. Les rouges sont plus légers que ceux de l'appellation contiguë : Bourg. Si on les compare par dégustation, par exemple à la Maison du vin de Blaye-Bourg, on les trouvera moins distingués quoique plus moelleux et plus souples.

Séparé du Médoc par la Gironde, le site de Blaye a un aspect romanesque avec ses collines arrondies coiffées d'une immense forteresse en forme d'étoile bâtie d'abord aux XIe et XIIe siècles et reconstruite par Vauban, sous Louis XIV. Cet ouvrage est à peu près en ruine actuellement. Des postes de garde, au toit en forme de dé à coudre, situés aux angles des murailles, la vue s'étend sur la Gironde jusqu'à Pauillac, sur l'autre rive. Dans l'estuaire même on voit trois grandes îles plantées de vigne.

C'est également à proximité du site de Blaye qu'on pêchait, en Gironde, l'esturgeon pour ses œufs ; le seul véritable caviar produit ailleurs qu'en Iran, Russie ou Roumanie.

Bleichert

Mot allemand désignant le vin rosé.

Blending

En anglais : mélange.

Voir COUPAGE

Blush wine

En Californie, un rosé pâle très populaire provenant des cépages rouges comme le Pinot Noir et surtout le Zinfandel.

Bõa Vista

Une des meilleures Quintas du Haut-Douro, au Portugal, appartenant depuis bien des années à la famille Forrester.

Boal, Bual

Type de Madère corsé, doux, riche en couleur et d'un bouquet extraordinaire.

Boca (D.O.C.)

Vin rouge du Piémont *(voir ce nom)*.

Bock

Voir BIÈRE BOCK

Bocksbeutel, Boxbeutel

Bouteille plate en forme de flasque, utilisée en Franconie (Allemagne) et Styrie (Autriche) et à peu près nulle part ailleurs sauf à Undurraga (Chili) où l'on s'en sert pour le Riesling. Enfin, certains vins australiens et des rosés portugais sont commercialisés en flacon de ce genre. Quoique nombre de vins de Franconie soient vendus dans des Bocksbeutel en Allemagne, c'est surtout le Steinwein d'or vert qu'on trouve à l'étranger dans ces bouteilles.

On explique l'origine de ce flacon de diverses manières. Selon toute évidence, il ressemble à la gourde de cuir. On cite aussi certain fourre-tout suranné cher aux Allemandes qui suivent les modes anciennes, enfin certain organe du bouc présente à peu près la même forme. En tout cas, on utilise ces flasques depuis longtemps et il est même possible de préciser que, dès 1728, on s'en servit pour les vins du Burgespital de Wurzbourg.

Voir FRANCONIE

Bocoy

Fût de noyer utilisé pour l'expédition des vins espagnols. Il contient généralement 650 à 700 l. Il existe une media bocoy ou demi-bocoy qui contient en général 350 l. Ces contenances sont les mêmes que celles des Halbstück (demi-pièce) et Viertelstück (quart de pièce) allemands.

Bodega

En Espagne, lieu où l'on conserve le vin et qui n'est pas une cave mais un chai bâti au-dessus de la surface du sol. Dans le langage familier ce mot désigne aussi le marchand de vins et l'entreprise vinicole.

En Angleterre et ailleurs : un café où l'on vend du vin.

Bois ordinaires

Voir COGNAC

Bolivie

La Bolivie n'est pas le plus important pays producteur de vin d'Amérique du Sud. La superficie plantée en vigne à vin est de 1 600 ha, à laquelle s'ajoutent le même nombre d'hectares de vigne à raisin de table. La production de vin est négligeable : 20 000 hl (environ 200 000 caisses) par an environ, ce qui ne permet évidemment pas d'exporter. Les importations sont aussi négligeables. La Bolivie produit à peu près autant d'eau-de-vie que de vin. Comme au Pérou et au Chili, l'eau-de-vie, en Bolivie, est généralement du Pisco *(voir ce nom).*

Bombom Crema

Liqueur au goût de miel, faite à Cuba.

Bonarda

Raisin utilisé pour faire des vins rouge foncé, principalement autour d'Asti en Italie. Ces vins sont parfois mousseux.

Voir PIÉMONT

Bonde

Bouchon de fût. Il peut être fait en bois, en poterie, en verre ou en caoutchouc. Ceux de ces deux derniers types sont en général utilisés pour obturer les fûts de vin nouveau dans lesquels peut se produire une fermentation secondaire. Certains comportent une soupape qui permet au gaz carbonique de s'échapper. Durant la seconde année de maturation, le vin soutiré est conservé dans des fûts clos plus hermétiquement avec des bondes en bois souvent entourées de tissu ou bien avec une bonde dénommée bonde bordelaise de sûreté. Le fût est alors tourné de telle sorte que le vin mouille la bonde.

Voir CHAPITRE V

Bonded Spirits, ou Wines

Spiritueux ou vins entreposés sous le contrôle des douanes ou du fisc jusqu'à ce que les droits soient payés par l'acheteur. Aux États-Unis, cette pratique régit un certain système d'appellation : le whisky doit rester entreposé ainsi pendant quatre ans au moins pour pouvoir s'appeler « Bonded Rye » (whisky de seigle) ou « Bonded Bourbon » (whisky de maïs). Jusqu'en 1958, il n'était permis de laisser mûrir les whiskys de cette manière que pendant huit ans au bout desquels le fisc exigeait le paiement de la taxe de régie intérieure.

Bonnes Mares (Appellation Contrôlée)

Bourgogne rouge. Côte de Nuits. Communes de Chambolle-Musigny et Morey-Saint-Denis. Classement officiel : Grand Cru.

L'origine du nom est obscure, mais nul ne suggère sérieusement qu'il ait un rapport quelconque avec des eaux stagnantes, bonnes ou mauvaises. La superficie de ce cru est étendue par rapport aux normes de Bourgogne : 15,55 ha, dont 1,8 ha à Morey-Saint-Denis et le reste à Chambolle. Il est contigu au Clos de Tart, de Morey, et longe la route tortueuse conduisant au sommet de la colline. Normalement le nom des deux communes sur lesquelles il se trouve ne figure pas sur les étiquettes. Bonnes Mares est un Grand Cru. Or il n'y en a que 31 en Bourgogne sur des centaines de vignobles classés. Son nom suffit donc à lui tout seul sur les étiquettes qui doivent porter également le millésime, le nom du propriétaire dont les vignes ont servi à faire le vin, ou de l'expéditeur et son adresse, voire les deux. Toute autre mention est superflue.

Comme la plupart des crus de Bourgogne, Bonnes Mares est divisé entre maints propriétaires (l'auteur de ce livre fut l'un d'eux) qui cultivent leur propre vigne. Ce très grand vin est peu connu à l'étranger, on ignore pourquoi. Meilleur que la plupart des Côte de Beaune, il est parmi les meilleurs de la Côte de Nuits — à l'exception du Corton. Néanmoins, bien des vins de moindre intérêt ont une plus grande réputation. Peut-être a-t-il été éclipsé par le fabuleux Musigny, dont les vignes se trouvent à l'autre extrémité de Chambolle, ou

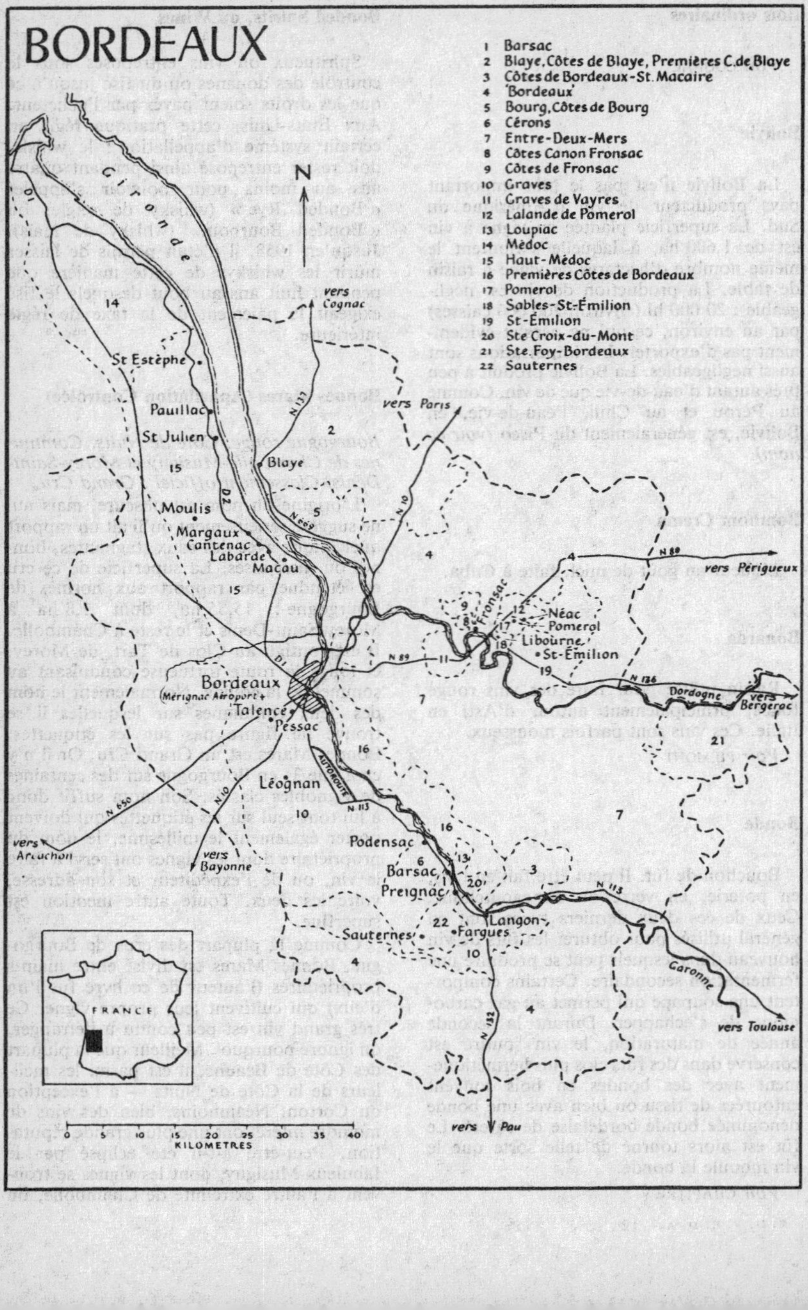
BORDEAUX
1 Barsac
2 Blaye, Côtes de Blaye, Premières C. de Blaye
3 Côtes de Bordeaux-St. Macaire
4 'Bordeaux'
5 Bourg, Côtes de Bourg
6 Cérons
7 Entre-Deux-Mers
8 Côtes Canon Fronsac
9 Côtes de Fronsac
10 Graves
11 Graves de Vayres
12 Lalande de Pomerol
13 Loupiac
14 Médoc
15 Haut-Médoc
16 Premières Côtes de Bordeaux
17 Pomerol
18 Sables-St-Émilion
19 St-Émilion
20 Ste Croix-du-Mont
21 Ste. Foy-Bordeaux
22 Sauternes
N
Gironde
vers Cognac
vers Paris
N 137
N 10
N 669
D2
D1
St Estèphe
Pauillac
St Julien
Blaye
Moulis
Margaux
Cantenac
Labarde
Macau
Fronsac
Néac
Pomerol
Libourne
St-Émilion
N 89
vers Périgueux
N 136
Dordogne
vers Bergerac
Bordeaux
(Mérignac Aéroport+)
Talence
Pessac
Autoroute
Léognan
N 113
N 650
vers Arcachon
vers Bayonne
Podensac
Barsac
Preignac
Sauternes
Fargues
Langon
Garonne
vers Toulouse
N 132
vers Pau
FRANCE
0 5 10 15 20 25 30 35 40
KILOMETRES

bien négligé par les amateurs de vin qui traversent la Bourgogne trop rapidement vers Gevrey-Chambertin.

De même que tous les vins rouges du département de Côte-d'Or, le Bonnes Mares est fait avec du Pinot Noir. Sur le sol de ce cru, il produit des vins généralement plus moelleux que les grands Morey et qui partagent l'élégance ainsi que la délicatesse du Musigny. Plus riches en tanin que la plupart des Bourgogne, ils sont d'une vigueur durable qui leur permet de vieillir et de s'arrondir merveilleusement. Arrivés à maturité, ils conservent leurs qualités plus longtemps que les autres Bourgogne rouges.

Production minime : environ 300 hl par an ou l'équivalent de 3 100 caisses.

Bonnezeaux

Petit secteur privilégié des coteaux du Layon en Anjou qui a droit à une appellation contrôlée particulière.

Voir ANJOU

Bons Bois

Voir COGNAC

Bor

Nom du vin en hongrois.

Bordeaux

Rouges, blancs, rosés. Sud-Ouest de la France.

Le Bordelais est la plus importante région viticole de France. Plus de la moitié des vins fins du monde proviennent de France, et environ le quart de Bordeaux.

Bordeaux existait déjà au temps de l'Antiquité et connut bien des vicissitudes au cours de sa longue histoire. Quand les Romains arrivèrent dans la région, en 56 av. J.-C., Bordeaux s'appelait Burdigala. C'était déjà un port, mais pas encore le plus important de la Gironde. Il était en contact commercial avec la Grande-Bretagne et d'autres pays du Nord. Routes et fleuves reliaient Bordeaux à la province romaine de Gaule. Selon l'écrivain bordelais Gaston Marchou, la domination romaine ne pesa guère sur Burdigala et ses habitants, les Bituriges Vivisci, se romanisèrent sans peine et même avec bonheur. La cité prospéra et les vignobles des environs aussi. Pline parle des vins qu'on y faisait au Ier siècle de notre ère. Au IVe, Ausone écrivait ses œuvres dans son agréable villa, hors de la cité. Cette prospérité ne dura guère. Vinrent les Wisigoths et les siècles d'obscurantisme pesèrent sur la ville et les vignes. Par bonheur le christianisme avait précédé les invasions barbares. A Bordeaux comme ailleurs l'Église conserva les vestiges des anciennes connaissances et sauva la viticulture, mais non sans nombre de revers successifs au cours des siècles.

En 1152, Éléonore d'Aquitaine épousa Henri Plantagenêt, comte d'Anjou et roi d'Angleterre. Elle lui apportait en dot le Poitou, la Guyenne, la Gascogne ; la ville de Bordeaux en faisait évidemment partie. D'abord les Bordelais boudèrent leur nouveau maître. Mais le fils d'Éléonore, Richard Cœur de Lion, passa un certain temps dans la ville et semble en avoir charmé les habitants. Néanmoins, dans un édit de son successeur au sujet des vins français vendus en Angleterre vers 1200, on n'en trouve aucun du Bordelais. Mais ils ne tardèrent pas à être envoyés de Bordeaux en Angleterre en dépit de lourdes taxes, au départ comme à l'arrivée. A la fin du règne d'Henri III (1216-1272) les négociants de Bordeaux avaient acquis bien des privilèges : impôts réduits, droit de vendre leur marchandise sur les marchés anglais, de constituer un conseil (Jurade) municipal et d'élire leur maire. Les bateaux partaient encore de Soulac et d'autres ports, maintenant de petite importance. Mais Bordeaux (le port de la Lune) grandissait et prospérait. Les mâts des navires marchands se dressaient nombreux comme les arbres d'une forêt au fond de la Gironde. Les Graves furent à la mode en Angleterre mais, jusqu'au XVIe siècle, on considérait le Médoc comme un pays sauvage et ses vins ne furent vraiment connus qu'à partir du XVIIe siècle.

Les bourgeois bâtirent ; la ville s'étendit. Au XIVe siècle, la Jurade était très puissante. Nul n'avait le droit de vendre son vin avant que les riches bourgeois, membres de ce conseil, aient disposé du leur. Des familles aristocratiques dont les domaines se trouvaient hors de la ville sollicitaient le titre de bourgeois. En ce qui concerne les vins des autres cités (Libourne, Bergerac, Cahors), on ne pouvait les introduire à Bordeaux pour les vendre à des étrangers qu'après la fin de la foire vinicole d'automne. En ces temps-là, on buvait le vin frais tiré du tonneau durant sa première année. Il fallait que les bateaux anglais aient débarqué les vins de la nouvelle vendange avant Noël. Au début, les fûts des sous-privilégiés étaient relégués au quai des Chartrons qui fut plus tard réservé aux seuls grands marchands de Bordeaux.

Quand la guerre de Cent Ans (1337-1453) éclata, les Bordelais, qui se trouvaient fort heureux sous un régime aussi favorable à leur commerce, se rangèrent dans le camp anglais. En 1356, le Prince Noir fit prisonnier le roi de France et l'amena à Bordeaux. « On ne saurait décrire les banquets et les fêtes que les gens de la ville et son clergé offrirent au prince », dit le chroniqueur Froissart. Le roi Jean semble avoir pris sa bonne part des réjouissances avant d'être conduit en Angleterre. L'année suivante fut celle de la peste noire. Dès que l'épidémie s'apaisa, la guerre reprit. Vers la fin de sa vie, le Prince Noir, épuisé, malade, ne rappelait guère le magnifique vainqueur de Poitiers. Il lançait dans la campagne avoisinant Bordeaux des raids de destruction. Ce qui subsistait était ensuite ravagé par les armées françaises dans leurs efforts pour reconquérir toute la Gascogne. Cependant les vignobles restèrent longtemps intacts et le commerce maritime continua. Même quand le malheureux Henri VI devint roi d'Angleterre, Bordeaux et son célèbre archevêque Pey Berland croyaient encore que les Anglais pourraient conserver la ville. Ils demandèrent du secours. Il en vint peu : une petite armée sous les ordres du vieux John Talbot, comte de Shrewsbury. Courageuse mais inférieure en nombre, elle fut vaincue à Castillon. Talbot y périt, mais son nom survit par le Château-Talbot, dans le Médoc. Bordeaux redevint française. La guerre de Cent Ans prenait fin. D'abord les bourgeois n'en furent nullement enchantés. Ils perdirent leurs privilèges municipaux et le commerce maritime cessa presque entièrement. Or, en ce temps de mauvaises routes et de lents charrois, les transports par voie de terre étaient fort difficiles.

Quand il succéda à Charles VII, le roi Louis XI réalisa l'intérêt du commerce des vins et rendit à la ville bien des privilèges au détriment des agglomérations avoisinantes qui étaient restées fidèles au roi de France pendant la guerre. Bordeaux devint le siège d'un parlement et le roi autorisa les Anglais à revenir y chercher du vin.

Le siècle suivant fut celui des guerres de Religion. Le calvinisme se répandit dans le Sud-Ouest de la France. Il y eut des persécutions, des soulèvements et, en 1572, Bordeaux connut sa propre version du massacre de la Saint-Barthélemy. En accordant l'édit de Nantes aux huguenots, Henri IV ramena la paix. Au XVIIe siècle, les vins de Bordeaux étaient connus à Paris et à la cour. Quand le cardinal de Richelieu planta un vignoble au bord de la Loire, il envoya chercher des ceps à Bordeaux. Mme de Sévigné prédit que la mode de ce vin passerait « comme le café et Racine ». Elle se trompa sur les trois points. On dit que Louis XIV arrosait d'énormes quantités de viandes au Saint-Émilion et au Chambertin. Mais la rigueur de son gouvernement déplaisait aux grands bourgeois de Bordeaux dont tous les pouvoirs passaient à l'intendant du roi. Les guerres de Louis XIV nuisaient aussi au commerce. Ses mauvaises relations avec l'Angleterre et l'avènement dans ce pays de rois, hollandais d'abord, allemands ensuite, amenèrent la signature du traité Methuen qui favorisa sur le marché anglais les vins portugais au détriment des vins français. Pourtant, les membres de la classe dominante anglaise tenaient à leur Clairet et la contrebande leur en fournissait.

Le milieu du XVIIIe siècle fut la *belle époque* pour Bordeaux, quoique à un certain moment un intendant ait ordonné aux vignerons d'arracher leurs vignes pour cultiver des céréales. Des ordonnances de ce genre ne sont guère observées. Un de ceux qui refusèrent d'obéir fut l'écrivain-vigneron Montesquieu. Le commerce du vin passait toujours en premier, mais d'autres industries débutaient : distillation, construction navale, verrerie, raffinage de sucre. L'Amérique du Nord était alors un important client et les Antilles un fournisseur de choix pour Bordeaux. La ville s'enrichit. Hôtels particuliers et bâtiments publics apparurent de-ci, de-là : place de la Bourse, allées de Tourny et le splendide théâtre de Victor Louis en sont encore les témoignages. Quand le duc de Richelieu succéda à Tourny comme intendant, il fit venir des troupes d'acteurs pour jouer dans ce théâtre et invita volontiers les actrices à dîner. Le moins qu'on puisse dire, c'est qu'il était frivole, à la différence des riches bourgeois bordelais parmi lesquels il y avait des protestants qui menaient une vie plutôt austère. C'est à cette époque que s'installèrent à Bordeaux bien des étrangers dont les noms sont désormais fortement enracinés : Barton, Lawton et Johnston par exemple.

En 1797, au château Lafite, on mit pour la première fois du vin rouge à vieillir dans une bouteille assez bien tournée pour être couchée sur le côté. Une vieille bouteille poussiéreuse de ce millésime subsiste encore de nos jours dans les caves du château.

La Révolution et les guerres napoléoniennes furent néfastes à Bordeaux. Coupés de l'Angleterre, des États-Unis, des Antilles, certains commerçants en furent réduits à vendre des pruneaux au lieu de vin. En 1808, le port était paralysé. Napoléon lui rendit visite et promit des subventions mais il n'en résulta rien, sauf que les Bordelais d'ardents partisans de la Restauration.

Dès que les guerres cessèrent, le commerce reprit. L'Angleterre diminua ses droits de douane au cours des années 1820 à 1839. Mais, après 1850, s'abattit sur le Bordelais la terrible épidémie du mildiou. En 1855, on procéda à la classification des crus du Bordelais fondée sur des classifications antérieures et des prix courants. C'est ainsi qu'au cours de l'exposition internationale de cette année-là, les grands vins de Bordeaux furent à l'honneur. En 1860, le gouvernement Gladstone abaissa encore les droits de douane sur les vins entrant en Angleterre et permit aux épiciers de les vendre au détail. Il en résulta un commerce plus actif à des prix plus bas et une exportation massive de Bordeaux vers l'Angleterre. Les vingt années qui précédèrent la catastrophe du phylloxéra (1878) connurent des millésimes mémorables. Notamment : 1858, 1864, 1865, 1870, 1875. Les connaisseurs qui ont goûté à ces vins affirment qu'on n'en boira plus jamais de pareils. Même si nous ne sommes pas d'accord, nous devons admettre que les vins fins d'aujourd'hui ne sont plus les mêmes qu'autrefois, parce que désormais les vignes sont greffées sur des souches américaines alors qu'autrefois elles étaient des *Vitis vinifera* à l'état pur. Quoi qu'il en soit, 1893 et 1899 sont considérés comme d'excellents millésimes pour le Bordeaux, de même que 1904, 1906 et 1914. L'entre-deux-guerres connut aussi des millésimes dont tout le monde se rappelle : 1924, 1928, 1929, 1934 et 1937. Ceux qui achetèrent ces vins avant la dernière guerre pour les conserver eurent la main heureuse car le Bordeaux était exceptionnellement bon marché durant les dix années qui précédèrent la Seconde Guerre mondiale. Grâce aux *Notes sur un livre de cave* du professeur Saintsbury, nous savons que les Bordeaux mis en bouteille au château se vendaient alors en francs Poincaré au même prix qu'en 1960 en francs Pinay qui valaient sensiblement le triple.

Appellations d'origine du Bordelais

Après d'interminables disputes et litiges, on fixa, en 1911, les limites de la région vinicole de Bordeaux en décidant qu'elles coïncideraient avec celles du département de la Gironde, sauf pour la bande de dunes côtières qui n'en fait pas partie.

Le plus vaste des départements français, la Gironde, produit environ 5,6 millions d'hl par an sur plus de 100 000 ha de vigne, ce qui représente 1/8 de sa superficie totale. Le nom du département dériverait d'un ancien nom de l'hirondelle. La Dordogne et la Garonne confluent un peu en amont de Bordeaux, dans l'estuaire de la Gironde où la marée de l'Atlantique se fait sentir et qui coule sur 80 km avant de se déverser dans l'océan. Le confluent des deux fleuves a en effet l'aspect d'une queue d'aronde. Les limites du département de la Gironde englobent les côtes de l'estuaire et tous les environs de Bordeaux qui en occupent à peu près le centre. Tous les grands Bordeaux sont des vins issus de régions très proches des rivières, sauf en ce qui concerne Saint-Émilion et Pomerol où l'on ne voit de l'eau courante que lorsqu'on se trouve dans les vignes et qu'il y pleut.

La région de Bordeaux comporte au moins trois douzaines d'appellations contrôlées désignant des catégories de vin différentes les unes des autres. Ceux qui portent cette seule appellation : Bordeaux, la plus générale, sont moins distingués que ceux qui ont droit à une appellation plus précise. Tous les vins faits à partir de vignes cultivées dans cette région n'ont d'ailleurs pas droit à cette appellation mineure qui exige l'application de normes minimales, tant en viticulture qu'en viniculture (*voir* APPELLATION D'ORIGINE CONTROLÉE). Les appellations d'origine régionales plus restreintes — Haut-Médoc, Saint-Julien, etc. — seront presque toujours celles de vins provenant de différents vignobles situés dans la région portant ce nom et achetés par un négociant qui les mélange entre eux. La réputation de ce négociant peut donner une indication quant à la valeur du vin. En général elle est bonne. Le Monopole Bordeaux de diverses maisons d'expédition est un vin de ce type auquel l'expéditeur entend donner son nom. Presque tous ces vins régionaux sont des coupages. Si le millésime figure sur la bouteille, tous les vins qui ont servi au mélange devraient être ceux de cette même année. Quand le millésime n'est pas indiqué, il y a coupage non seulement entre le produit de différents vignobles, mais aussi de différentes années. Les meilleurs expéditeurs procèdent à ces mélanges dans l'intention d'offrir un vin de bonne qualité suivie d'une année à l'autre. Tel est le principe des meilleurs coupages de vins et spiritueux. Une qualité constante signifie une qualité moyenne, réduite à un dénominateur commun.

Les rouges et les blancs mis en bouteille par un négociant ou au château sont ceux qu'on trouve le plus couramment sur le marché. Les derniers cités sont ceux d'un certain vignoble déterminé ou bien de quelques vignobles de moindre intérêt, voire de plusieurs petits châteaux. Presque tous les crus bordelais portent le nom de « Château » même si la propriété ne comporte ni château, ni manoir ; ce sont souvent de modestes maisons de campagne, voire de simples pavillons. Le vin portant sur son étiquette la mention « Château » n'est jamais un mélange : il est toujours fait avec les raisins des vignes cultivées sur le domaine de ce château et de nul autre. Il porte presque toujours un millésime. C'est donc le vin d'une certaine vendange de vignes cultivées sur un certain terroir. Étant donné les différents facteurs variables influant sur la qualité du vin, notamment le temps durant l'été où le raisin mûrit, ces vins n'auront certainement pas une qualité suivie d'une année à l'autre, comme les mises en bouteille régionales. Mais, les bonnes années, ils atteindront des sommets qu'on n'imagine même pas avant d'y avoir goûté. Les vins mis en bouteille au château en portent la mention sur leur étiquette. Cette étiquette permet au propriétaire de garantir l'authenticité du vin.

Sur plus de trois mille châteaux du Bordelais, environ deux cents seulement ont fait l'objet d'une classification officielle à un moment quelconque depuis le XVIe siècle. Trois de ces listes sont encore en vigueur : celle des Médoc et Sauternes datant de 1855 ; des Graves, classés en 1953 ; enfin celle des Saint-Émilion en 1955, 1969 et 1986 (*voir* MÉDOC, SAUTERNES, GRAVES, SAINT-ÉMILION).

Tous les châteaux classés comme exceptionnels sont traités en particulier (*voir* LAFITE, LATOUR, YQUEM, CHEVAL-BLANC, etc.). Voici la liste des subdivisions régionales ou communales donnant droit à une appellation contrôlée du Bordelais :

Subdivisions régionales de qualité les plus importantes		
Sauternes	Vins blancs doux	1 450 ha
Barsac	Vins blancs doux	560 ha
Médoc	Vins rouges	3 400 ha
Haut-Médoc	Vins rouges	3 200 ha
Saint-Estèphe	Vins rouges	1 100 ha
Pauillac	Vins rouges	1 000 ha
Saint-Julien	Vins rouges	800 ha
Margaux	Vins rouges	1 100 ha
Listrac	Vins rouges	500 ha
Moulis	Vins rouges	350 ha
Pomerol	Vins rouges	835 ha
Saint-Émilion	Vins rouges	5 000 ha
Saint-Émilion Les Satellites	Vins rouges	3 500 ha
Graves	Vins blancs	1 450 ha
Graves	Vins rouges	2 120 ha

Caractéristiques

La multiplicité des noms impose à l'évidence une extrême variété parmi les vins de Bordeaux. Nulle part ailleurs on ne trouve autant de différences entre les divers vins. Grosso modo il est possible de dire que les vins rouges sont faits au nord de la ville et les blancs au sud où se trouve aussi la subdivision de Graves autour de l'agglomération qui porte ce nom et où l'on fait aussi bien du blanc que du rouge, parfois à partir des mêmes vignes, sur le même terrain. Quoiqu'il y ait des exceptions, les vins blancs passent du sec au doux en traversant le secteur de Graves à partir de Bordeaux jusqu'au Sauternes, à l'extrême sud de la région. A la manière qui lui est propre — délicate, et parfois très ferme — le Bordeaux rouge est le meilleur au monde en son genre. Pourtant ses caractéristiques de moelleux et de subtilité ne s'épanouissent qu'avec l'âge. Sa teneur en tanin — qui, avec l'alcool, décide si le vin sera plein, corsé ou léger — est plus élevée dans le Bordeaux que dans le Bourgogne authentique et naturel. Nous précisons cela par opposition à la théorie selon laquelle les Bordeaux seraient légers et les Bourgogne lourds. Il n'en est rien. Pourtant il faut tenir compte de nombreuses exceptions à toute règle. La délicatesse des Bordeaux légers apparaît de manière exemplaire chez les Margaux (centre du Médoc) qui ont un goût nettement tranché, mais un tissu moelleux. En règle générale cependant, les Bordeaux naturels sont vigoureux jusqu'à une certaine dureté dans leur jeunesse, mais ils mûrissent merveilleusement pour devenir moelleux avec l'âge. Plus le Bordeaux est grand, plus celui qui le conserve sera largement récompensé de sa patience, surtout en ce qui concerne celui des vignes cultivées autour de Pauillac et les très robustes Saint-Estèphe qui ne doivent pas être consommés avant d'avoir suffisamment mûri. Les Graves rouges aussi sont rustiques et pleins dans leur jeunesse et n'atteignent la splendeur que plus tard. D'autre part, les vins de Bourgogne ont tendance à vieillir plus vite et ceux du Beaujolais comptent parmi les vins les plus légers de France, sinon du monde entier. Un Côte de Nuits peut fort bien être plus délicat qu'un Saint-Émilion, vin très corsé et qu'on appelle parfois le « Bourgogne du Bordelais ». Certains Bordeaux ne partagent pas la caractéristique générale de leur région. Étant donné leur extrême variété, c'est parfaitement normal.

Blanc ou rouge, sec ou doux, le vin de château est exempt de toute addition, donc absolument naturel. Pour cette raison et aussi à cause de leur teneur en fer, ces crus sont magnifiquement sains et donnent la santé. (De temps à autre on autorise la chaptalisation dans le Bordelais — notamment en 1980 et 1984 pour ne citer que les années récentes — cependant c'est une tendance de plus en plus fréquente. Néanmoins les abus sont plus rares qu'ailleurs où cette pratique est courante). Une des caractéristiques des Bordeaux, c'est leur formidable longévité, tout à fait exceptionnelle pour des vins naturels. Certains des plus grands Médoc vivront jusqu'à cent ans en bouteille (l'opiniâtre 1870 ne tint ses promesses qu'à partir de l'âge de 50 ans et pour certains même, celui de 70 ans). Parmi les vins blancs doux, il en est également qui durent jusqu'à 100 ans, notamment le Château-Yquem. En dépit de leur énorme multiplicité et variété, les Bordeaux ont généralement en commun quelque chose de très particulier : leur parfum, plus nettement perceptible chez les rouges âgés : une fraîcheur de sous-bois ou bien un parfum de violette profondément dissimulée sous l'herbe, bref un arôme délicat que l'on ne trouve dans aucun autre vin.

Sol et climat

Une telle diversité de vins dénote une variété équivalente de sols. De ce point de vue, l'élément le plus caractéristique, très répandu, consiste en la présence de pierrailles en surface et dans le sous-sol. Elles se présentent sous la forme de gravier ou *graves* qui donnent leur nom à quelques-uns des plus beaux crus de la région ; ou bien sous l'aspect de cailloux gros comme un œuf, voire comme le poing, qui figurent fièrement dans le nom de certains crus, tels que Château-Caillou en Barsac, Château-Beaucaillou à Saint-Julien, et qui contribuent largement au caractère du vin, par exemple à Château-Latour, à Château-Margaux, Château-Lascombes ou Château Prieuré-Lichine. A quelques exceptions près, les meilleurs vins proviennent de vignes cultivées sur des apports du Quaternaire. A l'inverse, mais en vertu du même principe, les sols formés d'alluvions récentes n'ont droit à aucune appellation contrôlée de Bordeaux. Ces derniers apports des fleuves, encore marécageux, sont appelés *palus*. Cette particularité projette une lumière intéressante sur l'évolution des goûts : voici quelques centaines d'années les palus étaient les plus recherchés dans les quatre subdivisions du Bordelais alors reconnues.

Pas tous au même degré, mais tous les Bordeaux subissent l'influence du climat humide et doux provenant de la proximité des fleuves, de l'estuaire, de l'océan et de la forêt de pins qui adoucit le contact avec l'océan. Les étés sont chauds, mais à proximité de l'océan cette chaleur provoque souvent des orages soudains ; les longues périodes de sécheresse sont donc rares. L'hiver est court, généralement doux. Le pire danger qui pèse sur la vigne, c'est la grêle ; durant les dernières années elle a frappé la région de Barsac-Sauternes plus que les autres et détruit plus d'une vendange à Château-d'Yquem, à Château-Rayne-Vigneau et les crus contigus.

Les gelées aussi sont à craindre, mais il s'en produit moins souvent dans le Bordelais que dans la plupart des autres régions viticoles. C'est précisément pour cette raison que les rigueurs sans précédent de février 1956 anéantirent des hectares de vigne. Nullement habituées à résister au froid, les ceps périrent et la récolte fut réduite de quelque 50 %, soit environ 2 630 000 hl. Il est vrai que la région de Bordeaux n'avait pas connu un hiver aussi froid depuis 1709.

Encépagement

Les Bordeaux rouges doivent être faits avec certaines variétés de Cabernet (Cabernet Sauvignon et Cabernet Franc) ainsi que des raisins suivants : Merlot, Malbec et Petit-Verdot. Les vins blancs, avec les suivants : Sémillon, Sauvignon et Muscadelle. Très rares sont les vins faits avec du raisin d'une seule variété. Presque tous résultent d'un mélange des variétés autorisés ; la proportion de chaque cépage varie selon les idées de chaque vigneron ; cependant tous respectent en général les règles qui se sont révélées les mieux adaptées à tel ou tel cru particulier.

Jusqu'en 1953, on ne tolérait des raisins moins nobles que jusqu'à concurrence maximale de 10 %. Mais à partir de mars 1953, toutes ces vignes ont été systématiquement arrachées. Montesquieu nous indique que la situation était fort différente de son temps. Selon lui, en 1785, on faisait du rouge à partir de 27 variétés différentes et de 22 pour le vin blanc.

Millésimes

On accorde beaucoup trop d'importance aux millésimes en ce qui concerne les vins de Bordeaux. De 1795 à 1870, 40 % des années furent mauvaises ou médiocres et 60 % bonnes ou très bonnes. Depuis 1870 la proportion s'améliore : 80 % de millésimes bons ou excellents et 20 % de médiocres. Il apparaît donc qu'avant 1870, on comptait deux fois plus de mauvaises années. La science moderne a permis d'éliminer les facteurs qui donnent trop d'importance aux millésimes car elle diminue les « bas ».

Cela ne signifie nullement que la qualité du vin ne change pas d'une année sur l'autre, sauf en ce qui concerne les zones de vins ordinaires, mais cela veut dire que la terminologie employée pour décrire les millésimes — surtout dans des textes extrêmement abrégés, donc prêtant à confusion, voire comportant un certain parti pris — ne donne pas une idée exacte de la réalité. Sur ces listes, l'inverse de « grande » année est toujours année « pauvre » ou « petite ». En réalité, il y a de nombreuses petites années, mais ce mot ne concerne nullement les caractéristiques ou la qualité du vin. Dire d'un vin « léger » qu'il est « petit » est un grave abus de langage. Un « grand » Bordeaux rouge est simplement un Bordeaux fait au cours d'une « grande » année : c'est une année durant laquelle le soleil n'a cessé de briller tout l'été pour donner un vin qui se développera lentement et durera longtemps. Une « petite » année est tout simplement une année de moindre ensoleillement et dont les vins se feront plus rapidement.

Trompés par des tableaux de millésimes, trop de gens s'imaginent qu'ils ne doivent acheter que les vins des « grandes » années, généralement indiquées en gros caractères. Ce faisant, ils achètent surtout ce qu'on devrait appeler des vins de longue durée. Trop souvent ils les boivent avant que ces vins aient atteint leur plénitude en bouteille. S'ils avaient choisi du vin d'années plus légères, ils auraient payé moins cher et auraient eu une meilleure bouteille *au moment où ils la burent*.

Néanmoins, dire que les grands millésimes sont surévalués serait incorrect. Quand on les conserve convenablement, quand on sait attendre, ils atteignent des sommets sublimes.

D'autre part il est exact que les années légères, moins riches en tanin, sont sous-évaluées car les vins de ces années-là, prêts à être consommés plus tôt, ne sont pas toujours inférieurs mais vont seulement

APPELLATIONS CONTROLÉES DE LA RÉGION DE BORDEAUX*				
Appellation	*Date d'inscription*	*Rendement maximal hl/ha*	*Production moyenne*	
			Blanc	*Rouge*
Barsac	11 sept. 1936	25	15 000	
Blaye ou Blayais	22 mars 1983 blanc	65	26 000	
	rouge	55		165
Bordeaux Blanc	14 nov. 1936	65	600 000	
Bordeaux Clairet ou Rosé	13 sept. 1951	55		9 500
Bordeaux Rouge	14 nov. 1936	55		790 000
Bordeaux Côtes de Francs	26 mai 1967	50	200	10 000
Bordeaux Côtes de Castillon	15 juillet 1955	50		120 000
Bordeaux sec	14 déc. 1977	65	530 000	
Bordeaux Blanc Supérieur	22 mars 1983	50	15 000	
Bordeaux Rouge Supérieur	14 oct. 1943	50		300 000
Bordeaux Mousseux	16 mars 1943	chiffres non disponibles		
Cadillac	13 mars 1969	40	2 300	
Canon Fronsac	1er juillet 1949	47		10 500
Cérons	11 sept. 1936	40	30 000	
Côtes de Blaye	11 sept. 1936	60	11 000	
Côtes de Bordeaux Saint-Macaire	31 juillet 1937	50	3 700	
Côtes de Bourg, Bourg, ou Bourgeais	14 mai 1941 blanc	60	5 000	
	11 sept. 1936 rouge	50		140 000
Entre-Deux-Mers	31 juillet 1937	60	120 000	
Fronsac	14 mars 1938	47		27 000
Graves	4 mars 1937	50	43 000	67 000
Graves Supérieures	4 mars 1937	45	19 000	
Graves de Vayres	31 juillet 1937 blanc	60	12 000	
	rouge	50		6 600
Haut-Médoc	14 nov. 1936	48		105 000
Lalande de Pomerol et Néac	8 déc. 1936	42		35 000
Listrac-Médoc	8 juin 1957	45		20 000
Loupiac	11 sept. 1936	40	10 500	
Lussac-Saint-Émilion	14 nov. 1936	45		39 000
Margaux	10 août 1954	45		34 000
Médoc	14 nov. 1936	50		110 000
Montagne-Saint-Émilion	14 nov. 1936	45		65 000
Moulis	14 mai 1938	45		12 500
Pauillac	14 nov. 1936	45		42 000
Pessac-Léognan	9 sept. 1987 blanc	45	chiffres non disponibles	
	rouge	48		
Pomerol	8 déc. 1936	42		24 000
Premières Côtes de Blaye	11 sept. 1936 blanc	60	200 000	
	rouge	50		130 000
Premières Côtes de Bordeaux	31 juillet 1937	50	30 000	70 000
Puisseguin-Saint-Émilion	14 nov. 1936	45		23 500
Sainte-Croix-du-Mont	11 sept. 1936	40	15 000	
Saint-Émilion	14 nov. 1936	45		246 000
Saint-Émilion Grand Cru	7 oct. 1954	40		170 000
Saint-Estèphe	14 nov. 1936	45		56 000
Sainte-Foy-Bordeaux Blanc	31 juillet 1937	55	6 500	
Sainte-Foy-Bordeaux Rouge	31 juillet 1937	50		3 500
Saint-Georges-Saint-Émilion	14 nov. 1936	45		6 000
Saint-Julien	14 nov. 1936	45		26 000
Sauternes	30 sept. 1936	25	29 000	

* Les chiffres peuvent varier du simple au double d'une année sur l'autre.

Les vendanges

Dans le Bordelais, on vendange généralement fin septembre, parfois début octobre, presque jamais en août ou en novembre. En règle générale, plus l'été est chaud, plus on vendange tôt. En guère plus d'un siècle et demi, voici les millésimes des années au cours desquelles on vendangea exceptionnellement tôt ou tard : en août, 1822 et 1893 ; en novembre, 1816.

On cueille d'un seul coup toutes les grappes de toutes les vignes pour les vins rouges et la plupart des blancs. Mais pour les vins très doux de Barsac et de Sauternes, on cueille grappe à grappe et parfois grain à grain, au fur et à mesure de la maturation du raisin. Les vendanges durent donc à peu près trois fois plus longtemps dans le Barsac et le Sauternais et elles se terminent parfois en novembre. Le tableau suivant expose le cycle de la vigne au cours des années les plus marquantes pendant plus d'un siècle.

Maturation de la vigne
au Château Mouton-Rothschild
(grandes années seulement)

Année	*Floraison*		*Début de la véraison*	*Début des vendanges*
	Début	*Fin*		
1986	9 juin	19 juin	11 août	6 oct.
1985	3 juin	17 juin	6 août	3 oct.
1982	25 mai	8 juin	21 juil.	17 sept.
1979	12 juin	28 juin	6 août	1er oct.
1978	10 juin	26 juin	10 août	10 sept.
1976	30 mai	12 juin	4 juil.	15 sept.
1975	3 juin	21 juin	21 juil.	23 sept.
1970	5 juin	19 juin	22 juil.	28 sept.
1966	25 mai	15 juin	25 juil.	26 sept.
1961	15 mai	5 juin	25 juil.	2 oct.
1952	19 mai	5 juin	8 juil.	18 sept.
1947	26 mai	15 juin	15 juil.	17 sept.
1945	11 mai	1er juin	2 juil.	7 sept.
1929	24 mai	25 juin	22 juil.	21 sept.
1921	19 mai	13 juin	18 juil.	10 sept.
1900	29 mai	14 juin	26 juil.	25 sept.
1893	28 avr.	20 mai	23 juin	22 août
1870	18 mai	5 juin	12 juil.	10 sept.
1822	13 mai	31 mai	3 juil.	24 août

Maturation du vin

Autrefois conservés en jarres ou en amphores, les Bordeaux commencèrent à être vieillis en fûts sur les conseils de Charlemagne. Des siècles plus tard (un peu avant la Révolution française) on imposa l'usage uniforme de la *barrique bordelaise* qui est encore en usage de nos jours : elle fut alors interdite à tous les autres vins. Ses dimensions sont idéales pour la maturation des Bordeaux rouges. Toutefois on est en train de procéder à des expériences afin de savoir si un fût de plus grande capacité ne ralentirait pas la maturation des Bordeaux blancs pour leur conserver plus longtemps fraîcheur et fruité afin de répondre à la demande sans cesse croissante de vins blancs secs toujours plus jeunes.

Le prix de la barrique a augmenté de manière spectaculaire, à Bordeaux comme ailleurs, et devient un des éléments constitutifs capitaux du prix auquel le vin est livré sur le marché. Au moment où nous écrivons cet ouvrage, les barriques en chêne du Limousin, de l'Allier ou de Nevers coûtent 1 900 francs hors taxe. On employait du chêne importé de Pologne, de Suède et des États-Unis. Depuis la guerre il en vient quelques-uns de Yougoslavie et la plupart des forêts du Limousin (auxquelles recourent surtout les producteurs de Cognac), de l'Allier et Nevers. Enfin, pour en avoir assez, on emploie aussi du bois de moins bonne qualité venant d'Alsace.

Les vins blancs fermentent et mûrissent en fûts. Les vins rouges fermentent dans de vastes cuves, autrefois en chêne, et aujourd'hui en ciment ou en acier inoxydable dans la plupart des domaines. Ensuite, ils mûrissent en fûts comme les blancs.

Traditionalistes et modernistes se disputent âprement au sujet des cuves de ciment dans le Bordelais. Nul n'a pu démontrer que la fermentation dans de telles cuves, plus faciles à nettoyer, implique une perte de qualité et ce matériel conquiert rapidement de nouveaux partisans. Dans quelques crus on a commencé à expérimenter prudemment la maturation du Bordeaux rouge dans les tonneaux de chêne où il fermente. Cette innovation, si elle réussit, réduirait les prix en éliminant les barriques coûteuses et donnerait un vin plus léger, consommable plus tôt. Les grands crus de Bordeaux rouge ne seront jamais faits selon cette méthode car une part du tanin qui assure leur longévité leur est donnée par le chêne neuf des barriques renouvelées chaque année. Mais peut-être des vins plus légers et plus jeunes y trouveront-ils leur place.

On comprend que, depuis la guerre, les Bordelais aient de plus en plus tendance à avancer la mise en bouteille grâce à des soutirages plus nombreux (quatre par an) qui activent le développement du vin. Il y a 40 ans, le Bordeaux rouge restait au moins 3 ans dans le bois. De nos jours, on met en bouteille dans la plupart des châteaux 18 à 30 mois après les vendanges.

Les bouteilles de Bordeaux

La bouteille type de Bordeaux a des épaules carrées pour retenir le dépôt quand elle est couchée et un goulot bien adapté au long bouchon qui protège les meilleurs vins. Le vin mûrit plus vite en petites bouteilles qu'en grandes, en partie à cause de l'oxygène qui passe à travers le bouchon en quantité égale mais relativement plus grande par rapport à la quantité de vin. Pour cette raison, un vin que l'on doit boire jeune (tout spécialement un vin blanc sec) pourra être bon en demi-bouteille (appelée *fillette*) ; mais, dans ce même contenant, un vin vieux sera « passé ». Le magnum est le contenant idéal pour les grands Bordeaux destinés à vieillir ; sa contenance s'élève à 1,5 l, soit l'équivalent de deux bouteilles de Bordeaux (75 cl) ; dans le magnum, le vin vieillira plus lentement. Double magnum (3 l) et Jéroboam (4,5 l) sont rares. Quant à l'impériale (6 l), qui contient autant que 8 bouteilles normales, on n'en voit plus souvent depuis la guerre. Certains experts assurent que les Bordeaux rouges vieillissent mieux dans des flacons plus gros que le magnum, toujours pour la même raison : proportion entre vin et section du bouchon. D'autres estiment que le magnum présente la capacité optimale. On ne discute de cette question que dans le Bordelais, et le problème est impossible à résoudre puisqu'il concerne des vins ayant déjà plus de 30 ans de bouteille et dont la maturation est soumise à des douzaines de facteurs d'influence divers et subtils.

Classification personnelle des bordeaux

Révisée à dater de 1986 et fondée sur la réputation des crus de Bordeaux en 1977. Les crus sont classés par ordre alphabétique dans chaque catégorie de chaque subdivision régionale. Tous les châteaux Saint-Émilion et Pomerol classés ci-dessous portent respectivement le nom des communes de Saint-Émilion et Pomerol.

Crus hors classe

Haut-Médoc
- Château Lafite-Rothschild *(Pauillac)*
- Château Latour *(Pauillac)*
- Château Margaux *(Margaux)*
- Château Mouton-Rothschild *(Pauillac)*

Graves
- Château Haut-Brion *(Pessac, Graves)*

Saint-Émilion
- Château Ausone
- Château Cheval-Blanc

Pomerol
- Château Pétrus

Crus exceptionnels

Haut-Médoc
- Château Brane-Cantenac *(Cantenac-Margaux)*
- * Château Cos d'Estounel *(Saint-Estèphe)*
- * Château Ducru-Beaucaillou *(Saint-Julien)*
- Château Gruaud-Larose *(Saint-Julien)*
- Château Lascombes *(Margaux)*
- Château Léoville-Barton *(Saint-Julien)*
- * Château Léoville-Las-Cases *(Saint-Julien)*
- Château Léoville Poyferré *(Saint-Julien)*
- * Château Lynch-Bages *(Pauillac)*
- Château Montrose *(Saint-Estèphe)*
- Château Palmer *(Cantenac-Margaux)*
- * Château Pichon-Longueville, Comtesse de Lalande *(Pauillac)*
- Château Pichon-Longueville-Baron *(Pauillac)*

Graves
- * Domaine de Chevalier *(Léognan)*
- * Château La Mission-Haut-Brion *(Talence)*
- Château Pape-Clément *(Pessac)*

Saint-Émilion
- * Château Figeac
- Château Magdelaine

Pomerol
- Château La Conseillante
- Château L'Évangile

Château Lafleur
Château La Fleur-Pétrus
Château Trotanoy

GRANDS CRUS

HAUT-MÉDOC
Château Beychevelle *(Saint-Julien)*
Château Boyd-Cantenac *(Cantenac-Margaux)*
Château Branaire-Ducru *(Saint-Julien)*
Château Calon-Ségur *(Saint-Estèphe)*
Château Cantemerle *(Haut-Médoc)*
Château Cantenac-Brown *(Cantenac-Margaux)*
* Château Giscours *(Labarde-Margaux)*
Château d'Issan *(Cantenac-Margaux)*
* Château La Lagune *(Haut-Médoc)*
Château Malescot-Saint-Éxupéry *(Margaux)*
Château Mouton-Baronne-Philippe *(Pauillac)*
* Château Prieuré-Lichine *(Cantenac-Margaux)*
Château Rausan-Ségla *(Margaux)*
Château Rauzan-Gassies *(Margaux)*
Château Talbot *(Saint-Julien)*

GRAVES
* Château Haut-Bailly *(Léognan)*

SAINT-ÉMILION
Château Beau-Séjour-Bécot
* Château Bélair
* Château Canon
Clos Fourtet
Château La Gaffelière
Château Pavie
Château Trottevieille

POMEROL
Château Gazin
Château Latour-Pomerol
Château Nénin
* Château Petit-Village
* Vieux-Château-Certan

CRUS SUPÉRIEURS

HAUT-MÉDOC
Château Batailley *(Pauillac)*
Château Chasse-Spleen *(Moulis)*
Château Clerc-Milon-Rothschild *(Pauillac)*
Château Duhart-Milon-Rothschild *(Pauillac)*
Château Durfort-Vivens *(Cantenac-Margaux)*
Château Gloria *(Saint-Julien)*
Château Grand-Puy-Lacoste *(Pauillac)*
* Château Haut-Batailley *(Pauillac)*
* Château Kirwan *(Cantenac-Margaux)*
Château Lagrange *(Saint-Julien)*
Château Langoa-Barton *(Saint-Julien)*
Château Marquis d'Alesme-Becker *(Margaux)*
Château Marquis de Terme *(Margaux)*
Château Pontet-Canet *(Pauillac)*
Château La Tour-Carnet (Haut-Médoc)

GRAVES
* Château Carbonnieux *(Léognan)*
Château de Fieuzal *(Léognan)*
Château La Louvière *(Léognan)*
* Château Malartic-Lagravière *(Léognan)*
* Château Saint-Pierre *(Saint-Julien)*
Château Smith-Haut-Lafitte *(Martillac)*

SAINT-ÉMILION
Château l'Angélus
* Château Balestard-La-Tonnelle
Château Beauséjour-Duffau-Lagarrosse
Château Cadet-Piola
Château Canon-la-Gaffelière
Château La Clotte
Château Croque-Michotte
Château Curé-Bon-La-Madeleine
Château La Dominique
* Château Larcis-Ducasse
Château Larmande
Château Soutard
Château Troplong-Mondot
Château Villemaurine

POMEROL
Château Beauregard
Château Certan-Giraud
* Château Certan-de-May
Clos l'Église
Château l'Église-Clinet
Château Le Gay
Château Lagrange
Château La Pointe

BONS CRUS

HAUT-MÉDOC
Château D'Agassac *(Haut-Médoc)*
* Château Angludet *(Cantenac-Margaux)*
Château Beau-Site *(Saint-Estèphe)*
Château Beau-Site Haut-Vignoble *(Saint-Estèphe)*
Château Bel-Air-Marquis d'Aligre *(Soussans-Margaux)*
Château Belgrave *(Saint-Laurent)*
* Château de Camensac *(Haut-Médoc)*
Château Citran *(Haut-Médoc)*
Château Cos-Labory *(Saint-Estèphe)*
* Château Croizet-Bages *(Pauillac)*
Château Dauzac *(Margaux)*

Château Ferrière *(Margaux)*
Château Fourcas-Dupré *(Listrac)*
Château Fourcas-Hosten *(Listrac)*
Château Grand-Puy-Ducasse *(Pauillac)*
Château Gressier-Grand-Poujeaux *(Moulis)*
Château Hanteillan *(Haut-Médoc)*
Château Haut-Bages-Libéral *(Pauillac)*
Château Haut-Marbuzet *(Saint-Estèphe)*
Château Labégorce *(Margaux)*
Château Labégorce-Zedé *(Margaux)*
Château Lafon-Rochet *(Saint-Estèphe)*
Château Lamarque *(Haut-Médoc)*
Château Lanessan *(Haut-Médoc)*
Château Lynch-Moussas *(Pauillac)*
Château Marbuzet *(Saint-Estèphe)*
Château Maucaillou *(Moulis)*
* Château Les Ormes-de-Pez *(Saint-Estèphe)*
Château Pédesclaux *(Pauillac)*
* Château de Pez *(Saint-Estèphe)*
Château Phélan-Ségur *(Saint-Estèphe)*
Château Pouget *(Cantenac-Margaux)*
Château Poujeaux *(Moulis)*
Château Siran *(Labarde-Margaux)*
Château du Tertre *(Arsac-Margaux)*
Château La Tours-de-Mons *(Soussans-Margaux)*
Château Villegeorge *(Haut-Médoc)*

GRAVES

Château Bouscaut *(Cadaujac)*
Château Larrivet-Haut-Brion *(Léognan)*
Château La Tour-Haut-Brion *(Talence)*
Château La Tour-Martillac *(Martillac)*

SAINT-ÉMILION

Château L'Arrosée
Château Bellevue
Château Berliquet
* Château Cap-de-Mourlin
Domaine du Châtelet
Clos des Jacobins
Château Corbin *(Giraud)*
Château Corbin *(Manuel)*
Château Corbin-Michotte
Château Coutet
Château Dassault
Couvent-des-Jacobins
Château La Fleur-Pourret
Château Franc-Mayne
Château Grâce-Dieu-Les Menuts
Château Grand-Barrail-Lamarzelle-Figeac
Château Grand-Corbin
Château Grand-Corbin-Despagne
Château Grand-Mayne
Château Grand Pontet
Château Guadet-Saint-Julien
Château Laroque
Château Moulin-du-Cadet
Château Pavie-Decesse
Château Pavie-Macquin
Château Saint-Georges-Côte-Pavie
Château Tertre-Daugay
Château La Tour-Figeac
Château La Tour-du-Pin-Figeac
Château Trimoulet
Château Yon-Figeac

POMEROL

Château Bourgneuf-Vayron
Château La Cabanne
Château Le Caillou
* Château Clinet
Clos du Clocher
Château La Croix
Château La Croix-de-Gay
Clos de l'Église
Château L'Enclos
Château Gombaude-Guillot
Château La Grave-Trignant-de-Boisset
Château Guillot
Château Moulinet
Château Rouget
* Clos René
Château de Sales
Château du Tailhas
Château Taillefer
Château Vraye-Croix-de-Gay

* Ces vins sont jugés meilleurs que leurs pairs dans la présente classification.

EXPORTATION

L'exportation des vins de Bordeaux d'appellation d'origine contrôlée s'élevait en 1985 à environ 1,6 million d'hl (17,5 millions de caisses), ce qui représente une augmentation de 33 % par rapport à 1982. Sur la totalité : 250 000 hl (2,5 millions de caisses) furent exportés aux États-Unis.

CRUS DE BORDEAUX. CLASSIFICATION

Il y eut une grande exposition internationale à Paris en 1855. Ses organisateurs demandèrent aux Bordelais des échantillons de leurs produits les plus remarquables. Cet événement incita les notabilités locales à classer leurs meilleurs crus. Ils ne s'intéressèrent alors qu'aux Médoc et aux Sauternes. Les Graves, qui avaient autrefois été en tête, étaient alors tombés au-dessous des deux autres régions produisant les vins les plus typiques du Bordelais. Il est vrai que les négociants en vin, en partie par snobisme, dédaignaient leurs confrères de Libourne et des crus voisins : Saint-Émilion et Pomerol. C'est ainsi que Château-Pétrus en Pomerol, Château-Cheval-Blanc et Château-Ausone (révéré comme le plus vieux des fameux vignobles de la région) à Saint-Émilion furent omis lors de la classification des vins de la Gironde en 1855. Il leur fallut attendre un siècle pour être dans une classification différente et avoir droit à un classement officiel. Les courtiers bordelais, qui vendent le produit des divers vignobles aux expéditeurs et sont donc considérés comme connaissant les vins mieux que quiconque, furent chargés de cette tâche. Ils fondèrent leur jugement sur trois critères : le sol, le prestige et les prix.

Décision fort avisée comme l'a prouvé la longévité de la classification de 1855. Climat, sol et exposition de la vigne ne changent guère et ces éléments exercent la même influence bénéfique depuis toujours. Mais hélas ! les propriétaires changent. Certains cultivent leurs vignes eux-mêmes et produisent un vin meilleur que d'autres. On ne saurait donc douter que la hiérarchie établie il y a plus de cent ans est au moins en partie surannée. Rares sont les châteaux dont le domaine est resté immuable. On achète et revend sans cesse des parcelles de vigne.

La classification reste valable cependant pour les Premiers Crus : les trois grands Médoc : Château-Lafite, Château-Margaux et Château-Latour, ainsi que Château-Haut-Brion qui a toujours été sur la liste. Remarquons cependant qu'il est situé dans les Graves, mais son vin était trop bon pour que les jurés de 1855 le tinssent à l'écart. En dépit de la géographie, ils le classèrent dans les Médoc. Le Château-Mouton-Rotschild, en tête de liste des Seconds Crus en 1855, fut enfin classé Premier Cru en 1973.

Quand on considère la classification de 1855, on doit souligner que Second, Troisième, Quatrième ou Cinquième Cru ne signifie pas que le vin soit de seconde, troisième, quatrième ou cinquième qualité. En réalité, 62 seulement des quelque 4 000 crus du Bordelais se virent attribuer le titre de Grand Cru — de Premier à Cinquième — et c'est la crème des vignobles, qui, dans leur ensemble, produisent les plus grands vins rouges du monde. Venir après les Lafite, Latour, Margaux et Haut-Brion, ce n'est pas être dans une seconde catégorie, loin de là ! En outre, les Premiers ne sont les meilleurs qu'en moyenne ; certaines années les autres valent autant et même mieux. Quiconque achète une bouteille d'un des meilleurs millésimes de ces célèbres crus (à son prix) est certain d'acquérir quelque chose de superbe. Mais l'aventure commence quand on cherche parmi les autres années et les autres crus dans la somptueuse liste des vins de Bordeaux.

Les Crus Exceptionnels *ne sont pas* supérieurs aux Grands Crus, mais ce sont ceux qui furent déjà classés en 1855, *après* les 62 grands vignobles. Ils étaient eux-mêmes suivis par les Crus Bourgeois et les Crus Artisans. Parmi ceux-là se trouvent quelques grands vins qui méritent désormais d'être élevés à un grade supérieur.

Bien que valable, la vieille classification ne l'est pas entièrement car, si elle dit la vérité, elle ne dit pas toute la vérité. Les opinions exprimées dans la presse et ailleurs nous prouvent que, même à Bordeaux, il règne dans certains milieux un malaise croissant à ce sujet. On en arrive à cette situation : tout en reconnaissant que la réglementation de 1855 présente des défauts, il semble impossible de l'améliorer quoique certains des crus qui y figurent n'existent plus.

En 1959, on chargea un comité d'étudier comment améliorer le travail fait en 1855. Il discuta deux propositions : amender l'ancienne nomenclature pour tenir compte des changements, ou bien la laisser en l'état et en dresser une nouvelle. Estimant qu'il fallait modifier bien des choses, l'auteur de cette encyclopédie fit partie d'un des premiers comités composé des principaux vignerons, négociants et courtiers bordelais. En 1959, il publia son classement personnel de tous les vins rouges de Bordeaux, selon les mêmes critères que ceux du classement récent des Saint-Émilion et des Graves (Pomerol n'était pas classé et ne l'est toujours pas). Révisée à plusieurs reprises, la classification la plus récente date de 1986 (classification des Saint-Émilion).

Pendant que ce travail était en préparation, chaque expert fut consulté en privé et « sans procès-verbal ». Il en résulte qu'aucune opinion personnelle n'est citée. Pourtant il apparut bientôt à l'évidence que, sur certains points, les avis concordaient. Des enquêtes sur les cadastres de diverses communes révélèrent que les vignes de certains châteaux n'occupent plus le même terrain qu'en 1855. Dans bien des cas il s'agissait de modifications insignifiantes. Mais, dans d'autres cas, on avait procédé à d'importants transferts de parcelles. Le critère essentiel de qualification — un sol de première qualité — perd donc sa validité dans ces cas-là.

D'autres châteaux, classés parmi les Troisièmes Crus, ne font plus de vin du tout. Leur nom subsiste parmi les Grands Crus de 1855, comme une ruine rappelle un monument disparu. De telles absurdités nuisent au commerce du vin de Bordeaux. L'absurdité inverse apparaît aussi quand un vignoble classé Cinquième Cru, voire Cru Bourgeois, mérite d'être vendu avec le titre de Second ou Troisième Cru. Le vigneron et le client sont lésés autant l'un que l'autre par cette classification qui induit en erreur.

On convint en général qu'en appliquant les critères de 1855, il faudrait ranger dans les Premiers Crus le Château-Pétrus, qui n'était pas encore classé du tout, dans la région de Pomerol ; il faudrait promouvoir Château-Mouton-Rothschild de Second à Premier Cru, ce qui fut fait en 1973, et Cheval-Blanc de Premier Saint-Émilion à Grand Cru de Bordeaux. Bref, tant de vignobles de Saint-Émilion, Graves et Pomerol réclament leur place légitime que, selon toute évidence, une nouvelle classification devrait englober tous les vins du Bordelais. Il ne faut donc plus recourir à la nomenclature de 1855, car tout guide qui n'est pas rigoureusement exact trompe le public et lui fait perdre confiance. C'est ce qui est en train de se produire.

Quant à la forme que devrait prendre une nouvelle classification, on convient presque unanimement qu'il ne faudrait pas répéter l'erreur de 1855 en rangeant les crus en Premier, Second, etc. En un temps où la publicité et l'art de vendre sur un marché concurrentiel prévalent, tout vin classé Second, Troisième ou Quatrième serait injustement handicapé. Les classifications récentes des Saint-Émilion et des Graves ont évité cet écueil et adopté le canevas suivant : trois catégories, « Premiers Crus », « Grands Crus » et « Autres Principaux Crus » (*voir* APPENCICE A, III et VII). Dans la classification révisée qu'il suggérait, l'auteur avait adapté et étendu ce système comme suit : *Crus Hors Classe, Crus Exceptionnels. Grands Crus, Crus Supérieurs et Bons Crus.*

Enfin, la plupart des experts consultés estimèrent que, pour fixer la position de chaque cru, le prix devrait rester le plus sûr critère, comme en 1855. C'est donc en fonction de la valeur, de la qualité et du prestige de chaque vin que la classification suivante fut préparée. On tint compte du fait que, convenablement traité, un grand sol donnera des grands vins ; certains crus n'ont donc pas été rétrogradés autant que leur direction actuelle le justifierait, parce que leur sol est resté intact et que, sous une nouvelle direction, ces vignobles peuvent se relever.

En procédant à un tel classement, on doit envisager une durée de 25 à 50 ans, pour le moins. L'état actuel de la liste de 1855 démontre qu'un classement quelconque ne peut garder sa validité indéfiniment. Mais, à l'inverse, des changements trop fréquents sémeraient la confusion et entameraient la confiance des acheteurs.

En 1960, quand le comité eut formellement demandé la révision de la Classification de 1855, l'Institut national des appellations d'origine fut appelé à arbitrer. Deux années plus tard cependant, on décida à Bordeaux que les attributions de cet organisme étaient trop limitées pour lui permettre de trancher en une matière aussi complexe et controversée. La Chambre de commerce de Bordeaux et l'Académie des vins de Bordeaux prirent en main le problème de la réforme. Au moment où ce livre est mis sous presse, aucune des modifications nécessaires n'a encore été apportée à la Classification de 1855, pourtant désuète. Ces changements exigent un courage et un esprit d'initiative qui font encore défaut dans la région de Bordeaux. Les problèmes que pose la Classification de 1855 se font toujours plus évidents. Nous avons vu que, en 1973, le Mouton-Rothschild fut classé Premier Cru par décret du ministre de l'Agriculture. La Classification de 1855 est la propriété exclusive du Comité des Grands Crus Classés et ne peut en aucun cas être modifiée officiellement. La Classification ci-dessus, révisée en 1986, est la seule qui « ose » réunir les meilleurs vins rouges des quatre régions bordelaises importantes.

Voir CLASSIFICATION DES BORDEAUX

Bordeaux : Mousseux supérieur

Vin d'appellation contrôlée, légèrement mousseux, de la région de Bordeaux.
Voir BORDEAUX

Borderies

Moindre région de Cognac qui produit des eaux-de-vie au goût et à la finesse considérables.
Voir COGNAC

Bosa

Malvasia di Bosa (D.O.C.) est un vin rouge, richement coloré, de Sardaigne.
Voir SARDAIGNE

Bota

1. Gourde, en espagnol. La gourde espagnole courante est faite avec de la peau de chèvre non tannée et contient à peu près 1 l. Son bec, en os ou en bois, est mince. On fait jaillir le vin en pressant la gourde. Plusieurs personnes peuvent donc boire tour à tour sans que leurs lèvres touchent le bec.

2. Fût espagnol de 500 l, très utilisé pour conserver et faire mûrir les vins. Contenant normal du Xérès. Il existe une media bota ou demi-bota, contenant 250 l.

Botrytis cinerea

Cryptogame, autrement dit moisissure, qui attaque les raisins, lesquels deviennent gris, moisissent, se rident et se ratatinent. Dans certains cas, c'est la pourriture grise et la vendange en souffre parfois jusqu'à être perdue. Mais dans d'autres cas, quand le phénomène est étroitement surveillé, il s'agit de la pourriture noble. Elle donne les vins de dessert très doux tels que, en France, Barsac, Sauternes, Monbazillac et certains crus d'Anjou et Touraine ; en Allemagne : Auslese, Beerenauslesen et Trockenbeerenauslesen et, en Hongrie, le Tokay. Nulle part ailleurs on n'a réussi à faire du vin en cueillant tardivement des raisins trop mûrs. Certaines conditions climatiques doivent être remplies. Des résultats plus que satisfaisants ont été atteints aux États-Unis, en Australie et dans d'autres pays du monde.

Le champignon microscopique pénètre dans le fruit mais sans entailler la peau ni la faire éclater. Il n'expose donc pas la pulpe à l'air. Si tout se passe bien, le raisin flétrit, perd une partie de son eau, par une espèce de dessication naturelle mais, comme la moisissure ne supprime que peu de sucre, la teneur de ce dernier s'élève proportionnellement. Le fruit perd plus d'acidité que de sucre. Il en résulte que la proportion de solides solubles — sucre et glycérine — augmente plus vite que l'acidité. Quand on vinifie, le produit de la fermentation devient presque huileux, très sucré et très fortement alcoolisé. Les conditions climatiques doivent être telles que le raisin en mûrissant trouve suffisamment d'humidité dans l'air pour que la moisissure se développe. Il faut ensuite une alternance de sécheresse, permettant à l'eau du raisin de s'évaporer et empêchant la moisissure de se développer trop vite, puis d'humidité qui ranime son activité. Si la température s'élève trop, le champignon meurt. A la fin de cette culture difficile et hasardeuse, il reste peu de jus dans le raisin et on obtient peu de vin, c'est pourquoi il est extrêmement cher.

Botticino (D.O.C.)

Vin rouge italien ; à boire jeune.
Voir LOMBARDIE

Bouché

Se dit d'une bouteille fermée par un bouchon de liège. A ne pas confondre avec *bouchonné* (goût de bouchon).

Bouchet

Une des variétés de vigne cultivée en Saint-Émilion et Pomerol, synonyme de Cabernet Franc et Cabernet Sauvignon.

Bouchonné

Bouteille dégradée par un mauvais bouchon ; le vin prend alors un goût de bouchon.

Bouillie Bordelaise

Mélange de sulfate de cuivre et de chaux amortie utilisé sous forme de vaporisation fongicide dans de nombreuses partie d'Europe. Appliquée pendant les mois d'été pour combattre le mildiou et l'oïdium, cette vaporisation donne aux vignobles français et allemands une teinte d'un bleu-vert caractéristique.

Voir CHAPITRE V

Bouquet

Qualité organoleptique du vin due à son acidité volatile. Le bouquet doit être net, sans le moindre défaut. Cette odeur est produite par la dissipation des esters et éthers, composants évanescents du vin. Quand on débouche une bouteille froide, le bouquet est à peine perceptible. A bonne température, on sent d'abord le bouquet. Le parfum qui subsiste plus longtemps est l'arôme.

Bourbon

Whiskey américain *(voir* WHISKEY : BOURBON)

Bourg, Bourgeais, Côtes de Bourg (Appellation Contrôlée)

Rouges et blancs. Région de Bordeaux.

Appellation d'origine s'appliquant aux vins rouges et blancs provenant des collines de Bourg qui dominent le confluent de la Garonne et de la Dordogne se confondant pour donner la Gironde. Ce cru est presque entièrement environné par celui de Blaye. Les deux anciennes villes fortifiées de Bourg et de Blaye ne sont guère qu'à 10 km l'une de l'autre et on peut considérer leurs vins comme presque semblables. Toutefois, le Bourg rouge est plus corsé que le Blaye rouge et, dans l'ensemble, supérieur. A l'inverse, le blanc des Premières Côtes de Blaye est le meilleur des deux régions.

Bourgogne

Vins rouges et blancs. Centre-Est de la France.

L'ancien domaine des ducs de Bourgogne n'est, sur le plan économique, ni la plus vaste ni la plus importante région vinicole du monde. Mais c'est de loin l'une des plus grandes quant à la qualité et la diversité. Nulle part ailleurs le vin ne s'intègre autant à la vie quotidienne, et nulle part ailleurs en général (sauf à Bordeaux) on n'éprouve un tel amour du vin ni une telle fierté de sa perfection.

Voilà plus de 2 000 ans que les Bourguignons cultivent la vigne sans interruption sur le même sol, consacrent leur vie à la soigner, à en faire des vins magnifiques, qu'ils boivent et expédient vers les quatre coins du monde. la tradition est passée de père en fils et des nobles aux prêtres, puis aux paysans. Au long des siècles, on a discerné les sites les plus propices à la culture de la vigne, les variétés convenant le mieux à ces sols ; on les a plantées et on les a chéries. Il en résulte la Bourgogne telle qu'elle est aujourd'hui.

On accuse toutefois la grande région vinicole d'avoir considérablement nui à la qualité du Bourgogne en pratiquant une taille trop intense sous prétexte d'obtenir une plus grande quantité, et en plantant de nouvelles vignes dans des terres qui ne sont pas propices. Il est certain que, vers la fin des années 60 et 70 ainsi que dans les années 80, la production s'est montrée plutôt inégale.

Hélas ! il est vrai que le Bourgogne de l'un est l'ordinaire de l'autre car aucun autre nom n'a été aussi obstinément employé de manière abusive. En bien des pays du monde, Bourgogne est devenu presque synonyme de vin rouge, foncé et lourd, parfois trop âpre, parfois trop doux ; l'acheteur (voire le vendeur) ignorent souvent que bien des Bourgogne sont des vins légers, fins et subtils et que quelques-uns des plus grands vins de cette province sont blancs.

Les vins rouges du Beaujolais — subdivision régionale de la Bourgogne — par exemple, atteignent leur maximum de qualité lorsqu'ils sont légers, frais et fruités. Les vins de la Côte-d'Or, surtout ceux des communes de Volnay, Pommard et Beaune, peuvent être d'une finesse et d'une délicatesse exquises. La confusion qui règne à ce sujet est encouragée par les commerçants du monde entier qui n'hésitent pas à coller une étiquette Bourgogne sur n'importe quel vin rouge, quelle que soit son origine. En réalité, les seuls vins ayant le droit

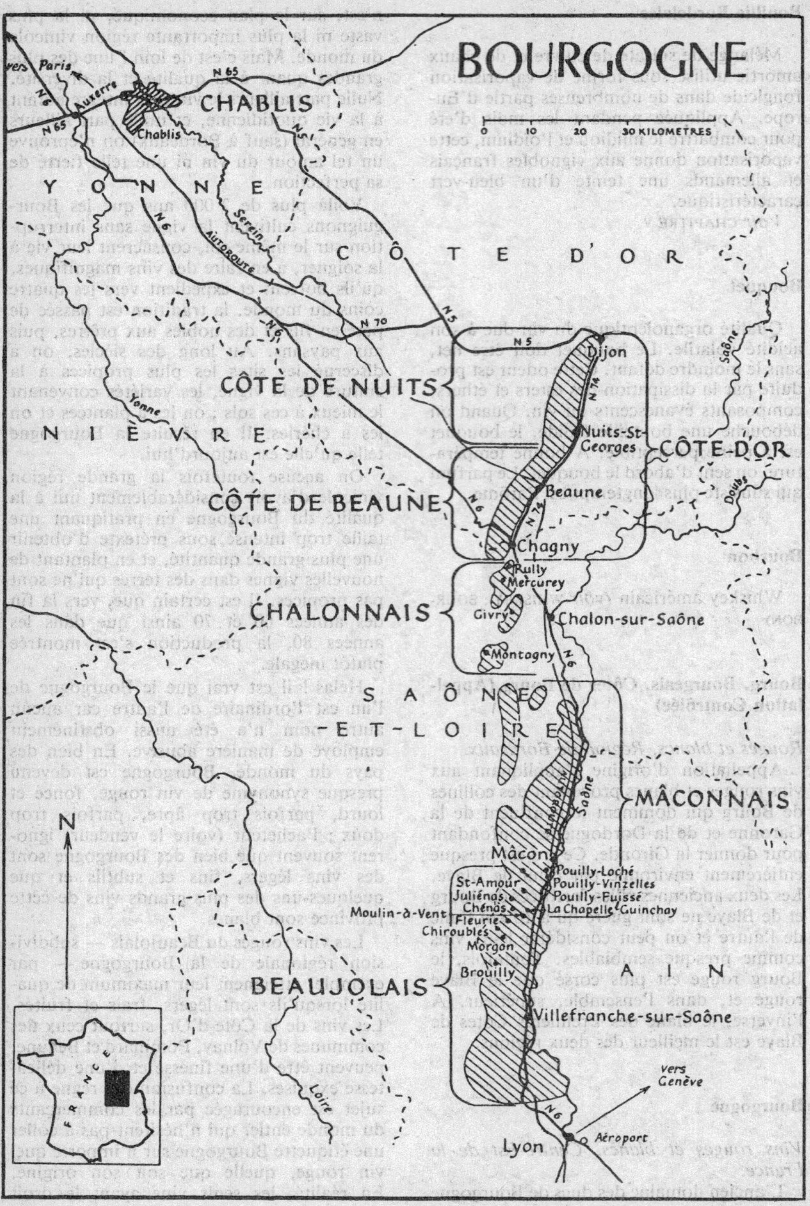
BOURGOGNE
0 10 20 30 KILOMETRES
vers Paris
N 65
N 6
Auxerre
CHABLIS
Chablis
Y O N N E
Serein
AUTOROUTE
C Ô T E D'O R
N 5
N 70
Dijon
N 74
CÔTE DE NUITS
Nuits-St-Georges
CÔTE-D'OR
N I È V R E
Yonne
Saône
Doubs
CÔTE DE BEAUNE
Beaune
Chagny
Rully
Mercurey
Givry
CHALONNAIS
Chalon-sur-Saône
Montagny
S A Ô N E
-E T- L O I R E
MÂCONNAIS
Mâcon
Pouilly-Loché
Pouilly-Vinzelles
Pouilly-Fuissé
La Chapelle Guinchay
St-Amour
Juliénas
Chénas
Moulin-à-Vent
Fleurie
Chiroubles
Morgon
Brouilly
BEAUJOLAIS
A I N
Villefranche-sur-Saône
vers Genève
Aéroport
Lyon
Loire
FRANCE
N

historique, géographique, moral (et, même légal, dans le Marché Commun) de porter ce nom sont ceux de certains secteurs clairement définis des départements de Côte-d'Or, Yonne, Sâone-et-Loire ainsi que de l'arrondissment de Villefranche-sur-Sâone, dans le département du Rhône. Comme il en va pour tous les vins français d'appellation contrôlée, les variétés de vignes sont définies légalement, la quantité de vin produite à l'hectare est également limitée, les méthodes de culture, de taille, d'amendement du sol, ainsi que celles de vinification et de maturation sont contrôlées légalement ; enfin, si le vin qui résulte de l'ensemble de ces opérations n'atteint pas certaines normes minimales, ce n'est pas un Bourgogne. (Ces contrôles ne sont pas appliqués seulement au Bourgogne, mais à tous les vins français d'appellation contrôlée). C'est pourquoi, malgré leurs mérites, les bouteilles qui portent sur leur étiquette bourgogne californien, bourgogne sud-africain, bourgogne chilien ne sont pas des Bourgogne. Le vignoble de Bourgogne ne couvre que 40 000 ha.

Voir APPELLATION D'ORIGINE CONTRÔLÉE

HISTOIRE DU VIN

On ne sait pas qui introduisit la vigne en Bourgogne, mais on sait que les Romains en trouvèrent quand ils conquirent le pays et que sous leur infuence la culture s'accrut et prospéra sûrement. Les premiers Barbares qui envahirent l'Empire romain, et la Bourgogne notamment, détruisirent probablement les plantations. Mais les Burgondes — envahisseurs barbares eux aussi — durent recommencer à en planter à la fin du IVe siècle.

En 581, le roi des Burgondes, Gontran, donna les vignobles de Dijon à l'abbé de Saint-Bénigne, événement qui devait avoir des conséquences à longue échéance. Les moines se réjouirent de ce présent qui leur assurait une source constante de vin pur pour les services religieux. Au cours des siècles qui suivirent, le royaume des Burgondes devint le duché de Bourgogne. Suivant l'exemple de Gontran, ses souverains offrirent à différents ordres religieux des vignobles tels que ceux d'Aloxe, Fixey, Fixin, Santenay, Auxey, Comblanchien, Chassagne, Savigny, Pommard et Meursault.

Dans le monde médiéval, le vin représentait la richesse. Emportés par ce soudain afflux de biens terrestres, certains moines oublièrent les strictes règles monastiques et menèrent trop bonne vie. Au XIIe siècle, saint Bernard de Clairvaux dénonça cet esprit de luxe et d'envie. En 1112, il arriva au monastère de Cîteaux et le réforma. C'est de cette réforme que naquit l'ordre des cisterciens. Saint Bernard ne s'entendit pas avec les bénédictins du monastère de Cluny. Cluny avait été une des communautés les plus puissantes de l'Église de France et possédait une abondance considérable de biens fonciers plantés de vignes. Les cisterciens adoptèrent la devise *Cruse et aratro* (par la croix et l'araire) et entreprirent de cultiver les terres à l'abandon. En Bourgogne, rien ne prospère mieux que la vigne et la viticulture devint une des principales occupations de l'ordre. Une de ses plus belles réalisations fut la fondation du Clos de Vougeot, constitué lentement, lopin par lopin, grâce aux donations de seigneurs impressionnés par la sainteté et l'esprit industrieux des moines. L'ordre frère des cisterciens fonda le Clos des Dames de Tart, qui devint plus tard le Clos de Tart.

Les siècles se succédant, le Moyen Age approchant de sa fin, la vigne prospéra et couvrit de plus grandes superfices. Mais la variété des raisins s'accrut. En 1395, le duc de Bourgogne, Philippe le Hardi, bannit des vignobles de son duché, le raisin, qu'il désigne par ces mots : « le Gaamez déloyal ». Cette variété de vigne donnait du vin en abondance, mais plein de « très grande et horrible âpreté ». Le Gamay dont parle le fils de Saint Louis survit en Bourgogne de nos jours ; c'est une de ces variétés qui donnent l'excellent Beaujolais ; mais, dans le département de la Côte-d'Or, le vin fait avec ce même raisin ressemble beaucoup à celui dont parlait Philippe le Hardi, voilà plus de cinq siècle. Un autre édit ducal tenta d'interdire la détention de vins provenant de n'importe quelle autre région.

Les vins de Bourgogne, particulièrement le Beaune, plaisaient aux rois de France. On dit que, lorsqu'il dut affronter les armées impériales à Bouvines, Philippe-Auguste fit venir un baril de Beaune. Lors du sacre de Philippe VI à Reims, le vin coulait à flots des narines d'un étalon de bronze devant la cathédrale. Louis XI adorait le Volnay et il eut le bonheur de ramener au cours de son règne le duché rebelle de Bourgogne dans le domaine de la couronne.

Libérée enfin des guerres féodales, la

Bourgogne fut encore ravagée au cours des guerres de Religion. Là, comme dans le Bordelais, on ordonna de temps en temps d'arracher les vignes pour semer des céréales, mais il ne semble pas que le commerce du vin en souffrit. A la fin du XVIIe siècle et au début du XVIIIe, le Bourgogne, qu'appréciait Louis XIV, connut une nouvelle vogue. Ce n'était pas encore le vin que nous connaissons. Il était beaucoup plus léger. Parfois on mêlait du raisin blanc au rouge, ce qui donnait un vin rosâtre, de la teinte de l'œil de perdrix, qu'on préférait alors. Les étrangers — particulièrement les Allemands et les Hollandais — réclamaient, dit-on, des vins plus forts. On aurait alors sucré le moût à leur intention quand la vendange ne suffisait pas : il s'agissait donc d'une chaptalisation longtemps avant Chaptal.

On a raconté trop d'histoires au sujet de Napoléon et des divers crus de Bourgogne pour les répéter dans cet ouvrage. Il semble toutefois que le train de ses maréchaux transportait des barriques de vin d'un bout à l'autre de l'Europe. Le Chambertin était le cru préféré de Talleyrand dont on cite la phrase suivante : « Monsieur, quand on vous sert un tel vin, vous prenez le verre respectueusement, vous l'admirez, vous le humez, vous le reposez et vous en discutez ». Dumas disait du même vin : « Rien ne projette sur l'avenir une teinte plus rose ».

Quand la Révolution française éclata, une bonne part du vignoble bourguignon appartenait à l'Église. Le canevas de la viticulture fut donc complètement bouleversé dans cette province par la vague d'anticléricalisme qui balaya la France à partir de 1790. Les biens de l'Église furent saisis par l'État, servirent de gage aux assignats et passèrent aux mains des acquéreurs de biens nationaux. Puis, à partir du Premier Empire et du code Napoléon, les vignobles se morcelèrent de génération en génération : c'est ainsi que s'établit l'état actuel de la viticulture bourguignonne. Le vigneron dont toutes les vignes se touvent sur un seul terrain pourrait être ruiné par la grêle ; mais s'il ne possède qu'une parcelle d'une vigne et une parcelle d'une autre, à quelques kilomètres de là, l'orage épargnera vraisemblablement une partie de sa récolte. Chaque grand cru continue à exister en tant qu'entité, mais il est partagé entre un certain nombre de propriétaires. Deux bouteilles de vin provenant de la même vendange du même vignoble peuvent être différentes l'une de l'autre car leurs caractéristiques dépendent dans une certaine mesure du savoir-faire de celui qui a vinifié leur contenu. Le système bordelais des grands domaines réunis entre les mains d'un seul propriétaire est pratiquement inconnu en Bourgogne. A de très rares exceptions près, il n'existe pas de château en Bourgogne dans le sens qu'on donne à ce mot dans la région bordelaise. En Bourgogne, chaque domaine est constitué de pièces et de morceaux, de parcelles dispersées entre divers vignobles et qui n'ont d'autre lien les unes avec les autres que leur appartenance à un seul homme. On compte cependant plus de cent appellations d'origine en Bourgogne. A première vue, ce système semble compliqué et confus. En réalité il n'est ni l'un ni l'autre.

Appellations d'origine en Bourgogne

Les vins de Bourgogne sont répartis entre différentes appellations d'origine contrôlée, tout simplement parce qu'il existe autant de types distincts de vin. Comme dans tous les systèmes français d'appellation contrôlée, les noms vont du général au particulier. Chambertin nous donne un exemple de la manière dont fonctionne ce système.

Chambertin est un des meilleurs crus bourguignons. Par bonnes années, quand il est bien fait, ce vin est inégalable. Le vignoble ne couvre même pas 13 ha (12,95) : il a légalement droit au titre de Grand Cru avec 30 autres des centaines de vignobles bourguignons. Son vin peut prendre le nom de Chambertin ; celui de la commune : Gevrey-Chambertin ; celui d'une subdivision plus vaste : Côte de Nuits ; ou le nom général de Bourgogne. Mais il porte toujours le célèbre nom de Chambertin, pourvu qu'il soit conforme à certaines normes minimales élevées. Plus le nom est précis, plus les normes minimales sont élevées et meilleur est le vin. Ce système est assez bien établi pour assurer aux vignerons un prix plus élevé pour le meilleur vin, dont la qualité se reflète dans le nom. Nous voyons ici nettement l'enchaînement des appellations : nom de cru — nom de commune — nom du secteur — nom de la région ; soit : Chambertin — Gevrey-Chambertin — Côte de Nuits — Bourgogne. Le même canevas se reproduit dans toutes les communes de la Côte-d'Or et dans les autres secteurs de la Bourgogne (quoiqu'il puisse y avoir de-ci, de-là, quelques exceptions mineures à la règle).

Le fait que les 13 ha de Chambertin appartiennent à plusieurs vignerons a engendré une manière particulière de traiter le vin et de le vendre. Ce système a été mis au point pour diminuer la confusion. Il consiste en ceci : un négociant achète les vins de divers vignerons — à Chambertin, par exemple — il les mélange et les vend sous l'étiquette de Chambertin et celle de sa firme. Le résutat d'un tel mélange sera assez constant d'année en année. L'avantage de ce procédé est qu'on ne verra pas chaque vigneron offrir sur le marché des vins différents sous la même appellation. Le client apprend aisément le nom du vin et du négociant qu'il préfère. Il se sentira assez sûr de la marchandise qu'il achète chaque année et dont les qualités resteront toujours assez constantes. Le système n'est pas sans inconvénients : quels que soient les soins du négociants, le produit du mélange ne sera peut-être pas identique au meilleur vin du cru ; quand celui d'un vigneron talentueux est mêlé à celui d'un viticulteur maladroit, la qualité du meilleur est noyée par celle du moins bon.

La Bourgogne n'est pas très étendue, elle ne produit pas plus de 2 millions d'hectolitres par an, alors que la région de Bordeaux en produit près de 5 millions. En outre, le Bourgogne authentique n'est pas bon marché et ne peut pas l'être. Le temps est souvent mauvais pour le vigneron qui ne peut pas compter sur une bonne vendange tous les ans ; le produit de la vente des bonnes années doit lui permettre de vivre durant les mauvaises. Quand la quantité est basse, les ressources du vigneron baissent en proportion ; il doit pourtant manger et la vigne exige des soins coûteux. Tout cela ne fait pas baisser les prix.

Étant donné les prix élevés et le fait que les vins sont très divers, il importe de savoir ce que l'on achète en fait de Bourgogne, plus que dans toute autre bonne région. Des négociants sans scrupule se permettent depuis des siècles d'acheter hors de Bourgogne des vins à bon marché pour allonger leurs stocks quand ils baissent, ce qui leur permet de maintenir des prix accessibles, tout en faisant des bénéfices élevés. Cette fraude fit fureur immédiatement après la Première Guerre mondiale et continua au cours des années 1930 et suivantes, jusqu'à ce que des esprits éclairés unissent leurs efforts pour amender et parfaire les lois sur les appellations d'origine, ce qui donna des pouvoirs plus étendus aux inspecteurs des fraudes. Les lois n'ont pas complètement éliminé la tromperie mais elles l'ont rendue beaucoup plus difficile. Certains vignerons eux-mêmes sont en train d'adopter un système dérivé de celui des châteaux du Bordelais pour rendre la fraude pratiquement impossible. Un vin mis en bouteille au domaine est celui qui a été fait et mis en bouteille par le même homme, généralement un viticulteur, qui cultive la vigne avec les raisins de laquelle ce vin a été fait, vigne qui ne couvre guère en général que de 1 à 5 ha. Dans un tel cas, l'étiquette indiquera : le nom du vin, le millésime, le nom du viticulteur et le fait que le vin fut mis en bouteille au domaine. Parfois cette mention s'exprime de cette façon : « Mise du domaine » ou encore autrement « mis en bouteille par le propriétaire ».

Les plus grands crus proviennent des coteaux dorés de la Côte-d'Or : longue chaîne de collines couronnées de broussailles et qui roulent au long de la bordure est de la plaine bourguignonne. Cette chaîne part de Dijon (au temps jadis il existait aussi un Côte de Dijon et on s'est efforcé de le ressusciter, surtout pour les rosés de Marsannay) et se termine juste au sud de Santenay. On voit sur la carte qu'elle est divisée en deux secteurs : au nord, Côte de Nuits, qui fait les vins royaux de Chambertin, de Musigny et de La Romanée (le premier grand vignoble qu'aperçoit l'automobiliste le long de la route est le Clos de Vougeot) et, au sud, la Côte de Beaune, d'où viennent les rouges plus délicats (Beaune, Pommard, Volnay) ainsi que les blancs somptueux de Meursault et de Montrachet.

Un certain nombre d'appellations communales bourguignonnes n'apparaissent que rarement, voire jamais, sur les étiquettes hors de Bourgogne. L'appellation la plus générale s'applique aux vins qui sont souvent agréables à boire si on les saisit jeunes, à proximité des vignes d'où ils proviennent, mais qui ne vieilliront ni ne voyageront bien. On trouvera dans les tableaux ci-dessous et les pages suivantes, un certain nombre de ces appellations.

Appellations contrôlées de la région de Bourgogne				
Appellation	*Date d'institution*	*Rendement maximal hl/ha*	*Production (hl) Blanc*	*Production (hl) Rouge*
Bourgogne (Vins Fins des Hautes Côtes)	31 juillet 1937	r/ros 55 bl 60	10 698	120 000
(C'est l'appellation la plus générale. Elle est accordée à tout vin provenant de la région délimitée de Bourgogne, pourvu que les rouges soient faits avec du Pinot Noir, avec certaines tolérances pour le Pinot Liebault et le Pinot Beurot, ainsi que le César et le Tressot dans l'Yonne ; et les blancs avec du Chardonnay et du Pinot Blanc. Les rouges doivent titrer au minimum 10º et les blancs 10,5º).				
Bourgogne Passetoutgrains	31 juillet 1937	55		42 500
(Jadis fait en quantités énormes, par cuvage en commun de Pinot Noir et de Gamay (au moins 1/3 de Pinot), ce vin doit titrer au moins 9,5º. Quoique agréable sur place dans sa jeunesse, il ne supporte pas bien le transport et se conserve mal).				
Bourgogne Aligoté	31 juillet 1937	60	58 000	
(Vin blanc produit exclusivement avec du raisin Aligoté. Le Chardonnay est autorisé aussi, mais il n'est pratiquement pas utilisé. Teneur minimale en alcool : 9,5º).				
Bourgogne ordinaire **Bourgogne Grand Ordinaire**	31 juillet 1937	r/ros 55 bl 60	8 000	
(Qu'un vin puisse être à la fois « grand » et « ordinaire » indique combien l'I.N.A.O. tient habilement compte des susceptibilités. Ces deux appellations portent sur les vins rouges et rosés faits avec du Pinot et du Gamay (du César et du Tressot dans l'Yonne) et les vins blancs avec du Pinot Blanc, du Chardonnay, de l'Aligoté, du Melon de Bourgogne (et du Sacy, dans l'Yonne). Titre au moins 9º pour les rouges et rosés et 9,5º pour le blanc).				
Bourgogne mousseux	16 mars 1943	ros 55 bl 60		
(Parfois assez agréable mais trop souvent médiocre ou pire, ce vin est la version « mousseux » de n'importe quel blanc ou rouge ayant droit à une appellation de Bourgogne, mais évidemment, dans la pratique, on ne traite presque jamais ainsi ceux qui méritent une appellation de haute qualité. Étant donné qu'en Angleterre et aux États-Unis les droits de douane sont aussi élevés que sur le Champagne, ce dernier est plus intéressant à l'achat).				

Le tableau suivant donne les mêmes renseignements sur les appellations d'origine contrôlée de Bourgogne concernant des vins plus distingués que les précédents et qui se répartissent entre les 5 secteurs suivants : Côte-d'Or (rouges et blancs) : Chablis (blancs) ; Beaujolais (rouges et très peu de blancs) ; Mâconnais (rouges et blancs) ; Chalonnais (rouges et blancs). *(Voir* chacune de ces appellations à sa place dans l'ordre alphabétique).

APPELLATIONS CONTRÔLÉES DE LA RÉGION DE BOURGOGNE
(Les crus qui ont droit à une appellation sont classés par commune.
Les meilleures communes sont marquées d'un astérisque.)

Appellation	*Date d'inscription*	*Rendement maximal hl/ha*		*Production moyenne hl*	
		Blanc	*Rouge*	*Blanc*	*Rouge*
I — CÔTE-D'OR					
* Aloxe-Corton	11 mars 1938	45	40	25	5 250
Corton	31 juillet 1937	40	35	25	2 000
Corton-Charlemagne	31 juillet 1937	40		1,300	
Auxey-Duresses	21 mai 1970	45	40	1,150	3,200
* Beaune	5 déc. 1972	45	40	600	15 000
Blagny	21 mai 1970		40		225
* Chambolle-Musigny	11 sept. 1936		40		6 500
Bonne Mares	8 déc. 1936		35		500
Musigny	11 sept. 1936	40	35	10	300
* Chassagne-Montrachet	21 mai 1970	45	40	3,750	6 200
Bâtard-Montrachet	31 juillet 1937	40		450	
Chevalier-Montrachet	31 juillet 1937	40		200	
Criots-Bâtard-Montrachet	31 juillet 1937	40		50	
Montrachet	31 juillet 1937	40		120	
Cheilly-lès-Maranges	21 mai 1970	45	40	3	400
Chorey-lès-Beaune	21 mai 1970	45	40	7	4 000
Côte de Beaune	5 déc. 1972	45	40	170	2 500
Côte de Beaune-Villages	21 mai 1970		40		6 800
Côtes de Nuits-Villages	20 août 1964	45	40	5	6 500
Dezize-lès-Maranges	21 mai 1970	45	40	10	60
* Fixin	8 déc. 1936	45	40	20	900
* Gevrey-Chambertin	11 sept. 1936		40		15 500
Chambertin	31 juillet 1937		35		500
Chambertin-Clos-de-Bèze	31 juillet 1937		35		850
Chapelle-Chambertin	31 juillet 1937		37		210
Charmes-Chambertin	31 juillet 1937		37		1 000
Griotte-Chambertin	31 juillet 1937		37		100
Latricières-Chambertin	31 juillet 1937		37		200
Mazis-Chambertin	31 jtuillet 1937		37		350
Mazoyères-Chambertin	31 juillet 1937		37		200
Ruchottes-Chambertin	31 juillet 1937		37		100
Bourgogne Hautes-Côtes-de-Beaune	31 juillet 1937	60	*55*	150	8 500
Bourgogne Hautes-Côtes-de-Nuits	31 juillet 1937	60	*55*	1 490	1750
Ladoix	21 mai 1970	45	40	200	3 500
Bourgogne Marsannay-la-Côte	31 juillet 1937		*55*		1 500
* Meursault	21 mai 1970	45	40	12,500	800
Monthélie	21 mai 1970	45	40	50	3 000
* Morey-Saint-Denis	8 déc. 1936	45	40	40	3 000
Clos de la Roche	8 déc. 1936		35		500
Clos Saint-Denis	8 déc. 1936		85		200
Clos de Tart	4 janv. 1939		35		200
Clos des Lambrays	27 avril 1981		35		200
* Nuits-Saint-Georges	5 déc. 1972	45	40	50	12 000
Pernand-Vergelesses	21 mai 1970	45	40	800	2 600
* Pommard	11 sept. 1936		40		11 000
* Puligny-Montrachet	21 mai 1970	45	40	11 000	300

Appellation	*Date d'inscription*	*Rendement maximal hl/ha*		*Production moyenne hl*	
		Blanc	*Rouge*	*Blanc*	*Rouge*
Bienvenue-Bâtard-Montrachet	31 juillet 1937	40		125	
Saint-Aubin	21 mai 1970	45	40	1 400	2 700
Saint-Romain	21 mai 1970	45	40	1 100	750
Sampigny-lès-Maranges	21 mai 1970	45	40	150	100
Santenay	21 mai 1970	45	40	230	14 000
Savigny-lès-Beaune	21 mai 1970	45	40	400	11 000
* Volnay	9 sept. 1937		40		9 000
* Vosne-Romanée	11 sept. 1936		40		6 500
Échezeaux	31 juillet 1937		35		1 400
Grands-Échezeaux	31 juillet 1937		35		350
La Tâche	11 sept. 1936		35		250
Richebourg	11 sept 1936		35		250
Romanée-Saint-Vivant	11 sept.1936		35		190
Romanée-Conti	11 sept. 1936		35		40
La Romanée	11 sept. 1936		35		30
* Vougeot	8 déc. 1936	45	40	75	650
Clos de Vougeot	31 juillet 1937		35		2 100
II — CHABLIS					
Chablis	13 janv. 1938	45		60 000	
Chablis Grand Cru	13 janv. 1938	45		4 500	
Petit Chablis	5 janv. 1944	50		6 000	
Chablis Premier Cru	13 janv. 1938	50		25 000	
III — BEAUJOLAIS					
Beaujolais	12 sept. 1937	55	55	2 500	500 000
Beaujolais-Supérieur	12 sept. 1937	55	55	1 000	10 000
Beaujolais-Villages	12 sept. 1937	55	*50*	2 000	350 000
Brouilly	19 oct. 1938		48		70 000
Chénas	11 sept. 1936		48		18 000
Chiroubles	11 sept. 1936		48		15 000
Côte de Brouilly	19 oct. 1938		48		13 000
Fleurie	11 sept. 1936		48		40 000
Juliénas	11 mars 1938		48		30 000
Morgon	11 sept. 1936		48		55 000
Moulin-à-Vent	11 sept. 1936		48		30 000
Saint-Amour	6 janv. 1946		48		13 000
IV — MACONNAIS					
Mâcon	31 juillet 1937	60	*55*	500	5 000
Mâcon-Supérieur	31 juillet 1937	60	*55*	13 000	47 000
Mâcon-Villages	31 juillet 1937	60		125 000	
Pouilly-Fuissé	11 sept. 1936	45		43 000	
Pouilly-Loché	27 avril 1940	50		1 500	
Pouilly-Vinzelles	27 avril 1940	50		2 500	
Saint-Véran	1er juin 1971	55		25 000	
V — CHALONNAIS					
Givry	8 fév. 1946	45	45	600	6 000
Mercurey	11 sept. 1936	45	40	1 000	20 000
Montagny	11 sept. 1936	45		6 000	
Rully	13 juin 1939	40	40	4 000	3 500

Les chiffres en italique correspondent au vin rouge et rosé.

L'encépagement de la Bourgogne

Pour les vins rouges

Pinot Noir. C'est la plus noble de toutes les vignes. Chef d'une famille distinguée, le Pinot Noir, aussi appelé Noiren ou Noirien en Bourgogne, surpasse en excellence ses parents et rejetons. Il s'adapte aux sols variés de la Côte-d'Or pour donner les raisins dont sont faits les vins les plus grands. Phénomène curieux : dans le granit du Beaujolais, il ne donne que des vins plats, sans distinction et y cède la place au Gamay.

Gamay. Sauf en Beaujolais — où il donne un vin fruité, léger et éminemment délicieux — le Gamay a tendance à être vulgaire, acide et âpre en Bourgogne. On en cultivait beaucoup autrefois en Côte-d'Or, mais il est en train de disparaître en Bourgogne et le Gamay qu'on y conserve est réservé au vin consommé par le personnel. Néanmoins, une très petite quantité de Passe-Tout-Grain est encore livrée au commerce : il est produit par le cuvage en commun de Gamay et de Pinot Noir.

Pinot Liebault. Sauf pour un spécialiste, il est impossible de le distinguer à n'importe quel point de vue du Pinot Noir.

Pinot Gris. Aucun Bourgogne n'est fait qu'avec du Pinot Gris comme le sont tant d'Alsace. On en cultive pourtant et les vignerons assurent qu'en ajouter une certaine quantité au Pinot Noir fournit un vin plus élégant, fin et délicat.

César et Tressot. Autorisés seulement dans l'Yonne pour les vins qui ne prennent que l'appellation d'origine la plus générale.

Pour les vins blancs

Chardonnay (aussi appelé *Aubaine* ou *Beaunois)*. On le crut autrefois de la famille du Pinot et on l'appelait alors Pinot Chardonnay. C'est le raisin qui donne tous les plus grands vins blancs de Bourgogne. Sur des sols crayeux, comme ceux de Côte-d'Or, Chablis, Mâconnais, il donne des vins divers selon les conditions locales et qui, lorsqu'ils atteignent leur apogée, ont tendance à être à la fois corsés et délicats, à conserver le parfum du raisin. Ils sont merveilleusement équilibrés et également dotés d'une extraordinaire finesse.

Pinot Blanc. C'est le blanc de la famille Pinot. On l'ajoute au Chardonnay pour faire les meilleurs vins blancs.

Aligoté. Ce raisin fournit les vins blancs banals de Bourgogne qui n'ont guère de race, ne supportent pas bien le transport, mais peuvent être extrêmement agréables quand ils sont consommés sur place. Parfois on les rend légèrement mousseux, ou plutôt pétillants.

Sacy. Autorisé seulement dans l'Yonne, pour les vins qui portent l'appellation d'origine la plus générale.

Melon de Bourgogne. Autorisé dans toute la Bourgogne, mais seulement pour les vins qui prennent l'appellation d'origine la plus générale, c'est-à-dire : Bourgogne.

La viniculture en Bourgogne

Le temps de cuvage de tous les vins de Bourgogne est bref. Ici, les vins rouges fermentent avec la peau du raisin : les vins blancs, au contraire, sont débarrassés des peaux avant fermentation. Mais, en Bourgogne, les vins rouges restent seulement en contact avec les peaux pendant six à douze jours (optimum dix jours). Cette pratique contraste nettement avec celle du Bordelais où les rouges cuvent de douze à vingt jours. La différence de méthode donne des vins différents.

Les Bordeaux cuvés longuement absorbent plus de tanin provenant des peaux et pépins que ne le font les Bourgogne. Ils sont donc plus durs au début et atteignent un point culminant plus élevé grâce à leur longévité ; les grands Bordeaux rouges n'arrivent à la plénitude de leur gloire qu'avec l'âge. D'une plus faible teneur en tanin, les Bourgogne rouges seront consommables bien plus tôt, souvent dans les deux à cinq ans après les vendanges. En outre, le Cabernet Sauvignon du Bordelais donne des vins plus lourds, plus corsés que le Pinot Noir de Bourgogne. Ainsi, par sa légèreté, le Bourgogne naturel contredira le préjugé selon lequel tous les Bourgogne sont corsés et tous les Bordeaux légers.

Hormis ce qui concerne la durée de cuvage, la vinification en Bourgogne est sensiblement celle que nous avons décrite au CHAPITRE V. Pourtant la chaptalisation est très répandue en Bourgogne parce que l'été n'est en général pas assez ensoleillé dans cette région pour donner au raisin le sucre nécessaire pour avoir des vins parfaitement équilibrés. Cette addition de sucre avant fermentation n'a lieu que sous un contrôle sévère des autorités. Ce sucre fermente avec celui du raisin et il en résulte un vin d'un plus fort degré alcoolique, ce qui lui donne parfois en même temps force et corps. Malheureusement, on constate actuellement une tendance à chaptaliser à l'excès les meilleurs vins.

Les vins de Bourgogne vieillissaient entre 18 et 24 mois dans des récipients de contenances diverses. Ceux de consommation courante sont conservés dans de grandes cuves, mais les meilleurs exigent des futailles plus petites. Le fût normal est la *pièce* qui contient 228 litres. Il arrive que l'on parle d'une ancienne mesure de capacité, la *queue,* équivalant à deux pièces, mais il n'existe plus de tonneaux de cette dimension. La demi-pièce s'appelle *feuillette* (114 l) et le quart de pièce *quartaut* (57 l). Pour le Chablis, cependant, on utilise une autre feuillette d'une capacité de 132 l et la pièce traditionnelle du Mâconnais en contient 215 , alors que celle du Beaujolais a une capacité de 216 l. Heureusement cette ancienne futaille est en train de céder la place à la pièce courante de Bourgogne.

On vieillit moins qu'autrefois les vins de Bourgogne : 12 à 20 mois est maintenant pratique courante. Il en résulte un breuvage plus net, frais et plus fruité ; les experts estiment que ce changement est parfaitement justifié. Les Bourgogne sont ensuite mis dans des bouteilles aux épaules tombantes et plus trapues que celles du Bordelais.

Quoique maints Bourgogne soient consommables à n'importe quel moment entre 5 mois et 5 ans après la mise en bouteille, d'autres conservent parfois leur excellence jusqu'à un demi-siècle et même plus. Malheureusement ces vieilles bouteilles deviennent excessivement rares. Le vin de Bourgogne absorbait naturellement plus de tanin au contact des peaux et du bois neuf, ce qui lui assurait une plus grande longévité. Il arrive que certains négociants ajoutent du tanin aux vins jeunes, ce qui n'a pas le même effet et n'aboutit qu'à dénaturer le goût du vin. Autre adultération subie par bien des Bourgogne dans les caves des négociants : un coupage avec des vins lourds d'autres régions, dans le but de lui donner un caractère plus bourguignon. Depuis une centaine d'années, la demande de Bourgogne s'est tellement accrue qu'on a importé illicitement des vins de degré élevé du Rhône, du Midi et d'Algérie pour allonger une production devenue insuffisante. Des vins d'Italie de fort degré ont maintenant pris la place de ceux venant d'Algérie. Le contenu des bouteilles de Bourgogne s'éloignait de plus en plus des caractéristiques du véritable vin de la région. Ainsi se constitua un marché à l'usage des buveurs de vin sans expérience à qui on enseigna que, si le vin n'avait pas la consistance épaisse et trop alcoolisée qu'ils associaient mentalement au vin de Bourgogne, il était déficient. On en arriva à cette situation paradoxale : quand ces amateurs parvenaient à mettre la main sur un vin mis en bouteille au domaine ou par un honnête négociant, ils s'en plaignaient parce qu'il ne ressemblait en rien à leur Bourgogne habituel. Pour ceux qui jugent le vin au goût plutôt qu'à l'étiquette, déguster un tel vin est bien souvent une révélation.

Voir CÔTE DE BEAUNE : CÔTE DE NUITS ; CÔTE-D'OR ; CHABLIS ; MÂCONNAIS ; BEAUJOLAIS ; CHALONNAIS

Bourgogne Mousseux (Appellation Contrôlée)

Bourgogne rouge, blanc ou rosé que l'on champagnise dans d'énormes cuves ou en bouteille. Pour cela, on n'utilise jamais les vins fins de la région, ce qui explique que le Bourgogne mousseux soit presque sans exception un vin assez commun et parfois même désappointant. Actuellement, les Bourgogne mousseux sont blancs pour la plupart.

Voir CRÉMANT DE BOURGOGNE ; BOURGOGNE

Bourgueil et Saint-Nicolas-de-Bourgueil (Appellation Contrôlée)

Rouges et rosés de la Loire. Touraine.

Ces deux crus sont distincts mais contigus et leurs vins se ressemblent tellement qu'on les classe généralement ensemble. Ils ont aussi en commun cette particularité d'être les seuls vignobles de la Loire dont l'appellation d'origine ne porte que sur les rouges et les rosés ; les blancs de Bourgueil ne portent que l'appellation générale Touraine. Ce sont des vins légers, tendres et délicats, d'un fruité prononcé et d'un fort bouquet qui évoque l'idée de framboise et peut-être de violette. Le vin étiqueté Saint-Nicolas-de-Bourgueil n'est fait qu'avec des raisins cultivés en ce lieu et il est généralement meilleur que le Bourgueil dont les vignes sont réparties sur huit localités. Partout le sol est sablonneux, semé de cailloux, enrichi de calcaire et d'argile. Seul le Cabernet Franc est autorisé. Les vins doivent titrer au moins 9,5°. La production annuelle s'élève à environ 45 000 hl.

Bourru (vin)

Vin reposant encore sur sa lie ou à peine tiré du tonneau. Appliqué à certains vins comme le Beaujolais, qui doit être bu jeune, ce terme désigne plus une qualité qu'un défaut.

Bouscaut (Château-)

Bordeaux rouges et blancs. Commune : Cadaujac, en Graves.

Classé en 1953 parmi les cinq Premiers Graves pour le vin blanc, et les onze Premiers Graves pour le vin rouge, Château-Bouscaut est le premier grand domaine sur la route Graves-Sauternes conduisant de Bordeaux à Toulouse. Beau bâtiment où le Moyen Age se mêle au moderne ; tapisseries remarquables, piscine, immense parc muré. Le chai est divisé en deux pour y faire des vins rouges — qui fermentent dans des cuves énormes de chêne — et des blancs qui sont pressurés au pressoir électrique. Mis le premier jour dans un réservoir puis soutirés directement dans des barils, l'un et l'autre y fermentent et mûrissent. Dans le chai de conservation, vins rouges et blancs vieillissent côte à côte.

Un petit groupe d'Américains amateurs de vins, animé par Charles Wohlstetter, président du conseil d'administration de *Continentel Telephone,* et par Howard Sloane, acheta le vignoble en 1968. Le domaine Wohlstetter-Sloan vendit Château Bouscaut en 1979 à Lucien Lurton, propriétaire du Château Brane-Cantenac, du Château Durfort ainsi que du Château Climens, à Barsac.

Le vin rouge est fait avec 45 % de Merlot, 40 % de Cabernet Sauvignon, 10 % de Cabernet Franc et 5 % de Malbec ; les blancs avec 60 % de Sémillon et 40 % de Sauvignon blanc.

Caractéristiques : Les vins blancs n'ont pas donné l'exemple du caractère de qualité, de finesse et de fruit qu'on trouve dans beaucoup de très bons Graves. Le vin rouge est loin des meilleurs Graves.

Superficie : rouge 39 ha ; blanc 5 ha.

Production moyenne : 1 500 caisses de blanc ; 10 000 caisses de rouge.

Bouteille (demi-)

Bouteille dont la capacité représente approximativement la moitié du contenu d'une bouteille normale, soit 37,5 cl pour la plupart. La demi-bouteille américaine contient environ 12,5 onces liquides américaines, la demi-bouteille anglaise, 12 onces liquides anglaises, soit 35 cl.

Bouteille (Nouvelle réglementation de la)

Voir APPENDICE C

Bouzy

Localité située sur la hauteur de Reims, qui produit des raisins rouges servant à faire un des Premiers Crus de Champagne ainsi qu'un vin rouge non mousseux.

Voir CHAMPAGNE

Boxbeutel

Voir BOCKSBEUTEL

Boyd-Cantenac (Château-)

Bordeaux rouges. Commune de Cantenac-Margaux, Haut-Médoc.

Il n'y a pas de château sur ce domaine qui est un Troisième Cru du Médoc selon la classification de 1855. Il appartient à M. P. Guillemet et le vin de ses vignes est fait au château Pouget, appartenant au même propriétaire. Jusqu'en 1961, ce cru ne méritait pas sa haute classification. Mais M. Guillemet a fait d'énormes efforts et le vin est redevenu digne de la classification de 1855. On cultive dans ce vignoble, maintenant bien entretenu, 70 % de Cabernet Sauvignon, 20 % de Merlot, 6 % de Cabernet Franc et 4 % de Petit Verdot. La vinification est supervisée par le docteur Peynaud, ancien professeur d'œnologie à l'université de Bordeaux.

Caractéristiques : Soutenu, rond et élégant.
Superficie : 18 ha
Production moyenne : 80 tonneaux (7 000 caisses).

Brachetto

Raisin rouge d'Italie qui donne un vin fortement coloré et de goût agréable.
Voir PIÉMONT

Brachetto d'Acqui (D.O.C.)

Vin rouge piémontais légèrement pétillant.
Voir ITALIE

Branaire-Ducru (Château-)

Bordeaux rouge. Commune de Saint-Julien, en Haut-Médoc.
En face du Château-Beychevelle, de l'autre côté de la route du Médoc, à l'endroit où elle pénètre au sud dans Saint-Julien, Château-Branaire-Ducru, Quatrième Cru selon la classification de 1855, appartint à M. Jean Tapie et à sa sœur Madame Tari.

Les vignes sont plantées à souhait sur une éminence plate. Le vaste chai est excellent pour les vieux vins car il est enterré jusqu'aux deux tiers de sa hauteur, ce qui lui assure une humidité bénéfique. Madame Tari, l'épouse du propriétaire du Château Giscours, et Monsieur Tapie, son frère, ont vendu le vignoble à un groupement d'assurance en 1987.
Caractéristiques : Grand vin parfois dur au début, mais doué d'une grande longévité. C'est un des meilleurs de Saint-Julien.
Superficie : 48 ha.
Production moyenne : 25 000 caisses.

Brandy

Employé seul, ce mot anglais ne désigne que l'eau-de-vie obtenue par la distillation du vin, mais par extension il signifie aussi eau-de-vie de tout autre fruit dont le nom précède le mot brandy. L'eau-de-vie de vin est exclusivement un produit du raisin ; on le distille dans le monde entier.

Les meilleurs brandys français sont l'Armagnac et le Cognac. Le Cognac est probablement l'exemple le plus exquis au monde des alcools de ce type, suivi de l'Armagnac. La plupart des pays vinicoles produisent des brandys, qui sont parfois de très grande qualité et parfois médiocre. Le secret d'un bon brandy réside en partie dans le vin distillé, dans le processus de distillation (le meilleur brandy est fait dans des alambics en terre), mais aussi dans son âge et le bois dans lequel il est vieilli. Le Cognac, par exemple, vieillit dans le chêne du Limousin. Rappelons qu'une fois que le brandy est mis en bouteille, non seulement il cesse de s'améliorer mais peut même se détériorer après un certain temps. Ainsi des étiquettes comme « Brandy Napoléon » n'ont aucun sens, car tout brandy conservé en barrique depuis l'époque napoléonienne serait maintenant évaporé ; il en serait de même pour le brandy en bouteille, qui serait probablement moins bon que lorsqu'il était conservé dans du verre. De toute façon, il n'en resterait plus une goutte.

Toutes sortes de fruits peuvent être utilisés pour le brandy aux fruits.

Les autres grands brandys internationaux sont le *Calvados :* eau-de-vie française à base de pomme de Normandie ; le *Marc :* eau-de-vie obtenue par distillation du marc de raisin ; la *Grappa :* nom italien du marc ; et l'*Applejack :* eau-de-vie américaine à base de pomme.
Voir ces noms

Brane-Cantenac (Château-)

Bordeaux rouge. Commune de Cantenac-Margaux, en Haut-Médoc.
Jadis célèbre sous le nom de Château-Gorce, ce vignoble fut acquis par le « Napoléon des vignes », le baron Brane. En 1820, il lui donna son nom, geste hardi pour l'époque. « Gorce est très connu, écrivit-il à la presse, mais j'ai confiance dans le nom de Brane ». Il acheta aussi un vignoble à Pauillac, nommé Pouyallet et le baptisa Brane-Mouton. C'est celui qui est devenu Mouton-Rothschild. En ce temps-là, on considérait Brane-Cantenac comme supérieur et le baron vendit Brane-Mouton pour consacrer tous ses soins au premier. Lucien Lurton, énergique viticulteur, est actuellement le propriétaire de cet énorme Second Cru, ainsi que de Durfort-Vivens à

Margaux, Château-Climens à Barsac, et Château-Bouscaut en Graves.

Brane a longtemps langui dans une zone de qualité crépusculaire. On fit, avec les produits de ce très grand vignoble, des vins médiocres qui déçurent bien des fervents du Médoc. Malgré quelques bons millésimes, il a beaucoup de déceptions.

Caractéristiques : Souvent une belle souplesse et de la finesse, malheureusement ce vin est souvent surpassé par ses voisins.

Superfice : 85 ha.

Production moyenne : 30 000 caisses.

Brännvin

Autre nom de l'Aquavit *(voir ce mot).*

Brauneberger Falkenberg

Un des meilleurs vins élégants du village de Brauneberg en Moselle allemande.

Voir MOSELLE

Brauneberger Juffer et Juffer-Sonnenuhr

Les plus célèbres des meilleurs vins du secteur viticole de Brauneberg et un des meilleurs de toute la Moselle allemande. Fleuris, fins et élégants.

Voir MOSELLE

Brède (Château de La)

Bordeaux blanc. Commune de la Brède, en Graves, France.

Le château de La Brède fut la résidence de Montesquieu à la fin du XVIIe siècle et au début du XVIIIe. Montesquieu ne fut pas seulement un grand écrivain, mais aussi un grand vigneron. Son vignoble était plus vaste que celui du château actuel. Il s'étendait sur des lieues carrées de terre des Graves et englobait bien des crus devenus, depuis lors, célèbres sous d'autres noms. Le grand écrivain travaillait sa vigne aussi activement qu'il travaillait de la plume et négociait énergiquement ses vins, tant en France qu'en Angleterre. De nos jours, La Brède n'a plus qu'un intérêt historique quoiqu'il reste un des plus beaux châteaux du Bordelais. Ce cru ne fut pas mentionné dans la classification des Graves de 1959.

La petite quantité de vin fournie par les vignes de La Brède n'a aucune distinction ; sa qualité est loin d'aller de pair avec la beauté du château.

Superficie : 6 ha.

Production moyenne : 900 caisses.

Breganze

Vins rouges ou blancs italiens de Vicence.

Voir VÉNÉTIE

Brenner (D.O.C.)

Maladie cryptogamique de la vigne qui sévit particulièrement en Allemagne.

Voir CHAPITRE IV

Brésil

Avec ses 7 770 000 km², le Brésil est le plus vaste pays de l'Amérique du Sud. Environ 690 km² (plus de 60 000 ha) seulement sont plantés en vigne. Au cours des dernières années, la production du vin s'est développée considérablement et la demande intérieure s'est accrue. Les viticulteurs recourent désormais aux engrais modernes ainsi qu'à des méthodes plus efficaces pour traiter et purifier leurs vins dont la qualité s'est améliorée. La production qui était tombée en 1964 à 1 million d'hectolitres, s'est accrue pour atteindre de nos jours environ 2,5 millions d'hectolitres (27 millions de caisses).

Le Brésil fut colonisé par des Portugais habitués à boire du vin, mais au début, les premiers colons ne s'intéressèrent guère à la vigne. C'est au cours des premières années de notre siècle qu'on commença seulement à planter des vignes dans ce pays, mais le mouvement ne prit une réelle extension que lorsque des Italiens immigrèrent après la Première Guerre mondiale.

L'État méridional de Rio Grande do Sul (39 000 hectares) est la principale région vinicole. Située entre l'Atlantique, l'Argentine et l'Uruguay à l'extrémité sud du pays, c'est-à-dire la plus tempérée, elle jouit du climat le plus favorable au vin. Les autres centres sont São Paulo (9 000 hectares), Paraná (2 000 hectares) et Minas Gerães (700 hectares), à une altitude variant de 700 à 1 800 mètres. Le vignoble s'étend aussi à Santa Catarina (6 000 hectares) d'où l'on expédie la vendange à São Paulo pour qu'elle y soit vinifiée. Pernambuco a environ 700 hectares.

70 % des vignes plantées au Brésil sont des hybrides de la variété *Vitis labrusca* et malheureusement 30 % seulement sont des *Vitis vinifera*. La première variété supporte en effet beaucoup mieux le climat chaud et humide que la *Vitis vinifera*. Autres raisins : Duchesse (aussi appelé Riesling de Caldas) ; Niagara, Folha de Figo (feuille de figuier) ; Black July, Seibel, Deux 10096, 6905, quelques variétés du type Couderc, Delaware, Jacques Gaillard et diverses espèces de Bertille-Seyve. A Santa Catarina : Concord, Cintiana, Herbemont, Gothe, Trebbiano, Poverella et quelques types de Muscat sont également cultivés. Enfin des souches européennes fournissent des vins de qualité.

Les principaux types de vins brésiliens sont les suivants :

Vins de table à bon marché. Rouges du genre bourgogne et bordeaux rosés et blancs, secs, demi-doux, doux et mousseux.

Bons vins de table. Rouges faits avec des vignes Barbera, Bonarda, Cabernet, Merlot et d'autres bonnes variétés. Vins blancs avec Trebiano Poverella, Malvasia, Riesling et Sémillon.

Vins chers. Mousseux fermentés en cuve et en bouteille : Muscat et Malvoisie.

Un des meilleurs vins brésiliens est fait par la firme portant le nom étourdissant de l'Indústria, Comércio e Navegaçâo, Sociedade Vinicola Rio Grandense, Ltda. Elle commercialise ses vins sous l'étiquette Granja União. Ils sont rouges et blancs. Certains rouges sont faits avec du Merlot, du Cabernet et du Gamay. Les blancs avec du Trebbiano du Chardonnay, du Gewurztraminer, du Pinot Blanc, et du Riesling. Trebbiano est le nom italien de l'Ugni blanc. Sa culture dénote l'influence italienne au Brésil. Si depuis quelque temps le Brésil voit son industrie vinicole en pleine expansion, c'est en grande partie à la Central Vinicola do Sul (VINOSUL S/A) qu'il le doit.

La plus grande partie des vins brésiliens est vendue sur le marché intérieur. São Paulo et Rio de Janeiro sont les plus gros consommateurs. On importe aussi du vin d'Europe et des pays américains voisins, notamment du Chili. Les Brésiliens boivent peu. Une baisse des droits de douanes encouragerait les importations et par là même la création d'un marché pour les vins du pays. Parmi les quelque 60 entreprises vinicoles du Brésil, la plus importante est celle que nous avons déjà citée. Compte aussi : Luiz Antunes et Cia ; Luiz Michielon, S.A. ; Sociedade Vinhos Unico, Ltda ; Carlos Dreher Neto, e Mosele, S.A. ; Societade Brasiliera de Vinhos Ltda, et Amalden.

Distillats. Conhaques et liqueurs diverses.

Breton

Nom donné en Touraine au Cabernet Franc.

Voir CABERNET

Bristol Cream

Vieux Xérès Oloroso, doux, mis en bouteille à Bristol, Angleterre.

Bristol Milk

Xérès Oloroso sucré, moins riche que le « Cream », mis en bouteille à Bristol, Angleterre.

British Compounds

Nom donné par le fisc britannique aux spiritueux redistillés, rectifiés ou épicés.

Brizard

La maison Marie-Brizard, liquoriste bordelais.

Brolio

Excellent Chianti classique ; le meilleur n'est pas vendu dans la fiasque (fiasco) populaire, mais en bouteille du genre de la bordelaise.

Voir TOSCANE

Brouilly

Voir BEAUJOLAIS ; CÔTE DE BROUILLY

Broustet (Château)

Bordeaux blanc. Commune de Barsac, en Sauternes.

Ce domaine produit un vin assurément doux, classé parmi les Seconds Crus de Sauternes en 1855.

Superficie : 16 ha.

Production moyenne : 30 tonneaux (3 000 caisses).

Brown Sherry

Xérès Oloroso foncé et doux.

Voir XÉRÈS

Brunello di Montalcino (D.O.C.G.)

Ce vin de *Denominazione di Origine Controllata e Garantita* est l'un des meilleurs vins rouges d'Italie, doué d'une très grande longévité.

Voir TOSCANE

Brunissure

Maladie de la vigne due à la surproduction et à la taille insuffisante. Une peau brune apparaît sur la feuille, qui tombe.

Voir CHAPITRE IV

Brut

Sur l'étiquette d'une bouteille de Champagne ce mot indique que le vin est très sec. Il l'est même plus que celui qui est étiqueté Extra Sec ou Extra Dry.

Voir CHAMPAGNE

Bual ou Boal

Madère corsé et doux.

Bucelas

Bon vin portugais *(Denominação de Origem)* produit en petite quantité.

Voir PORTUGAL

Buchu

Cette liqueur sud-africaine est pratiquement inconnue ailleurs. On verra pourquoi en lisant ce qu'en dit C. de Boscari dans son livre *Wines of the Cape* (Vins du Cap) : « L'herbe avec laquelle les sauvages d'Afrique soignaient tous leurs maux, depuis la douleur d'estomac jusqu'à la piqûre de serpent, depuis le genou de la bonne jusqu'au mauvais sort, pendant des siècles avant l'apparition de l'homme blanc. Greffé sur la pharmacopée européenne, le buchu est désormais cultivé autour de Paarl. On se sert de l'extrait de cette plante en usage externe comme embrocation et en usage interne mélangée à de l'eau-de-vie, pour les désordres du transit digestif. On lui attribue des pouvoirs curatifs miraculeux et son goût est assez affreux pour qu'il les possède ».

Bulgarie

Peu de pays peuvent se vanter de posséder de plus vieilles traditions en matière de vins que la Bulgarie : la commercialisation de la viticulture et du vin trouverait son origine en ancienne Thrace, dont une partie est maintenant dans les frontières de la Bulgarie. Comme dans tous les États balkaniques, les frontières bulgares n'ont cessé d'avancer et de reculer au fil des siècles. Aujourd'hui, le pays est délimité au nord par le Danube, sa frontière roumaine ; à l'est 150 km de côtes longent la mer Noire ; au sud et à l'ouest, elle voisine avec la Turquie, la Grèce, la Serbie et la Macédonie. Près de la moitié du pays est montagneux, avec les montagnes des Balkans à l'ouest et le massif Rhodope au sud. Mais les riches terres du Danube et des vallées de Meritza dotent la Bulgarie d'une agriculture qui forme la base de l'économie nationale. Sa situation géographique, qui correspond à la latitude de l'Espagne et des régions italiennes de Toscane et d'Ombrie, en fait une terre idéale pour la culture du raisin et la production de vins.

HISTOIRE

La viticulture bulgare sommeilla pendant les cinq siècles que dura la dictature turque musulmane, mais survécut comme partout ailleurs en Empire ottoman. Le pays ne se libéra totalement de l'influence turque qu'à la fin de la Première Guerre mondiale. A partir de ce moment, la superficie des vignobles et le total annuel de sa production en vins ne firent qu'augmenter. En 1940, la production atteignait 2 000 000 d'hl dont environ 300 000 hl étaient destinés à l'exportation, principalement vers l'Allemagne. La Seconde Guerre mondiale et les remous de l'après-guerre furent la cause majeure de l'effondrement de la viticulture bulgare. En 1948, une entreprise d'État, Vinprom, fut chargée de diriger l'ensemble de la production et de la commercialisation des vins. Aujourd'hui, la Bulgarie est probablement l'exemple le plus intéressant et le plus réussi d'application de méthodes modernes de production commerciale à d'anciennes traditions d'agriculture fondamentalement paysanne. Il en est de même dans tous les États balkaniques. Les quelque 450 000 paysans-vignerons ont déjà une solide expérience des coopératives, qui sont à la source de la « collectivisation » de la production existante. En outre, Vinprom créa de nouveaux grands vignobles et la production annuelle de vins en Bulgarie dépasse maintenant 4 millions d'hl (environ 40 millions de caisses). Des projets visant à doubler ce chiffre d'ici les dix prochaines années peuvent sembler ambitieux, mais la Bulgarie s'affirme de plus en plus dans le marché de l'exportation, surtout vers la Russie — où, semble-t-il, la demande est insatiable —, la République Fédérale allemande — son plus ancien client —, mais aussi vers tous les autres pays importateurs de vins. Les Bulgares affirment aujourd'hui que 60 % de leur production est exportée, dont la moitié en Union Soviétique. Ils disent en outre être les plus gros exportateurs du monde de vins en bouteille — ce qui est surprenant mais difficile à réfuter. Lors de la grande réorganisation de l'après-guerre, des experts occidentaux furent appelés — principalement d'Allemagne — pour prodiguer leurs conseils. Aussi le réseau national de caves et centres vinificateurs est-il équipé du matériel allemand, français et italien le plus moderne.

Si la Bulgarie ne produit pas de vins fins et n'en n'a jamais produit, elle est maintenant en mesure de fournir d'énormes quantités de bons vins aptes à satisfaire une demande mondiale en plein essor. Vins blancs et rouges sont produits en quantité égale, les rouges étant les meilleurs. Les vins bulgares peuvent être divisés en quatre catégories : les vins ordinaires, les vins « supérieurs », les meilleurs vins qui jouissent d'une situation géographique favorable et les vins contrôlés, équivalents à une *Appellation Contrôlée*. Les Européens en général ne les apprécient pas. Pourtant, depuis la réorganisation — et certainement grâce aux conseils prodigués par les experts allemands —, la Bulgarie parvient à produire des blancs étonnamment bons, légers et riches en acide, susceptibles de satisfaire la demande croissante en vins plus secs. Les Bulgares consomment 22 l de vin par personne et par an (ce qui n'est pas énorme pour cette partie de l'Europe), mais apprécient aussi la bière et surtout cette eau-de-vie de prune typique de toute l'Europe du Sud-Est.

Encépagement et types de vins

Vins blancs

Dimiat était la vigne indigène la plus cultivée. On l'utilise aussi bien pour la production de vins que de raisins de table. Dimiat correspond au Smederevka slave et est probablement étroitement apparenté au Chasselas. Le vin fait avec du Dimiat ne se distingue pas particulièrement. Le rouge Misket, une variété de la grande famille des Muscat, donne un vin beaucoup plus intéressant. Ce vin, riche de l'arôme et du goût de ce raisin, abonde dans la région de Karlovo en Bulgarie centrale, ainsi que dans la vallée de Sangulare située à proximité de la Mer Noire, et en général dans tout le nord du pays. Quoique la Bulgarie compte plus de vingt régions vinicoles d'importance variée, les noms de lieux ont peu d'importance. En effet les vins bulgares doivent de plus en plus leur nom à la variété de raisin, spécialement en ce qui concerne les vins d'exportation. Les approvisionnements des grandes caves — celles où l'on fait la plus grande partie des vins — proviennent de régions très vastes. Ceci est particulièrement vrai pour les vins faits avec des variétés plantées dans les grands vignobles d'État : le Rhin, Waelschriesling, Sylvaner et Chardonnay d'Europe occidentale, Furmint de Hongrie, et le Rczaziteli géorgien d'Union Soviétique. Ils ont, quant à eux, quelques noms bien établis : « Hemus », un Misket doux de Karlovo ; « Rosenthaler Riesling », vin issu d'un mélange des deux sortes de Riesling et originaire de la Vallée des Roses, toujours dans la région de Karlovo ; « Euxinograd », mélange de Dimiat, Misket et Waelschriesling ; « Sonnenkueste », un Dimiat. Ces deux derniers vins proviennent de la région de la mer Noire, près de Varna. Les vins faits avec du Chardonnay et du Sylvaner, importés par la Grande-Bretagne, sont agréables, suffisamment secs et étonnamment légers. En outre, la Bulgarie produit une quantité abondante de vin mousseux *(Champanski)* vendu sous la marque « Iskra ». La production est centrée sur la ville de Ljaskovec, au nord du pays. On y utilise les deux méthodes de fabrication russe et champenoise, 15 % du total étant encore produit selon la méthode champenoise.

Vins rouges

Nombreux sont les bons vins rouges en Bulgarie. Gamza — vigne semblable à la variété Kadarka des Balkans —, la vigne la plus couramment cultivée, produit un vin qui doit être bu jeune, comme un Beaujolais. La meilleure vigne indigène — Mavrud (signifie « noir »), donne un vin à la couleur et au goût profonds, mais qui gagne à vieillir avant d'être buvable. Le meilleur vin de ce type est produit à Asenovgrad, près de Plodiv, deuxième ville de Bulgarie. Au sud, on cultive le Pamid (semblable au raisin serbe Plovdina, utilisé pour faire un vin *Siller* de consommation locale), ainsi que le Saperavi russe. Comme pour les vins blancs, les Bulgares ont obtenu d'excellents résultats en plantant de nouvelles vignes d'Europe occidentale, notamment du Cabernet Franc et du Cabernet Sauvignon, grâce auxquelles ils produisent maintenant des vins dont la qualité rappelle un peu celle des Bordeaux.

SPIRITUEUX

On distille de la bonne eau-de-vie à Preslav, ville des montagnes des Balkans ; celle-ci est faite avec du vin Dimiat. La meilleure production est principalement destinée à l'exportation sous la marque « Pliska ». Ici comme dans tous les États balkaniques, on fait également un alcool de prune très fort, le Slivova. On produit aussi une version de la Mastika grecque, qui rappelle vaguement le pastis. Mais la spécialité bulgare est le Rosa, une liqueur sucrée extraite de pétales de roses de Damas, ces mêmes fleurs qui, depuis des siècles, donnent l'essence de rose.

Bulk Gallon

Mesure de capacité équivalant à 4,5496 l en Angleterre et à 3,785 l aux États-Unis, utilisée pour le vin et les alcools, sans se soucier de leur teneur en alcool, donc à ne pas confondre avec le *Proof Gallon (voir ce mot)*.

Burdin

Botaniste français qui obtint par croisements de plants un raisin à vin rouge nommé Burdin 4503, à partir d'un raisin à vin blanc, comparable au Sylvaner et nommé Burdin 5201.

Burgenland

Blancs et rouges, Sud-Est de l'Autriche.

Région vinicole d'Autriche dont les principales localités sont : Rust, Oggau, Sankt Margarethen et Mörbisch. Le Burgenland se trouve sur la frontière de Hongrie. On y cultive surtout le Furmint qui donne aussi le Tokay.

Voir AUTRICHE

Burgunder

C'est le raisin Pinot de Bourgogne transplanté dans les pays de langue allemande où les vins faits avec cette variété de raisin s'appellent Spätburgunder (bourguignon tardif), Frühburgunder (bourguignon hâtif), Weissburgunder (blanc) ou Grauerburgunder (gris). Néanmoins le nom le plus courant du Pinot Gris est Ruländer *(voir ce mot)*.

Butt

Barrique normalisée britannique. Elle contient 491 l de bière blonde, Xérès ou Malaga, et 573 l de n'importe quel autre vin. Malgré ces précisions légales, le mot *butt* désigne couramment n'importe quel tonneau ou fût servant à contenir vin, bière ou eau de pluie.

Buza

Breuvage alcoolique égyptien obtenu par la distillation de dates fermentées.

Voir ÉGYPTE

Buzet (Côtes de Buzet jusqu'en 1986)

Appellation Contrôlée, d'environ 1 200 ha dont 80 % sont plantés, pour le rouge, de Merlot, Cabernet Sauvignon, Cabernet Franc et 20 %, pour le blanc, de Sauvignon, Semillon et Muscadelle. Les 70 000 hl (750 000 caisses) sont presque entièrement produits par une coopérative.

Voir CÔTES DE BUZET

Byblin

Vin doux de Phénicie, cité dans les œuvres littéraires de l'Antiquité. Originaire de Byblos il fut probablement produit par la suite en Thrace.

Voir CHAPITRE I et ANTIQUITÉ (VINS DE L')

Byrrh

Marque d'un apéritif très populaire en France, à base de vin épicé à la quinine et additionné d'eau-de-vie de vin. On le fait à Thuir, près de la côte de la Méditerranée et de la frontière espagnole.

C

Cabernet

Remarquable variété de raisin qui donne les meilleurs rouges du Médoc, les vins supérieurs de Californie, d'Australie, du Chili, et d'autres pays. Le meilleur et le plus répandu est le Cabernet Sauvignon. Le Cabernet Franc, cultivé dans le Médoc, à Saint-Émilion, en Graves, dans la vallée de la Loire, est considéré de moindre qualité. Ces deux-là sont les seuls Cabernet qui comptent réellement en viticulture.

Cabrières

Voir LANGUEDOC

Cachiri

Liqueur faite en Guyane à partir du manioc dont on tire aussi le tapioca.

Cadillac (A.O.C.)

Bordeaux blanc. Région du Sud-Ouest.

Située sur la rive droite de la Garonne, face aux vignobles de Graves et de Sauternes, cette Appellation Contrôlée cultive du Sémillon et du Sauvignon Blanc. Le vin est très semblable à ceux de la proche Sainte-Croix-du-Mont.

Cahors

1. Variété de raisin rouge vulgaire, autorisé seulement en quantité limitée dans la région de Bordeaux entre autres. On l'appelle aussi Malbec et Cot.

2. *Région du Sud-Ouest.* Suivant son cours vers l'embouchure de la Garonne, le Lot sillonne le grand plateau du Causse, ce pays calcaire qui produit davantage de truffes que le Périgord. Situés sur les deux berges du Lot, les vignobles de l'Appellation Contrôlée de Cahors s'étendent sur 50 km entre la pittoresque ville de Cahors et le village de Soturac. Cette région délimitée de près de 40 000 ha est située à 160 km à l'est de Bordeaux et à 100 km au nord de Toulouse. La majeure partie de sa superficie ne produit pas de vins. La production annuelle de 180 000 hl (environ 2 millions de caisses) provient de petits lopins de terre dispersés le long des rives du fleuve ; ils ne totalisent qu'environ 3 200 ha. Les meilleurs vignobles donnent au sud et au sud-est.

Le raisin du Cahors est le Malbec ou Cot, connu dans la région sous le nom d'Auxerrois. Utilisé seul, il donne un vin couleur encre, profond et dur ; c'est pourquoi on cultive aussi des Merlot et Jurançon, ainsi qu'un peu de Tannat et Syrah ; néanmoins ces vins contiennent toujours 70 % de Cot. Les vignes poussent sur les vieilles terres alluviales qui ont formé des terrasses et de petites collines sur les rives escarpées du Lot. Environ un tiers des raisins sont cultivés en bordure du Causse, où le sol est principalement formé de dépôts kimmeridgiens typiques de la zone de Chablis. La fine terre rouge de Cahors est entièrement couverte de cailloux calcaires, d'où l'impression que donnent les vignes de pousser dans la pierre. Le sol peu terreux est très peu profond, mais le sous-sol fissuré permet un enracinement très profond, ce qui explique la vigueur et l'extraordinaire longévité des vignes.

Les vins de Cahors ont souvent été décrits comme étant des vins « noirs ». Le Malbec donne ici un vin très dense et très foncé, qui a toujours été utilisé pour colorer et remonter les Bordeaux, vins plus légers. Depuis que les vignobles ont été ravagés par le phylloxéra, les vins ne sont pas terriblement forts en alcool ou en tanin, mais demandent toujours à être longuement vieillis en barrique et en bouteille. Après une bonne maturation, ce vin peut être velouté et dégager un parfum doux, mais il garde toujours sa couleur foncée. Ce vin de qualité a su mériter une Appellation d'Origine Contrôlée.

A Parnac, près du centre de la zone délimitée, se trouve la grande coopérative Les Caves d'Olt, qui contrôle près de la moitié de la production régionale. Le Château Haute-Serre de Georges Vigouroux et le Château de Cayrou de Jean Jouffreau sont parmi les meilleurs Cahors mis en bouteille au domaine.

Caillou (Château-)

Bordeaux blanc. Commune de Barsac, en Sauternais.

Classé Second cru en 1855, Château-Caillou est contigu aux deux Premiers Crus de Barsac : Château-Climens et Château-Coutet. Peut-être doit-il son nom au sol à gros cailloux qui donne tant de qualité aux vins de Bordeaux. Son propriétaire, M. Bravo, possède deux autres crus du Bordelais ; Château-Baulac et Château-Petit-Mayne.

Caractéristiques : C'est un vin liquoreux agréable.

Superficie : 17 ha.

Production moyenne : 4 000 caisses.

Cairanne

Une des meilleures communes des Côtes du Rhône. On y produit des vins rouges, blancs et rosés.

Voir RHÔNE

Caisse

Une caisse de vin contient 12 bouteilles de 75 à 80 cl chacune ; ou 24 demi-bouteilles ; ou 48 quarts (de Champagne) ; 6 magnums ou 3 jéroboams. Autrefois ces caisses n'étaient faites qu'en bois. Quoique aujourd'hui bien des vins soient expédiés en cartons, ces derniers portent encore couramment le nom de caisses.

Cajuada

Breuvage de l'Afrique occidentale fait à partir de noix de cajou fermentées.

Calabre

Vins blancs et rouges. Sud de l'Italie.

La Calabre est le pied de la botte italienne. Ce pays montagneux et chaud est une terre de misère sauf le long de la côte où la fraîcheur marine et le sol plus fertile permettent la culture de l'oranger et du citronnier. Le sol est surtout volcanique et la vigne y croît aussi bien que n'importe quelle autre plante. Pourtant, la plupart des vins de Calabre ne sont pas de premier ordre, en règle générale ils sont plutôt médiocres.

Ciró est une D.O.C. applicable aux vins rouges, blancs et rosés de Ciró, Ciró Marina et d'une partie des communes de Crucoli et Melissa, situées à l'est de Cosenza. Le blanc est fait avec du Greco Bianco ainsi qu'un peu de Trebbiano Toscano, le rouge et le rosé de Gaglioppo, mais aussi de Greco et de Trebbiano. Le Ciró blanc est un vin de couleur paille. Les rouges et rosés sont chaleureux et pleins de corps.

On peut accorder une mention exceptionnelle au Greco di Bianco (D.O.C.), vin jaune et doux à forte teneur en alcool (17°). Il vient de Gerace, dans les Apennins de Calabre. On en fait très peu. Ce vin était tenu en haute estime dans la Rome antique.

Les deux rouges les plus abondants sont le Savuto (D.O.C.) et le Ciró di Calabria. Quoique faits avec des raisins différents, ils ont certaines caractéristiques communes, notamment leur âpreté, leur saveur vigoureuse et capiteuse.

Le premier est fait avec du raisin Gaglioppo, ainsi qu'une certaine quantité de Greco Néro, et le second avec les raisins

Arvino, Pecorello, Greco et une certaine quantité de Malvoisie. Lacrima di Castrovillari et Moscato di Cosenza (parfois Moscato di Calabria) complètent la liste des vins calabrais les mieux connus.

Le premier est un vin de table rouge produit évidemment dans la région de Castrovillari. Le second est l'inévitable Muscat fait parfois avec des raisins secs et qui ne compte pas parmi les meilleurs Muscats d'Italie. Donnici, Lamezia, Melissa, Pollino et Sant'Anna di Isola Capo Rizzuto sont tous des vins D.O.C.

Caldaro (Lago di) (D.O.C.)

Vin rouge d'Italie septentrionale au goût d'amande.

Voir TRENTIN-HAUT ADIGE

Californie

Voir ÉTATS-UNIS : CALIFORNIE

Calisaya

Liqueur espagnole qui a un goût amer de quinine.

Calon-Ségur (Château-)

Bordeaux rouge. Commune de Saint-Estèphe, en Haut-Médoc.

Ce vignoble est classé Grand Cru. Comme à Château-Latour, on laisse les vignes de Château-Calon-Ségur aller au terme de leur longévité ; on ne les arrache donc pas secteur par secteur, mais on les remplace une par une ; c'est ainsi qu'elles produisent jusqu'à l'âge de 90 ans et même plus. Cette méthode favorise évidemment la qualité aux dépens de la quantité : la vigne produit mieux et du meilleur vin mais de moins en moins à partir de la quinzième ou vingtième année. Pourtant, étant donné l'étendue du vignoble, on ne manque pas de vin à Calon-Ségur.

Autrefois, ce château était un des trois seuls crus de Saint-Estèphe. Ironie de la classification de 1855, Calon-Ségur fut coté Troisième Cru et Château-Montrose, Second Cru. Or, en 1825, Montrose n'était qu'une parcelle de bois du domaine de Calon-Ségur. Aujourd'hui Calon-Ségur pourrait fort bien figurer comme Second Cru. Avec Palmer c'est l'un des meilleurs des Troisièmes Crus et il surpasse quelques Seconds.

Le mot « Calon » fut jadis le nom d'une petite embarcation utilisée au Moyen Age pour transporter du bois de construction d'une rive à l'autre de la Gironde. Plus tard, ce nom s'étendit à tous les environs de Saint-Estèphe qui s'appela jusqu'au XVIIIe siècle Calones ou Saint-Estèphe-de-Calon. A ce moment il échut par mariage au président de Ségur, marquis de Ségur-Calon, qui possédait aussi les grands Château-Lafite et Château-Latour, mais préférait probablement Calon car il disait : « Je fais du vin à Lafite et à Latour, mais mon cœur est à Calon. » Cette phrase figure comme devise au-dessus d'une voûte de la cour. Elle explique aussi le cœur qui est représenté sur l'étiquette.

Le sol du cru appartient à trois types : gravier sablonneux qui donne au vin de la finesse et du nez ; gravier gras, autrement dit sol calcaire granuleux, contenant des déchets sédimentaires organiques qui, s'ils n'étaient pas mêlés aux autres sols, donneraient un vin corsé mais vulgaire ; enfin, gravillon mince qui seul produit des vins racés mais d'une certaine âpreté. L'ancien propriétaire, Édouard Gasqueton, joua sur cette gamme de sols pour produire son remarquable vin. Depuis sa mort, en 1962, Château-Calon-Ségur appartient à son neveu Philippe Gasqueton.

Caractéristiques : La plus éminente est son corsé, quoique cette vigueur soit contenue dans des éléments d'une certaine souplesse. Les vins de Saint-Estèphe sont les plus corsés des Médoc et Calon-Ségur produit souvent l'un des vins les plus puissants de Saint-Estèphe. C'est aussi un de ceux qui vit le plus longtemps.

Superficie : 50 ha.

Production moyenne : 200 tonneaux (20 000 caisses).

Caluso (D.O.C.)

Vin blanc doux de différents types, produit autour de Turin.

Voir PIÉMONT

Calvados

La meilleure eau-de-vie de pomme du monde. Elle est obtenue par la distillation du cidre, en Normandie, et doit son nom au département du Calvados. La meilleure vient de la vallée d'Auge qui produit le plus de cidre. Quand il est assez âgé, le Calvados est un alcool magnifique, mais on trouve rarement les meilleurs hors des caves normandes. Pendant la production du cidre, on distille les résidus du pressurage des pommes. C'est ce qu'on appelle généralement eau-de-vie de Marc de Cidre.

Camensac (Château de)

Bordeaux rouge. Commune de Saint-Laurent, en Haut-Médoc. (Saint-Laurent n'est pas une appellation d'origine et les vins de cette commune portent l'appellation Haut-Médoc.)

Classé Cinquième Cru en 1855, c'est un vignoble peu connu et presque oublié. Ces dernières années de nouvelles plantations ont accru la superficie du vignoble dont le rendement est relativement faible.

Caractéristiques : Qualité en net progrès.

Superficie : 62 ha.

Production moyenne : 260 tonneaux.

Campanie

Rouges et blancs. Sud-ouest de l'Italie.

Les vins de Campanie sont l'essence même de la province ensoleillée qui les produit. Nulle part ailleurs la vigne n'est aussi exubérante qu'à Naples — capitale de la Campanie — mais sans ses vins, cette ville perdrait une partie de sa gaieté. Ses plages et ses îles — Sorrente, Capri, Ischia — sont d'une beauté tellement légendaire que ce sont des lieux de plaisir depuis l'Antiquité.

Toute la côte de la baie de Naples pourrait être le paradis terrestre et c'est précisément ce qu'elle est d'après la mythologie napolitaine.

Le Lacrima (ou Lacryma) Christi (Larme du Christ) (D.O.C.) est un vin d'or pâle, assez sec, fait avec les raisins cultivés sur le flanc sud du Vésuve. L'histoire qu'on raconte à son sujet pourrait avoir été inventée pour damer le pion de son rival du Latium : « Est ! Est !! Est !!! » Mais les Napolitains jurent qu'elle est vraie. Ils disent que lorsque Lucifer tomba en disgrâce, ses compagnons et lui arrivèrent sur terre dans un tel fracas que le sol s'effondra pour former la baie de Naples. L'ange déchu comprit rapidement qu'il se trouvait à l'endroit le plus proche de son paradis perdu, aussi peupla-t-il de démons Naples et ses environs. La ville devint donc une citadelle de malice. Abaissant son regard vers la terre, le Sauveur souffrit de voir son paradis terrestre aussi profondément englouti dans le péché. Il pleura et Sa larme tomba sur le Vésuve. De cette larme jaillit une vigne qui proliféra et donna un vignoble. Chaque année, la larme se reproduit elle-même dans la cuve où fermente le vin pour rappeler à l'honnête vigneron la gloire qui l'attend au paradis. Tout cela arriva, bien sûr, il y a très longtemps et on a planté du Greco et du Fiano pour remplacer les vignes originelles, mais la légende survit et on la répète avec chaque verre de Lacrima Christi. Précisons en outre que ce vin n'a aucun rapport avec le Lagrima Christi espagnol (*voir* MALAGA), sauf qu'Italiens et Espagnols s'accusent réciproquement de plagiat.

Le Falerne (Falerno) est aussi un vin dont l'histoire remonte très loin. Les Romains l'appelaient Falernum et semblent presque l'avoir considéré comme une des merveilles de leur monde. Malheureusement nous ne savons pas avec quels raisins on le faisait en ce temps-là et nous n'avons qu'une idée confuse au sujet du goût qu'il avait alors. Le Falerne actuel vient de Campi Flegrei, Capoue, Sessa Aurunca et Mondragone. Fait avec du raisin Falanghino, il est généralement d'un jaune doré, demi-sec et d'une qualité inférieure. On en exporte beaucoup. On fait aussi du Falerne rouge, surtout avec du raisin Aglianico, et il est assez agréable tant que son prix reste raisonnable.

Capri. Ce vin blanc D.O.C. représente plus typiquement la Campanie que ne le font le Lacrima Christi et le Falerne. Le Capri est fait avec des raisins Greco et Falanghina que l'on cultive sur l'île. Ils donnent un vin blanc capiteux, vif, sec (ou parfois demi-doux) qui convient aux fruits de mer de la baie. On peut le consommer aussi avec un sandwich en apéritif, sur une terrasse ombragée par une treille. Ce vin délicieux est introuvable ailleurs qu'à Capri car il est fait en si petite quantité qu'il ne suffit même pas à apaiser la soif des habitants de l'île. Ils importent donc des vins assez semblables pour les déguiser sous l'étiquette Capri. On peut en dire autant du vin fort ressemblant de l'île voisine, Ischia, dont une partie est vendue sous le nom d'Arturi. Capri produit aussi du rouge et du rosé mais en plus petite quantité encore que du blanc.

Ischia. Les vins blancs (Ischia Bianco) et rouges (Ischia Rosso) produits entièrement sur l'île sont des D.O.C. L'Ischia blanc est fait avec des raisins Forastera et Biancolella ; il est de couleur paille dorée, avec un bouquet délicat et un goût assez agréable. Une partie du vin, produit dans l'un des meilleurs secteurs de l'île, peut être appelée Ischia Bianco Superiore. Ce vin reste en cuve plus longtemps pour acquérir du corps et du goût. Le vin rouge peut provenir de n'importe quelle partie de l'île ; il est fait avec des raisins Guarnaccia, Piedirosso et Barbera. Le goût est sec et légèrement tannique.

Greco di Tufo. Vin blanc D.O.C. de la région d'Avellino. C'est avec les raisins Greco di Tufo et Coda di Volpe que l'on fait ce vin sec et d'une bonne couleur jaune dorée. Mais cette appellation peut également s'appliquer au vin pétillant produit dans la même région.

Taurasi (D.O.C.). Vin rouge fort et vigoureux fait avec des raisins Aglianico, Piedirosso, Barbera et Sangiovese. Jeune, ce vin est souvent trop âpre ; il ne peut être vendu qu'après quatre ans de vieillissement.

Moindres vins de Campanie

Conca. Fait avec des raisins San Giovese, Canaiolo, Malvasia et Aglianico, sur les coteaux qui dominent la baie de Sorrente. Ce vin est rouge, parfois un peu grossier et généralement d'une forte teneur alcoolique. Typiquement italien, il convient parfaitement aux pâtes et autres plats du pays, mais il déçoit en général avec des mets plus subtils.

Fiano di Avellino (D.O.C.). Léger, blanc, fleuri, ce vin est fait avec les raisins de Fiano cultivés 50 km à l'est de Naples.

Gragnano. Le plus mineur des vins rouges de la Campanie provient des terres d'Amalfi, dans la péninsule entre Naples et Sorrente. D'une contexture légère, il a une teinte riche et profonde. Son charme le plus remarquable est sa fraîcheur et son bouquet qui rappelle la violette ou la fraise nouvelle. Ce sont les caractéristiques du vin jeune qui doit être consommé assez rapidement. Par tradition il est fait avec des raisins Jaculillo, Piede di Palumbo et Aglianico. De temps en temps on le rend *frizzante* (pétillant) mais on ne saurait dire si c'est volontairement ou l'effet du hasard.

Ravello. Des vins rouges, blancs et rosés sont faits dans cette localité fleurie sur la côte d'Amalfi dont ils portent le nom. Le rosé (rosato) est le plus attrayant. Le blanc provient de raisins Greco et Fiano ; le rouge et le rosé de l'Aglianico sont les meilleurs de cette région.

Solopaca (D.O.C.). Des vins rouges et rosés viennent de cette petite ville du nord de la Campanie et en portent le nom. Raisins : Mangiaguerra, Olivoto et Aleatico. Le vin blanc est fait avec du Trebbiano et du Malvasia, le rouge avec du Sangiovese, du Piedirosso et de l'Aglianico.

Vesuvio (D.O.C.). Le Lacryma Christi del Vesuvio est un Vesuvio supérieur. Vins rouge et rosé à base d'Aglianico de Piedirosso et d'Olivella et aussi vin blanc fait avec du Colpa di Volpe, raisins cultivés sur les pentes du Vésuve. Ce vin servirait à arrondir la production de Capri rouge, avec une nette majoration de prix.

Campari

Bitter d'un brun roussâtre parfumé aux herbes et à l'écorce d'orange, produit par la maison Fratelli Campari de Milan. On s'en sert pour faire les cocktails Americano et Negroni. Ou bien on le boit sec, avec un zeste de citron, ou encore à l'eau de Seltz.

Campbeltown

Un des deux principaux centres de fabrication du whisky de malt dans les Western Highlands. L'autre est sur l'île voisine d'Islay. Campbeltown est située sur la péninsule de Kintyre qui s'étend en direction du sud sur le Firth of Clyde. Voilà encore deux siècles on prenait Kintyre pour une île.

Voir WHISKY : SCOTCH

Canada

Les vignobles du Canada sont situés surtout sur la péninsule du Niagara, au sud de l'Ontario et dans la vallée d'Okanagan en Colombie britannique. La première de ces deux régions est de loin la plus importante.

HISTOIRE DU VIN CANADIEN

Selon les sagas nordiques, Leif L'Heureux fut le premier qui découvrit l'Amérique du Nord. Il la baptisa Vineland en raison de la profusion de vignes sauvages qu'il croyait y avoir trouvées et qui en réalité auraient été des baies de myrtilles. ce furent sans doute les missionnaires français qui y firent les premiers vins, pour la messe. On lit en effet dans *Relation des jésuites en 1636* de Lejeune : « En certains endroits, il y a beaucoup de vignes sauvages, chargées de raisin. Certains en ont fait du vin par curiosité. J'y ai goûté et il m'a paru très bon. » Telle est la première trace écrite de viticulture au Canada. Mais c'est beaucoup plus tard qu'elle prit une importance commerciale, grâce à l'influence d'un Allemand et non d'un Français. En 1811, en effet, John Schiller, ancien caporal, s'établit à Cooksville, près de Toronto, dans l'Ontario. Il y planta des vignes et s'organisa pour faire du vin. Les Canadiens acceptent cette date comme celle du début de leur industrie vinicole. En 1890, les vignes couvraient déjà plus de 2 000 ha sur la péninsule du Niagara. Elles couvrent maintenant 11 000 ha. On trouve 6 000 ha de vignobles dans la vallée d'Okanagan, dans la région centrale de la Colombie britannique, où un négociant en vins hongrois, Eugène Rittich, planta ses vignes dans les années 1920.

Les vinificateurs de l'Ouest ne durent pas leur prospérité à leurs raisins locaux, mais aux fruits importés de Californie. Jusque dans les années 1960, la quasi-totalité du vin « canadien » de la Colombie britannique était fait avec du raisin californien. A cette époque, il fut décidé de spécifier le pourcentage de raisins Okanagan qui devait nécessairement être présent dans les vins portant l'étiquette locale. Ce pourcentage est maintenant fixé à 80 %. Les deux régions vinicoles les plus importantes produisent à elles deux 800 000 hl (près de 9 millions de caisses) de vin, en outre, certains vinificateurs des provinces de l'est produisent une quantité regrettable non négligeable de vins faits avec des concentrés de jus de raisin mais heureusement on y recourt de plus en plus rarement.

Les vignobles étaient principalement peuplés de variétés nord-américaines, celles-ci restent l'épine dorsale de l'industrie vinicole canadienne, mais on leur substitue petit à petit des hybrides européens et certaines variétés de *Vitis vinifera*. Dans l'Ontario, 45 % de la production sont assurés par la *vinifera* et des raisins hybrides. Ce pourcentage augmente chaque année car les producteurs sont soucieux de répondre aux demandes des consommateurs. Toute la production de la Colombie Britannique est en *vinifera* et en raisins hybrides. On pensait d'abord que la *Vitis vinifera* ne pouvait être cultivée au Canada, jusqu'à ce que des recherches et expériences viennent prouver le contraire. Les vignobles qui possèdent des plants de cette espèce sont peu étendus mais déjà en pleine expansion. Le foyer de la recherche viticole canadienne est la station expérimentale de Vineland, du ministère de l'Agriculture d'Ontario, où plus de trois cents variétés de vignes à vin ont été expérimentées. Beaucoup d'entreprises vinicoles, et plus particulièrement de petits centres récents, consacrent leur recherche à la culture de *Vitis vinifera* et aux techniques de vinification. Alors qu'auparavant la majeure partie de la production canadienne consistait en vins de liqueur du genre porto, la demande en vins de table est en pleine augmentation et ces derniers représentent maintenant 90 % de la production totale. A l'exception de ces vins de table, la plupart font des mélanges, de différentes années et de différents vignobles, qui sont vieillis dans des fûts de bois. Contrairement à l'usage européen, les vins doivent être commercialisés par ceux qui les vinifient. Dans toutes les provinces, sauf l'Ontario, les vinificateurs ne doivent vendre qu'aux Bureaux de contrôle des alcools ou régies des alcools qui possèdent le monopole de la vente au détail aux consommateurs, hôtels et restaurants à travers leur chaîne de magasins. Dans l'Ontario, les vinificateurs peuvent vendre leurs vins soit au Bureau de contrôle des alcools qui dirige une chaîne de 600 magasins, soit aux consommateurs, par l'intermédiaire d'un nombre limité de magasins gérés en coopérative.

En 1916, huit des provinces du Dominion votèrent en faveur de la prohibition des boissons alcooliques, mais les vinificateurs de l'Ontario — car l'Ontario ne bannit jamais l'alcool — continuèrent de prospérer. (Le Québec s'opposa jusqu'en 1919 à la vente des alcools puis ne bannit que les spiritueux).

Régions vinicoles canadiennes

Environ 85 % des raisins cultivés au Canada proviennent des terres alluviales de la fertile péninsule du Niagara, encadrée par le lac Ontario, le lac Érié et la rivière Niagara. Les principaux vignobles se trouvent à l'ouest des chutes du Niagara et de l'autre côté du lac Ontario en partant de Toronto. La plupart des vignes sont plantées au-dessus des 100 m d'escarpement du Niagara, quoique de nombreux vignobles aient été récemment transférés au sommet, où les terres sont plus généreuses. Bien que le climat du pays soit en général froid et âpre, la région du Niagara a une saison viticole moyenne de 173 jours. Proche des grands artères d'eau, le Niagara a en fait plus de jours sans gel que beaucoup d'autres régions situées plus au sud. Les hivers y sont doux, avec une température moyenne de —4° à —1°. Les pluies modérées, un été chaud et un automne prolongé fournissent toutes les conditions requises pour la viticulture et de bonnes vendanges.

Près des trois quarts du vin canadien sont produits sur la péninsule pàr 8 des 60 vinificateurs du pays. La production de raisin de la péninsule du Niagara est seulement inférieure à celle des pommes, qui constituent la récolte de fruits la plus importante du Canada. Les raisins Labrusca tels que Concord, Niagara, Elvira — au goût madré — y prédominent. Les cépages de type Labrusca sont progressivement remplacés par des hybrides français et de la *Vitis vinifera* comme les Seyval Blanc, Maréchal Foch, de Chaussac, Riesling et Chardonnay. Cette évolution est accélérée par la demande du marché, ce qui permet aux producteurs d'hybrides tels que le Seyval Blanc d'obtenir deux fois le prix du Labrusca et plus de trois fois le prix des variétés de *Vitis vinifera.* A la périphérie de la ville de Niagara-Falls se trouve T.G. Bright and Co., le plus gros producteur de vins du Canada ; c'est là, après la Seconde Guerre mondiale, qu'un chimiste français, Adhémar de Chaunac, importa des plants de *Vitis vinifera* et certaines variétés d'hybrides, avant même que celles-ci soient introduites dans l'Est des États-Unis. Le vignoble de Bright cultive du Pinot Noir et du Pinot Chardonnay, avec lesquels on fait un vin blanc mousseux depuis la fin des années 50. La firme a aussi produit un Gewürztraminer qui a donné de bons résultats. Les autres centres de vinification importants de la région sont Château-Gai à Niagara Falls, qui achète ses raisins chez les producteurs locaux, et la firme Andres à Winona. La Jordan Winery, avec son musée du vin à Twenty Mile Creek, est également intéressante. Plusieurs centres vinicoles récents se spécialisent avec succès dans la production de *Vitis vinifera* et d'hybrides français. Inniskillin et Château des Charmes, par exemple, ont brillamment réussi à fabriquer des vins à partir de Chardonnay et de Riesling. Quelques expériences ont été faites pour produire des « vins glacés » atteints de pourriture noble *(Botrytis)* à partir de raisins Vidal. Bien que les vignobles soient concentrés sur la péninsule du Niagara, on trouve d'autres vignobles épars dans la partie sud de l'Ontario. Toronto abrite deux établissements vinicoles : les maisons Cartier, Turner, Charal, Pelee Island Vineyards, et même jusqu'à Windsor, à l'ouest, de l'autre côté du fleuve en partant de Detroit, où la Charal Winery fut fondée en 1975 et où Cholio Wines s'établit en 1981.

A 2 500 km à l'ouest des vignobles de l'Ontario, se trouve la région vinicole de la vallée Okanagan, en Colombie britannique. Située entre le Plateau Trepanier et les Montagnes Monashee à l'est de Vancouver, cette vallée s'étend sur 100 km au sud du Lac Okanagan. Comme à l'est, la proximité du lac tempère le climat, et la saison viticole dure 185 jours. L'irrigation avec l'eau du lac et les fleuves des montagnes permet d'augmenter le maigre taux de pluie, qui ne dépasse pas 20 à 30 cm par an. Les Riesling, Chardonnay, Seyval Blanc et Gewürztraminer prédominent actuellement car de nombreux viticulteurs d'Okanagan ont été encouragés à planter des hybrides français de *Vitis vinifera*. Ils produisent avec succès des vins vendangés tardivement.

L'industrie vinicole canadienne a atteint un tel niveau qu'elle a cessé de produire une quantité aussi importante de vins de liqueur fortifiés pour se consacrer davantage aux vins de table de qualité supérieure. Avec l'augmentation de la demande en vins de table, particulièrement aux États-Unis, l'avenir de l'industrie canadienne consiste dorénavant à produire des vins de qualité, fait avec de bonnes variétés de raisin.

Voir également WHISKY CANADIEN

Canadian Whisky

Whisky du Canada.

Voir WHISKY CANADIEN

Canaiolo

Un des raisins rouges qui servent à faire le Chianti.

Voir TOSCANE

Canaries

Voir ESPAGNE

Canasta

Grand panier dans lequel on portait le raisin à la saison des vendanges dans la région de Jerez.

Voir XÉRÈS : MONTILLA

Candie

Le nom de cette ville de Grète figure parfois sur l'étiquette des vins provenant de l'île.

Voir GRÈCE

Cannelle

Liqueur de cannelle.

Cannonau di Sardegna

Vin rouge ou rosé D.O.C. de Sardaigne *(voir cette région).*

Canon (Château-)

Bordeaux rouge. Commune de Saint-Émilion.

Classé Premier Grand Cru en 1955, ce vignoble est planté exactement sur l'emplacement des anciennes carrières d'où l'on tira les pierres qui servirent à construire Saint-Émilion au Moyen Age. Le château lui-même n'a aucun style.

Le Château-Canon 1982 est considéré comme l'une des plus grandes bouteilles de cette année-là. Ce cru a toujours été un des premiers de Saint-Émilion et la classification officielle récente n'a fait qu'entériner une réputation solidement acquise depuis bien des générations.

Caractéristiques : Vin souple, généreux, doté d'une finesse considérable.

Superficie : 18 ha.

Production moyenne : 6 500 caisses.

Canteiro

Type de Madère plutôt rare. Désigne le vin qui a mûri à la chaleur du soleil.

Cantemerle (Château-)

Bordeaux rouge. Commune de Macau, en Haut-Médoc (Macau n'est pas une Appellation Contrôlée et ses vins portent celle de Haut-Médoc).

Classé Cinquième Cru en 1855, Cantemerle est actuellement considéré dans le monde entier comme très supérieur à ce titre officiel. En réalité il mérite d'être promu au rang de Second ou Troisième Cru. En partant de Bordeaux, sur la route du Médoc, Cantemerle est le second grand vignoble du Haut-Médoc (le premier étant La-Lagune) et il se trouve à quelque 3 km du premier groupe de crus célèbres qui ont droit à l'appellation d'origine Margaux, disséminés sur plusieurs communes. Le château est entouré par un des plus vastes et somptueux parcs du Médoc et les vignes plantées de part et d'autre de la partie boisée produisent un vin excellent.

Cantemerle existait bien avant la fondation de maints crus d'aujourd'hui. Au Moyen Age, c'était le site d'une forteresse nommée Sauves qui joua un grand rôle au cours des turbulences de ce temps. Portion de la baronnie de Cantemerle, acquise en

1759 par la famille de Jehan de Villeneuve, il resta entre ses mains jusqu'en 1892, année où le domaine fut acheté par le père de feu M. Pierre J. Dubos, puis, par un groupe d'assurances en 1980.

La haute réputation de ses vins est due en grande partie aux efforts de feu M. Dubos, petit homme sémillant aux jambes solides, toujours guêtrées, qui se rappelait encore l'anglais appris en Angleterre bien des dizaines d'années plus tôt et qu'on respectait comme l'un des plus dévoués vignerons du Médoc. Son *Livre de Cru* fut légendaire dans le Bordelais ; il y consigna inlassablement la direction du vent, la température, la pression atmosphérique, le comportement de la vigne, sa floraison, sa maturation, etc., chaque matin, chaque après-midi, chaque soir, pendant plus de 65 ans. A l'approche de l'automne, M. Dubos notait chaque jour la récolte de chaque secteur, le nombre de comportes mises à fermenter dans telle et telle cuve, la température de la journée, l'état des raisins au moment de la cueillette. Une attention aussi formidable a donné des fruits splendides : les bons vins de Cantemerle. Depuis 1981, le vignoble s'est considérablement étendu : 34 ha de nouvelles vignes ont été plantés sous la surveillance des Domaines Cordier qui dirigent le vignoble.

Caractéristiques : Beau vin léger, souple, qui vieillit rapidement, Cantemerle est encore un exemple du caractère suranné de la classification 1855 : voilà en effet un Cinquième Cru qui a produit bien des bouteilles superbes. Fût très populaire en Hollande.

Superficie : 55 ha.

Production moyenne : 280 tonneaux (25 000 caisses).

Cantenac

Parfois dénommé Cantenac-Margaux, ce village est situé dans le Haut-Médoc. Ces vins sont vendus sous l'appellation d'origine de la commune contiguë : Margaux. Il n'y a d'ailleurs pas de différence appréciable en fait de qualité et de type entre les vins des deux localités.

Six crus de Cantenac furent classés en 1855 : Château-Brane-Cantenac (Second Cru) ; Château-Kirwan, Château-Issan, Château-Palmer, Château-Boyd-Cantenac et Château-Cantenac-Brown (Troisièmes crus) ; enfin Château-Prieuré-Lichine et Château-Pouget (Quatrièmes Crus).

Voir chacun de ces noms à sa place dans l'ordre alphabétique.

Cantenac-Brown (Château-)

Bordeaux rouge. Commune de Cantenac-Margaux, en Haut-Médoc.

Classé Troisième Cru en 1855, le vignoble fut établi par M. John Lewis Brown, un marchand de Bordeaux, qui le vendit en 1860 au propriétaire de Léoville-Poyferré, M. Armand Lalande. Le vignoble était alors deux fois plus grand qu'à présent. La famille du Vivier, ex-propriétaire de la firme de négoce de Luze à Bordeaux, racheta le vignoble en 1969 à M. Jean Lawton, le jovial patron de la firme concurrente Lalande.

Quelques années plus tard, les du Vivier achetait le château, gigantesque construction de brique rouge semblable aux pensionnats de l'époque Tudor, à M. André de Wilde. En 1987, la famille du Vivier vendit le domaine à un groupe d'assurances français.

Caractéristiques : Grands vins pleins, faits avec les variétés Médoc typiques : Cabernet Sauvignon, Merlot et Cabernet Franc. Grand vin corsé, un peu plus corsé que celui des châteaux voisins. Le nouveau propriétaire devrait améliorer qualité et réputation.

Superficie : 42 ha.

Production moyenne : 150 tonneaux (13 000 caisses).

Cap Corse

Apéritif fait avec les vins capiteux du cap Corse (péninsule la plus septentrionale de l'île) que l'on additionne de quinquina et d'herbes.

Capbern-Gasqueton (Château-)

Bordeaux rouge. Commune de Saint-Estèphe, en Haut-Médoc.

La propriété couvre plus de 30 ha, dont plus de la moitié est plantée en vigne sur des hauteurs caillouteuses au bord du village de Saint-Estèphe, au-dessus de la Gironde. De l'autre côté de l'agglomération, se trouve Château-Calon-Ségur qui produit actuellement un des très bons Bordeaux rouges ; ces deux châteaux appartiennent à la famille de Philippe Gasqueton qui les exploite personnellement. Les vins de Capbern sont donc aussi bien soignés par ces viticulteurs experts que le célèbre Calon-Ségur et méritent d'être promus au rang de Grands Crus.

Caractéristiques : Vin rond et corsé qui associe harmonieusement dureté et finesse. Meilleur que certains crus classés.

Superficie : 36 ha.

Production moyenne : 12 000 caisses.

Cape Smoke

Littéralement : Fumée du Cap. L'une des eaux-de-vie les moins chères et les pires de l'Afrique du Sud. Une sage politique fiscale, favorisant les eaux-de-vie de bonne qualité au détriment des pires, est en train de provoquer la disparition de cet alcool.

Cape Wines

Vins du Cap.

Voir AFRIQUE DU SUD

Caperitif

Apéritif d'un jaune d'or profond, fabriqué en Afrique du Sud, à partir de vin additionné d'alcool et d'herbes. Son amertume rappelle celle du vermouth.

Capri (D.O.C.)

Vin blanc sec fait dans l'île de Capri mais dont une certaine partie vient aussi de l'île voisine d'Ischia, et d'autres localités des environs. On fait aussi à Capri une petite quantité de rouge et de rosé.

Voir CAMPANIE

Caque

Grand panier contenant 70 à 80 kg de raisin, dans lequel on déverse le contenu des hottes à l'extrémité de chaque sillon pendant les vendanges en Champagne. Dans cette région on dit indifféremment caque ou mannequin.

Carafe

Dans l'usage courant, le vin servi au restaurant en carafe ne présente pas d'autre garantie que la bonne foi et le bon goût du restaurateur.

Le vin servi de la même manière chez les connaisseurs est celui qui a été décanté un bon moment avant le repas, voire la veille. Les meilleures carafes sont faites de verre clair comme du cristal pour permettre aux convives d'apprécier pleinement la couleur du vin. Dans les très bons restaurants, quand on sert ainsi des vins décantés, la coutume exige qu'on apporte en même temps le bouchon pour que le client se rende compte de son état.

Caramel

Sucre brûlé qu'on ajoute aux spiritueux pour les colorer. Tous les alcools sortent incolores de l'alambic. S'ils ne se colorent pas dans des barriques de bois pendant leur maturation, on doit leur ajouter du caramel : substance insipide et pratiquement inodore.

Carbonated Wine

Littéralement : vins au gaz carbonique. Il s'agit de vins rendus artificiellement mousseux par addition de gaz carbonique.

Voir MOUSSEUX

Carbonique (Gaz)

CO_2. La fermentation du sucre sous l'effet des levures le tranforme à peu près en parts égales d'alcool et de gaz carbonique. Normalement ce gaz se dissout. Mais si on le maintient dans le liquide, on obtient un breuvage mousseux : vin mousseux, bière, cidre.

Carbonnieux (Château-)

Bordeaux rouge et blanc. Commune de Léognan, en Graves.

Ce vin charmant est à l'origine d'une

anecdote aussi charmante. Pour vendre leur vin en Turquie, malgré la prohibition islamique, les moines de l'abbaye Sainte-Croix de Bordeaux, alors propriétaires du cru, étiquetaient leur vin : Eau minérale de Carbonnieux. Le sultan y goûta et dit : « Si les eaux minérales françaises sont aussi bonnes, pourquoi ces gens-là prennent-ils la peine de faire du vin ? ».

Bâti dans les anciens vignobles, quand seuls les coteaux et les crêtes étaient plantés de vignes, le château date du XIVe siècle. En 1953, le Carbonnieux, tant rouge que blanc, fut classé parmi les principaux Graves. Antony Perrin fait un très bon vin rouge plein corsé. Le blanc a fait la grande célébrité de ce cru.

Caractéristiques : Vin doué à la fois de légèreté et de finesse. La prépondérance du Sauvignon, dans le blanc, lui donne un goût particulièrement agréable.

Superficie : 40 ha de rouge ; 40 ha de blanc.

Production moyenne : de blanc : 14 000 caisses ; de rouge : 14 000 caisses.

Carboy

Grosse bouteille de verre (parfois de terre cuite) enveloppée de rotin ou de lamelles de bois. Le nom dérive du persan *garabana,* signifiant gros flacon ou dame-jeanne.

Carema (D.O.C.)

Vin frais fait avec du raisin Nebbiolo, originaire de la région de Turin.

Voir PIÉMONT

Carignan

Variété de raisin cultivée surtout dans le sud de la France et dans les autres pays à climat chaud, pour faire des vins de table et de dessert robustes et capiteux. On l'a aussi transplanté aux États-Unis où l'on écrit son nom : Carignane.

Cariñena

Vins rouges et blancs les plus connus d'Aragon.

Voir ESPAGNE

Carmel

Quelques-uns des vins d'Israël portent ce nom, suivi de la variété de raisin ou du type de vin, par exemple : Carmel muscat, Carmel porto.

Voir ISRAËL

Carpano

Le plus ancien producteur de vermouth italien, dont il produit maintenant deux types à Turin : le vermouth traditionnel, ainsi qu'un autre vermouth amer et doux appelé Punt e Mes.

Carta Blanca

Littéralement Carte Blanche. Rhum légèrement corsé de Porto Rico et de Cuba. Plus léger, plus pâle et plus sec que le Carta Oro.

Voir RHUM : CUBA ; PORTO RICO

Carta Oro

Littéralement Carte d'Or. Rhum légèrement corsé de Porto Rico et de Cuba. L'addition de caramel le rend un peu plus foncé que le Carta Blanca. En général il est aussi un peu plus lourd et légèrement plus doux.

Voir RHUM : CUBA ; PORTO RICO

Caséine

Cette protéine est employée dans le traitement des vins blancs, tant pour les clarifier que pour les protéger contre la madérisation. Cette substance, qui contient du phosphore, est en général extraite du lait où elle est présente sous forme de sel calcaire. Après lavage, séchage, broyage et tamisage, elle peut être utilisée à la dose de 5 à 20 g par hectolitre pour le collage du vin ou à celle de 25 à 30 g/hl tant pour prévenir que pour guérir l'oxydation.

Cask

Un des nombreux noms anglais du tonneau, qui n'en manque pas non plus en français : barrique, fût, baril, etc.

Voir APPENDICE B : CONTENANTS ET MESURES

Casse

Désordre du vin qui se manifeste par une coloration trouble et une précipitation dont souffre la présentation et le goût du breuvage. La casse est due à une oxydation trop importante ou à un excès d'air, de protéines, de fer ou de cuivre.

Voir CHAPITRE V

Cassis (Appellation Contrôlée)

1. Appellation d'origine de certains vins de Provence. Les vignes qui donnent droit à ce nom sont plantées sur les coteaux dominant un pittoresque village de pêcheurs, Cassis, situé à quelque 20 km de Marseille.

Voir PROVENCE

2. Liqueur d'un rouge foncé, sucrée, faite avec les baies de cassis. Le plus connu est celui de Dijon. Mais on en fait aussi ailleurs. Dans cette ville et aux environs on le prend en apéritif en le mélangeant au vin blanc, selon une recette attribuée à feu le chanoine Kir qui fut maire de Dijon ; mais avant que sa vogue se soit répandue sous le nom de Kir, on le consommait déjà sous celui de Rince Cochon.

Castel del Monte (D.O.C.)

Vins frais italiens, rouges et blancs, originaires des Pouilles *(Voir cette région)*.

Castelli di Jesi

Vin blanc D.O.C. de la province des Marches.

Voir VERDICCHIO DI CASTELLI DI JESI

Castelli Romani

Vin bon marché, très populaire dans les restaurants de Rome.

Voir LATIUM

Catalogne

Provinces du nord de l'Espagne où l'on parle le Catalan — Barcelone, Gerone, Lérida et Tarragone. Elles produisent une grande variété de vins plutôt ordinaires, allant du Priorato, un vin lourd et doux, au Penedès, vin mousseux léger et pâle, produit selon les mêmes procédés que le Champagne. Cette région offre également de nombreux vins de table dont la plupart sont bons, et quelques grands vins.

Voir ESPAGNE

Catawba

Raisin rose américain d'origine incertaine, qui devrait son nom à un cours d'eau de la Caroline du Nord. Son jus est blanc, sec et très savoureux. On l'utilisa largement au XIXe siècle, surtout pour faire des vins mousseux. « Sparkling Catawba » (Catawba mousseux), le plus célèbre, fait par la firme Longworth Vineyards de Cincinnati, Ohio, était extrêmement populaire.

Cava (Méthode champenoise)

Terme utilisé pour des vins supérieurs espagnols, fermentés en bouteille en Catalogne.

Caviste

Nom donné dans les restaurants à celui qui s'occupe de la cave où l'on conserve le vin, et que l'on devrait plus correctement nommer sommelier. En Bourgogne le responsable du vin gardé en cave s'appelle caviste alors que dans le Bordelais on lui donne le titre de maître de chai.

Cellier

Local où l'on conserve le vin, appelé aussi chai. Il s'agit dans ce cas de bâtiments construits au-dessus de la surface du sol. Dans certaines régions les vins sont conservés en cave.

Voir CHAPITRE IX

Centerbe

Liqueur italienne faite avec une centaine d'herbes différentes où l'on distingue surtout le goût de la menthe. On l'appelle aussi Silvestro en l'honneur d'un moine italien, Fra San Silvestro, qui aurait eu l'idée de ce mélange.

Central Valley

Cette vallée, située au centre de la Californie, est une région vinicole. Principalement Escalon-Modesto (canton de San Joaquin) et diverses agglomérations des cantons de Stanislaus et Merced.

Voir ÉTATS-UNIS : CALIFORNIE ET OUEST

Cep

Pied de vigne.

Cépage

Plant de vigne. Mot employé pour indiquer la variété de vigne ; par exemple : Pinot, Riesling, etc.

Cerasella

Liqueur italienne rouge foncé et sucrée. Elle est faite avec des cerises et sa saveur est enrichie par un certain nombre d'herbes.

Cerasuolo d'Abruzzo (Montepulciano) (D.O.C.)

Vin rouge italien, léger.

Voir ABRUZZES

Cerise d'Alsace

Eau-de-vie blanche faite avec des cerises, beaucoup plus souvent appelée Kirsch.

Voir ALSACE

Cérons (Appellation Contrôlée)

Vins blancs. Bordeaux.

La route des crus qui suit la rive gauche de la Garonne au-delà des châteaux de Graves, puis des coteaux du Sauternes, serpente ensuite dans un pays plat aux vignes bien entretenues, aussi touffues qu'un tapis de haute laine. C'est la région de Cérons. De-ci, de-là, des petites constructions en forme de bouteille ou de château minuscule vantent le vin et vous invitent à entrer pour goûter.

Les Cérons, ni aussi secs que les Graves blancs, ni aussi doux que les Sauternes, sont faits selon des méthodes impeccables avec les mêmes raisins que les Sauternes : Sémillon, Sauvignon et Muscadelle. Comme pour le Sauternes, on laisse les raisins dépasser la pleine maturité pour les enrichir en sucre et on les cueille grain à grain. En fin de compte, comme l'indiquent les petits stands alignés au long des routes, les vins blancs de Cérons sont beaucoup plus populaires en France qu'on ne l'imaginerait, vu leur faible réputation à l'étranger. (A Bordeaux on suppose que si ce vin ne s'est pas taillé sa place sur le marché mondial, c'est à cause de son caractère intermédiaire, ni doux ni sec).

Pour répondre à la tendance actuelle du marché on fait cependant une quantité considérable de Cérons sec. Mais le Cérons typique est un vin doux, un peu moins sucré que le Barsac dont la région est contiguë et dont il faisait autrefois partie, de même que le Barsac est un Sauternes un peu moins doux. On produit 4 000 hl (40 000 caisses) de Cérons, 14 000 hl (150 000 caisses) de Barsac, 30 000 hl (300 000 caisses) de Sauternes.

Certan-de-May (Château-)

Bordeaux rouge. Commune de Pomerol.

Ce château faisait autrefois partie de la propriété des Barreau, qui comprenait également Vieux-Château-Certan. Il produit un Pomerol typique, quoique ces dernières années il soit nettement inférieur à certaines grandes propriétés voisines.

Superficie : 4 ha.

Production moyenne : 2 000 caisses.

Certosa

Liqueur italienne rouge, analogue à la Chartreuse.

Cesanese

Variété italienne de raisin.

Cesanese di Piglio (D.O.C.)

Remarquable vin rouge du Latium, fait avec du raisin Cesanese
Voir LATIUM

Chablis (Appellation Contrôlée)

Vins blancs. Environs d'Auxerre, Bourgogne.

Chablis est un des noms de vin parmi les plus célèbres au monde mais il désigne surtout un des vins les plus rares au monde. Ces blancs, d'une sécheresse de silex, sont produits avec les raisins cultivés sur les collines avoisinant Chablis, à quelque 180 km au sud-est de Paris.

L'agglomération est située dans la vallée d'un petit cours d'eau, le Serein, dans le département de l'Yonne. Des collines arrondies bordent cette rivière. C'est sur leurs flancs qu'on cultive les vignes, mais en quantité réduite bien que le vignoble de Chablis soit actuellement en pleine reconstitution. Toutes appellations confondues, il y a plus de 2 500 hectares de vignes à Chablis et la tendance actuelle est à la plantation des terres d'appellation.

Le sol est dur et pénible à travailler. La surface arable est mince, et en bien des endroits le sous-sol blanc, riche en calcium (terre connue sous le nom de glaise de Kimmeridge), transparaît. Pis encore, la mince couche supérieure est facilement entraînée par les eaux le long des pentes et il faut la remonter car les meilleurs vins ne proviennent que des vignes cultivées à mi-hauteur.

Autre danger : le climat peu clément. Chablis est une des régions vinicoles les plus septentrionales de France, guère moins que la Champagne ou l'Alsace. Plantée aussi loin au nord, la vigne dépense une grande part de sa vigueur rien que pour survivre aux durs hivers, aux étés incertains et aux gelées tardives, fréquentes en mai, qui sont les plus périlleuses car elles peuvent ruiner toutes les espérances d'une année. Les meilleurs vignobles, souvent les plus susceptibles de geler, utilisent aujourd'hui des *chaufferettes* à fuel pour réchauffer l'air. Il existe par ailleurs des systèmes de pulvérisation ou d'aspersion qui, en vaporisant les vignes, permettent de protéger les bourgeons par la formation d'une couche de glace. De telles pratiques ont complètement transformé l'économie de Chablis.

Le vigneron de Bourgogne est passionnément attaché, non seulement à sa terre, mais à son vin. Pour les plus âgés, il n'est pas de sacrifice trop grand si l'on obtient un grand vin, ne serait-ce qu'en années très favorables. Les plus jeunes restent maintenant à Chablis et ont presque tous suivi les cours d'écoles viti-vinicoles à Beaune ou ailleurs. Comme leurs parents, ils cherchent la meilleur qualité (celle-ci s'est constamment améliorée depuis vingt ans). Les fils des agriculteurs des alentours abandonnent d'ailleurs leurs cultures au profit de la vigne dans la zone de l'appellation.

Les plus grands crus de Chablis se trouvent sur une colline visible de la grand-place de la ville. Ils couvrent 90 ha intégralement cultivés. Tous les vins qu'ils produisent sont vendus sous l'appellation Grand Cru suivi du nom des sept climats. La plus grande partie des Chablis Premier Crus est maintenant plantée sur les quelque 450 autres ha et les vignes sont intégralement en production. Il est difficile actuellement de trouver une parcelle de Chablis Premier Cru qui ne soit pas plantée. Ce sont des vins excellents, qui, de temps en temps, atteignent un degré de qualité aussi élevé que les Grands Crus. Enfin le Chablis et le Petit Chablis viennent au troisième rang ; on ne peut les appeler vins mineurs que par comparaison avec leurs splendides compagnons de cave.

La totalité des vignobles est concentrée dans une zone de 16 km de long sur 10 km de large et, sur cette surface, un peu plus de 2 500 ha seulement sont plantés de vigne, dans les communes de Chablis, Chichée, Chemilly-sur-Serein, Poilly-sur-Serein, Préhy, Fyé, Fleys, Rameau, Courgis, Beines, Poinchy, Maligny, Milly, Béru, La Chapelle-Vaupelteigne, Villy, Lignorelles, Ligny-le-Châtel, Fontenay et Viviers.

Mais ces noms apparaissent rarement sur les étiquettes.

Le Chardonnay est utilisé à Chablis où on l'appelle parfois Beaunois. Le Pinot Blanc est aussi autorisé. Il fut un temps où prévalaient les raisins Sacy, Melon et Aligoté, mais ces variétés ont été arrachées car leur usage est interdit. Les vignes d'aujourd'hui sont taillées très bas pour que le sol de craie, brun et blanc, reflète les rayons du soleil sur les grappes et hâte ainsi leur maturation. Cette taille sévère restreint évidemment la quantité de fruits, même au cours des meilleures années.

Chaque vigneron du Chablis possède en général un certain nombre de parcelles dispersés dont la surface totale varie de 5 à 15 ha (il y a maintenant à Chablis une vingtaine d'exploitations de plus de 20 hectares. Les plus vastes s'étendent sur 70, 90 et 115 ha dans les différentes appellations). Les crus célèbres, si petits soient-ils, sont souvent partagés entre une demi-douzaine de propriétaires et chacun travaille sa part à sa façon. Les négociants ont donc adopté la pratique, commune en Bourgogne, qui consiste à mélanger les produits de plusieurs vignobles d'une même appellation et de leur apposer leur propre étiquette. Nombre de vignerons ont pourtant commencé à mettre eux-mêmes leur vin en bouteille. Ils soignent la vigne, vendangent, font fermenter le vin, le traitent et le vendent sous leur propre nom.

Les vignes de petite taille sont désormais plantées en rangées perpendiculaires à la ligne de crête, alors qu'autrefois on les plantait parallèlement à cette ligne. La nouvelle méthode facilite la culture et le drainage mais provoque l'érosion.

Généralement on vendange en Chablis durant les 15 premiers jours d'octobre et le temps est alors frisquet. Dès que le raisin est mûr, on le cueille et on le presse le jour même car la fermentation pourrait commencer du jour au lendemain, ce qui donnerait du tracas au vigneron.

De grosses masses de raisin arrivent à la propriété. On ne presse que légèrement et le jus est immédiatement versé dans des cuves de grandes capacités soit verrées ou émaillées ou bien en inox. Une petite minorité de producteurs passe le vin dans des fûts de bois avant la mise-en-bouteille.

Dans tous les chais et caves du Chablis, il règne en automne, juste après les vendanges, un fort parfum douceâtre auquel se mêle l'odeur désagréable du gaz carbonique produit par la fermentation. Pendant les premiers jours, ceux de fermentation tumultueuse, les vignerons prennent garde, comme ailleurs, de ne pas rester trop longtemps dans la cave car ils pourraient y succomber à l'asphyxie par le gaz carbonique.

La plupart des années, le soleil ne donne pas assez de sucre au raisin pour fournir la quantité d'alcool indispensable aux grands vins. Le vigneron ajoute du sucre au moût, autrement dit, il le chaptalise, selon les années, c'est nécessaire, conseillé ou inutile. La chaptalisation reconnue par la loi se fait sous contrôle administratif.

Quand le moût a fermenté, le vin est prêt pour le premier soutirage, qui a lieu généralement au cours du mois de février qui suit la vendange. Un pompage lent et prudent aère et clarifie le vin qui laisse derrière lui le dépôt appelé lie. Une partie de la récolte est vendue par les petits vignerons en « moûts » aussitôt après le pressurage soit aux négociants de Chablis, soit aux négociants de Beaune. Une autre partie est vendue au bout de quelques mois en vin fini aux mêmes négociants. Les vignerons, de plus en plus nombreux qui commercialisent leurs vins en bouteilles, étalent leurs mise-en-bouteilles de 8 à 18 mois après la vendange.

La plus grande partie des vins de Chablis est vendue à l'exportation.

Histoire du vin de Chablis

La célébrité du vin de Chablis remonte à des temps très anciens. C'est un des vins qui ont conservé leur renom alors que d'autres, aussi bien connus jadis, sont oubliés maintenant. Le département de l'Yonne a produit jusqu'aux 2/3 de tous les Bourgogne, mais seule la région de Chablis y conserve quelque importance. (On fait encore des vins rouges de moindre qualité dans les villages d'Irancy, Saint-Bris-le-Vineux, Chitry et Joigny, mais en petite quantité et ils ne méritent ni acclamations ni prix élevés).

Nul ne sait quand on planta les premières vignes à Chablis. On ignore aussi s'il y en avait dans la région quand Jules César y arriva, mais on sait à coup sûr qu'elles étaient là à la fin de l'Empire romain. L'effondrement de l'Empire marqua un déclin des vignobles. Mais vers le XIIe siècle, ils ressuscitèrent grâce aux moines.

L'abbaye cistercienne de Pontigny (15 km de Chablis) possédait des vignes dans toute la région et on pense que le raisin Chardonnay y date de cette époque. La plupart des moines venaient de la Côte-d'Or où le Chardonnay est roi pour le vin blanc. Le nom de Beaunois qu'on donne au Chardonnay confirme cette hypothèse. D'autres couvents et chapitres possédaient des vignes dans la région de Chablis, notamment Saint-Martin de Tours, à qui elles avaient été données, au IXᵉ siècle, par Charles le Chauve, frère de son abbé. L'association entre Tours et Chablis dura jusqu'en 1790, moment où la Révolution confisqua les biens de l'Église.

La compensation insuffisante pour la somme énorme de travail exigée par la culture de la vigne dans la région de Chablis ne fût alors que l'un des facteurs du dépérissement de ce grand cru. Il y en eut un autre : le phylloxéra qui commença à s'y manifester en 1893. Il sévissait déjà dans d'autres régions et ne tracassait guère les gens du Chablis jusqu'à ce qu'un été exceptionnellement chaud lui donnât les circonstances favorables à sa prolifération. Les autres vignerons français avaient déjà découvert le moyen de combattre ce mal : greffer les variétés locales de *Vitis vinifera* sur des hybrides ou des souches américaines. Beaucoup de vignobles du Chablis furent rapidement reconstitués sur des souches portant les numéros suivant : 161-49, 3 309, 41-B et B-31. Mais la dépense était si élevée que certains vignerons succombèrent à la tentation de se livrer à une autre activité. Après 1930, le Chablis avait retrouvé une part de sa prospérité mais il connut de nouvelles difficultés. Sa réputation provoquait une grosse demande. Pour la satisfaire on livra du vin, blanc et sec, mais qui n'avait rien d'autre en commun avec le Chablis. Depuis 1936, la loi sur les Appellations Contrôlées a commencé à y remédier. On trouve désormais sur le marché beaucoup moins de faux Chablis qu'autrefois.

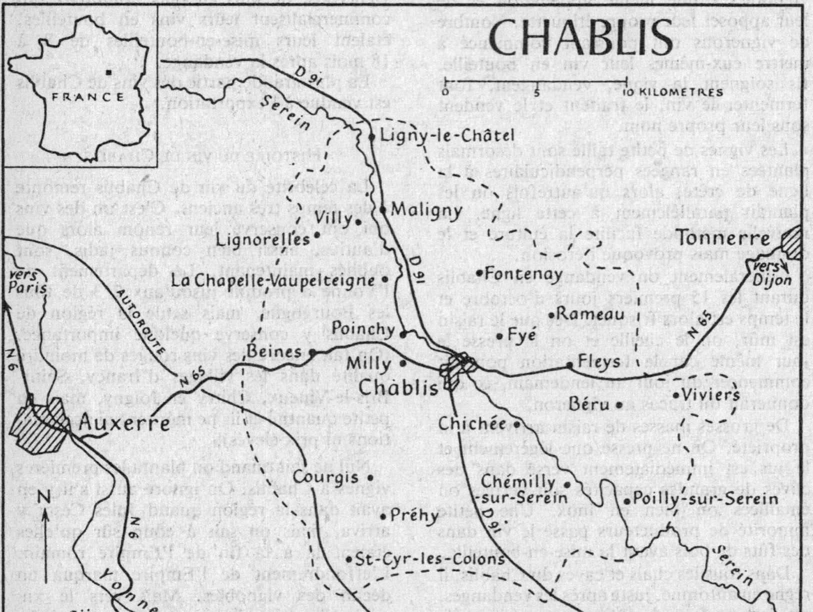

LES GRANDS CRUS

Sept vignobles couvrant 90 ha composent les Grands Crus de Chablis. Ils sont contigus, à mi-hauteur, sur le coteau sud-ouest et, à une exception près (Blanchots, aux environs de Fyé), ils sont tous sur le territoire de la commune de Chablis. On les vend presque toujours sous une étiquette portant le nom du cru : Blanchots, Les Clos, Valmur, Grenouilles, Vaudésir, Les Preuses et Bougros. Un autre aurait pu être inclus : La Moutonne. Mais il n'a jamais été reconnu officiellement quoique l'on ait considéré la question.

La confusion commença au sujet de La Moutonne dès la Révolution française ; ce vignoble fut alors confisqué par l'État et passa entre les mains d'un vigneron du pays. Le document qui sanctionna la vente semble avoir été extrêmement vague et ne situait pas le vignoble d'une manière précise quoique les gens de Chablis puissent en indiquer le lieu sans difficulté : environ 2 ha situés entre Vaudésir et Les Preuses. En 1951, les autorités vinicoles françaises recommandèrent de lui conférer le titre de Grand Cru du Chablis. Mais comme la qualité était décevante, cette recommandation n'eut pas de suite et le décret mourut d'une paisible mort bureaucratique.

Il est impossible de définir ce qui rend ces crus nettement supérieurs aux autres et même à ceux qui leur sont contigus. L'interaction du sol, de l'ensoleillement et d'on ne sait quels facteurs mystérieux y produit, d'une manière trop complexe pour qu'on puisse l'analyser, exactement le raisin qui convient pour faire un certain vin déterminé. Mais ce qui est clair, c'est la différence qui existe effectivement entre ces vins et les autres.

Les vins de ces Grands Crus sont des Chablis, mais différents des autres car tous sont d'un jaune d'or, légèrement teinté d'un vert particulier, d'un sec impeccable qui s'assortit d'un parfum délicat et léger. Les plus grands, plus variés et plus riches, possèdent au superlatif cette qualité inexprimable qu'on appelle l'élégance, la finesse ou la race. Étant donné que les vins de ces sept crus déterminés sont toujours supérieurs aux autres, ils ont seuls droit à l'appellation Grand Cru. Ils doivent en outre titrer au moins 11°. Ceux des bonnes années conservent la plénitude de leur qualité pendant dix ans ou davantage : longévité considérable pour un blanc sec. Dans la plupart des cas, on ne gagne pas grand-chose à les conserver plus de cinq ans. Ces crus ne produisent que 4 500 hl (50 000 caisses) environ par an, la plus grande partie exportée dans le monde entier.

Rive droite du Serein		*Rive gauche du Serein*	
Cru	*Commune*	*Cru*	*Commune*
Chapelot	Fyé	Beauroy	Poinchy
Côte de Fontenay	Fontenay (en partie)	Beaugnon	Chablis
	Fontenay	Beauregards	Courgis
Vaupulent	La Chapelle-Vaupelteigne (en partie)	Butteaux	Chablis
		Châtain	Chablis
Fourchaume	La Chapelle-Vaupelteigne et Maligny	Côte de Cuissy	Courgis
		Côte de Jouan	Courgis
Mont de Milieu	Fyé et Fleys	Côte de Léchet	Milly
Montée de Tonnerre	Fyé	Forêts ou Forests	Chablis
Pied d'Aloup	Fyé	Les Lys	Chablis
Vaucoupin	Chichée	Mélinots	Chablis
Vaulorent	Poinchy	Montmain	Chablis
		Séchet	Chablis
		Troesme	Beines
		Vaillon et Côte de Vaillon	Chablis
		Vaux de Vey	Beines
		Vaux Lignot	Beines
		Vosgros ou Vogiras	Chichée

PREMIERS CRUS

Un peu plus de trente vignobles situés dans diverses communes aux alentours de Chablis, sur les deux rives du Serein, ont droit à l'appellation Premiers Crus. Leurs vins viennent immédiatement après les Grands Crus, leur sont souvent semblables bien que, en général, légèrement inférieurs et les dégustateurs les plus chevronnés ne les distinguent pas aisément les uns des autres. On les vend d'habitude sous le nom de Chablis suivi de celui du cru, par exemple : Chablis-Montée de Tonnerre.

Si ce vin ne titre pas 10,5° au moins, il perd son droit à l'appellation Premier Cru. La production anuelle s'élève à environ 25 000 hl (1 million de caisses) par an.

Voici le nom de ces 27 vignobles et des communes sur lesquelles ils se trouvent.

CHABLIS *(Appellation Contrôlée)*

La mention Chablis sans autre qualification sur une étiquette désigne un vin originaire des coteaux de la région, mais qui n'est ni Grand Cru ni Premier Cru. Ce vin titre au moins 9,5°. On en produit environ 60 000 hl par an, une bonne partie est vendue en vrac et le reste en bouteille.

PETIT CHABLIS *(Appellation Contrôlée)*

Les vins portant cette appellation proviennent aussi des coteaux du Chablis, situés dans les différentes communes du vignoble chablisien. Ils sont généralement vendus en vrac, surtout en France et en Grande-Bretagne. La production annuelle s'élève en moyenne à 6 000 hl.

Chai

Du poitevin *quai*, et probablement du gaulois *caio*. Les Gaulois auraient eu l'habitude de conserver leur production de vin dans les tonneaux *(voir ce mot)*, près des quais. Le chai est un cellier construit audessus de la surface du sol et où l'on conserve le vin en fûts. Dans le Bordelais où il existe peu de caves, tous les vins sont conservés en chai.

Chalonnais

Vins rouges et blancs. Bourgogne.

La chaîne des coteaux du Chalonnais semble prolonger celle de la Côte de Beaune et les vins des deux régions se ressemblent nettement. Pourtant ceux du Chalonnais sont de moindre qualité, et atteignent rarement le même niveau d'excellence. Ils sont cependant bien connus : produits en grande quantité, relativement bon marché et souvent très bons.

Le nom vient de celui de Chalon-sur-Saône, petite ville paisible, sise à quelque 8 km à l'ouest des vignobles. On cultive aussi des vignes plus près de la ville mais, si bizarre que cela paraisse, leur vin n'est pas assez chalonnais pour avoir droit à l'appellation. A cet effet, les raisins doivent avoir été cultivés au flanc de certains coteaux déterminés dans les quatre communes de Givry, Mercurey, Montagny et Rully. Tous les autres vins du voisinage n'ont droit qu'à l'appellation générale de Bourgogne.

Les coteaux privilégiés sont généralement orientés à l'est, quelques-uns au sud-est, et très peu en plein sud. Le sol est pratiquement le même qu'en Côte de Beaune, mais plus fertile.

Les normes fixées pour ces vins ne diffèrent pas notablement de celles qui sont appliquées aux autres secteurs de la Bourgogne. Les rouges doivent être faits principalement avec du Pinot Noir ainsi que du Pinot Liebault et du Pinot Beurot. Quant aux blancs, seuls le Pinot Blanc et le Chardonnay sont permis. La production ne doit pas excéder 40 hl par hectare pour Rully, 45 pour Givry et Montagny, enfin pour Mercurey 40 hl pour les rouges et 45 hl pour les blancs. Ces normes sont d'ailleurs sujettes à modifications les années exceptionnelles. Les rouges doivent titrer au minimum 10,5° et les blancs, 11°. On ne fait pas de Chalonnais rosé.

Les Chalonnais rouges sont généralement plus légers et ne durent pas aussi longtemps que les Bourgogne de Côte-d'Or, et d'autre part, ils ont souvent un fort arôme. Il se peut qu'une certaine bouteille âgée de cinq à huit ans, soit excellente. Les vins blancs sont assez agréables en général, mais un peu délicats à l'exportation. On fait dans le Chalonnais une grande quantité de Bourgogne mousseux, vin qui a ses partisans mais qu'il ne faut pas prendre au sérieux.

APPELLATION D'ORIGINE

Rully (Appellation Contrôlée)

Située à l'extrême nord du Chalonnais

(donc à partir de Chagny), cette commune est le centre de production de Bourgogne mousseux depuis 1830 et pendant longtemps elle a vécu presque entièrement de la vente de ce vin qui n'est d'ailleurs pas fait avec les meilleurs sélections de Bourgogne.

A la fin de la Première Guerre mondiale, les vignerons se trouvèrent une fois de plus en difficulté. Aucune disposition législative ne protégeait les noms des bons vins et, dans le chaos qui suivit la conflagration mondiale, bien des négociants succombèrent à la tentation du bénéfice rapide et le marché fut inondé de gros vins ordinaires vendus sous le nom de crus fameux. C'est alors qu'on manifesta pour exiger des contrôles sévères. Les vignerons de Rully eurent des ennuis. Leurs vins étaient — et sont encore — supérieurs à la moyenne, mais ils les vendaient sous le nom de Mercurey et les vignerons de cette appellation n'étaient pas enchantés par une telle pratique. Quand ils se mirent d'accord sur leurs normes de contrôle, ils exclurent de l'appellation d'origine tous les vins de Rully.

Restaient trois ressources aux vignerons de Rully : obtenir des gens de Mercurey qu'ils admettent de nouveau leur vin ; organiser eux-mêmes leur propre contrôle ; se contenter de l'appellation générale Bourgogne, avec la réduction de prix que cela impliquait. Plutôt que de réclamer leur propre appellation d'origine, ce qui les aurait obligés à accepter certaines normes minimales et aurait pris longtemps, les vignerons préférèrent la première solution et ils cherchèrent à se faire donner le nom de Mercurey. Mais la question du Bourgogne mousseux compliquait les choses, et les autorités vinicoles se montrèrent aussi opiniâtres que les vignerons de Mercurey. Enfin, en 1939, Rully abandonna la partie, adopta ses propres normes pour avoir son appellation d'origine, tout en continuant à produire du mousseux de Bourgogne. La production de Rully est de 7 500 hl (plus de 80 000 caisses) par an dont 50 % de blanc et 50 % de rouge.

Des vins rouges et blancs produits à Rully, ces derniers sont les plus appréciés et on les considère comme les meilleures productions du sud de la Bourgogne, immédiatement après les blancs du Mâconnais. Le Rully blanc est caractérisé par un bouquet prononcé et un goût vineux appelé « vinosité ». Mais comme la plupart des blancs secs, il devrait être consommé jeune. Le vin produit par les meilleurs vignobles est promu au rang de Premier Cru à condition qu'il titre un demi-degré de plus que la norme minimale. Ces vignobles — dont quelques-uns produisent aussi bien du blanc que du rouge — sont : Vauvry, Mont-Palais, Meix-Caillet, Les Pierres, La Bressande, Champ-Clou, La Renarde, Pillot, Cloux, Raclot, Raboursay, Ecloseaux, Marisson, La Fosse, Chapître, Préau, Moulesne, Margoty, Grésigny.

Mercurey (Appellation Contrôlée)

Ce sont les plus connus et les meilleurs vins du Chalonnay. Ils sont faits avec des raisins cultivés dans les communes de Mercurey, Saint-Martin-sous-Montaigu et Bourgneuf-Val-d'Or. Quoique la loi permette de cultiver des raisins à vin blanc et à vin rouge, ceux de Mercurey sont des raisins pour le rouge dans la proportion de 95 % environ.

Ces vins ressemblent souvent beaucoup aux Côte de Beaune : plus légers, mais parfois d'une richesse surprenante, et généralement d'une moindre finesse quoiqu'ils s'en rapprochent étonnamment les meilleures années. Ils doivent indiscutablement être consommés jeunes : entre deux et cinq ans d'âge. Sains et agréables, ils manquent généralement de race.

Une des meilleures organisations de la commune est la cave coopérative dirigée avec une compétence hors du commun. Elle respecte les vins de chacun de ses membres et constitue plutôt une réserve qu'une usine à coupages. Chaque membre de la coopérative possède son propre vin, son propre outillage et son équipement propre. Un des grands avantages de la coopérative, c'est qu'elle permet de se procurer les fournitures à meilleur marché, parce qu'elle achète en quantité, au prix de gros.

La célébrité de Mercurey est si grande qu'elle lui épargna, avec quelques rares autres communes, les méventes qui suivirent les deux guerres mondiales. Le renom des vins et le fait qu'ils sont généralement vendus moins cher que leurs voisins de la Côte-d'Or contribuent à la prospérité constante de Mercurey. On y cultive surtout le Pinot Noir. La production annuelle avoisine 20 000 hl (plus de 200 000 caisses).

Comme ailleurs, certains vignobles de Mercurey ont droit au titre de Premier Cru sur leur étiquette s'ils titrent un demi-degré de plus que la norme minimale dans ce cas, le nom de cru s'ajoute à celui de Mercurey. Ce sont les : Clos du Roi, Les Voyens, Clos Marcilly, Clos des Fourneaux, Clos des Montaigus.

Givry (Appellation Contrôlée)

Le rouge prévaut à Givry, où l'on fait aussi un peu de blanc. Selon la tradition, le vin de ce cru était un des préférés d'Henri IV. Mais l'on croit toutes les communes qui émettent cette même prétention, ce roi devait être affligé d'une soif colossale et partager son cœur entre à peu près tous les vins de France. Les Givry rouges sont un peu plus légers et généralement plus communs que ceux de Mercurey, quoique souvent ceux des meilleurs vignobles (Clos-Saint-Pierre, Clos-Saint-Paul, Cellier-aux-Moines et Clos-Salomon) les valent presque. Un des plus importants propriétaires de Givry est la famille du baron Tenard qui possède nombre de vignobles, y compris le Cellier-aux-Moines, à Givry et le célèbre Montrachet dans la Côte-d'Or. Ils entreposent les vins de toutes leurs propriétés dans leurs caves de Givry, profondément enfoncées sous la ville. Les énormes salles souterraines suggèrent l'idée d'un décor pour un film d'Hollywood.

Quelque 6 500 hl (plus de 70 000 caisses) produits chaque année à Givry sont vendus sous le nom de la commune.

Montagny (Appellation Contrôlée)

Seul nom du Chalonnais (ou Côte chalonnaise) qui s'applique uniquement à des vins blancs. Les vignes sont situées dans les agglomérations de Montagny, Buxy, Saint-Vallerin et Jully-lès-Buxy, mais seulement sur les sols désignés par les experts comme aptes à produire du vin portant cette appellation d'origine. Au total, la zone autorisée couvre à peine plus de 300 ha.

Avec quelques exceptions peu des vins de Montagny sont de première qualité. « Agréables », tel est le mot qu'on emploie le plus souvent pour les décrire et il est particulièrement approprié, à condition de les boire jeunes. Cépage : Chardonnay. Production annuelle : environ 6 000 hl (environ 65 000 caisses).

Des vignobles en nombre étonnant ont été sélectionnés comme supérieurs. Leurs vins ont droit à la désignation de Premier Cru et à porter leur propre nom en plus de celui de la commune. Les bouteilles portant ces trois indications sont rares ; voici ces crus :

Sous-les-Roches	Les Treuffères
Les Combes	Les Bouchots
Les Saint Ytages	Les Vignes-sur-le-Clou
Les Vignes-Saint-Pierre	Les Vignes-Couland
Les Charmelottes	Les Vignes-du-Soleil
Les Champs-Toizeau	Les Marais
(ou Chantoiseau)-	Les Perrières
Les Garchères	La Pallue
Les Chacolets	Le Varignys
Les Clouseaux	Les Thilles
Les Carlins	La Vigne-Devant
Le Breuil	La Corvée
Les Champs-de-Coignée	Les Vignes-Dessous
	Les Maroques
Les Burnins	La Thi
Les Montcuchots	Les Macles
Les Crets	La Condemine
Les Beaux-Champs	Les Vignes-Longues
Les Pandars	Les Vignes-Blanches
Les Jardins	Cornevent
Les Saint-Morille	Le Mont-Laurent
Le Clou	Les Bonneveaux
Les Vignes Serrières	Les Basses
Les Resses	La Mouillère
Le Perthuis	Les Paquiers
Les Gouresses	Les Coères
Les Bordes	Les Thillonnés
Les Las	Les Chandits
Clos-Chaudron	Les Chazelles
La Grande Pièce	Le Vieux-Château
Les Pidans	Les Vignes-du-Puits

Chambertin (Appellation Contrôlée)

Bourgogne rouge. Commune de Gevrey-Chambertin, en Côte de Nuits. Classification officielle : Grand Cru.

Le Chambertin est le grand seigneur de la Bourgogne, tant à cause de sa magnificence et de sa noblesse indiscutables que par déférence pour Napoléon qui le préférait à tous les autres vins. On ne s'étonnera donc pas que la commune de Gevrey se soit adjointe ce nom pour devenir Gevrey-Chambertin

— quoique cela puisse susciter la confusion chez les amateurs inexpérimentés. Si vous achetez du Chambertin, assurez-vous que l'étiquette indique simplement : Chambertin. Si elle porte la mention Gevrey-Chambertin, il peut provenir de n'importe quel vignoble de la commune et sera évidemment de moindre qualité (mais attention ! moindre par rapport à son éminent voisin seulement). Il semble inutile de signaler qu'une bouteille de Chambertin doit toujours porter indication du millésime.

La vigne de Chambertin s'étend sur un coteau en pente douce, à mi-hauteur, au sud du village, près de la route des Grands Crus qui conduit à Morey-Saint-Denis. Elle est contiguë à celle du Clos de Bèze : la seule autre qui ait le droit au titre de Chambertin. Cette clause fut insérée dans la loi parce que, tout aussi remarquable, le Clos de Bèze est moins connu que son voisin. Dans la pratique, une partie du vin de cette vigne se vend comme du Chambertin-Clos de Bèze et le reste, simplement comme Chambertin. Inversement, Chambertin n'a aucun droit au nom de Clos de Bèze.

Les deux vignobles couvrent une superficie approximative de 24 ha : 13 pour Chambertin et 11 pour Clos de Bèze. Cette surface, relativement minime, est partagée entre plus de deux douzaines de vignerons. Chacun cultive ses propres vignes, vendange ses propres raisins, fait son propre vin et le vend à qui lui plaît. Il y a donc toujours une certaine diversité entre les bouteilles de Chambertin. Des soins scrupuleux d'une part, plus de légèreté d'autre part, voilà qui suffit à créer des différences entre les vins provenant la même année du même vignoble. Néanmoins, tous se ressemblent plus que les membres d'une même famille, de même que se ressemblent le Chambertin et le Clos de Bèze. Certains experts de la localité affirment que les vins de ces deux vignes sont tellement semblables qu'il est impossible de les distinguer.

A son apogée, le Chambertin est un grand vin robuste, à l'arrière-goût prononcé, tenace et racé. La couleur profonde de sa robe est une de ses caractéristiques les plus distinctives. Ce vin a un nez formidable. (Le dégustateur, en effet, attribue souvent son propre organe de perception sensorielle au vin lui-même). Ce nez est si remarquable que le terme habituel de bouquet perd sa signification quand il s'agit de Chambertin. Dans un Chambertin bien fait, représentant une bonne année, toutes les caractéristiques se marient en une harmonie équilibrée et le vin s'améliore avec l'âge pour atteindre une virilité austère. Alors le novice s'exclame : « Grand vin ! » Quant à l'expert il murmure : « Chambertin... » La production est minime quoique plus importante qu'on ne le croirait étant donné la superficie du vignoble, et cela est dû au fait que Clos de Bèze en fournit une bonne partie.

Chambertin-Clos de Bèze (A.O.C.)

Bourgogne rouge. Commune de Gevrey-Chambertin, en Côte de Nuits. Classification : Grand Cru.

En l'an de grâce 630, le duc Almagaire de Bourgogne fonda l'abbaye de Bèze, près de Dijon et la dota de terres et champs avoisinants pour assurer sa subsistance. L'une de ces parcelles consistait en un bois de quelque 15 ha à un endroit qui se trouve être aujourd'hui la commune de Gevrey-Chambertin. Les moines défrichèrent, plantèrent des vignes et créèrent ainsi le Clos de Bèze. Ils le cultivèrent jusqu'au XIIIe siècle, puis il passa aux mains d'un autre ordre. La vigne ne devint exceptionnelle qu'au XVIIIe siècle, lorsqu'un certain Jobert — secrétaire de l'intendant du roi et probablement homme d'affaires avisé — en prit possession avec la vigne voisine de Chambertin et entreprit de les rendre célèbres. Le cru était si bon que sa réputation dura. Si bien que lorsque les autorités classèrent les vins de Bourgogne, il eut droit au titre de Grand Cru. Remarquons qu'il n'y en a que 31 dans toute la région de Bourgogne.

Le Clos de Bèze est situé immédiatement au sud de Gevrey-Chambertin, au bord d'un chemin sinueux parmi les vignobles. Chambertin est contigu et ces deux crus sont les meilleurs de la commune. Les vins des deux vignes ont également droit à l'appellation Chambertin, quoique Clos de Bèze soit considéré comme légèrement supérieur ; mais nombre de ses propriétaires profitent de la loi et le vendent sous le nom le plus connu et le plus simple, donc le plus demandé.

L'appellation officielle, celle qu'on trouvera sur les étiquettes, est Chambertin-Clos de Bèze. On n'en produit pas beaucoup.

En une année moyenne la quantité ne dépasse guère 500 hl ou l'équivalent de 5 500 caisses, sans compter les bouteilles qui sont vendues sous le seul nom de Chambertin.

Les caractéristiques des deux vins sont pratiquement les mêmes et nous en traitons sous le nom de Chambertin.

Chambéry

Cette vieille ville de Savoie est célèbre pour le Vermouth extra-sec qu'elle produit et qui bénéficie d'une Appellation d'Origine Contrôlée.

Chambolle-Musigny (Appellation Contrôlée)

Bourgogne rouge, ainsi que du blanc. Commune de Chambolle en Côte de Nuits.

Ces vins rouges sont délicats, élégants, d'un arôme exaltant et ils ont le charme à la fois fragile et résolu des vins fins en dentelle. Les blancs — produits en très petite quantité — partagent le même charme, mais ont tendance à manquer d'une partie de la finesse qui fait la grandeur des rouges.

Ces vins sont célèbres depuis des siècles et ils ont longtemps réussi à éclipser leurs voisins de Morey-Saint-Denis avec lesquels ils n'ont d'ailleurs rien de commun. Ceux de Morey, en effet, ont tendance à être grands, forts, fougueux, alors que ceux de Chambolle ont les qualités diamétralement opposées, à peu près dans tous les domaines. Pourtant, une bonne part de la production de Morey était naguère commercialisée sous le nom de Chambolle. La loi sur les appellations d'origine interdit cette pratique et conféra à Morey sa propre appellation. Un des crus les plus remarquables — Les Bonnes Mares — est partagé entre les deux communes ; mais ses vins ont les caractéristiques familiales des Chambolle plutôt que celles des Morey.

Les Bonnes Mares et les Musigny *(voir chacun de ces mots dans l'ordre alphabétique)* situés chacun à une extrémité de l'agglomération, sont les meilleurs vins de Chambolle. Tous deux ont légalement droit au titre de Grand Cru et ne portent que le seul nom du vignoble sur l'étiquette, ce qui est la marque de l'excellence hors classe.

D'autres très bonnes vignes sont classées Premiers Crus. Leurs vins ont stature et race, mais viennent immédiatement après les deux chefs de file. Ils portent sur l'étiquette le nom de la commune avec celui du cru. Le meilleur est Les Amoureuses, situé immédiatement au-dessous des vignes des Musigny, sur la frontière qui sépare Chambolle-Musigny de Vougeot. Les Bourguignons estiment que ce vin mérite bien son nom. Il est légèrement — légèrement, nous insistons — moins caractérisé que celui de Musigny et, les bonnes années, celui du vigneron capable, a une délicatesse féminine, une grâce enjôleuse et un bouquet captivant vraiment chaleureux.

GRANDS CRUS

Cru	*Superficie (ha)*
Les Musigny	10,1
Les Bonnes Mares (en partie)	13,7

QUELQUES PREMIERS CRUS

Les Amoureuses	5,35
Les Charmes	9,29
Les Cras	4,21
Les Borniques	1,5
Les Baudes	3,5
Les Plantes	2,6
Les Hauts-Doix	1,75
La Combe d'Orveau	5
Les Chatelots	2,6
Les Gruenchers	3
Les Groseilles	1,51
Les Fuées	6,2
Les Lavrottes	1
Derrière-la-Grange	0,73
Les Noirots	2,9
Les Sentiers	4,94
Les Fousselottes	4
Aux Beaux-Bruns	2,4
Les Combottes	0,65
Aux Combettes	2,27
Les Carrières	0,7
Les Chablots	2,03
Aux Échanges	2,58
Les Grands Murs	0,75

D'autres crus sont classés dans la même catégorie que Les Amoureuses. Quoique leur production parvienne rarement à la même excellence extraordinaire elle peut souvent être d'une parfaite magnificence.

Les vins qui ne viennent ni des deux grands Crus, ni des Premiers Crus, ni d'autres crus classés, mais qui ne sont pas énumérés ici faute d'avoir été expérimentés, ont droit à la seule appellation générale de Chambolle-Musigny. Mais il est évident qu'ils ne se conforment pas aux normes minimales extrêmement rigoureuses imposées aux autres. Mais ils en possèdent bien des caractéristiques, quoique à un degré moins sublime.

La superficie plantée en bonnes vignes de Chambolle-Musigny ne s'élève qu'à quelque 175 ha et sa production moyenne (rien qu'en rouge) à quelque 6 500 hl par an (quelque 70 000 caisses).

Chambrer

Opération consistant à amener lentement le vin à la température de la pièce dans laquelle il sera consommé. C'est celle qui convient le mieux à la plupart des vins rouges. Le chauffer en plongeant la bouteille dans de l'eau chaude ou en la posant devant le feu n'est pas recommandé : ce choc soudain est capable de bouleverser l'équilibre chimique du vin et d'en détruire, ou pour le moins affaiblir, l'excellence. Si le vin est trop froid, on peut le réchauffer en tenant le verre entre les mains, mais une élévation brusque de température le ruine.

Voir CHAPITRE VIII

Champagne (Appellation Contrôlée)

Principalement des vins blancs mousseux ; une petite quantité de blancs, de rouges et de rosés non mousseux. Est de la France.

Les vins délicieusement mousseux de Champagne sont les plus célèbres du monde. Il existe certes des gens selon lesquels on devrait réserver le Champagne au lancement des bateaux et des débutantes ; d'autres qui voudraient en boire à tous les repas, avant les repas, après les repas, au milieu de la matinée ou au milieu de la nuit, mais la plupart éprouvent un frisson de joie quand le bouchon jaillit du goulot, qu'une volute de buée s'élève et que le vin d'or pâle mousse dans les grands verres. Il n'est de Champagne que de la région champenoise et on l'ignore trop hors de France.

Le seul vin qui ait un droit quelconque à l'appellation Champagne est fait avec certains raisins précisés légalement dans un secteur limité et bien défini de la province de Champagne. Les vignes qui produisent ces raisins sont cultivées conformément à des règles locales strictes, et la vinification s'accomplit également selon des règlements précis. Le Champagne est ce qu'il est, en partie par le sol sur lequel pousse la vigne, en partie par le climat, en partie par les vignes, en partie par le labeur des vignerons et leurs traditions. Des vins mousseux faits n'importe où au monde peuvent être bons, mais aucun ne sera jamais du Champagne — quoique certains aient l'audace d'en porter le nom, comme un masque. On sait moins dans le monde qu'il existe quelques vins de Champagne non mousseux ; on en fait pourtant, dans cette province et ils obtiennent un certain succès en dépit de leurs prix élevés. L'appellation « vin nature de Champagne » a été remplacée par l'appellation Coteaux Champenois, qui doit nécessairement figurer sur toute bouteille de vin non mousseux destinée à la vente. Depuis cinq ans, les ventes de ces vins se situent autour de 1 million de bouteilles. La région de Champagne commence à 150 km à l'est et légèrement au nord de Paris, c'est une vaste plaine, calcaire, cultivée avec soin, coupée de-ci, de-là, par un cours d'eau et dominée par la montagne de Reims. Entre la ville d'Épernay sur la Marne, et celle de Reims sur la Vesle, se dresse une bosse informe, au milieu du dos solide de la Champagne. Quand on la voit du haut des airs, elle apparaît comme une excroissance crayeuse en forme d'énorme point d'interrogation posé sur la plaine. Cette montagne de Reims n'est montagne que sur un pays plat car son altitude moyenne avoisine 200 m et n'en atteint 300 qu'en quelques rares endroits. Le jambage du point d'interrogation s'étend au-delà de Reims, vers le nord, en direction de la Petite Montagne et sa boucle s'enroule autour d'Épernay, au sud, pour se terminer dans le secteur appelé Côte de Bouzy. La région des grands crus se partage à Épernay. Une branche longe le cours de la Marne en direction du Château-Thierry et l'autre s'oriente droit au sud, pour former la célèbre Côte des Blancs, où le Pinot Noir cède la place au Chardonnay Blanc. Ces secteurs sont les meilleurs de la Champagne, mais pas les seuls. Ils sont entièrement dans le département de la Marne, mais les limites de l'appellation Champagne débordent les frontières de ce département. Les 3/4 du Champagne viennent de la Marne, le reste de ses voisins : Aube, Aisne et Seine-et-Marne. C'est de ces trois derniers départements que coulent à flot les Champagne à bon marché vendus dans le monde entier.

Plus de 200 millions de bouteilles sont expédiées, dont 75 millions sont exportées : États-Unis et Royaume-Uni en importent chaucun 15 millions, Allemagne 8 millions, Italie 6 millions et Belgique 5 millions.

Histoire du vin de Champagne

Les vignes de Champagne figurent parmi les plus anciennes d'Europe. La paléontologie prouve qu'il y en avait déjà à l'ère tertiaire, que les géologues situent entre un million et soixante millions d'années avant notre époque. Il se pourrait qu'on ait fait du vin avec les raisins de ces vignes avant l'arrivée des Romains, mais rien ne le prouve. Les Romains encouragèrent la viticulture en Champagne comme partout ailleurs en Gaule.

A l'origine, le vin de Champagne n'était pas mousseux et concurrençait celui de Bourgogne. Les deux provinces rivalisèrent et leur dispute finit par se résumer en cette question : lequel des deux vins est le meilleur pour la santé ? Le problème fut enfin résolu par les médecins de la cour de Louis XIV qui se prononcèrent en faveur du Bourgogne. Les mousseux ne progressèrent guère en Champagne jusqu'au XVIIe siècle. C'est alors, dit-on, que les découver-

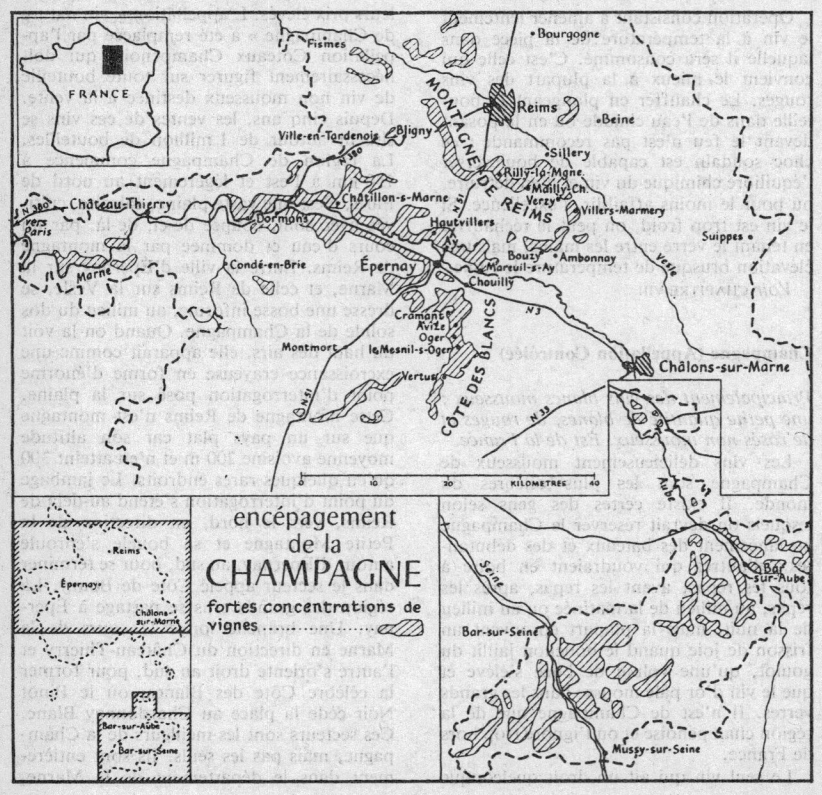

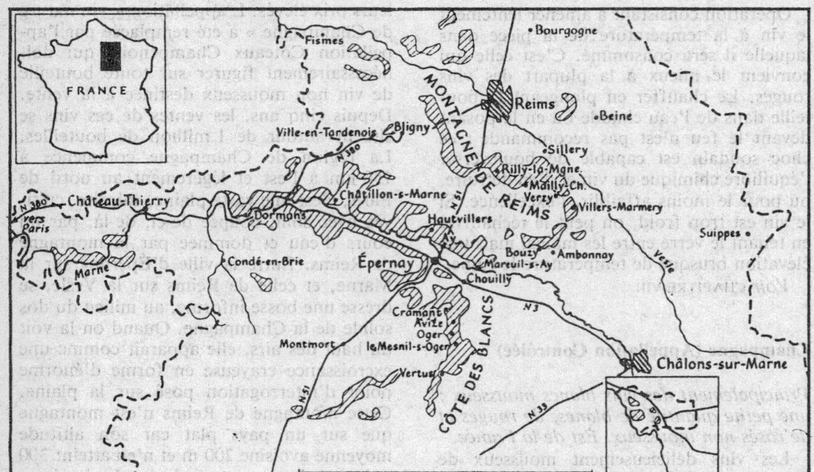

tes d'un moine bénédictin, Dom Pérignon, bouleversèrent les méthodes de vinification.

Tous les vignerons ont remarqué que certains vins fermentent de nouveau au printemps et que, si leur gaz ne peut s'échapper, ils moussent et en général font éclater le récipient qui les contient. On appelait ces vins *saute-bouchon,* ou *vin diable*.

Dom Pérignon (ou l'un de ses contemporains) comprit que la pression qui s'élevait dans le breuvage était due à la présence de gaz carbonique. Il recommanda d'utiliser des bouteilles plus solides. Jusqu'alors, en général, les bouchons n'étaient pas en liège, mais en coton ou en tissu imbibé d'huile. On se mit alors à en faire de plus épais et à les lier avec une ficelle. On lui attribue aussi le mérite d'avoir été un des premiers à mélanger les vins de Champagne qui, pour la plupart, ont besoin des qualités que seul le coupage peut leur donner. Ce moine bénédictin était maître de chai à l'abbaye d'Hautvillers depuis 47 ans quand il mourut en 1715.

Il faut souligner également les travaux réalisés à la même époque par Dom Oudart, cellérier de l'abbaye de Saint-Pierre-aux-Monts à Pierry, qui permirent alors des progrès considérables dans la vinification du vin de Champagne. Jean Oudart fut un des premiers à préférer les bouchons de liège espagnol aux vieux bouchons de bois et d'étoupe. Il est plausible que les deux moines se soient connus et qu'ils aient pu confronter leurs expériences œnologiques.

Classification particulière des crus de Champagne

Les petites agglomérations de Champagne et les vignobles qui se trouvent sur leur territoire sont classés selon une échelle complexe de pourcentages. Le grade accordé à chaque localité détermine le prix du Champagne, en quelque année que ce soit. Chaque automne les vignerons rencontrent les négociants qui vont acheter la vendange et ils établissent le prix par marchandage. Le prix doit être décidé à l'avance car, lorsque la vendange a commencé, les raisins souffriraient du moindre retard. Le prix décidé est celui des tout premiers crus qui ont officiellement droit à 100 % du tarif convenu. Le prix du raisin des autres localités sera déterminé par le pourcentage attribué à ces crus. Dans certains secteurs moindres, on accorde des primes à certains types de raisin pour encourager les vignerons qui plantent des vignes donnant de meilleurs fruits mais en moins grande quantité. Depuis 1966, le prix de base du kilo de raisin a été augmenté par le paiement de diverses primes aux producteurs. En 1986, le prix de base était d'environ 20 F plus une petite prime pour les raisins Chardonnay et Pinot Noir. A cette somme s'ajouta une prime de 6 % versée aux vignerons s'engageant par contrat à fournir du raisin durant plusieurs années. Soit un total approximatif de 22 F par kilo pour les meilleurs vignobles.

La montagne de Reims se targue de six crus à 100 % : Beaumont-sur-Vesle, Mailly, Sillery (à une certaine époque, le nom de vin le plus renommé en Angleterre), Puisieulx, Verzenay et Verzy. En se dirigeant vers le sud, dans la direction de la vallée de la Marne, c'est-à-dire en quittant la montagne pour s'engager dans la Côte de Bouzy, les meilleurs crus sont : Ambonnay, Ay, Bouzy, Louvois et Tours-sur-Marne. Sur la Côte des Blancs se trouvent Avize, Chouilly, Cramant, Le Mesnil-sur-Oger et Oger.

Dans les agglomérations où l'on cultive du raisin rouge et du blanc, chacun aura droit à un pourcentage différent et, sauf dans la Côte des Blancs, le plus élevé est toujours attribué au rouge ; les plants qui donnent des raisins blancs sont plus ou moins considérés comme des curiosités dans les autres secteurs.

Presque tous les mousseux de Champagne sont faits avec un mélange de raisins noirs et blancs. Certains sont des Blancs de Noirs, autrement dit des vins blancs faits avec du raisin noir ; quelques-uns sont des Blancs de Blancs, ou vins blancs faits avec des raisins blancs ; ces derniers proviennent presque uniquement de la Côte des Blancs, au sud d'Épernay.(La plupart des Champagne ne portent aucune autre appellation que Champagne, quoiqu'il soit assez courant d'indiquer le cru sur l'étiquette de ceux qui ne sont pas mousseux.) Certains fabricants de Champagne disent que les raisins blancs ont tendance à améliorer la qualité du mélange. La vogue actuelle se porte donc vers les Blancs de Blancs, d'où la demande croissante de Chardonnay, soit pour mélanger avec les raisins noirs, soit pour les vinifier seuls, et ils sont devenus plus chers que les Pinot Noirs. On fait aussi une petite quantité de vin rosé en Champagne ainsi que divers vins non mousseux dénommés Coteaux Champenois (dont fait partie le Bouzy Rouge). Le Rosé de Riceys est une appellation spécifique qui désigne les vins rosés tranquilles issus de raisins récoltés sur le seul terrain de la commune de Riceys dans l'Aube. Mais l'appellation Champagne sans autre mention désigne toujours la variété mousseuse.

ARRONDISSEMENT DE REIMS

Canton d'Ay	%
Ambonnay	100
Avenay	93
Ay	100
Bisseuil	95
Bouzy	100
Champillon	93
Cormoyeux	85
Cumières	93
Dizy	95
Hautvillers	90
Louvois	100
Mareuil-sur-Ay	99
Mutigny	93
Romery	85
Tauxières	99
Tours-sur-Marne rouge	100
Tours-sur-Marne blanc	90

Canton de Beine	
Berru	84
Cernay-les-Reims	85
Nogent-l'Abbesse	87

Canton de Bourgogne	
Brimont	83
Cauroy-les-Hermonville	83
Cormicy	83
Merfy	84
Pouillon	84
Saint-Thierry	87
Thil	84
Villers-Franqueux	84

Canton de Reims	
Ormes	85
Reims	88
Taissy	94
Trois-Puits	94

Canton de Verzy	
Beaumont-sur-Vesle	100
Chamery	90
Chigny-les-Roses	94
Ludes rouge	94
Ludes blanc	86
Mailly-Champagne	100
Montbré	94
Puisieulx	100
Rilly-la-Montagne	94
Sermiers	89
Sillery	100
Trépail	95
Verzenay	100
Verzy	100
Villers-Allerand	90
Villers-Marmery	95

Canton de Châtillon-sur-Marne	
Baslieux	84
Belval-sous-Châtillon	84
Binson-Orquigny	86
Champlat-Boujacourt	83
Châtillon-sur-Marne	86
Courtagnon	82
Cuchery	84
Cuisles	86
Jonquery	84
Montigny-sous-Châtillon	86
La Neuville-aux-Larris	84
Olizy-Violaine	84
Passy-Grigny	84
Pourcy	84
Reuil	86
Sainte-Gemme	84
Vandières	86
Villers-sous-Châtillon	86

Canton de Fismes	
Châlons-sur-Vesle	84
Chenay	84
Crugny	86
Hermonville	84
Hourges	86
Pévy	84
Prouilly	84
Trigny	84
Unchair	86
Vandeuil	86

Canton de Ville-en-Tardenois

Bligny	83
Bouilly	86
Bouleuse	82
Branscourt	86
Brouillet	86
Chambrecy	83
Chaumuzy	83
Coulommes-la-Montagne	89
Courcelles-Sapicourt	83
Courmas	87
Écueil	90
Faverolles	86
Germigny	85
Gueux	85
Janvry	85
Jouy-les-Reims	90
Lagery	86
Les Mesneux	90
Marfaux	84
Pargny-les-Reims	90
Poilly	83
Rosnay	83
Sacy	90
Sainte-Euphraise	86
Sarcy	83
Savigny-sur-Ardres	86
Serzy-et-Prin	86
Tramery	86
Treslon	86
Villedommange	90
Ville-en-Tardenois	82
Vrigny	89

ARRONDISSEMENT D'ÉPERNAY

Canton d'Avize

Avize		100
Brugny-Vaudancourt		86
Chavot-Courcourt		88
Cramant		100
Cuis	rouge	90
	blanc	95
Grauves	rouge	90
	blanc	95
Le Mesnil-sur-Oger		100
Mancy		88
Monthelon		88
Morangis		84
Moslins		84
Oger		100
Oiry		100

Canton de Dormans

Boursault	84
Champvoisy	84
Cerseuil	84
Comblizy	83
Courthiézy	83
Dormans (Try, Vassy, Vassieux, Chavenay)	83
Festigny	84
Le Breuil	83
Le Mesnil-le-Hutier	84
Leuvrigny	84
Mareuil-le-Port	84
Nesle-le-Repons	84
Œuilly	84
Port-à-Binson	84
Soilly	83
Troissy-Bouquigny	84
Verneuil	86
Vincelles	86

Canton d'Épernay

Chouilly	rouge	95
	blanc	100
Damery		89
Épernay		88
Fleury-la-Rivière		85
Mardeuil		84
Moussy		88
Pierry		90
Saint-Martin-d'Ablois		86
Vauciennes		84
Venteuil		89
Vinay		86

Canton d'Esternay

Bethon	rouge	85
	blanc	87
Chantemerle	rouge	85
	blanc	87

Canton de Montmort

Baye	85
Beaunay	85
Broyes	85
Cogny	85
Coizard-Joches	85
Courjeonnet	85
Étoges	85
Fèrebrianges	85
Oyes	85
Talus-Saint-Prix	85
Villevenard	85

Canton de Sézanne

Barbonne-Fayel	rouge	85
	blanc	87
Fontaine-Denis-Nuisy	rouge	85
	blanc	87
Saudoy	rouge	85
	blanc	87
Sézanne	rouge	85
	blanc	87
Vinedey	rouge	85
	blanc	87

ARRONDISSEMENT DE CHÂLONS

Canton de Vertus

Bergères-les-Vertus	rouge	90
	blanc	95
Coligny	rouge	87
	blanc	90
Étrechy	rouge	85
	blanc	87
Givry-les-Loisy		85
Loisy-en-Brie		85
Soulières		85
Toulon-la-Montagne		85
Vert-la-Gravelle		85
Vertus		95
Villeneuve-Renneville		95

Canton de Suippes

Billy-le-Grand	95
Vaudemanges	95

Tous les crus de la Marne sont classés à 80 %.

ARRONDISSEMENT DE CHÂTEAU-THIERRY

Canton de Condé-en-Brie

Barzy-sur-Marne	85
Baulne-en-Brie	85
Passy-sur-Marne	85
Trelou-sur-Marne	85
Aisne (moins les 4 communes du canton de Condé-en-Brie ci-dessus mentionnées)	80

Tous les crus de l'Aube (environ 60) sont classés à 80 % sauf Villenauxe-la-Grande.

Environ 28 000 ha sont plantés de bonnes vignes en Champagne, dont environ 21 000 dans le département de la Marne ; 5 000 dans celui de l'Aube ; 2 000 dans l'Aisne et moins de 30 en Seine-et-Marne. Il y a moins d'un siècle, la superficie plantée ne s'élevait guère à plus de 15 000 ha, mais l'épidémie de phylloxéra, qui arriva en Champagne vers 1890, et les ravages de la Première Guerre mondiale, durant laquelle le pays fut pendant quatre ans un des principaux théâtres d'opérations, réduisirent la superficie du vignoble. Selon les récoltes, de 1 à 2 millions d'hl de vin sont traités en mousseux. Quant aux autres vins, leur production est très réduite. Quant au Bouzy Rouge (non mousseux), sa production dépasse rarement 900 hl et celle du Rosé de Riceys est pratiquement négligeable.

Plus de la moitié du Champagne est traité dans les caves des gros négociants dont la plupart se trouvent à Reims et Épernay. On a creusé sous ces deux villes, dans le sol calcaire, d'énormes chambres souterraines. Une firme possède environ 18 km de caves si profondes qu'il faut descendre un escalier de 116 marches pour les atteindre. La plupart de ces caves sont taillées en larges avenues portant les noms des principales villes consommatrices de Champagne. Des statues taillées dans les murs de craie leur donnent une certaine ressemblance avec les galeries d'art. Elles servirent pendant la guerre d'abris souterrains, mais offrent un meilleur abri aux vins qu'aux hommes. Leur température reste constamment à 10 °C d'un bout de l'année à l'autre. Fraîches, sèches, propres, elles négligent aucun soin particulier pour rester aptes à la conservation des vins.

Épernay et Reims, où les rois de France étaient autrefois sacrés dans la magnifique cathédrale deux fois détruite, deux fois reconstruite, sont les deux centres principaux d'expédition et nombre de négociants ont des bureaux dans les deux villes. Voici les noms des plus importantes maisons de Reims : Veuve Clicquot-Ponsardin, Heidsieck Monopole, Charles Heidsieck, Mumm, Piper-Heidsieck, Pommery et Greno, Louis Roederer et Taittinger. Parmi celles d'Épernay on compte : Mercier, Moët et Chandon, Perrier-Jouet, Castellane et

Pol Roger. Il y a en outre à Ay, petite ville qui domine la Marne, quelques entreprises parmi lesquelles Ayala et Bollinger.

Climat, sol et vigne

Les vignobles de Champagne sont les plus septentrionaux de France. Quand on cultive la vigne aussi près de la limite nord de son domaine, il faut prendre des soins extrêmes pour la protéger contre les conditions climatiques défavorables, non seulement en raison des dommages qu'elle peut subir de ce fait mais aussi parce que la vitalité de toute plante est diminuée par son combat pour survivre, ce qui la rend moins apte à combattre la maladie que les vignes cultivées sous des cieux plus cléments. Pourtant, c'est précisément les rigueurs du climat qui donnent au Champagne son exquise délicatesse. La situation et l'exposition des vignobles sont importantes et presque tous sont orientés soit au sud soit au sud-est, à l'exception de ceux de la Côte des Blancs qui regardent vers l'est, et ceux de l'agglomération de Verzenay (coté 100 %) qui font face au nord. L'exposition au sud implique que la colline abritera la vigne des durs vents d'hiver et qu'elle jouira pleinement du soleil estival. Gelées et vagues de froid hivernales ont tendance à s'appesantir sur les vallées et les dépressions : les vignes sont donc surtout plantées à mi côte où elles sont relativement à l'abri quoique les gelées désastreuses n'y soient pas inconnues. L'humidité n'est pas excessive et ce facteur est important, étant donné que la plupart des maladies cryptogamiques de la vigne se développent dans l'humidité. Le Chardonnay, qui importe tellement, est très sujet à la pourriture grise, type de moisissure qui sévit particulièrement sous les climats humides.

Le climat n'est pas le seul facteur qui contribue à faire du Champagne ce qu'il est. Le sol exceptionnel, d'où la vigne tire sa nourriture et dont les qualités se reflètent dans les raisins et les vins, joue aussi un rôle important. L'élément principal de ce sol est la craie, mais il y en a d'autres. La silice et la marne lui donnent une consistance qui permet de le travailler et on y trouve aussi des traces minimes de divers éléments. Presque toute la craie de Champagne se présente sous la forme de glaise de Kimmeridge — même formation que dans le Chablis *(voir ce nom)* — d'après le nom du village d'Angleterre où l'on a étudié et identifié ce mélange. Sa composition, d'un grain grossier, élimine l'excès d'humidité, mais en retient assez pour abreuver la vigne. Les cailloux blancs reflètent les rayons du soleil sur le fruit en voie de maturation et conservent suffisamment de chaleur pour continuer à rayonner longtemps après que le soleil ait disparu à l'horizon. Sans ce supplément de chaleur les raisins ne mûrissent pas du tout en certaines années.

Enfin, troisième facteur : les vignes plantées en Champagne font l'objet d'une surveillance attentive. Les cépages Meunier et Pinot Noir prédominent ; ce dernier est une vigne dont les raisins noirs donnent des vins de l'or le plus pur. Le Chardonnay est un cépage noble important. On appelle parfois ce dernier Pinot Chardonnay quoique les spécialités aient établi qu'il n'appartient pas à la famille Pinot. Enfin, on cultive aussi en Champagne un peu de Meslier et d'Arbanne. Il subsistait dans l'Aube quelques plants de Gamay après la guerre, mais leur produit n'était pas particulièrement heureux. Tout le Gamay aurait dû être arraché en 1942, mais la guerre fit remettre l'échéance jusqu'en 1962. Aujourd'hui, les vignes plantées en Gamay ont toutes été arrachées et replantées en Pinot Noir ou Meunier.

En général, les ceps sont plantés en rangs espacés d'un mètre l'un de l'autre. Sur chaque rang les plants sont séparés par 40 à 50 cm et leurs sarments liés à des fils de fer qui vont d'une extrémité à l'autre du sillon. On compte généralement deux ou trois rangs de fil de fer auxquels s'accrochent les vrilles de la vigne dont les grappes pendent vers le sol. La taille est déterminée par la loi et les seules méthodes autorisées sont les suivantes : Chablis, Cordon de Royat, Guyot. Toutes ces mesures tendent à assurer que la vigne fournira d'année en année une quantité modérée de raisin de haute qualité.

En général, les raisins sont petits et assez acides. Le climat relativement froid de Champagne ne les mûrit que lentement et certaines années incomplètement. Au fur et à mesure que l'été s'écoule, l'acidité diminue et la teneur en sucre augmente, mais elle ne s'élève jamais autant que dans les régions plus chaudes. Pourtant, certaines années, ces raisins fortement acides sont capables de produire 12° d'alcool.

En temps normal, les vins sont vinifiés en un breuvage mousseux, délicat, qui offre la plus subtile combinaison de couleur, d'arôme et de goût.

Comme tous les grands vins, les Champagne dépendent du temps et comme tous les grands vins ils sont magnifiques en certaines années. Quelques-unes des meilleures pour le Champagne furent (les plus grandes en italique) : *1928,* 1929, 1934, 1937, 1945, *1947,* 1949, *1952, 1953,* 1955, *1959,* 1961, 1962, *1964,* 1966, 1969, 1970, *1971,* 1973, 1975, 1976, *1978,* 1979, 1981, 1982 et 1985.

Vendange et vinification en Champagne

Comme ceux de tous les vins, les travaux de vinification commencent pour le Champagne dès la vendange. Autrefois sa date était fixée par la loi et quiconque commençait à vendanger trop tôt était traduit devant les fonctionnaires régionaux qui infligeaient un châtiment. Le ban des vendanges — proclamation officielle — survit, mais désormais c'est une formalité plus qu'une obligation. De nos jours le facteur décisif est le raisin qui doit être mûr, mais pas trop. On vendange assez tard en Champagne, d'habitude à partir du début de la seconde ou de la troisième semaine d'automne. La teneur minimale du raisin en sucre, donc du vin en alcool après fermentation, est décidée chaque année par le Comité interprofessionnel du vin de Champagne, organisme semi-officiel qui siège à Épernay et régit toutes les activités vinicoles de la région, y compris la défense de l'appellation.

Pour protéger les plus de 5 000 travailleurs saisonniers qui participent à la cueillette des raisins en Champagne, les machines à vendanger étaient encore interdites en 1988. Les vendangeurs coupent les lourdes grappes de raisin mûr. Les hommes les plus vigoureux vont et viennent le long des sillons en portant des paniers où est jeté le raisin récolté ; puis ces porteurs déversent leur charge à l'extrémité du sillon. Les raisins y sont examinés : les trop mûrs ou ceux qui présentent un défaut quelconque sont éliminés et les autres mis en cagette ou en mannequin : grand panier large et profond, contenant quelque 60 à 80 kg de raisin. Ces cagettes sont transportées rapidement jusqu'au *vendangeoir* le plus proche afin d'éviter l'oxydation du raisin.

Les viticulteurs de Champagne vendent toute une partie de leur récolte en raisins à des négociants. Ce sont les firmes commerciales qui font le vin et le mènent d'un bout à l'autre d'une longue série d'opérations d'où résulte le Champagne. La plupart de ces entreprises commerciales possèdent leurs propres vignobles pour s'assurer au moins une partie de la récolte annuelle. On estime que quelque 3 000 à 3 400 des 28 000 ha de vignes leur appartiennent. Elles ont des *vendangeoirs* dans toutes les communes importantes et pressurent le raisin sur-le-champ.

Il existe néanmoins des coopératives qui assurent le pressurage, la vinification et parfois la chaptalisation. Tel est le cas de la coopérative de Mailly-Champagne (cru côté à 100 %). Pendant la crise économique de l'entre-deux-guerres, les grandes firmes commerciales refusèrent d'acheter les raisins des vignerons de Mailly qui s'associèrent et fondèrent une coopérative. Ne possédant aucun capital au début, ils construisirent leurs vendangeoirs et les équipèrent eux-mêmes durant leurs heures de loisir. Actuellement cette coopérative groupe 70 vignerons. Elle produit des Champagne millésimés, rosés et blancs, et les expédie dans le monde entier.

Pendant toutes les vendanges, des véhicules circulent sur les routes, entre vignes et pressoirs. Le raisin est pressé dès qu'il arrive. La majorité des raisins de Champagne sont noirs et, si le jus restait en contact avec les peaux colorantes, le vin prendrait une teinte indésirable. C'est pourquoi les vinificateurs pressent le raisin immédiatement c'est-à-dire avant qu'il ait le temps de se colorer.

Quant au Champagne rosé, on le fait parfois en ajoutant du vin rouge au blanc : pratique tenue en piètre estime, sauf en Champagne où elle donne des résultats qui semblent la justifier. Mais la méthode la plus courante de vinification en rosé consiste à laisser cuver les raisins rouges avec leur peau pendant un temps limité pour lui donner seulement la coloration désirée. Quel que soit le procédé employé, les fabricants de Champagne considérent la variété rose comme une bizarrerie qui n'appartient pas à la même classe que le célèbre blanc.

Les pressoirs de chêne sont ronds, larges

et bas et comportent un réceptacle à leur base pour recueillir le jus à mesure qu'il s'écoule. Leurs formes et leurs dimensions sont telles qu'ils contiennent exactement 4 t de raisins, uniformément répartis en minces couches. Les première, deuxième et troisième serres donnent un vin de haute qualité. Un dernier pressurage, appelé rebêche, donne un vin ordinaire qui sera consommé par les ouvriers de l'entreprise. La première serre produit 2 000 l (soit dix « pièces » ou barriques) de vin de première qualité, appelé « vin de cuvée ». La deuxième serre donne environ 2 pièces de vin appelé « première taille ». La troisième donne encore une pièce et demi de « deuxième taille ». Ces deux dernières tailles serviront à la fabrication du vin ordinaire destiné aux ouvriers.

Le jus qui s'écoule du pressoir est généralement versé dans d'énormes cuves, puis dans des barriques, pour être expédié aux caves de l'entreprise, à Ay, Épernay et Reims. Le pressurage a lieu à proximité de la vigne, mais tout le reste est fait par le négociant dans ses propres locaux. On administre au jus de raisin frais une légère dose de soufre pour empêcher que la fermentation ne commence avant que le vinificateur soit prêt à la diriger. Dès que le jus arrive à la cave, on le goûte et on l'étudie pour évaluer sa consistance. En mainte année il faut lui ajouter du sucre : pratique répandue en Bourgogne et qui, certaines années, s'étend même vers le sud, jusqu'à Bordeaux. En Champagne cette chaptalisation a pour but d'obtenir un vin titrant entre 10 et 12° et d'une acidité modérée. Selon l'année, le vinificateur ajoutera du sucre ou bien diminuera l'acidité du moût (jus de raisin non fermenté). Parfois aussi il ajoutera de l'acide citrique ou tartrique. Hormis ce qui concerne le sucre, qu'on ajoute assez fréquemment, les autres additions sont exceptionnelles et peu désirables, sauf en années difficiles.

Après ces traitements, le vin se met à fermenter. Il bout vigoureusement dans les barriques. Pendant 8 à 10 jours, après cette phase tumultueuse, il se calme nettement et continue encore 10 à 20 jours à faire tranquillement et sereinement des bulles. Pendant cette fermentation, l'action des levures convertit le sucre en alcool et en gaz carbonique. Ce gaz s'échappe librement à travers la bonde de la barrique. Quand la fermentation est terminée, on laisse le vin reposer et se clarifier.

Au mois de décembre de l'année de vendange, le vin s'est stabilisé : toutes les particules de raisin subsistant après pressage ainsi que les levures épuisées sont tombées au fond du tonneau. Le vin est alors prêt pour le premier soutirage. On le tire donc du baril en y laissant lies et autres impuretés. Après ce premier soutirage, on procède à l'*assemblage* des vins provenant de différents vignobles et qui ont fermenté séparément dans la même cave. Ce coupage des vins de plusieurs crus — par exemple d'Ay, de Sillery ou de Verzenay — donne un produit uniforme et durable.

Après un second soutirage, à la fin de janvier, et un troisième, juste avant la mise en bouteille, les vins sont prêts pour une seconde fermentation qui en fera de parfaits Champagne.

Ceux qui ne doivent pas être champagnisés sont également soutirés, mais leur évolution s'arrête là et ils sont vendus sous l'appellation « Coteaux champenois ».

Champagnisation

Champagnisation, tel est le nom de la méthode traditionnelle par laquelle on fait mousser le vin en lui permettant de fermenter une seconde fois en bouteille. On s'y prépare d'ordinaire dès après le second soutirage — celui de janvier — quand le coupage (ou assemblage) est fait. Quelques firmes se spécialisent en vins de cru : ceux qui ne proviennent que d'une seule agglomération. Mais la plupart des Champagne sont des assemblages de divers vins provenant des vignobles qui donnent droit à ce nom.

La délicate opération de mélange commence par le prélèvement d'échantillons dans les divers tonneaux de la firme. Ces échantillons sont emportés dans une salle de dégustation. D'une propreté immaculée, aérée, aseptique, exempte de toute odeur et de quoi que ce soit qui puisse distraire l'attention du dégustateur, telle est cette pièce. Ces précautions ont une grande importance, étant donné que ce spécialiste travaille sur des vins jeunes et qu'il doit être capable de déceler le moindre défaut ou la plus petite impureté avant qu'elle ne se développe. Le résultat désiré est un Champagne qui ressemblera à celui que la firme a mis en vente au cours des années précédentes. C'est cette dégustation qui permet de choisir les vins à mélanger et dans quelles proportions. Les autres sont laissés à part pour être mis en bouteille sous une autre étiquette : celle de la seconde qualité vendue par la même firme.

Quand le vin est fait, soutiré et mélangé, il est prêt pour être mis en bouteille et subir la fermentation secondaire qui le rendra mousseux. En général la mise en bouteille commence à peu près en avril et dure jusqu'en juillet. La première opération consiste à ajouter au mélange la *liqueur de tirage :* généralement une solution de sucre de canne dissoute dans du vin, à laquelle on ajoute très exceptionnellement un peu d'acide citrique, ce qui hâtera la transformation du sucre de canne en sucres hexoses fermentables.

La quantité de cette liqueur de tirage est calculée de telle sorte qu'elle ajoutera 20 à 26 g de sucre à chaque litre de vin traité. Parfois, on ajoute moins de liqueur et le Champagne qui en résulte est crémant ou légèrement mousseux. Le mot *crémant* ne doit pas prêter à confusion avec Cramant, une des premières villes de la Côte des Blancs.

Le sucre ajouté sous forme de liqueur de tirage fermente et va rendre le vin mousseux. Cette fermentation a lieu sous l'action de levures qui peuvent être déjà présentes dans le vin ou qui peuvent y être ajoutées à cet effet. Dans ce cas on choisit des variétés particulière de levures. La fermentation qui se produit en bouteille est la réplique exacte de la première. Elle produit de l'alcool (la teneur en alcool du vin augmentera d'environ un degré) et du gaz carbonique. Mais cette fois le vin n'est plus dans une barrique à bonde ouverte. Il est emprisonné dans une solide bouteille obturée par un fort bouchon maintenu au goulot par du fil métallique.

Pour des raisons mystérieuses, au moment où la sève commence à monter dans la vigne, le vin commence sa seconde fermentation, comme s'il existait encore un lien secret entre eux. Les caves sont fraîches et empêchent la température de précipiter l'action du levain. L'expérience a montré, en effet, que le vin est d'autant meilleur que la fermentation s'est produite plus lentement. Les bouteilles de vin sont empilées, couchées, au fond des caves. Tous les six mois ou à peu près, on défait et refait les piles en donnant à chaque bouteille une vigoureuse secousse pour libérer quelque dépôt qui a pu s'être formé. Une marque peinte sur le cul de la bouteille indique dans quelle position elle est couchée et on la repose toujours sur le même côté. Quand on les remet en piles, celles qui étaient au milieu sont posées à l'extérieur et vice versa parce que la chaleur de la fermentation est plus élevée au centre qu'à la périphérie.

Pendant la fermentation, le gaz carbonique qui ne peut s'échapper provoque une pression. Finalement cette pression s'élèvera jusqu'à 5 à 6 fois celle de l'atmosphère. De temps en temps il arrive qu'une bouteille se brise (parce que la pression dépasse sa résistance). La fermentation elle-même ne durera qu'environ trois mois. Mais on laisse les vins en cave pendant plusieurs années pour qu'ils vieillissent et on continue à secouer les bouteilles de temps en temps pour empêcher le dépôt de prendre une forme consistante.

A la fin de la période de vieillissement, les vins sont prêts pour le *remuage* et le *dégorgement :* longue série d'opérations qui débarrassera la bouteille du dépôt.

Le remuage pourrait s'appeler secouage car le Champagne doit être secoué d'une certaine manière. D'abord on procède petit à petit à la *mise sur pointe* qui consiste à poser la bouteille goulot en bas. On y procède sur des casiers spéciaux appelés *pupitres :* planches inclinées qui ressemblent un peu à des chevalets de peintre. Des trous percés des deux côtés du pupitre permettent d'y introduire le goulot de la bouteille qui y tiendra fermement dans n'importe quelle position : horizontale ou verticale. Les planches sont munies de charnières et on peut les faire pivoter pour que la bouteille d'abord horizontale prenne un certain angle avec l'horizontale : d'ordinaire quelque 30°. Très lentement, en prenant largement son temps, on fait pivoter la planche pour que la bouteille soit littéralement tête en bas. Chaque jour, un spécialiste hautement qualifié, le remueur, secoue soigneusement chaque bouteille et la repose à un angle légèrement plus ouvert en la faisant tourner d'un quart de tour sur son axe. Cette opération fait s'agiter légèrement le dépôt glissant dans le goulot au fur et à mesure que la bouteille s'approche de la verticale, si bien qu'à la fin il repose sur le bouchon. Le remueur travaille à une vitesse incroyable pour le profane, et à deux mains : il est capable de manipuler 32 000 bouteilles par jour. Pour être sûr que tout le vin est absolument sain, on lui donne une prime pour chaque bouteille défectueuse qu'il découvre. Quand il a terminé, les bouteilles sont la tête en bas sur le pupitre, le dépôt repose sur le bouchon et le vin est prêt pour l'opération suivante : le dégorgement qui chassera ce sédiment. Aujourd'hui, le remuage est mécanisé.

Le dégorgement est une opération délicate surtout si elle est effectuée selon la vieille méthode traditionnelle. On prend chaque bouteille, on la débouche lentement et la pression chasse le dépôt. L'astuce consiste à perdre le moins de vin possible tout en ne laissant rien du dépôt dans la bouteille. Il faut évidemment une pratique et une habileté exceptionnelles pour accomplir un tel tour de force. La méthode moderne consiste à glacer le goulot de la bouteille. Le sédiment et une petite quantité de vin gèlent. Quand on débouche, la pression chasse un bloc solide. On ramène la hauteur du vin a ce qu'elle était à l'origine en en prélevant un peu dans une autre bouteille. Le Champagne est alors prêt pour le dosage et le bouchage définitif.

Le dosage du Champagne varie selon la clientèle éventuelle. Les clients éclairés préfèrent le Champagne *brut,* c'est-à-dire aussi sec que possible. Mais quand il doit être servi avec le dessert, il faut choisir un Champagne plus ou moins doux. A cet effet, on ajoute au vin du sucre dilué dans une certaine quantité de *vin de réserve.* En général les Champagne de meilleure qualité sont livrés au commerce à l'état brut, car les défauts que les autres pourraient présenter seront masqués par l'addition de sucre.

La *liqueur d'expédition* consiste en une petite quantité de sucre dissoute dans un peu de Champagne identique à celui qui doit être traité et à laquelle on ajoute parfois un peu d'eau-de-vie de vin. Les proportions sont en général les suivantes :

Nom français	*%*	*Nom anglais*
Brut	0 à 2	Brut
Extra-Dry	2 à 3	Extra-Dry
Sec	3 à 6	Dry
Demi-sec	6 à 8	Semi-Dry
Doux	8 à 10	Sweet

Après cette addition, les bouteilles sont prêtes pour le bouchage final. Quoique le bouchon change, le vin reste dans la même bouteille pendant toute son évolution, sauf s'il doit être transvasé dans de plus grands contenants. Étant donné que sur chaque récolte 2 à 3 % des bouteilles éclatent, il serait périlleux d'utiliser des bouteilles d'une capacité supérieure à celle du magnum. C'est donc au moment du dégorgement, c'est-à-dire après la seconde fermentation, qu'on transvase le Champagne dans les bouteilles de grande capacité allant du jéroboam (3,2 l) au nabuchodonosor (15 l). Mais on rebouche alors les bouteilles avec des bouchons neufs. Les meilleurs viennent d'Espagne ou du Portugal et sont faits avec le liège de chênes âgés de 12 à 15 ans.

Selon la loi française, tous les bouchons utilisés pour le Champagne doivent porter le mot Champagne imprimé dessus. Si ce mot n'est pas visible, la bouteille ne contient pas du Champagne. Les bouchons de liège sont imbibés d'eau pour les ramollir et on les enfonce dans le goulot, puis on ramène les bouteilles dans les caves où elles passeront encore un certain temps à vieillir sous surveillance. On vérifie attentivement si la liqueur d'expédition est bien mélangée au vin et s'il ne commence pas une troisième fermentation qui serait indésirable. Ce temps de probation dure jusqu'à deux ans. Finalement, les meilleurs Champagne vieillissent six à sept ans avant d'être prêts à la consommation et chaque bouteille aura subi entre 150 et 200 manipulations avant de quitter la cave.

CONTENANCE DES BOUTEILLES

Nom	*Contenance*
Quart	18,7/20 cl
Demie	37,5 cl
Bouteille	75 cl
Magnum	1,5 l
Jéroboam	3,2 l
Réhoboam	4,5 l
Mathusalem	6 l
Salmanazar	9 l
Balthazar*	12 l
Nabuchodonosor*	15 l

* Ces bouteilles ne sont plus guère utilisées.

Voir APPENDICE B

Servir le Champagne

On considère en général que le Champagne est meilleur servi frappé, mais pas glacé. Les fabricants de Champagne sont un peu plus tolérants que certains amateurs en ce qui concerne la manière de déboucher la bouteille. Les puristes suggèrent qu'il faut recueillir le bouchon dans la main plutôt que de lui laisser traverser la pièce ou heurter le plafond à grand bruit et qu'il ne faut surtout pas laisser perdre les premières gouttes jaillissant de la bouteille. Selon eux, si le bouchon saute trop vivement, la pression baisse trop brusquement en dissipant une part des bulles qu'on a pris tant de soin et tant d'années à mettre en réserve dans le vin. En tout cas, le fouet à Champagne élimine en effet les bulles au détriment du véritable goût de ce vin. De même, mettre de la glace dans le verre est une abomination aux yeux des connaisseurs.

Bien des vignerons de Champagne et des négociants estiment que la coupe largement évasée est moins appropriée à leur vin que le verre long et haut en forme de flûte. Ils conseillent même de grandes tulipes contenant près d'un quart de litre. « Les bulles disparaissent trop vite dans la coupe et ce sont les bulles qui font le Champagne », disent-ils. Le choniqueur Art Buchwald exprime à peu près la même idée autrement : « J'aime le Champagne parce que son goût me donne toujours l'impression d'avoir le pied endormi. »

Chantepleure

Nom donné en Vouvray et quelquefois en Bourgogne à la pipette dont on se sert pour prélever un peu de vin dans une barrique ou tout autre contenant de grande capacité.

Chapeau

Croûte solide que forment la pulpe et les peaux à la surface du moût dans les cuves, pendant la fermentation.

Voir CHAPITRE V

Chapelle-Chambertin (Appellation Contrôlée)

Bourgogne rouge. Commune de Gevrey-Chambertin, en Côte de Nuits. Classement officiel : Grand Cru.

La Chapelle est un des vins les plus délicats de cette commune située au nord de la Côte de Nuits. En général, les vins de Gevrey sont charnus, robustes, affirmatifs et strictement virils ; quoiqu'il partage ces qualités, le Chapelle-Chambertin y ajoute une légèreté, un fruité et parfois une certaine finesse qui le font ranger à part.

Les neuf crus qui constituent la famille Chambertin sont groupés autour du noyau : Le Chambertin et Chambertin-Clos de Bèze. Ils sont tous contigus à la petite route qui traverse le vignoble en allant de Gevrey à Morey-Saint-Denis et ceux qui ne la jouxtent pas en sont visibles. Quand on quitte Gevrey par cette route, Chapelle-Chambertin est la première vigne importante qu'on trouve sur la gauche. Pourtant, le nouveau venu ne la remarquera probablement pas, à moins qu'un habitant du pays ne la lui désigne. Dans ces communes renommées il n'y a pas grand-chose qui distingue un grand cru d'un autre. Les différences ne deviennent apparentes que dans les vins eux-mêmes. Classé Grand Cru, le vignoble de Chapelle-Chambertin couvre une surface d'environ 5,37 ha qui est partagée entre plusieurs propriétaires. Ils produisent ensemble environ 200 hl par an, soit l'équivalent de 2 000 caisses.

Chaptalisation

Addition de sucre au moût, avant ou pendant la fermentation, afin d'assurer au vin une teneur en alcool en harmonie avec celle de ses autres composants. Ce procédé a été suggéré par Chaptal, d'où son nom.

Voir CHAPITRE V

Charbono

Raisin à vin vraisemblablement originaire d'Italie mais maintenant surtout cultivé en Californie, particulièrement dans la vallée du Napa. Il donne un vin rouge agréable et plein de corps, mais sans finesse.

Chardonnay

Excellent raisin blanc, cultivé surtout en Bourgogne. Il ressemble au Pinot Noir mais n'est pas un vrai Pinot, quoique autrefois on l'ait pris pour une variété blanche de cette vigne et qu'on l'ait donc appelé Pinot Chardonnay. Selon la région, on le nomme aussi Arnoison, Aubaine, Beaunois, Melon blanc. Il fournit du vin riche, bien équilibré, à l'arôme exceptionnel, et dont le superbe arrière-goût reste longtemps dans la bouche. On trouve du Chardonnay en Californie où il donne de très bons résultats.

Charente (Vin de)

Il s'agit surtout des vins légers, maigres, âpres, qu'on distille pour faire du Cognac. Cependant, cette même région produit aussi du vin rouge (avec lequel on ne fait jamais de Cognac) et du vin blanc qui n'est pas non plus transformé en Cognac.

Voir COGNAC

Charlemagne (Appellation Contrôlée)

Bourgogne blanc. Commune d'Aloxe-Corton, en Côte de Beaune. Classement officiel : Grand Cru.

La surface plantée en vigne n'est que de 32,38 ha et les vins blancs sont excellents, mais on utilise rarement seule l'appellation Charlemagne, étant donné que les vignerons de ce cru ont aussi droit à celle de Corton-Charlemagne, plus connue, donc préférée.

L'empereur Charlemagne aurait été personnellement propriétaire de ce vignoble qui porte son nom et il l'aurait donné à l'église ou plutôt à l'abbé de Saulieu. Au XVIe siècle, cette terre fut louée à un aubergiste de Beaune qui justement s'appelait Charles. Au XVIIe siècle le domaine fut morcelé et une partie échut aux Hospices de Beaune.

Charmat

En 1910, le savant œnologue français Eugène Charmat imagina un procédé permettant de faire du vin mousseux en grosse quantité. On l'emploie encore, plus ou moins modifié.

Le procédé conçu par Charmat exige quatre cuves : trois pour le vin et une autre pour la levure. Le vin non encore mousseux est mis dans la première cuve où on le vieillit artificiellement en le chauffant pendant 12 à 16 heures. Grâce à une pompe, on le transvase dans l'autre cuve ; on y ajoute levure et sucre et on le laisse fermenter pendant 10 à 15 jours. Puis on le pompe dans la troisième cuve où on le clarifie par réfrigération. Enfin on le filtre et il est mis en bouteille. Pendant tout ce processus le vin reste à l'abri de l'air et ne perd jamais la pression qu'il prend pendant la fermentation.

Certes, le système Charmat ne saurait remplacer la fermentation secondaire en bouteille, employée pour faire le Champagne. Il permet seulement au viniculteur de produire un flot continu de vin mousseux à bon marché, sain, mais dont la qualité ne suscite pas l'enthousiasme.

Charmes-Chambertin (Appellation Contrôlée)

Bourgogne rouge. Commune de Gevrey-Chambertin, en Côte de Nuits. Classement officiel : Grand Cru.

Charmes-Chambertin et Mazoyères-Chambertin constituent une association dans laquelle le premier est le partenaire muet. Selon la règle, les vins de Charmes et de Mazoyères peuvent être vendus sous le nom de Charmes, mais Charmes n'a pas droit à l'appellation Mazoyères. Dans la pratique, tout est Charmes.

Les deux crus, contigus, se trouvent à gauche de la route des vignobles quand on se dirige de Gevrey vers Morey-Saint-Denis sur la route des Grands Crus. On voit d'abord Charmes ; le plus petit, juste en face de Chambertin, et ensuite Mazoyères, en face de Latricière-Chambertin. Ils couvrent ensemble une surface de 31,61 ha.

Les vignerons du pays considèrent les deux vins comme à peu près identiques. Toutefois Charmes a un peu plus de corps et Mazoyères un peu plus de finesse. Toujours selon les gens du pays, Mazoyères serait le cru supérieur mais, comme il est vendu sous le nom de Charmes, il n'y a pas moyen de les distinguer l'un de l'autre.

Le Charmes est plus léger que ses voisins,

les Premiers Crus de Gevrey, et il est délicat pour cette commune dont le style naturel de vins est fait de caractère viril.

Classé Grand Cru en 1937 — la plus haute cote des vins de Bourgogne — par l'Institut national des appellations d'origine des vins et eaux-de-vie, le Charmes doit se conformer à des normes strictes imposées par la loi et les traditions *(au sujet de ces normes voir* CÔTE DE NUITS).

Le cru appartient à un nombre raisonnable de propriétaires.

La production moyenne du vin des deux vignobles est sensiblement inférieure à 1 000 hl par an, au chiffre assez représentatif et qui équivaut à environ 11 500 caisses.

Charnu

Qualité du vin fortement corsé.

Chartreuse

Célèbre liqueur faite à Tarragone (Espagne) et à Voiron (France) par des moines de l'ordre des chartreux. Ces moines fondèrent leur distillerie espagnole quand celle de la Grande-Chartreuse fut saisie, en 1903, lors de la séparation de l'Église et de l'État. Depuis 1932, ils ont repris la fabrication de leur liqueur à Voiron. Au début de notre siècle, il régna une grande confusion au sujet de cette liqueur parce que les biens de l'ordre avaient été nationalisés et vendus. La marque commerciale était donc tombée dans le domaine public, mais on ne connaissait pas la recette. La « Chartreuse » vendue en France n'était alors qu'une pâle imitation de la véritable liqueur. Les moines, n'ayant plus droit à cette appellation, étiquetèrent leur produit ainsi : Liqueur fabriquée à Tarragone par les pères chartreux. L'étiquette a changé depuis qu'en 1932 les moines ont repris leur activité en France et l'appellation n'appartient plus qu'à eux seuls.

Cette liqueur est faite avec de l'eau-de-vie de vin et des extraits de nombreuses herbes et plantes qui lui donnent sa saveur. La recette est encore un des secrets des chartreux. Elle aurait été donnée en 1605 par le père Jérôme Maubec qui la perfectionna par la suite. Mais les moines n'en expédièrent pas hors de leur monastère jusqu'en 1848, quand quelques officiers de l'armée y goûtèrent et furent tellement impressionnés qu'ils entreprirent de la faire connaître. A l'origine, c'était un élixir blanc, plus fort que la liqueur d'aujourd'hui, mais sa fabrication a cessé. Désormais la Chartreuse est verte ou jaune : la verte, plus forte ; la jaune, moins alcoolisée, est plus douce.

Chassagne-Montrachet et Chassagne-Montrachet-Côte de Beaune (A.O.C.)

Bourgogne rouge et blanc. Commune de Chassagne, en Côte de Beaune-Montrachet.

A l'extrémité sud de la Côte de Beaune se trouve la Côte des Blancs qui produit les meilleurs vins blancs de Côte-d'Or. Le meilleur, et de beaucoup, provient du vignoble de Montrachet qui s'étend en parts égales sur les communes de Chassagne-Montrachet et Puligny-Montrachet. Ceux qui viennent immédiatement après sont, à coup sûr, des vins magnifiques. On fait aussi à Chassagne de très bons vins rouges qui, malgré leur valeur exceptionnelle, sont parfois moins cher que leurs voisins des Côtes de Beaune parce que peu connus et plutôt éclipsés par la célébrité des blancs. Il n'en a pas toujours été ainsi. Au XVIIIe siècle Chassagne était célèbre pour ses vins rouges. On dit que le rouge de la vigne de Morgeot était tellement estimé qu'on échangeait deux bouteilles de Montrachet pour une de Morgeot. Le sort a ainsi tourné qu'aujourd'hui on ne fait plus de rouge à Morgeot dont les vins blancs — quoiqu'ils ne méritent plus l'ancien taux d'échange — n'en sont pas moins parmi les meilleurs de la commune. Chassagne est la dernière des communes de quelque importance de la Côte de Beaune. Plus au sud se trouve Santenay dont les vins sont souvent bons, mais rarement extraordinaires. Au-delà de Santenay, la colline s'incline vers la Côte chalonnaise. Mais les vins blancs de Chassagne sont souvent exceptionnels.

Le principal cru est évidemment l'incomparable Montrachet, mais Bâtard-Montrachet et Criots-Bâtard-Montrachet sont aussi classés tous deux parmi les plus hauts crus. *(Voir chacun de ces crus à sa place dans l'ordre alphabétique).* Ce sont tous de Grands Crus selon la classification officielle qui les place donc à égalité avec les meilleurs Bourgogne. Légèrement après eux dans la hiérarchie officielle, mais souvent leurs égaux en qualité, on trouve Morgeot, Ruchottes et Caillerets.

GRANDS CRUS	
Vins blancs	*Superficie (ha)*
Montrachet (en partie)	3,99
Bâtard-Montrachet (en partie)	5,84
Criots-Bâtard-Montrachet	1,57
(*Voir* PULIGNY-MONTRACHET)	

PREMIERS CRUS	
Vins blancs et rouges	*Superficie (ha)*
Les Grandes Ruchottes (blanc seulement)	2,13
Morgeot	4,29
Les Caillerets	5,11
Clos Saint-Jean	5,08
Les Rebichets (Clos Saint-Jean)	5,45
Les Murées (Clos Saint-Jean)	1,61
Chassagne du Clos Saint-Jean	2,02
Clos de la Boudriotte	2,23
La Maltroie	8,70
Champs-Gain	4,62
La Romanée	3,35
Les Brussanes	2,87
Les Chaumées	7,43
Les Vergers	9,41
Les Macherelles	5,19
L'Abbaye de Morgeot	8,56
La Grande Montagne	7,86
Bois de Chassagne	8,39

N.B. : De par la configuration du cadastre, les sous-sections cadastrales portaient le nom d'un lieu-dit. C'est pourquoi de nombreux lieux-dits sont rattachés à un nom de climat, ex. : Morgeot ou Clos Saint-Jean ou... Les Brussonnes... ou La Boudriotte.

Le blanc de Chassagne possède bien des caractéristiques communes avec celui de Puligny : sec, ferme, mais jamais dur, corsé, richesse fleurie, arrière-goût durable. Montrachet, quant à lui, a une vivacité étonnante pour un vin blanc sec, mais les autres ont tendance à madériser assez vite. Parfois, dix ans est trop pour eux et ils sont dans leur meilleure forme entre trois et huit ans.

Les rouges de Chassagne sont en général meilleurs que ceux de Puligny et souvent plus connus que ceux de Santenay. Assez durs, bien ronds, ils ont un goût de terroir caractéristique et présentent une transition entre les autres rouges de Côte-d'Or et ceux des secteurs méridionaux de la Bourgogne. Boudriotte est le plus viril en sa jeunesse, mais en vieillissant il prend une rondeur et une richesse parfois trop affirmative. Le Clos Saint-Jean arrive plus vite à son apogée, il a plus de finesse et développe son bouquet beaucoup plus tôt. En général les vins rouges de Chassagne atteignent leur plein épanouissement au bout de cinq ans. Mais ils donnent quand même une joie considérable à ceux qui les boivent plus jeunes.

Quelque 350 ha sont plantés en vigne sur le territoire de Chassagne. Le vin qui se conforme aux normes minimales légales a droit au nom de la commune comme appellation contrôlée et, s'il provient de 332 ha déterminés, il peut s'y ajouter la désignation : Côte de Beaune.

Après les trois Grands Crus qui portent seulement leur propre nom, il y a les Premiers Crus qui ont le droit d'être étiquetés à leur propre nom plus celui de la commune. La production moyenne de Chassagne s'élève à quelque 6 200 hl (plus de 65 000 caisses) de rouge et 7 000 hl (plus de 75 000 caisses) de blanc.

Chasselas

Un des bons raisins de table européens qu'on utilise aussi pour faire des petits vins légers au bouquet délicat mais qui ne se conservent pas faute d'acidité suffisante.

Les variétés de cette famille sont le Gutedel (Allemagne), le Fendant (Suisse) et le Chasselas Doré (Californie). Ce sont là les principales, mais le spécialiste distingue aussi le Chasselas du Moissacais ou de Thomery, de Fontainebleau, de Montauban, les Chasselas précoces, à bois vert, à bois rouge, etc.

Chasse-Spleen (Château-)

Bordeaux rouge. Commune de Moulis, en Haut-Médoc.

La commune de Moulis a droit à sa propre appellation d'origine. Elle s'étend un peu au nord et à l'ouest de Margaux. Son meilleur vin est le Chasse-Spleen, classé Cru Exceptionnel en 1855. Une nouvelle classification des vins de Médoc lui accorderait un rang supérieur. Servi souvent au cours des dernières années aux banquets de la Commanderie du Bontemps *(Voir ce mot)*, il tient son rang parmi les vins les meilleurs de cette région exceptionnelle du Bordelais et mérite sa réputation mondiale. M. Merlot est le copropriétaire du Château-Chasse-Spleen.

Caractéristiques : Un des meilleurs de sa classe. Rond et corsé. Très bonne race.

Superficie : 70 ha.

Production moyenne : 20 000 caisses.

Château

Dans le monde du vin, ce mot ne désigne pas un grand et beau château comme ceux de la Loire, mais une propriété où l'on cultive la vigne et fait du vin. Ce mot est employé dans ce sens surtout dans la région de Bordeaux où les vignes et les chais sont en général dirigés à partir d'une maison de campagne située au centre de la propriété. Il arrive que ce bâtiment ait l'aspect d'un petit château, mais ce peut être une villa de proportions moyennes. Le vin fait et mis en bouteille à la propriété porte la mention *Mise en bouteille au château*. Ils sont toujours plus appréciés que les vins génériques qui peuvent être des coupages. Pour les noms des meilleurs châteaux à vin du Bordelais voir à leur place dans l'ordre alphabétique.

Château (Mise en bouteille au)

Vin mis en bouteille au château où il a été fait, avec le raisin des vignes cultivées sur le domaine de ce château. Cette appellation garantit qu'il n'a fait l'objet d'aucun mélange ou trafic quelconque et qu'il est authentique. En ce qui concerne la plupart des principaux crus, cette mention est en même temps une garantie de très haute qualité. Si la récolte d'une année n'est pas conforme aux normes du cru, le propriétaire cédera son vin à des négociants qui le vendront sous l'étiquette régionale.

Château-Chalon (Appellation Contrôlée)

Vin jaune du Jura français.

Ce vin a effectivement une couleur jaune. Il s'apparente au Xérès et peut durer jusqu'à 60 ou 70 ans.

Voir JURA

Châteauneuf-du-Pape (Appellation Contrôlée)

Surtout rouge et aussi du blanc. Vallée du Rhône.

Le vignoble de Châteauneuf s'étend sur un peu plus de 3 000 ha, à mi-chemin entre Avignon et Orange, sur la rive gauche du Rhône. Ce cru se targue des normes et contrôles les plus stricts du monde. Sans Châteauneuf et sa personnalité la plus éminente — feu le baron Le Roy de Boiseaumarié — les réglementations seraient moins nombreuses et moins sévères en France actuellement car, en 1936, les autorités françaises calquèrent les règles déjà appliquées par le baron et d'autres propriétaires de Châteauneuf depuis 1923. Feu Philippe Dufays, qui abandonna la médecine pour la viticulture, était un des animateurs de la commune.

Les gens de Châteauneuf appliquèrent leur réglementation par nécessité. Après la Première Guerre mondiale il n'y avait pas nécessairement de rapport entre l'étiquette et le contenu des bouteilles de vin. La bouteille vendue sous le nom de Châteauneuf pouvait très bien contenir n'importe quoi, mais pas forcément du vin de ce cru. Depuis 1923 néanmoins, le tableau a changé du tout au tout et si la fraude n'a pas été complètement extirpée, elle a reçu un coup presque mortel.

La plupart des Côtes du Rhône sont faits avec un seul raisin, mais à Châteauneuf on en cultive treize variétés. Il en résulte que les vins produits par les divers vignerons seront différents les uns des autres car chacun d'eux soutient que tel ou tel type de raisin donne certaines caractéristiques particulières et que le Châteauneuf-du-Pape n'atteint la plénitude de ses qualités que si l'on sait jouer sur la gamme des variétés de raisin.

Grenache apporte du moelleux et de l'alcool ; Mourvèdre, Syrah, Muscardin et Vaccarèse ajoutent corps, couleur et fermeté ; Counoise, Picpoul et Cinsault donnent bouquet et fraîcheur ; finesse et chaleur viendront de Clairette et de Bourboulenc. Terret noir, Picardan et Roussanne sont aussi autorisés à Châteauneuf-du-Pape. Les pieds sont plantés à l'écart l'un de l'autre, parfois jusqu'à 1,50 m entre chaque et entre les rangs. Le sol est couvert de galets qui atteignent la taille d'une petite noix de coco. Les grappes de raisin mûrissent entre les rayons torrides du soleil et la chaleur réfléchie par ces pierres. Cette chaleur de four et de nouvelles méthodes de cuvage plus brèves donnent des vins qui dépassent d'habitude les 12,5° exigés (minimum réglementaire appliqué à bien peu de vins français et qu'aucun ne dépasse) et atteignent parfois 14°, voire 15°. Ce vin charnu, de couleur profonde, n'a pas la fermeté de l'Hermitage ou du Côte Rôtie, et mûrit plus vite que la plupart des Côtes du Rhône. Souvent il est consommable au bout de trois ou quatre ans. Quoique moins intense que celui de Côte Rôtie son bouquet est remarquable et il a un goût particulier dit « vinosité ».

On y fait également des vins blancs très agréables qui, tout en ayant le même goût particulier que les rouges, sont beaucoup moins connus et appréciés.

Le nom de Châteauneuf-du-Pape est celui d'un vieux château en ruine construit au temps de la « captivité de Babylone » (1305-1377), quand les papes étaient français et qu'Avignon remplaçait Rome comme siège de la papauté. C'était alors le château neuf qui devait servir de résidence d'été au souverain pontife. Sa construction commença sous Clément V, ancien évêque de Bordeaux et grand amateur de vin (son nom survit dans le Bordelais grâce à Château-Pape-Clément). Elle se termina sous Clément VI, mais les vignes furent sans doute plantées sous le pontificat de Jean XXII, c'est-à-dire entre Clément V et Clément VI. Le domaine fut attaqué pendant les guerres de Religion et le château brûlé en 1552.

Le vin de cette région ne prit sans doute le nom de Châteauneuf-du-Pape que vers le XIXe siècle ; auparavant on l'appelait vin d'Avignon. La production varie considérablement d'année en année car, sous un climat aussi sec, le raisin reste souvent petit par manque d'eau. Mais par bonne année elle s'élève à environ 3 500 hl (38 000 caisses) de bon vin blanc et quelque 95 000 hl (1 million de caisses) de vin rouge (plus d'un million de caisses).

CRUS IMPORTANTS DE CHÂTEAUNEUF-DU-PAPE	*Superficie (ha)*
Domaine des Fines-Roches	47,35
Domaine de la Nerthe	46,54
Clos Saint-Jean	44,49
Domaine de Nalys	46,54
Château de Vaudieu	29.70
(Environ 40 % seulement de ces superficies sont actuellement en production mais la totalité a droit à l'appellation d'origine contrôlée).	
La Gardine	24,44
Château-Fortia	25,86
Domaine des Sénéchaux	23,59
Clos des Papes	13,51
Domaine de Saint-Prefert	14,16

Châtillon-en-Diois (Appellation Contrôlée)

A.O.C. du département de la Drôme. Le rouge et le rosé doivent titrer au minimum 10° ; le blanc, 10,5°.

Voir A.O.C.

Chauché Gris

On cultive ce raisin dans les régions de Livermore et de Santa Cruz, en Californie. Le vin qui en provient est vendu sous le nom de « Grey Riesling » ou « Rhine Wine » (quoiqu'il ne soit pas un Riesling et que la Californie ne soit pas non plus sur le Rhin). On le baptise même parfois « chablis » !

Chaud (Vin)

Vin rouge, plus ou moins coupé d'eau, bouilli, épicé, sucré et servi très chaud. Ce breuvage présente une aptitude extraordinaire à enrayer dès leur début tous les maux provenant d'un coup de froid.

Chaume (Quarts de)

Voir ANJOU : COTEAUX DU LAYON

Chautauqua

Région vinicole de l'État de New York.
Voir ÉTATS-UNIS : ÉTATS DE L'EST

Cheilly-les Maranges et Cheilly-les-Maranges-Côte de Beaune (A.O.C.)

Bourgogne rouge et blanc. Côte de Beaune.

La commune de Cheilly et ses voisines, Sampigny et Dezize, qui ont, toutes trois, ajouté le nom du cru qu'elles possèdent en commun à leur propre nom, sont les plus méridionales de la Côte de Beaune.

Les vins de Cheilly sont d'habitude mélangés avec ceux des autres communes de ce célèbre coteau et vendus comme Côte de Beaune-Villages. La superficie plantée en vigne couvre quelque 125 ha, mais les vins provenant de quelque 43 ha privilégiés, enclavés dans l'ensemble de cette zone, ont droit d'ajouter le nom de Côte de Beaune à celui de la commune. Les Maranges, Plantes de Maranges et La Boutière sont les meilleurs crus de la commune et, quoiqu'ils n'en profitent presque jamais, ont le droit de porter sur l'étiquette leur propre nom outre celui de la localité.

Chenas (Appellation Contrôlée)

Vin du Beaujolais produit en faible quantité avec des raisins cultivés à l'intérieur de la célèbre zone de Moulin-à-Vent. Sans avoir l'excellence du Moulin-à-Vent ils n'en sont pas moins de première classe et moins chers. Ils offrent donc des prix intéressants aux amateurs avisés.
Voir BEAUJOLAIS

Chêne

Les meilleurs tonneaux et barriques dans lesquels on vieillit le vin sont faits en chêne. Un bon tonneau de chêne ne peut qu'améliorer le vin, même si celui-ci manque de tanin et de caractère, à l'origine ; mais, laissé trop longtemps en tonneau, le vin risquerait d'être séché et prendre le goût du bois. Les meilleurs chênes pour la tonnellerie viennent du Limousin et de Nevers, ainsi que de Yougoslavie. Aux États-Unis, on utilise plus couramment le chêne blanc du Tennessee, quoique la Californie importe quelques espèces européennes pour y vieillir ses bons vins rouges.

Chenin Blanc

Raisin prédominant dans la basse vallée de la Loire. Il sert à faire du Vouvray et d'autres vins de Touraine ainsi que la plupart des blancs d'Anjou. On l'utilise également aux États-Unis. On l'appelle parfois Pineau de la Loire, Blanc d'Anjou, etc.
Voir ANJOU, TOURAINE, CALIFORNIE

Cherry Brandy

Ce devrait être une eau-de-vie obtenue par la distillation du jus de cerise fermenté. En réalité, elle contient une certaine quantité de noyaux de cerise écrasés qui lui donnent un goût d'amande amère.

Cherry Heering

Cette liqueur de cerise est produite par la maison Peter Heering de Copenhague au Danemark. Connue dans le monde entier, elle a un goût authentique de cerise. Faite selon la formule du fabricant, elle n'est pas trop douce en raison de la proportion de noyaux utilisés dans la distillation. C'est un des cordiaux les plus populaires des États-Unis.

Cherry liqueur

Cordial obtenu en faisant macérer des cerises dans de l'eau-de-vie de vin sucrée. Le Cherry Rocher est célèbre en France. Thomas Grant and Sons en font une variété anglaise.
Voir CHERRY HEERING ; MARASQUIN

Cheval-Blanc (Château-)

Bordeaux rouge. Commune et appellation Saint-Émilion.

Considéré en général comme le plus grand Saint-Émilion d'aujourd'hui, Cheval-Blanc fut classé officiellement parmi les douze Premiers Grands Crus de ce secteur en 1955 puis en 1986. Il a en outre le privilège de figurer en tête de liste avec Château-Ausone, alors que les dix autres suivent dans l'ordre alphabétique. Le sol est surtout caillouteux quoique pas uniformément. La vigne est plantée sur terrain plat à la limite nord-est de Saint-Émilion, au bord de Pomerol. En tant que bâtiment, le château n'a rien de remarquable.

Monsieur Fourcaud-Laussac était propriétaire et c'est maintenant Jacques Hébrard qui suppervise ce Grand Cru.

Caractéristiques : Indiscutablement, c'est un des plus grands crus de Bordeaux. Par très bonne année, avec plus de rondeur, il est de la même qualité exceptionnelle des plus grands Médoc. Sa notoriété s'est considérablement accrue au cours des dernières années. Trois qualités distinctives ont contribué à ce succés. Pour 1/3, c'est du Pomerol, car les vignes sont contiguës à celles de Pomerol ; pour 1/3, du Graves, car le sol est caillouteux ; pour l'autre tiers, c'est un Saint-Émilion type. Cette combinaison donne un excellent vin, souple et vigoureux.

Superficie : 35 ha.

Production moyenne : 14 000 caisses.

Chevalier (Domaine de)

Bordeaux, rouges et blancs. Commune de Léognan, en Graves.

L'une des rares propriétés du Bordelais qui s'appelle domaine au lieu de château. En 1959, ce cru fut classé parmi les onze premiers Graves rouges et parmi les cinq meilleurs pour le blanc, qu'il produit en quantité moindre. Ce classement brillant va tout à l'honneur des Ricard, qui furent propriétaires de ce riche domaine pendant près d'un siècle jusqu'à son achat en 1983 par la Cie Bernard. Le Domaine Chevalier rouge reste un Graves exceptionnel, dont la qualité est souvent comparée à celle du cru La Mission-Haut-Brion. Le blanc fait le ravissement de tous les vrais connaisseurs.

Caractéristiques : Un vin très fin et plein de vigueur, même dans les années moins intéressantes. L'un des meilleurs Graves rouges. Le blanc est également excellent.

Superficie : rouge : 13 ha ; blanc : 3 ha.

Production moyenne : rouge : 50 tonneaux ; blanc : 10 tonneaux (5 000 caisses).

Chevalier-Montrachet (Appellation Contrôlée)

Bourgogne blanc. Commune de Puligny-Montrachet, en Côte de Beaune. Classement officiel : Grand Cru.

Ces vins sont les plus proches du grand Montrachet lui-même. Ils ont la même richesse enveloppante sans aucune trace de douceur, le même parfum pénétrant et la même magnificence de finesse. Rien de surprenant à tout cela étant donné que les vignobles sont contigus. Chevalier est plus léger et moins puissant que Montrachet mais, selon l'habileté du vigneron, il peut parfois être aussi grand, voire plus grand. Une superbe finesse, telle est l'attrait caractéristique de ce beau vin blanc.

Les vignes de Chevalier sont immédiatement au-dessus de celles de Montrachet dans la commune de Puligny-Montrachet. De l'autre côté, il y a celles de Cailleret — bon mais pas de la même classe que les deux autres — et, de part et d'autre, il n'y a pas de vigne du tout.

Couvrant plus de 6 ha, Chevalier est partagé entre plusieurs propriétaires dont Mme Boillereault de Chauvigné et, pour une bonne part du reste, Bouchard Père et Fils, Jadot et Latour (propriété commune), Le Flaive et Chartron.

Production moyenne : plus de 200 hl (2 000 caisses).

Cheverny

Face à Blois sur la Loire, en plein cœur de la Touraine, se trouvent le village de Cour-Cheverny et son beau château. Les vignobles des alentours produisent le V.D.Q.S. Cheverny. Les vins blancs sont faits principalement avec les raisins Chenin Blanc et Pineau de la Loire, les rouges avec du Gamay Noir du Cabernet Sauvignon et du Cabernet Franc, que l'on utilise également pour produire une petite quantité de rosé.

Chian

Vin grec célèbre dans l'Antiquité, provenant de l'île de Chio.

Voir ANTIQUITÉ (VINS DE L')

Chianti (D.O.C.G.)

Chianti est un des noms dont on abuse le plus dans le monde entier. Presque tous les pays producteurs de vin l'utilisent et l'appliquent à n'importe quel vin rouge, pourvu qu'il soit vendu dans des flacons paillés. Le vrai Chianti n'est produit que dans une toute petite zone de Toscane, province du centre de l'Italie. Il est vendu aussi bien en bouteille qu'en fiasque. Quel que soit le contenant, il portera sur le goulot un sceau à l'effigie d'un petit coq noir sur fond d'or s'il contient du Chianti « classique ». Le Chianti toléré, produit dans un secteur plus vaste de Toscane, sera scellé à l'image d'un chérubin blanc. Les neuf associations de Chianti appelées consorzios ont chacune un sceau différent.

Voir ITALIE ; TOSCANE

Chiaretto

Rosé italien du lac de Garde.

Voir ITALIE

Chicha

Breuvage fait par les Indiens de l'Amérique du Sud, en brassant du maïs.

Chili

Le Chili produit les meilleurs vins d'Amérique du Sud. En fait de quantité il figure au 8e rang parmi les pays vinicoles du monde entier. Sol et climat sont favorables à la viticulture, avec l'aide de l'irrigation. Les vignerons français qui plantèrent les meilleurs vignobles ont laissé derrière eux une haute tradition de viniculture, mais les Espagnols cultivèrent la vigne dès les premiers temps de la conquête. Le gouvernement chilien portait une attention éclairée sur la vigne et le vin. Après la prise de pouvoir par le président Allende, on s'attendait à la nationalisation de certains grands domaines.

Avec ses quelque 130 000 ha de vignobles, le Chili produit environ 9 millions d'hl de vin par an. A peine 72 000 hl (800 000 caisses) — soit 0,8 % du total — sont exportés, principalement vers les pays d'Amérique du Sud, certains pays d'Europe et les États-Unis. Avant le coup d'État de 1973, le Chili exportait également à Cuba. Le vin chilien est universellement apprécié : quoique n'étant pas un grand vin, il est indubitablement bon, et le rapport qualité-prix est généralement très avantageux. La quantité de vin consommée annuellement a été limitée à 40 l par habitant, mais la consommation moyenne reste bien au-dessous de cette limite. Celle-ci fut fixée il y a quelques années par le gouvernement dans le cadre d'une campagne contre l'alcoolisme. 2 % des terres arables du pays sont couvertes de vignes, et l'industrie vinicole emploie constamment 35 000 ouvriers, soit quatre fois plus de main-d'œuvre que les grandes mines de cuivre.

Le Chili produit trois types de vin : des vins de liqueur dans le nord, de bons vins de table dans le centre et des vins de table ordinaires dans le sud. Ceux du centre présentent une nette ressemblance avec les Bordeaux de moindre classe. Ce n'est pas surprenant car sol et climat des deux régions sont très semblables. Quant aux vignes et aux pratiques vinicoles, elles ont été importées directement du Bordelais. Les vins chiliens ne sauraient évidemment égaler un rouge de bonne année mis en bouteille au château, mais ils égalent ou surpassent les vins régionaux et présentent l'avantage d'être bien moins chers. Outre les vins faits avec du Cabernet et qui ont le genre bordelais, on fait aussi au Chili des vins de type bourguignon, à partir du Pinot Noir, mais avec beaucoup moins de succès.

Un des meilleurs vins chiliens est le Riesling ; sa production a diminué, non en raison de sa qualité, mais parce que les vignerons trouvent son prix de revient trop élevé. Désormais on fait du vin blanc avec du Pinot Blanc, du Sauvignon et du Sémillon. Le vin ordinaire rouge provient du sud du pays où l'on cultive tant les variétés d'origine française que le País, vigne originaire d'Espagne, mais acclimatée depuis si longtemps au Chili qu'on la considère comme un enfant du pays. Le País est très semblable à la prolifique variété Mission, si courante en Californie. Le País est utilisé dans 70 % des vins chiliens.

SOL ET CLIMAT

Le Chili jouit d'une situation si heureuse qu'il a jusqu'à présent échappé aux ravages du mildiou — la maladie cryptogamique la plus destructrice — et au phylloxéra, quoique ce pou de la vigne ait prélevé son tribut sur les vignobles d'Argentine à l'est et du Pérou au nord. Les Chiliens disent que la chaîne des Andes, qui les sépare de l'Argentine, a empêché cette peste de se propager de ce côté-là et que le désert d'Atacama lui a barré la frontière du Pérou ; enfin, les vents soufflant généralement de l'océan, il n'arrivera pas par la voie des airs. Cet optimisme semble d'ailleurs justifié car, même les variétés de vignes européennes les plus vulnérables n'ont pas besoin d'être greffées sur des souches américaines. Pourtant on en a déjà fait l'expérience et la reconstitution du vignoble chilien pourrait être menée à bien avec le minimum de confusion si jamais le phylloxéra envahissait le pays. Les nombreuses précautions prises aux frontières rendent d'ailleurs cette possibilité peu probable.

De même qu'il y a trois types de vin au Chili, on y compte trois zones de viticulture :

La région nord : Elle commence au désert d'Atacama et s'étend jusqu'au fleuve Choapa. On y cultive surtout du Muscat et c'est de là que proviennent les meilleurs raisins de table chiliens. L'irrigation est une nécessité vitale, étant donné qu'en général les pluies sont négligeables. Mais la pénurie de précipitations atmosphériques est étroitement liée à la présence du courant froid de Humboldt qui longe la côte du Pérou. Quand ce courant est déplacé par un afflux d'eaux plus chaudes, il en résulte des pluies diluviennes qui détruisent les vignes et d'ailleurs à peu près tout dans la région. Les vignes sont surtout cultivées dans les vallées qui coupent le pays d'est en ouest et l'irrigation est précisément fournie par ces fleuves. Les vins de la zone nord sont forts, et ont un degré d'alcool élevé. Parfois on les traite à la manière des Xérès, Madère et Porto en leur rajoutant encore un peu d'alcool.

La région centrale : C'est la plus importante du point de vue de la qualité ; elle s'étend du nord au sud entre le fleuve Aconcagua et le Maulé. L'influence dominante et presque exclusive est celle du Bordelais, tant au point de vue viticole qu'en ce qui concerne la vinification. On y cultive surtout : Cabernet Franc, Cabernet Sauvignon, Merlot, Malbec (écrit au Chili : Malbeck), Petit-Verdot, pour les vins rouges ; Sémillon et Sauvignon pour les blancs. Tous proviennent de la région de Bordeaux. Les autres vignes qui comptent sont le Pinot Noir et le Pinot Blanc. Riesling et País ont moins d'importance. Les vignes sont soignées et traitées selon les méthodes traditionnelles de Bordeaux à ceci près : presque tous les vignobles sont irrigués et leur rendement dépasse celui des vignes qui comptent seulement sur la pluie. Ce facteur ne nuit pas à la qualité des vins. Étant donné que les meilleurs vins du Chili proviennent de vignes irriguées, il est impossible actuellement de déterminer s'ils seraient meilleurs dans d'autres conditions.

Les deux meilleurs secteurs de la zone centrale (donc du Chili) sont les vallées de l'Aconcagua et du Maípo, toutes deux spécialisées dans le Cabernet ; leurs vins ont une vigoureuse finesse, un bel équilibre et plus de longévité que la plupart des crus chiliens. La haute vallée du Maípo, au sud-est de Santiago — capitale du Chili — jouit de la meilleure réputation qu'elle mérite. Plus calcaire qu'ailleurs, le sol contient un pourcentage généralement plus élevé de sable et d'ardoise. Cabernet Franc et Cabernet Sauvignon y prospèrent en donnant des vins forts et stables, d'une coloration foncée et d'un riche arôme. Le fort rendement à l'hectare est attribué en partie à l'irrigation.

La région vinicole méridionale : Elle va du fleuve Maulé au Bío-Bío. A quelques exceptions près dans l'extrême nord, les vignes ne sont pas irriguées. Le sous-sol est dur et la couche supérieure est constituée par un mélange d'ardoise et de boue, parfois riche en fer, avec de-ci, de-là, des calcaires sédimentaires qui émergent à la surface. Les vins sont nettement moins intéressants que ceux du centre. Quoiqu'on y cultive des vignes d'origine française (Cabernet, Malbec, Sémillon) et un peu de Riesling, la région sud est surtout plantée de País à gros rendement. Certains mélanges sont faits avec une partie de ces vins, le reste constitue le breuvage quotidien des Chiliens. Bien que le produit soit probablement inférieur en qualité aux vins faits plus au nord, la viticulture est importante dans cette région du Chili, où elle fait vivre environ 13 000 petits vignerons. Au sud du fleuve Bío-Bío, le climat est trop rigoureux pour y cultiver des raisins à vin.

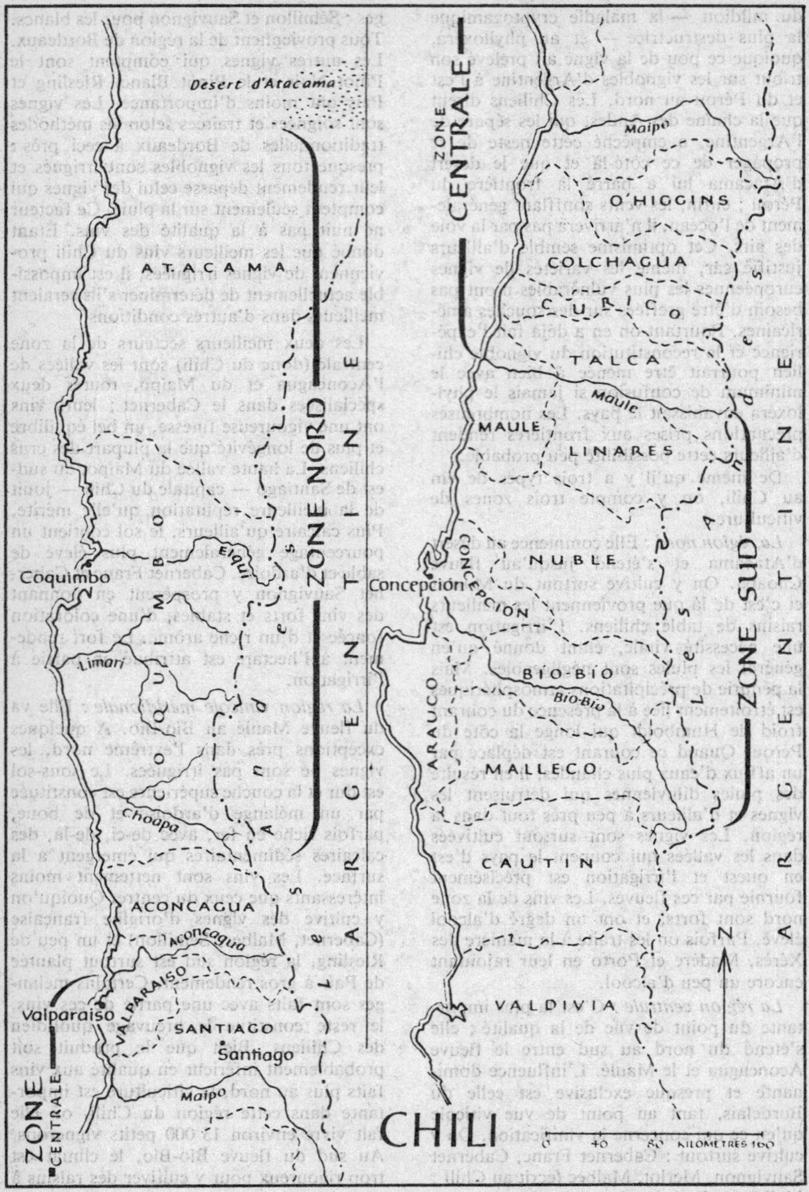
Desert d'Atacama
ATACAMA
ZONE NORD
COQUIMBO
Elqui
Coquimbo
Limari
Choapa
ACONCAGUA
Aconcagua
VALPARAISO
Valparaiso
SANTIAGO
Santiago
Maipo
ZONE CENTRALE
ARGENTINE
Les Andes
ZONE CENTRALE
Maipo
O'HIGGINS
COLCHAGUA
CURICO
TALCA
Maule
MAULE
LINARES
NUBLE
Concepción
CONCEPCION
BIO-BIO
Bio-Bio
ARAUCO
MALLECO
CAUTIN
VALDIVIA
ZONE SUD
ARGENTINE
Les Andes
CHILI
0 40 80 KILOMETRES 100

Histoire du vin au Chili

Quoique conquis et peuplé par des Latins habitués à boire du vin, la plupart des pays d'Amérique du Sud, durent attendre l'afflux d'immigrants italiens, après la Première Guerre mondiale, pour avoir leurs propres vignobles de quelque importance. Mais le Chili et le Pérou font exception, car on y cultive la vigne presque depuis l'arrivée des Espagnols.

Les missionnaires qui suivirent immédiatement les conquistadores plantèrent la vigne pour s'assurer une source suffisante de vin de messe. On croit que les premiers ceps furent importés au Chili soit par Francisco de Carabantes, soit par Bartoloméo de Terrazas. L'un des deux, mais on ne sait pas à coup sûr lequel, prit part à l'expédition au Chili de Diego de Almagro, entre 1535 et 1537. Les vignes qu'il y apporta donnaient, dit-on, des raisins rouges de petite taille extrêmement savoureux.

La culture du vin reçut son premier élan vers 1556, aux environs de Santiago d'où elle se répandit dans le pays voisin qui est devenu, de nos jours, l'Argentine. On y cultiva alors surtout des Muscat, en particulier du Muscat d'Alexandrie. Faute d'autre nom, les Chiliens appellent le second : País. On sait qu'il vient d'Espagne, mais à part cela, ses origines sont enveloppées de mystère. Les vins étaient alors surtout destinés à la messe ou bien on les traitait à la manière espagnole. La véritable industrie du vin dut encore attendre jusqu'au milieu du XIXe siècle pour naître.

En 1851, le père de la viticulture chilienne, Silvestre Ochagavia, comprit que ce pays pouvait devenir une des meilleures régions vinicoles du continent américain. Poussé par cette conviction, il fit venir de France un bon nombre d'experts en viticulture. En outre, il importa diverses boutures des meilleures vignes françaises qu'on planta surtout dans la vallée centrale du Chili où se trouvent encore les vignobles les plus réputés du pays. Son expérience eut un tel succès que le gouvernement chilien s'en mêla et fit venir d'autres plants de France. C'est ainsi qu'une nouvelle industrie nationale fut lancée au Chili.

De nos jours, le vignoble type du Chili est très petit. Sur 32 000 propriétés, plus de 26 000 ont 5 ha ou moins. Ce morcellement soulève divers problèmes de culture et a une influence directe sur la qualité du vin. Le petit vigneron chilien, qui n'a ni capital ni équipement, ne peut espérer produire un vin de très haute qualité, car il s'y ruinerait. Mais le gouvernement chilien a affecté une part de son budget à des prêts permettant aux coopératives de construire des caves et d'acquérir du matériel. Chaque vigneron n'est donc pas obligé d'acheter les machines coûteuses dont il a besoin. Ces organisations coopératives paient des experts techniques qui conseillent les vignerons sur les dernières et les meilleures méthodes.

La vallée du fleuve Maipo est une région qui possède quelques-uns des meilleurs vignobles et entreprises de vinification du Chili. Concha y Toro possède 1 500 ha de vignes à Pirque, Torconal, Maípo, Cachapoal et San Juan de Peteroa ; ses deux centres de vinification se trouvent à San Miguel et Pirque. On y fait du bon vin, particulièrement avec du Merlot, Cabernet Sauvignon, Sauvignon Blanc, Sémillon et Riesling. A Pirque, on produit du « champagne » en vrac à partir d'un assemblage de Pinot Blanc, Pinot Gris, Riesling et Chardonnay.

L'entreprise de vinification Canepa a Valparaiso produit un vin fait avec des raisins cultivés dans le bassin de Maípo, au sud-ouest de la capitale. La plupart des vignobles, peuplés de Cabernet Sauvignon et de Riesling, se trouvent le long des berges sablonneuses et très caillouteuses du fleuve Puangue, endroit qui ne manque pas d'évoquer le Bordelais.

A Santa Ana, située à l'ouest de Santiago, se trouve Vina Undurraga, dont le fondateur fut le premier à exporter en 1912 les vins chiliens aux États-Unis. Ses vignes prospèrent aujourd'hui dans un climat modéré, sur un sol irrigué par l'eau du fleuve. On y cultive la plupart des bonnes variétés de *Vitis vinifera* courantes au Chili, ainsi que du Pinot Noir. On y produit également du vin mousseux.

Dans le Llano del Maípo — le bassin Maípo —, au sud de Santiago, se trouvent Viña Santa Rita et, plus à l'est, Viña Cusiño-Macul. Dans certains bons vignobles chiliens, on cultive des vignes importées des grands vignobles français. C'est le cas de Cusiño-Macul, où l'on trouve des pieds originaires de Pauillac dans le Haut-Médoc, et de Martillac, dans le Graves. Plus de la moitié de ses 260 ha produit des raisins à vins rouges particulièrement du Cabernet Sauvignon. Le vin blanc est fait principalement avec du Sémillon. Ici et à Undurraga, entre autres *viñas*, les meilleurs vins vieilliront dans des barriques de chêne américain.

Deux autres centres de vinification importants se trouvent au sud de la région de Maípo. Dans la province de Talca, à Molina, fut fondée en 1865 Viña San Pedro, d'une superficie de 400 ha. A Curicó, une famille espagnole, les Torres, exploite depuis 1979, 150 ha de vignobles ainsi qu'une grande *bodega* bien équipée. Miguel Torres fait appel à toute la technologie moderne et produit des fûts à partir de chênes américains et français. Son Cabernet Sauvignon Santa Digna y vieillit ensuite. Les deux principales coopératives chiliennes de cette région sont : Curicó et Talca.

Contrôle administratif

L'industrie du vin chilien est une des mieux réglementées du monde ; peut-être est-ce surtout pour lutter contre l'alcoolisme. Il en résulte qu'on y encourage la production des vins de haute qualité.

Une quantité maximale de production est imposée à chaque vigneron. S'il lui arrive par hasard de la dépasser, il doit se débarrasser du surplus. Pour cela les deux méthodes les plus courantes consistent à essayer d'exporter, ou bien à distiller pour faire de l'alcool industriel. Chaque année le vigneron doit déclarer la quantité de vin qu'il a faite. Si la production du pays dépasse le maximum légal, chaque viticulteur doit se débarrasser d'une certaine quantité de sa production variant proportionnellement, d'une part avec le surplus national, d'autre part avec le rendement à l'hectare de chaque propriété. Le vigneron doit ensuite déclarer comment il a disposé de son excédent et en quelle quantité. Pour éviter que les vins médiocres écrasent le marché de l'exportation, le Conseil national du commerce extérieur impose des restrictions. Pour être exportés les blancs doivent titrer au moins 12° et les rouges 11,5° ; les uns comme les autres doivent être clairs, d'une coloration nette, être sains et avoir au moins un an d'âge.

Le contrôle administratif des vins du Chili porte sur l'âge. Il y a quatre classes de vin d'exportation : le *courant*, qui a un an ; le *spécial*, qui en a deux ; la *réserve*, de quatre ans ; l'appellation *Gran Vino* s'applique aux vins de six ans ou plus. Dans bien des cas les vins de *réserve* peuvent être parmi les meilleurs du Chili.

Spiritueux

Une partie non négligeable de la production de vins de Muscat de la région nord est distillée pour produire la bonne eau-de-vie du Chili et celle de quelques autres pays d'Amérique du Sud.

Voir PISCO

Chinchón

Spiritueux à goût d'anis fait en Espagne et que l'on boit additionné d'eau, dans de grands verres.

Chine

Depuis les temps les plus anciens, on a fait du vin en Chine. Aujourd'hui des vignes sauvages poussent dans le sud. On y voit des stations vinicoles expérimentales, et un petit nombre de vignobles coopératifs. Ses vignes européennes (telles que Pinot et Riesling) ont été introduites dans le pays, et des vignes de type américian issues de *Vitis labrusca*, ainsi que de variétés indigènes y ont été plantées. Certaines sont cultivées sur des terres irriguées d'après un système de taille bizarre qui les fait lier sur des treillages en forme d'éventail. D'autres vignobles, non irrigués ceux-là, recourent à la méthode dite « de la pergola »

Toutefois le vin semble être réservé aux grandes occasions, la limonade et la bière étant apparemment les boissons qui accompagnent les repas quotidiens. Mais le vin semble destiné à un avenir prometteur. D'anciens centres de vinification ont été remis en fonction et l'on en projette de nouveaux. Les officiels confirment que le pays produit actuellement du raisin, des fruits, des vins de riz, ainsi qu'une variété de boissons distillées.

Histoire du vin en Chine

D'après l'histoire de Chine on aurait commencé à y faire du vin dès l'année 2140 av. J.-C. En ce temps-là, il s'appelait *li* ou *chang* au lieu de *chiu*, son nom actuel. Le vin serait aussi venu des pays méditerranéens et de la Perse, au long de la route suivie à pas lents par les caravanes qui transportaient de la soie en sens inverse. De temps à autre les guerres contre les Barbares mettaient un terme à ce commerce pendant des dizaines d'années consécutives. Mais vers 130 av. J.-C. on aurait importé des vignes de Perse et on les aurait plantées près du palais de l'empereur. Pourtant c'est seulement au VIIe siècle de notre ère, à l'époque où les Chinois dominaient toute l'Asie centrale, que l'art de la vinification se répandit largement dans leur pays. Le vin n'était pas la boisson des masses, mais poètes et mandarins l'appréciaient. Sous la brillante période de la dynastie T'ang, l'art et la poésie fleurissaient et les courtisans, comme les artistes, buvaient du vin. Le poète Li Po — sorte de Villon errant qui écrivait et récitait ses poèmes à la louange du vin — se noya de manière très poétique : ivre, il voulut étreindre le reflet de la lune dans une rivière, y plongea et ne reparut pas.

De nos jours on fait du vin de raisin : rouge et blanc, sec, doux, mousseux ou non, ainsi que du rosé. Le nom chinois du vin de raisin est *p'u t'ao chiu*. La superficie actuelle est d'environ 30 000 ha. Les principales variétés de raisin « ou ancien raisin chinois » [le *Longyon* (œil de dragon), le *Niunai* (pis de vache) et le *Wuhebai* (raisin épépiné Thompson)] peuvent être largement améliorées. Les vignes sont cultivées au Nord-Ouest dans la région de Sinkiang au nord du Yangtse, en Chine Centrale et de l'Est (notamment dans la région du Yantai qui couvre environ 10 000 hectares de vignes), au nord et au sud de la Grande Muraille, près du fleuve Liao. La production est particulièrement abondante dans les provinces du Sinkiang, Shanxi, Hebei, Henan, Shandong et Jiangsu. On trouve également certains vins en retrait du continent, notamment les rouges et blancs doux Chefoo, les rouges et blancs secs Tsingtao et un vin mousseux appelé Tahsiang-pinchiu. Le Chefoo rouge ressemble plutôt à un Porto léger, le blanc est un vin fort et aromatique. Les Tsingtao se rapprochent davantage de la conception occidentale du vin de table. On produit également un peu de vin dans le célèbre vignoble de Lung Yen, à Pékin, jadis, on y cultivait des vignes qui donnaient un vin fort apprécié des empereurs Ming.

Dans les années 70, le groupe Rémy-Martin fut le premier parmi les Occidentaux à passer un accord avec la Chine pour faire, dans la région de Tianjin, un vin appelé « Dynastie » à partir de raisins de Muscat, et produit à raison de 15 à 18 000 caisses par an. On trouve également un autre vin chinois vendu sous le nom de « La Grande Muraille ». La production s'accroît d'environ 5 % tous les ans et le gouvernement chinois espère dépasser les 80 000 tonneaux actuels. Ce résultat semble prometteur aux groupes Rémy-Martin, Pernod-Ricard et Martini-Soprex qui, à l'origine, se sont associés à ce gouvernement. D'autre part, le centre de vinification Huadong, dans la Péninsule de Shandong (nord-est de la Chine), près de Tsingtao, fût terminé en 1988. Le vignoble et les locaux sont sous la direction de Michael Parry, un importateur de vins et spiritueux à Hong Kong, et Charles Whish du centre viticole Rosemount dans le Hunter Valley, en Australie.

VIN DE RIZ

Ce breuvage traditionnel de la Chine est obtenu en sucrant et en faisant fermenter du riz ou du millet riches en gluten. Ces vins de riz dorés titrent entre 6 et 9°. Appelés Shaohsing, originaires de la ville située dans la province de Chekiang où l'on produisait du vin pendant la période des « Royaumes combattants » (430-221 après J.-C.), leur teneur en alcool varie entre 15 et 19° et leur teneur en sucre peut atteindre 20 %.

Le vin de riz est consommé dans toute la Chine, mais plus particulièrement dans les provinces qui longent le Yangtse. Les marques les plus connues sont Yen Hung, Shan Niang, Chia Fan, Hsiang Hsueh et Hua Tiao. Fukien Loh Chiu et Mi Lao Chiu sont également deux vins de riz faits avec du riz jaune dans la province de Shantung.

SPIRITUEUX

On fait de l'eau-de-vie de vin en Chine, mais ce n'est pas la boisson distillée la plus typique. Ce sont en effet les eaux-de-vie de céréales, qui sont les plus populaires en Chine. Appelées *pai chiu*, elles eurent un grand succès sous la Dynastie Yuan (1280-1368) ; elles sont faites avec des céréales augmentées de levures, puis adoucies et fermentées. La plus célèbre entre toutes est l'ardent Mao-t'ai, produit dans la ville du même nom, dans la province de Kweichow, au sud-ouest de la Chine. Le Mao-t'ai s'obtient par distillation du millet et du blé ; il est généralement vieilli pendant une période considérable avant d'être consommé, généralement lors de grandes occasions. Il titre 53° ou plus. Un autre *pai chiu* célèbre est Fen Chiu, produit dans le village Sing Hua de la ville de Fen, dans la province de Shansi. Il s'obtient par distillation de millet, blé, haricots. C'est une eau-de-vie parfumée, au goût clair et vif.

Enfin Ta Chu de Szechwan, Si Fen de Shensi et Wu Liang Yu, également de Szechuan, sont d'autres spiritueux chinois connus.

Chinon (Appellation Contrôlée)

Vins rouges, blancs, rosés de la Loire ; mousseux, demi-mousseux et non mousseux. Touraine.

La forteresse médiévale en ruine de Chinon se dresse au bord de la Vienne, sur une colline escarpée au flanc de laquelle s'accrochent les maisons pittoresques de la vieille ville. Centre vinicole depuis longtemps, Chinon se réclame de son admirateur le plus exubérant : Rabelais qui cultiva une vigne des environs : la Devinière. Il y aurait fait ce qu'il appela du « vin taffetas » doux et velouté. Les paroles de Rabelais survivent à Chinon et sont encore justifiées.

On y fait du rouge, du rosé et du blanc. Le rouge est le plus intéressant. Le Chinon blanc est presque toujours éclipsé par le Vouvray et le Montlouis ; ses rosés par ceux d'Anjou. Mais les rouges peuvent être souples, fleuris, d'un bon bouquet qui rappelle souvent la framboise. Pour être bon, le Chinon doit être celui d'une grande année, mais on n'en compte que deux par décennie dans la région, ou à peu près. Le rouge et le rosé — ce dernier frais et d'un goût net, quoique pas exceptionnel — sont faits avec du Cabernet Franc, sur un sol silicieux ; le blanc avec du Chenin Blanc cultivé sur un sol crayeux. Tous doivent titrer au moins 9,5°. La production moyenne est de 55 000 hl par an (en 1970 : 175 hl de blanc et 35 000 de rouge).

Chiraz

Ville du sud-ouest de l'Iran, proche du golfe Persique, qui a donné son nom aux vins persans les plus connus. Avant Mahomet et jusqu'à Khomeiny, on buvait librement du vin en Perse. La viticulture persista dans la région montagneuse de Chiraz. Elle prospérait déjà au Moyen Age, car Marco Polo en fait une description fabuleuse. Il explique notamment comment les vignes sont palissées sur des palans qui les soulèvent pour les faire passer par-dessus les maisons.

Voir IRAN

Chiroubles (Appellation Contrôlée)

Village de Beaujolais où l'on fait un excellent vin rouge léger qui est en train de devenir l'un des plus populaires de tous les Beaujolais rouges, à Paris et dans la France entière.

Voir BEAUJOLAIS

Chlorose

Maladie de la vigne due à un excès de calcium dans le sol, ce qui empêche l'assimilation du fer. On traite ce mal en ajoutant du fer à la terre. Parfois aussi on remplace les vignes atteintes par des plants greffés sur des souches résistant au calcium.

Voir CHAPITRE IV

Chopine

Petite cruche ou bouteille de vin équivalent à peu près à l'ancienne pinte et qui contient environ un demi-litre.

Chorey-lès-Beaune (Appellation Contrôlée)

Bourgogne rouge et blanc. Côte de Beaune.

Village vinicole bourguignon où il y a plus de village que de viticulture. Comme bien des communes sœurs, Chorey peut soit vendre ses vins sous sa propre appellation, soit les mélanger avec ceux d'autres localités déterminées pour les vendre comme Côte de Beaune-Villages. Il en résulte que certaines années elle déclare

4 000 hl de vin d'appellation communale et d'autres, guère plus d'une centaine.

Dans toute la Côte-d'Or les collines s'abaissent doucement vers une plaine dont la limite est marquée par la route nationale N° 74. En roulant vers le sud, vous voyez des vignes des deux côtés de cette route, mais les vignobles ne sont vraiment bons que sur le côté escarpé à droite. A gauche, sur la plaine qui s'étend jusqu'au chemin de fer, ils sont nettement inférieurs. Or, presque tous ceux de Chorey sont à gauche. C'est à peine si une parcelle de 167 ha se trouve de l'autre côté de la route mais elle ne monte pas assez haut pour que cela présente une réelle importance. Aucun des vignobles de Chorey n'est classé Premier Cru. On pourrait y faire des rouges et des blancs, mais on n'y fait pratiquement que des rouges.

Chromatographie

Procédé d'analyse par absorption sélective d'un mélange de la substance par une matière poreuse. On y recourt en vinification et la substance poreuse employée alors est généralement du papier. La chromatographie permet de vérifier efficacement la présence de certains acides organiques dans le vin. Elle sert aussi en viticulture pour discerner entre *Vitis vinifera* et des hybrides.

Chusclan

Une des bonnes communes des Côtes du Rhône pour les vins rosés et rouges.

Voir RHÔNE

Chypre

Bordée par des plages en dent de scie, l'île de Chypre s'allonge à l'extrémité orientale de la Méditerranée, à quelque 100 km de la côte de Syrie. Ses plaines rôtissent au soleil, mais de janvier à avril le sommet de ses montagnes est couvert de neige et la plupart des vignes sont plantées sur leurs flancs.

La viticulture est une des activités importantes de l'île. Sur quelque 64 000 familles agricoles, environ 30 000 dépendent dans une certaine mesure de la viticulture ou de la viniculture qui se sont développées considérablement durant les vingt dernières années. Le vignoble de Chypre couvre maintenant plus de 30 000 ha, soit 10 % des terres cultivables.

Les touristes qui parcourent l'île ont l'occasion d'admirer les vignobles de Chypre, qui abondent surtout sur les contreforts méridionaux des monts Troodos, aux environs de Limassol et de Paphos, ainsi qu'au pied de la chaîne des Cérines, autour de Nicosie. Ces étendues plantées en vignes qui semblent vastes sont en réalité divisées en un grand nombre de petites parcelles. La route conduisant de Limassol à Paphos est bordée de vignes soigneusement ordonnées — de doux raisins de table mêlés aux raisins à vin, de jeunes vignes poussant sur le sol couleur de cendre, des plants plus âgés, hauts et touffus. A la saison des vendanges, lorsque des cargaisons entières de raisin sont transportées par camion vers les grands centres de vinification, la route est glissante de jus rouge. Les routes de montagne en lacet offrent une vue spectaculaire : une vaste mosaïque de vignes qui s'étendent sur les versants de montagne pour diminuer à perte de vue en petites parcelles autour de vieux villages. Les paysans gardent leur vin pour leur propre consommation — parfois un de ces vins traditionnels, épais, sombres, et très concentrés —, mais la plus grande partie du raisin est vendue aux grands négociants.

Avec une récolte moyenne de plus de 200 000 t de raisin, la production par habitant est proportionnellement supérieure à celle des différents pays vinicoles d'Europe. Chypre produit environ 1 000 000 hl de vin par an (11 millions de caisses).

HISTOIRE DU VIN A CHYPRE

Chypre était l'île d'Aphrodite, déesse de l'Amour, que les Anciens adoraient en particulier dans son temple de Paphos. On sait à coup sûr que l'île était habitée à l'époque mycénienne et que ses habitants étaient en relations commerciales avec les autres populations de la mer Égée. Grecs et Phéniciens y fondèrent des colonies. On voit au musée de Chypre une superbe amphore qui daterait d'environ 900 av. J.-C. ; de récentes excavations ont mis au jour des mosaïques et autres vestiges indiquant qu'on faisait du vin à Chypre dans l'Antiquité. On sait que ces vins étaient bus en Égypte, en Grèce et à Rome. Mainte légende locale concerne le culte d'Aphrodite en l'honneur de laquelle les Cypriotes célébraient de grandes fêtes, notamment à l'occasion du pèlerinage annuel au temple de Palaïpaphos ; Hésiode raconte comment on faisait à Chypre le vin nommé Nama, avec des raisins séchés au soleil.

Beaucoup plus tard, en 1191, Richard Cœur de Lion donna l'île aux Chevaliers du Temple. Cet ordre s'intéressa, comme tous les autres, à la vigne et au vin. Les Templiers apprécièrent le superbe vin doux de l'île, monopolisèrent sa vente et le baptisèrent Commanderie. Le Nama de l'Antiquité porte encore de nos jours le nom de Commandaria. Aucun autre vin au monde ne peut se targuer d'une appellation aussi ancienne. Dans la chronique de la croisade que fit Richard Cœur de Lion, on lit que, à sa première arrivée à Chypre, on lui offrit un banquet au cours duquel « les meilleurs vins des vignobles de Chypre furent servis et ils seraient, dit-on, différents de ceux de tous les autres pays ». Des siècles plus tard, en 1743, Richard Pococke écrivait à Londres : « ... les riches vins de Chypre qui sont tellement estimés partout au monde, qui proviennent seulement des environs de Limassol et sont très chers. En certains endroits on fait, en effet, du bon vin rouge. » Au temps des Plantagenêts, on importait du vin de Chypre en Grande-Bretagne. On but du Commanderie à un grand banquet donné à Londres en 1352, par Henry Richard, maître de la Compagnie des vignerons, en l'honneur du roi Pierre Ier de Chypre. Quatre autres monarques assistaient à ce dîner : Édouard III d'Angleterre, David d'Écosse, Jean II de France et Valdemar de Danemark. L'événement est resté célèbre sous le nom de Banquet des rois. Plus de deux cents ans plus tard, la reine Élisabeth Ire accorda à sir Walter Raleigh le monopole de l'importation des vins de Chypre par le port de Southampton où prospéra une petite colonie de commerçants cypriotes.

On raconte que le sultan turc Soliman II conquit Chypre en 1571 parce qu'il aimait ses vins. Connu pour son intempérance (on le surnomma même le Poivrot), il convoqua son commandant en chef et lui ordonna d'envahir l'île, en ces termes : « Il s'y trouve un trésor que seul le roi des rois est digne de posséder. »

Les Turcs n'abolirent pas complètement la viticulture, mais elle languit et la production se réduisit à peu de chose. C'est seulement en 1878, quand les Anglais prirent en main l'administration de l'île, que la vie reprit dans les vignobles. Par miracle, le phylloxéra n'atteignit pas Chypre, et les vignes de jadis continuent à y pousser sur leurs anciennes souches. Les vignes de Chypre ont joué un rôle dans la création de quelques vins célèbres hors de l'île. On en implanta à Madère au XVe siècle et c'est à elles que l'on doit le célèbre Madère d'aujourd'hui. On attribue la même origine au Marsala de Sicile et au Tokay hongrois.

M. F. Rossi établit de Londres les premières règles du commerce extérieur. En 1956, dans un rapport sur l'industrie vinicole chypriote, il proposa diverses améliorations et expérimentations. Chypre se fit donc envoyer des boutures de nouvelles variétés et depuis le gouvernement s'efforce de suivre les conseils de M. Rossi. On créa un Conseil œnologique, représentatif de tous les secteurs de l'industrie vinicole. De nouvelles recherches furent entreprises par des spécialistes comme M. J. Branas, ancien professeur de viticulture à l'université de Montpellier. Par la suite, les centres vinificateurs furent modernisés et dotés de l'équipement le plus moderne, y compris d'unités de fermentation contrôlée. Le gouvernement effectua des contrôles et des études systématiques sur la viniculture, le choix des sites, les sols et les maladies. Une assistance technique fut fournie à ceux qui en avaient besoin. Chypre n'ayant jamais eu de phylloxéra, il fallut d'abord isoler soigneusement les nouvelles variétés et les planter en quarantaine à la station de Ayia Irini. Ces variétés se sont peu à peu introduites dans la production, contribuant considérablement à la qualité du Xérès et des vins de table chypriotes.

Les vignes européennes ont permis d'enrayer la tendance naturelle qu'ont les vins blancs cultivés en climat chaud d'être un peu plats et de manquer d'acidité et de fraîcheur.

Variétés de raisins

Environ 80 % du raisin à vin sont du Mavron rouge ; 10 % du Xynisteri blanc, 7 % du Soultana et du raisin de table et environ 2 à 3 % du Muscat. On cultive le Mavron dans la plupart des vignobles de

Chypre ; et la meilleure variété au flanc d'une colline nommée Afames, tandis que d'autres se trouvent dans la région de Panayia à Paphos et Pitsilia au flanc du massif du Troodhos. Certains des vins les plus renommés de Chypre sont faits dans cette région. Les vignes traditionnelles de Xynisteri sont répandues dans toute l'île notamment autour de Pitsilia et de Paphos, à l'ouest. Elles produisent du vin blanc.

Types de vins

Vins rouges

Ils sont faits surtout avec des raisins indigènes. Mais on implante à Chypre d'autres variétés qui donnent acidité, couleur et un meilleur équilibre, notamment un raisin ovale nommé Opthalma et du Maratheftika, qui doit son nom à son pays d'origine Marathassa.

Le Mavron sert aussi à faire du rosé appelé, dans l'île et en Grèce, Kokkineli. D'une couleur prononcée pour un rosé, frais au palais, il est d'habitude assez sec. Frappé, il se marie avec à peu près n'importe quel aliment. Parmi les rouges les plus connus, citons l'Afames et l'Othello, tous deux secs, et le Kykko et l'Olymbos. Il importe toutefois de se rappeler qu'une bonne partie du vin se conforme au goût des Cypriotes : rouges très corsés, de couleur foncée et à forte teneur en tanin, ce qui convient avec les mets savoureux et très épicés de Chypre.

Vins blancs

Arrivés à maturité les blancs sont charnus et ont un goût très particulier. En général, ils sont assez secs. Les gens du pays les aiment ainsi et les levures locales sont capables de fermenter, même en présence de la forte proportion d'alcool propre aux vins cypriotes, pourvu que le moût contienne assez de sucre. Parmi les plus connus, citons l'Aphrodite et l'Arsinoé, tous deux secs.

Commanderie

Ce vin de dessert très sucré, celui qui a rendu Chypre célèbre chez les amateurs de vin, est fait depuis des centaines d'années dans des villages de montagne, notamment : Kalokhorio, Zoopiyi et Yerassa. Les variétés les plus employées sont le Mavron et le Xynisteri. Aujourd'hui encore, comme dans la Grèce antique, les vignerons mélangent raisins rouges et blancs. Certains font encore leur vin comme au temps d'Homère, dans d'énormes jarres de terre cuite, enduites de poix mêlée de cendre de vigne et poils de chèvre. Ils les enterrent pour les conserver pendant plusieurs années. Pourtant, dans la propriété voisine, vous trouverez peut-être des cuves modernes en ciment mais les raisins sont toujours étalés au soleil auparavant, comme aux temps d'Hésiode. Traditionnellement, le Commanderie était fait selon le système Mana, la jarre la plus vieille n'étant jamais laissée vide mais toujours remplie de vins plus jeunes, comme dans la solera à Xérès.

Aujourd'hui, toutes les opérations de mélange et de vieillissement du Commanderie s'effectuent par les grandes firmes qui achètent les vins aux fermiers, et le liquide marron et sucré a bien peu à voir avec le concentré — tellement épais qu'il peut être gratté au couteau sur les bords de la cuve — que l'on trouve encore dans certains villages. La qualité est variable et dépend essentiellement du mélange. Mais avec un peu de chance, les hôtes des négociants pourront se voir offrir un verre de Commanderie vieux d'un siècle : ce sera alors un vin sombre, velouté, moelleux, plein de la douceur riche et cuivrée des raisins cuits par le soleil. A Limassol, le port qui exporte le plus de vin, les grands négociants vinifient selon les procédés les plus modernes.

Le Commanderie varie de village à village, selon les méthodes de vinification et la proportion de raisin rouge et blanc qui entre dans sa préparation. Après une longue maturation, il est parfois si concentré que, même pour le consommer sur place, on le mélange à certains autres vins qui ne nuisent pas à sa saveur caractéristique. L'art du coupage est donc un facteur important dans la production du Commanderie.

Vins du type Xérès

On fait une grande variété de Xérès à Chypre, tant pour la consommation intérieure que pour l'exportation. Le principal importateur, la Grande-Bretagne, en a reçu qui titrait autant que le Xérès espagnol clarifié et mis en bouteille en Angleterre. Celle-ci importe aussi des vins de divers degrés d'alcool servant à des coupages, ainsi qu'un vin doux de moindre degré et le moins cher parmi tous ceux du type

Xérès qui sont en général bon marché. Récemment pourtant les Cypriotes portèrent leurs efforts sur les Xérès très forts et la phase suivante de cette évolution mène à l'exportation d'un vin se rapprochant d'autant plus du produit authentique qu'il est fait par la méthode de la *flor (voir ce mot)*. Ils sont en train de constituer des stocks sur leur île et il est permis de prévoir que ce vin gagnera du prestige et atteindra des prix plus élevés sur le marché. Le type très sec est maintenant également exporté, quoiqu'en bien moins grande quantité que le populaire type doux. Dans la *bodega* Keo, les « Xérès crème », une fois mis en tonneaux, mûrissent au soleil pendant deux ou trois ans avant d'être transférés dans un autre entrepôt, où ils achèveront de vieillir dans le bois.

Exportations

Les Cypriotes ont donné à Limassol, port animé où règnent les négociants en vins, le nom de « Bordeaux de Chypre ». Limassol possède plusieurs grands centres de vinification équipés de tous les procédés modernes de pressurage, refroidissement, filtrage et examen des vins. Les tonneaux sont empilés dans des entrepôts en bord de mer et dans des hangars en plein air. A Kéo, les bouteilles sont expédiées dans des conteneurs d'une capacité de 850 cartons chacun, ce qui permet une économie considérable de frais de transport. Les quatre firmes principales sont Kéo, Sodap et Haggipavlu (la plus ancienne maintenant fusionnée avec Étko) et Loel. En 1985, 400 000 hl (4,5 millions de caisses) environ de vin de table, de Commandaria et de Sherry furent exportés, dont plus de la moitié au Royaume-Uni et en U.R.S.S. Chypre s'affirme de plus en plus dans la production de vins de table bon marché que l'évolution de l'industrie a permis d'améliorer. On les exporte davantage et, le plus souvent, les restaurants les servent en carafe. Avant que la Grande-Bretagne n'entre dans le Marché commun, Chypre jouissait d'un tarif douanier préférentiel accordé dans tous le Commonwealth par ce pays, son plus gros client pour les vins. Par la suite, des accords spéciaux furent passés pour préserver les intérêts cypriotes, du moins dans les premiers temps. La Grande-Bretagne est restée le plus gros client de Chypre.

Spiritueux

Chypre produit environ 30 000 hl (plus de 300 000 caisses) d'eau-de-vie par an et en exporte environ un neuvième. La proportion des exportations d'eau-de-vie a baissé par rapport à celle des vins durant les dernières années. Les habitants de l'île boivent volontiers l'eau-de-vie additionnée d'eau glacée. On fait aussi à Chypre un « V.S.O.P » selon les méthodes de Cognac.

Les deux principales liqueurs du pays sont le Pilfar qui ressemble au Curaçao et le Kéo, spécialité du genre Cointreau. En général le gouvernement achète tout l'alcool de raisin dénommé Zivania. Additionné de gomme et de graines d'anis, cet alcool devient une boisson locale nommée Masticha et Ouzo. L'île produit de grandes quantités de moût de raisin, concentré par des méthodes modernes d'évaporation sous vide. Les exportations annuelles de ce moût, vers le Royaume-Uni, s'élèvent à 5 ou 10 000 tonnes, tandis que des quantités moins importantes sont exportées en U.R.S.S.

Cidre

Breuvage produit par la fermentation du jus de pomme, en France, en Angleterre et dans d'autres pays d'Europe. Les colons britanniques importèrent cet art en Amérique du Nord.

Autrefois on commençait par écraser les pommes, en les battant avec des masses en bois, dans des cuves de pierre ou de bois pour en faire une pâte. Mais voilà longtemps qu'on a adopté le pressoir à cidre ressemblant en tous points au pressoir à vin. Depuis peu, on utilise une machine constituée par deux cylindres munis de lames aiguës ; ils tournent sur eux-mêmes à grande vitesse et les pommes qu'on jette entre eux sont réduites en fine pâte beaucoup plus rapidement qu'avec un pressoir. La pâte ainsi obtenue, qu'on appelle parfois le « fromage », était disposée en plusieurs couches séparées par de la paille. On faisait attention à ce que la paille ne soit pas seulement répartie au-dessous et au-dessus du « fromage », mais qu'elle entoure également les côtés de façon à en préserver la forme et servir de filtre pendant le pressurage. Quand ce fromage atteignait à peu près la hauteur d'un mètre, on le pressait pour en extraire tout le jus. De nos jours on se sert de moules qui mettent le fromage en forme et des tissus remplacent la paille. Mais dans l'ensemble le procédé reste le même. Autrefois le résidu du pressage servait à l'alimentation des porcs. Il est désormais humecté et sert à la fabrication d'alcool de marc.

Dans les fermes du Somerset, en Angleterre, et de Normandie, en France, on laisse vieillir le cidre pendant un an ou plus et il devient alors étonnamment fort. Pour les cidres livrés au commerce on se sert parfois de levures sélectionnées en plus de celles qui sont présentes à l'état naturel sur la pomme. Pour faire du cidre doux, on le filtre avant que tout le sucre ait fermenté et on le met en bouteille. Il se produit alors une fermentation secondaire pareille à celle du Champagne. Pour faire des cidres mousseux à bon marché, on y infuse du gaz carbonique.

Cinque Terre (D.O.C.)

Vin blanc italien fait avec des raisins Vernaccia.

Voir LIGURIE

Cinsault (ou Cinsaut)

Variété de raisin cultivée dans le sud-ouest et le midi de la France, la vallée du Rhône et l'Algérie. On lui donne divers noms selon la localité : Picardan Noir, Espagne, Malaga, etc. Associé au Grenache, il donne au vin chaleur et corps.

Ciró (D.O.C.)

Un des vins rouges de Calabre les plus connus.

Voir CALABRE

Citrique (acide)

Bien qu'on en trouve en abondance dans les agrumes et qu'il soit présent dans la plupart des autres fruits, le raisin, et partant le vin, n'en contiennent qu'une infime quantité. $COOH - CH_2 - C (OH) (COOH) - CH_2 - COOH$.

Clairet

Nom donné autrefois en France à un mélange léger de blanc et de rouge et parfois à un vin rouge très léger. C'est de ce mot que dérive l'appellation « claret » par laquelle Anglais et Américains désignent le vin rouge de Bordeaux (*voir* CLARET).

De nos jours le Clairet n'est plus un rosé mais un vin rouge léger, souple et fruité, manquant de tanin et qui peut être bu frais et jeune. Un bon Clairet est fait avec des variétés de raisin qui ont tendance à fournir des vins délicats et qui, en raison de leur faible acidité, ont pu atteindre une pleine maturité. On ne laisse les peaux du fruit qu'un ou deux jours dans la cuve de fermentation. Pour assurer la fermentation malolactique on administre un léger traitement au soufre. Quand les fermentations malolactique et alcoolique sont terminées, on stabilise le vin par collage et sulfitage.

Clairette de Bellegarde (A.O.C.)

Vin blanc. Sud de la France.

Située à quelque 15 km de Nîmes, la commune de Bellegarde fait un petit vin léger et jaune, avec du raisin Clairet. Les vignes sont cultivées sur un sol pierreux, balayé par un bras du Rhône. Clairette de Bellegarde est une des rares appellations d'origine contrôlée de vin blanc du Languedoc. Son emploi est soumis aux limitations géographiques habituelles, ainsi qu'à des normes de taille. Ce vin doit titrer au moins 11,5° et recevoir l'approbation d'un comité de dégustateurs qui lui accordent leur sceau d'approbation figurant sur la bouteille. Cette mesure n'est pas générale en France. C'est dans ces conditions seulement que le vin pourra s'appeler Clairette de Bellegarde. Production moyenne de la commune : environ 4 000 hl par an.

Voir LANGUEDOC

Clairette de Die (Appellation Contrôlée)

Vin blanc. Sud de la France.

Vin demi-mousseux et également vin non mousseux d'un jaune doré, fait dans 32 communes du département de la Drôme.

Produit des raisins Clairette et Muscat, la Clairette de Die date de la Gaule romaine :

l'agglomération s'appelait alors Dea Augusta.

Le vin tranquille doit être obtenu uniquement avec le cépage Clairette.

En faisant leur vin mousseux, les vignerons doivent adopter une des deux méthodes suivantes : le procédé de fermentation secondaire en bouteille à la manière champenoise, avec une proportion de vin de Clairette ne pouvant être inférieure à 75 % ; le procédé rural traditionnel (aussi appelé méthode dioise), avec une proportion de vin de Muscat ne pouvant être inférieure à 50 %. Selon cette dernière méthode, on laisse le vin fermenter lentement en le filtrant souvent et en lui administrant des petites quantités de soufre pour ralentir l'action des levures. Ce soufre a aussi un effet purifiant et tue les bactéries nocives. Quand la première fermentation est terminée, le vigneron obture sa barrique aussi hermétiquement que possible et laisse fermenter le sucre qui subsiste dans le vin. Il le fait ensuite passer par un filtre à pression qui met efficacement un terme à toute fermentation et purifie le vin. Mais le gaz carbonique reste dans le liquide, ce qui le rend mousseux. Cette méthode, quoique ancienne, est encore, de nos jours, la plus utilisée.

Plus ou moins mousseuse, la Clairette de Die a un goût rappelant le Muscat et titre au moins 10,5°.

La production s'élève en moyenne à quelque 40 000 hl (près de 450 000 caisses), produits pour la plupart par la Cave coopérative de Die.

On estime que pour apprécier pleinement ce vin, il faut en avoir l'habitude.

Clairette du Languedoc (A.O.C.)

Vin blanc. Sud de la France.

La grande plaine du Languedoc s'étend depuis Arles jusqu'à la frontière d'Espagne et produit près de la moitié des vins français. Mais ce sont presque tous des vins ordinaires. De-ci, de-là, toutefois, quelques vignobles méritent une Appellation d'Origine Contrôlée. La Clairette du Languedoc en est un exemple. On fait ce vin dans onze communes : Adissan, Aspiran, Paulhan, Fontès, Cabrières, Péret, Le Bosc, Lieuran-Cabrières, Nizas, Saint-André-de-Sangonis et Ceyras, dans le département de l'Hérault. Le raisin de variété Clairette donne deux types de vin sur ces coteaux brûlés par le soleil.

Le premier est celui qui porte simplement l'étiquette Clairette du Languedoc, avec en plus parfois le nom de la commune d'origine. C'est un blanc sec, lourd, qui titre au moins 12°.

Le second ajoute à son nom la qualification « rancio ». Pour avoir droit à ce titre, ce vin désagréable doit être fait avec des raisins laissés sur la vigne longtemps après maturation, titrer au moins 14° et vieillir au moins trois ans pendant lesquels il madérise. Enfin, il doit avoir le goût caractéristique du rancio (ou vin oxydé) *(voir ce mot)*.

Les vignes donnant la Clairette du Languedoc couvrent environ 1 130 ha et la production est inférieure à 11 200 hl (120 000 caisses).

Voir LANGUEDOC

Clape (La)

Voir LANGUEDOC, COTEAUX DU LANGUEDOC

Claret

En Grande-Bretagne, tout spécialement, et souvent aussi aux États-Unis, on appelle ainsi le Bordeaux rouge. Dès que commença en Angleterre l'importation des vins de Bordeaux, c'est-à-dire tout au début du XIIIe siècle, la préférence des Anglais alla aux rouges légers de couleur claire, presque roses, et cette préférence subsiste de nos jours. Les Français les appelaient vin clairet ou Clairet. Moins subtils sur la prononciation des voyelles, les Anglais prononcèrent Clarett.

Mais ce n'était pas le Claret d'aujourd'hui. Certes on faisait déjà vieillir les vins de Bordeaux au temps de la Gaule romaine, mais cette pratique se perdit pour ne reprendre qu'à l'époque moderne. Pendant des siècles le Bordeaux ne fut que du « vin de l'année ». On le consommait parfois quinze jours après les vendanges : à peu près le temps qu'il fallait aux bateaux pour retourner en Angleterre et y débarquer les barriques. La fermentation de ce vin était très courte. D'ordinaire quelqu'un restait l'oreille collée à la cuve de fermentation pour percevoir le bouillonnement du moût. On soutirait le vin peu après qu'elle avait cessé.

De nos jours encore on fait certains vins par le procédé de fermentation courte qui dure moins de quatre jours. Le goût s'orientant vers les vins jeunes et légers, on a recommencé à faire du Clairet à Bordeaux. Mais les Bordelais n'aiment pas ce mot. Il ressemble trop à « Claret » qui désigne désormais les Bordeaux rouges, même vieux. Ils préfèrent donc l'appeler rosé et, ces temps derniers, ce rosé de Bordeaux est devenu assez populaire.

Le Clairet ou rosé de Bordeaux n'est pas un mélange de vins blanc et rouge. Autrefois on confondait facilement le Claret léger (*vinum claratum* : vin clarifié) avec le vin léger et clair par nature (*vinum clarum* : vin clair). Ce vin clarifié n'était que du vin rouge trop foncé auquel on ajoutait du blanc ordinaire. De nos jours la loi interdit dans toute la France de faire du Clairet ou rosé en mélangeant blanc et rouge.

Voir BORDEAUX

Clarete

Terme espagnol utilisé principalement dans la région de La Rioja pour tout vin rouge léger en corps et en couleur.

Clarification

Opération destinée à donner au vin une limpidité de bon aloi exigée par la clientèle. Elle consiste essentiellement à faire disparaître les éléments en suspension dans le liquide. On y procède par collage et/ou filtrage *(voir ces mots)*.

Clarke (Château-)

Bordeaux rouge. Commune de Listrac, en Haut-Médoc. Classement officiel : Cru Bourgeois.

Un connaisseur, le baron Edmond de Rothschild, acquit ce domaine en 1970 et le planta de vignes en 1973. Le nouveau chai, entre Moulis et Listrac, est à visiter.

Caractéristiques : Vin assez dur, bien vinifié et qui a du corps.

Superficie : 131 ha.

Production moyenne : 500 tonneaux (50 000 caisses).

Classification de 1855

Voir BORDEAUX

Clerc-Milon-Rothschild (Château-)

Bordeaux rouge. Commune de Pauillac, en Haut-Médoc.

Contigu aux Château-Lafite et Mouton-Rothschild, ce vignoble est un Cinquième Cru du Médoc, selon la classification de 1855. La propriété fut achetée en 1970 par le baron Philippe de Rothschild, déjà propriétaire de deux autres crus de Pauillac, Mouton-Rothschild et Mouton-Baronne-Philippe.

Caractéristiques : Vin bien vinifié, présentant les caractéristiques typiques de Pauillac : dur au début, mais corsé et riche.

Superficie : 25 ha.

Production moyenne : 125 tonneaux.

Climat

En Bourgogne, ce nom signifie *vignoble*, l'équivalent de *cru* à Bordeaux.

Climens (Château-)

Bordeaux blanc. Commune de Barsac, en Sauternais.

Un des deux meilleurs Barsac (l'autre est Château-Coutet situé à quelque 200 mètres), Climens se dresse au bord d'un vieux chemin tortueux qui sinue entre des murs de pierre aux carrefours marqués de flèches d'or indiquant au touriste la route du Sauternes. Le vin de ce château a droit aux deux appellations d'origine, Barsac et Sauternes, et utilise les deux : Barsac-Sauternes. (Autrefois, Barsac était une zone célèbre, mais depuis 1936, l'appellation Sauternes qui est plus connue a été accordée aux vins de cette commune. Les Barsac sont d'authentiques Sauternes quoiqu'ils tendent à être plus légers et moins doux.)

En 1855, l'année où Climens fut classé Premier Cru de Sauternes, M. Henri Gounouilhou acheta la propriété. Elle appartient actuellement à M. Lucien Lurton, également propriétaire du Château Brane-Cantenac à Margaux, du Château Durfort-Vivens à Margaux, et du Château Bouscaut en Graves. Le propriétaire n'habite pas le château, bâtisse de bois, chartreuse sans prétention. Mais les chais, situés au-delà de la cour couverte de gravier, sont vastes et impressionnants. Les 4/5 des vignes sont du Sémillon et le reste du Sauvignon et du Muscadelle.

Caractéristiques : Un vin bien meilleur quand il est jeune. Par grandes années, il atteint le sommet de la finesse. Les superbes 1929, 1947, 1949, 1971 et 1983 sont des classiques en fait de liquoreux avec une grande finesse. Dans le passé, Climens pouvait surpasser Château-Yquem : il était plus léger, avec moins de vinosité et de corps, mais miraculeusement subtil.

Superficie : 33 ha.

Production moyenne : 65 tonneaux (6 000 caisses).

Clinet (Château-)

Bordeaux rouge. Commune de Pomerol.

Traditionnellement un des meilleurs crus de Pomerol, Château-Clinet appartient maintenant à Georges Audy et produit un vin sain mais sans grande distinction.

Superficie : 9 ha.

Production moyenne : 36 tonneaux.

Clinton

Vigne américaine qui donne des petits raisins noirs de goût épicé. Quoique de fort rendement, elle ne permet de faire que des vins bons pour le coupage. On la cultive surtout pour ses souches qui servent de porte-greffes à d'autres variétés.

Clone

Ensemble formé par un individu végétal et par tous les descendants qui en sont issus par multiplication asexuée.

Clos

Vigne entourée de murs ou qui le fut autrefois. On en trouve surtout en Bourgogne. Certains vins de ces clos méritent une appellation d'origine particulière. Certains peuvent ne pas jouir de ce privilège mais sont néanmoins célèbres, notamment : Le Clos (Pouilly-Fuissé) ; Les Clos (Chablis) ; Les Clos (Côte-Rôtie) ; Clos des Arlots (Nuits-Saint-Georges-Prémeaux) ; Clos Blanc (Pommard) ; Clos de la Boudriotte (Chassagne) ; Clos du Chapitre (Fixin) ; Clos de la Commaraine (Pommard) ; Clos des Corvées (Nuits-Saint-Georges-Prémeaux) ; Clos des Ducs (Volnay) ; Clos des Forêts-Saint-Georges (Nuits-Saint-Georges-Prémeaux) ; Clos de la Maréchalle (Nuits-Saint-Georges-Prémeaux) ; Clos des Mouches (Beaune) ; Clos du Papillon (Savennières-Loir) ; Clos des Perrières (Meursault) ; Clos des Porrets-Saint-Georges (Nuits) ; Clos des Réas (Vosne) ; Clos du Roi (Aloxe-Corton) ; Clos du Roi (Beaune) ; Clos Saint-Jacques (Gevrey) ; Clos Saint-Jean (Chassagne) ; Clos Saint-Paul (Givry) ; Clos Saint-Pierre (Givry).

Clos de Bèze

Voir CHAMBERTIN-CLOS DE BÈZE

Clos Fourtet

Voir FOURTET

Clos Haut-Peyraguey

Voir HAUT-PEYRAGUEY

Clos de la Roche (Appellation Contrôlée)

Bourgogne rouge. Commune de Morey-Saint-Denis, en Côte de Nuits. Classement officiel : Grand Cru.

Le Clos de La Roche est un des moins connus de ce secteur de la Côte de Nuits ; comme il est bon, parfois exceptionnel, il offre une valeur intéressante à l'acheteur avisé.

Depuis des siècles, il est éclipsé par Bonnes Mares, par Clos de Tart et par Clos des Lambrays. Pour son malheur aussi, les vins de Morey étaient le plus souvent vendus sous l'appellation d'une des deux communes voisines (Gevrey-Chambertin et Chambolle-Musigny) probablement plus à l'avantage de ces derniers qu'à leur détriment.

Le vignoble est un des plus vastes des crus de Morey. Il couvre une superficie de quelque 15 ha au sommet d'une colline qui domine la route passant à travers les vignobles sur la limite séparant Gevrey de Morey. Sa noblesse est telle que c'est un des rares Grands Crus de Bourgogne dont les bouteilles ne portent pas le nom de la commune car celui du clos suffit. Pour avoir droit à cette appellation, évidemment, le vin doit se conformer aux normes rigoureuses des Grands Crus. Comme la plupart des vins de Morey, il est gaillard et riche quoique étrangement délicat, comme le Clos de Tart. Si on trace une droite partant de la vigoureuse noblesse de Chambertin et aboutissant à l'élégance de Musigny, on trouvera Clos de La Roche peut-être juste en dessous de Chambertin, dont il n'a pas l'austère majesté ; mais il possède une grâce enjoleuse.

Comme la plupart des vignobles de Bourgogne, le Clos de La Roche appartient à plusieurs vignerons.

La production moyenne est de 500 hl (5 500 caisses) de de vin par an.

Clos Saint-Denis (Appellation Contrôlée)

Bourgogne rouge. Commune de Morey-Saint-Denis, en Côte de Nuits. Classement officiel : Grand Cru.

Les vignes de Clos Saint-Denis bordent la route des Grands Crus qui serpente au milieu des vignobles de la Côte-d'Or, un peu avant le village de Morey quand on roule vers le sud. En 1927, Saint-Denis décida d'ajouter à son nom celui du vignoble quoique le clos ne fût pas alors classé parmi les meilleurs de l'agglomération. C'est seulement en 1937 que le Saint-Denis fut classé Grand Cru : c'est en effet un des très bons vins de la Bourgogne.

Le vin qui est produit par les vignes du Clos Saint-Denis est un des plus légers des Grands Crus de Côte de Nuits. Délicatesse et finesse, telles sont les caractéristiques sur lesquelles il faut porter son attention par bonnes années, car il n'aura jamais la robustesse charnue de ses pairs : Clos de Tart, Clos de La Roche, Clos des Lambrays (ce dernier est un vin remarquable classé Grand Cru). Nombre de vignerons cultivent les quelque 6,5 ha du Clos Saint-Denis et déclarent ensemble environ 200 hl en année moyenne, ce qui fait environ 2 200 caisses.

Clos de Tart

Bourgogne rouge. Commune de Morey-Saint-Denis, en Côte de Nuits. Classement officiel : Grand Cru.

Jusqu'en 1141, ce vignoble s'appelait Climat de La Forge. Il changea de nom quand les bernardines (version féminine des cisterciens) de l'abbaye de Notre-Dame l'achetèrent. En 1184, une bulle du pape entérina la transaction et, depuis, cette vigne a gardé le nom de Clos de Tart. Les sœurs la cultivèrent en l'accroissant légèrement en 1240, jusqu'à ce que la Révolution la fît passer à l'État qui la revendit. Contrairement à ce qui s'est passé dans la plupart des vignobles de Bourgogne, le Clos de Tart est resté intact et il est actuellement tout entier entre les mains de la Maison J. Mommessin, de Mâcon.

Le Clos de Tart est situé juste au nord de Morey, à droite de la route des vignobles quand on roule vers le sud, entre Bonnes Mares et le Clos des Lambrays. Ses 7 ha sont entièrement clos par un vieux mur qui borde la chaussée à mi-hauteur de colline. On dit souvent qu'il produit un vin pour les dames, mais c'est par référence pour ses anciennes propriétaires, car il est gaillard. Toutefois, à cette caractéristique de vigueur propre aux vins de Morey, il ajoute une délicatesse et une subtilité particulières ; en vieillissant il devient extrêmement gracieux. Ce vignoble est classé Grand Cru : la plus haute appellation en Bourgogne. Quoiqu'il n'ait pas l'enthousiasme brûlant de son voisin, le Clos des Lambrays, il mérite parfois son renom considérable.

Par année moyenne, la production s'élève à quelque 200 hl, soit l'équivalent d'environ 2 200 caisses.

Clos de Vougeot (Appellation Contrôlée)

Bourgogne rouge. Commune de Vougeot, en Côte de Nuits. Classement officiel : Grand Cru.

Les 50 ha du Clos de Vougeot (ou Clos-Vougeot) sont tellement célèbres que ce vignoble est pratiquement inscrit à l'actif du bilan national. Par tradition, les régiments de l'armée française qui passaient à proximité saluaient les vignes. Des moines cisterciens commencèrent à planter au XIIe siècle sur les coteaux au-dessus de leur monastère et le vignoble resta entre les mains du clergé jusqu'à la Révolution. Les moines ne plantèrent pas toute la surface actuelle ; une bonne part leur fut offerte par de pieux Bourguignons qui s'appelaient Hugues le Blanc, Eudes le Vert et Wallo Gile : ils en prirent soin et l'entourèrent d'un mur. Au XVIe siècle, les vignes s'étendaient déjà tellement qu'on jugea bon d'y construire un château ou tout au moins un bâtiment pour abriter le pressoir à l'intérieur de l'enclos. On confia à un jeune moine zélé le soin d'en dresser les plans. Il y travailla avec ferveur mais succomba au péché mortel d'orgueil en le signant de son nom. L'abbé lui reprocha ce péché et ordonna à d'autres moines de remanier complètement le plan. Ces derniers conçurent une bâtisse désolante. Selon la légende, le premier architecte se repentit de son péché et en mourut de chagrin, ce qui était bien porté au Moyen Age dans un tel cas. Quant au bâtiment, il fut construit avec tous ses défauts pour rappeler le péché et la disgrâce encourue par le coupable.

Depuis lors, il a subi mainte addition et rénovation. La dernière en date, mais il y en aura peut-être d'autres encore, fut l'œuvre de la Confrérie des chevaliers du Tastevin de Bourgogne : société qui veille à ce que le reste du monde n'oublie pas les vins de sa province. Les membres de la Confrérie — négociants en vin, vignerons, touristes et invités de marque — se rassemblent tous les mois ou à peu près dans la grande salle à manger du « château ». Ainsi les salles où résonna jadis le plain-chant des moines retentissent maintenant du bruit, du tumulte et des chansons à boire des chevaliers qui louent les vins de Bourgogne. Cinq cents personnes peuvent s'asseoir dans la grande salle des banquets dont les piliers de pierre sont décorés d'armoiries et de hottes qui ont servi aux vendanges. On y lit aussi les millésimes les plus célèbres depuis 1108.

Depuis la confiscation des biens de l'Église au temps de la Révolution, le Clos de Vougeot n'a que rarement appartenu à un seul propriétaire. Le dernier vécut au XIXe siècle ; sa tombe est située à côté de la terrasse qui conduit au grand portail du « château ». Depuis sa mort, le clos est de plus en plus morcelé et désormais une centaine de personnes cultivent les vignes encore entourées de murs.

Chacun soigne sa propre part et replante à son gré. Les vignes ont donc divers âges. Or, l'âge a un effet considérable sur la qualité. Chacun aussi soigne ses plants à sa façon, vendange quand il lui plaît et fait son vin à son gré, son talent, sa conscience et ses aptitudes. Enfin chacun vend à l'acquéreur de son choix : certains en pièce (fût) à des négociants, d'autres mettent en bouteille sous leur nom.

Hormis ces diversités dues au système de propriété, le vignoble est partagé en trois sections qui donnent des vins différents. Il est donc difficile de définir un ensemble de caractéristiques convenant à tous les Clos de Vougeot. S'il fallait le faire, on pourrait dire honnêtement que, par bonne année, un Clos de Vougeot sera relativement charnu avec beaucoup de nez ; il n'aura pas la majesté austère du Chambertin ni la grâce délicate du Musigny ou du Romanée-Saint-Vivant, mais inclinera plutôt vers ce dernier. En tout cas, ce vin réjouira toute la bouche et laissera un somptueux arrière-goût durable.

Sur guère moins de 50 ha, Clos de Vougeot produit à peu près 2 000 hl (plus de 20 000 caisses) par an.

Sur les trois secteurs du Clos tels que le constituèrent jadis les moines, celui qui se trouve immédiatement derrière le château et s'étend en direction du mur est le meilleur ; le secteur du milieu vient immédiatement après, enfin, celui d'en bas, proche de la route nationale, est nettement inférieur. La différence est due en partie à une variation de pente du coteau : très plat en bas et de plus en plus incliné à mesure que l'on approche du château. Et en partie au sol : une marne crayeuse, d'un brun roux, mêlée de cailloux s'étend en haut ; le bas, plus brun que roux, contient plus d'humus et moins de pierres ; le sol du bas a tendance à conserver l'humidité. C'est donc par année sèche que les vignes y donnent la même production que celles qui sont plantées plus haut.

A une certaine époque le vignoble fut divisé en parcelles qui conservent leurs noms traditionnels : au sommet, Musigny de Clos de Vougeot (c'est le plus proche de Chambolle-Musigny), Garenne, Plante Chamel, Plante Abbé, Montiottes Hautes, Chioures, Quartier de Marci-haut, Grand Maupertuis et Petit Maupertuis. A mi-côte on trouve Dix Journaux, Baudes Bas et Baudes Saint-Martin. En bas, où le vin est généralement moins bon mais se vend quand même à un prix aussi élevé, il y a Montiottes Bas, Quatorze Journaux et la partie inférieure de Baudes Bas et de Baudes Saint-Martin.

On fait aussi du vin blanc dans la petite commune de Vougeot, mais il n'a pas droit à la même appellation et il est vendu comme Clos Blanc de Vougeot.

Cobblers

Traduit littéralement, la boisson des cordonniers. Aux États-Unis, ce sont des cocktails composés de jus de fruits, vin ou alcool, et décorés de fruits ou de baies.

Cochenille

Chenille qui attaque la vigne.

Voir CHAPITRE IV

Cochylis

Ce papillon dépose ses œufs sur les raisins et les enveloppe dans un cocon. C'était autrefois un des plus redoutables ennemis de la vigne. On l'a vainement combattu à la nicotine et à l'arsenic. Mais désormais des produits suisses — Nirosan et Gésarol — pulvérisés seuls ou avec de la bouillie bordelaise, viennent à bout de cette plaie.

Voir CHAPITRE IV

Cocktail

Mélange contenant en général au moins un spiritueux et servi glacé, à l'apéritif. Cette boisson d'origine américaine est encore beaucoup consommée aux États-Unis, notamment le Manhattan : 2 parts de whisky de seigle et 1 de Vermouth italien, avec un rien de bitter ; et le Dry Martini : 4 parts de gin ou Vodka, 1 part de Vermouth français, qui est parfois pulvérisé dans le verre avec un atomiseur.

Cocuy

Liqueur faite au Venezuela avec une plante du désert nommée *sabila.*

Coffey

Tous les appareils à distillation continue dérivent de celui qui fut mis au point par un Irlandais, inspecteur général des impôts : Coffey. Ces alambics spéciaux permettent la production à grande échelle de l'alcool de grain, notamment le whisky. Désormais l'appareil de Coffey fait place à celui de Barbet et Ilye.

Cognac

Eau-de-vie de vin. Sud-Ouest de la France.

En 1860, un géologue français nommé Coquand fit un voyage dans les Charentes : région côtière brumeuse, éclairée par des rayons solaires d'une teneur exceptionnelle en rayons ultraviolets. Un étrange compagnon était avec lui lors de cette excursion scientifique, c'était un dégustateur professionnel de vins et eaux-de-vie. Ils allèrent de ferme en ferme, de cellier en cellier, de vigne en vigne. Le géologue prélevait des échantillons de sol pour les analyser et le dégustateur flairait et sirotait l'eau-de-vie. Ensuite, ils comparèrent leurs notes sur les qualités et caractéristiques de chaque Cognac et le sol de chaque vignoble. Leurs notes coïncidaient rigoureusement.

Coquand prouvait ainsi sa théorie sur le rapport qui existe entre les sols et les eaux-de-vie.

La division de la région de Cognac en six zones — Grande Champagne, Petite Champagne, Borderies, Fins Bois, Bons Bois et Bois ordinaires — dérive de ses travaux, mais n'explique quand même pas la qualité exceptionnelle des eaux-de-vie de Cognac.

Spéculer sur l'excellence unique du Cognac et ses causes ne manque pas d'intérêt. D'abord, le sol contient de la craie en proportion décroissante depuis la Grande Champagne jusqu'aux Bois ordinaires. Qualité et valeur du Cognac décroissent de même. Mais la craie ne produit pas un bon vin rien qu'autour de Cognac. On lui doit aussi le Champagne et le Xérès. Les calcaires sédimentaires sont la terre d'élection des vignes exceptionnelles.

Le vin de Cognac (ou plus exactement des Charentes, car le nom de la ville n'avait pas encore éclipsé celui de la région) était plutôt acide. Pourtant, autrefois, on ne le distillait pas et son acidité n'était donc pas encore devenue une vertu. Les marins anglais et scandinaves ne venaient pas chercher du vin en Charente mais du sel. Toutefois, lorsqu'ils se trouvaient à quai, ils achetaient aussi du vin de la région. Ce débouché encouragea la culture de la vigne et on arriva à la surproduction. Alors, pour occuper moins d'espace dans les cales des bateaux, pour fortifier le vin avant de l'expédier sur les mers septentrionales, et enfin pour payer moins d'impôts car les vins étaient alors taxés à la quantité, on fit bouillir le vin des Charentes. On voulait réduire le volume que l'acheteur aurait rétabli à l'arrivée par addition d'eau. Personne n'imaginait alors quelle essence miraculeuse donnerait la distillation du vin de Charente.

Quand on commença à distiller du Cognac, peu après 1600, on faisait déjà d'autres eaux-de-vie en France. Mais alors que le vin des Charentes donnait une eau-de-vie consommable à l'état naturel, toutes les autres devaient être additionnées d'herbes ou de fruits pour leur donner de la saveur ou masquer leur mauvais goût. (Il en alla ainsi jusqu'à l'invention de la distillation multiple, un siècle plus tard). La zone montagneuse du Limousin, célèbre pour ses chênes, se trouve immédiatement à l'est de la région Charentaise, dans les premiers sommets du Massif Central sur lesquels le fleuve Charente prend sa source.

Quand la distillation du Cognac était encore un art domestique datant de 200 ans, on pensa à le conserver dans des tonneaux en chêne du Limousin qui se trouvaient à portée de la main. De nos jours, le chêne coûte cher et on a cherché partout des forêts dont les bois auraient sur les eaux-de-vie le même effet que le chêne du Limousin. Mais on n'en a pas trouvé. Les gens du pays n'hésitent pas à vous dire : « Il est difficile de préciser ce qui importe le plus du bois ou du vin ». On ne s'en étonnera pas en apprenant que, sur un hectolitre d'alcool vieilli pendant 25 ans dans un fût de chêne, on trouve 500 g d'extrait de bois qui contribue énormément au bouquet du vieux Cognac. On a beaucoup utilisé aussi les chênes de la forêt de Tronçais, dans l'Allier, en raison de son grain fin. Il donna d'excellents résultats, mais le Cognac vieillissait plus lentement que dans celui du Limousin. En raison de son prix extrêmement élevé, on s'en sert de moins en moins.

Jusqu'en 1860, on n'expédiait pas le Cognac en bouteille et il ne s'appelait même probablement pas Cognac. Les traditionalistes du métier s'opposaient à la mise en bouteille en disant : du moment que l'eau-de-vie ne vieillit bien que dans le bois, mieux vaut qu'elle voyage en barriques. C'était vrai, pourtant la vente en bouteille permet au fabricant de savoir ce qu'il y aura dedans quand elle atteindra le consommateur. C'est d'ailleurs un exemple d'une loi fondamentale au sujet des vins et alcools : la bouteille la plus sûre est celle qui passe bouchée entre les mains des intermédiaires. En outre, le nom sur l'étiquette et le lieu d'origine de l'eau-de-vie devinrent célèbres et c'est ainsi que Cognac fut connu dans le monde entier.

De nos jours, il peut y avoir du coñac, du koniak (contrefaçon grecque désormais supprimée) et des conhaques, mais il n'y a qu'un Cognac d'après la loi française et celle de bien d'autres pays. Il s'agit d'une eau-de-vie obtenue par la distillation de vins provenant de certaines variétés de raisin, cultivées dans une région délimitée de la Charente et de la Charente-Maritime (et, pour une très petite quantité, de deux autres départements), qui a subi deux distillations successives dans un alambic — jamais dans un appareil à distillation continue — et qui a vieilli dans du chêne.

Il y a quelque 90 ans, tout le vignoble des Charentes fut balayé par le phylloxéra et l'industrie du Cognac dut repartir de zéro. Tout en y procédant, les négociants réalisèrent que bien des alcools neutres, produits par distillation multiple, les concurrençaient sur leur propre marché et que, étant donné la tendance croissante à vendre en bouteille, ils ne pouvaient plus expédier le Cognac en barriques. Ils décidèrent donc de faire vieillir eux-mêmes leur produit. On se fera une idée de ce que cela leur coûte en considérant qu'actuellement les ventes de Cognac s'élèvent à 6 billions de francs par an. Celui qui vend du Cognac âgé de 5 ans doit évidemment avoir en cave le produit de cinq vendanges successives. S'il se spécialisait dans le Cognac de 40 ans d'âge, il lui faudrait stocker la distillation de quarante vendanges, ce qui exigerait un capital astronomique et des entrepôts qui couvriraient la moitié du département. Avec un stock de vieil alcool relativement minime, deux firmes, actuellement, ont investi dans ces réserves environ 25 milliards de francs chacune, représentés par quelque 104 000 barriques pour les deux.

Types de Cognac

De nos jours la plupart des firmes concentrent leur activité sur le Cognac Trois-Étoiles, qui représente environ 65 % des ventes de Cognac. Diverses légendes expliquent l'histoire de ces trois étoiles ; on commença à étiqueter ainsi l'eau-de-vie voilà à peu près 75 ans, lorsque se répandit la mode des mélanges de Cognac typiques. Les premières bouteilles ainsi marquées auraient été expédiées sur le marché australien. N'allons surtout pas croire que ces trois étoiles désignent de l'eau-de-vie âgée de trois ans, mais seulement du Cognac plus vieux que celui qui est destiné à être consommé avec de l'eau de Seltz, et toujours plus jeune que le V.S.O.P. En général, le Trois-Étoiles des négociants les plus importants a passé plusieurs années en fût (l'alcool ne vieillit pas comme le vin dans le verre ; un Cognac de 1860, mis en bouteille en 1900 et un Cognac de 1900 mis en bouteille en 1940, ont exactement le même âge).

Le V.S.O.P. (initiales de Very Superior Old Pale), ce qui est assez curieux puisque, en vieillissant en fût, le Cognac absorbe du tanin qui le rend foncé. A l'origine, c'est un liquide incolore ; c'est le tanin qui le hâle. Very Superior Old Dark serait une appellation plus logique.

En réalité, le V.S.O.P. est un type d'eau-de-vie mais pas un Cognac d'un âge plus précis que celui du Trois-Étoiles.

Le plus vieux type commercialisé par de nombreuse firmes peut s'appeler : Réserve, Extra, X.O., Cordon Bleu, etc., et l'on peut trouver, dans les cas exceptionnels, de l'eau-de-vie millésimée. Ces exceptions portent sur des quantités relativement faibles.

Dans la pratique, le V.S.O.P. livré par les maisons de confiance peut avoir passé de 5 à 10 ans en fût. Mais il importe de comprendre que V.S.O.P. indique un type, car le Cognac — sauf celui d'un cru et d'une année déterminés qui ne sont plus désormais que rarement commercialisés — est toujours un mélange d'eaux-de-vie provenant de divers secteurs et de diverses années. Chaque firme établit elle-même le modèle de son V.S.O.P. — de même que de son Trois-Étoiles — et procède, d'année en année, à des coupages adroits pour vendre un Cognac conforme au modèle initial, ce qui lui permet de l'offir dans la même bouteille, sous la même étiquette. Elle conserve des échantillons originaux ; lorsqu'il s'agit de les reproduire par mélange, on les « flaire » car on se fie plutôt à l'arôme qu'au goût. Étant donné que le vin d'une année n'est jamais identique à celui de la précédente, on conçoit combien il est difficile d'obtenir un produit constant en mélangeant dans des proportions à déterminer l'eau-de-vie produite par les divers vins de l'année. Un « Cognac de dix ans » peut vraisemblablement être composé de diverses eaux-de-vie qui ont plus et moins de dix ans.

La mention V.S.O.P. indique ce qu'est l'eau-de-vie : l'interprétation par telle ou telle firme du type V.S.O.P. On voyait autrefois sur le marché des États-Unis du V.S.E.P. (E pour Extra). Il disparaît aujourd'hui.

Il faut signaler que l'acheteur en a plus pour son argent quand il achète un V.S.O.P. ou quelque autre vieux Cognac que lorsqu'il achète un Trois-Étoiles. La mise en bouteille, mise en caisse et les droits de douane et impôts sont les mêmes. En proportion ils sont donc moins élevés pour un Cognac cher que pour un Cognac bon marché, ce qui peut augmenter le plaisir du consommateur.

Millésime et âge

L'âge est considéré comme une grande vertu du Cognac. Actuellement il y a quatre critères qui permettent d'évaluer cet âge et ils sont fondés sur des faits vérifiables.

1. En Angleterre, la loi exige que le Cognac ait au moins trois ans d'âge.

2. Aux États-Unis, le Cognac doit avoir au moins deux ans, selon la loi.

3. Selon la loi française, le V.S.O.P. ne peut être exporté que s'il a au moins quatre ans d'âge.

4. Enfin il existe sur les quais de Londres des entrepôts soumis à un contrôle strict. Le Cognac expédié en fûts en Angleterre y

vieillit dans le chêne. La date de son arrivée est scrupuleusement notée. Quand il est livré au commerce, il porte l'indication « British Bonded ». On en trouve non seulement en Angleterre, mais aussi aux États-Unis. Son âge certain permet en effet de le vendre à un prix suffisamment élevé pour couvrir les frais de réexpédition. Dans le métier, on l'appelle aussi « Old Landed » parce qu'il est débarqué avant d'être mis en bouteille. Le climat de Londres n'étant pas celui de Cognac, l'eau-de-vie qui y vieillit n'a pas exactement le même goût. Il semble plus net et en même temps plus fondu, ce que certains préfèrent et d'autres pas. En outre, il perd un peu de sa vigueur dans un lieu humide. Pourtant quelques-uns des plus grands Cognac accessibles aujourd'hui sont des eaux-de-vie mises en bouteille à Londres, qui n'ont fait l'objet d'aucun mélange en provenance d'un certain cru, en une année bien définie. Ils peuvent être superbes. L'âge leur donne de la délicatesse ; ils deviennent les prototypes du grand Cognac. Depuis la guerre, l'expédition en fût vers l'Angleterre a beaucoup diminué.

Le Cognac jeune, qui vient d'être distillé, est d'autant plus âpre et dur que le vin était clair et acide. Compte 00 désigne son âge officiel. Au 1er avril suivant la fin officielle de la distillation, 2 mois après celle-ci, le compte d'âge devient 0, puis change à nouveau chaque année au 1er avril. Actuellement l'âge minimum d'un Cognac Trois-Étoiles ou d'un alcool équivalent est compte 2 ; il est compte 4 pour un V.S.O.P. ou son équivalent et compte 6 au minimum pour un vieux Cognac. En raison des stocks importants de Cognac que possèdent les compagnies, et du volume énorme des ventes (110-120 millions de bouteilles par an), le Bureau national du Cognac, agence locale de régulation des marchés, ne suit les Cognac que jusqu'au compte 6. Ensuite, toutes les règles et techniques de conservation de la qualité et de la pureté par le vieillissement relèvent de la responsabilité de la société productrice et constituent tout son prestige et toute sa fierté. Négociants, cultivateurs et coopératives le font vieillir. Or on compte 322 firmes expéditrices de Cognac, de nombreuses coopératives de distillation et, sur les quelque 50 000 agriculteurs qui cultivent la vigne et font du vin destiné au Cognac, un peu plus de 20 000 le font distiller eux-mêmes et veillent sur le vieillissement de leur propre production. Outre cette multiplicité d'individualités diverses, les entrepôts des grandes maisons de Cognac sont éparpillés un peu partout à Cognac, Jarnac et à la campagne. Elles divisent leurs stocks pour empêcher qu'un éventuel incendie ne le

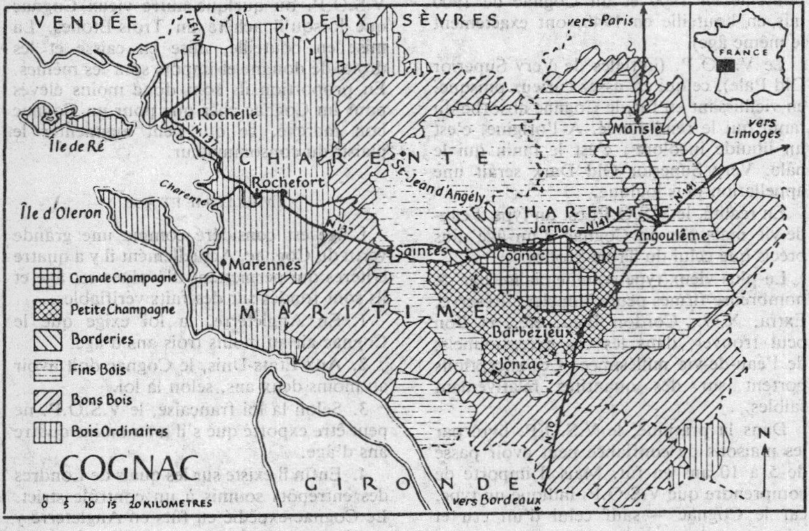

détruise entièrement. L'assurance rembourserait bien sûr le prix de la marchandise disparue, mais la firme qui perdrait toute sa réserve de Cognac mettrait des années pour disposer d'assez de vieilles eaux-de-vie afin de restaurer sa marque. Devant un tel nombre de propriétaires et de distillateurs, de barriques éparses aussi, les autorités de Cognac sont assez réalistes pour comprendre qu'un contrôle des très vieilles eaux-de-vie est impossible. « Nous tenons par-dessus tout à la confiance du public et nous préférons donc ne rien certifier dont nous ne pouvons pas être absolument certains », disent-elles.

Puisqu'il en est ainsi, il est impossible de certifier qu'une bouteille quelconque contient du Cognac de plus de 5 ans, sauf s'il s'agit d'un « British Bonded ». Distillateurs et négociants eux-mêmes aiment de moins en moins parler d'âge. « Nous prenons la peine de mettre en vente des Cognac de plus de 20 ans, ça coûte cher et c'est vain car nous n'en sommes nullement récompensés : le public le trouve trop jeune s'il n'a pas fait l'aller et retour de Russie avec Napoléon ». Quoi qu'il en soit, si ces eaux-de-vie étaient vraiment allées en Russie avec la Grande Armée, elles ne seraient pas plus vieilles que le jour où on les a mises en bouteille. En réalité, il n'existe pas sur le marché d'eaux-de-vie datant de cette époque. Indiscutablement les pires tromperies en matière de Cognac furent les eaux-de-vie vendues sous les étiquettes affirmant ou laissant seulement entendre qu'elles dataient du temps de Napoléon. Ce n'était que fraude et contrefaçon. Toutefois, il faut faire une distinction entre ces faux et les eaux-de-vie dont l'étiquette indique ou laisse entendre qu'elle seraient du genre Napoléon. Cette indication s'apparente à Trois-Étoiles et V.S.O.P. Le Cognac contenu dans une bouteille ainsi étiquetée aura au moins 6 ans.

Le vieillissement optimal se situe à environ 40 ans et dépend à la fois de l'eau-de-vie et de la manière de l'entreposer. Audelà, la maturation en fût cesse de l'améliorer. On peut encore déguster des Cognac de 1815 et de 1850, dans les paradis (le saint des saints où sont conservés les plus vieilles barriques) à Jarnac et à Cognac. Mais ce ne sont plus que des échos de symphonies éteintes. Ils servent toutefois aux coupages avec de très vieux Cognac parce qu'ils conservent leur bouquet après avoir perdu tout le reste.

A Cognac, il semble, de l'avis de tout le monde, que d'ici à une douzaine d'années les V.S.O.P. auront plus de 10 ans et que les Trois-Étoiles domineront le marché. Les taux d'intérêt, les taxes, les droits de douane multiplient par 2 ou 3 le prix du Cognac dans la plupart des pays. Les négociants ne peuvent donc pas augmenter le prix déjà élevé de la bouteille en y ajoutant les frais réels de vieillissement. Le V.S.O.P. de 5 à 10 ans d'âge est déjà considéré comme une mauvaise affaire par bien des firmes.

Et maintenant, une question se pose : les petites firmes qui vendent du très vieux Cognac à une clientèle de choix pourront-elles survivre ? Il est déjà regrettable que le Trois-Étoiles des maisons de moindre importance soit chassé du marché par les campagnes publicitaires des grandes marques. Certains distillateurs estiment que, dans une génération, il ne restera plus qu'une demi-douzaine de maisons gigantesques ; les autres, tout en admettant que les marques monopoliseront le Trois-Étoiles et peut-être le V.S.O.P., n'en estiment pas moins que la demande de Cognac trop vieux pour être produit à grande échelle, suffira à faire vivre les petits négociants spécialisés dans les eaux-de-vie de luxe.

En fait de Cognac, la question du millésime est controversée. En règle générale, qui ne supporte pratiquement pas d'exception, le Cognac produit avec le vin d'un seul secteur et d'une seule année n'est pas vendu dans le commerce. On n'en trouve guère qu'à la campagne chez les bouilleurs de cru. Tous les Cognac qui se vendent sont des coupages de plusieurs crus et plusieurs récoltes. On accuse cette pratique d'écrêter les sommets pour remplir les ravins. Si c'était vrai, tous les mélanges de Cognac ne seraient que des compromis : des concessions commerciales destinées à satisfaire la demande de produits suivis. La plupart des négociants en Cognac affirment qu'il n'en est rien. Selon eux, aucun secteur de la région ne produit jamais, en aucune année, une eau-de-vie parfaitement équilibrée, complète et harmonieuse. Tout en convenant que la Grande Champagne est la meilleure région, tant pour le bouquet, la finesse et l'élégance que pour le charme, ils font remarquer que le Cognac du secteur des Borderies, qui vieillit rapidement, a un goût de violette et aussi une pointe de finesse qui manque en général à la Grande Champagne, trop lourde bien que princière.

SECTEURS GÉOGRAPHIQUES ET APPELLATIONS

Le cru en tant que tel ne joue aucun rôle en Cognac et ne figure pas sur l'étiquette. Mais il importe de connaître les secteurs dont le nom est indiqué sur les bouteilles des eaux-de-vie de classe. Le vignoble de Cognac, entre les limites duquel sont faits tous les vins destinés au Cognac, est partagé géographiquement dans les proportions suivantes :

	%
Grande Champagne	14,65
Petite Champagne	15,98
Borderies	4,53
Fins Bois	37,82
Bons Bois	22,19
Bois ordinaires	4,83

La qualité va en décroissant depuis la Grande Champagne jusqu'aux Bois ordinaires et elle donne une idée de la situation géographique du secteur : la Grande Champagne est au centre et les autres s'en éloignent en cercles concentriques ou à peu près.

Dans tous ces secteurs on produit du vin rouge dont on ne fait jamais du Cognac et des vins blancs qui ne sont pas distillés non plus. En règle générale, plus le secteur est pauvre, plus on y fait du vin qui ne devient pas du Cognac.

Grande Champagne (A.O.C.)

C'est le secteur qui produit les Cognac les plus chers et les meilleurs. Mais la différence de prix n'a aucun rapport avec celle qui existe entre les vins de Grand Cru et de moindre appellation des grandes régions vinicoles. La Grande Champagne est douée d'une remarquable finesse, de bouquet et d'élégance ; mais elle est dure en sa jeunesse et doit vieillir 15 ans ou plus ; elle a moins de corps que les Borderies, mais plus que la Petite Champagne. On l'appelle aussi Grande Fine Champagne. (« Champagne », quand ce mot ne désigne pas la province, signifie en français zone de sol crayeux).

Petite Champagne (A.O.C.)

Semblable à la Grande Champagne, sauf que ses caractéristiques se manifestent à un moindre degré et qu'elle vieillit plus rapidement. La différence est due à une teneur légèrement inférieure en craie dans le sol.

Fine Champagne et Fine Maison (A.O.C)

Vieux mélange d'eau-de-vie de Cognac et de Grande et Petite Champagne exclusivement. Le mot fine vient de l'usage français d'appeler fine « tout produit de distillation ». La Fine Maison est simplement une eau-de-vie dont un restaurant fait sa spécialité. La Fine Maison peut donc être médiocre, passable ou excellente, selon que le restaurateur aura les connaissances nécessaires et le désir d'en faire une spécialité.

Borderies (A.O.C)

Quoi qu'on en pense souvent, ce secteur ne borde pas ceux de Petite et de Grande Champagne. Il leur fait face ainsi qu'à la ville de Cognac et se trouve simplement au nord de la Charente. Les Cognac des Borderies sont les plus corsés.

Fins Bois (A.O.C.), Bons Bois (A.O.C), Bois Ordinaires (A.O.C.)

Secteurs de qualité moyenne, de plus grande superficie, mais où les vignes sont aussi denses. La zone des Fins Bois est la meilleure des trois. La plus grande partie se trouve à proximité de la côte et l'air marin a une influence sensible sur l'eau-de-vie. Les eaux-de-vie issues du secteur des Fins Bois sont la base de Cognac Trois-Étoiles.

RÉGIONS OFFICIELLES DE COGNAC : Communes ayant droit aux noms les plus importants

La région dont l'eau-de-vie a droit au nom de Cognac est divisée en six secteurs dont Grande Champagne, Petite Champagne et Borderies sont les plus importantes. Ils englobent les communes suivantes :

Grande Champagne (ou Grande Fine Champagne)

Communes : Ambleville, Angeac-Champagne, Bonneuil, Bourg-Charente (rive droite de la Charente), Bouteville, Château-

Bernard, Cognac (rive gauche de la Charente), Criteuil-Magdeleine, Éraville, Gensac-la-Pallue, Genté, Gimeux, Gondeville, Juillac-le-Coq, Lignières-Sonneville, Mainxe, Malaville, Merpins, Salles-d'Angles, Saint-Brice (rive gauche de la Charente), Saint-Fort-sur-le-Né, Saint-Même, Saint-Preuil, Segonzac, Touzac, Verrières, Viville.

Petite Champagne

Communes du département de la Charente : Angeac-Charente, Ars, Barbezieux, Barret, Birac, Bourg-Charente (rive droite), Châteauneuf, Graves, Guimps, Jurignac, Lachaise, Ladiville, Lagarde-sur-le-Né, Montchaude, Mosnac, Nonaville, Saint-Amand-de-Graves, Saint-Bonnet, Saint-Hilaire-de-Barbezieux, Saint-Médard-de-Barbezieux, Saint-Palais-du-Né, Salignac-de-Pons, Salles-de-Barbezieux, Vignolles.

Communes du département de Charente-Maritime : Allas-Champagne, Archiac, Arthenac, Biron, Bougneau, Brie-sous-Archiac, Brives-sur-Charente, Celles, Chadenac, Champagnac, Cierzac, Coulonges, Clam, Échebrune, Germignac, Jarnac-Champagne, Jonzac, Lonzac, Meux, Moings, Montils, Neuillac, Neulles, Pérignac-de-Pons, Reaux, Rouffiac, Saint-Ciers-Champagne, Saint-Eugène, Saint-Germain-de-Lusignan, Saint-Germain-de-Vibrac, Saint-Martial-de-Coculet, Saint-Marcial-de-Vitaterne, Saint-Maurice-de-Tavernoles, Saint-Lheurine, Saint-Seurin-de-Palenne, Saint-Sever.

Borderies

Communes : Burie, Chérac, Cherves, Cognac (rive droite de la Charente) Javrezac, Louzac, Saint-André, Saint-Laurent-de-Cognac, Saint-Sulpice, Richemont.

La vigne et le vin

La vigne utilisée pour le Cognac est surtout le Saint-Émilion des Charentes ou l'Ugni Blanc. Selon la loi, le Cognac des subdivisions régionales qui a droit aux noms de Grande Champagne, etc., ne peut être produit que par la distillation de vin fourni par des vignes de Folle Blanche, Colombard et Saint-Émilion. Aucun autre raisin n'est autorisé. La loi est très stricte et, depuis 1955, tout vigneron qui plante des vignes non autorisées dans son vignoble se voit refuser la totalité de sa vendange.

Désormais Colombard et Folle Blanche ne représentent plus ensemble que 6 % de l'encépagement et presque tout le reste est du Saint-Émilion : une sous-variété de l'Ugni Blanc. A Cognac, il n'y a pas directement de rapport inverse entre la qualité et la quantité. Néanmoins, pour maintenir un plus haut standard, un maximum de 100 hl/ha est imposé.

Cette particularité nous donne une indication sur les relations étranges entre vin et eau-de-vie. On dit volontiers à Cognac que la meilleure eau-de-vie est faite avec les pires vins. C'est exact dans une certaine mesure. Le vin des Charentes est âpre et ne peut guère être bu qu'avec des coquillages et, encore, si l'on n'a rien de meilleur sous la main. D'autre part, il doit être *sain*. La distillation ne supprime ni perfection ni imperfection mais au contraire les accentue. Si le vin présente un défaut, son distillat sera imbuvable. Néanmoins les vertus du vin destiné à la consommation ne sont pas les mêmes que celles des vins dont on fait le Cognac. Au point de vue technique le Saint-Émilion est une vigne de « troisième époque ». En Italie on l'appelle « Trebbiano » et en Algérie, dans le Midi et en Californie, « Ugni Blanc ». Dans ces régions plus chaudes, les raisins de « troisième époque » sont dans leur élément. Mais à Cognac, beaucoup plus au nord, ils ne mûrissent jamais parfaitement et donnent des raisins surs, de forte teneur en acide et faible teneur en alcool : ce qui convient parfaitement à la meilleure eau-de-vie du monde.

Le cycle de vie d'un Cognac

Dans la région de Cognac, la campagne doucement vallonnée, brumeuse, jouit d'un ensoleillement actinique qui contribue à donner son goût au Cognac ; 85 000 ha sont cultivés dont la moitié de la production est distillée. L'unité d'habitation n'est pas le château, mais l'enclos. Un haut mur entoure maison, cour, granges, étables, basse-cour ; il n'est coupé que par deux ouvertures voûtées qui peuvent parfois être fermées par de grandes portes de bois. A l'intérieur de ces forteresses domestiques dispersées sur le vignoble, on a un peu l'impression que le temps s'est arrêté depuis des siècles, et ce n'est peut-être pas une illusion. Aucun paysan n'est plus individualiste et indépendant que le vigneron de Cognac. Tout compte fait, il peine pour produire quelque chose de bien plus stable que le franc d'après guerre.

On apporte le raisin de la vigne et on fait le vin comme dans les autres régions. C'est le processus suivi lors de la distillation qui diffère.

On chauffe le vin dans un chaudron de cuivre posé sur son lit : un four carré en briques. Au bout d'un certain temps, les essences d'alcool s'élèvent en vapeur dans une tubulure gracieusement incurvée en col de cygne. Condensée par rafraîchissement, cette vapeur devient le brouillis : liquide d'aspect laiteux qui titre de 27 à 28°. On le distille à son tour, exactement de la même manière, mais cette fois on élimine le premier produit de la distillation, la « tête », et le dernier, la « queue », et on ne conserve que le « cœur ». C'est le Cognac en son enfance : cru, pur, incolore, titrant 70° par volume.

Quoique le temps ne semble pas agir dans ces forteresses domestiques, le mode de vie a changé comme partout ailleurs. Pendant tout l'hiver, hommes et femmes doivent veiller patiemment sur l'alambic. Les gens âgés le font plus volontiers que les jeunes. De plus en plus, les négociants sont obligés de distiller eux-mêmes parce que les fils et filles des viticulteurs ne veulent plus passer leur hiver auprès de l'alambic.

Dès sa distillation, le Cognac est versé dans un fût en chêne du Limousin qu'on ne remplit pas trop parce que le liquide doit être en contact avec l'oxygène. Ce fût est conservé à un endroit où il est soumis aux effets de la température extérieure. Théoriquement, le Cognac passe un an dans un fût neuf. Puis on le tranfère dans un autre, plus vieux, auquel il reste encore du tanin. A ce stade, il est intéressant de constater que le fût délaissé a absorbé 12 l de Cognac. Dans la pratique, pour éviter cette perte, on répartit par moitié le Cognac de l'année dans des barils neufs et des barils usagés. De cette manière l'eau-de-vie absorbe assez de tanin dans le chêne neuf sans rester trop longtemps en contact avec lui. L'idéal serait un fût fait avec le bois d'un chêne de 80 à 100 ans, qui aurait vieilli au moins cinq à six ans à l'air libre pour perdre ses tanins les plus amers. Voilà encore un des facteurs qui font passer l'élaboration du Cognac des mains du vigneron à celles du négociant. Comme nous l'avons déjà dit, on ne peut utiliser que des fûts en chêne du Limousin ou de la forêt de Tronçais dans l'Allier, encore doivent-ils auparavant passer cinq ans en plein air. Leur prix est désormais si élevé que le vigneron-distillateur a de plus en plus tendance à utiliser ses vieux fûts, et le Cognac est moins vieux.

Pendant sa maturation le Cognac subit plusieurs transformations : son volume diminue ainsi que sa teneur en alcool ; il dissout et absorbe le tanin du bois. Mais on ne constate pas, comme pour le vin, des réactions chimiques telles qu'hydrolyse et acétification. Le Cognac ne s'évente pas non plus de la même manière que le vin.

Les coupages sont toujours effectués dans les locaux des négociants. Certains de ceux-ci sont immenses et sinistres comme des prisons ; d'autres, installés dans de vieux châteaux. Les barriques des différentes eaux-de-vie sont versées sur des gouttières à l'étage au-dessus de celui où se trouve la cuve de mélange. Le liquide s'écoule et tombe dans la cuve où des pales, mues par un mécanisme, l'agitent lentement. Le coupage est fait par étapes successives séparées par de longues pauses pour laisser reposer l'alcool. Les différents Cognac se marient lentement.

Il faut un demi-siècle pour que l'évaporation réduise la teneur en alcool de 70° aux 40° qui conviennent pour expédition et consommation. Économiquement, il n'est pas possible d'attendre aussi longtemps. Il faut donc réduire artificiellement la teneur en alcool. On y procède en ajoutant de l'eau distillée, soit directement, soit indirectement. Étant donné que l'addition directe d'eau « choque » le Cognac, les meilleures firmes recourent à la méthode indirecte en ajoutant du *faible* au lieu d'eau. Ce *faible* est un Cognac dont la teneur en alcool a été réduite à 27° par addition d'eau distillée mais qu'un long repos a remis de son choc. On ne l'ajoute au mélange que petit à petit, pour n'en réduire la teneur que de 8 à 9° à chaque fois. Après chacune de ces opérations, on filtre et on laisse le Cognac se reposer.

L'addition de *faible* et les autres procédés plus compliqués accroissent l'amertume et la perte par évaporation. Voilà un des facteurs qui rend coûteuse la fabrication du Cognac. De même, la porosité des chênes du Limousin qui permet à l'eau-de-vie de vieillir permet aussi à l'air d'entrer dans le fût et aux vapeurs d'eau-de-vie de s'évaporer. La quantité d'alcool qui se dissipe dans le ciel des Charentes équivaut presque exactement à la consommation française et à un quart de la consommation mondiale de Cognac.

Les fûts dans lesquels mûrit le Cognac sont entreposés dans des chais, c'est-à-dire des bâtiments construits au-dessus de la surface du sol. On les distingue aisément à leurs murs noircis, non par de la suie, mais par une moisissure du vin. Ces fûts sont des *tierçons* qui contiennent entre 350 et 450 l chacun. Certains négociants assurent que le Cognac vieillit mieux dans de gros tonneaux et d'autres, au contraire, préfèrent les plus petits. A l'extrémité de chaque rangée se trouve le *chanteau* (généralement marqué CH) : fût dont le contenu sert à maintenir le niveau des autres. Quoiqu'elle soit coûteuse, on ne fait rien pour empêcher l'évaporation car, sans elle, il n'y aurait pas de vieillissement. Les chais sont donc ventilés.

Quand le Cognac est prêt, on le met dans des bouteilles qui ont été rincées au Cognac et dont le bouchon lui aussi a trempé dans du Cognac. Alors, la bouteille est prête à s'en aller au bout du monde.

EXPORTATION

On exporte environ 90 % du Cognac. Les États-Unis restent le plus gros client, suivis par l'Angleterre. Aucun autre produit de la terre ne rapporte à la France un revenu aussi important. Les ventes augmentent tant en Angleterre qu'aux États-Unis. 1,5 million de caisses environ dans le premier pays et plus de 2,6 millions dans le second.

Ne serait-ce que pour le transporter d'un entrepôt à l'autre du même propriétaire, tout vin ou spiritueux qui circule en France doit être accompagné d'un *acquit* ou *congé (voir ces mots),* ainsi l'administration peut en suivre tous les mouvements. Un document analogue, l'*acquit jaune d'or,* accompagne les exportations de Cognac. Conçu à l'origine pour faciliter les formalités d'exportation, ce certificat garantit en même temps les normes de l'eau-de-vie.

Cohobation, Cohober

Cohober, c'est redistiller un distillat pour augmenter sa teneur en alcool. Cette opération s'appelle cohobation.

Cointreau

Marque célèbre d'une liqueur du genre Curaçao faite à Angers et aussi aux États-Unis, par la famille Cointreau. Quoique les bouteilles et étiquettes soient identiques, la teneur en alcool varie d'un pays à l'autre. A l'origine, cette liqueur s'appelait Curaçao blanc, triple sec. Mais tant de fabricants utilisèrent la locution triple sec que la famille Cointreau donna son propre nom à sa liqueur.

Voir CURAÇAO

Colares, Collares

Hormis le Porto, le Colares est le vin le plus remarquable du Portugal. Les vignes sont cultivées sur des terrains sablonneux dominant l'Atlantique, à une cinquantaine de kilomètres de Lisbonne. Ce vin acquit sa célébrité pendant l'épidémie de phylloxéra qui dévasta les vignobles du monde entier il y a maintenant près de cent ans. Les vignes poussant sur des sols sablonneux ne furent pas atteintes et leurs vins se vendirent à des prix fabuleux, car il n'y en avait presque plus d'autres.

Le Colares murissait dans des fûts en acajou d'Angola ou des États-Unis, pendant une quinzaine d'années. Pour l'aimer, il faut en avoir l'habitude car il a un goût tellement particulier qu'il choque parfois le profane.

Voir PORTUGAL

Collage

Opération ayant pour but de clarifier le vin avant de le mettre en bouteille.

Voir CHAPITRE V : CLARIFICATION

Collage bleu

Clarification du vin avec des cristaux de ferrocyanure de potassium permettant de l'épurer du casse cuivreux. Ceci est efficace pour stabiliser les vins blancs, mais les risques d'un dosage trop fort sont tels que les pays qui l'autorisent l'ont soumis à des règlements très stricts. Le collage bleu est autorisé en Allemagne mais interdit en France et aux États-Unis. Aux États-Unis, on utilise un produit commercialisé appelé Cufex qui, tout en détruisant le casse cuivreux, donne de plus grandes garanties de sécurité.

Voir CHAPITRE V : COLLAGE

Collerette

Petite étiquette collée sur le goulot de la bouteille.

Colli Albani (D.O.C.)

Vins blancs, parfois pétillants, du Latium *(voir ce nom)*.

Colli Euganei (D.O.C.)

Vins rouges ou blancs légers du nord de la Vénétie (Italie).

Voir VÉNÉTIE

Colli Orientali del Friuli (D.O.C.)

Vins du nord-est de l'Italie.

Voir FRIOUL-VÉNÉTIE-JULIE

Collio (D.O.C.)

Vins rouge ou blanc sec légèrement pétillant, du nord de l'Italie. Ils sont également connus sous le nom de Collio Goriziano..

Voir FRIOUL-VÉNÉTIE-JULIE

Collioure (A.O.C.)

Vin rouge. Côtes de Roussillon.

L'Appellation Contrôlée de Collioure est donnée aux vins rouges « naturels » de la région de Banyuls, au nord immédiat de la frontière espagnole, sur la côte méditerranéenne. Ce vin de table ne doit pas être confondu avec l'apéritif fortifié assez doux ou vin de liqueur produit dans la même région : celui-ci possède son propre nom d'origine : Banyuls *(voir ce nom)*. Les raisins Grenache Noir et Carignane sont cultivés sur 100 ha (ce qui justifie la deuxième appellation de ce vin : Grenache de Collioure) : la production annuelle moyenne est de 2 000 hl.

Colmar

Ville vinicole d'Alsace.

Voir ALSACE

Colombard

Variété de raisin cultivée en Dauphiné où on l'appelle Bon Blanc ; en Charente on le baptise Pied-Tendre, et, dans le Tarn-et-Garonne, Blanquette.

Colombie

La vigne couvre 2 000 ha et la production atteint 38 000 hl par an de vins dont certains sont doux, d'autrés servent à la distillation. Ceux-ci s'appellent en général vermouth, muscat, ou encore, plus à tort, manzanilla, voire porto. On fait aussi quelques vins de table légers, mais ils sont également doux.

Pommes, cerises et mûres sont la principale source d'aromatisation des boissons alcooliques. La distillation est un monopole des gouvernements provinciaux. *Aguardiente* (aromatisé à l'anis), rhum, alcools du genre vodka et gin sont produits dans diverses parties du pays. Les classes les plus favorisées consomment de la vodka et le reste de la population préfère le *guarapo* et l'*Aguardiente*. Le premier est obtenu par la fermentation de canne à sucre et de citron. L'anisado est une eau-de-vie de canne à sucre parfumée aux grains d'anis. Le *guarapo* n'est pas commercialisé. Les cultivateurs de certaines régions du pays le font chez eux pour leur propre consommation. Frais il ressemble au cidre nouveau.

Comète (Vin de la)

Il arrive parfois qu'une année de bonne vendange coïncide avec l'apparition d'une comète. On sait qu'il en fut ainsi en 1630. Plus proche de nous, 1811 était plus connu et c'est à ce millésime qu'on fait allusion quand on parle de vin de la comète.

Commandaria

Vin qui a la plus grande longévité et qui est l'un des meilleurs de Chypre.

Voir CHYPRE

Commanderie du Bontemps de Médoc et de Graves (Bordeaux)

Société locale d'amateurs de vin de Médoc et de Graves qui est en réalité une organisation vouée à la promotion de ce vin. Ses membres — vignerons, négociants, notables de toutes sortes — portent des capes médiévales et de longues robes au cours de leurs réunions : banquets, cérémonies d'initiation de nouveaux membres.

Commonwealth (Vins du)

Vins des pays du Commonwealth britannique, notamment Australie, Canada et Nouvelle-Zélande *(voir ces noms)*. Ils n'ont pas la même qualité que les bons vins d'Europe, mais sont aussi moins chers. Quoique jamais exceptionnels, ils peuvent être extrêmement agréables et ce sont des breuvages bon marché.

Commune

Dans les régions de bon vin, les crus groupés sur le territoire d'une ou plusieurs communes en prennent généralement le nom comme Appellation d'Origine Contrôlée. Cela signifie qu'on leur reconnaît certaines caractéristiques similaires et que les mêmes normes de qualité leur sont imposées. A titre d'exemple citons Margaux, Saint-Julien et Saint-Émilion parmi les plus importants noms de communes servant d'Appellation d'Origine Contrôlée à des Bordeaux rouges.

Comporte

Récipient (sorte de cuveau) placé, lors des vendanges, à l'extrémité des sillons de vigne et dans lequel on verse le contenu des baquets ou des hottes.

Coñac

Appellation abusive utilisée en Espagne pour l'eau-de-vie de vin.

Voir ESPAGNE

Concord

Le raisin bleu-noir le plus cultivé dans l'est des États-Unis. Robuste et productif, il s'adapte à une variété étonnante de sols et de climats, mais ne donne que des vins extrêmement médiocres qui se vendent pourtant très bien aux États-Unis, soit en coupage, soit en vin kasher : doux, fort, et parfaitement sans intérêt. S'il a quelque célébrité, le Concord la doit à son goût et son arôme foxé (de l'anglais *fox* : renard).

Condrieu (Appellation Contrôlée)

Vin blanc, Vallée du Rhône.

Fortement parfumé et d'un goût de terroir très prononcé dû au sol granitique du vignoble, ce vin est pratiquement inconnu ailleurs que dans les parages de Condrieu. La production de vin est faible (moins de 15 000 caisses par an, fabriquées à partir de la variété Viognier). Des méthodes modernes de vinification et la mise en bouteille précoce ont donné du fruit à ce vin. Cette modernisation est due en partie à feue Mme Vve Point, propriétaire du grand restaurant La Pyramide, à Vienne, qui lança le Condrieu, vignoble blanc le plus proche de ce haut-lieu gastronomique.

Voir RHÔNE (VINS DU)

Confrérie

Association d'amateurs de vin *(voir ce mot)*.

Confréries

Diverses régions vinicoles françaises ont chacune leur propre confrérie, survivance des temps médiévaux, mais aussi organe de promotion des ventes. Leurs membres, viniculteurs et négociants, portent les costumes historiques qui leur ont été attribués lors d'une longue cérémonie d'inauguration suivie d'une fête. Certaines des confréries les plus célèbres étaient ou sont encore la Commanderie du Bontemps du Médoc et de Graves *(voir ce nom)*, la Connétablie de Guyenne, la Jurade de Saint-Émilion, les Chevaliers du Tastevin de Nuits-Saint-Georges, les Compagnons du Beaujolais, la Commanderie de Champagne de l'Ordre des Coteaux, la Confrérie des Chevaliers de la Chantepleure de Vouvray et la Confrérie Saint-Étienne, en Alsace. D'autres sont la Confrérie des Compagnons de la Capucine, de Toul, les compagnons Hauts-Normands du Gouste-Vin, le Conseil des Échansons de France, à Paris, la Commanderie des Vins et Spiritueux de France (également à Paris), le Nouvel Ordre Hospitalier, Curieux et Courtois des Chevaliers de Saint-Bacchus, à Paris, l'Ordre Bachique et Épicurien du Gay Savoir en Bien Manger et Bien Boire, les Compagnons du Pintou en Auvergne, la Confrérie Vineuse des Piliers Chablisiens, la Confrérie des Trois Ceps, dans l'Yonne, la Cousinerie de Bourgogne, la Confrérie des Vignerons de Saint-Vincent, à Mâcon, la Confrérie du Gosier-Sec de Clochemerle, dans le Beaujolais, la Confrérie des Chevaliers de la Syrah et Roussette, dans la vallée du Rhône, l'Ordre Illustre des Chevaliers de Méduse, en Côtes de Provence, la Confrérie des Échansons de Vidauban, la Confrérie des Comtes de Nice et de Provence, l'Échansonnerie des papes, à Châteauneuf-du-Pape, la Commanderie de Tavel, l'Ordre de la Boisson de la Stricte Observance des Costières du Gard, Antica Confraria de Saint-Andu de la Galiniera, dans l'Hérault, le Consulat de Septimanie, dans les Coteaux du Languedoc, l'Illustre Cour des Seigneurs de la Corbière, la Commende Majeure de Roussillon pour Garder le Devoir et le Droit de la Vigne et du Vin, l'Ordre de la Dive Bouteille, à Gaillac, la Confrérie du Vin de Cahors, La Viguerie Royale du Jurançon, la Viguerie du Madiran, la Commanderie des Chevaliers de Tursan, le Grand Conseil de Bordeaux, l'Académie du Vin de Bordeaux, les Compagnons de Bordeaux, le Club des Amis du Vin de Bordeaux, la Commanderie du Bontemps de Sauternes et Barsac, la Commanderie du Bontemps de Sainte-Croix-du-Mont, les Compagnons du Loupiac, la Confrérie des Hospitaliers de Pomerol, les Gentilshommes de Fronsac, le Consulat de la Vinée de Bergerac, la Principauté de Franc-Pineau, en Charentes, l'Ordre des Chevaliers Bretvins, la Confrérie des Chevaliers du Sacavin, en Anjou, la Confrérie des Vignerons de la Canette, à Bouille-Loretz (Deux-Sèvres), la Confrérie des Vins Gousiers d'Anjou, la Commanderie du Taste-Saumur, la Confrérie des Hume-Piot du Loudonois, la Confrérie Vineuse de Tiré-Douzils, dans le Poitou, les Entonneurs Rabelaisiens, à Chinon, la Confrérie des Fripe-Douzils, à Bourgueil, la Confrérie des Chevaliers des Cuers du Baril, en Touraine, la Coterie des Closiers de Montlouis, la Commanderie des Grands vins d'Amboise, la Confrérie des Compagnons de Grandgousier, la Confrérie des Baillis de Pouilly-sur-Loire, le Collège des Chanoines de Tannay, les Chevaliers de Sancerre, la Compagnie des Vignerons d'Honneur, la Compagnie d'Honneur des Sorciers et Birettes, en Anjou, la Confrérie des Chevaliers du Cep, à Verdigny, l'Ordre des Chevaliers du Paissiau, la Maîtrise des Échansons à Reuilly, le Cercle des Chevaliers du Cep, à Châteauroux, l'Ordre des Vins Palais, à Saint-Pourçain, la Confrérie des Compagnons du Bousset d'Auvergne, la Confrérie de Saint-Verny, la Confrérie de Bacchus et d'Icare, à Lyon, la Compagnie du Sarto, en Savoie, la Commanderie des Nobles Vins du Jura et Gruyère de Comté, et la Pairie des Vins d'Arbois. Il existe également des confréries consacrées aux grandes eaux-de-vie de vin françaises : la Confrérie des Alambics Charentais, à Cognac ; et la Compagnie des Mousquetaires d'Armagnac, à Condom.

En Suisse, on trouve la Confrérie des Vignolants de Neufchâtel, l'Ordre de la Channe, et la Confrérie de Guillon ; en Belgique, la Gilde de Saint-Vincent de Belgique et la Confrérie des Chevaliers Rabelaisiens de Belgique ; en Italie, la Confraternita della Cheer, Les Cavaliers d'Asti et de Montferrato, et la Confraternita d'la Tripa. Il y a plusieurs confréries aux États-Unis dont le Universal Order of the Knights of the Vine of California.

Congé

Document officiel français qui accompagne tous les transports de vins et spiritueux pour indiquer que les taxes ont été payées. On s'en sert pour envoyer vins et alcools aux détaillants et aux consommateurs, sur le territoire du pays, mais pas à l'exportation.

Il y a six types différents de congés qui se distinguent par leurs initiales et leur couleur.

Les transports de boissons sur lesquelles les taxes n'ont pas été payées sont accompagnés d'un acquit *(voir ce mot)*.

Congénères, Congénériques

On appelle caractéristiques congénères de goût et d'arôme celles que le distillat reçoit de la matière distillée. Plus la distillation est poussée, moins le spiritueux conservera de caractéristiques congénères et plus il deviendra neutre, c'est-à-dire insipide et inodore. (On peut dire congénère ou congénérique.)

Connétablie de Guyenne

Société qui se consacre à la promotion des vins blancs doux de Bordeaux. Leurs membres se réclament des connétables de Bordeaux qui, au Moyen Age, estimaient les vins traversant le fleuve et décidaient s'ils étaient dignes d'être livrés au commerce.

Voir PREMIÈRES CÔTES DE BORDEAUX

Conseillante (Château-La-)

Bordeaux rouge. Commune de Pomerol.

Seul un chemin charretier sépare les vignobles de ce grand cru de Pomerol — appartenant à la famille Nicolas depuis 1871 — de ceux de Château-Cheval-Blanc à Saint-Émilion. C'est l'un des vignobles les plus respectés de Pomerol.

Superficie : 11 ha.

Production moyenne : 4 000 caisses.

Consorzio

Nom italien d'associations de vignerons et négociants qui s'efforcent de promouvoir un contrôle des appellations d'origine des vins. L'adhésion est volontaire et les membres s'imposent de respecter les délimitations géographiques ainsi que certaines normes minimales de qualité. A ces conditions, ils ont le droit d'apposer le sceau de leur consorzio sur le goulot de leurs bouteilles. Ces labels de l'association sont numérotés et chaque consorzio à son label.

Voir un bref exposé sur les consorzi à ITALIE, et sur la manière dont fonctionne un consorzio type, à TOSCANE.

Constantia

Célèbres vins du Cap, déjà exportés par l'Afrique du Sud au début du XIXe siècle.

Voir AFRIQUE DU SUD

Coopérative

Centre vinificateur ou cave possédés et gérés en commun. Cette pratique est courante en Europe comme dans le reste du monde. La coopérative démarre généralement à petite échelle, entre quelques producteurs qui ont besoin du coûteux équipement indispensable à la production et à la commercialisation de leurs vins. Certaines coopératives restent toujours modestes d'envergure, mais d'autres sont parmi les plus grands centres vinificateurs du monde.

Corbières (Appellation Contrôlée)

Les Corbières sont la dernière région de vignobles de la province du Languedoc, avant le début des vignobles du Roussillon. Au nord, ses 13 000 ha de vignes s'étirent de Narbonne à la proche cité fortifiée de Carcassonne, et au sud, jusqu'à la bordure nord du Roussillon. En 1986, les vins de Corbières réussirent à être promus du rang de V.D.Q.S. (Vins Délimités de Qualité Supérieure) au rang d'Appellation d'Origine Contrôlée ; environ 500 000 hl sont produits annuellement, dont 95 % de vin rouge, 4 % de rosé et 1 % de blanc.

Les Corbières se divisent approximativement en deux types de terrains de vignobles : d'abord, la vaste plaine plate située au nord et à l'ouest de Narbonne, de chaque côté de l'autoroute de Carcassonne, qui, plus au sud, donne les vins les moins bons de la région. La région des *coteaux*, au sud et au sud-ouest de Narbonne, a des sols plus légers et un microclimat plus frais que les vignobles de la plaine et les vins sont en conséquence supérieurs. Les sols riches en ardoise des villages de vignobles tels ceux de Castelmaure, Cascastel, Tuchan, Bizanet, Embresset-Castelmaure et Cucugnan, font des vins pleins, avec du corps, et d'une qualité bien supérieure à la moyenne, souvent banale.

Quelques-uns parmi les meilleurs villages ont fait des efforts intenses, par l'intermédiaire des collectivités agricoles locales, pour améliorer la qualité, en remplaçant les variétés de raisins les plus pauvres (comme l'Aramond), et en perfectionnant les variétés semblables au Carignan qui est le raisin prédominant. Des expériences effectuées à partir de meilleurs raisins, peu typiques du Languedoc, ont grandement contribué à la qualité des vins de Corbières. Le Syrah du Rhône, le Mourvèdre et le Merlot ont donné de bons résultats et ont permis d'améliorer les vins. La *macération carbonique*, une technique utilisée pour rehausser l'arôme et la vinosité des vins, a également relevé la qualité.

Certains villages ont obtenu des subventions du gouvernement pour améliorer les méthodes de production et de vinification. Parmi ces améliorations : la réunion de parcelles de vignobles disparates afin d'obtenir une plus grande mécanisation pour une meilleure efficacité ; l'amélioration de l'équipement et la technique des cuveries.

Une autre évolution de nature à changer le profil des Corbières est l'accroissement des petits domaines dirigés par des cultivateurs qui veulent faire des vins de Corbières des vins de haute qualité. Une récolte limitée, une vinification experte, et un vieillissement en tonneau avant la mise en bouteilles, ont produit un bon nombre de vins avec du corps et un fruité remarquable. Parmi les meilleurs domaines on peut citer Château-Beauregard, Domaine Fontsainte, Domaine des Ollieux, Domaine Saint-Maurice, Domaine Montjoie, Domaine de Villemajou, Domaine de la Voulte, Le Prieuré de Saint-Amand, Château des Palais, Château de Cabriac et Domaine Saint-Joseph.

Cordial

Breuvage à base d'alcool, additionné de fruits ou de substances aromatiques suivant diverses méthodes : macération, infusion ou simple mélange. Il est toujours sucré. Ce mot est presque devenu synonyme de liqueur.

Cordon

Méthode de taille de la vigne consistant à incliner le cep pour qu'il pousse aussi parallèlement que possible au sol. A cet effet, il est soutenu par du fil métallique ou par un tuteur. Les vignes donnant des vins de certaines appellations contrôlées sont soumises à une réglementation portant sur le nombre de sarments verticaux ascendants ou descendants, ainsi que sur le nombre de bourgeons de chaque flèche sarment.

Voir CHAPITRE IV

Cornas (A.O.C.)

Vin rouge. Vallée du Rhône.

Le Cornas n'est jamais grand, il est souvent bon et rarement cher. C'est un rouge fait avec du raisin Syrah. Il possède les caractéristiques que l'on attend en général des vins du Rhône, mais avec moins d'exubérance que ses voisins (l'Hermitage par exemple). Par rapport à son prix, sa qualité en fait une bonne affaire.

Comme souvent dans les Côtes du Rhône, les vignes sont cultivées sur des terrasses aménagées à flanc de collines tellement abruptes que l'usage du tracteur y est impossible et que tout travail doit être fait à la main. Le vignoble de Cornas est assez vaste pour fournir jusqu'à 2 500 hl par an (plus de 25 000 caisses).

Coronata

Vin italien léger et clair.

Voir LIGURIE

Corps, corsé

Le vin qui a du corps emplit la bouche, c'est-à-dire que la sensation du goût d'une seule goutte de ce vin est perçue par la bouche entière. Cette caractéristique est donnée par l'alcool et le tanin. Tous les grands vins ont du corps, à l'exception de quelques grands blancs comme ceux de la Moselle. Dans leur jeunesse, les grands vins sont souvent trop corsés, mais quand leur vieillissement évolue ils deviennent d'une rondeur charnue. Un vin très corsé est dit charnu.

Corse

Le climat de celle île (département français) est presque idéal pour la culture de la vigne. Malheureusement, sur ses 8 540 km², seuls 12 000 ha sont plantés de vignes.

Les vins de ces vignes n'atteignent pas un quelconque degré de qualité, sauf ceux qui proviennent des environs d'Ajaccio, de Sartène et de Patrimonio. La plupart des vins corses sont rudes et vulgaires, vinifiés au petit bonheur et mal soignés mais des progrès notables ont été faits. De gros apports de capitaux et l'immigration de centaines de pieds-noirs courageux et compétents venus d'Algérie en 1960 ont aidé à la plantation de près de 1 500 ha en appliquant des méthodes modernes. Mais ces vignes essentiellement plantées dans la plaine orientale et destinées à produire des vins de table ont été pour la plupart arrachées. Une grande quantité du vin est bue par les touristes qui envahissent la Corse pendant les vacances d'été et qui pourtant s'intéressent plus à la beauté sauvage du décor qu'aux crus du pays.

Parmi les meilleurs vins blancs de l'île, citons cependant ceux du cap Corse : la péninsule qui fait face à la Côte d'Azur. Les Corses ne manquent pas de dire que Napoléon Bonaparte, dont les parents avaient une vigne à Ajaccio, préférait le vin corse à tous autres.

Cette péninsule a aussi donné son nom à un des principaux articles d'exportation corses : un vin de liqueur bu en apéritif dont la France consomme quelque 4 000 hl par an : le Cap Corse.

Les autres vins, surtout blancs, viennent du voisinage de Corte, au centre de l'île (rouges et blancs), de Cauro (blancs et rosés), et des villes méridionales de Sartène, Santa-Lucia-di-Tallano, Bonifacio (rouges et blancs). Les meilleurs vins de Corse sont les vins d'Ajaccio et Patrimonio, ces deux appellations ayant été récemment promues au rang de Grand Cru. Le Cru Ajaccio doit à son cépage le Sciaccarello une originalité certaine ; au Domaine Péraldi, le comte de Poix fait à partir de ce cépage le vin rouge le plus prometteur, si ce n'est le meilleur, de l'île. Tous ont un goût caractéristique et une teneur en alcool souvent supérieure à celle qu'en attend le consommateur sans expérience. On les compare souvent à ceux des Côtes du Rhône et des Côtes de Provence, mais ils sont généralement moins bons.

La plupart des vignes cultivées dans le nord de l'île sont d'origine italienne, notamment : Niellucio (le Sangiovèse italien), Moscata, Aleatico, Vermentino (de la famille Malvoisie), Genovese, Biancone et Biancolella. Dans le sud et notamment à Ajaccio le cépage dominant pour les rouges et rosés est le Sciaccarello, d'origine inconnue. La plus grande partie du vin est consommée sur place et on peut évaluer la production aux environs de 900 000 hl dont 70 000 hl en Appellation Contrôlée (770 000 caisses).

Cortaillod

Le meilleur vin rouge de Neuchâtel. Son vignoble le plus connu s'appelle Cru de la Vigne du Diable.

Voir SUISSE

Cortese

Raisin blanc d'Italie qui donne un vin sec et léger : Cortese dell'Alto Monferrato (D.O.C).

Voir PIÉMONT

Corton (Appellation Contrôlée)

Bourgogne rouge et blanc. Commune d'Aloxe-Corton, en Côte de Beaune. Classement officiel : Grand Cru.

En partant de la petite ville d'Aloxe (prononcer Alosse), la route des vignobles sinue vers Beaune. Ce petit secteur produit les meilleurs vins rouges de la Côte de Beaune. Ses crus les plus réputés sont : Corton, Corton-Bressandes et Corton-Clos du Roi. On y fait aussi un grand vin blanc plus vigoureux, élégant et parfumé que le Meursault au sud : c'est le Corton-Charlemagne, un des Grands Crus blancs de la Côte de Beaune.

Comme presque tous ceux de Bourgogne, les vignobles de Corton sont morcelés et certaines des plus grandes parcelles appartiennent à l'excellent négociant Louis Latour et au prince de Mérode. Les vins de cinq parcelles d'Aloxe sont vendus aux enchères aux Hospices de Beaune comme Cuvée du Dr Peste et Cuvée Charlotte-Dumay, en l'honneur de ceux qui donnèrent les vignes aux Hospices. Sur les étiquettes, le grand nom de Corton précède celui du cru : Corton-Bressandes, Corton-Clos du Roi et Corton-Charlemagne. Les grands vins prennent les noms des vignobles célèbres plutôt que celui de la commune. Le Corton s'étend sur à peu près 78 ha. Environ 1/3 de la production est du blanc.

Corton-Charlemagne (Appellation Contrôlée)

Bourgogne blanc. Commune d'Aloxe-Corton, en Côte de Beaune. Classement officiel : Grand Cru.

Voilà un des grands Bourgogne blancs. Quand il jouit de la plénitude de ses qualités, il est de la classe de l'illustre Montrachet. Étant donné que la production est minime par comparaison à la demande mondiale, le Corton-Charlemagne est rare. Riche, de grande race, moins moelleux que les Meursault blancs, il a une fermeté d'acier. Il fut un temps où les secteurs de moindre importance pouvaient être plantés en Aligoté, mais désormais les normes ne tolèrent plus que le noble Chardonnay.

Le vignoble est partagé en trois parts : deux des principaux propriétaires sont les estimables négociants Louis Latour et Louis Jadot ; le reste appartient à environ une demi-douzaine d'excellents vignerons dont le mieux pourvu produit environ 200 caisses et celui qui possède la moins grande surface, 14 caisses seulement. Malheureusement ce vin splendide, d'une couleur dorée, se raréfie. Les vignes sont plantées sur un coteau si incliné qu'elles devaient être traitées à la main et, après les fortes pluies, il fallait remonter de la terre à dos d'homme car ni chevaux ni bœufs ne pouvaient le faire. Ce travail de forçat n'a pas d'attraits pour les enfants de vigneron, même si le problème semble en partie résolu par l'emploi de tracteurs.

Voir ALOXE-CORTON

Cos d'Estournel (Château-)

Bordeaux rouge. Commune de Saint-Estèphe, en Haut-Médoc.

Ce château appartient à Bruno Prats propriétaire de Château-Petit-Village.

Les vignes sont plantées juste en face de Château-Lafite de l'autre côté de la route des vignobles qui sépare Pauillac de Saint-Estèphe. Classé Second Cru en 1855, Cos d'Estournel est selon toute évidence un des plus grands de la catégorie. Il a les qualités typiques du Saint-Estèphe : grandeur, vigueur et finesse.

Sous l'habile direction de Bruno Prats (petit-fils de M. Fernand Ginestet) il est devenu l'un des plus populaires parmi les crus classés du Médoc. Selon M. Bernard Ginestet, les Chevaliers du Temple donnèrent au vignoble le nom de Cos à leur retour des Croisades qui les avaient amenés à Rhodes et à l'île voisine de Cos. Selon M. Prats, ce nom proviendrait d'une déformation phonétique de « Caux » comme l'indique une carte du XVIIe siècle. Les vignes sont plantées assez haut, au-dessus de Pauillac, et le château proprement dit — charmante fantaisie gothique et chinoise, unique dans le Médoc — domine le décor. Pendant la guerre, les petites pagodes qui ornent le mur de la propriété étaient occupées par des batteries antiaériennes allemandes. Elles furent alors détruites puis restaurées par la suite. Les propriétaires actuels ont donné son aspect exotique au château en ajoutant à l'entrée principale une porte sculptée ayant appartenu jadis au sultan de Zanzibar. Bruno Prats possède aussi à 1 500 m de Cos, toujours sur la commune de Saint-Estèphe, le ravissant château Marbuzet.

Caractéristiques : Les qualités de ce vin reflètent la situation du cru : à mi-chemin entre Saint-Estèphe et Pauillac. Il est plus léger et plus souple que les autres Saint-Estèphe tout en restant charnu et riche et surtout excellent en finesse.

Superficie : 65 ha.

Production moyenne : 250 tonneaux (25 000 caisses).

Cos Labory (Château-)

Bordeaux rouge. Commune de Saint-Estèphe, en Haut-Médoc.

Seul Cinquième Cru de Saint-Estèphe

selon la classification de 1855, Cos Labory est très bien situé sur les hautes collines en pente douce qui séparent Pauillac de Saint-Estèphe. Ses deux plus proches voisins sont Château-Lafite à Pauillac et Château-Cos d'Estournel à Saint-Estèphe. Autrefois, les deux Cos appartenaient au même propriétaire : M. Martyn, de Londres. Désormais, Labory appartient à Cécile Audoy, assistée de son fils Bernard.

Caractéristiques : Bon vin sans atteindre la qualité de la plupart des autres Grands Crus classés de Saint-Estèphe et de ses voisins.

Superficie : 15 ha.

Production moyenne : 60 tonneaux (6 000 caisses).

Cosecha

En espagnol : récolte et vendange ou millésime. Les vins espagnols portent l'indication : *Cosecha 1982, cosecha 1987...*

Costière du Gard (Appellation Contrôlée)

Vins rouges, rosés ou blancs produits dans 24 communes du département du Gard. Ces vins doivent titrer 11° minimum. Les 3 450 hectares produisent 2 millions de caisses annuellement.

Voir V.D.Q.S.

Cot

Autre nom de cépage Malbec aussi appelé Pied-Rouge, Cahors, etc.

Côte

Flanc de colline. En fait d'appellation, le mot Côte — Côtes du Rhône, Côte de Nuits, etc. — désigne en général des vins de qualité moindre que Clos, Château ou toute autre indication précise de cru.

Côte de Beaune (Appellation Contrôlée)

Bourgogne rouges et blancs. Département de la Côte-d'Or.

Quoique 80 % des 150 000 hl produits par an soient des rouges, cette côte est surtout célèbre pour ses blancs secs dont les plus grands proviennent de l'extrémité méridionale dite familièrement, mais non officiellement, Côte de Meursault ou Côte des Blancs. En réalité, on fait du blanc et du rouge partout en Côte de Beaune et les uns comme les autres peuvent être remarquables.

La Côte de Beaune est la moitié méridionale et basse du département de la Côte-d'Or. Elle commence à Ladoix à proximité de la fin de la Côte de Nuits et s'étend sur moins de 25 km jusque vers Santenay. Elle doit son nom à la ville principale, Beaune, « capitale des vins de Bourgogne », nom aussi familier aux négociants, importateurs et exportateurs de vin, que Chicago aux fabricants de conserves de viande. Ce mot est simple et même les langues les plus opiniâtrement réfractaires à la prononciation française le disent aisément alors que d'autres appellations d'origine bourguignonnes leur paraissent rébarbatives. Selon une histoire, d'ailleurs assez controversée, un grand marchand de vins londonien donnait comme première leçon à ses apprentis l'avis catégorique suivant : « Il y a deux sortes de Bourgogne : le Beaune et le reste. Nous vendons du Beaune. » Néanmoins tout le Côte de Beaune n'est pas du Beaune.

La côte englobe 19 communes dont les vins vont de l'ordinaire à l'incomparable et sont commercialisés sous des noms divers. Certaines bouteilles ne portent que le seul nom d'un cru exceptionnel. C'est une indication précise. Elle signifie que le vin a été fait avec des raisins cultivés dans le seul vignoble qui porte ce nom, que les autorités le considèrent comme un des plus grands Bourgogne et qu'il est conforme à des normes de qualité appropriées au nom. Il n'y a que huit crus de cette catégorie en Côte de Beaune. Légèrement au-dessous dans la hiérarchie des Appellations Contrôlées viennent les vins qui portent le nom de la commune, suivi par celui d'un vignoble. Leurs normes minimales de qualité sont légèrement moins sévères que celles des précédents. Mais souvent il est impossible de déceler la différence et dans bien des cas ces vins égalent ou surpassent leurs compagnons de cave plus renommés. Les vins les moins racés de cette côte sont vendus avec le seul nom de la commune et rien d'autre. Cette hiérarchie est conforme aux règles générales du système d'Appella-

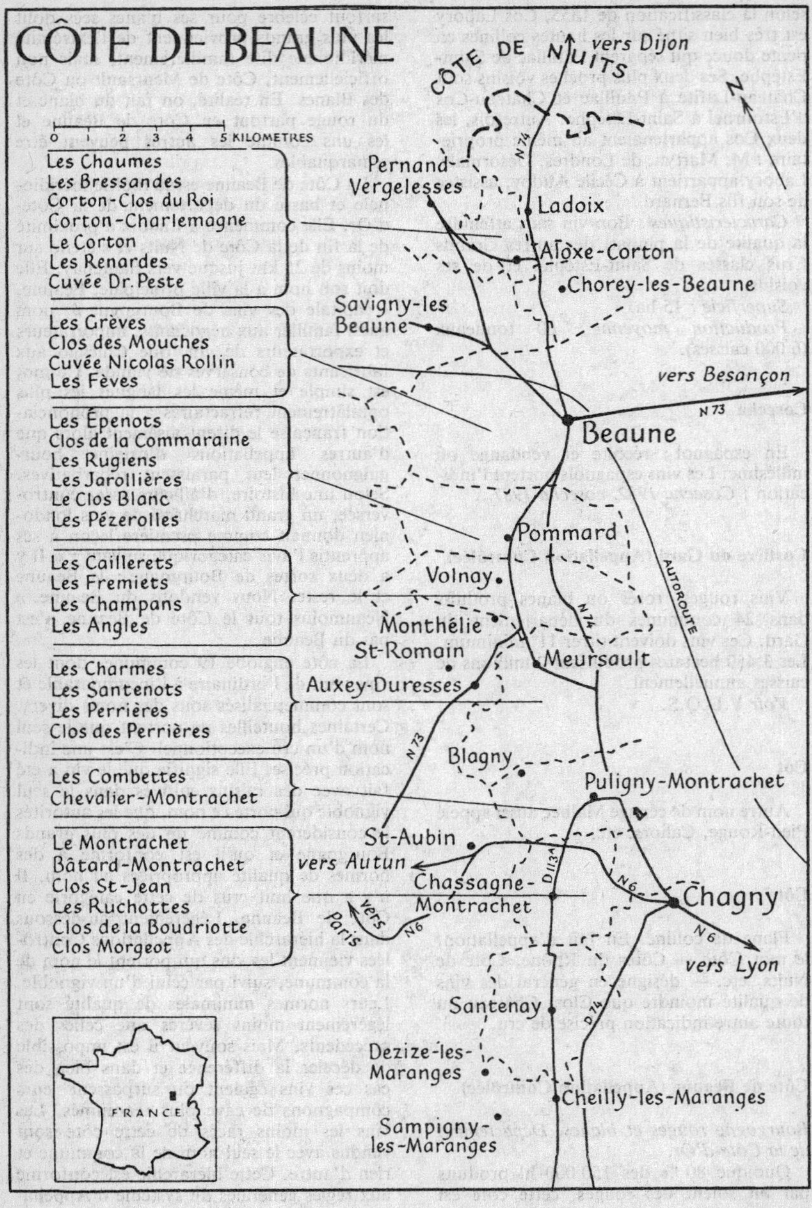
CÔTE DE BEAUNE
0 1 2 3 4 5 KILOMETRES
Les Chaumes
Les Bressandes
Corton-Clos du Roi
Corton-Charlemagne
Le Corton
Les Renardes
Cuvée Dr. Peste
Les Grèves
Clos des Mouches
Cuvée Nicolas Rollin
Les Fèves
Les Épenots
Clos de la Commaraine
Les Rugiens
Les Jarollières
Le Clos Blanc
Les Pézerolles
Les Caillerets
Les Fremiets
Les Champans
Les Angles
Les Charmes
Les Santenots
Les Perrières
Clos des Perrières
Les Combettes
Chevalier-Montrachet
Le Montrachet
Bâtard-Montrachet
Clos St-Jean
Les Ruchottes
Clos de la Boudriotte
Clos Morgeot
FRANCE
CÔTE DE NUITS
vers Dijon
N
N74
Pernand-Vergelesses
Ladoix
Aloxe-Corton
Chorey-les-Beaune
Savigny-les Beaune
vers Besançon
N73
Beaune
Pommard
Volnay
AUTOROUTE
N74
Monthélie
St-Romain
Meursault
Auxey-Duresses
N73
Blagny
Puligny-Montrachet
St-Aubin
vers Autun
D113A
Chassagne-Montrachet
N6
Chagny
vers Paris
N6
N6
vers Lyon
Santenay
D74
Dezize-les-Maranges
Cheilly-les-Maranges
Sampigny-les-Maranges

tion d'Origine Contrôlée. Mais il faut toujours compter avec certaines variantes et exceptions.

On trouvera parfois des bouteilles portant le mot « Cuvée » suivie par un nom de personne. Cette indication signifie que le vin provient des Hospices de Beaune ou de l'Hôpital de la Charité et qu'il a été fait avec les raisins d'un vignoble offert par la personne dont le nom est indiqué sur l'étiquette *(voir* HOSPICES DE BEAUNE*)*.

Lorsque ce vin arrive au consommateur, il est en général beaucoup plus cher que n'importe lequel de ses pairs, et même parfois trop cher. Les enchères annuelles des Hospices de Beaune ont lieu le troisième dimanche de novembre, et servent de critère traditionnel pour établir le barème des prix de toute la Côte-d'Or. L'acheteur se consolera parce qu'il aura le plaisir de consommer un très bon vin et d'avoir contribué à une œuvre de charité. Mais il arrive parfois, hélas ! que des étiquettes soient falsifiées.

Certaines étiquettes portent aussi l'appellation Côte de Beaune-Villages. Elles indiquent que le contenu de la bouteille est un mélange de vin produit dans deux communes ou plus de la côte. Il arrive rarement qu'une étiquette donne le nom de la commune suivi par la mention Côte de Beaune. Ces derniers mots n'ont guère de sens et le vin entre dans la catégorie de ceux qui portent seulement le nom de la commune.

Comme partout en Bourgogne, il est difficile de généraliser au sujet des Côte de Beaune. La plupart des rouges sont assez légers, délicats, très parfumés et vieillissent vite. Encore faut-il faire exception pour le Corton rouge de la commune d'Aloxe-Corton : vin noble et charnu, d'un rouge à la fois resplendissant et profond, l'un de ceux qui durent le plus longtemps de toute la Bourgogne. Les blancs sont toujours secs, mais il y a tout un monde de différence entre les grands blancs d'Aloxe-Corton, à l'extrémité nord de la côte, et ceux de la Côte de Meursault, au sud. Même sur cette dernière (qui n'est pas une Appellation Contrôlée, répétons-le), le Meursault diffère nettement du Puligny-Montrachet et de son voisin Chassagne-Montrachet : le premier tend vers une délicatesse féminine et le second vers la virilité. Pourtant ils sont tous faits avec les mêmes raisins et sensiblement de la même manière. A lui seul ce détail suffirait à montrer pourquoi les vins de Bourgogne portent tant de noms différents. Deux vignes de la même variété, en effet, plantées à quelques centaines de mètres l'une de l'autre, ne donneront pas des fruits identiques.

S'il fallait résumer les caractéristiques des Côte de Beaune on dirait ceci : arrivés à leur plein épanouissement les blancs ne sont égalés nulle part au monde ; quant aux rouges, ils le cèdent en excellence à leurs frères de Côte de Nuits.

Le sol en Côte de Beaune

Au point de vue géologique, le sol comprend trois éléments distincts remontant à différentes phases du jurassique ; mais deux seulement importent au point de vue du vin. Le sol de la période bathonienne, consistant en une base de roche dure couverte d'une mince couche de terre, parfois de la marne blanchâtre, se trouve dans une certaine mesure dans les secteurs de Beaune et de Pommard. La marne blanche prend plus d'importance sur la Côte de Meursault où elle constitue le sol qui convient le mieux aux raisins destinés à faire du vin blanc. Le sol de l'ère oxfordienne a tendance à accumuler au pied du coteau des oolithes riches en fer ; les raisins qui y sont cultivés donnent des vins rouges au bouquet prononcé. Au fur et à mesure que l'on s'élève sur ces mêmes coteaux, le sol tourne au grisâtre ; son contenu argileux augmente et les raisins donnent après fermentation des vins prodigieux quant à la finesse, l'élégance, la richesse et le corps ; le tout magnifiquement équilibré. Le Corton en est le meilleur exemple. Même aux endroits où le sol est le plus gris, il conserve la proportion de fer qui donne un goût caractéristique aux rouges.

Il résulte de ce qui précède que la couleur du sol elle-même indique celle du vin qui réussira le mieux sur le terrain. Nulle part ailleurs au monde la différence n'apparaît d'une manière aussi spectaculaire.

Normes légales des vins

Comme tous les autres vins français d'Appellation Contrôlée, les Côte de Beaune doivent atteindre certaines normes minimales pour avoir droit à une appellation d'origine. Elles varient en fonction du lieu où est cultivée la vigne. Six vignobles seulement ont droit de ne porter que le seul nom du cru avec la mention Grand Cru, à condition de se conformer aux normes exigées. (Ils sont marqués d'un astérisque dans la liste qui suit.) Les autres sont des Premiers Crus ou des vins communaux selon qu'ils proviennent des meilleurs vignobles ou de n'importe quelle vigne cultivée sur le territoire de la commune. Le vin qui ne se conforme pas aux normes de son appellation tombe dans la catégorie immédiatement inférieure. Mais s'il peut y avoir déclassement, il n'y a jamais de promotion. Sans modification du classement officiel, aucun Premier Cru ne peut être vendu comme Grand Cru, quelle que soit son excellence.

Voici les normes donnant droit aux Appellations d'Origine Contrôlée.

Vins rouges

Grands Crus

1. Le vin ne doit être fait qu'avec du Pinot Noir, Pinot Liebault et Pinot Beurot. Une proportion de 15 % au maximum de Pinot Blanc et de Chardonnay est tolérée, à la discrétion de celui qui fait le vin.
2. La production ne doit pas dépasser 50 hl/ha.
3. Chaque année un quota spécial est défini et déterminé par la quantité et la qualité de la vendange.

Premiers Crus

1. Mêmes variétés de raisin que pour les Grands Crus.
2. Production limitée à 35 hl/ha.
3. Teneur minimale en alcool : 11°.

Vins communaux

1. Mêmes variétés de raisin que pour les appellations précédentes.
2. Production limitée à 50 hl/ha.
3. Teneur minimale en alcool : 10,5°.

Vins blancs

Grands Crus

1. Ces vins ne doivent être faits qu'avec du Chardonnay (dit aussi Beaunois et Aubaine), à l'exclusion de tout autre raisin.
2. Production maximale : 50 hl/ha.
3. Suite à la demande importante de vins de Bourgogne blancs, le quota de 50 hl/ha est changé en fonction de la vendange.

Premiers Crus

1. Cépage : Chardonnay exclusivement.
2. Production maximale : 35 hl/ha.
3. Teneur minimale en alcool : 11,5°.

Vins communaux

1. Cépage : Chardonnay exclusivement.
2. Production maximale : 50 hl/ha.
3. Titre minimal 11°.

Crus les plus réputés - Vins rouges

Cru	*Commune*
Le Corton*	Aloxe-Corton
Le Clos du Roi	Aloxe-Corton
Les Renardes	Aloxe-Corton
Les Chaumes	Aloxe-Corton
Les Bressandes	Aloxe-Corton
Clos Saint-Jean	Chassagne-Montrachet
Clos de la Boudriotte	Chassagne-Montrachet
Clos Morgeot	Chassagne-Montrachet
Les Vergelesses	Savigny-lès-Beaune
Les Marconnets	Savigny-lès-Beaune
Les Santenots	Meursault
Les Fèves	Beaune
Les Grèves	Beaune
Les Marconnets	Beaune
Les Bressandes	Beaune
Les Clos des Mouches	Beaune
Aux Cras	Beaune
Les Champimonts	Beaune
Les Épenots	Pommard
Les Rugiens	Pommard
Les Jarollières	Pommard
Le Clos Blanc	Pommard
Les Pézerolles	Pommard
Clos-de-la-Commaraine	Pommard
Les Caillerets	Volnay
Les Champans	Volnay
Les Fremiets	Volnay
Les Angles	Volnay

CRUS LES PLUS RÉPUTÉS - VINS BLANCS

Cru	*Commune*
Le Montrachet* *(en partie)*	Puligny-Montrachet
Le Montrachet* *(en partie)*	Chassagne-Montrachet
Chevalier-Montrachet*	Puligny-Montrachet
Bâtard-Montrachet* *(en partie)*	Puligny-Montrachet
Bâtard-Montrachet* *(en partie)*	Chassagne-Montrachet
Bienvenue-Bâtard-Montrachet*	Puligny-Montrachet
Criots-Bâtard-Montrachet*	Chassagne-Montrachet
Les Combettes	Puligny-Montrachet
Les Pucelles	Puligny-Montrachet
Les Chalumeaux	Puligny-Montrachet
Blagny-Blanc	Puligny-Montrachet
Les Grands Ruchottes	Chassagne-Montrachet
Clos des Perrières	Meursault
Les Perrières	Meursault
Les Charmes	Meursault
Les Genevrières	Meursault
Corton-Charlemagne	Aloxe-Corton
Le Corton	Aloxe-Corton

Voir à leur place dans l'ordre alphabétique : ALOXE-CORTON ; SAVIGNY-LÈS-BEAUNE ; BEAUNE ; POMMARD ; VOLNAY ; CHASSAGNE-MONTRACHET ; PULIGNY-MONTRACHET ; MEURSAULT. *Voir aussi les communes de :* PERNAND-VERGELESSES ; LADOIX-SERRIGNY ; CHOREY-LÈS-BEAUNE ; SAINT-ROMAIN ; MONTHELIE ; AUXEY-DURESSES ; SAINT-AUBIN ; SANTENAY ; DEZIZE-LÈS-MARANGES ; SAMPIGNY-LÈS-MARANGES ; CHEILLY-LÈS-MARANGES.

Côte de Beaune-Villages (Appellation Contrôlée)

Appellation d'origne très générale de certains vins de Bourgogne. Pour y avoir droit, le vin doit être issu d'une des localités énumérées ci-dessous et titrer 10,5° minimum. Le mélange de deux ou plusieurs communes ne lui fait pas perdre son appellation. La production de ces vins varie considérablement d'année en année, au gré des négociants qui effectuent les coupages et en fonction de la récolte des communes en question. Les écarts vont presque du simple au double ; par exemple : 5 000 hl à 7 000 hl. Voici les localités dont le vin a droit à cette appellation d'origine :

Auxey-Duresses	Meursault-Blagny
Blagny	Monthélie
Chassagne-Montrachet	Pernand-Vergelesses
Cheilly-lès-Maranges	Puligny-Montrachet
Chorey-lès-Beaune	Saint-Aubin
Côte de Beaune	Saint-Romain
Dezize-lès-Maranges	Sampigny-lès-Maranges
Ladoix-Serrigny	Santenay
Meursault	Savigny-lès-Beaune

Côte des Blancs

Chaîne de collines de la région champenoise plantées de Pinot Blanc et de Chardonnay. Principales agglomérations : Avize, Cramant et Mesnil.

On appelle souvent de la même manière, mais à tort, le secteur de Meursault. En fait d'Appellation d'Origine Contrôlée, Côte des Blancs est de Champagne *(voir ce mot).*

Côte de Brouilly

Les vins rouges portant cette appellation proviennent du cœur du Beaujolais dont le meilleur secteur est celui de Brouilly.

Voir BEAUJOLAIS

Côte de Nuits

Bourgogne rouges et blancs. Département de la Côte-d'Or.

La Côte de Nuits s'étend sur quelque 20 km à partir du sud de Fixin et jusqu'à proximité de carrières situées immédiatement au-dessous de Nuits-Saint-Georges, ville principale de ce secteur auquel elle donne son nom. Certains des vignobles plantés sur ce coteau dans des secteurs soigneusement délimités comptent parmi les meilleurs au monde.

Dans ce petit secteur, le Pinot Noir

produit le meilleur vin si les circonstances s'y prêtent. Plus au nord, il donnerait un vin plus mince et plus dur ; plus au sud, le vin serait plus mou et moins robuste. Même en Côte de Nuits, ce raisin délicat n'est pas facile à cultiver et toute la côte n'a pas le même sol, idéal pour son épanouissement. Voilà pourquoi les grands vignobles de cette région sont tellement exigus et aussi pourquoi ils produisent des vins exceptionnels alors que leurs voisins les plus proches sont parfois médiocres. Dans cette zone, les vignobles, comme dans toute la Côte-d'Or, s'appellent climats : chaque « climat » variant selon son exposition, son sol et son drainage.

En Côte de Nuits, tous les climats sont exposés au sud-est et les rayons du soleil levant aspirent l'humidité le long des pousses de vigne. Plus au sud, le soleil serait trop chaud et la vigne flétrirait. Dans une zone climatique où il faut si peu pour gâcher une récolte, la tâche du vigneron est pénible, épuisante, mais chacun donne à son vin une part de ses caractéristiques. Si lors d'une dégustation, l'on compare l'un de ces vins, on peut déceler, si l'on est expérimenté, la différence entre un Côte de Nuits et un Côte de Beaune, et même entre un Charmes-Chambertin et son voisin Clos de Bèze.

Le sol de la Côte de Nuits est une marne rougeâtre contenant des cailloux calcaires d'une teneur variable en lave et en terre de Fuller (un type d'argile riche en silicates de calcium et de magnésium), sels de calcium, potassium et phosphore. Le sous-sol, qui date de la période jurassique, est une argile schisteuse contenant du fer et de la craie. Les défonçages (labours profonds) mélangent ce sous-sol au sol de surface.

Les quelque 1 500 ha de vignes sont plantés surtout en Pinot Noir. Mais on y trouve aussi du Chardonnay. Quelques secteurs sont plantés en Gamay, Melon et Aligoté, pour la consommation des ouvriers de la propriété et de leur famille. La plus grande partie des vins sont rouges, mais on fait aussi du blanc dans les communes de Vougeot et de Chambolle-Musigny, toujours avec le même Pinot Noir. (Deux autres variétés sont tolérées : Pinot Liebault et Pinot Beurot ; ces vignes sont des variantes du Pinot Noir et lui ressemblent énormément. Il y en a d'ailleurs fort peu en Côte de Nuits.)

Les Côte de Nuits sont classés en trois catégories : Grands Crus, Premiers Crus et vins communaux, en fonction de leur origine et des normes minimales suivantes :

Grands Crus

1. Seules variétés de raisin autorisées : Pinot Noir, Pinot Liebault et Pinot Beurot pour les rouges ; Chardonnay pour les blancs. Pour les rouges : tolérance de 15 % au maximum de Pinot Blanc et Chardonnay, à la discrétion du vigneron.

2. Production maximale : 35 hl/ha (un surplus de 20 % est toléré) sauf pour les crus de Latricières-Chambertin, Charmes-Chambertin, Mazis-Chambertin, Ruchottes- Chambertin, Chapelle-Chambertin dans la commune de Gevrey-Chambertin où le maximum autorisé s'élève à 37 hl/ha.

3. Les rouges doivent titrer au minimum 11,5° et les blancs, 12°. Production autorisée : 50 hl/ha.

Premiers Crus

1. Mêmes cépages que pour les Grands Crus.

2. Production maximale : 40 hl/ha.

3. Teneur minimale en alcool : rouges 11°, blancs, 11,5°.

4. Ces vins peuvent être vendus sous le nom de la commune et du cru ou sous celui de la commune suivi de la mention Premier Cru. S'ils ne se conforment pas aux normes ci-dessus, ils tombent dans la catégorie des vins communaux.

Vins communaux

1. Mêmes variétés de raisins que pour les appellations ci-dessus.

2. Production maximale : 50 hl/ha.

3. Les rouges doivent titrer au moins 10,5° et les blancs 11°.

4. Les vins qui ne se conforment pas aux trois normes ci-dessus sont déclassés et vendus sous une appellation plus générale, telle que Bourgogne.

La réglementation indiquée ci-dessus s'applique à tous les bons vins de la Côte de Nuits, sauf ceux qui portent l'appellation Côte de Nuits-Villages, qui sont supérieurs au simple Bourgogne mais n'ont pas la même classe que les trois catégories : Grands Crus, Premiers Crus, vins communaux.

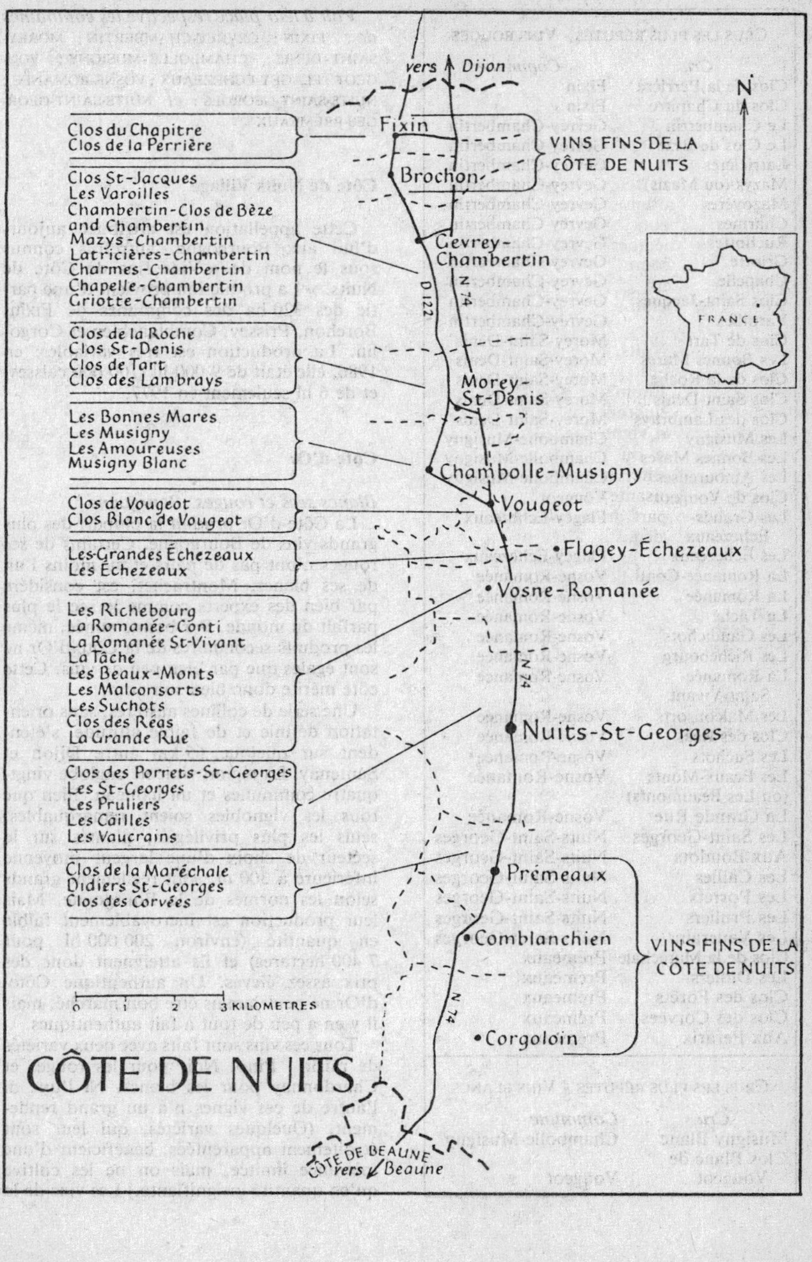
vers Dijon
N
Fixin
Brochon
Gevrey-Chambertin
D 122
N 74
Morey-St-Denis
Chambolle-Musigny
Vougeot
Flagey-Échezeaux
Vosne-Romanée
N 74
Nuits-St-Georges
Prémeaux
Comblanchien
N 74
Corgoloin
VINS FINS DE LA CÔTE DE NUITS
VINS FINS DE LA CÔTE DE NUITS
FRANCE
Clos du Chapitre
Clos de la Perrière
Clos St-Jacques
Les Varoilles
Chambertin-Clos de Bèze and Chambertin
Mazys-Chambertin
Latricières-Chambertin
Charmes-Chambertin
Chapelle-Chambertin
Griotte-Chambertin
Clos de la Roche
Clos St-Denis
Clos de Tart
Clos des Lambrays
Les Bonnes Mares
Les Musigny
Les Amoureuses
Musigny Blanc
Clos de Vougeot
Clos Blanc de Vougeot
Les Grandes Échezeaux
Les Échezeaux
Les Richebourg
La Romanée-Conti
La Romanée St-Vivant
La Tâche
Les Beaux-Monts
Les Malconsorts
Les Suchots
Clos des Réas
La Grande Rue
Clos des Porrets-St-Georges
Les St-Georges
Les Pruliers
Les Cailles
Les Vaucrains
Clos de la Maréchale
Didiers St-Georges
Clos des Corvées
0 1 2 3 KILOMETRES
CÔTE DE NUITS
CÔTE DE BEAUNE
vers Beaune

CRUS LES PLUS RÉPUTÉS - VINS ROUGES

Cru	*Commune*
Clos de la Perrière	Fixin
Clos du Chapitre	Fixin
Le Chambertin	Gevrey-Chambertin
Le Clos de Bèze	Gevrey-Chambertin
Latricières	Gevrey-Chambertin
Mazys (ou Mazis)	Gevrey-Chambertin
Mazoyères	Gevrey-Chambertin
Charmes	Gevrey-Chambertin
Ruchottes	Gevrey-Chambertin
Griotte	Gevrey-Chambertin
Chapelle	Gevrey-Chambertin
Clos Saint-Jacques	Gevrey-Chambertin
Varoilles	Gevrey-Chambertin
Clos de Tart	Morey-Saint-Denis
Les Bonnes Mares	Morey-Saint-Denis
Clos de la Roche	Morey-Saint-Denis
Clos Saint-Denis	Morey-Saint-Denis
Clos des Lambrays[1]	Morey-Saint-Denis
Les Musigny	Chambolle-Musigny
Les Bonnes Mares	Chambolle-Musigny
Les Amoureuses	Chambolle-Musigny
Clos de Vougeot	Vougeot
Les Grands-Échezeaux	Flagey-Échezeaux
Les Échezeaux	Flagey-Échezeaux
La Romanée-Conti	Vosne-Romanée
La Romanée	Vosne-Romanée
La Tâche	Vosne-Romanée
Les Gaudichots	Vosne-Romanée
Les Richebourg	Vosne-Romanée
La Romanée-Saint-Vivant	Vosne-Romanée
Les Malconsorts	Vosne-Romanée
Clos des Réas	Vosne-Romanée
Les Suchots	Vosne-Romanée
Les Beaux-Monts (ou Les Beaumonts)	Vosne-Romanée
La Grande Rue	Vosne-Romanée
Les Saint-Georges	Nuits-Saint-Georges
Aux Boudots	Nuits-Saint-Georges
Les Cailles	Nuits-Saint-Georges
Les Porrets	Nuits-Saint-Georges
Les Pruliers	Nuits-Saint-Georges
Les Vaucrains	Nuits-Saint-Georges
Clos de la Maréchale	Prémeaux
Les Didiers	Prémeaux
Clos des Forêts	Prémeaux
Clos des Corvées	Prémeaux
Aux Perdrix	Prémeaux

CRUS LES PLUS RÉPUTÉS - VINS BLANCS

Cru	*Commune*
Musigny Blanc	Chambolle-Musigny
Clos Blanc de Vougeot	Vougeot

Voir à leur place respective les communes de : FIXIN ; GEVREY-CHAMBERTIN ; MOREY-SAINT-DENIS ; CHAMBOLLE-MUSIGNY ; VOUGEOT ; FLAGEY-ÉCHEZEAUX ; VOSNE-ROMANÉE ; NUITS-SAINT-GEORGES ; *et* NUITS-SAINT-GEORGES-PRÉMEAUX

Côte de Nuits Village

Cette appellation est attribuée aujourd'hui aux Bourgogne, autrefois connus sous le nom de « Vins fins de Côte de Nuits. » La production provient d'une partie des 320 ha des communes de Fixin, Borchon, Prissey, Comblanchien et Corgolin. La production est très variable : en 1986, elle était de 9 000 hl (100 000 caisses) et de 6 hl seulement en 1977.

Côte-d'Or

Blancs secs et rouges. Bourgogne.

La Côte-d'Or produit la plupart des plus grands vins de Bourgogne. Certains de ses rouges n'ont pas de pairs et au moins l'un de ses blancs, Montrachet, est considéré par bien des experts comme le sec le plus parfait du monde. Par bonne année, même les produits secondaires de la Côte-d'Or ne sont égalés que par bien peu de vins. Cette côte mérite donc bien son nom.

Une série de collines austères, sans orientation définie et de faible altitude, s'étendent sur quelque 65 km entre Dijon et Santenay. La région vinicole englobe vingt-quatre communes et un hameau. Bien que tous les vignobles soient remarquables, seuls les plus privilégiés, plantés sur le secteur de choix d'une largeur moyenne inférieure à 300 m, sont réellement grands selon les normes de la Bourgogne. Mais leur production est incroyablement faible en quantité (environ 200 000 hl pour 7 400 hectares) et ils atteignent donc des prix assez élevés. Un authentique Côte-d'Or ne peut jamais être bon marché, mais il y en a peu de tout à fait authentiques.

Tous ces vins sont faits avec deux variétés de raisin : Pinot Noir pour les rouges et Chardonnay pour les blancs. Ni l'une ni l'autre de ces vignes n'a un grand rendement. (Quelques variétés, qui leur sont étroitement apparentées, bénéficient d'une tolérance limitée, mais on ne les cultive qu'en quantité insignifiante.) Les vins de la

Côte-d'Or qui proviennent d'autres variétés de vignes n'ont pas droit à une appellation spécifique et tombent dans la désignation plus générale de Bourgogne.

Outre le faible rendement des vignes nobles, leur culture à une latitude aussi élevée, donc sous un climat rigoureux, présente bien des aléas. C'est pourtant ce même climat qui donne aux vins leur finesse en année favorable. Il implique un effort maximal de la part de la vigne, rien que pour amener son fruit à maturité et il assure en même temps que le raisin, si péniblement mûri, est d'une qualité superbe. Toutes les années, évidemment, ne sont pas celles de succès parfaits, mais dans cette région aussi on a attribué trop d'importance aux tables de millésimes. Certes les Bourgogne varient plus d'année en année que les vins de régions relativement plus ensoleillées, comme celle de Bordeaux. Néanmoins, une bouteille de Côte-d'Or d'une des moins bonnes années procurera des délices pourvu qu'elle soit authentique et vendue à un prix honnête. Même par année « désastreuse » on fait souvent de bons vins. Cela nous prouve que le vin refuse d'obéir aux règles établies par les statisticiens et par ceux qui dressent des tables de millésimes. Le cru compte beaucoup plus que l'année, encore faut-il le choisir à bon escient.

Les vins de la Côte-d'Or se répartissent en trois catégories : 1. ceux qui portent le nom de la commune ; 2. ceux qui ajoutent le nom du vignoble à celui de la commune (Nuits-Saint-Georges-Les-Porrets) ; 3. ceux qui portent uniquement le nom du vignoble, Chambertin et Montrachet, par exemple.

Les vins qui ne portent d'autre Appellation d'Origine que celle de la commune (Gevrey-Chambertin, par exemple) peuvent être faits avec les raisins de n'importe quelle vigne cultivée sur le territoire de la commune et les normes qui leur sont imposées sont les moins rigoureuses de la Côte-d'Or. Ils sont souvent excellents, parfois distingués, mais jamais grands. La seconde catégorie est celle des vins provenant uniquement du vignoble indiqué sur l'étiquette et leurs normes sont plus sévères. On compte parmi eux quelques-uns des plus splendides Bourgogne.

Le troisième groupe, qui porte seulement le nom d'un vignoble réputé, est celui des Grands Crus ; il n'y en a que trente et un en Bourgogne. En général, ils sont inégalables, quoique parfois ceux de la seconde catégorie leur soient supérieurs. Ce qui compte pour l'acheteur c'est d'être capable de distinguer le nom d'une commune de celui d'un cru. Ce n'est pas toujours aussi simple qu'il semble.

Bien des débutants ont acheté par inadvertance une bouteille de Gevrey-Chambertin en croyant avoir affaire à un Chambertin, ou de Chambolle-Musigny en croyant acquérir un Musigny. Erreur parfaitement excusable du fait que les Bourguignons ajoutent au nom de leur commune celui de son plus célèbre vignoble. Mais ce n'est pas une règle : Pommard, Volnay et Beaune, par exemple, considèrent que leur propre nom a beaucoup plus de valeur que celui de n'importe quel cru de leur territoire. Pour compliquer les choses, quelques vignobles portent des noms doubles. Ainsi, Gevrey-Chambertin est une commune, rien de plus ; Chambertin, Latricières-Chambertin, Charmes-Chambertin et quelques autres sont des crus, et des plus réputés. Heureusement il n'y a que vingt-quatres communes viticoles en Côte-d'Or dont treize seulement présentent une importance réelle. (On trouvera à la fin de ce chapitre une liste des crus les plus renommés de la Côte-d'Or. En outre, dans l'article BOURGOGNE, on trouvera l'énumération de ces mêmes communes avec leur production annuelle.)

La Côte-d'Or est nettement divisée en deux parties : Côte de Nuits au nord, et Côte de Beaune au sud. Dans l'ensemble, il est permis de dire que la première donne les plus grands Bourgogne rouges et la seconde, les plus grands blancs. Mais il y a des exceptions. Au temps jadis, il existait une Côte de Dijon qui s'étendait au nord de la Côte de Nuits. Mais l'expansion de la ville de Dijon et la baisse de qualité des vins de cette côte en ont réduit l'intérêt à presque rien, quoiqu'elle ait joui d'une grande estime.

Dans la commune de Chenôve, qui produit encore de nos jours quelques vins mineurs, se trouve un pressoir qui passe pour le plus grand du monde : le Pressoir du Duc, tel est son nom officiel, mais les gens du pays l'appellent la Grosse Margot, par affection pour la duchesse Marguerite qui, disent-ils, au XVe siècle, accordait ses faveurs aux vignerons et vendangeurs les plus adroits et les plus habiles. Chenôve, Marsannay et Couchay produisent quelques vins, mais la première commune qui compte, c'est celle de Fixin, à l'entrée de la Côte de Nuits.

Le secteur central des collines, entre Fixin et Santenay, est devenu la grande région vinicole de la Côte-d'Or. Les facteurs déterminants sont la vigne, l'exposition de la colline et son ensoleillement, la quantité de pluie et le drainage de l'eau superflue. Mais le sol est peut-être encore plus important : c'est l'élément le plus critique quant à la production de n'importe quel grand vin. Les collines de Bourgogne datent de la même époque et appartiennent à la même formation que les monts du Jura qui ont donné leur nom à l'époque où ils se formèrent, le jurassique, il y a quelque 130 à 155 millions d'années. Pendant les quelque 130 millions d'années qui séparent leur soulèvement de la première apparition d'un être humain tenant à peine sur ses jambes, les collines furent alternativement rôties au soleil, couvertes de glace, inondées, fouettées par des vents sauvages. Le résultat net de toutes ces épreuves, c'est un sol calcaire, semé d'oolithes riches en fer. Le Bourguignon est fermement convaincu que toute cette succession d'événements était prédéterminée et que l'ensemble des conditions climatiques et géologiques de ces collines fut expressément prévu pour ses vignes et rien d'autre. Il n'est pas besoin de le pousser beaucoup pour qu'il avoue : « La création du monde n'avait pas d'autre but ». Que pourrait-il croître d'autre que de la vigne sur la Côte-d'Or ? Où pourrait-on trouver des vins qui vaillent ceux de cette côte ?

Quoique les Bourgogne de la Côte-d'Or comptent parmi les rares grands vins du monde, il y en a de meilleurs les uns que les autres. Toute classification n'a qu'une valeur éphémère, car l'homme contribue beaucoup à la qualité de son vin ; or les hommes changent et meurent. Il est cependant permis d'esquisser une grande classification d'ensemble. L'ordre dans lequel les crus sont énumérés ci-dessous est fondé sur l'opinion personnelle de l'auteur qui consacra des années à déguster des vins de Bourgogne en les comparant les uns aux autres. Cette liste peut donc ne pas être approuvée unanimement. Pour qu'elle donne une évaluation exacte de la qualité des vins, il faut qu'ils reflètent les caractéristiques du sol et soient *mis en bouteille à la propriété*.

VINS ROUGES

Cru	*Commune*
La Romanée-Conti	Vosne-Romanée
Chambertin-Clos de Bèze et Chambertin	Gevrey-Chambertin
La Tâche	Vosne-Romanée
Les Richebourg	Vosne-Romanée
Musigny	Chambolle-Musigny
Clos de Vougeot	Vougeot
Les Bonnes Mares	Chambolle-Musigny
Grands-Échezeaux	Flagey-Échezeaux
La Romanée-Saint-Vivant	Vosne-Romanée
Corton-Clos du Roi	Aloxe-Corton
Les Saints-Georges	Nuits-Saint-Georges
Latricières-Chambertin	Gevrey-Chambertin
Le Corton	Aloxe-Corton
Les Bressandes	Aloxe-Corton
Cuvée Nicolas Rolin	Beaune (Hospices de Beaune)
La Grande Rue	Vosne-Romanée
Les Renardes	Aloxe-Corton
Cuvée Dr. Peste	Aloxe-Corton (Hospices de Beaune)
Clos des Porrets-Saint-Georges	Nuits-Saint-Georges
Mazis-Chambertin	Gevrey-Chambertin
Les Amoureuses	Chambolle-Musigny
Clos de Tart	Morey-Saint-Denis
Les Pruliers	Nuits-Saint-Georges
Les Cailles	Nuits-Saint-Georges
Les Caillerets	Volnay
Clos de la Perrière	Fixin
Clos Saint-Jacques	Gevrey-Chambertin
Les Varoilles	Gevrey-Chambertin
Les Échezeaux	Flagey-Échezeaux
Les Beaux-Monts (ou Beaumonts)	Vosne-Romanée
Les Malconsorts	Vosne-Romanée
Clos de la Roche	Morey-Saint-Denis
Les Fremiets	Volnay
Les Champans	Volnay
Les Suchots	Vosne-Romanée
Clos des Réas	Vosne-Romanée
Chapelle-Chambertin	Gevrey-Chambertin

Charmes-Chambertin	Gevrey-Chambertin
Griotte-Chambertin	Gevrey-Chambertin
Clos du Chapitre	Fixin
Clos des Lambrays	Morey-Saint-Denis
Les Rugiens	Pommard
Les Épenots	Pommard
Les Jarollières	Pommard
Clos de la Maréchale	Nuits-Prémeaux
Didiers-Saint-Georges	Nuits-Prémeaux
Clos des Corvées	Nuits-Prémeaux
Les Vaucrains	Nuits-Saint-Georges
Les Santenots	Meursault
Les Fèves	Beaune
Les Grèves	Beaune
Clos des Mouches	Beaune
Clos de la Boudriotte	Chassagne-Montrachet
Clos Saint-Jean	Chassagne-Montrachet
Clos Morgeot	Chassagne-Montrachet
Clos de la Commaraine	Pommard
Les Angles	Volnay
Le Clos blanc	Pommard
Les Pézerolles	Pommard
Clos Saint-Denis	Morey-Saint-Denis

VINS BLANCS

Cru	*Commune*
Le Montrachet	Chassagne et Puligny-Montrachet
Chevalier-Montrachet	Puligny-Montrachet
Clos des Perrières	Meursault
Bâtard-Montrachet	Chassagne et Puligny-Montrachet
Corton-Charlemagne	Aloxe-Corton
Les Perrières	Meursault
Les Ruchottes	Chassagne-Montrachet
Musigny Blanc	Chambolle-Musigny
Les Charmes	Meursault
Les Combettes	Puligny-Montrachet
Clos Blanc de Vougeot	Vougeot

Voir également CÔTE DE NUITS ; CÔTE DE BEAUNE ; BOURGOGNE

Côte Rôtie (Appellation Contrôlée)

Vin rouge. Vallée du Rhône.

Le Côte Rôtie — généreux, riche en couleur, d'un goût de truffe et de framboise — vient immédiatement après le plus célèbre vin de la vallée du Rhône : le Châteauneuf-du-Pape. Vraiment rôtie par le soleil, cette côte s'étend sur environ 3 km de long. Elle est si agreste que les vignes y sont cultivées sur des terrasses soutenues par de vieux murs de pierre. Sur ces parcelles exiguës, les raisins s'ensoleillent durant tout l'été. La Côte Rôtie est située sur la rive droite du Rhône, à l'extrémité nord de la région vinicole. Les vignobles sont partagés entre les communes d'Ampuis et de Tupin-et-Semons. Ils sont orientés au sud-sud-est. Leurs vins aux caractéristiques astringentes concentrées ont une forte teneur alcoolique.

La Côte Rôtie est divisée en deux parties : Côte brune et Côte blonde. On voit la différence à la couleur du sol et on la perçoit au goût des vins. En Côte brune, la terre est brunâtre, riche en glaise et contient une forte proportion d'oxyde de fer. En Côte blonde, le sol est d'une couleur plus claire parce que la craie domine sur la marne. Les vins de Côte brune sont plus tendres au début mais prennent de la vigueur avec l'âge, alors que leurs voisins de la Côte blonde ont une jeunesse gaie et vivace mais fanent beaucoup plus vite. Selon la légende, Maugiron (un des premiers seigneurs d'Ampuis) offrit chacun de ses vignobles à chacune de ses deux filles, une brune et une blonde. L'influence de ces dames du temps jadis continue à se manifester dans les caractéristiques des vins. Les deux côtes donnent des vins rouges, charnus au point d'en être chaleureux, doués d'une longévité appréciable ; ils ont un bouquet plein d'assurance et un fini satiné. Pour éviter un excès de vigueur, le vigneron pouvait ajouter des raisins blancs au moment de la fermentation, mais jamais plus de 20 %. Cette addition arrondit les angles et donne une certaine finesse. Le raisin rouge est du Syrah et le blanc du Viognier, cultivés côte à côte au flanc de la côte.

La surface plantée en vigne a diminué durant les dernières années en raison des difficultés de travail sur une côte où l'usage des engins mécaniques est impossible. Paradoxalement, la réputation de ce vin augmente au fur et à mesure que la surface du vignoble diminue. Il en résulte, hélas ! qu'on n'a pas toujours résisté à la tentation d'allonger ce bon vin. Selon des chiffres officiels des plus récents, la Côte Rôtie a environ 125 ha de vignes et une production annuelle d'environ 4 000 hl (près de 40 000 caisses).

Voir RHÔNE (VINS DU)

Coteau

Versant d'une colline. Ce mot peut apparaître dans les noms de certaines régions vinicoles, par exemple Coteaux de la Loire.

Coteaux d'Aix-en-Provence, Coteaux d'Aix-en-Provence-Les Baux (Appellation Contrôlée)

Vins rouges, blancs et rosés. Provence.

Les vins de cette appellation sont faits avec les raisins cultivés sur les territoires de la commune d'Aix et des environs, en un certain secteur délimité. Ils avaient droit à la mention V.D.Q.S. (Vins Délimités de Qualité Supérieure), qui représente le second rang dans la hiérarchie officielle des vins français. Ils peuvent être rouges, blancs ou rosés, et doivent titrer au moins 11°. Variétés de vignes autorisées pour les rouges : Cabernet Sauvignon, Syrah, Grenache, Carignan, Cinsault, Mourvèdre et Counoise ; pour les blancs : Bourboulenc, Clairette, Grenache, Blanc, Sauvignon, Sémillon, Ugni Blanc et Vermentino.

En 1986, les Coteaux des Baux et les Coteaux d'Aix reçurent chacun la distinction d'« Appelation Contrôlée ». Les 300 ha de coteaux des Baux, produisant quelque 10 000 hl (110 000 caisses), furent rattachés aux Coteaux d'Aix auxquels ils appartenaient précédemment grâce à la qualité exceptionnelle de douze de leurs vignobles.

Coteaux de l'Aubance (Appellation Contrôlée)

Vins blancs et du rosé. Anjou.

Petite rivière au cours paresseux, l'Aubance s'écoule vers le nord, et se jette dans la Loire à quelque 50 km en aval de Saumur. Elle traverse un paysage doucement vallonné. Les vignes cultivées à flanc de coteau sont d'une qualité légèrement inférieure à celle des Coteaux de la Loire et des Coteaux du Layon. Les blancs d'Aubance sont généralement doux, parfois demi-doux et comptent parmi les Anjou que l'on trouve le plus souvent à l'étranger. On ne discerne aucune différence appréciable entre les rosés des Coteaux de l'Aubance et les autres rosés de l'Anjou. Seul le Chenin Blanc est autorisé pour les vins blancs — les plus doux sont faits avec des raisins cueillis après qu'ils ont été atteints par la pourriture noble *(voir ce mot)* — et le Cabernet Franc domine pour le rosé. Production annuelle du blanc : environ 2 500 hl (plus de 25 000 caisses). Rouge et rosé inclus, le total s'élève à une moyenne annuelle d'environ 2 300 hl (25 000 caisses).

Voir ANJOU

Coteaux du Languedoc (Appellation Contrôlée)

Vins rouges et rosés. Sud de la France, région du Languedoc (Vins du Midi).

Voir LANGUEDOC

Coteaux du Layon (Appellation Contrôlée)

Vins blancs de la Loire. Anjou.

Ces vins sont surtout les plus doux, les plus riches et les plus moelleux des Anjou blancs. Il leur faut une année ensoleillée pour que leur richesse se manifeste. Quoique moins fleuris que les Sauternes, ils ont un bouquet inimitable et une alacrité qui dément leur teneur en alcool s'élevant parfois jusqu'à 13°. Ils vieillissent lentement mais vivent longtemps. On fait aussi quelques blancs secs dans ce secteur.

Voir ANJOU

Coteaux du Loir (Appellation Contrôlée)

Rouges, blancs et rosés de la Loire.

Petit secteur septentrional de la région vinicole de la Loire. Il produit des rouges, des rosés et des blancs que l'on confond aisément avec ceux des coteaux de la Loire. Le Loir est un affluent de la Loire.

Comme partout dans la vallée de la Loire, les blancs ont tendance à surpasser les rouges. Faits avec du Chenin Blanc ou du Pineau de la Loire, ils doivent titrer au moins 9,5°. Ce sont des vins secs sauf lorsqu'un été exceptionnellement chaud donne assez de sucre aux raisins pour produire des vins doux ou demi-doux. Contrairement aux secs qui mûrissent vite, les vins plus doux doivent vieillir un certain temps en bouteille pour être prêts à la consommation.

Pour les rouges et les rosés, le Pineau d'Aunis est en train de disparaître rapidement devant les Cabernet. Sont aussi autorisés le Gamay et le Cot. Le Groslot n'est permis que jusqu'à concurrence de 25 % pour les rosés.

Les vignes sont plantées sur des sols allant de la marne calcaire (en général pour les vignes à vin blanc) à un mélange de glaise et de schiste. De temps à autre, les vins sont demi-mousseux ou pétillants. La production annuelle est de 1 500 hl (16 000 caisses) environ.

Coteaux de la Loire

Vins blancs. Anjou.

Légèrement plus durs et pas tout à fait aussi doux que les Coteaux du Layon faits au-delà du fleuve, ces vins n'en sont pas moins agréables au dessert. Les meilleurs titrent jusqu'à 12 et même 13° et conservent une certaine quantité de sucre non réduit. Cette douceur et cette richesse sont obtenues par le même procédé que pour les Sauternes : en laissant la pourriture noble *(voir ce mot)* se développer sur la vigne en automne avant la vendange.

Le meilleur cru sec de se secteur — Savennières — a droit, à une Appellation d'Origine Contrôlée particulière.

Tous les vins de ces coteaux ne sont pas doux car la zone des Coteaux de la Loire s'étend partiellement jusqu'à la région du Muscadet, près de Nantes, où les vins — les plus robustes de leur genre — sont pâles et secs. Production d'Anjou-Coteaux de la Loire : 3 000 hl (plus de 30 000 caisses).

Voir ANJOU

Coteaux de la Mejanelle

Voir LANGUEDOC ; COTEAUX DU LANGUEDOC

Coteaux de Saumur

Voir SAUMUR ; ANJOU

Coteaux de Saint-Christol

Voir LANGUEDOC ; COTEAUX DU LANGUEDOC

Coteaux de Touraine et Coteaux de Touraine mousseux

Voir TOURAINE

Coteaux du Tricastin (Appellation Contrôlée)

Vins rouges, blancs et rosés de la vallée du Rhône.

Les automobilistes empruntant l'autoroute Paris-Nice traverseront les vignobles de cette Appellation Contrôlée, située à environ 50 km au sud de Valence, dans la Drôme. C'est sur la gauche de l'autoroute que se trouvent les coteaux où poussent ses raisins. Tricastin touche la région bien plus grande des Côtes du Rhône, et les variétés de raisins sont en effet les mêmes dans les deux régions : Grenache, Mourvèdre, Syrah, Picpoul, Carignan, Clairette, Bourboulenc, Ugni Blanc et Cinsault. La production annuelle s'élève à 85 000 hl (près de 950 000 caisses) essentiellement de vin rouge.

Coteaux de Vérargues

Voir LANGUEDOC ; COTEAUX DU LANGUEDOC

Côtes d'Agly

Vins vinés doux. Roussillon.

Peu distante de la frontière espagnole dans les Pyrénées Orientales. Côtes d'Agly produit une moyenne annuelle de 100 000 hl (1 million de caisses) de vin blanc fort et doux. On y fait également une petite quantité de vin rouge, mais il est généralement inférieur au vin produit dans la proche Corbières et quitte rarement la zone de production.

Voir VINS VINÉS DE FRANCE

Côtes de Bergerac (A.O.C.)

Voir BERGERAC

Côtes de Blaye (A.O.C.)

Voir BLAYE

Côtes de Bordeaux

Voir PREMIÈRES CÔTES DE BORDEAUX

Côtes de Bordeaux-Saint-Macaire (A.O.C)

Secteur du Bordelais qui produit de bons vins secondaires.
Voir BORDEAUX

Côtes de Bourg (A.O.C.)

Voir BOURG

Côtes de Buzet (A.O.C.)

Vins rouges et blancs. Région du Sud-Ouest.

C'est entre les grandes régions du Bordelais et de l'Armagnac, en Aquitaine, que se trouve cette importante zone fruitière, dont les produits sont connus dans toute la France. L'appellation contrôlée de Buzet est au cœur même de cette région, sur la rive gauche de la Garonne. La totalité du vin — environ 80 000 caisses par an — est produite par la coopérative que dirige un ancien gérant de Château-Lafite. Les rouges sont bons et supérieurs aux blancs et sont heureusement produits en plus grande quantité.
Voir BUZET

Côtes Canon-Fronsac, Côtes de Fronsac Aujourd'hui Canon-Fronsac et Fronsac (A.O.C.).

Vins rouges. Région de Bordeaux.

La ville médiévale de Fronsac, près de laquelle Charlemagne posséda jadis un château, située au confluent de l'Isle et de la Dordogne, à quelque 25 km à l'est de Bordeaux, a droit pour ses vins à deux Appellations d'Origine Contrôlée du Bordelais. On y fait du blanc, mais seul le rouge est un vin d'appellation. Fronsac englobe une zone plus restreinte : Canon-Fronsac, qui produit les meilleurs vins. L'I.N.A.O. a récemment réduit l'appellation en abandonnant « Côtes ». Canon-Fronsac est situé sur la crête élevée des Côtes Canon : grande falaise verte qui domine la Dordogne. Le plus petit secteur s'enorgueillit de son nom et de deux Château-Canon distincts ainsi que de huit autres crus dans le nom desquels figure celui de Canon. Il ne faut pas les confondre avec *le* Château-Canon de Saint-Émilion.

Les vins de ces secteurs sont assez pleins pour des Bordeaux. La délicatesse, qu'on ne trouvait autrefois que chez ses rares meilleurs crus, est en train de descendre lentement vers les moins importants qui n'étaient pas faits auparavant comme ils auraient dû l'être. Corsés, chaleureux, les rouges sont particulièrement appréciés dans les pays de la Manche et de la mer du Nord.

Par une meilleure commercialisation de leurs vins et grâce à l'amélioration de leurs méthodes de vinification, les producteurs de Fronsac sont en train de gagner du respect.

Côtes de Fronsac produit environ 25 000 hl (270 000 caisses) de vin par an, dont une grande partie est un grand vin fruité. Canon-Fronsac représente environ la moitié de ce chiffre.

Côtes de Castillon (Appellation Contrôlée)

Vins rouges. Bordeaux.

Agréable vin secondaire de la région bordelaise. En choisissant bien les crus de ce secteur, qui est contigu à Saint-Émilion, on peut faire d'excellents achats.
Voir BORDEAUX

Côtes de Duras (Appellation Contrôlée)

Vins rouges et blancs. Sud-Ouest de la France.

Vins rouges et blancs provenant de 15 communes entourant la ville de Duras, située à quelque 110 km au sud-est de Bordeaux. Les blancs sont fait avec des raisins Sémillon, Sauvignon, Muscadelle Mauzac, Rouchelain (ou Pineau de la

Loire) et Ondenc ; les rouges avec des raisins Cabernet Sauvignon, Cabernet Franc, Merlot et Cot. Teneur minimale en alcool : 10° pour les rouges et 10,5° pour les blancs. Les vignes de ce secteur couvrent une surface d'un millier d'hectares. On y fait surtout du vin blanc et la production totale (rouges et blancs) varie de 10 000 à 50 000 hl (entre 110 000 et 550 000 caisses) par an.

Côtes du Jura ou Côtes du Jura mousseux

Voir JURA

Côtes-du-Marmandais

Vins V.D.Q.S. produits dans une petite région située aux alentours de la commune de Marmande, au sud-est du Bordelais sur la Garonne. Les rouges comme les blancs sont d'intérêt purement local.

Côtes de Montravel (A.O.C.)

Voir BERGERAC

Côtes de Nuits Villages (A.O.C.)

Voir CÔTES DE NUITS

Côtes de Provence

Appellation Contrôlée de Provence.
Voir PROVENCE

Côtes du Rhône (Appellation Contrôlée)

Nom d'une région viticole et vinicole, et de ses vins, située au bord du Rhône, dans le sud-est de la France.
Voir RHÔNE

Côtes du Roussillon (A.O.C.)

Vins rouges et blancs. Sud-Est de la France.

Ce secteur, situé à l'est des Pyrénées, est un des plus romanesques de l'histoire de France. On y produit actuellement des vins rouges et rosés fort intéressants, auxquels on a reconnu le statut d'Appellation Contrôlée.

Voir ROUSSILLON

Côtes de Toul

Une des deux appellations d'origine lorraine dont la production consiste en vins délimités de qualité supérieure (V.D.Q.S.). La plupart sont des « vins gris » qui sont une des traditions de la Lorraine *(voir ce nom)*.

Côtes du Ventoux (A.O.C.)

Vins rouges et rosés de la vallée du Rhône. Midi de la France.

Situé entre la Provence et la vallée du Rhône, le plateau du Vaucluse — au sol sec — s'élève à 40 km à l'est d'Avignon. Les vignobles des Côtes du Ventoux, qui s'étendent sur plus de 5 000 ha au-delà du plateau, se trouvent directement à l'est de Carpentras — ville célèbre par ses melons — et juste au sud du mont Ventoux.

On y cultive principalement du Grenache Noir — variété de base pour tout le sud des Côtes du Rhône —, ainsi que du Syrah, du Cinsault, du Mourvèdre et du Carignan. Tous ces raisins s'accommodent bien du sol rouge et pauvre de la Méditerranée formée du calcaire dur du mont Ventoux, de talus et de pierres. Les quelques 4 000 vignerons des cinquantes et une communes de cette Appellation Contrôlée produisent environ 250 000 hl (plus de 2,5 millions de caisses) par an de vin en majorité rouge. 60 % de la production est un vin solide, fruité et d'un rouge tannique, et 20 % de la production des Côtes du Ventoux est appelée « vin primeur », autrefois connus sous le nom de « vin de café » ou « vin d'une nuit ». De caractère moins consistant et plus faible en alcool que les autres rouges, ces vins primeurs sont décuvés et pressurés après une très courte fermentation. Ils sont de loin les vins les plus célèbres de cette Appellation Contrôlée. La production de rosé représente 15 %. Celle de blanc est insignifiante.

Couché

On appelle parfois vin couché du vin conservé dans une bouteille couchée. Couché est aussi la position du tonneau ou de la barrique lorsqu'on les tourne de telle sorte que la bonde soit humectée par le vin.

Couderc, Georges

Œnologue français qui a obtenu des vignes hybrides fournissant des vins sains mais qui n'ont guère d'autres vertus. On les cultive tant en France qu'ailleurs.

Couhins (Château-)

Bordeaux blanc. Commune de Villenave-d'Ornon, en Graves.

Contigus aux Château-Carbonnieux et Château-Bouscaut, Couhins et l'ancien Pont de Langon (maintenant un seul vignoble) appartinrent jusqu'en 1969 aux mêmes propriétaires que Château-Calon-Ségur, en Médoc. Les propriétaires précédents furent un ambassadeur d'Espagne en France et un évêque d'Alger.

Le domaine fut racheté en 1969 par l'État, qui projetait d'en faire un centre œnologique expérimental. Aujourd'hui, André Lurton loue Couhins et produit un bon vin avec 50 % de Sauvignon, 25 % de Muscadelle et 25 % de Sémillon. En 1959, ce vin fut classé parmi les très bons Graves blancs.

Caractéristiques : Léger mais plein de caractère, avec un goût charmant. Vin blanc sec, très bien vinifié.

Superficie : rouge 6 ha, blanc 1 ha.

Production moyenne : rouge 25 tonneaux (2 000 caisses), blanc 5 tonneaux (400 caisses).

Coule (Vin de)

Vin fait avec le premier jus de raisin qui sort du pressoir. On dit indifféremment vin de coule ou vin de tête.

Couleur des alcools

Les spiritueux sont incolores à la sortie de l'alambic. On leur donne de la couleur après distillation. Certains alcools prennent une coloration brune en fût, mais cette même coloration leur est souvent donnée artificiellement par addition de caramel. La teinte verte de la crème de menthe est aussi obtenue par une addition.

Couleuse

Lorsque l'air entre en contact avec le vin, celui-ci suinte par le bouchon de la bouteille, produisant ainsi une oxydation prématurée susceptible d'endommager le vin.

Coulure

Maladie, ou plutôt trouble fonctionnel, de la vigne. Elle se manifeste soit par la flétrissure d'une partie des fleurs ou des raisins, soit par leur développement inégal. Au pire, fleurs ou fruits ne se développent pas du tout.

Voir CHAPITRE IV

Coupage

Pratique consistant à mélanger des vins ou des spiritueux pour obtenir une qualité uniforme d'une année sur l'autre ou un produit de meilleure qualité que n'importe quel composant du mélange pris isolément. Dans certains cas, le coupage est un moyen pratique d'augmenter la quantité mais pas du tout la qualité. Si le breuvage original était de première qualité, il en perd une partie par mélange et se voit ainsi privé de son originalité et de sa distinction.

Tous les Xérès sont des coupages, de même que la plupart des Champagne, des Cognac et des whiskys. Dans ces cas particuliers, le coupage est bénéfique.

Il ne faut surtout pas confondre couper et mouiller. Cette dernière opération consiste à ajouter de l'eau à un alcool ou à un vin.

Coupe

Verre — ou tasse — à pied.

Court noué

Autre nom de la dégénérescence infectieuse de la vigne.
Voir CHAPITRE IV

Coutet (Château-)

Bordeaux blanc. Commune de Barsac en Sauternais.

Le vin de Château-Coutet a droit, comme tous les Barsac, à deux Appellations Contrôlées : soit Sauternes, soit Barsac. Commune du secteur de Sauternes, Barsac est en effet une Appellation d'Origine Contrôlée. En 1855, Coutet, qui se trouve à 1 500 m au-dessous de la ville de Barsac, fut classé Premier Cru de Sauternes.

Il existe tout un réseau de liens entre ce château et celui d'Yquem. Les parties les plus anciennes des deux bâtiments, qui datent tous deux du XIIIe siècle, sont identiques au point de vue architectural. Le puits dans la cour du Château-Coutet est la réplique exacte de celui qui se trouve dans la cour du château d'Yquem, à une dizaine de kilomètres plus loin. Jusqu'en 1923, le Château-Coutet appartenait à la famille de Lur-Saluces qui possède le château d'Yquem depuis deux siècles.

Le château appartient actuellement à M. Marcel Baly de Strasbourg qui l'acheta en 1977 à M. Edmond Rolland. C'est le père de Mme Rolland — de l'importante maison Guy et Mital, fabricants de pressoirs à Lyon — qui acheta ce domaine au groupe qui l'avait lui-même acheté au père de feu le marquis de Lur-Saluces.

Les chais se dressent en face du château, de l'autre côté de la cour intérieure. On y apporte les raisins après les avoir laissé mûrir jusqu'à la pourriture noble, selon la norme du Sauternes et du Barsac. Le pressurage est fait dans de grands pressoirs électriques. La pâte qui en résulte est jetée à la fourche dans une cheminée à succion qui la précipite dans un gigantesque cylindre rotatif. La centrifugation élimine les rafles. Ensuite on represse deux fois de suite la pulpe. Le jus s'écoule par des trappes dans les cuves placées au-dessous du plancher. De ces cuves, on transfère chaque soir le moût dans des barils où il fermente, puis reste trois ans pour arriver à maturation.

Considéré par nombre de gens comme le meilleur des Barsac, le Château-Coutet résulte d'une viticulture extrêmement attentive. Quand M. Baly estime que sa production n'est pas conforme à ses propres exigences, il lui refuse le nom du château et la vend anonymement comme un Barsac quelconque.

L'étiquette actuelle de Château-Coutet est la même que celle de Château-Filhot qui appartient à la famille de Lur-Saluces.

Caractéristiques : Ce Barsac plus nerveux que ses congénères du Sauternes présente une gracieuse trace d'acidité. Cette particularité exceptionnelle expliquerait, dit-on, le nom du château. (En gascon, *coutet* signifie couteau). Le vin doit ses caractéristiques au sous-sol de roches calcaires. Quoique les Barsac soient aussi liquoreux (variant habituellement entre 3° et 6° Beaumé) que ses voisins du Sauternes, ils sont plus secs au goût en raison de leur caractère coupant. Vin de grande race, Château-Coutet conserve longtemps son fruité.

Superficie : 38 ha.
Production moyenne : 7 500 caisses.

Cowra

Région viticole de la Nouvelle-Galles du Sud.
Voir AUSTRALIE

Cramant

Localité du secteur d'Épernay, en Champagne. On y produit un des plus grands vins de la Côte des Blancs.
Voir CHAMPAGNE

Cream Sherry

Xérès Oloroso, lourd et doux. Inconnu en Espagne, lancé en Angleterre, il est devenu vraiment populaire aux États-Unis.
Voir XÉRÈS

Crémant

Vin blanc fait avec des raisins blancs et noirs et très légèrement mousseux, seulement pétillant. Ce vin fait en Champagne ne doit pas être confondu avec le village vinicole champenois appelé Cramant.

Crémant de Bourgogne (A.O.C.)

Autrefois connu sous le nom de Bourgogne mousseux *(voir ce nom)*, le Crémant de Bourgogne est un mousseux fait avec une ou plusieurs variétés de raisins à Bourgogne (Chardonnay, Pinot Gris, Pinot Blanc, Pinot Noir, Gamay, Melon, Sacy) selon le procédé utilisé pour le Champagne. Ces mousseux étaient indifféremment rouges, rosés ou blancs, mais la nouvelle appellation « Crémant de Bourgogne » ne s'applique aujourd'hui qu'aux blancs et aux rosés. La production annuelle atteint une moyenne de 5 000 hl.

Crème

Sur l'étiquette d'une bouteille de liqueur, ce mot indique seulement qu'il s'agit d'une liqueur sucrée, et sert à la différencier d'une eau-de-vie naturelle telle que le Cognac ou l'Armagnac. Selon l'usage contemporain, ce mot couvre toutes les liqueurs sucrées faites à base de n'importe quel fruit, grain ou feuille : ananas, banane, cacao, café, cassis, chocolat, cumin, fraise, framboise, mandarine, menthe, moka, noyau (cerise), prunelle, rose, thé, vanille, violette.

Crème Yvette

Ancienne liqueur américaine très sucrée et parfumée à la violette de Parme. Elle doit son nom à Yvette Guilbert, l'incomparable diseuse française.

Crépy (Appellation Contrôlée)

Vin blanc léger titrant au moins 9° et qui provient des coteaux crayeux s'élevant sur les berges sud du lac de Genève dans le département de Haute-Savoie. Quelque 60 ha de vigne qui ont droit à une Appellation Contrôlée y produisent environ 2 000 hl. Certains Crépy sont naturellement pétillants. Fait avec du raisin de Chasselas, tous sont secs et aromatiques. En raison de sa faible production, Crépy n'exporte pratiquement jamais son vin.

Crescenz

Orthographe défectueuse mais courante de *Kreszenz*, mot allemand signifiant cru.

Criollas

Vignes descendant de celles que les jésuites importèrent en Argentine et qui fournissent encore la plus grande partie des vins blancs et rosés de ce pays.

Criots-Bâtard-Montrachet (Appellation Contrôlée)

Bourgogne blanc. Commune de Chassagne-Montrachet, en Côte de Beaune. Classement officiel : Grand Cru.

Encore un des splendides vins de la famille des Montrachet. Les vins de Chassagne ont un goût caractéristique au sujet duquel on ne peut se tromper. Secs sans être durs ils ont tendance à être très fruités, sans laisser d'arrière-goût sucré.

Superficie : 2 ha.

Production : 80 hl (environ 880 caisses) par grandes années.

Voir BATARD-MONTRACHET ; CHASSAGNE-MONTRACHET.

Croizet-Bages (Château-)

Bordeaux rouge. Commune de Pauillac, en Haut-Médoc.

Un des quelques Cinquièmes Crus d'après la classification des grands vignobles de 1855. Les vignes du vieux domaines de Bages sont plantées sur les terres vallonnées qui entourent Pauillac. On l'appelait parfois Château-Clavé-Croizet-Bages. La famille Quié, propriétaire de ce château, possède aussi le vignoble de Rausan-Gassies (Deuxième Cru) à Margaux, et le Château-Bel-Orme-Tronquoy-de-Lalande (Cru Bourgeois supérieur) près de Saint-Estèphe.

Caractéristiques : Bon, mais pas exceptionnel.

Superficie : 25 ha.

Production moyenne : 100 tonneaux (8 000 caisses).

Croûte, Croûté

Dépôt qui se forme dans les goulots des bouteilles de vieux Porto et qu'on appelle ainsi parce qu'il laisse un cercle de croûtes à l'intérieur de la bouteille.

Quant au Porto Croûté (Crusted Port), il est plus fort et plus charnu que la plupart des Tawny et des Ruby, rappelle le Porto millésimé et s'améliore en bouteille. Ce Porto n'est pourtant jamais millésimé et n'est jamais non plus celui d'une grande année car, s'il en était ainsi, il porterait sa date. Le Crusted Port n'aura jamais la magnificence d'un Porto millésimé. Il faut le décanter.

Voir PORTO

Crozes-Hermitage

Vins blancs et rouges.

Voir HERMITAGE, RHÔNE

Cru

Vignoble de grande qualité auquel on donne généralement un statut particulier d'après les lois de la classification. Un vignoble classé officiellement devient un *Cru Classé.*

Cru Artisan

Classe mineure de crus de Bordeaux de qualité inférieure au Cru Bourgeois et supérieure au Cru Paysan. Ce sont les vins ordinaires de Bordeaux ; coupés généralement et rarement mis en bouteille au château, ils portent peu souvent le nom d'un vignoble. Actuellement, ces vins sont pourtant de plus en plus souvent mis en bouteille et vendus sous étiquette brevetée.

Cru (Bouilleur de)

Celui qui fait bouillir sa récolte pour obtenir de l'eau-de-vie ou qui la fait distiller pour sa consommation personnelle.

Crust, Crusted Port

Voir CROÛTE, CROÛTÉ

Cruzan Rum

Rhum de Sainte-Croix (archipel des îles Vierges).

Voir RHUM : ILES VIERGES

Cryptogames

Tous végétaux sans fleurs ni fruits. En ce qui concerne la viticulture et la viniculture, les cryptogames intéressants sont des champignons ou moisissures microscopiques qui, en général, sont causes de maladies de la vigne, mais dont l'action peut aussi parfois être bénéfique (pourriture noble).

Voir CHAPITRE IV

Cul

Le fond de certaines bouteilles est garnie de dentelures servant à retenir la lie pour l'empêcher de se répandre dans toute la bouteille.

Culaton

Mot piémontais qui désigne le fond de la bouteille et le résidu qui s'y dépose. Selon une vieille superstition de cette province italienne, il faut conserver le fond de la bouteille jusqu'au lendemain du jour où on l'a débouchée pour le donner alors à des amis. Quand on considère l'épaisseur du dépôt des vins du Piémont, ce présent semble bizarre.

Cumin liquidum optimum castelli (CLOC)

Il s'agit d'une liqueur danoise blanche qui doit son goût à des graines de cumin. Ce nom signifie : « La meilleure liqueur de cumin du château. » C'est une espèce de kummel.

Curaçao

A l'origine il s'agissait d'une liqueur hollandaise faite avec l'écorce des oranges qui poussent sur l'île de Curaçao aux Antilles néerlandaises, au large du Venezuela. Ce breuvage est devenu tellement populaire que bien des distillateurs en vendent sous les noms les plus divers. Cointreau et Grand Marnier sont deux exemples de marques commerciales de Curaçao, alors que le Curaçao triple sec est produit par de nombreuses firmes.

Cuve

Grand réservoir de dimensions variables, en chêne, acier inoxydable ou ciment (et parfois doublé de verre), dans lequel les vins sont fermentés et coupés.

Cuvée

Contenu de la cuve. Ce mot signifie couramment tout le vin provenant d'une cuve ou tout le vin fait à un certain moment et dans les mêmes conditions. Dans certaines régions de France, cuvée signifie aussi parcelle de vigne. En Champagne, il a deux autres significations : le vin de cuvée est celui du premier pressage et une cuvée est un certain mélange de Champagne ou une fraction déterminée du vin en stock. La *Cuvée anglaise* est un Champagne très sec, préparé spécialement par coupage pour l'Angleterre. *Voir* CHAMPAGNE

D

Dame-jeanne

N'importe quelle grosse bouteille qui contient plus de 2 l, et généralement enrobée de vannerie. La dame-jeanne sert à conserver ou transporter vins ou spiritueux. Dans le Bordelais, la dame-jeanne a une contenance plus précise : plus que le magnum, et moins que le double magnum, soit l'équivalent de 2,5 l environ. L'usage de ce récipient dans cette région en rapports constants avec l'Angleterre doit dater de longtemps car son nom en anglais *(demi-john)* est visiblement une déformation du mot français. N'est plus fabriquée.

Dampierre

Commune productrice de vin rosé et rouge sur les coteaux de Saumur.

Voir ANJOU

Damson Gin

Gin britannique qui doit son goût aux petites prunes noires dites Damson.

Danemark

Le climat du Danemark ne lui permet pas de produire du véritable vin, mais on y fait un commerce actif de « vins de fruits ». Les plus populaires sont faits avec des baies : cassis, mûres et surtout, des cerises.

Le Danemark produit également des liqueurs dont la plus connue est probablement le Cherry Heering. La plupart des cerises servant à la distillation proviennent de Seeland (île danoise où se trouve la capitale du pays et située entre la Suède et le continent).

Autre liqueur très consommée : le Cloc brun (*voir* CUMIN LIQUIDUM OPTIMUM CASTELLI), breuvage épicé au léger goût de cumin et titrant 38,5°.

SPIRITUEUX

Depuis des années, les Danois s'ingénient à produire du whisky. En 1952, le premier whisky distillé au Danemark fut lancé sur le marché par la firme qui commercialise le Cumin liquidum optimum castelli ou Cloc brun.

Les fabricants se servent de malt d'orge séché au-dessus d'un feu de tourbe ; le whisky est distillé en alambic et mûri dans des fûts de chêne.

La plus forte production de spiritueux danois est l'aquavit (Akvavit en danois). Il est bu au cours des repas, en dépit de son fort parfum de cumin.

Voir AQUAVIT

Danziger Goldwasser

Liqueur blanche anisée et parfumée aussi au cumin. On ajoute à ce liquide des paillettes d'or qui flottent dans la bouteille. On fait aussi une Silberwasser dans laquelle des paillettes d'argent remplacent celles d'or. A l'origine, ces liqueurs étaient produites dans le vieux port de Danzig. Puis nombre de firmes en firent de semblables. La plus connue est sans doute la Liqueur d'or, produite en France.

Dão

Vins portugais *(Denominação de Origem)*, surtout rouges, provenant des vignobles situés au sud du Douro.

Voir PORTUGAL

Dauzac (Château-)

Bordeaux rouge. Commune de Labarde-Margaux, en Haut-Médoc.

Les vignes de ce Cinquième Cru poussent sur un bon sol plat et caillouteux aux confins sud de la zone délimitée ayant droit à l'appellation d'origine Margaux. Elles appartenaient autrefois à la firme bordelaise de Nathaniel Johnston — négociant en vins — puis à M. H. Bernet. Les premiers propriétaires, les Lynch, quittèrent leur Irlande natale au XVIIIe siècle pour venir s'installer en France. Ils laissèrent leur empreinte sur plusieurs châteaux du Médoc et constituent un exemple de la grande influence des Irlandais dans cette région. M. A. Miailhe, propriétaire de Château-Siran contigu à Dauzac, l'acheta en 1966. Il planta une superficie considérable, plus que doublant la production primitive. M. Félix Chatellier, arboriculteur et propriétaire depuis 1978, a construit de nouveaux chais et installé un équipement moderne de cuverie.

Caractéristiques : M. Chatellier a réalisé de remarquables progrès qui font d'un vin laissant à désirer un vin supérieur à son classement.

Superficie : 55 ha.

Production moyenne : 20 000 caisses.

Debröi Hárslevelü

Un des meilleurs vins blancs secs de Hongrie. Il est fait avec des raisins Hárslevelü, qui entrent aussi pour partie dans la vinification du Tokay.

Voir HONGRIE

Décanter

Verser du vin de sa bouteille d'origine dans un autre contenant qui sera apporté sur la table. Cette opération (décantation ou décantage) a pour but, soit de séparer le vin de son dépôt, soit de l'aérer.

Déclassement

Rétrogradation d'un vin dans la hiérarchie des appellations d'origine contrôlée, c'est-à-dire passage, après dégustation, à une appellation moins précise (par exemple de Pauillac à Haut-Médoc ou de Nuits-Saint-Georges à Bourgogne) ou à une appellation moins appréciée (par exemple de Bordeaux Supérieur à Bordeaux ou de Bourgogne à Bourgogne Grand Ordinaire), ou encore, perte de toute appellation d'origine pour devenir simplement : vin rouge, vin blanc ou vin rosé.

Cependant avec le PLC, ou plafond limite de classement, un propriétaire peut déclasser un vin sous un autre nom, tout en respectant les normes et les limites de l'appellation d'origine. Château Lafite est à Pauillac ainsi que château Latour. Dans le cas du PLC, une certaine partie de leur production peut être respectivement appelée Moulin des Carruades et Les Forts de Latour et ces vins gardent l'appellation Pauillac.

Voir à ce sujet les tableaux d'appellation d'origine contrôlée d'origine contrôlée aux articles BORDEAUX et BOURGOGNE.

Dégénérescence infectieuse

Maladie de la vigne due à un virus, appelée aussi court noué.

Voir CHAPITRE IV

Dégorgement

Opération consistant à éliminer le dépôt des bouteilles de Champagne et autres vins mousseux.

Voir CHAMPAGNE

Dégustation

Permet de juger la qualité et les caractéristiques d'un vin par le goût et l'odorat. La dégustation à l'aveugle consiste à garder secrètes l'origine ou l'identité d'un vin avant de le présenter au dégustateur.

Deidesheimer Grainhübel

Un des meilleurs vins de Deidesheim, en Palatinat.

Voir PALATINAT

Deidesheimer Leinhöhle

Vin remarquable de Deidesheim, en Palatinat.

Voir PALATINAT

Delaware

Une des meilleures variétés de vigne de l'Est des États-Unis. Probablement originaire du Delaware, elle est surtout cultivée dans l'Ohio et dans le secteur vinicole de Finger Lakes (État de New York). Le raisin de cette vigne donne un vin net, frais, épicé, qui n'a pas trop le goût de foxe et qu'on traite généralement en mousseux.

Delicat, Delikat

Mots français et allemand désignant le goût subtil d'un vin titrant moins de 12°, ce qui est le cas de bien des vins allemands, lesquels titrent aussi peu que 8°.

Delicatessen

Vigne hybride sans qualités remarquables et qui produit des vins rouges. Obtenue par T.V. Manson, du Texas, elle devrait son nom au grand nombre de variétés diverses d'où elle provient et qui donne une idée de charcuterie.

Demi, demie

Le demi n'est pas un demi-litre, mais fut autrefois une demi-pinte. Légalement, le demi de bière servi à la pression contient 25 cl. Quant à la demie (demi-bouteille), il s'agit d'un flacon couramment appelé chopine. (Contenance variant entre 37,5 et 50 cl).

Voir APPENDICE B

Demi-queue

Étant donné que la queue désigne en Bourgogne deux pièces, la demi-queue équivaut à une pièce, c'est-à-dire à une barrique qui contient 228 l.

Demi-john

Grosse bouteille enrobée de sparterie et d'une contenance variant entre 1 et 50 l. On s'en sert couramment pour conserver et transporter le vin. Selon toute évidence, ce nom est une corruption du français : dame-jeanne. Cette particularité a éveillé la curiosité des amateurs d'étymologie qui se sont efforcés de faire remonter le mot à l'arabe ou au persan. Il semble pourtant que le mot arabe désignant cette grosse bouteille vienne de l'italien.

Demi-sec

Porté sur l'étiquette d'une bouteille de Champagne, ce mot ne désigne pas un vin sec, mais au contraire plutôt doux.

Voir CHAMPAGNE

Dénaturant, dénaturé, dénaturer

Le dénaturant est une substance que l'on ajoute à l'alcool pour le rendre impropre à la consommation afin d'éviter les lourdes taxes imposées aux spiritueux.

Denominación de Origen

Garantie de validité des étiquettes des vins espagnols.

Voir CHAPITRE X

Denominazione di Origine Controlata

Équivalent en Italie de l'appellation contrôlée. La loi qui l'organisa prévoit trois degrés : appellation d'origine simple *(semplice)* ; appellation d'origine contrôlée *(controlata)*, D.O.C. ; appellation d'origine contrôlée et garantie pour les meilleurs vins *(controlata e garantita)*, D.O.C.G.

Voir ITALIE

Densimètre, densimétrie

Le densimètre est un instrument fondé sur le principe d'Archimède, qui sert à mesurer la densité du moût de raisin. Il consiste en un cylindre creux, lesté et gradué, qui s'enfonce plus ou moins dans le liquide, en fonction de la densité de ce dernier.

Voir ARÉOMÈTRE, MUSTIMÈTRE

Dépôt

On observe fréquemment la précipitation d'un dépôt dans de nombreux vins rouges et certains blancs au cours de leur vieillissement en bouteille. Dans les vins blancs, il s'agit généralement d'une parcelle de cristal d'acide tartrique incolore, sans goût et sans danger, mais dans les vins rouges ce dépôt contient généralement un tanin amer et un pigment et doit être laissé tel quel dans la bouteille. Les vieux vins rouges de classe, qui contiennent parfois une quantité considérable de ce dépôt, sont alors décantés pour séparer le vin de la couche présente au fond de la bouteille. C'est pourquoi certaines bouteilles de vins rouges de qualité, tels les Bordeaux ou Bourgogne, ont des « dentelures » permettant de séparer le dépôt du reste du vin.

Desmirail (Château-)

Bordeaux rouge. Commune de Margaux, en Haut-Médoc.

Classé Troisième Cru en 1855, ce vignoble a été absorbé par Château-Palmer. En 1981, la marque fut achetée par M. Lurton de Brane-Cantenac. Le bâtiment appartenait à feu M. Paul Zuger, ancien propriétaire du Château-Malescot-Saint-Exupéry et fut rebaptisé Château Marquis-d'Alesme par Jean-Claude, son fils, en 1981. Le fait que le Château-Desmirail figure encore parmi les crus classés du Bordelais démontre combien la classification de 1855 est périmée.

Dessert (Vins de)

Vins doux, charnus, parfois additionnés d'alcool, qui conviennent au dessert ou sont bus ensuite. Aux États-Unis, le vin de dessert, bu n'importe quand, est tout simplement un vin de liqueur (additionné d'eau-de-vie, ou un vin auquel on a ajouté un spiritueux quelconque). Les vins de table naturels considérés comme vins de dessert sont les Barsac, Sauternes, Vouvray ou vins doux de la Loire, le Vin Santo d'Italie, les Beerenauslesen et Trokenbeerenauslesen du Rhin et de la Moselle, ou les vins de Californie ou d'Alsace, vendangés plus tard.

Dézaley

Vin blanc bien connu de Lavaux, dans le canton de Vaud.

Voir SUISSE

Dezize-les-Maranges et Dezize-les-Maranges-Côte de Beaune (Appellation Contrôlée)

Bourgogne rouge et blanc. Côte de Beaune.

Commune de vins mineurs, située à l'extrémité sud de la Côte de Beaune. Ses vins sont très légers, vieillissent vite et ont parfois un bon fruité. On les mélange habituellement à ceux d'autres communes de la même côte pour les vendre sous l'appellation de Côte de Beaune-Villages. Mais, de temps en temps, certains sont vendus sous le seul nom de la commune. Cette différence d'étiquette n'est pas à la discrétion des producteurs. Il s'agit de géographie et de qualité. Le vin qui porte le nom de la commune doit seulement avoir été produit avec n'importe quel raisin cultivé sur les 60 ha de vignes de Dezize-les-Maranges. Pour y ajouter le nom Côte de Beaune, il doit provenir des 30,4 ha privilégiés.

Dhroner Hofberg

Vin remarquable de Dhron, situé sur la Moselle.
Voir MOSELLE

Diamond (Moore's Diamond)

Raisin hybride américain obtenu par Jacob Moore. Ce raisin fut autrefois très utilisé pour faire du vin blanc, mais convient mieux comme raisin de table.

Diana

Une des premières vignes hybrides des États-Unis, obtenue dans le but d'améliorer la célèbre Catawba. Le raisin Diana est assez répandu dans l'Ohio et l'État de New York. Il sert à faire des vins blancs mais présente le défaut de varier considérablement en qualité d'une année à l'autre.

Diastase

Ferment produit par la levure et qui convertit l'amidon en dextrine, puis en sucre et enfin transforme le sucre en alcool et en gaz carbonique.

Die

Voir CLAIRETTE DE DIE

Dimyat

Raisin à vin blanc, cultivé en Bulgarie sur la côte de la mer Noire.
Voir BULGARIE

Dionysos

Dieu grec du vin.
Probablement originaire de Thrace, Dionysos était une divinité de la nature symbolisant autant la fécondité que le vin. Selon la mythologie grecque, il était fils de Zeus et de Sémélé, était doué de dons prophétiques et parcourait le monde connu en ce temps-là en répandant la culture de la vigne. Il imposa, conjointement aux rites bacchiques, le culte de sa propre personnalité. Selon Euripide, Panthée, roi de Thèbes, voulut interdire les rites bacchiques et en périt. Bacchos, autre nom du dieu Vin, fut plus tard adopté par les romains sous le nom de Bacchus *(voir ce mot)*.

Distillation

Art ou science fondés sur le principe que, l'alcool étant plus léger que l'eau, il s'évapore à une température plus basse, ce qui fait que, lorsqu'un liquide légèrement alcoolisé est chauffé à une température comprise entre les deux points d'ébullition, les vapeurs qui s'en élèvent peuvent être retenues et condensées pour former un liquide de teneur alcoolique plus élevée. Selon la qualité et les caractéristiques que l'on désire obtenir, la distillation se fait soit dans des alambics, soit dans des appareils à distillation continue.

Dans la troisième édition de son ouvrage, *The Engineers'Handbook*, J. H. Perry définit la distillation comme étant « la séparation des constituants d'un mélange liquide par vaporisation partielle de celuici et récupération indépendante de la vapeur et des résidus. Les constituants les plus volatils du mélange primitif seront retenus de façon plus concentrée dans la vapeur, les constituants moins volatils seront en plus grande concentration dans le résidu liquide. La perfection de la séparation dépend de certaines propriétés des composantes présentes et des modalités du processus de distillation. En général, on appelle « distillation » les processus de vaporisation par lesquels on obtient la vapeur, habituellement par condensation. On appelle « évaporation » la disparition de l'eau de la solution aqueuse de substances non volatiles par la vaporisation. La vapeur développée, c'est-à-dire l'eau, est éliminée. La majorité des applications de la distillation se trouvent dans la séparation d'une ou de plusieurs des composantes d'avec les mélanges de corps composés organiques.
Voir CHAPITRE II

Distillation (seconde)

Elle permet d'améliorer le goût et la vigueur d'une eau-de-vie.

Dizy

Commune proche d'Ay, dans la vallée de la Marne. On y produit un Champagne coté à 95 %.
Voir CHAMPAGNE

D.O.C. ou D.O.C.G.

Voir DENOMINAZIONE DI ORIGINE CONTROLATA ; ITALIE

Doisy-Daëne (Château-)

Bordeaux blanc. Commune de Barsac, en Sauternes.
Classé Second Cru en 1855, ce domaine produit un vin doux typique de la région, ainsi qu'une petite quantité de vin blanc sec fait en partie avec du Riesling, mais qui ne porte pas le nom du château.
Superficie : 15 ha.
Production moyenne : 30 tonneaux (2 000 caisses).

Doisy-Védrines (Château-)

Bordeaux blanc. Commune de Barsac, en Sauternes.
Classé Second Cru en 1855, cette propriété est située entre Château-Coutet et Château-Climens, tous deux Premiers Crus de la même classification. On y fait un vin liquoreux. Château Doisy-Védrines appartient à Pierre Casteja, frère d'Émile Casteja, propriétaire d'un vignoble du Médoc.
Superficie : 20 ha.
Production moyenne : 40 tonneaux (4 000 caisses).

Dolceacqua ou (Rossese)

Vin rouge D.O.C. fait avec du raisin Rossese, le long de la côte de Ligurie *(voir ce nom).*

Dolcetto

Raisin italien donnant des vins secs génériques.
Voir PIÉMONT

Dole

Bon vin rouge fait dans le Valais avec du raisin Gamay qu'on appelle Dole dans ce pays. Cas très exceptionnel parmi les vins, celui-ci est féminin. Dans le Valais, on l'appelle la Dole. Il entre aussi dans sa composition du Pinot Noir à jus blanc du Beaujolais.

Dom

« Cathédrale », en allemand, certaines d'entre elles étant dotées de vignobles. La plus notoire est la cathédrale de Trier, qui possède des vignobles au sud de la commune d'Avelsbach ainsi qu'à Wiltingen, sur la Sarre.

Dom Pérignon

Père légendaire du Champagne tel que nous le connaissons de nos jours.
Voir CHAMPAGNE

Domaine

Propriété foncière. En ce qui concerne le sujet de cette encyclopédie, il s'agit d'un domaine viticole. On le trouve surtout dans l'expression : *mise en bouteille au domaine.*

Donnaz (D.O.C.)

Vin rouge du Val d'Aoste, au nord de l'Italie.
Voir PIÉMONT ; ITALIE : VAL D'AOSTE

Dop Brandy

Eau-de-vie de marc sud-africaine. Des impôts incroyablement élevés en ont rendu la production dénuée d'intérêt au point de vue économique et on n'en trouve presque plus, ce qui n'est pas une grande perte étant donné sa qualité.

Dosage

Addition de sirop de sucre au Champagne et autres vins mousseux avant bouchage final et expédition.

Voir CHAMPAGNE

Douro

L'un des trois fleuves les plus importants du Portugal.

Voir PORTO

Dousico

Breuvage grec capiteux, à goût d'anis.

Doux

Appliqué aux vins, ce mot signifie qu'ils ont un goût sucré, par exemple, Sauternes et Barsac.

Sur l'étiquette d'une bouteille de Champagne, le mot doux indique un vin très sucré qui n'est guère consommé en Grande-Bretagne ni aux États-Unis, et que dédaignent partout les véritables amateurs de ce vin.

Doux (Vins doux naturels)

La différence entre les vins doux et les vins doux naturels, c'est que ces derniers sont produits d'une manière artificielle par addition d'alcool, après ou pendant la fermentation. Ce qu'il y a de naturel, c'est que l'alcool ne doit être que de l'eau-de-vie de vin.

Voir VINS VINÉS

Douzico

Spiritueux turc dans le genre du kummel.

Downy Mildew

Mildiou cotonneux, appelé faux mildiou en Amérique et mildiou en France.

Ne pas confondre avec le mildiou poudreux : une des maladies qui fait le plus de mal aux vignes.

Voir CHAPITRE IV

Draff

Matière résiduelle solide qui subsiste dans la cuve après la fermentation du grain dont on fait le whisky.

Drambuie

Liqueur composée de scotch, de miel de bruyère et d'herbes, dont la formule secrète appartient à la famille Mackinnon de la banlieue d'Edimbourg, en Écosse. On dit que la formule aurait été donnée par Bonnie Prince Charlie à un lointain Mackinnon qui l'aurait aidé à s'enfuir en France.

Le nom serait une corruption de l'expression gaélique *an dram buidheach*, signifiant : la liqueur qui satisfait. C'est une des liqueurs les plus populaires aux États-Unis.

Dreimännerwein

Sobriquet familier du vin de Reutlingen et qui signifie « vin de trois hommes », non qu'il fasse voir triple, mais parce que ce vin est si mauvais, dit-on, qu'il faut un homme pour tenir le buveur, un second pour lui verser le vin dans la bouche et enfin le troisième pour l'avaler.

Dry

Voir SEC

Dubonnet

Apéritif rouge foncé populaire consistant en un vin doux naturel additionné d'écorces amères et de quinquina qui lui donnent son goût caractéristique. On en fait aux États-Unis du rouge et du blanc. Consommé aussi en Angleterre.

Ducru-Beaucaillou (Château-)

Bordeaux rouge. Commune de Saint-Julien, en Haut-Médoc.

Le vignoble forme un tapis continu avec celui du Château-Beychevelle. Son nom actuel lui a été donné par le propriétaire précédent, M. Ducru, et il est bien nommé en raison de la proportion élevée de pierres que l'on trouve sur le sol où sont plantées les vignes. Ces cailloux contribuent à la grandeur de bien des vins du Médoc, notamment Château-Latour. A Beaucaillou la couche pierreuse est très épaisse.

Le bâtiment est à l'écart de la route, en bordure du coteau qui domine la Gironde.

Au cours des années trente et au début des années quarante de notre siècle, ce cru était tombé si bas que bien des Bordelais trouvaient injustifié son rang de Second Cru.

Mais, au cours des années cinquante, son propriétaire actuel, M. Jean-Eugène Borie, lui rendit la vie et c'est actuellement un vignoble qui mérite d'être très prisé.

Caractéristiques : Souple mais charnu ; typiquement un grand Saint-Julien. Excellent vin. On peut compter sur une constance de qualité d'année en année. Ce grand vin surpasse en qualité la plupart des Seconds Crus classés.

Superficie : 50 ha.

Production moyenne : 220 tonneaux (20 000 caisses).

Duhart-Milon-Rothschild (Château-)

Bordeaux rouge. Commune de Pauillac, en Haut-Médoc.

Seul Quatrième Cru de Pauillac, selon la classification de 1855. Une partie des vignes est contiguë à celles de Château-Lafite, qui a d'ailleurs acheté Duhart-Milon.

Caractéristiques : Ce vin partage certaines des caractéristiques propres aux vins de Pauillac mais sa qualité n'était pas ce qu'elle aurait dû être. Les nouveaux propriétaires l'ont déjà beaucoup améliorée et la réputation de ce vin grandira certainement.

Superficie : 58 ha.

Production moyenne : 230 tonneaux (20 000 caisses).

Dulce

Signifie « doux » en espagnol, surtout en matière de vins. Vins doux ajoutés au Xérès sec pour mieux le vendre à l'étranger.

Dunder

Lie de canne à sucre utilisée pour déclencher la fermentation du rhum.

Dur

Un excès de tanin rend le vin dur. Mais il ne s'agit pas forcément d'un défaut, car il disparaît avec l'âge, et la dureté contribue à conserver le vin. Celui qui fut dur dans sa jeunesse devient ferme. En fin de compte, la dureté est un signe de vigueur juvénile. Les Bordeaux rouges de 1975, par exemple, restèrent durs jusque vers les années 90.

Se dit d'un vin manquant de « moelleux ».

Voir FERMÉ

Duras

Voir CÔTES DE DURAS

Durfort-Vivens (Château-)

Bordeaux rouge. Commune de Margaux, en Haut-Médoc.

Classé Second Cru en 1855, ce château appartint à M. Pierre Ginestet. A l'origine, il appartenait à M. Durfort de Duras. Il porte son nom actuel depuis son achat en 1924 par M. Vivens. Il est situé à l'entrée de l'agglomération de Margaux, près des Château-Margaux, Château-Palmer, Château-Rauzan-Ségla et Château-Rausan-Gassies qui sont très souvent supérieurs aux Durfort. En 1963, les vignes et les chais furent achetés par M. Lucien Lurton. Propriétaire de Brane-Cantenac, du Château Climens, et depuis 1979 du Château Bouscaut, M. Lurton a plus que doublé la superficie du vignoble, qui est passé de 10 à 42 ha. Le château appartient actuellement à Bernard Ginestet, qui y vit depuis les années soixante plutôt qu'au Château-Margaux qui appartint à la famille jusqu'en 1977.

Superficie : 25 ha.

Production moyenne : 90 tonneaux (8 000 caisses).

Duriff

Cépage de Californie, autre nom du Petit-Syrah *(voir ce nom).*

Dürkheim (Bad Dürkheim)

Le Wurstmarkt qui se tient en septembre dans cette ville est un des plus grands festivals du vin (en dépit de son nom qui signifie : marché de la saucisse). Dürkheim produit une grande quantité de blanc et le rouge, le plus renommé du Palatinat.

Voir PALATINAT

Dutchess

Vigne américaine obtenue dans le canton Dutchess (État de New York) vers le milieu du XIXe siècle. Elle donne des vins légers et secs. On la cultive encore plus ou moins dans l'État de New York.

E

East India

Voir INDES ORIENTALES

Eau-de-vie

A l'origine : alcool de vin. Désormais : tout alcool consommable, produit par la distillation de n'importe quoi. Les eaux-de-vie les plus connues sont l'Armagnac et le Cognac, produits par la distillation de vin et le Calvados, par la distillation du cidre.
Voir APPLEJACK ; AQUAVITAE ; AQUA VITE ; ARMAGNAC ; CALVADOS ; COGNAC ; DISTILLATION

Eau-de-vie d'artichaut

Alcool distillé en France, fait avec l'artichaut de Jérusalem. Il existe en Italie un apéritif appelé Cynar, également produit avec des artichauts.

Eau-de-vie de cidre

Toute eau-de-vie obtenue par distillation du cidre.
Voir APPLEJACK ; CALVADOS

Eau-de-vie de Danzig

Équivalent français de la Danziger Goldwasser *(voir ce mot)* ; appelé aussi Liqueur d'Or.

Eau-de-vie de lie

Spiritueux produit par la distillation de la lie récupérée au moment du lavage des fûts.

Eau-de-vie de marc

Voir MARC

Eau-de-vie de vin

Voir EAU-DE-VIE

Ébullioscope

Appareil servant à déterminer la teneur en alcool des vins et spiritueux. Fondé sur le fait que, à la pression atmosphérique normale (760 mm de mercure), l'eau bout à 100° et l'alcool à 78°C, le point d'ébullition du liquide mis à l'épreuve indiquera la proportion d'alcool et d'eau qu'il contient. Ce point se situera évidemment entre 78 °C et 100 °C.

Échezeaux (Appellation Contrôlée)

Bourgogne rouge. Commune de Flagey-Échezeaux, en Côte de Nuits. Classement officiel : Les Échezeaux du Dessus Grand Cru.

Échezeaux est une appellation d'origine contrôlée, mais ni un vignoble ni un cru : cas exceptionnel qui n'est concevable qu'en

Bourgogne. Cette appellation d'origine englobe tout ou partie de onze vignobles différents, dont l'un, auquel on a accordé le titre de Grand Cru, le plus élevé de Bourgogne.

Ci-dessous la liste des vignobles d'où proviennent ces vins :

Crus	*Superficie (ha)*
Les Grands-Échezeaux	9,2
Les Échezeaux :	
En Orveaux	9,7
Les Treux	4,9
Clos Saint-Denis	1,8
Les Cruots (ou Vignes blanches)	3,3
Les Rouges-du-Bas	4,0
Champs-Traversins	3,6
Les Poulaillières	5,2
Les Loachausses	3,8
Les Quartiers de Nuits	2,6
Les Échezeaux du Dessus	3,6

Comme s'il ne leur suffisait pas d'avoir jeté leur filet et baptisé Échezeaux tous les vins des alentours et tout ce qu'elles y trouvaient, les autorités viticoles choisirent le nom de Flagey, localité où il n'y a pas d'autre vignoble important (sauf le Grand Cru Grands-Échezeaux qui est aussi une appellation, mais celle-ci distincte de l'appellation Échezeaux — *voir* Grands-Échezeaux). Flagey-Échezeaux est situé du mauvais côté de la grand-route (du côté est) qui va de Dijon à Lyon, c'est-à-dire sur la plaine où l'on ne fait aucun vin qui mérite d'être cité. Une petite partie seulement de son territoire s'étend à l'ouest de la route, sur le coteau. Il en résulte que, si les vins des onze vignes en question n'atteignent pas leurs normes minimales, ils sont vendus sous le nom de Vosne-Romanée.

En réalité, on vend très peu de vin sous l'appellation d'Échezeaux et presque tout ce vin est livré au commerce sous l'étiquette Vosne-Romanée, d'ailleurs tout proche. Il y a au moins une raison à cela : bien peu de gens connaissent le nom d'Échezeaux ou de Flagey-Échezeaux qui n'est pas facile à prononcer.

La superficie et la diversité des vignobles ayant droit à cette appellation impliquent que, lorsqu'on trouve des Échezeaux sous leur propre nom, ils peuvent différer considérablement les uns des autres. Certains seront magnifiquement arrondis et propres à combler la différence existant entre les Vougeot, charnus et vigoureux, et les Vosne-Romanée, légers et délicats ; d'autres auront moins de distinction qu'ils le devraient. Faute d'être connus dans le monde, ils sont vendus à des prix intéressants. La demande est, en effet, si minime qu'on les vend à des prix inférieurs aux vins présentant des qualités similaires, mais de plus grande réputation.

La production moyenne varie autour de 1 400 hl, soit à peu près 15 500 caisses.

Echt

Kummel russe ou polonais contenant des cristaux de sucre.

Voir KUMMEL

Écologie viticole

Étude de la relation existante entre la vigne et les sol et climat dans lequels elle prospère, également de la qualité du vin que ses fruits produisent.

Edelfäule

Pourriture noble, en allemand.

Edelweiss

Liqueur italienne faite avec des extraits de fleurs des Alpes. Il s'agit d'une marque particulière de la liqueur nommée Fior d'Alpi.

Edelzwicker

Sur une bouteille de vin d'Alsace, le mot Edelzwicker indique un coupage de raisins nobles.

Voir ALSACE

Égrappage

Séparation des raisins et des pédoncules avant de verser le moût dans la cuve de fermentation et de pressurer. L'égrappage est nécessaire parce que les pédoncules contiennent des huiles et tanins qui rendraient le vin amer et âpre. On égrappe à la main ou avec une machine nommée égrappoir. Égrappage se dit aussi éraflage ou plus simplement séparation *(voir ce mot).*

Egri Bikavér

Sans doute le vin hongrois le plus connu, Tokay excepté. C'est un vin rouge dont le nom signifie « Sang de taureau d'Eger ».

Voir HONGRIE

Égypte

De temps en temps, on trouve des jarres dans un tombeau et, quand on les ouvre, elles contiennent des traces tout à fait sèches de ce qui fut du vin, voilà quelque cinq mille ans sans doute. Mais l'art égyptien de l'Antiquité nous révèle comment on cueillait les grappes, comment on les pressurait et comment on enterrait le vin dans les tombeaux. On serait même naïvement tenté de croire que ce vin était destiné uniquement aux morts.

Les aventures de l'Égyptien Nestor Gianaclis, au XXe siècle, sont peut-être les plus fascinantes de notre époque. En s'appuyant sur toutes les connaissances scientifiques modernes, il s'est ingénié à reconstituer un passé disparu depuis plus de 2 000 ans.

Dans l'Antiquité, les vins égyptiens jouissaient d'une excellente réputation. Cléopâtre servit à César du Maréotique qui provenait, dit-on, de Méroé, près de la quatrième cataracte, sur le Nil supérieur. D'autres vins égyptiens connaissaient une grande vogue dans tout le monde méditerranéen.

Au début de notre siècle, il n'y en avait pratiquement plus et les rares vins d'Égypte étaient indiscutablement mauvais. Nestor Gianaclis entreprit de rechercher les sols sur lesquels on pourrait cultiver les bonnes vignes à vin. Parallèlement, il essaya de découvrir quel était vraiment le goût des vins égyptiens antiques. Conviendraient-ils encore aux gens du XXe siècle ? D'après les œuvres de Virgile, Horace, Pline et d'autres auteurs qui écrivirent au sujet des vins consommés par les Grecs et les Romains de l'Antiquité, Gianaclis conclut que leur goût ne devait pas différer sensiblement du nôtre. S'ils aimaient les vins égyptiens, nous les aimerions aussi.

Sous le sable qui le recouvrait, il trouva, au seuil du désert, un sol totalement différent des alluvions apportées par le Nil et qui constitue désormais la terre arable de sa vallée. L'analyse chimique confirma qu'il s'agissait de terres calcaires exemptes de sel, presque identiques à celles de la Champagne. Ce début était prometteur, et Gianaclis planta ses premières vignes en 1903.

Les difficultés commençaient seulement. Les livres les plus complets sur le vin antique n'indiquaient presque rien quant à la variété des vignes cultivées dans l'ancienne Égypte.

A longueur d'année, on essaya 73 variétés de vignes avec la collaboration d'experts français, italiens, hongrois et d'autres pays vinicoles ; Gianaclis obtint vingt autres nouveaux types qui furent soumis à des analyses de laboratoire. Les grands vins exigent du soleil, un sol, une vigne appropriée à ce sol et, surtout, la bonne combinaison de ces trois éléments. Gianaclis dut faire en quelques années ce qui avait nécessité des siècles d'expérience dans la plupart des pays vinicoles : harmoniser la bonne technique et la bonne vigne au climat et au sol.

En 1931, après plus d'un quart de siècle d'efforts, il sembla que Gianaclis avait réussi. Cette année-là, il présenta à la Chambre syndicale des courtiers gourmets de Paris des vins du vignoble de Mariout, situé à l'ouest du delta du Nil. Deux années plus tard, on disait en France que le vin des Pharaons avait ressuscité et que le monde pourrait boire de nouveau le nectar vanté par Virgile, mais la qualité laissait beaucoup à désirer.

De nos jours, ces vins tiennent en partie leurs promesses et sont intéressants. Les vins blancs se boivent plus facilement que les rouges, qui peuvent encore s'améliorer. On s'efforce de les orienter vers des types super-californiens et super-algériens pour les lancer sur le marché mondial. On a envoyé des échantillons aux grandes expositions internationales et la production qui s'accroît (quelque 15 000 hl — plus de 1 000 caisses — chaque année à partir d'un encépagement de 30 000 ha) dépasse la capacité d'absorption du marché intérieur. L'exportation s'est développée, particulièrement en direction de l'Union Soviétique. Une coopérative d'État, la « Egyptian

Vineyards and Distillers Co », possède, près d'Alexandrie, des vignobles produisant plusieurs vins, dont un rouge : le Omar Khayyam, qui doit s'améliorer.

SPIRITUEUX

La différence de prix entre les spiritueux égyptiens et étrangers est faible. Cognac, whisky d'importation concurrencent fortement les rhums, araks, et eaux-de-vie domestiques qui sont taxés à 55 %. Le rhum produit par la distillation de la mélasse provenant de canne à sucre égyptienne est de bonne qualité. Néanmoins, l'Égypte produit à peu près deux fois plus de *tafia* : spiritueux plus grossier obtenu par distillation des résidus de la fabrication de sucre. La production annuelle de cet alcool s'élève à quelque 8 300 hl (92 000 caisses) et celle du rhum à environ 2 800 (31 000 caisses). Le tafia titre plus de 50°. Enfin, on fait un autre alcool consistant en un mélange de rhum et de tafia, additionné de 30 % d'eau-de-vie de vin et dans lequel le rhum n'entre que pour 10 % (production annuelle quelque 12 500 hl ou plus de 135 000 caisses). Quelques Égyptiens consomment aussi un alcool de datte nommé *Buza*. La fermentation et la distillation de ce fruit (souvent à moitié pourri) sont livrées au hasard. Peut-être est-ce ce qui le rend populaire car, fabriqué dans de telles conditions, son prix est à la portée des paysans du pays.

Eiswein

Vin fait à partir de raisins doux et gelés, sélectionnés fin novembre et au mois de décembre. Le jus, en gelant, se sépare du sucre. D'une qualité similaire au Beerenauslese.

Eitelsbacher Karthäuserhofberg

Cru remarquable d'Eitelbach, dans la Ruhr.

Voir RUHR

Elbling

Vigne cultivée au Luxembourg, en Lorraine et en Allemagne qui produit de grosses quantités de vin.

Elefantenwein (Vin d'Éléphant)

Surnom d'un vin de Tübingen (Allemagne), fait avec des raisins si durs, dit-on, que l'homme ne pourrait pas les fouler et que seul l'éléphant en exprimerait le jus. On faisait la même plaisanterie au sujet du Reutlinger de la région du Neckar.

Élixir d'Anvers

Marque de liqueur faite par F.X. de Beukelaer, d'Anvers, avec des herbes et plantes macérées dans de l'eau-de-vie de vin. Ce spiritueux doré, assez doux, est très parfumé.

Élixir Longae Vitae.

Autre nom des Pommeranzen Bitters.

Voir BITTER

Eltviller Sonnenberg

Le plus élégant des vins d'Eltville. L'autre cru remarquable de la localité s'appelle Eltviller Langenstück.

Voir RHEINGAU

Elvira

Vigne hybride américaine obtenue à la fin du XIXe siècle dans le Missouri. On la cultive encore pour faire des vins blancs, généralement mousseux.

Émilie-Romagne

Vins blancs et rouges. Italie.

Au sud du Pô, une grande plaine s'étend des Apennins jusqu'à la côte Adriatique. Une montagne s'y dresse, au sommet de laquelle se trouve la république de Saint-Marin et sur les flancs de laquelle on cultive la vigne.

Cette région constitue la province d'Émilie-Romagne. Dans l'ensemble, son sol est plat. Elle est surtout agricole et on y cultive le blé et le maïs. Les vignobles d'une certaine superficie sont rares, mais on voit partout de la vigne. Elle se faufile entre les autres cultures, s'accroche à n'importe quel support. Apparemment, elle ne bénéficie d'aucun soin et ignore le couteau du vigneron. Cette viticulture hors du commun donne un charme étrange au décor, mais ne contribue pas à la qualité des vins. Cependant, aujourd'hui, les vignobles sont remarquablement soignés et le palissage des vignes est fait avec grand soin. On estime que le vignoble compte 5 000 ha.

San Giovese di Romagna

Lambrusco et Albana donnent les vins les plus fameux de l'Émilie-Romagne, mais le San Giovese est le plus répandu. Il varie à l'extrême ; parfois amer et dur, parfois moelleux et chaleureux. Cependant on en trouve toujours. Il est toujours rouge et toujours sec. Cette dernière caractéristique suffit à charmer bien des visiteurs de la région. Le San Giovese fournit la plus grosse partie de la production annuelle d'Émilie-Romagne : environ 9 millions d'hl.

Lambrusco

Il n'y a que de lointains rapports d'étymologie entre Lambrusco et *Vitis labrusca*, espèce de vigne originaire d'Amérique. Peut être est-ce le meilleur exemple d'un secteur vinicole portant le nom de son raisin. Le vin qu'il produit est rouge, parfois désagréable, tantôt sec, tantôt douceâtre, pétillant, avec une mousse d'un rouge brillant qui déconcerte. L'appellation Lambrusco regroupe quatre D.O.C. : Lambrusco di Sorbara, Lambrusco Grasparossa di Castelvetro, Lambrusco Salamino di Santa. Croce et Lambrusco Reggiano. Les trois premiers sont produits dans la région de Modène, le dernier près de Reggio-Emilia. Dans le meilleur des cas, ce sont des vins très prisés par la population locale, mais ils n'ont rien d'exceptionnel, surtout lorsqu'ils sont trop doux et mousseux. Néanmoins le Lambrusco est le vin importé le plus vendu aux États-Unis.

Albana di Romagna (D.O.C.)

Vin d'un jaune d'or qui peut être sec ou demi-sec et dont même le type sec conserve souvent des traces de sucre non réduit. Ce vin est produit avec de l'Albana qui se cultive dans la région montagneuse située entre Bologne et Rimini.

On dit que Galla Placidia, régente de l'Empire romain d'Occident (435 de notre ère), aurait été l'une des premières ferventes de l'Albana. Alors qu'elle voyageait à travers ce pays, elle s'arrêta dans une petite localité pour étancher sa soif à l'auberge. On lui servit du vin dans une cruche grossière. Quand elle l'eut goûté, elle s'exclama : « Tu mérites d'être bu dans de l'or ! » Depuis, cette localité porte le nom de Bertinoro (Te boire-en or).

Colli Piacentini

D.O.C. d'un vigoureux vin rouge produit à Ziano et dans six autres communes de la province de Plaisance, avec des raisins Barbera et Bornarda. C'est un vin sec avec un léger arrière-goût douceâtre.

Trebbiano di Romagna

D.O.C. fait avec du Trebbiano di Romagna dans une grande région faisant partie des provinces de Bologne, Forli et Ravenne. C'est un vin de couleur paille, au goût sec et au bouquet agréable. On fait aussi un vin mousseux qui peut être sec, doux ou demi-doux.

Il existe également un D.O.C. s'appliquant au Trebbiano val Trebbia, vin fait principalement avec du Trebbiano et qui ne mérite pas grande attention.

Monterosso val d'Arada (D.O.C.)

Vin blanc fait avec les variétés Trebbiano, Belverdino et Santamaria. Légèrement pétillant, il gagne à être bu jeune et frais.

Bianco di Scandiano (D.O.C.)

Vin blanc douceâtre, souvent pétillant, produit dans les vallonnements de Reggio-Emilia.

Colli Bolognesi (Monte San Pietro et Castelli Medioevali)

Ce vin D.O.C. produit sur les coteaux situés entre Modène et Bologne comprend huit variétés. Il est un vin supérieur à la moyenne régionale, fait avec du Pinot Blanc, du Sauvignon Blanc et du Barbera.

Encaveur

Celui qui encave : qui met en cave son propre vin, ou le vin de vignerons qui ne possèdent pas de cave. Ce mot est surtout utilisé dans le Valais. Ailleurs on dit plutôt négociant.

Encépagement

1. Cépages ou variétés de vignes qui composent un vignoble. 2. Superficie plantée de vignes.

Enfer d'Arvier

Vin du Val d'Aoste, en Italie septentrionale.
Voir PIÉMONT

Entonnage

Mise en tonneaux.

Entre-deux-Mers (Appellation Contrôlée)

Bordeaux blancs. Sud-Ouest de la France.
Vins blancs de carafe, légers, nets et fruités, qui avaient tendance depuis quelques années à être secs et doivent l'être maintenant pour satisfaire aux obligations administratives de l'I.N.A.O. Selon la tradition, ils étaient autrefois moelleux et parfois doux. Le vin rouge de la région n'a pas droit à l'appellation d'Entre-deux-Mers et on le vend sous le nom de Bordeaux. Ce secteur vinicole ne comporte aucun Grand Cru. Une bonne partie de son vin est faite par quinze coopératives admirablement équipées et capables de traiter 410 000 hl par an.

Cette région doit son nom à sa situation géographique : Garonne et Dordogne étant, en l'occurrence, considérées comme des mers. Elle est aussi située entre Bordeaux, Libourne, Pomerol et Saint-Émilion. La chaîne de coteaux qui longe la Garonne en face de Graves, Barsac et Sauternes et une petite enclave de sol pierreux, au bord de la Dordogne, près de Libourne, sont les meilleurs secteurs de cette région. Ils ont donc droit à des appellations d'origine distinctes : Loupiac, Sainte-Croix-du-Mont, Cadillac et Premières Côtes de Bordeaux, sur la Garonne, et Graves de Vayres sur la Dordogne. Ce sont les meilleurs vins de la région d'Entre-deux-Mers (A.O.C. pour les vins blancs uniquement).

Entreprise vinicole

Firme faisant son propre vin.

Enzian

Liqueur obtenue par la distillation des racines de gentiane jaune qui, dans la montagne, atteignent jusqu'à 1 m de long. C'est un des types de schnaps les plus aristocratiques. L'Enzian provient des pays alpins et avoisinants.
Voir ALSACE : GENTIANE

Enzymes

Grandes protéines produites par des organismes pour catalyser des réactions chimiques. Les enzymes peuvent être extraits et purifiés, puis ajoutés à une solution de façon à provoquer une transformation chimique. L'enzyme pectinase — que l'on ajoute parfois aux raisins blanc fraîchement pressurés — favorise la décomposition des pectines gélatineuses, ce qui facilite le pressurage. On ne l'utilise jamais pour faire de très bons vins.
Voir CHAPITRE V

Épernay

Important centre commercial situé en Champagne et qui, avec Reims, possède les plus grandes caves de cette région. Moët et Chandon, Pol Roger, Mercier et De Venoge sont les vins les plus importants et les plus réputés. Le siège du Comité Interprofessionnel des Vins de Champagne (C.I.V.C.) se situe à Épernay.
Voir CHAMPAGNE

Épesses

Vin blanc de Lavaux (canton de Vaud).
Voir SUISSE

Équilibre

Degré d'harmonie atteint par les diverses composantes d'un vin jugé dans son ensemble. Ceci revient à dire qu'un vin équilibré contrôle tous ses différents aspects sans qu'aucun ne soit particulièrement décelable ou déficient. Un vin équilibré peut ne pas être un grand vin, mais un grand vin est toujours équilibré.

Éraflage

Synonyme d'égrappage, (*voir ce mot et* SÉPARATION).

Erbacher Markobrunn

Voir MARKOBRUNN ; RHEINGAU

Erdener Treppchen

L'un des vignobles les plus connus d'Erden (Moselle allemande), et un vin remarquablement sec.
Voir MOSELLE

Érinose

Maladie due à de très petits insectes. Elle ne détruit que certaines variétés de vigne.
Voir CHAPITRE IV

Ermitage

Voir HERMITAGE

Erzeugerabfuellung

Mot allemand signifiant « mis en bouteille » au domaine.

Espagne

L'Espagne compte la plus grande superficie de vignes d'Europe, mais n'est pas le premier pays producteur de raisins : l'Italie et la France la devancent largement. Ses 1 700 000 ha de vignobles — qui représentent plus d'un cinquième de la totalité des vignobles d'Europe — produisent 28 millions d'hl par an (plus de 310 millions de caisses). Ici comme ailleurs, ces dernières années ont marqué la soudaine expansion de la viticulture et l'adoption progressive des méthodes modernes de vinification. L'Espagne, fort contrastée dans son climat, son paysage et son sol, produit des vins de tous les types : des délicats (Xérès, Fino) aux riches vins de dessert, des frêles vins vieux aux rouges forts et puissants, aux délicieux vins de Alella et aux âpres vins verts du Nord-Ouest. La plaine centrale produit une quantité énorme de vin ordinaire *(vino corriente)* que l'on utilise comme vin de carafe et comme coupage.

La plus grande partie du pays est un vaste plateau, la *meseta*, coupé de-ci de-là de chaînes montagneuses agrestes dont les pics sont couverts de neiges éternelles.

Le climat est dur : étés secs et torrides ; hivers d'un froid mordant. Vue d'avion, l'Espagne apparaît comme une carte en relief, colorée de marron et ridée de vallées souvent asséchées quoique, de-ci de-là, un cours d'eau étincelle parfois. Celui qui voyage par le train ou la route découvre un décor moins monotone. Après une étendue d'herbe roussie, apparaît un bosquet de pins ou de chênes-lièges, puis une lande tapissée de romarin et de lavande odorants, puis une oliveraie. Quand il arrive au bord d'un fleuve, il se trouve sur une terre presque luxuriante où le maïs pousse entre des rangées de peupliers. Audelà de la sierra Morena, c'est la province de Cordoue, où l'air est plus doux. Au printemps, toute l'Andalousie est verte. Figuiers, orangers, oliviers y foisonnent. Les hivers sont doux et, sur toute la côte de la Méditerranée, le climat est tempéré par la mer. Une bande de terrains côtiers est plantée d'arbres fruitiers, d'oliviers et de vignes. La vigne pousse et produit partout, au bord de la Méditerranée comme sur les coteaux abrités au creux de certaines vallées. Les régions les plus productives sont la Nouvelle-Castille, La Mancha, la Catalogne et toute la côte Est.

Les meilleurs vins ne proviennent pourtant pas de ces contrées mais de l'Andalousie, pays du Xérès, des vignobles de Rioja, en Logroño, Alava et Navarre, et de la région de Penedès en Catalogne.

HISTOIRE DU VIN ESPAGNOL

Les vignobles d'Andalousie sont très anciens. Dès l'an 1100 avant notre ère, les Phéniciens fondèrent Cadix et y plantèrent probablement des vignes importées de l'Orient. Puis vinrent les Grecs, les Carthaginois et les Romains qui répandirent la vigne et la science de la viticulture à travers toute l'Espagne. Les Romains consommaient du vin de ce pays et Cicéron vante les crus de Tarragone et de Catalogne. Quand s'écroula l'Empire romain, les Barbares envahirent le pays. Les Vandales ont laissé leur nom à l'Andalousie. Les Wisigoths régnèrent ensuite sur l'Espagne. Sans doute ces envahisseurs détruisirent-ils des vignobles, mais la vigne subsista.

Quand les Arabes arrivèrent à leur tour, en 711 de notre ère, ils protégèrent la viticulture pour consommer du raisin de table.

Petit à petit, les chrétiens reconquirent le pays et y firent du vin. Puis, en 1492, le dernier roi maure fut chassé de Grenade.

Dès le début du XIVe siècle, l'Angleterre importait des vins espagnols. Au temps de l'apogée de l'Espagne, quand Charles Quint régnait sur un empire sur lequel le soleil ne se couchait jamais, toute l'Europe du Nord consommait du *Sack* (Xérès) du *Tent* (Alicante) et du vin des Canaries.

Au début de notre siècle, moins ravagée par le phylloxéra que bien d'autres pays européens, l'Espagne exportait abondamment. Mais, à partir de 1930 et pendant quelques années, la France contingenta les importations de vins étrangers pour favoriser la production locale et celle d'Algérie ; l'Espagne fut alors durement touchée. Puis éclata la guerre civile. Négligées, les vignes succombèrent au phylloxéra et des vignobles entiers disparurent complètement, notamment autour de Madrid et de Tolède. Le vin se fit alors rare et son prix doubla. La Seconde Guerre mondiale aggrava la situation. Le mildiou se répandit à partir de 1940, puis vinrent de nombreuses années de sécheresse. La production de vin ne reprit sérieusement qu'à partir de 1952-1953 et les prix commencèrent à baisser. Depuis 1959, la vigne gagne du terrain, surtout en Nouvelle-Castille. Cela explique l'augmentation du taux d'exportation. En 1970, il était plus élevé qu'au cours des six années précédentes ; il augmenta encore de 90 % en 1976, atteignant ainsi 6 000 000 hl. Cette augmentation concerne tous les vins à l'exception des types plus légers, non fermentés, portant la Denominación de Origen.

Les premiers clients de vins espagnols sont, par ordre décroissant, le Royaume-Uni, la Suisse, les Pays-Bas, l'Allemagne

fédérale, la Suède et la Hongrie. A en croire les populaires images espagnoles représentant des buveurs fort occupés à vider à la régalade leurs *porrones* de verre soufflé, il semblerait que les Espagnols font une grande consommation de leur vin. En réalité, celle-ci est tout à fait modérée : elle était de 57 l par personne en 1984 alors qu'en 1970 elle s'élevait à 92 l. Les sombres *bodegas*, avec leurs fûts de bois et leurs sols de pierre, sont encore fréquentées. Mais nombreux sont également les Espagnols qui leur préfèrent les supermarchés, qui offrent un plus grand choix de vins en bouteilles de toutes les régions. Une grande quantité de ces bouteilles sont produites par les nouvelles coopératives agricoles, mais on trouve également des vins aussi fins que les bons vins de Rioja.

ÉVOLUTION RÉCENTE DE L'INDUSTRIE VINICOLE EN ESPAGNE

	1963	*1978*	*1984*
Superficie plantée en vigne (1)	1 698	1 719	1 469
Production (2)	25 824	39 900	35 500
Exportations (2)	1 854	3 751	11 100
Importations (2)	1,2	35	15
Consommation totale	19 100	25 000	19 500
Consommation par tête (3)	63,6	70	57

1. Milliers d'hectares. 2. Milliers d'hectolitres. 3. Litres.

LÉGISLATION DES VINS EN ESPAGNE

La législation espagnole évolue lentement vers un plus grand contrôle des vins, depuis la plantation des vignes jusqu'à la mise en bouteille et l'étiquetage ; cependant il reste encore beaucoup à faire dans la plupart des régions. La région de Jerez et celle de Rioja sont d'heureuses exceptions. L'ambitieux programme visant à réglementer les appellations d'origine (Denominaciòn de Origen ou D.O.) par des normes sévères et des contrôles de qualité, est mis en œuvre avec efficacité dans les régions suivantes :

Andalousie : Jerez-Xérès-Sherry, Condado de Huelva, Málaga, Montilla-Moriles.

Rioja : Rioja.

La Mancha et Nouvelle-Castille : Almansa, La Mancha, Mentrida, Valdepeñas.

Levante : Jumilla, Utiel-Requena, Valencia, Alicante, Yecla.

Vieille Castille : Rueda, Ribera del Duero.

Catalogne : Alella, Penedés, Priorato, Tarragona, Ampurdán Costa Brava.

Aragon : Cariñena, Campo de Borja.

Navarre : Navarra.

Galice : Ribeiro, Valdeorras.

Sur le marché intérieur aussi, le Rioja domine toutes les listes de vins de première classe. Il en résulte que certains Valdepeñas et autres vins respectables peuvent être éclipsés. Les clients en sont venus à croire que seul le Rioja est digne d'arroser un bon repas. En général, les blancs ne sont pas à la hauteur des rouges, quoiqu'il y ait évidemment des exceptions ; l'Alella en est une : vin blanc très agréable.

L'Espagne, avec ses montagnes et ses contrastes violents, est un pays de vins d'une grande diversité : mais la main du vigneron aplanit les différences.

Voir MÁLAGA ; MONTILLA-MORILES ; RIOJA ; XÉRÈS

AUTRES RÉGIONS VINICOLES

Centre : Manche et *Nouvelle-Castille.*

Dans le secteur de La Manche, une immense étendue de vignes taillées court rompt la monotonie de la plaine. Les vignes, plantées à 3 m de distance les unes des autres, poussent sur un sol brûlé par le soleil, ombragées par les quelques oliviers qui s'y mêlent çà et là. Cette région, pays de Don Quichotte, a bien peu changé, bien moins que de nombreuses autres régions d'Espagne. Aujourd'hui, on y fait de l'industrie légère, et les méthodes agricoles ont quelque peu évolué, mais l'on vit encore dans ces fermes aux murs de terre battue, aux cheminées en forme de cloche et aux fours extérieurs. C'est un sol rouge, crayeux ou schisteux, une région riche en blé, en moulins et en vin.

Les hivers y sont rigoureux ; les vignes s'en ressentent et donnent un vin vigoureux. L'été, les raisins mûrissent à souhait sous le soleil écrasant et, après les vendanges, le vin, rouge et blanc, coule à flot dans les carafes des cafés de Madrid et, plus loin, jusqu'en France. On pratique également la distillation, mais les vins ne sont pas souvent mis en fûts pour un long vieillissement : dans la région, on aime les vins jeunes, vifs, brillants et frais. Le vin en vrac est un vin ordinaire *(vino corriente)* ; une partie de celui-ci portera, à tort d'ailleurs, l'étiquette Valdepeñas, qui est censée être la marque du vin le plus distingué de la région.

Voisine de la Nouvelle-Castille (dont Madrid est le centre), La Manche est divisée en deux secteurs : Haute-Manche (La Mancha Alta) et Basse-Manche (La Mancha Baja). Le premier secteur embrasse les provinces de Albacete et Cuenca ; le second, plus grand, celles de Tolède et Ciudad Real. A l'est, La Manche est délimitée par Valence et Alicante ; à l'ouest, elle touche l'Estremadure, pays d'origine de la plupart des conquistadores ; au sud, elle s'étend jusqu'à la Sierra Morena. La région que l'écrivain espagnol José de Castillo décrivait comme étant le cœur du pays du vin rouge, est celle où se rejoignent les quatre secteurs de la Manche, Levante, Murcie et Albacete. C'est là qu'on boit les « vaillants » rouges à forte teneur en alcool. Toutefois, un bon Cabernet Sauvignon est produit par le Marqués de Griñon à Malpica de Tajo.

C'est au sud de la région, à 200 km au sud de Madrid, sur la route de Grenade, que l'on produit le Valdepeñas, le meilleur et le plus connu des vins de Manchega. La ville de Valdepeñas, avec ses innombrables *bodegas*, se consacre tout entière au vin. On y voit encore des *pellejos*, sorte d'outres faites avec la peau d'un cochon entier. Ce procédé quelque peu macabre permet pourtant d'obtenir des récipients parfaitement étanches à l'air, dans lesquels le vin se conserve bien. Les *tinajas*, énormes jarres bombées en grès, existent encore. Le procédé est simple et traditionnel : le vin rouge fermenté séjourne dans la *tinaja* et bientôt, les dépôts précipitent au fond du récipient, où le vin clarifié s'affinera jusqu'au printemps prochain. Il sera alors transvasé dans des fûts puis vendu. Quant aux blancs et aux rosés *(rosado)*, on les soutire dans une autre amphore après la première fermentation, de façon à les séparer de leurs peaux. On fabrique des *tinijas* à Toboso et Villanobelo — deux villages où la légende de Dulcinée et de Don Quichotte est encore vivante — mais la plupart sont décoratifs car, là aussi, les fûts de bois et les cuves de fermentation doublées de verre les remplacent peu à peu.

Les rouges *(tintos)* n'ont pas la couleur profonde, noirâtre, de la plupart des vins espagnols, mais sont plus clairs, d'un rouge rubis. Un bon rouge Valdepeñas se doit d'être moelleux et harmonieux ; il évoque les vins du Nord, mais en plus soutenu. L'appellation, pourtant protégée par la Denominaciòn de Origen, est encore trop souvent utilisée abusivement. Les vins blancs de Valdepeñas sont d'une couleur pâle tirant sur le vert, ou encore d'un jaune doré intense. Les autres vins de Manchega ayant droit à la Denominación de Origen sont : Mancha, pâles vins blancs et *claretes* (rouges légers) d'Albacete ; La Manchuela, qui s'étend d'Albacete à Cuenca jusqu'à Valence et produit des *tintos, claretes et rosados* robustes ; Almansa, proche de la zone côtière d'Alicante et dont les vins *(claretes et tintos)* atteignent parfois 17° ; enfin Mentrida, située à proximité de Tolède, qui produit des rouges forts et secs, plutôt ordinaires.

Les principales variétés plantées dans le secteur de La Manche sont rouges — Cencibel, Tinto Basto, Garnacha, Aragon et Castellana, ainsi que quelques autres variétés de blancs — principalement Arién et Jaén, ainsi que Pardillo et Cirial. Le mélange Cencibel-Arién donne les forts bons *claretes* de Valdepeñas, favorisés par un sol riche en craie et en schiste. En 1971, la superficie et la production des différentes appellations étaient les suivantes :

Almansa (D.O.) : 15 000 ha, pour 180 000 hl (2 millions de caisses) de vins blancs et rouges.

Mancha (D.O.) : 200 000 ha pour 2 900 000 hl (32 millions de caisses) de rouge et de blanc.

Manchuela : 60 000 ha pour 1 million d'hl (11 millions de caisses) de rouge et de blanc.

Valdepeñas (D.O.) : 30 000 ha pour 340 000 hl (3,7 millions de caisses) de rouge et de blanc.

Mentrida (D.O.) : 21 000 ha pour 300 000 hl (plus de 3 millions de caisses) de rouge et de blanc.

Levante et Alicante

Sur la côte orientale, la longue et fertile bande de terre irriguée qui longe la méditerranée entre Alicante et Benicarlo — la Costa Blanca éclaboussée de soleil, avec son immense jardin irrigué par les Arabes, riche en palmiers, figuiers, orangers, mais aussi en champs de coton et en rizières — ne représente qu'une partie de cette région vinicole. Les deux grands ports de Valence et d'Alicante assurent son activité. C'est l'un des secteurs les plus arides d'Espagne, avec des hivers doux et ensoleillés, et le deuxième producteur de raisin après La Manche. En retrait, se trouve la zone de Cheste, plus tourmentée encore, au climat continental, derrière laquelle s'élèvent les hauts sommets déserts de Utiel-Requena. Les vins de ces trois Denominaciónes de Origen (Valencia, Alicante, Utiel-Requena) ont toutes les caractéristiques du sol qui les produit. C'est en effet une région de vins simples, à boire rapidement : plutôt doux que secs, plutôt rouges que blancs ; ils accompagnent fort bien paellas, poissons et crevettes roses, ainsi que le gibier, très abondant dans la région. Le vin est ici une industrie importante, et un peu partout de nouvelles coopératives modernes remplacent les petites caves individuelles.

Valence

Autrefois célèbre pour ses vins doux, Valence fait aujourd'hui des *tintos, blancos et claretes* doux et secs, ainsi que les *mistelas*, vins de couleur ambrée. Les raisins utilisés sont le Moscatel et le Malvasia, le Planta Nova, le Garnache, le Merseguera, le Bobal et autres variétés. Il existe également un apéritif très populaire, aromatisé et fait de mélanges de vieilles *soleras*. Les rouges douceâtres de Valence sont des vins robustes et capiteux titrant entre 12 et 16°. L'un des plus savoureux est le Fondillon, pour lequel la demande dépasse de loin l'offre, assez réduite. On consomme ces rouges, ainsi que les *rosados*, aux repas ; à environ deux ans d'âge, ils acquièrent les caractéristiques de vins millésimés.

Cheste (ce n'est pas une Denominación de Origen)

Cette zone centrale possède des vignes autour des agglomérations de Chivas et de Turia. La majorité des vins sont blancs secs, doux et demi-doux, d'une couleur pâle ou encore d'un jaune intense et doré. Les deux variétés de raisin principales sont Planta Nova et Merseguera, les vignes couvrent 7 500 ha.

Utiel-Requena

Cette zone montagneuse où Valence touche la Castille produit des vins rouges pour la plupart, qui sont à la fois plus légers, plus rudes et de couleur plus vive que ceux de la plaine. Les *tintos, claretes* et *rosados* titrent tous entre 10 et 13°. Les vignes couvrent 50 000 ha. C'est une Denominación de Origen.

Jumilla

Cette autre appellation d'origine du Levante se trouve en fait en Murcie septentrionale, où l'arrière-pays est fort pauvre, quoique la province ait été jadis riche en mines. Mais en direction de la mer, on trouve, là aussi, une *huerta*, où les vignobles dévalent les vallées du fleuve jusqu'à Valence. Les rouges sont des vins ordinaires mais agréables, ils doivent leur légère douceur au raisin Monastrel. Dans le même secteur, une autre agglomération vinicole florissante porte le nom de Yecla. Jumilla couvre 50 000 ha de vignes.

Yecla

Yecla, qui possède sa propre Denominaciòn de Origen, se trouve dans le même secteur que Jumilla, dans la région du Levante, à proximité de la Murcie septentrionale. Ses 27 000 ha de vignobles sont plantés principalement de Monastrel, qui donne des vins rouges. Comme Jumilla, c'est un centre riche en *bodegas*, où les raisins des vignobles environnants deviennent des vins blancs ou sombres en couleur.

Catalogne

A l'instar du Levante, cette région est contrastée : on distingue l'étendue fertile et ensoleillée qui longe la Costa Brava et, plus haut, les terres rocailleuses de l'intérieur. Ses vignobles datent de l'époque gréco-romaine, et ses vins étaient célèbres au Moyen Age ; la production actuelle — vins en vrac mais aussi vin d'appellation contrôlée — est encore élevée. Torres à Penedès fait d'excellents vins à bon prix.

Tarragone

Cette petite région qui encercle Priorato possède sa propre Denominaciòn de Origen. Le Tarragone est traditionnellement considéré à l'étranger comme un rouge fort, doux et dépourvu de toute finesse. Cette conception est aujourd'hui totalement dépassée car il existe actuellement une grande variété de vignes et de vins : lourds et légers, doux et secs, pour les blancs comme pour les rouges. C'est surtout à Reus qu'on produit le Tarragone.

Ampurdàn-Costa Brava

Ces vignobles de la Catalogne septentrionale possèdent leur propre Denominaciòn de Origen. Ils sont situés dans la province de Gérone, à l'intérieur du pays et à proximité de la frontière française. Les 6 800 ha de Carinena et de Garnacha donnent d'assez agréables blancs et rosés. Dans le même secteur se trouve Castello de Perelada — dont l'œnothèque et le musée œnologique sont dignes d'intérêt —, qui produit des rouges, des blancs et des rosés, ainsi qu'un mousseux célèbre. Après celles de Perelada, les bouteilles les plus connues sont celles du baron de Terrades.

Alella

Situés à environ 12 km au nord de Barcelone, ces vignobles des temps romains couvrent les coteaux d'un grand massif, un vignoble face à la mer, l'autre tourné vers l'intérieur des terres.

Les vignes cultivées sur un sol granitique autour de la ville d'Alella ainsi que dans plusieurs autres villages environnants donnent des raisins aux qualités différentes et complémentaires : ainsi, les vignes tournées vers le nord produisent des raisins riches en acide, qui contrebalancent la faible acidité des raisins donnant vers le sud. 600 ha de terres, plantées principalement de Xarel-Lo, Picpoule, Macabeo, Pansa Blanca et Red Sumoll, produisent des vins blancs, rouges et rosés. Il existe également un vin de dessert d'une couleur dorée appelé Lacre Violeta. La vinification a lieu selon les méthodes traditionnelles (le vin séjourne habituellement trois ans dans les fûts en chêne avant d'être mis en bouteilles) et le vin ne perd rien de ses qualités naturelles. Le Marqués de Alella, vin souple et fruité, est le plus apprécié. Les blancs sont des vins légers, au bouquet fort agréable.

Priorato

Avec en toile de fond la Sierra de Montsant et les ruines de son vieux prieuré, les vignobles de Priorato s'étendent en terrasses jusqu'à la vallée ocre du fleuve Ciurana. Les vignes et les oliviers poussent pêle-mêle sur ce promontoire rocailleux, où l'huile est tout aussi importante que le vin. La nature schisteuse du sol volcanique et la légère brise du mistral favorisent d'abondantes récoltes en vins fortement alcoolisés. Les villages environnants consacrent la plus grande part de leur activité à leurs vignobles. C'est à Gandesa et à Falset qu'on en vend le produit : des vins secs et doux, bons mais très forts et d'un rouge vif. Certains des vins ordinaires peuvent titrer entre 19 et 24°. Les blancs sont des vins clairs et brillants, au parfum fruité. La plus haute parcelle de ce secteur est Conca del Barbara, qui s'élève jusqu'à la crête d'une colline ; elle produit de vigoureux vins rouges et de chaleureux vins blancs au bouquet caractéristique. Les raisins les plus importants pour le rouge sont le Carinena et le Garnacha, pour le blanc le Macabeo et le Pedro Ximenez.

Dans la plus haute parcelle de la région de Priorato, les vignes perchées sur la colline, donnent de vigoureux vins rouges et de chaleureux vins blancs au bouquet caractéristique. Le district a demandé à être reconnu comme Denominación de Origen. Les vignobles couvrent 7 000 ha de Macabeo, Parellada, Pansa, Sumoll tinto et Bobal.

Penedés

C'est l'une des deux appellations contrôlées de la région de Barcelone. Ce secteur est divisé, lui aussi, en trois zones : zone côtière (Baja), zone centrale et vignobles de montagne (Alta), qui sont parmi les plus haut perchés d'Espagne. Le sol crayeux, riche en *albariza*, se prête parfaitement à la viticulture. Les vignobles de la plaine, situés autour de Sitges et de Vilafranca del Penedés, donnent des vins forts et colorés ; l'un des principaux cépages est le Malvasia. Les vignobles d'altitude donnent un vin blanc léger et plein de charme avec du Parellada, du Macabeo et du Chardonnay. La plus grande maison d'exportation de vins de la région est celle de la famille Torres, elle offre un vaste assortiment de très bons vins rouges et blancs et possède un centre de vinification à Vilafranca del Penedés. Les vins de Torres sont de loin les meilleurs vins blancs d'Espagne et du monde. La zone centrale de la Catalogne produit les meilleurs mousseux d'Espagne : Codorniu et Freixenet sont deux marques mondialement connues. Seules les caves produisant ces vins selon la méthode champenoise ont droit à l'appellation *cavas*. Jean Léon produit un bon Cabernet Sauvignon.

Grandesa Terralta (voir Priorato)

Souvent cité avec Priorato, cette région est maintenant candidate pour sa propre appellation. Ses 11 500 ha de vignobles plantés principalement de Garnacha, Macabeo et Carinena, donnent des vins d'un rouge vif, fortement alcoolisés, ainsi que des vins d'un blanc transparent.

Aragon

Cet ancien royaume d'Aragon est depuis toujours réputé pour ses vins. Les vignobles cuits par le soleil sont protégés par la Sierra de la Muela et irrigués par le fleuve Ebro. Ses vins sont de tout style et de toute nuance, particulièrement le Cariñena et le Campo de Borja qui ont tous deux droit à la Denominaciòn de Origen. Comme les vins ordinaires ou *corrientes*, ils peuvent être rouges et blancs, doux et secs ; ce sont des vins de caractère, fortement alcoolisés, certains d'entre eux, plus légers (un peu capiteux), sont agréables. Les principaux raisins utilisés sont le Garnacha, le Cariñena et le Bobal.

Navarre

L'appellation Navarra couvre quatre secteurs : Montana, Valdizarbe, Ribera Alta et Ribera Baja. La Navarre est un pays au décor romantique, qui s'étend sur 22 500 ha, depuis les bois et les fleuves de montagne des Pyrénées jusqu'à Logroño, où certains vins ont droit à l'appellation Rioja. C'est au nord qu'on fait les *vinos verdes*, vins verts et piquants. Au sud, les vignobles sont situés à proximité de Pampelune (où les *corrientes* rappellent les vins produits du côté français) et surtout dans les vallées de l'Ebro et de Ribera, où les vins sont plus forts et parfois plutôt verts. Les principaux cépages sont le Carasol et le Secano.

Galice

Sur la côte atlantique, le pays présente un aspect verdoyant caractéristique, où le climat tempéré favorise d'abondantes récoltes et vendanges. A l'intérieur des terres, les vignes sont taillées court, à la manière castillane ; mais à proximité de la mer, elles grimpent le long de poteaux et s'entortillent autour de treillis disposés de façon à les protéger de l'humidité venant du sol ; ce système est appelé *parrales*. La région possède trois appellations : Valdeorras, Valle de Monterrey et Ribeiro. Valdeorras jouit d'un micro-climat, ses 5 000 ha produisent des vins blancs et rouges de qualité moyenne. Le Godello donne le blanc, et le rouge est fait avec du Mencia et de l'Alicante. Ces vignobles, situés dans la paisible vallée de Sil, sont divisés en nombreuses parcelles ; la vallée de Monterrey, qui traverse le sud d'Orense en direction du Portugal, est une zone moins pluvieuse que le reste de la région : ses coteaux produisent d'agréables vins rouges faits avec les raisins Alicante, Albarello et d'autres variétés, ainsi que des vins blancs faits avec la vigne Jerez. Les vins blancs de la province d'Orense sont souvent plus forts et plus parfumés que les rouges. Les vins de Ribeiro proviennent en partie d'Orense et d'Avia — ces derniers étant très prisés localement. Les rouges sont agréables mais toujours moins soutenus que les blancs. Les méthodes traditionnelles de vinification ont été léguées par les anciens monastères. Parmi les raisins utilisés, on trouve l'Albarino, le Treixadura, le Palomino et le Godello. Ce secteur de la côte atlantique, proche du Portugal, donne souvent des vins qui sont aussi légers, piquants, frais et verts que les *Vinos Verdes* de la région de Minho. Dans le secteur de Pontevedra, les vignes sont cultivées sur *parrales* dans les zones Contado, Albarino et Rosal.

Condado de Huelva

Située à l'extrême sud de l'Espagne, à la frontière du Portugal, séparée de la province de Cadix par le fleuve Guadalquivir, Huelva est un pays de vignes et de camargue, de chevaux, de taureaux, et aussi de raisins, qui donnent des vins fort réputés dans leur région d'origine. La Denominación Condado de Huelva couvre le secteur Condado de Niebla, où les vignes poussent à proximité du fleuve. Les 19 000 ha de vignobles produisent 650 000 hl (plus de 7 millions de caisses) de vin par an. Les types *palido* (pâle) et Olorosso sont appelés *Condado viejo* (vieux). Les vins Condado sont fabriqués selon le système solera.

Extremadoure

Située en bordure du Portugal, cette province longue et étroite, riche en vertes forêts, en profondes vallées et en gibier, ne possède pas de Denominación de Origen mais a du vin en abondance, pour la plupart agréable, fort, et d'une belle couleur lumineuse. Caceres produit des vins blancs corsés et de valeureux rouges. La zone d'Almendralejo produit également une bonne quantité de vins courants qui accompagnent bien les plats régionaux, viande de porc, ragoûts savoureux et solides gazpachos.

Léon et Castille. Rueda. Ribera del Duero

Les deux Denominación de Origen en progression sont Rueda pour les blancs et Ribera del Duero pour les rouges. Les blancs de Rueda, produits avec le Verdejo Blanco, sont des vins à l'arôme prononcé. Les meilleurs sont ceux du Marqués de Griñon et du Marqués de Riscal. C'est dans cette région, plus précisément à Valbuena de Duero, près de Valladolid, que se trouve l'intéressant petit vignoble de Vega Sicilia (100 ha seulement) dont les cépages furent importés de Bordeaux par le propriétaire, Don Eloy Lecanda, après que le phylloxéra eut détruit ses vignes. Il se compose de 50 % de Tempranillo, 25 % de Cabernet Sauvignon et le reste de Malbec et de Merlot. Le vin y est traité à la manière du Bordeaux : il vieillit dans des barriques de chêne et n'est jamais mis en bouteille avant d'avoir atteint cinq ans d'âge ; Vega Sicilia et Pesquera ont la réputation de figurer parmi les meilleurs vins rouges espagnols.

Provinces basques

Vizcaya et Guipucoa, situés dans les environs de Bilbao et de San Sebastian, ne présentent que peu d'intérêt pour les vins. On y boit surtout du cidre et le Chacolí local.

Les Canaries et les Baléares

Dès l'époque élisabéthaine, les Sack des Canaries et de Palma (ces derniers provenant de Las Palmas, port de la Grande Canarie) étaient célèbres en Angleterre. On donna le nom de l'oiseau à la couleur et celui des îles à l'oiseau ; or, les îles étaient autrefois parcourues par des chiens *(canes)*. La coïncidence de nom entre l'oiseau et le vin donna lieu à maints jeux de mots, notamment dans *Twelfth Night* de Shakespeare : « Jamais de la vie... sauf si tu vois un canari m'abattre ».

Voilà un siècle, l'oïdium fit perdre aux vins des Canaries leur place sur le marché mondial. On produit encore pourtant environ 60 000 hl (660 000 caisses) de *corriente* qui sont consommés sur place : surtout du blanc et un peu de *clarete*.

Les Baléares cultivent le raisin en petites parcelles et produisent du vin selon les méthodes traditionnelles. A Majorque, la région de Benisalem produit des rouges sombres et lourds, alors qu'à Felanitx on trouve des vins plus légers et assez plats. A Ibiza et Formentor, où le vin est plus fort, quelques coopératives modernes sont établies.

Espalier

Genre de taille de la vigne. Le tronc diverge en deux flèches principales et plusieurs sarments, tous sur le même plan et soutenus par un treillage ou des fils parallèles. Ce système donne lieu à plusieurs variantes dont celles de la treille et du guyot, plus pratiques, comportent le tronc et une seule branche.

Voir CHAPITRE IV

Espumoso

Signifie mousseux en espagnol.

Voir CAVA

Est ! Est ! ! Est ! ! ! (D.O.C.)

Vin sec de Montefiascone, Italie.

Voir LATIUM

Esters

Composé organique provenant d'une réaction lente entre les acides du vin et l'alcool.

Voir CHAPITRE V

Estufades

Immenses étuves dans lesquelles on « cuit » le vin de Madère.

Étampe

Vin de marque.

États-Unis

Avec 44 États producteurs sur 50, les États-Unis se placent au 6e rang mondial. La Californie, à elle seule, produit plus de vin que les régions de Bordeaux et de la Bourgogne réunies. Le B.A.T.F. (Bureau of Alcohol, Tobacco and Fire-arms) est en train d'instaurer un système pour normaliser et contrôler les appellations pour la protection du consommateur. Aux États-Unis, on trouve deux types de vignes : les indigènes, qui prospèrent à l'état sauvage dans l'Est, et diverses variétés de *Vitis vinifera* européennes importées en Californie. *Vitis vinifera* constitue la base de toute vraie viniculture, tant en Europe qu'en Californie. En Californie, comme sur la totalité du territoire des États-Unis, les viticulteurs s'expriment en tonnes par acres, alors que dans le Bordelais, en Bourgogne et dans les autres régions vinicoles d'Europe, la production est exprimée en hl/ha.

HISTOIRE DU VIN AMÉRICAIN

Ce seraient les Vikings qui auraient les premiers traversé l'Atlantique depuis l'Europe jusqu'au Nouveau Monde. Ce qu'ils y virent était sans doute des vignes car ils appelèrent ce nouveau pays Vineland. Les premiers vins auraient été faits à base de Scuppernong, par les Huguenots français, en 1562, près de Jacksonville en Floride. Cependant, d'aucuns pensent que les premiers vins ont été faits à base de *Vitis aestinalis* à Paris Island en Caroline du Sud, en 1570. Les premiers colons avaient le projet de faire du vin dans leur nouveau territoire. Les colons du Jamestown firent du vin à Jamestown en Virginie aux environs de 1609 et les pèlerins du *Mayflower* burent probablement leur première production en 1623 lors du premier *Thanksgiving*.

Les premiers vins furent le produit de raisins sauvages et s'avérèrent radicalement différents des vins que les colons avaient laissés derrière eux en Europe. Ils importèrent des vignes européennes (notamment Thomas Jefferson et lord Baltimore) mais celles-ci périrent rapidement à cause de maladies, de parasites et du climat. Le premier raisin qui rencontra quelque succès tant au niveau de la vigne que du vin fut l'Alexander, croisement accidentel entre une variété américaine et un plant européen. On lui donna le nom de celui qui le découvrit : John Alexander, jardinier de William Penn.

En 1600, des moines franciscains firent passer du Mexique au Nouveau-Mexique, voire en Californie, une technique de vinification pour un usage sacramentel. Il ne fallut pas attendre longtemps pour voir une douzaine d'autres États se mettre à faire du vin.

En Californie, les viticulteurs commencèrent à importer d'Europe des vignes *vinifera* de qualité et avec le chemin de fer transcontinental, la Californie devint un élément majeur dans les marchés de l'est. Alors que les vagues d'immigrants européens débarquaient, le marché du vin s'accrut rapidement ainsi que les maisons de vins.

Dans les années 1860 le phylloxéra, puceron dont les piqûres sont fatales à la vigne, commença à se répandre dans les vignobles tant en Californie qu'en Europe, et les viticulteurs entamèrent activement des travaux en vue de développer des espèces résistantes avant que les vignes ne soient décimées. En 1880 l'Université de Californie de Davis institua son département de viticulture et d'œnologie, en partie pour résoudre le problème du phylloxéra. En 1900 on perfectionna la technique de greffage des vignes *vinifera* à de solides rhizomes, et les vins américains commencèrent à gagner des médailles dans les compétitions européennes.

Cependant un fléau bien plus grave menaçait la production de vin américaine. Petit à petit le mouvement prohibitionniste gagna les États et en 1920 lorsque le Congrès américain vota la loi Volstead et le 18e amendement interdisant la fabrication et la consommation de boissons alcolisées sur le plan national, plus de trente États étaient déjà passés sous le régime local de la prohibition.

Bien que celle-ci ait décimé l'industrie du vin américain, ce fut une aubaine pour les vignerons car le prix du jus, du concentré et des grappes de raisins pour la fabrication du vin maison augmentèrent considérablement. Cela donna aussi naissance à cette tradition typiquement américaine du *quick shot*, boisson très alcoolisée consommées avec un plaisir illicite derrière des portes closes.

Le 18e amendement fut abrogé le 5 décembre 1933 et plus de 1 000 maisons de vins surgirent l'année suivante. Les Américains portèrent un toast à l'abrogation avec la dernière vendange qui avait à peine trois mois et le goût de ce toast produit hâtivement, détourna nombre d'Américains du vin pour toujours.

Pendant les trois décades suivantes, le vin resta principalement le domaine du snob et de l'ivrogne. Les snobs écrivirent sur la manière de le boire et les ivrognes buvaient des portos et muscats élevés en alcool et bon marché, plus pour l'effet que pour le goût.

Lors de la Seconde Guerre mondiale, quelques soldats américains postés en Europe furent confrontés à l'usage de boire du vin pendant les repas. Ils rentrèrent en ayant contracté cette habitude et donnèrent un coup de pouce aux maisons de vins américaines.

Dans les années 1950 l'Université de Californie de Davis et l'Université de Cornell commencèrent à conférer un diplôme aux viticulteurs, chimistes et vignerons à l'issue d'une instruction technique.

Avec l'ère des avions à réaction virent les vols transcontinentaux et les Américains voyageant en Europe découvrirent le plaisir de boire du vin en mangeant.

Développements récents

En 1968, le vin de table devint, pour la première fois depuis la prohibition, plus populaire aux États-Unis que les portos, sherry et muscats plus alcoolisés, marquant ainsi le début de l'expansion du vin.

Au cours de la décennie suivante, plus d'une douzaine d'États votèrent des lois encourageant les vignerons à faire du vin à partir du raisins cultivés sur place, et le nombre de maisons de vins aux États-Unis passa d'environ 400, en 1968, à presque 1 000 en 1983.

En 1976, l'Amérique célébrait son bicentenaire et au milieu de cette manifestation patriotique parvint la nouvelle d'une dégustation de vins, en France, organisée par un éminent marchand de vins, pendant laquelle des Chardonnay et Cabernet Sauvignon de Californie avaient été confrontés à des Bourgogne blancs et des Bordeaux rouges ; les experts français ayant voté, la Californie l'avait emporté quoique de peu. Soudainement, les vins de Californie devinrent en vogue aux États-Unis, et en 1980 la consommation de vin des Américains dépassa, pour la première fois, celle du whisky.

L'essor du vin américain est maintenant un fait établi.

Avant que la valeur du dollar ne monte en 1982, et que les vins français ou tout autre vin importé ne deviennent abordables pour les États-Unis, les consommateurs américains dédaignèrent les vins européens, et commencèrent à étudier et à vanter les mérites de leurs productions.

Un groupe hétéroclite d'individualistes de toutes conditions sociales, attirés par des perspectives de profit ou simplement par amour du vin, contribuèrent à la création de nombre de nouvelles maisons de vins établies dans les années 1970. Des médecins, des architectes, des ingénieurs, des industriels, des pilotes de ligne, des publicitaires investirent individuellement ou en groupes et préparèrent les terrains, plantèrent la vigne, construisirent des cuveries et se mirent à faire du vin. Leur énergie et leur dévouement ainsi que la curiosité et la réceptivité des amateurs de vin américains furent le fer de lance d'une amélioration générale des vins américains. Les plus grandes maisons de vins telles que Gallo, Almadén et Paul Masson qui s'étaient spécialisées auparavant dans des marques de vins en pichets, mirent de plus en plus l'accent sur les variétés de leurs lignes de production. En 1976 l'entreprise Coca-Cola d'Atlanta acheta plusieurs maisons de vins, leur appliquant son savoir-faire en matière de marketing ainsi que ses capitaux, et devint rapidement l'un des dix premiers producteurs des États-Unis.

La diversité des formations et des tempéraments des nouveaux fabriquants de vins conduisit à une période d'expérimentation de la fabrication du vin et du traitement des vignes. On se souviendra des années 1970 comme à une période d'intense créativité œnologique alors que des tentatives nouvelles et souvent osées étaient faites pour assortir des variétés de raisins (et leurs clones et hybrides) aux vicissitudes du climat et du sol qui n'avaient jamais été exploité auparavant pour faire pousser de la vigne.

Les problèmes, qui pouvaient être résolus technologiquement, furent les plus simples. Pour cette raison, les vins blancs (par nature moins complexes et dépendant plus d'une technique de cuvage à lumière que le vin grouge) et plus particulièrement les Chardonnay ont atteint un niveau de qualité relativement plus élevé que la plupart des rouges.

Les problèmes rencontrés dans la fabrication du vin en Amérique ne seront résolus qu'après une patiente expérimentation. Un problème chronique pour les meilleurs vins rouges et blancs réside dans le fait que la Californie a un climat trop clément et trop ensoleillé et ainsi les raisins mûrissent trop vite pour avoir les éléments aromatiques secondaires qui font toute la distinction entre un grand vin et un assez bon vin. La plupart du temps les taux de sucre font monter le degré en alcool au-delà de 13 % et 14 %, ce qui est beaucoup trop si l'on veut obtenir légèreté et raffinement. Seuls un essai et une erreur dans la sélection des clones et des différents microclimats à l'intérieur des zones de températures adéquates pourront résoudre ce problème.

La majorité des autres États sont envahis d'amateurs et de fermiers convertis en viticulteurs sans expérience ni talent qui essayent de produire du vin dans des climats, des sols et avec un marché difficiles. Au-delà de l'amélioration du traitement du vignoble et des techniques de vinification se pose le problème trop souvent minimisé de la commercialisation de la vaste quantité des nouveaux vins américains. Au début des années 1980, comme les prix européens baissaient et que le dollar américain devenait plus fort, le prix des vins américains devint excessif. Comme la révolution vinicole n'a plus l'attrait de la nouveauté et qu'un marché plus compétitif devient une réalité, les faillites et les fusions sont monnaie courante et plus particulièrement au sein des maisons de vins les plus récentes. Ces maisons de vins aux soutiens financiers solides et dont les programmes de prix et de marketing sont agressifs et bien conçus sont les plus susceptibles d'échapper à des crises économiques et à une compétition galopante avec l'étranger. La chute du dollar en 1987 a renforcé la demande de vins américains par rapport aux vins importés.

Législation de l'étiquetage

Comme cette nouvelle génération d'Américains qui se sont passionnés pour le vin atteint sa majorité, il reste à standardiser et à codifier les lois américaines concernant le vin et à ne donner aux vins américains que des noms américains. Le B.T.A.F. (Bureau des Tabacs, Alcools et Armes à feu), division du ministère des Finances des États-Unis, amorce le développement d'un système d'étiquetage et d'appellation approprié à la viticulture et au commerce des États-Unis.

Une fois ces formalités accomplies, les vins américains pourront être considérés à part entière dans le monde vinicole.

Cépages des États

Aux États-Unis, les vins sont produits principalement à partir de quatre espèces : *Vitis vinifera*, *Vitis labrusca*, des hybrides « franco-américains », et *Vitis muscadinae*. Les États à l'ouest des Montagnes Rocheuses, y compris la Californie, utilisent presque exclusivement des croisements des espèces *Vitis vinifera* et *vinifera-vinifera*. La plupart des États à l'est des Rocheuses font aussi pousser l'espèce *vinifera*, mais celle qui est de loin la plus populaire est l'espèce *Vitis labrusca*. Dans le sud l'espèce *Vitis muscadinae* est assez répandue.

Vitis vinifera

La majorité des variétés de *Vitis vinifera* qui pousse aux États-Unis sont des clones en provenance directe du vignoble européen ; ce sont fondamentalement les mêmes variétés que celles qui sont utilisées en Europe. Les espèces *Vitis vinifera* produisent les plus grands vins des États-Unis, voire du monde. La plupart des espèces vinifera sont greffées sur des rizhomes résistant au phylloxéra tels que S04, Rupestris Saint-George, et 5BB.

Principaux cépages à vin rouge

Cabernet Sauvignon. Sur la grande variété de cépages à vin rouge connus dans le monde entier, on n'en a recommandé qu'un petit nombre pour la Californie. Parmi ceux qui ont passé des tests rigoureux, le Cabernet Sauvignon est le plus estimé. Il s'adapte mieux aux parties les plus fraîches des vallées côtières, mûrit généralement à mi-saison, plus lentement que dans la région de Bordeaux. Il fournit des vins plus corsés et plus lourds. En Californie, il manque souvent de bouquet, pourtant on sait qu'il a donné en très petite quantité de remarquable grands vins qui peuvent d'ailleurs se comparer aux meilleurs du monde.

Pinot Noir. On recommande ce cépage pour les régions les plus fraîches. C'est une des variétés les plus cultivées en Bourgogne. En Californie on le confond parfois avec Pinot Meunier, Pinot Pernand et Pinot Saint-Georges qui n'est d'ailleurs pas un vrai Pinot. Il mûrit tôt, mais il n'est pas toujours facile de contrôler sa fermentation ni son vieillissement. Bien qu'excellente, cette variété qui donne du très bon vin ailleurs réussit moins bien en Californie que le Cabernet Sauvignon. Les meilleurs Pinot Noirs de Californie viennent des climats frais des comtés de Napa, Sonoma, Monterey, Mendocino et Lake.

Gamay et Gamay Beaujolais. Ce Gamay est en réalité une variante de la famille Pinot Noir. Quoique plus facile à traiter que ce dernier, il exige une grande attention. Comme le Pinot Noir, il mûrit tôt et la moindre erreur de manipulation gâterait le vin. Le véritable Gamay, de la variété qui donne le Beaujolais rouge en France, est surtout cultivé à Napa où il fournit des vins légers délicieux qui, dans certains cas, possèdent le bouquet manquant à bien des vins de Californie.

Grenache. Ce cépage est très recherché en raison de son rendement, de sa vigueur et de sa résistance à la maladie. C'est celui qui sert à faire le Tavel rosé dans la vallée du Rhône. On en fait aussi des rosés en Californie, en raison de sa couleur.

Barbera. En Californie, il est très acide, d'une vigueur et d'un rendement moyens. Il réussit surtout dans les vallées côtières et le milieu de la vallée centrale où il produit d'honnêtes vins corsés.

Zinfandel. C'est une des variétés de raisin les plus répandues en Californie. On ignore son origine exacte. Il n'est d'ailleurs guère cultivé dans d'autres pays. Vulnérable au mildiou ; une humidité excessive ou simplement l'irrigation peut l'amener à pourrir. En général on le vendange tôt. Pratiquement toutes les régions de Californie lui conviennent, mais dans les plus fraîches, il donne ses meilleurs vins secs. Le Zinfandel est une variété à très bon rendement. Ses vins sont agréables, honnêtes et séduisent par un bouquet composite. Leur belle couleur, leur goût et leur arôme chaleureux expliquent leur popularité. Un Zinfandel de qualité produit par un bon centre vinicole est supérieur à bien des Cabernet Sauvignon que l'on trouve aujourd'hui. Cette variété mériterait plus d'attention et de respect qu'on n'en lui prête actuellement hors des frontières de la Californie. Le Zinfandel produit des rouges et des rosés.

On cultive aussi deux autres variétés de raisin à vin rouge intéressantes — Ruby Cabernet et Grignolino — mais on n'a pas encore réalisé toutes leurs possibilités.

Ruby Cabernet. C'est une variété hybride obtenue par la station d'agriculture expérimentale de Californie. Elle s'est révélée de bon rendement et ses raisins ont une forte teneur en acide, particulièrement dans la région d'Escalon-Modesto.

Cépages à vin rouge de moindre qualité

Alicante-Bouschet, Carignane, Petite-Syrah et Refosco sont d'autres variétés à vin rouge de gros rendement, mais sans grande qualité. L'Alicante-Bouschet fournit de grandes quantités de vin ordinaire ; malheureusement on en cultive encore trop en Californie ; dans les régions centrale et méridionale on en fait des faux bourgognes, des bordeaux rouge, des chianti. La qualité du Carignane n'est pas mauvaise sur un bon sol. On le cultive beaucoup dans les régions chaudes et il sert souvent à des coupages. A Napa et dans les comtés de Sonoma, Monterey, Kern et San Joaquin, on préfère une variante de qualité supérieure de la Petite-Syrah.

Principaux cépages à vin blanc

Les meilleures variétés de vignes qui donnent du bon vin blanc sec sont surtout cultivées dans la région côtière nord et dans les autres secteurs les plus frais de Californie.

Pinot Chardonnay ou *Chardonnay*. Ce n'est pas une variété à grand rendement en général, mais en France elle donne le Chablis et les plus splendides Bourgogne, tels que Meursault et Montrachet. Elle a toutes les vertus qu'il faut pour faire de bons vins et mûrit bien dans les régions les plus fraîches pour atteindre un excellent équilibre de sucre et d'acidité. Le Chardonnay donne les meilleurs vins blancs de Californie dans les secteurs les plus frais de Napa, San Benito, Sonoma et Monterey où il s'adapte bien. Sa culture n'est pas une tâche aisée, mais les résultats qu'il donne en valent la peine. En Californie il produit un vin moins riche qu'en France et n'a pas non plus le même bouquet.

Sauvignon Blanc. C'est la variété qui sert à faire les Graves blancs et, de pair avec le Sémillon, elle constitue la base de tous les grands Sauternes. On l'utilise énormément pour le Pouilly-Fuissé, le Sancerre, le Chavignol (Cher). En Californie, elle réussit particulièrement dans la région de la côte nord. C'est une vigne à maturation précoce qui s'améliore en vieillissant et devient aussi plus vigoureuse.

Sémillon. Voilà encore une autre variété qui convient mieux à la région de la côte nord. La sécheresse du climat californien ne permet pas à la pourriture noble de se manifester comme dans le Sauternais à la fin de la maturation du raisin.

Pinot Blanc. Cette variété sert à faire bien des Bourgogne blancs et quelques Alsace. Elle semble conserver ses vertus ancestrales en Californie, mais jusqu'à récemment on ne l'avait pas encore assez plantée en général. Son raisin de bonne qualité résiste vigoureusement aux maladies et a une distinction qui lui est propre. Son rendement est supérieur à celui du Pinot Chardonnay mais dépasse rarement 6,80 t à l'ha. On a souvent confondu le Pinot Blanc avec le Chardonnay mais bien des experts considèrent que le Chardonnay est une variété tout à fait différente qui n'appartient pas à la famille Pinot.

Chenin Blanc. Malgré son nom il ne faut pas le confondre avec le Pinot Blanc car c'est en réalité le *White Pinot*. Ce White Pinot s'adapte et produit bien dans les zones variant du légèrement frais au chaud. En France on l'appelle aussi Pineau de la Loire et c'est lui qui fournit les délicieux Vouvray et Saumur, entre autres. Bien que d'une qualité supérieure à la moyenne, il n'a pas la distinction du Pinot Blanc.

Riesling. Ce Riesling, dit aussi White Riesling ou Johannisberg Riesling, donne aux célèbres vins du Rhin et de la Moselle, ainsi qu'à la plupart des bons vins alsaciens, leur réputation exceptionnelle. C'est l'une des meilleures variétés du monde et on le cultive partout en Europe (sauf au bord de la Méditerranée) pour faire des vins excellents. C'est dans les régions relativement froides qu'il se comporte le mieux, mais la Californie, au climat semblable à celui des pays riverains de la Méditerranée, ne peut lui offrir ces conditions. Toutefois, dans les secteurs les plus frais, il produit un vin supérieur à la moyenne, auquel manquent malheureusement l'équilibre et la délicatesse des Riesling européens. Dans la région de la côte nord, il produit un peu plus que le Chardonnay et mûrit plus tard.

Traminer. On le compare souvent, à son avantage, aux meilleurs Riesling quand on le cultive dans les meilleurs secteurs de l'Alsace et du Jura. Dans les parties les plus fraîches de Californie, il donne un vin bien équilibré, d'un arôme caractérisé et délicat. On l'appelle aussi Red Traminer, en raison de la teinte rouge que le grain prend en mûrissant. La Krug Winery de Sainte-Hélène, dans la vallée de Napa, produit des petites quantités de Traminer supérieur. En Alsace et en Allemagne, certains plants choisis de Traminer s'appellent Gewürz-Traminer ou Gewürztraminer. Celui qui le connaît sait distinguer infailliblement son bouquet et sa saveur épicée. Les firmes Stony Hill, Château St-Jean et Hacienda produisent également de bons Gewürztraminer.

Vitis labrusca

Les raisins sauvages découverts par les Vikings qui nomèrent le Nouveau Monde « Vineland » étaient probablement des *Vitis riparia, Vitis rupestris* et des *Vitis labrusca*. Des trois, l'espèce *Labrusca* donna les vins les plus satisfaisants quand les variétés européennes de *Vitis vinifera* ne poussèrent plus à cause de circonstances défavorables telles que des virus, l'humus, le mildiou et un climat inapproprié. Les *labruscas* aussi appelés variétés « du pays » ou « américaines », résistent en général à l'hiver, vieillissent bien et supportent de grandes quantités de grappes de raisins aux peaux épaisses. Les vins sont très parfumés et facilement identifiables grâce à un arôme distinctif dérivé de plusieurs composants rares. On dit souvent de cet arôme qu'il est « foxé » (de *fox* : renard), terme dont l'origine est encore controversée mais qui vient probablement des premières vignes *labruscas* dites « vignes renard ». Pour éviter que cet arôme ne se développe par trop, on coupe généralement les *labruscas* assez tôt. En raison de leur faible taux de sucre et de leur acidité la plupart des *labruscas* sont améliorés (dilués avec de l'eau), coupés avec des hybrides ou du vin de Californie ou resucrés pour obtenir un arôme agréable.

Des *labruscas* tels que Concord ou Niagara sont beaucoup utilisés pour faire des jus de raisin non fermentés, des gelées, des boissons non alcoolisées et des bonbons en Amérique du Nord ; on les trouve rarement en Europe sauf dans certaines régions d'Italie. Des chercheurs ont découvert plusieurs moyens de supprimer l'arôme foxé de certains *labruscas* mais dans la plupart des cas ce goût de « gelée » persiste.

Les *labruscas* convrent encore la grande majorité du territoire à l'est des Montagnes Rocheuses bien que les hybrides franco-américains et les *viniferas* soient de plus en plus utilisés dans les maisons de vins. Les variétés qui tendent à donner les meilleures vins sont Delamare, Dutehess, Isabella et Niagara qui sont tous des croisements de *labrusca.*

Hybrides franco-américains

Cherchant toujours à améliorer les matières premières pour la fabrication du vin et à développer des variétés adaptées aux climats et aux sols, les viticulteurs croisent des espèces et des variétés depuis environ deux siècles. Le besoin d'hybrides s'est accru avec l'épidémie de phylloxéra dans les dernières décades du XIXᵉ siècle. Les viticulteurs français et américains commencèrent à croiser l'espèce *vinifera* avec une espèce américaine, cherchant un hybride qui produirait un bon vin à partir de vignes résistant aux insectes nuisibles et aussi robustes que celles d'origine. Au début on désignait les hybrides par des numéros mais récemment on leur a donné des noms. Les hybrides sont souvent appelés « producteurs directs » car ils n'ont pas besoin d'être greffés à des rhizomes résistant au phylloxéra. Malgré cela, certains viticulteurs préfèrent toujours greffer ces vignes à des souches très adaptées au sol et au climat.

Les hybrides blancs tendent à être meilleurs que les rouges et certains tels que des Seyval Blanc, Vignoles, Vidal Blanc, Cayuga White poduisent un aussi bon vin rouge que des *viniferas* quand ils sont bien faits.

Chimiquement les hybrides rouges ont une pigmentation légèrement différente de celle des *viniferas* et un arôme qui ne ressemble pas à celui des *viniferas* communs. Cependant ils n'ont pas un arôme « foxé » à moins qu'ils ne soient coupés avec des *labruscas* ou vieillis dans des cuves ayant contenu des *labruscas.* Les hybrides rouges donnent un meilleur vin lorsque leur taux de sucre n'est pas trop élevé au moment des vendanges, quand on les chaptalise et lorsqu'on les coupe avec d'autres vins. Les meilleurs semblent être le Baco Noir, Chancellor et Léon Millot bien qu'il ne soient toujours pas comparables aux *vinifera.*

Les œnologues les plus connus en matière d'hybridation furent Baco, Kuhlman, Seibel, Villard, Ravat et Couderc. On trouve la plupart des hybrides franco-américains à l'est des Montagnes Rocheuses.

APÉRITIFS

On classe les apéritifs avec les vins de dessert en raison de leur teneur en alcool, néanmoins on les distingue car, contrairement aux vins de dessert, ils sont consommés avant le repas. Aux États-Unis, comme ailleurs, les deux principaux apéritifs à base de vin sont des xérès et des vermouths. Gardons-nous bien, évidemment, de confondre le xérès américain avec le Xérès qui ne peut provenir que de la seule région de Jerez de la Frontera, en Espagne.

« Xérès » (ou sherry) américain

Les procédés de vieillissement et la température élevée donnent à ce faux xérès un goût caractéristique de noix. Bien des régions de l'État de Californie produisent du vin de ce type. Le raisin qui lui convient le mieux est le Palomino ou Napa Golden Chasselas, qui n'est d'ailleurs pas un Chasselas. Le véritable Xérès espagnol est presque entièrement fait avec ce même Palomino. Malheureusement bien des vignerons utilisent encore d'autres variétés — Flame, Tokay, Mission, Thompson Seedless et Feher Szagos — qui donnent de moins bons vins.

On trouve aux États-Unis trois catégories de xérès : un apéritif sec, contenant de 0 % à 2,5 % de sucre ; le xérès californien (appelé sherry), avec 2,5 % à 4 % de sucre ; enfin, un xérès Crème doux qui contient plus de 4 % de sucre. Tous titrent entre 17 % (minimum) et 20 %.

La plupart de ces vins sont faits dans des cuves de bois, de béton ou d'acier où ils vieillissent, après addition d'alcool, pendant deux à six mois, à une température variant de 49° à 60 °C. Ensuite, on les met dans des petits tonneaux de chêne où ils mûrissent 6 mois de plus et plus longtemps encore dans le cas des vins de la meilleure qualité.

On ne fait pratiquement aucun xérès selon la méthode de la *flor* (*voir ce mot* et XÉRÈS), c'est-à-dire à l'espagnole, pourtant on a mis au point une nouvelle méthode pour les xérès destinés au coupage et qui s'appelle « flor submergée ». Les meilleurs xérès de la région vieillissent très longtemps dans leurs fûts de chêne.

Vermouth américain

On distingue deux genres de vermouth : le genre français, sec, couleur d'ambre clair ; et le genre italien, doux, ambre foncé. Aux États-Unis, pour faire du vermouth, on commence par choisir et faire vieillir des vins blancs neutres. Puis on les traite avec des herbes et autres substances aromatiques (généralement importées) qui sont mises directement dans le vin ou bien en les faisant infuser au préalable. Ensuite, le vin additionné d'alcool vieillit en fûts. Chaque producteur opère selon une formule secrète comportant parfois jusqu'à 50 herbes, racines, graines, écorces, fleurs, fruits séchés, voire de l'absinthe, etc. Le vermouth titre entre 15° et 20°. Un vermouth léger est récemment devenu populaire aux États-Unis.

VINS DE DESSERT

Ceux des États-Unis titrent au minimum 14° et vont du demi-doux ou doux. On les divise en quatre genres : porto, porto blanc, tokay et Muscat. Malheureusement on ne contrôle que négligemment les appellations des vins de dessert en Californie. Cependant, quelques-uns portent des noms de raisin — Muscat de Frontignan et Tinta — et sont généralement de meilleure qualité. Les chaudes vallées de l'intérieur de la Californie produisent les meilleurs raisins convenant à ces types de vins.

« Porto » américain

Bien des raisins servent à faire ce vin mais ce sont rarement ceux que l'on emploie au Portugal pour le vrai Porto. En Californie on se sert de Carignane, Petite-Syrah Trousseau, Grenache, Valdepeñas et Zinfandel auxquels on ajoute Alicante-Bouschet, Alicante Ganzin et Salvador, pour leur couleur foncée.

Le porto américain est généralement d'un rouge profond fruité, lourd et corsé. Le sucre naturel du raisin lui donne entre 8° et 14° d'alcool et il est plus foncé et plus doux que le véritable Porto. On en fait aussi du plus clair et moins lourdement corsé, qu'on appelle le porto roux.

Comme les autres vins de dessert, les portos américains réussissent mieux dans les régions les plus chaudes. Les meilleurs sont faits avec des raisins Tinta Madeira, Tinta Cão et Touriga : trois variétés portugaises de choix. Il faut reconnaître le mérite du Ficklin Vineyard de Madéra, dans la vallée de San Joaquin, qui produit le meilleur vin californien du genre porto en employant les méthodes portugaises (*voir* PORTO).

« Porto » blanc

On fait ce vin avec du Thompson Seedless qui est en réalité un raisin blanc de table, c'est un vin doux couleur de paille.

Muscat américain

Ce vin de dessert est fait avec des raisins Muscat qui servent aussi à faire un vin de table léger. Les Muscat ont un goût et un arôme caractéristiques qui les rendent rarement agréables et font plutôt figure de parents pauvres sur le marché. Leur couleur va du doré à l'ambre foncé et jusqu'au rouge. Ils contiennent 10 à 15 % de sucre naturel. Étant bon marché, ils sont souvent vendus à la place du whisky et d'autres alcools beaucoup plus chers.

Les meilleures variétés de raisins servent à faire des vins de table Muscat qu'on peut considérer comme les meilleurs. Comme blanc on se sert du Muscat de Frontignan (appelé parfois Muscat Canneli en Californie) et du Malvasia bianca ; pour le rouge, de Malvasia et d'Aleatico.

La plupart des Muscat sont faits avec du Muscat d'Alexandrie (qui est aussi un raisin de table). Ils ont une couleur dorée. Mais on utilise aussi sept autres genres de Muscat en Californie. Dans la vallée de Santa Clara les vignerons cultivent un Muscat noir dit Muscat Hamburg. Le climat chaud de la vallée de San Joaquin, où les raisins atteignent une forte teneur en sucre, est celui qui convient le mieux pour les Muscat de Californie.

« Tokay » californien

On le fait en mélangeant d'autres vins de dessert tels que porto, xérès et angelica. Il n'a aucun rapport avec le véritable Tokay et n'est même pas fait avec le Flame Tokay : raisin de table cultivé dans la région de Lodi. Ce Tokay contient de 7 à 10 % de sucre naturel de raisin et son léger goût de noix rappelle celui du Xérès. Sa couleur est d'un rose ambré. C'est le vin de dessert dont on produit la moins grande quantité et sa qualité est inférieure à la moyenne.

L'*Angelica* est un vin original de Californie qui n'a d'ailleurs pas à en être fier. Il existe néanmoins quelques bons Angelica, mais en faible quantité. Couleur de paille, très doux, additionné d'eau-de-vie, c'est plutôt un cordial qu'un vin de dessert. On le fait avec du raisin Mission et du Grenache à meilleur marché (variété espagnole du Grenache). Il est très fruité. Les « winos » (ceux qui s'enivrent avec des vins de dessert à bon marché) achètent en général l'Angelica en petites bouteilles.

L'*Aleatico* est un vin épicé et fruité qui ressemble au Muscat rouge. On le fait avec le raisin Aleatico auquel il doit ses qualités. On trouve également un autre Aleatico : vin de table assez rare et de qualité inférieure.

Le « *malaga* » des États-Unis est un vin apéritif sans moindre rapport avec le véritable Malaga d'Espagne.

Les *vins de baies* (cassis, framboise, etc.) sont, en Californie, produits surtout aux environs de Elk Grove, dans la vallée du Sacramento.

Comme autres vins de dessert, la Californie produit aussi un grenache fait avec du raisin Grenache, dans la vallée de San Joaquin, un marsala qu'on trouve rarement sur le marché et qui n'a rien de commun avec le Marsala de Sicile ; enfin le madère californien n'est qu'une piètre imitation du Madère.

Un des obstacles majeurs à la production en Californie de vins de type Xérès acceptables, était l'ancienne loi stipulant que les xérès locaux devaient titrer 19,5 % d'alcool. Depuis 1971, ils peuvent légalement titrer 17 %, soit la même teneur que les Xérès espagnols.

Les vins naturels spéciaux ne font pas exactement partie de la classe des vins de dessert, mais ils semblent avoir bénéficié de la récente expansion de l'industrie des vins de baies. Le docteur Maynard Amerine donne un bon aperçu de l'origine des vins : « L'idée des vins aromatisés remonte aux civilisations grecques et romaine. A ces époques, les vins servaient surtout à masquer les goûts et odeurs désagréables ; on prit ainsi l'habitude de leur ajouter des aromates, le vin leur faisant fonction de « véhicule », il remplissait ainsi le même rôle que les épices et parfums. Certaines civilisations, plus anciennes encore, ajoutaient des herbes aux vins pour des raisons médicales ou mystiques et firent grande consommation de vins aromatisés. Lorsqu'on découvrit la distillation, vins et liqueurs aromatisés furent faits de préférence avec des vins vinés ou des eaux-de-vie de vin. »

Les vins « spéciaux » des États-Unis sont faits avec du vin, auquel on ajoute herbes, épices, jus de fruit, aromates, essences, et autres parfums. En tout cas, on n'y ajoute aucun alcool ou eau-de-vie de vin, on ne peut donc, à juste titre, leur donner le nom de vin.

Vins mousseux

Les États-Unis fournissent des rouges, des rosés et des blancs mousseux titrant entre 10 et 14°. Les plus populaires sont le « champagne » et le « bourgogne mousseux ». Quoique aucun vin fait en France hors de Champagne n'ait droit à ce nom, il faut reconnaître que certains mousseux américains sont faits conformément à la méthode champenoise de fermentation secondaire en bouteille. Dans ce cas-là, la loi fédérale accorde au vin le droit de porter sur son étiquette la mention « champagne fermenté en bouteille » à condition que le mot « américain » (ou le nom de l'État) y soient ajoutés. Cette étiquette doit aussi expliquer qu'il s'agit d'un mousseux fait à la manière de la Champagne française, dans l'État de la Californie, celui de New York ou n'importe quel autre État. En Californie, on fait aussi du mousseux selon le procédé Charmat : fermentation secondaire en masse dans d'énormes cuves enduites intérieurement de verre et hermétiquement closes. En France, seuls les mousseux fermentés en bouteille et produits dans la région de Champagne ont droit à l'appellation « Champagne » *(voir ce mot)*.

On fait des champagnes dans tout l'État de Californie. Les meilleurs dans les régions les plus fraîches : cantons de Sonoma, Santa Clara, Napa et Alameda. Les plus doux, dans le district de Cucamonga, au sud. Dans ces deux régions on use de la méthode de fermentation secondaire en masse. Ce système est aussi employé dans la vallée intérieure. Ceux qui fermentent en bouteille proviennent surtout des zones où l'on produit de bons vins de table. Vignobles d'Almadén à Los Gatos (vallée de Santa Clara), F. Korbel et Bros., à Guerneville (canton de Sonoma), Weibel Champagne Vineyards de Mission San José (sud du canton d'Alameda) ainsi que les vignobles Hans Kornell, Beaulieu, le Domaine Chandon (groupe Moët-Hennessy), et récemment les vignobles plantés par Roederer dans le canton de Mendocino et par Deutz près de Santa Barbara sont probablement les meilleurs producteurs de mousseux californien.

Le Pinot Noir et le Pinot Chardonnay, c'est-à-dire les raisins qui servent à faire le Champagne, donnent les meilleures qualités de mousseux californien ; on utilise aussi en Californie d'autres bons raisins : Pinot Blanc, Sémillon, Sauvignon Blanc, White Riesling et Folle Blanche, et des variétés de qualité inférieure : Sauvignon Vert, Burger, French Colombard et Green Hungarian. Les champagnes de Californie vont du sec au doux et sont additionnés de sucre, de la même manière qu'en Champagne, mais on n'y trouve pas de vrai brut.

Les mousseux rosés qui portent le nom de champagne peuvent être fermentés en bouteille ou en cuve close : la loi exige que l'étiquette indique lequel de ces deux procédés a été utilisé.

Parmi les mousseux, le bourgogne mousseux est le plus consommé après le champagne. C'est un vin rouge rendu gazeux par l'une des deux méthodes qui servent également à faire les champagnes. Faits avec des raisins Pinot Noir, Carignane, Mondeuse et Petite-Syrah, ces vins vont du demi-doux au doux.

Des vins de table portant les noms de Moselle, Sauternes, etc., sont parfois traités en mousseux, comme les champagnes. On fait des muscats mousseux avec des Muscat légers provenant généralement de Muscat canelli (Muscat de Frontignan). Ils ont tendance à être doux et on les vend souvent sous un nom italien : « Moscato spumante. » Le Malvasia bianca donne un vin doux à goût de Muscat qui est parfois champagnisé.

Pour faire d'autres mousseux on les gazéifie artificiellement. La loi de Californie et d'autres États exige qu'ils soient désignés comme tels. Parfois on les appelle aussi vins effervescents. Produits en masse et à meilleur marché, ils sont plutôt moins bons que les mousseux fermentés naturellement.

Les « champagnes » de New York et de l'est sont produits à base de divers raisins. On utilise plus fréquemment des hybrides et des *Viniferas* mais on a encore largement recours aux *labruscas* (Delanare, Catanba et Aurora). Bully Hill et Wagner à Finger Lakes font un bon Seyval Blanc mousseux en utilisant la méthode champenoise, Glenora fait des expériences avec du Chardonnay, Gold Seal utilise du Chardonnay pour son Blanc de Blanc et Herman Wiemer du Riesling. Plusieurs autres producteurs de l'est entament ou poursuivent des essais sur des vins mousseux. Taylor, Great Western et Gold Seal sont les principaux producteurs de champagne.

Les Bourgogne mousseux et les champagnes rosés proviennent aussi d'une grande variété de raisins. Récemment plusieurs maisons de vins ont produit des vins de type « spumante » à partir de Muscats et de *labruscas* qui ont fait l'unanimité chez les consommateurs.

États-Unis : Arkansas

Cela peut paraître surprenant, mais l'État d'Arkansas produit près de 40 000 hl (440 000 caisses) de vin par an. La plupart des vignobles se trouvent dans les comtés de Franklin et de Johnson, ainsi qu'à l'extrémité nord-ouest de l'État, autour de Tontitown. Ils couvrent une superficie totale d'environ 2 000 ha. Quatre des plus importants centres vinificateurs (il y en a dix en tout) se trouvent dans la petite ville d'Altus : Wiederkehr, Post, Sax et Mount Bethel. C'est dans la région d'Altus que l'on produit la quasi-totalité du vin d'Arkansas. On fait des vins de table et, s'ils ont tendance à être un peu trop doux, ils ne pourront que s'améliorer au fur et à mesure que les hybrides franco-américains et que les vignes *vinifera* remplaceront les médiocres variétés indigènes, qui sont prépondérantes depuis la deuxième moitié du XIXe siècle.

États-Unis : Californie et Ouest

Climat, sol et autres conditions permettant la production de bon vin sont réunis en Californie à l'égal de ceux qui prévalent dans la plupart des bonnes régions vinicoles du monde. Qualité et quantité ont fait de la Californie l'une des premières régions vinicoles du monde. Le pire handicap qui nuisit à la production de grands vins, c'était, en bien des secteurs, l'énorme encépagement de variétés médiocres ou mauvaises.

Les plantations de bonnes vignes étaient plutôt limitées alors qu'abondaient les raisins à vin rouge tels que Zinfandel, Carignane, Alicante-Bouschet ; et à vin blanc comme Frenche Colombar, Thompson Seedless et Sauvignon vert qui, tous, ne produisent que des vins ordinaires. Les vins variétaux de type *Vitis Vinifera* étaient rationnés en raison de leur rareté. Aujourd'hui les choses ont changé. Ils sont produits en grosses quantités et sont souvent très bien vinifiés. En gros, les régions les plus fraîches, au nord de l'État — vallées de Napa, Sonoma, Livermore, Valley, Santa Cruz et Santa Clara, Mendocino —, produisent des vins de table ; certains présentent un goût d'une excellente distinction. Les régions les plus chaudes donnent des vins de dessert. Jusqu'en 1965, 60 % des vins californiens étaient malheureusement des vins doux ou additionnés d'alcool plutôt que des vins de table. Depuis, ces derniers ont supplanté les faux Porto et Xérès et représentent aujourd'hui 80 % de la totalité des vins produits dans l'État de Californie. Des chiffres récents indiquent que la vente des vins de table progresse deux fois et demi plus vite que celle des vins de liqueur.

Aujourd'hui, 67 % des vins vendus aux États-Unis viennent de Californie. En 1985, la production totale de vins de table, de liqueurs et vins mousseux s'élevait à environ 158 millions de caisses, soit l'équivalent de la production moyenne annuelle de tous les vins d'appellation contrôlée français (bien sûr, les vins d'appellation contrôlée ne représentent qu'un sixième de tous les vins produits en France). La production des vins vinés, qui ne représentait que 8 % du marché, déclina régulièrement au début des années 80. Les vins mousseux atteignirent 7 % de la production totale avec 11,3 millions de caisses — quinze ans plus tôt, les « champagnes » représentaient à peine 2 % du volume total. Dans les années 80, la croissance de la production a été constante dans le segment « blush » des vins de table. Les « Coolers », concoctions à base de jus de fruit et de vin sont emballés et vendus de la même façon que la bière. Ils ne se sont développés qu'à partir de 1980 et atteignent aujourd'hui une part de marchés surprenante de 15 %.

Histoire du vin en Californie

L'histoire du vin en Californie remonte à Cortès, qui conquit le Mexique. Dès 1524, il décida que la viticulture serait une des industries du Nouveau Monde. Les vignes importées alors étaient probablement d'origine espagnole. Mais on n'est pas certains que boutures et graines arrivèrent directement d'Espagne. Au bout d'un certain temps, le vin du Mexique concurrença celui d'Espagne. Comme l'avait fait longtemps avant eux l'empereur Domitien, les Espagnols ordonnèrent d'arracher toutes les vignes de la colonie. Néanmoins la viticulture survécut pendant bien des années en diverses régions du Mexique et tout particulièrement en Basse-Californie, à l'insu des fonctionnaires espagnols.

Un jésuite, le père Juan Ugarte, planta probablement les premières vignes à vin de la côte Ouest vers 1697, à la mission Saint-François-Xavier, située en Basse-Californie. C'étaient des variétés européennes, les seules que plantèrent les jésuites et on les nomma « Mission », nom qu'elles portent encore aujourd'hui. Les missions espagnoles s'étendant lentement vers le nord, le raisin Mission apparut en Haute-Californie. Sous la conduite du père Junipero Serra, les franciscains plantèrent du Mission à leur mission de San Diego de Alcala, peu après leur installation en 1769. Les vignes prospérèrent et les vendanges se révélèrent, dit-on, meilleures que tout ce que l'on avait jusqu'alors connu au Nouveau Monde. Les franciscains du père Serra établirent 21 missions, qui avaient presque toutes leurs vignobles, entre San Diego et Sonoma, le point le plus septentrional du Camino Real (Route royale) qui est encore aujourd'hui une grande route. Mais la plupart de ces missions étaient groupées dans le sud de la

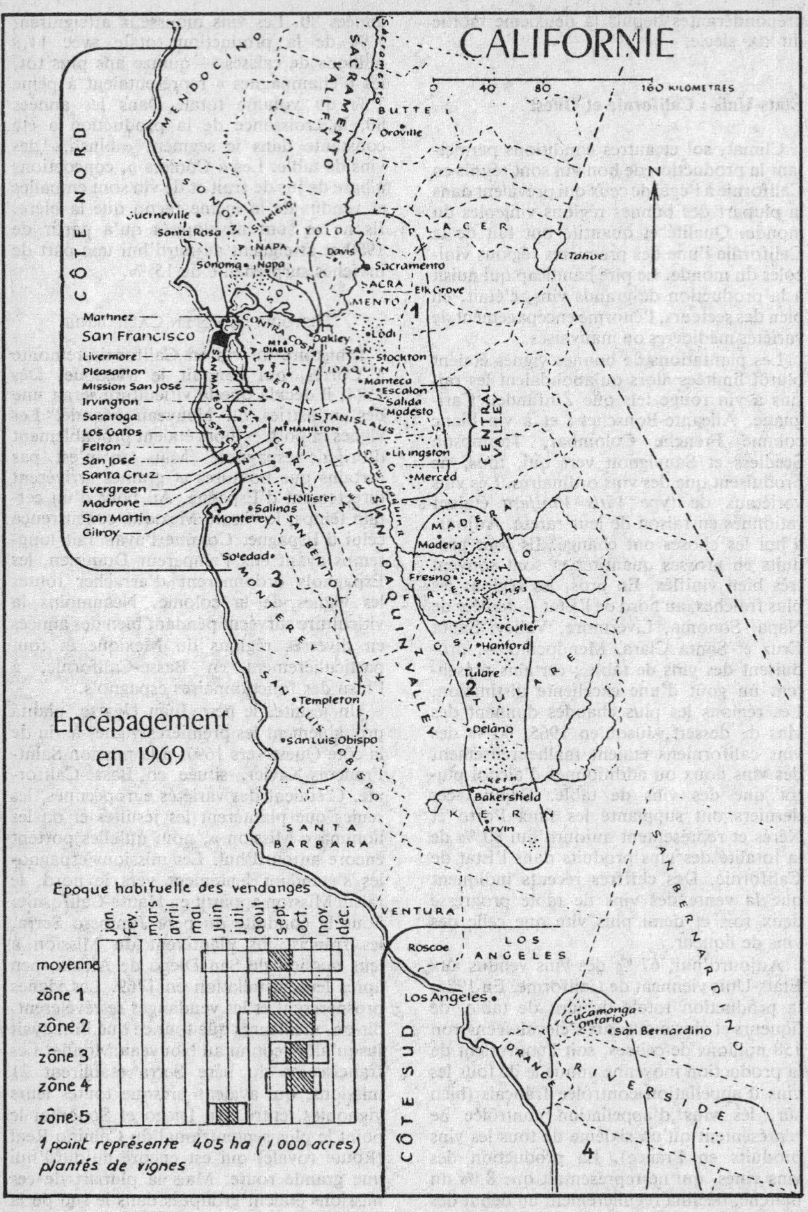
CALIFORNIE
0 40 80 160 KILOMETRES
N
MENDOCINO
SACRAMENTO VALLEY
Sacramento
BUTTE
Oroville
SONOMA
St Helena
Guerneville
Santa Rosa
NAPA
YOLO
Davis
Sonoma
Napa
SOLANO
Sacramento
SACRAMENTO
Elk Grove
PLACER
L. Tahoe
CÔTE NORD
Martinez
San Francisco
CONTRA COSTA
MT DIABLO
ALAMEDA
SAN MATEO
STA. CRUZ
STA. CLARA
Oakley
Lodi
SAN JOAQUIN
Stockton
Manteca
Escalon
Salida
Modesto
STANISLAUS
MT HAMILTON
Livingston
MERCED
Merced
CENTRAL VALLEY
Livermore
Pleasanton
Mission San José
Irvington
Saratoga
Los Gatos
Felton
San José
Santa Cruz
Evergreen
Madrone
San Martin
Gilroy
Hollister
Salinas
Monterey
SAN BENITO
Soledad
MONTEREY
3
1
MADERA
Madera
Fresno
FRESNO
Kings
Cutler
Hanford
KINGS
TULARE
Tulare
2
Delano
SAN JOAQUIN VALLEY
Templeton
SAN LUIS OBISPO
San Luis Obispo
Bakersfield
KERN
Arvin
SANTA BARBARA
SAN BERNARDINO
VENTURA
Roscoe
LOS ANGELES
Los Angeles
Cucamonga
Ontario
San Bernardino
ORANGE
RIVERSIDE
CÔTE SUD
4
Encépagement en 1969
Epoque habituelle des vendanges
jan. fev. mars avril mai juin juil. août sept. oct. nov. déc.
moyenne
zône 1
zône 2
zône 3
zône 4
zône 5
1 point représente 405 ha (1 000 acres) plantés de vignes

Californie. Des descendantes des vignes que les franciscains cultivèrent alors vivent encore. Ils choisirent la mission de Saint-Gabriel-Archange, près de Los Angeles, pour y installer leur principal centre de viniculture. On voit encore à cette mission le petit bâtiment d'*abobe* (pisé) où les Indiens foulaient le raisin pour en exprimer le jus. De nos jours, des touristes viennent de loin et de partout pour voir la vigne de la Trinité qui fut probablement plantée avant 1780.

Entre 1770 et 1830, alors que les missions fleurissaient, on y produisait du vin selon les besoins des pères. En 1850, le gouvernement mexicain sécularisa les missions, dont les vignobles furent laissés à l'abandon. Mais on savait désormais qu'il était possible de faire du vin et de l'eau-de-vie en Californie.

Nouveaux propriétaires de vignobles

La décadence des missions, la ruine de leurs vignobles, le délabrement de leurs installations et de leurs pressoirs marquent la fin d'une époque et le début de la viticulture moderne. Avant 1830, les vignes appartenant à des personnes privées étaient rares. Pourtant, dès 1824, Joseph Chapman — un des premiers Américains qui s'installèrent sur le site de l'actuelle Los Angeles — planta 4 000 pieds de vigne. Puis vint Jean-Louis Vignes, un Bordelais qui se lança dans une aventure commerciale consistant à faire du vin pour le vendre, à peu près à l'endroit où se trouve actuellement la principale gare de Los Angeles. Dès 1833, on acclamait son vin et son eau-de-vie. Ces deux pionniers firent école ; la viticulture s'étendit. En une génération elle devint la principale activité du district de Los Angeles. Vignes fut un des premiers à conseiller de planter des variétés de raisin nobles. Peu après 1830, il importa des boutures de vignes européennes de choix. On les emballa délicatement, pour les envoyer d'abord de France à Boston, puis en Californie par le cap Horn. Ce long voyage n'endommagea pas les boutures qu'on planta. Quelques-unes donnèrent des fruits dont on fit des vins de Californie. William Wolfskill, trappeur du Kentucky, créa lui aussi une importante entreprise de viticulture et de viniculture peu après 1830. Dès 1858, deux ans avant sa mort, le vignoble de Wolfskill s'étendait déjà sur près de 58 ha et comptait 55 000 pieds de vigne. Il possédait une cave d'une capacité de 2 300 à 3 800 hl.

Outre Vignes et Wolfskill, Charles Kohler et John Frohling méritent aussi d'être cités parmi les pionniers des vins de Californie. Tous deux d'ascendance allemande, ils achetèrent une vigne en commun, de 300 pieds, près le Los Angeles, et ouvrirent en même temps une boutique de marchands de vin à San Francisco, dans un sous-sol — la première de ce genre — avec moins de 2 500 l dans leur cave. En 1862, ils avaient déjà près de 25 000 l de vin, et environ 910 l d'eau-de-vie dans leurs caves voûtées.

Les raisins Mission furent introduits dans les premiers vignobles commerciaux par Chapman, Vignes et les autres pionniers, qui plantèrent cette variété d'abord au sud, puis au nord de la Californie. Vigne robuste et de haut rendement, ses fruits manquaient toutefois de caractère et convenaient mal à la fabrication de vin de table. Pourtant, elle continua à dominer la viticulture californienne pendant plus de 80 ans.

Augmentation des cépages européens par le colonel Haraszthy

La transition entre le cépage Mission et les belles variétés européennes fut due à un nouveau venu en Californie, quelque douze ans après que Jean-Louis Vignes eut réussi avec ses boutures importées de France. Ce pionnier extraordinaire fut Agoston Haraszthy, aristocrate hongrois, considéré depuis comme le père de la viticulture californienne. La première importation à grande échelle de vignes étrangères commença en 1851, quand le colonel Haraszthy planta 100 boutures et 6 pieds de vigne de choix à San Diego. Parmi ces plants, il y avait le célèbre Zinfandel qui servit plus tard à faire un rouge sec très populaire. Au début les vignerons s'entêtèrent à cultiver leur Mission et ne se décidèrent que lentement à acheter de nouvelles variétés de vignes, car ils croyaient que le colonel spéculait simplement sur la vente de ses boutures. C'est seulement en 1878 que l'encépagement en Zinfandel prit de l'extension. Convaincu que les meilleurs raisins étrangers pouvaient prospérer en Californie, Haraszthy chercha à déterminer les sols convenant le mieux à chaque variété sur le territoire de l'État. Il croyait aussi obtenir de meilleurs résultats, et plus rapidement, en important un plus grand nombre de variétés.

Dès 1861, le gouverneur de Californie — John G. Downey — le chargea d'une mission viticole consistant à rassembler à l'étranger toutes les variétés de vigne qui pouvaient donner des résultats satisfaisants. Il choisit 100 000 boutures de 300 variétés qui furent toutes expédiées en Californie dans le courant d'une année. Il en planta un certain nombre sur son vignoble de Buena Vista, à Sonoma. Mais la plus grosse part fut vendue à des vignerons de toutes les parties de l'État. En 1863, Haraszthy fonda la Buena Vista Vinicultural Society à laquelle il apporta son ranch de 2 400 ha dont 160 ha plantés en vigne. C'est ce don d'un large assortiment de cépages et ses recherches constantes qui stimulèrent l'expansion de la viticulture contemporaine en Californie. La plupart des variétés de qualité supérieure qu'il importa à cette époque furent plantées autour de la baie de San Francisco. Cette région profita énormément de la démonstration que fit Haraszthy : on peut produire des vins de haute qualité sur des terrains non irrigués.

Nombre de cultivateurs et toutes sortes de gens qui cherchaient simplement un profit immédiat se lancèrent sans expérience dans la viticulture. Ils ne se soucièrent ni de choisir leurs variétés de vigne, ni du sol, ni des autres conditions dans lesquelles ils les plantaient. Ce désordre remit à plus tard la réalisation de l'idéal qui avait animé Haraszthy. De nos jours encore il n'est pas atteint.

Entre 1860 et 1870, Los Angeles, Anaheim et Sonoma se distinguaient comme les trois principaux secteurs de production de vin et de raisin. Les vignobles y étaient plus nombreux et plus vastes que partout ailleurs.

C'est la découverte des filons d'or qui suscita à l'origine la prospérité de l'or liquide — le vin — en Californie. Le marché du vin s'étendit au fur et à mesure qu'on découvrait de l'or. Les chercheurs d'or de 1849 considéraient le Los Angeles comme un luxe. Puis quand se termina la ruée vers l'or, les prix s'écroulèrent. Pour permettre à la viticulture de survivre, le parlement de Californie exempta d'impôts les nouveaux vignobles. En 1870, l'avenir semblait plus rose : le succès obtenu par Haraszthy avec les nouvelles variétés européennes, les législations bienveillantes de l'État et de la Fédération provoquèrent l'expansion de la viniculture et la qualité des vins de Californie fut reconnue dans tout le pays. Mais cette prospérité ne dura pas. Une crise économique s'appesantit sur les États-Unis de 1875 à 1877 et l'industrie du vin en pâtit aussi. Après 1878, les choses commencèrent à aller mieux. La crise avait éloigné les simples amateurs et spéculateurs, et ceux qui persévérèrent dans l'industrie vinicole produisaient maintenant des vins issus de meilleures variétés de raisin. Ceux-là n'échappèrent pas seulement à la crise, mais aussi à l'épidémie de phylloxéra.

Néanmoins, depuis l'abrogation, l'histoire de la viniculture californienne est surtout celle du progrès. On a planté bon nombre de bonnes variétés de vigne qui peuvent fournir les meilleurs vins de table rouges et blancs.

L'apparition du phylloxéra

Le phylloxéra — pou térébrant de la vigne — se manifesta en Californie avant 1870. En 1876 il devint une véritable plaie et ravagea encore pendant au moins trois ans les vignes des cantons de Sonoma, Napa, Yolo, El Dorado et Placer, comme il avait déjà dévasté celles d'Europe. Les Français furent les premiers qui réussirent à enrayer la catastrophe en greffant leurs vignes *Vinifera* sur des souches de variétés indigènes de l'Est des États-Unis résistant au phylloxéra. Peu de temps après, les vignerons californiens adoptèrent la même méthode.

Le début de la législation

Les commissaires du Bureau viticole de l'État de Californie contribuèrent à éliminer le phylloxéra et à stabiliser la viticulture. Institué en 1880, cet organisme aida les vignerons à choisir les sols et climats convenant le mieux à chaque variété de vigne et à combattre leurs maladies. Une station viticole expérimentale, dirigée par le collège d'agriculture de l'université de Californie, contribua aussi à ces progrès. Ce collège continue encore de nos jours ses recherches et son enseignement de la viticulture et de l'œnologie, sous l'impulsion du professeur A.J. Winkler et du docteur Maynard Amerine, respectés par les œnologues et viticulteurs du monde entier. Quant au Bureau viticole d'État, il fit adopter les lois qui imposèrent les premières normes de qualité aux vins de Californie.

Viticulture et commerce du vin s'accrurent encore de 1900 à 1915. Puis commença à se dessiner un mouvement vers la prohibition totale des boissons alcooliques. Enfin, cette prohibition fut imposée d'abord en 1919 par la loi Volstead, puis comme 18e amendement à la Constitution des États-Unis en novembre 1920. La viticulture de Californie en fut durement frappée. Bien des nouvelles entreprises de vinification cessèrent de fonctionner. La production du vin tomba d'à peu près 2 275 000 hl à environ 1 200 000 hl en 1919.

Pourtant la prohibition ne fut pas totalement désastreuse. Il était encore permis de faire du vin à usage médicinal et pour la messe. Une partie de l'industrie commerciale du vin subsista donc. Quand, treize ans plus tard, on reconnut enfin que la prohibition se soldait par un échec, une campagne dans le sens inverse amena le vote du 21e amendement constitutionnel, en décembre 1933. A partir de ce moment-là, chaque État, chaque canton, chaque municipalité fut libre d'imposer sa propre prohibition. Alors les vignerons qui n'avaient pas perdu courage purent reprendre à grande échelle et presque immédiatement la production de vin. Pendant un certain temps la demande dépassa l'offre et les prix montèrent exagérément ; on vendit des vins de qualité inférieure. C'est seulement en 1938 que le marché se stabilisa sur une tendance générale à l'extension.

La mesure la plus importante qui fut prise dans toute l'histoire du vin californien fut l'effort des gens du métier pour choisir les variétés de vigne et pour produire de bons vins qui portent le nom du raisin : Cabernet Sauvignon, Pinot Chardonnay. Malheureusement on n'a pas tout à fait réussi à éliminer le Mission des régions les plus froides, ni à diminuer la proportion d'Alicante-Bouschet. La viniculture de Californie ne s'est pas complétement remise de la prohibition au temps de laquelle le marché exigeait des raisins à peau dure qui supportaient le voyage jusqu'aux États de l'Est. Une vigne de haute qualité comme le Cabernet Sauvignon ne produit guère plus de 50 hl à l'ha ; on la dédaigna en faveur du Carignane et de l'Alicante-Bouschet d'un rendement cinq fois supérieur. La qualité des vins produits a été énormément améliorée.

Parmi les producteurs qui se firent connaître entre les années 1940 et 1950, il faut citer Louis M. Martini, doyen des viticulteurs de la vallée du Napa, viennent ensuite feu Herman Wente, John Daniel Jr. de Inglenook, Madame de Latour des vignobles Beaulieu, Chaffee Hall de Hallcrest, Peter Mondavi de la Maison Charles Krug et Robert Mondavi, feu Martin Ray qui possédait jadis les vignobles Paul Masson, enfin Louis Benoist, ancien propriétaire de Almadén. Tous ont employé des méthodes d'affaires à grande échelle et contribué de même à maintenir la qualité des vins américains, en dépit de la pression de la demande qui incline à une production de masse. Enfin, feu Frank Schoonmaker, négociant en vins new-yorkais, qui introduisit les bons vins d'Amérique, à l'est des Montagnes Rocheuses, avec l'aide de l'auteur de cette encyclopédie, est encore un de ceux qui ont combattu plus pour la qualité que pour la quantité.

On compte quelque 676 entreprises de vinification en Californie. La situation évolue d'année en année. De nouvelles entreprises apparaissent, telles que les Weibel Champagne Vineyards et le Domaine Chandon. D'autres se retirent des affaires, comme le Fountaingrove Vineyard, par exemple. Certaines deviennent trop commerciales et sacrifient la qualité à la quantité. Paul Masson et Cresta Blanca, qui produisaient autrefois de bons vins, en sont des exemples quoiqu'ils fassent actuellement de remarquables efforts pour atteindre des normes plus élevées. Quelques entreprises seulement insistent pour que les vins de Californie portent leur nom d'origine ; à ce point de vue, feu Paul Rossigneux, président de la Napa et Sonoma Wine Co, Robert Mondavi et feu Carl Wente ont toujours été respectés pour leur attachement sans compromis à des normes élevées.

Aujourd'hui, les vignerons de Californie ont une tâche à accomplir : amener leur industrie à un niveau tel qu'elle puisse concurrencer sur un pied d'égalité celles d'Europe. Ce n'est possible qu'avec des vins de bonnes variétés, mais pas avec des imitations. Le Xérès vient d'Espagne ; le Porto, du Portugal ; Bourgogne, Chablis et Sauternes, de France. Donner un de ces noms à un vin de Californie, c'est admettre son infériorité.

De bons cépages, avec l'aide de sols et

de climats appropriés, donneront de bons vins. Planter de bonnes variétés de vigne sur la terre de Californie doit certainement donner des vins qui mériteront d'être jugés selon leurs propres qualités.

Développements récents

Aujourd'hui les raisins et le vin californiens représentent une industrie valant des milliards de dollars. Entre 1970 et 1987, les plantations se sont accrues dans une proportion de 250 %. De nouvelles régions viticoles ont été créées pour remplacer les régions dévorées par l'expansion des villes de cet État le plus peuplé du pays. Un jour, 1/6 de l'immense superficie consacrée à l'agriculture sera couvert de vignobles. Pour l'instant, la superficie totale des vignobles est de 300 000 ha, dont un peu plus de la moitié est plantée exclusivement de raisins à vin. Parallèlement, on observe un développement semblable des centres de vinification : des millions de dollars sont investis chaque année dans de nouvelles constructions, dans l'équipement et la recherche. L'expansion de l'industrie vinicole n'a pas affecté l'état des centres déjà existants : les très grosses entreprises coexistent toujours côte à côte avec les très petits centres. Les quelques centres importants produisent plus de 65 % des vins californiens. Outre ces entreprises géantes, il en existe trois ou quatre, moins importantes, qui offrent dans tout le pays un large éventail de vins sélectionnés. Celles qui ont réussi dans ces dix dernières années sont pour la plupart des entreprises de taille moyenne, proposant, à des prix raisonnables, des produits de qualité supérieure à la moyenne. C'est à ces producteurs et à certaines des petites entreprises que l'on doit les vins fins de Californie.

Depuis 1965 environ, le « boom » du vin californien attire de grandes sociétés, d'immenses firmes de boissons et comestibles et des institutions financières. Heublein, Inc, qui rachetèrent United Vintners, Inglenook, et Beaulieu ; National Distillers qui racheta les Vignobles d'Almadén en 1967 et les revendit à Heublein Inc. en 1987, Seagrams qui sont les propriétaires de Paul Masson ; Italian Swiss Colony, Lejon, Vet, depuis 1983, Wine Spectrum (Sterling Vineyards, The Monterey Vineyard, Taylor California Cellars et Taylor Wine Company) racheté à Coca-Cola d'Atlanta. Seagram, en 1987, revendit quelques-unes de ses entreprises viticoles à Vintners International. En 1973, la société Moët-Hennessy fonda Domaine Chandon Vineyards. Elle acheta 320 ha de vignobles dans les comtés de Napa et Sonoma et lança avec succès en 1975 des vins mousseux produits selon la traditionnelle méthode champenoise. Domaine Chandon acheta également Simi Winery à Sonoma. Piper-Heidsieck s'associa à Sonoma Vineyards. Nestlé possède Beringer depuis 1972. De même des sociétés allemandes comme Peter Eckes et A. Racke, producteurs des vins mousseux Kupferberg, achetèrent respectivement Franciscan Vineyards et Buena Vista Vineyards en 1979.

Freixenet, le plus important vendeur de mousseux aux États-Unis, lança en 1983 un projet de production de 100 000 caisses de Gloria Ferrer, chiffre prévisible à partir de 1988. La maison Louis Roederer a acquis 160 ha de Anderson Valley à Mendocino en 1982. La première production était de 100 000 caisses, chiffre atteint en 1987. Distillers Company Ltd, le plus grand producteur de whisky mondial, acheta Concannon Vineyards en 1983. Aujourd'hui Distillers est détenu par les Guiness Brewers.

Plantations

En 1969, après plusieurs années de déclin, le nombre d'ha plantés exclusivement de raisins à vin recommença à augmenter régulièrement. 19 000 ha furent plantés en 1972, soit plus que pour toute la période 1965-1970. Les plantations de 1973 et 1974 furent plus importantes encore et, début 1975, les vignobles de raisin à vin couvraient une superficie totale de 129 000 ha. En 1986, la superficie des vignobles de Californie atteignit 136 000 ha, représentant plus d'un tiers de celle des régions de Bordeaux et Bourgogne réunies.

La nouvelle tendance qui consiste à planter des raisins à vin de qualité supérieure est plus significative encore que la fantastique augmentation de la superficie des vignobles. Pour prendre un exemple, en 1959, le Cabernet Sauvignon, ce noble raisin de Bordeaux, couvrait seulement 250 ha, en 1981, il s'étendait sur une surface de plus de 12 000 ha. Le Pinot Chardonnay et le Pinot Noir ont augmenté dans les mêmes proportions, sans compter d'autres variétés qui, bien que moins célèbres, n'en sont pas moins bonnes. Malgré tout, beaucoup de vins californiens sont encore faits avec le Thompson Seedless, une variété de raisin de table de qualité déplorable. Une bonne partie des plantations de ces grands plants de bonne qualité a été effectuée dans ces parties de l'État qui s'adonnent depuis peu à la viticulture. San Benito, Monterey, San Luis Obispo, Lake, Mendocino et Santa Barbara sont des secteurs où les vignobles se sont considérablement étendus. La firme Almadèn Vineyards fut la première à implanter des vignobles autour de San Benito, ainsi qu'à Paicines et Cienega. Dans les années 1960, Paul Masson, Mirassou et Wente Bros créèrent les vignobles de Monterey. Ceux de San Luis Obispo se sont étendus sur plus de 2 240 ha en moins de dix ans. On y fait des vins avec des variétés de Cabernet Sauvignon. Zinfandel, Sauvignon Blanc, Chardonnay, Merlot, Pinot Blanc et Gewürztraminer. La plupart des vignes sont situées autour de Paso Robles et de la ville de San Luis Obispo. Plus au sud de Los Angeles, à proximité de Riverside et de Temecula, on trouve ces mêmes variétés nobles ainsi que du Johannisberg Riesling et du Chenin Blanc, qui prospèrent dans un climat tempéré par des brises maritimes.

Travaux et recherches

Pendant près d'un siècle, les nouvelles plantations et autres aspects de la viniculture californienne ont toujours été conduits sous l'égide de l'université de Californie. Ses spécialistes ont prodigué leurs conseils aux négociants en vins d'Australie, de Nouvelle-Zélande, d'Espagne, du Portugal, de Yougoslavie, d'Argentine, du Brésil, du Chili, d'Afrique du Sud et même du Japon. Le campus de Davis, situé à 110 km au nord-est de San Francisco, accueille des étudiants en viticulture et en œnologie ainsi que des jeunes désireux de se spécialiser dans la recherche. Nombre des projets sont patronnés par les sociétés de vins californiennes. Cette étroite collaboration avec les producteurs locaux naquit en 1875, lorsque E.W. Hilgard fut nommé Professeur d'Agriculture par la nouvelle Université. Cinq ans plus tard la législature décidait de créer un département d'enseignement « des arts et sciences ayant trait à la viticulture, de la théorie et pratique de la fermentation, distillation et rectification, de la gestion des caves..., ces enseignements étant illustrés par des travaux pratiques ».

Trois savants de l'université (de renommée internationale) ont joué un rôle essentiel dans l'amélioration des vins californiens au cours des vingt dernières années ; il s'agit de H.P. Olmo : généticien et pathologiste des plantes, Maynard A. Amerine que ses recherches et ouvrages sur les vins amènent à voyager dans le monde entier, enfin Harold W. Berg : expert conseil des problèmes du vin, qui a éclairé de sa science des viticulteurs de tous les pays.

Les travaux, réalisés par le docteur Olmo — qui a consacré quarante ans de sa vie à produire de nouvelles souches hybrides qui ont donné un vin de qualité dans de nombreuses régions du pays —, étaient en application dans certains vignobles californiens. Le docteur Amerine, estimé dans le monde entier pour sa science, fut président de la Société Américaine des œnologues, il remporta de nombreux prix de diverses organisations étrangères, il écrivit de nombreux livres passionnants sur les vins et la viniculture et, surtout, contribua hautement à l'amélioration de la qualité des vins californiens. Le Professeur Berg, président sortant de la faculté d'œnologie, a mené de précieuses recherches sur le traitement du raisin, la stabilisation et le vieillissement du vin. Mais la grande réussite des chercheurs de l'université Davis fût avant tout la classification des secteurs viticoles californiens en cinq zones de température.

Dans les années 1930, les professeurs A.J. Winkler et Maynard Amerine se penchèrent sur la relation existant entre le climat et la qualité du vin produit avec les diverses variétés de raisin dans les différentes régions de Californie. Ils arrivèrent à la conclusion que la température était le seul facteur climatique fondamental qui affectait la culture des raisins à vin et que l'addition des températures quotidiennes était une donnée assez sûre pour permettre de prédéterminer les variétés de raisin convenant le mieux à chaque zone. Ce principe fut établi à partir du total des températures quotidiennes moyennes au-dessus de 10 °C entre le 1er avril et le 31 octobre. Une température de 10 °C fût évaluée à une température totale de 15 « journées-degrés ». Cinq régions climatiques furent ensuite établies en fonction des totaux de la saison :

Région I : moins de 2 500 journées-degrés.

Région II : de 2 501 à 3 000 journées-degrés.

Région III : de 3 001 à 3 500 journées-degrés.

Région IV : de 3 501 à 4 000 journées-degrés.

Région V : plus de 4 000 journées-degrés.

En connaissant la région climatique à laquelle appartenait son vignoble, un viticulteur pouvait donc déterminer quelles vignes étaient les plus appropriées. Lorsque le total était au-dessous de 1 800 journées-degrés, la plupart des variétés de raisin ne mûrissaient pas assez pour produire un vin ayant la teneur en alcool minimum légale. Dans les régions plus chaudes, les raisins mûrissaient plus vite et donnaient d'abondantes récoltes, mais les vins manquaient d'acidité, de couleur et d'arôme. C'est dans ces régions que l'on fait les vins de liqueur ou vinés qui exigent une grande quantité de sucre de raisin naturel, ainsi que les vins de table courants. Dans les vignobles moins ensoleillés, où les vignes ne produisent qu'en quantité limitée, les raisins ont tout le loisir de mûrir lentement en gardant leur acidité et de réunir ainsi les qualités de couleur et d'arôme qui font la finesse des bons vins de table.

Les zones californiennes productrices de vins primés étaient les régions I, II et III, alors que les régions IV et V produisaient surtout des raisins de table, du vin en vrac, des vins vinés et de liqueur cités plus haut. Ces zones furent établies exclusivement en fonction du climat et ne recouvraient donc pas nécessairement une région géographique. La présence des montagnes crée des microclimats différents. Aussi, les endroits appartenant à une catégorie climatique différente peuvent être séparés par une infinité de kilomètres, mais peuvent également se trouver sur un même flanc de montagne. Ainsi : les extrémités nord et sud de la longue vallée centrale furent classées dans la régions V, son centre dans la région IV. De même, la vallée de la Napa, principalement région III, avait quelques secteurs dans les régions I et II. Par contre, le tout proche secteur de Peachland, dans le comté de Sonoma, était presque entièrement région I.

Le concept d'addition de la chaleur pouvait être un instrument précieux pour les viticulteurs désireux de savoir quelles vignes étaient susceptibles de prospérer dans certaines contrées vierges de l'État. Il permettait également de donner approximativement la date à laquelle les raisins seraient mûrs. Cette classification fût faite en fonction du climat qui n'est, après tout, qu'un des facteurs influant sur la production de bons vins : pour certains viticulteurs de secteurs nouvellement exploités, les régions I, II et III ont une production de qualité ; seule, l'expérience acquise par les firmes dotées de techniques modernes pourra déterminer quels secteurs garantissent un bon vin.

Progrès technologiques

La vendange mécanique est née en Californie, où elle joue un rôle plus important que dans toute autre région productrice de vins fins du monde. Elle est couramment pratiquée dans les grands plateaux et bassins de l'intérieur, où l'on fait principalement du vin en vrac, mais aussi dans certaines parties de la côte septentrionale, d'où proviennent les meilleurs vins californiens. Ces vendangeuses géantes sont de deux types : l'une récolte le fruit par aspiration avec la plupart des feuilles de vigne, l'autre secoue le plant et récolte les raisins qui en tombent. De l'avis des œnologues, la vendange mécanique exige que les raisins soient pressurés dans les plus brefs délais. Plusieurs vignobles ont d'ailleurs des machines permettant le pressurage et l'égrappage sur place, certains ont même installé des projecteurs pour le travail de nuit.

Une autre machine, plus petite que ces vendangeuses, réduit également le travail humain ; elle permet : de remuer en même temps et doucement un grand nombre de bouteilles pour éliminer le dépôt de tartrate logé dans le goulot et, d'augmenter la production des vins mousseux des caves à champagne de Korbel ; car, même pour les savants remueurs champenois, l'art du remuage est une longue opération.

Les viticulteurs californiens ont amélioré leurs techniques d'irrigation et ont également réussi à protéger les vignes du froid par le gel. L'anachronique fumigène, seul moyen connu jusqu'alors pour lutter contre les désastreuses gelées de printemps — qui peuvent détruitre 75 % d'une récolte —, a été remplacé dans de nombreux vignobles par des tourniquets automatiques qui arrosent les cépages dans les premières heures de la matinée, lorsque le froid est au plus vif. L'eau, déposée sur les pousses et les jeunes feuilles, gèle alors à une température de 0 °C, libérant ainsi la chaleur nécessaire à la protection de la vigne. En outre, la présence de la brume empêche la température de l'air de descendre trop bas. Ces systèmes requièrent au moins 400 l par minute pour chaque hectare à protéger et des réservoirs ont dû être installés pour garantir l'approvisionnement nécessaire. Mais avec les campagnes écologiques menées un peu partout pour le respect des fleuves et vallées, les vignerons ont de plus en plus de difficultés à trouver l'eau nécessaire pour combattre les gelées. De mêmes que les besoins en eau à des fins protectrices ne sont pas aussi pressants dans tous les secteurs de Californie, les besoins en eau pour l'irrigation ne concernent pas la totalité du pays. Dans les contrées de la côte septentrionale — où le taux de pluviosité atteint entre 75 et 100 cm par an — de nombreuses vignes ne sont pas irriguées, alors que d'autres doivent être généreusement arrosées en plein été. Dans ces plantations, l'irrigation ou la protection contre le gel sont souvent assurées par un système de tourniquets. D'autres parties de l'État ne jouissent pas d'un climat aussi généreux que celui des secteurs situés au nord de San Francisco, dans la vallée San Joaquin, par exemple, il ne faut pas moins de 1 220 000 m³ d'eau par saison pour assurer de bonnes vendanges.

Les méthodes d'irrigation varient d'un endroit à l'autre ; venu d'Israël, le nouveau système « égouttoir » arrose les cépages d'un mince filet d'eau provenant de tuyaux fixes au niveau du sol. Les mêmes systèmes de tourniquets couramment utilisés pour l'irrigation et le contrôle du gel, dans les parties les moins ensoleillées de l'État, sont également employés pour les climats chauds, où l'eau vaporisée modère la température d'un soleil ardent qui risquerait de brûler les raisins.

L'approvisionnement en eau posera de plus en plus de problèmes à l'avenir, et il est heureux que certains des nouveaux systèmes conçus pour lutter contre le froid du printemps et parfois de l'automne en aient tenu compte. Ainsi les ventilateurs : situés au niveau du sol, ils diffusent l'air au-dessus des vignes pour empêcher la température de descendre. D'autres appareils montés sur des tours brassent l'air frais du dessous avec l'air plus chaud du dessus. L'autre nouveauté est une combinaison sophistiquée du ventilateur et du *smudge pot* (?) : un appareil de chauffage au propane chauffe l'air, puis des ventilateurs soufflants distribuent le gaz chaud dans les rangs de vigne à travers de petits conduits de plastique gonflabes.

VARIÉTÉS DE CÉPAGES

Avec l'augmentation de la demande en bons vins de table, on n'a jamais planté autant de saines variétés de *Vitis vinifera* en Californie que maintenant. Malheureusement, certains vignerons cherchant à profiter rapidement des prix élevés des meilleurs raisins, se mettent à planter du Cabernet Sauvignon, du Pinot Noir ou d'autres variétés de qualité, dans des régions où le climat — bien trop chaud — n'est pas approprié à la culture de telles vignes. La plus grande étendue de plantations de vin de cépage se trouve à Monterey, au sud de la région vinicole de la côte nord. Dans les chaudes vallées internes telles que San Joaquin, de grands progrès ont été réalisés quant à la qualité des cépages. On cherche peu à peu à réduire la surface plantée de Thompson Seedless et autres raisins de table — trop souvent utilisés pour faire du vin — en faveur de bonnes variétés hybrides ou *vinifera*. Dans les parties les plus chaudes de l'État, les variétés européennes classiques ne donneront jamais de grands vins, mais avec des vignes soigneusement sélectionnées — en particulier certaines des vignes hybrides conçues à Davis — la qualité moyenne d'une bonne partie de vin en vrac pourrait être améliorée.

Les bonnes variétés de cépages se faisant plus courantes, de nombreux vins californiens adoptèrent le nom du cépage avec lequel ils étaient faits. Ainsi un « varietal », ou plutôt un vin de cépage, est un vin portant le même nom que celui du cépage avec lequel il est fait dans une proportion d'au moins 50 %. Selon la loi, un vin de Californie ne peut adopter le nom d'un raisin, ou plutôt d'une variété, que si la variété en question entre pour 75 % au moins dans la composition, à l'exception des cépages *labrusca*, leur goût étant si distinctement puissant qu'il suffit des 51 % légaux pour que leur caractère se reconnaisse dans le vin. L'expression *estate-bottled* (mis en bouteille à la propriété) indique que le vin a été vinifié dans la propriété vinicole qui possède les vignobles, ou qui en a le contrôle.

Les « régions viticoles » sont en cours

de classification : les appellations sont définies en fonction de leurs similitudes géographiques et climatiques selon le B.A.T.F. Les vins portant le nom d'une de ces régions viticoles doivent contenir au moins 85 % de cépage provenant de cette région. On en a déjà défini un grand nombre, y compris Napa Valley et Finger Lakes dans l'État de New York. D'autres encore sont en instance. De plus, le gouvernement des États-Unis envisage de faire voter des lois sur la composition, qui viseraient à rendre obligatoire l'énoncé des ingrédients. A l'heure actuelle plus de 50 additifs sont autorisés, allant de l'eau, sucre, acides de fruits (citrique, malique, tartrique) et dioxyde de soufre, aux colorants artificiels et conservateurs. La plupart de ces additifs sont autorisés dans d'autres pays. Les nouveaux règlements concernant l'étiquetage constituent un grand progrès mais sont encore insuffisants. Selon ces nouvelles lois, votées en 1978 et entrées en vigueur le 1er janvier 1983, un vin peut porter l'appellation Chardonnay et être mélangé avec 25 % de Thomson Seedless, Concord ou autres cépages communs de piètre qualité. De même, les définitions des régions viticoles manquent de rigueur. Par exemple Napa Valley comprend des raisins provenant de la région voisine de Pope Valley et des montagnes entourant la vallée. Le B.A.T.F. n'a pas défini des termes importants tels que « produit » ou « fabriqué ». Ainsi, une exploitation vinicole peut acheter du vin qui a été récolté, égrappé, fermenté et vieilli dans une autre propriété, et l'étiqueter comme ayant été « fabriqué » ou « produit » par elle. Il est malheureusement encore légal pour les *wineries* américaines de nommer leurs vins « Chablis », « Sauternes », « Champagne », « Bourgogne », « Rhin », « Sherry », « Porto » et « Madère », ce qui est une pratique déplorable.

Quelques variétés de cépages à vin rouge sont cultivées avec succès en Californie, notamment Cabernet Sauvignon (souvent appelé simplement Cabernet, mais il ne faut pas le confondre avec le Cabernet Franc), Pinot Noir, Gamay Beaujolais. Grenache, Barbera et Zinfandel. Parmi les variétés blanches, citons : Pinot Chardonnay ou Chardonnay, Sauvignon Blanc, Sémillon, Pinot Blanc, White Pinot, White Riesling (appelé aussi Johannisberg Riesling ou tout simplement Riesling), Sylvaner ou Franken Riesling et Traminer (aussi appelé Red Traminer).

Vignes hybrides

Si une superficie importante est aujourd'hui plantée de vignes hybrides, celles-ci n'en représentent pas moins un aspect intéressant dans l'avenir de la production de vins en Californie. En acceptant la récompense « Award of Merit » qui lui fut décernée en 1973 par la Société Américaine des Œnologues, le docteur Olmo, de l'Institut Davis, déclarait : « En Californie, on ressent vivement la nécessité de produire des vins qui soient d'origine exclusivement californienne. Nous ne pouvons espérer reproduire les grands vins d'autres pays simplement parce que nous avons importé leurs variétés de vignes et que nous utilisons leurs méthodes de vinification. Nos climats et nos sols sont bien trop différents. Mais nous pouvons et devons produire des vins qui soient aussi bons qu'ailleurs, en créant de nouveaux types de raisins qui donneront des produits de grande qualité, aux caractéristiques distinctes. La première étape consiste à éliminer certains défauts de nos propres vignes. Par la suite nous pourrions nous passer des variétés sélectionnées par les Français, les Allemands ou les Italiens parce qu'à travers les siècles elles se sont montrées appropriées à certaines régions. Or ces régions ne sont pas les nôtres, et plutôt que de les imiter, il serait bon de fonder notre industrie sur des variétés conçues par et pour les sols et climats californiens. »

Deux des hybrides les plus importants conçus par l'Université de Californie à Davis, sont le cépage à vin blanc Emerald Riesling et le Ruby Cabernet, variété à vin rouge. Au moins trois autres hybrides ont été cultivés avec succès et s'annoncent pleins de promesses : le Rubired, le Royalty, et le dernier-né, un raisin à vin appelé Carnelian. Le Ruby Cabernet est un croisement entre le Cabernet Sauvignon et le Carignane, variété extrêmement productive. Il produit en abondance et tolère des climats plus chauds. Le raisin lui-même possède certaines des caractéristiques du Cabernet Sauvignon, mais il ne donnera jamais un vin de la même qualité ou distinction. L'Emerald Riesling, un croisement entre le White Riesling (aussi appelé Johannisberg Riesling) et le Muscadelle de

Bordelais, donne un blanc de table qui rassemble à certaines caractéristiques du Riesling. Un autre espoir pour la production de bons vins est l'hybride, le Carnelian, conçu par le professeur Olmo. C'est un croisement entre le Cabernet Sauvignon, le Carignane et le Grenache qui produit un raisin au rendement élevé et s'adaptant bien aux régions les plus chaudes ; le vin est acceptable. Le Carnelian peut produire jusqu'à 180 hl par ha. Les vins obtenus jusqu'à présent sont d'un rouge moyen, légers et harmonieux. Ils peuvent être bus jeunes, mais vieillissent aisément. Le Rubired et le Royalty, conçus pour satisfaire les besoins en raisins riches en couleur et en acidité, sont assez résistants pour ne pas succomber à l'oïdium. Un hybride du XIXe siècle fut également croisé avec le raisin à Porto Tinta Cão, ce qui donna le Rubired. Le Rubired croisé avec un cépage peu connu appelé Trousseau, donna le Royalty. Les deux variétés furent introduites en 1964. De tous les hybrides californiens, l'Emerald Riesling et le Ruby Cabernet sont peut-être les plus réussis.

Régions viticoles de Californie

On compte six régions naturelles de viticulture en Californie : la côte nord, les vallées du Sacramento, du centre de San Joaquin, la côte sud et San Luis Obispo. Chacune a ses secteurs bien connus et on produit à peu près toutes les variétés de raisin et tous les types de vins dans au moins une de ces régions.

Côte nord

Cette région s'étend au nord et au sud de la baie de San Francisco dans plusieurs vallées parallèles à la chaîne côtière. Elle est caractérisée en général par des étés chauds et des pluies annuelles modérées. On y fait les meilleurs vins de table secs, rouges et blancs. Les principaux districts sont Napa, Sonoma, Mendocino, Livermore, Santa Clara, San Benito, Santa Cruz et Monterey.

1. *Napa.*

Voilà le district le plus célèbre de Californie pour les vins rouges, avec environ 150 entreprises commerciales de vinification et certains des plus beaux vignobles américains. Dans la langue des Indiens qui habitaient le pays, Napa signifie : abondance. Les terres riches et fertiles abondent en effet dans la vallée et les coteaux sont plantés de bonnes vignes. Environ 12 000 ha de vignobles ont produit les 80 000 t de raisins qui furent récoltés en 1986. La production moyenne était faible, 50 hl/ha, car une grande partie de la terre n'était pas productive. La récolte représenta plus de 150 millions de francs, soit 40 millions de plus que celle de Sonoma. Le Cabernet Sauvignon règne en souverain à Napa et produit mieux que le Pinot Noir. Le vin de Cabernet, de la même variété que celui des grands Bordeaux, vieillit très lentement dans la région de Napa ; on y laisse les vins en fût jusqu'à quatre ans. Les zones les plus fraîches de la vallée de Napa produisent le meilleur vin Cabernet Sauvignon d'Amérique. Depuis 1970, plus de 1 500 ha de vignobles de cette variété ont été plantés. Au total, Napa compte aujourd'hui plus de 2 640 ha de Cabernet Sauvignon ; seuls Sonoma et Monterey sont susceptibles d'en avoir plus.

Cette région se divise en haute et basse vallées. Sainte-Hélène, ville vinicole, se trouve au centre de la haute vallée, mais le district s'étend sur 11 km en direction de Calistoga et, au sud, il va jusqu'à Rutherford et Oakville. La basse vallée couvre les environs de la ville de Napa, à une heure de San Francisco par la route. Elle englobe le nord-ouest d'un large fond de vallée qui remonte jusqu'à la frontière du canton de Sonoma. Le sol est lourd à l'extrémité sud du canton de Napa mais ce secteur est le plus frais en raison de la proximité de la baie. La haute vallée est pierreuse. Les montagnes ont de l'influence sur le climat et sur l'exposition des vignes.

On estime en général à Napa qu'on ferait de meilleurs vins si les vignes étaient plantées sur les coteaux alors qu'actuellement les trois quarts sont cultivées sur terrain plat. C'est un des rares districts où les vignerons admettent qu'ils connaissent de bonnes et de mauvaises années, que certaines méritent d'être considérées comme des millésimes, mais pas les autres. Autre signe du progrès dans cette vallée : la fondation de nombreuses coopératives. En outre, depuis 1942, une association des professionnels du vin s'occupe des problèmes locaux.

Les plus importants propriétaires de vignobles sont : Baulieu, Beringer, Robert

Mondavi, les Frères Chrétiens, Inglenook, Charles Krug, la Compagnie Louis Martini, Freemark Abbey, Sterling Vineyards, Cuvaison, Clos du Val, Trefethen, Schramsberg, Joseph Heitz, Chappellet et le Domaine Chandon.

La basse vallée de Napa et le canton de Solano produisent relativement peu, mais ce secteur s'est étendu récemment sur la vallée voisine de Chiles. Toujours dans la vallée, le secteur de Carneros s'est avéré idéal pour les meilleurs raisins de vins de cépage.

Acacia Winery. Fondée en 1979, cette entreprise vinicole est spécialisée dans les vins produits à partir de Pinot Noir et de Chardonnay. Le groupe d'associés Chalone détient l'entreprise. Située au sommet d'une colline, dans le secteur de Carneros, Acacia possède une vue magnifique de la baie de San Pablo. Ses 20 ha de vignobles ainsi que des achats locaux sont utilisés pour produire environ 30 000 caisses chaque année. Larry Brooks est le maître de chai.

Beaulieu Vineyard. Le magnifique domaine de Beaulieu et ses vignobles furent fondés en 1900 par Georges de Latour. Ce Français importa de nombreuses boutures de sa terre natale et leur trouva un site idéal, non loin de Rutherford, où le sol perméable ne nécessite pas d'irrigation. Beaulieu n'a jamais cessé de produire : pendant l'époque de la prohibition, le domaine fournissait des vins de messe puis, à l'abrogation, il lança toute une gamme de vins à travers les États-Unis. Aujourd'hui il compte huit vignobles couvrant 400 ha de vignes ; tous sont situés au centre de la vallée du Napa, mis à part environ 60 ha dans la région de Carneros, à l'extrême sud de la vallée où la brise marine tempère le climat. On cultive principalement le Pinot Noir, le Chardonnay, le Cabernet Sauvignon, et le Sauvignon Blanc. Le Muscat de Frontignan — assez rare en Californie — est également prospère et donne un bon vin de cépage. Le vignoble fut vendu en 1969 à la Société Heublein. André Tchelistcheff, un des grands œnologues de la vallée du Napa, prit en main la production de Beaulieu de 1938, jusqu'à sa retraite, en 1973. Son Cabernet Sauvignon « Private Reserve » Georges de Latour est un des vins rouges de table des plus fins du pays. Le centre de vinification fut agrandi et la Société Heublein construisit, en 1973, un second pavillon de dégustation. Ainsi, depuis un quart de siècle, les vins de Beaulieu — et particulièrement la réserve personnelle — sont parmi les meilleurs vins produits aux États-Unis.

Beringer Brothers. Situé à Sainte-Hélène, cette célèbre entreprise vinicole, fondée en 1876, doit sa réussite à deux frères allemands, Frederick et Jacob Beringer. La construction d'inspiration rhénane est originale et spacieuse ; on y accède par la périphérie nord de la ville. Après avoir longtemps appartenu aux Beringer, le vignoble et le centre de vinification furent vendus en 1970 à la multinationale Nestlé International. Les magnifiques tunnels creusés dans le calcaire des collines derrière la vieille construction sont restés tels quels. Un nouveau centre de vinification fut construit sur la Highway 29 juste en face de la construction rhénane. Beringer est l'une des entreprises vinicoles les plus pittoresques de la vallée de Napa et attire chaque année des milliers de visiteurs.

Patrick Leon, œnologue français de Bordeaux, était, jusqu'en 1986, l'expert de Beringer. Un autre œnologue célèbre, originaire du Médoc, M. Boissenot, lui succéda. Il fut lui-même remplacé par M. Mondavi, autrefois du Château Latour. Les autres domaines vinicoles du groupe Nestlé sont : Souverain à Sonoma, Napa Ridge, Los Hermanos dans la vallée de Napa. Nestlé est aussi actionnaire de la Maison Deutz et des C & B Vintage Cellars.

Burgess Cellars. En 1972, Tom Burgess acheta ce beau vignoble de 10 ha, situé à 300 m sur le versant ouest de la montagne Howell, et commença à produire un Cabernet Sauvignon, un Zinfandel et un Petite Sirah. Son Chardonnay est fermenté dans des cuves de chêne suivant la tradition européenne. La production annuelle est d'environ 30 000 caisses.

Carneros Creek Winery. Balfour et Anita Gibson ont acheté ce vignoble en 1973 afin de produire un grand vin de Pinot Noir, cépage qui, jusqu'à présent, n'a donné que des vins décevants en Californie. En attendant que leurs jeunes vignes puissent produire du vin, la réputation qu'ils ont acquise pour leur Zinfandel, est d'être très tannique et fort.

Chappellet Vineyards. Située sur les hauteurs de Pritchard Hill, à 425 m au-dessus de la vallée du Napa, cette entreprise vinicole — l'une des plus représentatives qui aient été construites ces derniers temps sur la côte septentrionale de la Californie — fut conçue par Donn Chappellet, un Californien du Sud qui fit fortune en commercialisant des distributeurs automatiques de comestibles. C'est en 1967 qu'il acheta ces terres qui comprenaient plusieurs centaines d'hectares de vignobles ; par la suite, ceux-ci furent en grande partie replantés de Merlot, Pinot Chardonnay, Cabernet Sauvignon, Chenin Blanc et Johannisberg Riesling.

Situé au flanc d'une colline et entouré de chênes, l'élégant pavillon en forme de pyramide se fond à merveille dans le décor. Les cuves de fermentation en acier inoxydable contrastent avec la nouvelle tonnellerie en bois et le toit recouvert de lattes de métal. Ici opère l'œnologue Philip Togni, qui a travaillé dans trois pays différents et également en France pour l'auteur de cette encyclopédie.

Château Montelena. En 1974, le Chardonnay de Château Montelena a été préféré à de très grands Bourgogne blancs, par un jury d'experts à Paris. Depuis cette date, les vins de ce très beau vignoble jouissent d'une excellente réputation. Château Montelena produit quatre vins à partir de Johannisberg Riesling, Chardonnay, Zinfandel et Cabernet Sauvignon.

The Christian Brothers. Connu aux États-Unis sous le nom « Les Frères des Écoles Chrétiennes », cet ordre monastique voué à l'enseignement fut fondé en France au XVIIIe siècle par saint Jean-Baptiste de La Salle, et s'installa en 1868 en Californie. Cette entreprise vinicole est aujourd'hui l'une des plus importantes de toute la côte septentrionale de Californie. Les vignobles, fort étendus, sont situés à Mont La Salle, en bordure de la vallée du Napa et le long de Redwood Road, dans les Monts Mayacamas ; de nouveaux vignobles sont également dispersés dans les divers secteurs de la vallée du Napa. Plus de 520 ha sont consacrés à la viniculture, principalement dans les vallées du Napa et de San Joaquin, où l'on fait des vins de dessert et de l'eau-de-vie de vin.

Les vieilles caves « Greystone » sont situées au nord de Sainte-Hélène, non loin des entreprises Charles Krug et Beringer Brothers. Dans l'ensemble, les vins Christian Brothers (des vins de cépage millésimés, des vins de table, des mousseux et des vins de liqueur) sont parmi les meilleurs de la côte septentrionale ; Fromm et Sichel appelés aujourd'hui « The Christian Brothers Sales Co » en sont les distributeurs exclusifs. De plus, Christian Brothers vend plus d'eau-de-vie de vin que toute autre entreprise de distillation aux États-Unis. Les profits tirés de l'eau-de-vie et du vin sont distribués aux 13 écoles de la congrégation. Christian Brothers a pour vice-président et cellier Frère Timothy, dont la magnifique collection d'outils vinicoles et d'illustrations ayant trait au vin a fait le tour des musées d'Amérique.

Clos du Val. Nouveau venu à Napa, le Français Bernard Portet mérite le respect pour son travail au Clos du Val. Il produisit ses premiers vins en 1972 : un Cabernet Sauvignon et un Zinfandel puis, par la suite, un Chardonnay, un Merlot, un Sauvignon Blanc, un Sémillon et un Pinot Noir. La superficie du vignoble est de 120 ha et la production annuelle de 50 000 caisses.

Cuvaison Winery. Cette petite entreprise vinicole est située en bordure de la Silverado Trail, route parallèle au Highway 29, la « grande-route du vin ». Cuvaison fut créée en 1970 par deux amateurs : Thomas Cottrell et Thomas Parkhill, avec l'intention de ne produire, d'un unique cépage, qu'un nombre limités de vins de table millésimés. La société new-yorkaise Oakleigh Thorne en racheta des parts en 1973, et les revendit en 1979 au Suisse Alexander Schmidheiny. Les 120 ha de vignoble produisent du Cabernet Sauvignon, du Zinfandel, du Merlot et du Chardonnay. La Cuvaison espère atteindre les 40 000 caisses à la fin des années 80.

Conn Creek Winery. Autrefois à la sortie de la Highway 29, entre Sainte Hélène et Calistoga, Conn Creek s'installa en 1979 à Silverado, près de Rutherford. L'entreprise fut fondée en 1974 par Bill et Kathy Collins. Les familles DeWavrin-Woltner en furent les propriétaires partiels et, au cours de 1986, une grande partie de l'entreprise vinicole fut vendue à la firme américaine « U.S. Tobacco Company ». Les Collins y ont néanmoins conservé des parts, et Bill Collins en est le président. Conn Creek produit chaque année environ 25 000 caisses de Cabernet Sauvignon, Chardonnay et Merlot faits à partir des raisins du vignoble des Collins.

Diamond Creek Vineyards. Ce nouveau vignoble de 8 ha fondé en 1973 ne produit que du Cabernet Sauvignon à partir des variétés suivantes : Cabernet Sauvignon (88 %), Merlot (8 %) et Cabernet Franc (4 %). Le propriétaire, Al Brounstein, cherche à faire des vins concentrés et riches en tannin qui nécessitent un long vieillissement. Les 2 500 caisses annuelles consistent en trois Cabernet Sauvignon : Volcanic Hills, Gravelly Meadows et Red Rock Terrace.

Domaine Chandon. Contrôlé par le groupe français Moët-Hennessy, Domaine Chandon (600 ha) lança ses premiers vins sur le marché californien en mai 1977. On y produit principalement un vin mousseux qui, fort heureusement, ne porte pas l'appellation Champagne, le groupe Moët étant d'avis que seuls les vins provenant de la région française de Champagne y ont droit. 30 % des raisins du Domaine Chandon proviennent de ses propres plantations de Carneros — principalement du Pinot Noir et du Pinot Chardonnay — et le reste est acheté aux vignobles de Trefethen. La création d'une variété de vins de cépage est en cours.

Domaine Mumm. Au début des années 80, Seagram & Sons s'associèrent à la société française de champagne G.H. Mumm. Leur première production, Domaine Mumm Cuvée Napa, fut lancée au début 1986. Guy Devaux, originaire de Champagne, dirige l'opération en association avec Michel Budin, directeur de production chez Mumm, en France. Le Domaine Mumm est situé au pied de la Sterling Winery, propriété de Seagram dans la vallée de Napa.

Duckhorn Winery. Les premiers vins de cette exploitation dirigée par Dan et Margaret Duckhorn furent fabriqués en 1978 à Silverado, au nord de Sainte Hélène. 15 000 caisses de vin (Cabernet Sauvignon, Merlot et Sauvignon Blanc) sont produites chaque année à partir de raisins du domaine et de raisins achetés localement. Tom Rinaldi est le maître de chai.

Far Niente Winery. Gil Nickel, le propriétaire, produisit le premier Chardonnay de Far Niente en 1979. Le centre, construit en 1885 puis rénové, se trouve juste au sud d'Oakville. La production annuelle (11 000 caisses en 1982) devrait atteindre 28 000 caisses. En plus de son Chardonnay, Far Niente fabrique aussi un Cabernet Sauvignon.

Franciscan Vineyards. Cette exploitation vinicole fut vendue par ses fondateurs, Raymond Duncan et Justin Meyer, en 1979, à la société allemande Peter Eckes & Co le plus grand producteur mondial de Cognac, comprenant la marque Maria Krön. Le président de l'exploitation, Augustin Huneeus, est de nationalité chilienne. Sur cette exploitation, on cultive 500 ha de vignes et le centre de vinification, de taille moyenne, se trouve sur la grand-route du vin, à 9,50 km au sud de Sainte-Hélène, dans la localité de Rutherford. Les premiers raisins ont été vendangés en 1973 et les premiers vins blancs furent vendus en 1974. Les vins les plus fameux sont vendus sous l'étiquette Estancia.

Freemark Abbey Winery. Totalement restructurée par sept associés, cette entreprise vinicole située à la sortie nord de Sainte-Hélène, capitale vinicole de la vallée du Napa, est maintenant dotée d'un matériel des plus modernes. La vinification a lieu dans les étages inférieurs d'une vieille bâtisse fort pittoresque datant du XIXe siècle. Les étages supérieurs ont été transformés en magasins de bougies, d'articles de cuisine et de marchandises spécialisées. On y produit exclusivement des vins de table de pur cépage tels que le Pinot Noir et le Pinot Chardonnay, le Johannisberg Riesling et le Cabernet ainsi qu'un Cabernet Sauvignon. La production annuelle est d'environ 30 000 caisses. Les vins sont vieillis dans des tonneaux de chêne provenant d'un certain nombre de pays d'Europe. Lors d'une récente dégustation à l'aveugle à New-York, le jury attribua tous les honneurs à un certain Pinot Chardonnay de Freemark. Quelques-uns des propriétaires de Freemark Abey Winery possèdent aussi des parts du centre de Rutherford (*q.v.*) depuis 1976.

Grgich Hills Cellar. Autrefois maître de chai au Château Montelena, Mike Grgich s'unit en 1977 à Austin Hills, des cafés Hills Brothers, pour créer cette exploitation à l'intersection de l'autoroute 29 et Rutherford Road. Mike Grgich produisit le Chardonnay Montelena de 1973 qui surpassa quatre Bordeaux blancs français lors d'une dégustation à Paris en 1976. Aujourd'hui il fabrique son vin à partir de trois vignobles de la propriété : au sud de Napa, près de Rutherford et à Yountville. La superficie totale est de 88 ha. La production annuelle de 220 000 caisses est avant tout du Fumé Blanc et du Chardonnay. Un Zinfandel fut implanté en 1979 et un Cabernet en 1984.

Joseph Heitz Winery. Avec une surface vitifère de 50 ha à peine, Joseph Heitz fait appel aux autres viticulteurs de la vallée du Napa qui lui fournissent les raisins pour ses vins de cépage de qualité. Heitz, autrefois professeur d'œnologie et maître dans l'art du coupage, se mit à son compte au début des années 60. Il acheta d'abord la petite propriété de Leon Brendel à Sainte-Hélène puis, plus tard, un domaine vinicole sur la Taplin Road, à quelques kilomètres à l'est de la ville. Dix ans plus tard, ses vins avaient un tel succès que Heitz dut agrandir ses locaux. Il s'agit néanmoins d'une petite affaire, avec une production annuelle d'environ 15 000 caisses, ce qui équivaut à peu près au volume d'un château du Bordelais de taille moyenne. Joseph Heitz propose une grande variété de vins : Chardonnay, Cabernet, Pinot Noir, White, Riesling, Zinfandel et Grignolino, ainsi que quelques Porto et Xérès.

Inglenook Napa Valley Vineyards. Cette entreprise vinicole se trouve juste à la sortie du Highway 29 (surnommé la Grand-Route du Vin de la vallée du Napa) dans la localité de Rutherford. Ses vignobles, situés sur le Mont St-Jean, non loin du centre de vinification, furent fondés en 1879 par un certain capitaine Gustav F. Niebaum qui géra ses terres jusqu'à sa mort en 1908. Inglenook passa ensuite à son neveu, feu John Daniel, qui fit marcher l'affaire pendant la prohibition. Ensuite il perpétua les traditions familiales en cultivant des raisins de grande qualité sur les 90 ha de vignoble de Rutherford Ranch, qui fut entièrement replanté par les propriétaires actuels : Cabernet Sauvignon, Pinot Noir, Sémillon, Pinot Chardonnay, Pinot Blanc et Traminer parmi les meilleurs, une partie des terres étant également plantée de Gamay Beaujolais et de Merlot du Bordelais. Ce vieux domaine de famille fut entièrement racheté par l'entreprise vinicole Oakvill Vineyards. Les héritiers de Daniel sont encore très actifs aujourd'hui dans l'industrie des vins de la vallée de Napa. Huit ans plus tôt, la plus grande partie d'Inglenook avait été vendue au groupe United Vintners, qui, à son tour, fusionna avec Heublein en 1968. Si les nouveaux propriétaires n'hésitèrent pas à se lancer dans la production de vins courants, ils n'en continuèrent pas moins à produire les vins fins de cépage qui avaient forgé la réputation du domaine. La période dorée d'Inglenook commença vers la fin des années 30, lorsque ses propriétaires furent les premiers à limiter leur production aux vins de cépage. Les bouteilles de Cabernet Sauvignon et les vins de tonneau sélectionnés de cette époque sont maintenant rares et se paient très chers aux ventes aux enchères. John Richburg est le premier maître de chai dans l'histoire d'Inglenook, vieille de plus d'un siècle.

Hanns Kornell Champagne Cellars. Les caves de Hanns Kornell sont situées au nord de Sainte-Hélène, à l'est de l'autoroute 29. M. Kornell, Allemand de naissance et de formation, est un des rares producteurs de « champagne » indépendants de Californie, bien que son centre vinicole de Larkmead Lane ne produise du mousseux que depuis une trentaine d'années. Le centre lui-même date de la fin du XIXe siècle ; Kornell l'acheta lorsqu'il quitta Sonoma où il avait établi sa première affaire en 1952. Il n'y a pas de vignobles, car Kornell achète le vin à partir duquel il conçoit ensuite ses mousseux.

Ses caves comptent environ 4 millions de bouteilles, chacune ayant subi une opération individuelle. Un de ses derniers produits est un vin millésimé très sec dans le goût de Sekt allemand et, en 1983, un Blanc de Blancs, lui-même millésimé.

Charles Krug Winery. Fondée en 1861, Charles Krug Winery est la plus ancienne entreprise vinicole de toute la vallée du Napa. L'entreprise a ses locaux de vinification dans une vieille construction ornée de bois et d'or et située en bordure du Highway 29, au nord de Sainte-Hélène. En 1965, après une longue querelle familiale, Robert Mondavi abandonna Krug pour lancer sa propre exploitation vinicole (*q.v.*). Aujourd'hui, Krug appartient à l'entreprise C. Mondavi & Sons qui la dirige sous la présidence de Peter Mondavi et ses deux fils, Marc et Peter junior. Charles Krug, un des grands noms de l'histoire du vin en Californie, fut un valeureux disciple du colonel Haraszthy à Sonoma. C'est en 1858 dans le comté du Napa, qu'il produisit son premier vin commercial en utilisant un petit pressoir à cidre. En 1861 il fonda l'actuelle entreprise vinicole de Sainte-Hélène et y planta ses premières vignes ; ses vins ne tardèrent pas à se faire connaître à travers toute l'Amérique et même jusqu'en Europe. Il forma de nombreux grands viniculteurs de Californie, notamment C.H. Wente, Jacob Beringer, C.J. Wetmore et fit figure, jusqu'à sa mort, en 1892, d'autorité en matière de vins.

Depuis 1943, date à laquelle Charles Krug Winery fut rachetée par l'entreprise Mondavi, les locaux de vinification ont été augmentés, les vignobles se sont étendus et les caves ont gagné en surface et en importance : ce sont aujourd'hui les caves les mieux équipées et les plus actives de Californie. Les propriétaires ont également expérimenté de nouvelles techniques en matière de vinification. Les vignobles sont plantés de raisins blancs de grande qualité tels le Chardonnay, le Chenin Blanc, le Gewürztraminer, le Johannisberg Riesling, le Sémillon et le Sauvignon Blanc ; les variétés de raisins à vin rouge sont, entre autres, le Cabernet Sauvignon, le Gamay et le Pinot Noir. Le Chenin Blanc Krug fut le premier vin fait en Californie avec ce cépage. En 1962, les Mondavi achetèrent à Oakville, non loin de Sainte-Hélène, environ 200 ha du vignoble historique de To Kalon, qui passe pour être l'un des meilleurs de toute la vallée du Napa. Outre la propre production de To Kalon, d'autres raisins fins provenant d'autres vignobles du Napa contribuent à la fabrication des vins de cette entreprise.

Les vins primés de C. Mondavi et Fils portent deux étiquettes : Charles Krug pour les vins de cépage (400 000 caisses par an) et C.K. Mondavi pour les vins de table (1 million de caisses chaque année). Les vignobles de Sainte-Hélène, Yountville et Carneros s'étendent sur 480 ha. La production annuelle est d'environ 5 000 caisses.

Louis M. Martini Winery. Le fondateur de cette entreprise, Louis M. Martini, est un Italien né à Pietra Ligure en 1887, qui émigra aux États-Unis au début du siècle ; sa grande aspiration fut d'arriver à produire des vins d'excellente qualité et dès l'abrogation de la prohibition en 1933, il fit construire un grand centre vinicole à Sainte-Hélène, localité viticole située à 100 km environ au nord de San Francisco. Il acheta en dix ans trois autres vignobles importants et bien situés qu'il planta exclusivement de variétés de grande qualité. En 1941, l'auteur de cette encyclopédie puis son associé, Frank Schoonmaker (qui mérite la gratitude de tous les producteurs californiens de vins primés) se mirent à vendre des vins américains sous une appellation américaine. Pour la première fois, on put alors trouver à l'est des Rocheuses les vins de Louis Martini et bien d'autres encore. Les vignobles Martini couvrent actuellement 690 ha dans la région de Carneros, 110 ha sur les montagnes des alentours de Sonoma, 80 ha à Healdsburg et 110 ha près de Sainte-Hélène. Ces hectares comprennent la surface ajoutée à la fin des années 60 par Louis P. Martini fils. Les variétés principales à Sainte-Hélène sont le Cabernet Sauvignon, le Johannisberg Riesling, le Zinfandel et le Chenin Blanc ; les vignobles du Napa donnent surtout du Chardonnay et du Cabernet alors que les terres Martini à Sonoma sont riches en Gewürztraminer, Chardonnay, Folle Blanche, Zinfandel, Merlot et Gamay. Un Merlot de cépage vint d'être lancé sur le marché. A 86 ans, Martini père était le doyen des viticulteurs du Napa et sans doute l'une des personnalités les plus marquantes de l'industrie californienne. Ses vins sont réputés aux États-Unis pour leur qualité et la justesse de leur prix. Son fils Louis P. Martini est président de la compagnie. Une troisième génération de Martini s'intéresse maintenant à l'affaire familiale.

Mayacamas Vineyards. Ces magnifiques vignobles disposés en terrasses sont perchés sur les hauteurs des monts Mayacamas, à 300 mètres au-dessus de la propriété Christian Brothers de Mont La Salle par Lokoya Road, et à 19 km de la ville de Napa. Le premier propriétaire de Mayacamas, un certain Jack F.M. Taylor, y fit les premiers vins en 1945. Aidé de sa femme Mary, il fut l'un des premiers nouveaux producteurs de bon vin du Napa d'après-guerre. Leur production comptait alors dix-sept rouges et blancs de table ainsi qu'un remarquable Zinfandel Rosé. L'entreprise fut rachetée en 1968 par Robert Travers et son épouse. La qualité est toujours remarquable, mais la gamme des vins a été sagement réduite à quatre produits de cépage millésimés : Chardonnay, Chenin Blanc, Cabernet Sauvignon et Zinfandel Rosé. La surface exploitée est de 40 ha. La production est d'environ 5 000 caisses par an.

Robert Mondavi Winery. Robert Mondavi est aujourd'hui l'une des têtes de file de l'industrie californienne des vins primés. Avec l'aide de ses fils Michael et Timothy et de sa fille Marcia, il s'emploie à produire certains des meilleurs vins de cépage des États-Unis. Mondavi acquit chez Charles Krug l'expérience nécessaire pour lancer sa propre affaire en 1966. Le centre de vinification, situé au nord-ouest de la ville historique de Yountville, est l'un des plus actifs de Californie. Conformément à la philosophie des grands viticulteurs de la côte septentrionale. Mondavi est convaincu que cette région permet à une entreprise vinicole de taille relativement réduite de produire, en quantité limitée, des vins dont la texture et la qualité égalent les grands crus mondiaux. L'entreprise produit toute une gamme d'excellents vins de cépage : Chardonnay, Riesling, Traminer, Chenin Blanc, Fumé Blanc, Sauvignon Blanc, Gamay Rosé, Gamay Beaujolais et un bon Cabernet Sauvignon. Les vignobles s'étendent sur 320 ha. Lorsqu'elle commença à prospérer et après sa première récolte, une part de l'affaire fut rachetée par une société de Seattle (Washington), la Rainier Brewing Company. Actuellement Robert Mondavi se rend souvent en Europe pour s'informer des derniers équipements vinicoles et des nouvelles techniques en cours. Il fut l'un des premiers viticulteurs californiens à faire vieillir ses vins dans des tonneaux de différents types de bois de chêne. Le centre de vinification — une élégante construction de style espagnol ornée de boiseries — sert souvent à organiser des lunchs ou des séances de dégustation ; on y donne également des concerts. En 1979, Mondavi et le baron Philippe de Rothschild propriétaire du Château Mouton-Rothschild fondèrent l'association « Opus One ». Les raisins nécessaires à la fabrication du vin Mondavi-Rothschild sont vendangés sur un vignoble de 56 ha.

Moueix-Daniel. Christian Moueix, fils du copropriétaire de Château Petrus, de Pomerol et d'autres excellents vignobles dans la région de Saint-Émilion, s'est associé aux héritiers de John Daniel pour acheter une propriété de 50 ha à l'ouest de Yountville dans la vallée de Napa. Ils espèrent produire un vin rouge à base de Cabernet, « Dominus ». Une moitié des vignobles, dont le raisin est vendu, est planté de cépages produisant du vin blanc, l'autre de vignes ayant atteint leur maturité, Cabernet Sauvignon, Cabernet Franc et Merlot. La construction d'une exploitation vinicole est prévue. En attendant, sous l'égide de Christian Moueix, les raisins sont vinifiés par la nouvelle Rombauer Winery, petite exploitation et vignoble (*q.v.*), sur la Silverado Trail.

Niebaum-Coppola Estates. Francis Ford Coppola, metteur en scène, acheta en 1975 le domaine Niebaum, faisant ainsi son entrée dans le monde du vin. Situées à Rutherford, ces exploitations couvrent une superficie de 34 ha et produisent chaque année 4 000 caisses. Tous les efforts se concentrent aujourd'hui sur la fabrication d'un grand Cabernet Sauvignon en mélangeant trois vins de cépage du domaine. En 1985, le centre lança un Rubicon.

Oakville Vineyards. Sur la grand-route de Sainte-Hélène à Oakville, cette entreprise autrefois connue sous le nom de *Madonna Winery* appartenait aux Bartolucci qui la vendirent à Heublein en 1976.

Joseph Phelps Vineyards. Joseph Phelps, président d'une compagnie de construction, s'est intéressé à la viticulture lorsqu'il a construit les chais de deux grands vignobles voisins. Depuis 1973 Joseph Phelps Vineyards produit huit vins réputés pour leur équilibre et leur élégance dont un Sauvignon Blanc, différents Riesling et un vin de liqueur, le Scheurebe. Phelps produit aussi un vin à prix modéré, à partir de raisins récoltés sur les vignobles adjacents au centre viticole. Le maître de chai, Walter Schug, avait été formé à l'école d'œnologie de Geisenheim en Allemagne. Craig Williams lui succéda en 1983. La production est d'environ 70 000 caisses chaque année.

Pine Ridge Winery. Située dans une exploitation viticole rénovée, datant de l'avant prohibition, dans la région de Stag's Leap, Pine Ridge produit quatre vins : Merlot, Cabernet Sauvignon, Chardonnay et Chenin Blanc. Les associés Gary Andrus (fabricant de vins et directeur) et J.B. Haralson augmentèrent la production qui atteint aujourd'hui 40 000 caisses par an. Les propriétaires cultivent cinq variétés de vignes sur une superficie de 84 ha. Ils espèrent un jour produire entièrement à partir des vignes du domaine.

Remy Martin/Schramsberg. En septembre 1982, Jack et James Davis, propriétaires de Schramsberg Vineyards s'associèrent au plus grand fabricant de Cognac, Rémy Martin. Leur but : produire une eau-de-vie américaine unique en son genre, et de qualité comparable aux cognacs français. Ne regardant pas à la dépense, une magnifique distillerie munie de huit alambics et de deux caves pouvant contenir jusqu'à 7 000 limousines (fûts de chêne) fut construite dans le secteur de Carneros dans la vallée de Napa. 1985 vit la première production de RMS California Brandy.

Schramsberg Vineyards. Fondé par un pionnier allemand du nom de Jacob Schram, ce vieux centre vinicole menaçait de rendre l'âme jusqu'au jour où un certain Jack Davies, homme à l'esprit d'entreprise venu de Los Angeles, le racheta en 1965. Il intéressa un groupe d'associés à l'affaire, et avec son épouse J. Davies produisit lui-même son fameux vin mousseux, car Schramsberg ne produit que des vins mousseux ; en 1972, à l'occasion de son voyage en Chine, Richard Nixon en emporta une provision avec lui, car on en sert couramment à la Maison-Blanche. Davies a renouvelé les plantations de ses 16 ha de vignobles avec du Pinot Noir et du Pinot Chardonnay, avec lesquels il produit du Blanc de Blanc et un Blanc de Noir. En 1985, la famille Davies acquit un vignoble mitoyen, transformant ainsi leur domaine en une exploitation de 60 ha. La production annuelle est d'environ 50 000 caisses. Le centre de vinification se trouve entre Sainte-Hélène et Calistoga, en retrait du Highway 29. La construction date du milieu du XIXe siècle et a été classée monument historique.

Souverain Cellars. Construit en 1943 par Leland Stewart, Souverain est situé en pente sur la Silverado Trail et domine la vallée du Napa. La propriété fut rachetée à la fin des années 60 par la société Pillsbury, qui restaura les vieilles caves et fit construire d'élégants locaux connus sous le nom de Souverain of Rutherford, mais la propriété est à nouveau mise en vente. En outre, Pillsbury créa un immense et superbe centre vinicole à environ une heure de voiture de Souverain, au nord de Healdsburg, dans le comté de Sonoma. Connu sous le nom de Souverain of Alexander, ce centre est devenu le siège de toutes les activités vinicoles de l'entreprise et illustre toutes les qualités d'un centre viticole moderne. L'affaire de Rutherford fut vendue en 1976 à l'entreprise Freemark Abbey, qui y produit ses premiers vins dès 1977. La magnifique propriété de Healdsburg fut également vendue à l'Association des Viticulteurs de la côte septentrionale. Ce groupe continue à produire sous l'appellation Souverain ; les vins sont actuellement distribués par une division de la Standard Brands, la Société Julius Wile de New York.

Stag's Leap Winery. Warren Winiarski a étonné le monde lorsque son Cabernet Sauvignon a remporté le premier prix dans une dégustation à l'aveugle à Paris en 1976. Depuis, ses vins, qui sont caractérisés par l'élégance, la loyauté et le caractère du cépage, sont très demandés et difficiles à obtenir. Il produit aussi du Merlot, Sauvignon Blanc, Chardonnay et Petite Sirah. Le nombre de caisses est d'environ 30 000 chaque année. Le nom de Stag's Leap a été l'objet de procès entre plusieurs entreprises vinicoles rivales. C'est aujourd'hui un nom générique utilisé par sept sociétés de la région.

Sterling Vineyards. Ce domaine appartenait à un groupe d'administrateurs des Papeteries Sterling International. Créé en 1973, le centre de vinification — doté de locaux de taille moyenne et d'un équipement moderne — se trouve à 6 km au nord de Sainte-Hélène. Les 200 ha de vignobles ont été défrichés au début des années 60. La société Coca-Cola d'Atlanta, propriétaire de Monterey Vineyards, acquit Sterling en 1977 et le revendit en 1983 au groupe Joseph E. Seagram & Sons avec The Monterey Vineyard, Taylor California Cellars et la Taylor Wine Company de l'État de New York qui ensemble formaient The Wine Spectrum. On y produit du Chardonnay, du Cabernet Sauvignon, du Sauvignon Blanc et du Merlot. Tous les vins proviennent des vignes appartenant à Sterling et sont mis en bouteilles sur le domaine. Le nouveau centre vinicole est situé au sommet de la vallée ; on y accède par un funiculaire, ce qui constitue un point d'attraction pour les nombreux touristes qui font halte dans la vallée du Napa.

Sutter Home Winery se trouve au sud de Sainte-Hélène, non loin de certaines des meilleures entreprises vinicoles de l'État ; car nous sommes ici au cœur de la région vinicole de la côte septentrionale. Sutter Home, fondée en 1946 par la famille Trinchero, fut le premier centre à populariser le Zinfandel Blanc (créé en 1977). 2 millions de caisses environ sont produites chaque année à partir des vignobles de Central Valley ainsi que 60 000 caisses supplémentaires d'autres vins de cépage dont un Amador County Zinfandel. Tous les raisins sont achetés.

Trefethen Vineyards. Entreprise familiale depuis 1968, Trefethen produit d'excellents vins. Le Chardonnay clair et fruité, les Cabernet Sauvignon, Riesling Blanc et Pinot Noir sont pleins de finesse et d'élégance. Les 240 ha de vignes produisent 60 000 caisses chaque année. L'excédent de raisins, environ la moitié de la production totale du vignoble, est vendu à d'autres centres vinicoles de la vallée de Napa.

Vichon Winery. Acquis en 1985 par la famille de Robert Mondavi, ce centre vinicole fut fondé en 1980 par un groupe d'associés dont une douzaine de restaurateurs célèbres de la région. Le marché captif offert par les propriétaires fut une excellente introduction pour les trois vins de Vichon dont le style est plus subtil. Vichon produit du Chardonnay, du Cabernet Sauvignon et un vin, le Chevrignon, mélange de Sémillon et Sauvignon Blanc. Les 40 000 caisses sont toutes produites à partir de raisins achetés.

2. *Sonoma*

Ce district situé immédiatement au nord de San Francisco produit d'excellents vins de table et des mousseux qui sont parmi les meilleurs de l'État. Le canton de Sonoma est un des trois plus importants producteurs de vin en Californie. Au total, environ 12 400 ha y sont plantés de vigne. C'est dans ce canton qu'on trouve le plus grand nombre d'entreprises commerciales de vinification (environ 130). Malheureusement, quoique ce district semble parfaitement approprié à la production des bons vins, on y fait des quantités de vins de table plutôt ordinaires. Ceux du canton de Sonoma proviennent des vallées de la Sonoma, de la Santa Rosa et de la Russian River.

La vallée de Sonoma est parallèle à celle de la Napa dont la séparent les monts Mayacamas. C'est l'authentique « vallée de la Lune » de Jack London, qui écrivit et mourut dans ce beau pays. Les meilleurs vins de table sont produits par Buena Vista Vineyardo et Sebastiani ; au nord de Sonoma, ceux de Simi et Sonoma Vineyards, connus aujourd'hui sous le nom de « Rodney Strong », ont commencé à avoir bonne réputation.

Santa Rosa doit son nom à un petit affluent de la Russian River. C'est là que se trouvait le Fountain grove Vineyard depuis 1973, mais ses vignes ont été arrachées et cette propriété est actuellement un ranch d'élevage et un vrai complexe résidentiel de lotissement. On ne produit plus de vin dans cette vallée au nom si romantique.

C'est dans la vallée de la Russian River que se trouvent les entreprises vinicoles du secteur.

Parmi celles-ci, la plus importante est Korbel & Bros dont les vignobles sont situés sur les coteaux qui longent la Russian River. La production moyenne des vignobles de la Sonoma s'élève à un peu plus de 40 hl/ha. Il s'agit là d'un calcul effectué sur la totalité des vignobles, qui prend en compte un certain nombre d'hectares improductifs, ce qui explique une moyenne aussi basse.

Buena Vista Winery & Vineyards. Situés à environ 2 km à l'est de Sonoma et à 72 km au nord de San Francisco, ces vignobles historiques furent plantés par le colonel Agoston Haraszthy, grand viticulteur californien. Auteur d'un très sérieux rapport sur les vins et raisins de Californie, il prodigua en outre de précieux conseils en matière de viticulture à de nombreux vignerons californiens. A sa mort en 1869, l'affaire fut prise en main par ses deux fils Attila et Arpad. Une bonne partie des vignes européennes furent détruites par l'épidémie de phylloxéra qui s'abattit sur le pays et le tremblement de terre de 1906 acheva Buena Vista en dévastant le centre de vinification et les caves. Aussi la production resta-t-elle stagnante jusqu'en 1943, date à laquelle les deux centres de vinification furent restaurés et la surface vitifère augmentée. Aujourd'hui, les vignobles qui entourent la charmante construction de pierre de Buena Vista sont plantés de Pinot Noir, Cabernet Sauvignon, Riesling, Traminer et Sylvaner.

Buena Vista fut racheté en 1968 par la société Young's Market, qui le revendit en 1979 à A. Racke, une société allemande, propriétaire de Kupferberg, producteur de vins mousseux. La propriété détient aussi 330 ha dans le secteur de Carneros à Napa qui semble être très indiqué pour les cépages de Pinot Noir et de Chardonnay. Le maître de chai est Jill Davis. Environ 100 000 caisses de vin sont produites chaque année. Quant à l'ancien propriétaire de Buena Vista, Frank Bartholomew, il a ouvert un nouveau centre vinicole à Sonoma (*voir* HACIENDA WINE CELLARS).

Château Saint-Jean. Très jolie propriété (avec un très élégant château de style méditerranéen) fondé en 1973. Six variétés de raisins sont plantées sur 28 ha et comptent pour 10 % des 180 000 caisses produites chaque année. Le Château Saint-Jean est spécialisé en vins blancs et, avant tout, en Chardonnay. Le maître de chai, Richard Arrowood, tient à identifier ses vins par le nom de la parcelle du vignoble d'origine, ce qui donne, dès la première récolte : six Chardonnay et trois Riesling de différents terroirs, avec des goûts différents. Des vins botrytisés, faits à partir de Riesling, de

Gewürztraminer et de mélanges de Sauvignon Blanc-Sémillon représentent 2 % de la production. Tous ses efforts se sont surtout concentrés sur les variétés de Chardonnay et de Riesling, achetées au vignoble de Robert Young.

Domaine Michel. Un banquier de Genève, Jean-Jacques Michel, sa femme et quelques associés américains sont à l'origine de cette magnifique exploitation de style espagnol créée dans la Dry Creek Valley en 1985. La production atteint 25 000 caisses de quatre vins de cépage différents.

Foppiano Winery. Créé en 1896 par John Foppiano, un immigré italien, le vignoble est actuellement géré par Louis J. et Louis M. Foppiano, les troisième et quatrième générations. 80 ha de vignes produisent une gamme complète de bons vins à des prix modérés. La production annuelle est d'environ 200 000 caisses dont la plupart est vendue sous l'étiquette « Riverside Farm ».

Geyser Peak Winery. Un énorme vignoble de 245 ha, qui fut acheté en 1982 par la famille Trione à la Brasserie Stroh de Detroit, produit quatorze vins de cépage comprenant des crus millésimés et deux mousseux appelés « Opulence ». La production annuelle est d'environ 500 000 caisses. Les Trione possèdent 420 ha de vignobles et trois différentes appellations du comté de Sonoma.

Gloria Ferrer. Frexinet, premier vendeur de vins mousseux aux États-Unis, quitta l'Espagne en 1986 pour ouvrir dans la région de Carneros, au sud du comté de Sonoma, la sixième fabrique de mousseux de la compagnie. Les raisins provenant des 100 ha autour du centre de vinification fournissent l'essentiel de la production qui s'élève à 100 000 caisses. Le premier cru, un brut, fut fabriqué à partir de Pinot Noir dans un autre centre, tandis que leurs formidables installations de Ferrer étaient en construction. D'importantes caves et un magnifique site surplombant la baie de San Pablo feront de Ferrer une étape de choix pour les touristes amateurs de vins. Eileen Crane en est le maître de chai.

Hacienda Winery Cellars. Fondé en 1973 par l'ancien directeur de journal Frank H. Bartholomew, ce nouveau centre vinicole de 44 ha se trouve au cœur de la vallée de la Lune, à environ 14 km du centre de la ville. Ses caves ne se contentent pas de proposer ses propres vins, mais également les meilleures bouteilles des autres grands producteurs de la Sonoma. Ces vins ne peuvent être achetés que sur place. Hacienda produit six différents vins de cépages, le plus réputé étant un Chardonnay. La production annuelle est de 25 000 caisses.

Hanzell Vineyards. Lorsque dans les années 50, l'ambassadeur des États-Unis en Italie prit sa retraite, il s'installa à Sonoma avec l'idée de produire des vins de qualité égale aux meilleurs vins européens qu'il avait pu déguster. Ainsi, James D. Zellerbach conçut ses vins, ses vignobles et son centre de vinification sur le modèle français, en s'attachant plus particulièrement à l'exemple du Clos Vougeot et en ne produisant que des vins faits exclusivement avec des raisins de Bourgogne : Pinot Noir et Pinot Chardonnay. Dans son amour du détail, M. Zellerbach s'aperçut que les caractéristiques propres aux vins européens sont dues en grande partie aux méthodes de vieillissement : en effet les vins sont vieillis dans des barils en chêne, mais d'une variété qu'on ne trouve que dans certaines parties d'Europe. M. Zellerbach fut ainsi le premier à importer des barils français aux États-Unis, où cette pratique est aujourd'hui fort répandue. Le nom du vignoble, Hanzell, est né d'une combinaison du nom du propriétaire et du prénom de sa femme Hannah. A la mort de M. Zellerbach, la propriété fut achetée par Douglas Day. Aujourd'hui la propriété appartient à la comtesse Barbara de Brye ; elle produit environ 2 500 caisses de Pinot Noir et Chardonnay provenant des 12 ha de vignobles situés aux alentours dans la vallée de Sonoma.

Italian Swiss Colony. Située sur les paisibles collines d'Asti en Californie, cette colonie de Suisses et d'Italiens, fondée en 1881, possédait déjà plus de 600 ha de vignobles avant même le début du siècle. Elle fut achetée en 1983 au groupe Heublein Wines par l'association de viticulteurs Allied Grape Growers.

Un certain Andrew Sbarboro lança l'affaire et fit construire le centre de vinification en 1887, mais ses premiers vins furent un échec total, jusqu'au jour où un jeune pharmacien italien de San Francisco, Pietro Rossi, vint à Asti y dispenser les techniques de vinification qu'il avait apprises en Europe. Les vins eurent bientôt grand succès. La nouvelle génération des Rossi prend encore part à l'activité de l'entreprise. De 1940 à 1960, l'entreprise fut dirigée par Louis Petri qui en fit l'un des plus grands centres vinicoles du monde.

La capacité totale des six entreprises vinicoles d'Asti, de Madera, d'Oakville et de Stockton et enfin d'Inglenook à Rutherford, atteint 3,6 millions d'hl. On y produit une vaste gamme de vins de table et de dessert, de « portos », « xérès » et « champagnes », ainsi que de l'eau-de-vie de vin et des vins aromatisés. Parmi les nombreuses marques nationales on trouve Lejon, Petri, Annie Green Springs, Jacques Bonet et G. & D.

Jordan Vineyard & Winery. Thomas Jordan Jr, ancien homme d'affaires du pétrole, acheta cette très jolie propriété (avec un château de style français) en 1972 et la planta de Cabernet Sauvignon, Merlot et Pinot Chardonnay. Le vin principal de Jordan, un Cabernet Sauvignon, est élégant et bien équilibré. La production commença en 1979. Elle atteignait 25 000 caisses en 1982 et est aujourd'hui de 45 000 caisses par an.

F. Korbel & Bros., Inc. Cette entreprise vinicole est située en bordure du fleuve Russian River, à Guerneville, dans l'un des secteurs les plus pittoresques de Californie. Les frères Korbel quittèrent leur Tchécoslovaquie natale pour s'installer à Guerneville, dans le comté de la Sonoma ; il y produisirent leurs premiers « champagnes » à la fin du siècle dernier. A la fin de la Seconde Guerre mondiale, ils abandonnèrent complètement les vins de table pour se consacrer exclusivement à la production de champagnes. Au début de l'année 1954, Anton et Leo Korbel vendirent leur entreprise à la famille Heck. Adolf Heck, originaire de Saint-Louis, était l'ancien président de l'entreprise vinicole californienne Italian Swiss Colony of Asti (*q.v.*) ; son frère Paul étant lui, directeur de production. Adolf devint président et responsable de la vinification de l'entreprise Korbel... A la mort de M. Heck, en 1984, il fut remplacé par Robert Stashak, lui-même formé par M. Heck pendant douze ans.

Les grandes variétés utilisées pour la production des vins mousseux sont le Pinot Noir et le Chardonnay. Le centre de vinification propose les vins mousseux suivants : Korbel Rose, Korbel Brut, Korbel Extra Dry, Korbel Sec, un Blanc de Blanc, un Blanc de Noir et un mousseux naturel. 70 % de la production sont des mousseux et 30 % des eaux-de-vie. On fabrique néanmoins une très petite quantité de vins plats chaque année. Aujourd'hui, Korbel est, aux États-Unis, le plus grand producteur de vins mousseux selon la méthode champenoise. En 1942, Frank Schoonmaker et l'auteur ont fait connaître Korbel à l'est des Rocheuses. Korbel appartient depuis 1966 à l'entreprise de distillation Jack Daniels qui assure aussi la distribution des vins. Korbel produit également des vins de table ; une bonne partie des raisins à vins proviennent des 280 ha de cépages situés dans le secteur nord-occidental du comté.

J. Pedroncelli Winery. Quoique moins connue que certaines de ses voisines l'entreprise Pedroncelli produit des vins de cépage de qualité. Les vignobles et les locaux de vinification sont situés à environ 1 500 m au nord-ouest de Geyserville, en bordure du Highway 101. En achetant cette propriété en 1927, John Pedroncelli y retrouva le décor et le climat de son Italie natale. Les vignobles Pedroncelli couvrent aujourd'hui près de 50 ha et l'on y produit le premier Zinfandel Rosé de Californie. La production annuelle de cette entreprise est de 125 000 caisses.

Rodney Strong Vineyards. M. Strong, ancien danseur professionnel, commença à vendre des vins courants et de cépage sous l'étiquette Tiburon Vintners dans la région de San Fancisco. Son affaire devint la plus importante de Californie du Nord. En 1976, il fonda à Windsor une compagnie publique, Sonoma Vineyards et y employa tous ses talents de vinificateur comme maître de chai. Les importateurs new-yorkais Renfield achetèrent la compagnie en 1985 dont ils changèrent le nom. Elle devint Rodney Strong Vineyards. Renfield et Piper Heidsieck sont associés dans Piper-Sonoma (*q.v.*), le domaine voisin producteur de mousseux. Environ 50 % des raisins utilisés à la fabrication des vins de Strong proviennent de 500 ha de vignes. La production annuelle atteint presque 400 000 caisses.

Sebastiani Vineyards. Cette entreprise vinicole fut fondée en 1904 par l'Italien Samuele Sebastiani ; huit ans après son arrivée aux États-Unis, celui-ci réussit à réunir les fonds nécessaires pour s'installer à Sonoma et y lancer son affaire. Ses vins en vrac lui portèrent chance et peu à peu, son nom se répandit dans la ville.

Aujourd'hui la place historique de Sonoma — car c'est là que fut érigé, dans les années 1840, le drapeau de l'État qui fit de Sonoma la capitale de Californie — est entourée de nombreux buildings arborant le nom de Sebastiani. Depuis vingt-cinq ans, l'entreprise ne produit plus de vins en vrac et se consacre exclusivement aux vins de qualité, qui portent tous l'étiquette Sebastiani. Parmi ces vins, tous fort réussis, on trouve un Zinfandel, un Chardonnay, un bon Barbera et un Cabernet Sauvignon qui comptent parmi les meilleurs de Californie. Les vignobles couvrent 280 ha. A la mort d'August Sebastiani en 1980, son fils Sam lui succéda. Mais, en 1986, à la suite de querelles familiales, Don, son frère, reprit les rennes et fonda sa propre entreprise vinicole.

Simi Winery, Inc. Situé au nord de Healdsburg en bordure du spectaculaire Redwood Highway, cette agréable propriété, dont la cave de pierre est historique, fut construite en 1876 par les frères Simi, deux anciens négociants en vins de San Francisco. Elle fut rachetée en 1970 par Russell Green, qui la restaura et commença à y produire de bons vins de cépage avec les raisins de vignobles qu'il avait achetés en 1958. En 1976, Simi devint la filiale d'une entreprise d'importation de vins, Schieffelin & Co, elle-même rachetée par le groupe français Moët-Hennessy en 1981. Les 70 ha de vignobles dans le secteur de l'Alexander Valley ne suffisent pas à la fabrication des 145 000 caisses produites chaque année. Simi doit acheter la plupart des raisins aux comtés de Sonoma, Mendocino et Napa.

Piper-Sonoma. Cette exploitation est le résultat d'une entente franco-américaine entre les champagnes Piper Heidsieck et leurs importateurs Renfield Importers, société aujourd'hui vendue à Schenley Industries. Les caves, proches des vignobles de Sonoma, furent achevées juste à temps pour la première cuvée. En 1982, le centre fut ouvert aux visiteurs avec dégustation des mousseux bruts du domaine. Un Blanc de Noir est aussi fabriqué. La production annuelle est de 100 000 caisses de mousseux fait en majeure partie avec des raisins achetés au comté de Sonoma.

Sam Sebastiani. A la suite de différends familiaux, Sam Sebastiani lance sa propre affaire en 1986. Il produit du Sauvignon Blanc et du Cabernet Sauvignon à partir de raisins de première qualité provenant des comtés de Napa et de Sonoma ainsi que du Chardonnay dans une autre installation en attendant que la construction de son centre vinicole soit achevée.

Sonoma-Cutrer Vineyards. Les trois vignobles de Sonoma-Cutrer : les Pierres, Cutrer et Russian River Ranches sont spécialisés en Chardonnay. C'est Bruce Cutrer-Jones, ancien pilote de chasse, qui planta en 1972 180 ha de vignobles dans les secteurs de Russian River Valley et Carneros. Sonoma-Cutrer fournit du raisin à d'autres centres vinicoles jusqu'en 1981, année au cours de laquelle Jones construisit sa propre entreprise à l'ouest de Windsor, dans l'intention de ne produire que du Chardonnay. Le centre vinicole State of Art présente une table unique en son genre qui sélectionne les raisins avant qu'ils en soient pressurés et un tunnel réfrigérant qui recueille le moût sur le chemin du vignoble aux presses et aux réservoirs de fermentation. William Bonetti, l'un des experts en Chardonnay les plus réputés de Californie, est le maître de chai. Sonoma-Cutrer possède plusieurs terrains de championnat de croquet, tout proches du centre, où des tournois se déroulent chaque année.

Souverain of Alexander Valley. Construit en 1972, Souverain a appartenu pendant dix ans à un groupement de producteurs avant d'être racheté en 1986 par Wine World, la division vinicole de Nestlé International (qui comprend aussi les étiquettes Beringer Winery et Los Hermanos). Rebaptisé Château Souverain par le nouveau propriétaire, la production a été considérablement réduite : 40 000 caisses annuelles aujourd'hui, mais l'accent est mis sur des vins de cépage de meilleure qualité provenant de plusieurs appellations du comté de Sonoma. L'architecture incroyable de Souverain, souvenir des Hop Kilns, autrefois influents dans la région, comprend un magnifique restaurant.

3. *Mendocino*

Les vignerons de ce district ont depuis peu commencé à cultiver les meilleures variétés de raisins, et la superficie totale des vignobles, en pleine expansion, est passé de 480 ha à plus de 4 400 ha. Les coteaux dont l'irrigation était autrefois jugée impossible, et qu'on ne pouvait donc protéger contre le gel, reçoivent aujourd'hui l'eau de pluie des réservoirs situés dans les fermes. Le Cabernet Sauvignon et le Gamay Beaujolais sont les variétés les plus plantées, mais on s'intéresse également au Pinot Chardonnay et au solide Zinfandel. Mendocino est probablement une région de vins fins, qui a été pour le moins négligée jusqu'au début des années 70. Certains vignobles — surtout ceux situés dans la zone micro-climatique plus fraîche — produiront quelques-uns des meilleurs vins du nord de la Californie. En 1982, la maison champenoise Louis Roederer acquit 160 ha dans l'Anderson Valley, ce qui ne manquera pas d'impact pour Mendocino.

Cresta Blanca Winery. Autrefois célèbre, le nom de la première grande entreprise de Californie gagnerait à sortir de l'oubli. Aujourd'hui située au nord d'Ukiah, et non plus dans la vallée de Livermore près de San Francisco, Cresta Blanca se consacre à nouveau à la production de bons vins de cépage.

Cresta Blanca fut fondée en 1892 par un négociant innovateur, Charles Wetmore. Celui-ci avait effectué des voyages en Europe pour le compte du Comité viticole de Californie, et avait rapporté de France des boutures de bonnes vignes. Ainsi, sept ans après la création du domaine, les vins de Cresta Blanca remportaient des médailles à l'Exposition de Paris. Après quelques années médiocres, M. Schenley vendit l'entreprise à la Guild Wine Company en 1971. Cresta Blanca produit du Gamay Beaujolais, du Petite Sirah, du Cabernet Sauvignon, du Zinfandel, du Grignolino, du Sylvaner et du Pinot Chardonnay, ainsi que quelques vins de dessert et mousseux. Les vins de cépage, mis en bouteilles dans le comté de Mendocino, firent leur apparition sur le marché en 1983. La production annuelle est de 15 000 caisses environ.

Edmeades Vineyards. En 1972, Deron Edmeades hérita de son père cette propriété fraîche et humide de 40 ha ainsi que la détermination à la bien cultiver. Ses efforts et ceux du maître de chai ont porté leurs fruits. Les Cabernet Sauvignon, Zinfandel, Chardonnay et Gewürztraminer sont tout à fait satisfaisants. A cette production faite à partir du vignoble d'Anderson Valley s'ajoute les vins fabriqués à partir de raisins achetés. Au total 24 000 caisses par an.

Fetzer Vineyards. Située dans la solitaire vallée de Redwood, l'entreprise — et ses 280 ha de vignobles — appartient à Bernard Fetzer. C'est une affaire strictement familiale, dont le président est John Fetzer. Les Fetzer Vineyards ainsi que 120 ha de vignobles à Hopland produisent des vins de cépage. De plus, 70 % des raisins nécessaires à la production des 900 000 caisses annuelles sont achetés aux comtés de Lake, Mendocino, Sonoma et Monterey.

Parducci Winery. Ce centre vinicole, situé au nord d'Ukiah, fut fondé par Adolf Parducci à la fin de la prohibition. Ses fils, John et feu George, gérèrent l'affaire avant d'être remplacés par leurs familles. Parducci, l'une des meilleures entreprises de la côte nord, produit la plupart de ses vins avec des raisins cultivés dans les comtés de Mendocino et de Lake, ou vendangés sur ses 120 ha de vignobles. La production annuelle est de 300 000 caisses environ. Depuis 1969, des Cabernet Sauvignon ont été vinifiés à partir de raisins cultivés sur des parcelles différentes, afin de déterminer les qualités des nouveaux secteurs vinicoles. Parducci produit une grande sélection de vins de cépage. Bon Chenin Blanc à prix modéré.

Roederer U.S. C'est en 1986 qu'eut lieu la première presse de ce domaine, propriété des champagnes français Louis Roederer. Situé à 4 km au nord-ouest de Philo, Roederer cultive 160 ha de Chardonnay et de Pinot Noir dans l'Anderson Valley. On espère produire 100 000 caisses en 1988.

4. *Livermore*

Ce district mérite d'être noté pour sa production de plusieurs vins de bonne qualité. La vallée de Livermore dans le canton d'Alameda est connue dans tous les États-Unis pour ses bons vins du genre Sauternes, ainsi que pour d'autres blancs remarquables. Cette vallée doit son nom au pionnier Robert Livermore qui possédait, dès 1848, un vignoble près de la ville qui porte actuellement son nom.

C'est d'ailleurs plutôt un bassin qu'une vallée et il comporte deux secteurs distincts : les vignobles qui entourent la ville de Livermore et ceux de Pleasanton. En 1887, Charles A. Wetmore disait de cette vallée : « Il existe toutes les conditions connues pour être nécessaires à la production des vins et eaux-de-vie des plus hautes qualités, avoisinant les types français les plus nobles ». En 1882, Wetmore fonda, avec des boutures qu'il apportait directement de Margaux et de Château-d'Yquem, l'entreprise devenue célèbre sous le nom de Cresta Blanca, mais, malheureusement, elle n'a pas maintenu ses anciennes normes. Actuellement les deux entreprises remarquables de la vallée de Livermore sont Concannon Vineyard et Wente Bros.

Le sol de la plupart des vignobles de ce secteur est surtout d'aspect aride, grossier et pierreux comme celui de Châteauneuf-du-Pape et d'une partie des Graves et du Médoc. Il convient particulièrement à la production de blancs charnus allant du très sec au doux. On a réussi à faire récemment des vins plus légers. Une mise en bouteille précoce a beaucoup contribué à les améliorer car, voilà vingt ans, bien des gens les considéraient comme trop lourds. En raison du climat et de la nature du sol il est douteux que l'on puisse cultiver avec succès du Pinot Noir à Livermore.

En 1982, la vallée de Livermore fut désignée comme appellation par le B.A.T.F.

Au sud-ouest de Livermore et très près de l'extrémité de la baie de San Francisco se trouvent les centres vinicoles de Mission San José et d'Irvington, qui s'étendent presque jusqu'au canton de Santa Clara. Dans cette zone méridionale du canton d'Alameda, les vins rouges ont presque autant de succès que les vins blancs. On y produit également des mousseux, des apéritifs et des vins de dessert. Weibel Champagne, Vineyards et Llords et Elwood sont les plus importantes entreprises. Les vignobles d'Alameda n'ont cessé de diminuer jusqu'à atteindre une superficie d'environ 800 ha. Cependant, au sud de Pleasanton, Amaldén a acheté 104 ha qu'il a plantés avec dix bonnes et robustes variétés de raisins. La vallée de Sunol est devenue riche en vin.

Concannon Vineyard. En 1883, James Concannon acheta 19 ha de terrains graveleux situés au cœur de la vallée de Livermore, et fonda le vignoble qui porte son nom en y plantant des ceps de Sauvignon Blanc et de Sémillon rapportés de Bordeaux. En 1889, il réussit à convaincre le président du Mexique Porfirio Diaz de développer la viticulture. Diaz lui donna raison et l'Irlandais de Livermore put envoyer des boutures de ses vignobles au Mexique, où elles furent plantées dans les zones adéquates. La vallée de Livermore ne fut longtemps connue que pour ses vins blancs. Mais les Wente et les Concannon — deux familles voisines depuis plus d'un siècle — ont grandement contribué à améliorer les vins rouges de la région. L'innovation la plus intéressante de Concannon fut, en 1964, la création d'un cépage de Petite Sirah, donnant une autre dimension à ce raisin, autrefois destiné à être mélangé à leur « Bourgogne ». En 1983, la Distillers Company Ltd de Grande-Bretagne (qui produit plus de 50 % du whisky consommé dans le monde) acheta l'entreprise de vinification, dont Jim Concannon est resté le président.

Weibel Vineyards. Cette société est spécialisée dans la production de vins mousseux de type Champagne. Après avoir produit des vins en Suisse, puis des Champagne en France à partir de 1906, Rudolph Weibel vint ensuite s'établir à San Francisco, où il s'occupa d'importation de vins. En 1939, il produisit ses premiers vins et, en 1945, il fonda avec son fils, Frederick, la Maison Weibel Champagne Vineyards à Mission San José, dans le sud du comté d'Alameda. La propriété appartenait autrefois à Josiah et Leland Stanford, qui vendaient leurs vins sous l'étiquette Stanford. Les Weibel ont fait leur spécialité des vins de type Champagne fermentés en bouteilles ; pour leur Grand Cru Select, ils utilisent un coupage du très fin Pinot Chardonnay. Après la mort de son père, Frederick Weibel étendit la propriété en achetant des terres à Mendocino. En 1972, la construction d'un nouveau centre vinicole fut entreprise près d'Ukiah. Outre les vins mousseux, Weibel produit actuellement du Pinot Noir millésimé, du Chardonnay, et du Green Flungarian. Ces vins surprennent agréablement ceux qui ne connaissent les Weibel que pour leurs « champagnes ». Un « xérès » de type flor suscite un certain intérêt depuis quelque temps. La production totale de tous les vins Weibel avoisine aujourd'hui 1 000 000 de caisses par an. Weibel est le plus grand producteur de mousseux aux États-Unis.

Wente Bros. Propriété de vieille tradition située dans la vallée de Livermore : on y fait de bons vins de cépage, en particulier les meilleurs vins types Graves et Sauternes d'Amérique. Carl Wente, son fondateur, quitta l'Allemagne en 1880 pour s'établir aux États-Unis ; il acquit son expérience en vins californiens dans la vallée de Napa, chez Charles Krug, expérience qu'il mit en pratique en achetant, fin 1883, quelques vignobles dans la vallée de Livermore. L'entreprise s'est longtemps spécialisée dans la production de vins de table de première qualité, favorisée par un sol excellent. La propriété, vignobles inclus, est située sur la route de Tesla, en dehors de Livermore.

Carl Wente étendit sa propriété et ses fils, feu Herman et Ernest, y ajoutèrent les bons vignobles d'El Mocho. L'ancien propriétaire d'El Mocho, Louis Mel, avait planté des boutures de Sémillon, Sauvignon Blanc et Muscadelle du Bordelais qui provient du célèbre vignoble Château-d'Yquem à Sauternes. Aujourd'hui, ces excellentes propriétés sont judicieusement dirigées par les Wente, dont le Château Wente sauterne est apprécié pour sa grande qualité. Le domaine compte actuellement 600 ha de vignobles, dont 80 % sont plantés de variétés à vin blanc aussi excellentes que le Chardonnay, le Grey Riesling, le Sylvaner, le Sémillon, le Sauvignon Blanc et le Muscadelle. Parmi les 10 % de variétés à vin rouge on trouve du Pinot Noir, du Gamay et du Zinfandel.

La plupart des vins des Wente portent sur leur étiquette le nom de leur variété de raisin, et non pas — comme c'est trop souvent l'usage — une appellation d'origine empruntée aux régions d'Europe. L'urbanisation croissante de la vallée de Livermore a contraint le propriétaire actuel, Karl L. Wente, à poursuivre l'expansion des vignobles à Monterey suivant ainsi l'initiative de son père, Ernest. Aujourd'hui, la quatrième génération, Eric, Philip et Carolyn gèrent le domaine.

Aujourd'hui certains des meilleurs vins de la Maison Wente proviennent de ces 320 ha de vignobles plantés de Pinot Noir et de Chardonnay, nécessaires à la production de leurs mousseux.

5. *Santa Clara-San Benito-Santa Cruz*

La viniculture de ce district est surtout concentrée dans le canton de Santa Clara où se trouvent trente-neuf entreprises commerciales de viniculture. On distingue trois zones dans ce district totalisant environ 560 ha de vignobles. A l'ouest de la vallée de Santa Clara et au pied des monts Santa Cruz se trouve le Los Gatos et, un peu plus au nord-ouest, plus haut sur la montagne, Saratoga. La zone Los Gatos-Saratoga produit certains des meilleurs vins de table et mousseux de Californie dits « champagnes ». Almadén, Mount Eden, Ridge, Mirassou et Paul Masson *(voir ces noms)* sont les principaux vignobles de cette zone.

La deuxième zone de Santa Clara est à l'est de San José et les vignobles d'Evergreen s'étendent sur les pentes du mont Hamilton. On y produit des quantités raisonnables de vins généralement supérieurs.

La troisième zone comporte quarante-deux petites entreprises vinicoles qui font de bons vins moyens et pourvoient à la demande locale au sud du canton de Santa Clara, autour des agglomérations de Madrone, San Martin et Gilroy. C'est un des plus gros producteurs de fruits du monde entier et la culture du raisin y date du temps des missionnaires espagnols qui plantèrent les premières vignes.

Le canton de Santa Cruz est séparé de celui de Santa Clara par les monts de Santa Cruz. On y compte dix-neuf entreprises commerciales. Les vignes donnent des raisins bons et sains. Lors des dix dernières années, ce comté a pris une certaine importance grâce à ses bons vignobles de *varietal*. Mais il leur faut encore s'imposer, car la surface consacrée aux raisins à vin n'est que de 40 ha ; la plupart de ces raisins sont cultivés dans les parties plus fraîches et plus élevées.

Viennent enfin, au sud de ces deux derniers cantons, ceux de San Benito et San Luis Obispo qui produisent des quantités relativement minimes de vin de table. En grande partie grâce à Almadén, San Benito compte 1 800 ha de raisins *varietal,* et six caves où les vins sont entreposés. En 1982, les 920 ha de la Line Kiln Valley à San Benito furent agréés officiellement comme région viticole par le B.A.T.F., ainsi que l'appellation Chalone (3 460 ha) à San Benito County.

Almadén Vineyards. Les vignobles se trouvent toujours sur leur site original et font aujourd'hui partie de la ville de San José. Le domaine fut nommé d'après cet endroit historique (classé California State Historical Landmark n° 505) et situé à quelque 13 km au sud entre Los Gatos et l'ancienne ville minière d'Almadén. En 1852, Charles Le Franc effectua la première plantation commerciale de variétés européennes de qualité dans le comté de Santa Clara, et fonda les vignobles d'Almadén. On ne sait exactement qui, de Le Franc ou d'Étienne Thée — son compatriote bordelais — fut le vrai fondateur d'Almadén, mais on sait que ce fut Charles Le Franc qui planta de bonnes variétés européennes au pied des monts de Santa Cruz, où la chaleur de l'éternel soleil californien est tempérée par les fraîches brises nocturnes venant du Pacifique. Le sol rocailleux n'est pas assez fertile pour d'abondantes productions, mais les coteaux d'Almadén donnent des raisins de fort bonne qualité. Les vins d'Almadén sont presque tous des vins de cépage portant le nom du raisin prédominant. Le Pinot Chardonnay est un bon blanc américain, et le Cabernet Sauvignon local est un rouge qui ne manque pas de distinction.

Louis Benoist, un homme d'affaires de San Francisco qui fut exemplairement guidé par feu Frank Schoonmaker, acheta les vignobles en 1941 et augmenta la superficie de *varietals* en y ajoutant deux parcelles d'une surface totale de 120 ha. L'une d'entre elles, située dans les monts de Santa Cruz près d'Eagle Rock, est entièrement plantée de Johannisberg Riesling ; l'autre, le Foothill Vineyard, situé à environ 3 km de la propriété principale, cultive surtout du Cabernet Sauvignon et du Pinot Chardonnay. En 1956, Almadén Vineyards acheta Rancho Paicines, propriété de 1 400 ha située à 240 km au sud de San Francisco. Ses coteaux furent plantés de nombreuses variétés, parmi lesquelles le Pinot Noir, Cabernet Sauvignon, Johannisberg Riesling, Gewürztraminer et Pinot Chardonnay. La propriété, classé vignoble de montagne en raison de son altitude (200 à 300 m), offre différents types de sols et microclimats, tous particulièrement favorables à la culture de raisins produisant de bons vins de cépage ou *varietal*. Plus tard, Almadén loua puis acheta les locaux et 200 ha de vignes de la vieille entreprise Valliant appartenant à la société W.A. Taylor. Ce terrain situé à environ 200 km de San Francisco est devenu la « filiale » Cienega d'Almadén. D'autres vignobles ont été nouvellement achetés à Alameda et Monterey par Almadén Vineyards, qui fut elle-même rachetée, en 1967, par National Distillers ; c'est aujourd'hui l'un des plus grands producteurs du pays. Les vignobles Almadén furent achetés en 1986 par la société Heublein, puis revendus à l'« International Distillers and Vintners Co » (I.D.V.), compagnie du Royaume-Uni détenue par Grand Metropolitan P.L.C., société également du Royaume-Uni.

Felton-Empire Vineyards. Il y a 40 ans, les meilleurs vins de Santa Cruz venaient de Hallcrest Vineyards, fondée par un avocat de San Francisco, Chafee Hall. Après la mort de celui-ci en 1969, le vignoble fut d'abord loué au Concannon Winery et ensuite vendu en 1976 à Leo McCloskey, un œnologue, Jim Beauregard, un viticulteur, et John Pollard, un ancien pilote. Les trois ont rebaptisé le vignoble Felton-Empire, et ont repris la production d'une gamme complète de vins fins dont un excellent Riesling botrytisé qui rappelle un bon Auslese du Rheingau. La production annuelle est d'environ 20 000 caisses.

Martin Ray Vineyards. Ce vignoble fut fondé par Martin Ray et appartient aujourd'hui à une corporation vinicole. Son fils Pierre, professeur à l'université de Stanford, détient la majorité des parts. La production annuelle est de 4 000 caisses de Chardonnay, Merlot, Cabernet Sauvignon, Pinot Noir et une petite quantité de mousseux artisanaux. Ces vins sont faits à partir des raisins du vignoble ainsi que de raisins achetés aux comtés de Napa et Sonoma.

Paul Masson Vineyards. Fondée à Santa Clara dans les années 1880, l'entreprise Paul Masson limita longtemps son activité à cette région. Ce n'est que depuis une dizaine d'années qu'elle s'est transférée à Monterey, où le sol et le climat favorisent la production de bons vins de cépage. Les vins et champagnes Paul Masson sont mis en bouteilles à Gonzales près de Monterey.

Paul Masson était un Bourguignon qui arriva à San Francisco en 1878, muni d'une lettre de recommandation pour un compatriote, Charles Le Franc. Très vite, ils se mirent à produire un « champagne » qui remporta un grand succès. Masson fut l'associé de Le Franc, puis son gendre et enfin, lorsque Le Franc mourut en 1892, son successeur. En 1905, Masson fit construire un « château » et un centre de vinification, au cœur de ses vignobles, à même les coteaux des monts de Santa Cruz. En 1936, Martin Ray prit la direction de l'entreprise, mais il s'établit plus tard à son compte. Depuis 1942, Paul Masson Vineyards appartient à Seagram, une firme de distillation, qui acquit aussi plusieurs autres compagnies dont Taylor California Cellars en 1983. Paul Masson produit une sélection de quarante-trois vins, vins *varietal* ou de cépage, vins vinés, « champagne » et eaux-de-vie, ainsi que des coupages

« exclusifs » faits avec les vignes conçues par l'université de Californie, tels le Rubion, le Baroque et l'Emerald Dry.

Mirassou Vineyards. Les vignobles Mirassou sont situés dans le district d'Evergreen, à 8 km à l'est de San José et à 125 km au sud de Soledad, dans la région de Monterey. Les vins de Mirassou sont faits à Evergreen, où les visiteurs peuvent les déguster dans une nouvelle salle spécialement conçue. L'entreprise remonte aux temps de la Ruée vers l'Or. Elle commença à prospérer lorsque la fille du viticulteur Pierre Pellier épousa Pierre Mirassou. Dans les années 60, la cinquième génération des Mirassou commença à vendre les vins non plus en vrac, mais sous leur propre nom. Quelques années plus tard, les vins de Mirassou étaient connus dans tout l'État de Californie. La production annuelle est de 350 000 caisses de vins de cépage, de vins ordinaires et de mousseux.

Ridge Vineyards. Ridge fut fondé en 1959 par un groupe de chercheurs de l'université de Stanford et produit depuis plus de vingt-cinq ans le Cabernet classique de Monte Bello. Situés dans les monts de Santa Cruz, les vignobles et l'entreprise vinicole, vieille de plus de cent ans, dominent San Francisco et la baie. Les vins étaient fabriqués dans les années 60 par David Bennion. Paul Draper le remplaça en 1970. Les 40 000 caisses annuelles comprennent des Cabernet ainsi que les excellents Zinfandel de Geyserville, Lytton Springs, York Creek, Howell Mountain et Paso Robles.

6. *Monterey*

Ce district situé au sud de San Francisco s'apprêtait à devenir la plus grande région productrice de vins de cépage de Californie.

De nombreux vignobles furent plantés dans les années 70, mais ce ne furent que dix années plus tard que la région de Monterey fut implantée. Des 13 600 ha plantés en 1978, il n'en restait plus que 12 000 en 1985. Les plants improductifs furent arrachés et un plus grand effort fut fait pour adapter les différentes variétés de raisin aux sols et aux climats. Les principaux vignobles se trouvent dans la vallée de Salinas et les vallonnements des alentours de Soledad, ainsi que dans la région du Pinnacles National Monument. La vallée prend naissance à 210 km au sud-est de Monterey et dégringole jusqu'au comté de San Luis Obispo. Le sol est formé de granit en décomposition. Monterey dépasse aujourd'hui Napa et Sonoma en surface plantée.

Les zones climatiques appartiennent aux classes I, II et III, réparties sur deux zones bien distinctes. Le nord-ouest, Upper Monterey, a des terres légères et un microclimat frais (officiellement zones I et II) se prêtant à la culture du Riesling Gerwürztraminer et du Pinot Noir. Le sud-est de Monterey a des terres légèrement plus lourdes et des températures plus élevées (zone III) et est considéré par certains viticulteurs comme favorable au Cabernet Sauvignon, Zinfandel, Merlot et Sauvignon Blanc. En 1982, le district de Chalone, dont une partie est située dans le San Benito County, fut officiellement reconnu par le B.A.T.F. comme appellation.

Les terrasses fertiles qui s'étendent autour du sol de la vallée de Salinas souffrent rarement du gel. L'eau provient en abondance des sources souterraines, ainsi que de la grande rivière souterraine Salinas.

Chalone Vineyards. Fondés par Richard Graff et Philip Woodward, les vignobles Chalone sont perchés dans les monts Gavilàn, à l'est de la vallée de Salinas. Le groupe Chalone est une société publique possédant aussi les entreprises vinicoles des vallées d'Acacia, Carmenet et Edna. Les 150 ha de l'entreprise vinicole produisent de bons vins régionaux tels les Pinot Chardonnay, Pinot Noir, Chenin Blanc et Pinot Blanc, soit au total 20 000 caisses chaque année.

J. Lohr Winery. Jerry Lohr délaissa les affaires en 1972 pour s'adonner à la production de vin. 75 % des fruits nécessaires aux 250 000 caisses annuelles proviennent des 200 ha de vignobles situés à Monterey, dans la région de Sacramento Delta et à Napa. Douze *varietals* sont fabriqués au centre de San José. Lohr a su adapter les cépages à leur environnement et obtenir les meilleurs fruits dans chaque région.

Monterey Peninsula Winery. Les amateurs de vins vinifiés sans filtration ni collage recherchent les vins du Monterey Peninsula Winery. Chaque vin porte le nom de sa parcelle de vignes. Les maîtres de chai sont Dick Nuckton et Roy Thomas. Quelques vins, foncés et intenses, ont été fabriqués à partir de Zinfandel, Cabernet Sauvignon, Barbera et Chardonnay. Tous les raisins sont achetés aux comtés de Monterey et Amador. Peter Watson-Graff produit 15 000 caisses de vin chaque année au centre vinicole qui se trouve à Sand City.

Vallée du Sacramento

Cette région commence dans la partie nord du canton de San Joaquin et s'étend au nord jusqu'à Oroville, dans le canton de Butte. Elle englobe en outre les cantons de Sacramento, Placer, Yolo, Amador. C'est seulement une prolongation de la grande vallée centrale qui représente le cœur de la Californie agricole. La diversité de ses sols, de son relief, de son climat en fait une des trois importantes subdivisions vinicoles de la Californie. L'influence modératrice de la baie de San Francisco s'y fait sentir : les étés ne s'échauffent que lentement et les hivers sont plus frais. Certains secteurs, surtout ceux où les gels sont négligeables et les étés doux, deviendront les terroirs des meilleurs vins. Au nord, un relief trop accidenté rend la viticulture impossible. Le comté de Butte est assez prometteur, et on y cultive de plus en plus de vignes. Pendant des années, la vallée du Sacramento se limita à donner quelques bonnes variétés, mais aujourd'hui, sa surface plantée s'élève à quelque 1 200 ha.

La plupart des centres vinicoles sont groupés dans les cantons de San Joaquin et de Sacramento. La majorité des entreprises produisent en masse. Vins de table ordinaires et de dessert y abondent.

Les environs de Lodi-Sacramento dominent ce secteur. En partant de Sacramento — capitale de l'État — en direction du sud vers la ville d'Elk Grove, on se trouve dans un pays de grosse production : vins de table et de dessert, faux bourgognes et faux portos faits avec des raisins de bonnes variétés ou de variétés inférieures. On produit aussi à Elk Grove des vins de fruits et de baies, des vins de dessert et des apéritifs plutôt que des vins de table.

Au nord du canton de San Joaquin, les nombreuses entreprises de la petite ville animée de Lodi produisent presque exclusivement des vins de dessert. Néanmoins le secteur de Lodi, qui s'étend autour de la ville en toutes directions, produit une quantité substantielle de vins de table. La plupart sont faits avec de nouveaux hybrides conçus pour des climats plus chauds. Le comté de San Joaquin compte 15 200 ha de vignes et a le rendement par hectare le plus élevé de Californie. Étant donné leur abondance, ses vins ne sont évidemment pas les meilleurs de l'État. Le comté possède vingt-trois entreprises vinicoles et quatorze distilleries. On produit en effet une grande quantité d'eau-de-vie.

D'Agostini Winery. C'est le plus ancien domaine du Shenandoah Valley. Fondé en 1856 par un Suisse, Adam Uhlinger, et acheté en 1911 par Enrico D'Agostini, le domaine fut géré par les quatre fils d'Enrico jusqu'en 1984 où un négociant en vins de Sacramento, Armagan Ozdiker, racheta l'entreprise vinicole. Les raisins produits par les 51 ha de vignobles ainsi que des raisins achetés assurent environ 35 000 caisses de vin chaque année. Le domaine est aujourd'hui un site historique.

Guild Wineries. Cette coopérative fut mise sur pied en 1934 par feu Lawrence Marshall ; trente ans plus tard la Guilde acheta les firmes Alta, Garrett et Cribari & Sons, les intérêts vinicoles Schenley y compris Roma, Cresta Blanca et les champagnes Cook. La Guilde est probablement surtout connue pour son Vino da Tavola, un rouge de table. On y fait néanmoins quelque cinquante autres produits, commercialisés sous vingt étiquettes différentes. La coopérative compte aujourd'hui huit entreprises vinicoles dont les organes de direction se trouvent à Lodi, centre offrant de grandes possibilités pour mettre le vin en cuvée puis en bouteilles. Guild appartient à 500 vignerons. En plus de ses vins, Guild fabrique aussi différentes eaux-de-vie et la « Silverado California Vodka ».

Vallée centrale

Le principal secteur de cette vallée, celui d'Escalon-Modesto, est le siège de quelques-unes des plus grandes entreprises vinicoles commerciales de Californie. Escalon et Manteca se trouvent au sud de Stockton, dans la partie méridionale du canton de San Joaquin. Les vignobles s'étendent d'est en ouest entre ces deux petites agglomérations. Cette région couvre le sud de San Joaquin, le canton Stanislaus, le nord de celui de Merced, aux environs de Livingston. On y produit une grande quantité de raisins de table — Flame, Tokay et Thompson Seedless ou Sultanina — et, par malheur, on en utilise une bonne partie pour faire du vin. Néanmoins l'usage de bons Zinfandel se fait plus courant. Les entreprises vinicoles les plus importantes se trouvent à Modesto et à Salida dans le canton de Stanislaus.

Une des plus grandes entreprises vinicoles

du monde, E. et J. Gallo, se trouve à Modesto. La vallée centrale produit des quantités énormes de vin médiocre, surtout de dessert, et quelques vins de table ordinaires ainsi que des mousseux avec des variétés de raisins à gros rendement. Même ses raisins de table sont de qualité inférieure aux normes. On y pressure environ 500 000 t de raisin par an. Cette région présente une ressemblance marquée avec le sud de la France et, à un moindre degré, avec l'Algérie, non seulement au point de vue du climat, mais aussi en ce qui concerne les vins. On y plante de plus en plus de raisin à vin, si bien qu'aujourd'hui les deux tiers des 36 000 h de vignobles sont plantés de variétés qui produiront un vin acceptable.

E. et J. Gallo Winery. Ernest et Julio Gallo sont deux des noms les plus connus dans l'industrie vinicole américaine. Leur centre principal de Modesto est le plus grand du monde en son genre. Ils en possèdent trois autres à Fresno, Livingston et dans le comté de Sonoma. L'entreprise à une capacité de fermentation de 18 millions d'hl et met en bouteille jusqu'à 150 000 caisses par jour au centre de Modesto qui sont exportées vers les Caraïbes, le Canada, le Royaume-Uni et d'autres pays européens. Gallo fabrique aussi ses propres bouteilles et produit essentiellement des vins de table. Néanmoins, vers 1975, une nouvelle ligne de *varietals*, vendue sous l'étiquette « Wine Cellars of Ernest & Julio Gallo » est commercialisée. Huit vins de cépage sont fabriqués, y compris du Cabernet Sauvignon, du Chardonnay et du Sauvignon Blanc. Une cave récemment construite, équipée de fûts de chêne français et yougoslaves, accueille cette nouvelle ligne. A une époque où les entreprises fusionnent ou font faillite, Gallo Winery est toujours demeurée une affaire familiale.

Grâce à une commercialisation ingénieuse de produits convenant aux goûts de l'Américain moyen, les vins de Gallo sont aujourd'hui appréciés un peu partout. Il y a bien sûr un sérieux travail d'expertise derrière cette politique de production massive de vins bon marché, mais sains. La société expérimente chaque nouveau vin, elle possède le plus important personnel de chercheurs spécialisés en chimie, œnologie et microbiologie, de Californie.

Vallée de San Joaquin

Secteur central de la grande vallée intérieure, c'est aussi le plus chaud. Son climat est typiquement celui des vallées intérieures où ne se fait pas sentir l'influence des brises marines. Pluies annuelles négligeables, température moyenne en juillet et août (27 °C) rendent l'irrigation nécessaire. On y produit une grande quantité de raisins secs ainsi que des vins de liqueur et vins doux naturels de qualité supérieure à la moyenne. Les vins de table secs manquent de qualité parce que les raisins qu'on y cultive présentent un mauvais équilibre entre sucre et acidité.

Le principal secteur de cette région est celui de Fresno-San Joaquin Valley, qui englobe cinq cantons, à savoir, du nord au sud, Madera (au sud de Merced County), Fresno, Kings, Tulare et Kern.

Les vignobles du canton de Madera entourent la ville de ce même nom. Le plus important quant à la quantité est celui de Ficklin.

On compte vingt et une entreprises vinicoles dans la seule ville de Fresno. Nombre d'entre elles produisent de faux portos, sauternes, xérès, etc. : grave handicap pour une activité économique qui pourrait être prometteuse. On peut améliorer les vins de cette vallée intérieure en y plantant de meilleures variétés de vignes. D'autres importantes entreprises ont leur siège en diverses villes aux environs de Fresno : Fowler, Selma, Reedley, Parlier et Sanger.

Hanford est le centre viticole du canton de Kings ; Tulare et Cutler sont ceux du canton de Tulare.

Les vastes vignobles du canton de Kern s'étendent de Delano à Arvin, autour de Bakersfield. Les cent dix entreprises de Kern ne livrent pas directement leur production au détail mais fournissent du vin aux principales firmes des autres régions. On pressure environ 1,5 million de t de raisin par an dans la vallée de San Joaquin. Plus de la moitié des 36 000 ha de vignes ont été plantés durant les trois dernières années.

J.F.J. Bronco Winery. Précédemment propriétaires de Franzia Winery, les deux frères Franzia et un de leurs cousins fondèrent le Bronco Winery en 1973. Cet énorme centre vinicole (capacité de 2,5 millions d'hl) est l'un des plus grands producteurs de vins de table et de mousseux.

Giumarra Vineyards. Cet énorme domaine de 6 000 ha dont 3 200 sont plantés en vignes, fut fondé en 1906 par un immigré Sicilian, « Papa Joe » Giumarra. En dépit d'un climat tropical, le vignoble est planté en cépages nobles : Johannisberg Riesling, Chardonnay, Chenin Blanc et Cabernet Franc, ainsi qu'en Colombard et Carignane. Les vins sont bien vinifiés et d'un degré en alcool pas trop élevé. En 1986 Giumarra commença l'importation de raisins portant l'appellation « Central Coast » nécessaires à la production d'un Chardonnay vieilli dans des fûts de chêne et de trois autres vins blancs. La production annuelle moyenne s'élève à 1 million et demi de caisses.

Côte sud

Ce secteur se divise en trois districts : canton de Los Angeles, canton de San Diego et Cucamonga-Ontario. Situés au sud de la vallée côtière, les deux premiers sont rafraîchis par les brises marines alors que le district intérieur de Cucamonga-Ontario (synonyme de canton de San Bernardino) est une prolongation de la zone désertique dont les étés sont comparables à ceux de la vallée de San Joaquin. Ce secteur plus chaud convient moins bien à la production des vins de table secs, mais on y fait d'assez bons vins doux.

Dans le petit district d'Escondido (canton de San Diego) on fait surtout du muscat avec du raisin Muscat d'Alexandrie.

Le district le plus célèbre de la Californie du Sud se trouve aux environs de Cucamonga. On y produit de grandes quantités de vins légers à consommer jeunes car le climat torride ne permet pas d'obtenir un vin corsé durable. Le vin de table rouge est fait avec des variétés de raisins vinifiés en faux chianti, bourgogne et claret (bordeaux rouges). Quelques vignobles de cette région donnent un honnête Grignolino rosé. Dans ce district de Cucamonga-Ontario, on produit des vins de toutes sortes allant des rouges pour la table au faux champagne mousseux, ainsi que des apéritifs et des vins de dessert. Sous un climat aussi ensoleillé, la qualité dépend de l'habileté du vigneron : une quantité excessive nuisant toujours à la qualité. Les raisins cultivés dans la partie la plus chaude, celle du désert — notamment les vallées de Coachella et Imperial —, ne conviennent pas pour faire du vin, et on ne les utilise pas pour cela ; on y fait des raisins de table à maturation précoce.

La Californie du Sud ne joue pas un grand rôle dans la production de vins : elle ne représente en effet que 5 % de la production totale de l'État. Il existe néanmoins trente centres vinificateurs, dont six appartiennent à la firme Brookside Vineyards. Certains secteurs de comtés de San Diego et de Santa Barbara s'affirment à nouveau dans la production de vins et de raisins. Santa Barbara arrive en tête avec 3 600 ha de raisins à vin ; San Bernardino en compte un peu plus de 1 400 et San Diego, environ 52. Les vignobles de toute la région South Coast Mountain sont plantés de *vitifera* génériques, ce qui est contraire à la pratique dans le reste de la Californie (à l'exception de la moitié du comté de Monterey).

Callaway Vineyard and Winery. 128 ha plantés sur un plateau à Rancho California bénéficient d'un microclimat particulièrement favorable à la viticulture : bonne humidité sans trop de chaleur, et une période de culture très longue. Dirigé par Dwayne Helmuth, Callaway ne produit que du vin, environ 100 000 caisses chaque année. C'est aujourd'hui le premier centre vinicole du sud de la Californie. 65 % des raisins nécessaires à la fabrication du Fumé Blanc, Sauvignon Blanc, Chenin Blanc sec, Chardonnay, Riesling Blanc, Vin Blanc et d'un vin de dessert, « Sweet Nancy », sont achetés.

Callaway fut racheté par les distillateurs canadiens Hiram Walter en 1981 puis par les brasseurs irlandais Guinness en 1986.

États-Unis : États de l'Est

Maryland

Le climat de cet État convient éminemment à la culture de la vigne à vin. Mais, à une exception près, on n'en tire guère profit. Cette exception est la firme Boordy Vineyard, à Ryderwood, près de Baltimore, où J. et J. Wagner (M. et Mme Philip M. Wagner) non seulement faisaient du vin, mais procédaient à des expériences sur différents types de raisin. Les sols consacrés à ces expériences sont plantés de diverses hybrides. Ce sont les Wagner qui introduisirent à l'échelle commerciale des hybrides français. Néanmoins ils font aussi du vin, ne serait-ce que pour montrer les grandes qualités que l'on peut tirer des vins de l'est des États-Unis fait avec des raisins hybrides à condition qu'on les traite comme il convient. Jusqu'à présent les résultats sont louables et la contribution des Wagner à la viniculture américaine est importante. En 1980, les Wagner vendirent l'entreprise vinicole à un viticulteur de la région et cessèrent de produire du vin. Ils continuent néanmoins à cultiver des vignes dont le raisin est vendu aux Vins de Boordy, à vendre des plants de vigne et à donner des conférences sur le vin. Concurremment avec la Seneca Foods Corporation, les Vins de Boordy sont produits sur une bien plus grande échelle à Penn-Yan, État de New York, et Proser, État de Washington.

Michigan

On cultive la vigne au sud de cet État, à Benton Harbor et à Paw Paw, près du lac Michigan. Le Concord occupe la plus grande place dans les vignobles avec du Catawba et du Delaware. On y fait des vins secs, doux, mousseux et non mousseux qui sont malheureusement inférieurs à ceux produits ailleurs aux États-Unis. La première entreprise vinicole, pour la quantité, est le Michigan Wineries, qui produit des vins faits avec des variétés indigènes et hybrides. Dans le comté de Berrien, à proximité du lac, se trouve le vignoble Tabor Hill qui donne du bon vin de table ; on y trouve également des plantations expérimentales de *Vitis vinifera* tels que le Chardonnay et le Riesling. Ici comme ailleurs, les variétés *vinifera* et certains hybrides — Chelois, Cascade ou Foch, par exemple — assureront l'avenir des bons vins de table. L'appellation à l'étude pour cette région est *Lake Michigan Shores.*

New York

L'État de New York, avec ses soixante-quinze entreprises vinicoles, vient en deuxième place après la Californie. La production en 1985 était de 1,2 million d'hl de vin (plus de 13 millions de caisses) environ 6 % de la production des États-Unis. D'après les derniers chiffres disponibles, qui datent de 1980, la superficie des vignobles serait de 16 600 ha dont 7 700 ha produisent des raisins à vin. Le reste est destiné à la fabrication de jus, gelées et autres produits. En 1986, environ 75 000 tonnes de raisin furent utilisées pour fabriquer du vin à New York, dont 50 % de *labrusca* (utilisé essentiellement pour les « wine coolers »), 40 % d'hybrides et 10 % de *vinifera.*

Les vins de l'Est des États-Unis ont peu de chose en commun avec ceux d'Europe. Il ne faudrait pas toutefois considérer cette différence comme un signe immédiat d'infériorité. Les vins indigènes de n'importe quel pays au monde ont leurs propres mérites pour être consommés en certaines occasions ; quand le vigneron prend conscience de la fonction et produit des vins qui jouent leur rôle, ces derniers ne peuvent pas être remplacés par des produits d'autres pays. Évidemment certains de ces vignerons comprennent la situation mieux que d'autres. Cela explique la rivalité entre les réalistes qui s'efforcent d'adapter leur production aux conditions de sol et de climat, et ceux qui s'échinent en vain à imiter des vins qui ne peuvent provenir que d'Europe ou de Californie.

Pour aggraver la confusion, il existe une autre rivalité entre les vignerons les plus réalistes : certains prônent les variétés de vignes indigènes et d'autres tendent de plus en plus à utiliser des hybrides. Actuellement, les premiers ont plus de partisans, mais les hybrides pourraient fort bien être les vignes de l'avenir.

A quelques exceptions près, les partisans des hybrides entrent en fureur au sujet de tels coupages. Même une petite addition de jus de raisin indigène donne au vin un goût caractéristique (le foxe, de *fox* : renard) ; on dit aussi qu'il est noahté (de *noah* : variété américaine au gout de foxe très prononcé) ; ce défaut provient vraisemblablement du goût et de l'arôme prononcés des vignes sauvages dites « vignes renard ». Les amateurs de vin qui n'aiment pas cette caractéristique — et ils sont nombreux — assurent qu'il faut l'éliminer, sinon l'Est des États-Unis ne produira jamais de vin dont il puisse être fier. Ceux que le foxe ne dérange pas — et il y en a — le considèrent comme la marque traditionnelle des vins américains et estiment que le faire disparaître serait priver le pays d'une part de son patrimoine. L'histoire sera seul juge.

Histoire du vin

New York fut un des premiers États à planter de la vigne, au milieu du XVIIe siècle, à Long Island et Manhattan.

La première maison de vins, Brotherhood Winery, ouvrit en 1839 dans la région de l'Hudson River. Brotherhood et Thomas Vineyards de Californie furent fondées la même année et sont les plus anciennes des États-Unis.

Pendant des décennies les vins de New York eurent la réputation d'être doux et « foxé » et produits principalement à base de Concord. En 1952, Charles Fournier de Gold Seal, éminent œnologue d'origine française, employa Konstantin Franck, un immigrant russe, pour planter et expérimenter des vignes *vinifera*.

Après la prohibition, l'industrie du vin à New York se développa lentement, atteignant le chiffre de trente-neuf maisons de vins en 1976. Cette même année dans un effort pour encourager cet important business agricole, l'État passa une loi « Farm Winery Act » qui facilita l'ouverture de maisons de vins. L'État compte aujourd'hui environ soixante-dix maisons de vins.

Au moment où la loi « Farm Winery Act » fut votée on avait fait suffisamment de recherches pour identifier un certain nombre de candidats susceptibles de remplacer Concord comme pivot de l'industrie du vin de New York. De nouvelles maisons de vins mettant l'accent sur ces *vinifera* et hybrides sortirent de terre en même temps que la vigne. Les progrès furent étonnants et l'avenir est peut-être même plus grand qu'en Californie.

Les variétés de blanc correspondaient le mieux au climat frais et vif de New York. Cependant un travail sérieux a été effectué dans l'État pour améliorer les variétés de rouge. Les vins mousseux connaissent une renaissance, certaines maisons de vins expérimentent la méthode champenoise. Des vins de type porto ou sherry sont aussi prometteurs, et sans perdre de vue leurs livres de comptes, les maisons de vins mettent au point des vins simples, agréables et qui se boivent bien, mousseux et semblables au Lambrusco, pour inviter la jeune génération aux plaisirs du vin.

Cependant le climat pose quelques problèmes. Il faut souvent chaptaliser (sucrer) le jus non fermenté pour obtenir un vin stable. En automne, la pluie gêne souvent les vendanges, provoque la pourriture et allonge le vin. Les hivers rigoureux font « mourir les pousses », les pieds, les souches et même les plants et de plus la vigne peut contracter la galle. Un dégel prématuré peut provoquer la sortie des bourgeons et les exposer au gel. Pour élever de la vigne dans l'État de New York il faut être téméraire, mais la qualité du vin en vaut la peine.

Jusqu'ici les meilleures variétés de rouges ont été le Baco Noir, Chancellor, Chelois et Léon Millot.

Quand aux meilleures variétés de blancs ce sont le Riesling, Chardonnay, Gewürztraminer, Seyval Blanc, Vignoles, Vidal Blanc et Cayuga White. C'est sans doute à cause du climat frais et du sol ardoisier que le Riesling semble avoir été si prometteur. Le Riesling de New York a un arôme qui rappelle la pomme et la fraise et que l'on retrouve dans les bons Riesling allemands, avec même plus de piquant et de tonus que les Riesling de Californie.

Régions vinicoles de l'État de New York et des autres États américains

Les quelque 16 200 ha de vignobles à vin sont répartis en quatre régions distinctes ; la plus célèbre est de loin le secteur des Finger Lakes, suivie de la prometteuse vallée de l'Hudson. Viennent ensuite la partie américaine du Lake Erie et la partie est de Long Island.

1. *Finger Lakes.* Les vignobles les plus importants sont au bord des lacs Keuka et Canandaigua, et, dans une moindre mesure, des lacs Seneca et, Cayuga. Les Finger Lakes forment un ensemble de fentes creusées par quelque ancien glacier et qui s'étendent en s'écartant comme les doigts d'une main ouverte, dans un paysage doucement vallonné. Le climat habituellement dur au nord de l'État de New York est tempéré par ces lacs qui se remplissent au printemps et devient presque idéal pour la culture de la vigne. On y fait surtout du mousseux, sans dédaigner les autres vins. Le sol pierreux, volcanique, est riche en minéraux et les racines des vignes y pénètrent assez profondément pour ne pas souffrir du gel pendant l'hiver ; les eaux souterraines les nourrissent pendant les mois d'été arides. Bien que les premières vignes aient été plantées en 1829 à Hammondsport par le révérend épiscopal James Bostwick, on ne commença à produire du vin à grande échelle que plusieurs dizaines d'années plus tard. Lorsque de nombreuses entreprises vinicoles s'établirent dans la région après la Guerre de Sécession, elles produisirent surtout du mousseux. On y fait surtout encore des mousseux de différents types, sans négliger pour autant les autres vins.

La zone Hammondsport-Pleasant Valley, à l'extrémité sud du lac Keuka, est le siège de plusieurs firmes, notamment de la grande Taylor Wine Company et de sa filiale, Pleasant Valley Wine Company — qui produit le célèbre Great Western New York State, sorte de champagne. Pleasant Valley et Taylor font des coupages avec plus de trente variétés de raisin, dont la moitié sont des hybrides. On les cultive dans des vignobles situés à 190 km des centres vinificateurs, situés l'un à côté de l'autre dans la ville de Hammondsport.

A quelques kilomètres au nord de ces deux entreprises, se trouve la Gold Seal Winery, agréablement située sur la rive ouest du lac Keuka. Gold Seal, autrefois appelée Urbana Wine Company, est surtout connue pour ses mousseux produits sous la marque Charles Fournier. La plupart des mousseux de Finger Lakes sont faits encore avec des raisins Catawba, Delaware, Elvira et un peu d'Isabella, et coupés dans la plupart des cas avec des vins de Californie neutres ou à goût plat. Ce coupage est nécessaire : il sert à diminuer l'insupportable goût de foxe des variétés indigènes. La plupart de ces mousseux fermentent en bouteille. Un ancien directeur de Gold Seal, M. Fournier, se distingua par son efficacité en engageant un des spécialistes en vins les plus intéressants des États-Unis, le docteur Konstantin Frank, et lui permit de mettre en application certaines de ces idées.

2. *Vallée de l'Hudson*. C'est la plus ancienne région vinicole qui produit du vin sans interruption depuis que des huguenots y plantèrent des vignes en 1677. Bien que le fleuve Hudson ne tempère guère la région, la vallée très encaissée reçoit l'air maritime. Il y a 400 ha de vignobles, ils ne sont pas tous plantés sur les coteaux de la rivière. Certains se répandent jusqu'à la frontière de l'État du Connecticut. Le sol est complexe, avec des strates argileuses, de l'ardoise, du schiste et du calcaire. La plupart des entreprises vinicoles (environ 15) sont postérieures au Winery Act de 1976. La popularité des *vinifera* est en recul. Les hybrides prospèrent et les vins rouges y sont meilleurs qu'à Finger Lakes.

3. *Lake Erie*.Ce secteur commence près de Buffalo, longe la rive du lac Erie,

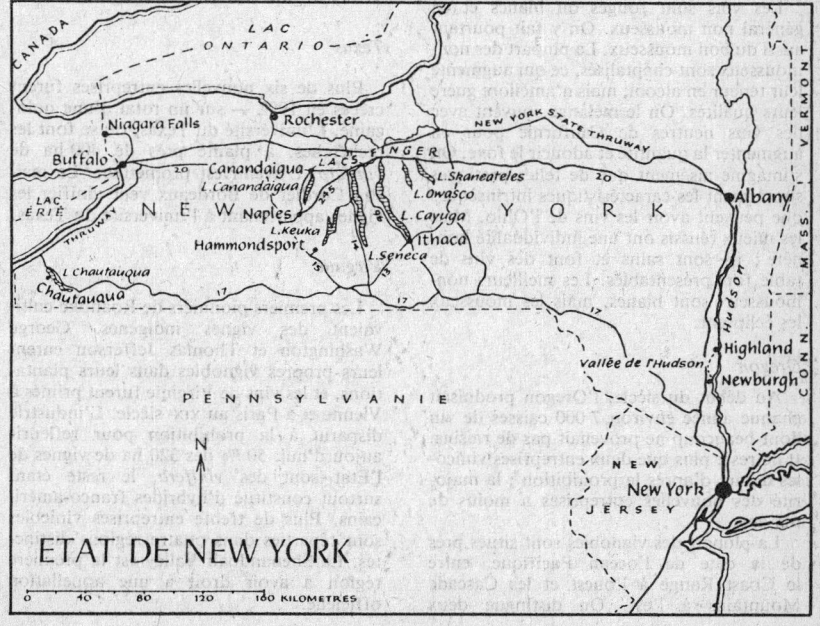

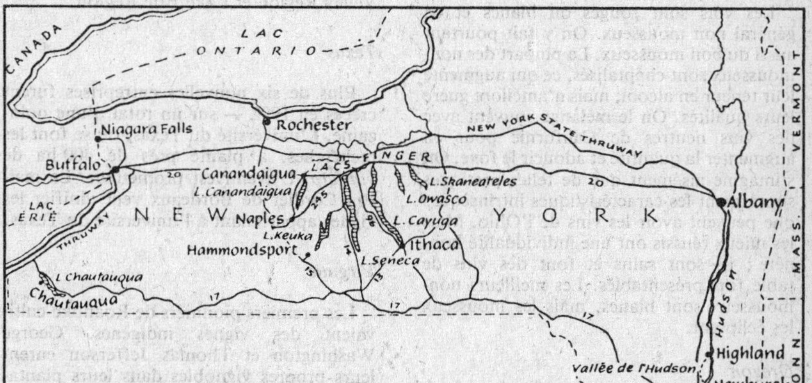

pénètre en Pennsylvanie et finit en Ohio. Le Concord abonde dans ses vignobles. On le consomme surtout comme raisin de table. Le vin de Chautauqua est Kascher.

4. *Long Island*. Les vignes s'étendent sur les deux rives du Niagara, entre les lacs Erié et Ontario, tant dans l'État de New York qu'au Canada. Du côté américain on fait des quantités considérables de vin de table, en partie avec des hybrides et en partie avec des raisins indigènes qui sont cultivés en général à l'est de Buffalo (*voir aussi* CANADA).

Ohio

La plus grande zone vinicole de cet État borde le lac Erie entre Vermillon et Port Clinton. Sandusky en constitue le centre géographique et économique. Les vignobles les plus importants se trouvent sur Middle Bass Island — talonnés de très près par ceux de Kelley — et sur les îles North Bass et South Bass (ou Put-in-Bay). Le Catawba y est préféré par tradition bien qu'il ait été remplacé récemment dans une certaine mesure par d'autres variétés indigènes et quelques hybrides.

Les vins sont rouges ou blancs et en général non mousseux. On y fait pourtant aussi du bon mousseux. La plupart des non-mousseux sont chaptalisés, ce qui augmente leur teneur en alcool, mais n'améliore guère leurs qualités. On le mélange souvent avec des vins neutres de Californie pour en augmenter la quantité et adoucir le foxe. On s'imagine aisément que de telles pratiques suppriment les caractéristiques intrinsèques que peuvent avoir les vins de l'Ohio. Mais les mieux réussis ont une individualité honnête ; ils sont sains et font des vins de table fort présentables. Les meilleurs non-mousseux sont blancs, mais les mousseux les éclipsent.

Oregon

Au début du siècle, l'Oregon produisait chaque année environ 7 000 caisses de vin dont beaucoup ne provenait pas de raisins. Il ne reste plus que deux entreprises vinicoles datant d'après la prohibition ; la majorité des nouvelles entreprises a moins de dix ans.

La plupart des vignobles sont situés près de la côte de l'océan Pacifique, entre le Coast Range à l'ouest et les Cascade Mountains à l'est. On distingue deux régions viticoles : l'une au nord sur la rivière Willamette près de Portland, l'autre au sud sur les berges des rivières Umpqua et Rouge, près de Roseburg. La vallée Willamette est une région de 8 000 m² entourée de frontières naturelles : la rivière Columbia au Nord, la chaîne montagneuse de Gast Range à l'ouest, les montagnes Calapooya au sud et les montagnes Cascade à l'est. On y trouve la majorité des vignobles et entreprises vinicoles de l'Oregon. L'Oregon produit l'un des meilleurs Pinot Noir des États-Unis, ainsi que du Gewürztraminer, Chardonnay, Riesling et Riesling botrytisé. Il y a plus de soixante *wineries* ou viticulteurs en Oregon qui est un des meilleurs sites au monde, en dehors de la Côte d'Or en Bourgogne, pour la plantation de Pinot Noir.

Pennsylvanie

La plupart des entreprises vinicoles (plus de 55) se trouvent soit au sud-est, de Philadelphie à Harrisburg, soit au nord-est, autour du lac Erie. Les appellations officielles sont respectivement Lancaster Velley Region et Lake Erie Region.

Texas

Plus de six nouvelles entreprises furent créées en 1982 — sur un total d'une quinzaine. L'université du Texas, où se font les recherches, a planté près de 400 ha de *vinifera*. L'avenir est prometteur. La maison Cordier de Bordeaux veut vinifier les vignes appartenant à l'université du Texas.

Virginie

Les premiers pionniers de Roanoke cultivaient des vignes indigènes. George Washington et Thomas Jefferson eurent leurs propres vignobles dans leurs plantations, et les vins de Virginie furent primés à Vienne et à Paris au XIXᵉ siècle. L'industrie disparut à la prohibition pour refleurir aujourd'hui. 50 % des 320 ha de vignes de l'État sont des *vinifera*, le reste étant surtout constitué d'hybrides franco-américains. Plus de trente entreprises vinicoles sont réparties dans quatre régions distinctes. La Shenandoah Valley est la première région à avoir droit à une appellation officielle.

Washington

D'ici à quelques années, l'État de Washington pourrait bien produire plus de raisins que tous les autres, la Californie exceptée. On compte environ soixante entreprises vinicoles, dont huit se sont lancées depuis 1975. Columbia Valley est l'appellation B.A.T.F. pour les vignobles de l'État répartis entre la vallée de Yakima et celle de Wallawalla. Les plantations de *vinifera* couvrent actuellement quelque 5 000 ha mais le vignoble s'accroît régulièrement.

Le climat des secteurs vinicoles de Washington est aussi favorable que celui des meilleures régions de Californie. Les vallées sont fraîches, assez peu touchées par le gel, et la saison dure assez longtemps pour donner des raisins mûris à point, bien équilibrés en sucre et acidité. Ces conditions font des vignobles de Washington un terrain d'élection pour les meilleures variétés de *Vitis vinifera* (qui sont les raisins à vins utilisés en Europe). On trouve les variétés Pinot Noir, Cabernet Sauvignon, Gewürztraminer, Riesling, Sémillon et Chardonnay dans les parcelles expérimentales et à la station d'expérimentation agricole de l'État de Washington, ainsi que dans les nombreux vignobles privés récents.

Washington se consacre plus à la production de raisin qu'à la viniculture et approvisionne des entreprises vinicoles de la Californie du Sud, de la Colombie britannique du Sud au Canada. La firme American Wine Growers, de l'État de Washington, fait ses vins (sous l'appellation Ste Michelle) avec des raisins cultivés dans l'État, de même que la firme Associated Vintners of Kirkland maintenant appelée Columbia Winery. Les Boordy Vineyards de Philip Wagner ont planté des raisins *vinifera* et construit un grand centre vinificateur à Prosser, dans la vallée de Yakima. Les hybrides sont également courants. L'État voisin d'Idaho offre sur une échelle plus réduite de bonnes perspectives. La firme Troy Winery produit déjà des vins avec ses propres raisins, dont le Pinot Noir, l'Aurora et le Riesling.

Autres états viticoles des États-Unis

Arizona, Colorado, Connecticut, Delaware, Floride, Géorgie, Idaho, Indiana, Illinois, Iowa, Kentucky, Louisiane, Massachusetts, Minnesota, Mississippi, Missouri, Montana, New Hampshire, New Jersey, New Mexico, Oklahoma, Rhode Island, Caroline du Sud, Tennessee, Utah et Wisconsin.

Éthers

Corps chimiques composés qui comptent parmi les composants importants des vins et spiritueux, auxquels ils confèrent bouquet ou arôme.

Éthiopie

Quoique plusieurs nations d'Afrique soient productrices de vin, l'Éthiopie n'en fait pas partie. Si on le compare aux quantités produites par l'Algérie, l'Afrique du Sud, le Maroc, la Tunisie et l'Égypte, le total annuel moyen — environ 50 000 hl (555 000 caisses) — était plutôt minime. Les trois principales régions viticoles — productrices de raisins à vin comme de raisins de table — sont Abadir-Dukem, Guder et Érythrée au nord du pays. Les variétés Sultana et Muscat Noir prédominent dans les quelque 500 ha de vignobles, mais une grande partie du vin est également faite avec des concentrés. Parmi les quelques centres vinificateurs, citons le Domaine Elaberet, Makanissa, Altavilla et Alexandrakis ; la plupart de leurs vins accusent encore aujourd'hui l'influence mussolienne.

Étiquette

Spécifie les caractéristiques d'un vin.

Etna (D.O.C.)

Vins rouges, blancs ou rosés de Sicile *(voir ce nom)*.

Étoile

Un des meilleurs vins blancs du Jura français produit dans la partie la plus méridionale de cette région.

Voir JURA

Eudémis

Microlépidoptère, c'est-à-dire papillon microscopique, qui détruit le raisin.
Voir CHAPITRE IV

Eumelan

Raisin à vin rouge de l'est des États-Unis. Rendement faible, sans intérêt pour les producteurs de vin.

Évangile (Château l')

Bordeaux rouge. Commune de Pomerol.
Voisin de Château Cheval-Blanc en Saint-Émilion, ce cru fait un vin excellent. Les Ducasse en sont les heureux propriétaires.
Superficie : 13 ha.
Production moyenne : 40 tonneaux (4 000 caisses).

Excoriose

Maladie cryptogamique extrêmement rare de la vigne.
Voir CHAPITRE IV

Expédition (liqueur d')

Terme champenois désignant une solution de sucre, de vin et parfois d'eau-de-vie, que l'on ajoute au mousseux après avoir enlevé le bouchon, juste avant de l'expédier.
Voir CHAMPAGNE

Exportation de vin

Les chiffres varient inévitablement d'année en année selon les vendanges et les fluctuations industrielles et politiques. Le taux d'exportation pour les deux premiers pays producteurs — Italie et France — augmente régulièrement, alors que l'Algérie — qui était jusqu'à présent le plus gros exportateur — est en baisse. Si l'Argentine, les États-Unis et l'Union Soviétique sont d'importants producteurs, ils n'exportent pas grand-chose.

Extra-Dry

Mention qui figure sur certaines étiquettes de Champagne. Elle désigne seulement un Champagne assez sec. Le Champagne vraiment sec sera étiqueté brut.

Ezerjó

Variété de raisin à vin blanc cultivée en Hongrie. Elle donne son nom à un vin charnu, de couleur or, fait à Mór, près de Budapest.

EXPORTATIONS DE VIN DANS LE MONDE
(en hectolitres)

Italie	14 800 000
France	8 800 000
Espagne	5 400 000
Bulgarie	2 400 000
Hongrie	2 400 000
Allemagne fédérale	2 000 000
Portugal	1 600 000
Algérie	1 300 000
Yougoslavie	1 100 000
Grèce	650 000
Roumanie	550 000
U.R.S.S.	490 000
Chypre	375 000
Tunisie	360 000
Autriche	330 000
Maroc	300 000
Argentine	200 000
États-Unis	175 000
Belgique	170 000
Grande-Bretagne	150 000
Albanie	115 000
Afrique du Sud	85 000
Luxembourg	81 000
Australie	75 000
Chili	72 000
Pays-Bas	66 000
Malte	50 000
Israël	49 000
Tchécoslovaquie	44 000
Turquie	40 000
Égypte	25 000
Suisse	8 000
Total	40 260 000

Les chiffres ci-dessus représentent les moyennes des dernières années, corrigées de façon à projeter les tendances des années à venir. Dans certains cas, notamment pour la Grande-Bretagne et les Pays-Bas, les statistiques comprennent les vins réexportés.

F

Factory House

Club et immeuble où siège ce club, à Vila Nova de Gaia près de Oporto (Portugal). On y boit les meilleurs Porto du monde. De nos jours il est plus correct de l'appeler British Association, mais tout le monde continue à dire Feitoria Inglesa (Factorerie anglaise). Jadis le système des factoreries était un des privilèges d'extraterritorialité dont jouissaient les Britanniques en pays étranger. C'est par courtoisie envers les Portugais que le nom de club a changé. De nos jours encore, pourtant, les entreprises britanniques de commerce du Porto jouissent de faveurs particulières accordées à aucune autre au Portugal.

Tous les associés anglais des entreprises de Porto, à Oporto, étaient autrefois membres de ce club, sauf si un Portugais faisait partie de la firme.

Falerno

Vignobles où l'on fait le Falerne contemporain sur les flancs du mont Massico (à peu près à mi-chemin entre Rome et Naples). Leurs vins sont généralement blancs, demi-secs et pas trop forts.

Le Falerne était le vin le plus célèbre de la Rome antique. Il venait déjà des monts Massico, mais nous ne savons pas avec quels raisins on le faisait et nous ne pouvons nous faire qu'une idée approximative du goût qu'il avait.

Voir CAMPANIE ; ANTIQUITÉ (VINS DE L')

Falernum

Sirop ne titrant guère que 6° d'alcool, fait aux Bermudes et aux Antilles britanniques, avec du sucre, du citron, des amandes, du gingembre et d'autres épices. Il sert à améliorer le goût des punchs et autres breuvages à base de rhum.

Fan Leaf

Nom en langue anglaise du court noué : dégénérescence infectieuse de la vigne.

Voir CHAPITRE IV

Fara (D.O.C.)

Vin rouge du Piémont *(voir ce nom)*, en Italie.

Fass

Nom allemand du fût, du tonneau.

Fassle

En allemand : petit tonnelet utilisé à peu près de la même manière que la gourde en France et le *porrón* en Espagne, c'est-à-dire en faisant jaillir le liquide directement dans la bouche, la tête rejetée en arrière. Le Fassle contient environ 5 l et un *Spitzle* remplace le fausset. Il faut une certaine adresse et une main sûre pour ne pas s'arroser la figure en buvant.

Faugères

Voir LANGUEDOC ; COTEAUX DU LANGUEDOC

Fausset

Trou dans une des deux faces plates d'un fût, par lequel on soutire le vin. Ce trou est obturé en général par un simple bâtonnet de bois dur et, quand le tonneau est « en perce », par un robinet.

Faye d'Anjou

Commune des coteaux du Layon, en Anjou, qui a droit à une appellation contrôlée particulière.
Voir ANJOU

Federweisser

Littéralement : blanc comme plume (laiteux). C'est le nom qu'on donne en Allemagne au vin nouveau servi dans les auberges après la vendange.

Feher Bor

En hongrois : vin blanc.

Feints

Résidu de la seconde distillation du malt servant à faire du Scotch.

Fendant

Les vins les plus populaires du Valais (Suisse) faits avec du Fendant : variété de Chasselas connu en Allemagne sous le nom de Gutedel.
Voir SUISSE

Fermé

Se dit d'un vin de qualité qui s'obstine à rester dur pendant de nombreuses années avant d'atteindre son sommet. Ces vins sont généralement très riches en tanin ; l'année 1975 produisit de tels vins.

Fermentation

Décomposition du sucre en deux composants essentiels : alcool éthylique et gaz carbonique. Gay-Lussac en a donné la formule :

$$C_6H_{12}O_6 \rightarrow 2\ C_2H_6O \quad 2\ CO_2$$
$$(180\ g) \quad (92\ g) \quad (88\ g)$$

Malheureusement, cette équation n'est pas tout à fait exacte. Des mesures précises ont démontré que, si l'alcool devrait représenter 51 % du sucre, il n'équivaut en réalité qu'à 47 %. Les 4 % restants sont composés de divers produits : alcools plus volatiles, composés azotés, glycérine, etc.

La fermentation est provoquée par les enzymes des levures. Il existe diverses espèces de levures qui ont chacune un effet différent sur les sucres offerts à la fermentation (surtout ceux du raisin, de la canne à sucre et du lait). Pour que la fermentation ait lieu de manière satisfaisante, il faut contrôler la température et l'aération.
Voir CHAPITRE V

Fernet Branca

La marque la plus connue de bitter italien. On le consomme comme apéritif. Il est recommandé pour les estomacs fatigués et les lendemains d'excès alcooliques.
Voir BITTER

Ferrière (Château-)

Bordeaux rouge. Commune de Margaux, en Haut-Médoc.

Situé au cœur du village de Margaux, ce bon vignoble — classé Troisième Cru en 1855 — est actuellement loué aux propriétaires de Château-Lascombes qui en tirent chaque année une quantité limitée de vin rouge.

Ferrocyanure

Vulgairement appelé bleu de Prusse, le ferrocyanure de potassium sert au collage du vin.
Voir COLLAGE ; CHAPITRE V

Fiano

Le raisin avec lequel on fait les vins légers et peu âpres d'Avellino, près de Naples.

Fiasco

En français : fiasque. Bouteille de vin enrobée de sparterie et contenant à peu près 2 l. Utilisée en Italie, surtout pour le Chianti.

Fieuzal (Château de)

Bordeaux rouge et blanc. Commune de Léognan, en Graves.

Ce vignoble, qui appartint jadis à la famille La Rochefoucauld, planté sur un bon coteau pierreux était bien géré par son ex-propriétaire M. Érik de Bocke. Impresario autant que vigneron, M. de Bocke vendit, en 1974, son vignoble à M. Negrevergne, un fabricant de produits pharmaceutiques bordelais et il est bien géré par M. Gribelin. Fieuzal est un Cru classé des Graves depuis 1959.

Caractéristiques : en fait de qualité, ces vins peuvent tenir tête à peu près à n'importe quel Graves. Le rouge est généreux, velouté et a un charmant bouquet ; le blanc est sec et racé.

Superficie : rouge 29 ha ; blanc 3 ha.

Production moyenne : rouge 100 tonneaux (10 000 caisses) ; blanc 12 tonneaux (1 200 caisses).

Figeac (Château)

Bordeaux rouge. Commune et secteur de Saint-Émilion.

Un des Saint-Émilion les plus connus depuis longtemps, classé parmi les Premiers Grands Crus en 1955, Figeac ne doit pas être confondu avec d'autres crus de Saint-Émilion qui emploient ce nom en diverses combinaisons. Six crus entourent Château-Figeac (Charles de Figeac était un jurat noble de Saint-Émilion), mais ce nom employé sans aucune association quelconque appartient au meilleur, qui est aussi un des plus vastes de Saint-Émilion. Touchant Cheval-Blanc, près de la limite de Pomerol, les vignes entourent un château et un chai reliés par une large avenue qui coupe à travers un parc splendide. Le propriétaire actuel, Thierry Manoncourt, est un viticulteur ardent et épris de progrès, qui a récemment fait construire un nouveau chai de toute beauté.

Caractéristiques : Ce vin a retrouvé et dépassé sa forme durant ces quelque quinze dernières années. C'est un des meilleurs Saint-Émilion en dépit de son prix élevé ; très caractéristique, il est robuste et bien arrondi.

Superficie : 40 ha.

Production moyenne : 130 tonneaux, 13 000 caisses.

Filhot (Château-)

Bordeaux blanc. Commune et secteur de Sauternes.

Ce vignoble appartient à Henri de Vaucelles. Il produit des vins un peu plus secs qu'Yquem. En général on considère qu'il mérite mieux que le titre de Second Cru de Sauternes datant de 1855 et qu'une nouvelle classification en ferait un Premier Cru. Belle construction du XVIIIe siècle, le château, entouré de gazon, a plutôt l'air d'une maison de campagne anglaise que française. Il se trouve d'ailleurs que Château-Filhot a toujours de nombreux partisans en Angleterre.

Caractéristiques : Forte teneur en alcool ; un des Sauternes les plus secs et, à ce titre une exception.

Superficie : 50 ha.

Production moyenne : 100 tonneaux (10 000 caisses).

Fillette

En langage familier : demi-bouteille de vin. Surtout employé en Anjou.

Filtrage

Procédé de clarification du vin qui consiste à le faire passer à travers un filtre (en général de papier) afin de le débarrasser des particules en suspension. Dans maintes régions de grands vins on recourt à des méthodes plus anciennes de clarification. Facile et pratique, le filtrage peut priver le bon vin d'une partie de sa qualité. C'était surtout vrai lorsqu'on utilisait les filtres à amiante Seitz, aujourd'hui abandonnés.

De trop nombreuses couches, ou bien la négligence, peuvent détruire toute distinction, laissant un vin insipide et sans aucun caractère.

Fine Champagne

Il ne s'agit pas de Champagne mais de Cognac. On obtient la Fine Champagne par coupage d'eaux-de-vie de la Petite et de la Grande Champagne.

« Une fine », c'est ainsi qu'on commande généralement du Cognac en France : quelle qu'en soit son origine, mais c'est une erreur, car la Fine, comme indiqué ci-dessus, est une eau-de-vie provenant des meilleurs secteurs de la région de Cognac, les plus crayeux.

Finesse

Qualité du vin doué d'élégance ou de race exceptionnelles.

Finger Lakes

Région vinicole du nord de l'État de New York. L'une des plus importantes de l'est des États-Unis. On y fait quelques-uns des meilleurs mousseux d'Amérique. Les vignobles les plus favorisés sont situés au bord des lacs Keuka et Canandaigua, et les autres autour de lacs Seneca et Cayuga. Quelques-unes des firmes vinicoles les plus importantes ont leur siège dans le district de Pleasant Valley-Hammondsport. Outre d'excellents mousseux on y fait d'autres types de vin.

Voir ÉTATS-UNIS : ÉTAT DE L'EST

Fino

Le type de Xérès le plus sec.

Fins Bois

Un des secteurs de la région de Cognac moins réputé que Grande Champagne ou Petite Champagne mais dont les eaux-de-vie sont la base des Trois-Étoiles « *** ».

Voir COGNAC

Fior d'Alpi

Littéralement Fleurs des Alpes. Liqueur italienne sucrée, jaune, et qui contient en général des cristaux de sucre. On la vend dans une bouteille caractéristique, haute et étroite.

Fitou (Appellation Contrôlée)

Vin rouge du Midi. Sud de la France.

Région vinicole française d'une importance plus historique qu'actuelle. Située juste au nord du Roussilon et de la frontière espagnole, Fitou comprend neuf communes : Fitou, Leucate, Caves-de-Treilles (divisée en deux régions : Lapalme, près de la côte méditerranéenne, entre Narbonne et Perpignan, à la sortie de l'autoroute A9, la Languedocienne, et Tuchan), Paziols, Cascatel, Villeneuve-des-Corbières et Treilles, qui sont situées à 25 km à l'intérieur du pays. Le soleil chaud de la Méditerranée tombe brutalement sur les coteaux presque stériles dont 2 000 ha environ sont plantés de vignes.

Pour avoir droit à l'appellation Fitou, le vin doit être fait avec au moins 90 % de Grenache et/ou de Lldoner Pelut et/ou de Carignan (maximum 75 %). Les autres 10 % peuvent être un ou plusieurs des suivants : Cinsault, Terret noir, Maccabeo, Mourvèdre et Syrah. Production maximale à l'hectare : 40 hl, sauf en années exceptionnelles. Foncé, plein, très savoureux, d'une forte teneur en alcool, le Fitou est un des meilleurs vins du Midi. La qualité du Fitou varie énormément selon la vocation des caves coopératives dans la sélection de leur cuve, du goût désagréablement herbacé à une satisfaisante plénitude.

Pour avoir droit à l'appellation contrôlée, le Fitou doit vieillir en fût pendant neuf mois. La production moyenne annuelle est de 80 000 hl (près de 900 000 caisses).

Fixe (Acidité)

L'acidité du vin est due à deux catégories d'acides : les fixes et les volatiles. Le principal acide fixe est le tartrique qui donne au vin une âpreté agréable. Les acides fixes ne peuvent être éliminés par la distillation par vapeur.

Fixin (Appellation Contrôlée)

Bourgogne rouge. Côte de Nuits.

Fixin est la commune vinicole située le plus au nord de toutes celles de la Côte de Nuits. L'appellation Fixin englobe le territoire de Fixey qui lui fut rattaché en 1850. Situé à 10 km au sud de Dijon, sur la route des Grands Crus le village de Fixin compte près de 160 ha de vignes.

La plus grande partie des vins de Fixin (sur une superficie de 110 ha environ) peut être vendue sous l'appellation Côte de Nuits Village. D'autre part un peu plus de 22 ha de vignes de la commune ont droit à l'appellation d'origine Fixin Premier Cru. Les meilleurs de ces vins proviennent du Clos de la Perrière. Selon la classification, désormais périmée, des vignobles de la Côte-d'Or datant de 1860, ce cru était une Tête de Cuvée et avait seul cet honneur sur le territoire de Fixin. La classification plus récente faite par l'Institut national des appellations d'origine des vins et eaux-de-vie en a fait un Premier Crus de Fixin, honneur qu'il partage avec cinq autres vignes. Les vins du Clos de la Perrière sont colorés et fermes. Ils acquièrent en vieillissant une grande finesse et beaucoup de bouquet. Ils ressemblent beaucoup à ceux de la commune voisine, Gevrey-Chambertin. Certaines années ils peuvent surclasser les crus secondaires de Gevrey et se classer immédiatement après le grand Chambertin.

Les quelque 30 ha restants sont en appellation contrôlée Bourgogne.

PREMIERS CRUS

Cru	*Superficie (ha)*
Clos de la Perrière	16,53
Clos du Chapitre	4,70
Les Hervelets	3,64
Les Meix-Bas	1,88
Clos Napoléon	1,82

Flagey-Échezeaux

Flagey-Échezeaux est une localité mais pas une appellation d'origine. Pourtant deux de ses vignobles ont droit à leur propre appellation contrôlée. L'agglomération se trouve à gauche de la grand-route qui traverse la Côte de Nuits. Les limites de la commune s'enclavent entre Vougeot et Vosne-Romanée.

Les deux vignobles d'Échezeaux qui ont droit au titre de Grand Cru sont Échezeaux et Grands-Échezeaux *(voir ces noms)*. Les années où leurs vins ne se conforment pas aux normes rigoureuses, ils sont déclassés au rang de Premiers Crus de la commune voisine Vosne-Romanée, ils ont alors seulement droit à l'appellation Vosne-Romanée, sans autre indication d'origine.

Voir ÉCHEZEAUX

Flagon

Grosse bouteille ayant en général la forme d'un globule aplati et d'une capacité quelconque, ou bien bouteille trapue semblable à la Bocksbeutel *(voir ce mot)* de la Franconie. Utilisée pour les faux bourgognes du Commonwealth, surtout d'Australie.

Fleur

Pellicule qui se forme à la surface du vin ou du vinaigre, au contact de l'air. Elle se compose de moisissures appelées mycodermes.

Fleuri

On dit d'un vin qu'il est fruité et fleuri quand sa saveur rappelle le parfum des fleurs. Les vins fleuris le sont davantage dans leur jeunesse. Rares sont les grands vins qui sont doués de cette qualité.

Fleurie (Appellation Contrôlée)

Longtemps vendus sous l'appellation de Beaujolais, ces vins sont parmi les Beaujolais les plus typiques, ceux qui manifestent le mieux la fraîcheur et le charme fruité de ces vins rouges.

Voir BEAUJOLAIS

Flip

En anglais, boisson chaude composée de vin et/ou eau-de-vie, de glace pilée, de sucre, d'un œuf, auxquels on ajoute de la noix de muscade et divers arômes.

Floc

Apéritif d'Armagnac. Il est à l'Armagnac ce que le Pineau des Charentes est au Cognac. C'est un vin doux, non fermenté, à base d'Armagnac.

Flor

En espagnol : fleur. Il s'agit d'une pellicule blanche qui se forme, comme les fleurs, à la surface des Xérès. Quand cette « flor » apparaît, le vin devient un Fino. Dans le cas contraire, c'est un Oloroso. Certains vins du Jura sont sujets à cette flor.

Voir XÉRÈS ; CHAPITRE V

Floraison

Apparition des fleurs sur la plante. En viticulture, ce mot désigne la période pendant laquelle la vigne est en fleur et à la fin de laquelle apparaissent les petites baies vertes qui deviendront des raisins.

Fluid Ounce

Aux États-Unis, elle est égale à 1/16 de la pinte américaine standard (0,568 l) ; en Grande-Bretagne, elle désigne le volume d'une once standard d'eau pure mesurée à une température de 17°C et à une pression atmosphérique de 760 mm. Dans le système métrique, une once américaine correspond à 2 957 cl, et une once liquide anglaise à 2 841 cl : l'once américaine est donc d'environ 4 % supérieure à l'once anglaise.

Flûte

En France, bouteille longue et mince semblable à celles que l'on utilise pour les vins d'Alsace et du Rhin, mais en verre transparent. Les rosés sont de plus en plus fréquemment expédiés dans des flûtes.

La flûte est également un verre dans lequel on sert traditionnellement le vin mousseux et spécialement le Champagne. Sa forme élancée en V permet de retenir les précieuses bulles.

Folle Blanche

Variété de raisins la plus employée autrefois pour faire les vins maigres des Charentes que l'on distille pour obtenir du Cognac. La variété Saint-Émilion l'emporte maintenant sur la variété Folle Blanche (quoiqu'on en cultive encore dans la région de Cognac).

Fond

Voir CUL

Fontaine de vin

Pendant des siècles, les fontaines d'où s'écoulait du vin furent en honneur pendant les fêtes des vendanges ou autres réjouissances. Les vieilles chroniques allemandes attribuent la plus grande ancienneté à celle d'Urach (1474) ; le vin rouge et le vin blanc y alternèrent pendant trois jours et trois nuits à l'occasion d'un mariage royal. C'était également une coutume française. Lors de la première entrée d'un certain roi à Paris, une fontaine de vin s'écoulait dans une vasque si grande que des demoiselles y nageaient en costume d'Ève.

Égyptiens, Grecs et Romains connurent aussi les fontaines de vin. De nos jours on en reconstitue à l'occasion des vendanges dans de nombreux pays d'Europe.

Forbidden Fruit

Littéralement : fruit défendu. Liqueur américaine sans doute plus connue à l'étranger qu'aux États-Unis. Elle était faite avec du shaddock (espèce de gros pamplemousse en forme de poire à pulpe sèche et peu agréable à consommer : *Citrus maxima*) infusé dans de l'eau-de-vie de vin. De couleur brun-roux, elle était vendue dans des bouteilles rondes qui avaient la forme et la taille du shaddock.

Foreshots

« Tête » du distillat qui apparaît lorsqu'on fait bouillir du grain pour faire du whisky.

Forster Jesuitengarten

Le plus connu des vins remarquables de Forster, en Palatinat.

Voir PALATINAT

Forster Kirchenstück

Le meilleur des vins remarquables de Forster, en Palatinat.

Voir PALATINAT

Fortifiés (vins)

Vins additionnés d'eau-de-vie de vin. Il peut s'agir de mistelles, de vins doux naturels ou de vins de liqueur, selon le moment auquel l'alcool a été mis dans le moût ou dans le vin. Porto, Xérès, Malaga, Madère sont des vins fortifiés. Aux États-Unis, la loi interdit l'appellation « Fortified Wine » et les vins ainsi traités doivent être étiquetés : « Dessert Wine ». (En français, la désignation la plus correcte est « vins vinés ».)

Voir PORTO ; XÉRÈS ; MADÈRE ; MALAGA ; MISTELLE ; VINS DE LIQUEUR, VINS DOUX NATURELS, VINS VINÉS

Forzato

Nom que donnent les Italiens au vin fait avec des raisins plus que mûrs.

Foudre

Gros fût dans lequel on fait mûrir et on transporte le vin. Ce mot vient de l'allemand *Fuder*. On s'en sert surtout en Alsace où il a une capacité imprécise mais avoisinant le millier de litres.

Fourcas-Hosten (Château-)

Bordeaux rouge. Commune de Listrac, en Haut-Médoc.

La colline de Fourcas, à l'extrémité nord de Listrac, est le point culminant du plateau de Listrac que deux châteaux, également excellents, se partagent : Fourcas-Hosten et Fourcas-Dupré. Classé Bourgeois supérieur en 1855, Château-Fourcas-Hosten mérite sans doute mieux et pourrait être considéré comme un Grand Cru du Médoc. Jusqu'en 1951, il existait deux Fourcas-Hosten appartenant à des cousins. Ils sont désormais réunis entre les mains d'un seul propriétaire. En 1971, sous la direction de Bertrand de Rivoyre, la propriété fut cédée à un groupe d'amateurs de vin américains. Depuis, un vaste programme de plantation et d'amélioration a été déclenché. Monsieur Peynaud, ex-doyen de l'Institut œnologique de Bordeaux, supervise actuellement la vinification. Château-Fourcas-Hosten est donc en train de se constituer une solide réputation.

Caractéristiques : Vin charnu, un peu dur, mais pourtant distingué.

Superficie : 46 ha.

Production moyenne : 200 tonneaux, 18 000 caisses.

Fourtet (Clos)

Bordeaux rouge. Commune et secteur de Saint-Émilion.

Un des douze Premiers Grands Crus de Saint-Émilion selon la classification officielle de 1955 et celle de 1986. La vigne est plantée le long du mur d'enceinte de Saint-Émilion qui date du XIe siècle et qui est un des villages viticoles les plus pittoresques de France. Les caves, taillées dans le roc dur, sous les vignes, méritent d'être visitées. Le domaine appartient à la famille Lurton.

Caractéristiques : Ce bon vin charnu est le type même des Saint-Émilion. Néanmoins, selon des critiques récentes, la qualité aurait quelque peu décliné.

Superficie : 18 ha.

Production moyenne : 6 700 caisses.

Fox-grape, Foxe, Foxy

Nom familier de la *Vitis labrusca* qui pousse à l'état sauvage au nord-est et au nord-centre des États-Unis. Ses raisins ont une saveur bizarre, vaguement framboisée au premier contact avec la bouche, mais suivie par un arrière-goût très âcre. On peut en faire du vin, mais on y retrouve le même goût et le même arôme. Ces particularités gustatives n'ont rien de commun avec le « renard » et on appelle cette variété de vigne Fox-grape parce qu'elle vit à l'état sauvage, comme l'animal. C'est pourquoi les Français ont fort pertinemment traduit dans ce cas précis fox, par foxé, pour désigner la saveur et l'odeur particulières des raisins de ce genre et du vin qu'on en fait. Les Américains appellent cette particularité, foxy. On dit aussi en France que le vin est *noahté*, dérivé de Noah : la variété de *Vitis labrusca* la plus connue en Europe.

Une des variétés les plus courantes de *Vitis labrusca* cultivée aux États-Unis pour faire du vin est le cépage Concord.

Fraîcheur

Ce qui fait le charme engageant et brillant de tous les rosés, de la plupart des blancs et de quelques rouges ; cette qualité se révèle lorsque le vin est jeune, et disparaît avec l'âge. La plupart des vins blancs et tous les rosés d'aujourd'hui sont à leur sommet lorsque bus jeunes, avant que leur « vivacité » — un de leurs atouts majeurs — ne s'éteigne.

Fraise

Eau-de-vie ou alcool blanc fait par distillation de ce fruit.

Framboise

Eau-de-vie ou alcool blanc fait par distillation de ce fruit.

Franc de goût

Qualité d'un vin au goût nettement caractérisé.

France

Apprécier les bons vins est un des plaisirs des sociétés, milieux et individus les plus civilisés ; les plus grands vins du monde viennent de France, centre de la civilisation moderne, non seulement pour les beaux-arts, mais aussi pour les arts mineurs mais délicieux du manger et du boire. Le vin inspire les artistes ; il fait le bonheur des consommateurs ; il symbolise l'art de vivre français et c'est une de ses principales ressources agricoles économiques.

Les mystères de la vinification ne sauraient être réduits à des statistiques, pas plus qu'on ne peut définir un tableau en indiquant la surface de la toile ou le temps qu'il fallut pour le peindre. Néanmoins les statistiques ne sont pas à dédaigner.

Plus de 1 000 000 hectares, soit 3,35 % des terres cultivées sont plantées de vignes en France. La plus grande partie de ces raisins sont destinés à faire du vin. La production annuelle se répartit ainsi : 700 000 hl de jus de raisin non vinifié ; 13 000 000 de quintaux de raisins consommés en fruits et 66 000 000 hl de vin. Ce vin est en grande partie ordinaire, quoiqu'environ 20 000 000 d'hl soient classés comme vin d'appellation contrôlée. Pour pallier la surproduction, la superficie viticole, maintenant stabilisée, fût réduite progressivement de 100 000 ha.

Des millions de Français tirent directement ou indirectement leur subsistance ou avantages du vin. Ils sont vignerons, négociants, expéditeurs, ouvriers employés régulièrement sur les vignobles, fabricants de bouteilles, de matériel de viticulture et de viniculture, techniciens de laboratoire et une nuée de fonctionnaires dont la tâche ne consiste pas simplement à tenir à jour des statistiques, mais aussi à veiller à l'application des règlements qui assurent la qualité du vin. Si on y ajoute ceux qui transportent le vin avec d'autres marchandises, les boutiquiers qui ne vendent pas que du vin, on peut dire que bien d'autres Français vivraient moins bien sans cette denrée.

La France exporte environ 11,5 millions d'hl de vin et en importe à peu près autant, surtout des pays méditerranéens. Les États-Unis sont le plus gros client, suivis de l'Angleterre, du Bénélux et de l'Allemagne. La famille française moyenne dépense environ 1 % de son budget nourriture en vins ; la consommation par personne est l'une des plus importantes du monde : 82 l par an.

Cette quantité ne porte que sur les vins taxés. La consommation est beaucoup plus grande si l'on tient compte du vin consommé par le vigneron et qui, n'étant pas taxé, échappe aux statisticiens.

Le vin représente donc un secteur économique d'une importance capitale pour la France, un élément d'une valeur incalculable à son actif et une énorme source de devises étrangères. Mais le vin est beaucoup plus que ça en France : presque un genre de vie.

Histoire du vin en France

Les Gaulois faisaient du vin avant la conquête romaine, surtout autour de la colonie grecque de Massilia (Marseille). Les Romains répandirent la connaissance du vin dans toute la Gaule et enseignèrent aux Gaulois soit à planter les vignes qu'ils leur apportaient, soit à tailler et cultiver les vignes sauvages qui poussaient probablement dans certaines régions du pays.

La province (aujourd'hui Provence) romaine de Gaule conquise bien avant Jules César était reliée par des routes commerciales allant l'une de Béziers à la Garonne (déjà en contact maritime avec la Bretagne : aujourd'hui Grande-Bretagne), et l'autre, par le Rhône et la Saône jusqu'à la Moselle d'une part, et la Loire d'autre part. Les marchandises étaient transportées par voie fluviale jusqu'au port de Chalon-sur-Saône et de là par charrois. Le vin voyageait dans des amphores de terre cuite. On a retrouvé des fragments de ces grandes jarres dans le lit des cours d'eau et le long des routes. On a récupéré sur les fonds de la Méditerranée, parmi les épaves de bateaux coulés, des amphores encore bouchées, contenant toujours les restes d'un liquide : le vin nouveau de centaines d'années avant notre ère. C'est en Gaule qu'on inventa le tonneau dès l'époque gallo-romaine. Des siècles plus tard, Saint-Louis aimait à faire des fûts à ses heures de loisir. Allant d'un monastère à l'autre, il ne manquait pas de goûter le vin fait par les moines.

Petit à petit, on trouva et sélectionna de nouvelles variétés de vignes plus robustes, et les surfaces plantées de vignes s'étendirent vers le nord. D'abord le long des rives du Rhône, puis jusqu'à la Loire, la Bretagne et l'Ile-de-France. Dès le début du Moyen Age, avant les vins de Gascogne, Londres recevait des vins du Rhin et des *Vins de France* — c'est-à-dire des environs de Paris — qui étaient très estimés. Puis, la demande croissant, les bateaux anglais allèrent chercher du vin à La Rochelle, Angers, Saumur. Rouen aussi était alors un port très actif. Argenteuil, auquel les impressionnistes de la fin du XIXᵉ siècle ont donné une nouvelle célébrité, était déjà renommé six cents ans plus tôt pour ses vins qui figuraient sur la table de Philippe Auguste. Avant de devenir mousseux, les vins de Champagne suivaient sans doute le même destin que ceux d'Ile-de-France. Vers la fin du XVIIIᵉ siècle, Saint-Evremont et d'autres auteurs vantèrent les crus de Reims, Ay et Épernay.

Les vins de cette époque contenaient moins d'alcool et duraient moins que ceux auxquels nous sommes habitués. Le rouge léger de Gascogne, le Clairet, était expédié au XIVᵉ siècle en barrique et on le consommait dans l'année qui suivait les vendanges. En 1352 les Londoniens lurent sur un édit : « ... mélanger le vieux vin de Bordeaux avec le jeune vin de Bordeaux et faire passer le mélange pour du jeune Bordeaux est interdit, comme un dommage causé au roi et au peuple. » Étant donné qu'en ce temps-là on conservait le vin dans des fûts de bois poreux, on ne pouvait le faire vieillir car il ne tardait pas à être éventé, donc d'un goût désagréable.

Bien des vignobles de France appartenaient à l'Église ; les moines prenaient presque autant de peine à répandre la viticulture que l'Évangile et leurs vins en vinrent à leur fournir une importante source de revenus. En Bourgogne, le duc veillait sur la vigne autant que les moines. Bien des ducs de Bourgogne surent faire la publicité de leurs vins. Pendant de nombreuses années on les consommait surtout en France et en Flandres (alors rattachées à la Bourgogne avec une cour à Bruxelles). Longtemps plus tard, les Huguenots, qui quittèrent la France à la révocation de l'édit de Nantes, firent connaître les vins de Bourgogne en Suisse et en Allemagne. Vers 1750, ils fondèrent en Hollande les premières maisons de commerce et de courtage en vins.

A Bordeaux, la bourgeoisie vinicole s'enrichit et gagna en pouvoir. Pendant toute la guerre de Cent Ans et par la suite, l'Angleterre resta leur principal client. Puis la Hollande prit la seconde place pour les vins blancs. Au temps des Tudors, les Anglais se mirent à boire plus de bière et de Sack (vin d'Espagne). Le Bordeaux n'entrait plus aussi librement en Angleterre et coûtait plus cher. Mais la contrebande pourvoyait aux besoins des amateurs de Clairet, même lorsque leur furent imposés de lourds droits de douane comme conséquence du traité de Methuen qui accordait des faveurs particulières aux vins portugais. Les guerres qui se déroulèrent sur le territoire français ravagèrent les vignobles, mais aussitôt la paix revenue, on les reconstitua opiniâtrement. Au cours des siècles les vignerons connurent des hauts et des bas. En dépit des batailles, du passage des armées, moines et paysans (et les nobles aussi) continuaient à veiller sur leurs vignes et à faire du vin en adaptant toujours mieux leurs procédés aux conditions locales. On taillait court à Bordeaux, long sur le Rhône ; on laissait les raisins pourrir sur pied avant de les cueillir dans le Sauternais ; Dom Pérignon, dit-on, découvrit que le liège peut faire un excellent bouchon, et aussi la manière de rendre le vin mousseux ; les vignerons de Château-Chalon étalèrent les raisins sur des lits de paille pour les faire sécher au soleil d'automne. En d'autres parties du monde, d'autres vignerons trouvèrent parallèlement des procédés du même genre, mais nulle part on n'appliqua ces techniques avec autant de foi et de persévérance qu'en France. Les régions vinicoles d'aucun autre pays au monde ne sont dotées de sols et de climats aussi divers. On ne s'étonnera donc pas que la France produise la plus grande variété de vins fins du monde.

Ce n'est pas sans peine ni reculs que la tradition des vins français de qualité parvint à s'établir. Les efforts que fit le duc de Bourgogne pour bannir le « gaamez déloyal » (le Gamay qui convient au Beaujolais mais qui ne fait pas honneur aux vins de la Côte-d'Or) sont une des péripéties de ce combat constant. La lutte contre les fraudes les plus diverses en est une autre. La stricte application des lois sur l'appellation contrôlée devrait y mettre fin, mais le nombre de condamnations prononcées pour fraude chaque année montre que tous les Français ne sont pas animés par le même désir de peiner pour la meilleure qualité. Néanmoins, dans les régions de grands vins, la majorité des vignerons engagent toutes leurs ressources pour produire chaque année le meilleur vin possible.

De nos jours, on réclame toujours plus de toutes choses, faites plus vite et à meilleur marché. S'il en est une qui ne peut répondre à cette demande, c'est bien le vin. On peut le faire à bon marché, mais alors, ce ne sera pas un vin fin ; on peut le produire en masse, mais il ne pourra plus être un grand vin. Les vignes à rendement relativement faible et celles que l'on taille le plus court pour orienter toute l'énergie du plant vers la qualité au détriment de la quantité sont celles qui donnent les meilleurs vins. Les vignerons savent que quantité et qualité ne vont pas de pair. Autre tendance actuelle qui va à l'encontre du vigneron : la confiance du public pour les produits constants. Tous les vins diffèrent d'année en année ; on peut les standardiser par coupage, mais on ne trouvera jamais dans une cuve de mélange un vin standard de la plus haute qualité. Les vins ordinaires du Midi de la France et de l'Algérie peuvent certes être agréables pour arroser les repas de tous les jours, mais s'en servir pour couper de meilleurs vins ne leur rend pas justice... ni au consommateur.

Voici la question qui se pose : les grands vins survivront-ils à cette tendance ? Les vignerons français estiment qu'ils peuvent persévérer dans la tradition ; l'admirable législation sur les appellations d'origine contrôlée les conforte dans cette conviction. Bien des amateurs de vin, en France et à l'étranger, soutiennent leurs efforts destinés à maintenir les vieilles normes de qualité élevée, en manifestant, comme ils ne l'avaient jamais fait jusqu'à présent, un intérêt pour les grands vins. D'autres, plus pessimistes, rappellent que les salaires augmentent et que le matériel devient plus cher, ce qui rendra peut-être économiquement impossible de faire des grands vins et d'autant plus qu'une courte période de temps inclément peut ruiner les vignerons et dévaster les meilleurs vignobles.

Par bonheur pour la France, la réputation de ses vins — admirablement préservée par les lois d'Appellation Contrôlée — est si bien établie dans le monde entier qu'elle peut faire payer la prime nécessaire pour protéger leur suprématie. Les prix considérablement élevés que peuvent atteindre les meilleurs vins français semblent être une forte garantie de leur survie à l'ère du machinisme.

Régions vinicoles de France

La France est divisée en 95 départements, et, à peu près dans les 2/3, on cultive la vigne pour en vendre le produit. Chaque vin est le résultat d'un climat et d'un sol déterminés, de la variété de raisin avec lequel il est fait, des hommes qui le font et de leurs traditions professionnelles. Tous ces facteurs diffèrent. L'histoire du vin de Bourgogne ne serait pas la même sans les Cisterciens et la Révolution ; le développement du vignoble bordelais dépendit pendant longtemps de ses liens étroits avec l'Angleterre ; le Champagne est lié depuis son origine à la découverte — par Dom Pérignon ou un autre — de la fermentation secondaire en bouteille ; les vins de la vallée du Rhône doivent une bonne part de leurs succès actuels à un homme d'exception : le baron, Le Roy de Boiseaumarié. Si les vins français sont nombreux, les grandes régions vinicoles le sont, elles, beaucoup moins. Voici les plus importantes *(les voir aussi chacune à sa place dans l'ordre alphabétique)* :

Alsace

Plus que les autres régions, l'Alsace perfectionne ses vins. Supérieurs aux crus secondaires allemands, les meilleurs Alsace sont en train d'atteindre la qualité de leurs rivaux des meilleurs domaines du Rheingau, du Palatinat et de la Moselle.

Bordeaux

La plus vaste et la plus productrice des grandes régions vinicoles de France. Les rouges (Clairet jadis et Claret en anglais) du Haut-Médoc, des Graves, de Saint-Émilion et de Pomerol ; les blancs, liquoreux, avec de la sève, de Sauternes et de Barsac, les plus secs de Graves, ont été imités dans le monde entier, mais les meilleures de ces contrefaçons ne les valent jamais.

Bourgogne

Ses vins sont si divers qu'il serait absurde d'essayer d'en décrire un « type ». Les rouges peuvent être austères et aristocratiques comme le Corton et le Chambertin, ou légers et délicats comme devraient toujours l'être ceux de Chambolle. Les blancs sont toujours secs, mais les qualités du Chablis, du Montrachet, du Meursault sont si diverses que, pour les connaître, il faut les goûter.

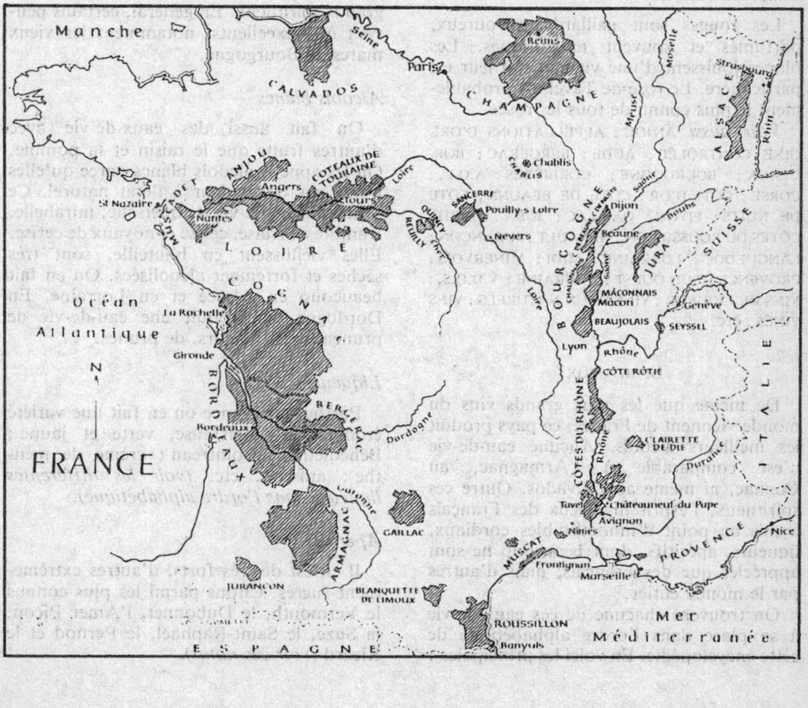

Champagne

Ce nom d'un vin mondialement célèbre a été tellement imité à l'étranger que bien des gens ne savent pas ce qu'il signifie et s'imaginent à tort qu'il désigne n'importe quel vin blanc « qui fait des bulles ». Pourtant la signification de Champagne est strictement définie en France et la fabrication de ce vin est soumise à des règles précises et rigoureuses. Loin de s'appliquer à n'importe quel mousseux, ce nom est réservé à un vin unique, fait avec certains cépages, selon certains procédés, dans une certaine partie de la province à laquelle il doit son nom.

Vallée de la Loire

Les blancs peuvent être secs, demi-doux ou doux et sont généralement meilleurs que les rouges. Tous sont enjôleurs, mais il existe de grandes différences de région en région, de viticulteur en viticulteur et d'un millésime à l'autre.

Vallée du Rhône

Les rouges sont gaillards, savoureux, parfumés et souvent magnifiques. Les blancs jouissent d'une vigueur qui leur est particulière. Le rosé de Tavel est probablement le plus connu de tous les rosés.

Voir aussi ANJOU ; APPELLATIONS D'ORIGINE CONTRÔLÉE ; AUDE ; BERGERAC ; BORDEAUX ; BOURGOGNE ; CORBIÈRES A.O.C. ; CORSE ; CÔTE-D'OR ; CÔTE DE BEAUNE ; CÔTE DE NUITS ; FITOU ; GAILLAC ; JURA ; GARD ; CÔTES DU ROUSSILLON ; HÉRAULT ; JURANÇON ; LANGUEDOC ; LORRAINE ; MIDI ; MINERVOIS ; PROVENCE ; SUD-OUEST ; TOURAINE ; V.D.Q.S. ; VINS DE LIQUEUR ; VINS DOUX NATURELS ; VINS VINÉS ; etc.

SPIRITUEUX

De même que les plus grands vins du monde viennent de France, ce pays produit les meilleurs alcools. Aucune eau-de-vie n'est comparable à l'Armagnac, au Cognac, ni même au Calvados. Outre ces spiritueux, l'esprit ingénieux des Français a mis au point d'innombrables cordiaux, liqueurs, apéritifs, dont beaucoup ne sont appréciés que des Français, mais d'autres par le monde entier.

On trouvera chacune de ces eaux-de-vie à sa place dans l'ordre alphabétique de cette encyclopédie. En voici les principales :

Armagnac

Eau-de-vie d'une région strictement délimitée de la Gascogne, berceau du turbulent mousquetaire d'Artagnan.

Calvados

Eau-de-vie de cidre d'une région délimitée de Normandie. Bien fait, et correctement vieilli, il peut devenir remarquable.

Cognac

Ce n'est pas le nom de n'importe quelle eau-de-vie de vin, mais d'une certaine eau-de-vie de vin bien déterminée. Le Cognac est tellement célèbre qu'on abuse de son nom plus que d'aucun autre. Le vrai n'est fait que dans les environs de la ville de Cognac.

Marc

Les marcs ne sont pas faits avec le jus de fruit, mais avec les résidus du pressurage. Beaucoup sont trop durs, surtout dans leur jeunesse, pour être mentionnés parmi les grands spiritueux. En général, certains peuvent être excellents, notamment les vieux marcs de Bourgogne.

Alcools blancs

On fait aussi des eaux-de-vie avec d'autres fruits que le raisin et la pomme. On les appelle alcools blancs parce qu'elles n'ont pas de couleur à l'état naturel. Ce sont les eaux-de-vie de quetsche, mirabelle, framboise, fraise, cerise et noyaux de cerise. Elles vieillissent en bouteille, sont très sèches et fortement alcoolisées. On en fait beaucoup en Alsace et en Lorraine. En Dordogne on produit une eau-de-vie de pruneaux, et, ailleurs, de prunes.

Liqueurs

Partout en France on en fait une variété étonnante : Chartreuse, verte et jaune ; Bénédictine ; Cointreau ; crème de menthe ; anisette, etc. *(voir les différentes liqueurs dans l'ordre alphabétique).*

Apéritifs

Il en est de très forts, d'autres extrêmement sucrés. Citons parmi les plus connus le Vermouth, le Dubonnet, l'Amer Picon, la Suze, le Saint-Raphaël, le Pernod et le Ricard *(voir ces noms).*

Franciacorta

Agréable vin rouge, blanc ou rosé de Brescia.
Voir LOMBARDIE

Franconie

État allemand de Bavière, Superficie : 5 200 ha. Vins blancs : 97 %, vins rouges : 3 %.

C'est la région viticole la plus orientale d'Allemagne. La plupart des vignobles s'étendent sur des coteaux abruptes, le long des méandres du Main et de ses affluents. Würzburg en est la capitale régionale, culturelle et viticole. Elle est non seulement renommée pour son architecture splendide mais aussi pour ses trois domaines d'excellente réputation : les caves de l'État de Bavière « Staatlicher Hofkeller » (initialement créées par l'Église en 1128, aujourd'hui situées dans le magnifique palais baroque dessiné par Balthasar Neumann et anciennement résidence des Princes Évêques) et les Bürgerspital et Juliusspital (tous deux institutions de charité, datant respectivement de 1319 et 1576). La forteresse Marienburg, qui surplombe la ville, abrite un intéressant musée du vin et une grande collection d'œuvres du XVIe siècle, réalisées par le sculpteur Riemenschneider. La région est formée de 3 districts (Bereiche) et administre le Bereich Bayerischer Bodensee, petite zone située sur les bords du lac de Constance.

Variétés cultivées : Müller-Thurgau (50 %), Silvaner (20 %), Kerner (6 %), Scheurebe (3 %), Riesling (2,5 %).

Vins : pleins, charnus, puissants, profonds, plus lourds que vigoureux (excepté le vin de Moselle léger et racé), excellents au cours d'un repas grâce à leur caractère rude et sec (assez semblables aux Chablis, mais d'une teneur en alcool moins élevée).

Des statistiques remontant loin dans le temps nous montrent combien la viniculture de Franconie a décliné. Avant la guerre de Trente Ans (1618-1648), la vigne ne couvrait guère moins de 40 000 ha dans cette province ; en 1870, quelque 9 000 ha ; en 1900, moins de 7 000 ha et de nos jours, à peu près 5 000 ha. Les guerres y sont pour beaucoup. La guerre de Trente Ans détruisit des vignobles entiers et la Seconde Guerre mondiale les dévasta, surtout autour de Würzburg. Le climat joua un rôle tout aussi désastreux ; les hivers sont rigoureux et les étés très chauds en Franconie, mais le plus grave c'est qu'il gèle souvent à la phase critique de la floraison et en octobre, saison des vendanges. Dans de telles conditions, la vigne a reculé vers les coteaux les plus élevés où rien d'autre ne pousserait. Les terres plus basses, plus fertiles aussi, sont consacrées à d'autres cultures.

50 % environ des 6 600 viticulteurs adhèrent à des coopératives. La superficie moyenne des vignobles est de 70 ares. En plus des coopératives locales de taille moyenne, il existe une coopérative régionale très moderne à Kitzingen-Repperndorf. Les vins sont bien faits et présentent de bonnes caractéristiques régionales à un prix abordable (même si les vins de Franconie ne sont pas bon marché).

La partie occidentale de la région s'étend sur le district de Mainviereck, hormis la zone de Aschaffenburg où le sol est un mélange de roches anciennes, et de micaschiste, avec une prédominance de grès coloré. Les variétés rouges (Spätburgunder et Portugieser) y produisent bien même si elles sont aussi cultivées dans d'autres parties de la région. Le climat y est maritime.

Le district de Maindreieck, qui inclut Würzburg, est le cœur de la région. Ici, le terrain sablonneux produit des Silvaner charnus et vigoureux. Dans les bonnes années, ils font preuve d'élégance et leur parfum est très nuancé. Le Scheurebe (croisement de Silvaner et de Riesling), dont le bouquet légèrement acide rappelle le cassis, offre un contraste intéressant. Depuis des siècles, des vins exceptionnels ont été produits sur le vignoble de « Stein » à Würzburg, détenu conjointement par les trois domaines cités ci-dessus.

Le vin de Stein (vin de pierre) ne provient que du Würzburger-Stein, un coteau situé à proximité de Würzburg. Les vignes y sont orientées au sud et poussent sur un sol fortement incliné surtout constitué de calcaire. Ce vin est si célèbre qu'à l'étranger on donne son nom inconsidérément à tous ceux qui se présentent dans la bouteille caractéristique de Franconie. D'un vert doré, le véritable Steinweine a des qualités exceptionnelles que les connaisseurs savent apprécier.

Avant la promulgation de la loi allemande sur les vins en 1971, « Steinwein » était utilisé comme terme courant pour tous les vins de Franconie, vendus en Bocksbeutel (bouteille en forme de flacon). Les autres villages importants sont : Escherndorf, Nordheim, Randersacker, Sommerach, Sommerhausen, Thüngersheim et Volkach.

Le district le plus oriental tire son nom de la forêt de Steiger qui l'abrite. Très terreux et parfumés, les vins fabriqués à partir de Müller-Thurgau sont produits sur un sol de gypse et de marne rouge. Bacchus, croisement de (Silvaner × Riesling) × Müller-Thurgau donne des vins pleins, fruités et légèrement acides. La spécialité Rieslaner (croisement de Silvaner × Riesling) produit des vins tardifs, particulièrement élégants, de type Auslese, riches en extraits, au fruité noble et à l'acidité racée. Comme dans le district central, le climat est ici continental, avec des hivers très froids (risques de gelées) et des étés chauds permettant aux raisins d'acquérir une plus grande maturité. Dans les années chaudes, l'acidité est moins forte et les vins sont très secs mais harmonieux. En Franconie, « sec » signifie moins de 4 g/l de sucre résiduel. Dans les autres régions, le maximum légal est de 9 g/l. Castell, Iphofen, Rödelsee et Wlesenbronn sont d'importants villages.

Producteurs : Fürstl, Castell'sches Domänenamt Ernst Gebhardt, Fürst Löwenstein-Wertheim-Rosenberg, Schloss Sommerhausen-Steinmann, Dr Hans Wirsching.

Pour une liste plus complète des districts (Bereiche), des vignobles collectifs (Grosslagen = Gl) et des vignobles individuels (Einzellagen), *voir* APPENDICE B.

Frappé

On a trop souvent tendance à confondre frappé et glacé. Frappé signifie seulement rafraîchi. Certaines liqueurs, comme la crème de menthe, peuvent être frappées en y versant de la glace pilée.

Frascati

Vin blanc sec D.O.C. de Castelli Romani, en Italie.

Voir LATIUM

Frecciarossa

Bon vin léger de Lombardie *(voir ce nom).*

Fredonia

Cépage rouge de bon rendement, servant à faire du vin rouge, surtout dans le New Jersey.

Free-Run

Expression anglaise désignant la première coulée de vin après fermentation du moût, ou le premier jus qui s'écoule dès le premier pressurage léger. On en fait les meilleurs vins et, dans maintes régions, il est mis en bouteille séparément. En France, c'est le « vin de tête » ou le « vin de coule » (*voir* TÊTE ET COULE).

Freisa (d'Asti, di Chieri)

Cépage utilisé en Italie, surtout au Piémont, pour faire un vin rouge (D.O.C.) vivace parfois pétillant, au bouquet délicieux.

Voir PIÉMONT

Frioul-Vénétie-Julie

Vins rouges, rosés et blancs. Nord-est de l'Italie.

Située à la frontière de l'Autriche et de la Yougoslavie, cette région est plutôt petite et montagneuse. Une grande quantité de vins (environ 1 000 000 hl, soit 11 000 000 caisses) est produite, pour les rouges, à partir des variétés de Merlot, Cabernet Franc ou Sauvignon, Refosco, Pinot Noir, quelques Malbec, Schioppettino, Ribolla Nera et Tazzelenghe ; pour les blancs, à partir de Pinot Blanc et Chardonnay, de Pinot Gris, Riesling Renano, Sauvignon, Malvasia, Ribolla, Tocai Friulano, Traminer, Müller-Thurgau, Picolit et Verduzzo. La plupart des vins, qu'ils soient Vino di Tavolo ou D.O.C. sont vendus sous le nom de l'une des variétés de raisins citée ci-dessus. Les principales D.O.C. sont :

Aquileia, région plate du nord de la Côte adriatique.

Collio, Collio Goriziano, agglomération proche de la Yougoslavie, située près de

Gorizia et dont le micro-climat convient très bien aux vins blancs.

Colli Orientali del Friuli, qui tout comme d'autres D.O.C. du Frioul, est souvent vendu sous le nom de sa variété de raisin.

Grave del Friuli, produit près d'Udine et connu sous le nom de Grave.

Isonzo : région située sur le cours de la rivière Isonzo et très favorable aux vins rouges.

Latisana : plaines côtières longeant la rivière Tagliamento et très appropriée pour les vins rouges.

Frizzante

Nom italien des vins légèrement mousseux appelés « pétillants » ou « perlés ».

Fronsac

Nouvelle dénomination, ne s'appelle plus Côtes de Fronsac.

Voir CÔTES CANON FRONSAC

Frontignan-Muscat (Appellation Contrôlée)

Secteur méditerranéen célèbre pour son muscat. Ce nom désigne souvent aussi la bouteille de 75 cl.

Voir VINS VINÉS FRANÇAIS

Fronton, Côtes du Frontonnais

Bons vins produits dans la région de Fronton, en Haute-Garonne. Ils ont mérité le titre d'« Appellation Contrôlée ».

Fruité

La première expression printanière de bien des vins, innocente et fraîche, perceptible surtout à l'odorat. Cette caractéristique est due à la haute volatilité des esters qui donnent le goût et l'arôme. Elle disparaît rapidement chez les vins qui ne sont pas riches en sucre. Les vins fruités, secs ou demi-secs, doivent être bus jeunes, avant qu'ils ne commencent à faner. Le rouge fruité n'a pas fermenté longtemps sur la lie mais, mis en bouteille jeune, il manquera de tanin. Les Beaujolais rouges sont un bon exemple de vin fruité, de même que les Moselle blancs.

Fuder

Gros fût allemand contenant environ 1 000 l.

Voir FOUDRE

Fumarium

Cellier dans lequel les Romains *amélioraient* leurs vins en les exposant à la fumée.

Fumigation

Opération consistant à faire brûler une mèche de soufre dans une cuve ou un fût, pour détruire bactéries et les levures indésirables. Parfois elle consiste à remplacer l'air en contact avec le vin par de l'anhydride sulfureux. Trop de soufre gâterait le vin. A Bordeaux on considère en général qu'un quart de mèche suffit pour une barrique (225 l). On dit couramment : méchage (de mèche), pour fumigation.

En Californie, là où le chêne a proliféré, le sol doit être désinfecté par fumigation avant que des vignes ne puissent y être plantées.

Voir ANHYDRIDE SULFUREUX, CHAPITRE V

Funchal

Port et chef-lieu de Madère où une grande partie du vin est entreposé et vieilli, et d'où il est ensuite expédié.

Furfurol

Aldéhyde présent en quantité infime dans le vin et les spiritueux et en quantité nettement plus grande dans les alcools de grain. On l'écrit parfois furfural : son nom en anglais.

Furmint

Beau raisin blanc dont on fait le Tokay. Il entre aussi dans la vinification de certains crus allemands.

Fusel Oil

Alcool amylique, en anglais. Il s'agit d'alcool volatile, nauséeux, que la rectification élimine des spiritueux.

d'alcool volatile, nauséeux, que la rectification élimine des spiritueux.

Fût, futaille

Récipients en planches de bois cintrées (douves) et jointes, servant à conserver et expédier vin, cidre, eau-de-vie.

Voir TONNEAU, TONNELLERIE ; APPENDICE B

G

Gaffelière (Château La)

Bordeaux rouge. Commune de Saint-Émilion.

Certains experts le considèrent comme l'un des meilleurs Saint-Émilion. Le domaine remarquablement situé, se trouve sur la petite route sinueuse qui traverse la grand-route Bordeaux-Bergerac pour grimper jusqu'aux sommets de la commune de Saint-Émilion. Il appartient au comte de Malet-Roquefort et fut classé Premier Cru en 1955 et en 1986. On abandonna le nom Naudes en 1963, et depuis cette date, il ne s'appelle plus que Château La Gaffelière. Il est anormalement cher pour certains.

Caractéristiques : des vins fins bien que variables. Dans les bonnes années, c'est l'un des bons Saint-Émilion.

Superficie : 22 ha.

Production moyenne : 90 tonneaux (8 500 caisses).

Gaillac (Appellation Contrôlée)

Vins blancs mousseux et non mousseux. Sud de la France.

Le Tarn coule dans le département du même nom. Ce n'est pas un grand cours d'eau, mais c'est une des plus belles rivières de France. Les truites abondent dans ses eaux écumantes qui bondissent à travers des rochers et que dominent des falaises majestueuses.

Aux alentours de Gaillac les vignes plantées à flanc de collines fournissent les vins de deux appellations : Premières Côtes de Gaillac et Gaillac mousseux.

Les vignobles de Gaillac semblent avoir donné de meilleurs vins au Moyen Age que leurs rouges, rosés et blancs douceâtres et sans intérêt d'aujourd'hui (mais les goûts évoluent). Les Plantagenêts étaient amateurs de Gaillac, de même qu'Henri VII. Dans ses *Mémoires de Languedoc* (1633), Catel écrit que ce vin, très apprécié par les princes étrangers, laissait dans la bouche un goût de rose.

Depuis 1938, une série de décrets précise dans quelles conditions ont doit faire le Gaillac. Six variétés de raisins seulement sont autorisées pour les vins blancs : Mauzac, l'Enc de l'El, Ondenc, Sémillon, Sauvignon et Muscadelle. Le Mauzac représente de 80 à 100 % des vignobles. Les rouges et les rosés sont faits principalement avec les raisins Duras, Fer, Syrah et Gamay Pour avoir droit à l'appellation d'origine Premières Côtes de Gaillac, le vin doit titrer 12° dont 10,5° au moins d'alcool acquis pour être étiqueté simplement Gaillac.

Le Gaillac mousseux doit être fait selon la méthode champenoise de fermentation secondaire en bouteille ou par la méthode gaillacoise — légèrement différente — qui consiste à mettre le vin en bouteille alors qu'il contient encore du sucre non transformé, ce qui provoque une fermentation en vase clos et laisse souvent aussi un dépôt assez épais au fond de la bouteille.

Galgenwein

Littéralement : vin de gibet. Il s'agit de vin tellement dur qu'il n'est plus besoin de gibet pour celui qui l'a bu.

Gallisation

Terme ayant trait à une addition de sucre liquide au moût du raisin avant la fermentation, afin d'augmenter le taux d'alcool d'un vin. La chaptalisation est le procédé similaire utilisant du sucre sec (de betterave ou de cane).

Gallon

Mesure de capacité des pays anglo-saxons. Celui de Grande-Bretagne (British Imperial Gallon) équivaut à 4,54596 l et celui des États-Unis (U.S. Gallon) à 3,78531 l.
Voir PROOF GALLON ; WINE GALLON

Gamay

Raisin rouge servant à faire du vin rouge. Sauf en Beaujolais, où il donne des vins admirables, ce raisin présente peu d'intérêt. Il est assez bon en Touraine, capricieux en Californie où il s'adapte aux vignobles montagneux de Santa Cruz, mais donne un vin ordinaire dans la vallée du Napa.

Gambellara (Recioto, Vin Santo) (D.O.C.)

Vin blanc sec semblable au Soave.
Voir VÉNÉTIE

Gamza

Une des principales variétés de raisin bulgare avec laquelle on fait du vin rouge et du blanc.
Voir BULGARIE

Gard

Un des trois départements qui produisent le plus de vin, les deux autres étant l'Aude et l'Hérault. Hormis le rouge et robuste Costières *(voir Costières du Gard)* et la Clairette de Bellegarde *(voir ce nom)*, blanc, le Gard ne produit que des vins ordinaires.

Garda

Nom de plusieurs vins des environs du lac de Garde : Chiaretto del Garda, Moniga del Garda et le D.O.C. Riviera del Garda-Bresciano.
Voir LOMBARDIE

Garrafeira

Sur les bouteilles de vin portugais, cette mention désigne un vin qui a vieilli quelques années en bouteille avant d'être mis en vente. C'est à peu près l'équivalent de « réserve » ou de « réserve spéciale ».

Gattinara (D.O.C.)

Populaire vin rouge plein de corps, fait dans le Piémont *(voir ce nom)*.

Gay-Lussac

Chimiste français auquel on doit la formule chimique de la fermentation *(voir ce mot)*. Ses travaux sur l'alcoométrie et l'acide sulfurique ont apporté une importante contribution aux progrès de la viniculture.

Gazéifié

Mention qui désigne les vins rendus artificiellement mousseux par insufflation de gaz carbonique.

Gazin (Château)

Bordeaux rouge. Commune de Pomerol.
M. de Baillencourt est le propriétaire de ce cru — l'un des plus grands domaines de la région — qui ne mérite pas toujours sa haute réputation.
Superficie : 25 ha.
Production moyenne : 7 000 caisses.

Gean Whisky, Geen Whisky

Liqueur écossaise faite avec du whisky et des cerises noires.

Gebiet

Région en allemand. Plus spécifiquement, une des onze régions vinicoles reconnues par les lois de la R.F.A.

Geisenheim

La plus importante école de viticulture allemande se trouve dans cette ville du Rheingau. Ses vignobles produisent de bons vins, notamment le Rothenberger et le Fuchsberg.

Voir RHEINGAU

Gemarkung

Ville ou village d'Allemagne qui donne son nom à un vin, de même qu'en France certaines appellations contrôlées se réduisent simplement au nom d'une commune.

Généreux

On dit d'un vin qu'il est généreux quand il possède à la fois chaleur, richesse, vitalité et forte teneur en alcool.

Geneva

Orthographe anglaise de Jenever, nom que les Hollandais donnent au gin.

Voir GIN

Genièvre

Quoique le gin soit, à proprement parler, un alcool de grain (orge maltée ou seigle, notamment), il a souvent un goût de genièvre parce que cette plante lui donne de la saveur. C'est le cas du gin hollandais qu'on appelle Jenever aux Pays-Bas.

Voir GIN

Gentiane

Liqueur française et suisse obtenue par la distillation des racines de gentiane. L'apéritif le plus populaire de ce genre en France est celui de la marque Suze.

Voir ENZIAN

Gentil

Nom que les Alsaciens donnent au raisin Riesling *(voir ce nom).*

Geropiga, Jeropiga

Sirop de raisin utilisé au Portugal pour sucrer le Porto.

Gers

Département du Sud-Ouest. Il produit un vin plutôt quelconque, souvent utilisé comme coupage avec d'autres vins blancs. On en distille une petite quantité pour en faire de l'Armagnac.

Gevrey-Chambertin (Appellation Contrôlée)

Bourgogne rouge. Commune de la Côte de Nuits.

Gevrey-Chambertin est une commune de la Côte-d'Or, en Bourgogne, et plus particulièrement du secteur le plus septentrional de la Côte-d'Or : la Côte de Nuits. Gevrey-Chambertin est aussi la plus au nord des communes de la Côte de Nuits. Comme bien d'autres agglomérations de cette célèbre chaîne de collines, la commune a ajouté à son nom celui de son meilleur cru, un des plus célèbres du monde. Jusqu'en 1847, l'appellation légale était Gevrey. Depuis, elle est devenue Gevrey-Chambertin. Les édiles de la commune n'étaient pas les seuls qu'impressionnait la réputation de leur célèbre cru ; il fut un temps, en effet, ou à peu près tous les propriétaires de vignobles ajoutaient « Chambertin » au nom de leur propre cru, peut-être parce qu'ils espéraient naïvement qu'une partie au moins de ses qualités déteindrait par magie sur leur production, et aussi pour le vendre plus cher. En 1936, les autorités intervinrent pour désigner ceux qui ont désormais légalement droit à cette appellation.

Vers l'an 630, le duc de Bourgogne fit don d'une terre de Gevrey à l'abbaye de Bèze. Les moines y plantèrent de la vigne et découvrirent qu'elle donnait un vin extraordinaire. Selon les anecdotes qu'on raconte encore dans le pays, un terrain voisin de l'abbaye appartint à un certain moment à un nommé Bertin et on l'appela le « champ de Bertin ». Constatant le succès que les moines obtenaient avec leur vin, Bertin planta aussi de la vigne sur son champ dont le nom fut bientôt abrégé en Chambertin.

Mais ce ne sont ni Bertin ni les moines de l'abbaye qui rendirent célèbre ce vignoble. L'honneur doit en revenir à un nommé Jobert qui fut propriétaire de Chambertin et du Clos de Bèze. A une certaine époque, il changea son nom pour s'appeler Jobert-Chambertin. De nos jours, les deux vignobles ne sont plus réunis comme au temps de Jobert. Ils sont non seulement séparés mais en outre parcellés en terrains appartenant à plus de deux douzaines de vignerons.

Étant donnée la réputation du Chambertin, on ne s'étonnera pas que les propriétaires de vignes des environs aient cherché à en tirer parti. Selon la loi actuelle, seuls quelques-uns des vignobles qui lui sont immédiatement contigus ont le droit d'ajouter le nom de Chambertin à celui de leur cru. En ce qui concerne le Clos de Bèze, considéré comme l'égal de Chambertin, il peut être vendu sous le nom de Chambertin s'il plaît aux propriétaires. Il a aussi le droit de placer le mot magique *avant* le sien, alors que les autres doivent l'écrire *après*. Chambertin-Clos de Bèze est son nom exact et le cru est englobé dans le décret visant Chambertin. Les autres sont régis par un autre décret. En ce qui concerne les normes, la différence essentielle entre les deux décrets porte sur la production maximale, à savoir : Chambertin et Chambertin-Clos de Bèze, 35 hl/ha ; Latricières-Chambertin, Mazoyères-Chambertin, Charmes-Chambertin, Mazis- (ou Mazys-) Chambertin, Ruchottes-Chambertin, Griotte-Chambertin et Chapelle-Chambertin, 37 hl/ha. Voilà les Grands Crus de la commune et chacun est traité dans cette encyclopédie à sa place dans l'ordre alphabétique.

Les vignes sont plantées à mi-hauteur de coteau entre Gevrey-Chambertin et Morey-Saint-Denis, situé plus au sud. On les aperçoit de la route nationale 74, qui longe le pied des collines. Un chemin pavé permet de s'élever à flanc de coteau et d'avoir une vue d'ensemble plus précise. Quand on quitte Gevrey-Chambertin, le premier vignoble qui tombe sous les yeux est celui de Mazis (dans la conversation courante on ne prononce pas la seconde partie du nom, mais elle doit toujours figurer sur les étiquettes). Ruchottes est juste au-dessus. Les deux se trouvent sur la droite, contigus au Clos de Bèze alors que Griotte et Chapelle sont juste en face, de l'autre côté de la route. Une petite cabane se dresse sur le Clos de Bèze ; elle porte le nom de Pierre Damoy, décédé en 1971, un des plus gros propriétaires du cru et un des meilleurs vignerons. A part cet unique détail, rien ne distingue un vignoble de l'autre. Quand on a dépassé le Clos de Bèze, une grande pancarte annonce : « Ici commencent les vignes de Chambertin. » On a à peine le temps de digérer cette information qu'une autre indique : « Ici finissent les vignes de Chambertin. » 500 m environ les séparent, et la largeur du vignoble correspond à peu près à la moitié de la longueur. A part ces deux pancartes, rien n'indique qu'on se trouve à proximité d'un sol qui donne un vin prodigieux, et quand on regarde les vignobles les uns après les autres, on ne saurait dire lequel donne le meilleur nectar. Le nouveau venu serait incapable de les identifier. Pour cela, il faut goûter le vin.

Comme la plupart des villages de la Côte-d'Or, Gevrey-Chambertin est tapi entre deux collines au fond de ce que l'on appelle une Combe. Tous les Chambertin sont sur la colline sud, mais il y a d'autres excellents vignobles du côté nord.

Selon la classification de 1860 des vins de la Côte-d'or, seuls Chambertin et Clos de Bèze avaient le titre de Têtes de Cuvée ; les autres, y compris ceux qui ont été promus au rang de Grands Crus, étaient alors classés en dessous comme Premiers Crus. En ce temps-là, certains avaient droit au titre de Grand Cru, notamment : Clos Saint-Jacques, Varoilles, Fouchère, Étournelles, et Cazetiers ; ils sont classés aujourd'hui Premiers Crus, et peuvent être vendus sous une des deux étiquettes suivantes, au choix du vigneron ou du négociant : leur nom plus celui de la commune, ou le nom de la commune plus la mention Premier Cru. Bien des experts regrettent que Varoilles et Clos Saint-Jacques n'aient plus droit au titre de Grand Cru, comme les autres meilleurs vignobles de la commune. En bien des années, leurs excellents vins peuvent se comparer avec avantage aux cinq autres Grands Crus Chambertin, mais peut-être pas avec les deux anciennes Têtes de Cuvée.

La commune produit aussi des vins de

Grands Crus		
Vignoble	*Superficie (ha)*	*Production moyenne annuelle*
Chambertin (cru exceptionnel)	17,7	500
Chambertin-Clos de Bèze (cru exceptionnel)	15,17	850
Latricières-Chambertin	6,23	200
Mazoyères-Chambertin	19,18	200
Charmes-Chambertin	12,42	1 000
Mazis- (ou Mazys-) Chambertin	9,47	145
Ruchottes-Chambertin	8,45	100
Griotte-Chambertin	3,18	100
Chapelle-Chambertin	4,06	210

Premiers Crus	
Vignoble	*Superficie (ha)*
Varoilles	5,94
Clos Saint-Jacques	6,92
Aux Combottes	4,9
Bel-Air	3,72
Les Cazetiers	9,11
Combe-au-Moine	4,78
Étournelles	2
Lavaut	9,43
Poissenot	2,19
Champeaux	6,76
Les Goulots	1,82
Issarts (ou Plantigone)	1,82
Les Corbeaux	3,12
Cherbaudes	2,19
La Perrière	2,47
Clos-Prieur (partie supérieure seule)	1,98
Le Fonteny	3,80
Champonnet	3,32
Au Closeau	0,53
Craipillot	2,75
Champitennois (ou Petite Chapelle)	3,97
En Ergot	1,17
Clos du Chapitre	0,97

moindre qualité qui n'ont droit qu'à l'appellation Gevrey-Chambertin ; nombre d'entre eux peuvent être fort agréables. Ils ne sont pas tous faits avec les seuls raisins cultivés sur le territoire de la commune, mais aussi avec ceux des meilleurs vignobles de l'agglomération voisine : Brochon. La superficie totale plantée en vigne ne s'élève qu'à quelque 200 ha. Voir ci-contre la liste des meilleurs crus *(voir aussi séparément les Grands Crus à leur place dans l'ordre alphabétique).*

Gewächs

Synonyme de *Kreszenz* : cru, en allemand.

Gewürztraminer

Variété de vigne et nom du vin que l'on fait avec ses raisins. On le dit plus épicé que le Traminer. Il entre dans la composition de bien des vins alsaciens et allemands. En réalité, les deux noms, Traminer et Gewürztraminer, peuvent être pratiquement interchangés, et, s'il y avait vraiment quelque différence entre eux, l'usage l'a fait disparaître.

Voir ALLEMAGNE ; ALSACE

Ghemme (D.O.C.)

Vin rouge sec du Piémont *(voir ce nom)*, en Italie.

Gigondas (Appellation Contrôlée)

Une des meilleures communes vinicoles des Côtes du Rhône. On y produit des vins rouges, blancs et rosés. La production annuelle s'élève à environ 350 000 hl (plus de 380 000 caisses).

Voir RHÔNE

Gill

Mesure de capacité anglaise équivalent à 1/4 de la pinte britannique ou 14,206 cl, environ. On dit aussi *quatern*.

Gin

Alcool à goût de genièvre obtenu par distillation et rectification d'orge maltée ou de seigle et parfois de maïs. Néanmoins la définition « le gin est un esprit de grain » n'est pas tout à fait exacte. On peut en faire en distillant et rectifiant théoriquement n'importe quoi. Pendant la dernière guerre le gin anglais était fait avec de la mélasse brute ; certains gins secs de Londres, destinés à la consommation anglaise, sont encore faits de cette manière. Néanmoins, la plus grande partie est désormais produite par la distillation de céréales, comme pour l'exportation. Le prix du gin est pratiquement le même quelle que soit l'espèce de grain avec lequel il est fait.

Il y a deux différents types de gin : le britannique et le hollandais. Aux États-Unis, on le fait de la même manière qu'en Angleterre. Le gin hollandais s'appelle Jenever ; en Angleterre on le nomme Hollands ou Schiedam : nom d'une des villes où l'on en fabrique. Les Anglais l'appellent aussi Geneva (Genève), corruption inadmissible de Jenever et de Genièvre.

Hollandais et Anglais se targuent, et parfois se défendent, d'avoir inventé le gin. A coup sûr, on en faisait au XVIIe siècle en Angleterre avec de l'orge, du houblon et des baies de genièvre. Gin Lane, du dessinateur Hogarth, nous montre ce qu'il en résultait. En 1736, le Gin Act en interdit la fabrication et la consommation. Comme la plupart des prohibitions, celle-ci ne fut pas efficace et on l'abrogea en 1742 parce que le gin clandestin était pire que l'autre.

Les progrès en fait de distillation, et surtout la découverte de la rectification, ont permis d'éliminer les caractéristiques les plus nocives des spiritueux et d'obtenir de l'alcool presque absolument pur. Néanmoins la rectification ne fait pas partie des processus de fabrication des gins hollandais, pas plus que des rhums et des whiskies les plus forts. Ils conservent donc en partie le goût de l'orge, du malt et autre céréales.

Le gin hollandais est souvent vendu en cruches de grès et les Hollandais le boivent sec dans des petits verres étroits et hauts. Pour le faire on commence par laisser macérer de l'orge grillée, du seigle ou parfois du maïs. Puis on le fait fermenter avec des levures, ce qui prend deux ou trois jours. On distille ensuite. Le produit de cette première distillation est additionné de baies de genièvre et de divers autres ingrédients selon la recette de chaque fabricant, puis on distille de nouveau le mélange. (Dans certains cas, les baies de genièvre sont écrasées et brassées avec le malt.)

Si l'on redistille une fois de plus le produit de la deuxième distillation, il en résulte ce qu'on appelle le Double Gin. Les gins hollandais titrent moins que les anglais et veillissent généralement sous contrôle. La loi exige qu'ils titrent 35° d'alcool.

Pour la fabrication des gins britanniques et américains, on prend un alcool hautement rectifié — ou neutre — donc incolore et insipide. On le redistille avec des baies de genièvre, de la coriandre ou d'autres éléments propres à lui donner du goût. En cas de seconde distillation, ce gin prend le nom de London Dry. Il est si facile de faire du gin sec qu'on peut considérer sa fabrication comme un art culinaire ; étant donné qu'il s'agit seulement de donner du goût à un alcool neutre, il y a de quoi tenter l'amateur. Quelques-uns se contentent d'acheter de l'alcool et de le traiter à leur façon. Les gins de qualité inférieure sont faits en ajoutant des huiles essentielles à l'alcool sans prendre la peine de distiller une seconde fois. Toutefois, les gins secs sont tellement rectifiés qu'ils ne contiennent plus d'alcool amylique et qu'il est inutile de les laisser vieillir pour éliminer ce produit nocif. Le vieillissement ne les améliore donc nullement et ils peuvent être bus immédiatement.

Le gin prend les caractéristiques des ingrédients figurant dans la recette du fabricant. Après rectification de l'alcool de base, ces ingrédients sont ajoutés d'une manière ou d'une autre. Parfois, on les fait macérer dans l'alcool. Une autre technique pratiquée notamment par Burrough's Beefeater, à Londres, consiste à faire passer l'alcool dans un alambic « de goût ». C'est un petit alambic en forme de boîte dans lequel les vapeurs d'alcool et celles de genièvre, angélique, coriandre, etc., entrent en contact. Tous les distillateurs de gin emploient du genièvre auquel ils ajoutent les éléments les plus divers : fenouil, réglisse, écorce d'orange, anis, cumin, iris de plusieurs variétés, amandes, etc.

Outre ces diversités entre les différentes marques de gin, il y en eut deux types distincts. L'Old Tom Gin est sucré par simple addition de sucre au gin sec. Le Plymouth Gin est fait dans la ville de ce nom, en Angleterre, par une seule firme et c'est un intermédiaire entre le gin ordinaire anglais et celui de Hollande. Le Sloe Gin *(voir ce nom)* est fait avec du gin mais n'en est pas. Aux États-Unis, les gins London Dry peuvent être de trois sortes : gin importé d'Angleterre ; gin fait aux États-Unis par licence ou concession du distillateur anglais ; ou tout gin sec fait aux États-Unis ayant les caractéristiques du London Dry. Dans tous les cas, les principes généraux de préparation sont identiques.

On fait vieillir en baril certains gins qui prennent la teinte dorée du bois, mais c'est rare. Aux États-unis ont préfère de beaucoup les gins neutres parce qu'on les utilise dans des cocktails auxquels ils apportent de l'alcool sans intervenir dans l'harmonie des goûts. La plupart des gins sont consommés en effet dans les « dry martinis », les collins ou encore avec de la « tonic water » : eau de Seltz parfumée à l'écorce d'orange. Cette dernière est connue sous le nom de Gin-Tonic.

Les gins au citron ou à l'orange sont en général parfumés artificiellement avec des essences de ces fruits, mais quelques-uns sont faits par addition de jus avant la distillation.

Gin Fizz

Breuvage frais et effervescent, servi dans des grands verres. Il se compose de gin, de jus de citron, d'un peu de sucre, avec de l'eau de Seltz et de la glace. Ces *Fizzes* peuvent être préparés selon d'autres recettes dans lesquelles l'eau-de-vie remplace le gin.

Gingembre

Le gingembre sert à faire divers breuvages très appréciés par les Anglos-Saxons, notamment les suivants :

Ginger Ale

Il s'agit d'une eau minérale pétillante, de couleur rousse. Souvent on y ajoute du gin ou du whisky pour en faire un breuvage comparable au « Gin-Tonic ». Ce succédané de bière n'est que de l'eau gazéifiée à laquelle on ajoute une matière colorante, quelques gouttes d'essence de poivre ou de gingembre ou de glucose. Pour que le breuvage soit plus mousseux, ont peut aussi y ajouter du « froth heading ».

Ginger Beer

Breuvage pâle et mousseux, vendu en bouteille et très consommé en Angleterre. On le fabrique en faisant fermenter, dans de l'eau, du sucre, du gingembre et de la crème de tartre. On le met en bouteille avant la fin de la fermentation. Le gaz carbonique qui reste enfermé dans la bouteille rend cette « bière » gazeuse.

Ginger Wine

Breuvage vendu en Angleterre, obtenu avec du gingembre, de la levure, du sucre, des rondelles de citron, des raisins secs et de l'eau. Souvent on le fortifie à l'alcool et on l'épice au poivre.

Ginger Brandy

Spiritueux auquel on a donné un goût de gingembre. De couleur rousse, il est fabriqué en Grande-Bretagne.

Giródi di Cagliari (D.O.C.)

Vin de Sardaigne semblable au Porto.

Giró di Sardegna

Vin de dessert rouge et sucré de la Sardaigne *(voir ce nom)*.

Gironde

Département dans lequel est située la ville de Bordeaux. Également, estuaire de la Garonne, en aval de sa confluence avec la Dordogne au nord de la ville.

Giscours (Château-)

Bordeaux rouge. Commune de Labarde-Margaux, en Haut-Médoc.

Après être tombé très bas, Château-Giscours, l'un des meilleurs Troisièmes Crus du Médoc, selon la classification de 1855, fut acheté en 1954 par M. Tari qui produisait du vin de façon intensive dans le département d'Oran. Il trouva le vignoble planté en partie de vignes hybrides qui le dégradaient. En 1955 et 1956, il les fit arracher et reconstitua un cru de première qualité. Les derniers millésimes montrent un grand progrès.

Les archives de Château-Giscours remontent à 1552. Cette année-là, un seigneur de La Bastide le vendit à un certain Pierre de L'Horme. Le domaine passa ensuite entre les mains de la famille Saint-Simon qui en fut dépossédée par la Révolution. En 1793, un nommé Jacob l'acheta pour le compte de deux Américains : John Gray et Jonathan Davis, de Boston.

Le château actuel fut construit sous Napoléon III par un banquier, le comte Pescatore. En 1852, Édouard Cruse l'acheta et il resta entre les mains de sa famille jusqu'en 1913. Il comporte deux grandes ailes et se trouve à l'entrée d'un des parcs les plus beaux du Bordelais, avec un lac, des canaux dont la surface disparaît sous les plantes aquatiques, un bosquet de rhododendrons dans lequel se trouve un séquoia géant de Californie. Depuis 1973 le groupe anglais I.D.V., propriétaire de Gilbey's, est le distributeur exclusif mondial de ce vin.

Caractéristiques : Vin plein et délicat cependant supérieurement parfumé et souvent élégant.

Superficie : 80 ha.

Production moyenne : 350 tonneaux (35 000 caisses).

Givry (Appellation Contrôlée)

Commune de la Côte chalonnaise qui produit surtout des vins rouges.

Voir CHALONNAIS

Glogg

Boisson chaude à base de vin auquel on ajoute de l'eau-de-vie ou de l'aquavit, des amandes et des raisins secs. En Suède, c'est une boisson hivernale traditionnelle.

Gloria (Château-)

Bordeaux rouge. Commune de Saint-Julien, en Haut-Médoc.

Le vignoble comporte des parcelles de Château-Léoville-Poyferré et de Château-Gruaud-Larose qui sont des Seconds Crus ; de Château-Saint-Pierre et de Château-Duhart-Milon, Quatrièmes Crus. A l'origine, les chais étaient ceux du Château-Saint-Pierre. Le propriétaire actuel de Château-Gloria, M. Henri Martin, maire de Saint-Julien, gère avec son gendre son domaine. C'est une des personnalités les plus marquantes du Médoc et du Bordeaux vinicoles. En 1956 il devint président du Comité interprofessionnel des vins de Bordeaux (C.I.V.B.). Les qualités du terrain, la gestion intelligente et énergique ont élevé les vins de Château-Gloria bien au-dessus de leur titre actuel : Cru bourgeois du Médoc. Ils méritent largement d'être promus au rang de Grand Cru.

Caractéristiques : Rond et subtil, le Château-Gloria présente certaines des meilleures caractéristiques de Saint-Julien : une combinaison de plénitude et de délicatesse notamment. Généralement, un vin très bien vinifié.

Superficie : 50 ha.

Production moyenne : 200 tonneaux (18 000 caisses).

Gluco-œnomètre

Instrument servant à évaluer la teneur en sucre du moût frais ; utilisé surtout par les fabricants de Porto.

Glycérine

Trialcool liquide se formant à partir du sucre pendant la fermentation du jus de raisin. Lorsque produite en quantité, elle donne des vins d'une douceur et d'une « épaisseur » caractéristiques (manque de corps). Formule : CH_2OH — $CHOH$ — CH_2OH.

Gobelet

Méthode de taille de la vigne : le tronc court diverge en plusieurs branches qui donnent à l'ensemble une forme de vase ou de gobelet.

Goldwasser

Voir DANZIGER GOLDWASSER

Gourmet

Nom que les Alsaciens donnent aux courtiers en vins.

Goût américain

Ce terme peut prêter à confusion : il désigne les Champagne doux, alors que ceux-ci ne sont, en fait, pas expédiés aux États-Unis.

Goût anglais

Désigne les Champagne secs destinés au marché anglais.

Goût de pierre à fusil

Se dit d'un vin très sec, tel le Chablis.

Goût de terroir

Il ne s'agit évidemment pas du goût du sol lui-même, mais du goût particulier que certains sols donnent au vin.

Goutte (Vin de)

Vin fait avec le jus du raisin obtenu par dernier pressurage. A l'inverse du vin de tête ou vin de coule (*voir à* TÊTE et à COULE), c'est le vin le moins bon de la vendange.

Graacher Himmelreich

Un des vins réputés de Graach sur la Moselle allemande. Le Josephshof est un autre délicieux vin de Graach et l'un des rares en Allemagne à être vendu sans la mention du nom spécifique de son site viticole.

Voir MOSELLE

Gragnano

Un des principaux vins rouges de la Campanie (Italie).

Voir CAMPANIE

Graisse

Altération du vin plus couramment appelée dégénérescence graisseuse. Le vin gras devient visqueux et huileux.

Voir CHAPITRE V

Grand cru

Vignoble de qualité.

Grand Cru classé

Désignation spéciale réservée aux meilleurs des quelque 3 000 châteaux vinicoles de la Gironde. Les Médoc, les Sauternes et les Barsac furent classés en 1855 ; les Graves, en 1953 ; les Saint-Émilion en 1955 et 1986. En 1965, l'appellation Grand Cru classé fut exclusivement réservée par la loi aux Bordeaux.

Grand-La-Lagune (Château-)

Voir LAGUNE

Grand Marnier

Liqueur du type Curaçao à base d'eau-de-vie de vin et à goût d'orange. Cette marque appartient aux Établissements Marnier-Lapostolle de Neauphle-le-Château et Château de Bourg.

Cette liqueur douce se présente sous deux espèces : la rouge est la plus forte et la jaune la plus douce.

Grand-Pontet (Château-)

Bordeaux rouge. Commune de Saint-Émilion.

Situé sur le plateau parmi les grands vignobles du Saint-Émilion, ce cru fait un des vins les plus honnêtes de la région. Il appartenait jusqu'en 1979 à la maison Barton et Guestier, qui elle-même appartient à Seagrams, depuis 1981 il est la propriété de M. Bécot.

Superficie : 14 ha.

Production moyenne : 60 tonneaux (6 000 caisses).

Grand-Puy-Ducasse (Château-)

Bordeaux rouge. Commune de Pauillac, en Haut-Médoc.

Un tiers du vignoble est une partie de l'ancien Château-Grand-Puy ; le reste de cette vigne constituant maintenant le Château-Grand-Puy-Lacoste. Un autre tiers se trouve près de Château-Batailley, au sud de Pauillac ; et le troisième tiers, au nord, près des Château-Pontet-Canet et Château-Mouton-Rothschild.

D'après la classification de 1855, Grand-Puy-Ducasse est un Cinquième Cru. Le château se trouve sur une large artère qui borde les quais de Pauillac. C'était, jusqu'au début des années 80, un musée du vin et le siège de la Commanderie du Bontemps, association vinicole du Médoc.

Caractéristiques : Bonne race, mais plus léger et moins bien constitué que le Grand-Puy-Lacoste.

Superficie : 36 ha.

Production moyenne : 140 tonneaux (14 000 caisses).

Grand-Puy-Lacoste (Château-)

Bordeaux rouge. Commune de Pauillac, en Haut-Médoc.

La plus grande partie de ce vin est exportée vers l'Angleterre, les États-Unis et l'Allemagne. Cinquième Cru du Médoc. le vignoble est planté sur un des points les plus élevés de Pauillac (en vieux français, *puy* signifiait *hauteur*). L'histoire de ce domaine remonte à la fin du XVe siècle. Après la Révolution, un certain M. Lacoste l'acheta et lui donna son nom. Comme Château-Calon-Ségur, c'est un des rares domaines vinicoles du Médoc d'un seul tenant, indivis et resté intact depuis la classification de 1855.

Caractéristiques : Excellent vin corsé, un peu rude en sa jeunesse mais qui, en vieillissant, devient extrêmement plaisant et de grande race. M. Dupin, propriétaire de ce cru depuis 1934, a beaucoup contribué à la belle réputation acquise par ce grand vin et il en est légitimement fier. Il gardera longtemps la réputation d'avoir été un des plus grands gastronomes du Médoc pour la période de l'après-guerre. Actuellement, Grand-Puy-Lacoste appartient à Eugène Borie (propriétaire de Ducru-Beaucaillou) et mériterait mieux que son cinquième rang datant de 1855.

Superficie : 45 ha.

Production moyenne : 180 tonneaux (17 000 caisses).

Grand-Saint-Bernard

Liqueur suisse d'un vert pâle.

Grande (Fine) Champagne (A.O.C.)

Le meilleur secteur des vignobles de Cognac. Ce nom sur une étiquette indique la marque d'une eau-de-vie de la meilleure qualité au point de vue origine. D'après certains, il faut ajouter un pourcentage déterminé de vin des Borderies (autre versant de la Charente) pour donner de la chaleur à la splendide finesse de la Grande Champagne. Cette région doit sa distinction à son sol crayeux.

En français, le mot *champagne* désigne cette nature de sol, seul élément qui soit commun à la Grande Champagne et à la Petite Champagne de la région de Cognac et aux vins de Champagne.

Voir COGNAC

Grands-Échezeaux (Appellation Contrôlée)

Bourgogne rouge. Commune de Flagey-Échezeaux, en Côte de Nuits. Classement officiel : Grand Cru.
(Flagey-Échezeaux n'est pas une appellation et quand les vins de cette commune ne se conforment pas aux normes minimales, ils sont vendus comme vins communaux de Vosne-Romanée.)

Le mythe largement répandu selon lequel tous les Bordeaux sont légers et tous les Bourgogne puissants peut aisément être démenti par celui qui met côte à côte une bouteille de Grands-Échezeaux et une bouteille de bon Saint-Émilion.

Grands-Échezeaux se trouve entre Vougeot et Vosne-Romanée. Ses vins se situent logiquement à mi-chemin entre la vigueur charnue des premiers et l'aisance, l'élégance aristocratique des seconds. Leur corps, bien équilibré, en fait des breuvages bien arrondis, dotés d'une délicatesse et d'une finesse dont les Bourguignons disent qu'ils sont *en dentelle*. Bien que peu connus, ils comptent indiscutablement parmi les plus grands de tous les Bourgogne rouges.

Le vignoble couvre une superficie de 9,15 ha sur une colline d'où l'on aperçoit toute l'étendue de Clos-Vougeot. Il est partagé entre plusieurs propriétaires dont le Domaine civil de la Romanée-Conti et quelques excellents vignerons fort capables, notamment les fils de René Engel et de Louis Gros.

La production annuelle s'élève à quelque 350 hl (3 800 caisses).

Grand vin

Terme utilisé librement sur les étiquettes ; il n'est donc pas une garantie légale de qualité supérieure.

Granja Uniao

Marque commerciale de certains des meilleurs vins brésiliens, rouges et blancs.

Voir BRÉSIL

Granjo

Vin blanc naturellement doux du Portugal, obtenu en laissant la pourriture noble attaquer le raisin avant la vendange, selon la méthode des Sauternes et des Spätlese allemands.

Grappa

Nom italien du marc : alcool obtenu par la distillation du résidu de pressoir. On use aussi de ce mot en Californie et dans les pays de langue espagnole. La plupart des Grappa sont durs, grossiers, jeunes et, en fin de compte, médiocres.

Gras

Gros vin doux manquant de cette dureté qui lui donnerait du corps, et riche en glycérine naturelle. Les Bordeaux, Pomerol et certains Saint-Émilion en sont un exemple typique.

Graves (Appellation contrôlée)

Vins blancs et rouges. Région de Bordeaux.

Bien des étrangers qui n'ont goûté que des coupages médiocres de ce secteur prenaient les Graves tout simplement pour des blancs douceâtres. En réalité, les meilleurs blancs des Graves sont secs et les plus grands Graves sont rouges. Ce secteur s'étend sur une longueur de 65 km et atteint presque 20 km en sa plus grande largeur, entre le Sauternes et le Médoc. Une grande variété de sites et de sols est à l'origine, évidemment, des vins de types différents.

La ville de Bordeaux se trouve en Graves. l'extension de ses faubourgs fait reculer la vigne. Seuls de grands domaines comme Haut-Brion et la Mission-Haut-Brion ont trop de valeur pour succomber sous l'invasion de la pierre et du béton. Ils subsistent à l'état insulaire au milieu des bâtiments et des magasins en bordure d'une grand-route. Néanmoins, au Moyen Age, quand les bourgeois vignerons de Bordeaux retournaient précipitamment à l'abri des murs de leur vigne, cette proximité offrait un grand avantage. Dans les deux sens du mot, les Graves sont le premier secteur de Bordeaux. En Angleterre d'ailleurs, où l'on consommait la plus grande partie de ces vins, Graves et Bordeaux étaient synonymes. Il en était encore ainsi au XVIIIe siècle lorsque Pepys décrivit le bon vin de Haut-Brion. Mais au siècle suivant, la mode fut au Médoc. Quelque temps après les guerres napoléoniennes, Haut-Brion tomba dans la médiocrité en raison d'une mauvaise gestion. Après 1850, l'épidémie d'oïdium sévit durement en Graves dont les vignerons ne reconstituèrent que lentement leurs vignobles. Est-ce pour cela ou pour des raisons de politique locale qu'en 1855 les Graves ne furent pas compris dans la classification des vins de la Gironde ? Cependant Haut-Brion, qui avait recouvré son ancienne splendeur, ne pouvait être ignoré, on le classa Premier Cru du Médoc, sans se soucier de la géographie. En réalité, tous les grands vins rouges des Graves — vigoureux, charnus et durables — ont toujours eu leurs partisans. Les viticulteurs reprirent une activité normale et, en 1864-65 — avant que le phylloxéra ne fasse ses ravages —, les expéditeurs purent négocier à nouveau avec profit avec eux.

Le mot Graves dérive de gravier ; le sol de ce secteur est en effet fort pierreux, et convient donc aux raisins rouges Cabernet Sauvignon, Cabernet Franc, Merlot, Malbec et Petit-Verdot. On retrouve le même sol en Pomerol, Saint-Émilion et Médoc. Les vignes sont aussi les mêmes qu'en Médoc et les vins rouges des deux secteurs ont un air de famille.

Les Médoc (surtout les Margaux) sont plus féminins et délicats ; les Graves ont plus de corps, un caractère particulier et une netteté très agréable.

En réalité, les Graves rouges sont plus nombreux que les blancs. Dans la partie sud du secteur, à proximité du Sauternais, le sol devient sablonneux et les raisins à vin blanc dominent : Sémillon, Sauvignon et très peu de Muscadelle, comme en Sauternes. Les Graves blancs sont surtout secs, principalement au nord (le meilleur de tous est le Haut-Brion blanc, produit en petite quantité) mais ceux qui avoisinent Sauternes sont suaves, pleins et moelleux.

C'est le pays des châteaux les plus romanesques du Bordelais ; des petits cours d'eau sinuent entre vignes et bois.

Parmi les châteaux, citons : Olivier, qui se reflète dans les eaux calmes de ses fossés et fut jadis un pavillon de chasse du Prince Noir ; Labrède, entouré aussi de fossés, est encore plus beau. C'est là que vécut Montesquieu et qu'il cultiva ses vignes ; Labrède est cependant plus fameux pour sa bibliothèque que pour ses vins.

En 1953, on classa enfin les meilleurs

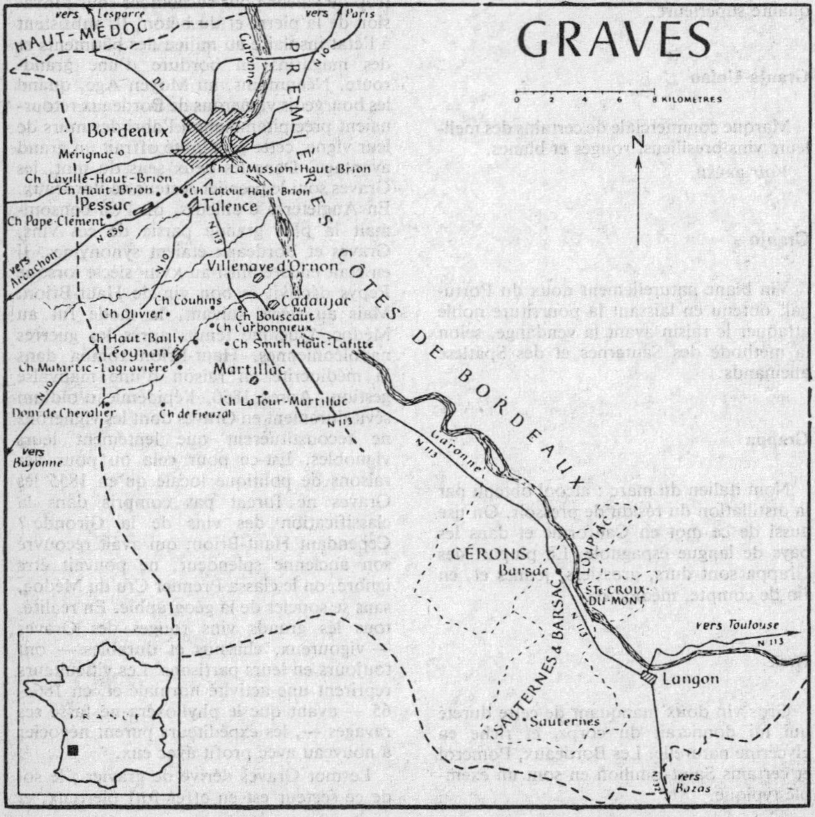

crus de Graves : rouges et blancs. La classification souleva tant de critiques qu'il fallut la réviser en 1959. On n'y ajouta que deux rouges et trois blancs, ce qui ne donna guère de satisfactions.

Voir le tableau de la classification 1959 des Graves.

CLASSIFICATION OFFICIELLE DES GRAVES EN 1959

(Voir chacun de ces crus à sa place dans l'ordre alphabétique, ainsi que la liste de tous les crus de Graves à l'appendice A, VII.)

CRUS CLASSÉS POUR LEUR VINS ROUGE ET BLANC

	Commune
Château-Bouscaut	Cadaujac
Château-Carbonnieux	Léognan
Château de Chevalier	Léognan
Château-Haut-Brion	Pessac
Château-La Tour-Martillac	Martillac
Château-Malartic-Lagravière	Léognan
Château-Olivier	Léognan

CRUS CLASSÉS POUR LEUR VIN ROUGE

	Commune
Château-de-Fieuzal	Léognan
Château-Haut-Bailly	Léognan
Château-Haut-Brion	Pessac
Château-La Mission-Haut-Brion	Pessac
Château-La Tour-Haut-Brion	Talence
Château-Pape-Clément	Pessac
Château-Smith-Haut-Laffite	Martillac

CRUS CLASSÉS POUR LEUR VIN BLANC

	Commune
Château-Couhins	Villenave-d'Ornon
Château-Laville-Haut-Brion	Talence

Dans ces deux classifications, le Château-Haut-Brion figure parmi les vins rouges des Graves, tout en restant un Premier Cru du Médoc. Une des erreurs les plus flagrantes des premières classifications des Graves fut l'omission du Château-Haut-Brion blanc. C'est pourtant un des meilleurs vins blancs secs de Bordeaux. Notons que cette erreur fut réparée en 1960.

En 1987, l'Appellation d'Origine Contrôlée Pessac-Léognan fût reconnue. Elle s'étend sur dix communes et les crus classés de Graves font tous partie des 55 châteaux de la nouvelle appellation.

Voir BORDEAUX

Graves de Vayres (Appellation Contrôlée)

En face de Libourne, sur l'autre rive de la Dordogne, une enclave de sol pierreux pénètre dans la vaste région d'Entre-deux-Mers spécialisée dans les blancs secs de qualité moyenne. La qualité de ce terrain pierreux est nettement supérieure et mérite sa propre appellation : Grave de Vayres. Vayres en est l'agglomération la plus importante et Graves désigne dans la région ce genre de sol. Cette appellation est plus célèbre que de raison en Allemagne où les Graves de Vayres à bon marché sont vendus pour des Graves quoiqu'ils ne leur ressemblent guère.

Le Graves de Vayres rouge vieillit rapidement. Très attrayant et souple, il soutient la comparaison avec les Pomerol et Saint-Émilion d'au-delà de la Dordogne, qui ne sont pas les meilleurs. Leur production s'élève à environ 6 000 hl par an (environ 65 000 caisses).

Suaves et moelleux, les blancs (guère plus de 12 000 hl, soit 130 000 caisses) se distinguent par leur tendance à la graisse.

Graves supérieur (Appellation Contrôlée)

Vins blancs de Bordeaux.

Appellation d'origine contrôlée attribuée à tous les vins blancs du secteur délimité des Graves qui titrent au minimum 12°C, par fermentation naturelle. Bien que les Graves produisent des vins rouges et des blancs, seuls ces derniers ont droit à cette appellation particulière. On fait souvent remarquer à juste titre que la mention « supérieur » n'indique pas une supériorité de qualité, mais seulement de teneur en alcool. Néanmoins, les crus classés et les plus réputés des Graves blancs sont des

Graves supérieur. La production annuelle s'élève à quelque 19 000 hl, soit plus de 210 000 caisses.

Voir GRAVES

Gray Riesling, Gray Dutchess

Raisin blanc de Californie qui n'est d'ailleurs pas du tout un Riesling mais un descendant du Chauché gris français.

Gray Rot

Maladie du raisin qui se manifeste par une altération du fruit et par des taches sur les feuilles.

Grèce

La culture de la vigne est une des principales activités agricoles de la Grèce. Le sol et le climat de ce pays le destinèrent, dès les temps les plus reculés, à la viticulture sur laquelle on trouve bien des références dans l'*Iliade* et *l'Odyssée*. La terre calcaire de la Grèce continentale, de la Crète et d'autres îles, et le sol volcanique d'îles connues pour leurs vins, comme Santorin, conviennent à la vigne. Des 165 000 ha de vignobles, 90 000 sont consacrés à la vigne à vin.

Le climat sec donne des raisins très sucrés et les vins ont un goût fruité caractéristique, surtout ceux qui sont très doux. Les vins destinés à l'exportation sont faits selon les méthodes les plus modernes, dans de véritables usines à vin, par de gros manufacturiers. Mais les viticulteurs n'en sont pas là et continuent à cultiver leur vigne comme au temps où leurs ancêtres adoraient Dionysos.

Après la guerre gréco-turque qui suivit la Première Guerre mondiale, les Grecs réfugiés, originaires des régions vinicoles d'Asie Mineure, étendirent le vignoble grec et le pays exporta de grandes quantités de vin, surtout entre 1926 et 1929. Durant les années qui suivirent la Seconde Guerre mondiale, la guerre civile et les réapparitions du phylloxéra ainsi que du mildiou endommagèrent beaucoup les vignes. On prit des mesures contre le phylloxéra et on reconstitua le vignoble qui couvre maintenant une surface égale à celle d'avant-guerre.

Placée en neuvième position dans la production européenne et quatorzième dans la production mondiale, la Grèce occupe maintenant une place importante sur le marché mondial. Elle produit en moyenne 5 200 000 hl de vin par an (environ 55 millions de caisses), dont 450 000 d'hl (5 millions de caisses) sont exportés, principalement en Allemagne Fédérale, Suisse, Suède, au Bénélux et aux États-Unis.

Jusqu'à récemment on n'avait fait que de rares tentatives pour contrôler la qualité et appliquer des lois d'appellation. Insouciant, le consommateur grec n'exigeait pas grand-chose du producteur. Il en résultait que les vignobles étaient menés à la va-comme-je-te-pousse. En général on considère le vin comme une chose aussi nécessaire que l'eau et l'air, et sa consommation comme un droit acquis. Il y en a d'ailleurs assez pour la population et il est souvent bon marché. La plus grande partie du vin grec n'est même pas mise en bouteille et vieillit dans d'énormes cuves. On ne saurait parler d'un commerce de vins fins ; rares sont les petits propriétaires qui embouteillent un minimum de vin.

Néanmoins on a mis au point certaines lois de contrôle qui furent promulguées dans les années 70 et sont mises en vigueur progressivement. Depuis 1976, une nouvelle législation vinicole adaptée aux exigences modernes de la production des vins et conforme aux lois du Marché Commun est entré en vigueur. 26 régions viti-vinicoles ont été délimitées et reconnues avec des appellations d'origine. Un Institut de Vin qui dépend du ministère de l'Agriculture est chargé du contrôle de la qualité des vins grecs. Toutefois, un nombre insuffisant d'œnologues qualifiés rend très difficile l'application des contrôles. Depuis 1970, les prix sont contrôlés par l'État.

Tel qu'il se présente maintenant, le négoce du vin grec peut se diviser en trois principaux secteurs : 1. les coopératives ; 2. les grandes entreprises privées ; 3. les producteurs agissant pour leur propre compte sur une plus petite échelle. Il existe cinquante-cinq coopératives (disposant de 40 % de la capacité totale en cuves) et 250 entreprises privées. Les sept plus importantes sont Botrys, Boutari, C.A.I.R., Kourtakis, Porto Carras, Cambas et Achaia-Clauss, qui fournit près de 80 % de la totalité du vin grec consommé sur le territoire, soit 15 millions de bouteilles et une quantité encore plus impressionnante de vin en vrac. La consommation annuelle par habitant est d'environ 44 l : une grande partie de ce vin est d'ailleurs fait par les paysans-vignerons, pour être presque immédiatement consommé.

Les maisons de négoces et les coopératives ont beaucoup investi ces dix dernières années afin de moderniser leurs installations vinicoles ; elles tendent à augmenter la mise en bouteilles, et font des efforts renouvelés pour promouvoir les vins grecs à l'étranger.

Régions vinicoles de Grèce

Le Péloponnèse

C'est la région vinicole grecque la plus importante (66 000 ha) et qui produit le plus : 25 % soit plus de 1 113 000 hl (12 millions de caisses). Une des plus importantes firmes, la coopérative de Patras, est située à l'extrême nord, en face de Messolonghi. C'est là que Byron mourut de fièvre (mais depuis, on est venu à bout des moustiques vecteurs de malaria). Aux environs de Patras, port important du pays, sont installées plusieurs maisons vinicoles dont Achaia-Clauss S.A., Beso S.A., et Transetcom S.A.

On atteint Patras par une ravissante route côtière le long du golfe de Corinthe ou par une voie de chemin de fer parallèle. La ville niche au pied d'une montagne abrupte. Sur 8 km de large, la vigne couvre ses flancs. Elle se compose des variétés Mavrodaphni, Muscat, Aghiorghitico et Phileri. On n'y voit quelques sillons et rangées de plants bien taillés. D'autres poussent à la diable, comme de la broussaille, sous un soleil ardent. Certaines des meilleures appellations grecques viennent de cette région : quelques rouges, mais surtout des blancs secs. On y produit aussi

un Muscat doux et, plus important encore, le Mavrodaphni extrêmement sucré (on en fait aussi sur l'île de Céphalonie). Le Mavrodaphni de Patras est un des rares vins de dessert qui semble mieux s'exprimer quand il n'est pas frappé mais chambré. C'est un rouge cher, lourd, sucré, qui titre de 14 à 16ºC. Parmi les autres vins de la région, citons le Tegée, léger et rosâtre ; le souple Mantinée, le Nemée ou « sang d'Hercule », sec, si foncé qu'il en est presque noir.

L'Attique

Avec 15 % de la production nationale du vin, l'Attique, qui jouit d'un climat très chaud, vient au second rang des régions vinicoles grecques. Au sud d'Athènes, les vignobles produisent une grande quantité de vins ordinaires pour la consommation domestique. Ils s'étendent à proximité des plages, au-delà d'une route bien pavée. On y cultive du Savatiano blanc, cépage à partir duquel on prépare les meilleurs vins résinés, appelés Retsina, et également du Mandilaria, pour les vins rouges et du Rhoditis, pour le rosé. C'est cette région qui produit le Marco et aussi l'Hymette au pied de la montagne du même nom. Ce vin doit être bu entre sa deuxième et sa quatrième année.

Citons encore le Pallini, l'un des meilleurs vins grecs, préparé avec soin sur un petit domaine qui porte ce nom.

La Macédoine

Les parties occidentale et centrale de cette région sont particulièrement favorables à la viticulture et sont devenues un véritable centre de production de vins rouges. Sur les coteaux méridonaux et ensoleillés du mont Velia, l'appellation Naoussa provient de Xynomavro. Du côté est, à Chalkidiki, on prépare de nouvelles plantations de cépages nobles. La famille d'armateurs grecs Carras, planta un vignoble important dans les années soixante, près de leur station touristique.

La vinification du vin, appelé Porto Carras, était surveillée par le professeur Émille Peynaud, l'éminent œnologue de Bordeaux.

L'île de Rhodes

Célèbre jadis pour son Colosse, cette île était déjà un centre de civilisation à l'époque mycénienne. Longtemps plus tard les chevaliers de l'Hôpital s'y installèrent.

On fait du vin à Rhodes depuis des siècles et peut-être des millénaires. La coopérative C.A.I.R. est le principal producteur. Le vin blanc sec le plus connu est produit à partir de la variété de raisin Athiri, et le rouge à partir de l'Amorgiano. Le Lindos, est un blanc sec qui provient des vignes cultivées autour de la ville de Lindos qui abrite les ruines célèbres.

L'île de Samos

Séparée de la Turquie par un étroit bras de la mer Égée, l'île de Samos fut complètement privée de ses vignes que les Turcs rasèrent l'année où ils conquirent Constantinople (1453). Pourtant, lorsque les Grecs la reconquirent, en 1912, ils y trouvèrent des vignobles et des vins aussi bons qu'avant.

Durant les 25 années suivantes, une succession de lois fit de Samos une des rares appellations contrôlées de Grèce. Aucun vin qui n'est fait sur cette île, avec des raisins cultivés sur cette île, n'a droit au nom de Samos. D'autre part, il est interdit de mêler le vin de Samos à n'importe quel autre, alors que les vins grecs de toute autre origine ont droit à un coupage atteignant 30 %. Afin d'assurer l'exécution de cette loi, il est interdit d'importer à Samos des vins d'une autre partie de la Grèce.

Le Muscat de Samos, vin doux, est un des deux vins grecs que l'on trouve le plus souvent à l'étranger et que l'on aime le plus (l'autre est le Mavrodaphni). Le raisin Muscat blanc, planté sur 2 300 ha, fournit la plus grosse partie des vins de Samos.

Le relief accentué de cette île montagneuse aux coteaux si abrupts qu'il faut souvent y tailler des terrasses convient bien à la vigne. Le raisin jaune d'or y prospère sous un climat doux, mais l'époque de la vendange varie beaucoup d'un vignoble à l'autre : sur la plaine, elle commence en août ; pour les vignes plantées haut sur la montagne, en octobre.

Outre le Samos naturellement doux, on fait à Samos des vins de liqueur et chez tous on retrouve le goût et le bouquet accentué du Muscat.

L'île de Santorin

Les vignes cultivées sur le sol volcanique de cette île appartiennent à diverses variétés et donnent des vins secs et doux, parfois fort agréables.

Le bon vin sec porte toujours l'étiquette Santorin ; le doux (de moins en moins produit) soit la même, soit la mention Vino Santo. Sur les collines rôties au soleil de cette île magnifique, le raisin atteint une telle teneur en sucre que le vin titre souvent jusqu'à 17°C.

La Crète

Cette grande île est un centre important de la viticulture grecque. Ses collines ensoleillées assurent un bon rendement. Les vignes qu'on y cultive appartiennent aux variétés Romeiko, Kotsifali, Mandilari et Liatico. Elles fournissent des vins de table robustes et charnus, riches en alcool.

De sérieux efforts ont été faits en Crète pour protéger les quatre appellations : Sitia, Dafnès, Archanes et Peza. Certains sont étiquetés Candie (ou Archanes). Les grandes coopératives de production s'appellent Chania, Heraklion, Archanes et Peza. A. Cambas, S.A. et Achaia-Clauss possèdent des vignobles en Crète, mais une petite partie seulement des vins que vendent ces firmes provient de leurs propres crus. Les 45 000 ha produisent environ 1 million d'hl (11 millions de caisses).

L'Épize

Région montagneuse du nord-ouest. La zone vinicole de Zitsa, près de la ville de Yannina, produit des vins semi-pétillants faits à partir du Debina. Metsovo et Cabernet Sauvignon sont ses deux vins les plus réputés.

Autres régions

L'île de Céphalonie produit un vin blanc à partir du Robola, cépage blanc. Les environs de la ville de Rapsani, au centre-est du pays, produisent de bons vins rouges à partir du Mauroudi.

AUTRES VINS GRECS

Retsina

C'est le plus populaire des vins de Grèce, mais ce nom ne désigne pas un type particulier de vin, il en couvre toute une variété : ceux à qui on a donné artificiellement la saveur de la résine de pin. C'est le cas de la plupart des vins grecs blancs et rosés clairs (Kokkineli), mais pas des rouges. Dans les régions méridionale et centrale du pays, presque tout le monde — surtout à la campagne — préfère ce vin à goût résineux. Plus de 80 % des vins de l'Attique, faits avec du raisin Savatiano, sont traités de cette manière.

Maintes histoires hypothétiques cherchent à expliquer comment on en est venu à résiner ainsi le vin. Selon une de ces théories, les Grecs de l'Antiquité se servaient de résine pour enduire les jarres de terre cuite dans lesquelles ils conservaient leurs vins ; ils y prirent goût et continuèrent plus tard à ajouter de la résine, délibérément. Selon une autre, cette coutume résulte d'un incident : le manque de chêne obligea les vignerons à utiliser des fûts de pin. Toutefois, cette théorie est contredite par le fait que les jarres trouvées dans des tombes égyptiennes, antérieures à la période classique de l'Antiquité grecque, sont enduites de résine et de bitume. On peut considérer que, dès cette époque, les Anciens estimaient que la résine améliorait le goût du vin. Nous savons que les Romains ajoutaient aussi de la poix et d'autres ingrédients au vin, que l'on ne pouvait boire que coupé d'eau, mais cet usage n'a plus court en Italie de notre temps.

Le Restina doit être bu frais. Les Grecs disent que le meilleur vient des environs d'Athènes. Les paysans qui en font pour leur propre consommation opèrent selon des méthodes ancestrales ; souvent ils le boivent peu après la fermentation.

Le Restsina titre entre 12,5 et 13°C. Contrairement à la plupart des vins, il ne s'améliore pas avec l'âge.

Monemvasia ou Malvoisie

De nos jours, le nom Monemvasia désigne n'importe quel vin de n'importe quelle région de la Grèce possédant plus ou moins les caractéristiques du Malvoisie. Jadis pourtant, Monemvasia — port d'eau profonde du sud de la Grèce — était un centre actif d'exportation de vin. Cette ville donna son nom aux vins qu'elle expédiait, mais qui étaient produits à Naxos et sur d'autres îles des Petites Cyclades, ainsi qu'en Crète, notamment autour de Candie.

Le Monemvasia circula sur toute la Méditerranée. On l'appela Malvagia en Espagne ; Malvasia en Italie ; Malvoisie en France et Malmsey en Grande-Bretagne (pays importateur). Il y était célèbre au temps de Shakespeare et même avant. Tout le monde se souvient aussi de l'anecdote selon laquelle le duc de Clarence se serait noyé dans une barrique de Malmsey.

On est resté longtemps sans comprendre que Malvoisie n'est pas une appellation d'origine mais simplement un type de vin ou encore un vin fait avec du raisin Malvoisie et qu'il provient aussi bien d'Espagne que de Grèce, de Madère que de Crète.

Parmi les autres vins grecs qu'on trouve parfois à l'étranger, il y a le Mantinée, vin blanc sec des hauteurs de l'Arcadie qu'il est bon de consommer aux environs de sa cinquième année et bien rafraîchi ; le Mavro Naoussis, vin rouge de couleur foncée, provient de Naoussa, au centre de la Macédoine.

SPIRITUEUX GRECS

Eaux-de-vie

Les meilleures eaux-de-vie de vin grecques sont faites avec du Savatiano et les raisins de variétés rouges et blanches cultivés sur le continent ou sur l'île de Samos. Elles se présentent sous trois espèces : les plus jeunes qui, l'on suppose, ont cinq ans d'âge ; les Cinq-Étoiles qui en ont paraît-il vingt-cinq et les Sept-Étoiles plus de quarante (ce qui est faux). Couleur et arôme dérivent naturellement du vieillissement en fût. D'autres eaux-de-vie peuvent être douces et additionnées d'ingrédients, qui leur donnent du goût, pour être consommées en apéritif ou en digestif. Les marques les plus populaires de ces alcools secs et clairs sont Metaxa, Botrys, Cambas et Lizas.

Ouzo et Mastika (ou Masticha)

Ce sont les principaux apéritifs. L'Ouzo est un breuvage au goût d'anis qu'on prend généralement froid, additionné d'eau ou « on the rocks ». Comme l'absinthe, les pastis et les Pernod, l'eau trouble sa couleur et le rend brumeux.

Faite à base d'eau-de-vie à laquelle on ajoute de la gomme de *Pistacia lenticus,* la Mastika provient de l'île de Chio surtout, mais, comme l'Ouzo, elle est aussi originaire de la Grèce continentale. Le Tsipouro est aussi une eau-de-vie fermenté aromatisée à l'anis.

Raki

C'est un spiritueux du même genre que l'Arrack, consommé au Proche-Orient. Les Grecs en font surtout sur la côte est, à partir de vins neutres dans lesquels macèrent des figues et autres fruits. D'un blanc clair, fort et ardent, on le consomme sans se soucier du temps durant lequel il a vieilli. C'est un breuvage rustique.

Tsipouro

C'est une eau-de-vie fermentée aromatisée à l'anis.

Greco

Raisin qui sert à faire le Greco di Bianco, certains vins de Calabre et d'autres régions d'Italie.

Greco di Bianco (D.O.C.)

Un des meilleurs vins de Calabre. Doux et doré, il est doté d'un bouquet fleuri.
Voir CALABRE

Greco di Tufo (D.O.C.)

Vin blanc sec italien
Voir CAMPANIE

Greffage sur place

Pour une description de cette méthode de greffage.
Voir CHAPITRE IV

Grenache

Raisin sucré qui donne des vins de forte teneur en alcool et au bouquet caractéristique. Il sert à faire le Grenache doux (un vin de dessert) à Banyuls, dans la région du Roussillon. On le cultive ailleurs en France, sous le nom d'Alicante, Carignane rousse, Tinto, etc. En Espagne, on le nomme Alicantina ou Garnacha. Implanté au nord de la Californie il y donne d'excellents rosés.

Grenadine

Sirop rouge sucré qui en général ne contient pas du tout d'alcool et parfois très peu. On s'en sert pour sucrer et parfumer d'autres breuvages. A l'origine, la grenadine était faite avec des grenades.

Grignolino

Raisin italien qui, au Piémont, donne un vin rouge sec, soit capiteux, soit demi-doux et pétillant. La culture de cette vigne décline malheureusement en Italie. Les deux D.O.C. sont Grignolino d'Adi et Grignolino del Monferrato Casalese.

Grillet (Château-) (Appellation Contrôlée)

Vin blanc de la vallée du Rhône.

Situé sur les coteaux qui longent le Rhône, ce cru couvre environ 2,7 ha des communes de Verin et de Saint-Michel-sous-Condrieu. Il produit près de 1 000 caisses (100 hl) de vin par an. C'est un blanc sec capiteux, harmonieux et plein, avec parfois un léger arôme de Muscat, quoiqu'il soit entièrement fait avec du Viognier. Dans les grandes années, il peut être superbe, parmi les meilleurs blancs de la vallée du Rhône, et même surpasser les Hermitage blancs, mais il est produit en quantité si réduite qu'il sort rarement de la région. On en vend beaucoup au restaurant de la Pyramide, à Vienne, où les vins subissent une sélection très sévère avant d'être admis dans les caves de la maison. Pourtant, le vin est plus connu pour sa rareté que pour sa qualité.

Grinzing

Coteau viticole et faubourg de Vienne. C'est là qu'on boit le Heurige : vin nouveau.

Voir AUTRICHE

Griotte-Chambertin (Appellation Contrôlée)

Bourgogne rouge. Commune de Gevrey-Chambertin, en Côte de Nuits. Classement officiel : Grand Cru.

Vin charnu, parfois splendide, mais rarement vendu sous sa propre appellation. Le vignoble est partagé entre un nombre de propriétaires relativement restreint pour la Bourgogne. Ces vins sont généralement vendus à divers négociants dont quelques-uns ont la fâcheuse habitude de les utiliser pour allonger des crus plus réputés. Malgré cette habitude regrettable, les 2 ha de Griotte-Chambertin produisirent 100 hl de vin par an, équivalant à 1 000 caisses environ.

Gris (Vin)

Le vin gris est un rosé souvent attribué à l'Asace mais qui, en réalité, provient de Lorraine.

Voir LORRAINE ; ALSACE

Grk, Gerk

Vin blanc sec, d'un jaune clair, fait en Dalmatie. Il a un arrière-goût caractéristique.

Voir YOUGOSLAVIE

Grog

Mélange d'eau chaude, de rhum et de citron, très apprécié par temps froid pour combattre rhume ou grippe. A l'origine c'était seulement un rhum dilué baptisé ainsi d'après le surnom (Old Grog) de l'amiral Vernon (1684-1757) qui aurait le premier ordonné de mouiller le rhum de la British Navy. Dans les pays anglo-saxons, on donne parfois ce nom par extension au rhum consommé pur.

Grolleau (Groslot)

Raisin cultivé en France surtout pour faire des rosés d'Anjou. On l'appelle aussi Pineau de Saumur.

Grombalia

Région qui produit 90 % des vins tunisiens.

Gros Plant du Pays Nantais

V.D.Q.S. de la Loire-Atlantique, dans la composition duquel entre exclusivement du raisin Gros Plant. Il n'existe qu'en blanc et titre au minimum 8,5 °C.

Voir V.D.Q.S.

Gros rouges

Les « Bourgognes » californiens ordinaires et la plupart des vins ordinaires français, italiens et espagnols sont de ceux-là. Ils ont du corps mais sont totalement dénués de finesse.

Gruaud-Larose (Château-)

Bordeaux rouge. Commune de Saint-Julien en Haut-Médoc.

Le domaine — alors appelé Fond-Bedeau — fut acheté en 1757 par un certain M. Gruaud, qui en changea le nom. Trente ans plus tard, la fille de M. Gruaud épousait un M. Larose, lequel racheta les terres et apposa son nom à celui de feu son beau-père. Les étiquettes antérieures à 1934 indiquent soit Gruaud-Larose-Sarget, soit Gruaud-Larose-Faure. A l'origine, il n'y avait qu'un seul vignoble qui fut partagé en deux il y a un peu plus de cent ans, quand les héritiers Sarget en vendirent la plus grande partie à un certain M. Faure.

En 1925, le vignoble fut acheté par Désiré Cordier. Son fils, Georges réunit Gruaud-Larose-Sarget et Gruaud-Larose-Faure en 1934. Depuis le Château Gruaud-Larose produit constamment de bons vins. Les Cordier, qui furent propriétaires d'une des maisons les plus prospères de Bordeaux, possédaient également le Château Talbot, aussi à Saint-Julien (ces vignobles furent rachetés en 1983 par le groupe « La Hénin », propriétaire, dans le Midi, des vins de table « Listel »).

Gruaud-Larose est un Second Cru du Médoc d'après la classification de 1855.

Caractéristiques : Vin bien équilibré qui vieillit rapidement et qui est le type même des meilleurs Saint-Julien. Finesse remarquable et parfum léger.

Superficie : 76 ha.

Production moyenne : 250 tonneaux (22 000 caisses).

Gruenberg

Petite région vinicole isolée des alentours de Grünberg, en Silésie, Allemagne orientale.

Grumello

Vin rouge de la Valteline (Italie), fait avec du raisin Nebbiolo.

Voir LOMBARDIE

Grünfer Veltliner

Principale variété de raisin cultivée en Basse-Autriche.

Guebwiller

Agglomération vinicole alsacienne des environs de Colmar.

Guignolet

1. Eau-de-vie de cerise noire. On la produit surtout en Anjou, en Touraine et en Vendée.

2. Marque d'apéritif consommé partout en France, le Guignolet a un goût de cerise, titre 16° et on y ajoute du kirsch au moment de le boire.

Guiraud (Château-)

Bordeaux blanc. Commune et secteur de Sauternes.

Château-Guiraud et Château-d'Yquem sont les seuls Sauternes classés officiellement en 1855 qui sont réellement à Sauternes. A cette époque-là on estimait que la commune de Sauternes était trop petite pour fournir une quantité de vin capable de lui assurer une réputation mondiale. Les experts étendirent donc l'appellation à quatre communes avoisinantes où se trouvent les autres douze meilleurs crus.

Le château est un bâtiment caractéristique du XIXe siècle, style chartreuse, niché au milieu des arbres. Devant lui se trouve un chai long, en forme de L, avec à une extrémité une tour en forme de moulin à poivre, coiffée d'un toit conique. Les vignes bien tenues s'étendent dans le prolongement du chai.

En 1981, Guiraud fut vendu à un Canadien, Hamilton Narby. Ce vin a fait de grands progrès. M. Narby fait également un bon vin sec : le « G de Guiraud ».

Caractéristiques : Assez doux, pourrait

être racé. Quelques millésimes remarquables.

Superficie : 52 ha.

Production moyenne : 90 tonneaux (8 000 caisses).

Gumpoldskirchner

Vin blanc délicat, un des meilleurs d'Autriche, provenant des vignobles de Gumpoldskirchen.

Voir AUTRICHE

Gunflint Taste

Littéralement : goût de pierre à fusil.

Gutedel

Variante allemande de la famille des Chasselas. Elle est également cultivée en Australie.

Gutsname

Nom allemand des propriétés vinicoles, équivalant à Château, en Bordelais, et à Clos, en Bourgogne.

Gutturnio dei Colli Piacentini (D.O.C.)

Bon rouge sec d'Italie.

Voir ÉMILIE-ROMAGNE

Guyenne (Connétablie de)

Voir PREMIÈRES CÔTES DE BORDEAUX

Guyot

Variété de taille en espalier. Elle consiste à ne conserver qu'une seule branche et à laisser se développer le tronc. Cette méthode est très utilisée dans les régions de grand vin tel que le Médoc.

Voir CHAPITRE IV

Gyöngyös

Les vins blancs mousseux de Gyöngyös figurent parmi les meilleurs de Hongrie. On fait aussi des rouges dans la même région, et en plus grande quantité.

Voir HONGRIE

H

Halbrot

Nom que les Suisses donnent au vin rosé et qui signifie littéralement : demi-rouge.

Halbstueck

Tonneaux utilisés pour le vieillissement et le stockage des vins du Rheingau, d'une capacité de 600 l.

Half-on-half

Liqueur hollandaise de couleur rousse faite de Curaçao et de Bitter d'orange, en parties égales.

Hallgartner Schönell

Vignoble exceptionnel de Hallgarten, d'où provient un des meilleurs vins de Rheingau. Jungfer, autre cru important des environs de cette ville, mérite également d'être cité.

Voir RHEINGAU

Happocras

Vin aromatisé consommé au Moyen Age. Probablement était-il fait de vinaigre sucré et épicé ; filté à travers de la laine, ce filtre s'appelait manche d'Hippocrate.

Haro

Petite ville espagnole située sur le fleuve Ebro. Haro est le centre du commerce des vins de Rioja.

Voir RIOJA

Harriague

Raisin cultivé en Uruguay surtout.

Voir TANNAT

Hárslevelü

Variété hongroise de raisin qui sert à faire le Tokay et d'autres vins.

Hattenheimer Nussbrunnen

Un des plus grands vins du Rheingau.

Voir RHEINGAU

Hattenheimer Wisselbrunen

Un des plus grands vins du Rheingau qui, avec Hattenheimer Nussbrunnen et Steinberg, forme le superbe triumvirat des vins d'Hattenheim.

Voir RHEINGAU

Haut, Haute

Ajouté à un nom de lieu, sur une étiquette de vin, cet adjectif ne signifie absolument rien en ce qui concerne la qualité et n'a qu'un sens purement géographique : plus élevé, ou en amont. Par exemple, le secteur bordelais du Haut-Médoc s'appelle ainsi parce qu'il est en amont du Médoc, sur le cours de la Gironde. Que son vin soit meilleur n'est qu'une coïncidence. Il existe des exemples inverses. Le Haut-Armagnac est inférieur en qualité au Bas-Armagnac. Quant à l'appellation d'origine Haut-Sauternes, elle ne signifie rien parce qu'il n'existe pas de région géographique qui porte ce nom et, en ce qui concerne la qualité, cette appellation est dénuée de sens.

Haut-Bages-Libéral (Château-)

Bordeaux rouge. Commune de Pauillac, en Haut-Médoc.

Ce vignoble divisé en deux parties — l'une attenante à Pontet-Canet, l'autre proche de Château Latour — fut classé Cinquième Cru de Médoc en 1855. Il fut racheté et remis en état en 1960 par les Cruse qui, en 1983, vendirent la propriété à Jacques Merlot, déjà propriétaire de Chasse-Spleen.

Caractéristiques : Assez charnu et peu commun. Le vin est en train de s'améliorer.

Superficie : 23 ha.

Production moyenne : 80 tonneaux (8 000 caisses).

Haut-Bailly (Château-)

Bordeaux rouge. Commune de Léognan, en Graves.

Contrairement à la plupart des Grands Crus des Graves, Haut-Bailly ne produit pas de vin blanc, et son rouge figure parmi les onze crus classés du secteur en 1953 et 1959.

Restauré voilà quelque soixante-quinze ans, après les ravages du phylloxéra, par M. Ballot des Minières, qui avait en ce temps-là la réputation d'être le roi des vignerons, ce cru connut une excellente période puis tomba en décadence. Dans l'espoir de faire mieux que son prédécesseur, le propriétaire suivant poussa si loin la modernisation qu'il en vint à mettre son vin en bouteille huit mois après les vendanges au lieu de deux ans et ensuite à le pasteuriser. Il appartient maintenant à M. Sanders et depuis que Haut-Bailly a été libéré de ces entreprises progressistes, il a recouvré son ancien prestige. Bien équilibrés et charnus ses vins se distinguent des Graves et ressemblent plutôt à certains Médoc. On y cultive 70 % de Cabernet Sauvignon, 20 % de Merlot et 10 % de Cabernet Franc.

Caractéristiques : Vin charnu, bien arrondi, avec une grande finesse.

Superficie : 25 ha.

Production moyenne : 80 tonneaux, (8 000 caisses).

Haut-Batailley (Château-)

Bordeaux rouge. Commune de Pauillac, en Haut-Médoc.

Jusqu'en 1924, ce vignoble faisait partie du domaine de Château-Batailley et partage donc avec ce dernier le titre de Cinquième Cru de Médoc d'après la classification de 1855. Il appartient maintenant à Mme des Brest-Borie, sœur de Jean-Eugène Borie, qui fit beaucoup pour hausser Château Ducru-Beaucaillou au niveau de qualité qu'il a aujourd'hui. Les chais se trouvent à Saint-Julien, non loin de ceux de Château Ducru-Beaucaillou.

Caractéristiques : Très semblable à Château-Batailley, avec une petite robustesse et très bien vinifié.

Superficie : 22 ha.

Production moyenne : 60 tonneaux (6 000 caisses).

Haut-Brion (Château-)

Bordeaux rouge et blanc. Commune de Pessac, en Graves.

Ce château, dont l'histoire est vieille de près de cinq siècles, est aujourd'hui indiscutablement l'un des plus grands vignobles producteurs de vins rouges du monde. Il appartient actuellement à M. Douglas Dillon, ancien Secrétaire d'État au Trésor des États-Unis, et à sa famille. Plus que tout autre vignoble, Haut-Brion a été considéré comme le symbole de la qualité des vins de Bordeaux et comme le producteur du Bordeaux le plus traditionnel.

Depuis cinq siècles, le nom de ce cru figure, sous des orthographes diverses, dans les archives du Bordelais. Nous savons que

Jean de Ségur l'acheta en 1509. Il passa entre les mains de l'amiral Philippe de Chabot en 1525 ; la carrière de Chabot étonna, dit-on, Brantôme ; il était auprès de François Ier quand ce dernier fut fait prisonnier à Pavie. Chabot ne garda pas longtemps Haut-Brion qui passa à la famille Pontac, dans la dot de Jeanne de Bellon. Puis une autre Pontac l'apporta en dot à un membre de la famille Fumel qui posséda aussi Château-Margaux pendant un certain temps alors que d'autre part les Pontac étaient propriétaires à Blanquefort d'un autre vignoble qui produisait les vins blancs appelés Pontac, célèbres au XVIIe siècle, en Angleterre. Ce nom figurait aussi alors sur les étiquettes du rouge de Haut-Brion. En 1666, François-Auguste de Pontac acheta une participation dans une taverne londonnienne connue sous le nom de Pontac's Head et très fréquentée par la noblesse. On y buvait du Haut-Brion à discrétion. Ce serait la première fois dans l'histoire qu'un vin de Bordeaux fut appelé par son nom à l'étranger, et non pas vendu comme simple « Bordeaux ». Il y avait en ce temps-là, dans la cité de Londres, une autre taverne tenue par un cuisinier français : le Royal Oak de Lombard Street, où Pepys allait boire « une sorte de vin français appelé Ho Bryen qui avait un bon goût très particulier ». En 1683, John Evelyn notait dans son journal qu'il s'était entretenu avec M. Pontac, fils du célèbre président au parlement de Bordeaux, et propriétaire de l'excellent cru de Haut-Brion, d'où venait le plus grand vin de Bordeaux. Dryden, Swift et de Foë dînèrent à leur tour dans cette taverne et Swift estima que, à 7 shillings le flacon, son vin était cher. En 1677, Locke, le philosophe, rendit visite à Haut-Brion et remarqua que ses prix avaient augmenté « en raison des commandes envoyées par de riches Anglais qui tiennent à en avoir, coûte que coûte ».

C'est pendant les années prospères du XVIIIe siècle que les vins du Médoc l'emportèrent en popularié sur ceux des Graves. Mais Haut-Brion conserva tout son prestige. En 1770, le comte de Fumel divisa le domaine en deux. Il conserva le château avec une partie de la vigne et vendit le reste, appelé Chai Neuf, au marquis de Latresne. Quand éclata la Révolution, le château appartenait à son cinquième fils, Joseph, maire de Bordeaux qui fut guillotiné en 1794. Une partie du château fut saisie par l'État, et une autre resta entre les mains de la famille qui racheta ensuite la part de l'État et la revendit, en 1801, à Talleyrand qui la garda jusqu'en 1804.

Rien n'indique que Talleyrand ait vécu à Haut-Brion, mais ne doutons pas qu'il sut se servir de son vin. Ses succès de diplomate étaient dus non seulement à sa vivacité d'esprit, au charme de sa conversation et au talent de son cuisinier, mais aussi à l'excellence de ses bouteilles. Au congrès de Vienne il vint à bout de tout le monde et ce fut, dit-on, en invitant les autres diplomates à des dîners somptueux.

Après 1804, Haut-Brion connut la phase la moins glorieuse de son histoire sous une série d'hommes d'affaires. Enfin, en 1836, J.-E. Larrieu acheta ce château. Quatre années plus tard, il put acquérir aussi « le chai neuf » et remembrer le domaine en son état antérieur. En peu de temps il restaura aussi la qualité du vin. C'est ainsi qu'en 1855, lors de la classification des prestigieux vins de la Gironde, Haut-Brion fut classé Premier Cru (alors qu'on omit d'autres grands Graves) avec les trois grands Médoc : Lafite, Latour et Margaux.

Quand le reste des Graves fut enfin classé, en 1953 et encore en 1959, le somptueux rouge de Haut-Brion fut évidemment mentionné à la première place. Ainsi ce Château est à la fois Premier Cru des Graves et de Médoc. Haut-Brion blanc, moins célèbre que le rouge (surtout parce qu'il ne représente que dix pour cent de la production du château), est pourtant en général un des blancs secs les plus caractéristiques et les meilleurs de tout le Bordelais. Alors que les autres Premiers Crus ont vu leur production ou leur taille s'accroître, Haut-Brion est resté à une production d'environ 140 tonneaux par an, celle-ci étant limitée par la proximité des banlieues environnantes.

Le vignoble est situé dans la banlieue de Bordeaux. Les immeubles de la grande ville et ceux de Pessac l'entourent de tous côtés. On y cultive essentiellement les vignes à vin rouge sur les collines qui entourent les principaux chais et le château. Tout à fait au sommet, poussent, sur un terrain plat, les vignes de Sémillon et de Sauvignon qui donnent le vin blanc. Haut-Brion fut le premier des grands châteaux du Bordelais à utiliser des cuves de fermentation en acier inoxydable, que tous les œnologues modernes préfèrent (non seulement du point de vue de la fermentation et du contrôle des températures, mais aussi pour des raisons d'hygiène) aux anciennes cuves de bois que l'on trouve encore dans les chais de certains Grands Crus. Cette modernisation ambitieuse fut entreprise au début des années 1960 sous la direction de feu Seymour Weller, alors président de Haut-Brion depuis près de quarante ans. Le château et ses terres offrent aujourd'hui un aspect fort soigné et superbement digne. Vers la fin des années 1960, la magnifique entrée de pierre fut restaurée. En 1973, on entreprit la construction d'une magnifique cave souterraine. Enfin, en 1974, Haut-Brion fut magnifiquement redécoré, ses vieux murs décapés pour montrer toutes la beauté des anciennes pierres. Cette transformation est l'œuvre de l'actuelle propriétaire du Château, la princesse Joan de Luxembourg, fille de Douglas Dillon et aujourd'hui Duchesse de Mouchy.

Le sol sur lequel on cultive les vignes à vin blanc est assez argileux alors que celui des vignes à vin rouge est constitué par une épaisse couche de graves (le nom du gravier dans la région). Ce gravier, qui a donné son nom à tout le secteur des Graves, atteint à Haut-Brion une épaisseur de 15 à 20 m. On dit que cette terre poreuse, dont les cailloux réfléchissent le soleil, retiennent la chaleur et laissent fuir l'eau, serait le facteur qui assure la haute qualité de Haut-Brion, même en moins bonnes années. L'eau n'y séjourne pas et la terre a l'aridité qui plaît à la vigne.

Caractéristiques : Le rouge est un très grand vin, souvent très charnu, avec le goût particulier qu'il doit au sol pierreux des Graves. Il atteint une grande élégance et, même les moins bonnes années, il est capable de mieux réussir que les vins du voisinage, parce que le raisin, en raison de sa situation, y mûrit un peu plus tôt. Il est aussi plus facile de recruter des ouvriers saisonniers dans les faubourgs de Bordeaux où le personnel disponible abonde et peut aisément suspendre le travail durant la pluie.

Le Haut-Brion blanc est un des meilleurs vins secs de toute la région de Bordeaux. Contrairement aux Château-Lafite, Latour, Margaux et Mouton, Haut-Brion ne peut étendre la superficie de ses vignobles ; c'est pourquoi la quantité de Haut-Brion produite reste relativement faible, alors que la production des autres Premiers Crus ne fait qu'augmenter ces dernières années.

Superficie : rouge, 66 ha ; blanc 3 ha.

Production moyenne : rouge, 130 tonneaux (13 000 caisses) ; blanc, 14 tonneaux (1 400 caisses).

Haut-Comtat

V.D.Q.S. du département de la Drôme, dans la région de Nyons. Le rouge et le rosé titrent 11° au minimum. Pas de blanc.

Haut-Médoc

Vins rouges. Région de Bordeaux.

Le meilleur secteur du Médoc pour la production du vin rouge et aussi une appellation d'origine contrôlée, limitée à la fraction du Médoc qui est le plus en amont au long de la Gironde. Ce secteur comporte des subdivisions qui sont aussi des appellations d'origine : Margaux, Pauillac, Saint-Julien, Saint-Estèphe et tous les plus célèbres châteaux du Médoc.

Voir MÉDOC

Haut-Montravel

Voir MONTRAVEL

Haut-Peyraguey (Clos)

Bordeaux blanc. Commune de Bommes, en Sauternais.

Le vignoble, en déclivité, entoure un « château » qui ressemble plutôt à une habitation rurale peinte à la chaux. Le sol se compose d'une marne semée de pierres. Selon la classification de 1855, le vin de Haut-Peyraguey a droit au titre de Premier Cru.

Caractéristiques : Vin doux, distingué, racé, fait avec soin.

Superficie : 11 ha.

Production moyenne : 25 tonneaux (2 000 caisses).

Haute-Savoie

Ce département de France compte deux appellations contrôlées de vin blanc : Crépy et Seyssel *(voir ces noms et* SAVOIE).

Hectare

Mesure de superficie égale à 10 000 m².

Hectolitre

Unité de mesure égale à 100 l. Tous les vins ordinaires français sont vendus à l'hl.

Heidelberg Tun

Tonneau construit en 1751 par le maître tonnelier Jacob Engler le Jeune, pour l'Électeur Karl Theodor, et qui se trouve au château d'Heidelberg. D'une contenance de 200 000 l, il n'a été rempli que trois fois et voilà longtemps qu'il fuit. La pompe qui servait à en soutirer le contenu est encore exposée dans la salle royale (Königsaal) du château.

Hérault

Un des trois départements qui produisent la plus grande quantité de vin en France. Les deux autres sont l'Aude et le Gard. Les environs de Montpellier et Béziers fournissent une très grande quantité de vin ordinaire, ainsi qu'un blanc sec, de qualité supérieure : la Clairette du Languedoc (A.O.C.). Un des meilleurs vins rouges de l'Hérault est le Minervois (A.O.C.).

Voir VINS DE LIQUEUR FRANÇAIS

Hermitage, Ermitage
(Appellation Contrôlée)

Vins rouges et blancs de la vallée du Rhône.

Célèbre depuis longtemps les vins de l'Hermitage proviennent des vignes cultivées sur les coteaux qui dominent Tain, petite agglomération des bords du Rhône, située à quelque 80 km au sud de Lyon, et guère plus de 20 km au nord de Valence. Des petites vignes en terrasses soutenues par des murs de pierre couvrent la colline qui se dresse, abrupte, derrière la ville. Une chapelle en ruine, dédiée à Saint-Christophe, construite jadis sur l'emplacement d'un temple élevé par les Romains à Mercure, est un des traits caractéristiques du paysage. D'après une légende du pays, Saint-Patrice y aurait planté des vignes durant son premier séjour en France. Le cru doit son nom à un ermite, le chevalier Gaspard de Stérimberg, qui se serait retiré au sommet du coteau dans le but d'y faire pénitence après la croisade contre les Albigeois en 1224. Il termina sa vie en méditant et en cultivant la vigne. Il offrait son vin aux pèlerins qui venaient le voir car il ne possédait rien d'autre. Et c'est ainsi que la réputation de l'Hermitage se répandit.

Sur 220 ha de sol maigre (une mince couche de calcaire sur un dur sous-sol de granit) la vigne ne donne que 40 hl/ha. En outre, elle est vulnérable à la coulure *(voir ce mot),* on ne s'étonnera donc pas que l'authentique Hermitage soit rare et cher.

Le raisin à vin rouge est du Syrah qui, d'après certains, serait originaire de la province de Shiraz, en Perse, et que Stérimberg aurait rapporté lui-même d'une croisade. D'après d'autres ce serait les Romains qui auraient introduit cette vigne en France. En tout cas, Hermitage serait un des plus anciens vignobles français.

Pour le vin blanc, on cultive surtout du Marsanne et une petite proportion de Roussanne au centre du coteau. La production de blanc est inférieure à 12 000 caisses par an, mais il s'agit de vin nettement caractérisé, charnu, avec un goût de pierre à fusil qui convient aux plats aussi fortement épicés que le curry. Il compte parmi les blancs secs qui durent le plus longtemps et garde ses qualités jusqu'au-delà de vingt ans d'âge. Mais il finit par madériser et il est en général préférable de le consommer entre ses six et quinze ans.

Le blanc et le rouge ont tendance à la dureté dans leur jeunesse.

Rugueux à ses débuts, le rouge devient moelleux et velouté, grand et généreux à la maturité et il se forme au fond de la bouteille un dépôt épais. Avec l'âge, il acquiert un riche arôme, de l'arrière-goût et un bouquet qui évoque la framboise et la giroflée. Sa robe somptueuse passe du violet foncé à la pelure d'oignon.

En Angleterre, au XIXᵉ siècle, l'Hermitage était fort estimé et le professeur Saintsbury le considérait comme « le plus viril des vins ».

On fait trois fois plus d'Hermitage rouge que de blanc. Les meilleurs crus rouges sont : Les Bessards, Le Méal, L'Hermitage, La Varogne, Les Diognières, Les Greffieux et La Pierelle.

Chante-Alouette est parmi les plus célèbres Hermitage blanc. Tous sont secs, délicats, quoique corsés et dotés de bouquet. Chante-Alouette est à la fois le nom d'une terre à vigne et la marque de l'entreprise Chapoutier. Ce vin est en général un mélange du produit des meilleurs vignobles tels que Beaumes, Les Murets, Les Rocoules, La Chapelle, Maison-Blanche et, évidemment, Chante-Alouette.

Certains vignerons doués du sens de la publicité ont peint leur nom à la chaux sur les murs qui soutiennent les terrasses. On y lit : Chapoutier et Paul Jaboulet Aîné, proprétaires de vignes et négociants. La production s'élève à environ 4 500 hl (50 000 caisses).

L'Hermitage est situé juste au-dessus du groupe de vignobles qui produit les vins vendus sous le nom de Crozes-Hermitage (près de 450 000 caisses sont produites annuellement) : vins agréables mais qui ne sauraient être comparés à ceux qui ont droit à l'appellation Hermitage.

Hesse

Voir RHEINHESSEN

Heurige

Vin jeune, léger, parfois fait avec les raisins des treilles qui couvrent les façades des maisons de Grinzing, dans la banlieue de Vienne.

Heurige signifie littéralement « vin de l'année », mais on l'appelle plus généralement vin de mai.

Highball

Breuvage glacé qu'on prend dans un grand verre et qui se compose généralement de whisky à l'eau de Seltz.

Hochheimer-Domdechaney (Hocks)

Ce grand vin fruité est probablement le meilleur de Hochheim, agglomération située sur le Main, au-delà de Wiesbaden. Mais parce qu'il ressemble aux vins du Rheingau, on le classe en général parmi ces derniers. C'est à cet Hochheimer qu'on doit le nom de Hock par lequel les Anglais désignaient autrefois les vins du Rheingau, et, par extension, tous ceux de la vallée du Rhin.

Voir RHEINGAU

Hogshead

Fût de capacité variable et le plus utilisé pour l'expédition en gros de vins et spiritueux. Le nom, utilisé en Angleterre, dériverait du scandinave *ox-hoft,* tonneau d'une capacité variant de 256 à 264 l. La capacité standard du hoghshead varie selon le liquide qu'il contient, à savoir :

Vins français	:	225 à 228 l
Bières, cidres et Xérès	:	246 l
Whiskies	:	250 l
Porto	:	259 l
Eau-de-vie	:	273 l

Voir BARRIQUE ; TONNEAU ; APPENDICE C

Hollande

Voir PAYS-BAS

Hollands

Genre de gin que l'on trouve d'habitude en Hollande, où on l'appelle Jenever (genièvre). On le vend souvent dans des cruches de grès. Il diffère du London Dry (le gin britannique et américain courant) du fait qu'il est moins redistillé. Comme celle du Scotch, du Cognac et du rhum de la Jamaïque, la distillation du Jenever est assez légère pour que le goût de la matière distillée se retrouve dans le distillat alors que celle du London Dry est tellement poussée qu'il est incolore et insipide à la sortie de l'alambic et qu'on doit ensuite le consommer en mélanges qui lui donnent du goût. Les Hollands ne sont donc pas des composants neutres de cocktails et les Hollandais le boivent sec.

Voir GIN

Homeburn

Nom que les Norvégiens donnent aux spiritueux distillés au foyer.

Honey Brandy

Littéralement eau-de-vie de miel, obtenue par la distillation de l'Hydromel.

Voir HYDROMEL

Hongrie

Le plus célèbre vin hongrois, vin des empereurs et des rois, c'est le Tokay *(voir ce nom)* et les autres vins du pays sont plus ou moins éclipsés par la réputation de cet aîné prestigieux. Pourtant certains sont excellents. Les Hongrois se targuèrent des normes de vinification les plus élevées et de contrôles stricts. La Hongrie fût, en effet, un des pionniers (la première loi fût passée en 1893) des appellations d'origine portant sur le lieu de provenance et la variété du raisin.

On a toujours fait du vin en Hongrie. Les 3/4 de ses vignobles furent détruits en 1875 par le phylloxéra et, en 1891, par le pernospora, maladie cryptogamique de la vigne. On reconstitua les vignobles comme en France, en greffant les variétés locales sur des souches américaines. On sabla plus de 100 000 ha de vignobles, le sol sablonneux rendant les vignes moins vulnérables au phylloxéra. Il y a en Hongrie de nombreuses fermes d'État (exploitant 15 % des régions viticoles) ; des entreprises de viniculture (qui disposent de peu de vignobles mais d'un réseau national de caves vinicoles — vinification, stockage, embouteillage —) ; des coopératives agricoles (qui vendent la majeure partie de leur raisin aux entreprises de viniculture et aux fermes d'État) ; et de petites entreprises (qui procèdent à la transformation du raisin selon les méthodes traditionnelles ou bien en vendant leur récolte au secteur d'État ou aux coopératives. La participation de ces petites entreprises dépassent 50 %). La production moyenne s'élève maintenant à environ 5 millions d'hl (55 millions de caisses) par an dont 75 % de vin blanc et le reste en vins rouges et « Siller ». En outre, la Hongrie produit plusieurs vins rouges de grande qualité. La moitié de la production est exportée principalement vers les pays socialistes. Cependant, la République Fédérale d'Allemagne est un des marchés traditionnellement importants. Monimpex, société d'exportation hongroise à Budapest, est la seule agence autorisée à exporter du vin de Hongrie. La Hongrie est un pays où la consommation de vin annuelle *per capita* s'élève à 25 l environ.

RÉGIONS VITICOLES DE LA HONGRIE

La Hongrie est découpée en quatre régions naturelles et délimitées géographiquement : I - La région principale de la Grande Plaine/Alföld ; II - La région principale de la Transdanubie du Nord ; III - La région principale de la Transdanubie du Sud et IV - La région principale de la Hongrie Septentrionale.

La Grande Plaine/Alföld couvre près de la moitié des terres, de l'est du Danube à la frontière roumaine. La Transdanubie, la Pannonie romaine, se trouve entre le Danube et le Drava, divisée par le lac Balaton en deux zones, Nord et Sud. La région de la Hongrie Septentrionale, près des Carpathes, qui longe à l'est de Budapest la frontière slovaque, est une région vraiment montagneuse.

I - LA RÉGION PRINCIPALE DE LA GRANDE PLAINE		
		ha
1.	Alföld/La Grande Plaine	70 000
II - LA RÉGION PRINCIPALE DE LA TRANSDANUBIE DU NORD		
2.	Ászár-Neszmély	2 800
3.	Badacsony	2 500
4.	Balatonfüred-Csopák	2 250
5.	Balatonmellék	2 550
6.	Mór	1 300
7.	Somló	500
8.	Sopron	1 750
III - LA RÉGION PRINCIPALE DE LA TRANSDANUBIE DU SUD		
9.	Dél-Balaton	3 500
10.	Mecsekalja	1 500
11.	Szekszárd	1 850
12.	Villány-Siklós	1 500
IV - LA RÉGION PRINCIPALE DE LA HONGRIE SEPTENTRIONALE		
13.	Bükkalja	4 000
14.	Eger	3 400
15.	Mátraalja	7 550
16.	Tokajhegyalja	7 000

Tous les vignobles hongrois furent recensés au cadastre viticole entre 1948 et 1953. La superficie actuellement plantée en vignes de la Hongrie est de 160 000 hectares qui se répartissent maintenant en seize régions vinicoles, la région de Tokajhegyalja constitue une région naturelle (*voir* Tokay). Il existe également des terrains non classés mais favorables à la production du vin.

Les régions viticoles se classent selon leur production et la qualité des vins, en :

1) Régions produisant des vins blancs de « qualité supérieure » : Tokajhegyalja, Badacsony, Balatonfüred-Csopak, Somló. 2) Régions produisant principalement des vins blancs « d'excellente qualité » : Ászár-Neszmély, Balatonmellék, Bükkalja, Dél-Balaton, Mátraalja, Mecsekalja, Mór. 3) Régions produisant principalement des vins rouges « d'excellente qualité » : Eger, Sopron, Szekszárd, Villány-Siklós. La Grande Plaine/Alföld produit la grande majorité du vin commercial hongrois, et notamment, les vignobles sablonneux cités ci-dessus.

VARIÉTÉ DE RAISINS

La Hongrie possède de nombreuses variétés de raisins d'origine, dont quelques-uns fournissent les vins les plus appréciés. En ce qui concerne les vins blancs, les variétés les plus importantes sont le Furmint, élément principal du Tokay (Tokaj) ; le Hárslevelű (ce qui signifie « feuille de tilleul » à cause de la forme caractéristique de ses feuilles) ; c'est le second élément, par son importance, du Tokay ; le Kéknyelű (ce qui signifie « tige bleue », caractéristique du vin) et le Szürkebarát (« moine gris »), une sorte de Pinot Gris. Parmi les autres vins d'origine, il faut citer l'Ezerjó (« mille bienfaits »), le Leányka (« jeune fille »), le Mézesfehér (« miel blanc »), le Juhfark (« queue d'agneau »), le Budai Green et le Piros Cirfandli. Parmi les variétés d'autre origine européenne, citons le Olaszrizling (Wälschriesling ou Riesling italien), qui est aujourd'hui le cépage blanc le plus répandu en Hongrie ; un peu de Rheinriesling ; le Sylvaner (Szilváni), le Traminer, le Pinot Blanc (Fehérburgundi), le Sauvignon, le Grüner Veltliner, Müller-Thurgau et Bouvier en provenance d'Autriche, et deux muscats, l'Ottonel et le Sárgamuskotály (« Muscat jaune ») — dont on utilise une petite quantité dans la fabrication de Tokay.

En ce qui concerne les vins rouges, la Hongrie élève surtout le Kadarka des Balkans et, en provenance d'Europe occidentale, le Pinot Noir, le Kékfrankos, le Merlot, le Cabernet Franc et le Cabernet Sauvignon, ainsi que quelques Portugais bleu autrichien et des variétés de Zweigelt.

Le Tokay (produit dans la région naturelle de Tokajhegyalja), le plus grand vin hongrois — et assurément l'un des plus grands vins du monde — est décrit en détail sous une rubrique à part.

Badacsony, Balatonfüred-Csopak et *Balatonmellék,* les districts 3, 4 et 5 énumérés ci-dessus, recouvrent les vignobles des collines orientées au sud-est sur le rivage nord du lac Balaton. La vigne a été cultivée

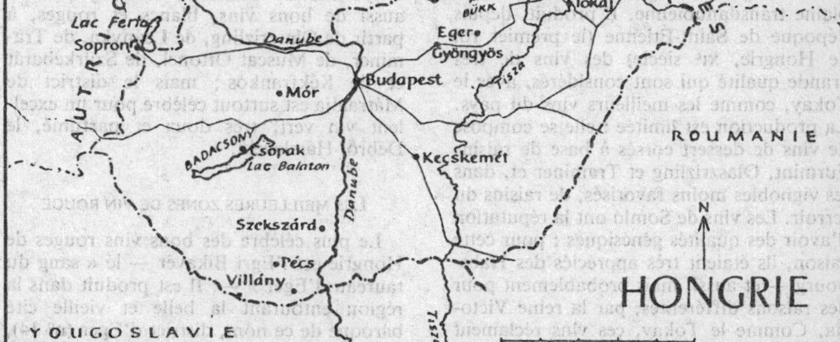

ici, et le vin a été produit, depuis plus de deux millénaires ; sous l'occupation romaine, les excellents vins du Balaton étaient transportés dans les caves impériales à Rome. Le sol du district de Badacsony est constitué de roche basaltique absorbant la chaleur avec un revêtement de loess ; si l'on ajoute cette caractéristique à l'aspect et au micro-climat des alentours du lac Balaton, on obtient des vignobles en terrasses sur les pentes des collines, produisant des vins blancs de la plus haute qualité, à base de Szürkebarát et de Kéknyelű — et, depuis les plantations nouvelles qui on suivi l'épidémie de phylloxéra, d'Olaszrizling.

Les vins hongrois sont souvent étiquetés du nom de leur lieu d'origine suivi du suffixe possessif *i* et du nom de la variété de raisin utilisé — par exemple Badacsonyi Kéknyelű.

Les collines voisines de Balatonfüred-Csopak sont d'une structrue géologique différente (ardoise cristalline avec un revêtement de grès rouge) et elles jouissent d'un climat particulièrement chaud. Les vins, plus doux et plus riches que ceux de Badacsony, sont à base de raisin Olaszrizling, mais aussi de Traminer, Muscat et Sylvaner. Ils sont d'une excellente qualité, ont une très forte personnalité et, à leur façon, ils supportent la comparaison avec les meilleurs vins blancs de France et d'Allemagne. Les autres régions du district de Balaton donnent des vins blancs de qualité, légers, très agréables, d'un style populaire, faits à base de raisins Olaszrizling, Sylvaner Rheinriesling et Traminer.

Somló, le septième des grands districts viticoles, est une petite montagne volcanique couverte de vignes et dominant la plaine transdanubienne. Il produit, depuis l'époque de Saint-Étienne (le premier roi de Hongrie, XIe siècle) des vins de très grande qualité qui sont considérés, avec le Tokay, comme les meilleurs vins du pays. La production est limitée : elle se compose de vins de dessert corsés à base de raisins Furmint, Olaszrizling et Traminer et, dans les vignobles moins favorisés, de raisins du terroir. Les vins de Somló ont la réputation d'avoir des qualités génésiques ; pour cette raison, ils étaient très appréciés des Habsbourg — et aussi, mais probablement pour des raisons différentes, par la reine Victoria. Comme le Tokay, ces vins réclament du temps pour se faire et pour mûrir ; la production étant limitée, ils sont toujours assez chers.

Les districts de Ászár-Neszemély et de Mór (nº 2 et nº 6, page 456), sont, selon les normes hongroises, des vignobles très récents et la plus ancienne partie en a été plantée par des émigrants bavarois au milieu du XVIIIe siècle dans les clairières. Ils sont surtout intéressants pour le vin Ezerjó (Móri Ezerjó) produit par les vignes qui poussent sur le sol sableux, riche en quartz et en mica, du district de Mór. Le phylloxéra ne pouvant survivre sur des sols de cette nature, les ceps poussent sur leurs propres racines. L'Ezerjó, qui, dans d'autres régions de l'Europe du Sud-Est produit des vins sans grande distinction, donne, dans ces conditions particulières, un vin sec d'excellente qualité au bouquet fin et parfumé.

Le district de Mecsekalja (nº 10) fait partie d'un vignoble du sud de la plaine transdanubienne, qui remonte à l'époque romaine et qui était autrefois connu sous le nom de Pécs-Villány. Les collines de Mecsek forment un vignoble de vin blanc autour de la ville de Pécs et de cinq autres villages. Il produit surtout d'excellents vins blancs faits à partir de Olaszrizling, de Furmint et de Cirfandli ; ce sont des vins agréables, bien équilibrés et en grande partie exportés en vrac vers la Grande-Bretagne où ils sont très appréciés.

La grande zone de Mátraalja, ou Mátravidék (nº 15) est, après la grande plaine, le plus vaste vignoble de Hongrie. Au pied des montagnes de Matra, s'étendaient jadis deux zones, Gyöngyös-Visonta et Debrő. La majorité du raisin de table de Hongrie est cultivée dans cette région à partir d'hybrides de Chasselas et on y produit aussi de bons vins, blancs et rouges, à partir de Olaszrizling, de Leányka, de Traminer, de Muscat Ottonel, de Szürkebarát et de Kékfrankos ; mais le district de Mátraalja est surtout célèbre pour un excellent vin vert, très doux et parfumé, le Debrői Hárslevelű.

Les meilleures zones de vin rouge

Le plus célèbre des bons vins rouges de Hongrie est l'Egri Bikavér — le « sang du taureau d'Eger » —. Il est produit dans la région entourant la belle et vieille cité baroque de ce nom, district d'Eger (nº 14), sur un sol d'argile recouvrant une roche volcanique — bonne terre à vin rouge. Bien entendu, ce vin n'a rien à voir ni avec les taureaux ni avec le sang et il est fait à base de raisins Kékfrankos, Merlot connu sous le nom de Médoc Noir, Oporto ou Cabernet Franc. A son apogée, c'est un vin plein, moelleux, foncé, qui se bonifie en vieillissant en bouteille, ce qu'il fait rarement. La légende de son nom vient d'une histoire qui remonte au XVIe siècle, lorsque les puissantes armées turques qui attaquèrent la ville furent repoussées par les troupes locales encouragées par les larges rasades d'Egri Bikavér, meilleur vin rouge hongrois, que leur versaient leurs femmes. L'Egri Kadarka peut également être excellent et il se bonifie aussi en vieillissant en bouteille. Cette région produit de bons vins blancs, riches vins de dessert faits à partir des raisins hongrois Leányka et Mézesfehér, les vins de table plus secs étant faits à partir d'Olaszrizling.

Un des meilleurs vins rouges hongrois est probablement le Kékfrankos qui est produit dans la région de Villány et qui est connu sous le nom de Villányi-Burgundi. Il a nombre de qualités des raisins de Bourgogne et, comme la plupart des autres vins rouges hongrois, il s'améliore en vieillissant quelques années en bouteille. On fait aussi d'excellents vins rouges dans le district de Villány-Siklós (nº 12), avec du raisin Kadarka et des vins plutôt rudes avec de l'Oporto, et du Cabernet. C'est en fait un très bon district pour le vin rouge. Szekszárd (nº 11), un peu au nord-ouest, produit également, avec du raisin Kadarka, un bon vin corsé, plutôt dans le style du Bordeaux. Ces régions sont de vieux vignobles, remontant à l'époque préromaine, avant l'empereur Probus, qui vint de Pannonie et qui encouragea la viticulture. On y cultive aussi le Cabernet Franc et le Kékfrankos.

Sopron (nº 8), le quatrième des districts hongrois pour le vin rouge, est situé à l'extrême nord-ouest du pays, dans le Burgenland hongrois, à la frontière autrichienne. La viticulture remonte ici aux Celtes, à l'époque pré-romaine, et c'est le nom de Sopron qui, il y a des siècles, répandit à travers l'Europe occidentale la renommée des vins de Hongrie. On produit ici des vins de toutes sortes, rouges et blancs, mais la célébrité de ce district est fondée sur un vin fait à partir d'un raisin voisin du Gamay bourguignon ; le Soproni Kékfrankos, qui rappelle le Beaujolais et qui doit être bu jeune et frais.

Les terrains sablonneux

La grande plaine est, en général, la région des vaste fermes d'État, sur des terrains sablonneux que les Magyars ont, au cours des siècles, soumis et transformé en terres arables. Ce fut, et c'est toujours, une lutte épique, mais la vigne, avec ses racines allongées, peut y pousser. Cela fut d'une grande importance lors de l'épidémie de phylloxéra, car le puceron du phylloxéra ne peut survivre sur des sols de cette nature. La plupart du vin produit dans l'Alföld n'est pas d'une grande qualité, mais il satisfait les exportations vers l'Allemagne par exemple ; il sert à la fabrication du Sekt, à la distillation et il constitue la base du vermouth. Mais on trouve dans l'Alföld d'anciennes oasis, surtout entre le Danube et la Tisza : Kecskemét, vieille localité de vignobles et de vergers ; Jászberény, Csengőd, Solt, Iliskorős, Kiskunhalas et Szeged, dans l'extrême-sud. L'Olaszrizling, l'Ezerjó, le Leanyka, le Cirfandli, le Veltliner, le Hárslevelű, le Kadarka, le Kékfrankos, le Merlot, et le Cabernet sont les principales variétés de cette région, particulièrement dans les vastes et nouvelles plantations, encore que la plupart des vins du terroir, dont quelques-uns sont de grande qualité, soient produits par de vieux vignobles. On produit aussi, à Hajós et Kadarka, un remarquable Cabernet ; un bourgogne à Vaskur.

Types de bouteilles et étiquetage

Le Tokay Aszu et le Tokay Szamorodni sont livrés au commerce dans des bouteilles blanches typiques d'un demi-litre *(voir une description de leur étiquetage par degré de qualité au mot* TOKAY). La plupart des autres vins hongrois d'exportation, y compris d'autres types de Tokay, sont vendus dans des bouteilles hautes et minces, pareilles à celles des vins allemands. Mais l'Egri Bikavér et un ou deux autres figurent sur le marché dans des bouteilles à épaules étroites et carrées, semblables à celles du vin de Bordeaux. Cependant de grandes quantités de vin sont exportées en vrac pour être mises en bouteille par le pays importateur.

SPIRITUEUX HONGROIS

La Hongrie produit une grande variété de liqueurs et d'eaux-de-vie. La plus célèbre est le Barack Pálinka (eau-de-vie d'abricot) non sucrée, produite par la distillation d'abricots frais des vergers de Kecskemét. Elle est vendue dans des bouteilles normalisées de 70 cl et de 35 cl, ainsi que dans le *Fütyülős* (flacon de 50 cl à très long goulot). La même région produit aussi la Kecskeméti Barack, liqueur douce d'abricot qui conserve le riche parfum du fruit.

Les meilleures autres liqueurs de fruit sont faites avec des cerises et des poires de couleur dorée (Császárkorte en hongrois). Autre liqueur intéressante, l'Hubertus, faite à base d'herbes, et d'un goût un peu plus amer.

Parmi les autres eaux-de-vie non sucrées, citons Szilva Pálinka ou Szilvorium (eau-de-vie de prune), vodka, kirsch d'Eger et rhum Casino. Toutes sont plus ou moins connues en Grande-Bretagne, au Canada, aux États-Unis, en Amérique du Sud. Les meilleures Szilva Pàlinka viennent du comté de Szatmár et sont faites avec trois variétés de prunes différentes.

Hops

Nom anglais du houblon.
Voir HOUBLON

Hospices de Beaune

L'antique façade de l'hôpital de la Charité se dresse au centre de Beaune. La vente aux enchères des vins de ces hospices fixe chaque année le barème des prix de base de tous les vins de la Côte-d'Or. Elle dicte donc la valeur de la vendange qui est le sang des Beaunois et elle précède les *Trois Glorieuses :* les trois banquets somptueux au cours desquel les Bourguignons se rassemblent pour boire et glorifier leurs vins préférés.

Les Hospices furent fondés en 1443 par Nicolas Rollin, le chancelier du duc de Bourgogne, et sa femme Guigone de Salins. Il semble qu'à cette époque Beaune était entièrement peuplée de mendiants (vingt-quatre seulement des familles de la ville étaient considérées comme solvables). On n'aurait donc pu trouver de site mieux choisi pour un établissement charitable. Selon certains, Rollin - qui entre autres choses était chargé de la perception des impôts - pouvait se permettre de faire construire un asile pour les pauvres qu'il avait contribué à réduire à la misère. Toujours est-il que sa donation dura et qu'au cours des siècles les Hospices reçurent des dons nombreux, notamment sous forme de lopins plantés de vignes.

Un portail voûté s'ouvre dans le mur d'enceinte et donne accès à une cour pavée de pierres arrondies dans laquelle on aperçoit des groupes de visiteurs et où circulent les sœurs hospitalières : l'administration est néanmoins laïque depuis la fondation. Précisément parce qu'ils étaient gérés par des laïques, les Hospices ne furent pas confisqués à la Révolution, période pendant laquelle un bouillonnement anticlérical amena l'État à saisir les biens de l'Église. Les bâtiments qui entourent cette cour datent du Moyen Age. Des colonnes soutiennent un balcon qui fait tout le tour du quadrilatère. Le toit superbe est couvert de tuiles multicolores et des fenêtres mansardées y pointent, ornées de bois sculpté. Au-delà de cette première cour il y en a d'autres que voient rarement les visiteurs et c'est sur la dernière qu'ouvent les bâtiments dans lesquels on fait le vin.

La vente aux enchères des vins des Hospices de Beaune marque le plus grand événement de l'année bourguignonne. Les négociants y affluent du monde entier. Elle a lieu habituellement le troisième dimanche de novembre. Trois jours avant, déjà la foule grouille dans la ville et, la veille, tout le monde envahit les chais pour goûter le vin. A la fin de cette journée, le premier banquet des *Trois Glorieuses* a lieu au Clos de Vougeot.

La vente proprement dite a lieu au marché de Beaune qui a été aménagé en vue de cette manifestation. Elle est, par exemple, présidée par une personnalité, récemment par le prince Bernhardt des Pays-Bas, l'ambassadeur du Royaume-Uni et celui des États-Unis. Les enchères ont lieu selon un rite traditionnel : « à la chandelle ». On place trois petites bougies dans des bougeoirs et les enchères commencent quand on allume la première : lorsqu'elle se meurt on allume la seconde puis la troisième et le dernier prix entendu avant que la dernière bougie s'éteigne est celui de l'adjudication.

Les enchérisseurs se livrent à une concurrence fiévreuse car posséder ne serait-ce qu'une petite quantité de vin des Hospices de Beaune assure un prestige considérable tant au négociant en vins qu'au restaurateur. Les prix dépassent donc souvent la valeur réelle du vin, mais l'acheteur a au moins la consolation d'apporter sa contribution à une bonne œuvre.

Malheureusement tout le vin est emporté en tonneaux dans les mois qui suivent la vente et tous les acheteurs n'en prennent pas le soin qu'il mérite. Pis encore, les prix sont si élevés et la demande si grande que certains sont tentés d'allonger leur vin.

Les vignes de l'hôpital sont éparpillées partout en Côte de Beaune. Les vins ont bien sûr une appellation mais ils sont plus connus par le nom du donateur des vignes qui les ont produits. La Cuvée du Dr Peste, par exemple, provient des raisins cultivés dans un vignoble de Corton ; plus précisément dans la partie d'Aloxe-Corton appelée la Maréchaude ; mais étant donné que cette parcelle de terre fut donnée aux Hospices par le docteur Peste, le vin est encore vendu sous son nom. Les Hospices possèdent 52 ha de vigne et produisent plus de 2 000 hl (22 000 caisses) par an, dont 75 % de rouge.

En outre, ils mettent à la vente du marc de Bourgogne. Après la vente du vin vient celle du marc de l'année précédente : environ 300 hl par an. Comme pour les vins, les prix sont légèrement plus élevés que pour les marcs de qualité identique distillés n'importe où ailleurs en Bourgogne.

A la fin des enchères, le second banquet des *Trois Glorieuses* a lieu dans les caves des Hospices. Le lendemain cette trilogie se termine par la Paulée : un banquet au village de Meursault ; les vignerons sont censés y apporter une bouteille de vin le meilleur et le plus rare et la faire passer autour de la table. A la fin de ce dernier repas chacun retourne chez soi pour se remettre.

Les résultats des ventes récentes sont les suivants (une pièce équivaut à une barrique de 228 l) :

Pommard — Dames de la Charité *18 pièces,* Savigny-les-Beaune-Arthur Girard *22 pièces,* Beaune-Maurice Drouhin *55 pièces,* Beaune-Dames Hospitalières *44 pièces,* Volnay-Santenots-Gauvain *28 pièces,* Pernand-Vergelesses *13 pièces,* Beaune-Nicolas Rolin *40 pièces,* Savigny-lès-Beaune-Borneret *37 pièces,* Beaune-Clos des Avaux *54 pièces,* Volnay-Santenots-Jehan-de-Massol *25 pièces,* Corton-Docteur Peste *33 pièces,* Monthélie-Lebelin *17 pièces,* Beaune-Brunet *32 pièces,* Volnay-Général Muteau *33 pièces,* Meursault-Genevrières-Baudot *33 pièces,* Meursault-Humblot *6 pièces,* Meursault-Charmes-de Bahèzre de Lanlay *20 pièces,* Beaune-Guigone de Salins *30 pièces,* Savigny-lès-Beaune-Fouquerand *28 pièces,* Auxey-Duresses-Boillot *5 pièces,* Beaune-Rousseau-Deslandes *32 pièces,* Pommard-Billardet *39 pièces,* Beaune-Hugues et Louis Bétault *34 pièces,* Volnay-Blondeau *13 pièces,* Corton-Charlotte Dumay *31 pièces,* Corton-Charlemagne-François de Salins *4 pièces,* Meursault-Charmes-Albert Grivault *11 pièces,* Meursault-Goureau *11 pièces,* Meursault-Loppin *11 pièces,* Meursault-Genevrières-Philippe-le-Bon *11 pièces,* Beaune-Cyrot-Chaudron *16 pièces,* Mazis-Chambertin-Madeleina-Collignon *23 pièces.*

Hotte

Panier d'osier porté à dos d'homme entre les rangs, lors des vendanges. On les fait maintenant en tôle galvanisée ou en matière plastique.

Houblon

Plante grimpante, vivace, aux feuilles rugueuses et lobées comme celles de la vigne. Les cônes couverts du lupulin amer et odorant des fleurs femelles servent à donner du goût à la bière.

On cultive le houblon en Europe, en Asie centrale et en Amérique.

Houghton

Vignoble remarquable de l'Australie occidentale, il appartient à l'Emu Wine Company.

Voir AUSTRALIE

Houx

Alcool blanc fait en Alsace en distillant des baies de houx.

Voir ALSACE, SPIRITUEUX

Hudson (vallée du fleuve)

Région viticole qui s'étend sur la rive droite du fleuve Hudson, entre Newburg et Kingston, dans l'État de New York. Les principaux vignobles sont High Tor Benmarl et ceux de la Hudson Valley Wine Company. On y cultive des cépages américains de *Vitis labrusca* et des hybrides dont le meilleur est Seyval. Cette région produit des vins rouges, blancs et rosés.

Voir ÉTATS-UNIS : ÉTATS DE L'EST

Huelva (Condado de Huelva)

Province d'Espagne qui produit des vins fortement alcoolisés et lourds. Condado de Huelva est une *Denominación de Origen*.

Voir ESPAGNE

Hunter (vallée du fleuve)

Région vinicole de la Nouvelle-Galles du Sud (Australie). On y trouve les vignobles les plus anciens du pays et quelques-uns des rares qui produisent presque exclusivement des vins de table.

Ils sont groupés autour de Pokolbin et de Cessnock.

Voir AUTRALIE

Hybride

Croisement de deux variétés différentes de vigne : généralement l'une appartient à l'espèce européenne *Vitis vinifera* et l'autre, à une espèce américaine. Le but de ces croisements est d'obtenir un plant doté de la rusticité et de la résistance aux maladies propres aux vignes américaines mais qui donnent des fruits de même qualité que ceux des variétés de *Vitis vinifera*. Il existe un certain nombre de bonnes vignes hybrides ; quelques-unes conviennent à certaines localités ; mais il y a encore beaucoup à faire dans ce domaine.

On a procédé à des expériences d'hybridation aux États-Unis (États de New York, du Maryland et de Californie), au Canada et en Europe. Les hybrides obtenus en France portent en général le nom de celui qui les obtint, plus un numéro. Parmi ces noms, les plus connus sont : Baco, Couderc, Siebel, Seyne-Villard et Seyval.

Philip Wagner, de Baltimore, a contribué grandement à améliorer, grâce à ses hybrides, les vignobles de l'Est des États-Unis. Il a réussi de nombreux croisements entre vignes indigènes qui s'accommodent du sol et du climat de l'Est des États-Unis et commencent à diminuer le goût de foxe propre aux vins de cette région.

Voir CHAPITRE IV ; ÉTATS-UNIS

Hydromel

Boisson des anciens Gaulois et Anglo-Saxons, à base de miel fermenté. C'est un liquide pâle, clair et doré au goût de miel, avec environ 8 % d'alcool en volume. L'Hydromel (eau de miel) était aussi connu chez les Romains. Le Metheglin est son équivalent gallois, en plus épicé. Lorsque l'Hydromel est distillé, on l'appelle alors Eau-de-vie de miel.

Hydromètre

Instrument servant à mesurer la teneur en sucre des moûts. Il se présente sous la forme d'une ampoule lestée dont l'extrémité contient une échelle calibrée en grammes de sucre pour 100 g de solution. Le moût est ensuite versé dans un cylindre calibré. On y plonge l'hydromètre qui, s'immobilisera une fois le niveau d'équilibre atteint, celui-ci variant selon la densité de la solution. Le sucre étant la cause première de l'augmentation de la densité du moût au-delà de la densité de l'eau, l'instrument peut être calibré de façon que l'échelle montre directement le pourcentage de sucre à une température établie.

Hydromètre de Sikes

L'hydromètre de Sikes est reconnu légalement comme instrument de mesure de la teneur en alcool des liquides, en Grande-Bretagne.

Voir APPENDICE C : tableau comparatif du degré des alcools entre les mesures françaises, britanniques et américaines.

Voir PROOF SPIRIT.

Hymette

Vins légers, rouges et blancs, produits en Attique, près du mont Hymette.

Voir GRÈCE

I

Immiscible

Qui ne peut se mêler à une autre substance. L'exemple classique de liquides immiscibles est celui de l'huile et du vin. C'est pourquoi avant l'utilisation du bouchon on mettait le vin à l'abri de l'air en versant de l'huile d'olive qui formait à sa surface une pellicule protectrice.

Impériale

Bouteille de taille exceptionnelle, utilisée pour la conservation des grands vins de Bordeaux. Elle contient environ 6 l, soit l'équivalent de huit bouteilles habituelles de Bordeaux.

Importation de vin

On ne peut pas vraiment tirer de conclusions de la quantité de vin qu'un pays importe. Certains grands producteurs en importent des quantités considérables, d'autres pas du tout. Certains pays qui sont relativement pauvres en vins en importent beaucoup, d'autres pas du tout. Ainsi l'Union Soviétique, qui se limitait auparavant à importer des quantités très moyennes, est maintenant devenu le second importateur de vins, en grande majorité algériens. La liste ci-contre représente les moyennes réalisées pour l'importation de vin durant ces dernières années. Ces moyennes ont été rajustées afin d'illustrer les tendances qui semblent se dessiner pour les prochaines années.

Importations de vin dans le monde

Pays importateurs	*hectolitres*
Allemagne Fédérale	9 450 000
U.R.S.S.	6 780 000
France	5 580 000
Grande-Bretagne	5 400 000
États-Unis	5 185 000
Belgique	2 180 000
Pays-Bas	2 130 000
Suisse	1 990 000
Allemagne de l'Est	1 540 000
Canada	1 475 000
Danemark	950 000
Suède	930 000
Japon	550 000
Pologne	485 000
Tchécoslovaquie	300 000
Hongrie	265 000
Autriche	200 000
Italie	165 000
Luxembourg	150 000
Finlande	125 000
Irlande	110 000
Australie	85 000
Bulgarie	85 000
Nouvelle-Zélande	29 000
Mexique	20 000
Afrique du Sud	19 000
Espagne	15 000
Roumanie	12 000
Brésil	4 000
Total	46 209 000

Incrustation

Formation d'une croûte sur le vin, particulièrement le Porto.

Inde

On sait que le vin était déjà connu en Inde voilà 2 000 ans et que les gens du pays en buvaient encore au temps des Mogols. La principale région viticole était alors le Cachemire. Une pièce de monnaie datant de 1628 nous montre le Grand Mogol Jahanjir un gobelet de vin à la main. Il y avait aussi en ce temps-là des vignobles autour de Golconde, Kandahar et Surate. Mais, voilà cent ans, ne survivaient que les vins du Cachemire dont certains furent présentés à l'exposition de Calcutta de 1888. Mais les vignes (importées de Bordeaux) furent alors attaquées par le phylloxéra et il fallut les greffer sur des souches américaines.

On voit encore quelques vignobles autour de Madras. Les vins sont consommés sur place. Les vignobles furent plantés par des missionnaires français, aux environs de 1889. Au cours des dernières années ils se sont étendus autour de Kodaikanal, Dharmapour et Penoukanda. Néanmoins la culture de la vigne y est plutôt une distraction qu'une entreprise sérieuse.

Outre ceux des environs de Madras, on trouve des vignobles dans l'État de Maharashtra. Piper-Heidsieck a conclu un contrat très important (5 millions de dollars) visant à implanter, dans cet État, la première « winerie » de l'Inde. Elle devrait produire chaque année 1 million de bouteilles de vins mousseux et 2 millions de bouteilles de vins tranquilles. Piper-Heidsieck se charge de la plantation du vignoble (en cépages européens : Pinot Noir, Ugni Blanc, Chardonnay) et également de la formation en France du personnel indien.

Bien que la demande en vin soit faible dans un pays où les gens ne s'intéressent guère aux boissons alcoolisées — soit parce qu'ils ne les apprécient pas, soit parce que leur religion les leur interdit — l'Inde produit néanmoins des alcools : jus de palmes fermentés, alcool de riz, mais aussi eaux-de-vie de vin, gin, rhum et whisky. En 1972, ces diverses productions s'élevaient aux chiffres suivants :

PRODUCTION D'ALCOOL EN INDE

	hectolitres
Eaux-de-vie	46 000
Gin	40 000
Whisky	115 000
Rhum et bitters	75 000

Indes orientales

Au temps de la navigation à voile, quand les bateaux doublaient le cap de Bonne-Espérance, on mettait souvent à bord des barils de Xérès et de Madère en guise de lest. Le long voyage aller et retour avec balancement de roulis et tangage améliorait ces vins et les vieillissait. On les appelait alors East India Sherry et Madeira (Xérès et Madère des Indes orientales). Certains négociants donnent encore cette appellation à leurs bons coupages de vin de dessert. On trouve des Xérès Amoroso (Oloroso doux) étiquetés ainsi.

Inferno (D.O.C)

Vin rouge de la Valteline (Italie) fait avec du raisin Nebbiolo.

Voir LOMBARDIE

Ingelheimer

Avec l'Assmannshauser, l'Ingelheimer est un des meilleurs — et peut-être le meilleur — des vins rouges allemands, mais il ne figure certainement pas parmi les meilleurs du monde. Même au sommet de leur plénitude, les vins rouges allemands sont médiocres selon les normes mondiales.

Voir RHEINHESSEN

Institut national des appellations d'origine

Connu couramment sous le sigle de l'I.N.A.O.

Voir APPELLATION D'ORIGINE CONTRÔLÉE (A.O.C.)

Iona

Vigne hybride obtenue par le croisement de deux variétés américaines de l'État de New York où on la cultive actuellement surtout pour faire du vin blanc mousseux. Son fruit d'un rouge foncé est sucré. Sa fermentation fournit un vin sain et nettement sec. L'Iona est un exemple typique de raisin rouge qui sert à faire du vin blanc. Il doit son nom à l'île d'Iona sur le fleuve Hudson près de Peekskill.

Iran

L'Iran fut un des premiers pays où l'on pratiqua viticulture et viniculture. Selon une légende, un souverain de Perse aurait découvert incidemment ce breuvage produit par la fermentation du jus de raisin. Hérodote accusait les Perses de boire à l'excès. La littérature ancienne fourmille de références au vin et à la fécondité des vignes de Perse.

Même après la conquête par les Arabes musulmans, Omar Khayyam continua à chanter les louanges des vins de son pays. Le plus célèbre était le Chiraz. Selon une hypothèse le raisin Syrah, cultivé actuellement dans la vallée du Rhône et ailleurs, aurait été apporté de Chiraz en Europe occidentale par les chevaliers du Moyen Age, au retour des croisades.

Les vignes couvraient 135 000 ha : on les cultivait surtout au pied des montagnes et particulièrement dans les provinces de l'Azerbaïdjan oriental, de l'Azerbaïdjan occidental, de Khorassan, Téhéran, Farse, Hamédan, Lourestan et Zanjan. La production annuelle s'élevait à environ 4 000 hl, dont la quasi-totalité était consommée dans le pays. Pourtant l'Iranien moyen consommait moins d'un demi-litre de vin par an.

Le Thompson Seedless était l'une des variétés de raisins les plus couramment plantées ; il donne des raisins de table de qualité, mais il n'en est pas de même pour le vin. Parmi les villes possédant des centres de vinification, on pouvait trouver : Téhéran, la capitale ; Shiraz *(voir ce nom) ;* Hameadan, situé à 320 km à l'ouest de la capitale ; Malayer, près de Hameadan ; Shiravan, au nord-est ; Shahrooh au nord et Aladeh, à environ 160 km au nord de Shiraz.

Depuis 1979, les mouvements en faveur d'un État islamique ont entraîné une prohibition de toutes boissons alcooliques.

SPIRITUEUX

La Perse produisait 80 000 hl d'Arrak par an. La bière y était également beaucoup plus populaire que le vin ; on la remontait parfois avec du raki et du sucre.

Voir ARRACK

Irancy

Vins rouges et rosés plutôt ordinaires, produits dans le département de l'Yonne, à environ une quinzaine de kilomètres au sud de Chablis, dans le nord de la Bourgogne.

Irouléguy (Vins d')

Vins rouges, blancs et rosés. Pyrénées-Atlantiques.

A l'extrême sud-ouest de la France, perchées dans les sommets des Pyrénées, se trouvent les communes de Saint-Jean-Pied-de-Port et de celle de Saint-Étienne-de-Baïgorry, toutes deux proches de Biarritz, haut-lieu de villégiature, et de Bayonne, célèbre pour ses jambons. Ces deux villages se trouvent au centre des vignobles qui produisent l'Appellation Contrôlée Irouléguy. Les vins blancs sont très semblables aux vins naturellement doux produits non loin de là, dans le Jurançon. Mais les rouges — légers en couleur mais ne manquant pas de goût — leur sont certainement supérieurs.

Isabella

Cépage américain prolifique dont on pensa grand bien un certain temps, mais qui n'est plus utilisé désormais qu'en coupage pour la production de mousseux dans l'État de New York. De couleur bleue, il donne un vin pâle de goût légèrement foxé, et sans caractéristiques prononcées. On le trouve aussi, hélas ! dans le sud de la Suisse, sous le nom d'Americano.

Ischia (D.O.C)

Ile de la baie de Naples, qui produit des vins blancs secs dont une bonne partie est vendue sous l'étiquette « Capri ».

Voir CAMPANIE

Isinglass

Substance gélatineuse blanchâtre et translucide, provenant de la vessie de certains poissons d'eau douce, particulièrement de l'esturgeon. On utilise l'isinglass pour le collage des vins et des bières. En français : ichtyocolle.

Voir CHAPITRE V

Islay

Une des Hébrides, au large de l'Écosse, près de la péninsule de Kintyre. Islay et Kintyre produisent tout le whisky de malt de l'ouest des Highlands.

On trouve à peu près deux fois plus de distilleries à Islay qu'à Campbeltown, qui est le centre industriel de Kintyre.

Voir WHISKY, MALT.

Israël

Israël fait des vins d'à peu près tous les genres : vin de table, rouge et blanc ; vin perlé ; mousseux pour tous les goûts — brut, extra dry, semi-sec et doux — produits selon la méthode champenoise de fermentation secondaire en bouteille. Tous ceux qui sont destinés à l'exportation sont préparés sous contrôle religieux, car les communautés juives de l'étranger peuvent l'utiliser à des fins sacramentelles et comme boisson. Israël produit aussi eaux-de-vie et liqueurs.

Les principaux vins d'Israël, jusqu'à ces dernières années, étaient des rouges et des blancs charnus et doux, des Muscat dorés et un vin doux du genre Tokay. Mais ces derniers temps les vins de table secs et demi-secs, rouges et blancs, deviennent de plus en plus populaires. En 1985 les vins de table représentaient 70 % de la production. Autrefois les Israéliens empruntaient les noms de vin des pays étrangers et des bouteilles étaient étiquetées malaga du Carmel ou bien porto du Carmel. Ils sont en train d'abandonner cette pratique et désormais la plupart de ces vins portent un nom hébreu. Voici les plus intéressants :

Vins doux de dessert

Muscat, Partom, Porath, Porath Atic, Ashdod, Poriah et Vered (autrefois porto). Topaz, Tokeah, Tivon et Savion (autrefois tokay). Almog, Gilon et Nalagenia (autrefois malaga). Sharir (« sherry » : xérès). Yakeneth (« alicante »). Yashan Noshan. Yenon. Moriah. Atzmauth. Château Rishon.

Vins de table secs et demi-secs

Rouges : Adom Atic. Primor (autrefois pommard). Vin Rouge Supérieur. Château Windsor. Carmelith. Atzmon. Mont Rouge. Cabernet Sauvignon. *Blancs :* Carmel Hock. Mont Blem. Massadah. Château Montagne. Levanan. Doron. Yarden. *Rouges et Blancs :* Avdad. Ashkalon. Ben-Ami. Montford.

Vins mousseux

Président, Château de la Montagne, Sambation

HISTOIRE DU VIN

La Palestine a probablement été un des premiers pays dont les habitants jouirent du vin. On suppose en général que les premiers vignobles furent ceux d'Anatolie, de Perse, de Mésopotamie et d'Égypte et que l'on cultivait la vigne dans ces pays voilà déjà 3 000 ans. Les communications entre la Palestine et l'Égypte datent de temps très reculés. Une lettre écrite aux environs de 1800 avant notre ère rapporte que « figues et vignes abondent en Palestine en plus grande quantité que l'eau » et que « chaque enfant d'Israël se repose sous son figuier près de sa vigne ». Selon l'auteur d'une autre lettre datant d'environ 1 500 av. J.-C., les vignes donnaient des fruits dans chaque jardin de Palestine et le vin coulait en cascade dans ses caves. Dès que les eaux du déluge se retirèrent, Noé s'empressa « de planter la vigne » et d'en boire le vin. Selon la tradition, il y eut réellement un « déluge » qui se situerait aux environs de l'an 2800 av. J.-C. Les Égyptiens conquirent la Palestine sous leur XVIIIe dynastie (1555-1325 av. J.-C.), puis de nouveau en 917 av. J.-C. où les soldats de Sheshang Ier pillèrent Jérusalem et arrachèrent les vignes dans les agglomérations dont ils s'emparèrent. Elles furent cependant replantées et ne tardèrent pas à produire de nouveau.

En ce qui concerne Canaan, nous savons que le miel et le lait y coulaient en abondance ; le vin devait y couler aussi. Nous voyons au chapitre XIII du Livre des Nombres que les hommes, envoyés en reconnaissance dans ce pays par Moïse, en revinrent avec une grappe de raisin sur leurs épaules. Ils l'avaient cueillie à un endroit nommé Val Eshkol (ce mot signifiant grappe en hébreu).

Les vignerons des temps bibliques connaissaient la vinification (de même que Magon de Carthage) et nombre de leurs coutumes sont encore connues et respectées de nos jours. Dans un pays où il y avait parfois plus de vin que d'eau, on ne l'utilisait pas seulement comme breuvage et comme médicament. Il servait à nettoyer les maisons, teindre les tissus. On estime que des Israélites en consommaient à ces divers usages 3 à 4 l par jour et par tête.

La vigne poussait partout dans le pays : sur les collines, dans les vallées, sur les plaines et même sur les rives de la mer Morte. Aux vendanges on choisissait soigneusement les raisins selon un procédé assez semblable à celui de certaines régions de Chypre (*voir ce nom*). Il y avait de nombreux types de vin : du blanc ; du rouge ou « vin joli » ; du vin foncé ou vin « nègre » ; du vin doux fait avec des raisins séchés ; du vin de lait (peut-être un mélange de vin et de lait chaud) ; du vin d'asperges (bouilli avec le légume). Les Israéliens préparaient diverses mixtures : miel et poivre avec des vins doux ; herbes et poivre avec les vins secs. Certains vins devaient être bus en leur première année, d'autres après trois ans de cave ou plus. Avant les grandes fêtes on soutirait trois fois le vin et, à la fête des Tabernacles, des jarres de vin décoraient les niches du temple. Les vins du Liban étaient fort prisés. Le célèbre Helbon, qu'il fallait acheter à Damas (Ézéchiel, chap. XXVII), était un vin blanc cuit. Sans doute y avait-il plus de blanc que de rouge.

La production de vin atteignit son point culminant en Palestine au temps du Second Temple détruit en l'an 70 de notre ère, à la fin d'une guerre contre les Romains. Bien des vignobles célèbres furent alors anéantis. Les juifs en reconstituèrent quelques-uns et continuèrent à les cultiver de manière épisodique pendant quelque temps. Mais la viticulture ne recommença à prospérer qu'à notre époque. Cependant, au cours du Ier siècle de notre ère, des auteurs romains décrivent différents vins de Palestine — Chechem, Lydda, Césarée, Achkelon et Gaza — qui étaient fort estimés et qu'on exportait vers la Syrie, l'Égypte et même la Bretagne (Angleterre). Après la conquête arabe, la plupart des vignes de Palestine furent arrachées. La prohibition coranique était alors appliquée avec une telle rigueur que les musulmans bannissaient même les raisins de table par crainte qu'ils fussent pressés pour en faire du vin.

Au Moyen Age pourtant les croisés trouvèrent quelques vignobles près du mont Carmel, de Bethléem et de Nazareth. Quelques-uns restèrent assez longtemps dans le pays pour cultiver les vignes à leur propre usage. On lit qu'en 1280 il y avait « près de Bethléem des vignes magnifiques. Les musulmans ne les cultivent pas, mais les chrétiens en font du très bon vin ».

Il semble que certains musulmans qui vivaient près des agglomérations chrétiennes faisaient eux-mêmes du vin pour le vendre à leurs voisins.

Le vin en Israël de nos jours

L'histoire contemporaine du vin de Palestine commence en 1870, avec la fondation de la première école d'agriculture. Dès le début, elle posséda à Mikveh un vignoble qui donnait quelques raisins de table, mais beaucoup plus de raisins à vin, tous de l'espèce *Vitis vinifera,* à savoir : Alicante, Bordeleau, Carignan, Petit Bouchet, etc. En ce temps-là, des monastères chrétiens possédaient aussi des terres plantées de *Vitis vinifera,* mais de petite surface. En 1880, les templiers allemands plantèrent une superficie considérable dans la région du Carmel ; ils importèrent des vignes de la vallée du Rhin et firent du bon vin.

Quand les premiers sionistes arrivèrent en Israël, en 1882, ils plantèrent leurs premiers vignobles sous le patronage du baron de Rothschild et encore avec des variétés de l'espèce *Vitis vinifera.* Bientôt de vastes celliers s'emplirent de tonneaux et les vignes donnèrent du vin à Chomrom ainsi qu'en divers points de la Galilée. Dès 1890, les immigrants juifs cultivaient plus de 2 800 ha et la surproduction commença à poser un problème. Les vignerons cherchaient à exporter leur vin quand survint le phylloxéra qui détruisit nombre de ceps et mit fin à la surproduction pour un certain temps. Le baron Rothschild conseilla aux vignerons israéliens de planter des vignes greffées sur des souches américaines.

En 1906, la viticulture israélienne de Palestine fut de nouveau capable de subvenir à ses besoins et Rothschild donna aux vignerons ses celliers de Richon-le-Zion, près de Tel-Aviv, et de Zikhron-Yaacov, au sud de Haïfa. Ce sont encore les principaux centres de production de vin. La coopérative qui se constitua alors adopta le nom de *Société coopérative vigneronne des grandes caves Richon-le-Zion et Zikhron-Yaacov*[1]. Elle opère encore actuellement et produit 75 % du vin d'Israël, selon les méthodes françaises introduites par le baron de Rothschild. L'organisation se tient au courant des progrès et les applique : gigantesques cuves de béton, derniers procédés de stabilisation des vins et de mise en bouteille mécanique.

Au début, la viticulture travaillait à perte. En 1948, lors de la fondation d'Israël, des milliers de nouveaux immigrants affluèrent ; bon nombre venaient de pays vinicoles et la culture de la vigne connut une nouvelle expansion. Dès 1953 la surface cultivée en vignes avait doublé et depuis on y a encore ajouté 2 000 ha. Actuellement, la consommation intérieure de vins s'élève à environ 180 000 hl (2 millions de caisses). Près de 40 000 hl (plus de 400 000 caisses) d'excédent sont destinés à l'exportation.

Quoiqu'une si grande superficie d'un aussi petit pays soit plantée de jeunes vignes, la qualité du vin ne s'est pas encore nettement manifestée. Certaines variétés européennes produisent des vins agréables et satisfaisants dans des secteurs déterminés et quelques vins israéliens remportent des prix à des concours et expositions internationaux. Ils continueront certainement à s'améliorer, grâce au bon matériel répandu dans le pays et à l'assistance technique. Israël est donc destiné à devenir un bon pays vinicole, tant pour la qualité que pour la quantité. Depuis 1957, l'Institut du vin israélien procède à des recherches scientifiques, des études de marché et à la mise à l'épreuve par dégustation des vins destinés à l'exportation.

1. Raison sociale en français.

Régions vinicoles israéliennes

Zikhron-Yaacov

Sur les côtes du Mont Carmel, cette région vinicole est la plus vaste et la plus importante (40 % de la production israélienne) du pays. Des vignes y furent plantées à la fin du XIXe siècle. La région est connue pour ses blancs et rosés.

Galilée

Au nord du pays. Région montagneuse, située de 600 à 1 000 m au-dessus du niveau de la mer, de température modérée, voire fraîche. Ce vignoble nouveau produit de bons vins secs, blancs et rouges. Le Gamla et le Yarden ont acquis depuis peu une réputation internationale.

Sydoon-Gezer

Au centre du pays, ce vignoble important (deuxième en superficie après Zikhron-Yacoov) produit de bons vins rouges.

Environs de Jérusalem

Vignobles neufs et petits plantés ces vingt-cinq dernières années et produisant de bons vins blancs et rouges.

La production récente de vin en Israël

Depuis une dizaine d'années, la production annuelle moyenne de vin en Israël est d'environ 350 000 hl pour 3 000 ha plantés. Environ 60 % de cette production provenaient de la Société coopérative vigneronnne des grandes caves Richon-le-Zion et Zikhron-Yacoov. Il existe d'autres entreprises viticoles importantes, notamment : Hamartef, Eliaz et Carmel Zion. Quelque 500 vignerons sont actuellement membres de la Société coopérative, qui assure environ 75 % des exportations de vin.

En 1952, cette coopérative fonda une filiale aux États-Unis sous le nom de Carmel Wine Co., Inc., New York. Celle-ci la représente à l'exportation aux États-Unis et au Canada. Il existe aussi une filiale en Grande-Bretagne : The Carmel Wine Company. Cette dernière est presque aussi ancienne que la viticulture en Israël.

Elle fut en effet fondée en 1897, quinze ans seulement après la résurrection de la viticulture juive en Palestine. Les vins et spiritueux sont importés tant en bouteilles qu'en fûts, pour être ensuite mis en bouteille à Londres. La Grande-Bretagne et les États-Unis sont les principaux clients d'Israël, qui expédie également du vin vers vingt-six autres pays, quoiqu'en plus petite quantité.

Actuellement la plupart des vins sont faits avec des raisins Carignan, Alicante, Grenache, Sémillon, Muscat, ainsi qu'avec une variété locale appelée Dabuki. Les vignerons s'efforcent d'améliorer la qualité de leurs vins en limitant l'encépagement du Carignan, variété médiocre et trop répandue, au profit de raisins bien meilleurs tels que le Cabernet Sauvignon, le Colombard français et le Sauvignon Blanc. On plante en outre des Cabernet Rubis et des Riesling Émeraude, qui ne peuvent qu'amener les Israéliens à produire des vins de table raisonnablement bons, pour la consommation intérieure comme pour l'exportation.

Israël est désireux de produire de meilleurs vins et doit donc acquérir un peu plus de savoir-faire. Les grands progrès effectués sont cependant tout à fait prometteurs.

Issan (Château d')

Bordeaux rouge. Commune de Cantenac-Margaux, en Haut-Médoc.

Avant l'effondrement de l'Empire austro-hongrois, à la fin de la Première Guerre mondiale, le Château d'Issan était le vin préféré à la cour de Vienne. L'empereur n'en voulait pas boire d'autre et chacun suivait son exemple.

« Pour la table des rois et les autels de Dieu », telle est la fière devise de ce vignoble et on la voit gravée dans la pierre au portail. Le superbe château du XIVᵉ, commençait à se délabrer quand on entreprit de le restaurer en 1952.

Les vignes sont situées en bordure de la route, en face du Château-Prieuré-Lichine, au nord du village de Cantenac. Château-d'Issan appartient à Mme Marguerite E. Cruse, veuve de Emmanuel Cruse, et à son fils Lionel, qui était le président de la maison Cruse et Fils, Frères. Le magnifique domaine se rapproche de Château-Palmer et a droit à l'Appellation d'Origine Margaux.

Caractéristiques : Quoique la délicatesse et le goût typique des Margaux soient présents, ce vin est d'un corsé charnu qui rappelle les crus situés plus au nord dans le Médoc, par exemple ceux de Pauillac.

Le vin a maintenant recouvré dans le monde entier l'ancien prestige qu'il avait perdu dans les années 60 et 70.

Superficie : 35 ha.

Production moyenne : 130 tonneaux (11 000 caisses).

Italie

L'Italien aime que son vin soit capiteux, robuste et surtout abondant. C'est un des buveurs de vin les plus spontanés du monde et il consomme avec la plus grance satisfaction ses 82 l de vin par an, qu'il soit bon, mauvais ou quelconque. Son vin ordinaire peut être grossier, insuffisamment fermenté, épais, dénué de finesse, il sera toujours bien accueilli à la table du repas.

On a décrit l'Italie sous l'aspect d'un vaste vignoble et c'était exact. La vigne s'y répandait partout. Elle grimpait aux arbres et les enveloppait, courait le long des routes, pendait comme des franges aux haies et aux barrières, fleurissait dans un désordre magnifique auprès des oliviers et des champs de céréales. Elle poussait avec aisance et ses fleurs donnaient de grosses grappes. On ne voyait pas en Italie autant de vignobles disciplinés, traités avec soin qu'en France et en Allemagne. Quant à la production de vin proprement dite elle était en proie au même laisser-aller que la culture de la vigne. En vérité, il semblait souvent que le vigneron se souciait surtout de transférer son vin le plus rapidement possible de la cuve de fermentation à sa table. Toutefois un changement radical est intervenu dans la plupart des vignobles, et les vins sont maintenant bien vinifiés.

L'Italie est le premier producteur et exportateur de vin du monde. Sa production annuelle moyenne s'élève à envi ı 77 millions d'hl (850 millions de caisses), dont 14,8 millions d'hl (160 millions de caisses) vont à l'exportation (presque 20 %). Mais l'Italie importe également quelque 165 000 hl (près de 2 millions de caisses) de vin par an. De toutes les grandes régions productrices de vin, l'Italie, les États-Unis et l'Australie ont fait les progrès les plus révolutionnaires : d'une médiocrité rétrograde à de véritables sommets œnologiques. Vers 1975, le facteur humain, l'un des quatre facteurs essentiels

ITALIE
SUISSE
AUTRICHE
HONGRIE
YOUGOSLAVIE
FRANCE
VAL D'AOSTE
PIEDMONT
LIGURIE
LOMBARDIE
TRENTIN HAUT ADIGE
FRIOUL-VENETIE-JULIENNE
VENETIE
EMILIE ROMAGNE
TOSCANE
OMBRIE
MARCHES
ABRUZZES
LATIUM
CAMPANIE
BASILICATE
POUILLES
CALABRE
SICILE
MARSALA
ADRIATIQUE
MER TYRRHENIENNE
MER IONIENNE
ILE D'ELBE
ISCHIA
CAPRI
PANTELLERIA
MT ETNA
L Majeur
L Come
L Caldaro
L Trasimène
Turin
Asti
Gattinara
Milan
Bergame
Bolzano
Trente
Verona
Padoue
Venise
Gênes
Bologna
Ravenne
Forli
Pise
Livourne
Florence
Sienne
Montepulciano
Pérouse
Portoferraio
Montefiascone
Rome
Foggia
Naples
Potenza
Brindisi
Tarente
Reggio
Messine
Palerme
Syracuse
Po
Adige
Arno
Tibre
Ticin
N
0 20 40 60 80 100 200 KILOMETRES 300
vins renommés
Aglianico del Vulture 1
Albana 2
Aleatico di Portoferraio 3
Asti Spumante 4
Barbera 5
Barbaresco 6
Bardolino 7
Barolo 8
Capri 9
Castelli Romani 10
Chianti 11
Cinque Terre 12
Cirò 13
Est! Est!! Est!!! 14
Frascati 15
Gattinara 16
Gragnano 17
Lacrima Christi 18
Lago di Caldaro 19
Lambrusco 20
Marsala 21
Moscato di Pantelleria 22
Orvieto 23
Sangiovese 24
S. Maddalena 25
Soave 26
Valpantena 27
Valpolicella 28
Verdicchio 29

de qualité, s'est développé en Italie, région après région et les méthodes traditionnelles — le plus souvent mauvaises — ont fait place à la science moderne de la viticulture. Ceci est surtout vrai pour les vins blancs. De nouvelles variétés de raisin, le contrôle de la fermentation et une mise en bouteille précoce ont permis de produire des vins frais et séduisants qui ont remplacé des vins auparavant sujets à l'oxydation.

Les parcelles où l'on mélange la vigne à d'autres cultures se font de plus en plus rares. Aujourd'hui, la polyculture ne représente plus que 700 000 ha contre plus de 2 millions d'ha en 1964. 1 400 000 ha sont consacrés exclusivement à la viticulture intensive. Après des années d'exode rural, la tendance s'inverse, et on constate un accroissement des jeunes revenant travailler la terre. On recense environ deux millions d'ouvriers viticoles, sans compter les propriétaires de petites parcelles qui pourraient faire monter ce chiffre à trois millions.

Certains vins italiens peuvent être très bons. Citons, parmi les meilleurs, le Barolo et le Barbaresco du Piémont, le Valpolicella et le Soave de Vénétie, le célèbre Chianti de la Toscane, le Brunellos di Montalcino et le Vino Nobili di Montepulciano. Les meilleurs vins italiens sont souvent faits par des petits vignerons pour leur usage personnel et ils vendent leur surplus à des clients attitrés dont ils ont souvent hérité en même temps que de la vigne. Le touriste de passage n'a guère de chance de rencontrer un tel viticulteur et de goûter son vin. Il boira plutôt le produit amélioré et commercialisé par de grandes firmes, c'est-à-dire standardisé. La qualité de ce breuvage dépendra entièrement de l'entreprise qui le fait et le vend.

Les contrôles de qualité

Jusque vers la fin des années 60, les vins italiens ont souffert de l'absence de méthodes de la viticulture et du laisser-aller en ce qui concerne la réglementation, poussé si loin que des vins qui ne méritent même pas l'Appellation d'Origine toscane ont été étiquetés Chianti avant la réglementation d'Appellation Contrôlée. A l'origine de ce désordre il y a l'échec du gouvernement pour protéger les Appellations d'Origine de la même manière qu'en France. Certes, la France n'y est pas parvenue sans difficulté, mais elle a résolu ce problème de manière satisfaisante beaucoup plus tôt que l'Italie. Redoutant de voir son marché submergé par des vins italiens à bon marché au fur et à mesure que s'abaissaient les barrières douanières entre pays du Marché commun, le gouvernement français pressa le gouvernement italien d'appliquer des lois de contrôle du même genre que celles sur lesquelles veille l'I.N.A.O. Ce qui fut fait.

Denominazioni di Origine

En 1963, la réglementation des *Denominazioni di Origine* prit force de loi. Elle comporte trois degrés.

— Simple
  Par exemple, Rosso Toscano est un vin fait avec des raisins Rosso, n'importe où en Toscane.
— Contrôlée
  Par exemple, Dolcetto d'Alba est un bon vin du Piémont provenant uniquement de Dolcetto d'Alba, Neive, Treiso, Rodello, Sinio et de tous les secteurs de Montforte d'Alba, La Morra, Verduno et Monchiero.
— Contrôlée et garantie
  Par exemple, un Barolo ou un Barbaresco authentique portant le sceau et le label officiels.

L'Appellation Simple *(Denominazione di Origine Semplice, D.O.S.)* est accordée aux vins ordinaires faits avec les raisins cultivés par tradition dans une région. Cette D.O.S. a été abolie car les lois de la C.E.E. (Marché commun) s'imposent aux États membres et les vins, qui auparavant relevaient de cette catégorie, sont aujourd'hui connus comme *vini da tavola con indicazione geografica*, c'est-à-dire vins de table portant une indication géographique.

Le souhait de la C.E.E. était qu'en dépit d'une grande confusion l'Italie crée des noms de lieu dans le cadre de règles strictes. Ainsi, c'est avec un plus grand respect que l'on considère le caractère individuel et l'identité des vins italiens. On peut trouver de très bons *vino da tavola* (tels le Tignanello et le Sassicaia) qui n'ont pas respecté les contraintes imposées aux raisins classés D.O.C. et D.O.C.G.

L'Appellation Contrôlée *(Denominazione di Origine Controlata, D.O.C.)* est réservée à 11 % des vins italiens qui sont conformes à des normes précises. Les vignes qui produisent ces vins sont recensées sur un registre officiel.

Enfin, l'Appellation Contrôlée et Garantie *(Denominazione di Origine Controllata e Garantita, D.O.C.G.)* n'est accordée qu'aux vins conformes à certaines normes de qualité et vendus à des prix déterminés, sur recommandation du ministère de l'Agriculture et des Forêts. Ces vins doivent être vendus dans des récipients d'une contenance ne dépassant pas 5 l. L'étiquette doit indiquer que leur origine est contrôlée et garantie ; elle doit préciser aussi la contenance de la bouteille, le nom du vigneron et de celui qui a mis en bouteille, le lieu de cette mise en bouteille et la teneur en alcool. Les vignerons qui désirent faire classer leur vin dans cette catégorie supérieure doivent présenter une requête au ministère de l'Agriculture et des Forêts dont un inspecteur fera analyser le vin. Ces requêtes doivent être étayées par une abondante documentation concernant la région, la production moyenne annuelle, les variétés de vignes cultivées, les caractéristiques du vin, etc. Cette appellation supérieure n'est accordée qu'avec l'approbation d'un certain nombre de vignerons de la même région. En fin de compte, c'est le président de la République italienne qui décide, sur avis des ministères concernés. A partir de ce moment-là, celui qui fait le vin de cette dénomination doit se conformer strictement aux règles suivantes :

1. Inscription du vignoble sur le registre approprié et déclaration obligatoire de la production et des stocks ;
2. Étiquetage correct des bouteilles et flacons ;
3. Inspection par des membres d'organisations bénévoles délégués par le ministère de l'Agriculture ;
4. Collaboration aux mesures préventives prises pour réprimer la fraude et affermir le contrôle des appellations d'origine ;
5. Paiement des pénalités en cas d'infraction aux règlements.

L'Institut national pour la surveillance des appellations d'origine *(Istituzione del comitato nazionale per la tutela delle denominazioni di origine)* est formé par le ministère de l'Agriculture et des Forêts, conjointement à celui de l'Industrie et du Commerce qui en nomment le président et les vingt-huit membres représentant les ministères intéressés ainsi que l'I.C.E. Sa fonction consiste à promouvoir et surveiller les vins d'Appellation Contrôlée et Garantie, et à stimuler des recherches tendant à leur amélioration. L'appartenance à cette catégorie d'appellation est volontaire ; les meilleurs producteurs tiennent à vendre avec ce certificat pour leurs exportations et sont prêts à soumettre leurs vins à l'inspection et à l'analyse. Le caractère non obligatoire de cette réglementation implique que certains vins exportés ne sont pas contrôlés. Il appartient donc au client de vérifier avant d'acheter. Cette nouvelle législation mérite des encouragements surtout quand on compare la situation actuelle à celle qui prévalait auparavant. Tous ceux qui sont mêlés à la production et au commerce du vin doivent comprendre qu'il vaut la peine de sacrifier la quantité à la qualité. La loi du 12 juillet 1963 a été modifiée, les règlements qui étaient devenus périmés et qui manquaient d'efficacité ont été abrogés ou amendés. Il appartient désormais au gouvernement de promulguer certains décrets permettant le contrôle des moûts, des vins et vinaigres et de continuer à établir les règlements interdisant la fraude dans la préparation et la vente de ces produits

Les consorzi et D.O.C.

Chaque *consorzio* peut veiller au contrôle des vins de son secteur et appliquer les règlements. Avant que la loi ne réglemente les appellations d'origine, seuls les vins portant l'estampille d'un *consorzio* local présentaient une certaine garantie de qualité. Dans les régions où existe un *consorzio*, certains vignerons et négociants peuvent en faire partie, mais aucun n'y est obligé. Malheureusement ceux qui n'appartiennent pas au *consorzio* ont les mêmes droits à l'appellation d'origine locale et les membres du *consorzio* n'ont droit en plus qu'à l'estampille de leur organisation. Après les *consorzi*, la réglementation des D.O.C. a stimulé l'amélioration de la qualité des vins. Seuls les vins faits à partir de cépages traditionnels avaient droit à cette appellation, en dépit des cultivateurs qui obtenaient de très bons résultats à partir de variétés telles que Cabernet Sauvignon et Chardonnay et qui ne pouvaient espérer qu'en la seule dénomination *vino da tavola* (vin de table). Il est permis d'espérer que la loi sur les *Denominazione di Origine* parviendra à protéger de bons vins et à contrôler leur commercialisation.

En ce qui concerne les *consorzi*, chacun

détermine ses propres normes de qualité qui, de ce fait, sont susceptibles de varier de l'un à l'autre. Certains sont tellement rigoureux que le vin doit forcément toujours être excellent. D'autres se contentent d'une moyenne de qualité assez minime. En général, le règlement du *consorzio* définit les variétés de raisins autorisées, les limites du secteur, la teneur minimale en alcool et indique si d'autres vins peuvent être importés d'autres zones. Dans tous les cas, le vin doit être goûté par un comité élu dont l'approbation donne droit à l'estampille du *consorzio*. Cette dernière est disposée de telle façon qu'on ne peut ouvrir la bouteille sans briser le sceau.

Chaque *consorzio* impose ses règles à sa façon. En cas d'infractions grossières et répétées, le châtiment peut aller jusqu'à l'exclusion.

Un minimum de collaboration entre les *consorzi* et l'Institut pour l'inspection des appellations d'origine pourrait apporter de très grosses améliorations à l'ensemble des vins d'Italie.

Les régions vinicoles

La péninsule italienne est caractérisée par une extrême diversité de paysages. Les Alpes le cèdent aux Apennins et les plaines alternent avec les montagnes d'un bout à l'autre de la botte. En règle générale les meilleurs vins sont ceux du Nord, mais on en trouve d'intéressants dans le Sud, surtout quand on les boit sur place. Les Italiens ont divisé leur pays en régions ou subdivisions administratives et il convient de discuter de leurs vins en les rangeant dans ces mêmes catégories. Ces régions et leurs vins sont les suivantes *(voir aussi les principales régions, chacune à sa place dans l'ordre alphabétique)* :

Les Abruzzes

Située immédiatement au sud de l'Italie centrale, au bord de l'Adriatique, cette région produit quelques vins sans prétention mais souvent agréables. Le Montepulciano di Abruzzo, rouge, le Trebbiano di Abruzzo, blanc, sont les noms des principales variétés de raisins. Le Montepulciano est également produit en rosé sous l'appellation Cerasuola d'Abruzzo. Les vins qu'on en fait sont tous agréables consommés sur place, et lorsqu'ils ne souffrent pas du voyage, les meilleurs gardent leur charme. *Voir* p. 117.

L'Apulie (Pouille)

C'est le talon de la botte. Cette région plate produit de grandes quantités de vins ordinaires dont une bonne part est utilisée en coupages ou sert à faire du vermouth. *Voir* p. 627.

Le Basilicate

Cette région méridionale, la Lucanie des Romains, ressemble à un chaos de montagnes, de vallées inaccessibles où l'on fait du vin. Le plus connu est l'Aglianico del Vulture. La première partie de ce nom est celui de la variété de vigne et la seconde celui de la montagne sur laquelle on la cultive. Cette région produit aussi d'assez grandes quantités de Muscat et de Malvoisie. *Voir* p. 197.

La Calabre

Située à l'extrême pointe de la botte, cette province produit un vin blanc doux, le Greco di Gerace (fait avec les raisins du même nom), et un rouge foncé, le Ciró di Calabria (fait surtout avec des raisins Gaglioppo, cultivés à Ciró). Les amateurs de Muscat apprécieront aussi cette région. *Voir* p. 252.

La Campanie

C'est la région de Naples. Ses vins les plus populaires sont le Vesuvio rouge, fait surtout avec des cépages Aglianico, Piedirosso et Olivella cultivés sur les terres d'origine volcanique au pied du mont Vésuve, et le Ravello, rouge et blanc, qui provient du charmant village de ce nom sur la côte d'Amalfi, et est aussi très apprécié. Le vin blanc Greco di Tufo, près d'Avellino, vient aussi de cette région ainsi que le Lacrima Christi, vin blanc doux, et le vin fort Taurasi. Le Gragnano rouge du voisinage d'Amalfi est aussi délicieux à boire sur une terrasse fleurie donnant sur la baie de Naples. Enfin, les vins gais et légers connus sous le nom de Capri et faits tant à Capri qu'à Ischia, sont aussi des produits de cette région. *Voir* p. 254.

L'Émilie-Romagne

Cette vaste région agricole du centre de l'Italie ne produit pas de vins de qualité.

Le Lambrusco rouge, en général assez doux et pétillant, est le vin d'importation le plus vendu aux États-Unis ; l'Albana convient à ceux qui aiment le vin blanc pas trop sec et ils semblent avoir un certain avenir dans l'exportation. Les collines de Romagne produisent une grande quantité de Sangiovese rouge et de Trebbiano. Bien que longtemps destinés exclusivement à la consommation locale, les vins de Frioul-Vénétie-Italie se forgent peu à peu une réputation de qualité. Les blancs sont faits principalement avec du Pinot Gris, du Pinot Blanc, du Tokay, du Riesling et du Sauvignon Blanc ; les rouges avec du Merlot, du Cabernet Franc et du Pinot Noir. Il existe également, quoique en petite quantité, un bon vin de dessert appelé Picolit. *Voir* p. 357.

Friuli-Venezia-Giulia

Située dans le nord-est de l'Italie à la frontière de l'Autriche et de la Yougoslavie, c'est la nouvelle région ascendante en Italie pour les vins blancs. Les cépages du soi-disant Tocai, Picolit, Sauvignon, Riesling, Traminer, Pinot Gris, Pinot Blanc, ainsi que quelques cépages de Chardonnay ont prospéré sous ce microclimat qui est un mélange des vents de l'Adriatique avec l'air des Alpes. Friuli, qui produit plus de rouge que de blanc, a acquis une réputation pour ses bons Merlot, Cabernet Sauvignon et Franc et son Refosco indigène.

Le Latium

Les vins des Castelli Romani (châteaux de Rome), surtout les blancs secs, comptent parmi les meilleurs d'Italie. Le Frascati et le Marino sont les plus connus. Nombre de ces vins supportent les rigueurs des voyages océaniques. Blanc, sec ou demi-doux, l'Est ! Est !! Est !!! de Montefiascone est celui qui fait l'objet de la plus belle légende italienne au sujet du vin. *Voir* p. 493.

La Ligurie

Prolongement de la Côte d'Azur française, cette province ne produit pas de vins remarquables. Le Cinqueterre blanc sec ou légèrement doux est le mieux connu quoi qu'il y en ait d'autres tels que le Dolceacqua (rouge).

La Lombardie

Les rouges de la Valteline — Sassella, Grumelo, Valgella, Fracia et Inferno — sont hautement estimés. Les vins de la rive ouest du Lac de Garde comme le Franciacorta sont souvent délicieux. On fait des rouges, des blancs et des roses. Ces derniers sont probablement les meilleurs, surtout le Chiaretto.

Les Marches

Cette région, située entre les Apennins et l'Adriatique, ne produit pas de vins de grande qualité. Les principaux vins sont le Piceno rouge et le célèbre Verdicchio dei Castelli di Jesi, un blanc généralement très bien fait que l'on trouve souvent à l'étranger.

Molise

Région vinicole de la côte Adriatique la moins importante d'Italie dont le Montepulciano del Molise et le Ramitello rosso sont les deux vins les plus connus.

Le Piémont

Région de deux des meilleurs rouges italiens devenus D.O.C.G. en 1981 : le Barolo et le Barbaresco, cette région produit aussi l'Asti Spumante, un mousseux doux et sec. Les autres bons vins non mousseux sont : Freisa, Barbera, Gattinara, Grignolino d'Asti, Nebbiolo d'Alba, Dolcetto et Ghemme. C'est aussi à Turin qu'est fabriqué le Vermouth, apéritif à base de vins bon marché et d'extraits d'herbes.

La Sardaigne

Les vins de cette belle île accidentée, sont toujours des blancs très secs et très agréables ; les rouges ont moins d'attrait. Ces vins de table constituent un changement bienvenu après les vins doux et corsés traditionnels.

La Sicile

On avait l'habitude d'associer la Sicile à la production de vins doux et corsés. De nos jours, l'œnologie moderne et les coopératives viticoles ont transformé la production sicilienne et de nombreux vins de table, bons et appréciés, ont peu à peu remplacé le Marsala qui était le vin le plus célèbre de l'île. En effet, la Sicile exporte environ 25 % du vin italien. Parmi les meilleurs vins, citons le Marmertino blanc, le Faro rouge, les vins rouges et blancs des pentes de l'Etna et surtout les blancs secs et les rouges corsés de Corvo. Le Marsala, vin traditionnel de Sicile, peut être bon, mais il est devenu difficile à trouver.

Trentin-Haut-Adige (Tyrol méridional)

Administrativement dépendantes de l'Italie, les régions septentrionales du Trentin et du Haut-Adige s'en détachent toutefois nettement par leur culture et leur langue germaniques. Les vins rouges de la région (y compris le Cabernet, le Merlot, le Pinot Noir et le Santa Maddalena) sont en grande partie distribués en Allemagne et en Autriche. Les vins blancs (y compris le Riesling, le Traminer, le Pinot Gris et le Pinot Blanc) sont appréciés dans leur région d'origine et l'étranger. Les coopératives de la région ont jusqu'à présent amélioré la qualité.

La Toscane

Son vin le meilleur et le plus célèbre, le Chianti (D.O.C.G.), se présente dans le commerce sous divers types, mais les vignerons qui cultivent les vignes dans la zone du Chianti Classico soutiennent qu'ils ont seuls droit à l'appellation. S'ils portaient d'autres noms, en effet, quelques autres Chianti seraient des vins magnifiques, mais ce ne sont pas toujours de vrais Chianti. Le très onéreux Brunello di Montalcino est le meilleur vin de la région et reçut le premier l'appellation D.O.C.G.

L'Ombrie

Découvrir l'Orvieto blanc, le meilleur vin de l'Ombrie, est sans doute stimulant mais seule l'exploration des merveilles artistiques et antiques des villes, à mi-chemin entre Rome et Florence, vaut le voyage. Dans cette province viticole riche d'histoires sont produits les vins blancs et rouges de Colli del Trasimeno autour du lac Eponyme. L'Ombrie produit également le Torgiano, un vin D.O.C. rouge fort et rond. Le blanc est fait principalement avec du Trebbiano.

Val d'Aoste

Dans la plus petite région viticole d'Italie, les vignobles sont cultivés en terrasses. Les vins les plus connus sont le Donnaz et l'Enfer d'Arvier, des versants de montagne.

La Vénétie

Les meilleurs vins de ce secteur sont les célèbres vins des environs de Vérone, notamment les rouges secs Valpolicella, Recioto et Bardolino ainsi que le blanc sec Soave.

Ives

Variété indigène de vigne américaine rustique et vigoureuse mais sans grand intérêt car son raisin à peau grossière donne un vin fortement foxé (*voir* FOX-GRAPE, FOXÉ, FOXY).

Izarra

Liqueur du Pays basque semblable à la Chartreuse. Comme son célèbre modèle, l'Izarra se présente en deux couleurs : la jaune, douce, et la verte, d'une plus forte teneur en alcool. Fabriquée à Bayonne.

J

Japon

De l'île Kyu-Shu, à l'extrême sud, jusqu'à celle d'Hokkaido, située le plus au nord, quelque 30 000 ha du territoire japonais sont plantés de vignes qui produisent raisins de table et raisins à vin. La production totale des vins de raisins dépasse 160 000 hl (plus de 1,5 millions de caisses). Cependant, pour un Japonais qui prend un verre de vin, il y en a cent qui prennent du saké ou de la bière. La bière représente 65 % de la consommation totale, le saké (obtenu par le brassage du riz) 19 %, et d'autres breuvages à base de grain, atteignent des proportions tellement importantes que le public a été mis en garde contre le danger de diminuer ainsi les disponibilités de grain alimentaire. Le vin constitue donc un produit de remplacement possible ; les boissons alcoolisées importées au Japon deviennent néanmoins très populaires chez les gens aisés.

Les régions vinicoles japonaises sont celle de Yamanashi ainsi que, dans une moindre mesure, celles de Yamagata et Nagano qui produisent des vins encore plus médiocres. Toutes sont situées sur l'île principale de Hondo, la seule qui produise une quantité importante de vin.

L'humidité du climat et le sol acide rendent la viticulture difficile. Il faut donc choisir des raisins qui mûrissent tôt, c'est-à-dire avant que les pluies torrentielles de septembre n'anéantissent le travail d'une année entière. Les vignes sont plantées à raison de 400 ceps à l'hectare, séparés les uns des autres par 6 m environ. Elles poussent aussi en treille ou dans les potagers.

Le Japon est un des rares pays au monde où prospèrent les trois familles de vignes : européenne, américaine et asiatique. Pourtant aucune ne donne des produits de qualité sur le sol japonais. Les variétés de *Vitis labrusca* (américaine) et quelques hybrides, seuls ou à peu près, fournissent des vins convenables et parfois même agréables. Les variétés Delaware, Muscat Bailey et Campbell's Early représentent une bonne part de l'encépagement quoiqu'on utilise de plus en plus le Sémillon, le Chasselas, le Chardonnay et le Riesling pour les vins blancs et que le Cabernet Sauvignon avec un peu de Merlot fournissent 75 % des rouges. En général les vignes européennes sont très vulnérables aux maladies cryptogamiques telles que le mildiou et l'oïdium qui sévissent particulièrement sous le climat humide du Japon.

Quoique la culture de la vigne au Japon remonte au XIIe siècle, l'histoire du vin de ce pays ne commence qu'au XIXe. Les vignes étaient utilisées auparavant pour la décoration et le jus de raisin à des fins médicinales. Quant au vin, il ne prospéra qu'avec l'afflux des Européens et des Américains. Très curieux dans le domaine de l'agriculture, les Japonais s'intéressèrent à l'idée du vin et envoyèrent des missions étudier cette production en France et en Californie. Au XXe siècle la viticulture s'est accrue et elle prospère, mais est encore loin de présenter un intérêt économique réel.

Trop de vignobles japonais ne sont que des parcelles ; leur personnel manque d'expérience et ils sont dirigés de façon rudimentaire. Il existe de nombreuses coopératives mais elles ne sont en général ni mieux équipées ni mieux dirigées que les entreprises privées. 60 % du marché sont contrôlés par trois entreprises géantes — Mercian, Manswine et Suntory. La plupart de ces firmes ont des plantations dans la région vinicole la plus prospère, la vallée de Kofu, située dans la préfecture de Yamanashi à 120 km à l'ouest de Tokyo. Cette vallée est moins touchée par l'humidité et les pluies que beaucoup d'autres régions, les journées y sont chaudes et les nuits fraîches, ce qui explique qu'elle produise des raisins supérieurs à la moyenne. Les meilleurs vins de la vallée sont faits avec du Cabernet Sauvignon, du Merlot, du Sémillon, mais on en fait aussi d'agréables avec la variété indigène Koshu. Nombre de ces vins sont semblables à ceux de la Hunter Valley en Australie, où la température, le taux de pluie, le sol graveleux rappellent précisément la région de Kofu. Les meilleurs vins sont légers et secs ; la quasi-totalité est consommée à Kofu, on en trouve difficilement même dans des centres tels que Tokyo et Kyoto, et l'exportation est pratiquement nulle.

Le Japon importe environ 200 000 hl (2,2 millions de caisses) de vin et de spiritueux par an. Malgré les frais de douane élevé et une consommation annuelle moyenne de vin par personne de 0,73 l, les optimistes en déduisent que le Japon représente un des grands marchés de l'avenir. Isama Yokosuka, savant japonais, écrivit au sujet du porto japonais dans l'*American Journal of œnology* : « On ne fait pas du porto par la méthode de fermentation naturelle mais en ajoutant à un vin quelconque 1 à 15 % d'alcool éthylique, de l'eau du robinet, des colorants, des parfums, du sucre et des acides organiques. Le produit qui en résulte est d'une qualité extrêmement basse. » Une grande quantité de vin est fabriquée à partir de concentrés importés.

Japonica (Popillia)

Minuscule coléoptère qui s'attaque aux vignes de l'Est des États-Unis et couramment appelé la bestiole japonaise.

Voir CHAPITRE IV

Jasnières (Appellation Contrôlée)

Vins blancs de la région de la Loire.

Petit secteur vinicole des coteaux du Loir, sur la rive nord de la Loire. Ses vins sont blancs et moelleux ou demi-doux. On les fait avec du Pineau de la Loire (ou Chenin) qui pousse sur un sol où domine le calcaire. Les vignes s'étendent sur les communes jumelles de Lhomme et de Ruillé-sur-Loir. Leur production n'est pas élevée : sur plus de 20 hectares elle est de 1 200 hl (13 000 caisses).

Jauge

Instrument de mesure graduée permettant d'évaluer le contenu des tonneaux.

Jaune (Liqueur)

Nom donné à des imitations de la Chartreuse jaune.

Voir CHARTREUSE

Jaune (Vin)

Vin jaune de la région du Jura, en France, fait avec des raisins cueillis tardivement, conservé en fût pendant un temps exceptionnellement long et durant lequel une pellicule blanche se forme à la surface du liquide, pareille à la *flor* du Xérès.

Voir JURA ; XÉRÈS

Jean-Faure (Château-)

Voir RIPEAU

Jenever

Nom que les Hollandais donnent au gin de leur pays et que dans les pays anglo-saxons on appelle généralement Hollands. Le nom Jenever est produit par la combinaison du mot genièvre en français et en hollandais. Le Jenever a, en effet, goût de genièvre. Quoique certains Anglais appellent à tort ce breuvage Geneva, il n'a aucun rapport avec la ville suisse de Genève.

Jerez de la Frontera

Ville d'Andalousie au sud-ouest de l'Espagne qui produit le Xérès ou le Sherry.

Voir XÉRÈS

Jeriñac

Marque déposée de l'eau-de-vie de vin de Jerez de la Frontera, en Espagne, et qui s'écrivait parfois Xereñac ou Cherinac. Il s'agissait en réalité d'une imitation à peine déguisée de l'appellation désormais interdite Coñac.

De toute façon, quelle que soit la manière d'écrire ou de prononcer Cognac, ce nom ne s'applique qu'à la seule eau-de-vie de vin faite en France dans la région de Cognac. *Voir* ESPAGNE ; XÉRÈS.

Jéroboam

En Champagne, l'équivalent de quatre bouteilles ; à Bordeaux, de six bouteilles. En Angleterre, le jéroboam équivaut généralement, mais pas nécessairement, à six bouteilles.

Jeropiga

Voir GEROPIGA

Jigger

Nom familier du petit verre de spiritueux aux États-Unis, équivalant à 4,25 cl.

Johannisberg

1. Grand cru du Rheingau dont le vin le plus connu est le Schloss Johannisberger.
Voir RHEINGAU

2. Vin suisse fait avec du raisin Sylvaner et qui doit probablement son renom au fait qu'il porte le même nom que les grands Johannisberg allemands.
Voir SUISSE

Johannisberg Riesling

Nom utilisé en Californie pour désigner le raisin Riesling authentique.

Johanniswein

Comme l'indique la Chronique des *Minnesinger* du XIIIe siècle, l'apôtre Jean, qui était assis auprès du Christ à la Cène et qui but sans en être affecté un verre de vin empoisonné sur lequel il avait fait avec une prescience méritoire le signe de la croix, est évoqué en Allemagne au sujet de la bénédiction du vin. A Deidesheim, le 27 décembre, jour de la Saint-Jean-l'Évangéliste, les fidèles apportent à la messe la meilleure bouteille de leur cru pour la faire bénir. Ce vin de la Saint-Jean est considéré comme bon pour la santé et la fécondité ; il apporterait la paix et on le boit souvent dans un bol à deux anses qui passe de main en main autour de la table pour assurer la concorde et l'amour réciproque des convives. On boit aussi du Johanniswein aux mariages. Dans bien des régions d'Allemagne on n'en boit pas d'autre pour le « coup de l'étrier » et Martin Luther lui-même, dit-on, respectait cette tradition.

Jordanie

Aux temps jadis, la vigne prospérait dans ce pays et le vin y était d'usage courant. Actuellement les 2 000 ha plantés de vigne ne produisent pratiquement plus que du raisin de table.

Les habitants de la Jordanie ne boivent guère de vin. Comme dans les pays du Proche-Orient, on y fait plus d'Arrack que de vin.

Josephshof

Dans le monde entier (sauf en Allemagne où l'Himmelreich est plus célèbre) le Josephshof est l'un des crus les plus connus du secteur de Graach, dans la vallée allemande de la Moselle. Comme tous les autres vins de Graach, il est doté d'une grande longévité et sa saveur emplit immédiatement la bouche. C'est l'un des rares vins à être vendu sans le nom d'un terroir bien spécifique. Josephshorf correspond au nom de l'ancienne communauté près de Graach.
Voir MOSELLE

Journal

Vieille unité de mesure bourguignonne égale à 1/3 d'ha.

Julep

Boisson que l'on sert froide dans de grands verres et qui consiste en spiritueux (souvent du Bourbon), sucre, feuilles de menthe et glace pilée. Boisson traditionnelle très populaire dans l'État du Kentucky de même que dans les autres États du sud des États-Unis.

Juliénas (Appellation Contrôlée)

Vins très connus du Beaujolais. Ils ont eu malheureusement tendance à vivre sur leur réputation et ne la méritèrent pas toujours autant que ceux des autres villages célèbres de la région : Fleurie, Brouilly et Moulin-à-Vent.

Voir BEAUJOLAIS

Jura

Vins rouges, blancs, rosés et jaunes. Franche-Comté.

Située à mi-chemin entre la Côte-d'Or et la frontière suisse, cette région produit plusieurs vins qui compensent la faible quantité par une grande variété. Il y a des mousseux et des non-mousseux, des rouges, des blancs, des rosés, des vins de paille et les étranges vins jaunes. Presque tous ces vins de Franche-Comté portent les appellation générales Côtes du Jura ou Côtes du Jura mousseux. Arbois, Château-Chalon et l'Étoile sont trois appellations plus précises. Ceux de l'Étoile ne peuvent être que blancs ou jaunes. Les meilleurs sont ceux d'Arbois.

Le relief accentué de la région, où les plaines ensoleillées alternent avec des pentes abruptes, s'assortit d'une grande variété de sols. Dans les terres les plus basses on trouve de l'argile presque pure ; sur les contreforts des montagnes, la marne contient des cailloux ; enfin, plus en altitude, du calcaire se mêle à des sédiments organiques. Ces hauteurs produisaient autrefois de grandes quantités de vin. L'épidémie de phylloxéra y a sévi cruellement et le vignoble n'a été reconstitué que très partiellement. De 18 600 ha en 1836, sa superficie est tombée à quelque 1 400 ha qui sont plantés de variétés de haute qualité.

Le produit le plus caractéristique du Jura pourrait être le vin jaune. On le fait exclusivement avec du raisin Savagnin, qui serait, croit-on, le Traminer d'Alsace. Ce vin blanc est doué d'une longévité extraordinaire : les bouteilles encore bonnes à boire au bout de cinquante ans et plus ne sont pas rares. Pour faire du vin jaune on vendange tard et on presse le raisin comme pour faire du vin blanc. Le moût est ensuite mis dans des fûts hermétiquement clos et il y reste de six à dix ans (six ans est le minimum légal de l'appellation). Peu après la mise en barrique, il se forme à la surface une pellicule qui le protège encore plus efficacement de l'air. Cette pellicule, composée de micro-organismes, absorbe tout l'oxygène et interdit donc l'oxydation du vin. Elle donne au vin son étrange couleur jaune et son parfum qui évoque la noix. Cette pellicule est la même que celle du Xérès et on l'appelle *flor (voir ce mot)* en Espagne. Elle n'est pas sans rapport avec la maladie du vin provoquée par la bactérie acétique qui combine l'oxygène et l'alcool. Toutefois, la bactérie du vinaigre gâte complètement le vin, alors que celle qui apparaît dans le vin du Jura ne le modifie que légèrement d'une manière bénéfique. La pellicule conserve la même couleur blanche jusqu'à ce qu'on la fasse disparaître par soutirage.

Un autre produit typique du Jura est le vin de paille. Il doit son nom à une pratique ancienne qui consistait à faire sécher les raisins sur un lit de paille avant le pressurage et aussi à sa couleur de paille. En réalité on fait aujourd'hui ce vin en suspendant les grappes dans des chais bien aérés. Cette méthode de séchage dure longtemps. Les normes de l'appellation exigent un minimum de deux mois. Elles donnent au vin sa richesse et sa longévité.

La vinification de ces deux vins exceptionnels présente des difficultés et implique des frais ; ils sont donc vendus cher. Les vignerons du Jura s'en détournent actuellement et il est fort à craindre que vin jaune et vin de paille disparaissent.

On exporte fort peu de Côtes du Jura. L'Alsace et la Suisse en consomment mais ce sont des proches voisins et la plus grande partie de la production est consommée sur place. Il est vrai que des vins aussi exceptionnels sont mieux appréciés par ceux qui les font et les connaissent. En outre, on les considère en général comme des *vins de pays* : excellents quand on les consomme dans leur pays d'origine, mais incapables de soutenir la comparaison avec les grands vins de France. Il ne se vend donc guère que 20 000 hl (220 000 caisses) de blanc et 5 000 hl (55 000 caisses) de rouge portant l'appellation la plus générale : Côtes du Jura, sans compter les ventes d'Arbois, Château-Chalon et l'Étoile.

Arbois (Appellation Contrôlée)

L'Arbois est sans doute le vin le plus connu du Jura. On le fait dans les agglomérations situées au pied des montagnes et groupées autour de la ville charmante d'Arbois, dans le canton d'Arbois. Sous ce nom figurent tous les types de vins décrits cidessus (c'est-à-dire des vins rouges, rosés, blancs, des vins jaunes et des vins de paille).

Le Savagnin ne sert pas qu'à faire le vin jaune. Il entre aussi dans la vinification des blancs avec le Melon d'Arbois (ainsi appelle-t-on le Chardonnay dans cette région) et le Pinot Blanc Vrai. Pour les rouges et les rosés, les vignerons du Jura cultivent le Plousard, le Trousseau et le Gros Noiren (Pinot Noir de Bourgogne).

Certains blancs peuvent être extrêmement plaisants. En général on ne considère pas les rouges comme exceptionnels mais bien des Français — surtout ceux de la région — affirment que le rosé d'Arbois vaut le Tavel. Les experts ne sont pas d'accord à ce sujet.

Outre la célébrité de ses vins, la ville d'Arbois est connue parce que Louis Pasteur s'y livra à ses expériences sur le vin. Il y procéda lorsque les vignerons s'inquiétèrent parce que leur production ne supportait pas l'exportation au-delà des océans. Les travaux de Pasteur à ce sujet allèrent beaucoup plus loin et eurent des répercussions mondiales.

Château-Chalon (Appellation Contrôlée)

Au sud, légèrement à l'ouest d'Arbois, se trouve la petite ville de Château-Chalon qui donne son nom au vin de la localité et des communes voisines. Seul le vin jaune de ce secteur a droit à l'appellation Château-Chalon. Il passe au moins six ans en fût : durée extrême pour un blanc. La production annuelle n'atteint pas les 1 500 hl (16 000 caisses).

Cette ville doit son nom à un vieux château qui domine la région mais qui n'a aucun rapport avec le vignoble. Le Château-Chalon n'est donc *pas* un vin de château. On le vend en bouteille de section presque carrée appelée clavelin. Aucun autre vin n'y a droit. Le Château-Chalon est considéré comme le meilleur de ces vins très extraordinaires.

L'Étoile (Appellation Contrôlée)

Quelques-uns des meilleurs vins du Jura sont faits à l'extrémité sud de la région, autour de l'Étoile, sur le territoire de trois communes seulement. La production n'atteint pas 2 000 hl (plus de 20 000 caisses) par an en moyenne. Cette quantité minime n'exclut pas la variété car elle comprend des vins de différents genres autorisés dans le Jura : blanc, jaune, paille et mousseux.

Jurançon (Appellation Contrôlée)

Vins blancs. Sud-Ouest.

On cultive les vignes sur des coteaux extrêmement abrupts au pied des Pyrénées. Leur déclivité est même si accentuée que c'est à peine s'il est permis de-ci, de-là, d'utiliser des animaux, encore moins des tracteurs et en général tout le travail doit être fait par l'homme seul. Dans de telles conditions, la région ne produit qu'une quantité limitée de vin, surtout autour de Pau. Il s'agit uniquement de blanc, d'un teinte dorée, généralement doux et d'un parfum très particulier.

Autrefois, les vignobles occupaient une superficie plus étendue et produisaient davantage. Mais depuis la plaie du phylloxéra ils n'ont été que partiellement reconstitués et n'ont pas recouvré leur productivité de jadis. Nombre de vignerons du cru auraient manifesté un fort préjugé contre le greffage de leurs vignes traditionnelles sur des souches américaines, quoique ce fût le seul moyen efficace pour restaurer le vignoble.

Les gelées de printemps ont un effet mortel sur les jeunes pousses. Pour y parer on laisse croître les vignes jusqu'à une grande hauteur (entre 1,50 m et 1,80 m). Des traverses clouées sur les piquets leur donnent une forme de croix et l'hiver le vignoble prend un aspect de cimetière. Les sarments producteurs sont palissés sur des fils de fer entre 90 cm et 1,20 m du sol et on ne les libère de leurs liens que lorsque le danger de gel est passé.

Les vignes nobles du Jurançon appartiennent à des variétés locales très anciennes :

Gros Manseng, Petit Manseng et Courbu. Pour avoir droit à l'appellation Jurançon, le vin doit être fait avec au moins 85 % de ces variétés et pas plus de 15 % des deux variétés secondaires tolérées : Camaralet et Lauzet. Le vigneron ne laisse qu'un à quatre longs sarments à chaque vigne. Elles ne doivent pas donner plus de neuf à quinze grappes chacune. La taille courte qui ne laisse que deux ou trois yeux est interdite. Si une vigne produit trop, ce qui l'empêche de croître, on lui laisse moins de pousses l'année suivante. Quatre ans après la plantation, la vigne produit déjà des raisins qu'il est permis d'employer pour faire du Jurançon. La production maximale est fixée à 40 hl/ha pour l'appellation Jurançon et à 50 hl/ha pour l'appellation Jurançon sec.

On vendange très tard dans le Jurançon, car les vignerons attendent que la pourriture noble dessèche les raisins pour ne laisser à la place de l'eau qu'il contiennent qu'une très petite quantité de jus ressemblant à du miel. Parfois on laisse le raisin sur la vigne jusqu'après la Toussaint. On a vendu trop de Jurançon sec médiocre, ce qui a nui à la réputation de la région. La production atteint à peine 15 500 hl (170 000 caisses) par an en moyenne. Une grande partie est consommée dans les Pyrénées, mais on en trouve aussi à Paris et ailleurs.

Voir production à SUD-OUEST (VIN DU)

K

Kabinettwein (vin de Cabinet)

Terme appliqué principalement aux vins allemands du Rhin. Il désignait autrefois la réserve spéciale du propriétaire du vignoble. Le terme serait né à Kloster Eberbach sur le Rhin, où les meilleurs Steinberger étaient stockés dans une petite cave spéciale appelée « Das Kabinett », qui existe encore aujourd'hui. L'importance des vins de Cabinet était et reste fondée sur le fait que les grands vins allemands ne sont pas seulement vendangés et mis en tonneau séparément des autres éléments du vignoble, mais aussi à des dates différentes. Dans la plupart des vignobles le terme « Kabinett » s'appliquait à un vin et était inscrit sur son étiquette si la barrique dépassait un certain prix à la vente. Aujourd'hui, le terme de Kabinettwein peut s'appliquer à un vin qui atteint un certain niveau de qualité. La chaptalisation de ces vins est interdite.

Voir ALLEMAGNE

Kadarka

Variété de raisin la plus cultivée en Hongrie. Les Roumains en produisent également sous le nom de Codarcà.

Käfferkopf

Important vignoble d'Ammerschwihr.

Voir ALSACE

Kaiserstuhl

Un des meilleurs crus du pays de Bade *(voir ce nom)*.

Kallstadt

Agglomération vinicole voisine de Bad-Dürkheim.

Voir PALATINAT

Kampthal (Vallée de Kamp)

Région vinicole située au bord du Kamp, en Basse-Autriche. Heiligenstein et Gnisberg comptent parmi les coteaux de ce pays qui conviennent le mieux à la vigne.

Voir AUTRICHE

Kanyak

Alcool de vin turc, dont le nom ressemble trop à Cognac, du moins pour les esprits soupçonneux.

Karthäuserhofberg

Vignoble remarquable d'Eitelsbach.

Voir MOSELLE (MOSEL-SAAR-RUWER)

Kascher (Vin)

Également cascher ou cawcher ; kocher aux États-Unis.

Dans son acception stricte, ce mot désigne le vin fait selon la loi rabbinique pour être utilisé durant les services religieux juifs. Par extension il s'applique aussi à ce qui est essentiellement le vin de la pâque, de loin le plus vendu aux États-Unis actuellement.

Le rituel juif exige la présence de vin au service du vendredi soir précédant les jours saints et pendant la saison de la pâque. Ce vin doit être pur, naturel, exempt de tout mélange, sain, et fait selon des normes de pureté strictes sous la surveillance d'un rabbin. A part ça, il ne diffère en rien du vin de consommation courante et sert souvent à cet usage. Quant au vin de la pâque, fait autrefois à la maison, il est plus épais et plus doux que les vins ordinaires. C'est par extension qu'il est devenu synonyme de vin kocher presque partout aux États-Unis.

Le vin kocher américain est fait presque entièrement avec du Concord des vignobles de l'État de New York où ce raisin atteint désormais un tel prix qu'il élimine les meilleures variétés.

Les centres de fabrication du vin kocher américain sont les villes de New York et de Chicago où l'on ne trouve guère de vignes. En règle générale, les raisins du nord de l'État de New York sont achetés par des entreprises de conservation de fruits qui les mettent en frigorifiques et les expédient aux vinificateurs urbains, au fur et à mesure des besoins. Ces derniers les dégèlent, les font fermenter en y ajoutant du sucre de canne tant pour augmenter leur douceur que pour combattre la désagréable acidité du Concord. Enfin, ils les traitent au soufre pour empêcher la fermentation en bouteille. Grâce à cette chaîne, la vinification se poursuit tout au long de l'année et ne dépend plus de facteurs périmés tels que l'époque des vendanges.

Kasel

Village vinicole de la Ruhr. Son meilleur cru est le Kaseler Nies'chen. (Éviter toute confusion avec la ville de Kassel, en français Cassel.) *Voir* MOSELLE (MOSEL-SAAR-RUWER).

Kava, Ava-ava

Breuvage fait en Polynésie avec les racines d'un buisson appelé kava. C'est le vin des îles du Sud. « La liqueur qu'ils font avec la plante nommée ava-ava est le jus obtenu par le pressurage des racines. Leur manière de préparer ce breuvage est aussi simple que répugnante pour un Européen. La voici : plusieurs personnes prennent des racines et les mâchent jusqu'à ce qu'elles deviennent molles et pulpeuses : puis ils les crachent sur un plateau ou dans un récipient, tous dans le même ; quand ils en ont mâché une plus ou moins grande quantité, ils y ajoutent de l'eau, beaucoup ou peu selon qu'ils désirent un breuvage léger ou fort ; le jus ainsi dilué est filtré à travers une matière fibreuse ressemblant à des poils fins ; il est alors prêt à la consommation, à laquelle on procède, d'ailleurs, immédiatement. D'un goût plat, presque insipide, à peine relevé par une saveur de poivre, tel est cet ava-ava. » — Capitaine Cook, 1774, à Tahiti.

De nos jours on écrase les racines dans un pressoir à vis.

Kaysersberg

Agglomération vinicole d'Alsace *(voir ce nom).*

Kefir ou Képhir

Breuvage alcoolisé obtenu au Caucase par la fermentation du lait de vache (*voir* KOUMISS) et auquel on ajoute des grains de sorgho.

Keg

Petit fût de bois ou de métal, contenant en général moins de 45 l, utilisé en Angleterre.

Kéknyelü

Un des meilleurs crus de vin blanc de Badacsony (lac Balaton).

Voir HONGRIE

Kellerabfüllung, Kellerabzug

Littéralement : remplissage à la cave ou tirage de cave. Cette formule allemande pouvait équivaloir à nos mise en bouteille au château ou mise en bouteille au domaine.

Kintyre

Péninsule de la côte d'Écosse qui, avec l'île d'Islay, produit tout le whisky de malt des Highlands occidentales. Jusqu'à la fin du XVIIIe siècle on prenait Kintyre pour une île : la principale des Hébrides intérieures. *Voir* WHISKY, MALT.

Kir

Apéritif très populaire généralement composé d'un Bourgogne blanc léger et d'un doigt de Cassis. Il doit son nom au chef de la Résistance lyonnaise et ex-maire de Dijon, le chanoine Félix Kir.

Kirsch, Kirschwasser

Alcool obtenu par la distillation de cerises entières avec leurs noyaux. Ce Kirsch mûrit dans des fûts enduits de paraffine ou dans des jarres de terre cuite car il ne doit pas prendre la couleur du bois. Le Kirsch authentique apparaît toujours parfaitement incolore.

On fait du Kirsch surtout en Alsace, en Allemagne et en Suisse. Le Kirsch allemand est souvent vendu sous le nom de Schwarzwalder (de la Forêt-Noire). Celui de Suisse est surtout produit dans le voisinage de Bâle et porte le nom de Basler Kirschwasser.

Kirwan (Château-)

Bordeaux rouge. Commune de Cantenac-Margaux, en Haut-Médoc.

Ce vignoble est planté sur un terrain en légère déclivité derrière Cantenac : la première agglomération importante que l'on traverse sur la route du vin de Médoc. Kirwan se trouve entre Château-Brane-Cantenac et Château-Prieuré-Lichine. Depuis février 1954, tous les vignobles de Cantenac ont droit à l'Appellation d'Origine Margaux, célèbre agglomération vinicole située à 1 500 m de là, et qui produit des vins d'un genre très semblable.

Kirwan est classé Troisième Cru dans la classification de 1855. Il appartenait alors à M. Godard, maire de Bordeaux. A sa mort, celui-ci en fit don à la ville de Bordeaux, laquelle le revendit à Daniel et Georges Guestier. La fille de Daniel épousa Alfred Schyler, dont l'entreprise — Schröder et Schyler — racheta le domaine en 1924. Ils en sont toujours les propriétaires. Le vignoble était en piteux état et la production subissait une baisse considérable. Jean-Henri Schyler, l'actuel président de Schröder et Schyler et propriétaire du beau château, s'associa avec Jean-Marie Moueix, cousin de Jean-Pierre Moueix, le producteur et négociant de Saint-Émilion. A eux deux, ils firent un travail exemplaire : en 1972, le vignoble fut remis en état à grand renfort de tracteurs et, en 1973, quelques vignes y furent plantées. Ces dépenses auraient été impensables si Jean-Marie Moueix, le nouvel associé, n'avait contribué aux investissements nécessaires, et si, en 1970, les Crus Classés n'avaient atteint des prix qui les justifiaient largement.

Caractéristiques : Fruité et plein de distinction, le Kirwan est l'un des Margaux les plus féminins et élégants. Il s'affirme d'autant plus que, depuis 1970, sa mise en bouteille au château est devenu obligatoire.

Superficie : 30 ha.

Production moyenne : 120 tonneaux (10 000 caisses).

Kislav

Spiritueux russe fait avec des pastèques.

Kloster Eberbach

Ancien monastère cistercien, proche d'Hattenheim, qui appartient actuellement à l'État et produit le célèbre Steinberg.

Voir RHEINGAU

Knipperlé

Cépage à vin blanc cultivé en Alsace où on l'appelle aussi Kleinergelber et Kleiner Rauschling.

Königsbacher

Un des vins du Mitteelhaardt, en Palatinat. *Voir* PALATINAT.

Konsumwein

Vin ordinaire en allemand.

Kontuszowka

Liqueur polonaise au goût d'huile de lavande.

Kornbranntwein

Spiritueux fait en Allemagne et en Hollande, avec des céréales fermentées. Étant donné qu'il s'agit surtout de seigle, cet alcool est presque l'équivalent européen du whisky de seigle (rye).

Kornschnapps

Liqueur européenne faite avec du grain fermenté.

Koumiss, Kumiss

Breuvage sibérien ou caucasien, fait avec du lait fermenté de jument, de vache ou de chamelle.

Voir KEFIR

Krajina

Vin yougoslave, surtout rouge, mais aussi parfois blanc, produit près de la frontière de Roumanie et de Bulgarie. Krajina signifie frontière.

Voir YOUGOSLAVIE

Krampen

Secteur vinicole situé autour de Cochem, dans la vallée de la basse Moselle, en Allemagne, et qui doit son nom au coude brusque (Krampe) que fait la rivière pour contourner des falaises d'ardoise dure. Ces vins comptent parmi les bons vins de la Moselle, précisément en raison de la dureté du sol.

Voir MOSELLE

Kreszenz

Synonyme de Gewächs. Ce mot allemand signifie cru, mais il désignait plutôt le propriétaire d'un vignoble ou d'une parcelle que le vignoble lui-même. Ainsi, la mention « Kreszenz Hans Müller » sur une étiquette indiquait que la bouteille contenait du vin fait avec du raisin de vignes appartenant au nommé Hans Müller. Ce détail était intéressant car, en Allemagne, au moment de la vendange, chaque propriétaire mettait dans des barriques particulières le produit de chaque parcelle et les vignobles étaient souvent partagés entre plusieurs propriétaires qui employaient des méthodes différentes et obtenaient aussi des résultats divers.

Kriska

Vin de palme d'Afrique occidentale.

Kummel

L'Allemagne et la Hollande prétendent l'une et l'autre avoir inventé cette liqueur, mais Russes, Polonais et Baltes ont toujours été ses plus fervents amateurs. C'est de l'alcool de céréale auquel les graines de cumin donnent du goût ; il est doux et parfaitement incolore. Dans le passé, on laissait le sucre se cristalliser dans la bouteille et, dans ce cas, on l'appelait Kummel de Cristal. Un des plus célèbres Kummel est celui d'Allasch, non loin de Riga, située en Union soviétique. *Voir* LIQUEURS

Kvass

Bière russe rafraîchissante, brassée à la maison, à partir de seigle et d'orge. On lui donne du goût avec de la menthe ou des groseilles.

L

Labrusca (Vitis)

Espèce de vigne qui pousse à l'état sauvage en Amérique du Nord.

Lacrima (ou Lacryma) Christi del Vesuvio

Vin D.O.C. moelleux quoique assez sec, fait avec les raisins des vignes cultivés sur les flancs sud du mont Vésuve et qu'il ne faut pas confondre avec la Lágrima Christi de Malaga. Il existe aussi un Lacrima Christi rouge.

Voir CAMPANIE

Ladoix (Appellation Contrôlée)

Bourgogne rouge et blanc. Côte de Beaune.

La commune de Ladoix-Serrigny a droit à une appellation propre, mais peu de vins portent ce nom sur leur étiquette. Le produit ordinaire de cette localité est vendu sous les appellations plus générales de Côte de Beaune et Côte de Beaune-Villages et les meilleurs (La Maréchaudes, La Topeau-Vert, La Courière, Les Grandes-Lottières, les Petites-Lollières, Les Lollières, Les Basses-Mourottes, Le Rognet-et-Corton, Les Vergennes) sous celle de la localité voisine : Aloxe-Corton. En raison de cette liberté de choix la quantité de vin étiquetée Ladoix varie considérablement.

Cette localité est la plus septentrionale de la Côte de Beaune. La route nationale qui va de Dijon à Lyon et, au-delà, vers la Côte d'Azur coupe Ladoix-Serrigny en deux. Le premier de ces deux noms dérive du celtique *doix*, qui signifie fontaine.

Quant à Serrigny, un ancien hameau, il est situé du mauvais côté de la route nationale. Il se trouve en effet qu'en Côte-d'Or les vignes situées à l'ouest de la R.N. 74 ont droit aux grandes appellations et celles qui sont à l'est à l'appellation générique : Bourgogne.

Les vignobles Les Vergennes et Le Rognet, contigus à Aloxe-Corton, ont officiellement droit à l'Appellation d'Origine Corton et Corton-Charlemagne ; et ceux qui leur sont plus proches, à celle d'Aloxe-Corton.

Ces vins privilégiés de Ladoix-Serrigny ressemblent à leurs voisins à tous points de vue. Quant aux autres, ils sont légers, mûrissent vite et ont souvent un bouquet charmeur. En Appellation Contrôlée, la vigne couvre une superficie de 140 ha sur le territoire de la commune.

Production moyenne : rouge 3 500 hl (38 000 caisses) ; blanc : 200 hl (plus de 2 000 caisses).

Lafaurie-Peyraguey (Château-)

Bordeaux blanc. Commune de Bommes, en Sauternes.

Ce château mauresque, entouré de murs, fut construit au XIIIe siècle sur une petite colline en face du château d'Yquem. Il domine la mer de vignes qu'il semble protéger. Le chai est bâti dans la cour. Il fut classé Premier Cru en 1855.

Caractéristiques : Malgré sa distinction, il est moins riche que bien des meilleurs Sauternes.

Superficie : 26 ha.

Production moyenne : 70 tonneaux (7 000 caisses).

Lafite (Château-)

Bordeaux rouge. Commune de Pauillac, en Haut-Médoc.

Château-Lafite — un des meilleurs vins rouges de Bordeaux, donc un des plus élégants du monde entier — date de huit siècles. En 1234, il appartenait à un certain Gombaud de Lafite et cent ans plus tard ses vins étaient déjà célèbres. Mme de Pompadour en servait au XVIIIe siècle, et Mme Dubarry disait que, puisque le roi préférait le Bordeaux, elle n'en boirait aucun autre. Au château on assure que ce Bordeaux ne pouvait être que le Lafite, et c'est peut-être vrai.

Pendant un certain temps ce vignoble appartint à Alexandre de Ségur qui possédait aussi Château-Latour et Château-Calon-Ségur. Il tomba dans le domaine de l'État en 1794, après que son propriétaire du moment (un président au parlement de Guyenne) eut été guillotiné. Ensuite un syndicat hollandais l'acheta. C'est à cette époque-là qu'on utilisa les premières bouteilles pour conserver le vin. Puis Château-Lafite passa entre les mains d'un banquier anglais : Sir Samuel Scott. Il fut mis en vente aux enchères en 1868 et c'est alors que la famille Rothschild en fit l'acquisition à un prix tellement élevé que, selon les plaisanteries de l'époque, seuls les Rothschild pouvaient se l'offrir. Le château alla en effet au baron James de Rothschild pour une somme qui équivalait à plus de 15 millions de F. Par une étrange coïncidence — mais peut-être n'est-ce pas totalement involontaire — la banque Rothschild avait établi son siège rue Laffite à Paris.

Sur les premières étiquettes on voit Lafite écrit avec 2 t ou 2 f, voire les deux. Ce nom dérive du gascon *la hite* qui signifie la hauteur. Lafite est situé sur la colline la plus élevée de Pauillac, aux confins de Saint-Estèphe et domine les marais qui s'étendent au bord de la Gironde. De ses fenêtres on voit passer de grands bateaux glissant vers l'Atlantique et par temps de brouillard on entend leurs sirènes de brume.

Éric de Rothschild et Élie de Rothschild, cousins de Philippe de Rothschild de Château-Mouton-Rothschild, sont deux des nombreux propriétaires de Lafite. Les deux vignobles de Lafite et de Mouton-Rothschild sont contigus. Lafite est fait avec des raisins Cabernet Sauvignon, Cabernet Franc, Petit Verdot et une bonne quantité de Merlot qui lui donne souplesse. D'autre part, Mouton, où l'on cultive très peu de Merlot, est fait pour 70 % avec du Cabernet Sauvignon, ce qui le rend plus dur.

Lafite est très fier de son grand nom et ne le donne qu'à ses vins de tout premier choix (celui des jeunes vignes n'y a jamais droit), les vins de moindre valeur étant vendus sous le nom de Moulin des Carruades. Cette branche des Rothschild possède également le Château-Duhart-Milon-Rothschild à Pauillac *(voir ce nom)*, le château La Cardonne dans ce qui s'appelait le Bas-Médoc, et aussi le Château-Rieussec à Sauternes. Actuellement sous la direction d'Éric de Rothschild, le domaine de Château-Lafite s'étend sur quelque 120 ha dont les trois quarts sont consacrés à la viticulture.

Les chais sont groupés autour du château et les 24 cuves en chêne de la grande cuverie contiennent chacune 12 500 l. Le château bâti sur une belle terrasse du XVIIIe siècle figure sur les étiquettes. Les vignes poussent jusqu'au pied des murs du jardin. Le bâtiment en pierre claire donne du relief à deux magnolias verts et à un vieux cèdre.

Les caves froides et voûtées comportent des galeries éclairées par des lustres de fer forgé. C'est la partie la plus impressionnante du château. Le plus ancien millésime est celui de 1797 ; d'autres pancartes indiquent : 1801, 1805, 1811, année de la Comète, le meilleur millésime du début du XIXe siècle. Les nouvelles caves souterraines, construites en 1987, s'harmonisent avec les anciennes.

Étant donné que le vin vieillit plus lentement, donc mieux, dans les grosses bouteilles, il y a de nombreux magnums, doubles magnums et impériales entreposés dans les caves de Lafite.

Caractéristiques : Les grandes années, quand le Lafite réussit pleinement, c'est un vin suprême, doué d'une grande finesse à laquelle le Merlot donne une souplesse particulière. Il est à la fois ferme, délicat et souple. Mais les années moins bonnes donnent encore des vins excellents, plus légers que ceux des meilleurs millésimes, quoique quelques crus, produits dans les années 70, furent décevants.

Superficie : 88 ha.

Production moyenne : 250 tonneaux (22 000 caisses).

Lafleur (Château-)

Bordeaux rouge. Commune de Pomerol.

Ce superbe petit vignoble a longtemps appartenu aux sœurs Robins, également propriétaires de Château-Le Gay à Pomerol. Son sol très graveleux produit un vin au goût décidé.

Superficie : 4 ha.

Production moyenne : 12 tonneaux (1 000 caisses).

Lafleur-Pétrus (Château-)

Bordeaux rouge. Commune de Pomerol.

Adjacent au célèbre Château-Pétrus, ce cru de qualité fait honneur à son nom. J.-P. Moueix, autrefois le plus gros négociant de Saint-Émilion, en est l'heureux propriétaire.

Superficie : 9 ha.

Production moyenne : 35 tonneaux (3 500 caisses).

Lafon-Rochet (Château-)

Bordeaux rouge. Commune de Saint-Estèphe, en Haut-Médoc.

Seul Quatrième Cru de Saint-Estèphe selon la classification de 1855, Lafon-Rochet appartient à M. Tesseron qui a récemment augmenté la superficie du vignoble et a amélioré le vin. Il est aussi propriétaire du Château-Pontet-Canet à Pauillac qui a été depuis des générations la propriété de la maison Cruse.

Le château (belle construction restaurée en 1973) est situé au milieu du grand plateau qui surplombe les vignobles. De nouvelles caves souterraines ont été construites.

Caractéristiques : Le vin s'est amélioré lors des dernières années. Les vendanges récentes ont donné des résultats encourageants.

Superficie : 42 ha.

Production moyenne : 110 tonneaux (11 000 caisses).

Lager

Voir BIÈRE

Lagrange (Château-)

Bordeaux rouge. Commune de Saint-Julien, en Haut-Médoc.

Ce vaste domaine s'étend sur les coteaux qui s'élèvent à quelque 2 500 m de la Gironde. Il fut classé Troisième Cru en 1855. Vers la fin du XIXᵉ siècle, le vignoble était le plus grand Cru Classé du Médoc, avec près de 300 ha de vignes.

En 1983, la maison japonaise de vins et d'alcools Suntori l'acheta à une famille espagnole.

Caractéristiques : Bien que les sols permettent d'attendre une production de grande qualité, jusque vers la moitié des années 70 le vignoble ne produisit que des vins médiocres qui n'étaient pas à la hauteur de leur rang de Troisième Cru. Depuis quelques années, Lagrange s'améliore. On y vinifie maintenant de meilleurs vins. Les caves ont été refaites en 1986 avec des chais à air conditionné.

Superficie : 110 ha.

Production moyenne : 500 tonneaux (40 000 caisses).

Lagrange (Château-)

Bordeaux rouge. Commune de Pomerol.

Ce château situé sur le plateau de Pomerol au cœur des meilleurs vignobles, produit un bon vin typique de la région. On l'appelle parfois Lagrange-Pomerol pour le distinguer du Château Lagrange de St Julien.

Superficie : 8 ha.

Production moyenne : 30 tonneaux.

Lágrima

Vin de liqueur de Malaga, qu'il ne faut pas confondre avec le Lacrima Christi fait en Campanie aux environs de Naples bien qu'ils soient tous deux de couleur dorée et que leur nom signifie : larme.

Voir MÁLAGA

Lagune (Château-La-)

Bordeaux rouge. Commune de Ludon, en Haut-Médoc.
(Ludon n'est pas une Appellation d'Origine et le vin est classé parmi les Haut-Médoc.)

Ce Troisième Cru, selon la classification de 1855, est le premier vignoble classé qu'on atteint en quittant Bordeaux par la route du vin en direction du Médoc. Sa production était excellente et célèbre au début du siècle. A cette époque, pour le distinguer des autres crus nommés La Lagune, on l'appela Grand-La-Lagune. Il appartient actuellement à la famille de feu M. Chayoux, de la société de Champagne Ayala.

Caractéristiques : Ce vin est un vin de qualité. Les efforts actuels lui ont permis non seulement de recouvrer son ancien prestige mais de le dépasser. Charnu, d'un goût profond, il a une bonne part de la race propre au Margaux (11 km plus au nord) tout en présentant quelques traits des Graves.

Superficie : 70 ha.

Production annuelle : 250 tonneaux (25 000 caisses).

Lait de poule

Cordial composé d'un jaune d'œuf battu avec du rhum ou de l'eau-de-vie de vin, sucrés et additionnés de noix muscade ou autres épices.

Lake Erie (Lac Érié)

Importante région vinicole de l'Est des États-Unis. Les vignobles s'étendent autour de Sandusky et aussi sur les Iles Kelley, North Bass, South Bass et Middle Bass. On y cultive de bonnes variétés américaines de vigne dont les préférées sont Catawba et Delaware. Cette région produit des vins rouges et blancs et quelques mousseux intéressants.

Voir ÉTATS-UNIS : ÉTATS DE L'EST

Lalande de Pomerol (Appellation Contrôlée)

Bordeaux rouge. Région de Bordeaux.

Cette commune, dont l'appellation englobe maintenant Néac, touche à la célèbre région de Pomerol. La production moyenne est de 35 000 hl (380 000 caisses). Quoique similaires aux Pomerol, ses vins ont un goût qui leur est particulier et quelques-uns soutiennent la comparaison avec leurs plus grands voisins. Le Château-Bel-Air, situé au-delà de la ligne de démarcation de Pomerol, est remarquable.

Voir POMEROL

Lambrusco (D.O.C. : di Sorbara, Grasparossa, Reggiano, Salamino)

1. Vin rouge, douceâtre et pétillant de l'Émilie-Romagne.
2. Variété de vigne à vin rouge, cultivée surtout en Émilie et dans le Haut-Adige.

Lamothe (Château-)

Bordeaux blanc. Commune de Sauternes.

Classé Second Cru des Sauternes en 1855, le renom de ce vin ne dépasse pas nos frontières.

Superficie : 19 ha.

Production moyenne : 25 tonneaux.

Lanessan (Château-)

Bordeaux rouge. Commune de Cussac, en Haut-Médoc.
(Cussac n'est pas une Appellation d'Origine et ce vin porte le nom de Haut-Médoc.)

Classé Cru bourgeois du Médoc en 1855, ce vaste vignoble mérite une promotion comme le prouve le prix de son vin. Le château abrite un musée de harnais et de véhicules hippomobiles anciens qui attire des visiteurs.

Caractéristiques : Ce bon vin est fait avec soin par M. Bouteiller, qui était propriétaire du Château-Pichon-Longueville-Baron. C'est un vin charnu.

Superficie : 40 ha.

Production moyenne : 220 tonneaux (20 000 caisses).

Langoa-Barton (Château-)

Bordeaux rouge. Commune de Saint-Julien, en Haut-Médoc.

De la route, on aperçoit ce château, derrière ses grilles, juste avant le tournant brusque qui précède l'arrivée à Saint-Julien. Ses caves et chais ne servent pas qu'à son propre vin de Troisième Cru, mais aussi à ceux d'un Second Cru : le Château-Léoville-Barton. Les deux domaines sont contigus. Anthony Barton, descendant de Hugh Barton qui acheta Langoa en 1821 et un tiers du grand vignoble de Léoville en 1826, habite à Langoa et est responsable de ces deux bons vins.

Caractéristiques : Très semblable à son voisin Léoville-Barton, mais plus léger et sans atteindre tout à fait le même degré d'excellence.

Superficie : 15 ha.

Production moyenne : 60 tonneaux (6 000 caisses).

Languedoc (Coteaux du Languedoc A.O.C.)

Le Languedoc est la plus grande région de vignobles de France et, avec sa sœur méridionale, le Roussillon, il couvre 380 000 ha, 38 % de la totalité des vignobles de France. C'est une bande de vignobles parmi les plus grandes et les plus intensivement cultivées dans le monde.

Viticolement parlant, le Languedoc commence là où les Côtes du Rhône et les Côtes de Provence finissent — à la jonction du Gard et du Rhône, environ à 15 km au sud d'Avignon. Il recouvre les départements méditerranéens du Gard (en partie), de l'Hérault et de l'Aude, finissant au sud, là où les collines du Corbières se profilent dans le Roussillon, dans le département des Pyrénées-Orientales.

De la grande quantité de vin produit par le Languedoc, moins de 10 % est classé comme *Appellation d'Origine Contrôlée*, et la plus grande partie consiste en vins de table.

Les trois classifications de vin ci-dessous représentent le volume de la production de la région : *Appellation d'Origine Contrôlée* (A.O.C.), *Vin Délimité de Qualité Supérieure* (V.D.Q.S.), *Vin de pays* et Vin de Consommation Courante (V.C.C.).

Jusqu'en 1985, bien qu'ils représentaient moins de 10 % de la production totale du Languedoc, les vins V.D.Q.S. du Languedoc constituaient presque la moitié des vins V.D.Q.S. produits annuellement en France. Il n'y a que deux V.D.Q.S. (les autres étant passés en A.O.C.) : Côte du Cabardès et de l'Orbiel ou Cabardès et Côte de la Malepère.

Les vins de pays sont de moins bonne qualité que les vins V.D.Q.S., mais ils sont produits en plus grande quantité. Le Languedoc est en France le premier producteur avec plus de 60 vins de pays produisant en moyenne presque 6,5 millions d'hl de vin par an, soit près de 25 % de la totalité de la récolte du Languedoc. Ils sont généralement appelés d'après le nom de la vallée ou du versant où ils ont poussé : « Vin du Pays du Val de Cesse (Aude) ou Vin du Pays des Coteaux Cevenols », par exemple. La qualité de ces vins (et la quantité produite) dans chacun de ces « pays » peut varier énormément : agréable, s'il s'agit de vins locaux, sans distinction et destinés à une consommation immédiate rapide et, parfois, de qualité discutable. La production de vin du Pays de Languedoc représente près de 70 % de tout le vin de pays produit en France.

La dernière catégorie de vin produit dans le Languedoc est le Vin de Consommation courante (V.C.C.). Sur les 28,5 millions d'hl de vin produit dans le Languedoc chaque année, approximativement 300 millions de caisses de douze bouteilles (environ 4 milliards de bouteilles), près de 18 millions d'hl font partie de la catégorie des V.C.C. La surproduction des V.C.C. dans le Languedoc a eu un effet économique désastreux sur la région. Des milliers d'ha de terrains impropres sont plantés de variétés de cépages de pauvre qualité. On trouve peu de stimulants économiques pour parvenir à produire de meilleurs vins. Les dépenses et la difficulté à trouver de l'eau pour les travaux d'irrigation ont ralenti la reconversion de la production viticole en productions maraîchères et arboricoles.

Ces problèmes semblent être plus aigus dans les départements du Gard et de l'Hérault. Dans l'Hérault et l'Aude méridionaux, de grands efforts ont été faits pour améliorer les vins de Fitou, Corbières et Minervois qui sont maintenant tous des A.O.C. Des sociétés locales d'intérêt collectif agricole (SICA) ont rassemblé des groupements de producteurs. Les caves coopératives et les particuliers, de leur côté, replantent les vignobles avec des cépages de meilleure qualité, améliorent leur technique œnologique (la macération carbonique — *voir ce mot* —, entre autre) et modernisent leur équipement. Si le Languedoc a un avenir, c'est certainement dans ces vins d'appellation que l'on trouve dans le sud.

Bien que le Languedoc, situé entre Nîmes et Narbonne, produise les agréables vins d'Appellation Contrôlée, Muscat de Frontignan et Clairette du Languedoc, etc., ce sont, en fait, les vins A.O.C. des coteaux du Languedoc qui sont produits en plus grande quantité. L'appellation Coteaux du Languedoc fut créée en 1985, comme un nom générique sous lequel on peut vendre des petits vins locaux d'appellation A.O.C. ; les principaux sont : Cabrière, Coteaux de la Méjanelle, Coteaux de Saint-Christol, Coteaux de Vérargues, La Clape, Montpeyroux, Picpoul-de-Pinet, Pic-Saint-Loup, Quatourze, Saint-Drézery, Saint-Georges-d'Orgues et Saint-Saturnin qui sont donc considérés comme faisant partie des Coteaux du Languedoc. A l'exception des Coteaux du Languedoc-La Clape et Coteaux du Languedoc-Picpoul de Pinet, seuls les vins rouges et rosés sont acceptables pour acquérir le *label* « Coteaux du Languedoc ». Lorsqu'ils sont qualifiés, ils peuvent être vendus avec ou sans le nom de la commune. La superficie totale couvre environ 7 000 ha. Le montant total de vin vendu en tant que Coteaux du Languedoc dépend de la quantité qui porte le label, celle-ci est de l'ordre de 300 000 hl (environ 3 millions de caisses) par an. Les vins sélectionnés du Languedoc, dont la liste est établie du nord au sud, sont les suivants :

Pic-Saint-Loup (A.O.C.) : Petite région de vin rouge, rosé et un peu de blanc (mais non en A.O.C.) dont le nom vient d'un sommet situé à 25 km au nord-ouest de Montpellier. La production moyenne s'élève à environ 35 000 hl (plus de 350 000 caisses).

Cabrières (A.O.C.) : Entre Pézenas et Clermont-l'Hérault, une région connue spécialement pour la Clairette du Languedoc. La production annuelle de Cabrières s'élève à près de 6 500 hl (70 000 caisses).

Coteaux de la Méjanelle (A.O.C.) : Situé entre Montpellier et la côte ; une minuscule quantité de vin blanc (non en A.O.C.) sur les 10 000 hl (110 000 caisses) de la production totale.

Coteaux de Saint-Christol (A.O.C.) : Une petite région de vin rouge entre Montpellier et Nîmes.

Coteaux de Vérargues (A.O.C.) : En bordure de Saint-Christol, produisant environ 15 000 hl (160 000 caisses) par an d'un vin rouge léger.

Faugères (A.O.C.) : Une région montagneuse au nord-ouest de Béziers, produisant des vins rouges au goût marqué de terroir (50 000 hl, soit 550 000 caisses).

Saint-Chinian (A.O.C.) : Grande région de vins rouges au nord-ouest de Béziers, sur la Nationale 112. La production annuelle s'élève à 85 000 hl (près de 950 000 caisses).

Saint-Saturnin (A.O.C.) : Petite région de vin rouge à l'est de Lodève qui produit un peu plus de 20 000 hl par an (220 000 caisses).

Montpeyroux (A.O.C.) : Une région voisine, à l'est de Saint-Saturnin, produisant un type similaire de vin rouge (15 000 hl, soit 160 000 caisses).

Saint-Drézéry (A.O.C.) : Petite région de vin rouge au sud-est de Pic-Saint-Loup.

Saint-Georges-d'Orques (A.O.C.) : Région de vin rouge à l'ouest de Montpellier.

La Clape et Quatourze (A.O.C.) : Dans l'Aude, produisant des vins rouges, rosés, et un peu de blancs (La Clape seulement). Probablement les meilleurs Coteaux du Languedoc. La Clape produit plus de 10 000 hl annuellement (110 000 caisses) et Quatourze seulement 250 hl (2 700 caisses).

Les meilleurs sols pour les vignes sont ceux de types schisteux tels qu'on les trouve à Faugères et, par endroit, à La Clape.

Le nom Cabrières s'applique exclusivement aux rosés. Les rouges et les rosés sont faits principalement avec un mélange de Carignan, Cinsault, Grenache Noir, Mouvèdre, Syrah et Lladoner Pelut. Le sol, le climat et le mode de vinification étant à peu près les mêmes pour chacun de ces vins, c'est le mélange de raisins qui seul les distingue les uns des autres.

La production maximum légale pour tous les vins est de 50 hl par ha. Même dans ce vignoble le plus productif de France dont les variétés de vignes peuvent donner des récoltes gigantesques, la production autorisée se situe bien en-deçà des quantités vendangées dans les régions vinicoles primées de Californie. Si la France parvient peu à peu à contrôler la qualité de certains de ses vins les moins connus, les viticulteurs et législateurs américains pourraient faire de même pour les vins américains les plus célèbres.

AUTRES VINS D'APPELLATION D'ORIGINE CONTRÔLÉE DU LANGUEDOC

Clairette de Bellegarde : Un vin blanc d'Appellation situé entre Nîmes et Arles. Le cépage utilisé est la Clairette locale, et ces vins secs ont tendance à être anodins.

Voir CLAIRETTE DE BELLEGARDE

Clairette du Languedoc : De style similaire et fait avec le même cépage que la Clairette de Bellegarde ; situé au sud-ouest de Nîmes, dans une région dont le centre est la ville d'Aspiran.

Voir CLAIRETTE DU LANGUEDOC

Corbières : Une très grande production de rouge. Les blancs et les rosés sont faits en petite quantité.

Voir CORBIÈRES

Costières du Gard : Des vins rouges, blancs et rosés provenant de la chaîne de collines et de la plaine, entre Nîmes et Arles. Ces vins, dont 90 % sont rouges, ont tendance à être légers et moins intéressants que ceux du sud du Languedoc. La plupart du vin est vinifié dans les caves coopératives de la région.

Voir COSTIÈRES DU GARD

Fitou : C'est peut-être le meilleur vin rouge sec du Languedoc. Autrefois, on produisait des vins *herbacés* assez lourds ; on retrouve d'ailleurs le caractère de ces vins dans les Fitou plus pauvres. Grâce à des méthodes de vinification améliorées, le nombre des bons vins de Fitou, bien tournés et satisfaisants, a augmenté.

Voir FITOU

Minervois : Producteur de vins rouges, blancs et rosés, le Minervois s'étend sur la bordure de l'Hérault et de l'Aude, bien à l'intérieur des terres de la côte méditerranéenne, limité à l'ouest par la Montagne Noire. Plus pauvre — et plus typique — le Minervoisare est assez astringent et manque de charme, avec un goût de terroir trop prononcé. Actuellement, les meilleures coopératives fournissent des vieux vins plus intéressants. Ces vins généreux qui remplissent la bouche, sont agréablement et naturellement fruités. Toutefois, ils restent moins remarqués que leur voisin méridional, le Corbières.

Voir MINERVOIS

Blanquette de Limoux : Un vin pétillant provenant des vignobles situés au sud de Carcassonne, autour de la ville de Limoux. C'est certainement l'un des meilleurs vins blancs produit dans le Languedoc. La règle générale du Languedoc veut que les vins blancs soient trop riches en alcool et rapides à « oxyder » à cause d'un manque d'acidité suffisante ; cependant la Blanquette de Limoux et le « Limoux Nature » (vin non pétillant) sont généralement frais et bien faits, mais, manquant de caractère, ils ne retiennent pas longtemps l'attention. La Blanquette de Limoux ressemble à un Champagne quelconque.

VINS DÉLIMITÉS DE QUALITÉ SUPÉRIEURE DU LANGUEDOC

Côtes du Cabardès et de l'Orbiel ou Cabardès : Des vins rosés et rouges vendus en grande partie aux fabricants de Vermouth de Sète et Marseille.

Côtes de la Malepère : rouges et rosés produits dans l'Aude (10 000 hl, soit 110 000 caisses).

AUTRES VINS DU LANGUEDOC

Vins de Sables : Ce n'est pas du tout, en fait, un vin d'appellation, mais un type de vin de consommation courante, bien fait, qui a poussé sur le sable du littoral de la Méditerranée, entre la Camargue et le Cap d'Agde. Le plus grand producteur de ce vin de sable, ainsi nommé, est la Compagnie des Salins du Midi, qui produit les vins sous la marque Listel.

Vins Doux Naturels : Ce sont des vins vinés d'apéritif, faits avec le raisin de Muscat. Pendant la fermentation, avant que tout le sucre ne se soit converti en alcool, on ajoute de l'eau-de-vie pour arrêter la fermentation, laissant au vin un haut niveau d'alcool (15 %) et beaucoup de sucre à l'état résiduel. Il y a quatre V.D.N. dans le Languedoc, tous situés dans le département de l'Hérault. Ce sont le Muscat de Frontignan, le Muscat de Lunel, le Muscat de Saint-Jean-de-Minervois et le Muscat de Mireval qui sont tous des A.O.C.

Voir VINS VINÉS : CLAIRETTE DE BELLEGARDE ; CLAIRETTE DU LANGUEDOC ; MINERVOIS

Lascombes (Château-)

Bordeaux rouge et rosé. Commune de Margaux, en Haut-Médoc.

Domaine féodal des ducs de Duras, Lascombes doit peut-être son nom au chevalier de Lascombes qui le posséda au début du XVIIIe siècle, ou à sa situation géographique. Les gens du pays disent en effet que Lascombes dérive de Lascote, contraction de « la côte » et le vignoble se trouve effectivement sur une éminence arrondie. En 1855, il fut classé Second Cru du Médoc.

Par une succession de ventes, parcelle par parcelle, le vignoble était réduit à 16 ha de parcelles disséminées quand les Ginestet (qui furent propriétaires de Château-Margaux) l'achetèrent en 1920. L'amélioration du vignoble et son remembrement commencèrent alors et furent poursuivis sous la tutelle de l'auteur de ce livre et d'un groupe de ses amis qui achetèrent Château-Lascombes en 1952. Désormais le vignoble reconstitué couvre plus de 100 ha, au nord-est de Margaux. L'auteur n'a plus rien à voir ni avec la firme de négoce qui porte son nom, ni avec le Château-Lascombes.

En 1971, l'auteur et ses associés vendirent Lascombes à Bass-Charrington, une firme de vins, alcools et bières britannique, qui avait déjà acheté la firme de distribution de l'auteur à Bordeaux, quelques années auparavant.

Le château de pierre grise, sis à la limite du village, en est le principal monument. Il fut construit au XIXe siècle par Me Chaix d'Est-Ange, alors bâtonnier de l'ordre des avocats et célèbre pour avoir gagné le procès du canal de Suez pour la France contre l'Égypte. Les bariques reposent dans un chai neuf et moderne, éclairé par des torchères électriques faites avec des ceps tourmentés. Un nouveau cuvier fût bâti en 1986.

Caractéristiques : Le Château-Lascombes est un vin fin. Il possède un bouquet léger et indéfinissable qui souligne les qualités « féminines » du Médoc et qui, d'après certains, rappellerait la violette.

Superficie : 110 ha.

Production moyenne : 375 tonneaux (35 000 caisses).

Latium

Vin blancs et rouges. Environs de Rome, Italie.

Si les vins des Castelli Romani perdent jamais leur place parmi les merveilles éternelles de Rome, c'est qu'il n'y a pas de justice. Plus de 90 % du Latium produit des vins blancs alertes, secs ou demi-secs. A en juger par la quantité qui en est vendue, les Romains doivent les apprécier autant que les visiteurs. Ils proviennent de Frascati, Colonna, Castel Gandolfo, Grottaferrata, Montecompatri et Marino. On trouve aussi parfois les noms de Velletri, Colli Albani et Colli Lanuvini, mais l'étranger avisé prend rarement la peine de spécifier le cru qu'il désire. Chaque propriétaire de *trattoria* qui se respecte a son propre fournisseur ; que vous demandiez un Frascati, un Colonna ou un *vino bianco,* le garçon acquiescera probablement et vous apportera ce qu'il a sous la main. En tout cas ce vin sera presque à coup sûr éminemment buvable. Le meilleur est sans doute le Frascati qui tend à être plus vigoureux et à durer plus longtemps que les autres. Malgré une légèreté apparente, sa teneur en alcool le rend extrêmement insidieux.

Colli Albani est un D.O.C. fait avec du Malvasia Rossa, Trebbiano Toscano, Malvasia del Lazio et Bovino. On le produit dans les communes de Albano et Aricca, ainsi que dans certaines parties de quatre autres villages adjacents à Rome. Ce vin demi-doux, de couleur paille, a un bouquet délicat. Lorsqu'il titre plus de 12,5 % d'alcool, le Colli Albani peut être appelé *Superiore.* Cette Dénomination d'Origine est aussi appliquée à un vin blanc mousseux fait avec les mêmes raisins. Il existe un autre vin blanc D.O.C. très semblable, le Colli Lanuvini, produit dans les communes de Genzano et Lanuvio, entre le Lac Nemi et Aprilia.

Le Cesanese di Affile (D.O.C.), appelé Affile, est fait avec les raisins du même nom que l'on cultive dans la commune d'Affile, près de Rome. C'est un vin rouge qui peut être sec, demi-doux ou même doux. Il vieillit modérément bien et ressemble quelque peu à deux autres vins D.O.C., le Cesanese del Piglio et Cesanese di Olevano Romano.

Le Frascati (D.O.C.) est fait avec des Malvasia, Greco et Trebbiano cultivés sur un sol particulièrement riche en potassium et en phosphore mais pauvre en nitrogène et en calcium. C'est ce qui donne à ce vin sa touche caractéristique. Il en existe trois types : sec, demi-doux et doux, ce dernier étant connu sous le nom de *canellino.*

Marino est une ville ravissante assez célèbre pour ses vins : ainsi la décrivait Bacci, médecin du pape Sixte V, en l'an

1500. Les vins de Marino (D.O.C.) sont toujours produits entre le lac Albano et Rome. Ils sont généralement blancs, délicats et fruités.

La D.O.C. Velletri s'applique aux vins rouges faits avec des raisins Sangiovese, Montepulciano et Cesanese, et aux vins blancs faits avec du Trebbiano et du Malvasia. L'excellent Velletri blanc est plus connu et plus apprécié, quoique le rouge soit assez agréable.

Zagarolo, un autre D.O.C. s'appliquant aux vins blancs du Latium, doit son nom à la ville de Zagarolo, situé au sud-est de Rome. Il est fait avec du Malvasia et du Trebbiano et est généralement sec ou légèrement doux. Lorsqu'il titre au moins 12,5 % d'alcool, il peut être appelé *Superiore*. Les vins rouges et blancs de Cori, semblables aux vins de Velletri et de Zagarolo, sont également classés D.O.C.

Les vins des Castelli Romani faits essentiellement avec du Malvasia et du Trebbiano, ont une teinte jaunâtre, et peuvent être secs, doux ou demi-doux. On en produit une quantité énorme. Cette province produit également des vins rouges.

Plus célèbre peut-être que ces produits des alentours de Rome, l'Est ! Est !! Est !!! est un vin blanc de Montefiascone, près du lac Bolsena. Le nom de ce vin remonterait à l'an 1111 au cours duquel un certain évêque Fugger fit un voyage d'Allemagne à Rome. Très pointilleux sur le chapitre du vin et craignant de boire en chemin des crus indignes de lui, il envoya un homme de confiance goûter le vin de toutes les auberges et tavernes de la route. S'ils lui semblaient bons, cet homme devait écrire près de la porte « est » et dans le cas contraire « non est ». Tout se passa normalement jusqu'à ce que le serviteur atteignît Montefiascone. A peine eut-il goûté le vin qu'il ressortit en trombe pour écrire sur le mur : « Est ! Est !! Est !!! » Il retourna dans l'auberge et s'installa confortablement dans la cave.

Ce vin parfois sec, plus souvent un peu doux, n'est pas un grand vin. D'un jaune foncé, il offre peu au palais du connaisseur. Néanmoins il mérite d'être goûté.

Les autres vins blancs D.O.C. sont : le Bianco Capena, juste au nord de Rome ; le Cerveteri, produit à partir de Trebbiano, Malvasia et Verdicchio ; le Cori, au sud-est de Rome et Montecompatri-Colonna. Les vins rouges D.O.C. sont : le Cerveteri ; le Cori, fait à partir de Montepulciano ; Nero Buono di Cori et Cesanese ; les trois Aprilia, faits de Merlot, Sangiovese et Trebbiano, tous au sud de Rome. Les bons vins sans D.O.C. sont : le Castel San Giorgio, rouge et blanc ; le Colle Picchioni et le Torre Ercolana.

Le nord du Latium donne enfin un bon vin quoique peu connu, *l'Aleatico di Grapoli* (D.O.C.). Une fois séché à souhait, ce raisin Aleatico donne un vin rouge de dessert, riche et doux, titrant environ 16°. On le sert généralement très frais, accompagné de fruits.

Citons parmi les moindres vins les Muscat, les Malvoisie (les meilleurs viennent de Grottaferrata qui produit aussi un vin assez léger et plutôt sec). Le Malvoisie est un vin blanc doux qu'on vend parfois tout frais, à la sortie de la cave de fermentation. Terracina — ville située à quelque 120 km au sud de Rome, sur la célèbre voie Appienne — est connue pour son Muscat un peu plus faible en alcool et en sucre que la plupart de ses semblables. On le recommande à juste titre pour accompagner l'exquise pâtisserie romaine.

Latour (Château-)

Bordeaux rouge. Commune de Pauillac, en Haut-Médoc.

Montaigne, qui cultivait lui-même la vigne au XVIe siècle dans le Bordelais, parle de Château-Latour dans ses *Essais*. Ce vin était donc déjà célèbre dès cette époque. Vers la fin du XVIIe siècle, le domaine passa par mariage des mains de Chavanas, secrétaire conseiller du roi Louis XIV, à celles de la famille Ségur. Le second Ségur dans la lignée des propriétaires mérita le surnom de Prince du Vin. Il possédait en même temps Château-Lafite, Château-Latour et Château-Calon-Ségur. La propriété fut divisée pendant la Révolution et la famille ne recouvra la moitié perdue qu'en 1841. La Société civile de Château-Latour fut fondée en 1842. En ce temps-là, c'était un cas unique, mais, depuis, on l'a beaucoup imité. Seuls les membres de la famille pouvaient en faire partie. En 1963, la famille de Beaumont vendit 77 % de ses intérêts au groupe Pearson de Londres. La firme Harveys en acheta alors un tiers. L'honorable Alan Hare représentant le groupe Pearson est le nouveau président de Latour et Jean-Paul Gardère administrait le domaine. Christian Le Sommer prit la responsabilité de l'administration et de la production.

La tour — Latour — se dresse au centre du vignoble. Elle faisait partie d'une muraille construite par les gens du Médoc au Moyen Age pour se défendre contre les pirates. Ces fortifications furent rasées durant la guerre de Cent Ans. Louis XIII ordonna de restaurer la tour et depuis elle est restée exactement dans le même état que sous son règne. Les chais se dressent à l'emplacement du reste de la forteresse. On raconte qu'en ce temps-là une grande quantité de pièces d'or fut jetée dans les fossés, d'où la légende d'un trésor enterré à Château-Latour. En réalité ce n'est peut-être pas une légende. Il y a quelques décennies on a trouvé à la Tour de Londres une carte indiquant la présence d'or à Château-Latour. Des sociétés se sont formées pour le retrouver, mais jusqu'à présent toutes leurs recherches furent vaines.

La grande qualité du Château-Latour doit être attribuée en grande partie au sol composé pour moitié de pierres grosses comme des œufs. Il fallait aiguiser les fers des charrues de Château-Latour deux fois par jour ; le sol est si dur qu'un bœuf ne suffisait pas pour traîner la charrue, et il fallait en atteler une paire. Toutefois, les tracteurs en viennent à bout. Ces cailloux contiennent du quartz. Certains peuvent être taillés et polis. Jadis un marquis de Ségur étonna la cour de Versailles par son gilet orné de ces faux diamants « Messieurs, se serait exclamé Louis XV, voici l'homme le plus riche de mon royaume. Sa terre produit du nectar et des diamants ! »

Comme dans beaucoup d'autres vignobles, on pratique encore à Latour une méthode de remplacement des vignes appelée *jardinage* et qui consiste à laisser chaque cep vieillir jusqu'à son âge maximal ; on le remplace alors sans se soucier de ses voisins, tandis que dans la plupart des vignobles on procède au remplacement parcelle par parcelle, à un âge de retraite fixe, allant de vingt-cinq à quarante ans. Il en résulte que jusqu'à ces derniers temps Latour avait le vignoble à la moyenne d'âge parmi les plus anciennes, d'où un vin plus charnu et d'une plus forte teneur en alcool. Plus la vigne vieillit, plus la qualité du vin augmente et plus sa quantité diminue. Les 7/10 des raisins de Château-Latour sont du Cabernet Sauvignon ; Merlot, Cabernet Franc et Petit-Verdot se partagent le reste.

Château-Latour est un Premier Cru, avec Lafite, Margaux, Haut-Brion et Mouton-Rothschild.

Caractéristiques : Vin charnu et dur dans sa jeunesse, Latour devient un miracle de fermeté, de richesse et de noblesse. Il a besoin d'une longue maturation pour atteindre à sa plénitude, mais il mérite cette attente. A ne pas boire dans sa jeunesse. Ce cru réussit parfois les années où les autres n'y parviennent pas. Comme c'est le cas pour tous les bons Grands Cru, la sévère sélection des cuves est un autre facteur contribuant à la qualité des vins. Le second vin est vendu sous le nom Les Forts-de-Latour, et le troisième, sous la simple appellation Pauillac.

Superficie : 60 ha.

Production moyenne : 250 tonneaux (22 000 caisses).

Latour-Pomerol (Château-)

Bordeaux rouge. Commune de Pomerol.

C'est à J.-P. Moueix que l'on doit ce vin très velouté produit pendant quelque temps dans la propriété de Mme Lacoste, également copropriétaire de Château-Pétrus.

Superficie : 8 ha.

Production moyenne : 35 tonneaux (3 500 caisses).

Latricières-Chambertin (Appellation Contrôlée)

Bourgogne rouge. Commune de Gevrey-Chambertin, en Côte de Nuits. Classement officiel : Grand Cru.

Latricières est classé officiellement Grand Cru de la Côte-d'Or *(voir la signification de ce titre et ses normes à* CÔTE DE NUITS). A tous points de vue, c'est le plus proche du Chambertin.

Chambertin et Latricières se trouvent à droite de la route des vignobles quand on quitte Gevrey-Chambertin en direction du sud pour aller au village suivant de Morey-Saint-Denis. Ils ne sont séparés que par un étroit sentier. Un vieux mur délabré, au sommet du coteau, sépare Latricières d'un bois touffu et difficilement pénétrable.

L'auteur de cette encyclopédie possédait en partie le secteur de Latricières qui se trouve au pied de ce mur. Comme la plupart des grands crus de Bourgogne, celui-ci appartient à de nombreux propriétaires qui possèdent, seuls ou en association, des parcelles de surface variable. Latricières produit les meilleurs vins de la commune après Chambertin et Clos de Bèze. Quoiqu'il n'ait pas en général la même plénitude ni la même noblesse que ces deux crus, il partage leur vigueur, leur couleur d'un foncé viril et surtout leur race. Sa caractéristique principale c'est qu'il excelle en finesse, et parfois plus que Chambertin et Chambertin-Clos de Bèze.

Les vignes de Latricières couvrent une superficie de 7,35 ha. Une année moyenne produit à peine plus de 200 hl (plus de 2 000 caisses).

Latte

Sarment mûr de la vigne.

Laudun

Une des meilleures communes des Côtes du Rhône. Elle produit des vins rouges, blancs et rosés.

Voir RHÔNE

Lavaux

Les vignes, cultivées en terrasses, de cette localité du canton de Vaux produisent un tiers de tout le vin suisse. Le Lavaux blanc est fait avec du Chasselas.

Voir SUISSE

Laville-Haut-Brion (Château-)

Bordeaux blanc. Commune de Talence, en Graves.

Ce vignoble ne produit que du vin blanc et se classe parmi les cinq Premiers Crus des Graves blancs. Comme Château-La-Mission-Haut-Brion et Château-La-Tour-Haut-Brion, Château-Laville-Haut-Brion appartenait aux héritiers Woltner, et fut acheté en 1983 par le Château Haut-Brion.

Caractéristiques : Excellent Graves sec, typique.

Superficie : 6 ha.

Production moyenne : 20 tonneaux (2 000 caisses).

Layon

Voir COTEAUX DU LAYON ; ANJOU

Lazio

Nom italien de la région du Latium *(voir ce nom).*

Leaf Reddening

Maladie de la vigne. En français : rougeau (*voir* CHAPITRE IV ; ROUGEAU).

Léger

Appliqué à un vin rouge, cet adjectif signifie petit, sans intérêt, de faible teneur en alcool et en tanin. De tels vins peuvent cependant être très agréables. En ce qui concerne les vins blancs, léger n'a pas le même sens. Un Moselle léger, par exemple, peut être un très grand vin.

Léoville-Barton (Château-)

Bordeaux rouge. Commune de Saint-Julien, en Haut-Médoc.

Second Cru dans la classification de 1855 ; avec les deux autres Léoville, ce vignoble représente un quart de l'ancien domaine de Léoville, divisé d'ailleurs en trois parties. A la mort de Ronald Barton, le vignoble fut repris par son neveu Anthony Barton, descendant de Hugh Barton qui avait acheté Longoa-Barton en 1821 et Léoville-Barton cinq ans plus tard. Il habite à Langoa et dirige le domaine avec sa femme Éva et leur fille Lillian. Ce magnifique château devrait être appelé Léoville car le Langoa et le Léoville sont tous deux vinifiés et conservés sur la même propriété. Il a produit récemment un des meilleurs de tous les Saint-Julien.

Caractéristiques : Un des meilleurs Léoville. Bien équilibré et racé.

Superficie : 45 ha.

Production moyenne : 180 tonneaux (18 000 caisses).

Léoville-Las Cases (Château-)

Bordeaux rouge. Commune de Saint-Julien, en Haut-Médoc.

Léoville-Las Cases représente la moitié de l'ancien domaine de Léoville dont l'autre moitié est partagée entre Léoville-Barton et Léoville-Poyferré. Il s'étend des limites du bourg de Saint-Julien jusqu'à celles de Château-Latour. Autrefois, l'ensemble du vignoble Léoville allait de Château-Beychevelle à Château-Latour. Un des monuments les plus remarquables sur la route des vignobles du Médoc est le portail de Las Cases, juste après le village de Saint-Julien. Il figure sur les étiquettes du vin.

Comme les autres Léoville, Las Cases est un Second Cru depuis 1855. Sa qualité a baissé dans les années 1950. Mais en 1959, 1961 et 1964, ce fut un des meilleurs Médoc. La vigne est maintenant gérée par Michel Delon ; jusqu'en 1900 il appartenait au marquis de Las Cases auquel il doit le nom de son principal cru et de son second vin étiqueté Clos du Marquis.

Caractéristiques : Pendant un certain temps, ce vin fut trop léger et même un peu maigre. On constate un progrès très net : 1959 fut superbe ; 1961, un classique du genre et 1970 et 1985 excellents. C'est un bon exemple de vignoble replanté. Les jeunes vignes produisent des vins légers mais acides ; en 1959, celles de Las Cases, atteignaient une certaine maturité à laquelle s'ajouta une nouvelle méthode de vinification — conçue par le professeur Peynaud, ancien professeur d'œnologie à l'université de Bordeaux — pour métamorphoser considérablement ce vin.

Superficie : 80 ha.

Production moyenne : 260 tonneaux (25 000 caisses).

Léoville-Poyferré (Château-)

Bordeaux rouge. Commune de Saint-Julien, en Haut-Médoc.

Ce Second Cru du Médoc, d'après la classification de 1855, ne formait qu'un seul vignoble avec les deux autres Léoville : Léoville-Barton et Léoville-Las-Cases. Ce vignoble date du XVIIe siècle et fut acheté par M. Léoville, président du parlement de Bordeaux, qui lui donna un nouveau nom. M. Léoville mourut en 1769. Pendant la Révolution, toute la propriété fut mise sous séquestre et finalement en 1830, le baron Poyferré racheta un quart du vignoble. Le domaine appartient actuellement aux Cuvelier. Il arriva occasionnellement que son vin fût le meilleur des trois, ce qui n'est plus le cas. Le 1929, en particulier, fut considéré comme l'un des meilleurs du siècle en Médoc, mais ce n'est plus qu'un souvenir. Son second vin est commercialisé sous le nom de Château-Moulin-Riche-Poyferré.

Caractéristiques : Moins bon que son voisin Léoville-Las Cases et surtout moins racé, ce vin n'est pas moins souple, Il avait en partie perdu sa distinction en raison de la jeunesse de ses vignes.

Superficie : 60 ha.

Production moyenne : 220 tonneaux (22 000 caisses).

Levures

Champignons unicellulaires de taille microscopique, se trouvant sur la peau des raisins, et qui provoquent la fermentation alcoolique. L'un d'eux, le *Saccharomyces cereviseae,* est l'agent vinificateur par excellence, car il donne au vin son caractère et sa constitution. Cette levure disparaît lorsque les derniers grammes de sucre ont été convertis en alcool. Le *Saccharomyces bayanus,* variété mineure mais importante dans les Bordeaux blancs, les Pomerol et les Saint-Émilion, résiste mieux à l'alcool que la première variété et se multiplie au cours de la fermentation. Le *Saccharomyces acidifaciens,* autre variété, est souvent cause de troubles dans les vins blancs. Dans de nombreuses entreprises vinicoles modernes, les levures sont sélectionnées et cultivées avec un soin particulier.

Les raisins mûrs peuvent souvent avoir des levures indésirables. On peut les détruire en soufrant le moût et en y ajoutant des levures de culture.

Voir CHAPITRE V

Liban

Voir SYRIE ; LIBAN

Lie

Dépôt ou résidu consistant en tartre que le vin laisse au fond de la barrique quand on le soutire.

Liebfrauenstift-Kirchenstueck

C'est du vignoble, situé aux environs de Liebfrauenkirche (Église Notre-Dame) à Worms qu'est issu le nom de Liebfraumilch, vin courant du Rhin.

Voir RHEINHESSEN

Liebfraumilch

Vin de qualité, *Qualitaetswein,* cher aux Allemands, et originaire de Rheinhessen, Rheinpfalz, Nahe ou du Rheingau. En tant que vin de qualité, il fait l'objet de contrôles stricts de la part du gouvernement et sa production est déterminée par la loi. C'est un vin de tous les jours, doux et fruité, fabriqué à partir de Riesling, Mueller-Thurgau, Sylvaner ou Kerner. La qualité varie en fonction du producteur ou de l'expéditeur, ce qui prouve que son prix n'est pas un critère de choix suffisant.

Voir RHEINHESSEN

Liechtenstein

Les vins de cette petite principauté indépendante, située entre la Suisse et l'Autriche, sont d'un rouge clair, presque rosé. On les désigne généralement du nom de la capitale : Vaduz. *Voir* VADUZER

Ligurie

Vins rouges et blancs. Nord-Ouest de l'Italie.

La Ligurie est le prolongement de la Côte d'Azur et présente le même aspect : un chapelet de plages adossées aux Alpes. Le décor est ravissant mais le travail effarant. Il faut descendre les raisins des vignes presque inaccessibles sur des espèces de traîneaux. Néanmoins, si le spectacle de ces vendanges distrait le touriste, il fera mieux d'aller boire du vin ailleurs. La Ligurie produit environ 400 000 hl (environ 4 millions de caisses) par an de vins pour la plupart très ordinaires.

Dolceacqua (Rossese di Dolceacqua) (D.O.C.)

La plupart du vin étant fait dans les vignobles de Dolceacqua, c'est de ceux-ci qu'il tient son nom, éventuellement précédé du nom de la variété de raisin — Rossese. Bien que ce nom signifie « eau douce » en italien, Le Dolceacqua, a généralement assez d'acidité pour être un vin de table tout à fait acceptable. A son mieux, il ressemble au Beaujolais. Ce vin d'une teneur en alcool solide (12 % à 14 %) jouissait des faveurs de Napoléon.

Cinqueterre, Cinqueterre Sciacchetra (D.O.C)

On dit souvent grand bien de ce fameux vin blanc. Il doit son nom (Cinq Terres) au fait qu'il provient de cinq agglomérations : Vernazzi, Campiglia, Riomaggiore, Monterosso et Biassa. Généralement sec, demi-sec, rarement tout à fait doux, il est fait avec des raisins Vernaccia. Quoique sain, il n'a rien d'émouvant. Il n'en est pas moins — et de loin — le vin le plus célèbre de la région. Il existe un type de ces vins faits avec des raisins à demi secs, le Sciacchetra de couleur ambrée, au bouquet profond et légèrement aromatique, à consommer en apéritif ou au dessert et qui titre au moins 17 % d'alcool.

Vermentino Ligure, Coronata et Polcevera

Vins légers et même minces aux caractéristiques semblables, tous faits surtout avec du raisin Vermentino quoique l'on cultive aussi du Bosco et Brachetto, principalement dans le secteur de Coronata. Il ne devrait pas être cher. Le Vermentino Ligure peut parfois être mousseux.

Lillet

Apéritif français, demi-sec, fait de 85 % de vin blanc et 15 % de jus de fruits. Bruno Borie en est le président et parmi les commanditaires figurent Jean Eugène Borie, son père, les compagnies Duclot, Dubos et Merlau de Bordeaux, et Robert Drouhin de la Bourgogne.

Limoux (Appellation Contrôlée)

Petite ville, proche de Carcassonne. On y fait un peu de vin non mousseux (vin de Blanquette) et un bon mousseux plus connu : la Blanquette de Limoux *(voir ce nom)*.

Liqueur d'Hendaye

Liqueur basque provenant des environs d'Hendaye.

Liqueurs

Ces breuvages doux et généralement d'une forte teneur en alcool sont servis dans de petits verres, après le repas. Faits de sucre, sirop et alcool, ils doivent leur goût à des fruits, des plantes ou des herbes et ils facilitent souvent la digestion, d'où leur nom courant : digestifs. Les eaux-de-vie de fruits, produites surtout en Alsace (avec des framboises, des quetsches, des cerises, etc.) sont parfois maladroitement appelées liqueurs et devraient être classées comme eaux-de-vie.

HISTOIRE DES LIQUEURS

On connaissait la distillation de l'eau et des liquides aromatiques dès les temps anciens puisque Hippocrate, Galien et Pline la mentionnent dans leurs écrits. Cependant, c'est seulement vers l'an 900 de notre ère que les Arabes inventèrent le procédé permettant d'obtenir de l'alcool par distillation. Il se pourrait toutefois qu'on en ait fait avec des céréales fermentées, dans le nord de l'Europe, un peu plus tôt. L'invention des liqueurs vint encore plus tard. D'abord, il s'agissait seulement d'adoucir des alcools trop grossiers en les additionnant de sirop, puis on y ajouta des herbes tant pour leur donner du goût qu'à des fins thérapeutiques. Comme nous le savons, le vin (et plus tard l'alcool) était au Moyen Age le principal antiseptique pour panser les blessures. Cependant, plantes, racines et herbes fournissaient le remède à la plupart des maladies. Les moines en cultivaient dans les jardins de leurs monastères et les expérimentaient. Puis vinrent les alchimistes, qui poussèrent ces recherches plus loin. Arnaud de Villeneuve, savant catalan né vers 1240, fut « l'inventeur des teintures modernes dans lesquelles les vertus des herbes sont extraites par l'alcool ». Avec son disciple Raymond Lulle, il fut le premier à écrire un traité sur l'alcool et à faire connaître des recettes de liqueurs curatives. Ils commencèrent avec de l'alcool sucré, puis y mêlèrent citron, rose, fleur d'oranger. Par la suite, ils auraient peut-être ajouté des pépites d'or à leurs mixtures, on les considérait comme une panacée. Villeneuve eut des ennuis avec l'Inquisition en raison de ses idées avancées. Mais il avait sauvé la vie du pape grâce à une potion de vin, d'herbes et d'or. C'est pourquoi le Saint-Père le protégea. Quand la peste sévit en Europe, les liqueurs associées aux baumes végétaux et toniques devinrent des médicaments précieux.

Au XVe siècle, les Italiens étaient fort avancés en ce qui concerne la fabrication des liqueurs. Catherine de Médicis en apporta quelques recettes en France. Plus tard, Louis XIV aimait beaucoup une liqueur qui contenait de l'ambre, des grains d'anis, de la cannelle et du musc. D'autres alcools que l'eau-de-vie de vin servirent à faire des liqueurs, notamment le rhum importé des nouvelles colonies.

Souvent, les ménagères fabriquaient leurs propres liqueurs et, comme aujourd'hui, les utilisaient pour la cuisine et la pâtisserie. Mais, durant le siècle dernier, l'industrie de la distillation fit de tels progrès et il apparut sur le marché une telle variété de liqueurs que ratafias et liqueurs de ménage commencèrent à disparaître.

FABRICATION DES LIQUEURS

Mélanger de l'alcool, du sirop de sucre, de l'essence de menthe vendue dans le commerce et quelque autre ingrédient savoureux, voilà un procédé de fabrication simple et auquel on peut procéder dans une cuisine. Les distillateurs qui livrent des liqueurs au commerce font à peu près la même chose, mais d'une manière plus compliquée. Dans les deux cas, il en résulte une liqueur grossière.

Les meilleures liqueurs sont généralement celles dont tous les composants ont été distillés, mais certains fruits et certaines herbes ne supportent pas la distillation ; ils se mêleront d'ailleurs fort bien au spiritueux par macération ou infusion.

En distillant une liqueur, on cherche l'inverse du résultat souhaité en distillant de l'alcool pur.

Dans le second cas, il faut séparer tous

les autres constituants de l'alcool, alors que, dans le premier, on cherche à conserver les substances qui donnent du goût. Parmi les nombreux fruits, noyaux, feuilles et racines, fleurs et graines utilisés dans ces mélanges mystérieux, bon nombre d'entre eux peuvent être distillés.

Il suffit à cet effet de les laisser séjourner dans l'alcool pendant un temps plus ou moins long. Puis, quand cet alcool est bien imprégné, de le redistiller. Ensuite, on sucre avec du sirop. Le produit obtenu est normalement incolore. Quelques liqueurs le restent, tels par exemple, le Kummel et le Cointreau. Mais, étant donné que nombre de bonnes marques de liqueur sont par tradition vertes, ambrées, rouges ou jaunes, la plupart des distillateurs ajoutent une matière colorante inoffensive à leurs produits. Qu'elles soient claires ou colorées, toutes les liqueurs sont filtrées afin de leur assurer une parfaite limpidité. Avant la mise en bouteille, on les conserve de nos jours dans de grandes cuves.

Quant aux composants qui ne supportent pas la distillation, on les fait infuser dans de l'eau, pourvu qu'ils ne soient pas trop volatiles. S'ils se dissolvent aisément dans l'eau et ne supportent pas la chaleur, on procède par infusion prolongée à froid. Dans d'autres cas on fait macérer ces substances dans l'alcool jusqu'à ce qu'elles lui donnent goût et parfum. Après ces opérations, le liquide peut fort bien être épais et il faudra le filtrer. Quoique les liqueurs de fruits faites sans distillation conservent en général leur couleur naturelle, la macération de plusieurs substances peut leur donner une teinte bourbeuse qu'il faudra rectifier. En général, dans ce cas-là, on y ajoute avant filtrage une teinture insipide et inodore, dissoute dans de l'alcool. La cochenille, certains sels d'aluminium et la crème de tartre, dissous dans de l'eau et de l'alcool, donneront à la liqueur une belle teinte cramoisie.

L'addition de sucre ne fait pas qu'adoucir le breuvage, elle lui donne en même temps suavité et corps. Parfois le sucrage est simplement fait avec du sirop de sucre. Parfois aussi avec un mélange de sucre, voire avec du miel. Lorsqu'un des ingrédients est le jus d'un fruit sucré, la dose de sucre à ajouter sera évidemment plus faible.

La qualité de la liqueur dépend du choix des substances qui se mélangeront harmonieusement et aisément entre elles, ainsi qu'avec l'alcool et le sucre. C'est là que réside le secret de la fabrication et chaque fabricant garde le secret de sa recette. Dans certains cas, tout le monde sait quels sont les principaux composants d'une liqueur. Nul n'ignore, par exemple, que le Cointreau est fait à partir d'écorces d'oranges macérées dans de l'eau-de-vie de vin, mais d'autres composants inconnus entrent également dans sa fabrication. On sait aussi que les liqueurs anisées sont faites avec des grains d'anis ; le Kummel avec du cumin ; la crème de menthe avec de la menthe. De même, la Mentuccia italienne, appelée aussi Centerbe, est obtenue grâce au mélange d'une centaine d'herbes. La célèbre Bénédictine, elle, est élaborée en vertu d'une recette secrète que personne ne connaît.

Parmi les fleurs, fruits, épices, plantes, dont on extrait la saveur pour la faire passer dans des liqueurs, citons : lavande, rose, orange, citron, genièvre, vanille, angélique, thym, fenouil, iris, camomille, cannelle, amande, écorce d'orange de Curaçao, clous de girofle, gingembre, etc.

Voir BÉNÉDICTINE ; GRAND MARNIER ; IZARRA ; etc.

Liquor

Au États-Unis, ce mot désigne sans précision tout spiritueux ou breuvage alcoolisé, mais, dans certains cas particuliers, il conserve son sens original : liquide.

Liquoreux

Savoureux et très sucré

Lirac (Appellation Contrôlée)

Vin rosé et blanc. Vallée du Rhône.

La commune de Lirac est proche de Tavel et ses vignobles ressemblent aux crus de sa célèbre voisine. Mais alors qu'à Tavel on ne fait que du rosé, Lirac produit aussi une petite quantité de vin blanc et de vin rouge. Le sol est plus sablonneux à Lirac qu'à Tavel et ses rosés sont donc moins charnus, moins caractérisés.

Quant à son vin blanc il est agréable, mais pas extraordinaire. Lirac produit environ 20 000 hl (plus de 200 000 caisses) de vin par an.

Voir RHÔNE

Listofka

Apéritif russe à base de cassis.

Listrac-Médoc (Appellation Contrôlée)

Bordeaux, surtout rouge et un peu de blanc. Haut-Médoc.

Commune du Haut-Médoc, qui bénéficie d'une appellation contrôlée. Elle produit une grande quantité de vin, mais aucun château classé ne s'y trouve. Ses quelques 500 ha de vignes plantées sur une bonne bande de terrain pierreux à faible déclivité et exposition favorable donnent des vins charnus : une quantité respectable de vins « fins » et des rouges classés Bourgeois Supérieurs ou Crus bourgeois. Parmi les Supérieurs, citons Château-Fonréaud, Château-Fourcas-Dupré et Château-Fourcas-Hosten. Il y a aussi à Listrac une cave coopérative. La récolte annuelle s'élève à quelque 20 000 hl (plus de 200 000 caisses).

Voir BORDEAUX

Litre

Unité de capacité métrique pour les liquides ; le volume d'un kg d'eau distillée à la température de 4 °C, sous une pression atmosphérique de 760 mm. Le litre équivaut à 1,0567 quart américain, 1,9531 pinte anglaise, 33,8146 onces liquides américaines, 35,1961 onces liquides anglaises, et 100 ml.

Livermore Valley

La vallée de Livermore est une région vinicole de Californie qui produit notamment de très bons vins blancs, dans le canton d'Alameda.

Voir ÉTATS-UNIS : CALIFORNIE ET OUEST

Liversan (Château-)

Bordeau rouge. A Saint-Sauveur dans les environs de Pauillac.

Dans les années 80, les princes de Polignac ont acquis ce Cru bourgeois (46 ha) d'un bon rapport qualité-prix, après avoir vendu la maison de champagne Pommery.

Ljutomer

Orthographe serbe du vin yougoslave le plus connu. Sur l'étiquette des bouteilles destinées à l'exportation, on supprime habituellement le « j ». Les vins blancs de Lutomer (en français : Lutomir) appartiennent à plusieurs types selon la variété de raisin qui les fournit et cette variété est indiquée sur l'étiquette.

Voir YOUGOSLAVIE ; LUTOMER

Lobe

Division d'un organe foliacé. Une feuille de vigne tyique en a cinq.

Locorotondo (D.O.C.)

Vins blancs secs de la région italienne des Pouilles *(Voir ce nom).*

Lodge

Littéralement : loge, en français et *loja,* en portugais — ce qui équivaut à cellier ou chai. Néanmoins, les Anglais (qui ont fait le renom et le succès du Porto, et qui ont même beaucoup contribué à ses progrès) ne mettent, c'est connu, aucune bonne volonté à adopter les mots des autres idiomes. C'est ainsi que les *lojas* où l'on conserve le Porto le long du Douro, surtout à Vila Nova de Gaia, au Portugal, ont fini par s'appeler les « lodges ».

Logroño

Importante agglomération vinicole du secteur de Rioja-Alta, qui produit un des meilleurs vins espagnol.

Voir RIOJA

Loir

Affluent de la Loire sur les rives duquel on fait plusieurs vins agréables.

Voir COTEAUX DU LOIR ; JASNIÈRES ; LOIRE

Loire

Vins blancs, rouges et rosés. Vallée de la Loire.

Le titre de cet article comporte déjà une bizarrerie car on ne vend guère de vin sous l'appellation Loire, sauf peut-être un peu de Muscadet, et les crus des Coteaux de la Loire : Anjou, Vouvray, Sancerre, Pouilly, Muscadet, etc., sont des appellations beaucoup plus connues.

Pourtant tous ces vins sont rassemblés sous l'appellation générale « Loire ». Cet usage est justifié par le fait qu'ils ont certaines caractéristiques communes qui sont la marque de la Loire.

« Charmants », voilà l'adjectif qui les qualifie le mieux. S'ils n'ont pas tous la race magnifique des grands Bordeaux et Bourgogne, ils ont quand même quelque chose d'indéfinissable qui leur est propre : une grâce et une gaieté qui les rend merveilleusement rafraîchissants. La vallée de la Loire produit toutes sortes de vins : rouge sec et blanc doux, rosé et blanc sec, mousseux pétillant. On en trouve à l'étranger en assez grande quantité. Mieux vaut les boire quand ils sont jeunes — aussi bien le rouge que le blanc, sauf les vins liquoreux — étant donné qu'ils ont tendance à décliner après trois ou quatre années de bouteille, surtout si on les fait voyager. Cette règle ne s'applique pas aux blancs doux car le sucre qui leur est ajouté et leur forte teneur en alcool leur permettent de vieillir avec grâce et de supporter les chocs qui seraient fatals au vin qui a une constitution moins robuste. Le millésime importe davantage dans la vallée de la Loire que dans les autres régions vinicoles de France car, si le soleil n'a pas brillé assez généreusement, une acidité excessive peut déséquilibrer les vins.

La Loire prend sa source au sud du Massif Central, coule droit au nord, décrit une boucle entre Nevers, Orléans et Blois, pour se diriger ensuite vers l'ouest et se jeter dans l'Atlantique, à Nantes, après un parcours d'un millier de kilomètres. Elle a déjà parcouru près de la moitié de son trajet quand apparaissent sur ses rives les premiers crus ayant droit à l'appellation d'origine : Menetou-Salon, Pouilly-sur-Loire et Sancerre dont les vignes s'étendent sur des collines en pente douce. Dès lors, les vignobles abondent, sinon sur ses berges, au moins sur celles de ses tributaires, notamment le Cher (vin de Quincy) et l'Arnon (vin de Reuilly). A partir de Tours commencent les deux secteurs contigus de Touraine et d'Anjou, avec les Coteaux du Loir et la petite enclave de Jasnières, sur le Loir. Et le fleuve continue jusqu'à la région du Muscadet, autour de Nantes.

Histoire des vins de la Loire

On ne sait pas avec certitude si on cultivait la vigne au bord de la Loire avant la conquête romaine ou si ce sont les Romains qui l'ont amenée dans la région. A coup sûr les conquérants développèrent et étendirent le vignoble en Gaule.

Mais nous sommes certains que, dès ses débuts, l'Église contribua aux progrès de la viticulture et de la vinification sur la Loire comme partout ailleurs. Saint-Martin de Tours possédait de grands biens fonciers plantés de vigne jusqu'en Bourgogne, mais encore beaucoup plus sur les rives de la Loire. Les vignerons du pays racontent d'ailleurs que l'art de la taille fut découvert par l'âne de saint Martin.

Selon cette légende, Saint Martin parcourait régulièrement ses vignobles. Il aimait le vin nouveau, aidait les vignerons de la vallée et les mettait au courant de ce que faisaient ceux des autres régions. En 345, un beau matin, il arriva en Anjou pour voir un vignoble appartenant à l'Église. Là, il attacha sa monture à l'extrémité d'une rangée de vignes. Son inspection se prolongea ; il s'arrêta de-ci, de-là, pour poser des questions et donner des conseils aux moines qui soignaient les vignes et peut-être alla-t-il au cellier, goûter le vin de l'année. A son retour, il constata que l'âne avait brouté les feuilles et que certaines des jeunes pousses étaient dévorées jusqu'au tronc. Mais, l'année suivante, ces mêmes vignes produisirent de meilleurs raisins, en plus grande abondance. Les moines ne laissèrent pas échapper la leçon de l'âne, mais trouvèrent une méthode de taille plus sûre.

Pendant les siècles tourmentés du Moyen Age, les vignobles de Touraine et d'Anjou prirent une importance considérable dans le commerce entre la France et l'Angleterre car les Plantagenêts étaient à la fois comtes d'Anjou et rois d'Angleterre. Mais, avant que les Anglais ne perdent leurs possessions en France, leur goût s'orienta vers les vins de Bordeaux. Les Hollandais leur succédèrent ; leurs bateaux remontaient la Loire pour charger le vin jusqu'à Tours et même Blois. Puis, sous Louis XIV, la guerre entre la France et la Hollande (1672) mit un terme à ce commerce. Ayant perdu successivement leurs deux meilleurs marchés, les vignerons de la Loire furent obligés de chercher un nouveau débouché en France. Or, en ces temps des mauvaises routes, des nombreuses douanes intérieures à tarif élevé, et des brigands de grands chemins, il était beaucoup plus facile d'expédier le vin en bateau par le fleuve, puis par l'océan. Cependant, les gens de la Loire y parvinrent et, depuis lors, la France et la Belgique sont les plus grands consommateurs de leurs vins. Les récents progrès en vinification permettent d'expédier plus sûrement les vins outre-mer et on les trouve en bonne quantité aux États-Unis, en Angleterre et ailleurs.

Types de vin

On fait tous les types de vin non mousseux le long de la Loire ainsi qu'une bonne quantité de mousseux et de pétillants ; ce mot est devenu presque synonyme de Vouvray. C'est au XIXe siècle, lorsque le Champagne devint à la mode, qu'on commença à faire des mousseux au bord de la Loire ; ce sont presque tous des blancs et ils viennent surtout de Saumur, ainsi que des environs, mais pas tous.

Les meilleurs vins de la Loire sont les blancs, doux et secs, non mousseux. Les secs doivent être consommés assez jeunes : entre 9 mois et 5 ans, en règle générale ; certains doux ne satisfont le palais exigeant des vignerons du pays qu'après avoir vieilli jusqu'à 15 ans. Mieux vaut toutefois les acheter jeunes parce que c'est le moment où ils sont le moins cher et l'économie ainsi réalisée compense les frais de conservation. Il en va d'ailleurs de même en ce qui concerne tous les bons vins.

Le rosé est en quelque sorte une spécialité de la Loire. Il y en a de deux sortes : le rosé léger et un autre d'une couleur et d'un caractère plus robuste, fait principalement avec du Carbernet Franc et qui est plus doux. Ce dernier est le meilleur des deux.

Les vins rouges sont en général secs, assez moelleux, fruités. Ils mûrissent vite et sont exquis quand on les consomme jeunes.

Encépagement

La variété de raisin ne figure pas toujours sur l'étiquette des vins de la Loire, comme sur ceux des vins d'Alsace par exemple. Mais, pour les connaisseurs, le nom du cru indique quand même le type de raisin. Ce sont :

Cabernet Franc. Cépages les plus utilisés par ceux qui font du vin rouge et qui s'en servent aussi en partie pour le rosé. En Touraine, on l'appelle : Breton.

Il aurait été implanté dans la Loire au XIIe siècle. Au XVIIe siècle, l'abbé Breton planta dans le pays un vignoble pour le cardinal de Richelieu, ce qui explique ce surnom. A l'origine, on le cultivait en Gironde pour faire du vin rouge. Dans la vallée de la Loire on lui donne d'autres noms : Veron, Bouchy, Bouchet, etc.

Carbernet Sauvignon. On le trouve surtout en Anjou, où la surface des vignobles s'est étendue au cours des dernières années. Il y sert surtout à faire du rosé.

Chasselas. Raisin qui fournit les 3/4 de la production de blanc sec de Pouilly-sur-Loire : celui de qualité mineure. Le meilleur Pouilly, Blanc Fumé de Pouilly ou Pouilly-Fumé, est fait avec du Sauvignon Blanc cépage aussi appellé Blanc Fumé.

Chenin Blanc. Sa culture est limitée à l'Anjou, la Touraine et Jasnières. C'est le raisin à vin blanc le plus cultivé sur les rives de la Loire. En Touraine on l'appelle Pineau de la Loire. On sait qu'il fut cultivé en Anjou dès les temps les plus reculés. A n'en pas douter, il fut obtenu par sélection de ceps autrefois sauvages. On s'en sert pour faire du blanc sec ou doux, selon la température : les étés chauds donnent des doux et les frais, des secs. Autre facteur contribuant à cette diversification : la méthode de fermentation. Les meilleurs vins produits à partir de cette variété sont les : Savennières, Coulée-de-Serrant et Roche-aux-Moines.

Cot. Variété secondaire de vigne, cultivée en Touraine, dans la vallée du Cher, et qui donne des vins rouges sans intérêt. On l'appelle aussi Pied-Rouge, Malbec ou Malbeck, Cahors.

Gamay. Cette vigne du Beaujolais est cultivée dans une mesure limitée sur les coteaux de la Loire et en Touraine. Sauf dans la zone d'Ancenis, elle sert à faire des rosés plutôt que du rouge.

Groslot ou Grolleau. En Anjou, ce raisin sert à faire du rosé.

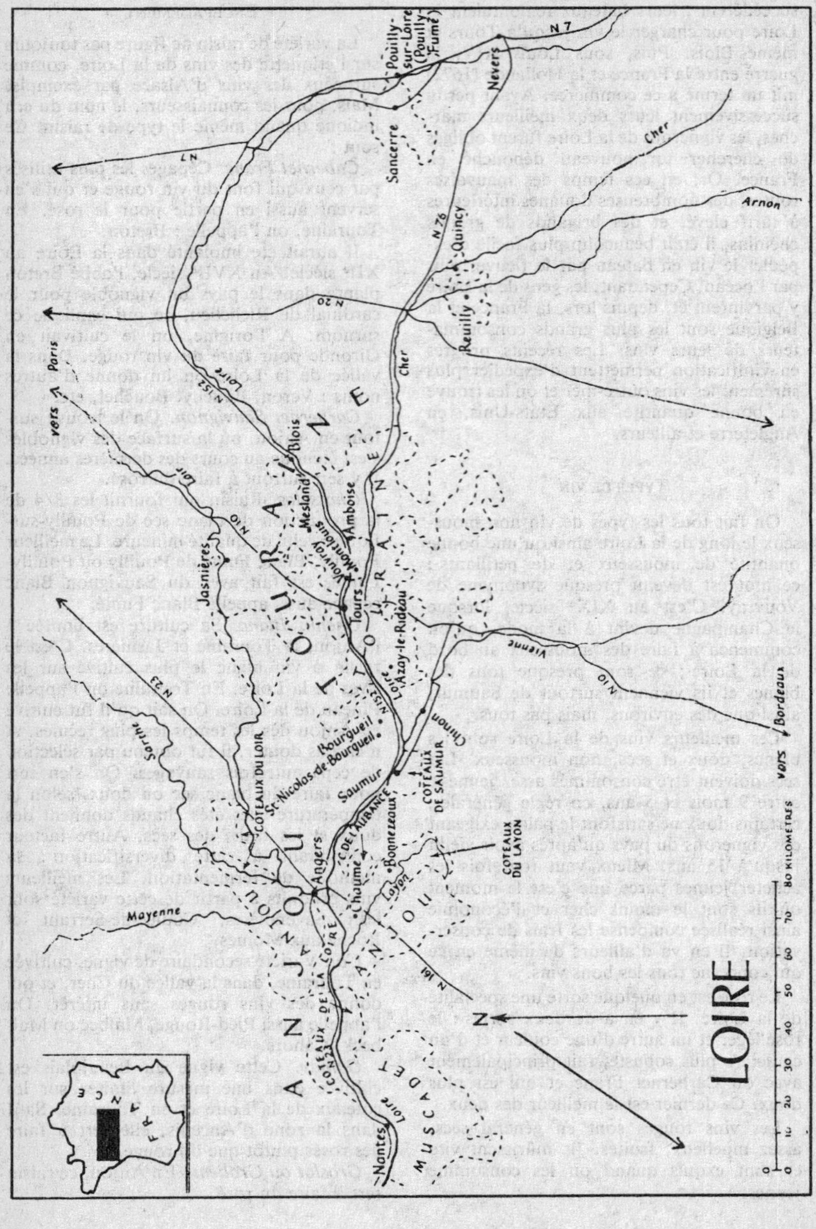
LOIRE
ANJOU
TOURAINE
Nantes
Angers
Saumur
Tours
Blois
Amboise
Chinon
Azay-le-Rideau
Bourgueil
St-Nicolas-de-Bourgueil
Vouvray
Montlouis
Mesland
Jasnières
COTEAUX DU LOIR
COTEAUX DE SAUMUR
COTEAUX DU LAYON
COTEAUX DE LA LOIRE
C. DE L'AUBANCE
MUSCADET
Bonnezeaux
Chaume
Layon
Sancerre
Pouilly-sur-Loire (Pouilly-Fumé)
Nevers
Quincy
Reuilly
Cher
Vienne
Indre
Arnon
Loir
Sarthe
Mayenne
Loire
vers Paris
vers Bordeaux
N 7
N 10
N 20
N 23
N 76
N 152
0 10 20 30 40 50 60 70 80 KILOMETRES
FRANCE

Gros Plant du pays nantais. Cultivé en bordure de la région du Muscadet, cette vigne donne des vins blancs frais, parfois un peu acides et consommés plus spécialement sur place.

Muscadet. C'est en réalité le Melon de Bourgogne qui changea de nom quand on l'implanta à l'embouchure de la Loire. Les vins blancs secs que l'on fait avec ces raisins sont légers, frais, un peu âpres, acides et excellents avec le poisson et les fruits de mer.

Noble. Synonyme de Pinot, utilisé en petite quantité pour le vin rouge de Touraine.

Pineau d'Aunis. Autrefois le plus utilisé pour les vins rouges, ce raisin est presque entièrement remplacé par le Cabernet Franc. On le trouve encore sur des surfaces restreintes en Anjou, où on le cultivait dès le XIIe siècle.

Pinot Noir. On cultivait abondamment cette variété de vigne à Sancerre au début du XIIe siècle. Depuis lors, elle a été remplacée petit à petit par le Sauvignon.

Récemment, on a constaté dans certains vignobles du Sancerrois une forte tendance à replanter du Pinot Noir car, les bonnes années, il donne un excellent rosé. En raison de ses qualités et de la mode, le vin rouge fait avec ce raisin est en train d'acquérir un nombre important de partisans.

Sauvignon Blanc. Ce raisin du Bordelais donne des résultats exceptionnellement bons dans les meilleurs vignobles de la Loire. Les blancs secs de Pouilly, Sancerre, Quincy, Reuilly sont fait exclusivement avec le Sauvignon.

SUBDIVISIONS VINICOLES DE LA LOIRE

On compte neuf principales subdivisions régionales le long de la Loire, dont trois — Anjou, Muscadet et Touraine — sont vastes et se subdivisent elles-mêmes en nombreux secteurs alors que les autres présentent moins d'importance et couvrent des superficies plus réduites.

Anjou

Cette province produit des vins rouges et des blancs. Ces derniers peuvent être secs ou doux. Les doux sont les meilleurs. On y fait aussi des rosés, secs ou demi-doux.

L'Anjou se subdivise en : Anjou-Coteaux de la Loire, Savennière, Bonnezeaux, Coteaux de l'Aubance, Coteaux de Layon, Quarts de Chaume, Saumur et Coteaux de Saumur (qui sont aussi les principales Appellations Contrôlées).

Coteaux du Loir

Petit secteur d'importance mineure, situé sur les rives du Loir. Vins rouge, blanc et rosé. Le blanc est doux ; le rosé et le rouge ne sont pas toujours très bons. Rappelons que le Loir n'est qu'un affluent de la Loire et ne doit pas être confondu avec celle-ci. Coteaux du loir est une Appellation d'Origine Contrôlée.

Jasnières

Petit secteur situé au cœur des Coteaux du Loir, qui produit des vins de qualité supérieure, tous blancs et qu'on dit généralement moelleux : légèrement doux, veloutés et d'un riche tissu. Jasnières est une Appellation d'Origine Contrôlée.

Menetou-Salon

Nouvelle appellation de vins blanc, rouge et rosé, situés en amont sur le cours de la Loire, au sud de Pouilly.

Muscadet

A l'embouchure de la Loire, les 9 800 ha de vignobles produisent des vins blancs secs, frais et délicieux. Ils se divisent en trois appellations d'origine : Muscadet de Sèvre-et-Maine, le plus célèbre, dont la région délimitée s'étend à une quinzaine de kilomètres au sud de Nantes ; Muscadet-Coteaux de la Loire ; Muscadet.

Pouilly-sur-Loire

Dans ce secteur, situé le plus en amont sur le cours de la Loire, on pressure du Sauvignon Blanc pour faire l'excellent vin blanc sec nommé Pouilly-Fumé ou Blanc Fumé de Pouilly. Le Chasselas donne un blanc similaire mais moins distingué, appelé Pouilly-sur-Loire. Les Appellations d'Origine Contrôlées sont : Pouilly-sur-Loire, Blanc Fumé de Pouilly ou Pouilly-Fumé.

Quincy

Quoique situé à quelque 50 km de la Loire, sur les rives du Cher, ce secteur produit des vins classés parmi ceux de la Loire. Ce blanc sec ressemble beaucoup au Pouilly-Fumé, au Sancerre et au vin de

Reuilly avec, en outre, un léger goût de terroir caractéristique. Quincy est une Appellation d'Origine Contrôlée.

Reuilly

Vin blanc sec — souvent maigre, dur et acide — de Reuilly, sur l'Arnon, un affluent du Cher. Les vins de ce secteur ressemblent à ceux de Quincy. Reuilly est une Appellation d'Origine Contrôlée et produit aussi des vins rouges et rosés.

Sancerre

Un des secteurs vinicoles les plus connus parmi ceux qui sont en amont de la Loire. Son célèbre blanc sec n'est fait qu'avec du Sauvignon.

Il existe aussi un très bon rosé sec de Sancerre et parfois on y fait du rouge, ces deux derniers avec du Pinot Noir. Sancerre est une Appellation d'Origine Contrôlée.

Savennière, Coulée-de-Serrant, Roche-aux-Moines

Le Chenin Blanc, planté sur la rive droite de la Loire, produit ces vins blancs secs, considérés comme les meilleurs vins de Loire. Savennière est l'Appellation Contrôlée principale.

Touraine

Ce secteur produit des vins rouges, blancs et rosés. Les blancs peuvent être doux ou secs. La Touraine englobe les zones de Bourgueil, Saint-Nicolas-de-Bourgueil, Chinon, Montlouis, Touraine-Amboise, Touraine-Azay-le-Rideau, Touraine Mesland et enfin le Vouvray, de réputation mondiale.

Voir chacune de ces appellations à sa place dans l'ordre alphabétique.

Lombardie

Vins rouges, blancs et rosés. Nord de l'Italie.

Depuis les Alpes, à sa frontière nord, jusqu'aux villes climatiques du lac de Garde et pratiquement jusqu'aux faubourgs de Milan, la Lombardie est une région de vignes et de vin. De-ci, de-là, évidemment, on trouve des espaces sans vignobles : les confins septentrionaux, trop montagneux ; les basses terres du centre au sol humide, consacrées à la culture du riz. Mais, en général, on y voit de la vigne partout. Elle fournit les meilleurs vins en Valteline, région alpestre proche de la frontière suisse, à une trentaine de kilomètres au sud de Saint-Moritz. Les cépages cultivés près du lac de Garde donnent aussi des vins très appréciés par les Italiens.

Valteline

Dans ce secteur, dont le centre est Sondrio, on fait quatre vins rouges presque identiques — Fracia, Sassella, Grumello et Inferno — avec du raisin Nebbiolo cultivé sur les pentes les plus arables des Alpes. Le Valgella est assez semblable, quoique moins intéressant.

Si le montagnard n'est pas le même homme que celui de la plaine, il semble que ni la vie ni le vin n'aient changé depuis des siècles en Valteline. Le paysan, qui vous sert un verre de vin et vous recommande de ne pas rester dehors trop tard parce que les loups-garous hantent encore les sommets, semble un homme d'un autre âge et on n'imagine guère qu'il puisse modifier ses méthodes de viticulture et de vinification. La mécanisation est rare dans ce pays dont bien des pentes sont trop abruptes même pour les animaux ; l'homme doit donc cultiver la terre sans aide. Pour cette raison, et aussi parce que le Nebbiolo n'a qu'un rendement assez modeste, la Valteline ne produit guère plus de 27 000 hl (300 000 caisses) par an pour ses quatre crus. Ses vins semblent résumer non seulement les vertus, mais aussi les défauts de tous ceux d'Italie. Ils ont une fraîcheur agréable et sont parfois un peu pétillants, comme bien d'autres en Italie. En fin de compte, quand les vins de la Valteline sont bien réussis, ils sont bons et chaleureux. Ils sont faits avec un minimum de 95 % de raisins Nebbiolo, connus localement sous le nom de Chiavennasca. On les cultive sur de hautes terrasses donnant sur le sud, autour de Fracia, Sassella, Inferno, Grumello et Valgella. Ce sont en fait des *Valtellina Superiore* et, outre la D.O.C. Valtellina, leur étiquette indique également leur lieu précis d'origine. L'un des meilleurs est le Sfursat, vin fait avec des raisins partiellement séchés, ce qui explique une teneur en alcool d'au moins 14,5 %. Après avoir vieilli pendant quatre ans, ce vin peut être appelé *riserva* et devient alors un vin de table qui ne manque pas de finesse si de caractère.

Lugana

Ce vin de Lombardie est fait avec du raisin Trebbiano auquel on ajoute parfois du Vernaccia. Quel que soit le tapage publicitaire que l'on fasse à son sujet, c'est un petit vin, généralement jaunâtre, titrant de 11 à 12,5°. Malheureusement, les viniculteurs italiens font vieillir trop longtemps leur blanc, contrairement à ce qui se fait ailleurs. Si on les mettait en bouteille plus tôt, les Lugana seraient probablement bien meilleurs.

Frecciarossa

Domaine vinicole de la province de Pavie, contigu au Piémont. Tous ses vins proviennent d'un seul vignoble de 28 ha, planté sur une colline couronnée par un château à proximité de Casteggio. Ils se présentent sous quatre aspects : Bianco (blanc sec), Ambrato (blanc demi-doux), Rosso (rouge sec) et Saint-Georges (rosé sec). Les blancs sont fait avec du Riesling. Le rouge et le rosé avec du Pinot Noir, du Bonarda di Gattinera, du Barbera et du Croatina. La production s'élève à un peu moins de 2 000 hl (plus de 20 000 caisses) par an, répartis à peu près à égalité entre les quatre catégories, soit un rendement dépassant 67 hl/ha. Cas extrêmement rare en Italie : ils sont mis en bouteilles au domaine. On fait aussi, dans les mêmes parages, deux vins rouges : Barbacarlo et Buttafuoco (D.O.C.).

La Lombardie produit un Muscat et un Muscat mousseux en quantité assez importante quoique insuffisante. Ils sont commercialisés sous le nom de Moscato di Casteggio et Moscato di Casteggio Spumante. Le premier est un muscat doux, typique, et le second ressemble à l'Asti Spumante (*voir* PIÉMONT). Tous ces vins ont maintenant leur appellation d'origine. D'autres vins de Lombardie moins connus méritent notre attention. Ainsi Riviera del Garda Chiaretto et Rosso, deux D.O.C. produits sur la rive sud-occidentale du lac de Garde. Tous deux sont faits avec des raisins Groppello et Sangiovese et ont en commun un arrière-goût persistant et amer. Le Rosso est d'un rouge rubis très profond, alors que le Chiaretto est un rosé plutôt foncé. Parmi les bons vins D.O.C. de Lombardie, on peut citer : dans la région du Lac de Garde, les Riviera del Garda Bresciano rouge et rosé, et le vin blanc Tocai di San Martino della Battaglia ; proche de Milan, le San Columbano, vin rouge, et les vins blanc et rouge de Valcalepio. Un très bon vin blanc, fait à partir de Pinot Noir et Pinot Gris, comme le Frecciarossa dans le district de Oltrepó Pavese, est vendu par Angelo Ballabio. Un autre bon rouge D.O.C. est le Botticino. Son nom vient d'une commune située près du Lac de Garde. Ce vin, qui gagne à être bu jeune, est fait avec les variétés Barbera, Schiava, Gentile, Marzemino et Sangiovese. Oltrepó Pavese est la Dénomination d'Origine Contrôlée de six vins provenant d'une zone spécifique de la province de Pavia, au sud du Pô. Le nom est généralement suivi de celui de la variété de raisin principalement utilisé dans le vin — Barbera, Bonarda, Riesling, Cortese, Moscato, etc. Lorsque seul le nom est indiqué, le vin contient essentiellement du Croatina et du Barbera. Enfin, La Lombardie offre deux agréables D.O.C. appelés Franciacorta Rosso et Franciacorta Chardonnay, que l'on produit dans 21 communes de la province de Brescia. Le Rosso est fait avec du Cabernet, du Barbera, du Nebbiolo et du Merlot ; c'est un vin sec et même robuste. Le blanc est évidemment fait principalement avec du Chardonnay, auquel il doit son nom ; il est parfois pétillant et doit toujours être bu jeune.

London Dry Gin

Un des deux types essentiels de gin (l'autre s'appelle Hollands en Angleterre et aux États-Unis ; genièvre en France ; et Jenever en Hollande). Le London Dry est celui des États-Unis et d'Angleterre. Il s'agit d'un alcool distillé jusqu'à en devenir insipide et auquel on ajoute par la suite différentes herbes et surtout du genièvre. Moins distillé, le genièvre conserve ses caractéristiques originelles.

Voir GIN

Lorraine

Vins blancs, rouges et rosés. Est de la France.

Depuis les années 50, les vins de Lorraine, qui avaient pratiquement disparu, refont petit à petit surface. Jadis célèbre pour son *vin gris* (un rosé fait avec du

Gamay) et pour ses mousseux, cette province a été ravagée par trois guerres et le phylloxéra ; enfin la loi protégeant l'appellation Champagne lui porta un coup fatal pour de nombreuses années. Actuellement deux vins de Lorraine — Côtes de Toul et Vins de Moselle — sont des *vins délimités de qualité supérieure*.

La Lorraine a toujours été une des provinces les plus maltraitées de France. Après la guerre de 1870, elle fut partagée en deux. L'Allemagne annexa le nord et le sud resta français. C'est alors que ses vins connurent la plus grande vogue. Ceux de la partie allemande furent vinifiés en Sekt : vin mousseux allemand, et ceux de la partie française étaient des vins gris ou bien des mousseux vendus sous le nom de Champagne par les négociants de Champagne eux-mêmes. En 1908, les vendanges furent désastreuses en Champagne et les entreprises vinicoles de la province firent venir tout leur vin de Lorraine. Les vignerons de Champagne réagirent si violemment, il y eut tant de désordres et même d'émeutes, qu'une loi protégea le nom de leurs vins à partir de 1908 et fut renforcée en 1911. Dès lors les vins de Lorraine durent trouver un autre débouché.

Les vignerons ne s'étaient pas encore remis de cette épreuve que la Première Guerre mondiale éclata. Les quelques vignobles qui lui survécurent furent ensuite ravagés par une résurgence du phylloxéra. On se contenta de planter des vignes hybrides pour faire des vins très ordinaires à l'usage des seuls Lorrains.

C'est seulement après la Seconde Guerre mondiale que les vignerons de Lorraine se mirent à replanter d'une manière suivie des vignes de qualité.

Les vins de Lorraine sont, de nos jours, ce que l'on peut espérer de mieux d'une région aussi froide et aussi septentrionale. Les raisins vendangés tard (fin octobre) donnent un vin titrant peu et fort acide. Les rouges sont nettement moins agréables que les blancs et les rosés ; l'excès d'acidité étant un défaut indiscutable chez les rouges.

Côtes de Toul

La plupart des vins portant cette appellation sont *gris*, c'est-à-dire qu'il s'agit des rosés légers traditionnels de Lorraine. Leur origine délimitée englobe certains secteurs des communes de : Lucey, Bruley, Pagney-derrière-Barine, Écouvres, Dongermain, Mont-le-Vignoble, Charmes-la-Côte, Blénod-les-Toul et Bulligny. Gamay de Toul, Gamay de Liverdun, Pinot Noir et Pinot Meunier sont les seuls raisins autorisés pour l'appellation et doivent entrer dans la composition du vin dans la proportion d'au moins 85 % ; Aubin Blanc, Auxerrois et Aligoté ne sont que tolérés et seulement jusqu'à un maximum de 15 %. Le rendement maximal à l'hectare est limité à 60 hl.

Le Côtes de Toul ne titre que 8,5° (degré minimum autorisé) par année moyenne, mais peut atteindre 10°, voire 11° par année exceptionnellement chaude, cependant il est toujours nettement acide. On n'en produit guère plus de 3 500 hl (environ 38 000 caisses) par an. Étant donné que le vignoble des Côtes de Toul s'accroît, cette production peut s'élever.

Vins de Moselle

Les vins de cette appellation sont faits dans trois secteurs distincts qui ont chacuns leurs caractéristiques. Autour de Metz, ce sont surtout des rosés légers, souvent étiquetés Clairet de la Moselle. Ceux des environs de Sierck-les-Bains sont généralement blancs. Enfin on fait le traditionnel vin gris surtout autour de Vic-sur-Seille. Tous doivent être fournis par les mêmes vignes, à savoir : Gamay (maximum 30 %), Auxerrois, Meunier, Pinot Noir, Pinot Blanc, Pinot Gris, Riesling et Gewürztraminer. Comme les Côtes de Toul, ces vins ont tendance à une extrême acidité mais n'en sont pas moins agréablement fruités dans leur jeunesse.

Pour avoir droit à l'appellation, la production doit être limitée à 60 hl/ha. La production totale s'élève à 380 hl (plus de 4 000 caisses) par an. Comme pour les Côtes de Toul, cette quantité a tendance à augmenter.

Spiritueux

Parmi les alcools blancs de la Lorraine, la Mirabelle est la plus connue.

Louche

Se dit d'un vin troublé par la présence de petites particules en suspension. Ceci se produit parfois lors d'une variation de température excessive et trop rapide.

Loupiac (Appellation Contrôlée)

Vin blanc. Région de Bordeaux.

Ce secteur est le prolongement vers le nord de celui de Sainte-Croix-du-Mont, sur la rive droite de la Garonne, en face de Sauternes. Il produit approximativement la même quantité de vin que Sainte-Croix-du-Mont, dans des conditions identiques, et la seule différence entre les produits des deux communes est une différence d'appellation. Pourtant ces vins peuvent être considérés comme des Sainte-Croix-du-Mont.

Voir SAINTE-CROIX-DU-MONT

Low Wines

Littéralement ; vins bas. Il s'agit du whisky entre la première distillation et la redistillation.

Lugana (D.O.C.)

Le principal vin blanc de Lombardie. Il est fait avec du Trebbiano auquel on ajoute parfois du Vernaccia.

Voir LOMBARDIE

Lunel (Muscat de)

Voir VINS DE LIQUEUR FRANÇAIS

Lussac-Saint-Émilion

Commune ayant droit à une appellation contrôlée. On y fait des vins rouges.

Voir BORDEAUX

Lutomer

Orthographe de Ljutomer telle qu'elle figure sur les vins de cette région destinés à l'exportation. L'étiquette indique aussi la variété de raisin : par exemple, Lutomer Riesling, Lutomer Sylvaner, etc.

Voir YOUGOSLAVIE ; LJUTOMER

Luttenberger

Nom allemand donné aux vins yougoslaves de Ljutomer pendant l'occupation autrichienne précédant la Première Guerre mondiale. Les vins blancs firent une brillante carrière sous ce nom, que l'on utilise encore à l'occasion. En fait, ils s'appellent aujourd'hui Ljutomer, ou Lutomer sur les étiquettes de langue anglaise.

Voir YOUGOSLAVIE ; LJUTOMER ; LUTOMER

Luxembourg

Les vins blancs des jolies collines arrondies qui se dressent au Luxembourg, le long de la Moselle, ressemblent à ceux d'Alsace. Légers et fruités, ils sont faits pour être consommés sur place et on n'en trouve guère hors du Benelux.

Les quelque 1 000 ha de vignes luxembourgeoises produisent une moyenne annuelle de 170 000 hl (plus de 1,8 millions de caisses) de vin.

Le Grand-Duché consomme à peu près 55 % de ses vins, ce qui représentent les 2/3 de la consommation luxembourgeoise. Le reste est importé de France ou d'Italie. Les Luxembourgeois consomment en

moyenne 27 à 28 bouteilles de leur vin chaque année, ce qui les place très bas sur l'échelle de la consommation européenne. Quant au quart de ses propres vins, que le Luxembourg ne consomme pas lui-même, il est envoyé en Belgique. Hollande et Allemagne n'en importent que des quantités si faibles qu'on peut les considérer comme symboliques et, sur le reste du marché mondial, la production luxembourgeoise peut être comparée à ce que représente une goutte d'eau dans un seau. Pour goûter le vin luxembourgeois il faut aller au Grand-Duché ou, au moins, en Belgique.

Histoire du vin au Luxembourg

Jusqu'à la Révolution française, au Luxembourg, les moines cultivaient la vigne. Ce pays fut annexé par la Première République française et fit ensuite partie de l'empire de Napoléon Ier. Les Français chassèrent les moines, sécularisèrent les vignobles et les divisèrent en parcelles. Ils sont restés dans cet état puisqu'on en compte 1 000 dans ce petit pays. Leur superficie moyenne avoisine 0,5 ha et c'est à peine si une demi-douzaine s'étendent sur 6 ha. Ce morcellement est contrebalancé par les coopératives ; il en existe une dans chaque agglomération vinicole et elles vinifient au total 65 % de la récolte.

Au début de notre siècle, le vin luxembourgeois servait presque entièrement à des coupages commercialisés sous le nom imprécis de Elbling, englobant les vins médiocres du Palatinat et de la basse Moselle, ainsi que du Luxembourg. La Première Guerre mondiale mit fin à cette pratique en isolant le Luxembourg de l'Allemagne. Les vins du Grand Duché, dénués de caractère, durent chercher un autre débouché. Il s'ensuivit une crise qui dura de 1918 à 1925. Alors le gouvernement établit une station viticole à Remich, sur la Moselle. Il paya des primes pour l'arrachage des vignes médiocres. Les vignerons luxembourgeois acceptaient le principe qui est encore le leur : le vin est un produit de qualité, pas de quantité. La station viticole est à la fois un enseignant et un policier. Un de ses services procède à des analyses, donne des conseils, aide les vignerons, mène campagne contre les maladies de la vigne. Un autre surveille les appellations d'origine figurant sur les bouteilles de vin.

On cultive la vigne au Luxembourg depuis le temps des Romains. Les archives vinicoles de ce pays remontent à 370, qui fut une année catastrophique au point de vue vinicole. Le vin de 1866 fut de nouveau tellement aigre que les bourgeois le baptisèrent Bismarck. Autre année dure pour les vignerons du Luxembourg : 1944, quand la vallée de la Moselle servit de champ de bataille durant la dernière contre-offensive de von Rundstedt. Mais, l'année suivante, les vignobles prospéraient de nouveau au Luxembourg.

Appellations des vins luxembourgeois

Toutes les vignes du Luxembourg sont cultivées sur la rive gauche de la Moselle, qui coule sensiblement du sud au nord, entre l'Allemagne et le Grand-Duché. Elles reçoivent donc les premiers rayons du soleil matinal, avantage auquel s'ajoute la protection que leur donnent les forêts plantées au sommet des coteaux et qui arrêtent le vent d'ouest soufflant presque toute l'année. Les bords de la Moselle luxembourgeoise forment un damier où la vigne alterne avec les cerisiers et les pruniers dont les fruits donnent les alcools blancs distillés au Luxembourg. Selon la loi du Grand-Duché, les appellations correspondent au type suivant :

Moselle Luxembourgeoise, Appellation Contrôlée utilisée en complément de la variété de raisin. Moselle Luxembourgeoise Riesling, Appellation Contrôlée. Localité d'origine avec ou sans le site du vignoble, et la variété de raisin : Wormeldange Riesling, Riesling du vignoble d'Elterberg près de Wormeldange.

Dans les catégories de vins fins, l'étiquette doit indiquer le millésime, la variété de raisin, le nom du vigneron ainsi que son adresse.

Aujourd'hui, la tendance va aux vins de qualité ; la répartition était récemment la suivante :

— Vins de table : 35 %.

— Marque nationale (vin qui a subi des tests analytiques et organoleptiques par douze experts) : 45 %.

— Vin classé : 7 %.

— Premier Cru : 3 %.

— Grand Premier Cru : 10 %.

Le traitement et le type de la vigne font l'objet d'une réglementation stricte et les vins d'une dégustation officielle par la Commission de la Marque nationale.

Depuis l'établissement de cette Marque nationale par le gouvernement en 1935, son label figure de plus en plus souvent sur les vins du Luxembourg. Il s'agit d'un petit sceau portant l'indication : *Marque nationale*, et fixé au goulot des bouteilles garanties. Des fonctionnaires d'État surveillent la mise en bouteille de ces vins.

VARIÉTÉS DE RAISINS SERVANT A FAIRE LES MEILLEURS VINS

Les meilleurs vignobles se trouvent sur le sol calcaire de Remich et sur celui de Grevenmacher, composé d'argile et de calcaire et semé de pierres. Ce genre de terrain, surtout sur un sous-sol marneux, est considéré comme bon pour le Riesling, alors que l'argile d'une teinte allant du vert au rouge est celle qui convient au Pinot.

Les variétés de raisin cultivées au Luxembourg sont les suivantes : Riesling, Traminer, Ruländer (Pinot Gris), Pinot Blanc, Auxerrois, Sylvaner, Rivaner, Elbling, Muscat Ottonel.

Avec ces raisins on fait les meilleurs vins, qui sont les suivants :

Rivaner. Vin de table léger, ayant un peu le goût de Muscat, provenant de toutes les localités luxembourgeoises de la Moselle. Le cépage est plus connu sous le nom de Müller-Thurgau.

Pinot Auxerrois, Pinot Blanc et *Ruländer* (ou Pinot Gris). Vin plus charnu, plus généreux et plus corsé que le précédent, mais qui a souvent moins de bouquet. Meilleures localités d'origine : Wellenstein, Remerschen et Schengen.

Riesling. Élégant et très distingué, mais avec une tendance à l'acidité en années humides. Meilleures localités d'origine : Wormeldange, Stadtbredimus, Wintrange, Schengen, Remiche, Grevenmacher, Ehnen.

Traminer. Gros vin velouté, au goût et au parfum typiquement épicés. Meilleurs localités : Ahn, Wellenstein, Schwebsingen, Schengen, Machtum.

SPIRITUEUX

Cerises et prunes des vergers luxembourgeois fournissent kirsch, quetsche et mirabelle. Le nombre des distilleries varie, mais se situe aux environs de 950.

Lynch-Bages (Château-)

Bordeaux rouge. Commune de Pauillac, en Haut-Médoc.

Bien que classé Cinquième Cru du Médoc en 1855, le Lynch-Bages se vend en réalité à des prix de Second Cru. Il est situé à Bages, soit à moins de 400 m au sud de Pauillac et on le voit nettement de la route du vin lorsqu'on se dirige vers cette localité.

Un propriétaire d'origine irlandaise, M. Lynch, qui fut maire de Bordeaux, lui donna son nom. Depuis 1933, il appartient à la famille Cazes et, durant ces dernières années, à l'énergique maire de Pauillac, M. J.-C. Cazes et à son fils, Michel. Sous sa direction efficace, le cru a rapidement affermi sa qualité et sa réputation. Le lancement de la renommée de Lynch-Bages débuta dans les années 50 quand, deux fois de suite, les principaux vignerons de Cantenac-Margaux, les courtiers et négociants en vin de Bordeaux, réunis au Château-Prieuré-Lichine, dégustèrent à l'aveugle les principaux vins du Médoc, et chaque fois Lynch-Bages fut classé premier. Que ce bon cru soit encore relégué au cinquième rang montre combien la classification de 1855 est périmée.

Caractéristiques : Il peut être riche, corsé, rond et superbe dans les grandes années. D'un goût flatteur dans sa jeunesse, il sait vieillir aussi.

Superficie : 76 ha.

Production moyenne : 300 tonneaux (28 000 caisses).

Lynch-Moussas (Château-)

Bordeaux rouge. Commune de Pauillac, en Haut-Médoc.

Le vin de ce petit vignoble, classé Cinquième Cru du Médoc en 1855, est surtout vendu en Hollande et en Belgique. De même que le Château-Lynch-Bages, il appartint autrefois à M. Lynch. Les propriétaires actuels, Émile Casteja et son fils ont replanté une grande partie du vignoble.

Caractéristiques : A boire quand il est jeune.

Superficie : 40 ha.

Production moyenne : 175 tonneaux (17 000 caisses).

M

Macadam (Vin de)

Nom que les Parisiens donnaient autrefois aux vins doux expédiés tout droit de la cuve de fermentation jusqu'aux boulevards de Paris, où on les consommait à la terrasse des cafés, c'est-à-dire sur le macadam. Le plus célèbre de ces vins venait de la région de Bergerac *(voir ce nom).*

Macération carbonique

Une méthode de macération de raisins à vin rouge dans la cuve avant la fermentation est utilisée pour rehausser le *fruité* et l'*arôme* du vin. En bref, la méthode comprend les étapes suivantes : lorsque les raisins ont été ramassés et égrenés, ils sont placés dans une cuve sans *être foulés.* La cuve est ensuite remplie de *gaz carbonique.* L'absence d'oxygène et la condition relativement sèche de la cuve retarde le début de la fermentation, la faisant démarrer en même temps que les raisins eux-mêmes, plutôt que dans le jus contenu normalement dans la cuve. La période de macération conduit automatiquement à la fermentation. Ce lent déclenchement de la fermentation et le contact prolongé du jus et de la peau permettent d'obtenir un plus grand arôme et une meilleure vinosité. Les vins faits entièrement ou partiellement à la macération carbonique sont remarquables par leur arôme fortement fruité et par une plus grande profondeur de couleur. Les cépages utilisés le plus souvent pour la macération carbonique sont le Carignan, le Grenache et le Gamay.

Mâché

On dit d'un vin qu'il est mâché quand le soutirage ou le transport a détruit son équilibre.

Mâcon

Centre de commerce du vin en basse Bourgogne.

Voir MÂCONNAIS

Mâcon Supérieur

Appellation d'Origine Contrôlée des vins de la région du Mâconnais *(voir ce nom).*

Mâconnais

Vin blanc surtout, ainsi que du rouge et du rosé. Sud de la Bourgogne.

La région du Mâconnais s'étend au sud de la Bourgogne, le long de la Saône, au-dessous du Chalonnais et au-dessus du Beaujolais. La limite entre Beaujolais et Mâconnais est confuse. On voit en effet sur la carte de la Bourgogne que La Chapelle-Guinchay, commune du Mâconnais se trouve au sud de Saint-Amour, Juliénas et Chénas, célèbres crus du Beaujolais. Les vins de La Chapelle sont habituellement vendus sous le nom de Beaujolais s'ils sont rouges, et de Mâconnais s'ils sont blancs. C'est un des cas où vignerons et négociants choisissent l'appellation qui leur semble la meilleure.

Le meilleur et le plus célèbre des Mâconnais est le blanc sec de Pouilly-Fuissé. Il s'est déjà assuré une bonne place sur nombre de grandes tables depuis des années et sa popularité ne cesse de croître. Mais il existe d'autres Pouilly, notamment ceux des crus voisins de Pouilly-Loché et Pouilly-Vinzelles. Nous avons déjà vu aussi qu'il existe sur la Loire un Pouilly-Fumé *(voir ce nom)* qui ressemble au Pouilly du Mâconnais par le nom et la couleur mais n'est pas fait avec la même variété de raisin et n'a pas le même goût.

Parmi les vins blancs de la Bourgogne méridionale, le Mâcon occupe la même place qu'un cru du Beaujolais chez les rouges. Ni l'un ni l'autre ne sont jamais de très grands vins. Tous deux sont souvent excellents et généralement extrêmement agréables. L'intérêt que le public porte au Pouilly-Fuissé et aux autres vins du Mâconnais date de beaucoup plus longtemps que la popularité du Beaujolais, dont le cercle des partisans ne s'est élargi que durant ces dernières années.

Le Mâconnais exporte ses vins, très demandés depuis le XVIIe siècle, et cela, dit-on, grâce à l'esprit d'initiative d'un certain vigneron nommé Claude Brosse. Vers 1660, Brosse estima qu'il était grand temps de faire connaître hors de la Bourgogne l'excellence des vins du Mâconnais. Géant sans peur, il chargea sa charrette de deux barriques et prit la route de Paris. On ne voyageait guère en ce temps-là sur les 400 km de route bourbeuse, mal entretenue, et où les brigands de grand chemin tendaient des embuscades. Mais Brosse arriva sain et sauf à Paris, ce qui lui prit environ trente jours. Sa stature imposante attira l'attention du roi qui voulut savoir ce que faisait ce Bourguignon si loin de sa province. Puisque Brosse s'occupait de vin, Louis XIV y goûta. A peine en eut-il bu une gorgée qu'il passa une commande à Brosse. Ce qui, par hasard, plaisait au roi correspondait exactement à ce que la cour avait toujours souhaité. C'est ainsi que Brosse lança les vins du Mâconnais sur le marché de Versailles et de Paris.

Actuellement les vignerons du Mâconnais ne produisent pas seulement du vin blanc mais aussi une bonne quantité de rouge. Quant au rosé, ils en font peu. La proximité du Beaujolais, où la vigne noble est le Gamay, incite les viticulteurs du Mâconnais à en planter, mais avec des résultats moins heureux. Par tradition, le raisin à vin rouge fut toujours le Gamay à jus coloré, ou, plus exactement, Gamay Teinturier, gros fruit, abondant, qui donne un jus foncé, contrairement à la plupart des raisins à peau colorée. Parmi tous les membres de la famille Gamay, ce Teinturier est à l'origine de nombreux abus. C'est précisément ce cep « déloyal » que dénonçait Philippe le Hardi et qui a été condamné et interdit sans cesse en Bourgogne. Pourtant, dans le Mâconnais, il est encore permis d'utiliser jusqu'à 15 % de Gamay Teinturier pour le vin rouge. Ces vins sont pour la plupart faits avec du Pinot Noir, dont un peu de Gamay Noir à jus blanc. Et c'est de Pinot Noir que l'on replante ces vignes.

Si le Gamay donne de biens meilleurs vins en Beaujolais qu'en Mâconnais, c'est que le sol des deux régions n'est pas le même. Nulle part en Mâconnais on ne trouve le granit qui donne au Beaujolais un attrait particulier. Pour une raison inverse, les coteaux crayeux du Mâconnais permettent au Chardonnay — seule vigne noble à vin blanc de Bourgogne — de donner des résultats exquis. Pour être plus précis, disons que le Mâconnais possède trois catégories distinctes de sol. Le meilleur est celui de Pouilly-Fuissé, un peu au sud-ouest de Mâcon. Le vallonnement datant du jurassique — c'est-à-dire de quelque 150 millions d'années — a rapproché le sous-sol de la surface et le calcaire s'y est mêlé à l'ardoise. Au nord-ouest de Mâcon, on trouve une formation géologique différente : une longue vallée où la désintégration d'oolithes calcaires donne une couche superficielle assez profonde pour que la vigne y prospère. Ces deux secteurs conviennent parfaitement aux vignes à vin blanc. Vers l'extrémité nord du Mâconnais, le terrain présente un aspect plus varié et confus. Ici domine la craie, ailleurs, l'ardoise, et les vins ont la saveur que leur donne le terroir. Certains sont bons, d'autres le sont moins.

La terre de certaines parties du Mâconnais a toujours passionné les géologues. Non seulement on y trouve plusieurs couches successives de formations rocheuses souterraines, mais encore chacune date d'une période géologique différente. L'ensemble du secteur s'est révélé un excellent terrain de chasse au trésor pour ceux qui cherchent des reliques d'un passé révolu. Des excavations ont permis de déterrer des fossiles datant de 6 000 ans, dans le voisinage de Solutré — une des communes qui ont droit à l'appellation

Pouilly-Fuissé — et à peu près tous les laboureurs du pays ont, un jour ou l'autre, trouvé sur leurs terres un vestige datant souvent de l'époque gallo-romaine. Mais l'histoire du Mâconnais n'est pas inscrite seulement dans le sol et le sous-sol. Le grand monastère médiéval de Cluny fut construit dans la ville qui porte ce nom, à quelque 15 km au nord-ouest de Mâcon. Ses moines contribuèrent beaucoup à maintenir les connaissances anciennes pendant les siècles de ténèbres et, durant un certain temps, Cluny fut une des communautés les plus puissantes de l'Église française. Ces mêmes moines contribuèrent aussi à répandre d'autres connaissances plus pratiques : la viticulture et la vinification. Ils conseillèrent aux paysans du voisinage d'augmenter la superficie de leurs vignobles et leur apprirent à soigner correctement leurs ceps. Les archives n'indiquent pas si les moines inspirèrent le vin ou si le vin inspira les moines, mais il est certain que la viticulture de Bourgogne doit son existence à l'esprit industrieux de Cluny.

Dans cette région méridionale de la Bourgogne, on applique des méthodes particulières de viticulture. Le soleil y est plus chaud qu'en Côte-d'Or, et l'été un peu plus long. Le Chardonnay, en particulier, peut y être cultivé à plus haute altitude que partout ailleurs dans la province. En raison de ce plus grand ensoleillement, les vignerons disent qu'il n'est pas nécessaire de tailler la vigne court pour qu'elle profite de la chaleur réfléchie par le sol pierreux. En outre, on peut se permettre en Mâconnais d'accorder aux raisins quinze jours de plus pour mûrir que dans la Côte-d'Or.

La plupart des vins du Mâconnais sont surtout vendus sous l'appellation Mâcon-Villages, puis loin derrière sous l'appellation Mâcon Supérieur ou bien Mâcon suivi par le nom de la commune où fut cultivée la vigne. Une quantité moins grande est vendue simplement sous le nom de Mâcon, sans autre indication d'origine. Mais les meilleurs portent une des trois appellations Pouilly. Comme partout ailleurs en France, ces appellations n'impliquent pas seulement une origine, mais aussi certaines normes.

Appellations d'origine du Mâconnais

Pouilly-Fuissé (Appellation Contrôlée)

C'est le roi des vins blancs du Mâconnais. En général il est assez léger et très sec. Le meilleur a une rondeur charnue très nette qui le distingue de ses congénères de moindre qualité : vins légers mais trop acides et manquant de caractère. Le Pouilly-Fuissé est moins dur que le Chablis, mais aussi moins fruité, et le sol sur lequel pousse la vigne lui donne un léger goût de terroir. Dans sa jeunesse, il présente un bouquet très léger et une couleur d'or pâle légèrement teintée de vert. C'est alors qu'il est dans sa plénitude. Il faut donc le boire jeune. Les Pouilly-Fuissé atteignent, en effet, leur point culminant après six mois de bouteille et n'y restent que pendant trois à cinq ans. Quelques-uns ont une teneur suffisante en alcool pour durer plus longtemps. Mais ils ne s'amélioreront plus. Les conserver présente donc peu d'intérêt.

Pour être un vrai Pouilly-Fuissé, le vin doit provenir d'une des quatre communes suivantes : Solutré-Pouilly, Fuissé, Chaintré et Vergisson. Il ne doit être fait qu'avec du Chardonnay à raison de 50 hl/ha. La teneur en sucre naturel du moût doit s'élever à 170 g/l, ce qui donne au vin, après fermentation, une teneur en alcool de 11°. Précisons qu'il s'agit de sucre naturel car, dans le Mâconnais, comme ailleurs en Bourgogne, les vignerons ont le droit d'ajouter une certaine quantité de sucre au moût : procédé appelé chaptalisation *(Voir ce mot)*. Cette pratique n'est pas sans danger. Quand on ajoute trop de sucre, on adultère finesse et élégance ; même si on obtient un vin plus corsé et plus lourd, on le rend parfois grossier.

Les quatre communes qui produisent le Pouilly-Fuissé ont au total plus de 750 ha de vigne et produisent en moyenne 40 000 hl (plus de 440 000 caisses) de vin par an. Le meilleur est vendu sous l'appellation Pouilly-Fuissé suivie du nom de cru. Pour y avoir droit, il doit présenter une teneur en sucre de 178 g par litre de moût et titrer 12° au moins.

Les meilleurs noms de vignobles qu'on peut trouver sur les étiquettes sont les suivants : pour la commune de Solutré-Pouilly : Les Chailloux, Les Boutières, Les Chanrue, Les Prâs, Les Peloux, Les Rince ; pour la commune de Fuissé : Château-Fuissé, Le Clos, Clos de Varambond, Clos de la Chapelle, Menetrières, Versarmières, Les Vignes Blanches, Les Châtenets, Les Perrières, Les Brûlets ; pour la commune de Chaintré : Le Clos Reissier.

En général, les vins de Solutré-Pouilly

ont tendance à plus de féminité et de délicatesse que ceux des autres communes, alors que ceux de Fuissé peuvent être plus forts. La coopérative de Chaintré produit certains des meilleurs Pouilly-Fuissé, de qualité supérieure à ceux de Vergisson.

Pouilly-Loché, Pouilly-Vinzelles (A.O.C.)

Ce sont les deux moindres Pouilly du Mâconnais. Les normes de ces appellations (sauf l'origine évidemment) sont rigoureusement identiques à celles des Pouilly-Fuissé. Néanmoins ils n'atteignent jamais tout à fait le même degré d'excellence. En règle générale, ils sont plus légers, moins racés, mais souvent plus fruités que les Pouilly-Fuissé.

Selon le règlement de ces appellations, le Pouilly-Loché doit provenir des vendanges du territoire de la commune de Loché (la plus proche de Fuissé) et le Pouilly-Vinzelles de celles de Vinzelles (immédiatement au sud de Loché) et Loché. Ensemble, ces deux communes produisent au maximum quelque 4 000 hl (près de 45 000 caisses) par an.

Saint-Véran (A.O.C.)

Saint-Véran est une appellation assez récente qui dût son succès croissant à la hausse des prix du Pouilly-Fuissé. Bien que ce blanc sec soit délicat, sa qualité n'est cependant pas comparable à celle des meilleurs Pouilly-Fuissé. Les villages Chânes, Saint-Amour, Saint-Vérand, Prissé, Chasselas, Leynes et Davayé revendiquant l'Appellation d'Origine Contrôlée Saint-Véran produisent annuellement environ 25 000 hl (plus de 250 000 caisses).

Mâcon Supérieur ou Mâcon suivi du nom de la comune d'origine (A.O.C.)

Cette appellation, très peu utilisée, comme celle de Beaujolais Supérieur d'ailleurs, porte théoriquement sur les vins blancs, rouges et rosés. Pratiquement, plus de la moitié est blanc et à peu près tout le reste rouge. Il n'y a donc presque pas de rosé. Les rouges sont des petits vins, en général sans qualités remarquables et, même à Mâcon, on consomme plus volontiers du Beaujolais que du Mâcon rouge. Quant au blanc, il n'a peut-être pas la distinction du Pouilly-Fuissé. Mais, de temps en temps, un des meilleurs vignerons en produit un qui égale et même surpasse les Pouilly de moindre qualité.

Le vin qui porte cette appellation doit provenir de l'arrondissement de Mâcon pour les vins blancs, ou des communes de Boyer, Bresse-sur-Grosne, Champagny-sous-Uxelles, Champlieu, Étrigny, Jugy, Laives, Mancey, Montceaux-Ragny, Nanton, Sennecey-le-Grand et Veres pour les vins rouges. Le vin rouge doit être vinifié à partir des cépages suivants : Gamay Noir à jus blanc, Pinot Noir et Pinot Gris et 15 % au maximum des cépages blancs : Pinot Blanc et Chardonnay, Aligoté et Gamay Blanc (dit Melon). La production ne doit pas dépasser 55 hl/ha.

Le moût doit contenir un minimum de 62 g de sucre par litre, ce qui lui assure 10° d'alcool après fermentation.

Pour les blancs, les cépages utilisés sont le Pinot Blanc et le Chardonnay. Le moût doit contenir un minimum de 70 g de sucre par litre qui donnent, après fermentation, 11°.

Ces mêmes vins blancs peuvent tout aussi légitimement être vendus sous l'appellation Bourgogne, mais les rouges n'y ont droit que s'ils sont faits exclusivement avec du raisin Pinot. Toutefois, cette appellation est trop générale pour présenter un attrait quelconque. Actuellement, on vend environ 60 000 hl (plus de 660 000 caisses) par an de Mâcon Supérieur, dont plus de la moitié de blanc.

Mâcon-Villages (A.O.C.)

Quarante-trois villages situés dans l'arrondissement de Mâcon bénéficient de cette appellation qui ne produit pratiquement pas de vin rouge. La production moyenne annuelle s'élève à 125 000 hl (près de 1,5 million de caisses).

Mâcon ou Pinot-Chardonnay-Mâcon (A.O.C.)

Tout en bas de l'échelle du Mâconnais se trouvent les vins vendus simplement comme Mâcon rouge, Mâcon blanc ou Pinot-Chardonnay-Mâcon (appellation inexacte étant donné que ce vin peut être fait aussi bien avec du Pinot Blanc qu'avec du Chardonnay et qu'il est semblable au Mâcon blanc dont le nom est moins compliqué). Ces appellations couvrent les vins de moindre qualité, aussi bien blancs que rouges, mais surtout rouges.

Pour y avoir droit, les vins doivent être produits à raison de 55 hl/ha pour les rouges et rosés et 60 hl/ha pour les blancs, c'est-à-dire en quantité plus importante que les précédents.

On constate une fois de plus que, en fait de vin, la quantité et la qualité ne vont jamais de pair. En ce qui concerne l'origine, ces vins proviennent exactement de la même zone délimitée que le Mâcon Supérieur. Mais la teneur en sucre des rouges ne s'élève qu'à 144 g/l, donnant 9° d'alcool et celle des blancs à 153 g/l, donnant 10°.

Sous cette appellation on fait environ 6 000 hl (plus de 65 000 caisses), avec une production de blanc inférieure à celle de rouge.

Madagascar

Cette grande île, située au large de la côte sud-est de l'Afrique, produit une certaine quantité de rhum.

Voir RHUM FRANÇAIS

Madère

Jusqu'au début du XVIIIe siècle, le vin de Madère était exporté à l'état naturel. Nous savons que, dès 1704, on brûlait le surplus de Madère pour faire de l'eau-de-vie. Néanmoins, selon les archives, c'est seulement en 1753 qu'« on ajouta un seau d'eau-de-vie à chaque pièce de vin avant de l'expédier ». C'est ce « seau d'eau-de-vie » qui donna au Madère la caractéristique et l'excellence unique qu'il a encore aujourd'hui. Quelque vingt années plus tard, cette pratique s'étendait à tous les vins d'exportation. A cette même époque, on commença à charger des tonneaux de ce vin sur des bateaux remontant en direction des Indes orientales, pour que le vin ait tout le loisir de s'affiner pendant le voyage, jusqu'au retour des bateaux. Déjà, le Madère avait la caractéristique et l'excellence unique qu'il a encore aujourd'hui, et il devint extrêmement populaire au Royaume-Uni et dans ses colonies d'Amérique où le commerce fut florissant jusqu'en 1852, date à laquelle les vignobles furent ravagés par l'oïdium.

On faisait alors de grands Madère — on en fait encore — mais les débouchés que ce vin s'était assurés au temps de la navigation à voile et des explorations se sont fermés. Les ventes n'ont cessé d'augmenter depuis que les négociants se sont regroupés en une association du vin de Madère visant à en promouvoir le nom.

Aujourd'hui, environ 500 000 caisses de Madère sont produites chaque année. Les vins nécessaires à sa fabrication représentent 1/3 de tous les vins produits par les 1 600 ha plantés de vignes. Le reste est consommé dans l'île comme vin de table. Les expéditeurs ne possèdent qu'une très petite partie du vignoble de Madère, qui est divisé entre les milliers de producteurs ; aussi achètent-ils, à la période des vendanges, raisins et vins à un prix fixé à l'avance.

Histoire du vin de Madère

L'histoire de cette île est presque celle de ses vins. Au point de vue politique, Madère fait partie intégrante du Portugal ; géographiquement, c'est une île de l'Atlantique située à 575 km au large de la côte marocaine et à 850 km de Lisbonne. Longue de 57 km et large de 13 km, elle offre un paradis à ceux qui y passent leurs vacances. La vigne y pousse sur des terrasses taillées au flanc de déclivités abruptes et ses vallées ombragées sont couvertes de fleurs.

Madère était déjà connue par les Phéniciens et les Grecs. Plus tard Génois et Portugais y abordèrent. Mais les forêts étaient si denses que les marins n'osèrent pas y pénétrer jusqu'à ce qu'Henri le Navigateur envoyât l'intrépide capitaine João Gonsalves Zarco en prendre possession pour le Portugal en 1418. Il baptisa cette île « Bois », nom qui lui convient. Des arbres serrés les uns contre les autres, aux branchages enchevêtrés, couvraient toute sa surface et leur densité rendait vain l'usage de la hache. Pour résoudre le problème, Zarco y mit le feu et remonta à bord pour assister au spectacle. Selon la légende, il attendit longtemps : l'incendie aurait fait rage pendant sept ans ! Quand il s'éteignit enfin, les arbres avaient disparu, mais ils laissaient sur la roche volcanique, pour des siècles, de l'humus qui offraient un des sols les plus fertiles du monde.

Des pionniers arrivèrent du Portugal, d'Espagne, de Hollande et d'Italie. Ils plantèrent canne à sucre et vigne de Malvoisie. La terre riche et le climat subtropical transformèrent Madère en un jardin luxuriant, en plein Atlantique. Les marins relâchaient à Funchal pour embarquer eau et vivres frais et pour remplir leurs tonneaux de vin. Les traités de commerce entre le Portugal et la Grande-Bretagne firent la fortune des vins de Madère autant que celle des Porto. Les Anglais qui s'installaient dans leurs colonies d'Amérique gardèrent la nostalgie des vins portugais et bientôt ils en importèrent.

Quand les colons d'Amérique s'apprêtèrent à rompre avec l'Angleterre, le Madère devint de plus en plus leur vin favori et ils considérèrent qu'en boire était un devoir patriotique, équivalant à faire le pied-de-nez au roi et à son parlement. Les Anglais avaient, en effet, décidé alors que seuls les navires britanniques avaient le droit d'apporter des marchandises européennes aux colonies du Nouveau Monde. Inutile de dire que les capitaines anglais faisaient payer leur monopole au prix fort. Mais Madère étant en Afrique, ses vins pouvaient arriver sur les bateaux battant n'importe quel pavillon. Les Américains s'avisèrent de cette particularité et on vit des bouteilles de Madère sur leurs tables. La popularité du Madère sur la côte Atlantique des États-Unis dura aussi longtemps que la navigation à voile.

Le capitaine Frederick Marryat, écrivain anglais, remarque dans son *Diary in America* (1839, 10) : « Le Claret et les autres vins français vont fort bien en Amérique. Mais le terrain sur lequel les Américains nous battent est celui du Madère, qui est chez eux d'une qualité que l'on ne peut pas se procurer en Angleterre. C'est dû à l'extrême chaleur et aux grands froids du climat qui font vieillir ce vin ; je peux presque dire que je n'avais pas encore goûté de bon Madère avant d'arriver aux États-Unis. Si l'on considère les droits de douane infimes qu'ils paient, le prix des vins est en général extrêmement élevé, mais celui du bon Madère est étonnant. Vendues aux enchères, certaines marques atteindront, à coups sûr, de 12 à 20 dollars et j'ai même entendu parler de bouteilles payées 40 dollars pièce. »

Au XVIIIe siècle et au début du XIXe, la fortune du vin de Madère arriva probablement à son apogée. Les guerres de la Révolution et de l'Empire diminuaient l'exportation des vins français. Madère n'y étant pas mêlée, son commerce prospéra. Le « seau d'eau-de-vie » ajouté à chaque barrique permettait au vin de voyager et le long transport par mer le faisait mûrir. Madère exportait en grande quantité vers l'Angleterre et l'Amérique dont les ports méridionaux recevaient la plus grosse part des chargements : Savannah, La Nouvelle-Orléans, Charleston et Baltimore.

Un désastre s'abattit sur Madère en 1852, quand l'oïdium ravagea ses vignes. Elle se relevait à peine quand le phylloxéra apparut en 1872. Déjà affaiblies par la plaie précédente, les vignes de Madère succombèrent au pou qui s'en prenait à leurs racines. Bien des négociants britanniques, établis depuis longtemps sur l'île, la quittèrent. Le peu de vin de Madère produit actuellement, nous le devons au courage et à la persévérance des quelques-uns qui restèrent sur place. Ils importèrent des souches de vignes américaines immunisées contre le phylloxéra. Il fallut attendre bien des années pour qu'elles entrent en pleine production. Mais quand on eut assez de vin pour en exporter, il se révéla de très mauvaise qualité, quoique produit en grande quantité car les vignes américaines ont un gros rendement. Il fallut les couper pour y greffer des vignes européennes datant d'avant l'épidémie de phylloxéra.

Vinification du Madère

Les vendanges sont probablement aussi pittoresques à Madère que partout ailleurs, mais elles durent sûrement plus longtemps. Elles commencent au milieu du mois d'août au niveau de la mer et se poursuivent sur les hauteurs au fur et à mesure de la maturation du raisin pour se terminer en octobre. Les vignerons de Madère commencent à écraser leurs raisins en les foulant au pied en dansant et en chantant dans des *lagares* : grandes cuves de bois oblongues. Cette danse sur les raisins est suivie par un pressurage plus rigoureux, après quoi le jus de raisin ou *mosto* est porté aux « lodges » *(voir ce mot)* des négociants, à Funchal, dans des outres en peau de chèvre ou des barriques posées sur des traîneaux attelés de bœufs qui sont plus nombreux que les tracteurs.

Ce moût fermente et devient d'abord le *vinho claro*. On y ajoute de l'alcool et on le met en *estufa* (étuve) pour y subir un traitement particulier au Madère : l'*estufagem* (étuvage). Ce procédé date du temps où le Madère faisait le tour du monde ou bien l'aller-retour des Indes, pour mûrir, soumis aux roulis et tangage des bateaux, sous la chaleur des tropiques. Mais, pendant les guerres napoléoniennes, le fret étant trop rare, on inventa l'étuvage, opération qui consiste à maintenir le vin à une température élevée, dans une espèce de « chambre chaude ».

De nos jours, l'*estufa* est un vaste cellier à chauffage central dans lequel les fûts de vin passent six mois. On amène progressivement la température entre 40 et 46°C, puis on la laisse retomber à la normale en six mois, ce qui donne à peu près le même effet qu'un voyage autour du monde.

Les Madère plus doux sont remontés à l'eaux-de-vie avant d'être chauffés en chambre, alors que pour les Madère secs, ce n'est qu'après fermentation et après avoir reposé en *estufa* que l'on y ajoute l'eau-de-vie.

Le vin qui n'a pas été *estufado* s'appelle *Canteiro*. A la sortie de l'*estufa*, le Madère subit un *estagio* (stage), c'est-à-dire dix-huit mois de repos, pour se remettre du traitement. Ensuite on le mélange au vin des années précédentes pour obtenir divers « lots » appelés *soleras*. Après ce coupage, on lui laisse encore un temps de repos pour que les divers éléments se marient. Puis un dernier mélange précède l'exportation.

Le vin de Madère est celui qui vit le plus longtemps. On trouve encore des bouteilles millésimées qui datent de l'ère préphylloxérienne. A vrai dire, y goûter procure moins de plaisir que la satisfaction d'une expérience inoubliable.

Types de vins de Madère

On compte quatre types distincts de Madère ; chacun porte le nom du raisin dont il provient et peut être sec ou richement sucré, avec toute une gamme intermédiaire. Ce sont :

Sercial. C'est le meilleur des Madère secs, excellent avec la soupe de tortue, compagnons traditionnels dans les pays anglophones. Parfois pâle, parfois doré, il manque souvent de corps, mais est toujours sec, avec un nez magnifique. Le célèbre écrivain œnologue André Simon l'a défini ainsi : « Une âme dotée d'un nez. »

Verdelho. Plus sucré et plus fort que le Sercial, il laisse dans la bouche un goût sec et net. Il est excellent servi avec une soupe et, comme chacun sait, accompagne merveilleusement le consommé de tortue. A l'époque victorienne, il était d'usage d'offrir aux visiteurs du matin une tranche de gâteau et un verre de ce Madère.

Bual ou *Boal*. Plus corsé et plus doux que les deux précédents, il a un bouquet caractéristique et sa couleur va du marron roussâtre au brun très foncé. C'est décidément un vin de dessert.

Malmsey. Fait avec des raisins de Malvoisie, c'est un vin extrêmement riche et généreux, doué d'un équilibre remarquable et d'un bon bouquet. Il est très corsé. Ce type de Madère est excellent après le repas.

Madère a un passé très ancien et ses quelques vins sont rares ou ont disparu ; le Terrantez, demi-doux, en est un exemple typique. On trouve aussi les noms suivants sur les bouteilles de Madère :

Rainwater (eau de pluie). C'est un coupage. A l'origine, c'était le nom d'une marque ; il est devenu, à l'usage, celui d'un type de vin pâle et léger comme l'indique son nom. Mais, quant au goût, il peut être sec ou un peu sucré.

Soleras millésimeos. De même que bien des bouteilles de vins français portent leur année de vendange sur l'étiquette, de même on trouve du Madère portant la date d'une *solera*. Ce mot, écrit avant ou après une date, ne signifie pas que le vin fut fait seulement en cette année-là, car de temps à autre le fût fut ouillé avec un vin plus jeune, choisi parce qu'il possède des qualités et des caractéristiques similaires. L'âge moyen d'une *solera* peut être évalué à quelque 80 ans. Il s'agit toujours de très bon vins.

Les grands négociants de l'association du vin de Madère sont Blandy's Madeiras Lda., Leacock & Co. (Wine) Lda. (dont le fondateur s'installa à Madère en 1741), Rutherford and Miles Ltd., Cossart Gordon and Co. Ltd., T.T.C. Lomedino Lda. (firme qui possède une réserve remarquable de vieux vins), Shortridge Lawton and Co. Ltd., F.F. Ferraz Lda., Luis Gomes (Vinhos) Lda., & Freitas Martins Caldeira Lda. Il y a d'autres firmes importantes ne faisant pas partie de l'association : Henriques & Henriques, H.M. Borges, Vinhos Barbeito, Marcel Gomes and Cia Lda., ainsi que Veiga Franca & Co. Ltd.

Dans son ouvrage des plus sérieux, *Le Vin portugais*, Raymond Postgate mentionne Avery de Bristol qui, bien que n'étant pas un expéditeur mais un négociant importateur, « possède un choix unique de Madère provenant de nombreuses sources différentes... Le plus vieux est un Verdelho d'environ 1846 ».

Madérisation

Soit parce qu'ils ont passé l'âge de leur plénitude, soit parce qu'ils sont conservés dans de mauvaises conditions, les vins blancs peuvent perdre leur fraîcheur et leur fruité en prenant une teinte brunâtre. Ce changement de couleur résulte de leur oxydation et on l'a appelé madérisation parce que ces vins prennent une saveur que le Madère doit à la présence d'un aldéhyde éthylique résultant soit de l'oxydation de l'alcool, soit de la dissociation de l'aldéhyde acide sulfureux par oxydation progressive de cet acide. Mais la madérisation peut aussi être due à un vieillissement en fût trop prolongé avant la mise en bouteille.

Pour certains Madère, Marsala, Xérès et le Château-Chalon du Jura français, la madérisation est une qualité qui ajoute à la grandeur du vin et lui donne un goût appelé *rancio*. Pour les autres vins blancs c'est un défaut, particulièrement désagréable chez les Montrachet, les Meursault, les Côtes de Beaune et encore plus désagréable chez les Graves que chez les Sauternes parce que la douceur des Sauternes dissimule la saveur plate de ce moisi brunâtre.

Un traitement à l'anhydride sulfureux et à la caséine permet de protéger les vins contre la madérisation, et l'acide sulfureux supprime le goût plat.

Madiran (Appellation Contrôlée)

Vin rouge fait à Madiran, dans les Pyrénées-Atlantiques et les Hautes-Pyrénées. Charnu, très corsé, avec un bouquet prononcé, il provient surtout de Tannat (40 %) et de Cabernet Sauvignon, Bouchy (Cabernet Franc) et Pinenc (Fer), pour le reste. Il titre 11°. Le blanc de la même partie de la vallée de l'Adour s'appelle Pacherenc du Vic Bilh *(voir ce nom)*. La production moyenne est de 40 000 hl (plus de 400 000 caisses) par an.

Magdelaine (Château-La)

Bordeaux rouge. Commune et région de Saint-Émilion.

Ce vin fut classé Premier Grand Cru de Saint-Émilion en 1955, puis en 1986. Le vignoble appartient à Jean-Pierre Moueix, il est contigu à ceux d'Ausone et de Belair, situés sur les hauteurs de Saint-Émilion.

Caractéristiques : Les vignes bien entretenues donnent un vin charnu et velouté, à l'arrière-goût caractéristique.

Superficie : 11 ha.

Production moyenne : 40 tonneaux (3 500 caisses).

Magistrats de la vigne

Ces prédécesseurs des inspecteurs de l'I.N.A.O, contrôlaient rigoureusement la qualité des vins d'Alsace dès le XVIIIe siècle.

Voir ALSACE

Magnum

Bouteille contenant deux fois la capacité normale (0,75 cl). Certains vins rouges vieillissant mieux lorsqu'ils sont dans des bouteilles de grande contenance.

Mai (Vin de)

Boisson traditionnelle de la région du Rhin, faite avec du vin de ce pays dans lequel ont infusé des feuilles d'aspérule. On le sert frappé, dans un bol, avec une grande cuillère qui sert à pêcher les fraises et autres fruits qui y flottent. C'est une boisson rafraîchissante et joyeuse. On peut la préparer partout et, faute de vin du Rhin, n'importe quel blanc sec et léger convient.

Mailly

Agglomération proche de Reims. Elle produit un Champagne de très bonne qualité.

Voir CHAMPAGNE

Maípo (Vallée du)

Une des meilleures régions vinicoles du Chili (l'autre est la vallée de l'Aconcagua) spécialisée dans le Cabernet et le Malbec qui fournissent des vins de longue durée, dotés de finesse et d'équilibre.

Voir CHILI

Maître de chai

Titre de celui qui est chargé de la vinification et de surveiller le vieillissement des vins d'un château, dans le Bordelais. Cette expression, en usage ailleurs que dans le Sud-Ouest, s'applique aussi à celui qui dirige la vinification et le vieillissement des vins chez un négociant. C'est, à l'évidence, un homme expérimenté et un bon dégustateur. Dans d'autres régions vinicoles on l'appelle plus simplement caviste.

Maladie de la bouteille

Indisposition temporaire qui affecte parfois le vin, peu après sa mise en bouteille. Elle dure peu et guérit d'elle-même.

Málaga

Vins de desserts espagnols. Andalousie orientale.

Située sur la côte espagnole, pays de chaleur et jadis d'indolence — où les raisins mûris par le soleil donnent un jus sucré, et où la douceur du climat a bien pu provoquer une certaine léthargie chez ses habitants — l'Andalousie vit maintenant à l'ère moderne : sa capitale a été urbanisée, et sa vie transformée par le tourisme de Torremolinos, Marbella, et du reste de la Costa del Sol. Autrefois, Málaga était célèbre pour ses vins doux, qui eurent un grand succès à l'étranger. La littérature anglaise est riche de références au « Moutains » et au Xérès de Málaga, et pourtant on en boit bien peu aujourd'hui dans les pays anglo-saxons. Mais on continue à faire du Málaga — et le Málaga produit selon les méthodes traditionnelles, n'a jamais été meilleur — et à en exporter. Parmi ses plus gros clients, l'Allemagne vient en tête, suivie par la Suisse, les pays scandinaves, et la France. Les 5 000 ha de vignobles détenant la « Denominaciòn de Origen » produisent 55 000 hl de ce vin qui a perdu et continue de perdre une partie de sa clientèle.

Les vignobles, à peine visibles de la côte, sont situés sur les flancs de montagne, et c'est autour de Archidona, Antequera, et Velez-Málaga que se trouvent les meilleurs lots. Le cépage Pedro Ximénez, riche, lourd et onctueux, est le cépage majeur utilisé comme coupage avec du Lairen, du Moscatel, et d'autres raisins locaux. C'est cet assemblage qui donne à ce vin sa force, sa richesse et sa couleur sombre. Cette région a une longue histoire et la grande variété de ses raisins — aussi bien sous forme de vin que de fruits de table — reçut les louanges des anciens Grecs, des Romains, ainsi que des écrivains de la Renaissance. Les conquérants maures, s'ils ne buvaient pas le vin interdit, appréciaient du moins les succulents raisins que l'on cultive encore aujourd'hui, et dont une bonne partie, une fois séchée, produira les savoureux raisins secs qui font l'orgueil de la région. Des caisses de vin auraient été envoyées à Tamerlan le Grand et Catherine la Grande ; l'histoire du Pedro Ximenez fut tracée dans *Cosmografia* de Merula, ouvrage publié à Amsterdam en 1636. Et Columella qui, au Iᵉʳ siècle, disserta sur les vins dans sa *Re Rustica*, était lui-même d'origine andalouse. Contrairement aux Xérès sombres, le Málaga est un vin naturel contenant environ 16 % d'alcool et n'est pas enrichi à l'eau-de-vie. Autrefois, l'on faisait le célèbre Lagrima Christi (à ne pas confondre avec le Lacrima Christi italien qui est bien différent) en laissant les raisins exprimer leur suc goutte à goutte sans aucun pressurage. Ces vins sont maintenant commercialisés et sont plutôt moyens, douceâtres et de couleur marron. Mais il y a aussi d'innombrables petits vignobles (dont certains donnent un excellent « Mountains » pur, que les vignerons gardent pour leur usage personnel) produisant des vins rouges et autres ; quant au Málaga caractéristique, ce vin dont la qualité est protégée par la « Denominación de Origen », il est fait selon des méthodes traditionnelles dans les grandes *bodegas* de la petite ville, avec du vin, du moût ou des raisins fournis par les petits fermiers. Les meilleurs sont veillis selon le système de la *solera* (*voir* XÉRÈS).

Avant le pressurage, les raisins sont étalés sur des nattes de paille, où le soleil les mûrira et les adoucira au maximum. Ils fermenteront ensuite dans de grandes cuves en chêne (dans les grandes *bodegas*, celles-ci ont parfois des dimensions énormes, compte tenu du peu de distribution dont ce vin jouit de nos jours).

Enfin le jeune vin sera transvasé dans des barriques de chêne, où il mûrira pendant deux ou trois ans. Après quoi, il pourra être vendu aux négociants en vins ou placé dans la *solera* des vins fins de la *bodega*. Ceux-ci, riches en nuances de couleur et de douceur, se classent ainsi :

Málaga dulce color. Très doux, très sombre (marron noir).

Málaga blanco dulce. Très doux, couleur pouvant aller du jaune doré au topaze.

Málaga semi-dulce. Assez doux, jaune doré ou rouge.

Málaga Lagrima et Lagrima Christi. Très doux, vieil or ou sombre, quelconque.

Málaga blanco seco. Plutôt sec, ou pâle, arrière-goût agréable.

Málaga Moscatel. Couleur ambrée, un goût certain de raisin.

Pedro Ximenez. Douceur liquoreuse, très sombre avec des reflets rougeâtres.

Málaga Rome. Vin fort, rouge et blanc doré.

Málaga Pajarete. Vin fort (de 15 % à 20 %), couleur ambrée, pâle ou sombre.

Tintillo de Málaga. 15 % à 16 % d'alcool, couleur rouge.

Suffisamment mûri, un bon Málaga peut-être d'une grande distinction. A propos d'un de ces vins, qu'il goûta dans la *bodega* Scholtz Hermanos, M.H.X. Yoxall écrivit : « Comme lorsqu'au contact de quelque chose de froid, vous vous demandez si ce quelque chose vous gèle ou vous brûle, il en va de même lorsque vous goûtez les grands Málaga où le sucre est sublimé jusqu'à en être presque astringent. » Pourtant, en Angleterre, les Málaga sont bien rares aujourd'hui, et surtout les meilleurs. Ici comme ailleurs, on trouve des vins ordinaires et fades ; il y en a d'autres, tels le Rome et le Pajarete, et certains vins demi-doux, que l'on mélange souvent au vino tinto. Les vins classés ci-dessus titrent tous entre 14 % et 23 % d'alcool.

Les principaux producteurs et exportateurs de Málaga sont : Hijos de A. Barcelo, S.A. ; Luis Barcelo, S.A. ; Flores Hermanos, S.A. ; Felix Garcia Gomez ; José Garijo Ruiz ; Carlos J. Krauel ; Larios, S.A. ; Lopez Hermanos, S.A. ; Compania Mata, S.A. ; Juan Mory et Cia., S.A. ; Pérez Texeira, S.A. ; Guillermo Rein Segura ; Casa Romero, S.L. ; Scholtz Hermanos, S.A. ; Hijos de José Suarez Villalba ; Vinicola Andalucia, S.A. ; et Manuel Pacheco Moron.

Malartic-Lagravière (Château-)

Bordeaux rouge et blanc. Commune de Léognan, en Graves.

La réputation du Château-Malartic-Lagravière rouge est fort ancienne et il fut compris dans les onze crus rouges classés des Graves en 1953 et 1959. Ce même domaine produit aussi un excellent blanc sec qui est beaucoup moins connu que le rouge.

Caractéristiques : Le rouge est un grand vin dont le goût emplit la bouche et qui doit probablement ses qualités particulières à la prépondérance du Cabernet Sauvignon. Le reste est fait de Merlot. Quant au vin blanc, il est fait exclusivement avec du Sauvignon Blanc.

Superficie : rouge, 11 ha, blanc, 1,5 ha.

Production moyenne : rouge, 4 000 caisses, blanc, 550 caisses.

Malbec

Raisin de grand rendement qui entre dans la composition des Bordeaux rouges. On le cultive aussi ailleurs, où il est connu sous le nom de Cot.

Malescot-Saint-Exupéry (Château-)

Bordeaux rouge. Commune de Margaux, en Haut-Médoc.

Ce cru doit son nom au comte de Saint-Exupéry qui l'acheta en 1827. Quant au château — grand manoir de pierre grise en plein village de Margaux — il n'en restait plus qu'une carcasse après la Seconde Guerre mondiale. Roger Zuger, le propriétaire actuel, le restaura en 1964.

Jusqu'en 1955, ce domaine appartenait aux distillateurs britanniques Seager Evans qui le vendirent cette année-là à feu Paul Zuger. Jusqu'alors administrateur du vignoble et expert en vinification, M. Zuger était président de l'Association des appellations contrôlées de Margaux, fondée en 1955.

Le vignoble fut classé Troisième Cru du Médoc en 1855.

Caractéristiques : Très plein pour un Margaux, très élégant aussi et parfois légèrement dur à ses débuts. Les qualités de ce vin reflètent la forte proportion (80 %) de Cabernet Sauvignon qui entre dans sa composition.

Superficie : 32 ha.

Production moyenne : 160 tonneaux (16 000 caisses).

Malle (Château de)

Bordeaux blanc. Commune de Preignac, en Sauternes.

Un vin léger, frais et net, au moins aussi agréable que le très beau château amoureusement entretenu par la propriétaire, la comtesse Pierre de Bournazel. Le château possède aussi plus de 25 ha en Graves, produisant quelques 100 000 bouteilles (8 000 caisses).

Le vignoble fut classé Second Cru dans la Classification de 1855.

Superficie : 25 ha.

Production moyenne : 50 tonneaux (5 000 caisses).

Acide malique

L'un des acides les plus abondants dans les raisins verts, mais qui disparaît en partie au fur et à mesure que le fruit mûrit ; COOH-CH2-CHOH-COOH.

Malmesbury

Région vinicole sur la côte de la province du Cap.

Voir AFRIQUE DU SUD

Malmsey

Corruption du nom d'un vin qui, à l'origine, était exporté de Monemvasia, en Grèce, et devint Malvasia en Italie, Malvoisie en France, Malvagia en Espagne. Malmsey désigne aussi une variété de vigne ainsi que les vins qui en proviennent. De nos jours le plus célèbre est fait à Madère *(voir ce nom)*.

Le Malmsey était célèbre en Angleterre au temps de Shakespeare et on le trouve souvent cité dans les écrits de cette époque. L'anecdote la plus connue sans doute au sujet de ce vin a trait à la mort du duc de Clarence qui se noya dans un fût de Malvoisie. Sans doute le vin provenait-il alors de Grèce plutôt que de Madère.

Malolactique (Fermentation)

Fermentation secondaire due à la conversion de l'acide malique en acide lactique et gaz carbonique. Quand elle se produit lorsque le vin est en fût, il en résulte simplement une diminution de l'acidité. Mais si, malheureusement, le vin est en bouteille, la fermentation malolactique le rend gazeux et sa pression augmente. Ce phénomène se produit plus souvent chez les Bourgogne que chez les Bordeaux il peut être dû à une mise en bouteille prématurée. La fermentation est causée par certaines espèces de bactéries résistant à l'acide, les *Lactobacillus* et *Leuconostoc*. La caractéristique de différentes espèces de ces bactéries malolactiques propres à certaines caves peut être un facteur important permettant d'établir le caractère individuel des vins produits.

Voir CHAPITRE V

Malte

On cultive la vigne sur cette île, surtout sur sa côte sud. Mais, étant donné que des pluies torrentielles sont suivies par un été torride, ses raisins ne donnent que des vins ordinaires, généralement durs et âpres, qu'ils soient blancs ou rouges. Les Maltais s'efforcent actuellement de produire un Muscat, riche et doux, pour le dessert, afin de l'exporter surtout vers le Royaume-Uni. Environ 1 000 ha sont plantés de vignes, mais la plus grande partie donne des raisins de table, surtout autour de Burmarrad, Rabat et Siggiewi. Les raisins Gellewza, Gannaru, Nigruwa et Dun Tumas sont parmi les variétés les plus connues. La production de vin, est évaluée à quelque 19 000 hl (plus de 210 000 caisses) et est surtout consommée localement.

Malvoisie

Vin et raisin originaires de la région de Monemvasia en Grèce. Depuis, cette variété de vigne s'est répandue dans tout le monde viticole sous divers noms : Malvoisie en France, Malgavia en Espagne, Malvasia en

Italie. Le vin lourd et doux qu'elle donne était célèbre il y a longtemps en Angleterre sous le nom de Malmsey *(voir ce nom)*.

Mandarine

Liqueur dorée et douce, au goût de mandarine, faite en Belgique.

Manganèse

Élément qui est présent dans à peu près tous les vins, en quantité infime mais variant selon le sol du vignoble. On en trouve plus dans le Beaujolais que dans le Bordeaux et davantage dans le rouge que dans le blanc. La plus grosse partie du manganèse des raisins se trouve dans les pépins.

Mannequin

Grand panier contenant 70 à 80 kg de raisin, dans lequel on déverse le contenu des hottes à l'extrémité de chaque sillon pendant les vendanges en Champagne.

Voir CHAMPAGNE

Mannitique (Fermentation)

Fermentation qui se produit lorsque la température dans la cuve dépasse 35 °C et que le vin manque d'acidité : les bonnes levures meurent et d'autres bactéries entrent en action. Le vin dépose, se trouble et prend une saveur douce-amère de moisi.

Voir CHAPITRE V

Manzanilla

Bon vin sec de Sanlúcar de Barrameda, en Espagne. On y ajoute parfois de l'eau-de-vie et on le vend comme un type de Xérès.

Voir XÉRÈS ; MONTILLA

Marasquin

Liqueur faite avec des cerises amères appelées marascas et qui provenaient uniquement de Dalmatie. Avant que l'enclave italienne de Dalmatie soit intégrée à la Yougoslavie, on ne faisait du Marasquin (Maraschino) qu'à Zadar (nom actuel de l'ancienne Zara en Italie). Titrant quelque 25°, le Marasquin est vendu dans des flacons d'un demi-litre enrobés d'osier. Le principal distillateur est Luxardo. Après la guerre, il transféra son entreprise de Trieste à Padoue. Pour s'assurer une quantité suffisante de marascas, il en planta 80 ha. Drioli, entreprise moins importante, est l'autre distillateur de Marasquin bien connu en Italie.

Marc

1. Résidu de pressurage du raisin, de la pomme et d'autres fruits.

2. Eau-de-vie obtenue par la distillation du marc de raisin. En général, la distillation est poussée jusqu'à une forte teneur en alcool. En vieillissant, cette eau-de-vie prend un goût caractéristique où l'on retrouve celui du raisin, avec un soupçon de cuir. La plupart des région vinicoles produisent du marc. Celui de Bourgogne est le plus connu, notamment celui de Romanée-Conti, Musigny, Chambertin, Nuits-Saint-Georges, Meursault et Montrachet. Les marcs des secteurs de Bourgogne où l'on fait du vin blanc sont plus légers et ont un peu plus de finesse que ceux des zones de vin rouge. Le marc des Hospices de Beaune est le plus cher. Un des plus légers et des plus fins est fait en Champagne. Le marc d'Auvergne a aussi bonne réputation. En Italie et en Californie on appelle cet alcool *grappa*.

Marches (Les)

Vins rouges et blancs. Centre-Est de l'Italie.

Comme toutes les régions de la péninsule italienne, Les Marches sont riches de souvenirs historiques. Elles devraient leur nom aux temps où elles étaient une province frontière de l'empire de Charlemagne. Comme partout en Italie, la vigne abonde et Les Marches produisent plus de 2 millions d'hl (plus de 22 millions de caisses) de vin par année, pour la plupart consommés par le pays parce qu'ils ne méritent pas d'être exportés.

Le Verdicchio di Castelli di Jesi (D.O.C.) fait exception. Léger, sec ou demi-sec, ce blanc, couleur d'or clair ou de paille, peut atteindre une teneur en alcool étonnante :

14°. On le fait à Cupramontana, Monteroberto et Castelbellino, dans la province d'Ancône. C'est un des vins mineurs d'Italie qui supporte le transport. Le Classico, un vin produit dans la zone archéologique ou *zona antica,* lui est supérieur. Le Verdicchio di Matelica est un autre vin D.O.C. semblable au Verdicchio du Jesi, mais il est produit un peu plus loin de la côte adriatique, à l'intérieur des terres. La production annuelle est d'environ 25 000 hl (plus de 270 000 caisses), soit seulement un quart du volume du di Jesi. Le Rosso Piceno (D.O.C.), fait avec les variétés de Sangiovese et Montepulciano, est souvent considéré comme le meilleur vin rouge de la province. Le Rosso Conero (D.O.C.) doit son appellation au nom que les Grecs donnèrent au cerisier marin qui pousse encore aujourd'hui sur les pentes du mont Conero. C'est un vin rouge, sec, assez acide tout en étant fruité ; il est produit près d'Ancône avec des raisins Montepulciano et Sangiovese. Également D.O.C., le Rosso Piceno est un autre vin rouge fort semblable au Rosso Conero, mais peut-être encore plus raffiné. Le Bianchello del Metauro est un vin blanc D.O.C. fait avec du Bianchello et un peu de Malvasia, cultivé sur les collines du Métaure, où eut lieu l'une des plus grandes batailles de l'antiquité lorsque les Romains vainquirent les Carthaginois. Le vin léger et sec s'allie bien avec la cuisine locale à base de poisson. Le Bianco Falerio, vin blanc fait avec du Trebbiano, et le Sangiovese dei Colli Pesaresi (D.O.C.), vin rouge fait avec du Sangiovese et du Montepulciano, sont deux autres vins agréables, sans plus.

Les Marches produisent, quant à elles, un vin rouge sec ou doux et pétillant appelé Vernaccia di Serrapetrona (D.O.C.).

Marcottage

Méthode traditionnelle de propagation de la vigne. En réalité on procède plutôt par provignage, ce qui est une variante du marcottage.

Voir CHAPITRE IV

Maréotique

Grand vin de l'Égypte antique, très connu dans le monde méditerranéen. Cléopâtre en aurait servi à Jules César pour le séduire.

Voir ÉGYPTE

Mareuil-sur-Ay

Village du département de la Marne, proche d'Épernay. Les parcelles produisent des raisins qui donnent un excellent Champagne *(voir ce nom).*

Margaux

Bordeaux rouge. Haut-Médoc.

Les vins de Margaux constituent une famille royale. Grands Crus et aussi plus modestes vignobles y partagent tous les mêmes caractéristiques.

Aucune commune du Bordelais, ni même du Médoc, ne présente une telle gamme de vins similaires.

C'est le grand soleil de l'été qui donne aux Margaux leur splendeur. Par bonne année, les plus grands crus des bons secteurs, situés un peu au nord, à Saint-Estèphe et Pauillac, peuvent se surpasser, mais, dans tous les cas, il faudra attendre assez longtemps pour qu'ils soient prêts à la consommation. Mais à Margaux, un fort ensoleillement aura éveillé les vertus subtiles latentes dans la vigne. En de telles années, les vignobles de Margaux peuvent surclasser tous les autres Médoc. Ces vins sont les plus féminins, les plus délicats, les plus élégants. Mais, par année moins favorable, un Saint-Estèphe plus hardi ou un Pauillac typique réussiront mieux.

Le nom de Margaux dérive de Marojallia, ainsi que l'appelait Ausone, poète latin du IVe siècle auquel Château-Ausone de Saint-Émilion doit son nom.

L'agglomération de Margaux proprement dite est située à environ 25 km au nord-ouest de Bordeaux. C'est un village paisible, presque endormi.

Mais il y a aussi le vin ! A la saison de la fermentation, on sent le vin partout, comme ailleurs à la campagne on sent, à la même saison, l'odeur d'herbes et de feuilles brûlées. De hauts châteaux aux toits pointus se dressent en plein village et des lopins de vigne s'insinuent entre logements et boutiques. Tout autour, il n'y a que de la vigne : un océan calme, brun l'hiver, vert l'été, toujours légèrement caressé par la brise. De-ci, de-là, un château apparaît au loin au milieu de son parc, pareil à l'écume sur la crête des vagues.

Cinq villages, et non un seul, ont droit à l'appellation d'origine Margaux. Voilà un quart de siècle, on considérait que leurs vins provenaient d'un seul cru : le Margaux. Ces communes sont : Margaux, Arsac, Soussans, Cantenac et Labarde. Elles produisent des vins semblables sur un sol partout léger et graveleux.

CRUS CLASSÉS DE MARGAUX 1855

Premier Cru
Château-Margaux

Seconds Crus
Château-Rausan-Ségla
Château-Rauzan-Gassies
Château-Lascombes
Château-Durfort-Vivens
Château-Brane-Cantenac

Trosièmes Crus
Château-Kirwan
Château-d'Issan
Château-Giscours
Château-Malescot-Saint-Exupéry
Château-Boyd-Cantenac
Château-Cantenac-Brown
Château-Palmer
Château-Desmirail
Château-Ferrière
Château-Marquis d'Alesme

Quatrièmes Crus
Château-Prieuré-Lichine
Château-Pouget
Château-Marquis de Terme

Cinquièmes Crus
Château-Dauzac
Château du Tertre
(Voir chacun de ces crus au nom de chaque château).

Il y a plus de cinquante ans, un procès fut engagé contre un certain propriétaire de Soussans. Ce vigneron possédait un terrain le long de la Gironde dont le sol, une terre d'alluvions bourbeuse, n'était pas le vrai sol de Margaux et son vin n'avait donc pas droit à cette appellation d'origine. Le résultat du procès ne fut probablement pas celui escompté. La justice décida que ni le vin de ce vignoble particulier, ni aucun autre fait à Soussans n'avait droit à l'appellation Margaux. En quelques années, des jugements similaires refusèrent le nom de Margaux aux communes d'Arsac, Labarde et Cantenac. Ce fut la consternation, car seul un important vignoble de Margaux et quelques petits avaient toutes leurs vignes sur le territoire même de la commune. Tous les autres, par contre, s'étendaient sur celui des communes parias. Il suffisait d'un arpent seulement pour que tout le cru perde droit à l'appellation, parce qu'une partie de son vin au moins ne provenait pas de la région délimitée. Margaux vécut dans une atmosphère de guerre civile car les petits vignerons dont les parcelles se trouvaient bien à l'abri dans les limites de la commune avaient intérêt à s'opposer à tout nouveau changement.

Pendant des années, il n'y eut rien à faire. Puis, en 1953, quelqu'un eut une brillante idée : puisque Margaux ne pouvait pas signifier ce qu'il aurait dû vouloir dire, pourquoi subsisterait-il un Margaux ? A partir de cette question, on put agir. Du moment que l'appellation d'origine Margaux ne pouvait pas recouvrer ses limites légitimes, on la supprima complètement. Même les vins de la commune perdirent le droit de porter ce nom. De nouveau ce fut la consternation. Les vignerons de Margaux qui s'étaient opposés à une révision constatèrent qu'ils ne pouvaient plus vendre leur vin parce que les documents nécessaires à l'exportation sous le nom de Margaux leur étaient refusés. Ils réclamèrent une décision et l'I.N.A.O. suggéra qu'il valait mieux, sans doute, reconsidérer tout le problème.

Il en résulta une nouvelle réglementation d'après laquelle les vins de Margaux sont ceux des communes de Margaux, Soussans, Arsac, Cantenac et Labarde, mais seulement s'ils proviennent de vignes cultivées sur un certain sol approuvé par l'I.N.A.O. et présentant les caractéristiques typiques de Margaux ; la production est limitée à 45 hl/ha ; variétés de raisin, méthodes de taille, de culture et de vinification sont réglementées afin d'assurer des normes de qualité élevées. En outre, les vins doivent passer un examen : une dégustation à l'aveugle (la première de ces dégustations pour l'appellation contrôlée Margaux eut lieu en 1956). 1 000 ha environ, produisant 4,5 millions de bouteilles par an, ont actuellement droit à l'appellation.

En général, le principal cru d'un secteur

ne résume pas les caractéristiques des vins du voisinage amenés à leur plus haut degré de perfection, mais présente plutôt une excellence qui lui est particulière. Or, dans le secteur de Margaux, Château-Margaux est le type même de tous les Margaux.

Margaux (Château-)

Bordeaux rouge et blanc sec. Commune de Margaux, en Haut-Médoc.

Avec son portique à colonnes et sa décoration intérieure de pur style Empire, le château Margaux est situé au milieu d'un vaste parc. Au XVe siècle, son vin était déjà connu sous des noms tels que Margou et Margous. Un château fort occupait l'emplacement du bâtiment actuel et s'appelait Lamothe. Remarquons qu'un des propriétaires de Lamothe était le seigneur de Durfort, alors que, jusqu'au début des années 60, le propriétaire de Margaux, Pierre Ginestet, possédait également le proche Château-Durfort.

En 1750, on améliora le vignoble en le replantant. Quant au château actuel, il fut construit au début du XIXe siècle par un élève de Victor Louis, architecte de l'opéra de Bordeaux. En 1836, le vicomte d'Aguado l'acheta. Son fils le vendit en 1879 au comte Pillet-Will qui apporta diverses améliorations vinicoles. En 1925, le château appartenait au duc de La Trémoille auquel l'acheta une société dont faisait partie M. Fernand Ginestet, alors propriétaire du domaine contigu : Château-Lascombes. Entre 1935 et 1949, M. Ginestet acheta les parts de ses associés et devint seul propriétaire. Château-Margaux passa ensuite à Bernard et Pierre Ginestet qui le gérèrent jusqu'en 1977 puis le vendirent à Laura et feu André Mentzelopoulos, alors propriétaires de la chaîne de magasins Félix Potin. Le château a été superbement restauré, les vignobles sont beaucoup mieux entretenus et administrés avec une grande efficacité.

Avec Lafite, Latour et Haut-Brion, Château-Margaux fut classé au premier rang parmi les vins de Médoc, en 1855.

Château-Margaux produit aussi une petite quantité de très bon blanc sec (entre 2 000 et 4 000 caisses par an), ce qui est exceptionnel en Médoc ; il ne porte pas le grand nom de Château-Margaux mais celui de Pavillon Blanc du Château-Margaux. Aucune autre commune du Bordelais n'a un château qui porte son nom ; il n'y a pas de « Château-Sauternes », ni de « Château-Pauillac », par exemple.

En 1981, Laura Mentzelopoulos, aidée de sa fille Corine, entreprit la construction d'une immense cave souterraine, en dépit des problèmes techniques, pour obtenir de meilleures conditions d'entreposage.

Caractéristiques : Dans sa plénitude, c'est le vin le plus élégant et le plus délicatement féminin de la région. Parfaitement équilibré. Margaux et finesse sont synonymes.

Superficie : 75 ha de rouge, 12 ha de blanc.

Production moyenne : 250 tonneaux (23 000 caisses) de rouge, de 2 000 à 4 000 caisses de blanc.

Marino (D.O.C.)

En général, vins blancs du Latium *(voir ce nom).*

Markobrunn (ou Marcobrunn)

Ce vin d'Erbach, en Allemagne, sur le Rhin, était parfois étiqueté Markobrunner. Mais c'était un des rares vins d'Allemagne qui soit assez grand par lui-même pour se passer de l'appellation du village, de la ville ou du secteur. Peut-être n'est-ce pas le meilleur du Rheingau, mais c'est certainement le plus rond, le plus caractérisé et le plus épicé de tous les vins du Rhin et celui qui mérite le plus sa célébrité.

Voir RHEINGAU

Marne

Roche argileuse contenant une forte proportion de calcaire, que l'on utilise pour amender les sols acides.

Maroc

Viticulture et viniculture n'ont pas même un siècle au Maroc. Pourtant on y faisait déjà, dans l'Antiquité, du vin dont une partie était envoyée à Rome. Mais, avec l'invasion arabe et la prohibition islamique de tout breuvage alcoolisé, on cessa d'y cultiver de la vigne à vin pour ne plus produire que du raisin de table. Tout changea après l'établissement du protectorat français, en 1912. Les vignobles produisirent dès 1919, mais c'est seulement entre 1929 et 1935 que la viticulture marocaine connut, sous l'impulsion des colons français, une expansion telle que la vigne y couvrait quelque 45 000 ha. La superficie actuelle est de 20 000 hectares.

Il y a un certain nombre de crus intéressants au Maroc. Quelques appellations d'origine figurent sur les étiquettes comme indication de supériorité, mais elles n'ont rien de commun avec le système français des appellations contrôlée. Vins d'origine contrôlée ou non représentent un quart du revenu agricole marocain. Ce sont surtout des rouges et des rosés. On fait aussi, au Maroc, des quantités moins importantes de vin blanc, bien que, sous un climat aussi chaud, ils aient tendance à madériser trop vite. Les rosés posent à peu près le même problème, mais les viniculteurs en viennent plus facilement à bout. Au sud de Casablanca et à l'est de Marrakech, on produit aussi du vin gris. Des vins de dessert doux et d'une belle couleur rubis foncé sont exportés par le Maroc. On y fait aussi du vin mousseux selon la méthode champenoise. Depuis l'indépendance, en 1956, le ministère de l'Agriculture marocain a instauré un contrôle des vignobles, de la qualité des vignes ainsi que des vins, et réglementé le marché de cette boisson. Tout le vin doit être sain et vendable. Il doit titrer au moins 11°, ce qui n'est pas difficile sous ce climat quasi tropical. La loi marocaine, déjà en vigueur du temps des Français, interdit l'exportation de vins inférieurs aux normes. La plupart de ces réglementations étaient jadis entre les mains des Français. Et les Marocains n'avaient d'autre rôle que de fournir la main d'œuvre.

Le pays consomme environ 80 % de sa production annuelle, soit 400 000 hl (près de 4,5 millions de caisses). Le reste est exporté, surtout dans les pays du Marché Commun, où le vin marocain occupe une place laissée vide depuis que l'Algérie n'y envoie plus ses produits. Le Maroc expédie en Europe du vin rouge ordinaire bon pour le coupage. Après avoir nationalisé les vignobles au moment de l'indépendance, et « marocanisé » les sociétés de commercialisation des vins en 1973, le Maroc fait preuve maintenant de libéralisme économique en autorisant la location de vignobles par des étrangers. Le marché des vins marocains est actuellement géré par l'Office marocain de commercialisation et d'exportation à Casablanca.

Dans l'ensemble, les vins marocains sont des rouges capiteux mais frustes comme ceux d'Algérie et de Tunisie. Près de la moitié proviennent de Rabat-Rharb, Casablanca, Fez, Oudjda et Marrakech. On y cultive surtoût des vignes à fort rendement telles que Cinsault, Carignan, Cabernet, Mourvèdre, Grenache et Alicante-Bouschet pour le rouge. Les deux premiers sont les meilleurs et donnent aussi du rosé qui peut être très agréable dans sa jeunesse et est probablement le plus populaire dans le pays. Clairette, Macabeo, Ximenez, Plant X et Grenache sont les raisins les plus utilisés pour le vin blanc. On cultive encore par tradition des vignes de jadis, mais qui fournissent surtout des raisins de table, bien que le Rafsaï blanc du Rif soit maintenant utilisé en vinification. Malheureusement les vignes de ces anciens vignobles n'ont pas résisté au phylloxéra qui a exercé ses ravages dans le nord du pays.

Les autres anciens vignobles à raisin de table sont situés dans le nord (Zerhoun) et le sud (Atlas), à flanc de montagne. Le phylloxéra menace l'existence de toutes ces parcelles appartenant à de petits viticulteurs. Les vignobles modernes, où sont plantés des vignes importées, se trouvent dans les régions de plaine : Meknès-Fez, Oudjda-Taza et Rabat-Casablanca. On y pratique la culture intensive et le tracteur remplace les bêtes de somme. Dans le nord-est, on fait le Muscat de Berkane et les meilleurs rosés qui sont comparables à ceux de l'Ouest algérien. Au centre, Taza produit un vin rouge bon pour les coupages. Autour de Fez, on trouve du rouge, du rosé et des blancs couleur de paille. La région de Meknès fournit la plus grande partie du rouge marocain : vin de belle couleur, corsé et d'un goût caractérisé. Le Daïet (ou Roumi) aux vignes cultivées à flanc de coteau à l'est de Rabat produit aussi des vins rouges. Au nord de cette dernière région, autour de Sidi-Slimane, le principal vin est un rouge richement coloré : le Dar Bel Hamri. Malheureusement, on consomme si rapidement les vins de la région de Casablanca qu'ils n'ont pas le temps d'atteindre leur pleine maturité. Les meilleurs vins marocains laissent beaucoup à désirer. Les rosés de cette même région ressemblent au Pelure d'Oignon *(voir ce mot)*. Au sud de Casablanca, les vieux vignobles d'El-Jadida et de Demnate donnent un vin gris, sec et fruité, considéré comme une spécialité marocaine.

Marquis d'Alesme-Becker (Château-)

Bordeaux rouge. Commune de Margaux, en Haut-Médoc.

Planté de vignes depuis 1616, ce domaine fut acheté en 1803 par un nommé Becker et il en résulte une certaine confusion quant au nom du vin. Pendant longtemps Becker ajouta son patronyme à celui du marquis d'Alesme. Les bouteilles étiquetées jusqu'à ces dernières années portent vraisemblablement la mention Marquis d'Alesme. Mais aujourd'hui, Becker y figure à nouveau.

Ce petit vignoble occupe une des meilleures positions de la commune sur l'éminence nommée Margaux ou La Combe. Jean-Claude Zuger hérita de l'imposant château Desmirail (du bâtiment mais non des vignobles qui avaient été vendus à château Palmer), ainsi que des vignobles du château d'Alesme-Becker qui partageaient le château Malescot (aujourd'hui propriété de son frère Roger) et ses bureaux. Il donna à l'ancien château Desmirail (au bâtiment) le nom de son vignoble. Il est impossible de ne pas remarquer les panneaux d'Alesme-Becker, au cœur du village de Margaux. Château Desmirail a donc disparu. L'exploitation de Château-Marquis-d'Alesme-Becker est dirigée par Jean-Claude, le fils de feu Paul Zuger.

Selon la classification du Médoc en 1855, le Château d'Alesme-Becker est un Troisième Cru.

Caractéristiques : Bon vin peu connu, doué de la finesse des Margaux.

Superficie : 10 ha.

Production moyenne : 50 tonneaux (5 000 caisses).

Marquis de Terme (Château-)

Bordeaux rouge. Commune de Margaux, en Haut-Médoc.

Ce Quatrième Cru, selon la classification de 1855, était considéré par beaucoup comme un des vignobles les mieux entretenus du Médoc. Dans le passé, le vin n'a pas réalisé ce qu'on pouvait attendre de telles vignes. Depuis 1975, une taille judicieuse des vignes à diminué la quantité et amélioré la qualité des vins. Le domaine appartient aux Sénéclauze. Depuis 1981, un nouveau chai (méritant d'être visité) a été construit pour les stocks anciens et nouveaux.

Caractéristiques : Relativement charnu pour un Margaux. Bien qu'il ne figure pas parmi les meilleurs vins de la commune, il atteint souvent finesse et parfum en dépit de sa trop forte production.

Superficie : 38 ha.

Production moyenne : 150 tonneaux (14 000 caisses).

Marsala (D.O.C.)

Fait aux environs de la ville de Marsala, au nord-ouest de la Sicile, c'est le principal vin de dessert italien. John Woodhouse le fit connaître en Angleterre à la fin du XVIIIe siècle et sa famille ne tarda pas à prospérer grâce à ce négoce. Le Marsala, de couleur foncé, est aussi servi en apéritif. Il est fait avec un vin blanc aromatique nommé *Passito*, lui-même élaboré avec des raisins séchés. On y ajoute de l'eau-de-vie et du sirop de raisin. Il vieillit en fût pendant 2 à 5 ans.

Le Marsala all'uovo (ou Marsaluovo) est un breuvage d'hiver fait avec du Marsala, un jaune d'œuf et de l'alcool. Peut-être est-ce tout simplement une version du sabayon qu'on fait en Italie avec du Marsala et qui s'appelle dans ce pays Zabaione ou encore Zabaglione.

Voir SICILE

Marsannay, Marsannay-La-Côte

Agglomération située à l'extrême nord de la Côte de Nuits, au sud immédiat de Dijon. On y fait un blanc agréable appelé Chardonnay de Marsannay ainsi qu'une petite quantité de bon rouge sous le nom de Pinot Noir de Marsannay, mais son meilleur vin est indubitablement le Rosé de Marsannay. Également fait avec du Pinot Noir, c'est un des rosés les plus exquis et désaltérants que l'on puisse trouver en France. L'appellation contrôlée officielle est Marsannay ou Marsannay Rosé.

Marsanne

Cépage à vin blanc cultivé surtout en Provence, en Algérie et en Savoie.

Martina (D.O.C.)

Vins blancs des environs de Bari.
Voir POUILLE

Mascara

Importante région vinicole d'Algérie, près d'Alger. On y produit des vins blancs, rouges et rosés. Le rouge, de couleur foncée, était souvent utilisé en coupages avec certains vins français des plus connus, surtout en Bourgogne où il servait un peu de *vin teinturier* aux négociants.
Voir ALGÉRIE

Mash

Terme anglais. Céréale qui a macéré dans de l'eau chaude pour faire du whisky. Pendant cette macération, l'amidon du grain se transforme en sucre fermentable.

Mastika (ou Masticha)

Apéritif favori des Grecs, fait sur l'île de Chio avec de l'eau-de-vie de vin additionnée de résine de lentisque.
Voir GRÈCE

Mathusalem

Bouteille géante utilisée auparavant en Champagne. Elle contient l'équivalent de huit bouteilles normales mais n'est plus guère utilisée.

Maury (Appellation Contrôlée)

Petit secteur du Roussillon. On y fait un vin de liqueur d'appellation contrôlée.
Voir VINS VINÉS DE FRANCE

Mavrodaphni

Grec, ce vin rouge de dessert, lourd et sucré, est aussi le nom d'une variété de raisin.
Voir GRÈCE

Mavroud

Un des raisins les plus cultivés en Bulgarie. Il donne des vins de même teneur en acide et en alcool que ceux qui sont faits avec du Gamza. Mais le vin de Mavroud est de couleur rubis foncé.
Voir BULGARIE

Maximim Grünhäuser Abtsberg

Un des meilleurs vins de la Ruwer. Abtsberg est le cru supérieur de Mertesdorf-Grünhaus.
Voir MOSELLE

Mazis-Chambertin (Appellation Contrôlée)

Bourgogne rouge. Commune de Gevrey-Chambertin, en Côte de Nuits. Classement officiel : Grand Cru.

Mazis (parfois Mazys) est à peine au-dessous de Latricières-Chambertin dans la hiérarchie des vins qui ajoutent le nom du vignoble de Chambertin à leur propre nom. Accéder à cet honneur est un exploit. Les deux géants de la commune de Gevrey-Chambertin sont le Chambertin et Chambertin-Clos de Bèze. En général, on admet que Latricières vient immédiatement après.

La vigne de Mazis-Chambertin est contiguë à celle de Clos de Bèze sur le côté sud de Gevrey-Chambertin et ses vins ont quelque chose en commun avec ceux du vieux clos, quoiqu'ils soient généralement plus légers et n'aient pas la même vigueur austère. Mais ils ont une finesse prodigieuse. Les 9,10 ha plantés uniquement en Pinot Noir donnent environ 3 000 caisses.

Mazoyères-Chambertin (Appellation Contrôlée)

Bourgogne rouge. Commune de Gevrey-Chambertin, en Côte de Nuits. Classement officiel : Grand Cru.

Dans le classement officiel des vins de la Côte-d'Or, en Bourgogne, Mazoyères figure avec le titre de Grand Cru. La réglementation indique : Mazoyères ou Charmes, ce qui signifie que le Mazoyères peut être vendu pour du Charmes, et réciproquement. La plupart des vignerons profitent de ce règlement parce qu'ils estiment que Charmes est plus facile à prononcer et plus connu que Mazoyères.

Voir CHARMES-CHAMBERTIN

Mead

Nom anglais de l'hydromel *(voir ce mot).*

Mealie Beer

Bière indigène de l'Afrique du Sud, faite avec du maïs.

Meal-Moth

Nom anglais de la pyrale, petit papillon dont la larve s'attaque aux feuilles et aux fruits de la vigne.

Voir CHAPITRE IV

Méchage, mèche, mécher

Le méchage est l'opération qui consiste à assainir un fût en y faisant brûler une mèche de soufre. Mécher : assainir un tonneau.

Médicinal (Vin)

Le vin additionné d'épices ou d'autres substances a longtemps été utilisé par les médecins. Dioscoride, Galien et d'autres en ont laissé, de siècle en siècle, diverses recettes. Tous les traités de médecine du Moyen Age citent le vin comme remède curatif. Récemment, on pouvait trouver des vins rouges à bon marché, additionnés d'alcool et contenant aussi des extraits de viande ou de malt, ou autres produits destinés à en faire de prétendus fortifiants. On traite aussi du vin à l'ipéca ou avec des pepsines ; ils cessent alors d'être des breuvages pour être des médicaments.

Medford Rhum

Nom que les Américains donnaient à tous les rhums d'origine coloniale, lorsque l'Amérique appartenait aux Anglais.

Voir RHUM : NOUVELLE-ANGLETERRE

Médoc (Bas-)

Région, de 3 400 ha, située au nord du Bordelais et caractérisée par un sol plat et rocailleux moins propice à la culture des vignes que celui du Haut-Médoc *(voir ce nom).* Il n'y a pas d'appellation contrôlée Bas-Médoc, le vin de cette région est donc vendu sous la simple appellation Médoc ou sous l'un des nombreux noms de crus du Médoc.

Médoc (Haut-)

Vin rouge. Région de Bordeaux.

Le Médoc est au premier rang des grandes subdivisions vinicoles de la région de Bordeaux et bien des experts estiment que c'est la première du monde pour les vins rouges de haute qualité. Quand on considère à la fois la quantité de bon vin que produit le Médoc et les bouteilles incomparables de certains châteaux, cette opinion semble justifiée.

Le Médoc est le type même du Bordeaux rouge qui acquiert en vieillissant un bouquet subtil, évoquant la rose et la violette ou l'odeur indéfinissable des bois au printemps et celle de la terre fraîche. Ils sont féminins et délicats quand on les compare aux Saint-Émilion, plus charnus et plus chaleureux. On dit souvent d'eux que ce sont les reines plutôt que les rois des vins rouges. les Médoc ont une finesse prodigieuse lorsqu'ils ont été amenés à vieillir correctement. Même les crus secondaires du Médoc acquièrent de la qualité en vieillissant. Quant aux plus grands, on peut encore les boire lorsqu'ils ont atteint quatre-vingts ans d'âge, voir plus : la bouteille contient encore un vin plein de vie, moelleux, superbe.

A quelques exceptions près, on ne fait que du rouge dans ce secteur et aucun vin blanc n'a droit à l'appellation Haut-Médoc. Les vins des vignobles de Margaux — les Médoc les plus proches de Bordeaux — sont les plus féminins ; les Médoc deviennent de plus en plus corsés au fur et à mesure qu'on se rapproche de Saint-Estèphe (agglomération située à quelque 65 km de Bordeaux). Telle est la tendance générale du Haut-Médoc qui est la meilleure partie de ce secteur et qui constitue une Appellation d'Origine Contrôlée qu'on voit sur les étiquettes. Médoc est le nom qu'on donne aux vins provenant de la région située au nord de Saint-Estèphe, c'est-à-dire où la péninsule du Médoc se rétrécit progressivement en direction de Soulac-sur-Mer et de Verdon-sur-Mer, ville en face de laquelle la Gironde se déverse dans l'Atlantique. Ce secteur produit des vins de table de haute qualité. On y compte de nombreuses coopératives. L'une d'elles, situées à Bégadan (25 km de Pauillac), a une capacité dépassant 30 000 hl. Mais les vins les plus célèbres sont ceux du Haut-Médoc.

Outre ces deux appellations contrôlées — Médoc et Haut-Médoc — auxquelles ont droit tous les vins de la région conforme à des normes minimales sévères, cinq communes du Haut-Médoc ont droit à leur propre appellation : Margaux, Saint-Julien, Saint-Estèphe, Pauillac, Moulis et Listrac *(voir à sa place dans l'ordre alphabétique chacune des ces appellations).* Plus l'appellation est précise, et plus le vin risque d'être distingué. Un Margaux, par exemple, sera plus caractéristique et répondra à des normes de qualité plus élevées qu'un vin qui porterait l'appellation générale Médoc et même Haut-Médoc. L'usage veut que dans la conversation courante on appelle Médoc tout court même les vins les plus fins du Haut-Médoc. 54 des 62 crus classés se trouvent dans les quatre communes plus célèbres.

Par bonne année, les vins du Médoc atteignent des sommets extraordinaires, mais, par mauvaise année, ils ne tombent jamais beaucoup plus bas que leur grande qualité habituelle. Même les années défavorables, un Médoc bien fait sera un vin agréable, les grands châteaux faisant toujours bien leur vin. Après avoir été minutieusement sélectionnée cuve par cuve, la production des meilleures années prendra du temps pour vieillir, celle des autres années sera consommable beaucoup plus tôt.

Médoc serait une corruption du latin *in medio aquae,* ce qui correspond à sa situation géographique : au milieu de l'eau, entre l'Atlantique et la Gironde. Cette péninsule étale son sol sablonneux et pierreux sur quelque 100 km de longueur et sa largeur ne dépasse pas 25 km. La bande de territoire plantée de vignes est très étroite. Les grands vins ne proviennent que des bords de la Gironde sur une frange de 3 km de large. Le reste du Médoc est couvert de pinèdes, avec, çà et là, quelques champs et même des vignes dont le vin porte l'appellation générale Bordeaux. La forêt s'étend en direction de l'ouest jusqu'aux hautes dunes bordant l'Atlantique. Le long de la meilleure bande de terrain, les vignobles sont rassemblés en essaims. A la Maison du vin de Pauillac, une grande carte représente en miniature le panorama du Médoc ; tous les Châteaux classés et quelques autres y sont indiqués. On y voit immédiatement que la vigne se concentre autour de Margaux, ainsi que Saint-Julien, Pauillac et Saint-Estèphe et qu'elle est plus clairsemée entre ces quatre points. La raison en est simple. Margaux est sur une petite hauteur, Pauillac et Saint-Estèphe sur des éminences plus abruptes. Ailleurs un sol sans relief, où coulent des ruisseaux débouchant dans la Gironde, ne convient pas aussi bien aux bonnes vignes. L'étude d'une carte géologique explique ce phénomène. Le sol, datant du quaternaire, de nos jours, couvert de pierres et de gravier y apparaît en plages isolées par de nouveaux apports alluviaux déposés sur les basses terres. Les vignes qui poussent sur ce terrain n'ont droit à aucune des principales appellations d'origine du Médoc. Quant au sol caillouteux le plus ancien du Médoc, il date de la fin du tertiaire et des débuts du quaternaire. En ce temps-là, des glaciers glissant lentement depuis les lointaines Pyrénées auraient suivi le cours de la Gironde et raboté sa rive droite, plus abrupte. Quand ces glaciers fondirent, ils laissèrent sur le sol les pierres de leurs moraines. Ces petits cailloux ont une vertu particulière au Médoc : ils emmagasinent la chaleur du soleil pendant la journée et la restituent pendant la nuit aux vignes taillées bas.

Certes la qualité du sol importe en Médoc comme partout ailleurs. Ce sont ces terrains de graves qui donnent la race au vin. Mais d'autres éléments comptent aussi pour lui donner ses caractéristiques : climat, variété de vignes, méthodes de viticulture et de vinification. Le climat atlantique est nettement plus doux et plus humide en Médoc que dans les autres secteurs du Bordelais.

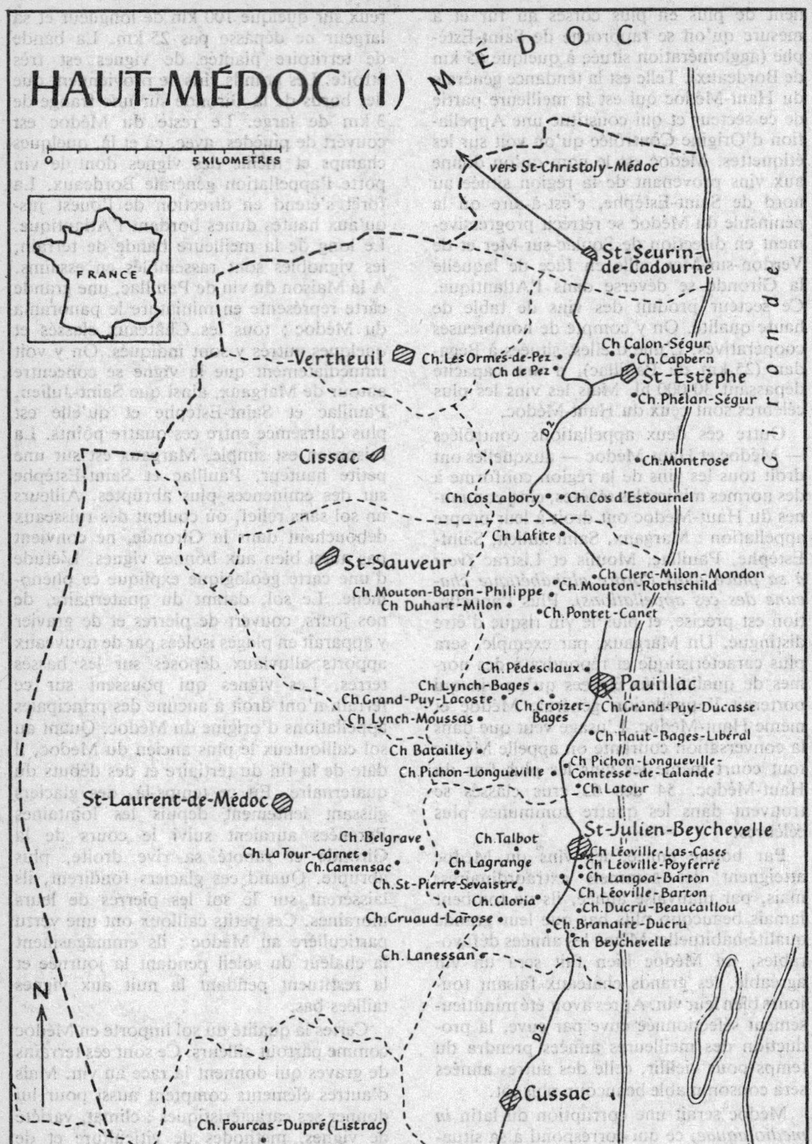
HAUT-MÉDOC (1)
MÉDOC
0
5 KILOMETRES
FRANCE
vers St-Christoly-Médoc
St-Seurin-de-Cadourne
Gironde
Ch Calon-Ségur
Ch.Capbern
St-Estèphe
Ch.Phélan-Ségur
Vertheuil
Ch.Les Ormes-de-Pez
Ch de Pez
D2
Cissac
Ch.Montrose
Ch Cos Labory
Ch.Cos d'Estournel
Ch Lafite
St-Sauveur
Ch Clerc-Milon-Mondon
Ch.Mouton-Baron-Philippe
Ch.Mouton-Rothschild
Ch Duhart-Milon
Ch.Pontet-Canet
Ch.Pédesclaux
Pauillac
Ch Lynch-Bages
Ch.Grand-Puy-Lacoste
Ch Croizet-Bages
Ch Grand-Puy-Ducasse
Ch Lynch-Moussas
Ch Haut-Bages-Libéral
Ch Batailley
Ch Pichon-Longueville-Comtesse-de-Lalande
Ch.Pichon-Longueville
Ch Latour
St-Laurent-de-Médoc
St-Julien-Beychevelle
Ch.Belgrave
Ch.Talbot
Ch.Léoville-Las-Cases
Ch.La Tour-Carnet
Ch Lagrange
Ch.Léoville-Poyferré
Ch.Camensac
Ch.Langoa-Barton
Ch.St-Pierre-Sevaistre
Ch.Léoville-Barton
Ch.Gloria
Ch.Ducru-Beaucaillou
Ch.Gruaud-Larose
Ch.Branaire-Ducru
Ch Beychevelle
Ch.Lanessan
N
Cussac
Ch.Fourcas-Dupré (Listrac)
vers Arcins

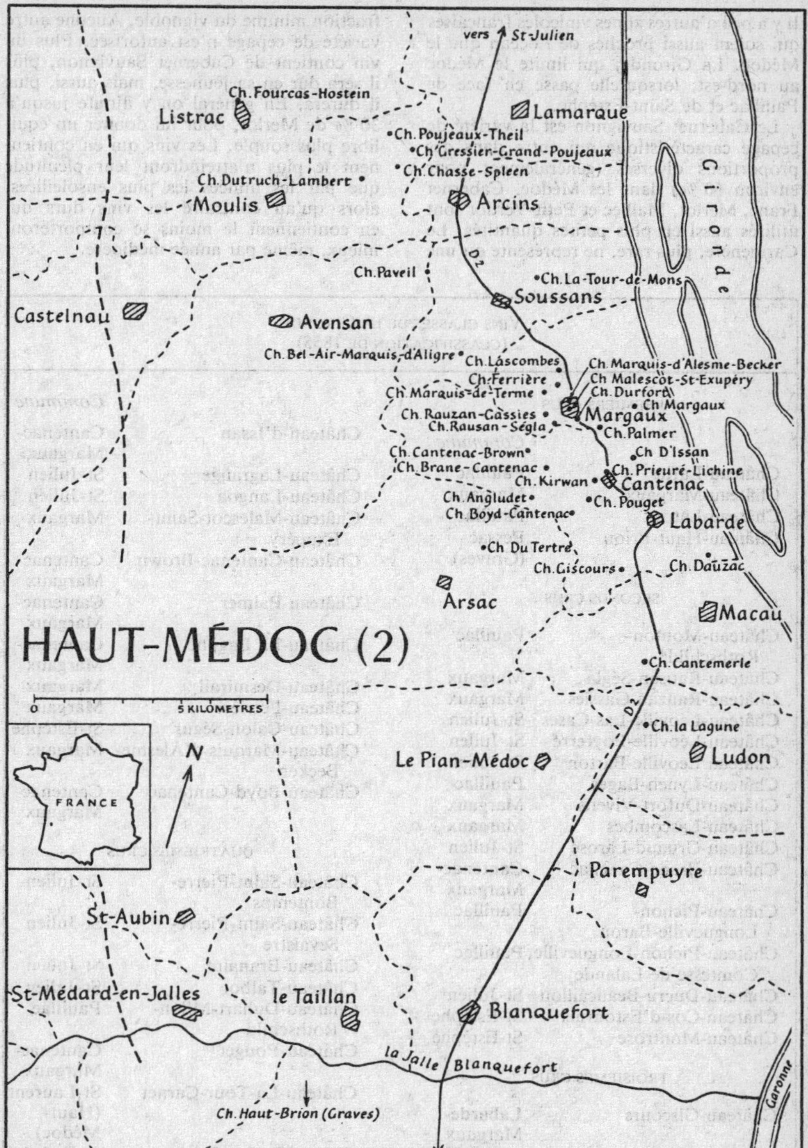
HAUT-MÉDOC (2)
vers St-Julien
Ch. Fourcas-Hostein
Listrac
Lamarque
Ch. Poujeaux-Theil
Ch. Gressier-Grand-Poujeaux
Ch. Chasse-Spleen
Ch. Dutruch-Lambert
Moulis
Arcins
Gironde
Ch. Paveil
D2
Ch. La-Tour-de-Mons
Soussans
Castelnau
Avensan
Ch. Bel-Air-Marquis-d'Aligre
Ch. Lascombes
Ch. Ferrière
Ch. Marquis-de-Terme
Ch. Marquis-d'Alesme-Becker
Ch. Malescot-St-Exupéry
Ch. Durfort
Ch. Margaux
Margaux
Ch. Rauzan-Gassies
Ch. Rausan-Ségla
Ch. Palmer
Ch. Cantenac-Brown
Ch. D'Issan
Ch. Brane-Cantenac
Ch. Prieuré-Lichine
Ch. Kirwan
Cantenac
Ch. Angludet
Ch. Pouget
Ch. Boyd-Cantenac
Labarde
Ch. Du Tertre
Ch. Giscours
Ch. Dauzac
Arsac
Macau
Ch. Cantemerle
0
5 KILOMETRES
Ch. la Lagune
Le Pian-Médoc
Ludon
FRANCE
N
Parempuyre
St-Aubin
St-Médard-en-Jalles
le Taillan
Blanquefort
la Jalle Blanquefort
Garonne
Ch. Haut-Brion (Graves)
vers Bordeaux

Il y a peu d'autres zones vinicoles françaises qui soient aussi proches de l'océan que le Médoc. La Gironde, qui limite le Médoc au nord-est, lorsqu'elle passe en face de Pauillac et de Saint-Estèphe.

Le Cabernet Sauvignon est la variété de cépage caractéristique qui entre dans des proportions diverses (généralement pour environ 60 %) dans les Médoc. Cabernet Franc, Merlot, Malbec et Petit-Verdot sont utilisés aussi en plus petites quantités. Le Carmenère, plus rare, ne représente qu'une fraction minime du vignoble. Aucune autre variété de cépage n'est autorisée. Plus un vin contient de Cabernet Sauvignon, plus il sera dur en sa jeunesse, mais aussi, plus il durera. En général on y ajoute jusqu'à 30 % de Merlot, pour lui donner un équilibre plus souple. Les vins qui en contiennent le plus n'atteindront leur plénitude que par les années les plus ensoleillées, alors qu'au contraire les vins durs qui en contiennent le moins se comporteront mieux, même par année médiocre.

VINS CLASSÉS DE LA GIRONDE
(CLASSIFICATION DE 1855)

PREMIERS CRUS	*Commune*
Château-Lafite	Pauillac
Château-Margaux	Margaux
Château-Latour	Pauillac
Château-Haut-Brion	Pessac (Graves)
SECONDS CRUS	
Château-Mouton-Rothschild*	Pauillac
Château-Rausan-Ségla	Margaux
Château-Rauzan-Gassies	Margaux
Château-Léoville-Las Cases	St-Julien
Château-Léoville-Poyferré	St-Julien
Château Léoville-Barton	St-Julien
Château-Lynch-Bages	Pauillac
Château-Dufort-Vivens	Margaux
Château-Lascombes	Margaux
Château-Gruaud-Larose	St-Julien
Château-Brane-Canenac	Cantenac-Margaux
Château-Pichon-Longueville-Baron	Pauillac
Château-Pichon-Longueville, Comtesse de Lalande	Pauillac
Château-Ducru-Beaucaillou	St-Julien
Château-Cos-d'Estournel	St-Estèphe
Château-Montrose	St-Estèphe
TROISIÈMES CRUS	
Château-Giscours	Labarde-Margaux
Château-Kirwan	Cantenac-Margaux
Château-d'Issan	Cantenac-Margaux
Château-Lagrange	St-Julien
Château-Langoa	St-Julien
Château-Malescot-Saint-Exupéry	Margaux
Château-Cantenac-Brown	Cantenac-Margaux
Château-Palmer	Cantenac-Margaux
Château-La Lagune	Cantenac-Margaux
Château-Desmirail	Margaux
Château-Ferrière	Margaux
Château-Calon-Ségur	St-Estèphe
Château-Marquis d'Alesme-Becker	Margaux
Château-Boyd-Cantenac	Cantenac-Margaux
QUATRIÈMES CRUS	
Château-Saint-Pierre-Bontemps	St-Julien
Château-Saint-Pierre-Sevaistre	St-Julien
Château-Branaire	St-Julien
Château-Talbot	St-Julien
Château-Duhart-Milon-Rothschild	Pauillac
Château-Pouget	Cantenac-Margaux
Château-La-Tour-Carnet	St-Laurent (Haut-Médoc)
Château-Lafon-Rochet	St-Estèphe
Château-Beychevelle	St-Julien

VINS CLASSÉS DE LA GIRONDE
(CLASSIFICATION DE 1855)

	Commune		Commune
Château-Prieuré-Lichine	Cantenac-Margaux	Château-Cos-Labory	St-Estèphe
Château-Marquis de Terme	Margaux	Château-Clerc-Milon-Rothschild	Pauillac
CINQUIÈMES CRUS		Château Croizet-Bages	Pauillac
Château-Pontet-Canet	Pauillac	Château-Cantemerle	Macau (Haut-Médoc)
Château-Batailley	Pauillac		
Château-Grand-Puy-Lacoste	Pauillac		
Château-Grand-Puy-Ducasse	Pauillac	CRUS EXCEPTIONNELS	
Château-Haut-Batailley	Pauillac	Château-Villegeorge	Avensan
Château-Lynch-Moussas	Pauillac	Château-Angludet	Cantenac-Margaux
Château-Dauzac	Labarde-Margaux	Château-Chasse-Spleen	Moulis (Haut-Médoc)
Château-Mouton-Armailhacq (maintenant Mouton Baronne-Philippe)	Pauillac		
Château du Tertre	Arsac-Margaux	Château-Poujeaux-Theil	Moulis (Haut-Médoc)
Château-Haut-Bages-Libéral	Pauillac	Château-la-Couronne	Pauillac
Château-Pédesclaux	Pauillac	Château-Moulin-Riche	St-Julien
Château-Belgrave	St-Laurent (Haut-Médoc)	Château-Bel-Air-Marquis-d'Aligre	Soussans-Margaux
Château-Camensac	St-Laurent (Haut-Médoc)		

* Déclaré 1er cru en 1973

On laisse produire les vignes pendant environ quarante ans. Après quoi on les arrache pour les remplacer. Comme dans la plupart des crus de qualité du Médoc, on s'en tient au vieil usage : laisser chaque cep atteindre son âge maximal et ne le remplacer qu'à sa mort. Mais dans d'autres cas on procède plus simplement en arrachant et replantant une petite parcelle de temps en temps. Presque tous les propriétaires s'efforcent de laisser vivre aussi longtemps que possible leurs vignes, ce qui améliore la qualité du vin car, plus la vigne est vieille, plus elle donne du bon vin.

Mais ce procédé coûte cher, non seulement parce qu'il exige plus de main-d'œuvre, mais surtout parce que, en gagnant en qualité, la vigne perd en rendement, et au cours de ses dernières années, sa production baisse très rapidement.

En Médoc, les vendanges commencent généralement aux derniers jours de septembre ; environ une année sur six, en octobre, et une année sur quatre-vingts, en août. Plus l'été est chaud, plus on vendange tôt, évidemment. L'égrappage (ou éraflage) est obligatoire. On y procède en recourant à de nouveaux engins : les manches de métal perforé qui tournent sur elles-mêmes ; le raisin et le jus s'écoulent par les trous et les rafles sont emportées vers l'extrémité de la manche. Il était de tradition de frotter les grappes sur une grille, les grains de raisin tombaient à travers un tamis et les rafles restaient entre les mains de celui qui opèrait. On a beaucoup discuté pour décider laquelle de ces deux méthodes est la meilleure, mais personne n'a jamais démontré que l'une ou l'autre donne des vins de qualité supérieure.

Après avoir été débarrassés des pédoncules et pédicelles, le jus et les peaux fermentent ensemble avec les pépins dans des cuves. Le moût prend alors sa couleur, car les pigments se trouvent dans la pellicule du raisin, et se charge de tanin qui lui donnera la longévité.

Dans la plupart des propriétés les vins sont laissés en cuve de 12 à 25 jours, après quoi on les fait s'écouler pour les débarrasser des peaux qui sont ensuite pressées pour faire un vin de presse qui, dans les vins de qualité, est l'âme du vin. Ils passent ensuite 18 à 28 mois en barrique avant d'être mis en bouteille (*voir* CHAPITRE IV). Quelques rares vignobles aristocratiques continuent à laisser le vin sur les peaux pendant 3 semaines à 1 mois, selon la tradition du Médoc, ce qui leur donne un maximum de tanin, parfois exagéré. Les grands vins de ce genre exigent un vieillissement prolongé qui les rendra consommables plus longtemps. Mais ce procédé n'est possible que pour les vins vendus à des prix élevés, car il coûte cher. C'est une habitude qui décroît car les consommateurs, même les plus avisés, recherchent des vins ayant une certaine souplesse. Ces vins très durs avec des cuvaisons prolongées ne sont plus de notre temps.

En 1855, les vins du Médoc (et du Sauternes) furent classés à l'occasion de l'Exposition internationale de Paris, par une commission de courtiers bordelais qui jugèrent surtout en fonction des résultats obtenus pendant les cent années précédentes. Ce classement en cinq catégories allant de Premier Cru à Cinquième Cru exige une révision. Il reste valable pour les Premiers Crus : Château-Lafite, Château-Margaux, Château-Latour. On y ajouta Château-Haut-Brion qui le méritait en ce qui concerne la qualité de ses vins, mais qui n'aurait jamais dû être classé parmi les Médoc puisqu'il est situé en Graves. En outre étant donné sa qualité, Château Mouton-Rothschild, classé en tête des Seconds Crus en 1855, fut reclassé Premier Cru en 1973. De même, on trouve, parmi les Seconds, Troisièmes, Quatrièmes et Cinquième Crus, des vins qui pourraient changer de catégorie *(pour un exposé plus complet de cette question, voir* BORDEAUX : CLASSIFICATION).

Aujourd'hui, ces vins sont devenus les plus chers et les plus recherchés du monde. A la fin des années soixante, les prix commencèrent à grimper et, bientôt, la plupart des très grands Médoc se vendirent à des prix plusieurs fois supérieurs au niveau qu'ils avaient atteint quelques années auparavant, le millésime 1970 battant tous les records. De toute évidence, un ensemble de facteurs en fut la cause : la prospérité générale associée à l'inflation et à la spéculation, la croissance spectaculaire du marché américain, l'essor de la demande des pays du Marché Commun, un intérêt plus marqué des Français pour leurs vins les plus fins (dans le cas des cinq plus grands crus) et un engouement nouveau des Japonais pour le luxe à la mode occidentale. La stabilité des prix jusqu'en 1969, en dépit d'une période d'inflation, a pu avoir un rôle important. Cependant en raison de la qualité exceptionnelle des millésimes 82, 83 et 85, les cours ont continué à grimper mais avec une acalmie à partir de 1986.

Les importateurs anglo-saxons et bien des Français se leurrent en ce qui concerne les Crus Exceptionnels qu'ils croient *meilleurs* que les Grands Crus ; *or il n'en est rien.* Les Crus bourgeois et les Crus artisans furent classés après les 62 plus grands, en 1855. On trouve pourtant parmi eux de très bons vins qui mériteraient une promotion dans la catégorie des plus grands crus. On trouvera la classification de 1855 en appendice. Une proposition de reclassement des crus de Bordeaux, faite par l'auteur en 1958, 1966, 1973 puis en 1986, figure à l'article BORDEAUX, après le paragraphe CLASSIFICATION. On y verra que la classification de 1855 ne représente plus la vérité dans bien des cas.

(Voir aussi les Crus Classés, à leur place dans l'ordre alphabétique.)

Meleto

Bon Chianti classique produit par l'entreprise Ricasoli.

Voir TOSCANE

Mendoza

Province d'Argentine qui produit les 3/4 du vin de ce pays.

Voir ARGENTINE

Menetou Salon (Appellation Contrôlée)

Commune située sur le cours supérieur de la Loire, au sud de Pouilly-sur-Loire. Ses 340 ha de Sauvignon Blanc produisent du vin blanc et ses quelque 50 ha de Pinot Noir, du vin rouge.

Meranese di Collina (D.O.C.)

Vin du Trentin Haut-Adige *(voir ce nom)*.

Mercurey (Appellation Contrôlée)

Bourgogne rouge et blanc. Chalonnais.

Un des quatre principaux vins du Chalonnais qui ressemblent aux Côte de Beaune, peut-être parce que les uns et les autres sont faits avec du Pinot Noir. Les meilleurs Mercurey sont les rouges.

Voir CHALONNAIS

Merlot

Raisin bleu-noir à peau épaisse, qui donne souplesse et rondeur aux vins de Médoc. On le cultive aussi en Italie, en Suisse et au Chili, en Californie, en Australie et ailleurs.

Mersin

Liqueur blanche à laquelle oranges et herbes donnent du goût ; c'est le curaçao turc.

Mescal, Mezcal

Un des noms du cactus mexicain avec lequel on fait le *pulque* et la tequila. On appelle aussi cette dernière boisson Mescal.

Voir PULQUE ; TEQUILA

Mesnil (-sur-Oger)

Agglomération champenoise qui produit un des meilleurs vins de la Côte des Blancs.

Voir CHAMPAGNE

Messe (Vin de)

Vin utilisé à fins sacramentelles. Il doit être pur et exempt de toute addition.

Metaxa

Eau-de-vie légèrement douce, de couleur foncée, faite en Grèce *(voir ce nom)*.

Metheglin

En irlandais : breuvage épicé. Ce mot désigne en général l'hydromel.

Meursault (Appellation Contrôlée)

Bourgogne blanc et très peu de rouge. Côte de Beaune.

Meursault est la « capitale du coteau des grands vins blancs ». Quoique la « Côte de Meursault » n'existe pas dans la terminologie officielle, cette expression est employée couramment et ne manque pas de justification. Ce secteur englobe les communes de Meursault et de Puligny-Montrachet ainsi que le hameau de Blagny, et forme un groupe de communes distinct du reste de la Côte de Beaune. Au nord, un défilé le sépare d'Auxey-Duresses et de Monthélie ; au sud, une autre dépression le sépare de Saint-Aubin ; à l'ouest, sa limite est au sommet des hauteurs et, à l'est, elle est marquée par la route de Beaune à Chagny, au-delà de laquelle s'étend la plaine de Bourgogne, région de vins plus ordinaires. Un autre secteur particulier : sol calcaire et sous-sol grossier, convenant parfaitement au Chardonnay. Certains vignobles de Meursault sont situés du mauvais côté de la limite nord et on y cultive surtout du Pinot Noir ; les vins qui en sont issus empruntent le nom de l'agglomération voisine : Volnay *(voir ce nom)* et sont vendus sous l'appellation Volnay-Santenots.

Meursault signifie « saut de souris », car les vignobles de vin rouge n'auraient autrefois été séparés de ceux de vin blanc que par un saut de souris. De nos jours, seule l'Hercule des souris pourrait passer de l'un à l'autre d'un seul saut. Pourtant, on trouve encore du Pinot Noir dans les vignobles et les viticulteurs de Meursault produisent environ 800 hl (plus de 8 500 caisses) de vin rouge par an. Les Meursault rouges sont vigoureux et ne révèlent leur flamme et leur excellent bouquet qu'au bout d'un certain temps de vieillissement. Toutefois ils n'égalent pas en qualité les rouges de la Côte de Nuits.

Par rapport aux autres localités de la Côte-d'Or, Meursault est assez grande et on ne saurait dire s'il s'agit d'un village trop développé ou d'une trop petite ville. Elle est légèrement dominée à l'ouest de collines arrondies qui s'élèvent vers le hameau de Blagny, isolé à l'extrémité sud-ouest, et dont les vins sont vendus sous les noms de Meursault, Blagny-Côte de Beaune et Meursault-

Côte de Beaune. Ils sont rouges et ceux qui portent les deux dernières appellations sont parfois mélangés aux vins de certaines autres communes de la Côte de Beaune pour être vendus comme Côte de Beaune-Villages. Meursault est une agglomération prospère où l'on trouve quelques monuments intéressants. La flèche délicate qui s'élève au-dessus de l'église plutôt trapue, suggère aux Bourguignons l'idée d'un bonnet sur la tête d'un paysan. A côté, il y a un bâtiment sinistre et gris qui servait de léproserie au Moyen Age. Grâce à des dons, les Hospices de Beaune possèdent plusieurs crus de Meursault qui, selon l'usage de ces hospices, sont vendus sous le nom des donateurs : dont voici les principaux : Loppin, Jehan Humblot, Baudot, Goureau, Albert Grivault et Bahèzre de Lanlay. Meursault a aussi son propre petit hospice plus ancien que celui de Beaune, dont le portail ouvre sur la route conduisant au village.

La plus grande partie du vin produit sous l'appellation Meursault est du blanc. Ce vin sec, rond, souple d'un tissu féminin, avec un bouquet ineffable. Sec, il n'a toutefois pas la dureté d'acier qu'on trouve dans le Chablis, mais, quand il provient des meilleures parcelles, une luxuriance et un arrière-goût à la fois durables et merveilleux. Ces vins arrivent rapidement à leur apogée et seuls les meilleurs réussissent à vieillir tandis que les autres tendent à madériser assez vite.

Les Perrières sont la meilleure parcelle et le vin provenant du cœur de ce cru — Clos des Perrières — est souvent capable de tenir tête à l'incomparable Montrachet. Après Les Perrières, vient Charmes, Genevrières, et La Goutte d'Or — vigne bien nommée. Tous comportent la même grâce séductrice et la même élégance. Très peu de choses les séparent. Le Blagny est peut-être légèrement supérieur au Meursault.

Compte tenu des vignes de Blagny, Meursault est la commune de la Côte-d'Or qui possède la plus grande surface plantée en vignes et chaque année elle rivalise avec Pommard et Beaune pour la première place quant à la quantité. Les 480 ha de vignes de Meursault (dont quelque 200 ha peuvent ajouter Côte de Beaune au nom de la commune) produisent en moyenne 12 500 hl (près de 140 000 caisses) de blanc.

Les meilleurs vignobles de la commune ont le titre de Premiers Crus et le droit d'ajouter leur nom à celui de la commune sur l'étiquette. Ce sont :

PREMIERS CRUS	
A Meursault	*Superficie (ha)*
Clos des Perrières et Les Perrières	13,7
Les Charmes-dessus	14,25
Les Charmes-dessous	16,80
Les Genevrières-dessus	10,65
Les Genevrières-dessous	5,40
La Goutte d'Or	5,30
Le Porusot-Dessus	5,30
Le Porusot	4,30
Les Bouchères	4,40
Les Santenots-Blancs	2,95
Les Santenots du Milieu	8
Les Caillerets	1,03
Les Petures	10,45
Les Cras	2,90
A Blagny	
La Jennelotte	5,04
La Pièce-sous-le-Bois	11,25
Sous le dos d'Ane	5,03

Mexique

On fait du vin au Mexique, surtout dans le nord du pays. Les zones viticoles couvrent une superficie de 60 000 ha. Le dixième environ est consacré à la production des vins ; le restant fournit de l'alcool. Ces zones sont réparties dans les endroits suivants : nord de la Basse Californie, région de Laguna à la frontière des États de Coahuila et Durango, Parras et Saltillo dans l'État de Coahuila, Aguascalientes, la région de San Juan del Rio à Queretaro, Delicias à Chihuahua et le secteur de Hermosillo dans l'État de Sonora. Il existe également des vignobles à San Luis Potosi, Zacatecas, Tlaxcala et Hidalgo.

HISTOIRE DU VIN MEXICAIN

Gouverneur du Mexique de 1521 à 1527, Hernando Cortez fit planter des vignes espagnoles dans les fermes de la Nouvelle Espagne. Avant ces plantations, les conquistadores faisaient du vin à l'aide de raisins sauvages. Le premier vignoble fut planté à Parras par un capitaine espagnol, Francisco de Urdiñola. Il y avait bien des vignes sauvages dans les coteaux et les vallonnements de la contrée, mais il n'existait jusqu'alors aucun vignoble de cépages cultivés. Parras, dont le nom signifie treilles, est encore un centre viticole et on cultive toujours la vigne, entre Monterrey et Torreón là où Don Francisco en planta. La viticulture mexicaine inspira la même jalousie aux Espagnols que 1 500 ans plus tôt, les vins gaulois aux Romains. Sur l'exemple de l'empereur Domitien qui ordonna en l'an 89, la destruction des cépages de Bourgogne, Philippe II publia en 1595 un édit interdisant de nouvelles plantations ou le remplacement des vignes sur le territoire du Mexique. Dans les siècles suivants, les vice-rois se gardèrent bien de déroger aux ordres de la couronne, et le vin resta un monopole espagnol. Malgré ces interdictions, la viniculture s'étendit du Mexique au Pérou et à l'Argentine au cours du XVIe siècle ; au XVIIIe siècle, elle arriva jusqu'aux territoires que nous connaissons aujourd'hui comme l'ouest des États-Unis.

Lorsque Miguel Hidalgo souleva le pays contre l'Espagne en 1810, un de ses buts était de mettre fin au monopole du vin et de renouveler la viticulture mexicaine. Pourtant l'industrie du vin ne bénéficia pas immédiatement du succès de l'insurrection. La variété de raisin Mission, appelée Criolla en Argentine ou Pais au Chili, apportée par les conquistadores d'Espagne trois cents ans plus tôt, était encore prédominante dans la plupart des vignobles mexicains. Le Mission est pourtant une *Vitis vinifera,* mais manque d'acidité et de couleur, les vins se conservant mal. Les premières expériences à grande échelle avec de bonnes variétés européennes furent entreprises à la fin du XIXe siècle. Un certain James Concannon (vigneron irlandais naturalisé américain et vivant à Livermore, Californie) expédia plusieurs milliers de boutures des meilleures variétés françaises dans tout le nord du territoire mexicain. En 1910, six ans après le séjour de Concannon au Mexique, la révolution éclatait. Quelques vignobles furent protégés pendant un certain temps par le général mexicain Pancho Villa et sa bande de brigands, mais la grande majorité furent ravagés ou abandonnés sous l'effet de la révolution. Depuis, la superficie des vignobles et la production de vins ont augmenté, cette dernière reste très réduite mais augmente régulièrement. Aussi la viniculture mexicaine ne pourra pas prospérer aussi longtemps que les Mexicains montreront peu d'intérêt pour les vins. En effet, ils boivent surtout du *pulque (voir ce nom),* de la bière et des boissons non alcoolisées, le vin restant inconnu à la plupart. Seuls les gens aisés en achètent lors d'occasions spéciales : ils choisissent alors les vins importés d'Europe (de France principalement) et des États-Unis. L'association des viticulteurs et les grandes marques du négoce ont lancé il y a quelques années une campagne en faveur de la consommation du vin. Cette action a porté ses fruits : la qualité s'améliore rapidement et la consommation augmente d'environ 15 % par an. Elle est estimée actuellement à 150 000 hl (plus d'1,5 million de caisses). Mais on produit des quantités bien supérieures de brandies ou *aguardiente.*

Régions vinicoles

Les vignobles de Basse Californie (Baja California) (environ 7 500 ha) sont situés dans les vallées fertiles du nord-ouest de cette presqu'île ailleurs aride et désolée. Les cinq régions importantes sont concentrées dans un rayon de 160 km de la frontière des États-Unis : Santo Tomás, à 40 km au sud de Ensenada ; Guadalupe, à 80 km au sud de la frontière américaine ; Ranchio Viejo, dans les terres d'Ensenada ; et les secteurs de Valle Redondo et de Tañama près de la ville de Tecate, presque à cheval sur la frontière américaine. Les plantations sont limitées par le taux de pluviosité assez bas : entre 12 et 45 cm par an, mais l'irrigation est de règle. Comme la côte californienne méridionale des États-Unis est tempérée par le Pacifique, ces vallées sont rafraîchies par les brises et les brumes de l'Océan.

Pour la production des vins de qualité, les principaux cépages suivant sont utilisés : Chenin Blanc, Sauvignon Blanc, Ugni Blanc et en moindre proportion, Chardonnay et Riesling pour les vins blancs ; Cabernet Sauvignon, Petite Syrah, Zinfandel et en moindre proportion, Barbera, Nebbiolo et Ruby Cabernet pour les vins rouges et rosés.

65 % de la production moyenne de Baja California sont destinés à la production de vins, 25 % à la distillation, et une quantité minime aux raisins de table (10 %), alors que dans le reste du pays le marché mexicain absorbe plus de 60 % de la production de raisins pour la fabrication de brandies. L'évolution de la qualité des vins de la Baja California est considérable.

Avec une prodution annuelle de 150 000 caisses, les Bodegas de Santo Tomás, à Ensenada, sont parmi les plus grands vignobles de Basse Californie. Fondées par un chercheur d'or italien puis rachetées par un ancien président du Mexique, les *bodegas* appartiennent aujourd'hui à la firme de vins d'importation Elias Pando, dont le siège est à Mexico. Le directeur technique, Dmitri Tchelistcheff (qui fut formé par son père dans les vignobles de Beaulieu de la vallée du Napa, en Californie) a considérablement amélioré la qualité des vins. Les vins de Tomás sont aujourd'hui parmi les meilleurs et les plus réputés du Mexique. La moitié de la superficie de Santo Tómas est plantée de vignes ordinaires telles que Mission, Rosa de Perú et Palomino ; on y cultive également les variétés Valdepeñas, Grenache, Carignan, ainsi que le Colombard français, Cabernet Sauvignon, Pinot Noir, Johannisberg Riesling, Sémillon et Chenin Blanc. Tchelistcheff a introduit quelques bonnes techniques de viniculture : la fermentation à froid des vins blancs, le vieillissement en bouteilles des vins rouges et la fermentation en bouteilles des vins mousseux. Une bonne partie des raisins servant à faire ces vins viennent de vignerons particuliers. Bien que le centre vinificateur soit à Enseñada, les vignobles de Santo Tomás se trouvent dans la vallée du même nom au sud de la ville et dans la région de Guadalupe au nord-est. On trouve deux autres centres modernes dans le secteur de Guadalupe : les Productos Vinicola, producteurs de vins « Terrasola » et un vaste complexe technique production-vinification conçu pour les vins de qualité, faisant partie de la division mexicaine de Pedro Domecq, énorme firme espagnole productrice de Xérès et de brandies, que la filiale mexicaine a dépassée en importance. Là et dans les vignobles de Luis Cetto, on cultive avec les méthodes les plus modernes, les cépages nobles européens fournissant les vins de Los Reyes, de Calafia, parmi les vins mexicains les plus réputés.

A Saltillo, à 200 km au sud-ouest de Larredo, Texas, se trouve le quartier général de Nazario Ortiz Garza, un des plus gros producteurs de vin et d'eau-de-vie du Mexique. A Saltillo, les 180 ha de vignobles ont du être réduits de moitié en raison des nouveaux besoins de la ville en pleine expansion. Le plus grand vignoble de Don Nazario se trouve dans l'État de Aguascalientes, à 300 km au nord-ouest de Mexico. Ses Viñedos San Marcos couvrent 3 200 ha de terres surplombant l'autoroute qui relie El Paso et le Texas à la capitale. D'autres entreprises sont les Bodegas de San Ygnacio, dont le propriétaire est Filemon Alonzo ; les Bodegas de Monte Casino, propriétaire Victor Manuel Castelazo ; les Productos de Uva Aguascalientes, appartenant à la famille Cetto ; et les Industrias de la Fermentación, dont le propriétaire est un certain David Alonzo.

A une cinquantaine de kilomètres à l'ouest de Saltillo se trouve Parras de la Fuente. C'est là qu'en 1593 les premières vignes espagnoles furent plantées à côté des cépages indigènes. La plus ancienne entreprise de vinification du Mexique, la Vinícola del Marqués de Aguayo, se consacre aujourd'hui à la production de bons vins de table mousseux et non mousseux. Il ne reste aucun vestige des anciennes installations de Francisco de Urdiñola si ce n'est un adobe dans un des nouveaux bureaux. Non loin du plus ancien vignoble du Mexique se trouvent les énormes Bodegas de San Lorenzo de Casa Madero, appartenant au cousin de l'ancien président Madero. Ce sont les deuxièmes vignobles en âge. Depuis l'acquisition des vignobles de Parras en 1870, les Madero ont constamment étendu leurs possessions. Vers la fin du XIXe siècle, Evaristo Madero Elonzindo ramena d'un voyage en Europe d'excellents cépages et du matériel de distillation. Ses vins remportèrent de nombreux prix lors des expositions internationales du début du siècle. Les Madero replantèrent leurs vignobles après les ravages causés par le phylloxéra et la révolution et, depuis 1962, Casa Madero est un des meilleurs centres du monde. Le climat de Parras est semblable à celui de Lodi, en Californie, mais à cause de son altitude (1 600 m) les vignes sont souvent menacées par de sévères gelées. D'autres maisons de Parras sont les Bodegas del Delfín, propriété de Aguirre Benavides ; les Bodegas del Rosario, propriété de Antonio Benavides et Elias T. Tejada ; les Bodegas de Perote, propriété de Arturo Perez de Yarto ; et les Bodegas del Vesubio appartenant à Nicolas Minonàs. Le premier vignoble d'État a été planté à Torreón, à l'ouest de Parras, afin de fournir aux viticulteurs des souches de bonnes variétés produites par le département œnologique de l'université de Californie de Davis. Dans le même secteur, mais en marge de Durango, à Gomez Palacio, se trouve la Vinicola del Vergel. Fondée en 1943, on y découvre aussi bien d'anciennes caves voûtées de marbre à l'européenne que des nouveaux réservoirs d'extérieur en acier inoxydable venus des États-Unis. Une grande partie des vignobles de Vergel est consacrée à la culture de raisins de table et de cépages inférieurs, mais depuis quelque temps on y cultive également d'assez bonnes variétés telles que l'Ugni Blanc, le Ruby Cabernet et le Colombard.

La région vinicole la plus méridionale du Mexique se trouve dans la vallée de Rio de San Juan, à 150 km au nord de Mexico. Avec une altitude de près de 2 000 m, cette vallée est de loin la région vinicole la plus haute du pays. Les Cavas de San Juan y cultivent du Cabernet Sauvignon, du Pinot Noir, du Gamay et du Pinot Gris, ainsi que des variétés inférieures ; on y fait des vins « Hidalgo ». A Tequisquiapan, au nord de San Juan del Rio, la maison française des Cognac Martell produit du vin de table et du brandy.

SPIRITUEUX

Tequila, *pulque* et *mescal (voir ces mots)* sont des spiritueux typiquement mexicains faits avec le jus de la plante séculaire. D'autres alcools sont fait avec la canne à sucre. Le Mexique produit également du *ron* (rhum), de l'anis et de l'eau-de-vie de vin. Celle-ci s'est imposée, au détriment de la tequila et du rhum, comme l'alcool distillé le plus populaire du Mexique. Son succès a une origine en partie sémantique. Le mot *coñac* est l'équivalent espagnol de l'eau-de-vie de vin vieillie mais après la Deuxième Guerre mondiale, le gouvernement mexicain limita l'utilisation du nom aux eaux-de-vie importées provenant de la seule région de Cognac. Les distillateurs mexicains adoptèrent alors l'appellation anglaise brandy quoique ce mot n'existe pas dans le vocabulaire espagnol. Le succès fut fulgurant et aujourd'hui près de 80 % des raisins cultivés sur le territoire du Mexique servent à la fabrication d'eau-de-vie de vin.

Michigan

État et région vinicole des États-Unis. Les principaux vignobles sont situés dans la partie sud de l'État. On y fait des vins doux et mousseux, malheureusement de qualité moyenne.

Voir ÉTATS-UNIS : ÉTATS DE L'EST

Midi

Vaste région vinicole de France qui s'étend à l'ouest du Rhône, jusqu'aux Pyrénées, englobe les départements de l'Aude, de l'Hérault, du Gard *(voir ces noms)* et une partie des Pyrénées-Orientales. C'est cette région qui fournit la plus grande partie des vins ordinaires français.

Mildiou

Maladie de la vigne, originaire d'Amérique.

Voir CHAPITRE IV

Millefiori

Liqueur italienne, couleur d'or clair, qui serait faite avec des extraits d'un millier de fleurs alpestres. En général, la bouteille contient une menue branchette autour de laquelle du sucre s'est cristallisé. Cette liqueur est fabriquée par Vigevanese.

Millerandage

Maladie de la vigne qui se manifeste par une grande différence entre les grains de raisin de la même grappe ou par leur insuffisance sur les grappes. Le millerandage est une séquelle de la coulure, due soit à une floraison insatisfaisante, soit à une mauvaise fécondation des fleurs.

Voir CHAPITRE IV

Millésime

Année de la vendange dont provient un vin. A travers le monde, cette date figure sur presque toutes les bouteilles de vin fin.

Voir TABLES DE MILLÉSIMES

Minervois (Appellation Contrôlée)

Vins rouges, rosés ou blancs. Région du Languedoc.

Le Minervois se trouve juste au nord de la région vinicole des Corbières, à 100 km au sud-est de Toulouse. Ses vignobles — situés dans les départements de l'Aude et de l'Hérault, au nord-est de Narbonne et au nord-ouest de Carcassonne, la célèbre ville médiévale — couvrent une superficie de 18 000 ha. Son sol rude et accidenté s'étend en une série d'immenses steppes veinées de schiste, de lignite et de gneiss. La plupart des vignobles se trouvent sur un sol alluvial riche en minéraux. Extrêmement caillouteux il favorise la captation des eaux. Le nom Minervois vient de Minerve, une des places fortes érigées au temps où le Midi de la France était sous l'égide des Romains. Le Minervois et Les Corbières étaient connus des Romains : la 10ᵉ Légion, ayant installé ses campements dans la ville de Narbonne et ses alentours, fit une grande consommation de vins locaux et les introduisit en Italie. C'était un vin fort apprécié, semble-t-il, de Pline le Jeune et de Cicéron. Certains affirment que les vins trouvés dans les épaves d'anciens navires échoués en Méditerranée occidentale seraient des Minervois et des Corbières.

Seule une trentaine de kilomètres sépare les vignobles de la côte, qui est récemment devenue un haut lieu de villégiature. Mais le centre de vinification se trouve à l'intérieur des terres, dans la petite ville d'Olonzac. On y fait du Minervois rouge avec une majorité de Carignan, du Lladoner Pelut Noir, du Syrah Noir, du Mourvèdre, du Grenache Noir et aussi du Cinsault. C'est un vin fort et plein qui gagne à vieillir quelques années en bouteille. La production annuelle s'élève à environ 300 000 hl (plus de 3 millions de caisses). La quasi-totalité est produite par plus de 40 coopératives car c'est un vin trop courant et bon marché pour assurer la subsistance des petits producteurs indépendants.

La production de Minervois blanc est tout-à-fait minime (près de 6 000 hl, soit environ 65 000 caisses).

Voir LANGUEDOC

Mirabelle de Lorraine

Eau-de-vie obtenue par la distillation de la mirabelle, en Lorraine et en Alsace. Mais seule celle des prunes des régions de Nancy et de Metz a légalement droit à l'appellation réglementé Mirabelle de Lorraine.

L'alcool fait avec les mirabelles du secteur de Metz est le meilleur. La Mirabelle Fine du Val de Metz est une bonne étiquette à rechercher.

Les mirabelles (Mirabelle de Nancy et Mirabelle de Metz exclusivement, pour l'appellation réglementée) sont cueillies par temps sec. On les fait fermenter pendant au moins 15 jours avec des levures spécialement choisies puis on les conserve en fût pendant quelques mois avant de procéder à deux distillations successives, comme pour le Cognac. Ensuite, l'eau-de-vie est conservée en fût.

Voir ALSACE

Mise en bouteille au château

Cette mention (mise ou mis en bouteille) sur une étiquette indique que le vin a été mis en bouteille par le propriétaire de la vigne dont il provient et garantit son authenticité. Cette formule est celle du Bordelais.

Voir MISE EN BOUTEILLE AU DOMAINE

Mise en bouteille au domaine

Pratique d'importance fondamentale selon laquelle le propriétaire d'un vignoble met individuellement le pur produit de ses vignes en bouteille. Imprimé sur l'étiquette, ce terme devrait toujours être une garantie d'authenticité d'un vin et, dans une certaine mesure, de qualité supérieure. L'étiquette doit spécifier que le vin a été mis en bouteille au domaine qu'il provient indiscutablement du propriétaire du vignoble, et indiquer clairement qu'il a été mis en bouteille par la personne qui le produit (ou du moins dans sa propriété). En France, la mise en bouteille au domaine, est virtuellement la même chose que la mise en bouteille au château. On l'appelle le plus souvent : *Mise du domaine, Mise au domaine, Mis en bouteille au Domaine, Mise du Propriétaire, Mis en Bouteille par le Propriétaire, ou Mise à la Propriété.* En Allemagne, le terme correspondant était *Original-Abfüllung,* mais il a été remplacé par *Auseigenem Lesegut ou Erzeugerabfüllung.*

Mise en bouteille à la propriété

Même signification et même garantie que « mise en bouteille au château » ou « au domaine ».

Mission-Haut-Brion (Château-La)

Bordeaux rouge. Commune de Talence, en Graves.

Le château est bâti derrière des rangs symétriques de vignes, juste en face de Haut-Brion, au bord de la route Bordeaux-Arcachon. Les vignes à vin rouge entourent le château ; elles bordent la voie de chemin de fer de Bordeaux à Irun passant dans une tranchée à une centaine de pas des chais. Le vin rouge fut classé parmi les onze meilleurs Graves en 1953 et 1959.

Ce vignoble fut fondé au XVIIIe siècle par les frères de la mission Saint-Vincent-de-Paul. Une perle de l'art monastique rappelle les fondateurs : petite chapelle pointue sur le plafond de laquelle on écrivit autrefois, en lettres d'or, les grands millésimes. Pendant la Première Guerre mondiale, on donna cet or à la Banque de France.

Quand les raisins arrivent de la vigne, on les précipite d'abord dans une cuve de bois datant du XVIe siècle. Le moût fermente ensuite dans les cuves. La famille Dewavrin-Woltner, qui était propriétaire de La Mission-Haut-Brion, de La Tour-Haut-Brion et de Laville-Haut-Brion (blanc), vendait le vin de la mission à un prix élevé, justifié car son vignoble produit de remarquables bouteilles. Ces trois propriétés furent achetées en 1983 par le Château Haut-Brion.

Caractéristiques : Un superbe rouge. Bien des courtiers avisés lui attribuent le même caractère qu'au Château Haut-Brion qui se trouve de l'autre côté de la route ; il affine cependant plus vite. Il atteint une belle rondeur charnue avec une race remarquable.

Superficie : 17 ha.

Production moyenne : 70 tonneaux (6 000 caisses).

Mistelle

Boisson obtenu en ajoutant de l'alcool au jus de raisin avant qu'il ne fermente. La présence de cet alcool interdit la fermentation et tout le sucre naturel reste dans le moût. Ce produit sert surtout à faire des vermouths et autres apéritifs. Autrefois, l'Algérie produisait et expédiait chaque année d'énormes quantités de mistelle.

Mittelhaardt

Le meilleur secteur vinicole du Palatinat *(voir ce nom).*

Mittelrhein

États allemands du Palatinat et de nord-Westphalie. Superficie : environ 800 ha. 98 % de vins blancs, 2 % de vins rouges.

Situation : Avec ses rivages rocailleux, ses vieux châteaux et son immortelle légende de la Loreleï, cette partie du Rhin descendant de Bingen jusqu'à Coblence et au-delà est un parcours passionnant à effectuer en bateau à vapeur.

Le Mittelrhein (Rhin moyen) est l'une des plus petites régions vinicoles d'Allemagne. Elle est située dans une zone très pittoresque qui s'étend du nord de Bingen et pratiquement jusqu'à Bonn, soit 100 km environ de part et d'autre du Rhin. Bacharach, charmant village médiéval, est un centre vinicole important aux nombreux bons producteurs. Koblenz est le centre commercial moderne pour le négoce du vin. Citons aussi quelques villages : Boppard, Braubach, Oberwesel et Steeg. La région se divise en 3 districts : Bereich Bacharach, Bereich Rheinburgengau qui regroupe aussi un petit nombre de vignobles dans la vallée de la rivière Lahn et Bereich Siebengebirge près de Bonn.

Variétés de raisin : Riesling (74 %), Müller Thurgau (11 %), Kerner (6 %).

Vin : Aciéreux, terreux à l'acidité austère. Dans les mauvaises années, il convient mieux à la fabrication du Sekt *(voir ce nom).* Les vignes ne poussent pas seulement sur les coteaux du Rhin, mais aussi sur les vallonnements des montagnes environnantes, où les conditions sont particulièrement défavorables à la viticulture. Les vents froids qui descendent du massif Hunsrück rencontrent l'air chaud du Rhin et provoquent des gelées soudaines à la fin du printemps et en début d'automne. D'autre part, la partie du Mittelrhein située sous Saint-Goarshausen est une des rares régions vinicoles du monde où le phylloxéra n'ait pas encore fait de ravages. Les conditions de culture sur les falaises d'ardoise argileuse (graywacke) sont améliorées par le microclimat hérité du Rhin. Les meilleures années sont celles où il pleut suffisamment pour humidifier le sol poreux. On n'y fait aucun grand vin et on en trouvera très peu à l'étranger. 500 des 1 000 viticulteurs de la région fabriquent leur propre vin. Il est consommé sur place par les touristes lorsqu'ils viennent visiter les magnifiques ruines des châteaux et le Loreleï. Le reste est vendu en vrac aux producteurs de Sekt.

Voir APPENDICE B

Moelleux

Qualité d'un vin doux et fruité. On l'applique généralement aux blancs, surtout aux Sauternes. Ce terme peut parfois décrire des vins qui ne sont pas nécessairement doux.

Molise

Située sur la côte Adriatique, cette petite province vinicole italienne ne produit que des vins sans importance.

Monbazillac (Appellation Contrôlée)

Vin blanc et doux de dessert, fait dans la région de Bergerac *(voir ce nom).*

Monica di Sardegna (D.O.C.)

Vin de liqueur fait en Sardaigne *(voir ce nom).*

Monimpex

Office national d'exportation des vins et spiritueux hongrois.

Monopole

Cette mention, qu'on trouve fréquemment sur les étiquettes de vin, indique qu'il est produit exclusivement par un viniculteur ou qu'un certain négociant s'est assuré l'exclusivité de sa vente. Il peut s'agir aussi de vins de coupages de la même appellation contrôlée. Dans ce cas le millésime est rarement indiqué.

Les négociants qui mettent en vente ces « Monopole » s'efforcent d'entretenir une qualité constante d'année en année en sacrifiant les millésimes de pointe de façon à obtenir un produit moyen.

Montagne-Saint-Émilion (A.O.C)

Grande commune dans laquelle se trouvent quelques respectables propriétés de Saint-Émilion.

Voir PARSAC-SAINT-ÉMILION ; SAINT-ÉMILION

Montagny

Commune du Chalonnais, en Bourgogne, qui a droit à sa propre Appellation d'Origine Contrôlée.

Voir CHALONNAIS

Montagu

Subdivision de la région de Little Karoo, en Afrique du Sud *(voir ce nom).*

Montefiascone (D.O.C.)

Vin blanc provenant des coteaux s'élevant au flanc des monts Volsini, en Italie. C'est à son sujet qu'on raconte l'histoire d'Est ! Est !! Est !!!

Voir LATIUM

Montepulciano (D.O.C.G.)

Connu sous le nom de Vino Nobile di Montepulciano, ce vin rouge léger provient de vignes plantées en terrain argileux entre 300 et 600 mètres d'altitude.

Montepulciano di Abruzzo (D.O.C.)

Vin rouge léger d'Italie.

Voir ABRUZZES

Monthélie et Monthélie-Côte de Beaune (A.O.C.)

Bourgogne rouge et blanc. Côte de Beaune.

Monthélie est le frère bâtard de Volnay. C'est une des communes vinicoles les plus pittoresques de Bourgogne, avec ses rues en pente, ses petites maisons d'âge vénérable. Les vins rouges peuvent être de qualité comparable à ceux de Volnay lorsqu'ils proviennent du terroir contigu aux Caillerets, comme aux Champs Fulliot, ou proches du Clos des Chênes et des Santenots comme le Cas Rougeot, la Taupine, le Clos Gautey. Ce sont là les meilleurs des Premiers Crus de Monthélie.

Monthélie produit essentiellement des vins rouges et des vins blancs (à partir de Chardonnay et de Pinot Blanc), dont certains sont mousseux. On y cultive le Pinot comme partout en Côte-d'Or, sur un sol si pauvre que, selon les Bourguignons, « une poule mourrait de faim à Monthélie pendant les vendanges ». Les vestiges d'un cimetière gaulois témoignent de l'ancienneté de cette commune. Un peu plus d'une centaine d'hectares y sont plantés de vignes. Elles produisent en moyenne près de 3 000 hl (plus de 30 000 caisses) de vin par an, la quasi-totalité étant du vin rouge. Ces vins peuvent être vendus à volonté sous l'appellation Monthélie ou comme Monthélie-Côte de Beaune-Villages. Un calcul assez exact suggère que le Monthélie devrait coûter les 3/4 du prix du Volnay de la même année. Les meilleurs vignobles ont le titre de Premiers Crus et peuvent ajouter leur nom à celui de la commune sur l'étiquette, en voici la liste :

PREMIERS CRUS

	Superficie (ha)
Sur la Velle	6,03
Les Vignes Rondes	2,71
Le Meix Bataille	2,28
Les Riottes	0,74
La Taupine	1,50
Le Clos-Gauthey	1,80
Le Château-Gaillard	0,49
Les Champs-Fulliot	8,11
Le Cas-Rougeot	0,57
Duresse	6,72
Le Village (Monthélie)	0,22

Montilla-Moriles

Apéritif et vins de table. Sud de l'Espagne.

Proches parents du Xérès, les vins de Montilla-Moriles (plus connus sous le nom de Montilla) n'en n'ont pas moins des caractéristiques et un climat bien particuliers ; ils ont en outre leur propre *Denominación de Origen*. Ils sont cultivés dans la province de Cordoue, sur une immense surface clairsemée de tournesols, d'oliviers et d'amandiers au sud de la vieille ville de Cordoue dont le nord s'étend en une vaste plaine, mais c'est dans le sud de la province que se trouve la partie la plus prospère de la région. Dans ce décor de coteaux et de plateaux qui se dressent au-dessus des oliveraies et des terres ocres de l'Andalousie méridionale, on fait une grande quantité de bons vins ordinaires *(vinos corrientes) ;* le sol calcaire *(Albariza)* des coteaux de la Sierra de Montilla et de Montilla Alto donnent de grands vins de *solera*. Ce sont ces mêmes sols qui, autour de Jerez, donnent le Xérès. Les Finos de Montilla sont des vins d'une belle couleur légèrement dorée, légèrement acerbes ; les Amontillados sont des vins moelleux au léger parfum de pomme ; les Olorosos sont des vins naturels profonds, au goût de noisette, eux aussi très secs. Il y a également un vin sombre et extrêmement doux, mis en bouteille sous de nombreux noms différents, qui peut être comparé à un Cream Sherry mais en plus sucré.

La province de Córdoba — qui, dans sa longue histoire fut occupée et conquise par les Phéniciens, les Romains, les Maures puis les rois d'Espagne — est la région la plus torride d'Espagne. Le climat est de type continental avec, dans les Sierras, des hivers doux et des étés ardents. Les vignes sont taillées bas et profondément enracinées dans le sol blanc et ridé ; on les paille soigneusement afin qu'elles retiennent les pluies hivernales qui nourriront les racines pendant les chaleurs de l'été. La variété la plus plantée est le Pedro Ximénez (on trouve également environ 20 % de Lairen, Baladi et Moscatel) ou P.X., comme on l'appelle à Jerez, qui ne produit ici que des vins doux ; mais à Montilla-Moriles, où les raisins mûrissent rapidement et sont vendangés tôt, ils sont si riches en sucre qu'ils sont immédiatement fermentés, ce qui donne un vin fort et extrêmement sec. Les Finos titrent entre 14,5 % et 15,5 % d'alcool et les Olorosos entre 18 % et 20 % ; il n'est donc pas besoin de les viner si l'Oloroso dépasse ses 15 % naturels. Le vin doux P.X. produit dans la région est le seul vin dont la fermentation soit interrompue alors que la teneur en sucre du moût est encore élevée.

Les villes et villages jouant un rôle important dans la production de Montilla sont Montilla, Moriles, Aguilar de la Frontera, Baena, Fernan Nuñez, Lucena, Cabra, Doña Mencia et Puente Genil. La méthode de vinification, à quelques différences près, est fort semblable à celle employée à Jerez : à l'exception du P.X., les raisins ne sont pas séchés au soleil avant le pressurage, leur longue fermentation ne se fait pas dans des fûts, mais dans des *tinajas :* ce sont des jarres semblables à celles de Valdepeñas, mais plus grandes et faites en béton ou parfois en inox plutôt qu'en terre glaise. Dans ces jarres le jeune vin est affiné à l'aide de blanc d'œuf et de bentonite *(voir ce mot)*. On l'en extrait lorsqu'il est clair et bien filtré ; il commencera alors sa lente maturation dans les fûts de chêne des grandes et hautes *bodegas.* A ce stade, on pourra juger si le Montilla est un futur Oloroso ou — s'il se développe à sa surface la substance écumeuse appelée *flor* — un futur Fino. La *flor* se forme au printemps, réduit en été et en hiver pour réapparaître au moment des vendanges. Au bout d'un an, 1/3 du jeune vin est vendu aux débits de boisson pour la consommation locale. La meilleure partie de la production poursuivra son vieillissement en fût *(criadera)* dans les *bodegas.* Au bout de cinq ans, ils pourront être admis à la *solera* (*voir* XÉRÈS). Certaines *soleras* possèdent des fûts vieux de plusieurs siècles ; selon le système propre à la *solera,* une petite quantité du précieux liquide est versée dans le fût voisin, qui à son tour donnera un peu de contenu à son voisin, et ainsi de suite. Ces vins ont une longue histoire : des amphores de Munda (nom romain de Montilla) ont été découvertes en Italie ; il reçurent des louanges de Columella dans son œuvre *Re Rustica.*

Avant la mise en vigueur de la sévère législation des appellations d'origine (*Denominación de Origen*), une grande partie du vin de Montilla était expédiée à Jerez et réapparaissait ensuite sous le nom de Xérès. Il est possible que ce manège n'ait pas encore tout à fait cessé, mais les vins de Montilla sont maintenant appréciés pour eux-mêmes, surtout localement ; les Finos et les Amontillados sont servis comme apéritif avec des crevettes et de savoureuses *tapas ;* ils peuvent même accompagner le premier plat d'un repas. Les Amontillados sont de vieux Finos qui prennent une belle couleur d'ambre avec l'âge. L'emploi du terme Amantillados à Jerez a parfois été discuté : ce serait, d'après certains, une utilisation abusive du nom de Montilla ; de fait, l'appellation Amantillados désigne un type de vins de cette région, dont les meilleurs sont probablement faits à Jerez.

A quelques kilomètres de Montilla, le village de Doña Mencia produit un bon vin. A Rute, un autre village plus étendu, on fait du Montilla ainsi qu'une quantité considérable d'*aguardientes* et *anisados.* Les Montilla sont des vins assez courants en Angleterre, particulièrement ceux des grandes *bodegas* Alvear, Vinsur, Carbonell et Montulia.

D'après des chiffres récents, l'appellation contrôlée Montilla-Moriles s'étend sur 16 000 ha de vignobles, qui produisent 1 million d'hl (11 millions de caisses) de vin par an. Les entreprises d'exportation sont : Alvear, S.A. (Montilla) ; Aragon y Cia, S.A. (Lucena) ; Carbonell y Cia, S.A. (Cordoue) ; Espejo, S.A. (Montilla) ; Cia Vinicola del Sur, S.A. (Montilla) ; Crismona, S.A. (Doña Mencia) ; Montisol, S.A. (Montilla) ; Montulia, S.A. (Montilla) ; Moreno, S.A. Luis Ortiz Ruiz (Montilla) ; Perez Barquero, S.A. (Montilla) ; Miguel Velasco Chacon (Montilla) ; Conde de la Cortina (Montilla).

Montilla Sierra

Vin semblable aux Xérès Fino. Un des deux meilleurs Montilla.

Voir MONTILLA

Montlouis (Appellation Contrôlée)

Vin blanc mousseux et non mousseux. Touraine, vallée de la Loire.

C'est le jeune frère du Vouvray. On le fait dans un secteur situé de l'autre côté de la Loire, juste en face de celui du Vouvray. Les deux vins se ressemblent tellement que parfois, même les experts ne peuvent les distinguer l'un de l'autre. Mais si le meilleur Montlouis peut souvent être classé dans la même catégorie que le bon Vouvray, le Montlouis ordinaire ne saurait lui être comparé. Or, la plus grande partie des quelque 9 000 hl (100 000 caisses) de vin produit à Montlouis n'atteint pas les normes du Vouvray.

Tout le Montlouis est blanc, fait avec du Chenin Blanc, cultivé à Montlouis, Lussault et Saint-Martin-le-Beau. Il se situe dans la gamme des blancs qui ne sont jamais tout à fait doux ni vraiment secs. Une partie est traitée en mousseux, mais le non mousseux et le pétillant sont meilleurs et plus typés. Pour avoir droit à l'appellation, le non mousseux doit titrer 10,5° et le mousseux 9°.

Montpeyroux

Voir LANGUEDOC

Montrachet (Appellation Contrôlée)

Bourgogne blanc. Commune de Puligny-Montrachet et de Chassagne-Montrachet, en Côte de Beaune. Classement officiel : Grand Cru.

Peu connu jusqu'au XVIIe siècle, ce vin commença à se faire une réputation entre le milieu et la fin du XVIIIe. Désormais bien des connaisseurs le considèrent comme le plus grand vin blanc du monde. « Divin », « magnifique », « formidable », « à boire à genoux, chapeau bas », « somptueux avec un brio martial ». On a dit tout ça et bien d'autres choses au sujet du Montrachet. Quoi qu'il en soit, le Montrachet est un vin d'une race et d'une élégance exceptionnelles. Tout à fait sec, il a la profondeur et un bouquet séduisant. Le vignoble s'étend à mi-côte, partie sur la commune de Puligny-Montrachet, partie sur celle de Chassagne-Montrachet. Hormis les vignes on ne voit que des taches de sous-sol calcaire maigre qui affleurent et de-ci, de-là, des herbes folles, par opposition aux broussailles qui couronnent en général les collines des autres parties de la Côte-d'Or. Tout autour des vignes de Montrachet se trouvent d'autres crus fameux tels que Chevalier-Montrachet, Bâtard-Montrachet et Les Caillerets qui s'appelaient jadis Les Demoiselles. Tous donnent des vins exceptionnels qui sont considérés comme les plus grands vins blancs secs du monde.

Les vignes de Montrachet ne s'étendent que sur 7,99 ha et ne produisent même pas 300 hl (plus de 3 000 caisses) par an. Ce vin magnifique est donc rare. Autrefois les acheteurs réservaient la récolte des années à l'avance, et les prix étaient si élevés qu'ils ne signifiaient presque plus rien. Une bouteille de Montrachet authentique est encore une rareté et elle le restera toujours.

En 1962, le gouvernement français paya 600 millions d'anciens francs pour sauver les quelques arpents de Montrachet en déviant le projet d'autoroute Paris-Lyon qui sans cela serait passé par Puligny et aurait coupé le vignoble.

On sait peu de chose au sujet des débuts de la vigne à Montrachet et des vignerons qui les premiers y firent du vin blanc, puis le perfectionnèrent ensuite. Pendant de nombreuses années, la plus grande partie du vignoble appartint au marquis de Laguiche et les héritiers actuels en possèdent encore un quart qui leur donne 8 pièces environ par an (quelque 1 800 l). La famille de feu le baron Thénard en possède aussi une part, moins grande que celle de Laguiche. Quoiqu'ils possèdent d'autres biens, dans le vignoble et dans d'autres secteurs, les Thénard déclarent que leur part de Montrachet est leur plus grande fierté.

Selon les millésimes, on préférera la production de Puligny-Montrachet [dont la superficie représente à peine plus de la moitié (4,01 ha) des vignes de Montrachet] à celle de Chassagne-Montrachet, ou inversement. Toujours est-il que leur réputation peut varier en raison d'une combinaison subtile d'impondérables qui font des vins ce qu'ils sont.

De nos jours quelques vins bien faits, provenant des vignes avoisinant Montrachet, rivalisent parfois avec ce souverain.

Voir CHASSAGNE-MONTRACHET ; PULIGNY-MONTRACHET

Montravel (Appellation Contrôlée)

Vin sec et demi-doux de Bergerac.

Voir BERGERAC

Montrose (Château-)

Bordeaux rouge. Haut-Médoc. Commune de Saint-Estèphe.

Tapi dans les vignes, loin de la grand-route, le château Montrose est une agréable villa, avec une annexe extraordinaire dont les balcons rappellent un chalet suisse. Le domaine s'étend jusqu'au fleuve dont il est séparé par des rangées de petites maisons numérotées où habitent les ouvriers. Trait curieux, ces alignements ont des noms de rues qui rappellent la nostalgie d'un ancien propriétaire alsacien : rue d'Alsace, rue de Mulhouse, etc. Le vignoble, classé Second Cru en 1855, est divisé en carrés séparés par des allées. Il appartient à M. Charmolue qui dirige l'exploitation.

Caractéristiques : Corsé, vieillissant lentement pour atteindre la grandeur et la plénitude qui caractérisent tant de Saint-Estèphe. Pourtant on le comparait parfois au Château-Latour de la commune voisine, Pauillac. Un charnu profond avec parfois des tannins agressifs donnaient à Montrose sa caractéristique distincte. La qualité était constante d'année en année. Depuis les années quatre-vingt, un changement de vinification a contribué à donner des vins plus souples et moins taniques.

Superficie : 79 ha.

Production moyenne : 320 tonneaux (30 000 caisses).

Morey-Saint-Denis (Appellation Contrôlée)

Bourgogne rouge et blanc. Côte de Nuits.

Les vins de Morey-Saint-Denis sont plus divers que ceux de la plupart des communes de la Côte-d'Or. Certains reflètent la situation des vignobles, à mi-chemin entre l'austère majesté de Gevrey-Chambertin et l'élégance délicate de Chambolle-Musigny. D'autres, excellents en virilité opiniâtre sont considérés comme les plus corsés de la côte mais ne sont pas aussi connus que le Gevrey-Chambertin, au nord, et que le Chambolle-Musigny, au sud.

Autrefois, on ne vendait presque pas de vin sous le nom de Morey bien qu'on en produisît une grande quantité. La production de la commune était généralement mélangée à celle des voisines et vendue tout simplement comme Gevrey-Chambertin ou comme Chambolle-Musigny. Il en résulte que, dans le passé, Morey n'était pas reconnu à sa juste valeur. Même aujourd'hui, un nombre insuffisant d'amateurs connait cette appellation et ce vin. Il est moins demandé et donc moins imité.

L'agglomération elle-même ne présente guère d'attraits et les rares visiteurs ne voient qu'une place triste au-delà de laquelle sinue la route des vignobles. Près de cette place, entourée de hauts murs, se trouve le Clos des Lambrays (un des crus les plus remarquables de Morey) et, à côté de ce dernier, le Clos de Tart. Les autres grands crus sont dans les environs.

On a classé les meilleurs vignobles de Bourgogne en 1860, puis on a fait une définition des appellations en 1936. Le classement des cuvées de 1860 ne correspond pas forcément aux appellations actuelles. Selon le premier classement, les meilleurs vins de Morey étaient ceux du Clos de Tart, du Clos des Lambrays et des Bonnes Mares (quoique ce dernier soit le territoire de Chambolle-Musigny pour sa plus grande part et n'en ait qu'une toute petite à Morey). Selon la définition des appellations, les meilleurs vins étaient ceux de Clos de Tart, Clos de la Roche, Clos Saint-Denis et Bonnes Mares qui devinrent donc des Appellations Contrôlées *(voir chacun de ces noms à sa place dans l'ordre alphabétique).*

Le Clos des Lambrays ne figurait plus parmi les meilleurs et on ne lui accorda qu'un statut légèrement moindre. Bien des connaisseurs estimèrent que c'était une erreur car ses vins étaient toujours faits de manière impeccable et par bonnes années ils valaient les meilleurs du coteau. Cependant, au moment où l'on définit les appellations, la propriétaire du Clos des Lambrays, M. Cosson, ne défendait pas son bien aussi énergiquement que ses voisins et le prestige de son cru en souffrit.

Depuis la fin des années 1940, l'auteur a aidé la fervente Madame Cosson a faire connaître le Clos des Lambrays. L'erreur de 1936 fût finalement rattrapée : en 1982, le Clos des Lambrays eut droit à sa propre Appellation Contrôlée.

Lambrays et Tart sont les vins les plus robustes de la commune, suivis en général par Clos de la Roche. Souvent Bonnes Mares incline vers la délicatesse de Chambolle tout en conservant une ferme vigueur et un allant estimables. Clos Saint-Denis est le plus léger et le plus fragile.

Outre ces Grands Crus, d'autres vins sont vendus chaque année sous l'appellation Morey-Saint-Denis, suivie ou non par leur propre nom. Ce sont les Premiers Crus de la commune, choisis pour la qualité supérieure de leurs vins. Ils sont habituellement excellents sans avoir la magnificence des Grands Crus qui ne portent que leur nom sur l'étiquette.

Hormis la superficie des cinq Grands Crus, on compte près de 100 ha plantés de vignes dans la commune de Morey et leur production s'élève à quelque 3 000 hl (plus de 30 000 caisses) de rouge.

En année normale, Morey ne produit guère plus de 50 hl (plus de 550 caisses) de blanc.

GRANDS CRUS	*Superficie (ha)*
Bonnes Mares (en partie) *(voir aussi à Chambolle-Musigny)*	1,51
Clos de la Roche	16,80
Clos Saint-Denis	6,6
Clos de Tart	7,5
Clos des Lambrays	8,8
PREMIERS CRUS	
Les Rochots	2,58
Les Sorbets	2,68
Clos Sorbet	3,32
Les Millandes	4,21
Le Clos des Ormes (en partie)	3,15
Monts-Luisants	5,36
Clos Bussière	2,59
Aux Charmes	1,17
Les Charrières	2,27
Côte-Rôtie	1,32
Les Genevrières	1,19
Les Chaffots	2,62
Les Chénevery (en partie)	1,90
Aux Cheseaux	1,49
La Riotte	2,47
Clos Baulet	0,87
Les Gruenchers	0,50
Les Faconnières	1,66
Les Blanchards	1,99

Morgon

Le plus corsé des bons vins que sont le crus de Beaujolais. Parfois, il est même tellement chaleureux qu'il ressemble au Bourgogne situé à quelques kilomètres plus au nord.

Voir BEAUJOLAIS

Móri Ezerjó

Vin fait dans le village de Mór, avec du raisin Ezerjó et dont le nom s'écrit parfois Moriezerjó.

Voir HONGRIE

Moriles

Secteur de la zone où l'on fait le Montilla, pas loin de Cordoue, au sud de l'Espagne. Le vin qu'on y produit est un Fino sec.

Voir MONTILLA

Mort noire

Nom populaire de l'aquavit en Islande et boisson nationale de ce pays. Cette eau-de-vie est parfumée aux graines de carvi.

Voir AQUAVIT

Mocastel de Setúbal

Vin de liqueur fait dans les environs de Lisbonne.

Moscato

Nom italien du raisin Muscat.

Moselblümchen

« Petite Fleur de la Moselle ». Vin léger, de consommation quotidienne, à boire lorsque l'on a soif. C'est un vin de Moselle très ordinaire équivalent, en terme de qualité, au Schwarze Katz de Traben-Trarbach.

Moselle (Mosel-Saar-Ruwer)

États allemands du Palatinat et de la Sarre. Superficie : 12 800 ha environ. 100 % de vins blancs.

Situation : Les vignobles sont plantés le long des vallées de la Moselle et de ses deux affluents les plus importants, la Sarre et la Ruwer. La région se divise en cinq districts (Bereiche) : le district de Zell/Untermosel s'étend du confluent de la Moselle et du Rhin jusqu'à Coblence et au village de Zell. Il est célèbre pour ses « chats noirs » (Schwarze Katz) vignobles produisant des vins assez ordinaires. En amont, de Briedel à Kenn, se situe le district de Bernkastel, connu aussi sous le nom de Mittelmosel (moyenne Moselle), qui regroupe les plus fameux villages viticoles d'Allemagne : Erdig, Urzig, Zeltingen, Wehlen, Graach, Bernkastel, Brauneberg et Piesport. Le district de la Sarre et la Ruwer comprend les vignobles des deux vallées ainsi que ceux situés autour de l'ancienne cité romaine de Trèves. Du sud de Trèves à la frontière luxembourgeoise s'étendent les districts d'Obermosel et Moseltor. Ce dernier signifie littéralement « Seuil de la Moselle ».

Variétés cultivées : Riesling (54 %), Müller-Thurgau (23 %), Elbling (9 %), Kerner (6 %). Depuis 1986, mais avec une permission spéciale, quelques viticulteurs ont eu l'autorisation de planter des variétés rouges.

Vin : très parfumés, racés, piquants, élégants, fruités et délicats.

La moselle : 2 000 ans de viticulture

Le secret des vins de la Moselle peut s'expliquer en deux mots : ardoise et Riesling. Comme les syllabes d'une formule magique, leur mariage engendre des produits variés, de telle sorte que chaque vin diffère de son proche voisin mais qu'ils ont tous la qualité délicate et légère d'un bouquet incomparable qui proclame l'appellation Moselle et ne sauraient être imités.

Aux temps préhistoriques, la mer Dévonienne couvrait toute la zone à travers laquelle, de nos jours, coule la Moselle depuis les Vosges, en France, jusqu'à son confluent avec le Rhin, en Allemagne. Quand cette mer disparut, sa faune et sa flore se fossilisèrent en une sorte d'ardoise que les Allemands appellent *schiefer.*

Serrée entre deux murs de cette ardoise, la Moselle creuse son lit de plus en plus profondément. On ne sait pas s'il existait des vignes sur ses rives avant l'arrivée des Romains, mais en ce temps-là, le cañon de la Moselle était déjà assez profond pour ne plus être soumis à l'action du vent. Cette rivière, en outre, décrit d'innombrables boucles qui contribuent aussi à mettre ses berges à l'abri du vent. Large et encaissée

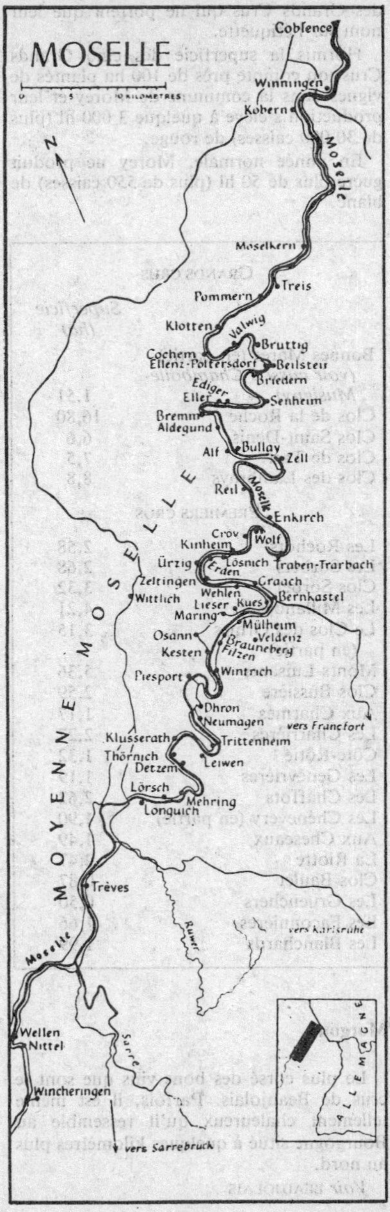

dans une vallée étroite, elle tempère l'atmosphère et reflète les rayons du soleil. L'ardoise elle-même a lentement cédé à l'érosion par l'eau et les rives sont désormais à la fois usées et abruptes. Là où les vignes sont enracinées, le cours d'eau met en réserve humidité et chaleur et les réfléchit vers ses berges.

Voilà encore un des secrets de la Moselle. Il explique encore pourquoi on n'a pas cessé de faire du vin depuis 2 000 ans dans cette région vinicole la plus septentrionale du monde : la Moselle est située sur le même parallèle que Terre-Neuve. Mais le gel n'atteint pas la vallée avant la fin de novembre, mois où, dans les bonnes années et sur les coteaux les meilleurs (abruptes), les Riesling tardifs sont encore vendangés.

Les gens qui s'échinent opiniâtrement dans leurs vignobles aux déclivités vertigineuses relèvent de diverses ascendances et aujourd'hui encore on distingue des Celtes et des Romains de type pur qui pourraient figurer sur d'anciennes pièces de monnaie.

Dans leur isolement, ils sont restés prudents, pieux, laborieux, voués depuis des siècles à une tâche éreintante : cultiver la vigne sur des aires d'aigle et en ramener les fruits par des sentiers presque verticaux.

Les vignerons de la Moselle expliquent aisément qu'aucune machine, aucun animal ne peut travailler sur leurs falaises. Cette tâche est réservée à l'homme seul qui doit tout monter et descendre sur son dos. Néanmoins la mécanisation se développe d'année en année : terre, engrais, bidons d'insecticide et même socs de charrue peuvent être hissés grâce à des câbles qui s'enroulent sur des tambours de treuils. Souvent les ouvriers eux-mêmes vont au travail et en reviennent dans des wagonnets semblables à ceux des téléphériques.

L'ardoise, telle est la moitié du secret de la Moselle. Le nom des crus se termine souvent par « lay » ou « ley », indiquant simplement que le sol est schisteux. Le meilleur secteur s'étend des environs de Trèves jusqu'à un peu au dessous de Zell. C'est celui de la Moselle moyenne. La qualité de ses vins est due au fait que l'ardoise se désagrège à une cadence qui maintient toujours une couche suffisante de sol cultivable. Il ne s'épuise donc pas et reste vierge. En aval de Zell, sol et microclimat changent : les vins sont plus légers. Dans la haute Moselle, au contraire, le sol n'est pas schisteux mais calcaire et donne de moins bons vins. A lui seul cet élément prouverait que la race des vins de la Moselle leur est conférée par l'union de Riesling et de l'ardoise, car la variété du raisin est l'autre moitié du secret.

On n'a pas toujours cultivé du Riesling sur la Moselle. Les Romains y implantèrent la *Vitis elvenea,* vigne ressemblant à l'Elbling, ancienne variété, elle aussi plantée par les Romains, qui est toujours cultivée dans l'Obermosel. Elle produit des vins blancs, légers et neutres, qui, en raison de leur grande acidité, sont souvent utilisés pour fabriquer des mousseux. Aux XVe et XVIe siècles on cultiva en Moselle des raisins blancs de Bourgogne. Le Riesling ne commença à y apparaître qu'au XVIIe siècle, mais il lui fallut longtemps pour conquérir le terrain puisqu'en 1787 seulement le prince évêque Clément Vinceslas de Trèves rendit sa culture obligatoire.

Le Riesling n'explique quand même pas tout et en particulier les diversités de qualité entre chaque parcelle puisque, sauf dans la haute Moselle, le Riesling est la grande variété de raisin de cette région. Quatrième zone viticole d'Allemagne (après le Rheinhessen, le Palatinat et Bade), la Moselle en est le plus grand vignoble. Un quart de la région environ, et plus principalement les sites plats, sont plantés de Müller-Thurgau (croisement de Riesling et de Silvaner). On y cultive aussi le Kerner, raisin semblable au Riesling, et l'ancienne variété Elbling ; mais c'est le Riesling noble qui est le mieux adapté aux pentes des coteaux d'ardoise, secs et pierreux.

La variété infinie des vins qui rend la consommation du Moselle tellement exquise est due à l'exposition au soleil et au côté de la rivière sur lequel est plantée la vigne. Étant donné que la nature de l'ardoise a dicté à la rivière la manière de creuser son lit, on en revient encore une fois à la cause première : le sol, ainsi qu'à l'influence des micro-climats.

Les Mosellans vous expliqueront tout cela de manière fort intéressante dans leurs tavernes en rondins, au long des berges de la rivière. Ils étaleront sur la table une carte et suivront du doigt le cours d'eau en s'arrêtant à chaque courbe. Partout où la Moselle s'est heurtée au schiste le plus dur, elle a changé d'orientation, mais a rongé la rive à laquelle elle se heurtait. Il en résulte que l'intérieur de la courbe est abrupt et que la couche cultivable y est mince, alors que l'extérieur est toujours en promontoires relativement bas que la rivière disloque et sur lesquels elle dépose du limon lors de ses crues. D'un côté, la vigne donne un vin paresseux et charnu, parce qu'elle pousse sur un sol d'alluvions ; de l'autre, elle fournira un vin plus sec et racé, comme toujours quand elle dispose à peine de quoi vivre. Piesport, Bernkastel, Graach, les vignobles de Wehlen, qui se trouvent sur l'autre côté, en face de ces vignes, Zeltingen, Urzig, sont tous à l'intérieur d'une courbe. Par bonheur, ces excellentes sections sont orientées soit à l'est, soit à l'ouest (Piesport, au sud-est ; de Graach à Zeltingen au sud-ouest ; Urzig au sud-est). C'est ainsi qu'elles reçoivent le maximum de soleil. Or il y a une seule exception : Bernkastel, qui produit pourtant les vins les plus célèbres. Cette agglomération se trouve à l'ouverture d'une petite vallée tranchant entre deux collines et qui s'ouvre en fourche autour de la base d'une troisième. Le Doktorberg, sur la rive basse, en amont de la ville, s'incurve à partir du bord de la rivière, de telle sorte que le cru de Bernkasteler Doktor est orienté au sud avec une légère déviation vers l'ouest. C'était l'un des vins les plus chers d'Allemagne, mais il n'est pas certain que ses qualités soient à la hauteur des prix fabuleux qu'il lui arrive parfois d'atteindre.

Les grands événements de l'histoire de la Moselle sont très espacés dans le temps : fondation des vignobles, à peu près au début de l'ère chrétienne ; promotion de la viticulture et de la vinification par les cisterciens qui s'installèrent sur la Moselle en 1134 ; adoption du Riesling comme variété quasi unique à la fin du XVIIIe siècle ; enfin, énorme accroissement de la production durant les cinquante dernières années.

La Moselle est la seule région à posséder une grande proportion de vignes européennes originales (non greffées). Le sol de pierre et de gravier semble les avoir protégées de la destruction par le phylloxéra. Beaucoup pensent que la qualité exceptionnelle des vins fins de Moselle est due au caractère original de ses vignes. Les développements de la science et les progrès de la technologie ont profité à la fois à l'amélioration qualitative et quantitative des vins allemands. C'est aussi en transformant les vergers des plaines en vignobles plantés de variétés précoces, plus productrices que le Riesling, que la production de la région s'est accrue. Ces progrès ont permis à de nombreux viticulteurs de survivre financièrement aux années où le Riesling mûrissait à peine, ce qui n'a pas nécessairement rehaussé la réputation des vins de Moselle. La production à l'hectare est fonction de la région, de la variété et de la maturité de la récolte. En année moyenne, la production de Riesling s'élève entre 90 et 130 hl/ha, ce qui est beaucoup ; entre 130 et 150 hl/ha pour le Müller-Thurgau et l'Elbling, ce qui n'est pas compatible avec la qualité. La production annuelle de la Moselle est très supérieure à celle qu'elle était. Cet accroissement est dû à une amélioration des méthodes viticoles, à l'utilisation d'engrais du commerce, de plants hautement productifs d'Elbling et Kerner ainsi qu'à la pression d'une demande croissante.

Sur les quelque 11 000 viticulteurs de Moselle, la plupart sont de petits exploitants qui ne possèdent guère plus d'1,5 ha et 1 % seulement en ont plus de 5. La moitié, environ, des vins de la région est commercialisée par des entreprises vinicoles ; un quart est directement vendu par de petits et gros vignerons ; le reste revient aux coopératives vinicoles dont la plupart se sont associées à la fin des années 60 pour constituer les Caves Centrales de Moselle (Zentralkellerei rebaptisée « Moselland Cooperative » en 1986). « Moselland » regroupe plus de 5 000 membres.

L'unité de vente traditionnelle est le *Fuder* de 1 000 litres, fût de chêne qui contient 1 333 bouteilles, soit un peu plus de 100 caisses de vin. Bien que l'on se serve de plus en plus de réservoirs en acier inoxydable et en fibres de verre, beaucoup plus pratiques et permettant d'obtenir une qualité plus constante, le *Fuder* est toujours utilisé par de nombreux domaines, petits et grands, pour faire vieillir leurs meilleurs vins.

Les vins régionaux très plaisants des villages de Zell, Bernkastel et Piesport ont fait connaître la Moselle au-delà de ses frontières. Mais c'est surtout grâce à ses bons Riesling, vendangés tardivement, qu'elle s'est forgée une réputation mondiale.

C'est dans cette région vinicole exceptionnellement pittoresque : les auberges médiévales en rondins de Bernkastel, secteur surexploité de Cochem (dont les tours évoquent une fantaisie de fabricant de jouets), que s'accomplissent certaines des réussites les plus sensationnelles de la viniculture allemande. Il s'agit, entre autres, du Trockenbeerenauslese, étonnant vin d'or d'une rondeur qui emplit toute la bouche. C'est un concentré incomparablement riche de tout ce que la Moselle peut offrir de meilleur à l'amateur. Malheureusement, au niveau des prix actuels, les vignerons le produisent à perte. Cependant, lorsque le temps le permet, le Trockenbeerenauslese est produit par fierté dans l'art et la tradition de la viticulture de la Moselle-Sarre-Ruwer.

On ne peut le faire qu'en passant et repassant sans cesse entre les rangs de ceps sur les déclivités escarpées pour cueillir un à un chaque grain à l'instant où il atteint le maximum, non pas de maturité, mais de surmaturité. Dans un pays où l'élévation du prix de la main-d'œuvre est le trait saillant de l'économie depuis la dernière guerre mondiale, un tel raffinement devient impossible.

Moyenne Moselle (Bereich Bernkastel)

La portion moyenne de la Moselle commence juste en aval de Trèves, la plus vieille ville d'Allemagne. Elle se termine, de l'avis général, immédiatement au-dessous d'une grande courbe de la Moselle, à Zell, là où les agglomérations d'Alf et de Bullay se font face, séparées par la rivière. Les plus grands vins sont, dans le sens du courant : les Piesporter, les Brauneberger, les Bernkasteler, les Graacher, les Wehlener, les Zeltinger, les Urziger et les Erdener. Les meilleures parties de la Moselle ont une telle valeur que les parcelles y coûtent 60 à 70 fois et parfois jusqu'à 200 fois le prix d'une parcelle de surface équivalente en haute Moselle. Le district de Bernkastel regroupe les vignes collectives suivantes (Grooslagen) : Vom Heissen Stein, Schwarzlay, Nacktarsch, Badstube, Kurfürstlay, Michelsberg, St. Michael et Probstberg.

Crus et appellations d'origine

Bernkastel-Kues

Bernkastel, qui compte aujourd'hui 10 000 habitants, fut fondée en 1291 et reçut ses franchises de Frédéric Barberousse. Nichée entre le Doktorberg et le Schlossberg, couronnée par les ruines du château de Landshut, cette petite ville, avec sa place centrale médiévale, ses maisons de torchis aux poutres apparentes, ses enseignes en fer forgé, est presque trop nette, peinte à neuf comme un décor de cinéma ; pourtant tout y est authentique, soigneusement entretenu et fourbi pour accueillir les milliers de touristes dont les grandes vagues affluent au premier weekend de septembre, attirés par le festival des vendanges au cours duquel des stands de dégustation de vin sont dressés autour des fontaines baroques.

Le sol riche en ardoise donne aux vins leurs caractéristiques particulières. En un certain sens, la terre leur procure la rondeur et le goût d'un vin méridional mais en outre et beaucoup plus, c'est l'ardoise qui leur confère un goût de pierre à fusil et d'épices qui est la marque de la Moselle. L'ardoise de Bernkastel est la plus dure de toutes, comme le prouvent les chênes du pays. On se sert de ces chênes pour tanner le cuir des chaussures : ceux de Bernkastel pour le cuir des semelles, ceux de Wehlen, et des secteurs voisins pour le reste. L'influence du sol joue de la même façon pour les vins et leur donne leur race. Certains prétendent que Bernkasteler et plus spécialement ceux du site Doktor ont un petit soupçon de fumé, comme ceux de Bingen, sur le Rhin. Les vins ont un parfum particulier ; les sites les plus favorables, très pentus et plantés de Riesling, produisent des vins élégants qui ont du corps. Les vignobles de Bernkastel constituent l'ensemble du *Grosslage* de Badstube et d'une partie de celui de Kurfürstlay. Les meilleures parcelles sont à Badstube.

Les vignobles de Bernkastel

Bernkasteler Doktor. C'est le vin le plus célèbre de la Moselle. Quoique indiscutablement de première classe, il est vendu de nos jours à un prix ridiculement trop élevé. Au XIVe siècle, il aurait guéri le prince évêque Bohémond II de Trèves. Voilà ce qui explique son nom ainsi que d'innombrables plaisanteries, chansonnettes et poèmes. Le coteau est orienté au sud-sud-ouest, audessus de la ville. On dit que le vin profite du soleil réfléchi par les toits autant que de la réverbération sur la surface de la rivière. Le Bernkasteler Doktor Feinste Auslese fut choisi par le Dr Adenauer comme cadeau à Eisenhower : 50 bouteilles de ce que l'on considérait comme le plus grand produit d'Allemagne.

Parmi les principaux propriétaires figurent la veuve du docteur Hugo Thanisch, Deinhard et Cie et Lauerburg ; d'autres vignerons n'en possèdent que de petits lopins. Quand la part de Deinhard fut achetée en 1902 à Herr Kunst, maire de Bernkastel, le paiement eut lieu en pièces d'or ; on n'avait jamais payé une vigne aussi cher jusqu'alors.

Badstube. Le *Grosslage* Badstube, avec ses 58 ha de vignes, fut créé en 1971 pour aider à maintenir la grande réputation des vins de Doktor. Dans les années difficiles, les vignerons vendent leur vin Doktor sous le nom de Badstube. Cependant, les meilleurs vignobles individuels (Einzellagen) de Bernkastel font tous partie du Badstube. Ce sont : Doktor, Lay, Graben, Bratenhöfchen et Matheisbildchen.

Certains endroits du Schlossberg sont excellents. Les vignobles mineurs de Bernkastel (dans le Kurfürstlay *Grosslage*) sont Johannisbrünnchen et Stephanus Rosengärtchen.

Les vignobles de Kues en face de Bernkastel

Située de l'autre côté de la rivière, Kues fut intégrée à Bernkastel en 1905. Le site célèbre où le large pont de Bernkastel touche la rive est l'hôpital Nikolaus, fondé en 1448. Il devait à l'origine héberger 33 vieillards pauvres, jamais plus, jamais moins, et la règle a toujours été observée depuis lors. Kues est moins charmante que Bernkastel et ses vins provenant de vignes cultivées sur la rive extérieure de la courbe, donc sur un sol où la rivière dépose plus d'alluvions lors de ses crues, sont moins distingués.

Kardinalsberg est le plus réputé des vignobles de Kues ; mais certains pensent que la qualité des vins de Weisenstein est meilleure car les vignes bénéficient d'une exposition au sud. L'autre vignoble qui mérite d'être cité est Rosenberg. Les vins de Kues sont plus ronds et moins élégants que ceux de Bernkastel.

Brauneberg

Depuis des siècles, le village et son vignoble majestueux, de l'autre côté de la Moselle, sur le coteau de Braune Berg (colline brune), s'appelait Dusemond, nom dérivé d'une appellation romaine signifiant mont doux.

Les vins de Brauneberg sont très estimés ; ils sont pleins, élégants, parfumés et fruités. D'ailleurs, quand Napoléon avait fait évaluer les vignobles de la Moselle en 1806 afin de les taxer, ceux de Brauneberg furent considérés comme les plus précieux. Les vignobles de Brauneberg font partie du *Grosslage* Kurfürstlay.

Les meilleurs crus sont ceux de Juffer et Juffer-Sonnenuhr. (Juffer signifie littéralement vierge et fait ici allusion aux sœurs franciscaines qui possédaient autrefois ces vignobles).

Autres crus : Kammer, Mandelgraben et Klostergarten.

Erden

On appelle le coteau d'Erden « la Montagne d'Or de la Moselle », et cet hommage est justifié. C'est celui qui donne les meilleurs vins de toute la Moselle après le Doktorberg. Ils sont particulièrement fruités et de grande race car ils proviennent d'ardoise plus dure qu'ailleurs comme dans le cas de Bernkastel. Dans la région, on dit volontiers que les vins de Wehlen sont plus *Mädel* (jeune fille) et ceux d'Erden plus *Bube* (gars). Les Erdener sont certainement plus corsés que les délicats Wehlener.

Prälat est peut-être le meilleur de ces excellents vignobles ; il appartient presque exclusivement aux héritiers de la famille Berres. Treppchen (ou petites marches) décrit ironiquement par son nom les vignes cultivées en terrasses étagées les unes au-dessus des autres. C'est le vignoble le plus connu d'Erden qui produit des Riesling remarquables.

Autres vignobles : Bussley, Herrenberg. Tous font partie du *Grosslage* Schwarzlay.

Graach

« Graach » vient du mot gallois « gravos » ce qui signifie « gravier ». Le sol est ici pierreux, argileux et à forte teneur en ardoise. L'argile, qui se situe sous une couche de 5 m d'ardoise, donne aux vins plus de corps (ils sont plus ronds que les Wehlener), un parfum épicé et les fait vieillir plus lentement. Comme les vins de Piesport, ils sont meilleurs dans les années sèches.

Presque tous les vignobles sont situés à flanc de coteaux, exposés au sud-ouest, et sont plantés de Riesling : Himmelreich, Domprobst (ou encore Dompropst, ce qui signifie littéralement « prévost ou chef de cathédrale »), Josefshöfer et Abstsberg.

Josefshöfer, tout comme Schloss Vollrads et Schloss Johannisberg, est une des rares appellations à être vendues sans indication d'origine. Il appartenait au monastère Saint-Martin à Trèves et était connu sous le nom de Martinshof. Il prit son nom actuel quand un certain Joseph Hain l'acheta après la sécularisation des biens de l'Église au début du XIXe s. En 1858 il le vendit au comte Kesselstatt et il appartient encore entièrement au Domaine Kesselstatt. Les autres principaux crus sont ceux des familles Prüm et Bergweiler ainsi que celui de Friedrich Wilhelm Gymnasium, célèbre lycée communal de Trèves. Les vignobles de Graach font partie du *Grosslage* Münzlay.

Quand il ne pleut ni en septembre ni en octobre, Graach produit des vins merveilleux et, d'une manière générale, plus l'année est sèche, meilleurs ils sont.

Presque tous les vignobles appartenaient jadis à l'Église, de nos jours Prüm, Thanisch, Deinhard et Kesselstatt en possèdent la plus grosse part. Les petits vignerons du pays en ont moins et dans les terres les moins bonnes.

Piesport

Tout comme Bernkastel, Piesport est un des villages les plus importants de la Moselle, aussi bien au niveau qualitatif que quantitatif. Derrière la ville et sur ses deux côtés, les vignes s'étendent sur une colline pentue qui s'incurve comme un large bol, orienté plein sud, et situé à merveille pour capter les rayons du soleil réfléchis sur la rivière.

Un expert a décrit les Piesport comme « les reines de la Moselle ». Ils sont merveilleusement délicats et parfumés, jamais lourds ni corsés, d'une distinction incomparable. Dans les bonnes années, ils font de grands vins de Moselle. Dans les années humides, ils peuvent être quelconques car les sommets boisés retiennent l'humidité et les vignobles situés en-dessous ne peuvent sécher.

Pour des raisons commerciales, une grande quantité de vin est vendue sous le nom du *Grosslage* Michelsberg. Mais les vins les plus fins sont nommés d'après les vignobles individuels dont le plus connu est celui de Goldtröpfchen. Günterslay, Falkenberg, Grafenberg, Domherr, Schubertslay, Gärtchen et Kreuzwingert entourent Goldströpfchen. Treppchen, vignoble important situé sur la rive opposée, est l'autre cru principal de Piesport.

Ürzig

Les vignes poussent sur un coteau incroyablement abrupt par endroits, très abrité et exposé au sud. La structure du sol est très différente de celle des autres secteurs de la Moselle. Il s'agit de strates profondes de roches volcaniques, mélangées à de l'ardoise avec des taches de calcaire coloré. C'est ce terrain particulier qui donne aux vins leur goût spécial. Ils sont très fruités mais plus épicés que les autres. Ces vignobles, ainsi que tous les meilleurs domaines de Moselle, sont plantés exclusivement de Riesling. Par année chaude, ils atteignent à la magnificence et d'après certains experts, ils sont même bons par année pluvieuse. Il existe deux crus : Würzgarten qui littéralement signifie « jardin d'épices » (würzig : épicé), et Goldwingert. Tous deux font partie du *Grosslage* Schwarzlay.

Wehlen

Village banal et sans prétention si on le compare à ses voisins, Wehlen est situé sur le cours de la Moselle, en face du vignoble qu'en Allemagne on considère comme le meilleur de la Moselle : Wehlener Sonnenuhr. Son vin atteint parfois, et pour des raisons justifiées, les prix très élevés du Berkasteler Doktor, mais les Allemands le considèrent comme supérieur. Les traits caractéristiques des Wehlener sont une élégance et une finesse. Les vins sont riches et ronds ; leur goût et leur bouquet uniques et délicats. De 1084, date de sa fondation, jusqu'en 1802 où il fut sécularisé, le monastère cistercien de Kloster Machem possédait la plupart des vignobles de Wehlen. Beaucoup de leurs noms, d'ailleurs, en sont un souvenir : Klosterberg, Nonnenberg, Klosterhofgut, Abtei. Les autres vignobles sont · Hofberg et Rosenberg. Sonnenuhr est le cru le plus remarquable. Tout comme dans la région voisine de Graach, les parcelles les meilleures et les plus réputées appartiennent aux familles Prüm et Bergweiler. Les vignobles de Wehlen font partie du *Grosslage* Münzlay.

Zeltingen

En raison de l'étendue de la région viticole de Zeltingen, la qualité et l'élégance des vins varient suivant les vignobles et les producteurs. Les vignobles de Himmelreich, avant qu'ils ne soient agrandis par le remembrement, s'étendaient derrière le village, sur des coteaux abruptes orientés au sud, et produisaient de très bons vins. Zeltinger Himmelreich, situé dans les nouvelles sections plus en amont et sur la rive opposée, est souvent moins distingué. Il en est de même de Deutscherrenberg. Les deux meilleurs crus sont : Schlossberg et Sonnenuhr. Le Zeltinger Sonnenuhr jouxte et est en fait le prolongement du site réputé de Wehlen qui porte le même nom. Les vins, leurs prix mis à part, sont très semblables ; toutefois, les Zeltinger ont peut-être plus de corps que les Wehlener. La plus longue étendue ininterrompue des meilleurs vignobles de Moselle, plantés de Riesling, commence à Bernkastel et finit à Zeltingen. Les vignobles font partie du *Grosslage* Münzlay.

Les vins de cette agglomération présentent plus de diversité que n'importe où dans la région et ce n'est pas toujours à leur avantage. Par bonne année, Zeltingen produit environ 2,5 millions de bouteilles. Aucun autre secteur de la Moselle ne s'approche d'un tel chiffre. Il en résulte qu'on voit bien des bouteilles de Zeltinger ordinaire éclipser les quelques vins splendides du secteur. Il est difficile de définir le type du Zeltinger, en raison de son extrême variété, allant du vin léger et fleuri à d'autres très corsés. Les meilleurs ont un charme féminin.

Secteurs moins importants et leur valeur

Hormis Zeller Schwarze Katz, ne sont connus à l'étranger que les vins provenant du cœur même de la moyenne Moselle. Les grands noms ont atteint leur notoriété parce que les vignobles appartiennent en tout ou partie à de gros propriétaires ou à des producteurs remarquables qui ont acquis leur réputation depuis des générations. Les prix records réalisés lors des fameuses ventes aux enchères de Grosse Ring ont aussi rendu célèbres de nombreux villages et domaines. Néanmoins, il y a bien d'autres villages encore dont les vins gagneraient à être connus. Mais précisément parce qu'ils sont moins renommés, donc moins chers, de bonnes affaires sont à réaliser. Les villages cités ci-dessous ne jouissent pas encore de la réputation internationale de ceux que nous venons de décrire. Cependant, ils offrent, eux aussi, une large gamme de bons vins à des prix raisonnables pour la consommation quotidienne ou en des occasions spéciales.

Enkirch

Village pittoresque. La vaste zone viticole est essentiellement plantée de Riesling. Les vins sont fleuris, racés et vigoureux. *Grosslage* Schwarzlay.

Kersten

Très vieux village dont les vignobles appartenaient autrefois à la congrégation de Saint-Paulin-de-Trèves, d'où les noms des deux meilleurs crus : Paulinshofberger et Paulinsberg. Tous deux sont plantés de Riesling, cultivé à flancs de coteaux. *Grosslage* Kurfürstlay.

Klüsserath

Village viticole typique aux coteaux abruptes orientés au sud et plantés de Riesling. Les vins sont délicats mais non racés. Bruderschaft est le cru le plus renommé. *Grosslage* St Michael.

Kröv

Village ancien ayant appartenu autrefois aux royaumes Mérovingien et plus tard Carolingien. Il est aujourd'hui fameux pour ses étiquettes : elles dépeignent le nom de son célèbre vignoble de Nacktarsch (qui signifie littéralement « fesses à l'air »). On y voit un petit garçon recevant une fessée sur son postérieur nu. Les vignobles abruptes, plantés de Riesling, produisent de bons vins fruités à l'acidité moyenne. *Grosslage* Nacktarsch.

Leiwen

Le domaine viticole s'est régulièrement accru par la conversion de vergers en vignobles. Laurentiuslay, coteau abrupt planté de Riesling, produit, dans les années favorables, de bons vins fruités et de caractère.

Lieser

Site nommé d'après la petite rivière qui se jette dans la Moselle. Le cru de Schlossberg tire son nom du château (Schloss), datant du XIXe siècle et appartenant à la famille Schorlemer. Süssenberg et Niederberg sont des vignobles abrupts, plantés de Riesling. *Grosslage* Kurfürstlay.

Mülheim

Situé au sud de Bernkastel, ce village produit des vins élégants délicatement fruités et alertes, vinifiés à partir du Riesling. Dans les années 20, le Mülheimer Sonnenlay était connu sous le nom de « vin Zeppelin », car assez léger et délicat pour voyager sur les fameux dirigeables. Un cru en particulier, celui d'Helenenkloster, produit souvent de l'Eiswein. *Grosslage* Kurfürstlay.

Neumagen

C'est le plus ancien village viticole d'Allemagne. On y a retrouvé de nombreux objets relevant de la viticulture et datant de l'époque romaine, ainsi que la tombe d'un négociant en vins romain. Elle avait la forme des bateaux qui servaient au transport du vin. On peut la voir au Landesmuseum à Trèves. *Grosslage* Michelsberg.

Traben-Trarbach

Ces deux villages situés le long de la Moselle, sont depuis le XVIe siècle un centre important du commerce vinicole. C'est aussi un lieu touristique et populaire. Les vignobles plantés de Riesling sont abrupts. Bons vins fruités à l'acidité prononcée. *Grosslage* Schwarzlay.

Trittenheim

Vignoble sur la Moselle où le Riesling fut planté pour la première fois. C'est aussi le lieu de naissance du grand humaniste Trithemius. Les vignobles sont situés dans une boucle du fleuve de 180°. Très bons vins élégants et fruités. Les crus les plus célèbres sont : Altärchen et Apotheke. *Grosslage* Michelsberg.

Veldenz

Ville extrêmement pittoresque, surplombée d'une petite colline coiffée de ruines, et située en retrait de la Moselle dans une vallée adjacente. Elle produit des Riesling et des Müller-Thurgau plaisants, au bouquet et à la fraîcheur agréables.

Wintrich

Vignobles abrupts plantés de Riesling et produisant des vins de bonne qualité. Le Müller-Thurgau, cultivé dans les régions plates, donne des vins plaisants, légers et fruités.

Wittlich

Site historique important où les moines cisterciens, arrivant du monastère voisin de Himmerode en 1134, ont introduit la viticulture et l'ont étendue dans une grande partie de la Moselle et de la Ruwer. Les Riesling sont racés et piquants, les Müller-Thurgau simples et légers. *Grosslage* Schwarzlay.

Basse Moselle (Bereich Zell-Mosel)

La partie basse de la Moselle s'étend de Zell jusqu'à Coblence, au confluent de la Moselle et du Rhin. Les nombreux coteaux sont souvent plantés de Riesling. Dans les régions plus plates, on cultive du Müller-Thurgau, du Kerner et quelques variétés précoces. Les vins de cette région sont en général moins élégants et moins remarquables que ceux de la moyenne Moselle. Ils sont néanmoins plaisants, fruités, à l'acidité piquante et rafraîchissante.

Ce district tire son nom du village de Zell, l'un des plus grands centres viticoles situé sur la Moselle et planté principalement de Riesling. Ses vins et leurs étiquettes au chat noir (Schwarze Katz) sont mondialement connus. La légende veut qu'un groupe de commerçants d'Aix-la-Chapelle, incapable de décider quel Fuder (fût) de vin était le meilleur, s'en remit au chat du négociant en choisissant celui sur lequel il s'était endormi. Zeller Schwarze Katz est un vin populaire pour la consommation quotidienne. Il est exporté en grande quantité, mais la qualité est inégale. Le prix le plus bon marché ne doit pas être un critère de sélection et, pour éviter d'être déçu, il convient de se fier au nom d'un producteur ou d'un expéditeur sérieux.

En plus du Schwarze Katz, le district comprend les vignobles collectifs suivants : Weinhex (qui signifie littéralement « sorcière du vin » et fait allusion aux procès des sorcières qui eurent lieu dans les années 1650), Goldbaümchen, Rosenhang et Grafschaft.

Voici quelques-uns des villages les plus populaires : Alf, Beilstein, Bremm (réputé pour être le vignoble le plus abrupt d'Europe), Cochem, Ediger-Ellenz, Kobern-Gondorf, Neer, et Winningen (qui abrite le plus ancien festival des vins allemand). Presque toujours pittoresques avec leurs maisons médiévales à colombage, leurs nombreuses églises, fontaines, monuments de tous styles (romanesque, gothique, Renaissance et baroque) et leurs châteaux majestueux, ces villages et leurs paysages exceptionnels sont le décor magique dans lequel on peut jouir du charme des vins de Zell.

Haute-Moselle (Bereich Obermosel et Bereich Moseltor)

On considère que les vignobles situés en amont de Trèves appartiennent à la région de haute Moselle. Ils sont très différents des grands Riesling de Moselle, cultivés sur de l'ardoise. Dans ces deux districts, les sols crayeux désagrégés (terrain calcaire et glaiseux, parsemé cà et là de marne et de sable) sont mieux adaptés à la culture de l'Elbling et aux variétés de Bourgogne telles que le Ruländer ou le Pinot Gris. L'Elbling est une variété ancienne, apportée en Moselle par les Romains il y a 2 000 ans ; le Müller Thurgau en est une autre importante. Ces vins ont souvent un charme particulier, mais ils ne sont pas de la race et de la lignée des vins de Moselle moyenne ou de la Sarre et la Ruwer. Mais leurs liens avec ceux des deux autres régions ne sont qu'une affaire de nom car il leur manque les éléments essentiels propres aux véritables vins de la Moselle : ardoise et Riesling. En haute Moselle, on cultive presque exclusivement de l'Elbling, étroitement apparenté à la variété que les Romains introduisirent dans ces parages voilà 2 000 ans. On y trouve aussi un peu de Müller-Thurgau (croisement de Riesling et de Sylvaner) et les vignerons ont planté récemment du Ruländer. Le sol n'est plus schisteux mais calcaire. Pourtant, les vins de haute Moselle ont parfois un charme qui leur est particulier. En moyenne ils sont même sans doute meilleurs que ceux de basse Moselle, mais aucun ne saurait concurrencer ceux de moyenne Moselle. Bien des bons vins de haute Moselle ont assez de qualités pour offrir de bonnes affaires car peu connus, ils ne sont pas chers. Le district d'Obermosel regroupe deux vignobles collectifs : Gipfel (qui était autrefois le nom d'une bonne parcelle de Nittel) et Königsberg. Nittel est le *Weinbauort* (agglomération vinicole) le plus important et le plus célèbre. Wellen et Winchering sont également de quelque importance.

Le district de Moseltor (qui signifie littéralement « seuil de la Moselle ») comprend un vignoble collectif, Schloss Bübingen, nommé d'après le château cerné de douves de Bübingen, construit en 1340 par Gabriel von Remich.

Sarre-Ruwer (Bereich Saar-Ruwer)

Composé de trois secteurs regroupés par la nouvelle réglementation vinicole : la vallée de la Sarre, la vallée de la Ruwer est une grande étendue de vignobles situés autour de Trèves sur les coteaux qui surplombent les méandres du confluent de la Sarre, de la Ruwer et de la Moselle.

Les meilleures années, les Sarre peuvent surclasser les Moselle. L'été chaud et sec produit de grands vins le long de cette rivière. Ils sont légers, épicés et ont une saveur unique qui rappelle le cassis, ainsi qu'un bouquet ressemblant à celui du Muscat. En général, les Sarre durent plus longtemps et prennent plus de temps à mûrir que les Moselle. Ils sont habituellement faits avec du Riesling cultivé sur le sol caractéristique de la basse Sarre, identique à celui de la Moselle : ardoise qui s'effrite lentement pour constituer une couche arable. En amont de Sarrebourg, la teneur en ardoise diminue

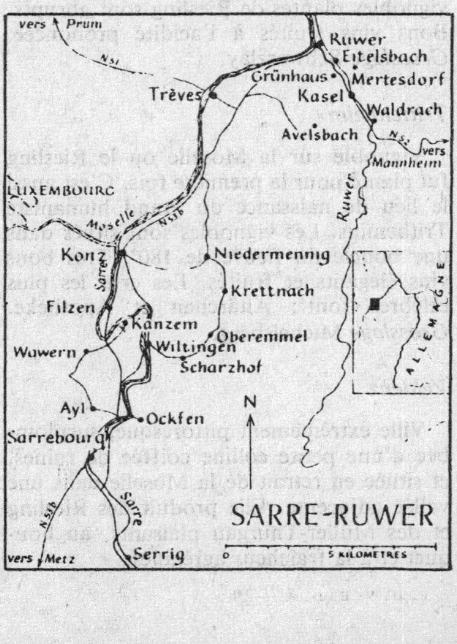

dans le sol. De Serrig à Konz-Karthaus, où la Sarre se déverse dans la Moselle, on ne voit guère que de la vigne sur ses rives. Les vins de la Sarre, qu'on pourrait presque considérer comme des super Moselle quant à la race et à l'élégance d'acier, sont toujours classés avec les Moselle. Ockfen fournit probablement la plus haute moyenne de bons vins mais, selon l'opinion générale, le meilleur cru est le célèbre Scharzhofberg, situé légèrement en amont, au-delà du village de Wiltingen.

Dans leur plénitude, les vins de la Ruhr sont les plus maigres d'Allemagne : plus légers que ceux de la Sarre et de la Moselle. Les meilleures années ils ont un bouquet qui rappelle les épices, durant les années médiocres ils peuvent être trop acides pour la plupart des gens. En général, plus la Ruhr se rapproche de la Moselle et plus la qualité de ses vins augmente. Les vins de la Ruhr (et ceux de la Sarre) sont toujours classés avec ceux de la Moselle et l'étiquetage des vins allemands rassemble les trois régions sous la formule Moselle-Sarre-Ruwer. Sarre et Ruwer sont des affluents de la Moselle. Mais si la Sarre est une rivière respectable, la Ruwer est un ruisseau assez étroit pour être franchi d'un bond. La région se réduit à une étroite vallée qui débouche dans celle de la Moselle, un peu en aval de Trèves. Elle s'élargit en amont et c'est là, sur un vallon proche du cours d'eau, que se trouvent, les vignobles d'Avelsbach plantés de Riesling ; c'est également là que le vin est produit.

Le district regroupe deux vignobles collectifs : Römerlay (vignobles de Trèves et de la Ruwer) et Scharzberg (vignobles de la Sarre).

MEILLEURS VILLAGES
(R = Ruwer, S = Sarre)

Avelsbach (R). Les vignobles sont plantés dans l'angle formé par la Moselle et la Ruhr. Lorsque les étés sont chauds, ils produisent des vins d'une excellente qualité ; dans les mauvaises années, ils sont plus rudes et trop aciéreux ou durs, au goût de la plupart des consommateurs.

Ayl (S). Ses vins rivalisent de près en qualité avec ceux d'Ockfen. Herrenberg et Kupp (vins pour connaisseurs, exquis par été chaud, provenant d'un vignoble abrupt) sont les meilleurs crus.

Eitelsbach (R). Karthäuserhofberg est le cru remarquable. C'était autrefois un monastère. Il fut donné aux Chartreux par un ecclésiastique nommé Baudouin au milieu du XIVe siècle et passa intégralement entre les mains de la famille Rautenstrauch lors de la sécularisation des biens de l'Église en 1802. Les descendants de cette même famille en sont les propriétaires actuels. Leur étiquette est originale. C'est une petite étiquette courbée, fixée simplement au goulot de la bouteille. Les vins sont étiquetés Eitelsbacher Karthäuserhofberg, suivi du nom d'un vignoble : Kronenberg, Sang, Burgberg, Orthsberg, Stim.

Filzen (S). Village viticole situé dans la région septentrionale, au confluent de la Sarre et de la Moselle. Les Riesling sont racés. Pulchen, Urbelt et Herrenberg sont de bons crus.

Kanzem (S). Tout comme dans les villages situés sur le cours de la Sarre et de la Ruwer, la viticulture remonte ici au temps des Romains. Les vignobles sont plantés sur des coteaux abruptes, exposés au sud. Dans les bonnes années, ils produisent d'excellents vins au parfum épicé et à l'acidité superbement fruitée.

Cassel (Kasel) (R) est le plus important *Gemarkung* de la Ruwer. Avec ses 75 ha de vignes à l'embouchure de la vallée, il a une superficie double de celles des autres de la même région. La seule localité qui lui équivaut en quantité — Waldrach, plus en amont — ne fait que des petits vins. Le meilleur Cassel est sans doute le Kaseler Nies'chen, somptueusement souple et léger quand il atteint sa plénitude. Principaux crus : Kehrnagel, Hitzlay, Dominikanerberg, Paulinsberg, Kohlenberg et Timpert.

Mertesdorf (R). Les vins de Maximin Grünhaus sont toujours d'excellents vins de la Ruwer, surtout dans les années sèches. C'est la perle du Gemarkung Mertesdorf. Il doit son nom au fait que, avant la sécularisation des biens de l'Église allemande par Napoléon, il appartenait à l'abbaye Saint-Maximim de Trèves. Il appartient actuellement à Herr von Schubert. Les vins sont étiquetés Maximin Grünhaus et, suivi du nom d'un vignoble (Abtsberg, Herrenberg, Brudersberg).

Oberemmel (S). Ce village, non loin de Wiltingen, produit de très bons vins, racés avec les grands Riesling.

Ockfent (S). Parmi les meilleurs vins de la Sarre. Le premier cru, Bockstein, rivalise avec le Scharzofberger de Wiltingen, comme roi de la Sarre. Il est plus charnu mais moins élégant et le surclasse en certaines années. Geiberg est l'autre cru important.

Sarrebourg (Saarburg) (S). Ville très pittoresque et touristique. C'est le centre vinicole important de la Sarre. Dans les grandes années, les Saarburger sont stylés et de bonne qualité.

Serrig (S). Région située à l'extrémité des vignobles sarrois. Le climat y est moins fiable que dans les villes plus proches de la Moselle. Les vins de Serriger peuvent néanmoins être remarquables dans les bonnes années.

Trèves (Trier) (R et S). C'est la plus grande ville de la Moselle. C'est aussi un centre vinicole important. Elle regroupe de grands et importants domaines et des parcelles dans la plupart des meilleurs crus des régions de Moselle-Sarre-Ruwer. C'est une petite cité fascinante dont le slogan « En 2 000 pas, vous vivez 2 000 ans d'histoire » mérite d'être suivi. Une collection exceptionnelle d'objets viticoles, datant de l'époque romaine, est exposée dans le musée régional.

Waldrach (R). Produit de bons vins fruités, dont le caractère est plus affirmé dans les bonnes années.

Wawern (S). Herrenberg et Goldberg sont les crus les meilleurs. Les vins ne sont pas aussi remarquables que ceux d'Ayl, mais ceux produits par les Riesling, cultivés sur des coteaux abrupts, sont de haute qualité.

Wiltingen (S). Excellent village viticole dont les vins sont comparables aux meilleurs crus de la Moselle moyenne. Scharzhofberg est le cru qui donne presque toujours le meilleur vin de la Sarre. Il est doué d'une élégance suprême. Les vignes sont orientées au sud et à l'ouest, sur une haute colline, au-delà de Wiltingen. Leur histoire est curieuse. Plantées il y a 200 ans par le monastère de Trèves, elles échappèrent à la sécularisation des biens de l'Église par Napoléon car un prêtre nommé Muller les fit passer pour son bien personnel. Napoléon vint et repartit. Muller conserva le vignoble, épousa une jeune femme et fonda une famille. Son descendant actuel, l'affable Herr Egon Muller, est probablement le meilleur vigneron de la Sarre. Le Scharzhofberger peut être vendu sans le nom du village. Wiltinger Braune Kupp, Kupp et Braunfels font partie des autres bons crus.

PRINCIPAUX DOMAINES DE MOSELLE-SARRE-RUWER

Voici les noms de quelques producteurs traditionnels. Tous possèdent des parcelles des meilleurs vignobles, situés sur des coteaux abrupts exposés au sud et plantés de Riesling. Les vins vieillissent en fûts de chêne selon la méthode traditionnelle. Si l'on en juge d'après les prix atteints lors des ventes aux enchères, tous les vins profitent du vieillissement en bouteilles.

Moyenne Moselle

Prüm et Bergweiler. On rencontre d'Urzig à Brauneberg plusieurs domaines magnifiques au nom de Prüm, de Bergweiler, ou portant un nom composé dans lequel figure l'un de ces deux noms. Les Prüm sont viticulteurs à Wehlen depuis des siècles, mais leur renommée bien méritée remonte au XIXᵉ siècle, à Sebastian Alois Prüm (1794-1871), fondateur de tous les domaines portant son nom (S.A. Prüm Erben). Son frère, Jodocus, fit construire en 1842 les cadrans solaires de Wehlen et Zeltingen afin que les travailleurs, trop pauvres pour s'acheter une montre, puissent savoir quand faire une pause, déjeuner ou terminer leur journée de travail. A la fin du siècle, l'exploitation familiale atteignait 17 ha pour devenir l'un des plus grands domaines privés anonymes de moyenne Moselle. En 1911, la propriété fut divisée entre les sept enfants de Matthias, fils de Sebastian Alois :

1) Johann Josef le plus âgé, qui fonda le domaine J.J. Prüm et acquit une grande parcelle des biens de son frère (3) Matthias. Son fils, aussi prénommé Sebastian Alois, entra dans l'affaire en 1920 et s'appliqua à produire des vins de qualité. Son succès est reconnu lors de ventes aux enchères. Son petit-fils, le Dʳ Manfred Prüm, est l'actuel propriétaire et s'applique à maintenir cette qualité. Il possède les meilleures parcelles du Wehlener Sonnenuhr, Graacher Himmelreich ainsi que d'excellents crus à Bernkastel et dans le Zeltinger Sonnenuhr. Ce domaine est l'un des plus considérés d'Allemagne.

2) Sebastian Alois, second fils, qui a transmis son héritage aux domaines S.A. Prüm Erben et S.A. Prüm, Wehlen (dont le propriétaire est Raimund Prüm) et S.A. Prüm Erben, Christoffel-Prüm, Urzig.

4) Peter Prüm. Ses propriétés ont été

transmises à deux domaines qui portent son nom : Peter Prüm Erben, M. Engelberting-Prüm, Wehlen, et Peter Prüm Erben, St. Studert-Prüm, Wehlen.

5) Anna Prüm, mariée au Dr Weins. Les domaines actuels sont : Dr Weins-Prüm Erben (Selbach-Weins) et Dr Weins (Willi Weins).

6 et 7) Maria et Katharina Prüm, épouse de Zacharias Bergweiler, producteur fabuleux. Il étendit considérablement ses vignobles, connus aujourd'hui sous le nom de Zach. Bergweiler-Prüm Erben fut divisé entre ses cinq enfants : *Dr Zach Bergweiler*, Wehlen, le domaine fut hérité par son fils unique et est loué actuellement à Deinhard ; *Dr Heidemanns-Bergweiler*, Bernkastel, *Dr Adams-Bergweiler* : deux domaines dont l'un porte le nom de la famille Loosen d'Urzig ; *Licht-Bergweiler* (Brauneberg), et *Dr Pauly-Bergweiler*, aujourd'hui dirigé par son fils, le Dr Peter Pauly, qui possède des crus excellents à Bernkastel, Graach, Weheln, Zeltingen et Brauneberg. Il est marié à Helga Berres, autre famille de viticulteurs célèbres en moyenne Moselle et propriétaire du petit domaine remarquable, *Peter Nicolay/C.H. Berres Erben* à Urzig.

Le propriétaire des crus de *Bernkastel Doktor* est Gutsverwaltung Deinhard à Bernkastel — les vignobles, plantés de Riesling, s'étendent sur 27 ha à Bernkastel, Graach, Wehlen, Lieser, Kesten (Moselle) et Kasel (Ruwer). Il y avait, à la fin du XIXe siècle, tant de vins vendus sous le nom de Bernkasteler Doktor que l'on pouvait douter de leur authenticité. Pour sauvegarder ce produit, Deinhard acheta la moitié du domaine au prix incroyable de 100 marks or la vigne. Il possède la majeure partie du cru.

Weingut WWe. Dr H. Thanisch. Domaine traditionnel de Riesling. Les vignes s'étendent sur 13 ha à Bernkastel, Brauenberg, Graach et Lieser. Une bouteille de Bernkasteler Doktor Trockenbeerenauslese, du millésime de 1921, battit tous les records mondiaux en 1978 en atteignant le prix de 7 500 DM. 7 ans plus tard, toujours au cours d'une vente, le même vin se vendit au prix de 11 100 DM.

Weingut J. Lauerburg. Propriété traditionnelle de Riesling s'étendant sur 4 ha et dont les vignobles exceptionnels sont situés à Bernkastel, Graach et Wehlen. Lauerburg est le plus ancien propriétaire d'une parcelle du cru de Doktor.

Trèves

Weingut Reichsgraf von Kesselstatt. C'est le plus grand vignoble privé de la Moselle, détenu par la famille Günther Reh. Ce domaine est mentionné pour la première fois dans des documents datant de 1349 et 1377 et relatant que Friedrich von Kesselstatt fut nommé administrateur des caves royales de Trèves. Les 100 ha de vignobles sont situés près de quatre domaines historiques ayant autrefois appartenu à un monastère : Josephshof/Graach, Domklausenhof/Piersport, Saint Irminin-hof/Kasel sur la Ruwer et Abteihof/Oberemmel sur la Sarre. Les bureaux administratifs et les caves se trouvent dans le palais baroque Kesselstatt à Trèves, qui abrite aussi un restaurant pour gourmets et une galerie au rez-de-chaussée. En 1986, le domaine introduisit une garantie de 10 ans pour ses vins (uniquement valable en Allemagne) dans le but d'encourager les consommateurs à laisser vieillir les Riesling de Moselle. Le domaine est particulièrement fier de sa médaille d'Honneur en or, décernée pour l'excellence de sa vinification. Il figure ainsi parmi la poignée de domaines à avoir reçu cette récompense.

Güterverwaltung Vereinigte Hospitien. Fondation charitable créée par Napoléon en 1805 et qui regroupait des hôpitaux et des institutions sociales de Trèves. On estime que les caves à vin sont les plus anciennes d'Allemagne : les murs et fondations faisaient jadis partie d'un camp romain qui abritait le plus grand entrepôt romain au nord des Alpes. Les 55 ha de vignobles sont situés en moyenne Moselle et sur la Sarre. Leurs coteaux abrupts sont plantés avant tout de Riesling. Les propriétés regroupent : Schloss Saarfelser Schlossberg à Serrig, Wiltinger Hölle, Piesporter Schubertslay et Trierer Augenscheiner. L'étiquette représente saint Jacques, en souvenir de l'hôpital Saint-Jacques, autrefois hospice pour les pèlerins qui se rendaient sur la tombe de l'apôtre à Saint-Jacques-de-Compostelle. Le Vereinigte Hospitien est une corporation, à but non lucratif, qui utilise ses revenus (dont 10 % lui viennent de la viticulture) pour le fonctionnement d'un hôpital, de 500 maisons de retraite, d'un home d'enfants et d'un centre pour malades souffrant de scléroses multiples.

Friedrich Wilhem Gymnasium. Exploité grâce aux dons versés à l'école. Elle fut fondée par les Jésuites en 1563. Ses 45 ha de vignobles sont situés sur la Moselle et la Sarre. Ce sont des coteaux abrupts plantés de Riesling. Les vins vieillissent en fûts de chêne. L'étiquette porte le blason des Jésuites.

Verwaltung der Bischöflichen Weingüter. Regroupement en 1966 de 3 grands domaines ecclésiastiques, de nombreuses parcelles appartenant à l'Église, notamment sur la Sarre et la Ruwer, et de quelques sites sur la Moselle. Cependant, les vins portent toujours les étiquettes traditionnelles du domaine dont ils sont issus. *Bischöfliches Priesterseminar* est un séminaire catholique de Trèves qui reçut ses vignobles du prince évêque Clemens Wenzeslaus en 1773. Comme tous les autres biens de l'Église, ses domaines furent sécularisés en 1794, puis rétablis par édit spécial en 1809. Ses 34 ha de vignobles se situent sur la Moselle, la Sarre et la Ruwer. *Bischöfliches Konvikt* est une école préparatoire qui possède quelque 40 ha de vignobles et une partie du fameux Piesporter Goldtröpfchen. *Hohe Domkirche*, domaine qui appartenait à la cathédrale de Trèves. Il couvre approximativement 22 ha de vignobles sur la Sarre (Scharzhofberg) et la Ruwer (Avelsbach).

Sarre et Ruwer

Karthäuserhof. Domaine important d'Eitelsbach. C'est le seul propriétaire des vignobles situés sur le Karthäuser Hofberg qui domine la Ruwer et regroupe Burgberg, Kronenberg, Sang, Orthsberg et Stim. Ses 20 ha de Riesling s'étendent sur les collines abruptes. Le Karthäuserhof a appartenu à l'archevêque et aux électeurs de Trèves au XIIIe siècle et aux moines chartreux de 1335 à 1803. Après avoir été sécularisé en 1794, il fut vendu aux enchères à la famille Rautenstrauch. Ses descendants en sont les propriétaires actuels. L'étiquette est unique : l'une des plus petites étiquettes du monde pour l'une des Appellations d'Origine les plus longues.

Maximin Grünhaus. Ce domaine de tout premier ordre appartient à la famille von Schubert depuis 1882 et est situé près de Mertesdorf. Le magnifique manoir était autrefois la propriété de l'abbaye Saint-Maxime de Trèves. Les 33 ha de vignobles sont divisés en 3 crus : Abtsberg, Herrenberg et Brudersberg. L'étiquette traditionnelle, dessinée en 1900, est toujours la même. Les Prädikats sont mentionnés sur le goulot de la bouteille par une étiquette triangulaire.

Scharzhof. Région viticole de renommée internationale située près de Wiltingen. Autrefois propriété du monastère de Sainte-Marie aux martyres de Trèves, elle fut sécularisée en 1794, puis rachetée lors d'une vente aux enchères par Jean-Jacques Koch, l'arrière-arrière grand-père du propriétaire actuel Egon Müller. Le domaine regroupe environ 8,5 ha de crus dans le site Braunfels de Wiltingen et au cœur de Scharzhofberg, l'un des noms les plus célèbres de la viticulture allemande. Egon Müller possède la plus grande parcelle de ce coteau abrupt, toujours plantée de pieds de Riesling européen originel (non greffés). Depuis 1954, il est le copropriétaire et directeur d'un autre magnifique domaine viticole, le Gallais (Kanzem) d'une superficie de 2,5 ha à Wiltingen et Wawern.

Autres bons producteurs : Dieter Ebert, Serrig ; Robert Eymael, Urzig ; Dr Fischer, Ockfen ; Forstmeister Geltz Erben-Zilliken, Saarburg ; Ferd. Haag Erben et Fritz Haag, tous deux à Brauneberg ; von Hövel, Oberemmel ; Milz-Laurentiushof, Trittenheim ; Georg Fritz von Nell, Trèves ; von Othegraven, Kanzem ; Okonomierat Piedmont, Konz-Filzen ; Max Ferd. Richter, Mülheim ; Hubert Schmitz, Wiltingen ; Selbach-Oster, Zeltingen ; Bert Simon, Serrig ; Tobias, Piesport.

Moselle (Vins de la)

Vins lorrains délimités et de qualité supérieure.

Voir LORRAINE et LUXEMBOURG

Moseltaler

« Moseltaler » est pour la Moselle ce que l'Edelzwicker est pour l'Alsace : c'est un vin de Moselle typique au caractère léger et fruité, et à l'acidité prononcée. Lancé en 1986, ce Qualitätswein (vin de qualité) régional peut être fabriqué à partir d'une ou plusieurs variétés de Riesling, Müller-Thurgau, Elbling et Kerner, cultivées dans les régions de Moselle-Sarre-Ruwer. Ni la variété de raisin ni la plus petite appellation d'origine ne peuvent figurer sur l'étiquette. Le sucre résiduel est limité à 15 g à 30 g/l et l'acidité doit être d'au moins 7 g/l.

Mother Wine

Littéralement : vin mère. Il s'agit de vin concentré par ébullition et utilisé pour donner plus de vigueur aux vins jeunes. Une peinture murale dans le tombeau de Menopth, en Égypte, nous montre que ce procédé date au moins de 4 000 ans.

Mou

Concernant un vin, cet adjectif indique qu'il est dénué de corps.

Mouillage, vin mouillé

Mouiller un vin consiste à l'additionner d'eau.

Moulin-à-Vent (Appellation Contrôlée)

Le Beaujolais le plus corsé et le plus connu sur certains marchés.

Voir BEAUJOLAIS

Moulis

Bordeaux rouge. Commune de Moulis, en Haut-Médoc.

Cette commune de 350 ha bénéficie de sa propre Appellation Contrôlée.

Voir MÉDOC

Moutain

Vieille appellation anglaise du vin de Málaga *(voir ce nom).*

Mourisco

Raisin qui entrait en proportion importante dans la vinification du Porto *(voir ce nom).*

Mourvèdre

Raisin à vin rouge, cultivé en France (surtout dans le Midi), en Algérie et en Espagne. Citons les nombreux noms qu'on lui donne ici et là : Négron, Espar, Mataro, Catalan, Beni Carlo et Tinto.

Voir PROVENCE

Mousseux

Vins pétillants. Tous les vins français de ce type portent ce nom, à l'exception des mousseux produits dans la région de Champagne qui sont les seuls à avoir droit à l'appellation Champagne. C'est la présence de gaz carbonique dans la bouteille qui rend ces vins effervescents. Les meilleurs sont faits selon la méthode champenoise de fermentation secondaire en bouteille *(voir* CHAMPAGNE). On en fait d'autres selon le procédé Charmat de fermentation en cuve close et de mise en bouteille sous pression *(voir* CHARMAT). Enfin, le procédé le moins recommandable consiste à diffuser du gaz carbonique dans le vin, comme dans certains jus de fruits pétillants.

Voir BOURGOGNE MOUSSEUX.

Moût

Jus de raisin qui n'a pas encore fermenté ou qui est en cours de fermentation.

Mouton-Baronne-Philippe (Château-)

Bordeaux rouge. Commune de Pauillac, en Haut-Médoc.

Voilà environ 200 ans, Château-Mouton-d'Armailhacq et l'actuel Château-Mouton-Rothschild ne constituaient qu'un seul domaine. En 1855, Mouton-Rothschild fut classé premier parmi les Seconds Crus du Médoc. D'autre part, Mouton-d'Armailhacq fut classé Cinquième Cru et, juste avant la dernière guerre, il était plus connu que certains Quatrièmes Crus et même Troisièmes Crus.

Mouton-Baronne-Philippe est situé entre les célèbres vignobles de Mouton-Rothschild et de Pontet-Canet, au nord de Pauillac. Ses vins sont excellents et l'honneur en revient au baron Philippe de Rothschild, propriétaire de Mouton-Rothschild qui fait ce vin depuis 1930 et donna son prénom au vignoble en 1950. Il en modifia à nouveau le nom en 1977 en hommage à son épouse Pauline décédée. On l'appelle donc désormais, en général : Château-

Mouton-Baronne-Philippe. Le baron Philippe s'est révélé un des vignerons et promoteurs les plus intelligents de i'histoire contemporaine des vins de Bordeaux et du Médoc. Quoique les deux vignobles soient contigus, les vins sont traités séparément. Sa fille Philippine, ancienne actrice est souvent à Mouton-Rothschild.

Caractéristiques : Un très bon Pauillac, plus léger que Mouton-Rothschild, mais également avec un bouquet d'une finesse caractéristique.

Superficie : 50 ha.

Production moyenne : 190 tonneaux (18 000 caisses).

Mouton-Rothschild (Château-)

Bordeaux rouge. Commune de Pauillac, en Haut-Médoc.

Plusieurs interprétations sont données pour l'origine de ce nom. Le baron Philippe de Rothschild, son propriétaire actuel, en donne deux : en vieux français, un terrain vallonné se serait appelé *mothon ;* en outre, une succession de petits vallonnements suggère à l'esprit le verbe moutonner. Mais autour de Pauillac, on dit que Mouton est tout simplement un endroit où paissaient jadis des moutons. Avant d'appartenir aux Rothschild, ce domaine était la propriété du baron de Brane, seigneur de Mouton (c'était au XVIIIe siècle et ce nom nous apporte une explication supplémentaire quant à l'origine de l'appellation). Le domaine s'appelait Château-Pouyallet. Entre le XVIe siècle et 1853, date à laquelle les Rothschild l'achetèrent, on compte parmi ses propriétaires des célébrités telles que le duc de Gloucester (1430), Jean Dunois, Gaston de Foix. Depuis quatre générations désormais, soit plus d'un siècle, le vignoble est passé de Nathaniel Rothschild à James puis à Henri et enfin, aujourd'hui, à l'arrière-petit-fils de l'acquéreur, Philippe de Rothschild. La qualité et le renom de son vin n'ont cessé de grandir. Mouton était déjà hautement estimé en 1855 quand on classa les crus du Médoc. Étant donné qu'à cette époque il ne se vendait pas tout à fait au prix des Premiers Crus, mais plus cher que les Seconds Crus, on lui accorda une place exceptionnelle de premier parmi les Seconds. Ce compromis ne plut pas et c'est depuis lors que Château-Mouton a adopté une devise imitée de l'ancienne boutade des Rohan : *Premier ne puis, second ne daigne, Mouton suis.* Les Rothschild l'ont scrupuleusement observée et depuis l'amandement à la classification de 1855, réalisé en 1973 par le ministère de l'Agriculture, Mouton-Rothschild est enfin reconnu comme Premier Cru. Ceci marque peut-être le premier pas vers une remise à jour de l'ancienne classification.

Cette prééminence est due à la haute qualité du vin lui-même, surtout depuis que, en 1926, Philippe de Rothschild en assuma la direction et devint plus tard propriétaire. Il fut assisté dans sa gestion par un homme fort capable : M. Marjary. La gestion du domaine est aujourd'hui placée sous la responsabilité du directoire de Philippe Cottin, de Patrick Léon, de la fille de Philippe de Rothschild, Philippine et prochainement peut-être de son fils : Philippe Sereys de Rothschild. Une production moyenne de 900 barriques provient exclusivement de Cabernet Sauvignon et cuve longtemps. Patrick Léon, l'actuel œnologue chargé de la vinification, ainsi que l'ex-maître de chais Raoul Blondin, dont le père exerça cette fonction avant lui pendant plus d'un demi-siècle, sont convaincus qu'on ne peut faire un grand vin sans cuvage prolongé. Actuellement, presque partout en Médoc, on ne laisse le jus de raisin en contact avec les peaux et pépins que pendant 9 à 15 jours. Mais à Mouton, le moût dans sa totalité macère en cuve pendant tout un mois, c'est-à-dire encore 20 jours après la fin de la fermentation. Ce procédé et l'usage de Cabernet Sauvignon à raison de 85 % ont pour but de produire un grand vin vigoureux qui exige une longue maturation en bouteille, mais donne alors un breuvage splendide et d'une grande longévité.

Le grand chai des vins de la dernière récolte à Mouton-Rothschild est le plus spectaculaire du Bordelais. Les fûts rangés en bon ordre, sur cinq ou six rangs, longs d'une centaine de mètres, offrent un spectacle impressionnant. Lors des banquets, on en ouvre les grandes portes doubles. Le chai proprement dit est au-dessus du niveau du sol. Mais, au-dessous, dans des caves aux murs noircies par des mousses, plus de 100 000 bouteilles de Mouton sont entreposées à une température constante de 11 °C. C'est là aussi que se trouve la fabuleuse « bibliothèque » vinicole dont les pièces rares sont des bouteilles couvertes de poussières et de toiles d'araignée qui datent de 100 ans et plus. Le long du mur du fond se trouve un casier contenant les bouteilles de tous les millésimes depuis l'achat du château par les Rothschild.

Le talent déployé pour initier et sensibiliser le public à l'art des grands vins ne se manifeste pas que sur le domaine. Les étiquettes des bouteilles, par exemple, sont illustrées chaque année par un artiste différent. Salvador Dali, Henry Moore, Jean Cocteau, Marc Chagall, Picasso. Pendant des années le baron Philippe, avec l'aide avisée de sa femme maintenant décédée, a collectionné tableaux, verres, tapisseries, vases et d'autres objets ayant un rapport avec le vin. Ils les ont rassemblés dans un musée admirablement éclairé qui ouvrit en 1962 et offre aux amateurs de vin une collection dont ils peuvent être reconnaissants. Ce n'est là qu'un des nombreux accomplissements du baron Philippe de Rothschild qui plus que tout autre s'est consacré à la recherche de la qualité et à l'expression artistique du vin. A ce titre, son nom figure dans les annales des vins.

Caractéristiques : Toujours puissant, et corsé, presque charnu, avec une saveur particulière presque métallique qui a disparu dans les récents millésimes et que les gens du Bordelais appelaient goût de capsule. La forte proportion de Cabernet Sauvignon rend son viellissement très lent.

Superficie : 65 ha.

Production moyenne : 26 000 caisses.

Müller-Thurgau

Variété de vigne obtenue par croisement de Riesling et de Sylvaner. C'est aussi le vin fait avec le raisin de cette variété. On cultive de plus en plus le Müller-Thurgau en Allemagne.

On en trouvait aussi une certaine quantité en Alsace.

Ce nom figure rarement sur les étiquettes de vin.

Voir ALLEMAGNE ; ALSACE

Munson (Thomas V.)

Arboriculteur américain qui a obtenu plusieurs vignes hybrides, notamment la Delicatessen. Munson a presque révolutionné l'art de l'hybridation à partir de son vignoble expérimental de Denison, au Texas, mais ses propres travaux n'ont qu'un intérêt limité pour les viticulteurs puisqu'ils sont plutôt orientés vers la production de nouvelles variétés de raisins de table.

Murray Valley

La plus grande région vinicole d'Australie située à la frontière des États de Victoria et d'Australie méridionale. On y produit essentiellement de très bons vins de table, des vins de liqueur et de l'eau-de-vie.

Voir AUSTRALIE

Murrumbidgee

Vignoble irrigué au bord du Murrumbidgee, affluent du fleuve Murray, en Nouvelle-Galles du Sud. On y produit à la fois des vins de table et des vins de liqueur.

Voir AUSTRALIE

Muscadel

Un des noms donnés en pays anglo-saxons aux vins doux vinés généralement additionnés d'alcool et produits avec du raisin Muscat *(voir ce nom).*

Muscadelle

Raisin à vin blanc, cultivé dans la région de Bordeaux. Il entre dans la vinification des Sauternes doux et des Graves secs.

Au cours du siècle dernier, on cultivait un excellent Muscadelle en Afrique du Sud, où il donnait un bon vin du Cap nommé Constantia.

Muscadet (Appellation Contrôlée)

Vins blancs. Basse-Loire.

Les vignobles de Muscadet — les seuls de Bretagne qui soient classés — s'étendent à l'embouchure de la Loire, près de Nantes. Le raisin qui sert à faire ce vin est l'ancien Melon de Bourgogne (il n'existe plus dans cette région) rebaptisé Muscadet ; il fut introduit dans la région par des moines au

XVIIe siècle. C'est un vin léger et frais, dont le bouquet comporte une trace de musc, et qui accompagne admirablement poissons et fruits de mer. Depuis la dernière guerre il a considérablement gagné en popularité en France comme à l'étranger. Les vendanges de Muscadet sont les plus précoces de France ; elles donnent un vin qui doit être bu jeune. Mûris plus que nécessaire les raisins donnent un vin qui, n'ayant plus la fraîcheur et l'acidité qui le caractérisent, perd les qualités du Muscadet.

Les bons Muscadet sont mis en bouteille immédiatement après le décuvage. C'est la seule région à posséder un système de cuves souterraines placées sous des caves, dans le sol frais et rocailleux. Ces vins sont mis en bouteille alors qu'ils contiennent encore du gaz carbonique (le soutirage les oxyderait et les aplatirait), ce qui les rend légèrement pétillants ou perlés : c'est ce qu'on appelle la méthode « sur lie ». Néanmoins de nombreux Muscadet de qualité inférieure sont perlés artificiellement ; ils peuvent également contenir des traces de sucre non fermenté qui couvrent leur goût naturellement acide.

Exploitée après la guerre, la région du Muscadet ne produit des vins fins que depuis quelques années. Elle compte environ 6 000 métayers, dont certains cultivent des vignobles d'à peine 2 ha. La plupart des vignerons restent inorganisés alors que les négociants contrôlent un tiers de la production des 10 000 ha de vignobles. La production globale s'élève à quelque 600 000 hl (plus de 6 millions de caisses) par an, dont 80 % produits sur les coteaux du Sèvre-et-Maine (A.O.C.) situés entre les rives des deux fleuves. 10 % proviennent des terres rocailleuses des Coteaux de la Loire (A.O.C.). Les derniers 10 % portent la simple appellation « Muscadet », sans autre mention. Les amateurs à la recherche du meilleur cru de la région rencontrent bien des difficultés car le Muscadet ne classifie pas la production de ses différentes communes ; le Beaujolais, par exemple, opère une distinction entre l'Appellation Contrôlée Beaujolais, le Beaulolais-Villages et la production de ses meilleurs villages, Fleurie, Brouilly et Morgon. Il n'en va pas de même dans le Muscadet, où aucune distinction ne sera faite entre les crus de Saint-Fiacre, La Haie-Fouassière ou Le Pallet. Les meilleurs Muscadet viennent de Sèvres-et-Maine et surtout du sud de cette région. Vallet (capitale sinon de droit, du moins de fait, du Muscadet), Mouzillon, Le Pallet, Saint-Fiacre, La Haie-Fouassière, Vertou, Monnières, Haute-Goulaine et Gorges sont des noms d'agglomérations les plus dignes d'attention.

Le Gros Plant (ou Gros Plant du Pays Nantais) est un V.D.Q.S. (Vin délimité de qualité supérieure, label qui désigne des vins de qualité inférieure à celle des Appellations Contrôlées) au goût légèrement plus acide que le Muscadet de Sèvre-et-Maine ; on le fait avec du Gros Plant exclusivement, de la famille de la Folle Blanche, variété autrefois cultivée dans la région de Cognac, au nord de Bordeaux, désormais, on ne la trouve plus que dans la région de Nantes. Le Gros Plant est un vin plus gros et plus vulgaire que le Muscadet, bon pour la consommation locale mais pas pour l'exportation.

Muscadine

Vignes indigènes du sud de l'Amérique du Nord. La variété la plus connue est la Scuppernong ; les autres, James et Mish.

Ces raisins ne plaisent guère aux vinificateurs parce qu'ils contiennent peu de sucre et beaucoup d'acide, et aussi en raison de leur arôme désagréable et très prononcé après vinification.

Voir CHAPITRE IV

Muscat

1. Raisin sucré, le plus souvent blanc, dont il existe de nombreuses familles. Il donne des vins lourds, de saveur et d'odeur prononcées, ainsi que des vins de dessert très doux. On les consomme aussi comme raisins de table. En Californie, le Muscat d'Alexandrie est cultivé pour faire du vin, mais ce n'est pas un raisin de bonne qualité.

2. Muscat de Beaumes-de-Venise, Muscat de Frontignan, Muscat de Lunel, Muscat de Saint-Jean-de-Minervois Muscat de Mireval et Muscat de Rivesaltes sont des vins de liqueur français et tous des Appellations Contrôlées *(voir à cette appellation).*

Muscat d'Alsace

Muscat sec et fruité, fait en Alsace *(voir ce nom).*

Muscat de Samos

Voir SAMOS : GRÈCE

Muscatel

Ces vins, faits avec le raisin Muscat, peuvent être blancs, rouges, de dessert ou mousseux. Deux des plus connus sont le Muscat de Frontignan et le Muscat de Samos.

En Californie on vend comme succédané de spiritueux une quantité malheureusement trop importante de vins vinés baptisés Muscatel.

Muselétage

Action de placer un muselet sur le goulot des bouteilles de Champagne ou encore de mousseux.

Musigny (Appellation Contrôlée)

Bourgogne rouge et blanc. Commune de Chambolle-Musigny, en Côte de Nuits. Classement officiel : Grand Cru.

« Si notre coteau n'était pas le plus riche du monde, ce serait le plus pauvre ». Il suffit de voir Musigny pour comprendre cette boutade. Le vignoble s'étend au long d'une petite route de terre battue au-delà de laquelle il n'y a qu'une bande de brousailles et de roc. D'un côté la terre ne vaut pratiquement rien. De l'autre, on sait qu'elle s'est vendue jusqu'à 600 000 francs l'hectare.

Ce vignoble comporte trois parties : Les Musigny, Les Petits Musigny et La Combe d'Orveau. Elles se succèdent dans cet ordre le long du coteau. Sur un plateau, au-dessous, se dresse le château du Clos de Vougeot au milieu de ses vignes. A Musigny, le Pinot Noir domine, mais on y trouve aussi du Pinot Blanc et du Chardonnay qui ne servent pas qu'à faire du vin blanc.

En général, les vignerons qui possèdent des parcelles de Musigny font du vin rouge. Quant au vin blanc, on n'en produit qu'occasionnellement et jamais plus de 7 hl par an. Les rouges sont connus pour leur délicatesse, leur élégance et surtout leur finesse. Les Bourguignons assurent qu'ajouter un peu de Pinot Blanc ou de Chardonnay au moût accroît considérablement ses qualités. La loi autorise 16 % de vigne à vin blanc, mais les vignerons se contentent en général de 10 %. Par bonne année, outre leur délicatesse féminine incomparable, les Musigny ont un bouquet qui rappelle la violette et la fraise. Ils sont prêts à la consommation au bout de deux ans ou à peu près. Mais les bons Musigny, mis en bouteille au domaine, peuvent continuer à vieillir pendant des années et profiter énormément de leur séjour dans le verre.

La superficie de ce vignoble d'exception s'étend sur quelque 10 ha qui produisent par années moyennes 300 hl, soit l'équivalent de 3 600 caisses.

Mustimètre ou saccharomètre

Selon la définition du *Dictionnaire du vin*, un mustimètre ou saccharomètre est un densimètre vulgarisé par Salleron et gradué selon l'échelle centésimale de Gay-Lussac. Il indique le poids en grammes du litre de liquide dans lequel on le plonge. Cet instrument présente une importance capitale en vinification et presque tous les viticulteurs français s'en servent.

TABLEAU DE CORRECTION

Température °C	*Correction*	*Température* °C	*Correction*
10°	— 0,6	21°	+ 1,1
11°	— 0,5	22°	+ 1,3
12°	— 0,4	23°	+ 1,6
13°	— 0,3	24°	+ 1,8
14°	— 0,2	25°	+ 2,0
15°	0	26°	+ 2,3
16°	+ 0,1	27°	+ 2,6
17°	+ 0,3	28°	+ 2,8
18°	+ 0,5	29°	+ 3,1
19°	+ 0,7	30°	+ 3,4
20°	+ 0,9		

La graduation du centre de l'échelle marquée 1 000, représente l'équivalent de la densité de l'eau distillée (1 000 g par litre) ; les graduations situées au-dessus indiquent des densités inférieures, et celles qui sont situées au-dessous, des densités supérieures, par exemple celle d'un litre du moût (ou tout autre liquide) dans lequel l'instrument est plongé.

Pour déterminer la densité d'un moût, on presse quelques grappes de raisin, on filtre le jus à travers un tissu et on le met dans une éprouvette assez large, dans laquelle on plonge successivement un thermomètre et un mustimètre. Supposons qu'on lise 1 065 sur le mustimètre et 18 ºC sur le thermomètre, on se rapporte d'abord au tableau de correction ci-dessous pour corriger la lecture faite sur le mustimètre afin de savoir ce qu'elle serait si la température était de 15 ºC.

Précisons cet exemple. Le moût est testé à une température de 18 ºC. Le mustimètre indique 1 065. Le tableau de correction indique qu'il faut ajouter 0,5 à la donnée du mustimètre pour connaître la densité du moût à la température normale de 15 ºC.

Si la température n'était que de 12 ºC au lieu de 18, le tableau de correction nous indique qu'il faudrait déduire 0,4 des 1 065 indiqués par le mustimètre dont l'indication exacte, après correction, serait : 1 064,6. Cette correction étant faite, nous consulterons les tableaux ci-après pour voir quel est le poids de sucre contenu dans un litre de moût et quelle sera la teneur en alcool du vin après fermentation.

Un instrument semblable est utilisé en Californie : l'hydromètre *(voir ce mot)* Brix ou Balling, qui indique le poids de sucre contenu dans 100 g de solution.

TABLEAU D'ÉQUIVALENCE DE DENSITÉ DES VINS ET DES MOÛTS NORMAUX OU ANORMAUX D'UNE TENEUR PERSPECTIVE INFÉRIEURE A 10º D'ALCOOL

(Avec leur teneur en sucre et leur teneur probable en alcool ainsi que le poids de sucre qu'il faut leur ajouter pour obtenir un vin de 10º).

(Selon SALLERON.)

Densité ou degré du mustimètre	*Degré Baumé de l'aréomètre*	*Grammes de sucre par litre de moût*	*Teneur en alcool du vin qui en résulterait*	*Poids en grammes de sucre cristallisé à ajouter par litre de moût pour obtenir un vin de 10º*
1 000	0			
1 001	0,1			
1 002	0,3			
1 003	0,4			
1 004	0,6			
1 005	0,7			
1 006	0,9			
1 007	1,0			
1 008	1,1			
1 009	1,3			
1 010	1,4			
1 011	1,6			
1 012	1,7	2	0,1	168
1 013	1,8	5	0,2	166
1 014	2,0	7	0,4	163
1 015	2,1	11	0,6	159
1 016	2,3	13	0,7	157
1 017	2,4	15	0,9	154
1 018	2,6	18	1,1	151
1 019	2,7	21	1,2	149
1 020	2,8	23	1,4	148
1 021	2,9	26	1,5	146
1 022	3,1	29	1,7	142
1 023	3,2	31	1,8	139
1 024	3,4	34	1,9	137
1 025	3,5	37	2,1	134
1 026	3,7	39	2,3	130
1 027	3,8	42	2,4	127
1 028	3,9	45	2,6	124
1 029	4,1	47	2,8	122
1 030	4,2	50	3,0	120
1 031	4,3	53	3,1	119

TABLEAU D'ÉQUIVALENCE DE DENSITÉ DES VINS ET DES MOÛTS NORMAUX OU ANORMAUX D'UNE TENEUR PERSPECTIVE INFÉRIEURE A 10° D'ALCOOL *(suite)*
(Avec leur teneur en sucre et leur teneur probable en alcool ainsi que le poids de sucre qu'il faut leur ajouter pour obtenir un vin de 10°).
(Selon SALLERON.)

Densité ou degré du mustimètre	*Degré Baumé de l'aréomètre*	*Grammes de sucre par litre de moût*	*Teneur en alcool du vin qui en résulterait*	*Poids en grammes de sucre cristallisé à ajouter par litre de moût pour obtenir un vin de 10°*
1 032	4,5	55	3,2	115
1 033	4,6	58	3,4	112
1 034	4,7	61	3,5	110
1 035	4,9	63	3,7	107
1 036	5,0	66	3,9	104
1 037	5,2	69	4,0	102
1 038	5,3	72	4,2	99
1 039	5,4	74	4,4	95
1 040	5,5	76	4,5	93
1 041	5,7	80	4,7	90
1 042	5,8	82	4,8	88
1 043	6,0	84	5,0	85
1 044	6,1	87	5,1	83
1 045	6,2	90	5,3	80
1 046	6,3	92	5,4	78
1 047	6,5	95	5,6	75
1 048	6,6	98	5,7	73
1 049	6,7	100	5,9	70
1 050	6,9	103	6,0	68
1 051	7,0	106	6,2	65
1 052	7,1	108	6,3	53
1 053	7,3	111	6,5	59
1 054	7,4	114	6,7	56
1 055	7,5	116	6,8	54
1 056	7,7	119	7,0	51
1 057	7,8	122	7,2	48
1 058	7,9	124	7,3	46
1 059	8,0	127	7,5	42
1 060	8,2	130	7,6	41
1 061	8,3	132	7,8	37
1 062	8,4	135	7,9	37
1 063	8,6	138	8,1	32
1 064	8,7	140	8,2	31
1 065	8,8	143	8,4	26
1 066	8,9	146	8,6	24
1 067	9,0	148	8,7	22
1 068	9,2	151	8,9	19
1 069	9,3	154	9,0	17
1 070	9,4	156	9,2	13
1 071	9,6	159	9,3	12
1 072	9,7	162	9,5	8
1 073	9,8	164	9,6	7
1 074	9,9	167	9,8	3
1 075	10,0	170	10,0	

TABLEAU D'ÉQUIVALENCE DE DENSITÉ DES MOÛTS
D'UNE TENEUR PERSPECTIVE INFÉRIEURE A 10° D'ALCOOL

(Avec leur teneur en sucre et leur teneur probable en alcool et le volume d'eau qu'il faut leur ajouter pour réduire le vin à une teneur en alcool de 10°).
(Selon SALLERON.)

Densité ou degré du mustimètre	*Degré Baumé de l'aréomètre*	*Grammes de sucre par litre de moût*	*Teneur en alcool du vin qui en résulterait*	*Volume d'eau (en l) à ajouter par litre de moût pour ramener sa densité à 1 075 et obtenir un vin de 10°*
1 076	10,2	172	10,1	0,01
1 077	10,3	175	10,3	0,02
1 078	10,4	178	10,5	0,04
1 079	10,6	180	10,6	0,05
1 080	10,7	183	10,8	0,06
1 081	10,8	186	10,9	0,08
1 082	10,9	188	11,0	0,09
1 083	11,1	191	11,2	0,10
1 084	11,2	194	11,4	0,12
1 085	11,3	196	11,5	0,13
1 086	11,4	199	11,7	0,14
1 087	11,6	202	11,9	0,16
1 088	11,7	204	12,0	0,17
1 089	11,8	207	12,2	0,18
1 090	11,9	210	12,3	0,20
1 091	12,0	212	12,5	0,21
1 092	12,2	215	12,6	0,22
1 093	12,3	218	12,8	0,24
1 094	12,4	220	12,9	0,25
1 095	12,5	223	13,1	0,26
1 096	12,6	226	13,3	0,28
1 097	12,7	228	13,4	0,29
1 098	12,9	231	13,6	0,30
1 099	13,0	234	13,8	0,31
1 100	13,1	236	13,9	0,33
1 101	13,2	239	14,0	0,34
1 102	13,3	242	14,2	0,36
1 103	13,5	244	14,4	0,37
1 104	13,6	247	14,5	0,38
1 105	13,7	250	14,7	0,40

La première colonne des tableaux (p. 568, 569 et 570) indique la densité du moût, c'est-à-dire celle qu'on lira sur le mustimètre. La seconde colonne montre quelles seraient les valleurs équivalentes sur l'aréomètre (ou gluco-œnomètre) Baumé et le densimètre ou saccharomètre Gay-Lussac. La troisième colonne indique le poids du sucre naturel de raisin contenu dans un litre de moût. La quatrième donne la teneur probable en alcool du vin après fermentation du moût, en supposant que tout le sucre fermente (ce qui ne se produit pas toujours particulièrement au-dessus de 14° à 15° d'alcool). La cinquième colonne indique le poids de sucre cristallisé pur qu'il faut ajouter à chaque litre de moût pour que le vin après fermentation titre 10° d'alcool. Par l'expression sucre cristallisé pur, nous désignons du sucre blanc normalisé à 100°. Si on utilisait des sucres moins purs, blancs ou bruns, les chiffres indiqués par le tableau seraient insuffisants et il faudrait les majorer proportionnellement au degré du sucre utilisé. Au tableau 2, la cinquième colonne indique le volume d'eau en litres à ajouter à chaque litre de moût pour ramener ce dernier à la densité normale de 1 075.

Pour en revenir à l'exemple du début de cet article nous trouvons :

1. Qu'un moût de 1 065 en densité correspond à 8,8 degrés Baumé ;

2. Que ce moût contient 143 g de sucre de raisin par litre ;

3. Qu'après fermentation, ce sucre donnera 8,4 degrés d'alcool, ce qui signifie que le vin contiendra 8,4 l d'alcool par hectolitre ;

4. Qu'il faudra ajouter 26 g de sucre cristallisé par litre pour élever la teneur en alcool du vin à 10°.

Mutage

Opération qui consiste à interrompre artificiellement la fermentation soit en utilisant de l'anhydride sulfureux, soit en ajoutant de l'alcool au moût. Il en résulte que le vin contiendra une partie de sucre non convertie en alcool. C'est une pratique courante en Entre-Deux-Mers mais aussi dans d'autres districts de la région de Bordeaux.

Muté

Vin que l'on additionne d'eau-de-vie pour arrêter ou empêcher la fermentation. Les vins mutés sont souvent utilisés pour les apéritifs et le coupage de vins manquant de corps et de douceur.

Mycoderma aceti

Bactérie qui sûrit le vin ou le transforme en vinaigre. On l'appelle couramment *acetobacter*.

Mycoderma vini

Levure à laquelle on attribue la formation d'une pellicule sur certains vins.

Voir FLEUR ; FLOR ; XÉRÈS ; VINS DU JURA

Myrat (Château de)

Bordeaux blancs. Commune de Barsac, en Sauternes.

Classé Second Cru en 1855, ce domaine (qui ne produit plus de vin de nos jours) appartient à la famille de Pontac.

N

Nabuchodonosor

Bonbonne de Champagne plus que bouteille, d'une capacité de 16 l ou 20 bouteilles. A cette contenance, on ne l'utilisait auparavant qu'en Champagne.

Nackenheimer Rothenberg

Un des meilleurs Nackenheimer, un cru célèbre de Rheinhessen, en Allemagne.
Voir RHEINHEISSEN

Nahe

État allemand du Palatinat. Superficie approximative : 4 600 ha. 98 % de vins blancs, 2 % de vins rouges.

Situation : la Nahe (7e des 11 régions viticoles d'Allemagne de par sa taille) s'étend entre les vallées de la Moselle et du Rhin. Elle tire son nom d'une rivière, la Nahe, qui se verse dans le Rhin à Bingen, juste en face de Rüdesheim — point de rencontre de quatre régions : Mittelrhein, Nahe, Rheingau et Rheinhessen. En amont, les vins sont extrêmement légers, faits en général avec du Riesling et rappellent les crus de la Sarre, sans toutefois en avoir la finesse. Ce n'est pas surprenant, la Sarre et la Nahe sont proches l'une de l'autre et autrefois on appelait les vins de la haute Nahe vins de la Sarre.

La Nahe se verse dans le Rhin à Bingen, en face de Rüdesheim. De même que les vins de la haute Nahe ressemblent à ceux de la Sarre, ceux qui sont faits en aval de Bad Kreuznach rappellent les vins du Rheingau. Ils sont produits dans la même zone climatique. Néanmoins, il ne faut pas prendre strictement à la lettre ces subdivisions territoriales ; dans un domaine aussi capricieux et varié que le vin, ce serait absurde. Récemment, lors d'une dégustation dans la région de la Nahe, on constata que certains Roxheimer et Gutenberger étaient plus légers que les Moselle.

Le secteur de la Nahe englobe les vallées de deux cours d'eau plus petits : l'Alzenz et le Glan, mais ces vallées ne produisent pas de vins intéressants.

Si la viticulture se modernise dans cette région, c'est parce qu'il a fallu reconstituer des vignobles entièrement détruits par les maladies de la vigne. L'État vint alors au secours des vignerons ruinés. S'il ne l'avait pas fait, il n'y aurait plus aujourd'hui de vin de la Nahe. Les améliorations qui en résultèrent eurent des effets contradictoires. Le prix de revient du vin s'est accru et par conséquent seul le domaine de l'État et un nombre relativement faible d'assez grands propriétaires peuvent se permettre de courir les risques qu'implique la production de vins de qualité. Les gelées du mois de mai, assez fréquentes dans la Nahe, peuvent détruire toute la récolte d'une année. Pour les autres, le problème a été résolu en partie par les coopératives agricoles auxquelles on doit à peu près 1/5 de la production annuelle totale. Bad Kreuznach est la ville la plus importante de la région. Station thermale très populaire, c'est aussi le centre de la viticulture où se sont installés les principaux producteurs. La région se divise en deux districts : le district Schloss Böckelheim qui regroupe les vignobles de la haute et moyenne Nahe au sud et au sud-ouest de Bad Kreuznach, et le district de Kreuznach qui se situe dans la basse Nahe, au nord de la ville.

Variétés de raisin : Müller-Thurgau (27 %), Riesling (22 %), Silvaner (14 %), Kerner (8 %), Scheurebe (7 %), Bacchus (6 %). On trouve également de petits vignobles de deux variétés rouges : Spätburgunder (Pinot Noir) et Portugieser.

Vins : Ils sont riches en nuances. Ce sont des Riesling piquants, racés et élégants ; des Silvaner ronds, des Müller-Thurgau, Kerner, Scheurebe, Bacchus et autres, parfumés et fruités.

Salle de dégustation de l'Allemagne

Ce sont les Romains qui ont apporté, il y a 2 000 ans, des ceps de vigne dans la vallée de Nahe comme le prouvent les anciens outils viticoles et les pichets de vin excavés autour de Bad Kreuznach (et exposés au musée local). Mais c'est la géologie plus que l'histoire qui a influencé le caractère des vins de Nahe. La variété extraordinaire des sols et les compositions multiples que l'on trouve dans cette petite région expliquent la grande diversité des vins que l'on y produit, d'où son surnom de « salle de dégustation de l'Allemagne ».

Les strates de grès rouge — semblables aux « Rotliegendes » qui donnent aux meilleurs Niersteiner toute leur élégance — serpentent la région comme un large ruban. Dans la partie inférieure de la Nahe (toute proche du Rhin), le sol, à forte teneur en quartz et en ardoise, produit des vins racés au fruité agréable, semblables de par leur style aux vins du Rheingau. Plus loin, en amont, les sols changent. Ils sont constitués d'argile, de terreau, de loess et de marne, et produisent des vins plus généreux, plus doux et souvent plus fleuris. Dans la moyenne et haute Nahe (sites les plus remarquables), le sol est un mélange d'ardoise gris vert et de roches pyrogènes comme le mélaphyre et le porphyre. Le paysage de la Nahe y est des plus spectaculaires avec notamment le précipice de porphyre (d'une hauteur de 200 m) à Rotenfels — qui est aussi la falaise la plus abrupte au nord des Alpes. Les vins, en particulier les Riesling, sont parmi les plus fins d'Allemagne. Parce qu'ils sont très distingués, complexes et élégants (qualités typiques des vins cultivés sur sols d'ardoise) on les a souvent comparés aux vins de la Sarre.

En dépit de sa situation au nord, le climat de la Nahe est doux grâce à l'abri naturel de la chaîne de l'Hunsrück qui la protège contre les vents froids et la pluie. Les sommets sont coiffés de la forêt Soon qui retient la chaleur dans la journée et la laisse filtrer la nuit, maintenant ainsi une température égale dans les vignobles — facteur important pour l'assimilation et l'obtention d'une maturité continue et homogène des raisins.

Producteurs

L'habileté et le dévouement des hommes change d'une génération à l'autre, cependant parmi les noms suivants figurent ceux de quelques producteurs traditionnels. Cette liste n'est pas exhaustive :

Weingut Paul Anheuser (Bad Kreuznach), Weingut Ökonomierat August E. Anheuser (Bad Kreuznach), Weingut Hans Crusius (Traisen), Schlossgut Diel (Burg Layen), Weingut Carl Finkenauer (Bad Kreuznach), Weingut Dr. Josef Höfer (Burg Layen), Reichsgräflich von Plettenberg'sche Verwaltung (Bad Kreuznach), Prinz zu Salm-Dalberg'sches Weingut (Schloss Wallhausen), Weingut Jacob Schneider (Niederhausen), Weingut Erbhof Tesch (Langenlonsheim), Vereinigte Weingüter Schlink-Herf-Gutleuthof (Bad Kreuznach), Winzergenossenschaft Rheingrafenburg (Meddersheim), Zentralkellerei der Nahe Winzer (Bretzenheim).

Environ 55 % des 2 300 viticulteurs de la Nahe sont producteurs de vin. La taille moyenne de leur vignoble est de 3 ha environ. La moitié de la production régionale est vendue directement par les viticulteurs, l'autre moitié étant commercialisée par le négoce et les coopératives. La production annuelle, calculée sur une moyenne de dix années est de 360 000 hl (4 millions de caisses).

Villages et Crus importants

Dans le district de Schloss Böckelheim, le village du même nom et les villages voisins de Niederhausen ont une réputation de qualité grâce aux vins exceptionnels produits par le prestigieux Domaine Vinicole d'État (Verte waltung der Staatlichen Weinbaudomänen). L'aigle noir stylisé sur l'étiquette est un souvenir de ses origines prussiennes. Deux crus sont particulièrement bons : Kupfergrube (créé au début du XXe siècle, lors d'une campagne contre le chômage) et Hermannshöhle. Felsenberg et Hermannsberg sont aussi excellents. Autres villages qui méritent d'être cités : Altenbamberg (Rotenfels), Norheim (Dellchen), Roxheim (Berg, Höllenpfad), Traisen (Bastei), Meddersheim et Monzingen, Rüdesheim/Nahe à ne pas confondre avec Rüdesheim/Rheingau.

Dans le district de Kreuznach, le village du même nom possède d'excellents vignobles qui produisent des crus très stylés et de toute première classe. Ces grands crus comprennent : Krötenpfuhl, Brückes, Narrenkappe, Kahlenberg et Hinkelstein. Citons aussi les villages de : Burg Layen (Schlossberg), Dorsheim (Burgberg, Goldloch), Langenlonsheim, Münster-Sarmsheim (Dautenpflänzer, Pittersberg) et Wallhausen (Johannisberg, Felseneck).

Voir APPENDICE B

Nairac (Château)

Bordeaux blancs. Commune de Barsac, en Sauternes.

Après avoir été négligé pendant de longues années, ce petit domaine situé à l'entrée de Barsac a été repris en main par ses nouveaux propriétaires, Thomas Heeter, un Américain, et maintenant son ex-femme, Nicole Tari, fille du propriétaire de Château-Giscours. Nicole Tari est aujourd'hui seule responsable. Les vignobles ont été replantés et la magnifique maison du XVIIIe siècle est tout à fait restaurée. Le vin, un Barsac-Sauternes typique, est classé Second Cru, bien qu'il compte de loin parmi les meilleurs Barsac.

Superficie : 16 ha.

Production moyenne : 25 tonneaux (2 000 caisses).

Napa-Solano

Région vinicole de Californie. On y produit de bons vins de table rouges. Bien des bons vins blancs proviennent aussi de la vallée de Napa.

Voir ÉTATS-UNIS : CALIFORNIE ET OUEST

Cagliari (Nasco di) (D.O.C.)

Vin de liqueur de Sardaigne *(voir ce nom).*

Natural Wine

Vin auquel rien n'a été ajouté qui aurait pu avoir de l'influence sur son goût ou sa vigueur (en anglais).

Nature

Vin nature, c'est-à-dire sans addition de sucre. En Champagne cette même expression désigne le vin non mousseux du pays.

Néac (Appellation Contrôlée)

Bordeaux rouges. Bordelais.

L'aire d'Appellation Contrôlée Lalande de Pomerol s'est étendue à l'aire d'Appellation Contrôlée Néac en 1954.

Voir LALANDE DE POMEROL

Nebbiolo

Raisin servant en Italie à faire des vins rouges, par exemple le Sassella et l'Inferno, en Lombardie.

Nectar

La boisson des dieux grecs de l'Antiquité. On utilisa plus tard ce nom pour des vins de qualité exceptionnelle, et de nos jours on trouve encore en Grèce des bouteilles de Nectar.

Negus

Boisson chaude très ancienne composée de Porto, sucre, citron et épices.

Nerveux

Ce qualificatif désigne des vins au goût net, prononcé et ayant une acidité fixe assez élevée.

Net

Se dit d'un vin rafraîchissant et agréable, sans faux goût.

Neuberger

Cépage cultivé en Autriche.

Neuchâtel

Canton suisse qui produit des vins blancs secs, légers et vivaces.
Voir SUISSE

Neutre (Alcool)

Eau-de-vie de vin distillée à un très haut degré. Si elle était tout à fait neutre, elle titrerait 100°, n'aurait aucune caractéristique particulière. Dans la pratique, toute eau-de-vie titrant plus de 85° est considérée comme neutre. De même pour l'alcool neutre utilisé en coupages pour les whiskies.

New Jersey

Région vinicole peu importante des États-Unis, dont le centre est Egg Harbor.

Nez (avoir du)

Se dit du bouquet d'un vin.

Niagara

1. Région vinicole de l'État de New York. Le cru le plus important est Château-Gai, au Canada, dont le meilleur vin est un mousseux, exempt de coupages, fait avec du raisin Delaware.
2. Un des plus vieux raisins hybrides américains qui produit du vin blanc ayant un goût de foxe prononcé.
Voir ÉTATS-UNIS : ÉTATS DE L'EST

Niederhäuser Hermannshöhle

Un des vins les plus connus de la vallée de la Nahe, en Allemagne. *Voir* NAHE

Niersteiner

Le meilleur vin de Rheinhessen. Élégance et bon nez. Les plus fins des Niersteiner sont des Riesling. *Voir* RHEINHESSEN

Nip

Nom que les Anglais donnent à une bouteille contenant environ 1/4 de litre et dont la véritable contenance devrait toujours être une demi-pinte (28,412 cl).

Noah

Raisin de couleur verte qui donne du vin blanc. C'est un hybride américain qui fut d'abord connu dans l'Illinois. Après que le phylloxéra eut ravagé l'Europe, à la fin du XIXᵉ siècle, on adopta le Noah en France, mais les vignerons ne tardèrent pas à l'abandonner en raison du goût de foxe qu'il donnait au vin. Il a même été interdit. On en trouve pourtant encore, de-ci, de-là. C'est du nom de ce raisin que dérive l'adjectif « noahté », synonyme de « foxé ».

Noble

Terme généralement appliqué à toutes variétés de raisins, tout vignoble ou tout vin de supériorité durable et indiscutable. Un raisin noble dans un bon vignoble donnera un vin remarquable.

Noble Rot

Littéralement : pourriture noble *(voir ce mot et* BOTRYTIS CINEREA).

Noblejas

Vin de Tolède, généralement des rouges vigoureux, assez semblables aux crus mineurs des Côtes du Rhône.

Noggin

Autre nom du *gill* ou quart de pinte britannique (14,206 cl).

Norheim

Village viticole de la vallée de la Nahe en Allemagne.
Voir NAHE

Norton

Peut-être est-ce la meilleure vigne indigène américaine pour le vin rouge. Elle donne des vins corsés, bien équilibrés, exempts de foxe.

Norvège

Au temps jadis, c'est-à-dire pendant tout le Moyen Age et jusqu'au début du XVIIe siècle, les Norvégiens ne buvaient que bière et hydromel en fait de breuvages alcoolisés. Bien qu'ils fussent depuis longtemps en contact par mer avec des pays où l'on buvait du vin, les Norvégiens ne l'adoptèrent qu'au bout de plusieurs siècles. La révolution, en fait de boisson, se produisit quand on importa des spiritueux. Elle n'eut lieu qu'au XVIIe siècle car, jusqu'alors, on ne trouvait en Norvège, dans le commerce, aucun alcool consommable. Puis il y en eut beaucoup. Sauf entre 1756 et 1816, chacun était libre de distiller au foyer. L'aquavit était alors l'alcool préféré des Norvégiens. En 1830, on dénombrait 11 000 alambics en activité. En 1845, un bouleversement se produisit. La pomme de terre était devenue la matière première la plus utilisée pour la fabrication des spiritueux. Or les distillateurs non professionnels ne s'en servaient pas facilement. Et cette année-là donc, une loi interdisait les alambics d'une capacité inférieure à 200 l. Ces deux facteurs contribuèrent à diminuer le charme de la distillation à domicile.

Petit à petit, deux grosses entreprises s'assurèrent un quasi-monopole de la distillation : Jorgen b. Lysholm, de Trondjheim, et Løiten Braenderis Distillation, de Christiania, aujourd'hui Oslo. En 1927 cependant, le monopole du vin (A/s Vinmonopolet) prit en main les distilleries et contrôle encore de nos jours l'achat et la vente de tous les spiritueux consommables en Norvège. Le conseil d'administration de cet office est nommé par son directeur : le roi. L'instauration du monopole avait pour but de réglementer la vente et de lutter contre l'alcoolisme. A/s Vinmonopolet est l'unique organisme chargé de rectifier les alcools distillés indépendamment, d'importer des vins et spiritueux, de les vendre en gros et au détail. Il contrôle même l'alcool utilisé à des fins médicales. L'importation en gros de la bière est contrôlée de la même manière mais on peut la vendre librement dans certains magasins qui en ont la licence. Actuellement on vend près de 200 000 hl (plus de 2 millions de caisses) de vin en Norvège. Ni le vin, ni les spiritueux ne sont taxés à la douane mais les impôts intérieurs sont très élevés. La vente annuelle des spiritueux s'éleve à plus de 185 000 hl, à savoir :

Spiritueux mis en bouteille à l'étranger.

Spiritueux importés et mis en bouteille par A/s Vinmonopolet.

Spiritueux importés et mélangés à de l'alcool norvégien.

Alcool produit en Norvège.

Selon les statistiques officielles, les Norvégiens âgés de plus de 15 ans consomment annuellement 6 l d'alcool pur par tête.

Les marques d'aquavit norvégienne Løiten et Lysholm sont exportées vers la plupart des marchés du monde.

La Norvège produit aussi une « Linie Aquavit » spécialité unique. C'est l'eau-de-vie qui a « traversé la ligne », c'est-à-dire l'équateur. Pour maintenir une ancienne tradition, l'aquavit déjà vieillie en fût fait l'aller et retour Norvège-Australie sur les cargos Wilhelmsen et franchit donc deux fois la ligne. Le balancement du bateau pendant ce voyage fait subir à l'alcool une maturation supplémentaire. L'air salé et les variations de température y contribuent aussi.

L'A/s Vinmonopolet garantit sur l'étiquette que le voyage a bien eu lieu, en indique la date ainsi que le nom du bateau. « Linie Aquavit » est bonne avec les hors-d'œuvres et les mets épicés.

Nouvelle-Zélande

La Nouvelle-Zélande doit la naissance et la prospérité de sa viticulture à quelques hommes remarquables : Samuel Marsden — missionnaire anglican et chef aumônier du gouvernement de la Nouvelle-Galles du Sud — il importa les méthodes agricoles européennes ; James Busby, premier résident britannique en Nouvelle-Zélande ; l'évêque Pompallier, missionnaire catholique français. Ces trois hommes introduisirent les premières boutures de vignes, en Nouvelle-Zélande. Plus tard, un certain Roméo Bragata, diplômé de l'école italienne d'œnologie de Comegliano, premier œnologue du gouvernement néo-zélandais, consolidait les bases de l'industrie vinicole naissante et enseignait aux colons l'art de faire du bon vin.

On trouve dans le journal de Samuel Marsden, à la date du 25 septembre 1819, la première indication de plantations de vignes : « J'ai planté (à Kerikeri) environ 100 pieds de vigne de variétés différentes, achetées à Port Jackson (Sydney). Pour autant que j'en puisse juger, la nature du sol et du climat néo-zélandais semble promettre de bons résultats. »

Le journal du célèbre explorateur français Dumont d'Urville de l'Astrolabe — qui visita la baie des îles pour la deuxième fois en 1840 — contient les premières observations écrites sur le vin produit en Nouvelle-Zélande. Hôte de Busby à Waitangi, il se vit offrir « un léger vin blanc très mousseux et d'un goût exquis. A juger de cet échantillon, je ne puis qu'être certain que la vigne sera amplement cultivée sur les collines sablonneuses de ces îles ».

En 1838, l'évêque introduisit des vignes françaises en Nouvelle-Zélande. Les colons français firent de même à Akaroa en 1840 et les Allemands à Nelson en 1843.

En 1894, de nombreux secteurs de l'île du Nord et de l'île du Sud étaient plantés de vignes, toutes de la variété *Vitis vinifera*. Mais le phylloxéra et la montée de la prohibition ne tardèrent pas à compromettre la nouvelle industrie. Le phylloxéra eut de graves conséquences ; de nombreux fermiers furent contraints d'abandonner complètement la viniculture, d'autres, arrachant les plants de *vinifera*, se mirent à cultiver des variétés hybrides américaines résistant au phylloxéra, mais produisant des vins de qualité bien inférieure aux *vinifera*. Ces souches dérivées de *Vitis labrusca* se révélèrent très prolifiques grâce au climat humide du nord ; mais leur production — raisins à vin et raisins de table — peut aisément être écoulée.

En 1906, la superficie plantée s'élevait à 220 ha. En 1909 — date à laquelle Bragata quitta le ministère de l'Agriculture —, elle atteignait 268 ha. Cependant en 1923, elle n'était plus que de 179 ha : le désintérêt du gouvernement, la montée de la prohibition, la menace constante du phylloxéra, de l'oïdium et de la pourriture, contraignirent de nombreux colons à abandonner la viniculture au profit d'autres travaux agricoles plus rentables. On ne comptait plus que trois classes principales de vignerons : les immigrants yougoslaves et quelques autres dans la province d'Auckland ; les occupants des terres jadis plantées par les gentlemen-farmers de la baie de Hawke ; enfin les Pères maristes, descendants spirituels de l'évêque Pompallier, qui établirent définitivement leur vignoble à Greenmeadows dans la baie de Hawke.

L'industrie continua à s'affaiblir pendant la Première Guerre mondiale. Il y avait pénurie de main-d'œuvre. La prohibition fut renforcée, privant ainsi les viniculteurs de débouchés pour leurs produits.

Le gouvernement instauré en 1935 contribua considérablement à la relance en prenant certaines mesures : il réduisit l'importation de vins de 50 % par l'octroi de licences, et décida d'augmenter de 50 % les taxes sur les vins importés. Le véritable coup de fouet fut donné par l'explosion de la guerre en 1939 ; les approvisionnements étrangers se réduisant considérablement, la Nouvelle-Zélande dut vivre sur ses propres ressources.

La superficie de vignobles doubla presque pendant la guerre et elle augmenta progressivement durant les années suivantes. En 1973, la Nouvelle-Zélande comptabilisait quelque 2 000 ha de vignes produisant au moins 300 000 hl (plus de 3 millions de caisses) de vin par an. Près de 500 ha de *vinifera* furent plantés par une firme associée à une entreprise américaine et de nouveaux vignobles ont permis d'atteindre une superficie totale de plus de 4 500 ha en 1986. Aujourd'hui 95 % de la superficie est plantée de *Vitis vinifera* et des cépages blancs comme le Chardonnay, le Riesling, le Sauvignon et le Sémillon ont eu une augmentation de plus de 100 % depuis le début des années 80.

Entre Auckland et Christchurch, on peut distinguer différentes régions où la vigne est cultivée : les districts de Hawkes Bay et de Poverty Bay, autour des villes de Napier et Gisborne sur la côte est de North Island, représentent 2/3 des vignobles plantés de la Nouvelle-Zélande ; 20 % de la superficie totale plantée se trouve dans la province de Marlborough, aux alentours de Blenheim, dans le nord-est de South Island ; pratiquement tout le reste se trouve autour des villes de Auckland et de Hamilton dans le nord-ouest de South Island.

Pendant longtemps — pratiquement du début du siècle à nos jours — l'industrie vinicole néo-zélandaise s'est trouvée confrontée à un grave dilemme. La demande portait essentiellement sur les vins vinés — Porto, Xérès, Madère, etc. Or les experts ont toujours déclaré que le climat tempéré du pays ne permettait pas de produire des vins de liqueur naturels. En 1946, la Commission royale pour les licences déclare : « Le climat n'est pas suffisamment chaud pour produire des raisins assez riches en sucre ». La même commission fit remarquer que cette déficience était compensée par l'addition de sucre de canne, certains vins doux contenant jusqu'à 30 % de leur poids de sucre ajouté.

Donc, la demande est en faveur des vins vinés, alors que le climat convient à la production de vins de table légers. Le viniculteur a toujours fait face à la situation, et comprend l'intérêt de se consacrer à la production de vins de table, plus appropriée au climat et au sol. Le climat de la baie de Hawke est très semblable à celui de certaines parties de la Bourgogne et du Bordelais. Blenheim est la région la plus ensoleillée et la moins pluvieuse de tout le pays, particulièrement à l'époque des vendanges, bien que les sols aient parfois à souffrir du gel. Contrairement à ce que pensent certains, les régions vinicoles néo-zélandaises jouissent d'un climat beaucoup plus chaud et ensoleillé — comme le témoignent les chiffres annuels — que celui de la Suisse et de l'Allemagne.

Bien que le Cabernet Sauvignon de la baie de Hawke se soit régulièrement distingué dans les concours internationaux, un nombre croissant de vins se popularisent à l'étranger tels que le Chardonnay, le Riesling et le Gewürztraminer. Les vignerons plantent de nouvelles vignes au fur et à mesure que le ministère de l'Agriculture lève la quarantaine qui les frappe. On faisait déjà du bon Cabernet Sauvignon en Nouvelle-Zélande il y a près de soixante-dix ans. Les variétés Pinot Noir, Pinot Meunier, Hermitage (Shiraz) et Pinotage donnèrent elles aussi de bons vins rouges.

En ce qui concerne les vins blancs, on découvre le Pinot Chardonnay et le Traminer. Jusqu'à présent ces variétés sont produites en quantité réduite, mais les viticulteurs ont du Riesling-Sylvaner (Müller-Thurgau) en abondance, variété qui donne l'un des blancs les plus populaires de Nouvelle-Zélande vendu sous le nom de « Riesling ». Quant au vrai Riesling, on le plantait déjà bien avant l'épidémie de phylloxéra, et s'il est prospère en Australie, il ne devrait pas l'être moins ici.

Certaines parties de la Nouvelle-Zélande ont un sol et un climat tout à fait favorables à la production de très bons vins de table en quantité abondante. Il faudrait planter plus de cépages européens au lieu des types hybrides américains, particulièrement prolifiques, mais ne pouvant pas produire de vins de qualité dans ce climat tempéré. La Nouvelle-Zélande est un des plus gros producteurs mondiaux de Müller-Thurgau après l'Allemagne et la plus grande partie de ses vins sont faits avec du Müller-Thurgau. Depuis, la plantation de variétés *vinifera* de vins de table rouges et blancs a augmenté.

Pour la période 1985-86, sur 30 viticulteurs détenant une licence, 120 étaient opérationnels. La production totale pour la saison 1985 s'élevait à 600 000 hl (6,5 millions de caisses) de vin.

Selon l'Association de viniculture, la consommation annuelle de vins locaux et étrangers serait de 16,5 l par personne, alors qu'elle s'élèverait à 132 l pour la bière. A l'heure actuelle, Montana Wine Ltd à Auckland est le plus gros producteur de vin, il appartient en partie à la maison Joseph Seagram & son, Inc. et couvre environ 2 500 ha de vignobles produisant plusieurs vins de cépages. McWilliams et Corbans sont deux autres producteurs dignes d'attention. On estime que le vin blanc de table représente environ 47 % de la production totale, les vins de table rouges et rosés 6 %, le vin en vrac 6 %, les vins mousseux 12 %, et les vins vinés environ 29 %.

Noyau

Liqueur incolore ou rosâtre sucrée artificiellement, et qui peut avoir un goût d'huile d'amande ou de pêche.

Nu

Le prix nu est celui du vin sans barrique ni bouteille, c'est-à-dire du vin parfois appelé vin en vrac.

Nuits (Côte de)

Voir CÔTE DE NUITS

Nuits-Saint-Georges (Appellation Contrôlée)

Bourgogne rouges ainsi que des blancs. Côte de Nuits.

L'ancienne ville de Nuits, qui, en 1892, adopta le nom de son cru le plus chéri pour devenir Nuits-Saint-Georges, se trouve presque à l'extrémité sud de la côte à laquelle elle donne son nom. Contrairement à la plupart des autres appellations de Côte de Nuits, celle-ci couvre non seulement les vignobles de Nuits, mais aussi ceux de Prémeaux situés un peu plus au sud. Ces deux communes sont les dernières qui comptent dans ce secteur avant que le sol ne change pour prendre les caractéristiques de la Côte de Beaune. En réalité la Côte de Nuits s'étend un peu plus au sud et englobe les agglomérations de Comblanchien et de Corgoloin, mais ni l'une ni l'autre ne donne des vins remarquables et elles ont seulement droit à l'appellation Vins fins de la Côte de Nuits *(voir* CÔTE DE NUITS).

Aucun vignoble de Nuits ne figure parmi les 31 Grands Crus classés par l'I.N.A.O. Néanmoins certains sont très grands. Quand on arrive dans cette agglomération par le nord, on aperçoit les premières vignes sur la droite de la vieille route des vignobles, en bas de la colline qui descend en pente douce de Vosne-Romanée vers le Meuzin (petit cours d'eau presque à sec pendant une bonne partie de l'année). Un autre vignoble commence de l'autre côté, sur une pente abrupte, rocheuse et couverte en son sommet d'arbres et de broussailles. Seul le tiers inférieur de cette éminence est planté de vignes ; on y trouve même celles des meilleurs crus de Nuits :

Les Pruliers, Les Porrets, Les Cailles, Les Saint-Georges et, un peu au-dessus de ce dernier, Les Vaucrains. Les Saint-Georges s'étendent le long de la limite de Nuits et au sud, Les Didiers, Clos des Forêts et Clos de la Maréchale se trouvent dans la commune de Prémeaux dont ils sont les meilleurs crus.

PREMIERS CRUS	
A Nuits-Saint-Georges	*Superficie (ha)*
Les Saint-Georges	7,5
Les Vaucrains	6,2
Les Cailles	3,8
Les Pruliers	7,7
Les Porrets (ou Porets)	7,1
Aux Boudots	6,4
Les Hauts-Pruliers	0,2
Aux Murgers	3,9
La Richemone	2
Les Chabœufs	2,8
Les Perrières	3,4
La Roncière	2,2
Les Procès	1,3
Rue-de-Chaux	2,1
Aux Cras	3
Aux Chaignots	5,9
Aux Thorey *(en partie)*	5
Aux Vignes Rondes	3,8
Aux Bousselots	4,2
Les Poulettes	2,1
Aux Crots	4
Les Vallerots	3,6
Aux Champs-Perdrix	0,7
En La Perrières-Noblet	0,3
Aux Damodes	8,5
Chaines-Carteaux	2,5
Aux Argillas	1,9
Les Crots (Château-Gris)	2,88
A Prémeaux	
Clos de la maréchale	9,5
Clos Arlot	5,4
Clos des corvées	5,1
Clos des Forêts Saint-Georges	7,1
Les Didiers	2,5
Aux Perdrix	3,5
Les Corvées-Paget	1,5
Les Clos Saint-Marc	0,93
Clos des Argillières	4,2
Clos des Grandes-Vignes *(en partie)*	2,2
Les Argillières	0,2

Nuits, la plus grande agglomération de la côte à laquelle elle a donné son nom, n'est cependant pas très importante. Sa population est légèrement inférieure à 5 000 âmes. Pratiquement tous les habitants de Nuits — hommes, femmes, enfants — vivent du vin d'une manière ou d'une autre. Nuits est célèbre aussi pour son Marc de Bourgogne *(voir* MARC), son Cassis *(voir ce nom),* son jus de raisin et son Bourgogne mousseux *(voir* BOURGOGNE). Malgré toutes ces activités complémentaires, la célébrité de Nuits demeurera toujours attachée à ses vins. Si l'I.N.A.O. n'a pas considéré, en 1936, les crus de la commune comme dignes de figurer au premier rang de la Bourgogne, en 1860, une classification antérieure reconnaissait neuf Têtes de Cuvée, le meilleur titre de l'époque, à savoir : Les Saint-Georges, Aux Boudots, Les Cailles, Aux Cras, Aux Murgers, Les Porrets, Les Pruliers, Aux Thorey et Les Vaucrains. Tous sont actuellement des Premiers Crus et produisent des vins superbes (partout en Bourgogne les Premiers Crus portent sur leur étiquette le nom de l'agglomération d'origine et celui du vignoble, par exemple : Nuits-Saint-Georges Les Porrets. Les Grands Crus ne portent que le seul nom du vignoble, par exemple : Chambertin).

La caractéristique la plus remarquable des vins de Nuits est leur fermeté. Plus corsés que la plupart des Bourgogne, il leur faut parfois des années pour vieillir. Le plus ferme est en général Les Vaucrains. C'est un des meilleurs de la commune et même de toute la Côte de Nuits et c'est un vin de garde, qu'il faut savoir conserver et ne pas boire dans sa jeunesse. Le bouquet aussi caractérise les Nuits qui sont parfois très odorants. La plupart du temps, le vin des Saint-Georges sera le plus coté en raison de sa finesse et il pourra aussi être d'une couleur plus foncée et d'un goût plus « vineux » que les autres. Les Pruliers débutent souvent dans la vie avec un léger goût métallique, mais ce goût passe et le vin vieillit merveilleusement. Les Porrets, et encore plus le Clos des Porrets, sont les plus fruités. Le Clos des Porrets est un petit secteur des Porrets, et le meilleur. Il appartient tout entier aux héritiers de M. Henri Gouges, un des plus fervents et opiniâtres défenseurs du Bourgogne authentique et aussi un des vignerons les plus respectés de Bourgogne. Ses fils continuent à produire aussi un bon vin blanc mais seulement en petite quantité et en vendent la quasi-totalité à Paris, particulièrement au restaurant Taillevent. Aux Boudots est aussi un bon cru. Quant à Aux Cailles, il possède toutes les caractéristiques des Nuits avec en outre un velouté qui lui est propre.

Les vignobles de Nuits-Saint-Georges couvrent au total une superficie d'environ 320 ha. Ils produisent à peu près 12 000 hl (plus de 130 000 caisses) de vin rouge et une très petite quantité de vin blanc.

Au total 151,2 ha de Premiers Crus pour une superficie de 318 ha en Appellation Contrôlée Nuits-Saint-Georges.

O

Oberemmeler

Bon vin de la Sarre, dont les crus Karlsberg, Raul, Rosenberg et Hütte sont bien connus. Scharzberg est le nom du site viticole collectif.

Voir SARRE

Ockfener Bockstein

Toujours parmi les meilleurs et en certaines années *le* meilleur vin de la Sarre. Il est fort et corsé pour un des vins de cette région qui en général tendent à être légers.

Voir SARRE

Octave

Petit fût d'une capacité équivalent à 1/8 de pipe (*voir ce mot*). Étant donné que la capacité de la pipe varie elle-même considérablement, l'octave peut contenir entre 54,5 l et 81,8 l. Mais en général il en contient environ 63,6 l.

Oechsle

Le degré Oechsle est l'équivalent allemand de l'échelle Balling ou Brix (*voir* BALLING) américaine : elle mesure le poids spécifique du jus de raisin déterminé par son taux de sucre.

Œil-de-perdrix

Expression dérivée de la teinte rosâtre que présente l'œil de perdrix et qui désigne parfois cette même teinte chez les vins blancs ou quasi rosés. Elle se manifeste dans certains Bourgogne et Champagne. Cette ancienne expression est de moins en moins employée en raison de la popularité des vins rosés.

Œnologie

La science du vin. Dans leur *Traité d'œnologie,* J. Ribéreau-Gayon et E. Peynaud définissent l'œnologie également comme la science qui traite de la préparation et de la conservation du vin et de ses éléments par l'application des règles de la chimie. Dans ce traité, les auteurs ont aussi indiqué que le but de l'œnologie consiste à prévenir les maladies du vin et, en général, à contribuer à la production des meilleurs vins possibles avec le minimum de pertes et de dépenses inutiles. Il n'est pas question de transformer un mauvais vin en bon vin car la qualité est régie par le sol, le temps et la variété de raisins. Mais, si on laissait vieillir les vins selon les fantaisies de la nature, ils seraient gâchés. L'homme doit donc intervenir pour ménager au vin les conditions dans lesquelles ses caractéristiques naturelles de goût et de bouquet atteindront la perfection.

L'œnologue est un technicien qui conquiert son diplôme dans la pratique scientifique de la vinification.

Œsterreicher

Le raisin Sylvaner ou Franken Riesling.

Off-Licence

En Angleterre, licence autorisant la vente de vin, bière et spiritueux à emporter et, par extension, le comptoir du débit de boisson où l'on vend des breuvages alcoolisés à emporter. Il existe une autre expression : « on-licence », pour les débits de boisson à consommer sur place. Les Américains disent : « off-premises » au lieu de « off-licence ».

Oggau

Agglomération vinicole du Burgenland, en Autriche, et l'une des appellations d'origine les plus importantes.

Voir BURGENLAND

Ohio

Voir ÉTATS-UNIS : OHIO

Oïdium

Maladie cryptogamique de la vigne, originaire d'Amérique et que les Américains appellent *mildew* (mildiou). Mais en France, l'oïdium est une autre maladie que le mildiou.

Voir CHAPITRE IV

Okaolehao ou Oke

Breuvage hawaïen obtenu par la distillation d'un mélange de mélasse, lie de riz et jus de racines de taro rôties. De couleur trouble et foncée, cette eau-de-vie est généralement mise en bouteille à 40° d'alcool.

Old Tom Gin

Gin qui a subi une addition de sucre.

Oléron (Maladie d')

Maladie de la vigne qui sévit plus ou moins en Afrique du Sud mais rarement ailleurs.

Voir CHAPITRE IV

Olivier (Château-)

Bordeaux rouge et blanc. Commune de Léognan, en Graves.

Bien que le rouge et le blanc soient tous deux classés parmi les meilleurs crus des Graves depuis 1953, le blanc sec est généralement préféré. Datant du XIIIe siècle, le château proprement dit est entouré de murailles avec tours et fossés. Il n'a plus de rapport avec le vin. Depuis bien des années, la maison Eschenauer de Bordeaux s'occupe de la commercialisation. Au XIVe siècle, ce château était un pavillon de chasse du Prince Noir.

Caractéristiques : Ce vin agréable a du caractère et il en existe de bonnes bouteilles.

Superficie : rouge, 18 ha, blanc, 16 ha.

Production moyenne : rouge, 90 tonneaux (8 000 caisses), blanc, 65 tonneaux (6 000 caisses).

Oloroso

Xérès à goût de noix, fortement savoureux et parfumé, plus riche que le Fino. Pour une comparaison entre Oloroso et Fino, *voir* XÉRÈS.

Oltrepò Pavese (D.O.C)

Vins rouges ou blancs de Pavie, en Italie.

Voir LOMBARDIE

Ombrie

Vins blancs et rouges. Centre de l'Italie.

L'Ombrie — véritable mélange d'art, d'antiquité étrusque et de vins — est située à mi-chemin entre Florence et Rome et est traversée par l'autoroute du Soleil. Cette région jouit d'un climat chaud et sec l'été, frais et humide l'hiver. Les 12 000 ha de vignobles produisent 1 000 000 hl (11 millions de caisses) de vins, dont 50 % par des coopératives.

L'Orvieto blanc (D.O.C.) est le vin le plus réputé d'Ombrie. C'est un vin très agréable ; généralement sec, on le trouve aussi en demi-sec. Autrefois doux et souvent oxydé, les méthodes de vinification actuelles l'ont transformé en un vin blanc très sec, de couleur jaune paille. Il est fait essentiellement à partir de Trebbiano Toscano (50 à 65 %) et pour le reste de Verdello, Grechetto, Drupeggio et Malvasia. L'Orvieto classique compte pour environ 1/3 des 90 000 hl (1 million de caisses) produits, L'Orvieto vieillit dans des caves creusées à flanc de falaises calcaires.

Colli Perugini est la D.O.C. de vins rouges, rosés et blancs. Les 1 100 ha sont plantés de Sangiovese et de Merlot pour les rouges et rosés, de Trebbiano Toscano et Grechetto pour les blancs.

Sagrantino di Montefalco est la D.O.C. de vins rouges. La production annuelle, de 10 000 hl (plus de 110 000 caisses) environ, provient d'une petite région vinicole de 155 ha. Le vin de Sagrantino est sombre et haut en couleurs. Ce sont à la fois des vins doux ou *passito* et des vins rouges secs.

Colli Altotiberini : planté à flanc de coteaux, ce vignoble est situé au nord des Apennins. La D.O.C. vient des 350 ha qui produisent en moyenne 25 000 hl (plus de 250 000 caisses) de vins rouges et blancs. Les variétés de raisins sont le Trebbiano pour les blancs, le Sangiovese traditionnel et le Merlot pour les rouges.

Colli del Trasimeno est la D.O.C. de vins rouges et blancs produits autour du lac Trasimeno, proche de Pérouse. Les blancs, des cépages Trebbiano, Malvasia, Verdicchio et Grechetto sont de couleur jaune paille et de goût harmonieux ; les rouges des cépages Sangiovese, Gliegiolo et Gamay, sont plutôt secs et légèrement tanniques, avec une agréable senteur de violette.

Torgiano est la D.O.C. de vins rouges et blancs produits au sud-est de Pérouse, dans le secteur adjacent à la médiévale Turris Janis (Tour de Janus, dieu romain à double visage). Les 100 000 hl (plus d'un million de caisses) de rouges produits par cette petite région vinicole sont des vins pleins faits avec du Sangiovese, Cenaiolo et Montepulciano. Les blancs sont produits à partir de Trebbiano Toscano, Malvasia et Grechetto.

Lungarotti est l'un des plus grands exportateurs d'Ombrie qui vend l'essentiel de ses meilleurs vins sous la marque de Rubesco. Le Riserva est l'un des plus fameux vins rouges d'Italie.

Once

En anglais *ounce*. Mesure de poids = 28,35 g ; mesure de capacité *(fluid ounce) = 2,841 cl.*

Aux États-Unis, mesure de capacité = 2,957 cl.

Opimien

Un des cinq ou six noms connus de grands vins de l'Antiquité. Contrairement aux autres (Pramnien, Falerne, etc.) il n'était pas appelé ainsi en raison de son origine géographique, mais par référence à l'année de vendange. Sous le consulat d'Opimius, en l'année 121 av. J.-C., l'été fut tellement splendide dans les environs de Rome qu'on fit de grands vins, particulièrement du Falerne. Sans doute en exagérant, on prétendit que les Opimiens conservèrent la plénitude de leurs qualités pendant cent ans.

Oporto (Porto)

Ville située à l'embouchure du Douro, au nord du Portugal. Selon la loi portugaise, pour avoir droit à l'étiquette Oporto (Porto), les vins doivent être expédiés par le port d'Oporto.

Voir PORTO

Oppenheimer

Vin de Rheinhessen. En certaines années chaudes et sèches, il surclasse le Niersteiner.

Voir RHEINHESSEN

Or (Liqueur d')

Liqueur d'herbes française, d'un jaune pâle, avec de petites particules dorées flottant dans la bouteille ; une variante de la Danziger Goldwasser.

Orange

L'orange sert à faire divers breuvages, à savoir :

Bitter d'orange
Alcool très populaire en Angleterre où on l'utilise en mélange dans des cocktails. Il doit son goût aux écorces d'orange aigrelette de la région de Séville.
Voir BITTERS

Eau-de-vie d'orange
Liqueur dont André Simon donne la recette comme suit : 4,5 l de la meilleure eau-de-vie ; les écorces de 8 oranges de Séville ; 2 citrons coupés très fin ; 1 pain d'un kilo de sucre ; mettre le tout dans un récipient de grès ; boucher et sceller ; secouer pendant quelques minutes tous les jours durant trois semaines ; filtrer, mettre en bouteille et boucher.

Vin d'orange
Breuvage obtenu au Brésil par la fermentation de jus d'orange.

Ordinaire

Appellation du vin consommé couramment en France.

Oregon

État et région vinicole des États-Unis, l'une des rares qui convienne parfaitement à la *Vitis vinifera* et surtout au cépage Pinot Noir qui a obtenu de meilleurs résultats qu'en Californie.
Voir ÉTATS-UNIS : CALIFORNIE ET OUEST

Orgeat

Sirop fait avec de l'orge mais maintenant par émulsion d'amandes.

Originalabfüllung

Littéralement : remplissage (mise en bouteille). A l'origine, cette expression désignait en Allemagne le vin mis en bouteille par le producteur.
Voir ALLEMAGNE

Originalabzug

Littéralement : tirage originel. Expression, toujours utilisée, équivalent à la précédente *(Originalabfüllung)*.
Voir ALLEMAGNE

Orvieto (D.O.C.) et Orvieto Classico

L'Orvieto est un blanc agréable et l'un des vins italiens dont la qualité est la plus constante. Généralement sec, il se présente aussi en demi-sec. Actuellement on le traite pour qu'il soit sec, en raison de l'évolution du goût. Les vignerons d'Orvieto furent parmi les premiers à remarquer cette tendance et à traiter leur vin de telle sorte qu'il satisfasse la demande. Mais cette nouveauté suscita des controverses. Les traditionalistes, tels que l'austère baron toscan Ricasoli, soutinrent que l'Orvieto doux est un des plus beaux échantillons de la viticulture italienne ; traité en sec il devient agréable mais ce n'est plus de l'Orvieto. A cela les vignerons répondirent, avec raison, que le marché de l'Orvieto *Amabile* ou *Abboccato* (comme on appelle le demi-sec) a tellement diminué qu'il n'est plus possible de se spécialiser dans sa production. « Notre vin traditionnel est aussi bon qu'il l'a toujours été, disent-ils, mais, en outre, nous produisons un vin sec sous le même nom. Peut-être des caractéristiques légèrement différentes, mais il n'en conserve pas moins la qualité de l'Orvieto ».

L'Orvieto doux possède un charme et une délicatesse qui lui sont propres. On le fait surtout avec les raisins suivants : Trebbiano, Malvasia, Grechetto, Drupeccio, Verdello et Procanico. Pour le sec, c'est le Trebbiano qui domine.

L'Orvieto vieillit dans des caves creusées au flanc de falaises semblables à celles que l'on trouve dans la région du Vouvray en France. Ces cavernes contribueraient à donner au vin ses caractéristiques exceptionnelles si l'on en croit les vignerons.

L'Orvieto sec contient une plus grande proportion d'alcool que le doux (jusqu'à 13° contre 11° pour le doux) parce que, dans ce dernier, on interrompt la fermentation pour conserver une part de sucre non résolu. Néanmoins, le sec conserve le charme du doux. Il est d'ailleurs rarement tout à fait sec, mais semble équilibrer une trace de sucre résiduel et un arrière-goût très légèrement âpre. A peu près la moitié des quelque 90 000 hl d'Orvieto produits par an sont traités en sec et environ 30 000 ha de vignes sont plantés.

Voir OMBRIE

Osaka

Une des principales régions vinicoles du Japon *(voir ce nom).*

Ouillage, ouiller

L'ouillage est le vide que l'évaporation crée dans la barrique. Ouiller désigne l'opération qui consiste à combler ce vide en versant du vin dans le tonneau. Par extension, ouillage est devenu le nom de cette opération.

Voir CHAPITRE V

Ouillère, Ouillière ou encore Oullière

Vigne dans laquelle les rangs de ceps sont séparés par des cultures intercalaires.

Ouvrée

Vieille mesure bourguignonne de superficie, correspondant à environ 1/24 d'ha.

Ouzo

Spiritueux à base d'anis très prisé en Grèce et qu'on trouve parfois à l'étranger, notamment aux États-Unis et en Angleterre. L'Ouzo est un proche parent des apéritifs anisés français appelés Ricard et Pernod. On le boit froid et additionné d'eau. Cette addition trouble sa couleur.

Voir GRÈCE : SPIRITUEUX

Oxhoft

Mesure de capacité scandinave variant entre 254 et 264 l.

Oxydation

Expression employée pour désigner l'influence souvent néfaste de l'oxygène de l'air sur le vin. Elle est synonyme d'évent lorsqu'elle est faible, de madérisation, de rancis lorsqu'elle est forte. Elle est surtout dommageable pour les vins blancs ; elle intervient après un séjour trop prolongé en fût ou en bouteille ; le vin blanc fonce de couleur, devient brunâtre et perd la fraîcheur de sa dégustation.

En revanche, pour certains types de vins — Madère, Xérès, vin de Paille du Jura — l'oxydation est à la base de leurs caractères et elle est même très appréciée.

Une substance s'oxyde quand elle fixe de l'oxygène ou perd de l'hydrogène ou, plus exactement, quand ses atomes acceptent des électrons. Par exemple l'oxydation de l'anhydride sulfureux (SO_2) donne de l'acide sulfurique (SO_4H_2).

Les substances oxydables du vin sont surtout les tanins, les matières colorantes. Le fer joue un rôle important dans les phénomènes d'oxydation.

Le contraire de l'état d'oxydation est l'état de réduction.

Voir MADÉRISATION ; CHAPITRE V

P

Paarl

Agglomération et vallée de la province du Cap en Afrique du Sud. On y fait des vins de table légers.

Voir AFRIQUE DU SUD

Pacherenc du Vic Bilh (Appellation Contrôlée)

Vin blanc des Pyrénées françaises produit pratiquement dans le même secteur que le Madiran *(voir ce nom)*, c'est-à-dire dans la vallée de l'Adour. Les raisins qui entrent dans sa composition sont principalement : Arrufiac, Mansenc, Courbu, Sémillon et Sauvignon.

Voir SUD-OUEST DE LA FRANCE

Paille (Vin de)

On fait dans le Jura (et en moins grande quantité ailleurs) du vin de paille qui doit son nom à la méthode consistant à laisser sécher les raisins sur de la paille avant de les pressurer. Ce vin a aussi une couleur de paille.

Voir JURA

Paillon

Fourreau de paille dans lequel on met les bouteilles pour les protéger. Le paillon n'est plus beaucoup utilisé.

Les vins expédiés aux États-Unis ainsi que sur d'autres marchés d'exportation sont protégés par un emballage en carton parce que les lois interdisent l'utilisation de la paille qui pourrait abriter maladies, insectes malfaisants ou microbes.

País

Raisins et vins d'origine espagnole, cultivés et produits depuis si longtemps au Chili qu'on les considère comme indigènes.

Palatinat (Pfalz, Rheinpfalz)

État allemand du Rheinland-Pfalz. Superficie : 23 000 ha. 89 % de vins blancs, 11 % de vins rouges.

Le Palatinat est une des provinces les plus attrayantes et les plus ensoleillées d'Allemagne. Les petits villages pimpants comme ceux des cartes postales, avec leurs enseignes aux vives enluminures et leurs pots de fleurs aux fenêtres, sont tapis au milieu de vergers et de vignobles que les gens du pays appellent Weingarten. L'hiver y est si doux et l'été si chaud que figues et citrons y prospèrent ; cerises, abricots, pêches, y abondent et le raisin mûrit tôt pour donner des vins doux et corsés. Situé à l'ouest du Rhin et au nord de l'Alsace, le Palatinat est couvert de forêts qui s'élèvent d'un côté vers le massif de la Hardt et descend de l'autre côté vers la plaine du Rhin. La campagne est plutôt plate, ensoleillée, à peine accidentée, avec d'un côté la Hardt et de l'autre, le Rhin, parfois visible au loin. Les villages ont toujours l'air ancien qui caractérise ceux d'Allemagne du sud, avec des rues étroites, tortueuses, pavées de pierres arrondies et des maisons aux poutres apparentes souvent sculptées de pampres ou autres motifs rappelant la vigne. Partout sur la Weinstrasse on ne vit presque que du vin qui donne de grandes joies par bonne année et tristesse quand les vendanges sont mauvaises.

Cette province doit son nom au latin *palatium*. Le premier palais des empereurs romains était en effet situé sur le mont Palatin et, par la suite, toutes les résidences impériales conservèrent ce nom. Le fonctionnaire chargé de l'administration du palais portait le titre de *comes palatinus*. Ce titre se transmit pendant des siècles d'un souverain du Palatinat à son successeur et devint en allemand *Pfalzgraf* (c'est-à-dire comte palatin).

Situation : Région viticole la plus importante en terme de production et deuxième après le Rheinhessen par la taille, le Palatinat est bordé par le Rheinhessen au nord et la France au sud et à l'ouest. Les vignobles s'étendent sans interruption sur 80 km comme un large ruban chevauchant la route des vins (la Deutsche Weinstrasse) et parallèle aux montagnes de la Haardt. A l'origine la région se divisait en haute, moyenne et basse Haardt. Aujourd'hui, elle regroupe deux districts (Bereiche) : Bereich Mittelhaardt-Deutsche Weinstrasse, situé dans la moitié nord de la région et dont Bad Dürkheim et Neustadt sont les deux centres de négoce de vins les plus importants, et le Bereich au sud dont Landau est le principal centre commercial.

Variétés de raisin : Müller-Thurgau (24 %), Riesling (15 %), Kerner (11 %), Silvaner (9 %), Portugieser (8 %), Morio-Muskat (7 %), Scheurebe (6 %).

Vins : Élégants, ronds, au bouquet superbe. Les Müller-Thurgau et Silvaner sont doux et ont du corps. Les vins rouges varient du Spätburgunder stylé (Pinot Noir) au Portugieser léger et fruité. Quelque 30 à 40 % des vins sont secs ; ils sont agréables et harmonieux en raison de leur maturité acide et de leur corps.

Le climat du Palatinat est chaud et ensoleillé grâce aux montagnes de la Haardt qui protègent les régions viticoles des vents froids et de la pluie. 3 % des vignobles sont plantés sur des coteaux abrupts ou des parcelles en terrasse. Le reste est cultivé sur des pentes douces et 2/3 en plaines. Les sols des vignobles situés à l'est de la route des vins sont un mélange d'alluvions, de sable et de graviers sans calcaire. On y trouve aussi de riches dépôts de loess. Du nord au sud, une bande calcaire traverse la région ; elle part de Grünstadt, passe par Herxheim, Kallstadt, Forst, Deidesheim et réapparaît plus au sud, près de Siebeldingen et Frankweiler. 40 à 45 % des vignobles sont plantés sur des zones de terreau, de sable gras et d'argile ; 15 % sur des taches calcaires de marne rouge, de basalt (Forst) et de grès rouge disséminées çà et là.

Sur les 11 500 viticulteurs du Palatinat, 40 % fabriquent eux-mêmes leurs vins et en vendent la majeure partie en direct. La taille moyenne de leurs vignobles est de 3,25 ha. Elle est de 1 ha pour ceux qui livrent leurs raisins et leur moût aux coopératives ou au négoce. Calculée sur dix ans, la production moyenne annuelle est de 2,4 millions d'hl (soit plus de 25 millions de caisses). 30 % des raisins vendangés vont aux coopératives ; 45 % sont vendus au négoce et le reste est acheté par les domaines qui produisent leur vin. Les viticulteurs du sud vendent généralement une bonne partie de leur récolte aux coopératives ou au négoce qui à leur tour approvisionnent les supermarchés, les grandes surfaces et les grossistes. Les ventes directes et la production de vin mis en bouteilles au domaine sont plus fréquentes dans le nord.

Villages, vignobles et producteurs

Voici la liste des plus importants villages viticoles, classés, non par ordre alphabétique, mais d'après leur situation géographique si l'on suit la route des vins du nord au sud, juste après Grünstadt. Forst, Deidesheim, Wachenheim, Ruppertsberg et Ungstein sont cinq villages qui produisent régulièrement des vins de qualité — mais de très bons vins sont fabriqués dans toute la région — et si les conditions climatiques et le sol sont des facteurs importants, le producteur est aussi responsable de la qualité finale et du caractère de son vin. Les producteurs suivants sont des coopératives et des viticulteurs fiables et traditionnels.

Herxheim, Freinsheim, Grosskarlbach et Dackenheim

Bien que ces villages ne jouissent pas d'une réputation nationale, les vins sont de très grande qualité. Les blancs sont fabriqués à partir des 3 variétés classiques : Riesling, Müller-Thurgau et Silvaner, et les bons rouges à partir de Spätburgunder et Portugieser. Herxheim coiffe majestueusement une colline et la vue de la vallée y est magnifique. Freinsheim est une localité particulièrement ravissante avec sa ville fortifiée, son église gothique, sa mairie baroque et ses maisons à colombages.

Parmi les meilleurs crus figurent : Herxheimer Himmelreich, Freinsheimer Goldberg et Musikantenbuckel, Grosskarlbacher Burgweg, Dackenheimer Kapellgarten.

Producteurs : Herxheim, Winzergenossenschaft, Freinsheim, Lehmann-Hilgard, K. Neckerauer, Grosskarlbach, Lingenfelder, Dackenheim : Winkels-Herding, et près de Kirchheim, Emil Hamel.

Kallstadt

Les vins de ce secteur sont généralement charnus et lourds. Les vignes sont cultivées sur une certaine colline calcaire dont le sol est considéré comme « chaud ». De très bons Riesling et des Silvaner exceptionnellement stylés y sont produits ainsi que des rouges agréables. Le village situé au-dessus des vignobles fut considéré, il y a quelques années, comme le plus beau de la route des vins. L'un des sites les plus remarquables est Saumagen (qui signifie littéralement « panse de truie »). Un festival original y est organisé chaque année au printemps et les touristes peuvent y apprécier « le Saumagen deux fois : dans le verre et dans l'assiette ». Le Saumagen est une spécialité régionale très populaire faite d'un mélange épicé de viande et de pommes de terre cuites dans une poche, d'où son nom.

Meilleurs crus : Saumagen, Annaberg, Kronenberg, Steinacker.

Producteurs : Stumpf-Fitz, Koehler-Ruprecht, Eduard Schuster, Henninger, Stauch et une bonne coopérative locale.

Ungstein

« L'Ungsteiner réveille les morts », telle est la devise des vins d'Ungstein. Les blancs ronds, qu'ils aient ou non une telle vertu, provenant des coteaux orientés au sud et à l'est, riches, parfumés et qui se gardent longtemps. C'est dans cette région qu'une grande villa romaine et son pressoir furent excavés ainsi que des outils et instruments viticoles, des bouteilles et des verres à boire. Mérite le détour.

Meilleurs crus : Herrenberg, Weilberg, Nussriegel. Du très bon vin est aussi vendu sous le nom du Grosslage Honigsäckel.

Producteurs : Weingut Pfeffingen-Fuhrmann.

Bad Dürkheim

Le Feuerberg de Dürkheimer est le rouge le mieux connu du Palatinat. Mais dans ce secteur on fait trois fois plus de blanc que de rouge. La Dürkheim Wurstmarkt (Foire aux saucisses), qui a lieu durant la seconde et la troisième semaines de septembre depuis plus de cinq cents ans, est la plus importante manifestation vinicole d'Allemagne. Un foudre gigantesque destiné à l'origine à contenir 1 700 000 litres, a été converti en restaurant dans le faubourg nord de cette ville.

Des quantités considérables de Dürkheimer sont vendues sous le nom des trois crus collectifs : Feuerberg, Hochmess et Schenkenböhl.

Crus uniques : Michelsberg, Spielberg, Fuchsmantel, Fronhof, Abtsfronhof, Rittergarten, Hochbenn, Nonnengarten, Steinberg et Herrenmorgen.

Producteurs : Fitz-Ritter, Karl Schaefer, Joh. Karst et une excellente coopérative, Winzergenossenschaft Vier Jahreszeiten.

Wachenheim

On raconte à Wachenheim que voilà quelques générations le maire lança à l'abbé de Limburg un défi : lequel boirait le plus. Tous deux étaient opiniâtres. Mais le maire tenait encore brillamment debout quand l'abbé, succombant au bon vin de Wachenheim, glissa sous la table. Pour marquer l'estime que lui inspirait le vin de cette commune, l'abbé fit grâce de la dîme que Wachenheim payait au cloître de Limburg. D'après les experts, les vins sont bons, riches, capiteux, charnus, très fins et d'une grande substance. Les éloges et l'excellente réputation des vins de Wachenheim sont l'œuvre d'un grand nom du monde vinicole allemand, feu le Dr Albert Bürkin-Wolf.

Meilleurs crus : Gerümpel, Rechbächel, Goldbächel et Luginsland.

Producteurs : Dr Bürklin-Wolf, J.L. Wolf Erben et une très bonne coopérative Winzergenossenschaft Wachtenburg-Luginsland.

Schloss Wachenheim, fondé en 1888, est très connu pour ses excellents Riesling Sekt.

Forst

Forst est une jolie ville dont les grandes maisons baroques prouvent que la viticulture peut être aussi une activité lucrative. Une éminence de basalte volcanique, nommée Pechstein ou Basaltsteinbruch, située à l'ouest de l'agglomération, fournit un sol particulier qui emmagasine la chaleur solaire et la restitue aux vignes durant la nuit. Cette constance de température permet aux raisins de mûrir plus complètement que partout ailleurs en Allemagne et on y produit de nombreux vins vendangés tardivement. Le sol lourd et argileux de Forst, riche en minéraux, retient l'eau. C'est pourquoi dans les années de sécheresse, les vins sont meilleurs que ceux de Deidesheim, la région voisine. Ils sont puissants, très parfumés et riches en bouquet.

Meilleurs crus : Jesuitengarten, Kirchenstück et Ungeheuer. Une grande quantité de vin est aussi vendue sous le nom du Grosslage Mariengarten.

Producteurs : Wilhelm Spindler, Weingut Mossbacher Hof, Acham-Magin et une bonne coopérative.

Deidesheim

Les Forster et les Deidesheimer rivalisent entre eux ; ce sont certainement ceux qui viennent la plupart du temps en tête de tous les vins du Palatinat. Le sol, plus léger que celui de Forst, produit des vins plus élégants et les raisins semblent y mûrir plus vite. C'est un avantage non négligeable dans les mauvaises années. Dans les années de sécheresse, les vignes peuvent souffrir d'un manque d'humidité. Les meilleurs vignobles s'étendent entre la route des vins et le versant d'un coteau boisé. L'agglomération de Deidesheim est ancienne et attrayante. Son auberge, Gasthaus Zur Kanne, fondée en 1160, vaut la peine d'être visitée. Chaque mois de mai, au cours d'un célèbre festival du vin, on vend aux enchères une chèvre primée à l'hôtel de ville de style baroque. Cette coutume date de près de 600 ans ; le petit village de Sankt Lambrecht dut alors payer une chèvre en guise d'amende parce que ses troupeaux avaient brouté sur les terres de Deidesheim et, depuis, il continue à livrer une bête de prix par an.

Meilleurs crus : Hohenmorgen, Herrgottsacker, Leinhöhle, Kieselberg, Mäushöhle et Grainhübel. Le Grosslage Hofstück est utilisé pour de nombreux vins. La qualité dépendra du producteur.

Producteurs : Bassermann-Jordan et Reichsrat von Buhl, deux grands noms du vin allemand, ont la réputation internationale d'être de beaux domaines traditionnels. Weingut Dr Deinhard et Gutsverwaltung Deinhard-Deidesheim, Josef Biffar, Herbert Giessen, Dr Kern, Jul. Ferd. Kimich, Helmut Mehling, Weingut Georg Siben Erben, et une bonne coopérative locale. Weinbau Hahnhof, domaine viticole d'une importante société qui dirige une chaîne de restaurants coquets (Hahnhof) où sont servis les spécialités et les vins du Palatinat, y possède ses bureaux.

Ruppertsberg

Vins forts et fruités avec beaucoup de race, qui proviennent des meilleurs vignobles de cette vieille agglomération vinicole fondée avant la naissance du Christ et située à un important carrefour dès le temps des Romains. Elle se trouve au sud de Deidesheim et deux vignobles s'étendent sur les deux territoires.

Meilleurs crus : Hoheburg, Linsenbusch, Reiterpfad, Nussbien et Gaisböhl.

Producteurs : Une bonne coopérative locale. Tous les domaines importants de Deidesheim, Forst et Wachenheim ont des propriétés à Ruppertsberg.

Gimmeldingen

Sur deux collines arrondies au pied de la Hardt, les sols sablonneux produisent de bons vins plaisants.

Meilleur cru : Mandelgarten. La plupart de son vin est vendu sous l'étiquette du Grosslage Meerspinne.

Producteurs : Kurt Mugler et une coopérative (avec comme voisine Mussbach).

Mussbach

La plus importante institution viticole, l'Institut de Recherche et d'Enseignement d'État s'y est installée récemment. Elle possède aussi le plus vieux domaine du Palatinat (VIIIe siècle), le Johannitergut, et est la propriétaire exclusive du cru Johannitergarten.

Neustadt an der Weinstrasse

Située au milieu de la Weinstrasse, à l'extrémité sud de la Mittelhardt, Neustadt est la plus grande communauté vinicole (les villages voisins y compris) du Palatinat avec plus de 2 000 ha de vignobles. Elle abrite chaque automne un festival populaire du vin où la reine du vin allemand est couronnée.

Crus : Grain, Erkenbrecht, Mönchgarten.

Producteurs : Weingut Müller-Catoir (Neustadt-Haardt) et F. & G. Bergdolt.

Le district de Südliche Weinstrasse (district méridional) commence juste au sud de Neustadt. Le paysage y est plus exceptionnel car les coteaux sont plus abrupts. La région est humide car la barrière des montagnes de la Haardt, interrompues par des vallées latérales et pentues, ne fait plus obstacle aux pluies. Les sols sont plus riches et les récoltes très importantes. Ce district était autrefois connu pour les grosses quantités de vins courants au goût terreux. Aujourd'hui, après la réorganisation du vignoble et grâce aux coopératives en quête de qualité, le district produit des vins bien faits et attrayants qui révèlent de bons caractères variétaux.

Maikammer, Saint-Martin, Edenkoben, Edesheim

Très jolis villages situés au pied de Kalmit, point culminant des Monts de la Haardt.

Grosslage : Mandelhöbe, Schloss Ludwigshöhe et Ordensgut.

Producteurs : Weingut Ernst Minges, Klaus Erath.

Rhodt unter Rietburg

Ville très pittoresque dont le vignoble de Traminer est ancien (vieux d'environ 300 ans). Schloss Ludwigshöhe, autrefois résidence d'été de Louis Ier de Bavière, domine la ville.

Grosslage : Ordensgut.

Producteur : Une très grande et moderne coopérative régionale, Gebietswinzergenossenschaft Rietburg.

Siebeldingen et Birkweiler

L'Institut National de la viticulture de Geilweilerhof à Siebeldingen est très réputé pour ses recherches sur les essences. C'est ici que furent créés les nouveaux croisements de Morio-Muskat, Bacchus et Optima.

Grosslage : Königsgarten.

Producteurs : Weingut Ökonomierat Rebholz, Weingut Hohenberg.

Ilbesheim

Secteur de l'autre importante coopérative de la région, Gebietswinzergenossenschaft Deutsches Weintor. Les vins sont bons, bien faits et pas trop chers.

Grosslage : Herrlich.

Schweigen

Dernier village de la route allemande des vins. Son gigantesque portail de pierre (Deutsches Weintor) marque la frontière française. On y trouve un parcours éducatif de viticulture ainsi que des comptoirs de dégustation.

Quelques domaines vinicoles importants			
Propriétaires des domaines	*Siège social*	*Superficie (ha)*	*Désignation des biens (par localités)*
Bassermann-Jordan Certains des vignobles datent d'avant 1360. Le domaine actuel a été arrondi par la famille Bassermann-Jordan depuis qu'il est entre ses mains, c'est-à-dire depuis la fin du XVIIIe siècle. Dans ses caves aux murs noirs qui s'étendent sur une longueur de quelque 800 m sous Deidesheim, on trouve certains des vins les plus merveilleux du Palatinat, par exemple le presque invraisemblable Forster Jesuitengarten Trockenbeerenauslese de 1900 où le Forster Jesuitengarten Riesling Trockenbeerenauslese 1950 qui atteignit le prix le plus élevé au Palatinat depuis la Seconde Guerre mondiale, soit l'équivalent de 75 F la bouteille prise au vignoble avant toute majoration. A la vente aux enchères des vins de qualité de 1955, le Deidesheimer Hohenmorgen Riesling Trockenbeerenauslese de 1952 ne fut traité qu'à quelque 4 F au-dessous de ce prix record. Ce domaine historique, dont le livre d'or est signé par des célébrités allant du compositeur Mendelsshon au boxeur Max Schmeling, appartient au vénérable patriarche des vins du Palatinat, le Dr Friedrich von Bassermann-Jordan, âgé actuellement de plus de quatre-vingts ans et ancien président de l'Association des vignerons allemands. Le gigantesque ouvrage en trois volumes sur l'histoire du vin dont il est l'auteur fait autorité. Son fils, le Dr Ludwig von Bassermann-Jordan est aujourd'hui propriétaire du domaine.	Deidesheim	40	Forst : Forster Kirchenstück, Forster Jesuitengarten, Pechstein, Ungeheuer, etc. Deidesheim : Deidesheim Hohenmorgen, Grainhübel, Geheu, Kalkofen, Leinhöhle, etc. Ruppertsberg : Ruppertsberg, Reiterpfad, Nussbien, Spiess, Hoheburg, etc. Bad Dürkheim Ungstein
Josef Biffar	Deidesheim	11	Deidesheim ; Ruppertsberg
Reichsrat von Buhl	Deidesheim	100	Deidesheim : Deidesheimer Leinhöhle, Kieselberg, etc. Forst : Forster Freundstück, Kirchenstück, Pechstein, Ungeheuer, etc. Wachenheim : Wachenheimer, Luginsland, etc. Ruppertsberg : Ruppertsberger Hoheburg, Reiterpfad, etc. Königsbacch : Königsbacher Rolandsberg, Idig, etc.
Weingut Dr Bürklin-Wolf Les propriétés Bürklin-Wolf appartiennent à la	Wachenheim	105	Wachenheim : Wachenheimer Gerümpel, Gold-

Quelques domaines vinicoles importants *(suite)*			
Propriétaires des domaines	*Siège social*	*Superficie (ha)*	*Désignation des biens (par localités)*
même famille depuis 1790. Un grand foudre ovale et sculpté qui servit lors de vendanges antérieures se trouve encore en bas de l'escalier abrupt conduisant à l'une des deux grandes caves de ce domaine à Wachenheim. Dans ces antres humides on trouve des éléments plus récents : chaque fût porte le nom de la parcelle avec les raisins de laquelle fut fait le vin qu'il contient, et une pancarte peinte en blanc donne tous les autres détails sur l'origine du contenu. La dernière guerre mondiale y a laissé ses traces : le cratère d'une bombe, qui fut cimenté depuis. Le Dr Bürklin-Wolf était un des plus ardents promoteurs et défenseurs des vins allemands. Il fut nommé président de l'Association des vignerons allemands en 1964. Son nom est synonyme de la qualité qu'il exigea et qu'il créa. Sa fille Bettina et Georg Racquet, autrefois membre du Domaine d'État de Nahe à Niederhauser, poursuivent la tradition familiale de ce grand domaine.			bächel, Odinstal, Böhlig, Rechbächel (seul propriétaire), Luginsland, etc. Forst : Forster Kirchenstück, Jesuitengarten, Pechstein, Ungeheuer, etc. Desdesheim : Desdesheimer Hohenmorgen, Kalkofen, etc. Ruppertsberg : Ruppertsberger Hoheburg, Gaisböhl (seul propriétaire), Reiterpfad, Nussbien, etc. Bad Dürkheim
Weingut Dr Deinhard et Gutsverwaltung Wegeler -Deinhard	Deidesheim	37	Deidesheim : Deidesheimer Leinhöhle, Kalkofen, Kieselberg, Grainhübel, Herrgottsacker, etc. Forst : Forster Kirchenstück, Ungeheuer, etc. Ruppertsberg : Ruppertsberger Hofstück, Spiess, Nussbien, etc.
Weingut Dr Kern	Deidesheim	5	Deidesheim ; Ruppertsberg
Weingut Köhler Ruprecht	Kallstad	8	Kallstadt
Weingut Eugen Spindler	Forst	15	Forst ; Deidesheim ; Ruppertsberg ; Wachenheim
Weingut Stumpf-Fitz	Annaberg (près de Bad Dürkheim)	1	Kallstadt ; Bad Dürkheim

Palette

Appellation contrôlée de vins provençaux.

Voir PROVENCE

Palma

Appellation utilisée à l'exportation pour un Xérès Fino très net et délicat.

Voir XÉRÈS

Palmer (Château-)

Bordeaux rouge. Commune de Cantenac-Margaux, en Haut-Médoc.

Situé entre la route des vins et Château-Margaux, juste en face de Château-Rausan-Ségla et de Château-Rauzan-Gassies, Palmer est un des Troisièmes Crus les plus connus et les plus recherchés. Il doit son nom au général anglais Palmer qui le posséda au début du XIXe siècle. Les vins de ce château méritent leur réputation mais ce nom facile à prononcer dans les pays anglo-saxons n'y est peut-être pas pour rien. Appelé alors Château de Gasq, ce cru, ainsi que Château-Lafite, était fort prisé à la cour de Versailles sous Louis XV.

Les propriétaires sont internationaux : Français, Hollandais et Anglais. 60 % du vignoble appartient à la firme bordelaise Mähler-Besse. M. Mähler-Besser fut longtemps consul honoraire de Hollande à Bordeaux. 30 % appartiennent à Sichel and Co., firme dirigée par l'Anglais Peter Sichel qui réside au Château-Angludet. Enfin 10 % appartiennent à la famille médocaine de M. Bouteiller. Ces trois propriétaires ont conjugué leurs efforts pour vendre leurs produits sur les marchés où ils se trouvent dans une situation de force ; aussi Palmer atteint-il des prix élevés, tout à fait justifiés. Avant la Seconde Guerre mondiale, les propriétaires du Château-Palmer achetèrent le Château Desmirail, autre Troisième Cru classé de Margaux, gardèrent les vignes et supprimèrent ce nom de cru.

L'encépagement du vignoble de Palmer est constitué de 40 % de Cabernet Sauvignon, 40 % de Merlot, 10 % de Cabernet Franc et 10 % de Petit Verdot.

Caractéristiques : Vin très fin, bien arrondi et corsé.

Durant les vingt dernières années, en raison de ses excellentes qualités, ce vin est devenu une des mises en bouteille au château les plus recherchées du Médoc.

Superficie : 40 ha.

Production moyenne : 140 tonneaux (12 000 caisses).

Palo Cortado

Xérès rare qui associe les caractéristiques de l'Oloroso et du Fino.

Voir XÉRÈS

Palomino

Raisin blanc le plus utilisé pour la production du Xérès à Jerez, Espagne. Il sert aussi à faire des vins de moindre qualité dans diverses autres régions du pays. On le cultive aussi en Californie où il donne non seulement du vin du type Xérès, mais aussi des vins de table secs. On l'appelle aux États-Unis Golden Chasselas (Chasselas doré).

Palus

Terre à vigne sur les berges de la Dordogne, de la Garonne et de la Gironde, dans la région de Bordeaux, ainsi que sur les îles de la Gironde. Le sol des palus est trop lourd et humide pour donner des vins fins mais n'en produit pas moins une grande quantité de bons vins ordinaires dont une importante partie est la boisson quotidienne des travailleurs du vignoble bordelais, ces vins se vendent sous l'appellation de Bordeaux rouge supérieur.

Panay

Ile de l'archipel des Philippines et marque du rhum que produit cette île.

Voir RHUM : PHILIPPINES

Panier (ou panier de service)

Corbeille oblongue où l'on couche une bouteille de vin qui est légèrement inclinée, afin de l'agiter le moins possible en versant son contenu.

Quand on apporte avec soin la bouteille de la cave à la table sur laquelle on la débouche et qu'on la pose doucement dans le panier, cet objet est utile. Mais si on secoue plusieurs fois la bouteille dans le panier pour servir, mieux vaut décanter le vin au préalable.

Pape-Clément (Château-)

Bordeaux rouge. Commune de Pessac, en Graves.

Fondé en 1300 par Bertrand de Goth, archevêque de Bordeaux, ce vignoble prit son nom actuel quand son fondateur devint le pape Clément V. En 1953, lors de la classification des Graves, ce cru ne fut pas classé ; mais, certains propriétaires s'étant efforcés d'améliorer leur vignoble et leurs techniques de vinification, Pape-Clément fut inclus dans la classification de 1959. Les vins n'ont d'ailleurs pas cessé de s'améliorer et comptent maintenant parmi les bons vins rouges de Graves. Ils atteignent souvent des prix aussi élevés que les meilleurs Seconds Crus du Médoc ce qui n'est pas toujours justifié.

Caractéristiques : Un très bon vin, avec toutes les qualités d'un Graves typique. Certaines bouteilles des grandes années étaient tout simplement superbes.

Superficie : 30 ha.

Production moyenne : 140 tonneaux (14 000 caisses).

Parfait amour

Liqueur sucrée, très épicée, rouge ou violette, faite en France et en Hollande.

Paris

On cultivait jadis la vigne à Paris et dans sa banlieue. Les plus célèbres vignobles étaient ceux de Montmartre où subsiste la rue de la Goutte-d'Or en souvenir d'une excellente vigne à vin blanc. A Passy, où des sources d'eau chaude offraient des cures thermales aux citadins, il existe encore une rue des Vignes où les curistes allaient boire quelques gorgées de vin. Mais l'apogée de la viticulture parisienne date du XIIIe siècle, et, depuis lors, le vignoble n'a cessé de rétrécir. Il ne reste plus aujourd'hui que les vignes de Montmartre dont on vend le vin aux enchères par amour de la tradition, à des prix ridiculeusement élevés par rapport à la qualité.

Parras

Un des centres de la viticulture mexicaine et siège social des Bodegas del Marqués de Aguayo.

Voir MEXIQUE

Parsac-Saint-Émilion (Appellation Contrôlée)

Bordeaux rouge. Saint-Émilion.

Commune dont les vignes, plantées sur des coteaux calcaires, produisaient des vins corsés, de belle couleur. Depuis 1975, les vins de Parsac-Saint-Émilion peuvent être vendus sous l'appellation Montagne-Saint-Émilion, maintenant couramment utilisée.

Voir SAINT-ÉMILION

Passe

Petite étiquette ajoutée à l'étiquette principale de certaines bouteilles de vin pour donner les renseignements qui ne sont fournis ni sur cette dernière ni sur la collerette.

Passeriller

Ancien terme. Opération consistant à faire sécher des raisins sur un lit de paille. On pratique le passerillage surtout dans le Jura pour le raisin Savagnin que sa peau épaisse rend peu vulnérable à la pourriture. Les vins de paille du Jura sont faits avec des raisins passerillés.

Pour faire le Muscat de Frontignan vraiment naturel, on pratique une autre sorte de passerillage consistant à pincer ou tordre le pédoncule de la grappe avant la vendange. En interrompant ainsi la circulation de la sève, on provoque un dessèchement prématuré du raisin, donc un accroissement de sa teneur en sucre.

Voir JURA ; VINS VINÉS DE FRANCE ; FRONTIGNAN

Passetoutgrains (Appellation Contrôlée)

Honnêtes Bourgogne rouges faits avec un mélange de Pinot et de Gamay ainsi que d'autres moindres cépages.

Voir BOURGOGNE

Passion Fruit Liqueur

Liqueur australienne d'un doré foncé et très sucrée, faite avec de la grenadille.

Passito

Vin italien fait avec des raisins séchés. D'ordinaire, il s'agit de vin de dessert, mais parfois on ajoute de ces raisins à ceux qui servent à faire les vins secs.

Pâque (vin de)

Le vin de la pâque juive.
Voir KACHER (VIN)

Pasteur (Louis)

Célèbre chimiste français qui découvrit la pasteurisation lors d'expériences sur les vins du Jura. Avant lui (1822-1895), les méthodes de vinification étaient surtout traditionnelles car elles échappaient à toute théorie scientifique. Pasteur isola les micro-organismes qui font fermenter le jus de raisin, mais ses travaux n'apportèrent guère de changements dans les pratiques vinicoles. L'œuvre de Pasteur a certainement contribué à augmenter la production du vin en quantité mais extrêmement peu en qualité.

Pasteurisation

Procédé de stérilisation du vin et d'autres liquides par la chaleur.

La stabilisation du vin, du lait ou d'autres liquides consiste à les débarrasser de la plupart des micro-organismes qu'ils contiennent, en les élevant rapidement et pour un temps limité à une température de 60 à 66 °C. Elle est parfois efficace pour les vins ordinaires mais n'est pas recommandée pour les vins fins. La pasteurisation ne détruit pas seulement les bactéries, mais aussi les autres micro-organismes et, après l'avoir subie, les vins cessent d'évoluer. La pasteurisation peut avoir lieu avant ou après la mise en bouteille.
Voir CHAPITRE V

Pastis

Apéritif favori des Marseillais, mais consommé dans toute la France. Le pastis est un alcool parfumé avec des herbes et plus particulièrement la réglisse. Il ressemble beaucoup aux anis, quoique son goût soit moins distingué. Quand on y verse de l'eau, le pastis devient nuageux et laiteux mais n'a pas la teinte verdâtre de l'anis. L'anis et le pastis présentent certaines caractéristiques de l'absinthe (ancien apéritif interdit), mais ils contiennent moins d'alcool et surtout l'absinthe (herbe) n'entre pas dans leur composition : c'est cette herbe qui fit interdire l'absinthe dans la plupart des pays civilisés. Les trois marques les plus connues de pastis sont Pernod, Ricard et Berger.

Patent Still

Nom anglais de l'appareil à distillation continue, plus économique que le vieil alambic qui devait sans cesse être ouvert et rempli. On appelle aussi cet appareil alambic de Coffey car il dérive de celui qui le fit breveter en 1832, Aeneas Coffey. Ce dernier engin était d'ailleurs une amélioration de celui de Robert Stein (en 1826). La plupart des meilleurs rhums et des meilleurs whiskies sont encore distillés à l'alambic qui permet aux distillats de conserver une plus grande partie de la saveur et de l'arôme du liquide distillé. Sauf pour ceux qui préfèrent les breuvages légers, la distillation à l'alambic reste synonyme de qualité pour les eaux-de-vie et autres spiritueux.

Patras

Ville et région vinicole de Grèce qui produit surtout de bons vins blancs. Nombre d'entreprises vinicoles et de coopératives ont leur siège à Patras.
Voir GRÈCE

Patrimonio (Appellation Contrôlée)

Vin produit entre Bastia et l'Ile-Rousse. C'est l'un des meilleurs vins de Corse.
Voir CORSE

Pauillac (Appellation Contrôlée)

Bordeaux rouge. Haut-Médoc.

En superficie, la plus importante des quatre grandes communes viticoles (Margaux, Pauillac, Saint-Estèphe, Saint-Julien) de la péninsule du Médoc, Pauillac est aussi la moins connue. Ce paradoxe s'explique par le fait que les crus célèbres de son territoire (Château-Lafite, Château-Latour, Château-Mouton-Rothschild et d'autres) jouissent d'une célébrité exceptionnelle et leur nom suffit largement à les identifier.

La hiérarchie des crus de ce secteur est étrangement inégale. Pauillac compte trois Premiers Crus ; deux Seconds Crus, les deux Châteaux-Pichon-Longueville ; pas de Troisième Cru ; un Quatrième Cru bien connu, Château-Duhart-Milon, et douze (!) Cinquièmes Crus sur les 18 qui figurent sur la liste des crus classés. Le petit nombre de Troisièmes Crus et de Quatrièmes Crus à Pauillac illustre combien la classification officielle de 1855 est périmée ; en effet, plusieurs Cinquièmes mériteraient un titre plus élevé.

Les vins de Pauillac ne présentent guère de similitudes quant à leur genre et n'ont en commun que le charnu des Médoc. A part cela, chacun a ses caractéristiques propres. Ils sont plus vigoureux que les délicats Margaux et, hormis un ou deux, moins chaleureux que les Saint-Estèphe. On ne peut guère faire des généralisations tant soit peu exactes au sujet de vins aussi divers que Lafite et Latour, par exemple, un choix spécial de raisins donnant au premier plus de finesse et au second plus de fermeté.

Le secteur commence au sud, à Château-Latour, contigu à Saint-Julien. Le territoire est doucement accidenté et les vignes sont plantées sur les pentes qui s'étendent vers les terrains marécageux qui bordent la Gironde. A la vieille enclave de Bages, juste avant Pauillac, se dresse une éminence plus élevée. Au-delà de la ville, les coteaux les plus hauts sont ceux de Pontet-Canet, Mouton-d'Armailhacq (connu aujourd'hui sous le nom de Baronne-Philippe) et Mouton-Rothschild, tous côte à côte sur le même plateau. Puis vient Château-Lafite, contigu à Saint-Estèphe sur la pente la plus prononcée de Pauillac. C'est le seul secteur du Médoc que l'on puisse considérer comme légèrement accidenté.

Pendant des siècles Pauillac fut un port actif. De nos jours encore il s'y trouve un bureau de douane, mais les seuls navires qui y accostaient étaient les pétroliers venant d'Afrique et d'Amérique. Ils alimentaient la très importante raffinerie au nord de la ville, aujourd'hui fermée, qui nuisait tant à la beauté du paysage qu'à la qualité de l'air et surtout à celle des vins. La navigation a réduit la distance qui sépare Bordeaux de l'océan et, depuis lors, le port de Pauillac s'endort. Peu de Pauillacais se rappellent que La Fayette quitta la France de leur port pour aller porter secours aux *Insurgents* d'Amérique.

La Commanderie du Bontemps de Médoc — confrérie vineuse locale de promotion commerciale qui rassemble vignerons, négociants et personnalités s'intéressant au vin — a son quartier général à la Maison du Vin, sur le fond du fleuve. Ses cérémonies sont les événements les plus sensationnels de la ville où jadis on réservait un brillant accueil aux pirates de la Gironde et où l'on combattit durant la guerre de Cent Ans.

Les vignobles de Pauillac, qui ont droit au titre de Crus Classés depuis la classification des vins du Médoc en 1855, sont les suivants :

PREMIERS CRUS

Château-Lafite-Rothschild
Château-Latour
Château-Mouton-Rothschild*

* Déclaré Premier Cru par le ministère de l'Agriculture en 1973.

SECONDS CRUS

Château-Pichon-Longueville-Baron
Château-Pichon-Longueville, Comtesse de Lalande

QUATRIÈME CRU

Château-Duhart-Milon-Rothschild

CINQUIÈMES CRUS

Château-Batailley
Château-Haut-Batailley
Château-Croizet-Bages
Château-Clerc-Milon
Château-Grand-Puy-Ducasse
Château-Grand-Puy-Lacoste
Château-Haut-Bages-Libéral
Château-Lynch-Bages
Château-Lynch-Moussas
Château-Mouton-Baronne-Philippe
Château-Pédesclaux
Château-Pontet-Canet

Voir aussi chacun de ces crus à sa place dans l'ordre alphabétique.

Pavie (Château-)

Bordeaux rouge. Commune et secteur de Saint-Émilion.

Bien que très morcelé au cours des dernières années, Château-Pavie n'en reste pas moins le plus vaste des grands vignobles de Saint-Émilion. Il est magnifiquement situé sur le flanc sud d'une colline entièrement couverte de vignes. Château-Ausone et l'agglomération de Saint-Émilion se trouvent sur l'autre versant. Toutes les vignes de Pavie sont orientées au sud. Des changements trop fréquents de propriétaire expliquent peut-être pourquoi les vins de ce cru ont décliné pendant un certain temps. Mais sous la direction efficace de M. Valette, ils ont retrouvé leurs qualités de 1955 et 1986, année où Château-Pavie fut classé parmi les onze Premiers Grands Crus, alors que ses satellites — Château-Pavie-Decesse et Château-Pavie-Macquin — furent rangés seulement dans la catégorie des Grands Crus de Saint-Émilion.

Caractéristiques : Une grande production et un grand Saint-Émilion typique. Vin généreux très bouqueté.

Superficie : 35 ha.

Production moyenne : 200 tonneaux (15 000 caisses).

Pays (Vin de)

Ils répondent à une classification réglementée de vins faits dans différentes régions de France. Dans la hiérarchie des vins français, ils se situent, du point de vue technique, juste au-dessus de la catégorie la moins distinguée qui sont les *vins de consommation courante*. Leur niveau de qualité apparaît inférieure à celle de la plupart des vins V.D.Q.S. (*Vin Délimité de Qualité Supérieur*). Les *vins de pays* sont produits dans des régions spécifiques avec des cépages, des méthodes de vinification précisées par le ministère de l'Agriculture et contrôlées par des associations locales de cultivateurs. Ils portent le nom des *pays* qui les produisent comme des vins du pays des Vals d'Agly dans les Pyrénées Orientales ou les vins d'Hauterive en Pays d'Aude. Leur qualité peut varier : agréable (sans être exceptionnelle) à franchement pauvre. La plus grande région productrice de *vins de pays* en France est le Languedoc-Roussillon qui produit plus de soixante types différents. Ces vins de pays ont souvent une faible teneur en alcool. Ils peuvent être fort agréables quand on les boit sur place dans leur jeunesse. Citons par exemple un restaurant de Savoie qui recommande le vin de Pays d'Allobrogie. Ce petit vin blanc est consommé par au moins 80 % des clients qui ont bien raison de le faire. On peut en dire autant de maints petits vins de l'Anjou et du Jura, surtout autour d'Arbois. Mais ils décevraient s'ils vieillissaient et s'ils avaient subi un transport prolongé. Néanmoins la science a grandement amélioré la qualité de la plupart de ces « vins de pays » qui, autrefois mal vinifiés, sont aujourd'hui appréciés dans beaucoup de régions françaises, parfois même à l'étranger. La production moyenne annuelle de *vins de pays* dépasse les 7 millions d'hl (plus de 75 millions de caisses).

Pays-Bas

On ne cultive pas la vigne à vin aux Pays-Bas, mais la fabrication des spiritueux y date d'environ 1500 et on la considère comme une « vieille industrie nationale ». A l'origine, les Hollandais distillaient du vin pour faire de l'eau-de-vie, mais à partir de la seconde moitié du XVIe siècle, ils se mirent à traiter des grains. L'industrie de la distillation hollandaise ne se développa pleinement qu'à partir de 1670, quand le gouvernement interdit l'importation de l'eau-de-vie de vin française et imposa de lourds droits de douane aux alcools allemands. Elle prospéra surtout le long de la Meuse, notamment à Rotterdam, Delfshaven et Schiedam. Au moins 40 des 140 distilleries des Pays-Bas sont situées à Schiedam.

Genièvre

Ce produit original de la distillation hollandaise passe souvent pour être identique au gin. Il existe pourtant une différence considérable de goût et de composants entre ces deux alcools. Le genièvre type est obtenu en distillant du vin de malt ou un mélange de vin de malt et d'eau-de-vie avec des baies de genièvre et, si possible, d'autres végétaux aromatiques, avec ou sans addition de sucre. Par tradition, le genièvre se boit sec, légèrement rafraîchi. On ne l'avale pas d'un coup, on le déguste. Actuellement les jeunes Hollandais le consomment en *long drink* c'est-à-dire largement coupé d'eau.

Brandewijn (Brandevin)

Un des plus anciens spiritueux, encore populaire en certaines régions du pays. Le facteur essentiel de sa préparation consiste à le faire vieillir sur du charbon de bois et à y ajouter des substances diverses pour lui donner de la saveur. Ce brandevin sert aussi à faire de l'Advocaat et diverses liqueurs de fruits : cerise, prune, ainsi que les liqueurs typiquement hollandaises obtenues en y ajoutant raisins secs et abricots.

Bessenjenever ou gin de cassis

Autre produit typiquement hollandais obtenu en ajoutant de l'extrait de cassis à un alcool neutre.

Advocaat

Ce breuvage est si épais qu'il faut le prendre à la cuillère. On le fait en ajoutant de l'œuf, du sucre et de la vanille à de l'eau-de-vie de vin. Il titre 15 à 18° d'alcool. Un Advocaat plus léger est exporté vers l'Angleterre.

Raisins secs en brandevin

Ce breuvage, qui titre environ 15°, est obtenu en ajoutant des raisins secs, du sucre candy et de la cannelle à de l'eau-de-vie de vin.

Liqueurs

Les distillats préférés des Hollandais sont l'anisette, les eaux-de-vie d'abricot et de cerise, le curaçao, la crème de cacao, la kummel, le marasquin et le persico, ce dernier obtenu en distillant des noyaux de pêche.

Whisky

Les Pays-Bas produisent une certaine quantité de whisky à base d'orge, maïs et seigle séchés sur des feux de tourbe qui donnent une saveur de fumée.

Élixirs (Bitters)

Ces breuvages sont obtenus en faisant infuser herbes, graines et écorces dans de l'eau-de-vie et parfois en les distillant, mais pas toujours. En général on y ajoute une forte quantité de matière colorante et très peu de sucre. Ces élixirs sont moins en vogue qu'ils ne l'étaient voilà cinquante ou soixante ans.

Les Hollandais préfèrent le Pommeranz rouge ou vert qui est le plus alcoolisé, surtout le rouge qui sert à faire le Schilletje ou Voorburg.

Citons aussi Longae Vitae Catz bitters, Angostura, Boonekamp, etc.

Voir ADVOCAAT ; GIN

Pécharmant (Appellation Contrôlée)

Le meilleur vin rouge de Bergerac, qui ressemble au Saint-Émilion de second ordre.

Voir BERGERAC

Pêche (Eau-de-vie de)

Eau-de-vie obtenue par la distillation de la pêche, mais souvent les Anglo-Saxons donnent ce nom *(Peach Brandy)* à une liqueur consistant en eau-de-vie de vin sucrée dans laquelle ont macéré des pêches.

Pecsenyebór

Catégorie de qualité concernant les vins hongrois.

Pédesclaux (Château-)

Bordeaux rouge. Commune de Pauillac, en Haut-Médoc.

Classé Cinquième Cru en 1855, ce petit domaine appartient actuellement à M. Lucien Jugla.

Caractéristiques : Petit vin de qualité inégale. La vinification n'a pas toujours été ce qu'elle pourrait être.

Superficie : 30 ha.

Production moyenne : 12 000 caisses.

Pedro Ximénez

Raisin très sucré cultivé en Andalousie et dans d'autres régions de l'Espagne. Il sert surtout à faire des vins doux ou à adoucir les Xérès.

Pelure d'oignon

Ce terme désigne la couleur brûnatre pris par certains vins vieux. On appelait autrefois ainsi les vins rosés, mais cette dernière expression l'a emporté.

Perlada

Juste au nord de Figueras sur le versant espagnol des Pyrénées, se trouve cette petite agglomération vinicole que domine un château impressionnant. Son rosé est assez apprécié et bien meilleur que les rouges et blancs produits dans les mêmes vignobles. Mais le plus célèbre des vins de Perlada est un « champagne espagnol » exporté à Londres et dont l'appellation fut d'ailleurs interdite par les tribunaux anglais lors d'un procès intenté par l'Institut français des Appellations d'Origine. Cette décision confirma en Grande-Bretagne le droit exclusif des producteurs de Champagne français à l'appellation Champagne.

Perlant, Perlé

On appelle ainsi des vins légèrement pétillants, particulièrement certains Vouvray, Muscadet et vins suisses.

Voir PÉTILLANT

Perlwein

Vin mousseux obtenu par gazéification et qui est très apprécié en Allemagne.

Pernand-Vergelesses et Pernand-Vergelesses-Côte de Beaune (Appellation Contrôlée)

Bourgogne rouges et blancs. Côte de Beaune.

Le village de Pernand-Vergelesses est un des plus anciens de la Bourgogne vinicole. Il est situé derrière la « montagne » : la colline qui s'élève au-delà d'Aloxe-Corton et qu'entourent Ladoix-Serrigny et Savigny-les-Beaune. Cette agglomération est composée de maisonnettes tassées les unes contre les autres et où habitent la plupart des producteurs de Corton-Charlemagne : un des plus grands crus de Bourgogne blanc. Presque tous ne possèdent qu'une superficie très restreinte et leur production annuelle varie de 3 à 12 barriques, voire moins.

Aucun vignoble célèbre n'est entièrement situé sur le territoire de la commune, mais plusieurs vignes qui ont droit à l'Appellation d'Origine Corton, Corton-Charlemagne et Charlemagne *(voir ces noms)* s'étendent partiellement en deçà des limites de Pernand-Vergelesses. Elles ont légitimement droit à l'appellation d'Aloxe-Corton. Quant aux autres, elles donnent surtout des rouges vendus sous l'appellation plus générale de Côte de Beaune. Ce sont des vins légers qui ont parfois un bouquet remarquable et sont souvent fruités. Certains Bourguignons disent que ces vins brûlent d'une flamme chaude et intense, mais ce n'est que feu de paille. Les blancs sont à la fois souples et lourds, sans partager la race des grands blancs d'Aloxe.

La commune produit environ 800 hl (plus de 850 caisses) de vin blanc par an ; la production de vin rouge, variable, se situe cependant toujours aux environs de 2 500 hl (plus de 25 000 caisses) par an. Ces vins sont vendus indifféremment sous le nom de Pernand-Vergelesses ou de Pernand-Vergelesses-Côte de Beaune. (Aucune différence de qualité ni de goût entre ces deux appellations.) Si on les mélange aux vins de certaines autres communes du même coteau, ils sont étiquetés Côte de Beaune-Villages. Les Premiers Crus couvrent une surface d'environ 57 ha et peuvent être vendus sous une étiquette portant à la fois le nom de la commune et celui du vignoble. On a accordé le titre de Premiers Crus aux vignobles qui suivent :

PREMIERS CRUS

Crus	*Superficie (ha)*
Ile des Hautes Vergelesses	9,40
Les Basses Vergelesses	18,05
Creux de la Net	3,45
Les Fichots	11,22
En Caradeux	14,38

Pernod

Marque d'un apéritif à l'anis produit et commercialisé par la firme Pernod Fils.

Comme les autres anis et pastis, il se boit additionné d'eau qui le rend trouble comme tous les anis.

Voir PASTIS

Pérou

Le Pérou est un des plus anciens producteurs de vin d'Amérique du Sud, mais il en produit peu et de qualité moyenne. La viticulture y date au moins de 1566, année où Francisco de Carabantes planta quelques vignes aux environs d'Ica, oasis située au sud de la capitale : Lima.

Le sol et le climat du Pérou ne permettent à la vigne de subsister que dans certaines régions côtières, convenablement irriguées. Les Andes enneigées sont trop froides et trop arides ; quant au nord du pays, il convient mieux à d'autres cultures. Dans ces régions du Pérou l'industrie minière et l'élevage, surtout celui du lama, sont les principales activités.

La plupart des vignes péruviennes sont d'origine européenne. Elles donnent bon nombre de vins naturels, tant rouges que blancs. Un des meilleurs cépages est le Malbec. Mais le Pérou produit aussi des vins vinés dans le genre du xérès, du porto et du madère.

Quant aux vins de table vineux et chauds, ils ressemblent à ceux d'Espagne. Le Pérou ne produit qu'environ 80 000 hl (plus de 850 000 caisses) de vin par an et ses 14 000 ha de vignobles se trouvent autour de Ica, où se trouve le célèbre vignoble Facama, Lima et des anciennes villes Inca de Cuzco et Arequipa. Dans le sud, la production des vignobles de Moquega est également assez importante.

SPIRITUEUX

Alors que les descendants des Espagnols boivent volontiers du vin, les Indiens préfèrent la *chicha*, obtenue par brassage de maïs et de mélasse, ou un des alcools distillés dans le pays.

Le meilleur de ces alcools péruviens est le Pisco *(voir ce nom)* obtenu par distillation du vin de Muscat incomplètement fermenté. Cette eau-de-vie additionnée de blanc d'œuf et d'Angostura sert à faire un breuvage typiquement péruvien.

Perry

Nom anglais du poiré : espèce de cidre de poire, qui peut être mousseux ou non mousseux.

Perse

Voir IRAN

Pessac

Bonne commune vinicole du secteur des Graves, dans le Bordelais, où se trouvent notamment Haut-Brion et Pape-Clément.

Voir GRAVES

Pessac-Léognan (Appellation Contrôlée)

Située dans la partie septentrionale des Graves, aux abords sud et sud-ouest de la ville de Bordeaux, cette appellation récente s'étend sur les communes de Mérignac, Pessac, Talence, Canejan, Cadanjac, Gradignan, Léognan, Martillac, Saint-Médard d'Eyrans et Villenave d'Ornon.

Malgré une urbanisation désordonnée qui a contrarié et contrarie toujours son développement, l'appellation Pessac-Léognan produit annuellement près de 35 000 hl de vin (plus de 350 000 caisses) et atteind le quart de la superficie et du volume produit en Graves mais représente près de 50 % de la valeur globale de cette dernière appellation : les crus classés de Graves font tous partie des 55 châteaux d'appellation Pessac-Léognan. Environ 80 % des vins rouges sont produits à partir des cépages Merlot, Cabernet Franc, Cabernet Sauvignon, Cotlou Malbec), Petit Verdot et Carnemère et 25 % des vins blancs à partir de Sauvignon, Sémillon et Muscadelle.

Pétillant

Adjectif qui s'applique aux vins légèrement mousseux. On dit aussi : perlant ou perlé pour certains Vouvray. Il s'agit uniquement de vins rendus légèrement gazeux en raison de la présence de sucre non fermenté au moment de la mise en bouteille. La pression maximale autorisée en France pour les vins pétillants est de deux atmosphères à 20 °C.

Petit-Chablis (Appellation Contrôlée)

Chablis agréable mais de moindre qualité produit à Lignorelles, Ligny-le-Châtel et d'autres localités qui ont droit à l'appellation Chablis.

Voir CHABLIS

Petite Champagne

Aucun rapport avec le vin de Champagne. Il s'agit de la seconde région de Cognac. L'alcool produit dans ce secteur portera le nom de Petite Champagne ou de Fine Champagne.

Voir COGNAC

Petite-Sirah (Syrah)

Raisin cultivé en Californie où il produit un assez bon vin rouge et qu'on appelle aussi Duriff. Selon certains experts, ce raisin descendrait du Syrah avec lequel on fait en France l'Hermitage. D'autres autorités soutiennent qu'il n'en est rien.

Petit-Verdot

Raisin cultivé dans la région de Bordeaux pour les vins rouges.

Voir VERDOT

Petit-Village (Château)

Bordeaux rouge. Commune de Pomerol.

Ce vin au prix élevé que produit la famille Prats contient bien plus de Cabernet Sauvignon que les Pomerol moyens. Les frères Prats possèdent également Cos d'Estournel, à Saint-Estèphe, en Haut-Médoc.

Superficie : 9 ha.

Production moyenne : 42 tonneaux (4 000 caisses).

Pétrus (Château-)

Bordeaux rouge. Commune et secteur de Pomerol.

Vin le plus remarquable de Pomerol et l'un des huit premiers du Bordelais, le Château-Pétrus atteint des prix comparables (et souvent plus élevés) à ceux des Premiers Crus du Médoc. Les vignes sont plantées sur un sol caillouteux, un peu plus élevé que ses alentours, mais pas assez pour être appelé coteau, à quelque 1 500 m de Libourne et à peu près 3 km de Saint-Émilion, en bordure de la route qui réunit ces deux célèbres agglomérations vinicoles. Le chai, situé dans un petit bâtiment attrayant, est décoré des clés symboliques de saint Pierre (Petrus) dont la statue en bois monte la garde au portail. Ce château appartenait à Mme Loubat, octogénaire énergique qui conduisait elle-même sa voiture et dirigeait l'exploitation du vignoble. Déguster le vin dans son chai, en sa compagnie, offrait un double délice : sa vieille courtoisie française charmait autant que son vin. Le vignoble appartient actuellement à M. J.-P. Moueix et à la famille de Mme Loubat. Il est merveilleusement supervisé par Christian Moueix.

Caractéristiques : Vin superbe, bien rond et fruité, parfois velouté. On peut le boire avant qu'il ne soit très vieux.

Superficie : 12 ha.

Production moyenne : 40 tonneaux (4 000 caisses).

Pez (Château de)

Bordeaux rouge. Commune de Saint-Estèphe, en Haut-Médoc.

Par tradition un des Premiers Crus Bourgeois Supérieurs du Médoc, le Château de Pez mérite en réalité un classement plus élevé. Les vignes sont situées juste en face de Château-Calon-Ségur, dans le village de Saint-Estèphe. Il appartient à Xavier Gardinier qui, pendant quelques années, fut propriétaire des champagnes Lanson Pommery.

Caractéristiques : Moins charnu que bien de ses voisins, il n'en a pas moins les qualités caractéristiques des Saint-Estèphe : dureté initiale et maturation lente. C'est un des crus secondaires du Médoc qui produisait des vins à la fois bons et bon marché.

Superficie : 25 ha.

Production moyenne : 100 tonneaux (9 000 caisses).

Pfalz

Nom allemand du Palatinat.

Voir PALATINAT ; ALLEMAGNE

Phylloxéra

Maladie de la vigne due à un parasite, *Phylloxera vastatrix,* pou térébrant de la famille des aphididés. Il prospéra probablement pendant longtemps dans les vignes indigènes de l'est des États-Unis auxquelles il causa moins de dommages qu'à celles des autres pays et régions. Au cours de la seconde moitié du XIXe siècle, le phylloxéra ravagea d'abord les vignobles de Californie. Puis il passa en Europe avec des vignes importées des États-Unis et causa des dommages sans précédent dans la plupart des pays vinicoles. La France fut particulièrement frappée. Le phylloxéra y sévit à partir de 1870. Les plus vieux connaisseurs de vin discutent encore des mérites respectifs des Bordeaux rouges d'*avant* et d'*après* cette plaie. La mesure préventive consiste à greffer des variétés de *Vitis vinifera* sur des souches venant d'Amérique qui résistent mieux à ce fléau car le pou s'attaque surtout aux racines. La greffe n'affecte pas le raisin de *Vitis vinifera* mais diminue sa longévité.

Les vignes ne vivent donc plus aussi longtemps qu'autrefois. Or, les vieilles vignes donnent peu de raisins, mais de qualité supérieure, alors que les vignes jeunes donnent plus de raisins, mais de moins bonne qualité.

Autre conséquence du phylloxéra, probable mais non encore scientifiquement prouvée : c'est seulement depuis cette épidémie que la vigne peut être atteinte de court-noué ou dégénérescence infectieuse. Maints savants éminents en concluent que le phylloxéra est l'agent de cette maladie.

Voir CHAPITRE IV

Pic-Saint-Loup

Voir LANGUEDOC ; COTEAUX DU LANGUEDOC

Piceno (Rosso) (D.O.C.)

Vin rouge italien des collines de Piceno, au pied des Apennins. *Voir* MARCHES

Pichet

Petit récipient en bois, en terre ou en grès, utilisé pour servir le vin ou le cidre.

Pichon-Longueville,
Baron de Pichon (Château-)

Bordeaux rouge. Commune de Pauillac, en Haut-Médoc.

Voilà plus d'un siècle, les deux vignobles Pichon-Longueville, situés aujourd'hui chacun d'un côté de la route des vins, ne formaient qu'un seul domaine. Certaines bouteilles de Pichon-Longueville (Baron) sont étiquetées simplement Pichon-Longueville ; quant au vin du vignoble Comtesse de Lalande, il était toujours étiqueté Pichon-Longueville-Lalande ou Pichon-Lalande, et récemment, Pichon-Longueville, Comtesse de Lalande. Jacques de Pichon, baron de Longueville, fut le premier président du parlement de Bordeaux au XVIIe siècle et devint propriétaire des deux vignobles.

Le château de Pichon-Longueville-Baron, construit au XIXe siècle, avec ses tourelles « Renaissance », conviendrait admirablement aux étiquettes. Pichon est malheureusement un autre de ces vignobles qui furent achetés en 1987 par un groupe d'assurances. On craint que cette série de reprises par des groupes d'assurances, ne dépersonnalise en partie le Médoc.

Ce vignoble est un Second Cru du Médoc.

Caractéristiques : Bon vin très plein avec une bonne matière, parfois irrégulier.

Superficie : 30 ha.

Production moyenne : 120 tonneaux (11 000 caisses).

Pichon-Longueville,
Comtesse de Lalande (Château-)

Bordeaux rouge. Commune de Pauillac, en Haut-Médoc.

Ce vignoble représente environ les 3/5 de l'ancien domaine de Pichon-Longueville, divisé il y a un peu plus de cent ans, et il forme une enclave en demi-cercle dans les vignes de Château-Latour. Le caractère du vin de certaines parties de ce vignoble est très proche de celui du Château-Latour. Second Cru selon la classification de 1855, ce vin fut d'abord étiqueté Pichon-Longueville-

Lalande ou Pichon-Longueville, puis Comtesse de Lalande, son nom actuel. Celui qui porte seulement la mention Pichon-Longueville sera du Pichon-Longueville-Baron *(voir ci-dessus)*. L'héritier de M. Miailhe, Mme de Lencquesaing, est la propriétaire de Pichon-Lalande — comme on appelle communément ce cru à Bordeaux.

Caractéristiques : Plus souple et fin que Pichon-Longueville-Baron, cet excellent vin l'emporte en qualité et en popularité sur Pichon-Baron qui venait en tête au cours des années 1950. Le Pichon-Lalande 1982, 1983 et 1985 est de si grande qualité qu'il devrait encore stimuler la demande.

Superficie : 72 ha.

Production moyenne : 26 000 caisses.

Picpoul, Picpoule

Raisin à vin blanc cultivé dans le Sud de la France. Il donne des vins plutôt minces et sert aussi à faire du vermouth. Les Catalans l'appellent Avillo.

Piémont

Vins rouges et blancs. Nord-Ouest de l'Italie.

Comme son nom l'indique, le Piémont est situé au pied des Alpes, à l'extrémité nord-ouest de l'Italie. Sa capitale, la ville prospère et active de Turin, est le centre de l'industrie du vermouth, et la région autour d'Alba produit deux des meilleurs vins italiens : le Barolo et le Barbaresco. Blancs secs, ou parfois excessivement sucrés, l'Asti Spumante et le Moscato d'Asti, moins recherché, sont aussi des produits de cette province. Tous les producteurs de ces vins font partie d'un *consorzio* qui veille à la qualité et à l'authenticité des produits mis sur le marché.

Le centre du Piémont est une vaste plaine qui commence à la vallée sinueuse du Pô supérieur. Il est entouré par les Alpes au nord et à l'ouest, les Apennins à l'est et au sud-est et les hauteurs de Langhe et Monferrato, au sud. Malgré les déclivités vertigineuses de certaines de ses montagnes, le Piémont vient au cinquième rang des provinces italiennes pour la production du vin (après la Pouille, la Sicile, l'Émilie-Romagne et la Vénétie). On y fait plus de 5 millions d'hl (55 millions de caisses) de vin par an, dont 80 % proviennent du secteur situé au sud, au flanc des hauteurs de Monferrato. D'une altitude assez faible et d'une déclivité incroyable, ces coteaux ressemblent un peu à ceux du Beaujolais. Dans cette région on voyait partout de hautes vignes cultivées côte à côte avec du maïs, du blé et d'autres produits de la terre. De nos jours la vigne est plantée d'une façon intensive. La vigne prospère aussi dans le reste du Piémont. Toutefois elle n'y produit que de bons vins mais d'une qualité inférieure à ceux du secteur de Monferrato et Langhe. On cultive surtout dans cette province le Nebbiolo ainsi que diverses qualités de Muscat, de Barbera,. Bonarda, Freisa, Brachetto, Cortese, Dolcetto, Erbaluce et Grignolino, depuis l'extrémité inférieure de la vallée du Pô jusqu'aux hauteurs voisines du val d'Aoste : le secteur montagneux et austère qui s'élève jusqu'aux frontières suisse et française.

BAROLO ET BARBARESCO (D.O.C.G.)

Barolo et Barbaresco sont des bons vins complets, vigoureux et robustes d'une grande profondeur et d'une saveur prononcée. Leur grande qualité a été reconnue par les autorités vinicoles italiennes qui leur ont attribué la plus grande appellation, celle de D.O.C.G. (*Denominazione di Origine Controllata e Garantita*). Le Barolo vieillit plus lentement. Mais on préférait souvent le Barbaresco plus léger et beaucoup plus fin. Tous deux sont d'une virilité exempte de tout compromis, certains y découvrent parfois un arrière-goût qui rappellerait le goudron, ce qui ne plaît pas à tous. Les deux sont d'une couleur riche et profonde. Le meilleur Barolo est presque noir mais avec l'âge il prend au contact de l'air, quand on le verse, la teinte brunâtre de la pelure d'oignon.

Ces deux vins sont les rejetons du Nebbiolo qui, par tempérament, s'accommode parfaitement du bon climat piémontais ainsi que de ses déclivités rocheuses abruptes. Tous deux fermentent pendant 15 à 18 jours avant d'être soutirés et versés dans les cuves de chêne où ils vieilliront : le Barolo pendant 2 à 4 ans et le Barbaresco pendant moins longtemps. Ces cuves de taille variée peuvent atteindre des proportions énormes. Les meilleures sont faites avec des chênes de Slovénie, noircis par l'âge. Pendant son long vieillissement, le vin se débarrasse d'un lourd dépôt et perd sa dureté, ce qui n'empêche pas qu'un long séjour en bouteille est nécessaire, surtout aux meilleurs, afin de leur donner de la souplesse. Mais, même après un long vieillissement, les deux vins restent lourds : ils conviennent parfaitement à la viande rouge, la venaison et les pâtes.

Leur zone de culture pénètre presque dans les hauteurs de Langhe et de Monferrato. Celle du Barolo comporte 1 300 ha de vignes autour de Barolo, Castiglione, Falletto, Monforte d'Alba, Serralunga et La Morra. Moins vaste, celle du Barbaresco (500 ha) se trouve légèremement au nord-ouest de Barbaresco et de trois autres communes de la province de Cuneo.

Certaines bouteilles portent le label d'un *consorzio* local qui lui a donné son approbation. Y figure le nom de l'organisation : *Consorzio per Tutela del Barolo e Barbaresco*. Pour le Barolo il est bleu, orné d'un lion d'or, pour celui du Barbaresco il représente la vieille tour qui se dresse dans cette ville. Les meilleurs producteurs de Barolo sont Moscarello Bartolo, Rinaldi Francesco, Renato Ratti, Cordero di Montezemolo et Giacoso. A Barbaresco, Angelo Gaja est un producteur modèle d'où la qualité de ses vins. D'autres vins sont produits par quelque 70 viticulteurs, appartenant tous à la coopérative : Produttori Barbaresco.

GATTINARA (D.O.C.)

Vin plein de corps d'un rouge grenat fait avec des raisins Nebbiolo (connus dans la région sous le nom de Spauna) et cultivés autour de la commune de Gattinara, au nord de Turin. Après le Barolo et le Barbaresco, c'est l'un des meilleurs vins du Piémont, riche en tanin et d'un bouquet exquis.

ASTI SPUMANTE (D.O.C.) ET MOSCATO D'ASTI (D.O.C.)

On incline la bouteille à l'angle qui convient, une serviette blanche entoure le goulot, le sommelier dégage lentement le bouchon qui tout à coup jaillit de la bouteille avec une forte détonation. Alors la légende voulait qu'on crie au sommelier de « retourner à Asti », quel que soit le vin qu'il servait et le lieu où cela se passait, car l'Asti Spumante était certainement le vin qui faisait le plus de bruit quand on le débouchait.

Quand Charles Gancia ramena le secret de sa fabrication à son entreprise de Canelli, peu avant 1860, on vendait ce vin sous le nom de champagne d'Asti, champagne de Muscat ou champagne italien produit dans la province piémontaise qui porte le même nom que sa capitale. Asti, situé sur les rives du Tanaro, compte 68 900 habitants. Mais la réaction des Français et l'amour-propre national obligèrent les Piémontais à choisir une appellation originale ; ils se décidèrent finalement pour Asti Spumante. Phénomène qui peut faire sourire mais n'étonnera pas : il arrive parfois qu'un viniculteur, à l'autre bout du monde, baptise son vin Asti Spumante quand il veut le différencier d'un mousseux plus sec de sa région plus proche du Champagne ou autres vins mousseux.

L'Asti Spumante est un Muscat mousseux, sec ou doux et légèrement fruité. Avec sa modeste teneur en alcool (7 à 9°), sa forte teneur en sucre non fermenté et sa mousse réjouissante, il convient parfaitement aux festivités sans prétention, et c'est le préféré des Italiens en de telles circonstances. Il est bon marché en Italie quand on le compare aux mousseux des autres parties du monde. Mais les droits de douane majorent tellement

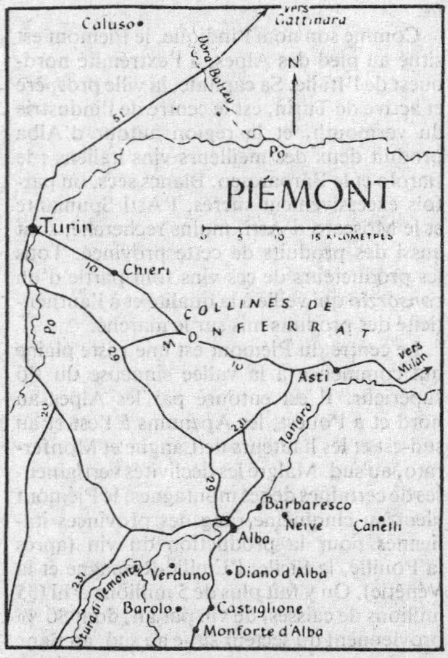

son prix qu'on le paye plus cher qu'il ne le mérite.

Le Moscato d'Asti est un vin similaire mais encore plus faible puisqu'il titre en général 7°. On le fait selon le procédé Charmat en cuve close plutôt que selon la méthode champenoise employée par les meilleures firmes pour leurs bons vins (*voir* CHAMPAGNE *et en particulier le paragraphe intitulé* CHAMPAGNISATION). Ce vin provient de 52 communes groupées autour de la petite ville d'Asti, dans le secteur des hauteurs de Monferrato et Langhe ; il est fait exclusivement avec des raisins Muscat.

Malgré sa célébrité, l'Asti Spumante se vend moins qu'autrefois. Le public change de goût et se détourne des vins doux pour se porter vers les secs. Petit à petit les producteurs de vin suivent et se mettent à traiter une partie de leur production en sec, surtout en ce qui concerne les mousseux. Ils utilisent alors les raisins Riesling et Pinot, mais rarement les variétés cultivées jusqu'alors dans leur propre secteur ou aux environs.

Les meilleures entreprises vinicoles ont planté des vignes destinées spécialement à cette nouvelle production et vinifient aussitôt que possible après la vendange. D'autres maisons importent des raisins de n'importe où, là où elles peuvent en acheter. Le mousseux sec d'Asti ne porte pas en général le nom de la ville, qui est réservé au doux, plus célèbre. Il est donc vendu en général sous l'appellation Pinot, Pinot Spumante, Gran Spumante.

On en exportait quelques-uns sous le label « Méthode Champenoise ».

Ces mousseux secs sont en général fluets et dénués de distinction, mais en Italie ils sont si bon marché que l'acheteur ne risque pas grand-chose.

Parmi les vins mousseux, seuls l'Asti Spumante et le Moscato d'Asti jouissent de la protection d'une D.O.C. Les bouteilles jugées, par le *consorzio*, dignes de porter leur appellation, sont estampillées d'un label représentant San Secondo, saint patron d'Asti, à cheval, et la mention : *Consorzio per la Tutela del Moscato d'Asti e Asti Spumante.*

AUTRES VINS

Presque tous les vins mineurs du Piémont sont étiquetés en fonction de la variété de raisins avec lesquels ils sont faits. En général, on peut les considérer comme variant à l'extrême, selon leur lieu d'origine — rarement indiqué — et l'habileté du vinificateur. Néanmoins, ils partagent tous certaines qualités plus ou moins typiques.

Dans la liste suivante les vins marqués d'un astérisque portent le nom du raisin dont ils proviennent.

Barbera *

Vin rouge, lourd, très plein, souvent dur, fait en grande quantité dans tout le Piémont et même dans toute l'Italie, mais surtout dans les secteurs d'Asti, Alessandria et Cuneo. Il y a quatre Dénominations d'Origine pour le bon Barbera : Barbera del Monferrato, d'Alba, d'Asti et Dei Colli Tortonesi.

Bonarda *

Vin rouge foncé, provenant surtout des environs d'Asti, il est parfois traité en mousseux.

Caluso Passito (D.O.C.), Caluso Passito Liquoroso (D.O.C.) et Erbaluce di Caluso (D.O.C.)*

Ce *passito* (vin fait avec des raisins séchés) est fourni par des vignes de la variété Erbaluce, cultivée autour de Caluso, à quelque 65 km au nord-nord-est de Turin. Il est blanc et doux et on ne le fait qu'en petite quantité. Le *liquoroso* est un vin vinifié. L'*Erbaluce* est un vin blanc sec.

Carema (D.O.C.)

Vin rouge, léger et frais, fait avec du Nebbiolo cultivé dans la vallée d'Asti, au bord de la rivière Dora Baltea, dans la province de Turin.

Cortese di Gavi ou Gavi, Cortese dell'Alto Monferrato, Cortese Colli Tortonesi (tous D.O.C.)

Vin blanc sec, peu remarquable, parfois mousseux mais plus souvent non mousseux. Il faut le boire très jeune.

Dolcetto *

Ce vin, généralement doux, comme son nom le suggère, ne l'est pas au Piémont. C'est un rouge de teinte foncée et de corps plutôt léger. Ce vin a les D.O.C. suivantes : Dolcetto d'Acqui, di Ovada, di Diano d'Alba, delle Langhe Monregalesi, d'Asti, Dogliani et Albas.

Freisa d'Asti et Freisa di Chieri (D.O.C.)*

Vin rouge vivace, relativement léger, d'un fruité charmeur et d'un bouquet délicieux. Le meilleur est celui de Chieri (près de Turin, au sud-est, au pied des hauteurs de Monferrato). C'est peut-être le meilleur des vins secondaires du Piémont. Certains Freisa sont vendus avec la mention *frizzante*, ce qui équivaut au « pétillant » français.

Grignolino d'Asti (D.O.C.)*

Vin rouge clair, sec, légèrement amer, manquant de la profondeur et de la densité propres à la plupart des Piémontais rouges.

Boca (D.O.C.)

Vin rouge fait principalement avec du Nebbiolo ainsi qu'un peu de Vespolina et de Bonarda. Il est produit à Boca et dans quatre autres villages autour de Novare. Avec son bouquet fleurant la violette et sa couleur d'un beau rouge rubis, ce vin sec rappelle vaguement le fruit du grenadier.

Brachetto d'Acqui (D.O.C.)*

Produit à Acqui même et dans plusieurs autres communes de la province d'Alessandria et d'Asti, ce vin d'un rouge pâle est délicatement sucré et *frizzante*, ou demi-mousseux.

Ghemme (D.O.C.)

Vin rouge grenat, avec un bouquet assez agréable suggérant la violette. Vin sec et légèrement amer qui vieillit bien, il est fait avec du Nebbiolo et un peu de Vespolina et de Bonarda, dans les communes de Ghemme et de Romagnano Sesia.

Rubino di Cantavenna (D.O.C.)

C'est un vin d'un rouge pâle, sec mais qui emplit la bouche, fait avec des raisins Barbera, Grignolino et Freisa cultivés à Cantavenna et dans trois autres villages d'Alessandria.

Sizzano (D.O.C.)

Vin sec et d'un rouge rubis fait à Sizzano (dans la province de Novara) avec du Nebbiolo, Vespolina et Bonarda. Ce vin doit vieillir au moins trois ans — dont deux ans en tonneau — avant d'être vendu.

Fara (D.O.C.)

Vin assez semblable au Sizzano mais au bouquet plus fin et fait à Fara et Briona.

Nebbiolo d'Alba (D.O.C.) et Roero (D.O.C.)*

Cette vigne noble du Piémont donne un vin d'un rouge clair au parfum de violette. Autres vins : Lessona (D.O.C.), Bramaterra (D.O.C.) et Gabiano (D.O.C.)

Malvasia di Casorzo d'Asti (D.O.C.)

Vin doux mousseux, couleur cerise, produit le plus souvent en cuves, selon la méthode Charmat. Également D.O.C., le Malvasia di Castelnuovo don Bosco (D.O.C.) lui ressemble beaucoup.

Val d'Aoste (D.O.C.)

Région autonome située au-dessus du Piémont, le val d'Aoste est aussi un D.O.C. comprenant quinze types différents. Les vins Donnaz et Enfer d'Arvier sont les deux vins les plus importants.

Donnaz est un vin rouge fait avec des raisins Nebbiolo (connus dans la région sous le nom de Picoutener) dans certaines parties de Donnaz, Perloz, Bard et Pont Saint-Martin.

On le produit sur les berges du fleuve Dora Baltea, juste au-dessus de la commune de Carema, donnant elle-même son nom à un autre vin. Donnaz est un vin doux dont le bouquet suggère l'amande, surtout lorsqu'il a atteint une certaine maturité : sa couleur est rouge grenat.

Enfer d'Arvier est fait avec des raisins Petit-Rouge, un peu de Vien du Nus, Neyret et Dolcetto. Produit autour de la commune d'Arvier, ce vin de bonne qualité est comme le Donnaz, d'une belle couleur grenat et a un arrière-goût amer qui n'est pas pour déplaire. Enfer d'Arvier doit vieillir au moins un an dans les tonneaux de bois d'une capacité maximum de 300 litres.

Les raisins sont cultivés sur de belles terrasses si élevées qu'elles font de la viniculture un véritable sport.

Pierce (Maladie de)

En anglais : *Pierce's disease.*
Maladie qui sévit dans les vignes de Californie.
Voir CHAPITRE IV

Pierre à fusil

Goût particulier de certains vins blancs provenant de vignes cultivées sur un sous-sol crayeux. Le Chablis est le principal exemple des vins qui ont le goût de pierre à fusil.

Piesporter Goldtröpfchen

Généralement le meilleur (malheureusement trop cher) des très grands vins de Piesporter, en Moselle allemande. Après un été sec, les Piesporter sont incomparables *(Goldtröpfchen* = petite goutte d'or).
Voir MOSELLE

Pimm's Cup

Il existe quatre sortes de Pimm's Cup. On raconte qu'ils furent conçus à l'origine par un barman du restaurant Pimm's, à Londres. Ils plurent tant aux clients que ces derniers demandaient sans cesse aux serveurs d'en vendre à emporter. C'est pour cela qu'on commença à les produire à une échelle commerciale. Vendus en bouteille, ils ressemblent à de vigoureux cordiaux, mais quand on les mélange à des jus de fruits, qu'on y ajoute de la bourrache et des rondelles de concombre pour les servir glacés dans de grands verres, ils deviennent des boissons rafraîchissantes fort agréables en été. Voici les quatre sortes de Pimm's Cup : le numéro 1, à base de gin ; le numéro 2, à base de whisky ; le numéro 3, à base de rhum ; le numéro 4, à base d'eau-de-vie de vin.

Pinard

Se dit en argot d'un gros rouge bon marché.

Pineau d'Aunis

Raisin qui entre dans la composition du rosé d'Anjou et des vins rouges de la Loire, où il est remplacé petit à petit par le Cabernet Franc.

Pineau des Charentes

Vin viné de la région de Cognac, consommé en apéritif.

Voir VINS VINÉS DE FRANCE

Pineau ou Pinot de la Loire

Autre nom du Chenin Blanc *(voir ce nom).*

Pinot ou Pineau

Une des familles de vignes à vin les plus distinguées, qui fournit à elle seule ou avec d'autres variétés les plus grands Bourgogne et Champagne ainsi que bien d'autres vins fins. Mais le Pinot est capricieux : par exemple, il ne s'adapte pas bien dans les régions situées au nord de la Loire. Le plus remarquable de la famille est le Pinot Noir (*voir ce nom*) ou Noirien (ou Noiren), qui donne les Bourgogne rouges. Pinot Liebault et Pinot Meslière entrent aussi dans la composition des Bourgogne, mais ils sont pratiquement identiques au Noirien. Pinot Gris et Pinot Blanc, vignes éminemment nobles, entrent dans la composition des Bourgogne blancs. Tous les Pinots abondent dans les meilleurs vignobles de Champagne. Quant à Pinot Chardonnay il est mal nommé car ce n'est pas un Pinot et il est préférable de l'appeler Chardonnay.

Pinot Blanc

Raisin blanc de la famille Pinot. Il sert à faire quelques Bourgogne blancs et d'autres vins. A ne pas confondre avec le Chardonnay. Les Allemands l'appellent Klevner et quelquefois Weissburgunder (Bourguignon blanc).

Pinot Chardonnay

Voir CHARDONNAY

Pinot Gris

Raisin de la famille Pinot, qui donne de bons vins blancs en Alsace où on l'appelait aussi Tokay d'Alsace. Dans d'autres parties de la France, on le nomme Pinot Beurot, Fauvet, Malvoisie, Auxerrois Gris. En Allemagne, son nom devient Rülander *(voir ce nom).*

Pinot Noir

Le Pinot Noir ou Noirien est un des plus grands raisins à vin de qualité. C'est lui qui donne les rouges fabuleux de Bourgogne, et le Champagne lui doit une bonne part de ses caractéristiques. Mais cette vigne est capricieuses et d'un rendement modéré. Pourtant, sur un sol et sous un climat appropriés, elle produit de manière splendide. Quoique moins intensément, on cultive aussi le Pinot Noir dans d'autres pays d'Europe, aux États-Unis, dans les États de Californie et en Oregon où on le confond parfois avec le Pinot Meunier et le Pinot Saint Georges qui n'est pas un vrai Pinot ; il est aussi cultivé en Australie. En Allemagne où on l'appelle Spätburgunder, il donne les meilleurs vins rouges du pays. Synonymes : Pineau, Savagnin, Klevner (Alsace), Clevner (Suisse orientale).

Pinte

Mesure légale de capacité anglo-saxonne, égale à 1/8 de gallon. La pinte britannique équivaut à 0,568 l ou à 20 onces fluides britanniques. La pinte de 16 onces fluides américaines équivaut à 0,473 l.

Pipe

Gros fût de section ovale dont la capacité varie selon le pays, la région et le contenu. On l'utilise surtout pour le Porto. Voici la capacité la plus courante des pipes :

Madère : 418 l. Marsala : 423 l. Vin : 477 l. Porto et Tarragone : 523 l. Lisbonne : 532 l.

Piquant

Adjectif appliqué aux vins âpres, acides et mordants.

Piqué

Adjectif désignant les vins qui ont tourné au vinaigre ou sont en train de le faire en raison d'une acidité volatile excessive.

Piqué (vin)

Vin dont la fermentation a été stoppée avant que la totalité du sucre ait pu être convertie en alcool.

Piquets

Solides pieux, de préférence en bois d'acacia, plantés en rangés et réunis par des fils de fer sur lesquels on palisse la vigne.

Piquette

Boisson obtenue en versant de l'eau sur le résidu de pressurage. D'un faible degré alcoolique, mais d'un goût frais, la piquette fut la boisson quotidienne des ouvriers agricoles au moins depuis l'époque romaine. Par extension, piquette désigne n'importe quel vin médiocre ou mauvais.

Piqûre (ou acescence)

Désordre qui se produit dans le vin et se manifeste par l'apparition d'une pellicule grise.

Voir CHAPITRE V

Pisco (Eau-de-vie de)

Eau-de-vie obtenue par la distillation du vin de Muscat, au Pérou, au Chili, en Argentine et en Bolivie. A l'origine, le Pisco était péruvien et provenait de la vallée d'Ica, le meilleur secteur vinicole du pays, près du port du Pisco.

Après distillation, l'eau-de-vie est mise

dans des récipients en terre cuite. En général, on la boit jeune.

Plat

Champagne ou vin mousseux ayant perdu ce qui le caractérise, c'est-à-dire les bulles. Également, vin non mousseux terne, peu attrayant et manquant d'acidité.

Plâtrage

Addition de plâtre de Paris aux moûts d'une acidité insuffisante. Sauf dans quelques rares cas exceptionnels, cette pratique ne donne pas des vins de haute qualité.

Plavac

Raisin indigène yougoslave qui sert à faire les vins rouges de Dalmatie.
Voir YOUGOSLAVIE

Plein

Un vin « plein » a plus de goût, de corps, et d'alcool que la moyenne. Ce n'est pas nécessairement un signe délégance, car un vin « plein » a tendance à être lourd et grossier.

Plummer

Rhum de la Jamaïque, modérément corsé.
Voir RHUM : JAMAÏQUE

Plymouth (Gin de)

Type de gin fait à Plymouth, en Angleterre, intermédiaire entre celui de Hollande et le London Dry, consommé presque exclusivement en Grande-Bretagne et aux États-Unis.
Voir GIN

Pointe (Château-la-)

Bordeaux rouge. Commune de Pomerol.
Ce domaine appartenant à M. d'Arfeuille, négociant en vins de Lisbourne, est l'un des plus grands de Pomerol. Il produit un grand vin ne manquant pas de goût.
Superficie : 20 ha.
Production moyenne : 80 tonneaux.

Pointe (Vin de)

Traduction du mot allemande *Spitzenwein.* Il s'agit des vins de toute première qualité.

Pointe (Mise sur)

Longue opération qui prend plusieurs mois et qui consiste à amener lentement chaque bouteille de Champagne dans la position verticale : goulot en bas. Pour y parvenir on se sert d'un pupitre. La mise sur pointe à lieu en même temps que le remuage.
Voir CHAMPAGNE

Poiré

Jus de poire fermenté obtenu par les mêmes procédés que le cidre. En Suisse et dans certaines régions de la France, l'eau-de-vie de poire est parfois remarquable.

Polcevera

Vin blanc italien, mince et léger.
Voir LIGURIE.

Pologne

On fait de la vodka en Pologne depuis des centaines d'années et les Polonais affirment que cet alcool est originaire de leur pays et non de Russie. Au Moyen Age, on distilla d'abord la vodka comme médecine, puis comme boisson dans les monastères et les petits manoirs de la campagne. Quand cet alcool devient populaire, le mot *woda* (eau) prit une terminaison diminutive affectueuse qui le transforma en *wodka* ou *vodka.* Chacun le distillait selon sa recette qui faisait partie du patrimoine familial et certaines de ces formules sont encore utilisées par ceux qui distillent la vodka de nos jours.

Actuellement on ne fait plus guère de vodka avec des pommes de terre, sauf celle de la marque Wodka Luksusowa (Vodka de luxe). En général il s'agit d'un alcool de grain, le plus souvent du seigle. Après filtrages répétés, le distillat est conservé pendant longtemps dans de hautes cuves d'acier, puis pompé dans une machine qui le brasse avec de l'eau distillée. Enfin on le raffine par un nouveau filtrage. Le produit fini doit être neutre, d'une teneur modérée en alcool et incolore, comme l'est la célèbre Vyborowa. Contrairement à la vodka russe, celle de Pologne est toujours mise en bouteille chez celui qui la fait. Durant ces dix dernières années, les exportations polonaises de vodka se sont accrues considérablement. Pour celle qui est destinée aux pays occidentaux, les Polonais appliquent un système d'étiquetage de couleur : bleu pour 45°, rouge pour 37,75°. Peut-être parce qu'elle est coûteuse, la vodka polonaise est considérée en France comme une boisson chic. Les connaisseurs recommandent de la boire glacée. Le Polonais la conserve volontiers dans le compartiment le plus froid de son réfrigérateur et la sert dans un seau à glace. Il la boira aussi bien pendant tout le repas que comme apéritif. Pour cet usage, la vodka Krabus — alcool de haute qualité, fait selon des vieilles recettes traditionnelles — serait la meilleure.

On produit divers types de vodka en Pologne. Certaines doivent leur goût à des fruits, des fleurs ou des herbes. Citons parmi ces dernières la Zytnia, spiritueux de couleur claire qui conserve le goût du seigle ; la Soplica, à laquelle de l'eau-de-vie de vin et de la vieille eau-de-vie de cidre donnent un goût et un arôme particuliers ; Jarzębiak, vodka de sorbes, si âpre qu'elle est parfois adoucie par addition de sucre et d'eau-de-vie de vin ; la Tarniówka, eau-de-vie de prunelle. La Zubrówka, particulièrement caractéristique de la production polonaise et très appréciée à l'étranger, porte sur son étiquette l'image d'un auroch. Quand c'est de l'authentique Zubrówka, elle a le goût d'une certaine herbe « sainte » dont raffole le zubra (ure de Pologne). Cette vodka, d'un vert olive clair, a un goût et un arôme à la fois étranges et subtils. Un brin de l'herbe « sainte » flotte dans chaque bouteille. La tradition exige qu'on en offre un verre à ceux qui reviennent de chasser dans la forêt de Bialowieza. Désormais l'État a le monopole de toutes les vodkas consommées sur place ou exportées.

On fait de la vodka en U.R.S.S., en Finlande, dans les pays scandinaves et, comme le gin, la vodka est fabriquée localement à travers le monde.

Liqueurs de vodka et d'eaux-de-vie.

Vieux type de vodka, la Starka est obtenue par la distillation du seigle, à un degré moins élevé que pour la Vyborowa, puis coupée de vin après maturation dans des fûts de chêne. Ce breuvage sec a un goût caractéristique et une couleur marron clair. La Pologne produit aussi sa propre Śliwowica (Slivovitz ou eau-de-vie de prune) et une Winiak Luksusowy, eau-de-vie pure et rectifiée, obtenue par la distillation de vins importés.

Autres liqueurs et cordiaux

La Viśniówka, cordial fait avec des cerises noires, est la plus populaire à l'étranger. La Pologne exporte d'autres cordiaux à base de fruits : liqueur de cerises, eau-de-vie de cerises, une espèce de liqueur d'or appelée Zlota Woda ; une liqueur forte à base d'herbes, la Likier Ziolowy, et une spécialité, la Krupnik liqueur, hydromel distillé, rectifié et épicé. Cette boisson qui nous vient du Moyen Age a la particularité d'être toujours servie chaude. Selon la légende, Giedymin, un prince lithuanien du XIVe siècle, serait mort de froid si l'un de ses chevaliers ne l'avait sauvé in extremis grâce à une tasse de Krupnik bouillant.

Polychrosis botrana

Microlépidoptère dont les chenilles s'attaquent aux inflorescences de la vigne et au raisin. Plus couramment appelé eudémis.

Voir CHAPITRE IV

Pomace

Nom anglais du marc : ce qui reste du fruit après pressurage. Pomace Brandy est le nom de l'eau-de-vie de marc de raisins, distillée en Californie et plus couramment désignée sous son nom italien : *Grappa*.

Pombo, Pombe

Breuvage des populations bantoues (Afrique), fait avec du millet ou du sorgho.

Pomerol (Appellation Contrôlée)

Bordeaux rouges.

Les Pomerol ressemblent aux Saint-Émilion et aux Médoc les mieux charpentés, dont ils partagent la subtilité et la finesse. C'est pourquoi on dit souvent à Bordeaux qu'ils sont intermédiaires entre ces deux types de grands vins rouges. Le secteur de Pomerol est contigu à celui de Saint-Émilion et on y cultive les mêmes variétés de raisin que dans le Médoc. Ces deux facteurs expliquent la qualité du vin. Il est exact que les Pomerol provenant d'un sol pierreux, proche de Saint-Émilion, pierreux lui aussi, ressemblent beaucoup à leurs voisins. Néanmoins ils ont des qualités qui leur sont propres, notamment une onctuosité veloutée. Les assimiler aux Médoc ou aux Saint-Émilion crée donc une confusion. Intermédiaires, quant au corps, ils doivent leur goût particulier au sous-sol ferrugineux de

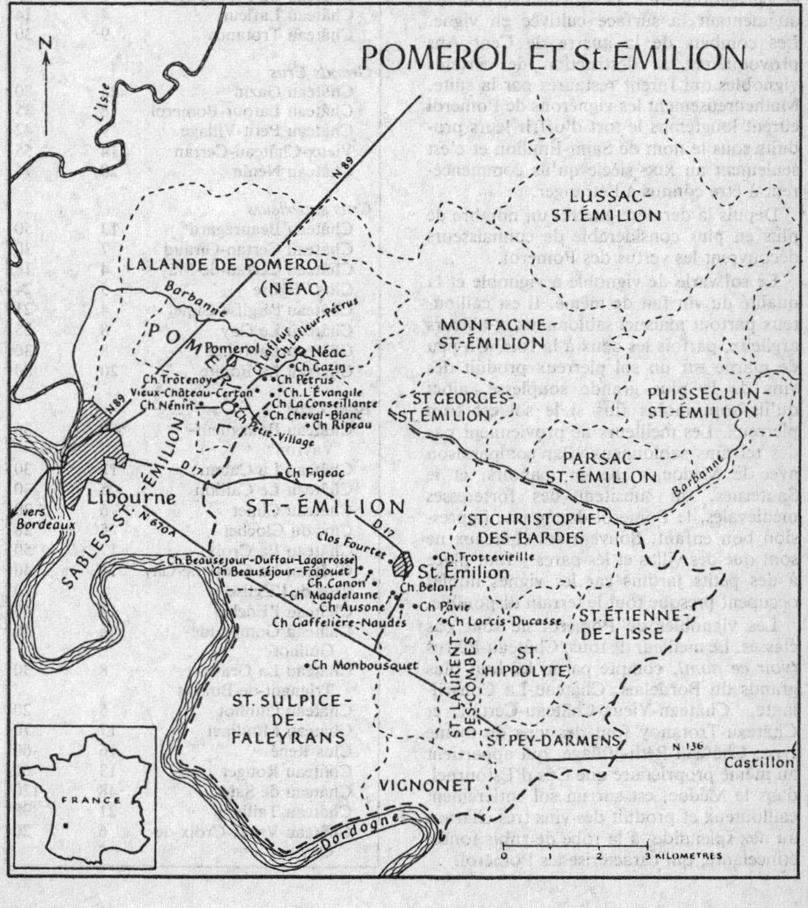

leur secteur. Ils comptent donc parmi les rouges les plus caractéristiques de la région de Bordeaux.

Le secteur de Pomerol couvre plus de 800 ha, presque entièrement sur le territoire de la commune de Pomerol, avec une petite partie sur celle de Libourne, et constitue un plateau peu élevé. Comme Saint-Émilion, situé à une dizaine de kilomètres, cette zone était un carrefour au temps des Romains alors que presque tous les transports s'effectuaient par voie fluviale.

La vigne prospérait à Pomerol, comme à Saint-Émilion, dès l'époque gallo-romaine. Au XIIe siècle, les templiers s'y installèrent et perfectionnèrent la viticulture, tout en augmentant la surface cultivée en vigne. Les combats de la guerre de Cent Ans provoquèrent la destruction de certains vignobles qui furent restaurés par la suite. Malheureusement les vignerons de Pomerol eurent longtemps le tort d'offrir leurs produits sous le nom de Saint-Émilion et c'est seulement au XIXe siècle qu'ils commencèrent à être connus à l'étranger.

Depuis la dernière guerre, un nombre de plus en plus considérable de connaisseurs découvrent les vertus des Pomerol.

Le sol varie de vignoble à vignoble et la qualité du vin fait de même. Il est caillouteux partout mais ici sablonneux et ailleurs argileux, parfois les deux à la fois. Un peu de marne sur un sol pierreux produit des vins de la plus grande souplesse, alors qu'ils sont moins fins si le sol est trop pierreux. Les meilleurs ne proviennent pas des terrains sablonneux. Par comparaison avec le Médoc, riche en manoirs, et le Sauternes, où subsitent des forteresses médiévales, le Pomerol donne une impression bon enfant. Souvent ses châteaux ne sont que des villas et les parcs y font place à des petits jardins car les vignes nobles occupent presque tout le terrain disponible.

Les vignobles de Pomerol ne sont pas classés. Le meilleur de tous, Château-Pétrus *(voir ce nom)*, compte parmi les huit plus grands du Bordelais. Château-La Conseillante, Château-Vieux-Château-Certan et Château-Trotanoy font des vins du même type. Château-Petit-Village, qui appartient au même propriétaire que Cos d'Estournel, dans le Médoc, est sur un sol entièrement caillouteux et produit des vins très charnus au nez splendide, à la robe de rubis foncé, étincelante, qui caractérise les Pomerol.

En l'absence de classification officielle, voici dans quel ordre on range couramment les Pomerol :

POMEROL : ESQUISSE D'UNE CLASSIFICATION PERSONNELLE

Production annuelle moyenne

	Ha	*Tonneaux*
Cru hors classe		
Château Pétrus	12	40
Crus exceptionnels		
Château La Conseillante	11	40
Château l'Évangile	13	36
Château La Fleur-Pétrus	9	35
Château Lafleur	4	14
Château Trotanoy	9	30
Grands Crus		
Château Gazin	25	80
Château Latour-Pomerol	8	35
Château Petit-Village	9	42
Vieux-Château-Certan	14	55
Château Nénin	20	76
Crus supérieurs		
Château Beauregard	13	50
Château Certan-Giraud	7	30
Château Certan-de-May	4	18
Clos l'Église	5	24
Château l'Église-Clinet	4	21
Château Le Gay	8	25
Château Lagrange	8	30
Château La Pointe	20	80
Bons Crus		
Château Bourgneuf-Vayron	9	36
Château La Cabane	12	30
Château Le Caillou	5	30
Château Clinet	6	20
Clos du Clocher	5	28
Château La Croix	17	50
Château La Croix-de-Gay	11	40
Clos de l'Église	5	20
Château l'Enclos	11	40
Château Gombaude-Guilhot	6	30
Château La Grave-Trignant-de-Boisset	8	30
Château Guilhot	5	20
Château Moulinet	17	70
Clos René	16	60
Château Rouget	13	60
Château de Sales	48	120
Château Taillefer	21	90
Château Vraye-Croix-de-Gay	6	20

Pommard (Appellation Contrôlée)

Bourgogne rouge. Côte de Beaune.

Pommard vient au second rang parmi les communes de la Côte de Beaune et produit plus de 10 000 hl (plus de 110 000 caisses) de vin par an. Avant que les lois sur les appellations d'origine aient mis un peu d'ordre dans le commerce du vin, un chroniqueur bourguignon estimait qu'on vendait dans le monde entier chaque semaine plus de Pommard que la commune pouvait produire en dix ans. L'étonnante célébrité de ce vin entraîne les pires abus commerciaux et les experts sont assez perplexes à ce sujet. A leur avis, le Pommard, même authentique, est presque toujours un vin extrêmement agréable, mais ne saurait être considéré comme un des plus grands Bourgogne.

Immédiatement au sud de Beaune, la grand-route diverge en deux branches. L'une va vers Chagny, l'autre serpente sur les collines vers Autun, par Pommard, Volnay et Monthélie. Elle contourne les agglomérations entourées de vignes. Bon nombre de vignobles sont clos de murs sur lesquels sont inscrits les noms de divers négociants. Si vous prenez cette route, vous trouverez Les Petits-Épenots à votre droite, aussitôt après la fourche, puis Les Grands-Épenots, Le Clos Blanc et enfin l'agglomération elle-même.

Petit village endormi, coupé à peu près en deux par un ruisseau paresseux, Pommard est orné d'un curieux beffroi. On y est à peine entré qu'on en sort déjà pour plonger dans une mer de vignes qui conduit alors à Volnay.

Les différents crus de Pommard présentent moins de différence entre eux que ceux des autres agglomérations de Bourgogne. Cependant, Les Épenots est en général extrêmement souple et arrondi, avec un beau bouquet ; Les Rugiens est le plus ferme ; En Argilières, le plus léger. Citons aussi un cru exceptionnel : Les Chaponnières. Tous les vins partagent les mêmes caractéristiques : fermeté, couleur foncée et bouquet. Plus résolus que ceux de Beaune, ils emplissent la bouche et laissent un arrière-goût agréable. Mais la plupart des vins de la Côte de Nuits sont plus charnus, tant pour le corps que pour la texture.

La chaptalisation (addition de sucre au moût en fermentation) augmente à la fois

Premiers Crus	*Superficie (ha)*
Les Rugiens-Bas	5,83
Les Rugiens-Hauts	6,83
Les Grands-Épenots	10,15
Clos des Épenots	5,23
Les Petits-Épenots	15,14
Clos de La Commaraine	3,74
Le Clos Blanc	4,18
Les Arvelets	8,46
Les Charmots	9,65
En Argilière	3,99
Les Pézerolles	5,91
Les Boucherottes	1,85
Les Saussiles	3,84
Les Croix-Noires	1,28
Les Chaponnières	2,87
Les Fremiers	5,13
Les Bertins	3,54
Les Jarolières	3,24
Les Poutures	4,13
Le Clos Micot	2,83
La Refène	2,31
Clos du Verger	2,11
Derrière Saint-Jean	0,28
La Platière	2,53
Les Chanlins-Bas	4,43
Les Combes-Dessus	2,80
La Chanière	2,78
Plante aux Chèvres	1,87
Les Bœufs	14,92
Les Vignots	15,41
Les Petits Noisons	15,58
Les Noisons	9,10
En Brescuil	5,31
Le Bas de Sausilles	4,25
Les Porrières	8,65
Les Lavières	4,38
Les Riottes	3,97
Les Tavannes	3,68
La Croix Blanche	3,22
La Croix Planet	3,73
Le Poisot	3,30
Les Cras	11,18
Les Combes Dessous	3,98
Les Chanlins Hauts	3,28
Les Lambots	2,76
Les Vaumuriens Hauts	11,72
Les Vaumuriens Bas	6,60
La Combotte	3,76
En Moigelot	0,41
Trois Follots	3,83
La Vache	8,74
En Mareau	5,23
En Chiveau	3,78
Village de Pommard	25,83
Clos Beaudes	1,49
Rue Aux Porcs	8,79
En Chaffaud	1,12

leur corps et leur teneur en alcool. Malheureusement, certains expéditeurs abusent de ce bon procédé pour obtenir des vins plus charpentés, mais aussi plus grossiers.

Pommard fut mieux traité lors de la première classification importante ayant eu lieu en Côte-d'Or en 1860 que lors de la seconde en 1936. En effet, dans la première, trois climats[1] avaient été considérés parmi les meilleurs de la Bourgogne, alors que dans la seconde ils ont été rétrogradés au rang de Premier Cru. Cela signifie que tous les vins de Pommard porteront le nom de l'agglomération et que les meilleures bouteilles y ajouteront celui d'un cru particulier, par exemple : Pommard-les-Épenots ou Pommard-Rugiens.

Une des raisons pour lesquelles le Pommard est si bien connu, c'est que ses vignobles sont vastes et la production élevée. Plus de 300 ha de la commune sont consacrés aux vignes nobles. Une bonne partie appartient à de gros négociants qui ont su faire connaître le nom de leur vin.

La liste précédente est celle des Premiers Crus de Pommard.

Pommeranzen Bitters

Bitters qui doivent leur goût aux oranges Pommerans. On les appelles parfois Élixir de longue vie.

Ponsigue

Cordial vénézuélien à base de rhum et auquel les cerises Ponsigue donnent un goût particulier.

Pontet-Canet (Château-)

Bordeaux rouge. Commune de Pauillac, en Haut-Médoc.

Classé Cinquième Cru en 1855, c'est un des vignobles du Médoc bien connus. Comme dans les autres grands crus classés, son vin est fait surtout avec des cépages Cabernet Sauvignon et Merlot. Situés près de l'entrée de Château Mouton-Rothschild, ses coteaux dévalent les collines jusqu'au port de Pauillac. C'est au début du XIXe siècle qu'un certain M. Pontet établit ce cru sur des terres connues sous le nom de Canet.

De nombreuses années plus tard, en 1865, les héritiers de M. Pontet vendirent les vignobles à Hermann Cruse, directeur de la firme de négoce Cruse et Fils Frères, qui en fut propriétaire jusqu'en 1976, date à laquelle M. Guy Tesseron l'acheta. Son fils, Alfred, est le responsable du château.

Les caves souterraines contiennent la production. C'est chose rare en Médoc, où seuls Château Mouton-Rothschild, Château-Lafite, Château-Margaux, Château-Beychevelle et quelques autres crus, peuvent se vanter d'avoir de telles caves. Le Pontet-Canet de l'année est entreposé dans un chai au toit très haut.

Caractéristiques : Parfois distingué et lent à vieillir. Dans les années 70, son caractère commun fut critiqué.

Superficie : 75 ha.

Production moyenne : 250 tonneaux (25 000 caisses).

Pony

1. Mesure de capacité anglaise égale à une once fluide, soit 2,84 cl.

2. Petit verre contenant à peu près 4 onces fluides, soit 11,36 cl, utilisé particulièrement pour l'eau-de-vie.

Porrón

Ustensile dérivant de la *bota* ou gourde espagnole. L'adresse et la bonne humeur avec laquelle les experts font jaillir en l'air un mince filet de vin et le recueillent en bouche ajoutent au pittoresque de l'Espagne. On ne saurait toutefois recommander l'usage du porrón ou de la *bota* aux dégustateurs car ces ustensiles obligent à avaler constamment pour ne pas briser l'arc de vin. En Espagne, certains disent que cette manière de boire augmente les qualités organoleptiques du vin.

Porter

Bière britannique amère, brune et très foncée qui a pratiquement disparu. Elle est obtenue par le brassage de malt séché à une température si élevée qu'il en est roussi. C'est contre la consommation de ce breuvage que

1. Noms des vignobles en Bourgogne.

s'éleva si vigoureusement Élizabeth Barrett Browning, femme de lettres anglaise du XIXᵉ siècle.

Voir BIÈRE

Portland

Vigne hybride américaine, de peu d'importance, à rendement moyen, qui donne des raisins de table et des raisins à vin. Ses fruits, de couleur verte, sont vinifiés en blancs.

Porto

Vin viné portugais.

Selon la loi portugaise, le Porto est le vin du haut Douro (Cima de Douro, Alto Douro) viné par addition d'eau-de-vie de vin et qui est expédié de Porto, ville qui se trouve à l'embouchure du Douro et qui a donné son nom à ce vin. Selon la loi britannique, seuls les vins corsés du Portugal, et non leurs copies, peuvent s'appeler Porto. Cette loi permet cependant l'utilisation de la dénomination *port-style* pour les vins du type Porto d'Australie, d'Afrique du Sud et même de Grande-Bretagne, fabriqués à partir de moûts importés.

Aux États-Unis, les vins du type Porto ont le droit de porter le nom Port à condition que leur véritable origine soit indiquée (par exemple : Californian Port). Le Porto d'origine est reconnu par les lois américaines avec l'appellation « Porto » (désignation portugaise pour le vin de Porto) et non pas « Port Wine » qui est considéré par les autorités américaines comme une désignation générique. Les portos faits en Afrique du Sud, en Australie, en Californie, en Amérique du Nord ou du Sud, ne sont pas des Porto.

Quand on parle de Porto tout court, il s'agit, ou tout au moins il devrait s'agir, du véritable Porto de Portugal qui est généralement rouge. Le schiste du sol est probablement le facteur qui, avec le climat et les méthodes de vinification mises au point au cours de longues années, donne à ce vin ses caractéristiques exceptionnelles. Il tombe moitié moins de pluie dans la haute vallée du Douro qu'à Porto et c'est la région la plus sèche du Portugal septentrional.

Il y a peu de grandes régions vinicoles dans le monde qui exportent autant que Oporto : il est plus facile d'obtenir un Vintage Port (Porto millésimé) en Grande-Bretagne et aux États-Unis que dans un bon restaurant de Lisbonne.

A l'origine, le vin Douro n'était pas viné, mais il était presque toujours dur, âpre et supportait mal le voyage. Quand les relations entre le Royaume-Uni et le Portugal, pays maritimes l'un et l'autre, se resserrèrent, les Anglais importèrent du Porto qui leur plut beaucoup. C'est alors qu'on commença à le viner, sans doute pour l'aider à supporter le voyage et peut-être aussi pour le rendre plus attrayant. L'addition d'eau-de-vie arrête la fermentation du sucre naturel, ce qui conserve au vin une partie de sa douceur. Il semble intéressant de savoir que le Porto est viné jusqu'à concurrence de 20 %.

L'histoire du développement de la région vinicole du Porto montre le rôle qu'y joue le schiste. Comme en Moselle allemande, c'est lui qui donne au vin sa race. Voilà deux cents ans, la région délimitée du haut Douro était beaucoup plus petite qu'aujourd'hui. Elle s'accrut graduellement jusqu'à atteindre son étendue actuelle, s'étirant sur une centaine de kilomètres en longueur à partir de Régua, jusqu'à la frontière espagnole. C'est une région schisteuse ; le schiste est une roche cristalline qui s'effrite facilement. Dans la zone du Porto les miettes de schiste couvrent le sous-sol granitique d'un pays qui serait désolé si on n'y cultivait pas la vigne. Là où le granit n'est pas couvert de schiste effrité, la vigne ne donne que des vins de table, comme dans la basse vallée du Douro ou autour de Dão, mais pas de Porto.

Le Porto doit aussi son succès à l'esprit d'entreprise, au climat, ainsi qu'au « palais » anglais. Les négociants britanniques jouèrent un rôle capital dans la promotion de ce vin et leurs entrepôts, appelés *lodges,* abritent près de la moitié du Porto en voie de vieillissement à l'embouchure du Douro, à Vila Nova de Gaïa. Ils possèdent aussi bon nombre des plus vastes *quintas* (domaines vinicoles). Avant la Seconde Guerre mondiale, les Britanniques achetaient la moitié de toute la production de Porto. Le déclin brusque de ces importations est dû principalement au fait que de nombreux autres vins vinés moins chers se sont imposés sur le marché, mais il indique aussi sans doute un changement de goût, et le Royaume-Uni a perdu la place de premier consommateur de Porto (qu'elle occupait par tradition) et qui revient maintenant à la France, celle-ci consommant près de 40 millions de bouteilles par an d'un Porto de qualité moyenne. La France couvre à elle seule plus de 40 % des exportations portugaises de Porto. Le Royaume-Uni se maintient au quatrième rang, et bien que le Porto rouge bon marché ait cessé d'être une boisson populaire dans les pubs, la demande de Porto d'origine augmente ; le marché a repris depuis le début des années 1960. Environ 90 % des expéditions des vins de Porto sont absorbées par la C.E.E. Au Portugal même, on s'intéresse de plus en plus au Porto — y compris au Porto blanc sec (genre d'apéritif que l'on trouve seulement au Portugal) et les chiffres montrent que les Portugais viennent au troisième rang après la France et le Bénélux.

La production annuelle moyenne est d'environ 600 000 hl (6,5 millions de caisses) de vin pour environ 25 000 ha de vignobles.

Comment fait-on le Porto

Les vignes sont cultivées sur des coteaux abrupts ou en terrasses accrochées aux falaises qui constituent les gorges du Douro. Si on n'avait pas aménagé et consolidé les terrasses à grand-peine durant des générations, presque tous les vignobles seraient emportés par le fleuve durant les brèves mais violentes pluies de décembre et de mars. Le climat est dur — étouffant l'été et glacial l'hiver.

Pour planter les vignes on est souvent obligé de faire sauter la roche pour que les racines s'enfoncent assez profondément afin de s'assurer un minimum d'humidité durant les étés secs. Depuis l'épidémie de phylloxéra bien des terrasses ont été abandonnées. On les appelle des « mortórios ». Leurs ruines chancelantes offrent un spectacle vraiment tragique, surtout quand on pense aux énormes efforts qu'exigea leur aménagement. Certaines de ces terrasses sont tombées dans un tel état de délabrement qu'on a préféré en constituer d'autres, plus larges, plutôt que de les remettre en état.

Dans une certaine mesure au moins, tout Porto est un coupage, car on reconnaît unanimement que certaines variétés de raisin donnent un meilleur vin dans des conditions climatiques déterminées et d'autres, dans des conditions différentes ; par conséquent, chaque type de vigne apporte une qualité particulière au vin et aucune ne peut donner un Porto qui soit nettement supérieur aux autres. On cultive le Touriga Nacional qui ressemble au Cabernet Franc, le Roriz et Barroca. Quatre ou cinq raisins foncés appelés Tintas et Sousão donnent à la robe du Porto un rouge profond. Ce sont en particulier le Tinto Cão et le Touriga Francesca qui est sans doute un proche parent du Pinot Noir. Les Porto blancs sont faits avec divers raisins, notamment Verdelho, Malvasia, Rabigato et Esgana-Cão. Traditionnellement, les vendangeurs coupaient les grappes et les jetaient dans de grandes hottes d'osier accrochées aux épaules d'autres vendangeurs et retenues par une lanière frontale. Si la vigne était proche du chai, les raisins y étaient portés dans ces hottes par des hommes marchant en longue file indienne. Quand la distance le justifie, les vendangeurs vident leurs hottes dans des comportes transportées au chai par des tracteurs. Dans quelques *quintas,* la tradition survit. Les cuves à pressurage, appelées *lagares,* sont généralement faites avec des lames de granit. Quand on y verse le raisin, la fête commence. Les fouleurs y sautent, les pieds nus, forment la chaîne en se tenant par les bras pour ne pas glisser sur la masse visqueuse et tournent en écrasant le raisin sous leurs pieds. Ils font ce travail en chantant des mélopées dont le ton est parfois donné par quelques instruments. Chaque équipe travaille pendant quatre heures jusqu'à ce que tout le jus ait été exprimé. Il commence à fermenter dès le début, en raison de la chaleur et du mouvement. Aujourd'hui, cette pratique se fait rare et le foulage est de plus en plus remplacé par un pressurage mécanique ; toutefois, la *vindima* est encore aujourd'hui agrémentée de musique et de danses.

Lorsque le contremaître estime que la fermentation a atteint le point approprié (son saccharomètre lui indique la quantité de sucre qui n'a pas encore été convertie en alcool), le jus, qui est un vin cru, est déversé dans de vastes récipients nommés *toneis* ou *cubas.* C'est alors qu'on y ajoute de l'eau-de-vie de vin dans une proportion égale à environ 20 %. Étant donné que la fermentation cesse lorsque la teneur en alcool approche de 16,5°, cette addition y met un terme. Le sucre qui aurait fermenté si on n'avait pas arrêté le phénomène reste dans le vin. C'est pour cela que la plupart des Porto sont des vins doux. Le degré de douceur est déterminé par le point auquel on arrête la fermentation et évidemment par les coupages effectués ensuite.

Au début du printemps, suivant la vendange, le vin additionné d'eau-de-vie, c'est-à-dire le jeune Porto encore vert, est mis dans des fûts d'une contenance de 600 l que l'on expédie alors par la voie ferrée. Dans le passé, on l'expédiait sur un *rabelo,* bateau à fond plat gréé d'une voile unique et gouverné à la perche ou bien par camion citerne. Dans ce cas, le vin faisait un voyage mouvementé avant d'atteindre l'embouchure du Douro. Au printemps, en effet, le fleuve, grossi par les pluies, est rapide et bouillonne sur les hauts-fonds. Maintenant un barrage empêche ce moyen de transport.

En réalité, le vin ne va pas à Porto mais à Vila Nova de Gaia de l'autre côté du fleuve. C'est là que se trouvent les entrepôts dont l'emplacement fut attribué par la loi.

VINTAGE PORT (PORTO MILLÉSIMÉ)

Si l'année a été exceptionnelle le vinificateur mettra une partie du vin à part pour le livrer au marché sous étiquette vintage. En général, il n'y procède que lorsque les principaux expéditeurs sont d'accord, mais pas toujours. A cela il y a une raison : les Porto non millésimés sont des mélanges de vins faits au cours de diverses années ; le négociant qui doit satisfaire une grosse demande d'excellent Porto déjà vieilli répugnera à en distraire une partie pour la millésimer. En moyenne, on ne millésime le Porto que deux ou trois fois dans une décade. Les « Oporto » 1934, 1942, 1945, 1947, 1948, 1950, 1955, 1960, 1966, 1967, 1970, 1972, 1975, 1977, 1980, 1983 et 1985 sont des exemples typiques de grandes années. On parle volontiers également des 1878, 1896, 1908 et 1912.

De toutes les grandes années, 1927 et 1945 sont incontestablement considérées comme exceptionnelles. Parmi les dernières années, 1963, 1970 et 1977 sont excellentes. Parfois aux enchères à Londres, on peut encore en trouver, mais avec d'extrêmes difficultés en ce qui concerne les deux plus anciens.

Le vin choisi pour être millésimé était presque toujours expédié en Angleterre deux ans après les vendanges, ou un peu plus, et mis en bouteille presque immédiatement. Le Porto millésimé vieillit dans le verre ; l'autre, dans le bois. Depuis 1974, tous les Vintage Port doivent être mis en bouteille au Portugal. Pendant la guerre, les Vintage Port étaient mis en bouteille au Portugal, mais en général cette opération avait lieu dans le pays importateur où les bouteilles sont couchées pour que le vin y mûrisse. Le Porto dépose toujours beaucoup. Son dépôt s'appelle « croûte ». Si l'on agite la bouteille, cette croûte mettra un certain temps à déposer de nouveau. Il est donc préférable de mettre la bouteille dans une position verticale pendant au moins 24 heures et de la décanter avant de servir le vin.

Les Vintage Port exigent habituellement de 10 à 15 ans pour atteindre leur plénitude et, dans certains cas, plus longtemps. Comme tous les vins de haute qualité, ils doivent être consommés longtemps après les vendanges car ils s'améliorent grandement en bouteille.

Le Porto devrait être servi chambré, c'est-à-dire à la température de la pièce dans laquelle il sera consommé. On y parvient en l'apportant dans cette pièce plusieurs heures avant de le boire. Le Vintage Port se dégrade s'il reste trop longtemps à l'air libre. Certains habitants de Vila Nova de Gaia affirment qu'il se conservera jusqu'à 10 jours, à condition que la carafe soit à peu près pleine. Le Porto doit être bu en digestif. Toutefois, les plus légers, pris en apéritif, peuvent être servis frappés.

Les petits « verres à porto » nuisent au vin, surtout au Vintage Port qui a plus de bouquet que n'importe quel autre et exige donc de l'espace pour se manifester. Rien ne s'oppose d'ailleurs à la consommation du Porto dans des verres limpides en forme de tulipe qui conviennent si bien à la plupart des autres vins et il y a de bonnes raisons d'en recommander l'usage. Le bord supérieur de la tulipe se refermant légèrement, le nez du vin se développera pleinement et ne se dispersera pas. L'amateur et le connaisseur se réjouiront pleinement en admirant la couleur du breuvage à travers le cristal.

Il faut décanter soigneusement le Vintage Port pour le débarrasser du dépôt qui se sera formé au fond de la bouteille. Ce n'est pas difficile. Il suffit d'opérer avec douceur pour ne pas troubler le vin. Certains millésimes, par exemple le 1935 mis en bouteille par Sandeman, offrent une facilité supplémentaire : des granules de granit couvrent le fond de la bouteille pour accrocher le sédiment.

La nouvelle tendance est de libérer des crus de Porto millésimé, issus d'une seule *quinta,* surtout lors des années où il n'y a pas de déclaration de production.

Crusted Port

Le Crusted Port (Porto croûteux) ne provenait pas d'une seule vendange mais avait été traité de la même manière que le Vintage Port et évolua de façon identique. On trouvait le même dépôt au fond de la bouteille. Il était fait avec un mélange de quelques bons vins et mis en bouteilles après environ 4 ans ; il vieillissait ensuite en bouteille pendant 6-8 ans avant de pouvoir être consommé. Il pouvait évoquer la qualité d'un Vintage Port à moindre prix. Il pouvait être excellent : il était plus corsé et avait plus de nez que les Porto mûris en fût, mais il n'atteignait pas les mêmes sommets que les Vintage Port parce qu'on avait employé à l'origine des vins de moindre qualité. La production de Crusted Port est terminée et l'I.V.P. (Institut des Vins Portugais) n'autorise plus aujourd'hui la mention de « Crusted Port » sur les étiquettes.

Tawny Port

Dans les *armazems* (chais) de Vila Nova de Gaia, on mélange la production de diverses années de Porto. Ces coupages sont vieillis en fûts de chêne (néanmoins, ceci n'est pas fait pour les vins mis en bouteille sous l'appellation Porto millésimé) ; chaque négociant s'efforce de livrer à sa clientèle un vin présentant des qualités constantes d'une année à l'autre. C'est à cela que servent les coupages qu'on peut considérer comme une orchestration de plusieurs instruments pour obtenir la meilleure symphonie. On conçoit donc que ce genre de Porto diffère selon la marque, tout en restant un produit authentique. Le mot employé à Vila Nova de Gaia à ce sujet donne une idée du soin et de l'art qu'exige l'élaboration de ce vin. On ne parle pas de coupage ou mélange mais d'éducation.

En vieillissant le vin change de couleur. Il passe du violet au rubis, puis petit à petit, à un brun doré : la teinte appelée *tawny* (roux). Le bon Porto Ruby est la version la plus jeune de ce vin. On le met en bouteille alors qu'il est encore rouge, frais et fruité. Le Porto Tawny met longtemps à vieillir dans le bois. Des années s'écoulent avant que l'on puisse l'embouteiller et le vendre. Il ne peut donc être bon marché. On devrait le boire tôt après sa mise en bouteille car, si c'est un vieux Tawny, il aura déjà acquis une grande élégance. C'est un digestif qui n'aura jamais la puissance d'un grand Vintage Port, mais il pourra être d'une extrême finesse. Un grand Porto millésimé convient aux climats froids ; un splendide vieux Tawny, plus léger, à un climat chaud.

Malheureusement on produit du Tawny selon d'autres méthodes qui donnent des vins, bons peut-être, mais certainement moins raffinés que les véritables vieux Tawny. Les Porto Ruby et blancs mélangés prennent une couleur rousse qui en fait de faux *tawny.* A l'exception des Vintage Port, tous les Porto mûris en fût sont expédiés « prêt à boire », et ne gagnent rien à rester en bouteille. Le bon Tawny n'est jamais bon marché. Vous comprendrez pourquoi si vous visitez un des grands *armazems* de Vila Nova de Gaia. Plus de 2 % du vin s'évaporent du fût chaque année. En voyant un millier de barriques alignées sur trois rangées de hauteur, vous frémirez en pensant qu'il s'en dissipera l'équivalent de 15 000 bouteilles avant votre retour si vous y allez de nouveau l'année suivante.

Porto Ruby

Jeune Porto mûri en fût, riche en couleur, fruité et doux. Un mélange de vins vieux de plusieurs années ne s'améliore pas beaucoup en bouteille. On l'utilisait jadis dans les pubs anglais pour faire le célèbre Port-and-Lemon (Porto au citron).

Porto Blanc

Vin viné doux, d'une belle couleur topaze, fait avec des raisins blancs. Cet apéritif fut aussi populaire en France que le Porto Ruby l'était en Angleterre, et certains Français continuent de l'apprécier. Dans les années 1950, on tenta de relancer un marché faiblissant en exportant un Porto blanc sec qui remportait déjà comme apéritif un certain succès au Portugal et que l'on obtenait en laissant le sucre se transformer en alcool avant de viner le vin. Toutefois, ce Porto blanc fut peu apprécié à l'étranger.

Porto millésimé mis en bouteille tardivement

Lorsqu'un vin d'une bonne année mûrit plus longuement en fût que le Porto millésimé classique — soit cinq ans ou plus —, il se forme une croûte sur les bords du fût et la couleur rubis du vin commence à s'éclaircir, sans pour autant prendre une couleur rousse. Une fois mis en bouteille, il sera clair et buvable presque immédiatement. C'est un vin plus léger que le Vintage Port connu sous la désignation L.B.V.

L'avenir du Porto

Aujourd'hui, la France qui boit le Porto en apéritif, est le grand client d'Oporto. Lorsque la Grande-Bretagne ralentit considérablement ses importations de Porto après la Seconde Guerre mondiale, on pensa à en faire du moins doux. Étant donné que la douceur de ce vin est due à la présence de sucre encore non converti au moment où l'on arrête la fermentation, il est évidemment possible de le traiter en sec : on se contentera à cet effet de laisser le sucre se transformer en alcool. Le vin qui en résultera sera absolument naturel. Mais sera-ce encore du Porto ? Cette nouvelle tendance est totalement ignorée en Grande-Bretagne, quoique les Portugais apprécient ce vin comme apéritif.

De nos jours, on s'efforce de produire les Porto traditionnels les plus fins possible et on applique à cet effet des contrôles de qualité de plus en plus sévères. La région du Porto fut la première au monde à être délimitée strictement. C'est le marquis de Pombal qui y procéda en 1756. Quant à Vila Nova de Gaia, on l'a choisie comme centre d'exportation à l'origine parce qu'il s'y trouvait déjà des entrepôts de conservation où, depuis des siècles, on gardait des vins venus du Douro qui bénéficiaient des conditions climatiques idéales pour y vieillir. Ces entrepôts sont étroitement gardés. Dans le passé, des surveillants armés y faisaient des rondes et auraient tiré à vue sur quiconque aurait été aperçu dans la zone interdite en dehors des heures de travail.

L'Institut du vin de Porto, que tout le monde à Porto appelle *Instituto*, organise des séances de dégustation à l'aveugle dans ce qui est sans doute la plus belle salle de dégustation du monde entier. Des eaux courantes y absorbent toutes les odeurs. Les dégustateurs n'ont pas le droit de répondre au téléphone pendant les opérations, ce qui pourrait les troubler et favoriserait peut-être aussi des tricheries. Tous les Porto sont appréciés à l'aveugle par des experts qui passent d'abord un examen puis agissent pendant quatre ans en qualité de dégustateur-assistant avant d'avoir le droit de vote. Un tiers seulement des quelque 250 000 pipes (fûts de quelque 550 l) produites chaque année acquièrent le droit d'être vendues sous l'étiquette Vin de Porto. Quant au reste, on le boit à Porto et dans les environs, mais sous une autre appellation et la majorité est distillée pour fournir l'eau-de-vie de vin qui servira à viner le Porto ou le vin de table.

Les chiffres de vente de Porto ont dépassé les chiffres d'avant-guerre. En ce qui concerne le vin en tant que vin, en écartant toute considération commerciale, la réponse à cette question se trouve peut-être dans ce que disait feu José Joaquin da Costa Lima, l'ardent et optimiste ex-directeur de l'*Instituto*. Selon lui, le Porto doit s'efforcer d'être plus Porto que jamais ; il lui faut de l'alcool parce que les plus grands vins de Porto sont les plus corsés mais aussi les plus déséquilibrés. S'ils ne l'étaient pas, ils ne pourraient assimiler les 20 % d'eau-de-vie de vin et s'effondreraient. Mais un vin aussi déséquilibré accepte cette eau-de-vie qui lui *rend* son équilibre. Les Porto secs existent, c'est un fait, mais ils ne pourront jamais égaler ces vins uniques et somptueux.

Comme l'écrivit Raymond Postgate dans son livre *Les Vins portugais*, chaque négociant détermine le caractère et la qualité de son Porto. L'histoire des vieilles maisons fondées au début du XIXe siècle est passionnante et richement documentée (le livre de Sarah Bradford, *The Englishman's Wine*, en donne un résumé utile). Certaines maisons ont peu à peu élargi leur champ d'action et un nombre suffisant ont su conserver leur indépendance. Les principaux négociants en Porto sont les suivants : Sandeman ; Croft (avec Delaforce, racheté récemment) ; Warre ; Calem ; Ferreira ; Tuke Holdsworth ; Offley ; Taylor (y compris Guimaraens, négociant de la maison

Fonseca, reprise en 1949) ; Silva et Cosens (qui fusionna avec Dow's en 1877 et continue d'expédier ses vins en Angleterre sous l'étiquette Dow) ; Cockburn et Martinez ; Gonzalez Byass ; Kopke ; Barros Almeida ; et Real Companhia Velha ; Quinta da Noval ; Ramos-Pinto. Symington's possède maintenant la maison Warre (fondée en 1680), ainsi que Silva et Cosens, Graham's Dows, Smith-Woodhouse, et Quarles Harris. La première compagnie à avoir été fondée ces 50 dernières années est une compagnie anglaise du nom de « Churchill ».

Voir PORTUGAL

Porto Rico

Ile des Antilles qui vient en tête pour la production de rhum.

Voir RHUM : PORTO RICO

Portugal

Selon leur nature, les vins du Portugal appartiennent à trois catégories : les célèbres vins vinés Porto et Madère ; et aussi les vins de table d'appellation d'origine contrôlée *(Denominação de Origem)* provenant de certaines régions délimitées ; enfin les vins ordinaires *(consumo)*.

HISTOIRE DU VIN PORTUGAIS

La viticulture existait probablement avant même l'arrivée des Romains, et le nord du pays, où l'hégémonie musulmane ne dura pas très longtemps, produisit du vin presque sans interruption. Dès le XIIe siècle, on expédiait du port de Viana do Castelo le vin de Monção — produit dans la région de Minho au nord-ouest du pays — en Angleterre, où il était fort apprécié. Vers le milieu du XIVe siècle, Édouard III encouragea les échanges — le vin portugais contre la laine anglaise — en signant des accords commerciaux avec le Portugal et un traité qui permit aux pêcheurs portugais de pêcher au large des côtes anglaises. Le Monção, les vins du Douro et les vins d'Algarve, restèrent populaires, mais dès 1580 — date à laquelle Philippe II d'Espagne annexa le Portugal et ses territoires d'Extrême-Orient, puis il interrompit le commerce avec l'Angleterre —, les vins de Charneca, vraisemblablement produits dans la région de Lisbonne, commencèrent à s'imposer. Dans une scène du *Henry VI* (IIe partie, Acte II, scène 3) de Shakespeare, on voit les rebelles porter des toasts à grand renfort de Sack, de Charneca et de bière.

La domination espagnole dura jusqu'en 1640. Entre-temps, les navires hollandais et britanniques combattaient les Portugais, s'ingérant dans leur commerce avec leurs comptoirs des Indes et d'Asie. L'ancienne alliance anglo-portugaise fut enfin restaurée par le mariage de Charles II avec Catherine de Bragance, mais les vins portugais ne recouvrèrent pas immédiatement leur ancienne popularité. Comparés aux vins français, ils étaient plutôt primitifs, vulgaires et inachevés. Les vins français furent proscrits sous le règne de Guillaume d'Orange lorsque l'Angleterre et la Hollande entrèrent en guerre avec la France ; cette mesure, quoique peu efficace, obligea néanmoins les Anglais à augmenter les importations de vins portugais qu'ils appréciaient peu ; mais le gouvenenement maintint son interdit sur les vins français ; de plus, le traité Methuen de 1703 portant sur les échanges anglo-portugais restait toujours en vigueur.

Depuis au moins un siècle, une « factory » (association de facteurs ou agents de commerce à la vente) s'était créée à Porto, où des Anglais ainsi que d'autres étrangers s'étaient établis dans différents commerces dont le commerce des vins. Toutefois le vin de Porto d'alors n'était pas celui que nous connaissons aujourd'hui ; c'est seulement vers la seconde moitié du XVIIIe siècle que le Porto — et, à la même époque, le Madère — prit son caractère définitif. Il remporta immédiatement un grand succès en Angleterre et sur le territoire des États-Unis, juste après la guerre de Sécession. Ces vins vinés prospérèrent au détriment des vins de table portugais qui ne furent plus consommés qu'à l'intérieur du pays. Avec la réorganisation de l'industrie vinicole et les nouvelles lois passées dans les années 1930 et 1960, ils purent s'imposer à nouveau sur le marché.

Avec l'Italie, la France, l'Espagne et l'Allemagne occidentale, le Portugal est aujourd'hui un des importants pays producteurs d'Europe occidentale (cependant loin derrière les trois premiers) et le onzième mondial. Sa production de vins de table s'élève à

8 300 000 hl (plus de 92 millions de caisses) environ par an. Les appellations d'origine représentent environ la moitié de ce chiffre. Il y a beaucoup plus de rouges que de blancs et une grande quantité de rosés. La production de grands vins vinés est nettement moins importante : 600 000 hl (6,5 millions de caisses) de Porto et seulement quelque 50 000 hl (plus de 550 000 caisses) de Madère par an. Les vignobles du pays couvrent une superficie totale de 350 000 ha, dont 3 000 ha situés sur l'île de Madère. Le Portugal compte plus de 300 000 parcelles ; aussi le vignoble moyen dépasse-t-il à peine un hectare. Plus de 235 000 personnes (soit 20 % de la population active agricole) vivent de la viniculture. La consommation locale est très élevée : chaque Portugais boit en moyenne 85 l de vin par an, soit au moins 9 fois plus que l'Américain moyen.

Le total des exportations de vins portugais (1 600 000 hl, soit 17 millions de caisses) a considérablement décru quand le Portugal a perdu ses colonies, l'Angola et le Mozambique. Au nombre de ses bons clients figurent : les États-Unis, la Grande-Bretagne, le Danemark et la France. Cette dernière est le pays qui achète le plus grand volume de vin de Porto.

Législation des vins au Portugal

Tous les vins portugais ont des certificats d'origine et sont produits dans des conditions déterminées en des régions officiellement délimitées. Le Porto est de loin le plus important d'entre eux. Hormis le Porto et le Madère, les vins qui ont droit à l'appellation d'origine *(Denominação de Origem)* sont les suivants : Vinhos Verdes, Dão, Colares, Douro, Bairrada, Algarve, Bucelas, Carcavelos et Moscatel de Setúbal. Les deux derniers sont des vins sucrés que l'on trouve rarement, sinon jamais à l'étranger. *(Pour* PORTO et MADÈRE, *voir rubriques des mêmes noms).*

La réglementation portugaise prescrit des contrôles extrêmement rigoureux que l'on s'applique aujourd'hui à faire respecter. Le commerce des vins est entièrement contrôlé par l'une des deux organisations officielles suivantes : l'Instituto do Vinho do Porto siégeant dans la ville du même nom, en ce qui concerne le Porto ; l'Intituto da Vinha e do Vinho à Lisbonne, pour les autres vins. Sous leur égide, des commissions supervisent la vinification dans ses différents stades, depuis le vignoble jusqu'à l'étiquetage et l'expédition des bouteilles. Chaque vigneron reçoit un certificat indiquant le montant de sa production et le nombre de ses fûts ; éventuellement un autre certificat lui sera délivré si ces vins réunissent les qualités requises pour avoir droit à l'appellation d'origine. Ils seront préalablement soumis à des experts pour la dégustation. Le troisième certificat est un permis octroyant des cachets — le nombre exact suffisant à la quantité de vin contenue dans les cuves de chaque vigneron — aux vins en cours de vinification *(estagio).* Lorsque le vin est tranféré en entrepôt, il est à nouveau noté par la commission locale ou par l'organisme gouvernemental compétent. Avant qu'ils soient expédiés à l'étranger, les vins devront subir un dernier contrôle de qualité se concluant par l'octroi d'un permis qui les autorisera à être exportés sous l'appellation de leur lieu d'origine.

Vins d'origine certifiée

Vinhos Verdes

La zone de Vinhos Verdes s'étend au nord-ouest du Portugal entre les fleuves Minho et Douro, c'est-à-dire dans la province d'Entre-Douro-e-Minho, appellation que portent parfois les vins. La contrée a un aspect souriant mais ridé. Elle a la forme d'un grand bol aux bords relevés du côté de la mer. Les montagnes retiennent les vents marins humides, ce qui assure à Minho un climat doux et pluvieux. Bien des rivières la sillonnent et sectionnent le terrain en de nombreuses zones, suffisamment différentes les unes des autres pour que six d'entre elles aient été reconnues comme des subdivisions régionales : Lima, Basto, Braga, Amarante, Penafiel et Monção ; enfin Lafões, secteur assez semblable aux précédents, au sud du Douro. Les vignobles couvrent une superficie totale de près de 35 000 ha, soit presque 10 % de la surface viticole nationale, et produisent plus de 2 millions d'hl (22 millions de caisses), soit 20 % de la production nationale.

Les Vinhos Verdes sont des vins verts par leur vivacité et non par leur couleur. On les fait avec des raisins vendangés précocement, avant d'être mûrs. Après environ un an, ce sont des vins légers, vifs et légèrement mordant ; versés dans des

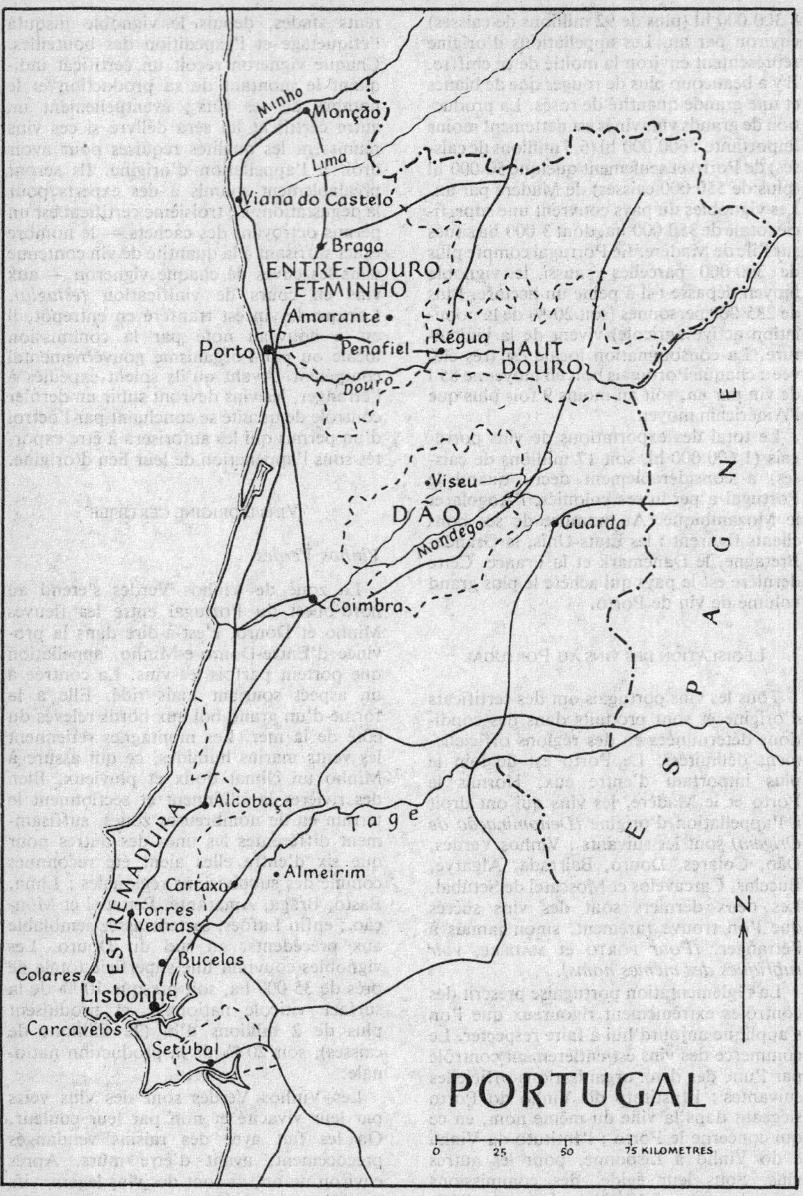
Minho
Monção
Lima
Viana do Castelo
Braga
ENTRE-DOURO
-ET-MINHO
Amarante
Porto
Penafiel
Régua
HAUT
DOURO
Douro
Viseu
DÃO
Mondego
Guarda
Coimbra
E S P A G N E
Alcobaça
Tage
ESTREMADURA
Almeirim
Cartaxo
Torres
Vedras
Bucelas
Colares
Lisbonne
Carcavelos
Setúbal
N
PORTUGAL
0 25 50 75 KILOMETRES

verres, ils donnent une écume mousseuse qui, en se déposant, révèle une fraîcheur piquante. Cette caractéristique vient du fait que les vins subissent une légère fermentation secondaire en bouteille. La région de Minho est verdoyante et boisée ; les hivers y sont rigoureux, les étés souvent humides et parfois extrêmement chauds. Dans ce pays principalement aride, cette région agricole fertile est une véritable oasis plantée d'arbres fruitiers, de légumes et d'autres cultures. Les vignes poussent librement autour de ces plantations, grimpant autour des arbres et des haies. Dans ce climat généreux qui leur épargne les grandes chaleurs et l'humidité, les raisins donnent des vins plus fluets, moins alcoolisés que ce qu'on pourrait attendre de cette partie du sud. Les blancs sont les plus agréables : servis bien froids en apéritif ou avec le poisson, ces vins désaltérants sont faits pour être consommés en été. Les rouges sortent de l'ordinaire : riches en tannin, de couleur sombre. Quoiqu'intéressants, ils ne sont pas aussi avenants que les blancs. Les principales vignes à Vinhos Verde sont Azal Branco, Avesso, Loureiro, Trajadura et Pedernã pour les vins blancs ; Bastardo, Alvarelhão et Verdelho Tinto pour les rouges ainsi qu'Azal Tinto, Espadeiro Tinto, Boaracal et Vinhão.

Avec leur charme tout en fraîcheur et en jeunesse, les Vinhos Verdes étaient jadis introuvables à l'étranger ; depuis, avec l'amélioration des conditions d'expédition, on les trouve maintenant hors des frontières du Portugal, mais aux États-Unis (où le vin mousseux est très taxé) les bouteilles arrivent privées de leur pétillement caractéristique.

Les meilleurs Vinhos Verdes d'appellation comprennent :

Agulha. Sec et légèrement pétillant, c'est un vin caractéristique vendu dans des bouteilles de pierre.

Alvarinho de Monção, Cepa Velha. Particulièrement bon dans son genre ; légèrement plus fort et de goût plus prononcé que la plupart des vins, il vieillit aussi un peu plus longtemps ; on le vend dans de sveltes bouteilles de verre brun ; produit à Monção.

Casa da Calçada. Très sec, peu pétillant et avec un léger piquant, c'est décidément un vin vert ; produit à Amarante.

Casa da Seara. Il existe deux types de ce vin blanc : le type plus sec *(meio seco)*, plus riche en saveur et en pétillement, est vendu dans de hautes bouteilles vertes ; produit à Louro.

Casa de Vilacetinho. C'est un vin typiquement vert vendu dans de hautes bouteilles brunes.

Aveleda. Produit près de Penafiel, cet agréable vin blanc pétillant est maintenant couramment exporté ; c'est peut-être le plus populaire des Vinhos Verdes à l'étranger.

Casa Mendes. Vif et agréable vin blanc typiquement vert ; produit à Aliança.

Casal Miranda. Vin typique de la région ; produit à Louro.

Casalinho. Un vin très léger, pas vraiment sec, produit à Felgueiras.

Gamba. Vin vert pétillant typique ; il est vendu en fiasques.

Gatão. Un Vinho Verde typique.

Lagosta. Un vin plein pétillant, fort connu et apprécié à l'étranger.

Meireles. Un bon exemple de Vinho Verde, désaltérant et délicatement pétillant.

Mirita. Un autre vin d'Aliança, légèrement plus doux.

Moura Basto. Vin assez pétillant mais moins plein que certains autres ; il est fait avec le raisin Azal ; produit à Amarante ou Basto.

Souto Vedro. C'est un vin difficile ; vert, très piquant, sec et pétillant ; produit à Amarante.

Tâmega. C'est un vin au goût prononcé, mais il contient moins d'acide que le Souto Vedro.

Tres Marias. Vin douceâtre et assez mou ; produit à Vizela.

Quinta de Curvos. Vin spécial d'Esposende mis en bouteilles au domaine.

Dão

Les vins de Dão (prononcer « daung ») proviennent du centre de la région nord du Portugal, où le climat est froid et humide en hiver et très chaud en été. Le décor est sauvage, boisé et montagneux. Une bonne partie des vignes sont plantées en terrasses comme dans la haute vallée du Douro où l'on fait le Porto. Le granit affleure sur une grande partie du terrain, et il est impossible d'y cultiver quoi que ce soit. Les meilleurs vignobles sont situés dans les clairières des forêts qui forment des vallées dont le sol est jonché de granit et de schiste mis en miettes par l'érosion. Aux alentours de la ville de Viseu, on produit du vin depuis au moins sept siècles. Mais ce n'est que depuis ce siècle que la région de Dão a été limitée dans un triangle dont les angles sont Viseu, Guarda et Coimbra.

Cette région produit plusieurs centaines de fois plus de vin rouge que de blanc. Une bonne partie des raisins blancs connaissent un triste sort en étant mêlés avec les rouges pour donner au vin une vive couleur rubis. Pour le rouge on y cultive principalement le Bastardo, l'Alvarelhão, le Tourigo, le Tinta Carvalha, le Boga de Couro ainsi qu'un raisin appelé Tinta Pinheira, dérivant probablement du Pinot français. Pour le blanc, les variétés les plus importantes sont le Dona Branca, le Cerceal, le Fernão Pires, le Barcelo et l'Arinto qu'on suppose descendre du Riesling allemand. La plupart des parcelles cultivées par les paysans sont de proportions assez réduites, et leur production ne dépasse peut-être pas 50 hl en année moyenne. Dans les vignobles plus prospères de Dão, les vignes sont taillées court et les rangées espacées, mais ailleurs elles poussent plus librement le long d'échalas ou autour de jeunes arbres arqués. La culture y est pénible et il faut souvent faire sauter la roche avant de planter les vignes. Le décor désolé fait survivre un mode de vie primitif. Aux vendanges ce sont souvent des femmes qui portent les raisins aux cuves dans des paniers d'osier ou de plastique posés sur leur tête. Mais, sauf quelques rares exceptions, les *trabalhadores* ne foulent plus les raisins sous leurs pieds nus.

Les principales caractéristiques des vins de Dão, pris dans leur ensemble, sont la souplesse et la suavité, qualités qu'explique l'analyse chimique car elle révèle une teneur exceptionnellement élevée en glycérine. Toutefois certains crus plus vulgaires peuvent avoir un goût de terroir prononcé. A la différence des Vinhos Verdes voisins, ces vins sont aussi forts que les vins du Rhône, titrant en moyenne 12 % d'alcool. Souvent le nez comporte un soupçon de levure car, dans cette région, les levures sont habituellement forcées. Certains rouges foncés peuvent évoquer le Pinot Noir. Les blancs sont des vins nets, secs, parfois durs et au goût prononcé, qui peuvent être fort agréables. Bien qu'ils puissent supporter trois ou quatre ans en bouteille, leur intérêt réside dans leur jeunesse et leur fraîcheur. Les vins rouges, quant à eux, sont encore bons après dix ans mais n'atteignent jamais la maturité des vieux clairets.

La région délimitée de Dão comprend quelque 16 communes, parmi lesquelles Nelas, Penalva do Castelo, Mortàgua et Oliveira do Hospital sont particulièrement dignes d'intérêt. Bien qu'il puisse y avoir une différence marquée entre les vins de ces différents villages, celle-ci tend à être éliminée par le coupage ; il n'en reste pas moins que certains coupages seront meilleurs que d'autres. La mise en bouteilles au domaine est une pratique peu courante ici. Les firmes locales et les grands négociants sont contrôlés par la Fédération des viniculteurs de Dão qui a monté avec succès plusieurs coopératives dans la région, où leur nombre augmente. Chaque coopérative produit son vin puis en laisse la vente à l'Union des coopératives et à des groupes de vente qui disposent d'une réglementation pour le contrôle de la qualité des vins au moyen de la dégustation et l'analyse chimique. Malheureusement l'Union n'a aucun pouvoir sur les plantations des parcelles paysannes : elle peut seulement recommander certaines variétés de raisin, les vignerons restant libres de refuser ses conseils. La région produit un des meilleurs vins de table d'exportation ; avec quelques efforts et un contrôle plus sévère, ceux-ci pourraient aisément devenir des vins fins.

Les entreprises de vinification locales sont : Vinicola do Vale do Dão (Viseu), Sociedade Vinicola do Dão (Viseu), J.P. da Ferreira dos Santos (Povolide, Viseu), J.M. Fonseca, União Comercial da Beira (Oliveirinha) et Vinicola de Nelas (Nelas).

Parmi les bons négociants en vins de Dão qui n'ont pas de caves dans la région délimitée, on trouve : Sociedade dos Vinhos de Porto Constantino, S.A.R.L. ; Caves Aliança-Vinicola de Sangalhos, S.A.R.L. ; Real Companhia Vinicola do Norte de Portugal, S.A.R.L. ; Caves Solar das Francesas, S.A.R.L. ; Imperial Vinicola, Limitada ; Sociedade dos Vinhos Vice-Rei, S.A.R.L. ; Sociedade dos Vinhos Borges et Irmão ; Caves do Casalinho, Limitada ; João T. Barbosa, Limitada, J. Serra & Son, Limitada.

Colares

Le véritable Colares bénéficia du phylloxéra. Quand, à la fin du siècle dernier, ce pou dévastateur arriva en Europe avec des vignes américaines, il dévasta à peu près tous les vignobles du continent. Plus bas, se trouvent les vignobles plantés en terrasses sur le sol ferme *(chão rijo)* des vallonnements montagneux. Le phylloxéra sévit ici comme partout ailleurs et actuellement toutes les vignes sont greffées sur des souches américaines, plus résistantes. Sur un sol — sablonneux en surface et argileux en profondeur — de Colares, particulièrement réfractaire à la vigne, le phylloxéra n'a pu faire ses ravages. A 32 km de Lisbonne, sur un promontoire boisé et sillonné de fleuves qui s'élève jusqu'aux hauteurs de Sintra, la vigne couvre des dunes côtières quadrillées de coupe-vent faits de roseaux et de tiges de bruyères tissés ensemble.

Planter la vigne est difficile. Il faut creuser une tranchée de la taille d'un homme afin que la vigne puisse s'agripper au sol ferme et argileux. Les souches sont étayées avec le sable mais n'y prendront pas racine. C'est un travail harassant et dangereux, car ces murs de sable risquent constamment de s'affaisser pendant que l'on creuse la tranchée. Avant le phylloxéra, ce travail pénible n'en valait pas la peine, et une grande partie de la région n'était qu'une étendue de sable et de pins rabougris ; lorsque le phylloxéra réduisit de moitié la production européenne, il redevint intéressant d'exploiter les terres arides de Colares. Par la suite ses vignobles argileux furent replantés de vignes européennes greffées sur des souches américaines. Mais les vins atteignirent des prix trop élevés pour être rentables. Une grande partie du véritable Colares est maintenant consommé localement ; seul ce vin a droit à la marque d'origine légale. Certains le considèrent comme l'un des meilleurs vins de table portugais, d'autres lui préfèrent le Dão. Il se fait de plus en plus rare, surtout depuis que les terres sont consacrées au tourisme balnéaire en pleine expansion.

Tout le vin de dunes fait à Colares provient du raisin Ramisco et Santarem. João Santaren, variété qu'on croit originaire de Bordeaux. Pour faciliter la plantation, les vignes sont encouragées à se développer horizontalement ; les extrémités des souches, enfouies dans le sol produisent alors de nouvelles racines. Le Ramisco donne un vin à maturation lente. Parfois le Colares mûrit pendant 14 ans dans de grands fûts en acajou de l'Angola ou en séquoia des États-Unis. Malheureusement cette pratique n'est pas toujours observée, aussi les vins de Colares n'ont pas une qualité constante. Un bon Colares doit être d'un rouge sombre et avoir un grand nez ; quoique robuste, il ne sera probablement jamais aussi corsé qu'un vin du Rhône, auquel il peut être comparé par certains côtés. Il existe également un Colares blanc, vinifié à partir du cépage Malvoisie, sans grand intérêt d'ailleurs.

De toutes les firmes ayant leurs cuves dans la coopérative régionale (Adega regional) de Colares, une seule produit d'authentiques vins millésimés. Les bouteilles des autres firmes portent l'appellation Vindima ou Colheita suivie d'une date. Mais le vin qu'elles contiennent est un coupage dans lequel la vendange de l'année citée n'entre que pour une partie. La date devrait indiquer celle du vin prédominant, mais il ne s'agit que d'une information vague et quelque peu douteuse.

Caractéristique des vins portugais en général et des Colares en particulier : l'usage de la mention *Garrafeira* ou *Reserva*. Le mot Garrafeira figurant sur une bouteille indique que le vin est conservé en fûts et en bouteilles pendant un certain nombre d'années avant d'être mis en vente. Ces vins sont également millésimés. Quant au Vindima, faute d'indication contraire, il est vendu aussitôt sa mise en bouteille.

Carcavelos

Situés près de l'embouchure du Tage sur la Costa do Sol, ce vieux vignoble producteur de vins secs et doux est menacé comme ceux de Bucelas par l'extension de la banlieue de Lisbonne et du centre balnéaire d'Estoril qui empiètent peu à peu sur ses terres. Carcavelos fut fort célèbre au XVIIIe siècle lorsque le marquis de Pombal, après avoir réorganisé différents secteurs du pays s'en prit aux vignobles de sa propre région. Ses méthodes de vinification — tout à fait révolutionnaires pour l'époque — furent appliquées dans des centres pilotes, où le contrôle de la qualité des vins était rigoureux. Mais en raison de sa popularité croissante, le nom de Carcavelos commença à être utilisé pour des crus mineurs, à la suite de quoi le vin tomba peu à peu dans l'oubli.

En 1908, les autorités locales prirent l'affaire en main, délimitèrent le secteur et instaurèrent des contrôles de qualité. Carcavelos est la zone ayant droit à l'appellation. Aujourd'hui la production se limite au seul vignoble de Quinta do Barão. On y produit des blancs et des rouges, mais les premiers (faits avec le raisin Galego Dourado ainsi qu'un peu d'Arinto et de

Boal) sont de loin les plus importants. Ces vins doux, ambrés, additionnés d'environ 19 % d'alcool, ont un arôme de noisette. Ils gagnent à vieillir quatre ou cinq ans avant d'atteindre leur bouquet et leur finesse optimaux. Au Portugal, on le boit en apéritif ou, tel le Sauternes en France, comme vin de dessert ; on l'accompagnera volontiers d'un biscuit en fin d'après-midi.

Bucelas

Le vin de Bucelas — localité située immédiatement au nord de Lisbonne — était fort connu il y a un siècle à peu près et exporté en grande quantité, mais de nos jours on n'en trouve plus guère à l'étranger. Avec l'extension de Lisbonne, les vignobles des environs ne manquent pas de se rétrécir, ce qui diminue leur production. Le Bucelas que savouraient les troupes durant les guerres napoléoniennes et que les Anglais prisèrent tant par la suite, était à l'origine un vin doux et viné. Néanmoins il était parfois connu sous le nom de Hock portugais. En 1911, l'addition de sucre et d'alcool fut interdite et le Bucelas actuel est un vin sec et riche en acide, plutôt léger et évanescent, avec parfois un certain goût de terroir, mais dans l'ensemble très agréable, surtout servi avec le poisson. L'appellation Bucelas est octroyée à onze villages, dont Charneca et bien sûr, Bucelas ; les principaux vignobles se trouvent dans la vallée de Trancão ; les raisins prédominants sont l'Esgana Cão et l'Arinto, ce dernier est probablement parent du Riesling. La production annuelle est d'environ 35 000 caisses.

Moscatel de Setùbal

Fourni par des vignes taillées irrégulièrement, dont les sarments tordus jaillissent du sol comme des bras dressés vers le ciel, et rarement plantées en rangées, ces vins de liqueur doux et dorés ne sont produits qu'en petite quantité dans une région située en face de Lisbonne. Leurs vignobles s'étendent sur les charmants coteaux de la Serra da Arràbida, à proximité de deux villages — Palmela et Azeitão — situés en retrait du port de Setùbal, qui donne son nom à la région. Le Moscatel de Setùbal est un vin viné et très doux, évoquant fortement le raisin Muscat avec lequel il est fait ; jeune, c'est un vin fruité qui prend une couleur sombre et s'adoucit avec l'âge. On fait également un vin rouge ordinaire qui jusqu'à présent ne porte pas l'appellation régionale.

Bairrada

Située au sud d'Agueda, entre le littoral et les montagnes de Caramulo et de Buçaco, c'est une zone de grande production dont le centre se situe à Anadia. On y fait de bons vins de table : des blancs assez agréables, mais surtout des rouges pleins de corps (faits avec le raisin Baga). Il existe également des rosés, dont certains sont vendus pétillants sur le marché anglais, alors que les Portugais et les Américains les apprécient non-mousseux. Les bons blancs mousseux du Portugal viennent eux aussi de cette région ; ce sont des vins propres et pétillants au goût bien particulier — et bien différent de celui du Champagne —, vinifiés selon la méthode champenoise. La région de Bairrada produit quelque 5 millions de caisses par an.

Depuis maintenant plusieurs années, le gouvernement portugais s'intéresse particulièrement à l'exportation de ses vins et le Comité de promotion de l'exportation encourage les plus grandes firmes à se faire concurrence en produisant de nouvelles marques. En outre, on ne devrait pas tarder à instaurer de nouvelles zones délimitées d'appellation contrôlée. Les secteurs susceptibles d'être retenus sont les suivants :

Lafóes. Non loin de la région de Dão, ses vignes poussent sur un sol granitique appartenant plus ou moins à la contrée de Vinhos Verdes ; les raisins sont palissés contre des treilles et vendangés avant d'être entièrement mûrs. Les principaux raisins à vin blanc sont l'Arinto et le Sercial ; la variété utilisée pour les rouges est l'Amaral et le Tourigo. On fait quelques rouges légers ou *claretes* agréables. Certains des vins les plus célèbres sont Evelita, Allegro et Grandjo.

Águeda. Les vignobles se trouvent au centre du nord du pays, près des fleuves Vouga et Águeda. Les vignes poussent en bordure de terres labourées ; elles sont parfois taillées court ou entortillées autour des treilles. Certains vins légers rappellent les Vinhos Verdes, en plus plein et en moins vif ; d'autres ressemblent plutôt aux Dão.

Alcobaça. Située à proximité de la côte, à l'ouest du massif qui la sépare du bassin du Tage, cette région centrale au climat variable produit des vins provenant de sols différents et variés. Les rouges comme les blancs sont connus depuis le XIIe siècle ; les premiers sont des vins d'une couleur éclatante au parfum caractéristique et les meilleurs blancs sont produits autour d'Obidos, magnifique ville entourée de hauts murs.

Torres Vedras. Situé au sud d'Alcobaça et au nord de Colares, Torres Vedras est le plus gros producteur de vins ordinaires. Ce sont pour la plupart des rouges pleins, colorés et fortement alcoolisés.

Ribatejo. A l'est de Torres Vedras, les vignobles, situés autour d'Almeirim et Cartaxo, produisent des blancs vigoureux (près de 8 millions de caisses par an) et des rouges plein de corps.

Lagoa, Portimão. Chauffés par le soleil du sud, les vignobles d'Algarve (Appellation d'Origine) produisent de robustes rouges et blancs secs ordinaires.

Rosados. Les rosés portugais n'ont pas d'appellation d'origine. L'un d'entre eux, le Mateus Rosé, produit dans de populaires bouteilles ventrues à l'étiquette suggestive, est un des vins les plus vendus au monde, suivi de près par le Lancers. Les vins doux étant plus appréciés des Anglais, les Mateus Rosés sont additionnés de sucre avant d'être exportés. Le Lancers est très populaire aux États-Unis, et le Mateus dans le monde entier ; le Faisca, plus mousseux que la plupart des autres est particulièrement apprécié au Portugal ; enfin, la Casa de Cerca. Tous ces vins sont pétillants.

SPIRITUEUX

Les eaux-de-vie portugaises (connues dans leur pays sous le nom *d'aguardentes*) existent depuis les temps de la conquête musulmane. Ils ont un goût et un parfum caractéristiques et ressemblent peu au Cognac. La plupart des *aguardentes* sont additionnés de sucre et aromatisés de caramel comme de nombreuses eaux-de-vie.

Pot

1. Petite bouteille sympathique et fort utile du sud de la Bourgogne, notamment du Beaujolais. Elle contient à peu près 1/2 l. On l'emplit au robinet du fût pour servir le vin dans les restaurants et les cafés. Plus grand que la demi-bouteille et plus petit que la bouteille, le pot de Beaujolais est devenu très populaire en France depuis 1958 ; l'auteur de cette encyclopédie s'est ingénié avec succès à le faire adopter aux États-Unis. On en trouve aussi en Angleterre.

2. Ancienne mesure de capacité française utilisée pour le vin.

Poteen, Potheen

Whisky fait ou vendu dans des conditions illicites en Irlande.

Pottle

Ancienne mesure de capacité anglaise utilisée pour le vin et qui équivalait à un demi-gallon, soit environ 2,27 l.

Pouget (Château-)

Bordeaux rouge. Commune de Cantenac-Margaux, en Haut-Médoc.

Jusqu'à la Révolution, le vignoble appartint aux moines du Prieuré, château qui appartient actuellement à l'auteur de cette encyclopédie. Quatrième Cru selon la classification de 1855, ce château est actuellement exploité parallèlement à celui de Boyd-Cantenac, Troisième Cru, par M. Guillermet qui possède les deux domaines. Les deux vins sont faits au château Pouget et se sont considérablement améliorés depuis la fin des années 60.

Caractéristiques : Généralement assez plein et harmonieux avec une finesse de Margaux.

Superficie : 12 ha.

Production moyenne : 50 tonneaux (4 000 caisses).

Pouille

Vins blancs et rouges. Sud-Est de l'Italie. Sur l'Adriatique.

Cette province, souvent appelée Les Pouilles et qui est l'ancienne Apulie (en italien : Puglia), constitue le « talon » de la « botte » italienne. La plaine à blé, écrasée par le soleil, totalement dénuée d'ombrage, se transforme au fur et à mesure que l'on s'engage plus loin vers le sud, pour devenir une immense mer moutonnante de vignes et d'oliviers noueux qui trop souvent cohabitent sur le même terrain. Le sol est aussi pauvre que le soleil est chaud et la vigne s'y adapte tellement bien que le pressurage des raisins de la Pouille donne 11 millions d'hl de vin par an. La plus grosse partie est du rouge vendu en fût, aussitôt après la fin de la fermentation, dans toute l'Italie où il est consommé comme vin ordinaire. On en utilise une partie à des coupages et à l'élaboration du vermouth ainsi qu'à celle de divers apéritifs à base de vin, consommés en grande abondance. Toutes ces utilisations s'expliquent par sa fermeté et sa forte teneur en alcool. En Pouille comme dans le Midi de la France, les vignerons s'intéressent plus à la quantité qu'à la qualité et personne, ni dans une région ni dans l'autre, ne prétend produire des vins fins. Néanmoins nous devons citer quelques délicieuses exceptions.

Le *San Severo* est une D.O.C. s'appliquant aux blancs, rouges et rosés produits dans la commune de San Severo ainsi que dans sept autres communes de la province de Foggia. Le vin blanc, de couleur paille claire, léger, sec, éminemment buvable, est produit à l'extrémité nord de la Pouille, sur le *tavoliere* (échiquier), autrement dit le plateau sur lequel se trouve Foggia. C'est un vin moyennement fort fait avec du raisin Bombino, Trebbiano et certains experts le classent parmi les meilleurs blancs des Pouilles.

Le *Tavoliere* offre d'autres vins : les Locorotondo, Martina Franca, Castel del Monte et Matino, tous des D.O.C.

Locorotondo et *Martina Franca* sont tous deux des vins blancs faits avec des proportions différentes de Verdeca et Bianco di Alessano, raisins cultivés dans les régions avoisinantes, au sud-est de Bari. Tous deux ont un bouquet délicat, un goût sec, une couleur vert pâle, et titrent environ 12° d'alcool.

Castel del Monte est la D.O.C. des blancs et rouges faits respectivement avec du Pampanuto et de l'Uva di Troia, raisins de la région de Bari. Le Castel del Monte blanc est un vin sec et frais de bon caractère, mais pas aussi bon que le rouge, qui s'améliore en vieillissant et peut mériter le cachet « riserva » au bout de trois ans. C'est un vin excellent, bien équilibré en tanin et acidité.

Le *Matino* est produit à l'extrême sud des Pouilles, aux environs de Lecce, ville célèbre pour son architecture baroque. Les vins prennent leur nom d'un village appelé Matino. Les rouges et rosés peuvent contenir jusqu'à 30 % de Malvasia et de Sangiovese. Mais c'est le raisin Negro Amaro qui donne à ces vins leur léger goût de brûlé tellement caractéristique.

Moscato di Trani est la D.O.C. de vins naturellement doux faits avec du Moscato Bianco et produits dans les environs de Bari. On donne aussi ce nom à un vin « liquoroso » de la zone, mais il est nettement plus alcoolisé.

Parmi les autres D.O.C., citons : l'Aleatico di Puglia (vin rouge doux), l'Ostuni (vin blanc sec), le Gravina (demi-sec) et les vins rouges : Alezio, Brindisi, Cacc'e mmitte di Lucera, Copertino, Orta Nova, Primitivo di Manduria (légèrement doux), Rosso Canosa, Rosso di Cerignola et Salice Salentino. Les principales variétés de raisin utilisées pour les vins rouges sont : Malvasia Nera di Brindisi, Sussumaniello, Montepulciano, Sangiovese, Trebbiano Toscano, et Uva di Troia. Pour les vins blancs : Malvasia del Chianti, Greco di Tufo, et Bianco d'Alessano. Bari et Brindisi sont les deux villes les plus importantes d'Apulie, ce sont aussi les deux ports principaux de l'Adriatique ouverts sur la Grèce avec Tarante sur la mer ionienne.

Le *Primitivo di Mandurio* est un vin rouge à deux visages : la première vendange donne un vin lourd et grossier servant à fortifier certains rouges plus légers du Nord de l'Italie ; une seconde vendange des mêmes raisins donne, par contre, un vin fin et au goût agréable, qui vieillit avec profit.

Rosso Barletta et Squinzano sont les vins D.O.C. de moindre importance produits par cette province. Ils portent le nom de la localité autour de laquelle ils sont produits, tous en quantité énorme. Ce sont des vins nettement mineurs.

Pouilly-Fuissé (Appellation Contrôlée)

Le meilleur vin blanc sec du sud de la Bourgogne et qui, depuis la dernière guerre mondiale, jouit enfin du renom qu'il mérite en Angleterre et aux États-Unis. Le Pouilly-Fuissé s'est taillé une bonne part du marché qui était autrefois réservé au Chablis. Il est fait avec du Chardonnay dans quatre communes du Mâconnais *(voir ce nom)*.

Pouilly-Fumé (Appellation Contrôlée)

Excellent vin blanc sec de la vallée de la Loire.

Voir POUILLY-SUR-LOIRE

Pouilly-Loché (Appellation Contrôlée)

Vin blanc sec du Mâconnais, au sud de la Loire. Quoique mineur, le Pouilly-Loché ressemble beaucoup au célèbre Pouilly-Fuissé, mais n'est pas tout à fait aussi bon.

Voir MÂCONNAIS

Pouilly-sur-Loire (Appellation Contrôlée)

Vins blancs de la vallée de la Loire, Nièvre et Berry.

A Pouilly, en aval de Nevers, sur la Loire, la terre s'élève doucement, presque imperceptiblement quand on s'éloigne du fleuve souvent paresseux, mais la déclivité suffit à la vigne qui se plaît toujours plus en pente qu'à plat. On cultive deux variétés de raisins à Pouilly et on en fait deux vins blancs, secs l'un et l'autre, mais entièrement différents à tout point de vue.

Le Pouilly-Fumé (ou Blanc Fumé de Pouilly) est le meilleur. Fait avec du Sauvignon, il est léger mais rond, ferme, éminemment agréable et rafraîchissant. La similitude de type et de nom le fait confondre avec le Pouilly-Fuissé du Mâconnais, mais ces deux vins diffèrent totalement. Même les vins légèrement inférieurs de cette région de la Loire ont tous une sécheresse de pierre à fusil et un goût indescriptible qui fait parfois évoquer la truffe. Quoiqu'ils puissent être délicieux ces vins manquent généralement de grande race.

Le vin de Pouilly-sur-Loire est fait avec du Chasselas, qu'on cultive surtout sur terrain argileux. Ce vin est presque aussi sec que son fier compagnon, mais dure moins et a des tendances à la vulgarité.

Bref, c'est un blanc respectable, en carafe, dans le pays où il est né, mais peu intéressant ailleurs.

Environ 600 ha du territoire de Pouilly sont consacrés à la vigne : le Chasselas est planté sur 80 ha et le Pouilly-Fumé prédomine sur 520 ha. La production annuelle approche les 35 000 hl (plus de 350 000 caisses) pour le Pouilly-Fumé et 4 000 hl (près de 45 000 caisses) pour le Pouilly-sur-Loire.

Pouilly-Vinzelles (Appellation Contrôlée)

Vin blanc sec du Mâconnais qui par très bonne année ressemble au Pouilly-Fuissé — son proche voisin — mais ne le vaut jamais.

Voir MÂCONNAIS

Pourriture noble

Dégradation bénéfique du raisin provoquée par *Botrytis cinerea (voir ce nom)* dans des conditions favorables. Le raisin semble moisir parce qu'il rétrécit et sa peau se ride, mais c'est seulement parce qu'il perd son eau, d'où un accroissement proportionnel de sa teneur en sucre. Dans des conditions défavorables la même moisissure devient la pourriture commune ou pourriture grise souvent aussi appelée en France par son nom dérivé de l'anglais *grey rot.*

Pramnien

Vin grec célèbre dans l'Antiquité *(voir ce nom).*

Précipitation

Un dépôt de bitartrate de potassium (crème de tartre) peut apparaître dans les vins jeunes sous la forme de petits cristaux. Ce phénomène se présente chez les vins rouges et blancs qui ont été exposés au froid. Le remède consiste à chauffer prudemment la bouteille et à la faire tourner sur elle-même jusqu'à ce que les cristaux se dissolvent. En Europe (pour les vins ordinaires) et en Californie, les vins sont exposés à des températures inférieures à 0 °C pendant une période de 3 jours à 4 semaines afin de précipiter le bitartrate de potassium avant la mise en bouteille.

Premières Côtes de Blaye (A.O.C.)

Appellation d'origine contrôlée du Bordelais attribuée à des vins blancs et rouges. Les blancs sont les meilleurs du Blayais.

Voir BLAYE

Premières Côtes de Bordeaux (A.O.C.)

Vins blancs et rouges.

Appellation d'origine contrôlée accordée aux vins blancs et rouges d'un secteur situé en bordure de la rive droite de la Garonne, en face des Graves, de Barsac et de Sauternes. La zone des Premières Côtes de Bordeaux commence immédiatement en amont de Bordeaux et s'étend sur une cinquantaine de kilomètres en remontant le cours du fleuve mais ne dépasse guère quelque 3 km de large. Dans sa partie sud elle englobe les bonnes communes à vin blanc doux de Loupiac et de Sainte-Croix-du-Mont.

Le vin blanc est meilleur en qualité que le vin rouge. En général, on y cultive la vigne à vin rouge en aval au plus près de Bordeaux et la vigne à vin blanc en amont. Les raisins prescrits pour le rouge sont les mêmes que dans le Médoc : Cabernet Sauvignon et Franc, Merlot, Malbec, Petit-Verdot et Carménère ; pour le vin blanc, les mêmes que dans le Sauternais, à Loupiac et à Sainte-Croix-du-Mont : Sémillon, Sauvignon et Muscadelle. Les blancs allaient du sec au doux en passant par le demi-sec. Les vins doux ne valaient pas tout à fait ceux de Loupiac et de Sainte-Croix-du-Mont, mais il ne faut pas oublier que ces derniers soutiennent la comparaison avec beaucoup de Sauternes. De nos jours, on produit essentiellement des blancs secs. En appellation Premières Côtes de Bordeaux, la production moyenne annuelle de vin blanc s'élève à plus de 35 000 hl (350 000 caisses) et à 70 000 hl (près de 800 000 caisses) pour le vin rouge.

Sur la rive droite du fleuve les coteaux sont abrupts alors que, sur la rive Graves-Barsac-Sauternes, le terrain est plat. Par endroits, les berges révèlent la craie blanche et la glaise qui donnent au vin des Premières Côtes de Bordeaux ses caractéristiques. Les vignes sont généralement exposées au sud.

Située dans la zone des vignes à vin blanc, Cadillac héberge une des principales confréries vinicoles du Bordelais : la Connétablie de Guyenne, qui consacre son activité à la promotion des vins blancs de cette région de Bordeaux. Elle a adopté ce nom en souvenir des connétables de Bordeaux qui, au Moyen Age, jugeaient les vins circulant sur le fleuve et leur accordaient ou non l'accès au marché. Le siège de la société se trouve dans le très beau château médiéval des ducs d'Épernon.

Presse (Vin de)

Après la fermentation alcoolique, les cuves sont écoulées et on fait un pressurage des peaux, qui contiennent, en dehors des pigments et des tannins, l'âme et le caractère du vin. Le vin de presse résultant du pressurage est ajouté au vin qui a fermenté. C'est une contribution tout à fait positive.

Pression

Boisson, notamment bière, en vrac ou en tonneau dont elle est tirée pour être consommée immédiatement.

Preuve

Très petit récipient de verre, semblable à une éprouvette, que l'on descend au bout d'une chaînette dans les barils de Cognac pour en prélever afin de le faire goûter et d'offrir la *preuve* de sa qualité. Dans la région de Cognac on l'appelle plus familièrement topette.

Prieuré-Lichine (Château-)

Bordeaux rouge. Commune de Cantenac-Margaux, en Haut-Médoc.

A l'origine, ce château était un prieuré des bénédictins, qui furent les premiers à prêcher l'évangile de la vigne dans la région de Bordeaux. Château Prieuré-Cantenac fut acheté en 1951 par l'auteur de cette encyclopédie. Le changement de son nom fut sanctionné et approuvé en 1953 par le président des Grands Crus Classés, le marquis de Lur-Saluces. Château Prieuré-Lichine est situé juste derrière l'église de Cantenac, qui fut en partie construite au XVIIe siècle et brûlée sous la Révolution, mais dont la façade fut reconstruite en 1802. Le prieuré était placé sous la surveillance de l'abbaye de Vertheuil, sise plus haut dans le Médoc. Depuis plus de 30 ans, les vignes ont été remembrées et reconstituées sur les meilleurs terroirs, à peine accidentés, de Cantenac, Arsac, Labarde, Soussans et Margaux qui forment l'Appellation Contrôlée Margaux. Parmi les acquisitions se trouve la parcelle La Bourgade qui appartint à la famille La Chapelle du XVe siècle jusqu'en 1867. En 1667, Guy de La Chapelle offrit les vins de sa vigne à

Louis XIV ; ils furent mis en concurrence avec les Bourgogne recommandés par Fagon, médecin du roi. Pendant bien des années, Louis XIV préféra ceux de La Bourgade.

C'est en procédant à des échanges, souvent à raison de 2 m² pour 1 m², et en sacrifiant la quantité à la qualité (les parcelles les moins bonnes, les plus basses, les plus sablonneuses ont été troquées contre des terres plus élevées et mieux drainées), que Prieuré-Lichine a pu acquérir depuis 1951 des parcelles de Margaux (Premier Cru), Palmer, Ferrière, Kirwan, Giscours d'Issan et Boyd-Cantenac (tous Troisièmes Crus) et Brane-Cantenac (Seconds Crus). 10 ha adjacents à Château-Margaux ont récemment été achetés et plantés. Prieuré-Lichine fut classé Quatrième Cru en 1855. Son propriétaire, grâce à l'acquisition de ces excellentes parcelles, et à des replantations extensives, ainsi qu'à l'amélioration vinicole et du matériel, a créé un vin très supérieur à sa classification. Un vignoble subsidiaire est le Cru Bourgeois de Château de Clairefont, dans le village de Margaux.

Le Prieuré-Lichine est très apprécié en France et aux États-Unis. Le château abrite beaucoup de souvenirs glanés dans les pays vinicoles du monde entier. Des panneaux saluent, en caractères élégants, les passants sur la route des vignobles par Margaux.

Comme tous les crus de Cantenac, Château-Prieuré-Lichine bénéficie, depuis 1954, de l'Appellation d'Origine Margaux, en raison de la proximité des deux communes et de la grande similitude de leurs vins.

Caractéristiques : Beau vin qui vieillit assez rapidement, souple et relativement plein de caractère il possède la délicatesse et surtout la finesse à laquelle la commune de Margaux doit sa juste réputation. Le propriétaire, auteur de ce livre, est fier du vin produit.

Superficie : 62 ha.

Production moyenne : 250 tonneaux (25 000 caisses).

Primeur (Vin de)

Vin jeune. Cette expression était souvent utilisée comme synonyme de vin bourru.

Depuis la demande importante pour les Grands Crus de Bordeaux, une partie de la production est mise en vente, pendant la période du vieillissement en barrique, pour être livrée après la mise en bouteille. On dit que ces vins sont vendus en primeur.

Production de vin

Il est permis de dire sans risque d'erreur qu'à peu près la moitié de la production

PRODUCTION DE VIN DANS LE MONDE

	Hectolitres
Italie	77 000 000
France	66 000 000
U.R.S.S.	34 500 000
Espagne	33 400 000
Argentine	20 000 000
États-Unis	17 900 000
Allemagne Fédérale	10 500 000
Chili	9 000 000
Afrique du Sud	9 000 000
Roumanie	8 700 000
Portugal	8 300 000
Yougoslavie	7 400 000
Hongrie	5 700 000
Grèce	5 200 000
Bulgarie	4 300 000
Australie	4 000 000
Autriche	3 700 000
Brésil	2 800 000
Algérie	1 800 000
Tchécoslovaquie	1 700 000
Suisse	1 300 000
Chypre	950 000
Uruguay	760 000
Tunisie	600 000
Japon	590 000
Nouvelle-Zélande	500 000
Canada	470 000
Maroc	400 000
Turquie	390 000
Albanie	220 000
Israël	190 000
Luxembourg	170 000
Mexique	150 000
Pérou	90 000
Liban	50 000
Madagascar	50 000
Libye	30 000
Bolivie	20 000
Malte	19 000
Égypte	15 000
Pays-Bas	10 000
Syrie	8 000
Jordanie	5 000
Iran	4 000
Belgique	2 000
TOTAL	337 893 000

totale de vin dans le monde est fournie par la France, l'Italie, l'U.R.S.S. et l'Espagne, quoique les quantités varient d'année en année et de pays en pays, en raison de la température, des aléas résultant des variations climatiques et des maladies qui sévissent dans les vignobles, malgré les découvertes scientifiques contemporaines qui ont résolu bien des problèmes de viticulture et de viniculture, mais non pas tous. Il faut considérer le vin comme un phénomène naturel et toujours imprévisible. Il est donc difficile de chiffrer la production exacte de chaque pays, d'autant plus à une époque où les vignobles augmentent sans cesse dans de nombreuses parties du monde. Le tableau page 631 indique les moyennes des dernières années, mais certains chiffres ont été volontairement majorés pour tenir compte de nouvelles et importantes plantations qui ont été faites récemment et qui seront en pleine production dans un avenir proche.

Prohibition

La prohibition des vins, spiritueux et autres breuvages alcooliques a été promulguée à des époques diverses dans différents pays. En général, ces mesures se sont révélées vaines et illusoires, à la seule exception d'une certaine phase de l'histoire ancienne chinoise et des pays musulmans où le Coran interdit absolument la consommation d'une seule gorgée de boisson alcoolisée quelconque, même s'il en fallait des barriques pour commencer à en ressentir quelques effets.

Aux États-Unis, le 18e amendement constitutionnel interdit partout « la fabrication, la vente ou le transport de breuvages intoxiquants » et sur tous les territoires soumis à leur juridiction, ainsi que leur importation et exportation. Ratifié par 46 États sur 48, cet amendement entra en vigueur le 16 novembre 1920. Il avait été précédé de peu par la loi Volstead (octobre 1919) votée en dépit du veto du président Wilson. Cette loi interdisait fabrication, vente et transport de tout breuvage titrant plus d'un degré d'alcool.

Cette prohibition provoqua le chaos. Pendant toute sa durée, les débits de boisson clandestins proliférèrent, le « gin de baignoire » devint la boisson nationale (ce terme était plus pittoresque qu'exact), les contrebandiers firent fortune ainsi que les distillateurs illicites dits « au clair de lune ». On vendit même des bouteilles sur l'étiquette desquelles on mettait en garde l'acheteur contre le méfait qu'il commettrait en ajoutant telle proportion d'eau à leur contenu ou en les laissant pendant tel ou tel temps à telle ou telle température car ils le transformeraient en breuvage alcoolique.

On entendait dans les caves du pays éclater des bouteilles de bière brassée par des amateurs. Bien des citoyens, qui à tout autre point de vue respectaient la loi de leur pays, considéraient la contrebande de l'alcool comme un devoir et en ramenaient au pays quand ils allaient à l'étranger. L'absurdité atteignit son point culminant lorsque le gouvernement fédéral ouvrit à New York un débit clandestin sous prétexte que, en enfreignant la loi, il pincerait plus aisément les contrevenants.

L'affaire fut réglée le 5 décembre 1933, quand le 21e amendement constitutionnel proclama l'échec de cette expérience déplorable et abrogea le 18e amendement. Depuis lors, chaque État, chaque canton, chaque commune est libre d'interdire fabrication, vente et transport de boissons alcooliques ou alcoolisées ou de les ignorer. Le Mississippi fut le dernier État qui accepta l'abrogation : en 1961. Ce qui se passe dans les villes restées « sèches » rappelle souvent une réflexion de George Bernard Shaw au sujet d'une ville sèche d'Irlande : « Ses habitants ne sacrent ni ne s'enivrent et ils semblent avoir grande envie de faire les deux ».

Prohibitionnisme musulman

Principe musulman interdisant la consommation de boissons alcoolisées en Islam. Avec les décrets des anciens empereurs de Chine, c'est la seule interdiction qui ait eu un effet durable. Elle porta un coup mortel à la viniculture dans tout l'Islam. Seuls quelques non-croyants continuèrent de s'y adonner et les musulmans se limitèrent à la production de raisin de table. Depuis, les Européens — notamment les Français en Afrique du Nord — ont réintroduit la viniculture dans les pays musulmans.

Prokupac

Le « cépage national de Serbie ». Il était autrefois une importante variété de Yougoslavie mais il est de moins en moins utilisé.

Proof Gallon

Un gallon de spiritueux à la teneur « proof » équivalant à 57,14 degrés sert d'unité de compte pour les impôts et droits de douane.

Voir GALLON

Proof Spirit

« Je dois expliquer pour l'information de M. Snowden, que, lorsque nous parlons de ces degrés nous voulons dire : degrés de spiritueux « proof » et que, lorsque nous parlons de degrés spiritueux « proof », nous voulons dire : degré. » Telle fut l'explication de sir Winston Churchill lorsqu'on l'interrogea, à la Chambre des communes, sur le sens de l'expression « proof spirit ». Cette réponse dénote combien il est difficile d'expliquer une notion aussi confuse.

Lorsque Clark inventa l'hydromètre, à la fin du XVIIIe siècle, il n'avait aucune idée de ce que peut être l'alcool absolu (100°). Il savait seulement que, s'il mettait cet instrument dans un liquide alcoolisé, il pourrait en déterminer la densité et en calculer la teneur en alcool d'après la profondeur à laquelle s'enfoncerait l'appareil. Il choisit arbitrairement une certaine teneur qu'il baptisa « proof » (preuve, étalon). Toute teneur alcoolique inférieure fut décrétée U. P. : *under proof* (au-dessous du niveau étalon) et toute teneur supérieure, fut décrétée O. P. : *over proof* (au-dessus du niveau étalon). Trente ans plus tard, Bartholomew Sikes (parfois orthographié Sykes) mit au point un hydromètre qui reste en usage aux États-Unis depuis 1816. Mais Sikes décida que son niveau étalon équivaudrait à 50° d'alcool à la température de 16 °C. En Angleterre, le niveau-étalon correspond à 49,28 % en poids, ou à 52,10 % en volume, d'alcool pur. Chaque 0,5% d'alcool au-dessous ou au-dessus du niveau-étalon correspond à un degré U.P. (au-dessous du niveau-étalon) ou O.P. (au-dessus du niveau-étalon). La teneur en alcool d'un spiritueux est exprimée en degrés « proof » de la façon suivante : 70° « proof » correspondent à 30° U.P., ce qui donne dans le premier cas une densité supérieure de 70 « proof » au niveau-étalon et, dans le second cas, une densité inférieure de 30 « proof » au niveau-étalon. Remarque importante : un volume de 100 % d'alcool pur n'est pas égal au niveau « proof » ou étalon, mais à 75,35° O.P. ou au-dessus du niveau-étalon.

Voir en APPENDICE *la table de conversion*

Provence, Côtes de Provence

Vins rosés, rouges et blancs.

Pays des troubadours et des chantres, de la gaieté et du soleil, cette région du sud-est donne sur la Méditerranée. Marseille à l'ouest, le grand port naval de Toulon, qui se prolonge jusqu'à Saint-Raphaël, la délimitent. Les vignes prospèrent, non loin des plages encombrées, sur un sol pauvre qui leur convient fort bien : sable, calcaire sédimentaire et schiste.

Les premières vignes importées en Gaule auraient été plantées en Provence par les Phocéens, dans la région de Marseille. La culture dut s'étendre après la conquête romaine, très antérieure à César car, depuis les guerres puniques, les Romains occupaient tout le territoire gaulois, le long de la Méditerranée, des Alpes aux Pyrénées. César aurait choisi les vins de Provence pour les donner à ses légionnaires à leur retour de la conquête des Gaules. Un des villages où l'on cultive encore la vigne aurait été baptisé par César lui-même. Il s'agit de La Gaude, au-dessus de Cannes. Après avoir goûté le vin de ce cru, César aurait claqué la langue et clamé : *Gaudeamus !* (Réjouissons-nous !).

L'ancienne province n'existe plus aujourd'hui ; elle est officiellement divisée en cinq départements : Bouches-du-Rhône, Var, Vaucluse, Basses-Alpes et Alpes-Maritimes. Mais elle restera toujours la Provence dans le cœur des Français amoureux de la tradition et dans tous les cœurs. Avec sa mer d'un bleu d'azur, son soleil et son mistral — vent bienfaiteur venant du nord, qui souffle toujours pendant trois, six ou neuf jours — la Provence garde tout son caractère, qu'elle doit pour beaucoup aux vins provençaux.

Cette région vinicole produit près de 2 000 000 hl (22 millions de caisses) de vin par an. Ils ont tous un certain caractère provençal. On peut les boire à grandes gorgées, sans se soucier de les savourer. Quoique assez rudes, ils parviennent à combiner vivacité et gaieté ; leur teneur en alcool est telle que la consommation peut rapidement partager leurs qualités.

La Provence produit surtout du rosé, mais aussi du blanc et du rouge. Ces derniers ressemblent à ceux d'Italie.

Les rosés de Provence comptent parmi les meilleurs de France et conviennent parfaitement aux spécialités régionales où poissons et fruits de mer abondent. Il faut les boire assez jeunes. Quelques-uns des meilleurs rouges peuvent profiter d'un vieillissement de quelques années, mais rares sont ceux qui conservent leur plénitude au-delà de plus de cinq ans.

Au point de vue de la quantité, rouges et rosés surclassent les blancs que l'on trouve rarement hors de France. La vigueur des vins blancs de Provence incita un vigneron à les définir ainsi : « De la toile cirée bordée de dentelle. » Les rosés sont frais, nets et gracieux ; les meilleurs ont perdu leur goût d'orange depuis qu'ils sont mieux vinifiés.

Appellations d'origine provençales

Bandol (Appellation Contrôlée)

Située à environ 32 km à l'est de Marseille le long de la côte, cette zone délimitée, plantée de quelque 680 ha de vignobles, a droit à l'appellation d'origine Bandol. Elle englobe la commune de ce nom et celles de Sanary, La Cadière d'Azur, le Castellet et quelques parties des communes d'Ollioules, Évenos, Saint-Cyr-sur-Mer et Beausol. Partout le sol est surtout composé de calcaire siliceux.

Une des caractéristiques les plus originales de la Provence, c'est la grande variété de raisins autorisés pour faire ses divers vins. En appellation Bandol on en cultive quatre pour les blancs et sept pour les rouges et rosés. Pour compliquer les choses, il est permis de mêler 20 % en volume de raisin à vin blanc pour vinifier des rouges et des rosés, mais à condition qu'ils fermentent ensemble et ne soient pas mélangés par la suite. Cette mesure donne des vins plus légers mais sans affecter leur qualité.

Clairette, Ugni Blanc et Bourboulenc sont les raisins utilisés pour les blancs dans la proportion minimum de 60 % de l'encépagement. Le Sauvignon est aussi utilisé mais dans la proportion maximum de 40 % de l'encépagement. Pour les rouges et rosés, on cultive, dans la proportion minimum de 80 % de l'encépagement, du Mourvèdre (dont le pourcentage minimum est de 50%), Grenache et Cinsault ; accessoirement : Carignan, Pécoui-touar, Tibouren et Syrah.

Pour jouir de l'Appellation Contrôlée Bandol, les vins doivent titrer au moins 11°. Sous un climat aussi ensoleillé, ils dépassent habituellement cette norme. En outre, ils ne peuvent être vendus qu'après avoir vieilli en fût pendant 8 mois s'ils sont blancs ou rosés, et 18 mois s'ils sont rouges.

Ces vins sont étiquetés Bandol ou Vin de Bandol, ce qui signifie exactement la même chose. La production moyenne annuelle s'élève à quelque 30 000 hl (plus de 300 000 caisses) pour les rouges et les rosés, et à près de 1 500 hl (150 0000 caisses environ) pour les blancs. Certains sont exportés mais on les vend surtout en France.

Bellet (Appellation Contrôlée)

Le Bellet, comme le Bandol et le Cassis, est cultivé sur la côte. La production réduite, qui se consomme sur place, provient de Nice et de ses agglomérations environnantes.

Le sol est formé de poudingue, étrange conglomérat formé d'innombrables cailloux arrondis et usés par l'action du vent et de la pluie. Il est riche en silice, et ceci explique peut-être que ces vins soient de loin les meilleurs de tout le Midi de la France. Le sol de poudingue, qui s'étend sur les lieux-dits de Les Séoules, Le Pilon, Le Grand-Bois, Golfan, les Cappan, Saint-Romain-de-Bellet, La Tour, Candau, Saquier, Saint-Sauveur, Gros-Pin, Serre-Long, Crémat, Mont-Bellet, Li Puncia et Lingestiera, couvre l'Appellation d'Origine Bellet. Ici comme dans le reste de la Provence, un grand nombre de vignes sont autorisées ; elles sont divisées en deux types : le type principal et le type secondaire.

Le Folle (ou Fuella), le Braquet et le Cinsault sont les variétés principales pour les Bellet rouges et rosés ; le Rolle, le Rousan et le Spagnol sont celles du vin blanc. (Les vignes accessoires sont le Carignan, le Bourboulenc, le Grenache, le

Roussan, la Rolle, le Spagnol, la Clairette et le Pignerol pour les rouges et rosés ; la Clairette, le Bourboulenc, le Chardonnay, le Muscat à petits grains et le Pignerol pour les blancs.) Ces cépages ne doivent pas dépasser 40 % de l'encépagement.

Les blancs, rouges et rosés titrent tous 10,5 % d'alcool. La production annuelle n'atteint que 650 hl (plus de 7 000 caisses) de rouges et rosés, les blancs ne présentant à peine plus d'un tiers de cette récolte.

Cassis (Appellation Contrôlée)

Une des meilleures appellations de vin rosé, en Provence, est celle de Cassis, petit port de mer situé à quelque 25 km de Marseille et un des principaux fournisseurs de poisson de cette grande ville. Le poisson et le Cassis se marient parfaitement car le rosé, sec et musclé, et le blanc, corsé et capiteux, conviennent à la bouillabaisse, succulente spécialité à base de rascasse et de homard dont tout le monde vous dira justement que seuls les Marseillais savent la préparer correctement.

Toutes les vignes qui fournissent l'Appellation d'Origine Cassis sont cultivées sur le seul territoire de cette commune. Les vignerons affirment que la constance des brises de la Méditerranée leur assure une température presque invariable. Ils expliquent ainsi les très faibles variations quantitatives de leurs vendanges, qui produisent environ 5 000 hl (55 000 caisses) de vin par an. Dans la région de Cassis, les blancs (près de 4 000 hl par an) sont plus abondants que les rouges, ce qui est assez inhabituel en Provence. On cultive principalement Ugni Blanc, Doucillon, Sauvignon, Clairette, Marsanne et Pascal Blanc, pour les vins blancs ; Grenache, Carignan, Mourvèdre, Cinsault et Barbaroux, pour le rouge et le rosé.

Tous les vins, quelle que soit leur couleur, doivent titrer au moins 11°.

Malheureusement, on les sert souvent trop froids, même à Cassis, ce qui tue leur goût. Mais ils n'en sont pas moins justement renommés car ils sont pleins, fins, capiteux et robustes. Les blancs et les rosés sont les meilleurs.

Palette (Appellation Contrôlée)

Près d'Aix-en-Provence, les collines s'élèvent rapidement vers des hauteurs rocheuses qui conduisent au secteur délimité du vin de Palette. C'est le seul cru exceptionnel de Provence qui ne provienne pas de la zone côtière. Il s'étend sur les communes de Meyreuil, Tholonet et Aix-en-Provence, sur les sols dérivés de la formation géologique dite « Calcaire de Langesse ».Les blancs comptent parmi les meilleurs de cette région ; les rouges sont bons et de bonne durée.

Les variétés de raisins autorisées et tolérées à Palette sont encore plus nombreuses qu'ailleurs en Provence et dépassent 25. Le Clairette doit entrer pour au moins 55 % dans la composition des blancs. Le reste

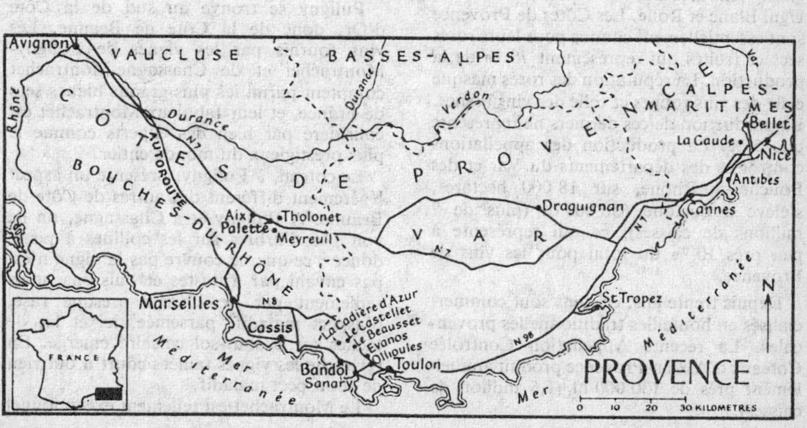

peut être du Grenache Blanc, du Muscat Blanc (de tous types cultivés dans le pays : Frontignan, Die, Ponse Muscade, etc.) et Terret-Bourret, dans une proportion maximale de 20 %, auxquels s'ajoutent Picpoul, Pascal, Aragnan, Colombard, Ugni Blanc ou Ugni Rosé. Quant aux rouges et aux rosés, Grenache, Mourvèdre et Cinsault doivent entrer dans leur composition pour au moins 50 % ; quant au reste, il se répartit entre une douzaine de variétés.

Cette tolérance extrême explique que les vins diffèrent considérablement selon les raisins utilisés et les proportions dans lesquelles on les mélange. Mais les vins de Palette doivent recevoir l'approbation d'un comité de dégustateurs experts, mis en place par l'I.N.A.O. Ils présentent les mêmes vertus et les mêmes défauts que tous ceux de Provence. Très agréables quand on les boit dans la vieille ville d'Aix-en-Provence, ils perdent leur vivacité charmante et leur gaieté si on les exporte. La production moyenne annuelle est extrêmement réduite : 400 hl pour les rouges et les rosés (plus de 4 000 caisses) et près de 200 hl pour les blancs (plus de 2 000 caisses).

Provence (Côtes de)
(Appellation contrôlée)

La zone de ces vins se subdivise en cinq secteurs, allant de Marseille à Draguignan vers l'intérieur des terres, et de Marseille au Var le long de la côte. On y cultive surtout les variétés suivantes : Grenache, Cinsault, Carignan, Syrah, Cabernet Sauvignon, Mourvèdre, Tibouren, Clairette, Ugni Blanc et Rolle. Les Côtes de Provence sont essentiellement connus pour leurs rosés secs et fruités qui représentent 70 % de la production. La réputation des rosés masque celle des vins rouges et celle des vins blancs. La production de ces derniers ne représente que 5 %. La production des appellations contrôlées des départements du Var et des Bouches-du-Rhône, sur 18 000 hectares, s'élève à quelque 650 000 hl (plus de 7 millions de caisses), ce qui représente à peu près 10 % du total pour les vins de Provence.

Depuis trente ans, ces vins sont commercialisés en bouteilles traditionnelles provençales. La récente Appellation Contrôlée Coteaux d'Aix-en-Provence produit annuellement près de 130 000 hl (1,5 million de caisses).

Provignage

Méthode de propagation de la vigne.
Voir CHAPITRE IV

Prune

Eau-de-vie obtenue par la distillation de la prune.
Voir QUETSCHE ; MIRABELLE ; SLIVOVITZ

Prunelle ou Prunellia

Liqueurs vertes faites en France avec des noyaux de prunelle.

Puglia

Voir APULIE ; ITALIE

Puisseguin-Saint-Émilion (Appellation Contrôlée)

Commune qui produit des vins rouges charnus de Saint-Émilion.
Voir SAINT-ÉMILION

Puligny-Montrachet
et Puligny-Montrachet-Côte de Beaune

Bourgogne rouge et blanc. En Côte de Beaune.

Puligny se trouve au sud de la Côte d'Or, donc de la Côte de Beaune. Les vins fournis par les vignes de Puligny-Montrachet et de Chassagne-Montrachet comptent parmi les plus grands blancs secs de France, et leur fabuleux Montrachet est considéré par bien des experts comme le plus prestigieux du monde entier.

Le coteau, à Puligny, présente un aspect légèrement différent des autres de Côte de Beaune. A Puligny et à Chassagne, on ne voit pas d'arbres sur les collines à pente douce ; ce que ne couvre pas la vigne n'est pas envahi par arbustes et buissons, mais seulement par de l'herbe presque rase, d'aspect maladif, parsemée, ici et là, de taches où le sous-sol calcaire émerge. En revanche les vignes taillées court n'ont rien de cet aspect maladif.

Le Montrachet est tellement exceptionnel

qu'il faut le considérer comme un cas entièrement à part parmi les vins de Bourgogne. Outre Montrachet, Puligny partage un autre Grand Cru avec Chassagne : Bâtard-Montrachet. A ces deux géants de la viticulture s'ajoutent quelques autres vignobles situés uniquement à Puligny. Chevalier-Montrachet et Bienvenue-Bâtard-Montrachet sont deux des plus merveilleux et les autorités françaises leur ont accordé le titre de Grand Cru. Théoriquement cela signifie que ces autorités les considèrent comme égaux aux 29 autres crus les plus grands de toute la Bourgogne. Sur un plan plus pratique, ce titre signifie que le vin ne portera sur son étiquette que le seul nom du cru alors que les autres portent soit le nom de la commune suivi de celui du cru, soit seulement celui de la commune *(voir chacun des Grands Crus à sa place dans l'ordre alphabétique).*

Bien que les Grands Crus soient, de l'avis unanime, considérés comme les meilleurs, d'autres vins de Puligny sont superbes et, dans les mains d'un vinificateur talentueux, ils peuvent égaler les plus prestigieux. Citons parmi ceux-là : Les Pucelles, situé juste au nord de Bienvenue-Bâtard-Montrachet ; Le Cailleret, au-dessus des Pucelles et contigu à Chevalier (Cailleret s'appelait autrefois Les Demoiselles, mais sa proximité avec Chevalier donnait lieu à tant de plaisanteries, parfois si mauvaises, qu'on en changea le nom). De l'autre côté de l'agglomération, vers Meursault, se trouvent les excellentes Combettes, coupées en deux par la route qui constitue la limite entre Charmes et Meursault. Plus haut sur le coteau, en direction du petit hameau de Blagny — qui s'étend du point le plus élevé de Meursault jusqu'au point le plus élevé de Puligny — on trouve un autre vignoble exceptionnel, Les Chalumeaux.

Tous les vins blancs de Puligny partagent à peu près les mêmes caractéristiques. Ils sont éminemment secs, moins onctueux et moins luxuriants que les Meursault, mais peuvent avoir un bouquet charnu, riche, fleuri et parfois fruité. Leur robe d'or vert prend des teintes et des luminosités diverses. Ils ont une vigueur et une virilité peu communes pour des blancs. Ils laissent dans la bouche une sensation fraîche et pleine. Et, plus le vin est bon, plus son arrière-goût persiste.

En plus des vins blancs, on fait à Puligny une petite quantité de rouge, mais pas avec les raisins des crus les mieux cotés. Il est moins bon en général que le rouge de la commune voisine, Chassagne, quoiqu'il ait souvent une bonne charpente et un bouquet expressif qui lui est propre.

235 hectares de la commune sont consacrés à la vigne, dont 140 fournissent des vins vendus sous l'appellation Côte de Beaune, ils sont souvent de qualité remarquable. Les vins les meilleurs portent simplement le nom du cru (Grands Crus) ou le nom du cru plus celui de la commune (Premiers Crus). Puligny produit environ 11 000 hl (plus de 120 000 caisses) de vin par an, et seulement quelques centaines d'hl en vin rouge.

GRANDS CRUS	*Superficie (ha)*
Montrachet *(en partie)*	4,01
Bâtard-Montrachet *(en partie)*	6,02
Chevalier-Montrachet	7,36
Bienvenue-Bâtard-Montrachet	3,69
PREMIERS CRUS	
Les Combettes	6,76
Les Pucelles	6,78
Les Chalumeaux	5,80
Le Cailleret	3,93
Les Folatières	16,63
Clavaillon	5,58
Le Champ-Canet	5,58
Les Referts	5,52
Sous le Puits	6,79
Garenne	11,40
Hameau de Blagny	4,28

Pulque

Spiritueux obtenu au Mexique par la distillation du jus d'un cactus aux noms divers : pulque, agave, plante centenaire, aloès américain et mescal. Très apprécié des Mexicains, ce breuvage fermenté est en général bu aussitôt après son élaboration. On en vend des millions de litres dans les fermes de la campagne et dans les *pulquerias* des villes.

Voir TEQUILA

Punch

1. Boisson sucrée à base de rhum très populaire aux Caraïbes.

2. Breuvage cordial que l'on boit chaud en hiver. Il se compose d'eau-de-vie épicée dans laquelle baignent des rondelles de fruits et qu'on flambe.

3. Punch de Norvège : digestif à base d'arack indonésien qui titre 26 à 27°. A/S Vinmonopolet — monopole d'État des vins et spiritueux norvégiens — est le producteur de ce punch norvégien.

4. Punch suédois : cordial épicé à base de rhum. Parfois on le boit dans un petit verre, comme une liqueur, parfois on l'additionne d'eau chaude pour en faire un grog. Il date du XVIIIe siècle, époque à laquelle la Suède entra en relations commerciales avec les Indes orientales d'où elle importa, entre autres, du riz et de la canne à sucre, ainsi que du rhum.

Puncheon

Gros fût de capacité variable, autrefois généralement, 264 l environ ; aujourd'hui, plus couramment 378 l. Utilisé surtout aux Indes occidentales pour le rhum.

Pupitre

Casier servant à amener progressivement les bouteilles de vin mousseux dans la position verticale, goulot en bas, pour les préparer au dégorgement ou éjection du dépôt accumulé pendant la seconde fermentation.

Voir CHAMPAGNE

Puttonyos

Seau utilisé en Hongrie afin de mesurer la quantité de raisins choisie spécialement pour la vinification du Tokay. La collerette de chaque bouteille de Tokaji Aszu porte la mention : 3 puttonos, 4 puttonos, et ainsi de suite (l'Office d'exportation a simplifié l'orthographe en supprimant l'y).

Voir TOKAY

Pyrale

Papillon dont les chenilles s'attaquent aux végétaux et surtout à la vigne dont elles consomment les feuilles et les pédoncules floraux.

Voir CHAPITRE IV

Q

Quart

1. En France : *a)* grosse tasse de fer blanc ou d'aluminium faisant partie de l'équipement du soldat et contenant 1/4 de litre ; *b)* petite bouteille contenant entre 18 et 25 cl ; *c)* par extension, une quantité à peu près équivalente de vin servi en carafe.
2. En pays anglo-saxons : 1/4 de gallon. S'il s'agit du gallon impérial (britannique), le quart équivaut à 40 onces liquides ou 1,136 l. S'il s'agit du gallon U.S., il équivaut à 32 onces liquides U.S. ou 0,946 l.

Quarter-Cask

A l'origine, fût d'une capacité égale au quart de celle de la *pipe (voir ce mot)*. Pratiquement, sa capacité actuelle varie de 25 à 35 gallons britanniques, soit environ 113 à 160 l.

Quarts de Chaume (Appellation Contrôlée)

Appellation d'origine contrôlée, subdivision de la région vinicole des Coteaux du Layon, en Anjou.
Voir ANJOU : COTEAUX DU LAYON

Quatourze

Voir LANGUEDOC : COTEAUX DU LANGUEDOC

Quetsche

Prune bleue cultivée en Alsace et en Lorraine.
Voir ALSACE : SPIRITUEUX

Queue (Vin de)

Vin de qualité inférieure, obtenu par pressurage de tout raisin disponible : vert, voire avarié.

Quincy (Appellation Contrôlée)

Vins blancs. Vallée de la Loire.

Secteur vinicole d'importance mineure qui produit des vins blancs secs que l'on classe parmi ceux de la Loire quoique Quincy soit situé sur le Cher, à quelque 50 km de ce fleuve. Ces vignes s'étendent sur les collines de Quincy et Brinay. Elles sont plantées dans un sol calcaire et leurs vins ressemblent à ceux de Reuilly, Sancerre et Pouilly-sur-Loire, comme dans ces régions, l'encépagement est surtout du Sauvignon. Les quelque 115 ha de vignes de ce secteur produisent en moyenne 4 000 hl (plus de 40 000 caisses) par an.
Voir LOIRE

Quinquina

Dans le langage courant : vin apéritif contenant une certaine proportion de quinquina qui lui donne une saveur légèrement amère. Le quinquina est l'écorce d'un arbre tropical, *chinchona*, qui fournit également la quinine et la cinchonine.

Quinta

Littéralement, ce mot signifie en portugais « domaine agricole », et, par extension, au Portugal, il désigne un vignoble ou cru.

R

Rabaud-Promis (Château-)

Bordeaux blanc. Commune de Bommes, en Sauternais.

A l'origine, le domaine de Rabaud était un des plus anciens du Sauternais. En 1660, il produisait énormément et couvrait une superficie dépassant 80 ha. Le château proprement dit fut construit par Victor Louis, l'architecte du théâtre de Bordeaux. Le domaine passa entre les mains de M. de Sigalas en 1864 et une partie fut vendue en 1903 à M. Promis. Après 1930, les vignes de Rabaud-Promis et de Sigalas-Rabaud se trouvèrent réunies pour être séparées de nouveau en 1952. Depuis Sigalas-Rabaud est devenu bien supérieur à Promis et il peut être considéré comme un des bons Sauternes. Lorsqu'ils ne constituaient qu'un seul vignoble, leurs vins furent classés Premier Cru de Sauternes, en 1855, et ce titre vaut actuellement pour Rabaud-Promis *(voir* SIGALAS-RABAUD).

Caractéristiques : Ce n'est pas un des plus grands. Doux, manque un peu de race.

Superficie : 33 ha.

Production moyenne : 50 tonneaux (5 000 caisses).

Rabigato

Une des principales variétés de raisin utilisé pour faire du Porto blanc.

Rablay-sur-Layon

Commune vinicole ayant droit en y ajoutant son nom, à l'Appellation Contrôlée Coteaux du Layon, en Anjou.

Voir ANJOU ; COTEAUX DU LAYON

Race

Pour les vins, synonyme de finesse. Cette supériorité doit certainement être attribuée au sol ou terroir. Elle se manifeste par la délicatesse et la discrétion.

Rafle

La grappe sans ses raisins — autrement dit, l'ensemble pédoncule et pédicelles de la grappe.

Rainwater

Mot anglais. Littéralement : eau de pluie. A l'origine, marque commerciale, et maintenant nom général des Madère légers et secs.

Raisin

Fruit de la vigne. Il existe de nombreuses variétés. Le vin est fait avec le jus de raisin fermenté.

Ramisco

Variété de raisin avec laquelle on fait le vin de dune à Colares, au Portugal *(voir ce nom).*

Rancio

En Espagne, ce mot désigne la saveur de noisette particulière au Xérès. En Californie, il s'applique au goût que prennent après cuisson les vins doux de dessert. Dans un sens presque identique, il désigne la saveur accentuée des Madère, Marsala, Malaga et autres vins vinés. En France, cet adjectif s'applique en particulier au goût caractéristique des vins doux de Banyuls après maturation et aussi du Château-Chalon du Jura.

Raspail

Liqueur de couleur jaune à laquelle des herbes donnent sa saveur. Elle aurait été mise au point en 1847 par François-Vincent Raspail.

Ratafia

A l'origine, ce nom s'appliquait à n'importe quel breuvage bu lors de la ratification d'un traité ou d'un accord quelconque. Actuellement, il désigne des apéritifs doux à base de vin, par exemple : ratafia de Bourgogne, ratafia de Champagne, ce dernier est l'équivalent du Pineau des Charentes, dans la région de Cognac.

Rauchbier

En allemand, littéralement : bière de fumée. Il s'agit d'une bière faite avec du malt fumé.

Rauenthal

Certains Rauenthaler — tels que le Baiken — sont probablement les meilleurs du Rheingau et, à l'exception de Schloss Johannisberg, ceux qui atteignent les prix les plus élevés. Ils sont charnus, fruités, épicés, à l'acidité prononcée et très aptes à vieillir.

Voir RHEINGAU

Rausan-Ségla (Château-)

Bordeaux rouge. Commune de Margaux, en Haut-Médoc.

Contigu à Rauzan-Gassies, avec lequel il ne formait jadis qu'un seul domaine, Rausan-Ségla se trouve en retrait de la route des vignobles, en face de Château-Margaux et Château-Palmer, au sud de l'agglomération de Margaux. Selon la classification de 1855, c'est un Second Cru.

Acquis par Pierre des Mesures de Rausan, en 1661, il resta dans la famille Rausan pendant 200 ans. A ce propos, Thomas Jefferson écrivait : « ...Rozan-Margau, fait par Mme de Rozan... voilà le vin que je fais importer pour moi... » Outre les vins du vignoble qui porte leur nom, les Rausan — ou Rauzans — louèrent pendant un certain temps Château-Margaux et Château-Latour où ils firent du vin. En 1866, Rausan-Ségla fut vendu au grand-père maternel de la famille Cruse, négociant en vins à Bordeaux qui le revendit en 1956 à M. de Mesnom, lequel le céda, en 1962, au groupe britannique Holt, propriétaire de la firme Eschenauer, négociant en vins à Bordeaux. Holt appartient maintenant au groupe Lonhro de Londres.

Caractéristiques : Les vins de Rausan-Ségla ont beaucoup perdu de leur qualité, mais la situation a commencé à s'améliorer en 1983. En 1986, une salle des cuves et de nouveaux chais furent construits. En raison du renouvellement des plants, il ne faut pas s'attendre à une grande qualité du vignoble avant les années 2 000.

Superficie : 43 ha.

Production moyenne : 150 tonneaux (15 000 caisses).

Rauzan-Gassies

Bordeaux rouge. Commune de Margaux, en Haut-Médoc.

Rauzan-Gassies ne formait autrefois qu'un seul domaine avec Rausan-Ségla. Actuellement les deux vignobles sont contigus, au sud de Margaux. Son vin était déjà fort connu en 1530. Parmi les nombreux propriétaires de ce château au cours de quatre siècles et plus, aucun ne fut plus extravagant, semble-t-il, que le chevalier de Rauzan. Faute d'obtenir le prix qu'il espérait de son vin, il l'embarqua sur un bateau et mit le cap sur Londres. Arrivé à destination, il annonça qu'il vendrait sa production lui-même sur le pont et attendit les clients. N'obtenant pas encore le prix qui lui convenait, il annonça qu'il verserait un fût par jour dans la Tamise jusqu'à ce qu'il obtînt satisfaction ou n'ait plus de vin. On raconte que, le troisième jour, la population de Londres se rassembla sur les quais pour assister à un événement aussi inouï et que le bruit s'en répandit, de telle sorte qu'on lui offrit le prix qu'il voulait pour les barriques subsistant à bord.

Actuellement, Rauzan-Gassies appartient aux héritiers de feu M. Paul Quié qui possèdent aussi Château-Croizet-Bages. Rauzan-Gassies est un Second Cru selon la classification de 1855, comme Rausan-Ségla. Les critiques estimaient que le vin n'était pas à la hauteur du vignoble tel qu'il était cultivé alors. Sur le marché de Bordeaux, Rauzan-Gassies était un des Seconds Crus les moins chers, ce qui est moins le cas depuis les progrès faits dans les années 1970.

Caractéristiques : Dans les années 50 et au début des années 60, bien des critiques bordelais remarquèrent, à juste titre, que la qualité de ce vin n'était pas à la hauteur de son classement. Certains de ses millésimes étaient même affligés d'un excès d'acidité volatile. Grâce à l'action d'Émile Peynaud, doyen d'œnologie de Bordeaux, la vinification s'est améliorée depuis 1969.

Superficie : 33 ha.

Production moyenne : 150 tonneaux (15 000 caisses).

Ravat

Français dont la plus grande réussite fut sans doute le porte-greffe Ravat 262, qui donne aux États-Unis un vin rouge léger rappelant un petit Beaujolais. La Ravat 6 est son meilleur cépage à vin blanc, mais sa vulnérabilité au froid rend son utilisation hasardeuse aux États-Unis.

Ravello

Magnifique petit village de l'Italie méridionale, proche de Naples et d'Amalfi, qui produit une quantité modérée de blancs et rosés ; ils ne sont toutefois pas aussi intéressants que le village.

Rayne-Vigneau (Château de)

Bordeaux blanc. Commune de Bommes, en Sauternais.

Classé Premier Cru de Sauternes en 1855. Les vignes, cultivées sur un plateau qui s'étend à partir du sombre château à tourelles, ne sont pas le seul trésor que produit leur sol. Pour une raison qui échappe aux experts, c'est le seul secteur du Bordelais où l'on trouve des pierres précieuses ou rares. Saphirs, opales, jaspes, onyx et topazes provenant de ce vignoble figurent dans bien des musées de France et d'autres pays. Le principal propriétaire est Mestrezat-Preller, négociant à Bordeaux.

Caractéristiques : Ce grand cru est capable de progrès.

Superficie : 67 ha.

Production moyenne : 150 tonneaux (11 000 caisses).

Rebate Brandy

Littéralement, eau-de-vie de rabais. Locution commerciale de l'Afrique du Sud désignant l'eau-de-vie faite selon des règles strictes imposées par le gouvernement et vieillie en fût pendant au moins trois ans. Cette mesure fut prise pour encourager les distillateurs à augmenter la qualité de leurs produits. Le gouvernement accorde un abattement *(rabais)* fiscal sous certaines conditions. Les spiritueux de moindre qualité, d'autre part, sont taxés encore plus lourdement.

Rebêche ou Recoupe

Émiettement du marc pour un nouveau pressurage.

Récolte

Action de recueillir les produits de la terre. Quant à la récolte des raisins, le mot spécifique est *vendange*.

Rectification des spiritueux

Distillation qui consiste à séparer les substances en jouant sur la diversité de leur degré de volatilité. Un mélange est chauffé jusqu'à atteindre les points d'ébullition successifs de ses composants. La vapeur de chacun d'eux est ainsi recueillie séparément. Si la substance est déjà purifiée ou d'une composition constante, c'est-à-dire si tous ses composants se volatilisent à la même température, l'opération n'est plus distillation mais rectification.

Voici la définition de la rectification par J.H. Perry dans *The Engineer's Handbook* (Manuel de l'ingénieur), troisième édition : « La rectification est une distillation à laquelle on procède de telle sorte que la vapeur s'élevant de l'alambic entre en contact avec une certaine quantité de vapeur condensée provenant du même alambic. De ce contact résulte un transfert de substances et un échange de chaleur, ce qui procure un plus grand enrichissement de la vapeur du composant le plus volatile qui ne pourrait être obtenu par une seule distillation en consommant la même quantité de chaleur. Les vapeurs condensées utilisées à cette fin s'appellent reflux.

« L'appareil utilisé en général dans lequel les vapeurs émanant d'un alambic se déplacent à contre-courant des vapeurs précédemment émises par ce même alambic s'appelle colonne de rectification ou tours ».

Voir CHAPITRE VI ; GIN

Régional

Se dit de tout vin dont le nom vient d'une région ou d'un département et non pas d'un vignoble en particulier. Ces vins sont généralement des coupages bon marché ; Bordeaux, Provence, Californie aux États-Unis et Rioja en Espagne sont des exemples de ces noms régionaux.

Réhoboam

Énorme bouteille utilisée pour le Champagne et qui contient l'équivalent de 6 bouteilles, soit 4,8 l.

Voir APPENDICE B

Reims

Principal centre de commerce du Champagne, avec Épernay.

Voir CHAMPAGNE

Remuage

Opération qui précède le dégorgement au cours de la vinification en Champagne. Les bouteilles sont placées sur un appareil spécial et on les secoue légèrement chaque jour pendant quatre mois, tout en les faisant pivoter sur elles-mêmes jusqu'à ce que le dépôt repose contre le bouchon. Ensuite, on arrachera rapidement le bouchon, d'un mouvement habile, pour chasser le dépôt, opération qui s'appelle le dégorgement. Auparavant les bouteilles étaient placées, col incliné vers le bas, sur un pupitre *(voir ce mot)*, et remuées à la main.

Voir CHAMPAGNE

Reputed pint

Nom de la pinte légale britannique. Elle équivaut à un peu plus d'une demi-bouteille. Le gallon britannique en contient 12. La pinte équivaut à 56,8245 cl et correspond à 1,2009 pinte U.S.

Reputed quart

Capacité légale de la bouteille de vin et de spiritueux en Angleterre. Elle équivaut à 1/6 de gallon, soit environ 75 cl.

Reserva

Mention qui, sur les étiquettes du vin de Rioja, indique qu'il a vieilli. Elle dénote parfois la qualité et parfois un vin usé...

Voir RIOJA

Respiration

Un vin « respire » ou s'oxyde lorsqu'il entre en contact avec l'air. En général, les vins rouges ont besoin de plus d'aération que les blancs, surtout les jeunes rouges en raison de leur teneur élevée en tanin. Pour apprécier au mieux tout le bouquet d'un bon vin, il convient de déboucher la bouteille et de laisser un vin respirer pendant une heure ou deux, car c'est lui donner toutes les chances de donner le meilleur de lui-même.

Voir CHAPITRE VIII

Retsina

Vin grec ordinaire, blanc ou rosé, traité à la résine de pin. On en consomme une grande quantité en Grèce. Dans le centre et le sud de ce pays, presque tout le monde, surtout les paysans, préfère ce vin à goût de résine.

Voir GRÈCE

Reuilly (Appellation Contrôlée)

Vins blancs, rosés et rouges. Région de la Loire.

Petit secteur vinicole peu connu, baigné par l'Arnon, affluent du Cher. On y produit une petite quantité de blanc sec, avec du raisin Sauvignon. On y cultive aussi du Pinot Noir (approximativement 90 ha) et du Pinot Gris qui donnent quelque 600 hl (plus de 6 500 caisses) annuellement de vins rouges et rosés. Les quelque 40 ha de Sauvignon produisent chaque année près de 1 000 hl (plus de 10 000 caisses). Le Reuilly blanc ressemble au Sancerre et au Pouilly-sur-Loire, mais il est en général plus acide et plus léger.

Voir LOIRE

Réunion (Ile de la)

Département français d'outre-mer, situé dans l'océan Indien. On y fait du rhum *(voir ce mot).*

Rhein

Orthographe allemande du mot Rhin.

Voir PALATINAT ; RHEIGAU ; RHEINHESSEN ; RHIN-MOYEN

Rheingau

État allemand du Hesse. Superficie : 3 000 ha environ. 94 % de vins blancs et 6 % de vins rouges.

Les vins du Rheingau sont les meilleurs d'Allemagne lorsqu'ils atteignent la plénitude de leurs qualités. En tant que tels, avec leurs pairs de la Moselle et les grands vins blancs de Bourgogne, ce sont les meilleurs du monde pour la variété de leurs caractéristiques organoleptiques.

Par année moyenne ou mauvaise, les vins du bas Rheingau, depuis le secteur de Rüdesheim jusqu'à Hochheim, dans le haut Rheingau, tendent à être meilleurs que les vins des plus grandes régions vinicoles, lesquels peuvent être trop légers. Mais par grande année, les célèbres et délicieux Riesling de la portion du Rhin allant d'Eltville à Winkel, vendangés tardivement, atteindront des sommets incomparables. Pour merveilleux que puissent être les Moselle les plus charmants, ils n'auront jamais le tempérament et la race des grands Rheingau. Quelques Bourgogne blancs ont assez de caractère et de vigueur pour défier les Rheingau secs. On peut même avancer que, dans un certain sens, un vin tel que le Château-Yquem, en Sauternes, est leur équivalent en tant que vin doux mais, en raison du climat plus clément de la région de Bordeaux, il les dépasse énormément en quantité. Néanmoins, les grands crus du Rheingau, faits avec des raisins vendangés tardivement, qui vieillissent lentement et durent longtemps, sont les véritables rois du royaume des vins. Riches et d'une race exquise, après un été ensoleillé et un automne brumeux, bénéficiant des brouillards du Rhin, ils conserveront leurs qualités pendant trente ou quarante ans.

Situation : Il se trouve à 30 km environ à l'ouest de Francfort, près d'Hochheim où le Main se verse dans le Rhin et où commence la région des vignobles en coteaux, exposés au sud. Ils s'étendent le long du Rhin de Wiesbaden, où le fleuve se courbe vers l'ouest, jusqu'à Lorchhausen, ville frontière de l'État du Hesse. Le long de ce parcours, le Rhin s'élargit jusqu'à atteindre 600 m de large, ce qui le fait ressembler à un grand lac. La chaleur du soleil qui se réfléchit sur la surface du fleuve, maintient jour et nuit une température constante dans les vignobles. Les coteaux orientés nettement au sud sont protégés du vent du nord par les collines du Taunus couvertes de forêts ; en outre, les courbes du Rhin les mettent à l'abri des vents de l'est et de l'ouest. Plantés sur des terrains accidentés à forte pente, les vignobles courent en vagues parallèles, le long du fleuve. « Là où va la charrue, la vigne ne doit pas aller », tel est un proverbe de Rheingau qui exprime une rude vérité. La déclivité, l'exposition au sud et la protection climatique dont jouissent les coteaux permettent de vendanger tard ; parfois on laisse la pourriture noble se développer jusqu'en décembre.

Presque tous les villages du Rheingau jouissent d'une réputation internationale, de Hochheim — d'où est tiré le mot « Hock » — à Rüdesheim, aussi renommé pour sa « Drosselgasse » bordée d'une multitude de buvettes que pour ses vins. La région est entièrement comprise dans un district — celui de Johannisberg — et est divisée en 10 crus collectifs (Grosslagen ou GL).

Variété de raisin : Riesling (80 %), Müller-Thurgau (6 %), Spätburgunder ou Pinot Noir (5 %), Ehrenfelser (3 %) et Kerner (2 %).

Les habitants du Rheingau sont très fiers du fait que le pourcentage de Riesling cultivé dans leur région soit plus élevé que partout ailleurs en Allemagne. Riesling est synonyme de haute qualité. Et c'est uniquement grâce à la production de vins du plus haut standard qu'une région aussi petite a acquis une haute position dans le monde du vin.

On dit que le Riesling est originaire du Rheingau. La plus vieille référence à cette variété remonte au 13 mars 1435, à une facture de l'entreprise Klaus Kleinfisch pour la livraison de Riesling à la forteresse de Rüsselsheim, aux portes du Rheingau. C'est grâce aux propriétaires des domaines — principalement l'Église et l'aristocratie — dont les efforts visèrent à améliorer la qualité, que la culture du Riesling devint obligatoire dans le Rheingau. En 1672, par exemple, le monastère Sainte-Claire de Mainz ordonna à ses vignerons du Rheingau de remplacer les variétés rouges par des vignes de Riesling de la plus haute qualité. En 1803, un prêtre bénédictin et un maître de chai de l'abbaye de Fulda écrivaient : « Le Riesling est aujourd'hui la seule variété qui puisse être plantée dans tout le Rheingau ». C'est à cette époque que naquit la réputation du Riesling et avec elle la renommée des vins du Rheingau en Allemagne et à l'étranger. La station de sélection viticole à Geisenheim mérite une mention spéciale pour les efforts développés au cours du siècle dernier dans le but d'améliorer les Riesling. Par la sélection et la propagation des meilleures souches, les chercheurs de Geisenheim ont développé des clones de Riesling plus résistants au gel, aux insectes et à la maladie. Le Rheingau est la première région viticole du monde à cultiver exclusivement des vignes de Riesling résistant aux virus. Les viticulteurs de la région peuvent ainsi pratiquer des méthodes saines et écologiques de production. La longévité accrue des vignes augmente la qualité de leurs vins.

Le Spätburgunder, autre grande variété de raisin de la région, fut rapporté de Bourgogne dans le Rheingau il y a des siècles. Au XVIe siècle, Lorch possédait plus de vignes de Spätburgunder que n'importe quel autre village du Rheingau. Le centre de production du vin rouge s'est progressivement déplacé vers les collines voisines de Assmannshausen, où les vignes étaient moins sujettes aux gelées précoces. Aujourd'hui Assmannshausen est toujours réputé

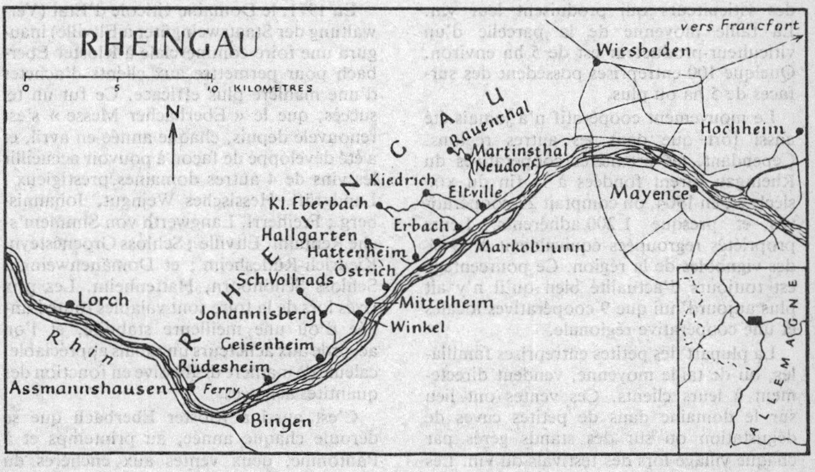

pour ses bons Spätburgunder, mais grâce à la qualité des clones de Geisenheim, le Spätburgunder est à nouveau planté à Lorch et dans toute la région.

Production et Ventes

Bien que les vignes y furent cultivées à l'époque romaine, c'est avant tout sous l'influence des archevêques de Mainz, du xe au xive siècle, que la viticulture prospéra vraiment dans le Rheingau. Les rives du Rhin furent déboisées et replantées de vignes. Les paysans qui participèrent à ces gros travaux gagnèrent leur liberté. Le Rheingau fut alors connu comme la terre où les fermiers possédaient des droits civils, où « celui qui respire l'air de Rheingau est un homme libre ». L'Église et l'aristocratie jouèrent un rôle vital dans le développement de l'industrie du Rheingau. Leur recherche absolue de la qualité et leur désir de découvrir de nouvelles et meilleures méthodes de viticulture, de technologie de cave et de vente fit du Rheingau l'exemple pour beaucoup d'autres régions viticoles. Aujourd'hui 1 940 viticulteurs ont ce même esprit d'entreprise. Le concept de propriété privée a ici une longue tradition et explique pourquoi les habitants du Rheingau sont si indépendants et individualistes.

La production moyenne annuelle du Rheingau, est d'environ 200 000 hl (plus de 2 millions de caisses). Près de 85 % des vignobles de la région appartiennent à 65 % des viticulteurs qui produisent leur vin. La taille moyenne de la parcelle d'un viticulteur-producteur est de 5 ha environ. Quelque 100 entreprises possèdent des surfaces de 5 ha ou plus.

Le mouvement coopératif n'a jamais été aussi fort que dans les autres régions. Cependant, les premières coopératives du Rheingau furent fondées à la fin du xixe siècle et, en 1904, on comptait 27 coopératives et presque 1 200 adhérents. Leurs propriétés regroupées équivalaient à 19 % des vignobles de la région. Ce pourcentage est toujours d'actualité bien qu'il n'y ait plus aujourd'hui que 9 coopératives locales et une coopérative régionale.

La plupart des petites entreprises familiales, ou de taille moyenne, vendent directement à leurs clients. Ces ventes ont lieu sur le domaine dans de petites caves de dégustation ou sur des stands gérés par chaque village lors des festivals du vin. Les viticulteurs ouvrent fréquemment, durant quelques semaines ou quelques mois, de petites buvettes dans leurs locaux. Certains possèdent même des restaurants et leurs vins figurent sur la carte. De nombreux clients vivent à proximité et apprécient leurs contacts avec le vigneron — en fait, une grande proportion de ces relations amicales remonte à des générations.

Sur le marché international, les grands domaines très réputés sont prédominants. Des courtiers en vin, hautement qualifiés, ont aidé à maintenir la stabilité du marché et à entretenir la réputation de ces domaines lors de leurs transactions en Allemagne et à l'étranger. Bien qu'une guilde des courtiers remonte au xive siècle, la profession n'a réellement commencé à s'épanouir qu'à la fin du xixe siècle avec l'introduction des ventes aux enchères à travers le Rheingau. La sélection des vins disponibles est devenue plus large depuis que les noms de crus individuels figurent sur les étiquettes — ceci contrastant avec la pratique traditionnelle qui consiste à appeler les vins par le nom de leur village — et il fut plus facile aux agents d'acheter et de vendre de manière efficace. Les domaines — tenant compte de l'expertise des agents et des conditions du marché — leur donnèrent le droit exclusif de vendre leurs vins aux enchères. Même aujourd'hui cette tradition est respectée lors de foires commerciales et ventes aux enchères dans le Rheingau, dont deux sont spécialement intéressantes.

En 1971, le Domaine viticole d'État (Verwaltung der Staatsweingüter à Eltville) inaugura une foire commerciale à Kloster Eberbach pour permettre aux clients d'acheter d'une manière plus efficace. Ce fut un tel succès, que le « Eberbacher Messe » s'est renouvelé depuis, chaque année en avril, et a été développé de façon à pouvoir accueillir les vins de 4 autres domaines prestigieux : Landgräfl. Hessisches Weingut, Johannisberg ; Freiherrl. Langwerth von Simmem'sche Rentamt, Eltville ; Schloss Groenesteyn, Kiedrich-Rüdesheim ; et Domänenweingut Schloss Schönborn, Hattenheim. Les prix fixés lors de la foire sont valables toute l'année d'où une meilleure stabilité, et l'on accorde aux acheteurs un rabais appréciable, calculé de manière dégressive en fonction des quantités achetées.

C'est aussi à Kloster Eberbach que se déroule chaque année, au printemps et à l'automne, deux ventes aux enchères du

Domaine viticole d'État où sont adjugées des spécialités (meilleurs tonneaux), des vins rares et des sélections du Schatzkammer (cave pour vins précieux). Les ventes ne sont plus le forum commercial qu'elles étaient et ceci en raison du nombre croissant d'acheteurs privés (non-négociants) mais aussi parce que la taille d'un lot moyen est aujourd'hui considérablement plus importante que les 600 litres traditionnels d'un Halbstück (800 bouteilles ou environ 66 caisses). La vente de 1964 fut la dernière au cours de laquelle un Halbstück fut adjugé. Depuis, tous les vins sont vendus en bouteilles. Néanmoins, les ventes d'Eberbach sont une tradition du Rheingau et cela depuis 1806. De nos jours, les prix records mondiaux qui y sont atteints ne contribuent pas seulement à augmenter le prestige du Domaine viticole d'État, mais aussi à attirer l'attention internationale sur le fait que les meilleurs vins blancs allemands figurent au haut niveau mondial, et se conservent particulièrement longtemps. En novembre 1986, le Dr. Hans Ambrosi, grande personnalité de l'industrie viticole allemande et directeur du Domaine viticole d'État, accueillit plus de 900 invités internationaux pour la vente d'automne au cours de laquelle un prix record fut atteint par une bouteille de vin blanc : 35 000 DM pour un Neroberger Riesling Trockenbeerenauslese Cabinet de 1983 (Neroberger est le coteau qui domine Wiesbaden). Le record antérieur fut pulvérisé : l'année précédente, lors d'une vente de la Verband Deutscher Prädikatsweingüter (Association des domaines de vin Prädikat allemand, dont le Domaine viticole d'État est membre), une bouteille de Steinberger Trockenbeerenauslese de 1983 atteignit 22 000 DM.

Une douzaine de villages organisent en été et à l'automne des festivals du vin, le plus remarquable étant celui du Rheingauer Weinwoche (semaine du vin du Rheingau) qui se déroule durant neuf jours consécutifs à Wiesbaden. Ces manifestations sont une source importante de contacts et de revenus supplémentaires pour les domaines d'une taille petite ou moyenne. Une centaine de producteurs de la région y ont des stands de dégustation, offrant chacun une gamme de 14 vins différents (du Qualitätswein de chaque jour aux spécialités rares, telles que les Beerenauslese, Trockenbeerenauslese, Eiswein et vieux millésimes) que l'on peut échantillonner. Les vins sont vendus en petits verres de 0,1 litre ; la quantité est suffisante pour que l'on puisse apprécier physiquement et financièrement le large éventail des vins du Rheingau. De plus, chaque village possède une buvette communale (Probierstand, stand de dégustation) qui propose les vins d'un domaine chaque semaine et qui est tenue par un viticulteur, sa famille ou son personnel. Un chemin de randonnée bien indiqué (Rheingauer Riesling-Pfad) et un itinéraire routier (Rheingauer Riesling-Route) permettent d'explorer facilement les beautés de la région et d'en apprécier les vins.

Principaux crus du Rheingau

Lorsque l'on regarde une carte plate du Rheingau, nous passons à côté d'une dimension importante — le relief — qui, avec la structure du sol et les micro-climats, influence directement le caractère des vins du Rheingau, de Hochheim vers le nord du Rheingau (de Wiesbaden à Hattenheim), les vignobles les plus proches du fleuve sont plantés sur des pentes douces qui deviennent plus raides dans le Rheingau moyen et sont très abruptes à Rüdesheim et autour de la courbe du fleuve (Assmannshausen, Lorch). Parallèlement, il existe un nombre important de villages et vignobles situés plus près du sommet boisé des monts du Taunus, et qui ne sont pas toujours visibles à cause des pentes très abruptes (Rauenthal, Kiedrich, Steinberg, Hallgarten, Schloss Vollrads et Johannisberg). Les coteaux pentus produisent des vins souvent décrits comme maigres, lisses, racés, à l'acidité prononcée et au caractère piquant. Au contraire, les vignobles plantés sur des pentes plus douces, produisent des vins charnus, fruités et moins acides. Dans les années sèches, les crus situés à proximité des forêts (qui retiennent l'humidité) sont les plus favorisés et les plus productifs. Les sols changent aussi d'est en ouest. Dans la partie septentrionnale et centrale de la région, gravier, sable, terreau, argile, marne forment la couche la plus profonde, souvent recouverte de loess. La partie extrême ouest est formée, quant à elle, de grès, de quartzite et surtout d'ardoise argileuse. Les vignes de ces sites poussent bien, même par années fraîches et humides. Par années très chaudes, les vins ne sont cependant pas aussi élégants et ont une teneur en alcool plus élevée. Bien des experts estiment que les meilleures localités en fait de qualité, et par bonne année, sont les suivantes, en allant d'est en ouest :

premièrement, les meilleurs crus de Rauenthal ; deuxièmement, les meilleurs crus du triangle Erbach-Hattenheim-Hallgarten ; troisièmement, les meilleurs crus de Johannisberg avec Schloss Vollrads et Winkler Hasensprung, à Winkel ; quatrièmement, les meilleurs crus de Rüdesheim. Par année moyenne, ce dernier passe en tête de liste par rapport aux autres crus. Dans les années de sécheresse, les vignobles situés à proximité de l'humidité des forêts donneront les meilleurs vins.

Les facteurs géologiques et climatiques déterminent la qualité de la production, mais le caractère ultime et la distinction d'un vin sont l'œuvre du producteur habile. Grâce aux institutions de recherche et d'éducation très vénérées de Geisenheim et Eltville, les viticulteurs du Rheingau sont bien formés aux méthodes actuelles d'entretien du vignoble et à la technologie de la cave, d'où la qualité des vins du Rheingau. Les producteurs mentionnés ci-dessous sont nommés d'après le village de leur domaine, car de nombreuses entreprises très vastes et traditionnelles ont des parcelles dans plusieurs villages. Il est intéressant de souligner que presque tous les grands domaines nobles et le Domaine viticole d'État possèdent des parcelles à Hattenheim, au cœur de la région. Par manque de place, de nombreux producteurs valables ne peuvent être mentionnés.

Assmannshausen

On dit souvent qu'Assmannshausen produit le meilleur vin rouge d'Allemagne. La vigne à vin rouge qui prospère sur les terres sédimentaires d'un rouge bleuâtre appartient à la variété Spätburgunder, ainsi appelée parce que son raisin mûrit tardivement et qu'elle fut apportée de Bourgogne au XIIe siècle par les cisterciens. Le vin qu'elle donne est doux, velouté, avec un léger arrière-goût d'amande qui rappelle un léger Bourgogne.

Grosslage : Steil.

Meilleur cru : Höllenberg.

Autres sites : Frankenthal, Hinterkirch.

Producteurs : Eulberg, Hufnagel, Schön.

Eltville

Cette localité des bords du Rhin porte un nom d'origine latine : *alta villa.* Jusqu'à la fin du XVe siècle, ce fut la résidence d'été du prince-électeur de Mayence et on y voit encore les ruines de son palais.

Johannes Gutenberg, l'inventeur de l'imprimerie rotative, y a vécu et travaillé à la fin du XVe siècle. Aujourd'hui, Eltville est un centre important pour le commerce du vin et des mousseux (Sekt) dans le Rheingau. Les vins sont de bonne qualité dans l'ensemble, un peu plus doux que ceux des vignobles voisins de Erbach et Kiedrich.

Grosslage : Heiligenstock, Steinmächer.

Meilleurs crus : Sonnenberg, Langenstück, Taubenberg.

Producteurs : C. Belz Erben, Oek. Rat, J. Fischer Erben, Freiherrl. Langwerth von Simmen, Egon Mauer, Richter-Boltendahl et le Verwaltung der Staatsweingüter (Domaine viticole d'État), mondialement connu.

Erbach

En général, vins charnus aux caractéristiques viriles. Le meilleur est le célèbre Markobrunn.

Markobrunn

Le nom de cette localité s'écrit tantôt Markobrunn, tantôt Marcobrunn. Elle donne un vin qui est l'un des meilleurs et des plus connus du Rheingau. Il n'atteint pas la superbe élégance des meilleurs Rauenthaler, mais il est plus corsé, et caractérisé par une vivacité épicée. Lors de son voyage au Rheingau en 1788, Thomas Jefferson le préféra à tous les autres vins de la région. Il doit son nom à un puits (*Brun* signifie source ou puits) que l'on voit encore au pied d'un mur délabré creusé dans du grès et portant le nom de Markobrunnen : sources de saint Marc. Le fait que cette source et le vignoble célèbre se trouvent sur la ligne de démarcation entre Erbach et Hattenheim a donné naissance à une légende comme on en raconte tant le long du Rhin. Pendant des générations les deux localités se disputaient ce site. Enfin, grâce à de vieilles archives, les gens d'Erbach prouvèrent que la source se trouvait sur leur territoire et ils s'en réjouirent à grand tapage. Mais quatre ou cinq matins plus tard, ils ne dirent plus rien. Pendant la nuit, un farceur d'Hattenheim avait écrit en grosses lettres sur le mur :

So ist es recht und
So soll es sein,
Nach Erbach das Wasser,

Nach Hattenheim den Wein.
(Tout va bien
Il doit en être ainsi
Vers Erbach, l'eau
Vers Hattenheim, le vin.)

Grosslage : Deutelsberg.

Autres grands crus : Hohenrain, Siegelsberg, Rheinhell.

Producteurs : Jakob Jung, Freiherr zu Knyphausen, Oetinger, Prinz Friedrich von Preussen (Schloss Reinhartshausen) et Tillmanns Erben.

Geisenheim

Ce secteur situé entre Rüdesheim et Johannisberg n'est pas aussi connu que le méritent ses vins. Le château de Schönborn, l'un des plus importants, est situé dans la localité, il présente par lui-même un grand intérêt historique. C'est là qu'en 1648 un ancêtre du propriétaire actuel rédigea le traité qui mit fin à la guerre de Trente Ans. Geisenheim est aujourd'hui très connu grâce à l'Institut de recherche d'État pour la viticulture, l'horticulture, l'œnologie et le paysagisme. Il regroupe 14 instituts dont le fameux Institut pour la culture viticole et le greffage de la vigne, dirigé par le Dr. Helmut Becker, expert reconnu mondialement dans son domaine et défenseur actif des vins de son Rheingau natal. C'était ici, en 1882, que le Dr. Hermann Müller de Thurgau (en Suisse) créa la variété qui porte son nom, en croisant du Riesling et du Silvaner. L'institut est le plus grand fournisseur, en Allemagne, de pieds résistants. En plus de ses installations de recherche, de ses 30 acres environ de vignobles expérimentaux et d'une entreprise vinicole moderne équipée pour la microvinification, c'est la seule école d'œnologie allemande de niveau universitaire comprenant une faculté de 30 professeurs. L'Allemagne ne produirait pas la qualité et la quantité s'il n'y avait eu les efforts d'institutions comme celle-ci. Le domaine viticole de cet institut produit des vins de haute qualité qui sont vendus à la fois en Allemagne et à l'étranger.

Les vignobles de Geisenheim fournissent des vins de bonne qualité, même dans les années moyennes. Ils ont un goût terreux bien particulier.

Grosslage : Burgweg, Erntebringer.

Meilleurs crus : Klaüserweg, Mäuerchen, Kilzberg, Klaus.

Producteurs : Erbslöh'sches Weingut, Graf von Francken-Sierstorpff, Schumann-Nägler, Freiherr von Zwierlein.

Hallgarten

De nombreux vignobles sont extrêmement abrupts et produisent des vins particulièrement mûrs, charnus et riches. La qualité peut être superbe dans les années sèches.

Grosslage : Mehrhölzchen.

Meilleur cru : Schörhell.

Autres sites : Hendelberg, Jungfer, Würzgarter

Producteurs : Karl Franz Engelmann, Fürst Löwenstein, Adam Nass. Il y a, en plus, deux coopératives importantes : Winzergenossenschaft Hallgarten et Vereinigte Weingutsbesitzer Hallgarten.

Hattenheim

Ce très joli petit village, aux maisons à colombages, a toujours été étroitement lié à l'ancien monastère cistercien de Kloster Eberbach. On raconte qu'au XIIIe siècle les premières vignes plantées sur le célèbre Steinberg furent celles intelligemment achetées par des moines aux producteurs d'Hattenheim. Hattenheim était aussi le siège de la plus vieille guilde de « Weinschröter » (littéralement rouleurs de barriques, débardeurs du Moyen Age) dans le Rheingau.

Les vins sont très fins et délicats. Les meilleurs d'entre eux sont de grands Rheingau.

Grosslage : Deutelsberg.

Meilleur cru : Steinberg (voir ci-dessous).

Autres sites : Mannberg, Nussbrunnen, Wisselbrunnen, Engelmannsberg.

Producteurs : Hans Barth, Hans Lang, « Georg Müller Stiftung », Balthasar Ress, Dömänenweingut Schloss Schönborn.

Steinberg et Kloster Eberbach

Le cru de Steinberg, près de Kloster Eberbach, est situé quelques collines plus loin, après Hattenheim. Comme Marcobrunn, c'est l'un des plus grands noms du vin en Allemagne. Les moines cisterciens, du monastère d'Eberbach, ont planté le vignoble à flanc de coteau il y a 700 ans. Comme Clos de Vougeot en Bourgogne, c'est une parcelle unique ceinturée d'un immense mur de pierre. Aujourd'hui, le vignoble de 31 ha appartient et est exclusivement dirigé par le Domaine viticole d'État (*voir aussi* ALLEMAGNE). Les vins sont fermentés dans les installations modernes du domaine à Eltville, mais vieillis dans les caves anciennes de Kloster Eberbach. Dans les meilleures années, les Steinberger sont charnus, puissants, à l'acidité aciéreuse et au parfum très profond. Ils vieillissent merveilleusement bien (ce qui est confirmé par les prix records mondiaux lors des ventes aux enchères). Le monastère de Kloster Eberbach fut fondé il y a près d'un millier d'années par des augustins qui adoptèrent la règle de Cîteaux : ils furent les premiers à appliquer cette règle en Allemagne. C'est alors que commença réellement le travail de la vigne et du vin.

Les cisterciens plantèrent en 1135 le terrain qui est devenu de nos jours le cru Steinberg. On ne s'étonnera pas d'apprendre que ces moines détruisirent les forêts pour y faire prospérer la vigne si on se rappelle leur devise : « Ora et Labora » (prie et travaille). Ils entendaient accroître la surface des terres arables et, comme ils avaient appris la viticulture en Bourgogne, la vigne les intéressait particulièrement. Au XIIIe siècle, leur flotte de vin naviguait sur le Rhin jusqu'à Cologne. A son apogée, Kloster Eberbach posséda jusqu'à plus de 200 ha dans le Rheingau et dans ce qui est devenu le Rheinhessen.

De nos jours, la basilique romane construite entre 1150 et 1185 est utilisée pour des concerts magnifiques de musique classique (l'acoustique est excellente) et autres cérémonies, comme par exemple la superbe célébration de Erntedankfest (actions de grâces), qui a lieu le premier dimanche de décembre. La basilique, éclairée aux chandelles, s'emplit des sons profonds du chœur des cuivres et des voix du millier de personnes présentes au service œcuménique. 4 000 bouteilles de Riesling sont offertes à cette occasion, à un organisme charitable — façon pour les viticulteurs du Rheingau d'exprimer leurs remerciements pour la nouvelle vendange. Aujourd'hui, Kloster Eberbach est le centre viticole culturel du Rheingau : siège de l'Académie du vin allemand et de la Société vinicole du Rheingau, qui organise des séminaires et des dégustations de vin ainsi que d'importantes foires et ventes aux enchères. Un musée consacré à l'histoire des cisterciens et du vin, des installations permettant des dégustations et des séminaires scientifiques ainsi que des chambres d'hôtes sont actuellement en construction et font partie du grand programme de rénovation commencé en 1986.

Le Prädikat allemand, appelé Kabinett, est, dit-on, originaire du Rheingau, peut-être bien de Kloster Eberbach. La facture d'un charpentier datant de 1730, pour des travaux effectués à Kloster Eberbach dans le « Cabernedt Keller », fait figurer une des mentions les plus anciennes du mot « Cabinet », qui signifie « petite cave » où sont entreposés séparément des vins de qualité supérieure. Les documents du monastère révèlent que le Cabinet Keller d'Eberbach commença avec un nombre choisi de vins du cru de 1712 et que, entre 1732 et 1782, 112 caisses du Cabinet Keller furent vendues. L'habitude était prise. Lorsque le monastère fut repris par les ducs du Nassau en 1803, un édit fut promulgué : il déterminait l'entreposage dans la cave Cabinet d'Eberbach des vins les plus exquis produits sur le domaine, pour fournir la Cour. Aujourd'hui, le terme Kabinett est attribué à un vin Prädikat allemand pour désigner sa très haute qualité.

Hochheim

A l'extrême est du Rheingau, nom du lieu où le Main se jette dans le Rhin, se situe la jolie ville d'Hochheim. Ses vignobles sont plantés en terrain plus plat ou sur des pentes douces. Grâce au micro-climat agréable, les vignes mûrissent souvent une ou deux semaines plus tôt que partout ailleurs dans le Rheingau. C'est un avantage dans les années fraîches ou pluvieuses. Les Hochheimer figurent parmi les plus grands vins du Rheingau. Ils sont très fruités, parfumés et, aux dires de certains, ils ont un goût terreux bien distinct. L'appellation Hock, qui désigne en anglais les vins du Rheingau et s'étend souvent à tous ceux du Rhin, dérive de Hochheim.

Grosslage : Daubhaus.

Meilleurs crus : Domdechaney et Kirchenstück.

Autres bons sites : Stein, Hölle.

Producteurs : Aschrott, Domdechant Werner. Weingut Königin Viktoriaberg est le propriétaire exclusif du vignoble nommé d'après la reine Victoria, qui, dit-on, apréciait par-dessus tout les vins d'Hochheim.

Johannisberg

On dit qu'un jour d'hiver, Charlemagne, qui de son palais d'Ingelheim regardait au-delà du Rhin, vit combien la neige avait fondu sur les pentes de l'actuel Johannisberg. Il ordonna que les premières vignes y furent plantées. Les raisins vendangés dans le vignoble de Johannisberg en 817 produisirent 6 000 litres de vin, comme le rapporta le fils de Charlemagne, Louis le Pieux.

Schloss Johannisberg.

A l'origine cette éminence s'appelait *Mons Episcopi*. Elle fut donnée, à la fin du XIe siècle, aux Bénédictins par l'archevêque de Mayence. Les Bénédictins y érigèrent un monastère à la mémoire de Jean-Baptiste, et depuis ce mont s'appelle Johannisberg. Après la sécularisation décrétée par Napoléon en 1803, le vignoble appartint successivement au prince d'Orange, à Napoléon, à l'empereur d'Autriche, qui le donna à Metternich en 1816, au congrès de Vienne, en récompense des services diplomatiques qu'il avait rendus. Son descendant, le prince de Metternich, est toujours le propriétaire bien que le domaine appartienne désormais à un groupe contrôlé par Rudolph Oetker, magnat dans l'alimentaire, qui possède aussi le domaine voisin de von Mumm.

Schloss Johannisberg est l'un des plus grands domaines viticoles traditionnels du monde, non seulement pour ses Riesling typés et de caractère, mais aussi pour le rôle qu'il a joué dans l'histoire du vin allemand. Le terme de « Premiers Crus » lui est très souvent associé. Lorsqu'il appartenait à l'abbaye de Fulda, il devint obligatoire de planter du Riesling. En 1720, Schloss Johannisberg, avec ses quelque 38 500 vins produits à partir de Riesling, fut le premier vignoble du Rheingau exclusivement planté du raisin noble. En 1775, le courrier qui devait apporter la permission de l'abbé de commencer les vendanges, fut retardé. Lorsqu'il arriva, les raisins pourrissaient dans les vignes. Ils furent néanmoins récoltés, et, à la surprise de tous, produisirent un vin exceptionnellement bon. Le Schloss Johannisberg est le premier domaine du Rheingau à avoir reconnu la valeur d'un Spätlese (littéralement, vendange tardive). La même année, en dépit du coût, il mettait en bouteilles quelques-uns de ses vins.

Schloss Johannisberg mérite la visite. Ses caves, qui remontent à 1100 et 1716-1721, figurent parmi les plus importantes du monde, et son trésor, la bibliothèque souterraine, possède des volumes très rares remontant à 1748. La vue de la terrasse est magnifique. Le 50e degré de latitude traverse le vignoble situé face au Rhin — c'est aussi la latitude du nord du Labrador et du nord de la Mongolie. Cependant, il jouit d'un climat doux, non seulement pour la vigne mais aussi pour les figues, les amandes et les citrons qui mûrissent dans les jardins du palais.

Grosslage : Erntebringer.

Autres bons crus : Hölle, Hansenberg.

Producteurs : G.H. von Mumm, Landgräfl ; Hessisches Weingut, . Weingut Johannishof.

Kiedrich

Les vignobles sont plantés assez haut sur les contreforts des monts Taunus au-delà d'Erbach. La vigne y est cultivée depuis 1131. La ville est considérée comme « le joyau gothique du Rheingau » en raison de sa belle église Saint-Valentin et de ses bancs minutieusement gravés de très beaux motifs de grappes et de vignes. Elle possède le plus vieil orgue qui fonctionne encore en Allemagne. Les vins sont très prisés grâce à leur grand style. Ils ne sont cependant pas aussi connus à l'étranger qu'ils le mériteraient.

Grosslage : Heiligenstock.

Meilleurs crus : Gräfenberg, Sandgrube, Wasseros, Klosterberg.

Producteurs : Schloss Groenesteyn et Weingut Dr. Weil.

Lorch

Les vignobles sont plantés sur des coteaux d'ardoise très abrupts qui demandent un travail manuel intensif. Les vins sont spécialement vigoureux et « spritzig » — l'ardoise permet à l'acidité du Riesling de ressortir. Dans d'autres régions du Rheingau, les meilleurs crus sont souvent moyens ou pauvres.

Grosslage : Burgweg.

Meilleurs Crus : Bodenthal-Steinberg, Krone, Pfaffenwies, Kapellenberg et quelques endroits du Schlossberg.

Producteurs : Weingut Friedrich Altenkirch, Graf von Kanitz, Fritz Perabo.

Oestrich

Une énorme tour de 1652 marque l'emplacement d'Oestrich, l'un des plus vieux établissements du Rheingau. Il possède la plus grande étendue ininterrompue de vignobles de la région. Les vins sont pleins et fruités, mais ils n'ont pas la classe de ceux du cru voisin d'Hattenheim. Schloss Reichartshausen fait exception. Situé à mi-chemin entre les deux villages, c'est un petit vignoble qui produit des vins au caractère bien particulier.

Grosslage : Gotteshal, Mehrhölzchen.

Meilleurs crus : Doosberg, Lenchen.

Producteurs : Un nombre de viticulteurs nommés Eser, Wegeler Erben (Deinhard). Aux alentours de Mittelheim : Hupfeld Erben, Reitz'sches Weingut Christian Reis.

Rauenthal

Avec les meilleurs crus de Hattenheim et d'Erbach ainsi que les Johannisberg et les Steinberg, ces vins comptent parmi les plus grands par bonne année. Le village est repoussé dans les collines du Taurus. Les vignobles s'étendent sur des coteaux abrupts et en terrasse. Dans les années chaudes, les Rauenthaler figurent sans aucun doute parmi les meilleurs d'Allemagne. Ils sont extrêmement fruités, épicés et à l'acidité très prononcée. Vieillissent bien. En général, partout au Rheingau, les meilleures terres à vigne appartiennent aux grands domaines vinicoles qui appliquent les meilleures méthodes viticoles avec le plus grand soin et font les meilleurs vins. Mais dans le secteur de Rauenthal, même les petits vignerons produisent des vins excellents. L'État est le plus gros propriétaire (28 ha), puis vient le Freiherr Langwerth von Simmern avec 3 ha. En moyenne, les vignes de Rauenthal ont un rendement inférieur d'un tiers à celles des autres secteurs, mais elles gagnent en qualité ce qu'elles perdent en quantité. La zone la plus intéressante a toujours été le Rauenthalerberg : coteau cultivé depuis 700 ans. Les vins ne peuvent plus être vendus sous ce nom, bien que Rothenberg et Gehrn soient effectivement situés sur le coteau.

Grosslage : Steinmächer.

Meilleur cru : Bailken.

Autres bons sites : Gehrn, Rothenberg, Wülfen, Langenstück.

Rüdesheim

Les vignes de Rüdesheim sont plantées sur un coteau à forte déclivité qui s'élève au bord même du Rhin. Cette situation particulière rend leurs vins exceptionnellement constants en qualité. Par mauvaise année on peut en principe compter sur eux, mais par bonne année ils sont juste au-dessous de la moyenne élevée du Rheingau. Ce coteau bénéficie du maximum d'ensoleillement et de la chaleur réfléchie par le fleuve ; même par été frais les raisins y mûrissent donc mieux qu'ailleurs. D'autre part, le soleil rôtit la vigne et le sol, et les dessèche ; par été chaud les vins manqueront donc de parfum et de rondeur. Bien que Rüdesheim soit une localité vinicole du Rhin fort connue en Allemagne, elle y est moins célèbre qu'à l'étranger où elle partage le renom de Nierstein en Rheinhessen. Les touristes en croisière sur le Rhin y font étape en grand nombre.

La plus belle collection du monde de verres, gobelets, coupes et autres ustensiles à boire se trouve sans doute dans le château délabré de Brömserburg, le plus vieux de toute la vallée du Rhin ; il date des IXe, Xe et XIIe siècles. On y voit du matériel vinicole utilisé au Rheingau au temps où vivait le Christ, des petites tasses de terre cuite datant de l'âge de pierre et aussi l'évolution de ces récipients à travers les âges jusqu'aux verres à long pied typiquement allemands. L'évolution de la bouteille allemande y est aussi exposée et on constate qu'elle est arrivée à sa forme actuelle aux environs de 1790.

Grosslage : Burgweg.

Meilleurs crus : Berg Rottland, Berg Schlossberg, Berg Roseneck.

Autres bons sites : Bischofsberg et Magdalenenkreuz.

Producteurs : G. Breuer, Dr. Heinrich Nägler.

Walluf

La plus ancienne mention de viticulture dans le Rheingau se trouve dans une donation datée de 779 où deux vignobles de Walluf étaient offerts au Kloster Lorsch. A l'origine deux villages (le haut et le bas Walluf), Walluf produit aujourd'hui des Riesling racés, typiques du Rheingau ainsi que de bons Spätburgunder, peu connus hors de la région.

Grosslage : Steinmächer.

Meilleurs crus : Walkenberg, Oberberg, Berg-Bildstock.

Producteurs : J.B. Becker, Arent Erben.

Winkel

Petit village dont l'excellente réputation pour ses vins fins est largement due au prestigieux domaine de Schloss Vollrads, situé derrière la ville. On dit que la « Maison grise » (Graues Haus) est la plus vieille maison de pierre de toute l'Allemagne. Elle fut probablement construite en 850 et servit de dernière résidence à l'archevêque et grand universitaire Rhabanus Maurus de Mainz. C'est aussi la demeure ancestrale des Greiffenclaus (de Schloss Vollrads) qui la possèdent encore à ce jour. Ils l'ont restaurée avec soin et transformée en lieu d'exposition pour tous les vins du Rheingau. C'est depuis 1981, un restaurant pour gourmets qui essaie de montrer combien les Riesling du Rheingau et les vins de Spätburgunder s'accordent à ravir avec la nourriture. Au début du XIXe siècle, la demeure Brentano à Winkel était le lieu de rendez-vous favori de tous les romantiques rhénans, y compris Goethe qui fut particulièrement inspiré par la vendange fabuleuse de 1811.

Schloss Vollrads

Comme ses voisins, le Schloss Johannisberg et Steinberg, ce cru est l'un des plus grands noms du vin allemand. C'est la famille Greiffenclaus qui a la plus longue tradition de viticulture — non seulement dans le Rheingau mais probablement aussi dans le monde. Les traces les plus anciennes de vin de Vollrads remontent à 1211. Vers 1300, les terres du domaine actuel furent libérées et la famille quitta la Maison Grise pour s'installer dans la tour du château fortifié, achevée en 1330. Le magnifique palais baroque, construit vers la fin du XVIIe siècle, est la demeure du propriétaire actuel, Erwein comte Matuschka-Greiffenclau. Comme feu son père, le comte Matuschka est une des têtes très respectées de l'industrie du vin allemand. Il se consacre totalement à la recherche de la meilleure qualité et veut aussi démontrer combien les vins de Riesling du Rheingau s'harmonisent avec la nourriture. Dans ce dessein, outre les nombreuses dégustations qu'il organise dans le monde entier, il en anime régulièrement dans ses magnifiques salles de réception qui sont appelées « Dégustations de Lucullus ». Ses efforts ont beaucoup contribué à valoriser l'image des vins allemands sur les marchés d'exportation.

UNION DES VINICULTEURS DU RHEINGAU

Négociants	*Siège*	*Ha*
Verwaltung der Staatsweingüter	Eltville	760
Freiherrl. Langwerth v. Simmern'sches Rentamt	Eltville	150
Rentmeister Egon Mauer	Eltville	15
Weingut Oek. Rat Jak. Fischer Erben	Eltville	31
Weingut C. Belz Erben	Eltville	30
Weingut Richter-Boltendahl	Eltville	51
Weingut Freiherr zu Knyphausen	Erbach	80
Weingut Dr. Weil	Kiedrich	80
Robert v. Oetinger'sches Weingut	Erbach	30
Weingut Eberhard v. Oetinger	Erbach	33
Gräfl. von Schönborn'sches Rentamt	Hattenheim	200
Gemeinde-Weingut « Georg Müller Stiftung »	Hattenheim	40
Weingut K.F. Engelmann	Hallgarten	16
Weingut Adam Nass	Hallgarten	16
Gutsverwaltung Geh. Rat Wegeler Erben	Ostrich	400
Reitz'sches Weingut	Ostrich	12
Graf Matuschka-Greiffenclau'sche Schloss Vollrads	Winkel	188
Weingut Fürstl. Loewenstein, Schloss Vollrads	Hallgarten	80
Weingut Jakob Hamm	Winkel	18
A.v. Brentano'sche Gutsverwaltung	Winkel	35
Geromont'sche Gutsverwaltung	Winkel	16
Fürst v. Metternich	Johannisberg	160
Landgräfl. Hess. Weingut	Johannisberg	160
Weingut Freiherr v. Zwierlein	Geisenheim	92
Erboslöh'sches Weingut	Geisenheim	40
Freiherr v. Ritter zu Groenesteyn	Kiedrich	120
Gräfl. v. Kanitz'sche Weingut	Lorch	60
Domdechant Werner'sches Weingut	Hochheim	52
Geh. Rat Aschrott'sche Gutsverwaltung	Hochheim	80
Weingut Dr. H. Nägler	Rüdesheim	23
Weingut Georg Brewer	Rüdesheim	32
August Eser	Mittelheim	35
H. Hupfeld Erben	Mittelheim	42
Administration Schloss Rheinhartshausen	Erbach	270
Weingut H. Tillmann's Erben	Erbach	40
		3 487

On distingue les vins de Schloss Vollrads par leur style fruité, piquant et élégant. Ils s'améliorent en vieillissant en bouteilles. Les crus les plus remarquables sont produits durant les années chaudes et ensoleillées. Dans les mauvaises années, les vins sont vendus en vrac, et ne sont pas autorisés à porter le Schloss Vollrads. Le comte Matuschka est aussi propriétaire du domaine Fürst Löwenstein à Hallgarten.

Grosslage : Honigberg, Erntebringer.

Meilleur cru : Hasensprung.

Autres bons sites : Bienengarten, Dachsberg, Klaus et Jesuitengarten.

Producteurs : Baron von Brentano, Geromont, Jacob Hamm, Mehrlein, Schönleber-Blümlein.

Association des domaines de la Charte des vins

Dans les années 80, un groupe de viticulteurs du Rheingau, en quête de qualité, ont créé cette association pour promouvoir les vins de Riesling de type classique du Rheingau. Les vins de la Charte se présentent tous dans la bouteille traditionnelle brune, grande et fine du Rheingau, gravée à l'emblème de la Charte : une double arche romane. Seuls les vins de Riesling du Rheingau, spécialement sélectionnés (grâce aux dégustations aveugles par un panel d'experts) conformes aux critères stricts de l'association, peuvent être mis en bouteilles. Ils doivent aussi être conservés dans les caves du producteur jusqu'au 1er octobre au moins de l'année suivant la vendange.

Rheinhessen

État allemand du Palatinat. Superficie : 25 000 ha. 94 % de vins blancs, 6 % de vins rouges.

Situation : La plus grande région vinicole d'Allemagne est située dans un paysage vallonné, bordé par la Nahe à l'ouest et le Rhin à l'est. Les « quatre coins » de la région : Mainz, Worms, Bingen et Alzey, sont les villes importantes pour le commerce du vin. Une ancienne route romaine traverse le Rheinhessen en diagonale de Mainz à Alzey, ce qui prouve que les vignes y sont cultivées depuis plus de 2 000 ans. La région est divisée en trois districts (Bereiche) : le Bereich Wonnegau, qui regroupe la partie sud et la ville de Worms, le Bereich Bingen qui se situe à l'ouest et comprend aussi les vignobles s'étendant de Beingen à Mainz. Le troisième district tire son nom du célèbre village de Nierstein et regroupe une succession de petites villes charmantes sur le bord du Rhin, connues sous le nom de « Front Rhénan » ou « Terrasse du Rhin ».

Cette région est l'ancien grand duché de Hesse où les rois hanovriens d'Angleterre recrutaient les mercenaires qui combattirent les *Insurgents* des États-Unis. Elle constitue actuellement la plus grosse partie de la province de Hesse qui donne son nom aux vins de la région. Ceux qui sont produits dans cette province sont des Rheinhessen et aucun de ceux provenant d'ailleurs n'ont droit à cette appellation.

Principales variétés de raisin : Müller-Thurgau (24 %), Silvaner (13 %), Scheurebe, croisement de Silvaner et de Riesling, nommé d'après le viticulteur Georg Scheu (10 %), Bacchus, croisement de (Silvaner × Riesling) et Müller-Thurgau (8 %), Kerner, croisement de Trollinger et de Riesling (8 %), Faberrebe, croisement de Weissburgunder, Pinot Blanc et Müller-Thurgau (7 %) et Riesling (6 %).

Vins : Une description nous en est donnée par Carl Zuckmayer, écrivain originaire du village de Nackenheim (près de Nierstein) qui parle de « vin du rire... charmant et attrayant ».

Cette région produit des vins souples, sans caractère nettement tranché mais d'un type tellement évident qu'ils sont les plus faciles à reconnaître parmi les crus allemands. Peut-être précisément est-ce en raison de leur simplicité et de leur douceur qu'ils ont toujours été les mieux connus à l'étranger. Ce ne sont pas des vins de garde, car ils s'améliorent très peu en bouteille et inclinent à faner au bout de huit ou dix ans. Hormis l'infime quantité provenant de raisins vendangés tardivement, les Rheinhessen de plus de dix ans sont rarement intéressants. Les vins du Rheinhessen sont doux, pleins et agréables. Les Riesling produits autour de Bingen et sur la Terrasse du Rhin sont élégants et stylés.

« Si tu n'es pas vigneron, tu n'es pas du pays ». Tel est un dicton du Rheinhessen. On y fait du vin depuis deux milliers d'années et on y cultive la vigne dans presque toutes les localités. La plupart des vignobles sont de dimensions réduites, sauf autour de Nierstein, d'Oppenheim et de Bingen (les meilleurs secteurs), il y a peu de grands domaines et 50 % des vignerons du Rheinhessen ne possèdent pas plus d'un hectare chacun. Ils vivent en partie du vin et en partie d'autres activités agricoles ; c'est un

0
5
10 KILOMETRES
RHEINGAU
Wiesbaden
54
Main
Rhin
42
455
Mayence
9
Rüdesheim
BAC
Bingen
9
Ingelheim
Gau-Algesheim
40
Laubenheim
Büdesheim
Ockenheim
41
Bodenheim
Dromersheim
Elsheim
Gau-Bischofheim
Nackenheim
Harxheim
Hahnheim
Nierstein
Schwabsburg
Bosenheim
Oppenheim
420
Dexheim
Wörrstadt
Friesenheim
Dienheim
9
Dalheim
Ulversheim
Ludwigshöhe
Guntersblum
RHEINHESSEN
Alzey
Mettenheim
ALLEMAGNE
40
Bechtheim
Westhofen
271
Rhin
Osthofen
Dalsheim
47
47
Worms
N
9
RHEINHESSEN
E12
PALATINAT
(RHEINPFALZ)
vers Sarrebrück

des grands avantages de la région qui lui permet de subsister pendant les mauvaises années. Cependant, sur les 11 000 viticulteurs du Rheinhessen, près des 2/3 cultivent du raisin et produisent leurs vins. 70 % sont vendus en vrac aux grandes entreprises vinicoles afin d'y être mis en bouteilles. Le mouvement coopératif n'est pas aussi développé dans le Rheinhessen que dans les autres régions. Néanmoins, on compte une coopérative centrale et de nombreuses coopératives locales qui ont contribué à stabiliser le marché et à améliorer le niveau de vie des viticulteurs. Pour l'ensemble de la région, les efforts de la station expérimentale viticole d'Oppenheim ont été exemplaires pour perfectionner les méthodes de culture et de vinification.

Sous les auspices de l'office de promotion des vins régionaux du Rheinhessen, un nouveau concept a été créé pour favoriser la renaissance des Silvaner qui étaient autrefois la variété la plus plantée de la région. Sous le slogan « Rheinhessen Silvaner — vin sec classique », quelque 100 producteurs ont décidé de restaurer des critères spécifiques de production, de vente ainsi que la commercialisation de leur Silvaner sec dans un conditionnement uniforme. Le vin ne doit être fabriqué qu'avec du Silvaner, contenir au maximum 4 g de sucre résiduel par litre, avoir au minimum une acidité totale de 5 g par litre ainsi qu'une bonne teneur moyenne en extraits. En tant que vin de qualité (Qualitätswein) il doit, selon la loi, subir les tests officiels de contrôle de qualité et se livrer également à un deuxième test, celui de la Société allemande d'agriculture. On contrôle aussi les vins pour s'assurer qu'ils répondent au caractère typique des Silvaner. Le millésime est obligatoire, mais le vin ne peut être commercialisé avant le 1er mars de l'année suivant la vendange. L'emballage est étonnant — la bouteille marron traditionnelle, utilisée pour les vins du Rhin, porte une simple étiquette jaune et noire qui met en évidence l'inscription « Rheinhessen Silvaner Trocken » (sec).

Le sol, la vigne, le temps et l'homme collaborent à la qualité du vin. Le climat du Rheinhessen est doux, sec, assez ensoleillé et relativement exempt des gels de printemps et d'automne qui terrorisent les vignerons des autres régions, surtout ceux de la Moselle. Mais en contrepartie, les vins de Rheinhessen manquent du caractère que leur donnerait un climat plus précaire car, plus la vigne peine pour survivre, meilleur est son vin. Bref, leur qualité reflète la douceur du climat.

En plus des trois variétés allemandes classiques utilisées pour les vins blancs, il existe de nouveaux croisements plantés dans le Rheinhessen, et, plus principalement, sur les coteaux intérieurs de la région. A Alzey, à la station régionale de production de plants, de nouveaux croisements ont été développés, essentiellement dans les années 20 sous la direction du Dr. Georg Scheu, afin de découvrir une variété qui offre tout d'abord le goût et l'élégance du Riesling, mais qui soit aussi précoce. On développe également d'autres variétés pour couper les vins et donner du corps, du bouquet ou un parfum particulier à des vins normalement neutres ou pour adoucir une acidité âpre et désagréable dans les mauvaises années.

Le vin rouge est de plus en plus populaire en Allemagne. Le Rheinhessen a été longtemps connu pour ses « îlots de vin rouge » autour d'Ingelheim. Le Spätburgunder (Pinot Noir) et le Portugieser sont les principales variétés, le premier produisant des vins très élégants (mais légers), le deuxième, un petit vin de tous les jours très agréable. La « philosophie » allemande concernant les méthodes de vinification des vins rouges diffèrent énormément de celles de ses voisins plus méridionaux. Le fruité est une vertu, et les vignerons, en général, ne mélangent pas les crus pour obtenir un goût stable d'année en année. Ils préfèrent laisser le caractère de chaque récolte révéler son influence sur le fruit. Les vins rouges allemands ont une acidité faible en tanin, et, comparés aux vins rouges produits dans d'autres régions, ils ont une teneur en alcool relativement faible. On les remarque en partie pour leur acidité fruitée, semblable à celle des vins blancs.

Le sol du Rheinhessen se compose de calcaire, marne et quartz, souvent le calcaire au-dessus et la marne en dessous. Il varie considérablement de vignoble à vignoble. Le long du Rhin, autour de Bingen, on trouve du schiste pareil à celui de la Moselle. Entre Nackenheim et Nierstein, et un peu plus loin, subsiste une étrange pierre calcaire rouge déposée par les glaciers de l'ère glaciaire. La perméabilité du sol explique que les vins de Nierstein, Nackerheim et Schwabsburg souffrent moins des années humides.

Principaux crus du Rheinhessen

Voici la liste des crus les plus intéressants du Rheinhessen. Les noms des propriétaires, qui s'élèvent à plusieurs centaines, ne peuvent pas être énumérés ici. Néanmoins, pour les meilleurs vins nous citons le nom du producteur ou celui du domaine tel qu'il apparaît sur l'étiquette, précédé de *Wachstum, Weingut* ou autre locution similaire. Nous nous sommes efforcés de donner les noms des meilleurs vignerons, mais notre liste n'est pas exhaustive.

Alsheim

Chaîne de collines basses situées à 1 500 m du Rhin, entre Worms et Oppenheim. Plus gros producteur de l'arrondissement de Worms pour la qualité, compte parmi les quatre premiers du Rheinhessen. Grande quantité de Riesling. Fait partie de la fameuse Terrasse du Rhin.

Crus : Fischerpfad, Goldberg, Römerberg, Sonnenberg, Frühmesse.

Domaine vinicole : Weingut Rappennof-Dr. Muth.

Alzey

Ville ancienne datant de 223 et aujourd'hui cité rurale. En plus de la station de production de plants, un centre gouvernemental de contrôle de qualité y a été installé. Il est chargé de tester la qualité de tous les vins du Rheinhessen.

Vignobles : Les vins vendus sous le nom de leur Grosslagen (GL) ou sous des noms collectifs : Pettersberg ou Sybillenstein.

Domaines vinicoles : Weingut der Stadt Alzey (propriété de la ville). C'est aussi à Alzey que l'on trouve deux importantes entreprises vinicoles : Leoff et H. Sichel Söhne.

Bechtheim

Vins de coteau à 3 km des terres plates et sans vignes qui se perdent dans le Rhin.

Crus : Geyersberg, Rosengarten, Stein.

Domaines vinicoles : Dr Blum'sches Weingut, Ferdinand Kœhler, Weingut Wilhelm Schœneck.

Bingen

Situé sur la rive gauche du Rhin, en face de Rüdesheim, en Rheingau, à l'endroit où la Nahe se jette dans le fleuve, Bingen couvre une éminence célèbre depuis l'époque romaine pour ses vignobles. Bengen-Dempten, faubourg de la ville, et Bingen-Büdesheim, situé un peu au-delà, où des collines arrondies bordent la Nahe, forment un seul secteur avec Bingen et leurs vins peuvent être considérés comme des Binger.

Bingen est relié à Rüdesheim par un ferry-boat qui peut tournoyer comme une plume tant le courant du fleuve peut être violent et qui semble alors sur le point de dériver loin des quais quand il va aborder. Agglomération tassée aux rues enchevêtrées, sur un terrain varié, Bingen mérite les noms de ville du vin et ville du Rhin.

Bingen a survécu aux épidémies, à la guerre de Trente Ans et à d'autres désastres. A la fin du siècle dernier, 130 cafés et 120 marchands de vin fournissaient à boire à ses 6 000 citoyens. Depuis lors, la population a triplé mais on s'y amuse toujours autant. Il arriva jadis qu'un évêque de Mayence, parlant aux membres du clergé de Bingen, leur demanda incidemment un crayon. Tous plongèrent la main sous leur soutane et en sortirent un tire-bouchon. Depuis, cet ustensile s'appelle « crayon de Bingen ». Quoique séparé du Rheingau par la seule largeur du Rhin, Bingen produit des vins qui sont nettement des Rheinhessen : ils ont la vivacité que confère le sol schisteux. Ceux qui proviennent des bords du Rhin ont parfois un goût de fumé qu'on attribue à l'intensité de la circulation ferroviaire et de la navigation fluviale. En fait, l'alimentation se faisant à l'électricité et au gas-oil, ce goût ne peut-être attribué qu'au sol.

Crus : Rosengarten, Schwätzerchen, Schlossberg, Budenstück, Kapellengerg, Kirchberg, Osterberg, Pfarrgarten, Schlemenstück et Scharlachberg.

Domaines vinicoles : Villa Sachsen et Jung et Junghof.

Bodenheim

Propriété d'un monastère au Moyen Age. Vins épicés, corsés, avec beaucoup de bouquet, qui n'atteignent pourtant pas les mêmes sommets que ceux de Nierstein et d'Oppenheim, provenant de quelques kilomètres plus au sud. Fait partie de la fameuse Terrasse du Rhin.

Crus : Ebersberg, Burgberg, Hoch, Leidhecke, Silberberg, Westrum, Heiterbrünnchen, Kapelle, Kreuzberg, Mönchspfad et Reichritterstift.

Domaines vinicoles : Peter Kerz III, Oberstleutnant Liebrecht'sche Weingutsverwaltung, Anton Riffel, et Weingut Kühling-Gillot.

Dalheim

Vins plutôt forts et très nets.
Crus : Altdörr, Kranzberg et Steinberg.

Dalsheim (-Florsheim)

Le phylloxéra obligea à replanter, à un coût énorme, des souches américaines. Le Sylvaner y fut toujours le plus cultivé mais, introduit depuis une quarantaine d'années, le Müller-Thurgau convient au sol argileux. Les vins se sont nettement améliorés, et nombreux sont ceux faits avec ce nouveau croisement.
Crus : Steig, Bürgel, Frauenberg, Hubacker et Sauloch.
Domaine vinicole : Docteur Becker, H. Müller et Schales.

Dexheim

Considéré, depuis le Moyen Age, comme l'égal d'Oppenheim, de Schwabsburg et de Nierstein qui est contigu. Mais actuellement ce vin ne vaut pas ceux des localités voisines.
Crus : Doktor.
Domaines vinicoles : Adolf Dahlheim, August Dahlheim, Sander.

Dienheim

Contigu à Oppenheim, au sud. Les vignes plantées au bord du Rhin produisent des vins de première qualité. La « Pierre Silius », preuve d'un passé romain à Dienham, atteste que ces vignobles produisent du vin depuis plus de 2 000 ans.
Crus : Falkenberg, Siliusbrunnen Tafelstein, Herrenberg, Höhlchen, Kreuz, Herrengarten, Paterhof et Schloss.

Dittelsheim-Hessloch

Petit village non loin d'Alzey et situé au pied d'une haute colline, le Kloppberg. Les viticulteurs locaux ont ouvert au sommet un charmant restaurant, excellente façon de goûter la cuisine et les vins locaux tout en jouissant d'une vue magnifique. On accède au sommet par un chemin piétonnier.
Crus : Kloppberg, Geiersberg, Leckerberg, Liebfrauenberg, Pfaffenmütze, Mönchube, Mondschein et Edle Weingarten.

Dromersheim

Vallée abritée. Un des plus vieux villages vinicoles du Rheinhessen qui englobait autrefois Kloster Fulda.
Crus : Honigberg, Kapellenberg, Mainzweg et Klosterweg.

Friesenheim

Encépagement : Müller-Thurgau, et aussi Sylvaner.
Crus : Altdörr, Bergspfad et Knopf.

Gau-Algesheim

Sur le front du Rhin, entre Bingen et Ingelheim, en face du Rheingau, Un célèbre festival du vin nouveau a lieu le second week-end d'octobre, sur l'historique place du marché. Ce fut, au Moyen Age, une grande foire annuelle du vin.
Crus : Rothenberg, Goldberg, Johannisberg, Steinert et Saint-Laurenzikapelle.
Domaine vinicole : Averanius'sche Gutsverwaltung.

Gau-Bickelheim

Siège des caves centrales de la région (Zentralkellerei Rheinischer Winzergenossenschaften), entreprise extrêmement moderne et bien tenue.
Crus : Bockshaut, Kapelle, Saukopf.

Gau-Bischofheim

Coteaux orientés au sud, en aval de Nierstein.
Crus : Glockenberg, Herrnberg, Pfaffenweg et Kellersberg.
Domaine vinicole : Oberst Schultz H. Werner.

Guntersblum

Vin habituellement fruité. Sur le front du Rhin. Au troisième rang pour la quantité en Rheinhessen. Vignoble très morcelé. Coteau à pente faible. Vignobles d'un seul tenant sur 1 500 m de chaque côté de la route. La plupart des caves de la ville sont situées le long d'un chemin d'un kilomètre, connu sous le nom de « Kellerweg », au pied des vignobles. Ici se déroule l'un des festivals du vin les plus populaires.
Crus : Autental, Bornpfad, Eiserne Hand, Himmelthal, Steinberg, Sankt Julianenbrunnen, Kreuzkapelle, Steig-Terrassen, Sonnenberg et Sonnenhang.
Domaines vinicoles : Emil Schätzel, Schlossgut, Schmitt, Ernst Küstner, Friedrich Frey et Schmitt-Dr. Chnacker.

Hahnheim

Vignobles de coteaux orientés au sud, situés au centre de la région.

Crus : Knopf, Moosberg.

Domaine vinicole : Walter Heinz.

Harxheim

Coteaux à forte pente, contigus au secteur de Nierstein, mais leurs vins n'atteignent pas les mêmes sommets que ceux des collines riveraines du Rhin à Nierstein.

Crus : Schlossberg, Lieth et Börnchen.

Domaines vinicoles : August Böll, Peter Lotz.

Ingelheim

Dans cette localité le rouge éclipse le blanc, à l'inverse de ce qui se passe partout en Allemagne et particulièrement en Rheinhessen. Les blancs sont de bons vins de table. Les rouges, faits avec du Portugieser sont légers et plaisants, tandis que ceux faits avec du Spätburgunder ont réellement de la qualité. Selon certains experts, les meilleurs crus d'Ingelheim produisent les meilleurs rouges d'Allemagne et méritent d'être classés parmi les plus grands du monde. Ingelheim, Weinheim et une demi-douzaine de localités voisines portant des noms du même genre et diverses subdivisions du secteur adoptent la même appellation en raison de la célébrité d'Ingelheim. Tous proviennent d'un point quelconque de la zone vallonnée qui entoure cette ville médiévale dominant le Rhin. Charlemagne y avait une forteresse. On raconte que par un jour d'hiver, regardant au-delà du Rhin, il remarqua que la neige avait commencé à fondre sur les coteaux de ce qui est aujourd'hui le Schloss Johannisberg. Il ordonna alors que les premières vignes y furent plantées. Ingelheim offre un panorama magnifique du Rheingau central. Les excellentes asperges récoltées en mai et en juin dans la région sont aussi très réputées.

Crus : Horn, Pares, Rheinhöle, parmi de nombreux autres.

Domaine vinicole : J. Neuss (rouges).

Ludwigshöle

Quand on atteint ce petit village, en avant d'Oppenheim, le coteau s'abaisse pour faire place à une vaste plaine. Une bonne part du vin de Ludwigshöhe est étiqueté Liebfraumilch.

Crus : Honigsberg et Teufelskopf.

Domaines vinicoles : Weingut Brüder Dr Becker, Johann Gräf.

Mainz

Centre vinicole pendant des siècles et capitale de la Rhénanie-Palatinat, Mainz est une ville universitaire vivante. Ses maisons à colombages et ses tavernes accueillantes sont situées dans une zone ravissante, derrière la cathédrale. La cathédrale, comme ses semblables à Worms et Speyer, est l'un des plus beaux exemples en Allemagne de l'architecture romane-rhénane.

Johannes Gutenberg, inventeur de l'imprimante rotative, est né à Mainz. Le musée Gutenberg est à visiter. Le Mainzer Weinbörse (fête vinicole commerciale) se déroule chaque année au mois d'avril et est patronnée par l'Association allemande des producteurs de vins Prädikat.

Vignobles : Les vins sont généralement vendus sous les noms des deux vignobles collectifs : Domherr et St. Alban.

Mettenheim

Les vignes sont cultivées en bordure d'une plaine, sur une vaste courbe du Rhin, un peu au sud de l'excellente zone qui s'étend de Bodenheim jusqu'à Guntersblum. Bons vins moyens mais aucun de pointe. Mettenheim est le seuil méridional de la fameuse Terrasse du Rhin. On peut retrouver traces de la viticulture depuis la période carolingienne où le nom allemand « Kloster Lorsch » est mentionné.

Crus : Michelsberg, Schlossberg, et aussi Goldberg.

Domaine vinicole : Gerhard Koch.

Nackenheim

On fait des vins blancs de première classe sur le sol rouge de glaise et de schiste de cette localité située immédiatement en amont de Nierstein. Autrefois les vins de Nackenheim étaient utilisés à des coupages, mais on a fini par reconnaître leur haute qualité. Certaines années le rendement à l'hectare est le plus bas du Rheinhessen, ce qui est toujours un indice de qualité. Dominé par une église baroque, le village surplombe presque le Rhin, du sommet d'une hauteur couverte de vignes, auxquelles l'influence modératrice du fleuve sur le climat facilite l'existence. La plus grosse usine de capsules pour bouteilles de vin de toute l'Europe se trouve à Nackenheim. C'est aussi le lieu de naissance de Carl Zuckmayer (auteur et dramaturge allemand), grand promoteur des vins de la région. Nackenheim fait partie de la fameuse Terrasse du Rhin.

Crus : Engelsberg, Rothenberg (exceptionnel), Schmitts-Kapelle.

Domaines vinicoles : Gunderloch-Lange, Gunderloch-Usinger.

Nierstein

Nierstein produit les meilleurs vins du Rheinhessen. Dans cette localité tout le monde possède des vignes célèbres depuis des centaines d'années. Sur 550 parcelles, deux douzaines produisent le vin onctueux, élégant, charnu qui, dans le monde entier, porte le nom de Niersteiner. Veillez à la mention Riesling sur l'étiquette car les meilleurs sont faits avec ce cépage. Les Nackenheimer ont un bouquet merveilleux.

Le nom de Nierstein dérive de celui d'une source d'eau minérale que les Romains appelaient Neri et d'une borne qui marqua jadis la frontière entre le territoire des Francs et celui d'autres tribus germaniques. La ville s'appela d'abord Neri am Stein qui se transforma en Nierstein. Quand on quitte Mayence par la route, avec le Rhin à sa gauche, on aperçoit une éminence assez abrupte, le Weinberg, entièrement couverte de vignes. Des panneaux avec des grosses lettres indiquent le nom des secteurs tels que HIPPING, KRANZBERG, etc. Nierstein est le plus vaste *Weinbauort* du Rhin et surtout du Rheinhessen.

Crus : les meilleurs sont Glöck, Heiligenbaum, Kranzberg, Ölberg, Orbel, Hipping, Pettenthal, Bildstock, Hölle et Paterberg. Suivent Bergkirche, Schloss Schwabsburg, Zehnmorgen, Pfaffenkappe, Brudersberg, Goldene Luft, Brückchen, Kirchplatte, Klostergarten, Rosenberg et aussi Schloss Hohenrechen. Les sites viticoles de Spiegelberg, Rehback et Auflangen sont fameux et les vins sont très souvent expédiés sous ces noms plutôt que celui d'un domaine individuel.

Domaines vinicoles : Weingut Balbach Erben, Weingut J. et H.A. Strub, Emil Förster, Frh. von Heyl zu Herrnsheim, Gustav Gessert, Weingut Louis Guntrum, Gorg Harth, Fritz Hasselbach, Weingut Friedrich Kehl, Franz Karl Schmitt (veuve de), Hermann Franz Schmitt-Hermannshof, Geschwister Schuch, Georg Albrecht Schneider, Reinhold Senfter, Weingut Heinrich Schalmp Jr. La coopérative régionale Rheinfront produit de très bons vins provenant des propriétés de ses adhérents situées dans la plupart des meilleurs sites de Nierstein. Elle offre de bonnes affaires.

Ockenheim

Peut être très bon les années très ensoleillées qui permettent de faire une bonne quantité de Spätlese sur les coteaux orientés au sud. On y utilise de plus en plus le Müller-Thurgau parce que le public apprécie de plus en plus le vin aromatique qu'il fournit.

Crus : Hockenmühe, Klosterweg, Kreuz, Laberstall, St. Jakobsberg et Schönhölle.

Domaine vinicole : Wihelm Merz.

Oppenheim

En général, l'Oppenheimer est plus corsé et plus moelleux que le Niersteiner, alors que ce dernier a plus d'élégance. Par année chaude et sèche, l'Oppenheimer surpassera vraisemblablement le Niersteiner, alors que par année humide et froide, ce dernier sera meilleur. Le sol d'Oppenheim retient l'eau tandis que le coteau de Nierstein, plus incliné, la laisse s'écouler. Dans l'église Sainte-Catherine à l'intérieur austère et nu, on voit quelques pierres tombales datant des XVe et XVIe siècles, ornées de pampres et d'autres symboles viticoles. Oppenheim est aussi le siège de la plus importante institution viticole de la région. Un centre de recherche et de formation de haut niveau y a beaucoup amélioré les méthodes de culture et de vinification. Il possède aussi 20 ha de vignobles à Oppenheim et Nierstein. Le musée viticole allemand possède une collection intéressante d'outils.

Crus : Daubhaus, Herrengarten, Paterhof, Herrenberg, Kreuz, Sackträger, Schlossberg, Zuckerberg, Schloss, Schützenhütte et Gutleuthaus.

Domaines vinicoles : Friedrick Baumann, Adam Becker, Franz Josef Gallois, Louis Guntrum, J. A. Harth et Co., Ernst Jungkenn, Karl Koch (Erben), Franz Josef Senfter, Carl Sittmann, Weingut der Stadt Oppenheim, Dr L. Winter.

Osthofen

Crus : Goldberg, Kirchberg, Hasenbiss, Klosterberg, Rheinberg, Neuberg, Leckzapfen et Liebenberg.

Schwabsburg

Avec sa tour sans fenêtres et son château construit pour Frédéric Barberousse, Schwabsburg est un joli village entouré de vignes, dans un petit vallon à quelque 1 500 m de Nierstein. Les vignobles sont orientés au sud et au sud-ouest. Ils bénéficient du même sol rougeâtre de schiste et de glaise que celui des crus généralement plus intéressants situés au bord du Rhin. Les vignobles de Schwabsburg font partie du *Weinbauort* de Nierstein.

Selzen

Crus : Osterberg, Gottesgarten et Rheinpforte.

Domaine vinicole : Weingut Schätzel (Erben).

Ülversheim

Vin généralement fort et corsé. Vignes presque toutes cultivées sur la face sud du front du Rhin.

Cru : Schloss Aulenberg.

Westhofen

Crus : Brunnenhaüschen, Kirchspiel, Benn, Aulerde, Morstein, Rotenstein et Steingrube.

Worms

On aperçoit, de-ci de-là, un petit lopin de vigne en pleine ville, parmi les bâtiments ou les ruines accumulées par la guerre. La ville ancienne est célèbre pour sa cathédrale où Martin Luther fut déclaré hérétique en 1521. L'autre église renommée est la Liebfrauenkirche, d'où le vin réputé Liebfraumilch tire son nom.

Liebfraumlich et Liebfrauenstift

Le 29 avril 1910 — jour néfaste dans l'histoire du vin allemand —, la Chambre de commerce de Worms décida que l'appellation Liebfraumilch pouvait désormais être utilisée par n'importe quel vin de bonne qualité fait en Rheinhessen, ce qui était le comble du paradoxe. Le Liebfraumilch est un *Qualitätswein* — vin de qualité — et peut être fait dans sa région d'origine Rheinhessen, le Rheingau, le Palatinat ou Nahe. En tant que vin de qualité (*Qualitätswein*), il doit satisfaire aux tests gouvernementaux de contrôle de qualité et sa production est déterminée précisément par la loi. Son moût doit essentiellement provenir de Riesling, Müller-Thurgau, Silvaner ou Kerner, mais aucune de ces variétés ne doit être mentionnée sur l'étiquette. Il ne doit pas être sec (trocken) ou demi-sec (halbtrocken), mais doit contenir au moins 18 g/l de sucre résiduel. Le Liebfraumilch est très ancien et demeure toujours aujourd'hui l'un des vins régionaux allemands les plus populaires. Pour toute cuvée, le résultat doit être d'une qualité aussi bonne que les composants utilisés à sa fabrication. Il est donc préférable de se fier au nom d'un producteur ou d'un expéditeur sérieux inscrit sur l'étiquette, plutôt qu'à un prix incroyablement bas. Plusieurs marques anciennes, telles Madonna, Crown of Crowns, Blue Nun, Hans Christof et Goldener Oktober pour n'en nommer que quelques-unes, offrent une bonne qualité.

Le sol du vignoble Liebsfrauenstift, qui entoure une haute église grise dans un faubourg de Worms, est plat et couvert par des alluvions qui donnent au vin un goût fade. Néanmoins, entre le XVIe et le XVIIe siècles, avant que les appellations d'origine soient d'un usage courant, le nom Liebfraumilch avait acquis petit à petit une célébrité mondiale. La production du vignoble originel, qui entoure la Liebfrauenkirche, n'a jamais dû dépasser 2 000 caisses, même l'année la plus favorable. Il n'aurait donc pas suffi à satisfaire la demande. Le nom s'étendit donc à d'autres vins. La plupart des parcelles cultivées derrière un haut mur, tout autour de l'église, appartiennent au Domaine Valckenberg et à celui de J. Langenbach, mais des petits lopins sont la propriété d'Eberhard, de W. Mahler et de E. Rieth.

Rheinriesling

Variété de Riesling cultivée en Autriche.

Rhenish

Nom que les Anglais donnaient aux vins du Rhin et, par extension, à tous ceux d'Allemagne. Il a été remplacé par Hock.

Rhin (Vins du)

Nom donné à tous les vins du Rhin en général.

Voir RHEINGAU ; RHEINHESSEN ; PALATINAT

Rhône (Côtes du)

Vins rouges, blancs et rosés. Sud de la France.

Le Rhône est un fleuve à vin. Il draine les vignobles qui s'étendent sur la vaste plaine de son delta ou s'étagent sur ses rives abruptes, au-dessus d'Avignon, en bordure des Cévennes, à l'extrémité du Jura et autour du lac Léman. Pourtant, les seuls vins qui portent son nom : Côtes du Rhône, sont ceux qui proviennent de la portion de son cours située entre Lyon et Avignon.

C'est un pays de cocagne pour la gastronomie dont Lyon passerait aisément pour une des capitales. A l'est du fleuve on élève les célèbres poulets de Bresse ; à l'extrémité sud abondent fruits et poissons et les grands restaurants servent d'excellents poulets en vessie, des quenelles de Nantua, de succulentes charcuteries et maints autres plats régionaux. Les habitants de cette région mangent de bon cœur et arrosent leurs repas d'un solide vin du Rhône ou de Beaujolais.

Les vignobles des Côtes du Rhône s'étendent sur quelque 220 km sur les rives les plus escarpées et fortement ensoleillées du fleuve. L'élément dominant du sol est le granit. Les vins doivent leurs caractéristiques à cette roche, à la forte déclivité des rives, au climat ensoleillé. Ils ne sont pas subtils, mais solides, gaillards même, et capiteux. Ils ont un parfum presque entêtant. Pour les dompter il faut leur faire subir une longue peine de bouteille. Ils rivalisent rarement en quantité et jamais en qualité avec les plus grands Bordeaux et Bourgogne, mais dans leur pleine forme ils peuvent être excellents. Pourtant le destin a voulu que ces vins, cependant nettement caractéristiques, soient souvent classés parmi les Bourgogne : confusion qui nuit aux deux régions, peut-être est-ce parce que l'extrême nord des Côtes du Rhône est proche du Beaujolais, donc du sud de la Bourgogne, et peut-être encore plus à cause de l'usage de la solide bouteille bourguignonne pour commercialiser les vins du Rhône.

Sauf les Tavel, Châteauneuf-du-Pape et Hermitage, les vins du Rhône n'étaient guère connus jusqu'à ces temps derniers. Cette situation a évolué, grâce surtout aux efforts de feu le baron Le Roy de Boiseaumarié, et désormais les vins des Côtes du Rhône se vendent hors de leur propre région. Le baron gérait son propre vignoble à Châteauneuf-du-Pape. Il fut un des fondateurs de l'I.N.A.O. et président de l'Office international du vin. Commandeur de la Légion d'honneur, il dirigea aussi l'Association des vignerons des Côtes du Rhône. Il formula lui-même les règlements qui firent des Châteauneuf-du-Pape des vins honnêtes alors que jusqu'à cette époque cette appellation était une de celles qui donnait le plus lieu à la fraude. Plus tard, il étendit son activité à tous les vins du Rhône, puis à ceux de la France entière.

La région des Côtes du Rhône est longue et étroite. Les vins diffèrent considérablement d'une extrémité à l'autre. Les progrès en viticulture et viniculture sont plus marqués ici que là, et les secteurs les plus avancés donnent évidemment de meilleurs vins. Dans son ensemble, la qualité s'est énormément améliorée au cours des dernières années, mais elle reste inégale. Bien des producteurs ont encore besoin d'être aidés, surtout dans les secteurs les moins connus. La région dans son ensemble produit en moyenne plus de 2 millions d'hl (plus de 20 millions de caisses) de vin par an, vendus sous l'appellation Côtes du Rhône. D'autres — supérieurs en qualité et quantité — sont vendus sous des noms plus précis. Les meilleurs figurent dans le tableau ci-dessous :

PRODUCTION MOYENNE

Crus	*Hl*	*Vins*
Châteauneuf-du-Pape	100 000	blancs, rouges, rosés
Condrieu	400	blancs
Cornas	2 600	blancs, rouges, rosés
Côte Rôtie	4 000	rouges, rosés
Crozes-Hermitage	72 000	blancs, rouges, rosés
Gigondas	35 000	rouges, rosés
Château Grillet	65	blancs
Hermitage	4 500	blancs, rouges, rosés
Lirac	20 000	blancs, rouges, rosés
Saint-Péray	2 000	blancs
Saint-Joseph	12 000	blancs, rouges, rosés
Tavel	30 000	rouges, rosés

Les vins secondaires de la région sont vendus sous l'appellation Côtes du Rhône parfois suivie d'une autre mention. Alors qu'en règle générale, plus l'appellation d'un vin français est précise et plus on peut espérer qu'elle couvre le produit d'un meilleur cru, il n'en est pas toujours absolument ainsi dans la région du Rhône. Si l'appellation générale est suivie du nom d'une des communes — par exemple, Vinsobres, Vacqueyras, Rasteau, et Laudun (ces quatre communes devraient d'ailleurs avoir droit assez rapidement à leur propre appellation) —, les vins seront conformes à des normes plus élevées et pourront souvent être délicieux. Mais, si la mention Côtes du Rhône est utilisée seule, les normes étant plus larges, le vin risque d'être simple et sans grand apport de qualité. Un des éléments les plus importants au sujet de ces normes, c'est la teneur minimale en alcool qui est toujours précisée, au niveau de la production pour les vins fins, en France. Elle importe toujours et encore beaucoup plus pour les vins du Rhône car l'alcool ajoute corps et rigueur : deux caractéristiques qui sont précisément celles de ces vins. Comme le Beaujolais produit le Beaujolais-Villages, le Côtes du Rhône produit également une Appellation Contrôlée plus connue appelée Côtes du Rhône-Villages, dont les meilleurs sont faits à Cairanne, Vinsobres, Chusclan, Vacqueyras, Rasteau, Laudun et Beaumes de Venise.

La plupart des meilleurs Côtes du Rhône sont faits avec une seule variété de raisin, parfois deux ou trois — à l'exception du seul Châteauneuf-du-Pape pour lequel treize variétés sont utilisées. Le cépage le plus employé est le Syrah qui donne des vins solides, bien charpentés, d'une belle couleur et d'un bon bouquet, mais inclinent à la dureté. Le Grenache Noir est lui aussi beaucoup utilisé. Le cépage blanc Viognier confère onctuosité et fraîcheur. Les autres variétés à vin blanc les plus cultivées sont le Roussanne, qui donne des vins onctueux sur les coteaux ensoleillés ; le Marsanne, raisin plus vigoureux et de meilleur rendement, plus courant que le Roussanne. Pour l'appellation générale Côtes du Rhône, les vignerons peuvent faire entrer dans la composition de leur vin n'importe lequel ou tous les cépages principaux suivants : Grenache, Clairette, Syrah, Mourvèdre, Picpoul, Terret Noir, Bourboulenc, Carignan, Roussanne, Picardan, Cinsaut, Marsanne et Viognier. Environ une dizaine de cépages accessoires sont autorisés.

Sur le Rhône les étés sont longs et presque invariablement très chauds. Les vins diffèrent donc peu d'une année à l'autre. Mais si faible qu'elle soit, cette différence est perceptible. Les meilleures années furent 1978, 1982, 1983, 1984 et 1985.

Caractéristiques des vins du Rhône

Beaumes-de-Venise. Très bon vin doux fabriqué à partir du Muscat ayant droit à sa propre appellation contrôlée. Les autres vins produits n'ont droit qu'à l'appellation Côtes du Rhône-Village.

Côte Rôtie (A.O.C.). Vins rouges, robustes et capiteux, riches en couleur. Un soupçon de violette dans le bouquet. Certains trouvent en outre une pointe de framboise dans la saveur.

Condrieu (A.O.C.). Vin blanc légèrement teinté de rose, robuste et parfumé. On en fait du sec et du demi-doux qui sont l'un et l'autre dans leur meilleure forme quand on les boit jeunes et frais. Le Condrieu est un des vins blancs préférés des Lyonnais.

Château-Grillet (Appellation contrôlée). Vin blanc, qui ressemble au Condrieu. Il est robuste et vigoureux, peut-être avec un peu plus de finesse que le Condrieu. Étant donné que la production est très faible, on voit rarement ce vin hors de sa région.

Hermitage (Appellation Contrôlée). Rouge, charnu et vigoureux, avec une certaine délicatesse et du moelleux quand il est mûr. Le bouquet a une fragrance d'iris. Il vieillit bien. Le blanc a une teinte dorée. Il est sec et fruité, avec un parfum caractéristique et peut durer longtemps sans madériser.

Crozes-Hermitage (Appellation Contrôlée). Vin rouge dont la teinte plutôt violette est moins profonde que celle de l'Hermitage dont il n'a pas non plus le moelleux. Léger goût de terroir. Une faible quantité de blancs est aussi produite en Appellation Contrôlée.

Saint-Joseph (A.O.C.). Les rouges sont délicats et parfumés, d'une belle couleur rubis, mais moins corsés que les Hermitage. Ils sont prêts à la consommation au bout de quelques années de bouteille. Les blancs sont plus légers que ceux de l'Hermitage.

Cornas (A.O.C.). Vin rouge, un peu dur au début, d'un beau grenat. Il vieillit bien et devient moelleux et velouté à sa maturité, mais jamais aussi parfumé que l'Hermitage.

Saint-Péray (A.O.C.). Blanc corsé, plein d'esprit, de belle couleur avec un bouquet

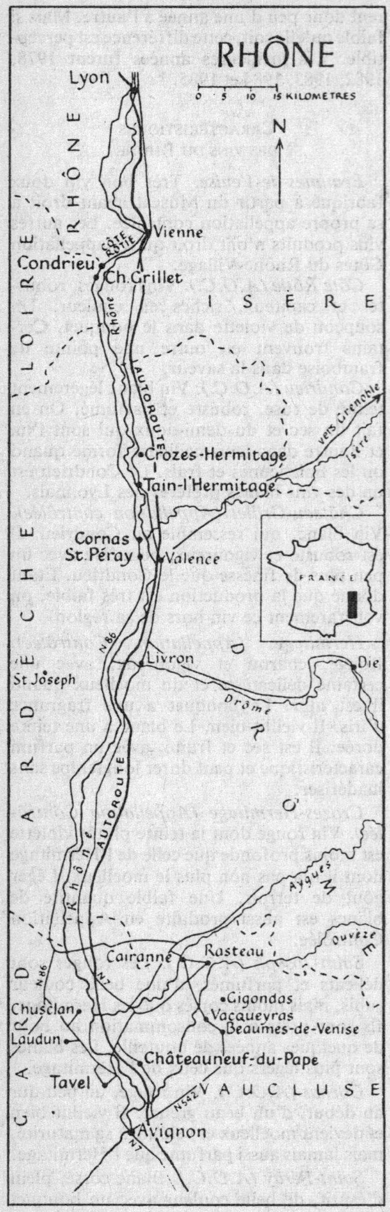

caractéristique. En vieillissant il madérise parfois prématurément. Certains sont faits en mousseux sec ou demi-sec.

Clairette de Die (A.O.C.). Blanc légèrement mousseux fait avec des raisins Clairette et Muscat, autour de Die, sur la Drôme.

Châteauneuf-du-Pape (Appellation Contrôlée). Ce vin, très connu, est corsé, d'une couleur foncée, plus souple et à maturation plus rapide que la plupart des vins du Rhône. Il existe aussi un Château-neuf-du-Pape blanc agréable mais moins intéressant.

Tavel (A.O.C.). Un des meilleurs rosés de France. Fait surtout avec du raisin Grenache. Rose clair, sans la moindre teinte d'orange, léger et rafraîchissant. Doit être frappé.

Vaucluse et *Gard*. Provenant de sols divers, les vins de ces deux départements appartiennent à des types très différents. En général, les vignes plantées en terrasses sur du sol argileux et pierreux, sont destinées aux rosés. Ceux de Lirac et de Chusclan ne sont guère inférieurs au Tavel. Laudun fait des vins blancs ainsi que des rosés et des rouges. Gigondas, Cairanne et Vacqueyras produisent des vins souples, d'un fort degré d'alcool. Ils sont rouges, blancs ou rosés. Beaumes-de-Venise et Rasteau sont des vins de dessert (*voir* VINS VINÉS DE FRANCE).

Rhum

Le rhum est obtenu par distillation de canne à sucre fermentée. Parmi tous les spiritueux, c'est celui qui conserve le plus le goût du produit distillé. Les eaux-de-vie dérivant de l'amidon, comme la vodka de pomme de terre et le whisky de céréales, doivent être cuits ou maltés. Dans le cas du rhum, fait à partir du sucre, il est inutile de transformer l'amidon en sucre. La distillation du rhum n'a pas besoin d'être très poussée comme celle du gin ou de la vodka. C'est l'alcool qui subit le moins d'opérations chimiques. On peut le mettre à vieillir dans des fûts qui ont déjà servi, parce qu'il n'a pas besoin du tanin que le chêne donne à d'autres alcools, comme le Cognac, par exemple. On peut ajouter au rhum divers éléments pour modifier son goût, mais ce n'est pas indispensable. On peut aussi l'additionner d'eau, mais ce n'est pas nécessaire et, quand il s'agit d'un bon rhum, mieux vaut ne pas le faire. Il peut être aussi incolore que l'eau ou d'une teinte qui va de l'ambre à l'acajou. Le seul colorant qu'on lui ajoute est le caramel, qui ne modifie en rien son goût. Les véritables caractéristiques du rhum sont déterminées par les facteurs suivants :

La matière dont il est fait

La grande majorité des rhums est faite avec de la mélasse : résidu incristallisable qui reste après la formation du sucre ; parfois, il est fait directement avec le jus du sucre de canne, ou avec des mélasses de seconde catégorie et autres résidus. Ce dernier type est généralement appelé *tafia* plutôt que rhum, et vaut rarement la peine d'être exporté ou même d'être mis en bouteille. Les rhums les plus fins sont faits avec de la mélasse, à quelques exceptions près ; ainsi, l'un des meilleurs rhums de Haïti est fait directement avec du jus de canne, quant au rhum martiniquais, il est obtenu par la distillation de ce jus concentré en sirop.

Modification du goût en fait de rhum

On appréciait surtout autrefois les rhums corsés au goût riche et nettement tranché. Depuis trente-cinq ans le goût des consommateurs du monde entier a évolué. Bien des gens préfèrent désormais le rhum plus léger, au goût plus subtil et d'un arôme plus délicat. On le distille donc de plus en plus dans des appareils à colonne.

Fermentation lente ou rapide

La fermentation d'un rhum de type léger peut être achevée en douze heures. En général elle dure entre un jour et un jour et demi. La Jamaïque et quelques autres pays produisent actuellement une bonne quantité de rhum léger. Mais Porto Rico et Cuba en sont les principaux producteurs depuis longtemps. Après fermentation lente on obtient un rhum plus lourd par addition de *dunder* (dépôt resté au fond de l'alambic après distillation). Ceux qui préfèrent le rhum savoureux au goût nettement distinctif prétendent que les autres ont une saveur de lait écrémé. La fermentation lente peut durer jusqu'à douze jours. Les rhums des types Wedderburn et Plummer, qui sont des produits traditionnels de la Jamaïque, résultent de la fermentation lente. Ceux de la Martinique, dits « de grand arôme », sont aussi des breuvages lourds obtenus par fermentation lente.

Enfin, les rhums à haute teneur en esters sont faits de la même façon que les Wedderburn en poussant plus loin la recherche de ces substances.

Type de levures

Les levures utilisées pour la fermentation du rhum sont cultivées ou naturelles. Il est essentiel, dit-on, que la recette des levures cultivées reste secrète pour en préserver toute l'individualité. Un certain producteur de rhum à Haïti est convaincu que le succès de sa production est dû à la parfaite harmonie entre la canne et la levure qu'il emploie parce qu'elles sont de la même origine. De même, tous les distillateurs de Porto Rico sont convaincus unanimement que les vertus de leur rhum (magnifique ! disent-ils) sont dues aux lignées de levures que chacun cultive.

Distillation en alambic ou en appareil à colonne

Comme le whisky, le rhum peut être distillé soit en alambic, soit en appareil à distillation continue. Ce dernier convient mieux aux rhums légers qui sont de plus en plus demandés. Le rhum d'alambic conserve plus des éléments de la matière première. Il est plus lourd, et comme on peut toujours l'additionner d'eau, il convient à tout le monde.

Notons que le vieux rhum de la Jamaïque est le type même de l'alcool corsé provenant de l'alambic.

Teneur en alcool, à la distillation

Si étrange que cela paraisse, plus le rhum est léger, plus sa distillation est poussée. A la sortie de l'alambic, celui de la Jamaïque par exemple, titre 96° ; alors que les rhums plus corsés du même pays ne sont distillés qu'à 86°.

Appellations d'origine

Ce sujet est assez confus. Aux États-Unis, l'administration fédérale des alcools a décrété que « Porto Rico, Cuba, Demerara, La Barbade, Sainte-Croix, Saint-Thomas, les îles Vierges, La Jamaïque, La Martinique, La Trinité, Haïti et Saint-Domingue ne désignent pas des types de rhum ». Sans être des appellations générales, ces noms n'en conservent pas moins leur signification géographique. Ils ne peuvent donc pas être donnés à des rhums produits ailleurs que dans les régions ou pays indiqués par ce nom. Or chaque centre de production fait des rhums de type différent, et certains types s'identifient avec certains pays. Aujourd'hui encore, la Jamaïque s'identifie avec un rhum lourd et savoureux quoiqu'elle produise de nos jours des alcools plus légers. A l'inverse, les rhums légers sont attribués à Porto Rico et à Cuba, bien que ces deux îles produisent des alcools d'autre type. Les différences qui existent entre les divers rhums résultent des méthodes de préparation, du sol, du climat et encore plus de l'eau.

Origine du Rhum

A l'origine, le rhum était déjà ce qu'il est resté foncièrement : l'alcool des Indes occidentales, provenant de la canne à sucre et de l'eau dévalant des montagnes. Il se pourrait que la canne à sucre ait été importée des Açores aux Antilles par Christophe Colomb lors de son second voyage. La première trace écrite du rhum à la Barbade date de 1600, et voici la description d'un bol à faire du punch au rhum aux Indes occidentales, au XVIIIe siècle :

« Un bassin de marbre, construit au milieu d'un jardin dans ce but précis, tel est le bol. On y versa 1 200 bouteilles de Rhum, 1 200 bouteilles de vin de Malaga, 500 l d'eau bouillante auxquels on ajouta 300 kg du meilleur sucre de canne et 200 kg de noix muscades pulvérisées. Puis on y pressa 2 600 citrons. On lança à la surface un joli canot d'acajou manœuvré par un gamin de douze ans qui rama pendant quelque temps puis accosta afin de servir les 600 convives, lesquels absorbèrent l'océan sur lequel il flottait. »

Le rhum jouissait d'une énorme popularité aux colonies anglaises d'Amérique avant 1775. Elles en consommaient 450 000 hl par an, soit plus de 18 l par tête, alors que de nos jours la consommation s'élève à 6 l par personne, tous spiritueux compris. Selon un historien, la loi britannique de 1763, conçue pour amener les Américains à abandonner les rhums des Antilles espagnoles en faveur des produits britanniques, provoqua l'insurrection des colonies. Cette hypothèse ne plaît pas à tous. Pourtant est-il tellement plus noble de se révolter pour une affaire de thé que pour une affaire de rhum ? L'histoire de Paul Revere, telle qu'on l'enseigne aux enfants des États-Unis, est amputée d'un détail. Revere commença sa chevauchée en silence et le cœur serré. Puis il s'arrêta chez un distillateur de rhum nommé Isaac Hall, capitaine de Minute Men, et but deux bonnes rasades de rhum. C'est seulement ensuite qu'il se mit à hurler à tue-tête que les Habits-Rouges arrivaient. George Washington fut à coup sûr lancé par le rhum. Il fut élu en 1758, non à la suite d'une campagne électorale, mais parce qu'il avait distribué 340 l de rhum aux électeurs de la Virginia House de Burgesses, ce qui lui valut d'être envoyé plus tard au Continental Congress.

Le rhum servait pratiquement de monnaie d'échange dans le trafic des esclaves. Les marchands de « bois d'ébène » quittaient les Antilles avec un chargement de rhum. Cet alcool apparaît dans toutes les histoires de pirates (« Quinze hommes sur le coffre d'un mort / yo-ho-ho ! et une bouteille de rhum ! ») Entre 1920 et 1930, le rhum revint à la piraterie lorsque des vedettes rapides transportaient en contrebande l'alcool de Cuba jusqu'à la pointe de la Floride,

Quand la prohibition fut abrogée aux États-Unis, les Américains contractèrent l'habitude de boire divers mélanges de rhum agrémentés de tranches de fruits et servis glacés. Cette mode survit, mais on emploie en général des rhums de marque.

Les procédés de distillation sont à peu près les mêmes pour le rhum que pour le whisky, sauf que la matière première n'a pas besoin d'être maltée (*voir* DISTILLATION, GIN, WHISKY).

D'une manière générale, les Britanniques boivent le rhum de leurs anciennes colonies des Antilles, les Français celui de leurs départements d'outre-mer. Les États-Unis importent surtout de Porto Rico, moins des îles Vierges, encore beaucoup moins de la Jamaïque et des Barbades et des quantités minimes des Antilles françaises, de Haïti et d'autres îles.

Voir RHUM : PORTO RICO ; RHUM : JAMAIQUE ; RHUM : INDES OCCIDENTALES ; RHUM : ANTILLES FRANÇAISES ; RHUM : HAITI ; RHUM : MARTINIQUE, ETC.

Rhum : La Barbade

Les magnifiques îles-jardins antillaises, ou Windward Islands, sont composées de calcaire, corail, cendres volcaniques : mélange qui donne au sol un caractère poreux convenant très bien à la culture de la canne à sucre. Quoique le climat y soit idéal, le manque de cours d'eau rend l'irrigation nécessaire, on procède par pompage de nappes souterraines.

La canne à sucre étant la principale production de ces îles, on y fait beaucoup de rhum. On en produit même de plus en plus et les exportations s'accroissent encore plus rapidement. Les dernières statistiques dénotent une élévation d'un tiers jusqu'à un chiffre de plus de 30 000 hl (plus de 530 000 caisses) de rhum.

Le rhum de la Barbade est fait à partir de mélasse, sous-produit de la fabrication du sucre, soit en alambic, soit en appareil à distillation continue. Assez légers comme corps et comme teinte, ils ont une saveur onctueuse avec une touche de fumé ou de cuir. Il y a 5 distilleries : Hanschell Inness (Cockspur Rum) ; West India Rum Refinery, Alleyne, Arthur & Hunt, R.L. Seale & Co. et Mt. Gay Distillers. Certains vieux rhums de cette dernière firme peuvent être bus secs comme les bonnes eaux-de-vie de vin.

Rhum : Cuba

Le rhum léger et délectable de Cuba est la boisson courante des Cubains, qui tiennent à la légèreté. La distillation et le vieillissement de l'alcool sont faits selon des méthodes tendant à obtenir cette qualité. On le traite même avec du charbon de bois pour le rendre plus léger.

Canne à sucre, levure, eau limpide des torrents dévalant des montagnes composent les bons rhums antillais. Ceux de Cuba et de Porto Rico sont généralement faits avec de la mélasse — sous-produit de la fabrication du sucre de canne — fermentée avec des levures cultivées et, enfin, avec de l'eau pure. Souvent le rhum cubain est traité par coupage avec des spiritueux plus âgés et filtré au sable pendant sa maturation.

Cuba produit deux types de rhum : Carta Blanca (étiquette blanche) qui était la base des cocktails Daiquiri, et Carta Oro (étiquette d'or) auquel on ajoute du caramel pour lui donner une couleur moelleuse ; il est donc un peu plus foncé et plus doux que le Carta Blanca. Les meilleurs rhums provenaient des environs de Santiago, au sud de l'île. Avant la prise du pouvoir par Fidel Castro, voici quels étaient les principaux distillateurs : Compañia Ron Bacardi, Alvarez Camp y Co, Santiago ; Arechabaia, Cadenas, Matanzas. Désormais toute exportation vers les pays occidentaux a cessé, une bonne partie du rhum cubain est maintenant exportée en U.R.S.S. et ses satellites.

Rhum : Demerara

Nom du rhum exporté de Guyane (ancienne Guyane britannique).

Voir RHUM : GUYANE

Rhum français

On a toujours bu du rhum en France, où sa consommation s'accroît. Les Français consomment surtout celui des Antilles françaises et, dans une moindre mesure, de l'île de la Réunion. Hormis deux ou trois marques de la Martinique, ces rhums sont rarement exportés vers d'autres pays que la France et ne figurent donc pas sur le marché mondial.

Antilles françaises

La Martinique et la Guadeloupe fournissent une grande quantité de rhums corsés dont certains de bonne classe. Si l'on se rappelle que ces îles ne sont pas des colonies, protectorats ou territoires soumis à la France, mais des départements français au même titre que la Gironde et les Bouches-du-Rhône, on comprendra que les rhums des Antilles soient consommés en France de préférence aux autres. Des deux îles, la Martinique (*voir* RHUM : LA MARTINIQUE) est celle qui compte le plus au point de vue du rhum.

La Réunion

Comme la Martinique et la Guadeloupe, la Réunion est un département français, mais de l'océan Indien, au large de Madagascar. En fait de spiritueux elle ne fabrique que du rhum dont la production s'est beaucoup accrue récemment : 100 000 hl (plus d'un million de caisses) par an. Il s'agit de rhum blanc, qui n'a donc guère vieilli. Mais la Réunion exporte aussi une petite quantité de rhum plus coloré, vieilli en fût.

Guyane française

Dans ce département français de l'Amérique du Sud, deux distilleries — Prévot et Mirande — produisent chaque année un peu moins de 7 500 hl (plus de 80 000 caisses) d'un rhum blanc sans distinction particulière. La Guyane ne produit aucun autre spiritueux.

Rhum : Guyane

L'ancienne Guyane britannique produit deux types de rhum, l'un par distillation continue, l'autre en alambic.

La caractéristique distinctive du rhum de la Guyane est sa fermentation rapide : généralement de 36 à 40 heures.

Outre le rhum d'exportation, la Guyane en produit pour la consommation de ses 400 000 habitants. En général, ce rhum n'est consommé qu'après macération de divers fruits et épices dans le produit d'une distillation continue. On teinte ensuite légèrement le distillat avec du caramel et on le met en bouteille vers 43°. Le produit qui résulte de ces opérations est moins corsé que le Demerara, beaucoup plus connu à l'étranger. Le Courantin se rencontre parfois en Angleterre. C'est aussi un rhum fruité et épicé, dans le genre de celui que consomment les Guyanais.

Le Demerara, qui porte le nom du cours d'eau le long duquel on cultive la canne à sucre, est le rhum le plus exporté par la Guyane.

On le fait, en alambic ou en appareil à distillation continue, avec de la mélasse. Il fermente spontanément dans des cuves de bois. On y ajoute une quantité infime d'acide sulfurique pour tuer les bactéries et un peu de sulfate d'ammonium pour nourrir les levures. Le Demerara a généralement une couleur foncée, qu'il doit au caramel fait en brûlant de la canne à sucre. Il n'est pas aussi lourd que la suggérerait sa couleur. En raison de la fermentation rapide, il n'a pas une saveur aussi prononcée que les rhums à fermentation lente.

Certains Demerara sont distillés en alambic et conservent un tiers de plus d'esters : substances qui donnent le goût. Ils titrent aussi deux fois plus.

Le Demerara exporté titre environ 82°. La Guyane est le principal producteur de rhum des pays d'influence britannique de la mer des Antilles.

Rhum : Haïti

La canne à sucre pousse partout sur l'île d'Haïti, mais c'est seulement dans le nord, au-delà du petit port de Cap-Haïtien, qu'on trouve les cannes convenant le mieux à la fabrication d'un rhum de première catégorie. Une chaîne de montagnes court parallèlement à la côte et, au-delà, dans les vallées, la pluie est moins abondante qu'ailleurs. La citadelle de l'Empereur Noir Henri Christophe — qui perdit la raison et se suicida avec une balle d'argent — jaillit vers le ciel, dominant les équipes de coupeurs de canne qui balancent en cadence leurs *machettes* en s'accompagnant d'un chant rythmé.

Il y a plus d'un siècle et demi, Haïti se révolta et se libéra de la France. Néanmoins, traditions, attitudes, coutumes sont encore nettement françaises et l'adresse avec laquelle les Français font de bons alcools continue à se faire sentir dans les rhums du pays. Ils sont produits par deux distillations successives en alambic, exactement comme le Cognac. Toutefois, le rhum de première distillation est souvent vendu à bon marché, mais jamais exporté. Il est tout à fait incolore, d'où son nom : Clairin.

Les jours de fête à Haïti, ce rhum est vendu frais, au verre, sur des petits stands dressés le long des rues et des routes, éclairés par des lampes qui brillent comme des étoiles. Les Haïtiens croient que le Clairin a la vertu de rendre propices les divinités vaudou. C'est pourquoi, et aussi peut-être parce qu'il est bon marché, l'on en verse sur le sol lors des cérémonies de ce culte. La majorité des habitants de cette île adorent encore les divinités africaines introduites par les esclaves et leur offrent quelques gorgées de leur boisson favorite avant de boire.

Le Barbancourt est le rhum d'Haïti le plus connu et aussi l'un des meilleurs du monde. Modérément corsé, il est équilibré de manière exquise. Selon M. Jean Gardère, qui fabrique le Barbancourt, sa qualité serait due, dans une certaine mesure, à la levure naturelle de la zone où l'on cultive les cannes qui servent à le faire. Cette origine commune de la canne et de la levure, ainsi que le sol et les méthodes de fabrication ont une influence subtile sur le jus de canne et la levure, d'où l'harmonie qui règne visiblement dans ce rhum.

Le jus de canne, pasteurisé pour paralyser ses vitamines naturelles pendant la distillation, est traité aussitôt après le pressurage des cannes et il ne produit pas de fermentation secondaire. La distillerie qui produit le Barbancourt — et qui fut fondée en 1862 — a actuellement une capacité atteignant environ 25 000 hl (plus de 250 000 caisses). On y fait du rhum Trois-Étoiles et Cinq-Étoiles de réserve. Autrefois, le dernier n'était vendu qu'à Haïti, mais désormais on les exporte tous.

Jusqu'à l'indépendance d'Haïti, la France était le marché du rhum de cette colonie et les importations françaises atteignirent jusqu'à près de 700 000 hl (près de 8 millions de caisses). Actuellement, le rhum de la Martinique domine le marché français. Selon Jean Gardère, les liens qui persistent entre Haïti et la France sont dus à une parenté de sol : le calcaire sur un fond sédimentaire qui donne le rhum d'Haïti est pratiquement identique à celui des meilleurs produits vineux de France : Cognac et Champagne.

Voici les principaux distillateurs de rhum à Haïti :

Propriétaire	*Marque du rhum*	*Distillerie*
Jean Gardère	Barbancourt	Damiens (Port-au-Prince)
Hermann Colas	Citadelle	Cazeau (Port-au-Prince)
Max Nazon	Nazon	Port-au-Prince
Raymond Nazon	Larue	Cap-Haïtien

Rhum : West Indies (Indes occidentales)

Anciennes possessions britanniques, la Barbade, La Jamaïque, la Guyane et Trinidad constituent cet ensemble situé dans la mer des Antilles ou des Caraïbes. Il produit environ 7 millions de *proof gallons* de rhum par an. La Barbade et la Jamaïque en font environ 1,5 million chacune ; Trinidad et la Guyane, environ 2 millions. Le principal exportateur (environ 1,5 million de gallons) est la Guyane, suivie par la Jamaïque (1 million), la Barbade (700 000) et Trinidad (300 000). Le rhum est la boisson traditionnelle de la marine britannique. D'après les archives, un équipage de sir George Summer se réfugia aux Bermudes en 1609 pour échapper à un ouragan et s'y consola en buvant des « eaux confortantes », autrement dit, du rhum. Pendant la guerre d'Indépendance des États-Unis, l'armée anglaise consomma des centaines de milliers de gallons de rhum. Depuis le XVIIe siècle jusqu'à nos jours, les marins de la Royal Navy ont droit à une ration quotidienne de rhum.

Voir RHUM : LA JAMAIQUE ; LA BARBADE ; GUYANE ; TRINIDAD

Rhum : la Jamaïque

Aucun producteur de rhum n'a été aussi durement touché par la récente évolution des goûts que ne le fut la Jamaïque. Par tradition, cette île produisait un rhum lourd, riche en saveur, obtenu par fermentation lente et distillation peu poussée en alambic, puis addition de *dunder (voir ce mot).*

Aujourd'hui encore, bien que les rhums de la Jamaïque aient encore tendance à présenter une saveur et un arôme plus caractérisés que les autres, ils sont plus légers qu'autrefois et dans cette île on a abandonné la méthode de la fermentation lente. Les rhums de la Jamaïque peuvent être divisés en quatre catégories : 1. légers, obtenus par distillation continue et appelés *Common Clean* ; 2. légers et moyennement corsés, distillés en alambic ; 3. Wedderburn et Plummer, plus lourds ; 4. rhums à forte teneur en esters.

Ceux de la première catégorie sont faits avec de la mélasse, en appareil à distillation continue, comportant deux ou trois colonnes. Leur distillation est parfois poussée jusqu'à 96°. On prend grand soin de ne pas éliminer les véritables composants du rhum subsistant dans les résidus.

Ceux de la deuxième catégorie sont faits à partir d'un mélange de jus de canne, de mélasse de première qualité, d'eau et d'acides. La distillation en alambic permet de conserver saveur et odeur de la canne.

Les Wedderburn et Plummer ont plus de corps que les deux précédents. Ils sont faits selon les méthodes traditionnelles et quiconque désire savourer un véritable Jamaïque, robuste comme ceux d'autrefois, doit goûter un de ces deux-là. Leur distillation en alambic est poussée jusqu'à 86° en général.

Les rhums à haute teneur en esters sont fermentés et distillés à peu près de la même manière que les Wedderburn, mais leur teneur en esters doit être plus élevée.

La majeure partie de la production jamaïcaine (et des autres rhums des Antilles autrefois britanniques) était envoyée en fûts à Londres pour y vieillir et c'est là-bas qu'avait lieu la mise en bouteille. Cette opération a toujours lieu mais est de moins en moins effectuée.

Rhum : London Dock

Nom donné au rhum des Indes occidentales autrefois britanniques, expédié en gros à Londres pour vieillir et mûrir dans les entrepôts des quais.

Rhum : la Martinique

La grosse production de rhum martiniquais soit plus de 90 000 hl (1 million de caisses) par an se répartit approximativement ainsi : 55 % faits à partir de mélasses et 45 % par la distillation du jus de canne à sucre.

On compte à peu près cent grandes plantations de canne à sucre et 14 grandes distilleries. Le chef-lieu, Fort-de-France, est typiquement une ville de rhum. La place poussiéreuse sur laquelle se dresse la statue de Joséphine de Beauharnais est bordée sur toute la longueur d'un de ses côtés par des bureaux et magasins d'expéditeurs de rhum où les caisses s'empilent jusqu'au plafond. Le principal bassin du port s'engage étrangement dans la ville et les superstructures des transatlantiques en croisière se dressent au milieu des maisons de manière incongrue, comme sur une avenue maritime. De temps en temps, on voyait s'élever paresseusement des volutes de vapeur au-dessus d'un cargo qui allait emporter du rhum à l'autre bout du monde.

Jusqu'au début du XXe siècle, la Martinique s'enorgueillissait d'une capitale fort différente de la clinquante et chaotique Fort-de-France : Saint-Pierre, la ville la plus riche de toutes les Antilles. On en voit encore les ruines : belles rues pavées dans lesquelles courent désormais, en bouillonnant et chantant, les ruisseaux qui dévalent de la montagne ; maisons écrasées sur lesquelles poussent bananiers sauvages, vignes et manguiers. En quelques secondes, une éruption de la montagne Pelée toute proche effaça cette ville et ses 40 000 habitants. Dans cette désolation, quelques firmes se sont réinstallées à Saint-Pierre, le long d'une plage de sable volcanique noir. Les plantations du rhum Saint-James, un des mieux connus du monde, sont à proximité.

Si quelque 50 distillateurs font du rhum, on raconte à la Martinique que cette industrie appartient à dix familles. Voilà une trentaine d'années, cette situation aboutit à un événement probablement unique dans l'histoire : « la grève des dix familles ». Les propriétaires de plantations estimaient alors que les impôts trop élevés les ruinaient. Quand les cannes arrivèrent à maturité, l'unique récolte de l'île était prête à être traitée. Les représentants des dix familles déclarèrent aux députés et au préfet : « Nous nous mettons en grève. Nous, nous pouvons subsister des années sans profits. Croyez-vous que l'État puisse en faire autant ? Sans sucre ni rhum, il n'y aura pas d'impôts. Il serait donc temps de nous entendre sur des bases raisonnables. »

Les rhums faits à partir du jus de canne à sucre sont parfois additionnés de *dunder* (résidu qui reste dans l'alambic après distillation et qu'on traite généralement par fermentation lente) mais pas toujours. Ceux qui ne se colorent pas par vieillissement en fût sont appelés : Grappe Blanche. On les consomme surtout dans l'île et ils servent à faire le célèbre punch de la Martinique.

Ce punch martiniquais est probablement d'origine britannique. En voici la recette : rhum, sirop de canne à sucre et un zeste de citron. Mais les prix ont changé. En exportant vers la France du sirop de canne à sucre, la maison Duquesne a rendu le punch martiniquais populaire dans la métropole.

Un seul rhum de la Martinique est fait à base de *dunder* fermenté pour 60 % et de sirop de jus de canne concentré pour le reste. C'est le rhum Saint-James, vendu dans des bouteilles à section carrée, bien connues. Sa couleur foncée et son arôme le distinguent d'à peu près tous les autres.

Les rhums faits avec de la mélasse fermentent avec le *dunder* et sont colorés au caramel. Le plus coté de ce genre s'appelle Grand Arôme (utilisé pour parfumer). Il est préparé par fermentation lente qui dure de huit à douze jours. Lourds et riches, ils soutiennent la comparaison avec ceux du genre Wedderburn faits à la Jamaïque.

Bien des gens considéraient le rhum Clément, blanc ou noir, comme le prince des produits de la Martinique. Proche de l'agglomération nommée François, la distillerie n'avait aucune prétention. On y apportait la canne dans des wagonnets poussés par des ouvriers noirs sur des chemins de fer à voie étroite, ou tirés par une petite locomotive. Un tapis roulant les entraînait vers les rouleaux qui les écrasaient. Le jus épais s'écoulait dans des cuves et les cannes pressurées glissaient dans un toboggan. Le jus obtenu par ce procédé était transformé en rhum de diverses qualités. M. Charles Clément — petit homme pimpant et des plus charmants — expliquait personnellement que les meilleurs vieillissaient jusqu'à douze ans en fût.

Le rhum Duquesne — autre bonne marque — était distillé au sud de l'île. Une partie — le rhum blanc — était vendue sous la marque Genippa ; le reste, vieilli en entrepôt, sous l'appellation Grand'Case (étiquette d'argent, 3 ans d'âge) et « Val d'Or » (étiquette dorée, 10 ans). L'entreprise Duquesne était une affaire de famille dirigée par M.O. des Grottes.

Les rhums obtenus par distillation de la mélasse sont toujours faits dans des distilleries proches de grandes raffineries de sucre. Il n'y en a pas beaucoup. Les distilleries qui traitent le jus de canne sont plus nombreuses.

Rhum : Nouvelle-Angleterre

Le rhum, surtout le rhum fort, lourd, cordial, fut un des éléments qui contribuèrent à la formation de la Nouvelle-Angleterre. Connecticut, Rhode Island et Massachusetts importaient la mélasse des Indes occidentales et en faisaient du rhum, vendu dans les tavernes du nord des futurs États-Unis et expédié vers celles du sud par des bateaux qui ramenaient coton et tabac. Ces colonies exportaient aussi vers l'Europe en échange des marchandises que le Nouveau Monde n'était pas encore à même de fabriquer.

Un des aspects les plus intéressants de ce commerce fut son caractère « triangulaire » qui fit la fortune de bien des armateurs et capitaines de navire de Nouvelle-Angleterre. Les bateaux emportaient le rhum d'Amérique vers l'Afrique, en ramenaient des esclaves qui servaient à payer la mélasse aux Indes occidentales et cette mélasse revenait en Nouvelle-Angleterre pour être convertie en rhum. Les tentatives que fit George III pour taxer la mélasse donnèrent de la vigueur à l'esprit d'indépendance tout autant que la taxe du timbre. C'est devant des verres de rhum, dans les tavernes, qu'on s'enflamma contre « la taxation sans représentation ». Le rhum de la Nouvelle-Angleterre représentait, il y a plus d'un siècle, la plus grosse industrie de spiritueux des États-Unis. On le fait toujours dans l'État du Massachusetts où on en vend environ 7 500 hl (plus de 80 000 caisses) par an. C'est un rhum lourd, très savoureux et corsé. Distillé à 80°, il vieillit dans des barriques de chêne roussies au feu. Ce procédé lui donne sa couleur foncée. Il n'existe plus que trois fabricants de rhum en Nouvelle-Angleterre de nos jours.

En outre, on trouve encore de magnifiques vieux rhums dans les caves personnelles des vieilles familles de Nouvelle-Angleterre. Au goût, ils soutiennent la comparaison avec les vieux bourbons américains et les Cognac français.

État relativement peu peuplé, le New Hampshire se distingue par la plus forte consommation par tête, de rhum, de tous les États-Unis.

Rhum : Panay

Voir RHUM : PHILIPPINES

Rhum : Philippines

Les Philippines produisent deux marques distinctes de rhum qui portent le nom de deux îles de cet archipel : Tanduay et Panay. Ils ont un goût différent. Le Tanduay se vend considérablement plus que l'autre et il est aussi plus cher.

Rhum : Porto Rico

Porto Rico est le premier producteur de rhum du monde entier. 70 % du rhum consommé aux États-Unis proviennent de cette île. Il se présente en deux types : White Label (étiquette blanche) très légèrement corsé et Gold Label (étiquette d'or) à peine moins léger. Les États-Unis absorbent environ trois fois plus de White Label que de Gold Label, alors qu'à Porto Rico la production est inverse. Cependant les Portoricains en consomment moins car ils disposent de variétés à meilleur marché telles que Palo Viejo et Ron Llave.

Cuba *(voir* RHUM : CUBA), célèbre aussi pour ses rhums légers, produit également ces deux types : étiquette blanche et étiquette d'or.

L'économie portoricaine a toujours dépendu de la canne à sucre dont la récolte est riche et abondante sur cette île. L'industrie du rhum lui doit son existence. Le premier gouverneur de l'île, Ponce de Léon, distilla la canne à sucre. Une dépêche de 1526 signale déjà que les indigènes s'enivrent avec du rhum. Ce Ponce de Léon était un homme d'affaires. Un historien va jusqu'à dire qu'en prétendant chercher la fontaine de Jouvence, il ne s'intéressait qu'à un distillat négociable.

Le raffinage de la canne à sucre donne du sucre et, comme sous-produit : la mélasse. Les rhums de Porto Rico sont obtenus en distillant cette mélasse fermentée, grâce à l'addition de levures cultivées et d'eau de montagne. Ils vieillissent sous contrôle du gouvernement et sont expédiés en bouteille. Pendant la dernière guerre, le whisky manqua aux États-Unis. On fit alors à Porto Rico des rhums de toute sorte et pas toujours bons. Les Américains consommèrent même du mauvais rhum portoricain. Après la guerre, ces produits de mauvaise qualité devinrent invendables et pesèrent sur le marché. C'est alors que des lois strictes assurèrent la haute qualité des rhums exportés avec l'estampille de l'île. Le gouvernement dirige lui-même une distillerie modèle par le truchement de l'université de Porto Rico. C'est le seul endroit où un programme de ce genre ait été subventionné par le gouvernement.

Le rhum de Porto Rico est généralement assez léger, peu corsé et sec, contrairement aux produits plus épais et aromatiques de la Martinique. En général, la mélasse fermente grâce à des levures de culture et on la distille dans des appareils à colonnes.

Les distilleries sont largement dispersées sur l'île, sous des climats nettement différents. Ici pluies constantes, là sécheresse permanente. Le sol varie aussi. Enfin, chaque distillateur cultive sa propre levure à partir d'une cellule unique. Ces facteurs contribuent aux caractéristiques de chaque marque. Tous les manufacturiers cultivent constamment des levures afin d'en avoir toujours suffisamment pour leurs opérations quotidiennes et surtout pour que la lignée ne s'éteigne pas. A Porto Rico, on considère cette activité comme un des secrets du rhum. Levure, sol et climat, imposent au rhum leur marque indélébile. De même que les dégustateurs de vin français, certains connaisseurs de rhum se targuent de pouvoir dire exactement d'où vient le breuvage dont ils ont goûté un verre.

Au temps de la prohibition, nombre d'anciennes distilleries cessèrent de fonctionner. Citons parmi les exceptions la Puerto Rican Distilling Company, qui fabrique le Ronrico, en général léger quoique certains, titrant 75°, soient plus lourdement corsés.

Actuellement, 14 distilleries fonctionnent légalement à Porto Rico. La Distileria Bacardi se vante d'avoir la plus grosse capacité de production du monde entier. Voici, dans l'ordre alphabétique, le nom des marques les plus exportées : Bacardi, Boca Chica Carioca, Don Q, Maraca, Merito, Ronrico.

Rhum : Tanduay

Un des principaux types de rhum fait aux Philippines.

Voir RHUM : PHILIPPINES

Rhum : Trinidad (La Trinité)

Les rhums de cette île, d'un type assez léger, sont obtenus par la distillation de la mélasse en appareil à colonnes. Avant fermentation, la mélasse est diluée dans l'eau et clarifiée, ce qui permet de mieux contrôler la fermentation. On y ajoute de la levure. La conversion en alcool est achevée en 36 ou 48 heures. Le rhum qui en résulte est sain mais moins distingué que ceux des autres types. La distillation est poussée jusqu'à 83 et même 96°.

Rhum : îles Vierges

Le rhum des îles Vierges est généralement de type moyen : un peu plus lourd que celui de Porto Rico. La plus grande partie est exportée en fûts. Sainte-Croix convient mieux à la canne à sucre que Saint-Thomas et Saint-John, et par conséquent à la production du rhum. Saint-Thomas est fort petite : quelques pitons rocheux se dressant sur la mer des Antilles. Sainte-Croix, beaucoup plus vaste, consiste presque uniquement en un chapelet de superbes plages entourant un immense champ de canne à sucre. Les rhums de cette île portent l'appellation Cruzan, mention qui figure fréquemment sur les étiquettes. La distillerie appartient au gouvernement local et fonctionne en régie directe.

Ribeauvillé

Agglomération vinicole d'Alsace *(voir ce nom).*

Ricard

Apéritif français au goût d'anis très populaire. Fort et assez chargé en alcool, il doit être dilué avec de l'eau, ce qui lui donne un aspect laiteux et trouble.

Riceys (Rosé des) (A.O.C.)

Vin rosé de Champagne, non mousseux.
Voir CHAMPAGNE

Richebourg (Appelation Contrôlée)

Bourgogne rouge. Commune de Vosne-Romanée, en Côte de Nuits. Classement officile : Grand Cru.

Richebourg est un géant dans sa commune, en partie parce que son vin est classé Grand Cru — le titre le plus élevé en Bourgogne — et en partie aussi parce que, avec ses 8,03 ha de vignes (qui débordent d'ailleurs sur le climat voisin de Les Verroilles), il possède un des plus vastes vignobles de Vosne. Seul Romanée-Saint-Vivant le dépasse en superficie parmi les meilleurs crus de la commune.

Les vignes sont plantées assez haut sur le coteau, au nord de La Romanée et de La Romanée-Conti. La Romanée-Saint-Vivant est situé en face, de l'autre côté de la route. Après 1930, un décret du ministère de l'Agriculture autorisa le vignoble situé légèrement au-dessus, à flanc de coteau, et connu sous le nom de Verroilles ou Richebourg, à porter l'appellation d'origine contrôlée. Cette mesure légalisait une très ancienne pratique.

Elle ajoutait plus de 3 ha à l'appellation Richebourg. Contrairement à d'autres Grands Crus de Vosne, Richebourg n'est pas le monopole d'un seul propriétaire. Il appartient à huit propriétaires différents. Trois seulement en possèdent des parcelles d'une superficie relativement importante : Domaine des fils de Louis Gros, Domaine de La Romanée-Conti et Charles Noellat.

Inutile de dire que ce morcellement détermine de grandes différences entre les Richebourg d'une même année. En règle générale cependant, ce sont tous des vins de velours de Vosne. Tous ceux de cette commune ont ce velouté, mais il est plus prononcé chez le Richebourg que chez les autres. Il est doté en outre d'une robuste plénitude et acquiert un admirable parfum avec l'âge. La production moyenne annuelle dépasse à peine 250 hl, soit l'équivalent de près de 3 000 caisses.
Voir VOSNE-ROMANÉE

Richon-le-Zion

Un des principaux centres vinicoles d'Israël *(voir ce nom).*

Riesling

Variété de raisin qui donne les vins les plus distingués et les plus nobles d'Alsace, de la Moselle et du Rhin. Petit, jaunâtre, pas très juteux, ce fruit n'en est pas moins un des plus grands raisins du monde. Les Riesling d'Alsace portent généralement cette appellation sur leur étiquette. Mais elle n'apparaît pas toujours sur celles des Riesling du Rhin et de la Moselle. On cultive aussi ce cépage en Allemagne, en Autriche, en Californie, au Chili, en Australie, en Suisse et ailleurs.

Rieussec (Château-)

Bordeaux blanc. Commune de Fargues, en Sauternais.

Après de nombreux changements de propriétaire, Rieussec a été remembré par l'acquisition de parcelles voisines qui en avaient été séparées. Le vin est différent de son voisin : Château-Yquem. Rieussec est en effet plus corsé et moins subtil. Une partie de la propriété seulement est plantée de vignes. Le vin fut officiellement classé Premier Cru de Sauternes en 1855. Le vignoble fut acheté en 1971 par M. Albert Vuillier, qui en 1984 vendit la majorité de ses parts à un groupe bancaire présidé par Château Lafite-Rothschild. Le vignoble de Rieussec à l'avantage considérable d'être situé sur un plateau ce qui permet à ses vins de mûrir avant d'autres Sauternes. Dans les années 70, Rieussec commença à commercialiser un vin sec, appelé « R », fait de raisin provenant de la partie du vignoble classée Sauternes ainsi que de 8 ha qui n'ont droit qu'à l'appellation « Bordeaux supérieur ».

Caractéristiques : Très liquoreux car riche en sucre non converti. Un des meilleurs Premiers Crus.

Superficie : 61 ha.

Production moyenne : 100 tonneaux (8 000 caisses).

Rio Negro

Province vinicole d'Argentine (*voir ce nom*).

Rioja

Vins rouges. Nord de l'Espagne.

Au cours des cinquante dernières années, les meilleurs Rioja se sont classés parmi les premiers vins espagnols. Néanmoins — bien qu'ils viennent nettement en tête de la liste et soient intéressants à acheter — ils s'échelonnent, en général, entre les très bons vins et les moyens. Il arrive, de temps à autre, qu'une bouteille d'une des meilleures firmes présente des qualités exceptionnelles et égale les meilleurs vins rouges, à l'exception toutefois des grands Bordeaux et Bourgogne. La vinification du Rioja est dominée par des grandes entreprises qui s'efforcent de commercialiser des produits constants et de qualité moyenne. Elles dominent le marché et comprennent — à quelques exceptions près — les seules maisons autorisées à produire les vins de Rioja ayant droit aux Certificats d'Origine. En outre, on peut espérer une amélioration de la qualité, bien que les grandes firmes d'exportation aient malheureusement tendance à considérer la valeur d'un vin en fonction de son âge, aussi le vin est-il souvent vieilli trop longtemps en fût, puis vendu immédiatement après la mise en bouteille. Le vin perd alors beaucoup de sa clarté, de sa vigueur, de sa fraîcheur et de son fruité, précisément parce que la maturation en bouteille est insuffisante. Les vins blancs, qui subissent parfois le même traitement, deviennent plats et madérisent. Il arrivait que le vin en bouteille soit plus jeune que l'année imprimée sur l'étiquette ; ceci pouvait s'expliquer soit par la surestimation de la valeur de l'âge du vin, soit par une certaine négligence de l'exactitude, mais aussi par le système de la demi-*solera*, qui consistait à ajouter de temps en temps une petite quantité de très vieux vin de la réserve (*gran reserva*).

Il y a pourtant quelques heureuses exceptions à cette règle : parmi les meilleurs producteurs, la *bodega* du Marquès de Riscal à Elciego. Là aussi, il y a eu de nouvelles plantations de raisins à vin blanc, et le docteur E. Peynaud, œnologue de Bordeaux, a été consulté sur les procédés modernes de vinification du vin blanc. Toutefois, d'une manière générale, les Espagnols sont enclins à croire que les vins faibles, suroxydés et frêles, sont plus distingués que les gros vins forts et assez quelconques produits dans le pays. De toute façon, la durée du vieillissement en fût — parfois 5 et même 10 ans — est excessive. Le jour où ce défaut sera éliminé (il semble que ce soit en bonne voie), les vins de Rioja, qui sont potentiellement de très beaux vins, ne pourront qu'y gagner en qualité.

Le Certificat d'Origine, délivré récemment pour l'exportation, a amélioré la qualité de ces vins. Le terme *crianza* signifie que le vin a au minimum trois ans d'âge et qu'il a vieilli une année au moins en fût. *Reservas* et *gran reservas* indiquent un vieillissement en bouteille.

Les vins de Rioja participèrent à l'épanouissement vinicole espagnol au moment où la découverte de l'Amérique ouvrit de vastes marchés aux exportations du pays.

Outre le climat difficile, le développement de la région de Rioja a été freiné par un autre facteur : l'absence de bonnes routes pour écouler la marchandise. Pendant plus d'un siècle, et dès 1790, la construction d'une route fut le but de ceux qui voulaient ramener l'industrie des vins espagnols à la splendeur des jours passés.

Le succès des Rioja commença, en 1892, avec la fondation d'une station viticole à Haro, au centre de cette région en forme de haricot. A peu près simultanément s'engagea une campagne pour interdire aux autres vins espagnols d'en porter le nom. Ce combat n'est d'ailleurs pas encore gagné. Haro est devenu un centre de première importance, doté d'un institut vinicole.

Après un long retard par rapport aux autres régions d'Espagne, celle de Rioja a fait reconnaître la qualité de ses vins et on convient désormais qu'elle est due à sa situation géographique exceptionnelle. La zone délimitée des vins de Rioja se divise en trois secteurs : Rioja Alta, Rioja Alavesa, Rioja Baja. Seule la haute vallée du cours d'eau (haute Rioja : Rioja Alta) est soumise à un climat septentrional et de type atlantique, c'est là que l'on produit les vins les plus fins. Ceux de Alava sont plus lourds mais indiscutablement bons. D'autre part, la basse Rioja (Rioja Baja) ne produit que des vins ordinaires, rarement vendus en bouteille et peu exportés. Les vins portant la *Denominación de Origen* sont cultivés sur 40 000 ha de vignobles, qui donnent 1 million d'hl (plus de 11 millions de caisses) de vin rouge, blanc et rosé (*rosado*).

Appellations d'origine et vinification

Environ 60 firmes ont le droit de faire du Rioja et de le vendre sous cette appellation d'origine, avec un certificat de garantie et un petit timbre dentelé sur la bouteille. Le nombre n'est pas officiellement limité à deux douzaines, mais pour en faire partie le producteur doit avoir un minimum de 500 fûts en stocks. Cela représente un gros investissement et le petit vigneron n'en a pas les moyens. Les autorités admettent qu'il s'agit là d'un système empirique tendant à limiter le nombre des producteurs pour pouvoir surveiller leurs opérations et améliorer une situation encore imparfaite. D'ailleurs, quelques vignerons et producteurs, qui ne possèdent pas le minimum de 500 fûts, ont été admis sur la liste en raison de l'excellence de leur vin.

La loi qui contrôle et protège les vins de Rioja ne saurait se comparer à la législation française, ni même à celle qui régit l'appellation Xérès, mais elle est quand même beaucoup plus efficace que celle qui concerne les autres vins de table espagnols. L'appellation Rioja (ou celle d'un des villages situés dans cette région) ne peut être accordée qu'aux vins qui possèdent certaines caractéristiques précises et atteignent des normes minimales de qualité. Quand le vin produit dans la région est inférieur aux normes, le nom du village peut figurer sur la bouteille, mais avec la mention suivante : « Ce vin a été fait dans la localité de X, mais n'a pas le droit à l'appellation Rioja. »

La région des vins de Rioja est englobée dans les limites de la province de Logroño et dans certains secteurs de Alava et Navarre. Les vins qui ont vieilli ou ont été « élaborés » hors de la zone n'ont pas droit à l'appellation Rioja.

La vinification des Rioja est faite, en principe, selon les méthodes françaises. A cela, rien d'étonnant, étant donné qu'il y a près d'un siècle lorsque le phylloxéra détruisit les vignobles de Bordeaux, des Français prirent en main viticulture et vinification dans la région de Rioja qui n'était pas encore atteinte par le fléau.

L'afflux des Français dans la région de Rioja en ce temps-là a laissé une marque nettement perceptible : les vins cuvent et fermentent à peu près de la même façon qu'en France ; ceux qui ne sont pas vendus dans le courant de l'année comme vins légers ordinaires vieillissent en fûts de chêne dont certains ont la même contenance que la barrique bordelaise. Conservés dans les caves de certaines *bodegas* (entreprises vinicoles) qui ressemblent à celles de la France jusqu'au plus petit détail. Il y a néanmoins une grande différence : alors que les bons vins de Bordeaux sont produits individuellement par un seul propriétaire de vignobles, les Rioja sont des mélanges produits dans les grandes *bodegas* à partir de raisins cultivés — en partie et même presque entièrement — par les paysans-vignerons de la région. Ceci est plus courant en Californie et dans certaines parties du Rhône. Quant au vin régional de moindre importance, une bonne partie est maintenant produite avec succès par 40 coopératives, puis vendue comme *vinos corrientes* de bonne qualité.

Types de vins de Rioja : étiquettes des bouteilles

La région de Rioja, telle qu'elle est délimitée actuellement, s'étend sur les deux rives de l'Èbre, au nord de l'Espagne un peu à l'est de Burgos. Le petit secteur qui n'est pas compris dans la province de Logroño est une espèce de poche dans la province d'Alava où l'Èbre, beaucoup plus étroit, coule entre des collines plus élevées. Cette différence géographique se reflète dans les vins car les Rioja d'Alava sont plus lourds, corsés et sanguins, alors que dans la plaine de l'Èbre, ils ont une légèreté qui rappelle les Bordeaux rouges.

La région est extrêmement découpée, mais dans l'état actuel de l'évolution des vins on peut ne considérer que trois principales divisions.

Rioja Alta

La haute Rioja est située au nord-ouest et englobe la ville de Logroño. Le climat y est le même que sur la côte basque et le golfe de Gascogne. Il ressemble donc à celui de Bordeaux : printemps agréable, automne doux et prolongé favorable aux vendanges. Il gèle et neige l'hiver, mais le climat n'est pas très rigoureux. Deux dangers pèsent néanmoins sur la vigne : gelées tardives fin avril ou au début de mai, alors que le réchauffement de la température a déjà stimulé la montée de la sève ; et le *solano* : vent d'est chaud qui brûle les vignes. Malgré cela, le climat de Rioja est assez stable et les années assez régulières pour n'avoir pas à recourir à la chaptalisation.

Alavesa

Les vins d'Alava (dont la superficie est de 800 ha) sont classés parmi les meilleurs avec ceux de la haute Rioja. Parfois l'étiquette des bouteilles indique que le vin est un Alavesa. En général il sera plus chaleureux que le Rioja Alta. On le compare habituellement au Bourgogne mais, goûté sur place, il rappelle plutôt les bons vins du Rhône.

Rioja Baja

Les vins de la basse Rioja sont rarement mis en bouteille. Lorsque l'Èbre s'écoule vers la Méditerranée, en aval de Logroño, le climat change. Il ressemble plus à celui de l'Aragon qu'à celui du golfe de Gascogne : le temps y est plus chaud. Alors que la haute Rioja est relativement sèche, la basse Rioja est aride. En raison du climat plus chaud, la saison y est toujours de deux semaines en avance et, pourtant, dans la vaste plaine de l'Èbre, on vendange plus tard qu'en amont. Ce prolongement de la maturation du raisin produit des vins d'une teneur nettement plus élevée en alcool : 15 à 16° en Rioja Baja et 11 à 12,5° en Rioja Alta.

Les Rioja sont vendus en bouteille et en fût. On en fait vieillir une partie dans des fûts de chêne américain, soit de 600 l (*bocoyes*), soit de 225 l (*barricas bordelesas :* barriques bordelaises). Ces vins vieillis sont en général les seuls qui atteignent les marchés étrangers ou que l'on trouve dans les meilleurs restaurants d'Espagne.

Les vins millésimés portent la mention *Cosecha* (vendange) suivie de l'année (par exemple, *Cosecha 1978* ou *Cosecha 1982*). D'autres portent la mention *Reserva* ou *Reserva Especial,* parfois suivie de l'année et parfois non. *Reserva* indique que le vin a été conservé plus longtemps (presque toujours en fût, pas en bouteille) que celui qui porte seulement la mention *Cosecha*. *Reserva Especial* indique une conservation encore plus prolongée.

Il n'est pas toujours facile de choisir entre ces trois types de vin. Les plus vieux le sont parfois trop et la conservation trop poussée en fût les a amollis. Et pourtant, ce sont en général les meilleurs vins des meilleures années qui sont mis de côté pour subir ce mauvais traitement. Quant au millésime, il faut le considérer comme une approximation. Il indique seulement que la plus grande partie du vin contenu dans la bouteille ou la barrique provient de telle ou telle vendange. Les plus grandes années de ce siècle pour le Rioja sont : 1904, 1920, 1922, 1924, 1925, 1928, 1934, 1935, 1942, 1948, 1953, 1954, 1957, 1962, 1964, 1966, 1970, 1976, 1978, 1981 et 1982 pour le début de cette décennie.

Les vins blancs sont doux (*dulce*) ou sec (*seco*). Ils ne sauraient rivaliser avec les rouges car ils sont trop souvent *pasados* (madérisés). Les rouges sont classés par âge, comme *Finos de mesa* (vins fins de table) ou comme *Reservas,* et par couleur : *Rosado, Clarete, Ojo de Gallo et Tinto,* allant du rose pâle au rouge foncé. *Clarete* et *Tinto* sont les types que l'on rencontre le plus souvent. Parfois on fait le *Clarete* en mélangeant du blanc et du rouge. Mais cette pratique est moins courante à Rioja que dans la Manche, par exemple, et en général le *Clarete* est un honnête vin rosé résultat d'un bref contact entre le jus et la peau du raisin. Enfin, *Tinto* désigne le vin rouge. En effet, les Espagnols n'emploient jamais l'adjectif *rojo*, alors qu'ils utilisent *blanco* pour les vins blancs.

Comme en Californie, les vins sont généralement plus connus par le nom de l'expéditeur que par celui du cru. On admet volontiers à Rioja que les crus diffèrent beaucoup les uns des autres. L'exposition au sud ou au nord importe énormément ; le sol des coteaux est surtout schisteux et plus ancien que le terrain d'alluvions du fond de la vallée et des bords du fleuve. Ces facteurs ont une influence sur le vin. La fermentation dans des cuves distinctes des produits de différents crus en est à ses débuts. Si le vin porte le nom d'un vignoble — Zaco, Tondonia et Paceta sont les plus connus — cette mention a un caractère symbolique. Certaines *bodegas* de haute tradition, comme celles du Marquès de Riscal, Marquès de Murrieta, la Compañia Vinicola del Norte de España et Cune, peuvent utiliser principalement leurs propres raisins et sélectionner une petite quantité d'autres raisins de viticulteurs moins importants ; mais la plupart font leurs assemblages avec les récoltes de nombreux petits vignobles.

Autrefois, chaque Rioja portait un nom de *cepa* : Cepa sauternes, Cepa chablis, Cepa rhin, Cepa barsac, Cepa médoc et ainsi de suite. Parfois aussi, estilo sauternes, estilo médoc ou encore especial sauternes, graves, barsac, et même plus simplement chablis, sauternes, etc. Cet étiquetage imitatif fut interdit en 1960, et confirmé par le Marché Commun.

Encépagement

Protégée des excès climatiques par de hautes montagnes, au-delà de l'horizon, la Rioja Alta, au sol brun tacheté de roux, rappelle l'Arizona et l'Afrique du Nord. Quant aux coteaux couverts de vignes, ils évoquent ceux de Chablis. Les grands domaines ont adopté des techniques modernes de vinification, et quelques *bodegas* et coopératives ont pu acquérir les installations les plus récentes. Les coins les plus reculés de la province restent primitifs et pittoresques. Les vieux villages juchés sur les collines sont tous à l'écart des grandes routes. Cet isolement leur a permis de conserver leur originalité. D'innombrables maisons sont encore ornées de blasons sculptés dans la pierre. La région doit son nom à la prononciation défectueuse du nom d'un petit affluent de l'Èbre, le rio Oja. C'est une terre pauvre, en grande partie aride et rocailleuse avec quelques coins fertiles et magnifiques. L'aspect de désolation n'a pas grand-chose à voir avec le vin qui est exclusivement produit — du moins en théorie — par les quelques grandes *bodegas* de la Rioja, dont voici les principales :

La Rioja Alta, S.A. ; R. López de Heredia, Viña Tondonia, S.A. ; Bodegas Martínez Lacuesta, Hnos., Ltda ; Bodegas Franco Españolas ; Bodegas Ramón Bilbao ; Rioja Santiago, S.A. ; Campo Burgo, S.A. ; Compañia Vinícola del Norte de España ; Bodegas Marqués de Cáceres ; Bodegas Bilbainas ; Bodegas Riojanas ; Bodegas Montecillo ; Vinos de los Herederos del Marqués de Riscal, S.A. ; Federico Paternina, S.A. ; Viñas Salceda ; Alavesas ; Beronia ; Martinez Bujanda ; Campillo ; Marqués de Ciria ; Corral ; El Coto ; Domecq ; Lan ; Sociedad Vinicola Laserna ; Laturce ; Muga ; José Palacios ; Marqués del Puerto ; La Granja Nuestra Señora de Remelluri ; Carlos Serres ; Velazquez ; Bodegas Berberana ; AGE, Bodegas Unidas, S.A. ; Bodegas Gurpegui ; Bodegas Lagunilla, S.A. ; Bodegas Marqués de Murríeta ; Bodegas Muerza, S.A. ; Bodegas Olarra ; Bodegas Palacio, S.A. ; Bodegas Faustino Martínez ; Vinícola Vizcaina, Rojas y Cia, S.R.C. ; Bodegas Campo Viejo de Savin, S.A. ; Bodega Coop. Del Valle de Ocón ; Bodega Coop. Nuestra Señora de la Anunciación ; Bodega Coop. Nuestra Señora de Valvanera de Cuzcurrita, Tirgo y Sajazarra ; Bodega Coop. Nuestra Señora de Vico ; Bodega Coop. San Isidro ; Bodega Coop. San Miguel ; Bodega Coop. San Pedro Apóstol ; Bodega Coop. Santa Daria ; Bodega Coop. Sonsierra ; Bodega Coop. Virgen de la Vega ; Bodega Coop. La Bastida.

Les vins rouges sont produits avec des cépages des variétés suivantes : Garnacha, Tempranillo, Graciano et Mazuelo. Aucune espèce de vigne de Rioja, blanche ou rouge, n'est capable de donner un vin satisfaisant à elle seule. Toutes manquent d'un ingrédient essentiel : acidité ou richesse, ou encore finesse. Tous les bons vins sont donc faits avec des raisins de plusieurs variétés. On verra bientôt du Cabernet Sauvignon.

Le Garnacha ressemble au Grenache

français. C'est un raisin à gros rendement qui donne du vin ordinaire, faible de bouquet. Il ne mûrit pas complètement en Rioja Alta, sauf année exceptionnellement chaude. C'est lui qui donne la masse des vins de Rioja Baja et des autres parties de l'Espagne, notamment autour de Madrid où on l'appelle en général Aragon, ou Tinto aragonés, parce qu'il provenait à l'origine d'Aragon. On le cultive largement dans le secteur de Rioja en raison de sa résistance à l'oïdium qui, avec le mildiou, est une des pires plaies de la région.

Le moût du Tempranillo est tout à fait neutre. Les autres raisins utilisés en mélange avec celui-ci sont ceux qui donnent le goût au vin. Il mûrit rapidement quoiqu'il se conserve mal et la couleur qu'il confère au vin constitue à peu près son seul intérêt.

Le Graciano possède un parfum nettement distinct. Le Mazuelo — variété proche du Carignan de Provence et du Rhône — n'est que peu cultivé car il est vulnérable à l'oïdium.

Les vins blancs sont en général faits avec un mélange de Malvasia, Viura.

Ripeau (Château-)

Bordeaux rouge. Commune et secteur de Saint-Émilion.

Autrefois réuni à Château-Jean-Faure, qui lui est contigu et qui appartenait depuis longtemps au même propriétaire, Ripeau était un des gros producteurs de Saint-Émilion. Proche du Château-Cheval-Blanc, presque sur les limites de Pomerol, le vignoble appartint à Michel de Wilde, gendre de feu Mme Loubat qui, avec son mari, fonda les deux vignobles réunis aujourd'hui sous le nom de Château-Ripeau. Actuellement, le château appartient à la fille de M. de Wilde, mariée à M. Janoueix, propriétaire, négociant à Libourne. Château-Ripeau est un Grand Cru de Saint-Émilion classé en 1955 puis en 1986.

Caractéristiques : Vin généreux au bouquet personnel. Le type du bon Saint-Émilion.

Superficie : 14 ha.

Production moyenne : 70 tonneaux (7 000 caisses).

Ripley

Vigne hybride américaine, obtenue à la station agricole de l'État de New York, servant à la fois comme raisin de table et comme raisin à vin. Le Ripley donne un blanc sec, mais vinifié seul, son vin tend vers la platitude. S'il trouve un partenaire approprié, ce raisin, employé en mélange, pourrait donner un produit de bonne qualité.

Riquewihr

Agglomération vinicole d'Alsace *(voir ce nom)*.

Rivesaltes (Appellation Contrôlée)

Secteur ensoleillé du Roussillon, célèbre pour ses vins de Muscat.

Voir VINS VINÉS DE FRANCE

Riviera del Garda Bresciano (D.O.C.)

Vins rouge ou rosé de la Lombardie *(voir ce nom)*.

Riz (vin de)

Liqueur japonaise obtenue par la fermentation du riz.

Voir SAKÉ

Robertson

Secteur vinicole de la région de Little Karoo, dans la province du Cap.

Voir AFRIQUE DU SUD

Roche

Voir CLOS DE LA ROCHE

Rochefort-sur-Loire

Commune vinicole des Coteaux du Layon, en Anjou *(voir ces noms)*.

Rodo (Vinho do)

Vin mousseux, en portugais.

Romanée (La)

Bourgogne rouge. Commune de Vosne-Romanée, en Côte de Nuits. Classement officiel : Grand Cru.

La Romanée est le plus petit (moins d'un hectare) des grands vignobles de Vosne. Elle est située immédiatement au-dessus de la Romanée-Conti dont la sépare un simple sentier. Malgré la proximité et la similitude de noms et de vins, il s'agit de deux crus séparés et distincts.

A Vosne, on admet en général que le vin de ce terroir n'a pas toute la finesse et toute l'élégance de celui de La Romanée-Conti ; La Romanée est peut-être le plus robuste des deux. Il gagnerait en corps et en chair ce qu'il cède en finesse.

Ce vignoble appartenait à l'abbé Juste Liger-Belair, puis fut racheté par la Société civile du Domaine de la Romanée-Conti. Sa production atteint à peine 30 hl, soit l'équivalent de 350 caisses. Désormais, sa commercialisation a été confiée à un négociant. Il n'est jamais mis en bouteille au domaine, ce qui est regrettable.

Voir VOSNE-ROMANÉE

Romanée-Conti (La)

Bourgogne rouge. Commune de Vosne-Romanée, en Côte de Nuits. Classement officiel : Grand Cru.

La Romanée-Conti, un des crus les plus célèbres du monde, ne couvre qu'une superficie extrêmement limitée. Il ne s'en écoule donc qu'un mince filet de vin, vendu à des prix très élevés, et l'amateur qui parvient à s'en assurer une bouteille estime qu'il a de la chance. Si ce vin est tellement surestimé c'est par la faute des snobs qui l'achètent pour impressionner et font ainsi monter le prix.

Contrairement à la pratique habituelle en Bourgogne, *tout* le vin de La Romanée-Conti est mis en bouteille au domaine et chaque bouteille porte sur l'étiquette et sur le bouchon le sceau de la Société civile de La Romanée-Conti qui possède cette vigne ainsi que la Tâche et des parties d'autres crus. En réalité cette société est une affaire de famille, celle de M. Duvaut-Blochet, qui l'acheta en 1869. Le vignoble n'avait changé de main que neuf fois depuis le XIIIe siècle et depuis il continue à être transmis par héritage. Ses propriétaires actuels sont M. de Villaine, descendant de M. Duvaut-Blochet et directeur de banque à Moulins, et Mme Bise-Leroy. En 1760, le prince de Conti l'acheta en dépit des protestations de Mme de Pompadour qui le convoitait elle aussi.

Puisqu'il est mis en bouteille au domaine, on trouve de vieilles bouteilles de La Romanée-Conti à la cave du domaine. Visiter cette cave est une expérience dont le souvenir fait monter l'eau à la bouche. Elle est pourtant primitive et modeste, mais les bouteilles qu'elle abrite contiennent ce qu'on a défini ainsi : « L'union du satin et du velours. »

En réalité, les vins de La Romanée-Conti se divisent en deux catégories : les millésimes antérieurs à 1945 et ceux d'après. Jusqu'à cette année-là, les propriétaires conservaient leurs vignes françaises au lieu de les greffer sur des souches américaines comme le faisaient les autres vignerons depuis le phylloxéra. Ils assuraient leur survivance par provignage : opération qui consiste à enterrer un vieux cep en ne laissant dépasser hors de terre qu'une seule jeune pousse. Celles de La Romanée-Conti étaient donc issues en ligne directe de celles que les moines avaient plantées plus de douze siècles auparavant. Mais le pylloxéra demeurait une menace constante et il fallait traiter ces vignes à grand-peine et lourde dépense. Pendant la dernière guerre mondiale les produits chimiques nécessaires à ce traitement disparurent, la main-d'œuvre manqua, les vignes dépérirent et ne donnèrent plus que 50 caisses par an. En 1945, les propriétaires abandonnèrent leurs traditions, arrachèrent leurs vignes, plantèrent des porte-greffes d'origine américaine résistants au phylloxéra.

Il en résulta que la quantité de La Romanée-Conti descendit brusquement. Quand les vignes étaient jeunes, la qualité n'était pas celle du nectar d'autrefois. Dans leur plénitude, les vins de La Romanée-Conti ont un équilibre parfait, associé à une race et une finesse extraordinaires. Les experts du pays assurent que c'est le vin le plus corsé de Vosne, ce qui signifie sans doute « qu'il a une mains de fer dans un gant de velours ».

Son goût reste dans la bouche pendant un temps étonnamment long.

Quoique la production soit nettement plus élevée qu'autrefois, elle n'est pas considérable. La vendange moyenne donne 40 hl ou moins de 450 caisses.

Voir VOSNE-ROMANÉE

Romanée-Saint-Vivant (La)

Bourgogne rouge. Commune de Vosne-Romanée, en Côte de Nuits. Classement officiel : Grand Cru.

Comme les deux autres La Romanée, ce vignoble est un Grand Cru, c'est-à-dire un des 31 mieux classés de la Bourgogne (la commune de Vosne en compte cinq). Avec ses 9,43 ha, La Romanée-Saint-Vivant est le plus vaste Grand Cru de la commune. Il doit son nom à l'abbaye de Saint-Vivant à laquelle il appartint pendant longtemps mais qui n'existe plus.

La Romanée-Saint-Vivant est située sur le coteau, juste au-dessous de La Romanée-Conti et de Richebourg, au-dessus de l'agglomération de Vosne. Malgré sa grande superficie, il n'appartient qu'à quatre propriétaires. Son vin a les qualités et les caractéristiques des Grands Crus de Vosne : grâce veloutée et parfum expansif, mais la qualité pourrait être meilleure si les vignes n'étaient pas taillées de façon à donner le maximum de quantité. Malheureusement de mauvais millésimes ont été mis en bouteille et cela n'améliore pas l'image de marque de ce cru. A coup sûr il mérite de figurer parmi les plus grands vins de Bourgogne.

La production annuelle s'élève à près de 190 hl (près de 2 000 caisses).

Romer-du-Hayot (Château-)

Bordeaux blanc. Commune de Fargues, en Sauternes.

Ce château, second cru de Sauternes peu connu est situé dans un bois de la commune de Fargues, dont les vins ont droit à l'appellation Sauternes. Les vins ont tendance à être un peu lourds.

Superficie : 12 ha.

Production moyenne : 60 tonneaux (3 000 caisses).

Rond

Pour être rond, un vin doit être à la fois grand et harmonieux. Alors, il atteint un équilibre parfait et la manière dont son goût se répand dans toute la bouche suggère une idée de rondeur.

Rosato

Nom que les Italiens donnent au vin rosé.

Rosé

Quand il est fait correctement, le vin rosé provient de raisins de cépages rouges qui fermentent pendant deux ou trois jours, quelquefois moins, avec la peau et les pépins qui lui donnent la couleur. Ces éléments sont éliminés par soutirage à l'instant critique où le vin a pris exactement la coloration rose que l'on souhaite. Le rosé ne devrait jamais être un mélange de vins rouges et de vins blancs, quoique ce soit parfois le cas. Il doit toujours être servi frais. En France le meilleur rosé est le Tavel, mais on en fait aussi d'excellents à Bordeaux, en Anjou et dans la plupart des régions vinicoles. Aux États-Unis, le rosé jouit d'une popularité prodigieuse.

Rosé de Béarn

Vin rosé produit en appellation Béarn, dans les Basses-Pyrénées.

Rosé de Riceys (Appellation Contrôlée)

Vin rosé, non mousseux, fait en Champagne (*voir ce nom*).

Rosette

Vin blanc demi-doux et rarement distingué, provenant de Bergerac (Appellation Contrôlée) (*voir ce nom*). C'est aussi le nom d'une variété hybride franco-américaine qui manque de couleur et est donc souvent utilisée pour vinifier un rosé.

Rosolio

Liqueur italienne rouge, au goût de rose. On produisait autrefois en France une version de cette liqueur appelée Rossolis.

Rossese ou Dolceacqua (D.O.C.)

Vin rouge fait avec des raisins Rossese cultivés sur la Riviera italienne.

Voir LIGURIE

Rosso

Signifie « rouge » en italien. En Californie, ce mot s'applique maintenant aux rouges légèrement doux, mais les *vini rossi* courants d'Italie sont toujours secs.

Rosso Conero ; Conero (rouge) (D.O.C.)

Vin rouge fruité mais un peu acide, produit dans les Marches italiennes.

Voir MARCHES

Rosso Piceno ; Piceno (rouge) (D.O.C.)

Vin rouge italien des collines de Piceno, au pied des Apennins.

Voir MARCHES

Rougeau

Maladie de la vigne due à une blessure qui empêche la sève de circuler.

Voir CHAPITRE IV

Rouget (Château-)

Bordeaux rouge. Commune de Pomerol.

Ce domaine, dont Jean Brochet est le propriétaire, est l'un des plus vieux de la région, et a produit jusqu'ici des vins très agréables, typiques du Pomerol.

Superficie : 13 ha.

Production moyenne : 60 tonneaux (6 000 caisses).

Roumanie

On cultivait la vigne en Roumanie longtemps avant l'époque contemporaine. Il y avait des vignobles en Scitia Minor (aujourd'hui la Dobroudja) avant même que les Grecs aient fondé leurs colonies de l'Helespont (mer Noire) au début du VIIe siècle avant notre ère. Au flanc des contreforts des Carpates il existait de vastes plantations de vignes depuis des temps immémoriaux dans la région des Cotnari, Uricani, Husi, Odobesti, Panciu, Nicoresti, Dealul-Mare et Drăgăsani. Les grecs expédiaient leurs amphores à vin vers tous les points du monde civilisé de leur temps. Plus tard leurs négociants des ports du nord apportaient de gros fûts à leurs foires, ce qui n'était possible que grâce aux tonnelleries de Cotnari, Odobesti et Drăgăsani. La Roumanie produit actuellement 8,5 millions d'hl (près de 95 millions de caisses) de vin, ce qui la classe cinquième producteur d'Europe, entre le Portugal et l'Allemagne fédérale. Les vignobles se sont considérablement étendus et couvrent maintenant 300 000 ha. Le Roumain consomme environ 28 l de vin par an. Le gouvernement encourage l'industrie vinicole, notamment en projetant d'augmenter la superficie des vignobles à 1 million d'ha dans les dix années à venir. Il est indéniable que le gouvernement joue un très grand rôle, pourtant seulement 20 % des cépages appartiennent à l'État. Plus de la moitié du vin est produite par de grosses coopératives, et un tiers de la production est encore assuré par les parcelles individuelles.

Récemment, on a aussi planté de la vigne à Tîrnave, Simburesti et Segarcea et elle y prospère à souhait. L'extension du vignoble sur presque toute la surface du pays est due au fait que la Roumanie est située dans sa quasi-totalité au-dessous de la limite septentrionale de culture de la vigne et que son relief est constitué de coteaux en pente douce. En dehors des vins non mousseux, on tend à produire et à vendre davantage de vins pétillants.

PRINCIPALES RÉGIONS VINICOLES

Le vignoble de Cotnari

Ce vignoble couvre les contreforts des Carpates, au nord-est de la Roumanie, près de la ville historique de Jassy. Il jouit de conditions climatiques (automnes longs et secs) et géologiques (sols riches en calcaire). Cotnari est un des plus vieux vignobles du pays. En 1646, le père jésuite Marcus Bandinus en parla dans son compte rendu d'un séjour en Moldavie. Malgré son grand âge ce vignoble de 5 000 ha prospère encore. Ses nouvelles plantations, résultant des connaissances scientifiques modernes, promettent un grand avenir, à brève échéance.

Encépagement : Grasă de Cotnari, Fetească Albă, Tămîioasa Românească Frîncuşa.

Type de vin : Le Cotnari est un vin de dessert naturel titrant 13 à 15° d'alcool par volume et contenant plus de 50 g/l de sucre résiduel. Bien équilibré, il est doté d'une saveur et d'un bouquet très fins.

Le vignoble de Murfatlar

Situé près de la mer Noire, sur les collines de Murfatlar, ce vignoble constitue une seule vigne de plus de 7 000 ha sur des coteaux ensoleillés caressés par une douce brise marine. La viniculture y est conduite par des techniciens qualifiés, selon les méthodes scientifiques les plus récentes.

Encépagement : Les cépages qui prévalent dans ce secteur sont le Pinot Chardonnay et le Pinot Gris. D'autres variétés telles que Muscat Ottonel, Pinot Noir et Cabernet Sauvignon donnent aussi des résultats satisfaisants.

Type de vin : Le Murfatlar est principalement un vin de dessert dont le fin bouquet comporte une nuance à peine perceptible mais unique et délectable de fleur d'oranger.

Le vignoble de Tîrnave

Situé sur les deux rives du cours d'eau qui porte ce nom, ce vignoble est bien connu pour la qualité de ses vins. Les zones les plus intéressantes sont : Blaj, Medias, Richis, Jidvei, Seuca, Valea, Lungă, Atel, Tigmandru.

Encépagement : Riesling italien, Fetească, Ruländer, Traminer, Sauvignon, Neuburger, Muscat Ottonel.

Type de vin : On produit en Tîrnave des vins secs, obtenus à partir des cépages Fetească et Riesling ; des vins demi-secs et doux à partir de Traminer et Sauvignon, et un vin célèbre, le Muscat Ottonel.

Le vignoble de Dealul-Mare

C'est un des secteurs vinicoles les plus étendus de Roumanie : 20 000 ha de vignes s'étendent sur plus de 60 km.

Situé à l'endroit où les contreforts extrêmes des Carpates se fondent avec la plaine et les coteaux, sous les chauds rayons du soleil, ce vignoble produit les vins préférés des Roumains : Valea Călugărească, Tohani, Săhăteni, Urlati, Pietroasele.

Encépagement : Cabernet Sauvignon, Pinot Noir, Merlot, Riesling italien, Fetească Albă, Tamîioasa Românească, et Muscat Ottonel.

Type de vin : L'orgueil du cru de Valea Călugăreasca sont les rouges faits avec du Pinot noir et du Cabernet Sauvignon. Ils sont riches et foncés, au goût agréable, harmonieux, velouté, plein de caractère.

Le vignoble de Vrancea

C'est la plus vaste région viticole de Roumanie. Elle s'étend sur un territoire au relief et aux sols divers. Elle est soumise aussi à des conditions climatiques qui diffèrent d'un point à un autre.

Les vins de Vrancea diffèrent donc aussi les uns des autres.

Voici leurs principaux types :

Odobesti : Vins de table blancs et vins de qualité faits avec Fetească, Muscat Ottonel, Aligoté et Galbenăçt.

Cotesti : Vins de table rouges et blancs et vins de qualité faits avec Riesling, Fetească, Muscat, Pinot Noir et Cabernet Sauvignon.

Panciu : Vins de table blancs, particulièrement appréciés pour leur fraîcheur.

Nicoresti : Vins de table rouges et vins de qualité faits avec le raisin Băbească de Nicoresti et Fetească Neagră.

Le vignoble du Banat

Cette région comporte deux centres de production : celui de la plaine — Teremia, Mare, Tomnatec — qui produit en grande quantité des vins de table blancs d'une teinte verdâtre et d'une qualité constante ; celui des collines dont les crus les plus connus sont : Buziaş, Recaş, Miniş, Ghioroc, Baratke, Pîncota et Şiria.

Encépagement : Les vins blancs de Teremia et Tomnatec sont faits avec : Creaţa (Riesling du Banat) Majărcă et Steinschiller. Les vins rouges de Miniş et de Recaş sont faits avec Kadarka et Cabernet.

Type de vin : Les terrasses pierreuses de

Minis fournissent le célèbre Kadarka du Banat : vin rouge apprécié pour son goût et son arôme caractéristiques.

Autres vignobles

Les vins blancs de Drăgasani Stefăneşti, Jasi, Husi et Galati ; les rouges et les blancs de Segarcea (Mehedinti, Sîmbureşti et Uricani) ; les blancs demi-secs d'Alba Julia, Aiud, Lechinţa et de Bistriţa, complètent la vaste gamme des productions vinicoles roumaines.

On a estimé que le développement des stations viticoles, où l'on cultive les jeunes vignes servant aux plantations des viticulteurs, et l'application de méthodes scientifiques modernes, tant en viticulture qu'en viniculture, doivent permettre au vignoble roumain de s'étendre sur plus de 330 000 ha. Le plan économique actuel vise à planter 50 000 ha supplémentaires en variétés qui assureront la production essentielle des grands combinats de vinification que le gouvernement roumain a créé afin d'exploiter au mieux le grand potentiel vinicole du pays.

EXPORTATION DES VINS ROUMAINS

Le vin n'est devenu un produit d'exportation de quelque importance qu'après la Seconde Guerre mondiale. En moyenne, la Roumanie expédie annuellement vers l'étranger environ 550 000 hl (plus de 6 millions de caisses) de diverses variétés de vin pour satisfaire les goûts des différents marchés : vers la République fédérale allemande, des vins de table blancs et rouges faits avec des raisins Riesling, Fetească, Kadarka, Cabernet Sauvignon et Rotburgunder ; vers l'Autriche, outre des blancs ordinaires, des vins de qualité, faits avec Riesling, Fetească, Rulănder, Muscat Ottonel, Tămîioasa, Romînească, ainsi que des rouges Rotburgunder et Cabernet Sauvignon. La Roumanie exporte aussi ses vins vers la Suisse, la Belgique, la Hollande, la Suède, le Danemark, la France, la Grande-Bretagne, les États-Unis, et, évidemment en plus grande quantité, vers la Pologne, la Russie, la Tchécoslovaquie, l'Allemangne de l'Est.

En 1959, la Roumanie participa au concours vinicole organisé à Montpellier. Selon un dégustateur enthousiaste, ses vins étaient « ... une surprise agréable... un somptueux Merlot de Nicoreşti, couleur de rubis et au goût délicat... Réserve de Ploieşti, léger, d'une finesse agréable. Les blancs secs et demi-secs de Coteşti rappellent un de nos crus alsaciens et peuvent être classés parmi les meilleurs du monde. Le Riesling avec sa fraîcheur et le Fetească avec son arôme à la fois délicat et précis ont reçu une approbation unanime. Dans le même groupe, le Fetească de Tîrnave justifie son titre : Perle de Tîrnave... L'épais Chardonnay de Murfatlar au goût de miel... et le subtil Cotnar... ont fait les délices des dégustateurs ».

Voici les principaux vins mis en bouteille en vue de l'exportation par « Vinexport » :

Vins de table blancs	
Perla de Tîrnave	Aligoté
Fetească de Tîrnave	Riesling de Dealul-Mare
Riesling de Tîrnave	Vin de table ordinaire
Grünsilvaner	Vin de table supérieur
Rulända	
Furmint	
Sauvigon	
Vins de dessert	
Cotnari	Murfatler
Vins rouges	
Pinot Noir	Cabinet
Cabernet	Băbească de Nicoreşti
Kadarka	

Roussette de Savoie (A.O.C.)

Principale production vinicole de Seyssel, en Haute-Savoie. Blanc, sec comme du silex, il est fait avec du raisin Roussette.

Voir SEYSSEL ; SAVOIE

Roussillon

Le Roussillon, région vinicole méridionale de la France, appartient au département des Pyrénées-Orientales. Mais cette belle région — aux pics enneigés des Pyrénées, aux contreforts sauvages profondément entaillés et traversés par les torrents montagneux — n'occupe que depuis peu de temps une place significative sur la carte des vins français.

Jusqu'au milieu des années 60, les vins du Roussillon étaient de deux types : les vins vinés (*q.v*) appelés *vins doux naturels* (V.D.N.) et les vins rouges secs sans qualité particulière. Considérés comme vin d'apéritif, les V.D.N. ont toujours été populaires en France, ils sont cependant moins appréciés à l'étranger. Jusqu'à ce que les vins rouges des Côtes du Roussillon prédominent, les V.D.N. ont permis aux producteurs de vivre dans cette région.

Les V.D.N. d'appellation contrôlée du Roussillon sont Maury, Banyuls (et Banyuls Grand Cru), Rivesaltes, Muscat de Rivesaltes et Grand Roussillon. Dans les années 50, on employait les vins rouges secs du Roussillon comme vins de coupage. L'intense effort fait depuis les années 60 pour les améliorer a permis d'obtenir l'Appellation Contrôlée de Côtes du Roussillon, vins rouges, rosés et blancs. La production a été limitée à 50 hl/ha, et le contenu minimum d'alcool fixé à 11,5° pour les vins rouges et rosés, 10,5° pour les blancs.

Les vins rouges des meilleurs villages des Côtes du Roussillon peuvent se qualifier pour l'appellation « Côtes du Roussillon-Villages ». Parmi les meilleurs de ces villages, citons : Caramany, Montner, Latour-de-France, Vingrau et Estagel. Caramany et Latour-de-France peuvent indiquer le nom de leur village sur l'étiquette.

Dans la région, le cépage dominant a toujours été le Carignan qui produit ses meilleurs vins dans le riche sol schisteux du nord du Roussillon, le long de la côte d'Agly et des villages mentionnés ci-dessus. Les autres cépages importants sont : le Grenache — réputé pour sa vinosité —, le Syrah, le raisin du Rhône, et le Mourvèdre. La macération carbonique, technique utilisée pour rehausser l'arôme et la vinosité des vins, se répand de plus en plus.

Les meilleurs vins des Côtes du Roussillon possèdent un arôme attirant, proche de celui des baies, une riche et agréable structure tannique et un fruité prolongé. Dans les bonnes années, les meilleurs de ces vins s'améliorent en bouteilles pendant une période pouvant aller jusqu'à trois ans. Les Côtes du Roussillon blancs et les très bons rosés sont également produits en petite quantité. L'un des meilleurs lieux d'origine du vin rosé est la coopérative du village de Rasiguères. La production de vin blanc n'est pas d'une aussi bonne qualité que les rouges ou les rosés. On procède actuellement à des expériences pour utiliser le cépage blanc du Sauvignon et en améliorer sa qualité.

La production de *vins doux naturels* et des Côtes du Roussillon, plus les « Villages », est d'environ 600 000 hl de vin par an (6,5 millions de caisses).

Voir VINS VINÉS DE FRANCE

Royaume-Uni

L'Angleterre possède des vignes et produit du vin à un niveau commercial mais encore à une échelle extrêmement limitée. Il n'en reste pas moins que depuis une vingtaine d'années, la viticulture s'est considérablement développée. En 1986, on comptait environ 480 ha de vignes, plus de 100 centres de vinification, et plus de 270 viticulteurs qui vendaient leurs vins. Feu M. Jack Ward et son associé Ian Howie du Merry-down Company ont fondé une coopérative dotée des équipements les plus modernes où une trentaine de propriétaires envoient leurs raisins pour le pressurage. Il existe également un nombre non négligeable de vignobles privés qui, comme autrefois, sont le violon d'Ingres de propriétaires de domaines campagnards des XVIIIe et XIXe siècles. Le dernier de ces domaines Castle Coch, Glamorgan, appartenait au marquis de Bute et fut abandonné pendant la Première Guerre mondiale.

Rappelons que les Normands et, au début du Moyen Age, les Anglais produisaient beaucoup de leur vin. Selon Bède le Vénérable, des vignobles prospéraient en Angleterre dès l'an 730 ; plus tard, une ordonnance d'Alfred le Grand (849-901) indemnisa les vignerons pour les éventuels dommages causés à leurs vignes. Après la conquête normande, la viticulture continua de s'étendre, particulièrement dans les monastères. Des vignobles se créaient à l'ouest et au sud de l'Angleterre, ainsi que dans le Pays de Galles, l'Essex et le Suffolk ; on en trouva plus tard également au nord, aussi loin que Lincolnshire et York. Vers la moitié du XIVe siècle, il y eut un déclin de la viticulture (mais elle ne cessa jamais complètement) : il arrivait une telle quantité de vin du continent — surtout des domaines gascons des Plantagenêts — qu'il devenait plus intéressant de l'importer que de le cultiver.

Après la Deuxième Guerre mondiale, l'intérêt pour les vins s'accrut peu à peu dans le pays, et des vignobles furent implantés dans le Lincolnshire, l'East Anglia, le Sud et quelques-uns dans le Pays de Galles. Parmi les producteurs qui méritent d'être cités, feu Sir Guy Salisbury-Jones, de Hambledon, dans le Hampshire, fait figure de pionnier : il y implanta son vignoble en 1952. D'autres noms sont également importants : M. Nigel Godden, Pilton Manor, Somerset (autrefois, sa terre était cultivée par les abbés de Glastonbury) ; Lady Montagu, de Beaulieu ; M. et Mme J. G. Barrett : Felsted, Essex ; M. Colin Gillespie de Wooten, Somerset ; M. Kenneth Barlow du vignoble d'Adgestone, île de Wight. Une Association des vignobles anglais fut fondée en 1967 pour encourager la viticulture.

Les nouveaux vignerons sont particulièrement encouragés par les progrès réalisés dans la création de nouvelles espèces de vignes mieux adaptées à un climat qui fut longtemps considéré comme peu favorable à la viticulture. On fait un peu de vin rouge avec du Pinot Noir et autres variétés ; mais comme en Allemagne, le climat est plus propice aux vins blancs. Le Müller-Thurgau (ou Riesling × Sylvaner) est la variété la plus couramment utilisée. On cultive aussi du Seyval Blanc, Chardonnay, Triomphe d'Alsace, du Pinot Blanc, ainsi que du Reichensteiner, Huxelrebe, Madeleine Angevine, Schonburger, Ortega, Kerner et autres variétés allemandes. La plupart des vendanges sont assez satisfaisantes. Les vignobles les plus renommés se situent pour la plupart dans les comtés du sud et en East Anglia. Ce sont : Lamberhurst dans le Kent, propriété de Kenneth McAlpine ; Richard Barnes Biddenden et Carr Taylor dans le Sussex. C'est aussi à partir du Sussex que Gay Biddlecombe commercialise ses St. Georges. Notons ailleurs : Tom Day du Three Choirs Vineyard dans le Gloucestershire et Richard Bache d'Astley dans la vallée de la Servern.

Le terme Vin britannique (pour le distinguer du Vin anglais) s'applique à des vins forts et bon marché faits de raisins secs ou de jus de raisin concentré d'importation, vinifiés en Angleterre. Cela donne effectivement du vin douceâtre, mais certainement pas du bon vin. Il est assez regrettable que le gouvernement anglais ait choisi d'imposer plutôt les vins naturels anglais de 11,5° que les vins de 15°.

Voir WHISKY ; SCOTCH

Rubino di Cantavenna (A.O.C.)

Vin rouge, léger, mais plein, du Piémont italien.

Voir PIÉMONT

Ruby Port

Jeune Porto fait de coupages, d'une belle couleur rubis, fruité et doux ; il vieillit dans le bois.

Ruchottes-Chambertin (A.O.C.)

Bourgogne rouge. Commune de Gevrey-Chambertin, en Côte de Nuits. Classement officiel : Grand Cru.

On trouve bien des bouteilles excellentes, voire extraordinaires, de ce vin qui n'en est pas moins une sorte de parent pauvre dans la famille Chambertin. Quelques critiques sévères le trouvent banal et l'accusent de manquer de race. En réalité, s'il n'arrive généralement pas au même niveau de magnificence que le Chambertin, un Ruchottes bien fait n'est ni banal ni vulgaire.

Le vignoble est contigu au Clos de Bèze au sud du village de Gevrey-Chambertin. Il est situé plutôt haut sur le coteau pour un grand vin exceptionnel. Il couvre à peine plus de 3 ha et sa production s'élève habituellement à environ 100 hl (plus de 1 000 caisses).

Voir GEVREY-CHAMBERTIN

Rüdesheimer Berg

Le Rüdesheimerberg (littéralement : mont de Rüdesheimer) est un coteau escarpé qui s'élève sur la rive du Rhin. Il produit les meilleurs vins de Rüdesheimer. Leur étiquette mentionnera le nom du village, Rüdesheimerberg, suivi de celui du cru, tels que Berg Rottland, Berg Schlossberg ou Berg Roseneck.

En raison de la forte déclivité, le drainage du sol est excellent et, par année humide, les vins de ce coteau comptent parmi les meilleurs du Rheingau. Mais, par année chaude, les raisins rôtissent au soleil, c'est pourquoi ce village populaire produit un vin souvent inférieur à la moyenne de la région.

Voir RHEINGAU

Rufina

Jolie petite commune du Chianti, située à environ 32 km au nord-est de Florence, dans la vallée du fleuve Sieve. Ses vins sont parmi les meilleurs crus auxquels on n'ait pas octroyé l'appellation Classico.

Ruländer

Raisin grisâtre, originaire de Bourgogne (Pinot Gris), introduit en Allemagne par un certain Ruland. On le cultive aussi en Alsace et en Suisse. Il s'appelle également Grauerburgunder ou Tokaier.

Rully

Commune de la Côte du Chalonnais, en Bourgogne, qui a droit à sa propre appellation d'origine contrôlée. On y produit des vins rouges et blancs.
Voir CHALONNAIS

Rumbullion, Rumbustion

Deux mots employés au XVIIe siècle, dans les Antilles britanniques, pour désigner le rhum. Leur origine exacte est obscure. Certains suggèrent qu'ils dérivent d'un dialecte du Devonshire.

Ruppertsberger

Bons vins de la moyenne Haardt, en Palatinat. Ses meilleurs crus sont : Hoheburg, Gaisböhl, Linsenbusch, Nussbien.
Voir PALATINAT

Russie

Voir U.R.S.S.

Russian River Valley

Secteur vinicole du canton de Sonoma, en Californie, sur la côte du Pacifique, à quelque 80 km au nord de San Francisco.
Voir ÉTATS-UNIS : CALIFORNIE ET OUEST

Ruster Ausbruch

Vin autrichien très doux, fait avec des raisins cueillis tardivement sur les vignes de Rust, en Burgenland. *Voir* AUTRICHE

Rutherglen

Célèbre région vinicole de la province de Victoria, en Australie.

On produit, dans le Rutherglen, certains des meilleurs vins vinés et vins de dessert ainsi que des vins de table rouges et charnus, mais en quantité nettement moins importante qu'autrefois. *Voir* AUSTRALIE

Ruwer

Voir MOSELLE (SARRE-RUWER)

S

Sables-Saint-Émilion

Autrefois appellation d'origine située près de Saint-Émilion, ses vins ont été intégrés dans l'appellation plus connue de Saint-Émilion.

Voir SAINT-ÉMILION

Saccharomètre

Voir MUSTIMÈTRE

Saccharomyces Cereviseae

Levure naturelle du vin qui se trouve sur la pruine : pellicule grise couvrant les peaux de raisin à la fin de l'été et en automne.

Voir LEVURES ; CHAPITRE V

Sack

Un des premiers noms donnés en Angleterre aux vins de Xérès (*voir*, par exemple, Shakespeare, *Henry IV*, 2ᵉ partie, acte IV, scène 3). Pendant un certain temps on crut que ce mot dérivait de l'espagnol *seco* (sec). Mais en ce temps-là, le Xérès était probablement doux et pas du tout tel que nous le connaissons de nos jours. On accepterait donc facilement l'hypothèse de M. H. Warner Allen selon laquelle *sack* dérive bien de l'espagnol, mais du mot *sacar* (sortir, exporter). Le nom de ce vin doux fut ensuite appliqué à celui de vins du même genre : Canary Sack et Malaga Sack.

Sacramentel

Vin utilisé au cours de certains sacrements de certaines Églises chrétiennes. Au Moyen Age le besoin de s'assurer des vins sacramentels incita les moines à participer activement à la viticulture. Le terme sacramentel s'applique aussi au vin utilisé lors de la pâque et d'autres fêtes religieuses juives.

Sacramento Valley

Région vinicole de Californie.

Voir ÉTATS-UNIS : CALIFORNIE ET OUEST

Saint-Amour (Appellation Contrôlée)

Vin rouge du Beaujolais. Saint-Amour est la localité la plus septentrionale de ce secteur, contiguë à celle de Pouilly-Fuissé en Mâconnais. Le Saint-Amour est un des Beaujolais les plus charnus.

Voir BEAUJOLAIS

Saint-Aubin
Saint-Aubin-Côte de Beaune

Bourgogne rouges et blancs. Côte de Beaune.

Saint-Aubin est situé sur les coteaux derrière Puligny-Montrachet et Chassagne-Montrachet, mais ses vins ne valent pas ceux de ces deux crus. D'abord les vignes de Saint-Aubin sont plantées un peu trop haut, c'est-à-dire au-dessus de la zone qui, à mi-hauteur du coteau, donne vraiment les vins de première classe. En raison de la différence de qualité, le Saint-Aubin devrait être beaucoup moins cher que les autres vins de la Côte de Beaune. Acheté assez jeune et à bon prix, il peut offrir un excellent placement.

Les vins de Saint-Aubin sont vendus sous cette seule appellation ou sous celle de Saint-Aubin-Côte de Beaune. Mélangés aux vins d'autres communes, ils portent l'appellation Côte de Beaune-Villages. N'importe quel vin, qui a droit à l'une de ces appellations, peut porter les deux autres.

Les vignobles de Saint-Aubin ont une étendue de 236 ha dont 156 ha sont classés Premier Cru.

Par année moyenne la production s'élève à plus de 2 500 hl (plus de 25 000 caisses) de rouge et à près de 1 500 (plus de 15 000 caisses) de blanc sans compter celui qui est vendu sous l'appellation Côte de Beaune-Villages.

PREMIERS CRUS

Crus	*ha*
La Chatenière	8,4
Les Murgers-des-Dents-de-Chien	16,1
En Remilly	29,7
Les Frionnes	12,6
Sur-le-Sentier-du-Clou	18
Sur Gamay	14,9
Les Combes	24,9
Champlot	10,9

Saint-Chinian (Appellation Contrôlée)

C'est un vignoble, situé à flanc de coteaux du Languedoc, qui produit des vins rouge et rosé faits d'au moins 50 % de Carignan.

Voir LANGUEDOC ; COTEAUX DU LANGUEDOC

Saint-Christol (Coteaux de)

Petite localité de l'Hérault ayant droit à l'appellation Coteaux du Languedoc suivie de son propre nom.

Voir LANGUEDOC

Saint-Denis

Voir CLOS SAINT-DENIS ; MOREY-SAINT-DENIS

Saint-Drézéry

Voir LANGUEDOC

Saint-Émilion (cépage)

Cette variété d'Ugni Blanc fournit la plus grande partie des vins de la Charente distillés pour faire du Cognac *(voir ce nom)*. On la cultive aussi dans d'autres parties de la France, où on l'appelle Clairette à grains ronds, Clairette de Vence, Graisse, Queue de renard, Roussan. En Italie, ce raisin s'appelle Trebbiano ; en Corse, Rossola.

Saint-Émilion (Appellation Contrôlée)

Vin rouge. Région de Bordeaux.

Saint-Émilion est une des Appellations Contrôlées les plus connues du Bordelais. Le vin de Saint-Émilion est généralement le plus charnu, rond et plein des Bordeaux rouges. Comme dans le Médoc, certains grands millésimes exigent un très long temps de vieillissement. Ceux qui connaissent mal les Bourgogne nature le compare souvent à ces vins. Les vignobles de Saint-Émilion peuvent aisément être divisés en deux catégories : ceux de la plaine et ceux des coteaux. Mais dans chaque catégorie les vins diffèrent d'un cru à l'autre en raison des différences de sol et d'exposition du terrain. Les coteaux de Saint-Émilion entourent l'agglomération comme une couronne. Ce secteur est très accidenté, sauf au voisinage de celui de Pomerol. La distinction entre plaine et coteau se manifesta de manière spectaculaire à la fin de février 1956, lorsque la viticulture bordelaise subit son pire hiver depuis 1709. Le gel frappa les vignes de la plaine et tous les crus de cette catégorie, y compris Château-Cheval-Blanc, le plus grand Saint-Émilion, perdirent leur récolte de 1956 et de 1957.

Les vignobles des coteaux, au contraire, survécurent. Château-Ausone (probablement le meilleur d'entre eux) s'en tira indemne.

On estime que Saint-Émilion est la plus

vieille agglomération vinicole de France (probablement à l'exception de celles de Provence). C'est certainement la plus pittoresque. Construite sur une colline de pierre douce, facile à travailler, elle semble faite d'une seule pièce. Les caves de bien des châteaux sont d'anciennes carrières exploitées au Moyen Age pour construire la ville. Il n'est pas de site plus agréable pour consommer un grand vin que l'endroit où on le fait. La terrasse du principal restaurant de la ville (Hostellerie de Plaisance) se trouve sur le dôme d'une église : l'église monolithe creusée dans le rocher. Il s'agit en réalité d'une église construite au IXe siècle, mais c'est aussi le plus vaste lieu de culte taillé dans le roc.

Les initiations solennelles de la Commanderie Vinicole — la Jurade — à la lueur des bougies, dans la crypte, sont un spectacle inoubliable. Du belvédère de l'Hostellerie de Plaisance, où vous pouvez déguster votre vin, vous voyez les toits rougeâtres de la Tour du Roi, bâtie sous Louis VI en 1124, les arcades en ruine du cloître des Cordeliers et les vignes qui couvrent les coteaux de Saint-Émilion et s'étalent sur la plaine.

Ausone, qui écrivit un poème épique sur la Moselle, vécut dans une luxueuse villa romaine qui pourrait avoir été située à proximité du lieu où se trouve aujourd'hui Château-Ausone. En son temps (le IIIe siècle), Saint-Émilion était déjà entouré de vignes.

Quant à saint Émilion, il n'apparaît qu'au VIIIe siècle. Il s'arrêta dans cette localité alors qu'il se rendait en pèlerinage à Saint-Jacques-de-Compostelle (Espagne). Si vous visitez son ermitage proche de l'église, vous y verrez sa couchette et son tabouret, sculptés dans la pierre. On vous dira alors que Saint-Émilion, était en ce temps-là un désert et que le saint, séduit par une source miraculeuse, y fonda une colonie. Sans manquer de respect à la religion, on peut suggérer que cette source était celle du vin de Saint-Émilion car la région n'avait rien d'un désert. Elle avait prospéré sous les Romains et n'avait rien perdu de son florissant passé. En tout cas, le saint s'attarda à Saint-Émilion mais il n'alla jamais jusqu'à Saint-Jacques-de-Compostelle.

L'agglomération de Saint-Émilion est située à quelque 38 km au sud-ouest de Bordeaux.

Outre Saint-Émilion, sept communes ont droit à cette appellation. Ce sont : Saint-Laurent-des-Combes, Saint-Christophe-des-Bardes, Saint-Hippolyte, Saint-Étienne-de-Lisse, Saint-Pey-d'Armens, Saint-Sulpice-de-Faleyrens et Vignonet. Leurs territoires constituent un demi-cercle au sud et à l'ouest de Saint-Émilion. Aucune ne produit de vin atteignant le niveau des crus de première catégorie. Mais Château-Larcis-Ducasse, à Saint-Laurent-des-Combes, où se prolonge le coteau de Château-Pavie, mérite d'être cité. Château-Monbousquet, à l'écart d'un petit chemin vicinal, au-delà de la route Bordeaux-Périgueux, sur la plaine de Saint-Sulpice-de-Faleyrens, est un domaine où vins et chevaux de race étaient élevés par une des personnalités les plus dynamiques de Saint-Émilion et un des plus importants producteurs de vin : feu M. Daniel Querre. Du sommet d'une tour datant du XIIe siècle, c'est cet homme de 135 kg qui, de sa voix claironnante, donnait le signal aux vendangeurs lors de la cérémonie annuelle de la Jurade, appelée *Ban des Vendanges*. Son exemple est maintenant suivi par son fils Alain Querre.

Trois communes situées au nord de Saint-Émilion et à l'ouest de Pomerol ont le droit d'ajouter à leur nom celui de Saint-Émilion. Leurs appellations contrôlées sont les suivantes : Saint-Georges-Saint-Émilion, Montagne-Saint-Émilion et Puisseguin-Saint-Émilion. Les vins de Parsac et Saint-Georges peuvent être vendus sous l'étiquette Montagne-Saint-Émilion qui est souvent la plus utilisée. Château-Saint-Georges et, dans une moindre mesure, les autres vins de Saint-Georges-Saint-Émilion ne se distinguent du Saint-Émilion proprement dit que par la tradition et l'usage. Au point de vue de la qualité, ils ont les mêmes caractéristiques : longévité et splendeur ne se manifestant qu'après maturation suffisante en bouteille.

Enfin, Sables-Saint-Émilion est l'appellation contrôlée des vins d'un petit secteur contigu d'un côté à Saint-Émilion, de l'autre, à Libourne, et situé entre Pomerol et la Dordogne. Les vignes de Sables-Saint-Émilion, comme le nom l'indique, sont plantées dans du sable. Les vins mineurs qu'elles produisent sont plus proches des moindres Pomerol que des Saint-Émilion.

Durant l'été 1955, l'Institut national des appellations d'origine procéda au classement officiel des vins de Saint-Émilion. Auparavant on avait toujours considéré Château-

Cheval-Blanc et Château-Ausone comme les premiers crus hors classe. En 1955 on leur accorda seulement de figurer en tête de liste des Premiers Grands Crus, mais sans autres droits particuliers. Les 10 autres Premiers Grands Crus sont classés ensuite dans l'ordre alphabétique. Sachant quelles difficultés avait soulevée la classification des vins de Médoc un siècle plus tôt, les experts de l'I.N.A.O. se gardèrent de diviser les Crus classés en Premiers, Seconds, Troisièmes, Quatrièmes, Cinquièmes, car cette hiérarchie peut suggérer à tort qu'un Troisième Cru, par exemple, n'est qu'un vin de troisième catégorie. Les crus de Saint-Émilion furent donc divisés en 1986, comme ils le furent en 1955, en deux groupes seulement : celui des Premiers Grands Crus (ils sont 11) et des Grands Crus (environ 70).

PREMIERS GRANDS CRUS (classification de 1986)	
Château-Ausone	Château-Figeac
Château-Cheval-Blanc	Clos-Fourtet
Château-Beau-séjour-Duffau-Lagarrosse	Château-La Gaffelière
Château-Bélair	Château-La-Magdelaine
Château-Canon	Château-Pavie
	Château-Trottevieille

En 1986, Château-Beau-Séjour-Bécot fut injustement omis des Grands Crus classés, alors qu'il en faisait partie lors de la classification de 1955.

On trouvera en appendice l'ensemble de la classification. Chacun de ces Premiers Grands Crus est traité, en outre, à sa place dans l'ordre alphabétique.

A l'unanimité, Château-Cheval-Blanc est considéré comme le meilleur des Saint-Émilion et, avec Château-Pétrus, en Pomerol, l'égal des quatre grands Médoc : Lafite, Latour, Margaux, Château-Mouton-Rothschild et de Haut-Brion (classé dans les Graves). Le cas de Château-Ausone n'est pas aussi certain. La plupart des gens soutiennent qu'il suit immédiatement Cheval-Blanc et mérite donc une place particulière au sommet de la hiérarchie. D'aucuns cependant trouvent que, durant les dernières années, Figeac, situé juste au-dessous sur le même coteau, a parfois égalé Ausone.

Saint-Estèphe (Appellation Contrôlée)

Bordeaux rouge. Haut-Médoc.

Saint-Estèphe est la quatrième dans la liste des grandes communes productrices du grand Médoc rouge. Elle est située le plus au nord du Haut-Médoc. Sa production annuelle (près de 9 millions de bouteilles ayant droit à l'appellation d'origine contrôlée) est la plus élevée de toutes les communes du Médoc. Mais, dans son ensemble, elle n'atteint pas la qualité des vins de Margaux, Pauillac et Saint-Julien. Certains des moindres Saint-Estèphe offrent une transition entre les Bas-Médoc et les Haut-Médoc, plus aristocratiques. On ne s'en étonnera pas en considérant que cette commune est située à la limite des deux régions.

Alors que certains Saint-Estèphe peuvent manquer de finesse, par contre Château-Cos-d'Estournel, Château-Montrose et Château-Calon-Ségur sont trois crus parmi les plus distingués du Médoc. La gamme de qualité est plus large chez les Saint-Estèphe que chez les vins des trois autres célèbres communes. C'est pourquoi il faut les choisir avec soin.

CRUS CLASSÉS DE SAINT-ESTÈPHE
Seconds Crus
Château-Cos-d'Estournel
Château-Montrose
Troisième Cru
Château-Calon-Ségur
Quatrième Cru
Château-Lafon-Rochet
Cinquième Cru
Château-Cos-Labory
(*Voir* chacun de ces crus à sa place dans l'ordre alphabétique.)

Corsés et avec beaucoup de bouquet, en général, les Saint-Estèphe diffèrent les uns des autres. Calon-Ségur, situé à l'extrémité nord, est le plus Saint-Estèphe des Saint-Estèphe. A l'opposé des vins délicats et féminins de Margaux, les Saint-Estèphe sont souvent assimilés par les Bordelais aux Saint-Émilion, plus lourds que les Médoc. Dans leur jeunesse ils se distinguent par leur corps fruité. Selon la classification en 1855 des vins de Médoc, Saint-Estèphe ne compte que cinq Crus classés, c'est-à-dire beaucoup moins que les autres principales communes.

Sainte-Foy-Bordeaux (Appellation Contrôlée)

Bordeaux blancs et rouges.

Vins blancs doux, faits selon la méthode du Sauternes, avec des raisins cueillis après qu'ils ont dépassé leur maturité et qu'ils sont atteints de pourriture noble, et avec des raisins de la même variété qu'en Sauternais : Sémillon, Sauvignon et Muscadelle. Ce secteur est situé à l'extrémité est de la région vinicole de Bordeaux. Il serait mieux à sa place si on le classait avec les Monbazillac qui sont également blancs et doux. Une petite quantité de vin rouge porte également cette appellation, mais elle ne représente qu'environ 40 % de la production totale.

Saint-Gall

Ancien nom d'un apéritif français à base de vin rouge additionné d'eau-de-vie.

Saint-Georges-d'Orques

Voir LANGUEDOC ; COTEAUX DU LANGUEDOC

Saint-Georges-Saint-Émilion

Une des quatre communes situées au nord de Saint-Émilion et qui partagent le droit à l'Appellation Contrôlée de Saint-Émilion en complément de leur lieu d'origine *(voir ce nom).*

Saint-Jean-de-Minervois (Muscat de)

Voir VINS VINÉS DE FRANCE

Saint-Joseph (Appellation Contrôlée)

Vins blancs et rouges des Côtes du Rhône.

Voir CÔTES DU RHÔNE

Saint-Julien (Appellation Contrôlée)

Bordeaux rouge. Haut-Médoc.

Une des quatre principales communes qui produisent le vin rouge de Médoc ; les autres étant Pauillac, Margaux et Saint-Estèphe. La production de Saint-Julien est aussi faible que celle de Margaux. Elle dépasse à peine 5 500 000 bouteilles par an, le vin ayant droit à l'appellation d'origine contrôlée. Comme vin régional (appellation communale), c'est probablement avec Margaux la plus connue des six appellations du Haut-Médoc sur le marché mondial.

Les vignes de Saint-Julien (775 ha) poussent sur un sol pierreux contenant une proportion considérable de glaise. Le vin présente des affinités avec ceux de Pauillac, situé immédiatement au nord de la commune, et avec ceux de Margaux qui se trouve à une quinzaine de kilomètres au sud, au-delà d'une bande de terre trop basse et trop humide pour les vignes de qualité.

De robe un peu plus foncée et de saveur plus corsée que les Margaux typiques, les Saint-Julien ressemblent à cet égard aux Pauillac, mais ils sont moins charnus que ces derniers et vieillissent plus rapidement. D'autre part, leur finesse, leur délicatesse féminine les rapprochent des Margaux.

L'agglomération est un petit village situé entre les célèbres Léoville, sur une courbe de la route des vignobles qui va de Bordeaux en direction du nord. On l'appelle parfois Saint-Julien-Beychevelle pour marquer son rapport avec le célèbre et ancien domaine de Beychevelle.

Après avoir traversé des pâturages, la route des vignobles grimpe tout à coup et, au sommet de la côte, commence le territoire de Saint-Julien, avec Château-Beychevelle, puis Château-Ducru-Beaucaillou du côté de la Gironde, et Château-Branaire-Ducru de l'autre côté de la route, en face des deux premiers. Au tournant, une bouteille de 10 m de haut attire le regard à l'angle des vignes de Beychevelle. En pénétrant dans cette région on voit un panneau qui demande aux passants de saluer l'ancien et célèbre vignoble de Saint-Julien.

La célébrité de Saint-Julien, qui date de loin, a été ressuscitée par son maire M. Henri Martin, propriétaire de Château-Gloria et Château Saint-Pierre qui présida le C.I.V.B. (Comité interprofessionnel des vins de Bordeaux) dans les années 65, et la Commanderie du Bontemps du Médoc.

Par année moyenne, à peu près une soixantaine de vins différents portent l'Appellation d'Origine Contrôlée Saint-Julien à laquelle ils ont droit s'ils proviennent de la région délimitée, s'ils sont traités conformément à certaines normes et si une séance annuelle de dégustation leur a permis d'affirmer leurs qualités.

La liste des vignobles de Saint-Julien qui ont droit au titre de Cru classé selon la classification officielle des vins du Médoc en 1855 montre qu'il n'y a ni Premier ni Cinquième Crus à Saint-Julien.

CRUS CLASSÉS DE SAINT-JULIEN

Seconds Crus
Château-Ducru-Beaucaillou
Château-Gruaud-Larose
Château-Léoville-Barton
Château-Léoville-Las Cases
Château-Léoville-Poyferré

Troisièmes Crus
Château-Lagrange
Château-Langoa-Barton

Quatrièmes Crus
Château-Beychevelle
Château-Branaire
Château-Saint-Pierre
Château-Talbot

(*Voir* chacun de ces Crus classés à sa place dans l'ordre alphabétique.)

Saint-Lambert-du-Lattay

Commune des Coteaux du Layon, en Anjou, qui produit des vins blancs doux.
Voir ANJOU

Saint-Laurent

Raisin à vin rouge cultivé principalement en Autriche et en Tchécoslovaquie.

Saint-Marin (San Marino)

Ce tout petit pays couvre une superficie inférieure à 59 km² dont la plus grande partie est tellement en pente qu'elle semble presque verticale. Il produit un vin de table rouge, nommé Sangiovese, et un Muscat mousseux de dessert, nommé Moscato. Sa production totale s'élève à 20 hl par an. Tout le Sangiovese (plutôt dur) et tout le Moscato (liqueur digestive, nommée Titanium) sont consommés par le million de touristes qui visitent chaque année cette république indépendante, connue pour ses timbres, enclavée sur le territoire italien. La liqueur Titanium doit son nom au Monte Titano, pic qui jaillit de la plaine italienne à 15 km de Rimini, sur l'Adriatique, sur le sommet duquel est perchée la ville de Saint-Marin.

La liqueur est faite avec des fleurs de montagne, selon une recette qui n'a pas changé depuis un siècle. La savourer ou boire un verre de Saint-Marin, attablé à une terrasse en plein air, en admirant l'Adriatique ou les franges bleutées des Apennins, laisse un souvenir inoubliable. Soyez certain qu'un citoyen de Saint-Marin trouvera toujours un prétexte pour vous raconter comment son pays est resté indépendant en dépit des convoitises de conquérants aussi redoutables que César Borgia et Napoléon Ier. Il est exact que cette république est un îlot de liberté depuis 1 600 ans.

Saint Martin

Saint Martin (env. 345) fut un des premiers saints patrons des vignerons de la vallée de la Loire. Une légende attribue à son âne la découverte de la taille des vignes.
Voir LOIRE

Saint-Nicolas-de-Bourgueil (A.O.C.)

Vins rouges et rosés de Touraine, dans la vallée de la Loire. Ses quelque 17 000 ha de vignes sont plantés en Cabernet Franc.
Voir BOURGUEIL, TOURAINE

Saint-Péray et Saint-Péray mousseux (A.O.C.)

Vins blancs secs et doux, mousseux et non mousseux. Vallée du Rhône.

Les vins de Saint-Péray étaient fort prisés en France durant le Second Empire, puis ils tombèrent en disgrâce ; mais ils redeviennent à la mode. Tout comme autrefois, le mousseux corsé semble le plus recherché.

Les vignes de Saint-Péray (Roussanne et Marsanne) sont cultivées sur une hauteur abrupte qui domine le Rhône sur sa rive droite. Parfois les vignerons attendent que la pourriture noble ait desséché les raisins et augmenté proportionnellement à la perte d'eau leur teneur en sucre pour faire des vins très doux. En général pourtant les raisins sont cueillis dès qu'ils sont mûrs et vinifiés en sec. Une bonne part de la production subit une fermentation secondaire en bouteille, selon la méthode champenoise, pour donner du mousseux. Les quelque 40 ha de vignes de Saint-Péray donnent annuellement, plus de 2 000 hl (plus de 20 000 caisses) de vin.

Voir RHONE

Saint-Pierre (Château-)

Bordeaux rouge. Commune de Saint-Julien, en Haut-Médoc.

Ce vignoble est un Quatrième Cru selon la classification de 1855 et doit son nom à un certain baron Saint-Pierre qui l'acheta en 1767. En 1892, une partie du vignoble fut vendue à M. Léon Sevaistre et prit le nom de Château-Saint-Pierre-Sevaistre, alors que le reste du domaine se fit connaître sous le nom de Château-Saint-Pierre-Bontemps. Il fut remembré par ses anciens propriétaires anversois : Castelein et Van der Busshe Fils. Récemment les vins se sont beaucoup améliorés. En 1982, M. Henri Martin, propriétaire du Château Gloria, aussi à Saint-Julien, acquit Château Saint-Pierre et rétrocéda quelques parcelles à ses voisins les Château Ducru-Beaucaillou et Gruaud-Larose.

Caractéristiques : Plutôt léger et généralement sans grande distinction. Une meilleure vinification pourrait élever la qualité.

Superficie : 17 ha.

Production moyenne : 50 tonneaux (5 000 caisses).

Saint-Raphaël

Apéritif français, rouge, délicat et doux-amer, à base de vin viné et qui doit sa saveur surtout à la quinine. Le Saint-Raphaël fut longtemps très populaire en France.

Saint-Romain (Appellation Contrôlée)

Bourgogne rouge et blanc. Côte de Beaune.

Situé sur les collines au-delà de Meursault et d'Auxey-Duresses, Saint-Romain fait un petit vin qui mérite une petite réputation. Mais il est d'une valeur raisonnable par comparaison aux autres crus de la célèbre Côte de Beaune. Une partie de la production — tant en vins rouge que blanc — est vendue sous l'Appellation d'Origine Contrôlée Saint-Romain. Une autre partie, mélangée au vin d'un certain nombre limité de communes de la Côte de Beaune, porte légitimement l'étiquette Côte de Beaune-Villages. Quelque 100 ha de la commune ont droit aux appellations et, dans les bonnes années, la production s'élève à environ 2 000 hl (plus de 20 000 caisses), dont environ près de la moitié de vin blanc. Une quantité non précisée est affectée aux Côte de Beaune-Villages.

Saint-Saturnin

Voir LANGUEDOC ; COTEAUX DU LANGUEDOC

Saint Véran (Appellation Contrôlée)

Bourgogne blanc. Région du Mâconnais.

Proche de la plus célèbre Appellation Contrôlée de Pouilly-Fuissé, cette région viticole de 330 ha produit également du vin blanc avec du raisin Chardonnay. La production annuelle est de 25 000 hl (plus de 250 000 caisses).

Saint Vincent

Saint patron des vignerons français. Selon une légende, il eut soif en paradis et demanda la permission de retourner sur terre pendant quelque temps pour goûter de nouveau les bons vins de France. L'autorisation lui fut accordée et il entendait évidemment remonter au ciel au moment prévu. Mais le vin rouge des Graves le perdit. On le trouva dans la cave de La Mission-Haut-Brion, ne sachant plus ce qu'il faisait sur terre et ne se rappelant pas qu'il devait regagner le paradis. En guise de châtiment, il fut transformé en statue de pierre. On voit encore sa statue dans cette cave. Il tient une grappe à laquelle il ne reste plus guère de raisins et porte sa mitre de travers. Des processions et des festivités ont lieu en son honneur tous les 22 janvier, surtout dans les villages de Côte-d'Or, chacun de ceux-ci ayant l'organisation de cette fête à tour de rôle. Cette manifestation est connue sous le nom de « Saint-Vincent-Tournante ».

Sainte-Croix-du-Mont (Appellation Contrôlée)

Bordeaux blanc.

Petit secteur du sud de Bordeaux, séparé du Sauternais par la Garonne. Ses vins blancs sont doux et rappellent beaucoup leurs voisins d'au-delà du fleuve. Ils sont d'ailleurs faits avec les mêmes variétés de raisins — Sémillon, Sauvignon et une certaine quantité de Muscadelle — cueillis tardivement, après pourriture noble comme pour le Sauternes.

Si ces vins n'ont pas toute l'élégance et toute la finesse des meilleurs Sauternes, ils n'en sont pas moins les meilleurs blancs doux de la rive droite de la Garonne. Leur prix relativement modique leur donne un intérêt certain.

La hauteur de Sainte-Croix-du-Mont est couverte de vignes comme d'une cape qui tomberait des épaules. Au sommet se dresse l'église de Sainte-Croix-du-Mont à la flèche délicate et, à une centaine de mètres, un château fort datant du Moyen Age. Illuminés les soirs d'été, ces deux monuments rayonnent comme des phares au-dessus de la mer de vignes des Graves et de Sauternes.

La production moyenne s'élève à quelque 15 000 hl (plus de 150 000 caisses), soit environ la moitié de celle du Sauternes. Pour avoir droit à l'appellation d'origine contrôlée, les vins doivent titrer au moins 13°, mais en réalité, ils en atteignent souvent 15.

Nulle part ailleurs on ne peut les déguster plus agréablement que sur la terrasse en plein air aménagée juste au-dessous du château fort. Les tables posées sur l'herbe dominent les vignobles qui dévalent comme un torrent vert jusqu'aux basses terres bordant le fleuve. Au-delà, un rideau de saules masque Sauternes, mais à l'horizon on distingue confusément la silhouette du château d'Yquem.

Saints patrons des vignerons allemands

Les Allemands ont emprunté aux Français saint Urbain, évêque d'Autun, dont ils ont fait le saint patron le plus honoré du raisin et du vin. Sa fête, qui tombe le 25 mai, est célébrée dans bien des agglomérations vinicoles d'Allemagne. Bon nombre de chapelles portent son nom et sa statue est très répandue dans les régions où l'on fait du vin.

Les vignerons de Franconie ont leur propre patron : saint Kilian. Ceux des bords du lac de Constance, saint Otmar, évêque du monastère de Saint-Gall auquel la légende attribue un fût qui se remplit miraculeusement de vin médicinal aussi vite qu'on consomme son contenu.

D'autres saints et personnages bibliques ayant quelque rapport avec le vin sont révérés en Allemagne : saint Cyriaque en Palatinat, sainte Geneviève et sainte Madeleine, saint Walter et saint Werner, sainte Élisabeth et même la Sainte Vierge Marie de même que saint Pierre. Pour chacun de ces saints, on raconte une légende qui justifie la dévotion particulière que leur portent les vignerons.

Voir aussi SAINT MARTIN (San Marino) ; SAINT VINCENT

Saké

Boisson japonaise titrant entre 12 et 16°. Elle est faite avec du riz lavé, cuit à la vapeur, puis fermenté. Vers la fin de la fermentation on lui ajoute encore du riz, puis on soutire, on filtre et on fait vieillir en fût.

Incolore et plutôt doux, le saké laisse un arrière-goût amer. Les Japonais le servent tiède dans des petites tasses de porcelaine. Les indigènes d'Okinawa font aussi un saké, mais il est plus dur et en général ils le servent froid. Il y a plus d'une douzaine de types différents de sakés, qui se regroupent en trois grandes catégories : le *mirin,* utilisé pour la cuisine ; le *toso,* un alcool doux et épicé que l'on boit au Nouvel An ; le *seishu,* le vin totalement raffiné que l'on connaît en Occident.

Le premier saké s'appelait *Kuchikam* (ou « maché dans la bouche »). Ce type de saké était fait en machant du riz, des marrons ou du millet, puis en les crachant dans un bol afin qu'ils puissent y fermenter, ce rituel peu appétissant trouve son origine en Chine. Le procédé est maintenant industrialisé. La marque Gekkeikan Saké, produite à Kyoto, vend plus de 25 millions de caisses à travers le monde.

Salmanazar

Bonbonne plus que bouteille (utilisée en Champagne) servant davantage à l'exposition qu'à la conservation du vin. Elle contient 9 l, soit l'équivalent de 12 bouteilles de Champagne (*voir ce nom et* APPENDICE B).

Salta

Province vinicole d'Argentine *(voir ce nom).*

Saltillo

Agglomération vinicole du Mexique où se trouve le siège social de la Compañia Vinicola de Saltillo.
Voir MEXIQUE

Samogon

Vodka de contrebande, en Russie.

Samos

Le Muscat de Samos est un des vins les plus connus de Grèce. Son appellation d'origine est contrôlée.
Voir GRÈCE

Sampigny-les-Maranges et Sampigny-les-Maranges-Côte de Beaune (A.O.C.)

Bourgogne rouges et blancs. Côte de Beaune en Bourgogne.
Sampigny est une commune vinicole mineure, située à l'extrémité sud de la Côte de Beaune. En général ses vins sont mélangés à ceux d'autres communes du voisinage et vendus sous l'appellation Côte de Beaune-Villages. Mais on en trouve aussi étiquetés sous leur propre nom. Les vignes de Sampigny couvrent environ 44 ha et quelques vins ont droit à l'appellation Côte de Beaune suivie du nom de la commune. Quelques rares vins exceptionnels peuvent être étiquetés Sampigny-les-Maranges ou Sampigny-les-Maranges-Clos du Roi. Dans les deux cas, la mention ajoutée est le nom d'un des meilleurs crus de la commune. Seuls les Maranges et le Clos du Roi sont classés Premier Cru. D'ici peu, l'appellation Sampigny-les-Maranges, de même que celles de Cheilly-Les-Maranges et Dezize-Les-Maranges, seront supprimées et regroupées sous le nom de Maranges.

Samchou

Saké chinois.
Voir SAKÉ

San Joaquin Valley

Région chaude de Californie, qui produit des raisins secs et des vins doux vinés. Ses principaux secteurs sont les cantons de Madera, Fresno, Kings, Tulare et Kern.
Voir ÉTATS-UNIS : CALIFORNIE et OUEST

San Juan

Province d'Argentine où l'on pratique la culture extensive de la vigne.

San Marino (Sangiovese)

Voir SAINT-MARIN

San Michele

Liqueur danoise à goût de mandarine.

Sancerre (Appellation Contrôlée)

Vins blancs. Vallée de la Loire. Nièvre et Berry.
Petit mais bien connu, l'appellation de Sancerre, sur le cours supérieur de la Loire occupe 1 600 ha qui donnent par an, environ 600 000 caisses de vin blanc et 180 000 de rouge et rosé. L'agglomération, qui donne son nom à ce secteur, compte 500 récoltants et offre un panorama magnifique

sur les coteaux dont quelque 300 ha sont plantés de Sauvignon. Les vignes s'étendent non seulement sur le territoire de Sancerre mais sur celui de treize localités environnantes. Les meilleurs crus sont Bué, Champtin et Chavignol.

Ce vin doit sa saveur au sol calcaire. Il est nettement sec et, après un été humide, il lui arrive d'être trop acide. Mais si l'été est chaud une teneur suffisante en alcool équilibre l'acidité et le vin prend un goût rafraîchissant, presque piquant. Jamais grand, le Sancerre n'en est pas moins un des blancs les plus agréables et les plus populaires de France.

Les vins rouges et rosés, faits avec du Pinot Noir, représentent environ 17 000 hl (près de 200 000 caisses) de vin par an.

Voir LOIRE

Sandweine

Ce vin de sable du Burgenland (Autriche) doit son nom au sol sur lequel on cultive les vignes qui le fournissent. Comme le phylloxéra évite le sable, ces vignes comptent parmi les rares qui n'ont pas été greffées sur des souches américaines. Les vins de sable sont étiquetés Seewinkel, suivi par l'indication de la variété du raisin.

Voir AUTRICHE

Sangiovese

Raisin à vin rouge utilisé pour le Chianti, le Montepulciano et beaucoup d'autres vins italiens.

Voir ITALIE

Sangria

Boisson espagnole rafraîchissante composée de vin rouge, de jus de citron et d'orange, de sucre, d'eau gazeuse ou plate, et qui peut être, parfois, agrémentée de baies, de fruits, etc.

San Severo (D.O.C.)

Vins secs italiens, blanc, rosé et rouge, assez ordinaires.

Voir POUILLE

Santa Maddalena (D.O.C.) et Classico (D.O.C.)

Vin rouge du Haut-Adige fait à partir des raisins de Schiave, qu'on appelle aussi quelquefois Sankt-Magdelener.

Voir TRENTIN-HAUT-ADIGE, ITALIE

Santa Rosa

Centre du canton vinicole de Sonoma, en Californie.

Voir ÉTATS-UNIS : CALIFORNIE ET OUEST

Santarem-João Santarem

Raisin bleu-noir cultivé sur les coteaux de Colares, au Portugal *(voir ce nom)*.

Santenay et Santenay-Côte de Beaune (A.O.C.)

Bourgogne rouge et blanc. Côte de Beaune.

Santenay est la dernière des communes vinicoles importantes de la Côte de Beaune avant qu'elle ne se perde au sud dans le secteur de Cheilly-les-Maranges, Dezize-les-Maranges et Sampigny-les-Maranges. Ces vins sont en majeure partie rouges, légers, à vieillissement rapide et parfois extraordinairement fruités. Souvent très bons, on peut les acheter pourvu qu'ils soient moins chers que certains autres Côte de Beaune. Par bonne année, l'authentique Santenay rouge rivalise avec les vins de Chassagne-Montrachet et de Volnay, mais jamais avec les plus grands Bourgogne.

Mélangé avec celui d'autres communes de la même côte, il est vendu sous l'appellation Côte de Beaune-Villages dont une partie porte en outre la mention précise de certaines communes. Le Santenay est exporté vers la Suisse et les Pays-Bas où on apprécie ce vin en raison de sa qualité et de son prix plus ou moins avantageux. Le vignoble de Santenay s'étend sur une superficie à peine inférieure à 400 ha et, par année moyenne, produit environ 14 000 hl (plus de 150 000 caisses) de rouge. Les principaux Premiers Crus sont les suivants : Gravières (23,4), Clos de Tavannes dit « les Gravières » (5,3), la Comme (21,6), Beauregard (20,4), La Maladière (13,6), Clos Rousseau (23,8).

Santo (Vin) (D.O.C. pour certains secteurs de Toscane)

Voir TOSCANE

Santo (Vino)

Vin blanc doux de dessert fait en Grèce et en Vénétie (Italie) avec des raisins qu'on a laissé sécher sur pied ou sur treillis. Le Vino Santo a une belle couleur d'or.

Santorin

Vin grec provenant de l'île portant ce nom. S'il est doux il peut aussi être étiqueté Vino Santo.

Voir GRÈCE

Sapin (Bière de)

Cette bière noire, appelée parfois bière de Dantzig, est faite dans cette ville avec des jeunes pousses et de la sève de sapin fermentées.

Sardaigne

Vins rouges et blancs. Ile italienne de la mer Tyrrhénienne.

Cette île montagneuse située au large de la côte d'Italie centrale est la plus grande de toute la Méditerranée, Sicile exceptée. Elle fut habitée depuis les temps préhistoriques et il semble probable que ses premiers habitants cultivèrent la vigne.

La Sardaigne présente un décor étrange et sauvage. L'origine de ses habitants — gens de petite taille et très individualistes — est un mystère. D'énormes monuments de pierre permettraient de l'élucider, mais on n'en a pas encore déchiffré la signification. Tombes de géants ? repaires de magiciens ? ces *nuraghi* — tours de forme conique — semblent avoir servi à l'origine de refuge, tour de guet et forteresse aux premiers habitants de l'île où l'on en trouve partout.

L'île de la Sardaigne produit environ 2 000 000 hl (plus de 20 millions de caisses) de vin par an. Certains vins sont doux, exceptionnellement forts et d'un goût qui provient, à l'évidence, du sol granitique.

Depuis les années 1960, la production viticole de la Sardaigne a subi une révolution œnologique. De nouvelles variétés de raisin, récoltées de bonne heure afin d'en préserver l'acidité, le contrôle de la température de fermentation et une mise en bouteilles précoce sont les principaux signes d'une vinification moderne qui a transformé le style et la qualité des vins de Sardaigne. Le plus grand domaine italien, Sella et Mosta, au nord d'Algherro, produit, à partir du cépage espagnol Torrelata, un vin léger et parfumé. A la place des vins doux et corsés d'antan, l'île produit à présent de bons vins rouges ou blancs (particulièrement blancs) qui sont frais et secs. Ces vins légers, légèrement piquants (CO_2) sont appréciés des nombreux touristes qui fréquentent en masse la Sicile et surtout la Costa Smeralda, centre de vacances et station balnéaire construits par l'Aga Khan près de Porto Cervo, de Porto Rotondo et de Cala di Volpe, et qui est peut-être, de nos jours, un des plus beaux lieux de séjour d'été en Europe.

Vernaccia di Oristano (D.O.C.)

Le mieux connu des vins de Sardaigne. Il est fait avec les raisins cultivés principalement autour d'Oristano, dans la vallée du Tirso qui coule du centre de l'île en direction de l'ouest et débouche dans la Méditerranée au fond du golfe d'Oristano, là où l'île est la plus large. Ce vin sec, d'une couleur d'ambre, ressemble au Xérès et titre jusqu'à 16° et même plus. Il laisse un arrière-goût un peu amer qui s'efface rapidement. Le *liquoroso* viné Vernaccia se distingue en deux types : le type doux, titrant 16,5°, et le type sec, à 18°. Ces vins peuvent être appelés Riserva après avoir vieilli 4 ans dans le bois.

Nuragus di Cagliari (D.O.C.)

Un des meilleurs vins de table fait avec des raisins qui portent le même nom, cultivés autour de Cagliari. Ce vin capiteux, d'une couleur jaune paille, représente annuellement environ 10 % de toute la production vinicole sarde.

Vermentino di Gallura (D.O.C.)

Ce vin provient des vignes cultivées autour de Santa Teresa di Gallura, localité la plus septentrionale de l'île, à flanc de montagne, sur un terrain qui ne promet guère. Sec, couleur d'ambre, titrant entre 13 et 14° d'alcool, il manque de distinction.

Malvasia di Bosa (D.O.C.)

D.O.C. produit en très petites quantités — à peine 150 hl dans une année moyenne — avec les raisins Malvasia et Seberu cultivés autour de Bosa, sur la côte occidentale de l'île, légèrement au nord du centre. Le vin qui titre entre 15 et 17,5° d'alcool a un agréable goût de noisette ; comparé au Vernaccia, il est un peu moins sec et d'une couleur plus riche et sombre. Un autre vin fait avec le même raisin est le Malvasia di Cagliari (D.O.C.), au goût légèrement amer d'amandes grillées.

Oliena

Fait avec des raisins Cannonau et Monica, dans la région de Nuoro, ce vin, plutôt sec, a une couleur grenat.

Cannonau di Sardegna (D.O.C.)

Vin sec ou demi-doux d'un beau rouge rubis, fait avec des raisins Cannonau ; il existe également un rosé. Lorsqu'il est viné, le Cannonau, qui rappelle le Porto, donne un excellent vin de liqueur (Cannonau Liquoroso Dolce Naturale) ainsi qu'un apéritif *(liquoroso secco).*

Vins de dessert

Autrefois, les Sardes portaient le gros de leurs efforts sur la production de vins de dessert. Il est évident que le climat chaud de leur île permet aux vignes de donner des raisins riches en sucre, donc corsés et doux. Le Girò di Cagliari rouge, doux, rappelle un peu le Porto ; il est fait avec du raisin Girò, cultivé dans le voisinage de Cagliari. Le Monoca di Sardegna et le Monica di Cagliari (D.O.C.) assez semblables mais d'une couleur plus foncée, presque violette. Ces deux vins titrent jusqu'à 17°. Le Nasco — vin blanc ou plutôt d'une couleur dorée très marquée — est réputé pour son bouquet, qui rappellerait le parfum de la fleur d'oranger, et aussi pour sa saveur un peu amère. On trouve également des Muscat de Sardaigne, notamment le Moscato di Sorso-Sennori (D.O.C.) et Moscato di Cagliari (D.O.C.), deux vins qui sont souvent vinés.

Voir ITALIE

Sarre (Saar)

Voir MOSELLE

Sassella

Vin rouge de la Valteline fait avec du raisin Nebbiolo.

Voir LOMBARDIE

Saumur et Coteaux de Saumur (A.O.C.)

Vins blancs mousseux, pétillants et non mousseux, généralement secs. Du rosé et du rouge aussi. Anjou.

La différence entre les deux appellations n'a jamais été précisée clairement. Pour le moment elles ont presque la même signification. Actuellement, on ne vend sous l'appellation Coteaux de Saumur qu'une petite quantité de vin blanc et on ne trouve aucun rouge sous cette appellation. Pour l'appellation Saumur, les vins sont rouges, blancs et rosés, mais on ne trouve guère de Saumur rouge hors de la région. Ils peuvent être mousseux, pétillants ou non mousseux. La plus grande partie de la vendange est traitée en mousseux. Un peu plus lourd et plus banal que le Vouvray, le Saumur mousseux n'en est pas moins fort présentable mais ne saurait se comparer au Champagne. La plus grande partie du Saumur mousseux est vinifiée et vieillie dans les énormes cavernes creusées dans les falaises entourant la ville. La loi exige que ces vins soient traités selon la méthode champenoise (*voir* CHAMPAGNE) de fermentation secondaire en bouteille, avec un pourcentage de Chenin Blanc. D'ordinaire le reste provient de Chardonnay, de Groslot avec une certaine quantité de Cabernet Franc. L'amélioration du vin mousseux est due à la création de l'appellation « Crémant de Loire ».

Le Saumur non mousseux est, en certaines années, un des très bons vins blancs d'Anjou. Généralement sec — quoiqu'il conserve parfois un léger vestige de douceur — il se révèle souvent plus robuste que les autres vins secs de cette province. Il existe deux rosés. Le meilleur est fait exclusivement avec du Cabernet. Ils ne diffèrent pas nettement des autres bons rosés d'Anjou. Une partie des blancs est pétillante ou demi-mousseuse. La production annuelle s'élève environ à 60 000 hl (plus de 650 000 caisses).

Voir LOIRE

Saumur-Champigny (A.O.C.)

Vin rouge, Anjou.

Là où confluent la Loire et la paisible Vienne et jusqu'à l'est de Saumur, s'étendent les coteaux crayeux où l'on cultive les Cabernet Franc qui donneront le Saumur-Champigny rouge. C'est un vin frais, généreux, d'un rouge rubis, dont le parfum rappelle celui des violettes. Les connaisseurs le jugent un peu plus rude que les rouges de Touraine. Cette appellation contrôlée de près de 800 ha étant située à l'extrême nord, limite à laquelle le Cabernet Franc peut donner encore de bons résultats, l'année importe particulièrement. Dans les très mauvaises années, une partie du raisin ne mûrit pas complètement et doit être vinifié, par conséquent, comme simple Rosé d'Anjou. La production annuelle moyenne des vins rouges d'appellation contrôlée s'élève à 40 000 hl (près de 450 000 caisses).

Saussignac (Appellation Contrôlée)

Vins blancs, pas très intéressants, de la Dordogne, produits à Gageac-et-Rouillac, Monestier, Razac-de-Saussignac et Saussignac. Les vins en appellation Saussignac peuvent aussi bénéficier de l'appellation Bergerac.

Sauternes (Appellation Contrôlée)

Vin blanc. Bordeaux.

L'atmosphère qui règne au moment des vendanges dans le Sauternais rappelle celle d'un film de Hitchcock. Pour faire un vin doux *réellement* naturel, le raisin doit atteindre un excès de maturité appelé pourriture noble. S'il n'y parvient pas, le vin n'aura pas sa richesse de sucre et d'alcool qui atteint parfois 16 et même 17°, avec 6 degrés de sucre résiduel, et il n'aura pas droit à l'appellation Sauternes. Mais, d'autre part, si l'on dépasse le point précis de surmaturation désirable, la suavité et la richesse du vin augmentent au point d'en oblitérer le bouquet. Ajoutons à cela que le moment propice vient tard dans une saison où le gel peut frapper la vigne à tout instant. Alors on compendra pourquoi les vignerons du Sauternais font les cent pas dans leurs vignes plusieurs fois par jour afin de décider quand ils vendangeront.

Aucun autre vin liquoreux au monde n'est fait à une telle échelle par un procédé aussi délicat et hasardeux. Seule une partie de la récolte de certains crus du Rhin et de la Moselle est traitée de la même manière pour donner les *Trockenbeerenauslese*, mot qui décrit parfaitement le procédé : « Raisins desséchés choisis spécialement » — et se compose lui-même comme un jeu de Meccano. La méthode du Sauternes est la seule qui puisse donner des vins aussi riches sans addition de sucre ni arrêt prématuré de la fermentation, ni par aucun autre artifice. La pourriture noble dont il s'agit est l'œuvre d'un champignon microscopique, *Botrytis cinerea,* qui attaque en automne la peau du raisin et fait évaporer l'eau. Cette moisissure n'augmente pas la teneur absolue en sucre mais seulement sa proportion par rapport à la masse totale du moût dont 80 % environ sont composés d'eau. En même temps, *Botrytis cinerea* provoque des transformations encore mal définies dans le raisin : augmentation de la teneur en glycérines et en pectines. Ce sont ces éléments qui donne au Sauternes sa suavité et son velouté et aussi ses célèbres « jambes » : lentes coulées du vin le long du verre quand on l'a incliné.

Quand elle est prête pour la vendange, la grappe a rapetissé et ses raisins sont ridés. Même si cette comparaison peut être désagréable, elle est exacte : cette grappe ressemble alors à une chauve-souris qui dort pendue par les pattes. La pourriture noble, d'une couleur grisâtre, ne semble pas promettre le nectar qu'elle donnera. L'eau s'étant évaporée, le raisin ne donne pas une grande quantité de jus. Cette perte de volume s'ajoute aux frais plus élevés de vendange. Le champignon se développe au hasard sur la vigne et il faut passer et repasser jusqu'à six fois, voire plus, entre les rangs pour choisir les raisins qui sont à point. On comprendra que le vrai Sauternes ne peut pas être bon marché.

Vrai Sauternes. Aucun autre vin, en effet n'est aussi souvent flatté par ceux qui volent son nom. Le Sauternes n'est pas un quelconque vin blanc doux, mais le vin blanc doux du Sauternais, dans la région de Bordeaux, en France. Les vins qu'on

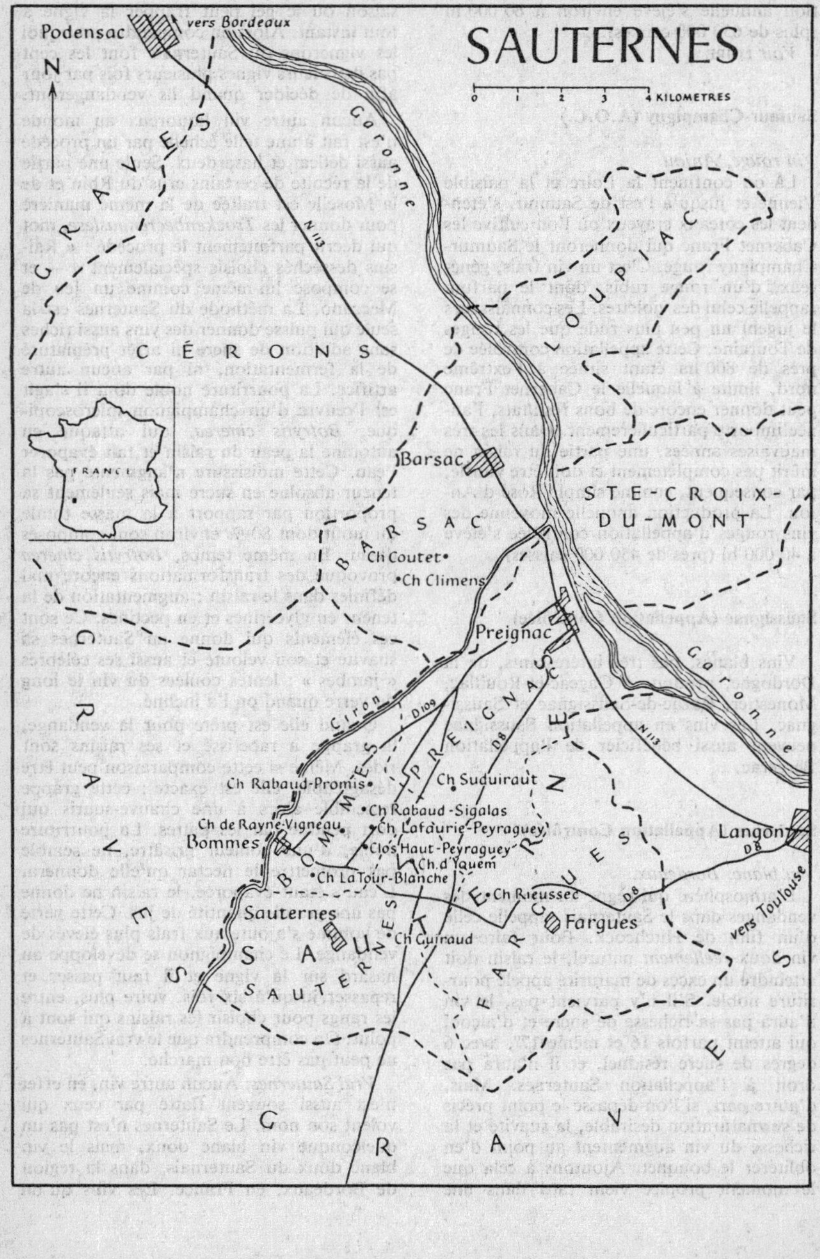
SAUTERNES
0 1 2 3 4 KILOMETRES
Podensac
vers Bordeaux
N
GRAVES
Garonne
N113
CÉRONS
LOUPIAC
FRANCE
Barsac
BARSAC
STE CROIX DU-MONT
Ch Coutet
Ch Climens
Preignac
PREIGNAC
Garonne
N113
Ciron
D109
D8
Ch Suduiraut
Ch Rabaud-Promis
Ch Rabaud-Sigalas
Ch de Rayne-Vigneau
Ch Lafaurie-Peyraguey
Bommes
BOMMES
Clos Haut-Peyraguey
Ch d'Yquem
Ch La Tour-Blanche
Ch Rieussec
Sauternes
SAUTERNES
Fargues
FARGUES
Ch Guiraud
Langon
D8
vers Toulouse
GRAVES

trouve en bien d'autres parties du monde et qui s'appellent sauternes — et même sauterne, comme si une mauvaise orthographe apaisait les mauvaises consciences — ne sont pas des Sauternes.

Les caractéristiques de chaque vin sont déterminées par divers facteurs parmi lesquels le sol, le temps, dans une certaine région géographique, ont une importance capitale. Des vignes de la même variété, même issues les unes des autres, ne produiront pas le même vin sur des sols et sous des climats différents. Quand on a trouvé la vigne (ou les vignes) qui convient à une certaine région propice à la viticulture, on obtiendra un vin magnifique, mais seulement après des dizaines d'années de travail : plusieurs générations. On ne trouve pas, sur toute la surface du globe, deux régions où tous les facteurs s'allient de la même manière pour produire deux vins identiques.

Le Sauternais comprend cinq communes : Sauternes, Barsac, Bommes, Preignac et Fargues. On y fait partout le vin d'une manière parfaitement identique, principalement avec du Sémillon et du Sauvignon. Le Muscadelle n'entre dans cette composition que pour une très faible proportion. Étant donné qu'en Sauternes on ne vendange pas rang par rang, mais au fur et à mesure de la surmaturation, chaque producteur obtient un vin différent selon la date à laquelle il a vendangé.

Lorsqu'elles arrivent au chai, les grappes passent d'abord dans un long cylindre rotatif qui remplace l'ancien fouloir. Il exprime le premier jus. Ensuite on procède à l'éraflage, puis les raisins sont pressurés trois fois de suite. Autrefois, les produits de ces quatre pressurages étaient traités séparément. De nos jours, on les mélange dans de grandes cuves où la vendange du jour ne reste que quelques heures. Puis on verse le moût dans des fûts où il fermente et vieillit. La vendange d'un jour n'étant jamais identique à celle de la veille ni à celle du lendemain, chaque fût donne un vin différent. Lorsqu'il apparaît que le vin de certains fûts n'atteindra pas les normes souhaitées, on lui refuse le nom du château où il est fait et on le vend sous le nom d'un deuxième vin ou à des commerçants bordelais qui l'étiquettent alors simplement Sauternes. Dans ce cas il est formellement interdit aux négociants d'indiquer que la bouteille contient un vin d'un Cru Classé, car elle est vendue au prix — plus modique — d'un vin régional.

Le rendement maximum est de 3 000 bouteilles à l'ha (25 hl/ha) dans le Sauternais et la région produit, dans sa totalité, l'équivalent de 4 millions de bouteilles par an. Les Sauternes diffèrent d'un cru à l'autre, donc à plus forte raison de commune à commune mais ont tous, néanmoins, les mêmes caractéristiques générales. Les Barsac par exemple, ressemblent étrangement aux Sauternes. La seule différence que l'on puisse noter est que les Barsac sont parfois moins doux. Les Barsac ont droit à deux appellations au choix du producteur : Barsac ou Sauternes. Ils proviennent de vignes cultivées sur un terrain plus plat, moins pierreux, plus crayeux, à l'extrémité nord du Sauternais (*voir* BARSAC). Le Sauternais proprement dit — région plus accidentée autour des agglomérations de Sauternes, Bommes et Fargues — est plus pittoresque. La route des vignobles, guère plus large qu'un sentier, passe entre de vieux murs de pierre. Les grands crus couvrent les coteaux. Au sommet de chacun on voit généralement un château.

Les vignobles cultivés sur les terres les plus basses furent gravement endommagés par les gels de février 1956. Ceux des coteaux le furent moins. On ne trouve pas de 1956 ni de 1957, et fort peu du millésime des quelques années suivantes. La récolte de 1973 fut entièrement détruite par la grêle. Et les vins de 1974 sont rares.

Il faut servir le Sauternes frais, mais le glacer serait une hérésie car un froid excessif le paralyserait. On peut l'amener à une température propice dans un sceau à glace ou un réfrigérateur. Les Français servent parfois du vieux Sauternes madérisé en guise d'apéritif. L'oxydation aura légèrement atténué sa douceur mais ne l'aura pas fait disparaître.

Les Sauternes conviennent au foie gras, au saumon au début du repas ou au dessert. Le dessert avec lequel ils se marient le mieux est le fruit. Certains connaisseurs versent un verre de Sauternes en guise de dessert.

Le propriétaire de Château-d'Yquem n'est pas du tout de cet avis. Il soutient que depuis le XIXe siècle la tradition exige de boire le Sauternes non avec le dessert mais seulement avec certains poissons, avec du foie gras et du roquefort.

Crus classés de Sauternes et de Barsac (Classification de 1855)	
PREMIER GRAND CRU	
Château-d'Yquem (Sauternes)	
PREMIERS CRUS	
Château-La Tour-Blanche (Bommes)	Château-Climens (Barsac)
Château-Lafaurie-Peyraguey (Bommes)	Château-Guiraud (Sauternes)
Clos Haut-Peyraguey (Bommes)	Château-Rieussec (Fargues)
Château de Rayne-Vigneau (Bommes)	Château-Rabaud-Promis (Bommes)
Château de Suduiraut (Preignac)	Château-Sigalas-Rabaud (Bommes)
Château-Coutet (Barsac)	
SECONDS CRUS	
Château-Doisy-Daëne (Barsac)	Château-Nairac (Barsac)
Château-Doisy-Védrines (Barsac)	Château-Caillou (Barsac)
Château-d'Arche (Sauternes)	Château-Suau (Barsac)
Château-Filhot (Sauternes)	Château-de Malle (Preignac)
Château-Broustet (Barsac)	Château-Romer (Fargues)
	Château-Lamothe (Sauternes)

Voir CHATEAU-D'YQUEM et chacun des Premiers Crus à sa place dans l'ordre alphabétique. *Voir aussi* BARSAC

Sauvignon Blanc

Raisin blanc d'une qualité exceptionnelle, utilisé pour faire certains excellents vins blancs. Avec le Sémillon, et un peu de Muscadelle, il donne les meilleurs blancs de Bordeaux, depuis les Sauternes les plus doux jusqu'aux Graves les plus secs. Quelques blancs de la Loire, merveilleusement agréables, ne sont faits qu'avec ce seul raisin, notamment ceux de Sancerre. Le meilleur Pouilly-sur-Loire, qu'on appelle dans la région Blanc Fumé, a nettement le goût du Sauvignon Blanc. On cultive ce raisin en Californie où on le considère comme le meilleur pour le vin blanc, surtout dans les vallées de Livermore, San Benito et Santa Clara. Les vins qu'il fournit varient selon le sol, le climat et en fonction du traitement de la vigne et du raisin. Mais partout où les conditions sont favorables le vin aura une race et une distinction respectables. Dans certains secteurs de la vallée de la Loire, on l'appelle Surin ; en Allemagne, Muskat Sylvaner.

Sauvignon, Cabernet Sauvignon

Le meilleur raisin à vin rouge cultivé dans le Médoc. Petit, bleu-noir, la peau épaisse, il donne un jus abondant. Son vin, très ferme, vieillit lentement. Dans d'autres régions on l'appelle Bouchet et Vidure.

Voir CABERNET

Savagnin

Variété de raisin prévalant dans la composition des vins de Château-Chalon. Le Traminer Rouge d'Alsace s'appelle parfois Savagnin Rose, Savagnin Noir est un des noms régionaux du Pinot Noir.

Savatiano

Une des principales variétés de raisin utilisée en Grèce pour les liqueurs et les vins de table. Ces derniers sont souvent traités à la résine. On cultive le Savatiano surtout au centre de la Grèce et au Péloponnèse.

Voir GRÈCE

Savennières (Anjou-Coteaux de la Loire) (A.O.C.)

Un des meilleurs vins blancs vinifiés à partir du cépage Chenin Blanc. Les meilleures A.O.C. sont : Coulée-de-Serrant, Roche-aux-Moines.

Voir ANJOU ; LOIRE

Savigny-lès-Beaune et Savigny-lès-Beaune-Côte de Beaune (Appellation Contrôlée)

Bourgogne rouges et blancs. Côte de Beaune.

Au début du Moyen Age, les vignobles appartenaient à des moines. Mais la noblesse s'intéressait aussi à la viticulture. Un grand château entouré de fossés, construit en 1340, rasé en 1468, reconstruit en 1672, se dresse encore en bordure de la principale place de Savigny, entouré d'un parc un peu en désordre. Jadis demeure seigneuriale, il a perdu son opulence : les volets sont fermés et quelques poules grattent le sol de ce qui fut la cour d'honneur.

Quelque 360 ha de Savigny sont plantés de vignes et la production annuelle s'élève en moyenne à environ 12 000 hl (plus de 130 000 caisses) de vin presque totalement rouge, à l'exception de quelques centaines d'hectolitres.

Ce vin était très apprécié au temps jadis. Un duc de Bourgogne voulut élever un vigneron au rang de demi-dieu pour la qualité de son nectar. Mais la réputation du Savigny a beaucoup diminué. Léger et parfumé avec une grande finesse remarquable, ce n'est pourtant pas un vin de garde. L'agglomération se trouve entre Pernand-Vergelesses et Beaune. Les vins de ces trois localités sont fort semblables, mais ceux de Beaune sont meilleurs. Le Savigny se vend sous le nom de la commune, avec ou sans la mention Côte de Beaune, car si un vin atteint les normes d'une de ces appellations, il a aussi droit à l'autre. Assorti aux produits de certaines autres communes de la même Côte, il est vendu sous l'étiquette : Côte de Beaune-Villages. Les meilleurs vignobles de Savigny sont classés Premiers Crus, ce qui implique des normes minimales plus élevées et assure une plus haute qualité. Leurs vins peuvent être vendus sous le nom de la commune suivi de celui du cru. Voici la liste des principaux : Vergelesses, Marconnets, Dominode, Jarrons, Lavières, Serpentières, Peuillets et Aux Guettes.

Savoie (Haute-)

Cette région possède quatre appellations contrôlées de vins blancs : Crépy, Seyssel, Seyssel Mousseux et les vins de Savoie *(voir ces noms)*.

Scharlachberg

Bon vin blanc fait près de Bingen, sur le Rhin.

Voir RHEINHESSEN : BINGEN

Scharzholfberg

Généralement le meilleur vin de la Sarre. Il atteint fréquemment une élégance incomparable.

Voir SARRE

Schaumwein

Vin mousseux, en allemand.

Schiave

Raisin rouge cultivé en Italie, surtout dans le Haut-Adige.

Schiedam

Nom que les Hollandais donnent souvent à leur *genièvre,* parce que Schiedam est une des localités qui produisent le plus de cet alcool.

Schillerwein

Type de vin rouge produit en Europe centrale et dans le sud-est de l'Europe à partir de raisins rouges et blancs mêlés ensemble avant la vinification. Le jus fermente quelques jours avec ses peaux avant d'être soutiré : une partie du pigment et du tanin présents dans les peaux passent ainsi au moût, ce qui facilite grandement le travail du vinificateur et fait que le vin peut être bu beaucoup plus tôt.

Cette technique de vinification qui est vraisemblablement identique à celle des rosés, un typique Schillerwein d'Europe orientale a une couleur beaucoup plus profonde que celle des rosés français moyens.

Schloss

Littéralement : « château » en allemand, mais dans le jargon vinicole, ce terme est l'équivalent du château français, ou du domaine, qui comprend construction, vignobles, caves, etc.

Schloss Böckelheimer Kupfergrube

Bons vins de la vallée de la Nahe, en Allemagne. Les vignes qui les donnent sont cultivées au flanc d'un coteau nommé Kupfergrube (mine de cuivre).

Voir NAHE

Schloss Johannisberg

Le plus cher des Rheingau. Les courtiers et les vignerons les mieux informés de cette région le considèrent comme l'un de leurs meilleurs vins dont les qualités se maintiennent d'année en année, mais ils estiment qu'en certaines années d'autres le dépassent.

Voir RHEINGAU : JOHANNISBERG

Schloss Vollrads

Le meilleur vin du secteur de Winkel, dans la vallée du Rhin, en Allemagne, et un des meilleurs de toute cette région.

Voir RHEINGAU : SCHLOSS VOLLRADS

Schlossabzug

Les termes *Originalabfüllun* et *Schlossabzug* s'appliquaient à un vin naturel non chaptalisé mis en bouteille au domaine. Ils sont remplacés par *Erzeugerabfullung*.

Schnapps

En Allemagne et en Hollande : n'importe quel spiritueux fort et sec ; en Scandinavie, généralement l'aquavit. On fait un Schnapps aromatique avec du gin de type hollandais dans lequel ont infusé des herbes.

Schooner

Grand verre convenant particulièrement pour la bière et qui contient en général quelque 43 cl.

Schwarzwalder

Nom que les Allemands donnent indifféremment au Kirsch et au Cherry Brandy *(voir ces noms)*.

Scion

Segment d'une branche ou pousse, à un ou plusieurs bourgeons, greffée sur une souche pour former un pied complet. A la suite des ravages causés par le phylloxéra à la fin du XIXe siècle, on greffa des scions de *Vitis vinifera* européenne sur des souches américaines résistant à la maladie. Lorsque la bonne souche est sélectionnée pour la greffe, elle ne doit léguer aucune — ou très peu — de ses qualités personnelles au fruit du scion.

Sec

En matière de vin : contraire de doux. Un vin est sec quand tout le sucre du raisin a été converti en alcool par la fermentation. Les Bourgogne blancs, la plupart des Loire et Alsace, un bon nombre de Graves et Champagne, bien des vins de la Moselle et du Rhin sont secs, de même que des vins apéritifs tels que le Xérès, Fino et Amontillado. Le taux d'acidité du vin le rend aussi plus ou moins sec. La teneur en acide du vin en détermine également le caractère sec, à moins que celui-ci ne soit masqué par une teneur en sucre excessive.

Sur les étiquettes de Champagne, la mention « sec » n'indique pas que le vin soit vraiment sec, mais au contraire qu'il incline vers la douceur. De même, extra-sec (ou extra-dry) ne désigne pas un vin exceptionnellement sec, mais assez sec. Le Champagne vraiment sec est étiqueté « brut ».

Voir CHAMPAGNE

Secco

Pour le vin, sec, en italien.

Séché

Adjectif largement utilisé pour les vins âpres et plats à l'arrière-goût astringent. Cet état résulte d'une oxydation excessive.

Sédiment

Dépôt de matières solides qui apparaît au fond de la bouteille de vin au cours de son vieillissement. Bien qu'il soit amer, le sédiment n'a pas d'influence sur le goût du vin, pourvu qu'on le décante habilement avant de le servir.

Voir CHAPITRE V

Seeweine

Agréables petits vins du lac de Constance (Bodensee), sud de l'Allemagne.

Voir BADE

Seewinkel

Voir SANDWEINE

Seibel

Chercheur français qui obtint par hybridation une centaine de vignes aux caractéristiques diverses. Quelques-unes de ses réussites les plus notables ont été décrites par Philip Wagner, dans *A wine Grower's Guide.*

Sekt

Vin mousseux, en allemand. C'est Ludwig Devrient — célèbre acteur berlinois du XIXe siècle — qui lança ce mot en commandant sur scène du Sekt lorsqu'il jouait le rôle de Falstaff. Puis, comme il aimait le Champagne, il en usa de même pour en commander dans les cafés et les restaurants. Par la suite, le vin allemand du type Champagne prit le nom de Sekt.

Sémillon

Cépage à vin blanc utilisé pour les Sauternes et les Graves et assez répandu en Dordogne ainsi que dans le sud-est de la France. On le cultive aussi en Californie en Australie et ailleurs.

Séparation

Opération consistant à séparer les raisins des pédoncules et pédicelles de la grappe avant le transfer des raisins en cuves de fermentation. On dit aussi souvent : égrappage ou éraflage. Autrefois on éraflait à la main. Désormais, on se sert d'un égrappoir ou foulo-grappe. Tout le monde n'est pas d'accord au sujet de cette pratique, adoptée d'abord pour les vins fins de Bourgogne et de Bordeaux. De solides arguments militent pourtant en sa faveur. La séparation augmente la teneur en alcool des vins rouges d'environ 0,5°, en raison de l'abscence d'échanges qui se produisent normalement entre le moût et les rafles quand elles y baignent ensemble ; elle rend les vins moins astringents et les débarrasse de substances étrangères. Ils seront donc plus clairs, plus souples et vieilliront plus tôt que ceux qui ont absorbé le tanin de la rafle ainsi que des alcools non éthyliques. En outre, ce procédé économise le travail car le marc sera moins massif s'il ne contient pas de rafles.

En général on n'emploie guère l'égrappoir pour faire du vin blanc, sauf quelques-uns de haute qualité.

Seppeltsfield

Célèbre vignoble et centre viticole de la vallée de Barossa (Australie-Méridionale).

Voir AUSTRALIE

Sercial

Variété de raisin blanc qui fournit un des meilleurs Madère : sec, parfois pâle, parfois doré. Son bouquet est toujours immense.

Voir MADÈRE

Serre

Expression champenoise signifiant pressurage et résultat du pressurage. Dans la préparation du Champagne on appelle première serre, deuxième serre, etc., les produits successifs du pressurage. La première donne le vin de la plus haute qualité et la dernière — appelée aussi rebêche — un produit ordinaire destiné à la consommation du personnel de l'entreprise vinicole. La première serre donne le *vin de cuvée*, équivalant au *vin de tête* dans le Bordelais.

Sève

Liquide nutritif qui circule dans les plantes vasculaires, telles que la vigne. Mais en ce qui concerne le vin, on dit qu'il a de la sève pour suggérer charme, élégance, distinction féminines, c'est-à-dire une grâce qui ne s'impose pas comme celle des vins virils. On l'emploie aussi pour les Sauternes qui possèdent à un haut degré ces qualités, exquises certes, mais qui impliquent beaucoup de caractère perçant.

Seyssel (Appellation Contrôlée)

Vins blancs, mousseux et non mousseux. Haute vallée du Rhône. Vin des Alpes.

Peu après son entrée sur le territoire français, le Rhône traverse le secteur vinicole en forme de papillon de Seyssel, composé des deux communes qui portent ce nom (l'une en Haute-Savoie, l'autre dans l'Ain) et de celle de Corbonod (Ain). Les deux Seyssel et les deux départements sont séparés par le Rhône. Les vins de Seyssel sont blancs, parfois traités en mousseux.

Le secteur de Seyssel consiste en une série de collines et de dépressions, taillées jadis par les glaciers qui laissèrent sur leur passage de la marne siliceuse et du calcaire également siliceux. Tel est le sol sur lequel on cultive la vigne. Les collines offrent bon nombre de pentes exposées au sud et au sud-est.

Le Seyssel non mousseux n'est fait qu'avec de la Roussette. On ne sait pas si ce cépage fut cultivé dans l'Antiquité à Saint-Cornas et à Hermitage, sur le cours inférieur du Rhône, et si on le transporta à Seyssel sur les bateaux des marchands de sel, ou bien s'il fut importé de Chypre, ou encore si la Roussette descend de souches de Furmint, apportées de Hongrie par un duc de Savoie. Quelle que soit son origine, elle donne un vin léger, d'une sécheresse de silex, qui atteint sa plénitude très tôt et doit être bu jeune. C'est pourquoi on le met généralement en bouteille au mois d'avril qui suit les vendanges. La Roussette entre aussi dans la composition du Seyssel mousseux dans la proportion minimale de 10 %. Le reste est de la Molette et du Chasselas. A Seyssel, on appelle le mousseux du pays Bon Blanc.

Le secteur délimité de Seyssel comporte environ 60 ha de vignes et produit environ 2 500 hl (plus de 25 000 caisses) par an.

Seyval Blanc

Le Seyval Blanc (Seyval Seyve-Villard 5276) est l'une des meilleures variétés hybrides franco-américaines ; cette descendante du Chardonnay connaît un certain succès car elle s'acclimate facilement. Ce cépage mûrit tôt en grappes serrées que le mildiou attaque facilement. Ces grappes ont tendance à être trop chargées et nécessitent un éclaircissement au début de l'été. Le Seyval Blanc donne un vin blanc de bonne qualité qui va du demi-sec, semblable à certains vins allemands, au charpenté comme certains vins de la Loire et de Bourgogne. Cette variété est très répandue aux États-Unis.

Seyve-Villard

Bertille Seyve (1895-1959) était un hybrideur français qui développa un certain nombre de vignes hybrides. En 1919, il épousa la fille d'un autre hybrideur du nom de Villard, dès lors ses croisements, en particuliers ses blancs 5276 (Seyval Blanc) et 12.375 (Villard Blanc) furent connus sous le nom composé de Seyve-Villard.

Sherry

Xérès, en Anglais.

Voir XÉRÈS

Sherry Butt (ou Sherry Bota)

Fût d'une contenance de 600 l, s'il sert à la conservation, et de 500 l pour l'expédition. Dans le négoce espagnol, sa contenance totale est de 516 l, ce qui laisse une marge de 16 l pour évaporation, clarification, etc.

Voir XÉRÈS

Shot Berries

Nom anglais de la *coulure* : chute des fleurs avant leur fécondation ou apparition de grains de raisin de tailles très disparates sur la grappe.

Voir CHAPITRE III : COULURE

Sicile

Vins rouges et blancs. Ile de l'Italie méridionale.

La Sicile, séparée du bas de l'Italie par le détroit de Messine, est la plus vaste et la plus romantique des îles de la Méditerranée. Elle a de superbes plages, l'Etna et des étendues de maquis. Oranges, citrons et vignes y poussent et avec près de trois mille ans d'occupation par les Phéniciens, les Grecs, les Sarrasins, les Normands et les Espagnols, elle est devenue le « musée archéologique » de l'Europe. Temples, théâtres, cités de la Grande Grèce, ponts et aqueducs de la Rome antique, palais et églises normands attirent chaque année les amoureux d'art. Les étés y sont chauds et les vignes prolifiques : la contribution de la Sicile à la production vinicole totale de l'Italie est de 9 millions d'hl (100 000 caisses) par an, et représente près de 1/4 des exportations de vins italiens. La plupart des vins rouges sont exportés vers la France pour y être adjoints à de nombreux vins français.

Dans le passé, les vins corsés, tels que le fameux Marsala, prédominaient. Les ceps de vigne pour le Marsala, principalement le cépage Grillo, couvraient en abondance la partie occidentale de l'île. Depuis 1960 cependant, la Sicile est devenue un grand producteurs de vins de table, rouges et blancs, secs. Les vignobles jadis consacrés à la production du Marsala ont été replantés de variétés de Trebbiano, de Catarratto et d'Inzolia pour les vins blancs secs, de Sangiovese, de Nero Mascalise pour les vins rouges secs.

Une grande part des améliorations des vins siciliens est due aux efforts des œnologues et des coopératives viticoles. Pour préserver la fraîcheur et le fruité, les œnologues ont convaincu les propriétaires de vendanger plus tôt, début septembre. Ainsi, malgré les chaleurs de l'été, les vins peuvent préserver leur fruité et leur acidité et ne pas avoir un degré excessif d'alcool. En outre, les vins sont mis en bouteilles au cours du mois de décembre qui suit les vendanges au lieu de rester dans les cuves pendant 10 ou 14 mois.

Les coopératives ont fourni l'élément technologique et commercial qui a permis de supporter les modifications apportées dans la viticulture sicilienne. Aujourd'hui, 120 coopératives fournissent 80 % de la production viticole de la Sicile. Parmi les plus importants exportateurs de vins en bouteille, il faut citer Corvo près de Palerme et la coopérative Settesoli, à Menfi, près d'Agrigente. (La ville d'Agrigente possède des temples grecs du VIe et du Ve siècle avant J.-C.). Parmi les autres bons producteurs, citons la coopérative Enocarbj à Sciassa, Regaleali qui appartient au comte Giuseppi Tasca, Sclafabi près de Palerme et Villa Grande près de l'Etna.

TYPES DE VINS

Marsala. Vin d'apéritif et de dessert. Anciennement très populaire, le Marsala est obtenu par coupage du moût de vin blanc et de Passito : raisin sec fermenté avec de l'alcool de vin. Le type Vergine est généralement obtenu par système *solera*.

Corvo di Casteldaccia. Les vins rouges et surtout les vins blancs qui portent ce nom sont les vins siciliens les plus connus. Fondée par le duc de Salaparuta au début du XVIIIe siècle, la firme appartient aujourd'hui aux autorités siciliennes. Les vins blancs bonifiés, frais et secs ont quelque peu de la dureté du raisin de Trebbiano. Les rouges, à base de Nero Mascalese, de Perricone et de Calabrese sont bien vinifiés, forts et ils subsistent longtemps au palais.

Etna (D.O.C.). Les vins rouge, blanc et rosé proviennent des raisins cultivés sur les flancs frais et bien ensoleillés du volcan. Ces trois vins ont une teneur élevée en alcool. Le rouge est fait avec du Merello et de Mascalese, le blanc avec du Carricante et du Catarratto (le meilleur vient de Mils), et le rosé d'un rose profond proche du rubis.

Mamertino. Ce vin blanc, doré, est cultivé sur les coteaux avoisinant Messine, il est demi-doux, très fort, avec un bouquet aromatique.

Malvasia delle Lipari (D.O.C.). Vin jaune, doux, fait avec des raisins séchés, sur les îles de Salina, Stromboli et Lipari, satellites de la Sicile. On fait également des *passito* et des *liquoroso* avec les mêmes raisins séchés.

Moscato di Noto (D.O.C.). Vin jaune pâle, fleurant le miel, produit en petite quantité dans la région de Moscato di Siracusa.

Moscato di Pantelleria (D.O.C.). Vin de dessert couleur d'ambre et parfumé, produit sur l'île de Pantelleria, à mi-chemin entre la Sicile et la Tunisie.

Faro (D.O.C.). Vin rouge produit aux environs de Messine. Très bon pour la table, il n'est en général pas trop fort mais il peut titrer aussi parfois 14°.

Alcamo (D.O.C.). Également connu sous l'appellation Bianco d'Alcamo, ce vin est fait avec des raisins Catarratto et un peu de Trebbiano cultivés au nord-ouest de la Sicile, entre Palerme et Trapani. C'est un vin sec, frais, fruité et parfumé, de couleur jaune paille.

Cerasuolo di Vittoria (D.O.C.). Vin de couleur cerise particulièrement fort en alcool et pouvant vieillir très longtemps. C'est un excellent vin de table au bouquet de grenade et de jasmin.

Sigalas-Rabaud (Château-)

Bordeaux blanc. Commune de Bommes, en Sauternais.

Ce château appartient au comte et à la comtesse de Lambert ; la comtesse descend de la famille Sigalas (*voir* Rabaud-Promis au sujet des origines de ce domaine).

Caractéristiques : Meilleur que son voisin. Très distingué. Un des meilleurs Sauternes par bonnes années.

Superficie : 14 ha.

Production moyenne : 35 tonneaux (3 000 caisses).

Silvestro

Liqueur italienne dans la composition de laquelle entrent diverses herbes et parmi lesquelles domine la menthe. On attribue son invention à Fra San Silvestro.

Singlings

L'eau-de-vie de vin entre la première et la seconde distillation.

Šipon

Variété de raisin cultivée en Slovénie et dont on trouve le nom sur les étiquettes des vins de Ljutomer (Lutomer), par exemple : Lutomer Sipon. Ce mot s'écrit aussi parfois comme il se prononce : Chipon.

Voir YOUGOSLAVIE

Sirah

Raisin à vin rouge.

Voir PETITE-SYRAH

Siran (Château-)

Bordeaux rouge. Commune de Labarde-Margaux, en Haut-Médoc.

Le nom serait né en 1428, lorsqu'un certain Guillaume de Siran prêta serment d'allégeance à l'abbé de Saint-Croix en l'église de Macau.

Le domaine fut d'abord connu sous le nom de Saint-Siran. En 1809, la comtesse de Toulouse-Lautrec-Moufa, grand-mère du peintre, le reçut en héritage. Il appartient maintenant à Alain Miailhe qui était propriétaire d'un domaine attenant : Château Dauzac.

Caractéristiques : Le vin mérite mieux que d'être un simple Cru Bourgeois. Dans la classification personnelle de l'auteur des vins de Bordeaux, celui-ci place le Château-Siran au niveau et même au-dessus de certains crus classés. Dans les bonnes années, Siran a la finesse et le caractère d'un vin supérieur.

Superficie : 30 ha.

Production moyenne : 120 tonneaux (11 000 caisses).

Sitges

Vin doux de dessert exceptionnellement clair, produit dans l'agglomération catalane du même nom.

Voir ESPAGNE

Sizzano (D.O.C.)

Vin rouge du Piémont italien (*voir ce nom*).

Skhou

Koumiss distillé.

Voir KOUMISS

Sling

Breuvage servi glacé dans un grand verre, composé d'un mélange de spiritueux (généralement du gin), de cordial et de jus de fruit.

Slivovitz

Prononcer Chlivovitsa. C'est le nom le plus courant en Yougoslavie de l'eau-de-vie serbe et bosnienne. En serbo-croate *Slijiva* signifie prune. Cette eau-de-vie est faite avec les prunes bleues (variété Poregace ou Madjarka) cultivées dans la zone productrice de ces fruits qui est la seconde du monde pour la quantité. C'est la boisson nationale des Bosniaques et des Serbes qui l'appellent aussi Rakija.

Produit par double distillation, ce spiritueux est exporté vers l'Europe occidentale, les États-Unis, l'Australie, notamment, entre 35 et 43°, dans des bouteilles hautes et minces ou bien rondes et plates comme le tonnelet traditionnel de Yougoslavie. Célèbre depuis le Moyen Age, cette eau-de-vie est faite avec les fruits des arbres âgés au moins de vingt ans ; distillée deux fois, elle mûrit dans de petites barriques, on met alors l'eau-de-vie en bouteilles où elle peut rester au moins cinq ans.

D'autres pays des Balkans produisent diverses variétés de Slivovitz, mais c'est la Yougoslavie qui en est le producteur le plus important.

Sloe Gin

Cordial obtenu en faisant macérer des prunelles dans du gin (*voir ce mot*).

Smith-Haut-Lafite (Château-)

Bordeaux rouge. Commune de Martillac, en Graves.

Ce superbe château est à l'abandon au milieu d'un bosquet de châtaigniers. Son vin rouge, classé parmi les premiers Graves en 1953, est un monopole de la maison Louis ·Eschenauer. Depuis 1968, les vins blancs sont faits exclusivement avec du Sauvignon Blanc.

Caractéristiques : Ce vin a moins de caractère que la plupart des Graves de première catégorie, mais il récompense ceux qui lui permettent de vieillir jusqu'à sa plénitude. Depuis 1985, a fait de gros progrès.

Superficie : rouge, 45 ha ; blanc, 5 ha.

Production moyenne : rouge : 180 tonneaux, 17 000 caisses ; blanc : 20 tonneaux, 2 000 caisses.

Soave (D.O.C.)

Vin blanc italien des environs de Vérone. Sec et d'un bouquet agréable, il a une texture suave.

Voir VÉNÉTIE

Sochou

Spiritueux chinois obtenu par la distillation du saké (vin de riz).

Solera

Méthode par laquelle on fait les vins de Xérès et de Malaga ainsi que certaines eaux-de-vie espagnoles.

Voir XÉRÈS

Som

Nom que les Roumains donnent au raisin Furmint.

Somlói Furmint

Vin blanc fait avec du raisin de Furmint, à Somló, près du lac Balaton.

Voir HONGRIE

Sommelier

Personne qui, dans les restaurants, est chargée du service des vins et liqueurs. On dit aussi caviste.

Sonnenglanz

Un des principaux crus de Beblenheim, en Alsace.

Voir ALSACE

Sonoma

Région vinicole de Californie, au nord de San Francisco, qui produit. quelques excellents vins de table et des mousseux.

Voir ÉTATS-UNIS : CALIFORNIE ET OUEST

Sorbino

Liqueur de cerise finlandaise.

Souche

Vigne ou bouture de vigne sur laquelle un scion (partie d'une autre vigne destinée à être greffée) a été greffé. En se développant dans la terre, la souche donne à la vigne des racines fortes et saines, alors que le scion porte les fruits.

Soufrage

Quelquefois traitement des vins par l'anhydride sulfureux, mais surtout : pulvérisation de soufre sur la vigne pour lutter contre l'oïdium *(voir ce mot)*.

Sour

Breuvage américain composé de jus de fruit (généralement du citron) et de spiritueux, par exemple : whisky sour, brandy sour, etc. Littéralement, *sour* signifie « acide ».

Soutirage

Opération qui consiste à séparer le vin de sa lie, soit en le pompant, soit en le laissant s'écouler hors du fût. On répète plusieurs fois le soutirage au cours du vieillissement du vin en barrique.

Voir CHAPITRE V

Spätburgunder

Rejeton allemand du Pinot Noir qui fut importé de Bourgogne. Il fournit 4,5 % des vignobles allemands.

Voir ALLEMAGNE

Spätlese

Vins plus pleins et plus riches faits avec des raisins cueillis tardivement.

Voir ALLEMAGNE

Spätrot

Voir ZIERFANDLER

Spiritueux

Tout liquide alcoolique obtenu par distillation — eaux-de-vie, gin, whisky, vodka, etc. — ou liqueur contenant une forte proportion d'alcool.

Voir CHAPITRE II ; CHAPITRE VI

Spiritus Vini Gallici

Littéralement : « Esprit du vin de France ». Nom donné à l'eau-de-vie de vin dans la pharmacopée britannique.

Spritzer

Nom donné en Allemagne et dans les pays anglo-saxons à un breuvage composé d'un tiers de vin du Rhin et de deux tiers d'eau gazeuse. Byron l'appelait : *bock and seltzer*. C'est un breuvage rafraîchissant, agréable à boire l'été avec beaucoup de glace. N'importe quel vin honnête convient, mais blancs et rosés sont préférables.

Spritzig

Adjectif allemand qui s'applique aux vins rendus légèrement pétillants par un excès de CO_2.

Spumante

Mot italien désignant les vins mousseux. Le plus célèbre est l'Asti Spumante.

Steinweine

Littéralement : « vin de pierre ». Il s'agit des vins blancs d'un or vert de Franconie, en Allemagne, et de Styrie, en Autriche. Dans leur étrange flacon ovale, les Steinweine de Franconie ont des caractéristiques tellement particulières qu'ils sont destinés aux seuls connaisseurs.

Voir FRANCONIE ; AUTRICHE ; BOCKSBEUTEL

Steinberger

Un des meilleurs Rheingau par bonnes années. Tout le Steinberg appartient au Staatsweingut qui produit la plupart de ses vins à Eltville (leur siège) dans un domaine vinicole modernisé. Ce cru est situé près de Wiesbaden, derrière l'ancien et impressionnant monastère cistercien de Kloster Eberbach, à 3 km au nord d'Hattenheim. Le vignoble fut planté à flanc de coteau par les moines cisterciens il y a 700 ans. Tout comme le Clos de Vougeot en Bourgogne, c'est une parcelle unique, ceinturée par un énorme mur de pierre.

Voir RHEINGAU

Steinhaeger

Gin allemand de Westphalie qui ressemble au genièvre.

Voir HOLLANDS ; GENEVA ; GENIÈVRE

Stellenbosch

Secteur vinicole de la province du Cap.

Voir AFRIQUE DU SUD

Still Wines

Vins non mousseux, en anglais. La loi américaine stipule qu'ils doivent titrer moins de 14°. On emploie aussi cet adjectif pour le Champagne nature (non mousseux).

Stinger

Breuvage fait d'eau-de-vie et de crème de menthe, avec quelques gouttes de jus de citron. On le sert glacé et coupé d'eau.

Stoup

Intraduisible en français, le terme cruche ne rendant pas toutes les significations du mot anglais.

Stout

Bière britannique brune et forte.

Voir BIÈRE

Stravecchio

Mot italien désignant les très vieux vins.

Strega

Liqueur italienne, douce, de couleur jaune.

Stück

En Palatinat et Rheinhessen, fût de 1 200 l équivalant à quelque 1 550 bouteilles. La mesure la plus courante du Rheingau est le *Halbstück* ou demi-Stück, d'une contenance de 600 l.

Styrie

Province vinicole d'Autriche, d'ailleurs peu productrice. On y fait du blanc, du rosé et du rouge. Comme Vienne, Graz, capitale de la Styrie, a son Heurige ou Vin de mai, ainsi qu'un Steinwein d'or pâle qui ne manque pas d'intérêt.

Voir AUTRICHE

Suau (Château-)

Bordeaux blanc. Commune de Barsac, en Sauternes.

Vin bien mené mais peu connu. Classé en 1855 parmi les Seconds Crus de Sauternes.

Superficie : 7 ha.

Production moyenne : 15 tonneaux (1 300 caisses).

Suave

Un vin qui n'est ni ferme, ni dur, ni rude, est suave. Certaines variétés de raisin à maturation rapide donnent des vins suaves. Dans d'autres cas c'est l'âge du vin qui détermine la suavité. A partir du moment où un vin est suave, il ne durera guère.

Sucre (Vin de)

« Vin » fait en ajoutant du sucre et de l'eau aux rafles de raisin après séparation et en laissant fermenter cette mixture. On dit ausi piquette, comme pour le vin de marc.

Sucrage

Opération qui consiste à ajouter du sucre au moût avant fermentation, en général pour compenser une maturation insuffisante du raisin. Le sucrage, autorisé pendant la fermentation s'appelle en France, la chaptalisation (*voir* CHAPITRE V).

Sud-ouest de la France

Hors la grande région vinicole de Bordeaux, le sud-ouest de la France, qui s'étend de la Dordogne aux Pyrénées, comporte plusieurs secteurs producteurs de vin. Beaucoup de ces bons vins ont été promus de V.D.Q.S. à une appellation contrôlée. On trouvera la plupart de ces appellations à leur place dans l'ordre alphabétique : Béarn, Bergerac, Buzet, Cahors, Côtes de Duras, Fronton et Côtes du Frontonnais, Côtes de Montravel, Saussignac, Gaillac, Jurançon, Madiran, Monbazillac, Pacherenc du Vic Bilh, Pécharmant, etc.

D'autres vins du Sud-Ouest, agréables à boire sur place, sont rangés dans la catégorie V.D.Q.S. (Vins délimités de qualité supérieure). Ce sont les Côtes du Marmandais, Côtes de Saint-Mont, Côtes du Brulhois, Tursan, Vin d'Entraygues et du Fel, Vin d'Estaing, Vin de Lavilledieu et Vin de Marcillac.

Voir V.D.Q.S.

Suduiraut (Château-)

Bordeaux blanc. Commune de Preignac, en Sauternais.

Jadis fameux et classé Premier Cru en 1855, ce vignoble a presque cessé d'exister au début de notre siècle. Depuis lors il a été reconstitué et, durant les dernières années, il a produit à nouveau de bons vins. Autrefois dénommé Cru du Roy, il est contigu à Château d'Yquem et appartient aujourd'hui à la fille de M. Fonquernie.

Caractéristiques : Sauternes plutôt suaves, assez légers et harmonieux pour vieillir avec profit.

Superficie : 75 ha.

Production moyenne : 100 tonneaux (10 000 caisses).

Suède

Le climat septentrional de la Suède est trop froid pour la vigne et les Suédois consomment donc des vins d'importation. Comme leurs voisins scandinaves, ils produisent divers spiritueux, en consomment la plus grande partie et en importent aussi. Tout le commerce des vins et spiritueux est un monopole d'État géré par Aktiebolaget Vin et Spritcentralen, avec bureaux et entrepôts principaux à Stockholm.

L'industrie et le commerce de l'alcool furent nationalisés en Suède en 1917, pour éviter leur prohibition. Jusqu'alors les distilleries suédoises produisaient environ un million d'hectolitres de spiritueux par an (plus de 11 millions de caisses), pour une population de 3 millions d'âmes. Il est vrai que ces distilleries étaient au nombre de 175 000. On imagine aisément les résultats. La situation était devenue critique quand le parlement prit l'affaire en main. Les prohibitionnistes menaient une campagne tapageuse et non sans arguments. Cependant, grâce à l'esprit de prévoyance du Dr Ivan Bratt, et à son habileté, le monopole d'État fut adopté comme compromis. Il permit de contrôler et de rationner la vente des spiritueux. Le rationnement fut levé en 1955.

Actuellement la Suède consomme environ un peu moins de 1 500 000 hl (plus de 16 millions de caisses) de vin et spiritueux par an, mais sa population a presque triplé depuis la nationalisation de l'industrie en 1917 et la consommation d'alcool s'en est trouvée réduite. Depuis quelques années, on vend pour la première fois plus de vin que de spiritueux. Une grande partie de ce vin provient des réserves accumulées au fil des ans par le monopole. Néanmoins, la boisson la plus populaire est l'aquavit, suivi par le punch *(voir ce mot)* suédois, à base de riz et de canne à sucre. Sur les rayons d'environ 300 magasins de monopole, on trouve plus de 850 marques différentes de vins et spiritueux.

La Suède importe environ 900 000 hl (10 millions de caisses) de vin par an, dont une bonne moitié en vins de table et en vins fins et le reste en vins vinés tels que vermouth, Xérès et Porto. Une très grande partie du vin est mis en bouteille en Suède. Le monopole importe le vin dans d'immenses réservoirs débarqués à Stockholm, à proximité de la firme qui le met en bouteilles. Les vins courants portugais, espagnols, algériens et français sont les plus consommés et vendus à des prix raisonnables car cette organisation, le plus gros importateur de vin et de spiritueux du monde, réalise de grandes économies en expédiant le vin en vrac. On trouve de grands vins français dans les magasins, mais le choix limité à quelques Bordeaux s'est amélioré récemment. La plupart des bouteilles sont d'années antérieures à la brusque inflation des prix des vins français et certaines sont par conséquent des valeurs sûres. Le monopole suédois Spritcentralen distille, vend et expédie la vodka « Absolut » qui connaît un immense succès aux États-Unis.

Suisse

La Suisse est un pays producteur et consommateur de vin, divisé en trois parties, selon la langue (italienne, française ou allemande) qui coïncide avec le goût en fait de vin. Il y a cependant quelques exceptions remarquables : On fait du Johannisberg avec du Sylvaner vert dans le canton de langue française du Valais et on a importé le Merlot du Bordelais dans le Tessin, de langue italienne. En règle générale, les vins suisses offrent une gamme infinie de diversité. On imagine la différence entre le Dézaley fait avec des vignes cultivées sur les coteaux ensoleillés qui entourent le lac Léman, et les vins de Vispertermin, provenant de vendanges sur les monts du Valais, non loin du Matterhorn, à près de 1 100 m d'altitude. Les fortes déclivités imposent la culture en terrasse, donc une somme énorme de travail. La plupart des vignobles sont divisés en petites parcelles, mais leurs propriétaires ont actuellement tendance à partager le matériel et à se grouper en coopératives. Selon la région, le vin est tantôt vinifié par les coopératives ou les négociants, tantôt mis en bouteille directement à la propriété. Chaque année, en novembre, on met aux enchères le vin de la dernière vendange et les acheteurs affluent des alentours.

La vigne couvre 14 000 ha du territoire suisse. Sur 23 cantons, trois seulement n'en cultivent pas. Vaud, Valais, Genève et Neuchâtel (langue française) sont les plus importants producteurs. La vigne prospère autour des lacs de Genève et de Neuchâtel, sur les rives du Rhône en son cours supérieur et dans le Tessin (italien). La culture est moins dense à l'est et au centre et, comme dans le Tessin et aux environs de Genève, on consomme la production. La production annuelle dépasse 1 million d'hl (plus de 11 millions de caisses) ; les exportations, entre 5 000 et 10 000 hl (entre 35 000 et 110 000 caisses). Le préjugé selon lequel les vins suisses sont inaptes au transport est désormais battu en brèche car on en voit maintes bouteilles dans les vitrines des marchands de vin de nombreux autres pays. En général on admet qu'ils sont agréables mais un peu « courts » : leur goût s'efface rapidement. Ils sont chers par rapport aux vins français.

Suisse française

La Suisse française ou romande est un pays agréable, de collines ensoleillées s'abaissant vers les rives des lacs, de vergers et de châteaux.

Vaud

Ce canton était, il y a 25 ans, le plus gros producteur de vin de pays, mais il a perdu sa place au profit du Valais. La production provient des vignobles plantés à l'est et à l'ouest de Lausanne. Ce canton se divise en trois régions vinicoles : Lavaux et Chablais, à l'est ; La Côte à l'ouest et le Nord Vaudois.

Lavaux

Ce secteur s'étend sur une quinzaine de kilomètres, de Lausanne à Montreux, et Vevey en occupe presque exactement le centre *(voir* VEVEY). La déclivité générale est orientée au sud, ce qui offre la meilleure exposition au soleil et protège des températures extrêmes. On y aurait fait du vin dès le temps des Romains, et c'est probablement vrai.

A coup sûr, l'évêque de Lausanne prit, aux environs de 1137, un grand intérêt à la culture de la vigne et en aurait chargé les cisterciens, qui devinrent ainsi les principaux propriétaires d'une région s'étendant entre Lutry et Pully.

Pour le touriste, c'est une des zones vinicoles les plus charmantes de Suisse. Le château de Chillon y surplombe le lac d'un air contemplatif. La vigne s'élève au nord du lac Léman sur une succession de terrasses ; elle occupe la moindre crevasse du rocher ; le raisin mûrit à la chaleur du soleil et des rayons que reflète l'eau. Mais les vignerons y mènent une vie pénible. Les machines ne peuvent leur servir à rien dans un décor aussi chaotique. Les vignerons montent et descendent le long de sentiers vertigineux avec leur hotte sur le dos. Quand la pluie entraîne la terre, il faut la remonter à dos d'homme.

Principaux crus : Dézaley, qui produit un vin doré, que bien des gens considèrent comme le meilleur de Suisse ; Saint-Saphorin ; Rivaz ; Epesses ; Riex ; Villette ; Lutry ; Cully. La municipalité de Lausanne possède le Clos des Abbeyes et le Clos des Moines, tout proches de la ville et dont les vins sont mis aux enchères tous les ans début décembre.

Encépagement : Surtout le Chasselas, qui, comme dans ces cantons environnants, s'adapte bien au sol et au climat pour donner des vins secs, fruités et robustes tout à fait différents et supérieurs de ceux qu'il fournit en France.

La Côte

Ce pays de vignobles, sur la côte nord-ouest du lac Léman, a conservé intact son charme pastoral. Vergers, champs et vignes y alternent, ces dernières plantées au sommet des coteaux. La route du vin traverse des villages charmants : Féchy, Mont-sur-Rolle, Vinzel, Luins. D'autres vins agréables et vivaces proviennent de Bougy, de Begnins, de Bursins et de Perroy, situés dans le même secteur à côté de Chasselas, on cultive aussi le Gamay et le Pinot Noir qui donnent des vins agréables.

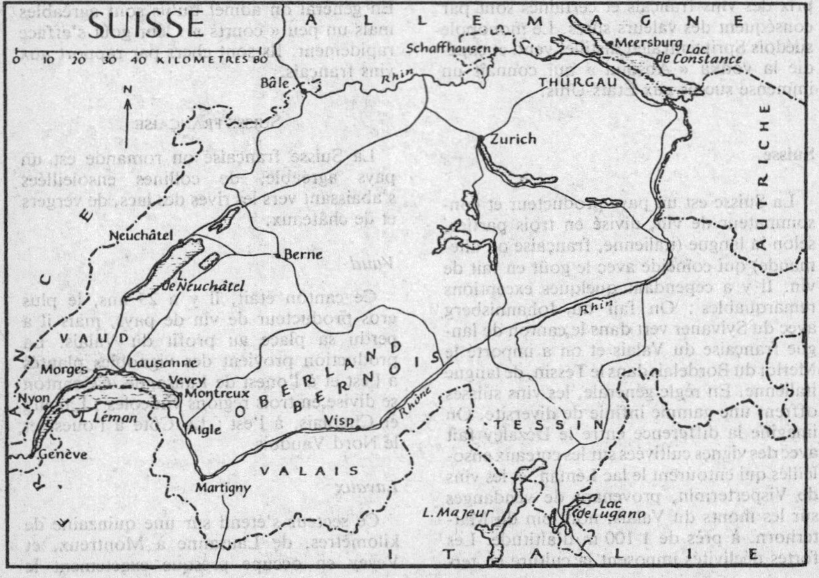

Chablais Vaudois

Ces vins blancs, plutôt capiteux et assez doux, proviennent des environs d'Aigle, au pied des Alpes. Les crus de Bex, d'Ollon, d'Yvorne, de Villeneuve et d'Aigle ont de la race, de l'acidité, une saveur nette où domine la véritable pierre à fusil.

Nord Vaudois

Ce petit secteur s'étend jusqu'à Concise, un peu au nord du lac de Neuchâtel. On y fait les vins blancs et rouges d'Orbe, de Grandson, de Bonvillars et de Concise. Quelques kilomètres à l'est, la région de Vully, dont les vignes s'étendent sur les rives du Lac de Morat et qui sont partagées entre les cantons de Fribourg et de Vaud, donnent un vin blanc pétillant. Le nord du canton de Vaud donne aussi des vins rouges peu connus, mais très plaisants.

Neuchâtel, Lac de Bienne

Ce canton est le plus septentrional de la Suisse française. La région du vin y commence un peu au-dessus du Lac à Vaumarcus, et se prolonge sans interruption jusqu'au Landeron, auprès du lac de Bienne. Un groupe de vignobles moins importants couvre les côtes de ce lac. Leurs meilleurs crus sont Schafis et Twann, qui donnent des vins vivaces.

Les vins blancs de Neuchâtel proviennent d'un sol crayeux. Ils sont très légers et vifs. Depuis plus d'un siècle les maisons Mauler et Bouvier pratiquent la méthode champenoise de fermentation secondaire en bouteille. Le vin rouge exclusivement fait de Pinot Noir est considéré comme l'un des meilleurs de Suisse. L'Œil-de-Perdrix — fait également avec du Pinot Noir après une brève cuvaison — est un rosé d'un charme particulier. La ville de Neuchâtel, capitale du canton, se trouve à l'extrémité nord-est du lac. Quand on la regarde du haut des collines, on voit un formidable château fort et l'église « La Collégiale ». Les vignes entourent l'agglomération. Le Neuchâtel était le plus exporté des vins suisses.

Principaux crus : Auvernier, Cormondrèche, Cortaillod, Cressier, Saint-Blaise. Ces vins sont parfois vendus sous l'étiquette d'un clos ou d'une localité, mais plus souvent sous l'appellation Neuchâtel.

Encépagement : Chasselas et Pinot Noir. Un peu de Pinot Gris et de Chardonnay fournissent les vins fermes et corsés.

Valais

C'est le « vieux pays ». Dans sa vallée haute, avant qu'il se jette dans le lac Léman, le Rhône est bordé de vergers et sur sa rive droite les vignes grimpent le long des contreforts des Alpes. Sur les moins élevés, les terrasses abritées s'étendent au soleil. On voit parfois, beaucoup plus haut, un vigneron juché à une altitude vertigineuse au-dessus de l'eau, en train de bêcher le sol ou de palisser les vignes à de hauts piquets. Les automnes du Valais sont longs et doux. On y cultive la vigne depuis l'époque romaine, par tradition. Au printemps, les montagnards d'Anniviers descendent de leur aire, au son des fifres et des tambours, pour faire la fête, entrecoupant leur long et dur temps de travail dans les vignes. Le vin fermente en cuve, passe l'hiver à Sierre, en fût de mélèze et n'est charroyé qu'après la fonte des neiges jusqu'au Val d'Anniviers où des caves sont creusées dans les pentes des Becs de Bossons. On les appelle Vins du Glacier. Ils sont blancs et en général durs.

Entre Loèche-les-Bains et Martigny, quelque 5 500 ha sont plantés de vignes et répartis parmi 20 000 propriétaires. En 1985, les cépages blancs fournirent 60 % ; les rouges 40 % ; leur part tend à croître. Les vieux ceps et les jeunes font l'ascension des coteaux et traînent dans les vallons. Des petits aqueducs (dans le pays : bisses) coupent à travers les terrains secs pour y apporter l'eau des glaciers et des murs séparent et soutiennent les terrasses. La plupart des vins du Valais portent le nom du raisin et non celui de la localité dont ils proviennent.

Principaux crus et variétés de raisin. En dépit de certaines apparences, l'encépagement du vignoble valaisan est principalement international. Quatre cépages monopolisent la quasi-totalité de la récolte. Ce sont le Fendant, nom régional du Chasselas, le Rhin ou Sylvaner, qui produit le Johannisberg, le Gamay (associé au Pinot Noir dans la Dôle) et le Pinot Noir : les deux premiers produisant du vin blanc, les deux autres du vin rouge. Viennent ensuite les cépages plus anciennement connus auxquels nous devons les spécialités : Amigne, Arvine, Hermitage, Pinot Gris (Malvoisie), Païen et Muscat. Ce sont tous des cépages à raisins blancs, sauf la Malvoisie qui donne du raisin rose, gris-rose, voire gris-violet (le vin pouvant être blanc ou même légèrement teinté). Le Fendant, nom donné au Chasselas en Valais, est un vin frais, pour la soif. Il allie la douceur à une certaine acidité, la distinction à la finesse. C'est un vin de type sec, jamais dur. Les Fendants les plus riches ont du moelleux et de la rondeur, mais trop riches, ils deviennent mous et capiteux. Le degré d'alcool, qui se situe habituellement entre 10,5 et 11,8, varie selon les circonstances. A l'origine, cette vigne pourrait avoir été importée par des mercenaires revenant de France. Étant donné que la terre était trop pauvre pour nourrir ses habitants, nombre d'entre eux se louaient à l'étranger comme soldats et revenaient ensuite chargés d'argent, d'honneur et de ceps. Un général qui combattit pour Louis XV aurait rapporté le Fendant et ramené avec lui un des jardiniers du roi pour qu'il veille à leur plantation. La Dôle est faite avec deux sortes de raisins, un Pinot Noir et un Gamay de qualité, qui sont cuvés, pressés et vinifiés ensemble. Le Pinot doit dominer dans ce vin rouge, puissant et parfumé, que certains connaisseurs considèrent comme le meilleur de la Suisse. Noble et généreux, il a une belle robe rubis. Le Pinot fut importé en 1848 et on commença à faire de la Dôle vers 1851. Plus de la moitié de l'encépagement en rouge est consacré au Pinot Noir et seulement une faible partie est vendue sous ce nom. Le Johannisberg se place au 2e rang de la production totale des vins blancs valaisiens (soit 10 à 15 % de cette production). On le fait avec le cépage Sylvaner, dit Rhin en Valais. C'est le seul qui se marie bien avec l'asperge du pays. Les années où l'on vendange tard il atteint une pointe de douceur qui le rend agréable au dessert. Le Riesling, importé de la vallée du Rhin, donne un petit vin agréable semblable à l'Hermitage blanc. Le colonel Dénéréaz apporta ce raisin blanc il y a plus d'une centaine d'années et, récemment, le Dr Wuilloud parvint à acclimater le Syrah de l'Hermitage rouge dans son domaine de Diolly. Le Pinot Gris, raisin tardif vendangé tard, donne du Malvoisie dans le Valais : vin doux de dessert dont l'arôme persiste. Arvine, Amigne, Humagne et Rèze sont depuis longtemps des vins du Valais. L'Amigne pourrait fort bien avoir été la *Vitis aminea* des Romains et le Muscat — cultivé aussi dans le Valais — leur *Vitis apiana*. A coup sûr, la Rèze et l'Humagne étaient connues au début du XIVe siècle. L'Arvine est un vin noble et plein d'esprit ; L'Amigne est agréable et parfumé ; l'Humagne est un vin sain, corsé et vivace. Quant à la Rèze, elle a presque complètement disparu, alors que le Fendant est le plus consommé. Le vin du pays, Vieux Rouge du Valais, se fait de plus en plus rare et il est grand temps d'y goûter. Dernier venu dans la gamme des appellations valaisannes, le Goron est né de l'extension de l'encépagement en rouges. On le considère à juste titre comme une Dôle déclassée. En effet, les vendanges de Pinot Noir et de Gamay n'ont pas la densité suffisante qui est déterminée par un comité interprofessionnel paritaire. Aussi, servent-elles à produire ce vin populaire le Goron qui reste relativement faible en alcool.

Genève

Les vignobles de ce tout petit canton suisse sont plantés en fer à cheval autour de la ville de Genève. Ils donnent des vins charmants et légers qui sont peu connus à l'étranger. En général plutôt secs et légèrement pétillants, ils ont un fin bouquet.

Principaux crus : Les plus connus sont ceux du secteur de Mandement, sur la côte ouest du lac. Le vin qui porte ce nom est léger et sec, avec un soupçon de noisette dans son bouquet. Les villages qui donnent leur nom aux vins de Genève sont Peissy, Russin et Satigny, la plus vaste commune viticole suisse. C'est là que se trouve le prieuré de Satigny qui date de la cinquantième année de notre ère. En 912, le prieur entra en possession du vignoble. Sur la rive gauche du lac et du Rhône, les crus de Jussy, Lully et Soral ont la meilleure réputation.

Encépagement : Chasselas pour les vins blancs avec quelques spécialités telles qu'Aligoté, Chardonnay, Pinot Gris. Récemment on a planté du Pinot et du Gamay car le sol révèle des possibilités intéressantes pour les vins rouges.

SUISSE ITALIENNE

Le soleil brille et les lacs sont bleus au Tessin. Sous les arcades des rues commerçantes, les éventaires regorgent de fruits. Quoique viticulture et viniculture ne soient pas une des principales activités, la vigne y pousse bien pour donner vins rouges et blancs. Le Nostrano du pays, fait avec du

Bondola et des raisins d'autres variétés, tend à la dureté. Pourtant, quand on le boit frais, à l'ombre d'un arbre — comme Keats aimait boire son Bordeaux rouge — il a un goût agréable et nettement caractérisé. Durant les dernières années on a planté du Merlot de Bordeaux dans le Tessin. Il donne un vin suave, fruité, vendu sous l'appellation officielle Viti et promet d'avoir une influence heureuse sur la viniculture de ce canton.

Suisse allemande

Les principaux cantons viticoles de la Suisse allemande, sont par ordre de grandeur (surface viticole) : Zurich, Schaffhouse, Argovie, Grisons, Thurgovie, Saint-Gall et Bâle-Campagne. Ces régions ont en fait un climat un peu moins favorable que celles du sud du pays. Elles produisent néanmoins des vins fort agréables, plutôt légers mais fruités.

Zurich

Le principal canton vinicole de Suisse allemande est moins favorisé en fait de sol et de climat que ceux du sud. Néanmoins il produit quelques vins agréables. On plante actuellement du Klevner (Pinot Noir) et la production s'améliore.

Principaux crus : Herrliberg, Meilen et Erlenbach produisent des vins rouges plutôt doux. On fait du vin blanc principalement sur les côtes du lac de Zurich alors que les rouges viennent du Weinland.

Encépagement : Klevner, Riesling-Sylvaner, Rauschling et Muller-Thürgau.

Schaffhausen

Le plus important secteur vinicole de ce canton — le plus septentrional de la Suisse — est celui de Klettgau. Le vignoble y est admirablement situé. Le raisin Klevner y fournit un vin frais et très agréable. On en fait également une certaine quantité à Steinam-Rhein. Les vins de Stein sont faits avec du Blaurock et du Kefersteiner. Plus près de la ville de Schaffhausen, le Pinot Gris donne un vin agréable.

Autres cantons

D'autres cantons — Argovie, Saint-Gall, Thurgovie, les Grisons et Bâle — produisent également du vin mais à une moindre échelle et en consomment la plus grande partie.

Sulfatage

Traitement des vignes contre divers parasites par aspersion de sulfate.

Sulfate de cuivre

Sel cuivreux également appelé pierre bleue. On l'utilise dans les vaporisateurs fongicides $CuSO_45H_20$.

Sulfurisation

Le traitement du moût ou du vin à l'anhydride sulfureux (SO_2) ou à l'acide sulfureux (H_2SO_2) a pour but de ralentir la fermentation quand c'est nécessaire, de tuer des micro-organismes indésirables et de contribuer ainsi à la production d'un vin sain. Il importe de ne jamais sulfiter à l'excès, erreur qui donnerait au vin une odeur désagréable, un goût de soufre. La quantité d'anhydride sulfureux qui convient varie en raison directe de la teneur en sucre du pH et de la température. Le pH détermine la dose correcte de SO_2 sous la forme active : H_2SO_2. Plus le pH est élevé, plus il faut ajouter de SO_2 pour en avoir une quantité équivalente sous sa forme active. La loi détermine d'ailleurs les doses maximum de ces substances. Elles varient de pays en pays, étant donné que le besoin de sulfiter dépend du climat. Les levures résistent mieux au SO_2 quand elles sont les plus actives (ce qui se produit lors de la fermentation tumultueuse qui a lieu par temps très chaud) et, en de telles circonstances, on recourt à une dose plus élevée qu'à l'ordinaire comme lorsque se produit quelque désordre dans le moût ou le vin. Lorsque la fermentation est lente (par exemple lorsqu'il a beaucoup plu au début de la vendange ou sous un climat froid), 100 mg/l d'anhydride sulfureux suffiront à ralentir la vinification. Quand la température atteint ou dépasse 10 °C, la dose peut aller jusqu'à 150 mg/l. Ajouté aux raisins à vin rouge ou au moût de vin blanc en doses parfaitement appropriées, l'anhydride sulfureux aide à parer aux désordres biologiques, tout en laissant proliférer les levures qui convertissent le sucre en alcool.

Le tableau sur l'action purificatrice de l'anhydride sulfureux (p. 151) indique comment SO_2 agit en qualité de purificateur, comment il tue les bactéries et comment il prévient la casse brune en détruisant les oxydases. Les vins qui ont été traités à l'anhydride sulfureux ont des chances d'être mieux équilibrés et plus riches en certains éléments que ceux qui ne l'ont pas été. La teneur en alcool peut augmenter l'acidité volatile. Cette augmentation résulte d'une fermentation exempte d'autres réactions chimiques, donc d'une meilleure utilisation du sucre. L'addition d'anhydride sulfureux ne provoque qu'un affaiblissement momentané de la couleur. Pour le rouge, la perte de couleur ne sera que temporaire et le vin reprendra sa teinte normale dès que l'action de l'anhydride sulfureux cessera. Dans des conditions normales, la robe du vin sera embellie et débarrassée des traces de brun et de jaune. La teneur en SO_2 diminue à chaque soutirage.

Voir ANHYDRIDE SULFUREUX

Sur, Suret

Se dit d'un vin ayant tourné à l'aigre et qui, partant, n'est pas buvable. Le contraire d'un vin doux est un vin sec, et non pas un vin sur.

Süssdruck

Légers rouges ou rosés faits en Suisse avec du Pinot Noir.

Suze

Suze est la marque appartenant à Pernod Ricard d'un apéritif à la gentiane fait en France, où il est le plus consommé. D'une couleur jaune, la Suze a un goût légèrement amer.

Sweet

En anglais ; doux, en particulier pour les vins. En l'occurrence doux signifie sucré et un vin d'une très forte teneur en alcool peut être doux, par exemple les Sauternes et encore plus les vins vinés, dits vins doux naturels.

Sylvaner

Cépage blanc, de bon rendement, cultivé en Alsace, Autriche, Suisse, Allemagne et récemment en Australie, Californie, Nouvelle-Zélande et Afrique du Sud. Il donne des vins légers et plaisants. Dans les pays de langue allemande, on l'appelle aussi Oesterreicher (Autrichien) ou Franken.

Synthétique (Vin)

Décoction de moût de fruits concentré, levure et eau.

Syrah, Sirah

Raisin cultivé dans la vallée du Rhône, pour l'Hermitage rouge. Il aurait été ramené du Proche-Orient par les croisés, d'après certains, ou bien aurait été apporté bien plus tôt de Syracuse par les légions de Probus. En tout cas, ce raisin prospère surtout sous climat chaud. Il mûrit tardivement et craint les gelées d'automne. On a planté le Syrah en Suisse, Californie, Australie et Afrique du Sud.

Syrie et Liban

La vigne prospère depuis les temps les plus anciens sur les côtes orientales de la Méditerranée et cette région fut probablement une des premières à faire du vin. La Bible cite Damas comme centre vinicole. Les vins d'Helbon et le célèbre Chalybon étaient exportés vers tous les pays connus dans l'Antiquité (*voir* CHAPITRE I).

De nos jours, on trouve les vignobles surtout dans les zones montagneuses éloignées de la côte. En Syrie, la région de Latakieh mise à part, on cultive la vigne dans les secteurs accidentés d'Alep, Homs et Damas. Quelque 100 000 ha, en tout. Au Liban, en dépit de la guerre, la superficie plantée de vigne a dépassé 19 000 ha, dont une grande partie dans la vallée de Bekaa. Dans ces deux pays, le gros de la vendange est destiné à la table, soit en raisins frais, soit en raisins secs, ou converti en jus de fruit. Cela ne laisse qu'une faible quantité de raisin à pressurer pour faire du vin. On fait aussi de l'Arak dans ce pays. La distillation est généralement entre les mains des chrétiens qui produisent et consomment le vin : vin de table ordinaire titrant 9 à 10°, provenant de variétés de raisin françaises. On y fait également un peu de mousseux.

Pendant la dernière guerre, les troupes françaises cantonnées en Syrie exigèrent évidemment du vin. La production augmenta alors et les procédés de vinification firent des progrès. Quand les troupes françaises se retirèrent la production baissa considérablement. Elle est maintenant plus faible en Syrie qu'au Liban.

Szekszárdi Kadarka

Un des bons vins rouges, charnu, du sud de la Hongrie.

Szemelt

Mot hongrois signifiant : cueillette du raisin grappe à grappe au moment où chacune atteint le degré de maturité ou de surmaturation désiré, et le vin obtenu par ce procédé.

Voir ALLEMAGNE ; AUSLESE ; SAUTERNES

T

Table (Vin de)

Dans le sens le plus étroit, cette expression désigne le vin ordinaire consommé couramment pendant les repas. Mais on l'emploie de plus en plus pour les vins naturels non mousseux, afin de les différencier des mousseux, des vins vinés et des vins ayant une appellation. Aux États-Unis, la loi fédérale spécifie que l'appellation « table wine » s'applique aux vins titrant moins de 14°.

Tables de millésimes

Le millésime équivaut à l'année de vendange ou récolte du raisin. Il désigne donc le vin fait avec les raisins d'une certaine année qui figure sur l'étiquette.

En matière de Champagne et de Porto, le mot millésime (en anglais : *vintage*) prend une acception particulière et signifie : très bonne année. Dans ces deux régions, les années moins favorables, le vin nouveau est mélangé aux produits d'autres récoltes et l'étiquette n'indique aucun millésime. Champagne et Porto millésimés sont donc des vins d'années exceptionnellement bonnes. Dans le Bordelais, en Bourgogne, sur le Rhin, tous les vins de bon cru portent la date de vendange sur leur étiquette, que l'année soit bonne ou passable.

Les tables de millésimes sont des listes récapitulatives, généralement chronologiques et comprenant un plus ou moins grand nombre d'années de références auxquelles une note de valeur a été attribuée. Ce système est utile dans les pays de climat tempéré où, malgré tous les soins des viticulteurs, les variations météorologiques ont une telle influence sur la vendange que celle d'une année peut donner un vin excellent ; la suivante, un vin à peine moyen ; et la troisième, un vin tout à fait médiocre par manque de maturité du raisin. Mais ces jugements, imprimés en tables et diffusés parmi les consommateurs, peuvent les induire en erreur, au moins partiellement, parce qu'ils n'en disent pas assez.

Ces tables sont établies sur ce fait : dès le moment des vendanges, les viticulteurs peuvent préjuger grosso modo quelle sera la qualité de leur vin. Ensuite interviennent les statisticiens qui rassemblent et résument l'opinion générale et la traduisent en notes. Mais cette note s'applique à la qualité qu'aura le vin quand il atteindra sa pleine maturité par exemple dans le bordelais, c'est-à-dire dans cinq ans, dix ans et même quinze, voire plus. Les tables de millésimes, par exemple, indiquaient et indiquent toujours que 1945 était une grande année ; mais elles ne disaient pas que les vins à vieillissement lent, tels que certains Bordeaux, n'atteindraient la plénitude de leurs qualités que vingt ans plus tard. Ceux qui burent ce vin de grande année furent donc déçus, car une grande partie de ce vin fut consommée prématurément.

Pour la même raison, si l'on considère deux vins jeunes, le plus agréable peut fort bien être celui qui a été le moins bien coté sur la table de millésimes, parce qu'il n'est pas destiné à durer longtemps et qu'il aura atteint son maximum de qualité en deux ou trois ans, alors que les vins mieux cotés demanderont plus longtemps.

En outre, les tables de millésimes ne donnent que des généralités sans tenir compte d'innombrables exceptions. 1947 fut par exemple un grand millésime pour les Bourgogne. Mais plusieurs crus de cette province ne donnèrent cette année-là que des vins rouges médiocres. D'autre part, il y a toujours un ou plusieurs crus qui offrent de magnifiques réussites, même dans les très petites années. Ces vins sont de bonnes affaires pour l'acheteur, parce que les prix, influencés par la réputation de l'ensemble du millésime, sont généralement bien plus bas que ceux des bonnes années. Dans l'ensemble, les vins rouges des meilleurs crus, des meilleurs secteurs tombent rarement au-dessous de certaines normes, même si l'été a été déplorable.

Dans les pays et les régions où les étés sont toujours d'une chaleur torride, le temps ne fait pas varier la qualité du vin dans de grandes proportions aussi les tables de millésimes présentent peu d'intérêt.

Malgré toutes les erreurs que présente toute généralisation, *voir* APPENDICE F : TABLEAU DES MILLÉSIMES.

Tâche (La)

Bourgogne rouge. Commune de Vosne-Romanée, en Côte de Nuits. Classement officiel : Grand Cru.

Saura-t-on jamais si ce cru doit son nom au fait que jadis les ouvriers y étaient peut-être payés à la tâche et non à l'heure, ou bien s'il y a eu déformation d'un autre mot inconnu ?

L'appellation d'origine contrôlée englobe plus que le vignoble de La Tâche proprement dit — qui couvre seulement 1,43 ha — et s'étend à quelque 4,61 ha de parcelles avoisinantes qui étaient regroupées sous le nom du lieu-dit Les Gaudichots. Cette extension date de 1936, année où les lois couvrant les appellations contrôlées de Bourgogne furent mises au point. On décida alors que la qualité des parcelles voisines méritait ce nom.

Comme La Romanée-Conti, La Tâche appartient à un seul propriétaire : la Société civile de La Romanée-Conti. Les vins ressemblent à ceux que cette société tire de son cru le plus célèbre, mais sont plus délicats, tout en étant cependant arrondis et pleins, avec une étonnante profondeur de goût.

Au cours des dernières années, La Tâche a souvent produit des vins supérieurs à ceux de La Romanée, mais ni l'un ni l'autre ne donnent de grandes quantités. La Tâche produit environ 1 700 caisses.

Tafia, taffea

Les premiers Noirs des Indes occidentales françaises désignaient ainsi le rhum et ce fut le premier nom que porta cet alcool. Les Créoles l'écrivirent d'abord *taffia*. Actuellement, le Tafia n'est plus qu'un rhum de seconde qualité fait avec de la mélasse impure, alors que le rhum proprement dit provient de la distillation de mélasse de première catégorie ou de jus de canne à sucre.

Voir RHUM ; ÉGYPTE

Taglio

Nom italien des vins de coupage

Tahbilk

Vignoble du Victoria (Australie, *voir ce nom*), qui produit surtout du blanc et quelques vins de tables rouges, tous étiquetés en variété de raisin.

Taille

Opération qui consiste à couper les tiges, qui ont produit du raisin, partant du tronc de la vigne et de laisser un bras pour l'année à venir. En France, la taille commence au mois de novembre et se termine fin mars, début avril.

En Champagne, produit du second pressurage du raisin et des pressurages suivants, sauf le dernier. La première taille équivaut à la deuxième serre et la deuxième taille à la troisième serre (*voir ce mot*). Le vin de taille sert à faire le vin de seconde qualité de chaque fabricant de Champagne. Seul, celui de la première serre est vendu sous la meilleure marque de chaque producteur.

Voir CHAPITRE IV ; CHAMPAGNE

Talbot (Château-)

Bordeaux rouge. Commune de Saint-Julien, en Haut-Médoc.

Classé Quatrième Cru en 1855, le Talbot se vend cependant à des prix équivalents à ceux de certains Seconds Crus. Il est fait surtout avec du Cabernet Sauvignon et du Petit Verdot. Château-Talbot doit son nom à John Talbot, comte de Shrewsbury, qui perdit la dernière bataille de la guerre de Cent Ans et y périt, à quatre-vingts ans, en 1453. Mais on ignore s'il posséda jamais cette propriété personnellement. M. Jean Cordier, le propriétaire actuel, obtint un vif succès avec son chai qui était parmi les premiers à être d'une propreté, d'une netteté et d'un modernisme spectaculaires. De grandes cuves et des foudres y remplacent en partie les barriques traditionnelles. Il vendit une partie de ses parts au groupe « La Hénin » en 1983.

Quand on considère la qualité du Château-Talbot et celle d'autres crus mieux classés, on a le droit de dire qu'il mérite une promotion.

Caractéristiques : Grand vin charnu, pourtant souple, généralement bien vinifié.

Superficie : 100 ha.

Production moyenne : 400 tonneaux (35 000 caisses).

Tanin

Un des principaux composants du vin, provenant des pellicules et pépins des raisins et dissous dans le liquide pendant sa fermentation. Le tanin donne au vin son caractère et sa longévité. Sa combinaison avec les aldéhydes provoque la précipitation d'un dépôt. Le tanin est une substance astringente qui se trouve aussi dans l'écorce d'arbres et certaines noix. Il a également des qualités antiseptiques.

Voir CHAPITRE V

Tannat

Principal cépage du Madiran (sud-ouest de la France). On le considère comme identique à l'Harriague, cultivé intensément en Uruguay.

Tarragone

Une demi-douzaine d'appellations d'origine officielles espagnoles.

Voir ESPAGNE

Tarragona Port

Littéralement : porto de Tarragone. Il s'agit d'un vin rouge épais et lourd, fait autour de cette agglomération, au sud de Barcelone, en Espagne, et qui prétend indûment au nom de Porto. Le vrai Porto ne provient que d'une région délimitée avec précision dans la haute vallée du Douro, au Portugal. L'imitation tarragonaise a été exclue du marché britannique, par une loi datant de 1916. Il est aussi interdit de la vendre sous ce nom aux États-Unis et dans quelques autres pays.

Tartrate

Les tartrates sont des sels de l'acide tartrique. Ce sont aussi des composants du vin.

Voir CHAPITRE V

Tartre

Ce sous-produit de vin comprend la plus grande partie du dépôt cristallin qui reste, après soutirage, dans les cuves et fûts. A l'état presque pur, c'est de la crème de tartre. Mais quand il est en contact avec une matière calcaire, il donne un tartrate neutre de calcium. Le citrate de sodium et la congélation remédient à la précipitation des tartres.

Tartrique (acide)

Le principal acide fixe qui compose le vin. Il est présent en plus forte proportion dans le raisin que dans les autres fruits.

Voir CHAPITRE V

Tastevin

Tasse d'argent servant à déguster le vin, surtout en Bourgogne, mais aussi dans le

Midi. Elle est plate et à bords godronnés, pour réfléchir la couleur du vin.

Tatachilla

Grand vignoble du McLaren Vale en Australie-Méridionale. Ces vins se vendaient en partie en Angleterre sous l'appellation Keystone burgundy (bourgogne de Keystone).

Voir AUSTRALIE

Taupette

Nom donné familièrement dans la région de Cognac à l'ustensile appelé preuve : petit tube de verre lesté qu'on laisse couler dans les fûts de Cognac au bout d'une chaîne afin de prélever un peu d'eau-de-vie pour dégustation.

Taurasi (D.O.C.)

Vin de Campanie, rouge et vigoureux

Tavel (Appellation Contrôlée)

Vin rosé. Vallée du Rhône.

Les millésimes signifient peu de chose en ce qui concerne les vins du Rhône et sans doute encore moins pour le Tavel. Il n'existe, en effet, que du Tavel rosé et le rosé dépend beaucoup plus du sol et de la variété de raisins que de la température. La proportion d'alcool et d'acidité variera légèrement d'année en année, mais l'habileté du vigneron y palliera : il vendangera tôt les années chaudes et tard les années fraîches. En outre, le millésime ne signifie pas grand-chose tant que le vin n'a pas vieilli. Par sa nature même, le rosé doit être bù dans le premier rayonnement de sa jeunesse. Le millésime peut donc être négligé à ceci près, toutefois, que l'année marquée sur l'étiquette indique si le vin est encore jeune et frais. Un an au minimum, cinq ans au maximum, voilà la bonne règle.

Compte tenu du fait que c'est un rosé, le Tavel est un vin gouleyant et corsé. C'est aussi un des mieux connus du monde entier parmi tous les vins de cette couleur. Il n'a droit à son appellation d'origine contrôlée que s'il titre un degré alcoolique minimum de 11°, mais en général il en atteint 12, voire plus. Plusieurs raisins entrent dans sa composition, surtout le Grenache. Le vin ne doit pas contenir plus de 60 % de Grenache, et au moins 15 % de Cinsault.

Les vignes de Tavel poussent sur un sol varié où dominent la craie et une argile crétacée. La zone délimitée de culture s'étend sur 750 ha environ.

Elle comprend toute la commune de Tavel située à moins de 10 km de Châteauneuf-du-Pape d'une part, et d'Avignon d'autre part, sur la rive droite du Rhône. Un petit secteur du territoire de Roquemaure, commune voisine, a aussi droit à l'Appellation d'Origine Tavel. La production moyenne annuelle s'élève à un peu plus de 30 000 hl (plus de 300 000 caisses), qui sont expédiés non seulement vers tous les horizons de France, mais vers tous les pays du monde. 60 % du volume total est produit par la coopérative Les Vignerons de Tavel.

Tawny Port

Littéralement, Porto roux. Il s'agit d'authentique Porto, vieilli en fût pendant quatre à dix ans et coupé d'autre Porto avant la mise en bouteille. Moins lourd et moins resplendissant que le Porto de grand millésime (*vintage*), le Tawny Port a plus de finesse. Une fois mis en bouteille le Tawny Port ne doit plus être conservé mais bu le plus tôt possible.

Voir PORTO

Tchécoslovaquie

La Tchécoslovaquie produit du vin mais en importe beaucoup plus. Les douze régions viticoles se trouvent en Bohême, en Moravie et en Slovaquie. La récolte suffit presque maintenant à satisfaire la demande nationale. Dans ces conditions, on exporte un peu de vin et de mousseux.

La viticulture date d'il y a fort longtemps chez les Tchèques, mais elle a connu plus de vicissitudes qu'ailleurs. A coup sûr on faisait du vin en Bohême dès le IXᵉ siècle. Au cours de la seconde moitié du XIVᵉ siècle, on y importa et planta systématiquement des vignes de Bourgogne, sous l'impulsion de l'empereur Charles IV. Surtout autour de Prague, la viticulture prospérait au XVIᵉ siècle et au début du XVIIᵉ. Puis vint la guerre de Trente Ans et ses dévastations. On replanta, mais les nouveaux vignobles furent anéantis à deux reprises aux XVIIᵉ et XIXᵉ siècles. On peut donc dire que la viticulture tchèque actuelle ne date que de 1920, lorsqu'on reconstitua le vignoble national.

D'après les statistiques, la production se situe aux environs de 1 500 000 hl (18 millions de caisses), dont plus de 85 % de blanc. La majeure partie des vins est consommée sur place. Néanmoins, quelques vins et quelques mousseux sont exportés, principalement vers l'U.R.S.S. et l'Allemagne de l'Est. En fait, les Tchécoslovaques doivent même importer du vin pour satisfaire à la demande. Chaque individu boit 14 litres de vin par an. Les vignobles couvrent plus de 46 000 ha. La Slovaquie produit 2/3 des vins, la Moravie la plupart du tiers restant car la Bohême n'en produit que très peu. Les viticulteurs vendent la majorité de leurs fruits à des entreprises d'État pour être vinifiés et ne fabriquent que très peu de vin eux-mêmes.

Les vins de Bohême ont évidemment des affinités avec ceux d'Allemagne. Prague est a la même latitude que le Rheingau et le Palatinat et on y cultive presque les mêmes raisins : Riesling du Rhin, Traminer et Sylvaner pour les vins blancs ; Blauer Burgunder, Portugieser et Saint-Laurent, pour les rouges. Les vins de meilleure qualité proviennent d'un petit secteur situé au nord de Prague et englobant Litoměřice, Roudnice et Mělník, sur l'Elbe ; Velké Zernoseky, un peu plus à l'ouest.

La plus grande partie du vin de Moravie provient du sud de la région centrale du pays, au-dessous de Brno et de la frontière, juste en face du secteur vinicole autrichien de Krems-Vienne.

L'ensemble de ces secteurs vinicoles moraves est limité à l'ouest par la localité de Znojmo, par Mikulov sur la frontière autrichienne et par Hustopeče-Hodonín au nord-est. On y cultive du Veltliner qui produit des vins blancs, le long du Danube, en Autriche, ainsi que d'autres variétés de raisin, telles le Riesling du Rhin et le Riesling italien Walsh, ce dernier comptant pour plus de 20 % de la superficie des vignobles. Importants aussi sont les Sylvaŋer, Traminer, Sauvignon, Weiss Burgunder et une variété que les Tchèques appellent Rulandské et qui pourrait bien être le Ruländer-Pinot Gris. Les vins de Mikulov sont légers et parfumés, avec une assez forte teneur en acidité.

A l'extrémité orientale de la Tchécoslovaquie, en face de la région hongroise du Tokay, on fait un vin de ce type avec les cépages Furmint et Lipovina. Ces deux variétés de raisins sont parmi les plus utilisées en Hongrie. Les meilleures appellations d'origine tchèque sont Malá Trňa, Viničky et Streda nad Bodrogom. Partout ailleurs en Tchécoslovaquie, surtout au pied des monts Carpates, on produit de grandes quantités de vin. A l'ouest se trouve le plus grand secteur vinicole de Tchécoslovaquie,

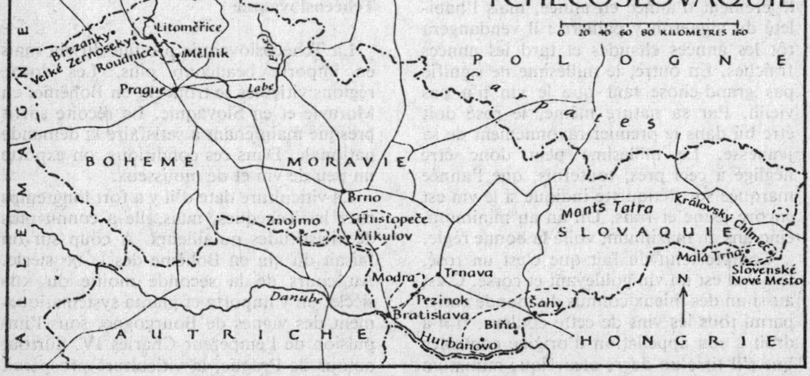

celui des petites Carpates et de Nitra, planté surtout en Veltliner, Riesling italien, Sylvaner, Müller-Thurgau, Frankovka, Saint-Laurent, Blauer Burgender, Portugieser, Feteasca Regale, Feteasca Alba, Traminer et Sauvignon. Les variétés utilisées pour les vins rouges représentent environ 14 % de la récolte. 8 millions de bouteilles de mousseux sont produites en Tchécoslovaquie selon les procédés de « charmat » et de « méthode champenoise ».

Teinturier

Nom donné au raisin à jus coloré. Quelle que soit leur couleur, la très grande majorité des raisins donnent un jus incolore ou légèrement doré car les pigments de couleur ne se trouvent que dans la peau et pas dans la pulpe. Les teinturiers sont une exception.

Tent

Nom que les Anglais donnaient jadis couramment aux vins rouges d'Alicante et qui dérivait très probablement de Tinto (*voir ce nom*).

Tequila

Des trois breuvages obtenus au Mexique par la fermentation du jus de mescal — tequila, mescal et pulpe — la tequila est le plus civilisé. Aussi incolore que de l'eau pure, gobé d'un seul trait à la manière mexicaine, après avoir léché du sel sur sa main, ce liquide enflamme la gorge. On le consomme aussi beaucoup aux États-Unis, surtout sur la côte ouest.

Voir MESCAL ; PULQUE

Terlaner (D.O.C.)

Vin blanc du Tyrol méridional.

Voir TRENTIN-HAUT-ADIGE

Teroldego

Raisin à vin cultivé dans le Trentin (Italie) et qui donne des vins rouges, particulièrement dans les secteurs de Mezzolombardo et Mezzocorona.

Terroir (Goût de)

Saveur particulière que le sol sur lequel on cultive la vigne confère au vin.

Tertre (Château du)

Bordeaux rouge. Commune d'Arsac-Margaux, en Haut-Médoc.

Abandonné pendant quelques années, le château, situé sur la route vicinale joignant Arsac à Margaux, a droit, depuis 1954, à l'Appellation Contrôlée Margaux, comme d'autres vins d'Arsac. Un groupe belge, sous la direction de Philippe Gasqueton de Château-Calon-Ségur, a replanté le vignoble. Le Château du Tertre se vend bien en Belgique et également en Hollande. Cinquième Cru selon la classification de 1855, Château du Tertre dans son état actuel prouve à quel point la qualité dépend de la direction d'une propriété.

Caratéristiques : La qualité du vin avait décliné jusqu'à néant, mais depuis 1966, elle a fait des progrès considérables surtout dans les années 80.

Superficie : 47 ha.

Production moyenne : 200 tonneaux (18 000 caisses).

Tête (Vin de)

Dans le Sauternais, vin provenant du premier pressurage : le meilleur. En 1921, Château-Yquem étiqueta même une *crème de tête*. En général, erreur de marketing car des clients veulent la petite quantité supérieure et dédaignent le reste.

Thermomètre

Il ne devrait pas exister de chai sans thermomètre, indispensable tant pendant la fermentation que pendant la conservation du vin. Le maître de chai ne cesse de vérifier la température du moût pendant la fermentation et, par température très élevée, il parviendra sans doute à la modérer pour sauver le vin. C'est ici qu'intervient l'habileté du spécialiste car, par temps chaud, tel cru donnera du vin meilleur que tel autre. Le thermomètre sert aussi à corriger les données du mustimètre et de l'alcoomètre.

Le monde, avec toutefois l'exception des États-Unis, s'est converti au système Celsius où la température est mesurée en centigrades. D'autres pays, en raison des accords du Marché Commun, se sont aussi convertis au système Celsius.

Le thermomètre de Celsius indique zéro à la température de congélation de l'eau et 100 à la température de son ébullition. Réaumur indique zéro degré à la température de congélation de l'eau et 80° à sa température d'ébullition. Le Fahrenheit indique 32° à la température de congélation de l'eau et 212° à sa température d'ébullition.

Certes, le thermomètre réagit rapidement, mais pour prendre la température d'un liquide il faut l'y laisser quelque temps.

On trouvera à l'appendice D un tableau de conversion de degrés centésimaux en Fahrenheit. Voici en outre les calculs à faire pour convertir le Réaumur et le Fahrenheit en centésimaux.

Pour convertir le centésimal en Réaumur, on multiplie la température centésimale par 4/5. Pour convertir le Réaumur en centésimaux on multiplie la température Réaumur par 5/4.

Pour convertir le centésimal en Fahrenheit, on multiplie la température centésimale par 1,8 et on lui ajoute 32. Pour convertir le Fahrenheit en centésimaux on commence par en soustraire 32, puis on le divise par 1,8.

Pour convertir le Fahrenheit en Réaumur, on en soustrait 32 et on multiplie par 4/9. Pour convertir le Réaumur en Fahrenheit, on le multiplie par 9/4 et on ajoute 32.

Thief

Littéralement : voleur. C'est le nom anglais de la pipette : tube servant à prélever une petite quantité de vin ou de liqueur dans un fût ou autre contenant. La pipette est généralement en verre, parfois en argent.

Tia Maria

Marque de liqueur de la Jamaïque, vendue internationalement à base de rhum auquel on ajoute du café et des épices.

Tierno (Vino)

Voir VINO TIERNO

Tinta

Famille de raisins à vin : Tina Cão, Tinta Francisca, etc., servant à faire le Porto. On a planté certains de ces raisins en Californie.

Tintara

Vignoble du Val McLaren, en Australie méridionale.
Voir AUSTRALIE

Tinto

Pour le vin rouge, les Espagnols n'emploient pas le mot *rojo*, mais disent *vino tinto*.

Tirage

Synonyme de soutirage.

Tirage (Liqueur de)

Solution de sucre et de vin vieux qu'on ajoute au Champagne et à d'autres mousseux pour assurer une fermentation secondaire.
Voir CHAMPAGNE

Tire-bouchon

Tout instrument servant à déboucher une bouteille. Dans sa forme la plus traditionnelle, il se présente comme une spirale en métal pourvue d'un manche. Les variations sur cette présentation de base sont bien sûr infinies, tout comme il existe une quantité considérable de substituts modernes du tire-bouchon.

Bien plus important que l'accessoire est le bouchon lui-même. Pour les bonnes bouteilles — dont le bouchon est généralement plus long que la moyenne —, il est essentiel que la spirale ait entre 60 et 80 mm environ de longueur, afin de traverser le bouchon dans toute sa longueur. Le métal doit être fin et taillé en spirale ouverte ; le bord ne doit pas être trop effilé, car il pourrait déchiqueter le bouchon en le tirant. La pointe doit être assez aiguë et façonnée de manière à ne pas être centrée dans la spirale.

Les tire-bouchons à leviers et les tire-bouchons doubles peuvent être utiles à condition que la spirale soit parfaitement conçue. On peut également utiliser une aiguille pour percer le bouchon ; en injectant du gaz par le dessous, le bouchon sautera. Mais ceci est efficace à condition que l'aiguille soit assez longue pour traverser le bouchon dans toute sa longueur. Ces inventions peuvent sembler quelque peu fantaisistes, mais elle permettent en fait d'extirper d'un seul coup un bouchon relativement friable.

Tischwein

Littéralement « vin de table », en allemand. Il s'agit bien du vin destiné à la consommation courante lors des repas. Ne pas confondre avec *Tafelwein.*

Toddy

Breuvage consommé chaud, fait de spiritueux (souvent de rhum), de sucre, de rondelles de citron, de clous de girofle et d'eau. Dans certains pays tropicaux, on le boit aussi froid ; il est alors fait avec la liqueur tirée du jus de palme fermenté.

Tokaier

Voir RULANDER

Tokaji

Un des mots qui apparaissent sur l'étiquette du Tokay et qui est suivi par l'indication du type de Tokay, par exemple : Tokaji Edes Szamorodni.

Voir TOKAY

Tokay (Tokaj)

Le Bodgrog et Tisza dévalent des Carpates et confluent à Tokaj, puis ils s'écoulent vers le Danube et leurs eaux se perdent dans la mer Noire.

Nul ne sait depuis quand on cultive la vigne sur le sol volcanique situé entre ces deux cours d'eau. Elle était déjà là quand les Magyars (Hongrois) arrivèrent il y a un millier d'années. Le vin provenant de la région hongroise proche de l'Ukraine et de la Slovaquie était célèbre au temps des croisades, pour le moins. Au XVIIIe siècle, l'écrivain Szirmay de Szirma disait pourtant que la réputation du Tokay ne datait que de la découverte de la méthode Aszu, c'est-à-dire une cinquantaine d'années auparavant. Les écrivains modernes la font remonter plus haut dans le temps, mais les propos d'un quasi-contemporain semblent plus véridiques. Le Tokay tel que nous le connaissons est du Tokaji Aszu.

Certains Hongrois affirment que les vins doués d'une fermeté d'acier et de grande race faits autour du lac Balaton sont les meilleurs du pays. Mais le reste du monde n'est pas d'accord. Le Tokay, vin que l'on peut considérer comme le plus concentré de tous, semble contenir sa mélodie mieux qu'aucun autre. Même le Champagne n'égale pas cet aristocrate doré qu'une compagnie entière de cosaques gardait jadis, autour de la table de Catherine II. Le plus superbe Trockenbeerenauslese du Rhin ou de la Moselle ou même un Château-d'Yquem du meilleur millésime manqueront au moins d'un des éléments qui ennoblissent le Tokay. Voltaire disait que le Tokay donnait de la vigueur à la moindre fibre de son cerveau et ranimait, au plus profond de son âme, les étincelles enchanteresses de l'esprit et de la bonne humeur.

La région vinicole du Tokaj-Hegyalja se trouve au nord-est de la Hongrie et touche la Tchécoslovaquie et l'Ukraine soviétique. Ses quelque 7 000 ha de vignobles produisent annuellement environ 200 000 hl (plus de 2 millions de caisses) de Tokay divers.

La région de Tokajhegyalja est un territoire clos. Vingt-huit agglomérations ont droit à l'appellation Tokaji pour leur vin. Tokaji signifie vin de Tokaj, car le i est en hongrois la marque du génétif. Les vignes de Tokaj sont cultivées sur un sol volcanique, fait de feldspath, de kaolin et de porphyre, qui contribue à donner au vin ses caractéristiques ; la surface du sol est formée de lave ancienne et de lœss. Toutes les agglomérations ayant droit à l'appellation sont situées dans les contreforts méridionaux — Hegyalja signifie précisément « contrefort » — du massif Eperjes-Tokaj, protégé au nord par les hauteurs des monts Carpates. Les agglomérations les plus importantes sont Tokaj, Tallya, Tarcal, Olaszliszka, Erdöbénye, Tolcsva, Mád ainsi que les centres culturels et politiques de la région, Sàrospatak et Satoraljaújhely. Une petite partie de la région vinicole se trouve en Tchécoslovaquie.

Comme pour tous les grands vins, la situation géographique et la conformation du sol sont deux des nombreux facteurs contribuant à leur originalité. Le climat, les variétés de raisins et la méthode de vinification sont d'autres facteurs importans. A Tokaj, les étés chauds et secs, les automnes particulièrement longs, permettent aux raisins, dans les bonnes années, de mûrir à souhait sous le soleil. Seul un nombre limité de variétés est autorisé : Furmint est de loin la variété la plus importante et la plus apte à la surmaturation et à la pourriture noble. Il fut introduit dans la région, au XIIIe siècle, après une invasion tartare, par des viticulteurs wallons. Hàrslevelvü est le second cépage le plus utilisé.

Le procédé utilisé pour faire ces vins exceptionnellement concentrés est semblable à la méthode employée pour les Sauternes ou les Trockenbeerenauslesen allemands, mais il reste unique en son genre. Le raisin Furmint, qui sert à faire le Tokay, est une variété d'un jaune terne, à peau épaisse. Sous l'action du chaud soleil d'automne, il mûrit excessivement et le *Botrytis cinerea (voir ce nom)* entame alors son processus de réduction des acides naturels et de concentration du sucre. Ces raisins ayant perdu toute leur eau étaient appelés *aszu,* ce qui signifie précisément « desséché ». Sous la dynastie des Habsbourg qui appréciait particulièrement ces vins, on les appelait *Ausbruch,* traduction allemande du terme hongrois.

Comme en Sauternes ou sur les coteaux du Rhin et les terrasses de la Moselle, les raisins sont donc vendangés tard, après avoir été desséchés par le soleil. En France et en Allemagne, les vendangeurs passent et repassent à plusieurs reprises le long des rangs de vigne, pour choisir les raisins grain à grain, lorsqu'ils sont à point, c'est-à-dire desséchés comme il se doit. En Hongrie aussi, le Furmint mûrit inégalement : certains grains sont prêts plusieurs jours avant les autres. Mais la méthode utilisée pour le Tokay étant différente, il en résulte des vins de style différent. Au moment des vendanges, les raisins arrivés à la surmaturation désirée sont mis à part dans des seaux appelés *puttony* en hongrois.

Les grands noms de Tokay

Les raisins sélectionnés sont vinifiés séparément ou avec d'autres raisins et leur jus, chaque mélange donnant un des célèbres Tokay. C'est à ce stade de la vinification que la méthode *aszu* se distingue des techniques propres aux régions du Sauternes ou du Rheingau allemand.

Tokaji Eszencia

L'essence est la plus précieuse des spécialités des vins de Tokay. Elle est faite exclusivement de grains *aszus.* On cueille un à un les grains surmaturés et atteints par la pourriture noble. Ces grains de raisin sont conservés dans des cuves jusqu'à la fin des vendanges. Le poids des fruits entassés suffit pour que le sirop dégoutte. Ce nectar est ensuite fermenté pendant plusieurs années dans de petites fûts appelés *gönci* dont la mesure originale est 136-140 litres. Il n'existe sur terre aucun vin comparable à cette essence de Tokay, aux vertus magiques sur lesquelles on a tant disserté. Le Tokaji Eszencia traditionnel est resté introuvable à l'étranger pendant de longues années. Les caves d'État produisent une quantité infime de ce vin fabuleux, et lorsqu'on réussit à trouver une bouteille d'Eszencia récente, il s'agit probablement d'un vin contenant surtout du vin Aszu courant pour une très petite quantité de Eszencia.

Tokaji Aszu

Une fois qu'ils ont donné leur part d'Eszencia, les raisins Aszu sont écrasés pour former une sorte de pâte ; les pépins doivent rester entiers alors que les peaux se dissolvent presque entièrement. Pendant cette opération, les raisins qui n'ont pas été touchés par le *Botrytis cinerea* sont vendangés et pressurés de la façon habituelle. On les laisse macérer quelques heures. On mélange ensuite le moût et la pâte Aszu et on laisse le tout macérer quelques jours dans des cuves ouvertes. On filtre enfin la pulpe solidifiée, et le moût enrichi est versé dans les fûts *gönci* (ou *Szerennyei*), où il terminera sa lente maturation de 4 à 6 ans. Ce lent vieillissement, à une température de 8 à 12ºC, lui donne le fin bouquet si caractéristique des Tokay. On voit donc que, comme pour certains Xérès et pour le Château-Chalon d'Arbois, le caractère particulier du bouquet est dû à une oxydation contrôlée. Les caves de Tokaj possèdent une microflore spéciale, caractérisée par le *Cladosporium cellare*. Cette moisissure forme une couche noire presque ouatinée, sur les murs de la cave. Elle absorbe par microcondensation les esters, les aldéhydes volatils, les vapeurs des alcools et les acides volatils provoqués par l'évaporation du vin et présents dans l'air de la cave.

Le caractère du Tokaji Aszu sera indiqué par la présence du mot *puttonyos* sur le goulot de la bouteille. Le nombre de *puttonyos* ou seaux, contenant chacun 25 kg, de cette pulpe concentrée de raisins secs versée dans la cuve de fermentation des autres raisins du même vignoble, figure sur chaque bouteille de chaque cuvée. Ainsi, la collerette de chaque bouteille portera la mention : 3 *puttonyos*, 4 *puttonyos*, 5 *puttonyos*, etc. Plus la proportion de grains Aszu sera élevée, plus le vin dans son ensemble sera concentré. Les bouteilles indiquant 5 ou 6 *puttonyos* sont des vins faits presque entièrement avec du moût aszu, la quantité de moût de raisin normal étant infime. Les grandes années donnent bien sûr un vin plus riche que les années médiocres ; et la grandeur de l'année dépend de l'état de maturation des raisins le jour même des vendanges.

La teneur en alcool et les autres caractéristiques varient évidemment avec le nombre de *puttonyos*, mais le Tokay titre en général entre 13 et 15°. Le cépage Furmint n'atteint l'état convenant pour faire de l'Aszu que planté au-dessus d'une altitude de 100 m et les meilleurs vins proviennent des vignes plantées sur les coteaux à une altitude variant entre 130 et 250 m. On estime que la proportion d'Aszu entrant dans la composition de tous les vins d'une vendange ne s'élève qu'à 1/3 000, mais bien des années, il arrive même qu'on ne puisse pas faire d'Aszu du tout.

Tokaji Szamorodni

Szamorodni est un mot slave et non pas magyar, ce qui montre bien l'intérêt que les Russes et les Polonais ont pu porter aux vins Tokay. Le mot signifie « tel qu'il a été cultivé » et désigne les vins faits avec les raisins qui n'ont pas été sélectionnés pour devenir des grains Aszu. Ainsi, lorsque les conditions générales favorisent le développement du *Botrytis cinerea,* seules quelques grappes restent bonnes pour le Tokaji Szamorodni. Inversement, une année pauvre en Aszu sera riche en Tokaji Szamorodni. La vinification est semblable à celle du Aszu ; la fermentation se fait aussi en deux étapes : les raisins sont d'abord écrasés puis macèrent quelques heures pour s'oxyder ; on les presse ensuite et ils sont laissés à fermenter. Ils doivent enfin vieillir entre deux et quatre ans, juste le temps nécessaire, comme disent les Hongrois, « pour laisser les grains Aszu dégorger leur sucre » ; puis, dans les *gönci* entreposés dans les typiques caves à voûte basse. D'autre part, pour se mettre à la portée des acheteurs anglo-saxons, étiquettes et collerettes indiquent en anglais si le vin est sec ou doux. Le doux évidemment proviendra d'une vendange où le nombre de raisins *Aszu* fut important. Dans ce cas, Szamorodni aura un nez formidable. Si le mot doux *(sweet)* ne figure pas sur la bouteille, la mention Edes y suppléera. Le Tokaji Edes Szamorodni est donc un Tokay du type Szamorodni comportant une forte proportion de raisins ayant dépassé la maturité et il sera doux.

Le Tokaji Aszu et le Tokaji Szamorodni ne sont vendus que dans des bouteilles de verre transparent contenant environ un demi-litre. Très longues et minces, elles ressemblent à des matraques. Les autres variétés de Tokay, telles que le Tokay Furmint, sont vendues dans des bouteilles sveltes et hautes du même type que celles du vin du Rhin et d'Alsace et qui sont très courantes en Hongrie et qui portent la marque du monopole d'État.

Tokaji Máslás

Après avoir soutiré l'Aszu ou le Szamorodni de son fût, on y verse du vin de Tokay ordinaire et on le laisse sur la lie du précédent pendant plusieurs mois. C'est ainsi qu'on obtient le Tokaji Máslás.

Tokaji Forditás

Après avoir fait de l'Aszu, on en ressuscite le marc en y ajoutant du moût frais. Une seconde fermentation se produit alors et c'est ainsi qu'on obtient le Tokaji Forditás.

AUTRES MENTIONS
FIGURANT SUR LES ÉTIQUETTES DE TOKAY

Tokaji Aszú-eszencia : excellent Aszú. Une essence très sucrée ayant un faible degré alcoolique et vendu très rarement. *Tokaji Edes :* Tokay doux. *Tokaji Száraz :* Tokay sec. *Monimpex :* monopole d'État d'exportation.

Magyar Állami Pinçegazdaság : caves d'État hongroises.

Tokay d'Alsace

L'emploi du terme Tokay n'est pas autorisé par les réglementations du Marché Commun. Le raisin doit être appelé Pinot Gris.

Tom Collins

Breuvage qu'on consomme glacé et qui se compose de gin, parfois remplacé par la vodka, de sucre de jus de limon et de citron, le tout largement coupé d'eau de Seltz.

Tom and Jerry

Lait de poule fait de jaune d'œuf, lait ou eau chaude, sucre et eau-de-vie ou rhum.

Tonneau

Barrique à vin, généralement en bois et cerclé. Sa taille et sa capacité sont très variables, selon les usages traditionnels de chaque localité (pour tonneaux et conteneurs normaux, *voir* APPENDICE C). Les tonneaux sont utilisés pour la maturation, l'emmagasinage et le transport des vins, spiritueux et bières. En Europe, le vin ordinaire est toujours vendu en tonneau, ce qui permet de consommer le vin au fur et à mesure des besoins. Dans la région de Bordeaux, cette mesure théorique équivaut à 4 barriques, soit 900 l. Le tonneau de 900 l doit donner 100 caisses de 12 bouteilles.

Le tonneau est une invention absolument gauloise qui conquit le monde. Les Gaulois y conservaient leur boisson nationale originelle, la bière, en attendant d'y faire vieillir le vin, alors que les Romains conservaient leur vin dans des amphores.

Tonnelage

Ce qui concerne la tonnellerie, notamment la fabrication et la réparation des tonneaux ou barriques ; honoraires perçus par un tonnelier pour un travail effectué.

Voir APPENDICE C

Tonnelier

1. Artisan qui confectionne des tonneaux ;

2. Négociant s'occupant de l'échantillonnage et de la mise en bouteille des vins ;

3. Boisson anglaise faite d'un mélange des deux bières brunes Stout et Porter.

Torgiano (A.O.C.)

Bon vin rouge ou blanc italien d'Ombrie *(voir ce nom).*

Toro

Vin rouge auparavant nommé Toro, produit à Zamora, en Espagne *(voir ce nom).*

Toscane

Vins rouges et blancs, Italie centrale.

La Toscane était le pays du Chianti. Cette région produit aussi une grande quantité d'autre vin qui est vendue sous le nom de chianti sans en être et d'autres encore qui ne sont pas vendus sous cette appellation. Inutile sans doute de préciser que les océans de chianti qui déferlent sur toute la surface du globe ne proviennent pas seulement de Toscane ni même d'Italie. Mais le vrai Chianti vient de Toscane et il est parfois excellent.

CHIANTI (D.O.C.G.)

Le secteur délimité du Chianti Classico couvre à peu près 70 000 ha entre Florence et Sienne. Il est aussi accidenté, rocheux et apparemment aride que n'importe quelle autre région de vignobles. Quittez Florence par la grande route au-delà de la Porta Romana, dépassez le cimetière militaire américain bien entretenu, puis tournez à gauche et vous vous trouverez dans un autre monde. Les collines sont grisâtres, peu élevées mais abruptes. Vignes et cyprès sont dispersés sur la roche dure. Vous n'êtes plus sur une autoroute, mais sur un chemin étroit, sinueux, où vous trouverez peu de voitures automobiles, mais par contre, de temps en temps, une charrette ou un cheval trottant lentement. Des panneaux indicateurs délavés signalent la proximité de localités historiques dont les rues généralement désertées donnent une impression d'abandon : Greve, Radda, Castellina, Gaiole. Du haut des collines les plus élevées, de massives forteresses vous écrasent. Vous êtes dans un pays où se déroulèrent les combats entre Florence et Sienne. Les Florentins bâtirent ces châteaux forts pour mettre un terme aux incursions des Siennois. En 1376 les châtelains s'unirent dans la ligue du Chianti pour tenir les assaillants en respect le temps que Florence puisse venir à leur secours. Vous êtes dans le secteur du Chianti Classico, le seul qui ait vraiment droit à l'appellation Chianti. Les vignerons de ce secteur affirment que, selon l'histoire, personne d'autre qu'eux, ni en Toscane ni ailleurs, n'a le droit d'user de cette appellation. La géologie corrobore d'ailleurs l'histoire car le sol n'est pas le même que dans le voisinage. Argile schisteuse, recouverte de calcaire et, pardessus, d'un sable pierreux, cette terre ne se retrouve nulle part ailleurs.

Étant donné que le sol est l'un des facteurs essentiels — peut-être le plus important — qui donne au vin ses caractéristiques, il apparaît que rien de ce que l'on fait hors du secteur du Chianti Classico n'est véritablement du Chianti. Paradoxe : la plus grande partie du Chianti ne vient pas de là.

Cette appellation est peut-être trop célèbre. Peut-être aussi le flacon à cul rond a-t-il trop attiré l'attention à force de circuler partout. Toujours est-il que les vignerons d'une douzaine de secteurs circum voisins, appâtés par la douce odeur du succès, se mirent à vendre leur vin sous le nom de Chianti. Certes ils y ajoutaient une autre mention, mais le mot magique figurait sur leurs étiquettes. Dans chaque secteur on forma avec raison un *consorzio* pour protéger l'appellation acquise et chacun de ces syndicats fit valoir son bon droit à l'utiliser, en vertu d'un usage datant de longues années.

Il faut reconnaître que certains Chianti subsidiaires sont magnifiques. On dit souvent que le Chianti Rufina (ne pas confondre avec Ruffino qui est une marque déposée) est mieux équilibré que le Chianti Classico. Mais malheureusement d'autres ne sont pas de la même classe. Malgré cette confusion et ces proliférations de noms, on peut néanmoins trouver du Chianti authentique et le reconnaître aisément. Il suffit de vérifier si l'estampille du *Consorzio per la Difesa del Vino Tipico di Chianti* figure sur la bouteille. Elle représente un jeune coq noir sur fond d'or, entouré d'un cercle rouge sur lequel est inscrit le nom de l'organisation.

Voici les bons vins qui ont droit à l'appellation d'origine : Chianti Colli Aretini, Chianti Colli Fiorentini, Chianti Colli Senesi, Chianti Colli Pisane, Chianti Montalbano, Chianti Rufina. Les Chianti Classico, Ruffina et Colli Fiorentini doivent indiquer leur zone de production sur la bouteille.

Contrairement à ce que croient bien des gens le Chianti n'est plus vendu en *fiasco* et les meilleurs le sont en bouteilles ordinaires où ils vieillissent mieux. L'enveloppe de paille de la fiasque avait tendance à pourrir. En outre, ce type de bouteille avait le désavantage d'être coûteux.

Ajoutons incidemment que le *fiasco* n'est plus aussi bon marché de nos jours, par rapport à la bouteille, qu'il l'était voilà une cinquantaine d'années. En ce temps-là, on pouvait faire souffler les flacons à cul rond et les faire habiller de paille par des femmes, pour presque rien. Actuellement la main-d'œuvre coûte davantage et les bouteilles classiques, fabriquées en série, attirent moins le regard du client mais reviennent nettement moins cher. Le *fiasco* bulbeux appartient désormais au passé.

Même après avoir vieilli pendant des années le véritable Chianti n'est jamais très subtil. Une bonne part de son charme réside dans sa vigueur capiteuse et gaillarde, à laquelle s'ajoute une légère trace d'amertume, voire de dureté qui lui est tellement caractéristique. Si les meilleurs Chianti perdent la plus grande partie de cette amertume en vieillissant et deviennent moelleux, il en subsiste toujours quelque chose.

Certains Chianti jeunes peuvent être rendus *frizzante* c'est-à-dire pétillants et même un peu piquants, en ajoutant en cours de fermentation du jus de raisins à maturation tardive au vin déjà fermenté. Cela augmente son caractère rafraîchissant et sa gaieté. Très rares sont les grands Chianti, mais à peu près tous peuvent être agréables.

Selon la tradition, ce vin est fait avec cinq variétés de raisins dans une proportion déterminée : le Sangiovese (70 % à 90 %) lui donne corps et alcool ; le Canaiolo (5 % à 10 %) tempère sa dureté et fournit le bouquet ; le Trebbiano et le Malsavia (5 % à 10 % ensemble) rendent sa couleur plus claire car ce sont des raisins blancs ; enfin, le Colorino (environ 5 %) contribue à donner au vrai Chianti sa brillante robe de rubis.

Malheureusement les grandes entreprises vinicoles ont adopté des normes très basses pour la qualité des vins qu'elles exportent. Comme presque partout en Italie, les Chianti hors classe ne sont faits qu'en petite quantité et on ne les trouve guère que dans les hôtels et restaurants italiens dont le propriétaire n'hésite pas à payer le prix de la qualité. Dans un tel cas, boire du Chianti est un plaisir alors que trop souvent la bouteille ne contient qu'un vin ordinaire.

Vino Santo
(D.O.C. pour certains secteurs seulement)

Ce nom signifierait : vin pour les saints. Le vrai Vino Santo est demi-doux, doré, fait par les vignerons de Toscane — et pratiquement dans toute l'Italie — mais en très petite quantité. Certaines firmes de Florence et des environs commencent à en vendre, mais on exporte rarement les meilleurs.

Le Vino Santo est un agréable vin de dessert quoique moins doux que la plupart des autres. Il est produit (au moins en Toscane) par la vinification de raisins Trebbiano et Malvasia séchés avec soin à l'ombre, suspendus auparavant aux poutres des greniers. Le séchage prend plusieurs mois au bout desquels à peu près les 2/3 du jus se sont évaporés, et la teneur en sucre s'est proportionnellement élevée. On presse ces raisins et on verse le jus dans des fûts d'une capacité toujours inférieure à 125 l, emplis aux 3/4 seulement. Ensuite on les bouche et on les laisse à la chaleur pendant 4 ans. En règle générale la chaleur tue le vin. Mais, dans ce cas particulier, on recherche une certaine forme de madérisation. Le vin change de couleur et devient ambre foncé ; il prend un goût et un arôme de noix qui ressemblent à ceux du Xérès. A la fin de ce vieillissement le vin est filtré et prêt à la consommation. On choisit les raisins pour leur goût plus que pour leur teneur en sucre, ce qui donne au Vino Santo un caractère exceptionnel : sa douceur est masquée et équilibrée par sa teneur alcoolique élevée et austère.

Autres vins de Toscane

Aleatico di Portoferraio

• Vin rouge, doux de dessert, fait autour de la capitale de l'île d'Elbe, que Napoléon ne trouva pas assez vaste pour son génie. L'Aleatico de cette île — fait avec des raisins du même nom — est un vin chaleureux, corsé, riche et parfois excellent. Sa célébrité pourtant lui fait peut-être du tort, car il y a tout lieu, en effet, de soupçonner que la totalité du vin ainsi étiqueté n'est pas authentique.

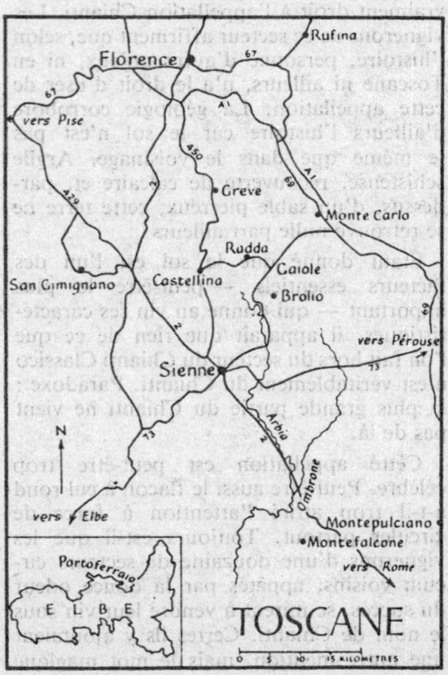

Elba (D.O.C.)

Vin léger, couleur de paille, fait avec du raisin Procanico cultivé sur l'île d'Elbe. Les fervents de vins italiens le còmparent au Chablis, mais il ne faut pas les prendre trop au sérieux. L'Elba rouge est un vin sec, profond, d'un rouge rubis, au goût légèrement aromatique. Il est fait principalement avec du Sangiovese, mais aussi avec du Procanico et du Canaiolo. La D.O.C. Elba peut également être appliquée aux rouges et blancs naturellement mousseux de l'île. Les étiquettes faisant de quelque manière allusion aux temps napoléoniens sont autorisées, à condition d'avoir été en usage depuis dix ans au moins avant juillet 1967.

Bianco Vergine della Valdichiana (D.O.C.)

« D'une blancheur virginale » en partie par sa couleur et en partie parce qu'il n'est fait qu'avec le premier jus recueilli avant pressurage. Sec, titrant environ 11°, agréablement frais en raison d'une acidité légèrement supérieure à la normale par rapport aux autres vins italiens.

Brolio (marque de Ricasoli)

Excellent Chianti Classico de la firme Ricasoli, qui porte le nom de la forteresse médiévale où il est vinifié par le Barone Ricasoli.

Brunello di Montalcino (D.O.C.G.)

Un des grands centres des bons vins italiens se situe sur les coteaux près de la belle petite ville de Montalcino au sud de Sienne. Le chai le plus respecté, le plus coûteux et le plus connu est « Il Greppo » de Biondi-Santi. Le *Brunello* de Bondi-Santi, produit exclusivement à partir de la transformation du Sangiovese, a acquis l'appellation D.O.C.G., titre le plus honorifique d'Italie. Ce vin est dur, tanique et vieillit très lentement (il faut attendre plusieurs dizaines d'années avant de le boire avec plaisir). On parle dans le monde entier de son prix excessivement élevé. Les 12 ha de vignes qui se trouvent sur les coteaux produisent 3 sortes de vins : le *Riserva* (qui provient de vieilles vignes de plus de 25 ans et doit avoir au moins 5 ans d'âge), l'*Annata* et le *Greppo* (qui est un vin de table provenant de vignes âgées de moins de 10 ans) ; le propriétaire actuel est Franco Biondi-Santi. En contraste avec le style classique des vins de Biondi-Santi, *Altesino* est le champion des vins modernes et légers ; depuis 1970, le propriétaire de ce vin est Giulio Consonno, un industriel milanais mais le centre de vinification est dirigé par Claudio Basla et Antonio Cossisti. A cause de l'appellation D.O.C.G. du Brunello, tous les vins issus du Sangiovese doivent vieillir en fûts pendant 4 ans, ce qui réduit le fruit du vin. Cependant, il y a une tendance vers un nouveau style de vin tel le *Rosso di Montalcino*, qui a droit à l'appellation D.O.C. Plus léger, moins cher il est fait uniquement de Sangiovese Grosso et ne doit vieillir qu'une année en fûts. Cette tendance vers des vins plus légers a également été adoptée par un producteur local : Angelo Solci. Les autres Brunellos sont Fattoria dei Barbi, Emilio Costanti, Carpazo, Camigliano, Il Poggione, Argiano, Col d'Orcia, Case Basse, Santa Restituta, Grieppone, Capanna, Baricci et Val di Suga. Le renom de *Montalcino* sera très aidé par une énorme exploitation viticole voisine qui se trouve à Sant'Angelo Scalo qui a été inaugurée à la fin de 1984 par John et Harry Mariani, propriétaires de la Sté américaine Villa Banfi, importateurs de « Lambrusco ». Plus de 800 ha de différentes variétés ont déjà été plantés. Les vins de cépages provenant de ce château Castello Banfi des vignobles avoisinants, sont Brunello, Chardonnay, Cabernet Sauvignon et moscadello.

Carmagnano (D.O.C.)

Producteur d'un excellent vin rouge, de quelques rosés et d'un bon Vino Santo.

Castello di Ama

Situé au sud de Gaiole et au nord de Sienne, ce domaine de Chianti Classico devient un modèle d'excellence. Les vins sont exclusivement faits à partir de ses 45 ha de vignobles, comme dans les crus classés du Médoc, avec un équipement qui pourrait bien être un exemple pour de nombreux excellents châteaux de Bordeaux.

Lacrima d'Arno (marque commerciale)

La traduction littérale est « Larme du Fleuve Arno ». Fait principalement avec du raisin Pinot, c'est un agréable vin blanc sec.

Meleto et *Castello di Rampolla*

Bons Chianti Classico.

Montecarlo (D.O.C.)

Bons vins, blanc ou rouge, de la localité portant ce nom. Fait principalement avec du Trebbiano et du Sangiovese c'est un vin sec et délicat.

Moscadello di Montalcino (D.O.C.)

Vin mousseux de Toscane, généralement plus *frizzante* (pétillant) que *spumante* (mousseux). Il n'est produit qu'en petite quantité par une cave coopérative.

Vernaccia di San Gimignano (D.O.C.)

Vin blanc fait avec du raisin Vernaccia, généralement traité en sec et plus rarement en doux. Plus connu, le sec a une robe d'ambré clair avec un léger bouquet et un arrière-goût un peu amer. Le doux est encore très utilisé comme vin de messe, ce qui était sa destination originelle.

Vino Nobile di Montepulciano (D.O.C.G.)

Vin rouge qui connut une célébrité littéraire au XVIIIe siècle lorsque le poète Francesco Redi l'invoqua en ces termes dans son *Bacchus en Toscane* : *Montepulciano d'ogni vini é il Re.* (« Le Montepulciano de tous les vins est le roi. ») Peut-être par déférence pour la République italienne d'aujourd'hui, ce roi est tombé dans la roture. Il est fait surtout avec du Sangiovese. Ce vin — produit par les familles nobles de Montepulciano, ville située à 48 km au sud de Sienne — s'exportait déjà dès le début du XIVe siècle. Il porte maintenant l'appellation Denominazione di Origine Controllata e Garantita. Beaucoup d'excellents vins de Toscane ne sont pas D.O.C. : le Tignanello d'Antinori, fait de Sangiovese et d'au moins 10 % de Cabernet Sauvignon et le Sassicaia fait de Cabernet Sauvignon sont des exemples de très bons vins qui souffrent de discrimination depuis que le D.O.C. n'accepte que des vins produits à partir du traditionnel cépage Sangiovese.

Bianco di Pitigliano (D.O.C.)

Trebbiano Blanc produit dans la petite commune de Pitigliano. C'est un vin acide, d'un jaune pâle, à boire jeune et frais.

Parrina (D.O.C.)

Vins blancs et rouges produits dans le sud de la Toscane avec les principales variétés des raisins de la région. Le blanc, fait avec du Trebbiano et du Malvasia, est un vin moelleux et agréable. Le rouge, fait avec du Sangiovese, du Canailo et du Montepulciano, est un vin réputé qui vieillit avec profit.

Rosso della Colline Lucchesi (D.O.C.)

Vin rouge fait avec les raisins traditionnels du Chianti ; on le produit dans les environs de la ville de Lucques, région célèbre pour son huile d'olive. C'est un vin frais et fruité, souvent pétillant, à boire jeune.

Toul (V.D.Q.S.) (Appellation Contrôlée)

Voir CÔTES DE TOUL ; LORRAINE

Tour-Blanche (Château-La)

Bordeaux blanc. Commune de Bommes, en Sauternais.

Depuis un demi-siècle, ce cru appartient à l'État français. Le vin a été fait par des locataires qui payaient à l'administration des domaines un loyer d'environ 30 barriques par an. Il a décliné de la splendeur qui le fit classer en 1855 en tête des Premiers Crus de Sauternes, juste après le seul Château d'Yquem. Depuis 1955, le ministère de l'Agriculture gère le vignoble et le Château-La-Tour-Blanche actuel, nettement plus léger et moins doux que ses voisins de Bommes-Sauternes, a des partisans. Quant au château proprement dit, il abrite une importante école de viticulture et c'est pour cela que Daniel Osiris en fit don à l'État en 1907.

Caractéristiques : Léger avec une petite tendance au sec qui le différencie légèrement des autres Sauternes. Du nerf et de la vigueur.

Superficie : 27 ha.

Production moyenne : 35 tonneaux (3 500 caisses).

Tour-Carnet (Château-La)

Bordeaux rouge. Commune de Saint-Laurent, en Haut-Médoc. (Saint-Laurent n'est pas une appellation d'origine et le vin est légitimement étiqueté Haut-Médoc.)

La tour carrée, donjon d'un château du XIIIe siècle, qui donne son nom au vin, domine une des plus belles propriétés du Médoc. Classé Quatrième Cru du Médoc en 1855, il était déjà célèbre et atteignait les plus hauts prix dès 1354. Cette splendeur passée n'était, hélas ! qu'un souvenir jusqu'à ces dernières années. Vers le milieu des années 60, le nouveau propriétaire, M. Lipschitz, fit des efforts pour redonner leur splendeur aux vignobles, au chai et au château. Ce cru a su retrouver sa place dans la classification de 1855.

Caractéristiques : S'est amélioré ces dernières années. Vin bon et sain.

Superficie : 42 ha.

Production moyenne : 150 tonneaux (15 000 caisses).

Tour-Haut-Brion (Château-La)

Bordeaux rouge. Commune de Talence, en Graves.

La Tour-Haut-Brion est un des trois Haut-Brion des faubourgs de Bordeaux. Les autres sont La Mission-Haut-Brion et La-Ville-Haut-Brion. Comme La Mission-Haut-Brion, La Tour-Haut-Brion fut classé Premier Cru de Graves en 1953 et 1959. Tous deux appartenaient à la famille Woltner jusqu'en 1983, quand ces trois Châteaux furent achetés par le Château-Haut-Brion, le grand Premier Cru appartenant à la famille Dillon.

Caractéristiques : Corsé, plutôt dur, semblable à celui de La Mission-Haut-Brion, mais moins fin.

Superficie : 4 ha.

Production moyenne : 20 tonneaux (1 500 caisses).

Tour-Martillac (Château-La)

Bordeaux blanc et rouge. Commune de Martillac, en Graves.

La tour qui donne son nom à ce vin est le vestige d'un fortin du XIIe siècle et se dresse devant une chartreuse du XVIIIe siècle, sur la colline de Martillac. C'est tout ce qui reste du château détruit lors de la Révolution française.

Le vin rouge de ce château a été classé parmi les onze Graves les plus intéressants en 1955 et en 1959.

Le blanc aussi a été classé parmi les autres meilleurs Graves blancs en 1955.

En 1928, La-Tour-Martillac a été achetée par Alfred, gérant de la maison de négoce Kressmann à Bordeaux. Son fils, Jean, qui dirigeait l'exploitation depuis 1940 en a hérité en 1955 et l'exploite depuis 1977 avec ses enfants Tristan et Loïc.

Caractéristiques : Très bon vin, agréable à boire.

Superficie : rouge - 20 ha ; blanc - 5 ha.

Production moyenne : rouge - 105 tonneaux (10 500 caisses) ; blanc - 30 tonneaux (3 000 caisses).

Tour-de-Mons (Château-La)

Bordeaux rouge. Commune de Soussans-Margaux, en Haut-Médoc.

Château La Tour-de-Mons appartenait jusqu'au début des années 70 au propriétaire de Château Cantemerle et a bénéficié, pendant des années, des traitements viticoles attentifs qui ont hissé Château Cantemerle bien au-dessus de sa classification Cinquième Cru. Château-La Tour-de-Mons fut classé Cru Bourgeois du Médoc en 1855.

Le vignoble est géré actuellement par M. Bertrand Clauzel. Une vieille tour en ruine couverte de lierre se trouve sur ce domaine fondé en 1289 par un certain Jehan Colomb dont un cousin génois découvrit l'Amérique deux siècles plus tard. On veut bien le croire. Le second vin de Château-La-Tour-de-Mons est le Château-Richetère.

Caractéristiques : Vin fin et rond qui possède toute la délicatesse des Margaux. Quoique seulement Cru Bourgeois, c'est un des bons vins de cette catégorie surannée. Il mérite une meilleure classification car il produit des vins supérieurs à quelques Crus classés. Les bonnes qualités actuelles de son propriétaire garantissent que ce vin continuera à être bien vinifié.

Superficie : 30 ha.

Production moyenne : 120 tonneaux (10 000 caisses).

Touraine (A.O.C.)

Vins blancs, rouges et rosés. Vallée de la Loire.

Cette vaste région s'étend sur les deux rives de la Loire, aux environs de Tours. Elle est célèbre à la fois comme jardin de la France et comme pays des châteaux.

C'est là, en effet, que se trouvent les magnifiques palais de Blois, Amboise, Chenonceaux et Azay-le-Rideau. On affirme aussi que ses habitants parlent le français le plus pur et le plus clair. En outre, la Touraine produit environ 500 000 hl (5,5 millions de caisses) de vin par an. Certains sont assez ordinaires, mais quelques-uns se tiennent au premier rang des vins de France. Vieille ville non dénuée de charme, Tours est située sur la rive gauche de la Loire et les meilleurs crus, sur la rive droite, légèrement au nord. Quand on circule en Indre-et-Loire et en Loir-et-Cher (départements tourangeaux) on n'a pas l'impression d'être dans une région vinicole. La route qui sinue parallèlement au fleuve longe de hautes falaises ; des panneaux publicitaires indiquent qu'on peut acheter du vin ici et là, mais on voit rarement des vignes. Elles sont presque toutes plantées de l'autre côtés des hauteurs bordant le fleuve. Les caves sont creusées dans les falaises de calcaire, et il y règne une constance de température et d'humidité très favorable au vieillissement du vin. Rares sont les maisons qui ne possèdent pas une cave profonde, dans la colline sur laquelle elles se dressent, et rares aussi sont ces caves où du vin ne dort pas en attendant l'instant de vérité où on débouchera la bouteille en l'inclinant doucement au-dessus d'un verre limpide.

Pour les non-initiés, vin de Touraine signifie Vouvray, pourtant cette région produit des rouges et des rosés aussi bien que des blancs. Mais en Touraine les blancs sont plus fins. Ce secteur riche et fertile de la vallée de la Loire produit des vins mousseux et non mousseux, blancs, rouges, rosés. Certains ont une grande vigueur mais d'autres en manquent. Bon nombre d'entre eux, dans certains crus, ont une trop faible teneur en alcool pour supporter le transport, mais sont indiscutablement agréables quand on les déguste.

Une bonne part du sol de Touraine est trop argileuse et trop humide pour la vigne. Mais quand on gravit les collines, on trouve du calcaire à gros grains couvert de marne crayeuse, mélange nommé *aubuis*. Les vignerons de la Loire le disent idéal pour le Chenin Blanc : variété de raisin qu'ils cultivent le plus. Le Vouvray est le meilleur échantillon des vins qu'il produit. Dans d'autres localités le sol comporte moins de calcaire et plus de silex : par exemple, à Chinon, les cépages utilisés pour les vins rosés sont le Cabernet Franc et, en moindre quantité, les Gamay, Cot, Pinot Noir et Pinot Gris, ainsi que très peu de Groslot.

Les vins de cette région portent l'appellation générale Touraine ou l'appellation plus précise de secteurs plus réduits. L'appellation Touraine mousseux s'applique à des vins titrant de 8,5 à 9,5°, faits dans la région délimitée à raison de 60 hl par ha de vigne. Les vins portant une appellation plus précise doivent atteindre des normes plus élevées. Les secteurs qui subdivisent la Touraine sont : Bourgueil, Saint-Nicolas-de-Bour-

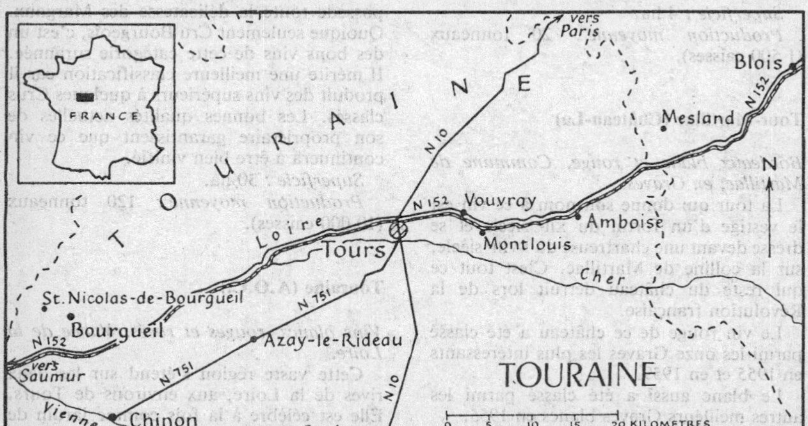

gueil, Chinon, Montlouis, Touraine-Amboise, Touraine-Azay-le-Rideau, Touraine-Mesland, Vouvray.
(Voir chacun de ces noms à sa place dans l'ordre alphabétique.)

Touraine-Amboise (Appellation Contrôlée)

Vin rouge, blanc et rosé.

Cette petite subdivision de la Touraine produit de petites quantités de vin légèrement supérieur à ceux qui ont droit à la seule appellation générale Touraine, mais inférieur aux plus célèbres secteurs de la même province. Rouge et rosé sont faits avec du Cabernet Franc, du Cabernet Sauvignon, du Cot et du Gamay ; le blanc, avec du Chenin Blanc. Le rouge et le rosé doivent titrer 9,5° et le blanc, 10°.

Voir TOURAINE

Touraine-Azay-le-Rideau (Appellation Contrôlée)

Vin blanc et rosé.

Depuis 1953 cette agglomération célèbre par son château a le droit de vendre son vin sec sous sa propre appellation d'origine qui s'applique également aux sept communes avoisinantes. Ce vin doit être fait avec du Chenin Blanc et titrer au moins 10°. Il est bon mais n'a rien d'exceptionnel pour un Touraine. Les rosés sont faits principalement avec le raisin Groslot et doivent titrer au moins 9°.

Voir TOURAINE

Touraine-Mesland (Appellation Contrôlée)

Vins blanc, rouge et rosé.

Cette petite subdivision de Touraine jouit d'une appellation d'origine propre depuis 1955. Rouge et rosé sont faits surtout avec du Gamay ; le blanc avec du Chenin Blanc et du Sauvignon. Le rosé et le rouge doivent titrer 9,5° ; le blanc 10°.

Voir TOURAINE

Touriga

Raisin rouge le plus cultivé dans la région de Dão, au Portugal. Il sert aussi à faire le Porto.

Tourne

Désordre qui se produit dans le vin. Il devient gazeux, d'une odeur et d'un goût désagréables, se trouble et perd sa couleur.

Voir CHAPITRE V

Traben-Trarbach

Agglomérations jumelles situées face à face sur la Moselle, en Allemagne. Chacune possède de bons crus de vin blanc.

Voir MOSELLE

Traminer

Variété de vigne qui donne les vins d'Alsace les plus épicés. On l'appelle aussi Gewürztraminer, nom qui figure fréquemment sur les étiquettes de vins allemands faits avec ce raisin. On le cultive aussi dans le sud du Tyrol.

Voir ALLEMAGNE ; ALSACE ; GEWÜRZTRAMINER.

Trappistine

Liqueur vert-jaune, très claire, faite avec de l'Armagnac et diverses herbes à l'abbaye de la Grâce-de-Dieu, dans le Doubs.

Trasfugado (Vinho)

Le vinho trasfugado (portugais) est le Madère après le soutirage qui l'a séparé de sa lie.

Trebbiano

Nom italien de l'Ugni Blanc. L'un des raisins à vin blanc les plus répandus en Italie, notamment dans le Latium et en Toscane. Il prospère aussi en France sous le nom de Saint-Émilion des Charentes.

Trebbiano di Abruzzo et Trebbiano di Romagna

Vins blancs italiens (D.O.C.).

Voir ABRUZZES ; ÉMILIE-ROMAGNE

Trentin-Haut-Adige

Vins blancs et rouges du Trentin-Haut-Adige (appelé aussi Tyrol méridional), en Italie.

Les possibilités du Haut-Adige pourraient en faire l'une des meilleures régions productrices de vins blancs italiens, mais actuellement ces possibilités ne se sont pas encore complètement manifestées. Le sol, le climat, les vignes de cet angle nord-est des Alpes sont capables de produire des vins qui rivaliseraient avec ceux d'Autriche et d'Alsace. Mais les quelque 6 000 vignerons, eux, s'en tiennent aux rouges légers traditionnels, qui sont un compromis entre les rouges légers d'Allemagne et les rouges plus pleins de l'Italie méridionale.

Heureusement, et en particulier dans le Trentin, certaines coopératives investissent dans la technologie moderne, au grand bénéfice de la qualité des vins.

Avant 1919, le Haut-Adige faisait partie du Tyrol autrichien. A la fin de la Première Guerre mondiale, le traité de Saint-Germain l'attribua à l'Italie, mais ses habitants sont des Germains et l'Autriche continue à boire leurs vins. Ceux qu'elle n'importe pas s'en vont vers la Suisse et l'Allemagne. Le Haut-Adige produit 3,8 millions hl (plus de 40 millions de caisses) de vin par an, dont la plus grande partie est du rouge. Si bon qu'il soit, il est surclassé par le meilleur blanc. En règle générale, les meilleurs vins blancs proviennent de la partie située le plus au nord du Haut-Adige, et les rouges, du Trentin, qui s'étend au sud, autour de la ville de Trente et jusqu'aux rives ensoleillées du lac de Garde.

Encépagement

La viniculture du Trentin-Haut-Adige a un aspect cosmopolite. L'influence autrichienne se manifeste dans le Riesling et le Traminer ; la française, dans le Pinot, le Cabernet, le Merlot ; les Italiens y ont apporté, entre autres, les raisins Schiave, Lambrusco, Teroldego et Garganega, appelé Terlano dans le pays.

Les vignes Riesling sont les plus intéressantes. Cultivées sur des coteaux au climat plutôt froid, elles donnent des raisins dont la fermentation fournit un vin merveilleux. On peut en dire autant du Traminer, quoique le fruit du Riesling soit toujours meilleur dans les mêmes conditions de culture. Le Schiave, répandu dans la partie nord de la région, donne des vins rouges sains et parfois tout à fait délicieux. La culture du Merlot est développé. Il en résulte un vin d'une cordialité qui plaît aux Italiens et dont la juvénile rudesse est très adoucie dans ce pays.

Au Trentin, la variété locale la plus répandue est le Teroldego, parfois appelé Teroldico. Il donne généreusement des vins rouges ordinaires. Lambrusco et Merlot y abondent aussi. Mais ils sont le plus souvent vinifiés avec des raisins d'autres vignes pour obtenir un vin plus équilibré, qu'une unique variété ne pourrait fournir à elle seule.

Les meilleurs vins du Trentin-Haut-Adige

Riesling del Trentino (D.O.C.)

Pourrait être le roi de Haut-Adige, s'il n'était conservé en fût trop longtemps. Il faut admettre quelques exceptions car un grand nombre de bons Riesling font une impression assez favorable pour être exportés en Allemagne. Bien que ces vins n'atteindront jamais la race des meilleurs Riesling allemands, ils pourraient quand même occuper une bonne place au-dessous de ces derniers.

Santa Magdalener (Santa Magdalena) (D.O.C.)

Vin rouge du Haut-Adige qu'on appelle encore parfois aujourd'hui Sankt Magdalener. Il est fait avec du raisin Schiave et, en moindre quantité, avec du Lagrein, cultivés tous les deux sur les beaux coteaux avoisinant Bolzano. La Santa Magdalena est un vin sain, onctueux et agréable au léger arôme d'amandes.

C'est probablement le vin rouge le plus fin de toute la région, plus riche en couleur et en goût que le Caldaro.

Teroldego Rotaliano (D.O.C.)

Vins rouge ou rosé du Trentin, produits en telle quantité qu'ils passent pour la seule ressource intéressante de la province. Ils sont secs, savoureux et vigoureux. Le rouge tend vers la rondeur, parfois avec une légère trace d'amertume due au tanin.

Traminer Aromatico del Trentino (D.O.C.)

Vin blanc sec épicé et parfumé. Le meilleur Traminer d'Italie vient du Haut-Adige.

Quoiqu'il ne soit pas encore remarquable, il peut devenir excellent et d'un prix raisonnable.

Caldaro (Lago di Caldaro, D.O.C.)

Vin agréable, d'un rouge grenat, avec un soupçon d'amande dans son bouquet. Il est fait avec du Schiave et du Rossara, cultivés autour du lac Caldaro (autrefois Kalterersee) à 15 km au sud de Bolzano. Léger et réjouissant, ce vin ne s'améliore guère avec l'âge.

Vino Santo del Trentino (D.O.C.)

Vin doux de dessert, fait avec des raisins (généralement Malvasia et Trebbiano) séchés avant vinification. Sans en avoir l'excellence, il ressemble au Vin Santo de Toscane.

VINS DE MOINDRE INTÉRÊT

Cabernet del Trentino (D.O.C.)

On cultive le Cabernet Franc et le Cabernet Sauvignon dans cette région, mais ni l'un ni l'autre à grande échelle. Son bouquet rappelle la senteur de l'herbe.

Val d'Adige (Valdadige Etschtaler) (D.O.C.)

Vin rouge fait avec les raisins Schiave, Lambrusco, Pinot et Teroldego, cultivés sur les rives de l'Adige, dans le Trentin. Du vin blanc y est aussi produit. Ce cours d'eau est long et passe sur des sols très divers. Les vins varient donc dans la même mesure. Le Val d'Adige fait fonction de vin rouge ordinaire.

Colline di Caldaro

Vin rouge fait avec du Schiave et du Pinot Noir cultivés sur les coteaux avoisinant le lac Caldaro.

Pinot Bianco (Weissburgunder et Chardonnay) (D.O.C.)

Les très bons résultats obtenus avec du Pinot Gris font de ces vins blancs du Trentin des vins prometteurs d'excellente qualité.

Lagarino Rosato (D.O.C.)

Bon vin rosé fait avec du raisin Lagrein. Avant 1919, il s'appelait Lagreinkretzer.

Marzemino del Trentino (D.O.C.)

Nom d'une variété de vigne à vin dont le fruit donne une grande quantité de rouge ordinaire au Trentin. Meilleur jeune.

Meranese di Collina (D.O.C.)

Vin rouge léger, fait avec du raisin Schiave, cultivé sur les collines Merano, à quelque 15 km au nord de Bolzano.

Merlot del Trentino (D.O.C.)

Ce cépage de Bordeaux sert à faire du rouge et du rosé pouvant être très agréables.

Moscato del Trentino (D.O.C.)

Ni aussi lourd, ni aussi doux que la plupart des vins de Muscat, il offre une diversité intéressante aux fervents de ce raisin. On produit aussi un Moscato Liquoroso viné.

Pino Nero del Trentino (D.O.C.)

Dans la région ce raisin porte parfois son vieux nom autrichien : Blauburgunder. On le cultive de-ci, de-là, mais il est rarement vinifié seul. Parfois on en fait du *spumante* (mousseux).

Lagrein del Trentino (D.O.C.)

Fait avec les raisins Lagrein, ce vin rouge sec et très fruité titre environ 12°.

Sorni (D.O.C.)

Vin rouge fait avec des raisins Merlot, Teroldego et des sous-variétés de Schiave, autour de Sorni, au nord de Trente. Le vin blanc peut être appelé *Scelto*.

Sylvaner

Petit vin blanc sec, convenant parfaitement à la carafe dans son pays d'origine. On le fait surtout autour de Bressanone (Brixen).

Terlano (D.O.C.)

Vin bien connu et fort présentable du Haut-Adige. D'une couleur légèrement verdâtre, il est fait avec du raisin Terlano qu'on appelle Garganega dans cette province. Mais plus souvent le Riesling et le Pinot Noir entrent dans sa composition.

Termeno d'Avio

Médiocre rosé, fait au sud du Trentin, avec des raisins Lambrusco, Merlot, Teroldego et Marzemino.

Trie

Triage des raisins à la vendange, afin d'en éliminer les grains verts ou pourris. Plus il s'agit de faire un vin de qualité, plus la trie est méticuleuse.

On appelle aussi trie le procédé de récoltes successives de raisins qui ont dépassé le degré de maturation normale.

Le mot trie désigne également les divers lots de raisins séparés par le triage. La première trie est celle des raisins de meilleure qualité. La dernière trie sert à faire le vin de queue *(voir ce mot).*

Trier

Très ancienne agglomération vinicole de la Moselle allemande. Outre son célèbre musée, on y trouve de bons vins blancs.

Voir MOSEL-SAAR-RUWER

Trinidad Rum

Rhum de l'île de la Trinidad.

Voir RHUM : INDES OCCIDENTALES

Triple Sec

Le Triple Sec, Curaçao blanc, était à l'origine l'appellation utilisée par les fabricants du Cointreau. Tant d'autres firmes adoptèrent ce nom que Cointreau le leur abandonna et dès lors cette maison surnomme sa liqueur, tout simplement : Cointreau. Triple Sec est actuellement utilisé par bon nombre de distillateurs dans divers pays et s'applique à des liqueurs du genre Curaçao *(voir ce nom).*

Trittenheim

Localité vinicole de la Moselle, en Allemagne. Parmi ses bons crus : Falkenberg, Laurentiusberg, Apotheke et Altärchen.

Voir MOSELLE

Trois Étoiles, Cinq Étoiles, etc.

S'applique aux Cognac et Armagnac. On pense souvent que le nombre d'étoiles indique un âge précis de trois, cinq années ou plus, alors qu'en réalité, le Trois-Étoiles représente un type bien précis d'Armagnac — qui sont généralement vieux de cinq ans — et de Cognac — généralement plus jeunes que les premiers ; mais ceci est loin d'être une règle. Rien n'est plus aisé que de dessiner une étoile, d'autant plus qu'à l'époque où l'usage des étoiles s'établit en Cognac, il existait un jeu en vogue qui consistait à dessiner une étoile sans jamais lever le crayon du papier. Le jeu s'étendit et il est probablement à l'origine du Trois-Étoiles. Si un brandy Trois-Étoiles n'est pas obligatoirement d'un âge particulier, il est toujours plus jeune qu'un V.S.O.P., qu'un X.O. ou qu'un Réserve et en tout cas, moins cher.

Les différents types d'étoiles et autres symboles sont étudiés de façon plus approfondie à la rubrique Cognac.

Voir V.S.O.P. ; X.O.

Trockenbeerenauslese

Littéralement : baies séchées choisies, dans le langage spécial des Allemands. Ce mot gigantesque décrit d'ailleurs exactement le procédé par lequel on obtient les vins doux du Rhin et de la Moselle dont certains comptent parmi les plus élégants du monde. On laisse le raisin se dessécher et se racornir du fait d'une maturation excessive et de l'action du champignon microscopique *Botrytis cinerea.* Ce phénomène élimine une bonne part de l'eau et la teneur en sucre s'accroît proportionnellement.

Les vendangeurs ne cueillent les raisins que grain par grain, au moment où ils ont atteint la maturation désirée. Dans l'Allemagne d'aujourd'hui le prix de la main-d'œuvre rend ces vins extrêmement coûteux.

Le Trockenbeerenauslese est l'homologue allemand du Sauternes français, à ceci près que, sous le climat clément du sud-ouest de la France, on peut produire des vins doux réellement naturels par cueillette des raisins grain à grain à un prix qui, quoique très élevé, n'est pas encore prohibitif.

Trotanoy (Château-)

Bordeaux rouge. Commune de Pomerol.

C'est à Jean-Pierre Moueix que l'on doit ce grand vin particulièrement riche et savoureux. Les vignes, des pieds anciens, poussent sur un sol argileux et graveleux.

Superficie : 9 ha.

Production moyenne : 30 tonneaux (3 000 caisses).

Trottevieille (Château-)

Bordeaux rouge. Commune et secteur de Saint-Émilion.

Toujours parmi les meilleurs Saint-Émilion, le Château-Trottevieille fut classé Premier Grand Cru en 1955. Il se vend bien à l'étranger, surtout en Belgique. Il appartenait à M. Marcel Borie, qui possédait aussi Château-Batailley, Cru classé du Médoc, et maintenant à son gendre, M. Castéja.

Caractéristiques : Vin fait avec soin ; du corps, du bouquet, une belle robe.

Superficie : 10 ha.

Production moyenne : 50 tonneaux (5 000 caisses).

Tuica

Spiritueux à base de prune, fait en Roumanie. Sa couleur varie du verdâtre au jaune. On le consomme parfois chaud, avec du sucre et du poivre ou du piment.

Tun

Fût contenant 210 gallons britanniques (955 l). Plein d'eau ou de vin, il pèse à peu près une tonne avoirdupois.

Tunisie

On cultivait la vigne en Tunisie autour de Carthage avant les guerres puniques. Des siècles plus tard, la prohibition musulmane fit interdire le vin pendant plus d'un millier d'années. Viticulture et viniculture reprirent sous le protectorat français et se pratiquent encore malgré les lois musulmanes. Les Français développèrent la viticulture sur le cap Bon qui ferme, à l'est, le golfe de Tunis, ainsi qu'autour de Tunis, dans les vallées de la Medjerda et de l'oued Miliane.

Les vignes de Tunisie couvrent actuellement une surface de quelque 38 000 ha qui ne sont pas tous en plein rendement. La production atteint une moyenne de 600 000 hl (6,5 millions de caisses). Les pointes des années passées sont maintenant courantes, bien qu'au moment de la reconstitution des vignobles, on ait tenté d'augmenter la qualité au détriment de la quantité.

La Tunisie produit des vins rouges, blancs et rosés, naturels et vinés, ainsi que des eaux-de-vie. La région vinicole se limite à un croissant étroit autour de Tunis, mais à bonne distance de la ville. Les principaux secteurs sont celui de Grombalia et le triangle Tunis-Mateur-Bordj Toum qui produisent plus de 90 % du vin tunisien. La question des crus ne présente pas d'importance particulière en ce qui concerne actuellement les vins de Tunisie. Néanmoins, les noms réputés sont : Carthage, Tébourda, Mornag, Muscat de Kelibia, Coteaux d'Utique, Khanguet et Sidi-Sâad, pour les vins naturels ; Byrsa et Rancio pour les vins vinés.

En Tunisie, on cultive surtout le Carignan, l'Alicante-Bouschet et le Cinsault pour le vin rouge ; la Clairette, le Beldi, Merseguera et Pedro Ximénez pour les blancs, l'Alicante-Grenache pour les rosés. Les vins ont une tendance nette à madériser, surtout les rouges qui sont faits avec l'Alicante-Bouschet ; ces raisins à maturation trop rapide sous ce climat donnent des vins de couleur faible qui tournent à la pelure d'oignon et prennent un goût amer. Pour y remédier, on a importé d'Espagne des vignes Pedro Ximénez. D'autre part on a aussi importé de France des vignes Sauvignon et Sémillon et d'Italie des vignes Merseguera pour les blancs ; Nocera, Pinot Noir, Cabernet et Mourvedre pour les rouges. Les rosés faits avec de

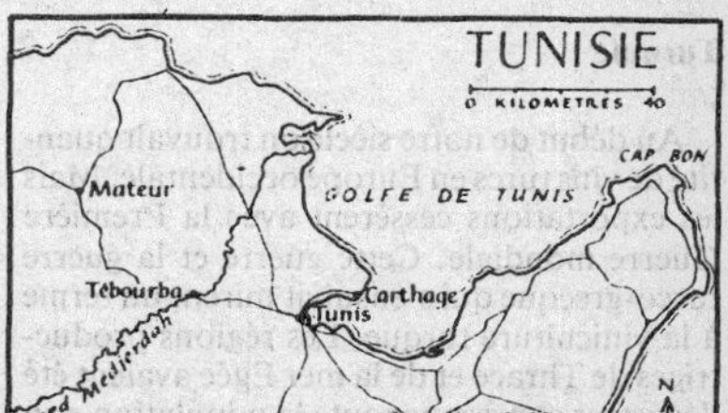

l'Alicante-Grenache se sont révélés les mieux réussis de ce genre. Ils comptent parmi les meilleurs rosés de l'Afrique du Nord, à condition qu'ils soient mis en bouteille dès qu'ils sont clarifiés et qu'on les boive jeunes, sinon, ils s'oxydent.

En 1957, un système d'appellation d'origine et de délimitation par région a été établi. Aussi trouve-t-on des vins de consommation courante, des vins supérieurs, des V.D.Q.S. et des A.O.C. Les vins proposés par les vignerons subissent une analyse chimique pour vérifier leur pureté, puis sont dégustés à l'aveugle par des experts de la Commission de classification. Les vins supérieurs de Tunisie sont vendus en bouteille. Diverses estampilles indiquent qu'ils appartiennent à cette catégorie. Le millésime doit y figurer. Ils doivent avoir au moins un an.

En 1945, on instaura l'Appellation Contrôlée « Vin Muscat de Tunisie ». Aucune restriction d'origine pourvu que le vin soit tunisien, mais il doit être fait avec des raisins des variétés suivantes : Muscat d'Alexandrie, Muscat de Frontignan, Muscat de Terracina. Les vins sont ensuite vinés de deux manières : on y ajoute de l'eau-de-vie de vin rectifiée jusqu'à en être insipide, avant que la fermentation ne commence, pour ainsi l'empêcher de se produire et conserver tout le sucre que contient le moût ; ou bien on arrête la fermentation par addition d'esprit de vin ou d'esprit rectifié insipide, afin d'obtenir un vin d'une teneur minimale de 17° et contenant environ 70 g de sucre par litre. Les vins faits selon la première méthode devraient en réalité s'appeler mistelles, car ce sont en réalité des jus de fruit additionnés d'alcool et n'ayant jamais subi de fermentation. La loi interdit de mélanger ces deux types de vin. On obtient une meilleure qualité par addition d'eau-de-vie de vin plutôt que par addition d'alcool complètement rectifié.

Turquie

Au début de notre siècle on trouvait quantité de vins turcs en Europe occidentale. Mais les exportations cessèrent avec la Première Guerre mondiale. Cette guerre et la guerre turco-grecque qui s'ensuivit mirent un terme à la viniculture turque. Les régions productrices de Thrace et de la mer Égée avaient été dévastées et presque toute la population non musulmane avait disparu. La terre tomba entre les mains de cultivateurs qui aimaient manger du raisin mais auxquels la religion interdisait de boire du vin, et ils étaient souvent persuadés que vendre leurs raisins à une entreprise vinicole était un péché. La renaissance de la viniculture turque incomba à la nouvelle république.

En 1927, quand on institua le monopole d'État de l'industrie des vins, la production totale était tombée à quelque 20 000 hl (200 000 caisses) par an. Aux environs de 1935, elle se développa petit à petit. L'État fit de sérieux efforts pour élever qualité et quantité sans majorer les prix, afin de s'assurer de nouveaux clients et de pouvoir concurrencer les pays producteurs traditionnels. On installa du matériel moderne dans les chais de l'État, on enseigna les nouvelles méthodes de viticulture et viniculture aux employés du monopole. Le décret de 1928, proclamant que la foi musulmane n'est plus la religion officielle, contribua à surmonter les scrupules de certains vignerons.

Par rapport à l'Occident, la Turquie fait figure de nouveau venu sur le plan vinicole. Pourtant la vigne prospérait dans ce pays bien avant que les Grecs ne plantassent les premiers vignobles de Gaule. On a tout lieu de croire, en effet, que les vignes les plus anciennes poussaient à l'état sauvage en Anatolie. Mais cette avance sur les autres pays fut freinée par l'invasion arabe puis réduite à néant lorsque les Turcs conquirent le pays, campagne qui aboutit à la prise de Constantinople en mai 1453. Les vignes continuèrent à donner du raisin, mais la plus grande partie de ceux-ci furent (et sont encore) réservés à la table, à la fabrication du vinaigre et du sucre de raisin. Au début de l'Empire ottoman la production du vin par les non-musulmans fut frappée d'impôts. En 1564, une nouvelle taxe sur toutes les boissons alcooliques ou alcoolisées fut instituée mais sa perception se révéla tellement difficile qu'on la supprima.

Vers la fin du XIXe siècle, bien qu'il y eut peu de buveurs de vin en Turquie, on y faisait 3 400 000 hl (plus de 35 millions de caisses) de vin, dont la plus grande partie était exportée.

La Turquie produit actuellement des vins secs, demi-secs, doux, vinés, mousseux. Les raisins destinés à faire des vins doux sont cueillis tardivement. Les vins vinés sont des Muscat doux ; les vins mousseux sont faits par addition de gaz carbonique. Les meilleurs crus sont situés au centre et au sud-est de l'Anatolie. La Thrace et la côte égéenne produisent des vins allant du très bon au moyen.

La viti-viniculture turque peut être répartie entre les régions suivantes : Thrace et Marmara ; Égée, mer Noire, Anatolie Moyenne, Méditerranée, sud-est de l'Anatolie.

MÉTHODES DE VINIFICATION

Les vignerons turcs font rarement leur propre vin, sauf quelques-uns dans les localités de Bozcaada et Mürefte. En général, ils vendent leurs raisins à des entreprises qui les traitent. Les entreprises vinicoles appartiennent à deux catégories : d'une part celles du monopole établi en 1927 et l'administration des fermes Atatürk ; d'autre part, les entreprises privées. Les chais de l'État sont équipés de matériel moderne où opère du personnel qualifié. Les entreprises privées, installées dans des échoppes, des granges, sont parfois minables ; leur matériel est en général primitif et ceux qui y travaillent manquent habituellement de qualification. Ces vinificateurs provoquent parfois des désordres en offrant aux paysans des prix ridiculement bas pour des raisins qui sont d'ailleurs, quel que soit l'acheteur, toujours vendus très bon marché.

On pressure les raisins soit dans des pressoirs hydrauliques, soit dans des pressoirs à vis manœuvrés à la main, selon l'importance de l'entreprise. Souvent on commence par un pressurage à la main et on passe ensuite le marc dans un pressoir électrique. Les jus ainsi obtenus ne sont pas mélangés et le premier donne les meilleurs produits équivalent à nos « vins de tête ». Dans les entreprises les mieux organisées, le moût fermente dans les cuves en ciment et dans des salles où la température est maintenue constamment basse. Au bout d'une semaine on les transfère dans d'autres cuves et on les y laisse évoluer. La plupart des vins sont plutôt légers et ne vieillissent que huit à douze mois. Seuls les plus grands crus restent en fût deux ou trois ans. Étant donné que les vins turcs n'ont en général qu'une faible acidité, il faut les traiter, pour les conserver, à l'anhydride sulfureux dont les doses sont cependant réglementées par une loi datant de 1954. Il faut aussi les soutirer plus tôt qu'ailleurs. Le collage a lieu avant la mise en bouteille, généralement

RÉGIONS VINICOLES TURQUES ET CÉPAGES PLANTÉS (BLANC)

Région	*Cépage*	*Localité*
Thrace et Marmara	Clairette	Tekirdag
	Chardonnay	Tekirdag
	Riesling	Tekirdag-Canakkale
	Sémillon	Tekirdag-Canakkale
	Beylerce	Bilecik
	Yapincik	Tekirdag
	Vasilaki	Canakkale-Balikesir
Égée	Sémillon	Manisa-Izmir
	Bornava Misketi	Manisa
Anatolie Moyenne	Émir	Nevsehir-Kayserie-Nigde
	Hasandede	Ankara
Méditerranée	Dökülgen	Hatay
Anatolie (Sud-Est)	Dökülgen	Gaziantep
	Morozkaraso	Gaziantep
	Rumi	Gaziantep
	Kabarcik	Gaziantep-Urfa

RÉGIONS VINICOLES TURQUES ET CÉPAGES PLANTÉS (ROUGE)

Région	*Cépage*	*Localité*
Thrace et Marmara	Pinot Noir	Tekirdag
	Adakarasi	Balikesir
	Papazkarasi	Edirne-Kiklareli
	Kuntra	Canakkale
	Gamay	Tekirdag
	Karalâhana	Tekirdag
	Cinsaut	Tekirdag
Égée	Carignane	Izmir
	Calkarasi	Denizli
	Grenache	Izmir
	Merlot	Izmir
	Cabernet Sauvignon	Maniza-Izmir
	Alicante Bouschet	Izmir
Anatolie Moyenne	Kalecik Karasi	Ankara
	Papazkarasi	Eskisehir-Nevsehir
	Dimrit	Nevsehir-Kayseri
Méditerranée	Sergi Karasi	Adana-Hatay
	Burdur Dimitri	Isparta-icel-Burdur
Anatolie (Sud-Est)	Horozkarasi	Gaziantep
	Oküzkarasi	Gaziantep-kilis
	Bogazkere	Gaziantep-kilis
	Sergi Karasi	Gaziantep

avec de la gélatine — le collage bleu est interdit. On filtre toujours le vin. La plupart des entreprises mélangent leurs vins pour obtenir une qualité constante et le vendent en bouteille. Plus rarement on le on le commercialise en fût. Les produits du monopole d'État sont en général meilleur marché que ceux des entreprises privées.

Production

En dépit des efforts de l'État, la production reste faible. Toutefois, l'emprise de la religion se desserrant, les Turcs commencent à répondre à la propagande en faveur du vin. Mais, pour la plupart, ils préféreraient manger leurs raisins, meilleur marché que la majorité des autres fruits car la vigne croît d'une manière luxuriante dans presque tout le pays. On évalue la consommation intérieure à près d'un demi litre par tête, et cependant, la Turquie vient au cinquième rang mondial pour la surface plantée en vigne, selon la liste de l'Office international du vin. La production de vin n'est nullement proportionnelle à la consommation. 3 % seulement des raisins étant prélevés à cet usage.

La situation s'améliore lentement. Actuellement les Turcs s'intéressent de près à leurs vignobles, on compte environ 700 000 ha dont la plupart sert à produire du raisin de table mais aussi à fabriquer du vin. La production, quoique variable d'année en année, atteint probablement 400 000 hl (près de 4,5 millions de caisses).

Le monopole d'État a naturellement pour objectif d'augmenter ses exportations. Quelque 40 000 hl (près de 450 000 caisses) de vin sont probablement exportés chaque année. La Suède est le principal acheteur des vins turcs (50 % des exportations), viennent ensuite la Suisse et l'Allemagne Fédérale. Pour améliorer ces statistiques d'une manière substantielle, les services d'État qui en sont chargés ont compris qu'il leur faudra réformer d'abord les normes de viticulture et la sélection des variétés de raisins. Pour ne pas décourager les vignerons, d'ailleurs peu enthousiastes, on n'appliqua d'abord les règlements qu'avec modération ; mais désormais les viticulteurs sont obligés d'apprendre des méthodes modernes et les entreprises privées de suivre l'exemple du monopole d'État. En outre, on cultive beaucoup trop de variétés de raisins en Turquie ; bien que certaines vignes soient autorisées dans chaque région cette normalisation n'a pas encore été imposée.

Cependant le phylloxéra qui atteignit la Turquie vers la fin du siècle dernier continue à sévir dans certains secteurs parce que les vignerons n'ont pas encore appris, aussi bien que ceux d'Europe, l'art de la greffe sur souche américaine résistant à cette maladie. Enfin, le gouvernement espère trouver des succédanés indigènes pour les bouchons et les douves à barrique qui coûtent trop cher à l'importation. Grâce à tous ces projets, il est permis d'espérer que les vins turcs deviendront des vins de consommation courante à l'étranger.

U

Ugni Blanc

Vigne fort répandue qui donne des raisins convenant aux vins blancs secs. On la cultive dans le Midi de la France, la région de Cognac, où on l'appelle Saint-Émilion, en Californie, en Italie, où, sous le nom de Trebbiano, il entre dans la composition de la plupart des vins blancs secs italiens.

Voir TREBBIANO ; SAINT-ÉMILION

Ullage

Littéralement : ouillage, mais en anglais ce mot a un sens plus étendu et désigne l'espace empli d'air qui s'étend entre la surface du vin et non seulement le sommet du fût mais aussi le bouchon de la bouteille, c'est généralement parce qu'elle a été trop exposée à la chaleur ou bien que le bouchon est défectueux.

Il faut alors s'en méfier car le vin peut fort bien être gâté.

U.R.S.S. (Union des républiques socialistes soviétiques)

L'U.R.S.S. (qui produit à peu près les mêmes quantités que l'Espagne) est le troisième pays producteur de vin du monde après l'Italie et la France ; le volume et la superficie de ses vignobles sont en constante expansion. Durant les dix années précédant les dévastations de la Seconde Guerre mondiale, la production était en moyenne de 5 millions d'hl, actuellement elle s'élève à environ 34 millions d'hl (près de 380 millions de caisses) par an, soit plus que la production américaine.

La production du vin fut toujours une activité économique importante en Russie, surtout sur les bords de la mer Noire. En outre, après 1930, le gouvernement entreprit d'augmenter la culture de la vigne dans les régions qui lui sont naturellement favorables, en particulier : Arménie, Azerbaïdjan, Géorgie, c'est-à-dire au Caucase, entre la mer Noire et la mer Caspienne, et en Crimée. En 1948, la surface cultivée en vigne était déjà le triple de celle d'avant la révolution et dépassait 4 000 ha, elle dépasse aujourd'hui 1 350 000 ha. Le pays importe près de 7 millions d'hl de vin — principalement d'Algérie — et il en exporte plus de 550 000 hl. La consommation par habitant est de 13 l par an, et l'État encourage le goût pour le vin afin de réduire la consommation impressionnante de spiritueux (vodka), car les Russes sont les plus gros consommateurs de spiritueux du monde.

La hausse de la production était due en partie aux accroissements territoriaux d'après guerre, comme l'annexion de la Moldavie soviétique qui fut, entre les deux guerres mondiales, la province roumaine de Bessarabie. On y a toujours produit de grandes quantités de vin, surtout autour de sa capitale Kichinef. Ce vin était autrefois connu sous l'appellation Bessarabie. On en faisait aussi une bonne partie aux environs des bouches du Dniestr, dans la région qui s'appelle maintenant Bielgorod Dniestrovskiy, et autrefois Akkerman, nom sous lequel on connaissait ses vins. Ce secteur fait partie de l'Ukraine.

APPELLATIONS D'ORIGINE AUTORISÉES EN U.R.S.S.

Variété de raisins et origine	*Secteur vinicole*	*Type de vin*
	VINS DU COMBINAT ABRAU-DURSSO, KRASNODAR	
Riesling Abrau	Abrau-Dursso	blanc sec
Riesling Anapa	Anapa	blanc sec
	VINS DU COMBINAT MASSANDRA, CRIMÉE	
Sémillon Oreanda	Crimée	blanc sec
Riesling Massandra	Crimée	blanc sec
Aligoté Ay-Danil	Crimée	blanc sec
Cabernet Livadia	Crimée	rouge sec
Bordo Ay-Danil	Crimée	rouge sec
Saperavi Massandra	Crimée	rouge sec
Muscat Blanc Massandra[1]	Crimée	doux de dessert
Muscat Blanc Livadia[1]	Crimée	doux de dessert
Muscat Rosé Gourzouf[1]	Crimée	doux de dessert
Muscat Noir Kuchuk-Lambat[1]	Crimée	rouge de dessert
Muscat Blanc Kastel[2]	Crimée	rouge de dessert
Muscat Rosé Alupka[2]	Crimée	rosé de dessert
Tokay Ay-Danil[1]	Crimée	dessert
Tokay Alouchta[2]	Crimée	dessert
Pinot Gris Ay-Danil	Crimée	dessert
Aiou-Dag[2]	Crimée	muscat rouge
Sou-Dag[2]	Crimée	blanc, genre Porto
Alupka[2]	Crimée	blanc, genre Porto
Livadia[2]	Crimée	rouge, genre Porto
Kuchuk-Lambat[2]	Crimée	rouge, genre Porto
Alouchta[2]	Crimée	rouge, genre Porto
Massandra[2]	Crimée	rouge, genre Porto
Kuchuk-Uzen[2]	Crimée	rouge, genre Madère
Massandra[2]	Crimée	rouge, genre Madère
	COMBINAT DE BESSARABIE	
Pinot	Moldavie	blanc
Aligoté	Moldavie	blanc
Bordo (probablement Cabernet)	Moldavie	rouge
Negru, Purkar, Cabernet, Saparvi	Moldavie	rouge
	VINS DU COLLECTIF TEMPELHOF	
Riesling	Tempelhof	blanc
Sylvaner	Tempelhof	blanc
	R.S.S. D'UKRAINE	
Riesling	Ukraine	blanc
Aligoté	Ukraine	blanc
Cabernet	Ukraine	rouge
	R.S.S. D'AZERBAIDJAN	
Matrassa	Azerbaïdjan	rouge
Akastafa[2]	Azerbaïdjan	blanc, genre Porto

1. Vin doux liquoreux.
2. Degré d'alcool dépassant 15 %, vin doux liquoreux.

Variété de raisins et origine	*Secteur vinicole*	*Type de vin*
Kara-Tachanakh[2]	Azerbaïdjan	blanc de dessert
Chemakha[2]	Azerbaïdjan	rouge de dessert
Kurdamir[2]	Azerbaïdjan	rouge de dessert
	R.S.S. DE GÉORGIE	
Tsolikohouri	Géorgie	blanc
Semillon	Géorgie	blanc
Kahouri	Géorgie	blanc
Tibaani	Géorgie	blanc
Téliani	Géorgie	rouge
Mukuzani	Géorgie	rouge
Napuréouli	Géorgie	rouge
Ousahelohouri	Géorgie	blanc de dessert
Tchakhavéri	Géorgie	blanc de dessert
Tvichi	Géorgie	blanc de dessert
Psou	Géorgie	blanc de dessert
Tetra	Géorgie	blanc de dessert
Ahméta	Géorgie	blanc de dessert
Hvantchkara	Géorgie	rouge de dessert
Kindzmaraouli	Géorgie	rouge de dessert
Ahachéni	Géorgie	rouge de dessert
Eniséli	Géorgie	eau-de-vie
Grémi	Géorgie	eau-de-vie
Vartsihé	Géorgie	eau-de-vie
Tbilisi	Géorgie	eau-de-vie
	R.S.S. D'ARMÉNIE	
Etchmiadzine[3]	Arménie	blanc
Voskévaz[3]	Arménie	blanc
Aréni[3]	Arménie	rouge
Norachéne[3]	Arménie	rouge
Achtaraque[3]	Arménie	blanc genre Xérès
Aigéchate[3]	Arménie	rouge genre Porto
Arévchate[3]	Arménie	rouge viné
Dvine	Arménie	eau-de-vie
Erévan	Arménie	eau-de-vie
Arménia	Arménie	eau-de-vie
Nairi	Arménie	eau-de-vie
	R.S.S. D'UZBÉKISTAN	
Uzbekiston	Uzbekistan	rouge
Aléatiko[3]	Uzbekistan	blanc de dessert
Umalak[3]	Uzbekistan	blanc de dessert
Bouaki[3]	Uzbekistan	blanc de dessert
Farkhad[3]	Uzbekistan	rouge genre Porto
	R.S.S. DE KAZAKHIE	
Ak-Kainar	Kazakhie	blanc mousseux
Issik	Kazakhie	blanc
Chirine	Kazakhie	vins vinés
Kazakhstane	Kazakhie	et vins de dessert
Tselinnoe	Kazakhie	

2. Degré d'alcool dépassant 15 %, vin doux liquoreux.
3. Degré d'alcool dépassant 15 %.

Variété de raisins et origine	*Secteur vinicole*	*Type de vin*
Ak-Boulak	Kazakhie	
Muscat Violet	Kazakhie	
	R.S.S. DE KIRGHISIE	
Muscat de Kirghisie[3]	Kirghisie	blanc de dessert
Muscat Violet[3]	Kirghisie	blanc de dessert
Cabernet	Kirghisie	rouge
Kirghistane	Kirghisie	rouge
Ala-Too[3]	Kirghisie	rouge genre Porto
	R.S.S. DE TADJIKISTAN	
Taifi	Tadjikistan	genre Porto
Tadjikistane	Tadjikistan	rouge genre Porto
Vakche[3]	Tadjikistan	rouge de dessert
Chirine[3]	Tadjikistan	vin de dessert
Gontchi[3]	Tadjikistan	vin de dessert
Guissare[3]	Tadjikistan	vin de dessert
Djaousse[3]	Tadjikistan	vin de dessert
	R.S.S. DE TURKMÉNIE	
Térbache[3]	Turkménie	vin de dessert
Yasman-Salik[3]	Turkménie	vin viné
Goulistane[3]	Turkménie	vin viné
Kopetdague[3]	Turkménie	vin viné

3. Degré d'alcool dépassant 15 %.

La production de vins mousseux occupe une grande place dans le plan d'expansion vinicole. On en fait 100 millions de bouteilles par an. Le meilleur est le Kaffia de Crimée. Une seconde catégorie, proche mais inégale, provient du collectif Abrou Dursso, à Krasnodar, près de la mer d'Azov, secteur qui eut toujours de l'importance dans la viticulture russe. Ce vin est le même que l'Abran blanc, parfois classé à tort parmi les vins de Crimée et qui provient d'une région plus à l'ouest.

Principales régions viticoles

A quelques médiocres exceptions près, tout le vin de l'Union soviétique est produit dans un vaste arc de cercle, au sud de la Russie, et qui s'étend de la frontière roumaine, à l'ouest, jusqu'au Caucase et à la mer Caspienne, voire jusqu'aux frontières de l'Iran, de l'Inde, de la Chine et de la Mongolie, à l'est. L'ensemble de cette zone prodigieusement vaste produit plus ou moins de vin. Les plus intéressants proviennent de l'ouest de la mer Caspienne, sur le cours inférieur du Don, au bord de la mer d'Azov, et plus particulièrement de Crimée. Arménie, Azerbaïdjan et Géorgie produisent aussi de bons vins.

Depuis les temps les plus reculés, la vigne prospéra dans ces régions et nous savons qu'on y faisait du vin très longtemps avant notre ère. On a trouvé des indices de viticulture au temps de l'ancien royaume de Van, c'est-à-dire un millier d'années avant Jésus-Christ. Ce royaume s'étendait jusqu'à la plaine d'Arménie et couvrait tout le sud de la Transcaucasie. Au temps d'Hérodote (460 av. J.-C.), les vins d'Arménie jouissaient déjà d'un grand renom. Deux cent cinquante ans plus tôt, quand les Assyriens prirent et pillèrent les villes de Van, ils y trouvèrent de vastes caves à vin. On se servait déjà du soufre en viniculture et on suppose que les vins étaient faits avec des raisins préalablement séchés au soleil. Les habitants de Géorgie apprirent aussi très tôt à cultiver leurs vignes. Des archéologues ont découvert des jarres et de grandes amphores à vin, qui datent du second millénaire av. J.-C. et dans l'Odyssée, Homère loue les « vins parfumés et vivaces de Colchide (Géorgie occidentale), pays de raisins dorés ». Xénophon relate que les habitants des bords de la mer Noire faisaient des vins robustes aromatiques et agréables quand on les coupait d'eau.

Crimée

On fait en Crimée surtout des vins doux et de dessert, tant rouges que blancs, mais aussi des vins secs, des vins vinés et des vins mousseux dont le bon Kaffia. La production n'est pas élevée, mais tout le secteur de Crimée produit les meilleurs vins de Russie, particulièrement au sud et à l'est. D'importants vignobles s'étendent le long de la côte à proximité des villes de Sébastopol et de Simféropol.

La viticulture contemporaine de Crimée se développa au début du siècle dernier sous l'impulsion d'un certain Pallas, expert français qui fit venir bon nombre de vignerons français pour créer et améliorer les vignobles. Le principal domaine, qui donna son nom au vin le plus célèbre, s'appelait Massandra et appartenait au prince Voronzof. Actuellement, plusieurs exploitations collectives vinicoles de Crimée utilisent cette appellation et il existe encore du Massandra rouge ainsi que du blanc sec. Le plus célèbre des vins de Crimée, encore aujourd'hui, est un vin viné, du type Madère, riche, couleur d'ambre, parfois considéré comme le meilleur de toute l'Union soviétique.

Les autres produits remarquables de Crimée sont : le Livadia, fait avec du Muscat (il y existe aussi un Livadia rouge fait avec du raisin Cabernet) ; le blanc sec Sémillon Oreanda (souvent appelé Orianda hors de Russie) ; le Saperadi ou, de nos jours, Saperavi Massandra, qui est le vin rouge sec et ne doit pas être confondu avec le grand Massandra doré de dessert, il n'en a pas moins de remarquables qualités de goût ; le rosé de dessert Alupka et un autre vin de dessert nommé Ay-Danil.

On cultive en Crimée bon nombre de variétés européennes, par exemple Riesling, Cabernet, Pinot Gris et surtout Muscat.

Vallée du Don

On produit des vins dans la vallée inférieure du Don, près de la mer d'Azov. Ils sont rouges ou blancs, et, en petite quantité, mousseux. Le plus connu porte l'appellation générale Dônski. Tsimliansk, Constantinowka et Novocherkassk sont les centres viticoles de la région. On y cultive des variétés locales, entre autres : Pletchistik, Krasnotop, Pukhliakovski ; tous donnant des vins blancs.

Moldavie

Nom que les Russes donnent à la Province roumaine de Bessarabie. C'est une des régions les plus productrices de l'U.R.S.S. : elle représente 8 % de la production totale du pays, soit plus de 2,8 millions d'hl. Elle possède 325 000 ha de vignobles dont plus de 200 000 ha sont productifs. On cultivait autrefois des vignes hybrides donnant des vins ordinaires ; aujourd'hui, on compte davantage de ceps de variétés européennes : Pinot, Aligoté, Riesling, Traminer, etc.

Ukraine

Après les dévastations causées par le phylloxéra à la fin du siècle dernier, une bonne part du vignoble ukrainien fut replantée en hybrides. On est en train de les remplacer systématiquement. Les vignobles sont de la même taille que ceux de Moldavie et produisent des vins rouges et blancs, peu alcoolisés, des mousseux et des vins de dessert. Les centres vinicoles sont Odessa, Ismalie et Carpates.

Stavropol

On fait des vins blancs — Riesling Bechtau et Sylvaner Bechtau — et des vins de dessert à base de Muscat, sur le flanc nord du mont Caucase, autour de Stavropol.

Krasnodar

Cette région porte le nom de sa ville principale qui se trouve à l'est de la mer Noire et de la mer d'Azov ; des fermes collectives de grande importance s'y sont créées. Riesling et Cabernet donnent de bons vins rouges et blancs secs autour d'Anapa et de Novorossivsk sur les bords de la mer Noire. La vallée du Kouban a toujours été connue pour sa grosse production de vins vinés et vins de dessert. Le collectif d'Abrau-Dursso, sur la mer Noire, l'un des meilleurs vins de l'Union Soviétique, produit un vin mousseux très célèbre. Cette région exporte deux autres vins mousseux dont l'un s'appelle simplement Krasnodar et l'autre Isimljanskoje Igristje.

Géorgie

Avec ses quelque 250 000 ha de vigne, la Géorgie est la plus grosse productrice de vin de première qualité. On y trouve certains des plus vieux vignobles de Russie.

Les vins de Géorgie exportés à l'étranger sont les blancs Myshako Riesling et Ghurdjurni. La région de Kakhétie est celle qui produit les meilleurs vins, notamment les Gourdjaani et Tsinandali blancs, ainsi que les Napureouli, Mukuzani et Mzvane ou Mzvane rouges. Cette région est également connue pour sa méthode de production : le moût fermente avec les rafles et les peaux dans des cruches d'argile, les vins ont un goût typiquement astringent. La variété de raisins Saperavi donne d'assez bons rouges. C'est la même qui produit les meilleurs vins de table de Crimée.

Le mot Mzvane qui s'applique à un vin de cette région est aussi celui d'une variété de raisins. Autre variété de vigne intéressante de la région, la Rkaziteli donne des vins blancs portant le même nom. Il y a aussi une production importante de vins mousseux et d'eaux-de-vie.

Azerbaïdjan

L'Azerbaïdjan soviétique (135 000 ha), situé à la frontière de l'Iran, produit des vins de table, des vins vinés et des eaux-de-vie. Le développement de la viticulture ne date que des années 1960 ; le vin de table Matrassa, renommé pour le cépage est le meilleur vin de cette région. Les centres principaux sont Kirovabad, Kurdamirsk, Chemakhinsk et Geokchai. L'Azerbaïdjan produit aussi des vins de dessert et des vins vinés.

Arménie

Le vin a toujours été un des produits essentiels de l'économie arménienne. Cette région se targue d'être la patrie de la vigne et sans doute avec raison. Actuellement on y fait des vins naturels, des vins vinés et des eaux-de-vie en grande quantité. Echmiadzin, Achtarak, Vedin et Oktemberian sont des centres vinicoles (43 000 ha).

Outre les principales régions vinicoles énumérées précédemment, la culture de la vigne s'étend, grâce à l'irrigation, au Turkménistan (à peu près 11 000 ha) où l'on fait des vins vinés, un prétendu tokay, ainsi que les Yasmansalik et Kara-Izium. En Ouzbékistan (environ 63 000 ha), les 3/4 de la surface cultivée en vigne sont plantés d'Iziun : un raisin de table, et 1/4 seulement de raisins à vin. On y fait surtout des vins de dessert. Le Tadjikistan, situé au nord du Pakistan et du Cachemire, possède actuellement près de 20 000 ha de vignes qui fournissent des vins de dessert. Enfin, dans l'immense Kazakhstan, qui s'étend de la Caspienne à la Mongolie, à peu près 20 000 ha ont été plantés voilà quelques années.

Les appellations d'origine autorisées en Union soviétique et précisées dans le tableau ci-avant sont extraites d'un bulletin de l'Office international du vin auquel l'auteur témoigne ici sa gratitude, de même que pour d'autres renseignements au sujet des vins soviétiques.

L'industrie russe du vin admet que l'on appelle certains de ses produits : porto, madère, tokay. Ces termes ne peuvent pas être corrects, car seul un vin de la vallée supérieure du Douro peut remplir les conditions nécessaires pour s'appeler Porto ; de même, aucun vin ne peut s'appeler Madère s'il ne provient pas de l'île de ce nom et n'est pas conforme aux normes de cette appellation.

Étant donné que, au moment où ce livre est imprimé, nous ne disposons que d'informations limitées au sujet de l'Union soviétique, nous avons indiqué : genre Madère, genre Porto, pour donner une idée approximative du type de vin.

Uruguay

Ce petit pays d'Amérique du Sud atteint une importance au point de vue vinicole qui est hors de proportion avec sa superficie. Il produit, en effet, environ 800 000 hl (près de 9 millions de caisses) de vin par an. Mais les Uruguayens boivent leur vin et n'en exportent guère. Un ruisselet, à peine, s'en écoule vers le Brésil. Si vous avez envie de boire un vin d'Uruguay, allez en Uruguay.

Les vins uruguayens sont rouges, blancs et rosés. Ces derniers ont une couleur plus foncée que dans les autres pays et tendent plus vers le *clarete* espagnol que vers le rosé français. On fait aussi du vermouth en Uruguay, ainsi que des vins de liqueur et des mousseux. En contradiction avec la règle générale, les vins vinés sont souvent étiquetés porto et les mousseux, champagne. Les Uruguayens préfèrent toutefois des vins qui portent des noms de leur pays, ou celui de la variété de raisin qui servit à les faire, ne serait-ce que la variété dominante dans un mélange.

La vigne la plus répandue en Uruguay est l'Harriague qu'il est permis d'assimiler au Tannat servant à faire le Madiran des Hautes-Pyrénées. Viennent ensuite les raisins Vidiella, dont l'origine est obscure et Cabernet, importé de la région de Bordeaux. Quand on mélange ces deux espèces de raisin, il en résulte un vin bien équilibré et agréable. On trouve aussi en Uruguay des vignes Barbera et Nebbiolo importées d'Italie et qui conservent leur nom d'origine. Les vins blancs sont faits surtout avec du Sémillon et du Pinot Blanc. 50 % de la production est en Frutilla et quelques vignes hybrides. On a également planté l'Isabella américaine. Comme toujours l'accroissement de la production s'assortit d'une baisse nettement marquée de la qualité.

La viticulture uruguayenne contemporaine ne remonte qu'aux dix dernières années du siècle dernier. Circonscrite d'abord aux alentours de Montevideo, elle s'étend désormais sur les collines basses et les plaines des départements de Montevideo, Canelones, San José et Maldonado (le long du rio de la Plata), Soriano et Paysandú (à la frontière de l'Argentine), et Florida (dans le centre du pays).

Au point de vue géologique, l'Uruguay n'est qu'un prolongement de la plaine brésilienne, et ses collines d'origine volcanique, à pente douce (*cuchillas*), ne dépassent jamais 600 m d'altitude.

Le climat est clément : température moyenne de janvier et février (mois de plein été), 22 °C ; du mois de juillet (mois du plein hiver), 10 °C. Il y pleut suffisamment, mais sans excès. Le vignoble couvre une superficie d'environ 16 000 ha.

Spiritueux

Les Uruguayens distillent les quantités d'eau-de-vie de vin qu'ils baptisent à tort cognac, et de la grappa, eau-de-vie de marc de raisin. Le Caña — un genre de rhum — est très populaire dans ce pays, de même qu'un apéritif nommé Amara ou Amargo. L'Anisette, le Gin, et le Guindado, obtenu par la fermentation de cerise et additionné d'alcool, y sont aussi assez répandus.

Le populaire Vino Seco est fait en ajoutant une bonne quantité de vin blanc à du rouge, puis en enrichissant la mixture avec de l'eau-de-vie de vin et en laissant le tout madériser au soleil. Ce procédé paraîtra sans doute déprimant à tous les amateurs de vins traditionnels.

Tous les vins et spiritueux de l'Uruguay sont sous le contrôle de l'État. Plusieurs écoles s'efforcent d'accroître les connaissances et d'améliorer les vins en envoyant des étudiants à l'étranger, particulièrement en Italie et en France.

Ürziger Würzgarten

Vin blanc. Moyenne Moselle.

Le meilleur cru d'Ürzig. Sol schisteux et volcanique. Vignoble tellement en pente que la viticulture devient un sport de montagne aux dangers mortels. Le vin est épicé et fruité. Outre le Würzgarten, se trouvent aussi à Ürzig les vignobles de Schwarzlay et Kranklay.

Voir MOSELLE

Usquebaugh

Forme anglicisée du *Uisgebeatha,* nom originel du whisky en langue celtique. *Uisgebeatha* signifie littéralement : eau-de-vie.

Voir WHISKY ; IRLANDE.

Utiel-Requena

Une appellation d'origine espagnole située au sud de Barcelone et à l'ouest de Valence. Les 50 000 ha de Trempanillo, Garnacha et Bobal produisent des rouges vigoureux et quelques rosés plus légers.

V

Vacqueyras

Une des meilleures communes vinicoles des Côte du Rhône. Elle produit des vins blancs, rouges et rosés et a droit à l'Appellation Contrôlée Côte du Rhône suivie de son propre nom.

Voir RHÔNE

Vaduzer

Vin rouge du Liechtenstein.

Les 2/3 du vin produit dans la petite principauté de Liechtenstein, située entre la Suisse et l'Autriche, portent l'appellation Vaduzer, dérivée du nom de sa capitale : Vaduz. Le reste provient de Schaan, Triesen et Balzers, d'où le nom des vins : Schaaner, Triesner et Balzner.

Les premiers vignobles furent probablement établis à Liechtenstein par les Romains et, plus tard, par des moines au début de l'ère chrétienne. En ce temps-là, le Liechtenstein n'existait pas encore. Son territoire fit d'abord partie de l'Empire romain, puis du Saint Empire romain germanique. En 1699 et 1712, les princes de Liechtenstein achetèrent la principauté sur laquelle ils règnent depuis lors. Toutes les vignes étaient alors cultivées par des moines, puis elles furent sécularisées voilà cent cinquante ans. De nos jours, la production annuelle se chiffre à quelque 800 hl (plus de 8 500 caisses).

Le Vaduzer est un vin rouge léger qui par sa teinte claire se rapproche du rosé. Il est fait exclusivement avec du Blauburgunder ; autrefois on cultivait aussi de l'Elbling (blanc), on essaya aussi Riesling et Sylvaner, mais on abandonna ces variétés. Les petits vignerons sont groupés dans une coopérative. Le seul domaine de Bockwingert comprend à peu près la moitié des vignes du secteur de Vaduz. Le cru le plus intéressant est Abtwingert, vignoble de la Rotes Haus.

En 1525, cette Maison Rouge appartenait aux bénédictins de Saint-Jean dont le couvent se trouvait à Togenberg. Elle datait déjà d'une centaine d'années, voire plus. Quiconque voit le pressoir gothique massif fonctionnant dans les caves comprend pourquoi la Rotes Haus est considérée comme la deuxième merveille du Liechtenstein, après le château du prince. Au milieu du XIXe siècle, Alois Rheinberger — les Rheinberger en sont encore propriétaires — émigra vers l'Illinois, planta le vignoble bien connu de Masberg Mansion à Nauvoo et y pratiqua les méthodes vinicoles de Vaduz.

Valdadige (Etschtaler) (D.O.C.)

Bons vins rouges et blancs provenant des rives de l'Adige, de Merano à Vérone en Vénétie.

Voir TRENTIN-HAUT-ADIGE

Val d'Aoste (D.O.C.)

Voir ITALIE

Valais

Région des Alpes suisses dont les vignobles sont situés sur les deux rives du haut Rhône, à l'est de Genève.
Voir SUISSE

Valdeorras

Voir ESPAGNE *(Galice)*

Valdepeñas

Vin le plus en vogue dans les cafés de Madrid. Il provient des vignes cultivées dans la Manche, au sud de la capitale. Ce sont des rouges vigoureux et parfois légers et des blancs secs. Jusqu'à ce que ceux de Rioja atteignent leur popularité actuelle, c'étaient les mieux connus des vins espagnols non vinés.
Voir ESPAGNE *(Centre)*

Valgella (D.O.C.)

Vins rouges de la Valteline, faits avec du Nebbiolo.
Voir LOMBARDIE

Valpantena

Un type de vin assez sembable au Valpolicella. L'un des plus grands propriétaires est la compagnie Bertani.
Voir VÉNÉTIE

Valpolicella (D.O.C.)

Le meilleur vin de Vénétie (Italie). D'un rouge rubis, odorant, fruité, il a un bouquet délicat et une riche texture.
Voir VÉNÉTIE

Valteline (D.O.C.)

Nom de plusieurs vins rouges italiens faits avec du raisin Nebbiolo.
Voir LOMBARDIE

Van der Hum

Liqueur sud-africaine dont le principal composant est l'écorce de *nartjie* (agrumes sud-africaines). Les autres ingrédients varient selon le producteur qui garde jalousement le secret de sa recette. De couleur rousse, cette liqueur a un fort goût d'orange. Van der Hum signifie : « Comment s'appelle-t-il ? » Le Brandy-Hum est obtenu en mélangeant par parts égales de l'eau-de-vie de vin et du Van der Hum dont on diminue ainsi la douceur.
Voir AFRIQUE DU SUD

Varietal Wine

Littéralement « vin de variété ». Il serait préférable de traduire par « vin de cépage ». Il s'agit de vin appelé, comme en Alsace, du nom de la variété de raisin qui domine dans sa vinification. Aux États-Unis, l'appellation des Varietal Wines est régie par la loi. Le raisin qui donne son nom au vin doit entrer au moins pour 75 % dans sa composition, pour une appellation simple, par exemple : California Pinot Noir, New York State Riesling, etc. et 85 % pour un vin provenant d'une A.V.A. (American Vinicultural Area) dont le nombre est croissant. Ces appellations sont régies par le B.A.T.F. (Bureau of Alcohol, Tobacco and Firearms). Cette réglementation fut adoptée dans le but de rompre avec des appellations dénuées de sens telles que Californian burgundy. La plupart des firmes productrices de bons vins l'ont adoptée.

V.D.N. (Vins doux naturels)

Vins vinés qui ont eu un rajout d'eau-de-vie de vin. Ils sont des apéritifs populaires en France mais ne s'exportent pas. Les principaux V.D.N. sont produits dans le Roussillon et dans quelques autres départements du Midi.
Voir ROUSSILLON

V.D.N.V. : Verband deutscher Naturwein-Versteigerer

Jusqu'à l'adoption de la Loi de 1971 sur le vin votée en R.F.A., le nom était Verband Deutscher Naturwein-Versteigerer, mais la nouvelle appellation V.D.P. (Verband Deutscher Prächtikats-und Qualitätsweingüter), fut adoptée pour se conformer à la réglementation abolissant l'utilisation du mot *Natur* à propos du vin.

Voir ALLEMAGNE

V.D.P. : Verband Deutscher Prädikats-und Qualitätsweingüter

Voir V.D.N.V.

V.D.Q.S. : Vins délimités de qualité supérieure

Cette mention figure sur l'étiquette de certains vins français considérés comme assez bons pour être soumis à un contrôle de qualité, mais n'ayant pas assez d'envergure pour entrer dans la catégorie des vins d'appellation d'origine contrôlée. Les V.D.Q.S. constituent donc une catégorie secondaire parmi les meilleurs vins de France.

La classification ci-après ne date que de 1949. Elle porte sur un assez grand nombre de vins dont quelques-uns sont très bons. A l'exclusion des plus grands vins français d'appellation d'origine, les meilleurs font partie de cette catégorie ainsi que, autrefois, les vins supérieurs d'Algérie. Les décrets portant sur les divers V.D.Q.S. indiquent les variétés de raisin autorisées et la teneur minimale en alcool ; ils délimitent la zone de production. Dans la plupart des cas le vin doit être dégusté par une commission d'experts constituée à cette fin et c'est seulement avec leur approbation que le produit a droit à la mention V.D.Q.S. Ces vins portent ces quatre lettres sur leur étiquette, ainsi que leur lieu d'origine et, dans le cas des vins mis en bouteille au domaine, le nom du producteur est aussi indiqué, ainsi que le numéro du label imprimé sur un timbre spécial.

Certains V.D.Q.S. présentent des valeurs vraisemblablement intéressantes à condition que la plus grosse part du prix représente le vin et non les droits de douane et frais de transport. Ce sont des vins honnêtes et sains dont la réputation ne doit pas provoquer la majoration du prix.

Quelques V.D.Q.S. sont traités dans cette encyclopédie à leur place dans l'ordre alphabétique.

APPELLATION DES V.D.Q.S.

Carbadès	*Aude*
Châteaumeillant	*Cher, Indre*
Cheverny	*Loir-et-Cher*
Côte Roannaise	*Loire*
Coteaux d'Ancenis *(suivi par un nom de cépage)*	*Loire Atl.*
Coteaux Pierrevert	*Alpes-de-Hte Provence*
Coteaux de Giennois	*Loiret, Nièvre*
Coteaux du Giennois Cosnes-sur-Loire	*Loiret, Nièvre*
Coteaux Varois	*Var*
Coteaux du Vendomois	*Loir-et-Cher*
Côtes d'Auvergne	*Puy-de-Dôme*
Côtes d'Auvergne *(suivi par un nom de lieu)*	*Puy-de-Dôme*
Côtes de Gien	*Loiret, Nièvre*
Côtes de Gien Cosnes-sur-Loire	*Loiret, Nièvre*
Côtes de la Malepère	*Aude*
Côtes de Saint-Mont	*Gers*
Côtes de Toul	*Meurthe-et-Moselle*
Côtes du Brulhois	*Lot-et-Garonne*
Côtes du Cabardès et de l'Orbiel	*Aude*
Côtes du Forez	*Loire*
Côtes du Lubéron	*Vaucluse*
Côtes du Marmandais	*Lot-et-Garonne*
Côtes du Vivarais	*Ardèche, Gard*
Côtes du Vivarais *(suivi par un nom de cru)*	*Ardèche, Gard*
Fiefs Vendéens	*Vendée*
Gros Plant ou Gros Plant du Pays Nantais	*Loire-Atl.*
Haut Comtat	*Drôme*
Mousseux du Bugey	*Ain*
Pétillant du Bugey	*Ain*
Roussette du Bugey	*Ain*
Roussette du Bugey *(suivi par un nom de cru)*	*Ain*
Saint-Pourçain	*Allier*
Sauvignon de Saint-Bris	*Yonne*
Tursan	*Landes*
Valençay	*Indre, Loir-et-Cher*
Vin du Bugey	*Ain*
Vin du Bugey mousseux	*Ain*
Vin du Bugey pétillant	*Ain*
Vin du Bugey *(suivi par un nom de cru)*	*Ain*
Vin du Bugey Cerdon mousseux	*Ain*
Vin du Bugey Cerdon pétillant	*Ain*
Vins d'Entraygues et du Fel	*Aveyron, Cantal*
Vins d'Estaing	*Aveyron*
Vins de Lavilledieu	*Tarn-et-Garonne*
Vins de Marcillac	*Aveyron*
Vins de Moselle	*Moselle*
Vins de l'Orléanais	*Loiret*
Vins du Haut-Poitou	*Vienne, Deux-Sèvres*
Vins du Thouarsais	*Deux-Sèvres*

Vega Sicilia

Voir ESPAGNE *(Rueda)*

Velouté

Qualité d'un vin qui, après vieillissement, conserve son corps, mais donne une sensation d'extrême suavité.

Vendange

Récolte des raisins ; signifie également : millésime.

Venencia

Coupe d'argent, de forme hémisphérique, dont l'anse est une baleine souple d'à peu près 1 m de long. On l'utilise en Espagne, particulièrement à Jerez de la Frontera, pour prélever un peu de Xérès dans les fûts.

Voir XÉRÈS

Vénétie (Veneto)

Vins rouges et blancs. Nord-est de l'Italie.

Les vins de Vénétie sont sans doute les plus charmants et de qualité la plus constante. On ne pourrait cependant guère les considérer comme grands. Cette région qui s'étend autour de Venise et de Vérone produit près de 8 500 000 hl (près de 95 millions de caisses) par an. Pour la quantité, c'est donc la troisième d'Italie.

Le Soave est un blanc sec et, comme l'indique son nom, nettement suave. Valpolicella, Valpantena et Bardolino exécutent de gracieuses variations sur un thème dont les trois notes dominantes sont : sec, rouge et léger. Forte saveur et dureté — qualités ou défauts habituels des vins italiens — semblent épargner ceux des environs de Vérone.

Promenez-vous autour de l'amphithéâtre romain de Vérone ou assistez à une représentation d'opéra, un soir d'été, errez le long des vieilles rues ou pénétrez dans une cour médiévale et alors les vins de Vérone, agréables à boire partout au monde, vous sembleront délicieux. Il est vrai que tous les vins ont meilleur goût dans leur pays d'origine. Mais ceux-ci par bonheur supportent le transport et semblent même emporter avec eux un peu de charme de Vérone.

LES MEILLEURS VINS DE VÉNÉTIE

Valpolicella, Recioto della Valpolicella, Amarone (tous D.O.C.)

Ce sont indiscutablement les meilleurs. Robe de rubis, 12 à 13°, bouquet délicat et riche, velours qui emplit la bouche. De temps en temps apparaît une bouteille qui contient une trace de sucre résiduel. Ce sucre se mettra à travailler dans la bouteille pour rendre le Valpolicella *frizzante* (pétillant) et même un peu piquant, ce qui n'a rien de désagréable. De même que pour les autres vins de Vérone, les meilleures bouteilles sont en général celles des plus petites firmes, car, hélas ! les plus importantes ont une tendance déplorable à étiqueter leurs produits selon la demande plutôt que selon la production.

Dans les vignobles des 19 communes produisant du Valpolicella, les principales variétés cultivées sont : Molinara, Rondinella, Rossignola, Negrara, Corvinon et Pelara.

Le Valpantena, nom d'une vallée de la zone, est un bon exemple du vin local ; sur ses étiquettes figureront le nom de la vallée : Valpolicella. Le Recioto della Valpolicella est fait dans 5 communes avec des raisins en partie séchés et sélectionnés, ce qui donne un type de vin de Vénétie particulièrement savoureux, à consommer dans les 2 ans. L'appellation dérive du mot *recia*, qui signifie « oreille » dans le dialecte local. C'est en effet de l'« oreille », c'est-à-dire de la partie supérieure de la grappe de raisin que les grains les plus mûrs sont

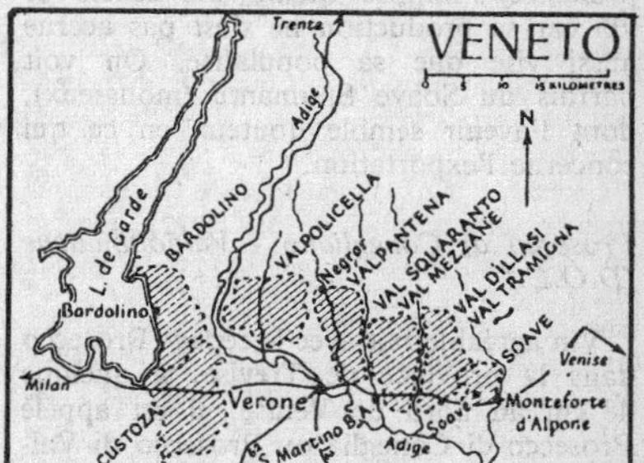

sélectionnés pour le Recioto. Il peut être sec, demi-doux ou doux et mousseux. Le Recioto sec s'appelle Amarone.

Bardolino (D.O.C.)

Vin qui porte le nom de son lieu d'origine et provient aussi des localités voisines situées sur la côte sud-est du lac de Garde. C'est un rouge sec, couleur de rubis clair. Dans sa prime jeunesse, il possède un charme ensorceleur, mais le perd généralement très vite. Le nouvel aspect de la viniculture italienne se manifeste ici car, désormais, le Bardolino fermente beaucoup moins longtemps que ne le voudrait la tradition. Il en résulte un vin plus léger, plus frais, plus net et beaucoup plus agréable. Il titre entre 10,5° et 13°. Corvina, Molinara, Negrara et Rondinella dominent dans sa composition.

Bianco di Custoza (D.O.C.)

Ce vin blanc sec provient des vignes situées au bord du lac de Garde.

Soave, Recioto di Soave et Soave Classico (tous D.O.C.)

Pas plus que ses congénères rouges, le Soave n'est un grand vin. Mais il est généralement bon. Dans sa meilleure forme, il a une légère teinte de paille avec des reflets verdâtres, et un goût très léger d'acide sec. Il est fait à partir des principales variétés de Garganega. Les 6 000 ha exploités, dont 2 000 sont plantés de Soave Classico, se situent aux alentours des localités de Soave et Monteforte d'Alpone, à 25 km à l'est de Vérone. La prudence s'impose quand on achète ce vin car sa production ne s'est pas accrue aussi vite que sa populairté. On voit parfois du Soave Spumante (mousseux), dont l'avenir semble douteux en ce qui concerne l'exportation.

Prosecco di Conegliano - Valdobbiadene (D.O.C.)

Vin agréable fait avec le cépage Prosecco dans la province de Trévise, à quelque 48 km au nord de Venise. Il est appelé Prosecco di Coneglia ou Prosecco di Valdobbiadene, mais ne change pas pour autant. C'est un vin délicatement sec et très fruité, qui existe également en mousseux et demi-mousseux.

Vins mineurs de Vénétie

Colli Euganei (D.O.C.)

Petits vins rouge et blanc des collines euganéennes, à 45 km au sud-est de Soave.

Breganze (D.O.C.)

C'est à 25 km de Vicenza que sont produits ces vins rouges et blancs. Le blanc est fait avec du Tokai, du Pinot et un peu de Vespaido ; le rouge, avec du Merlot et du Cabernet. Lorsqu'une seule variété est utilisée, l'appellation peut être suivie du nom de cette variété : ainsi, Breganze Çabernet, etc.

Cabernet di Lison-Pramaggiore (D.O.C.)

A proximité de Venise, la commune de Pramaggiore produit un rouge de table charnu, fait avec du Cabernet Franc et un peu de Merlot. C'est un vin sec, dont le bouquet évoque un parfum d'herbe fraîche. Au bout de trois ans de vieillissement, il peut être appelé Riserva.

Gambellara et Recioto di Gambellara Spumante (D.O.C.)

Le Gambellara est un blanc léger et sec qui ressemble au Soave, quoique ce dernier soit plus alcoolisé. On le fait avec du Garganega et un peu de Trebbiano, à l'est de la commune de Soave. Le Recioto di Gambellara Spumante est un mousseux doux fait de la même façon que les autres vins semblables de la région.

Merlot di Lison-Pramaggiore (D.O.C.)

Assez sec, mais plein, ce vin rouge de table est fait près de Venise avec du Merlot et du Cabernet.

Colli Berici (D.O.C.)

Au sud de la ville de Vicenzo, les coteaux de Berici produisent de légers rouges et blancs. Les premiers sont faits principalement avec du Cabernet Franc et du Merlot ; les blancs avec du Tokai, du Pinot Blanc, du Garganega et du Sauvignon Blanc. A l'instar des petits vins du Piave et du Breganze, les vins faits avec une unique variété de raisins peuvent ajouter le nom de celle-ci à leur appellation d'origine : ainsi, Merlot di Colli Berici, etc.

Venezuela

Pas de vignobles dans ce pays qui produit seulement des spiritueux, mais en petite quantité. Le principal spiritueux du Venezuela est probablement le Cocui (parfois Cocuy), fait avec l'agave cocui, homologue des spiritueux mexicains tequila et mescal. Il titre entre 40° et 50°, selon l'alambic utilisé et la pureté désirée. On le boit tel quel plutôt que de le panacher à la limonade et de se saler la bouche au préalable, comme cela se pratique au Mexique. Le Cocui a un goût particulier ressemblant à la tequila, mais légèrement plus dur. Le Venezuela produit aussi des rhums dont quelques-uns sont assez bons et des *aguardientes*. La fabrication de la bière s'accroît. On fait aussi quelques liqueurs dans les environs de Caracas. En plus de tous ces breuvages, les Indiens apprécient la *chicha,* obtenue par la fermentation du maïs. La Chicha est grossière, acide, d'une teneur exceptionnellement élevée en alcool et, dans l'ensemble, beaucoup trop rude pour plaire à de nombreux consommateurs. Environ 35 000 hl (plus de 350 000 caisses) sont exportés chaque année.

Vente sur souches

Vente de vin avant vendange, c'est-à-dire sur souche de vigne. Quand, pour les vins ordinaires, l'accord est fondé sur une certaine teneur en alcool du vin, le prix peut être majoré ou minoré selon que le vin titre plus ou moins une fois qu'il est fait.

Tout contrat de vente sur souches doit comporter une clause précisant que les deux parties connaissent cette règle (Code du vin, art. 320-332). Toute infraction à la loi est sanctionnée par taxation indirecte et amende (Code du vin, art. 1760). Jusqu'aux années 60, il y a parfois eu des ventes sur souches de Crus classés du Bordelais. Les quantités étaient indiquées en tonneaux.

Véraison

Moment de la maturation du raisin où il change de couleur pour passer du vert au rouge violacé ou au blanc verdâtre et translucide.

Voir CHAPITRE IV

Verdelho

Principale variété de raisin utilisée pour faire le Porto blanc. On la cultive aussi ailleurs, notamment en Australie.

Ce même nom sert d'appellation à un Madère doux et souple.

Verdes (Vinhos)

Vins légers, pétillants ou légèrement mousseux, faits au nord du Portugal, près de la frontière de la Galice espagnole. Extrêmement populaires dans leur pays d'origine, ils offrent, par été chaud, un rafraîchissement plein de charme.

Voir PORTUGAL

Verdicchio dei Castelli di Jesi (D.O.C.)

Vin blanc italien, léger, sec ou demi-sec.

Voir MARCHES

Verdot

Raisin appelé aussi Petit-Verdot, abondamment utilisé pour les vins rouges ordinaires de Bordeaux et parcimonieusement pour les meilleurs Médoc.

Vergennes

Cépage américain dont le fruit donne un vin sec, léger et agréable. Originaire du Vermont, il est cultivé dans l'État de New York.

Verjus

Raisin provenant d'une floraison tardive ou d'une seconde floraison de la vigne. Il ne mûrit pas et conserve une forte acidité. Par été très chaud on l'utilise pour compenser la déficience en acidité des raisins mûrs.

Vermentino

Ce raisin produit un bon vin blanc sur la Riviera (Côte d'Azur italienne) ; on le cultive aussi en Corse.

Voir LIGURIE ; CORSE

Vermetino Ligure

Vins blancs, minces et légers, parfois mousseux.

Voir LIGURIE

Vermouth

Le Vermouth n'est pas un vin. Certes, il est fait avec du vin, mais qui subit tant d'additions et de manipulations qu'il cesse d'être reconnaissable comme produit de la vigne. Il est très consommé et constitue un excellent apéritif, indispensable à certains cocktails, notamment le *Dry Martini*.

Ce nom dérive soit de l'allemand *Wermut,* soit de l'anglo-saxon *wermod,* qui signifient tous les deux absinthe. On faisait certainement du Vermouth en Italie dès le XVIIe siècle et on en produit maintenant dans le monde entier, sous deux espèces : le Vermouth français et le Vermouth italien. On en fait également en Californie et dans de nombreux autres pays vinicoles.

La fabrication du Vermouth est un art compliqué mais dénué de grandeur. Elle exige du vin, du sirop de sucre ou de la mistelle (jus de raisin non fermenté additionné d'eau-de-vie de vin), de l'alcool, un assortiment d'herbes et de plantes, un pasteurisateur, des cuves à réfrigération, des filtres, une table avec balances et poids pour doser les ingrédients : ce n'est plus qu'une affaire de fabrication industrielle.

Le composant essentiel c'est le vin : en général du blanc, assez insipide. Les transformations qu'il subira sont telles qu'utiliser un vin fin ou de caractère distinctif quelconque serait une dépense inutile. Une bonne part du Vermouth italien est faite avec le vin des plaines méridionales, et une bonne partie du Vermouth français avec des produits du Midi. Viennent ensuite les herbes et les substances qui donnent du goût : absinthe, hysope, quinquina, coriandre, genièvre, clou de girofle, camomille, écorces d'orange et même des pétales de rose. La liste et la proportion des ingrédients est un secret que chaque fabricant garde jalousement. On fera peut-être vieillir le vin pendant deux ans ou pas du tout. La première opération sera l'addition de sirop de sucre ou de mistelle, ensuite seulement de l'alcool et des substances organoleptiques. Les herbes macèrent dans l'alcool, parfois on les chauffe pour que leur saveur passe dans le spiritueux de la même manière que dans une infusion de thé. Quand l'alcool s'est suffisamment imprégné de saveur, on l'ajoute au vin sucré et on brasse la mixture pour que ces éléments se mélangent. Même dans les entreprises les plus modernes, on se sert en général de pales en bois pour ce brassage, afin de ne pas introduire un goût étranger dans le Vermouth. Vient alors l'addition de tanin, puis de gélatine pour clarifier le breuvage. Enfin, on le pasteurise. Après pasteurisation, le Vermouth est réfrigéré : il passe parfois deux semaines ou plus à — 10 °C. Pendant ce temps, tous les tartrates que contient le liquide se cristallisent et tombent au fond de la cuve. On fait passer ensuite le Vermouth par un filtre pour le débarrasser des dernières impuretés et tartrates qui subsisteraient. Après ce traitement rigoureux, le Vermouth se repose pendant quelques mois au bout desquels ont le met en bouteille pour expédition. On peut normalement espérer que le produit ainsi obtenu subira sans dommage le froid arctique et la chaleur tropicale ; mais les fabricants disent que des températures extrêmes trop prolongées nuiront à ce breuvage pourtant bien aguerri : elles l'oxyderaient et lui donneraient un désagréable goût de moisi. Il faudrait néanmoins pour cela une chaleur énorme.

On considère en général que le Vermouth français est sec et, l'italien, doux. C'est exact, mais on fait des Vermouth de l'un et l'autre genre dans les deux pays. Seuls les très doux sont italiens. Le Vermouth français de Chambéry, très sec, a droit à une appellation d'origine contrôlée. Il a des caractéristiques particulières, il est notamment plus léger que celui de Sète. Le Chambéry est fait avec des vins légers provenant surtout des vignes plantées sur les pentes des Alpes et les herbes qui entrent dans sa composition ne sont pas les mêmes que celles des manufacturiers qui fabriquent des Vermouth plus lourds. Un autre Vermouth très populaire est celui de la marque Noilly-Prat. Le Cinzano italien peut être rouge ou blanc, doux ou assez sec, de même que le Martini et le Gancia.

Vernaccia

Raisin à vin blanc utilisé en Italie, notamment en Marches et en Sardaigne.

Vernaccia di Oristano (D.O.C.)

Un des vins les mieux connus de la Sardaigne *(voir ce nom)*.

Vert

Se dit d'un vin qui n'est pas fait : trop riche en acide, rude et âpre, il manque de moelleux et de maturité. Ceci n'est pas dû nécessairement à l'âge, quoique les jeunes vignes soient plus fréquemment vertes que les autres. S'applique également à certains vins acides produits au nord d'Oporto, au Portugal, où les raisins sont vendangés avant d'être parfaitement mûrs.

Verte (Liqueur)

Nom qu'on donne souvent à des imitations de la Chartreuse verte.
Voir CHARTREUSE

Verveine du Velay

Liqueur faite au Puy, en Velay, avec de l'eau-de-vie de vin, de la verveine et d'autres herbes. Il y en a deux variétés, une jaune et une verte qui est plus forte.

Verzenay

Agglomération proche de Reims. On y produit un Champagne de Premier Cru.
Voir CHAMPAGNE

Verzy

Commune de la Montagne de Reims. On y produit un Champagne de Premier Cru.
Voir CHAMPAGNE

Vevey (Festival de)

Le plus important festival de vin du monde. Il a lieu épisodiquement depuis le XVIIe siècle dans la ville de Vevey, en Suisse, et perpétue la tradition de la Guilde médiévale des vignerons. Son nom officiel est Fête des Vignerons. Au cours de ce siècle elle a eu lieu approximativement tous les vingt-cinq ans et n'a été célébrée que quatre fois : en 1905, 1927, 1955 et 1977. La préparation du dernier festival dura cinq ans et ce fut un événement touristique sensationnel. Les spectacles, auxquels participèrent jusqu'à 3 500 personnes, célébrèrent le vin pendant quinze jours, devant un auditoire de 15 000 personnes.

Vieille (La plus vieille bouteille du monde)

Le musée du vin à Spire, en Palatinat, se targue d'exhiber la plus vieille bouteille du monde. On lui attribue environ 1 600 ans. Elle est scellée par l'huile utilisée autrefois pour isoler le vin de l'air et qui a durci. On a trouvé au fond de la Méditerranée des amphores plus anciennes encore scellées de la même manière.

Vieille Cure (La)

Cette liqueur très populaire en France, était faite à Cenon, près de Bordeaux, jusqu'en 1986, selon une recette qui comportait diverses eaux-de-vie et 52 herbes différentes. D'une couleur dorée, elle n'était pas sans similitudes avec la Bénédictine.

Vieux-Château-Certan

Bordeaux rouge. Commune de Pomerol.
Les héritiers des frères Thienpont, négociants en vin belges, produisent ce vin charnu, subtil et velouté.
Superficie : 14 ha.
Production moyenne : 55 tonneaux (5 500 caisses).

Vigne

Arbrisseau sarmenteux de la famille des ampélidacées, qui comprend la vigne vierge originaire de Virginie et d'autres variétés telles que la vigne à vin *Vitis* (avec ses sous-genres *Euvites* et *Muscadiniae),* la seule dont se sert le vigneron.

Voir CHAPITRE IV

Vignelaure (Château)

Vin rouge de Provence.

Situé à Rians à 30 km d'Aix-en-Provence, il a droit à l'Appellation Contrôlée Coteaux d'Aix-en-Provence, et est supérieur à la plupart des vins rouges des Côtes de Provence. Son propriétaire, Georges Brunet, possédait le Château La Lagune, dans le Haut-Médoc, qu'il vendit en 1960 pour acheter le domaine de Vignelaure, alors vierge. Il y planta 60 % de Cabernet Sauvignon, 30 % de Syrah et 10 % de Grenache. Son propriétaire vendit en 1987 la majorité de ses parts à un hôtellier américain.

Caractéristiques : Vins charpentés au vieillissement lent.

Superficie : 56 ha.

Production moyenne : 250 tonneaux (25 000 caisses).

Vigneron

Celui qui se livre à la culture de la vigne et à la fabrication du vin.

Vignoble

Terrain planté de vignes.

Vila Nova de Gaia

Agglomération située juste en face de Oporto, sur l'autre rive du Douro, à son embouchure, au nord du Portugal. La plupart des entrepôts de vin de Porto (appelés lodges) se trouvent à Vila Nova de Gaia et tout le véritable Porto, qui a droit à cette appellation, est expédié de cette localité.

Voir PORTO

Vilafranca del Penedès (Catalogne)

Vins de la province de Barcelone. Les meilleurs sont secs. *Voir* ESPAGNE

Vin

Ce terme devrait désigner exclusivement la boisson obtenue par la fermentation naturelle du jus de raisin mais, par extension, on l'applique trop souvent aux « vins » faits avec des légumes, des baies et d'autres fruits, particulièrement les cerises.

Les vrais vins — ceux qui sont le produit du raisin — peuvent être classés selon trois types principaux :

1. Boisson plate, ou vins de table accompagnant un repas. Ils se subdivisent en vins rouge, blanc et rosé (selon le raisin utilisé et le temps durant lequel les peaux restent avec le jus en fermentation), et en vins secs ou doux, selon que l'on laisse la totalité du sucre du raisin se convertir en alcool, ou qu'une partie du sucre reste en résidu.

2. Vins mousseux, dont le Champagne, vinifié par une seconde fermentation en bouteille, est le meilleur exemple.

3. Vins vinés, tels le Porto, le Xérès et le Madère, sont additionnés d'eau-de-vie.

Les différents pays vinicoles produisent, avec une grande variété de raisins, de nombreux vins de ces trois types, dont les plus importants sont étudiés dans l'encyclopédie par ordre alphabétique.

Pour une analyse de la nature du vin et de sa fabrication, *voir* CHAPITRE V.

Vinage

Addition d'alcool au vin. Dans certains secteurs on ajoute une petite quantité d'eau-de-vie aux vins bon marché pour les améliorer. Mais cette pratique ne peut qu'être condamnée quand il s'agit de vins de qualité.

Vinasse

Résidu des vins et liqueurs fermentés après leur distillation. Vinasse est aussi employé péjorativement pour désigner le gros vin ordinaire.

Vin chaud épicé

Vin rouge dilué porté à ébullition, épicé et sucré. Servi très chaud, c'est un remède souverain contre les débuts de rhume.

Vin de cuvée

En Champagne, désigne le vin fait avec le premier jus de raisin qui sort du pressoir.

Vin de garde

Grand vin de forte teneur en alcool et en tanin, qui mérite d'être conservé jusqu'à ce que le vieillissement ait aplani tout ce qu'il pouvait avoir d'agressivité dans sa jeunesse.

Vin du glacier

Vin blanc dur du Valais, ainsi dénommé parce qu'après la vendange il est conservé dans des agglomérations situées à une très haute altitude.

Voir SUISSE

Vin de goutte

Vin français fait avec le jus du raisin obtenu avant le pressurage.

Vins doux naturel

Voir V.D.N.

Vin gris

Le vin gris est un rosé souvent attribué à l'Alsace mais qui, en réalité, provient de la Lorraine.

Voir LORRAINE ; ALSACE

Vin d'honneur

Depuis les temps les plus reculés, on a offert des libations de vin aux dieux et le vin figurait sur la table des rois. Il est donc normal d'en offrir à ceux que l'on désire honorer. La pratique du vin d'honneur est encore courante de nos jours. Dans leur *Dictionnaire du vin,* Renouil et Traversay rappellent en quelles occasions on offrait et on offre encore du vin :

Vin de bourgeoisie. Offert, au Moyen Age, au maire et aux échevins, par toute personne qui devenait bourgeois de la ville.

Vin de couchier. Offert par les mariés à ceux qui avaient honoré le mariage de leur présence.

Vin de l'étrier. Offert à un hôte au moment où il s'en va. On dit maintenant « coup de l'étrier ».

Vin du curé. Offert au prêtre après un baptême.

Vin de veille. Que les officiers de la Maison du roi plaçaient auprès du lit du monarque, comme en-cas.

Vin du clerc. Offert par un plaideur au greffier du tribunal après un jugement favorable.

Vin fin

Cette locution devait être synonyme de vin de qualité, mais on en a beaucoup abusé. Ce sont parfois des vins supérieurs, comme dans le cas des Vins Fins de la Côte de Nuits, mais le terme est trop souvent improprement utilisé sur les étiquettes des marques déposées commerciales.

Vin jaune

Produit dans le Jura, c'est un vin fait avec des raisins vendangés sur le tard et conservé pendant un temps inhabituellement long ; mis en tonneau, il se forme une fine pellicule blanche à sa surface, connus dans la vinification du Xérès sous le nom de fleur.

Voir JURA

Vin de liqueur

Cette locution a deux sens : 1. un vin très doux tel qu'un riche Sauternes ; 2. un vin viné — additionné d'eau-de-vie de vin — titrant environ 18°, que l'on ajoute au Champagne avant de l'expédier.

Vin de marc

Vin obtenu en ajoutant de l'eau et du sucre au résidu du pressurage (marc). On dit indifféremment : vin de marc ou piquette.

Vinello, Vinettono

Diminutif appliqué en italien à certains vins pour exprimer le mépris qu'inspirent leur pauvreté ou leur maigreur. Ces mots signifient donc : vin petit ou fluet.

Vinexpo

Fondée au début des années 80, cette manifestation est devenue la foire du vin la plus importante du monde. Elle se tient au mois de juin tous les deux ans, sur les années paires, au parc des Expositions de Bordeaux.

Vinho liquoroso

Appellation portugaise du vin viné.

Vinho do Rodo

Appellation portugaise du vin mousseux.

Vinho trasfugado

Locution portugaise désignant le Madère après que le soutirage l'a débarrassé de sa lie.

Vinhos verdes

Voir VERDES (VINHOS)

Viniculture

Ensemble des opérations concernant la fabrication et la maturation du vin.

Alors que le terme Œnologie se réfère à l'aspect scientifique de la production du vin et à leur étude, la viniculture en couvre les aspects pratiques.

Vinifera (Vitis)

Espèce du genre *Vitis,* sous-genre *Euvites.* En font partie toutes les vignes européennes dont proviennent les plus grands vins du monde. On a aussi planté *Vitis vinifera* en Australie, Nouvelle-Zélande, Afrique du Sud, aux États-Unis et en Amérique du Sud.

Voir CHAPITRE IV

Vinification

Opération consistant à transformer le jus de raisin (moût) en vin.

Vino da Arrosto

Vin de race, en italien.

Vino de color

En Espagne, jus de raisin concentré utilisé pour colorer et adoucir les vins.

Vino corriente

Locution espagnole désignant le vin ordinaire (courant).

Vino dulce

En Espagne, vin très doux utilisé pour coupages.

Vino espumoso

Vin mousseux, en espagnol.

Vino de pasto

Vin de table, en espagnol qui désigne aussi un type de Xérès sans grande distillation.

Vino Santo

Voir SANTO (VINO)

Vino tierno

Locution espagnole désignant des vins lourds et doux utilisés en coupage.

Vino Tinto

Vin rouge, en espagnol.

Vinosité

Qualité essentielle ou cœur du vin : forte personnalité obtenue par l'accentuation des meilleures caractéristiques d'un type particulier. On utilise parfois ce mot pour suggérer une forte teneur en alcool, et c'est une erreur, car l'alcool n'est qu'un des éléments qui contribuent à donner au vin son caractère.

Vinprom

Entreprise d'État qui gère viticulture, viniculture et commerce du vin en Bulgarie (*voir ce nom*).

Vins délimités de qualité supérieure

Voir V.D.Q.S.

Vins de la Moselle

Une des deux appellations de vins de Lorraine classés dans la catégorie des vins délimités de qualité supérieure. Ils sont rosés ou blancs.

Voir LORRAINE

Vin nature de Champagne

Voir CHAMPAGNE

Vins vinés de France

Admirablement ensoleillée, la région de la côte méditerranéenne française s'est révélée depuis longtemps favorable à la culture des variétés de raisin qui donnent des vins à la fois doux et forts. C'est particulièrement vrai au pied des Pyrénées, dans le Roussillon. Ces vins ne présentent que peu d'intérêt dans les pays où il est facile de se procurer Porto et Xérès. Ce sont généralement des vins vinés, c'est-à-dire soit des vins doux naturels, soit des vins de liqueur (*voir* ces appellations à leur place dans l'ordre alphabétique). Dans les deux cas, on ajoute à ces vins de l'alcool ou de l'eau-de-vie de vin. C'est cette opération qui s'appelle le vinage et en fait des vins vinés. La locution « vin doux naturel » risque de créer une confusion, car elle peut s'appliquer très logiquement à des vins doux vraiment naturels, tels que les Sauternes de la région de Bordeaux.

Il n'y a guère de différence entre un vin de liqueur et un vin doux naturel et on les confond souvent à tel point que les deux expressions sont presque devenues synonymes. L'addition d'alcool a lieu avant fermentation et il en résulte simplement un mélange de jus de raisin et d'alcool, c'est-à-dire une espèce de mistelle de qualité supérieure. Cette dernière sert à la confection d'apéritifs et de liqueurs, alors que le vin doux naturel est fait exclusivement par le vigneron avec de meilleurs raisins et qu'il est consommé sans autre manipulation. Le vin doux naturel doit être fait avec au moins 90 % d'une seule variété de raisins ou bien un mélange des variétés suivantes : Muscat, Grenache, Maccabéo et Malvoisie ; l'alcool doit être ajouté en cours de fermentation pour l'arrêter et non pour l'empêcher.

Dans les deux cas, le vinage aboutit à ceci : le sucre cesse d'être converti en alcool dès que le mélange atteint un certain degré. Il restera donc une bonne part de sucre non converti, et l'alcool ajouté donnera au vin un fort degré. Selon les normes légales, ces vins vinés doivent titrer entre 14° et 21,5°. La plupart sont vendus à 18° ou à peu près. Un seul vin de liqueur fait exception : le Pineau des Charentes, fait dans la région de Cognac, avec du Cognac, et qui doit obligatoirement titrer entre 16 et 22°.

La production de ces vins doux naturels s'éparpille principalement sur une zone assez vaste allant du Roussillon, à l'extrémité sud-ouest de la côte, jusqu'au Rhône et même au-delà (Rasteau et Beaumes-de-Venise) en passant par Frontignan, Lunel, Mireval et Saint-Jean-de-Minervois à l'est. Par quelque extraordinaire miracle, les vignes de cette vaste région ont survécu au passage de nombreuses armées — Romains, Arabes, Francs, Espagnols entre autres — et au phylloxéra. Le système économique contemporain semble pourtant réussir ce que les envahisseurs de jadis et le pou térébrant n'ont pu faire : la production actuelle de ces vins varie aux environs de 500 000 hl (plus de 5,5 millions de caisses).

Zones productrices de vins vinés

Banyuls (Appellation Contrôlée)

Les vins de Banyuls, provenant de la pointe sud-ouest du Roussillon, sont considérés en général comme les meilleurs de cette zone. Le décor est celui de roches désolées coupées par des ravins abrupts et rôties par le soleil dont les rayons tombent dès le petit matin sur les pentes plantées de vignes. Banyuls est réputé pour ses vins naturels et ses vins vinés. On y fait notamment un rosé appelé Grenache parce qu'il est fait avec cette variété de raisins. Quoique assez bien connu en France, le Grenache de Banyuls n'est presque jamais exporté. Les vendanges sont tardives. Le 4/5 de la production annuelle (50 000 hl, soit 550 000 caisses) sont traités dans les neuf caves coopératives. 1 600 vignerons et ouvriers prennent soin des 2 800 ha de vignes.

Rivesaltes (Appellation Contrôlée)

Situé au nord du Roussillon le secteur de Rivesaltes bénéficie également d'un bel ensoleillement. On y cultive la vigne sur des terrasses caillouteuses. Ses vins étaient mieux connus et appréciés autrefois. Au temps où il était célèbre, le Rivesaltes était fait avec du raisin Muscat. La production de ces vins, appelés « Muscat de Rivesaltes », se situe autour de 100 000 hl (plus d'1 million de caisses) par an. Les vins portant la simple appellation Rivesaltes peuvent contenir d'autres variétés de raisin. Depuis une cinquantaine d'années, les vignerons se détournent du Muscat pour replanter de plus en plus en Grenache et en Malvoisie. A cela une raison : la vigne Muscat produit peu et le vin qu'elle donne exige de grands soins. D'autre part, les gens de Rivesaltes apprécient le doux vin de Malvoisie, couleur d'ambre. La production de Rivesaltes atteint environ 400 000 hl (plus de 4 millions de caisses) par an. Il est produit pour la plus grande partie par les nombreuses coopératives de la région.

Côtes d'Agly

Le dur sol de roche grise de ce secteur situé au nord-est du Roussillon est traversé par le cours supérieur de l'Agly en amont de Rivesaltes. D'autres petits cours d'eau arrosent le secteur des Côtes d'Agly. Ce sont presque des « oueds » qui enflent et dévalent rapidement après les rares pluies, mais restent à sec pendant la plus grande partie de l'année. Le cépage le plus cultivé est le Grenache.

Maury (Appellation Contrôlée)

Le petit secteur de Maury occupe l'extrême pointe nord-est du Roussillon, et c'est celui qui souffrit le plus des guerres et des invasions mais, même quand le vignoble y fut presque complètement détruit, les vignerons le reconstituèrent inlassablement sur un sol de pierres qui ne semble pourtant pas promettre grand-chose. Les vignes poussèrent au pied du château de Quéribus, dernier vestige cathare. On y cultive uniquement la variété Grenache Noir. Les vins rouges de Maury sont extrêmement foncés dans leur jeunesse, mais en vieillissant ils prennent une teinte brunâtre et un goût légèrement madérisé ou *rancio* ; ils peuvent alors être vendus sous le nom de Maury Rancio. A Maury la vigne couvre une superficie de 1 400 ha et produit près de 50 000 hl (environ 550 000 caisses) par an. La propriété est moins parcellaire que dans les autres secteurs du Roussillon puisque l'on compte seulement 530 propriétaires de vignes. A peu près tout le vin de Maury est traité en caves coopératives.

Frontignan (Appellation Contrôlée)

Dans ce secteur encore — situé face à la Méditerranée, à l'ouest du delta du Rhône —, l'origine de la vigne se perd dans la nuit des temps. Les vignerons du pays disent soit que leurs célèbres vignes Muscat de Frontignan datent de la Gaule romaine, soit qu'elles furent ramenées des croisades, ou encore qu'on les planta en 1204 à l'occasion d'un mariage royal. Il est fort probable que les croisés rapportèrent des vignes à vin du Proche-Orient et modifièrent ainsi l'assiette de la viticulture dans ces régions et dans les Pyrénées. Actuellement, quelque 350 vignerons exploitent 350 ha de vignes autour de la vieille ville de Frontignan, dans l'Hérault ; la production annuelle s'élève à 20 000 hl (plus de 200 000 caisses) 75 % du vin est vinifié dans la même coopérative. Frontignan est presque au bord de la mer, à mi-chemin entre le Grand-Roussillon et le Rhône.

L'appellation Muscat de Frontignan dérive du nom de la seule variété de vigne autorisée dans ce secteur. On y fait trois vins selon trois méthodes différentes. Le premier, un Muscat de Frontignan vraiment naturel, qui ne fait l'objet d'aucune addition d'alcool mais dont les raisins subissent avant la vendange un passerillage tout à fait exceptionnel. Quand il est mûr, on tord le pédoncule de la grappe ou on le pince pour empêcher la sève de circuler entre le fruit et le cep. Cette pratique, originaire d'Espagne, accroît la teneur en sucre en desséchant le raisin presque complètement. Grâce à ce passerillage, le vin atteint aisément le minimum de 15° d'alcool imposé par sa norme.

Les deux autres Muscat de Frontignan sont un vin doux naturel et un vin de liqueur. On en produit beaucoup plus. Nous avons déjà expliqué comment on élabore ces vins vinés. Les deux systèmes autorisés permettent au vin de conserver une bonne partie de son sucre naturel et de titrer entre 15 et 21°.

Afin de parer à toute fraude, le Muscat de Frontignan, le Frontignan et le Vin de Frontignan ne peuvent être vendus que dans une bouteille spéciale portant un sceau qui lui est accordé par un comité d'experts après dégustation.

Le secteur adjacent à Frontignan produit un Muscat de moindre renommée appelé Muscat de Mireval.

Saint-Jean-de-Minervois (Muscat de) (A.O.C.)

Petite localité du département de l'Hérault, Saint-Jean-de-Minervois produit un vin doux naturel et un vin de liqueur, selon les mêmes procédés qu'à Frontignan. La production atteint rarement les 2 000 hl (20 000 caisses) par an.

Lunel (Muscat de) (A.O.C.)

Comme celui de Frontignan, le Muscat de Lunel peut être un vin doux naturel ou un vin de liqueur, mais ce secteur ne produit pas de vin vraiment naturel (non additionné d'alcool). Autrefois riche d'attraits, Lunel n'offre plus grand intérêt aujourd'hui si ce n'est dans une perspective historique. Ses vignerons produisent près de 7 000 hl (plus de 75 000 caisses) de vin par an.

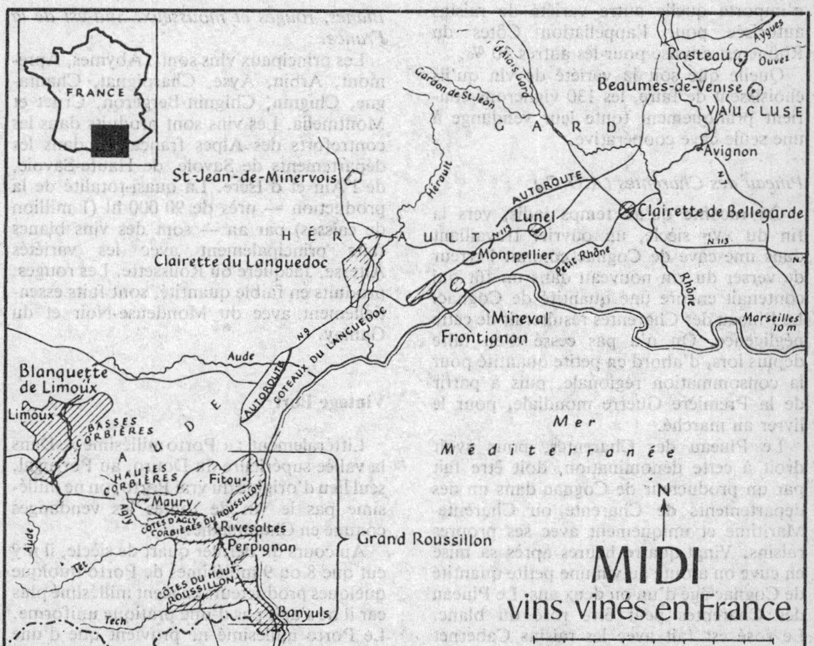

Beaumes-de-Venise (Muscat de) (A.O.C.)

Située sur la rive gauche du Rhône, dans le département du Vaucluse, Beaumes-de-Venise fait un excellent vin doux naturel et un vin de liqueur provenant uniquement de raisins de Muscat, comme à Frontignan. Cette zone produit seulement 9 500 hl (plus de 100 000 caisses) de vin par an.

Rasteau (Appellation Contrôlée)

La zone délimitée de Rasteau est située un peu au nord de Beaumes-de-Venise. Elle jouit d'un avantage exceptionnel, celui de produire et vendre des vins vinés de la même manière que ceux du Roussillon, et des vins naturels vendus sous l'appellation Côtes du Rhône. Il en résulte une production extrêmement variable qui peut, d'une année sur l'autre, comporter exclusivement des vins naturels ou, au contraire, passer à 3 000 hl (plus de 30 000 caisses) de vins vinés. Le facteur décisif est le temps, qui favorisera tel ou tel type de vin. Vin doux naturel et vin de liqueur de Rasteau doivent être faits avec au moins 90 % de Grenache ; n'importe quelle autre variété de raisins autorisée pour l'appellation Côtes du Rhône est admise pour les autres 10 %.

Quelle que soit la variété de vin qu'ils choisissent de faire, les 130 vignerons confient pratiquement toute leur vendange à une seule cave coopérative.

Pineau des Charentes (A.O.C.)

On raconte qu'au temps jadis, vers la fin du XVIe siècle, un ouvrier travaillant dans une cave de Cognac commit l'erreur de verser du vin nouveau dans un fût qui contenait encore une quantité de Cognac. Le Pineau des Charentes résulterait de cette négligence. On n'a pas cessé d'en faire depuis lors, d'abord en petite quantité pour la consommation régionale, puis à partir de la Première Guerre mondiale, pour le livrer au marché.

Le Pineau des Charentes, pour avoir droit à cette dénomination, doit être fait par un producteur de Cognac dans un des départements de Charente ou Charente-Maritime et uniquement avec ses propres raisins. Vingt-quatre heures après sa mise en cuve on ajoute au vin une petite quantité de Cognac âgé d'un ou deux ans. Le Pineau des Charentes peut être rosé ou blanc. Le rosé est fait avec les raisins Cabernet Sauvignon, Cabernet Franc, Malbec et Merlot Rouge : le blanc avec du Saint-Émilion, de la Folle Blanche, du Colombard, du Blanc Rosé, du Jurançon Blanc, du Montils, du Sémillon, du Sauvignon et du Merlot Blanc. Il ne peut être commercialisé qu'après avoir reçu l'approbation d'un comité de dégustateurs experts aux pouvoirs étendus qui peuvent approuver ou refuser l'approbation, exiger un vieillissement plus prolongé ou le mélange du Pineau soumis à leur expertise avec un vin de même type provenant d'un autre cru et dans la proportion qu'ils prescrivent. Ce dernier règlement a été adopté afin d'améliorer la qualité de certains vins provenant de la zone côtière et qui ont un goût légèrement salé quand ils sont exempts de mélange.

Devenu un apéritif très prisé en France, le Pineau doit titrer entre 16 et 22°. La production annuelle s'élève à environ 90 000 hl (1 million de caisses).

Vins de Savoie et Roussette de Savoie (A.O.C.)

Blancs, rouges et mousseux. Sud-est de la France.

Les principaux vins sont : Abymes, Apremont, Arbin, Ayse, Charpignat, Chautagne, Chignin, Chignin-Bergeron, Cruet et Montmelia. Les vins sont produits dans les contreforts des Alpes françaises, dans les départements de Savoie, de Haute-Savoie, de l'Ain et d'Isère. La quasi-totalité de la production — près de 90 000 hl (1 million de caisses) par an — sont des vins blancs faits principalement avec les variétés Altesse, Jacquère ou Roussette. Les rouges, produits en faible quantité, sont faits essentiellement avec du Mondeuse-Noir et du Gamay.

Vintage Port

Littéralement : « Porto millésimé ». Dans la vallée supérieure du Douro, au Portugal, seul lieu d'origine du vrai Porto, on ne millésime pas le vin de toutes les vendanges comme en Champagne.

Au cours du dernier quart de siècle, il n'y eut que 8 ou 9 millésimes de Porto quoique quelques producteurs en aient millésimé plus car il ne s'agit pas d'une pratique uniforme. Le Porto millésimé ne provient que d'une seule vendange et n'est pas mélangé avec celui d'autres années. Il doit vieillir au moins 10 ans et continue à s'améliorer encore en bouteille pendant de nombreuses années.

Voir PORTO

Vintage Wine

Littéralement « Vin millésimé » : vin provenant de la vendange dont la date est marquée sur l'étiquette.

Virginie

Région vinicole des États-Unis où les vignobles, rares mais de qualité, sont situés principalement dans les comtés d'Albemarle et de Clarke, avec Charlottesville au centre.

Voir ÉTATS-UNIS

Viticulteur

Personne qui cultive la vigne, généralement son propre vignoble. Le mot vigneron signifie presque la même chose, mais il s'agit plus souvent d'un métayer.

Viticulture

La culture de la vigne. C'est une science et un art.

Vitis

Espèce végétale à laquelle appartiennent toutes les espèces de vigne. *Vitis vinifera* est celle qui fournit à peu près tout le vin du monde, mais d'autres espèces en donnent également, soit à l'état naturel, soit en hybrides, c'est-à-dire par croisement de *Vitis vinifera* avec des vignes appartenant à d'autres espèces. Pour plus de détails sur *Vitis coignetia, Vitis labrusca, Vitis riparia,* etc. *voir* CHAPITRE IV.

Vitiviniculture

L'étude et la pratique de toutes les activités vinicoles et viticoles.

Vodka

Naguère boisson traditionnelle des Russes qui la buvaient sec, et même « cul sec », avant, pendant, et après les repas, la vodka est désormais un alcool international consommé et même fabriqué partout dans le monde. C'est tout de même encore avec le caviar qu'elle se manifeste traditionnellement. La véritable vodka n'a, en réalité, aucun goût. Elle est distillée jusqu'à insipidité. Peut-être est-ce pour cela qu'elle plaît tant à certains : certaines gens, en effet, boivent l'alcool pour le coup de fouet qu'il donne et sans se soucier de sa saveur. Insipide, ce spiritueux est aussi inodore, ce qui est une autre vertu selon certains.

La mode de la vodka en Occident débuta en Californie en 1945 et ne tarda pas à se répandre partout aux Etats-Unis puis à passer en Europe. D'aucuns préfèrent la couper d'eau minérale, gazeuse ou non, de jus de tomate (Bloddy Mary) ; d'autres la boivent sec. C'est aussi, évidemment, un bon élément de base pour les martinis et autres cocktails.

Native de Pologne et des pays baltes tout autant que de Russie, la vodka passait pour un alcool de pomme de terre. Actuellement elle est plutôt faite avec des céréales. Comme celle du gin, sa distillation à partir de grains est extrêmement poussée, puis elle est rectifiée pour obtenir un alcool qui ne conserve ni la saveur ni l'arôme de la matière première. La véritable vodka n'est pas additionnée de substances savoureuses. Mais certaines vodkas de marque sont traitées avec des herbes et vieillies pendant trois ans et plus, parfois dans des fûts qui ont contenu du vin.

Les diverses vodkas titrent toujours entre 32,5° et 49°.

Volatile (acidité)

En ce qui concerne le vin, l'acidité volatile est l'état provoqué par la présence d'acide acétique (l'acide du vinaigre, qui transforme le vin en vinaigre). Elle est causée par la présence de bactéries de déchets aérobiques et se présente souvent lorsque les tonneaux contenant du vin âgé d'un an ne sont pas complètement remplis ; le vin s'évaporant, les tonneaux doivent être remplis toutes les deux semaines environ.

Voir CHAPITRE V

Voleur (Thief)

C'est ainsi qu'en anglais on appelle la pipette utilisée pour prélever une petite quantité de boisson dans une barrique afin de la goûter.

Voleurs de raisins et contrefacteurs de vin

Depuis le début de l'histoire, les vignerons n'ont jamais manifesté d'indulgence envers ceux qui pillaient leurs vignobles ou trafiquaient leurs marchandises. En Allemagne, on obligeait les voleurs de raisins à parcourir leur localité les mains prises dans un étau en forme de violon et équipé d'une cloche qui sonnait au-dessus de leur tête pour attirer l'attention des villageois qui les raillaient et les houspillaient. Dans d'autres cas le voleur traversait l'agglomération à califourchon sur un âne, la tête tournée vers la queue, les raisins volés dans les mains, avec un placard sur la poitrine et le dos indiquant : « Il a volé des raisins ! ».

C'est aussi en Allemagne que les contrefacteurs de vin et ceux qui les trafiquaient étaient le plus sévèrement punis au Moyen Age. On allait jusqu'à les condamner à mort pour avoir falsifié l'honnête produit de la vigne.

Volnay (Appellation Contrôlée)

Bourgogne rouge. Côte de Beaune.

Les Volnay sont des vins assez délicats comparativement à d'autres Bourgogne. Ils vieillissent rapidement, ont plus d'élégance et une robe plus claire que les Beaune et les Pommard. Souples, arrondis, bien équilibrés, ils ont un bouquet particulièrement fin. La commune de Volnay est située au sud de Pommard, assez en altitude. Certains de ses vignobles sont mieux exposés que d'autres. Pour s'assurer contre le gel et la grêle, les vignerons préfèrent disperser leurs parcelles. La superficie cultivée en vignes à Volnay s'élève à quelque 243 ha qui produisent en moyenne 9 000 hl (100 000 caisses).

Au Moyen Age, le Volnay avait une légère teinte œil-de-perdrix. On en raffolait. Les ducs de Bourgogne offraient du Beaune et du Volnay aux rois, ainsi qu'aux papes d'Avignon. Louis XI finit par venir à bout des ducs de Bourgogne, annexa leur duché

Principaux premiers crus de Volnay	Superficie (ha)
Les Caillerets	12
Les Caillerets-Dessus ou Clos des 60 Ouvrées	2,4
Clos des Ducs	2,4
Les Brouillards	5,6
Les Mitans	4
En l'Ormeau	4,3
Les Angles	3,3
Pointes d'Angle	1,2
Frémiets	7,4
Champans	11,2
En Chevrets	6,4
Clos des Chênes	15,4
Clos de la Barre	1,3
Clos de la Bousse d'Or	2,1

et pris ainsi possession des vignes dont ils étaient si fiers. Volnay semble avoir été son vin préféré. Il fit transporter à son château de Plessis-lès-Tours toute la production de l'an 1477 de cette commune.

Seuls les vins rouges ont droit à l'Appellation Contrôlée Volnay et les blancs (Chardonnay), produits sur la commune de Volnay, sont vendus comme Meursault-Santenots. On répète volontiers dans le pays :

Entre Pommard et Meursault,
C'est toujours Volnay le plus haut.

Du point du vue topographique, c'est une vérité indiscutable. Le village domine ses vignes ; l'église, qui domine le tout, est le point de rencontre des chemins de vignoble, qui y descendent, et des rues de village, qui y grimpent.

Les Caillerets, cru le plus élevé, situé près du cimetière, est aussi le meilleur.

Du haut de la colline, le regard s'étend sur la grande vallée de la Bourgogne et, par beau temps, on aperçoit les crêtes enneigées du Jura. A droite de Volnay, se trouve le petit village de Monthélie, dont les vins de moindre intérêt et aussi moins connus que les Volnay présentent parfois l'avantage d'être moins chers. Les gens de Volnay disent couramment :

Qui n'a pas de vignes en Caillerets
Ne sait ce que vaut le Volnay.

Parmi les crus mineurs, citons : Les Aussy, Carelles dessus, la Gigotte, Lasolle,

Les Lurets, Piture dessus, Robardelle, Ronceret, Taillepieds, en Verseuil, Village.

Les crus de Volnay à Meursault : Les Caillerets, Les Santenots, Les Santenots du Milieu, Les Pétures, Les Cras.

Vöslau

Une des localités proches de Baden qui produit des vins rouges et aussi des Roten Sekt (rouges mousseux).

Voir AUTRICHE

Vosne-Romanée (Appellation Contrôlée)

Bourgogne rouge. Côte de Nuits.

Il n'est pas de cru qui ait été aussi louangé et avec une telle constance que les Vosne-Romanée. Par bonne année certains vins sont indiscutablement magnifiques et comptent aussi parmi les plus chers du monde. Même pour la Bourgogne, à la superficie restreinte, les plus grands crus de Vosne sont minuscules. Au total ils ne représentent que 26,2 ha et leur production annuelle ne dépasse guère 700 hl, soit à peu près l'équivalent de 7 500 caisses. La demande est si élevée pour le produit du plus vaste vignoble, la Romanée-Saint-Vivant, que jamais son propriétaire ne pourrait la satisfaire.

L'occasion de boire du vin de La Romanée ou de La Romanée-Conti est si rare qu'il faut toujours la considérer comme un événement exceptionnel.

Le Romanée-Conti est le grand vin de la commune en dépit de la surface infime du vignoble : 1,80 ha ! Les millésimes d'avant la Seconde Guerre mondiale — qui, désormais, ne sont plus guère que des souvenirs, — étaient parmi les plus magnifiques. Tout de suite après la guerre, on arracha et on replanta. Les vins produits maintenant sont aussi remarquables qu'avant. Perle de la couronne des vins bourguignons, La Romanée-Conti ne manque pas de gemmes dignes d'elle : La Romanée, La Tâche, Richebourg, La Romanée-Saint-Vivant *(voir chacun de ces crus à sa place dans l'ordre alphabétique).*

Souplesse et finesse veloutées, tels sont les traits communs de tous les Vosne qui, outre ces caractéristiques, sont légers, délicats, admirablement équilibrés. Ce sont des vins féminins, dénués d'agressivité et qui vieillissent avec une grâce extrême. C'est vrai non seulement en ce qui concerne les plus grands vignobles, mais aussi les crus classés dans la catégorie immédiatement inférieure, tels que : Grande Rue, Gaudichots, Beaux Monts et Malconsorts, qui produisent tous des vins merveilleux.

Crus classés de Vosne-Romanée	
Premiers Grands Crus	
Dans la commune	*Superficie (ha)*
La Romanée-Conti	1,8
La Tâche	6
Les Richebourg	8
La Romanée	0,83
La Romanée-Saint-Vivant	9,4
Premiers crus	
Les Gaudichots	1,02
Les Malconsorts	5,9
La Grande Rue	1
Les Beaux-Monts	11,4
Les Suchots	13,1
Clos des Réas	2,1
Aux Brûlées	3,8
Aux Petits-Monts	3,7
Aux Raignots	1,6
Les Chaumes	6,4
Grands Crus	
A Flagey-Échezeaux	
Grands-Échezeaux	9,1
Échezeaux	37,7

Les vignes qui donnent les vins commercialisés sous l'étiquette Vosne-Romanée sont presque toutes situées dans cette commune, mais quelques-unes se trouvent aussi dans celle de Flagey-Échezeaux. Les vins des deux meilleurs crus de Flagey — Grands-Échezeaux et Échezeaux — peuvent porter leur propre nom ou bien celui de Premier Cru de Vosne-Romanée.

Étant donné que leurs noms ne sont guère connus et assez difficiles à prononcer, surtout à l'étranger, les producteurs préfèrent utiliser la moindre appellation quoique, en règle générale, plus l'étiquette est précise, plus elle assure de qualité et implique également des prix plus élevés.

Au total pour l'Appellation Contrôlée

Vosne-Romanée, la superficie plantée en vignes est de 230 ha dont la production totale s'élève en une année moyenne à 6 500 hl (plus de 70 000 caisses).

Vougeot (Appellation Contrôlée)

Bourgogne rouges et blancs. Côte de Nuits.

Quand vous vous trouvez sur la route des vignes, sur la hauteur située au sud de Chambolle-Musigny, vous voyez une déclivité très prononcée en face de vous. Elle vous révèle le plateau situé au-dessous et où se trouve le célèbre château de Vougeot, entouré par les vignes du Clos de Vougeot *(voir ce nom),* l'ensemble clos par un mur de pierre qui a subi bien des intempéries.

Mis à part le clos — un des plus vastes vignobles de Bourgogne et aussi un des plus célèbres dans le monde entier — il ne reste plus grand-chose à Vougeot. Une petite agglomération nichée auprès du mur. On y pénètre par des portes voutées. Hors de ces fortifications se trouvent quelques vignobles dont les vins sont vendus sous l'appellation Vougeot suivie par le nom du cru, à condition qu'ils apparaissent conformes aux normes minimales.

Le nom de la commune et du clos dérivent de celui de la Vouge, petit cours d'eau qui descend en bouillonnant de la colline séparant Vougeot de Chambolle-Musigny. L'agglomération est fort ancienne et on y cultive la vigne depuis des siècles car, lorsque les cisterciens y arrivèrent au début du XIIe siècle, on leur donna ces terres. Les moines remembrèrent les divers crus qui se trouvent actuellement à l'intérieur des murs du clos, construisirent le château et rendirent son nom célèbre. Ils marquèrent de leur empreinte les vignobles voisins. Au cours des vingt derniers siècles, personne n'a autant œuvré pour les vins fins que les cisterciens. Leurs plus belles réussites sont le Clos de Vougeot et Kloster Eberbach, en Rheingau.

Les vignobles situés hors des murs sont Les Petits-Vougeot et Les Cras (tous deux, plantés de Pinot Noir, produisent des vins rouges) et Vigne Blanche ou Clos Blanc de Vougeot (planté de Chardonnay et Pinot Blanc, il donne du vin blanc). Le Clos Blanc appartient en sa totalité à l'entreprise, Les Héritiers Guyot, négociants à Dijon.

Le Clos de Vougeot est, évidemment, le trésor de la commune ; néanmoins, les autres sont agréables et souvent enchanteurs. Le Vougeot rouge est en général charnu et d'une agréable rondeur, mais il parvient toujours à conserver une certaine délicatesse et souvent son bouquet particulier s'impose. Le blanc est sec, parfois très fruité et fort ressemblant à ceux d'Aloxe-Corton, en Côte de Beaune. Il n'a pas la grande race des meilleurs Aloxe.

GRAND CRU	*Superficie (ha)*
Clos de Vougeot	50,59
PREMIERS CRUS	
Clos Blanc de Vougeot	3,04
Les Petits-Vougeot	5,64
Les Cras	2,99
Clos du Prieuré	1,6

A l'intérieur des murs du clos, il y a 50,59 ha de vignes et 12 ha à l'extérieur. Ces derniers produisent environ 450 hl (5 000 caisses) de vin rouge et guère plus de 60 hl (650 caisses) de blanc, en moyenne.

Les autres vignobles ont droit aux appellations Vougeot « Premier Cru », s'ils le sont, ou Vougeot.

Vouvray (Appellation Contrôlée)

Vin blanc sec, mousseux, pétillant et non mousseux. Touraine, dans la vallée de la Loire.

Le Vouvray est le vin le plus célèbre de la Touraine, province de la vallée de la Loire, paisible, semblable à un parc et qui constitue le cœur de la région des châteaux. Les vignobles gravissent les coteaux sur la rive droite du fleuve. La cour des Valois se tint souvent à Tours. Les meilleurs vignobles sont situés dans les escarpements, où des caves sont creusées à même les flancs de montagne. Seuls 500 vignerons cultivent le Vouvray. Huit communes ont droit à l'appellation contrôlée Vouvray ; ce sont : Chançay, Noizay, Paray-Meslay, Reugny, Rochecorbon, Sainte-Radegonde, Vernou et Vouvray. Même les moins bonnes années, leur vin est léger, délicieux, excellent à boire avec les rillons et les rillettes du pays sur les terrasses des restaurants de Vouvray.

Les vignobles de Vouvray datent du VIIIe siècle et n'ont cessé de produire depuis lors, sauf pendant les quelques années qui suivirent les dévastations par le phylloxéra à la fin du siècle dernier. On reconstitua alors les vignobles en greffant la vigne locale sur les souches américaines résistant au phylloxéra et la première vendange de ces nouveaux ceps eut lieu en 1900. Depuis 1936, seuls le Chenin Blanc et l'Artois sont autorisés à l'exclusion de tout autre variété de raisin.

Les vignes prospèrent sur un *aubuis* — mélange de marne et de calcaire sédimentaire — qui offre également une matière facile à creuser pour y faire des caves dans lesquelles vieillissent les vins. Les fûts sont entreposés dans le fond de cavernes et les vignerons habitent sur le devant de la même grotte où ils mènent presque une existence de troglodytes. Quand on roule le long de la Loire, en direction de Vouvray, on voit les façades de ces habitations dont les pièces sont enfoncées sous le rocher. Chez Marc Bredif il y a une vaste salle de dégustation circulaire au milieu de laquelle une ancienne meule de moulin sert de table et les bouteilles sont rangées dans des niches creusées dans le calcaire de la caverne.

Les Vouvray sont secs et souples, mais ils ont une tendance à la douceur qui peut être plus poussée quand l'été a été très ensoleillé et qu'on a vendangé tardivement, le soleil augmentant la teneur des raisins en sucre. Les vins doux durent plus longtemps que les plus secs et en général voyagent mieux. On en trouve des deux genres à l'étranger. Bien qu'on ne connaisse guère de mauvaises années en Vouvray, il arrive que les vins soient un peu acides si l'ensoleillement n'a pas été tout à fait suffisant. On compte un ou deux grands millésimes par décennie : ceux où abonde le vin doux et ensoleillé. Pourtant la plupart des Vouvray — mousseux, pétillants, ou ni l'un ni l'autre — sont secs (toutefois, les plus secs conservent toujours une trace de sucre résiduel). Leur caractéristique principale est une fraîcheur fruitée, bien que les années les plus riches fassent exception. Certains sont traités en mousseux ou en pétillant.

Si, pour bien des amateurs, Vouvray est synonyme de pétillant, on produit néanmoins dans ce secteur une bien plus grande quantité de vins tranquilles, ni mousseux ni pétillants.

Il est bien rare que le nom d'un cru figure sur une étiquette de Vouvray, parce que ces vins sont en général des mélanges effectués par les négociants du secteur qui les vendent sous leur propre nom. Mais il arrive que la localité soit précisée. Le millésime figure évidemment sur les meilleures bouteilles. Les plus recherchées sont 1947, 1949, 1955, 1957, 1959, 1961, 1964, 1966, 1967, 1969, 1970, 1971, 1973, 1976 et 1978. Il est impossible de mettre la main actuellement sur la plupart des millésimes de grandes années anciennes.

Tout Vouvray doit être fermenté en bouteilles et obligatoirement fait suivant le procédé champenois.

Le secteur de Vouvray produit en moyenne un peu plus de 100 000 hl par an (plus d'1 million de caisses).

Voir TOURAINE ; LOIRE

Vrac

La vente du vin en vrac comprend le vin seul. Quelquefois on emploie ce mot pour désigner des bouteilles non encore mises en caisses.

V.S.O.

Very Special Old, mention figurant sur certaines bouteilles de Cognac.

V.S.O.P.

Very Superior Old Pale. Cette mention, figurant sur certaines bouteilles d'Armagnac ou de Cognac, indique un type d'eau-de-vie d'un certain âge, mais n'a pas le même sens que le millésime sur les bouteilles de vin. La demande étant plus élevée en fait de Cognac, les V.S.O.P. de cette région se vendent plus rapidement et sont actuellement en moyenne plus jeunes que les Armagnac V.S.O.P.

Pour plus de précision sur l'âge des eaux-de-vie de vin, *voir* COGNAC.

V.V.S.O.P.

Very Very Special Old Pale. Mention figurant sur certaines bouteilles de Cognac.

W

Wachau

Importante zone vinicole de Basse-Autriche qui produit notamment les Kremser et les Dürnsteiner.

Voir AUTRICHE

Wachenheim

Bonne agglomération vinicole du Palatinat, dont les meilleurs crus sont : Gerümpel, Goldbächel, Rechbächel et Luginsland.

Voir PALATINAT

Wacholder

Spiritueux allemand ressemblant au gin.

Wachstum

Mot allemand synonyme de Kreszenz *(voir ce mot)*. L'un et l'autre équivalent au mot cru.

Waldmeister

Nom allemand de l'aspérule odorante, qui s'appelle aussi, familièrement, en français : petit muguet et reine des bois.

Cette herbe sauvage est un élément essentiel du vin de mai : punch populaire fait en Allemagne à base de vin nouveau. Le vin de mai est une tradition qui se perd.

Walluf

L'un des plus anciens villages vinicoles du Rheingau.

Voir RHEINGAU ; ALLEMAGNE

Walporzheim

Secteur de la vallée de l'Ahr, situé en Allemagne. On y produit du vin rouge.

Voir AHR

Wash

État intermédiaire de la matière première du whisky, après la fermentation et avant la distillation.

Washington

État producteur de vin aux États-Unis. C'est une des régions américaines autre que la Californie où prospère *Vitis vinifera*.

Voir ÉTATS-UNIS : CALIFORNIE ET OUEST

Wassail

La tradition anglaise en déclin du punch consommé à la veillée de Noël. Son nom dériverait de l'anglo-saxon : *Wes hál* (« Porte-toi bien »).

Wawern

Vin blanc allemand de la région de la Sarre. Herrenberg et Goldberg sont les meilleurs crus.

Voir SARRE

Wedderburn

Le type le plus lourd des rhums des Antilles britanniques. Produit par fermentation lente et distillé en alambic, on l'identifie au rhum de la Jamaïque par contraste avec les spiritueux légers de Porto Rico et de Cuba. De nos jours cependant on fait des rhums des deux types dans tous les pays producteurs. En Jamaïque notamment on distille de plus en plus de rhum léger en plus des Wedderburn et des Plummer.

Voir RHUM : WEST-INDIES ; RHUM : JAMAÏQUE

Wehlener Sonnenuhr

Les exportateurs de vin allemand considèrent à l'unanimité le Wehlener Sonnenuhr comme le meilleur Moselle, bien que le Bernkasteler Doctor soit mieux connu. Aucun autre Moselle et peu d'autre vin du monde entier n'a plus d'élégance ni une grande finesse que le Sonnenuhr au mieux de sa forme. Le meilleur porte l'étiquette de J.-J. Prüm, l'un des viticulteurs les plus renommés.

Voir MOSELLE

Wein

Vin, en allemand.

Weinbauer

Mot allemand désignant viticulteur et viniculteur.

Weinberg

Nom allemand des collines plantées de vignes à vin.

Weingut

Domaine vinicole, en allemand.

Weinviertel

Importante vallée et région vinicole d'Autriche, au nord du Danube.

Voir AUTRICHE

Weissbier

Littéralement : « bière blanche », nom que les Allemands donnent à une bière amère, populaire à Berlin.

Weissburgunder

Raisin le plus cultivé dans la province autrichienne du Burgenland.

Whiskey américain

Le whiskey américain et le peuple des États-Unis grandirent ensemble. Le pionnier avait besoin d'un breuvage aussi hardi et opiniâtre que lui-même et que la terre sur laquelle il s'installait à grand-peine. Il le lui fallait pour soigner les piqûres de serpent, prévenir la maladie et, parfois, se réjouir lorsqu'il quittait les plaines désolées et les forêts, pour passer un moment dans les saloons bruyants et louches. Le jeune whiskey, âpre et « vert », soutint les hommes qui conquirent le jeune continent américain, et il continue à dominer le goût de leurs descendants. L'adulte américain boit en moyenne ses 16 bouteilles de whiskey par an, ce qui représente au total pour le pays 60 millions de caisses, ou 6 millions d'hl de whiskey allant du spiritueux vieilli et parfois magnifique jusqu'aux plus durs mélanges. Il ne s'agit là que de statistiques officielles et on évalue entre 1 350 000 et 3 650 000 hl le whiskey vendu illégalement chaque année. Ce whiskey est appelé « whiskey de clair lune » (*moonshine*) ou de *bootleg* (« jambe bottée »). Un quart de tous les spiritueux fortement alcoolisés consommés aux États-Unis est fabriqué et vendu en contrebande. L'esprit indomptable du Far West survit.

A l'origine, le whiskey s'écrivait : whisky

et il était fait sur les pâturages brumeux de l'Écosse, mais probablement l'écrivait-on déjà whiskey autour des tourbières et des lacs d'Irlande. Aujourd'hui, il s'appelle whiskey aux États-Unis et en Irlande ; et whisky partout ailleurs, car on en fait à peu près dans tous les pays du monde. Mais les États-Unis sont le plus gros producteur. Le whiskey américain diffère de ses homologues européens non seulement par le goût et l'arôme mais aussi par la nature. Il ne varie guère d'une région à l'autre. Certes, le scotch est inimitablement écossais, le whiskey irlandais est le produit de la seule Irlande : mais les whiskeys américains sont classés par type et non par lieu d'origine. Le bourbon, le Rye (seigle) et autres genres de whiskey peuvent être faits n'importe où aux États-Unis. Pourvu qu'ils se conforment aux normes légales et qu'ils paient l'impôt, ils ont la bénédiction de l'État.

Comment grandit la popularité du whiskey

Les fondateurs de la République américaine n'étaient pas des buveurs de whiskey. Les pèlerins du nord et les gentilshommes de la Virginie penchaient plutôt pour la bière, le vin, le rhum et l'applejack (eau-de-vie de cidre). Pour que le whiskey devînt populaire, il fallut attendre l'établissement d'immigrants originaires d'Écosse et d'Irlande en Pennsylvanie et surtout la ruée vers l'Ouest. Comme celle de l'applejack, sa production se développa en raison du mauvais état des routes et de l'absence de moyens de transport. Les immigrants avaient apporté avec eux les secrets de la distillation et le sol était fertile : parfait pour les céréales, matières premières essentielles du whiskey. Mais le transport des produits de la terre posait un problème. Le peu de routes qui existaient étaient en mauvais état et inutilisables à la saison des pluies. Or, le cultivateur qui n'apportait pas sa récolte au marché était ruiné. Mais s'il laissait fermenter son grain et s'il le distillait, soit chez lui dans un petit alambic, soit dans celui de son voisin, le problème était résolu. Transformé en whiskey, le grain était moins volumineux, plus léger et plus facile à vendre. En Pennsylvanie et au Kentucky, la distillation commença chez les petits fermiers et devint une de leurs activités principales. Les fabricants new-yorkais de rhum s'efforcèrent de faire interdire le whiskey dans leur État, mais le whiskey l'emporta et remplaça le rhum comme breuvage courant. L'industrie du whiskey se développa et prospéra jusqu'à ce qu'un événement célèbre l'obligeât à émigrer vers l'Ouest.

En 1791, le gouvernement du président Washington eut des difficultés financières. Pour en venir à bout, il imposa une taxe sur le whiskey et ceux qui le fabriquaient protestèrent. La violence de cette rébellion du whiskey a été très exagérée. Néanmoins le président fut obligé d'envoyer la milice fédérale assurer l'ordre, la paix... et la perception de l'impôt. Les cultivateurs grognèrent, accusèrent le gouvernement de se mêler de leurs affaires privées et s'en allèrent vers l'Ouest : le sud de l'Indiana et l'Illinois, plus loin, dans le Kentucky et la Pennsylvanie. Les Peaux-Rouges hostiles étaient moins dangereux à leurs yeux que les percepteurs. Ce que les cultivateurs cherchaient et trouvèrent, c'était une bonne eau pure contenant peu de matières organiques mais riche en sulfate de calcium et carbonates minéraux : le genre d'eau qu'on trouve dans les veines de craie. A l'est des États-Unis, une longue zone de calcaire sédimentaire s'étend de l'ouest de la Pennsylvanie jusqu'au sud de l'Illinois, en traversant le Kentucky et l'Indiana ; puis elle plonge sous terre et refait surface au Maryland. De nos jours, 80 % des distillateurs légaux se trouvent dans ces cinq États et c'est là aussi que la distillation américaine atteignit sa majorité. Après ses premiers débuts, le whiskey devint une affaire, et même une grosse affaire. Dès 1911, les États-Unis produisaient plus de 3,7 millions d'hl, chiffre qui ne fut dépassé qu'en 1935. Entre ces deux dates s'étend l'ère d'obscurantisme des spiritueux américains, celle où les scellés avaient été apposés sur les distilleries, où contrebandiers et distillateurs marrons régnaient en maîtres.

Le 16 novembre 1920, la loi Volstead devint le dix-huitième amendement à la Constitution des États-Unis et instaura la prohibition. Jusqu'au 5 décembre 1933, les politiciens refusèrent d'avouer ouvertement que cette noble expérience aboutissait en réalité à un échec catastrophique. Mais aussitôt après l'abrogation, les distillateurs n'en eurent pas pour longtemps à épousseter leur matériel et reprendre la production ; en 1935, ils produisaient à pleine capacité. A partir de l'abrogation — hormis pendant les années de la Seconde Guerre mondiale —, l'industrie du whiskey prospéra vigoureusement, mais en dents de scie. 1951 fut une année record, avec plus de 7,8 millions d'hl. Depuis, la production s'est stabilisée aux environs de 3,7 millions d'hl par an, sans tenir compte d'une quantité équivalente qui vieillit en entrepôt.

La fabrication du whiskey

Le whiskey est un alcool de céréales. N'importe quel grain convient, mais aux États-Unis on utilise surtout le maïs et le seigle. Millet, sorgho et orge viennent après. Le grain macère d'abord dans l'eau pour former une pâte et on le cuit ensuite à haute pression puis on le laisse fermenter. Ce que l'on obtient alors n'est qu'une bière (*voir ce mot*) et on l'appelle en effet, « bière de distillateur ». On fait du whiskey *sweet mash* en utilisant des levures sélectionnées pour déclencher la fermentation ; le whiskey *sour mash* est obtenu en utilisant le résidu de fermentation antérieure appelé *spent beer* (bière épuisée) ou *draff*. Ensuite, bière et *draff* sont introduits, à la pompe, dans un énorme appareil à distillation continue et rectification.

Selon la loi américaine, la distillation-rectification ne doit pas être poussée au-delà de 95°. Au-dessus, le spiritueux perd toutes les caractéristiques et composants du grain utilisé et devient un alcool neutre dit *silent spirit* (esprit silencieux). La plupart des whiskeys ne sont distillés qu'à 70 ou 80° et quelques-uns à 62,5° seulement, ce qui est le cas des meilleurs bourbon et Rye (seigle). Après distillation, on le dilue avec de l'eau et on le met à vieillir. Le bourbon vieillit dans des fûts de chêne dont l'intérieur est brûlé. Après une deuxième dilution à l'eau qui amène l'alcool à 40 ou 50°, on le met en bouteille.

On ne sait pas exactement d'où vint l'idée d'utiliser des barils aux douves brûlées à l'intérieur. Selon une légende, un incendie d'entrepôts aux Indes occidentales laissa quelques barils partiellement brûlés. Faute de mieux on s'en servit de nouveau et le rhum qui vieillit dans ces fûts se révéla tellement meilleur que l'utilisation de barriques brûlées devint courante pour le rhum, puis pour le whiskey. Selon une autre histoire, cet usage serait originaire du Kentucky. On sait que pour incurver les douves de tonneau il faut les chauffer à la vapeur. Au cours de cette opération certaines furent atteintes par le feu qui chauffait l'eau. On s'en servit quand même et on eut la même révélation que dans l'histoire précédente. Il est toutefois difficile d'imaginer que des gens du Kentucky aient pu se montrer négligents dans une affaire aussi sérieuse que la fabrication de barriques destinées au whiskey. Quelle que soit l'origine de cette invention, le bois brûlé améliore et adoucit l'alcool auquel il donne corps et couleur.

Types de whiskey

La loi américaine définit de manière assez rigoureuse les divers types de whiskey du pays. Certaines de ces définitions n'ont guère d'intérêt pour le consommateur étant donné qu'elles concernent des types de wiskeys qui ne sont jamais mis en vente et servent de matière première à d'autres whiskeys. On verra chacun des types de whiskey par la suite dans l'ordre alphabétique, mais voici, au préalable, un résumé de leurs caractéristiques générales.

Bourbon Whiskey

A l'origine, le Bourbon Whiskey était fait dans le canton de Bourbon au Kentucky, avec du maïs. Désormais cette appellation s'applique à n'importe quel whiskey dont la distillation n'a pas été poussée au-delà de 80°, dans la composition duquel le maïs entre pour au moins 51 % et qui a vieilli au moins 2 ans dans un fût neuf, en chêne brûlé. La fermentation peut être déclenchée par de la levure sélectionnée ou par le résidu de fermentation antérieure. Les bouteilles seront étiquetées Straight Bourbon ou bien Blended Straight Bourbon.

Rye Whiskey (Whiskey de seigle)

Whiskey en voie de disparition. Le seigle doit représenter au moins 51 % du grain servant de matière première. La distillation ne doit pas être poussée au-delà de 80°. Le vieillissement de l'alcool doit avoir lieu dans des fûts neufs en chêne brûlé. On trouve du Straight Rye et du Blended Straight Rye, mais dans une moins large mesure que pour le bourbon.

Citons quelques-unes des autres définitions du terme whiskey :

Whiskey

C'est l'appellation la plus générale, mais on ne la trouve jamais seule sur les bouteilles. L'étiquette sur laquelle figurent d'autres mentions — Straight, Blended, Bourbon, etc. — doit évidemment répondre aux exigences particulières des types de whiskey en question, ainsi qu'à celles du whiskey en général. Selon la loi, le whiskey est « le distillat alcoolique d'une pâte fermentée de grain distillée à moins de 95°, de telle sorte que le distillat ait la saveur, l'arôme et les caractéristiques que l'on attribue en général au whiskey, qu'il quitte la salle des cuves de la distillerie à 55° au maximum et 40° au minimum et qu'il soit ensuite dilué avant mise en bouteille, mais pas au-dessous de 40° ». Étant donné que cette loi ne précise pas le temps de vieillissement, une bouteille qui ne porterait que le seul mot whiskey sur son étiquette contiendrait, selon toute vraisemblance, un breuvage cru et imbuvable.

Straight Whiskey

Whiskey dont la distillation n'est pas poussée au-delà de 80° et qui a vieilli au moins deux ans en fût neuf de chêne brûlé. Le Straight corn whiskey peut vieillir dans des fûts déjà utilisés et non brûlés. Les whiskey Straight qu'on trouve sur le marché sont en général des Straight Bourbon ou des Straight Rye. Ils représentent environ 27 % de la consommation.

Blended Whiskey

Mélange contenant au moins 20 % de Straight Whiskey à 50 %, soit avec un autre whiskey, soit avec un alcool neutre, ou encore avec les deux, et mis en bouteille à 40° au minimum. A peu près 25 % des whiskey vendus appartiennent à ce type. Ils présentent l'avantage d'être plus légers et moins chers que les Straight whiskeys. En outre, la teneur minimale de 40° (qui peut être obtenue par n'importe quelle combinaison d'un ou plusieurs whiskies, au besoin avec de l'alcool neutre) permet aux distillateurs de fabriquer un produit de qualité constante qui ne varie pas d'année en année. Quand il y entre une forte proportion d'alcool neutre, ce whiskey offre peu d'agréments à un palais cultivé. Le secret du Blended Whiskey de chaque distillerie réside dans l'art du maître mélangeur, capable de distinguer de quelles caractéristiques chaque alcool a besoin pour produire une réplique de l'alcool mis en vente précédemment par l'entreprise, de déterminer la nature et la proportion de chaque composant du mélange et de s'assurer que tous les ingrédients se marient correctement. Il est permis d'y ajouter une petite quantité de Xérès — jusqu'à 2,5 % — comme agent mélangeur.

Bottled-in-Bond Whiskey

Cette formule ne garantit pas obligatoirement une qualité supérieure, mais c'est pratiquement ce qu'elle fait en général. Elle n'est permise que pour les whiskey Straight de quatre ans d'âge au moins, mis en bouteille à 50°, produits par un seul distillateur, dans une seule distillerie, en une seule saison ou année. Ce whiskey vieillit durant le temps prescrit dans des entrepôts soumis au contrôle d'État et il paie l'impôt en les quittant. Le contrôle en question n'a qu'un caractère fiscal et, théoriquement, ne porte pas sur la qualité, mais sur la durée du séjour en entrepôt qui est aussi effectivement contrôlée.

Whiskey : Bourbon

Très tôt dans l'histoire coloniale de l'Amérique, un pasteur baptiste, Elijah Craig, installa un alambic à Georgetown, dans le Kentucky, et se mit à produire du whiskey de maïs. Cet alambic aurait été le premier instrument de ce genre apporté au Kentucky. Le pasteur baptisa son alcool : Bourbon Country Whiskey, d'après le canton d'origine. C'est beaucoup plus tard seulement que le Kentucky devint indiscutablement le centre de l'industrie du whiskey américain.

De nos jours, plus de la moitié des distilleries autorisées sont installées au Kentucky qui reste le plus gros producteur de bourbon. Cependant voilà bien longtemps que la fabrication du whiskey a franchi les limites du canton de Bourbon. Selon le règlement américain, le nom bourbon s'applique à n'importe quel whiskey obtenu par la fermentation de grain dont au moins 51 % de maïs (les autres céréales varient, mais on n'obtient un bon équilibre qu'avec du maïs, du seigle et de l'orge maltée) ; la distillation ne doit pas être poussée audelà de 80° (dans la pratique elle se situe généralement entre 62,5° et 70°) ; l'alcool doit vieillir en fût neuf de chêne brûlé. Ce whiskey, vieilli dans de telles conditions pendant 2 ans, s'appelle Straight Bourbon Whiskey, s'il n'a fait l'objet d'aucun coupage. S'il est mélangé avec d'autres bourbons straight, il porte soit l'appellation Bourbon, soit celle de Blended Straight Bourbon. C'est dans ce cas un mélange composé uniquement de bourbon.

Le Blended Bourbon (sans la mention Straight) est une mixture de bourbon et d'autres spiritueux, soit du whiskey, soit de l'alcool neutre de grain.

Le Straight Bourbon est en général sec, moelleux, corsé, alors que le Blended Bourbon sera rendu plus léger par l'addition d'esprits neutres. Straight Bourbon et Blended Straight Bourbon sont ceux qui se vendent le plus aux États-Unis : environ 3,5 millions d'hl, soit, à peu près, 30 millions de caisses par an. On les consomme surtout dans le Sud et dans l'Ouest.

Quand le maïs écrasé a été pesé et préparé pour la macération, on le mélange d'abord avec de l'eau que son passage sur un terrain de calcaire sédimentaire a filtrée, et on le chauffe. C'est alors qu'on ajoute les autres ingrédients tels que seigle et orge maltée. La levure (qui a la caractéristique du vinaigre) met 5 jours à se développer. On la mêle à la pâte de grain. Des pompes font passer le tout à travers des réfrigérateurs pour l'amener aux cuves de fermentation qui a lieu à 21 °C. Elle dure le temps voulu pendant lequel on alimente la levure avec des sucres de maltose. La partie du produit qui apparaît au moment où la température s'élève s'appelle « nouvelle bière » et on la sépare du reste pour la distiller. Cette nouvelle bière bout à une température moins élevée que l'alcool. On sépare donc les deux élements par chauffage. Le whiskey nouveau passe dans une cuve où il est dilué à l'eau, pour réduire sa teneur en alcool. Ensuite on le verse en fûts pour le faire vieillir en entrepôt soumis au contrôle d'État. De six mois en six mois, on vérifie et note ses caractéristiques. Avant de le mettre en bouteille on le compare à des échantillons standard de sa marque et on mesure à nouveau le volume au moment de payer l'impôt.

Whiskey : Corn

Whiskey obtenu par distillation d'une pâte de grain dans la composition de laquelle le maïs entre pour au moins 80 %. Il peut être vieilli ou non, en fût neuf ou usagé, brûlé ou non. En général, il ne vieillit guère, étant donné que la demande provient surtout de zones rurales où de jeunes enthousiastes régissent la mode des goûts. Le Corn Whiskey qui n'a pas vieilli est cru, incolore et, le moins qu'on puisse dire, c'est qu'il manque de subtilité. Ce whiskey de maïs diffère du bourbon à bien des points de vue. La loi lui impose 80 % de maïs dans sa pâte de grain, et au bourbon, 51 %, et il doit être vieilli dans des fûts neufs, en chêne brûlé.

Voir aussi WHISKEY AMÉRICAIN

Whiskey : Irish (Irlandais)

« De tous les vins, le vin irlandais est le meilleur », déclara naïvement le tsar Pierre le Grand. Il confirmait simplement ce que des générations d'Irlandais avaient toujours cru. Combien de générations ? La réponse est controversée. Selon certains on fait du whiskey en Irlande depuis au moins mille ans, selon d'autres, environ cinq cents ans seulement. Une chose est certaine : bien avant que whiskey et eau-de-vie de vin ne fussent commercialisés, les Gaëls — Irlandais et Écossais — faisaient fermenter le malt d'orge et le distillaient pour leur propre plaisir. Les Irlandais assurent que l'eau-de-vie de vin — nouvelle venue parmi les alcools consommables — naquit lorsque les missionnaires irlandais apportèrent en France le secret de la distillation et ils demandent comment on appliquerait autrement les similitudes en fait de méthodes de distillation et la coïncidence de nom : *uisge beatha* et eau-de-vie, qui signifient la même chose mot à mot.

Il y a encore un siècle, Écossais et Irlandais accordaient leurs faveurs au Scotch Whisky. Puis les Écossais apprirent à mélanger les produits des brassages successifs de malt, tout en conservant un scotch inimitable, et leurs brillantes capacités commerciales firent connaître ce produit dans le monde entier. Pendant un certain temps on se demanda si ces mélanges avaient le droit de s'appeler whisky. Une commission royale régla la question et le monde entier vint réclamer du whisky à la porte des Écossais. Il continue à le faire. Mais les Irlandais, restés fidèles à l'ancien whiskey, exempt de tout coupage, distillé en alambic, conservant une saveur caractéristique, ont du mal à élargir leur marché, quoique les perspectives s'améliorent et qu'ils aient de fidèles partisans dans le monde entier. La distillerie irlandaise supporte un autre handicap : ses produits sont lourdement taxés, si bien que l'Irlandais peut difficilement s'offrir sa juste part de la boisson nationale. Les contrebandiers s'efforcent de fournir du whiskey dont le prix n'est pas majoré par la taxe. On appelle familièrement leur produit *poteen,* nom emprunté au petit alambic, facile à démonter, dans lequel on le distille. Autour des lacs et des tourbières, dans les bogues, la fabrication du *poteen* est à la fois fort bien considérée et profitable. Il est rare que la police surprenne un distillateur clandestin. Quand elle arrive sur les lieux, il est déjà parti avec son alambic. Si dans sa hâte il a laissé derrière lui un peu de whiskey, celui qui le trouve économise l'équivalent de 15 francs par bouteille.

En dépit des impôts, l'Irlandais adore son whiskey. Même les chevaux, dit-il, s'en passent difficilement dans le pays. Cette boutade s'explique par un événement plus ou moins exact dont on parle encore à Dublin. Après une longue nuit de voyage, un cultivateur s'arrêta dans une petite agglomération pour faire boire son cheval à l'abreuvoir. Le cheval s'abreuva largement et quand, désaltéré, il s'éloigna de l'abreuvoir, on le vit tituber, tomber par terre, ivre-mort. L'abreuvoir était plein de bon vieux whiskey pur, prêt à la consommation. Tout le village s'en réjouit jusqu'à ce qu'un gardien prévînt la police qui à son tour appela le percepteur. L'enquête révéla qu'une distillerie du voisinage utilisait les conduites d'eau pour faire passer son whiskey d'un entrepôt contrôlé jusqu'au local où on le mettait en bouteille mais que cette nuit-là quelqu'un avait mal branché la tuyauterie. L'amende fut lourde et depuis lors les chevaux sont privés de whiskey dans cette région d'Irlande.

Les percepteurs ont rarement autant de chance. En dépit de leurs efforts, la distillation clandestine continue dans certaines régions, celles où, dit-on, aucun maquignon ne traiterait avec celui qui ne lui offrait pas un petit *deoch* pour chasser la fraîcheur du matin lors des foires d'animaux qui se tiennent l'hiver. Selon la qualité du *poteen* ainsi offert cette prise de contact aura ou n'aura pas d'influence sur le prix.

La fabrication du whiskey irlandais — tel que l'Old Buschmills' — se fait selon les mêmes principes que celle du scotch *(voir* WHISKY, SCOTCH). Mais il existe cependant certaines différences de procédés. Les whiskey irlandais, populaires et de prestige, sont distillés en alambic et exempts de tout mélange. Ils passent trois fois dans l'alambic, et deux fois seulement en Écosse. Le whiskey irlandais n'est fait qu'avec des céréales irlandaises, surtout de l'orge, maltée ou non, avec un peu de blé, d'avoine et de seigle. L'orge maltée n'est pas séchée comme en Écosse, au-dessus d'un feu de tourbe, combustible qui donne une saveur de « fumé » particulière au scotch. La distillation à lieu dans des alambics d'une contenance bien plus élevée que celle des alambics écossais, parfois plus de 750 hl, et elle est poussée jusqu'à 86°, alors qu'en Écosse elle ne va pas au-delà de 70°. Comme toujours dans la distillation en alambic, on ne conserve que le distillat obtenu au milieu de l'opération et « tête » et « queue » sont redistillées.

Les Irlandais calculent que le whiskey ne représente que 10 % de la pâte fermentée et qu'une bonne part encore s'évapore pendant le vieillissement.

Parlant de son whiskey national, un écrivain irlandais a dit que l'homme met sept jours à faire un whiskey qui se fait lui-même en sept ans. L'homme, en effet, consacre plus ou moins de temps à préparer le whiskey, mais ce dernier en a besoin de beaucoup plus pour avoir vraiment droit à ce nom.

La loi irlandaise n'impose qu'un vieillissement de cinq ans ; certains whiskeys vieillissent pourtant jusqu'à dix ans, et les meilleurs douze ou quinze, toujours en fût de bois, car dès qu'il est mis en bouteille, le whiskey, comme l'eau-de-vie de vin, ne vieillit plus.

Le scotch whisky est un mélange de lourd whisky de malt avec du whisky de grain, ce qui change les caractéristiques des deux composants et donne ce que le monde entier appelle scotch. D'autre part, le mélange qui sert à faire le whiskey irlandais comporte avant distillation de l'orge maltée et d'autres grains. Ajouter du whisky ou de l'alcool de grain après distillation en alambic n'a plus d'autre effet que d'affaiblir sa saveur. On colore le whiskey irlandais avec du caramel et on le dilue pour abaisser sa teneur en alcool à un niveau raisonnable. Il est généralement vendu à 40° ou à peu près. En outre, ce whiskey est distillé en alambic, comme le Cognac, et pas en appareil à distillation continue.

Les Irlandais s'efforcent de promouvoir un punch à leur façon (whiskey irlandais, écorce de citron, sucre et eau bouillante) et une espèce de café (whiskey irlandais, café et sucre avec une couche de crème fraîche par-dessus), afin de lancer leur marchandise. Ils ont aussi mis sur le marché quelques whiskeys obtenus par mélanges. On les a critiqués parce qu'ils ne s'adaptaient pas plus tôt à l'évolution du goût des acheteurs, mais ceux qui les critiquent ainsi ignorent peut-être la véritable nature du whiskey irlandais. Il n'y a pourtant aucun doute que le véritable Irish whiskey distillé en alambic et vieilli correctement pendant le temps voulu, est un très bon alcool.

Whiskey light (léger)

Au début des années 1960, la popularité des whiskeys écossais et canadiens augmentant aux États-Unis, les distillateurs américains eurent l'idée de produire un whiskey plus léger, ce qui s'avéra impossible, les lois fédérales contrôlant la teneur en alcool des whisky américains au moment de leur distillation. Selon ces lois les whiskeys en question — tels les bourbons et les whiskeys de seigle — devaient être distillés à moins de 160° « proof » *(voir ce mot)*, ou au-dessous d'une teneur en alcool de 80 %. Or plus de pourcentage d'alcool est bas, plus l'arôme du whiskey est retenu par les liqueurs spiritueuses. Pour réussir à faire un « whiskey léger », les firmes américaines auraient donc dû distiller leur alcool à plus de 160° « proof ». Distillé à 200°, le whiskey n'est plus qu'un alcool de grain sans aucun goût, semblable à la vodka.

Un nouvel obstacle qu'opposent les lois fédérales à la production de cet alcool : tous les whiskies de confection américaine (excepté ceux de maïs) doivent vieillir dans des fûts neufs en bois brûlé.

En 1967, les lois furent enfin révisées et le Light Whiskey fut défini comme « un alcool de céréales produit aux États-Unis à la date du 26 janvier 1968 et après, dont la distillation doit être poussée à plus de 160° et à moins de 190°, il doit être entreposé dans des fûts usagés en bois brûlé, ou dans des fûts de chêne neufs, aux douves non brûlées ». Plus loin, « Si le Light Whiskey est mélangé avec moins de 20 % de whiskey pur à un niveau de distillation donné, le mélange sera appelé Blended Light Whiskey ou Light Whiskey — A Blend. » Tous les whiskeys légers produits jusqu'ici n'ont pas atteint ce stade-là.

Whiskey Rye (seigle)

La plus grande partie du whiskey de seigle est faite en Pennsylvanie et au Maryland, et c'est dans cette même région qu'on le consomme. La production de Straight Rye a diminué et continue de décliner. Bien des consommateurs ont abandonné cet alcool pendant et après la guerre parce que plusieurs marques bien connues cessèrent de le faire Straight, pour vendre du whiskey de mélange.

Selon la loi, la pâte distillée pour faire du Rye Whiskey doit contenir au moins 51 % de seigle. La distillation ne doit pas être poussée au-delà de 80° et le distillat doit vieillir en fût neuf de chêne brûlé. Le Straight Rye doit être exempt de tout mélange et avoir vieilli pendant deux ans en fût. Le Blended Straight Rye, comme son nom l'indique, est un mélange de deux Straight Rye ou plus. Les bouteilles portant seulement l'étiquette Blended Rye contiennent un mélange de whiskey de seigle avec de l'alcool neutre et parfois d'autres whiskeys. Cet alcool, plus léger, de saveur moins caractéristique, est aussi moins cher. Les whiskeys de seigle sont en général plus lourds et un peu plus austères que les bourbons. Ils présentent certaines ressemblances avec les whiskeys irlandais, bien qu'ils soient faits en appareils à distillation continue et que l'irlandais soit distillé en alambic.

Whisky canadien

La caractéristique la plus distinctive du whisky canadien, en général, c'est la légèreté de son corps. Tout le whisky canadien ne doit être obtenu, selon la loi fédérale, qu'à partir de céréales. La proportion dans laquelle chaque céréale rentre dans la composition du mélange, le traitement du mélange, la surveillance particulière et sévère exercée par le distillateur pendant tout le processus de la fabrication mettent le whisky canadien hors classe parmi les autres distillats de grain.

Le whisky canadien est bien connu hors de son propre pays. Sa bonne réputation a été établie pendant plus de cent trente ans par une seule firme ; pendant plus de cent ans par quatre autres et par quelques distillateurs qui produisent depuis moins longtemps mais n'en respectent pas moins les traditions de leurs aînés.

Voici comment on procède pour faire le whisky canadien.

Le grain

Si longtemps qu'il dure, le vieillissement ne fera pas du bon whisky à partir de grain de qualité inférieure. Le grain amené à la distillerie n'est admis qu'après avoir été mis à l'épreuve consciencieusement par analyse chimique. Ensuite, maïs et seigle sont moulus pour en obtenir une farine grossière qui est versée dans d'immenses récipients contenant une certaine quantité d'eau. On chauffe cette pâte à la vapeur, afin de liquéfier l'amidon. Ensuite on ajoute de l'orge maltée pour convertir l'amidon en sucres fermentescibles. Cette opération, appelée saccharification, produit les maltoses, glucoses... que l'addition de levure fera fermenter, c'est-à-dire transformera en alcool.

La levure

La culture et le développement de la levure sont des soucis capitaux de chaque distillateur qui élève en éprouvette une lignée bien définie de germes soignés jalousement. Un des instants les plus critiques est l'apparition de la cellule vivante dans la levure. Étant donné qu'elle vit, elle est vulnérable. On recourt donc à des mesures extrêmes d'aseptie pour éviter toute contamination.

La fermentation

Après saccharification, la pâte de grain macérée dans l'eau est pompée hors des récipients où elle a chauffé, passe dans des serpentins où elle refroidit et se déverse dans des cuves où on lui inocule les cellules vivantes de levure. Ces dernières convertissent le sucre de la pâte d'une part en alcool et d'autre part en gaz carbonique. Ce processus dure environ trois ou quatre jours.

La distillation

Quand la fermentation est achevée, la pâte, qui contient désormais de l'alcool à la place du sucre, est pompée dans un appareil à distillation continue, comportant plusieurs colonnes et dont la température est contrôlée. En général les colonnes cylindriques comportent plusieurs étages. Cet équipement moderne et compliqué permet d'appliquer des procédés de distillation fort divers d'où résultent également des produits divers. Le distillateur peut notamment agir sur la concentration des ingrédients qui confèrent du goût au whisky.

Le vieillissement

Vient alors une opération capitale qui consiste à faire vieillir le whisky. Les distillateurs canadiens n'ont rien trouvé qui puisse adoucir et vieillir leur produit mieux que ne le fait la nature elle-même.

Le whisky cru, après distillation, est d'abord dilué pour l'amener à la teneur en alcool qui convient à la conservation en fût. Le whisky canadien vieillit dans des fûts de bois dont l'intérieur peut ou non être brûlé. Il y passera quatre, six, huit ou dix ans, dans des entrepôts dont la température est contrôlée. Pendant le vieillissement, un certain nombre de réactions lentes se produisent. Les composants les plus volatils du whisky s'évaporent à travers le bois qui lui-même agit sur les spiritueux pour l'adoucir. Certains sucres du bois et du tanin quittent le fût pour se mêler au liquide. Ce sont ces éléments qui entre autres donnent au whisky sa couleur dorée. Quand ils ont suffisamment vieilli, plusieurs lots de whiskies sont mariés, ce qui est tout un art. On goûte et on analyse le mélange pour apprécier sa qualité. S'il le mérite, ce whisky est filtré à plusieurs reprises, mis en bouteille, étiqueté. Il est alors prêt à être vendu.

Le whisky canadien destiné à la consommation au Canada, titre 39,9° à sa mise en bouteille et le whisky destiné à l'exportation est généralement mis en bouteille au degré d'alcool autorisé ou habituel dans le pays auquel il est vendu et cent cinquante quatre différents pays ou territoires du monde entier en importent.

Aucune entreprise privée au Canada n'est soumise à une surveillance et à un contrôle de l'État aussi sévères que le distillateur canadien. Quelque deux cents fonctionnaires du fisc opèrent dans les distilleries canadiennes elles-mêmes. Leur surveillance s'étend à la réception du grain par le distillateur, à toutes les phases de la production, à la mise en bouteille, à l'expédition, et elle ne s'arrête qu'au paiement de la taxe.

Mais l'État n'intervient absolument pas dans les techniques de distillation auxquelles recourt chaque distillateur, lequel est donc maître de la qualité et des caractéristiques de sa marchandise.

L'étiquette des bouteilles de whisky canadien sur laquelle on lit qu'il a été distillé, mélangé et mis en bouteille sous contrôle de l'État canadien n'est ni une formule publicitaire ni une fantaisie, mais l'affirmation d'un fait exact.

Whisky : Malt

Ce whisky de malt est un scotch fait en Écosse, dans 81 distilleries, avec de l'orge maltée, de l'eau et de la levure, à l'exclusion de toute autre substance. Il se distingue donc du scotch de grain dans la composition duquel entrent, outre l'orge maltée, du maïs, du blé, de l'avoine, du seigle.

Le whisky de malt est distillé en alambic. Le whisky de tous grains, en appareil à distillation continue.

Il existe quatre types de whisky de malt écossais : Highland, Islay, Lowland et Campbeltown. Le premier est produit à peu près partout dans les Highlands. De nombreuses distilleries se trouvent à proximité des rives de la Spey. On le considère comme le meilleur. Le second, Islay produit dans les Inner Hebrides et la péninsule de Kintyre, a généralement un goût plus prononcé. Il existe relativement moins de distilleries dans le sud et le Lowland Malt Whisky qu'elles produisent sert généralement à des coupages. Le West Islands Malt est souvent désigné par l'appellation Islay. Il y a huit distilleries sur l'île d'Islay. Elles produisent des malts d'Islay dont le « fumé » est célèbre. Ces distilleries sont Ardbeg, Bowmore, Bruichladdich, Bunnahabhain, Caol Ila, Lagavulin, Laphroaig et Campbell.

Le whisky de malt Macallan est exclusivement vieilli dans des fûts de Sherry. De tous les whiskies, seul le pur malt voit augmenter ses ventes.

Voir WHISKY : SCOTCH

Whisky : Scotch

On s'ingénie à imiter le Scotch Whisky partout au monde. Pendant un certain temps les Japonais en fabriquèrent dans une ville dont ils changèrent le nom pour pouvoir faire figurer Aberdeen sur leurs étiquettes. Avec leur méticulosité habituelle, des Allemands importèrent de l'eau de la Spey et n'obtinrent pourtant pas de scotch, qui fut et reste toujours inimitable.

Comment se fait-il que le scotch ne puisse être fait qu'en Écosse ? Voilà encore un mystère semblable à la combinaison impossible à analyser des ingrédients connus qui donnent aux grands vins leur véritable vertu. Apparemment, le scotch n'est qu'un produit de l'orge, de la levure, de l'eau écossaise, de l'air écossais et d'un procédé de distillation qui n'a rien de mystérieux. Il se trouve même que l'orge n'a pas besoin d'être écossaise. Elle peut venir de n'importe où. Les Écossais en ont importé de pays aussi lointains que l'Australie et les États-Unis (Californie). Ils considéraient même l'orge étrangère comme meilleure parce qu'elle est plus sèche, facteur important. Mais actuellement, presque tout le whisky est fait avec le l'orge de Grande-Bretagne. Si le scotch est du scotch, les matières premières ne sont pas seules en cause. Le *blending* (mélange) joue un rôle capital.

Il y a encore une centaine d'années, les Écossais consommaient du scotch exempt de coupage et qui avait une forte teneur en alcool. Puis les distillateurs se mirent à mélanger plusieurs whiskies et c'est ce procédé qui rendit leur produit célèbre dans le monde entier. On ne trouve plus guère qu'en Écosse même, en quantité notable, du scotch qui ne soit pas le produit de mélanges et qu'on appelle « single » (seul, unique, solitaire, célibataire).

Le secret du coupage réside dans le fait que tous les composants sont écossais et que le plus important est le whisky de malt écossais : élément de base irremplaçable. Pour produire leur scotch unique au monde, les distillateurs écossais recourent à des procédés qui semblent plus inspirés par la magie que par la science : la forme de l'appareil de distillation elle-même influe sur le whisky. Ayant construit un nouvel appareil à distillation, un distillateur ne parvint pas à recouvrer la splendeur perdue de son whisky et finit, en désespoir de cause, par faire copier son ancien appareil sans omettre un seul détail, y compris les pièces cloutées et martelées aux endroits usés ou perçés.

Avant de devenir le scotch que nous connaissons, le whisky d'Écosse mène une vie très remplie sous plusieurs identités. A son arrivée à la distillerie, l'orge est triée minutieusement pour en éliminer toute autre graine. En général elle est d'abord emmagasinée pendant un certain temps ; ensuite seulement, on la fait macérer : on la plonge dans de grandes cuves d'eau où elle passe un temps prédéterminé. Puis on la répand sur un sol de ciment où les malteurs l'étendent et la retournent. Au bout de deux ou trois jours, elle germe ; des embryons de racine apparaissent. Quatre ou cinq jours plus tard ces organes se dessèchent et le grain change d'aspect. Alors les malteurs considèrent que l'orge est « maltée ». Le malt est porté dans la salle du four où on l'étale sur des feuilles de métal perforé au-dessus d'un feu de tourbe qui le chauffe, l'assèche et le fume. Vers la fin de cette opération, quand on estime que le malt vert s'est imprégné de la saveur de la tourbe qu'il conservera jusqu'au moment où le whisky entrera en contact avec le palais du consommateur, on ajoute à la tourbe du coke et de l'anthracite pour obtenir une température de 71°C. Conçus pour laisser s'échapper la chaleur, les bâtiments où cette opération a lieu ont des bords de toit relevés qui leur donnent une allure de pagode, ce qui prête une grâce chinoise aux solides édifices de pierre écossais.

Après avoir subi l'épreuve du feu, le malt se repose pendant deux mois. Ensuite on en sépare les embryons de racine desséchés qui serviront à nourrir le bétail. Quant au malt proprement dit, il est écrasé et broyé dans un moulin circulaire de conception appropriée. On verse le malt pulvérisé dans la cuve à pâte : bassin circulaire dentelé. Des pales mues par un système d'engrenage y tournent sans fin pour brasser le malt dans l'eau bouillonnante. On y verse de l'eau quatre fois de suite, de plus en plus chaude, pour extraire les matières solubles du malt. Cette solution s'appelle *wort* (prononcer *wourt)*. Les deux premières eaux qui ont déjà servi à une extraction antérieure s'appellent *sparge*. L'eau infusée, à la sortie de la cuve, passe dans une machine réfrigératrice qui en abaisse la température à 24°C, celle qui convient à la levure. On la met alors dans des cuves de fermentation appelées « dos ». La troisième et la quatrième eau, serviront de *sparge* pour une extraction ultérieure. Le résidu qui subiste, le *draff*, servira aussi à l'alimentation du bétail.

C'est dans les bacs qu'on ajoute la levure au *wort*. Ces récipients sont des cuves à fermentation, parfois en pin ou en mélèze, mais plus souvent, de nos jours, en acier. La fermentation commence alors. Les éléments actifs de la levure transforment le sucre du *wort* en alcool et gaz carbonique. Ce dernier s'évapore et se dissipe dans l'air ambiant. L'alcool reste dans le *wort* qui titre alors quelque 5°. De nouveau la matière change de nom. Nous avons eu d'abord de l'orge, puis du malt, ensuite du *wort* et maintenant du *wash*.

Le *wash* s'écoule dans des alambics en cuivre, beaux engins rutilants qui, dans les grandes distilleries, dépassent de beaucoup la taille d'un homme. La distillation a lieu. Après la première distillation, le produit change encore de nom et devient *low wine* (bas vin, parce qu'il n'a pas encore atteint toute sa vigueur). Durant la seconde distillation, le distillat le plus clair et le plus fort est recueilli dans le *spirit receiver vat* (cuve à recueillir le spiritueux) et s'appelle enfin whisky. Ce whisky cru titre alors environ 58° et il lui faudra subir une dilution avec un peu d'eau pure de source. On le met en fût au titre de 55,5°. A ce moment-là, le distillateur a obtenu entre 11 et 14 l de whisky par boisseau d'orge (32,24 l). Mais son produit perdra une partie de sa teneur en alcool et de son volume pendant le vieillissement en fût. Sous un climat humide, la teneur en alcool diminuera plus vite que le volume et sous un climat sec il se produira l'inverse. Ces évaporations représentent une masse prodigieuse. Chaque année environ 11 millions de l de scotch s'évaporent dans l'air d'Écosse.

Le fût apporte la contribution finale à la splendeur du whisky qui s'améliore considérablement avec l'âge — en fût, pas en bouteille. En général, il vieillit dans des tonneaux en chêne d'Amérique. Il faut que ce soit du chêne. Quand il n'a pas à sa disposition des fûts précédemment imprégnés par du vin, le distillateur sera obligé d'utiliser un peu de caramel pour donner à son whisky la teinte rousse qu'attend le public.

Les fûts de whisky s'appellent *butts* s'ils contiennent plus de 364 l, et *hogsheads* s'ils contiennent entre 205 et 364 l ; *barrels* pour une capacité de 160 à 205 l ; enfin, *quarters* pour une capacité inférieur à 136 l. Les *octaves* contiennent entre 4 l et 68 l. Il existe trois types de *butts* dénommés, selon leur forme : *puncheon, pipe* ou tout simplement *butt*.

Ceux qui pratiquent les mélanges sont les grands artistes du whisky. On est fasciné quand on les voit au travail, se fiant plus à l'odorat qu'au goût, les narines dilatées sur de longs verres, étroits, en forme de tulipe. Quand l'expert a fait son choix, on mélange les divers ingrédients dans des cuves colossales où ils sont brassés par des pales, puis on les laisse se « marier ». Le mélange se composera d'environ 40 % de whisky de malt et 60 % de whisky de grain (céréales diverses). Mais parfois la proportion est à peu près inverse. Ces coupages donnent une gamme infinie de whiskies. Il n'est pas extraordinaire que 50 whiskies différents entrent dans la composition de celui qui sera livré au commerce. La plupart des experts conviennent que les meilleurs mélanges consistent en quantité égale de Highland Malt et de Lowland Malt, un peu d'Islay ou de Campbeltown, et le reste en whisky de grain non malté.

Dans l'ensemble, le whisky de malt des Highlands a un corps léger et une forte saveur. Le malt des Lowlands est aussi léger, mais moins nettement fumé. Quant au Campbeltown et à l'Islay, on les remarque pour leur lourdeur de corps et leur fort fumé.

Avant mise en bouteille, le whisky est dilué par addition de l'eau douce des *lochs* écossais, puis filtré.

La pénurie de scotch qui régna entre 1940 et 1950 résultait surtout des restrictions à la distillation au rationnement de l'orge attribuée à l'industrie pendant les premières années qui suivirent les hostilités (la quantité allouée pour la période s'étendant de 1945 à 1950 couvrait à peine une année de distillation). A cela, il faut ajouter le long temps nécessaire au vieillissement. Enfin un autre facteur fut l'accroissement de la demande mondiale, surtout aux États-Unis.

Actuellement, alors que la matière première ne manque heureusement pas, les Américains consomment 20 millions de caisses par an, voire plus, de cet alcool de grain qui est le plus prisé, il est aussi devenu l'apéritif et la dernière boisson de la journée les plus en vogue en France et dans d'autres pays d'Europe. La tendance actuelle indique un accroissement de la consommation des malts non mélangés.

White Port

Littéralement Porto blanc. Il s'agit de vin de Porto authentique fait avec du raisin blanc. En général il est un peu plus doux que le Porto rouge et c'est la France qui lui offre son plus grand débouché. Mais actuellement on constate une tendance croissante à faire du Porto blanc sec qu'on sert en apéritif au Portugal et que l'étranger commence à apprécier.

Voir PORTO

Wienerwald-Steinfeld

Bonne région vinicole d'Autriche, qui englobe Gumpoldskirchen et Baden.

Voir AUTRICHE

Wiltingen

Agglomération de la vallée de la Sarre, au sud-ouest de Trèves. Ses vignes produisent d'excellents vins blancs, dont le mieux connu est le Scharzhofberg.

Voir SARRE

Wine Cooler

L'un des vins qui monte en Amérique. Il est peu alcoolisé (moins de 8 %).

Wine Gallon

Mesure de capacité équivalent à 160 onces liquides britanniques de vin ou de spiritueux, quelle que soit leur teneur en alcool. On l'appelle aussi *bulk gallon*.

Voir PROOF GALLON

Winkel

Agglomération sur la rive du Rhin dans le Rheinhessen, où se trouvent quelques bons crus.

Wintrich

Bon secteur de vins blancs de la moyenne Moselle.
Voir MOSELLE

Winzer

Viniculteur, en allemand. La mention Winzerverein sur une étiquette indique que le vin a été produit par une coopérative.

Wood

Littéralement « bois » ; mais, s'agissant de vin, ce mot signifie : fût. On dit que le vin est dans le bois quand il est en tonneau.

Woody

Cet adjectif peut s'appliquer à deux états différents d'un vin ou d'un spiritueux : 1. forte odeur de chêne lorsque le liquide est resté trop longtemps en fût ; 2. une mauvaise teinte donnée par un bois défectueux. Ces deux inconvénients sont minimes et curables.

Worcester

District vinicole de la province du Cap.
Voir AFRIQUE DU SUD

Wort

L'extrait de malt dont la fermentation donne le whisky de malt. Prononcer *wourt.*
Voir WHISKY ; SCOTCH

Würtemberg

État allemand de Bade-Würtemberg. Superficie : 9 600 ha environ. 51 % de vins rouges, 49 % de vins blancs.

Situation : La région vinicole qui porte le nom de cet État est constituée par la vallée du Neckar (qui s'écoule vers le nord puis le nord-ouest, de Stuttgart à Mannheim, lieu de confluence avec le Rhin) et de la vallée de ses six tributaires.

Après bien des revers, les vins du Würtemberg s'améliorèrent en qualité durant le dernier siècle. Le remplacement des anciennes vignes par du Riesling et d'autres variétés nobles y contibuera également. L'expansion des villes et zones industrielles ont considérablement réduit la surface plantée en vignes. Les masses d'air tiède et humide venant des mers et océans rencontrent dans le Würtemberg les masses d'air froid venant du centre de l'Eurasie. Il en résulte des changements soudains et violents de température.

Les vignobles sont éparpillés entre les vallées du fleuve Neckar et de ses affluents. Stuttgart et Heilbronn sont les villes principales de la région. Mais, si l'on ne tient compte que du vin, Weinsberg est importante car la plus vieille école œnologique et station expérimentale d'Allemagne y est située. C'est aussi le plus grand domaine viticole de la région. Celle-ci se divise en 5 districts (Bereiche), dont deux sont très petits : le Württembergischer Bodensee et le Oberer Neckar. Le cœur traditionnel de la région s'étend entre les districts de Remstal-Stuttgart, Württembergisches Unterland et Kocher-Jagst-Tauber.

Variétés de raisin : Riesling (24 %), Trollinger, bonne variété rouge que l'on ne trouve que dans la région (23 %), Müllerrebe, appelé aussi Schwarzriesling (Pinot Meunier) (13 %), Müller-Thurgau (10 %), Kerner, croisement de Trollinger et Riesling développé à Weinsberg (9 %), Limberger (6 %).

Le produit le plus célèbre des viniculteurs du Würtemberg est certainement le Schillerwein, vin aromatique d'un rose clair. Son aspect ressemble aux autres rosés européens, mais il en diffère par sa vinification : le Schillerwein est fait à partir de raisins rouges et blancs mêlés ensemble avant d'être pressurés ; le mélange est ensuite fermenté. « Schillern » fait allusion à un jeu de couleurs. Ce vin est célèbre et fort demandé dans sa région de production.

Les sols sont variés : loess, argile, terreau, marne rouge et pierres calcaires dans la vallée du Neckar. Ils sont, en général, profonds, riches et produisent des vins qui se vantent d'être robustes.

Ici, comme dans les environs de Bade, les coopératives jouent un rôle très important dans la production du vin parce que la plupart des viticulteurs sont des négociants amateurs ou à temps partiel, dont l'exploitation ne dépasse pas 0,5 ha. Sur les 16 500 vignerons, 11 % fabriquent eux-mêmes leur vin. La majorité d'entre eux livrent leur raisin aux coopératives. La production moyenne annuelle est de 900 000 hl (10 millions de caisses). La consommation locale est élevée ; en conséquence, on trouve peu de vin du Würtemberg hors de la région et encore moins à l'étranger.

En plus des vins des Caves Centrales (Zentralkellerei) à Möglingen et des petites coopératives, les producteurs suivants offrent des vins de bonne qualité : Schlosskellerei Affaltrach, Weingut Graf Adelmann, Gräfl. von Bentzel-Sturmfeder'sches Weingut, Schlossgut Hohoenbeilstein, Fürst zu Hohenlohe-Öhringen'sche Schlosskellerei, von Stapf's-ches Weingut, Wüttembergische Hofkammerkellerei, et le Staatl. Lehr-und Versuchsanstalt à Weinsberg.

Voir APPENDICE B

Würzburg

Centre vinicole de Franconie *(voir ce nom)* qui produit les vins de Stein.

Wynberg

Secteur de la province du Cap qui produisit un des premiers vins d'Afrique du Sud *(voir ce nom)*.

X

Xérès (Sherry en anglais) (Jerez en espagnol)

Renommé et célébré depuis le temps de Shakespeare, le Xérès éclipse dans l'esprit de la plupart des gens tous les autres vins espagnols. C'est un vin viné : on lui ajoute de l'eau-de-vie de vin pour élever sa teneur en alcool à 15,5°, dans le cas des Finos et 18° dans celui des Olorosos. Les Espagnols eux-mêmes apprécient beaucoup mieux leur Xérès que les Portugais ne s'intéressent à leur Porto. Mais les Anglais et les Hollandais boivent beaucoup plus de Xérès que les Espagnols (cependant moins qu'autrefois) ; le Xérès s'exporte aussi de plus en plus en Europe jusqu'à la crise du Xérès au début des années 80. Les grandes maisons mondialement connues continuèrent à vendre alors que les moins importantes souffrirent.

Les vignobles de Xérès sont situés autour de la ville de Jerez de la Frontera, au sud de Séville dans la région la plus pittoresque d'Espagne. De même que Séville est une ville d'olives et de taureaux, Jerez (qui fut autrefois un centre de trafic d'or et de grands singes de Barbarie) est une ville de chevaux et de vin. Pendant le Festival de Pâques, les taureaux de combat et les matadors à cheval se rendent de Séville à Jerez et l'on voit de jeunes caballeros coiffés du chapeau gris de Cordoue, chevaucher avec de superbes filles en croupe, ou conduire des petites voitures découvertes tirées par des chevaux. Il y a seulement quelques années, malgré la grande activité de ses *bodegas,* Jerez, ville aux maisons blanches pleines de majesté et aux balcons en fer forgé, épargnée par l'expansion commerciale croissante, semblait sommeiller sous le soleil ardent. Aujourd'hui, la grande autoroute de Cadix-Séville a été construite dans les alentours et il règne partout une grande effervescence. La demande en Xérès fit un bond foudroyant et, avec la hausse des prix et des exportations, certaines des grandes firmes se développèrent. Pedro Domecq, par exemple, créa une société de contrôle au Luxembourg, la Domecq International, chargée de veiller sur ses nombreux intérêts — dont l'un était un investissement en participation avec Seagrams dans une grande firme de Rioja. En dépit de la demande croissante — et de l'amélioration de la qualité de certains produits concurrents à l'étranger — le Consejo Regulador, l'organe officiel qui contrôle le Xérès et sa Denominación de Origen, veille à ce que les stocks ne diminuent pas de plus de 40 % par an. Il espère empêcher la quantité de s'accroître au détriment de la qualité. Cependant les viniculteurs de Jerez ont encore la chance de pouvoir augmenter la superficie de leurs vignobles. Jerez compte officiellement 18 500 ha de vignes qui produisent près de 1,5 million d'hl (16,5 millions de caisses) du célèbre vin.

Aujourd'hui, le charme du Xérès et le mystère de son vieillissement restent toujours aussi vivants, les *bodegas* et *feria*, continuent d'attirer de nombreux visiteurs de Jerez. Le vin, l'élément essentiel de la vie économique de cette ville, doit son nom au latin *xeres* et à l'arabe *cherrisch* qui est devenu en anglais *sherry.* On cultive la vigne dans la région depuis que les Phéniciens y fondèrent une colonie plus de mille ans avant notre ère. Puis vinrent les Grecs, ensuite les Romains qui gouvernèrent le pays pendant des siècles. Plus tard, les envahisseurs Vandales donnèrent à toute la province le nom d'Andalousie. Les Maures arrivèrent en 711. Les chrétiens ne reconquièrent Jerez que vers 1264. Elle fut longtemps sur la ligne de démarcation entre chrétiens et musulmans et c'est à cela qu'elle doit son nom de Jerez de la Frontera.

Beaucoup plus tard, au XIXe siècle seulement, l'exportation du Xérès arriva à son apogée et la ville jouit alors d'une grande prospérité. Mais vers la fin du siècle la mode du Xérès déclina et le phylloxéra atteignit l'Andalousie. Cette maladie de la vigne — qui détruisit la plupart des vignobles d'Europe entre 1885 et 1900 — et les variations du goût public menacèrent la prospérité de Jerez. Pendant quelques années les exportations tombèrent lamentablement. Par bonheur elles devaient reprendre.

Le Xérès n'est qualifié ni par millésimes ni par crus. La notion d'âge disparaît dans le système de la *solera*, grâce auquel un vieil et bon Xérès éduque un vin plus jeune et cru. Les noms de crus n'existent pas pour deux raisons : 1) presque tous les Xérès sont obtenus par mélange de vins de plusieurs *pagos* (secteurs) différents ; 2) les secteurs intéressants sont divisés en tant de vignobles différents, donc entre tant de propriétaires, qu'aucun ne peut prétendre posséder un droit exclusif sur le vin.

Néanmoins, le lieu d'origine importe. 60 % du stock de toute firme doit avoir été acheté dans la Zona de Jerez Superior, qu'on appelle aussi le triangle et dont les pointes sont Jerez de la Frontera, Sanlúcar de Barrameda et Puerto de Santa Maria. C'est dans cette zone que se trouve le meilleur sol, nommé *albariza* : calcaire blanc dont le composant sédimentaire nourrit la vigne et la protège de la sécheresse estivale en formant à la surface une croûte dure sous laquelle subsiste de l'humidité. Les célèbres *pagos* de Macharnudo, Carrascal, Anina, Balbaina, Los Tercios et Miraflores, Martin Miguel et Charrudo à l'est qui produisirent les meilleurs Manzanillas, sont situés à l'intérieur de ce triangle. Les sols d'intérêt secondaire sont le *barro* et *l'arena*. Le premier contient aussi du calcaire, mais fortement mélangé à de l'argile et du sable ; le second est sablonneux et contient alumine et silice. On trouve ces sols dans les autres régions productrices de Xérès ; mais la zone supérieure produit le meilleur vin.

Tous les Xérès proviennent de la zone du Xérès qui comprend les villes de Jerez de la Frontera, Puerto de Santa Maria et Sanlúcar de Barrameda. Les vins de toutes les autres villes, dont les plus importantes sont Trebujena, Chipiona, Rota, Puerto Real et Chiclana de la Frontera (toutes situées dans la province de Cadix) doivent, pour avoir droit au nom de Xérès, vieillir dans les trois villes délimitant la zone supérieure de Xérès. La zone supérieure de Xérès.

Vignobles, vignes et vendanges

On dit volontiers à Jerez : « *Niñas y viñas son malas de guardar* », autrement dit : « Il est difficile de surveiller filles et vignes. »

Il y a à cela une bonne raison : le Palomino dont est fait 90 % du Xérès est un des rares raisins à grand vin du monde qui convienne aussi pour la table et pour la dégustation à la vigne même. Voilà pourquoi on trouve dans les vignobles de la région d'étranges *bien te veo* (« je te vois bien ») : petites huttes bâties comme des miradors, d'où un surveillant pouvait, autrefois, repérer quiconque volait du raisin.

Outre le Palomino, on cultive aussi

autour de Jerez les raisins Pedro Ximénez et Moscatel en quantité négligeable. Cette abondance apparente de variétés peut tromper le profane, d'autant plus que dans la région on ne donne pas moins de huit noms différents au Palomino. Listan est le plus courant : c'est celui qu'on utilise le plus généralement dans les crus de Manzanilla avoisinant Sanlúcar. On trouve aussi les noms Trempilla et Palomino de Jerez. Quel que soit son nom, cette vigne produit de grosses grappes de raisins clairs et gras qui pendent comme des essaims d'abeilles et mûrissent autant du fait de la réflexion de la chaleur par la croûte dure de l'*albariza* que du fait des rayons solaires qui les frappent directement. La taille de la vigne ne laisse qu'une seule branche, soutenue par un bâton fourchu en raison du poids des grappes. Pour faire durer la vigne et lui permettre d'attendre une quarantaine d'années, on limite la production en la taillant plus court qu'on ne le faisait dans la période pré-phylloxérienne. Si l'on s'efforce de prolonger l'existence des ceps, c'est parce que la replantation coûte cher. Les vignes sont plantées par lopins disséminés sur un relief légèrement accidenté où l'on cultive aussi céréales, tournesol et canne à sucre. On ne les voit pas des routes principales ni du chemin de fer. Les petites maisons peintes à la chaux, en bordure des sentiers conduisant à la vigne, sont groupées comme des annexes, autour des grands chais où l'on traite le vin. Au printemps on voyait jadis les mules marcher à pas lents dans les sillons, leurs bâts alourdis par des urnes arabes, en terre cuite, teintes en bleu brillant par le sulfate de cuivre. Aux vendanges, on ramasse les raisins avec des hottes en bois ou en plastique pour les porter sur de grandes nattes d'alfa, rondes, pareilles à des plateaux où ils s'amoncellent en tas et, pour certains vins, en une heure ou deux, toute la cour du chai est couverte de monticules de raisins qu'on laisse s'ensoleiller jusqu'à ce que le rapport du sucre et de l'eau atteigne le point voulu.

Il y a peu de temps encore, on pouvait voir les vendanges comme on les pratiqua pendant des siècles : pour presser les raisins, ceux-ci étaient foulés dans de grandes cuves de bois appelées *lagares* par des hommes chaussés de souliers spéciaux à semelle cloutée. Aujourd'hui, le pressurage automatique s'est substitué à cette ancienne coutume. La première fermentation du Xérès est extrêmement tumultueuse. Elle dure de trois jours à une semaine. La mousse bouillonne au-dessus de la bonde comme au goulot d'une bouteille de Champagne qu'on vient d'ouvrir. Après cette première phase, la fermentation se poursuit plus lentement pendant deux mois durant lesquels on laisse la bonde ouverte afin que le vin soit en contact avec l'air.

Quand la fermentation prend fin, le Xérès est absolument sec ; c'est-à-dire que la totalité des sucres fermentescibles a été convertie en alcool. En décembre ou janvier, on soutire le vin et on le hume, afin d'apprécier sa qualité et de décider en quel type de vin on le traitera. Le Xérès possède un attribut mystérieux : sans aucune intervention humaine, il tend rapidement à devenir soit un Fino sec et léger, soit un Oloroso, plus sain et plus sombre. C'est à la *flor* — ces fleurs de moisissures microscopiques forment une mousse pâle sur le vin — que l'on reconnaît le Fino. Un vin destiné à devenir un Oloroso n'a pas de *flor*, ou très peu et dans ce cas elle peut être éliminée par une injection d'eau-de-vie. Dès que le vin nouveau montre une nette tendance à devenir Fino ou Oloroso, il est soutiré (c'est-à-dire transvasé dans un fût), sa teneur en alcool testée, et si celle-ci s'avère inférieure au niveau requis, il sera légèrement viné avec de l'eau-de-vie de vin (jusqu'à environ 15,5 % pour un futur Fino ou Amontillado et 18 % environ pour l'Oloroso). L'addition d'eau-de-vie distinguera définitivement les deux types de Xérès. Après un court repos, le vin est de nouveau goûté et son fût marqué à la craie : un trait vertical (*raya*) signifie que le vin est bon pour un Fino ou Amontillado, qu'il a un bouquet net et assez de corps ; deux traits : le vin est assez bon pour un Oloroso ; trois traits : il présente un léger défaut ; deux traits verticaux et deux horizontaux, en croix : le vin n'est bon qu'à être distillé. Pendant un temps variable, un an maximum, le vin repose dans l'*añada* (fût de première année) ; ces fûts sont entreposés dans la *bodega*, chai spacieux et aéré. Le Xérès est placé sous la surveillance constante du *capataz* (maître de chai) qui, de nouveau, marque chaque fût à la craie : Y (*palma*, un Fino délicat) ; Ұ (*palma cortada*, un Fino plus plein) ; - (*raya*, type Oloroso) ; // - (*Dos rayas*, sélectionné à l'origine comme Fino et ayant perdu sa *flor*, devient un Oloroso). Lorsque le vin termine son séjour en añada, on le transfère dans la *criadera* (nursery), qui est le premier stade du système *solera*.

Solera

Outre la *flor* mystérieuse, ce qu'il y a de plus intéressant au sujet du Xérès, c'est la méthode particulière par laquelle on le maintient dans sa meilleure forme. Le très vieux et très bon Xérès a la vertu de pouvoir éduquer et améliorer le plus jeune. C'est pour cette raison qu'on conserve les vieux vins dans les plus vieux fûts du chai que les vignerons appellent *solera*. Les fûts y sont rangés par ordre d'âge et par catégorie. La plus vieille classe de la solera est celle qu'on appelle *solera*. La seconde en âge est la première *criadera*, celle qui vient immédiatement après la seconde *criadera*, et ainsi de suite. Quand on tire le vin de la solera, on prélève moins du tiers dans chaque fût. Puis on fait passer le vin de la première criadera dans la solera ; celui de la seconde criadera dans la première, etc. La merveille de ce système, c'est que les plus vieux fûts contiennent éternellement du vin de même qualité.

Prenons par exemple un fût de 1888. C'est à peine s'il y reste une cuillerée de vin de sa vendange initiale. Mais chaque vin qu'on y a versé au cours des années a subi une éducation et une transformation qui tend à prendre le caractère du vin en fût. Cela en fait un 1888, et ceux qui y viendront encore seront instruits de la même manière. Grâce à ce procédé il est possible non seulement de conserver au vin pendant des années la même qualité et les mêmes caractéristiques, mais en outre, en revigorant le Fino chaque année avec des vins plus jeunes, on l'empêche de perdre sa fraîcheur.

Dans les bodegas de Xérès

On conserve le Xérès (Sherry) dans des sanctuaires frais et obscurs, au-dessus de la surface du sol et tous orientés vers la mer. Telles sont les *bodegas* des firmes productrices de grands vins où tout le monde est le bienvenu. On ne demande à l'invité que d'aimer le Xérès et de désirer apprendre. On l'invitera à goûter un large échantillonnage de vins. Le guide ou le propriétaire lui-même maniera adroitement la souple *venencia* (tasse d'argent au long manche de baleine flexible). Le profane se fera ainsi une idée des mystères de la *flor*. Pour traverser cette croûte blanche il faut la frapper violemment avec la tasse d'argent afin que celle-ci atteigne le vin. La *venencia* disparaît dans la bonde du tonneau. Un instant après on entend nettement un « poc ». Ce bruit indique que la baleine s'est brusquement détendue en crevant la croûte. Verser le vin de la *venencia* dans un verre paraît simple ; en réalité ça ne l'est pas du tout. L'expert saisit l'anse flexible entre le pouce et l'index et laisse un long jet de vin décrire une parabole pour tomber dans le verre qu'il tient dans sa main libre. Quand l'amateur essaie d'en faire autant, le Xérès s'écoule infailliblement dans sa manche.

La *flor* (fleur, en espagnol) est la moisissure blanche qui se forme à la surface du vin en contact avec l'air. En vertu d'un lien mystérieux avec la vigne, elle épaissit par magie au printemps, quand le cep bourgeonne, et en automne, quand le raisin achève de mûrir. D'abord mince et floconneuse comme la neige, elle épaissit comme la pellicule qui se forme sur de la crème laissée trop longtemps à l'air libre. Après sa période de floraison, elle tombe au fond du vin.

L'air fait « tourner » les vins, les rend acides et en fait du vinaigre. Mais le Xérès et les vins du Jura en France se nourrissent d'air pendant leur vieillissement. S'ils en étaient privés, ils n'auraient pas leur saveur caractéristique. Les énormes bodegas voûtées de Jerez sont ouvertes aux deux extrémités pour que l'air y passe librement et nourrisse la *flor*. Deux micro-organismes différents forment cette croûte. L'un est la bactérie *Acetobacter* qui transforme le vin en vinaigre, et l'autre, la levure de la fermentation. Dans des conditions normales, c'est l'*Acetobacter* qui apparaît et voilà pourquoi tous les vins se dégradent au contact de l'air. Or il se trouve que dans la région de Jerez (comme dans le Jura) c'est le second de ces deux micro-organismes qui prend le pas et parvient à donner cette légèreté, cette sécheresse, ce mordant, qui fait le Xérès Fino. Le degré du vin varie entre 11,5° et 15,5° et la température de conservation entre 14 et 20°. Les Espagnols croient que cette levure est le même *Saccharomyces* qui fait fermenter le vin et en même temps forme la *flor* qui en voile la surface et absorbe tout le sucre subsistant après la fermentation. Aujourd'hui, les Finos sont soigneusement embouteillés sous nitrogène et les bouchons de lièges ont été remplacés par des capsules en acier pour empêcher l'oxydation.

Les types de Xérès

Tous les Xérès dérivent du type Fino, de l'Amontillado, et du type Oloroso. Le Fino ou Amontillado est celui sur lequel la *flor* s'est pleinement développée ; l'Oloroso, un vin qui n'a pas révélé de dispositions à nourrir une *flor* abondante. La petite pellicule à peine existante est alors supprimée par l'addition d'une plus forte dose d'eau-de-vie de vin que n'en a reçu le Fino. Certes l'action de l'homme se manifeste ici. Mais il n'opte pour le Fino ou pour l'Oloroso que selon une décision prise par le vin lui-même et nul ne sait pourquoi le contenu de tel baril entend être traité en Fino alors que celui du baril voisin — qui semble pourtant identique, provenant de la même vendange et du même vignoble — veut devenir Oloroso. A cela l'homme ne peut rien qu'attendre, observer et traiter le vin comme celui-ci en manifeste le désir.

Fino

Le Fino est un Xérès très clair, à peine doré et le plus léger de sa famille. Le nez du vin est prononcé et nettement caractérisé : pareil à l'odeur d'une pomme fraîchement cueillie ; on y perçoit aussi un soupçon d'amande. L'idéal serait de ne jamais mettre le Fino en bouteille car, lorsqu'on le boit frais tiré au fût, il n'a pas passé un seul instant de sa vie sans être au contact avec l'air. Moins viné que l'Oloroso, le Fino est d'un goût plus frais. Il peut survivre quelques années en bouteille, selon la température et les conditions de conservation. Mais il ne s'améliore pas du tout et finira par perdre sa fraîcheur. En raison de sa constitution délicate, le Fino est plus viné pour l'exportation que pour la consommation intérieure : il titre 16 à 17° dans le premier cas et 16 et 17° dans le second. Mais cette augmentation de sa teneur en alcool diminue son bouquet.

Quand vous achetez une bouteille de Fino, il vous est impossible de savoir son âge car le Xérès, toujours mis en bouteille juste au moment de l'expédition, n'est jamais daté quoique certains négociants estiment que la date de mise en bouteille devrait figurer sur l'étiquette afin de surveiller sa tendance à l'oxydation. Étant donné les circonstances, il vaudrait toujours mieux acheter le Fino juste au moment de le boire et à un fournisseur dont on peut être sûr qu'il ne l'aura pas gardé trop longtemps sur ses rayons. Aussitôt débouché, le Fino a tendance à faner. C'est pourquoi à Jerez on l'achète généralement en demi-bouteille.

Manzanilla

Le Manzanilla est à la fois un Xérès Fino — le plus léger des Finos — et un vin de type particulier. Il se forme en solera, développe sa *flor*, provient de raisin Palomino cultivé sur le même sol de calcaire sédimentaire que le Fino, mais à 23 km de Jerez, autour de la ville côtière de Sanlúcar de Barrameda. C'est le vent de la mer qui lui donne sa particularité : un rien d'amertume, surtout dans l'arrière-goût. Le Manzanilla est le plus clair des Finos. En Espagne, on le vend généralement au verre, tiré du baril. C'est alors un vin incroyablement léger et d'une sécheresse qui frise l'âpreté. Bien des Espagnols le préfèrent à tout autre. Dans tous les bars où l'on boit en piquant oignons, olives, et crevettes on peut entendre commander du Manzanilla. Phénomène qui démontre l'étroite parenté entre Manzanilla et Fino : si l'on porte un jeune Manzanilla dans une bodega de Jerez pour l'y mûrir, il devient un Xérès Fino ; par contre, un jeune Xérès Fino, emporté à Sanlúcar de Barrameda et éduqué dans une bodega de Manzanilla, ne devient pas un Manzanilla. Ce comportement étrange s'explique par l'influence de l'air marin à Sanlúcar. En soufflant à travers les bodegas de cette ville, il donne une pointe de sel à laquelle on reconnaît infailliblement le Manzanilla.

Dans la petite ville de Sanlúcar de Barrameda, aux maisons blanchies à la chaux, on distingue trois types de Manzanilla classés par âge : 1. Manzanilla Fino. 2. Manzanilla Pasada. 3. Manzanilla Olorosa. Bref, les Manzanilla sont classés à Sanlúcar exactement de la même manière que les Xérès à Jerez. Les 3 000 ha de vignes produisent environ 20 000 hl (plus de 200 000 caisses) de Manzanilla par an.

Palma

Nom utilisé très souvent en Espagne à la place de Fino, et dont on use depuis quelque temps pour le Fino d'exportation, de qualité particulièrement nette et délicate. La Palma est coté 1, 2, 3 ou 4. Plus ce chiffre est élevé, plus il est vieux. Néanmoins ces degrés ont une signification différente selon les bodegas.

Amontillado

Xérès de couleur plus foncée et titrant 1 à 3° de plus que le Fino, soit en moyenne 18° quoique, avec l'âge, il puisse aller jusqu'à 20 et 21°. Le Fino conservé en fût et qui n'est pas rafraîchi de temps en temps par un vin jeune peut devenir de l'Amontillado. Étant donné qu'il y a une forte demande pour l'Amontillado, on surveille les Fino : lorsque leur *flor* devient plus foncée et que leur goût de noix s'accentue, on marque le baril d'un signe indiquant qu'il ne faut pas le rafraîchir. Dans une certaine *bodega,* où l'influence anglaise est prédominante, on marque le baril d'un simple « no » à la craie.

L'Amontillado n'est pas toujours vendu à l'état pur. On en trouve à l'étranger qui a été sucré. On peut l'avoir coupé de Fino ou d'autre vin, mais ce mélange doit comporter une bonne part d'Amontillado, sinon le goût caractéristique de noix disparaîtrait. En général, plus cette saveur est perceptible plus l'Amontillado est un vin authentique. Ce vin est sec, net, vivace, tant pour le nez que pour le palais. Il existe des Amontillado Fino, qui se situent sur la ligne de démarcation entre les deux types. N'oublions pas que ces frontières ont un caractère assez arbitraire et qu'elles sont plutôt une nécessité du commerce car tous les types de Xérès se ressemblent et on passe d'une variété à l'autre par une gradation difficile à percevoir. Dans une des plus grandes bodegas de Jerez, on offre parfois aux visiteurs de marque une rangée de 34 verres contenant des Xérès dont la robe va de la couleur paille à l'acajou et qui titrent entre 15,2° et 21°. En fait de saveur, ils sont légers et frais à une extrémité et ont une saveur très prononcée à l'autre. Mais tous seront secs. A l'état naturel, aucun Xérès n'est doux.

Oloroso

L'Oloroso est un Xérès plus corsé, voire vineux, que l'Amontillado. Comme son nom l'indique, il a un fort bouquet : l'odeur de noix et la saveur sont très accentuées dans les meilleures bouteilles. Mais sa caractéristique la plus nette est la *gordura* : une riche vinosité et une opulence qu'on incline à traduire mot à mot par : grosseur. Cette sensation de richesse dure longtemps sur le palais et donne une illusion de douceur. En réalité — bien qu'on vende des Oloroso sucrés, soit sous le nom d'Oloroso, soit comme Amoroso ou Cream — le véritable Oloroso naturel est sec.

Voilà seulement quelque 150 ans que le public commença à s'intéresser au Xérès rendu plus léger par sa *flor.* Jusqu'alors, l'Espagne n'exportait que de l'Oloroso et la *flor* qui devait déjà apparaître sur le vin en ce temps-là était éliminée par addition d'eau-de-vie de vin.

L'attrait que le Fino exerça sur le public amena les gens de Jerez à produire deux types de vin différents selon qu'en sa prime jeunesse il présente une tendance plus ou moins marquée à fleurir. Dès qu'un vin manifeste l'intention de devenir Oloroso, on lui donne une plus forte dose d'eau-de-vie qu'au Fino. Elle supprime la *flor.*

Le nez de l'Oloroso authentique doit être absolument net. En général il titre entre 18 et 20°, mais avec l'âge il peut en atteindre 21 ou 22°.

Les Oloroso ont une belle teinte dorée et cet or devient plus foncé avec les années, indiquant ainsi que le vin a vieilli en fût. Plus corsé que le Fino, l'Oloroso supportera mieux la bouteille, mais pas plus que les autres Xérès, il ne s'y améliorera.

Palo Cortado

Le Palo Cortado est un Xérès rare : un Oloroso qui présente les caractéristiques du groupe Fino. En réalité il règne une certaine imprécision à son sujet et chaque *bodega* semble donner à cette appellation une signification différente. Chez l'un des plus importants producteurs de Xérès, le Palo Cortado est un Oloroso à nez d'Amontillado.

Un véritable Palo Cortado est un vin millésimé, ce qui est tout à fait exceptionnel. Précisons que c'est une chose qui se produit d'elle-même, spontanément, et ne peut pas être obtenue par coupage. On admet néanmoins que le vin authentique de ce type doit avoir vieilli au moins pendant 20 ans et qu'il n'est donc pas praticable au point de vue commercial. En fait, les vins de ce type qu'on trouve sur le marché ne font que ressembler au Palo Cortado.

Raya

Xérès très commun qu'on ne trouve pas à l'étranger. Raya signifie Oloroso de moindre qualité et grossier.

Amoroso

L'Amoroso est un Oloroso de couleur foncée, et sucré. On a créé ce style de vin pour complaire au goût anglais, mais il est inconnu en Espagne. (Quoiqu'en Espagne le Xérès soit toujours pris sec, il est d'usage d'ajouter un adoucissant à bien des types de Xérès destinés à l'exportation. Le meilleur de ces agents est le Pedro Ximenez ou P.X.)

L'Amoroso fort charnu, connu aussi sous le nom de East India, doit cette appellation à une pratique remontant aux temps de la navigation à voile : on envoyait le Xérès en fûts faire l'aller retour jusqu'aux Indes orientales. L'air marin, le roulis constant étaient considérés comme bénéfiques et l'on disait : « Quand il a le mal de mer, le Xérès vaut le double. »

Le Brown Sherry (Xérès marron) est un Amoroso très foncé et doux, vraisemblablement moins cher que l'East India. Les Xérès sont quelques fois rendus plus foncés par l'addition de *color* : un mélange de moût de raisin frais et concentré, qui donne la teinte la plus demandée sur certains marchés. Le Brown Sherry est en général un coupage de vieil Oloroso et de P.X. avec un soupçon de *color*.

Cream Sherry (Xérès crème)

Le Xérès de ce type est un Oloroso très doux. Il a été créé et produit à Bristol, en Angleterre, et il est aussi actuellement extrêmement propulaire aux États-Unis. Certains Cream Sherries sont mis en bouteille à Bristol ; il s'agit d'Oloroso expédiés de Jerez en fûts et traités en Angleterre. Mais désormais on produit aussi des crèmes en Espagne pour satisfaire une demande croissante. Toutefois, le Bristol Cream et le Bristol Milk sont, évidemment, mis en bouteille à Bristol.

En Angleterre, les Xérès foncés et doux peuvent ne pas être servis en apéritif mais à la fin des repas, pour remplacer le Porto.

Tio Pepe

Il ne s'agit pas de types mais de marques (comme La Ina) de Xérès sec, c'est-à-dire de Fino de même que le Dry Sack et le Double Century sont des marques de Xérès demi-sec. On sert la plupart des Xérès à la température ambiante : chambrés. Mais l'on doit rafraîchir légèrement l'Amontillado sec et frapper le Fino et le Manzanilla.

X.O.

Le type de Cognac le plus vieux que l'on trouve sur le marché en général. Cette mention est surtout utilisée par la Maison Hennessy, de Cognac. Les eaux-de-vie de vin millésimées sont des exceptions extrêmement rares. En général, la date inscrite sur l'étiquette d'une bouteille indique un type plutôt qu'un véritable millésime. Pourtant, les X.O. prétendent souvent avoir vingt ans de fût et ils les ont, en effet, fréquemment.

Comme les autres spiritueux, les eaux-de-vie de vin ne vieillissent pas en bouteille. Au sujet de leur âge, *voir l'article* Cognac, à sa place dans l'ordre alphabétique.

Xynisteri

Un des raisins qui dominent dans la vinification du Commandaria (Commanderie), le célèbre vin de dessert de Chypre. L'autre variété de raisin est le Mavron.

Y

Yakima (Vallée de)

Région vinicole de l'État de Washington où les vignes européennes prospèrent.

Yalumba

Célèbre vignoble de la vallée de l'Eden, en Australie du Sud, qui produit un vin blanc appelé Carte d'Or.

Voir AUSTRALIE

Yam (Vin de)

Breuvage obtenu en faisant fermenter des racines d'igname, en Afrique et en Amérique du Sud.

Yamanashi

Une des principales régions vinicoles du Japon.

Voir JAPON

Yayin

Mot qui, dans la Bible, désigne le vin. Il s'agit à coup sûr du véritable vin de raisin.

Yecla

Voir ESPAGNE

Yeso

Poudre riche en gypse utilisée en Espagne pour le plâtrage de certains vins.

Voir PLATRAGE

Yougoslavie

La Yougoslavie, république fédérale des Slaves du Sud, réunit Croatie, Slovénie (autrefois provinces de l'Empire austro-hongrois), Serbie (qui fut le centre d'attraction), Monténégro, Macédoine, Bosnie-Herzégovine. Elle vient au septième rang de l'Europe pour la superficie plantée de vignes.

En bien des régions de ce pays, le vin justifie le truisme selon lequel il n'a jamais aussi bon goût que là où il est fait. En Macédoine et au Monténégro — avec leurs montagnes presque inaccessibles et qui ont conservé leurs caractéristiques ancestrales presque intactes —, les vins que l'on boit sur place bénéficient du décor : coutumes locales, atmosphère pittoresque, légendes romanesques ; souvent aussi : les fûts dans lesquels on les conserve et les ustensiles employés pour les servir. Les fiasques rondes, en bois sculpté, les coupes ouvragées, entourées de lanières tressées et parfois munies d'une courroie qui permet de les porter sur soi, tout contribue à donner à la dégustation du vin un attrait exceptionnel. Il n'est pourtant pas indispensable de visiter les régions les plus reculées de la Yougoslavie pour connaître le charme de ses vins. Bien des milliers de touristes goûtent les rouges de Dalmatie à Dubrovnik : ville blanche entourée de murs, mais fort accessible. Ils peuvent boire aussi le rouge charnu, tirant 13 à 15°, du Sud comme le Dingač (prononcer Dinegatch) le Postup, le Plavac ou le blanc de Slovénie, dont on cultive les vignes au pied des alpes dans le nord du pays.

Les vins de Dalmatie n'ont probablement pas encore atteint toute la qualité dont ils pourraient faire preuve. Ceux de Slovénie sont mieux au point. On trouve d'ailleurs fréquemment en Grande-Bretagne, au Canada et aux États-Unis les blancs de Slovénie, les rouges, blancs et rosés de Serbie, quelques vins d'Istrie et, depuis peu, les rouges et blancs secs de Macédoine. La Yougoslavie exporte surtout vers les deux Allemagne, la Tchécoslovaquie, la Pologne et la Grande-Bretagne.

Histoire du vin yougoslave

L'origine du vin yougoslave remonte très loin dans le temps, comme celle du vin de tous les pays méditerranéens et balkaniques. Selon certains historiens, la culture de la vigne et la vinification furent apportées de Thrace au-delà des montagnes de Macédoine, il y a plus de 4 000 ans. D'autres prétendent que des marins apportèrent des vignes d'Asie Mineure par la Méditerranée. On sait à coup sûr que les habitants de la Dalmatie et de l'Istrie faisaient du vin sous la domination grecque, et les Slovènes sous celle des Romains. On trouve partout en Slovénie et en Croatie des vestiges de l'Empire romain. Souvent, pampres et grappes se retrouvent en motifs de décoration. Dans plusieurs des langues parlées en Yougoslavie, les termes courants de viticulture et viniculture dérivent du

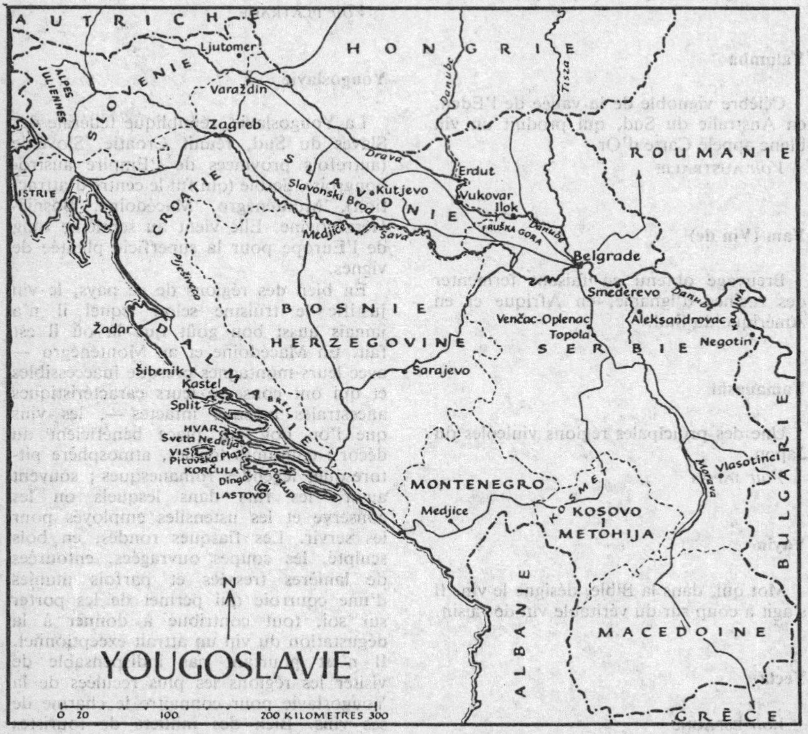

latin. Dans les musées de deux villes aussi éloignées l'une de l'autre que Dubrovnik, en Dalmatie, et Ptuj, en Slovénie — à moins de 80 km de la frontière autrichienne — le touriste peut admirer bien des amphores à vin grecques et romaines et d'autres objets usuels mis au jour à la suite de fouilles pratiquées dans les environs.

En Yougoslavie, comme dans bien d'autres pays d'Europe, la culture de la vigne et la vinification du jus de raisin furent encouragées par les seigneurs féodaux et les monastères pendant le Moyen Age. Au temps des croisades les vins d'Ohrid, à l'extrémité sud de la Yougoslavie, et ceux d'Albanie étaient fort appréciés en Europe.

Mais n'oublions pas que pendant des siècles la Yougoslavie appartint aux Turcs. Sarajevo, située à peu près au centre du pays, est encore aujourd'hui une ville typiquement turque. Les minarets en forme d'aiguille de ses quelque 70 ou 80 mosquées nous rappellent l'influence musulmane. Or le vin est interdit aux musulmans. Partout où les Turcs régnèrent, on abandonna la culture de la vigne qui ne reprit qu'après la libération de ces pays. Celle de la Yougoslavie dura de 1804 à 1912.

D'autre part, certains pays qui font actuellement partie de la fédération yougoslave ont appartenu pendant longtemps à l'Autriche. Ljutomer, par exemple, fit partie pendant des siècles de la province autrichienne de Styrie. Il en résulte que la viticulture et la viniculture du nord de la Yougoslavie sont typiquement autrichiennes. De nos jours encore il y règne une certaine confusion parce que certains vins de cette région se taillèrent autrefois une réputation mondiale sous leur nom allemand, qu'on remplace actuellement par des appellations yougoslaves. Ainsi, le Ljutomer-Ljutomerčan un des vins yougoslaves les plus célèbres, porte le nom de sa ville d'origine, située à l'extrémité nord du pays, près des frontières autrichienne et hongroise ; mais il a d'abord été connu sous son nom autrichien : Luttenberger car Ljutomer s'appellait autrefois Luttenberg. On a longtemps cru que ce vin était autrichien. On ignore souvent que Luttenberger et Ljutomer, Ljutomerčan sont les noms d'un même vin.

Vignes et statistiques

Plus de 250 000 ha du territoire yougoslave sont plantés de vignes qui produisent 7,4 millions d'hl (82 millions de caisses) de vin par an, c'est-à-dire presque autant que la Grèce, la Hongrie et la Roumanie. La consommation annuelle moyenne est de 28 l par personne, soit 3 fois plus que l'Américain moyen. Le marché de l'exportation s'est développé ces dernières années ; on expédie aujourd'hui à l'étranger environ 1 100 000 hl (12 millions de caisses) de vin. On en importe très peu.

On cultive de nombreuses variétés de vigne en Yougoslavie. Au nord, où l'influence autrichienne se fait encore sentir, Riesling, Traminer, Burgundy, Veltliner et Sylvaner dominent ; on y trouve aussi Merlot, Muscat, Pinot Blanc et Sauvignon. En Dalmatie, on cultive Plavac ; en Serbie, Prokupac ; en Bosnie-Herzégovine, Zilavka et Blatina ; au Monténégro, Vranac. On trouve aussi en Yougoslavie des vignes indigènes, ainsi que des hybrides dont bon nombre furent plantées après les ravages catastrophiques du phylloxéra qui atteignit la Yougoslavie aux environs de 1900.

Régions vinicoles

La Yougoslavie naquit de la Première Guerre mondiale par l'union de six différents pays de langue slave : Serbie, Croatie, Slovénie, Bosnie-Herzégovine, Monténégro et la partie septentrionale de la Macédoine. Quoiqu'ils constituent un ensemble harmonieux, chacun conserve ses anciennes coutumes, et les vins de l'un diffèrent de ceux des autres. Voici leur part respective dans la production totale de la Yougoslavie : Serbie, 38 % ; Croatie, 30 % ; Slovénie, 8 % ; Macédoine, 20 % ; Bosnie-Herzégovine, 3 % ; Monténégro, quantité négligeable.

Serbie

La Serbie, avec près de 80 000 ha, produit de grandes quantités de vins de consommation courante. Depuis ces dernières années, l'on commence à trouver ces vins à l'étranger. Ils portent le nom du secteur d'où ils proviennent. La plus grande partie des vins serbes est faite avec du raisin Prokupac (lentement remplacé par les cépages importés Gamay et Cabernet) considéré comme fruit de la « vigne nationale » serbe. Voici quelques-unes des appellation les mieux connues :

Župa (prononcer Joupa). Dans ce secteur situé au centre de la Serbie, les collines fortement ensoleillées produisent une grande quantité de vin rouge, charnu, riche, lourd, mais manquant de race et de distinction. On y fait aussi un rosé qui, comme le rouge, est dû au raisin Prokupac. Les vignobles couvrent une grande surface. L'agglomération d'Aleksandrovac est le centre de cette zone. (En yougoslave, la terminaison « ac » se prononce « ats ». Prononcer, par exemple « prokupats » et « Aleksandrovats ».)

Krajina (prononcer Kraillina). Situé autour de Negotin, ce secteur se trouve à proximité des frontières roumaines et bulgares. On n'y produit presque que du rouge, fourni par un mélange de Prokupac, Skadarka et Začinak. Ces vins furent à un certain moment bien connus en France où on les expédia quand les ravages du phylloxéra atteignirent leur point culminant, à la fin du siècle dernier. La petite quantité de vin blanc produite par ce secteur porte le nom de la variété de raisin avec laquelle elle est faite, Bagrina de Krajina.

Vlasotinci. Au sud de la Serbie. Presque tous les vins sont rosés et proviennent du Prokupac et du Plovdina.

Venčac-Oplenac (prononcer : Ventchats-Oplenats). Située au nord de Župa, sur la Morava, cette région est le cœur de la province serbe appelée Šumadija (Chumadilla) où commença l'insurrection contre la domination turque, au début du siècle dernier. On y cultive la vigne autour de Topola et surtout les variétés Prokupac, Pinot Noir et Gamay, qui donnent des vins rouges et rosés. Le rosé d'Oplenac est bien connu. On commence à cultiver également du Pinot Chardonnay.

Smerderevo. Énorme zone vinicole au relief doucement accidenté, située sur la rive droite du Danube, à proximité de la frontière roumaine. On y produit du bon vin blanc fait avec du raisin Smedervka et Wälschriesling.

Vojvodine (25 000 ha de vignobles). Province autonome de Serbie située à l'est de la Slavonie croate, limitrophe de la Hongrie et de la Roumanie. Dans ce centre agricole important, on cultive des raisins de table et, surtout, des vignes à vins ; dans nombre de nouvelles plantations, les anciennes variétés indigènes sont remplacées par des cépages occidentaux de meilleure qualité. La région compte trois secteurs : *Fruška Gora*, petit mont boisé situé entre le Danube et la Save où l'on trouve de grands vignobles et de gigantesques entreprises vinicoles modernes. On y cultive du Wälschriesling, du Sémillon, du Traminer, du Pinot Blanc et du Sauvignon Blanc. Les meilleures zones sont Erdevik, Irig, Petrouardin, Indjija et Sremski Karlovci, qui, au siècle dernier — lorsque le secteur appartenait à la Hongrie —, faisaient un vin rouge appelé Carlowitz (Karlovice Rothwein), fort apprécié en Grande-Bretagne, en Autriche et aux Pays-Bas. On y produit maintenant des blancs sains, dont la qualité peut être comparée à ceux de la région slovène de Maribor. Autrefois, Vojvodine faisait aussi de bons vins rouges avec les raisins Skadarka et d'autres cépages indigènes. La politique actuelle du gouvernement consiste à replanter les vignes à vin blanc, et à remplacer les variétés indigènes à vin rouge par les cépages bourguignons Gamay et Pinot Noir. Pour le moment, on n'insiste pas sur la production du vin rouge. Les vins blancs principaux sont : Riesling, Traminer, Nepplanta, Sirmium et Zupljanka. A Sremski Karlovici, on faisait un vermouth local, appelé Bermet, depuis le XVIIIe siècle.

Le deuxième secteur de Vojvodine, *Subotička Peščara* se situe entre les fleuves Danube et Tisza. C'est une étendue de sable amendée, l'extension de la Grande Plaine hongroise, Alföld. Les plantations ont été quelque peu améliorées et comprennent aujourd'hui du Grüner Veltliner autrichien, du Wälschriesling, du Ezerjó et du Muscat Ottonel hongrois, ainsi qu'une bonne variété locale à vin blanc, appelée Kevedinka. Les vins rouges sont faits avec du Kadarka, du Pinot Noir et du Blaufränkisch. On ne produit pas de vins de grande qualité dans cette région, et il serait intéressant d'examiner les résultats qu'obtiendront les nouvelles plantations, dont la plupart n'en sont qu'au stade expérimental.

Le secteur du *Banat* a un climat bien particulier ; il est situé à l'extrémité sud-est de la Plaine de Pannonie, là où les vallonnements s'élèvent pour devenir les Alpes transylvaniennes. Vrsač, située dans ces vallonnements, est encore aujourd'hui un centre vinicole ; certains de ses vins seraient même de bonne qualité. Cette zone produit essentiellement du vin blanc, et l'on y cultive les mêmes vignes qu'à Fruška Gora, ainsi qu'une vigne locale du genre Riesling, appelée Banatski Rizling Kreaca.

La petite quantité de vin rouge est également produite avec du Merlot, du Cabernet Sauvignon, du Gamay et du Pinot Noir.

Kosmet. Autre province autonome de Serbie, limitrophe à l'Albanie et à la Macédoine. Les anciens Grecs furent les premiers à planter des vignes sur les vallonnements de ses montagnes. Les nouveaux vignobles furent replantés dans les années 60, bien après les ravages du phylloxéra à la fin du siècle dernier. On y cultive du Cabernet Sauvignon, du Cabernet Franc, du Gamay et du Pinot Noir. Ces variétés produisent un vin rouge assez agréable et fort apprécié dans plusieurs pays d'Europe occidentale. On fait un peu de vin blanc avec du Žilavka et du Wälschriesling. La région de Kosmet s'unit à la Macédoine pour former un seul grand secteur vinicole. Les régions de Serbie, de Kosmet et celles de Macédoine totalisent 150 000 ha de vignes.

Croatie

Il est commode de partager les vins de Croatie, dont le vignoble couvre une superficie d'environ 40 000 ha en deux catégories principales : ceux qui proviennent de la région intérieure, s'étendant de la vaste plaine du Danube, jusqu'aux montagnes dominant Zagreb entre la Drave et la Save ; et ceux de la côte Adriatique qui comprennent les vins de la partie autrefois italienne de l'Istrie, ainsi que de la fabuleuse côte dalmate.

La zone intérieure comprend les vallées du Danube, de la Drave et de la Save et se prolonge jusqu'au flanc des Alpes, en Slovénie, c'est-à-dire tout près du célèbre secteur vinicole de Ljutomer, sans doute le meilleur de Yougoslavie. Mais, cultivées sur terrain plat, les vignes donnent des vins qui ressemblent plutôt à ceux de Serbie. Légers, un peu acides, ils sont agréables mais sans race marquée, ni prétention d'ailleurs. Ceux qu'on trouve le plus fréquemment sont ceux de Plješivica (Plyechivitsa), Vinica (Vinitsa), Varaždin (Varajdine) et Medjugorica (Medjugoritsa).

Au nord-est de la Croatie, l'influence autrichienne s'y fait sentir. Traminer, Riesling, Sauvignon, Sémillon, y occupent une bonne place ; quand ils sont bien faits, leurs vins blancs comptent parmi les meilleurs du pays. Ils offrent la richesse en alcool, la trace de sucre non converti et le parfum qu'on peut attendre de telles vignes. Les principaux centres viticoles sont Kutjevo, Erdut, Ilok, Vukovar, Belji, Djakoro, Slavonski Brod.

Les vignobles d'Istrie et de Dalmatie se trouvent en bordure de l'Adriatique. Dans cette région, les vignobles les plus célèbres sont plantés sur les îles Vis, Hvar, Brač, Korčula et sur la péninsule de Peljesac. Les collines s'écartent de la côte accidentée et le sol est jonché d'énormes rochers. Quant aux coteaux eux-mêmes, le vent permanent de l'Adriatique *borra* les dénude. Néanmoins les vignes poussent et produisent des vins du type méditerranéen : gaillards, charnus, d'un rouge foncé, avec une forte teneur en tanin et une très faible acidité. Les Dalmates coupent volontiers leur vin avec de l'eau, dans le verre, un peu de la même manière que procèdent certains consommateurs avec les vins ordinaires. Cette région produit aussi des blancs.

On y cultive diverses variétés de vignes. Certaines semblent inconnues ailleurs. Ce détail suggère que la viticulture date de très longtemps dans la région. Certains viticulteurs yougoslaves croient que l'une d'elles est une variété indigène.

Parmi les moins « dalmates » des vins de cette région, il y a ceux de Polja (Polya) qui font la transition entre ceux de l'intérieur et ceux de la côte. Plus légers, et d'une couleur plus claire que la plupart des vins dalmates, les blancs d'Imotski et de Promina sont les plus typiques.

La plupart des dalmates rouges (environ deux fois plus que de blancs) sont faits avec du mali Plavac, vigne indigène yougoslave. Les meilleurs proviennent des secteurs de Bol, Pitovske Plaže (Pitovski Plaza), Zveta Nedelja (Nedelia), Vis, Brela, Lastovo, Postup et Dingač (Dingache). La plupart de ces vins sont vendus sous étiquette indiquant et la variété de la vigne et le lieu d'origine, par exemple Plavac de Vis, signifie : vin fait avec du raisin Plavac, cultivé dans le secteur de Vis. Parfois, seul le lieu d'origine est indiqué.

Des vins rosés de la côte portent l'appellation Opol. Les meilleurs proviennent des agglomérations de Vis, Sibenik et Kaštel.

Les meilleurs vins blancs de Dalmatie ressemblent aux rouges car ils sont aussi lourds, de teinte foncée et d'une agréable rondeur. Les mieux connus sont les Grk (Gerk), Pošip (Pochip), Bogdanuša (Bogdanoucha), Vugava et Maraština (Marachtina). Jaune clair et sec, le Grk laisse un arrière-goût qui lui est absolument particulier ; il provient surtout de l'île de Korčula et des environs de Split (Spolète). Le Pošip provient aussi de l'île de Korčula. On cultive avec succès d'autres vignes sur les îles de Hvar et de Vis, près de Sbenik et Žadar (jadis Zara).

On fait aussi un vin doux, bizarre, appelé Prošek, avec des raisins à demi séchés ou avec du jus de raisin concentré, ou encore en faisant cuire le moût. Mais il est surtout consommé par les Dalmates et convient à leur palais.

Les vins de la péninsule d'Istrie sont très fréquemment faits à la manière italienne. Comme dans bien des régions d'Italie, on cultive d'autres plantes dans les vignobles. Teran fournit une petite partie de la production d'Istrie et son secteur va jusqu'à la partie slovène de la péninsule où il est plus connu. Un des meilleurs vins est le Malvazÿa, provenant d'un raisin appelé Malvasia en Italie, Malvoisie en France et Monemvasia dans son pays d'origine : la Grèce ; il donne, en Yougoslavie, des vins agréables. On y cultive aussi le Cabernet et le Merlot de la région de Bordeaux et quelques membres de la famille Pinot, importés de Bourgogne.

Slovénie (Ljutomer)

Toute la région vinicole de Slovénie subit l'influence de l'Adriatique à l'ouest et de l'immense plaine du Danube à l'est qui tempère le climat alpin en donnant des hivers assez doux et humides et d'assez beaux étés. Le climat est également tempéré par des vents atlantiques qui traversent les Alpes au col de La Porte de Vienne. Les Alpes juliennes crèvent le sol calcaire nommé *karst*, dans la direction de l'Adriatique. Tel est le terrain pierreux sur lequel prospère le vignoble qui couvre quelque 50 000 ha.

On peut diviser cette région en trois secteurs : côte Adriatique, bassin de la Drave et bassin de la Save. Le plus important est celui de la Drave d'où provient le célèbre Ljutomer. Parmi les crus intéressants citons : Ormož (Ormoj), Pohorje (Pohorie), Kozjak (Koziak), Slovenske, Gorice (Goritse) et Gornie-Radgona.

Les vins blancs de table de Ljutomer se trouvent à la disposition des consommateurs en Angleterre, en Scandinavie, aux États-Unis et sur d'autres marchés. Ils portent souvent l'appellation Lutomer, et l'étiquette indique en outre le nom de la variété du raisin, par exemple Lutomer Riesling, Lutomer Traminer, et Lutomer Sylvaner, Lutomer Sauvignon, Lutomer Šipon (Chi-pon). Sauvignon et Riesling sont secs ; le Sylvaner a une légère tendance à la douceur ; le Traminer est parfois doux, avec en outre, évidemment, la saveur épicée qui caractérise les vins faits avec cette variété du raisin. La couleur des vins de Ljutomer varie autour d'un bel or teinté de vert. Quoique de type allemand, et moins souvent français, selon la variété du raisin, ils n'atteignent jamais la subtilité ni la délicatesse de leurs contreparties allemande et française car ils sont moins hautement évolués et moins caractérisés. Néanmoins ils ont souvent un très beau bouquet et un goût nettement tranché qui peut même être parfois un peu trop prononcé. Les Riesling titrent souvent 14 et même 15° et la plupart des autres sont à peine un peu moins forts. Le Šipon est une variété de raisin locale. Il donne du vin sec ou doux selon la manière dont il est traité et tend à conserver une légère fraîcheur, même quand il a vieilli longtemps. Actuellement la plus importante production revient au Barbera, au Merlot et au Cabernet Sauvignon.

Les deux autres secteurs vinicoles de Slovénie présentent moins d'intérêt. Le mieux connu des vins de la Save est le Cviček (Tsvietchek), un rosé léger, frais, très recherché par les gens du pays pendant la canicule. Le vin le plus important de l'Adriatique est le rouge Kraški Teran (Krachkiteiran), du nord de l'Istrie. Il passe depuis longtemps pour avoir des vertus curatives, peut-être en raison de sa richesse en acide lactique, fer et tanin. Mais, pour apprécier son goût, il faut y être accoutumé.

Macédoine

La Macédoine, avec un vignoble d'environ 30 000 ha produit des vins rouges, blancs et rosés, ainsi qu'une certaine quantité de vins de dessert. Elle est devenue une importante région vinicole de Yougoslavie. L'occupation turque fit presque disparaître les vignobles. Ils étaient à peine reconstitués que vint le phylloxéra et ils n'ont pas encore leur superficie d'autrefois. Néanmoins, depuis la Seconde Guerre mondiale, le gouvernement yougoslave a fait avec succès de grands efforts pour restaurer le vignoble de Macédoine. On y produit une grande quantité de vin d'un caractère intermédiaire entre ceux de la Méditerranée et ceux du nord. Le Vranak joue un rôle prédominant pour les vins rouges ; Žilavartea et Smederevka, pour le blanc. Parmi les secteurs vinicoles actuels citons : Tikveš (Tikveche), Demir Kapija (Kapilla) et les villes de Tetovo, Ohrid, Bilota, Štip, Djeudyjelÿa, etc. Les experts yougoslaves observent avec satisfaction les progrès des vins de Macédoine.

Autres vins yougoslaves

Herzégovine et Monténégro, qui couvrent au total 7 500 ha sont les deux plus petits producteurs de vin en Yougoslavie. A elles deux ces républiques fournissent à peine plus de 2 % de la production totale. Les vins monténégrins se limitent presque exclusivement à ceux de Vranac. Deux vins de Herzégovine sont connus : Žilavka et Blatina. Le premier est le meilleur, surtout celui qui provient des environs de Mostar. Gaillard, riche, titrant 13 à 14°, il a un profond parfum. En général il est fait avec 70 % du raisin indigène Žilavka et d'autres variétés diverses. Actuellement, la culture de la vigne est en expansion en Herzégovine et à Monténégro.

Millésimes

Selon l'Institut de viniculture de Maribor, il n'y eut au cours du siècle dernier que deux millésimes exceptionnels : 1834 et 1890. En général le millésime a peu d'intérêt en Yougoslavie parce que la plus grande partie du vin fait l'objet de coupages. Quoique les exportations soient le monopole de quelques négociants autorisés, qu'il y ait de vastes domaines et des coopératives, le vignoble est étonnamment morcelé. 95 % appartiennent à des petits cultivateurs qui, selon la loi actuelle, ne peuvent posséder plus de 10 ha chacun. Le cultivateurs ont connu diverses vicissitudes, et, certaines années, des maladies de la vigne réduisirent la récolte de 65 % en Serbie et ailleurs, alors qu'en Istrie et tout le long de la côte de l'Adriatique, la production dépassa la moyenne pour les meilleurs vins. Plus récemment, leur sort s'est amélioré de façon générale, et la qualité de la production a suivi. Les vins yougoslaves sont de plus en plus consommés dans les pays d'Europe occidentale, on commence à réduire la production de coupages au profit de vins de cépage, vins mis en bouteilles et vendus sous le nom de la variété de raisin qui les compose, plutôt que sous l'appellation de la région d'origine.

Spiritueux

Voir MARASQUIN ; SLIVOVITZ

Yquem (Château-d')

Bordeaux blanc. Commune de Sauternes, en Sauternais.

Le Château-d'Yquem est le plus grand vin blanc doux, le seul qu'on puisse proclamer le meilleur en son genre sans craindre de contradiction. C'est à peine si par année exceptionnelle quelques Trockenbeerenauslesen peuvent lui être comparés. Cette suprématie fut d'ailleurs reconnue au siècle dernier. En 1855, en effet, quand on classa les Sauternes et les Médoc en fonction de leur excellence et de ce que l'on savait au sujet de leur vente, Château-d'Yquem fut le seul qui eut droit au titre de Premier Grand Cru. Distingué même parmi les plus fins Sauternes par plus d'onctuosité, d'une richesse qu'on peut qualifier d'opulence, d'une douce profondeur vineuse et d'une robe du plus bel or, le Château-d'Yquem doit ses qualités en partie aux normes les plus élevées de vinification et en partie à la magnifique exposition de ses vignes plantées sur une croupe qui domine tout le Sauternais ; enfin, le sol lui-même doit avoir une influence quasi magique. Dans chaque grande zone vinicole seuls un ou deux vignobles parviennent, bon an mal an, à produire des vins supérieurs à ceux de leurs voisins immédiats. Le cas de Château-d'Yquem en est l'exemple le plus remarquable.

Le domaine, qui produisait déjà du vin depuis deux ou trois siècles, passa par mariage entre les mains de la famille des marquis de Lur-Saluces, en 1885. Aujourd'hui encore, il appartient au comte Alexandre de Lur-Saluces. Feu le marquis Bertrand de Lur-Saluces le géra lui-même pendant de longues années. Militant pour la promotion des vins de France, il a dirigé plusieurs associations tendant à ce but, notamment celle des Crus classés de Bordeaux. Voilà plus d'un siècle et demi, Thomas Jefferson écrivait : « Sauterne. C'est le meilleur vin blanc de France et le meilleur est fait par M. de Lur-Saluces. »

Ajoutons un « s » à Sauterne et le mot doux après blanc, pour éviter des démêlés avec les partisans de certains blancs secs et l'opinion de Jefferson reste encore justifiée de nos jours.

Le Château-d'Yquem a toujours été cher et il l'est encore. Il est généralement vendu aux négociants bordelais en vrac, c'est-à-dire pris au château sans frais supplémentaires pour la mise en caisse à plus de 600 francs la bouteille. Il atteignit probablement le prix record au cours du siècle dernier quand le frère de l'empereur de Russie acheta quatre barriques du vin de 1847 pour la somme de 20 000 francs-or, soit très approximativement, 51 000 F. Si cher qu'il soit, son prix est justifié, non seulement par la demande, mais aussi par deux facteurs. En 1847 le Château-d'Yquem fut le premier Sauternes fait avec des raisins enrichis par la moisissure appelée pourriture noble. Ce procédé exige de repasser à bien des reprises dans les vignes pour cueillir les raisins grain à grain lorsque chacun atteint le degré de maturité propice, d'où un accroissement du prix de la main-d'œuvre. (Notons que cette pratique est en usage désormais dans tout le Sauternais.) En outre, seul le meilleur vin de ce cru est vendu sous le nom de Château-d'Yquem. Celui des mauvaises années ou des moins bonnes vignes par année médiocre est vendu seulement sous l'appellation Sauternes, ce qui représente un gros manque à gagner. En 1954, par exemple, on ne déclara que 336 barriques de Château-d'Yquem, et 172 de Sauternes ; en 1955, 480 barriques du cru et 100 d'appellation générique.

« Tous les vins de Château-d'Yquem sont mis en bouteille au château. Mais le cru ne donne son nom qu'à des vins rigoureusement choisis... » (marquis Bertrand de Lur-Saluces.) Jusqu'en 1876 les vins étaient choisis à la sortie du pressoir et vendus séparément en plusieurs catégories. Mais depuis cette année-là, toute la vendange a été uniformisée et plusieurs jours de vendange cuvent ensemble. Ce vin est doué d'une longévité extrême ; des bouteilles datant de cent ans, et même plus, contiennent encore du vin en pleine forme, à condition qu'elles aient été conservées correctement. Bien que ce grand vin doux soit apprécié comme il le mérite, la mode actuelle des vins secs est tellement irrésistible qu'on produit aujourd'hui à Château-d'Yquem du vin assez sec étiqueté Château-Y.

Quant au bâtiment, c'est un château fort à tours et murs d'enceinte, construit sur une colline. Il offre un des sites remarquables du sud-ouest de la France. Une des soirées les plus charmantes que l'on puisse passer en Europe, c'est au concert annuel donné dans la grande cour du château par des quatuors à corde de réputation internationale, au mois de mai, lors du festival musical de Bordeaux. Le château, inondé de lumière comme une forteresse de contes de fées, avec ses tours et ses murailles, resplendit sur des kilomètres à la ronde, dans la nuit du Sauternais.

La grêle est le grand ennemi de ce vignoble. Elle oblitéra les vendanges de 1951, 1952 et 1953. Aucun Château-d'Yquem ne fut produit en 1964, 1972 et 1974.

Caractéristiques : Liquoreux, d'une très longue vinosité et d'une finesse superbes, ce vin cher vaut largement son prix. Il vieillit merveilleusement car la madérisation qui se fait au cours des années devient une qualité et non un défaut.

Son extrême douceur annule les effets d'une oxydation excessive.

Superficie : 100 ha.

Production moyenne : 60 tonneaux. Elle varie beaucoup ; environ 5 500 caisses pour le Château-d'Yquem, et quelque 2 000 caisses pour le Château-Y (sous-marque).

Z

Zagarolo

Vins blancs des alentours de Rome.

Voir LATIUM

Zamora

Province espagnole située au nord de Salamanque. C'est de Zamora que provient le Toro, épais et foncé. Dans cette même province, on fait le Vega Sicilia à Quintanella de Abajo.

Voir ESPAGNE

Zeller Schwarze Katz

Ce « vin du Chat Noir », fait à Zell, sur la Moselle, en Allemagne, est beaucoup plus célèbre qu'il ne le mérite. Il doit sa renommée à son nom et à la publicité, mais pas à ses qualités. Le Zeller Schwarze Katz est un vin de consommation courante léger et rafraîchissant.

Voir MOSELLE

Zeltinger Sonnenuhr

Moselle d'une féminité ravissante, qui est souvent le meilleur du secteur de Zeltingen dont les vins offrent une large gamme des variétés de la région.

Voir MOSELLE-SAAR-RUWER.

Zierfandler

Variété de raisin cultivée en Autriche. On l'appelle aussi Spätrok (rouge tardif).

Zikhron Yaacov

Important centre de l'industrie du vin en Israël.

Voir ISRAËL

Zilavka

Raisin indigène yougoslave avec lequel on fait un vin blanc du même nom, aux environs de Mostar en Bosnie-Herzégovine. Gaillard, riche, d'une forte teneur en alcool, ce vin a un parfum qui lui est propre.

Voir YOUGOSLAVIE

Zimbabwe

Quand la Rhodésie déclara son indépendance en 1965, il était interdit d'importer du vin ; aussi quelques fermiers se lancèrent-ils dans l'exploitation de la vigne. Aujourd'hui ces domaines vinicoles s'étendent sur 1 000 ha environ et la production moyenne est de 180 000 caisses, principalement de blanc. Les grandes variétés de raisin sont : Colombard, Chenin Blanc et Sauvignon Blanc.

Zinfandel

Variété de raisin à vin rouge qui est sans doute le cépage noble le plus répandu en Californie et qui réussit merveilleusement bien.

Voir ÉTATS-UNIS : CALIFORNIE ET OUEST

Žubrowka

Type de vodka polonaise, très appréciée à l'étranger. D'une couleur vert pâle, elle doit son goût à l'herbe sauvage préférée du zubra (auroch polonais) qui figure sur l'étiquette. Chaque bouteille de Žubrowka authentique contient un brin de cette herbe.

Voir POLOGNE

Zupa

Région de Serbie qui produit une grande quantité de vins rouges et rosés.

Voir YOUGOSLAVIE

Zwack

Marque exclusive de liqueurs autrefois produites en Hongrie, fabriquées aujourd'hui en Autriche et en Italie. Les Zwack — particulièrement l'eau-de-vie d'abricot connue sous le nom de Barack Pàlinka — étaient les liqueurs les plus appréciées aux États-Unis avant la Deuxième Guerre mondiale.

Zwicker

Sur une étiquette de vin alsacien, cette mention indique un coupage de vin noble et de vin ordinaire. Les vins alsaciens qui portent une marque commerciale sont généralement des Zwicker.

Zymase

Enzyme ou diastase de la levure, qui convertit le sucre de raisin en alcool et gaz carbonique.

Voir FERMENTATION

Zymotechnologie

Technologie de la fermentation, particulièrement celle des levures.

Appendice A : Vins de Bordeaux

I. Classification officielle des Grands Crus de la Gironde (1855)

La production officielle est donnée en tonneaux, mesure courante à Bordeaux, équivalant à 4 barriques, soit 990 l qui doivent traditionnellement donner à la mise en bouteille 96 caisses de 12 bouteilles.

Ces données sur la production sont approximatives. Elles varient d'année en année. Elles sont estimées ici en tenant compte, dans la mesure du possible, de l'ouillage (évaporation) qui s'élève généralement à 15 %.

VINS DU HAUT-MÉDOC

Premiers crus		Production moyenne		
	Commune	*Ha*	*Tonneaux*	*Caisses*[1]
Château Lafite-Rothschild	*Pauillac*	88	250	22 000
Château Latour	*Pauillac*	60	250	22 000
Château Mouton-Rothschild	*Pauillac*	70	250	22 000
Château Margaux	*Margaux*	75	250	23 000
Château Haut-Brion[2]	*Pessac, Graves*	40	140	13 000
Seconds crus				
Château Rausan-Ségla	*Margaux*	43	150	15 000
Château Rauszan-Gassies	*Margaux*	43	120	15 000
Château Léoville-Las-Cases	*Saint-Julien*	80	260	25 000
Château Léoville-Barton	*Saint-Julien*	45	180	18 000
Château Léoville-Poyferré	*Saint-Julien*	60	220	22 000
Château Durfort-Vivens	*Margaux*	25	90	5 000
Château Lascombes	*Margaux*	110	375	35 000
Château Gruaud-Larose	*Saint-Julien*	80	350	32 000
Château Brane-Cantenac	*Cantenac-Margaux*	85	300	30 000
Château Pichon-Longueville-Baron	*Pauillac*	30	120	11 000
Château Pichon-Longueville-Comtesse-de-Lalande	*Pauillac*	72	280	25 000
Château Ducru-Beaucaillou	*Saint-Julien*	50	220	20 000
Château Cos-d'Estournel	*Saint-Estèphe*	60-65	250	25 000
Château Montrose	*Saint-Estèphe*	70	320	30 000

1. Les caisses sont toujours de 12 bouteilles.
2. Haut-Brion est unanimement considéré et classé parmi les cinq Premiers Crus du Médoc.

	Commune	*Ha*	*Tonneaux*	*Caisses*[1]
TROISIÈMES CRUS				
Château Giscours	*Labarde-Margaux*	80	350	35 000
Château Kirwan	*Cantenac-Margaux*	30	120	10 000
Château d'Issan	*Cantenac-Margaux*	35	130	11 000
Château Lagrange	*Saint-Julien*	110	500	40 000
Château Langoa	*Saint-Julien*	15	60	6 000
Château Malescot-Saint-Exupéry	*Margaux*	32	160	16 000
Château Cantenac-Brown	*Cantenac-Margaux*	42	150	13 000
Château Palmer	*Cantenac-Margaux*	40	140	12 000
Château La Lagune	*Ludon*	70	250	25 000
Château Desmirail	*Margaux*			
Château Calon-Ségur	*Saint-Estèphe*	50	200	20 000
Château Ferrière	*Margaux*		10	900
Château Marquis-d'Aslesme-Becker	*Margaux*	10	50	5 000
Château Boyd-Cantenac	*Cantenac-Margaux*	18	80	7 000
QUATRIÈMES CRUS				
Château Saint-Pierre	*Saint-Julien*	17	50	5 000
Château Branaire-Ducru	*Saint-Julien*	48	250	25 000
Château Talbot	*Saint-Julien*	100	400	35 000
Château Duhart-Milon-Rothschild	*Pauillac*	58	230	20 000
Château Pouget	*Cantenac-Margaux*	12	50	4 000
Château La Tour-Carnet	*Saint-Laurent*	42	120	11 000
Château Lafon-Rochet	*Saint-Estèphe*	42	110	11 000
Château Beychevelle	*Saint-Julien*	70	280	26 000
Château Prieuré-Lichine	*Cantenac-Margaux*	62	250	25 000
Château Marquis-de-Terme	*Margaux*	38	150	14 000
CINQUIÈMES CRUS				
Château Pontet-Canet	*Pauillac*	75	250	25 000
Château Batailley	*Pauillac*	55	220	20 000
Château Grand-Puy-Lacoste	*Pauillac*	45	180	17 000
Château Grand-Puy-Ducasse	*Pauillac*	36	140	14 000
Château Haut-Batailley	*Pauillac*	22	60	6 000
Château Lynch-Bages	*Pauillac*	76	300	28 000
Château Lynch-Moussas	*Pauillac*	40	175	17 000
Château Dauzac	*Labarde-Margaux*	55	220	20 000
Château Mouton-Baronne-Philippe	*Pauillac*	45	180	16 000
Château du Tertre	*Arsac-Margaux*	47	200	18 000
Château Haut-Bages-Libéral	*Pauillac*	23	100	8 000
Château Pédesclaux	*Pauillac*	30	130	8 000
Château Belgrave	*Saint-Laurent*	55	260	26 000
Château de Camensac	*Saint-Laurent*	62	260	25 000
Château Cos Labory	*Saint-Estèphe*	15	60	6 000
Château Clerce-Milon-Rothschild	*Pauillac*	25	125	9 000
Château Croizet-Bages	*Pauillac*	25	100	8 000
Château Cantemerle	*Macau*	55	280	25 000

1. Les caisses sont toujours de 12 bouteilles.

Crus exceptionnels	Commune		Commune
Château Villegeorge	*Avensan*	Château la Couronne	*Pauillac*
Château Angludet	*Cantenac-Margaux*	Château Moulin-Riche	*Saint-Julien*
Château Chasse-Spleen	*Moulis*	Château Belair Marquis d'Aligre	*Soussans-Margaux*
Château Poujeaux-Theil	*Moulis*		

II. Les Crus Bourgeois et Crus Artisans du Haut-Médoc

La production indiquée ci-dessous est approximative.

Les chiffres indiquent une production moyenne annuelle telle qu'elle est donnée par les communes d'après les déclarations de récolte.

CRUS DU HAUT-MÉDOC

	Commune	*Ha*	*Tonneaux*
Château l'Abbé Gorsse-de-Gorsse	*Margaux*	4	11
Château d'Agassac	*Ludon*	33	80
Château Andron-Blanquet	*Saint-Estèphe*	15	75
Château Aney	*Cussac*	22	100
Château Angludet	*Cantenac-Margaux*	30	120
Château Anthonic	*Moulis*	18	50
Château d'Arches	*Ludon*	4	17
Château d'Arcins	*Arcins*	82	300
Château Arnauld	*Arcins*	18	80
Château d'Arsac	*Arsac*	16	90
Château Balac	*Saint-Laurent*	11	50
Château Barateau	*Saint-Laurent*	7	31
Château Barreyres	*Arcins*	100	400
Château Beaumont	*Cussac*	57	350
Château Beauséjour	*Saint-Estèphe*	15	75
Château Beau-Site-Haut-Vignoble	*Saint-Estèphe*	19	80
Château Beau-Site	*Saint-Estèphe*	25	135
Château Bel-Air	*Saint-Estèphe*	4	25
Château Bel Air	*Cussac*	35	160
Château Bel-Air Lagrave	*Moulis*	12	46
Château Belair Marquis d'Aligre	*Soussans-Margaux*	17	50
Château Belgrave	*Listrac*	9	33
Château Belle Rose	*Pauillac*	6	30
Château Bellevue	*Cussac*	1	3
Château Bernones	*Cussac*	16	90
Cru Bergeron	*Moulis*	6	30
Château Bel-Orme-Tronquey de Lalande	*St-Seurin-de-Cadourne*	25	130
Château Bernores	*Haut-Médoc*	16	100
Cru Bibian Darriet	*Listrac*	2	9
Château Biston Brillette	*Moulis*	19	75
Château Bois du Monteil	*Cantenac*	5	30
Château Bonneau	*St-Seurin-de-Cadourne*	5	9

	Commune	*Ha*	*Tonneaux*
Château Bonneau-Livran	*St-Seurin-de-Cadourne*	7	40
Château Bouqueyran	*Moulis*	9	35
Château Bournac	*Saint-Estèphe*	3	8
Château Brame-les-Tours	*Saint-Estèphe*	6	30
Château Branas	*Moulis*	3	12
Château du Breuil	*Cissac*	25	100
Château Brillette	*Moulis*	27	40
Château de Cach	*St-Laurent*	14	80
Château Cambron	*Blanquefort*	5	20
Château Cambon La Pelouse	*Macau*	60	240
Château Canteloup et Commanderie	*Saint-Estèphe*	15	50
Château Capdelong	*Saint-Julien*	5	30
Château Cap du Haut	*Moulis*	7	35
Château Capbern-Gasqueton	*Saint-Estèphe*	36	75
Château Cap-Léon-Veyrin	*Listrac*	5	23
Château Caronne Sainte-Gemme	*Saint-Laurent*	42	200
Château du Cartillon	*Lamarque*	28	150
Château Chambert-Marbuzet	*Saint-Estèphe*	7	40
Château Charmail	*St-Seurin-de-Cadourne*	20	100
Château Charmant	*Margaux*	6	20
Château Chasse-Spleen	*Moulis*	66	210
Château Cissac	*Cissac*	45	220
Château Citran	*Avensan*	92	368
Château Clarke	*Listrac*	131	500
Château Colombier-Monpelou	*Pauillac*	14	90
Château de Côme	*Saint-Estèphe*	7	40
Château Constand Lesquireu	*Vertheuil*	61	350
Château Corconnac	*Saint-Laurent*	7	35
Domaine de Coudot	*Cussac*	6	35
Château Coufran	*St-Servin-de-Cordoue*	60	300
Château Coutelin-Merville	*Saint-Estèphe*	16	90
Château Deyrem-Valentin	*Soussans-Margaux*	7	30
Château Dillon	*Blanquefort*	38	150
Château Doyac	*St-Seurin-de-Cadourne*	12	70
Château Duplessis Fabre	*Moulis*	9	45
Château Duplessis Hauchecorne	*Moulis*	16	70
Château Dutruch Grand Poujeaux	*Moulis*	30	120
Château Fonbadet	*Pauillac*	15	100
Château Fonréaud	*Listrac*	50	300
Château Fontesteau	*Saint-Sauveur*	12	50
Château Fort de Vauban	*Cussac*	7	35
Château Fourcas-Dupré	*Listrac*	40	220
Château Fourcas-Hosten	*Listrac*	45	280
Château Gaudin	*Pauillac*	10	60
Château Glana	*Saint-Julien*	42	220
Château Gloria	*Saint-Julien*	50	200
Château Gobineau	*Listrac*	8	12
Château Grand Canyon	*Pauillac*	6	30
Château Grand Clapeau Olivier	*Blanquefort*	11	35
Château Grand Duroc Milon	*Pauillac*	5	25
Château Grand Moulin	*St-Seurin-de-Cadourne*	18	100
Château Grandis	*St-Seurin-de-Cadourne*	5	24
Château Grave La Cour	*Saint-Estèphe*	6	40
Château des Graviers	*Arsac*	7	45
Château Gressier Grand Poujeaux	*Moulis*	20	100

	Commune	Ha	Tonneaux
Château Hanteillan	*Cissac*	70	350
Château Haut-Bages-Monpelou	*Pauillac*	10	60
Château Haut-Brega	*St-Seurin-de-Cadourne*	7	40
Château Haut-Breton Larigaudière	*Soussans-Margaux*	5	30
Château Haut-Carmail	*St-Seurin-de-Cadourne*	5	25
Château Haut-Laborde	*Saint-Sauveur*	20	100
Château Haut-Logat	*Lissac*	9	45
Château Haut-Madrac	*St-Sauveur*	20	120
Château Haut-Marbuzet	*Saint-Estèphe*	40	200
Château Haut-Pauillac	*Pauillac*	5	30
Château Haut-Tayac	*Soussans*	6	25
Château Hennebelle	*Lamarque*	4	14
Château Houissant	*Saint-Estèphe*	20	100
Château Hourtin-Ducasse	*Saint-Sauveur*	30	150
Château du Junca	*Saint-Sauveur*	8	50
Château La Bécade	*Listrac*	22	115
Château La Bécasse	*Pauillac*	5	25
Château La Bridane	*Saint-Julien*	17	90
Château La Closerie-Grand-Poujeaux	*Moulis*	7	23
Château La Couronne	*Pauillac*	3	20
Château La Dame Blanche*	*Le Taillan*	5	20
Château La Fleur Milon	*Pauillac*	13	50
Château La Galiane	*Soussans-Margaux*	4	16
Château La Grave	*Saint-Sauveur*	8	45
Château La Gurgue	*Margaux*	10	35
Château La Haye	*Saint-Estèphe*	6	20
Château La Hontete	*St-Seurin-de-Cadourne*	8	45
Château La Houringue	*Macau*	27	150
Château La Mouline	*Moulis*	45	200
Château La Mothe	*St-Seurin-de-Cadourne*	18	100
Château de la Ronceray	*Saint-Estèphe*	5	30
Château La Rose Brana	*Saint-Estèphe*	11	60
Domaine La Rose Maucaillou	*Soussans-Margaux*	6	35
Coopérative de la Rose Pauillac	*Pauillac*	110	500
Château La Rousselière	*Saint-Estèphe*	8	45
Château La Tour du Haut Moulin	*Cussac*	24	100
Château La Tour-de-Mons, Château Richeterre, Château La Tour-de-Bessan	*Soussans-Margaux*	30	120
Château La Tour Pibran	*Pauillac*	7	25
Château La Tour du Roc	*Arcins*	9	30
Château La Tour des Ternes	*Saint-Estèphe*	12	13
Château Labégorce	*Margaux*	30	130
Château Labégorce-Zédé	*Soussans-Margaux*	21	100
Château Lachesnaye	*Cussac*	20	100
Château Ladouys	*Saint-Estèphe*	4	10
Château Laffitte-Carcasset	*Saint-Estèphe*	23	135
Château Lafon	*Listrac*	12	55
Château Lagorce	*Moulis*	3	7
Château Lagravette-Peyredon	*Listrac*	5	10
Château Lalande	*Listrac*	12	55
Château Lalande-Borie	*St-Julien*	18	100
Château de Lamarque	*Lamarque*	47	250
Château Lamothe-Bergeron	*Cussac*	60	300

* Le vin blanc du Château du Taillan s'appelle Château La Dame Blanche et n'a droit qu'à l'appellation Bordeaux Blanc Supérieur.

	Commune	*Ha*	*Tonneaux*
Château Lamothe-Cissac	*Cissac*	47	250
Château Landat	*Cissac*	30	150
Château Lanessan	*Cussac*	40	220
Cur Lauga	*Cussac*	3	4
Château Larose Trintaudon	*Saint-Laurent*	172	750
Cru Larragay	*Listrac*	2	6
Château Larrivaux	*Cissac*	21	100
Château Lavillotte	*Saint-Estèphe*	12	70
Château Le Boscq	*Saint-Estèphe*	13	65
Château Le Bourdieu	*Vertheuil*	32	180
Château Le Crock	*Saint-Estèphe*	32	180
Château Le Fournas Bernadotte	*Saint-Sauveur*	20	120
Château Le Meynieu	*Vertheuil*	15	80
Château Le Roc	*Saint-Estèphe*	1	5
Château Le Souley-Ste-Croix	*Vertheuil*	18	100
Château Lemone-Lafon-Rochet	*Ludon*	6	15
Château Les Baraillots	*Margaux*	5	30
Château Les Ormes-de-Pez	*Saint-Estèphe*	30	150
Cru Lescourt	*Listrac*	2	5
Château Lestage	*Listrac*	52	280
Château Lestage	*St-Seurin-de-Cadourne*	1	5
Château Lestage Darquier	*Moulis*	4	8
Château Lestage Darquier Grand Poujeaux	*Moulis*	5	30
Château Lestage Simon	*St-Seurin-de-Cadourne*	32	150
Château Leyssac	*St-Estèphe*	12	70
Château l'Ermitage	*Listrac*	5	30
Château L'Hôpital	*St-Estèphe*	5	30
Château Lieujean	*St-Sauveur*	12	70
Château Ligondras	*Arsac-Margaux*	7	35
Château Liouner	*Listrac*	13	70
Château Liversan	*St-Sauveur*	45	180
Domaine du Lucrabey	*Cissac*	5	7
Château MacCarthy	*St-Estèphe*	4	12
Château MacCarthy Moula	*St-Estèphe*	6	12
Château de Magnol	*Blanquefort*	17	90
Château Malescasse	*Lamarque*	25	90
Château Malleret	*Le Pian Médoc*	60	280
Château Malmaison	*Moulis*	4	5
Château Marbuzet	*St-Estèphe*	7	40
Château Marque	*St-Seurin-de-Cadourne*	1	6
Château Marsac-Seguineau	*Soussans-Margaux*	7	30
Château Martinens	*Cantenac-Margau*	30	120
Clos du Mas	*Listrac*	5	9
Château Maucaillou	*Moulis*	45	230
Château Maucamps	*Macau*	15	70
Château Mauvesin	*Moulis*	7	35
Château Médrac	*Moulis*	1	2
Château Meyney	*St-Estèphe*	50	300
Château Monbrison	*Arsac-Margaux*	14	70
Château Mongravey	*Arsac-Margaux*	5	30
Château Montbrun	*Cantenac-Margaux*	9	40
Château Morin	*St-Estèphe*	10	60
Château Moulin-à-Vent	*Moulis*	20	90
Château du Moulin du Bourg	*Listrac*	7	35
Château Moulin de Laborde	*Listrac*	16	90

	Commune	Ha	Tonneaux
Château Moulin Rose	*Lamarque*	3	9
Château Moulin de la Rose	*St-Julien*	4	14
Château du Moulin Rouge	*Cussac*	15	80
Château Moulis	*Moulis*	12	50
Château Nexon-Lemoyne	*Ludon*	16	75
Château Pabeau	*St-Seurin-de-Cadourne*	10	38
Château Padarnac	*Pauillac*	5	30
Château Paveil de Luze	*Soussans-Margaux*	24	120
Château Pey La Rose	*Pauillac*	6	30
Château de Peyrabon	*St-Laurent*	29	100
Château Peyrabon	*Pauillac*	5	30
Château Peyrabon	*St-Sauveur*	53	350
Château Peyredon	*Listrac*	3	9
Château de Pez	*St-Estèphe*	25	100
Château Phélan-Ségur	*St-Estèphe*	55	300
Château Pibran	*Pauillac*	7	30
Château Picard (*voir* Château Beauséjour)	*St-Estèphe*	12	60
Château Pichon	*Parempuyre*	23	130
Château Pierre Bibian	*Listrac*	14	60
Château Plantey	*Pauillac*	27	160
Château Pomeys	*Moulis*	7	25
Château Pomys	*St-Estèphe*	7	45
Château Pontac-Lynch	*Cantenac-Margaux*	9	60
Château Pontet-Chappez	*Arsac-Magaux*	4	20
Château Pontoise-Cabarrus	*St-Seurin-de-Cadourne*	24	125
Château Poujeaux	*Moulis*	50	280
Château Puy Castera	*Cissac*	25	120
Château Ramage La Batisse	*St-Sauveur*	54	300
Château du Raux	*Cussac*	15	70
Château Renouil Franquet	*Moulis*	4	8
Château du Retout	*Cussac*	25	120
Château Reverdi	*Listrac*	4	18
Château Reysson	*Vertheuil*	52	300
Château Richeterre			
Château Robert Franquet	*Moulis*	8	30
Château Rose Ste-Croix	*Listrac*	6	16
Château Ruat	*Moulis*	11	35
Château St-Ahon	*Blanquefort*	27	150
Château St-Estèphe	*St-Estèphe*	10	50
Château St-Marc	*Soussans-Margaux*	7	40
Château St-Martin	*Listrac*	2	8
Château St-Paul	*St-Seurin-de-Cadourne*	19	100
Château St-Sauveur	*St-Sauveur*	12	60
Château Saransot-Dupré	*Listrac*	10	40
Château Ségur	*Parempuyre*	30	140
Château Sémaillan-Mazeau	*Listrac*	12	50
Château Sénéjac	*Le Pian*	16	70
Château Senilhac	*St-Seurin-de-Cadourne*	14	65
Château Siran	*Labarde-Margaux*	30	120
Château Sociando-Mallet	*St-Seurin-de-Cadourne*	30	150
Château Soudars	*St-Seurin-de-Cadourne*	15	70
Château du Taillan*	*Le Taillan*	20	80

* Le vin blanc du Château du Taillan s'appelle Château La Dame Blanche et n'a droit qu'à l'appellation Bordeaux Blanc Supérieur.

	Commune	*Ha*	*Tonneaux*
Château Tayac	*Soussans-Margaux*	34	200
Château Terrey-Gros-Caillou	*St-Julien*	14	80
Château Teynac	*St-Julien*	5	19
Château Tour Granins	*Moulis*	9	50
Château Tour Marbuzet	*St-Estèphe*	8	45
Château Tour du Mirail	*Cissac*	18	100
Château Tour St-Joseph	*Cissac*	10	60
Château Tronquoy-Lalande	*St-Estèphe*	13	60
Château Verdignan	*St-Seurin-de-Cadourne*	48	200
Château Vieux Braneyre	*Cissac*	10	60
Château Vieux Coutelin	*St-Estèphe*	7	45
Château Villegeorge	*Avensan*	9	40

CRUS DU MÉDOC (ou BAS-MÉDOC)

	Commune	*Ha*	*Tonneaux*
Domaine des Anguilleys (Château Vieux Robin)	*Bégadan*	8	45
Beau Rivage de By	*Bégadan*	5	25
Château Bégadanet	*Bégadan*	4	12
Cru Bel-Air Mareil	*Ordonnac-et-Potensac*	3	12
Château Bellerive	*Valeyrac*	9	50
Château Bellevue	*Valeyrac*	9	45
Château des Bertins	*Bégadan*	25	125
Château Blaignan	*Blaignan*	45	200
Château Bois de Roc	*St-Yzans*	25	125
Château Brie Caillou	*St-Germain-d'Esteuil*	18	100
Château des Brousteras	*St-Yzans*	17	100
Château de By (Château Greysac)	*Bégadan*	8	40
Domaine de By	*Bégadan*	31	145
Château Carcanieux-les-Graves	*Queyrac*	20	100
Château Castéra	*St-Germain-d'Esteuil*	30	145
Cave Coopérative Belle Vue	*Ordonnac-et-Potensac*	130	700
Cave Coopérative St-Jean	*Bégadan*	500	2 300
Château Chantelys	*Prignac*	6	30
Château des Combes	*Bégadan*	4	20
Domaine de la Croix	*Ordonnac*	16	80
Coopérative La Chatellenie	*Vertheuil*	—	300
Coopérative de Prignac, Château Bensse	*Prignac*	200	950
Coopérative de Queyrac, Château St-Roch	*Queyrac*	56	300
Coopérative de St-Yzans, Cave St-Brice	*St-Yzans*	140	1 000
Cru des Deux-Moulins	*St-Christoly*	13	48
Château Gallais-Bellevue (*voir* Château Potensac)			
Château Greysac	*Bégadan*	52	250
Château Grivière	*Blaignan*	15	80
Château Haut-Blaignan	*Blaignan*	7	42
Château Haut Canteloup	*St-Christoly*	18	100
Château Haut Maurac	*St-Yzans*	25	120
Château Hauterive	*St-Germain-d'Esteuil*	75	350
Château Cru Hontane (*voir* Château Côtes de Blaignan)			
Château Hourbanon	*Prignac*	6	32

	Commune	Ha	Tonneaux
Château La Cardonne	*Blaignan*	55	300
Château La Clare	*Bégadan*	18	90
Château La Croix du Breuil	*Louqueques*	15	80
Château La France	*Blaignan*	6	30
Château La Gorce	*Blaignan*	37	180
Château La Gorre	*Bégadan*	7	40
Château Landon	*Bégadan*	25	150
Château La Ribeau	*St-Yzans*	18	100
Château La Rivière	*Blaignac*	12	60
Château La Rose Garamay (*voir* Château Livran)			
Château La Tour-Blanche	*St-Christoly*	26	150
Château La Tour de By	*Bégadan*	60	300
Château La Tour du Haut-Caussan (depuis 1987 : Château Haut-Caussan)	*Blaignan*	6	35
Château La Tour-St-Bonnet	*St-Christoly*	40	215
Château La Tour Seran	*St-Christoly*	18	100
Château Laujac	*Bégadan*	25	150
Château La Valière	*St-Christoly*	18	100
Château Le Boscq	*St-Christoly*	25	125
Château Le Tréhon	*Bégadan*	16	100
Clos Les Moines	*Couquéques*	18	110
Château Les Ormes-Sorbet	*Couquéques*	25	120
Château Les Tourelles	*Blaignan*	31	125
Château Les Tuileries	*St-Yzans*	15	80
Château L'Hermitage	*Couquéques*	6	15
Château Livran, Château La Rose Garamay	*St-Germain-d'Esteuil*	40	200
Château Loudenne	*St-Yzans*	28	150
Château Lugagnac	*Vertheuil*		
Clos Mandillot	*St-Christoly*		
Château Monthil	*Bégadan*	25	100
Clos du Moulin	*St-Christoly*	8	40
Château Panigon	*Civrac*	31	150
Château Patache d'Aux	*Bégadan*	42	350
Château Pay-de-Labo	*St-Germain-d'Esteuil*	2	7
Château Peymartin	*Ordonnac*	15	80
Château Plagnac	*Bégadan*	32	150
Château Potensac, Château Gallais-Bellevue	*Ordonnac-et-Potensac*	40	200
Château Preuillac	*Lesparre*	35	150
Château Reysson	*Vertheuil*	34	65
Château Roquegrave	*Valeyrac*	25	100
Château St-Bonnet	*St-Christoly*	40	300
Château St-Christoly	*St-Christoly*	18	100
Château St-Christophe	*St-Christoly*	18	100
Château St-Germain	*St-Germain-d'Esteuil*	2	8
Cru St-Louis (*voir* Coopérative de Queyrac)			
Château St-Saturnin	*Bégadan*	25	120
Château Sigognac	*St-Yzans*	56	250
Château Vernous	*Lesparre*	22	100
Cru du Vieux-Château Landon	*Bégadan*	27	110
Château Vieux Robin, Domaine des Anguilleys	*Bégadan*	15	100

III. Saint-Émilion. Classification officielle (1986)

En 1985, les meilleurs vins de Saint-Émilion furent classés, pour la troisième fois, en Premiers Grands Crus et Grands Crus.

Cette nouvelle classification devint légale le 27 mai 1986, les vins ne figurant plus sur cette nouvelle liste ont cependant le droit d'user de l'ancienne classification sur les étiquettes 1985. En revanche, les vins retenus pourront faire apparaître leur nouveau classement sur les étiquettes, à partir de la récolte de 1986.

PREMIERS GRANDS CRUS CLASSÉS

		Ha	*Tonneaux*	*Caisses*[1]		*Ha*	*Tonneaux*	*Caisses*[1]
A)	Château Ausone	7	35	2 800	Château Canon	18	75	6 500
	Château Cheval Blanc	35	160	14 000	Château Figeac	40	130	17 000
					Clos Fourtet	18	70	6 700
					Château La Gaffelière	22	90	8 500
B)	Château Beauséjour-Duffau-Lagarosse	7	25	2 000	Château La Magdelaine	11	40	3 500
					Château Pavie	35	200	15 000
	Château Bélair	13	50	4 000	Château Trottevieille	10	50	4 000

1. Le nombre de caisses indiqué est approximatif, mais les caisses sont toujours de 12 bouteilles.

GRANDS CRUS CLASSÉS

	Ha	*Tonneaux*		*Ha*	*Tonneaux*
Château L'Angélus	28	112	Château Corbin Michotte	7	35
Château L'Arrosée	9	35	Château Couvent-des-Jacobins	8	40
Château Balestard-la-Tonnelle	8	40	Château Croque-Michotte	10	50
Château Beau-Séjour-Bécot*	16,6	85	Château Curé-Bon-La-Madeleine	5	20
Château Bellevue	6	24	Château Dassault	26	130
Château Bergat	4	20	Château Faurie-de-Souchard	8,5	45
Château Berliquet	9	60	Château Fonplégade	17	100
Château Cadet-Bon	3	20	Château Fonroque	18	60
Château Cadet-Piola	7	30	Château Franc-Mayne	6,5	35
Château Canon-la-Gaffelière	22,5	125	Château Grand-Barrail-Lamarzelle-Figeac	23,5	150
Château Cap-de-Moulin (Jacques Capdemoulin)	15,5	90	Château Grand-Corbin	13,5	65
Château Chapelle Madeleine	1	1	Château Grand-Corbin-Despagne	25,5	160
Château Le-Châtelet	5	30	Château Grand-Mayne	17,5	70
Château Chauvin	12	60	Château Grand-Pontet	14	60
Château Corbin	12	60			

* On peut se demander si Château Beau-Séjour-Bécot doit figurer parmi les Grands Crus ou, comme il l'a été jusqu'en 1986, parmi les Premiers Grands Crus.

	Ha	*Tonneaux*
Château Guadet-St-Julien	5,5	25
Château Haut-Corbin	7	35
Château Haut-Sarpe	7	60
Clos des Jacobins	8	45
Château La Clotte	1	5
Château La Clusière	3	12
Château La Dominique	17	70
Clos La Madeleine	1	4
Château Lamarzelle	5,5	35
Château La Tour-Figeac	16	100
Château La Tour-du-Pin-Figeac-Moueix	8,5	65
Château La Tour-du-Pin-Figeac	7	45
Château Laniote	5	25
Château Larcis-Ducasse	11	60
Château Larmande	16	65
Château Laroze	28	100
Château La Serre	7	40
Château Le Couvent	18	70
Château Le Prieuré	4,5	25

	Ha	*Tonneaux*
Château Matras	16	60
Château Mauvezin	5	30
Château Moulin du Cadet	5	30
Clos de l'Oratoire	6	35
Château Pavie-Decesse	8,5	40
Château Pavie-Macquin	12	50
Château Pavillon-Cadet	1	5
Château Petit-Faurie-de-Soutard	9	50
Château Ripeau	14	70
Château St.-Georges-Côte-Pavie	6	21
Clos St.-Martin	2,5	10
Château Sansonnet	6,5	30
Château Soutard	22	120
Château Tertre-Daugay	8	45
Château Trimoulet	16	70
Château Troplong-Mondot	25	150
Château Villemaurine	6,5	35
Château Yon-Figeac	21	120

PRINCIPAUX CRUS

	Ha	*Tonneaux*
Domaine Allée-de-Lescours	4	11
Clos d'Armens	2	7
Château d'Arthus	5	13
Clos d'Arthus	12	23
Château Badette	8	23
Domaine de Badon-Patarbet	2	12
Château Barbey	2	9
Château Barbeyron	4	13
Château Barde-Haut	12	43
Château Bardoulet	2	7
Domaine de Bardoulet	3	15
Château du Basque	8	35
Château Béard	5	22
Château Béard La Chapelle	20	100
Château Beau-Mazerat (*voir* Grand-Mayne)		
Château Beausite	4	15
Château Bel-Horizon	2	5
Château Belair-Sarthou	5	19
Château Belle-Assise	16	100
Château Bellefont-Belcier-Guillier	11	42
Château Bellegrave	11	55

	Ha	*Tonneaux*
Château Belles-Plantes	3	9
Château Bellevue-Figeac	8	45
Château Bellevue-Mondotte	2	7
Château Bellevue-Puyblanquet	3	7
Château Belliste-Mondotte	26	120
Clos Bernachot	2	8
Clos Berthoneau (*voir* Château Du Roy)		
Château Bézineau	7	40
Cru Bibey	6	18
Château Bicasse-Lartigue	3	11
Château Bigaroux	31	150
Château Billerand	8	27
Cru Bicquet	4	19
Château Bois-Grouley	5	25
Château Bois-Redon-Grand-Corbin	4	16
Château Bord-Fonrazade	4	14
Château Bord-Lartigue	2	11
Château Boulerne	9	32
Château Bouquey	6	30
Domaine du Bourg	2	13
Château Boutisse	16	77

	Ha	*Tonneaux*
Château Brisson	4	13
Château Brisson, Château Destieux	9	30
Château Brun	6	20
Clos Brun	3	13
Château le Calvaire	12	60
Clos du Calvaire	2	7
Château Cantenac	12	60
Clos Cantenac	2	10
Clos Canterane	10	50
Château Caperot (*voir* Château Monbousquet)		
Clos Caperot	3	10
Château Capet	15	70
Château Capet-Guiller	15	80
Château Cardinal Villemaurine	12	60
Château Carteau-Bas-Daugay	6	30
Château Carteau-Côtes-Daugay	8	40
Château Carteau-Pin-de-Fleurs	3	16
Château Cassevert (*voir* Château Grand-Mayne)		
Château Castelot	10	43
Domaine de la Cateau	3	11
Château de Cauze	31	125
Château Cauzin	4	23
Clos de la Cavaille-Lescours	1	7
Cave Coopérative, Royal St-Émilion, Côtes Rocheuses	814	5 709
Château Côte de la Mouleyre	8	40
Château Champion	5	16
Château Chante-Alouette	6	23
Clos Chante-Alouette, Domaine Haut Patarabet	4	24
Château Chantecaille	3	17
Château Chantegrive	5	20
Domaine de la Chapelle	3	15
Château Chatelet (*voir* Château Larques)		
Château Cheval-Brun	5	14
Château Cheval-Noir	4	11
Château du Clocher	3	13
Domaine de la Clotte	5	15
Château du Comte	3	5
Clos Cormey	7	29
Château Comeil-Figeac	20	100

	Ha	*Tonneaux*
Château Côte-Mignon-la-Gaffelière	1	6
Château Côte de Rol-Valentin	3	9
Château Côtes Bernateau	12	70
Cru Côtes-Pressac	2	8
Cru Côtes-Roland	2	9
Clos Côtes-Roland-de-Pressac	2	9
Château Côtes-Veyrac	2	19
Château Coudert	3	12
Château Coudert-Pelletan	9	36
Château Croix-de-Figeac	3	12
Domaine de la Croix-Mazerat	2	5
Château Croix-du-Merle	3	8
Château Croix-Peyblanquet	4	9
Château de la Croix-Simard	1	7
Château Croix-Villemaurine	1	5
Clos Daupin	2	10
Château des Demoiselles	1	5
Domaine des Dépendances, Cru Jauguebland	6	30
Domaine Despagne	7	15
Château Despagnet	3	13
Château Destieu	4	15
Château Destieux	9	30
Château Destieux	7	25
Château Destieux (*voir* Château Brisson)		
Château Destieux-Berger	13	60
Château Destieux-Verac	11	36
Château l'Étoile-Pourret (*voir* Château La Grâce Dieu)		
Domaine des Escardos	7	12
Château Fagouet-Jean-Voisin	6	35
Château Faleyrens	5	12
Château Faugère	13	60
Château de Ferrand	30	148
Château Ferrandat	28	130
Cru Ferrandat	1	9
Château Pont-de-Figeac, Château Grangeneuve	25	79
Petit Clos Figeac	3	15
Château Fleurus	1	8
Château Flouquet	25	120
Château Fombrauge	50	200
Château Fond-Razade	4	8

	Ha	*Tonneaux*
Château Fond-de-Rol	1	5
Château Fonrazade	9	50
Clos Fonrazade	4	25
Clos Fontelle	1	5
Château Fougères	9	45
Château Fougueyrat, Château La Tour-Laroze, Cru Le Châtelet	19	87
Château de Fouquet	6	5
Château Fourney	39	160
Château Fourney (*voir* Château Vieux-Guinot)		
Château Franc (*voir* Château Franc-Patarabet)		
Château Franc-Beau-Mazerat	3	11
Château Franc-Cantenac	3	15
Château Franc-Cormey	2	4
Château Franc-Gros	4	14
Château Franc-Laporte	9	50
Clos Franc-Larmande	3	9
Château Franc-Mazerat	2	8
Château Franc-Patarabet, Château Franc	6	30
Château Franc-Peilhan	3	9
Château Franc-Petit-Figeac	3	22
Château Franc Pipeau	3	17
Château Franc Pourret	11	49
Château Franc-la-Rose	4	20
Château Franc-Rozier	3	15
Domaine de la Gaffelière	10	50
Château Gaillard	20	100
Château Gaillard-de-Gorce	8	40
Château Gastebourse (*voir* Château Pontet Clauzure)		
Château Gaubert, Clos des Moines	10	55
Clos Gerbaud	1	7
Château Godeau	3	8
Clos Gontey	2	13
Domaine Grand-Berc	10	55
Château du Grand-Bigaroux	9	50
Château Grand-Caillou-Noir	3	16
Château Grand-Corbin-Manuel	8	40
Château Grand-Faurie	1	5
Domaine du Grand-Faurie	4	17

	Ha	*Tonneaux*
Château Grand-Gontey	4	16
Clos Grand-Gontey	4	17
Domaine du Grand-Gontey	2	9
Château Grand Jacques	11	46
Château Cassevert, Château Beau-Marzeva	17	85
Château Grand-Mazerat (voir Château Grand-Mayne)		
Château Grand-Mirande	6	32
Château Grand Nauve	13	60
Château Grand-Peilhan-Blanc	7	34
Château Grand Pey-de-Lescours	31	150
Château Grand-Rivallon	3	9
Château Grangeneuve (*voir* Château Figeac)		
Château Grangey	5	22
Château des Graves	4	24
Cru des Graves	2	6
Château Graves-d'Armens	6	35
Château Graves d'Arthus	5	21
Château des Graves-de-Mondou	4	14
Château Gravet	12	60
Château Gravet-Renaissance	15	70
Clos Gravet	11	51
Clos du Gros	1	6
Château Gros-Caillou	17	100
Clos des Gros-Chênes	5	27
Cru Grotte-d'Arcis	3	14
Château Guadet-le-Franc-Grâce-Dieu	8	40
Château Gueyrot	6	27
Château Guillemot	7	17
Château Guinot	4	16
Clos Guinot	6	40
Domaine du Haut-Badon	3	8
Domaine de Haut-Barbey	2	7
Château Haut-Barbeyron	4	5
Château Haut-Benitey	5	13
Château Haut-Berthonneau	1	7
Clos Haut-Bibey	2	11
Château Haut-Brisson	13	65
Clos Haut-Cabanne	1	6
Château Haut-Cadet	13	36
Château Haut-Fonrazade, Cru La Tour-Fonrazade	11	43

	Ha	Tonneaux
Château Haut-Grâce-Dieu (*voir* Château Peyrelongue)		
Château Haut-Grand-Faurie	4	21
Cru Haut-Grand-Faurie	1	5
Château Haut-Gueyrot	9	50
Château Haut-Jauge Blanc	1	5
Château Haut-Jean-Faure Clos La Fleur-Figeac, Clos La Bourrue, Tauzinat-l'Hermitage	7	49
Château Haut-Jeanguillot	4	17
Château Haut-Lartigue	3	15
Château Haut-Lavallade	10	50
Château Haut-Mauvinon	8	28
Château Haut-Mazerat, Vieux Château Mazerat	8	35
Château Haut-Panet-Pineuilh	2	9
Château Haut-Peyroutas	11	60
Château Haut-Pontet	5	25
Château Haut-Pourret	5	30
Château Haut-Rabion	5	17
Château Haut-Renaissance	22	100
Domaine Haut-Trimoulet	5	20
Château Haut-Robin	4	14
Château Haut-Rocher	8	40
Château Haut-Segottes	7	42
Château Haut-Simard	20	150
Château Haut-Touran	3	8
Château Haut-Troquart, La Grace Dieu	4	19
Domaine Haut-Vachon	4	18
Château Haut-Veyrac	7	30
Château Haut-Nauve	8	40
Domaine Haute-Rouchonne	8	40
Château Hautes-Graves-d'Arthus	9	47
Château l'Hermitage-Mazerat	4	17
Château Jacques Blanc	17	100
Clos Jacquemeau	1	5
Château Jacqueminot	4	15
Château Jacques Noir	4	20
Château Jaubert-Peyblanquet	5	11
Château Jaugueblanc	5	21
Clos Jaumard	2	8
Château Jean Blanc	6	33
Clos Jean Guillot	7	35
Cru Jeanguillot	2	8
Château de Jean-Marie	4	20
Château Jean-Marie-Cheval-Brun	2	8
Château Jean-Voisin Carbonneyre	15	60
Château Jean Voisin	12	60
Grand Domaine Jean-Voisin	2	7
Château Joly	6	27
Cru Jubilé	2	9
Château Jupille et Château Carillon	22	100
Château Justice	3	15
Château La Barde	3	6
Clos La barde	15	70
Château La Barthe	9	50
Domaine La Beillonne	2	14
Château La Bouygue	3	17
Château La Chapelle	4	20
Château La Chapelle-Lescours	16	90
Château La Clotte-Grande-Côte	4	11
Château La Côte-Daugay	1	6
Clos La Croix	9	49
Château La Croix-Chantecaille	6	32
Clos La Croix-Figeac	3	18
Château La Croizille	4	9
Château La Fagnouse	5	37
Château La Fleur	5	28
Château La Fleur-Cadet	4	14
Clos La Fleur-Figeac (voir Château Haut-Jean-Faure)		
Château La Fleur-Pourret	6	30
Château La Fortine	2	6
Château La Garelle	9	50
Cru La Garelle	1	8
Clos La Glaye	4	17
Château La Gomerie	5	25
Château La Grâce-de-Dieu-les-Menuts	13	70
Château La Grange de Lescure	21	100
Château La Mauléone (*voir* Château Pontet Clauzure)		
Château La Mélissière	13	70
Château La Mouleyre	7	19
Château La Nauve	9	31

	Ha	*Tonneaux*		*Ha*	*Tonneaux*
Château La Rose-Côtes-Rol	4	19	Château Fougueyrat)		
Château La Rose-Rol	4	19	Château Le Freyche	4	13
Château La Rouchonne	9	50	Clos Le Freyche	4	9
Château La Sablière	6	28	Château Le Grand-Barrail	3	11
Château La Sablonnerie	10	35	Château Le Grand-Faurie	4	17
Château La Tour	7	27	Château Le Gueyrot	4	15
Château La Tour-Baladoz	7	40	Château Le Jurat	9	39
Château La Tour Bertonneau	2	8	Château Le Loup	6	5
Château La Tour-des-Combes	12	60	Château Le Merle	6	12
Château La Tour-Cravignac	3	16	Château Le Peillan	13	20
Château La Tour-Fonrazade	8	40	Château Le Poteau	4	17
Château La Tour-Puyblanquet	6	21	Château Le Rocher	3	10
Château La Tour-St-Émilion	4	18	Château Le Sable-Villebout	13	70
Château La Tour-St-Pierre	11	55	Château Le Tertre	4	13
Château La Tour-Vachon	4	21	Château Le Thibaut	9	33
Clos Labrit	3	19	Château Le Thibaut-Bordas	3	13
Château Lagaborite	2	8	Cru le Vignot	1	7
Château La Grave-Figeac	3	17	Château Les Bazilliques	6	30
Château Lapelletrie	9	54	Château Haut-Scarpe, Clos du Vieux, Château Les Grandes-Plantes-Haut-Béard	10	50
Château Lapeyre	13	65	Clos Les Graves	4	12
Château Larcis-Bergey	1	8	Château Les Jouans	12	90
Château Lardon-Jacqueminot	15	74	Château Les Moulins	4	19
Château Larmande	21	100	Château Les Moureaux	4	23
Château Laroque	44	200	Château Les Roquettes-Mondottes	3	10
Domaine Laroque, Château Nardon	3	19	Château Les Templiers	8	40
Clos Larose	2	10	Château Les Tuileries	3	18
Château Larques, Château Chatelet	19	36	Château Les Vieilles-Nauves	2	7
Château Lartigue	6	35	Château Les-Vieilles-Souches-La-Marzelle	4	18
Clos Lartigue	1	5	Château Lescours	32	160
Crus Lartigue	3	11	Château Lespinasse	16	80
Clos Lartigues	2	8	Domaine de Liamet	2	8
Château Lassègue	20	100	Château de Lisse	25	100
Château Latour-Blanche	1	4	Domaine du Logis-de-Moureaux	1	6
Château Latour-Pourret	6	16	Domaine de Longat	3	6
Château Lavallade	17	100	Château de Long-Champ	4	26
Château Lavergne	2	15	Château Magnan-la-Gaffelière	2	10
Clos Lavergne	9	46	Clos du Maine	2	10
Château Le Basque	18	47	Château Malineau	4	14
Château Le Bon-Pasteur	3	9	Château Mangot	20	66
Clos Le Bregnet	5	22	Château Marrin	19	100
Château Le Castelot	5	21	Château Maurillon	1	7
Château Le Cauze	20	130	Château Mayne-Vieux	5	17
Cru Le Châtelet (*voir*			Château Melun	14	75
			Château Menichot	5	18

	Ha	*Tonneaux*
Clos des Menuts	22	100
Domaine des Menuts	1	5
Château du Merle	6	18
Château Meylet-la-Gomerie	2	10
Château Millery-Lapelletrie	2	10
Château Milon	25	100
Château Milon-Feuillat	3	10
Château Mitrotte	1	6
Château des Moines	4	21
Château des Moines	4	23
Château Monbousquet, Château Caperot	31	144
Château Mondotte-Bellisle	6	16
Château Mondou	4	16
Clos Mondou	2	9
Château Monlot-Capet	8	37
Clos Monplaisir	2	8
Château Montbelair	18	100
Château Montlabert	10	40
Domaine de Montlabert	2	10
Château Montremblant	5	25
Château Morillon	2	8
Château de la Mouleyre	5	19
Château Moulin-Bellegrave	11	60
Château Moulin de Cantelaube	3	6
Château Moulin-de-Pierrefitte	3	14
Château Moulin-St-Georges	11	48
Château Moulin-St-Georges, Château Pindefleurs	13	65
Cru Mourens	2	7
Château Myosotis	3	10
Cru Napoléon	2	7
Château Nardon (*voir* Domaine Laroque)		
Clos de Naudin	2	6
Château de Neuville	1	7
Château Pailhas	12	51
Clos Pailhas	3	8
Clos du Palais-Cardinal	5	6
Château Panet	22	80
Château Paradis	15	80
Château Paradis, Château Patarabet	19	64
Château Parans	7	35
Clos Pasquette	3	15
Domaine de Pasquette	5	26
Château Patarabet	7	45
Château Patarabet (*voir* Château Paradis)		
Clos Patarabet	1	5
Cru Patarabet	1	4
Domaine Patarabet-la-Gaffelière	2	8
Clos Patarabet-Lartigue	2	9
Château Patris	5	29
Château Patris	9	50
Château Pavillon-Figeac	4	9
Château Peillan-St.-Clair	6	18
Château Pelletan	5	16
Château Pérey	2	10
Domaine de Pérey	2	10
Domaine Petit-Basque	2	6
Château Petit-Bigaroux	5	15
Château Petit-Bois-de-la-Garelle	3	14
Château Petit Bord	1	4
Domaine du Petit Clos	4	18
Château Petit-Cormey	6	25
Château Petit-Faurie	4	25
Château Petit-Faurie-Trocard	4	21
Clos Petit-Figeac, Clos Pourret	3	16
Château Petit-Fombrauge	2	6
Cru Petit-Gontey	2	9
Château du Petit-Gontey	3	9
Château Petit-Gravet	5	10
Domaine du Petit-Gueyrot	2	12
Château Petit-Mangot	16	70
Château Petit-Val	5	27
Château Peygenestou	2	10
Château Peymouton	3	10
Château Peyreau	18	75
Château Peyrelongue, Château Haut-Grâce-Dieu	11	52
Château Peyrouquet	24	120
Château Peyroutas	14	70
Clos Pezat	1	6
Château Picon-Gravignac	4	12
Château Pidoux	2	10
Clos Piganeau	1	8
Château Pindefleurs	9	50
(*voir* Château Moulin-St-Georges)		
Château Piney	9	50
Cru Piney	1	4
Château Pipeau	24	70
Château Pipeau-Menichot	10	50

	Ha	*Tonneaux*
Château Plaisance	9	50
Cru Plaisance	4	20
Cru Plateau-Jappeloup	3	6
Château Pointe-Bouquey	9	50
Château du Pont de Bouquey	3	11
Château Pont-de-Mouquet	12	40
Château Pontet	4	17
Domaine du Pontet	3	12
Château Pontet Clauzure	16	75
Clos Pourret (*voir* Clos Petit-Figeac)		
Château Pressac	24	90
Clos Pressac	7	32
Château Puyblanquet	18	100
Château Quentin	27	80
Château Quercy	4	22
Château Queyron	16	90
Château Queyron-Pin de fleurs	12	70
Château Rabat	3	10
Château Rabion	5	19
Domaine Rabion-Pailhas	4	14
Château Régent	4	20
Château Reine-Blanche	5	16
Château les Religieuses	2	9
Château Renaissance	5	24
Château de Rey	4	19
Château Reynard	4	14
Château Rivallon	8	24
Domaine de Rivière	5	21
Château Robin	9	50
Château Robin-des-Moines	5	7
Château Roc	4	20
Clos du Roc	3	8
Château Roc-St-Michel	4	18
Château Rochebelle	3	7
Château du Rocher	18	90
Château Rocher-Bellevue-Figeac	4	20
Château de Rol	5	24
Côtes de Rol	4	26
Domaine de Rol	3	13
Château Rol-de-Frombrauge	8	40
Clos Rol-de-Frombrauge	5	23
Cru Rol-de-Frombrauge	4	15
Château aux Roquettes	2	7
Domaine de la Rose	2	12
Château Roucheyron	6	28
Clos Roucheyron	1	5
Domaine du Rouy	2	9
Château du Roy, Clos Berthoneau	3	20
Royal St-Émilion (*voir* Cave Coopérative)		
Château Roylland	3	15
Château Rozier	17	90
Château Rozier-Béard	6	22
Clos du Sable	2	5
Château St-Christophe	7	29
Clos St-Émilion	8	44
Domaine St-Jean-de-Béard	4	11
Clos St-Julien	3	9
Château St-Lô	8	38
Château St-Martial	7	35
Château St-Pey	19	100
Château St-Pierre	4	11
Château St-Roch	3	9
Château St-Valéry	3	13
Château de Sarenceau	5	26
Château de Sarpe	6	12
Clos de Sarpe	3	10
Clos des Sarrazins	6	14
Château Saupiquet	1	9
Domaine Saupiquet	2	8
Domaine de Sème	4	20
Château Sicard	41	200
Château Simard	25	120
Clos Simard	3	13
Château Soutard-Cadet	3	11
Château Tarreyre	2	11
Château Tauzinat	3	5
Domaine Tauzinat	3	10
Château Teyssier	18	100
Château Toinet-Fombrauge	8	36
Château Tonneret	2	10
Château Tour des Combes	15	70
Château du Touran	4	25
Château Tour St-Christophe	45	225
Château Touzinat	7	40
Château Trapaud	11	94
Château Trapeau	8	47
Domaine de Trapeau	3	20
Château Trianon	5	21
Clos Trimoulet	4	21
Château Troquart (*voir* Château Ripeau)		
Château Truquet	4	18
Château Vachon	3	16
Château du Val-d'Or	20	100
Clos Valentin	4	21

	Ha	*Tonneaux*		*Ha*	*Tonneaux*
Clos Verdet-Monbousquet	5	11	Vieux-Château-Chauvin	4	18
Clos Vert-Bois	4	10	Vieux-Château-Fortin	5	16
Château Veyrac	3	25	Château Vieux Garouilh	12	60
Château Vieille-Cloche	13	65	Château Vieux-Guinot, Château Fourney	13	80
Château Vieille-Tour-La-Rose	3	16	Château Vieux-Larmande	4	11
Clos du Vieux (*voir* Château Les Eyguires)			Vieux-Domaine-Menuts	3	13
Château Vieux-Castel-Robin	4	17	Château Vieux-Moulin-du-Cadet	3	16
Château Vieux-Ceps, Château Badon	6	28	Vieux-Château-Peymouton	9	37
			Vieux-Château-Peyrou	1	7
			Clos Vieux-Pontet	2	6
			Château Vieux-Pourret	4	19

CRUS SECONDAIRES DE SAINT-ÉMILION ET DES LOCALITÉS AVOISINANTES

	Commune	*Ha*	*Tonneaux*
Château Ambois	*St-Georges-St-Émilion*	1	4
Domaine D'Arriailh	*Montagne St-Émilion*	4	6
Château Austerlitz	*Sables-St-Émilion*	5	18
Château Barbe-Blanche	*Montagne St-Émilion*	15	90
Château Barraud	*Montagne St-Émilion*	4	21
Domaine de Barraud	*Montagne St-Émilion*	4	11
Château Bayard	*Montagne St-Émilion*	11	50
Clos Bayard	*Montagne St-Émilion*	5	22
Domaine de Bayard	*Montagne St-Émilion*	8	19
Clos Beaufort-Mazerat	*St-Émilion*	2	9
Château Beauséjour	*Montagne St-Émilion*	14	60
Château Beauséjour	*Montagne St-Émilion*	14	80
Château Beausite	*Lussac-St-Émilion*	3	10
Château Belair	*Montagne St-Émilion*	8	50
Château Bel-Air	*Puisseguin-St-Émilion*	11	60
Château Bel-Air-Lussac	*Montagne St-Émilion*	19	105
Château de Bellevue	*Montagne St-Émilion*	11	60
Château Bellevue	*Montagne St-Émilion*	7	30
Château Béouran	*St-Émilion*	1	7
Cru Berlière	*Montagne St-Émilion*	4	15
Château de Berlière	*Montagne St-Émilion*	3	25
Château Berliquet	*St-Émilion*	7	19
Château Bertineau-Goby	*Montagne St-Émilion*	9	28
Château Binet	*Montagne St-Émilion*	9	19
Château Bonneau	*Montagne St-Émilion*	9	35
Domaine de Bonneau	*Montagne St-Émilion*	4	12
Château Branne	*Montagne St-Émilion*	6	35
Château Calon	*Montagne St-Émilion*	35	120
Château Calon-Montagne	*St-Georges-St-Émilion*	3	11
Château Calon-St-Georges	*St-Georges-St-Émilion*	3	25
Château Cap-d'Or	*St-Georges-St-Émilion*	5	26
Château de Cassat	*Puisseguin-St-Émilion*	13	65
Cave Coopérative des Côtes-de-Castillon	*St-Étienne-de-Lisse*	3	14

	Commune	Ha	Tonneaux
Cave Vinicole de Puisseguin	*Puisseguin-St-Émilion*	570	3200
Domaine du Chatain	*Montagne St-Émilion*	3	10
Château Chêne-Vert	*Montagne St-Émilion*	7	30
Château Chêne-Vieux	*Puisseguin-St-Émilion*	8	50
Domaine de la Clotte	*Montagne St-Émilion*	5	14
Coopérative de Montagne	*Montagne St-Émilion*	145	706
Clos des Corbières	*Montagne St-Émilion*	2	8
Château Corbin	*Montagne St-Émilion*	18	150
Domaine de Corniaud	*Montagne St-Émilion*	5	15
Domaine de Corniaud-Lussac	*Montagne St-Émilion*	3	10
Château Côte de Bonde	*Montagne St-Émilion*	7	55
Château Côtes-du-Fayan	*Puisseguin-St-Émilion*	8	20
Château Coucy	*Montagne St-Émilion*	18	85
Château du Courlat	*Montagne St-Émilion*	12	60
Domaine Croix-de-Grézard	*Montagne St-Émilion*	2	9
Château Croix-de-Justice	*Puisseguin-St-Émilion*	16	70
Château Cruzeau	*Sables-St-Émilion*	3	14
Château Daviau-La Chapelle	*Montagne St-Émilion*	5	30
Château Divon	*St-Georges-St-Émilion*	4	19
Clos l'Église	*Montagne St-Émilion*	4	17
Clos de l'Église	*Montagne St-Émilion*	13	46
Clos de l'Église (*voir* Château St-Georges)			
Château Faizeau	*Montagne St-Émilion*	10	45
Château Fongaban (*voir* Château Mouchet)			
Château Fontmurée	*Montagne St-Émilion*	1	3
Château de Font Murée	*Montagne St-Émilion*	10	39
Domaine Franc-Baudron	*Montagne St-Émilion*	6	20
Château Froquard	*St-Georges-St-Émilion*	3	15
Château Guadet-Plaisance	*Montagne St-Émilion*	4	30
Château Gaillard	*Sables-St-Émilion*	4	16
Château Garderose	*Sables-St-Émilion*	5	20
Château Gay-Moulins et Château des Moines	*Montagne St-Émilion*	18	80
Clos Gilet	*Montagne St-Émilion*	3	13
Château Gironde	*Puisseguin-St-Émilion*	4	5
Château Haut Goujon	*Montagne St-Émilion*	3	5
Domaine du Gourdins	*Sables-St-Émilion*	1	6
Domaine des Grands-Champs	*Montagne St-Émilion*	4	10
Domaine des Grands-Pairs	*Montagne St-Émilion*	2	8
Domaine de Grimon	*St-Georges-St-Émilion*	5	20
Château Gueyrosse	*Sables-St-Émilion*	4	15
Château Guibeau	*Puisseguin-St-Émilion*	41	200
Château Guillon	*St-Georges-St-Émilion*	13	40
Château Haute-Bastienne	*Montagne St-Émilion*	1	8
Domaine Haut-Caillate	*St-Georges-St-Émilion*	2	10
Château Haut-Chéreau	*Montagne St-Émilion*	2	5
Domaine Haut-Corbière	*Sables-St-Émilion*	2	11
Domaine Haut-Guillennay	*Sables-St-Émilion*	2	10
Château Haut-Guitard	*Montagne St-Émilion*	4	46
Château Haut-Langlade	*Montagne St-Émilion*	4	14
Château Haut-Larose	*Montagne St-Émilion*	5	30
Clos Haut-Listrac	*Puisseguin-St-Émilion*	4	14
Domaine de Haut-Marchand	*Montagne St-Émilion*	4	6
Clos Haut-Montaiguillon	*St-Georges-St-Émilion*	5	24
Château Haut-Musset	*Montagne St-Émilion*	5	45

	Commune	*Ha*	*Tonneaux*
Château Haut-Piquat	*Montagne St-Émilion*	16	80
Château Haut-Plaisance	*Montagne St-Émilion*	7	25
Château Haut-Poitou	*Montagne St-Émilion*	2	9
Château Haut-Pourteau	*Montagne St-Émilion*	2	8
Château Haut-St-Georges	*St-Émilion*	2	9
Château Haut-Sarpe	*St-Christophe-des-Bardes*	9	50
Château Haut-Troquard	*St-Georges-St-Émilion*	3	16
Clos Haut-Troquard	*St-Georges-St-Émilion*	1	6
Château La Haute-Faucherie	*Montagne St-Émilion*	8	35
Château l'Hermitage	*Montagne St-Émilion*	6	50
Château Jura-Plaisance	*Montagne St-Émilion*	8	30
Château -La-Bastienne	*Montagne St-Émilion*	17	80
Château la Cabanne	*Puisseguin-St-Émilion*	4	20
Château La Chapelle	*Montagne St-Émilion*	2	15
Château La Clotte	*Puisseguin-St-Émilion*	2	4
Château La Couronne	*Montagne St-Émilion*	4	50
Château La Croix-de-la-Bastienne	*Montagne St-Émilion*	2	12
Cru La Croix-Blanche	*Montagne St-Émilion*	2	7
Château La Croix-de-Blanchon	*Montagne St-Émilion*	5	40
Château La Faucherie	*Montagne St-Émilion*	3	6
Château La Fleur-Perruchon	*Montagne St-Émilion*	5	35
Château La Fleur-St-Georges (*voir* Château St-Georges)			
Château La Grande-Clotte	*Montagne St-Émilion*	5	40
Château La Grenière	*Montagne St-Émilion*	12	80
Château La Mayne	*Sables-St-Émilion*	3	8
Château La Paillette	*Sables-St-Émilion*	3	10
Château La Papeterie	*Montagne St-Émilion*	2	4
Château La Perrière	*Montagne St-Émilion*	5	35
Château La Picherie	*St-Georges-St-Émilion*	12	55
Château La Plante	*Sables-St-Émilion*	1	5
Clos La Rose	*Puisseguin-St-Émilion*	7	30
Château La Roseraie-du-Mont	*Puisseguin-St-Émilion*	4	9
Château La Tête-du-Cerf	*Montagne St-Émilion*	6	15
Château La Tour-Ballet	*Montagne St-Émilion*	1	5
Château La Tour-Blanche	*Montagne St-Émilion*	3	19
Château la Tour de Gillet	*Montagne St-Émilion*	6	50
Château la Tour-de-Grenet	*Montagne St-Émilion*	24	175
Château la Tour-Guillotin	*Puisseguin-St-Émilion*	15	75
Château la Tour-Paquillon	*Montagne St-Émilion*	8	35
Château La Tour-St-Georges (*voir* Château St-Georges)			
Château La Tour-de-Ségur	*Montagne St-Émilion*	12	70
Château La Vaisinerie	*Puisseguin-St-Émilion*	8	27
Clos La Vallée-du-Roi	*Montagne St-Émilion*	3	8
Domaine de Lamaçonne	*Montagne St-Émilion*	3	12
Château Langlade	*Montagne St-Émilion*	6	30
Domaine de Laplaigne	*Puisseguin-St-Émilion*	7	31
Château Larue	*Montagne St-Émilion*	4	13
Château Latour	*Montagne St-Émilion*	5	21
Château Latour-Musset	*Montagne St-Émilion*	10	35
Château Latour-de-Ségur	*Montagne St-Émilion*	8	45
Château Le Chay	*Puisseguin-St-Émilion*	13	58
Cru le Franc-Rival	*Montagne St-Émilion*	2	9
Château Le Gravier-Gueyrosse	*Sables-St-Émilion*	3	12

	Commune	Ha	Tonneaux
Château Le Mayne	*Puisseguin-St-Émilion*	10	45
Clos Le Pas-St-Georges	*St-Georges-St-Émilion*	6	31
Château le Pont-de-Pierre	*Montagne St-Émilion*	3	15
Château Le Puy-St-Georges (*voir* Château St-Georges)			
Château Le Roc-de-Troquard	*St-Georges-St-Émilion*	3	10
Château Le-Tertre-de-Perruchon	*Montagne St-Émilion*	3	7
Château Lenoir	*Sables-St-Émilion*	4	13
Château Léonard	*Puisseguin-St-Émilion*	9	30
Château Lépine	*Sables-St-Émilion*	2	7
Château Les Bardes	*Montagne St-Émilion*	3	13
Château Les Carrières	*Montagne St-Émilion*	2	20
Château Les Côtes-de-Gardat	*Montagne St-Émilion*	5	24
Château Les Eyguires	*St-Christophe-des-Bardes*		
Domaine Les Genêts	*Montagne St-Émilion*	3	9
Château Les Grandes-Vignes	*Montagne St-Émilion*	2	10
Château Les Jacquets	*St-Georges-St-Émilion*	5	22
Château Les Laurets	*Puisseguin-St-Émilion*	60	250
Château Les Renardières	*St-Georges-St-Émilion*	4	14
Château Les Tuileries-de-Laporte-Bayard	*Montagne St-Émilion*	45	225
Château Les Vieux-Rocs	*Montagne St-Émilion*	6	20
Château Lestage	*Montagne St-Émilion*	8	50
Château L'Ormeau-Vieux	*Puisseguin-St-Émilion*	7	23
Château Lucas et Château Rouzaud	*Montagne St-Émilion*	16	110
Château de Lussac	*Montagne St-Émilion*	20	140
Château du Lyonnat	*Montagne St-Émilion*	35	200
Château Lyon-Perruchon	*Montagne St-Émilion*	4	11
Château Macureau	*Montagne St-Émilion*	6	26
Clos des Magrines	*Puisseguin-St-Émilion*	3	6
Château Maison-Blanche	*Montagne St-Émilion*	30	150
Château de Maisonneuve	*Montagne St-Émilion*	7	20
Clos Maisonneuve	*Montagne St-Émilion*	2	8
Domaine de Maisonneuve, Château St-Georges-Macquin	*St-Georges-St-Émilion*	17	54
Château *Martinet*	*Sables-St-Émilion*	12	56
Clos Maurice	*St-Sulpice-de-Faleyrens*	1	6
Château Meynard	*Sables-St-Émilion*	6	11
Château Montaiguillon	*Montagne St-Émilion*	23	130
Château Montaiguillon	*St-Georges-St-Émilion*	3	16
Château Montesquieu	*Puisseguin-St-Émilion*	14	63
Clos Montesquieu	*Montagne St-Émilion*	3	12
Château Mouchet, Château Fongaban	*Puisseguin-St-Émilion*	10	35
Château Mouchique	*Puisseguin-St-Émilion*	4	17
Château du Moulin	*Puisseguin-St-Émilion*	6	30
Château Moulin-du-Jura	*Montagne St-Émilion*	3	10
Château de Musset	*Montagne St-Émilion*	7	40
Château Naguet-La-Grande	*Montagne St-Émilion*	5	12
Château Négrit	*Montagne St-Émilion*	12	60
Château Pavillon-Fougailles	*St-Émilion*	1	5
Château Petit-Clos du Roy	*Montagne St-Émilion*	8	50
Château Petit-Refuge	*Montagne St-Émilion*	2	15
Château Peyrou	*St-Étienne-de-Lisse*	5	24
Château Piron	*Montagne St-Émilion*	6	25
Château Plaisance	*Montagne St-Émilion*	20	100
Clos Plaisance	*Montagne St-Émilion*	9	28

	Commune	*Ha*	*Tonneaux*
Clos Plince	*Sables-St-Émilion*	1	6
Château du Puy	*Montagne St-Émilion*	6	35
Château Puy-Bonnet	*Montagne St-Émilion*	5	30
Château du Puynormond	*Montagne St-Émilion*	7	50
Domaine du Puynormond	*Montagne St-Émilion*	5	21
Château Quinault	*Sables-St-Émilion*	12	58
Domaine de Rambaud	*Montagne St-Émilion*	3	6
Clos des Religieuses	*Puisseguin-St-Émilion*	8	20
Château Rigaud	*Puisseguin-St-Émilion*	3	15
Château Roc-de-Puynormond	*Montagne St-Émilion*	6	10
Château Rocher-Corbin	*Montagne St-Émilion*	9	68
Château des Rochers (*voir* Château Bonneau)			
Domaine des Rocs	*Montagne St-Émilion*	8	40
Château Rocs-Marchand	*Montagne St-Émilion*	9	9
Château Roudier	*Montagne St-Émilion*	30	150
Château Roudier	*St-Georges-St-Émilion*	3	17
Domaine du Roudier	*Montagne St-Émilion*	10	50
Château des Roziers	*Montagne St-Émilion*	4	14
Château Sablons	*Montagne St-Émilion*	5	20
Château St-Georges, Château La Tour-St-Georges, Château Le Puy-St-Georges, Château La Fleur-St-Georges, Clos de l'Église	*St-Georges-St-Émilion*	35	250
Château St-Georges-Macquin (*voir* Domaine de Maisonneuve)			
Château St-Jacques-Calon	*Montagne St-Émilion*	6	45
Château St-Louis	*St-Georges-St-Émilion*	8	35
Château St-Michel	*Montagne St-Émilion*	2	9
Château St-Paul	*Montagne St-Émilion*	5	23
Château Samion	*St-Georges-St-Émilion*	4	20
Château Soleil	*Puisseguin-St-Émilion*	15	60
Château Taureau	*Montagne St-Émilion*	13	80
Château Teillac	*Puisseguin-St-Émilion*	20	100
Château Terrien	*Montagne St-Émilion*	7	35
Château Tetre-de-la-Mouleyre	*Montagne St-Émilion*	2	8
Clos Teynac-Rival	*Puisseguin-St-Émilion*	3	14
Château Teyssier	*Puisseguin-St-Émilion*	20	100
Château des Tours	*Montagne St-Émilion*	70	300
Château Vieux-Bonneau	*Montagne St-Émilion*	8	60
Vieux-Château-Calon	*Montagne St-Émilion*	5	35
Vieux-Château-Goujon	*Montagne St-Émilion*	2	10
Château Vieux-Guillou	*St-Georges-St-Émilion*	4	17
Vieux-Château-La-Beysse	*Puisseguin-St-Émilion*	4	6
Château Vieux-Logis-de-Cazelon	*Montagne St-Émilion*	2	8
Château Vieux-Montaiguillon	*St-Georges-St-Émilion*	3	13
Château Vieux-Mouchet	*Montagne St-Émilion*	1	6
Domaine du Vieux-Moulin-de-Calon	*Montagne St-Émilion*	1	6
Vieux-Château-Négrit	*Montagne St-Émilion*	5	40
Vieux-Château-Palon	*Montagne St-Émilion*	5	17

IV. Pomerol

Les vins de Pomerol ne sont pas classés officiellement. On considère Château Pétrus comme le Grand Cru hors classe.

La production indiquée ci-dessous est approximative. Elle indique une moyenne annuelle telle qu'elle est donnée par les communes d'après les déclarations de récolte.

PRINCIPAUX CRUS

	Ha	*Caisses*
Clos des Amandiers	2	1 000
Clos Barrail-du-Milieu, Clos du Pellerin	2	500
Château la Bassonnerte	4	2 000
Château Beauchêne	4	4 000
Château Beauregard	13	5 000
Château Beauséjour-de-Bonalgue	2	500
Château Beau-Soleil	3	2 000
Château Bel-Air, Vieux-Château-Boënot	13	5 000
Château Belle Brise	2	700
Château Bellegrave	6	2 000
Château Bellevue-Montviel	5	2 000
Château Boënot, Château Trintin	4	4 000
Château Bonalgue	3	900
Château Le Bon-Pasteur	6	2 000
Château Bourgneuf-Vayron	9	3 000
Château de Bourgueneuf	5	2 000
Château Brun-Mazeyres	3	2 000
Château de Cantereau	3	1 000
Château du Casse	2	700
Château du Castel	2	800
Château Certan-Giraud	7	3 000
Château Certan-Marzelle	4	2 000
Château Certan-de-May	4	2 000
Château Chêne-Liège	2	900
Château Clinet	6	2 000
Château Clos Bel-Air	2	900
Clos du Clocher, Château Monregard-Lacroix	5	3 000
Domaine des Clones	2	500
Château du Couvent	2	700
Château Deltour	2	700
Château Domaine de l'Église	7	3 000
Château Élisée	2	700
Château Enclos Haut-Mazeyras	7	3 000
Château du Fagnard	2	800
Château Ferrand	11	4 000
Château Ferron	2	700
Château Feytit-Clinet	6	2 000
Château Feytit-Guillot	1	500
Château Franc-Maillet	4	2 000
Château Gazin	25	7 000
Château Gombaude-Guilhot	6	3 000
Château Gouprie	3	2 000
Cru Grand-Mazeyres	2	500
Château Grand-Moulinet	2	500
Clos des Grands Sillons-Gabachot	3	2 000
Château Grange Neuve	4	2 000
Château Grate-Cap	9,5	4 000
Domaine des Graves de Maillet	1	400
Château Graves-Guillot	2	700
Château Guillot	5	2 000
Château Guillot-Trochaud	3	1 000
Château Haut-Cloquet	2	1 000
Cru Haut-Groupey	2	500
Château Haut-Maillet	5	2 000
Clos Haut-Mazeyres	9	2 000
Château de Haut-Pignon	2	500
Domaine de Haut-Trochaud	1	500
Domaine des Jacobins	1	500
Château La Cabanne	12	3 000
Château La Chichonne	2	500
Clos Lacombe	2	500
Château La Commanderie	5	2 000
Château La Conseillante	11	4 000
Château La Croix	17	5 000
Château La Croix-de-Gay	11	4 000
Château La Croix des Templiers	3	900
Château La Croix du Casse	9	4 000
Château La Croix-St-Georges	4	2 000
Château La Croix-Taillefer	2	600
Château Lafleur	4	1 000
Domaine de Lafleur	4	2 000

	Ha	*Caisses*
Château Lafleur-Gazin	7	2 000
Château La Fleur du Mayne	3	900
Château Lafleur-Pétrus	9	3 000
Château La Fleur-des-Rouzes	7	2 000
Château Lafleur du Roy	3	2 000
Château La Fleur-Treyssac	1	400
Château La Ganne	5	2 000
Château Lagrange	8	3 000
Château La Grave-Trigant de Boisset	8	3 000
Château La Patache	2	500
Château La Pointe	20	7 000
Domaine La Pointe, Clos Bel-Air	4	800
Château La Renaissance	5	2 000
Clos La Rose	3	2 000
Château La Rose-Figeac	5	2 000
Clos La Soulatte	2	500
Château Latour-Pomerol	9	4 000
Château La Truffe	2	700
Domaine de la Vieille École	2	400
Clos de la Vieille Église	2	500
Château La Violette	4	900
Château Le Bon Pasteur	7	2 000
Château Le Caillou	5	3 000
Château Le Carillon	4	2 000
Château Le Gay	8	2 000
Clos l'Église	5	2 000
Domaine de l'Église	7	3 000
Château de l'Église-Clinet	4	2 000
Château l'Enclos	10	4 000
Château Le Pin	1	500
Château Les Bordes	2	2 000
Clos Les Grands-Champs, Château Guillot	5	2 000
Château Les Grands-Sillons	2	1 000
Château Les Hautes-Rouzes	2	800
Clos Les Rouzes-Clinet	2	900
Château l'Évangile	13	3 000
Château Margot	1	500
Château Marzy	7	4 000
Château Mayne	3	900
Château du Mayne	2	900
Château Mazeyres	10	4 000
Clos Mazeyres, Château Beauchêne	6	2 000
Château Moulinet	17	7 000

	Ha	*Caisses*
Château Nénin	20	7 000
Château Nouvelle-Église	2	500
Clos du Pelerin		
Château du Petit-Moulinet	3	1 000
Château Petit Plince	3	900
Château Petit-Village	9	4 000
Château Pétrus	12	4 000
Château Pignon-Larroucaud	2	300
Château Plince	7	3 000
Château Plincette	1	400
Clos Plince	1	300
Château La Providence	3	600
Château Ratouin	3	700
Domaine des Ramparts	4	1 000
Clos René	16	6 000
Domaine de René	3	700
Château Rève-d'Or	5	2 000
Château de Robert	4	1 000
Château Rocher-Beauregard	2	700
Château Rouget	12	4 000
Clos du Roy	3	1 000
Château St-André	2	1 000
Château Saint-Pierre	3	2 000
Château Sainte-Marie	4	2 000
Château de Sales	47	12 000
Château Tailhas	9	800
Château Taillefer, Clos Beauregard, Château Toulifaut, Clos Toulifaut	21	9 000
Château des Templiers	3	2 000
Château Thibéaud-Maillet	2	2 000
Domaine Tour du Roy	1	400
Château Tristan	1	400
Château Tropchaud l'Église	3	1 000
Château Trotanoy	9	3 000
Château de Valois	6	3 000
Vieux-Château-Boënot (*voir* Château Bel-Air)	3	2 000
Vieux-Château-Bourgueneuf	5	2 000
Vieux-Château-Certan	14	5 500
Vieux-Château-Cloquet	2	600
Vieux Château Hautes Graves Veaulieu	1	500
Château Vieux-Maillet	4,5	500
Château Vieux Taillefer	2	500
Château Vieux Tressac	2	700
Château Vraye-Croix-de-Gay	6	2 000

APPELLATION LALANDE DE POMEROL

Commune de Lalande de Pomerol

Clos des Arnaud	Domaine de Grand Moine
Château de Bel Air	Château Grand Ormeau
Château Bourseau	Clos Haut Cavujon
Petit Clos de Brouard	Château Perron
Château de la Commanderie	Sabloire du Grand Moine
Château les Cruzelles	Château de Viaud
Clos de l'Église	Domaine de Viaud
Clos l'Étoile	Clos de la Vieille Forge

Commune de Néac

Domaine du Bourg	Château Gachet
Château Canon Chaigneau	Château Garraud
Clos du Carsel	Domaine des Grands Bois Chagneau
Château Chatain	Domaine du Grand Ormeau
Clos du Chatain	Château Haut Ballet
Domaine du Chatain	Château Haut Chaigneau
Château Laborde	Château Lafaurie
Château des Moines	Château Lavinot la Chapelle
Château Templiers	Château Les Grandes Versaines
Clos des Moines	Château Moncets
Château de Musset	Château Moulin à Vent
Château Perron	Château Siaurac
Château les Chaumes	Domaine de Surget
Château Chevrol Bel Air	Château de Teysson
Château Drouilleau Belles Graves	Château Tournefeuille
Château Fougeailles	

V. Fronsac

Les chiffres de production ci-dessous sont approximatifs. Ils donnent une moyenne annuelle telle qu'elle est indiquée par les municipalités d'après leurs déclarations de récolte.

PRINCIPAUX CRUS

	Commune	*Ha*	*Tonneaux*
Château d'Alem	*Saillans*	13	70
Château Arnauton	*Fronsac*	24	100
Au Tertre	*Fronsac*	4	20
Château Beauséjour	*Saillans*	8	40
Château Belair	*Saillans*	6	40
Château Bourdieu-La-Valade	*Fronsac*	10	50
Château Capet	*Fronsac*	4	20
Château du Carillon	*Saillans*	8	40
Château de Carles	*Saillans*	16	70

	Commune	*Ha*	*Tonneaux*
Château Chadène	*St-Aignan*	10	50
Château de Fronsac	*Fronsac*	7	30
Château Gagnard-et La Croix Bertrand	*Fronsac*	11	20
Château Hauchat	*St-Aignan*	6	25
Château Jeandeman	*St-Aignan*	23	100
Domaine Laborie	*Saillans*	6	10
Domaine du La Brand	*Saillans*	5	12
Château La Croix	*Fronsac*	20	100
Château La Croix Gandineau	*Fronsac*	5	12
Château La Croix-Laroque	*Fronsac*	5	25
Château La Dauphine	*Fronsac*	6	14
Château du Faure-Haut-Normand	*Saillans*	13	27
Château La Grave	*Fronsac*	3	7
Château La Lague	*Fronsac*	8	50
Château La Tour-Beau-Site	*Fronsac*	10	50
Château Lalande-Maussé	*Saillans*	8	45
Château Lambert	*St-Aignan*	3	15
Château La Valade (Roux)	*Fronsac*	12	50
Château La Vieille Curé	*Saillans*	14	32
Château Le Bosquet	*St-Aignan*	7	35
Château Les Abories de Meyney	*La-Rivière*	3	15
Château Les Roches-de-Ferrand	*St-Aignan*	12	60
Château Les Trois-Croix	*Fronsac*	12	60
Château Magondeau	*Saillans*	15	60
Domaine de Manieu	*La-Rivière*	6	20
Château Mayne-Vieille	*Galgon*	22	100
Château Meyney	*St-Aignan*	8	35
Château de Montahut	*Fronsac*	7	35
Château Moulin-Haut-Laroque	*Saillans*	12	50
Château Moulin des Tonnelles	*St-Aignan*	9	50
Château Moulin-Haut-Villars	*Saillans*	4	20
Château Musseau-Bellevue	*St-Aignan*	6	30
Domaine Normand	*Saillans*	6	30
Château Puyguilhem	*Saillans*	10	40
Château Peychez	*Fronsac*	4	8
Château Pipeau	*La-Rivière*	5	25
Château Plainpoint	*St-Aignan*	12	45
Château Pontus	*Fronsac*	8	40
Château Renard	*La-Rivière*	10	50
Château Richelieu	*Fronsac*	13	60
Château de la Rivière	*La Rivière*	40	160
Château Roc St-Bernard	*Saillans*	4	12
Château Rouet	*La-Rivière*	10	50
Château Saint-Cric-Les-Tonnelles	*St-Aignan*	10	50
Château du Tasta	*St-Aignan*	12	45
Château Les Tonnelles	*St-Aignan*	12	50
Château Tessendey	*Saillans*	5	25
Château Tour-Picot	*La-Rivière*	5	25
Château Vieille-Croix	*Saillans*	10	40
Château Vieux Moulin	*Fronsac*	8	35
Château Vieux-Vincent	*St-Aignan*	10	50
Château Villars	*Saillans*	24	100
Château St-Vincent	*St-Aignan*	7	30
Château Vincent	*St-Aignan*	10	50

VI. Canon-Fronsac

Les chiffres de production sont approximatifs. Ils donnent une moyenne annuelle telle qu'elle est indiquée par les communes d'après leurs déclarations de récolte.

PRINCIPAUX CRUS

Château Barrabaque	*Fronsac*	7	14
Château Belloy	*Fronsac*	5	10
Château Bodet	*Fronsac*	10	38
Château Canon	*Fronsac*	2	10
Château de Canon	*St-Michel*	10	30
Château Cassagne-Haut-Canon	*St-Michel*	8	40
Château Combes-Canon	*St-Michel*	2	7
Château Comte	*Fronsac*	3	10
Château Coustolle et Bourdieu-Lavalade	*Fronsac*	20	100
Château du Gaby	*Fronsac*	10	50
Château du Gazin	*St-Michel*	6	25
Château Grand Renouil	*St-Michel*	6	11
Château Caillou	*Fronsac*	3	9
Château Haut-Ballet	*St-Michel*	5	20
Château Haut-Gros-Bonnet	*Fronsac*	8	40
Château Haut-Lariveau	*St-Michel*	3	10
Château Haut-Mazeris	*St-Michel*	6	16
Château Haut-Panet	*Fronsac*	4	20
Château Junayme	*Fronsac*	16	75
Château La Chapelle-Lariveau	*St-Michel*	5	16
Château La Duchesse	*Fronsac*	3	15
Château La Fleur-Canon	*St-Michel*	4	30
Château La Marche-Canon	*Fronsac*	6	30
Château Larchevêque	*Fronsac*	5	10
Château Lariveau	*St-Michel*	7	18
Château Mausse	*St-Michel*	10	50
Château Mazeris	*St-Michel*	14	50
Château Mazeris Bellevue	*St-Michel*	12	50
Château Moulin-Pey-Labrie	*Fronsac*	8	40
Château Panet	*Fronsac*	4	8
Château du Pavillon-Gros-Bonnet	*Fronsac*	3	15
Château Perron	*Fronsac*	3	4
Château Pey-Labrie	*Fronsac*	8	40
Château Pichelebre	*Fronsac*	12	60
Château Queyran-de-Haut	*St-Michel*	3	10
Domaine de Roullet	*Fronsac*	3	5
Château Roullet	*Fronsac*	3	7
Château de Toumalin et Château Bourdieu-Panet	*Fronsac*	6	30
Château de Toumalin	*Fronsac*	8	40
Château Vrai Canon Bouché	*Fronsac*	12	55
Château Vrai Canon Boyer	*St-Michel*	7	22

VII. Graves. Classification officielle (1959)

Les crus du secteur des Graves furent classés officiellement en 1953 et en 1959. Château Haut-Brion, le plus grand de tous les Graves, est aussi classé officiellement parmi les grands Médoc.

Les chiffres de production sont approximatifs. Ils donnent une moyenne annuelle telle qu'elle est indiquée par les municipalités d'après leurs déclarations de récolte.

CRUS CLASSÉS DES GRAVES : VINS ROUGES

	Commune	*Tonneaux*	*Caisses*
Château Haut-Brion	*Pessac*	130	12 000
Château Bouscaut	*Cadaujac*	120	10 000
Château Carbonnieux	*Léognan*	130	12 000
Domaine de Chevalier	*Léognan*	50	5 000
Château Fieuzal	*Léognan*	100	9 000
Château Haut-Bailly	*Léognan*	80	8 000
Château La Mission-Haut-Brion	*Talence*	70	6 000
Château La Tour-Haut-Brion	*Talence*	20	1 500
Château La Tour-Martillac (Kressman La Tour)	*Martillac*	90	8 000
Château Malartic-Lagravière	*Léognan*	60	5 000
Château Olivier	*Léognan*	90	8 000
Château Pape-Clément	*Pessac*	140	14 000
Château Smith-Haut-Lafitte	*Martillac*	180	17 000

CRUS CLASSÉS DES GRAVES : VINS BLANCS

	Commune	*Tonneaux*	*Caisses*
Château Bouscaut	*Cadaujac*	400	4 000
Château Carbonnieux	*Léognan*	150	14 000
Domaine de Chevalier	*Léognan*	10	950
Château Couhins	*Villenave-d'Ornon*	5	400
Château La Tour-Martillac (Kressmann La Tour)	*Martillac*	20	2 000
Château Laville-Haut-Brion	*Talence*	20	2 000
Château Malartic-Lagravière	*Léognan*	10	900
Château Olivier	*Léognan*	65	6 000
Château Haut-Brion	*Pessac*	14	1 000

AUTRES PRINCIPAUX CRUS DES GRAVES

	Commune		*Ha*	*Tonneaux*
Château André-Lamothe	*Portets*	blanc	2	11
		rouge	4	15
Domaine Andron	*St.-Selve*	blanc	3	5
Clos d'Armajan	*Budos*	blanc	4	15
Château d'Arricaud	*Landiras*	blanc	20	80
		rouge	4	30
Château des Arrocs	*Langon*	blanc	3	10

	Commune		*Ha*	*Tonneaux*
Domaine Arzac	*St.-Selve*	blanc	2	5
Clos l'Avocat	*Cérons*	blanc	3	10
Château Bardins	*Cadaujac*	blanc	17	17
		rouge		2
Château Baret	*Villenave-d'Ornon*	blanc	13	45
		rouge		35
Domaine du Barque	*St.-Selve*	rouge	6	20
Cru Barrouet	*Pujols*	blanc	3	7
Domaine du Basque	*Pujols*	blanc	3	12
Château Batsères	*Landiras*	blanc	4	15
		rouge		
Château Beauchêne	*Beautiran*	blanc	3	7
		rouge	2	5
Domaine du Beau-Site	*Portets*	blanc	0,3	2
		rouge	3	9
Château Bel-Air	*Portets*	blanc	2	6
		rouge	3	10
Château Bel-Air	*St.-Morillon*	blanc	3	10
Château Bellefontaine	*St.-Pierre-de-Mons*	blanc	3	7
Domaine Bellevue	*Toulenne*	blanc	1	7
Domaine de Bellevue	*St.-Selve*	blanc	4	13
Château Belon	*St.-Morillon*	blanc	3	6
		rouge	4	30
Domaine de Bequin	*Portets*	blanc	5	11
		rouge	9	35
Château Bernard-Raymond	*Portets*	blanc	3	13
		rouge	2	11
Château Bichon Cassignols	*La Brède*	blanc	5	11
		rouge		2
Domaine de Biot	*Arbanats*	blanc	2	5
		rouge		4
Domaine de la Blancherie	*La Brède*	blanc	10	30
Château Boiresse	*Ayguemortes*	blanc	4	15
		rouge	5	20
Château de Bonat	*St.-Selve*	blanc	5	25
		rouge	13	50
Clos de la Bonneterie	*Portets*	blanc	2	6
		rouge		4
Clos de la Borderie	*Portets*	blanc	3	9
		rouge	2	8
Domaine du Boscq	*St.-Morillon*	blanc	2	5
Château Boyrein	*Roaillon*	blanc	6	16
		rouge	15	60
Domaine de Brochon	*Arbanats*	blanc	3	7
		rouge	2	3
Château Brondelles	*Lagon*	blanc	2	4
Domaine de Bruilleau	*St.-Médard-d'Eyrans*	blanc	7	19
Château Bruhaut	*St.-Pierre-de-Mons*	blanc	2	4
Château de Budos	*Budos*	blanc	14	55
		rouge	9	31
Clos Cabanes	*St.-Pierre-de-Mons*	blanc	4	11
Clos Cabanne	*St.-Pierre-de-Mons*	blanc	1	5
		rouge	2	10

	Commune		*Ha*	*Tonneaux*
Château Cabannieux	*Portets*	blanc	3	7
		rouge		6
Domaine de Calens	*Beautiran*	blanc	4	10
		rouge	6	20
Cru Camegaye	*Landiras*	Blanc	2	9
Clos Cantalot	*St.-Pierre-de-Mons*	blanc	7	22
Cru de Cap-de-Hé	*Pujols*	blanc	2	10
Château Carmes-Haut-Brion	*Pessac*	rouge	2	8
Domaine Carros	*St.-Selve*	blanc	2	9
Domaine de Casseuil	*Langon*	blanc	4	6
		rouge	3	10
Domaine Castelnaud	*St.-Pierre-de-Mons*	blanc	2	5
Château Catalas	*Pujols*	blanc	6	17
Château Cazebonne	*St.-Pierre-de-Mons*	blanc	7	
		rouge	6	25
Clos Chantegrive	*Podensac*	blanc	10	50
		rouge	5	25
Cru Chante l'Oiseau	*La Brède*	blanc	9	40
Château Chaviran	*Martillac*	rouge	4	16
Château Cherchy	*Pujols*	blanc	4	20
Cru Cherchy	*Pujols*	blanc	2	9
Château Chicane	*Toulenne*	rouge	6	25
Domaine du Ciron	*Pujols*	blanc	5	19
Château de Clare	*Landiras*	blanc	3	
		rouge	5	20
Cru du Couet	*St.-Pierre-de-Mons*	blanc	2	5
Domaine de Courbon	*Toulenne*	blanc	4	25
Domaine du Courreau	*St-Médard-d'Eyrans*	blanc		5
		rouge	3	3
Domaine du Courreau	*St.-Morillon*	blanc	3	11
Château Crabitey	*Portets*	blanc	2	4
		rouge	16	60
Domaine de la Croix	*Langon*	blanc	4	18
		rouge	2	8
Château de Cruzeau	*St.-Médard-d'Eyrans*	blanc	11	50
		rouge	36	160
Clos Darrouban	*Portets*	blanc		
		rouge	2	3
Domaine de Darrouban	*Portets*	blanc	3	15
		rouge	2	3
Château Despagne	*St.-Pierre-de-Mons*	blanc	4	14
Château Doms et Clos du Monastère	*Portets*	blanc	7	20
		rouge	18	70
Domaine du Druc	*Landiras*	blanc	2	6
Domaine de Durse, Domaine de Papoula	*Portets*	blanc	2	
		rouge	1	7
Domaine Étienne	*St.-Morillon*	blanc	2	6
Domaine de Faye	*Portets*	blanc	1	6
		rouge	2	7
Château Fernon	*Langon*	blanc	40	120
		rouge	4	15
Château Ferran	*Martillac*	blanc	6	11
		rouge	5	20
Château Ferrande	*Castres*	blanc	10	40
		rouge	32	180

	Commune		*Ha*	*Tonneaux*
Château Fieuzal	*Léognan*	blanc	1,5	15
		rouge	22	80
Château Foncla	*Castres*	blanc	3	10
Château Foncroise	*St.-Selve*	blanc / rouge	7	10
Château des Fougères	*La Brède*	blanc	2	5
Clos des Fougères	*Virelade*	blanc	4	11
Château de France	*Léognan*	blanc	4	15
		rouge	26	100
Domaine des Gaillardas	*St.-Selve*	blanc	4	10
Cru Galand	*Cérons*	blanc	1	4
Clos du Gars	*La Brède*	blanc	2	10
Château Gazin	*Léognan*	blanc / rouge	13	50
Clos de Gensac	*Pujols*	blanc	4	25
Domaine de la Girafe	*Portets*	blanc	5	22
		rouge	4	15
Cru de Gonthier	*Portets*	blanc	1	5
		rouge	2	7
Château Gorre	*Martillac*	blanc	1	1
		rouge	2	3
Château du Grand-Abord	*Portets*	blanc	5	18
		rouge	18	60
Château Grand Chemin	*Cérons*	blanc	2	8
Château Grandmaison	*Léognan*	blanc	3	10
		rouge	11	55
Château des Graves	*Portets*	blanc	3	6
		rouge	6	25
Domaine de Gravettes	*St.-Morillon*	blanc	4	15
		rouge	5	20
Château Graveyron	*Portets*	blanc	6	18
		rouge	4	10
Château de la Gravière	*Toulenne*	blanc	7	25
Château des Gravières	*Portets*	blanc	3	12
		rouge	19	120
Clos des Gravières	*Portets*	blanc	2	15
		rouge	1	5
Domaine des Gravières	*Portets*	rouge	2	6
Domaine de Guérin	*Castres*	rouge	4	6
Château Guillaumot	*La Brède*	blanc	2	10
Château des Guillemins	*Langon*	blanc	8	28
Domaine de Guirauton	*St.-Morillon*	blanc / rouge	6	12
Domaine des Guizats	*Pujols*	blanc	2	8
Hannetot Grand Maison	*Léognan*	rouge	5	15
Château Haut-Bergey	*Léognan*	rouge	13,5	70
Château du Haut-Blanc	*Pujols*	blanc	3	10
Domaine du Haut-Blanc	*Pujols*	blanc	4	12
Domaine Haut-Callens	*Beautiran*	rouge	3	12
Domaine du Haut Courneau	*Portets*	blanc	17	30
		rouge	5	60
Cru Haut-Gravette	*St.-Morillon*	blanc	3	6
Château Haut-Madère	*Villenave-d'Ornon*	rouge	2	3

	Commune		*Ha*	*Tonneaux*
Château Haut-Nouchet	*Martillac*	blanc	7	20
		rouge		30
Cru Hautes Plantes	*Landiras*	blanc	3	8
Château Haut-Reys	*La Brède*	blanc	3	15
Château Jamnets	*St.-Pierre-de-Mons*	blanc	2	5
		rouge		4
Clos Jamnet	*La Brède*	blanc	4	15
Cru Janot-Bayle	*Budos*	rouge	8	16
Domaine du Jau	*St.-Morillon*	blanc	3	5
Château Les Jaubertes	*St. Pardon de Congues*	blanc	6	35
		rouge	7	30
Clos Jean Dubos	*Pujols*	blanc	2	10
Château Jean-Gervais,	*Portets*	blanc	13	50
		rouge	22	45
Château Jean de Maye	*Portets*	blanc	4	15
		rouge	3	11
Clos de l'Abbaye-de-Larame	*Mazères*	blanc	6	12
Château La Garde	*Martillac*	blanc	6	30
		rouge	41	200
Clos Puyjalon				
Château Langueloup	*Portets*	blanc	2	6
		rouge		
Cru La Hounade	*Pujols*	blanc	2	9
Château La Louvière	*Léognan*	blanc	10	50
		rouge	37	170
Clos de la Magine	*St.-Pierre-de-Mons*	blanc	6	14
		rouge	5	20
Cru La Mainionce	*Pujols*	blanc	3	13
Cru Lamédecine	*St.-Pierre-de-Mons*	blanc	2	5
Cru de Lamoignon	*Pujols*	blanc	3	5
Château Lamothe-Bouscat	*Cadaujac*	rouge	4	15
Clos Lamothe	*Portets*	blanc	3	9
		rouge	8	25
Château Lamouroux	*Cérons*	blanc	8	37
Château Laouilley	*Roaillan*	blanc	3	3
Domaine La Payrère	*St.-Selve*	blanc	5	8
		rouge		2
Domaine de Larnavey	*St.-Selve*	rouge	2	8
Château Larrivet-Haut-Brion	*Léognan*	rouge	14	80
		blanc	1	5
Cru Larroucat	*Pujols*	blanc	2	8
Château Lassalle	*La Brède*	blanc	6	26
Cru La Salle	*Martillac*	blanc	3	8
Domaine La Solitude	*Martillac*	blanc	5	25
		rouge	19	40
Cru La Terce	*Budos*	rouge	2	3
Château La Tour-Léognan	*Léognan*	blanc	3	15
		rouge	7	30
Château La Tour Bicheau	*Portets*	blanc	4	12
		rouge	6	25
Château La Tour-de-Bayrein	*Langon*	blanc	13	40
		rouge	4	20
Château La Tourte	*Toulenne*	blanc	6	16
		rouge	4	10

	Commune		*Ha*	*Tonneaux*
Cru Le Bourut	*Pujols*	blanc	2	9
Cru de l'Église	*Virelade*	blanc	2	5
Château Léhoult	*Langon*	blanc	4	8
		rouge	3	10
Château Le Mayne	*Preignac*	blanc	9	30
Château Le Pape	*Légnan*	rouge	5	15
Château Lespault	*Martillac*	blanc	4	3
		rouge	0,5	2
Château de l'Espérance	*La Brède*	blanc	4	10
		rouge	8	25
Cru Lestage	*Landiras*	blanc	4	9
Domaine Lestang	*St.-Selve*	blanc, rouge	5	5
Château Le Thil	*Léognan*	rouge	3	4
Cru de l'Hermitage	*Budos*	blanc	9	35
		rouge	4	15
Clos de l'Hôpital	*Castres*	rouge	7	35
Château de l'Hospital	*Portets*	blanc, rouge	8	5
Château Liché	*St.-Pardon-de-Conques*	blanc, rouge	3	10
Château Limbourg	*Villenave-d'Ornon*	blanc, rouge	10	6
Château Liot-Moros	*Pujols*	blanc	5	15
Cru Liot	*Budos*	blanc	3	4
Château Lognac	*Castres*	rouge	15	30
Domaine de Louisot	*Virelade*	blanc	4	13
Clos Louloumet	*Toulenne*	blanc	3	8
Cru de Lubat	*St.-Pierre-de-Mons*	blanc	8	14
		rouge	4	15
Château des Lucques	*Portets*	blanc	2	11
		rouge	8	50
Domaine des Lucques	*Portets*	blanc	2	10
		rouge	12	60
Château Ludeman-La Côte	*Langon*	blanc	7	20
		rouge	3	10
Château Lusseau	*Ayguemortes*	rouge	4	10
Château Madélis	*Portets*	blanc	2	6
		rouge	13	10
Château Madran	*Pessac*	rouge	3	4
Château Magence	*St.-Pierre-de-Mons*	blanc	15	60
		rouge	11	45
Château Magneau	*La Brède*	blanc, rouge	5	11
Château Maillard	*Mazères*	blanc	5	13
		rouge	38	150
Clos de la Maison Blanche	*Budos*	blanc	2	5
Château Malleprat	*Martillac*	blanc	3	5
		rouge	4	
Domaine de Maron	*Landiras*	rouge	2	9
Cru Massiot	*Martillac*	blanc	2	6
Château de Mauves	*Podensac*	blanc	8	30
		rouge	12	50

	Commune		*Ha*	*Tonneaux*
Château de May	*Portets*	blanc	3	10
		rouge	2	5
Domaine du Mayne	*Langon*	rouge	3	8
Château Mayne-d'Imbert	*Podensac*	blanc	10	50
		rouge	5	25
Château Millet	*Portets*	blanc	20	90
		rouge	45	250
Château Mirabel	*Pujols*	blanc	3	14
Château du Mirail	*Portets*	blanc	5	16
		rouge	23	60
Château Moderis	*Virelade*	blanc / rouge	5	10
Château de Mongenan	*Portets*	blanc	2	5
		rouge	5	15
Clos de Mons	*La Brède*	blanc / rouge	3	8
Cru Morange	*Virelade*	blanc / rouge	2	7
Clos du Moulin-à-Vent	*St.-Pierre-de-Pons*	blanc	5	18
Cru du Moulin-à-Vent	*Landiras*	blanc	3	10
Château Mouteou	*Portets*	blanc	2	6
		rouge	1	4
Château Moutin	*Portets*	blanc / rouge	2	10
Château Mouyet	*Budos*	rouge	2	11
Cru Nodoy	*Virelade*	blanc / rouge	5	20
Clos de Nouchet	*Castres*	rouge	3	10
Château de Nouguey	*Langon*	blanc	2	6
Clos le Pape	*La brèche*	blanc	6	19
Domaine de Papoula (*voir* Domaine de Durce)				
Cru Patiras	*Toulenne*	blanc	2	4
Château le Pavillon-de-Boyrein	*Roaillan*	rouge	25	110
Château Peydebayle	*St.-Pierre-de-Mons*	blanc	2	5
		rouge		10
Château Péran	*Langon*	blanc / rouge	3	10
Cru Perran	*Landiras*	blanc	3	12
Domaine Perin de Naudine	*Castres*	rouge	5	15
Château Perron	*Roaillan*	blanc	14	37
Château Pesilla	*Landiras*	blanc	4	16
Château Pessan	*Portets*	blanc	2	10
		rouge	8	40
Château Péyran	*Landiras*	blanc	4	11
Château des Peyrères	*Landiras*	blanc	4	14
Cru Pezeau	*Beautiran*	rouge	3	10
Château Pingoy	*Portets*	blanc	1	5
		rouge	7	15
Château Picque-Caillou	*Mérignac*	blanc	18	75
Château Piron	*St.-Morillon*	blanc	15	50
		rouge	5	20
Château de Places	*Arbanats*	blanc	1	4
		rouge	6	25

	Commune		*Ha*	*Tonneaux*
Château des Places	*Arbanats*	blanc rouge	2 6	9 25
Château de Plantat	*St.-Morillon*	blanc rouge	3 6	10
Domaine des Plantes	*Landiras*	blanc rouge	6 4	25 15
Domaine des Plantes	*Landiras*	blanc	4	11
Domaine de Plantcy	*Castres*	blanc rouge	2	2 7
Château Pommarède	*Castres*	blanc rouge	3	10
Château Pommarède-de-Haut	*Castres*	blanc rouge	1 5	5 20
Château Pontac-Monplaisir	*Villenave-d'Ornon*	blanc rouge	6 8	30 45
Le Pontet	*St.-Médard-d'Eyrans*	rouge	5	20
Cru de Portail	*Landiras*	blanc	2	7
Château de Portets	*Portets*	blanc rouge	4 11	25 45
Cru de la Poste	*Virelade*	rouge	4	6
Château Poumey	*Gradignan*	rouge	4	7
Clos Puyjalon (*voir* Château Jean-Gervais)				
Château Queyrats, Clos d'Uza, Château St. Pierre	*St.-Pierre-de-Mons*	blanc	34	77
Château Rahoul	*Portets*	blanc rouge	3 15	15 50
Château de Respide	*Langon*	blanc rouge	65	55 40
Château Respide	*St.-Pierre-de-Mons*	blanc	4	5
Château Respide	*Toulenne*	blanc rouge	7 2	20 10
Château La Rocaille	*Virelade*	blanc rouge	9	13
Château Rochemorin	*Martillac*	blanc rouge	6 36	24 160
Domaine Roland	*Langon*	blanc	3	6
Château Roquetaillade- Roquetaillade	*Mazères*	blanc	3	9
Château Roquetaillade-la-Grange	*Mazères*	blanc rouge	38	130
Château Roubinet	*Pujols*	blanc	8	32
Cru Roudet	*Pujols*	blanc	2	10
Château de Rouillac	*Canéjean*	rouge	5	20
Cru Sadout	*Virelade*	blanc rouge	6	19
Château Saige-Fort-Manoir	*Pessac*	rouge	5	11
Château St.-Gérôme	*Ayguemortes*	blanc rouge	4 5	7 10
Clos St.-Hilaire	*Portets*	blanc rouge	3	12 8
Clos St.-Jean	*Pujols*	blanc	8	23
Château St.-Pierre (*voir* Château Queyrats)				

	Commune		*Ha*	*Tonneaux*
Château St.-Robert	*Pujols*	blanc	12	50
		rouge	16	65
Domaine du Sapeur	*Portets*	blanc	4	9
		rouge		10
Cru Sarraguey	*Virelade*	blanc	5	20
		rouge		
Domaine des Sarrots	*St.-Pierre-de-Mons*	blanc	2	5
Clos Sentouary	*St.-Pierre-de-Mons*	blanc	2	5
Domaine de Terrefort	*Landiras*	blanc	6	25
		rouge	12	50
Domaine de Teycheney	*Virelade*		2	4
Domaine de Teychon	*Arbanats*	blanc	4	16
		rouge	7	30
Château Toumilon	*St.-Pierre-de-Mons*	blanc	5	9
		rouge	6	25
Clos Toumilon	*St.-Pierre-de-Mons*	blanc	2	4
		rouge		10
Château Tourteau-Cholet	*Arbanats*	blanc	13	40
		rouge	21	
Clos de la Tuilerie	*Portets*	blanc	3	10
		rouge	2	
Cru La Tuilerie	*Landiras*	blanc	2	7
Château des Tuileries	*Virelade*	blanc	3	14
		rouge	2	10
Château Le Tuquet	*Beautiran*	blanc	26	100
		rouge		20
Château Tustoc	*Toulenne*	blanc	8	26
Clos d'Uza (*voir* Château Queyrats)				
Domaine des Vergnes	*Portets*	blanc	2	4
		rouge	1	
Clos Viaut	*St.-Pardon-de-Conques*	blanc	2	4
		rouge	7	30
Clos Viaut	*St.-Pierre-de-Mons*	blanc	9	25
Cru Videau	*Pujols*	blanc	6	25
Château La Vieille-France	*Portets*	blanc	16	25
		rouge		15
Château de Virelade	*Virelade*	blanc	3	9
		rouge	29	15

VIII. Sauternes et Barsac

Comme ceux du Médoc, les crus de Sauternes furent classés officiellement en 1855. Cette classification est connue comme la Classification officielle des Grands Crus de la Gironde de 1855.

La production officielle de ces crus représente approximativement 25 % de la production totale du Sauternais qui s'élève à environ 350 000 caisses par an.

Les chiffres de production sont approximatifs. Ils donnent une moyenne annuelle telle qu'elle est indiquée par les municipalités d'après leurs déclarations de récolte.

CRUS CLASSÉS DE 1855

Premier Grand Cru	Tonneaux	Caisses
Château d'Yquem	60	5 500
Premiers Crus		
Château Guiraud	90	8 000
Château La Tour-Blanche	35	3 500
Château Laufaurie-Peyraguey	70	7 000
Château de Rayne-Vigneau	150	11 000
Château Sigalas-Rabaud	35	3 000
Château Rabaud-Promis	50	5 000
Clos Haut-Peyraguey	25	2 000
Château Coutet	75	7 500
Château Climens	65	6 000
Château-Suduiraut	75	10 000
Château Rieussec	100	8 500

Seconds Crus Classés	Tonneaux	Caisses
Château d'Arche	50	4 000
Château Filhot	100	10 000
Château Lamothe	25	2 000
Château Myrat (ne produit plus de vin)		
Château Doisy-Védrines	35	6 000
Château Doisy-Daëne	20	2 000
Château Suau	15	1 000
Château Broustet	30	3 000
Château Caillou	40	4 000
Château Nairac	40	3 000
Château de Malle	50	5 000
Château Romer	5	1 000
Château Romer-du-Hayot	60	3 000

CRUS SECONDAIRES

	Commune	Ha	Tonneaux
Château d'Arche-Lafaurie	*Sauternes*	19	48
Château d'Arche-Pugnau, Château Peyraguey-le-Rousset	*Preignac*	15	32
Château d'Arche, Château Lamothe	*Sauternes*	15	40
Château d'Arche-Vimeney	*Sauternes*	5	11
Château d'Argilas le Pape	*Preignac*	2	4
Château d'Armajan-les-Ormes	*Preignac*	1	2
Cru d'Arrançon	*Preignac*	5	10
Cru Arrançon-Boutoc	*Preignac*	3	9
Château des Arrieux	*Preignac*	5	15
Château Augey	*Bommes*	10	26
Cru Baboye	*Fargues*	2	5
Château Barbier	*Fargues*	6	16
Cru de Barboye	*Bommes*	2	4
Château Barjuneau	*Sauternes*	6	15
Domaine Barjuneau-Chauvin	*Sauternes*	4	10
Clos Barreau	*Fargues*	1	4
Château Barrette	*Sauternes*	5	14
Cru Barrette	*Fargues*	1	2
Cru Bas-Peyraguey	*Preignac*	2	4
Château Bastor-Lamontagne	*Preignac*	38	90
Cru Bataille	*Bommes*	4	10
Château Batsalle	*Fargues*	4	9
Cru Batsalle	*Fargues*	1	3
Château Baulac-Dodigeos	*Barsac*	5	12
Cru Beylieu	*Fargues*	7	13

	Commune	*Ha*	*Tonneaux*
Château Béchereau	*Bommes*	8	25
Cru Bel-Air	*Preignac*	2	4
Château Bergeron	*Bommes*	8	20
Cru Bergeron	*Preignac*	4	11
Cru Bernisse	*Barsac*	1	4
Cru Bignon	*Bommes*	1	3
Cru Bordessoulles	*Preignac*	3	7
Château Bousclas	*Barsac*	3	8
Cru Bousclas	*Barsac*	4	12
Cru Boutoc	*Preignac*	5	10
Cru Boutoc	*Sauternes*	2	5
Château Bouyot	*Barsac*	6	15
Cru Bouyréou	*Preignac*	1	2
Château Brassens-Guitteronde	*Barsac*	5	14
Château Briatte	*Preignac*	8	20
Cru Camelong	*Bommes*	1	2
Château Cameron et Raymond-Louis	*Bommes*	9	35
Château Camperos	*Barsac*	3	10
Château Cantegril	*Barsac*	14	38
Cru Caplane	*Bommes*	2	5
Cru Caplane	*Sauternes*	3	10
Domaine de Caplane	*Sauternes*	5	25
Cru Carbonnieu	*Bommes*	10	30
Château de Carles	*Barsac*	6	16
Cru du Carrefour	*Sauternes*	1	2
Cru de la Cave	*Preignac*	2	5
Cru du Chalet	*Barsac*	2	5
Cru du Chalet	*Preignac*	1	3
Domaine de la Chapelle	*Preignac*	2	4
Château de la Chartreuse	*Preignac*	5	10
Cru Chauvin	*Sauternes*	2	4
Cru Claveries	*Fargues*	1	2
Château Closiot	*Barsac*	5	11
Cru Commarque	*Bommes*	4	10
Château Commarque	*Sauternes*	4	10
Cru Commarque	*Sauternes*	6	11
Château Commet-Magey	*Preignac*	4	8
Cru Commet-Magey-Briatte	*Preignac*	4	11
Domaine Cosse	*Fargues*	6	12
Domaine de Couite	*Preignac*	3	8
Cru Coussères	*Fargues*	1	2
Château Coustet	*Barsac*	6	21
Cru Coustet	*Barsac*	1	2
Domaine du Coy	*Sauternes*	3	8
Château de Coye	*Sauternes*	1	3
Cru Druenn	*Bommes*	2	4
Château Ducasse	*Barsac*	5	12
Cru Ducasse	*Fargues*	2	5
Château Dudon	*Barsac*	8	20
Domaine Duperneau	*Bommes*	3	9
Cru d'Espagnet (*voir* Château Esterlin)			
Château Esterlin, Clos d'Espagnet	*Sauternes*	3	7
Château de Fargues	*Fargues*	12	7
Château Farluret	*Barsac*	4	11
Cru Fillau	*Fargues*	4	10

	Commune	*Ha*	*Tonneaux*
Château Fleury, Château Terre-Noble	*Barsac*	2	4
Clos Fontaine	*Fargues*	9	25
Château Fontebride	*Preignac*	2	7
Domaine de la Forêt	*Preignac*	21	61
Cru Gavach	*Fargues*	3	7
Château Gilette, Domaine des Justices, Château Les Rochers, Château Les Remparts, Château Lamothe	*Preignac*	14	30
Clos Girautin	*Barsac*	1	3
Château Grand-Carretey	*Barsac*	1	2
Cru Grand-Carretey	*Barsac*	6	16
Cru Grand-Jauga	*Barsac*	2	6
Château Grand-Mayne-Qui-Né-Marc	*Barsac*	1	3
Cru Gravaillas	*Preignac*	2	4
Château Gravas	*Barsac*	8	20
Château Grillon	*Barsac*	6	18
Domaine Guilhem-du-Rey	*Preignac*	7	22
Château Guimbalet	*Preignac*	1	4
Château Guitteronde-Sarraute	*Barsac*	4	10
Château Guitteronde	*Barsac*	9	22
Château du Haire	*Preignac*	4	9
Cru du Haire	*Preignac*	6	18
Château Hallet	*Barsac*	10	24
Château Haut-Bergeron	*Preignac*	4	13
Château Haut-Bommes	*Bommes*	7	14
Château Haut-Claverie	*Fargues*	9	20
Château Haut-Fontebride	*Preignac*	6	20
Cru Haut-Laguerritte	*Bommes*	2	4
Château Haut-Mayne	*Fargues*	2	5
Cru Haut-Piquant	*Sauternes*	1	3
Cru du Hère	*Preignac*	2	2
Château Hourmalas (*voir* Château St-Marc)			
Cru Hourmalas	*Barsac*	2	6
Château Jany	*Barsac*	2	6
Cru Jauguet	*Barsac*	5	14
Château Jean-Galant	*Bommes*	6	15
Château Jean-Laive	*Barsac*	4	11
Clos de Jeanlaive	*Barsac*	5	11
Cru Jeannonier	*Bommes*	3	4
Domaine Jean-Robert	*Preignac*	1	3
Domaine du Juge	*Preignac*	4	10
Cru Junka	*Preignac*	3	4
Château Les Justices	*Preignac*	3	6
Domaine des Justices (*voir* Château Gilette)			
Cru La Bernisse	*Barsac*	3	7
Château La Bouade	*Barsac*	12	31
Clos La Bouade	*Barsac*	3	8
Domaine de Labouade-Rambaud	*Barsac*	1	3
Cru La Bouchette	*Preignac*	2	5
Château La Brouillère	*Bommes*	4	9
Cru Labrousse	*Barsac*	2	5
Château La Chapelle-St-Aubin	*Bommes*	3	6
Château La Clotte	*Barsac*	5	12
Cru Lacoste	*Barsac*	2	4
Cru La Côte	*Fargues*	5	9

	Commune	Ha	Tonneaux
Château Lafon, Château Le Mayne	*Sauternes*	6	19
Château Lafon-Laroze	*Sauternes*	3	5
Cru Lagardan	*Bommes*	3	10
Domaine de Lagauche	*Bommes*	2	4
Cru l'Agnet	*Bommes*	2	3
Château Lagravette	*Bommes*	2	5
Château La Gravière	*Preignac*	2	5
Cru Lahonade-Peraguey	*Bommes*	2	6
Château Lahouilley	*Barsac*	3	9
Château La Hourcade	*Preignac*	4	13
Cru Lalot	*Preignac*	3	8
Cru La Maringue	*Bommes*	1	2
Château Lamothe (*voir* Château d'Arches)			
Château Lamothe (*voir* Château Gilette)			
Cru Lamothe	*Sauternes*	6	14
Château Lamourette	*Bommes*	7	20
Cru Lanère	*Sauternes*	11	21
Château Lange	*Bommes*	5	12
Cru Lanusquet	*Fargues*	2	5
Clos Lapachère	*Barsac*	4	10
Château Lapelou	*Barsac*	6	16
Château Lapinesse	*Barsac*	16	44
Cru Lapinesse	*Barsac*	7	19
Cru La Pinesse	*Barsac*	2	5
Domaine de Laraude	*Sauternes*	2	5
Château Laribotte	*Preignac*	11	25
Château l'Arieste	*Preignac*	18	40
Clos l'Arieste	*Preignac*	3	8
Château La Tour	*Barsac*	2	4
Château Latrezotte	*Barsac*	7	20
Cru l'Aubépin	*Bommes*	10	26
Cru l'Aubépine	*Bommes*	2	4
Cru l'Aubépins	*Sauternes*	3	6
Château Lauvignac	*Preignac*	3	6
Château Laville	*Preignac*	15	35
Château Le Coustet	*Barsac*	5	10
Cru Le Haut Bommes	*Bommes*	0,5	2
Château Le Hère	*Bommes*	6	10
Château Le Mayne (*voir* Château Lafon)			
Château du Mayne	*Preignac*	9	25
Château Le Mouret	*Fargues*	6	6
Cru Le Pageot	*Bommes*	2	4
Château l'Ermitage	*Preignac*	7	13
Château Le Roc	*Preignac*	1	3
Château Larose-Monteil	*Preignac*	8	20
Cru Le Rousseau	*Bommes*	2	3
Château Le Sauhuc	*Preignac*	3	9
Cru Les Cailloux	*Bommes*	2	4
Cru Les Gravilles	*Barsac*	1	2
Château Le Sourd Béteille	*Bordeaux*	3	10
Château Les Plantes	*Barsac*	5	14
Château Les Remparts (*voir* Château Gilette)			
Château Les Rochers	*Preignac*	7	18
Château Les Rochers (*voir* Château Gilette)			
Cru Les Rochers	*Preignac*	2	4

	Commune	Ha	Tonneaux
Cru Les Tuileries	*Fargues*	1	3
Cru Le Tachon	*Bommes*	2	4
Château Leyret	*Preignac*	2	4
Château Liot	*Barsac*	11	29
Château de Luzies	*Barsac*	3	9
Cru Mahon	*Bommes*	3	10
Cru Mahon	*Preignac*	2	6
Cru de Mahon	*Preignac*	3	6
Clos des Maraings	*Preignac*	3	6
Château Masereau	*Barsac*	7	15
Château Mathalin	*Barsac*	11	35
Domaine de Mathalin	*Barsac*	1	3
Château Mauras	*Bommes*	13	36
Cru Mauras	*Bommes*	13	30
Cru Mauvin	*Preignac*	6	16
Château Du Mayne	*Barsac*	7	17
Château Du Mayne	*Preignac*	2	5
Château Mayne-Bert (*voir* Château Camperos)			
Clos Mayne-Lamouroux	*Barsac*	2	5
Cru Menate	*Barsac*	1	2
Château Menota, Château Menota-Labat	*Barsac*	17	54
Château Menota-Labat (*voir* Château Menota)			
Château Mercier	*Barsac*	2	4
Clos Mercier	*Barsac*	3	8
Cru Mercier	*Barsac*	1	4
Clos de Miaille	*Barsac*	1	2
Cru Miaille	*Barsac*	1	3
Cru Miselle	*Preignac*	3	7
Château du Mont	*Preignac*	4	11
Château Montalivert (*voir* Château Champeros)			
Château Monteau	*Preignac*	9	21
Cru Monteil	*Bommes*	3	7
Cru Monteil	*Preignac*	1	2
Domaine de Monteil	*Preignac*	7	19
Cru Montjoie	*Preignac*	2	4
Château Montjou (*voir* Château Terre Noble)			
Cru Mothes	*Fargues*	2	5
Clos du Moulin Neuf	*Preignac*	1	2
Château Mounic	*Fargues*	1	2
Domaine de Mounic	*Fargues*	1	2
Château Moura	*Barsac*	1	4
Cru Mouret	*Fargues*	3	7
Clos du Moynet	*Preignac*	2	4
Cru Moussotte	*Fargues*	1	3
Clos de Nauton	*Fargues*	4	7
Château Padouen	*Barsac*	10	20
Château Pageot	*Sauternes*	5	12
Cru du Pajot	*Bommes*	4	7
Château Paloumat	*Fargues*	2	2
Château du Pape	*Preignac*	3	12
Clos Le Pape	*Fargues*	5	11
Château Partarieu	*Fargues*	18	40

	Commune	*Ha*	*Tonneaux*
Cru Passérieux	*Barsac*	3	7
Château Pébayle	*Barsac*	5	15
Château Peillon-Claverie	*Fargues*	12	35
Château Pechon-Terre-Noble	*Barsac*	3	9
Château Pernaud	*Barsac*	17	35
Cru du Perret	*Bommes*	2	6
Château Perroy-Jean-Blanc	*Bommes*	7	17
Cru Petit-Grillon	*Barsac*	2	5
Cru Peyraguey	*Preignac*	2	5
Château Peyraguey-le-Rousset (*voir* Cru d'Arche-Pugnau			
Château de Peyre	*Fargues*	1	3
Clos Peyret	*Preignac*	1	3
Château Peyron	*Fargues*	4	17
Château Piada, Clos du Roy	*Barsac*	11	29
Cru Pian	*Barsac*	2	7
Château Piaut	*Barsac*	9	22
Château du Pick	*Preignac*	19	50
Clos de Pierrefeu	*Preignac*	4	10
Cru Pilote	*Fargues*	6	20
Cru du Piquey	*Bommes*	1	2
Cru de Pistoulet-Peyraguey	*Bommes*	2	4
Cru du Placey	*Barsac*	1	3
Cru Planton	*Barsac*	1	3
Château Pleytegeat	*Preignac*	12	51
Cru Pouteau	*Fargues*	6	20
Cru Pouton	*Preignac*	2	6
Clos des Princes	*Barsac*	2	6
Château Prost	*Barsac*	8	21
Château Pugneau	*Preignac*	3	8
Cru Puydomine	*Bommes*	2	4
Château Raspide	*Barsac*	5	16
Château Raymond-Lafon	*Sauternes*	20	37
Château des Remparts	*Preignac*	1	4
Cru Richard Barbe	*Bommes*	2	5
Cru Ripaille	*Preignac*	4	10
Château du Roc	*Barsac*	2	5
Clos des Rocs	*Preignac*	1	3
Château de Rolland	*Barsac*	14	39
Domaine de la Roudette	*Sauternes*	2	6
Château Roumieu	*Barsac*	18	46
Château Roumieu-Lacoste	*Barsac*	5	14
Château Rouquette	*Preignac*	6	17
Cru Rousset-Peyraguey	*Preignac*	5	15
Clos du Roy (*voir* Château Piada)			
Château St-Amand	*Preignac*	16	40
Château St-Marc, Château Hourmalas	*Barsac*	6	14
Château St-Michel	*Barsac*	1	3
Cru St-Michel	*Barsac*	1	3
Clos St-Robert	*Barsac*	1	3
Cru St-Sardeau	*Fargues*	2	6
Château Sahuc	*Preignac*	2	5
Château Sahuc-Latour	*Preignac*	9	25
Cru Saubade-Terrefort	*Sauternes*	2	3
Château Simon	*Barsac*	4	12

	Commune	*Ha*	*Tonneaux*
Château Simon-Carretey	*Barsac*	4	7
Château Solon	*Preignac*	4	13
Cru Soula	*Fargues*	4	9
Château Suau	*Barsac*	5	14
Domaine Tchit	*Fargues*	1	3
Cru Terrefort	*Bommes*	4	11
Domaine de Terrefort	*Bommes*	10	35
Château Terre Noble, Château Montjou	*Barsac*	9	24
Château Terre-Noble (*voir* Château Fleury)			
Cru des Terres Rouges	*Barsac*	2	4
Château Thibaut	*Fargues*	10	30
Cru Thibaut	*Fargues*	4	12
Château de Touilla	*Fargues*	3	4
Château Trillon	*Sauternes*	20	50
Cru Trinquine	*Preignac*	2	4
Cru Tucan	*Barsac*	2	3
Château Tucau	*Barsac*	3	9
Château Valmont-Mayne	*Barsac*	2	4
Château Veyres ·	*Preignac*	10	30
Cru Vigne-Vieille	*Barsac*	3	8
Château Villefranche	*Barsac*	6	13
Château du Violet	*Preignac*	11	30
Cru du Violet	*Preignac*	3	20
Cru du Violet-et-Lamothe	*Preignac*	5	12
Château Voigny	*Preignac*	6	18

IX. Cérons

Les chiffres de production sont approximatifs. Ils donnent une moyenne annuelle telle qu'elle est indiquée par les municipalités d'après leurs déclarations de récolte.

PRINCIPAUX CRUS

	Commune	*Ha*	*Tonneaux*
Château D'Anice	*Podensac*	12	50
Château Archambeau	*Illats*	4	34
Clos Avocat	*Cérons*	4	8
Clos de l'Avocat	*Cérons*	3	9
Château Balestey	*Cérons*	10	20
Clos de Barial	*Illats*	9	22
Clos du Barrail	*Cérons*	8	19
Château Beaulac	*Illats*	3	7
Château Beaulieu	*Cérons*	6	30
Cru Bel-Air	*Illats*	3	12
Clos de Bos-Lancon	*Illats*	4	12
Cru de Bouley	*Illats*	4	8
Domaine de Bourdac	*Illats*	7	40
Clos Bourgelet	*Cérons*	7	15
Cru de Boutec	*Illats*	5	20
Cru de Braze	*Illats*	7	18

	Commune	*Ha*	*Tonneaux*
Cru Brouillaou	*Podensac*	11	28
Cru de Cabiro	*Illats*	3	11
Château Cages	*Illats*	5	17
Domaine du Caillou	*Cérons*	5	10
Domaine Caillou Rouley	*Podensac*	8	15
Château Cantau	*Illats*	4	9
Clos Cantemerle	*Cérons*	3	7
Château de Cérons	*Cérons*	15	28
Château Chantegrive	*Podensac*	30	120
Domaine de la Citadelle	*Illats*	4	14
Cru Cleyrac	*Cérons*	5	15
Cru des Deux Moulins	*Illats*	4	8
Château Ferbos	*Cérons*	10	40
Domaine de Freyron	*Cérons*	3	5
Domaine de Gardennes	*Illats*	3	6
Château Grand Chemin	*Cérons*	4	8
Château des Grands Chênes	*Cérons*	3	6
Grand Enclos du Château de Cérons	*Cérons*	11	30
Château Hauret	*Illats*	4	9
Cru Haut-Buhan	*Illats*	7	18
Château du Haut-Gravier	*Illats*	11	22
Château Haut La Hontasse (P. Banos)	*Illats*	3	6
Cru Haut La Hontasse (R. Banos, J. Banos)	*Illats*	5	15
Château Haut-Mayne	*Cérons*	5	10
Cru de Haut-Mayne	*Cérons*	3	6
Château Haut-Rat	*Illats*	16	40
Château Huradin, Domaine du Salut	*Cérons*	8	30
Clos de Jaugua	*Illats*	4	8
Domaine de Jaussans	*Illats*	8	20
Château La Lanette Ferbos	*Cérons*	5	22
Château Lamouroux	*Cérons*	10	22
Château Lanette	*Cérons*	5	12
Château Laroche	*Illats*	14	45
Cru Larrouquey	*Cérons*	7	18
Château Larrouquey	*Cérons*	5	12
Château La Salette	*Cérons*	5	12
Domaine Le Cossu	*Podensac*	5	11
Château Le Huzet	*Illats*	7	18
Château de l'Émigré	*Cérons*	2	3
Cru Le Tintan	*Illats*	3	6
Cru de Lionne	*Illats*	7	18
Cru Madérot (Édouard Sterlin)	*Podensac*	9	18
Cru Majans	*Cérons*	3	6
Cru Marc	*Illats*	5	16
Château des Mauves	*Podensac*	7	16
Château Mayne d'Anice	*Podensac*	4	9
Cru Maynine	*Illats*	3	10
Domaine de Menaut Larrouquey	*Cérons*	12	32
Cru de Menjon	*Illats*	3	9
Château Moulin de Marc	*Cérons*	7	35
Château Moulin-à-vent	*Cérons*	4	12
Cru du Moulin-à-Vent (Baron)	*Illats*	2	6
Cru Moulin-à-Vent (Biarnes)	*Illats*	16	50
Clos des Moulins-à-Vent	*Cérons*	5	14
Cru des Moulins-à-Vent (Lafond)	*Cérons*	3	6

	Commune	*Ha*	*Tonneaux*
Cru des Moulins-à-Vent (Lapujade, Despujols)	*Cérons*	9	14
Domaine des Moulins-à-Vents	*Illats*	9	21
Château de Navarro	*Illats*	13	80
Cru du Noulin	*Cérons*	3	6
Cru des Parrajots	*Illats*	3	8
Cru des Perliques	*Illats*	3	8
Château du Peyrat	*Cérons*	14	45
Cru Peyroutene	*Cérons*	4	9
Cru Pinaud	*Cérons*	4	10
Domaine de Prouzet	*Illats*	7	13
Château du Roc	*Cérons*	5	8
Clos des Roches	*Illats*	2	6
Cru St-Roch	*Illats*	2	5
Domaine du Salut (*voir* Château Huradin)			
Château du Seuil	*Cérons*	3	13
Château Sylvain	*Cérons*	11	28
Château Thomé-Brousterot	*Illats*	8	18
Château Uferic	*Cérons*	6	14
Cru Voltaire	*Cérons*	4	7

X. Loupiac

Les chiffres de production sont approximatifs. Ils donnent une moyenne annuelle telle qu'elle est indiquée par les municipalités d'après leurs déclarations de récolte.

PRINCIPAUX CRUS

	Ha	*Tonneaux*		*Ha*	*Tonneaux*
Château Barbe Morin	5	16	Cru Marges Dusseau	4	17
Cru Barberousse	4	15	Château Mazarin	2	10
Château Bel-Air	5	16	Côtes de Mossac	2	7
Château Bertranon	2	5	Château Moulin Neuf	10	40
Château Bouchoc	2	4	Cru du Moulin Vieux	5	18
Château Caudiet	10	35	Château du Noble	7	15
Domaine du Chay	12	30	Château Peyruchet	12	34
Château Chichoye	2	7	Cru du Plainier	5	14
Clos de Ciron	4	9	Château Pontac	10	36
Château Clos Jean	14	45	Château Ricaud	15	60
Château Couloumet	5	12	Domaine de Roby	5	20
Château du Gros	4	20	Château Rondillon	12	40
Château Dauphine Rondillon	15	55	Cru de Rouquette	8	18
			Cru de la Sablière	4	13
Château de l'Ermitage	2	7	Cru St-Romain	4	11
			Château Terrefort	8	34
Château La Nève	9	40	Clos de Terrefort	3	6
Château Le Tarey	5	13	Cru de Terrefort	4	16
Château Le Pavillon	4	14	Cru de Terrefort Pierre Noire	3	11
Château Loupiac-Gaudiet	2	10	Château Turon Lanère (Dalas)	3	10
Château de Malendure	3	6			

	Ha	*Tonneaux*		*Ha*	*Tonneaux*
Château Turon Lanère (David)	5	18	Château du Vieux-Moulin	9	40

XI. Sainte-Croix-du-Mont

Les chiffres de production sont approximatifs. Ils donnent une moyenne annuelle telle qu'elle est indiquée par les municipalités d'après leurs déclarations de récolte.

PRINCIPAUX CRUS

	Ha	*Tonneaux*		*Ha*	*Tonneaux*
Cru Abraham	4	15	Château Lapeyrère	5	26
Cru Baret-les-Arrivaux	3	12	Clos L'Arabey	2	7
Château Bel-Air	3	15	Château La Rame	16	65
Clos Belle-Vue	4	17	Cru La Rame	6	27
Château de Bertranon	5	20	Clos Larrivat	3	13
Château Bouchoc	3	10	Château Laurette	15	66
Domaine du Bougan	3	6	Château Le Grand Peyrot	5	11
Domaine du Bugat	3	14	Clos Le Haut-Crabitan	2	8
Cru du Canet	3	6	Château Le Pin	3	13
Château des Coulinats	3	13	Château L'Escaley	5	23
Château Coulac	3	15	Clos Les Arrivaux	3	11
Domaine de Coullander	1	5	Cru Les Arroucats	2	7
Château du Crabitan	5	21	Domaine Les Marcottes	4	20
Domaine Damanieu	3	12	Cru Le Tarey	5	23
Domaine de d'Escaley	2	9	Château Loubens	10	34
Domaine du Gaël	2	10	Domaine de Louqsor	1	5
Cru de Gaillardet	1	4	Château Lousteau Vieil	7	33
Château Gensonne	2	5	Château des Mailles	6	24
Cru de Guerisson	3	7	Cru Medouc	4	8
Château Haut-de-Baritault	5	15	Clos du Médouc	2	7
			Cru Médouc La Grave	2	8
Cru Haut-Larrivat	3	12	Château Megnien	3	13
Cru Haut-Medouc	3	15	Château du Mont	7	30
Domaine de l'If	3	15	Cru de Montagne	5	19
Château Jean-Lamat	4	16	Domaine des Noyers	7	25
Château Laborie	6	24	Clos du Palmiers	3	12
Château La Caussade	5	20	Domaine de Pampelune	3	15
Domaine de Lacoste	2	9	Domaine de Parenteau	4	19
Cru de La Côte Doré	2	8	Château du Pavillon	11	40
Château Lafuë	4	15	Cru Peillot	2	9
Château La Grave	6	17	Cru du Pin	2	6
Cru La Grave	2	6	Château de la Princesse	2	9
Château La Gravière	11	51	Château Roustit	9	40
Château La Graville	4	10	Château de Tastes	6	18
Château Lamarque	15	25	Château Terfort	3	11
Château La Mouleyre	4	8	Cru du Terrefort	2	9
Clos La Mouleyre	4	16	Château Vertheuil	10	25
Cru La Mouleyre	3	12	Domaine du Vignots	2	7

XII. Côtes de Bourg ou Bourg

Les châteaux énumérés ci-dessous figurent parmi les châteaux les plus importants de la région.

	Commune		Commune
Château de Barbe	*Villeneuve*	Château Haut-Launay	*Teuillac*
Château Barrieux	*Samonac*	Château Haut-Rousset	*St-Ciers-de-Canesse*
Château Bégot	*Lansac*	Château La Barde	*Tauriac*
Domaine de Bel-Air	*St-Sevrin-de-Bourg*	Château La Croix-Davids	*Lansac*
Château Belair-Coubet	*St-Ciers-de-Canesse*	Château de La Croix de Millorit	*Bayon*
Château de Bousquet	*Bourg*	Château Lagrange	*Bourg*
Château Brulesécaille	*Tauriac*	Château La Grolet	*St-Ciers-de-Canesse*
Château de Bujan	*Gauriac*	Château Labilarde	*Bourg*
Château Camponac	*Bourg-sur-Gironde*	Domaine de Labilarde	*Bourg*
Château Caruel	*Bourg*	Château Lamothe	*Lansac*
Château Castel La Rose	*Villeneuve*	Château Laroche	*Tauriac*
Château du Castenet	*Samonac*	Château La Tour-Seguy	*St-Ciers-de-Canesse*
Domaine de Christoly	*Prignac-Marcamps*	Château Laurensanne	*St-Seurin-Bourg*
Château Civrac	*Lansac*	Château Le Sablard	*Lansac*
Château Colbert	*Comps*	Château Les Haumes	*St-Ciers-de-Canesse*
Château Coubert	*Villeneuve*	Château de Lidonne	*Bourg-sur-Gironde*
Château Croûte-Courpon	*Bourg*	Château Macay	*Samonac*
Château Donis	*Lansac*	Château de Marquisat	*Lansac*
Château Eyquem	*Bayon*	Château Mendoce	*Villeneuve*
Château Falfas	*Bayon*	Château Mercier	*Saint-Trojan*
Domaine de Fonbonne	*Teuillac*	Château Nodot	*Bayon*
Château Grand-Jour	*Prignac-Marcamps*	Domaine de Noriou-Lalibarde	*Bourg*
Château Grand Launay	*Teuillac*	Château Peychaud	*Teuillac*
Château de la Grave	*Bourg*	Château de Peyror	*Gauriac*
Château Gravettes-Samonac	*Samonac*	Château Plaisance	*Villeneuve*
Château de Grissac	*Prignac-Marcamps*	Château Poyanne	*Gauriac*
Château Groleau	*Monbrier et Teuillac*	Château Réty	*Tauriac*
Château Gros-Moulin	*Bourg*	Château Rousselle	*St-Ciers-de-Canesse*
Château Guerry	*Tauriac*	Château Rousset	*Samonac*
Château Guionne	*Lansac*	Château Sauman	*Villeneuve-de-Blaye*
Château Guiraud	*St-Ciers-de-Canesse*	Château Tayac	*St-Sevrin-de-Bourg*
Château de Haut-Castenet	*Bourg*	Château de Thau	*Gauriac*
		Château Tour de Tourteau	*Samonac*

XIII. Blaye

Ci-dessous quelques-uns des plus importants domaines vinicoles.

	Commune		*Commune*
Château Barbet	*Cars*	Château La Perotte	*Eyrons*
Château Bellevue	*Cars*	Château Lassale	*St-Genès*
Château Berthenon	*St-Paul*	Château La Taure Ste-Luce	*Blaye*
Château Chaillou	*St-Paul*	Château La Tour Gayet	*St-Androny*
Château Breuil	*St-Martin-Caussade*	Château Le Cone Moreau	*Blaye*
Château Cantemerle	*St-Genès*	Château Le Cone Sebilleau	*Blaye*
Château Cazeaux	*St-Paul*	Château Le Cone Taillasson	*Blaye*
Domaine du Chai	*Fours*	Château Le Menaudat	*St-Androny*
Château Charron	*St-Martin*	Château Les Alberts	*Mazion*
Château Chasselauds	*Cartelègue*	Château Les Bavolliers	*St-Christ-de-Blaye*
Clos d'Amières	*Cartelègue*	Château Lescadre	*Cadres*
Château Crusquet de Lagarcie	*Cars*	Château Les Chaumes	*Fours*
Château Crusquet Sabourin	*Cars*	Château Les Moines	*Blaye*
Château Dupeyrat	*St-Paul*	Château Les Petits Arnauds	*Cars*
Château Gadeau	*Plassac*	Château Les Ricards	*Cars*
Château Gigault	*Mazion*	Château Le Virou	*St-Girons*
Château Gontier	*Blaye*	Château Mayence	*Mazion*
Château Gontier	*Blaye-Plassac*	Château Mazerolles	*Cars*
Domaine de Graulet	*Plassac*	Château Monconseil	*Plassac*
Château Guillonnet	*Anglade*	Château Moulin de la Pitance	*St-Girons*
Château Haut-Cabat	*Anglade*	Château Pardaillan	*Cars*
Château Haut-Sociondo	*Cars*	Château Perrein	*Mazion*
Château La Bertonnière	*Plassac*	Château Peyrebrune	*Cartelègue*
Château La Brousse	*St-Martin-Caussade*	Château Pinet	*Berson*
Château La Cabane	*St-Martin-Caussade*	Château Pinet La Roquete	*Berson*
Château La Cave	*Blaye*	Château Puy Beney	*Mazion*
Château La Cure	*Cars*	Château Puy Beney Lafitte	*Mazion*
Château Lafont	*Cartelègue*	Château Rebouquet	*Berson*
Château La Garde	*St-Seurin-Cursac*	Château Ricadet	*Cartelègue*
Château La Garde Roland	*St-Seurin-Cursac*	Château Segonzac	*St-Genès-de-Blaye*
Château La Girouette	*Fours*		
Château Lagrange	*Blaye*		
Château La Hargue	*Plassac*		
Château Lamothe	*St-Paul*		

Nota : Outre les châteaux énumérés dans cet appendice, il en existe environ 1 500 autres dans les communes du Bordelais qui n'ont pas leurs propres appellations.

Appendice B : Vins Allemands

Les *Bestimmtes Anbaugebiet* sont des régions délimitées portant le nom officiel de chacun des onze secteurs vinicoles d'Allemagne. Chacune de ces régions appelées est divisée en une ou plusieurs sous-régions *Bereiche*. Chaque *Bereich* regroupe différents villages et les vignobles qui y sont associés. Ces agglomérations peuvent indifféremment être appelées *Weinbauort*, *Gemeinde* ou *Gemarkung*. Quant aux vignobles, chaque parcelle individuelle est appelée *Einzellage* ; les *Einzellagen* sont officiellement regroupés en sections de vignobles appelées *Grosslagen*. *Voir* ALLEMAGNE.

I. Anbaugebiet (région) : Ahr

BEREICH (sous-région) : WALPORZHEIM / AHRTAL

GROSSLAGE (SECTION DE VIGNOBLES) : KLOSTERBERG

*Weinbauort**	*Einzellage***	*Weinbauort*	*Einzellage*
Ahrweiler	Daubhaus	Kreuzberg	Übigberg
	Forstberg	Lohrsdorf	Landskrone
	Riegelfeld	Marienthal	Jesuitengarten
	Rosentahl		Klostergarten
	Silberberg		Rosenberg
	Ursulinengarten		Stiftsberg
Altenahr	Eck		Trotzenberg
	Übigberg	Mayschoss	Burgberg
Bachem	Karlskopf		Laacherberg
	Sonnenschein		Lochmühlerley
	Steinkaul		Mönchberg
Neuenahr	Kirchtürmchen		Schieferley
	Schieferley		Silberberg
	Sonnenberg	Pützfeld	Übigberg
Dernau	Burggarten	Rech	Blume
	Goldkaul		Hardtberg
	Hardtberg		Herrenberg
	Pfarrwingert	Reimerzhoven	Eck
	Schieferlay	Walporzheim	Alte Lay
Ehlingen	Kapellenberg		Domlay
Heimersheim	Burggarten		Gärkammer
	Kapellenberg		Himmelchen
	Landskrone		Kräuterberg
Heppingen	Berg und Burggarten		Pfaffenberg

* Weinbauort (village). ** Einzellage (vignoble).

II. Anbaugebiet (région) : Bade

BEREICH (sous-région) BADISCHE : BERGSTRASSE / KRAICHGAU

GROSSLAGE (SECTION DE VIGNOBLES) : HOHENBERG

Weinbauort	*Einzellage*	*Weinbauort*	*Einzellage*
Berghausen	Sonnenberg	Ersingen	Klepberg
Bilfingen	Klepberg	Grötzingen	Lichtenberg
Dietlingen	Keulebuckel		Turmberg
	Klepberg	Hohenwettersbach	Rosengarten
Durlach	Turmberg	Jöhlingen	Hasensprung
Dürrn	Eichelberg	Söllingen	Rotenbush
Ellmendingen	Keulebuckel	Weingarten	Katzenberg
Eisingen	Klepberg		Petersberg
	Steig	Wöschbach	Steinwengert

GROSSLAGE (SECTION DE VIGNOBLES) : MANNABERG

Bruchsal	Klosterberg	Obergrombach	Burgwingert
Dielheim	Rosenberg	Oberöwisheim, Unteröwisheim	Kirchberg
	Teufelskopf		
Heidelberg	Burg	Ostringen	Hummelberg
	Dachsbuckel		Rosenkranzweg
	Dormenacker		Ulrichsberg
	Herrenberg	Rauenberg	Burggraf
Heidelsheim	Altenberg	Rettigheim	Ölbaum
Helmsheim	Burgwingert	Rotenberg	Schlossberg
Horrenberg	Osterberg	Stettfeld	Himmelreich
Leimen	Herrenberg	Tairnbach	Rosenberg
	Kreuzweg	Ubstatd	Weinhecke
Malsch	Ölbaum	Untergrombach	Michaelsberg
	Rotsteig		Weinhecke
Malschenberg	Ölbaum	Wiesloch	Bergwäldle
Mingolsheim und Langenbrücken	Goldberg		Hägenich
			Spitzenberg
Mühlhausen	Heiligenstein	Zeutern	Himmelreich
Nussloch	Wilhelmberg		

GROSSLAGE (SECTION DE VIGNOBLES) : STIFTSBERG

Bahnbrücken, Gösheim und Oberacker	Lerchenberg	Hilsbach	Eichelberg
			Silberberg
		Kürnbach	Lerchenberg
Bauerbach	Lerchenberg	Landshausen und Menzingen	Spiegelberg
Berwangen	Vogelsang		
Binau	Herzogsberg	Menzingen, Münzesheim und Neuenbürg	Silberberg
Diedesheim	Herzogsberg		
Eberbach	Schollerbuckel		
Eichelberg	Kapellenberg	Michefeld	Himmelberg
Eichtersheim	Sonnenberg und Kletterberg		Sonnenberg
		Mühlbach	Lerchenberg
Elsenz	Spiegelberg	Neckarmühlbach	Hohberg
Eppingen	Lerchenberg	Neckarzimmern	Götzhalde
Eschelbach	Sonnenberg		Kirchweinberg
Flehingen	Lerchenberg		Wallmauer
Gemmingen	Vogelsang	Neudenau	Berg
Hassmersheim	Kirchweinberg	Odenheim	Königsbecher
Heinsheim	Burg Ehrenberg	Rohrbach a. G.	Lerchenberg
Herbolzheim	Berg		Steinsberg

Steinsfurt	Steinsberg		
Sulzfeld	Burg Ravensburger		Lerchenberg
	Dicker Franz	Tiefenbach	Schellenbrunnen
	Burg Ravensburger		Spiegelberg
	Hüsarenkappe	Waldangelloch	Sonneberg
	Burg Ravensburger	Weiler	Goldberg
	Löchle	Zaisenhausen	Lerchenberg

GROSSLAGE (SECTION DE VIGNOBLES) : RITTERSBERG

Dossenheim	Ölberg		Staudenberg
Grossachsen	Sandrocken	Lützelsachsen	Stephansberg
Heidelberg	Heiligenberg	Schriesheim	Kuhberg
	Sonnenseite ob der		Madonnenberg
	Bruck		Schossberg
Hemsbach	Herrnwingert		Staudenberg
Hohensachsen	Stephansberg	Sulzbach	Herrnwingert
Laudenbach	Sonnberg	Weinheim	Hubberg
Leutershausen	Kahlberg		Wüstberg

BEREICH (sous-région) : BADISCHES FRANKENLAND

GROSSLAGE (SECTION DE VIGNOBLES) : TAUBERKLINGE

Weinbauort	*Einzellage*	*Weinbauort*	*Einzellage*
Beckstein	Kirchberg		Nonnenberg
	Nonnenberg	Lindelbach	Ebenrain
Dertingen	Mandelberg	Marbach	Frankenberg
	Sonnenberg	Oberlauda	Altenberg
Gerlachsheim	Herrenberg		Steinklinge
Grossrinderfeld	Beilberg	Oberschüpf	Altenberg
Höhefeld	Kemelrain		Herrenberg
Impfigen	Silberquell	Recholzheim	First
Kembach	Sonnenberg		Kemelrain
Klepsau	Heiligenberg		Satzenberg
Königheim	Kirchberg	Sachsenflur	Kailberg
Königshofen	Kirchberg	Tauberbischofsheim	Edlberg
	Turmberg	Uissigheim	Stahlberg
	Walterstal	Unterschüp	Mühlberg
Krautheim	Heiligenberg	Werbach	Beilberg
Külsheim	Hoher Herrgott		Hirschberg
Lauda	Altenberg	Wertheim	Schlossberg
	Frankenberg		

BERECIH (sous-région) : BODENSEE

GROSSLAGE (SECTION DE VIGNOBLES) : SONNENUFER

Weinbauort	*Einzellage*	*Weinbauort*	*Einzellage*
Bermatingen	Leopoldsberg	Meersburg	Bengel
Bodman	Königsweingarten		Chorherrnhalde
Hagnau	Burgstall		Fohrenberg
Hilzingen	Elisabethenberg		Halnau
Immenstaad	Burgstall		Jungfernstieg
Kippenhausen	Burgstall		Lerchenberg
Kirchberg	Schlossberg		Rieschen
Konstanz	Sonnenhalde		Sängerhalde
Markdorf	Burgstall	Oberuhldingen	Kirchhalde
	Sängerhalde	Reichenau	Hochwart

Singen	Elisabethenberg		Lerchenberg
	Olgaberg		Sängerhalde
Stetten	Fohrenberg	Überlingen	Felsengarten

N'ont pas encore été affectés à un *Grosslage* (section de vignobles) :

Enzingen	Kapellenberg	Hohentengen	Ölberg
Gallingen	Ritterhalde	Nack	Steinler
	Schloss Rheinberg	Rechberg	Kapellenberg

BEREICH (sous-région) : MARKGRÄFLERLAND

GROSSLAGE (SECTION DE VIGNOBLES) : VOGTEI RÖTTELN

Weinbauort	*Einzellage*	*Weinbauort*	*Einzellage*
Bamlach	Kapellenberg	Huttingen	Kirchberg
Binzen	Sonnhohle	Istein	Kirchberg
Blansingen	Wolfer	Kleinkems	Wolfer
Efringen-Kirchen	Kirchberg	Lörrach	Sonnenbrunnen
	Öelberg	Ötlingen	Sonnhohle
	Sonnhohle		Stiege
	Steingässle	Rheinweiler	Kapellenberg
Egringen	Sonnhohle	Riedlingen	Steingässle
Eimeldingen	Sonnhohle	Rümmingen	Sonnhohle
Feuerbach	Steingässle	Schallbach	Sonnhohle
Fischingen	Sonnhohle	Tannenkirch	Steingässle
Grenzach	Hornfelsen	Weil am Rhein	Schlipf
Haltingen	Stiege		Stiege
Herten	Steinacker	Welmlingen	Steingässle
Hertingen	Sonnhohle	Wintersweiler	Steingässle
Holzen	Steingässle	Wollbach	Steingässle

GROSSLAGE (SECTION DE VIGNOBLES) : BURG NEUENFELS

Auggen	Letten	Liel	Sonnenstück
	Schäf	Lipburg	Kirchberg
Bad Bellingen	Sonnenstück	Mauchen	Frauenberg
Badenweiler	Römerberg		Sonnenstück
Ballrechten-Dottingen	Altenberg	Müllheim	Pfaffenstück
	Castellberg		Reggenhag
Britzingen	Altenberg		Sonnhalde
	Rosenberg	Niedereggenen	Röthen
	Sonnhohle		Sonnenstück
Dattingen	Altenberg	Neiderweile	Römerberg
	Rosenberg	Obereggenen	Röthen
	Sonnhohle	Schliengen	Sonnenstück
Feldberg	Paradies	Steinenstadt	Schäf
Hügelheim	Gottesacker		Sonnenstück
	Höllberg	Sulzburg	Altenberg
	Schlossgarten	Zunzingen	Rosenberg
Laufen	Altenberg		

GROSSLAGE (SECTION DE VIGNOBLES) : LORETOBERG

Bad Krotzingen	Steingrüble		Maltesergarten
Beingen	Maltesergarten	Ebringen	Sommerberg
Bollschweil	Steinberg	Ehrenstetten	Öelberg
Buggingen	Hölberg		Rosenberg

Eschbach	Maltesergarten	Pfaffenweiler	Batzenberg
Freiburg	Jesuitenschloss		Oberdürrenberg
Grunern	Altenberg	Schallstadt	Batzenberg
	Schlossberg	Scherzingen	Batzenberg
Heitersheim	Maltesergarten	Schlatt	Maltesergarten
	Sonnhohle		Steingrüble
		Seefeld	Maltesergarten
Kirchhofen	Batzenberg	Staufen	Schlossberg
	Höllhagen	Tunsel	Maltesergarten
	Kirchberg	Wettelbrunn	Maltesergarten
Mengen	Alemannenbuck	Wittnau	Kapuzinerbuck
Merzhausen	Jesuitenschloss	Wolfenweiler	Batzenberg
Norsingen	Batzenberg		Dürrenberg

BEREICH (sous-région) : KAISERSTUHL-TUNIBERG

GROSSLAGE (SECTION DE VIGNOBLES) : ATTILAFELSEN

Weinbauort	*Einzellage*	*Weinbauort*	*Einzellage*
Gottenheim	Kirchberg	Oberrimsingen	Franziskaner
Merdingen	Bühl	Opfingen	Sonnenberg
Munzingen	Kapellenberg	Tiengen	Rebtal
Niederrimsingen	Rotgrund	Waltershofen	Steinmauer

GROSSLAGE (SECTION DE VIGNOBLES) : VULKANFELSEN

Achkarren	Castellberg	Jechtingen	Eichert
	Schlossberg		Enselberg
Amoltern	Steinhalde		Gestühl
Bahlingen	Silberberg		Hochberg
Bickensohl	Herrenstück		Steingrube
	Steinfelsen	Kiechlinsbergen	Ölberg
Bischoffingen	Enselberg		Teufelsburg
	Rosenkranz	Königschaffhausen	Hasenberg
	Steinbuck		Steingrüble
Bötzingen	Eckberg	Leiselheim	Gestühl
	Lasenberg	Neuershausen	Steingrube
Breisach a. Rh.	Augustinerberg	Nimburg	Steingrube
	Eckartsberg	Oberbergen	Bassgeige
Burkheim	Feuerberg		Pulverbuck
	Schlossgarten	Oberrotweil	Eichberg
Endingen	Engelsberg		Henkenberg
	Steingrube		Käsleberg
	Tannacker	Oberrotweil	Kirchberg
Eichstetten	Herrenbuck		Schlossberg
	Lerchenberg	Riegel	St Michaelsberg
Ihringen	Castellberg	Sasbach	Limburg
	Fohrenberg		Lützelberg
	Kreuzhalde		Rote Halde
	Schlossberg		Scheibenbuck
	Steinfelsen	Schelingen	Kirchberg
	Winklerberg	Wasenweiler	Kreuzhalde
Ihringen (Ortsteil Blankenhornsberg)	Doktorgarten		Lotberg

BEREICH (sous-région) : BREISGAU

GROSSLAGE (SECTION DE VIGNOBLES) : BURG ZÄHRINGEN

Weinbauort	*Einzellage*	*Weinbauort*	*Einzellage*
Buchholz	Sonnhalde	Heuweiler	Eichberg
Denzlingen	Eichberg	Hochburg	Halde
	Sonnhalde	Lehen	Bergle
Freiburg	Schlossberg	Sexau	Sonnhalde
Glottertal	Eichberg	Wildtal	Sonnenberg
	Roter Bur		

GROSSLAGE (SECTION DE VIGNOBLES) : BURG LICHTENECK

Altdorf	Kaiserberg		Roter Berg
Bleichheim	Kaiserberg	Köndringen	Alte Burg
Bombach	Sommerhalde	Malterdingen	Bienenberg
Broggingen	Kaiserberg	Mundingen	Alte Burg
Ettenheim	Kaiserberg	Nordweil	Herrenberg
Hecklingen	Schlossberg	Ringsheim	Kaiserberg
Heimbach	Bienenberg	Tutschfelden	Kaiserberg
Herbolzheim	Kaiserberg	Wagenstadt	Hummelberg
Kenzingen	Hummelberg		

GROSSLAGE (SECTION DE VIGNOBLES) : SCHUTTERLINDENBERG

Friesenheim	Kronenbühl	Mietersheim	Kronenbühl
Heiligenzell	Kronenbühl	Münchweiler	Kirchberg
Hugsweier	Kronenbühl	Oberschopfheim	Kronenbühl
Kippenheim	Haselstaude	Oberweier	Kronenbühl
Lahr	Herrentisch	Schmieheim	Kirchberg
	Kronenbühl	Sulz	Haselstaude
Mahlberg	Haselstaude	Wallburg	Kirchberg

BEREICH (sous-région) : ORTENAU

GROSSLAGE (SECTION DE VIGNOBLES) : FÜRSTENECK

Weinbauort	*Einzellage*	*Weinbauort*	*Einzellage*
Berghaupten	Kinzigtäler	Lautenbach	Renchtäler
Bermersbach	Kinzigtäler	Nesselried	Renchtäler
Bottenau	Renchtäler		Schlossberg
Diersburg	Kinzigtäler	Niederschopfheim	Kinzigtäler
	Schlossberg	Nussbach	Renchtäler
Durbach	Bienengarten	Oberkirch	Renchtäler
	Josephsberg	Ödsbach	Renchtäler
	Kapellenberg	Ohlsbach	Kinzigtäler
	Kasselberg	Ortenberg	Andreasberg
	Kochberg		Franzensberger
	Ölberg		Freudental
	Plauelrain		Schlossberg
	Schlossberg	Rammersweier	Kreusberg
	Schloss Grohl	Reichenbach	Amselberg
	Steinberg		Kinzigtäler
Erlach	Renchtäler	Ringelbach	Renchtäler
Fessenbach	Bergle	Stadelhofen	Renchtäler
Gengenbach	Kinzigtäler	Tiergarten	Renchtäler
	Nollenköpfle	Ulm	Renchtäler
Haslach	Renchtäler	Zell-Weierbach	Abtsberg
Hofweier	Kinzigtäler	Zunsweier	Kinzigtäler

GROSSLAGE (SECTION DE VIGNOBLES) : SCHLOSS RODECK

Altschweier	Sternenberg		Eichwäldele
Baden-Baden	Eckberg	Obertsrot	Grafensprung
	Sätzler	Ottersweier	Althof
Bühlertal	Engelsfelsen		Wolfhag
	Klotzberg	Renchen	Kreuzberg
Eisental	Betschgräbler	Sasbachwalden	Alter Gott
	Sommerhalde		Klostergut
Kappelrodeck	Hex vom Dasenstein		Schelzberg
Lauf	Alter Gott	Sinzheim	Frühmessler
	Gut Alsenhof		Klostergut
Mösbach	Kreuzberg		Fremersberger
Neusatz	Burg Windeck		Feigenwäldchen
	Kastanienhalde		Sätzler
	Sternenberg		Sonnenberg
	Wolfhag	Steinbach	Stich den Buben
Neuweier	Altenberg		Yburgberg
	Gänsberg	Varnhalt	Klosterbergfelsen
	Heiligenstein		Sonnenberg
	Mauerberg		Steingrübler
	Schlossberg	Waldulm	Kreuzberg
Oberachern	Alter Gott		Pfarrberg
	Bienenberg	Weisenbach	Kestelberg
Obersasbach	Alter Gott		

III. Anbaugebiet (région) : Hessische Bergstrasse

BEREICH (sous-région) : STARKENBURG

GROSSLAGE (SECTION DE VIGNOBLES) : SCHLOSSBERG

Weinbauort	*Einzellage*	*Weinbauort*	*Einzellage*
Heppenheim	Eckweg		Steinkopf
(y compris Erbach	Guldenzoll		Stemmler
et Hambach)	Maiberg		

GROSSLAGE (SECTION DE VIGNOBLES) : WOLFSMAGEN

Bensheim	Hemsberg		Paulus
(y compris Zell	Kalkgasse		Streichling
et Gronau)	Kirchberg		

GROSSLAGE (SECTION DE VIGNOBLES) : ROTT

Alsbach	Schöntal	Zwingenberg	Alte Burg
Bensheim-Auerbach	Fürstenlager		Steingeröll
	Höllberg		
Bensheim-Schönberg	Herrnwingert		

N'ont pas encore été affectés à un *Grosslage* (section de vignobles) :

Seeheim	Mundklingen

BEREICH (sous-région) : UMSTADT

N'ont pas encore été affectés à un *Grosslage* (section de vignobles) :

Dietzenbach	Wingertsberg	Klein-Umstadt	Stachelberg
Gross Umstadt	Herrnberg	Rossdorf	Rossberg
	Steingerück		

IV. Anbaugebiet (région) : Franconie

BEREICH (sous région) : MAINVIERECK

GROSSLAGE (SECTION DE VIGNOBLES) : REUSCHBERG

Weinbauort	*Einzellage*	*Weinbauort*	*Einzellage*
Hörstein	Abtsberg		

N'ont pas encore été affectés à un *Grosslage* (section de vignobles) :

Aschaffenburg	Pompejaner	Rottenberg	Gräfenstein
Michelbach	Steinberg	Wasserlos	Schlossberg
	Apostelgarten		Luhmännchen
Obernau	Sanderberg		

GROSSLAGE (SECTION DE VIGNOBLES) : HEILIGENTHAL

Grossostheim	Reischklingeberg	Wenigumstadt	Wenigumstadt
	Harstell		

N'ont pas encore été affectés à un *Grosslage* (section de vignobles) :

Bürgstadt	Centgrafenberg	Klingenberg	Hochberg
	Mainhölle		Schlossberg
Dorfprozelten	Predigtstuhl	Kreuzwertheim	Kaffelstein
Engelsberg	Klostergarten	Miltenberg	Steingrübler
Erlenbach a. Main	Hochberg	Rück	Jesuitenberg
Grossheubach	Bischofsberg		Johannisberg
Grosswallstadt	Lützeltalerberg		Schalk

BEREICH (sous-région) : MAINDREIECK

GROSSLAGE (SECTION DE VIGNOBLES) : KIRCHBERG

Weinbauort	*Einzellage*	*Weinbauort*	*Einzellage*
Astheim	Karthaüser	Hergolshausen	Mainleite
Escherndorf	Berg	Köhler	Köhler
	Fürstenberg	Krautheim	Sonnenleite
	Lump	Neuses Am Berg	Glatzen
Fahr	Fahr	Neusetz	Neusetz
Hallburg	Rosenberg	Nordheim	Kreuzberg
	Kreuzberg		Vögelein

Obereisenheim	Höll		Höll
Odervolkach	Landsknecht		Sonneberg
Sommerach	Katzenkopf	Volkach	Ratsherr
	Rosennberg	Wipfeld	Zehntgraf
Stammheim	Eselsberg	Zeilitzheim	Heiligenberg
Untereisenheim	Berg		
GROSSLAGE (SECTION DE VIGNOBLES) : BURG			
Hammelburg	Heroldsberg	Rimbach	Landsknecht
	Trautlestal	Saaleck	Schlossberg
Ramsthal	St Klausen	Wirmsthal	Scheinberg
GROSSLAGE (SECTION DE VIGNOBLES) : ROSSTAL			
Arnstein	Arnstein	Karlstadt	Im Stein
Eussenheim	First	Laudenbach	Laudenbach
Gambach	Kalbenstein	Mühlbach	Mühlbach
Gössenheim	Homburg	Retzstadt	Langenberg
Himmelstadt	Kelter	Stetten	Stein
Karlburg	Karlburg		
GROSSLAGE (SECTION DE VIGNOBLES) : HONIGBERG			
Dettelbach	Berg-Rondell		Sonnenleite
GROSSLAGE (SECTION DE VIGNOBLES) : HOFRAT			
Alberstshofen	Herrgotsweg	Marktsteft	Sonnenberg
Buchbrunn	Heisser Stein	Repperndorf	Kaiser karl
Kitzingen	Eselsberg	Segnitz	Pfaffensteig
	Wilhelmsberg		Zobelsberg
Mainstockheim	Hofstück	Sulzfeld	Cyriakusberg
Marktbreit	Sonnenberg		Maustal
GROSSLAGE (SECTION DE VIGNOBLES) : EWIG LEBEN			
Randersacker	Marsberg		Teufelskeller
	Pfülben	Theilheim	Altenberg
	Sonnenstuhl		
GROSSLAGE (SECTION DE VIGNOBLES) : RAVENSBURG			
Erlabrunn	Weinsteig	Thüngersheim	Johannisberg
Güntersleben	Sommerstuhl		Scharlachberg
Oberleinach	Weinsteig	Unterleinach	Himmelberg
	Himmelberg	Veitshöchheim	Wölflein
Retzbach	Benediktusberg	Zellingen	Sonnleite
N'ont pas encore été affectés à un *Grosslage* (section de vignobles) :			
Böttigheim	Wurmberg		Pfaffenberg
Rimpar	Kobersberg		Schlossberg
Veitshöchheim	Sonnenschein		Stein
Würzburg	Abtsleite		Stein/Harfe
	Innere Leiste		

BEREICH (sous-région) : STEIGERWALD

Weinbauort	*Einzellage*	*Weinbauort*	*Einzellage*
GROSSLAGE (SECTION DE VIGNOBLES) : SCHILD			
Abtswind	Altenberg	Greuth	Bastel
GROSSLAGE (SECTION DE VIGNOBLES) : HERRENBERG			
Castell	Bausch		Kugelspiel
	Feuerbach		Reitsteig
	Hohnart		Schlossberg
	Kirchberg		Trautberg
GROSSLAGE (SECTION DE VIGNOBLES) : KAPELLENBERG			
Oberschwappach	Sommertal	Steinbach	Nonnenberg
Sand am Main	Kronberg	Ziegelanger	Ölschnabel
Schmachtenberg	Eulengrund		
N'ont pas encore été affectés à un *Grosslage* (section de vignobles) :			
Altmannsdorf	Sonnenwinkel	Unfinden	
Bamberg	Alter Graben	Krum	Himmelreich
Dingolshausen	Köhler	Michelau	Vollburg
Donnersdorf	Falkenberg	Mönchstockheim	Köhler
Eltmann	Schlossleite	Oberschwarzach	Herrenberg
Gerolzhofen	Arlesgarten	Prichenstadt	Krone
Handthal	Stollberg	Sand am Main	Himmelsbühl
Kammerforst	Teufel	Weiher	Weinberg
Königsberg in	Kinnleitenberg	Zell am Ebersberg	Schlossberg
Bayern Orsteil		Zeil am Main	Mönshang
GROSSLAGE (SECTION DE VIGNOBLES) : SCHLOSSBERG			
Grosslangheim	Kiliansberg	Sickershausen	Storchenbrünnle
Kleinlangheim	Wutschenberg	Wiesenbronn	Geissberg
Rödelsee	Küchenmeister		Wachhügel
	Schwanleite		
GROSSLAGE (SECTION DE VIGNOBLES) : BURGWEG			
Iphofen	Julius-Echte-Berg	Markt Einersheim	Vogelsang
	Kalb	Possenheim	Possenheim
	Kronsberg		
GROSSLAGE (SECTION DE VIGNOBLES) : SCHLOSSTÜCK			
Bullenheim	Paradies	Ingolstadt	Rotenberg
Ergersheim	Altenberg	Ippesheim	Herrschaftsberg
Frankenberg	Herrschaftsberg	Seinsheim	Hohenbühl
Hüttenheim	Tannenberg	Weimersheim	Roter Berg
N'ont pas encore été affectés à un *Grosslage* (section de vignobles) :			
Dietersheim	Burg Hoheneck		Sonneberg
Iphofen	Domherr		Wonne
Ipsheim	Burg Hoheneck	Tiefenstockheim	Stiefel
Martinsheim	Langenstein	Reusch	Hohenlandsberg
Neudorf	Hüssberg	Weigenheim	Hohenlandsberg
	Mönchsbuck		

BEREICH (sous-région) : BAYER. BODENSEE

Weinbauort	*Einzellage*
Nonnenhorn	Seehalde
	Sonnenbüchel

V. Anbaugebiet (région) : Mittelrhein

BEREICH (sous-région) : BACHARACH

GROSSLAGE (SECTION DE VIGNOBLES) : SCHLOSS REICHENSTEIN

Weinbauort	*Einzellage*	*Weinbauort*	*Einzellage*
Niederheimbach	Froher Weingarten	Oberheimbach	Klosterberg
	Reifersley		Römerberg
	Schloss Hohneck		Sonne
	Soonecker		Wahrheit
	Schlossberg	Trechtingshausen	Morgenbachtaler

GROSSLAGE (SECTION DE VIGNOBLES) : SCHLOSS STAHLECK

Bacharach	Hahn	Manubach	Heilgarten
	Insel Heylesern Wert		Langgarten
	Kloster Fürstental		Mönchwingert
	Mathias Weingarten		St Oswald
	Posten	Oberdiebach	Bischofshub
	Wofshöhle		Fürstenberg
Bacharach/Steeg	Hambusch		Kräuterberg
	Lennenborn	Rheindiebach	Fürstenberg
	St Jost		Rheinberg
	Schloss Stahlberg		

BEREICH (sous-région) : RHEINBURGENGAU

GROSSLAGE (SECTION DE VIGNOBLES) : BURG HAMMERSTEIN

Weinbauort	*Einzellage*	*Weinbauort*	*Einzellage*
Bad Hönningen	Schlossberg		Gartenlay
Dattenberg	Gertrudenberg		Rosenberg
Hammerstein	Hölle	Linz	Rheinhöller
	In den Layfelsen	Rheinbrohl	Monte Jup
	Schlossberg		Römerberg
Kasbach	Stehlerberg	Unkel	Berg
Leubsdorf	Weisses Kreuz		Sonneberg
Leutesdorf	Forstberg		

GROSSLAGE (SECTION DE VIGNOBLES) : BURG RHEINFELS

St. Goar	Ameisenberg		Kuhstall
	Frohwingert		Rosenberg

GROSSLAGE (SECTION DE VIGNOBLES) : GEDEONSECK

Boppard	Elfenlay		Weingrube
	Engelstein	Brey	Hämmchen
	Fässerlay	Rhens	König Wenzel
	Feuerlay		Sonnelay
	Mandelstein	Spay	Engelstein
	Ohlenberg		

GROSSLAGE (SECTION DE VIGNOBLES) : HERRENBERG

Dörscheid	Kupferfloz		Burg Gutenfels
	Wolfsnack		Pfalzgrafenstein
Kaub	Backofen		Rauschelay
	Blüchertal		Rosstein

GROSSLAGE (SECTION DE VIGNOBLES) : LORELEYFELSEN

Bornich	Rothenack	Patersberg	Teufelstein
Kamp-Bornhofen-Kestert	Liebenstein-Sterrenberg	St Goarshausen	Burg Katz
			Burg Maus
	Pilgerpfad		Hessern
Nochern	Brünnchen		Loreley-Edel

GROSSLAGE (SECTION DE VIGNOBLES) : MARSKBURG

Braubach	Marmorberg	Ehrenbreitstein	
	Mühlberg	Lahnstein	Koppelstein
	Koppelstein	Osterspai	Liebeneck-Sonnenlay
Filsen	Pfarrgarten		
Koblenz	Schnorbach	Urbar	Rheinnieder
	Brückstück	Vallendar	Rheinnieder
Koblenz-	Kreuzberg		

GROSSLAGE (SECTION DE VIGNOBLES) : LAHNTAL

Bad Ems	Hasenberg	Nassau	Schlossberg
Dausenau	Hasenberg	Obernhof	Gœtheberg
Fachbach	Pas encore défini	Weinähr	Giebelhöll

GROSSLAGE (SECTION DE VIGNOBLES) : SCHLOSS SCHÖNBURG

Damscheid	Frankenhell		Bienenberg
	Goldemund		Goldemund
	Sonnenstock		Ölsberg
Dellhofen	Römerkrug		Römerkrug
	St Wernerberg		St Martinsberg
Langscheid	Hundert		Sieben Jungfrauen
Niederburg	Bienenberg	Perscheid	Rosental
	Rheingoldberg	Urbar	Beulsberg
Oberwesel	Bernstein		

N'ont pas été encore affectés à un *Grosslage* (section de vignobles) :

Hirzenach	Probsteiberg

VI. Anbaugebiet (région) : Mosel-Saar-Ruwer

BEREICH (sous-région) : BERNKASTEL

GROSSLAGE (SECTION DE VIGNOBLES) : BADSTUBE

Weinbauort	*Einzellage*		*Einzellage*
Bernkastel-Kues	Bratenhöfchen		Lay
	Doctor		Matheisbildchen
	Graben		

GROSSLAGE (SECTION DE VIGNOBLES) : BEERENLAY

Lieser	Niederberg-Helden		Süssenberg
	Rosenlay		

GROSSLAGE (SECTION DE VIGNOBLES) : KURFÜRSTLAY

Andel	Schlossberg		Kirchberg
Bernkastel-Kues	Johannisbrünnchen		Klosterberg
	Kardinalsberg		Römerpfad
	Rosenberg		Sonnenuhr
	Schlossberg	Mülheim	Amtsgarten
	Stephanus-		Elisenberg
	Rosengärtchen		Helenenkloster
	Weissenstein		Sonnenlay
Brauneberg	Juffer	Osann-Monzel	Kätzchen
	Juffer-Sonnenuhr		Kirchlay
	Kammer		Paulinslay
	Klostergarten		Rosengarten
	Mandelgraben	Veldenz	Carlsberg
Burgen	Hasenläufer		Elisenberg
	Kirchberg		Grafschafter
	Römerberg		Sonnenberg
Kesten	Herrenberg		Kirchberg
	Paulinsberg		Mühlberg
Lieser	Niederberg-Helden	Wintrich	Grosser Herrgott
	Rosenlay		Ohligsberg
	Schlossberg		Sonnseite
	Süssenberg		Stefanslay
Maring-Noviand	Honigberg		

GROSSLAGE (SECTION DE VIGNOBLES) : MICHELSBERG

Hetzerath	Brauneberg		Gärtchen
Minheim	Burglay		Goldtröpfchen
	Günterslay		Grafenberg
	Kapellchen		Günterslay
	Rosenberg		Hofberger
Neumagen-Dhron	Engelgrube		Kreuzwingert
	Goldtröpfchen		Schubertslay
	Grosser Hengelberg		Treppchen
	Haschen	Rivenich	Brauneberg
	Hofberger		Geisberg
	Laudamusberg		Niederberg
	Nusswingert		Rosenberg
	Rosengärtchen	Sehlem	Rotlay
	Roterd	Trittenheim	Altärchen
	Sonnenuhr		Apotheke
Piesport	Domherr		Felsenkopf
	Falkenberg		Leiterchen

GROSSLAGE (SECTION DE VIGNOBLES) : MÜNZLAY

Graach	Abtsberg		Nonnenberg
	Domprobst		Rosenberg
	Himmelreich		Sonnenuhr
	Josephshöfer	Zeltingen-Rachtig	Deutschherrenberg
Wehlen	Abtei		Himmelreich
	Hofberg		Schlossberg
	Klosterberg		Sonnenuhr
	Klosterhofgut		

GROSSLAGE (SECTION DE VIGNOBLES) : NACKTARSCH

Kröv	Burglay		Herrenberg

	Kirchlay		Paradies
	Letterlay		Steffensberg
	GROSSLAGE (SECTION DE VIGNOBLES) : PROBSTBERG		
Fell	Maximiner Burgberg	Mehring	Vignobles de la rive droite de la Moselle
Kenn	Held		
	Maximiner Hofgarten	Riol	Römerberg
Longuich	Herrenberg	Schweich	Annaberg
	Hirschlay		Burgmauer
	Maximer Herrenberg		Herrenberg
	GROSSLAGE (SECTION DE VIGNOBLES) : SANKT MICHAEL		
Bekond	Brauneberg		Laurentiuslay
	Schlossberg	Longen	Zellerberg
Detzem	Maximiner Klosterlay	Lörsch	Goldkupp
			Zellerberg
	Würzgarten	Mehring	Blattenberg
Ensch	Mühlenberg		Zellerberg
	St Martin	Pölich	Held
	Sonnenlay		Südlay
Klüsserath	Bruderschaft	Schleich	Klosterberg
	Königsberg		Sonnenberg
Köwerich	Held	Thörnich	Enggass
	Laurentiuslay		Ritsch
Leiwen	Klostergarten		
	GROSSLAGE (SECTION DE VIGNOBLES) : SCHWARZLAY		
Bausendorf	Herzlay	Traben-Trarbach	Burgweg
	Hubertuslay		Gaispfad
Bengel	Klosterberg		Hühnerberg
Burg	Falklay		Königsberg
	Hahnenschrittchen		Kräuterhaus
	Schlossberg		Kreuzberg
	Thomasberg		Schlossberg
	Wendelstück		Taubenhaus
Dreis	Johannisberg		Ungsberg
Enkirch	Batterieberg		Würzgarten
	Edelberg		Zollturm
	Ellergrub	Traben-Trarbach (Ortsteil Starkenburg)	Rosengarten
	Herrenberg		
	Monteneubel		
	Steffensberg	Traben-Trarbach (Ortsteil Wolf)	Auf der Heide
	Weinkammer		Goldgrube
	Zeppwingert		Klosterberg
Erden	Busslay		Schatzgarten
	Herrenberg		Sonnenlay
	Prälat	Ürzig	Goldwingert
	Treppchen		Wünzgarten
Flussbach	Reichelbeg	Wittlich	Bottchen
Hupperath	Klosterweg		Felsentreppchen
Kinheim	Huberstuslay		Klosterweg
	Rosenberg		Kupp
Lösnich	Burgberg		Lay
	Försterlay		Portnersberg
Platten	Klosterberg		Rosenberg
	Rotlay		

GROSSLAGE (SECTION DE VIGNOBLES) : VOM HEISSEN STEIN

Briedel	Herzchen		Nonnengarten
	Nonnengarten		Rosenberg
	Schäferlay	Reil	Falklay
	Schelm		Goldlay
	Weisserberg		Moullay-Hofberg
Pünderich	Goldlay		Sorentberg
	Marienburg		

BEREICH (sous-région) : OBERMOSEL

GROSSLAGE (SECTION DE VIGNOBLES) : GIPFEL

Weinbauort	*Einzellage*	*Weinbauort*	*Einzellage*
Biltzingen	Pas encore défini		Römerberg
Fellerich	Schleidberg	Ondsdorf	Hubertusberg
Fisch	Pas encore défini	Palzem	Carlsfelsen
Helfant-Esingen	Kapellenberg		Lay
Kirf	Pas encore défini	Porz	Pas encore défini
Köllig	Rochusfels	Rehlingen	Kapellenberg
Kreuzweiler	Schloss Thorner	Soest	Pas encore défini
	Kupp	Temmels	Münsterstatt
Merzkirschen	Pas encore défini		St Georgshof
Meurich	Pas encore défini	Wasserliesch	Albachtaler
	Blümchen		Reinig auf der Burg
	Hubertusberg	Wehr	Rosenberg
	Leiterchen	Wellen	Altenberg
	Rochusfels	Wincheringen	Burg Warsberg
Oberbillig	Hirtengarten		Fuchsloch

GROSSLAGE (SECTION DE VIGNOBLES) : KÖNIGSBERG

Edingen	Pas encore défini	Liersberg	Pilgerberg
Godendorf	Pas encore défini	Mesenich	Held
Grewenich	Pas encore défini	Metzdorf	Pas encore défini
Igel	Dullgärten	Ralingen	Pas encore défini
Langsur	Brüderberg	Winersdorf	Pas encore défini

BEREICH (sous-région) : SAAR-RUWER

GROSSLAGE (SECTION DE VIGNOBLES) : RÖMERLAY

Weinbauort	*Einzellage*	*Weinbauort*	*Einzellage*
Franzenheim	Johannisberg		Heiligenhäuschen
Hockweiler	Pas encore défini	Riveris	Heiligenhäuschen
Kasel	Dominikanerberg		Kuhnchen
	Herrenberg	Sommerau	Schlossberg
	Hitzlay	Trier	Altenberg
	Kehrnagel		Andreasberg
	Nieschen		Augenscheiner
	Paulinsberg		Benediktinerberg
	Timpert		Burgber
Korlingen	Laykaul		Deutschherrenberg
Mertesdorf	Herrenberg		Deutschherren-köpfchen
	Johannisberg		
Mertesdorf (Ortsteil Maximin Grünhaus)	Abtsberg	Trier	Domherrenberg
	Bruderberg		Hammerstein
	Herrenberg		Herrenberg
Morscheid	Dominikanerberg		Jesuitenwingert

	Karthäuserhofberg Burgberg
	Karthäuserhofberg Orthsberg
	Karthäuserhofberg Sang
	Karthäuserhofberg Stirn
	Kupp
	Kurfürstenhofberg
	Leikaul
	Marienholz
	Maximiner
	Rotlei
	St. Martiner Hofberg
	St. Martiner Klosterberg
	St. Matheiser
	St. Maximiner
	Kreuzberg
	St Petrusberg
	Sonnenberg
	Thiergarten Felsköpfchen
	Thiergarten Unterm Kreuz
Waldrach	Doktorberg
	Ehrenberg
	Heilingenhäuschen
	Hubertusberg
	Jesuitenbarten
	Jungfernberg
	Krone
	Kurfüstrenberg
	Laurentiusberg
	Laurentiusberg
	Meisenberg
	Sonnenberg

GROSSLAGE (SECTION DE VIGNOBLES) : SCHARZBERG

Ayl	Herrenberger
	Kupp
	Scheidterberger
Falkenstein	Herrenberg
	Hofberg
Filzen	Altenberg
	Herrenberg
	Pulchen
	Steinberger
	Unterberg
	Urbelt
Hamm	Altenberg
	Liebfrauenberg
Irsch	Sonnenberg
Kanzem	Altenberg
	Hörecker
	Ritterpfad
	Schlossberg
	Sonnenberg
Kastel-Staadt	König Johann Berg
	Maximin Staadt
Kommlingen	Auf der Wittingerkupp
Könen	Fels
	Kirchberg
Konz	Euchariusberg
	Klosterberg
	Sprung
Krettnach	Altenberg
	Eucariusberg
Niedermenning	Euchariusberg
	Herrenberg
	Sonnenberg
Oberemmel	Agritiusberg
	Altenberg
	Hütte
	Karlsberg
	Raul
	Rosenberg
Ockfen	Bockstein
	Geisberg
	Heppenstein
	Herrenberg
	Kupp
	Neuwies
	Zickelgarten
Pellingen	Herrgottsrock
	Jesuitengarten
Saarburg	Antoniusbrunnen
	Bergschlösschen
	Fuchs
	Klosterberg
	Kupp
	Laurentiusberg
	Rausch
	Schlossberg
	Stirn
Schoden	Geisberg
	Herrenberg
	Saarfeilser Marienberg
Serrig	Antoniusberg
	Hellingenborn
	Hœppslei
	Herrenberg
	König Johann Berg
	Kupp
	Schloss Saarsteiner
	Schloss Saarfelser Schlossberg

	Vogelsang		Gottesfuss
	Würtzberg		Hölle
Wawern	Goldberg		Klosterberg
	Herrenberger		Kupp
	Jesuitenberg		Rosenberg
	Ritterpfad		Sandberg
Wiltingen	Braune Kupp		Schlagengraben
	Braunfels		Schlossberg

BEREICH (sous-région) : ZELL/MOSEL

GROSSLAGE (SECTION DE VIGNOBLES) : GOLDBÄUMCHEN

Weinbauort	*Einzellage*	*Weinbauort*	*Einzellage*
Briedern	Rüberberger		Rosenberg
	Domherrenberg		Übereltzer
Bruttig-Fankel	Götterlay	Müden	Funkenberg
Cochem	Bischofstuhl		Grosslay
	Hochlay		Leckmauer
	Klostergarten		St Castorhöhle
	Sonnenberg		Sonnenring
Ellenz-Poltersdorf	Altarberg	Pommern	Goldberg
	Kurfürst		Rosenberg
	Rüberberger		Sonnenuhr
	Domherrenberg		Zeisel
Ernst	Feuerberg	Senheim	Römerberg
	Kirchlay		Rüberberger
Klotten	Brauneberg		Domherrenberg
	Burg Coreidelsteiner	Treis-Karden	Dechantberg
	Rosenberg		Juffermauer
	Sonnengold		Münsterberg
Moselkern	Kirchberg		

GROSSLAGE (SECTION DE VIGNOBLES) : GRAFSCHAFT

Alf	Arrasburg-	Ediger-Eller	Bienenlay
	Schlossberg		Calmont
	Burggraf		Elzogberg
	Herrenberg		Engelströpfchen
	Hölle		Feuerberg
	Kapellenberg		Hasensprung
	Katzenkopf		Höll
	Kronenberg		Kapplay
Beuren	Pelzerberger		Osterlämmchen
Bremm	Calmont		Plaffenberg
	Frauenberg		Pfirsichgarten
	Laurentiusberg		Schützenlay
	Schlemmer-	Neef	Frauenberg
	tröpfchen		Petersberg
Bullay	Brautrock		Rosenberg
	Graf Beyssel-	Nehren	Römerberg
	Herrenberg	St Aldegund	Himmelreich
	Kirchweingarten		Klosterkammer
	Kroneberg		Palmberg-Terrassen
	Sonneck	Zell-Merl	Pas encore défini

GROSSLAGE (SECTION DE VIGNOBLES) : ROSENHANG

Beilstein	Schlossberg		Kloster Stuben
Bremm	Abtei	Briedern	Herrenberg

	Kapellenberg		Woogberg
	Römergarten	Mesenich	Abteiberg
	Servatiusberg		Deuslay
Bruttig-Fankel	Kapellenberg		Goldgrübchen
	Layenberg	Senheim	Bienengarten
	Martinsborn		Rosenberg
	Pfarrgarten		Vogteiberg
	Rathausberg		Wahrsager
	Rosenberg	Treis-Karden	Greth
Cochem	Arzlay		Kapellenberg
	Nikolausberg		Treppchen
	Rosenberg	Valwig	Herrenberg
Ediger-Eller	Stubener		Palmberg
Orsteil-Eller	Klostersegen		Schwarzenberg
Ellenz-Poltersdorf	Silberberg		
GROSSLAGE (SECTION DE VIGNOBLES) : SCHWARZE KATZ			
Zell	Burglay-Felsen		Römerquelle
	Domherrenberg		Rosenborn
	Geisberg	Zell-Merl	Adler
	Kreuzlay		Fettgarten
	Nussberg		Klosterberg
	Petersborn-	Zell-Merl	Königslay-Terrassen
	Kabertchen		Stefansberg
	Pommerell		Sonneck
Zell-Kaimt	Marienburger		
GROSSLAGE (SECTION DE VIGNOBLES) : WEINHEX			
Alken	Bleidenberg	Lay	Hubertsborn,
	Burgberg		Hamm
	Hunnenstein	Lehmen	Ausoniusstein
Burgen	Bischofstein		Klosterberg
Dieblich	Heilgraben		Lay
Güls	Bienengarten		Würzlay
	Im Röttgen	Löf	Godblume
	Königsfels		Sonnenring
	Marienberg	Moselweiss	Hamm
Hatzenport	Burg Bischofsteiner	Moselsürsch	Fahrberg
	Kirchberg	Niederfell	Fächern
	Stolzenberg		Goldlay
Kattenes	Fahrberg		Kahllay
	Steinchen	Oberfell	Brauneberg
Kobern-Gondorf	Fahrberg		Godlay
	Fuchshöhle		Rosenberg
	Gäns	Winningen	Brückstück
	Kehrberg		Domgarten
	Schlossberg		Hamm
	Uhlen		Im Röttgen
	Weissenberg		Uhlen

VII. Anbaugebiet (région) : Nahe

BEREICH (sous-région) : KREUZNACH

GROSSLAGE (SECTION DE VIGNOBLES) : KRONENBERG

Weinbauort	*Einzellage*		*Einzellage*
Bad Kreuznach	Berg		Brückes

	Forst	Orsteil Bosenheim	Galgenberg
	Galgenberg		Hirtenhain
	Gutental		Höllenbrand
	Hinkelstein		Paradies
	Hungrier Wolf	Orsteil Ippesheim	Himmelgarten
	Kahlenberg		Junker
	Kapellenpfad	Orsteil Planig	Höllenbrand
	Kauzenberg-Orionberg		Katzenhölle
	Kauzenberg-Rosenhügel		Nonnengarten
	Kauzenberg-In Den Mauern		Römerhalde
	Krötenpfuhl	Orsteil Winzenheim	Berg
	Mollenbrunnen		Honigberg
	Mönchberg		In den siebzehn Morgen
	Narrenkappe		Rosenheck
	Osterhöll	Bretzenheim	Felsenköpfchen
	Rosenberg		Hofgut
	St Martin		Pastorei
	Steinberg		Schlossgarten
	Tilgesbrunnen		Vogelsang
	Vogelsang	Hargeshein	Mollenbrunnen
			Straussberg
GROSSLAGE (SECTION DE VIGNOBLES) : PFARRGARTEN			
Dalberg	Ritterhölle		Sonnenberg
	Schlossberg		Steinrossel
	Sonnenberg	Spabrücken	Höll
Gutenberg	Felseneck	Wallhausen	Backöfchen
	Römerberg		Felseneck
	St Ruppertsberg		Hasensprung
	Schlossberg		Höllenpfad
	Schloss Gutenburg		Hörnchen
	Sonnenlauf		Johannisberg
Hergenfeld	Herrschaftsgarten		Johannisweg
	Mönchberg		Kirschheck
Schöneberg	Schäfersley		Laurentiusberg
	Sonnenberg		Mühlenberg
Sommerloch	Birkenberg		Pastorenberg
	Ratsgrund		Sonnenweg
GROSSLAGE (SECTION DE VIGNOBLES) : SCHLOSSKAPELLE			
Bingen-Bingerbrück	Abtei Ruppertsberg		Nixenberg
	Hildegardisbrünnchen	Dorsheim	Pittermännchen
			Trollberg
	Klostergarten	Eckenroth	Felsenberg
	Römerberg		Hölle
Burg Layen	Hölle	Genheim	Rossel
	Johannisberg	Guldental	Apostelberg
	Rothenberg		Hipperich
	Schlossberg		Hölle
Dorsheim	Burgberg		Honigberg
	Goldloch		Rosenteich
	Honigberg		St Martin
	Jungbrunnen		Sonnenberg
	Klosterpfad		Teufelsküche
	Laurenziweg	Laubenheim	Fuchsen

	Hörnchen	Schweppenhausen	Schlossgarten
	Junker		Steyerberg
	Karthäuser	Waldlaubersheim	Altenburg
	Krone		Bingerweg
	St Remigiusberg		Domberg
	Vogelsang		Lieseberg
Münster-Sarmsheim	Dautenpflänzer		Otterberg
	Kapellenberg	Weiler	Abtei Ruppertsberg
	Königsschloss		Klostergarten
	Liebehöll		Römerberg
	Pittersberg	Windesheim	Preiselberg
	Rheinberg		Fels
	Römerberg		Hausgiebel
	Steinkopff		Hölle
	Trollberg		Römerberg
Rümmelsheim	Hölle		Rosenberg
	Johannisberg		Saukopf
	Rothenberg		Schäfchen
Rümmelsheim	Schlossberg		Sonnenmorgen
	Steinköpfchen		
	GROSSLAGE (SECTION DE VIGNOBLES) : SONNENBORN		
Langelonsheim	Bergborn		Rothenberg
	Königsschild		St Antoniusweg
	Lauerweg		Steinchen
	Löhrer Berg		

BEREICH (sous-région) : SCHLOSS BÖCKELHEIM

GROSSLAGE (SECTION DE VIGNOBLES) : BURGWEG

Weinbauort	*Einzellage*	*Weinbauort*	*Einzellage*
Altenbamberg	Kehrenberg		Kertz
	Laurentiusberg		Klamm
	Rotenberg		Pfaffenstein
	Schlossberg		Pflingstweide
	Treuenfels		Rosenberg
Bad Münster a. St Ebernburg	Erzgrupe		Rosenheck
	Felseneck		Steinberg
	Feuerberg		Steinwingert
	Götzenfels		Stollenberg
	Höll		Herrmannsberg
	Köhler-Köpfchen	Norheim	Dellchen
	Königsgarten		Götzenfels
	Luisengarten	Norheim	Kafels
	Rotenfelser im Winkel		Kirschheck
			Klosterberg
	Schlossberg		Oberberg
	Steigerdell		Onkelchen
	Stephansberg		Sonnenberg
Duchroth	Felsenberg	Oberhausen an der Nahe	Felsenberg
	Feuerberg		Kielselberg
	Kaiserberg		Leistenberg
	Königsfels		Rotenberg
	Rothenberg	Schlossböckelheim	Felsenberg
	Vogeschlag		Heimberg
Niederhausen an der Nahe	Felsensteyer		
	Hermannshöhle		

	In den Felsen
	Königsfels
	Kupfergrube
	Mühlberg
Traisen	Bastei
	Kilckelskopf
	Nonnengarten
	Rotenfels
Waldböckelheim	Drachenbrunnen
	Hamm
	Kirchberg
	Königsfels
	Kronenfels
	Marienpforter Klosterberg
	Muckerhölle
	Mühlberg
	Römerberg

GROSSLAGE (SECTION DE VIGNOBLES) : PARADIESGARTEN

Alsenz	Elkersberg
	Falkenberg
	Hölle
	Pfaffenpfad
Auen	Kaulenberg
	Römerstich
Bayerfeld-Steckweiler	Adelsberg
	Aspenberg
	Mittelberg
	Schloss Stolzenberg
Boos	Herrenberg
	Kastell
Desloch	Hengstberg
	Vor der Hölle
Feilbingert	Bocksberg
	Feuerberg
	Höchstes Kreuz
	Kahlenberg
	Königsgarten
Gaugrehweiler	Graukatz
Hochstätten	Liebesbrunnen
Kalkofen	Graukatz
Kirschroth	Lump
	Widgrafenberg
Lauschied	Edelberg
Lettweiler	Inkelhöll
	Rheingasse
Mannweiler-Cölln	Rosenberg
	Schloss Randeck
	Seidenberg
	Weissenstein
Martinstein	Schlossberg
Meddersheim	Altenberg
	Edelberg
	Liebfrauenberg
	Präsent
	Rheingrafenberg
Meisenheim	Obere Heimbach
Merxheim	Hunolsteiner
	Römerberg
	Vogelsang
Monzingen	Frühlingsplätzchen
	Halenberg
	Rosenberg
Münsterappel	Grankatz
Niederhausen an der Nahe	Graukatz
Niedermoschel	Geissenkopf
	Hahnhölle
	Layenberg
	Silberberg
Nussbaum	Höllenberg
	Rotfeld
	Sonnenberg
Oberhausen an der Nahe	Graukatz
Obermoschel	Geissenkopf
	Langhölle
	Schlossberg
	Silberberg
	Sonnenplätzchen
Oberndorf	Aspenberg
	Beutelstein
	Feuersteinrossel
	Weissenstein
Oberstreit	Auf dem Zimmerberg
Odernheim	Klöster-Disibodenberg
	Hessweg
	Kapellenberg
	Langenberg
	Montfort
	Weinsack
Raumbach	Schlossbert
	Schwalbennest
Rehborn	Hahn
	Herrenberg
	Schikanenbuckel
Sobernheim	Domberg
	Marbach
Sobernheim-Steinhardt	Johannesberg
	Spitalberg
Staudernheim	Goldgrube
	Herrenberg
Unkenbach	Römerpfad
	Würzhölle
Waldböckelheim	Johannesberg
	Kastell
Weiler bei Monzingen	Heiligenberg
	Herrenzehntel
Winterborn	Graukatz

GROSSLAGE (SECTION DE VIGNOBLES) : ROSENGARTEN

Bockenau	Geisberg	Roxheim	Berg
	Im Felseneck		Birkenberg
	Im Neuberg		Höllenpfad
	Stromberg		Hüttenberg
Braunweiler	Hellenpfad		Mühlenberg
	Michaeliskapelle		Sonnenberg
	Schlossberg	Rüdesheim	Goldgrube
	Wetterkreuz		Wiesberg
Burgsponheim	Höllenpfad	St Katharinen	Fels
	Pfaffenberg		Klostergarten
	Schlossberg		Steinkreuz
Hüffelsheim	Gutenhölle	Sponheim	Abtei
	Mönchberg		Grafenberg
	Steyer		Klostergarten
Mandel	Alte Römerstrasse		Mühlberg
	Becherbrunnen		Mühlberg
	Dellchen	Weinsheim	Katergrube
	Palmengarten		Kellerberg
	Schlossberg		Steinkaut

VIII Anbaugebiet (région) : Rheingau

BEREICH (sous-régions) : JOHANNISBERG

GROSSLAGE (SECTION DE VIGNOBLES) : BURGWEG

Weinbauort	*Einzellage*	*Weinbauort*	*Einzellage*
Lorch	Bodenstal-Steinberg		Schlossberg
	Kapellenberg	Lorchhausen	Rosenberg
	Krone		Seligmacher
	Pfaffenwies		

GROSSLAGE (SECTION DE VIGNOBLES) : STEIL

Assmannshausen	Frankenthal		Schlossgarten
	Hollenberg	Rüdesheim	Berg Roseneck
	Hinterkirch		Berg Rottland
Aulhausen	Berg Kaisersteinfels		Berg Schlossberg
Geisenheim	Fuchsberg		Bischofsberg
	Klaus		Drachenstein
	Klauserweg		Kirchenpfad
	Kilzberg		Klosterberg
	Mäuerchen		Klosterlay
	Mönchspfad		Magdalenenkreuz
	Rothenberg		Rosengarten

GROSSLAGE (SECTION DE VIGNOBLES) : ERNTEBRINGER

Johannisberg	Goldatzel		Schwarzenstein
	Hansenberg		Schloss Johannisberg
	Hölle		Vogelsang
	Klaus		
	Mittelhölle		

GROSSLAGE (SECTION DE VIGNOBLES) : GOTTESTHAL

Öestrich	Doosberg		Schloss Reichhartshausen
	Klosterberg		
	Lenchen		

GROSSLAGE (SECTION DE VIGNOBLES) : MEHROLZCHEN

Erbach	Hohenrain		Siegelsberg
	Honigberg		Steinmorgen
	Marcobrunn	Hallgarten	Hendelberg
	Michelmark		Jungfer
	Rheinhell		Schönhell
	Schlossberg		Würzgarten

GROSSLAGE (SECTION DE VIGNOBLES) : HONIGBERG

Mittelheim	Edelmann		Hasensprung
	Goldberg		Jesuitengarten
	St Nikolaus		Klaus
Winkel	Bienengarten		Schlossberg
	Dachsberg		Schloss Vollrads
	Gutenberg		

GROSSLAGE (SECTION DE VIGNOBLES) : DEUTELSBERG

Hattenheim	Engelmannsberg		Pfaffenberg
	Hassel		Rheingarten
	Heiligenberg		Schützenhaus
	Mannberg		Wisselbrunnen
	Nussbrunen		Steinberg

GROSSLAGE (SECTION DE VIGNOBLES) : HEILIGENSTOCK

Kiedrich	Gräfenberg		Sandgrub
	Klosterberg		Wasseros

GROSSLAGE (SECTION DE VIGNOBLES) : STEINMACHER

Dotzheim	Judenkirch		Walkenberg
Eltville	Langenstück	Oberwalluf	Langenstück
	Rheinberg		Vitusberg
	Sandgrub	Rauenthal	Baiken
	Sonnenberg		Gehrn
	Taubenberg		Langenstück
Frauenstein	Herrnberg		Nonnenberg
	Homberg		Rothenberg
	Marschall		Wülfen
Martinsthal	Langenberg	Schierstein	Dachsberg
	Rödchen		Hölle
Niederwalluf	Berg-Bildstock	Wiesbaden	Neroberg
	Oberberg		

GROSSLAGE (SECTION DE VIGNOBLES) : DAUBHAUS

Boddiger	Berg		Reichesthal
Flörsheim	Herrnberg		Sommerheil
	St Anna Kapelle		Stein
Frankfurt	Lohrberger Hang		Stielweg
Hocheim	Berg	Mainz-Kostheim	Berg
	Domdechaney		Reichensthal
	Herrnberg		Steig
	Hofmeister		Weiss Erd
	Hölle	Wicker	König Wilhelmsberg
	Kirchenstück		Mönchsgewann
	Königin Viktoriaberg		Nonnberg
			Stein

IX. Anbaugebiet (région) : Rheinhessen

BEREICH (sous-région) : BINGEN

GROSSLAGE (SECTION DE VIGNOBLES) : ABTEY

Weinbauort	*Einzellage*
Appenheim	Daubhaus
	Drosselborn
	Eselspfad
	Hundertgulden
Gau-Amgesheim	Goldberg
	Johannisberg
	Rothenberg
	St Laurenzikapelle
	Steinert
Nieder-Hilbersheim	Honigberg
	Steinacker
Ober-Hilbersheim	Mönchpforte
Partenheim	Sankt Georgen
	Steinberg
Sankt Johann	Geyersberg
	Klostergarten
	Steinberg
Sprendlingen	Hölle
	Honigberg
	Klostergarten
	Sonnenberg
	Wissberg
Wolfsheim	Götzenborn
	Osterberg
	Sankt Kathrin

GROSSLAGE (SECTION DE VIGNOBLES) : ADELBERG

Weinbauort	*Einzellage*
Armsheim	Geiersberg
	Goldstückchen
	Leckerberg
Bermerscheim v.d.H.	Hildegardisberg
	Klostergarten
Bornheim	Hähnchen
	Hütte-Terrassen
	Kirchenstück
	Schönberg
Ensheim	Kachelberg
	Bingerberg
Erbes-Büdesheim	Geisterberg
	Vogelsang
Flonheim	Bingerberg
	Klostergarten
	La Roche
	Pfaffenberg
	Rotenpfad
Lonsheim	Mandelberg
	Schönberg
Nack	Ahrenberg
Nieder-Weisen	Wingertsberg
Sulzheim	Greifenberg
	Honigberg
	Schildberg
Wendelsheim	Heiligenpfad
	Steigerberg
Wörrstadt	Kachelberg
	Rheingrafenberg

GROSSLAGE (SECTION DE VIGNOBLES) : KAISERPFALZ

Weinbauort	*Einzellage*
Bubenheim	Honigberg
	Kallenberg
Engelstadt	Adelpfad
	Römerberg
Gross-Winternheim	Bockstein
	Burberg
	Heilighäuschen
	Höllenweg
	Horn
	Kirchenstück
	Klosterbruder
	Lottenstück
	Pares
	Rabenkopf
	Rheinhöhe
	Rotes Kreuz
	Schlossberg
	Sonnenberg
	Sonnenhang
	Steinacker
	Täuscherspfad
Heidesheim	Geissberg
	Höllenberg
	Steinacker
Ingelheim	Schloss Westerhaus
Jugenheim	Goldberg
	Hasensprung
	Heiligenhäuschen
	St Georgenberg
Schwabenheim	Klostergarten
	Sonnenberg
	Schlossberg
Wackernheim	Rabenkopf
	Schwalben
	Steinberg

GROSSLAGE (SECTION DE VIGNOBLES) : KURFÜRSTENSTÜCK

Gau-Bickelheim	Bockshaut	Gumbsheim	Schlosshölle
	Kapelle	Vendersheim	Goldberg
	Saukopf		Sonnenberg
Gau-Weinheim	Geyersberg	Wallertheim	Heil
	Kaisergarten		Vogelsang
	Wissberg		

GROSSLAGE (SECTION DE VIGNOBLES) : RHEINGRAFENSTEIN

Eckelsheim	Eselstreiber		Kletterberg
	Kirchberg	Pleitersheim	Sternberg
	Sonnenköpfchen	Siefersheim	Goldenes Horn
Frei-Laubersheim	Alte Römerstrasse		Heerkretz
	Fels		Höllberg
	Kirchberg		Martinsberg
	Reichskeller	Stein-Bockenheim	Sonnenberg
	Rheingrafenberg	Tiefenthal	Graukatz
Fürfeld	Eichelberg	Volxheim	Alte Römerstrasse
	Kapellenberg		Liebfrau
	Steige		Mönchberg
Hackenheim	Galgenberg	Wöllstein	Affchen
	Gewürzgarten		Haarberg-Katzensteg
	Kirchberg		
	Klostergarten		Hölle
	Sonnenberg		Ölberg
Neu-Bamberg	Eichelberg	Wonsheim	Hölle
	Heerkretz		Martinsberg
	Kirschwingert		Sonnenberg

GROSSLAGE (SECTION DE VIGNOBLES) : SANKT ROCHUSKAPELLE

Aspisheim	Johannisberg		Klosterweg
	Sonnenberg		Mainzerweg
Badenheim	Galgenberg	Gensingen	Goldberg
	Römerberg	Grolsheim	Ölberg
Biebelsheim	Honigberg	Horrweiler	Gewürzgärtchen
	Kieselberg		Goldberg
Bingen	Bubenstück	Ockenheim	Hockenmühle
	Kapellenberg		Klosterweg
	Kirchberg		Kreuz
	Osterberg		Laberstal
	Palmenstein		St Jakobsberg
	Pfarrgarten		Schönhölle
	Rosengarten	Plaffen-Schwabenheim	Hölle
	Scharlachberg		Mandelbaum
	Schelmenstück		Sonnenberg
	Schlossberg-Schwätzerchen	Sponsheim	Bingen Palmenstein
		Welgesheim	Kirchgärtchen
	Schwarzenberg	Zotzenheim	Johannisberg
Dromersheim	Honigberg		Klostergarten

BEREICH (sous-région) : NIERSTEIN

GROSSLAGE (SECTION DE VIGNOBLES) : AUFLANGEN

Weinbauort	*Einzellage*		*Einzellage*
Nierstein	Bergkirche		Heiligenbaum
	Glöck		Kranzberg

	Ölberg		Zehnmorgen
	Orbel		
	Schloss		
	Schwabsburg		
	GROSSLAGE (SECTION DE VIGNOBLES) : DOMHERR		
Budenheim	Pas encore défini		Pfaffengarten
Essenheim	Römerberg		Probstey
	Teufelspfad		Schlossberg
Gabsheim	Dornpfad	Schornsheim	Mönchspfad
	Kirchberg		Ritterberg
	Rosengärten		Sonnenhang
Klein-Winternheim	Geiershöll	Stadecken-Elsheim	Blume
	Herrgottshaus		Bockstein
	Villenkeller		Lenchen
Mainz-Finthen	Pas encore défini		Spitzberg
Mainz-Drais	Pas encore défini		Tempelchen
Ober-Olm	Kapellenberg	Udenheim	Golberg
Saulheim	Haubenberg		Kirchberg
	Heiligenhaus		Sonnenberg
	Hölle		
	GROSSLAGE (SECTION DE VIGNOBLES) : GÜLDENMORGEN		
Dienheim	Falkenberg		Gutleuthaus
	Herrenberg		Herrenberg
	Höhlchen		Kreuz
	Kreuz		Sackträger
	Siliusbrunnen		Schützenhütte
	Tafelstein		Zuckerberg
Oppenheim	Daubhaus		
	GROSSLAGE (SECTION DE VIGNOBLES) : GUTES DOMTAL		
Dalheim	Aldörr		Klosterberg
	Kranzberg		Sonnenberg
	Steinberg	Nierstein	Pfaffenkappe
Dexheim	Doktor	Selzen	Gottesgarten
Friesenheim	Altdörr		Osterberg
	Bergpfad		Rheinpforte
	Knopf	Sörgenloch	Moosberg
Hahnheim	Knopf	Undenheim	Goldberg
	Moosberg	Weinolsheim	Hohberg
Köngernheim	Goldgrube		Kehr
Lörzweiler	Königstuhl	Zornheim	Dachgewann
Mommenheim	Kloppenberg		Guldenmorgen
	Osterberg		Mönchbäumchen
	Silbergrube		Pilgerweg
Nackenheim	Schmittskapellchen		Vogelsang
Nieder-Olm	Goldberg		
	GROSSLAGE (SECTION DE VIGNOBLES) : KRÖTENBRUNNEN		
Alsheim	Goldberg		Sonnenhang
Dienheim	Herrengarten	Gimbsheim	Liebfrauenthal
	Paterhof		Sonnenweg
	Schloss	Guntersblum	Eiserne Hand
Dolgesheim	Kreuzberg		Sankt
	Schützenhütte		Julianenbrunnen
Eich	Goldberg		Sonnenberg
Eimsheim	Hexelberg		Sonnenhang
	Römerschanze		Steinberg

Hillesheim	Altenberg		Schloss
	Sonnheil		Schlossberg
Ludwigshöhe	Honigberg	Ülversheim	Aulenberg
Mettenheim	Goldberg		Schloss
Oppenheim	Herrengarten	Wintersheim	Frauengarten
	Paterhof		
	GROSSLAGE (SECTION DE VIGNOBLES) : PETERSBERG		
Albig	Homberg	Framersheim	Hornberg
	Hundskopf		Kreuzweg
Alzey	Schloss Hammerstein		Zechberg
		Gau-Heppenheim	Pfarrgarten
Bechtolsheim	Homberg		Schlossberg
	Klosterberg	Gau-Odernheim	Fuchsloch
	Sonnenberg		Herrgottspfad
	Wingertstor		Ölberg
Biebelnheim	Pilgerstein		Vogelsang
	Rosenberg	Spiesheim	Osterberg
	GROSSLAGE (SECTION DE VIGNOBLES) : REHBACH		
Nierstein	Brudersberg		Hipping
	Goldene Luft		Pettenthal
	GROSSLAGE (SECTION DE VIGNOBLES) : RHEINBLICK		
Alsheim	Fischerpfad	Dorn-Dürkheim	Hasensprung
	Frühmesse		Römerberg
	Römerberg	Mettenheim	Michelsberg
	Sonnenberg		Schlossberg
	GROSSLAGE (SECTION DE VIGNOBLES) : SANKT ALBAN		
Bodenheim	Burgweg		Pfaffenweg
	Ebersberg	Harxheim	Börnchen
	Heitersbrünnchen		Lieth
	Hoch		Schlossberg
	Kapelle	Lörzweiler	Hohberg
	Kreuzberg		Ölgild
	Leidhecke	Mainz	Edelmann
	Mönchspfad		Hüttberg
	Reichsritterstift		Johannisberg
	Silberberg		Kirchenstück
	Westrum		Klosterberg
Gau-Bischofsheim	Glockenberg		Sand
	Herrnberg		Weinkeller
	Kellersberg		
	GROSSLAGE (SECTION DE VIGNOBLES) : SPIEGELBERG		
Nackenheim	Engelsberg		Kirchplatte
	Rothenberg		Klostergarten
Nierstein	Bildstock		Paterberg
	Brückchen		Rosenberg
	Ebersberg		Schloss
	Findling		Hohenrechen
	Hölle		
	GROSSLAGE (SECTION DE VIGNOBLES) : VOGELSGÄRTEN		
Guntersblum	Authental		Kreuzkapelle
	Bornpfad		Steit-Terrassen
Wachenheim	Himmelthal	Ludwigshöhe	Teufelskopf

BEREICH (sous-région) : WONNEGAU

Weinbauort	*Einzellage*	*Weinbauort*	*Einzellage*
GROSSLAGE (SECTION DE VIGNOBLES) : BERGKLOSTER			
Bermerscheim	Hasenlauf		Sonnenberg
Eppelsheim	Felsen	Hangen-Weisheim	Sommervende
Esselborn	Goldberg	Westhofen	Aulerde
Flomborn	Feuerberg		Benn
	Goldberg		Brunnenhäuschen
Gudersheim	Höllenbrand		Kirchspiel
	Königstuhl		Morstein
	Hungerbiene		Rotenstein
	Mandelbrunnen		Steingrube
GROSSLAGE (SECTION DE VIGNOBLES) : BURG RODENSTEIN			
Bermersheim	Seilgarten		Steil
Flörsheim-Dalsheim	Bürgel	Mörstadt	Katzenbuckel
	Frauenberg		Nonnengarten
	Goldberg	Ober-Flörsheim	Blucherpfad
	Hubacker		Deutschherrenberg
	Sauloch		
GROSSLAGE (SECTION DE VIGNOBLES) : DOMBLICK			
Hohen Sulzen	Kirchenstück		Silberberg
	Sonnenberg	Offstein	Engelsberg
Mölsheim	Silberberg		Schlossgarten
	Zellerweg am schw.	Wachenheim	Horn
	Hergott		Rotenberg
Monsheim	Rosengarten		
GROSSLAGE (SECTION DE VIGNOBLES) : GOTTESHILFE			
Bechtheim	Geyersberg		Hasenbiss
	Rosengarten		Leckzapfen
	Stein		Neuberg
Osthofen	Goldberg		
GROSSLAGE (SECTION DE VIGNOBLES) : LIEBFRAUENMORGEN			
Worms	Affenberg		Lerchelsberg
	Am Heiligen-Häuschen		Liebfrauenstift-Kirchenstück
	Bildstock		Nonnenwingert
	Burgweg		Remeyerhof
	Goldapfel		Rheinberg
	Goldberg		Römersteg
	Goldpfad		Sankt Annaberg
	Hochberg		St Cyriakusstift
	Kapellenstück		St Georgenberg
	Klausenberg		Schneckenberg
	Kreuzblick		
GROSSLAGE (SECTION DE VIGNOBLES) : PILGERPFAD			
Bechtheim	Hasensprung		Mönchhube
	Heiligkreuz		Mondschein
Dittelsheim-Hessloch	Edle Weingärten		Pfaffenmütze
	Geiersberg	Frettenheim	Heil
	Kloppberg	Monzernheim	Goldberg
	Leckerberg		Steinböhl
	Liebfrauenberg	Osthofen	Kirchberg

	Klosterberg		Rheinberg
	Liebenberg		

GROSSLAGE (SECTION DE VIGNOBLES) : SYBILLENSTEIN

Alzey	Kapellenberg	Heimersheim	Sonnenberg
	Pfaffenhalde	Mauchenheim	Sioner Klosterberg
	Römerberg	Offenheim	Mandelberg
	Rotenfels	Wahlheim	Schelmen
	Wartberg	Weinheim	Heiliger Blutberg
Bechenheim	Fröhlich		Hölle
Dautenheim	Himmelacker		Kapellenberg
Freimerscheim	Frankenstein		Kirchenstück
	Rotenfels		Mandelberg

X. Anbaugebiet (région) : Rheinpfalz (Palatinat)

BEREICH (sous-région) SÜDLICHE WEINSTRASSE

GROSSLAGE (SECTION DE VIGNOBLES) : BISCHOFSKREUZ

Weinbauort	*Einzellage*	*Weinbauort*	*Einzellage*
Böchingen	Rosenkranz	Gleisweiler	Hölle
Burrweiler	Altenforst	Knöringen	Hohenrain
	St Annaberg	Nussdorf	Herrenberg
	Schäwer		Kaiserberg
	Schlossgarten		Kirchenstück
Dammheim	Höhe	Roschbach	Rosenkränzel
Flemlingen	Herrenbuckel		Simonsgarten
	Vogelsprung	Walsheim	Forstweg
	Zechpeter		Silberberg

GROSSLAGE (SECTION DE VIGNOBLES) : GUTTENBERG

Bad Bergzabern	Wonneberg[1]	Oberotterbach	Sonnenberg[2]
Dierbach	Kirchhöh	Schweigen-Rechtenbach	Sonnenberg[2]
Dörrenbach	Wonneberg[1]		
Freckenfeld	Gräfenberg	Schweighofen	Sonnenberg[2]
Kandel	Galgenberg		Wolfsberg
Kapsweyher	Lerchenberg	Steinfeld	Herrenwingert
Minfeld	Herrenberg	Vollmersweiler	Krapfenberg
Niederotterbach	Eselsbuckel		

GROSSLAGE (SECTION DE VIGNOBLES) : KLOSTER LIEBFRAUENBERG

Bad Bergzabern	Altenberg	Heuchelheim-Klingen	Herrenpfad[6]
Barbelroth	Kirchberg		
Billigheim-Ingenheim	Mandelpfad[3]	Kapellen-Drusweiler	Rosengarten
	Pfaffenberg	Klingenmünster	Maria Magdalena
	Rosenberg[4]	Niederhorbach	Silberberg
	Sauschwänzel	Oberhausen	Frohnwingert
	Steingebiss	Pleisweiler-Oberhofen	Schlossberg
	Venusbuckel		
Gleiszellen-Gleishorbach	Frühmess	Rohrbach	Mandelpfad[3]
	Kirchberg	Steinweiler	Rosenberg[4]
Göcklingen	Herrenpfad[6]	Winden	Narrenberg[5]
Hergersweiler	Narrenberg[5]		

GROSSLAGE (SECTION DE VIGNOBLES) : KÖNIGSGARTEN

Albersweiler	Kirchberg		Kalkgrube
	Latt	Godramstein	Klostergarten
Arzheim	Rosenberg		Münzberg
	Seligmacher[7]	Landau	Altes Löhl
Birkweiler	Rosenberg[8]	Ranschbach	Seligmacher[7]
	Kastanienbush	Siebeldingen	Im Sonnenschein
	Mandelberg		Mönchspfad
Frankweiler	Biengarten		Rosenberg[8]

GROSSLAGE (SECTION DE VIGNOBLES) : MANDELHÖHE

Kirrweiler	Mandelberg		Immengarten
	Oberschloss		Kirchenstück
	Römerweg	Maikammer-Alsterweiler	Kapellenberg
Maikammer	Heiligenberg		

GROSSLAGE (SECTION DE VIGNOBLES) : ORDENSGUT

Edensheim	Forst		Letten
	Mandelhang	Rhodt	Klosterpfad
	Rosengarten		Rosengarten
	Schloss		Schlossberg
Hainfeld	Kapelle	Weyher	Heide
	Kirchenstück		Michelsberg

GROSSLAGE (SECTION DE VIGNOBLES) : HERRLICH

Eschbach	Hasen	Impflingen	Abtsberg
Göcklingen	Kaiserberg	Insheim	Schäfergarten[10]
Herxheim bei Landau	Engelsberg	Leinsweiler	Sonnenberg[9]
		Mörzheim	Pfaffenberg
Herxheimweyher	Am Gaisberg	Rohrbach	Schäfergarten[10]
Ilbesheim	Rittersberg	Wollmesheim	Mütterle
	Sonnenberg[9]		

GROSSLAGE (SECTION DE VIGNOBLES) : SCHLOSS LUDWIGSHÖNE

Edenkoben	Bergel		Klostergarten
	Blücherhöhe		Mühlberg
	Heidegarten		Schwarzer Letten
	Heilig Kreuz	St Martin	Baron
	Kastaniengarten		Kirchberg
	Kirchberg		Zitadelle

GROSSLAGE (SECTION DE VIGNOBLES) : TRAPPENBERG

Altdorf	Gottesacker	Hochstadt	Roterberg
	Hochgericht	Knittelsheim	Gollenberg[11]
Bellheim	Gollenberg[11]	Lustadt	Klostergarten[12]
Böbingen	Ortelberg	Ottersheim	Kahlenberg
Bornheim	Neuberg	Römerberg	Alter Berg
Essingen	Osterberg		Narrenberg
	Rossberg		Schlittberg
	Sonnenberg	Schwegenheim	Bründelsberg
Freimercheim	Bildberg	Veningen	Doktor
Gross-u. Kleinfischlingen	Kirchberg	Weingarten	Schlossberg
		Zeiskam	Klostergarten[12]

BEREICH (sous-région) : MITTELHAARDT-DEUTSCHE WEINSTRASSE

Weinbauort	*Einzellage*	*Weinbauort*	*Einzellage*
GROSSLAGE (SECTION DE VIGNOBLES) : FEUERBERG			
Bad Dürkheim	Nonnengarten		Sonnenberg
	Steinberg	Gönnheim	Martinshöhe
Bobenheim am Berg	Kieselberg	Kallstadt	Annaberg
	Ohligpfad		Kreidkeller
Ellerstadt	Bubeneck	Weisenheim am Berg	Vogelsang
	Dickkopp		
GROSSLAGE (SECTION DE VIGNOBLES) : GRAFENSTÜCK			
Bockenheim	Burggarten		Katzenstein
	Goldgrube		Sonnenberg[14]
	Hassmannsberg		Vogelsang[13]
	Heiligenkirche	Obrigheim	Benn
	Klosterschaffnerei		Hochgericht
	Schlossberg		Mandelpfad
	Sonnenberg[14]		Rosengarten
	Vogelsang[13]		Schloss
Kindenheim	Burgweg		Sonneberg[14]
GROSSLAGE (SECTION DE VIGNOBLES) : HOCHMESS			
Bad Dürkheim	Hochbenn		Spielberg
	Michelsberg[15]	Ungstein	Michelsberg[15]
	Rittergarten		
GROSSLAGE (SECTION DE VIGNOBLES) : HÖLLENPFAD			
Battenberg	Schlossberg	Kleinkarlbach	Frauenländchen
Grünsdadt	Bergel		Herrenberg
	Goldberg		Herrgottsacker
	Honigsack		Kieselberg
	Hütt		Senn
Grünsdadt	Klostergarten	Mertesheim	St Martinskreuz
	Roth	Neuleiningen	Feuermännchen
	St Stephan		Schlossberg
	Schloss		Sonneberg
GROSSLAGE (SECTION DE VIGNOBLES) : HOFSTÜCK			
Deidesheim	Nonnenstück	Niederkirchen	Klostergarten
Ellerstadt	Kirchenstück		Osterbrunnen
Friedelsheim	Gerümpel		Schlossberg
	Rosengarten	Rödersheim-Gronau	Fuchsloch[16]
Gönnheim	Klostergarten	Ruppertsberg	Gaisböhl
	Mandelgarten		Hoheburg
	Sonnenberg		Linsenbusch
Hochdorf-Assenheim	Fuchsloch[16]		Nussbien
			Reiterpfad
Meckenheim	Neuberg		Spiess
	Spielberg		
GROSSLAGE (SECTION DE VIGNOBLES) : HONIGSÄCKEL			
Ungstein	Herrenberg		Weilberg
	Nussriegel		
GROSSLAGE (SECTION DE VIGNOBLES) : KOBNERT			
Dackenheim	Kapellgarten		Liebesbrunnen

	Mandelröth		Kirchenstück
Freinsheim	Musikantenbuckel	Leistadt	Herzfeld
	Oschelskopf		Kalkofen
	Schwarzes Kreuz		Kirchenstück
Herxheim am Berg	Himmelreich	Weisenheim am Berg	Mandelgarten
	Honingsack		Sonnenberg
GROSSLAGE (SECTION DE VIGNOBLES) : MARIENGARTEN			
Deidesheim	Grainhübel		Jesuitengarten
	Herrgottsacker		Kirchenstück
	Hohenmorgen		Musenhang
	Kalkofen		Pechstein
	Kieselberg		Ungeheuer
	Langenmorgen	Wachenheim	Altenburg
	Leinhöhle		Belz
	Mäushöhle		Böhlig
	Paradiesgarten		Gerümpel
Forst	Elster		Goldbächel
	Freundstück		Rechbächel
GROSSLAGE (SECTION DE VIGNOBLES) : MEERSPINNE			
Gimmeldingen	Biengarten		Ölberg
	Kapellenberg		Reiterpfad
	Mandelgarten	Mussbach	Bischofsweg
	Schlössel		Eselshaut
Haardt	Bürgergarten		Glockenzehnt
	Herrenletten		Johannitergarten
	Herzog		Kurfürst
	Mandelring		Spiegel
Königsbach	Idig	Neustadt an der Weinstrasse	Mönchgarten
	Jesuitengarten		
GROSSLAGE (SECTION DE VIGNOBLES) : PFAFFENGRUND			
Diedesfels	Berg	Geinsheim	Gässel
Duttweiler	Kalkberg	Hambach an der Weinstrasse	Kroatenpfad
	Kreuzberg		Langenstein
	Mandelberg		Lerchenböhl
GROSSLAGE (SECTION DE VIGNOBLES) : REBSTÖCKEL			
Diedesfeld	Johanniskirchel		Kirchberg
	Ölgässel		Schlossberg
	Paradies	Neustadt an der Weinstrasse	Erkenbrecht
Hambach	Feuer		Grain
	Kaiserstuhl		
GROSSLAGE (SECTION DE VIGNOBLES) : ROSENBÜHL			
Erpolzheim	Goldberg		Burgweg[18]
	Kieselberg		Goldberg[17]
Freinsheim	Goldberg[17]		Hahnen
Lambsheim	Burgweg[18]		Halde
Weisenheim/Sand	Altenberg		Hasenzeile
GROSSLAGE (SECTION DE VIGNOBLES) : SCHENKENBÖHL			
Bad Dürkheim	Abtsfronhof		Königswingert
	Fronhof		Mandelgarten
	Fuchsmantel[19]		Odinstal
Wachenheim	Fuchsmantel[19]		Schlossberg

GROSSLAGE (SECTION DE VIGNOBLES) : SCHNEPFENFLUG VOM ZELLERTAL

Albisheim	Heiligenborn	Niefernheim	Königsweg[22]
Bolanden	Schlossberg		Kreuzberg[20]
Budenheim	Hahnenkamm	Ottersheim/ Zellerthal	Bräunersberg
Einselthum	Kreuzberg[20]		
	Klosterstüch[21]	Rittersheim	Am hohen Stein
Gauersheim	Goldloch	Rüssingen	Breinsberg
Harxheim	Herrgottsblick	Stetten	Heilighäuschen
Immesheim	Sonnenstück	Zell	Klosterstück[21]
Kerzenheim	Esper		Königsweg[22]
Kirchheimbolanden	Schlossgarten		Kreuzberg[20]
Morschheim	Im Heubusch		Schwarzer Herrgott

GROSSLAGE (SECTION DE VIGNOBLES) : SCHNEPFENFLUG AN DER WEINSTRASSE

Deidesheim	Letten		Kreuz
Forst	Stift		Schlossgarten
	Süsskopf	Wachenheim	Bischofsgarten[23]
	Bischofsgarten[23]		Luginsland
Friedelsheim	Bischofsgarten[23]		

GROSSLAGE (SECTION DE VIGNOBLES) : SCHWARZERDE

Bissersheim	Goldberg	Kallstadt	Kronenberg
	Held		Steinaker
	Orlenberg		Saumagen
	Steig	Kirchheim	Geisskopf
Dirmstein	Herrgottsacker		Kreuz
	Jesuitenhofgarten		Römerstrasse
	Mandelpfad		Steinacker
Gerolsheim	Klosterweg	Kleinniedesheim	Schlossgarten
	Lerchenspiel		Vorderberg
Grosskarlbach	Burgweg	Lhaumersheim	Kirschgarten
	Osterberg		Mandelberg
Grossniedesheim	Schafberg		Kapellenberg
Hessheim	Lange Els	Obersülzen	Schnepp
Heuchelheim/ Frankenthal	Steinkopf	Ungstein	Osterberg
			Bettelhaus

XI. Anbaugebiet (région) : Württemberg

BEREICH (sous-région) : REMSTAL-STUTTGART

GROSSLAGE (SECTION DE VIGNOBLES) : HOHENNEUFFEN

Weinbauort	*Einzellage*	*Weinbauort*	*Einzellage*
Beuren	Schlossteige	Metzingen	Hofsteige
Frickenhausen	Schlossteige		Schlossteige
Kappishäusern	Schlossteige	Neuffen	Schlossteige
Kohlberg	Schlossteige	Weilheim	Schlossteige
Linsenhofen	Schlossteige		

GROSSLAGE (SECTION DE VIGNOBLES) : WEINSTEIGE

Esslingen	Ailenberg		Schenkenberg
	Burg	Fellbach	Gips
	Kirchberg		Goldberg
	Lerchenberg		Herzogenberg

	Hinterer Berg	(Ortsteil Obertürkheim)	Kirchberg
	Lämmler		
Fellbach	Mönchberg	(Ortsteile Hedelfingen, Rohracker)	Lenzenberg
	Wetzstein		
Gerlingen	Bopser		
Stuttgart	Kriegsberg	(Ortsteile Bad Cannstatt, Untertürkheim)	Mönchberg
	Mönchberg		
(Ortsteil Gaisburg)	Abelsberg	(Ortsteil Degerloch)	Scharrenberg
(Ortsteil Untertürkheim)	Gips	(Ortsteile Rotenberg, Uhlbach, Untertürkheim)	Schlossberg
(Ortsteil Uhlbach)	Götzenberg		
(Ortsteil Obertürkheim)	Ailenberg		
(Ortsteil Untertürkheim)	Altenberg	(Ortsteil Uhlbach)	Steingrube
(Ortsteile Bad Cannstatt, Feuerbach, Münster, Wangen, Zuffenhausen)	Berg	(Ortsteile Bad Cannstatt, Mühlhausen. Münster)	Steinhalde
		(Ortsteil Untertürkheim)	Wetzstein
(Ortsteil Bad Cannstatt)	Halde	(Ortsteile Bad Cannstatt, Hofen, Mühlhausen, Münster)	Zuckerle
(Ortsteile Bad Cannstatt, Untertürkheim)	Herzogenberg		
GROSSLAGE (SECTION DE VIGNOBLES) : SONNENBÜHL			
Kernen		(Ortsteil Endersbach)	Hintere Klinge
(Ortsteil Rommelshaussen)	Mönchberg	(Ortsteil Schnait)	Burghalde
(Ortsteil Stetten)	Mönchberg	(Ortsteil Strümpfelbach)	Altenberg
Weinstadt			
(Ortsteil Beutelsbach)	Burghalde		
GROSSLAGE (SECTION DE VIGNOBLES) : KOPF			
Beinstein	Grossmulde		Sommerhalde
Breuningsweiler	Holzenberg	Neustadt	Söhrenberg
Bürg	Schlossberg	Schorndorf	Grafenberg
Grossheppach	Wanne	Waiblingen	Hörnle
Grunbach	Berghalde	Winnenden	Berg
Hanweiler	Berg		Holzenberg
Kleinheppach	Greiner		Rossberg
Korb	Berg	Winterbach	Hungerberg
	Hörnle		
GROSSLAGE (SECTION DE VIGNOBLES) : WARTBÜHL			
Aichelberg	Luginsland		Zügernberg
Baach	Himmelreich	Grunbach	Klingle
Beutelsbach	Altenberg	Hanweiler	Maien
	Käppele	Hebsack	Lichtenberg
	Sonnenberg	Hertmannsweiler	Himmelreich
Breuningsweiler	Haselstein	Kleinheppach	Sonnenberg
Endersbach	Happenhalde		Steingrüble
	Wetzstein	Korb	Steingrüble
Geradstetten	Lichtenberg	Rommelshausen	Häder
	Sonnenberg	Schnait i. R.	Altenberg

Grossheppach	Steingrüble		Sonnenberg
Stetten i. R.	Brotwasser		Nonnenberg
	Häder	Waiblingen	Steingrüble
	Puvermächer	Winnenberg	Haselstein
Strümpfelbach	Gastenklinge		

BEREICH (sous-région) : WÜRTTEMBERGISCH UNTERLAND

GROSSLAGE (SECTION DE VIGNOBLES) : SCHALKSTEIN

Weinbauort	*Einzellage*	*Weinbauort*	*Einzellage*
Allmersbach a. W.	Alter Berg	Kleiningersheim	Schlossberg
Affalterbach	Neckarhälde	Löchgau	Felsengarten
Asperg	Berg	Ludwigsburg	Neckarhälde
Beihingen	Neckarhälde	(Ortsteil	Neckarhälde
Benningen	Neckarhälde	Hoheneck)	
Besigheim	Felsengarten	Marbach	Neckarhälde
	Wurmberg	Markgröningen	Berg
Bietigheim	Wurmberg		Sankt Johännser
Bissingen	Felsengarten	Mundelsheim	Käsberg
Erdmannhausen	Felsengarten		Mühlbächer
Gemmrigheim	Neckarhälde		Rosenberg
	Wurmberg	Murr	Neckarhälde
Grossingersheim	Schlossberg	Neckarweihingen	Neckarhälde
Hessigheim	Felsengarten	Poppenweiler	Neckarhälde
	Käsberg	Rielinghausen	Kelterberg
	Wurmberg	Rietenau	Güldenkern
Höpfigheim	Königsberg	Steinheim/Murr	Burberg
Kirschberg	Kelterberg	Walheim	Felsengarten
Kleinaspach	Kelterberg		Wurmberg

GROSSLAGE (SECTION DE VIGNOBLES) : STROMBERG

Bönnigheim	Kirchberg	Kleinsachsenheim	Kirchberg
	Sonnenberg	Knittlingen	Reichshalde
Diefenbach	König	Lienzingen	Eichelberg
Ensingen	Schanzreiter	Maulbronn	Eilfingerberg
Erligheim	Lerchenberg		Klosterstück
Freudenstein	Reichshalde		Reichshalde
Freudental	Kirchberg	Mühlhausen	Halde
Gründelbach	Steinbachhof	Obererdingen	Kupferhalde
	Wachtkopf	Ochsenbach	Liebenberg
Häfnerhaslach	Heiligenberg	Ötisheim	Sauberg
Hofen	Lerchenberg	Riet	Kirchberg
Hohenhaslach	Kirchberg	Rosswag	Forstgrube
	Klosterberg		Halde
Hohenstein	Kirchberg		Lichtenberg
Horrheim	Klosterberg	Schützingen	Heiligenberg
Illingen	Forstgrube	Spielberg	Liebenberg
	Halde	Sternenfels	König
	Schanzreiter	Vaihingen	Halde
Kirchheim	Kirchberg		

GROSSLAGE (SECTION DE VIGNOBLES) : HEUCHELBERG

Brackenheim	Dachsberg	(Ortsteil	Ochsenberg
	Mönchsberg	Botenheim)	
	Schlossberg	Cleebronn	Michaelsberg
	Wolfsaugen	Dürrenzimmern	Mönchsberg
	Zweifelberg	Eibensbach	Michaelsberg

Frauenzimmern	Kaiserberg		Schlossberg
	Michaelsberg	Niederhofen	Grafenberg
Güglingen	Kaiserberg	Nordhausen	Sonntagsberg
	Michaelsberg	Nordheim	Grafenberg
Haberschlacht	Dachsberg		Gräfenberg
Hausen/Z.	Jupiterberg		Ruthe
Heibronn (Ortsteil Klingenberg)	Schlossberg		Sonntagsberg
	Sonntagsberg	Pfaffenhofen	Hohenberg
Kleingartach	Grafenberg	Schwaigern	Grafenberg
Leingarten	Grafenberg		Ruthe
	Leiersberg		Sonnenberg
	Vogelsang	Stetten a. H.	Sonnenberg
Massenbachhausen	Krähenberg	Stockheim	Altenberg
Meimsheim	Katzenöhrle	Weiler/Z.	Hohenberg
Niepperg	Grafenberg	Zaberfeld	Hohenberg
	Steingrube		

GROSSLAGE (SECTION DE VIGNOBLES) : WUNNENSTEIN

Beilstein	Schlosswengert		Oberer Berg
	Steinberg		Süssmund
	Wartberg	Ludwigsburg (Ortsteil Hoheneck)	Oberer Berg
Gronau	Forstberg		
Grossbottwar	Harzberg		
	Lichtenberg	Oberstenfeld	Forstberg
Hof und Lembach	Harzberg		Harzberg
	Lichtenberg		Lichtenberg
Ilsfeld	Lichtenberg	Steinheim	Lichtenberg
Kleinbottwar	Götzenberg	Winzerhausen	Harzberg
	Lichtenberg		Lichtenberg

GROSSLAGE (SECTION DE VIGNOBLES) : SCHOZACHTAL

Abstatt	Burgberg	Ilsfeld	Rappen
	Burg Wildeck	Löwenstein	Sommerberg
	Sommerberg	Unterheinriet	Sommerberg
Auenstein	Burgberg		

GROSSLAGE (SECTION DE VIGNOBLES) : KIRCHENWEINBERG

Flein	Altenberg		Katzenbeisser
	Eselsberg		Riedersbückele
	Sonnenberg	Neckarwestheim	Herrlesberg
Heilbronn	Altenberg	Talheim	Hoche Eiche
	Sonnenberg		Schlossberg
Ilsfeld (Ortsteil Schozach)	Roter Berg		Sonnenberg
	Schelmenklinge	Untergruppenbach	Schlossberg
Lauffen	Jungfer		

GROSSLAGE (SECTION DE VIGNOBLES) : STAUFENBERG

Brettach	Berg	Horkheim	Stiftsberg
Duttenberg	Schön	Neckarsulm	Scheuerberg
Erlenbach	Kayberg	Œdheim	Kayberg
Gundelsheim	Himmelreich	Offenau	Schön
Heibronn	Stahlbühl	Talheim	Stiftsberg
	Stiftsberg	Untereisesheim	Vogelsang
	Wartberg		

GROSSLAGE (SECTION DE VIGNOBLES) : SALZBERG

Affaltrach	Dieblesberg		Sommerhalde
Eberstadt	Eberfürst	Eichelberg	Hundsberg

Ellhofen	Wildenberg	Sülzbach	Altenberg
	Steinacker	Weiler	Hundsberg
Eschenau	Paradies		Schlierbach
Grantschen	Wildenberg	Weinsberg	Wildenberg
Lehrensteinfeld	Steinacker	Wimmental	Altenberg
Löwenstein	Altenberg	Willsbach	Dieblesberg
	Wohlfahrtsberg		
Löwenstein (Ortsteil Hösslinsülz)	Dieblesberg		

GROSSLAGE (SECTION DE VIGNOBLES) : LINDELBERG

Adolzfurt	Schneckenhof	Obersöllbach	Margarete
Bretzfeld	Goldberg	Pfedelbach	Goldberg
Dimbach	Himmelreich	Siebeneich	Himmelreich
Geddelsbach	Schneckenhof	Schwabbach	Himmelreich
Harsberg	Dachsteiger	Unterheimbach	Schneckenhof
Heuholz	Dachsteiger	Untersteinbach	Dachsteiger
Kesselfeld	Schwobajörgle	Verrenberg	Goldberg
Langenbeutigen	Himmelreich		Verrenberg
Michelbach a. W.	Dachsteiger	Waldbach	Himmelreich
	Margarete	Windischenbach	Goldberg
Maienfels	Schneckenhof		

BEREICH (sous-région) : KOCHER-JAGST-TAUBER

GROSSLAGE (SECTION DE VIGNOBLES) : KOCHERBERG

Weinbauort	*Einzellage*	*Weinbauort*	*Einzellage*
Belsenberg	Heiligkreuz		Hofberg
Bieringen	Schlüsselberg	Niedernhall	Altenberg
Criesbach	Burgstall		Burgstall
	Hoher Berg		Engweg
Dörzbach	Altenberg		Hoher Berg
Ernsbach	Flatterberg	Siglingen	Hofberg
Forchtenberg	Flatterberg	Weissbach	Altenberg
Ingelfinden	Hoher Berg		Engweg
Künzelsau	Hoher Berg	Widdern	Hofberg
Möckmühl	Ammerlanden		

GROSSLAGE (SECTION DE VIGNOBLES) : TAUBERBERG

Elpersheim	Mönchsberg	Wermutshausen	Schafsteige
	Probstberg		

N'ont pas encore été affectés à un *Grosslage* (section de vignobles) :

Kressbronn am Bodensee	Berghalde		Probstberg
		Niederstetten	Schafsteige
Tübingen (Ortsteile Hirschau, Unterjesingen)	Sonnenhalden	Oberstetten	Schafsteige
		Reinsbronn	Röde
		Vorbachzimmern	Schafsteige
Haagen	Schafsteige	Weikersheim	Hardt
Laudenbach	Schafsteige		Karlsberg
Markelsheim	Mönchsberg		Schmecker

Appendice C : **Contenants et mesures**

I. Contenance des bouteilles

L'arrêté du 18 mai 1979 précise que les vins français conditionnés en vue de la vente au détail ne peuvent circuler, être mis en vente, ou vendus, que par quantités correspondant aux volumes repris dans le tableau ci-dessous :

VOLUMES RÉELS EN CENTILITRES		
Admis à titre définitif	Admis jusqu'au 31-12-83	Admis jusqu'au 31-12-83*
10 cl	18,7 cl	19 cl
25 cl	125 cl	20 cl
37,5 cl	300 cl	24 cl
50 cl		36 cl
75 cl		47,5 cl
100 cl		72 cl
150 cl		73 cl
200 cl		98 cl
500 cl		99 cl
		148 cl
		298 cl

*** à condition que les bouteilles correspondantes soient détenues par les utilisateurs à la date du 2-9-79.**

Cet arrêté précise, en outre, que ces dispositions ne s'appliquent pas aux produits mis en bouteilles avant le 2 septembre 1979.

Compte tenu de cet arrêté, la fabrication des bouteilles bordelaises contenant 75 cl ras bord va être progressivement stoppée au profit de bouteilles contenant réellement 75 cl, mais les bouteilles actuelles de 73 cl (gravées 75 cl dans le verre) pourront être utilisées jusqu'au 31-12-83, sauf pour l'exportation à destination des États-Unis et du Canada qui exigent déjà des capacités réelles de 75 cl, exprimées en ml depuis le 1er janvier 1979.

Cette nouvelle réglementation ne sera mise en place que progressivement et des délais d'application ont déjà été demandés au-delà du 2-9-79.

Tous les stocks de bouteilles 73 cl pourront donc être utilisés sans problème, y compris les étiquettes et les capsules correspondantes marquées 73 cl.

(Pour les équivalences britanniques et américaines ci-dessous, Gal. = gallon (4,5496 l) ; Qt. = quart (1,13649 l) : Pt. = pinte (56,8245 cl) ; Oz. = once (2,841225 cl), quand il s'agit de mesures britanniques (imperial gallon et ses subdivisions). Mais pour les mesures U.S. Gal. = gallon (3,785 l) ; Qt. = quart (0,94625 l ou 94,625 cl) ; Pt. = pinte (47,3125 cl) ; Oz. = once (2,95703125 cl.). Il s'agit évidemment dans les deux cas de l'once liquide (*fluid ounce*).

VIN	*Bouteilles*	*Capacités* *Système métrique*	*Once britannique*	*Once américaine*	*Équivalences* *britanniques* *Gal.*	*Qt.*	*Pt.*	*Oz.*	*américaines* *Gal.*	*Qt.*	*Pt.*	*Oz.*
ALSACE												
Demi-bouteille		36,00 cl	12,67	12,17				13				12
Bouteille		72,00 cl	25,34	24,34			1	5			1	8
ANJOU												
Demi-bouteille		37,50 cl	13,20	12,68				13				13
Bouteille		75,00 cl	26,40	25,36			1	6			1	9
BEAUJOLAIS												
Demi-bouteille		37,50 cl	13,20	12,68				13				13
Pot		50,00 cl	17,60	16,90				18			1	1
Bouteille		75,00 cl	26,40	25,36			1	6			1	9
BORDEAUX												
Fillette	1/2 bouteille	37,50 cl	13,20	12,68				13				13
Bouteille		75,00 cl	26,40	25,36			1	6			1	9
Magnum	2 bouteilles	1,50 l	52,79	50,71		1	–	13		1	1	3
Marie-Jeanne[1]	env. 3 bout.	2,50 l	88,00	84,53		2	1	8		2	1	4
Double magnum	4 bouteilles	3,00 l	105,59	101,42		2	1	6		3	–	5
Jéroboam	6 bouteilles	5,00 l	158,40	152,16		3	1	18	1	–	1	8
Impériale	8 bouteilles	6,00 l	211,18	202,85	1	1	–	11	1	2	–	11
BOURGOGNE												
Demi-bouteille		37,50 cl	13,20	12,68				13				13
Bouteille		75,00 cl	26,40	25,36			1	6			1	9
Magnum	2 bouteilles	1,50 l	52,79	50,71		1	–	13		1	1	3
CHAMPAGNE												
Quart	1/4 de bout.	20,00 cl	7,04	6,76				7				7
Demi-bouteille		37,50 cl	14,08	13,52				14				14
Bouteille		75,00 cl	28,16	27,05			1	8			1	11
Magnum	2 bouteilles	1,60 l	56,31	54,09		1	–	16			1	6
Jéroboam	4 bouteilles	3,20 l	112,63	108,19		2	1	13		3	–	12
Réhoboam	6 bouteilles	4,80 l	168,94	162,28	1	–	–	9	1	1	–	2
Mathusalem	8 bouteilles	6,40 l	225,25	216,37	1	1	1	5	1	2	1	8
Salmanazar	12 bouteilles	9,60 l	337,88	324,46	2	–	–	18	2	2	–	4
Balthazar[1]	16 bouteilles	12,80 l	450,51	432,74	2	3	–	10	3	1	1	1
Nabuchodonosor[1]	20 bouteilles	16,00 l	563,14	540,93	3	2	–	3	4	–	1	13
MOSELLE												
Demi-bouteille		35,00 cl	12,32	11,83				12				12
Bouteille		70,00 cl	24,63	23,67			1	5			1	8
PORTO												
Quart	1 bouteille	75,75 cl	26,66	25,61			1	7			1	10
Magnum	2 bouteilles	1,51 l	53,15	51,20		1	–	13		1	1	3
Tappit Hen	3 bouteilles	2,27 l	79,89	76,84		2	–	–		2	–	13
Jéroboam	4 bouteilles	3,03 l	106,64	102,45		2	1	7		3	–	6
RHIN												
Demi-bouteille		35,00 cl	12,32	11,83				12				12
Bouteille		70,00 cl	24,63	23,67			1	5			1	8

1. Ne se fait pratiquement plus.

VIN	*Bouteilles*	*Système métrique*	*Capacités* *Once britannique*	*Once américaine*	*Équivalences* *britanniques* *Gal.*	*Qt.*	*Pt.*	*Oz*	*américaines* *Gal.*	*Qt.*	*Pt.*	*Oz.*
XÉRÈS												
Pinte	1/2 bouteille	37,86 cl	13,32	12,80				13				13
Quart	bouteille	75,75 cl	26,66	25,61			1	7			1	10
ÉTATS-UNIS												
Tenth	1/2 bouteille	37,86 cl	13,32	12,80				13				13
Fifth	bouteille	72,72 cl	26,65	25,60			1	7			1	10
Magnum	2 bouteilles	1,51 l	53,15	51,20			1	13		1	1	3

Les contenances indiquées dans ce tableau sont celles qui sont fixées par la loi, mais le contenu réel de chaque flacon varie presque toujours aux environs de la contenance légale en raison de l'espace occupé par le bouchon.

II. Capacité des fûts

Pays, région et contenu	*Fût*	*Description*	*Litres*	*Gallons britanniques*	*Gallons américains*
FRANCE *Alsace*	*Foudre*	Comme en Allemagne, un gros fût pour conservation et vente du vin.	1 000, très approximativement. Il n'existe pas de tels fûts normalisés	220 env.	264,2 env.
	Aume	Utilisé surtout pour l'expédition. Même contenance que la feuillette de Bourgogne.	114	25,1	30,1
Beaujolais	*Pièce*		216	47,5	57,1
	Feuillette	Demi-pièce.	108	23,7	28,5
	Quartaut	1/4 de pièce.	54	11,9	14,3
Bordeaux	*Barrique*	Fût le plus courant du Bordelais. Donne 24 caisses de 12 bouteilles chacune.	225	49,5	59,4
	Tonneau	Mesure de compte équivalant à 4 barriques mais il n'existe pas de tels tonneaux dans la réalité.	900	197,9	237,8

Pays, région et contenu	*Fût*	*Description*	*Litres*	*Gallons britanniques*	*Gallons américains*
		La production des châteaux et les cours de leurs vins sont indiqués en tonneaux. Donne 96 caisses de 12 bouteilles.			
	1/2 barrique ou feuillette		112	24,6	29,6
	Quartaut	1/4 de barrique.	56	12,3	14,8
Bourgogne	*Pièce*	Fût normal de Bourgogne. Donne 24 à 25 caisses de 12 bouteilles chacune.	228	50,1	60,2
	Queue	Ancienne mesure de capacité équivalant à deux pièces. Il n'existe pas dans la réalité des fûts de cette contenance.	456	100,3	120,5
	Feuillette	Demi-pièce	114	25,1	30,1
	Quartaut	1/4 de pièce	57	12,6	15,1
Chablis	*Feuillette*	Fût normal du Chablis. Contenance supérieure à la feuillette du reste de la Bourgogne.	132	29	34,9
Champagne	*Queue*	Fût normal de Champagne. On dit aussi : pièce.	216	47,5	57
	Demi-queue		108	23,7	28,5
Vallée de la Loire					
Anjou					
Layon	*Pièce*	Capacité variable.	220 env.	48,4	58,1
Saumur					
Vouvray	*Pièce*	Même capacité que la barrique bordelaise.	225	49,5	59,4
Mâconnais	*Pièce*	Presque la même capacité que la pièce du Beaujolais.	215	47,3	56,8
Midi (et Algérie)	*Demi-muid*	Fût servant à la conservation.	env. 600-700	env. 143	env. 171,7
Vallée du Rhône	*Pièce*	Fût normal de la région de Châteauneuf-du-Pape. Contenance légèrement inférieure à celle de la pièce de Bourgogne.	225	49,5	59,4

Pays, région et contenu	*Fût*	*Description*	*Litres*	*Gallons britanniques*	*Gallons américains*
ALLEMAGNE *Rhin et Moselle*	*Ohm*	Ancienne mesure de capacité pour les vins du Rhin, périmée.	150	33	39,6
	Doppelohm	Double Ohm, équivalant à 1/4 de Stück.	300	66	79,2
	Fuder (Moselle)	Grand fût servant à la conservation.	1 000	219,9	264,2
	Stück (Rhin)	Grand fût servant à la conservation.	1 200	264	317
	Doppelstück (Rhin)	Double Stück.	2 400	527,8	634
	Halbstück (Rhin)	1/2 Stück	600	132	158,4
	Viertelstück (Rhin)	1/4 de Stück	300	66	79,2
AUSTRALIE ET AFRIQUE DU SUD	*Hogshead*		295,3	64,9	78
Lisbonne	*Pipe*		531,4	117	140,4
Madère	*Pipe*	Fût normal pour l'expédition du Madère. Donne en moyenne 44 caisses et demie de 12 bouteilles.	418	92	110,4
	Hogsead	Moitié de la pipe de Madère.	209	46	55,2
Marsala	*Pipe*	Contenance légèrement supérieure à celle de la pipe de Madère. Donne 45 caisses de 12 bouteilles.	422,6	93	11,6
	Hogshead	Même contenance que le Hogshead de Madère.	209	46	52,2
Porto	*Pipe*	Fût standard du Porto. Donne en moyenne 56 douzaines de « reputed quarts » (un « reputed quart » = environ 75 cl).	522,5	115	138
	Hogshead		259	57	68,4
	Quarter Cask	Env. 1/4 du fût standard.	127,2	28	33,6
Xérès	*Butt*	Fût standard du Xérès. Donne 52 caisses de 12 bouteilles.	490,7	108	129,6

Pays, région et contenu	*Fût*	*Description*	*Litres*	*Gallons britanniques*	*Gallons américains*
	Hogshead	1/2 butt. Donne 26 caisses de 12 bouteilles.	245,4	54	64,8
	Quarter Cask	1/4 du fût standard ou 1/2 hogshead.	122,7	27	32,4
	Octave	1/8 du fût standard de Xérès.	61,4	13,5	16,2
TARRAGONE	*Pipe*	Même capacité que la pipe de Porto.	522,5	114,9	138
	Hogshead		263,5	57,9	69,6
Eau-de-vie de vin	*Puncheon*	Fût le plus couramment utilisé pour les eaux-de-vie de vin.	545,2	120	144
	Hogshead	1/2 puncheon.	272,6	60	72
	Quarter Cask	1/4 de puncheon ou	136,3	30	36
Rhum	*Puncheon*	capacité extrêmement variable.	422,6-518	92,9-113,9	111,136,8
	Hogshead	Capacité également très variable.	245,4-272,6	54-59,9	64-8-72
Whisky-scotch	*Butt*	Fût standard de distillerie. Parfois il s'agit d'un puncheon de rhum en chêne, dont les douves ont été coupées à la longueur voulue pour obtenir la capacité.	env. 491	env. 108	env. 129,7
	Punchon	Capacité variable.	431,9-545,5	95-120	114,1-144,1
Whiskey américain	*Barrel*	Nouvelle barrique standard des whyskies Rye oú Bourbon exigée par la loi.	181,7	40	48
Whisky canadien	*Barrel*	Capacité variable qui dépasse généralement un peu celle du barrel standard des États-Unis.	env. 181,7	env. 40	env. 48
Spiritueux (*Vieillis*) américains	*Barrel*	Futaille usagée : mêmes dimensions et capacité que pour le Whiskey.	181,7	40	48
	Hogshead			45-80	54-96
	Barrel			35-45	42-54
	Quarter			15-30	18-36
	Octave			9-15	10,8-18

Pays, région et contenu	*Fût*	*Description*	*Litres*	*Gallons britanniques*	*Gallons américains*
CAISSE					
Bordeaux et Bourgogne			8,52	1,87	2,25
Champagne			9,23	2,0304	2,4375

Appendice D :

Tableau comparatif du degré des alcools

Sikes (G.-B.)	*U.S.A.*	*Gay-Lussac et Tralles*	*Sikes (G.-B.)*	*U.S.A.*	*Gay-Lussac et Tralles*
U.P.			35,0°	74,3°	37,1
(Under proof)*			34,4	75,0	37,5
60.0°	45,7°	22,9°	34,0°	75,4	37,7
59,8	46,0	23,0	33,5	76,0	38,0
59,0	46,9	23,4	33,0	76,6	38,3
58,9	47,0	23,5	32,6	77,0	38,5
58,0	48,0	24,0	32,0	77,7	38,9
57,1	49,0	24,5	31,8	78,0	39,0
57,0	49,1	24,6	31,0	78,9	39,4
56,3	50,0	25,0	30,9	79,0	39,5
56,0	50,3	25,1	30,0	80,0	40,0
55,4	51,0	25,5	29,1	81,0	40,5
55,0	51,4	25,7	29,0	81,1	40,6
54,5	52,0	26,0	28,3	82,0	41,0
54,0	52,6	26,3	28,0	82,3	41,1
53,6	53,0	26,5	27,4	83,0	41,5
53,0	53,7	26,9	27,0	83,4	41,7
52,8	54,0	27,0	26,5	84,0	42,0
52,0	54,9	27,4	26,0	84,6	42,3
51,9	55,0	27,5	25,6	85,0	42,5
51,0	56,0	28,0	25,0	85,7	42,9
50,1	57,0	28,5	24,8	86,0	43,0
50,0	57,1	28,6	24,0	86,9	43,4
49,3	58,0	29,0	23,9	87,0	43,5
49,0	58,3	29,1	23,0	88,0	44,0
48,4	59,0	29,5	22,1	89,0	44,5
48,0	59,4	29,7	22,0	89,1	44,6
47,5	60,0	30,0	21,3	90,0	45,0
47,0	60,6	30,3	21,0	90,3	45,1
46,6	61,0	30,5	20,4	91,0	45,5
46,0	61,7	30,9	20,0	91,4	45,7
45,8	62,0	31,0	19,5	92,0	46,0
45,0	62,9	31,4	19,0	92,6	46,3
44,9	63,0	31,5	18,6	93,0	46,5
44,0	64,0	32,0	18,0	93,7	46,9
43,1	65,0	32,5	17,8	94,0	47,0
43,0	65,1	32,6	17,0	94,9	47,4

Sikes (G.-B.)	*U.S.A.*	*Gay-Lussac et Tralles*	*Sikes (G.-B.)*	*U.S.A.*	*Gay-Lussac et Tralles*
42,3	66,0	33,0	16,9	95,0	47,5
42,0	66,3	33,1	16,0	96,0	48,0
41,4	67,0	33,5	15,1	97,0	48,5
41,0	67,4	33,7	15,0	97,1	48,6
40,5	68,0	34,0	14,3	98,0	49,0
40,0	68,6	34,3	14,0	98,3	49,1
39,6	69,0	34,5	13,4	99,0	49,5
39,0	69,7	34,9	13,0	99,4	49,7
38,8	70,0	35,0	12,5	Proof	50,0
38,0	70,9	35,4	12,0	100,6	50,3
37,9	71,0	35,5	11,6	101,0	50,5
37,0	72,0	36,0	11,0	101,7	50,9
36,0	73,1	36,6	10,0	102,9	51,4
36,1	73,0	36,5	10,8	102,0	51,0
35,3	74,0	37,0	9,9	103,0	51,5
9,0	104,0	52,0	15,5	132,0	66,0
8,1	105,0	52,5	16,0	132,6	66,3
8,0	105,0	52,6	16,4	133,0	66,5
7,3	106,0	53,0	17,0	133,7	66,9
7,0	106,3	53,1	17,3	134,0	67,0
6,4	107,0	53,5	18,0	134,9	67,4
6,0	107,4	53,7	18,1	135,0	67,5
5,5	108,0	54,0	19,0	136,0	68,0
5,0	108,6	54,3	19,9	137,0	68,5
4,6	109,0	54,5	20,0	137,1	68,6
4,0	109,7	54,9	20,8	138,0	69,0
3,8	110,0	55,0	21,0	138,3	69,1
3,0	110,9	55,4	21,6	139,0	69,5
2,9	111,0	55,5	22,0	139,4	69,7
2,0	112,0	56,0	22,5	140,0	70,0
1,1	113,0	56,5	23,0	140,6	70,3
1,0	113,1	56,6	23,4	141,0	70,5
0,3	114,0	57,0	24,0	141,7	70,9
Proof	114,29	57,14	24,3	142,0	71,0
O.P.			25,0	142,9	71,4
(Over proof)			25,1	143,0	71,5
0,6	115,0	57,5	26,0	144,0	72,0
1,0	115,4	57,7	26,9	145,0	72,5
1,5	116,0	58,0	27,0	145,1	72,6
2,0	116,6	58,3	27,8	146,0	73,0
2,4	117,0	58,5	28,0	146,3	73,1
3,0	117,7	58,9	28,6	147,0	73,5
3,3	118,0	59,0	29,0	147,4	73,7
4,0	118,9	59,4	29,5	148,0	74,0
4,1	119,0	59,5	30,0	148,6	74,3
5,0	120,0	60,0	30,4	149,0	74,5
5,9	121,0	60,5	31,0	149,7	74,9
6,0	121,1	60,6	31,3	150,0	75,0
6,8	122,0	61,0	32,0	150,9	75,4
7,0	122,3	61,1	32,1	151,0	75,5
7,6	123,0	61,5	33,0	152,0	76,0
8,0	123,4	61,7	33,9	153,0	76,5
8,5	124,0	62,0	34,0	153,1	76.6

Sikes (G.-B.)	*U.S.A.*	*Gay-Lussac et Tralles*	*Sikes (G.-B.)*	*U.S.A.*	*Gay-Lussac et Tralles*
9,0	124,6	62,3	34,8	154,0	77,0
9,4	125,0	62,5	35,0	154,3	77,1
10,0	125,7	62,9	35,6	155,0	77,5
10,3	126,0	63,0	36,0	155,4	77,7
11,0	126,9	63,4	36,5	156,0	78,0
11,1	127,0	63,5	37,0	156,6	78,3
12,0	128,0	64,0	37,4	157,0	78,5
12,9	129,0	64,5	38,0	157,7	78,9
13,0	129,1	64,6	38,3	158,0	79,0
13,8	130,0	65,0	39,0	158,9	79,4
14,0	130,3	65,1	39,1	159,0	79,5
14,6	131,0	65,5	40,0	160,0	80,0
15,0	131,4	65,7	40,9	161,0	80,5
			41,0	161,1	80,6
41,8	162,0	81,0	58,4	181,0	90,5
42,0	162,3	81,1	50,9	181,7	90,9
42,6	163,0	81,5	59,3	182,0	91,0
43,0	163,4	81,7	60,0	182,9	91,4
43,5	164,0	82,0	60,1	183,0	91,5
44,0	164,6	82,3	61,0	184,0	92,0
44,4	165,0	82,5	61,9	185,0	92,5
45,0	165,7	82,9	62,0	185,1	92,6
45,3	166,0	83,0	62,8	186,0	93,0
46,0	166,9	83,4	63,0	186,3	93,1
46,1	167,0	83,5	63,6	187,0	93,5
47,0	168,0	84,0	64,0	187,4	93,7
47,9	169,0	84,5	64,5	188,0	94,0
48,0	169,1	84,6	65,0	188,6	94,3
48,8	170,0	85,0	65,4	189,0	94,5
49,0	170,3	85,1	66,0	189,7	94,9
49,6	171,0	85,5	66,3	190,0	95,0
50,0	171,4	85,7	67,0	190,9	95,4
50,5	172,0	86,0	67,1	191,0	95,5
51,0	172,6	86,3	68,0	192,0	96,0
51,4	173,0	86,5	68,9	193,0	96,5
52,0	173,7	86,9	69,0	193,1	96,6
52,3	174,0	87,0	69,8	194,0	97,0
53,0	174,9	87,4	70,0	194,3	97,1
53,1	175,0	87,5	70,6	195,0	97,5
54,0	176,0	88,0	71,0	195,4	97,7
54,9	177,0	88,5	71,5	196,0	98,0
55,0	177,1	88,6	72,0	196,6	98,3
55,8	178,0	89,0	72,4	197,0	98,5
56,0	178,3	89,1	73,0	197,7	98,9
56,6	179,0	89,5	73,3	198,0	99,0
57,0	179,4	89,7	74,0	198,9	99,4
57,5	180,0	90,0	74,1	199,0	99,5
58,0	180,6	90,3	75,0	200,0	100,0

* *Voir* dans la partie alphabétique au mot PROOF SPIRIT

Appendice E : **Tables de conversion**

I. Mesures de longueur

Centimètres (cm)	*Pouces (Inches) (in.)*	*Mètres (m)*	*Pieds (Feet) (ft.)*	*Mètres*	*Yards (yds)*	*Kilomètres (km)*	*Miles * (m.)*
1	0,394	1	3,281	1	1,094	1	0,621
2	0,787	2	6,562	2	2,187	2	1,243
3	1,181	3	9,843	3	3,281	3	1,864
4	1,575	4	13,123	4	4,374	4	2,486
5	1,969	5	16,404	5	5,468	5	3,107
6	2,362	6	19,685	6	6,562	6	3,728
7	2,756	7	22,966	7	7,655	7	4,350
8	3,150	8	26,247	8	8,749	8	4,971
9	3,543	9	29,528	9	9,843	9	5,592
10	3,937	10	32,808	10	10,936	10	6,214
20	7,874	20	65,617	21	21,872	20	12,427
30	11,811	30	98,425	32	32,808	30	18,641
40	15,748	40	131,234	43	43,745	40	24,855
50	19,685	50	164,042	54	54,681	50	31,069
60	23,622	60	196,850	65	65,617	60	37,282
70	27,559	70	229,659	76	76,553	70	43,496
80	31,496	80	262,467	87	87,489	80	49,710
90	35,433	90	295,276	98	98,425	90	55,923
100 = 1 mètre	39,370	100	328,084	109	109,361	100	62,137

10 millimètres = 1 centimètre   10 mètres = 1 décamètre
10 centimètres = 1 décimètre   10 décamètres = 1 hectomètre
10 décimètres = 1 mètre   10 hectomètres = 1 kilomètre

I. Mesures de longueur *(suite)*

Pouces (in.)	*Centimètres (cm)*	*Pieds (ft.)*	*Mètres (m)*	*Yards (yds.)*	*Mètres (m)*	*Miles * (m.)*	*Kilomètres (km)*
1	2,540	1	0,305	1	0,914	1	1,609
2	5,080	2	0,610	2	1,829	2	3,219
3	7,620	3 = 1 yard	0,914	3	2,743	3	4,828
4	10,160	4	1,219	4	3,658	4	6,437
5	12,700	5	1,524	5	4,572	5	8,047
6	15,240	6	1,829	6	5,486	6	9,656

I. Mesures de longueur *(suite)*

Pouces (in.)	*Centimètres (cm)*	*Pieds (ft.)*	*Mètres (m)*	*Yards (yds.)*	*Mètres (m)*	*Miles * (m.)*	*Kilomètres (km)*
7	17,780	7	2,134	7	6,401	7	11,265
8	20,320	8	2,438	8	7,315	8	12,875
9	22,860	9	2,743	9	8,230	9	14,484
10	25,400	10	3,048	10	9,144	10	16,093
11	27,940	20	6,096	20	18,288	20	32,187
12 = 1 foot	30,480	30	9,144	30	27,432	30	40,280
20	50,800	40	12,192	40	36,576	40	64,374
30	76,200	50	15,240	50	45,720	50	80,467
40	101,600	60	18,288	60	54,864	60	96,561
50	127,000	70	21,336	70	64,008	70	112,654
60	152,400	80	24,384	80	73,152	80	128,748
70	177,800	90	27,432	90	82,296	90	144,841
80	203,200	100	30,480	100	91,440	100	160,934
90	228,600						
100	254,000						
*Mile terrestre (Le *Knot* ou mille marin [*nautical mile*] = 1 853 m).							

1 pouce divisé en $\frac{16}{16}$		= 0,0254 mètre
12 pouces (in.)	= 1 pied (ft.)	= 0,308 m
3 pieds	= 1 yard (yd.)	= 0,9143 m
1 760 yards	= 1 mile (m.)	= 1 609 m (1,609 km)

II. Aire ou superficie

Centimètres carrés (cm²)	*Pouces carrés (sq. in.)*	*mètres carrés (m²)*	*Pieds carrés (sq. ft.)*	*Hectares (ha)*	*Acres*	*Kilomètres carrés (km²)*	*Miles carrés (sq. m.)*
1	0,155	1	10,764	1	2,471	1	0,368
2	0,310	2	21,528	2	4,942	2	0,722
3	0,465	3	32,292	3	7,413	3	1,158
4	0,620	4	43,056	4	9,884	4	1,544
5	0,775	5	53,820	5	12,355	5	1,931
6	0,930	6	64,583	6	14,826	6	2,317
7	1,085	7	75,347	7	17,297	7	2,703
8	1,240	8	86,111	8	19,768	8	3,089
9	1,395	9	96,875	9	22,239	9	3,475
10	1,550	10	107,639	10	24,711	10	3,861
20	3,100	20	215,278	20	49,421	20	7,722
30	4,650	30	322,917	30	74,132	30	11,583
40	6,200	40	430,556	40	98,842	40	15,444
50	7,750	50	538,196	50	123,553	50	19,305
60	9,300	60	645,835	60	148,263	60	23,166
70	10,850	70	753,474	70	172,974	70	27,027
80	12,400	80	861,113	80	197,684	80	30,888
90	13,950	90	968,752	90	222,395	90	34,749
100	15,500	100	1 076,391	100 = 1 km²	247,105	100	38,610

10 000 cm²	= 1 m²
10 000 m²	= 1 hectare = 100 ares
100 hectares	= 1 km²

II. Aire ou superficie *(suite)*

Square inches (sq. in.)	*Centimètres carrés (cm²)*	*Square feet (sq. ft.)*	*Mètres carrés (m²)*	*Acres*	*Hectares*	*Square miles (sq. m.)*	*Kilomètres carrés (km²)*
1	6,452	1	0,093	1	0,405	1	2,590
2	12,903	2	0,186	2	0,809	2	5,180
3	19,355	3	0,279	3	1,214	3	7,770
4	25,806	4	0,372	4	1,619	4	10,360
5	32,258	5	0,465	5	2,023	5	12,950
6	38,710	6	0,557	6	2,428	6	15,540
7	45,161	7	0,650	7	2,833	7	18,130
8	51,613	8	0,743	8	3,238	8	20,720
9	58,064	9 = 1 sq yd.	0,836	9	3,642	9	23,310
10	64,516	10	0,929	10	4,047	10	25,900
20	129,032	20	1,858	20	8,094	20	51,800
30	193,548	30	2,787	30	12,141	30	77,700
40	258,064	40	3,716	40	16,187	40	103,600
50	322,580	50	4,645	50	20,234	50	129,499
60	387,096	60	5,574	60	24,281	60	155,399
70	451,612	70	6,503	70	28,328	70	181,299
80	516,128	80	7,432	80	32,375	80	207,199
90	580,644	90	8,361	90	36,422	90	233,099
100	645,160	100	9,290	100	40,469	100	258,999

144 pouces carrés (square inches) = 1 pied carré (square foot)
9 pieds carrés = 1 yard carré
4,840 yards carrés (square yards) = 1 acre ≠ 40 ares 1/2
640 acres = 1 mille carré (square mile)

III. Volumes

Centimètres cubes (cm³)	*Cubic inches*	*Décimètres cubes (dm³)*	*Cubic feet*	*Mètres cubes (m³)*	*Cubic yards*
1	0,061	1	0,035	1	1,308
2	0,122	2	0,071	2	2,616
3	0,183	3	0,106	3	3,924
4	0,244	4	0,141	4	5,232
5	0,305	5	0,177	5	6,540
6	0,366	6	0,212	6	7,848
7	0,427	7	0,247	7	9,156
8	0,488	8	0,283	8	10,464
9	0,549	9	0,318	9	11,772
10	0,610	10	0,353	10	13,080
20	1,220	20	0,706	20	26,159
30	1,831	30	1,059	30	39,239
40	2,441	40	1,413	40	52,318
50	3,051	50	1,766	50	65,398
60	3,661	60	2,119	60	78,477
70	4,272	70	2,472	70	91,557
80	4,882	80	2,825	80	104,636
90	5,492	90	3,178	90	117,716
100	6,102	100	3,531	100	130,795

1 000 centimètres cubes = 1 décimètre cube
1 000 décimètres cubes = 1 mètre cube = 1 stère

III. Volumes *(suite)*

Cubic inches	*Centimètres cubes*	*Cubic feet*	*Décimètres cubes*	*Cubic yards*	*Mètres cubes*
1	16,387	1	28,317	1	0,765
2	32,774	2	56,633	2	1,529
3	49,161	3	84,951	3	2,294
4	65,548	4	113,267	4	3,058
5	81,935	5	141,584	5	3,823
6	98,322	6	169,901	6	4,587
7	114,709	7	198,218	7	5,352
8	131,097	8	226,535	8	6,116
9	147,484	9	254,852	9	6,881
10	163,871	10	283,168	10	7,646
20	327,741	20	566,337	20	15,291
30	491,612	30	849,505	30	22,937
40	655,483	40	1 132,674	40	30,582
50	819,353	50	1 415,842	50	38,228
60	983,224	60	1 699,011	60	45,873
70	1 147,094	70	1 982,179	70	53,519
80	1 310,965	80	2 265,348	80	61,164
90	1 474,836	90	2 548,516	90	68,810
100	1 638,706	100	2 831,685	100	76,455

1,728 cubic inches = 1 cubic foot
27 cubic feet = 1 cubic yard

IV. Poids ou masse

Grammes	*Onces*	*Lb.*	*Oz.*	*Kilogrammes*	*Livres*	*Cwts.*	*Qtrs.*	*Sts.*	*Lb.*	*Oz.*
1	0,035			1	2,205				2	3
2	0,071			2	4,409				4	7
3	0,106			3	6,614				6	10
4	0,141			4	8,818				8	13
5	0,176			5	11,023				11	
6	0,212			6	13,228				13	4
7	0,247			7	15,432			1	1	7
8	0,282			8	17,637			1	3	10
9	0,317			9	19,842			1	5	13
10	0,353			10	22,046			1	8	1
20	0,705			20	44,092		1	1	2	1
30	1,058		1	30	66,139		2		10	2
40	1,411		1 1/2	40	88,185		3		4	3
50	1,764		1 3/4	50	110,231		3	1	12	4
60	2,116		2	60	132,277	1		1	6	4
70	2,469		2 1/2	70	154,324	1	1	1		5
80	2,822		2 3/4	80	176,370	1	2		8	6
90	3,175		3 1/4	90	198,416	1	3		2	7
100	3,527		3 1/2	100	220,463	1	3	1	10	7
150	5,291		5 1/4	150	330,69	2	3	1	8	11
200	7,055		7	200	440,92	3	3	1	6	15
250	8,818		8 1/4	250	551,16	4	3	1	5	3
300	10,592		10 1/2	300	661,39	5	3	1	3	6
350	12,346		12 1/2	350	771,62	6	3	1	1	10
400	14,110		14	400	881,85	7	3		13	14
450	15,873		15 3/4	450	992,08	8	3		12	1

IV. Poids ou masse *(suite)*

Grammes	*Onces*	*Lb.*	*Oz.*	*Kilogrammes*	*Livres*	*Cwts.*	*Qtrs.*	*Sts.*	*Lb.*	*Oz.*
500	17,637	1	1 1/4	500	1 102,31	9	3		10	5
550	19,401	1	3 1/2	550	1 212,54	10	3		8	9
600	21,164	1	5 1/4	600	1 322,77	11	3		6	12
650	22,928	1	7	650	1 433	12	3		4	
700	24,691	1	8 3/4	700	1 543,24	13	3		3	4
750	26,455	1	10 1/2	750	1 653,47	14	3		1	7
800	28,219	1	12 1/4	800	1 763,70	15	2	1	13	11
850	29,983	1	14	850	1 873,93	16	2	1	11	15
900	31,746	1	15 3/4	900	1 984,16	17	2	1	10	2
950	33,510	2	1 1/2	950	2 094,39	18	2	1	8	6
1 000 = 1 kilo.	35,274	2	3 1/4	1 000 = 1 tonne métrique	2 204,63	19	2	1	6	10

IV. Poids ou masse *(suite)*

Tonnes métriques	*Long ou gross tons*	*Tons*	*Cwts.*	*Qtrs.*	*Sts.*	*Lb.*	*Oz.*
1	0,984		19	2	1	6	9 3/4
2	1,968	1	19	1		13	3 1/2
3	2,953	2	19			5	13 1/4
4	3,937	3	18	2	1	12	7
5	4,921	4	18	1	1	5	3/4
6	5,905	5	18			11	10 1/4
7	6,889	6	17	3		4	4
8	7,874	7	17	1	1	11	11 1/4
9	8,858	8	17		1	3	1 1/2
10	9.842	9	16	3		10	4 3/4
20	19,684	19	13	2	1	6	6 1/4
30	29,526	29	10	2		2	
40	39,368	39	7	1		12	15 3/4
50	49,210	49	4		1	9	1 1/4
60	59,052	59	1		5		6
70	68,895	68	17	3	1	1	11
80	78,737	78	14	2	1	11	12 1/4
90	88,579	88	11	2		8	1
100	98,421	98	8	1	1	4	6

16 onces (oz.) = 1 livre
14 livres = 1 stone (st.)
28 livres = 1 quarter (qtr.)
112 livres = 1 hundredweight (cwr.)
20 hundredweight = 2,240 lb. = 1 ton (long)
2,000 lb. = 1 ton (short)

IV. Poids ou masse *(suite)*

Onces	*Grammes*	*Livre*	*Kilogrammes*	*Long ou gross tons*	*Tonnes métriques*
1	28,350	1	0,454	1	1,016
2	56,699	2	0,907	2	2,032
3	85,049	3	1,361	3	3,048
4	113,398	4	1,814	4	4,064
5	141,748	5	2,268	5	5,080
6	170,097	6	2,722	6	6,096
7	198,447	7	3,175	7	7,112
8	226,796	8	3,629	8	8,128
9	255,146	9	4,082	9	9,144
10	283,495	10	4,536	10	10,161
16 = 1 pound (livre)	453,592	14 = 1 stone	6,350	20	20,321
20	566,990	20	9,072	30	30,481
30	850,486	28 = 1 quarter*	12,701	40	40,642
40	1 133,981	30	13,608	50	50,802
50	1 417,476	40	18,144	60	60,963
60	1 700,971	50	22,680	70	71,123
70	1 984,467	60	27,216	80	81,284
80	2 267,962	70	31,751	90	91,444
90	2 551,457	80	36,287	100	101,605
100	2 834,952	90	40,823		
		100	45,359		
		112 = 1 hundred weight*	50,802		

* Ces mots n'ont pas d'équivalents en français

16 onces (oz.)	=	1 livre	
14 livres	=	1 stone (st.)	
28 livres	=	1 quarter (qtr.)	
112 livres	=	1 hundredweight (cwr.)	
20 hundredweight	=	2,240 lb. =	1 ton (long)
		2,000 lb. =	1 ton (short)

V. Capacités

Centilitres	*Onces britanniques*	*Équivalence britannique*		*Onces américains*	*Équivalence américaine*		
		Pts.	*Oz.*		*Qts.*	*Pts.*	*Oz.*
20	7,039		7	6,763			6 3/4
25	8,799		8 3/4	8,454			6 1/2
30	10,599		10 1/2	10,144			10 1/4
35	12,319		12 1/4	11,835			11 3/4
36	12,671		12 3/4	12,173			12 1/4
37,5	13,199		13-1/4	12,681			12 3/4
40	14,078		14	13,526			13 1/2
45	15,838		15 3/4	15,217			15 1/4

V. Capacités *(suite)*

Centilitres	*Onces britanniques*	*Équivalence britannique* *Pts.*	*Oz.*	*Onces américains*	*Équivalence américaine* *Qts.*	*Pts.*	*Oz.*
50	17,598		17 1/2	16,907	1		1
55	19,358		19 1/4	18,598	1		2 1/2
60	21,118	1	1	20,289	1		4 1/4
65	22,877	1	2 3/4	21,980	1		6
70	24,637	1	4 3/4	23,670	1		7 3/4
75	26,397	1	6 1/2	25,361	1		9 1/4
80	28,175	1	8 1/4	27,052	1		11
85	29,917	1	10	28,742	1		12 3/4
90	31,676	1	11 3/4	30,433	1		14 1/2
95	33,436	1	13 1/2	32,124	1		
100 = 1 litre	35,196	1	15 1/4	33,814	1		1 3/4

100 centilitres = 1 litre

V. Capacités *(suite)*

Litres	*Pintes britanniques*	*Gallons britanniques*	*Équivalence britannique* *Gals.*	*Qts.*	*Pts.*	*Oz.*
1	1,760	0,220			1	15 1/4
2	3,520	0,440			1	10 1/2
3	5,279	0,660		2	1	5 1/2
4	7,039	0,880		3	1	3/4
5	8,799	1,100	1			16
6	10,559	1,320	1	1		11 1/4
7	12,319	1,540	1	2		6 1/2
8	14,078	1,760	1	3		1 1/2
9	15,838	1,980	1	3	1	16 3/4
10	17,598	2,200	2		1	12
11	19,358	2,420	2	1	1	7 1/4
12	21,118	2,640	2	2	1	2 1/2
13	22,877	2,860	2	3		17 1/2
14	24,637	3,080	3			12 3/4
15	26,397	3,300	3	1		8
16	28,157	3,520	3	2		3 1/4
17	29,917	3,740	3	2	1	18 1/2
18	31,676	3,960	3	3	1	13 1/2
19	33,436	4,180	4		1	8 3/4
20	35,196	4,400	4	1	1	3 3/4
30	52,794	6,599	6	2		15 3/4
40	70,392	8,799	8	3		7 3/4
50	87,990	10,999	10	3	1	19 3/4
60	105,588	13,199	13		1	11 3/4
70	123,186	15,398	15	1	1	3 3/4
80	140,784	17,598	17	2		15 3/4
90	158,382	19,798	19	3		7 3/4
100 = 1 hl	175,980	21,998	21	3	1	19 3/4

V. Capacités *(suite)*

Litres	*Pintes américaines*	*Gallons américains*	*Équivalence américaine* *Gals.*	*Qts.*	*Pts.*	*Oz.*
1	2,113	0,264		1		1 3/4
2	4,227	0,528		2		3 1/2
3	6,340	0,793		3		5 1/2
4	8,454	1,057	1			7 1/4
5	10,567	1,321	1	1		9
6	12,681	1,585	1	2		11
7	14,794	1,849	1	3		12 3/4
8	16,908	2,113	2			14 1/2
9	19,021	2,378	2	1	1	1/4
10	21,134	2,642	2	2	1	2 1/4
11	23,248	2,906	2	3	1	4
12	25,361	3,170	3		1	5 3/4
13	27,475	3,434	3	1	1	7 1/2
14	29,588	3,699	3	2	1	9 1/2
15	31,702	3,963	3	3	1	1 1/4
16	33,815	4,227	4		1	13
17	35,928	4,491	4	1	1	14 3/4
18	38,042	4,755	4	3		3/4
19	40,155	5,019	5			2 1/2
20	42,269	5,284	5	1		4 1/4
30	63,403	7,925	7	3		6 1/2
40	84,538	10,567	10	2		8 1/2
50	105,672	13,209	13		1	10 3/4
60	126,806	15,851	15	3		13
70	147,941	18,493	18	1	1	15
80	169,075	21,134	21		1	1 1/4
90	190,210	23,776	23	3		3 1/4
100 = 1 hl	211,344	26,418	26	1	1	5 1/2

V. Capacités *(suite)*

Fluid ounces (G.B.)	*Centilitres*	*Fluid ounces U.S.A.*	*Équivalence américaine* *Qts.*	*Pts.*	*Oz.*
6	17,047	5,765			5 3/4
7	19,889	6,725			6 3/4
8	22,730	7,686			7 3/4
9	25,571	8,647			8 3/4
10	28,412	9,608			9 1/2
11	31,253	10,568			10 1/2
12	34,095	11,529			11 1/2
13	36,936	12,490			12 1/2
14	39,777	13,451			13 1/2
15	42,618	14,411			14 1/2
16	45,460	15,372			15 1/4
17	48,301	16,333		1	1/4
18	51,142	17,294		1	1 1/4
19	53,983	18,254		1	2 1/4
20 = 1 pt.	56,824	19,215		1	3 1/4
30	85,237	28,823		1	12 3/4

V. Capacités *(suite)*

Fluid ounces (G.-B.)	*Centilitres*	*Fluid ounces (U.S.A.)*	*Équivalence britannique* *Qts.*	*Pts*	*Oz.*
40 = 1 qt.	113,649	38,430	1		6 1/2
50	142,061	48,038	1	1	
60	170,473	57,646	1	1	9 3/4
70	198,885	67,253	2		3 1/4
80 = 2 qts.	227,298	76,861	2		12 3/4
90	255,710	86,469	2	1	6 1/2
100	284,122	96,076	3		

V. Capacités *(suite)*

Pintes britanniques	*Litres*	*Pintes américaines*	*Équivalence américaine* *Gals.*	*Qts.*	*Pts.*	*Oz.*
1	0,568	1,201			1	3 1/4
2 = 1 qt.	1,136	2,402				6 1/2
3	1,705	3,603		1	1	9 3/4
4 = 2 qts.	2,273	4,804		2		12 3/4
5	2,841	6,005		3		
6 = 3 qts.	3,409	7,200		3	1	3 1/4
7	3,978	8,407	1			6 1/2
8 = 1 gal.	4,546	9,608	1		1	9 3/4
9	5,114	10,809	1	1		13
10	5,682	12,010	1	2		1/4
11	6,251	13,210	1	2	1	3 1/4
12	6,819	14,411	1	3		6 1/2
13	7,387	15,612	1	3	1	9 3/4
14	7,955	16,813	2			13
15	8,524	18,014	2	1		1/4
16 = 2 gals.	9,092	19,215	2	1	1	3 1/2
17	9,660	20,416	2	2		6 3/4
18	10,228	21,617	2	2	1	9 3/4
19	10,797	22,818	2	3		13
20	11,365	24,019	3			1/4
30	17,047	36,029	4	2		1/2
40	22,730	48,038	6			1/2
50	28,412	60,048	7	2		3/4
60	34,095	72,057	9			1
70	39,777	84,067	10	2		1
80 = 10 gals.	45,460	96,076	12			1 1/4
90	51,142	108,086	13	2		1 1/2
100	56,825	120,095	15			1 1/2

20 fluid oz. britanniques = 1 pint
2 pints = 1 quart

V. CAPACITÉS *(suite)*

Fluid ounces (G.-B.)	*Centilitres*	*Fluid ounces (U.S.A.)*	*Équivalence britannique* Qts.	Pts	Oz.
6,245	17,744	6			6 1/4
7,286	20,701	7			7 1/4
8,327	23,658	8			8 1/4
9,368	26,615	9			9 1/4
10,408	29,573	10			10 1/2
11,449	32,530	11			11 1/2
12,490	35,487	12			12 1/2
13,531	38,445	13			13 1/2
14,572	41,402	14			14 1/2
15,613	44,359	15			15 1/2
16,653	47,316	16 = 1 pt.			16 3/4
17,694	50,274	17			17 3/4
18,735	53,231	18			18 3/4
19,776	56,188	19			19 3/4
20,817	59,145	20		1	3/4
31,225	88,718	30		1	11 1/4
41,634	118,291	40	1		1 3/4
52,042	147,864	50	1		12
62,450	177,436	60	1	1	2 1/2
72,859	207,009	70	1	1	12 3/4
83,267	236,582	80	2		3 1/4
93,676	266,154	90	2		13 3/4
104,084	295,727	100	2	1	4

V. CAPACITÉS *(suite)*

Pintes américaines	*Litres*	*Pintes britanniques*	*Équivalence britannique* Gals.	Qts.	Pts.	Oz.
1	0,473	0,833				16 3/4
2 = 1 qt.	0,946	1,665			1	13 1/4
3	1,419	2,498		1		10
4 = 2 qts.	1,893	3,331		1	1	6 1/2
5	2,366	4,163		2		3 1/4
6 = 3 qts.	2,839	4,996		2	1	
7	3,312	5,829		2	1	16 1/2
8 = 1 gal.	3,785	6,661		3		13 1/4
9	4,258	7,494		3	1	10
10	4,732	8,327	1			6 1/2
11	5,205	9,159	1		1	3 1/4
12	5,678	9,992	1		1	19 3/4
13	6,151	10,825	1	1		16 1/2
14	6,624	11,657	1	1	1	13 1/4
15	7,097	12,490	1	2		9 3/4
16 = 2 gals.	7,571	13,323	1	2	1	6 1/2

V. Capacités *(suite)*

Pintes américaines	*Litres*	*Pintes britanniques*	*Équivalence britannique* *Gals.*	*Qts.*	*Pts.*	*Oz.*
17	8,044	14,155	1	3		3
18	8,517	14,988	1	3		19 3/4
19	8,990	15,821	1	3	1	16 1/2
20	9,463	16,653	2			13
30	14,195	24,980	3			19 1/2
40	18,927	33,307	4		1	6 1/4
50	23,658	41,634	5		1	12 3/4
60	28,390	49,960	6		1	19 1/4
70	33,121	58,287	7	1		5 3/4
80 = 10 gals.	37,853	66,614	8	1		12 1/4
90	42,585	74,940	9	1		18 3/4
100	47,316	83,267	10	1	1	5 1/4

16 fluid oz. (U.S.A.) = 1 pint
2 pintes = 1 quart
4 quarts = 1 gallon

V. Capacités *(suite)*

Gallons britanniques	*Litres*	*Gallons américains*	*Équivalence américaine* *Gals.*	*Qts.*	*Pts.*	*Oz.*
1	4,546	1,201	1		1	9 3/4
2	9,092	2,402	2	1	1	3 1/2
3	13,638	3,603	3	2		13 1/4
4	18,184	4,804	4	3		7
5	22,730	6,005	6			3/4
6	27,276	7,206	7		1	10 1/4
7	31,822	8,407	8	1	1	4
8	36,368	9,608	9	2		13 3/4
9	40,914	10,809	10	3		7 1/2
10	45,460	12,010	12			1 1/4
11	50,006	13,210	13		1	11
12	54,552	14,411	14	1	1	4 1/2
13	59,097	15,612	15	2		14 1/4
14	63,643	16,813	16	3		8
15	68,189	18,014	18			1 3/4
16	72,735	19,215	19		1	11 1/2
17	77,281	20,416	20	1	1	5 1/4
18	81,827	21,617	21	2		15
19	86,373	22,818	22	3		8 3/4
20	90,919	24,019	24			2 1/2
30	136,379	36,029	36			3 3/4
40	181,838	48,038	48			4 3/4
50	227,298	60,048	60			6 1/4
60	272,758	72,057	72			7 1/4
70	318,217	84,067	84			8 1/2
80	363,677	96,076	96			9 3/4
90	409,136	108,086	108			11
100	454,596	120,095	120			12 1/4

V. Capacités *(suite)*

Gallons américains	*Litres*	*Gallons britanniques*	*Équivalence britannique* *Gals.*	*Qts.*	*Pts.*	*Oz.*
1	3,785	0,833		3		13 1/4
2	7,571	1,665	1	2	1	6 1/2
3	11,356	2,498	2	3		19 3/4
4	15,141	3,331	3	1		13
5	18,927	4,163	4		1	6
6	22,712	4,996	4	3	1	19 1/4
7	26,497	5,829	5	3		12 3/4
8	30,282	6,661	6	2	1	5 3/4
9	34,068	7,494	7	1	1	19
10	37,853	8,327	8	1		12 1/4
11	41,638	9,159	9		1	5 1/2
12	45,424	9,992	9	3	1	18 3/4
13	49,209	10,825	10	3		12
14	52,994	11,657	11	2	1	5
15	56,780	12,490	12	1	1	18 1/2
16	60,565	13,323	13	1		11 3/4
17	64,350	14,155	14		1	4 3/4
18	68,136	14,988	14	3	1	18
19	71,921	15,821	15	3		11 1/4
20	75,706	16,653	16	2	1	4 1/2
30	113,559	24,980	24	3	1	16 3/4
40	151,412	33,307	33	1		9
50	189,265	41,634	41	2	1	1 1/2
60	227,118	49,960	49	3	1	13 1/2
70	264,971	58,287	58	1		6
80	302,824	66,614	66	2		18 1/4
90	340,678	74,940	74	3	1	10 1/2
100	378,531	83,267	83	1		2 3/4

VI. Température

Degré centigrade	*Degré Fahrenheit*	*Degré centigrade*	*Degré Fahrenheit*
100,0	212,0	40,0	104,0
97,2	207,0	38,9	102,0
95,0	203,0	36,1	97,0
94,4	202,0	35,0	95,0
91,7	197,0	33,3	92,0
90,0	194,0	30,5	87,0
88,9	192,0	30,0	86,0
86,1	187,0	27,8	82,0
85,0	185,0	25,0	77,0
83,3	182,0	22,2	72,0
80,5	177,0	20,0	68,0
80,0	176,0	19,4	67,0
77,8	172,0	16,7	62,0
75,0	167,0	15,0	59,0
72,2	162,0	13,9	57,0
70,0	158,0	11,1	52,0
69,4	157,0	10,0	50,0
66,7	152,0	8,3	47,0

VI. Température *(suite)*

Degré centigrade	*Degré Fahrenheit*	*Degré centigrade*	*Degré Fahrenheit*
65,0	149,0	5,5	42,0
63,9	147,0	5,0	41,0
61,1	142,0	2,8	37,0
60,0	140,0	0,0	32,0
58,3	137,0	– 2,8	27,0
55,5	132,0	– 5,0	23,0
55,0	131,0	– 5,5	22,0
52,8	127,0	– 8,3	17,0
50,0	122,0	– 10,0	14,0
47,2	117,0	– 11,1	12,0
45,0	113,0	– 13,9	7,0
44,4	112,0	– 15,0	5,0
41,7	107,0		

Appendice F : **Tableau des millésimes**

Aucune table de millésimes ne saurait être un guide sûr car on ne peut standardiser les grands vins : produits d'une nature inconstante et d'hommes faillibles. Même par les pires années, n'importe quel secteur offre suffisamment de bouteilles agréables pour que ces exceptions invalident des jugements aussi dogmatiques que ceux qui figurent sur les tables de millésimes. On omet souvent un facteur pourtant capital lorsqu'il s'agit d'acheter des vins : le choix de ceux qui sont arrivés à un degré de vieillissement suffisant pour être consommés sur-le-champ. Souvent les produits des très grandes années ne vieillissent que lentement. Au moment de faire son choix, il importe donc de savoir si on achète du vin à consommer immédiatement ou à mettre en garde pour être bu plus tard.

ÉCHELLE DE VALEURS DES NOTES

20, 19 exceptionnellement grand	14, 13, très bon	7, 6 au-dessous de la moyenne
18, 17 très grand	12, 11, bon	5, 4 médiocre
16, 15 grand	10, 9, 8, passable	3, 2, 1 très médiocre

N.-B. — Bien des vins peuvent être trop vieux pour être consommés actuellement. Tous ceux qui sont dans ce cas sont cotés en italique. Tous les Bordeaux blancs antérieurs à 1961 qui ne sont ni Sauternes, ni Barsac, ni Sainte-Croix-du-Mont, doivent être considérés comme vraisemblablement madérisés.

Millésimes	*Bordeaux rouge*	*Bordeaux blanc*	*Bourgogne rouge (Côte-d'Or*	*Bourgogne blanc*	*Bourgogne rouge (Beaujolais)*	*Rhône*	*Loire*	*Alsace*	*Champagne*
1926	15	*14*	12	*12*	*11*	12	11	12	12
1927	*2*	*6*	*2*	*2*	*3*	7	*5*	*3*	*3*
1928	19,5	17	17	*16*	*17*	16	15	15	19
1929	19	19	19	*19*	*19*	19	*16*	*17*	18
1930	0	0	*4*	*4*	*4*	9	*6*	*4*	*4*
1931	*3*	*2*	*4*	*4*	*3*	*10*	*7*	*5*	*6*
1932	*1*	*1*	*3*	*4*	*5*	*11*	*7*	*5*	*6*
1933	10	*6*	*17*	*16*	*17*	*14*	*14*	*12*	*15*
1934	17	15	17	*16*	*17*	*16*	*15*	*16*	*15*
1935	*5*	*6*	*12*	*13*	*12*	9	*12*	*14*	*11*
1936	*8*	*8*	*8*	*6*	*9*	*14*	9	*10*	*10*
1937	15	18	15	*15*	*13*	*14*	*14*	*17*	*14*
1938	9	*8*	*14*	*13*	*10*	*13*	9	*10*	*12*
1939	*5*	*6*	*3*	*3*	*8*	*10*	*8*	*4*	*8*
1940	8	*9*	*9*	*9*	*8*	9	*8*	*11*	*8*

ÉCHELLE DE VALEURS DES NOTES *(suite)*

Millésimes	*Bordeaux rouge*	*Bordeaux blanc*	*Bourgogne rouge (Côte-d'Or)*	*Bourgogne blanc*	*Bourgogne rouge (Beaujolais)*	*Rhône*	*Loire*	*Alsace*	*Champagne*
1941	2	1	4	4	5	9	7	8	12
1942	12	15	12	15	14	15	11	13	15
1943	14	15	14	15	12	15	16	15	13
1944	11	9	4	5	7	9	7	5	9
1945	19	19	14	17	17	17	17	17	17
1946	8	7	12	9	10	15	10	10	11
1947	19	18	18	17	17	16	19	17	19
1948	15	16	13	10	10	8	10	12	14
1949	18	18	19	16	17	17	16	16	17
1950	14	15	12	18	12	15	10	8	9
1951	9	6	8	8	7	9	7	9	7
1952	15	15	16	16	16	17	14	15	17
1953	19	16	15	14	18	13	17	17	17
1954	12	9	10	11	10	14	10	13,5	10
1955	18	17	17	18	17	16	16	14,5	18
1956	12	10	9	14	9	12	12	10	12
1957	14	13	15	15	15	16	13	14	13
1958	11	13	13	17	13	15	15	14	12
1959	18	17	18	16	16	16	17	18	18
1960	13	13	10	14	10	16	14	13	14
1961	20	19	19	18	19	19	17	19	18
1962	17,5	18	16	16	16	15	16	16	16
1963	8	6	9	11	9	7	9	11	7
1964	16	13	17	15	17	14	15	18	16
1965	11	10	11	11	11	15	10	10	6
1966	18	18	16	16	16	14	15	16,5	18
1967	15	19	14	15	14	16	14	18,5	15
1968	9	7	11	6	11	13	10	10,5	9
1969	13	12	18	17	15	17	15	16	14
1970	18	16	14	16	14	15	15	15	16
1971	17	18	16	16	17	17	14	18,5	17
1972	13	13	14	11	12	15	12	11	12
1973	15,5	13	14	16	13	15	13	15,5	15
1974	14	9	14	15	13	13	13	15	13,5
1975	18,5	18,5	11	14	11	15	15	16	14
1976	17,5	17	17	16	19	17	18	19,5	15,5
1977	14	13	13	14	9	13	10	14	15
1978	18,5	16	18	17	17	18	16	15,5	16,5
1979	18	16	15,5	17	14	17	13	15,5	15
1980	15,5	18	13,5	15	12	14	13	12	13
1981	18	17,5	15	15	17	13	15	17	14
1982	19,5	16	16	17	13	17	14	15	16
1983	19	19,5	17	15	18	18	15	19,5	14
1984	15,5	16	15	16	14	13	13	13	13
1985	19	17	17	16	19	16	16,5	18,5	16
1986	19,5	18	16	17	18	15,5	14	16	13

Nota. – * 10 pour le sec, 13 pour le doux + 13 pour le sec, 19 pour le doux. ** 18 pour le sec, 13 pour le doux. *** 13 pour le sec, 15 pour le doux. □ 16 pour le sec, 18 pour le doux.

Bibliographie

Aaron, Sam, and Beard, James. *How to Eat Better for Less Money*, New York, 1970.

Aaron, Sam, and Fadiman, Clifton. *The Joys of Wine*, New York, 1975.

Adams, Léon D. *The Wines of America*, Boston, 1973.

Allen, H. Warner. *Claret*, Londres 1924 ; *A Contemplation of Wine*, Londres, 1951 ; *A History of Wine*, Londres, 1961 ; *Natural Red Wines*, 1951 ; *Run*, Londres, 1931 ; *Sherry and Port*, Londres, 1954 ; *White Wines and Cognac*, Londres, 1952 ; *The Wines of Portugal*, Londres, 1963 ; New York. 1964.

Ambrosi, Hans. *Wo Grosse Weine Wachsen*, Munich, 1973 ; *Deutscher Wein-Atlas*, Bielefed, 1973 ; *Welt-Atlas des Weines*, Bielefeld, 1983.

Amerine, Maynard A. and Joslyn, Maynard A. *Comercial Production of Table Wines*, Berkeley, 1940 ; *Dessert Appetizer Related Flavored Wines*, Berkeley, 1964 ; *Tables Wines : The Technology of their Production in California*. Berkeley et Los Angeles ; Londres, 1951.

Amerine, Maynard A., Berg, Harod W. and Cruess, William V. *The Technology of Wine Making* (seconde édition), Westport, Connecticut, 1967.

Amerine, Maynard A. and Singleton, Vernon L.*: Wine : An Introduction for Americans*, Berkeley et Los Angeles, 1966.

Anderson, Burton. *Vino : The Wines and Winemarkers of Italy*, Boston, 1980 ; *The Pocket Guide to Italian Wines*, New York,1982.

Balzer, Robert Lawrence. *The Pleasures of Wines*, New York, 1964.

Barbadillo, Manuel. *El Vino de la Alegria*, Jerez de La Frontera, 1951.

Barry, (Sir) Edward. *Wines of the Ancients*, Londres, 1775.

Benvegnin, Lucien, Capt. Émile and Piguet, Gustave. *Traité de Vinification*, (seconde édition) Lausanne, 1951.

Berry, Charles W. *In Search of Wine*, Londres, 1935.

Bertall. *La Vigne : Voyage autour des Vins de France*, Paris, 1878.

Bespaloff, Alexis. *Signet Book of Wine*, New York, 1980 ; *Guide to Inexpensive Wines*, New York, 1973.

Bijur, George. *Wines with Long Noses*, Londres, 1951.

Bode, Charles G. *Wines of Italy* Londres, New York, 1956.

Bourke, Arthur. *Winecraft : The Encyclopaedia of Wines and Spirits*, Londres, 1953.

Bradford, Sarah. *The Englishman's Wine*, Londres, 1969.

Bradley, Robin. *The Small Wineries of Australia*, Melbourne, 1982.

Bréjoux, Pierre. *Les Vins de Loire*, Paris, 1974.

Broedbent, Michael. *The Great Vintage Wine Book*, Londres et New York, 1980 ; *Wine Tasting*, 5e édition, Londres et New York, 1979 ; *The Complete Winetaster and Cellarman*, Londres, 1982, 1984 ;

Pocket Guide to Wine Tasting, Londres, 1982.

Brunet, R. *Dictionnaire d'Œnologie et de Viticulture*, Paris, 1946.

Bürklin, Albert ; Schultz, F.R. ; von Bassermann-Jordan ; von Diersburg, Rœder ; Weingarth, Otto. (Eds.) *Verband Deutscher Naturwein Versteigerer*, 1953.

Butler, Frank Hedges. *Wines and the Wine Lands of the World*, Londres, 1926.

Capus, Joseph. *L'Évolution de la Législation sur les Appellations d'Origine et la Genèse des Appellations Contrôlées*, Paris, 1947.

Carling, T.E. *The Complete Book of Drink*, Londres, 1951.

Carosso, Vincent P. *The California Wine Industry*, 1830-1895 Berkeley and Los Angeles, 1951.

Carter, Youngman. *Drinking Bordeaux*, New York ; Londres 1966.

Casabianca, A. *Guida Storica del Chianti* Florence, 1957.

Cassagnac, Paul de. *Vins de France (French Wines*, Trad. par Guy Knowles), Londres, 1930.

Chappaz, Georges. *Le Vignoble et le Vin de Champagne*, Paris, 1951.

Christie's Wine Publications. *Christies Wine Companion*, Londres, 1981.

Ciais, Adrien ; Quittanson, Charles ; Vanhoutte, René. *La Protection des Appellations d'Origine des Vins et Eaux-de-vie et le Commerce des Vins*, Montpellier, 1949.

Club des Gourmets. *Guía Practica de los Vinos de España*, Madrid, 1983.

Cornelssen, F.A. (Ed.). *Das Buch vom Deutschen Wein*, Mainz, 1954.

Croft-Cooke, Rupert. *Madeira*, Londres, 1961 ;
Port, Londres, 1957 ;
Sherry, Londres, 1955 ; New York ; 1956.

Croxby, Everette. *The vintage Years*, New York, 1973.

De Bosdari, C. *Wines of the Cape* (troisième édition), Cape Town ; Amsterdam ; 1967.

Degroot, Roy A. *The Wines of California*, New York, 1982.

De Kerdéland, Jean. *Historique des vins de France*, Paris, 1964.

Delamain, Robert. *Histoire de Cognac*, Paris, 1935.

Del Castillo, José, and Hallett, David R. *The Wines of Spain*, Bilbao, 1972.

Desgraves, Louis. *Bordeaux au cours des siècles*, Bordeaux, 1954.

Dettori, Renato G. *Vins et liqueurs d'Italie*, Rome, 1953.

Dion, Roger. *Histoire de la Vigne et du Vin de France*, Paris, 1959.

Doléris, J.-A. *Les Vignobles et vins de Béarn*, Pau, 1935.

Dumay, Raymond. *Guide du vin*, Paris, 1968 ;
Les Vins de Loire et les Vins du Jura, Paris, 1979.

Engel, Ferdinand. *Wirtschaftssicherung des österreichischen Weinbaus*, Vienna, 1946.

Enjalbert, Henri. *Histoire de la vigne et du vin*, Paris, 1975 ;
La seigrerie et le vignoble du Château Latour, Bordeaux, 1974.

Evans, Len. *The Australia and New Zealand Complete Book of Wine*, Sydney, 1973.

Eyland, J.M. *Ma Muse en vendanges*, Montpellier, 1960.

Faes, H. (Ed.). *Lexique viti-vinicole international : français, italien, espagnol, allemand*, Paris, 1940.

Faith, Nicholas. *The Winemasters*, Londres, 1978 ;
Château Margaux, Londres, 1980.

Fegan, Patrick W. *Vineyards and Wineries of America*, Brattleboro, Vermont, 1982.

Ferré, Louis. *Traité d'Œnologie Bourguignonne*, Paris, 1958.

Finigan, Robert. *Essentials of Wine*, New York, 1987.

Fisher, M.I. *Liqueurs : Dictionnary and Survey*, Londres, 1959.

Frolov-Gagreev, Anton M. *Ampelografia U.R.S.S.* (7 volumes), Moscou, 1946-1962.

Galet, P. *Cépages et Vignobles de France* (4 volumes), Montpellier, 1956, 1958, 1962, 1964.

George, Rosemay. *Chablis*, Londres, 1984 ;
Guía de los Vinos y Bodegas de Espana, Folio, Barcelone, 1984.

Ginestet, Bernard. *La Bouillie Bordelaise*, Paris, 1975 ;
Côtes de Bourg, Graves, Haut-Médoc, Margaux, Pauillac, Pomerol, St.-Estèphe, St.-Julien, 1984.

Gold, Alec (Ed.). *Wines and Spirits of the World*, Coulsdon, 1972.

Goldschmidt, Eduard (Ed.). *Deutschlands*

Weinbauorte und Weinberglslagen (sixième édition), Mainz, 1951.

Gonzalez Gordon, Manuel M. *Jerez — Xeres — Scheris*, Jerez de la Frontera, 1948.

Grossman, Harold J. *Grossman's Guide to Wines, Spirits and Beers* (édition mise à jour), New York, 1964.

Gunyon, R.E.H. *The Wines of Central and Southeasterne Europe*, New York, 1971.

György, Paul. *The Fine or Germany and all the World's Wine, Lore* Berlin, 1965.

Halasz, Zoltan. *Hungarian Wins Through the Ages*, Budapest, 1962.

Hallgarten, S.F. *Rhineland, Wineland*, 1951 ;
Alsace and Its Wine Gardens (édition mise à jour), Londres, 1965.

Harrison, Godfrey. *Bristol Cream*, Londres, 1955.

Hazan, Victor. *Italian Wine*, New York, 1982.

Healy, Maurice. *Stay Me with Flagons*, Londres, 1963.

Hedrick, Ulysses P. *The Grapes of New York*, Albany, 1908 ;
Grapes and Wines from Home Vineyards, New York, 1945.

Heinen, Winifried. *Rheinpfalz : Gesamtwerk Deutscher Wein*, Essen, 1980.

Henderson, Alexander L. *The History of Ancient and Modern Wines*, Londres, 1824.

Higounet, Charles. *Histoire de l'Aquitaine*, Toulouse, 1973.

Hyams, Edward. *Dionysos, A Social History of the Wine Vine*, Londres, 1965.

Ibar, Leandro. *El Libro del Vino*, Barcelone, 1982.

Isnard , Hildebert. *La Vigne en Algérie* (2 volumes), Gap, 1951-1954.

Jacquelin, Louis et Poulain, René. *Vins et Vignobles de France*, Londres/New York, 1962.

Jacques-Petit. F. *Les Appellations des Vins et Eaux-de-vie de France*, Angers, 1957.

James, Walter. *Wine in Australia* (nouvelle édition), Melbourne, 1963 ;
A World Bookof Wine, Londres, 1959, New York, 1960.

Jeffs, Julian. *Sherry*, Londres, 1961.

Johson, Hugh. *Wine*, Londres, 1966 ; *World Atlas of Wine*, Londres, 1977 ; New York, 1979, 1985 ;
Pocket Encyclopedia of Wine, ed. rev. Londres et New York, 1985 ;
The Atlas or German Wines, Londres, 1986.

Jones, Idwall. *Vines in the Sun*, New York, 1949.

Jung, Hermann. *Wein in der Kunst*, Munich, 1961.

Kaufman, William. *Champagne*, New York, 1973 ;
Pocket Encyclopedia of California Wines, San Francisco, 1982.

Keller, D. Joseph (Ed.) *Pfalzwein Almanach*, Neustadt, 1953.

Kittel, J.B. and Breider, Hans. *Das Buch vom Frankenweine*, Würzburg, 1958.

Kraemer, Ado. *Im Lande des Bocksbeutels* (troisième édition), Würzburg, 1961.

Krug, Henri et Rémi. *L'Art du Champagne*, Éd. Robert Laffont, Paris, 1979.

Laffet, H.E. *The Wine Industry of Australia*, Adelaïde, 1949.

Lafforgue, Germain. *Le Vignoble Girondin*, Paris. 1947.

Lafon, René ; Lafon, Jean ; Couillaud, Pierre. *Le Cognac : sa distillation* (quatrième édition), Paris, 1964.

Langenbach, Alfred. *German Wines and Vines*, Londres, 1962 ;
The Wines of Germany, Londres, 1951.

Larmat, Louis, (Ed.). *Atlas de la France Vinicole*, Les Vins de Bourgogne, Paris 1953 ;
Les Vins des Côtes du Rhône, Paris, 1943.

Layton, T.A. *Wines of Italy*, Londres, 1961.

Lebensfreude aus Rheinhessen (Collection d'articles), Mainz, 1954.

Léon-Gauthier, Pierre. *Les Clos de Bourgogne*, Beaune, 1931.

Lichine, Alexis. *Wines of France* (nouvelle édition), New York, 1951 ; Londres, 1969 ;
Les vins et vignobles de France,Éd. Robert Laffont, Paris, 1979, 1982, 1984, 1986.

Lucia, Salvatore P. *Wine as Food and Medicine*, New York ; Toronto, 1954 ;
A History of Wine as Therapy, Philadelphie et Montreal, 1963.

Lutz, H.F. *Viticulture and Brewing in the Ancient Orient*, Leipzig, New York, 1922.

Magistocchi, Gaudencio. *Tratado de Œnologia adaptado a la Republica Argentina*, Buenos Aires, 1955.

Malvezin, F. *Histoire de la Vigne et du Vin en Aquitaine*, Bordeaux, 1919.

Marchou, Gaston. *Bordeaux sur la Règne de la Vigne*, Bordeaux, 1941.
Marrison, L.W. *Wines and Spirits*, Londres, 1957.
Massee, William E. *Wines and Spirits, a Complete buying Guide*, New York, 1961.
Mayne, Robert, et les autres. *The Great Australian Wine book*, Nouvelle Galles du Sud, 1985.
Meinhard, Heinrich. *German Wines*, Londres, 1971.
Melville, John. *Guide to California Wines* (seconde édition), San Carlos California, 1960.
Mendelsohn, Ocar A. *The Earnest Drinker*, Londres, 1950.
Michel, Francisque. *Histoire du Commerce et de la Navigation à Bordeaux*, Bordeaux, 1867-1870.
Moore, Rodrigo Alvarado. *Chile, Tierra del Vino*, Santiago, 1985.
Morrix, Dennis. *The French Vineyards*, Londres, 1958.
Mouillefert, P. *Les Vignobles et les Vins de France et de l'Étranger*, Paris, 1891.
Muir, Augustus (Ed.). *How to Choose and Enjoy Wine*, Londres, 1953.
Müller, Karl. *Weinbau-Lexikon für Winzer, Weinhändler, Küfer une Gastwirte*, Berlin, 1930.
Office International de la Vigne et du Vin. *Lexique de la Vigne et du Vin : Français, Italiano, España, Deutsch, Portugues, English, Russk*, Paris, 1963.
Olney, Richard. *Iquem*, Suisse, 1985.
Pacottet, Paul and Guittonneau, L. *Vins de Champagne et Vins Mousseux*, Paris, 1930.
Parker, Robert Jnr. *Bordeaux*. New York, 1986.
Penning-Rowsell, Edmund. *The Wines of Bordeaux*, Londres, 1969 et 1979.
Peppercorn, David. *Bordeaux*, Londres, 1982 ;
Pocket Guide to the Wines of Bordeaux, London, 1986.
Perold, A. I. *A Treatise on Viticulture*, Londres, 1927.
Pestel, H. *Les Vins et Eaux-de-vie à appellations d'origine Contrôlées en France*, Mâcon, 1959.
Peynaud, Émile. *Le goût du vin*, Paris, 1980 ;
Œnologie pratique, connaissance et travail du vin, Paris, 1971 et 1981.
Pijassou, René. *Le Médoc*, Paris, 1980.
Ponsot, Maurice (Ed.). *Vins, Alcools et Spiritueux de France* (troisième édition), Paris, 1949.
Postgate, Raymond. *An Alphabet of Choosing and Serving Wine*, Londres, 1955 ;
The Plain Man's Guide to Wine, Londres, 1951.
Poupon, Pierre and Forgeot, Pierre. *Les Vins de Bourgogne* (nouvelle édition), Paris, 1964 et 1977 ;
Quelques Aspects du problème viti-vinicole luxembourgeois, Luxembourg, 1956.
Rainbird, George. *Sherry and the Wines of Spain*, Londres, 1966.
Ray, Cyril. *The Wines of Italy*, Londres ; New york, 1966.
Read, Jan. *The Wines of Spain and Portugal*, Londres, 1977 ;
Guide to the Wines of Portugal, Londres, 1978 ;
The Wines of Portugal, Londres, 1982 ;
The Wines of Spain, Londres, 1982 ;
Pocket Guide to Spanish Wines, Londres, 1983.
Reddings, Cyrus. *A History and Description of Modern Wines*, Londres, 1833 ;
French Wines and Vineyards, Londres, 1860.
Rendu, Victor. *Ampélographie française*, Paris, 1857.
Renouil, Yves. *Dictionnaire du Vin*, Bordeaux, 1962.
Ribereau-Gayon, Jean et Peynaud, Émile. *Traité d'Œnologie* (2 volumes), Paris, 1960.
Robb, J. Marshall. *Scotch Whisky*. Londres ; Édimbourg ; New York, 1950.
Rodier, Camille. *Le Vin de Bourgogne* (troisième édition), Dijon, 1948.
Roncarati, Bruno. D.O.C. *The New Image for Italian Wines*, Londres, 1971 ;
Viva Vino, D.O.C. *Wines of Italy*, Londres, 1976.
Roudie, Philippe. *Le Vignoble Bordelais*, Toulouse, 1973.
Roupnel, Gaston. *La Bourgogne*, Paris, 1946.
Rozet, Georges. *La Bourgogne Tastevin en main*, Paris, 1949.
Rudd, Hugh R. *Hocks and Moselles* (Constable's Wine Library), Londres, 1935.
Saintsbury, George. *Notes on a Cella-Book*, Londres 1920, 1963 ; New York, 1933.
Sandeman, Sons & Company, Ltd., George G. *Port and Sherry*, Londres, 1955.

Saunders, Peter. *A Guide to New Zealand Wine*, Auckland, 1982.

Schoonmaker. Franck. *Encyclopédia of Wine* (éd. rév.), New York, 1973 ;
The Wines of Germany (nouvelle édition), New York, 1966.

Schoonmaker, and Marvel, Tom. *American Wines*, New York, 1941 ;
The Complete Wine Book, New York, 1934 ;
Londres, 1935.

Scott, J.M. *Vineyards of France*, Londres, 1950.

Seely, James. *Great Bordeaux Wines*, Londres, 1986.

Seltman, Charles. *Wines in the Ancient World*, Londres, 1957.

Shand, P. Morton. *A book of French Wines*, Londres, 1960 ;
A book of Other Wines than French, Londres, 1929.

Simon, André L. *Champagne*, Londres ; New York, 1962 ;
The Commonsense of Wine, Londres, 1966 ;
Concise Encyclopaedia of Gastronomy (section VIII), Londres, 1946 ;
A Dictionary of Wines, Spirits and Liqueurs, Londres, 1958 ;
Known your Wines, Londres, 1956 ;
A Wine of the World, Londres, 1949.

Simon, Andrél. and Hallgarten, S.E. *The Great Wines of Germany*. Londres, New York, 1963.

Stein, Gottfried : *Reise durch di Deutschen Weigärten*, Munich, 1957.

Street, Julian L. *Wines* (troisième édition). New York, 1961.

Sutcliffe, Serena. *André Simon's Wines of the World*, 2ᵉ éd., Londres, New York, 1981 ;
Pocket Guide to the Wines of Burgundy, New York, 1986.

Thompson, Robert (Ed.). *California Wine*, Menlo Park, 1973.

Thorpy, Frank T. *Wine in New Zealand*, Auckland, 1971.

Thudichum, John L.W. and Dupré, August. *A Treatise on the Origin, Nature and Varieties of Wine*, New York, 1872.

Todd, W.J. *Tokay-Hegyalia*, Pest, 1867 ;
Port, Londres, 1926.

Torres, Miguel A. *Wines and Vineyards of Spain*, San Francisco, 1982 ;
Vino Español, un incerto futuro, Barcelone, 1978 ;
Los Vinos de España, Barcelone, 1983.

Tovey, Charles. *Wines and Wine Countries*, Londres, 1862.

Tucker, T. G. *Life in Ancient Athens*, Londres, 1912.

Union Générale de Syndicats pour la Défense des Grands Vins de Bourgogne. *Décrets définissant les Vins à Appellation d'Origine Contrôlée de la Région de Bourgogne*, Nuit-Saint-Georges, 1944.

Valente-Perfeito, J.C. *Let's Talk about Port*, Oporto, 1948.

Veronelli, Luigi. *I Vini d'Italia*, Londres, 1964.

Viala, Pierre et Vermorel, Victor. *Traité Général de Viticulture* (7 volumes), Paris, 1901-1910.

Wagner, Philip M. *American Wines and Wine-Marking*, New York, 1956 ;
A Wine-Crower's Guide (nouvelle édition), New York, 1965.

Wasserman, Sheldon. *The Wines or Italy. A consumer Guide*, New York, 1976 ;
The Wines of the Côtes du Rhône, New York, 1977.

Waugh, Alec. *In Praise of Wine*, Londres, 1959.

Weeks, C. C. *Modern Science and Alcoholic Beverages*, Manchester, 1921.

Weiss, Harry B. *The History of Applejack or Apple Brandy in New Jersey from Colonial Times to the Present*, Trenton, 1954.

Wilkinson, P. W. *First Steps in Ampelography* (1900) ;
Nomenclature of Australian Wines (1919).

Wilson, Rev. A. M. *Wines of the Bible*, Londres, 1877 ;
A Brief Discourse on Wines, Londres, 1961.

Wine and Spirit Trade Record. *Clarets and Sauternes*, Londres, 1920.

Winkler, Albert J. *General Viticulture*, Berkeley et Los Angeles, 1962.

Winroth, Jon. *Wine as you like it*, Neuilly, France, 1981.

Woon, Basil. *The Big Little Wines of France*, Londres, 1972.

Woutaz, Fernand. *Le Grand Livre des Confréries des vins de France*, Paris, 1971.

Xandri Tagüena, J. M. *Élaboration de Aguardientes Simples, Compuestos y Licores*, Barcelone, Madrid, 1958.

Yoxall, H. W. *The Wines of Burgundy*, Londres, 1968.

Zraly, Kevin, *Complete Wine Course*, New York, 1985.

Saunders, Peter. *A Guide to New Zealand Wine*, Auckland, 1982.
Schoonmaker, Frank. *Encyclopedia of Wine* (éd. rév.), New York, 1973.
The Wines of Germany (nouvelle édition), New York, 1980.
Schoonmaker, and Marvel, Tom. *American Wines*, New York, 1941.
The Complete Wine Book, New York, 1934 ;
Londres, 1935.
Scott, J.M. *Vineyards of France*, Londres, 1950.
Seely, James. *Great Bordeaux Wines*, Londres, 1986.
Seltman, Charles. *Wine in the Ancient World*, Londres, 1957.
Shand, P. Morton. *A Book of French Wines*, Londres, 1960 ;
A Book of Other Wines than French, Londres, 1929.
Simon, André L. *Champagne*, Londres, New York, 1962 ;
The Commonsense of Wine, Londres, 1966 ;
Concise Encyclopedia of Gastronomy (section VIII), Londres, 1946 ;
A Dictionary of Wines, Spirits and Liqueurs, Londres, 1958 ;
Know Your Wines, Londres, 1956 ;
Wines of the World, Londres, 1967.
Simon, André, and Hallgarten, S.F. *The Great Wines of Germany*, Londres, New York, 1963.
Stein, Gottfried. *Kreuzweg des Deutschen Weinbaues*, Munich, 1957.
Street, Julian. *Wines* (troisième édition), New York, 1961.
Sutcliffe, Serena. *André Simon's Wines of the World*, 2e éd., Londres, New York, 1981 ;
Pocket Guide to the Wines of Burgundy, New York, 1986.
Thompson, Robert (Ed.). *California Wine*, Menlo Park, 1973.
Thorpy, Frank. L. *Wine in New Zealand*, Auckland, 1971.
Thudichum, John L.W., and Dupré, August. *A Treatise on the Origin, Nature and Varieties of Wine*, New York, 1872.
Todd, W. J. *Port, How to Buy, Serve, Store and Drink It*, Londres, 1926.
Torres, Miguel A. *Wines and Vineyards of Spain*, San Francisco, 1982 ;
Vino Español, un nuevo futuro, Barcelone, 1983 ;
Los Vinos de España, Barcelone, 1983.
Tovey, Charles. *Wine and Wine Countries*, Londres, 1862.
Tucker, T. G. *Life in Ancient Athens*, Londres, 1911.
Union Générale de Syndicats pour la Défense des Grands Vins de Bourgogne. *Décrets définissant les Vins à Appellation d'Origine Contrôlée de la Région de Bourgogne*, Mâcon-Saint-Georges, 1944.
Valente-Perfeito, J.C. *Let's Talk about Port*, Oporto, 1948.
Veronelli, Luigi. *I Vini d'Italia*, Londres, 1964.
Viala, Pierre et Vermorel, Victor. *Traité Général de Viticulture* (7 volumes), Paris, 1901-1910.
Wagner, Philip M. *American Wines and Wine-Making*, New York, 1956 ;
A Wine-Grower's Guide (nouvelle édition), New York, 1965.
Wasserman, Sheldon. *The Wines of Italy. A consumer Guide*, New York, 1976 ;
The Wines of the Côtes du Rhône, New York, 1977.
Waugh, Alec. *In Praise of Wine*, Londres, 1959.
Weeks, C. C. *Modern Science and Alcoholic Beverages*, Manchester, 1921.
Weiss, Harry B. *The History of Applejack or Apple Brandy in New Jersey from Colonial Times to the Present*, Trenton, 1954.
Wilkinson, P. W. *First Steps in Ampelography* (1900) ;
Nomenclature of Australian Vines (1901).
Wilson, Rev. A. M. *Wines of the Bible*, Londres, 1877 ;
A Brief Discourse on Wines, Londres, 1861.
Wine and Spirit Trade Record. *Clarets and Sauternes*, Londres, 1920.
Winkler, Albert J. *General Viticulture*, Berkeley et Los Angeles, 1962.
Wise, John. *Wine as you like it*, Neuilly, France, 1961.
Woon, Basil. *The Big Little Wines of France*, Londres, 1972.
Woutaz, Fernand. *Le Grand Livre des Confréries des vins de France*, Paris, 1971.
Xandri Tavera, J. M. *Elaboración de Aguardientes Simples, Compuestos y Licores*, Barcelone, Madrid, 1958.
Yoxall, H. W. *The Wines of Burgundy*, Londres, 1968.
Zraly, Kevin. *Complete Wine Course*, New York, 1985.

Remerciements

Une œuvre aussi considérable n'aurait pu être réalisée sans l'assistance bienveillante et éclairée de personnes, institutions et associations qui s'identifient de mille manières avec les vins et spiritueux du monde entier.

J'entends d'abord remercier mes anciens assistants et les autres membres d'Alexis Lichine & Co ainsi que toutes les autres personnes qui ont collaboré à cette tâche, pour leur aide constante, en particulier, l'Honorable Julian Grenfell, Peter C. Handler, Philip I. Togni, Anthony Wood, Harold Jurgenson, Paul Zuckerman, Parker R. Reis, Martin Sinkoff, Katie Philson et le professeur Luccio P. Ruotola, Dominique Gayou, Élisabeth Schuman, Suzanne McEvoy, Catherine Currie, Jane Kettlewell et Élisabeth Lafargue.

Je suis profondémment reconnaissant envers tous ceux qui sont énumérés ci-dessous et à tous ceux qui ne figurent pas ici mais qui m'ont fourni données et informations indispensables sous forme de documents et brochures.

CHAPITRES PRÉLIMINAIRES

Dr Maynard A. Amerine, Department of Viticulture and Enology, University of California, Davis, California.
Feu James A. Beard, New York, auteur de *The Fireside Cookbook* et *Fish Cookery*.
Dr Charles A. Fox, New York.
Dr Herbert L. Gould, New York.
Dr Charles P. Mathé, San Francisco, Chairman of Board of Governors, The Society of Medical Friends of Wine.
Dr E. Peynaud, de la Station œnologique de Bordeaux.
Sénateur Professeur Georges Portmann de Bordeaux.

ENSEMBLE DU TEXTE

Sam Aaron, Sherry-Lehman, New York.
Leon Adams, Sausalito.
Mr. Agostini, I.N.A.O., Paris.
Rafael Aguilar, Spanish Embassy Commercial Office.
Samin Aksu, Forschungsinstitut des Turkischen.
Marcel Allard, Société des Alcools de Québec, Montréal.
José Duarte Amaral, Président, Junta Nacional do Vinho, Lisbonne.
Dr Hans Ambrosi, Eltville, Allemagne de l'Ouest.
E.C. Anagurstopoulos, Ambassade royale de Grèce, Londres.
E.T. Andersen, Vineland Station, Ontario.
José Ramón Garcia de Angulo, Président du Consejo Regulator, Jerez.
Abdelâziz, Ariji, Maroc.
Patricia Armstrong, Edimbourg.
Richard L. Arrowood, Sonoma, Californie.
Luigi Artusio, de la Stabilimento Fontanafredda.
Gerald Asher, Monterey Vineyard, San Francisco.
Prof. Dr Á. Asvány, Budapest.
Dr A. Asváry, Directeur, Institut des Recherches Viti-Vinicoles, Budapest.
Australian Wine Board.

S.P. Avakiants, Professeur, Institut des Industries Alimentaires, Moscou.
Raul Azparren, President, Camara de Comercio del Estado Lara, Barquisimeto.
André Balaresque, courier en vins, Bordeaux.
Fernando Aujusto Bandeira, la Casa do Douro, Regua.
Manuel Barbadillo, Sanlucar des Barrameda.
Jean-Luc Barbier, C.I.C.V., Épernay.
Catherine Bardy, Ambassade de France, New York.
M et Mme J.G. Barett, Felsted, Essex
Hayim S. Bar-Shai, Jerusalem.
Joseph Bartolo, Ambassade de Malte, Paris.
Dr Friedrich von Bassermann-Jordan, Deidesheim.
Joseph Baum,New York.
Ed Beard, St Helena, Californie.
Jean Beliard, Paris.
Comte Hubert de Beaumont autrefois de Château Latour, Pauillac.
Feu Son Excellence Joseph Bech, ancien premier ministre, Grand-Duché de Luxembourg.
Richard O. Becker, Northminster Winery, Wilmington, Delaware.
Alexis Bespaloff, New York.
Lennart Berenmark, de la Société Aktiebolaget Vin-Spritcentralen, Stockholm.
Alain Berger, I.N.A.O., Paris.
Paul Bergweiler, Bernkastel-Kues.
Cavalier Guglielmo Bertani, Véronne.
G. Biehler, Malaga.
Jochen G. Bielefeld, Deutsche Wein-Information, Main.
Max Bilan, Syndicat patronal des Chambres du Commerce et de l'Industrie Ankara.
Marcel Blanck, Alsace.
H. Blechner, Ambassade d'Autriche, Londres
Tansug Bleda, Délégation Turque à l'O.C.D.E., Paris
R.E. Boillot, Volnay.
D.I. Bonarjee, High Commission of India, Londres.
G.L. Bond, English Vineyards Association Ltd., Londres.
André Bonin, Fédération Internationale des Confréries Bachiques, Paris.
E. Bonvin, Association des Vignerons suisses, Londres.
Feu Sr. Bosch, Président de la Compañia Ron Bacardi, S.A., Santiago de Cuba et de San Juan Puerto Rico.
P.J. Botha, Zuider-Paarl, Afrique du Sud.
Julian Boyd, Princeton, New York.
Pierre Botineau, Bibliothèque Municipale de Bordeaux.
Pierre Bréjoux, de l'I.N.A.O., Paris.
Toni Bromser, Diplom Weinbauinspektor, Staatsweinkellerei, Kloster-Eberbach.
Maître Robert Brouillaud-Vickers, Bâtonnier, Bordeaux et Paris.
David Bruce, New York et Pékin.
Michel Brun, Romanèche-Thorins.
Feu Dr A. Burklin-Wolf, Wachenheim, President de la German Natural Wine Association.
W.D. Burnet, Distillers'Co. Ltd., Edinburg.
W. Bret Byrd, Byrd Vineyard, Myersville, Maryland.
Joachim Cálem, Oporto.
Colin Campbell, New York.
Inspecteur Canal, Institut National des Appellations d'Origine des Vins et Eaux-de-Vie, Armagnac.
Dorothy Cann, Institut Culinaire Française, New York.
Lucio Caputo, Institut Italien du Vin et de l'Alimentation, New York.
Manuel Casanueva, Ambassade du Chili, Paris.
Mario Castagna, Italian Trade Commission, New York.
R.E. Dejean de Castillo, Ambassade d'Argentine, Londres.
Dr J. Cavadias, de l'Ambassade de Grèce, Paris, Délégué à l'Office International du Vin.
Mlle Chabert, Présidente de la Cave Coopérative, Fleurie.
C. Chaillot, I.N.A.O., Paris.
Feu Georges S. Chappaz, Institut National des Appellations d'Origine des Vins et Eaux-de-Vie, Paris.
Pierre Chauveau, Cognac.
Chérif Chikhi, Ambassade d'Algérie, Washington.
Miss M. Clark, F. & E. May, Londres.
Guy Cloutier, Québec.
Ralph H. Cobbold, Director, Justerini and Brooks, Ltd., Londres.
Santiago Coello, Consejo Regulador, Rioja.
Aldo Contemo, Monteforte d'Alba, Piémont.
H.K.H. Cook, Australian Government Trade Commission, New York.

Henri Coquillaud, Directeur du Bureau National Interprofessionnel du Cognac.
Philippe Cottin, Pauillac.
Pierre Couillaud, centre vinicole, Cognac.
Jean Crettenand, Station Fédérale de Recherches Agronomiques de Changins, Nyon, Suisse.
Dr P. Cspregi, Budapest.
F. Jiménez Cuende, Madrid.
Feu Prof. Dalmasso, université de Turin et de l'Office international du vin.
Paul Damiens, conseiller technique de l'I.N.A.O.
N. Danilatos, Institut du Vin, Ministère de l'Agriculture, Athènes.
Virgilio Augusto Dantas, Lisbonne.
J. Dargent, Comité Interprofessionnel du Vin de Champagne, Épernay.
C.V. Dayns, New Zealand House, Londres.
Jean Delamain, Jarnac.
Jean Delmas, Président de Château Haut-Brion et directeur du Château-Brion.
G. Despagne, Président du Syndicat Viticole de Montagne St-Émilion.
Leonard A.T. Dennis, ex-Director, Grants of St. James', Bass Charrington Wintners, Londres.
Stanley Dennis, Director, Grants of St. James', Londres.
Marie-José Deshayes, O.I.V., Paris.
Deutsche Weinsiegel-Gesellschaft, Francfort.
Jorge D. Dias, Casa de Portugal, Londres.
Mauricio González Diez of Jerez.
J. Dolezal, Pilsner Urquell Co Ltd., Londres.
Beltrán Domecq, autrefois des Ets Williams et Humbert, Jerez de la Frontera.
José Ignacio Domecq, Ets Pedro Domecq, Jerez de la Frontera.
Brahim Douaouri, Directeur Général, Institut de la Vigne et du Vin, Alger.
Matthew W. Downer, Brown-Forman Distillers Corporation, Louisville, Kentucky.
Robert Drouhin, Beaune.
Georges Dubœuf, Romanèche-Thorins.
Feu Pierre J. Dubos, Château Cantemerle, Macau-Médoc.
Jean Ducamin, Secrétaire Général, Union des Coopératives de Bas-Armagnac Réans.
Jean Durup, Chablis.
Nico van Duyvenbode, Ottawa.
M. Eltaiej, Tunisie.
Jakob Graf zu Eltz, Eltville.
F.O. Emery, Londres.
Feu René Engel, Vosne-Romanée.
Mogador Empson, Londres.
Neil Empson, Milan, Italie.
André Enders, Directeur du C.I.V.C., Épernay.
J. Escoffier, Syndicat Général des Vignerons des Côtes du Ventoux.
M. Espinosa, Ambassade du Mexique, Paris.
H.B. Estrada, Président, Bacardi Imports, Inc., New York.
Len Evans, Sydney, Australia.
R.L. Exshaw, of John Jameson and Son, Ltd., Dublin.
Julio Faesler, Ambassade du Mexique, Londres.
Federal Press Service, Vienna.
J. Ferlay, Fédération des Syndicats de Producteurs de Chateauneuf-du-Pape.
Richard Figiel, Eastern Grape Growers and Winery News, Watkins Glen, New York.
Robert E. Fillet, U.S. China Chamber of Commerce, Washington, D.C.
Robert C. Finegan (Ed), *Finegan's Private Guide to Wine,* New York.
R.W. Finlayson, President, Toronto Wine and Food Society, Toronto (Ontario, Canada).
Don A. Fisher, Distilled Spirits Institute, New York.
Sir Guy Fison, Londres.
Peter Fleck, Zuider-Paarl, Afrique du Sud.
G.S. Foulds, Australian Wine Centre, Londres.
Georges Fouqier, courtier en vins, Bordeaux.
J. Fourcaud-Laussac, Château Cheval Blanc, Saint-Émilion.
M. Franchini-Netto, Ambassade du Brésil.
H.A.S. Fraser, Association des Distillateurs canadiens, Montréal.
M. Friedas, Office International du Vin, Paris.
Comte Gelasio Gaetani Lovatelli, Montalcino.
Angelo Gaja, Barbaresco, Piémont.
Edoardo Gancia, Directeur, Ets Gancia and Compagny, Canelli.
Fernando Garcia-Delgado, Consejo Regulador, Jerez de la Frontera.
Jean Gardère, Rhum Barbancourt, Haïti.
Jean-Paul Gardère, Château Latour.
Anna Gariazzo, Milan, Italie.
Prof. Pier G. Garoglio, Instituto di Industrie Agrarie, université de Florence.
Dr E. Ercole Garrone, Directeur du Consorzio, Asti.

Philippe Gasqueton, administrateur, Château Calon-Ségur, Saint-Estèphe.
Ing. C. Gavaneanu, Ambassade de Roumanie, Paris.
Gilbey Distillers & Vintners, Stellenbosch, Afrique du Sud.
Bernard Ginestet, Margaux.
Pierre Ginestet, ex-propriétaire du Château Margaux, Margaux.
Leftaris Glinavos, Union Nationale des Œnologues Grecs, Athènes.
Jean Godet, La Rochelle.
Pierre Goffre-Viaud, Contrôleur de l'I.N.A.O.
Graig Goldwyn, *International Wine Review*, Ithaca, New York.
Manuel Gonzalez Gordon, Jerez de la Frontera.
Feu Henri Gouges, Président de l'Association des vignerons de Bourgogne, Nuits-Saint-Georges.
G. Maxwell A. Graham, Oporto (Porto).
John A. Grant, Dumbarton, Écosse.
A.O. Grass, Canadian wine Institute, Ontario.
Feu Comte Matuschka V. Greiffenclau, de Schloss Volrads, ex-Président de l'Association des Vignerons allemands.
Feu Franz Greis, Bernkastel-Kues.
Feu Lord Grenfell, Londres.
Louis Gros et Fils, Vosne-Romanée.
Lester Gruber, Detroit.
Herman Guntrum, des Ets Weingut Louis Guntrum, Nierstein.
R.E.H. Gunyon, Sandwich, Kent.
Susan Hall, Powis, Pays de Galles.
Hassine Hammami, Chef de la Division Économique et Technique, Office du Vin, Tunis.
Bernard Haramboure, Pauillac.
A.J. Hasslacher, M.C., Madeira Association, Londres.
J. Hasting-Trew, ancien membre de la Cyprus Viticultural Board, Londres.
Thomas Heeter, Château Nairac, Sauternes.
Maurice Hennessy, Cognac.
Dr. Eva Herpay, Budapest.
Bernard Hine, Jarnac.
Feu François Hine, Jarnac.
Robert Hine, Jarnac.
P. Höhl, Section de la Viticulture et de l'Économie vinicole, Division de l'Agriculture, Berne.
J.H. Hopkins, John Jameson & Son, Ltd., Dublin.
Gaston Huet, Vouvray.
Jean Hugel, Riquewihr, Alsace.
Dr. Augusto Ippoliti, Florence.
Dr. Lorenzetto B.R. Luigi Ispettore, Consorzio de Chianti, Florence.
Carlos Garcia Izquierdo, Instituto Nacional de Denominaciones de Origen, Madrid.
Gérard Jaboulet, Tain l'Hermitage, Vallée du Rhône.
Michel Jaboulet-Vercherre, Pommard,
Julius L. Jacobs, San Francisco.
Pierre Janneau, Condom.
Japan Winiry Association, Tokyo.
Douglas Jooste, Vice-Président des Ets J. Sedgwick & Co. Ltd., Cape Town, Afrique du Sud.
Prue Judd, Ambassade de Grande-Bretagne, Paris.
Peter Jurgens, ex-Président, Almadén Vineyards, Sans Francisco.
The Honorable Kenneth Keating, Ambassade des États-Unis, Tel-Aviv.
Alfred A. Knopf, New York.
C. Kok, Stellenbosch, Afrique du sud.
Professor Kosinsky, Professeur de Viticulture, université de l'Agriculture, Budapest.
E. Kovalcicovà, Bratislava, Tchécoslovaquie.
Paul C. Kovi.
Vladimir Kovac, Novi Sad, Yougoslavie.
Édouard Kressmann, Bordeaux.
René Kuehn, Ammerschwihr.
Henry Lacoste, ancien Président, Syndicat Régional des Courtiers des Vins et Spiritueux de Bordeaux, de la Gironde et du Sud-Ouest.
M. Lahlon, Office marocain d'Exportations.
John W. Laird, New York.
Cathy Laloubère, Bordeaux.
Douglas Lamb, Sidney, Australie.
René Lambert, Bordeaux.
Don Antonio Larrea, chef de la station viticole de Haro, Rioja.
Louis Latour, Aloxe Corton.
L. Lavadoux, Centre de Recherches Agronomiques, Bordeaux.
Daniel Lawton, Bordeaux.
Hugues Lawton, Bordeaux.
Jerome J. Lehrer, Swiss Wine Bureau, New York.
Patrick Léon, Bordeaux.
Feu Baron LeRoy de Boiseaumarié, Châteauneuf-du-Pape, Président de l'Institut National des Appellations d'Origine des Vins et Eaux-de-Vie.

Raymond LeSauvage, Président du Syndicat des courtiers en vins de Bordeaux.
Henri Levèque, courtier en vins, Podensac, Gironde.
Juan Lewis, Beverage Testing Institute, Ithaca, New York.
José Joaquim da Costa Lima, Directeur de l'Institut du vin de Porto, Oporto.
O. Lindo, J. Wray et Naphew, Ltd., Kingston, Jamaïque.
Brett T. Lineham, New Zealand Trade Commission, New York.
Charles Loinger, Israel Wine Institute, Rehovot.
Feu Madame Edmond Loubat, Château Pétrus, Pomerol.
M. Luciano, Ambassade d'Italie, Paris.
Mlle Gesa Lundemann, Madrid.
Comte Alexandre de Lur-Saluces.
Feu Marquis de Lur-Saluces, Château d'Yquem, Sauternes.
André Lurton, Bordeaux.
Alexander McNally, New York.
M. Macici, Directeur Scientifique, Station Expérimentale, Prahova, Roumanie.
M. Maby,
Gérard Magrin, Comité Interprofessionnel des Vins des Côtes du Rhône.
Karel Masek, de Tchécoslovaquie, Cavaliere Capurso Marino, Consorzio de Vérone.
Feu Ed. Marjary, régisseur, Château Mouton-Rothschild, Pauillac.
Michel Firino Martell, Cognac.
John Marshall, Minnesota Grape Growers Association, Lake City.
Henri Martin, ex-président, Comité Interprofessionnel des Vins de Bordeaux, maire de Saint-Julien.
Gil Pires Martins, Vice-Président, Junta Nacional di Vinho, Lisbonne.
J.P. Mas, de l'I.N.A.O. à Bordeaux et Angers.
Diana Masieri, New York.
Sarah Matters, Bath, United Kingdom.
Egon Mauer, régisseur, Langwerth von Simmern, Eltville.
Fred May, Londres.
Roberto Mazzi, Negrar, Vénétie.
Abel Médard, Directeur, Comité Interprofessionnel du Vin de Champagne. Épernay.
D. Homen de Mello, Lisbonne.
E. Menia, O.N.C.V., Alger.
Pierre Meslier, régisseur, Château d'Yquem, Sauternes.
Prince P. von Metternich, de Schloss Johannisberg.
Dr. Franz Werner Michel, Deutsches Weininstitut, Mainz.
Ministère de l'Agriculture, Vienne.
Wallace Milroy, Londres.
Robert Mondavi, des Ets C. Mondavi and Sons, et de Charles Krug Winery, Napa, Californie.
Feu Duc Pierre de Montesquiou-Fezensac, Château de Marsan, Auch.
Renato Mora, Consultat du Chili, New York.
Christian Moueix, Libourne.
Jean-Pierre Moueix, Libourne.
Margaret Mountford, Australian Wine and Brandy Corporation, Adelaïde.
M. Ingéneiur Mujbaba, Directeur, Station Expérimentale, Constanza, Roumanie.
João Nicolau de Almeida, Vila Nova de Gaia, Portugal.
Dr. Antonio Niederbacher, Unione Italiana Vini, Milan.
Robert Niederman, Ica, Pérou.
Milos Nikolic, Yugoslav Information Center, New York.
Peter Nomikos, Santorini, Londres.
Ventura Nuñez, Felix Ruiz Y Ruiz, Jerez, Espagne.
Dr. Giorgio Odero, Propriétaire de Frecciarosso, Casteggio.
Président de Oliveira, Junta Nacional do Vinho, Lisbonne.
Alan Olson, German Wine Information Bureau, New York.
ONIVINS, Paris.
Julio Saro Diez Ordõnez, Instituto Nacional de Denominaciones de Origen, Madrid.
Caroline Ourvouai, Office National Interprofessionnel des Vins, Paris.
Raymond-Julien Pagès, Président, Fédération d'Auvergne des Vins et Spiritueux, Clermont-Ferrand.
José de Paiva, Trade Comission of Portugal, Paris.
H.F.M. Palmer, Australian Board, Adelaïde.
M. Paran, Ambassade d'Israël, Londres.
Andrès de Blas Pardilla, Madrid.
Anne-Marie Pargade, Bordeaux.
Colin Parnell, éditeur du *Decanter Magazine*.
Frank R. Passanante, Australien Trade Commission, New York.
Edouardo A. Diaz Peralta, Mendoza, Argentine.

Pierre Perromat, président de l'I.N.A.O. (Institut National de Appellations d'Origine des Vins et Eaux-de-Vie, Paris).
Émile Peynaud (professeur), directeur honoraire du Service de recherches de la Station agronomique et œnologique de Bordeaux, Bordeaux.
Katie Philson, New York.
Sp. Phylaktis, Cyprus Hight Commission, Londres.
Maurizio et Sol Piccioto, Bogota.
Alain Pineau, Bordeaux.
Comte de Poix, Domaine Péraldi, Ajaccio.
Jacques Pomerleau, Ambassade du Canada, Paris.
Bruno Prats, président du Comité des grands crus classés de Bordeaux.
R. Protin, Directeur, Office International du Vin, Paris.
Sebastian Prüm, des Ets Johann Josef Prüm, Wehlen.
Charles Quittanson, ex-directeur de l'inspection des Fraudes.
Renato Ratti, La Morra, Piémont.
Jean de Premio Real, Mexico.
Joachim Ress, Winkel.
Axel du Réau, C.I.V.C., Épernay.
Theodor Rettinger et fils, Wachenheim.
Peter Reynier, J.B. Reynier, Londres.
Dr Guglielmo Ricamdone, Directeur Général, Stabilimento Cinzano, S. Vittoria d'Alba.
Bettino Ricasoli, Florence.
Bertrand de Rivoyre, Ambares et Bordeaux.
Marie-Christine Rizzardi, Bardolino, Vénétie.
Gaspar Roca, Porto Rico.
Comte E. de Rohan-Chabot, Château de Saint-Martin, Taradeaux, Pdt du Syndicat de Défense des Côtes de Provence.
Ed. Rolland, Académie des Vins de Bordeaux et Château Coutet, Barsac.
Dr Bruno Roncarati, Londres.
Jaroslav Rosa, Tchécoslovaquie.
Pedro F. Rosell, Mendoza, Argentine.
Feu Baron Philippe de Rothschild.
Feu Jean-Pierre Rouff.
P. Rouvinet, Bureau Fédéral d'Agronomie, Berne, Suisse.
I.M. Roushdy, République arabe unie.
Alain Rousseau, Château du Cléray, Loire.
Professor Lucio P. Ruotola, de l'Université de Stanford, San Francisco.
Tadashi Sakuda, Suntory, Ltd., Osaka.
Francisco Salamero, Rioja.
Feu Maj. General Guy Salisbury-Jones, Hambledon, Hampshire, England.
Feu Joseph Salzmann, Kaysersberg.
Jean Samalens, Laujuzan.
Manuel Santolalla Lacalle, Consejo Regulador, Montilla-Moriles.
György Sárai, Monimpex, Budapest.
Jean-Ernest Sauvion, Château du Cléray, Loire.
Feu Étienne Sauzet, Puligny-Montrachet.
Noël Sauzet, Jarnac.
Miss Elliseva Sayers, Office d'Information du commerce Portugais, New York.
Jerry Schever, Remich, Luxembourg.
D.V. Schiazzano, Chambre de Commerce italienne, Londres.
Élizabeth Schwartz, *International Wine Review*, Ithaca, New York.
Guy Schyler, Château Lafite, Pauillac.
M.D.L. Scott, Heublein, Inc., Hartford, Connecticut.
R.I.C. Scott-Hayward, Johannesburg.
Tom Seabrook, W. et J. Seabrook, Melbourne.
Maurice Seignour, Président de l'Association des Négociants des Côtes-du-Rhône, Vacqueyras.
Feu Allan H. Sichel, Directeur des Ets Sichel et Compagnie, Bordeaux et Londres.
Peter Allan Sichel, Cantenac.
Peter M.F. Sichel, New York.
Freiherr Langwerth von Simmern, Eltville.
Martin Sinkoff, New York.
Werner Sitzmann, Málaga.
S. Sklar, Londres.
Évangelos Spanidis, Ambassade de Grèce, Paris.
Société d'Agronomie Allemande (D.L.G.), Francfort.
Société Civile de la Romanée-Comti.
Prof. Dr. Steingerg, Directeur du service de recherches et de l'École de Viticulture, Geisenheim.
Jane Stockwood, Londres.
Éric Stonyer, Ambassade de Nouvelle Zélande, Paris.
John Symms, Bass Charrington, Vintners, Londres.
Ing. Miroslav Synak, Bratislava, Tchécoslovaquie.
Syndicat Viticole de Fixin, Bourgogne.
Claude Taittinger, Reims.
Tari Pierre, président des Grands Crus de Bordeaux.
André Tchelistcheff, Napa, Californie.

Dimitri Tchelistcheff, Bodegas de Santo Thomas, Ensenada.
Richard et William Teltscher, Londres.
Jacques Théo, ex-Président Directeur Général Alexis Lichine & Co., Bordeaux, et ex-Président du C.I.V.B., Bordeaux.
H. Grégory Thomas, Grand maître Commanderie de Bordeaux, New York.
Carmel J. Tintle, Schenley Industrie, Inc, New York.
Dr. K.S. Tiwari, Directorate General et Technical Development, New Delhi.
Georgi Toromanov, Sophia, Bulgarie.
Miguel Torres, Barcelone, Espagne.
Jules Tourmeau, I.N.A.O., Dijon.
Nicolas Trambitsky, Paris.
Louis Trapet, Gevrey-Chambertin.
H. Vella, Pauillac.
Feu Jean Vermorel, Vaux-en-Beaujolais.
A. et P. de Villaine, Bougeron, Sâone-et-Loire.
Philip Wagner, Propriétaire, Boordy Vineyard, Riderwood, Maryland.
D.D. Ward, Mount Gay Distilleries, Ldt., Barbados.
Élizabeth Watts, Australian Wine and Brandy Corporation, Sydney.
Jack L. Ward, Horam Manor, Sussex.
Harry H. Waugh, ex-Administrateur de John Harvey, Ltd., Bristol, et du Château Latour, Pauillac.
H. Seymour Weller, Château Haut-Brion, Pessac.
Hildegard Weber, Deutsches Weininstitut, Mainz.
Jan Wells, Sans Francisco.
Dr. Franz Werner Michel, Mainz.
Odile Weltert, New York, Lyon.
William Widmer, Widmer's Wine Cellars, Naples, New York.
Prof. Albert J. Winkler, College of Agriculture, University of California, Davis, Californie.
Son Excellence Ardeshir, ancien Ambassadeur d'Iran, Washington, D.C.
V. Zanko, Produzece Industrijskih Vinarija, Zagreb.
Bruce Zoecklein, Œnologue, Université de Missori, Colombie.
Diego Zorilla de San Martin, Ministre, Ambassade d'Uruguay, Paris.

Index

A

C

D

E

F

G

H

I

J

K

L

M

N

P

Q

R

S

T

U

V

W

X

Y

Z

Tables des matières

APPENDICES

ACHEVÉ D'IMPRIMER POUR
LES ÉDITIONS ROBERT LAFFONT
SUR LES PRESSES DE
BPCC HAZELL BOOKS
AYLESBURY (GRANDE-BRETAGNE)
Printed in Great Britain

DÉPÔT LÉGAL : JANVIER 1991
Nº ÉDITEUR : S 1169